MW01254703

THE NEW INTERNATIONAL
GREEK TESTAMENT COMMENTARY

Editors
I. Howard Marshall
and
Donald A. Hagner

THE FIRST EPISTLE
TO THE CORINTHIANS

The First Epistle to the
CORINTHIANS

A Commentary on the
Greek Text

by

ANTHONY C. THISELTON

WILLIAM B. EERDMANS PUBLISHING COMPANY
GRAND RAPIDS, MICHIGAN / CAMBRIDGE, U.K.

THE PATERNOSTER PRESS
CARLISLE

© 2000 Wm. B. Eerdmans Publishing Co.

Published jointly 2000 in the United States of America by
Wm. B. Eerdmans Publishing Co.
2140 Oak Industrial Drive N.E., Grand Rapids, Michigan 49505
www.eerdmans.com
and in the U.K. by
Paternoster Press
P.O. Box 300, Carlisle, Cumbria CA3 0QS

Printed in the United States of America

13 12 11 10 09 08 07   9 8 7 6 5 4 3

Library of Congress Cataloging-in-Publication Data

Thiselton, Anthony C.
The First Epistle to the Corinthians: A commentary on the Greek text /
by Anthony C. Thiselton.
p.   cm.   (The new international Greek Testament commentary)
Includes bibliographical references and indexes.
ISBN 978-0-8028-2449-3 (alk. paper)
1. Bible. N.T. Corinthians — Commentaries.   I. Title.
II. New international Greek Testament commentary (Grand Rapids, Mich.)

BS2675.53.T45 2000
227'.2077 — dc21
                                        00-045321

British Library Cataloguing-in-Publication Data

A catalogue record for this book is available from the British Library.

ISBN 978-0-85364-559-7

CONTENTS

v

COMMENTARY

FOREWORD

Although there have been many series of commentaries on the English text of the New Testament in recent years, very few attempts have been made to cater particularly to the needs of students of the Greek text. The present initiative to fill this gap by the publication of the New International Greek Testament Commentary is very largely due to the vision of W. Ward Gasque, who was one of the original editors of the series. At a time when the study of Greek is being curtailed in many schools of theology, we hope that the NIGTC will demonstrate the continuing value of studying the Greek New Testament and will be an impetus in the revival of such study.

The volumes of the NIGTC are for students who want something less technical than a full-scale critical commentary. At the same time, the commentaries are intended to interact with modern scholarship and to make their own scholarly contribution to the study of the New Testament. The wealth of detailed study of the New Testament in articles and monographs continues without interruption, and the series is meant to harvest the results of this research in an easily accessible form. The commentaries include, therefore, extensive bibliographies and attempt to treat all important problems of history, exegesis, and interpretation that arise from the New Testament text.

One of the gains of recent scholarship has been the recognition of the primarily theological character of the books of the New Testament. The volumes of the NIGTC attempt to provide a theological understanding of the text, based on historical-critical-linguistic exegesis. It is not their primary aim to apply and expound the text for modern readers, although it is hoped that the exegesis will give some indication of the way in which the text should be expounded.

Within the limits set by the use of the English language, the series aims to be international in character, though the contributors have been chosen not primarily in order to achieve a spread between different countries but above all because of their specialized qualifications for their particular tasks.

The supreme aim of this series is to serve those who are engaged in the ministry of the Word of God and thus to glorify God's name. Our prayer is that it may be found helpful in this task.

I. HOWARD MARSHALL
DONALD A. HAGNER

PREFACE

I have tried to produce a commentary which is as close to being thorough, definitive, and at times distinctive and original as is possible within the limits of my ability, the space available, and the duties of head of a very active university department.

There may be two different reasons why someone might produce such an exceptionally detailed and lengthy commentary. One arises from what a writer may perceive as fair-minded thoroughness but others may view as the near-obsessiveness which characterizes most academics who pursue sources and issues to the bitter end. I should like to disclaim the latter since it usually suggests a lack of perspective and proportion. But others must judge. The second reason, however, plays a major part in shaping my aims. I am keenly aware of the sense of disappointment so often experienced when readers take up a substantial, scholarly commentary only to find that in the end it has failed to address precisely the questions to which they were seeking some kind of answer. I have therefore constantly set as my target reflection not only on every detail of the Greek text of Paul but also on the varied range of serious and responsible questions which readers of today will bring to the text. As a result, I offer six particular features.

1. I offer a new translation of the Greek. This has been revised a number of times in the light of exegesis and of all the major translations, versions, and commentaries. I have consistently explained and defended all differences from these standard versions, with a view to bringing out exegetical conclusions in the translation while retaining the translation as a translation and not as an exegetical paraphrase. When in doubt I have followed the consensus but elucidated my own view in the commentary.

2. In accordance with the format of this established series, I have sought to provide (in addition to a general Introduction) an introduction to each chapter or shorter section as appropriate, in part to suggest a preliminary overview of a passage; then I provide a verse-by-verse and often word-by-word commentary which includes Greek syntax and lexicography, textual criticism, issues of sociohistorical background and Pauline argument or rhetorical strategy, and theology. In the process, I seek to achieve an exegesis of the meaning of the word, phrase, sentence, verse, or extended passage in its theological and linguistic context.

3. To ensure that theological and sociohistorical issues are fully ad-

dressed from all angles, I have included numerous extended notes on issues and topics of special concern today. Examples include apostleship, issues of ethics, theology of grace and justification (no less prominent than in Romans), marriage, divorce and remarriage, Roman slavery, eschatological imminence, "headship" and gender differentiation, Paul and power, the Lord's Supper, prophetic utterance, speaking in tongues, other gifts of the Spirit, "Spirit-baptism," Christ's resurrection, and the future resurrection of the body.

4. I pay especially close attention to the sociohistorical background since it clarifies many issues. For example, the sociohistorical background of influence, wealth, patronage, and status at Corinth, together with research into civil proceedings at law, reveals that the central issue in 6:1-8 is not that of "a Christian going to law" but of a Christian with influence, power, and "the right connections" using this privilege to manipulate a vulnerable fellow believer for personal advantage. Similarly, research into the dress codes of respected and respectable married women in a Roman culture (to which Corinth aspired) sheds light on why such an issue as wearing or non-wearing of hoods in public worship should seem to be an issue of substance. This matter concerns the relative theological and ethical importance of self-respect and respect for others over against unqualified gender liberation in the gospel when the dual context is both public and that of divine worship (see the exegesis of 11:2-16). On the other hand, sociohistorical research into "rhetoric" remains more complex, while complexities about "headship" and mutuality in 11:2-16 cannot be solved by sociohistorical research alone.

5. I began to prepare extensive notes on the histories of effects of texts (*Wirkungsgeschichte* or textual "posthistory") which were more than merely a descriptive history of interpretation but which drew on the theoretical model proposed by H.-R. Jauss in reception theory. A dialectic between textual controls or constraints and interpretative creativity can most readily be sustained (as Jauss suggests) by comparing a stable core of continuity within tradition with more disruptive paradigms introduced by fresh hermeneutical questions. In consultation with General Editor I. Howard Marshall, however, it became clear that to pursue these throughout sixteen chapters would unduly strain the limits of an already long commentary. Hence much of the abbreviated material has become incorporated into the commentary, but half a dozen more explicit examples have been retained as Extended Notes, where they seem to perform their function most clearly. Both for this reason and because of their worth on their own merits, patristic, medieval, and Reformation exegesis feature in the exegetical discussion, together with some modern theology where this is appropriate. The specific Notes include, e.g., 2:6-16, where Basil and Athanasius emphasize the being and deity of the Holy Spirit, while Luther and Calvin call attention to the Spirit's agency in revelation. Both paradigms are legitimate, but each makes a different point. Another example arises from the role of the resurrection in the exegesis of the Fathers with their varied hermeneutical concerns (see the Note at the end of ch. 15).

6. Partly in the Introduction but also throughout the Commentary, I have made much of the impact of the culture of Corinth upon the developing faith of newly converted believers. At the risk of possible misunderstanding I have described their ever-ready move away from shared tradition and a tendency to elevate the self-constructed perceptions of peer groups above more rational reflection as anticipating a "postmodern" mood. Although premodern Corinth never passed through "modernity," Paul's respect for classical, rational argument alongside his acute awareness of the molding power of the cross and the Holy Spirit stood in contrast to the seductions of more fragmented peer-group pressures experienced by many at Corinth. To them Paul re-proclaims the noncompetitive gift of grace, the humbling "reversals" of the cross, and respect for the otherness of "the other" within a dialectic of ordered difference and unity. In so doing, he speaks powerfully to the world of today, emphasizing as well the christological criteria of "spirituality," love for the other in building the whole, and the transformative promise of the resurrection of the whole person when giftedness by the Holy Spirit will become unhindered, transparent, and complete. This destiny is certain, but it has not yet arrived. The transformative power of the cross operates in a present context of realism, but in a transformed world open to the future, characterized by the Holy Spirit, in which God is first and last.

I admit to embarrassment at the length of time taken to produce this work. However, it would have taken even longer if it were not for the generosity of the Humanities Research Board of the British Academy. A Competitive Award from the British Academy made possible the extension of a semester-long research leave granted by the University of Nottingham into a full year of research when only duties toward overseas Ph.D. candidates intervened. I am deeply grateful for this support, which also provided my Department with a Temporary Lecturer during my absence.

A substantial grant from the London Bible House Research Fund of the Bible Society in the United Kingdom also places me greatly in their debt. I should like to thank Dr. Martin Robinson and his committee for the provision of funding for research assistance, together with further support for typing. Their generous support also made possible certain other split funding for support in collaboration with the University of Nottingham.

I owe two different kinds of thanks to my wife Rosemary and my family. My wife typed in Greek and Hebrew from the very first (including several discarded drafts) as well as picking up typing for me at times when secretarial pressures were inordinate. I record my deep gratitude to her for her unfailing support and for sharing the vision for the work, among concurrent writing and conference demands. Further, my adult sons and daughter, Stephen, Linda, and Martin, suffered many responses of "very sorry, too busy" as well as longer absences from my four grandsons than should have occurred.

Mrs. Janet Longley transformed page after page of often almost illegible handwriting into a neat, accurate, and coherent set of discs for the publisher. Her competencies and skills far exceed such tedious work, although the reproduction of illegible German and French called on some of these. She has also assisted Mrs. Mary Elmer, our departmental secretary, in ensuring the smooth running of our Department of Theology. As head of the department since 1992, I owe my surviving sanity to their efficient and ever watchful support. I thank all of my colleagues, including my two fellow chairholders, Professor Alan Ford and Professor Maurice Casey, for their contributions to what is genuinely a happy and collaborative high-profile department in the United Kingdom and internationally.

Others to whom I owe debts of gratitude are too numerous to mention. I do, however, wish to thank church friends for their kindness and prayers. Then, too, I want to express my thanks to Professor I. Howard Marshall of the University of Aberdeen, who serves as a General Editor of the series. His judicious advice, his gentle reminder of some very recent articles which I had missed, and especially the speed and efficiency with which he processed some 2,000 pages of typescript are nothing short of remarkable. It is not always the custom, I understand, to thank one's publishers. However, over more than twenty years Eerdmans has handled several of my works, and I have received nothing but kindness, efficiency, care, and friendship from Mr. Jon Pott and other staff there. Finally, in the rush of correcting proofs and making the Subject Index to meet an agreed deadline, many (including Mrs. Janet Longley) helped me, but in particular Mr. Adonis Vidu, Mrs. Sheila Rees, and once again my wife Rosemary. They have given sacrificially of their time, for which I owe them heartfelt thanks.

ANTHONY C. THISELTON
Department of Theology,
University of Nottingham,
United Kingdom
Holy Week, 2000

ABBREVIATIONS

AARAS	American Academy of Religion Academy Series
AB	Anchor Bible
ABD	*Anchor Bible Dictionary*
ABenR	*American Benedictine Review*
ACNT	Augsburg Commentaries on the New Testament
ACR	*Australian Catholic Record*
AGJU	Arbeiten zur Geschichte des antiken Judentums und des Urchristentums
AGSU	Arbeiten zur Geschichte des antiken Spätjudentums und Urchristentums
AJA	*American Journal of Archaeology*
AJAH	*American Journal of Ancient History*
AnBib	Analecta Biblica
ANET	*Ancient Near Eastern Texts*
AnGr	Analecta Gregoriana
ANRW	*Aufstieg und Niedergang der römischen Welt*
ASeign	*Assemblees du Seigneur*
ATR	*Anglican Theological Review*
ATRSS	Anglican Theological Review Supplementary Series
AusBR	*Australian Biblical Review*
BA	*Biblical Archaeologist*
BAGD	Bauer, Arndt, Gingrich, and Danker, *A Greek-English Lexicon of the New Testament and Other Early Christian Literature*
BAR	*Biblical Archaeologist Reader*
BBET	Beiträge zur biblischen Exegese und Theologie
BDB	Brown, Driver, and Briggs, *Hebrew and English Lexicon of the Old Testament*
BDBG	Brown, Driver, Briggs, and Gesenius, *The New Hebrew and English Lexicon*
BDF	Blass, Debrunner, and Funk, *A Greek Grammar of the New Testament and Other Early Christian Literature*
BETL	Bibliotheca Ephemeridum Theologicarum Lovaniensium
BGBE	Beiträge zur Geschichte der biblischen Exegese
BGU	*Berliner Griechische Urkunden*
BHT	Beiträge zur historischen Theologie
Bib	*Biblica*
BibInt	*Biblical Interpretation*

ABBREVIATIONS

BibRev	*Bible Review*
BibTod	*Bible Today*
BJRL	*Bulletin of the John Rylands Library*
BK	*Bibel und Kirche*
BR	*Biblical Research*
BSac	*Bibliotheca Sacra*
BT	*Bible Translator*
BTB	*Biblical Theology Bulletin*
BU	Biblische Untersuchungen
BWANT	Beiträge zur Wissenschaft vom Alten und Neuen Testament
BZ	*Biblische Zeitschrift*
BZNW	Beihefte zur Zeitschrift für die neutestamentliche Wissenschaft
CBC	Cambridge Bible Commentary
CBQ	*Catholic Biblical Quarterly*
CD	*Church Dogmatics*
CIG	*Corpus Inscriptione Graecarum*
ClQ	*Classical Quarterly*
ComC	Communicators Commentary
ConB	Coniectanea Biblica
ConBNT	Coniectanea Biblica, New Testament
Conc	*Concilium*
ConNT	Coniectanea Neotestamentica
CSEL	Corpus Scriptorum Ecclesiastorum Latinorum
CT	*Christianity Today*
CTQ	*Concordia Theological Quarterly*
CV	*Communio Viatorum*
DPL	*Dictionary of Paul and His Letters*
Ebib	Etudes bibliques
EDNT	*Exegetical Dictionary of the New Testament*
EeT	*Église et Théologie*
EHST	Europäische Hochschulschriften Theologie
EKKNT	Evangelisch-katholischer Kommentar zum Neuen Testament
ETL	*Ephemerides Theologicae Lovanienses*
ETR	*Études theologiques et religieuses*
EvQ	*Evangelical Quarterly*
EvT	*Evangelische Theologie*
Exp	*Expositor*
ExpTim	*Expository Times*
FB	Forschung zur Bibel
FRLANT	Forschungen zur Religion und Literatur des Alten und Neuen Testaments
Grimm-Thayer	Grimm and Thayer, *A Greek-English Lexicon of the New Testament*
GTA	Göttinger theologische Arbeiten
GTJ	*Grace Theological Journal*
HALAT	*Hebräisches und Aramäisches Lexikon zum Alten Testament*
HNT	Handbuch zum Neuen Testament
HTR	*Harvard Theological Review*
HUCA	*Hebrew Union College Annual*

HUT	Hermeneutische Untersuchungen zur Theologie
IB	*Interpreter's Bible*
IBS	*Irish Biblical Studies*
ICC	International Critical Commentary
Int	*Interpretation*
ISBE	*International Standard Bible Encyclopedia*
ITQ	*Irish Theological Quarterly*
JAAR	*Journal of the American Academy of Religion*
JBL	*Journal of Biblical Literature*
JBR	*Journal of Bible and Religion*
JES	*Journal of Ecumenical Studies*
JETS	*Journal of the Evangelical Theological Society*
JHC	*Journal of Higher Criticism*
JR	*Journal of Religion*
JRE	*Journal of Religious Ethics*
JRH	*Journal of Religious History*
JRS	*Journal of Religious Studies*
JSNT	*Journal for the Study of the New Testament*
JSNTSS	Journal for the Study of the New Testament Supplement Series
JSOT	*Journal for the Study of the Old Testament*
JSS	*Journal of Semitic Studies*
JTS	*Journal of Theological Studies*
KD	*Kerygma und Dogma*
KNT	Kommentar zum Neuen Testament
Lampe	Lampe, *A Patristic Greek Lexicon*
LB	*Linguistica Biblica*
LCC	Library of Christian Classics
LCL	Loeb Classical Library
LD	*Lectio Divina*
Louw-Nida	Louw and Nida, *A Greek-English Lexicon of the New Testament Based on Semantic Domains*
LSJ	Liddell, Scott, and Jones, *A Greek-English Lexicon*
LV	*Lumière et vie*
LW	*Lutheran World*
MHT	Moulton, Howard, and Turner, *A Grammar of New Testament Greek*
MM	Moulton and Milligan, *The Vocabulary of the Greek New Testament Illustrated from Papyri and Other Nonliterary Sources*
Moule	Moule, *An Idiom Book of New Testament Greek*
MTZ	*Münchener theologische Zeitschrift*
NCBC	New Century Bible Commentary
Neot	*Neotestamentica*
NGTT	*Nederduitse gereformeerde teologiese tijdskrif*
NICNT	New International Commentary on the New Testament
NIDNTT	*New International Dictionary of New Testament Theology*
NIGTC	New International Greek Testament Commentary
NIVAC	New International Version Application Commentary
NovT	*Novum Testamentum*
NovTSup	Novum Nestamentum Supplements

NPNF	Nicene and Post-Nicene Fathers
NRT	*Nouvelle revue théologique*
NTA	*New Testament Abstracts*
NTD	Neue Testament Deutsch
NTR	*New Theology Review*
NTS	*New Testament Studies*
NTTS	New Testament Tools and Studies
PastPsy	*Pastoral Psychology*
Pauly	Pauly and Wissowa, *Real-Encyclopädie der classischen Altertumswissenschaft*
PG	*Patrologia Graeca*
PL	*Patrologia Latina*
PRS	*Perspectives in Religious Studies*
PSB	*Princeton Seminary Bulletin*
PSI	*Pubblicazione della Società Italiana*
RAC	*Reallexikon für Antike und Christentum*
RB	*Revue bibliques*
RechBib	*Recherches bibliques*
RefRev	*Reformed Review*
RevBib	*Revue biblique*
RevExp	*Review and Expositor*
RevistB	*Revista biblica*
RGG	*Religion in Geschichte und Gegenwart*
RHPR	*Revue d'histoire de philosophie religieuses*
Robertson	Robertson, *A Grammar of the New Testament in the Light of Historical Research*
RSR	*Recherches de science religieuse*
RTP	*Revue de théologie et de philosophie*
RTR	*Reformed Theological Review*
SacPag	Sacra Pagina
SBL	Society of Biblical Literature
SBLDS	Society of Biblical Literature Dissertation Series
SBLTT	*Society of Biblical Literature: Texts and Translations*
SBM	Stuttgarter biblische Monographien
SBS	Studies in Biblical Theology
ScEs	*Science et esprit*
SE	*Studia Evangelica*
SEÅ	*Svensk Exegetisk Årsbok*
SJT	*Scottish Journal of Theology*
SNT	Studien zum Neuen Testament
SNTSMS	Society for New Testament Studies Monograph Series
SR	*Sciences religieuses/Studies in Religion*
ST	*Studia Theologica*
TBei	*Theologische Beiträge*
TBü	*Theologische Bücherei*
TDNT	*Theological Dictionary of the New Testament*
TEH	*Theologische Existenz heute*
Theol	*Theology*

ABBREVIATIONS

ThEv	*Theologia Evangelica*
THKNT	Theologischer Kommentar zum Neuen Testament
TLG	*Thesaurus Linguae Graecae*
TLZ	*Theologische Literaturzeitung*
TNTC	Tyndale New Testament Commentaries
TQ	*Theologische Quartalschrift*
TrinJ	*Trinity Journal*
TRu	*Theologische Rundschau*
TS	*Theological Studies*
TTh	*Tijdschrift voor Theologie*
TToday	*Theology Today*
TTZ	*Trierer theologische Zeitschrift*
TynBul	*Tyndale Bulletin*
TZ	*Theologische Zeitschrift*
UBS	United Bible Societies
UBSGNT	United Bible Societies *Greek New Testament*
USQR	*Union Seminary Quarterly Review*
VC	*Vigiliae Christianae*
VoxEv	*Vox Evangelica*
VoxRef	*Vox Reformata*
VS	*Verbum Salutis*
VT	*Vetus Testamentum*
WA	*Weimarer Ausgabe*
WBC	Word Biblical Commentary
WTJ	*Westminster Theological Journal*
WUNT	Wissenschaftliche Untersuchungen zum Neuen Testament
WW	*Word and World*
ZKG	*Zeitschrift für Kirchengeschichte*
ZKT	*Zeitschrift für katholische Theologie*
ZNW	*Zeitschrift für die neutestamentliche Wissenschaft*
ZTK	*Zeitschrift für Theologie und Kirche*

BIBLIOGRAPHY

I. COMMENTARIES

Of the following eighty-six commentaries, the nine marked * (in one case **) are especially detailed and/or significant.

*Allo, E.-B., *Saint Paul. Première Épitre aux Corinthiens* (Paris: Gabalda, 2d ed. 1956 [1st ed. 1934]).

Ambrose, *Commentarius in epistolam B. Pauli ad Corinthios primam,* in J.-P. Migne (ed.), *PL* (Paris: Petit-Montrouge, 1857-86), vol. 17.

Ambrosiaster, *Ambrosiasti qui dicitur commentarius in epistolas Paulinus 2. In epistolas ad Corinthios,* in CSEL (Vienna corpus from 1866), 81:3-194.

Aquinas, *see* Thomas Aquinas.

Bachmann, P., *Der erste Brief des Paulus an die Korinther,* Kommentar zum Neuen Testament (Leipzig: Deichert, 1905 4th ed. with additions by E. Stauffer, 1936).

*Barrett, C. K., *A Commentary on the First Epistle to the Corinthians* (London: Black, 1968, 2d ed. 1971).

Barth, K., *The Resurrection of the Dead* (Eng. trans., London: Hodder & Stoughton, 1933).

Bengel, J. A., *Gnomon Novi Testamenti* (Stuttgart: Steinkopf and London: Dulau [from 3d ed. 1773], 1866).

Blomberg, C. L., *1 Corinthians,* NIVAC (Grand Rapids: Zondervan, 1994).

Bruce, F. F., *1 and 2 Corinthians,* NCBC (London: Oliphants, 1971).

Calvin, John, *The First Epistle of Paul to the Corinthians* (Eng. trans., Edinburgh: Oliver & Boyd and St. Andrew, 1960).

Chafin, K. L., *1, 2 Corinthians,* ComC 7 (Waco, Tex.: Word, 1985).

Chrysostom, John, *Homilies on the Epistles of Paul to the Corinthians* (1-44 on 1 Corinthians) Greek, in J.-P. Migne (ed.), *PG,* vol. 61, cols. 9-382; English, also NPNF (ed. P. Schaff; Edinburgh: T. & T. Clark, 1887-94; vol. 12, rpt. Grand Rapids: Eerdmans, 1989), 1-269.

*Collins, R. F., *First Corinthians,* SacPag 7 (Collegeville, Minn: Glazier/Liturgical Press, 1999).

*Conzelmann, H., *1 Corinthians: A Commentary* Hermeneia (Eng. trans., Philadelphia: Fortress Press, 1975).

Craig, C. T., "The First Epistle to the Corinthians," in *IB,* 10 (New York and Nashville: Abingdon Press, 1953), 3-262.

Cyril of Alexandria, *Fragmenta Varia, 3: In Epistolam 1 ad Corinthios* (ed. P. E. Pusey;

Brussels: Culture et Civilisation, 1965), 249-96; also in J.-P. Migne (ed.), *PG,* vol. 74, cols. 48-70.

Deluz, G., *A Companion to 1 Corinthians* (Eng. trans., London: Darton, Longman & Todd, 1963).

Didymus of Alexandria, *Fragments, 1 Cor 15–16,* in K. Staab (ed.), *Pauluskommentare aus der griechischen Kirche* (Münster: Aschendorff, 1933), 6-14.

Edwards, T. C., *A Commentary on the First Epistle to the Corinthians* (London: Hodder & Stoughton [Greek text], 2d ed. 1885).

Ellingworth, P., and H. A. Hatton, *Paul's First Letter to the Corinthians,* UBS Handbook (New York: United Bible Societies, 1994).

Erasmus Desiderius, *Epistola Pauli ad Corinthios prima,* in *Opera Omnia,* 6 (ed. J. Leclerc; Leiden, 1705), 661-747.

Evans, E., *The Epistles of Paul the Apostle to the Corinthians,* Clarendon Bible (Oxford: Clarendon Press, 1930).

Fascher, E., *Der erste Brief des Paulus an die Korinther, 1: Einführung und Auslegung der Kap 1–7,* HTKNT 7:1 (Berlin: Evangelische Verlagsanstalt, 1975; 3d ed. 1984).

*Fee, G. D., *The First Epistle to the Corinthians,* NICNT (Grand Rapids: Eerdmans, 1987).

Findlay, G. G., "St Paul's First Epistle to the Corinthians," in W. R. Nicoll (ed.), *The Expositor's Greek Testament* (Grand Rapids: Eerdmans [London, 1900], 1961).

Godet, F., *Commentary on St Paul's First Epistle to the Corinthians* (Eng. trans., 2 vols., Edinburgh: T. & T. Clark, 1886).

Goudge, H. L., *The First Epistle to the Corinthians,* Westminster Commentaries (London: Methuen, 1903, 4th ed. 1915).

Grosheide, F. W., *Commentary on the First Epistle to the Corinthians,* NICNT and New London Commentary (Grand Rapids: Eerdmans and London: Marshall, Morgan & Scott, 1953, 2d ed. 1954).

Hargreaves, J., *A Guide to 1 Corinthians* (London: SPCK, 1978).

Harris, W. B., *The First Epistle of St Paul to the Corinthians* (Serampore and Bangalore: Christian Literature Society, 1958).

Harrisville, R. A., *1 Corinthians,* ACNT (Minneapolis: Augsburg, 1987).

Hays, R. B., *First Corinthians,* Interpretation (Louisville: Knox, 1997).

Heinrici, C. F. G., *Das erste Sendschreiben des Apostel Paulus an die Korinther* (Berlin: Hertz, 1880); also 8th ed., *Der erste Brief an die Korinther* (Göttingen: Vandenhoeck & Ruprecht, 1896).

Héring, J., *The First Epistle of St Paul to the Corinthians* (Eng. trans., London: Epworth Press, 1962).

Hodge, C., *The First Epistle to the Corinthians* (London: Banner of Truth, rpt. 1958).

Horsley, R. A., *1 Corinthians* (Nashville: Abingdon Press, 1998).

Kistemaker, S. J., *1 Corinthians* (Grand Rapids: Baker, 1993).

Klauck, H.-J., *1 Korintherbrief,* Die Neue Echter Bibel (Würzburg: Echter Verlag, 1984).

Kling, C. F., "The First Epistle of Paul to the Corinthians," in J. P. Lange (ed.), *Commentary on the Holy Scriptures* (Eng. trans., Grand Rapids: Zondervan, 1960 [German 1861]), 5-864.

Kümmel, W. G. (*see* under Lietzmann).

Lang, F., *Die Briefe an die Korinther*, NTD 7 (Göttingen and Zürich: Vandenhoeck & Ruprecht, 1994), 1-250 (on 1 Corinthians).

Lias, J. J., *The First Epistle to the Corinthians,* Cambridge Greek Testament, earlier series (Cambridge: Cambridge University Press, 1892) (Greek text).

Lietzmann, H. (with W. G. Kümmel), *An die Korinther 1/2*, HNT 9 (Tübingen: Mohr, 4th ed. 1949), 1-96 (Lietzmann on 1 Corinthians) and 165-96 (Kümmel's supplement on 1 Corinthians).

Lightfoot, J. B., *Notes on the Epistles of St Paul* (London: Macmillan, 1895), 139-235 (on 1 Corinthians 1–7 only, Greek text).

Locke, John, *A Paraphrase and Notes on the Epistles of St Paul to the Galatians, 1 and 2 Corinthians, Romans, Ephesians* (1707) (ed. A. W. Wainwright; Oxford: Clarendon Press, 1987), 413-60 (on 1 Corinthians).

Luther, Martin, *Luther's Works* (American ed.), vol. 28: *Commentaries on 1 Corinthians 7 and 1 Corinthians 15* (St. Louis: Concordia, 1973), 9-214 (*WA,* 12:97-142 and 36:482-696).

MacRory, J., *The Epistles of St Paul to the Corinthians* (Dublin: Gill, 1915).

Mare, W. H., "1 Corinthians," in F. E. Gaebelein (ed.), *The Expositor's Bible Commentary* (Grand Rapids: Zondervan, 1976), 173-297.

Melanchthon, P., "Annotationes in epistulas Pauli ad Corinthios," in *Melanchthons Werke in Auswahl* (Gütersloh: Mohn, 1963), 4:16-84.

*Merklein, H., *Der erste Brief an die Korinther Kapitel 1–4,* Ökumenischer Taschenbuchkommentar zum Neuen Testament (Gütersloh: Gütersloher Verlagshaus and Mohn, and Würzburg: Echter Verlag, 1992).

Meyer, H. A. W., *Critical and Exegetical Handbook to the Epistles to the Corinthians* (Eng. trans., 2 vols., Edinburgh: T. & T. Clark, 1892 [vol. 1 and vol. 2, 1-124 on 1 Corinthians]).

Moffatt, J., *The First Epistle of Paul to the Corinthians,* Moffatt New Testament Commentary (London: Hodder & Stoughton, 1938).

Morris, L., *The First Epistle of Paul to the Corinthians,* TNTC (London: Tyndale Press, 1958).

Murphy-O'Connor, J., *1 Corinthians,* New Testament Message 10 (Wilmington: Glazier, 1979); and *1 Corinthians,* People's Bible Commentary (Oxford: Bible Reading Fellowship, 1997).

Oecumenius of Tricca (tenth cent.), "1 Kor," in K. Staab (ed.), *Pauluskommentare aus der griechischen Kirche* (Münster: Aschendorff, 1933), 432-43.

Origen (some 80 fragments of Greek text, in four parts), in C. Jenkins (ed.), "Documents: Origen on 1 Corinthians," *JTS* 9 (1908): 231-47, 353-72, 500-514; and 10 (1909): 29-51.

Orr, W. F., and J. A. Walther, *1 Corinthians,* AB 32 (Garden City, N.Y.: Doubleday, 1976).

Ortkemper, F. J., *1 Korintherbrief* (Stuttgart: Verlag Katholisches Bibelwerk, 1993).

Osty, C. E., *Les Épitres de Saint Paul aux Corinthiens* (Paris: Les Éditions du Cerf, 4th ed. 1964), 9-71 (on 1 Corinthians).

Parry, R. St. John, *The First Epistle of Paul the Apostle to the Corinthians,* Cambridge Greek Testament (Cambridge: Cambridge University Press, 1937).

Pelagius, "Commentary on 1 Corinthians," in J.-P. Migne (ed.), *PL,* 30:721-72; but on the originality of the text and the attributions to Pseudo-Jerome, cf. A. Souter (ed.), *Pelagius's Exposition of Thirteen Epistles of St Paul* (Cambridge: Cambridge University Press, 1926).

Peter Lombard, "Collectanae in epistolam 1 ad Corinthios," in J.-P. Migne (ed.), *PL,* vol. 191, cols. 1533-1696.

Photius of Constantinople (ninth cent.), "1 Kor," in K. Staab (ed.), *Pauluskommentare aus der griechischen Kirche* (Münster: Aschendorff, 1933), 544-83.

*Robertson, A. T., and A. Plummer, *A Critical and Exegetical Commentary on the First Epistle of St Paul to the Corinthians,* ICC (Edinburgh: T. & T. Clark, 2d ed. 1914 [Greek text]).

Robertson, A. T., *Word Pictures in the NT* (6 vols.), 4: *The Epistles of Paul* (Greek text) (New York: R. Smith, 1931), 68-207.

Robertson, E. H., *Corinthians One and Two* (London: Collins-Fontana, 1973), 10-101.

Ruef, J., *Paul's First Letter to Corinth,* Pelican New Testament Commentaries (Harmondsworth and Baltimore: Penguin, 1971).

Schlatter, A., *Paulus, der Bote Jesus. Eine Deutung seiner Briefe an die Korinther* (Stuttgart: Calwer, 4th ed. 1969 [1934]); also *Die Korintherbriefe Ausgelegt für Bibelleser* (Stuttgart: Calwer, 1962, 1984).

**Schrage, W., *Der erste Brief an die Korinther,* EKKNT 7/1-3 (Neukirchen-Vluyn: Neukirchener Verlag, and Zürich and Düsseldorf: Benziger Verlag, 3 vols. to date, 1991 [on 1:1–6:11]; 1995 [6:12–11:16]; and 1999 [11:17-14:40]).

Senft, C., *La Première Épitre de Saint Paul aux Corinthiens,* Commentaire du Nouveau Testament (Geneva: Labor et Fides, 2d rev. ed. 1990 [1979]).

Simon, W. G. H., *The First Epistle to the Corinthians,* Torch Bible Commentary (London: SCM, 1959).

Snyder, G. F., *First Corinthians: A Faith Community Commentary* (Macon, Ga.: Mercer University Press, 1992).

Strobel, A., *Der erste Brief an die Korinther,* Zürcher Bibelkommentare (Zürich: Theologischer Verlag, 1989).

Talbert, C. H., *Reading Corinthians: A Literary-Theological Commentary on 1 and 2 Corinthians* (New York: Crossroad, 1992).

Tertullian (brief fragmentary thematic exposition), *Against Marcion,* 5:5-10.

Theodore of Mopsuestia, "1 Kor," in K. Staab (ed.), *Pauluskommentare aus der griechischen Kirche* (Münster: Aschendorff, 1933), 172-96.

Theodoret, *Interpretatio primae epistolae ad Corinthios,* in J.-P. Migne (ed.), *PG,* vol. 82, cols. 225-376.

Theophylact, *Epistolae Primae Divi Pauli ad Corinthios Expositio,* in J.-P. Migne (ed.), *PG,* vol. 124, cols. 561-794.

Thomas Aquinas, *Super Epistolas S. Pauli Lectura. 1 ad Corinthios* (Taurin and Rome: Marietti, 1953). Note: 1-299, sects. 1-336, 1 Cor 1:1–7:9 are authentic; thereafter *postilla* from other sources are involved. The Eng. trans., *Aquinas Scripture* series (Albany, N.Y.: Magi Books, 1966-80), includes only Galatians, Ephesians, 1 Thessalonians, Philippians, and John 1–7.

Thrall, M. E., *The First and Second Letters of Paul to the Corinthians* (Cambridge: Cambridge University Press, 1965), 1-118.

Walter, E., *The First Epistle to the Corinthians,* New Testament for Spiritual Reading (Eng. trans., London: Sheed and Ward, 1971).

Watson, N., *The First Epistle to the Corinthians* (London: Epworth Press, 1992).

BIBLIOGRAPHY

*Weiss, J., *Der erste Korintherbrief* (Göttingen: Vandenhoeck & Ruprecht, 2d rev. ed. 1910) (rpt. 1977).

Wendland, H.-D., *Die Briefe an die Korinther,* NTD 7 (Göttingen: Vandenhoeck & Ruprecht, 1968 [1936])

Witherington, B. (*see* under General Bibliography).

*Wolff, C., *Der erste Brief des Paulus an die Korinther,* THKNT 7 (Leipzig: Evangelische Verlagsanstalt, 1996).

II. SELECT GENERAL BIBLIOGRAPHY

This short list of about a hundred further studies deliberately excludes both works which apply more appropriately to specific chapters (listed in full under sectional bibliographies) and with one or two exceptions works published before the early 1980s. A firm principle of selection (at the request of General Editor I. Howard Marshall) focuses upon works used regularly, mainly from the last fifteen years, to avoid replication of details in the sectional bibliographies, which list more narrowly specialist books and articles. For the same reason books predominate, while research articles are included in full in the sectional bibliographies and footnotes.

Adna, J., S. J. Hafemann, and O. Hofius (eds.), *Evangelium, Schriftauslegung, Kirche. Festschrift für P. Stuhlmacher* (Göttingen: Vandenhoeck & Ruprecht, 1997). (*See also* esp. under Gundry-Volf and under Hofius.)

Allenbach, J., A. Benoit, et al. (eds.), *Biblia Patristica. Index des citations et allusions Bibliques dans la littérature Patristique* (Paris: Éditions du Centre National de la Recherche Scientifique, 6 vols. to date, 1986-91).

Balch, D. L., E. Ferguson, and W. A. Meeks (eds.), *Greeks, Romans and Christians: Essays in Honor of A. J. Malherbe* (Minneapolis: Fortress, 1990). (*See also* under Stowers.)

Banks, R., *Paul's Idea of Community* (Peabody, Mass.: Hendrickson, rev. 2d ed. 1994 [1980]).

Bieringer, R. (ed.), *The Corinthian Correspondence,* BETL (Leuven: Leuven University Press, 1996).

Blasi, A. J., *Early Christianity as a Social Movement* (New York and Bern: Lang, 1988).

Bockmühl, M. N. A., *Revelation and Mystery in Ancient Judaism and Pauline Christianity,* WUNT 2:36 (Tübingen: Mohr, 1990).

Boer, M. C. de, *The Defeat of Death,* JSNTSS 22 (Sheffield: Sheffield Academic Press, 1988).

Brown, A. R., *The Cross and Human Transformation: Paul's Apocalyptic Word in 1 Corinthians* (Minneapolis: Fortress, 1995).

Bünker, M., *Briefformular und rhetorische Disposition im 1 Korintherbrief,* GTA 28 (Göttingen: Vandenhoeck & Ruprecht, 1984).

Cantarella, E., *Pandora's Daughters: The Role and Status of Women in Greek and Roman Antiquities* (Baltimore: Johns Hopkins University Press, 1987).

Carson, D. A., *The Cross and the Christian Ministry: An Exposition of Passages from 1 Corinthians* (Grand Rapids: Baker, 1993).

Castelli, E., *Imitating Paul: A Discussion of Power* (Louisville: Westminster/Knox, 1991).

xxix

Chow, J. K., *Patronage and Power: A Study of Social Networks in Corinth,* JSNTSS 75 (Sheffield: Sheffield Academic Press, 1992).

Clarke, A. D., *Secular and Christian Leadership in Corinth: A Socio-Historical and Exegetical Study of 1 Corinthians 1–6,* AGJU 18 (Leiden: Brill, 1993).

Combes, I. A. H., *The Metaphor of Slavery in the Writings of the Early Church,* JSNTSS 156 (Sheffield: Sheffield Academic Press, 1998).

Crafton, J. A., *The Agency of the Apostle: A Dramatistic Analysis of Paul's Responses to Conflict in 2 Corinthians,* JSNTSS 51 (Sheffield: Sheffield Academic Press, 1991).

Dunn, J. D. G., *1 Corinthians* (Sheffield: Sheffield Academic Press, 1995).

———, *The Theology of Paul the Apostle* (Edinburgh: T. & T. Clark, 1998).

Eckstein, H.-G., *Der Begriff Syneidesis bei Paulus,* WUNT 2:10 (Tübingen: Mohr, 1983).

Ellis, E. E., *Prophecy and Hermeneutic in Early Christianity* (Grand Rapids: Eerdmans, 1978).

Elliott, N., *Liberating Paul: The Justice of God and the Politics of the Apostle* (Maryknoll, N.Y.: Orbis, 1994).

Engels, D., *Roman Corinth: An Alternative Model for the Classical City* (Chicago: University of Chicago Press, 1990).

Eriksson, A., *Traditions as Rhetorical Proof: Pauline Argumentation in 1 Corinthians,* ConBNT 29 (Stockholm: Almqvist & Wiksell, 1998).

Fee, G. D., *God's Empowering Presence: The Holy Spirit in the Letters of Paul* (Carlisle: Paternoster and Peabody, Mass.: Hendrickson, 1994).

———, *Paul, The Spirit, and the People of God* (Peabody, Mass.: Hendrickson, 1996).

———, "Toward a Theology of 1 Corinthians," in D. M. Hay (ed.), *Pauline Theology, 2: 1 and 2 Corinthians* (Minneapolis: Fortress, 1993), 37-58.

Fitzgerald, J. T., *Cracks in an Earthen Vessel: An Examination of the Catalogues of Hardships in the Corinthian Correspondence,* SBLDS 99 (Atlanta: Scholars Press, 1988).

Forbes, C., *Prophecy and Inspired Speech in Early Christianity and Its Hellenistic Environment,* WUNT 2:75 (Tübingen: Mohr, 1995).

Furnish, V. P., "Theology in 1 Corinthians," in D. M. Hay (ed.), *Pauline Theology* (cited also below), 59-89.

Gardner, P. D., *The Gifts of God and the Authentication of a Christian: An Exegetical Study of 1 Corinthians 8–11* (Lanham, Md.: University Press of America, 1994).

Gillespie, T. W., *The First Theologians: A Study in Early Christian Prophecy* (Grand Rapids: Eerdmans, 1994).

Glad, C. E., *Paul and Philodemus: Adaptability in Epicurean and Early Christian Psychagogy,* NovTSup 81 (Leiden: Brill, 1995).

Gooch, P. W., *Partial Knowledge: Philosophical Studies in Paul* (Notre Dame: Notre Dame University Press, 1987).

Gooch, P. W., "'Conscience' in 1 Cor 8 and 10," *NTS* 33 (1987): 244-54.

Goulder, M., "σοφία in 1 Corinthians," *NTS* 37 (1991): 516-34.

Gundry-Volf, J. M., "Gender and Creation in 1 Cor 11:2-16: A Study in Paul's Theological Method," in J. Adna et al. (eds.), *Evangelium, Schriftauslegung, Kirche* (1997, cited above), 151-71.

———, *Paul and Perseverance,* WUNT 2:37 (Tübingen: Mohr, 1990).

Hainz, J., *Koinonia: "Kirche" als Gemeinschaft bei Paulus,* BU 16 (Regensburg: Pustet, 1982).

Hay, David M. (ed.), *Pauline Theology 2: 1 and 2 Corinthians* (Minneapolis: Fortress, 1993), esp. 1-131.

Hays, R. B., "Ecclesiology and Ethics in 1 Corinthians," *Ex Auditu* 10 (1994): 31-43.

————, *Echoes of Scripture in the Letters of Paul* (New Haven: Yale University Press, 1989).

————, *The Moral Vision of the NT: Community, Cross, New Creation* (San Francisco: Harper, 1996).

Hengel, M., *The Cross of the Son of God* (Eng. trans., London: SCM, 1986).

Hock, R. F., *The Social Context of Paul's Ministry: Tentmaking and Apostleship* (Philadelphia: Fortress, 1980).

Hofius, O., "Paulus — Missionar und Theologe," in J. Adna and S. J. Hafemann (eds.), *Evangelium, Schriftauslegung, Kirche* (1997, cited above), 224-37.

Hollemann, J., *Resurrection and Parousia,* NovTSup 84 (Leiden: Brill, 1996).

Horrell, D. G., *The Social Ethos of the Corinthian Correspondence* (Edinburgh: T. & T. Clark, 1996).

Horsley, R. A., "Consciousness and Freedom among the Corinthians: 1 Cor 8–10," *CBQ* 40 (1978): 574-89.

———— (ed.), *New Documents Illustrating Early Christianity* (5 vols., North Ryde, N.S.W.: Ancient History Documentary Research Centre, Macquarrie University, 1981-89).

———— (ed.), *Paul and Empire: Religion and Power in Roman Imperial Society* (Harrisburg: Trinity, 1997).

Hurd, J. C., *The Origin of 1 Corinthians* (London: SPCK, 1965; 2d ed. Macon, Ga.: Mercer University Press, 1983).

Jervis, L. A., and P. Richardson (eds.), "Gospel in the Corinthian Letters," in *Gospel in Paul: Studies on Corinthians, Galatians and Romans for Richard N. Longenecker,* JSNTSS 108 (Sheffield: Sheffield Academic Press, 1994), 38-164.

Kitzberger, I., *Bau der Gemeinde. Das paulinische Wortfeld οἰκοδομή ἐποικοδομεῖν,* FB 53 (Würzberg: Echter, 1986).

Kleinknecht, K. T., *Der Leidende Gerechtfertigte,* WUNT 2:13 (Tübingen: Mohr, 1984), esp. 208-304.

Litfin, D., *St Paul's Theology of Proclamation: 1 Cor 1–4 and Greco-Roman Rhetoric,* SNTSMS 79 (Cambridge: Cambridge University Press, 1994).

Lorenzi, L. de (ed.), *Charisma und Agape,* Benedictina 6 (Rome: Abbey St. Paul, 1983).

————, *Freedom and Love,* Benedictina 6 (Rome: Abbey St. Paul, 1981).

————, *Paolo a Una Chiesa Divisa (1 Cor 1–4)* (Rome: Abbey St. Paul, 1980), esp. essays by E. Best (9-41) and U. Wilckens (43-81).

Malherbe, A. J., "The Apostle Paul as Pastor," in Lung-Kwong Lo (ed.), *Jesus, Paul and John* (Hong Kong: Chung Chi Chinese University, 2000), 98-138.

Maly, K., *Mündige Gemeinde* (Stuttgart: Katholische Bibelwerk, 1967).

Marshall, P., *Enmity in Corinth: Social Conventions in Paul's Relations with the Corinthians,* WUNT 2:23 (Tübingen: Mohr, 1987).

Martin, D. B., *The Corinthian Body* (New Haven: Yale University Press, 1995).

————, *Slavery as Salvation: The Metaphor of Slavery in Pauline Christianity* (New Haven: Yale University Press, 1990).

Martin, R. P., *The Spirit and the Congregation: Studies in 1 Cor 12–15* (Grand Rapids: Eerdmans, 1984).

Meeks, W. A., *The Moral World of the First Christians* (Philadelphia: Westminster, 1986).

———, *The Social World of the Apostle Paul* (New Haven: Yale University Press, 1983).

Meggitt, J. J., *Paul, Poverty and Survival* (Edinburgh: T. & T. Clark, 1998).

Merk, O., *Handeln aus Glauben. Die Motivierungen der paulinischen Ethik* (Marburg: Elwert, 1968).

Merklein, H., "Die Einheitlichkeit des ersten Korintherbriefes," *ZNW* 75 (1984): 153-83.

Metzger, B. M., *A Textual Commentary on the Greek NT* (Stuttgart: UBS, 2d ed. 1994).

Mitchell, M. M., *Paul and the Rhetoric of Reconciliation: An Exegetical Investigation of the Language and Composition of 1 Corinthians* (Tübingen: Mohr and Louisville: Westminster/Knox, 1992).

Moores, J. D., *Wrestling with Rationality in Paul,* SNTSMS 82 (Cambridge: Cambridge University Press, 1995), 1-32 and 132-60.

Müller, U., *Prophetie und Predigt im NT,* SNT 10 (Gütersloh: Mohn, 1975).

Murphy-O'Connor, J., *Paul: A Critical Life* (Oxford: Oxford University Press, 1997).

———, *Paul the Letter-Writer: His World, His Options, His Skills* (Collegeville: Glazier/Liturgical Press, 1995).

———, *St. Paul's Corinth: Texts and Archaeology* (Wilmington: Glazier, 1983).

Neyrey, J. H., "Body Language in 1 Corinthians: The Use of Anthropological Models for Understanding Paul and His Opponents," *Semeia* 35 (1986 [1984]): 129-70.

Oster, R. E., "Use, Misuse and Neglect of Archaeological Evidence in Some Modern Works on 1 Cor (1 Cor 7:1-5; 8:10; 11:2-16; 12:14-26)," *ZNW* 83 (1992): 52-73.

Painter, J. (ed.), "Paul and the πνευματικοί at Corinth," in M. D. Hooker and J. G. Wilson (eds.), *Paul and Paulinism: Essays in Honour of C. K. Barrett* (London: SPCK, 1982), 237-50.

Pickett, R., *The Cross in Corinth: The Social Significance of the Death of Jesus,* JSNTSS 143 (Sheffield: Sheffield Academic Press, 1997), 37-84.

Pogoloff, S. M., *Logos and Sophia: The Rhetorical Situation of 1 Corinthians,* SBLDS 134 (Atlanta: Scholars Press, 1992).

Porter, S. E., and T. H. Olbricht (eds.), *Rhetoric and the NT,* JSNTSS 90 (Sheffield: Sheffield Academic Press, 1993).

Probst, H., *Paulus und der Brief: Die Rhetorik des antiken Briefes als Form der paulinischen Korintherkorrespondenz (1 Kor 8–10),* WUNT 2:45 (Tübingen: Mohr, 1991).

Richardson, N., *Paul's Language about God,* JSNTSS 99 (Sheffield: Sheffield Academic Press, 1994).

Rosner, B. S., *Paul, Scripture and Ethics: A Study of 1 Cor 5–7,* AGJU 22 (Leiden: P. Brill, 1994).

Sandnes, K. O., *Paul — One of the Prophets?* WUNT 2:43 (Tübingen: Mohr, 1991).

South, J. T., *Disciplinary Practices in Pauline Texts* (New York: Mellen Press, 1992).

Stanley, C. D., *Paul and the Language of Scripture,* SNTSMS 74 (Cambridge: Cambridge University Press, 1992).

Stowers, S. K., "Paul on the Use and Abuse of Reason," in D. L. Balch, E. Ferguson, and

W. A. Meeks (eds.), *Greeks, Romans and Christians: Essays in Honour of A. J. Malherbe* (Minneapolis: Augsburg, 1990), 253-86.

Theissen, G., *Psychological Aspects of Pauline Theology* (Eng. trans., Edinburgh: T. & T. Clark, 1987).

————, *The Social Setting of Pauline Christianity: Essays on Corinth* (Eng. trans., Philadelphia: Fortress, 1982).

Vanhoye, A. (ed.), *L'Apôtre Paul. Personalité, style et conception du ministère,* BETL 73 (Louvain: Louvain University Press, 1986).

Welborn, L. L., *Politics and Rhetoric in the Corinthian Epistles* (Macon, Ga.: Mercer University Press, 1997), esp. 1-94.

Wilckens, U., "Das Kreuz Christi als die Tiefe der Weisheit Gottes," in L. de Lorenzi (ed.), *Paolo a Una Chiesa Divisa* (cited above), 43-81.

Winter, B. W., "Gallio's Ruling on the Legal Status of Earliest Christianity (Acts 18:14-15)," *TynBul* 50 (1999): 213-24.

————, *Philo and Paul among the Sophists,* SNTSMS 96 (Cambridge: Cambridge University Press, 1997).

————, *Seek the Welfare of the City* (Grand Rapids: Eerdmans and Carlisle: Paternoster, 1994).

Wire, A. G., *The Corinthian Women Prophets* (Minneapolis: Fortress, 1990).

Wiseman, J., "Corinth and Rome 1: 228 BC–AD 267," in *ANRW* 2:7:1 (1979): 438-548.

Witherington, Ben, III, *Conflict and Community in Corinth: A Socio-Rhetorical Commentary on 1 and 2 Corinthians* (Grand Rapids: Eerdmans and Carlisle: Paternoster, 1995).

————, *Women in the Earliest Churches,* SNTSMS 59 (Cambridge, Cambridge University Press, 1988, rpt. 1991).

Yeo, Khiok-khing, *Rhetorical Interaction in 1 Corinthians 8–10,* BibIntMon 9 (Leiden: Brill, 1995).

Zaidman, L. B., and P. S. Pantel, *Religion in the Ancient Greek City* (Cambridge: Cambridge University Press, 1992).

Zuntz, G., *The Text of the Epistles* (London: Oxford University Press, 1953).

Introduction

I. ROMAN CORINTH IN THE TIME OF PAUL: GEOGRAPHY, ARCHAEOLOGY, SOCIOECONOMIC STATUS, PROSPERITY, AND CULTURE OF PRAGMATIC PLURALISM

A. Geography, Commercial Prosperity, and Roman Foundation

The first feature about the ancient city of Corinth which strikes the modern visitor, especially from the height of Acrocorinth above the ancient site, is its distinctive geographical situation at the crossroads or intersection between east and west and between north and south.[1] In the ancient world the significance of the strategic position not least for commercial prosperity was noted by Pausanias (c. AD 170) and by Strabo (c. 7 BC, slightly revised AD 18, in the case of Corinth on the basis of a visit perhaps c. 29 BC).[2] Strabo writes: "Corinth is called 'wealthy' because of its commerce, since it is situated on the Isthmus and is master of two harbours, of which one leads straight to Asia, and the other to Italy; and it makes easy the exchange of merchandise from both countries."[3] The harbor of Cenchreae faces east across the Saronic Gulf to Asia and Ephesus; the harbor of Lechaeum faces west (or north-west) across the Corinthian Gulf to Italy and the west.[4] Cenchreae lies c. 5 to 8 kilometers east of the ancient city; Lechaeum, 2 kilometers to the north.

Virtually all modern classical and archaeological studies confirm the commercial importance of the *diolkos,* a paved roadway built across the isthmus originally in the sixth century BC at its narrowest point of less than six kilometers.[5] It was used for the transportation of cargo or even light ships,

---

1. On Acrocorinth (1884 feet or 574 meters) and the geography of Corinthia (the *territorium* of Corinth) see Donald Engels, *Roman Corinth: An Alternative Model for the Classical City* (Chicago and London: University of Chicago Press, 1990), 8-14; and J. B. Salmon, *Wealthy Corinth: A History of the City to 338 BC* (Oxford: Clarendon Press, 1984).

2. Pausanias, *Journey through Greece,* bk. 2; Strabo, *Geography* 8.6.

3. Strabo, *Geography* 8.6.20. See further J. Murphy-O'Connor, *St Paul's Corinth: Texts and Archaeology* (Wilmington: Glazier, 1983), 6-10, 51-54.

4. Of multiple sources, cf., e.g., Pausanias, *Description of Greece* 2.1.5-7; in modern literature James Wiseman, "Corinth and Rome I 228 BC–AD 267," in *ANRW* 2.7.1 (Berlin: de Gruyter, 1979), 439-47 (cf. 438-548); map on 440; Engels, *Roman Corinth,* 8-21.

5. Wiseman, *Corinth and Rome,* 441; Engels, *Roman Corinth,* 50-52.

1

and parts can be seen today. Strabo referred to the crossing of the isthmus as "a welcome alternative for merchants both from Italy and Asia to avoid the voyage around Malea, and land their cargoes here."[6] Strabo quotes the sailors' maxim "When you double Maleae, forget your home."[7] Engels observes that treacherous winds made the six-day alternative route around the Southern Cape of the Peloponnese exceedingly dangerous for ships of the time, especially in winter. It was there that Paul experienced the storm which blew his vessel eventually to Malta (Acts 27, en route from western Crete). Today, Engels reports, the winds of Kythira in December and January may exceed Beaufort force 6, which would have been hazardous for ancient sailing ships.[8] It is no surprise, then, that ancient sources bear witness to the huge amount of trade and traders found in Corinth and its two parts as "the common emporium of Europe and Asia" and as "the market . . . and festival of the Greeks."[9]

Although the north-south axis could not match the east-west axis in commercial importance, the vertical direction held strategic political and cultural importance as well as some commercial significance.[10] The region north of the narrow isthmus, Perachora, is dominated by the Geranian Range (up to 1,351 meters) dividing Corinth from Megara. The city became the capital of the senatorial province of Achaea, and by the second century AD it became the largest city in Greece. The central region of the Corinthia (ancient Corinth and its wider surroundings) is dominated by Acrocorinth (height 574 meters), which in early times served as its citadel.

A fundamental turning point in the history of Corinth came with the colonization of the city at the direction of Julius Caesar shortly before his death in March 44 BC. In the mid-second century BC relations between Rome on one side and Corinth and the Achaean league on the other had seriously deteriorated. Issues of "freedom" coupled with a financial crisis led the Achaeans to declare war on Sparta, Rome's ally. Eventually a decisive battle led to the annihilation of the Achaeans under the Roman general Lucius Mummius in 146 BC. While other Achaeans were to be freed, the inhabitants of Corinth, as their leader, were sold, and the city looted and virtually demolished. Around 79-77 BC Cicero visited the site, and "the sudden sight of the ruins of Corinth had more effect on me than the actual inhabitants."[11] On the other hand, Wiseman

6. Strabo, *Geography* 8.6.20
7. Ibid.
8. Engels, *Roman Corinth*, 51.
9. Aristeides, *For Poseidon* 23; cf. Dio Chrysostom 37.8; Apuleius, *Metamorphoses* 10.35. Dio Chrysostom (Favorinus) called Corinth "the prow and stern of Greece" (37.36).
10. Wiseman, *Corinth and Rome*, 445-46.
11. Cicero, *Tusculanae Disputationes* 3.53. Many laments can be found, e.g., Polystratus, *Anthologia Graeca* 7.297, "Lucius has smitten the great Achaean Acrocorinth, the Star of Hellas, and the twin shores of the Isthmus; one heap of stones covers the bones of those felled by the spear. . . ." On the history of events from 195 BC to 146 BC see Wiseman, *Corinth and Rome*, 458-62.

insists that "the destruction of Corinth was far less extensive than scholars have preferred to believe."[12]

In 44 BC Julius Caesar refounded the city mainly from three sources of the *Roman* populace: (1) freedmen, (2) his own veterans, and (3) urban trades persons and laborers. The geographical position of Corinth ensured that they would prosper. Caesar took care to provide a setting and resources that would ensure a loyal strategic center for the advance of future eastern campaigns, perhaps to Dacia or Parthia. The formal name of the Roman colony was Colonia Laus Julia Corinthiensis, that is, colony of Corinth in Honor of Julius.[13] As a Roman *colonia* (Gk. πολίτευμα) Corinth's government was organized on a tripartite basis of an assembly of citizen voters, a city council, and annual magistrates. This reflected in miniature Roman government of the earlier Republican era. Colonists had the right to own property and to initiate civil lawsuits (cf. 6:1-8). They were aware of an identity and cultural inheritance that differed from the diversity of cultures that surrounded them (cf. Phil 3:20). The local civil senate had wide powers which enabled them to fund and to promote public building, roads, and other facilities. The chief magistrates of the colony were the two *duoviri iure dicundo,* elected annually by the *comitia tributa.* They also served as chief justices for civil cases, although imperial Provincial governors had jurisdiction in criminal cases (see exegesis of 6:1-8). Donald Engels shows convincingly the importance of the raw materials of soil and clay for cultivation, pottery, and above all the water of the Peirene Springs (which can be seen today) with "an average flow rate of 18 cubic metres per hour, enough in itself to supply the needs of a large city."[14] A vast deposit of marl, he continues, provided "an inexhaustible supply of clay for the manufacture of pottery, roof-tiles, and terra-cotta objects. . . . [Further] a lightweight sandstone with which much of the classical city was built" gave rise to "numerous traces of ancient quarrying activity" in addition to "a hard, white, crystalline limestone . . . ideal for paving the Lechaeum Road during the Roman era." There is no need to provide a comprehensive list. We may note, however (with Engels and Wiseman), that there is abundant evidence that "this coastal plain [Corinthia] was among the most productive regions in Roman Greece."[15]

All of these factors underline three fundamental points for our understanding of the epistle: (1) *the city community and city culture of Corinth*

---

12. Wiseman, *Corinth and Rome,* 494. He cites the archaeological reports of R. L. Scranton.

13. Wolfgang Schrage, *Der erste Brief an die Korinther,* EKKNT 7:1-3 (3 vols. to date, Zürich: Benziger and Neukirchen-Vluyn: Neukirchener, 1991, 1995, 1999), 1:25-29, summarizes evidence from ancient sources. On the importance of the *Roman* character of Corinth, see D. W. J. Gill, "Corinth: A Roman Colony in Achaea," *BZ* 37 (1993): 259-64.

14. Engels, *Roman Corinth,* 10.

15. Ibid., 11; see also Wiseman, *Corinth and Rome,* 444: "The land to the West of Corinth was proverbially fertile . . . the extensively cultivated coastal plain. Corinthian territory extended to the Nemea River. . . . The Saronic coastline of the Corinthia, then, from Epidauria to Megaris was a sea-distance of 300 stades [53-28 kilometers]" (445). Cf. also B. von Freyberg, *Geologie des Isthmus von Korinth* (Erlangen: Erlanger Geologische Abhandlungen, 1973).

were formed after a Roman model, not a Greek one, even if many immigrants came from Achaea, Macedonia, and the East to constitute an equally cosmopolitan superstructure; (2) *the city community and the city culture felt themselves to be prosperous and self-sufficient,* even if there were many "have nots" who were socially vulnerable or dependent on others; (3) *the core community and core tradition of the city culture were those of trade, business, and entrepreneurial pragmatism in the pursuit of success,* even if some paid a heavy price for business failures or for the lack of the right contacts or the right opportunities.

Donald Engels performs a useful service to scholarship by disengaging Roman Corinth from the versions of "primitivism" and "consumerism" that many associate with Max Weber's social theories. According to these theories, the city made its living from rents and taxes collected from the agricultural peasants of the Corinthia's rural economy. In this (inapplicable) sense the city was "consumerist." Further, a "primitivism" disengaged ancient classical cities from the kind of business market economies which characterize modern global capitalism. Allegedly "the classical world was innocent of many market values and institutions."[16] Engels shows convincingly that on the contrary "wealthy Corinth" was based on *an economy of market exchange of goods and services* in the traditions of keen business practices, including competition and the pursuit of pragmatic success.

"Goods and services" found a ready market in "travelers, traders and tourists" as well as other businesspersons.[17] "Corinth provided a huge market for agricultural supplies whose size had far outstripped the ability of its hinterland (territorium) to supply. . . . A market economy, therefore, influences to a large extent the price of land, the types of crops produced, the type of settlement pattern."[18] Even if we assume a high yield of 18 bushels per acre (16 hectoliters per hectare) of barley, 80 square miles (207 sq. km.) of cultivatable land would scarcely support 17,600 people per day (at about 2,600 calories).[19] As Engels concedes, however, given that agricultural workers needed to support themselves, the supply from the Corinthia *territorium* could never support more than around 10,800 from within the city.[20] Thus, with the pressures of market forces all that Bruce Winter and others have claimed about the dangers of famine for the poor is well corroborated.[21]

After 44 BC the new colonists from Rome (Caesar's veterans, manumitted slaves, and artisan or laboring classes) were soon joined by immigrants from

---

16. Engels, *Roman Corinth,* 1; cf. 1-7, 22-65, and throughout.
17. Ibid., 2.
18. Ibid., 25.
19. Ibid., 27.
20. Ibid., 28-33.
21. B. W. Winter, "Secular and Christian Responses to Corinthian Famines," *TynBul* 40 (1989): 88-106. See also B. W. Winter, *Seek the Welfare of the City: Christians as Benefactors and Citizens* (Grand Rapids: Eerdmans and Carlisle: Paternoster, 1994), 53-57.

the East, "including Jews and Syrians."[22] Archaeology has uncovered evidence of the prosperity and importance of the city in the period from Augustus onward through almost 1,200 inscriptions from the Roman period out of a total calculated by J. H. Kent (in 1950) to have reached 1,553 from all ancient periods. Many are "official documents," i.e., dedications to deities or emperors, records of gifts of buildings, monuments or other benefactions, gravestones, statues, or honors.[23] Further, these inscriptions in the Pauline era witness to the *Roman* character of much of the civic and higher-society life at Corinth. Of inscriptions from the period to be dated from Augustus to Nero, Greek inscriptions amount to only three, while inscriptions in Latin amount to 73.[24] The (Pauline) period of Claudius yields zero in Greek and 27 (19 certain) in Latin, while that of Nero (later Paul) yields one Greek and eleven Latin. Prior to Hadrian, 104 texts are in Latin and only four in Greek, but Greek again became common during Hadrian's reign (AD 117-138; 15 in Greek; 10 in Latin).

Evidence for the prominence of Roman, rather than Greek, patterns of culture in the most respected mores of the city becomes important for an understanding of a number of specific details of our epistle. One clear example concerns the wearing of hoods by women in public, especially in public worship, as well as the issue of head covering (just possibly an issue about hair) for men (1 Cor 11:2-16). Aline Rousselle and Dale Martin have shown that for a married woman in *Roman* society to appear in public without a hood sent out signals of sexual availability or at very least a lack of concern for respectability.[25] Similarly, in discussing 11:17-34 Murphy-O'Connor, Wiseman, Winter, Theissen, and others have shown how Roman dining customs, coupled with the architecture of the triclinium and the atrium in a Roman villa and conventions of Roman patronage, set the stage for meals among Christians, which "do more harm than good" (11:17).[26] Plutarch (c. AD 50-120) notes the role played by patronage in the Roman socioeconomic system as a key to acceptance, to fortune,

22. Wiseman, *Corinth and Rome,* 497.

23. John H. Kent, *Corinth: Results of Excavations Conducted by the American School of Classical Studies at Athens,* VIII:iii: *The Inscriptions 1926-1950* (Princeton, N.J.: American School of Classical Studies at Athens, 1966), 17-20. The number 1,553 includes collections by B. D. Meritt, *Greek Inscriptions 1896-1927* (*Corinth,* VIII:i; Cambridge, Mass.: Harvard University Press, 1931), and by A. R. West, *Latin Inscriptions 1896-1927* (*Corinth,* VIII:ii; Cambridge, Mass.: Harvard University Press, 1931).

24. Kent, *Corinth,* VIII:iii: *The Inscriptions,* 18-19.

25. A. Rousselle, "Body Politics in Ancient Rome," in G. Duby and M. Perot (eds.) *A History of Women in the West, I: From Ancient Goddesses to Christian Saints* (Cambridge, Mass.: Harvard University Press, 1992), 296-337; D. B. Martin, *The Corinthian Body* (New Haven: Yale University Press, 1995), 229-49; see below on 11:2-16.

26. Murphy-O'Connor, *St Paul's Corinth,* 154-55; Wiseman, *Corinth and Rome,* 528; B. W. Winter, "The Lord's Supper at Corinth: An Alternative Reconstruction," *RTR* 37 (1978): 73-82; W. J. Slater (ed.), *Dining in a Classical Context* (Ann Arbor: University of Michigan Press, 1991), esp. A. Booth, "The Age for Reclining . . .," 105-20; and G. Theissen, "Social Integration and Sacramental Activity," in *The Social Setting of Pauline Christianity: Essays on Corinth* (Eng. trans., Philadelphia: Fortress, 1982), 145-74.

and perhaps even to fame, and in modern research J. K. Chow, among many others, has collected evidence of the multiform implications of this for an understanding of Corinth and of our epistle.[27]

B. Archaeological Evidence of Extensive Trade and Cosmopolitan Pluralism

As with any other major city in Greece, however, the persistence of Greek influences in Graeco-Roman religion and cults finds confirmation in the coinage of the times as well as in the temples and religious sites identified through archaeological research. Greek temples were rededicated to the same Greek deities in the Roman period, notably at Corinth, to Poseidon, Aphrodite, Apollo, Demeter, Kore, and Asclepios.[28] Yet the dedications are very often inscribed through the medium of Latin rather than Greek in first-century inscriptions. Moreover, many (often on costly marble) relate to the Roman imperial cult or to abstractions linked with Roman rule (e.g., Victoria, Concordia, the Genius of the Roman Julian colony). "Fully twenty-five of the Latin dedications are to uniquely Roman gods or abstractions."[29]

Coinage provides abundant examples of the cosmopolitan character of Roman Corinth and the widespread extent of the trade and commerce which ensured its prosperity as a business center. Successive volumes of *Hesperia,* the official journal of the American School of Classical Studies at Athens, catalogue and evaluate excavations from 1930 to 1935 (Edwards), from 1941 (Harris), from 1970 to 1980 (Williams and Fisher), and from 1978 to 1990 (Williams and Zervos).[30] Thus, among coins issued by city mints, trade with the Peloponnese is evidenced by 81 coins from Argos and 45 from other Peloponnesian communities; 6 coins come from Megara; 30 come from mints in the Aegean, Asia Minor, and Syria. North-south trade from Macedonia and Egypt is also evidenced but in fewer numbers.

27. Plutarch, *Moralia* 805E, F; John K. Chow, *Patronage and Power: A Study of Social Networks in Corinth,* JSNTSS 75 (Sheffield: Sheffield Academic Press, 1992), throughout.

28. Cf. Engels, *Roman Corinth,* 93-101.

29. Ibid., 102; cf. 101.

30. K. M. Edwards, "Report on the Coins Found in the Excavations at Corinth during the Years 1930-1935," *Hesperia* 6 (1937): 241-56; J. Harris, "Coins Found at Corinth," *Hesperia* 10 (1941): 143-62; C. K. Williams and J. E. Fisher, "Corinth 1970: Forum Area," *Hesperia* 40 (1971): 45-46; *Hesperia* 41 (1972): 143-84; *Hesperia* 42 (1973): 1-44; (with J. MacIntosh), *Hesperia* 43 (1974): 1-76; C. K. Williams and J. E. Fisher, "Corinth 1974: Forum Southwest," *Hesperia* 44 (1975): 1-50; J. E. Fisher, "Coins: Corinth Excavations 1976," *Hesperia* 49 (1980): 1-29; C. K. Williams and O. H. Zervos, "Coins Excavated at Corinth," *Hesperia* 51 (1982): 115-63; *Hesperia* 55 (1986): 129-83; O. H. Zervos, *Hesperia* 55 (1986): 183-205; C. K. Williams and O. H. Zervos, "Excavations at Corinth, 1988: East of the Theater," *Hesperia* 58 (1989): 1-50; C. K. Williams and O. H. Zervos, "Excavations at Corinth, 1989: The Temenos of Temple E," *Hesperia* 59 (1990): 325-56. (*Hesperia* 60, 1991, celebrates the life and work of Charles K. Williams.)

The Corinth Archaeological Museum, which can be visited today, was built in 1931-32 by the American School of Classical studies and presented to the Greek state in 1934. Among the most striking exhibits are the large number of terra-cotta models of heads, hands, feet, arms, eyes, ears, and every part of the body which were excavated from the Asclepion, the temple of Asclepios god of healing, in prayer or in thanks for restoration of health or effective use of the part of the body concerned. Whether or note this sheds light on Paul's ready use of imagery concerning limbs or parts of the body (12:12-31; see below), the archaeological excavations on site of the Asclepion itself (dating from fourth century BC but restored after earlier damage by the colonists of 44 BC) shed a flood of light on issues about "dining" in the dining rooms which belonged to the temple complex. The sanctuary included a shrine, an *abaton* or sleeping quarters for those who were ill seeking the blessing and guidance of Asclepios, a courtyard with covered colonnades, and "behind the eastern colonnade were three dining rooms, each with 11 couches . . . and reservoirs."[31] The problem of eating meat associated with the "false gods" or "idols" of pagan temples when many non-Christian friends perceived such events as special occasions in normal social life (1 Cor 8:1–11:1) not only springs to life but also emerges as an issue of multidimensional ethical, cultural, and pastoral sensitivity.

The Corinth Museum also contains at the time of writing the mosaic which had formed the decorated floor of the triclinium (dining room) of the villa at Anaploga, a suburban site several hundred yards to the west of the formally bounded site of ancient Corinth, which is attributed broadly to the time of Paul (c. 50-75).[32] This not only attests the relative prosperity and sophistication of higher-class life at Corinth, but most especially provides data about the floor space available for meetings of Christians, especially for those who reclined on couches for "the Lord's Supper" (11:17-34). The triclinium measures 5.5 by 7.5 meters, while the atrium (hallway) measures 5 by 6 meters. Murphy-O'Connor calculates that the atrium might have held between 30 and 40 persons, with fewer in the triclinium where the couches occupied space.[33]

On 11:17-34 (see below) we argue that these facts probably provide an explanatory background for the tragic abuse of the Lord's Supper at Corinth whereby the meal in remembrance of Christ's death had become an occasion for dividing the Christian community into "first-class diners" (i.e., those who reclined in the triclinium and enjoyed the best food and quality of wine) and "second-class hangers-on" (who found room only in the atrium, where they were offered the leftovers and perhaps inferior wine). At all events, if this fol-

---

31. Wiseman, *Corinth and Rome,* 488; Wiseman provides a plan (fig. 9) of the Asclepion; see also J. Murphy-O'Connor, St Paul's Corinth, "Temple Banquets and the Body," 161-67, also with a plan (fig. 9; 163).

32. The earliest report was S. G. Miller, "A Mosaic Floor from a Roman Villa at Anaploga," *Hesperia* 41 (1972): 332-54; cf. more recently Wiseman, *Corinth and Rome,* 528, and Murphy-O'Connor, *St Paul's Corinth,* 153-61.

33. Murphy-O'Connor, *St Paul's Corinth,* 156.

lowed the regular pattern of Roman dining customs, such social distinctions on the basis of status and patronage might be expected. Pliny the Younger sets forth in detail a categorization of "the best dishes" for the host and his close friends; "cheap scraps of food" for the least esteemed; and "wine . . . divided into three categories. . . ."[34] Recently J. J. Meggitt has challenged the plausibility of such a reconstruction, but for the present it remains the majority view.[35]

The visitor to the site of ancient Corinth today will find two inscriptions, among others, of outstanding interest as windows on the socioeconomic status of some in Paul's time. A structure probably *in situ* in the ancient agora bears not one but two inscriptions concerning Babbius (one on the pedestal; the other on what was once the band above the columns of the structure) declaring: "Gnaeus Babbius Philinus, aedile and pontifex, had this monument erected at his own expense, and he approved it in his official capacity of duovir."[36] The Babbius monument is regarded on all sides today as a prime example of both benefaction and self-promotion. Such a monument and inscriptions illustrate "the ideas of self-promotion, publicity and recommendations written on stone."[37] The monument consisted of a circle of Corinthian columns set on a square pedestal, with a conical roof which was probably of pine. Babbius is likely to have risen from the ranks of nouveau-riche freedman to find himself with sufficient financial resources and appropriate social contacts entailing reciprocal obligations to have become a magistrate and finally one of the "chief magistrates," the *duoviri iure dicundo*.[38] These "chief justices" were "the executive officers of the city council."[39] Wiseman confirms that "the office of duovir at Corinth was open to freedmen."[40] This raises another side of the issue, however. Murphy-O'Connor and others agree that his direction to inscribe his name and benefaction twice and to confirm his own record of benefaction as duovir also revealed a deep sense of insecurity. He left nothing to chance: his name could not be ignored; nor could a subsequent chief magistrate refuse to authorize what he had confirmed in his dual capacity as aedile-donor and duovir-authorizer. Murphy-O'Connor observes, "The sense of insecurity of the successful freedman became a favourite topic in literature."[41]

The Babbius monument is located on the west side of the agora, north of

---

34. Pliny, *Letters* 2.6; Seneca, *Epistles* 95.24; Plutarch, *Quaestiones Romanae* 33; Suetonius, *Augustus* 64.3 and *Claudius* 43; cf. Winter, "The Lord's Supper at Corinth," *RTR* 37:73-82; and Theissen, *The Social Setting of Pauline Christianity,* 145-74.

35. J. J. Meggitt, *Paul, Poverty, and Survival* (Edinburgh: T. & T. Clark, 1998), 106-7, 118-22, and 189-93. Meggitt's view deserves respect.

36. Reconstructed with virtual certainty by J. H. Kent, *Corinth* VIII:iii, *The Inscriptions 1926-1950,* 73 (no. 155 and plate 14); 102 (no. 241, plate 19); see also Murphy-O'Connor, *St Paul's Corinth,* 171; and Wiseman, *Corinth and Rome,* 518.

37. Murphy-O'Connor, *St Paul's Corinth,* 171.

38. Wiseman, *Corinth and Rome,* 498.

39. Ibid.

40. Ibid.

41. Murphy-O'Connor, *St Paul: A Critical Life,* 270.

the temple of Apollo and the fountain, and probably derives from the period of Tiberius. To the north of the formal boundaries of the ancient site as it is currently defined lies a second inscription to fascinate modern visitors. An area paved with limestone from Acrocorinth contains the remains of an inscription once filled with bronze, *Erastus pro aedilit[at]e s[ua] p[ecunia] stravit:* "Erastus in return for his adileship laid [the pavement] at his own expense."[42] Kent records that this was found *in situ* east of the theater in April 1929. In 1966 Kent observed that "the original suggestion that Erastus is to be identified with the Corinthian Erastus of the NT (Rom 16:23) still seems sound."[43] Kent adds that "like his contemporary Cn Babbius Philinus, Erastus was probably a Corinthian freedman who had acquired considerable wealth in commercial activities."[44] In 1999 Collins still describes the identification of the Erastus whose greetings extend to Rome (Rom 16:23) with the city manager of the inscription as "a good possibility," while Merklein (1992) has little doubt; Winter (1994) builds up a very careful and convincing case covering several stages of argument; and Murphy-O'Connor (1997) appears to entertain no doubt.[45] One of the most detailed discussions, alongside that of Bruce Winter, is provided by Andrew Clarke (1993), who considers the argument of A. G. Roos (as Kent does) that the duovir, aedile, and quaestor were normally compelled to pledge an oath of loyalty *"per Jovem et divos imperatores et genium principis deosque Penates"* on taking office.[46] Yet he also notes Winter's argument concerning encouragement to Christian believers to be involved in city affairs (Rom 13:3; 1 Pet 2:14). Prior to his work of 1994, Winter had explicitly argued for the role of Christians as public benefactors to the secular city.[47] Horrell (1996) concludes that the identification is "highly likely," and would become almost a certainty if we accept Winter's latest proposal (1999) that the legal implications of Gallio's ruling in Acts 18 in effect places Christianity alongside Judaism as a *religio licita* with certain exemptions from imperial religious expectations. (On Winter's view of the Gallio ruling, see further below.)[48]

---

42. Kent, *Corinth* VIII:iii, *The Inscriptions,* 99 (no. 232, plate 21).

43. Ibid. With H. J. Cadbury, Kent argues that (1) the date is from almost the middle of the first century AD; (2) the name Erastus is uncommon, and not otherwise found at Corinth; (3) "Paul's word οἰκονόμος . . . with reasonable accuracy the function of a Corinthian aedile" (99-100; cf. 27).

44. Kent, *Corinth* VIII:iii, 100.

45. R. F. Collins, *First Corinthians,* SacPag 7 (Collegeville, Minn.: Glazier/Liturgical Press, 1999), 168; H. Merklein, *Der erste Brief an die Korinther Kap 1–4,* 38-39; Winter, *Seek the Welfare of the City,* 180-97; Murphy-O'Connor, *Paul: A Critical Life,* 268-70. Cf. also Theissen, *The Social Setting of Pauline Christianity,* 75-83 and 94; and Schrage, *Der erste Brief an die Korinther* 1:31-32, including n. 40.

46. A. D. Clarke, *Secular and Christian Leadership in Corinth: A Socio-Historical Study of 1 Cor 1–6,* AGJU 18 (Leiden and New York: Brill, 1993), 53; cf. 46-56. See further D. W. J. Gill, "Erastus the Aedile," *TynBul* 40 (1989): 146-51.

47. B. W. Winter, "The Public Honouring of Christian Benefactors: Rom 13:3-4 and 1 Pet 2:14-15," *JSNT* 34 (1988): 87-103.

48. D. G. Horrell, *The Social Ethos of the Corinthian Correspondence* (Edinburgh: T. & T.

The commercial and business prosperity of the city, as well as its competitiveness, pragmatism, and pluralism, brings us nearer to the heart of similarities with, and differences from, some twenty-first century contexts of gospel proclamation. We have already considered and accepted the compelling arguments of Donald Engels that the prosperity of Corinth rested not upon rents, taxes, and consumer items from its own territorium of Corinthia but upon its effectiveness as a service economy to tradespeople, merchants, travelers, and those seeking the resources of a well-equipped business center. Services included religious, educational, cultural, and judicial provisions, but also the availability of imports from a wide range of outlets, East and West.[49] Engels notes that the entire first [ground] floor of the 162-meter-long South Stoa was converted to administrative functions, together with three large halls or basilicas.[50] Murphy-O'Connor similarly observes that the provincial towns of Asia and Macedonia and even Athens itself were by comparison "sleepy oases of leisure. . . . Thus far he [Paul] had encountered nothing like it. . . . Corinth had more business than it could comfortably handle. The immense volume of trade was augmented by huge numbers of travellers. Profit came easily to those prepared to work hard, and cut-throat competition ensured that only the committed survived."[51]

Corinth's plentiful water supply permitted large bathing facilities as well as public latrines and other facilities, the remains of which can still be observed in the area of the Peirene Fountain today. The Isthmian Games were one of the three or perhaps four great pan-Hellenic festivals, were celebrated biennially, and provided considerable income for the city. The remains of the Games held in AD 49 shortly before Paul's arrival in Corinth (if he arrived in spring of AD 50; see below) and the huge crowds which came to Corinth during the Games, which took place while Paul was ministering in Corinth (AD 51), would have been a significant part of the world of the Corinth that Paul knew (see under 9:24-27, below).[52] Fascinating archaeological remains of the Games, including a relatively sophisticated scheme for starting runners on a curved track (*balbides*), can be seen at modern Isthmia in the area near the Museum representing the ancient site of the sanctuary of Poseidon. For a period their management was transferred to Sikyon, but Corinth recovered the management by

---

Clark, 1996), 97; see esp. B. W. Winter, "Gallio's Ruling on the Legal Status of Earliest Christianity (Acts 18:14-15)," *TynBul* 50 (1999), 213-24.

49. Engels, *Roman Corinth,* 43-65.

50. Engels, *Roman Corinth,* 44.

51. Murphy-O'Connor, *Paul,* 258. On Athens, see below, including Engels, *Roman Corinth,* 113-14, and Murphy-O'Connor, *Paul,* 108.

52. Murphy-O'Connor, *St Paul's Corinth,* 14-17 and 116-19; *Paul,* 258-59; Engels, *Roman Corinth,* 45-46, 51-52; and esp. O. Broneer, "The Apostle Paul and the Isthmian Games," *BA* 25 (1962): 2-31; O. Broneer, "The Isthmian Victory Crown," *AJA* 66 (1962): 259-83; and O. Broneer, *Isthmia,* 2: *Topography and Architecture* (Princeton: American School of Classical Studies at Athens, 1973). Cf. also O. Broneer, *Isthmia,* 1: *The Temple of Poseidon* (Princeton: American School of Classical Studies at Athens, 1971).

around AD 2.[53] From the period of Tiberius (before AD 37) the program of events expanded as time went on, including events in honor of the emperors (every four years), a poetry competition, musical competitions in trumpets, flutes, and lyres, and a range of athletic events and chariot races. In the *apobatikon* one rider would ride several horses, leaping from one to another. Kent observes that athletic contests for women were "a striking innovation in the Isthmian festival under the Empire."[54] The president *(agonothetes)* of the Games was elected by the City Council of Corinth.[55] Broneer, Murphy-O'Connor, and Engels call attention to the substantial revenue that accrued to Corinthian tradespeople and entrepreneurs from the huge crowds who stayed in the city and area during the Games every alternate spring.[56] Engels concludes: "The city of Corinth was a major tourist attraction in itself, and visitors regarded a stay there as a participation in a joyous, continual celebration."[57] Corinthian coins were used as promotional devices to advertise the games, and this may partly explain the preponderance of coins depicting Poseidon and his Isthmian sanctuary and coins depicting Aphrodite to hint at other attractions available in the city.[58]

The sheer volume of business and trade handled at Corinth becomes less surprising when we recall that a merchant would require goods and services not only for himself but often for those who had served as crew for his ship and other attendants. Rooms would be rented, taverns frequented, and the services of shops, entertainers, lawyers, laborers, dockers, warehousemen, leather workers, tentmakers, wagon repairers, pottery manufacturers, bankers, and presumably prostitutes would be in high demand. Those at Corinth who had begun to build a business empire or quasi-monopoly could demand tolls and special service fees. Ships would be repaired and refitted. Financial profit could be made at every level: by business profiteers who had charge of large commercial networks; by those who were moving rapidly up the ladder; by reliable and competent people who proved their worth as assistants or middle managers; by foremen, by salespersons, by craftsmen and craftswomen; indeed, by all who had skills or bodily health and muscle to offer in a competitive market. Engels comments, "The city offered migrants . . . opportunities to improve their social and economic status through employment in the bustling service economy of the city. The city's relatively high

53. See Kent, *Corinth* VIII:iii, *The Inscriptions 1926-1950*, 28-30; and B. D. Merritt, *Corinth* VIII:i, *Greek Inscriptions 1896-1927* (Cambridge, Mass.: Harvard University Press, 1931), e.g., nos. 14-16, and commentary.

54. Kent, *Corinth*, VIII:iii, 29.

55. Kent, *Corinth*, VIII:iii, 30, esp. n. 30. In AD 51 this was Lucius Rutilius (A. B. West, *Corinth VIII:ii, Latin Inscriptions 1896-1927* [Cambridge, Mass.: Harvard University Press, 1931], no. 82).

56. Broneer, "The Apostle Paul and the Isthmian Games," 2-31; see also Broneer's other works cited in n. 52 above; Engels, *Roman Corinth*, 52-53; see also under 9:24, below.

57. Engels, *Roman Corinth*, 51; cf. Aristeides, *Poseidon* 23.

58. Engels, *Roman Corinth*, 52.

death rates caused by the spread of infectious diseases would always ensure that positions would be available to newcomers. . . ."[59]

C. Status Inconsistency, Self-Promotion, Recognition, and a Postmodern Ethos

This feature led to the possibility of a rapid rise in socioeconomic status for many. Nevertheless it also led to what is often termed "status inconsistency." Wayne Meeks has very helpfully drawn upon a growing awareness in sociology that in a society preoccupied with concern for public status, honor, and self-promotion, it is a mistake to construe status in terms of any "single thing": "Most sociologists have come to see social stratification as a multidimensional phenomenon; to describe the social level of an individual or a group, one must attempt to measure their rank along *each* of the relevant dimensions" (Meeks's italics).[60] Thus "power (defined as the capacity for achieving goals in social systems)" may be *one* such dimension; "occupational prestige, income or wealth, education and knowledge, religious and moral purity, family and ethnic-group position, and local-community status (evaluation within some subgroup, independent of the larger society . . .)" provide other dimensions of variable status indicators.[61] Moreover, not all dimensions carry the same weight: "The weight of each dimension depends upon *who is doing the weighing*" (my italics).[62] This feature dramatically characterized the people of Corinth. Meeks concludes that this certainly applies to many of the Pauline circle: "We may venture the generalization that the most active and prominent members of Paul's circle (including Paul himself), are people of high *status inconsistency*" (my italics).[63] Meeks entitles his subsection on this theme "Mixed Strata, Ambiguous Status."[64]

Not surprisingly Meeks acknowledges the contribution of Gerd Theissen in underlining the phenomenon of social stratification at Corinth and its probable impact on the church as evidenced in 1 Corinthians.[65] More recently Witherington has provided an excellent account of these variations and incon-

59. Ibid., 49. See further Ben Witherington III, *Conflict and Community in Corinth: A Socio-Rhetorical Commentary on 1 and 2 Corinthians* (Grand Rapids: Eerdmans and Carlisle: Paternoster, 1995), 5-19 and 50-53.

60. Wayne A. Meeks, *The First Urban Christians: The Social World of the Apostle Paul* (New Haven: Yale University Press, 1983), 54.

61. Ibid.

62. Ibid.

63. Ibid., 73.

64. Ibid., 72.

65. Ibid., 68-70; and Theissen, *The Social Setting of Pauline Christianity,* esp. 69-120 and 145-74. Theissen takes as his point of departure the divergent assessments of the social status of the Corinthian church as represented, e.g., by A. Deissmann (low social status) and E. A. Judge (not socially depressed, some even pretentious). See *Social Setting,* 69.

sistencies in social status at Corinth, which included those who became Christian converts. He writes, "In Paul's time many in Corinth were already suffering from a self-made-person-escapes-humble-origins syndrome."[66] The phenomenon of boasting and self-promotion can be perceived not only in such examples as the double inscription of the Babbius monument (see above) but in a cultural mind-set also reflected in 2 Corinthians on the part of Paul's opponents at Corinth.[67] Paul's "self-humiliation, his assumption of a servant role" was directly at variance with the expected and accepted values of Corinthian city culture.[68] "In a city where social climbing was a major preoccupation, Paul's deliberate stepping down in apparent status would have been seen by many as disturbing, disgusting, and even provocative."[69] This comes to a head partly in definitions of "apostle" (see below on 1:1 and 9:1) but more especially in Paul's "foregoing his right" to receive maintenance (and hence patronage and reciprocal obligations) as a genuine professional in the sphere of religion and rhetoric (see below on 9:1-23).[70] Witherington concludes: "Corinth was a city where public boasting and self-promotion had become an art form. The Corinthian people thus lived with an *honor-shame* cultural orientation, where *public recognition was often more important than facts. . . .* In such a culture a person's sense of worth is based on *recognition by others* of one's accomplishments, hence the self-promoting public inscriptions (my italics).[71]

It is not entirely clear to me that as yet the implications of such an *honor-shame culture* for *epistemology and for social construction* have been sufficiently appreciated. Witherington is right to draw a contrast between (a) *recognition, perception, and interpretation* by a target following, and (b) *states of affairs, actual achievements, and the claims of truth.* Rhetoricians were employed, like some in the media or public relations today, to present a spin which shaped popular or public *perceptions* of what was *believed to be* the case. A number of New Testament scholars and social historians have provided the raw material on the basis of which a judgment may be reached. Those include, e.g., J. H. Neyrey, H. Moxnes, B. J. Malina, D. Gilmore, and M. Herzfield.[72] Here issues of social world, rhetoric, and a culture which effectively

---

66. Witherington, *Conflict and Community in Corinth,* 20.

67. Cf. T. B. Savage, *Power through Weakness: Paul's Understanding of the Christian Ministry in 2 Corinthians,* SNTSMS 86 (Cambridge: Cambridge University Press, 1996), 54-99; also Clarke, *Secular and Christian Leadership in Corinth,* 95-99.

68. Witherington, *Conflict and Community in Corinth,* 21.

69. Ibid.

70. Among other literature cited below, see Peter Marshall, *Enmity in Corinth: Social Conventions in Paul's Relations with the Corinthians,* WUNT 2:23 (Tübingen: Mohr, 1987), esp. 278-404.

71. Witherington, *Conflict and Community in Corinth,* 8.

72. J. H. Neyrey, "Honor and Shame in Luke-Acts: Pivotal Values in the Mediterranean World," in J. H. Neyrey (ed.), *The Social World of Luke-Acts: Models for Interpretation* (Peabody, Mass.: Hendrickson, 1991); J. H. Neyrey, *Paul in Other Words: A Cultural Reading of His Letters* (Louisville: Westminster-Knox, 1990); M. Herzfield, "Honor and Shame: Problems in the Compar-

embodies what we nowadays come to perceive as the "virtual reality" of the "soft" city of postmodernity (as against the "hard" city of sheer socioeconomic facts) overlap and merge to form a more complex and subtle counterpart to certain phenomena in our own time than may have been appreciated. The sense in which such social constructivism, which may owe more to the rhetoric of persuasion than to brute facts, may be regarded as a "soft" city of postmodern mood is well worked out by David Harvey.[73]

Witherington's comparison between "perceptions," "recognition," and "the facts" speaks volumes: *Corinthian culture has much in common with the social constructivism, competitive pragmatism, and radical pluralism which characterizes so-called postmodernity as a popular mood,* whether or not in strictly chronological terms it precedes, rather than follows, Western "modernity."[74] Indeed, as Stephen Pogoloff convincingly suggests, while the concern for *facts, truth, and rationality* remains central to the more "classical" Roman attitudes of Cicero and Quintilian, the reductive and contrived "instrumental" rationality and rhetoric *which looks not for truth but for applause and success* characterizes more readily the kind of competitive rhetoric which was most highly prized at Corinth.[75]

For Cicero and his later follower Quintilian (AD 40-95), rhetoric belonged to the area of liberal education, which trained the mind and searched for truth.[76] It concerned the expression of rational thought in communicative action. By contrast, Pogoloff associates the pragmatic rhetoric of nonclassical provincial Corinth with a parallel move today "in contrast to modernist epistemologies . . . to anti-foundational linguistic hermeneutics."[77] Pogoloff cites Stanley Fish's notion that in "anti-foundationalism" supposed truth-claims are inextricably

ative Analysis of Moral Systems," *Man* 15 (1980): 339-51; Cf. further H. Moxnes, "Honor, Shame, and the Outside World in Paul's Letter to the Romans," in J. Neusner et al. (eds.), *The Social World of Formative Christianity and Judaism* (Philadelphia: Fortress, 1988), 207-18; D. Gilmore (ed.), *Honor and Shame and the Unity of the Mediterranean* (Washington: American Anthropological Society, 1985); and less directly B. Malina, *Christian Origins and Cultural Anthropology* (Atlanta: Knox, 1986); J. G. Peristiany (ed.), *Honour and Shame: The Values of Mediterranean Society* (Chicago: University of Chicago Press, 1966); and *Semeia* 68: *Honor and Shame in the World of the Bible* (Atlanta: Scholars Press, 1996 [also dated 1994]), esp. 139-61.

73. David Harvey, *The Condition of Postmodernity* (Oxford: Blackwell, 1989 [1st ed. 1980]), 3-120. On the "soft city" that is "plastic by nature," "the soft city of illusion . . . aspiration" as against "the hard city one can locate in maps and statistics," see esp. 5-15. As a geographer Harvey underlines "fragmentation, indeterminacy . . . pragmatism . . . signals" (9).

74. To be sure, in some ways it is anachronistic to apply "postmodern" to a culture which has not experienced the Western rationalism of the Enlightenment. This issue was elaborated when I lectured in Singapore (November 1999) on "Postmodernity and the Crisis of Truth." However, participants from Indonesia and Malaysia recognized the "postmodern *mood* or *ethos*" as relevant to all cultures that experience it.

75. Stephen M. Pogoloff, *Logos and Sophia: The Rhetorical Situation of 1 Corinthians,* SBLDS 134 (Atlanta: Scholars Press, 1992), 7-196 and throughout.

76. Ibid., 37-69.

77. Ibid., 27.

tied to social construction; to "functions of the local . . . the contingent, the vari-able, the rhetorical . . . the argument which has been made . . . in philosophy by Richard Rorty. . . ."[78] Pogoloff agrees with Fish that "what is at stake . . . is a difference of world views" but perceives Paul as closer to Cicero than he is to Corinthian culture.[79]

The pragmatic criterion of becoming a winner in the marketplace, some-times with a sacrifice of personal integrity, made its impact on Corinthian rhet-oric. "Declamation increasingly became the major opportunity for oratorical displays. . . . In the classroom the competition might be over theory. But in dec-lamations . . . the contrast was . . . between rival performers. The drive for adu-lation, we learn from Seneca the Elder, often overcame the more basic goals of rhetoric."[80] Seneca observes that too many times the aim was "to win approval for yourself rather than for the case."[81] Quintilian laments that rhetoricians, like athletes or singers, were "greeted with a storm of ready-made applause . . . shouts of unseemly enthusiasm. . . . The result is vanity and empty self-sufficiency . . . intoxicated by the wild enthusiasm of their fellow-pupils."[82] The casualty is truth; the focus is "the speaker," as in the case of the twenty-first century chat-show host or participant in the mass media. It is of little surprise that party groups following their chosen leaders in the form of personality cults spring up (cf. 1:10-12, below). Pogoloff demonstrates the issues well in his chapters "Rhetoric and Status" and "Rhetoric and Divisions," while Clarke speaks of "personality-centred politics."[83]

Bruce Winter offers some broadly parallel comments in his work on the Sophists in relation to Philo and to Paul. The first-century sophistic movement, he observes, flourished at Corinth especially in terms of securing a public fol-lowing and attracting students to their schools.[84] "Winning admiration" was certainly part of what characterized their work. Although Winter distances him-self from Pogoloff's view that the Sophist movement at Corinth postdated Paul, nevertheless similarities emerge between these two works in their distancing of Paul from instrumental or pragmatic rhetoric alone, in contrast to the claims of truth embodied in the kerygma through the Spirit.

From yet another angle comes further confirmation of this contrast. John Moores argues that "Paul's use of argument can roughly be said to take two forms: they are (1) appeals to scripture; (2) appeals to reason, even though the

---

78. Ibid., 28, citing Stanley Fish, *Doing What Comes Naturally: Change, Rhetoric and the Practice of Theory in Literary and Legal Studies* (Durham: Duke University Press, 1989), 344-45.

79. Fish, *Doing What Comes Naturally,* 483; Pogoloff, *Logos and Sophia,* 30.

80. Pogoloff, *Logos and Sophia,* 175.

81. Seneca (c. 55 BC–AD 40), *Declamations: Controversiae* 9.1.

82. Quintilian, *Institutio Oratoria* 2.2.9-12.

83. Pogoloff, *Logos and Sophia,* respectively 129-72 and 173-96; Clarke, *Secular and Christian Leadership in Corinth,* 92; cf. 89-99; also L. L. Welborn, *Politics and Rhetoric in the Co-rinthian Epistles* (Macon, Ga.: Mercer, 1997), 1-42.

84. B. W. Winter, *Philo and Paul among the Sophists,* SNTSMS 96 (Cambridge: Cambridge University Press, 1997), 1-15 and 126-202.

latter depends often on 'enthymatic semiosis' (arguing from shared or partially unstated premises) rather than on purely deductive (or inductive) reasoning."[85] Moores distinguishes between a rhetorical interest shared by H.-D. Betz and M. M. Mitchell in which Betz rightly attacks the current "spell of the myth of Paul the non-thinker" and rhetoric as mere "persuasive strategy, psychological exploitation of the audience [in which persuasion] matters more than truth itself."[86]

Paul (in contradistinction to postmodern emphases upon textual indeterminacy) "does not think (as some . . . upholders of the importance of the reception factor do) that the identity of the message in a piece of communication is in any sense determined by what it means for those at the receiving end. For him it is rather *their* identity than that of the message which is determined by their response. To subject him to the criteria of present-day reception or reader response theory would be to turn *his* ideas on the subject upside down" (Moores' italics).[87] For him the Holy Spirit grants "the power of relating semantic and noetic fields."[88] With particular reference to rhetoric at Corinth and especially glossolalia in 1 Corinthians 14, however, Moores demonstrates what I am calling the "postmodern mood," in which market forces which give rise to social construction dominate the mind-set of Corinthian culture. This is "the view that can see meaning only as impact." This resonates with 1 Corinthians 1–2 on wisdom, and 1 Corinthians 14 on the inarticulate signal of the trumpet, i.e., of a melody without form which is mere noise, as witnessing to the mood in Corinth.[89]

Relevance to the Twenty-First Century

Given the issues of (1) status inconsistency, (2) religious pluralism, (3) cosmopolitan immigration and trade, (4) *priority of market forces not only in business but also in rhetoric,* and (5) the emphasis upon *recognition and perception of honor or shame within a socially constructed world,* Paul would have been surely astonished at *either* (a) early twenty-first century laments about the problems of *having to address a pluralist culture* supposedly for the first time; *or* (b) early twenty-first *celebrations over the demise of a transcontextual rationality in favor of "local," social constructions of truth.* With today's "post-

---

85. J. D. Moores, *Wrestling with Rationality in Paul,* SNTSMS 82 (Cambridge: Cambridge University Press, 1995), 10; cf. 5-32 and 132-60.

86. Ibid., 16 and 17; he cites H.-D. Betz, *Galatians,* Hermeneia (Philadelphia: Fortress, 1979), xiv.

87. Moores, *Wrestling,* 133-34.

88. Ibid., 135.

89. Ibid., 144; cf. 132-33 and 134-60. Although he examines Paul's use of rational argument mainly in Romans 1–8, Moores tends to cite Corinth as his major counterexample of pragmatic persuasion within the cultural settings of the NT.

modern" mood we may compare *the self-sufficient, self-congratulatory culture of Corinth coupled with an obsession about peer-group prestige, success in competition, their devaluing of tradition and universals, and near contempt for those without standing in some chosen value system. All this provides an embarrassingly close model of a postmodern context for the gospel in our own times, even given the huge historical differences and distances in so many other respects.* Quite apart from its rich theology of grace, the cross, the Holy Spirit, the ministry, love, and the resurrection, as an example of communicative action between the gospel and the world of given time, 1 Corinthians stands in a *distinctive position of relevance to our own times.*

II. THE CHRISTIAN COMMUNITY IN CORINTH: BEGINNINGS, NATURE, AND RELATIONS WITH PAUL

A. The Strategic Importance of Corinth for Paul and the Gospel and Paul's Strategy of Proclamation

Classical and New Testament historians alike agree that the founding of a Christian community held strategic importance for Paul. James Wiseman observes that Paul must have been attracted to Corinth for a number of reasons: "the large size of its Jewish community, swollen by the edict of Claudius" (although some disagree with this estimate of size); "the great size and importance of Corinth itself; perhaps even the reputation of the Isthmian Games (and the additional crowds they attracted). . . . The church of Corinth . . . became one of the largest and most important of the early churches."[90] Another classical historian, Donald Engels, writes: "Corinth was a logical place to establish a strong Christian church, for its numerous trade connections would assure the rapid propagation of the new religion, and quite soon it came to dominate the other churches of the province. Corinth also had an important Jewish community, and whenever Paul entered a new city, he would always begin preaching in the local synagogue."[91]

Engels cites a number of additional factors. Especially with the Isthmian Games and tourism, there was an abundant demand for Paul's trade and business as a tentmaker: "tents for sheltering visitors to the Spring games, awnings for the retailers in the forum, and perhaps sails for merchant ships. . . . He had come to stay and his economic independence did not make him a burden on his new converts in the city."[92] Further, we might add, it did not place him in a difficult position of financial dependence and hence of feeling obliged to offer some privilege to his benefactor or patron; he could pastor all without fear or favor

---

90. Wiseman, *Corinth and Rome,* 504.
91. Engels, *Roman Corinth,* 20.
92. Ibid., 112.

(see below on 9:1-23). Although Engels and Meggitt underline the effect of Paul's gospel mainly upon the urban poor, most writers emphasize the cross-section of social and ethnic mix whom Paul sought to win for the gospel (9:19-23).[93] The issue of the social constituency of the church is discussed below. Classical writers also draw on the striking comparison between vibrant, growing Corinth and stagnant, conservative Athens.[94] From within NT studies Murphy-O'Connor confirms this: "Corinth offered advantages which Athens lacked. . . . The latter was an old sick city whose past was infinitely more glorious than its present. . . . Athens was no longer either productive or creative . . . a mediocre university town. . . . As a centre of learning it had been surpassed even by Tarsus. The poverty of its economy is shown by the dearth of new buildings."[95]

By contrast Wiseman documents with reference to archaeological evidence the rapid urban development at Corinth in the early Roman period.[96] The Roman colonists displaced the center of the old Greek city, although such earlier structures as the South Stoa, the Well of Glauce, and necessarily the Peirene fountain were absorbed into a new central complex. Most if not all of the earlier temples and sanctuaries were restored, including the Sanctuary of Asclepios.[97] Oscar Broneer documents the program of remodeling, the construction of arched passageways to the forum on the south side of the temple hill, and the erection of civic and administrative halls and commercial areas of shops, while more recent excavations by Charles K. Williams reveal further developments east of the theatre.[98] The broad ramp and archway which leads to the Lechaeum road dates from the period of Augustus, and by the time of Paul's arrival a row of shops, a basilica, and a market area flanked the Lechaeum road. By this period (c. AD 50) ornate marble had been used for various purposes, perhaps (if not shortly afterward) the Babbius monument described above in the context of self-promotion and possibly also a sense of insecurity even on the part of freed persons who had won their way to the top.

---

93. Ibid., 113-16. On the economic life of the "urban poor" (*plebs urbana,* the poorer groups and slaves), see Meggitt, *Paul, Poverty, and Survival,* 53-73; D. G. Horrell, *The Social Ethos of the Corinthian Correspondence* (Edinburgh: T. & T. Clarke, 1996), 66-73 and 91-168; Merklein, *Der erste Brief an die Kor, Kap 1–4,* 31-42; Meeks, *The First Urban Christians,* 32-74. See also Meggitt, *Paul, Poverty, and Survival,* 101-7. Meggitt argues that very many of the urban poor lived barely on the bread line of sheer survival.

94. Engels, *Roman Corinth,* 113-14.

95. Murphy-O'Connor, *Paul,* 108.

96. Wiseman, *Corinth and Rome,* 509-21.

97. Ibid., 510-12.

98. O. Broneer, *Corinth,* I:iv: *The South Stoa and Its Roman Successors* (Princeton: America School of Classical Studies at Athens, 1954), 100-159; cf. more briefly Wiseman, *Corinth and Rome,* 513-21. See further C. K. Williams, "Corinth 1984: East of the Theater," *Hesperia* 54 (1985): 55-96; "Corinth, 1985: East of the Theater," *Hesperia* 55 (1986): 129-75; and works cited above up to *Hesperia* 59 (1990): and finally a cumulative tribute to his achievements in *Hesperia* 60 (1991).

If we follow the convention of describing Paul's missionary journey with Barnabas to Cyprus, Perga, Pisidian Antioch, Iconium, Lystra, and Derbe as his "First Missionary Journey" (cf. Acts 13 and 14), Paul's "Second Missionary Journey" eventually drew him to Corinth. With Silas (Silvanus, 1 Thess 1:1), Paul revisited the Christian churches in Syria and Cilicia, journeyed westward through South Galatia, and commissioned Timothy to join him from Lystra. According to the narrative in Acts, Paul had intended to visit the rich proconsular province of Asia but was "forbidden by the Holy Spirit" (Acts 16:6). Partly through a dream involving the urgent plea of "the man from Macedonia" (Luke; cf. Acts 16:10, where the "we" section begins), Paul crossed to Philippi and Thessalonica, which were to be his two main centers for work in Macedonia. If we are to draw any inference from the ending of the "we" section in Acts, Luke perhaps remained in Philippi, while Paul continued on to Thessalonica, the main city of Macedonia. According to the Acts account, after only a few weeks Jewish opponents forced Paul's departure ("they have turned the world upside down," 17:5-7). Then, after a stopover in Beraea, Paul moved on to Athens, sending Timothy to Thessalonica with some anxiety, hoping to receive news from the church there.

Everything that we have said about Corinth explains Paul's resolve to travel from Athens to Corinth, presumably with the conviction that Corinth would provide a more strategic center for the work of the gospel on the basis of the numerous factors which we have already set forth in some detail. Murphy-O'Connor offers an excellent and convincing reconstruction of events.[99] "The move is noted by Luke (Acts 18:1) and confirmed by 2 Cor 1:19," which suggests that Timothy and Silvanus (Silas) had rejoined him by now (although they were not necessarily with Paul during his initial weeks in Corinth). Murphy-O'Connor argues that Paul is no longer merely "traveling," but pursuing a conscious strategy of where best to plant churches (cf. 1 Cor 3:6, "I planted . . ."). He compares Corinth to "a wide-open boom town" like "San Francisco in the days of the Californian gold rush."[100] "The atmosphere was to Paul's advantage. He must also have been aware that the establishment of a church at Corinth would carry weight elsewhere as an argument for the value of Christianity. . . . The bustling emporium was no place for the gullible or timid; only the tough survived. What better advertisement for the power of the gospel could there be than to make converts of the pre-occupied and sceptical inhabitants of such a materialist environment (cf. 2 Cor 3:2)?"[101] We have already discussed its "superb communications," its role as a passageway "for all humanity," the presence of a Jewish community, and its opportunities for employment and for meeting with each class, race, and gender.

Paul would have traveled from Athens by land; sea voyages were avoided

---

99. Murphy-O'Connor, *Paul*, 108-10 and 256-73.
100. Ibid., 108.
101. Ibid., 109.

unless they were essential. The journey of some 50 miles would have taken Paul through Eleusis, but probably he would have aimed to reach Megara (26 miles) by the first nightfall.[102] The first part of the second lap of the journey brought him through relatively dangerous territory (cf. 2 Cor 11:26), but when he reached Schoenus he was in the Corinthian territorium and would have encountered the first jostling crowd of laborers and merchants. He would have encountered the paved *diolkos* (described above) and presumably passed through Isthmia, where perhaps traces of support structures for the Games of AD 49 could still be seen. Certainly he could have viewed the stadium and sanctuary of Poseidon. Finally, he would have turned south to join the Lechaeum road into Corinth.

Today the visitor to the site of ancient Corinth may proceed along the Lechaeum road toward the city forum and observe its paving edged with gutters that collected rainwater. Ahead stands the towering height of Acrocorinth, behind the center of the city and slightly to the west of due south. Stoas run parallel on either side of the road.[103] The traveler who arrived in the mid-first century would pass "through the mercantile suburb, beneath colonnaded sidewalks that protected from sun and weather. Ascending the terraces upon which the central city was located, he would see the Asklepieion, with its temple, colonnades and bathhouses, and the Old Gymnasium on his right. Nearby he might have stopped to refresh himself at the beautiful Fountain of Lerna. . . . The water could be clean and safe. . . . Moving closer to the Forum . . . large market buildings, basilicas and the law courts would line the colonaded street. On his left would be the Baths of Eurycles, public latrines, and the periobolos of Apollo with its famous works of art, and next the great Fountain of Peirene. . . . He would pass beneath the majestic triumphal arch surmounted by two gilded, horse-drawn chariots. . . . The forum itself was a vast open space thronged with merchants, street-hawkers, travellers, and local residents. Varicoloured tents covered the market stalls. . . . He would see . . . works of public art: paintings, marble sculpture and works of bronze . . . shrines, sanctuaries and temples . . . shops, stoas, and the administrative offices in the imposing South Stoa . . . dazzling colours."[104]

Paul made a firm decision (1:18) not to aspire to the status of a professional rhetorician, newly arrived to market the gospel as a consumer commod-

---

102. Ibid., 257 (all of Murphy-O'Connor's suggestions here are plausible).

103. Illustrations in color may be seen in many guides, e.g., Nicos Papahatzis, *Ancient Corinth: The Museums of Corinth, Isthmia and Sicyon* (Athens: Ekdotike Athenon, 1977), 58 (photograph in color); 49 (map); 113-14 (reconstruction of ancient Corinth); Wiseman, *Corinth and Rome,* 513 (map); Spyros Meletzis and Helen Papadakis, *Corinth* (Athens: Art Editions Meletzis, and Munich: Schnell & Steiner, 1997), 17 (photograph in color); P. G. Themelis, *Ancient Corinth: The Site and the Museum* (Athens: Hannibal, n.d.), 40 (photograph in color), 15 (map).

104. Engels, *Roman Corinth,* 13. On the probable location of the meat market *(macellum)* see D. W. J. Gill, "The Meat Market at Corinth (1 Cor 10:25)," *TynBul* 43 (1992): 389-93; and exegesis of 10:25.

ity designed to please the hearers and to win their approval. Whether or not such a strategy would have been successful, the nature of the gospel of Jesus Christ excluded its being treated as a market commodity tailored to the tastes and desires of market consumers. The power of the gospel lay in an utterly different direction, and to treat it as a commodity to be offered in a competitive market by manipulative rhetorical persuasion would be precisely to empty it of its power, i.e., its effectiveness to save and to transform those to whom it was proclaimed as kerygma (see below on 1:18-25).[105] He would earn his keep as a tentmaker and *proclaim the cross of Christ.*[106]

We have set forth above those many features of Corinthian culture which would not have fit readily with such a message: an obsessive concern to win reputation and status in the eyes of others; self-promotion to gain applause and influence; ambition to succeed often by manipulating networks of power; and above all an emphasis on autonomy and "rights." It is little wonder that the proclamation of the cross of Christ, entailing the shameful death of a person marginalized from society as an alleged criminal, was perceived by many as an affront (σκάνδαλον) and sheer folly (μωρία, 1:23), even if it held the currency of transformative power (δύναμις) and divine wisdom (θεοῦ σοφία, 1:24) to Christian believers on their way to salvation (τοῖς δὲ σωζομένοις, 1:18; τοῖς κλητοῖς, 1:24).[107] Hengel adduces the place of crucifixion in the Roman, Greek, and Jewish worlds, and concludes that "a crucified Messiah, son of God or God must have seemed a contradiction in terms to anyone, Jew, Greek, Roman or barbarian . . . offensive and foolish."[108] The sheer horror and degradation of death on a cross shouts aloud from almost every page of Hengel's vivid study.[109]

Hans-Ruedi Weber similarly underlines the unavoidable tension implicit in the situation at Corinth: "At Corinth Paul had deliberately preached his message without eloquence, in order not to empty Christ's cross of power (1:17, 2:1-5). The Corinthians in their quest for 'word-wisdom' [see on 2:1-3, below] blamed him for this. But it is in the nature of the cross that it cannot be preached

105. See also esp. Schrage, *Der erste Brief an die Korinther,* 1:165-203; Moores, *Wrestling with Rationality;* Pogoloff, *Logos and Sophia;* Winter, *Philo and Paul among the Sophists;* Merklein, *Der erste Brief an die Korinther, Kap 1-4,* 167-91; and Duane Litfin, *St Paul's Theology of Proclamation: 1 Cor 1-4 and Graeco-Roman Rhetoric,* SNTSMS 79 (Cambridge: Cambridge University Press, 1994), 137-228 and 244-61.
106. On "proclamation," see Litfin, *St Paul's Theology of Proclamation,* 196-97.
107. See Martin Hengel, *The Cross of the Son of God:* "Crucifixion" (Eng. trans., London: SCM, 1986), 93-103 and 138-82 (= *Crucifixion;* London: SCM, 1977, 1-11 and 46-90). The full title is *Crucifixion in the Ancient World and the Folly of the Message of the Cross* (91). See also Alexandra R. Brown, *The Cross and Human Transformation: Paul's Apocalyptic Word in 1 Corinthians* (Minneapolis: Fortress, 1995) throughout; and Raymond Pickett, *The Cross in Corinth: The Social Significance of the Death of Jesus,* JSNTSS 143 (Sheffield: Sheffield Academic Press, 1997), 58-84.
108. Hengel, *The Cross,* 102 (= *Crucifixion,* 10).
109. E.g., *The Cross* 150-55 (= *Crucifixion,* 58-63).

elegantly . . . only in weakness."[110] The judges find themselves judged, and those willing to receive encounter grace. Hence Moltmann, Weber, and Schrage perceive the cross in the context of Corinth as the "criterion" and the basis of a new identity.[111] H. Merklein also develops this theme: the cross constitutes both a "scandal" (1:23) and the center of Paul's theology.[112]

Paul himself recalls in our epistle that he did not come to Corinth to speak "with high-sounding rhetoric or a display of cleverness" (for the translation, see below on 2:1). He refused to place the criterion of "pleasing the audience," especially by a display of rhetorical performance above the content of the gospel, even though elsewhere he speaks of the different issue of pastoral sensitivity in meeting people where they are (9:19-23). Stowers may perhaps be right to infer a probable contrast between seeking public recognition by using street corners or public buildings, and Paul's preference where possible to speak in (where possible) a private household or in contacts through his own trade.[113] At all events, Paul also recalls that he came "in weakness with much fear and trembling" (2:3). We comment below (see under 2:2-3) that whether or not a hypothesis may be established about Paul's poor health (with A. Schweitzer and M. Dibelius), Paul disowned the protective veneer of rhetorical manipulation and adopted a communicative strategy entirely at odds with the confident self-promotion of the sophist or pragmatic rhetoricism who played to the gallery.[114] With T. Savage (see below on 2:3) we understand Paul's sense of weakness to derive from his awesome sense of responsibility in proclaiming with humble realism the awe-inspiring revelation of the sovereign, gracious, God made known through Christ and through the cross.[115] Paul disowns a rhetorical strategy which depends on cleverness and on enticing his hearers (2:4). Such a strategy would defeat its own purpose since it would contradict the very nature of the gospel.

---

110. H.-R. Weber, *The Cross: Tradition and Interpretations* (Eng. trans., London: SPCK and Grand Rapids: Eerdmans, 1979), 73; cf. 65-80 on the cross at Corinth.

111. Schrage, *Der erste Brief,* 1:165 (title of section); J. Moltmann, *The Crucified God* (Eng. trans., London: SCM, 1974); and Weber, *The Cross,* "For the Corinthians: The Cross as Criterion," 65-80: "it is essential . . . to use the cross as the criterion. . . . It is through the cross that God wishes to be perceived" (80).

112. K. Merklein, "Das paulinischen Paradox des Kreuzes," *TTZ* 106 (1997): 81-98; also Merklein, *Der erste Brief, Kap 1-4,* 167-91.

113. S. K. Stowers, "Social Status, Public Speaking, and Private Teaching: The Circumstances of Paul's Preaching," *NovT* 26 (1984): 59-82.

114. See below in 2:3; also Winter, *Philo and Paul,* 147-61, and M. A. Bullmore, *St Paul's Theology of Rhetorical Style: An Examination of 1 Cor 2:1-5 in the Light of First-Century Greco-Roman Rhetorical Culture* (San Francisco: International Scholars Publication, 1995), esp. 212-13.

115. Savage, *Power through Weakness,* 73.

B. Debates about the Socioeconomic Status of Paul and His Converts: Paul as a Tentmaker

If the details of Paul's earliest preaching in Corinth have not survived, we know that he plied his trade there as a tentmaker. Even if Paul began with other temporary arrangements, the picture which emerges from the Acts narrative (18:3, 11) coheres with the greeting in 16:19, namely, that Paul stayed for18 months in Corinth in the home of Aquila and Prisca (in Acts, Priscilla).[116] They may well have come to Christian faith earlier in Rome, and were probably freed persons of Jewish origin who left Rome in AD 49 when the Emperor Claudius closed down a Roman synagogue because of disturbances centering on the figure of Christ.[117] Suetonius speaks of an edict of Claudius leading to the expulsion of Jews "impulsore Chresto."[118] Murphy-O'Connor reasonably infers that they came directly to the Roman colony of Corinth with its well-known business opportunities to set up their small shop to sell perhaps leather craft among the commercial developments close to the Lechaeum road (see below under 16:19). Possibly they made their home in the loft above the shop (perhaps c. 13 feet by 13 feet by 8 feet), to judge from excavations of comparable commercial properties) "while Paul slept below amid the tool-strewn workbenches and rolls of leather and canvas. The workshop was perfect for initial contacts, particularly with women. While Paul worked on a cloak, or sandal or belt, he had the opportunity for conversation which quickly became instruction (cf. 1 Thess 2:9), and further encounters were easily justified by the need for new pieces or other repairs."[119] Murphy-O'Connor adds that different arrangements may have been needed if his ministry expanded so busily that actual work and trade in the shop became hindered.

A fuller reconstruction of Paul's work as an artisan and tradesperson emerges from two studies by R. F. Hock.[120] Paul spent many long, hot hours in a workshop (ἐργαστήριον). Hock argues that it was precisely Paul's working in a menial trade that is implied by the charge that he was widely regarded as "weak" (1 Cor 4:10-13) in the sense of socially inferior or unimpressive. At all events, this would be a predictable verdict among those of wealth and power.[121] He even suggests that "to boast in his weakness" relates to his paying his way to avoid placing a charge against the work of the gospel through humdrum, often

---

116. Cf. Gerd Lüdemann, *Paul Apostle to the Gentiles: Studies in Chronology* (Eng. trans., London: SCM, 1984), 160-62.

117. See Murphy-O'Connor, *Paul,* 263; F. F. Bruce, *Paul: Apostle of the Free Spirit* (Exeter: Paternoster, 1977), 250-51 and 381.

118. Suetonius, *Life of Claudius* 25.4.

119. Murphy-O'Connor, *Paul,* 263-64.

120. R. F. Hock, *The Social Context of Paul's Ministry: Tentmaking and Apostleship* (Philadelphia: Fortress, 1980), and "The Workshop as a Social Setting for Paul's Missionary Preaching," *CBQ* 41 (1979): 438-50.

121. Hock, *Social Context,* 60.

despised, labor (cf. 1 Cor 9:1-19 and 2 Cor 11:7-15; 12:13-16).[122] That Paul's work was arduous, uncomfortable, often hot, and always demanding can hardly be doubted. His was not the ideal associated with the professional "wise man," rhetorician, or established speaker-as-performer. As Pogoloff observes, many at Corinth who became Christian believers would have liked Paul to turn "professional"; to be like "the sophists, those 'visiting professional preachers' who relied upon . . . admirers, all expert talkers . . ." (like the chat-show hosts or media figures of the present day).[123]

In Paul's eyes, however, apostolicity entailed not a lofty stance based on prestige, but pointing to the cross and sharing in its shame and humiliation as God's chosen mode of self-revelation. The apostles were like bloodied fighters in the stadium, even if some Corinthian believers later came to perceive themselves as exempt from such struggle, sitting among the seats of the spectators who judged the quality of the apostolic performance (4:9-13). Paul became aware that some status-seeking people who became believers found Paul's status an embarrassment, even after they had come to faith. The apostles appeared like "the scum of the earth, the scrapings from people's shoes" (4:13; see commentary below).

"Paul repeatedly speaks of engaging in arduous physical labour (1 Thess 2:9; 2 Thess 3:7-8; 1 Cor 4:11-12; 9:6; 2 Cor 11:27). . . . It seems fair to deduce that he was some kind of manual worker . . . probably an artisan . . . probably all the more arduous given the peripatetic nature of his lifestyle."[124] Although he concedes that Hock's picture of Paul's communicating the gospel while making sales or repairs in his workshop, Meggitt rejects the view that Paul could readily combine these two activities to the extent claimed by Hock.[125] In support of a minority view among Pauline scholars, Meggitt urges that Paul spent much of his life in harsh poverty. Paul speaks of need and lack in the face of which he is willing to accept financial support in certain circumstances (Phil 4:16; 2 Cor 11:9). But 1 Corinthians 9 stresses that this was not his normal practice. Meggitt argues that such support as was received from individuals (Phoebe and Gaius; Rom 16:1, 23) may well have been very modest. "In the sight of others he remained one of the poor (2 Cor 6:8-10)."[126] If his rhetoric failed to impress (2 Cor 10:10), Meggitt argues (against E. A. Judge), Paul would not have been in the elitist category of the sophist who could charge the fees of a professional speaker.[127] Meggitt attacks the "myth" of Paul's affluent background.[128] Paul "shared fully in the destitute life of the non-elite in the Roman empire."[129]

---

122. Ibid., 62.

123. Pogoloff, *Logos and Sophia*, 191 and 203.

124. Meggitt, *Paul, Poverty, and Survival*, 75-76.

125. Ibid., 76-77.

126. Ibid., 78.

127. Ibid., 78-79; against E. A. Judge, "The Early Christians as a Scholastic Community," *JRH* 1 (1960): 4-15 and 125-37.

128. Meggitt, *Paul, Poverty, and Survival*, 80-97.

129. Ibid., 96.

Meggitt's account serves as a corrective to an overbland notion of Paul as a middle-class tradesperson. Yet on Meggitt's admission the actual data are meagre, and it is more plausible to discuss particular circumstances at Corinth which would make him less ready to become obligated (given the system of patronage and the reciprocal expectations of friendship in the Roman world) in the climate of self-promotion at Corinth than perhaps elsewhere. The two pictures presented by Meggitt on one side and by Hock and Murphy-O'Connor on the other must be permitted to complement and correct each other.[130] In the context of Corinth, Meggitt's comments carry weight, but as Paul's stay lengthened towards eighteen months it becomes implausible to imagine that the deep affection and respect of many of his converts would let him live a life of destitution, or even that someone capable of dictating such well-argued letters was as incompetent a speaker as Paul's own modesty and Meggitt's evaluation of it at face value would seem to imply. Moreover, Meggitt does not seem to take account of Paul's conscious status as a Roman citizen (cf. his consistent use of the name *Paul* as against the Jewish *Saul*).

The same ambivalence about the social status of Paul's converts at Corinth has characterized various eras of Pauline research. Meggitt observes that while Wuellner rightly notes the extent to which opposing theories have depended upon a certain exegesis of 1 Cor 1:26, "ironically the text has been intrinsic to both the 'Old' and ' New' consensuses, providing a keystone for their respective reconstructions of Christian origins."[131] The history of research into the social status of the earliest urban Christian churches is too well known to require detailed rehearsal, but an outline of its contours may be in order. In the early years of the twentieth century Adolf Deissmann's researches on the papyri led him to urge that the Greek of the NT was that used by ordinary people, not that of high literature. Paul's epistles were letters to everyday people in the everyday world. He inferred that Christianity in these years "came . . . from the lower class (Matt 11:25-6; 1 Cor 1:26-31)."[132] Deissmann did not claim that early urban Christians were exclusively lower class, but he assumed that they were predominantly so. A turning point emerged, however, in the work of E. A. Judge, who argued that specific evidence pointed to a mixed and socially diverse group. At Corinth, indeed, "the Christians were dominated by a socially pretentious section of the population. . . ."[133]

It would be a mistake to assume that the major commentators were all initially captivated by Deissmann and then later from 1960 by Judge. In 1910 J. Weiss noted that alongside Paul's statement that "not many of you were intel-

130. Murphy-O'Connor, *Paul,* 117-18, 261-67; Hock, *Social Context,* 66-68; also Bruce, *Paul,* 250-53.

131. Meggitt, *Paul,* 102.

132. A. Deissmann, *Light from the Ancient East* (Eng. trans., London: Hodder & Stoughton, rev. ed. 1927), 144.

133. E. A. Judge, *The Social Pattern of Early Christian Groups in the First Century* (London: Tyndale Press, 1960), 60. Cf. esp. 30-38.

lectuals . . . not many held positions of influence, not many were born to high status" (1:26), quite another social category included Stephanas, Gaius, Crispus, Quartus, Aquila, and Prisca.[134] Robertson and Plummer wrote in 1911 that Paul's earliest congregation would have included "a very mixed population" with sufficient independence and initiative for "each convert to choose his own leader."[135] We must therefore caution against the Hegel-like myth which simply places Judge's antithesis over against Deissmann's thesis, and perceives the work of Theissen and Meeks as the accepted synthesis. As a crude working sketch it has some validity: Theissen writes concerning Deissmann and Judge, "Both opinions are probably correct, because . . . the Corinthian congregation is marked by internal stratification. The majority of the members, who come from the lower classes, stand in contrast to a few influential members who come from the upper classes."[136] Theissen worked out his thesis in detail in his well-known essay "Social Stratification in the Corinthian Community."[137]

Some twenty years of intensive research into the social world of the New Testament and especially the Pauline communities have served to underline the radical diversity emphasized by Theissen, although in the case of Corinth the urban poor, including slaves, probably made up the majority of the community in sheer numerical terms. In an important contribution Blasi shares Theissen's view that a whole range of figures mentioned by Paul in the context of Corinth simply could not have fitted into Deissmann's category of "lower classes," and social diversity has been underlined by Banks, Gallagher, Stambaugh and Balch, Klauck, and others, even if Meggitt also calls attention to the precarious hold on sheer survival experienced by the *plebs urbana* and the near destitution of many agricultural laborers.[138] For those in a position to take advantage of the assistance of a patron, the utilization of patronage for self-advancement was not only understandable but generally expected. Chow, Judge, Yeo, P. Marshall, L. M. White, and Clarke have informed our understanding of the profound impact of their socioeconomic system upon a community such as typically belonged to Corinth.[139] In contrast to Meggitt's emphasis in his exegesis

134. J. Weiss, *Der erste Korintherbrief* (Göttingen: Vandenhoeck & Ruprecht, 1910), xvi. E..B. Allo adds that although "many" were from impoverished classes, some were persons of weight (Erastus and Crispus), with probably "a small number of wealthy people" (*Première Épitre aux Corinthiens* (Paris: Gabalda, 1956), 20 (citing also Weiss).

135. A. Robertson and A. Plummer, *A Critical and Exegetical Commentary on the First Epistle of St Paul to the Corinthians*, ICC (2d ed., Edinburgh: T. & T. Clark, 1914 [1911]), xv.

136. Theissen, *Social Setting,* 69.

137. Ibid., 69-120 (German, 1974).

138. A. J. Blasi, *Early Christianity as a Social Movement,* Toronto Studies in Religion 5 (New York: Lang, 1988), esp. 56-67; R. J. Banks, *Paul's Idea of Community* (Peabody, Mass.: Hendrickson, rev. ed. 1994), 1-25; J. E. Stambaugh and D. L. Balch, *The New Testament in Its Social Environment* (Philadelphia: Westminster, 1986); E. V. Gallagher, "The Social World of St Paul," *Religion* 14 (1984): 91-99; H. J. Klauck, "Gemeindestrukturen im ersten Korintherbrief," *Bibel und Kirche,* 40 (1985): 9-15; Meggitt, *Paul, Poverty, and Survival,* 53-73 and throughout.

139. J. K. Chow, *Patronage and Power: A Study of Social Networks at Corinth,* JSNTSS 75

of 1 Cor 1:26, those of Winter and Clarke underline the upper end of the spectrum of social diversity: "There can be no doubt that these descriptive terms used in 1 Cor 1:26 refer to the ruling class from which rhetors and sophists came . . . ," even if Paul acknowledges that "not many" (οὐ πολλοί) Christian believers were "intellectuals, as the world counts cleverness, not many held influence, not many were born to high status" (on the translation and exegesis, see below on 1:26).[140] A history of the debate in Pauline and classical scholarship is recounted by David Horrell.[141] The debate continues: Donald Engels (1990) tends to anticipate some of Meggitt's claims (1998), but not all of them: "Paul stayed in a private house" and shared in the regular trade of Priscilla and Aquila in making "awnings and sails which would be in great demand in the city."[142] John Elliott has compiled an extensive bibliography of "social-scientific" research on the NT up to 1993, and some emanates from particular "centers," especially from Yale (Wayne Meeks, A. J. Malherbe, and Dale Martin) and Macquarrie University (Edwin Judge, Peter Marshall, and Robert Banks).[143]

According to 16:15, "The Stephanas household were the first converts in Achaia, and they assigned themselves to the service of God's people" (on translation and exegesis see below). Stephanas very soon becomes a co-worker with Paul.[144] Not surprisingly, at this very initial stage Paul himself (as he soon ceased to do personally) baptized Stephanas and his household (1:16). Gaius and Crispus were probably also early converts (1:14), and neither Theissen nor Blasi hesitates to identify Crispus with the Crispus who held prominent office in the synagogue in Acts 18:8.[145] Theissen argues that the so-called "ruler" of the synagogue (ἀρχισυνάγωγος, Acts 18:8) led worship and also held responsibility for the building and fabric. Such were both "esteemed men" and financially prosperous.[146] Gaius is a Latin name which in Blasi's view suggests

---

(Sheffield: Sheffield Academic Press, 1992), esp. 12-37 and throughout; E. A. Judge, "'Antike und Christentum': Towards a Definition of the Field: A Bibliographical Survey," *ANRW* 2.23.1 (1979), 3-58, and esp. *Rank and Status in the World of the Caesars and St Paul* (Christchurch: University of Canterbury, 1982, and "Cultural Conformity and Innovation in Paul: Some Clues from Contemporary Documents," *TynBul* 35 (1984): 3-24; L. M. White (ed.), *Semeia 56: Social Networks in Early Christian Environment: Issues and Methods for Social History* (Atlanta: Scholars Press, 1992), esp. White (3-36), H. Hendrix (39-58); Marshall, *Enmity in Corinth;* Khiok-Khing Yeo, *Rhetorical Interaction in 1 Cor 8 and 10: A Formal Analysis with Preliminary Suggestions for a Chinese Cross-Cultural Hermeneutic,* Biblical Interpretation Series 9 (Leiden: Brill, 1995), 84-93; and Clarke, *Secular and Christian Leadership in Corinth,* esp. 25-39.

140. Clarke, *Secular and Christian Leadership,* 45; Winter, *Philo and Paul among the Sophists,* 200.

141. Horrell, *The Social Ethos of the Corinthian Correspondence,* 91-101.

142. Engels, *Roman Corinth,* 107; cf. 70-71.

143. J. Elliott, *Social-Scientific Criticism of the New Testament: An Introduction* (London: SPCK, 1995 [earlier Augsburg-Fortress, 1993]), 138-74.

144. R. Banks, *Paul's Idea of Community,* 164-65.

145. Theissen, *Social Setting,* 73; Blasi, *Early Christianity,* 56-59.

146. Theissen, *Social Setting,* 74-75.

higher status (cf. 1:14; Rom 16:23; cf. Acts 19:29), and his house must have been large enough to enable him to offer hospitality not only to Paul but also to a gathering of the church.[147] *Thus Gaius, Stephanas, and Crispus represent prominent persons of high rank, esteem, and probably wealth, respectively, within the Roman, Greek, and Jewish communities.* They were destined to assume leadership roles of various kinds as Paul's co-workers (e.g., 16:17).

As is now widely known, Theissen categorizes names of Christian believers at Corinth whom we may regard as being of high rank, influence, or in some cases wealth on the basis of their holding recognized offices (Crispus, Erastus); being heads of "households" (presumably an equivalent to Latin *familia,* which includes slaves and chattel: Crispus, Stephanas); having the resources and capacity to perform services to Paul or to the church (Phoebe from Cenchraea, Gaius, Titius Justus); and the leisure or business resources to travel (Stephanas, Fortunatus, Achaicus, Erastus, Phoebe, Aquila and Priscilla, and either Chloe or Chloe's people, depending on who financed the journey). Theissen lists and comments on sixteen names.[148] Nevertheless, some of his claims remain debated, and he himself notes that many of the Christians in Corinth were perceived as not merely inferior and without influence ("weak") but, worse, as "nothings," people "of no account" who did not merit attention or respect (τὰ ἐξουθενημένα, τὰ μὴ ὄντα, 1:28; on the translation and exegesis, see below).

The surprise comes not from the emergence of difficulty and conflict over social diversity ("because I am not a hand, I do not belong to the body," 12:15; "The eye cannot say to the hand, 'I have no need of you,'" 12:21); the surprise is, rather, that the transformative power of the gospel could provide a new common status and identity to all believers as "one body . . . whether Jews or Gentiles, whether slaves or free" (12:13). Murphy-O'Connor writes of the importance for Paul of "those with initiative, leisure and education [to] function as effective assistants in the spread of the gospel," but acknowledges that Paul's attitude to such people was complex: he availed himself of their services for the gospel, but "refused to permit himself to become dependent on them."[149] He needed to protect the socially vulnerable from feeling second class but also affirmed the freedom (within limits) of those in civic offices or positions of influence to retain their role as benefactors without unduly carping about such events as their dining with dignitaries in the precincts of a pagan temple.[150]

Most writers accept the claim in Acts 18:11 that Paul stayed in Corinth for eighteen months, if not slightly longer (18:18, unless this merely recapitulates v. 11). He is portrayed in Acts 18:19 as finally leaving by ship for Ephesus from the eastern port of Cenchraea (en route to Antioch) for the first stage of the journey, with Priscilla and Aquila. The widely agreed date of this ministry

147. Blasi, *Early Christianity,* 57.
148. Theissen, *Social Setting,* 73-95.
149. Murphy-O'Connor, *Paul,* 268.
150. See Winter, *Seek the Welfare of the City,* 105-22 (protection of the disadvantaged in 6:1-11); 165-77 (affirmation of those in positions of influence in 8:1–11:1).

in Corinth is from March AD 50 to around late September AD 51. The disturbance which resulted in a charge before Gallio seems to provide one of the few
fixed points in dating the chronology of Paul's ministry (see below). He left behind him a thriving church, throbbing with vitality and full of gifts and services
(1:4-8; 12:1–14:40). The problems which would emerge would be those of life,
not of decline. In Paul's eyes the prize of Corinth as a strategic center for the
spread of the gospel deserved and demanded close attention and pastoral care.
Hence there emerges a series of letters and delegations between Corinth and
Ephesus.

III. THE OCCASION OF THE EPISTLE:
DATES, REPORTS, LETTERS, AND INTEGRITY

A. Dates of Paul's Ministry in Corinth
and of the Writing of 1 Corinthians

Much of Pauline chronology revolves around the discovery of the Delphic letter
of Claudius which relates to Lucius Junius Gallio. The first four fragments
were discovered in 1905; three more in 1910, which were published in 1913; finally, two further fragments were excavated and published in 1967.[151] Sources
indicate that Roman officials would normally be chosen before the first of April
in time for preparation and travel to take up office from the first of July.[152] The
letter of Claudius which refers to Gallio is generally agreed to reflect a date of
April or May AD 52 (August 52, with Schrage, at the latest), and since it deals
with a report, the proconsulship of Gallio at Corinth must have run *either* from
July AD 51 to June AD 52 *or* from July AD 50 to June AD 51. An earlier date remains theoretically possible, but such a delay is scarcely likely. In AD 49 his
brother Seneca returned from exile in Corsica, and Seneca's return to favor may
have prompted the nomination of Gallio to office in March or April of AD 50.
However, both Murphy-O'Connor and G. Lüdemann argue that although either
AD 50-51 or AD 51-52 remains entirely possible, the earlier date hardly allows
adequate time for the report of the Delphi letter; hence 51-52 offers the more
probably date.[153] Schrage, Jewett, and Collins also argue for AD 51-52.[154] Sen-

---

151. See J. H. Oliver, "The Epistle of Claudius Which Mentions the Proconsul Junius
Gallio," *Hesperia* 40 (1971): 239-40; A. Plassart, "L'inscription de Delphes mentionnent le proconsul Gallion," *Revue des Études Greques* 80 (1967): 372-78 (the 1967 published inscription); Kent,
Corinth, VIII:iii, *The Inscriptions 1926-1959,* 55, no. 122 (plate 11, but before 1967 fragments);
B. W. Winter, "Gallio's Ruling on the Legal Status of Early Christianity (Acts 18:14-15)," *TynBul*
50 (1999): 213-24; Murphy-O'Connor, *Paul,* 16-21; and Schrage, *Der erste Brief,* 34-35.
152. Dio Cassius, *History* 57.14.5; cf. Murphy-O'Connor, *Paul,* 18-19.
153. Ibid., 21; Lüdemann, *Paul: Apostle to the Gentiles,* 163-64. This applies to Schrage's
date of August AD 52 also; see *Der erste Brief,* 34.
154. Schrage, *Der erste Brief,* 1:34; R. Jewett, *Dating Paul's Life* (London: SCM, 1979),

eca records that Gallio did not complete his term of office because of illness, and he would have been unlikely to begin the return journey to Rome after early September with the onset of more severe weather toward late autumn and fall.[155] In Murphy-O'Connor's view, Gallio's hearing of the charges brought against Paul (Acts 18:12-17) must have taken place between July (his arrival date) and September (his departure) of AD 51.[156] This would also cohere with a dating of Paul's arrival in Jerusalem in the latter part of AD 51 in Gal 2:1. On this basis Colin Hemer concludes: "Paul was in Corinth from autumn to early summer 52."[157]

Bruce Winter has examined the probable substance and implications of the accusation brought against Paul before Gallio. Paul's reasoning with the Jews after his arrival in Corinth, Winter argues, resulted in a breakaway group in which the prominent figures of Titius Justus (Acts 18:7), followed by Crispus (see above), were involved, and this constituted "a humiliating loss" with the suggestion of a "rival" synagogue.[158] The period following the edict of Claudius made the issue of Jewish identity a highly sensitive one (cf. Acts 16:21; 17:7). The Jews enjoyed certain distinctive immunities from prosecution for promoting un-Roman religion since their unique tradition was noted and respected as such. However, Winter argues, it would be intolerable for "mainline" Jews to see such immunity extended to the "messianic sect" of Christianity. Hence they sought a ruling from Gallio to this effect. Gallio, however, regarded the matter as one of internal Jewish self-definition, and treated it as a possible cause for disturbance. Perhaps the beating up of Sosthenes was perceived as an appropriate expression of general anti-Jewish feeling on the part of the current Claudian Roman establishment. The attempt to brand Christian faith at this stage as a *religio illicita* failed. Winter argues that the move so backfired that "Gallio's decision meant that all Christians in Corinth were thereby exempted from the annual obligation to worship the gods on the earth, i.e., the emperor and certain members of his family," even if it was no more than "the opinions of a leading jurist," which "could not be lightly disregarded."[159] While his argument cannot be demonstrated as conclusive or beyond question, Winter provides a detailed and largely convincing case, which has numerous implications for other aspects of 1 Corinthians and the NT more broadly. It may help to explain, for example, the position of certain Christians who held high office,

---

38-40 (alternative title, *A Chronology of Paul's Life* [Philadelphia: Fortress, 1979]; also Collins, *First Corinthians,* 23-24; cf. C. Wolff, *Der erste Brief des Paulus an die Korinther,* THKNT (Berlin: Evangelische Verlagsanstalt, 1996), 4-5; and Lüdemann, *Paul,* 163-64 (cf. also 162-75).

155. Seneca, *Epistulae Morales* 104.1.

156. Murphy-O'Connor, *Paul,* 21.

157. C. Hemer, "Observations on Pauline Chronology," in D. A. Hagner and M. J. Harris (eds.), *Pauline Studies: Essays Presented to F. F. Bruce* (Grand Rapids: Eerdmans and Exeter: Paternoster, 1980), 8; cf. 3-18.

158. B. W. Winter, "Gallio's Ruling on the Legal Status of Early Christianity," *TynBul* 50 (1999): 214 (cf. 213-24).

159. Ibid., 223.

which would otherwise put these positions under very difficult constraints (cf. 8:1–11:1).

According to the narrative of Acts 18:19-22 Paul spent only a short time in Ephesus before sailing on to Caesarea and then traveling on to Antioch. Meanwhile Priscilla and Aquila remained in Ephesus, where they met and instructed Apollos. A summary of related chronological events is provided by Murphy-O'Connor at various points in his *Paul: A Critical Life*.[160] In the summer of AD 52 (after the hearing before Gallio around late spring AD 51 and his departure from Corinth around early summer AD 52; see above), Paul traveled from Antioch to Galatia, while Apollos traveled from Ephesus to Corinth (cf. Acts 18:23 [Paul] and 18:27; 19:1a [Apollos]; 1 Cor 3:6). After he had revisited the congregations in parts of Galatia and Asia Minor in his role as apostolic pastor, Paul then returned to Ephesus, perhaps in September of AD 52. Over the following eighteen months through winter 52-53 to spring or summer of AD 54 Paul remained for the most part in Ephesus, where he consolidated the church and encouraged its outreach to Asia.

Murphy-O'Connor also believes that in spring 53 Paul received bad news from Galatia and wrote the Epistle to the Galatians. We cannot be certain about the date of Galatians: the earliest which some suggest would be AD 49-50; the very latest (if "Galatia" denotes the northern area rather than the southern province) would be 57-58. However, AD 53 offers a reasonable conjecture. Probably in the summer of the same year, Apollos returned from Corinth, and Murphy-O'Connor suggests that it was in response to news carried back to Apollos that Paul wrote the letter to Corinth that predated our "First Corinthians." The existence of a previous letter is clearly indicated by 1 Cor 5:9.[161] Murphy-O'Connor describes the spring and summer of AD 54 as a period of "intense contacts with Corinth," and the earlier part of AD 54 is widely accepted as the most likely date for the writing of 1 Corinthians, although further considerations arise (discussed below) from hypotheses relating to the integrity of the epistle.[162] Schrage proposes "either Spring of the year 54 or 55"; Collins argues

---

160. A summary is offered in Murphy-O'Connor, *Paul,* 184. See also the reconstructions by G. Lüdemann, Robert Jewett, and others cited below. The work carried out by Paul largely from Ephesus over the three years from AD 52 through to 55 has conventionally become known as "the Third Missionary Journey" and probably reflects such experiences as 2 Cor 1:8-10; 11:23; Rom 16:3 as well as snapshots from Acts 19. Cf. Bruce, *Paul,* 286-99; and *New Testament History* (London: Nelson, 1969), 301-18 and 333-37; and Jewett, *Dating Paul's Life* (= *Chronology*), 38-44, 75-87, 99-102; see further below.

161. Cf. Lüdemann, *Paul,* 103-8; also G. Lüdemann, *Antipaulinism in Early Christianity* (Philadelphia: Fortress, 1987), 202-12; Schrage, *Der erste Brief,* 1:36-37 and 385-87; J. C. Hurd Jr., *The Origin of 1 Corinthians* (London: SPCK, 1965), 213-39; Murphy-O'Connor, *Paul,* 184, 252-53, and 276-77. Most probably this letter became lost, although some think that 2 Cor 6:14–7:1 was part of it.

162. Murphy-O'Connor, *Paul,* 184; see assessments in the next note and, e.g., the reconstruction by M. C. de Boer, "The Composition of 1 Corinthians," *NTS* 40 (1994): 229-45 on the dual response to reports from Chloe's people and from the Stephanas delegation (see below).

for "certainly no later than 57, perhaps as early as 53-54"; Wolff, for "around AD 54"; Fee, for spring of around 53-55; Merklein for 54-55 or perhaps 55-56; Witherington, "early in 53 or 54"; Barrett, "the early months of 54, or possibly towards the end of 53," and Conzelmann and Allo, spring of 55.[163]

16:8 clearly indicates that the place of writing was Ephesus, and the time of year spring. If Paul left Corinth in September 51 after a ministry of a little more than eighteen months, *either two and a half years* (if 1 Corinthians dates from spring 54) *or perhaps three and a half years* (if the epistle derives from spring 55) *constitutes the probable period of development, expansion, and time for the emergence of the problems which Paul addresses in our epistle.* The visit of Apollos during this period may have constituted one contributory factor to these changes of emphasis, but Paul makes it abundantly clear that this had nothing to do with any divergence of vision between Apollos and himself (3:5-9; 16:12; see exegesis below) but rather with a group's manipulative appeal to a possible difference of style on the part of Apollos.

B. Oral Reports and Letter from Corinth: Sources and Issues

The occasion of writing may be understood in either or both of two ways: (a) *historically* or chronologically, the four distinct occasions of writing to which Paul responds are: (1) the oral report of "discords" (ἔριδες) and "splits" (σχίσματα) brought to Paul by "Chloe's people" (ὑπὸ τῶν Χλόης, 1:11).[164] It is likely that "Chloe's people" are business agents or responsible managerial slaves acting on Chloe's behalf (see exegesis below). Her agents may have belonged to the church at Ephesus and enjoyed regular links with Corinth, where they would have shared in the worship of the Christian community. (2) There is clear and explicit evidence that Christians in Corinth wrote a letter of inquiry to Paul (7:1, περὶ δὲ ὧν ἐγράψατε . . .). The proportion of 1 Corinthians which constitutes a response to the letter has been discussed in detail by Hurd and others (see below). (3) A number of Christians at Corinth wanted to receive a further visit from Apollos. Paul trusted Apollos to build faithfully on his own work

163. Schrage, *Der erste Brief,* 1:36; Collins, *First Corinthians,* 24; Wolff, *Der erste Brief,* 12-13; Merklein, *Der erste Brief,* 15; Witherington, *Conflict and Community,* 73; Gordon D. Fee, *The First Epistle to the Corinthians* (Grand Rapids: Eerdmans, 1987), 4-5; C. K. Barrett, *A Commentary on the First Epistle to the Corinthians* (London: Black, 2d ed. 1971 [1968]), 5; H. Conzelmann, *1 Corinthians: A Commentary on the First Epistle to the Corinthians,* Hermeneia (Eng. trans., Philadelphia: Fortress, 1975), 4-31 and 12-13; E.-B. Allo, *Saint Paul. Première Épitre aux Corinthiens,* Ebib (Paris: Gabalda, 2d ed. 1956), lxxxvi-lxxxix; also R. Jewett, *A Chronology of Paul's Life* (Philadelphia: Fortress, 1979), 104 (spring 55 or 56).

164. On these terms, see below on 1:10-12, and esp. Margaret M. Mitchell, *Paul and the Rhetoric of Reconciliation: An Exegetical Investigation of the Language and Composition of 1 Corinthians* (Tübingen: Mohr and Louisville: Westminster/Knox, 1992), esp. 65-99. See further, L. L. Welborn, *Politics and Rhetoric in the Corinthian Epistles.*

without rivalry or difference of vision (cf. 3:5-7; 16:12), but Apollos refused to go, no doubt not least out of disillusion that some had appealed to his manner and style as a manipulative lever for discord (see exegesis of 16:12). Paul therefore plans to visit them himself (4:21), but reports that while his plans are still fluid he may need to send Timothy on his behalf (16:10-11). (4) Better news may have come through Stephanas, Fortunatus, and Achaicus (16:17-18). At all events, they can amplify the report of Chloe's people and add further details to which Paul may respond.

(b) In *theological* terms an occasion of writing may be framed and defined differently. In the subapostolic age and in earlier patristic times it was often broadly assumed that the problem of discord and splits to which 1:10-12 alludes featured as the major issue which Paul felt called to address. Thus in his own letter to the Corinthian church (c. AD 96) Clement of Rome alludes to Paul's language "concerning himself and Cephas and Apollos because even then you had made yourselves partisans (προσκλίσεις ὑμᾶς πεποιῆσθαι)."[165] Being faithful (πιστός), loving, and long-suffering, and avoiding unstable or chaotic disorder (ἀταράχως) provide the antidote demanded by *1 Clement*.[166] Clement paraphrases 1 Cor 13:4, 7a: ἀγάπη καλύπτει πλῆθος ἁμαρτιῶν, ἀγάπη . . . ἀνέχεται . . . μακροθυμεῖ . . . (cf. 1 Cor 1:12; 4:2; 12:4-6; 13:1-7). Ignatius and Tertullian take up similar themes.[167] In recent scholarship in the modern era M. Mitchell declares, "Factionalism . . . is at issue throughout all sixteen chapters on the letter."[168] L. L. Welborn perceives the root problem as one of "personal adherents pledged to particular leaders," which becomes "a power struggle, not a theological controversy," while A. D. Clarke describes the issue in 1:10-12 as one of "personality-centred politics."[169]

Although such discord colors nearly all of the issues which the epistle addresses, it *would be a very serious mistake to imply that internal unity as an aspect of ecclesiology* dominated the subject matter of the epistle. To the degree to which Corinthian Christians imbibed secular Corinthian culture with an emphasis on peer groups and *local* value systems, the church had indeed become embroiled in what we have termed a *postmodern pragmatism of the market* with its related *devaluation of truth, tradition, rationality, and universals*. However, the value system is corrected not by reformulating an ecclesial polity, but by placing the community as a whole under the *criterion and identity of the cross of Christ*. Here a *reversal of value systems occurs* (cf. 1:26-31), and as recipients of the sheer gift of divine *grace* through the

165. *1 Clement, Ad Cor* 47:3.
166. *1 Clement*, 48:4, 5; cf. 49:1-6, on the need for love.
167. Ignatius, *Letter to the Philadelphians*, 3:3; 4:1; *Letter to the Ephesians*, 4:1, 2; *Letter to the Trallians*, 12:2; Tertullian, *Against Heresies*, 26 (citing 1 Cor 1:10); Cyprian, *Treatises*, 1:8 (also in 1 Cor 1:10).
168. Mitchell, *Paul and the Rhetoric of Reconciliation*, 67.
169. Welborn, *Politics and Rhetoric in the Corinthian Epistles*, 7 and 11 (cf. "Discord in Corinth," 1-42); Clarke, *Secular and Christian Leadership in Corinth*, 93.

cross, all stand on the same footing (cf. 4:7).[170] From this standpoint, *whether the issue of discord is dominant or merely a constituent component of a wider set of problems,* not ecclesiology but *a reproclamation of grace and the cross to Christian believers takes center stage.* A misunderstanding of this issue has often led to the overshadowing of 1 Corinthians by Romans when the central themes of Romans are no less central here and more explicitly applied to various areas of life.

Two opposite misreadings of the occasion of writing are possible. One is to recognize that a wide range and complexity of problems have arisen which call for urgent pastoral and theological address. While this perception is correct, it should not lead us to discount or to fail to discern coherence and unity within the epistle. It is not necessary, we shall argue, to postulate elaborate theories about "a collection of letters" which supposedly make up our "1 Corinthians."[171] On the other side, Paul does more than address a series of issues which arise as a result of factions and discord. There is more to the occasion of writing than this, even if this plays a role. It may well be the case, as our exegesis below demonstrates, that issues of "knowledge," the ministry, ethical laxity, advantages sought at law, marriage and celibacy, meat associated with pagan temples or worship, dress codes in public worship, the divisions at the Lord's Supper, misperceptions of the significance of what counts as "spiritual" in the context of "gifts" and Christ's Lordship, and perhaps a premature anticipation of eschatological "glory" all relate to the differing outlooks (some of them manipulative) on the part of specific groups. Nevertheless, to expound the underlying theology of these practical issues Paul advances the understanding of them that his addressees have reached. All are placed in the light of the cross, of divine grace, of the Lordship of Christ, and of a respect for "the other" that builds the whole community in mutuality and love. Much redefinition and "code switching" is entailed in the dialogue.[172]

To gain a clearer overview of the whole, it may be useful to trace J. C. Hurd's reconstruction of probable distinctions between material which responds to oral reports from Chloe's people, and material which replies to queries from Corinth by letter. Although Hurd's relatively early work dates from 1965, the arguments he advances concerning criteria for assessing the differences remain useful and still among the most detailed.[173] To be sure, serious modifications are also necessary, among which Margaret Mitchell's warning about the unreliability of the phrase "Now concerning . . ." (περὶ δέ) as a firm indicator of the topic raised by the letter from Corinth should be

---

170. Again, see Brown, *The Cross and Human Transformation,* in which apocalyptic underlines not only new creation but also the universal rather than the merely local.

171. W. Schmithals develops J. Weiss's partition theory in such a way as to attempt to identify nine letters for 1 and 2 Corinthians; Schmithals, "Die Korintherbriefe als Briefsammlung," *ZNW* 64 (1973), 263-88; cf. Weiss, *Der erste Korintherbrief,* xxxix-xliii.

172. See Moores, *Wrestling with Rationality in Paul,* 26-28; see also below.

173. Hurd, *The Origin of 1 Corinthians,* esp. 61-211.

noted.[174] In summary, (1) when he has to raise an issue about which no awareness has been expressed in a query from Corinth, Paul's tone is more emphatic, indignant, "aroused, even angry"; while in response to their questions or perceived difficulties, Paul's tone is calmer, gentler, and more carefully reasoned.[175] (2) There is a tendency for Paul to express issues more sharply ("all is black and white") when he has to bring a matter to their attention; he is more at pains to present both sides, or all sides, of a question which they have raised. (3) In the former case (i.e., where Paul initiates the issue) much emphasis is placed in the past and the present as this is reported; where they raise questions, the future and future policy receive primary attention. (4) A number of quotations from Corinth appear in 1 Corinthians. Hurd sees most of these as quotations from their letter (e.g., 6:12, 13; 7:1; 8:1, 4, 5, 6; 10:23; 11:2).[176] (5) He also cites the well-known supposed signal περὶ δέ, which occurs at 7:1, 25; 8:1; 12:1; 16:1; and 16:12. This coheres with his own analysis of the letter from Corinth as concerning (a) the married, 7:1-24; (b) unmarried men and women (7:25-38); (c) food offered to idols (8:1–11:1); (d) "spiritual gifts" (12:1–14:40); (e) the collection (16:1-4); and perhaps (f) Apollos (16:12).[177]

The first three criteria seem convincing, although they may not identify the only reason for such changes of mood or tone. The fourth may be valid in some cases; but Paul may at times well allude to what has been reported to him as a slogan or catchphrase in the life of the church. The fifth has already been called into question as a decisive criterion by Mitchell, but with caution it may serve as a broadly useful indicator of probability. Hurd then cites as responses to oral reports: (a) 1:10–4:21 on discord or splits and the ministry of Paul and Apollos; (b) 5:1-8 and 13a on the incestuous man; and (c) 11:17-34 on the divisions at the Lord's Supper. Hurd admits to uncertainty about whether the issue of immorality in 5:9-13a and the resurrection chapter (15:1-58) belong to the list of queries raised by the letter from Corinth.

Hurd's attempt to reconstruct the "previous letter" (to which 5:9 clearly alludes) remains in the nature of the case more speculative.[178] His hypothesis rests largely on identifying a tone of "counterarguments" to objections. Thus the previous letter would have stated (a) "Christians should be married because of the temptation to immorality"; to which the Corinthians would have voiced the objection "But it is best for a man *not* to touch a woman. Do you mean that married couples should forego the discipline of continence . . . ?" (b) "Avoid all association with immoral people, i.e., unbelievers." "But . . ." (c) "Avoid idola-

---

174. M. M. Mitchell, "Concerning περὶ δέ in 1 Corinthians," *NovT* 31 (1989): 229-56. Hurd's reconstruction of the "previous letter" may also invite some question.

175. See Hurd's summary in *The Origin of 1 Corinthians,* 82.

176. Ibid., 68, provides an extensive table of scholarly opinion up to 1965, listing some two dozen New Testament specialists.

177. Ibid., 65-74.

178. Ibid., 213-39.

try." "But an idol is nothing. There is no God but one." (d) "Women should wear veils." "But our woman never have been required to wear veils in the household of the church." (e) (f) (g) Similar counterarguments may relate to spiritual gifts, the resurrection, and the collection.

The most serious difficulty faced by the attempt to reconstruct the previous letter emerges from the last twenty years of research into classical and Pauline rhetoric. Whatever view one takes of Paul and diatribe style, there can be little doubt that Paul's awareness of the widespread use of deliberative rhetoric and its use within epistolary frameworks offers an alternative explanation to Hurd's explanations of the mood or tone of objections and counterarguments.[179] Some of his claims may be valid, but they cannot be demonstrated. The lasting contribution of Hurd's work lies in his formulation of criteria for distinguishing between Paul's responses to oral reports and responses to a letter, but even here only some of the criteria remain fully intact.

C. Controversy about the Integrity of the Epistle: Unifying Themes

To speak of the occasion of writing 1 Corinthians implies that we regard it as a single letter. R. F. Collins makes five initial points about the issue of the integrity of the epistle.[180] (1) It is remarkable that for almost the entire epistle (only 9:3, 14:15, and 15:16 are missing) we have a Greek MS which dates from around AD 200, namely Papyrus Chester Beatty II ($\mathfrak{p}^{46}$), no more than 150 years after Paul wrote the epistle. This is far older than any of the near complete MSS of the Gospels. The early $\mathfrak{p}^{45}$ is fragmentary. (2) On the other hand, Paul's letters are much longer than those of his contemporaries, and 1 Corinthians is especially long. Might it be a composite of more than one earlier letter? (3) Since 1876 when H. Hagge first raised this question, a number of scholars have argued that several letters are involved, of whom we should take account especially of J. Weiss (who argued for two letters in his commentary of 1910; for three letters in his *Earliest Christianity* of 1914, posthumously published 1917); W. Schmithals (three letters, 1956; nine letters for 1 and 2 Corinthians, 1973; thirteen letters, 1984); Robert Jewett (six letters, five from 1 Corinthians,

---

179. Cf. esp. Mitchell, *Paul and the Rhetoric of Reconciliation*, esp. 20-64; M. Bünker, *Briefformular und rhetorische Disposition im 1 Korintherbrief*, GTA 28 (Göttingen: Vandenhoeck & Ruprecht, 1984); Anders Eriksson, *Traditions as Rhetorical Proof: Pauline Argumentation in 1 Corinthians*, ConBNT 29 (Stockholm: Almqvist & Wiksell, 1998); Duane F. Watson (ed.), *Persuasive Artistry: Studies in New Testament Rhetoric in Honor of George A. Kennedy*, JSNTSS 50 (Sheffield: Sheffield Academic Press, 1991); and S. E. Porter and T. H. Olbricht (eds.), *Rhetoric and the New Testament*, JSNTSS 90 (Sheffield: Sheffield Academic Press, 1993), esp. 211-49.

180. Collins, *First Corinthians*, 10-14. On the integrity of the epistle see also Schrage, *Der erste Brief*, 1:63-71; H. Merklein, "Die Einheitlichkeit des ersten Korintherbriefes," *ZNW* 75 (1984): 153-83; and M. C. de Boer, "The Composition of 1 Corinthians," *NTS* 40 (1994): 229-45.

1978); Gerhard Sellin (three letters, 1987, 1991); and Khiok-kng Yeo (elements of four letters, 1995).[181] (4) Some of these theorists (e.g., Weiss and especially Schmithals) have changed their mind about the identity of the supposed letters, while the advocates of these partition theories seldom agree on where the partitions exist. (5) Strong arguments for the integrity of the epistle have been put forward by J. C. Hurd, H. Merklein, and M. M. Mitchell.[182]

Murphy-O'Connor is among those who advocate the unity of the epistle. Nevertheless, he urges, "the exaggerations of some practitioners . . . do not invalidate the method. Partition theories are never developed for their own sake; they are designed to account for observations that are made in good faith, and so they deserve to be taken seriously, even if ultimately they do not command assent."[183] Lang similarly regards such theories as understandable, but as necessary only if detailed exegesis forces such conclusions.[184] Thus Murphy-O'Connor concludes, with Fee, that "all the so-called contradictions in 1 Corinthians can be resolved by a more exacting exegesis."[185]

I have discussed some of the main partition theories elsewhere.[186] J. Weiss (1910) posited a first letter (Letter A) which remains extant in 10:1-23; 6:12-20; 10:23-30; 11:2-24 (together with 2 Cor 6:14–7:1); in contrast to a second (Letter B), namely 1:1–6:11; ch. 7 and 8; 9:1-23 (with ch. 13); and ch. 12, 14, 15, and 16.[187] Letter A seemed to Weiss to be more "rigorist," correcting unqualified freedom from the law, while Letter B examined a more balanced perspective. Several years later, however, Weiss revised his theory in terms of three letters (1 Corinthians 1–4 became B2 or C, together with 5:1–6:11, i.e., 1:1–6:11).[188] M. Goguel postulated three letters in 1926, but although he took account of Weiss, the outcome was significantly different.[189] J. Héring rejects the specific conclusions of Weiss and Goguel, but identifies two letters: Letter A is supposedly chs. 1–8, 10:23–11:1, and 16:1-4, 10-14; Letter B is the remainder, including ch. 15.[190]

W. Schmithals draws on the theories of J. Weiss and W. Schenk to pro-

---

181. The most extreme is W. Schmithals, "Die Korintherbriefe als Briefsammlung," *ZNW* 64 (1973): 263-88.

182. Mitchell, *Paul and the Rhetoric of Reconciliation,* 186-92 and throughout.

183. Murphy-O'Connor, *Paul,* 253.

184. F. Lang, *Die Briefe an die Korinther,* NTD 7 (Göttingen: Vandenhoeck & Ruprecht, 1994), 7.

185. Murphy-O'Connor, *Paul,* 253; Fee, *The First Epistle to the Corinthians,* 15-16.

186. A. C. Thiselton, "Luther and Barth on 1 Cor 15: Six Theses for Theology in Relation to Recent Interpretation," in W. P. Stephens (ed.), *The Bible, The Reformation and the Church: Essays in Honour of James Atkinson,* JSNTSS 105 (Sheffield: Sheffield Academic Press, 1995), 275-78; cf. 258-89.

187. Weiss, *Der erste Korintherbrief,* xl-xlii.

188. J. Weiss, *Earliest Christianity* (2 vols., Eng. trans., New York: Harper, 1959), 1:323-41.

189. M. Goguel, *Introduction au Nouveau Testament,* 4.2 (Paris: Leroux, 1926), 86.

190. J. Héring, *The First Epistle of St Paul to the Corinthians* (Eng. trans., London: Epworth Press, 1962), xii-xiv.

pose nine letters for the whole of Paul's correspondence.[191] Letter A is 1 Cor 11:2-34; Letter B ("the previous letter") is 1 Cor 6:1-11; 2 Cor 6:14–7:1; 1 Cor 6:12-20; 9:24–10:22; 15:11-58; 16:13-24; Letter C (the letter of response) is 1 Cor 5:1-13; 7:1–8:13; 9:19:22; 10:23–11:1; 12:1-31a; 14:1c-40; 12:31b–13:13; 16:1-12; and Letter D is 1 Cor 1:1–4:21. Since Letters E-I move from the "intermediate letter" (traditionally between our 1 and 2 Corinthians) onward, in theory these do not yet concern us, except that 1 Cor 9:1-18 is claimed to be part of Letter F. Schmithals offers variants in other writings, calling attention to the early theories of C. Clement (1894) and Weiss (1910).[192] Robert Jewett distinguishes six letters, of which five embody parts of 1 Corinthians. "Letter B" contains 1 Corinthians 15 together with 6:12-20; 9:24–19:22; 16:13-22 (with 2 Cor 6:14–7:1); "Letter C" is "the main frame" of eight blocks; "Letter D" embodies some fragments; "Letter E" contains 1 Cor 9:1-18 and 2 Corinthians 10–13.[193] G. Sellin offered a simpler but nonetheless comparatively still complex scheme in 1987.[194] In the same year W. O. Walker presented an overview of his proposals about non-Pauline interpolations.[195]

The most readily understandable and possible proposal is the modest suggestion of M. C. de Boer that Paul took up his pen (or rather resumed his dictation) twice, since after initial news from Chloe's people a second report arrived that caused him to address the situation with additional material.[196] First, Paul addressed the issue of discord in chs. 1–4. Then Stephanas arrived with the Corinthians' letter (7:25; 8:1; 12:1; 16:1, 12; cf. 16:16). But where do 11:2-end and ch. 15 fit in? "That Stephanas and Fortunatas and Achaicus remained mute as Paul read the letter from Corinth, out loud in their presence, is historically implausible. . . . They thus supplied him with further information. . . . Paul must have questioned them closely."[197] In de Boer's view it is "likely" that chs. 5–6 were occasioned by the Stephanas delegation.[198] "Breaks" occur between 4:21 and 5:1 and between 6:21 and 7:1. Moreover, 4:14-21 looks like a conclusion, but Paul does not close. He continues with an abrupt "it is actually reported that there is πορνεία among you . . . of such a kind that does not exist even among pagans" (5:1). De Boer finds H. Merklein's attempt to account for this stylistic break unconvincing.[199] He concludes, "Given the tone of incredulity, disgust

---

191. Schmithals, "Die Korintherbriefe als Briefsammlung," 263-88.

192. W. Schmithals, *Gnosticism in Corinth* (Eng. trans., Nashville: Abingdon, 1971 from 3d Ger. ed. [1st ed. 1956]), 87-113.

193. R. Jewett, "The Redaction of 1 Corinthians and the Trajectory of the Pauline School," *JAAR Sup.* 46 (1978): 398-444.

194. G. Sellin, "Hauptprobleme des ersten Korintherbriefes," *ANRW* 2.25.4 (1987): 2964-86.

195. W. O. Walker, "The Burden of Proof in Identifying Interpolations in the Pauline Letters," *NTS* 33 (1987): 610-18.

196. de Boer, "The Composition of 1 Corinthians," 229-45.

197. Ibid., 232.

198. Ibid., 233.

199. Merklein, "Die Einheitlichkeit des ersten Korintherbriefes," 159-60; cf. 153-83.

and shock that marks 5:1, . . . are we really to think that this information has come to Paul before he wrote chapters 1–4. . . ?"[200] This conclusion may also serve to explain why there may be some ambivalence about the purpose or certainty of Timothy's visit when we compare 4:17 with 16:10. Perhaps the one weakness in de Boer's argument is his contrast between a theology of the cross in chs. 1–4 and the "practical and behavioral" tone of chs. 5–6. The whole thrust of 5:1–14:40 concerns living out the identity of those who stand under the criterion of the cross and its implications of self-renunciation for the sake of "the other" and the whole community. Otherwise much of 8:1–11:1 and 12:1–14:40 loses its theological basis.[201]

Unless we accept the reasonable but not conclusive case of Martinus de Boer, what remain are the more convincing arguments of Fee, Lang, Mitchell, and Collins to the effect that such partition theories are needed *only if exegesis fails to reveal a genuine coherence* within the epistle. Schrage identifies the real issues: are the supposed tensions (1) between 11:18-19 and 1:10-12, (2) within chs. 8–10, or (3) between supposedly differing sources of information so great that we are forced into one of these theories?[202] E.-B. Allo carefully examined the claims of Weiss and Goguel, and convincingly concluded : "We do not hesitate to endorse the judgment of Godet, who sees an intellectual edifice admirably conceived and executed in spite of the diversity of the material."[203] Indeed, he has tart comments for Weiss and Goguel, over against the more generous observations noted above from Murphy-O'Connor. M. M. Mitchell convincingly demonstrates the rhetorical (or logical) coherence of the epistle subsequently to most of the partition theories.[204] The one weakness in Mitchell's argument is to underemphasize the theological basis of the unity which she demonstrates. The appeal of deliberative rhetoric "for advantage" is not only too vague a category; what counts as "advantage" is turned upside down by the cross, so that "advantage" now concerns (as she states) the "building up" of *the whole* and respect and concern for "the other." Even if he pre-dates most of the debate about partition and rhetoric, Karl Barth is right to insist: "the discourse of the whole epistle proceeds from a single point and harks back again to this point."[205] The resurrection which presupposes the cross and defines the cross from the side of eschatology (i.e., as grace, gift, and transformation into the mode of existence characterized by the Holy Spirit; see exegesis of 15:42-44) provides "the meaning and nerve of its [the epistle's] whole."[206]

---

200. De Boer, "The Composition of 1 Corinthians," 240.

201. Cf. again Brown, *The Cross and Human Transformation,* and Schrage, *Der erste Brief,* 1:165-203.

202. Schrage, *Der erste Brief,* 1:63-71.

203. Allo, *Première Épitre aux Corinthiens,* lxxxv.

204. Mitchell, *Paul and the Rhetoric of Reconciliation,* throughout.

205. Karl Barth, *The Resurrection of the Dead* (Eng. trans., London: Hodder & Stoughton, 1933), 113.

206. Ibid., 115.

Although I argued in 1978 that the unifying issue in 1 Corinthians was that of an overrealized eschatology, I should now wish to qualify this in spite of reaffirming this emphasis.[207] The triumphalism of many Christians at Corinth was certainly encouraged and supported by an overrealized eschatology which in turn led to a distorted view of what constitutes "being spiritual," or a "person of the Spirit." I stand by my conclusion of 1978 that the topics addressed in 1 Corinthians do not represent an almost random set of pastoral and ethical problems in relation to which Paul adopts a merely reactive stance, but that a "systematic and coherent" dimension characterizes both theological themes in Corinth and Paul's reproclamation of grace, the cross, and resurrection instantiated and actualized in terms of these contingent problems.[208] *Nevertheless I now perceive how this theological misperception combined with the seductive infiltration into the Christian church of cultural attitudes derived from secular or non-Christian Corinth as a city. Concerns about self-promotion, the psychological insecurity generated by status inconsistency, competitive pragmatism, and the radical pluralism which we have identified with David Harvey's "postmodern mood" of the social construction of a "virtual" reality, all encouraged concerns about "high status" as "people of the Spirit who were gifted" within a Christian subculture with its own autonomous value system.* Dale Martin's research into "higher-status gift[s]" and spiritual "status indicators" coheres well with the theological misperceptions that Paul also identifies.[209] With Pogoloff, Martin shows the associations between status-claims and rhetoric; status and places and provisions for dining in the context of the Lord's Supper; status and glossolalia; status, asceticism, and celibacy.[210]

As A. R. Brown and D. B. Martin, among others, argue, the unifying theme of the epistle is a *reproclamation of the different value system of grace, gifts, the cross, and the resurrection as divine verdict, criterion, and status bestowal within the new framework of respect and love for the less esteemed "other." Glorying in the Lord and receiving status derived from identification with the crucified Christ (1:30-31) lead to a new value system demonstrable in a wide array of life issues.* These range from attitudes toward "the less esteemed" in civil actions (6:1-11) to eating meat in the precincts of temples or bought at market (8:1–11:1); or from dress-codes in public worship (11:2-16)

---

207. A. C. Thiselton, "Realized Eschatology at Corinth," *NTS* 24 (1978): 510-26. The main thesis is affirmed by C. K. Barrett, *The First Epistle to the Corinthians,* 109; F. F. Bruce, *1 and 2 Corinthians,* NCBC (London: Oliphants, 1971), 49-50; and E. Käsemann, *New Testament Questions of Today* (Eng. trans., London: SCM, 1969), 125-26.

208. Thiselton, "Realized Eschatology at Corinth," 526; similarly, Thiselton, "Luther and Barth on 1 Cor 15," 275-78; cf. J. C. Becker, *Paul the Apostle* (Edinburgh: T. & T. Clark and Philadelphia: Fortress, 1980), 11-36 and 135-212; and Brown, *The Cross* (cited above).

209. D. B. Martin, *The Corinthian Body* (New Haven: Yale University Press, 1995), 86; and Martin, "Tongues of Angels and Other Status Indicators at Corinth," *JAAR* 59 (1991): 547-89.

210. Martin, *The Corinthian Body,* respectively 50-66, 73-76, 87-92, and 209-12.

or mutual respect for differing gifts (chs. 12–13) to the "ranking" and use of prophetic discourse and glossolalia (ch. 14). Yet "proclamation" does not fully indicate the wide range and subtlety of Paul's method of argument in this epistle. Part of what we have termed the "postmodern mood" at Corinth entailed the priority of the local over traditions of more universal currency; obsession with pragmatic success at the expense of devaluing truth; social recognition and manipulation by persuasion over against argument and rationality. This provides a reason (which emerges from more than mere fashion in New Testament studies) to conclude this Introduction with some comments on Paul's method of argument and rhetoric alongside his role as a letter writer.

IV. ARGUMENT AND RHETORIC: DOES PAUL AS LETTER WRITER, THEOLOGIAN, AND PASTOR USE RHETORICAL FORMS AND STRUCTURES?

A. The Need for a Balanced Assessment: Types and Levels of Appeal, Rhetoric, and Epistolography

There is no need to take up space listing the content of the epistle by themes, since the Contents pages of this commentary adequately perform this task. However, several unnecessary and unfortunate *polarizations* have distorted certain recent discussions of the role of rhetoric in Paul, in the context of which we try to adopt a middle way.

(1) First, *sheer argument alone* remains too often in the exclusively *intellectualist, didactic cognitive realm,* whereas, as M. M. Mitchell reminds us, *deliberative rhetoric in Paul's day also addressed the emotions, human desire, and future policies of action.*[211] As A. R. Brown and R. Pickett have argued in relation to the cross, and as I have consistently urged in my *New Horizons in Hermeneutics,* the function of much (although not necessarily all) biblical material is *transformative* (not simply informative).[212] For this reason "rhetoric," as a term, offers one advantage over the more traditional term "argument." It keeps in view an address to the whole person: reason, emotions, desires, attitude, will, and action; not simply the addressee as mere mind. This accords with Paul's view of the wholeness of human selfhood within the public domain, conveyed often by his use of σῶμα (1 Cor 6:20). Yet for all this there

---

211. Mitchell, *Paul and the Rhetoric of Reconciliation,* esp. 20-64; cf. Witherington, *Conflict and Community in Corinth,* 39-48 and 57-61; J. A. Crafton, "The Dancing of an Attitude: Burkean Rhetorical Criticism and the Biblical Interpreter," in S. E. Porter and T. H. Olbricht (eds.), *Rhetoric and the New Testament,* 429-42 (see further below).

212. Brown, *The Cross and Human Transformation,* esp. 13-64; R. Pickett, *The Cross,* 58-74; and A. C. Thiselton, *New Horizons in Hermeneutics: The Theory and Practice of Transforming Biblical Reading* (London: HarperCollins and Grand Rapids: Zondervan, 1992; rpt. Carlisle: Paternoster, n.d.), esp. 1-54 and 558-620.

remains a version of approach to rhetoric which encourages what Eriksson diagnoses as "the dichotomy between rhetoric and argumentation."[213]

Aristotle, Cicero, and Quintilian, we have already noted, saw "the art of persuasion" (Aristotle) or "the science of speaking well" *(bene dicendi scientia)* as the study of methods of articulation and expression, but not in such a way as to disengage this from rational argument and from passion (or at least concern) for truth.[214] As soon as provincial rhetoricians in such cultures as Roman Corinth came to stake everything on the approval and applause of the audience, "truth" lost its anchorage in the extralinguistic world and became a matter of social construction or "local" perception. It is noteworthy that Richard Rorty uses the term "local" with warm approval, as a strategy for avoiding what he openly concedes we should have to term "relativist."[215] At Corinth, similarly, "local" stands in contrast to Paul's summons to heed "the tradition" observed in "all the churches" (1:2; 3:13, 18, 22; 10:24; 11:2, 16, 17, 23; 14:36). "Rhetoric," however, *need* not be merely "instrumental, pragmatic or local." George Kennedy defines it as "the art of persuasion . . . of all who aim at some kind of attitude change on the part of their audience or readers."[216]

(2) A polarization between *audience-oriented rhetoric and tradition* should not stand without correction. Although we have endorsed the complaints of Pogoloff and Moores about the effects of audience-related criteria which Paul seems to reject, nevertheless Eriksson, again, points out how often Paul deliberately *begins* his argumentation from *Corinthian premises.*[217] Eriksson maintains a judicious balance by showing how *Paul consistently appeals to traditions* (as well as to OT scripture and rational or logical coherence), but that the eight specific instantiations of common Christian traditions to which Paul explicitly appeals "constitute *agreed-upon premises* which are the starting point for argumentation" (my italics).[218] These eight "Corinthian premises" include 1 Cor 15:3-5; 8:11b; 11:23-25; 10:16; 12:3; 16:22; 8:6; and 12:13.[219] Hence Eriksson would agree with Moores and Pogoloff that "the identity of the message" is betrayed if it is defined by the audience rather than by the kerygma of the cross.[220] Nevertheless the shared premises allow for what Moores calls "enthymematic semiosis," i.e., a productivity of sign recognition which remains within the horizons of the addressees while undergoing changes

---

213. Eriksson, *Traditions as Rhetorical Proof: Pauline Argumentation in 1 Corinthians* 7.

214. Quintilian, *Institutio Oratoria* 2.14.5; cf. 2.15.34, 38 and 2.15 as a whole. See further G. A. Kennedy, *The Art of Rhetoric in the Roman World* (Princeton: Princeton University Press, 1972).

215. R. Rorty, *Truth and Progress: Philosophical Papers* (Cambridge: Cambridge University Press, 1998), 3:10; cf. 1-15.

216. Kennedy, *The Art of Rhetoric,* 3.

217. Eriksson, *Traditions as Rhetorical Proof,* 7.

218. Ibid., 3.

219. Ibid., 73-134.

220. Moores, *Wrestling with Rationality in Paul,* 133-34.

and revaluations which constitute them into transformative speech-acts of various kinds.[221]

Along with Eriksson, Moores underlines Paul's uses of *argument* which embody (1) appeals to Scripture, and (2) appeals to reason.[222] However, the "open" or "unstated" aspects of premises and rational inference transform mere deduction or induction, which remains abstract and general, into contingent "enthymemes" which take up the "social" and "communicative" aspects of language to perform actions of attitude-change and persuasion, without sacrificing truth through "psychological exploitation of the audience" (cf. 1 Cor 2:1-5; see exegesis below).[223] "For Paul the power of the letter lies in the truth of what he is saying and his authority to proclaim it as such."[224] However, the "shared code" which allows intelligible communicative action to take place between the writer and the addressees thereby undergoes subtle modifications, corrections, and expansions. Moores derives from Umberto Eco the significance of "over-coding" and even "code-switching."[225] In an earlier study (1973) I anticipated this argument in terms of the simpler notion of "persuasive definition," which I applied to Paul's different definition of "being spiritual" from that widely used in Corinth.[226] I wrote, "Paul enters the horizons of the Corinthians only in order to transform them. Thus our language-games [Wittgenstein's term] are placed, once again, within . . . the framework of the message of the cross. And this, in turn, conditions once again the logic of their terms."[227] Thus the premise about the Spirit's prompting confession of Christ's Lordship is shared (12:3; cf. Eriksson's argument), but what "spirituality" inspired by the same Holy Spirit amounts to may *begin* with "a favorable emotive meaning" but *turn out to carry a cognitive content* which calls this into question.[228] Over the last twenty-seven years, however, I have come to lay increasing emphasis on this redefining or code switching as *transformative speech-acts.*

Alexandra Brown is entirely correct at this point to portray Paul's re-proclamation of the cross in this epistle as a speech-act in three particulars. First, it transforms perceptions and realities *in* the very utterance of this proclamation (J. L. Austin's definition of illocutionary acts); second, the epistle also constitutes "the correction of a prior speech-act that has misfired. To those who already think they already 'have it', the gospel must be preached again"; third, illocutions presuppose epistemological truth-claims and have "profound epistemological conse-

221. Ibid., 5-32.
222. Ibid., 10-11.
223. Ibid., 14-17.
224. Ibid., 22.
225. Ibid., 25-26; cf. 27-32.
226. A. C. Thiselton, "The Meaning of σάρξ in 1 Cor 5:5: A Fresh Approach in the Light of Logical and Semantic Factors," *SJT* 26 (1973): 204-28, esp. 216-18.
227. Ibid., 216.
228. The quotation, ibid., 217, is borrowed from John Hospers, *An Introduction to Philosophical Analysis* (London: Routledge, 2d ed. 1967), 53-54, on persuasive definition.

quences."[229] In other words, as against postmodern and "postliberal" attempts to appropriate J. L. Austin (ignoring his work on presuppositions), none of this operative language functions merely within an intralinguistic world of purely social construction. The truth of the gospel transcends this.

(3) In addition to all this, it is a mistake to polarize the genre used by *Paul as a letter writer (epistolography)* with genre used for *rhetorical purposes (rhetorical argument)*. Anders Eriksson provides an incisive and convincing exposé of this false and unhappy polarity in his excellent account of "Epistolography and Rhetoric" in 16:13-24.[230] Epistolary conventions, Eriksson argues, "shed light in the letter opening and the letter closing, which comprised a relatively large and highly standardized part of the short ancient letters." However, because letter forms shed less light on the main body of the Pauline letter, "many rhetorical critics here take the opposite stand."[231] Eriksson is able to shed considerable light on the *Maranatha* section as *both* rhetorical *peroratio* (recapitulation which takes up themes from *exordium* and *propositio,* 1:1-10) and the theme of "building up" from the body of the letter, with an eye to the future dimension characteristic of deliberative rhetoric. The details of Eriksson's proposals emerge in our exegesis of 16:13-24 (see below).[232]

For our part we have tried to hold together research from each of these two areas. Our bibliographies on 1:1-3, 4-9 and 16:13-24, as well as the exegesis which follows each, take seriously both standardized forms and epistolographic formulae, and Paul's creative use of conventions for his purposes without a countercultural undermining of the expected courtesies and customs. Some works rightly attempt to place equal weight on the epistolary and rhetorical in these sections.[233] There is no question whatever that Paul dictated his letters (see 16:21-24 as the exception), and this was the standard practice for most letter writers.[234] On its arrival it would be read aloud to the assembled Christians. We should avoid the historical anachronism of imagining that the majority at Corinth would have read his letter "privately" in silence as individuals. Hence Paul would have assumed its oral and aural impact, as well as its corporate context of understanding. Collins takes up Robert Funk's well-known work on letter reading as a way of extending Paul's "apostolic presence" to the community.[235]

---

229. Brown, *The Cross,* 8-30, esp. 30 (on correcting an earlier speech-act) and 8 (on epistemology).

230. Eriksson, *Traditions as Rhetorical Proof,* 280-84.

231. Ibid., 281.

232. Ibid., 279-98.

233. See D. L. Stamps, *The Rhetorical Use of the Epistolary Form in 1 Corinthians: The Rhetoric of Power* (Sheffield: JSOT Press, revised Durham Ph.D. thesis, 1992, still forthcoming for 2000). More than fifty works are cited on Paul as letter writer under 1:1-3 alone (see below).

234. Cf. the reference to Tertius as scribe or secretary for Romans (Rom 16:22).

235. Collins, *First Corinthians,* 3. Cf. R. W. Funk, "The Apostolic Presence: Paul," in Funk, *Parables and Presence* (Philadelphia: Fortress, 1982), also reprinted in W. R. Farmer, C. F. D. Moule, and R. R. Niebuhr (eds.), *Christian History and Interpretation: Studies Presented to John Knox* (Cambridge: Cambridge University Press, 1967), 249-68.

This makes it all the more important to evaluate the competing views set forth in our exegesis of 1:1, and especially of 9:1, about apostleship. In contrast to A. C. Wire and many others, I have argued (in part following Chrysostom, Best, Schrage, and Crafton) that Paul sees his apostleship not as an instrument of power but as a call to become a transparent agency through whom the crucified and raised Christ becomes portrayed through lifestyle, thought, and utterance (see below on 1:1 and 9:1).[236] In these terms Paul's extended correspondence of at least four letters to Corinth (the previous letter, 1 Corinthians, the letters of tears, and either 2 Corinthians or 2 Corinthians 1–9) should be seen as attempts to make transparent Christ (not Paul) to Corinth, through the medium of transformative speech-action. We have noted above that "the previous letter" (1 Cor 5:9) is sometimes identified with 2 Cor 6:14–7:1 (but not widely); and that his probable intention of visiting Corinth (1 Cor 16:5) may have had to be postponed, in which case many have argued that the "severe" letter of 2 Cor 2:4, 9 (which hardly seems to describe 1 Corinthians) may have served in place of this visit. Some identify this with 2 Corinthians 10–13; others believe that it has been lost; still others identify with a partition segment of 1 Corinthians. Whatever detailed conclusions about a series of letters we may adopt, the very least that the texts of 1 and 2 Corinthians demand is that Paul wrote no less than four letters to Corinth (cf. 1 Cor 5:9; 2 Cor 2:4, 9), whether or not he wrote more.

This phenomenon, together with such prolonged stays as not less than eighteen months at Corinth and no less than three years at Ephesus, serves *to underline Paul's concern as a pastor, or at least as a missionary-pastor,* who was no mere itinerant evangelist. Paul is neither simply the "theological thinker" (cf. J. Weiss) nor someone preoccupied with his own "experience" of being in Christ (cf. A. Deissmann), but a pastor whose "theology arises from his work as apostle," provided that we do not think of his theology as merely reactive.[237] Here the rhetorical emphasis of Anders Eriksson as arguments from Scripture and tradition reformulated in such a way as to constitute intelligible communicative acts from shared presuppositions offers a constructive emphasis.[238] Murphy-O'Connor also

---

236. See exegesis of 1:1 and 9:1. A. C. Wire, *The Corinthian Women Prophets* (Minneapolis: Fortress, 1990), sees the epistle as largely a conflict between "apostolic" authority (Paul) and "prophetic" authority or autonomy (especially liberated women at Corinth as prophets). Paul uses a rhetoric of power to dissociate thought (theirs) from reality (his); private from public to constrain women's freedom; self from community; and "flesh" from "Spirit" (ibid., esp. 12-23, but also throughout). From a postmodern perspective, Paul elevates his own "local" view particularly into "universal" truth on the basis of a perceived call to apostleship with a privileged role. In contrast see Chrysostom (*Homilies on the Epistles to the Corinthians,* 1:1); E. Best, "Apostolic Authority — ?" *JSNT* 27 (1986): 3-25; Schrage, *Der erste Brief,* 1:99-101; and J. A. Crafton, *The Agency of the Apostle,* JSNTSS 51 (Sheffield: JSOT Press, 1991), 62-63 and elsewhere. Cf. also Wolff, *Der erste Brief,* 14.

237. J. Munck, *Paul and the Salvation of Mankind* (Eng. trans., London: SCM, 1959), 67. Cf. also Beker, *Paul the Apostle.*

238. Eriksson, *Traditions as Rhetorical Proof;* cf. also H. Merklein, *Der erste Brief, Kap 1– 4,* 42-53 and throughout.

maintains a constructive balance between the pastoral concern shown corporately by Paul and his co-workers and his role as letter writer.[239] Like Eriksson, Murphy-O'Connor brings together epistolography and rhetoric as complementary aspects of a communicative whole.

B. The Decline and Rebirth of Rhetorical Approaches: The Basis of Transformative Speech-Acts in a Theology of the Cross

If rhetorical devices feature significantly in Paul's method of argument, however, how can we explain why, after a brief exploration of the subject by Weiss and others at the end of the nineteenth century, seventy years would elapse before the issue received renewed attention in biblical and Pauline studies? J. Weiss (1897) identified rhetorical features in Paul's epistles on the ground that these would play a role *in their public oral reading.* He insisted that we must approach the Pauline texts as *spoken* material. He endorsed the view of F. Blass that their style was lively, and embodied "asyndeton, antithesis, symmetry and rhythm."[240] He found parallelism in 1 Cor 1:21-22 (cf. also Rom 4:17); synonymous parallelism in 1 Cor 4:5; 15:50 (cf. Rom 1:21; 7:7; Gal 1:11-14; 3:14; Phil 1:9, 10); synthetic parallelism in 1 Cor 6:2-4 and 12:4-11 (cf. Rom 4:25; 10:9, 10); and antithetical parallelism in 1 Cor 12:3, 26; 15:42-44 (cf. 2 Cor 4:7-11, 16-18).[241] He also identified ascending rhetoric toward a climax, and "effects with sound" *(die Klangwirkung)* (e.g., πάντες . . . πάντες . . . πάντες . . . πλείοσιν in1 Cor 10:1-5 and the connectives in 10:6-11).[242] Weiss found chiasmus (abc-cba, in 1 Cor 9:19-22) and rhetorical "purple patches" *(Glanzstelle)* in Rom 8:31-39 and 1 Corinthians 13, of which the latter is also rhythmic and chiastic.[243] Finally, he detected numerous examples of symmetry (e.g., 1 Cor 3:1, but mostly in Romans).[244] In his last work, *Earliest Christianity* (1914), Weiss underlined Paul's originality as a writer, emphasizing his artistry, versatility, and use of the diatribe style.[245] In 1908 Weiss also reemphasized the shaping of the text for *public reading aloud.*[246] Rhetoric and epistolography, therefore, go hand in hand.

In 1908 Bultmann published his dissertation on similarities of style be-

239. J. Murphy-O'Connor, *Paul the Letter-Writer: His World, His Options, His Skills* (Collegeville: Glazier/Liturgical Press, 1995), esp. 1-41 and 64-101.

240. J. Weiss, "Beiträge zur paulinischen Rhetorik," in *Theologische Studien: Bernhard Weiss zu seinem 70 Geburtstage* (Göttingen: Vandenhoeck & Ruprecht, 1897), 166-67; cf. 165-247.

241. Ibid., 169-80.

242. Ibid., 186-88.

243. Ibid., 194-200.

244. Ibid., 207-44.

245. Weiss, *Earliest Christianity,* 2:399-419.

246. J. Weiss, *Die Aufgaben der neutestamentlichen Wissenschaft in dem Gegenwart* (Göttingen: Vandenhoeck & Ruprecht, 1908).

tween Paul and the Cynic-Stoic diatribe. Bultmann found examples of such diatribe style as rhetorical questions, paradoxes, parodies, and antitheses, and suggested parallels with Graeco-Roman writers from Bion to Epictetus.[247] Substantial modifications to his proposals about Paul's style in Romans, however, have more recently (1981) been suggested by Stowers.[248] Two major and influential works by E. Norden were ambivalent about Paul's rhetoric. In *Die antike Kunstprosa* Norden surveyed rhetorical prose from the sixth century BC to the Renaissance and found Paul "unhellenic."[249] Yet by common consent Norden paid most attention to the figurative, poetic, and rhythmic, which seemed to him to be largely lacking in Paul.[250] Thus in his second edition of 1909 Norden added a "Nachträge" in which he withdrew much of his earlier assessment, partly in dialogue with C. F. G. Heinrici. Yet his ambivalence returned in his later *Agnostos Theos*.[251]

It is widely agreed that in part the influence of Norden together with Deissmann's insistence that Paul's epistles were letters which presupposed the Greek of ordinary, everyday life as reflected in the papyri contributed much to the demise of rhetoric in Pauline studies. Apart from a careful suggestive and unduly neglected study by N. Schneider (1970), it is usually suggested that the reintroduction of serious attention to rhetoric in Pauline studies owes most to Hans-Dieter Betz, especially his work on Galatians.[252] Schneider, however, had already considered in some detail Paul's use of the classical rhetorical categories identified by Cicero, among others, of *inventio* (to find out what needs to be said); *dispositio* (to dispose and arrange the material); *elocutio* (its articulation or expression); and *actio* (its delivery); as well as such compositional elements now assumed in Pauline studies as *exordium* (opening to render the audience receptive); *narratio* (statement of a case); *confirmatio* (affirmative proof); *refutatio* or *confutatio* (refutation or rebuttal); and *peroratio* (conclusion).[253] In

247. R. Bultmann, *Der Stil der paulinischen Predigt und die Kynisch-stoische Diatribe* (Göttingen: Vandenhoeck & Ruprecht, 1910).

248. S. K. Stowers, *The Diatribe and Paul's Letter to the Romans,* SBLDS 57 (Chico: Scholars Press, 1981).

249. E. Norden, *Die antike Kunstprosa vom VI Jahrhundert vor Christus in die Zeit der Renaissance* (2 vols., Leipzig: Teubner, 1898).

250. Ibid., 1:50-55 and 499; cf. D. L. Clark, *Rhetoric in Graeco-Roman Education* (New York: Columbia University Press, 1957), 89-91.

251. E. Norden, *Agnostos Theos: Untersuchungen zur Formengeschichte religioser Rede* (4th ed., Leipzig: Teubner, 1923).

252. N. Schneider, *Die rhetorische Eigenart der paulinischen Antithese,* HUT 11 (Tübingen: Mohr, 1970); H.-D. Betz, "The Literary Composition and Function of Paul's Letter to the Galatians," *NTS* 21 (1975): 353-79; and his *Commentary on Paul's Letter to the Churches in Galatia,* Hermeneia (Philadelphia: Fortress, 1979).

253. The literature on this subject has now become breathtakingly immense. An excellent survey of major studies is offered by Stanley E. Porter, "The Theoretical Justification for Application of Rhetorical Categories to Pauline Epistolary Literature," in S. E. Porter and T. H. Olbricht (eds.), *Rhetoric and the New Testament: Essays from the 1992 Heidelberg Conference* (Sheffield: Sheffield Academic Press, 1993), 100-122, esp. 101, n. 4. However, the most comprehensive (even

our exegesis below we have found these categories to be especially constructive for our understanding of the rigorous logic of 15:1-58 on the resurrection and have often followed Eriksson on a variety of passages.[254]

In our exegesis of 1:1-3 and 1:4-9 we have paid most attention to Paul's simultaneous use of, and modification to, the standard letter form (see below), but we have also noted briefly their respective functions as prescript and *exordium*. Yet the genuineness of Paul's thanksgiving for the dynamic, even if also confused, Christian community in this vital strategic center (see above) should not become lost in observations about his winning audience-support by following the rhetorical convention of the *exordium* (vv. 4-9). Similarly we have accepted (below) Margaret Mitchell's rhetorical account of 1:10-12 as reflecting an appeal to deliberative rhetoric and a use of standard political terminology for the "advantage" of unity, but we have also qualified this firmly by noting Bjerkelund's research on the interpersonal uses of παρακαλῶ in 1:10 as denoting a request often based upon a personal or official relationship.[255] This does not prevent us from underlining Mitchell's understanding of 1:10 as functioning (at least in part) as a rhetorical *propositio* (see below), and Paul's "statement" about the report from Chloe's people (1:11-17) as sharing the function of a rhetorical *narratio* (see below).[256]

Our appeal to rhetorical categories also reflects some degree of caution, however, since we also believe that speculative hypothesis should not assume the status of proven facts. After all, Pogoloff, Winter, and many others have rightly stressed that Paul explicitly rejects the clothing of a professional rhetorician (cf. 2:1-5).[257] As is the case with the letter form, Paul uses the expected conventions and tools of the day when they serve, and do not conflict with, his

---

if insufficiently selective) bibliography is Duane F. Watson and Alan J. Hauser, *Rhetorical Criticism of the Bible: A Comprehensive Bibliography with Notes on History and Method,* Biblical Interpretation Series (Leiden: Brill, 1994), 101-15 and 120-25 (the New Testament and Paul, history); 126-42 (classical rhetoric by topic); and 178-201 (Paul), esp. 188-89 (1 and 2 Corinthians). See also S. E. Porter and T. H. Olbricht (eds.), *Rhetoric, Scripture, Theology and Essays from the 1994 Praetoria Conference,* JSNTSS 131 (Sheffield: Sheffield Academic Press, 1996), esp. 251-328 (Thessalonians, Ephesians, Colossians) and 393-422 (J. Smit on rhetoric and theology). On rhetoric in 1 Corinthians see esp. Mitchell, *Paul and the Rhetoric of Reconciliation;* Witherington, *Conflict and Community,* 39-48 and 55-61; Pogoloff, *Logos and Sophia;* and Eriksson, *Traditions as Rhetorical Proof.*

254. In addition to Eriksson, *Traditions,* throughout, D. F. Watson provides useful treatments, e.g., "Paul's Rhetorical Strategy in 1 Cor 15," in S. E. Porter and T. H. Olbricht (eds.), *Rhetoric and the New Testament,* 231-49.

255. Mitchell, *Paul and the Rhetoric of Reconciliation,* 1-99 and 198-201; cf. C. J. Bjerkelund, *Parakalô. Form, Funktion und Sinn der parakalô-Sätze in den paulinischen Briefen* (Oslo: Universitetsforlaget, 1967), 24-58, 109-10, and throughout.

256. We have also noted Mitchell's constructive use of G. A. Kennedy, *Classical Rhetoric and Its Christian and Secular Tradition* (London: Croom Helm, 1980) 129-60, especially on deliberative, epideictic, and judicial rhetoric (see exegesis and notes under 1:10) and her use of Betz.

257. Pogoloff, *Logos and Sophia,* and Winter, *Philo and Paul among the Sophists,* are both discussed above. See also the exegesis of 2:1-5 below.

purpose, but the subject matter always takes priority over the form, as Pogoloff convincingly demonstrates. We may sum up the advantages of attention to rhetoric in Paul by noting that (among other factors) this underlines (1) the reading aloud of his letter in public, for which letter forms and rhetorical tools both play a constructive role; (2) the importance of rationality and argument in Paul, of which Moores, Stowers, and Eriksson provide helpful reminders and 1 Corinthians 15 is an outstanding example; and (3) the priority of theological content and the reproclamation of the cross over the "clever" use of forms, which Pogoloff and Winter (among others) readily demonstrate.[258] Eriksson's work on traditions also underlines this.

Stanley Porter, following L. Thurén, helpfully distinguishes between three different types of approach to rhetoric in Paul.[259] (i) White, Doty, and Hübner continued to entertain doubts about the importance of rhetoric in the Pauline epistles, emphasizing instead the letter form and epistolography.[260] We have already argued, however, in common with Murphy-O'Connor, M. Bünker, and especially Eriksson that the two must be seen as complementary, and neither must be overemphasized at the expense of the other. Paul is a letter writer, but his letters are read publicly to a corporate audience who use their ears rather than their eyes. (ii) George Kennedy and Klaus Berger understand the letters primarily as rhetorical speeches, with almost incidental epistolary openings and closings, while H.-D. Betz emphasizes rhetoric but allows more weight to the epistolary forms.[261] Our first objection still applies, and too close a rhetorical analysis throughout may become speculative and at times even perhaps alien to Paul's strategy. (iii) M. Bünker and L. Thurén (with Eriksson, whose work postdates Porter's essay) rightly apply epistolary and rhetorical categories to different levels of exploration in complementary ways.[262]

In addition to this threefold classification of the relation between rhetoric and epistolography, it has also become customary to distinguish between (a) uses of the traditions of classical rhetoric associated with the work of Betz, Kennedy, Watson, and Mitchell, and (b) the so-called "new" rhetoric associated

---

258. In addition to Moores and Eriksson (cited frequently above), see also S. K. Stowers, "Paul on the Use and Abuse of Reason," in D. L. Balch, E. Ferguson and W. A. Meeks (eds.), *Greeks, Romans and Christians: Essays in Honor of A. J. Malherbe* (Minneapolis: Fortress, 1990), 253-86.

259. S. E. Porter, "Rhetorical Categories," in *Rhetoric and the New Testament,* 100-122; L. Thurén, *The Rhetorical Strategy of 1 Peter* (Abo: Abo Akademi, 1990), 57-64.

260. J. L. White, *The Body of the Greek Letter,* SBLDS 2 (Missoula: Scholars Press, 1972); W. G. Doty, *Letters in Primitive Christianity* (Philadelphia: Fortress, 1973); H. Hübner, "Der Galaterbrief und das Verhältnis von antiker Rhetorik und Epistolographie," *TLZ* 109 (1984): 241-50.

261. K. Berger, "Apostelbrief und apostolische Rede: Zum Formular frühchristlichen Briefe," *ZNW* 65 (1974): 190-231; Kennedy, *Classical Rhetoric* (cited above) and *New Testament Interpretation through Rhetorical Criticism* (Chapel Hill: University of North Carolina Press, 1984).

262. Bünker, *Briefformular und rhetorische Disposition im 1 Korintherbrief;* and L. Thurén, *The Rhetorical Strategy of 1 Peter,* 57-64.

with C. Perelmann and L. Olbrechts-Tytega, which finds some resonance with the work of A. C. Wire and K. Plank on 1 Corinthians.[263] The "new" rhetoric, however, tends to embrace quasi-postmodern assumptions and attitudes which presuppose precisely the audience-related social construction that Pogoloff and Moores identify as a target for Pauline attack and as more characteristic of rhetoric in Corinth and the Sophists than of the truth-concerns of Cicero, Quintilian, and Paul. In the new rhetoric, there is a tendency for rationality to become merely instrumental reason in the service of prior interests. A. C. Wire perceives such "manipulative" rhetoric as part of Paul's own strategy.

Even if we retain the emphasis of "classical" as against "pragmatic" or "postmodern" rhetoric, and even if we maintain a judicious balance between issues of rhetoric and issues of epistolography, the missing dimension remains too readily that of *Paul as theologian.* We have observed the importance of the theological "message" in a diversity of studies from W. Schrage's emphasis on "the word of the cross as ground and criterion of community and apostle"; Pogoloff's emphasis on the priority of content over form in Paul's speaking and writing; and Moores' emphasis on the identity of author and addressees as shaped by the message rather than by audience expectations and pragmatic perceptions.[264] Yet of all the works which take account of the relation between rhetorical method and *theology,* those by Eriksson and by A. R. Brown bring us closest to two fundamental points.

(a) Eriksson argues that as theologian Paul appeals to (1) *Scripture;* and (2) the common *theological traditions* which both he and the church in Corinth have inherited and share. Further, (3) Paul uses *rational argument* to apply these to the Corinthian situation, while (4) consciously utilizing *shared premises to work from within their own horizons of understanding.*[265] Thus *without compromising the theological givenness of the Christian message Paul promotes communicative action which engages with where the addressees are,* and, further, in ways that *include but are not restricted to the cognitive, intellectual, or rational.* Hence he does not despise the exploration of rhetorical *inventio,* and *avoids* "the dichotomy between rhetoric and argumentation."[266] "Speaking well" thus addresses the mind, the heart, and the will, and (especially in deliberative rhetoric) future policy.[267]

263. Wire, *The Corinthian Women Prophets;* and K. Plank, *Paul and the Irony of Affliction* (Atlanta: Scholars Press, 1987). On the distinction cf., e.g., Witherington, *Conflict and Community,* 57-61.

264. Schrage, *Der erste Brief,* 1:165; cf. 165-90; Pogoloff, *Logos and Sophia,* 37-70, 99-172; Moores, *Wrestling with Rationality,* 132-45.

265. Eriksson, *Traditions as Rhetorical Proof,* 7-80; cf. 81-134 and throughout. On the importance of Scripture for Paul in 1 Corinthians, see B. S. Rosner, *Paul: Scripture and Ethics. A Study of 1 Cor 5–7,* AGJU 22 (Leiden: Brill, 1994); on his use of reason, see esp. S. K. Stowers, "Paul on the Use and Abuse of Reason," in D. L. Balch et al. (ed.), *Greeks* (cited above), 253-86.

266. Eriksson, *Traditions as Rhetorical Proof,* 7.

267. Ibid., 48-53; and Mitchell, *Paul and the Rhetoric of Reconciliation,* 20-60 (on deliberative rhetoric).

(b) Eriksson's excellent work (1998) is well complemented by the approach of Alexandra R. Brown (1995).[268] Brown brings together Paul's communication of the transformative power of the proclamation of the cross with a concern for epistemology and an exposition of performative speech-acts. For thirty years I have consistently argued for the importance of speech-act theory as one of many ways of understanding the language of the New Testament.[269] In particular I distinguish between *"illocutionary" speech-acts,* which depend for their effectiveness *on a combination of situation and recognition,* and *"perlocutionary" speech-acts,* which depend for their effectiveness on *sheer causal (psychological or rhetorical) persuasive power.*[270] This also holds for the distinction between the nature of *apostolic* rhetoric and the *pragmatic, audience-determined rhetoric of Corinth and of a postmodern world* shaped by social construction alone.

Perlocutions can change people's perceptions and values merely by the orator's playing to the gallery. *Illocutions* transform worldviews not merely *by* rhetorical utterance but *in* the very utterance. The making of a promise provides a model example.[271] For the addressee to be *persuaded* that the promise is valid (perlocution) may depend on sheer causal rhetoric. For the promise to achieve *operative currency* the speaker must be able to fulfill the promise, address it to the appropriate hearer, and sincerely match words with deeds. Similarly, where in theology promise may entail such an "institutional fact" as the covenant, acts of commission, verdict, declaration, or direction (e.g., 1 Cor 7:17; 14:37-38; 16:1) may depend upon the derivative and delegated authority of apostolic status.

---

268. Brown, *The Cross and Human Transformation,* throughout.

269. A. C. Thiselton, "Thirty Years of Hermeneutics: Retrospect and Prospects," in J. Krašovec (ed.), *Interpretation of the Bible* (Ljubljana: Slovenian Academy and Sciences and Arts, and Sheffield: Sheffield Academic Press, 1998), 1,559-74; "The Parables as Language-Event," *SJT* 23 (1970): 437-68; "The Supposed Power of Words in the Biblical Writings," *JTS* 25 (1974): 283-99; *New Horizons in Hermeneutics* (1992, cited above), 31-54, 272-312, and 597-602; "Christology in Luke, Speech-Act Theory and the Problem of Dualism after Kant," in J. B. Green and M. Turner (eds.), *Jesus of Nazareth: Lord and Christ. Studies in Honour of I. H. Marshall* (Grand Rapids: Eerdmans and Carlisle: Paternoster, 1994), 453-72; and (with R. Lundin and C. Walhout), *The Promise of Hermeneutics* (Grand Rapids: Eerdmans and Carlisle: Paternoster, 1999), 200-240.

270. The terminology derives from J. L. Austin, *How to Do Things with Words* (Oxford: Clarendon Press, 1962), 99-105. However, the philosophical and linguistic issues are more complex than Austin allowed. On, e.g., the difference between "facts," "institutional facts," and the supposed irrelevance of extralinguistic states of affairs, see J. R. Searle, *Speech Acts: An Essay in the Philosophy of Language* (Cambridge: Cambridge University Press, 1969), 22-71; *Expression and Meaning: Studies in the Theory of Speech Acts* (Cambridge: Cambridge University Press, 1979), 1-57; and *The Construction of Social Reality* (London: Allen Lane, 1995), 1-126, 199-228; D. Vanderveken, *Principles of Language Use: vol. 1: Meaning and Speech Acts* (Cambridge: Cambridge University Press, 1990); and S. L. Tsohatzidis (ed.), *Foundations of Speech-Act Theory* (London: Routledge, 1994).

271. Thiselton in Lundin, Thiselton, and Walhout, *The Promise of Hermeneutics,* 223-40.

Illocutions may operate in ancient letters outside the context of theology. A. J. Malherbe has identified twenty-one functions of ancient letters in epistolary theory which set the stage for illocutionary speech-acts. In Pseudo-Demetrius, he notes, distinctions are drawn between (in our terminology) the following speech-acts: commanding, blaming, reproaching, rebuking, admonishing, congratulating, accusing, authorizing, and thanking.[272] I began from this starting point in a paper on speech-acts in 1 Corinthians.[273] Most of these acts depend for their currency on a given identity and status on the part of the speaker or letter writer.

A. R. Brown rightly speaks of the speech-act of the proclamation of the cross as having performative force in 1 Corinthians "to promote a new way of *being* in the world" (her italics).[274] In so doing she brings theology and ethical lifestyle together as one. As Brown observes, such language "not only says something but does something in the saying"; here the "reversals" of the cross in this epistle "transform perceptions and transform a world-view."[275] Supposed "wisdom" and "folly" change places. The result is that if any room is left to "boast," then "let him who boasts boast in the Lord" (1:31).[276] A. J. Malherbe concludes: "Paul's preaching consisted, then, in drawing a placard of Christ before people (Gal 3:1) . . . the message of Christ . . . of Christ's crucifixion (1 Cor 2:2)"; nevertheless, Malherbe adds, Paul "did not appear to make the distinction [between] 'pastoral' activities (1 Cor 14:5) and . . . the conversion of outsiders (1 Cor 14:24-25)."[277]

---

272. A. J. Malherbe, *Ancient Epistolary Theorists,* SBL Sources 19 (Atlanta: Scholars Press, 1988), 30-40. Malherbe lists a further forty-one from *Pseudo-Libanius* 66-80.

273. A. C. Thiselton, "Speech-Act Theory and 1 Corinthians," *SBL Greek Language and Linguistics Sections* (Philadelphia: Society of Biblical Literature, 1996).

274. Brown, *The Cross and Human Transformation,* 12.

275. Ibid., 15, 53-54, and 81.

276. Ibid., 87.

277. A. J. Malherbe, "The Apostle Paul as Pastor," in Lung-kwong Lo (ed.), *Jesus, Paul and John* (Hong Kong: Chung Chi Chinese University, 2000), 101-2; cf. 98-138.

COMMENTARY

I. Address, Greeting, and Thanksgiving (1:1-9)

A. ADDRESS AND GREETING (1:1-3)

(1) Paul, called to be an apostle of Christ Jesus through the will of God, and our Christian brother Sosthenes (2) to the church of God which is in Corinth, to those who are sanctified in Christ Jesus, called to be holy people, together with all who call on the name of our Lord Jesus Christ in every place, both their Lord and ours. (3) Grace and peace to you from God our Father and from the Lord Jesus Christ.

We reserve our main introduction to chs. 1–4 to its beginning immediately before the *propositio* of 1:10. Here we simply introduce briefly the Address and Greeting (1:1-3), also postponing an introduction to the Thanksgiving (1:4-9). Paul does not disdain the use of conventional formulae for the commencement and structure of a letter in the Graeco-Roman world of the first century. He does not discard the literary or social conventions of his time, as if the gospel were necessarily a counterculture which undermined expected conventions and courtesies when these are value-neutral.

Nevertheless, Paul fills the stereotypical form with a distinctively Christian content. To his own name, as the sender of the letter, he adds the designation **apostle** to indicate that he writes as one specially commissioned by God to perform an apostolic ministry.[1] Far from striking an authoritarian note (as many writers claim), the term points away from his own personal wishes or initiative to a given task which he has been called to undertake. His call to apostleship carries with it a dimension of necessity or compulsion (9:15-18; cf. Acts 26:14 and Gal 1:15 reflecting directly Jer 1:4-10; 20:7-9).[2] We argue below that the

1. J. Murphy-O'Connor, *Paul the Letter Writer* (Collegeville, Minn.: Glazier/Liturgical Press, 1995), suggests that whereas the earlier 1 Thess 1:1 (and 2 Thess 1:1) simply include the name of the sender(s), the fuller description "not by human persons but by God" (Gal 1:1) marks a new phrase which is reflected in 1 Cor 1:1 and thereafter (45-48).
2. See, e.g., J. Munck, *Paul and the Salvation of Mankind* (Eng. trans., London: SCM, 1959), 20-33; and H. Merklein, *Der erste Brief an die Korinther, Kap. 1–4* (Gütersloh: Gütersloher-Echter, 1992), 63-64. On the transparency of apostleship as pointing away from the person of the

term **apostle** entails a witness to Christ not simply in terms of knowledge or doctrine but also in living out Christ's death and resurrection in practice. The "lavish" filling out of the normally succinct "Sender to Recipient" formula is all the more striking in 1:1-3 in view of the limitations of space on a scroll for a papyrus letter.[3] Apart from the example of Paul's letter, it is rare in hellenistic letters of the period for the principal author **(Paul)** to name an associate co-worker, scribe, or secretary **(Sosthenes)** in the Address.[4]

The theme of being **called** by God finds expression equally in the designation of the sender, who is **called to be an apostle** (v. 1), and the designation of the recipients, who are **called to be holy people** (v. 2). From the first Paul begins the overture which will be developed: they are not a self-sufficient community; they share a common faith, a lifestyle and a tradition **with all who call on the name of our Lord Jesus Christ in every place.** Christ is not simply **their** (monopolized) **Lord** but also **ours.** "The Corinthians should not pretend to be unique (1 Cor 4:7) and thus a law unto themselves (cf. 1 Cor 11:16; 14:36)."[5]

Further Christian theological content within the conventional greeting formula finds expression in identifying the source of the **grace and peace** (χάρις ὑμῖν καὶ εἰρήνη, in contrast to the usual Greek greeting χαίρειν) as **God our Father and the Lord Jesus Christ.** Paul does not separate **God our Father** and **Jesus Christ** as co-sources of gifts, blessing, or divine presence.[6] For **Grace** (χάρις) often denotes not simply God's giving of a separable gift as such, but a gift which is inseparable from the self-giving of God's own presence and God's own self in and through Christ. When Paul discusses the Spirit of God, the same principle applies. To be "gifted" or "spiritual" cannot be separated from the activity of God's own Holy Spirit. Hence **peace** (εἰρήνη) is not simply a feeling of inner tranquility, but a harmonious relationship with God in intimate terms.

For the sake of convenience we place the main bibliography on apostle and apostleship at 9:1-3, where Paul uses the term more specifically. We distinguish between the following: (a) bibliography on letter forms for address and greeting, (b) bibliography on Paul's co-workers, (c) select bibliography on language about God and Christ, and (d) on the church as God's holy people, and (e) select works on Christ as Lord.

apostle, see esp. J. A. Crafton, *The Agency of the Apostle,* JSNTSS 51 (Sheffield: Sheffield Academic Press, 1991), esp. 61-66.

3. Cf. R. P. Collins, *First Corinthians,* SacPag 7 (Collegeville, Minn.: Glazier/Liturgical Press, 1999), 41-43.

4. E. R. Richards, *The Secretary in the Letters of Paul,* WUNT 2:42 (Tübingen: Mohr, 1991), 47, n. 138; also Collins, *First Corinthians,* 41-43.

5. J. Murphy-O'Connor, *Paul the Letter Writer,* 51.

6. N. Richardson, *Paul's Language about God,* JSNTSS 99 (Sheffield: Sheffield Academic Press, 1994), 243-73; cf. 95-137.

Bibliography on Opening Letter Forms and Greek Epistolography

Archer, R. L., "The Epistolary Form in the New Testament," *ExpTim* 68 (1951-52): 296-98.

Aune, D. E., "Opening Formulas," in *The New Testament in Its Literary Environment* (Cambridge: Clarke 1987), 184-86.

————, (ed.), *Greco-Roman Literature and the New Testament: Selected Forms and Genre,* SBL Sources for Biblical Studies 21 (Atlanta: Scholars Press, 1988), esp. J. L. White, "Ancient Greek Letters."

Beilner, W., "'ἐπιστολή," *EDNT,* 2:38-39.

Belleville, L. L., "Continuity or Discontinuity: A Fresh Look at 1 Corinthians in the Light of First-Century Epistolary Forms and Conventions," *EvQ* 59 (1987): 15-37.

Berger, K., "Apostelbriefe und apostolische Rede. Zum Formular frühchristlicher Briefe," *ZNW* 65 (1974): 190-231.

Boers, H., "The Form Critical Study of Paul's Letters: 1 Thessalonians as a Case Study," *NTS* 22 (1975-76): 140-58.

Botha, P. J. J., "Letter Writing and Oral Communication in Antiquity: Suggested Implications for the Interpretation of Paul's Letter to the Galatians," *Scriptura* 42 (1992): 17-34.

————, "The Verbal Art of the Pauline Letters: Rhetoric, Performance and Presence," in S. E. Porter and T. H. Olbricht (eds.), *Rhetoric and the New Testament: Essays From the 1992 Heidelberg Conference,* JSNTSS 90 (Sheffield: JSOT Press, 1993), 409-28.

Deissmann, A., *Light from the Ancient East* (Eng. trans., London: Hodder & Stoughton, 1927), 143-246.

Dewey, J. (ed.), *Semeia,* 65: *Orality and Textuality in Early Christian Literature* (Atlanta: Scholars Press, 1995), esp. R. F. Ward, "Pauline Voice and Presence . . . ," 95-107, and A. C. Wire, "Performance, Politics and Power," 129-37.

Doty, W. G., "The Classification of Epistolary Literature," *CBQ* 31 (1969): 183-99.

————, *Letters in Primitive Christianity* (Philadelphia: Fortress Press, 1973).

Exler, F. J. X., *The Form of the Ancient Letters: A Study in Greek Epistolography* (Washington, D.C.: Catholic University of America, 1923).

Friedrich, G., "Lohmeyers These über das paulinische Brief-Präskript kritisch beleuchtet!" *ZNW* 46 (1955): 272-74.

Kim, Chan-Hie, *Form and Function of the Familiar Letter of Recommendation,* SBLDS 4 (Missoula: Scholars Press, 1972).

Koskenniemi, H., *Studien zur Idee und Phraseologie des griechischen Briefes bis 400 n. Chr.,* C11, 2 (Helsinki: Annales academiae scientiarum Fennicae, 1956).

Lieu, J. M., "'Grace to You and Peace': The Apostolic Greeting," *BJRL* 68 (1985): 162-78.

Lohmeyer, E., "Probleme paulinischer Theologie, 1: Briefliche Grussüberschriften," *ZNW* 26 (1927): 158-73.

McGuire, M. R. P., "Letters and Letter Carriers in Ancient Antiquity," *Classical World* 53 (1960): 148-99.

Malherbe, A., *Ancient Epistolary Theorists,* SBL Sources for Biblical Study 19 (Atlanta: Scholars Press, 1988).

Meecham, H. G., *Light from Ancient Letters* (London: Allen and Unwin and New York: Macmillan, 1923).

Mitchell, M. M., *Paul and the Rhetoric of Reconciliation* (Louisville: Westminster-Knox, 1992), 184-94.

Mullins, T. Y., "Formulas in the New Testament Epistles," *JBL* 91 (1972): 380-90.

———, "Greeting as a New Testament Form," *JBL* 87 (1968): 418-26.

———, "Petition as a Literary Form," *NovT* 5 (1962): 46-54.

Murphy-O'Connor, J., "Co-Authorship in the Corinthian Correspondence," *RB* 100 (1993): 562-79.

———, *Paul and the Letter-Writer: His World, His Options, His Skills* (Collegeville, Minn.: Liturgical Press, 1995), 20-24, 42-64.

O'Brien, P. T., *Introductory Thanksgivings in the Letters of Paul,* NovTSup 49 (Leiden: Brill, 1977), 107-40 (on vv. 4-9).

Parkin, V., "Some Comments on the Pauline Prescripts," *IBS* 8 (1986): 92-99.

Prior, M., *Paul the Letter Writer and the Second Letter to Timothy,* JSNTSS 23 (Sheffield: JSOT Press, 1989).

Richards, E. R., *The Secretary in the Letters of Paul,* WUNT 2:42 (Tübingen: Mohr, 1992).

Rigaux, B., *Letters of St. Paul* (Eng. trans., Chicago: Franciscan Herald Press, 1968), 115-23 and 144-46.

Roller, O., *Das Formular der Paulinischen Briefe. Ein Beitrag zur Lehre vom antiken Briefe,* BWANT 58 (Stuttgart: Kohlhammer, 1933).

Sanders, J. N., "The Transition from Opening Epistolary Thanksgiving to the Body in the Letters of the Pauline Corpus." *JBL* 81 (1962): 348-65.

Schnider, F., and W. Stenger, *Studien zum neutestamentlichen Briefformular,* NTTS 11 (Leiden: Brill, 1987), 25-41.

Schubert, P., *Form and Function of the Pauline Thanksgivings* (Berlin: Töpelmann, 1939), mainly on vv. 4-9.

Stamps, D. L., *The Rhetorical Use of the Epistolary Form in 1 Corinthians: The Rhetoric of Power,* JSNTSS (Sheffield: JSOT Press, revised Durham University Ph.D. thesis, 1992, still forthcoming for 2000).

Stirewalt, M. L., "The Form and Function of the Greek Letter-Essay," in K. P. Donfried (ed.), *The Romans Debate, Revised and Expanded* (Peabody, Mass.: Hendrickson, 1991), 147-71.

———, *Studies in Ancient Greek Epistolography* (Atlanta: Scholars Press, 1993).

Stowers, S. K., *Letter Writing in Greco-Roman Antiquity* (Philadelphia: Westminster, 1986).

Traede, K., *Gründzüge griechisch-römischer Brieftopik* (Munich: Beck, 1970).

White, J. L., "The Ancient Epistolography Groups in Retrospect." *Semeia* 22: *Studies in Ancient Letter Writing* (1981): 1-14, and "The Greek Documentary Letter Tradition," *Semeia* 22 (1981): 89-106.

———, "Ancient Greek Letters," in D. E. Aune (ed.), *Greco-Roman Literature and the New Testament: Selected Forms and Genre,* SBL Sources for Biblical Studies 21 (Atlanta: Scholars Press, 1988).

———, "Epistolary Formulas and Clichés in Greek Papyrus Letters," *SBL Seminar Papers 2* (1978): 289-319.

———, *The Form and Function of the Body of the Greek Letter: A Study of the Letter-*

Body in Non-Literary Papyri and in Paul the Apostle (Missoula: Scholars Press, 1972).

———, "Introductory Formulae in the Body of the Pauline Letter," *JBL* 90 (1971): 91-97.

———, *Light from Ancient Letters* (Philadelphia: Fortress Press, 1986).

Wickert, U., "Einheit und Eintracht der Kirche im Präskript des ersten Korintherbriefes," *ZNW* 50 (1959): 73-83.

Bibliography on Paul's Co-Workers

Banks, R., *Paul's Idea of Community* (Peabody, Mass.: Hendrickson, 2d ed. 1994), 49-63 and 149-58.

Bruce, F. F., *The Pauline Circle* (Exeter: Paternoster, 1985).

Chow, J. K. M. *Patronage and Power: A Study of Social Networks in Corinth,* JSNTSS 75 (Sheffield: Sheffield Academic Press, 1992): 83-112.

Dodd, C. H., "New Testament Translation Problems, I." *BT* 27 (1976): 301-11 (on "brother" as one of an inner group).

Ellis, E. E., "Co-Workers, Paul and His," in G. F. Hawthorne and R. P. Martin (eds.), *Dictionary of Paul and His Letters* (Leicester: Inter-Varsity Press, 1993), 183-89.

———, "Paul and His Co-workers," in his *Prophecy and Hermeneutic in Early Christianity* (Grand Rapids: Eerdmans, 1978), 3-22.

Fiorenza, E. Schüssler, "Missionaries, Apostles, Co-Workers," *Word and World* 6 (1986): 420-33.

Frör, H., *You Wretched Corinthians!* (Eng. trans., London: SCM, 1995), throughout (but note that this draws on hypotheses about co-workers as part of a popular "docudrama" which draws on serious scholarship).

Harrington, D. J., "Paul and Collaborative Ministry," *NTR* 3 (1990): 62-71.

Holmberg, B., *Paul and Power: The Structure of Authority in the Primitive Church as Reflected in the Pauline Epistles,* ConBNT 11 (Lund: Gleerup, 1978), 58-69.

MacDonald, M. Y., *The Pauline Churches: A Socio-Historical Study of Institutionalisation in the Pauline and Deutero-Pauline Writings,* SNTSMS 60 (Cambridge: Cambridge University Press, 1988), 55-60.

Marshall, P., *Enmity in Corinth: Social Connections in Paul's Relation with the Corinthians,* WUNT 23 (Tübingen: Mohr, 1987), 133-37 and 143-47.

Meeks, W. A., *The First Urban Christians: The Social World of the Apostle Paul* (New Haven: Yale University Press, 1983), 133-34.

Ollrog, W. H., *Paulus und seine Mitarbeiter* (Neukirchen: Neukirchener, 1979).

Petersen, N. *Rediscovering Paul: Philemon and the Sociology of Paul's Narrative World* (Philadelphia: Fortress, 1985), 103-24.

Richards, E. R., *The Secretary in the Letters of Paul* (Tübingen: Mohr, 1991).

Theissen, G., *The Social Setting of Pauline Christianity: Essays on Corinth* (Eng. trans., Philadelphia: Fortress, 1982), 87-96.

Select Bibliography on Language about God and Christ

Cullmann, O., "Alle, die den Namen unseres Herrn Jesus Christus anrufen," in Cullmann, *Vorträge und Aufsätze 1925-1962* (Tübingen: Mohr, 1966), 605-22.

Dunn, J. D. G. *The Theology of Paul the Apostle* (Edinburgh: T. & T. Clark, 1998), 28-33 and 244-60.

Hurtado, L. W., *One God, One Lord* (Philadelphia: Fortress, 1988), esp. ch. 5.

Jüngel, E., *God and the Mystery of the World* (Eng. trans., Edinburgh: T. & T. Clark, 1983), 152-69 and 343-73.

Kramer, W., "'Lord Jesus Christ' in the Salutation," in his *Christ, Lord, Son of God* (Eng. trans., London: SCM, 1966), 151-55.

Kreitzer, L. J., *Jesus and God in Paul's Eschatology,* JSNTSS 19 (Sheffield: Sheffield Academic Press, 1987), 131-70.

Martin, F., "Pauline Trinitarian Formulas and Christian Unity," *CBQ* 30 (1968): 199-219.

Moltmann, J., *God in Creation* (Eng. trans., London: SCM, 1985), 1-19, 86-103.

———. *The Spirit of Life* (Eng. trans., London: SCM, 1992), 17-38, 132-38, and 248-67.

Morris, L., "The Theme of Romans," in W. Ward Gasque and R. P. Martin (eds.), *Apostolic History and the Gospel: Essays Presented to F. F. Bruce* (Exeter: Paternoster, 1970), 249-63.

Newman, C. C., *Paul's Glory-Christology: Tradition and Rhetoric,* NovTSup 69 (Leiden: Brill, 1992), 186-96 and 235-47.

Pannenberg, W. *Systematic Theology* (Eng. trans., Edinburgh: T. & T. Clark, 1991), 1:259-335.

Richardson, N. *Paul's Language about God,* JSNTSS 99 (Sheffield: Sheffield Academic Press, 1994), 95-138 and 240-307.

Van Linden, P., "Paul's Christology in First Corinthians," *BibTod* 18 (1980): 379-86.

Wanamaker, C. A., "Christ as Divine Agent in Paul," *SJT* 39 (1986): 517-28.

Bibliography on the Church as God's Holy People

Asting, R., *Die Heiligkeit im Urchristentum,* FRLANT 46 (Göttingen: Vandenhoeck & Ruprecht, 1930).

Bowers, P., "Church and Mission in Paul," *JSNT* 44 (1991): 89-111.

Barr, J., *The Semantics of Biblical Language* (Oxford: Oxford University Press, 1961), 119-29.

Berger, K., "Volksversammlung und Gemeinde Gottes. Zu den Anfängen der christlichen Verwendung von ekklesia," *ZTK* 73 (1976): 167-207.

Cerfaux, L., *The Church in the Theology of St. Paul* (Eng. trans., New York: Herder and Herder, 1959).

Chow, J. K., *Patronage and Power: A Study of Social Networks in Corinth,* JSNTSS 75 (Sheffield: Sheffield Academic Press, 1992).

Cullmann, O., "The Kingship of Christ and the Church in the New Testament," in *The Early Church* (Eng. trans., London: SCM, 1956), 105-40.

Dunn, J. D. G. *The Theology of Paul the Apostle* (Edinburgh: T. & T. Clark, 1998), 537-43.

Merklein, H., "Die Ekklesia Gottes: Der Kirchenbegriff bei Paulus und in Jerusalem," *BZ* 23 (1979): 48-70.

Robinson, J. A. T., *The Body: A Study in Pauline Theology* (London: SCM, 1952).

Roloff, J., "ἐκκλησία," *EDNT,* 1:410-15.

Schnackenburg, R., *The Church in the New Testament* (Eng. trans., Freiburg: Herder, 1965), 77-85.

Schöllgen, G., "Was wissen wir über die Sozialstruktur der paulinischen Gemeinden?" *NTS* 34 (1988): 71-82.

Schrage, W., "Ecclesia und Synagoge," *ZTK* 60 (1963): 178-202.

Schweizer, E., *Church Order in the New Testament* (Eng. trans., London: SCM, 1961), 89-105.

Snodgrass, K., "The Church," *Ex Auditu* 10 (1994), esp. 1-15 (D. G. Miller), 31-44 (R. B. Hays), and 45-54 (W. Liefeld).

Whiteley, D. E. H., *The Theology of St Paul* (Oxford: Blackwell, 2d ed. 1974), 186-99.

Wickert, U., "Einheit und Eintracht der Kirche im Preskript des ersten Korintherbriefs," *ZNW* 50 (1959) 73-82.

Select Bibliography on Christ as Lord

Beasley-Murray, P., "Romans 1:3f: An Early Confession of Faith in the Lordship of Jesus." *TynBul* 31 (1980): 147-54.

Bornkamm, G., "Christ and the World," in G. Bornkamm, *Early Christian Experience* (Eng. trans., London: SCM, 1969), 14-28.

Bruce, F. F., "Jesus Is Lord," in J. M. Richards (ed.), *Soli Deo Gloria: In Honor of W. C. Robinson* (Richmond: Knox, 1968), 23-36.

Bultmann, R., *Theology of the New Testament* (Eng. trans., London: SCM, 1952), 1:121-33, 331-36.

Cullmann, O., *Christology of the New Testament* (Eng. trans., London: SCM, 2d ed. 1963), 195-237.

Dahl, N. A., "Sources of Christological Language," in D. H. Juel (ed.), *Jesus the Christ* (Minneapolis: Fortress, 1991), 113-36.

Davis, C. J., *The Name and Way of the Lord,* JSNTSS 129 (Sheffield: Sheffield Academic Press, 1996).

de Lacey, D. R., "One Lord in Pauline Christology," in H. H. Rowdon (ed.), *Christ the Lord* (Leicester: Inter-Varsity Press, 1982), 191-203.

Dunn, J. D. G., *The Theology of Paul the Apostle* (Edinburgh: T. & T. Clark, 1998), 235-52.

Fitzmyer, J. A., "κύριος," *EDNT,* 2:328-31.

———, "The Semitic Background of the New Testament Kyrios-Title," in Fitzmyer, *A Wandering Aramean,* SBLMS 25 (Missoula: Scholars Press, 1979), 115-42.

Foerster, W., et al., "κύριος κτλ," *TDNT,* 3:1,039-98.

Gebauer, R., *Das Gebet bei Paulus* (Giessen-Basel: Brunnen, 1989).

Hahn, F., *The Titles of Jesus in Christology* (London: Lutterworth, 1969).

Hengel, M., *The Cross of the Son of God* (Eng. trans., London: SCM, 1986), 55-82 (rpt. from *The Son of God* [1976]).

Hurtado, L. W., "New Testament Christology: A Critique of Bousset's Influence," *TS* 40 (1979): 306-17.

———, *One God, One Lord: Early Christian Devotion and Ancient Jewish Monotheism* (Philadelphia: Fortress, 1988).

Kim, S., *The Origin of Paul's Gospel* (Grand Rapids: Eerdmans, 1982), 104-36.

Kramer, W., *Christ, Lord Son of God* (Eng. trans., London: SCM, 1966), 65-107 and esp. 151-82.

O'Collins, G., *Christology* (London: Oxford University Press, 1995).

Robinson, J. A. T., "The Earliest Christian Liturgical Sequence?" in *Twelve New Testament Studies* (London: SCM, 1962), 154-57 (rpt. from *JTS* 4 [1953]: 38-41).

Schweizer, E., *Lordship and Discipleship* (Eng. trans., London: SCM, 1960).

Stuhlmacher, P., *Biblische Theologie des NT* (Göttingen: Vandenhoeck & Ruprecht, 1992), 1:305-11.

Weiss, J., *Earliest Christianity* (Eng. trans., New York: Harper, 1959 [1937]), 2:458-63.

Whiteley, D. E. H., *The Theology of St. Paul* (Oxford: Blackwell, 2d ed. 1974), 99-123.

Ziesler, J. A., *Pauline Christianity* (Oxford: Oxford University Press, 2d ed. 1990), 35-48.

For Bibliography on Apostleship, see under 9:1-3.

1. Sender(s) (1:1)

1 (i) **Christ Jesus** follows the word order of the UBS *Greek New Testament,* 4th ed., which Metzger defends.[7] The sequence Χριστοῦ ᾿Ιησοῦ occurs in the very early p46 (about AD 200) as well as in B, D, F, G, and 33. The reverse sequence appears in א and in A, as well as in many later VSS, but this form usually occurs only in the context of the full title *Lord Jesus Christ.* (ii) κλητός, **called**, is omitted by A and D'. But this can be readily explained as providing a simplified, more succinct, version of a phrase which some scribes may have regarded as redundantly overloaded (cf. Rom 1:1; Gal 1:15).[8]

As the respective sections of the above bibliographies indicate, four or five sets of issues need to be considered separately. These include (1) the significance of Paul's use of, and modification to, stereotypical opening forms of ancient letters; (2) the force of ἀπόστολος, **apostle**, in its present context (otherwise cf. also 9:1-3); (3) the role played by Χριστοῦ ᾿Ιησοῦ διὰ θελήματος θεοῦ, and (4) Paul's unexpected insertion of the name of a co-worker, **Sosthenes**, into the standard letter form, together with his description as **brother**.

Commentators repeatedly begin their work on a Pauline epistle with the wholly predictable observation that in ancient Greek letters of Paul's era the formula "Sender to Addressee, greetings . . . I give thanks that . . ." remained as invariable as "Dear Sir . . ." or "Dear Mary . . ." today. Such a comment may tend to generate a sense of frustration not because it is wrong, but because usually it is offered only as a piece of historical or literary information, with little interest in its significance for today. Paul observes the customary etiquette and convention. He does not consciously project the Christian gospel and lifestyle as a counterculture within the Graeco-Roman world at every opportunity. It assumes countercultural patterns only when theological or ethical values run counter to some prevailing assumption or practice. However, Paul utilizes an accepted structure to insert within its frame distinctive components which bear his own stamp. The most familiar example of this concerns his modifying the word **to greet** (χαίρειν) to **grace to you and peace** (χάρις ὑμῖν καὶ εἰρήνη).

7. B. M. Metzger, *A Textual Commentary on the Greek New Testament* (Stuttgart and New York: United Bible Societies, 2d ed. 1994), 478.

8. H. Conzelmann, *1 Corinthians,* Hermeneia (Eng. trans., Philadelphia: Fortress, 1975), 19, n. 1 and 20, n. 16 (as against L. Cerfaux, *Christ in the Theology of St Paul* [Eng. trans., Freiburg and New York: Herder, 1959], 480-85).

From at least the time of Tertullian (c. 160–c. 225), interpreters have noted that more can be learned from Paul's distinctive and unusual changes within the formalized structure than from the structure itself. Today it would be unwise to evaluate degrees of endearment from "Dear Sir."

A mass of intensive research on the letter form is reflected in more than forty bibliographical items cited above. (See also the extensive bibliography on 16:13-24.) Otto Roller argued that epistolary convention during the three centuries before and after Paul came to constitute almost an invariable protocol.[9] On this basis, an otherwise odd comment from Tertullian becomes intelligible. Tertullian describes Paul's greeting as anti-Marcionite because he perceives that the unusual insertion of "and peace" sets up deliberate resonances of the standard Jewish form of greeting, thus offering explicit evidence that the God of Paul is the God of the Old Testament scriptures, as against the claims of Marcion. Even if in one sense he is "the destroyer of Judaism" Paul also consciously inserts "a formula which the Jews still use."[10]

Many commentators have suggested that the stylized forms and content of many ancient Greek letters betray a general Greek assumption that written letters or written texts were substantially inferior to the spoken word in oral discourse.[11] But Paul himself views the letter form as constituting an effective communicative event, and if, as is virtually certain, his letter or letters were read aloud to gathered assemblies, any disjunction between oral and written speech should not be exaggerated.[12] Research on the letter form may influence interpretations in practical and important ways. In 1:10, for example, Bjerkelund compares the function of **I appeal** or **I request** (παρακαλῶ) to **please** (as it is in modern Greek). This signals that the letter form has moved from thanksgiving to request. On the other hand, Ben Witherington follows Margaret Mitchell in placing the same word (παρακαλῶ) in the context of

---

9. W. Roller, *Das Formular der Paulinischen Briefe,* BWANT 58 (Stuttgart: Kohlhammer, 1933); W. G. Doty, *Letters in Primitive Christianity* (Philadelphia: Fortress, 1973) similarly speaks of "the extreme stereotyping found in Hellenistic letters . . . they are . . . amazingly stereotyped and bound to tradition" (11, 12).

10. Tertullian, *Against Marcion,* 5:5:1.

11. One of the most recent of a large number of discussions is Joanna Dewey (ed.), *Semeia, 65: Orality and Textuality in Early Christian Literature* (Atlanta: Scholars Press, 1995), esp. 95-138 (by R. F. Ward, A. J. Dewey, and A. C. Wire). See further, D. L. Stamps, *Rhetorical Use,* and A. Malherbe, *Ancient Epistolary Theorists.*

12. We find numerous examples of the "performance" of effective speech-acts through the medium of written texts both within the NT and in secular Greek. Abraham Malherbe has collected some valuable models of ancient epistolary principles and techniques (*Ancient Epistolary Theorists,* SBL Sources 19 [Atlanta: Scholars Press, 1988]). One of Malherbe's examples is Pseudo-Demetrius (c. AD 100). Pseudo-Demetrius observes that he has come across no fewer than twenty-one kinds of letter forms or "epistolary modes," which (with the two exceptions of "allegorical" and "ironic") all serve to perform actions. (On speech-acts see the Introduction, 41-43, 46, 50-52.) A commendatory letter (συστατικός) performs the act of commending someone; "blaming," "reproachful," and "consoling" letters (μεμπτικός, ὀνειδιστικός, παραμυθητικός) perform acts of consolation or blame no less than if they were oral speech.

Graeco-Roman rhetoric, and accords to it the status of the linchpin or *propositio,* which expresses the central argument of the whole epistle.[13] On the other hand, A. Eriksson rightly criticizes the unfortunate polarization between scholars too narrowly concerned with "epistolary form" and scholars concerned with rhetoric. Paul's letters embody *both,* and *both* illuminate exegesis.[14]

Paul alludes to his being **called** as an experience of compulsion. Like Jeremiah, he was set apart before birth (Gal 1:15; cf. Jer 1:5).[15] He exclaims, "Woe to me if I do not preach the gospel!" (1 Cor 9:16). It remains unlikely that Paul refers explicitly to Stoic notions of a *call* to maintain truth in the face of difficulty or persecution.[16] His being **called to be an apostle** provides a parallel with the addressees' being **called to be a holy people**[17] (see v. 2). Paul is not the only one "set apart, consecrated, and holy."[18] All Christian believers have a divine vocation.

We postpone a more detailed exploration of the literature on **apostle** until we reach 9:1-3. However, several questions arise already: Does Paul use the term to legitimate power over his readers, or to point beyond himself to God in Christ? Is the term in the first place an ecclesiological office or title, or is it a term which relates to proclaiming and living out the gospel in foundational witness to its basis and nature?

(a) A respectable history can be traced of careful writers who comment that Paul uses the word **apostle** here "to gain authority" (Calvin), "to affirm his authority" (Allo), to show that he has been "entrusted with authority" (Cerfaux and Ortkemper), or "to secure a leadership position" (MacDonald).[19] Perhaps before the work of F. Nietzsche and M. Foucault, such comments seemed more innocent. But these philosophers of critical theory drew to our attention the frequency with which in religion and society religious people, especially their leaders, made claims to truth about their relation to God or to absolutes in order

13. Ben Witherington III, *Conflict and Community* (Eerdmans: Grand Rapids and Carlisle: Paternoster, 1995), 94-97 and M. M. Mitchell, *Paul and the Rhetoric of Reconciliation* (Louisville: Westminster-Knox, 1992), 198-200. Witherington quotes Bjerkelund in his support; but although the latter stresses the importance of the content of the "appeal," its frame is epistolary rather than rhetorical; cf. C. J. Bjerkelund, *Parakalô. Form, Funktion und Sinn der Parakalô-Sätze in den paulinischen Briefen* (Oslo: Universitetsforlaget, 1967). See further under 1:10 below.

14. A. Eriksson, *Traditions as Rhetorical Proof: Pauline Argumentation in 1 Corinthians,* ConBNT 29 (Stockholm: Almqvist & Wiksell, 1998), 280-83.

15. J. Munck, *Paul,* 25-29; cf. 11-35.

16. K. L. Schmidt, "καλῶ," *TDNT* 3:493.

17. C. Wolff, *Der erste Brief des Paulus an die Korinther* (Leipzig: Evangelische Verlagsanstalt, 1996), 14.

18. A. C. Wire, *The Corinthian Women Prophets* (Minneapolis: Fortress, 1990), 30.

19. E.-B. Allo, *Saint Paul: Première Épitre* (Paris: Gabalda, 1956), 1; L. Cerfaux, *The Church in the Theology of St Paul* (Eng. trans., Freiburg: Herder, 1959), 251; M. Y. MacDonald, *The Pauline Churches* (Cambridge: Cambridge University Press, 1988), 48; F.-J. Ortkemper, *1 Korintherbrief* (Stuttgart: Katholisches Bibelwerk, 1993), 9. Merklein, *Der erste Brief Kap. 1–4,* also urges the "power and authority" aspect.

to dominate or to manipulate others.[20] Nietzsche certainly ascribed this strategy to Paul, and I have addressed his arguments elsewhere.[21] Recently, however, the debate has become all the more sensitive, not least on the basis of discussions in biblical studies about the "new" rhetoric and a rhetoric of power. P. J. J. Botha, for example, concedes that the new rhetoric emphasizes "playing-up-to-the-audience . . . and evoking authority."[22] A. C. Wire writes: "the writer's self-presentation *(ēthos)* is expected to dominate the introductory part . . . shaped for an effect."[23] Hence, rhetorical criticism raises the issue of whether Paul deliberately provides himself with a heightened profile as a basis for causal persuasion and even manipulative power play.

(b) Other writers from the patristic era to today, however, adopt a virtually opposite emphasis. Chrysostom, writing around A.D. 390, rejects notions of "self-presentation" in v. 1: "Here, of him that calls is everything; of him that is called, nothing. . . . Do you register the names of men as patrons?"[24] Chrysostom rightly notes that the surprising frequency of the name **Christ**, all within two or three verses, says it all.[25] Similarly, J. B. Lightfoot anticipated more recent arguments, urging that authorization is not the issue for Paul here; it is that of *lack of personal merit.* Paul writes as he does because *he has to do so,* with a "feeling of self-abasement."[26] If issues of authority are at all implied, these "must be . . . secondary."[27] J. A. Bengel attributes Paul's allusion to apostleship and to the will of God to *excluding personal merit.*[28]

In a seminal paper E. Best (1986) goes still further. He insists that the sign of apostleship is "Christ-like weakness."[29] The term in the NT, he urges, is used too variably to signify ecclesial office. It directs attention to God's grace: "**Called** to be an **apostle** . . . by the grace of God I am what I am" (1 Cor. 15:9, 10). Its association with lowliness also emerges in 1 Cor. 4:9. More recently, W. Schrage and C. Wolff find the key to the term here in Paul's perception of himself as the slave of Christ, who belongs to his Lord.[30]

---

20. F. Nietzsche, *The Complete Works* (18 vols., Eng. trans., London: Allen & Unwin, 1909-13), 9, *The Dawn of Day,* Aphorisms 66-71.

21. A. C. Thiselton, *Interpreting God and the Postmodern Self* (Edinburgh: T. & T. Clark and Grand Rapids: Eerdmans, 1995), 3-45 and 111-63.

22. P. J. J. Botha, "Verbal Art," in S. E. Porter and T. H. Olbricht, *Rhetoric and the New Testament* (Sheffield: JSOT Press, 1993), 413. Cf. also the respective rhetorical approaches of Ward, Dewey, and Wire in *Semeia 65, Orality and Textuality,* 95-135.

23. Wire, *The Corinthian Women Prophets,* 2.

24. Chrysostom, *Ep. Cor. Hom.,* 1:1.

25. Chrysostom, *Ep. Cor. Hom.,* 2:7.

26. Lightfoot, *Notes on the Epistles,* 143.

27. Ibid.

28. J. A. Bengel, *Gnomon Novi Testamenti* (Stuttgart: Steinkopf, 3d ed. 1866), 608, *humilis . . . animi* (first ed. 1742).

29. E. Best, "Apostleship Authority — ?" *JSNT* 27 (1986): 11; cf. 3-25.

30. W. Schrage, *Der erste Brief an die Korinther,* EKKNT 7.1 (3 vols. to date, Neukirchen: Neukirchener and Zürich: Benziger, 1991, 1995, and 1999), 1: 99-101; and C. Wolff, *Der erste*

(c) If this is valid, in what sense can apostleship remain "foundational" for the church (cf. 1 Cor 12:28)? Why are apostles "first" (12:28) as well as "last" (4:9 and 15:8)? V. P. Furnish perceives that apostleship points to "the truth of the gospel," not to some ecclesial structure, while Schrage also insists that it remains translocal.[31] Hence Barrett, Schütz, Jones, and others are right to see as the "sign" of apostleship *the living out of the gospel substance of dying and being raised with Christ.*[32] But should this not be the case for every committed believer? The "participatory" aspect can be shared among the community. But the "witness" aspect remains unique to the first-generation translocal apostles as witnesses to the resurrection. They occupy a unique place in salvation-history. Hence, following Fridrichsen, Barrett asserts, "The primary meaning of apostleship is eschatological."[33] Merklein, Wolff, and Schrage all stress the triple themes of call, Christocentric witness, and mission or proclamation.[34]

(d) I therefore propose a fresh nuance to the term *apostle* which seems not to have been noted. V. H. Neufeld and others urge that witness and confession carries with it two complementary aspects in the NT: on one side, objective witness that an event has occurred; on the other side, a participatory, self-involving act of nailing one's colors to the mast, of staking one's life or life-style on what is witnessed as true.[35] Hence on one side (i) *apostles witness uniquely to the "that" of Christ's death and resurrection* (1 Cor 15:3-9; cf. 9:1). Wilckens even argues that the "appearances" tradition originated as a sign of apostleship rather than initially as a witness more generally to the resurrection as such.[36] On the other side, (ii) apostleship entails a practical *experience of sharing in the weakness of the cross of Christ and in the transforming power of Christ's resurrection.* This twofold witness *constitutes a necessary* "sign of apostleship." As Schütz observes, if apostleship has anything to do with

---

Brief des Paulus an die Korinther, THKNT (Berlin: Evanglische Verlagsanstalt, 1996), 14. See further I. A. H. Combes, *The Metaphor of Slavery in the Early Church,* JSNTSS 156 (Sheffield: Sheffield Academic Press, 1998), 121-28.

31. V. P. Furnish, "On Putting Paul in His Place," *JBL* 113 (1994): 15; cf. 3-17; cf. Best, "Apostolic Authority," 17; Schrage, *Der erste Brief,* 1:99-101; and W. Beardslee, *Human Achievement and Divine Vocation in the Message of Paul* (London: SCM, 1961), 79-94.

32. C. K. Barrett, *The Signs of an Apostle* (London: Epworth Press, 1970), 11-84; and "Paul and the 'Pillar' Apostles," in J. N. Sevenster (ed.), *Studia Paulina in Honorem J. de Zwaan* (Haarlem: Bohn, 1953), 1-19; J. H. Schütz, *Paul and the Anatomy of Apostolic Authority,* JSNTSMS 26 (Cambridge: Cambridge University Press, 1975), 201; P. R. Jones, "1 Cor. 15:8: Paul the Last Apostle," *TynBul* 36 (1985): 3-34; and Schrage, *Der erste Brief,* 1:99-101.

33. Barrett, "'Pillar' Apostles," 19; cf. Fridrichsen, "The Apostle and His Message," UUÅ 3 (1947): 3:3-17; and Beardslee, *Human Achievement,* 83.

34. Merklein, *Der erste Brief,* 67; Wolff, *Der erste Brief,* 15-16; Schrage, *Der erste Brief,* 1:99-101.

35. V. H. Neufeld, *The Earliest Christian Confessions* (Leiden: Brill, 1963).

36. U. Wilckens, "Der Ursprung der Überlieferung der Erscheinungen des Auferstanden: Zur traditionsgeschichtlichen Analyse von 1 Kor 15:1-11," in W. Joest and W. Pannenberg (eds.), *Dogma und Denkstrukturen* (Göttingen: Vandenhoeck & Ruprecht, 1963), 56-95.

"power," it is the "power-through-weakness of the cross."[37] Apostleship thereby entails "the establishment of the kerygma (1 Cor 1:21) and indeed the proclamation of the kerygma," both in word and in lifestyle.[38] Thus P. R. Jones comments, "Paul's language is foundational. . . . [There is] the subjective side . . . 'in which *you* stand' . . . equally . . . objective content 'Christ died . . . and appeared to Cephas and last of all to me'."[39] Barrett sums it up: "As an apostle [Paul] refused to come down from the cross."[40] But this must be understood in the dual sense advocated above. (See under 4:9, 9:1-3, and 15:7-9 for corroboration and further discussion).

(e) One related point receives special illumination from these issues. Witherington points out, "The real complaint [from Corinth] against Paul may have been that he was not arrogant in his presentation, or did not engage in boasting, unlike the Sophists."[41] The Corinthians were "status-hungry people."[42] Some considered Paul unworthy on such grounds as we have discussed of the title *apostolos*.[43] Using "rhetoric" not in the widespread modern sense but in a Pauline way, Crafton urges that "divine presence is perceived not *in* but *through* agency. . . . Apostles are . . . windows on God's design. . . . An agent is intentionally visible; an agency is inherently transparent."[44] Bruce Winter provides a detailed appreciation of "Sophists" (including Corinthian Sophists).[45] This brings us back to the comments of Chrysostom and Lightfoot. Paul's apostleship points beyond his own presence to God as revealed in the cruciform shape of power-in-weakness. D. Litfin amplifies and clarifies Crafton's emphasis. As against a "rhetorical emphasis" (in the Corinthian or postmodern sense) "Paul's mission was to placard Christ, crucified."[46] Neil Richardson stresses the aspect of lifestyle when he observes, "The σκάνδαλον was re-enacted in the person of the apostle.[47]

Paul fills out his apostolic call by adding **apostle of Christ Jesus through the will of God** . . . Although he receives his commission from Christ, Paul seldom if ever isolates the agency *of Christ* from some corresponding allu-

37. Schütz, *Anatomy,* 187-20. Barrett, Best, and Holmberg share some of his emphases, while Schütz reflects the dual influence of Käsemann and Weber.

38. Schütz, *Anatomy,* 200.

39. Jones, "1 Cor. 15:8," 34.

40. Barrett, *Signs,* 44.

41. B. Witherington III, *Conflict and Community in Corinth* (Grand Rapids: Eerdmans and Carlisle: Paternoster, 1995), 123-24.

42. Witherington, *Conflict and Community,* 24.

43. Ibid., 21. Cf. 19-24, 46-48, 78-79, 123-29, and 136-50.

44. J. A. Crafton, *The Agency of the Apostle,* JSNTSS 51 (Sheffield: JSOT Press, 1991), 62 and 63 (his italics).

45. B. W. Winter, *Philo and Paul among Sophists,* SNTSMS 96 (Cambridge: Cambridge University Press, 1997).

46. D. Litfin, *St Paul's Theology of Proclamation: 1 Cor 1–4 and Greco-Roman Rhetoric,* SNTSMS 79 (Cambridge: Cambridge University Press, 1994), 196.

47. N. Richardson, *Paul's Language about God,* JSNTSS 99 (Sheffield: Sheffield Academic Press, 1994), 135.

sion to **the will of God**. Later in this epistle, more than in any other, he will attack any notion of "belonging to Christ" which might threaten to decenter the sovereign will of God as revealed in and through Christ.[48] The importance of this theme in Romans is expounded by Leon Morris, and noted for 1 Corinthians by Moffatt and Neil Richardson.[49] Even for Paul all salvific acts of God are, in an implicit, inferential, sense, already trinitarian, whether or not specific events or processes are associated more closely with God as Father, or with Jesus Christ, or with the Holy Spirit.[50] What a believing Christian is **called to be** depends not on what people might judge for themselves to be "fulfilling" or self-affirming but on the loving and purposive **will of God**.[51] Thus the pattern of Christ and the cross ("not my will but yours") reflects the sovereign centrality of the will of God for all life and every lifestyle.

Clearly the phrase recalls the more emphatic form in Gal. 1:1, "an apostle not of human origination or through some human channel" (οὐκ ἀπ' ἀνθρώπων οὐδὲ δι' ἀνθρώπου), where Paul also places the agency of God and Christ together: it is "through Christ and God the Father." Galatians, however, carries a polemical tone which (against F. C. Baur; see on 9:1-3) is not necessarily present in 1 Corinthians. Luther stresses the importance of a call according to the will of God for every vocation and for all Christians, but comments concerning Paul's call, "there is no greater danger than to assume such an office without a call of God. But, alas, many today are insensitive to all this. . . ."[52]

Through (as in Barrett and in Collins) translates διά with the genitive more accurately than *by* (NRSV, REB, NJB, NIV): **through the will of God** denotes not only agency, but mode, means, and efficient cause. Lexicographers and grammarians offer abundant evidence for this nuance in hellenistic Greek, including the NT (e.g., *through the law,* Rom 3:2; **through wisdom**, 1 Cor 1:21). These represent genitives of attendant circumstances as well as efficient cause.[53] The REB's *by God's call and God's will* is forceful but misses the nu-

---

48. See, e.g., J. Moffatt, *First Epistle of Paul to the Corinthians* (London: Hodder & Stoughton, 1938), 250-51, on 15:28, where he believes that Paul attacks "a form of Christ-mysticism which loosened the nexus between God and Christ" (251).

49. Moffatt, *First Epistle,* 250-51; Richardson, *Paul's Language,* 95-138 and 240-307; and L. Morris, "The Theme of Romans," in W. W. Gasque and R. P. Martin (eds.), *Apostolic History and the Gospel . . . Presented to F. F. Bruce* (Exeter: Paternoster, 1970), 249-63.

50. New Testament specialists do not always enter into constructive dialogue with such works as Pannenberg, *Systematic Theology,* 1:259-335; Jüngel, *God as the Mystery of the World,* 152-69, 343-73; J. Moltmann, *God in Creation,* 1-19, 86-103, and *The Spirit of Life,* 17-38, 132-8, and 248-67; and C. Gunton, *The Promise of Trinitarian Theology* (Edinburgh: T. & T. Clark, 1991). Such works explicate what is implicit in such a study as Neil Richardson's.

51. Hence the Church of England Doctrine Commission Report, *The Mystery of Salvation* (London: Church House Publishing, 1995), distinguishes salvation and vocation from "parallel notions of human fulfilment which make no reference to God. [Fulfilment] describes what secular people seek . . ." (32).

52. Luther, *Lectures on Romans,* LCC 15 (Eng. trans., London: SCM, 1961), 9.

53. Blass-Debrunner-Funk, *A Greek Grammar of the New Testament* (Chicago: University of Chicago Press, 1961) (hereafter abbreviated as BDF), 119-20, sect. 223; W. Bauer, W. F. Arndt,

ances of the Greek preposition. The syntax adds support to Munck's claim that in Acts 26:14 speculation about "kicking against the goads" by offering psychological explanations of repressed belief is irrelevant. Munck rightly interprets this allusion in Acts 26:14 to mean "From now on it will be hard . . . from now on you will have no discharge from the service which I, Christ, have now laid on you."[54] Merklein and Schrage follow Munck in comparing the compulsion experienced by Jeremiah ("Thou hast deceived me. . . . Thou art stronger than I . . . ," Jer 20:7-9) with Paul's account of his call in Gal 1:11-24.[55] The phrase also runs parallel with the sequence of thought in 2 Cor 5:11–6:2: "we are not commending ourselves" (5:12); "the love of Christ compels us" (v. 14); "we are ambassadors for Christ, God making his appeal through us" (v. 20). Behind the Greek κλητὸς ἀπόστολος . . . διὰ θελήματος θεοῦ lies the background of the Hebrew שׁלִיחַ (shaliach), which conveys the notion of one *sent* on behalf of another as that person's authorized representative, *sent* to perform a specific task.[56] (See, however, further under 9:1-3.)

The inclusion of a co-sender (here, **Sosthenes**) in the protocol of the opening letter form remains extremely rare in Greek letters apart from Paul's.[57] It is all the more remarkable, therefore, that Paul makes a recurring feature out of mentioning the names of co-senders: Timothy in 2 Cor 1:1; Timothy again in Phil 1:1 and in Col 1:1; Silvanus (Silas) and Timothy in 1 Thess 1:1 and 2 Thess 1:1; and Timothy yet again in Philem 1. Romans and Galatians reflect particular reasons of their own for Paul's omission of any allusion to a co-sender. *Paul does not perceive himself as commissioned to lead or to minister as an isolated individual, without collaboration with co-workers.* The role of *co-workers* emerges clearly in 1 Cor 16:13-20 (on which see bibliography and exegesis below).[58]

The identity of Σωσθένης ὁ ἀδελφός, especially whether he is the Sosthenes of Acts 18:15-17, cannot be determined, although Calvin asserts, "This is the Sosthenes who was the ruler of the synagogue at Corinth, and

---

F. W. Gingrich, and W. Danker, *A Greek-English Lexicon of the New Testament* (Chicago: University of Chicago Press, 2d ed. 1979) (hereafter BAGD), 179-81; cf. Barrett, *First Epistle,* 30; Collins, *First Corinthians,* 41 and 51.

54. Munck, *Paul,* 19-29, esp. 21.

55. Merklein, *Der erste Brief,* 1-4, 67-68; Schrage, *Der erste Brief,* 1:99-101.

56. Cf. Schrage, *Der erste Brief,* 1:99-100. But this should be developed into a more dubious hypothesis advocated initially by H. Rengstorf (1933) and then applied to ecclesial church order by Dom Gregory Dix (1946) and A. G. Hebert (1946, 1963) into a theory of "apostolic succession" based on the use of the term of rabbinic "ordination." See on 9:1-3.

57. Richards, *The Secretary in the Letters of Paul,* 47, n. 138, finds only six instances in 645 papyrus letters.

58. Among the numerous works cited, see esp. R. Banks, *Paul's Idea of Community* (Peabody, Mass.: Hendrickson, rev. ed., 1994), 139-69; W. A. Meeks, *The First Urban Christians* (New Haven: Yale University Press, 1983), 49-63 and 149-58; B. Holmberg, *Paul and Power,* ConBNT 11 (Lund: Gleerup, 1978), 58-69; and G. Theissen, *The Social Setting of Pauline Christianity* (Philadelphia: Fortress, 1982), 87-96.

whom Luke mentions in Acts 18:17."[59] This view may arise from three factors: (i) an established tradition (e.g., Theodoret, Erasmus et al.): (ii) the notion that the definite article before the word **brother** (ὁ ἀδελφός) may suggest that he is already known to the readers as a specific associate; and (iii) that the conversion of a former ruler of the synagogue at Corinth, presumably now with Paul in Ephesus, would provide a poignant reminder of the power of the gospel in the very opening of the letter. If this is the **Sosthenes** of Acts 18:17, we may recall that when Gallio dismissed the charges brought by Jewish spokespersons against Paul, Sosthenes became the object of physical assault. The crowd who attacked him may have been either a pro-Roman crowd attacking a perceived spokesperson of the Jews, or a pro-Jewish crowd attacking him in "transferred anger" in frustration at their lack of success. In either case, his conversion would constitute a spectacular witness to the transforming power of the gospel.

Nevertheless, there may be other reasons for including **Sosthenes** which would not involve any connection with Acts 18. He might be one of Paul's "staff" (to use Meeks's term), or one of the regular "co-workers," of whom Meeks mentions Timothy and Silvanus (Silas) as major examples.[60] In any case **Sosthenes** was a common Greek name in the first century. Judge, Meeks, and Theissen point out that "From the beginning the Pauline mission was a collective enterprise, with something that can loosely be called a staff."[61] These three writers, among others, portray how the planting, nurture, and interactive character of the local urban communities entailed a corporate leadership. Paul's "co-workers," however, in the sense ascribed to Timothy and Silvanus, performed a different role from that of, e.g., Prisca and Aquila (1 Cor 16:19-20), who lent Paul support, resources, and protection or patronage.[62]

We have translated ὁ ἀδελφός as **our Christian brother.** This is *not* merely a *paraphrase* since ἀδελφός (and more especially the feminine form ἀδελφή are used in this epistle to denote a Christian man or Christian woman respectively (see below esp. on 9:5). Sosthenes is described as one of the Christian family. Paul does, indeed, use the term **brother** as a term of affection and warmth for his co-workers (e.g., Tychicus, Col 4:7; Apollos, 1 Cor 16:12; and Quartus, Rom 16:23), and Banks perceives it as indicating "the kind of personal commitment to others" which invites the warmest, most intimate language.[63]

59. Calvin, *First Epistle of Paul to the Corinthians* (Edinburgh: St Andrew Press, 1960), 17.
60. Cf. Meeks, *The First Urban Christians*, 133-34; Ellis, *Prophecy*, 3-22; Petersen, *Rediscovering Paul*, 103-24; Banks, *Paul's Idea of Community*, 149-58; Holmberg, *Paul and Power*, 58-69.
61. Meeks, *First Urban Christians*, 133; cf. Theissen, *Social Setting*, 87-96.
62. It is often suggested that after Claudius expelled Jews from Rome in AD 49-50, Prisca and Aquila first assisted Paul at Corinth, then provided a house in Ephesus which he used as a base during the period when he wrote 1 Corinthians (along with their instruction of Apollos and hosting of a house congregation, 1 Cor 16:19) and then returned to Rome, where they again hosted a congregation (Rom 16:3-5). See on 16:19, below.
63. Banks, *Paul's Idea of Community*, 51.

But Paul does not restrict such "personal commitment to others" to his fellow workers only. In 1 Cor 8:11, 12, to damage "the brother or sister for whom Christ died" is tantamount to sinning against Christ (see under 8:11 and 12). If Christians are individually and corporately the shrine of the Spirit of God (1 Cor 3:16, 17; 6:19), to sin against a **brother** *or sister* is to desecrate God's holy temple. In Rom 8:29 the **brothers** *and sisters* of the Christian family cry to God as *"Abba,* Father," since they are co-heirs with Christ (Rom 8:14-17). It is therefore too restricted and too colorless to translate ὁ ἀδελφός here as *our colleague* (REB, while Phillips's *a Christian brother* (with the indefinite article) presupposes that he is not known to the addressees and misses the "co-worker" aspect. Collins rightly observes that in a period when the adjective "Christian" had not yet come into common use (cf. Acts 11:26) **brother** "had the connotation of fellow Christian."[64] Hence our translation underlines this point (as against NRSV's, NJB's, and NIV's *our brother).*

Two questions remain. (i) Was Sosthenes the scribe or amanuensis to whom Paul dictated this letter? (ii) Might he have been the one to whom Paul entrusted the carrying and reading of the letter? Tertius served as amanuensis for Romans (Rom 16:22), and H. G. Meecham argued in 1923 that Sosthenes "not improbably" acted in this capacity, as Timothy did for certain other epistles.[65] More recent Michael Prior has argued that **Sosthenes** was Paul's scribe.[66] Murphy O'Connor argues that in contrast to the earlier, more cooperative writing of 1 (or 2?) Thessalonians, 1 Corinthians was more specifically Paul's work. But Sosthenes' role as co-author, he argues, can be seen in the "we" of 1 Cor 1:18-31 and 2:6-16.[67] We cannot be certain, although the practice itself of dictating letters was common. All but a few were far more comfortable articulating arguments and ideas orally, leaving someone else to concentrate on the further task of translating this flow of thought and argument into writing.[68] The papyri offer abundant evidence of the practice at all levels of society.[69] We know that 1:1–16:20 was not in Paul's hand; he added 16:21-24 (see below on 16:21). The degree of secretarial freedom varied.[70] This would depend partly on the importance the author attached to precision of expression of their own thoughts, and how intimate or trustworthy the author regarded the amanuensis as closely understanding his or her mind and purposes.

---

64. Collins, *First Corinthians,* 51; cf. also 45.

65. H. Meecham, *Light from Ancient Letters* (London: Allen & Unwin, 1923), 104.

66. M. Prior, *Paul the Letter Writer and the Second Letter to Timothy,* JSNTSS 23 (Sheffield: JSOT, 1989), 39-42.

67. Murphy-O'Connor, "Co-Authorship in the Corinthian Correspondence," *RB* 100 (1993): 562-79; cf. also his *Paul the Letter-Writer,* 33-34.

68. Meecham, *Light from Ancient Letters,* 104.

69. For example, *Oxyrhynchus Papyri,* 245, 275, 479, where a signature in a different handwriting from that of the rest of the letter is appended.

70. P. J. J. Botha, "The Verbal Art," in Porter and Olbricht, *Rhetoric and the NT,* 415-16.

The second question remains even more difficult to answer. In recent rhetorical criticism it has become fashionable to speak of the "performance" of the letter by a public reading to the assembled congregation. Thus Botha writes: "In antiquity the letter carrier was . . . the vital link between sender and recipients. . . . Presentation (ὑπόκρισις actio) of the rhetorical act . . . is fundamentally the essence of rhetorical activity."[71] In 1 Thess 5:27 Paul requests "in a strikingly ceremonious way that his letter be read to all of the brethren."[72] It is idle to speculate whether Paul primed Sosthenes or some other representative to read the letter aloud to the whole church, or whether the letter carrier simply left the letter for a series of house-church leaders and others to read the text to groups of various sizes on more than one occasion. The principle of "performance" may assist us, on the other hand, to understand how certain aspects of Paul's "previous letter" (1 Cor 5:9) were so seriously misunderstood. A "hearing" is not the same as prolonged study, as Stamps implies.[73] We also need to bear in mind the debate about the integrity of the epistle. While Fee and Mitchell argue for the unity of the epistle, Weiss and Goguel propose that our epistle embodied three separate letters; Jewett, five or six; and Schmithals, thirteen or fourteen (see above in the Introduction, 36-39).[74] Hans Frör's recent popular "docu-drama" study divides our epistle into four, punctuated by "replies."[75]

2. Addressees (1:2)

2 (i) Early in the transmission of the Western text the phrase **which is in Corinth**, τῇ οὔσῃ ἐν Κορίνθῳ, became transposed to follow **to those who are sanctified in Christ Jesus** rather than to precede this phrase. The early MSS include p46, B, D*, as well as E, F, G. Meyer (and Lachmann) were among the minority who accepted this early Western reading, on the grounds of *difficilior lectio probabilior,* i.e., why should anyone change a

---

71. Ibid., 417 and 418. Botha continues: "To Cicero, the face, which he calls an *imago animi,* is a very important part of the body when it comes to relevant gestures. Crucial is the voice . . . the performative, dynamic essence of ancient communication" (419). Although we should beware of abusing accidents of word history, the fact that *actor* (ὑποκριτής) eventually became our English word *hypocrite* reminds us that the actor "plays out" the gestures and attitudes of the person in whose shoes the actor stands.

72. W. Beilner, "ἐπιστολή," *EDNT,* 2:39; cf. 38-39. See further J. Dewey (ed.), *Semeia 65: Orality,* 95-127, and also D. L. Stamps, *The Rhetorical Use of the Epistolary Form in 1 Cor* (Sheffield: Sheffield Academic Press; forthcoming [revision of Durham Ph.D. thesis, 1992]).

73. Stamps, *Rhetorical Use,* ch. 1.

74. Mitchell, *Paul and the Rhetoric of Reconciliation,* 184-304, offers an excellent sustained argument for the unity of 1 Corinthians; cf. Fee, *First Epistle,* 15; J. Weiss, *Der erste Korintherbrief,* xxxix-xliii; W. Schmithals, "Die Korintherbriefe als Briefsammlung," *ZNW* 64 (1973): 263-88 and his *Gnosticism at Corinth,* 87-113. See further A. Stewart-Sykes, "Ancient Editors and Copyists and Modern Partition Theories: The Case of the Corinthians Correspondence," *JSNT* 61 (1996): 53-64.

75. H. Frör, *You Wretched Corinthians!* (Eng. trans., London: SCM, 1995), 140-42.

reading to such poor style unless it was original?[76] Lightfoot thinks Paul quite capable of such awkward syntax. But Lietzmann, Conzelmann, Schrage, and others regard this sequence as (for Conzelmann) so "intolerable" as to be far more likely to reflect the repetition of an early scribal error.[77] Barrett suspects that the whole clause might be an addition because of its varied word order and its redundancy in the light of **called to be holy people**.[78] But as we shall note, Chrysostom and others see very good reasons for the deliberate repetition of **Christ Jesus** up to six times within a short compass. Paul wishes to draw the readers' attention away from themselves and even away from the writer *to Christ*.

(ii) Weiss thinks that the whole phrase **together with all who call on the name of our Lord Jesus Christ in every place, both their Lord and ours** was probably a scribal gloss; an interpolation by an early copyist who wishes to stress the universality of the church.[79] But this is groundless conjecture, and has no textual support. A more plausible suggestion would be that, against the self-importance of the church in Corinth, an indignant or wry copyist added "their Lord — and ours too!" in the margin, which was then assimilated into the text. But no evidence exists for this either.

The genitive in the phrase τῇ ἐκκλησίᾳ τοῦ θεοῦ, **of God**, τοῦ θεοῦ is possessive. From Chrysostom onward this assertion has been urged on the basis of language, but it also anticipates more recent work on social relations at Corinth. Chrysostom observes that the church is the possession "not 'of this person or that person' but of God."[80] The church does not "belong" to some local leader, group, or party, but is *God's*. Meyer construes the grammatical form as "genitive of the owner," followed by Edwards ("genitive of possession"), Robertson and Plummer, and Wendland.[81] More recently a number of writers who have adopted sociological or socio-rhetorical approaches to the epistle propose that Paul's chief concern arose from the undue influence of patrons or of "the strong," who exercised power on the basis of "wisdom" or of social status, and behaved as if they "owned" the church. This verse may begin an overture to this repeated theme. The church, Paul insists, belongs not to the wealthy, or to "patrons," or to some self-styled inner circle of "spiritual people who manifest gifts," *but to God*.[82] Both Paul and local patrons or "spirituals" are accountable

---

76. H. A. W. Meyer, *Epistles to the Corinthians* (2 vols., Eng. trans., Edinburgh: T. & T. Clark, 1892), 1:10.

77. Lietzmann, *An die Korinther,* 5; Conzelmann, *1 Cor,* 20-21; Schrage, *Der erste Brief,* 1:103; and more neutrally Lightfoot, *Notes,* 144.

78. Barrett, *First Epistle,* 32.

79. J. Weiss, *Der erste Korintherbrief* (Göttingen: Vandenhoeck & Ruprecht, 1910), 4.

80. Chrysostom, *1 Cor. Hom.,* 1:1.

81. Meyer, *Epistles,* 1:12; T. C. Edwards, *First Epistle to the Corinthians* (London: Hodder & Stoughton, 2d ed. 1885), 3; A. Robertson and A. Plummer, *First Epistle,* 2; H. D. Wendland, *Die Briefe an die Korinther* (Göttingen: Vandenhoeck & Ruprecht, 1936 [1968]), 14.

82. See e.g., Chow, *Patronage and Power,* 113-90; Witherington, *Conflict and Community,* 19-35; Marshall, *Enmity in Corinth,* 32-34, 68-69, 173-78, 246-58, 362-64, 388-404; S. M. Pogoloff, *Logos and Sophia: The Rhetorical Situation of 1 Corinthians,* SBLDS 134 (Atlanta: Scholars Press, 1992), 197-236; A. D. Clarke, *Secular and Christian Leadership at Corinth*

to God. The church is *God's* growing "field," *God's* planned "construction," *God's* inner shrine (1 Cor 3:9, where θεοῦ, **of God**, stands three times in an emphatic word order). Karl Barth captures the tone magnificiently: "The main defect" at Corinth was the belief of the addressees "not in God, but in their own belief in God and in particular leaders."[83] Barth's theological exegesis and Theissen's social-science approach point in the same direction here as the exegesis of Schrage, Strobel, and Wendland.[84] The church does not "belong" to any of its in-groups or leaders, but to God.

Regarding τῇ οὔσῃ ἐν Κορίνθῳ, Bengel drily speaks of the "paradox" of a church which is simultaneously **of God** and, of all places, at *Corinth: laetum et ingens paradoxon!*[85] We should not make an issue out of the redundant dative singular present participle τῇ οὔσῃ. The idiom occurs widely in hellenistic Greek, and with ὑπάρχω even in classical Greek.[86] Nevertheless Collins (as if in response to Bengel) argues that the participle is "not merely a copulative: it is a statement of existence as such. The church of God actually exists in Corinth."[87] However in a comment which has become notorious K. L. Schmidt sought to make particular play of this construction and this verse to support a "universal" as against a "congregational" doctrine of the church in Paul. He insists: "The sum of the individual congregations does not produce the total community of the church. Each community, how ever small, *represents the total* community of the Church. This is supported by 1 Cor 1:2; τῇ ἐκκλησίᾳ . . . τῇ οὔσῃ ἐν Κορίνθῳ . . . true rendering here is not 'the Corinthian congregation' but 'the congregation, church, assembly, *as it is in Corinth.*'"[88]

Schmidt overinterprets the grammar and exaggerates the implications of this verse. However, his faulty *method* may or may not invalidate his conclusions, since he also addresses wider considerations. An immediate allusion to **all who call on the name of our Lord Jesus Christ in every place** (v. 2) reinforces the thought that the church in Corinth is *not a self-contained autonomous entity: they are not a self-sufficient community; they are not the only pebble on the beach.* Their lifestyle and practices are monitored by translocal "fellow workers" of Paul's (notably by Timothy, 1 Cor. 4:17), and they are required to follow patterns of thought and lifestyle which characterize traditions or "order" (διατάσσομαι) "in all the churches" (ἐν ταῖς ἐκκλησίαις πάσαις,

(Leiden: Brill, 1993), 23-108; P. D. Gardner, *The Gifts of God and the Authentication of the Christian* (Lanham, Md. and London: University Press of America, 1994), 48-54; and Theissen, *Social Setting,* 121-43.

83. K. Barth, *The Resurrection of the Dead* (Eng. trans., London: Hodder & Stoughton, 1933), 17.

84. A. Strobel, *Der erste Brief an die Korinther* (Zürich: Theologischer Verlag, 1989), 21; Schrage, *Der erste Brief,* 103; Wendland, *Die Briefe,* 14; cf. Theissen, *Social Setting,* esp. 136; and Robertson and Plummer, *First Epistle,* 2.

85. Bengel, *Gnomon,* 608.

86. Xenophon, *Hellenica* 1.1.27.

87. Collins, *First Cor,* 52.

88. Schmidt, "ἐκκλησία," *TDNT,* 3:506 (both sets of italics mine); cf. 501-36.

1 Cor 7:17).[89] The importance of "order" (τάγμα) is seen not only from ecclesiology (τάξις, 14:40) but also from Christology and especially eschatology (15:23-24; cf. 27-28).[90]

Holmberg shows how in the Pauline churches networks of authority combine genuine leadership with genuine mutuality across local congregations and thus ensure a recognizable order, identity, and stability in a pluralistic society.[91] By contrast, in Corinth people wanted, even demanded, "the right to choose" (ἐξουσία, 8:9; πάντα μοι ἔξεστιν, 6:12; 10:23; see under 6:12 and 8:7-13). This obsession with autonomy colored both individual and corporate aspirations. Yet the notion of each community as an internally *self-contained autonomous* democracy finds no place in Pauline theology. Hence Paul will shortly ask indignantly: Has Christ been **apportioned out** or "parceled out" (μεμέρισται ὁ Χριστός; 1:13) into autonomous groups? It is possible to speak of the "catholicity" of the church of Paul's day, as well as its diversity. For its networks and shared commonality in Christ, in the gospel, and in a common apostolic witness to Christ amounted to more than a loose federation of autonomous communities. Whether a given local group genuinely reflects Christ and the apostolic gospel is not left to be determined by *criteria internal to the group in question,* but also relates to translocal counterchecks such as the *apostles,* Paul's *fellow workers,* and creeds, practices, and traditions followed *in all the churches.* Today the notion of criteria *internal to "local" or "ethnocentric" communities* brings us to the heart of the global debate about so-called *postmodernity.*[92]

We should also be cautious about overinterpreting the word **church,** ἐκκλησία. Hodge (1858) drew on word history to claim that the church is "called out from the world" (ἐκ-καλέω).[93] But the word was used in classical Greek to denote an assembly to which townspeople were "called" from their homes by a herald's cry or trumpet. It is often argued that the NT writers inherited the word later as the LXX translation of the Hebrew קהל (qahal). Although Hatch-Redpath cite sixty-six examples, Schrage argues that the LXX background does not fully account for the NT uses of ἐκκλησία, and returns to the Greek origins of the word.[94] Whatever the origin, the word stresses the call *to assemble together as a congregation* in God's presence.

---

89. See later discussions of "tradition," e.g., under 11:2, 23 and of common creeds, e.g., under 8:4-6, and bibliographies in these subjects. On the balance between "the one and the many" see also J. A. T. Robinson, *The Body,* 29-32 and 58-72.

90. Taken up in *1 Clement,* 40:1.

91. B. Holmberg, *Paul and Power,* throughout, esp. 58-69.

92. Richard Rorty consciously uses "local" or "ethnocentric" for criteria internal to specific communities, e.g., *Truth and Progress: Philosophical Papers* (Cambridge: Cambridge University Press, 1998) 3:1-15 and 19-42.

93. C. Hodge, *First Epistle to the Corinthians* (London: Banner of Truth, 5th ed. 1958 [1858]), 3.

94. Hatch-Redpath, *A Concordance to the Septuagint and the Other Versions of the Old Testament,* 1:433; and W. Schrage, "'Ekklesia' und 'Synagoge': Zum Ursprung des urchristlichen Kirchenbegriffs," *ZTK* 60 (1963): 178-202, and *Der erste Brief,* 1:102. Cf. further BAGD, 240-41.

Paul applies the cognate terms related to ἅγιος, **holy**, twice here: **sancti-fied, called to be holy people**, ἡγιασμένοις ἐν Χριστῷ Ἰησοῦ, κλητοῖς ἁγίοις. The words translated **sanctified** and **holy** derive from the verbal and adjectival cognate forms: (1) ἁγιάζειν, *to dedicate, to set apart, to make holy, to conse-crate* (cf. ἡγιασμένοις, perfect passive); and (2) ἅγιος, *holy person, one dedi-cated* and *set apart* to God. The latter may signify both status or role and char-acter. Hence *saints* are those set apart as God's own, and ideally *holy in life*, as a habituated pattern which has become reflected in a settled character.

The Greek again reflects an LXX translation, this time of the Hebrew קדוש *(qadosh)*, which means *separate* or *set apart* in contrast to *being in com-mon use*. The people of God and the things of God reflect their special status as serving God, who is awesomely Other, transcendent in majesty and purity. In this sense of the word, "Holiness is received, not achieved."[95] Even if this phrase were to be suspected of being a scribal insertion (which, we noted, is an extremely unlikely conjecture), Paul expresses this same thought in 1 Cor 6:11: **you have been washed, you were sanctified** (ἡγιάσθητε). The comparison with 6:11, however, does reveal one difference: the perfect passive of ἁγιάζειν in 1:2 denotes a past event with present effects which remain, whereas the aorist passive of the same verb in 6:11 may bring into focus more specifically the transitional and transformative event of the readers' coming to faith as an event of divine call.

Should ἐν be translated here as **in** (above, together with Barrett, REB, NRSV, ASV, NJB, AV/KJV, NIV) or as *by?* Paul regularly defines holiness or spirituality especially in this epistle in christological terms. The readers' status as those who belong to God and are called to live out this godly holiness *derives from their being-in-Christ*. On grammatical grounds alone ἐν Χριστῷ Ἰησοῦ could be translated **sanctified by Christ Jesus**, since ἐν followed by the dative case may include the notion of instrumentality. But elsewhere Paul places strong theological emphasis on being-in-Christ as a concept of corporate status which provides the ground for Christian life and destiny. The translation **sanc-tified in Christ Jesus** takes up this wider context. Thus Goodspeed translates ἐν as *by union with Christ Jesus*. Certainly ἐν with a dative of persons is broader than agency or instrumentality alone, often denoting mode, personal presence, or a close personal relation.[96] What counts as holy is perceived as *what counts as Christ-like*. Hence, just as Christ assumes the form of the "image" of God in public (εἰκών, 1 Cor 15:49), so a holy people *manifest* their consecration to God through the status and character which they derive from Christ.

The plural form of the dative participle ἡγιασμένοις, **to those sanctified**, provides an epexegetical gloss on the earlier singular form, **to the church**. The change from the singular to the plural is noteworthy. The singular stresses the solidarity of the readers as one united corporate entity; the plural calls attention

95. Conzelmann, *1 Cor,* 21.
96. BAGD, 258-61; also BDF, sect. 219, esp. (1) and (4).

to the individual responsibility of each member to live out his or her conse-crated status in Christ. (See further under the exegesis of 12:12-27.)

Just as Paul is **called** to apostolic witness, so every Christian believer is **called to be holy**. Because this call is to *every* Christian, Fee observes, the tra-ditional translation *saints* "contains too many misleading connotations to be of value."[97] J. W. C. Wand offers a memorable question: "Are only good people to be recognized as members of the divine society. . . ? Is the Church a museum for saints or a school for sinners?"[98] Nevertheless, just as Joshua was called to "possess" the land because he already "possessed" it as a divine gift (Josh 1:11-12), so believers are *called* to a lifestyle which reflects their *already* given sta-tus. Hence the theological and ethical make contact in this phrase in 1:2.[99] Cal-vin comments that the call is "to blamelessness of life," but "here God begins his work . . . and brings it to completion little by little."[100] The Corinthians, Paul repeatedly stressed, were far from having "arrived" (cf. 4:8-13, esp. 8b).

Paul now associates the other churches with Corinth: σὺν πᾶσιν τοῖς ἐπικαλουμένοις τὸ ὄνομα τοῦ κυρίου ἡμῶν Ἰησοῦ Χριστοῦ ἐν παντὶ τόπῳ, αὐτῶν καὶ ἡμῶν. Our translation (above) unavoidably presupposes a particular interpre-tation of **theirs and ours** (αὐτῶν καὶ ἡμῶν). Some ancient and modern commen-tators construe the meaning on the basis of the word order to mean **in their place and in our place**, applying it to *place* rather than to **Lord**. Thus Chrysostom un-derstands Paul to mean that Christ remains the one Lord of those separated in dif-ferent places: "One place helps them [has the effect of making them] not to be of one mind," but "though the place be separate, the Lord binds them together."[101] The Vulgate follows this path: *in omni loco ipsorum et nostro.* Cyril, Am-brosiaster, Pelagius and Thomas Aquinas read the particle τε after αὐτῶν, which Allo believes would then add a degree of strength to this possibility.[102]

97. Fee, *First Epistle,* 32.
98. J. W. C. Wand, *A History of the Early Church to AD 500* (London: Methuen, 3d ed. 1949), 145.
99. Barr takes up the question discussed by Schrenk concerning the exclusive choice of the ἅγιος, ἁγιάζω group to translate the Hebrew, rather than ἱερός, which occurs only once of the holy temple in the NT. Schrenk argues that this was because ἱερός had too many associations with the "holy" in pagan religion, especially Greek religions. But Barr rightly concludes that the chosen ἅγιος group offered "a Greek word with a suitable spread of meaning to fit the Hebrew words." Hence, like the Hebrew, the Greek word can denote things set apart for God's use or purpose (holy city, Matt 4:5; holy scripture, Rom 1:2; holy temple, 1 Cor 3:17; holy kiss, 1 Cor 16:20; 2 Cor 13:12); but also the process of transformation into Christ-like holiness of life (1 Cor 7:34; Col 1:22, 1 Thess 4:3), where ἁγιασμός is often translated **sanctification**. Cf. G. Schrenk, *TDNT,* 3:221-30, esp. 229, and less directly 231-83; and J. Barr, *The Semantics of Biblical Language* (Oxford: Ox-ford University Press, 1961), 282-86, esp. 286.
100. Calvin, *First Epistle,* 19.
101. Chrysostom, *Ep. Cor. Hom.,* 1:2.
102. Allo, *Première Épitre,* 3. This opens the door to speculation about "their place" and "our place": some take "ours" to mean Ephesus, and "theirs" to mean Corinth (which would invite "yours," not "theirs"). Others relate the phrase to the alleged "parties" of 1:12, interpreting "our" places as the Pauline house churches, and "theirs" as those of the Peter party or so-called Apollos or Christ parties.

Findlay, however, describes this whole approach, in spite of the word order, as "strained in various ways."[103] The key point is that the Corinthians, or at least those who cause the problems which Paul addresses, are self-absorbed and self-centered. They think and act as if they had a monopoly on Christ and the Spirit. They tend broadly to match the target of Nietzsche's telling aphorism: "The 'salvation of the soul', . . . in plain English 'the world revolves round me'."[104] Jesus Christ is not the exclusive "Lord" who serves only the interests of some specific group. He may indeed include them within wider Lordship, but he remains "both their Lord and ours." Anecdotal tradition tells how C. H. Spurgeon handled a similar problem when a self-centered church leader claimed his attention by insisting that he came as "the Lord's messenger." Spurgeon is said to have sent back the message that "he regrets that he is currently engaged with the Lord." In the sense conveyed by the anecdote, Christ is **their Lord and ours.**

The phrase **all who call on the name of our Lord** comes directly from Joel 3:5 (cf. Ps 98:6), from which it is taken up in Rom 10:13 and Acts 2:21. The LXX of Joel 3:5 reads πᾶς ὃς ἂν ἐπικαλέσηται τὸ ὄνομα κυρίου σωθήσεται, which is identical to Paul's quotation in Rom 10:13, and the vocabulary of the shorter phrase in 1 Cor 1:2 remains the same, allowing for the grammatical variations imposed by the context of reference. The allusion to **the day of the Lord** in 1:7-8 makes the allusion to Joel all the more probable.[105] Moffatt translates "invoke the name of the Lord," since the phrase ἐπικάλειν, "to call on" or "to invoke" (the gods) represents a standard phrase for the activity of worshipers toward their gods in classical and hellenistic Greek literature from Plato to Epictetus.[106] Thus Epictetus speaks of avoiding a task "except after invoking Demeter" (εἰ μὴ τὴν Δήμητρα ἐπικαλεσάμενοι).[107] If we place together the range of meanings of ἐπικαλεῖν in the LXX, the NT, the papyri, and the early Fathers, as well as the wider background in hellenistic literature, it becomes beyond doubt that "to call on the Lord" is to perform a self-involving commissive speech-act: Schrage calls it an "acclamation" performed as an "act."[108] It sig-

103. Findlay, *Expositor's Greek Testament,* 2:759.

104. Nietzsche, *The Complete Works* (cited above): *The Antichrist,* aphorism 43.

105. The resonance is perhaps too brief or unproblematic to receive apparent attention in C. D. Stanley, *Paul and the Language of Scripture,* SNTSMS 74 (Cambridge: Cambridge University Press, 1992) or in R. B. Hays, *Echoes of Scripture in the Letters of Paul* (New Haven: Yale University Press, 1989). But cf. Schrage, *Der erste Brief,* 1:105.

106. For example, Plato, *Timaeus* 27c; and Epictetus, *Dissertations* 2.7.12 (contemporary with Paul).

107. Epictetus, *Diss.* 3.21.12. As we might expect, the papyri, especially the magical papyri, offer too many examples to cite, including instances of second-century invocations at specific hours on special days, and cases where the noun ἐπίκλησις (*epiklesis,* as in the liturgical calling on the Spirit) means simply *spell* (e.g., a spell against becoming a slave, δούλων ἐπίκλησις, P. Lille 1.29[f27]).

108. Schrage, *Der erste Brief,* 1:105-6; on the papyri and other sources cf. Moulton and Milligan, *The Vocabulary of the Greek New Testament* (London, 1930), 239, and BAGD, 294,

nals an *act* of appeal and request which is simultaneously an *act* of commitment and trust on the part of the worshiper.

This explains why Paul can regard **calling on the name of our Lord** in 1:2 and confessing "Jesus is Lord" (Κύριος Ἰησοῦς) in 1 Cor 12:3 as the sign and test of what it is to be a Christian believer. It is not a matter of aiming appeals to a deity from some neutral stance; that does not capture the force of either ἐπικαλεῖν, "to call on," as Κύριος, "Lord." Weiss asserts that what **Lord** "means in a practical religious sense will best be made clear through the correlative concept of 'servant' or 'slave' of Christ (Rom 1:1; 1 Cor 7:22-23; Gal 1:10; Phil 1:1; Col 4:12)."[109] Bultmann similarly observes that only this self-involving dimension offers a sense of *freedom.* If "slaves" place themselves at the disposal of their Lord, their Lord has them in his care and they are no longer their own responsibility, but trustfully **call on the name of** [the] **Lord.** Such a person "lets this care go, yielding himself entirely to the grace of God."[110] See further especially under 8:6 and 12:3.[111] Combes notes the use of the correlative slave–Lord in a "positive" sense in 6:20, Rom 14:7-8, 14; 2 Cor 5:15.[112]

Paul uses Joel's phrase **the name of the Lord.** The name of the Lord stands as the guarantee that God's acts in and through Christ will accord with the revelation of his character as hitherto disclosed. **Name** in the OT often signifies character, position, and especially reputation. When Moses asked God's name (Exod 3:13) the LXX rendering "I am who I am" is probably better rendered on the basis of the Hebrew grammatical form "I will be who I will be" (3:14), i.e., *you will see* what constitutes my **name** by the sovereign and redeeming *acts which I shall perform,* and which will thereby disclose my identity in terms of *character.* When Psalmists praise **the name of the Lord** (Ps 9:2), this constitutes a recital of the saving acts which build his reputation and disclose his character: "Those who know your name put their trust in you" (Ps 9:10; cf. vv. 3-9 and Ps 20:1, 5, 7).[113] Hence to **call on the name of the Lord,** partly in Joel, but more fully here, means *not* to invoke *some shadowy, unknown, deity,* but *to commit oneself in trust to the one whose nature and character have been disclosed* as worthy of this trust.

In 1 Cor 1:2 **the name of the Lord** is applied to **our Lord Jesus Christ.** This christological application cannot be detached from the utterly familiar tradition that in the LXX κύριος translates and becomes "an expository equivalent

esp. under 2b. Cf. Josephus, *Antiquities* 4.222; *Oxyrhynchus Papyri* 1380:153; *1 Clement,* 52.3; 64:1; and numerous other instances. W. Kramer, *Christ, Lord, Son of God,* anticipates Schrage in emphasizing a possible liturgical context.

109. J. Weiss, *Earliest Christianity,* 2:458.

110. Bultmann, *Theology of the NT,* 1:331.

111. Cf. J. M. Bassler, "1 Cor 12:3: Curse and Confession in Context," *JBL* 101 (1982): 415-18, among a mass of other literature cited on 12:3 and 8:6.

112. I. A. H. Combes, *The Metaphor of Slavery in the Writings of the Early Church,* JSNTSS 156 (Sheffield: Sheffield Academic Press, 1998), 83; cf. 77-87.

113. Among other examples cf. Ps 23:3; 25:11; 54:1, 6; 66:2, 4; 96:2, 8; 106:8, 47; 113:1-3; 135:1, 3, 13; 145:1, 2, 21.

for the Divine Name," both the Hebrew unspoken proper noun יהוה (YHWH, no vowels used) and אדון (*'adon, lord) or* אדני (*'adonai*).[114] Cullmann comments, "*Adonai* was certainly the characteristic Jewish designation for God in the first century before and the first century after Christ."[115] On the other hand, Paul regularly applies the word κύριος to Christ. Bultmann observes, "For Paul 'Lord' and not 'Christ' is Jesus' title."[116] To proclaim Jesus as Lord (2 Cor 4:5) constitutes what Anderson Scott calls "a summary of Christian preaching."[117] Scott calls it "the one available profession of faith which Paul requires of a would-be Christian," and translates Paul's description of this confession τὸ ῥῆμα τῆς πίστεως (the word of faith) as "the formula which expresses faith."[118] Clearly therefore to invoke or to confess Christ as Lord is a *commissive act,* not a mere intellectual proposition, since Paul makes plain as 1 Corinthians unfolds that salvation entails more than having some correct head content (1 Cor 1:18-25; 8:1, 2; 7-13; and elsewhere. See especially under 8:7-13, on the limits of γνῶσις, "knowledge").

Paul was not the first to conceive of "invoking Christ as Lord" in prayer, trust, or self-commitment. The Aramaic form *Maranatha* (Μαράνα θά, 1 Cor 16:22), *Our Lord, come* (see under 16:22 in the translation), is difficult to explain unless, as Robinson argues, it stems from the early pre-Pauline Aramaic-speaking community.[119] A stronger argument is that such passages as Rom 1:3-4 show every sign of representing pre-Pauline confessions which Paul himself uses and endorses.[120] We refer readers to more detailed discussions and bibliography under 8:6 and especially 12:3, where "Jesus is Lord" assumes the dimension of a confessional formula or creed. There also it is both a truth-claim and a self-involving personal attitude of trust. The person who makes this confession belongs to Christ and is "his man" or "his woman." On the centrality of this title for Paul, Dunn elucidates various constructive comments.[121]

114. G. Quell, "κύριος," *TDNT,* 3:1,058.

115. Cullmann, *Christology of the NT* (Eng. trans., Louisville: Westminster John Knox, 1987), 200.

116. Bultmann, *Theology,* 1:80.

117. C. Anderson Scott, *Christianity according to St Paul* (Cambridge: Cambridge University Press, 1927), 250.

118. Ibid.

119. J. A. T. Robinson, "Earliest Christian Liturgical Sequence?" in his *Twelve NT Studies* (London: SCM, 1962), 154-57; also *JTS* 4 (1953): 38-41. However, under 16:22 we reject his supposedly "eucharistic" setting: it refers to the final parousia (see below).

120. P. Beasley-Murray, "Romans 1:3f.: An Early Confession of Faith in the Lordship of Jesus," *TynBul* 31 (1980): 147-54. It is noteworthy that in his *St Stephen and the Hellenists* Marcel Simon ascribes an early date to Stephen's acclamation of Jesus as Lord (Acts 7:59).

121. J. D. G. Dunn, *The Theology of Paul the Apostle* (Edinburgh: T. & T. Clark, 1998), 244-52. On the OT background, further, Wolff, *Der erste Brief,* 17.

3. Greeting (1:3)

3 It is entirely consistent with his practice that Paul both utilizes and trans-forms the conventional greeting form χαίρειν, *greetings* (cf. Acts 15:23; James 1:1) into a Christian greeting which simultaneously serves as a speech-act of *greeting* and a speech-act of *prayer:* χάρις ὑμῖν, **grace . . . to you**. Just as the thanksgiving form in 1:4-9 combines Greek, Jewish, and Christian elements, so this greeting-prayer also combines the conventional Graeco-Roman letter form with the Jewish greeting wish καὶ εἰρήνη, **and peace** (שלום, *shalom*). The dou-ble form occurs in Rom 1:7; 2 Cor 1:2; Phil 1:2; 2 Thess 1:2; cf. Gal 1:3; Eph 1:2. The Apostolic Fathers sometimes adopt the Pauline form (e.g., 1 Clem 1:1), and sometimes use *greetings* or *many* (i.e., "warm") *greetings* alone (πλεῖστα χαίρειν; Ignatius, *Letter to the Ephesians,* 1:1).

Is a wish which invokes the agency of God and Christ a greeting, or a prayer, or a greeting-prayer? Wishes which initially invoke God often histori-cally degenerate into sheer convention. Thus the English "Good-bye" origi-nates from the early form "God be wy you," "God buy'ye" as a contraction of "God be with ye." Paul prevents the assimilation of the two speech-acts of greeting and "wish-prayer" by solemnly expanding it to include the agency through whom the wish is fulfilled: **from God our Father and from the Lord Jesus Christ.**[122]

The emphasis here on **grace** (χάρις) is especially appropriate in the con-text of a church plagued by issues of competitive status seeking and "rights" (cf. 6:12; 10:23, Introduction and throughout). The word calls attention to God's unstintingly generous action regardless of the recipient's "achieve-ments." Bultmann's emphasis on **grace** as an "event" in Paul rather than a "quality" coheres with the logic here of that which is *given and received* and also with the views of Schrage and Dunn that it constitutes an event rather than a disposition: **grace** is therefore a "stronger" word than more general refer-ences to mercy.[123] **Grace** is not "timeless," but is bound up with God's action in Christ.[124] **Grace** is given by or in Christ (1:4). Paul declares: "by the grace of God I am what I am" (15:10); and asks: "What do you have that you did not re-ceive? And if you receive it, why do you boast as if it were not a *gift*" (4:7). Paul unfolds the grammar of the concept when he argues that if readers abstract

---

122. On "wish-prayer" in Paul, see G. P. Wiles, Paul's *Intercessory Prayers,* SNTSMS 24 (Cambridge: Cambridge University Press, 1974), 22-107, although Wiles ranks 1:3 here rather as a "blessing" (140-41). On the link between **God our Father** and the **Lord Jesus Christ**, see Rich-ardson, *Paul's Language about God,* esp. 95-138 and 308-15.

123. Bultmann, *Theology of the New Testament,* 1:288-92. Cf. further Barth, *Church Dog-matics,* 1/2, sect. 19; and 2/1, sects. 26 and 31; Schrage, *Der erste Brief,* 1:106; and J. D. G. Dunn, *Romans,* WBC (Dallas: Word, 1988), 1:17: "Grace is never merely an attitude or disposition of God. . . . Consistently it denotes something much more dynamic — the wholly generous *act* of God" (Dunn's italics).

124. Schrage, *Der erste Brief,* 1:106, n. 2.

grace from the language and actions of freely giving-and-receiving "then it is no more *grace*" (Rom 11:6; cf. further Rom 5:15; 12:3; 15:15; 2 Cor 6:1; Gal 2:9).

Grace is related closely to divine call or to divine choosing in vv. 2 and 3.[125] But if **grace**, like the divine word, is not separable from God's freely imparting *himself*, then Paul is introducing a refrain which he will repeat: "gifts" are not "possessions" which enhance status; gifts of **grace** entail God's own holy presence: "Your body is a temple of the Holy Spirit. . . . You are not your own" (1 Cor 6:19).[126]

The Hebrew-Jewish greeting εἰρήνη, שָׁלוֹם *(shalom),* often means **peace**, but since *shâlôm* can often entail "well-being" in a more generalized, nonspecific sense, it might be thought to convey only a dissipated greeting such as our English "Are you well?" (without pause for any answer). But the addition **from God . . . and from the Lord . . .** specifies a distinctive OT background which also spoke of the well-being which came from God (Num 6:22-26).[127] Thus, Moffatt sees this "peace or well-being" as "the outcome of his [God's] free favour," namely *grace.*[128] In the modern world we tend to internalize and subjectivize *peace* to mean "inner tranquility" or "an untroubled state of mind." But while it sometimes bears this meaning in classical Greek (especially in philosophical texts), the Hebrew and LXX background more often refer to a harmony of interpersonal relations. Gerhard von Rad urges that "no specific text" (i.e., in the OT) denotes a "spiritual attitude of inward peace."[129] Merklein endorses this view: "peace as a concept in opposition to 'war', . . . not a purely inner peace (as in the Stoics)."[130] Paul strikes this keynote in Rom 5:1, where "peace with God" describes an objective relationship between God and the new creation of the people of God in Christ.

The earliest commentators understood **grace and peace** in a profoundly theological sense. Tertullian (c. 210) comments that the conveying of **grace** presupposed a former need for reconciliation, while **peace** presupposes an earlier time of rebellion. He interprets both of these as aspects of an objective relationship to God.[131]

The Greek ἀπὸ θεοῦ πατρὸς ἡμῶν καὶ κυρίου Ἰησοῦ Χριστοῦ begins the piling up of consciously repeated allusions to **the Lord Jesus Christ** (which Chrysostom notes [see below]) and the correlation of the agencies of **God** as

125. Barth, *Church Dogmatics,* 1/1, sect. 5.148-49, and 1/2, sect. 16.212. Cf. further 1/2, sects. 17, 338-61, and 2/2, sects. 32-34.
126. Barth, *CD,* 1/1, sects. 5 (e.g., iii, 147-50), 8, 9 and 12; 2/1, sects. 27, 179, 217, and 288; cf. also sects. 28-31. Barth applies this principle to 1 Corinthians in *The Resurrection of the Dead* (Eng. trans., London: Hodder & Stoughton, 1933), 17-29 and throughout.
127. Gerhard von Rad, "εἰρήνη," *TDNT,* 2:402-6; and Wolff, *Der erste Brief,* 18.
128. Moffatt, *First Epistle,* 5.
129. Von Rad, "εἰρήνη," *TDNT,* 2:406, n. 11.
130. Merklein, *Der erste Brief,* 1:78.
131. Tertullian, *Against Marcion,* 5:5.

Father and **Jesus Christ** as **Lord**. In opening passages of this kind (cf. Rom 1:7; 2 Cor 1:3; Gal 1:1, 3, 4; Phil 1:2; 1 Thess 1:1; Philem 3) Paul brings together two major "defining" principles (if we may use this word loosely) for God. Neil Richardson writes, "The most important defining word used of God is πατήρ [Father]. . . . Paul only three times addresses or refers to God as 'Father of our Lord Jesus Christ'" (2 Cor 1:3; 11:31; Rom 15:6).[132] But Paul's references to God as πατήρ, Father, occur "either in opening salutations . . . or in prayers and doxological contexts. These contexts give the word a significance not immediately indicated by its relative infrequency. . . . For Paul it is *the* distinctively Christian way of referring to and addressing God.[133]

In these same opening and doxological contexts, Paul often also "defines God by reference to Christ," even if Richardson (perhaps overcautiously) adds "Paul does not often define God in this way."[134] The attractive view has been expressed that in his encounter with Christ on the road to Damascus, Paul found revealed the "Christlikeness" of **God**. This image is needed to complement accusations in our own day that Paul's use of **Father** leaves him open to the charge of "patriarchy" or "authoritarianism." The theme of the Christlikeness of God runs throughout the writings of Jüngel and Moltmann, who point to the decisiveness of the cross (1 Cor 1:18-25) for understanding God's being and identity.[135] This is entirely true to Paul. Paul asserts simultaneously the unconditioned "Almightiness" of God and the Christlikeness of God as known and revealed through the self-chosen "weakness" of the cross.[136] In this profound context the cross is no mere "instrument" of salvation, but a revelation of the cruciform identity of God.

The conjunction of the two terms, **Father** and **Lord Jesus Christ**, as co-agents provides the necessary context for understanding two complementary points. On one side, Pannenberg declares that **Father** is "by no means an arbitrary one [term, idea] for which others might be substituted," and is "much more a metaphor."[137] He resists current attempts to complement "Father" by "Mother" since "To bring sexual differentiation into the understanding of God would mean polytheism."[138] Already "Father" allows *room for a mother's love,* and "God transcends all sexual differences."[139] He concludes: "On the lips of

132. Richardson, *Paul's Language about God,* 271 (his italics).

133. Ibid.

134. Ibid.

135. For example, E. Jüngel, *Theological Essays* (Eng. trans., Edinburgh: T. & T. Clark, 1995), 2:120-44 and throughout, and *God as the Mystery of the World* (Eng. trans., Edinburgh: T. & T. Clark, 1983), 226-396; and J. Moltmann, *The Crucified God* (Eng. trans., London: SCM, 1974) and *History and the Triune God* (Eng. trans., London: SCM, 1991).

136. The conceptual difference between *Almighty* (used in the New Testament) and *omnipotent* is explored in G. van den Brink, *Almighty God* (Kampen: Kok Pharos, 1993).

137. W. Pannenberg, *Systematic Theology,* 3 vols. (Eng. trans., Edinburgh: T. & T. Clark, 1991), vol. 1.

138. Ibid.

139. Ibid. Pannenberg resists the modern stereotypical ascription of "caring" qualities ex-

Jesus 'Father' became a proper name for God. It thus ceased to be simply one designation among others."[140] Pannenberg appeals to Pauline thought, since God as Holy Spirit reenacts within believers Jesus' own address to God: "Abba, Father" (Rom 8:15; cf. Gal 4:5-6). Hence, he concludes, "the words 'God' and 'Father' are not just time-bound concepts. . . ."[141] Because God reveals himself as Christlike and because Christ in his earthly ministry, crucifixion, and resurrection is obediently one with God, Paul places *God in Christ* together as jointly the source of **grace** and **peace** for the readers. Pannenberg sees Irenaeus's image of Christ and the Spirit as "the 'two hands' of God" as accurately reflecting Paul's thought.[142]

On one side, the cross is "the power of **God**" (1 Cor 1:18); things are what they are "through the will of God" (1:1), through the decree, choice, or election of God (1:21, 27, 28; 2:7, 9); life and growth depend on the agency of God (3:6, 7); everything awaits the verdict of God (4:5); the assignment of varied "gifts" and even "modes of existence" (or "bodies") depends on God's decision (12:28; 15:10, 38). On the other side, Paul sees God's self-disclosure in the crucified Jesus."[143] Thus, "The collocation of the Father and Son in such texts as these [i.e., 1:3] must not be overlooked."[144]

B. THANKSGIVING (1:4-9)

(4) I give thanks to my God always for you on the ground of God's grace given to you in Christ Jesus, (5) because in every respect you were enriched in him, in every kind of speaking and with all kinds of knowledge, (6) as the witness to Christ was confirmed among you, (7) so that you fall short in no gift, while you wait for the public revealing of our Lord Jesus Christ. (8) He will keep you firm to the end, free from any charge, on the day of our Lord Jesus Christ. (9) Faithful is God, through whom you were called into communal participation in the sonship of Jesus Christ our Lord.

Paul's Distinctive Use of the Thanksgiving Form. In spite of hardships (4:8-12) Paul never hesitates to be thankful and to express thanks to God as to others. The Greek word-group εὐχαριστῶ occurs forty-six times in the Pauline corpus. We have already discussed Paul's use of literary forms and epistolary conven-

---

clusively to the motherly and discipline exclusively to the fatherly, and then of imposing these onto "God" to draw conclusions from a circular argument. *God in Christ* offers motherly nurture within his role as Father. Neither gender nor modern stereotypification entered into Paul's thought here, and merely confuses what Paul wishes to assert about divine co-agency.

140. Pannenberg, *Systematic Theology,* 1:262.
141. Ibid., 263.
142. Ibid., 270.
143. Jüngel, *God as the Mystery of the World,* 156-57.
144. Fee, *First Epistle,* 35. On the role of Christ as **Lord**, see below esp. on 12:3.

tions for the opening formulations of letters (see comments above and separate bibliography). However, two distinct issues arise here. (i) On one side much attention has been given recently to the role of the *exordium* in Graeco-Roman *rhetoric* and in Paul as a way of securing a "favorable attitude" on the part of the audience or addressees.[1] If the audience is not already strongly hostile, this goodwill may be gained in a straightforward or transparent way (a direct opening or *principium*). If there is prior hostility, a more subtle opening *(insinuatio)* may be used. Does such a strategy come within Paul's formulation of the conventional thanksgiving? (ii) The second distinct issue arises from *epistolary* research on *letter forms*. It concerns Paul's *distinctive* utilization of a standard thanksgiving form after the salutation or greeting. Broadly similar structures of opening thanksgivings occur in Rom 1:8-13; 1 Cor 1:4-9; Phil 1:3-11; 1 Thess 1:2-10; Philem 4-7; and in Col 1:3-14 and 2 Thess 1:3-12.[2] In addition to the act of giving thanks, most include an intercessory prayer and a reference to eschatological purpose or to future consummation. 1 Cor 1:8b and 9 reflect this eschatological reference, while Wiles classifies 1:8-9 as "a wish-prayer."[3] Paul thanks God for the readers and their gifts in spite of their evident shortcomings and even an implicit devaluation of his own work by many of them.

Considerable research has been undertaken on the form and function of the Pauline thanksgivings. We may distinguish four main stages of research. (i) Initially from A. Juncker (1905) to G. Harder (1936) attention focused largely on the OT and Psalmic background. (ii) However, in 1939 Paul Schubert examined Greek epistolary material. He paid particular attention to linguistic forms of the Greek εὐχαριστῶ as well as to the papyri and to Roman epistolography.[4] Schubert concluded after an exhaustive analysis of Pauline lexicography and grammar and the Greek social world that "the epistolary papyri convincingly attest a widespread conventional use of an epistolary, religious or non-religious introductory thanksgiving. [These] . . . are typical of normal social life."[5] Schubert also showed that these speech-acts usually presupposed some common "world" of interests. However, 2 Cor 1:3-7 follows the more explicitly Jewish pattern of a benediction: *Blessed be God* (εὐλογητὸς ὁ θεός). Hence (iii) James Robinson (1964) challenged Schubert's assumption that everything seems to be explained on the basis of the Graeco-Roman letter form. He explored a variety of Jewish sources, including the writings of Qumran, paying special attention to the ascription of blessings to

---

1. Among numerous examples, Mitchell, *Paul and the Rhetoric of Reconciliation,* 194-97; A. Eriksson, *Traditions as Rhetorical Proof: Pauline Argumentation in 1 Corinthians,* ConBNT 29 (Stockholm: Almqvist & Wiksell, 1998), 51-60; R. D. Anderson, *Ancient Rhetorical Theory and Paul* (Kampen: Kok Pharos, 1996); and Witherington, *Conflict and Community in Corinth,* 39-48.

2. This is evident from F. O. Francis and J. P. Sampley (eds.), *Pauline Parallels* (Philadelphia: Fortress and Missoula: Scholars Press, 1975).

3. Wiles, *Paul's Intercessory Prayers,* 97-101.

4. Schubert, *Form and Function of the Pauline Thanksgivings,* 24-27, 39-94, esp. table 2.

5. Ibid., 180 and 184.

God in hymns. He concluded that the Jewish blessing form of *berakah* offered a more fruitful comparison with Pauline thanksgivings than the stereotyped and often almost contentless forms of Greek epistolography.[6] (iv) However, Robinson underestimated the importance of the Greek epistolary sources. Hence in his work of 1977 Peter O'Brien argued that while Paul used the purely *formal structure* of the ancient Greek letter, the *content of the components* reflected Jewish influence as well as his own distinctive material and that of Christian theology.[7] O'Brien and Conzelmann both modify Schubert's thesis in this way.

O'Brien agreed with Schubert that the thanksgivings are no mere convention for Paul. Rather, he utilizes the prior convention to express "deep pastoral and apostolic concern," to perform "a didactic function" (as may occur in his intercessory prayers), and often to serve "a parenetic purpose."[8] This harmonizes with one shared characteristic of Greek epistolary literature, where a common function was to express thanks for some aspect of life which might well be taken up in the body of the letter. In other words, the thanksgiving form could function as a kind of overture embodying themes which would be developed more fully later in the main body of the work. Thus, whereas a "secular" Greek letter about trade might begin with a thanksgiving for safe travel, Paul thanks God for gifts or blessings which will feature in his subsequent material. Thus O'Brien notes the themes of grace (1:4), riches or abundance and "knowledge" (1:5; cf. 4:8; 8:1-11; 12:8; 13:2, 8), witness to the gospel (1:6; cf. 1:21; 2:4), eschatological waiting (1:7), and divine judgment and faithfulness (1:8-9).[9] On the other hand, Murphy-O'Connor thinks it "remarkable for what it does *not* say" (my italics).[10] He can allude only to "gifts of 'speech' and 'knowledge' of which he has no high opinion (1 Cor 8:1; 13:8-9, 14:2-5) and the fact that they were 'called into fellowship.'"[11] The absence of any reference to *love* speaks for itself.

Often, according to Schubert, an eschatological element may raise the eyes of the readers to a climax of divine blessing, e.g., 1 Cor 1:8, 9; Phil 1:10; 1 Thess 1:10; and 2 Thess 1:12. The "closure" assumes an almost credal form in 1:9.[12] In spite of Murphy-O'Connor's comments, the fullness of content of the thanksgiving is all the more impressive when we compare it with examples of non-Christian letters of the period.[13]

6. J. M. Robinson, "Die Hodajot-Formel," in *Apophoreta* (1964), 194-235.

7. P. T. O'Brien, *Introductory Thanksgivings in the Letters of Paul.*

8. Ibid., 13-14.

9. Ibid., 107-37. Cf. Schubert, *Form and Function,* 10-39.

10. Murphy-O'Connor, *Paul the Letter Writer,* 62.

11. Ibid. So also Héring, *First Epistle,* 3. See further below on v. 6.

12. O'Brien, *Introductory Thanksgivings,* 107-8; Schubert, *Form and Function,* 30-31; Roberts, "Transitional Techniques," 193, 198, 201.

13. Collins, *First Cor,* 55-56, provides some concrete examples from the papyri (as well as those in the more specialist literature).

A comparison, then, between the standard, *expected* convention of the thanksgiving form and Paul's *distinctive use* of it throws into relief five factors: (i) his lack of self-preoccupation with his own situation or his own welfare in contrast to that of the addressees; (ii) the emphasis on God and especially on the generosity of God's grace; and (iii) his eschatological perspective, which conveys the largest possible horizons of understanding within which the present assumes its true character in the light of God's promised future; (iv) in common with the Greek letter form, Paul's thanksgivings provide a point of contact, or renewed contact, with readers, and prepare the way, like an overture, for later developments of these; (v) Paul's pastoral concern shines out especially as he moves to its end. In these verses, P. Wiles observes, "Paul is moving from acknowledgement of the gifts of the readers to concern for that which is still lacking in them."[14] However, the emphasis on God's grace remains primary.[15] Thereby the speech-act of giving thanks operates at other levels also, e.g., embodying a didactic function, not least, as O'Brien observes, as a celebration of God's *undeserved grace in including Gentiles* among the new community of believers, and even celebrating "gifts" (e.g., "speech" and "knowledge") that were also sources of misperceptions and abuse at Corinth.[16]

1. Paul's Expression of Thanks for the Readers' Gifts (1:4-6)

On more general questions about the letter form, see above under 1:1-3.

Bibliography on Thanksgiving Forms

Arzt, P., "The Epistolary Introductory Thanksgiving in the Papyri and in Paul," *NovT* 36 (1994): 29-46.

Audet, J.-P., "Literary Forms and Contents of a Normal εὐχαριστία in the First Century," in F. L. Cross (ed.), *SE* (Berlin: Berlin Academy, 1959), 1:643-62.

Jewett, R., "The Form and Function of the Homiletic Benediction," *ATR* 51 (1969): 18-34.

Malherbe, A. J., *Ancient Epistolary Theorists,* SBL Sources 19 (Atlanta: Scholars Press, 1988), 30-40 (lists 21 letter forms).

Mitchell, M. M., *Paul and the Rhetoric of Reconciliation* (Louisville: Wesminster/Knox, 1992), 194-97.

Monloubou, L., *Saint Paul et la prière. Prière et évangélisation,* LD 110 (Paris: Cerf, 1982).

Murphy-O'Connor, J., *Paul the Letter Writer* (Collegeville, Minn.: Glazier/Liturgical Press, 1995), 55-64.

O'Brien, P. T., "Benediction, Blessing, Doxology, Thanksgiving," in *DPL,* 68-71.

---

14. Wiles, *Paul's Intercessory Prayers,* 98.

15. C. F. G. Heinrici, *Das erste Sendschreiben des Apostel Paulus an die Korinther* (Berlin: Hertz, 1880), 79-82.

16. O'Brien, *Introductory Thanksgivings,* 108-20 and 134-37. He compares the "riches" of 1:5 with the boastful allusion to "being rich" in 4:8, and "gifts" with 4:7 and 12:4-11.

————, *Introductory Thanksgivings in the Letters of Paul,* NovTSup 49 (Leiden: Brill, 1977), esp. 107-40.

————, "Thanksgiving and the Gospel in Paul," *NTS* 21 (1974-75): 144-55.

————, "Thanksgiving within the Structure of Pauline Theology," in D. A. Hagner and M. J. Harris (eds.), *Pauline Studies: Essays Presented to F. F. Bruce* (Grand Rapids: Eerdmans and Exeter: Paternoster, 1980), 50-66.

Roberts, J. H., "Transitional Techniques to the Letter Body in the Corpus Paulinum," in J. H. Petzer and P. J. Hartin (eds.), *A South African Perspective on the New Testament* (Leiden: Brill, 1986), 187-201.

Robinson, J. M., "Die Hadajot-Formel in Gebet und Hymnus des Früchristentums," in W. Eltester and F. H. Kettler (eds.), *Apophoreta: Festschrift für Ernst Haenchen,* BZNW 30 (Berlin: Töpelmann, 1964), 194-235.

Roller, O., *Das Formular der paulinischen Briefe* (cited under 1:1), 62-66.

Schubert, P., *Form and Function of the Pauline Thanksgivings,* BZNW 20 (Berlin: Töpelmann, 1939), esp. 39-94 and 158-85.

Wiles, G. P., *Paul's Intercessory Prayers,* SNTSMS 24 (Cambridge: Cambridge University Press, 1974), 97-122 and 156-73.

Bibliography on Grace, Charisma, and Gnosis
(But on Gnosis See More Especially under 8:1)

Arichea, D. C., Jr., "Translating 'Grace' *(charis)* in the NT," *BT* 29 (1978): 201-6.

Baumert, N., "Charisma und Amt bei Paulus," in A. Vanhoye (ed.), *L'Apôtre Paul. Personalité, style et conception du ministère* (Leuven/Louvain: Leuven University, 1986), 203-28.

————, "Zur Semantik von χάρισμα bei den frühen Vätern," *Theologie und Philosophie* 63 (1988): 60-88.

Berger, K., "χάρις," *EDNT,* 3:456-61.

Brockhaus, U., *Charisma und Amt die paulinische Charismenlehre* (Wuppertal: Brockhaus, 1972, 1987).

Bultmann, R., "γνῶσις," *TDNT,* 1:689-719.

————, *Theology of the New Testament* (London: SCM, 1952), 1:288-306 (on grace).

Cambe, M., "La *charis* chez saint Paul," *RB* 70 (1963): 193-207.

Conzelmann, H., "χάρις", *TDNT,* 9:359-415.

Doughty, D. J., "The Priority of Charis: An Investigation of the Theological Language of Paul," *NTS* 19 (1972-73): 163-80.

Dupont, J., *Gnosis. La connaissance religieuse dans les épitres de Saint Paul* (Paris: Gabalda, 1949).

Ellis, E. E., "'Spiritual' Gifts in the Pauline Community," *NTS* 20 (1973-74): 128-44.

Horsley, R. A., "Gnosis in Corinth: 1 Cor 8:1-6," *NTS* 27 (1980-81): 32-51.

Moffatt, J., *Grace in the New Testament* (London: Hodder & Stoughton, 1931).

Nolland, J., "Grace as Power," *NovT* 28 (1986): 26-31.

Potterie, L. de la, "Charis paulinienne et charis johannique," in E. E. Ellis and E. Grässer (eds.), *Jesus und Paulus. Festschrift für W. G. Kümmel* (Göttingen: Vandenhoeck & Ruprecht, 1975), 256-82.

Schmithals, W., *Gnosticism in Corinth* (Eng. trans., Nashville: Abingdon, 1971).

Schütz, J. H., *Paul and the Anatomy of Apostolic Authority,* SNTSMS 26 (Cambridge: Cambridge University Press, 1975), 249-80.

Silva, M., "The Pauline Style as Textual Choice: Γινωσκείν and Related Verbs," in D. A. Hagner and M. J. Harris (eds.), *Pauline Studies: Essays Presented to F. F. Bruce on His Seventieth Birthday* (Grand Rapids: Eerdmans and Exeter: Paternoster, 1980), 184-207.

Wilson, R. McL., "How Gnostic Were the Corinthians?" *NTS* 19 (1972-73): 65-74.

4 (1) ℵ*, B, and some other MSS omit μου, reading **to God** rather than **to my God**. This omission is followed by RSV, NJB, NIV, Barrett, and Fee, while Conzelmann places it in brackets. But Weymouth, NRSV, and UBS *Greek New Testament,* 4th ed., retain it, following ℵ*, A, C, D, G, 33, Vulgate and Syriac and Coptic VSS. Metzger argues convincingly for its retention.[17] (2) The plural ἡμῶν occurs in some MSS, but it is probably a scribal error. Many commentators, including Edwards, Meyer, Moffatt, and Allo, retain the singular pronoun. The pronoun may well underline the intimacy and genuineness of the thanksgiving, which might otherwise seem to go through the motions of the conventional letter form. Allo retains it on this basis.[18]

πάντοτε, *always,* carries the meaning of "at every opportunity" or "as a regular habit," as in 15:58, where it refers to working for the Lord "at all times" on the basis of the resurrection promise. Not only the churches which bring him unmixed joy, such as the Philippians, invite regular thanksgiving on Paul's part, but even troublesome Corinth. For the very existence of their faith as Christians outweighs any personal inconvenience, disappointment, or anguish which their less-than-appropriate attitudes and at times lifestyles also bring. The best Christian writings echo the thought: "Nothing is so acceptable to God as that people should be thankful, both for themselves and for others."[19] The use of the present tense εὐχαριστῶ underlines that for Paul "thanksgiving is an ongoing activity."[20]

Typically Paul addresses prayer and thanksgiving to *God,* prayer to Christ is rare, and prayer to the Spirit virtually absent. In the Pauline writings as a whole, prayer is addressed *to* God as Father *through* Christ prompted *by* the Holy Spirit. Although περί with the genitive usually means *about* or *concerning,* it fails to take account of the context to translate Latin *de* (Eng. *about, concerning*) with Beza, since it frequently occurs in contents of prayer or thanksgiving to mean *pray* **for**, or *give thanks* **for**, in Paul, Philo, Josephus, and others.

The preposition ἐπί has been translated **on the ground of** since with the dative it constitutes "the occasioning cause" (Findlay) or "the basis on which an action rests" (Edwards).[21] The aorist passive participle δοθείσῃ signifies the

17. B. Metzger, *A Textual Commentary on the Greek New Testament* (Stuttgart: United Bible Societies, 2d ed. 1994), 478.

18. E.-B. Allo, *Paul. Première Épitre aux Corinthiens,* 4.

19. Chrysostom, *1 Cor. Hom.,* 2:1.

20. Collins, *First Cor,* 57.

21. Findlay, *Expositor's Greek Testament,* 2:759; Edwards, *First Epistle,* 5; also Conzelmann, *1 Cor,* 26.

event of the gift of grace when the addressees became incorporated *into Christ.* The passive may reflect the Semitic use, which underlines God's agency, i.e., as giver. The focus of Paul's thanksgiving is the gracious deed of *God, not* the qualities which the recipients of this grace may possess in and of themselves.[22]

Two key principles emerge from Paul's use of **in Christ Jesus.** (i) In the first three verses Paul mentions *Christ Jesus* twice, and *Lord Jesus Christ* twice, i.e., *four* allusions in three verses. In 1:4-9 there are *five* references to Christ: **Christ Jesus** (v. 4), *Christ* (v. 6), *Lord Jesus Christ* (v. 7), *Lord Jesus Christ* (v. 8), and *Jesus Christ our Lord* (v. 9). In 1:10-13, the appeal (the *propositio*) is made through *our Lord Jesus Christ* (v. 10). *Thus there are ten references to Christ in the first ten verses.* Only overfamiliarity with biblical texts can obscure the remarkable nature of this repetition. Chrysostom hits the nail on the head: "Nowhere in any other epistle does the name of Christ occur so continuously in a few verses; by means of it he [Paul] weaves together the whole . . . not by chance or unwittingly. . . ."[23]

(ii) The second principle is that the addressees receive everything in **Christ** (1:4-7), even if in a proleptic sense. (See below on first-fruits of the resurrection harvest, 15:20.) The Corinthian addressees still **wait** (1:7) for final glory and for the consummation of the work of the Holy Spirit within their community (13:8-13; 15:44, 49). To be *in* **Christ** is to experience the eschatological tension whereby God has already showered his grace upon them and redeemed them from bondage (6:20); yet believers still sin, still die, and still need full transformation into the image of Christ (see on 15:50-54 and 4:8-13, below).[24] Christians experience *Christ* and his gift now; but there is immeasurably more to come when redemption is complete. Paul underlines the plenitude of God's gifts.[25]

5 Several issues of translation arise in v. 5. (i) Does ὅτι mean *because* or *that?* Grammatically either is equally possible, although if Schubert's analysis of thanksgiving forms is valid, *because* might be more likely. Collins similarly argues for **because** on the basis of parallels in Greek letter forms.[26] One way of avoiding the decision would be to follow Findlay and Schrage in viewing the whole clause as one of "explicative" apposition to that of the previous verse.[27] Hence the flow of thought could be rendered **given to you in Christ: I mean, you were enriched in him . . .** (v. 5).

---

22. This point is well made by Wolff, *Der erste Brief,* 20-21, and Schrage, *Der erste Brief,* 1:114-15.

23. Chrysostom, *1 Cor. Hom.,* 2:7.

24. The classic exposition of this eschatological tension can be found in O. Cullmann, *Christ and Time* (Eng. trans., London: SCM, 1951), 37-60, 81-93, 139-74, as well as N. Q. Hamilton, *The Holy Spirit and Eschatology in Paul,* SJT Occasional Paper (Edinburgh: Oliver & Boyd, 1957). Cf. also P. von der Osten-Sacken, "Gottes Treue bis zur Parusie . . . 1 Kor 1:7b-9," *ZNW* 68 (1977), 176-99, and Schrage, *Der erste Brief,* 1:114-24.

25. See David Ford's "economics of *abundance*," discussed under 16:1-4.

26. Collins, *First Cor,* 56.

27. Findlay, *Expositor's Greek Testament,* 2:759-60; Schrage, *Der erste Brief,* 1:114.

(ii) In what sense should we understand the three adjectival forms of πᾶς? The use here is *qualitative* rather than *quantitative,* i.e., **every kind . . . all kinds**. Frequently among the 1,244 uses in the NT the word is used loosely, broadly, or even generally rather than to mean *all* or **every** in the fully numerical sense of the term: e.g., *all* Jerusalem (Matt 2:3); *all* Judaea (Matt 3:5; cf. Mark 1:5), just as we might say "Everyone was there" in a broad sense. Thus Paul need not be implying that *all* speech at Corinth is the product of grace, and he resists any claim that the addressees "know it all." The probable meaning is "everything belonging, *in kind,* to the class designated by the noun *every kind of, all sorts of. . . .*"[28] *Knowledge* (γνῶσις) is not comprehensive in scope, for "now we know only in part" (1 Cor 13:9).

(iii) Does the aorist from ἐπλουτίσθητε, **you were enriched**, imply any lack of a continuing state which the use of the perfect might suggest? A perfect would have been less appropriate when, as O'Brien argues, the thanksgiving form in Paul lays emphasis on the dynamic action of God and of God's grace more strongly than on the state of the readers.[29] There is no thought, as some have suggested, that the addressees were endowed with riches (aorist) some of which they have now lost. πλουτίζω is a strongly causative verb pointing here in the passive to divine agency (cf. Rom 2:14; 11:33; Phil 4:19).[30]

(iv) **Speaking** or *speech* more properly conveys the semantic range of λόγος than, e.g., *word* (Collins) or *statement* (cf. *speech,* NRSV; *utterance,* NJB).[31] Many at Corinth focused on λόγος as "performance."[32] Certainly **speaking** and **knowledge** were the very gifts most prized by many in Corinth (cf. 12:8; 13:1, 2; 2 Cor 8:7), and when Paul later criticizes how these gifts are regarded and used, it is their misuse in relation to self-assertion, status, competitive division, and a devaluation of rational constraint which he has in view; he does not criticize *the gifts,* but people's *attitudes* toward them and their *misuse.* Hence it is for how they used and experienced ἐν αὐτῷ, in Christ, that Paul gives thanks. In practice **speaking** occurs in word and worship *in many modes,* all of which are included under λόγος in various contexts in Greek literature: in proclamation or preaching; in prophecy or preaching (see below on prophecy); in glossolalia *of various kinds* (γένη γλωσσῶν, 12:10); in confession of faith and

---

28. BAGD, 631, col. 2; also Grimm-Thayer, 4th ed., 491-93, esp. 491-92, category 1.1b. Luke's use of the LXX idiom for **all** *flesh* is characteristic: he means **all kinds** of people without reference to class, gender, or race, e.g., ἐπὶ πᾶσαν σάρκα in Acts 2:17, citing Joel 2:28 (LXX 3:1).

29. O'Brien, "Thanksgiving and the Gospel in Paul," *NTS* 21 (1974-75): 144-55; cf. also his *Introductory Thanksgivings,* 107-40; and comments by Wolff and Schrage under v. 4.

30. The probable use of the "divine passive" is confirmed by Collins, *First Cor,* 62.

31. Fee also translates **speaking** (*First Epistle,* 38).

32. S. M. Pogoloff, *Logos and Sophia: The Rhetorical Situation of 1 Corinthians,* SBLDS 14 (Atlanta: Scholars Press, 1992), 98-236, provides a masterly account of the issues. Pogoloff's work lies behind much of the rhetorical analysis in A. D. Clarke, *Secular and Christian Leadership at Corinth* (Leiden: Brill, 1993), and Witherington, *Conflict and Community,* which confirm much of his argument.

cries of acclamation (12:3).[33] **Every kind of speaking** may even reflect genuine gift of *versatility* in communication. Perhaps this is why Paul later tempers their enthusiasm for tongues by calling into question precisely their *communicative* effectiveness in worship or in the public domain rather than privately before God alone (see on 1 Cor. 14; 1-33 below). However, in the *exordium* or opening this is not the moment for criticism (on whether Paul follows rhetorical patterns of securing goodwill, see below under vii).

(v) γνῶσις, **knowledge**, calls for comment. Paul's evaluation of *knowledge* is generally positive, but with the fundamental qualification that love eclipses it in value and permanence (8:1, 7; 13:2).[34] Barrett relates it closely to σοφία, *wisdom,* but whereas "there is a different shade of meaning in the word σοφία (and σοφός) every time it occurs," against Schmithals he argues that γνῶσις, *knowledge,* "is most often used in a plain, non-technical, sense."[35] He concludes, "*Gnosis . . .* is evidently a good thing, but it is inferior to love, and may lead to an exaggerated individualism which loses concern for the neighbour."[36] We must seriously question whether Fee is too ready to associate γνῶσις with "the gift of special knowledge" in 12:8, for which there is insufficient exegetical evidence.[37]

That the Christians at Corinth made an issue out of γνῶσις is clear from statistics of word frequency alone: it occurs sixteen times in the Corinthian epistles (ten times in 1 Corinthians), but only five times in the other generally accepted Pauline epistles together, and only eight times in the rest of the NT as a whole, i.e., more times in 1 and 2 Corinthians than in the whole of the rest of the NT put together (1 Cor. 1:5; 8:1, 7, 10, 11; 12:8; 13:2; 14:6; cf. 2 Cor. 2:14, 4:6; 6:6; 8:7; 10:5; 11:6). In his substantial study of the subject, W. Schmithals argues that "the Corinthians' appeal to *Gnosis,* as it may be inferred from 8:1ff., is typically Gnostic in form and content."[38] Certainly there are points of affinity with later gnosticism. There seems to be simultaneously a libertarian outlook, **"all things are lawful for me . . . food for the stomach . . ."** (6:12, 13) and a probable asceticism about marriage alongside an apparent indifference to sexual license (5:1, 2; 7:1[b]).[39] But problems about the dating of "gnosticism" even as an incipient system are difficult to overcome, and other explanations can be offered for the outlooks displayed at Corinth.[40] If Schmithals were cor-

33. Cf. Schrage, *Der erste Brief,* 1:116-17, for this more inclusive force of ἐν παντὶ λόγῳ. Fee perhaps too narrowly perceives these "gifts" as relating closely to those of chs. 12 and 14 (*First Epistle,* 39-40).

34. Barrett, *First Epistle,* 36-37.

35. Barrett, "Christianity at Corinth," in *Essays,* 7; cf. 6-14.

36. Ibid.

37. Fee, *First Epistle,* 39. This assumption in some Pentecostal and neo-Pentecostal traditions invites challenge. See our exegesis of 12:8, below.

38. Schmithals, *Gnosticism in Corinth,* 229.

39. See below, including whether 7:1 represents a quotation from Corinthian theology.

40. R. McL. Wilson, "How Gnostic Were the Corinthians?" 65-74, offers a classic model of many possible responses to Schmithals.

rect, we should need to consider whether a translator should place *knowledge* in quotation marks in 1:5; but as it is, Barrett is probably correct in seeing a very generalized and nontechnical meaning, at least in this early verse.

Paul has an entirely positive approach to the verbal form *I know,* γινώσκω, in contrast to problems which beset the noun γνῶσις, *knowledge.* For the verb includes especially the notion of *coming to know,* i.e., it includes the principle expressed by Jesus, Socrates, and Paul that the first step toward knowledge is the recognition of ignorance: "Anyone who claims to 'know' . . . does not yet have knowledge" (8:2). "If you think that you are wise . . . you should become fools so that you may become wise" (3:18). The verb can refer positively to interpersonal relations with God (1 Cor 8:3; Phil 3:10), while the noun retains a degree of ambivalence. It becomes negative especially if it is regarded as *completed, comprehensive* knowledge (8:1; 13:9).

(vi) Two more general comments may be invited on this verse. We noted the comments (introduction to 1:4-6) of Murphy-O'Connor and Héring that what Paul omits from the thanksgiving says as much about the church at Corinth as what he includes. Parallels with other introductory thanksgiving forms throw this into sharp relief. Paul thanks God that faith at Rome and Thessalonica shines out like a beacon (Rom 1:8; 1 Thess 1:8); and that the Philippians affectionately share his partnership in the gospel (Phil 1:5, 8). Other grounds for thanksgiving emerge in 1 Thess 1:3 and elsewhere.[41] Yet we cannot doubt the sincerity of the thanksgiving. What Christians bring from their cultural backgrounds into the church has varying value. Paul respects and appreciates what he can, knowing that the transformative power of the cross transposes indifferent or ambivalent raw material into what becomes part of a genuine gift of God's grace for good. Paul places *everything* before God in a posture of thankful prayer and address.[42]

(vii) We return finally to the issue raised by research into ancient rhetoric, to which we have already alluded. To what extent is Paul influenced by the rhetorical conventions commended by Cicero, Quintilian, and earlier writers to provide *an "opening" (exordium) designed* to *gain the goodwill of the audience or addressees?* Cicero and Quintilian commend the strategy noted in our introduction to vv. 4-6: if an audience has a measure of goodwill the *exordium* may be "direct" *(principium)* to gain their favorable attention; if they are hostile, the *exordium* may need to take a subtle form *(insinuatio).*[43] These pave the way for the *propositio* or main thesis. Thus, e.g., Witherington, Mitchell, Eriksson, and Schrage believe that broadly (after the epistolary prescript of 1:1-3), the thanksgiving also forms a rhetorical *exordium* (1:4-9) which leads to the *propositio* of 1:10, followed by the explication of the *propositio* by an explana-

41. See F. O. Francis and J. P. Sampley, *Pauline Parallels,* SBL Sources 9 (Philadelphia: Fortress and Missoula: Scholars Press, 1975), sect. 2, 34-35.

42. Monloubou, *Saint Paul et la prière.*

43. Cicero, *De Inventione* 1.15.1; Quintilian, *Institutionis Oratoriae* 4.1.42.

tory *narratio* (1:11-17).[44] We suggest that if he was able to follow this rhetorical pattern in a nonmanipulative way which does not rely upon mere artifice, Paul might well adopt such a strategy. But he would do so, we suggest, only if this expresses his own genuine and sincere convictions. Otherwise it conflicts with his critique of *sophia logou* elsewhere in this epistle.[45]

6 καθώς, **as,** denotes, not measure *(just as)* but how **being *enriched*** relates to its *cause* in the *impact of the gospel* on the readers.[46] Conzelmann proposes *for indeed* in place of **as.** There is no doubt about the textual reading **witness** or *testimony* (μαρτύριον) here (in contrast to its occurrence in 2:1). On grammatical and contextual grounds alone it is difficult to decide whether Χριστοῦ represents a subjective genitive (of **Christ** in the sense that Christ does the witnessing) or an objective genitive (in the sense that **Christ** is the object of witness, i.e., the gospel and the Holy Spirit witness **to Christ** or *about* Christ).

The meaning of βεβαιῶ, **I confirm,** *I verify,* is clear.[47] But in what sense is the witness to Christ **confirmed**? Conzelmann rightly notes that in hellenistic texts the Greek word can relate to the founding and subsequent development of communities.[48] Presumably in this context **confirming** would mean stabilizing the corporate identity and structure of a community. If this is correct, ἐν ὑμῖν certainly means *among you* corporately, not *within you* individually as an experience. In Mark, however, βεβαιῶ is applied to preaching (τὸν λόγον) in the context of divine agency **confirming** its truth, reality, and operative effects. (Mark 16:20).[49] It also refers to confirming or ratifying promises, i.e., *proving them to be reliable* (Rom. 15:8). This coheres very well with what Paul would wish to note here. It includes the confirmation of Paul's work thereby.[50]

Although it is conceivable that **Christ** himself **confirms the witness** which he first gave in the earlier preaching, the regular Pauline pattern is for the Holy Spirit to bear **witness to Christ** through the message of the cross.[51] Christ is the focus of witness, and God through the Spirit *brings home* the truth of this witness as their Christian experience develops and as the Christian community lives out its lifestyle and grows. Others respond, and thereby further confirma-

---

44. Witherington, *Conflict and Community,* 44-48; Mitchell, *Rhetoric of Reconciliation,* 194-97; Eriksson, *Traditions,* 48-53; Schrage, *Der erste Brief,* 1:110-11.

45. See the decisive arguments of Pogoloff, *Logos and Sophia,* 99-128 (cf. also 129-96), and B. W. Winter, *Philo and Paul among the Sophists,* SNTSMS 96 (Cambridge: Cambridge University Press, 1997), esp. on 1 Cor 2:1-5.

46. Against Fee, *First Epistle,* 40, but with C. Senft, *La première Épitre des Paul aux Corinthiens* (Geneva: Labor et Fides, 2d ed. 1990), "καθώς est causal" (30).

47. BAGD, 38; Grimm-Thayer, 99-100; MM, 108.

48. Conzelmann, *1 Cor,* 27.

49. "In the NT 'testimony' (μαρτύριον) has become virtually a technical term for the proclamation of the gospel 'even if it is' rarely used by Paul (cf. 2:1; 2 Cor 1:12)" (Collins, *First Cor,* 62).

50. Senft, *La première Épitre,* 30.

51. Fee, *First Epistle,* 40, "'Testimony' refers to the gospel itself . . . the good news about Christ." Schrage, *Der erste Brief,* 1:117-19, also makes this point well, and it receives added force in his exposition of 1:18-25, "Das 'Wort vom Kreuz' als Grund und Kriterium . . ." (165-92).

tion of the witness to Christ occurs. The whole experience is no longer confined to a small group of individuals who may be similar in stature, mind-set, or culture, but the truth is cross-referenced among a widening and diversifying community in which the Holy Spirit is transparently at work. In this sense in multicultural, pluralist Corinth, each new experience of God and each new convert **confirms** as valid this **witness to Christ**.[52] Calvin observes, "God set his seal to the truth of His Gospel among the Corinthians."[53]

Some suggest that Paul alludes to quasi-tangible "signs" of the Spirit, such as prophecy and tongues (see above). But since the criteria for evaluating the genuineness of these turns out to be largely christological (see under 12:3; 13:1-13), it would constitute a circular argument to make such signs the primary basis for "confirming" a witness to Christ. Many appeals to "experience" beg the question of how we know what constitutes authentic experience. The epistle as a whole sets forth a network of criteria centered in the cross of Christ as the transformative and formative basis of Christian existence (see further under 1:18-31 and 2:1-5).

2. Paul's Thanksgiving: The Eschatological Focus (1:7-9)

Bibliography on Paul's Eschatology of Fulfillment and "Waiting" and Its Relation to Justification at the Last Day Appropriated Now

Baird, W., "Pauline Eschatology in Hermeneutical Perspective," *NTS* 17 (1971): 314-27.

Baumgarten, J., *Paulus und die Apokalyptik* (Neukirchen-Vluyn: Neukirchener Verlag, 1975).

Beker, J. C., *Paul's Apocalyptic Gospel: The Coming Triumph of God* (Philadelphia: Fortress, 1982), 61-78 and 105-22.

Bouttier, M., *Christianity according to St. Paul* (Eng. trans., London: SCM, 1966), 15-58.

Cullmann, O., *Christ and Time* (Eng. trans., London: SCM, 1951), 51-119, 139-215.

———, *Salvation in History* (Eng. trans., London: SCM, 1967), 150-85, 248-68.

Donfried, K. P., "Justification and the Last Judgement in Paul," *ZNW* 67 (1976): 90-110.

Ellis, E. E., *Paul and His Recent Interpreters* (Grand Rapids: Eerdmans, 1961).

Hamilton, N. Q., *The Holy Spirit and Eschatology in Paul,* SJT Occasional Papers 6 (Edinburgh: Oliver and Boyd, 1957).

Kümmel, W. G., *Promise and Fulfillment* (Eng. trans., London: SCM, 1957).

———, *The Theology of the New Testament* (Eng. trans., London: SCM, 1974), 141-46.

Ladd, G. E., "Eschatology and the Unity of New Testament Theology," *ExpTim* 68 (1957): 268-73.

---

52. Origen, *Fragments of Commentary on 1 Cor,* in C. Jenkins (ed.), *JTS* 9 (1908): 233, adopts this approach: experience of God confirms that "nothing can separate us from the love of God in Christ Jesus our Lord" (Rom 8:38-39). However, to stumble day by day will fail to bring such confirmation.

53. Calvin, *First Epistle of Paul to the Corinthians,* 21. Wolff also sees this as setting a seal on Paul's work (*Der erste Brief,* 21).

—————, *The Presence of the Future* (Grand Rapids: Eerdmans, 1974).

Lincoln, A. T., *Paradise Now and Not Yet: Studies in the Role of the Heavenly Dimension in Paul's Thought,* SNTSMS 43 (Cambridge: Cambridge University Press, 1981), 33-38, 52-54, 184-95.

Moltmann, J., *The Crucified God* (Eng. trans., London: SCM, 1974), 256-66.

—————, *Theology of Hope* (Eng. trans., London: SCM, 1967), 15-42, 102-20, and 197-229.

—————, *The Way of Jesus Christ* (Eng. trans., London: SCM, 1990), 334-40.

Osten-Sacken. *See* Von der Osten-Sacken.

Roberts, J. H., "The Eschatological Transitions to the Pauline Letter Body," *Neot* 20 (1986): 29-35.

Sampley, J. P., *Walking between the Times: Paul's Moral Reasoning* (Minneapolis: Fortress, 1991).

Shires, H. M., *The Eschatology of Paul in the Light of Modern Scholarship* (Philadelphia: Westminster, 1966).

Stuhlmacher, P., *Gerechtigkeit Gottes bei Paulus* (Göttingen: Vandenhoeck & Ruprecht, 1965).

Thiselton, A. C., "Realised Eschatology at Corinth," *NTS* 24 (1978): 510-26.

—————, *The Two Horizons* (Grand Rapids: Eerdmans and Carlisle: Paternoster, 1980), 415-22.

Von der Osten-Sacken, P., "Gottes Treue bis zur Parusie. Formgeschichtliche Beobachtungen zu 1 Kor. 1:7b-9," *ZNW* 68 (1977): 176-99.

Whiteley, D. E. H., *The Theology of St. Paul* (Oxford: Blackwell, 2d ed. 1974), 126-27 and 244-48.

Bibliography on Koinonia (See Overlapping Bibliography under 10:14-22)

Campbell, J. Y., "κοινωνία and Its Cognates in the New Testament," *JBL* 51 (1932): 352-80.

Hainz, J., *Koinonia. "Kirche" als Gemeinschaft bei Paulus,* BU 16 (Regensburg: Pustet, 1982).

Hauck, F., "κοινός, κοιωνός, κοινωνία κ.τ.λ.," *TDNT,* 3:789-809.

Maly, K., *Mündige Gemeinde. Untersuchungen zur pastoralen Führung des Apostels Paulus im 1 Korintherbrief* (Stuttgart: Katholisches Bibelwerk, 1967), 135-39.

Marion, D., "Communion. L'essence du christianisme en un seul mot." *Esprit et Vie* 102 (1992): 145-50 and 157-59.

Panikulam, G., *Koinonia in the New Testament: A Dynamic Expression of Christian Life,* AnBib 85 (Rome: Biblical Institute Press, 1979).

Schattenmann, J., "Fellowship, Share, Participate," *NIDNTT,* 1:635-44.

Seesemann, H., *Der Begriff κοινωνία im New Testament,* BZNW 14 (Giessen: Töpelmann, 1933).

Thornton, L. S., *The Common Life in the Body of Christ* (London: Dacre Press, 3rd edn. 1950), 1-187 and 253-355.

7 The grammatical construction has become a standard one for result by the later hellenistic period: ὥστε, **so that,** is followed by an accusative and an infinitive. Some have argued that the middle voice of ὑστερεῖσθαι denotes reflexive or subjective conditions, to be translated "causing you *not to feel behindhand* in any gift of grace."[54] The addressees should feel "a shower of spiritual energies of which they have a lively sense."[55] Nigel Turner, however, rightly questions whether the distinction between the reflexive middle and the more objective active remains as significant in Paul's day as it was in classical and in late pre-Christian hellenistic Greek. He allows that the reflexive use of the middle may occasionally occur in Paul (e.g., ἀπελούσασθε, probably, *you got yourself washed,* 1 Cor. 6:11), and that abundant instances occur in pre-Christian papyri. Nevertheless, "In our period there is not always any significance in the writer's choice of middle or active, and reflexive middle in the NT is relatively rare."[56]

Most commentators agree that *a state of affairs rather than a psychological perception or feeling* is at issue.[57] But Conzelmann points out that this still leaves a further choice: Does the verb mean *to suffer lack* or *to come behind?* Robertson urges that ὕστερος in the abjectival form simply means *late* or *behind,* and proposes the latter on this ground.[58] However, *to suffer lack* usually (not always) governs a genitive, whereas *to fall short* or *to come behind* most frequently precedes the preposition ἐν, **in,** as is the case here.[59] Hence **you fall short in no gift** represents the most appropriate translation. This is based on the promise of God, but also reflects 12:8-19 and parallels.[60]

The word translated **gift** (χάρισμα) has been variously translated in English versions. Moffatt translates *spiritual endowment;* REB, NJB, *gift* (as against JB, *gifts of the Spirit*), NRSV, NIV, *spiritual gift; spiritual* is not explicit in the Greek, for the word denotes simply "that which is freely given."[61] (Thus the German Bible Society [1984] *gift of grace* or *Gnadengabe.*) Calvin observes that "gifts" of any kind include "spiritual qualities which are, so to speak, means of salvation to believers."[62] Chrysostom, by contrast, believes that χάρισμα anticipates the gifts of 1 Corinthians 12–14 in particular, namely, "a psalm, a revelation, a tongue . . . the prophets," although he refuses to privilege these above others more broadly. The gifts include "the signs of the apostle."[63] In Chrysostom's view they represent the cumulative experience of God's gifts at Corinth, beginning with Paul's arrival and preaching and continuing up to the reception of the letter.

χάρισμα occurs only in Paul within the New Testament, except for 1 Pet.

---

54. Findlay, *Expositor's Greek Testament,* 2:760; Robertson and Plummer, *First Epistle,* 6; more recently BDF, sects. 101, 180, category 5, with a lengthy list of parallels.

55. Findlay, *Expositor's Greek Testament,* 2:760.

56. Moulton-Howard-Turner, *Grammar,* 3: *Syntax,* 54; cf. 53-57 (hereafter MHT).

57. For example, Barrett, *First Epistle,* 38; Conzelmann, *1 Cor,* 27; Fee, *First Epistle,* 41-42; Wolff, *Der erste Brief,* 22; cf. Wiles, *Intercessory Prayers,* 100.

58. A. T. Robertson, *Word Pictures in the NT, 4: The Epistles of Paul* (New York: R. R. Smith, 1931), 71 (hereafter, *Epistles*); also BAGD, 849.

59. Followed by Fee, *First Epistle,* 41; Conzelmann, *1 Cor,* 27; Schrage, *Der erste Brief,* 1:119.

60. Wolff, *Der erste Brief,* 22.

61. BAGD, 878; MM, 685.

62. Calvin, *First Epistle,* 22.

63. Chrysostom, *1 Cor. Hom.,* 2:4.

4:10. Philo uses χάρισματα to mean *gifts from God* (*Legum Allegoriae* 3.24), or *a favor* (3.78). In Rom 11:29 Paul uses the word of *God's gracious privileges* to Israel, and in 2 Cor 1:11 of God's special *favor* in delivering him from peril through much prayer. Typically in Rom 5:15, *the free gift of grace* stands in contrast to sin, which, earlier, pays its "wages" of death. Jerome perceives 1:7 as stressing *grace:* all is of God.[64]

The specific "gifts" in 1 Corinthians 12–14 are often called either *spiritual gifts* or *charismatic gifts*. But it goes against the grain of Paul's emphasis in the thanksgiving, as Chrysostom, Luther, and Barth in particular urge, to focus attention on the "religious experience" of 1 Corinthians 12–14 rather than on the generosity of God's sovereign gift of himself in a variety of ways as sheer, unmerited favor.[65] Although "One cannot say whether it was Paul himself who brought χαρίσματα into use as a term for πνευματικά," there can be no question about the difference of emphasis here between Paul and some of the "gifted spiritual people" at Corinth.[66] Indeed, the everyday use of "gifted" in modern English helps to make the point. "Gifted" people may be tempted to think of themselves as a cut above others. But, Paul responds, how can this be valid if "gifted" means *receiving a gift* (4:7)? Bittlinger therefore comments with justice "The term *charismata* denotes the source of gifts, i.e., divine *charis* (grace) becoming concrete."[67] It seems that the Corinthian church preferred to speak of *spiritual* gifts, or even "*spiritual* people" (12:1).

Gift, for Paul, draws attention to the free, generous, giving of the Giver instantiated in the noun χάρις, *grace,* and the verb χαρίζομαι, *freely give.*[68] In 1 Cor. 7:7 such a **gift** (χάρισμα) takes the form of contentment in vocation to the celibate life, or, as Luther defines it, the gift of chastity.[69] There is no suggestion in these contexts that such "gifts" need to be "spontaneous." (On this, see our exegesis of 12:8-10 and parallels.)

The second main theme in the verse qualifies any false optimism and corrects any complacency. Although they do not **fall short** of what God has freely given to them, the addressees **wait for the public revealing of our Lord Jesus Christ**. C. Anderson Scott expounds Paul's entire theology in terms of "three tenses of salvation."[70] The first part of the verse confirms that the addressees

64. Jerome, *Against the Pelagians,* 11:8.
65. Luther, *Works,* 28:16-17 and 84-95 (*WA,* 36:510-26); Barth, *Resurrection,* 16-26; Chrysostom, *1 Cor. Hom.,* 2:7.
66. Conzelmann, "χάρις," *TDNT,* 9:403, n. 11; cf. 402-6.
67. A. Bittlinger, *Gifts and Graces* (London: Hodder and Stoughton, 1967), 20; cf. Barrett, *First Epistle,* 38, for a similar view.
68. See Merklein, *Der erste Brief 1–4,* 91-92. Further, Lightfoot, *Notes,* 148-49, points out that in the papyri it may mean a gift from a friend.
69. Luther, *Works,* 28:16 (*WA* 12:105).
70. C. A. A. Scott, *Christianity according to St. Paul* (Cambridge: Cambridge University Press, 1927), 23-25; cf. 26-97 and 134-243. Chapter 2 bears the title "Salvation as a Fact of the Past" (26-97); ch. 4, "Salvation as a Progressive Experience," 134-235; ch. 5, "Salvation: Its Consummation in the Future," 236-43.

have decisively entered the realm of salvation. The second part adds the qualification that this is not the whole story. Corinthian triumphalism (at least on the part of the "strong") is excluded, for they still await the consummation. The well-known lifeboat analogy is well worn but still suggestive. Someone may have been saved (past) decisively from a sinking ship; but as the lifeboat brings him or her through choppy, uncomfortable seas (present), the final safe landing on the solid shore lies still ahead (future). Celebration comes then. The "strong" mistakenly act as if they have already "arrived" (4:8), and look down on the apostles and on others who seem still to struggle in blooded conflict and danger (4:9-13).[71]

Paul strikes the note in this overture which he will develop in 4:8-13: Christians have not yet "arrived" but **wait for the public revealing** (ἀπο-κάλυψις) **of our Lord Jesus Christ** and of realities that can now be grasped only in a context of faith, discipline, and obedient self-control (cf. 6:12; 8:7-13; 10:23). Cullmann provided the classic metaphor of this double perspective of "now" and "not yet" in the analogy of the contrast between winning a decisive battle ("D day") and the ending of the war ("V day"). God in Christ has won the decisive battle which assures victory for his people; but the war still drags on. Christians cannot yet behave as if sin and death were simply behind them.[72] Whiteley uses another analogy. Christians are like people who were once in the cold, freezing to death, but now have been transferred into a warm room. The forces of its heat will decisively overcome the forces of the cold; but in the present both sets of forces are active. Some limbs are already warm; but others have still to thaw out completely. The forces of heat are decisive, but are not yet the only operative forces. The decisive event has occurred, but the process which it set in motion takes time to reach completion.[73] Numerous other writers (e.g., Hamilton, Lincoln, and Sampley, among many others) explore this "double" eschatology.[74] G. E. Ladd views this double eschatology as a unifying or common thread in all the New Testament writings.[75]

This theme does more than prepare the way to damp down self-congratulation and encourage disciplined concern for others amidst the hazards of the journey. As Osten-Sacken notes, v. 7b comes as a surprise after

71. More fully, Thiselton, "Realised Eschatology at Corinth," 510-26. I still endorse most details, but I am more cautious about trying to reduce a complex of issues largely to a single problem.

72. Cullmann, *Christ and Time,* 75: "Man *is* that which he *will become* only in the future . . . already sinless, already holy, although this becomes reality only in the future" (his italics); cf. 71-77, 86-87, 154-57, and 235-38. Cf. further Cullmann, *Salvation in History,* 28-47.

73. Whiteley, *Theology of St. Paul,* 126-27.

74. Hamilton, *The Holy Spirit and Eschatology;* Lincoln, *Paradise Now and Not Yet,* 33-37 (cf. 184-95); Sampley, *Walking between the Times,* 5-34. Cf. further E. Käsemann, "Apocalyptic," in *New Testament Questions,* 108-37; Kümmel, *Promise and Fulfillment;* and Beker, *Apocalyptic Gospel,* 61-78 and 105-22. (See publication data in Bibliography.)

75. G. E. Ladd, esp. "Eschatology and the Unity of New Testament Theology," *ExpTim* 68 (1957): 268-73.

v. 7a.[76] The concern for others and image of the journey (chs. 8–10) place the church in its proper theological context. As against the claims of M. Mitchell and B. Witherington that the whole epistle turns on the *propositio* of an appeal for unity (see on 1:10), Paul's eschatology of promise and theology of salvation never allow the church to become an entity which fills our horizons, as if it existed, as it were, for its own sake.[77] Käsemann declares: "The apostle is not interested in the church *per se* . . . only in so far as it is the means whereby Christ reveals himself on earth . . . through the Spirit."[78] Bouttier observes that "in the poverty of one who is not yet master of his inheritance, the fellow heir with Christ awaits the hour. . . . Because Christ lives in him, he knows what is coming."[79]

We have translated **the revealing of our Lord Jesus Christ** with some freedom as **the public revealing**. Ἀποκάλυψις simply means *disclosure* or *revelation*. But it conveys the notion of revelation in more than one possible sense: revelation of truth (Rom 16:25; cf. Eph 1:17), or revelation through some specific means (Rev 1:1; cf. Gal 2:2); but also a further specific meaning when it refers to the last days. In Rom 8:19 Paul uses vivid, colorful language about creation's standing on tiptoe, craning its neck, in its yearning eagerness to see publicly the revealing of the sons of God or what God has made them to be (ἡ γὰρ ἀποκαραδοκία τῆς κτίσεως τὴν ἀποκάλυψν τῶν υἱῶν τοῦ θεοῦ ἀπεκδέχεται, 8:19). The eschatological act of revealing will be cosmic, public, and glorious.[80] The metaphor of night, in which things are hidden and invisible, turning to day, in which everything can be seen for what it is, governs Rom 13:12. In the light of all of this background we translate the Greek **public revealing**. Bengel succinctly observes that whether Christian character is authentic encourages either expectancy or dread at the prospect of this public revelation.[81] However, Christians are not "left to their own resources" **while** they **wait**.[82] Merklein calls attention to the consistent eschatological theme which continues to 16:22: *"Marana tha,"* "Our Lord, come!"[83]

8   (1) **Christ**, Χριστοῦ, is omitted by the early 𝔭46 and B, but retained by ℵ*, A, C, D, G, 33, the Peshitta, Syriac, and Coptic, and Origen, Cyril, and Chrysostom. Few, how-

---

76. Von der Osten-Sacken, "Gottes Treue bis zur Parusie . . . 1 Kor. 1:7b-9," 176-77; cf. 178-99.

77. This is well emphasized by E. Käsemann and J. Moltmann in different ways. Cf. Käsemann, "Apocalyptic," 108-37; cf. also *The Wandering People of God* (Eng. trans., Minneapolis: Augsburg, 1984; an earlier exposition of Hebrews written partly from prison); and Moltmann, *Theology of Hope,* 15-42, 102-20, 197-229 more generally, and *The Church in the Power of the Spirit* (Eng. trans., London: SCM, 1977) on the church.

78. E. Käsemann, *Perspectives on Paul* (Eng. trans., London: SCM, 1971), 117.

79. Bouttier, *Christianity according to St. Paul,* 37.

80. See Collins, *First Cor,* 64; and Héring, *First Epistle,* 3. Outside Paul, cf. 1 Pet 4:13.

81. Bengel, *Gnomon,* 609.

82. Moffatt, *First Epistle,* 7.

83. Merklein, *Der erste Brief 1–4,* 91.

ever, adopt the shorter reading, although Metzger shows how finely balanced the judg-ment is.[84] Many explain it as an early *accidental* omission. Three factors favor this. (i) **Christ**, as Chrysostom reminds us, occurs not less than once in every verse on aver-age since 1:1, and repetition makes such an accident all too possible. (ii) Paul regularly uses the three forms *Christ, Christ Jesus,* and *our Lord Jesus Christ* while *Our Lord Je-sus* would be uncharacteristic. (iii) The MS support for its inclusion is varied, embody-ing diverse traditions. (2) The Western tradition with its D, F, and G has two further vari-ants. It replaces ἕως with ἄχρι and **the day** with *at the parousia,* παρουσία. But variations in the Western text alone are often unreliable. They sometimes reflect theo-logical or pastoral concerns on the part of scribal redactors.

In the clause **He will keep you** (Gk. ὅς), does the pronoun refer to *God* or to *Christ?* We have translated the Greek relative pronoun by the nonspecific pro-noun **He** because, after reviewing the exhaustive discussions, we endorse Schrage's verdict that whether "ὅς at the beginning of v. 8 signifies Christ as God cannot be decided unequivocally."[85] Among English VSS, AV/KJV retains the Gk. *who;* REB, NIV, NJB, NRSV render **He**. Weiss, Conzelmann, and Fee argue that it is God who **confirms** the readers' eschatological security, probably here and certainly in 2 Cor. 1:21.[86] But Origen, Chrysostom, Meyer, and others insist that Paul wants to fill the minds of the addressees with Christ by constant repetition of his name and work.[87] It would be incautious explicitly to insert *God* into the translation as subject of the clause, when the antecedent *God* is as far back as v. 4. The Greek leaves the matter open. This need not trouble us since Paul's language here concerns the promises of God-in-Christ.[88]

The end, ἕως τέλους, clearly corresponds to **the day of our Lord Jesus Christ**. The eschatological context confirms the temporal reference, as against Schatter's adverbial interpretation *completely.*[89] Von der Osten-Sacken and Roberts note that in four cases (1 Cor 1:7-8; Phil 1:10; 1 Thess 1:10; 2 Thess 1:6-10) an eschatological theme provides the transition into the main body of the letter.[90] Paul assures the readers that at the last day they will be **free from any charge**, ἀνεγκλήτους. The Greek carries a range of meanings: *blameless, irreproachable,* and *unimpeachable.* In *Oxyrhynchus Papyri* of AD 20-50 a woman who has been deserted by her husband claims that she is *blameless.*[91] This well exemplifies the meaning that no charge can be brought by way of ac-

84. Zuntz, *Text,* 184, represents one of the few exceptions to the majority view; and Metzger, *Commentary* (2d ed. 1994), explains why his committee places *Christ* within square brackets "to indicate a certain amount of doubt concerning its originality" (479).

85. Schrage, *Der erste Brief,* 1:121.

86. Weiss, *Der erste Korintherbrief,* 10; Conzelmann, *1 Cor,* 28; Fee, *First Epistle,* 43-44.

87. Chrysostom, *1 Cor. Hom.,* 2:7; Meyer, *First Epistle to the Corinthians,* 1:20. Cf. further Allo, *Première Épitre,* 5.

88. Linguistic arguments favor *Christ;* theological arguments favor *God.*

89. A. Schlatter, *Die Korinther Briefe,* 9, does include a temporal aspect.

90. Roberts, "The Eschatological Transitions to the Pauline Letter Body," 29-35; P. von der Osten-Sacken, "Gottes Treue bis zur Parusie . . . 1 Kor. 1:7b-9," 176-99.

91. MM, 40; *POxy* 2.281.12.

cusation. This applies to the time which leads up to the day of the Lord as well as to being presented free from any charge on the day itself. Hence the word here belongs to the semantic domain of *accusation and declarative verdict.*[92] Robertson and Plummer rightly translate *unimpeachable,* but Edwards's **free from any charge** is a simpler form.[93] Fee tends to merge the issue into questions about the Corinthians' blameless "behavior."[94] But the primary emphasis falls upon the *verdictive* nature of the word. God *pronounces a verdict;* issues of the human moral condition remain secondary.

The final verdict occurs ἐν τῇ ἡμέρᾳ τοῦ κυρίου ἡμῶν Ἰησοῦ [Χριστοῦ]. Paul transfers to Christ language about the day of the Lord in Old Testament traditions (e.g., Amos 5:18 and Zeph 1:14-18; cf. Rom 13:12). This is portrayed in the OT as a day of judgment. But this is not a matter only of rewards or penalties. As the righteous judge God *puts all things right.* This has a social as well as a forensic dimension, both reversing the fortunes of the wicked and vindicating the cry of the oppressed.[95] But it is also forensic *and* personal: a public declaration of the verdict *unimpeachable,* i.e., of justification by grace. This can be anticipated by grace through appropriation (i.e., by faith), even in the present. Justification is an anticipation in advance of the verdict pronounced on the day of the Lord, in the faith-understanding that God keeps them **firm** and **free from any charge** up to and **on the day of our Lord Jesus Christ**.[96] It is extraordinarily wooden for Bultmann to claim that Paul inconsistently sees now God as judge, now Christ as judge.[97] If the language oscillates, this is because the work of salvation is (here) a joint work, which later emerges as a trinitarian work.[98] The main point is that as night dissolves into day (Rom 13:12) the hidden will become publicly visible and all that is wrong or that disrupts intimacy with God will be set right. It is unfortunate that the very clarity of this theme in Romans has tended to distract attention from its prominence in our epistle. The verdictive character of justification by grace is underlined by the role of definitive judgment on **the day of the Lord** in the OT, apocalyptic, and the NT.[99]

92. J. P. Louw and E. A. Nida, *Greek-English Lexicon of the NT Based on Semantic Domains* (2 vols., 2d ed., New York: United Bible Societies, 1988 and 1989), 1:438 (sects. 33-43; "Accuse, Blame," sects. 33-426 and 33-434).

93. Robertson and Plummer, *1 Cor,* 7; Edwards, *1 Cor,* 8.

94. Fee, *First Epistle,* 43-44.

95. Moltmann, *The Crucified God,* 256-66, and *The Way of Jesus Christ,* 334-40.

96. J. Weiss, *Earliest Christianity* (2 vols., Eng. trans., New York: Harper, 1959 [1937]), 502, speaks of justification by grace as a "pre-dating of what is really an eschatological act." A. Schweitzer declares that righteousness "belongs strictly speaking" to the future, although in practice it becomes effective in the present (*Mysticism of Paul the Apostle;* Eng. trans., London: Black, 1931, 205). Kertelge and Stuhlmacher also stress its eschatological context: Stuhlmacher, *Gerechtigkeit Gottes bei Paulus;* and K. Kertelge, *'Rechtfertigung' bei Paulus* (Münster: Aschendorff, 1967), 112-60. The "post-Sanders" debate leaves this issue intact; cf. Thiselton, *The Two Horizons,* 415-27.

97. Bultmann, *Essays Philosophical and Theological,* 283. Clearly this is to make his claim about "objectification" and myth more plausible.

98. Richardson, *Paul's Language about God,* 95-138.

99. See Schrage, *Der erste Brief,* 1:122-23.

9 Faithful is placed first to reflect its emphatic position in Gk. πιστὸς ὁ θεός. This takes up the notions of *confirming* and *calling* (v. 6). One who is **faithful** is trustworthy, reliable, consistent, and dependable. In the LXX the Greek word usually translates the niphal form of the *qal* אמן *('aman), confirm, support,* namely, נאמן *(ne'eman), trusty, faithful, to be trusted* (e.g., Prov 11:13). A dynasty can be *confirmed* or *established* (1 Sam 2:35; 1 Kings 11:38): belief can be *confirmed* (1 Kings 8:26), in the sense of βεβαιῶ *(confirm)* in 1:4-9. God is the faithful God (Deut 7:9). Hence the form אמן *('amen)* has the adverbial meaning *truly, surely, verily.*[100] Calvin observes, "whatever God begins, he will carry through to completion." In modern terms, everything rests on a divine commissive speech-act of *promise.* "God will never give them up"; the apostolic message to Corinth is a *promissory word* which affects and shapes *action in the present.*[101] It is natural to call those who place their trust in this word οἱ πιστεύοντες, believers.

This *commissive* dimension of the grammar of faithfulness is important for understanding Paul's theology of God, as well as certain modern dilemmas. In Rom 9:15-26, as well as in Romans 9–11 as a whole, Paul proclaims the sovereign will of God as free and unfettered: "I will have mercy on whom I have mercy. . . . Who can resist his will? Who are you, a human being, to argue with God?" (9:15, 19, 20). Yet if God is **faithful** he cannot lie or go back on his promises. Modern minds sometimes see this "cannot" as a contradiction of God's free sovereignty. But in Paul's theology this is a purely *logical* "cannot" in the sense of constituting a *logical entailment* of God's own free prior choice to be faithful. God himself chooses to constrain himself by his own pledges, promises, and commitments to his people. God *freely* chooses to *give himself* to his people as the trustworthy God. Clement of Alexandria calls this an "alliance by divine love" (Clement, *Stromata,* 5:1).[102]

The outcome of this **faithfulness** is that **through** Christ **you were called into the communal participation of the sonship of Christ our Lord.** καλεῖν in the aorist once again draws attention to the divine act (see Schrage and above, 1:1 and 1:2).[103] On the preposition **through** (διά with the genitive of the relative pronoun) see under 1:1, where it includes circumstances as well as efficient cause or agency. Héring comments, "God is not only the author of salvation, He also prepares the way for it."[104] Basil of Caesarea discusses whether the preposition in this passage is applied by Paul to the Father, Son, and Holy

---

100. Cf. Brown-Driver-Briggs-Gesenius, *The New Hebrew and English Lexicon* (1980 ed.; hereafter BDB), 52-53; Hatch-Redpath, *A Concordance to the Septuagint* (2 vols., Athens: Benefial Bask Publishers, 1977), 1:65 and 2:1,138-19.

101. Calvin, *First Epistle,* 22 and 23; and Von der Osten-Sacken, "Gottes Treue," 176-177. On Romans 9 see also R. H. Bell, *Provoked to Jealousy: The Origin and Purpose of the Jealousy Motif in Rom. 9–11,* WUNT 1 (Tübingen: Mohr, 1994), 63.

102. See further Clement, *Stromata,* 2:6.

103. Schrage, *Der erste Brief,* 1:123.

104. Héring, *First Epistle,* 4.

Spirit equally.[105] **Communal participation** may seem to make heavy weather out of Gk. κοινωνίαν, which is usually translated *fellowship*. But the use of *fellowship* in church circles may convey an impression quite foreign to Paul's distinctive emphasis. He does not refer to a society or group of like-minded people, such as a Graeco-Roman *societas*. Certain specific uses of the word may have this meaning (e.g., Rom 15:27), but not this type of passage.[106] Normally in Paul the word means **communal participation** in that of which all participants are shareholders, or are accorded a common *share*. It is not simply or primarily the experience of being together as Christians which is shared, but the status of being-in-Christ and of *being shareholders in a sonship derived from the sonship of Christ.*[107] Just as *the fellowship of the Holy Spirit* (2 Cor. 13:13) means participating in the sharing out of the Spirit (which then secondarily gives rise to fellowship experience within a community), so *the fellowship of his Son* (1 Cor. 1:9) means **communal participation in the sonship of Jesus Christ**. Godet rightly speaks of "participation in the life of Christ."[108]

Some writers have made this point by translating this passage as *participation in Christ's sonship:* Edwards insists vehemently, "not 'fellowship.'"[109] Thornton distinguishes two points about the word: first, its primary object is a sharing of Christ's life by his people; second, "but it is also 'in Christ' because it is a fellowship of Christians one with another."[110] Hence **communal** underlines the notion of a sharing community, of participation in a commonality. What believers share is not primarily one another's company (although this constitutes an entailment); they are *shareholders* (κοινωνοί) in Christ, in the Holy Spirit, and in Christ's sonship.[111] Thornton examines "the *koinonia* of the Holy Spirit" in 2 Cor 13:13 and concludes: "A genitive following the word *koinonia* expresses . . . that of which one partakes . . . the object shared."[112] Since Christians share also "the Messianic life," this means the experience of the cross (1:18-31) and of the resurrection (15:1-48).[113] "The Spirit of the anointed Messiah will produce in the messianic community effects which were produced in the Messiah.[114] Thornton concludes, "We are confronted with the impossibility of translating the word *koinonia*."[115]

Yet a translation is needed. The AV/KJV and NRSV translate *the fellow-*

---

105. Basil, *On the Spirit,* 1:10.

106. Sampley, *Pauline Partnership in Christ* (Philadelphia: Fortress, 1980), 96-97.

107. Lang, *Die Briefe an die Korinther,* 19, underlines this aspect.

108. Godet, *Commentary,* 1:60.

109. Edwards, *1 Corinthians,* 9, anticipates Lang.

110. Thornton, *The Common Life in the Body of Christ,* 77. Much of Thornton's discussion is very useful, even if flawed by overemphasis on Anglo-Catholic sacramentalism, which he reads into Paul.

111. These terms represent chapter titles, respectively 34-65, 66-95, and 156-87.

112. Ibid., 71.

113. Ibid., 79.

114. Ibid., 184.

115. Ibid., 157.

ship of his Son. This corresponds structurally to the Greek syntax, but it fails to address the issues set forth above. The NIV's *fellowship with his Son* underlines that the sharing is primarily with Christ; it risks a more subjective emphasis almost of "companionship" in view of modern uses of *fellowship* in the context of social groupings. NJB broadens the semantic area by rendering the phrase *has called you to be partners with his Son.* Yet while this allows for community as well as christological participation, *partners* conveys a symmetry of agency which *shareholder* or *participant* does not. The best of the major English VSS is REB's *to share in the life of his Son.* Moffatt's *to participate in his Son* is also acceptable, but without **communal** it could lose its corporate overtones. (Cf. Luther's *zur Gemeinschaft seines Sohnes.*)

A number of modern specialist studies have the effect of underlining Thornton's work. Panikulam and Schattenmann draw constructively on the earlier work of Seesemann.[116] Schrage takes up this work in a detailed exegesis of this passage.[117] Hainz undertakes a careful study and concludes that the meaning of κοινωνία in 1 Cor 1:9 can be seen fully only in the light of its *participatory and corporate* dimension explicated in "sharing in" the cup of the Lord in 1 Cor 10:16-17: "the cup of blessing which we bless, is it not a sharing (κοινωνία) of the blood of Christ? . . . one body are we, although many. . . ."[118] This provides introduction both to 1:10-17, the **one**, and to 1:18-25, for the shared cup and broken bread show forth the death of the Lord (11:26). Hainz shows that the same theological ground of communal participation in Christ and his messianic work underlies ecclesiology, the collection, the Holy Spirit as the source of unity, the wider relations between translocal communities, and baptism and the Lord's Supper. Panikulam adopts a broadly similar, although more sacramental, approach.[119] A recent study by Marion also confirms our approach.[120] The link with unity in 1:10-17 (cf. chs. 12–14) and with the cross in 1:18-25 seems thus to be established.[121] "The Corinthians are called to realize the fellowship into which they have been called by God."[122]

116. Panikulam, *Koinonia in the NT,* 17-30; Schattenmann, "Fellowship," 637-44; Seesemann, *Der Begriff κοινωνία im Neuen Testament,* esp. 34-56; and J. M. McDermott, "The Biblical Doctrine of κοινωνία," *BZ* 19 (1975): 64-77 and 219-33.

117. Schrage, *Der erste Brief,* 1:123-25.

118. Hainz, *Koinonia.*

119. Panikulam's work is Christocentric, but it may overemphasize the sacramental in comparison with Hainz's.

120. D. Marion, "Communion. L'essence du christianisme," *Esprit et Vie* 102 (1992): 145-50, 157-59.

121. Cf. the careful linking of "unity" and "harmony" in 1 Cor 1:1-10 with the later theme of the body of Christ in Ulrich Wickert, "Einheit und Eintract der Kirche im Präscript des ersten Korintherbriefes," *ZNW* 50 (1959): 73-82.

122. Collins, *First Cor,* 66.

II. Causes and Cures of Splits within the Community: Loyalty-Groupings or Status-Groupings in Conflict with the Nature of the Cross, the Spirit, and the Ministry (1:10–4:21)

As we have indicated, the end of the thanksgiving (1:4-9), especially with its eschatological conclusion (1:7b-9) alluding to waiting for the day of the Lord, marks the transition to the main body of the letter.[1] There is general agreement that 1:10 to 4:21 constitutes an identifiable section. Margaret Mitchell regards 1:10–4:21 as presenting the continuous theme of the whole epistle.[2] But whether or not such a view is accepted, this section does indeed turn on Paul's request for unity in the face of "splits" (σχίσματα, 1:10). Much has been made of the "political" nature of this vocabulary and its nature as a "power" struggle.[3] The facts concerning the splits have been conveyed orally to Paul by "Chloe's people" (ὑπὸ τῶν Χλόης, v. 11).[4] Paul's endeavor to provide a cure for them entails first of all the joint sharing of their being-in-Christ, of whom no single group has a monopoly (μεμέρισται ὁ Χριστός; **has Christ been apportioned out?** 1:13), and then an exposition of the nature of the gospel as centered in the cross of Christ (1:18-31; also 2:1-5). The specific role of rhetorical considerations (esp. in 1:10-17) is discussed below.[5]

Paul then proceeds to offer a diagnosis of why these two foundational themes have become obscured. The first concerns *the nature of preaching*. It is not of such a nature as to invite assessments of competing rhetorics. As such, its

---

1. See above on J. H. Roberts, "Eschatological Transitions," *Neot* 20 (1986): 29-35; and P. von der Osten-Sacken, "Gottes Treue bis zur Parusie," *ZNW* 68 (1977): 176-99.

2. Mitchell, *Rhetoric of Reconciliation,* 65-111. Over against the partition theories of J. Weiss, E. Dinkler, W. Schmithals, and others, this view coheres closely with her insistence on the unity of the whole epistle (see Introduction, 36-41).

3. See esp. Mitchell, *Rhetoric of Reconciliation,* 65-111, and Welborn, "Discord in Corinth."

4. On the reception of the oral report and criteria for reconstructing it, see esp. Hurd, *The Origins of 1 Corinthians,* 47-50 and 61-94, esp. 82.

5. One of the fullest but most succinct overviews can be found in Merklein, *Der erste Brief,* 3:1, "Rhetorische Analyse," 108-14 (on Betz, Bünker, Kennedy, Litfin, Lampe, et al.).

operative effectiveness depends on the force which it derives from God as authentic proclamation, not on artifices of persuasion or the consumer-oriented goals of rhetoricians. *The cross reverses* any strategy of manipulative power. Such a notion of "power" would prove to be counterproductive for genuinely christological proclamation since Christ points away from himself to the glory of God and the welfare of others in the cross (1:31–3:4, esp. 2:1-5). (See below on "illocutionary" acts of speech as against "perlocutions.")

A further factor can transform the causes of splits into their cures. This entails a *reappraisal of the role and nature of ministers and apostles.* Too high a view of ministry encourages a congregation or house group to place undue emphasis on particular human leaders. Perceiving allegiance to one leader as competing with loyalty to another can split the church. On the other hand, too low a view of ministry can lead to a do-it-yourself style of faith and conduct, and this can encourage a different kind of elitism. It may promote the interests of the self under the disguise of egalitarianism.[6] By breeding an attitude of "I am as gifted as he or she," it encourages a different kind of self-centeredness. Here assertion replaces the model of service and the cross. Hence Paul compares the self-sufficient attitude of those addressees who perceive themselves as spectators, observers, and assessors of others with the daily struggle and toil of the apostles, who live out the having-died of Christ as a public spectacle in the arena (4:1-13).

Too low a view of ministry overlooks the essential role of those who plant the church and of those who nourish it (3:5-9; cf. 3:10-23) as God's commissioned agents. Yet God alone gives the growth, and too high a view of ministry may ascribe life-giving properties to ministry as if it were almost an end in itself rather than a channel for life which derives entirely from God (3:6). A rounded, healthy Christian community draws on what God gives through a variety of channels and resources (3:6-22). Ministers are no more than examples of those who mediate gifts which come from God (3:21a, 23). Even Christ mediates the gifts and reign of God (3:23b).[7]

A. REPORT OF THE SITUATION AND ITS IMPLICATIONS (1:10-17)

(10) I ask you, brothers and sisters, through the name of our Lord Jesus Christ, that you all take the same side, and that there are no splits among

6. A simple but clear and nontechnical presentation of this point occurs in Rupert E. Davies, *Studies in 1 Corinthians* (London: Epworth Press, 1962), 42-43. Paul's words "save us from too high a doctrine of the Ministry — from supposing that the Minister is the person who makes the church . . . they save us from too low a doctrine of the Ministry. Ministers are not just full-time servants of the Church. . . . Ministers are God's agents . . ." (42).

7. Again, Richardson, *Paul's Language about God,* 95-138 and throughout, constructively conveys Paul's perspective as against views at Corinth.

you, but that you be knitted together again with the same mind-set and with the same consent. (11) For it was made clear to me about you, my dear Christian family, from Chloe's people that there are discords among you. (12) I mean this, that each of you says, "I, for my part, am for Apollos"; "I am a Peter person"; "As for me, I belong to Christ." (13) Has Christ been apportioned out? Surely Paul was not crucified for you, was he? Or were you baptized in the name of Paul? (14, 15) I give thanks that I baptized none of you except Crispus and Gaius, that none of you can say that you were baptized in my name. (16) Well, I did also baptize the household of Stephanas; for the rest, I do not recall whether I baptized anyone else. (17) For Christ did not send me to perform baptisms but to proclaim the gospel, not with clever rhetoric, lest the cross of Christ should be nullified.

The first three verses raise fundamental questions of interpretative judgments. One issue concerns the status and force of παρακαλῶ, variously translated *I beseech, I beg, I appeal,* or **I ask** (1:10). Carl J. Bjerkelund has written a full-length book on this one word, and English translations vary.[8] The crucial question is whether we follow Mitchell and Witherington in regarding the word as an *appeal* which introduces deliberative *rhetoric,* or follow Bjerkelund in viewing it as a *request* on the basis of Paul's particular relation to the readers. In the technical language of speech-act theory, the first view proposes that Paul uses only *perlocutionary force;* the second view proposes that the passage which follows 1:10 constitutes an example of *illocutionary* force. These terms are explained in the comments on 1:10 and receive attention in the Introduction, 43 and 51.

A second key issue concerns the meaning of the word σχίσματα, which we translate **splits**. We may distinguish three stages of research. (i) Ever since at least the work of F. C. Baur on "the Christ party" (*"die Christuspartei in der korinthischen Gemeinde,"* 1831), many have regarded the divisions as those of theological or doctrinal parties.[9] However, (ii) since the work of J. Munck, "The Church without Factions," and of N. A. Dahl (1967), a tendency emerges from the 1950s through to the 1980s to regard the splits as personality cults or "cliques" (Moffatt's translation, 1949).[10] (iii) During the 1990s various sociological approaches and proposals about analogues with Graeco-Roman political rhetoric have led to a third phase of discussion.[11] Unity is to "the advantage" of church

---

8. Bjerkelund, *Parakalô. Form, Funktion und Sinn.*

9. See below on 1:12.

10. Munck, *Paul and the Salvation of Mankind,* 135-67, and N. A. Dahl, "Paul and the Church at Corinth according to 1 Cor. 1:10–4:21," first published in W. R. Farmer et al. (eds.), *Christian History and Interpretation: Studies Presented to John Knox* (Cambridge: Cambridge University Press, 1967), 313-35, and revised in Dahl, *Studies in Paul,* 40-61.

11. Most notably Mitchell, *Paul and the Rhetoric of Reconciliation,* and Welborn, "On the Discord in Corinth: 1 Cor 1–4 and Ancient Politics," 85-111; revised in Welborn, *Politics and Rhetoric in the Corinthian Epistles,* 1-42. With a more theological modification see also Clarke, *Secular and Christian Leadership in Corinth,* 89-108; and in more sociological terms Marshall, *Enmity in Corinth: Social Conventions in Paul's Relations with the Corinthians.*

polity. We shall examine these in our commentary on 1:12, while we try to retain a translation which reproduces the imagery and metaphorical force of the Greek.

Bibliography on 1:10-12

Allo, E.-B., "Exc IV, Les partis à Corinthe, spécialement le parti 'du Christ,'" *Première Épitre aux Corinthiens,* 80-87.

Barrett, C. K., "Cephas and Corinth," in *Essays on Paul* (London: SPCK, 1982), 28-39.

Baur, F. C., "Die Christuspartei in der korinthischen Gemeinde," *Tübinger Zeitschrift für Theologie* 4 (1831): 61-206.

————, *Paul the Apostle of Jesus Christ* (2 vols., Eng. trans., London: Williams & Norgate, 1873-76).

Bjerkelund, C. J., *Parakalô. Form, Funktion und Sinn der parakalô Sätze in den paulinischen Briefen* (Oslo: Universitetsforlaget, 1967).

Brown, R. E., K. P. Donfried, and J. Reumann, *Peter in the NT* (London: Chapman, 1974 [1973]), esp. 32-36.

Carter, T. L., "Big Men at Corinth," *JSNT* (1997): 45-71.

Chow, J. K., *Patronage and Power: A Study of Social Networks in Corinth,* JSNTSS 75 (Sheffield: Sheffield Academic Press, 1992).

Clarke, A. D., *Secular and Christian Leadership in Corinth: A Socio-Historical and Exegetical Study of 1 Cor 1–6* (Leiden: Brill, 1993), esp. 89-105.

Dahl, N. A., *Studies in Paul* (Minneapolis: Augsburg, 1977), esp. "Paul and the Church at Corinth," 40-61.

Engberg-Pedersen, T., "The Gospel and Social Practice according to 1 Cor," *NTS* 33 (1987): 557-84.

Fitch, W. O., "Paul, Apollos, Cephas, Christ," *Theology* 74 (1971): 18-24.

Hock, R. F., *The Social Context of Paul's Ministry: Tentmaking and Apostleship* (Philadelphia: Fortress, 1980).

Horrell, D. G., *The Social Ethos of the Corinthian Correspondence* (Edinburgh: T. & T. Clark, 1996), 112-17 and 131-37.

Hurd, J. C., *The Origin of 1 Corinthians* (London: SPCK, 1965), 75-94, 101-7, and 126-42.

Hurst, L., "Apollos, Hebrews and Corinth," *SJT* 38 (1985): 505-13.

Kennedy, G., *Classical Rhetoric and Its Christian and Secular Tradition* (London: Croom Helm, 1980), 129-60.

Klauck, H.-J., *Hausgemeinde und Hauskirche in frühen Christentum* (Stuttgart: Katholisches Bibelwerk, 1981).

Lang, F., "Die Gruppen in Korinth nach 1 Kor 1–4," *TBei* 14 (1983): 68-79.

Lütgert, W., *Freiheitspredigt und Schwärmgeister in Korinth. Ein Beiträg zur Charakteristik der Christuspartie* (Gütersloh: Bertelsmann, 1908).

Manson, T. W., *Studies in the Gospels and Epistles* (Manchester: Manchester University Press, 1962), 190-209.

Marshall, P., *Enmity in Corinth: Social Conventions in Paul's Relations with the Corinthians,* WUNT 2:23 (Tübingen: Mohr, 1987).

Martin, D. B., *The Corinthian Body* (New Haven: Yale University Press, 1995), esp. 55-59 (cf. 59-68).

Meeks, W. A., *The First Urban Christians* (New Haven: Yale University Press, 1983), 117-19.

Meinertz, M., "σχίσμα und αἵρεσις im NT," *BZ* 1 (1957): 114-18.

Merklein, H., "Die Parteien in Korinth," in *Der erste Brief an die Korinther 1–4* (Gütersloh: Mohr, 1992), 134-52.

Mitchell, M. M., *Paul and the Rhetoric of Reconciliation: An Exegetical Investigation of the Language and Composition of 1 Corinthians* (Louisville: Westminster/Knox, 1992), esp. 1-99 and 198-201.

Munck, J., *Paul and the Salvation of Mankind* (Eng. trans., London: SCM, 1959), 135-67.

Murphy-O'Connor, J., *St Paul's Corinth* (Wilmington: Glazier, 1983), 153-61.

Neyrey, J. H., "Body Language in 1 Cor: The Use of Anthropological Models for Understanding Paul and His Opponents," *Semeia* 35 (1986): 129-70.

Perkins, P., *Peter: Apostle for the Whole Church* (Columbia: University of South Carolina Press, 1994), 111-15.

Sampley, J. P., *Pauline Partnership in Christ, Christian Community and Commitment in the Light of Roman Law* (Philadelphia: Fortress, 1980), 1-20, 79-102.

Schrage, W., "Exkurs: Die korinthischen 'Parteien,'" *Der erste Brief,* 1:142-48.

Senft, C., "Excursus: Les 'partis' à Corinthe," in *Première Épitre de S. Paul aux Corinthiens,* 33-35.

Theissen, G., *The Social Setting of Pauline Christianity* (Eng. trans., London: SCM, 1982), 54-68.

Vielhauer, P., "Paulus und die Kephaspartei in Kor," *NTS* 21 (1975): 341-52.

Welborn, L. L., *Politics and Rhetoric in the Corinthian Epistles* (Macon, Ga.: Mercer University Press, 1997), esp. "Discord in Corinth: First Cor 1–4 and Ancient Politics," 1-42 (rev. version of "On the Discord in Corinth," *JBL* 106 [1987]: 85-111).

Wilckens, U., *Weisheit und Torheit* (Tübingen: Mohr, 1959), 5-21.

Wuellner, W., "Haggadic Homily Genre in 1 Cor 1–3," *JBL* 89 (1970): 199-204.

1. The Nature of Paul's *Parakalō* Request (1:10)

10a Mitchell interprets 1:10 as the major statement of the rhetorical thesis of the whole epistle. The entire letter, she argues, "is throughout an argument for ecclesial unity as centred in the πρόθεσις or thesis statement of the argument in 1:10."[12] Witherington (with others) similarly writes that 1:10 constitutes "the *propositio* . . . the thesis statement of the entire discourse."[13] It introduces "a deliberative discourse," namely, the rhetorical argument or "the main advice the rhetor wants his hearer to heed, and is followed by arguments to persuade the audience."[14]

Both writers cite the work of Carl Bjerkelund with apparent satisfaction, since all three construe παρακαλῶ as the transitional hinge form between the end of the thanksgiving and the beginning of the main body of the letter.[15]

---

12. Mitchell, *Rhetoric of Reconciliation,* 1.

13. Witherington, *Conflict and Community,* 94; also Collins, *First Cor,* 69.

14. Witherington, *Conflict and Community,* 94.

15. Witherington, *Conflict and Community,* 94-95. Witherington even argues that Bjerkelund presses for the meaning "beseech," when Bjerkelund argues that its semantic area lies *be-*

Bjerkelund, however, offers a different account of the form and function of παρακαλῶ once its place within the sequence of the letter has been agreed upon. In his judgment it does *not* constitute a way of introducing a *rhetorical argument,* as much as replicating the style and form of official diplomatic letters or letters based on friendship. It functions as a request, to be translated **I ask** (sometimes also *urge* or *encourage*) and *depends not on rhetoric, but on some prior personal or official relationship between the writer and the addressees.*[16] A non-rhetorical use occurs, for example, in the Pastoral Epistles, "I ask (παρακαλῶ) that prayers, supplications . . . be made" (1 Tim. 2:1). Here it is ultimately **the name of our Lord Jesus Christ** rather than rhetorical persuasion that provides the ground for the request or plea.[17]

The contrast may be seen in terms of the difference between *illocutionary* speech-acts (on the basis of apostleship or friendship) and *perlocutionary* speech-acts (on the basis of rhetorical persuasion). J. L. Austin defined an illocutionary act as "the performance of an act *in* saying something."[18] Clear examples include *I promise, I name, I appoint, I free.* The operative effect of these utterances *as acts* depends not on rhetoric or persuasion, but on whether the speaker has the authority, status, or self-commitment to perform an illocutionary speech-act, e.g., to make a promise, to confer a name, to appoint to office. Luther and William Tyndale regarded *promising* as the most important speech-act of the biblical writings as Christian scripture.

By contrast, rhetoric constitutes a perlocutionary act. J. L. Austin describes perlocutions as "bringing about changes," typically by *persuading* and *convincing,* and through strategies such as that of *surprise.* To be sure, a perlocutionary act of transformation can result from an illocutionary promise or verdict.[19] But this is not what Mitchell and Witherington regard as the heart of their rhetorical approach. By contrast, Litfin approaches Pauline proclamation (1:14-17) as an operative act based on a relationship with Paul *as one commissioned and authorized to preach,* i.e., competent to perform illocutionary acts of proclamation. Litfin contrasts "the dynamic upon which the Graeco-Roman orator depended" with the "dynamic use of the cross" which derives its force and action from a different source and method.[20]

Mitchell and Witherington stand among a large number of writers who, following the researches of George Kennedy into Graeco-Roman rhetoric, seek

---

tween "commanding" on one side and "begging," "beseeching," "imploring," or even "appealing" on the other.

16. Bjerkelund, *Parakalô,* 74-58, 109-10, and throughout.

17. Rightly, Collins, *First Cor,* 68.

18. J. L. Austin, *How to Do Things with Words* (Oxford: Clarendon Press, 1962), 99; cf. 101 (his italics).

19. Austin, *How to Do Things;* cf. N. W. Wolterstorff, *Divine Discourse* (Cambridge: Cambridge University Press, 1995), 75-129.

20. Litfin, *St Paul's Theology of Proclamation,* SNTSMS 79 (Cambridge: Cambridge University Press, 1994), 191 and 192; cf. 181-210, esp. 185-92.

to uncover rhetorical patterns in the Pauline writings.[21] Mitchell perceives this as further demonstrating the unity of the epistle against a variety of partition theories. She writes "This investigation, through its understanding of 1 Corinthians as deliberative rhetoric, renders a fully coherent reading of the letter in its present literary form, and thus constitutes a sustained defense of the compositional integrity of 1 Corinthians."[22] Her criticisms of the partition theories of Weiss, Schmithals, Héring, and others are valid, and I have argued for the unity of the epistle in another study and in the Introduction.[23] This is one of several factors which vindicate explorations of rhetoric. However, as will emerge regularly, we need to heed Eriksson's valid point that *epistolography* and *rhetoric* are *complementary* approaches, not *competitive ones.*[24] Mitchell is rightly cautious about too readily utilizing the so-called new rhetoric of C. Perelman and L. Olbrechts-Tyteca. With good reason she suspects undue historical assimilations between ancient rhetoric and communicative theory in philosophy of language.[25] She also acknowledges that the risk which appeals to Graeco-Roman *Handbooks* of rhetoric may be too mechanical and indeed loose.

While Ignatius uses sociopolitical imagery to urge unity, Bjerkelund appeals to the same passages for his own interpretation of παρακαλῶ (Ignatius, *Letter to the Trallians,* 6:1; 12:2; cf. also *1 Clement* 47:1-3). He endorses the view that παρακαλῶ provides the point of transition between the thanksgiving and the main body of the letter.[26] But he insists that 1 Cor 1:10, 4:16, and 16:15 all reflect the *nonrhetorical* use of παρακαλῶ found consistently in papyri, in-

21. Kennedy, *Classical Rhetoric and Its Christian and Secular Tradition from Ancient to Modern Times,* esp. 129-32; on Jewish-Christian rhetoric more broadly, 120-60; in relation to philosophical rhetoric in Plato and Aristotle (41-85) and the Roman period of Cicero and Quintilian (89-105). Kennedy's exposition of deliberative rhetoric in Aristotle and others widens the distinction between illocutionary acts and perlocutionary acts. The deliberative speaker is fundamentally concerned to establish that a course of action will be *expedient* (my italics) for the audience" (Kennedy, *Classical Rhetoric,* 73; Aristotle, *Rhetoric* 1.8; 1358b.20-29; cf. Aristotle, *Rhetoric* 1.4-8 on deliberative rhetoric, and 1.10-15 on judicial rhetoric. By contrast, "epideictic" rhetoric relates to the present, just as deliberative rhetoric relates to the future, and judicial rhetoric to the evaluation of past acts (Aristotle, *Rhetoric* 1358b.18; cf. Kennedy, *Classical Rhetoric,* 73). Epideictic rhetoric thus stands near to, and overlaps with, illocutions, since it constitutes acts of praise or blame *in* the speaking of the utterance. Aristotle's use of the funeral setting matches Wittgenstein's instantiation of the first-person performative speech-act "We mourn" in a funeral oration. This, Wittgenstein declares, is an act or "expression of mourning — not to tell anything to those who are present" (*Philosophical Investigations;* Oxford: Blackwell, 2d ed. 1967), 2.10 (189); cf. Aristotle, *Rhetoric,* 1.9; 1366a.30; and further 3.12.

22. Mitchell, *Rhetoric of Reconciliation,* 2.

23. A. C. Thiselton, "Luther and Barth on 1 Cor. 15," in W. P. Stephens (ed.), *The Bible, the Reformation, and the Church: Essays in Honour of James Atkinson,* JSNTSS 105 (Sheffield: Sheffield Academic Press, 1995), 258-89, esp. 275-78.

24. A. Eriksson, *Traditions as Rhetorical Proof,* 280-83.

25. Mitchell, *Rhetoric of Reconciliation,* 7. Cf. C. Perelman and Olbrechts-Tyteca, *The New Rhetoric* (Notre Dame: University of Notre Dame Press, 1969).

26. Bjerkelund, *Parakalô,* 141.

scriptions, Graeco-Roman royal documents, and early Christian literature of the Pauline period. It *draws its force from a relationship of friendship, trust, or official status between the writer and the addressee(s),* not on sociorhetorical *causal* force. *I beg* (Moffatt, Barrett), *I beseech* (AV, KJV), even *I appeal* (REB, NIV, NRSV) are too causative and rhetorical for Bjerkelund.

Bjerkelund's citation of first-century examples is impressive.[27] When the request is for a personal favor, rhetorical argument has less prominence: παρακαλῶ σε οὖν πέμψαι . . . (*Papyrus Osloensis* 48:4). Moulton-Milligan also list **ask** as the first meaning for "a common formula in papyrus private letters."[28] Ignatius of Antioch offers examples which may support Bjerkelund's arguments (cf. *Trallians,* 6:1).[29]

Paul performs this act of request (1) as one member of a family to another (**brothers and sisters**); and (2) as one who speaks as Christ's commissioned agent to make a request (3) **through** (διά + genitive) **the name of the Lord Jesus Christ** (4) as if he were *present* (hence direct address) rather than absent (see on 16:13-24, esp. v. 21). It is difficult to know how best to translate ἀδελφοί, since the addition of **and sisters** adds to the text what it does not say explicitly. Nevertheless the male form regularly embodies a gender-inclusive meaning, and "Paul also . . . includes the women of the community" (cf. 11:2-16; 14:34-35).[30] It would be more misleading to translate ἀδελφοί as **brothers** (NJB, NIV) than as **brothers and sisters** (NRSV, Collins, and Fee).[31] Lightfoot rightly speaks of family bonds here, and classical Greek uses ἀδελφοί to refer to, e.g., a **brother** and *sister.*[32] The repetition of ἀδελφοί μου, **my brothers and sisters,** in the next verse clearly indicates (i) that within the same Christian family tensions and estrangements are inappropriate; (ii) that fellow believers deserve the mutual loyalty and respect which belongs within one family; and

27. *BGU* 665.19 (first cent. AD; *Michigan Papyri* 485.9; 499.15; *BGU* 850.5; 848.10; *Rylands Papyri* 695.11; *Aberdeen Papyri* 193.4. Abundant examples occur in the papyri cited by Bjerkelund, *Parakalô,* 34-58. In Philemon the semantic scope excludes *I command* (ἐπιτάσσειν) because the request for the return of "my child Onesimus, whose father I have become," is neither "by command" nor by rhetoric, but διὰ τὴν ἀγάπην μᾶλλον παρακαλῶ (Philem 8, 9), i.e., on the basis of a loving relationship.

28. MM, 484, e.g., *Paris Papyri* 42:8; Rylands Papyri 2.229.17 (AD 38); παρακληθείς "is used much as we use 'please' — *Fayyum Papyri* 109.3 (early 1 A.D.)" (484). Cf. further *Parakalô,* 59-72 and 88-108.

29. His well-known declaration of his *martyr-status,* "I am God's wheat, to be ground by the teeth of the wild beasts to be found Christ's pure head," follows *the act of request:* παρακαλῶ ὑμᾶς, μὴ εὔνοια ἄκαιρος γένησθέ μοι, ἄφετέ με θηρίων εἶναι βοράν: "I ask you, do not do me an untimely kindness; let me be food for the wild beasts" (Ignatius, *Romans* 4:1). Again closely following the form and function of 1 Cor 1:10, Ignatius *asks* the Philadelphians *to do nothing out of strife:* παρακαλῶ δὲ ὑμᾶς μήδεν κατ' ἐριθείαν πράσσειν (Ignatius, *Letter to the Philadelphians* 8:1). See further, e.g., Polycarp, *Letter to the Philippians* 9:1. All the same, Paul's ultimate ground of appeal remains **the name of our Lord Jesus Christ.**

30. Wolff, *Der erste Brief,* 25; also Collins, *First Cor,* 70.

31. Cf. Fee, *First Epistle,* 52, n. 22; Collins, *First Cor,* 67 and 76.

32. Lightfoot, *Notes,* 151; cf. LSJ, 30; *EDNT,* 1:28-30; BAGD, 16 (esp. [1]).

(iii) that the implicit rebuke has been softened through the signal of a bond of affection. Origen and Cyprian compare this with the "oneness" of John 10 and John 17:20-21.[33] Paul uses the term as a sign of affection especially for the Macedonian churches (twenty times in 1 Corinthians).[34] I have used a variety of translations since the word may denote *fellow Christians* or *dear friends* as well as **brothers and sisters**.

Paul's writing **in the name of our Lord Jesus Christ** to "heal" the splits (σχίσματα) may suggest an allusion to the Acts traditions of *healing in the name of Jesus* (Acts 3:6, 16; 4:7, 10; cf. 4:18; 5:28, 40; 16:18).[35] As I have argued elsewhere in relation to blessing and cursing, however, **the name** does not initiate *causal* force, as some theories about primitive word magic seem to imply, but *illocutionary authorization*.[36] This constitutes the tenth time that Paul names Christ in these first ten verses, and Chrysostom and Aquinas draw attention to this.[37] The Apostolic Fathers make their appeal on the same ground.[38] The **name** invokes the *character and reputation* of Jesus Christ as publicly known. In modern mass advertising, "the name" carries with it an image and a kind of guarantee, and this resonates with the ancient usage. To pray "in **the name** of Christ" means to ask that it be accepted for the sake of all that Christ is known to be and to have done. Grammatically διὰ τοῦ ὀνόματος, **through the name**, denotes *the means* of request.

10b Welborn sums up an important interpretative key to 1:10b-17 and the epistle as a whole. Paul alludes in v. 10b to "a power struggle, not a theological controversy."[39] A widespread current view arising from sociopolitical research suggests that Paul uses terminology drawn from the political vocabulary of the Roman or Graeco-Roman *polis*. In the Synoptic tradition the conjunction of σχίσματα, rents, tears or **splits**, with κατηρτισμένοι, *being mended, being repaired*, or **being knitted together again**, may recall the passage about James and John *mending* their nets (Mark 1:19; par. Matt 4:21). In 2 Cor 13:11 Paul instructs the local church *to put things back in order* (καταρτίζεσθε), "keeping the peace" (εἰρηνεύετε, being in harmony). Welborn notes that "A σχίσμα is a rift, a tear, as in a garment: it is used metaphorically of a cleft in political consciousness."[40]

The word σχίσμα, **split**, is also applied metaphorically to division of mind

33. Origen, *De Principiis*, 1:6:2, "that they may all be one . . ."; Cyprian, *Treatises*, 1.8, compares the "one flock" of John 10:16.

34. In 1 Corinthians it occurs at 1:10, 11, 26; 2:1; 3:1; 4:6; 7:24, 29; 10:1; 11:33; 12:1; 14:6, 20, 26, 39; 15:1, 31, 50, 58; 16:15.

35. Héring, *First Epistle*, 4. Also, e.g., Mark 9:38; 16:17; Luke 6:22.

36. A. C. Thiselton, "The Supposed Power of Words in the Biblical Writings," *JTS* 25 (1974): 283-99.

37. Allo, *Première Épitre*, 5.

38. Ignatius *Letter to the Ephesians*, 3:1; cf. *1 Clement* and Polycarp.

39. Welborn "Discord in Corinth," rev. version of earlier article (*JBL* 106 [1987]: 85-111) in Welborn, *Politics and Rhetoric in the Corinthian Epistles*, 7.

40. Welborn, *Politics*, 3. See further Schrage, *Der erste Brief*, 1:138-39.

or judgment, e.g., "there was a *split* in the crowd because of him [Jesus]" (σχίσμα οὖν ἐγένετο ἐν τῷ ὄχλῳ δι' αὐτόν, John 7:43; also 9:16 and 10:19). Jesus Christ constitutes for John the watershed which divides one stream into two. Paul calls attention to the problem in 1 Cor 11:18 as one of very serious proportions in the context of sharing the one bread and one cup of the Lord's Supper (1 Cor 11:18). The *tearing apart* of the limbs of a body precisely conveys Paul's language in 1 Cor 12:27: ἵνα μὴ ᾖ σχίσμα ἐν τῷ σώματι, a tear or *fracture within the body.* These cover the eight instances of σχίσμα (or σχίσματα) which occur in the New Testament, three of which (all the Pauline uses) come in 1 Corinthians. Paul's use of the present subjunctive in 1:10, μὴ ᾖ ... σχίσματα, denotes the request that splits *may not continue.* Plutarch (c. AD 46-120) points out that while brotherly love in family life is a huge support, *enmity within the family* is especially painful.[41]

When we turn from the metaphorical uses of σχίσμα to the phrase ἵνα τὸ αὐτὸ λέγητε πάντες, for which a wooden replication would be *that you all speak the same thing* (AV/KJV) the *political* nature of the language begins to emerge more clearly. The English versions offer a wide array of proposals, including *that all of you be in agreement* (NRSV); *that all of you agree* (NIV) *all to be in agreement in what you profess* (NJB); *agree(d) in what you say* (Barrett); *drop these party cries* (Moffatt); and be in *agreement* (Collins). It has long been recognized that this is the language of classical politics. Lightfoot (1895) writes: "We have here a strictly classical expression. It is used of political communities which are free from factions, or of different states which entertain friendly relations with each other."[42] He speaks therefore of "making up differences," although we should be cautious about implying any lack of difference that entailed bland uniformity. Robertson and Plummer rightly distinguish between musical harmony and a dull unison since Paul rejects the notion of unity as sheer replication in 12:4-30, replication or cloning implying redundancy.[43]

Welborn also elucidates further the political nature of σχίσματα. Thus Herodotus (fifth cent. BC) uses σχίσμα to denote a split or rift in political consciousness (7.219). Diodorus (first cent. BC) speaks of party divisions (σχιζόμενος) at Megara (Diodorus Siculus, 12.66.2). Clement of Rome speaks of "dissensions, divisions (σχίσματα), and war (πόλεμος) within the church at Corinth around AD 96" (*1 Clement* 46:5). He thus rejects F. C. Baur's notion that the differences of theology or doctrine were the primary issue of contention.[44] Just as many return to Lightfoot on "politics," so most scholars today have returned to the view of John Calvin: that the real problem being addressed in 1 Corinthians

41. Plutarch, *Moralia* 481 B-E; hence this perception was "in the air" in the first century. Differences *within* a close community or political party have always been more painful than differences from "outsiders."
42. Lightfoot, *Notes,* 151.
43. Robertson and Plummer, *First Epistle,* 10.
44. Welborn, *Politics,* 2-11.

1–4 is one of partisanship.[45] He notes that Paul deals in a different manner with false teaching in Galatians and Philippians. There "he engages in polemic."[46] The Corinthians are "inflated [with self-importance] on behalf of one against the other" (1 Cor 4:6).

Welborn convincingly points to numerous examples in Greek politics in which orators become inflated at their success and invite caricature as political windbags (e.g., Epictetus, *Dissertations* 2.16.10; Philo, *De Legatione ad Gaium* 86.154; Demosthenes, 19.314; 59.97; Thucydides, 1.132.1-3; Dio Chrysostom, 30.19; 58.5). Thus "It is a power struggle, not a theological controversy."[47] But although some earlier commentators perceived this, he argued, they failed to note how closely this trait mirrors parallel power struggles in the city-states of the Graeco-Roman world of Paul's day. Corinth represented an especially competitive and status-obsessed culture. Clearly their groupings within church life carried over these pre-conversion cultural traits.[48] As Dale Martin argues, "The problem of disunity at Corinth derives from issues related to status."[49]

Here two types of analysis of the language of Paul and the language used at Corinth come into play. On one side Ulrich Wickert shows the unity of theme which recurs from 1:1 through to 1:10 and beyond: as against competitive exclusivism and what Moffatt calls "cliques," Paul insists that Christ is Lord αὐτῶν καὶ ἡμῶν, **their Lord and ours** (1:2), the Lord of **all who call upon** [his] **name . . . in every place** (1:2), and he asks for harmony and unity through this one **name** under whose Lordship all stand equally.[50] On the other side, Welborn and Mitchell argue strongly that the same competitive concern for power and status marks church life at Corinth as that found in much secular life in Greek or Roman city-states. This governs the same political terminology. The following are the slogans and catchphrases found in Corinth: (1) τὸ αὐτὸ λέγητε, (2) μὴ ᾖ ἐν ὑμῖν σχίσματα, (3) ἦτε δὲ κατηρτισμένοι ἐν τῷ αὐτῷ νοΐ, and (4) ἐν τῇ αὐτῇ γνώμῃ. On these Mitchell writes: "Each contains a stock phrase in Greek literature for political order and peace: the use of four such phrases gives this πρόθεσις a vehemence and undeniable clarity."[51]

Those who say "the same thing," Mitchell continues, "are allies, compatriots, even co-partisans."[52] Following modern commentators since J. J. de Wette (1752), she cites Polybius, 2.62.4; 5.104.1 (second cent. BC), Thucyd-

45. Calvin, *First Epistle,* 8 and 25-27.
46. Welborn, *Politics,* 7 and 7, n. 20.
47. Ibid.
48. Witherington, *Conflict and Community,* 19-35; and Clarke, *Secular and Christian Leadership,* 89-108.
49. Martin, *The Corinthian Body,* 56; cf. 55-58.
50. Wickert, "Einheit und Eintracht" der kirche im Präscript des ersten Korintherbriefs," *ZNW* 50 (1959): 73-82.
51. Mitchell, *Rhetoric of Reconciliation,* 68.
52. Ibid.

ides, 5.31.6, and Dio Chrysostom, *Orations* 4.135 (first/second cent. AD). Hence I have proposed the translation **that you all take the same side** to embrace (i) the contemporary hellenistic Greek idiom of being political co-partisans; and, equally, (ii) the theological conception of sharing what they hold in common as those who share the same Lord (cf. 1:1-9 and Wickert). In chs. 8–11 and 12–14 Paul will attack any pattern of conduct which makes some Christians feel second class, as not belonging to an elite, or as "not on the same side" in liturgical or ethical practices. Mitchell is also correct to perceive that σχίσμα, **split** or *tear,* includes in a political context "a division or rift within the social fabric of the community."[53] She convincingly rejects the theories of Weiss and Schmithals that the meanings in 11:18 and 12:27 are so different as to invite or to confirm a partition theory of composition.

Munck rightly called into question Baur's theory that these σχίσματα represent "schisms" or theological parties based on differences of doctrine. Paul does not defend the "Paul group" (1:12), or attack other groups. All, equally, are told to forget their differences. In our comments on 1:12 we shall consider the evidence that small house groups had begun to develop separate climates, or a separate ethos, which led to self-sufficient independence and even competitiveness over against others.[54] If Mitchell is correct in claiming that "faction" may cover this meaning, then Munck's translated title "The Church without Factions" overstates the issue, even if his basic refutation of Baur remains sound. Theology and politics overlap since, as Martin urges, a rhetoric of status threatens the "one body."[55] Mitchell thus takes up Paul's application of the political imagery of **split** communities to "the term's most literal use for divisions of parts of the body and other natural phenomena."[56] For this moves us from politics to theology. A torn up plant or a seriously torn body *ceases to be a plant or a body.* "We murder, to dissect."[57] A restored order is needed: ἵνα . . . ἦτε δὲ κατηρτισμένοι . . . keeps open Sampley's claims about the church community as construed on the pattern of a mutually consenting Roman *societas.*[58]

Yet while he uses political language for the nature of the **splits**, Paul draws on Christology and theology for their cure. The rhetoric of status was part of "the factiousness which had been the curse of Greek democracy [and] had made its way into the local church, . . . even across the Aegean Paul seemed to hear shrill cries. . . ."[59] Yet he brings a theology of the Lordship of Christ and a Christology of the cross to bear on such politics: **"I ask through the name of our Lord Jesus Christ . . ."** For the σχίσματα denote not mere personal rivalry

---

53. Ibid., 70; cf. 71-80.

54. Cf. the discussions cited below (v. 12) by Theissen and Murphy-O'Connor.

55. Martin, *The Corinthian Body,* 55-56.

56. Mitchell, *Rhetoric of Reconciliation,* 73.

57. William Wordsworth, "Up, up, my friend, and quit your books," from *The Thorn* (1798).

58. Sampley, *Pauline Partnership in Christ, Christian Community and Commitment in the Light of Roman Law,* 1-20 and 79-102.

59. Moffatt, *First Epistle,* 9.

and quarrels, but also a diversity of *spiritualities* based on individualism, on loyalty to specific groups or factions as "spiritual." The issue is not *personal* rivalry, but rivalry among *"spiritual" groups* within the one church.[60]

Two more phrases remain to be examined in this pivotal verse: ἐν τῷ αὐτῷ νοῒ καὶ ἐν τῇ αὐτῇ γνώμῃ, **with the same mind-set and with the same consent**. The difficulty of an adequate English translation is indicated by the variety of proposals: *in the same mind and in the same judgment* (AV, KJV); *in the same mind and in the same purpose* (NRSV); *united in your beliefs and judgments* (NJB); *united in mind and thought* (NIV).

The varied translations well reflect the two types of difficulty which the translator encounters. First and foremost, the lexicographical and semantic range of both νοῦς (usually but not always *mind*) and γνώμη (*purpose, intention, mind, opinion, judgment,* **consent**) is exceptionally wide and context-dependent.[61] Second, interpretations of νοῦς as *mind, outlook, attitude,* or **mind-set** are bound up not only with contextual factors but also with detailed debates in the history of Pauline research.[62]

In the history of modern Pauline research, F. C. Baur interpreted νοῦς in accordance with nineteenth-century ethical idealism to denote self-consciousness which is capable of ethical reflection and decision. Here "the same mind" would convey a largely ethical category. In the era from Otto Pfleiderer to H. J. Holtzmann, νοῦς was interpreted primarily as human reason, and as providing a point of contact with God. But with the rise of the history-of-religions school, R. Reitzenstein and J. Weiss construed the term as virtually synonymous with πνεῦμα, as the "higher" or "religious" capacity of human persons.[63] But this conflicts entirely with Paul's emphasis in 1 Cor 2:6–3:4 and esp. 2:10-16, which concludes: "We have the *mind* of Christ" (2:16). In many passages the force varies.[64] In some passages the word appears to mean most naturally *outlook* or *attitude* (as in 1 Cor 2:16, "the mind of Christ"); while in others it means *mind* in the sense of *rational reflection* (1 Cor 14:14: "my mind is unproductive"). Hence we propose that **mind-set** in the present context draws out the meaning of *outlook, stance, orientation,* or *attitude,* without entirely losing the dimension of *rational judgment* which is nearly always implicit. This well accords with Jewett's final conclusion about this passage, that νοῦς here is "a complex of thoughts and assumptions which can make up the consciousness of

---

60. Schrage, *Der erste Brief,* 1:138-39.

61. The fullest range is BAGD, 163 (γνώμη, category 1, *purpose, mind* for this verse); and esp. 544-45 (νοῦς, category 3, *Christian attitude or way of thinking* for this verse). Cf. MM, 129 and 431; and Grimm-Thayer, 119 and 429.

62. R. Jewett, *Paul's Anthropological Terms* (Leiden: Brill, 1971), offers a masterly review of "conflict settings" and varied fashions in the history of research. See esp. 358-90 for 1:10.

63. R. Reitzenstein, *Hellenistic Mystery Religions: Their Basic Ideas and Significance* (Eng. trans., Pittsburgh: Pickwick, 1978); Weiss, *Der erste Korintherbrief,* 14 and 68-70.

64. Allo, *Première Épître,* 7 and esp. 105, rightly underlines the aspect of rationality in 1 Corinthians 14, while partition theories generate further plurality. See Jewett, *Paul's Anthropological Terms,* 375-84.

a person."[65] J. Weiss also notes that the preposition ἐν with νοΐ confirms the impression that the word here means something more than an organ of thought.[66] **Mind-set** approximates BAGD's proposal noted above: "the Christian *attitude* or *way of thinking*."[67]

The translation of γνώμη, **consent**, is less complex, but also determined largely by its context in view of its very wide semantic range. Here we diverge from BAGD, who place 1:10 under the categorization *purpose, intention, mind*. But if Welborn and Mitchell are right about Paul's use of political terminology, we may infer that the competitive corporate self-centeredness which characterize some of the "groups" stands most directly in semantic contrast to **consent**. The unity and harmony of the community depends on a voluntary willingness to respect the otherness of the other as having its place within the one community.[68] Josephus uses γνώμη of **consent** to a mode of government (*Antiquities* 18.336), while Paul tells Philemon that he does not wish to keep the services of Onesimus "without your consent" (χωρὶς δὲ τῆς σῆς γνώμης, Philem 14). In this sense "agreement" entails not uniformity but voluntary constraints of one's "rights" (cf. on 6:12, below) for the good of the whole. Paul expounds this as a key theme in 8:1–9:27. It further coheres with Wuellner's view that the whole of the first chapter, indeed the dominant thread in 1 Corinthians 1–3, is a homily which "concerns the divine judgment on human wisdom."[69] Such judgment is brought to a focus in the cross (1:18-25).

2. The Report and the Slogans (1:11-12)

11 The verb ἐδηλώθη, translated **it was made clear**, relates to the form δῆλος, *clear, evident*. With the active voice and an accusative noun it often means *to reveal*. The construction in the passive with a dative (here, μοι and περί) characteristically refers to conveying *information to* someone *about* something. Hence many translate *informed* or *reported*. But the word is "stronger than 'it was told me' (cf. 3:13). . . . The Apostle was reluctant to believe the reports which had come to his ears, [but] . . . the thing was undeniable."[70]

My dear Christian family is an alternative (with μου) for ἀδελφοί, used above in v. 10.[71] The repetition of the phrase underlines the point that this is no mere convention, but expresses the family unity and affection which is split apart by the reported situation.

65. Ibid., 378.
66. Weiss, *Der erste Korintherbrief,* 14; cf. 68.
67. BAGD, 163.
68. Further, Sampley, *Pauline Partnership,* and Martin, *Corinthian Body,* cited above.
69. W. Wuellner, "Haggadic Homily Genre in 1 Cor 1–3," 201; cf. 199-204.
70. Edwards, *First Epistle,* 18; cf. Chrysostom, *1 Cor. Hom.,* 3.3.
71. We vary the translation deliberately for reasons explained above. Women would be included in the Greek term (cf. Wolff, Collins, and BAGD, above).

That the phrase ὑπὸ τῶν Χλόης means **Chloe's people** is rightly the most widely accepted view (NRSV, NJB, Moffatt, and Collins), although NIV returns to "Chloe's household." Theissen reminds us that members of a *family* would normally be identified through the name of the father (not the mother), even if he was deceased.[72] An exception could be made if Chloe was well known at Corinth, but it remains more likely that **Chloe's people** are business associates, business agents, or slaves acting on her behalf. Perhaps they represented the business interests of this wealthy Asian woman, traveling between Ephesus and Corinth for her.[73] Whether or not Chloe had church connections, probably her agents belonged to the church at Ephesus and had regular links with the church at Corinth. On their last return to Ephesus, as Fee vividly expresses it, they gave Paul an "earful" about the state of the church at Corinth. "The mention of *Chloe's people* gives credence to the report received by Paul. The report was not hearsay."[74]

The term ἔρις would best be translated *strife* if it had occurred in the singular form. But to translate the plural ἔριδες as *strifes* would be awkward. *Quarrels* is favored by most English versions, but this seems to place undue emphasis on emotion and aggressive speech. *Strife* may include more subtle manipulative tactics.[75] Hence a more inclusive term such as *contentions* would be more appropriate, and **discords** may offer a more familiar English equivalent. Tertullian understands 1:10-11 to include the need for openness and mutual understanding: to speak more intimately with all who share the same faith.[76]

12 Paul unpacks and elucidates in what the reported **splits** and **discords** consist. The four names **Paul, Apollos,** *Cephas* (or **Peter**), and **Christ** occur in the same genitive singular forms.[77] Hence the English "I am of Paul, and I am of Apollos, and I am of Cephas, and I am of Christ" (AV, KJV) may at first seem correct. But "of Paul" hardly conveys the stylistic dynamic sociopolitical flavor which Paul seeks to convey, and Mitchell insists that this is not a genitive of possession.[78] The mood of staking personal loyalty to some group which finds its focus in one of the leaders with whom it has become closely associated may be conveyed by rendering *"I am for Paul"; "I am for Apollos"* . . . (REB). But "I belong to Paul" . . . "I belong to Apollos" (NRSV, NJB) must be considered (see further below).

If the form these "slogans" reflect is political, "personal adherence" becomes the issue.[79] Collins compares the citation of names with "the name of a

---

72. Theissen, *Social Setting,* 57.

73. Fee, *First Epistle,* 54.

74. Collins, *First Cor,* 78.

75. Cf. Welborn's phrase, "a struggle for power" (*Politics and Rhetoric,* 7).

76. Tertullian, *On Prescription against Heretics,* 26.

77. Paul regularly uses the Aram. *Cephas* in place of the Gk. **Peter**; cf. 3:22; 9:5; 15:5, Gal 1:18; 2:9.

78. Mitchell, *Rhetoric of Reconciliation,* 84-86.

79. Welborn, *Politics and Rhetoric,* 7.

person whose political interests they served."[80] But whereas Welborn speaks of allegiance to "political parties," Mitchell forcefully argues that the phraseology allows no more than a firm conclusion that the splits or factions had some (unspecified) connection with, or dependence on, some leading figure.[81] She insists that Welborn's argument cannot be supported by lexicographical and grammatical evidence. Most fundamentally of all, Dahl asserts: "there is no reason to think that either Apollos or Cephas was in any way responsible for the use made of their names by people at Corinth."[82] Hays goes further: these are not necessarily "clearly organized parties" but "inchoate dissensions and arguments brewing."[83]

Since Mitchell convincingly argues that the genitives cannot plausibly be construed as genitives of possession, we do not translate "I belong to Paul," "I belong to Apollos" . . . (NJB, NRSV). Equally, "I follow Paul," "I follow Apollos" (NIV) moves too closely to Welborn's hypothesis of political parties centered on persons. Mitchell proposes a *genitive of relationship,* on the analogy of "wife of," "husband of," "child of," which remains broader than the proposals of NIV or of Welborn.[84] Any proposed translation must also take full account of the contrastive particles μέν and δέ. It is impossibly pedestrian to retain the traditional schoolroom rendering "on the one hand . . . on the other hand . . . ," but the particles add color to the competitive mood. Hence, the translation proposed above varies and mixes constructions both for stylistic vigor and to show that no single pattern adequately translates the Greek: "**I, for one**" and "**I, for my part**" do justice to the particles μέν . . . δέ: "**I, for one, am one of Paul's people**"; "**I, for my part, am for Apollos**"; "**I am a Peter person**"; "**As for me, I belong to Christ.**"

Many exegetes argue for a lack of parallel between appeals to **Paul**, **Apollos**, and **Peter** on one side, and to **Christ** on the other. The translation reflects this. Tertullian shrewdly reconstructs a probable situation. "Dissensions," he observes, arose because "one attributes *everything* to Paul, another to Apollos. . . ."[85] By parity of reasoning, those who invoked the name of Christ in all probability thought of themselves as so completely owing "everything" to Christ alone that no room for ministerial support or agency was needed or wanted. This coheres with Paul's warning that some "cheat themselves" (3:18) out of the varied ministerial resources which are theirs: "all are yours, whether Paul, Apollos, or Cephas" (3:21). The general exclusion of the possessive genitive does not apply to "**I belong to Christ.**" This "slogan" is of a different order from the others.

80. Collins, *First Cor,* 79.
81. Mitchell, *Rhetoric of Reconciliation,* 84.
82. Dahl, *Studies in Paul,* 40-61.
83. Hays, *First Corinthians,* 22.
84. Mitchell, *Rhetoric of Reconciliation,* 85.
85. Tertullian, *On Baptism,* 14.

THE FOUR SO-CALLED GROUPS (1:12)

Since Paul does not attack or defend any specific group, as Fee observes, we can only speculate "as to how these four elements comprise a single issue."[86] A consensus has emerged that subsequent references in the epistle to *wisdom* (chs. 1–2), to *boasting* (1:29-31; 3:21; 4:7), and perhaps also to what counts as being *"spiritual"* (3:1-3; chs. 12–14) lie behind some or all of the factors involved. Merklein provides a careful account of the various ways in which a diversity of writers associate an overemphasis on hellenistic wisdom with the Apollos group, even if Apollos himself would not have given support to what was claimed in his name (see esp. exegesis under 16:12, below).[87]

Neyrey uses Mary Douglas's model from social anthropology to draw a contrast between a "conservative" stance of tight control over "the body," which entails a strong appeal to tradition (Peter group?) and uniformity (Paul group), as against a "weaker" bodily control which allows for more liberal social and sexual ethics (chs. 5–7) and greater charismatic freedom in such activities as prophecy and speaking in tongues (chs. 11–14), perhaps here the "Christ" group.[88] Wire has developed this kind of approach in detail, although from a broader base.[89] However, Carter explicitly responds with a more plausible emphasis on competitive individualism at Corinth. Class and patronage, he urges, model this status concern in ways which project *internal* boundaries *within* the church, whereas for Paul the major "boundary" divides the church as an integrated body *externally from* the world. To this extent he accepts Mary Douglas's emphasis on "boundaries."[90]

The Apollos Group

We know from both Acts and 1 Corinthians that Paul visited Corinth after his own first visit: "I planted; Apollos watered . . ." (1 Cor 3:6). Hurd and others defend and elaborate this assumption.[91] Largely on the basis of Acts 18:24, which coheres with the epistles, Apollos is associated with considerable skills of rhetoric and learning in the scriptures. At one stage he had confused Christian baptism with the purification baptism of John, or had appeared to know no theology of Christian baptism (Acts 18:25). Hence many have argued that he unwittingly lent his name to an overemphasis on rhetoric and "wisdom" at Corinth. Hurd points out that in 1 Cor 1:1–4:21, Paul gives most attention to "Apollos" (his name occurs six times), and following Weiss, believes that the group which used his name may well have espoused the "wisdom" theology which Paul calls in question in 1:18–4:21.[92] If in Acts 18:26-28 Apollos spoke "boldly"

86. Fee, *First Epistle,* 49.
87. Merklein, *Der erste Brief 1–4,* 134-48. On "wisdom" see B. A. Pearson (n. 96 below).
88. Neyrey, "Body Language in 1 Cor: The Use of Anthropological Models for Understanding Paul and His Opponents," 129-70.
89. A. C. Wire, *The Corinthian Women Prophets: A Reconstruction through Paul's Rhetoric* (Fortress: Minneapolis, 1990), esp. 40-43 and 182-93.
90. T. L. Carter, "'Big Men' in Corinth," *JSNT* 66 (1997): 45-71.
91. Hurd, *Origins of 1 Corinthians,* 97-99; also Schrage, *Der erste Brief,* 1:143-44; Wolff, *Der erste Brief,* 27; F. F. Bruce, *Men and Movements in the Primitive Church,* 65-70.
92. Weiss, *Der erste Korintherbrief,* xxx-xxxiv. See further L. Hurst, "Apollos, Hebrews and Corinth," *SJT* 38 (1985): 505-13.

and "powerfully," perhaps this stood in contrast to Paul's speaking "in fear and trembling" (1 Cor 2:3). Paul, however, distances both Apollos and himself from Corinthian triumphalism (1 Cor 4:6-13).

Some reconstructions, however, go beyond the evidence of the text. E. L. Titus presses connections between Apollos and Alexandrian traditions of allegorical interpretation to propose that Apollos constitutes Paul's "thorn on the flesh."[93] This view is against the evidence: "Paul betrays no hint of disapproval of Apollos."[94] R. M. Grant locates major differences in a different view of baptism, and earlier Heinrici ascribed Paul's reticence about baptism to a series of initiatory baptisms performed by Apollos.[95] But the allusion to John's baptism precedes the period of his further instruction by Priscilla and Aquila, and Heinrici acknowledges that Paul has no personal difference with Apollos. Birger Pearson traces to Apollos the language about wisdom, mystery, and Spirit in 2:6-16.[96] In the view of Paul, baptism and the Lord's Supper anchor salvation in the death and resurrection of Christ (Rom 6:3-11; 1 Cor 11:23-26), and any failure to place the cross at the center of Christian faith and experience as its sheet-anchor receives unqualified attack in 1 Cor 1:18-31 and 2:1-5. The group which used the name of Apollos may constitute part of Paul's target in these particular verses. As Wire comments, "How much can be read . . . about Apollos depends on the caution or boldness of the modern exegete."[97]

In the end, Barrett and Schrage identify the main point: "Paul never suggests any difference between Apollos and himself, but rather goes out of his way to represent Apollos as his colleague (3:6-9)."[98] Apollos himself was not responsible for the situation. But probably, as Witherington moderately states it, "Apollos had a following among some Corinthians. He had affected some Corinthians in the matter of *sophia*, both in its rhetorical form and as esoteric content. These influences had managed to stir up the pot. . . ."[99] Schrage concludes that while Apollos did not deviate substantially from Paul in theology, there were some at Corinth who found his rhetoric and personal style "especially attractive."[100] Schrage rejects the hypothesis of Heinrici, based on Paul's hesitations about administering baptism in 1:13-17 (see above). Bruce comments that in Paul's view "Apollos and he were 'fellow-workers for God' (1 Cor. 3:9)."[101] "Paul shows no trace of reserve" about Apollos.[102] Hence he encourages Apollos to visit Corinth again at an opportune time (1 Cor 16:12), even if Apollos does not wish to visit the church because of his probable disgust at the manipulation of his name (see below under 16:12).

93. E. L. Titus, "Did Paul Write 1 Cor 13?" *JBR* 27 (1959): 299-302.

94. Bruce, *Men and Movements*, 65.

95. Heinrici, *Das erste Sendschreiben*, 35-36 and 89-90.

96. B. A. Pearson, *The Pneumatikos-Psychikos Terminology in 1 Corinthians*, SBLDS (Missoula: Scholars Press, 1973), and "Hellenistic-Jewish Wisdom Speculation and Paul," in R. L. Wilken (ed.), *Aspects of Wisdom in Judaism and Early Christianity* (Notre Dame: Notre Dame University Press, 1975), 43-66. See further Litfin, *St. Paul's Theology of Proclamation*, 227-33.

97. Wire, *Corinthian Women Prophets*, 209.

98. Barrett, *First Epistle*, 43; cf. Schrage, *Der erste Brief*, 1:143-44; also Bruce, *Men and Movements*, 65; Fee, *First Epistle*, 56-57; Collins, *First Epistle*, 73.

99. Witherington, *Conflict and Community*, 96.

100. Schrage, *Der erste Brief*, 1:144.

101. Bruce, *Men and Movements*, 65.

102. Bruce, *Paul: Apostle of the Free Spirit* (Carlisle: Paternoster, 1977), 257.

Andrew Clarke convincingly argues that *secular* concepts of leadership were imported into the church at Corinth (see further below).[103] Clarke points out that "personality-centred politics within the church were characteristic of the surrounding Graeco-Roman society. . . . A secular understanding of the underlying distinctions in rank and status between those in the church and the 'apostolic' figures of Paul, Cephas, Apollos, demanded that it be politically advantageous to be associated with one or other of these figures."[104] Plutarch (c. AD 50-120) observes that just as young ivy twines itself around a strong tree to gain height, so an obscure person will seek a connection with a person of reputation to be "under the shelter of his power and grow great with him . . . in the affairs of State" (Plutarch, *Moralia* 805 E-F).

The implications of all this for the church's theology and unity today remain transparent. People may be motivated by the same interests as they turn well-known figures in preaching, in evangelism, or in theology into slogans which perceive them as the monopoly of some sub-group. Gaston Deluz reflects, might such figures as Thomas Aquinas, Luther, Calvin, or Wesley feel grave disquiet at the notion of a later age witnessing cries of "I am a Thomist"; "I am a Lutheran"; "I am a Calvinist"; or "I am a Wesleyan"?[105] However, this analogy would suggest too much emphasis on theological as well as personal differences. I Corinthians 1–4 reflects, as Clarke rightly calls them, "personality cults." The deep danger for the church then and now has been to make too much of *specific leaders and specific styles of leadership*. The lesson for leaders is that too high a personal profile, which substitutes too much personal history and personal style for gospel content, can sidetrack "followers" into "taking sides," even if this was far from the original intention.[106] On the specific nature and character of the theological stance of Apollos himself, Conzelmann refuses to speculate, while Wolff points out that, whatever the problem was, 1 Corinthians does not reflect the problem of "Judaism" or Jewish Christianity.[107]

The Paul Group

If Paul consciously renounces a style that focuses attention on himself (1:18–2:5), in what might the Paul group consist? The long tradition of modern scholarship since F. C. Baur associates this group with convictions about radical emancipation from the law (cf. 6:12), perhaps claiming Paul's own authority for a quasi-libertarian position. But is the "Paul" group a specific group or a rhetorical construct? Collins writes, "There is really no indication in the letter that there were three or four distinct factions."[108] Yet earlier modern scholarship reacted against F. C. Baur's polarization into "Pauline" and "Judaizing" parties. Thus H. A. W. Meyer writes, "There can be no

---

103. Clarke, *Secular and Christian Leadership in Corinth*, 89-105, esp. 90-95.

104. Ibid., 93.

105. Deluz, *Companion to 1 Corinthians*, 9: Héring draws a similar parallel.

106. Two powerful studies on this theme already cited are Karl Barth, *Resurrection*, 17-19; and Crafton, *Agency*, 53-102.

107. Conzelmann, *1 Cor*, 33; and Wolff, *Der erste Brief*, 28.

108. Collins, *First Cor*, 73.

reduction of the parties below *four.*"[109] Robertson and Plummer represent this "classical" approach. The Paul group reflects Paul's own preaching and teaching; the Apollos group, "hellenistic intellectualism"; the Cephas group, "the Gospel of the circumcision"; and the "Christ" group, perhaps "zealots for the law, hostile to the Apostleship of St. Paul."[110]

Nevertheless, shortly after the turn of the century a new mood entered the scene with the work of Wilhelm Lütgert (1908) and Johannes Weiss (1910), followed later by Reitzenstein, Wendland, Schmithals, Wilckens, and (with modifications) Conzelmann.[111] These perceived Paul and the Pauline group as standing in contrast to a gnostic or elitist style of "spiritual enthusiasm." The debate introduced at the beginning of this Note between J. H. Neyrey and T. L. Carter represents a more recent version of this contrast based on models drawn from social anthropology (see above, and below on the "Christ" group). Wendland pressed this thesis.[112] A. Schlatter attempted to expound a similar contrast in terms of prophetic outlooks drawn from more Jewish traditions. For Schlatter, Paul is strongly influenced by OT traditions.[113]

Neither Baur's theories (Paul versus Judaism) nor Lütgert's (Paul versus quasi-gnostic "spiritualism") reckon sufficiently with the demonstrable fact that Paul does not side with his own group against the others. They cannot overcome the arguments that we have insufficient evidence from this epistle or from other epistles to describe these "splits" as primarily doctrinal.[114] Yet, as Conzelmann urges, Paul expends such energy and concern on issues concerning pneumatic "enthusiasm" that we must not overreact, as if *no* theological emphasis whatever lay behind the protests of those who appealed to Paul as the one who first brought them to Christ.[115]

Two key factors may assist us in reconstructing the outlook of the Paul group. (i) As most agree, they almost certainly had as their nucleus Paul's first converts at Corinth. Presumably, as Apollos and other leaders visited Corinth, and as the church grew and expanded, the ethos of the whole began to shift. Murphy O'Connor convincingly argues that we may well imagine a house congregation of between thirty and forty persons, on the basis of archaeological evidence.[116] Expansion probably necessitated more than one group, each of which might well come to develop some distinctive social, liturgical, or group ethos. Eventually this might well generate a corresponding group loyalty.

If such a scenario carries weight, as surely it must, there would be affinities

---

109. Meyer, *First Epistle,* 1:26 (his italics).

110. Robertson and Plummer, *First Epistle,* 12.

111. Lütgert, *Freiheitspredigt und Schwärmgeister in Korinth;* Weiss, *Der erste Korintherbrief,* xxx-xxxix, 15-16, 73-75, 187-90; Wendland, *Die Brief an die Korinther,* 18-19; Schmithals, *Gnosticism in Corinth,* 199-206; cf. 119-24; Ulrich Wilckens, *Weisheit und Torheit* (Tübingen: Mohr, 1959), 5-41; cf. Conzelmann, *1 Cor,* "Excursus: The 'Parties,'" 33-34.

112. Wendland contrasts *Paul's* respect for order and tradition with the views of "pneumatics" who claim "direct revelation from Christ" (*Der Brief an die Korinther,* 19).

113. A. Schlatter, *Die Korinthische Theologie* (Gütersloh: Bertelsmann, 1914). Schlatter in effect attempts to understand Paul in isolation from hellenism.

114. Cf. Munck, *Paul and the Salvation of Mankind;* Dahl, *Studies in Paul,* 40-61; Welborn, *Politics and Rhetoric,* 1-42; and others cited above.

115. Conzelmann, *1 Corinthians,* 34.

116. Murphy-O'Connor, *St. Paul's Corinth,* 155-56; cf. 153-61.

between the Paul group and those in churches then and now who perceive themselves as maintaining faithfully the old, duly authorized, ways, in contrast to newer trends which emerge with more recent church members or visiting leaders. It also coheres with the conclusions of many social psychologists about the relation between the size of a group and intimacy and group loyalty. Finally, if this group appealed to authoritative rulings from the one who was the "planter" (3:6, 10) and spiritual "father" (4:15-17) of the whole church, other groups might plausibly seek some authority focus also. "Paul's people" may have been "the senior group"; "Peter's people" may have appealed to "the senior apostle"! At the same time we must also allow for an element of caricature in Paul's rhetorical description of the splits.[117]

(ii). Part of the "politics" surrounding Paul may have concerned his anxiety to discourage patronage on the part of "the influential" by being willing to accept financial support from Corinth (9:1-27). In 9:1-27 Paul feels the need to labor as his own free offering to God but also to avoid dependency on some patron who might manipulate the situation to exercise power. If Welborn is right about "power interests" at Corinth, this explains why Paul accepts such support at Philippi but not at Corinth. *Patronage* constitutes an important feature of Graeco-Roman social life.[118] It would be perceived, on one side, as a rebuff that Paul insisted on independence rather than allow himself to become a client. Hock goes further. He writes: "To those of wealth and power the appearance (σχῆμα) of the artisan was that befitting a slave (δουλοπρεπές). It is no wonder, then, that Paul thought it necessary to defend his practice of supporting himself (1 Cor. 9:1-27). . . . This lowly apostle seemed to have enslaved himself with the plying of a trade (cf. 9:19)."[119] Hock paints a vivid picture of the menial and uncomfortable nature of Paul's occupation in a small booth in the sweltering heat.[120] By contrast, "respected" rhetoricians and teachers, who were worthy to be treated as such, regularly gained the status and lifestyle of "middle-class professionals" by accepting patronage and support. To some at Corinth Paul's refusal to be "beholden" to anyone smacked of obstinate pride, and demeaned both him and them.[121]

Marshall takes this still further. To reject patronage, he argues, would be construed as a rejection of *friendship*. Paul did not want to accept a gift. This could only seem like gross ungraciousness if not sheer rudeness, and certainly as a slap in the face.[122] Finally, from the other side, as it were, Chow exposes the enormous power and influence wielded by patrons. For example, in the case of legal disputes in the Graeco-Roman world "improper influence could also be exercised in the administration of justice."[123] Hence the people who chose to initiate litigation were usually peo-

117. Collins, *First Cor,* 73, strongly emphasizes the features of rhetorical caricature, questioning whether there were indeed four or three groups rather than general discord.

118. Theissen, *Social Setting,* 1982, esp. 54-68 (originally *NTS* 21 [1975]: 192-221); Hock, *The Social Context of Paul's Ministry,* 26-68; Marshall, *Enmity in Corinth,* 1-35, 133-258; Meeks, *The First Urban Christians,* 117-19; Chow, *Patronage and Power;* and Clarke, *Secular and Christian Leadership in Corinth,* 89-107.

119. Hock, *Social Context,* 60.

120. Ibid., 26-49.

121. See the arguments especially of Meeks, Clarke, and others in sources cited.

122. Marshall, *Enmity in Corinth,* 1-34, 133-64, 165-258.

123. Chow, *Patronage and Power,* 129.

ple with the right friends or contacts. Perhaps the man who was guilty of incest was an especially influential patron: some within the church were "proud of him" (5:2, 6).[124] This also holds the key to issues about going to law in 6:1-11 (see below).[125]

If these scenarios carry weight, two characteristics might mark the Paul group (a) In socio-ethical-political terms they may have resisted (like Paul) the potential inequalities of allowing patronage, with its accompanying implicit returns of favors. This should not seep into church life. Paul cannot be seen to side with them because this will merely deepen the splits. (b) At a much deeper level, the Pauline lifestyle witnesses to identification with the crucified Christ and *a theology of the cross.* Paul's practical response is therefore to re-proclaim the centrality of the cross as "ground and criterion of the community and apostle" (1:18-25).[126] Fitzgerald may also be right to stress Paul's redefinition of "wisdom" in terms of a catalogue of hardships as the lot of an authentic "sage."[127] Engberg-Pedersen rightly modifies certain aspects of Theissen's approach on the ground that Theissen pins too much on social analysis alone, underplaying certain theological factors.[128]

The Peter Group

We cannot be certain whether Peter actually visited Corinth. Barrett argues for this possibility perhaps more strongly than any, although Donfried and Fitzmyer adopt a similar approach.[129] Paul regularly (but not invariably) uses the Aramaic "Cephas" for Peter, and mentions him in 1:12; 3:22; 9:5; and 15:5; but not in 2 Corinthians. Barrett surveys each of these references. In 1:12 he holds that the genitive case of the names is likely to signify agencies of conversion, since vv. 13-17 go on to allude to the administration of baptism in a way which suggests the baptism of converts by these named persons. Thus: "Converts tended to align themselves with the evangelist under whom they had been won to the faith."[130] Similarly, Barrett urges, the list of persons in 3:22 most probably represents teachers from whom the community could directly benefit. 9:5, he claims, most naturally alludes to Peter's receiving board and lodging from the community. He concedes that 15:5 was already part of a pre-Pauline tradition, but that it may hint at names with which the Corinthians were familiar. 9:5, Barrett sug-

---

124. Ibid., 130.

125. See B. W. Winter, *Seek the Welfare of the City: Christians as Benefactors and Citizens* (Grand Rapids: Eerdmans and Carlisle: Paternoster, 1994), 105-22.

126. Schrage, *Der erste Brief,* 1:165 (the phrase itself comes from J. Moltmann, *The Crucified God* [Eng. trans., London: SCM, 1974]).

127. John T. Fitzgerald, *Cracks in an Earthen Vessel: An Examination of the Catalogues of Hardships in the Corinthian Correspondence,* SBLDS 99 (Atlanta: Scholars Press, 1988), 117-32.

128. T. Engberg-Pedersen, "The Gospel and Social Practice according to 1 Corinthians," 557-84. Cf. also the argument that Philippi was the only church from which Paul chose to accept financial support in G. Lüdemann, *Paul, Apostle to the Gentiles: Studies in Chronology* (Eng. trans., London: SCM, 1984), 104.

129. Barrett, "Cephas and Corinth," in *Essays on Paul,* 28-39 (originally in *Abraham unser Vater,* Leiden: Brill, 1963); and K. P. Donfried and J. Fitzmyer in R. Brown, K. P. Donfried, and J. Reumann (eds.), *Peter in the NT* (London: Chapman, 1974 and Minneapolis: Augsburg, 1973), 32-36.

130. Barrett, "Cephas and Corinth," 29.

gests, even implies that Peter had visited Corinth with his wife, both of whom enjoyed their hospitality.

Barrett also appeals to some earlier, more speculative arguments put forward by Manson. Manson asks whether the allusion to someone's building on Paul's "foundation" (3:10-11) has any further implicit reference to Peter as the "rock" in the tradition reflected in Matt 16:18.[131] Manson also speculates about whether different "advice" about marriage and "spiritual" marriages (ch. 7), the legitimacy of certain foods (chs. 8–10), the Lord's Supper (11:17-34), and speaking in tongues (ch. 14) may have reflected different emphases or lines of approach on the part of Peter and of Paul respectively. Barrett is more reluctant than Manson to speak of "parties," but he concludes, "The evidence of 1 Corinthians shows the certain influence, and parallel presence, of Peter in Corinth."[132] His difficulty and embarrassment stemmed from "less scrupulous ecclesiastical politicians" who found Peter "useful as a figure head. He could not simply repudiate Peter; yet Peter, in the hands of those who made use of him, was on the way to ruining Paul's work at Corinth."[133]

A number of speculations tend to go further beyond hard evidence. Dahl, for example, suggests that the very decision to send a delegation with questions to Paul, rather than to Peter (or perhaps Apollos), itself sowed seeds of dissension at Corinth.[134] Dockx argues partly on the basis of Jerome's tradition that Peter arrived in Rome as early as the second year of Claudius (c. AD 42-43) for a chronology of Peter's career up to his martyrdom in 67, which allows for a visit to Corinth.[135] Fitch partly follows Manson in seeing a parallel between Paul, Peter, and a more Judaizing "Christ party" and the correlative groups represented at the Council of Jerusalem in Acts 15 (cf. Peter's "vacillation" to which Paul alludes in Gal 2:11-14).[136] Probably, Fitch speculates, the Peter group tried to follow Peter's "middle way."[137]

The "Christ" Group

No less than six possible explanations for the phrase have been suggested. We may classify them as follows before we evaluate them, although some of the groundwork for evaluation has already been covered in our comments above.

A "Judaizing" Group? From Baur to Later Formulations

Baur's well-known work "Die Christuspartei in der Korinthischen Gemeinde" (1831) summarizes its thesis in the remainder of its lengthy title, ". . . der Gegensatz des

131. T. W. Manson, *Studies in the Gospels and Epistles* (Manchester: Manchester University Press, 1962), 190-209.
132. Barrett, "Cephas and Corinth," 37.
133. Ibid., 37-38.
134. Dahl, *Studies in Paul*, 51.
135. S. Dockx, "Essai de chronologie pétrinienne," *RSR* 62 (1974): 221-41.
136. W. O. Fitch, "Paul, Apollos, Cephas, Christ," *Theology* 74 (1971): 18-24.
137. This view of a "middle way" on behalf of the Peter group might question Theissen's placing of Paul as a "middle way" between the concern for love for the weak and concern for "order," i.e., so-called "love-patriarchalism."

petrinischen und paulinischen Christentums in der ältesten Kirche, der Apostel Petrus in Rom."[138] Partly drawing on the Pseudo-Clementine *Homilies* of the second century (esp. *Homilies,* 17:13ff.), Baur begins with the argument that to be a true "apostle" entails having been a disciple of the earthly Jesus. But Paul was not an apostle in this sense, like the Twelve. The debate about Paul's claim to be an apostle therefore distinguishes the "Christ party," who held that true apostles had been disciples of Jesus of Nazareth, and the "Paul party," who accepted Paul's anti-Judaizing theology of emancipation from the law. In 2 Corinthians 3 Paul's opponents emerge, as they do in Galatians, as Judaizers. In Corinth, Baur argues, the focus of controversy moved from circumcision to apostolic authority, but supposedly the issue remains all of one piece. The allusions in 1 Cor 1:12 to "Christ's people" and "Peter's people" are the cries of Jewish or Judaizing Christians, while the "Paul party" is that of Gentile Christians.

We have seen that the attempt to distinguish "parties" on grounds of different theologies fails for various reasons.[139] Doctrine is not at issue (see above on Munck, Dahl, et al.); sociopolitical aspects of personality cults and social attitudes play a firm and substantial part (see above on Welborn, Mitchell, and Clarke). Furthermore, Weiss, Wendland, and others explain the "Christ party" (if such existed) in quite different terms (see below). However, it would be a mistake to dismiss Baur's work of 1831 as motivated by his interest in Hegel's view of history, as many writers claim. Hegel began to influence Baur some two years later, after initial reservations. Work in 1833 reflects a more positive interest in Hegel, and by 1838 Baur postulates a Jewish-Christian thesis, a Pauline antithesis, and a synthesis attempted in the mediating narrative theology of Acts, together with the Pastorals and 2 Peter. Finally, Baur produced a more systematic construct in his *Paulus* of 1845.[140] His argument of 1831 simply lacks adequate exegetical support and reads back too much from second-century material. His later engagament with Hegel seemed to confirm rather than to initiate his theories on 1 Cor 1:12, and historical anachronism should be avoided.

In spite of the difficulties of Baur's hypothesis, however, in 1869 Meyer refers to the view that the "Christ party" was "Jewish" or the one "commonly held."[141] But he also warns of the precarious status inferences about 1:12 from 2 Corinthians 10–13.[142] Even so, Robertson and Plummer call the "Christ party" "probably more advanced Judaizers than those who used the name of Kephas . . . 'zealots for the law.'"[143] Heinrici identifies the "Christ party" with Jewish-Christian extremists.[144] Weizsäcker specifies these as emissaries from James; while in Bacon's view they are those who "like Christ" accepted the constraints and teaching of the law.[145] Godet ascribes their identity to those who followed a former Pharisaic group and who "in virtue of their learning and high social position regarded themselves as infinitely supe-

138. Baur, "Die Christuspartei in der korinthischen Gemeinde," 61-206.

139. See, further, J. L. Sumney, *Identifying Paul's Opponents: The Question of Method in 2 Corinthians,* JSNTSS 40 (Sheffield: Sheffield Academic Press, 1990), 15-22; cf. 23-48.

140. Baur, *Paul the Apostle of Jesus Christ.*

141. Meyer, *First Epistle,* 1:30.

142. Ibid., 31.

143. Robertson and Plummer, *First Epistle,* 12.

144. Heinrici, *Das erste Sendschreiben,* 44-50 and 86-89.

145. B. W. Bacon, "The Christ-party in Corinth," *The Expositor* 8 (1914): 399-415; and Carl von Weizsäcker, *The Apostolic Age of the Christian Church* (2 vols., Eng. trans., London: Williams & Norgate, 1894-95).

rior to the apostles."[146] The more one explores the history of interpretation, the more the speculative and arbitrary nature of these hypotheses becomes apparent. Little hard evidence supports this approach.

"Ultraspiritual Pneumatics"? From Lütgert to Neyrey

A quite different and far more plausible view was formulated by Lütgert (see above) and advocated by Weiss, Wendland, Moffatt, and E.-B. Allo.[147] Wendland, Moffatt, and Allo argue that the "Christ party" were spiritualistic gnostics who recognized no authority and no source of revelation other than the glorified spiritual Christ. Moffatt calls them "ultra-spiritual devotees or high-flying gnostics who made a mystical Christ, no human leader, the centre of religion."[148] Wendland calls them "pneumatics who invoke for themselves special direct revelations from Christ, as against other groups."[149] Allo devotes a long appendix to the issue, and concludes that amid the perplexity of multiple interpretations, the notion of a group who included "spirituals," "antinomians," "libertines," and "gnostics" who had recently come from paganism and looked to no "human" teaching, offers the least difficult conjecture.[150] If Godet is correct, stripped of its technicalities this kind of view was earlier formulated by Schenkel in 1838.[151] In our introduction to the problem of these verses we also cited Neyrey's use of Mary Douglas's models in anthropology to explain a "grid" of greater or lesser emphasis respectively on "order" and "freedom" in the Spirit (see above).

In much broader terms, Manson, Bruce, and Barrett view this as a plausible explanation of the phrase.[152] Bruce also concludes that we reach it by "a process of elimination" of less probable hypotheses.[153] Exegesis of other parts of the epistle suggest that this has much to commend it. It coheres with "all are yours, whether Paul or Apollos or Cephas" (i.e., human leaders are a gift and resource; see under 3:21-22). Yet Paul also adds, "let no one boast in human leaders" (3:21). Weiss makes much of the influence of such a group at Corinth. Yet specifically on 1:12 he thinks the following explanation even more likely.

Interjection from a Copyist?

Weiss, followed by Héring, ascribes the phrase Ἐγὼ δὲ Χριστοῦ to an interjection from an indignant scribal copyist, or perhaps even to Sosthenes.[154] Perhaps the slogans "I

146. Godet, *First Epistle,* 1:75.
147. Lütgert, *Freiheitspredigt und Schwämgeister in Korinth,* has been discussed above; Wendland, *An die Korinther,* 18-19; Moffatt, *First Epistle,* 10; Allo, *Première Épitre,* 80-87.
148. Moffatt, *First Epistle,* 10.
149. Wendland, *An die Korinther,* 19.
150. Allo, *Première Épitre,* 86; cf. 80-87.
151. Godet, *First Epistle,* 1:70.
152. Barrett, *First Epistle,* 44-45; Manson, *Studies in the Gospels and Epistles,* 190-209. Their approach is not to be identified with the more specific theories of Neyrey and Wire (outlined above).
153. Bruce, *1 and 2 Corinthians,* 33.
154. Weiss, *Der erste Korintherbrief,* 15-16; cf. xxx-xxxix; Héring, *First Epistle,* 6.

am for Peter," "I follow Apollos," provoked the indignant marginal gloss "I am for Christ," or "I am Christ's," and was interpreted by the next copyist as an unintended omission to be incorporated into the text. This kind of explanation is sometimes put forward for τὸ μὴ ὑπὲρ ἃ γέγραπται in 4:6 (see below). But it cannot be more than conjecture. There is no textual evidence for the hypothesis.

Misreading for Crispus?

Perdelwitz proposed the equally speculative theory that the Greek Χριστοῦ originally read Κρίσπου.[155] A fourth group cried "I am for Crispus," who is mentioned in 1:14 as one of the three (alongside Gaius and the household of Stephanas, 1:15) whom Paul himself, unusually, personally baptized. Acts 18:7-8 refers to Crispus as a "ruler of the synagogue" who came to faith through Paul's ministry, and may have been succeeded in that office by Sosthenes (18:17). The Greek Uncials would make confusion between ΧΡΙΣΤΟΥ and ΚΡΙΣΠΟΥ. But Schrage reminds us that in addition to the theory's being mere conjecture, it would be difficult to explain why *I Clement* 47:3 alludes only to the *three* groups of Peter, Apollos, and Paul if the name Crispus stood on an equal footing as a fourth personal name, still within the first century.[156]

Pauline Rhetoric: Hypotheses and Declaration?

Chrysostom not only believed that the allusions to Paul, Apollos, and Peter were "masks" for groupings behind other names, but also that Paul added "I am Christ's," "of himself, wishing to make the accusation more grievous . . . although they were not using the Name themselves."[157] Tertullian does not comment explicitly on the verse, but leaves a clear implication that he understands it similarly: the respective groups, he observes, "attribute *everything* to Paul or to Apollos"; Paul attributes everything to Christ, as his subsequent allusions to the cross and to baptism (1:13-17) clearly indicate.[158] In modern scholarship Lake, Hurd, and, in broad terms, Mitchell, adopt this view.[159] Lake understands Paul's words in a contrastive sense: "as for me, I am Christ's." Hurd writes: "The whole thrust of Paul's argument . . . is that the separate designations 'Paul,' 'Apollos' and 'Cephas' ought to be replaced by the single affirmation 'I am of Christ.' The existence of a Christ-party at Corinth is extremely doubtful."[160] The greatest difficulty for this proposal is the implied dislocation of the same syntax. This raises a problem, for Fee rightly notes the symmetry of the constructions μέν, δέ, δέ, δέ, "with

155. R. Perdelwitz, *Die sogenannte Christuspartei in Korinth*, 1911 (cited by Allo, *Première Épitre*, 86, and Héring, *First Epistle*, 4; and by Hurd, *Origins of 1 Corinthians*, 103.
156. Schrage, *Der erste Brief*, 1:147.
157. Chrysostom, *1 Cor. Hom.*, 3:5.
158. Tertullian, *On Baptism*, 14.
159. Mitchell, *Rhetoric of Reconciliation*, 83, extended n. 101; K. Lake, *Earlier Epistles of Paul: Their Motive and Origin* (London: Rivingtons, 1911), 127.
160. Hurd, *Origins of 1 Corinthians*, 105; cf. 101-7 (see further 75-94 and 126-42 on issues about the "Paul" group).

no signal that there is a break."[161] Héring also sees the difficulty.[162] Although Schrage does not consider it decisive, Collins declares, "Were this the case one might have expected Paul to have employed a strongly adversative 'but' *(alla)*, but he does not do so."[163]

A Pauline Rhetoric of Irony?

Schrage agrees that it is Paul who uses the phrase "I am of Christ," but offers a variant of (e). Paul gives it an ironic twist: the slogans could be extended *ad absurdum* as if to point out that the exclusive claims to monopolize "Paul" or "Apollos" in a competitive way reaches the same degree of absurdity as applying a slogan of this kind to "Christ," as if Christ, too, could become the exclusive property of some specific group. The strength of this suggestion is that it leads most naturally to v. 13: **is Christ apportioned out?**[164] To postulate a "Christ group" would thus constitute an ironic touch added by Paul himself, countered by "You (all) are Christ's" in 3:23, as Mitchell emphasizes.

Fee may well be right in concluding that we have insufficient evidence to be certain of any clear conclusion. Nevertheless, of the six proposals outlined, (b) and (f) have most to commend them. However, negatively, the syntactical difficulty of (f), underlined by Héring and Fee, should not be brushed aside. Moreover, (b) coheres with a distinct trend throughout the epistle which suggests that some (not all) at Corinth chose to be "independent" of other ministries or churches, presumably on the ground that their Spirit-filled status gave them a hot-line to Christ. It would be not at all surprising if this element had faded out by the date (c. AD 96) at which *1 Clement* takes three groups relating to human personalities or traditions. As Bruce observes, probably this is the least difficult interpretation of 1:12.

This coheres well with the main arguments of the epistle. The relation between the various hypotheses about 1:12 and relevant allusions to later passages in the epistle is very well explored in detail by Merklein.[165] Ortkemper reminds us, "Paul himself gives us no closer information about the profile or programme of the groups of the time. This appears, on the contrary, not to interest him. Concrete particulars of the Corinthian groups emerge in Paul's arguments that follow, and are not expressed here."[166] Somehow a balance must be kept between Conzelmann's insight concerning the energy which Paul spends on addressing issues of "Spirit" and "spirituality," and Collins's warning about a possible rhetorical caricature of "groups" to make a more general point about "splits" which gathers around the manipulated names of leaders (Clarke) to facilitate a "power-struggle" (Welborn). All this forms the background to 1:18-25.

---

161. Fee, *First Epistle,* 58-59, n. 54.

162. Héring, *First Epistle,* 4; and Schrage, *Der erste Brief,* 1:146-48.

163. Schrage, *Der erste Brief,* 1:146-48, Collins, *First Cor,* 72.

164. Schrage, *Das erste Brief,* 148.

165. H. Merklein, "Die Parteien in Korinth," in *Der erste Brief 1–4,* 134-52. Merklein also details further literature up to 1992. Merklein himself emphasizes the disruptive impact of "wisdom" claims and of spiritual "enthusiasm."

166. F. J. Ortkemper, *1 Korintherbrief* (Stuttgart: Katholisches Bibelwerk, 1993), 23.

3. Further Explanations: The Splits Are Incompatible with Christology and the Centrality of the Cross (1:13-17)

A separate introduction to 1:13-17 is unnecessary since we introduced 1:10-17 at the beginning of the previous section. "Paul is aghast at what he has learned from Chloe's people; and often in such moments he turns to rhetoric, designed to help his readers/listeners to see the total absurdity of their own position."[167] Thus he formulates a series of rhetorical questions and statements which constitute a *reductio ad absurdum*. Could it be that **Christ** has been **apportioned out** in such a way as to give each "group" their very own Christ? Can there be any other basis for a common salvation except **a Christ crucified**? How can each, then, aspire to be a "church" independently of the others? Chrysostom writes, "Even those who said they were of Christ were at fault because they were implicitly denying this to others and making Christ the head of a faction rather than the head of the whole."[168]

We have divided the bibliographies on 1:13-17 into two: (a) On Wisdom, Preaching, and the Cross; (b) On Baptism and Its Possible Relation to Households. However, Paul's allusion to baptism in these verses occurs in passing, and does not provide "a theology of baptism." This is not Paul's aim here. A Helpful survey of the relevant passages for this can be found in R. Schnackenburg (cited in bibliography [b] below).

Wisdom, Rhetoric, Preaching, and the Cross

Bailey, K. E., "Recovering the Poetic Structure of 1 Cor. 1:17–2:2," *NovT* 17 (1975): 265-96.

Barbour, R. S., "Wisdom and the Cross in 1 Corinthians 1 and 2," in C. Andresen and G. Klein (eds.), *Theologia Crucis — Signum Crucis: Festschrift für E. Dinkler* (Tübingen: Mohr, 1979), 57-71.

Barrett, C. K., *Church, Ministry and Sacraments in the NT* (Exeter: Paternoster and Grand Rapids: Eerdmans, 1995).

Beaudean, J. W., Jr., *Paul's Theology of Preaching* (Macon, Ga.: Mercer University Press, 1988), 87-118.

Brown, A. R., *The Cross and Human Transformation: Paul's Apocalyptic Word in 1 Corinthians* (Minneapolis: Fortress, 1995), esp. 13-64 and 70-75.

Davis, James A., *Wisdom and Spirit: An Investigation of 1 Cor. 1:18–3:20 against the Background of Jewish Sapiential Traditions in the Greco-Roman Period* (Lanham, Md.: University Press of America, 1984).

Dunn, J. D. G., *The Theology of Paul the Apostle* (Edinburgh: T. & T. Clark, 1998), 163-69.

Goulder, M. D., "Sophia in 1 Corinthians," *NTS* 39 (1991): 516-34.

Grayston, K., *Dying We Live* (Oxford: Oxford University Press, 1990), 16-29.

Horsley, R. A., "Wisdom of Word and Words of Wisdom in Corinth," *CBQ* 39 (1977): 224-39.

---

167. Fee, *First Epistle*, 59-60.
168. Chrysostom, *1 Cor. Hom.*, 3:5.

Fitzmyer, J. A., *According to Paul* (New York: Paulist Press, 1993), 106-10.

————, "The Gospel in the Theology of Paul," *Int* 33 (1979): 339-50.

Lampe, Peter, "Theological Wisdom and the 'Word about the Cross': The Rhetorical Scheme in 1 Corinthians 1–4," *Int* 44 (1990): 117-31.

Litfin, Duane, *St Paul's Theology of Proclamation: 1 Cor. 1–4 and Greco-Roman Rhetoric,* SNTSMS 79 (Cambridge: Cambridge University Press, 1994), 109-35 and 174-212.

Ortkemper, Franz-Josef, *Das Kreuz in der Verkündigung des Apostels Paulus* (Stuttgart: Verlag Katholisches Bibelwerk, 1967), 43-46.

Penna, R., *Paul the Apostle: Wisdom and Folly of the Cross* (Eng. trans., Collegeville: Glazier/Liturgical Press, 1996), 45-60 and 135-64.

Pesce, M., "'Christ did not send me to baptize but to evangelize' (1 Cor 1:17a)," in L. de Lorenzi (ed.), *Paul de Tarse. Apôtre du notre temps* (Rome: Abbaye de S. Paul, 1979), 339-63.

Pickett, R., *The Cross in Corinth: The Social Significance of the Death of Jesus,* JSNTSS 143 (Sheffield: Sheffield Academic Press, 1997).

Plank, Karl A., *Paul and the Irony of Affliction,* SBL Semeia Series (Atlanta: Scholars Press, 1987), 16-26.

Pogoloff, Stephen M., *Logos and Sophia: The Rhetorical Situation of 1 Corinthians,* SBLDS 134 (Atlanta: Scholars Press, 1992).

Schnabel, E. J., *Law and Wisdom from Ben Sira to Paul,* WUNT 2:16 (Tübingen: Mohr, 1985).

Stowers, S. K., "Social Status, Public Speaking and Private Teaching: The Circumstances of Paul's Preaching Activity," *NovT* 26 (1984): 59-82.

Stuhlmacher, P., *Das paulinische Evangelium* (Göttingen: Vandenhoeck & Ruprecht, 1968).

Wedderburn, A. J. M., "ἐν σοφίᾳ τοῦ θεοῦ — 1 Kor. 1:21," *ZNW* 63 (1972): 132-34.

Wilckens, Ulrich, *Weisheit und Torheit. Eine exegetisch-religionsgechichtliche Untersuchung zu 1.Kor 1 and 2,* BHT 26 (Tübingen: Mohr, 1959), esp. 5-53.

Winter, Bruce W., *Philo and Paul among the Sophists,* SNTSMS 96 (Cambridge: Cambridge University Press, 1997), 182-94 and throughout.

Baptism and Its Possible Relation to "Households"

Aland, K., *Did the Early Church Baptize Infants?* (Eng. trans., London: SCM, 1963), 87-94.

Banks, R., *Paul's Idea of Community* (rev. ed., Peabody, Mass.: Hendrickson, 1994), 26-36, 77-85, 180-88.

Barth, M., *Die Taufe ein Sacrament?* (Zürich: Evangelischer Verlag, 1951).

Beasley-Murray, G. R., *Baptism in the NT* (London New York: Macmillan, 1962).

Carlson, R. P., "The Role of Baptism in Paul's Thought," *Int* 47 (1993): 255-66.

Cullmann, O., *Baptism in the NT* (London: SCM, 1950), 9-22.

Delling, G., *Die Zueignung des Heils in der Taufe: eine Untersuchung zum neutestamentlichen "taufen auf den Namen"* (Berlin: Evangelische Verlagsanstalt, 1961).

Dunn, J. D. G., *Baptism in the Holy Spirit* (London: SCM, 1970), 116-20.

————, *The Theology of Paul the Apostle* (Edinburgh: T. & T. Clark, 1998), 442-59, esp. 449-50.

Fascher, E., "Zur Taufe des Paulus," *TLZ* 80 (1955): 643-48.

Flemington, W. F., *The NT Doctrine of Baptism* (London: SPCK, 1948), 52-84.

Jeremias, J., *Infant Baptism in the First Four Centuries* (Eng. trans., London: SCM, 1960), 19-24 ("the *oikos* formula") and 25-48.

————, *The Origins of Infant Baptism* (Eng. trans., London: SCM, 1963), esp. ("The Baptism of 'Houses' ") 12-32.

Leenhardt, F., *Le Baptême chrétien: son Origine, sa signification* (Neuchâtel: Delachaux et Niestlé, 1946).

Schnackenburg, R., *Baptism in the Thought of St. Paul: A Study in Pauline Theology* (Oxford: Blackwell and New York: Herder, 1964).

Strobel, A., "Der Begriff des 'Hauses' im griechischen und römischen Privatrecht," *ZNW* 56 (1965): 91-100.

Voss, G., "Glaube und Taufe in den Paulusbriefen," *Una Sancta* 25 (1970): 371-78.

Wedderburn, A. J. M., *Baptism and Resurrection,* WUNT 1:44 (Tübingen: Mohr, 1987).

13 μεμέρισται occurs without a preceding μή in the overwhelming majority of early MSS (א A, B, C, D, G, 33, the Vulgate, syr harc, and Tertullian. But the very early p⁴⁶, Syriac (Paul and Peshitta), and Coptic (Boh) include μή before the verb. Whereas the 3d ed. UBS *Greek New Testament* evaluated the majority reading as "B" ("some degree of doubt"), the 4th ed. and Metzger now grade it as "A" ("virtually certain").[169] The main ground for virtual certainty is the probability that μή was inserted to underline the function of the sentence as a *question* anticipating a negative answer, rather than, as some interpret it, as a *statement* expressing what is entailed by the slogans of v. 12. Further, it may well represent a scribal anticipation of the second μή before **Paul**. Collins holds that the intrusion of μή rests on a misperception of the question as a statement: "Christ is not divided!"[170]

Bengel comments that Christ is not to be cut up to be divided out among different groups: *"neque corporis unitas scindenda";* "the unity of his body is not to be cut into pieces."[171] Clement similarly speaks of "tearing asunder (διαστῶμεν) the members of Christ (*1 Clement* 46:7), while Chrysostom paraphrases: "You have cut in pieces Christ and distributed his body."[172] Gregory of Nyssa suggests that this apportionment of Christ does violence to his unique divine nature.[173] Calvin protests that divided loyalties at Corinth entail the consequence that "Christ was being torn to pieces."[174] In modern commentaries this early tradition finds expression in Robertson and Plummer's question, "Does Christ belong to a section?" and their proposal, which we accept, "the probable meaning of μεμέρισται is **'has Christ been apportioned?'**, i.e., given to someone as his separate share."[175] Weiss, Schrage, and Conzelmann see an implicit

169. Metzger, *Textual Commentary* (2d ed.), 479.

170. Collins, *First Cor,* 81.

171. Bengel, *Gnomon,* 610.

172. Chrysostom, *1 Cor. Hom.,* 3:5.

173. Gregory of Nyssa, *Against Eunomius,* 6:1.

174. Calvin, *First Epistle,* 28.

175. Robertson and Plummer, *First Epistle,* 13.

reference to the church as Christ's body behind this verse.[176] Schrage more explicitly argues that if each group claims a monopoly of "Christ," then how could anyone conceive of Christ's being consequently "split up" *(zerspalten)* into fragments in his own Person?[177] The allusion to the body of Christ is confirmed, he suggests, by the use of the definite article in ὁ Χριστός, which is used "otherwise extraordinarily seldom." Indeed, one of the few places where the definite article occurs is precisely in the key passage about the one body: ἕν ἐστιν σῶμα, οὕτως καὶ ὁ Χριστός (1 Cor. 12:12).[178]

If, as seems certain, this sentence functions as a question, the vast majority of commentators assume that it anticipates the answer "no," just as the next rhetorical question does. *Christ cannot be apportioned out, can he?* The minority textual variant reflected in p^{46} assumes this interpretation. But if the question is understood as expressing a rhetorical entailment of v. 12, the anticipated answer would be "yes." Thus Lightfoot interprets the two questions as expecting different answers: "'Has Christ been divided?' This is only too true. 'Was Paul crucified for you?' This is out of the question."[179] Lightfoot retains the thought that the dissensions "rent Christ's body assunder, tearing limb from limb" (cf. 1 Cor. 12:12-13), but regards the question as one of accusation rather than warning. But although the minority textual reading probably represents an addition (μὴ μεμέρισται . . .), the intention of underlining the parallel between the two questions is very early and probably a valid interpretation.

Surely Paul was not crucified for you, was he? μὴ Παῦλος ἐσταυρώθη ὑπὲρ ὑμῶν; The English construction *surely . . . not . . . was he?* offers one of the best ways of conveying the use of μή in Greek (like *num* in Latin) as a way of formulating a question which emphatically invites a negative answer. To translate "Was Paul crucified for you?" (AV, KJV, NRSV, NIV) is simply too bland, and remains capable of being read as an open question, which the Greek explicitly excludes. A little better is "Was it Paul who [or that] was crucified for you?" (Moffatt, NJB). The reference to the crucifixion demonstrates beyond question the absurdity and indeed "sinfulness" of daring to put loyalty to human leaders on the same level as loyalty to Christ.[180]

The preposition ὑπέρ becomes especially important in the context of theologies of the work of Christ. We have translated it simply as **for** because with the genitive (ὑμῶν) the word can mean *for,* or *on behalf of,* or *for the sake of,* and either of the two more narrowly focused meanings risks excluding the other. A number of nuances occur in different contexts. In Greek contemporary with Paul writers could speak of ἀποθνῄσκειν ὑπέρ τινος, *to die for someone* (e.g., Josephus, *Antiquities* 13.6), and this idiom is perhaps among the closest

176. Weiss, *Der erste Korintherbrief* 16-17; Conzelmann, *1 Cor,* 35; and Schrage, *Der erste Brief,* 1:152.

177. Schrage, *Der erste Brief,* 152.

178. Ibid.

179. Lightfoot, *Notes,* 154.

180. Grosheide, *First Epistle,* 38-39.

parallels to *crucified for . . .* , even if it does not exclude richer nuances which may be drawn from other contexts.

Or were you baptized in the name of Paul? ἢ εἰς τὸ ὄνομα Παύλου ἐβαπτίσθητε; The key point for Paul was not who performed the baptismal rite, but in whose name the convert was baptized. Fee states a fundamental Pauline axiom when he observes, "The crucifixion of Jesus and the baptism of the believer are ideas that seem to flow together naturally in Paul (e.g., Rom. 6:2-3; Col. 2:12-15).[181] Rom 6:3-11 and 1 Cor 11:24-26 make it clear that the two dominical sacraments serve to anchor all Christian experience in the having-died and being-raised of Christ. Thus "Verses 14-16 . . . may best be interpreted as a sardonic rebuke of the Corinthians' proclivity to personality-centred ἔριδες."[182]

It is an issue of controversy whether to translate εἰς τὸ ὄνομα as **in the name** or as *into the name.* Strictly, the preposition εἰς most characteristically conveys the idea of *movement into,* with the accusative, *in contrast to location in* (ἐν) with the dative. But εἰς occurs in very many contexts with a multitude of nuances, and Moulton and Milligan illustrate "the interchange of εἰς and ἐν in late Greek . . . of AD 22."[183] Forceful arguments have been put forward by Schnackenburg to the effect that εἰς in baptismal contexts primarily signified *direction* rather than movement. He writes: "We ought to set βαπτίζειν εἰς in parallelism with πιστεύειν εἰς; the latter suggests the direction of faith, but it does not express any mystical movement to Christ. . . . The expression ἁμαρτάνειν εἰς Χριστόν [to sin against Christ] (1 Cor. 8:12) should also be compared."[184] In Gal 3:27 and Rom 6:3, Schnackenburg continues, "Christ is not a 'sphere' into which we are plunged, but the personal Christ with all that happened to him; our baptism 'to Christ' has the goal of uniting us with Christ and with everything that happened to him."[185] The issue is "the unity of the baptized with Christ."[186] Even baptism εἰς τὸν Μωϋσῆν (1 Cor. 10:2) is primarily "a 'sign of adherence to Moses.' "[187] The connection between εἰς and verbs of movement in other contexts "must not be made the norm for the entire linguistic use. . . ."[188]

Schnackenburg concludes that 1 Cor 1:13 and 1:15 should both be translated **"in the name"** since what is at issue is an "immediate relation to Christ

181. Fee, *First Epistle,* 61.
182. Litfin, *St Paul's Theology of Proclamation,* 186.
183. BAGD, 228-30; and esp. MM, 186-87, where the letter from Alexandria of AD 22 which demonstrates an interchange is cited on 186 at the foot of col. i and top of ii (*Oxyrhynchus Papryi* 2:294). See further Grimm-Thayer, 4th ed., 183-86, which equally stresses "direction" no less than motion; and Louw-Nida, 2:73-74, which lists 17 subcategories and some 20 idiomatic phrases embodying the word.
184. R. Schnackenburg, *Baptism in the Thought of Paul,* 23.
185. Ibid., 25.
186. Ibid., 29.
187. Ibid., 23.
188. Ibid., 22.

himself" in 1:13, and by implication an immediate relation to Paul in 1:15. He paraphrases the passage: "Christ is undivided. . . . Christ alone died for you. . . . You belong to Christ alone. . . . You were baptized in the name of Christ (and in the name of no other)."[189] Conzelmann develops this further: "'In the name' implies the *naming* of this name . . . , committed to the ownership of Christ, subjection to his lordship and protection."[190] This paraphrases Bengel: *"Crux et baptismus nos Christo asserit"* (claim us).[191]

Even if arguments of lexicography and syntax favor translating εἰς as **in**, we should not lose sight of one theological aspect which advocates of the other view stress: baptism represents an event of transition from one sphere to another.[192] Edwards compares Christ's passing through the cross with the Christian's passing through baptism, and this receives some plausibility from Paul's allusion to passing through the sea with Moses as a baptism (1 Cor 10:1-4).[193] On this basis Barrett translates *"into"* here (although he later speaks of "into or in").[194] Flemington declares, "Just as Christians are baptized *into Christ,* so the patriarchs were baptized *into Moses."*[195] Moreover, Paul does explicitly use the different preposition ἐν with the dative case for certain instances of usages: ἐδικαιώθητε ἐν τῷ ὀνόματι τοῦ κυρίου Ἰησοῦ Χριστοῦ (1 Cor 6:11). Conzelmann concludes that while we cannot exclude the idea of *into* as conveying transition, this translation alone unduly narrows the broader scope of **in the name**.[196] This is our view: *direction* remains primary, while movement becomes largely secondary.[197]

The aorist passive ἐβαπτίσθητε may perhaps carry a reflexive sense, *did you have yourselves baptized (in the name of Paul?).* If we were to adopt this view, the reflexive would further remove the content of baptism from the agency of the one who performed the rite, which becomes Paul's main concern in the next verses. But this reflexive aspect cannot be pressed in a first-century Greek passive.

14-15 ℵ*, B, and 1739 omit τῷ θεῷ in v. 14. This might suggest that τῷ θεῷ was inserted by a later corrector of ℵ in C and D (also the Vulgate, most other versions, Tertullian, and Chrysostom) on the basis of assimilation to 1 Cor 1:4; 14:18; Rom 1:8;

189. Ibid., 18-19.

190. Conzelmann, *1 Corinthians*, 35.

191. Bengel, *Gnomon*, 611. Cf. Cullmann *Baptism in the NT*, 9-22.

192. G. Delling, *Die Zueignung des Heils in der Taufe*, 75-76.

193. Edwards, *Commentary*, 21.

194. Barrett, *First Epistle*, 47.

195. W. F. Flemington, *NT Doctrine of Baptism*, 54.

196. Conzelmann, *1 Corinthians*, 36.

197. Schnackenburg, *Baptism in the Thought of Paul*, 3-61, convincingly distinguishes three main emphases in Paul: (1) a major emphasis on incorporation in Christ (Rom 6:3; 1 Cor 1:13; Gal 3:27); (2) a clear emphasis on salvation "with" Christ (Rom 6:5-11); and (3) a marginal element relating to washing or cleansing (minimal passages in Paul). On the preposition cf. further C. F. D. Moule, *Idiom Book* (2d ed. 1959), 67-71, and M. J. Harris, *NIDNTT*, 3:1184-88.

and other Pauline references. A, 33, and some Syriac and Coptic versions read τῷ θεῷ μου on a similar basis. But the words may have been accidentally omitted in scribal transcription. Metzger judges the scribal assimilation of μου (*my* **God**) as "obvious," but the decision about the inclusion of *to God* "more difficult."[198] The UBS *Greek New Testament,* 4th ed., substitutes a "C" categorization ("difficulty in deciding") for the 3d ed. "D," "a very high degree of doubt." Nothing of substance is at issue since Paul's stance of gratitude will implicitly be addressed to God, but it is probably implicit rather than explicit here. The translation **I give thanks** provides for this ambiguity: NJB and NIV omit **God**; NRSV and REB include it.

We have already examined the sociopolitical background which gives this verse particular point. A number of Christians at Corinth sought to acquire enhanced status by claiming some special connection with a major, esteemed figure. We recall the comment of A. D. Clarke: "Personality-centred politics within the church were characteristic of the surrounding Graeco-Roman society. . . . A secular understanding of the underlying distinctions in rank and status between those in the church and the 'apostolic' figures of Paul, Cephas and Apollos demanded that it would be personally advantageous to be associated with one or other of these figures."[199] We cited Plutarch's allusion to status seekers climbing like ivy by twining themselves around a strong tree (Plutarch, *Moralia* 805 E.-F). Chrysostom admirably conveys Paul's point: why are you so elated about your connections with those who performed your baptismal rites "when I for my part even give thanks that I have not done so!" (*Homilies,* 3:6). He adds: "Baptism truly is a great thing; but its greatness is not the work of the person baptizing, but of Him who is invoked in the baptism."

Tertullian, however, makes a complementary point. The fact that Paul did baptize Gaius, Crispus, and the household of Stephanas (v. 16) demonstrates that Paul did not belittle baptism or refuse to baptize converts. In the particular circumstances at Corinth, on the other hand, Paul expresses thankfulness that few, if any, could claim that *everything* came from or through him.[200] Ministry remains a shared partnership, and points away from itself to that to which it bears witness.

Weiss and Fee plausibly suggest that "the two exceptions are related to the fact that both men were very early converts in the city."[201] Crispus is "almost surely" the Jewish synagogue ruler of that name mentioned in Acts 18:8, while Gaius may well be the Gaius of Rom 16:23 to whom Paul alludes as "host to me and to the whole church" when he was likely to have been in Corinth. We cannot be certain about the identity of Crispus, especially since the name is so widespread, but Gaius is likely to be the person to whom Rom 16:23

198. Metzger, *Textual Commentary* (2d ed.), 479.
199. Clarke, *Secular and Christian Leadership,* 92-93.
200. Tertullian, *On Baptism,* xiv.
201. Fee, *First Epistle,* 62; and Weiss, *Der erste Korintherbrief,* 20-21 (also Findlay, *Expositor's Greek Testament,* 2:766; see n. 6).

alludes.[202] Both are Roman names; Stephanas (v. 15) is a Greek name (see also under 16:17, 18 and sources cited below).[203] If Crispus was "ruler of the synagogue" (Acts 18:8), this "was an honorific title awarded by a community in gratitude for a donation to their place of prayer." Such a one "was not a poor man."[204]

The clause ἵνα μή τις εἴπῃ refers back to the state of affairs concerning which it now introduces the consequence; it does not denote Paul's conscious purpose at the time. Bengel thus observes that a divine providence often reigns in events of which the reason is discovered only afterward.[205]

16 The word "Well" does not occur in the Greek, but the syntax requires a conjunction that introduces the notion of "on second thoughts. . . ." Lightfoot and Findlay consider the delightful possibility that in mid-dictation Paul's flow was interrupted by a tactful reminder from his amanuensis, who might just possibly have been either Stephanas himself or one of his household. 1 Cor 16:17 confirms that Stephanas was present with Paul when the letter was being written (see also under 1:1 [Sosthenes] and 16:21 [the postscript in Paul's own hand]).

There is an extensive literature on οἶκος, οἰκία, and "households" in the NT.[206] Modern writers are often too quick to assume that οἶκος, *household,* necessarily and in all cases denotes a standard "extended family" rather than a quasi-nuclear one with possible additions. In many cases "the household" may well include more than two generations, servants, slaves, clients, and/or lodgers. But we also know from funerary inscriptions since the Roman principate that even extended households under one roof left room for close relations between husbands and wives and between parents and children, which were not necessarily dissipated or made less intimate among the whole household.[207] We

202. As Schrage argues in *Der erste Brief,* 1:155.

203. See Banks, *Paul's Idea of Community,* 114-17; Meeks, *The First Urban Christians,* 51-63; Theissen, "Social Stratification," in *Social Setting,* 69-119, esp. 83-87 (houses), 87-91 (services, including Gaius); *Paul: A Critical Life* (Oxford: Oxford University Press, 1997), 265-68, "The First Converts" at Corinth; and Horrell, *Social Ethos,* 91-101.

204. Murphy-O'Connor, *St. Paul's Corinth,* 267.

205. Bengel, *Gnomon,* 610: Providentia Dei regnat saepe in rebus, quorum ratio postea cognoscitur.

206. See esp. Theissen, *Social Setting,* 83-87; Strobel, "Der Begriff des 'Hauses' . . .," 91-100; P. Wiegand, "Zur sogenannten 'Oikosformel,'" *NovT* 6 (1963): 49-74; G. Delling, "Zur Taufe von 'Häusern' im Urchristentum," *NovT* 7 (1965): 285-311; Banks, *Paul's Idea of Community,* 26-36; H.-J. Klauck, "Die Hausgemeinde als Lebensform im Urchristentum," *MTZ* 32 (1981): 1-15, and *Hausgemeinde und Hauskirche im Frühen Christentum,* Stuttgarter Bibelstudien 103 (Stuttgart: Katholisches Bibelwerk, 1981). Klauck sees the house community as the cornerstone of the local Christian community and the base of missionary activity in the first generation, but gives less attention to wider issues about the social structure of the οἶκος in Graeco-Roman society at large.

207. From among a wide variety of sources cf. those cited by M. B. Flory, "Family and '*Familia*' Kinship and Community in Slavery," *AJAH* 3 (1978): 78-95; and esp. R. P. Saller and B. D. Shaw, "Tombstones and Roman Family Relations in the Principate," *JRS* 74 (1984): 124-56, and

cannot be certain what size and what relationships were involved in any given instance of οἶκος in the absence of further information about the family or household in question. It is almost as vague as the English word *home,* except that less immediate relatives, slaves, and even associates of this or that kind often shared residence under one head of the house under the same roof, especially if the head of the house was well-to-do.

J. Jeremias has appealed to this verse in his defense of infant baptism.[208] But we cannot be certain that infants were included in the οἶκος even if it remains highly probable that they were. Numerous complexities mark the discussion. For example, A. Strobel tries to distinguish between the larger οἰκία (Lat. *familia*) and the smaller οἶκος (Lat. *domus*); but the terms can occur interchangeably (cf. οἰκία in 16:15), and Theissen regards his argument as problematic.[209] To manage a "house" means to have obedient children in 1 Tim 3:4. A well-to-do household, of which Stephanas's was probably an example, would probably have been mixed and relatively large.

For the rest translates λοιπόν, which functions as an adverbial accusative of λοιπός. Although οἶδα generally means *I know,* in the present context the nuance of "resultant" knowledge carries the force of **I do not recall**.[210]

17 It would be a mistake and also anachronistic to suppose that Paul draws a contrast between a sacramental ministry and a preaching ministry as such. Such a contrast is implied by C. T. Craig, among others.[211] In its context at Corinth, both βαπτίζειν and ἐν σοφίᾳ λόγου are aspects of potential ministry which, given the Corinthians' own presuppositions about both, call attention to the agency and status of the minister, and together these stand in contrast to εὐαγγελίζεσθαι, which from any viewpoint calls attention to the gospel (εὐαγγέλιον).[212] Schrage perceives this contrast as overdrawn to deliberate hyperbole.[213] Neither *preach* nor **proclaim** features in the Greek primarily to distinguish *modes* of communication. With the propensity of American English to transpose many nouns into verbs Beaudean has coined "gospelize" in his work

---

M. I. Finley (ed.), *Classical Slavery* (London: Cass, 1987), 65-87. Cf. further John H. Kent (ed.), *Corinth: Results of Excavations,* vol. 8. pt. 3 (Princeton, N.J.: American School of Classical Studies at Athens, 1966), e.g., 174-75; and D. B. Martin, *Slavery as Salvation: The Metaphor of Slavery in Pauline Christianity* (New Haven: Yale University Press, 1990), 1-7 and 140-45; I. A. H. Combes, *The Metaphor of Slavery in the Writings of the Early Church,* JSNTSS 156 (Sheffield: Sheffield Academic Press, 1998), 49-67; B. W. Winter, *Seek the Welfare of the City* (Grand Rapids: Eerdmans, 1994), 152-63. For an excellent survey of primary sources, see T. Wiedemann, *Greek and Roman Slavery* (London and New York: Routledge, 1981).

208. Jeremias, *Infant Baptism in the First Four Centuries,* and *The Origins of Infant Baptism.*

209. Strobel, "Der Begriff des 'Hauses' . . . ," 91-100; as against Theissen, *Social Setting,* 83-84.

210. BAGD, 556, followed also by Fee.

211. C. T. Craig, "First Corinthians," in *IB* (New York and Nashville: Abingdon, 1953), 10:24. See Merklein, *Der erste Brief 1–4,* 165-67, for a contextual approach.

212. Schrage, *Der erste Brief,* 1:157.

213. See Merklein, *Der erste Brief 1–4,* 165-67.

on this verse.[214] Since baptism and the Lord's Supper *also,* for Paul, **proclaim the gospel** of Christ's death and resurrection (Rom 6:3-11; 1 Cor 11:24-27), the contextual meaning of βαπτίζειν has been conveyed by translating it **to perform baptisms**, with its emphasis on ministerial agency.[215]

The first reference to σοφία, wisdom, raises a complex of issues in modern scholarship. How are we to translate οὐκ ἐν σοφίᾳ λόγου, which would be rendered in woodenly verbatim English as "by [or in] wisdom of speech"? Stephen Pogoloff devotes a careful chapter to this phrase.[216] As he shows, λόγος includes almost anything that is spoken (λέγω), including acts of speaking, speech, a word, discourse, sentence, statement, declaration, assertion, subject matter, looks of a word, and so on.[217] And BAGD confirms this, "The exact translation of λόγος depends on the context: *what you say* (Mt. 5:37); *statement* (PGM 4, 334, Lk. 20:20); *question* (Sext. Emp. Math. 8.295, 133; Diog. L. 2, 116); . . . *pastoral counselling with an individual* (1 Cor. 2:4a); . . . *preaching* (1 Ti. 5:17); *prophecy* . . . (Jn. 2:22; 18:32); *command* . . . (Lk. 4:36; 2 Pet. 3:5, 7); *report, story* . . . (Diod. 5.3: 40, 9). . . ."[218] The word may also extend to *reason, motive, reckoning, calculation,* and *computation* (Herodotus, 8.100; Josephus, *Antiquities* 16.120; *BGU* 164:21, et al.). Louw and Nida distinguish at least ten semantic fields or subcategories, including *statement, speech, gospel, reason, event,* and *accusation.*[219]

The reference to σοφία, then, must be the one which determines the nature and semantic range of λόγος in the present context. This word also has "extensive semantic ranges."[220] Given what we have already noted from a wide range of modern scholars about attitudes toward rhetoric in Roman Corinth, it is plausible to associate σοφία with practical instrumental cleverness or skill, and λόγος with calculative communication.[221] On this basis Paul may well mean *not by manipulative rhetoric.* Indeed, this might well be the best translation, except that it imposes on the English reader the interpretive judgment of the translator and makes the translation narrower and more specific than the Greek itself. Here is one of many cases where the fine line between interpretation and translation becomes virtually impossible to sustain. This kind of example offers one of many instances which encourage the serious student of the NT to learn Greek thoroughly, in order to arrive at a firsthand judgment on so com-

---

214. Beaudean Jr., *Paul's Theology of Preaching,* 92.

215. On the contrast between a prominent agent and transparent agency see J. A. Crafton, *The Agency of the Apostle,* 59-136 (cited and discussed above).

216. S. M. Pogoloff, *Logos and Sophia,* 99-127, provides an excellent discussion in a first-class study.

217. Pogoloff, *Logos and Sophia,* 111.

218. BAGD, 477; cf. Grimm-Thayer, 379-80.

219. Louw-Nida, *Greek-English Lexicon,* 2:153.

220. Pogoloff, *Logos and Sophia,* 109.

221. Following the work of M. Heidegger, the term "instrumental reason" has assumed an essential and growing importance as instantiated in the writings of J. Habermas and sociology of knowledge.

plex an issue. Pogoloff proposes the translation *sophisticated speech,* while BAGD suggest *cleverness in speaking.*[222]

James A. Davis stresses the *human* character of Paul's uses of σοφία in 1 Corinthians 1–4, especially in 1:18–3:20. It relates to "Israel's wisdom which had failed to perceive the pattern of God's activity in the course of contemporary events. . . . Paul also intends to critique the Corinthians with regard to the failure of this wisdom to perceive the meaning of God's activity in the cross of Christ."[223] Although Davis may perhaps overstress the part played here by the reference to Jewish traditions, support for the interpretation of 1 Corinthians 1–3 as "haggadic homily genre" of postbiblical Judaism comes from Wilhelm Wuellner; and, as Davis reminds us, Paul explicitly alludes to "the scribe" in parallel to the "wise" person in 1:20.[224] David Daube further identifies λόγος σοφίας with the דבר and חכמה *(dabar* and *chokmah)* of halakic discussions to which allusion is made in the Talmud.[225] Schnabel's work supports the connection between Wisdom and Law.[226] The close parallel between Jewish and Greek "wisdom" finds common expression in the phrase "the wisdom of the world." Witherington's emphasis on the expectations at Corinth of a Graeco-Roman orator's "success" or "impressiveness" offers a further parallel with Davis's stress on "levels of attainment with regard to the acquisition of wisdom . . . sapiential achievement" on which reliance is placed, and which occurs alongside "a stress upon eloquence."[227] For Davis this has resonances with Paul's critique of "achievement" through the law in postbiblical Judaism, even if this is to be qualified in the light of work by E. P. Sanders and others.[228] For Witherington, Paul's main aim in 1:17 is to distance himself from the so-called wisdom of the Sophist, who sets more store on winning arguments and impressing an audience by rhetorical display than on the actual content of what is at issue.[229] B. W. Winter shows how this Sophist tradition relates to Corinthian confessions of loyalty to specific religious spheres and thereby demonstrates the unity of thought in 1:10-17.[230]

222. Pogoloff, *Logos and Sophia,* 109; BAGD, 759.

223. Davis, *Wisdom and Spirit,* 71.

224. Davis, *Wisdom and Spirit* 72-74; cf. W. Wuellner, "Haggadic Homily Genre in 1 Cor. 1–3," *JBL* 89 (1970): 199-203. Wuellner takes as his point of departure Peder Borgen's thesis in his *Bread from Heaven* that John 6 reflects a homily pattern. Borgen finds such a homily pattern also in Gal 3:6-29, Rom 4:1-22, and in Palestinian Midrash of the first century. Wuellner sees the main theme of Paul's homily in 1 Corinthians 1–3 as "stated in 1 Cor. 1:19. It concerns divine judgment on human wisdom" (201).

225. D. Daube, *The NT and Rabbinic Judaism* (London: Athlone, 1956), 158-69. Daube's view is shared by S. Lieberman.

226. Schnabel, *Law and Wisdom from Ben Sira to Paul.* Schnabel traces connections between wisdom and law in Ben Sira, Qumran, Pauline Christology, and the ethics of moral conduct.

227. Davis, *Wisdom and Spirit,* 142-43; cf. Witherington, *Conflict and Community,* 46-48.

228. Davis, *Wisdom and Spirit,* 146.

229. Witherington, *Conflict and Community,* 103-4; see also Pogoloff, *Logos and Sophia* (throughout).

230. B. W. Winter, *Philo and Paul among the Sophists,* 182-94, esp. 185-86.

Both traditions and both critiques, therefore, come together in v. 17 as a transitional verse which introduces the main contrast between the "power" or operative effects of the cross and the "weakness" or inoperative attempts generated by "wisdom" on the part of the Gentile "Greeks" and Jews (1:18-31). Litfin describes v. 17 as "the nub of the issue."[231] The issue goes deeper than the traditional remark of many commentators that **clever rhetoric** merely stresses the importance of form at the expense of content.[232] Allo rightly points out that Loisy's "with eloquent wisdom" does not fully reach the heart of the matter, any more than Robertson and Plummer's "wisdom of language," unless these are understood to mean "with rhetorical artifice."[233] Paul is neither criticizing baptism nor devaluing eloquence, Senft urges, when each genuinely places the cross at the centre of the stage, but Paul attacks any use of them which *isolates* them from the cross as acts or events in their own right.[234] Similarly, Chrysostom argues that Paul does not attack a rhetoric (e.g., that of Apollos) which is grounded in his use of the scriptures (Acts 18:24, 27).[235]

In what sense would **clever rhetoric** entail the consequence that **the cross should be nullified**? Three levels at which the principle applies may be distinguished.

First, in accordance with the historical and rhetorical reconstruction convincingly put forward by Pogoloff and confirmed by others, σοφία in this context has nothing to do with "philosophical or religious speculation. Quite the contrary, σοφία was a matter of learning applied to *practical* accomplishment" (Pogoloff's italics).[236] Hence Pogoloff, as we have already noted, translates σοφία λόγου as "sophisticated speech," i.e., rhetoric enhanced by practical skills. But how does this make the cross *emptied* (κενωθῇ)? *If everything rests on human cleverness,* sophistication, or achievement, *the cross of Christ no longer functions as that which subverts and cuts across all human distinctions of race, class, gender, and status to make room for divine grace alone as sheer unconditional gift.* The connection between rhetoric and social class gives this the sharpest possible point. Pogoloff writes: "Paul claims that he did not preach in a status-conferring manner."[237] Neither he nor Apollos is a "status-indicator of eloquence." The Corinthians, or many of them, were *"hungry for status."*[238] (Witherington uses the same phrase.)[239] But *to treat the gospel of the cross of Christ as a vehicle for promoting self-esteem, self-*

231. Litfin, *St Paul's Theology of Proclamation,* 187.
232. Ortkemper, *1 Kor,* 24-25: "Form und Inhalt. . . ."
233. Allo, *Première Épître,* 12; cf. Robertson and Plummer, *First Epistle,* 15-16.
234. C. Senft, *Première Épître,* 36.
235. Chrysostom, *1 Cor. Hom.,* 3:7.
236. Pogoloff, *Logos and Sophia,* 109.
237. Ibid., 119.
238. Ibid., 124 (my italics).
239. Witherington, *Conflict and Community,* 22-24 and 100.

fulfillment, and self-assertion turns it upside down and "empties" it of all that it offers and demands.[240]

Second, rhetoric alone may win the emotions and even the mind and perhaps the will, but the human self is more than all of these modes of being. Today we may speak of a "psychological" conversion which may result causally from manipulative factors without touching the self's spiritual depths in an authentic turning *not simply toward a new set of beliefs and lifestyle, but to God.* This constitutes an authentic recognition of Christ's Lordship through the work of the Holy Spirit (1 Cor 12:3). Overreliance on **clever rhetoric** may in this sense provide an inauthentic shortcut to transformation by **the cross of Christ,** which becomes **nullified** as a means of restoring a relationship with God himself.[241]

Third, our distinction in speech-act theory between *perlocutionary* and *illocutionary* acts underlines the difference between two distinct sets of logical entailments or presupposed situations in each case. A. R. Brown urges, "Paul's Word of the Cross . . . not only says something but does something in the saying."[242] This is, in effect, J. L. Austin's definition of an illocutionary speech-act, and Brown implicitly and fruitfully explores this approach. **To proclaim the gospel** is initially an *illocutionary* speech-act which presupposes a call and commission from God on the part of the speaker and *the performance of divine promise,* based on the appropriation of God's covenantal pledge to limit his own freedoms in and through **the cross of Christ.**[243] Once again, even if this gives rise, in turn, to perlocutionary acts of persuasion, if the proclamation is transposed merely into the **clever rhetoric** of the sophist or the manipulative, self-appointed, preacher who is only "out for results," the transformative and promissory power of **the cross of Christ** becomes bypassed and thereby **nullified.** Thus, as we noted, Litfin calls v. 17 "the nub of the issue" for 1 Corinthians 1–4 and perhaps for the whole epistle.[244] Brown convincingly compares Paul's argument with J. L. Austin's criteria for rendering a performative speech-act "hollow or void."[245] She explicates "Paul's Performative Strategy"

240. On the issue in modern theology and in secular postmodernism, see A. C. Thiselton, *Interpreting God and the Postmodern Self: On Meaning, Manipulation and Promise* (Edinburgh: T. & T. Clark and Grand Rapids: Eerdmans, 1995), esp. 3-45 and 121-44. The Church of England Doctrine Commission Report *The Mystery of Salvation* (London: Church House, 1995) explicitly dissociates "fulfillment" from "salvation" as respectively secular and Christian notions (31-33).

241. Cf. Ortkemper, *Das Kreuz in der Verkündigung des Apostels Paulus,* 43-67.

242. Brown, *The Cross and Human Transformation,* 15.

243. See Brown, *The Cross,* 13-64, 70-75, and throughout. Also see our Introduction, 43, 52-53, and A. C. Thiselton, "Christology in Luke: Speech-Act Theory and the Problem of Dualism in Christology after Kant," in Joel B. Green and Max Turner (eds.), *Jesus of Nazareth: Lord and Christ* (Grand Rapids. Eerdmans, 1994), 453-72, and more esp. "Communicative Action and Promise," in R. Lundin, A. C. Thiselton, and C. Walhout, *The Promise of Hermeneutics* (Grand Rapids: Eerdmans, 1999), 133-240, esp. 209-40.

244. Litfin, *St Paul's Theology of Proclamation,* 187.

245. Brown, *The Cross,* 18.

in terms of his language.[246] Paul now has to re-proclaim the cross (1:18-31) since after his operative speech-action of founding the church he now has to correct what has begun to "misfire."[247]

B. THE CONTRAST BETWEEN HUMAN WISDOM AND THE TRANSFORMATIVE POWER OF THE CROSS AS GOD'S WISDOM (1:18–2:5)

(1) The **proclamation of the cross** opens up "a new way of *being* in the world" (Brown's italics).[1] "1:18–2.5 explains v. 17b — how genuine, full-orbed Christianity stands opposed to the fundamental values of a fallen, sinful world but provides the necessary antidote to the self-centered factionalism of the Corinthians."[2] In Paul's theology the cross is more than (but not less than) a remedy and atonement for past sins. It provides the basis for Christian identity and his transformative power to reshape Christian existence in the present and the future. Hence the *present* participles of 1:18 have a firm theological significance. Although he undervalues the aspect of sacrificial atonement and overstates his attack on "Lutheran" interpretations of Paul, it remains the case that Sanders is correct to assert that Paul's emphasis on the cross points "not [only] backwards to the expiation of past transgressions but [also] forwards . . . thinking more in terms of a change of lordship . . ." (his italics, my additions in brackets).[3]

(2) Since to the self-centered whose "world" has not yet been transformed, the proclamation of the cross takes the form of **folly** (μωρία, 1:18, 21, 23) or of what is **foolish** (μωρός, 1:25, 27), an *epistemological* dimension is involved. The most astonishing feature of 1:18–4:21 is its clear implication that even the self-styled "spiritual" who had presumably begun with the cross had come to regard it, in effect, as foolish. J. L. Martyn establishes Paul's connection between the cross, eschatology, and epistemology in this context. The "spiritual elite" monopolize and pre-empt the hitherto Pauline contrast between "secular" or *ordinary* (ψυχικός or κατὰ σάρκα) knowledge and *spiritual* (πνευματικός or κατὰ πνεῦμα) knowledge. But amidst the continuing struggles and realities of Christian existence *before* the eschaton (cf. 1:26-31; 2:1-5; 4:8-13) in Paul's judgment in the context of this letter "the implied opposite of knowing κατὰ σάρκα is not knowing κατὰ πνεῦμα, but rather knowing κατὰ σταυρόν. He who recognizes his life to be God's *gift* at the *juncture of the ages* recognizes also that until he is completely and exclusively in the new age, his knowing κατὰ πνεῦμα can occur only in the form of knowing κατὰ σταυρόν.

246. Ibid., 25-26.
247. Ibid., 30.
1. Brown, *The Cross in Human Transformation,* 12.
2. C. Blomberg, *1 Corinthians,* NIVAC (Grand Rapids: Zondervan, 1994), 52.
3. E. P. Sanders, *Paul and Palestinian Judaism* (London: SCM, 1977), 465 and 466; on 1 Cor 1:18, see 449.

For until the parousia, the cross is *and* remains *the* eschatological crisis" (Martyn's italics).[4] Alexandra Brown takes up this perspective: "1 Cor . . . the epistemological issues of the early chapters prepare for the explicitly ethical issues of later ones."[5] *Sophia* in 1:17–2:16 reflects "the Corinthians' ways of knowing," later reflected also in 8:1-3, but the transformative speech-act of proclaiming the cross sets up a series of polarities (perishing . . . being saved: folly . . . power of God; et al.) which "turns things upside down."[6] The cross projects a new world which Paul defines in terms of "having the mind of Christ" (2:16).[7]

Brown's emphasis on the transformative effects of the cross upon knowledge, behavior, and Christian identity finds close parallels with Pickett and Schrage. Pickett argues that the "word of the cross . . . in 1:10–4:21" concerns a recognition of "the event of Christ's death [as] the very ground of their being."[8] The cross brings into focus "an identity crisis which was the result of belonging to two discrepant universes of meaning . . . two polarized social worlds."[9] Thus the cross addresses directly the issue of Christian unity in 1:10–4:21, as well as other ethical and behavioral issues (5:1–14:42 and probably 15:1-58). We return to Schrage's excellent summary heading: the cross constitutes the "ground and criterion" of Christian and apostolic identity (his heading for 1:18–2:5).[10]

(3) The rhetorical structure of 1:18–2:5 clearly divides into three paragraphs, as the major commentators agree.[11] How can the gospel of Christ be a form of σοφία when (a) *the message* concerns a *crucified* Christ (1:18-25); (b) its *recipients* at Corinth are *far from "wise" or influential* in the sense understood by the world at large (1:26-31); and (c) Paul's own *preaching* when he came to Corinth was not characterized by *the kind of cleverness designed to impress an audience* (2:1-5)? (a) 1:18 begins with a rhetorical *partitio* which takes up the theme of v. 17, and revolves around five polarities of the theme *wise/wisdom* (σοφός/σοφία) and foolish/folly (μωρός/μωρία). Its closure comes in the interim or transitional v. 25, which sums up vv. 18-24 as an *inclusio* framed by vv. 17 and 25. (b) Arguably the coherent theme of vv. 26-31, *the status of the recipients* (as not relating to *sophia* in the usual sense of the term) is marked or framed by a biblical quotation at its beginning and end (1:26 alludes to Jer 9:26; 1:31, a more succinct version). (c) 2:1-5 is a self-contained unit which presses the argument of 1:18–2:5 with reference to Paul's preaching.

4. J. L. Martyn, "Epistemology at the Turn of the Ages: 2 Cor 5:16," in W. R. Farmer, C. F. D. Moule, and R. R. Niebuhr (eds.), *Christian History and Interpretation: Studies Presented to John Knox* (Cambridge: Cambridge University Press, 1967), 272; cf. 269-87.

5. Brown, *The Cross,* 12; cf. 8-11, 89-94, 97-104, and 150-54.

6. Ibid., 33, 76, 81.

7. Ibid., 139.

8. Pickett, *The Cross in Corinth,* 61; cf. 37-84.

9. Ibid., 62.

10. Schrage, *Der erste Brief,* 1:165; cf. 165-238.

11. For example, Fee, *First Epistle,* 66-68; Collins, *First Cor,* 90-92; Wolff, *Der erste Brief,* 34-35, 42-43, 47; Merklein, *Der erste Brief 1–4,* 108-14, 167-77; Schrage, *Der erste Brief,* 1:166-73. Cf. also Horrell, *Social Ethos,* 131-37.

The specific identification of rhetorical devices or methods is more problematic than tracing the structure. Schrage insists that 1:18-25 is not a rhetorical *narratio,* but the *argumentatio,* or "proof," of the explanation of the *propositio* (1:10), i.e., the *narratio* of 1:11-17.[12] However, Bünker identifies 1:18–2:16 as *narratio.*[13] Perhaps the most that can be said is that Cicero commended a pattern which Paul may follow loosely, albeit with what Litfin calls "adaptation" to his own purposes.[14] Cicero advocates a *summary thesis* or *propositio* (presumably 1:10 serves as this); then a brief *explanation* or *ratio* stating its basis (probably 1:11-17); followed by a *corroborative proof (rationis confirmatio* or *argumentio),* which 1:18–2:5 may function to serve.[15] Some writers have attempted to identify much smaller rhetorical units (e.g., Bailey on chiasmic units), but in general these have failed to command wide assent as more than possibilities rather than the result of a clear strategy.[16] Similarly, Wuellner's theory about a midrashic pattern in 1:19–3:21 loses force when he concedes that in rhetorical terms these verses represent "a major digression."[17] Most would probably follow Schrage and Witherington in placing the *narratio,* which explains the nature of what is disputed, earlier, and in identifying 1:18–2:5 as the *probatio* or *argumentatio,* which demonstrates the case.[18] This demonstration or proof elucidates three strands of mutually supportive corroboration.

It is tempting to be sceptical about some of the many rhetorical analyses which are currently in vogue, since they often oscillate between the obvious and the highly speculative. Yet they establish two things. First, granted Litfin's insistence that rhetoric remains Paul's servant, not his master, and that proclamation and argument remain his primary modes of discourse, Paul does not despise a judicious use of the resources of trained thought in the wider world of his day. Second, this emphasis helps to counter a widespread scepticism among some church people about the extent to which Paul would give such detailed attention to words, phrases, and sentences as biblical specialists tend to presuppose.

---

12. Schrage, *Der erste Brief,* 1:167.

13. Bünker, *Briefformular und rhetorische Disposition im 1 Korintherbrief,* 55-56. See further Merklein, *Der erste Brief 1–4,* 109-11.

14. Litfin, *St Paul's Theology of Proclamation,* 137-40, 174-201, 247-50.

15. Cicero, *Ad Herennium* 2.18.28, discussed in Eriksson, *Traditions as Rhetorical Proof,* 57-63.

16. Bailey, "Recovering the Poetic Structure of 1 Cor 1:17–2:2," 265-96.

17. W. Wuellner, "Haggadic Homily Genre in 1 Cor 1–3," 199-204; quotation from W. Wuellner, "Greek Rhetoric and Pauline Argumentation," in W. R. Schoedel and R. L. Wilken (eds.), *Early Christian Literature and the Classical Intellectual Tradition* (Paris: Beauchesne, 1979), 185; cf. 177-88.

18. Witherington, *Conflict and Community,* 44; and Schrage, *Der erste Brief,* 1:166-73.

1. The Limits of Human Wisdom in the Light of the Cross (1:18-25)

(18) For the proclamation of the cross is, for their part, folly to those who are on their way to ruin, but, for our part, the power of God to us who are on the way to salvation. (19, 20) For it is written, "I will destroy the wisdom of the wise, and the shrewdness of the shrewd will I nullify." Where is the sage? Where is the expert? Where is the debater of this world order? Has not God made a fool of the world's wisdom? (21) For since in God's wisdom it was not through wisdom that the world came to know God, it pleased God to save those who believe through the foolishness of what is proclaimed. (22-24) Since Jews asked for signs and Greeks seek wisdom, but we proclaim a crucified Christ: to the Jews an affront; to Gentiles, folly; but to those who are called, a Christ; God's power and God's wisdom. (25) For God's foolishness is wiser than human wisdom, and God's weakness is stronger than human strength.

Bibliography on 1:18-25

Bailey, Kenneth E., "Recovering the Poetic Structure of 1 Cor. 1:17–2:2," *NovT* 17 (1975): 265-96.

Beaudean, John W., Jr., *Paul's Theology of Preaching* (Macon, Ga.: Mercer University Press, 1988), 87-118.

Beker, J. C., *Paul's Apocalyptic Gospel:. The Coming Triumph of God* (Philadelphia: Fortress, 1982), 29-54.

Best, E., "The Power and the Wisdom of God. 1 Cor. 1:18-25," in L. de Lorenzi (ed.), *Paolo a uno chiesa divisa (1 Co. 1–4),* Monographica di "Benedictina" 5 (Rome: Abbazia di S. Paolo,1980), 9-39.

Bornkamm, G., "Faith and Reason in Paul," in *Early Christian Experience* (Eng. trans., London: SCM, 1969), 29-46.

Brown, A. R., *The Cross in Human Transformation: Paul's Apocalyptic Word in 1 Corinthians* (Minneapolis: Fortress, 1995).

Bünker, M., *Briefformular und rhetorische Disposition in 1 Korintherbrief* (Göttingen: Vandenhoeck & Ruprecht, 1984).

Carson, D. A., "The Cross and Preaching (1 Cor. 1:18–2:5)," in *The Cross and Christian Ministry* (Grand Rapids: Baker, 1993), 11-42.

Chevallier, M. A., "La prédication de la croix," *ETR* 45 (1970): 131-61.

Clement of Alexandria, *Stromata,* 1:18 and 5:1.

Cousar, C. B., *A Theology of the Cross: The Death of Jesus in the Pauline Letters* (Minneapolis: Fortress, 1990).

Crafton, J. A., *The Agency of the Apostle,* JSNTSS 51 (Sheffield : Sheffield Academic Press, 1991), 48-58, 163-69.

Davis, James A., *Wisdom and Spirit: An Investigation of 1 Cor. 1:18–3:20 against the Background of Jewish Sapiential Traditions in the Greco-Roman Period* (Lanham, Md. and New York: University Press of America, 1984), esp. 65-74.

Dunn, J. D. G., "Paul's Understanding of the Death of Jesus," in R. Banks (ed.), *Recon-*

ciliation and Hope: NT Essays on Atonement and Eschatology Presented to Leon Morris (Grand Rapids: Eerdmans, 1974), 125-41.

————, *The Theology of Paul the Apostle* (Edinburgh: T. & T. Clark, 1998), 163-81 and 207-33.

Ellis, E. Earle, "Christ Crucified," in Robert Banks (ed.), *Reconciliation and Hope: NT Essays on Atonement and Eschatology Presented to L. L. Morris* (Exeter: Paternoster, 1974), 69-75.

Fitzgerald, John T., *Cracks in an Earthen Vessel. An Examination of Catalogues of Hardships in the Corinthian Correspondence,* SBLDS 99 (Atlanta: Scholars Press, 1988), esp. 117-50 and 203-7.

Friedrich, G., "Die Verkündigung des Todes Jesu im Neuen Testament," *Biblisch-Theologische Studien* 6 (1982): 119-42.

Funk, R. W., "The Letter: Form and Style," in *Language, Hermeneutic and Word of God* (New York and London: Harper & Row, 1966), 250-74.

————, "Word and Word in 1 Cor. 2:6-16," in ibid., 275-306.

Grayston, Kenneth, *Dying We Live: A New Enquiry into the Death of Christ in the NT* (New York and Oxford: Oxford University Press, 1990), 21-27, and "The Power of the Cross," 27-29.

Hanson, Anthony T., "The Cross in the End Time," in *The Paradox of the Cross in the Thought of St. Paul,* JSNTSS 17 (Sheffield: JSOT Press, 1987), 11-24.

Hengel, M., *The Cross of the Son of God* (Eng. trans., London: SCM, 1986), 93-263.

Horrell, D. G., *The Social Ethos of the Corinthian Correspondence* (Edinburgh: T. & T. Clark, 1996), 131-37.

Jeremias, J., "Chiasmus in den Paulusbriefen," *ZNW* 49 (1958): 145-56.

Jervis, L. A., and P. Richardson, *Gospel in Paul: Studies Presented to R. N. Longenecker,* JSNTSS 108 (Sheffield: Sheffield Academic Press, 1994), 21-88 (see essays by Jervis, Hurd, and Mitchell).

Jüngel, Eberhard, *God as the Mystery of the World: On the Foundation of the Theology of the Crucified One in the Dispute between Theism and Atheism* (Eng. trans., Edinburgh: T. & T. Clark, 1983), 105-11, 122-26, 152-84, 199-232, 281-330.

————, "The World as Possibility and Actuality: The Ontology of the Doctrine of Justification," in *Theological Essays,* vol. 1 (Eng. trans., Edinburgh: T. & T. Clark, 1989), 95-123.

Käsemann, Ernst, "The Saving Significance of the Death of Jesus in Paul," in *Perspectives on Paul* (Eng. trans., London: SCM, 1971), 32-59.

Knox, W. L., "The Divine Wisdom," in *St. Paul and the Church of the Gentiles* (Cambridge: Cambridge University Press, 1939), 55-89.

Lampe, R., "Theological Wisdom and the 'Word about the Cross': The Rhetorical Scheme in 1 Cor 1–4," *Int* 44 (1990): 117-31.

Litfin, Duane, *St. Paul's Theology of Proclamation: 1 Corinthians 1–4 and Greco-Roman Rhetoric,* SNTSMS 79 (Cambridge: Cambridge University Press, 1994), 174-210.

Luz, U., "Theologie des Kreuzes als Mitte der Theologie im NT," *EvT* 34 (1974): 116-41.

McDonald, James I. H., *Kerygma and Didache: The Articulation and Structure of the Earliest Christian Message,* SNTSMS 37 (Cambridge: Cambridge University Press, 1980), 39-43 and 50-59.

McLean, B. H., *The Cursed Christ: Mediterranean Expulsion Rituals and Pauline Soteriology,* JSNTSS 126 (Sheffield: Sheffield Academic Press, 1996).

McNulty, T. Michael, "Pauline Preaching: A Speech-Act Analysis," *Worship* 53 (1979).

Merklein, K., "Die weisheit Gottes und die Weisheit der Welt (1 Kor 1:2): Zur Möglichkeit einer 'natürlichen Theologie' nach Paulus," in *Studien zu Jesus und Paulus,* WUNT 43 (Tübingen: Mohr, 1987), 376-84.

———, "Das paulinischen Paradox des Kreuzes," *TTZ* 106 (1997): 81-98.

Mitchell, Margaret M., *Paul and the Rhetoric of Reconciliation* (Tübingen: Mohr, 1991), 202-25.

———, "Rhetorical Shorthand in Pauline Argumentation: The Functions of 'the Gospel' in the Corinthian Correspondence," in L. Ann Jervis and Peter Richardson (ed.), *Gospel in Paul — Studies in Corinthians, Galatians and Romans for Richard N. Longenecker,* JSNTSS 108 (Sheffield: Sheffield Academic Press, 1994), 63-88.

Moltmann, J., *The Crucified God: The Cross as the Foundation and Criticism of Christian Theology* (Eng. trans., London: SCM, 1974).

———, *The Way of Jesus Christ: Christology in Messianic Dimensions* (Eng. trans., London: SCM, 1990).

Morris, Leon, *The Cross in the NT* (Grand Rapids: Eerdmans and Exeter: Paternoster, 1995).

Müller, K., "1 Kor. 1:18-25, Die eschatologisch-kritische Funktion der Verkündigung des Kreuzes," *BZ* 10 (1966): 246-72.

Neyrey, J. H., "'Despising the Shame of the Cross': Honor and Shame in the Johannine Passion Narrative," in *Semeia* 68 (1996) (*Honor and Shame in the World of the Bible,* 1994): 113-38.

O'Brien, P. T., *Gospel and Mission in the Writings of Paul* (Carlisle: Paternoster, 1995).

Oke, C. Clare, "Paul's Method Not a Demonstration but an Exhibition of the Spirit," *ExpTim* 67 (1955): 85-86.

Origen, "Fragments, sects. 6-8," in Claude Jenkins (ed.), *JTS* 9 (1908): 235-38.

Ortkemper, Franz-Josef, *Das Kreuz in der Verkündigung des Apostels Paulus* (Stuttgart: Verlag Katholisches Bibelwerk, 1967), 9-67.

———, "Wir verkünden Christus als den Gekreuzigten (1 Kor 1,23)," *Bibel und Kirche* 23 (1968): 5-12.

Pannenberg, W., "The Gospel," in *Systematic Theology,* vol. 2 (Eng. trans., Edinburgh: T. & T. Clark, 1994), 454-64.

Patte, Daniel, *Paul's Faith and the Power of the Gospel: A Structural Introduction to the Pauline Letters* (Philadelphia: Fortress, 1983), 281-87 and 301-12.

Peterson, E., "1 Cor. 1:18 und die Thematik des jüdischen Busstages," *Bib* 32 (1951): 97-103.

Pickett, R., *The Cross in Corinth: The Social Significance of the Death of Jesus,* JSNTSS 143 (Sheffield: Sheffield Academic Press, 1997), esp. 37-84.

Pogoloff, Stephen M., *Logos and Sophia: The Rhetorical Situation of 1 Corinthians,* SBLDS 134 (Atlanta: Scholars Press, 1992), 97-172.

Reese, James M., "Paul Proclaims the Wisdom of the Cross: Scandal and Foolishness," *BTB* 9 (1979): 147-53.

Ridderbos, H., *Paul: An Outline of His Theology* (Eng. trans., London: SPCK, 1977), 135-43.

Robinson, W. C., "Word and Power (1 Cor 1:17–2:5)," in J. McDowell (ed.), *Soli Deo Gloria: NT Studies in Honor of W. C. Robinson* (Richmond: Knox, 1968), 68-82.

Rood, L. A., "Le Christ ΔΥΝΑΜΙΣ ΘΕΟΥ (Puissance de Dieu)," in A. Descamps,

B. Rigaux, et al., *Littérature et Théologie Pauliniennes*, Recherches Bibliques 5 (Louvain: Desclée de Brouwer, 1960), 93-108.

Rosner, Brian S. *Paul, Scripture and Ethics: A Study of 1 Cor. 5–7* (Leiden: Brill, 1994), 3-17 and 81-194.

Schütz, John H., "The Cross as a Symbol of Power," in *Paul and the Anatomy of Apostolic Authority*, SNTSMS (Cambridge: Cambridge University Press, 1975), 187-203.

Schneider, Johannes, "σταυρός," *TDNT*, 7:572-85.

Stowers, Stanley K., "Paul on the Use and Abuse of Reason," in D. L. Balch, E. Ferguson, and W. Meeks (eds.), *Greeks, Romans and Christians: Essays in Honor of J. Malherbe* (Minneapolis: Augsburg, 1990), 253-86.

———, "Social Status, Public Speaking and Private Teaching: The Circumstances of Paul's Preaching Activity," *NovT* 26 (1984): 59-82.

Stuhlmacher, P., *Das paulinische Evangelium* (Göttingen: Vandenhoeck & Ruprecht, 1968).

Tertullian, *Against Marcion*, 5:5 and 6; *On the Resurrection*, 3.

Wedderburn, A. J. M., "ἐν τῇ σοφίᾳ τοῦ θεοῦ, 1 Kor 1:21," *ZNW* 64 (1973): 132-34.

Weder, H., *Das Kreuz Jesu bei Paulus* (Göttingen: Vandenhoeck & Ruprecht, 1981).

Wilckens, Ulrich, *Weisheit und Torheit. Eine exegetisch-religionsgeschichtliche Untersuchung zu 1 Kor. 1 und 2* (Tübingen: Mohr, 1959), 5-41 and 205-24.

Wilckens, Ulrich, "σοφία," *TDNT*, 7:465-528.

Winter, B. W., *Philo and Paul among the Sophists*, SNTSMS 96 (Cambridge: Cambridge University Press, 1997), 186-94.

Wood, H. G., "Didache, Kerygma and Euangelion," in A. J. B. Higgins (ed.), *NT Essays: Studies in Memory of T. W. Manson* (Manchester: Manchester University Press, 1959), 306-14.

Wuellner, W., "Haggadic Homily Genre in 1 Cor 1–3," *JBL* 89 (1970): 199-204.

18   We have noted that the semantic scope of ὁ λόγος is vast and needs to be contextually determined in most cases. Clearly *word* is possible as a translation only because *word of God* has become established in Christian tradition for any component (sentence, statement, utterance, message) of a communicative event ascribed to divine agency (see under 1 Corinthians 14:36, and also under 1:5). Since τῆς μωρίας describes τοῦ κηρύγματος in v. 21 where the two aspects of thought are parallel, we may justifiably assume that **proclamation** most adequately conveys the aspect of λόγος which Paul has in view. *Message of the cross* (NJB, NIV, Barrett) risks too narrow a concentration on cognitive or informational content. Such content is certainly included but it tends to point away from the transformative dimensions of **proclamation**.[19] Worst of all is *doctrine of the cross* (NEB, which REB has changed to *message*). *Doctrine* in this context may generate the very side effect which Paul attacks, namely, divisively drawing attention to itself in place of that to which it witnesses. D. Litfin's title, which he associates especially with this passage, exemplifies

---

19. Schrage describes the proclamation of the cross as the foundation of *transformed existence* (*Der erste Brief*, 1:165).

Paul's theme by using the term **proclamation**.[20] Semantically it stands here in contrast to σοφία λόγου (v. 17), which Litfin translates as **clever rhetoric**, and Pogoloff, with equal validity, as *sophisticated speech.*

Our translation **to those who are on their way to ruin** (also NJB) brings out the force of the articular *present* middle participle (in the dative of disadvantage). Most versions do mark the present (e.g., *to those who are perishing*, NRSV, NIV), but some such phrase as *on the way to* calls attention to the importance of the series of present tenses in connection with salvation. **Ruin** picks up the point that in the active voice ἀπόλλυμι means *to ruin* or *destroy*, while the middle voice, *perish, be lost, be ruined*, leaves open the issue of whether the agency is the self or another. JB's too gentle "not . . . salvation" remains insipid compared with the power of the imagery of **ruin**. **Ruin** also leaves open issues about annihilation and self-loss which are not a point of debate in these verses.

We have inserted **for their part** because although μέν . . . δέ often rightly remains untranslated, the force of the contrast *on the one hand* (μέν) . . . *on the other hand* (δέ) invites some explicit recognition in English in this verse, where antithesis constitutes the key to Paul's argument.[21] But, as Conzelmann correctly notes, the contrast between being **on their way to ruin** and being **on our way to salvation** does not correspond to the antithesis between human folly and human wisdom; it reflects the contrast between *human* folly (μωρία) and *divine* power (δύναμις θεοῦ).[22] This transposition from the expected is all the more remarkable because, as Wilckens argues, the wisdom-folly contrast played an important role in the Graeco-Roman world and almost certainly represented theological slogans or catchwords at Corinth.[23] "Folly" (μωρία) occurs in the NT only at 1 Cor 1:18, 21, 23; 2:14; and 3:19; while "fool" or "foolish" (μωρός) occurs within the epistles of Paul only in 1 Cor 1:25, 27; 3:18; and 4:10 (although twice in the Pastoral Epistles, at 2 Tim 2:13 and Tit 3:9). Hence *Paul transposes the wisdom-folly contrast* into that between *what is humanly self-defeating, stultifying, and foolish* on one side and *what becomes effective, operative, powerful, and transformative* by divine agency. Paul uses this rhetorical technique of transposition or "code-switching" elsewhere.[24]

The touchstone which gives rise to this contrast can be found in the **proclamation of the cross**. The genitive τοῦ σταυροῦ is an objective genitive, i.e., the object of the act of proclaiming, and the phrase serves, in effect, as Paul's definition of the gospel. In Peter Lampe's words, Paul presents "an absolute

---

20. Litfin, *St. Paul's Theology of Proclamation.*

21. See N. Schneider, *Die rhetorische Eigenart der paulinischen Antithese* (Tübingen, 1970). Further Collins, *First Cor,* 102, on the rhetorical device of *contradictio* for μέν . . . δέ. . . .

22. Conzelmann, *1 Corinthians,* 41; cf. Wolff, *Der erste Brief,* 36.

23. Wilckens, *Weisheit und Torheit,* 5-41 and 205-24. See further Merklein, *Der erste Brief,* 1-4, 170-75, and "Semantische Analyse"; and F. Lang, *Die Briefe an die Korinther.*

24. A. C. Thiselton, "The Meaning of σάρξ in 1 Cor. 5:5: A Fresh Approach in the Light of Logical and Semantic Factors," *SJT* 26 (1973): 204-28; J. D. Moores, *Wrestling with Rationality in Paul,* SNTSMS 82 (Cambridge: Cambridge University Press, 1995), 5-32 and 132-60.

contrast between *God* and the word about the *cross* on the one hand, and *the wisdom of the world* on the other hand" (my italics).[25] Such a contrast, Barth observes, "is clearly the secret nerve of this (and perhaps not only this) section."[26] We earlier considered the possibility that parts of vv. 1-3 reflect a homily pattern. If this is the case, and if Paul used the material elsewhere also, Barrett comments, then his "text" is 1 Cor 1:31: "If anyone is to glory, let him glory in the Lord."[27] The proclamation is **folly** unless God, not human wisdom, stands behind it to validate and to underwrite it. Hence Barth is entirely true to Pauline thought here when he speaks of "God by His activating, ratifying and fulfilling of the word of the Bible and of preaching lets it become true."[28] Barth continues: "The promise of the Word of God is not an empty pledge [cf. κενωθῇ, *emptied,* v. 17]. . . . It is the transposing of man into the wholly new state of one who has accepted and appropriated the promise."[29]

This helps us to see in what sense, for Paul, the proclamation of the cross is **the power of God**. It is that in virtue of which God's promise and transforming activity becomes *operative, effective, and actualized.* We need to distinguish between several distinct semantic domains in the occurrences of δύναμις in the NT.[30] In our mechanistic post-industrial age, we tend to think of *power* in terms of degrees of force, such as may be quantified by electrical voltage or by the influence of rhetoric or opinion polls. Louw and Nida place the reference to receiving power through the Spirit in this category in Acts 1:8, although this judgment may well be questioned. They are on firmer ground perhaps with "deeds manifesting great power," e.g., in Luke 1:51 and Acts 2:22, or possibly with the related domain of "authorities and powers" (Col 1:16; cf. Eph 2:12).[31] But from all of these they mark off uses of δύναμις as "pertaining to having special competence in performing some function." Apollos, for example, need not be regarded as "powerful" in the scriptures (δυνατὸς ὢν ἐν ταῖς γραφαῖς) but as especially "competent" (Acts 18:24).[32] Similarly δυναμόω may mean to em-

25. P. Lampe, "Theological Wisdom," *Int* 44 (1990): 120.

26. Barth, *The Resurrection of the Dead,* 18; cf. 15-29.

27. Barrett, First Epistle, 51; cf. C. D. Stanley, *Paul and the Language of Scripture,* SNTSMS 74 (Cambridge: Cambridge University Press, 1992), 186-88. Barrett cites H. St.-John Thackeray, *The Septuagint and Jewish Worship* (London: Oxford University Press, 1921), 97; but we have already cited the more recent proposals of Wuellner, "Haggadic Homily Genre in 1 Cor. 1–3," 199-204, the related suggestions of Davis, *Wisdom and Spirit,* 67-70, and the background cited by D. Daube.

28. Barth, *CD,* 1/1, *The Doctrine of the Word of God,* sect. 3.120.

29. Ibid., sect. 5.152.

30. Louw and Nida, *Greek-English Lexicon of the NT Based on Semantic Domains* (1988-89), 2.67; cf. 1.147-48, 479, 669, and 676.

31. Ibid., 147-48.

32. Ibid., 676. BAGD reserve their main category 2 for *ability, capability,* citing *Papyrus Oxyrhynchus* 1273.24; *BGU* 1050.14; Sir 29:20; Josephus, *Antiquities* 3.102; 10.54; Matt 25:15, and 2 Cor 8:3. But they tend to restrict examples to κατὰ δύναμιν, in the sense of *according to ability.* Although they categorize, e.g., 1 Cor 4:19-20 and 1 Thess 1:5 under "1. *power, might, strength,*" they rightly concede that in these last two occurrences δύναμις is "in contrast to mere word or ap-

power someone in the sense of giving them competence or authorization, while δύναμαι means to have the *ability* to carry something through, or to be *able* to do it.

The cross, then, constitutes the point at which, and/or the means through which, God's presence and promise becomes *operative* as that which *actualizes* and *transforms*.[33] It differs from human weakness and folly not in degree but in kind. For as we noted in our reading of v. 17, a merely rhetorical or psychological exercise in communicating some belief system remains empty if it fails to engage with **the cross** precisely as a saving proclamation, but reflects some *degree of human achievement in gaining and communicating "wisdom."* Such play with words may *seem* to be wise and sophisticated, but only to those who are **on their way to ruin**. Those who are **on our way to salvation** perceive it as sheer **folly**.

Davis and especially Pogoloff, we noted, associate *wisdom* with *degrees of human achievement.* This serves to underline why Paul so carefully uses a series of present participles and other forms of the present in this opening chapter when he describes or refers to salvation. The temptation to assume that Christians have already "arrived" nourishes a mood of self-congratulation which is entirely at odds with **the proclamation of the cross**: a Christ wounded, humiliated, and done-to-death. Hence "It is highly characteristic of Paul's soteriology that he does not speak of 'the saved' (which would be *'sesosmenoi'*) but of those who are being saved *(sozomenoi).* Salvation is not yet gained in its totality."[34]

Stowers and Fitzgerald convincingly argue that Paul stands alongside the best in the Greek philosophical tradition in attacking *not wisdom as such,* but rather *worldly* wisdom. In certain Socratic traditions the sage who serves others may perceive *hardship* as a sign of authenticity. But in some rhetorical schools only applause is perceived as a sign of "success."[35] Hence, Stowers insists, "Far from opposing faith . . . to reason, 1 Cor. 1:18–4:21 criticizes a lack of openness to that which is new and different, as well as epistemic vices

---

pearance." But this is precisely the point that we are making: the word means *operative validity* here and in several other places, in contrast to what is *null, void,* or *merely apparent.*

33. See Brown, *The Cross in Human Transformation,* and Pickett, *The Cross in Corinth* (discussed in our introduction to 1:18–2:5).

34. Héring, *First Epistle,* 8. The prominence of this future emphasis in 1 Corinthians does not support C. H. Dodd's hypothesis of a developing eschatology in Paul, in which his later writings stress the present and past ("The Mind of Paul," in *NT Studies* [Manchester: Manchester University Press, 1953], rpt. from *BJRL* 17 [1933]: 91-105). The article by J. Lowe which addresses Dodd's theory sufficiently answers any query of this kind ("An Examination of Attempts to Detect Development in St. Paul's Theology," *JTS* 42 [1941]: 129-42). As Lowe demonstrates, Paul's emphasis may shift in the light of the pastoral needs of his addressees, and especially in relation to which direction of their own theology invites correction or complementation.

35. John T. Fitzgerald, *Cracks in an Earthen Vessel — An Examination of Catalogues of Hardships in the Corinthian Correspondence,* SBLDS 99 (Atlanta: Scholars Press, 1988), 117-50 and 203-7; and Stanley K. Stowers, "Paul on the Use and Abuse of Reason," in D. L. Balch, E. Ferguson, and Wayne Meeks (eds.), *Greeks, Romans and Christians: Essays in Honour of J. Malherbe* (Minneapolis: Augsburg, 1990), 253-86.

such as conceit."[36] The latter brings illusion and self-deception which marks **their way to ruin**, for recognition of one's ignorance and one's need to continue to learn and to grow marks **our way to salvation**. However, unlike the tradition of the Greek sage, Paul bases everything on **the proclamation of the cross**. By its very nature this determines the pattern of Christian discipleship as living for others, at whatever personal cost.

In modern theology Bonhoeffer has given fresh currency to the ways in which **the cross** redefines what seems **folly** or what reflects **the power of God**. He writes: "If it is I who say where God will be, I will always find there a [false] God who . . . corresponds to me, is agreeable to me. . . . But if it is God who says where he will be . . . that place is the cross of Christ."[37] Hence, he observes, pinpointing a major point of resonance between Jesus and Paul, the beatitudes speak not of the happiness of the wise or the successful or the powerful, but of "those who grieve," "the poor," and "those who suffer persecution for doing right" (Matt 5:3, 4, 10).[38] Wisdom or grace without the cross is what is "sold on the market like a cheapjack's wares." "Cheap grace means the justification of sin without the justification of the sinner . . . forgiveness without requiring repentance, baptism without church discipline . . . the world goes on in the same old way . . . grace without the cross, grace without Jesus Christ."[39]

All of this now revolutionizes our understanding of the meaning of δύναμις θεοῦ, **the power of God**, still further. J. H. Schütz rightly comments on 1 Cor 1:10–4:21: "Paul's sense of power is cast in terms of one . . . very unusual image, the cross. . . . Power appears as weakness and weakness as power. . . . The apostolic life-style is scarcely an unambiguous display of power in the ordinary sense."[40] Many at Corinth seek the shortcut to "power" without the cross, seeking to become "already rich" (4:8) by a "transeschatological" route which avoids the humiliation of the apostolic cruciform lifestyle (4:9-13).[41] But this places *the gospel* at stake no less than it is in Galatians.[42] By rejecting the cry "I am for Paul" (1:12), Paul personally adopts a cruciform posture in relation to "power."

This has epoch-making consequences for the claims of Castelli and Wire about Paul's use of manipulative strategies for power, and with reformulations of the nature of sin in some feminist theologies.[43] Castelli appeals to the well-known

---

36. Stowers, "Paul on the Use and Abuse of Reason," 261.

37. D. Bonhoeffer, *Meditating on the Word* (Eng. trans., Cambridge, Mass: Cowley Publications, 1986), 45.

38. Cf. D. Bonhoeffer, *The Cost of Discipleship* (Eng. trans., London: SCM, unabridged ed. 1959), 93-176.

39. Ibid., 35-36; cf. 37-47.

40. Schütz, *Anatomy of Apostolic Authority,* 187.

41. Wilckens, *Weisheit und Torheit,* 17. See our citation above (introduction to 1:18–2:5) of Martyn, "Epistemology at the Turn of the Ages," and the related arguments of Brown.

42. Schütz, *Anatomy of Apostolic Authority,* 190.

43. E. Castelli, *Imitating Paul: A Discourse of Power* (Louisville: Westminster-Knox, 1991), 1-58, 89-118; A. C. Wire, *The Corinthian Women Prophets* (Minneapolis: Fortress, 1990),

principle expounded by M. Foucault that some assertions supposedly about truth can serve to enhance the speaker's power. She appplies this to Paul, arguing that his direction to imitate his apostolic example (4:16; 11:1) serves as a strategy for imposing Pauline "sameness" or "order" onto the church. Similarly, and more radically, Wire sees Paul as appealing to his own apostolic status as part of a manipulative rhetoric to constrain the new-found freedom and autonomy of women prophets in Corinth. We discuss these claims in more detail below (see, e.g., under 4:16 and esp. 11:1). Meanwhile, in the present verse it is difficult to reconcile such claims with Paul's redefinition of power as that of the cross, or with his earlier disowning of the "Paul" group (1:12), or with his renunciation of apostolic "rights" for the sake of "the other" and of "the weak" (9:12b-23). The cross is the paradigm of self-giving for the sake of the other.

Schütz therefore finds a double nuance in 1:18. **The cross** appears as **"folly"** or as **"the power of God"** *at one level in aspective terms:* from the viewpoint of **those on their way to ruin** it can be perceived or viewed only as **folly**, whereas in the eyes of **those on our way to salvation** it is revealed as what it is, namely, **the power of** the cruciform **God**, whose nature and *modus operandi* comes to light here. Yet **the cross** also appears *at a second level in* quasicausal or (better) transformative terms: "the word of the cross is in some sense response for their respective fates."[44] Schrage, Brown, and Pickett take up this latter theme, and Brown elucidates the relationship between the two themes in terms of epistemology and a world-creating speech-act.[45] Thus *"the wisdom of the world" is subjected to the critique of the cross* in both an *epistemic* sense (the cross defines in what reality consists) and in a *salvific* sense (the cross defines the pathway to life and well-being). We use the word "define" because these realities *count as* realities on the basis of a *definitive divine verdict* expressed through the cross in advance of the last judgment.

This theme in Paul finds particular expression in the work of Moltmann and Jüngel. "Christian identity can be understood as an act of identification with the crucified Christ."[46] It means sharing "the abuse of Christ" (Heb 11:26), even if this entails rejecting worldly "power," by leaving the security of "the camp" and sharing in solidarity with the humiliated and vulnerable; with those who at Corinth were often called "the weak."[47] For the Corinthians' "claim to sophia is in fact based on a misunderstanding of what sophia is (1:18ff.)."[48] Schütz concludes: "The cross itself has an eschatological, critical function

---

throughout. Compare feminist theologies of sin, e.g., in D. Hampson, *Theology and Feminism* (Oxford: Blackwell, 1990), esp. her critique of Niebuhr's notion of sin and pride, 121-25.

44. Schütz, *Anatomy of Apostolic Authority,* 192.

45. Schrage, *Der erste Brief,* 1:165; cf. 165-238; Brown, *The Cross in Human Transformation,* 8-11, 89-104, 150-54; Pickett, *The Cross in Corinth,* esp. 37-84.

46. Moltmann, *The Crucified God,* 19.

47. Moltmann, *The Way of Jesus Christ,* 210; and *Theology of Hope* (Eng. trans., London: SCM, 1967), 304-38.

48. Funk, "Word and Word in 1 Cor. 2:6-16," 278.

which, while it does not usurp God's final judgement in irrevocable fashion, anticipates and perhaps even determines it. It is this 'power' of the word of the cross which is in danger of being vitiated. . . . The polemical thrust of this idea touches on the 'judging' tendency in Corinth."[49] The consumer-oriented obsession with judgments *by an audience* about rhetoric and "consumer" judgments about social status is confronted by judgment *upon an audience* by the proclamation of the cross.

If **the cross** constitutes in some sense a criterion defined in terms of an act of God's judgment, the event of the cross cannot logically be separated from that anticipation of truth and reality which presupposes a finality or definitiveness otherwise reserved in principle for the revelation of God in the last days. Whether, in view of a difficult conceptual history, we prefer to speak of the context of apocalyptic, with Käsemann, Schweitzer, and Beker, or simply more broadly of a context of eschatology, the wisdom-folly, human wisdom versus divine act sets of contrast imply the "reversals" which in the Synoptic tradition characterize many eschatological pronouncements: the exalted will be brought low, and the humble will be exalted (Luke 1:52).[50] Under the title "Paul Proclaims the Wisdom of the Cross: Scandal and Foolishness," James M. Reese has little difficulty in relating "Christ, God's power and wisdom" (1 Cor 1:24) to the "reversals" of the Sermon on the Mount (Matt 5:1-12) and "the apocalyptic of the cross."[51] Earle Ellis further expounds this theme in terms of living for others.[52] The critical dimension finds expression in a number of other works, including especially Müller and Ortkemper.[53]

19-20   To the correct reading (last phrase of v. 20) τὴν σοφίαν τοῦ κόσμου, 𝔭[11] (seventh century), ℵ*, A, B, C*, D*, 33 et al. support the omission. The later gloss is to avoid the impression that Paul is attacking rationality but that which is considered wise within a pressing age. Since the late *Textus Receptus* adopted the longer reading, AV/KJV reads *wisdom of this world.*

This embodies the first of at least fourteen clear quotations from the OT in this epistle. The OT functioned as scripture for the early Christian communities

49. Schütz, *Anatomy of Apostolic Authority,* 192-93.

50. The parallels are transparent in the semantic analysis of Merklein, *Der erste Brief 1–4,* 171-75.

51. J. M. Reese, *BTB* 9 (1979): 147-53. See further J. C. Beker, "The Apocalyptic Character of Paul's Gospel," in *Paul's Apocalyptic Gospel,* 29-54.

52. Ellis, "Christ Crucified," in Banks (ed.), *Reconciliation and Hope,* 74. Earle Ellis writes, "In the present life they are called to actualize the 'crucifixion with Christ'. As imitators to Paul, they are to seek not their own benefit but that of others, to endure suffering. . . ." This coheres with what it is to live out the cross in 4:9-13, rather than relishing a wisdom of achievement as a spectator.

53. Ortkemper, *Das Kreuz in der Verkündigung des Apostels Paulus,* 9-67; and Müller, "1 Kor. 1:18-25. Die eschatologische-kritische Funktion der verkündigung des Kreuzes," 246-72" (see Bibliography above).

from the first, and the argument that Paul appeals to the OT only on an *ad hominem* basis when he addresses Jewish-Christian elements in Galatia or in Rome remains a precarious assumption. Brian Rosner among others has convincingly shown how strongly the OT, including the Deuteronomic decalogue, features behind Paul's ethics in 1 Corinthians, and special attention has been paid to the formula **it is written** by Metzger, Ellis, Moody Smith, and others.[54] Luther's German translation *Es steht geschrieben* ("it stands written") draws attention to the force of the perfect tense of γράφω as expressing the present, lasting, effects which result from a past action.

The place of the OT in Paul's theology remained a matter of deep concern in one of the first major theological controversies of the second century. Marcion attempted to drive a wedge between the two Testaments, and hence in his treatise *Against Marcion* Tertullian makes much of a passage such as this. The issue is not only that Paul appealed to the OT; even more profoundly the gospel constitutes no sudden turn-around from the purposes of the one God of Jews and Christians. The event of the cross publicly displays God's repeated judgment on the inadequacy of self-sufficient human wisdom. Tertullian therefore urges that Isa 29:14 (LXX, with one minor variant) constitutes "the Creator's words."[55] He then explicitly quotes 1 Cor 1:18-23, noting each single verse, to show that the way of the cross stems from the one God who is both creator and redeemer.[56] The "reasons" *(causae)* for the cross and for divine judgment on human wisdom lie "in the hands of him who gave us the scriptures," and the illusions and deceits of human wisdom were exposed "long before."[57] To quote Ulrich Luz, "For Paul, the OT is not in the first place something to understand, but it itself creates understanding."[58]

Is it clear that the OT quotation comes from the LXX of Isa 29:14? Paul quotes the LXX verse with the exception of the last word, where he uses ἀθετήσω, **I will nullify**, in place of the LXX κρύψω, *I will hide.*[59] Numerous explanations for the change have been proposed, including the use of a "free" rendering, a background combination with other texts, the currency of midrashic traditions, or the force of the Hebrew word סתר *(satar)* behind the Greek of the LXX or "adaptation" by Paul.[60] Calvin interpreted ἀθετήσω to mean "obliterate" *(obliterare),* which corresponds to the practical effect of hiding something

54. Rosner, *Paul, Scripture and Ethics: A Study of 1 Cor. 5-7,* 3-17, 81-194 et passim; cf. B. M. Metzger, "The Formulas Introducing Quotations of Scripture to the NT and the Mishnah," *JBL* 70 (1951): 297-307; Ellis, *Paul's Use of the OT,* 22-25; D. Moody Smith, "The Pauline Literature," in D. A. Carson and H. C. M. Williamson (eds.), *It is Written: Scripture Citing Scripture* (Cambridge: Cambridge University Press, 1988), 265-91.

55. Tertullian, *Against Marcion,* 5:5.

56. Ibid.

57. Ibid., 5:19.

58. Ulrich Luz, *Das Geschichtsverständnis des Paulus* (Munich: Kaiser, 1968), 134.

59. See Stanley, *Paul and the Language of Scripture,* SNTSMS 69 (Cambridge: Cambridge University Press, 1992), 185-86; cf. Wolff, *Der erste Brief,* 36, n. 71, κρύψω, not ἀθετήσω.

60. Stanley, *Paul and the Language of Scripture,* 185-86.

in the sense of making it *vanish from view*.[61] He argues (against the interpretation of Erasmus that ἀθετήσω means *I will reject*) that in Isaiah God does "reject" human wisdom, but he now brings about events which eclipse it and make
it useless and irrelevant. Fee argues that the rendering *to vanish* may indeed do
justice to the force of the Hebrew behind the LXX.[62] Robertson and Plummer
suggest that Paul quotes with his "usual freedom," while Héring leaves open the
possibility that Paul draws on memory perhaps of a *Vorlage* of the LXX or
some different version.[63] Senft simply declares, "Paul cites Isa 29:14 LXX
without doubt from memory."[64]

Collins helpfully frames four general principles about Paul's OT citations
which save us from losing sight of the whole because of the detail. (1) Paul
cites scripture frequently where hellenistic writers or rhetoricians might have
appealed to some classic "authority," and most often choose to quote from Isaiah (both in 1 Corinthians and in other epistles). (2) He generally quotes from
the Greek LXX. But he may sometimes depend on a minority textual tradition:
it is not always a "loose" quotation from the LXX texts that we know. (3) He
sees the scriptures as "actualized" in the context of his own situation and Corinth (whether or not we compare the *pesharim* of Qumran or rabbinic *midrash-
im*. (4) He sometimes ascribes OT references to God as applying to Christ as
Lord, and usually takes note of the original context.[65]

The context of Isa 29:14 bears out two points. First, as R. E. Clements's
exegesis makes clear, **the wisdom of the wise** includes what Pogoloff calls here
"the wise of this age" in the sense of that of "the learned or politically dominant
class." Hezekiah's political advisors urges the wisdom of seeking liberation
from the yoke of Assyria, and, as Clements notes, "the wise men here must be a
reference to the counsellors and political advisors of the King."[66] But, second,
in the wisdom of his own purposes God chose to reverse what was perceived as
wise in an event which appeared to consist in weakness and failure, but would
lead in the longer term to new beginnings and to a chastened, transformed, people. "Only when it failed would men come to realise that it was not . . . true wisdom at all."[67] Paul's appeal to Isaiah 29 therefore matches his own context. "It
makes precisely the point Paul wants to press here."[68]

The Gk. σοφία in Paul and in the LXX represents, as we should expect,
חכמה *(chokmah)* in the Hebrew in conjunction with the cognate forms σοφός,

61. Calvin, *First Epistle,* 36.
62. Fee, *First Epistle,* 69-70, n. 11.
63. Robertson and Plummer, *First Epistle,* 19; Héring, *First Epistle,* 8.
64. Senft, *Première Épitre,* 38.
65. Collins, *First Cor,* 94-96. He provides an excellent, succinct discussion. See also Hays,
First Cor, 28-30.
66. R. E. Clements, *Isaiah 1–39,* NCBC (Grand Rapids: Eerdmans and London: Marshall,
1980), 239; also Pogoloff, *Logos and Sophia,* 127.
67. Clements, *Isaiah 1–39,* 239.
68. Fee, *First Epistle,* 70; also Strobel, *Der erste Brief an die Korinther,* 46-47; Collins,
First Cor, 91, "deliberately chosen."

wise person, and חכם (chakam), which may mean skilled or clever in either learning, craft, or the practical affairs of daily life. Similarly, συνετός means *intelligent, sagacious, shrewd* (cf. today's "street-wise"), and σύνεσις denotes *intelligence, acuteness, shrewdness, insight.*[69] These terms translate the Hebrew בינת נבוני (binat nebonai) in Isa 29:14 where בינה (binah) and its cognate forms have comparable or parallel meanings, especially in this verse, and combine with חכמה (chokmah), *wisdom.*[70] **Shrewd . . . shrewdness** conveys the aspect of street-wise political life skills which may prove irrelevant in a context which transcends the original goal, without devaluing them as useful qualities in appropriate circumstances and in relation to instrumental goals.

Just as one part of the Hebrew parallelism finds expression in **the wisdom of the wise** and **the shrewdness of the shrewd**, so the verbal parallel finds expression in ἀπολῶ, **I will destroy** (future active of ἀπόλλυμι as against the middle voice in the previous verse), and ἀθετήσω, **I will nullify**, *bring to nothing, set aside, displace, or render invalid,* with a second distinct meaning of *reject.* Here the semantic contrast functions in relation to God as **power** (v. 18), as denoting that which is effective, valid, operative, and capable of achieving its goal. Against the background of Isaiah 29 the contrast suggests a parallel between the vulnerability and fragility of time spent devising strategies for self-preservation or self-enhancement as against seeking alignment of the self with the divine purpose.

Paul's dramatic rhetorical questions in v. 20 serve to drive home the point, rather than to cover new ground. **Where is the sage?** begins a triad of rhetorical questions which instantiate "his rhetorical use of *repetitio* or *expolitio*."[71] They hardly invite such a one to come forward to begin debate, as some have argued.[72] Paul invites his addressees to say what is left of a human wisdom which God's saving acts have left high and dry in the light of a cross. The cross places giving, receiving, and serving above achieving or "finding the right formula." If the question is not entirely rhetorical, a viable alternative is offered by Fitzgerald's work.[73] In the Socratic tradition, as against that of the Sophists, the path of the sage is marked by a catalogue of hardships, since, unlike the Sophists who serve themselves, the Socratic sage works for the benefit of others. Hence the thought

69. U. Wilckens, "σοφία," *TDNT,* 7:465-76 and 496-526; cf. further BAGD, 788; and Grimm-Thayer, 604.

70. BDBG, 108; G. Fohrer, "σοφία," *TDNT,* 7:476-96; and W. Zimmerli, "Zur Struktur des alttestamentlichen Weisheit," *ZAW* 51 (1933): 177-204.

71. Collins, *First Cor,* 103; cf. Wolff, *Der erste Brief,* 37, on the three groups, and Hays, *First Cor,* 29-30, on the rhetoric.

72. Cf. Fee, *First Epistle,* 70, who finds this "attractive," but concludes rightly that the questions serve rhetorically to "continue the point."

73. Fitzgerald, *Cracks in an Earthen Vessel,* 117-50 and 203-7. Fitzgerald comments: "The sage's sufferings, for example, serve to show both his serenity and his endurance. . . . In 1 Cor. 4 Paul presents himself as a model . . . like the philosophers, then, he uses *peristasis* catalogues. . . . Just as the sage's suffering plays a role in the divine plan, so does Paul's" (204). Cf. Stowers, "The Use and Abuse of Reason," 253-86.

may be: **Where is the sage?** In the case of the "clever" *Sophist,* even if *the Sophist's* attitude can be found in the church itself, this sophist stance brings the sage *nowhere.* But if **sage** is *redefined* in Socratic terms, *this* kind of sage lives a lifestyle which has resonances compatible with the cross, not least in beginning by admitting one's ignorance and need to begin anew. This accords with 3:18: *let him become a fool that he may become wise,* and is amplified and explicated in the identification of **the debater** (συζητητής) as a sophist (1:20). Bruce Winter explains: "Paul did not aim to persuade . . . , by use of the three *pisteis* in rhetoric, namely ἦθος, πάθος and ἀπόδειξις (cf. 1 Cor 2:1-5). . . . Attention would be diverted from the message of the crucified God."[74]

The translation and interpretation of γραμματεύς poses considerable difficulties. We have proposed **expert.** Héring and many others propose Jewish *scribe* in contradistinction to the Greek **sage** or Greek **debater.**[75] Senft, Conzelmann, and Barrett also focus on the OT or Jewish background, largely on the basis of the hypothesis that Paul has in mind as a background an anthology or *florilegium* of such biblical passages as Isa 19:11, 12; Isa 33:18; and probably Isa 44:25 and/or Job 12:17.[76] E. Peterson also argues for the use of a common homiletical fragment from which both 1 Cor 1:19 and parts of Bar 3:9–4:4 were derived perhaps based on Jer 8:13–9:24 (a possibility already hinted at by Edwards).[77] Peterson argues that on the Day of Atonement, Jewish traditions included a critique of the "great ones" of the world as part of a critique of triumphalism. Kenneth Bailey also endorses the conclusion of Wilckens that Paul's use of γραμματεύς forms part of his critique of Jewish theology, while συζητητής signals his polemic against Greek philosophy.[78] Bailey further proposes a chiastic structure in which **sage, person of letters,** and **debater** (or *wise man, scribe,* and *scholar*) correspond in the chiasmus to *"wise men, powerful, nobly born"* in 1:26.[79] Hays and Winter agree that "Much of the controversy at Corinth may have been stirred up by the tendency of new Christians to regard Paul and other Christian preachers as rhetors competing for public attention and approval alongside other popular philosophers. Paul's forceful rebuttal is designed to reframe the categories . . . and to put the gospel in a category apart. . . ."[80]

---

74. Winter, *Philo and Paul among the Sophists,* 187; cf. 186-94.

75. Héring, *First Epistle,* 9.

76. Senft, *Première Épitre,* 38; Conzelmann, *1 Corinthians,* 42-43; Barrett, *First Epistle,* 52-53. We know that such collections or *florilegia* existed and were widely used. Clement of Alexandria used *florilegia* of classical quotations.

77. E. Peterson, "1 Cor. 1:18 und die Thematik des jüdischen Busstages," *Bib* 32 (1951): 97-103; cf. Edwards, *First Epistle,* 26. Peterson depends primarily on H. St. J. Thackeray, *The Septuagint and Jewish Worship* (London: Oxford University Press, 1921, 3d ed. 1923), 95-100.

78. Bailey, "Recovering the Poetic Structure of 1 Cor. 1:17–2:2," 265-96 (esp. 278-79); and Wilckens, *Weisheit und Torheit,* 28.

79. Ibid., 279-81 et passim. In our introduction to this section, however, we queried whether Bailey's detailed listing of chiasmic forms could be established firmly.

80. Hays, *First Cor,* 27: cf. Winter, *Philo and Paul,* 187.

Plausible as these various chiasmic hypotheses are, allusions and chiasmic structures are usually difficult to demonstrate beyond doubt. Moreover, the appeal of Wilckens, Bailey, and many others to the distinction between Jews and Greeks in 1:22 is partially neutralized by Paul's associating *wisdom* with *Greeks* and *signs* with Jews. *Scribe* constitutes too specific a translation, even assuming a Jewish background, since the word in first-century Judaism means *teacher of the law* or *expert,* and is in process of developing into *rabbi.*[81] In the Graeco-Roman world the γραμματεύς is usually a *secretary* or a *clerk* to an official guild or public bureau.[82] Hence, if we allow for a blend of Graeco-Roman and Jewish nuances, we might translate *person of letters,* to preserve the connection with word history, or, perhaps less controversially, **expert**. Today we might well use some such term as *"the professional."* Whatever the original background of thought, we conclude with Schrage that Paul uses the term in his own way for the purpose of his argument, as it would also be understood by his addressees.[83]

The word συζητητής, translated **debater**, occurs only here in the whole of the NT. Ignatius therefore certainly quotes 1 Cor 1:20 when he writes: ποῦ σόφος; ποῦ συζητητής; and adds, ποῦ καύχησις τῶν λεγουμέν συνετῶν; where is the boasting of the so-called shrewd (Ignatius, *To the Ephesians,* 18:1)? The context in Ignatius has affinities with Paul's: the cross is σκάνδαλον τοῖς ἀπιστοῦσιν. Not only does the cross offend or invite ridicule; Ignatius refers further to the notion that "our God, Jesus, the Christ, was conceived by Mary from the seed of David, of the Holy Spirit" (18:2). Clearly in the reception of the text the scope of what eludes human wisdom has become broadened now to include not only the cross, which for Paul displays the heart of God's way of dealing with the world, but also the virgin birth.

The verb ζητέω, *to seek,* became a technical term for philosophical investigations, and in conjunction with the prefix συν- (with) came to mean to coexplore, hence to discuss and to debate especially issues of philosophy.[84] Bailey traces the meaning of "scholar as well as debater" through the Syriac Peshitta and Arabic versions, but concludes that, in accordance with his suggested chiasmus (discussed above), Paul chooses this un-Pauline word to correspond with εὐγενεῖς in 1:26. At all events, the συζητητής participated in a "dispute" or "issue." Hence "**'Debater'** is a good translation for the disputant families in Corinth, from law courts to lecture halls to dining rooms."[85] *Controversialist* might just convey the flavor, but may suggest a lack of seriousness. Further, as Pogoloff urges, both **expert** and **debater** reflect "the same social tendencies of status seeking which Paul perceives as related to the divisions in Corinth."[86]

---

81. Fee, *First Epistle,* 71; Pogoloff, *Logos and Sophia,* 160.
82. MM, 131-32; BAGD, 165-66.
83. Schrage, *Der erste Brief,* 1:175.
84. Cf. H. Greeven, "ζητέω," *TDNT,* 2:893.
85. Pogoloff, *Logos and Sophia,* 159.
86. Ibid., 162.

All of this is confirmed by Paul's use of the term τοῦ αἰῶνος τούτου, which we have translated **of this world order**. In Jewish and Christian eschatology the phrase occurs most characteristically to set in contrast "this age" from "the age to come." But if we translate *this age,* we encounter a lack of contextual understanding brought to the text by modern readers who may have little understanding of a Jewish eschatology of the two ages of apocalyptic. It would be even more misleading to render the term by some static equivalent such as *world* here. Apocalyptic contrasts express in temporal terms realities which in effect amount to a difference between two **world orders**. The present age is beyond mere reform or correction by "wisdom" or by prophetic word, but calls for a new creation. Yet continuities as well as differences lie between the old and new ages. Hence what appears as "folly" or "weakness" as it is judged within the values and frame of the old world order enters the new as what it is, but within the horizons of the new world order at once appears as "wisdom" and divine "power." The three status-related terms **sage, expert**, and **debater** receive a different evaluation within a different **world order**. In 1:26 Paul will repeat the thought in different terms: "Wise by human standards" (κατὰ σάρκα). Alexandra Brown's masterly exposition of the apocalyptic frame within which the performative speech-act of proclaiming the cross re-shapes "worlds" corroborates the unity of Paul's argument here.[87]

This is further corroborated by the parallelism of the last phrase of v. 20: οὐχὶ ἐμώρανεν ὁ θεὸς τὴν σοφίαν τοῦ κόσμου; **has not God made a fool of the world's wisdom**? As in the Fourth Gospel, so also in Paul, κόσμος may denote either the whole created order in a positive or neutral sense, or the world order as it has become through structural self-centeredness, status-seeking, and supposed self-sufficiency. Here it clearly functions in the second sense, for as we have seen from Stowers, Fitzgerald, and Pogoloff, it is not wisdom or reason as such which Paul attacks, but that which is status seeking, manipulative, or otherwise flawed in some way which diverts it from serving the purposes of God. The aorist active of μωραίνω, *I make foolish, I show to be foolish,* serves as an emphatic verb. The passive (Rom 1:22) means *to become* foolish. The phrase in modern English, **made a fool of,** usually applies to the unexpected disclosure of the foolishness of a self-important person or persons of assumed achievement or status whose assumption of importance, achievement, or status is exposed as illusory.

This matches the force of our passage. Schrage perceives it as the eschatological fulfillment in triumph through God's deed in Christ of the sure word of scripture about the self-styled achievements of the wise.[88] Wisdom refers not only to knowledge or expertise, which has limits, but also to "the attitude, in this case *hybris.*"[89] Chrysostom suggests several analogies: a sick person may

---

87. Brown, *The Cross,* esp. 13-30. Cf. Wendland, *Die Briefe,* 22; and more fully Weiss, *Der erste Kor,* 27-29, and Hays, *First Cor,* 28.

88. Schrage, *Der erste Brief,* 1:175.

89. Conzelmann, *1 Corinthians,* 42; and again the idea on 44.

be nauseated by health-giving food; a child, or people mentally disoriented, may think the important trivial, or the trivial important. Even so, the event of the cross is like the new frame of reference brought to the sick by health, or to children or to the unsound in mind by full, rational maturity.[90]

The valid notion of a new frame of reference places the notion of **the world's wisdom** (in contrast to the wisdom of the Holy Spirit, 2:6-16) in its proper context. Against virtually all other translations except the REB, the AV/ KJV translates *wisdom of this world* on the basis of the *Textus Receptus* (see Textual Note, above). The notion is presupposed, and presumably the REB includes it not because it represents a better textual reading (it does not), but because the later textual gloss explicates the implied contrast between *this* world, as the *present world order,* and the divine purposes which transcend it. The double force of τοῦ αἰῶνος τούτου, **this world order**, or *this* [present] *age* (v. 20a), and τοῦ κόσμου, **the world** (v. 20b), operates jointly to convey Paul's thought. Only within the broader frame of the purposes of God can the status of such reasoning be exposed as the folly of a limited wisdom, which sees only part of the picture from an inappropriate angle of vision.

Collins convincingly argues that in spite of a massive research literature on the subject "it seems unwarranted to try to identify one particular philosophical system as **the 'wisdom of the world'** to which Paul was making reference."[91] The Corinthian community was too diverse. Hence exclusively to identify this **wisdom** either with (1) the Jewish Wisdom tradition (Conzelmann, Windisch, Dupont), or (2) with hellenistic-Jewish traditions reflected, e.g., in Philo (Horsley, Pearson, Davis), or (3) with some early nascent form of gnosticism (Bultmann, Schmithals, Wilckens), remains too narrow: "each of them offers insights that shed some potential light on the situation of the Corinthian Christians."[92] The fundamental point, which is well argued by Stowers, is that Paul is *not* simply attacking the use of *human reason as such*. Reason can be flawed by "epistemic vices" of instrumental manipulation and selfdeception, and most certainly Paul sees human reason as having firm *limits*. However, his evaluation of reason is entirely positive when reason is rightly used for good and proper purposes within an appropriate framework.[93]

21 The Greek may at first seem more complex than it is because the word order cannot readily be translated in the same sequence. Paul uses ἔγνω (**came to know**) to bring out the "effective" force of the aorist, i.e., its eventful character as an act which gives rise to effects, just as the aorist infinitive σῶσαι, **to save**, also lets the emphasis fall on a single action of the divine de-

---

90. Chrysostom, *1 Cor. Hom.,* 4:1-4.

91. Collins, *First Cor,* 97.

92. Ibid.

93. Stowers, "Paul on the Use and Abuse of Reason," in *Greeks, Romans and Christians: Essays in Honor of J. Malherbe,* 253-86. (See further, Bornkamm, "Faith and Reason in Paul," in *Early Christian Experience,* 29-46.)

cree.[94] **Since** (ἐπειδή) is used in the causal sense. While εὐδοκεῖν may mean quite simply *to resolve, to determine, God chose* (Barrett), or *God decided* (NRSV), or **it pleased God** (AV, KJV) may perhaps more readily avoid any hint of a merely reactive or temporally conditioned divine action: "by God's design human wisdom did not lead to the saving experience of God."[95]

Two phrases stand in very sharp contrast to each other, both introduced by διά with the genitive: **through wisdom . . . through the foolishness of what is proclaimed**. Hence we have used the English idiom which offers a corresponding emphasis: **it was not through wisdom that**. . . . We have also explicated what is clearly the meaning of τοῦ κηρύγματος by rendering it **of what is proclaimed**. Commentators from Meyer (1869) to Wolff (1996) and Horsley (1998) emphasize that the phrase refers to *the substance of the preaching* (Meyer), or the proclamation of the crucified Christ (Wolff).[96] "The word *kērygma* (KJV 'preaching') here means not the act of preaching itself, but the content of that proclamation. This is confirmed by vv. 22-25, which go on to explicate 'the foolishness of what was preached.' "[97] The point is worth making, first because the emphasis falls on the limits of natural human inquiry and discovery. Second, Schrage places the emphasis on the divine decree and its basis, not on the mode of communication as such, and on the difference between gospel proclamation and human discovery. It has nothing to do with whether the mode of communication is in a pulpit rather than a variety of modes which may or may not include lectures, dialogue, disputation, or living the gospel out.[98]

The phrase ἐν τῇ σοφίᾳ τοῦ θεοῦ, **in God's wisdom**, has been interpreted in several different ways. The preposition ἐν with the dative has a wide semantic scope. BAGD list numerous subcategories of meaning, several of which are explored by Merklein.[99] Furthermore, the theme of divine wisdom has been un-

94. Cf. P. Bachmann, *Der erste Brief des Paulus an die Korinther* (Leipzig: Deichert, 1905; 4th ed. [with E. Stauffer] 1936), 86; Schrage, *Der erste Brief,* 1:178. See Nigel Turner on "perfective aorist" and subcategories of *Aktionsarten* (ingressive, perfective et al.) in MHT, 70-74, esp. 72.

95. Collins, *First Cor,* 105.

96. Meyer, *First Epistle,* 1:42; Wolff, *Der erste Brief,* 39; Horsley, *1 Cor,* 51.

97. Fee, *First Epistle,* 73; Robertson and Plummer describe "the foolishness of preaching" as "a bold oxymoron" (*First Epistle,* 21). Barrett also places the emphasis on the content, not the mode of presentation, when he comments of the *kerygma,* "it is focused on the cross" (*First Epistle,* 53).

98. Cf. Schrage, *Der erste Brief,* 1:181. Litfin's otherwise excellent discussion does sometimes verge on fusing the two distinct types of contrast, although we may readily admit that in practice they are often very closely related. Litfin writes, "The crucial term κήρυγμα in 1:21 again preserves Paul's dual emphasis on form and content" (*Proclamation,* 198). This observation remains valid particularly for the situation at Corinth, where the practice of rhetoric too often invited a competitive, status-seeking bid for applause and the applause of the audience (see Introduction, 20-21, and below).

99. BAGD, 258-61; Merklein, *Der erste Brief 1–4,* 180-82. Louw and Nida, *Greek-English Lexicon,* 2:84-85, list 21 "semantic domains": cf. also Grimm-Thayer, 209-13. Conzelmann shows how exegetes have drawn on many of these subcategories (e.g., temporal, instrumental, spatial, modal); (*1 Cor,* 45). Merklein enters into still more detail.

derstood in a variety of ways. This leaves room for more than one tradition of interpretation.

(1) *Wisdom revealed in the law and the prophets.* Clement of Alexandria, followed by a number of Church Fathers, takes **the wisdom of God** to refer to what was revealed "in what was spoken by the prophets."[100] Chrysostom includes also the design of the natural order "whereby it was God's will to make himself known."[101]

(2) *A Transformative wisdom which reverses the value systems of the world.* Origen takes up the second main line of interpretation in his treatise *Against Celsus.* Over against the distortions made of the Christian message and its scriptures by Celsus, Origen refers to the blindness which makes such distortions an aspect of "the wisdom of the world . . . not to be wondered at . . . since in the wisdom of God the world by wisdom did not come to know God."[102] Earlier he alludes to the accusation of Celsus that Christians say, "The wisdom of this life is bad, but foolishness is a good thing."[103] Origen interprets Paul's words as marking the *reversal of what counts as "wisdom"* (or what seems "folly") in the light of the cross and in the wisdom of God.

(3) *Divine Wisdom as God's Self-Disclosure.* After a careful consideration of wisdom in apocalyptic Jewish myths and the relation between God and the figure of Wisdom as God's "image" (εἰκών, Wis 7:22ff.; cf. Sir 1:9, 10), Conzelmann concludes, "Wisdom is 'his' [God's]. . . . The possibility of knowing God does not belong essentially to man (as a 'property'); it is bestowed on him by revelation."[104] Similarly Barrett writes, "there is no manifestation of God that man's essentially self-regarding wisdom does not twist until it has made God in its own image."[105] We are not in the abstract realm of discussing divine "attributes," but "God's free dealings with the world. Revelation is . . . an act of salvation."[106] Calvin observes, "It is the blindness of the human mind, which, surrounded by light, sees nothing."[107] Davis sees behind 1:18-21 Paul's appropriation of "the prophetic critique of Israel's wisdom which had failed to perceive the pattern of God's activity in the course of contemporary events," to which the failure of "wisdom" at Corinth constituted a close parallel.[108] God's *Self-disclosure,* however, is, as Barth points out, not simply *about* God, but "the Word of God is itself the act of God," an "address" which presupposes God's own presence.[109]

100. Clement, *Stromata,* 1:18.
101. Chrysostom, *1 Cor. Hom.,* 4:4.
102. Origen, *Against Celsus,* 5:16.
103. *Against Celsus,* 1:9.
104. Conzelmann, *1 Corinthians,* 46.
105. Barrett, *First Epistle,* 54.
106. Conzelmann, *1 Corinthians,* 46.
107. Calvin, *First Corinthians,* 40.
108. Davis, *Wisdom and Spirit,* 71.
109. Barth, *CD,* 1/1, 109 and 143.

(4) *Divine Wisdom as a Prophetic Critique of Instrumental Reason?* Wisdom in the later Jewish tradition, Beaudean asserts, became personified (cf. Proverbs 1–9) as "a prophetic voice summoning a person."[110] But in Graeco-Roman culture, especially at Corinth, it signified not only an achievement which invited applause but also "action to subjugate . . . and to master the various problems of life and life itself."[111] The cross reverses this principle: its "power" does not lie in the force of "mastery," but in a coming-to-nothing which awaits God's own transforming, creative, life and action. Beaudean accepts Horsley's analysis of the cross in hellenistic-Jewish traditions as "both eloquence and means of salvation."[112]

(5) *The Wisdom of God as Grace Freely Given.* This Wisdom, Litfin argues, precludes dependence on the "intellectual and verbal skills" of the rhetorician.[113] To press the connection between worldly wisdom in the hellenistic-Jewish tradition and "achievement" (Davis) is not an artificial "Lutheran" reading of these verses." The σοφία which Paul fears will undermine the community "is nothing other than rhetoric," but only in the special sense applicable to first-century Corinth.[114] It embodies the self-sufficient, self-confident *stance* which is at variance with the "weakness" and self-emptying of the cross and of the cruciform nature of God's dealings with the world in Christ. "The *Crucified One* must be the criterion for any possible concept of God."[115]

All of these five aspects play some part in assisting our understanding of Paul's use of the words **the wisdom of God** in this context. Above all, however, it stands in antithetical opposition to **the wisdom of this world order**, which is fallible, temporary, short-term, and self-absorbed. The links with apocalyptic verdict, whether in the cross or at the end time, cannot be avoided. For what some may perceive as *foolish* is in fact *definitive,* and will expose its transient opposite as deceptive and illusory. Merklein observes that the best commentary on v. 21a is Rom 1:18–3:20.[116]

22-24   In v. 23 the well-attested word ἔθνεσιν, **to the Gentiles** (e.g., ℵ, A, B, C*, D*, F, G, 33), is replaced by Ἕλλησι, *to Greeks,* in C3, D2, and the *Textus Receptus.* Hence **Gentiles** (NRSV, NIV, NJB, REB) is *Greeks* in AV/KJV. But the semantic contrast between Jew and Greek regularly denoted Jew and Gentile, so nothing of substance is at issue.

110. Beaudean, *Paul's Theology of Preaching,* 93.

111. Ibid.; cf. also U. Wilckens, "σοφία," *TDNT,* 7:476.

112. Beaudean, *Paul's Theology of Preaching,* 94, and R. Horsley, "Wisdom of Word and Words of Wisdom in Corinth," *CBQ* 39 (1977): 224-25; cf. 224-39.

113. Litfin, *St. Paul's Theology of Proclamation,* 198.

114. Welborn, *Politics and Rhetoric,* esp. 28-32; earlier, "On the Discord," 102; and Pogoloff, *Logos and Sophia,* 111.

115. Jüngel, *God as the Mystery of the World,* 184.

116. Merklein, *Der erste Brief 1–4,* 182. Further, U. Luz, "Theologie des Kreuzes . . .," *EvT* 34 (1994): 123-25 (cf. 116-41).

The *inclusive* aspect of the contrast between **Jews** and **Greeks** is more important than the exclusive: Paul examines the impact of the kerygma of the cross "in the presence of all humankind."[117] The introductory **since** (ἐπειδή) repeats the introductory syntax of v. 21, "a little loosely, to introduce a sharper restatement of the thought."[118] The respective role of **signs** and **wisdom** in relation to **Jews** and **Gentiles** is not accidental. **Jews** already had access to "wisdom" in the scriptures, but required **signs** to locate their situation within the promised purposes of salvation history. In one sense, they were right. For the resurrection of Christ constitutes the sign that the cosmic turning point has arrived and casts essential light on the christological and cosmic significance of Jesus of Nazareth.[119] Paul expounds **God's power** as an "eschatological motif."[120] On the other hand, the Gentile "Greeks" go on seeking what will bring success in politics, the courtroom, philosophy, or in everyday affairs of trade, love, or the household; what will bring "mastery" of life and especially the approval or admiration of patrons, masters, and their own peer group.[121]

Conzelmann perhaps underplays this distinctive contrast, but rightly comments that Paul's observation of the world of his day carries no hint of a moralistic judgmentalism here.[122] It is understandable that Jews should be careful about credulity concerning the fulfillment of the divine promise in an event which superficially seemed to contradict it. It was a "given" of Corinthian life and culture, as well as of much of the Graeco-Roman world, that people sought every means to gain esteem, honor, and success.[123] But this means that these very preoccupations, especially if pursued obsessively, will find **a crucified Christ an affront**: On one side it was **an affront** to those who **ask for signs**, since the disgraceful and humiliating execution of a Jewish teacher by the occupying power hardly seemed to constitute a sign of God's saving action. On the other side, it was **folly**, i.e., the very reverse of a "mastery" of life that brings success, honor, and esteem, for the figure whom Paul proclaimed passively accepted the kind of suffering and death which shouted failure, dishonor, and shame. Paul's *logos* was "speech about a person of the lowest status: a crucified criminal."[124] In the context of the final "reversals" expected in Jewish apocalyptic, the quest for "signs" of an imminent end is equally understandable, but in relation to the proclamation of the cross one which results in **affront**.

Paul does not use the definite article with Χριστόν here. The phrase

117. Collins, *First Cor,* 92; also Merklein, *Der erste Brief 1–4,* 187.

118. Barrett, *First Epistle,* 54.

119. Pannenberg, *Systematic Theology,* 2:343-79.

120. Müller, "I Kor 1:18-25," *BZ* 10 (1966): 246-72; and Collins, *First Corinthians,* 92.

121. Cf. Pogoloff, *Logos and Sophia,* 108-27, 129-72; and other literature cited above.

122. Conzelmann, *1 Corinthians,* 46-47.

123. See *Semeia* 68 (1996): *Honor and Shame in the World of the Bible,* esp. J. H. Neyrey, "Despising the Shame of the Cross," 113-38.

124. Pogoloff, *Logos and Sophia,* 156. See further Merklein, "Die Weisheit Gottes und die Weisheit der Welt (I Kor 1:21): Zur Möglichkeit und Hermeneutik einer 'natürlichen Theologie' nach Paulus," in Merklein, *Studien zu Jesus und Paulus,* 376-84.

should be translated either *a Christ crucified* (RV margin) or **a crucified Christ** (NJB). To translate simply Christ crucified (NRSV, RSV, Barrett) seems to lose some of the force of Paul's point. Some strongly emphasize this point, comparing 1 Cor 2:2 and Gal 3:1: "The Jews demanded a victorious Christ, heralded by σημεῖα. . . . Christ was not preached as a conqueror to please the one, nor as a philosopher to please the other."[125]

Paul would not conceal or accommodate **the affront** caused by his proclaiming **a crucified Christ**, in all the stark and offensive reality of the proclamation. The word σκάνδαλον, translated **affront**, has been variously rendered as *scandal* (Barrett, Fee), *stumbling block* (AV/KJV, NRSV, NIV, Collins, Moffatt), or *an obstacle they cannot get over* (NJB). All of these can be defended. The Greek word occurs only rarely outside the LXX and NT, but occurs six times in Matthew and Luke, six times in the Pauline epistles (once each in 1 Peter, 1 John and Revelation), i.e., 15 times in the NT. Hatch-Redpath list 21 occurrences in the LXX, where it translates four Hebrew words of which the two main nouns are מוֹקֵשׁ *(moqesh)* and מִכְשׁוֹל *(mikshol).*[126] These may relate to catching in a snare, but the meaning *trap,* or more strictly the tripstick of a trap, is not well attested in nonbiblical Greek, and offers only one of several possible meanings in most of the NT examples. In Gal 5:11 Paul speaks of τὸ σκάνδαλον τοῦ σταυροῦ, where a double **affront** is caused by the curse entailed for one who is hanged on the cross and by the nullification of the role of self-help.[127] Peter's suggestion in Matthew that Jesus should avoid the cross is itself a σκάνδαλον to Jesus (Matt 16:23). Barrett and Fee insist that it includes *scandal;* thus TEV translates *what is offensive.*[128] In several contexts the word denotes what may provoke someone to a negative or even rebellious reaction. No single English word seems to cover its various nuances, and much of the emphasis depends on the context. When we bear in mind Pogoloff's convincing picture of what it would be to proclaim a crucified criminal of modest status to those who sought honour, esteem, and success, to translate **an affront** seems to capture the mood and nuance most closely.

In certain religious circles then and now the absence of predetermined **signs** of God's action, leaving only the bare proclamation of *Christ,* also becomes **an affront.** We have already examined the force of **folly** (μωρία) in these verses. If "wisdom" smacks of achievement, success, and the path to esteem

---

125. Robertson and Plummer, *First Epistle,* 22.

126. Hatch-Redpath, 1268.

127. See H. Giesen, "σκάνδαλον," *EDNT,* 3:248-50 (H. Giesen); G. Stählin, "σκάνδαλον," *TDNT,* 7:339-58; Moulton and Geden, *Concordance to the Greek Testament,* 894-95, e.g., Matt 16:23; 18:7; Luke 17:1; Rom 9:33 (where the LXX reflects the Hebrew meaning); 11:9 (also LXX from Heb.); 14:13; 16:17; Gal 5:11; and 1 Pet 2:8 ("stone of stumbling"? rock of offense?). On Gal 5:11 cf. F. F. Bruce, *Commentary on Galatians,* NIGTC (Exeter: Paternoster and Grand Rapids. Eerdmans, 1982), 237-38. Bruce speaks both of the "curse" and of the "affront to all notions of proper self-pride or self-help" (238). Louw and Nida list *trap, sin,* and *offense* in distinct semantic domains (2:222).

128. Fee, *First Epistle,* 75, n. 38: it arouses opposition. Cf. Barrett, *First Epistle,* 54.

and honor in hellenistic-Jewish and Graeco-Roman traditions in the first century, the cross of Christ is perceived within such a culture and worldview as its very opposite. To renounce one's own powers in order to place one's trust entirely in the action of an Other constitutes the negation of all that "Greeks" or **Gentiles** understood about the path to success. Similarly, if "signs of the end" are understood to denote a reversal of Jewish political fortunes, a humiliated Messiah, again, is **an affront**. Jews and Gentiles stand on the same footing, each as self-styled "critic."[129]

Yet to those, both **Jews and Greeks** (τε καί . . .), whom God has **called**, the cross of Christ constitutes precisely the mode of action which conveys **God's power and God's wisdom**. It does not rest on human calculations about **signs** of the times, nor upon manipulative devices which entice belief, nor does it rest on self-defeating strategies to master life by techniques of human **wisdom**. **God's** manifestation of **power** and **wisdom** operates on a different basis, namely, the way of love which accepts the constraints imposed by the human condition or plight and the prior divine act of promise, and becomes effective and operative (has **power**) in *God's own way,* for it corresponds with God's own nature as revealed in Christ and in the cross. Any version of the gospel which substitutes a message of personal success for the cross is a manipulative counterfeit. Jüngel writes, "God defined himself as love on the cross of Jesus. If the cross, as the world's turning point, is the foundation and measure of metaphorical language about God, then such language itself has the function of bringing about a turning around, or change of direction. God cannot be spoken of as if everything remained as it was."[130]

In this sense, **God's power and God's wisdom** do indeed become actualized in, through, and even as **Christ: Christ, God's power and God's wisdom**. But because the cross is a turning point and criterion which may reverse assumptions and values, we should be cautious about applying without very careful qualifications the everyday meanings, or even theological meanings, of *power* and *wisdom* as they occur in other contexts. We have already seen from v. 18 that **God's power** refers to the effective operation of a power-in-weakness which operates under chosen and accepted constraints, namely, those of the cross, reflected in the cruciform lifestyle of apostolic hardships in 4:9-13.[131]

J. A. Davis's insistence that this divine wisdom stands in contrast to what is "achieved" in human wisdom coheres well with Dietrich Wiederkehr's exegesis of **to those who are called**, for whom *calling* is part of God's self-giving initiative, summed up in the phrase of v. 21, "**it pleased God**."[132]

25 This verse brings to a conclusion the force of the argument of vv. 18-

---

129. Schrage, *Der erste Brief,* 1:183, esp. as *"homines religiosi"* who *demand* signs or impose their own criteria; cf. also Collins, *First Cor,* 92-93 and 105-7.

130. Jüngel, *God as the Mystery of the World,* 220; and *Theological Essays* (Eng. trans., Edinburgh: T. & T. Clark, 1989), 1:65.

131. See above on Fitzgerald, *Cracks in an Earthen Vessel,* 117-50 and 203-7.

132. D. Wiederkehr, *Die Theologie der Berufung in den Paulusbriefen,* 112; cf. 123-25.

25, for which vv. 13-17 laid the groundwork, and following which 1:26-31 and 2:1-5 provide confirmation from two types of experience of church life. The force of ὅτι, translated **for**, remains causal. Although virtually all of the English versions translate τὸ μωρὸν τοῦ θεοῦ as **God's foolishness** or the *foolishness of God*, the definite article with the neuter single of the adjective μωρός strictly means *the foolish thing*. This has been taken in either of two possible senses. (1) Tertullian identifies the foolish thing *(Stultum)* as the cross; and the weak thing *(infirmum)* as the incarnation: "Quid est stultum Dei sapientius hominibus, nisi crux et mors Christi? Quid infirmum Dei fortius homine, nisi nativitas et caro Dei?"[133] Among modern commentators Weiss also interprets the neuter adjective as a reference to "the single act of God . . . namely the death of Christ on the cross, which is held by men to be a sign of foolishness and weakness."[134] (2) Meyer, Lietzmann, and others, however, interpret the article and adjectival form as virtually equivalent to modern quotation marks: "What appears to men absurd."[135] Typically TEV is so anxious to direct the understanding of the uninformed reader that it goes still further and translates: "what *seems to be* God's foolishness is wiser than human wisdom and what *seems to be* God's weakness is stronger than human strength." But this renders the reader passive and Paul's startling oxymoron insipid: the syntax, as reader-response theorists would insist, serves to provoke the reader into activity, and vv. 18-24 have given enough direction and sufficient clues to render Paul's clash of terms transparent to active readers.

Conzelmann speaks here of Paul's "epigrammatic form."[136] Jeremias and Funk also discuss the stylistic parallelism and the role of chiasmus in this section.[137] In a valuable and very fruitful research essay Margaret Mitchell recently addressed the issues of "Rhetorical Shorthand in Paul's Argumentation: The Functions of 'the Gospel' in the Corinthian Correspondence."[138] She takes up the rhetorical axiom expressed by Tryphon that "Brevity is an expression which has more meaning than just what is heard."[139] In terms of stylistic form, this may embody synecdoche; indeed, συνεκδοχή was a technical term in

---

133. Tertullian, *Against Marcion,* 5:5. This entire long chapter traces Pauline phrases in 1 Cor 1:3, in 1:18, 19, 20, 21, 22, 23, 24, 25, 27, 29, and 31, and in 1 Cor. 2:6, 7. Against Marcion, Tertullian insists that in the providence of the one God "nothing is found ignoble or contemptible . . . [except] in man's arrangement." The regulations in Leviticus about sacrifices and cleansing vessels, e.g., may be held in derision by those who glory in human wisdom rather than "glorying in the Lord" (1 Cor 1:31). But nothing in the OT compares for "foolishness" with the cross as God's mode of action.

134. Weiss, *Der erste Korintherbrief,* 34.

135. Meyer, *First Epistle,* 1:45; Lietzmann, *An die Korinther,* 10.

136. Conzelmann, *1 Cor,* 48.

137. Jeremias, "Chiasmus in den Paulusbriefen," 145-56; and R. W. Funk, "The Letter: Form and Style," in *Language, Hermeneutic and Word of God,* 260-61; cf. 250-74.

138. Mitchell, "Rhetorical Shorthand in Pauline Argumentation," in Jervis and Richardson (eds.), *Gospel in Paul,* 63-88.

139. Ibid., 67.

Graeco-Roman rhetoric.[140] Cicero similarly defines it as "when the whole is known from a small part, or a part from the whole."[141] Thus the gospel (τὸ εὐαγγέλιον) and the proclamation of the cross (ὁ λόγος τοῦ σταυροῦ) are shorthand instances of synecdoche *for the whole story of God's purposes which lead up to the cross and follow it.* They are "technical terms or titles which summarize the whole," and the reader must "fill in" what is implicit (as occurs in the "open" texts of Eco and Iser).[142]

Margaret Mitchell applies this approach to 1 Cor 1:18-25. In this passage, she comments, "The gospel story, as the exemplification of God's paradoxical logic, necessarily entails a re-evaluation of σοφία, δύναμις and εὐγένια ('wisdom, power and noble birth') which dismantles the 'human' constructs which are still so operative in the Corinthians' lives and dealings with one another. In place of all this, the gospel offers Christ crucified, a new kind of σοφία ('wisdom') as 1:30 recapitulates."[143] The proclamation of the cross is folly within the world order of human wisdom not least because Paul's *kerygma* constitutes "a paradigm of self-effacement" which contradicts the wisdom stance and wisdom posture which breeds the "splits" in the community.[144]

In line with the arguments noted in Schütz's interpretation of the power-in-weakness of the cross, Robert Funk shows how this abbreviated "word" generates a contrast between "two languages," one of which generates the world of human values, the other of which generates the world of effective reality summed up in Paul's use of the word δύναμις, *power.*[145] This real and effective "world" eclipses the limits of human wisdom and power, so that "God's foolishness is wiser than humans."[146] Hence Bengel sees the pretensions of human aspirations to wisdom and power as resting on wishful re-

---

140. LSJ, 1483, *"an understanding one thing with another:* hence in Rhetoric . . . an indirect mode of expression *when the whole is put for a part or vice versa;* Quintilian, *Inst. Or.* 8.6.19." Also in an adjectival form in Diodorus Siculus, 5.31.

141. Cicero, *Rhetorica ad Herennium* 4.33.44; This is more specific than "litotes" or understatement, suggested by Collins, *First Cor,* 108.

142. Mitchell, "Rhetorical Shorthand," 65. This suggests parallels at the "micro" level to the broader reader-response approach in literary theory of Wolfgang Iser, *The Implied Reader* (Baltimore: Johns Hopkins University Press, 1974), and esp. *The Act of Reading: A Theory of Aesthetic Response* (Baltimore: Johns Hopkins University Press, 1978 and 1980); Umberto Eco, *The Role of the Reader: Explanation in the Semiotics of Texts* (London: Hutchinson, 1981), and *Semiotics and the Philosophy of Language* (London: Macmillan, 1984). Both writers are expounded and evaluated in A. C. Thiselton, *New Horizons in Hermeneutics* (Grand Rapids: Zondervan, 1992), 516-29 (cf. 529-557), in a chapter devoted to reader-response theory.

143. Ibid., 71.

144. Ibid., 70. Cf. the arguments of J. A. Crafton and E. Best considered under 1:1 (on *apostle*).

145. Funk, "Word and Word in 1 Corinthians 2:6-16," in *Language, Hermeneutic and Word of God,* 281-88; cf. 275-305. See further Schütz, "The Cross as a Symbol of Power: 1 Cor. 1:10–4:21," in *Anatomy of Apostolic Authority,* 187-203.

146. Funk, "Word and Word," 275-76, 279-83, and 285-87.

definition: *definire velint quid sapiens et potens sit.*[147] Grammatically, we might understand τῶν ἀνθρώπων either as a straightforward genitive of comparison, *than humans,* or as a condensed comparison, *"wiser than human wisdom"* (cf. the idiom in Matt 5:20 and John 5:36).[148] Fee's paraphrase that God's wisdom "outsmarted" human wisdom in the cross destroys the qualitative differences between the notion of wisdom as a matter of being "smart" and the power-in-weakness which redefines power and wisdom in a difference of *kind,* not one of *degree.* Similarly his use of "overpowered" intensifies this problem.[149] Paul's marvelously succinct rhetorical parallelism both recapitulates vv. 18-24 (first paragraph or section of 1:18–2:5) and points forward to the next sections (1:26-31 and 2:1-5).[150]

2. The Contrast between Divine and Human Wisdom Further Demonstrated in Terms of the Corinthians' Own Human History and Social Status (1:26-31)

(26) Think about the circumstances of your call, brothers and sisters, that not many of you were intellectuals, as the world counts cleverness, not many held influence, not many were born to high status. (27-29) But the foolish things of the world God chose in order to shame the clever; and the weak things of the world God chose to shame positions of strength; and the insignificant of the world and the despised God chose, yes, the nothings, to bring to nothing the "somethings." So that all kinds of persons should not pride themselves before God. (30, 31) It is as a gift from him that you are in Christ Jesus, who became for us wisdom given from God: our righteousness and sanctification and redemption, in order that, as it is written, "Let the one who glories, glory in the Lord."

Little needs to be added to the general introduction (above) to 1:18–2:5. The contrast between the wisdom of God and so-called "human wisdom" is exposed in the light of the cross in its reality. This has transformative and epistemological implications as well as social and ethical consequences.[151] In terms of rhetoric, logical argument, and theological content, Paul expounds a coherent theme in terms of (1) the nature and transformative power of the

147. Bengel, *Gnomon,* 612.
148. Robertson and Plummer, *First Corinthians,* 23.
149. Fee, *First Epistle,* 77.
150. Merklein, *Der erste Brief 1–4,* 191 underlines this point, while BDF, sect. 490, consider it a model of Pauline parallelism; note also Collins, *First Cor,* 108: "the rhetorical technique of *sygkrisis,* rhetorical comparison, to highlight God's wisdom and power."
151. These are explored by many writers, but see especially references above to the work of Alexandra Brown and Raymond Pickett respectively, as well as more generally to Wolfgang Schrage's exegesis.

proclamation of the cross of Christ (1:18-25); (2) the nature and social status and composition of the church in Corinth (1:26-31); and (3) Paul's own experience and presentation of the gospel when he first came to Corinth (2:1-5). As Schrage suggests, the *propositio* of 1:10 had been explicated as a *narratio* in vv. 11-17, and then takes the form of a demonstration, proof, or *argumentio* of threefold force in 1:18–2:5.[152] Paul now unfolds the second strand of this *argumentio* (1:26-31)

The role of the cross as foundation and criterion of authentic wisdom has been demonstrated from the conflict between the very nature of the cross and human aspirations and evaluations concerning wisdom and folly. The act of God in Christ has brought about a reversal of human evaluations concerning status, achievement, and success.[153] This issue now receives practical demonstration first in the experience of the addressees concerning the origins and composition of their community (1:26-31) and then, further, from Paul's experience of how he proclaimed the gospel when he first arrived in Corinth (2:1-5).

Bibliography on 1:26-31

Bender, W., "Bemerkungen Übersetzung von 1 Kor 1:30," *ZNW* 71 (1980): 263-68.

Bowie, E. L., "The Importance of the Sophists," *Yale Classical Studies* 27 (1982): 29-59.

Brown, A. R., *The Cross in Human Transformation* (Minneapolis: Fortress, 1995), 80-97.

Bruce, F. F., *Paul: Apostle of the Free Spirit* (Exeter: Paternoster, 1977), 95-112.

Bultmann, R., *Faith and Understanding: Collected Essays* (Eng. trans., London: SCM, 1969), 220-46.

———, "The Term 'Flesh' *(Sarx)*," *Theology of the NT* (Eng. trans., London: SCM, 1952), 1:232-39.

Carson, D. A., *The Cross and the Christian Ministry* (Grand Rapids: Baker, 1993), 26-33.

Castelli, Elizabeth, "Interpretations of Power in 1 Corinthians," *Semeia* 54 (1991): 197-222.

Chow, John K., *Patronage and Power: A Study of Social Networks in Corinth*, JSNTSS 75 (Sheffield: Sheffield Academic Press, 1992).

Combes, I. A. H., *The Metaphor of Slavery in the Writings of the Early Church*, JSNTSS 156 (Sheffield: Sheffield Academic Press, 1998), 77-94.

Dahl, N. A., *Studies in Paul* (Minneapolis: Augsburg, 1977), 95-120.

deSilva, D. A., "'Let the One Who Claims Honor Establish That Claim in the Lord': Honor Discourse in the Corinthian Correspondence," *BTB* 28 (1998): 61-74.

Dunn, James D. G., "The Wisdom of God," in *Christology in the Making* (London: SCM, 1980), 163-94.

Engberg-Pedersen, T., "The Gospel and Social Practice according to 1 Corinthians," *NTS* 33 (1987): 557-84.

Fraser, J. W., *Jesus and Paul: Paul as Interpreter of Jesus from Harnack to Kümmel* (Appleford: Marcham Books, 1974), 11-32, 117-209.

---

152. Schrage, *Der erste Brief,* 1:167.
153. Witherington and Pogoloff in particular underlined this aspect (above).

Furnish, V. P., "Theology in 1 Corinthians," in D. M. Hay (ed.), *Pauline Theology, 2: 1 and 2 Corinthians* (Minneapolis: Fortress, 1993), 64-69.

Hengel, Martin, *Between Jesus and Paul: Studies in the Earliest History of Christianity* (Eng. trans., London: SCM, 1983), 1-29.

Holmberg, B., *Sociology and the NT: An Appraisal* (Minneapolis: Fortress, 1990), 21-76.

Horrell, D. G., *The Social Ethos of the Corinthian Correspondence* (Edinburgh: T. & T. Clark, 1996), esp. 91-101 and 132-37.

Horsley, R. A., "1 Corinthians: A Case Study of Paul's Assembly as an Alternative Society," in R. A. Horsley (ed.), *Paul and Empire Religion and Power in Roman Imperial Society* (Harrisburg, Pa.: Trinity Press International, 1997), 242-52.

Jewett, Robert, *Paul's Anthropological Terms: A Study of Their Use in Conflict Settings* (Leiden: Brill, 1971), 49-166, cf. 23-40.

Judge, E. A., "Paul's Boasting in Relation to Contemporary Professional Practice," *AusBR* 16 (1968): 37-50.

———, *The Social Pattern of the Christian Groups in the First Century* (London: Tyndale Press, 1960).

Jüngel, E., *Paulus und Jesus: Eine Untersuchung zur Präzisierung der Frage nach dem Ursprung der Christologie,* HUT 2 (Tübingen: Mohr, 1962).

Keck, L. E., "God the Other Who Acts Otherwise: An Exegetical Essay on 1 Cor 1:26-31," *Word and World* 16 (1996): 276-85.

Lohmeyer, E., *Probleme paulinischer Theologie* (Darmstadt: Wissenschaftliche Buchgesellschaft, 1954), 75-156.

Malina, Bruce J., *The NT World: Insights from Cultural Anthropology* (Atlanta: John Knox, 1981).

Martin, D. B., *Slavery as Salvation* (New Haven: Yale University Press, 1990), 50-85 and 117-35.

Matthews, V. H., et al. (eds.), "Honor and Shame in the World of the Bible," *Semeia* 68 (1994/1996).

Meeks, Wayne A., *The Moral World of the First Christians* (Philadelphia: Westminster, 1986), 32-38.

Meggitt, J. J., *Paul's Poverty and Survival* (Edinburgh: T. & T. Clark, 1998), esp. 75-107.

Moxnes, Halvor, "Honor, Shame and the Outside World in Paul's Letter to the Romans," in J. Neusner et al. (eds.), *The Social World of Formative Christianity and Judaism* (Philadelphia: Fortress, 1988), 207-18.

O'Day, G. R., "Jer 9:22-23 and 1 Cor 1:26-31: A Study in Intertextuality," *JBL* 109 (1990): 259-67.

Pogoloff, Stephen M., *Logos and Sophia: The Rhetorical Situation of 1 Corinthians,* SBLDS 134 (Atlanta: Scholars Press, 1992), 113-27, 153-72, 197-216.

Robinson, J. A. T., "The Concept of the Flesh (σάρξ)," in *The Body: A Study in Pauline Theology* (London: SCM, 1952), 17-26.

Sand, Alexander, *Der Begriff "Fleisch" in den paulinischen Hauptbriefen,* BU 2 (Regensburg: Pustet, 1967).

Sänger, D., "Die δυνατοί in 1 Kor 1:26," *ZNW* 76 (1985): 285-91.

Savage, Timothy B., *Power through Weakness: Paul's Understanding of the Christian Ministry in 2 Corinthians,* SNTSMS 86 (Cambridge: Cambridge University Press, 1996), 57-64, 74-80.

Schneider, N., *Die rhetorische Eigenart der paulinischen Antithese* (Tübingen: Mohr, 1970).

Schottroff, L., "'Nicht viele Mächtige,' Annäherungen an eine Soziologie des Urchristentums," in *Befreiungserfahrungen* (Munich: Kaiser, 1990), 247-56.

Schreiner, K., "Zur biblischen Legitimation des Adels: Auslegungsgeschichtliche zu 1 Kor 1:26-29," *ZKG* 85 (1974): 317-57.

Theissen, Gerd, *The Social Setting of Pauline Christianity: Essays on Corinth* (Eng. trans., Philadelphia: Fortress, 1982), 69-144.

Thiselton, Anthony C., "The Meaning of σάρξ in 1 Cor 5:5: A Fresh Approach in the Light of Logical and Semantic Factors," *SJT* 26 (1973): 204-28.

————, *The Two Horizons* (Exeter: Paternoster and Grand Rapids: Eerdmans, 1980), 407-11 (Korean trans. Seoul: Chongshin Publishing, 1980, 624-32).

Wedderburn, A. J. M. (ed.), *Paul and Jesus: Collected Essays*, JSNTSS 37 (Sheffield: Sheffield Academic Press, 1989), esp. 99-160.

————, "Some Observations in Paul's Use of the Phrases 'in Christ' and 'with Christ,'" *JSNT* 25 (1985): 83-97.

Winter, B. W., *Philo and Paul among the Sophists*, SNTSMS 96 (Cambridge: Cambridge University Press, 1997), 186-94.

Witherington, Ben, III, *Conflict and Community in Corinth: A Socio-Rhetorical Commentary on 1 and 2 Corinthians* (Grand Rapids: Eerdmans and Carlisle: Paternoster Press, 1995), 22-35 and 113-20.

Wuellner, W., "The Sociological Implication of 1 Cor 1:26-28 Reconsidered," *SE,* 6 (ed. E. A. Livingstone; Berlin: Berlin Academy, 1973), 666-72.

————, "Ursprung und Verwendung der σοφός-δυνατός-εὐγενής-Formel in 1 Kor 1:26," in E. Bammel, C. K. Barrett, and W. D. Davies (eds.), *Donum Gentilicium: NT Studies in Honour of D. Daube* (Oxford: Clarendon Press, 1978), 165-84.

————, "Tradition and Interpretation of the 'Wise-Powerful-Noble' Triad in 1 Cor 1:26," *SE,* 7 (ed. E. A. Livingstone; Berlin: Berlin Academy, 1982), 557-62.

Yeo, Khiok-khing, *Rhetorical Interaction in 1 Corinthians 8–10*, BibInt 9 (Leiden: Brill, 1995), 86-90.

26 The United Bible Societies *Greek New Testament,* 4th ed., follows all the earlier MSS in reading γάρ as the connective with v. 25. The Western D, F, G, substitute οὖν. Fee and Barrett rightly dismiss this later secondary reading as inverting Paul's argument.[154]

It is important to note how the three terms relating to **cleverness** (σοφοί), to **influence** (δυνατοί), and to **high status** (εὐγενεῖς) point forward to their inversion and redefinition in the later reference to *righteousness* (δικαιοσύνη), *holiness* (ἁγιασμός), and *redemption* (ἀπολύτρωσις) in Jesus Christ (v. 30).[155] Christ becomes the believers' sole ground of boasting (καυχάσθω, 1:31). DeSilva has recently shown how these verses embody "an honor discourse" in which honor is

154. Fee, *First Epistle,* 79; Barrett, *First Epistle,* 56.
155. On effective antithesis in rhetoric, see N. Schneider, *Die rhetorische Eigenart der paulinischen Antithese* (Tübingen: Mohr, 1970), and Winter, *Philo and Paul among the Sophists,* 193-94.

perceived to be dependent on the (public) evaluation of specific social groups. In the eyes of the world "not many" at Corinth received honor from those who "counted" in Graeco-Roman society. But honor, for believers, comes from a different source. "Let the one who claims honor establish that claim in the Lord."[156] Although Kenneth Bailey's proposals about a chiasmic structure extended more widely and are more elaborate, the inverted symmetry here is inescapable.[157] (See on v. 30.) The addressees have no reason to congratulate themselves on their intellectual, political, or social achievements as they are in themselves, and as the world assesses these achievements (κατὰ σάρκα, *according to the flesh*, or **as the world counts them**). Paul will set this assessment in contrast to a solid status exclusively based on Christ and an act of "reversal" brought about by God through Christ.

Several issues of translation call for comment. (1) βλέπω normally means *I see, I look at,* when used of physical sight, but is often extended metaphorically. It denotes *directing one's attention to something.* The present imperative active suggests the more forceful translation **Think about** (see further on κλῆσις).[158] Arguments for interpreting it as indicative are not convincing.[159] (2) γάρ (see Textual Note) is not primarily explanatory here but serves as a signal to introduce a fresh stage of argument.[160] The word often performs this function in first-century Greek, and is therefore best left untranslated. (3) κλῆσιν, *calling,* raises a difficulty. Especially in view of its use in 1:1 to denote *a called apostle* and in 1:2 to denote *a called holy people* who *call on the name of the Lord,* the word is likely here to carry its regular and frequent meaning in the NT as *called to faith* rather than the less common use of *calling* in the sense of vocation or profession. Apart from older commentators such as Olshausen, Witherington is one of the few to claim that it means "socio-economic status."[161] The emphasis falls clearly on God's calling to faith "to underscore both the dynamic nature of the call of God and God as the agent of the call."[162] In

---

156. D. A. deSilva, "Let the One Who Claims Honor Establish That Claim in the Lord": Honor Discourse in the Corinthian Correspondence," *BTB* 28 (1998): 61-74.

157. Bailey, "Recovering the Poetic Structure of 1 Cor 1:17–2:2," 265-96.

158. In strictly grammatical terms βλέπετε may be either second person plural present indicative active or second person plural present imperative active. The former is assumed by Valla, Erasmus, Beza, Bengel, and AV/ KJV. Bengel appeals to the use of γάρ for this view: "indicativum innuit *enim*" (*Gnomon,* 612). But we are about to note a different reason why Paul uses γάρ, and the vast majority of commentators interpret the form as imperative in this context, with the exception of Barrett's rendering *you can see what I mean* (*First Epistle,* 56).

159. Collins, *First Cor,* translates *ponder* (90, 109).

160. Fee, *First Epistle,* 79, rightly underlines this point.

161. Witherington, *Conflict and Community,* 113, asserts the conclusion apparently without argument. Among older commentators a few, including Krause and Olshausen, interpret *calling* in the sense of "profession" or "job," perhaps influenced by the regular modern use of Germ. *Beruf* for this purpose. The word hardly appears in everyday papyri (MM), and apart from odd uses in Philo and 1 Cor 7:20 BAGD offers few examples placing 1 Cor 1:26 firmly in the main category of "calling by God," esp. to faith.

162. Collins, *First Cor,* 109.

1:26, however, κλῆσις alludes not simply to the act of call but to its attendant circumstances. Allo and Barrett refer to "circumstances" and "conditions" relating to their call, and Senft and Grosheide to *the manner*" (Senft's italics) in which they were called.[163] Thus Robertson and Plummer paraphrase: "summon before your mind's eye what took place then; note the ranks from which one by one you were summoned into the society of God's people; very few came from the educated, influential, or well-connected class."[164] Anticipating Allo, they call this "an unanswerable *argumentum ad hominem,* clinching the result of the above passage." To make the point of emphasis clear, we have translated **Think about the circumstances of your call**, even though "circumstances" remains implicit rather than explicit in the Greek text.[165] (4) On ἀδελφοί see comments under 1:18–2:5 as well as Paul's family affection for fellow Christians who share the same grace, similar struggles, and the same destiny. (5) The phrase κατὰ σάρκα (*after the flesh,* AV/KJV) cannot be rendered directly into English without misunderstanding; most translators propose *by human standards* (NRSV, NJB, NIV, Moffatt, approximately REB, and Collins).

Detailed examinations of the use of σάρξ occur in Robert Jewett's useful study and in the very extensive work of Alexander Sand.[166] Earlier, a breakthrough occurred when Burton divided the occurrences of σάρξ in Paul into no less than seven distinct categories, refusing to subsume any under some generalized overarching meaning.[167] A diversity of meanings arise in a diversity of contexts. I argued for this in my two earlier studies, stressing the role of σάρξ as a term of evaluation of a stance within a given frame of reference.[168] Certainly "flesh and spirit are not two different 'parts' of a human person."[169] In some contexts a "fleshly" stance is one of "human self-sufficiency" (e.g., 1 Cor 3:21, "glorying in humankind"); while Bultmann calls it "the attitude of self-reliance [which] finds its extreme expression in man's 'boasting' (καυχᾶσθαι)."[170] It is no accident that 1:31 Paul concludes this section of argument by redirecting this καυχᾶσθαι to Christ as the sole ground on which to "glory" or "boast." In this passage, therefore, Paul compares the Corinthians' achievements in the realm of wisdom, influence, and status as humankind evaluates these on

163. Allo, *Première Épitre,* 19; Barrett, *First Epistle,* 57; Senft, *La première épitre,* 43; and Grosheide, *First Epistle,* 50.

164. Robertson and Plummer, *First Epistle,* 24.

165. Allo, *Première Epitre,* 19, entitles this whole section (1:26-31) *La preuve "ad hominem"* (19-22).

166. Jewett, *Paul's Anthropological Terms,* 23-40 and 49-166; and Sand, *Der Begriff "Fleisch" in den paulinischen Hauptbriefen.*

167. E. de W. Burton, *A Critical and Exegetical Commentary on the Epistle to the Galatians* (Edinburgh: T. & T. Clark, 1921), Appendix.

168. Thiselton, "The Meaning of σάρξ in 1 Cor 5:5," 204-28; and *The Two Horizons,* 407-11.

169. Sand, *Der Begriff "Fleisch,"* 144.

170. J. A. T. Robinson, *The Body,* 25; cf. 17-26; and R. Bultmann, *Theology of the New Testament,* 1:232-39, esp. 242.

grounds of *esteem, glory, or honour,* and the corresponding status which God has accorded them through Christ in his own eyes.[171] This paves the way for our translation (see further below).

Hence here Paul refers to the readers' relative *lack of public esteem, political power, and family status and influence from a sociopolitical viewpoint.*[172] From the earliest twentieth century (esp. with Deissmann) up to the period of Judge, Meeks, and Theissen, it was usually inferred from this passage that the vast majority of Christians at Corinth were of lowly social status.[173] Yet even in the third century Origen quotes Celsus as saying "let no one educated, no one wise, no one sensible draw near," while Calvin comments that "the Corinthians . . . had no great standing in the world," although they were "proud all the same."[174] Yet Origen himself used this verse as a reply to Celsus: *Not all* (**not many**) were influential as well educated (i.e., *some were*).[175] Prior to more recent work on the social history of the Pauline churches, it was recognized that too broad a generalization could not be drawn from this verse: "*Few* distinguished persons are in the ranks of the called" (my italics).[176]

Deissmann (1927) had argued for the lowly social status of Christians in NT times, and for their affinity with the language of the papyri. He cited Matt 11:25ff. and 1 Cor 1:26-31 as evidence for this.[177] In an influential essay of 1960, however, E. A. Judge argued to the contrary, "Far from being a socially depressed group, if the Corinthians are at all typical, the Christians were dominated by a socially pretentious section of the population of big cities."[178] He stresses the significance of the three institutions of *politeia, oikonomia,* and *koinonia.* Property-owning patrons help to sustain these. Evidence for some converts in high standing might well include Crispus, the synagogue ruler (Acts 18:8; cf. 1 Cor 1:14), and Erastus, who probably held some such office as city treasurer or perhaps the office of aedile (Rom 16:23). But are these more than a minority within the church?

Theissen agrees with part of Judge's argument, but stresses the *social diversity* of early urban churches: "the Corinthian congregation is marked by internal stratification."[179] The argument for the presence of those who held some

---

171. An illuminating parallel for an evaluative use of κατὰ σάρκα occurs in Rom 1:3-4: "of David's stock κατὰ σάρκα . . . Son of God . . . κατὰ πνεῦμα," i.e., the one person as seen with these two frames of evaluation and understanding. Again the epistemic and salvific are related, as in 1 Cor 1:18-25.

172. Senft, *La première Épitre,* 43.

173. The consensus review of the history of research is well known. For a brief summary, see Horrell, *Social Ethos,* 91-101; and, in more detail, Theissen, *Social Setting,* 69-120.

174. Origen, *Against Celsus,* 3:44; and Calvin, *First Epistle,* 44.

175. Origen, *Against Celsus,* 3:48.

176. Moffatt, *First Epistle,* 19-20.

177. Deissmann, *Light from the Ancient Near East* (London: Hodder & Stoughton, 2d ed. 1927), 144.

178. Judge, *The Social Pattern of the Christian Groups in the First Century,* 60.

179. Theissen, "Social Stratification in the Corinthian Community: A Contribution to the

status or influence may be drawn from references to officeholders (Crispus, Erastus); to heads of significant households (Crispus, Stephanas); to those who could render "services" to Paul or to others which presupposed a measure of wealth or influence (Epaphroditus, Gaius, Titius Justus); and to those who needed to travel, often as merchants or for business purposes (Aquila and Priscilla, Phoebe, Erastus, Stephanas, Chloe's people).[180] Most would now agree that Paul addresses the message of the cross to a community which experiences "status inconsistency."[181] "The social level of the Corinthian Christians apparently varied from quite poor to rather well-off . . . a fair cross-section of urban society. . . . They shared this 'status inconsistency' with others of their city. . . . Many . . . gained status not by lineage or sophistication. . . . Paul's words in 1 Cor 1:26 would have been a pointed reminder to such status-hungry people of their origins."[182] The message of pure grace through the cross of Christ contradicted any notion that "this new religion gave them status in their own eyes that they had been unable to obtain in the larger society."[183] Witherington comments on this passage, "Salvation in Christ is not a human . . . self-improvement scheme, but a radical rescue. . . . Grace is not only the great unifier but also the great leveler."[184]

This becomes all the more pointed in the light of Winter's reminder that "the terms mentioned in v. 26, σοφοί, δυνατοί and εὐγενεῖς, were used of those instructed by the sophists, and that the σοφοί are the sophists whose parents are δυνατοί and εὐγενεῖς."[185] This is confirmed from ancient sources and from a study by Bowie.[186] Philo censures those who imagine that generations of wealth and fame, the εὐγενεῖς who spring from great houses, deserve the highest honor because of their self-promotion in "boast and glory."[187] Sänger has argued that the δυνατοί were people whose wealth enabled them to exercise both social and political power (as 6:1-11 presupposes; see below).[188] This supports

Sociology of Early Hellenistic Christianity," in *The Social Setting of Pauline Christianity,* 69; cf. 69-120.

180. Ibid., 95. He lists Achaicus (16:17), Aquila and Priscilla (16:19; cf. Rom 16:3; Acts 18:2, 26), Erastus (Rom 16:23), Fortunatus (16:17), Gaius (1:14; cf. Rom 16:23), Jason (Rom 16:21), Crispus (1:14; cf. Acts 18:8), Lucius (Rom 16:21), Phoebe (Rom 16:1-2), Quartus (Rom 16:23), Sosipater (Rom 16:21), Sosthenes (1:1; cf. Acts 18:17?), Stephanas (1:16; 16:15), Titius Justus (Acts 18:7), Tertius (Rom 16:22), and Chloe's people (1:11) under the headings discussed above.

181. Meeks, *First Urban Christians,* 191-92.

182. Witherington, *Conflict and Community,* 23 and 24.

183. Ibid., 24.

184. Ibid., 118.

185. B. W. Winter, *Philo and Paul,* 189, following Munck and Theissen, although against Wuellner's theory that these allude to gifts of God in Genesis 1 according to Jewish tradition (see Wuellner in bibliography).

186. Plutarch, *Moralia* 58C; Diogenes Laertius, *Orations,* 29-32; E. L. Bowie, "The Importance of the Sophists," *Yale Classical Studies* 27 (1982): 28-59.

187. Philo, *De Virtutibus* 187-226 (cited by Winter, *Philo and Paul,* 190).

188. Sänger, "Die δυνατοί in 1 Kor 1:26," 285-91; also Strobel, *Der erste Brief,* 54.

our translation of δυνατοί as **those who held influence**. In harmony with De Silva's contention about establishing "honor" not in the eyes of social groups but in the eyes of the Lord (1:30-31) Keck presses the point that God as "the Other" acts otherwise from the prevailing wisdom of the world.[189] In the light of all this we have translated κατὰ σάρκα not simply as *by human standards* (NRSV et al.), but in conjunction with σοφοί **as the world counts cleverness**, which is more value-laden, as Paul intends.

In our Introduction (sect. 1c, on status inconsistency, and esp. sect. 2b, the socioeconomic status of Paul and his converts), we noted that the claims of Theissen, Judge, Clarke, and Winter needed to be qualified by the observations of J. J. Meggitt. Meggitt observes that 1:26 has been used to support "both the 'Old' and 'New' consensuses," i.e., both Deissmann's emphasis that "not many" held positions of significance and most were of lowly status, and claims from Judge to Winter and Murphy-O'Connor about some in positions of prominence.[190] Meggitt himself, we noted, stresses that *plebs urbana* lived on the breadline, at the very margins of survival, with many near destitution. While Meggitt may be accused of some posssible overstatements, the work of the classicist Donald Engels anticipates his conclusion about the severe poverty of many.[191] The wealth of research (cited in the Introduction) underlines the *range* of socioeconomic status likely to have characterized the church. Meeks's valid sociological insight into the psychosocial effects of "status inconsistency" (see above) underline Witherington's point about the transformative effect of the cross.[192] Christian "status" depends on the gift of grace and divine verdict, not upon compensatory self-esteem or self-promotion as "wise" or "spiritual" people.

27-29 **Before** τὰ μὴ ὄντα, **the nothings**, in v. 28, א², B, C³, D² Eusebius, Basil, and Chrysostom insert καί. The insertion matches the syntax of the previous clauses. But no issue of substance is involved. In English the string of nouns in apposition to one another invites some method of drawing breath as well as marking a climax (above, **yes, the nothings**). But Zahn and Metzger believe that the scribal insertion of καί has the opposite effect, namely, of construing τὰ μὴ ὄντα as a mere number of the series rather than as a summarizing climax.[193] The shorter reading is well supported (𝔭⁴⁶ א*, A, C*, D*, 33).

The threefold repetition of ἐξελέξατο ὁ θεός, **God chose**, dominates the flow of thought and syntax, and invites some method of translating the whole rhythmic utterance which will give it due prominence. For once, to follow in English the

189. Keck, "God the Other Who Acts Otherwise: An Exegetical Essay on 1 Cor 1:26-31," 437-43.

190. J. J. Meggitt, *Paul, Poverty and Survival* (Edinburgh: T. & T. Clark, 1998), 102; cf. 75-107. The material on Paul is more debatable (see above).

191. D. Engels, *Roman Corinth* (Chicago: University of Chicago Press, 1990), 70-71; but on Paul see 107.

192. Meeks, *The First Urban Christians*, esp. 54, 68-70, and 72-73; cf. Witherington, *Conflict and Community;* and Brown, *The Cross in Human Transformation*, 80-97.

193. Metzger, *Textual Commentary* (2d ed. 1994), 480.

broad order of the Greek phrases may well represent the most effective way of achieving this: **the foolish things of the world God chose . . . the weak things of the world God chose . . .** the mind experiences suspense until **God chose** offers the resolution of the accusatives. Godet observes, "The term ἐκλέγεσθαι does not here denote a decree of eternal predestination, but the energetic action whereby God has taken to Him (the Middle, λέγεσθαι) from the midst of the world (ἐκ) those individuals whom no one judged worthy of attention. . . . The strong, the wise . . . are thus covered with shame."[194] The key theological point not only concerns God's sovereign freedom *to choose* to love and to give himself regardless of human deserving or achievement, but also the discontinuity here between **God** and the **world**. God is no human construct, called in to legitimate human power interests, but the very reverse. His love for the nobodies and **the nothings** discounted as nonentities and as **insignificant** in the value system of the world puts the world to **shame** by its reversal of judgment. Hays heads this section (1:26-31) "God's Calling Excludes Human Boasting."[195]

A fundamental common feature between Paul and Jesus appears here.[196] Jesus shared table fellowship with the outcasts who were not among those whom religious and social Jewish society counted as "somebodies": those whose occupations prevented them from observing the finer minutiae of the Jewish laws, or the tax collectors regarded as renegades by many loyal religious Jews.[197] Many parables of Jesus about invitations to a great banquet turned on the primacy of grace over religious and social degrees of status and achievement (Matt 9:10-13; 11:25-27; 18:10-14; 20:1-16; 21:28-41; 22:1-10; Mark 2:15-17; 7:1-8; 10:23-27; 12:1-12; Luke 5:29-32; 7:36-50; 10:21-22, 29-37; 11:45-53; 14:12-24; 15:1-32; 18:9-13, 24-27). Jesus had "nowhere to lay his head" (Matt 11:20). His sayings about the ambiguity of "signs" (Mark 8:11), about wisdom (Matt 11:25-27; Luke 10:21-23), about rejection, suffering, and the cross (Mark 8:31-38), and above all about grace (Matt 20:1-16; Luke 15:1-32) offer very close affinities with Pauline themes in this and similar passages. They demonstrate the problematic nature of trying to drive a wedge between a theology of grace in Paul and Jesus' parables and deeds of grace, with his critical stance toward claims of socioreligious status. Jüngel puts forward a sustained argument for this fundamental parallel between Jesus and Paul. He also contends, surely rightly, that the theme of the grace of the gospel in Rom 1:16, 17 finds a parallel in 1 Cor 1:18-31. Paul's theology of grace "controls the theology of Paul's argument" in 1 Cor 1:18-31.[198] Although he will not go as far as

194. Godet, *First Epistle,* 1:112; cf. Findlay, *Expositor's Greek Testament,* 2:772; and Conzelmann, *1 Corinthians,* 50; and Strobel, *Der erste Brief,* 55.

195. Hays, *First Cor,* 31.

196. Grosheide, *First Epistle,* 50; and Jüngel, *Paulus und Jesus.*

197. Cf. Christian Wolf, "Humility and Self-Denial in Jesus' Life and Message and in the Apostolic Existence of Paul," in Wedderburn (ed.), *Paul and Jesus,* 145-60.

198. Jüngel, *Paulus und Jesus,* 31; cf. also R. Bultmann, *Faith and Understanding* (Eng. trans., London, SCM, 1969), 220-46.

Jüngel, Wedderburn recognizes that "the same fundamental experience underlies both his [Paul's] polemic against Jews and Judaizers in terms of righteousness, and his polemic against the supposedly wise Corinthians in terms of the truly wise folly of the cross of Christ."[199]

Wedderburn concludes, *"Both Jesus and Paul were in their lives and ministries characterized by what might be called an openness to the outsider, and that in the name of God"* (his italics).[200] In 1 Cor 1:26-31 Paul explains how "outsiders" in the eyes of the world could never become "insiders" *in the eyes of the world* through this new-found Christian status. Nevertheless through *God's* action they had become "insiders" *in the eyes of God,* on the basis of deriving their "wisdom," "acceptance," and "status" *from Christ's own* (1:30-31).[201] Many writers compare here the theology of reversal in the *Magnificat* (Luke 1:46-55).[202] The proclamation of the cross brings salvation and well-being to the "nothings" who had, in effect, "no being."[203]

Paul formulates the antithesis in terms of two triads: τὰ μωρά, **foolish things**, τὰ ἀσθενῆ, **weak things**, and ἀγενῆ, **the insignificant**, stand in contrast to τοὺς σοφούς, τὰ ἰσχυρά, and not εὐγενεῖς but τὰ ὄντα.[204] This is because ἀγενῆ has been glossed further as τὰ ἐξουθενημένα (perfect passive participle of ἐξουθενέω, the components of which include the intensive ἐκ ἐξ), i.e., *the thoroughly nothings, things set down as of no account,* i.e., **the despised**. This reflects its meaning in 1 Cor 6:4, concerning "those least esteemed in the church," and recalls the attitude of Jesus toward those whom the religious elite discounted. The phrase τὰ μὴ ὄντα, *the things that are not,* may best be translated **the nothings** because its force depends on a dual context: they are non-entities or **nothings** in socioreligious terms; but they also achieve the status of *somebodies* or **somethings** in God's eyes, while God **brings to nothing** (καταργήσῃ) those who supposed themselves to be significant by virtue of their status. Horrell underlines the point that in Roman society *"one's value is determined by education, wealth and breeding. The cross, on the other hand, turns the world upside down* [in] . . . a total transformation" (my italics).[205] Nothing

---

199. Wedderburn, *Paul and Jesus,* 103; cf. 99-160. See further, e.g., J. Blank, *Paulus und Jesus* (Munich: Kösel, 1968) and *Paulus: Von Jesus zum Christentum* (Munich: Kösel, 1982); Fraser, *Jesus and Paul;* F. F. Bruce, "Paul and the Historical Jesus," *BJRL* 56 (1974): 317-35, and *Paul: Apostle of the Free Spirit* (Exeter: Paternoster, 1977), 95-112; Hengel, *Between Jesus and Paul,* 1-29; E. P. Sanders "Jesus, Paul and Judaism," in W. Hasse and H. Temporini, *ANRW* 2:25:1 (Berlin: de Gruyter, 1982), 390-450; and Dahl, *Studies in Paul,* 95-120.

200. Wedderburn (ed.), *Paul and Jesus,* 131.

201. C. Wolf, "Humility and Self-Denial," in Wedderburn (ed.), *Paul and Jesus,* 145-60, shows how Paul's own "humiliation" (4:8-13) is a model drawn from the life of Jesus.

202. Hays, *First Cor,* 32 (who also cites Hannah's prayer in 1 Sam 2:1-10); and Horrell, *Social Ethos,* 134.

203. Merklein, *Der erste Brief 1–4,* 199: "*Gott . . . das 'Nicht-Seiende' erwählt.*"

204. τὰ μωρά and τὰ ἀσθενῆ are straightforward. BAGD lists ἀγενῆ as *base, low, or* **insignificant** (BAGD, 8; cf. Philo, *De Confusione Linguarum* 43; *Oxyrhynchus Papyrus* 79:3.

205. Horrell, *Social Ethos,* 134.

could be more relevant to the church then and now: *Are people "valued" according to their socioeconomic categorization?* *God* applies a different value system. Privative ἀργός, *idle, useless,* is very forceful: *to render utterly null,* i.e., to preserve the relation to τὰ μὴ ὄντα, **to bring to nothing**. The combination of stylistic rhythm, repetition, and emphatic word order makes this an especially powerful passage.

Can more be said about the social status of τὰ μὴ ὄντα and τὰ ἰσχυρά? Schreiner reviews patristic and medieval interpretations of vv. 26-29, and argues that Paul envisages a liberation of τὰ μὴ ὄντα who are *slaves*.[206] But this moves beyond Paul's point. Without reference to context τὰ ἰσχυρά simply means *the strong things*. But many recent writers identify "the strong" at Corinth as "the upper classes . . . those who are better off."[207] Since this interpretation depends largely on issues relating to "the strong" and the eating of meat dedicated to idols (8:1-13), we postpone discussion of this meaning until the later passage is considered. Meanwhile **positions of strength** allows for the possibility of an interpretation in terms of social status, without restricting it to this alone.

Verse 29 is introduced by ὅπως, which Edwards regards as introducing "the ultimate end, as ἵνα introduced the subsidiary purposes" of vv. 27 and 28.[208] Edwards can offer examples of ἵνα used for purposes subsidiary to a major expression of purpose, but the distinction is too fine to be pressed firmly in first-century hellenistic usage. His understanding of Paul's logic, however, remains valid. Conzelmann observes that the ἵνα clauses call attention to "the sovereignty of God" in purposes already in process of realization, while the ὅπως clause expresses the "ultimate aim."[209] This draws out "Christologically the Jewish idea of the overthrow of the lofty and the exalting of the lowly by God" in the Magnificat (διεσκόρπισεν ὑπερηφάνους διανοίᾳ καρδίας αὐτῶν· καὶ ὕψωσεν ταπεινούς . . . , Luke 1:51, 52), as well as in Josephus (e.g., *Antiquities* 1.227) and Philo (e.g., *De Somniis* 1.155).[210]

This cannot but be perceived as a σκάνδαλον, **an affront** (v. 23), to those in positions of power.[211] It is all the more so in a culture which prizes public *honor* and cannot live with public *shame* rather than the more individualistic "inner" concerns about *guilt* and *forgiveness* more characteristic of Western "Christendom." In Corinth **shaming** (καταισχύνειν) and *boasting* or **priding themselves** (καυχήσηται) was a public phenomenon of an "honor-shame" culture. The currency shifts in the Jewish-Christian *guilt-culture,*

206. Schreiner, "Zur biblischen Legitimation des Adels," 317-57.

207. Theissen, *Social Setting,* 136 and 139; cf. 121-43.

208. Edwards, *First Epistle,* 38.

209. Conzelmann, *1 Corinthians,* 50.

210. Ibid., 50-51.

211. R. Penna, *Paul the Apostle: Wisdom and Folly of the Cross* (Collegeville: Glazier/Liturgical Press, 1996), 3-9; Horrell, *Social Ethics,* 134; and Carson, *The Cross and Christian Ministry,* 27-31.

largely of the Latin West, if we decontextualize it from the *shame-culture* of Graeco-Roman and many oriental cultures.[212] *Shame* tends to relate to *corporate and social lack of honor* and to "losing face" among one's peers or in the sight of superiors or inferiors. *Guilt* tends to be more individualistic, relating to *individual moral failure*. Witherington declares, "The Corinthian people lived within an honor-shame orientation, where public recognition was often more important than facts, and where the worst thing that could happen was for one's reputation to be publicly tarnished. In such a culture a personal sense of worth is based on recognition by others of one's accomplishments, hence the self-promoting. . . ."[213]

The full force of μὴ καυχήσηται (aorist middle subjective with imperatival force) thus embodies two nuances. In the tradition of Israel (cf. the typical LXX phrases πᾶσα σάρξ, *all flesh,* and ἐνώπιον τοῦ θεοῦ, **before God**, and the intertextual allusion to Jer 9:23-24) moral and religious inadequacy remains the issue with the ensuing *pain of guilt: one has failed.*[214] In the tradition of Corinthian Graeco-Roman society (ἐνώπιον also occurs in the papyri of vernacular Greek in the Roman period) the issue becomes one of dishonored reputation, loss of face, and public humiliation which deprives the self of its social identity as a "someone." *The pain of shame* follows: *one has become a "nothing."* Yet Paul makes these negative points to highlight the glory of grace as sheer *gift:* God *bestows* self-acceptance and his own acceptance, setting aside guilt; and makes **all kinds of persons** (the regular generic meaning of πᾶσα σάρξ) **somethings** or *someones,* setting aside **shame.**

It is important to hold together the aspect of social status and the honor-shame contrast stressed in literature on the social history or sociology of the NT with the theological aspect of the achievement-acceptance contrast emphasized most characteristically in literature of a more Lutheran tradition.[215] Pogoloff carefully utilizes the best of Theissen's work without accepting all of his conclusions uncritically. He comments: "1 Cor 1:26-29 are key verses in Theissen's argument," referring "the nothings" largely to social status.[216]

212. Cf. Meeks, *The Moral World of the First Christians,* 36-38; E. A. Judge, *Rank and Status in the World of the Caesars and St Paul* (Christchurch, N.Z.:University of Canterbury, 1982); Moxnes, "Honor, Shame and the Outside World in Paul's Letter to the Romans," in Neusner et al. (eds.), *The Social World of Formative Christianity and Judaism,* 207-18; Dale B. Martin, *The Corinthian Body* (New Haven: Yale University Press, 1995), 58-61; Clarke, *Secular and Christian Leadership,* 95-99; Marshall, *Enmity in Corinth,* 180-84; Witherington, *Conflict and Community,* 6-9 and 19-24; "Honor and Shame in the World of the Bible," *Semeia* 68 (1994, also dated 1996).

213. Witherington, *Conflict and Community,* 8.

214. On the allusion to Jeremiah 9, see O'Day, "Jer 9:22-23 and 1 Cor 1:26-31: A Study in Intertextuality," 259-67; also Fee, *First Epistle,* 87; Clarke, *Secular and Christian Leadership,* 96; Collins, *First Cor,* 91, 100; and Schrage, *Der erste Brief,* 1:205-6.

215. Opposite ends of this spectrum might be represented, e.g., by Theissen, *Social Setting,* 70-73; and R. H. Bell in *Provoked to Jealousy: The Origin and Purpose of the Jealousy Motif in Romans 9–11,* WUNT 1:63 (Tübingen: Mohr, 1994), esp. 107-287.

216. Pogoloff, *Logos and Sophia,* 206.

The δυνατοί are "people of social influence."[217] Pogoloff agrees that "the Corinthians are competing because they are, in typical Greco-Roman fashion, both proud of whatever social status they have, and envious of those with higher status."[218] Even slaves within a household ranked themselves and other slaves as relative "somebodies" and "nobodies" within the household.[219] Availability of time for leisure commercial purchase power, and access to places of honor or privilege all constitute indicators of public status and esteem.[220]

Nevertheless, we should not forget that the earliest Christians also inherited the biblical traditions which molded their lives as believers. It is inconceivable that the polarity between exaltation and humiliation in the eyes of God played no part in their thought world. Paul therefore sharpens the focus of this biblical tradition with particular reference to the biblical theme of divine election as divine gift (cf. the threefold ἐξελέξατο) and the cross as the definitive critique and even possible reversal of human evaluations. These two dimensions *together* give v. 29 its full force: glorying is inappropriate in God's presence because whatever provides grounds for such glorying has come from God as his gift. Hence v. 30 begins ἐξ αὐτοῦ . . . *(It is from him that . . .).* "Paul disrupts the intuitive status expectations of his audience by invoking a belief he knows they share: the belief that in Christ, who was crucified, they have a common source of salvation and a common paradigm of leadership."[221] As with Greek traditions of *hybris,* the exclusion of καυχᾶσθαι, *boasting, self-glorying,* or **priding oneself** does away with "being full of oneself" in the presence of God.[222]

30-31 Almost no modern English translation of v. 30 follows the precise structure of the Greek, because the one-for-one rendering of each preposition, noun, and verb would leave an ambiguity or even the possibility of misunderstanding. We translate ἐξ αὐτοῦ δὲ ὑμεῖς ἐστε ἐν Χριστῷ Ἰησοῦ as **It is as a gift from him that you are in Christ Jesus** to meet two considerations. (1) Allo observes that the emphasis here lies on "the deed of God alone and his unfathomable election *(choix)*" together with the previous description of the emphatic ὑμεῖς (**you** *people*) as "**nothings**" apart from God's action (τὰ μὴ ὄντα).[223] (2) Weiss and Schrage further note that ἐξ in ἐξ αὐτοῦ conveys a force

217. Ibid., 209; cf. D. Sänger, "Die δυνατοί in 1 Kor 1:26," 285-91: J. Bohatec, "Inhalt under Reihenfolge der 'schlagworte der Erlösungsreligion' in 1 Kor 1:26-31," *Theology* 24 (1948): 252-71; E. A. Judge, "The Social Identity of the First Christians: A Question of Method in Religious History," *JRH* 11 (1980): 201-17, and *Rank and Status;* and Welborn *Politics and Rhetoric* ("the rich").

218. Pogoloff, *Logos and Sophia,* 211.

219. Meeks, *Moral World,* 32-34.

220. Ibid., 35-38.

221. Martin, *The Corinthian Body,* 59.

222. Marshall, *Enmity in Corinth,* 183; cf. Clarke, *Secular and Christian Leadership,* 96-99.

223. Allo, *Première Épitre,* 21.

parallel with that in Rom 11:36, *from him* (ἐξ αὐτοῦ) *and through him* (δι' αὐτοῦ) *and to him* (εἰς αὐτόν) *are all things.*[224] On this basis the preposition governs a *genitive of origin* (*from* him), but also carries an added *causal* nuance: God is the *ground* of all things as well as their origin. Hence NJB translates, *It is by him that you exist in Christ Jesus.*[225]

What does it mean to be **in Christ** (v. 30a)? Paul couples the concept of *new creation,* Schrage observes, with being "in Christ" (ἐν Χριστῷ). "One is *in* Christ only *through* Christ."[226] To be "in Christ" comes as a gift from "outside" us (*von dem extra nos,* cf. 1 Cor 1:4), although it also entails sharing in Christ's own identity and indeed becoming incorporated into "Christ's body."[227] Three phrases mark the history of research on being **in Christ** in Pauline theology. (1) Deissmann tended to stress the mystical, experimental, or "psychologizing" aspect. He explains Paul's experience of "Christ in me" and "I in Christ" in terms of "an inexhaustible religious 'energy' . . . in the soul of the convert. . . ."[228] (2) Weiss and Schweitzer, however, recognized the eschatological status of being-in-Christ as the mode of existence of God's new creation: "If anyone is in Christ, the person is a new creation" (2 Cor 5:17).[229] Schweitzer allows the term "mysticism" (in the positive sense of *Mystik*) only if due recognition is given to the corporate, eschatological, and objective status of being-in-Christ, which he derives from its apocalyptic background. Being-in-Christ is "assuming the resurrection mode of existence before the general resurrection of the dead takes place."[230] (3) Davies, Wikenhauser, and Tannehill combine these emphases on state and status, but stress the *derivative* nature of Christian "experience" resulting from the objective status of being-in-Christ.[231] Even Deissmann dissociates Paul's "response-mysticism" *(Mystik)* from a Corinthian "mysticism of intoxicated enjoyment."[232]

In other passages we may identify at least five different nuances of **in**

---

224. Weiss, *Der erste Korintherbrief,* 38-39; Schrage, *Der erste Brief,* 1:213.

225. Most translators and commentators restructure the English for the Greek, e.g., NRSV, *He is the source of your life in Christ;* NIV, *It is because of him that you are in Christ Jesus;* Conzelmann (*1 Cor,* 49), *By his act you are in Christ Jesus;* Barrett (*First Epistle,* 50 and 59), *But you are related to God in Christ Jesus.* A rare exception is Collins (*First Cor,* 90), *From him you are in Christ Jesus.*

226. Schrage, *Der erste Brief,* 1:214.

227. Ibid.

228. G. A. Deissmann, *Paul: A Study in Social and Religious History* (Eng. trans., London: Hodder & Stoughton, 2d ed. 1926), 161.

229. Weiss, *Earliest Christianity,* 2:466; and Schweitzer, *The Mysticism of Paul the Apostle,* 26-40, 52-74; cf. 75-100.

230. Ibid., 101. This also entails "Dying and Rising Again with Christ"; 101-59.

231. W. D. Davies, *Paul and Rabbinic Judaism: Some Rabbinic Elements in Pauline Theology* (London: SPCK, 2nd ed. 1958), 88; A. Wikenhauser, *Pauline Mysticism* (New York: Herder, 1960); and Robert C. Tannehill, *Dying and Rising with Christ,* BZNW 32 (Berlin: Töpelmann, 1966): "It is founded upon the past that the cross itself is an eschatological and inclusive event" (71). In relation to this verse, see Wolff, *Der erste Brief,* 45.

232. Deissmann, *Paul,* 153.

Christ.[233] Foremost among these distinct nuances in this verse is that of objective status and corporate solidarity. "Being-in-Christ" here is "no private Christian existence," but is to be a sharer in the status and state of "belonging" which finds expression in the way in which the limbs of a body belong to the body.[234] As Robinson points out, however, the notion of being "members" of a body has nowadays become an insipid metaphor for belonging to a social club, not that of a limb which constitutes part of the very being of the body in the solidarity of co-suffering or co-well-being.[235] Paul began to understand this *identity* when Christ as Lord described his persecution of the church as "persecuting *me*" (Acts 26:14; cf. 9:4, 5).[236] Paul will explicate this concept further in 12:12-27 (see exegesis below, esp. of v. 27). The new **wisdom**, in contrast to the cleverness of the Jewish or Greek sage in acquiring success in various enterprises, and thereby honor or esteem, derives from God's action through Christ which makes it possible to be **in Christ** as the Christian's objective status. Its content now manifests itself in sharing the gifts of **righteousness, sanctification, and redemption**. Yet ἐξ αὐτοῦ *remains fundamental: all this is "no product of human effort. . . . It is through the initiative of God"* without whom the Christian believers at Corinth would have remained the "nothings" *(Nicht-Sein)* of v. 28 (my italics).[237]

What is the specific relation between σοφία, δικαιοσύνη, ἁγιασμός, and ἀπολύτρωσις in v. 30b? Is Christ *characterized* by these qualities, or does he *impart or impute them* to believers? Controversy has emerged. Fee insists that the AV/KJV rendering *who of God is made unto us* **wisdom, and righteousness, and sanctification and redemption** treats this as a christological statement, and thereby sets subsequent interpretation on the wrong track. With Conzelmann he sees the bestowal of **wisdom** now redefined through the cross as a salvific act which brings **righteousness, sanctification, and redemption**.[238] J. Bohatec interprets the *four* terms **wisdom, righteousness, sanctifi-**

233. See Weiss, *Earliest Christianity,* 2:468-69; and Wedderburn, "Some Observations on Paul's Use of the Phrases 'in Christ' and 'with Christ,'" 83-97. Weiss distinguishes the following: (1) "In Christ" in an "objective" sense equivalent to "because Christ has come" (Rom 3:14; 8:39; 2 Cor 5:19); (2) "a more comprehensive, more inclusive or representative use" (1 Cor 7:14; 15:22); (3) instances where the phrase is merely part of a broader sentence construction, but often with such verbs as boasting, hoping, or trusting (1 Cor 1:31; 3:21; 2 Cor 10:17; Phil 2:19, 24; (4) passages where "in" has the instrumental force of "by" (1 Thess 4:1; Rom 15:30); and (5) "the full mystical sense" (1 Cor 1:30; 2 Cor 5:17; 1 Thess 3:8; Phil 4:1, 13). Some instances of (5) do not imply "a mystical temperament" (Gal. 3:28; Phil 4:3). (Schweitzer would call these "eschatological" examples.)

234. Schrage, *Der erste Brief,* 1:214. Similarly, Wolff, *Der erste Brief,* 45.

235. J. A. T. Robinson, *The Body: A Study in Pauline Theology* (London: SCM, 1957), 51.

236. Ibid., 58; cf. 8-9, Few doubt that Robinson overstates his case on resurrection and ecclesiology but that the broad approach is valid. Being "a member" has "ceased to be offensive" (51).

237. Merklein, *Der erste Brief 1-4,* 200.

238. Fee, *First Epistle,* 85. The AV/KJV, among other factors, has led to "a long history of misinterpretation in the church," together with reading 1 Cor 1:30 in the light of Col 2:2-3 and Jas 1:5. Cf. Conzelmann, *1 Corinthians,* 51-52.

cation, and **redemption**, as answering respectively to the *four* terms of vv.
27-28: τὰ μωρά *(foolish things)*, τὰ ἀσθενῆ *(weak things)*, τὰ ἀγενῆ *(things
despised as of no account),* and τὰ μὴ ὄντα *(the nothings).*[239] Some interpreters reject this as "artificial," arguing that neither the terms nor the parallels
are "systematically arranged."[240] But, given (1) the **wisdom-folly** contrast
(even recognizing the role of divine action versus human achievement here),
it is not at all fanciful or artificial to correlate further (2) *weakness* (i.e., lack
of *social influence and status*) with **righteousness** in the sense of "being of
accepted status"; (3) *being despised,* with **sanctification** (in the sense of having access to privileged places as one who "belongs"); and (4) **the nothings**
(those of no account) with **redemption** (as being transferred from a position
of no account to one of dignity and freedom). Although the theme of wisdom
(1:18-25) has become one of "power" (1:26-31), Paul still confronts "those
who consider themselves to be wise (see 3:18). . . . Divine wisdom is contrasted with human foolishness . . . which God will destroy."[241] "Righteousness looks to Jer 9:24, just as God's destroying illusory wisdom looks to Isa
29:14."

W. Bender lends some support, but also implies some modification, to the
view adopted by Fee by appealing first to the use of **wisdom** in 1:23-24, and
then to the triple terminology in 6:11: *"washed . . . sanctified . . . justified."* He
further cites 2 Cor 5:21, "so that **in him** we might become the **righteousness** of
God."[242] He then concludes with a proposal to translate 1:30 as follows: *From
him you are through Christ — who has been made into wisdom for us by God —
righteousness, sanctification, and redemption.* Thus the scriptural quotation becomes "fulfilled" (v. 31). This coheres also with Wedderburn's careful study of
uses of ἐν Χριστῷ: frequently God's action "in Christ" carries a meaning not
dissimilar from action "through" Christ (διά with the genitive).[243] Further, this
would also allow for resonances with the LXX of Wis 9:6, τῆς ἀπό σου σοφίας,
the wisdom that comes from you [God], which Weiss and others cite as background.[244] With Fee, we may regard ἡμῖν, **for us**, as meaning *on our behalf,* as a
dative of advantage.[245]

The four qualities, then, belong together, and *both characterize Christ
and are imparted by Christ.* Just as Barth insists rightly that *what real humanness consists in* appears only in the perfect "real man" Jesus Christ, so here
Paul redefines *what real wisdom consists in,* namely (in Moltmann's language),
The Way of Jesus Christ, as exhibited and made effective in God's own action in

239. Bohatec, "Inhalt und Reihenfolge der 'Schlagworte der Erlösungsreligion" in 1 Kor
1:26-31," 252-71.
240. Conzelmann, *1 Corinthians,* 52.
241. Collins, *First Cor,* 93.
242. Bender, "Bemerkungen zur Übersetzung von 1 Kor 1:30," 263-68.
243. Wedderburn, "Some Observations . . .," 90.
244. Weiss, *Der erste Korintherbrief,* 39.
245. Fee, *First Epistle,* 85.

Christ on the cross.[246] As against the obsession with status seeking and success at Corinth, **wisdom** is redefined and explicated as receiving the *gifts* of **righteousness, sanctification, and redemption** *freely bestowed through Christ and derivative from him.* It is only that for Christian believers. Hence **to glory in** their new-found status as *righteous, holy,* and *redeemed* is **to glory in the Lord**, and in no other person, no other thing. These other things are "**nothings**" not merely in a social sense, but, in isolation from God, also in an ontological sense. Thus Barrett comments, "Not only do your sources of supply — wisdom, strength, and so forth — come from God: your very being comes from him."[247]

It is difficult to be certain whether in any sense here Paul consciously identifies Christ with the figure of Wisdom as a quasi-personal entity in Prov 8:22-31 and Wis 7:22–8:1. Dunn sums up the issue judiciously. He writes: "Paul probably takes up wisdom language because it was already being used by the Corinthians. . . . It evidently gave rise to an elitist spirituality . . . (1 Cor 2:10–3:4). . . . Wisdom for the Corinthians had something to do with 'the rulers of this age' (2:6, 8). . . . However, there is no indication that the Corinthians thought of this wisdom as active in creation, as a personification of divine action . . . or as a personal being. . . . Still less can we conclude that the Corinthians had evolved anything properly to be called a Wisdom Christology."[248] But does Paul's own response go further? Christ, Dunn asserts, is "God's wisdom" for Paul, but "a wisdom in the sense of God's predetermined plan of salvation'. Christ is God's wisdom, then, not as a pre-existent being, but as the one who fulfilled God's pre-determined plan of salvation . . . through his death and resurrection. . . . There is no thought here of wisdom as a pre-existent divine hypostasis or person, either among the Corinthians or in Paul himself."[249] These terms provided "an important tool for asserting the finality of Christ's role in God's purpose."[250] Paul makes the "astonishing" claim that "the foolishness of the cross . . . is the real measure of divine wisdom (1:21-25)."[251]

Dunn's approach corroborates the point which Tertullian repeatedly makes against Marcion. The Christ of the New Testament fulfills the "wisdom" of God expounded in Proverbs and in Judaism as the way of bringing about the

246. Karl Barth, *CD*, 3/2, sects. 44, 55-202, esp. "(3) Real Man," mainly 132-52; cf. 153-202; also cf. J. Moltmann, *The Way of Jesus Christ* (Eng. trans., London: SCM, 1990). The connection with the redefinition of the human ἐν Χριστῷ is also suggested in J. D. G. Dunn's comment that "the whole thought here" (i.e., in Rom 6:11, ἐν Χριστῷ) "is still under the influence of 5:12-21: 'in Christ' as part of the eschatological humanity . . .," WBC (*Romans* [2 vols., Dallas: Word, 1988], 1:324).

247. Barrett, *First Epistle*, 59.

248. J. D. G. Dunn, *Christology in the Making: An Inquiry into the Origins of the Doctrine of the Incarnation* (London: SCM, 1980), 177 (2d ed., SCM, 1989; also Grand Rapids: Eerdmans, 1996).

249. Ibid., 178; cf. 176-87, 194-95.

250. Ibid., 194.

251. Dunn, *The Theology of Paul*, 274; cf. 272-77.

long-established purposes of the one God.[252] We shall return to further issues concerning **wisdom** when we take up 2:6-16; 8:6; and 10:1-4.

The noun δικαιοσύνη, **righteousness,** occurs only in 1:30 in this epistle, but the cognate verb δικαιόω, *I justify* or *deem righteous,* also occurs in 1 Cor 4:4 and 6:11. In 1 Cor 4:4 the sense is clearly *verdictive* or *declarative,* namely, *judge righteous, count righteous, deem righteous,* or *acquit,* since it relates to comparisons between human verdicts, which may not be valid, and the divine verdict (ὁ δὲ ἀνακρίνων με κύριός ἐστιν), which alone is definitive. Bender, Schrage, and Merklein also associate this verse with 2 Cor 5:21, "so that in him we might become the righteousness of God" (γενώμεθα δικαιοσύνη θεοῦ ἐν αὐτῷ). In 1:30 there is a corresponding identification: all is "from God" (ἀπὸ θεοῦ); "God is the sole originator also of righteousness, holiness *(Heiligung)* and redemption."[253] This righteousness of which God is "origin and active subject . . . is not *our* righteousness, but God's righteousness for us *(für uns)* which has become an effective reality. The δικαιοσύνη is thus clearly *iustitia aliena,* the righteousness from another and not our own, a work of God and not that of humankind" (Schrage's italics).[254]

We reject the claim that justification by grace is emphasized by Paul only in the more explicitly "anti-Jewish" or "Judaistic" contexts of Romans and Galatians.[255] In a judicious essay Barrett carefully weighs these issues about justification in the context of the Käsemann-Stendahl discussion, and concludes that while the doctrine is capable of being miscontextualized (i.e., assimilating Paul into Luther), nevertheless "justification by faith is a basic principle of God's dealings with his creatures, worked out in different ways in the story of a Paul and the story of a Luther."[256]

We have already discussed the meanings of ἁγιάζω and ἅγιος in 1:2. Craig succinctly summarizes the meaning of ἁγιασμός here in a way which recalls our discussions and clarifies its relation to **righteousness**. "*Righteousness* is not simply one of the moral virtues, but the divine acquittal, or will to save . . . (Rom 3:21). . . . **Sanctification** translates . . . an important Pauline term. From the same root came the adjective 'holy' and the noun 'saint'. The word has the cult significance of 'bringing into nearness to God' . . . through God's work. . . . In no passage in Paul does it describe an advanced state of Christian living."[257] Thus the "reversal" through the cross of lack of status and self-

---

252. Tertullian, *Against Marcion,* 5:6, and elsewhere.

253. Schrage, *Der erste Brief,* 1:216; Merklein, *Der erste Kor 1–4,* 203.

254. Ibid.

255. In addition to the Introduction, cf. A. C. Thiselton, "Luther and Barth on 1 Cor 15," in W. P. Stephens (ed.), *The Bible, the Reformation and the Church: Essays in Honour of James Atkinson,* JSNTSS 105 (Sheffield: Sheffield Academic Press, 1995), 258-89.

256. C. K. Barrett, "Paul and the Introspective Conscience," in Stephens (ed.), *The Bible, the Reformation and the Church,* 48; cf. 36-48.

257. C. T. Craig, "1 Corinthians: Exegesis," in *IB,* 10:34 See further BAGD, 9-10; Grimm-Thayer, 6-7; Wolff, *Der erste Brief,* 45-46; and Merklein, *Der erste Brief 1–4,* 195 ("das 'vor Gott' nut bestehen kann wem Gott Bestand gibt bzw wen er 'erwählt' . . .); see further ibid., 202-3.

esteem, whether in a shame-culture context or a guilt context finds expression in being clothed in the righteousness of Christ as divinely loved and accepted, and in being purified and set apart as one invited to the privileged place of intimacy with God, marked and identified by his name through Christ.

Redemption (ἀπολύτρωσις) also occurs only here in 1 Corinthians, only twice in Romans (Rom 3:24 and 8:23), once in Colossians (Col 1:14), and three times in Ephesians (Eph 1:7, 14; 4:30). The word λύτρον occurs only at Mark 10:45 (par. Matt 20:28, "a ransom for many"), and not in Paul. But we shall return to the concept in more detail in connection with ἀγοράζω in 1 Cor 6:20: "you were purchased [redeemed] with a price." ἠγοράσθητε γὰρ τιμῆς is also repeated in 7:23. The allusion to 6:20 reminds us that **redemption** is a term drawn from the slave market in the Graeco-Roman world. A slave may be purchased or "redeemed" from one situation under one master to a new situation under a new master if the new master pays the required price. Alternatively, as Deissmann demonstrates from ancient texts and inscriptions, ransom money could be paid at a temple, and the former slave liberated as a freedman under the protection of the deity.[258] "Sales" to Apollo, Athena, Asclepius, Serapis, and "to the most high God" (in AD 41 at Gorgippia) include "sure proofs of the influence of the pagan rite on Jewish hellenism in the time of the Apostle Paul."[259] Deissmann examined some thousand inscriptions at Delphi, and the value of his work in contextualizing the metaphor of **redemption** is recognized. Nevertheless, recent research demonstrates that his emphasis on "freedom" is misleading: the metaphor primarily refers to purchase *from* one owner *to* another, *by means of* a costly transaction.[260]

The three components which together constitute **redemption** are: (i) *liberation from some state of* bondage, jeopardy, suffering, or *humiliation;* (ii) *liberation by some act* which entails some dimension of personal *cost,* irrespective of the identity of the one who suffers the cost, and that of the precise form of the cost; and (iii) *liberation to a new situation of service,* free from oppression under a former master to serve the new "lord." In this sense, to borrow Dale Martin's title, this new lordship redefines "slavery" as salvation: believers do not belong to themselves (see under 6:19). Yet even this corrective to Deissmann should not be overpressed. Combes shows that *both* "new ownership" *and* "freedom" are nuances of the theology of redemption in Paul.[261]

It is important to note two further points. First, the theological background does not depend on Graeco-Roman socioeconomic imagery, for the life and faith of Israel was founded on an event of redemption *from* bondage in Egypt *by* saving acts of God which involved the shedding of blood (either

---

258. Deissmann, *Light from the Ancient East,* 318-32.

259. Ibid., 322.

260. See under 6:19-20; 7:23; also Martin, *Slavery as Salvation,* esp. 50-85, 117-35; and *Of Slavery in the Writings of the Early Church,* JSNTSS 156 (Sheffield: Sheffield Academic Press, 1998), esp. 77-94.

261. Combes, *The Metaphor of Slavery,* esp. 83-87.

among the firstborn of Egypt or among the animals of Passover) *to* a new life as God's own free and holy people *en route* to the promised land. Second, the three elements precisely match Paul's point to his addressees at Corinth: their **redemption** freed from a previous condition of being lowly "nothings" *by* a decisive act of God in Christ's costly death on the cross *to* whatever state of freedom and glory they now enjoyed. Hence, as those deemed righteous and holy and made free, their grounds for glory lay exclusively "**in the Lord**" (v. 31).[262]

The introduction of the quotation from the LXX by ἵνα is strictly an ana-coluthon, a broken construction for which several explanations of possible syntax have been offered. Lightfoot suggests "in order that it may be according to the langauge of scripture," but this is strained. If it is an ellipse from which a verb has been omitted, this is not the only instance where Paul hurries on, and the sense is perfectly clear: whether it fulfills or merely instantiates the principle already laid out, the climax of the argument finds expression in the ringing declaration, "**Let the one who glories, glory in the Lord**." Paul repeats the quotation in 2 Cor 10:17.

Most commentators see this as a free quotation from the LXX of Jer 9:23.[263] With Jer 9:22, the two verses (22, 23) trace the sequence of thought which Paul has been expounding and applying: μὴ καυχᾶσθω ὁ σόφος ἐν τῇ σοφίᾳ αὐτοῦ καὶ μὴ καυχάσφω ὁ ἰσχυρὸς ἐν τῇ ἰοχύι αὐτοῦ, καὶ μὴ καυχᾶσθω ὁ πλούσιος ἐν τῷ πλουτῷ αὐτοῦ ("let not the wise person glory in his/her wisdom, let not the strong glory in their strength; let not the rich glory in their riches"): all this expresses the point of the previous verses in Paul. Jeremiah now adds: ἀλλ᾽ ἢ ἐν τούτῳ καυχάσθω ὁ καυχώμενος, συνδιεῖν καὶ γινώσκειν ὅτι ἐγώ εἰμι κύριος ὁ ποιῶν ἔλεος ("but, rather, let the one who glories glory in this: to understand and to know [me], that I am the Lord, the One who executes mercy"). 1 Sam 2:10 also offers a part-parallel in the LXX to which several commentators appeal (mainly on the basis of its use in 1 Clement).[264]

The most convincing treatment, however, comes from Stanley.[265] The likelihood that Paul directly used Jer 9:22-23, he argues, is substantiated by the implicit parallel between 9:23 and 1 Cor 1:27-28 "where the categories τοὺς σοφούς . . . τὰ ἰσχυρά . . . τὰ ὄντα seem to have been modelled directly on ὁ σοφός . . . ὁ ἰσχυρός . . . ὁ πλούσιος of the Jeremiah passage."[266] It is easy to account for the omission of the introductory ἀλλ᾽ ἢ from the LXX. Paul regularly omits initial conjunctions. The one substantial change is the substitution of κυρίῳ for τούτῳ, but this "does not appreciably change the

262. On the controversy about "cost" see on 6:20.

263. See O'Day, "Jer 9:22-23 and 1 Cor 1:26-31: A Study in Intertextuality," 259-67.

264. *1 Clement* 13:1. Cf. the discussion of Lightfoot, *Notes,* 169.

265. Christopher D. Stanley, *Paul and the Language of Scripture: Citation Technique in the Pauline Epistles and Contemporary Literature,* SNTSMS 74 (Cambridge: Cambridge University Press, 1992), 186-88.

266. Ibid., 187.

meaning of the verse."[267] In any case, we may add, Paul does not use the quotation as a proof of something new, but as an instantiation of a principle which here receives climactic expression and corroboration. Karl Barth rightly identifies this verse as bringing to a sharp focus the theme of this first chapter, and indeed the theme of the whole epistle, not least of chapter 15 on the resurrection.[268]

THE POSTHISTORY, INFLUENCE *(WIRKUNGSGESCHICHTE)*, AND RECEPTION OF CHAPTER 1

In his excellent commentary on Matthew, Ulrich Luz notes that any account of "the History of Influence" of texts of the NT will inevitably be selective. This is "unavoidable."[269] In accordance with the work of H.-R. Jauss in this area, we select examples which instantiate (1) continuities and discontinuities of interpretation within specific traditions which influence interpretation; (2) the influence and history of effects *(Wirkungsgeschichte)* which shape the "pre-understandings" of subsequent generations of interpreters (i.e., predispose them to address a given agenda, but do not determine their agenda); and (3) identify those effects which have held particular influence in theology in the history of the daily life of the church, or more broadly in the history of ideas.[270]

An earlier, fuller, draft has been abandoned under pressure of space, and lest the above three points should become dissipated into a mere history of interpretation. (See the Preface, xvii, above.) In the case of ch. 1, it has seemed best to distinguish between the influence and effects of 1:18-25 and those of 1:26-31. Some of the earlier draft has been integrated into the exegesis as contributions from the patristic and other periods.

1:18-25

In the patristic period (1) writers facing persecution often underlined the aspect of the cross as **an affront** (σκάνδαλον, 1:23) or **folly** (μωρία, 1:18) to the world (e.g., Ignatius, Cyprian; (2) more "intellectual" apologists were sometimes at pains to point out that Paul does not attack all **wisdom** as such. (3) Some authors approach the passage differently, or use it to expound a broader theology (Origen, Augustine). (4) In Bernard and especially in Luther, the theological development focuses on a distinc-

267. Ibid., 188. Similarly Paul's ὁ καυχώμενος for Jeremiah 9 (LXX καυχάσθω may go back to an earlier Christian or Jewish usage, but more probably simply intensifies the force (ibid., 187).

268. Barth, *The Resurrection of the Dead,* 17-18.

269. U. Luz, *Matthew 1–7: A Commentary* (Eng. trans., Edinburgh: T. & T. Clark, 1990), 95.

270. H.-R. Jauss, *Literaturgeschichte als Provokation* (Frankfurt: Suhrkamp, 1970), and *Toward an Aesthetic of Reception* (Eng. trans., Minneapolis: University of Minnesota Press, 1982). On the importance and relevance of Jauss for biblical interpretation see R. Lundin, A. C. Thiselton, and C. Walhout, *The Promise of Hermeneutics* (Grand Rapids: Eerdmans/Carlisle: Paternoster, 1999), 191-99.

tive theology of the cross. In the modern period some writers (e.g., Pannenberg) offer a corrective in terms of a more integrated emphasis on the resurrection.

The Apostolic Fathers

Before AD 108 Ignatius quoted 1 Cor 1:20 in his reflection that the cross is "**an affront to unbelievers** (σκάδαλον τοῖς ἀπιστοῦσιν), but to us salvation." He continues: ποῦ σοφός; ποῦ σοζητύς; (where is the sage? where is the debater?).[271] Justin Martyr (AD 110-165) combines the two approaches set in contrast in our introduction. He argues that Christian truth does commend itself as truth to those of sound reason, but that widespread misinterpretation has placed the gospel within a frame where it appears (unjustly) as atheistic, foolish, incoherent, and irrational. Its "power" is revealed in a transformed lifestyle based on what is reasonable and true.[272]

The Patristic Era

Clement of Alexandria cites several verses from this passage to explain the need for a "higher" wisdom. For "has not God made foolish the wisdom of this world?"[273] Without such higher wisdom, human persons cannot apprehend Christ as Savior. While he underlines the benefit of culture and the germ of truth in many philosophical systems, Clement notes that in the end "those who in their own estimation are wise consider it fantastic that . . . God should have a Son, and especially that the Son should have suffered. . . . Has not God made foolish the wisdom of the world?" He compares the wisdom of God to the sun which, when it shines in splendor, virtually extinguishes the lamplight of human wisdom by its power.[274]

A clear contrast between the Alexandrian Clement and the "twice-born" Tertullian appears in their respective expositions of this same passage. Tertullian sees the contrast between human wisdom and divine action in 1 Cor 1:18-25 as more than a matter of "higher" wisdom. What one perceives as folly, another perceives as truth because "you are a different person from the heathen."[275] Paul has clearly declared here that "the wisdom of the world is foolishness." Moreover, against Marcion, he refuses to restrict this new wisdom to the God of Jesus Christ, as if to imply that the God of the OT scriptures did not also reveal purposes which find their fulfillment in Christ and the cross. It is not that the OT is lacking, but that in "seeking signs" the Jews "have already made up their minds about God, and 'the Greeks seek after wisdom' who rely on their own wisdom, not upon God's."[276]

In the fragments from his commentary, Origen the theologian appears, for he is perhaps the first to make much of the soteriology of the cross in this passage as a topic in its own right. Christ frees us in the destruction (καταλύσαι) of death, and of

271. Ignatius, *To the Ephesians*, 18:1.

272. Justin, *Apology*, 1:68.

273. Clement, *Stromata*, 1:3 (Against the Sophists); 1:18, 19; 5:1 (c. AD 202).

274. Ibid., 6:6.

275. Tertullian, *On the Resurrection*, 3 [c. AD 207].

276. Tertullian, *Against Marcion*, 5:5.

"ignorance, darkness and fatal pestilence (ἀγνοίας, καὶ τοῦ σκότους καὶ τῆς ἀπώλειας λοιμόν). The divine power (δύναμις) of the cross is for all (ὑπὲρ πάντων), and constitutes a victorious triumph over the devil. Hence, μὴ γένοιτο καυχάσθαι εἰ μὴ ἐν τῷ σταυρῷ.[277] On the divine decree and pleasure to save those who believe, Origen places together belief in Christ crucified with that of the resurrection of the body and future salvation.[278] This faith, however, comes from God, who destroys the cleverness of the wise.[279] Origen also contextualizes these verses in his treatise *Against Celsus.* He offers a lengthy quotation from 1 Cor 1:18-22 to substantiate the claims that Celsus's misinterpretation of a Christian doctrine of the last things rests quite simply on his approaching doctrine and scripture "with the wisdom of the world."[280] In *Against Celsus,* therefore, Origen is concerned with epistemology; in the fragments from his *Commentary,* with soteriology.

Cyprian of Carthage writes both as a former rhetorician and as a bishop forced to flee under the intense pressure of persecution under Decius (249). Cyprian's approach to our passage is christological: Christ is the Wisdom of God, by whom all things were made: "He is also both the wisdom and power of God, Paul proves in his First Epistle to the Corinthians: 'because the Jews require a sign, and the Greeks seek wisdom, but we preach Christ crucified, the power of God and the wisdom of God."[281] Lactantius also links epistemology with Christology. He alludes to the Socratic and Pauline theme of willingness to recognize one's ignorance as a condition for wisdom (1 Cor 3:18; cf. Rom 1:22) and the fallacy of seeking wisdom which is of a kind that counts as folly. Folly retains a disguise of "wisdom" only because there is a hiddenness about God's wisdom and truth which God can expose to view.[282] For in his allusions to the concept of Christ as "wisdom," he sees Christ as pre-emptying the dual role of *logos* and *sophia* in Greek thought: "He is both the voice and the wisdom of God."[283] Knowledge and wisdom (epistemology) are grounded in Christology.

Athanasius develops further the link between the wisdom-folly contrast and Christology. God has shown his wisdom in "What the Lord accomplishes in his body."[284] Yet this, as the anonymous "Ambrosiaster" (c. 370-80) points out, entails such supposed "folly" as the virgin birth and the resurrection, which many regard as irrational.[285] In the same vein Augustine quotes the entire passage in full, noting that "folly," for those who are blind, consists in "the body which Christ took of a woman and in the shame of the cross; for your lofty wisdom spurns such loss and contemptible things. . . . But God fulfils what the holy prophets predicted . . . 'I will destroy the wisdom of the wise' . . . ," followed by the full quotation of six verses.[286] Elsewhere, however, even in this passage about the "weakness" of the cross, Augustine associates God's power with his capacity to rule as the one who disposes all things as he wills,

277. Origen, "Fragments," *JTS* 9 (1908): 235, sect. 6 (Greek text ed. C. Jenkins).
278. Ibid., 236, sect. 7.
279. Ibid., 236-37, sect. 8.
280. Origen, *Against Celsus,* 5:16 (c. AD 240-250).
281. Cyprian, *Testimonies,* 2 (martyred in AD 258).
282. Lactantius, *Divine Institutes,* 4:2.
283. Ibid., 4:9; cf. 4:16.
284. Athanasius, *On the Incarnation,* 15.
285. Ambrosiaster, *Commentary on Paul's Epistles* (CSEL, 81:16).
286. Augustine, *The City of God,* 10:28.

and God's wisdom with his penetration of the cosmos.[287] The point of emphasis has shifted.[288]

Medieval and Reformation

In the medieval period the cross as divine wisdom finds a place especially in liturgical and devotional contexts. Bernard of Clairvaux, for example, writes, *"Ecce, enim in cruce est salus nostra": in the cross is our salvation;* and, he adds, it is also "our power."[289] I want "only to know Jesus, and him crucified." For Francis of Assisi the cross constitutes the subject matter of prayer, praise, and meditation.[290]

Luther expounds these verses as a major theme. The gospel is God's wisdom: "Paul says that the world considered our God a fool (cf. 1 Cor. 1:21)." Luther compares this with "claiming to be wise, they became fools" (Rom 1:22). "But we glory in God, that he alone is wise, and portions out his wisdom among his people. . . . The foolishness of God is wiser than men" (1:25).[291] Not only in the Heidelberg Catechism but also in his commentary work, Luther alludes to 1 Cor 1:17-25 and declares that Christ both is rejected by the world and is the **power** of God because "he emptied himself in order completely to hide his power, wisdom and goodness, disclosing only his weakness, foolishness and harsh suffering. . . . One who is powerful, wise and at ease must have these goods as if he had them not."[292] Luther returns, then, to Paul's notion of power-in-weakness, or the power of the cross, as Schütz, Pogoloff, and others have discerned it in this passage. Critics may claim that the resurrection polarity is insufficiently emphasized, but Luther offers a fine exposition of ch. 15 (see below).

Calvin underlines Paul's emphasis on "the blindness of the human mind" even when "surrounded by light." This helps us to understand the ambivalence of "knowledge of God" through his works in Rom 1:20-21.[293] Paul's positive affirmation about the gospel and salvation, Calvin observes, likewise anticipates Rom 1:16, "I am not ashamed of the gospel; it is the power of God for salvation to all who believe."[294] Bengel urges that the proclamation of the cross cuts across the achievements of religiosity or of wisdom because God is sheer grace: *"placitum est Deo, ex gratia"* (v. 21).[295]

---

287. Augustine, *On Faith and the Creed (De Fide et Symbolo),* 3 (4).

288. On Chrysostom and Gregory, see *1 Cor. Hom.,* 4:6, 11; and Gregory of Nyssa, *Against Eunomius,* 2:12:7, 12.

289. Bernard of Clairvaux, *Sermon on the Feast of St. Andrew,* 2:7; Migne, *PL,* 183:512 (AD 1090-1153).

290. Migne, *PL,* 183:1,000 (AD 1181-1226).

291. Martin Luther, *Luther's Works,* 28 (American ed.): 249-50 (*WA,* 26:28).

292. Luther, *Lectures on Romans* (ed. W. Pauck; LCC 15; London: SCM, 1961), 17.

293. Calvin, *First Epistle,* 40.

294. Ibid., 41. (This exegesis is confirmed by Francis and Sampley, *Pauline Parallels,* 106, sect. 74: "The Word of the Cross.")

295. Bengel, *Gnomon,* 612.

The Modern Period

"The word of the cross" in 1 Cor 1:18, Pannenberg observes, is "the gospel of God" in Rom 1:1, 1 Thess 2:2, and 2 Cor 11:7.[296] Like Margaret Mitchell, he sees it as a short-hand term for all that leads up to the story of Jesus, the cross, the resurrection, and what follows it. The proclamation is "power," then, not only in the "weakness" of the cross, but in its immediate entailment, namely the coming of God's "role" in the resurrection and eschatological future. "The power that fills the gospel is thus connected with the presence of the future of God in the coming of Jesus. . . ."[297]

Jüngel's view of how God's "wisdom" is disclosed in and through the cross profoundly addresses the problem of "modernity." If the act of God in the cross "destroys human wisdom," this entails the fruitlessness of the project of Descartes to "use" God as "a methodological necessity for the continuity of the 'thinking being' which is securing its existence."[298] Human wisdom reflects *about* God within issues of language as signification. Divine wisdom through the cross calls attention to "the address character of language."[299] Under the former mode of thinking, the death of Christ, or the death of God, is "a contradiction to the true deity of God," i.e., "folly." But "the word of the cross speaks in opposition to that."[300] Jüngel writes, "God defined himself as love on the cross of Christ . . . an event which in its uniqueness discloses the depths of deity. . . . God *is in and of himself* in such a way that he is *for* man" (Jüngel's italics).[301]

1:26-31

The Apostolic Fathers

Clement of Rome follows the theme of 1 Cor 1:26-31, and uses the quotation of v. 31, although he gives the argument a moralistic rather than a soteriological application.[302] The point, for Clement, is the exhortation "let us be humble-minded" (ταπεινοφρονήσωμεν). Hence the wise must not glory in their wisdom, but glory in the Lord. However, Clement does not appear to mean glorying in the mighty acts of the Lord, the cross of the Lord, or the grace of the Lord, but "remembering the words of the Lord Jesus . . . when he was teaching long-suffering: 'Be merciful, that you may obtain mercy'" (*1 Clement* 13:1-2). The emphasis lies on "injunctions" (13:3). This *hortatory* and moralistic use of Paul's words, however, does not remain characteristic of Tertullian, and most other Fathers.

---

296. Pannenberg, *Systematic Theology*, 2:455.
297. Ibid., 459; cf. "the Gospel," 454-64.
298. Jüngel, *God as the Mystery of the World*, 111.
299. Ibid., 11.
300. Ibid., 203-4.
301. Ibid., 221.
302. *1 Clement* 13:1 (c. AD 96).

The Patristic Era

Tertullian cites an interesting example of the quotation of 1 Cor 1:27 outside its context for manipulative purposes.[303] "God has chosen the foolish things to shame the wise" was supposedly used by Praxeas to argue that if it seems "foolish" for God, as a single being, "to make himself both a Father and a Son," such "foolishness" is part of the wisdom of God and undermines the attempt to draw any distinction of persons between the Father and the Son. This verse, Tertullian replies, does not allow us to defend any "foolish" view on the ground that God has reversed wisdom and folly in general. It must be understood in relation to God's specific purpose and acts. Tertullian himself quotes 1:27 in the context of the power of God to provide a new status, a new creation, and "a new nature" in place of the old at the resurrection.[304]

Origen also has to contend with misinterpretations or misuses of 1 Cor 1:26-28. He expresses the concern that "some have been led to suppose that no one who is instructed or wise or prudent embraces the Gospel."[305] He has two rejoinders. The first is exegetical: Paul does not say "none," but "not many." Second, other parts of the NT provide counterexamples. The qualifications for bishops or elders in the Pastoral Epistles, for example, require that they be judicious and convincing in argument as well as intelligent, prudent, and blameless in their lifestyle (Tit 1:9-10). In several passages Origen cites these verses to illuminate the contrast between Christian claims concerning revelation and the inspiration of scripture on one side and the aspirations of secular learning on the other. Deuteronomy, Origen argues, establishes the principle of divine election and calling, and prepares the way for what Paul declares in 1 Cor 1:26-31, namely, that Israel cannot find salvation if it glories in its own wisdom and becomes "Israel after the flesh"; for God upholds the decree that he reveals himself to the lowly whose glory is to glory in the Lord.[306] Similarly, Origen rejects the claim of Celsus about "the wise and learned among the Greeks," who "pride themselves on their own wisdom and theology." Both in 1 Cor 1:27-29 and in Rom 1:25 Paul shows that the "wise" have become foolish in the conceits of their hearts, reversing what is wise and what is foolish in their pride and in their worship of creatures in place of the Creator.[307] In his *Commentary on John,* Origen declares that Jesus Christ himself is the Gospel, whom to know as crucified and raised is to receive all good things: "for he is made to be from God righteousness and sanctification and redemption" (1 Cor 1:30).[308]

Augustine is concerned with Paul's dual emphasis on divine grace and divine sovereignty, for which he quotes 1 Cor 1:30-31. This righteousness of God, which is the gift of grace without merits, is not known by those who go about to establish their own righteousness."[309] Augustine then alludes to Rom 10:3 and to Ps 17:15;

303. Tertullian, *Against Praxeas,* 10.
304. Tertullian, *On the Resurrection,* 17.
305. Origen, *Against Celsus,* 3:48.
306. Origen, *De Principiis,* 4:1. The Greek and Latin vary in details, but substantially use the same quotations to make the same points.
307. Origen, *Against Celsus,* 4:4. On the "well-born" see Origen, *Fragments on 1 Cor,* sect. 8, lines 20 and 31.
308. Origen, *Commentary on John,* 1:11.
309. Augustine, *City of God,* 21:24.

God's righteousness is sweet: "taste and see how sweet the Lord is." But, he concludes, this does not deprive God of his sovereign choice concerning whether or not there are those who will remain condemned because they placed their hope only in themselves.

Augustine also turns to the earlier verses about wisdom (1 Cor 1:27). There is, he concedes, a genuine tradition of Wisdom in Proverbs. Christ is the "Wisdom of God ... co-eternal with the Father."[310] Such wisdom God makes accessible to the "simple," i.e., those in Proverbs who wish to learn, and those in 1 Cor 1:27 who do not boast of their own wisdom.

Chrysostom draws a very similar point from 1:26-27. He suggests the analogy of a physician who tries to teach his art to someone who thinks that he or she already knows it all.[311] "Arrogance" is a self-made barrier to knowing God; hence supposed wisdom is sheer folly. Chrysostom links this admirably with Paul's emphasis on God's sovereign and gracious action. "It is not possible we should be saved only by ourselves," and this was so "from the beginning."[312] This is sheer grace, for it serves "to show the copiousness of the gift ... ἐξ αὐτοῦ: we were made righteousness in him. 'Him who knew no sin He made to be sin for us that we might be made the righteousness of God in him' (2 Cor 5:21). . . . 'He who glories,' therefore, 'let him glory in the Lord' (1 Cor 1:31)."[313]

Medieval and Reformation Eras

This passage features in various writings of Bernard of Clairvaux. Bernard refers to the human plight of "not being able to help ourselves from not sinning." This is "loss of wisdom and power." But, Bernard asserts, "This is where Christ comes in. In Him humankind can possess the necessary 'power of God and the wisdom of God' (1 Cor 1:24). For as wisdom he can restore to humankind true wisdom. . . . As power, He is able to renew His free pleasure to human persons."[314] Christ, "who is our salvation," has also made the way to it, so that "no man can boast" (1 Cor 1:30).[315] In his work *On the Nature and Dignity of Love,* Bernard calls attention to the costly suffering of love by which Christ "became our wisdom."[316] On one side, Bernard urges, there is "vainglory; it has no basis of truth." On the other side, "the Apostle distinguishes clearly between true and false glory: 'He who boasts, let him boast in the Lord' (1 Cor 1:31; 2 Cor 10:7: cf. Jer 9:23-24). To boast in the Lord is to be in the truth."[317] The wider context of Bernard's thought here is that God is to be loved *for his own sake,* not for his "gifts."

Bernard's contrast between true and false glory corresponds with Luther's contrast in *The Heidelberg Disputation* of 1518 between a triumphalist, manipulative "the-

310. *City of God,* 17:20.

311. Chrysostom, *1 Cor. Hom.,* 5:2.

312. Ibid., 5:3.

313. Ibid., 5:4.

314. Bernard, *Life and Works of St Bernard* (ed. J. Mabillon; London: Hodges, 1896): *Treatise on Grace and Free Choice,* 26.

315. Ibid., 43.

316. Bernard, *Works: On the Nature and Dignity of Love,* 30.

317. Bernard, *Works: On Loving God,* 3.

ology of glory" and a truthful "theology of the cross": "The theologian of glory says bad is good, and good is bad. The theologian of the cross calls them by this proper name."[318] Luther relates this to the contrast between human wisdom and that of the cross. Indeed, "the foolishness of the cross" can be traced back to the faith of Moses in the Epistle to the Hebrews. He remarks: 'He chose the weak things. . . .' Moses chose the wisdom or rather the foolishness of the cross, and rejected the wisdom he had inherited."[319] Luther's confidence is expressed in his quotation of 1 Cor 1:30: "the righteousness which comes from faith in Christ is sufficient for him. Christ is his wisdom, his righteousness and all, as it says in 1 Cor 1:30: the justified man is surely the work and instrument of Christ."[320] Calvin declares that the gift of Christ as God's wisdom, righteousness, sanctification, and redemption constitutes the "mode of existence" *(modus subsistendi)* that Christian believers derive from being-in-Christ.[321] This becomes elaborated into a fully articulated doctrine of "imputed" righteousness: "We are accepted by God, because He [Christ] atoned for our sins by his death, and his obedience is imputed to us for righteousness."[322] But Calvin's approach is far from mechanical or theoretical. A new liberation takes place "when we are extricated from the labyrinth of sin and death."[323]

The Modern Period

Barth appealed to this passage for a renewed emphasis on the sovereignty of God. The word κλῆσις, he insists, "always means quite unambiguously the divine calling . . . by which a man is transplanted into his new state as a Christian. . . . Its sovereignty in the face of all human greatness is reflected in the fact that at Corinth only a few wise and mighty and noble . . . have received it (1 Cor 1:26, 27). Hence its sovereignty in the face of all differences in human origin and social position consists in the fact that we may and must become obedient to it whether we are circumcised or uncircumcised, slave or free. . . ."[324] Barth equally appeals to this passage for the inseparability of the experience of salvation from Christ. "Wisdom, righteousness, sanctification and redemption are not relevant conceptions in themselves, but only as predicates of the subject Jesus."[325] 1 Cor 1:30, he argues, would be "meaningless" without "the Subject Jesus Christ, on which it depends."[326]

A new and unusual turn has been taken with an emphasis on wisdom and even "wisdom Christology" in feminist theology since around 1980. Elisabeth Schüssler Fiorenza is the most widely known exponent of this approach, appealing to 1 Cor 1:24 and 1:30, Christ "God's Power and God's Sophia."[327] She perceives a Wisdom or

318. Luther, *The Heidelberg Disputation,* Thesis 21, in *Luther: Early Theological Works* (ed. J. Atkinson; London: SCM, 1962), 291.

319. Luther, *Epistle to the Hebrews,* in ibid., 220.

320. Luther, *The Heidelberg Disputation,* 25, in *Luther,* 294.

321. Calvin, *First Epistle,* 45.

322. Ibid., 46.

323. Ibid.

324. Barth, *CD,* 3/4, sect. 56.600.

325. Ibid., 1/2, sect. 13.10.

326. Ibid.

327. E. Schüssler Fiorenza, *In Memory of Her,* 189.

"Sophia-christology" especially in pre-Pauline material in Phil 2:6-11. She compares the "kenosis" of Phil 2:6-11 with *1 Enoch* 42:1-2: "Sophia found no place where she might dwell. Then a dwelling-place was assigned for her in the heavens. Wisdom went forth to make her dwelling among the children of humans, and found no dwelling place. Wisdom returned to her place, and took her seat among the angels." She comments, "Christ-Sophia has received his–her rulership over the whole cosmos."[328] We have noted the problems raised about "Wisdom Christology," and the issue remains at best complex; at worst problematic and speculative. It is instructive to note how radically this approach diverges from Barth's emphasis and the exegetical problems which it raises. However, it remains a formative influence in the history of the effects of the text *(Wirkungsgeschichte)*.

3. The Issue Demonstrated in Paul's Own Experience of Evangelism in Corinth (2:1-5)

(1) As for me, when I came to you, brother and sisters, I did not come with high-sounding rhetoric or a display of cleverness in proclaiming to you the mystery of God. (2) For I did not resolve to know anything to speak among you except Jesus Christ, and Christ crucified. (3) I came to you in weakness, with much fear and trembling. (4, 5) My speech and my proclamation were not with enticing, clever words, but by transparent proof brought home powerfully by the Holy Spirit, that your faith should not rest on human cleverness, but on God's power.

Paul has appealed to the experience of the Corinthians themselves concerning their own background and to what they owe their new status. This experience (1:26-31) substantiates the central issue about the act of God through the cross, which redefines wisdom and folly. Paul now shows how his own experience of events surrounding his proclamation of the gospel when he first came to Corinth confirms precisely the same point. As C. Clare Oke observes in his short article on 2:4, "The Divine and humbling non-contentious character of Christianity is shown, the Apostle submitted, in three ways: by the gospel's obvious independence of human intelligence (1:18ff.); by the lowly calibre of those called (1:26ff.); and by the manner in which he consistently introduced the gospel at Corinth (2:1-3), not humanly and self-confidently, but in an effacement of himself that allowed the Spirit to indicate His presence and power effectively."[329] We have indicated above that his first two clauses invite further clarification and modification, but Oke's perception of the structure and broad thrust of these verses remains valid.

Francis and Sampley's *Pauline Parallels* also remind us that 2:1-5 does not

328. Ibid., 190.

329. C. Clare Oke, "Paul's Method Not a Demonstration but an Exhibition of the Spirit," *ExpTim* 67 (1955): 85; cf. 85-86.

remain a theme peculiar to 1 Corinthians.[330] 2 Corinthians contains reference to the well-known accusation "his bodily presence is weak, and his speech of no account 'even if' his letters are weighty and strong (2 Cor 10:10)"; Galatians speaks of Paul's first preaching the gospel there as occasioned by "a bodily ailment" (Gal 4:14); while at Thessalonica his preaching constituted an occasion for "much affliction," but also for a communicative effect which was not empty but marked by "power and the Holy Spirit and with full conviction" (1 Thess 1:5-6). In a relatively recent monograph solely devoted to 2:1-5 Michael Bullmore contends that Paul both uses and opposes rhetoric in these verses: "It was against a particular strain of Graeco-Roman rhetoric that Paul set forth his own statement of rhetorical style."[331] The specific style which Paul opposed and disowned is described by Bullmore as "public display oratory" associated with the Second Sophistic. Stylistic virtuosity won audience approval, in contrast to Paul's conscious choice of "a simple and unaffected style which draws no attention to itself."[332] This harmonizes precisely with the issues about apostolic agency urged by Best and Crafton (and endorsed in our comments above) as well as perceptions of two types of rhetoric identified by Clarke, Winter, Witherington, and especially Pogoloff.[333] All of these writers, including Bullmore, cite primary sources, especially Plutarch, but also Dio Chrysostom, on the competitive showmanship of local provincial rhetoric at the Isthmian games. One could hear crowds of "wretched sophists" competing for applause, while rhetoricians were called in to entertain diners between courses at banquets.[334]

Bruce Winter confirms such a reconstruction of the situation behind 2:1-5. Paul's language is "anti-sophistic."[335] There were "sophistic conventions regarding the initial visit to a city by an orator seeking to establish a reputation as a professional speaker."[336] He would be "escorted with much enthusiasm and éclat (φιλοτιμία)."[337] Winter shows significant parallels between 2:1-5 and Dio's *apologia* of c. AD 102 (*Orations* 47), e.g., the use by Dio of μεγαλόφρων, "high-minded" address.[338] In 2:1-5 ἀπόδειξις and δύναμις presuppose rhetorical allusions, i.e., to *demonstration* and to *persuasiveness* respectively: "1 Cor 2:1-5 reveals a distinct constellation of rhetorical terms and allusions."[339] Nevertheless, "Paul repudiated the sophistic method of 'presenting himself' when he came to Corinth . . . [not] projecting an image of himself. . . ."[340]

330. Francis and Sampley, *Pauline Parallels,* sect. 76 (108-9).

331. Bullmore, *St Paul's Theology of Rhetorical Style,* 224.

332. Ibid., 225.

333. Again, Pogoloff, *Logos and Sophia,* is entirely convincing.

334. Bullmore, *St Paul's Theology of Rhetorical Style,* 62; Dio Chrysostom, *Discourses,* 8:9 (cf. 4:14); Plutarch, *Quaestiones Conviviales* 8.4.1.

335. Winter, *Philo and Paul among the Sophists,* 147-48.

336. Ibid., 148 and 151.

337. Dio, *Orations,* 47:22.

338. Winter, *Philo and Paul,* 152.

339. Ibid., 155.

340. Ibid., 157.

Bibliography on 2:1-5

A number of works cited under 1:18-25 and 26-31 are also relevant. Only some of these are cited below.

Beaudean, J. W., *Paul's Theology of Preaching* (Macon, Ga.: Mercer University Press, 1988), 87-118.

Best, E., "The Power and the Wisdom of God, 1 Cor 1:18–2:5," in L. de Lorenzi (ed.), *Paolo a Una Chiesa Divisa (1 Cor 1–4)* (Rome: Abbey St Paul, 1980), 9-41.

Bornkamm, G., "Faith and Reason in Paul," in *Early Christian Experience* (London: SCM, 1969), 29-46.

Bullmore, M. A., *St Paul's Theology of Rhetorical Style: An Examination of I Corinthians 2:1-5 in the Light of First Century Greco-Roman Rhetorical Culture* (San Francisco: International Scholars Publication, 1995).

Bünker, M., *Briefformular und rhetorische Disposition in I Korintherbrief* (Göttingen: Vandenhoeck & Ruprecht, 1984).

Carson, D. A., "The Cross and Preaching (1 Cor 1:18–2:5)," in *The Cross and Christian Ministry* (Grand Rapids: Baker, 1993), 11-42.

Clarke, M. L., *Higher Education in the Ancient World* (London: Routledge & Kegan Paul, 1971).

Friedrich, G., "Die Verkündigung des Todes Jesus im NT," *Biblisch-Theologische Studien* 6 (1982): 119-42.

Hartman, L., "Some Remarks on 1 Cor 1:1-5," *SEÅ* 39 (1974): 109-20.

Hengel, M., *The Cross and the Son of God* (Eng. trans., London: SCM, 1986), 93-263.

Horsley, R. A., "Wisdom of Word and Words of Wisdom in Corinth," *CBQ* 39 (1977): 224-39.

Koperski, V., "Knowledge of Christ and Knowledge of God in the Corinthian Correspondence," in R. Bieringer (ed.), *The Corinthian Correspondence,* BETL 125 (Leuven: Leuven University Press, 1996).

Lampe, P., "Theological Wisdom and the 'Word about the Cross': The Rhetorical Scheme of 1 Cor 1–4," *Int* 44 (1990): 117-31.

Lim, T. H., "Not in Persuasive Words of Wisdom but in Demonstrations of the Spirit and Power," *NovT* 29 (1987): 137-49.

Litfin, D., *St Paul's Theology of Proclamation: 1 Cor 1–4 and Greco-Roman Rhetoric,* SNTSMS 79 (Cambridge: Cambridge University Press, 1994).

Maly, K., *Mündige Gemeinde. Untersuchen zur pastoralen Führung des Apostels Paulus im I Kor* (Stuttgart: Katholisches Bibelwerk, 1967): 29-33.

Merklein, K., "Das paulinischen Paradox das Kreuzes," *TTZ* 106 (1997): 81-98.

Nielson, H. K., "Paulus Verwendung des Begriffes Dunamis. Eine Replik zur Kreuzestheologie," in S. Pedersen (ed.), *Die Paulinische Literatur und Theologie* (Arhus: Aros, 1980), 137-58.

Oke, C. C., "Paul's Method Not a Demonstration but an Exhibition of the Spirit," *ExpTim* 67 (1955): 85-86.

Ortkemper, F.-J., *Das Kreuz in der Verkündigung des Apostels Paulus* (Stuttgart: Katholisches Bibelwerk, 1967), 9-67.

Pickett, R., *The Cross in Corinth,* JSNTSS 43 (Sheffield: Sheffield Academic Press, 1997), esp. 37-84.

Pogoloff, S. M., *Logos and Sophia: The Rhetorical Situation of 1 Corinthians,* SBLDS 134 (Atlanta: Scholars Press, 1992), esp. 97-172.

Savage, T. B., *Power through Weakness,* SNTSMS 86 (Cambridge: Cambridge University Press, 1996), 54-99.

Stowers, S. K., "Paul on the Use and Abuse of Reason," in D. L. Balch, E. Ferguson, and W. Meeks (eds.), *Greeks, Romans and Christians: Essays in Honour of J. Malherbe* (Minneapolis: Augsburg, 1990), 253-86.

————, "Social Status, Public Speaking and Private Teaching: The Circumstances of Paul's Preaching," *NovT* 26 (1984): 59-82.

Wilckens, U., "Das Kreuz Christi als die Tiefe der Weisheit Gottes," in L. de Lorenzi (ed.), *Paolo a Una Chiesa Divisa (1 Cor 1–4)* (Rome: Abbey St Paul, 1980), 43-81.

————, *Weisheit und Torheit* (Tübingen: Mohr, 1959), 44-51.

Winter, B. W., *Philo and Paul among the Sophists,* SNTSMS 96 (Cambridge: Cambridge University Press, 1997), 113-244, esp. 147-61.

1 The word μυστήριον, **mystery** (of God), is ranked by the 4th ed. (1993) of the UBS *Greek New Testament* as "B," i.e., as "almost certain," although the 3d ed. (1975) had ranked it "C" (which in that edition meant "a considerable degree of doubt"). **Mystery** has the "probable" support of ℘46 (technically only a "probable" reading since the MS is not sufficiently well preserved to offer no margin of ambiguity; but the MS may be dated c. AD 200 as one of the earliest). It also constitutes the original reading ℵ, A, C, Syr P (Peshitta), cop[bo], and Slavonic VSS (also, e.g., Hippolytus and Ambrose). On the other hand, μαρτύριον, **witness** (of God), is attested by the ℵ2 and by B, D, F, G, 33, syr[h], cop[sa], Vulgate, and readings in Origen, Basil, Chrysostom, Jerome, Cyril, and Pelagius. The 4th ed. UBS reflects Metzger's note that μαρτύριον, **witness**, is probably to be explained as "a recollection of 1:6," whereas μυστήριον [**mystery**] here "prepares for its usage in vs 7."[341] Conzelmann believes that it is "impossible to decide" between the two readings, noting that if μαρτύριον (**witness**) could have been picked up from 1:6, no less could μυστήριον (**mystery**) have been picked up from 1:7, and that **mystery** depends largely on Egyptian MSS.[342] Fee and Wolff ask why any scribe might substitute the less-expected **witness** for the more familiar **mystery**, unless it was original, also appealing to Zuntz's view that μυστήριον here steals the thunder from its use later in the chapter.[343] He rejects Metzger's arguments "on all counts." Schrage is far more hesitant than Fee, noting that Fee does not consider a full range of uses of the terms in Paul or in the period of scribal traditions.[344] As the influence of mystery religions spread, this phenomenon provides an explanation for the very point which Fee considers inexplicable, namely, a good reason for Christian scribes "to avoid misunderstanding" about preaching by changing Paul's μυστήριον to μαρτύριον. No one can exclude either possibility, but with Collins we lean towards **mystery**.[345] *Both words,* although more especially **mystery**,

341. Metzger, *Textual Commentary* (2d ed.), 480. This is a well-known textual crux.

342. Conzelmann, *1 Corinthians,* 53, n. 6. Barrett calls it "difficult" to decide, but leans toward **testimony** (*First Epistle,* 62-63).

343. Fee, *First Epistle,* 88, n. 1; Wolff, *Der erste Brief,* 47.

344. Schrage, *Der erste Brief,* 1:226; also Moffatt, *First Epistle,* 23.

345. Collins (*First Cor,* 118) evaluates the issues with care: "Scrutiny of the textual witnesses and a closer reading of the text confirm . . . that 'mystery' is indeed the better reading." We agree.

emphasize that what is conveyed in Christian proclamation is *truth revealed by God, not human opinions.*

The Greek κἀγώ, **as for me**, is the regular ellipse at the beginning of a sentence for καὶ ἐγώ, and conveys a degree of emphasis. De Wette interpreted the emphasis as a contrast between Paul himself and other apostles, but clearly he is saying: "my own experience, too, like yours, confirms the same point." Bullmore and especially Winter have shown decisively that **as for me** stands in contrast to the "coming" to Corinth of sophists (see the introduction to 2:1-5). Once again, ἀδελφοί, **brothers**, raises all the problems of inclusive-language translation (see above on 1:10) and introduces a fresh section of argument (see on 1:26).

Translations of ὑπεροχὴν λόγου ἢ σοφίας, **high-sounding rhetoric or a display of cleverness** vary considerably. The unusual word ὑπεροχή occurs elsewhere in the NT only in 1 Tim 2:2, although the cognate verb appears in Rom 13:1. It has to do with *height,* and with the preposition ὑπέρ (hyper-) intensifying ἔχω, The word in effect corresponds with *preeminence,* which NRSV plausibly renders with λόγου as *lofty words.* Outside the NT Deissmann cites examples of inscriptions at Pergamon describing people "of high eminence."[346] The NIV tries to pick up the rhetorical context implicit in 1:18-31 with *brilliance of oratory* or *wise argument.* But this misses both the probable metaphor of height (although ὑπέρ can also signify *excess*) and the quasi-ironic hint that the demand for *cleverness* may result in what is *above people's heads.*[347] NIV overtranslates and narrows Paul's focus. Paul constantly strove for wise argument. His respect for reason precludes any anti-intellectualism as such.[348] His aim here is to expose the true basis and nature of Christian proclamation in contrast to the "self-presentation" of the visiting sophist. Christian proclamation does not allow for **high-sounding rhetoric or a display of cleverness** which could impede the gospel *by putting first what pleases the audience* and the personal "style" of the speaker. The apostle does not arrive with

---

346. Deissmann, *Bible Studies,* 255.

347. William Barclay's rendering "outstanding gifts of rhetoric or wisdom" verges on the possible with "out" in place of ὑπέρ, since the term is used in nonbiblical Greek for something "out of" the ordinary. Héring opts for the general impact in proposing "prestige of rhetoric," while Moffatt suggests "any elaborate words or wisdom." Lightfoot suggests "excellence of rhetorical display is of philosophical sublety," on the ground that ὑπέρ expresses *excess.*

348. See above on Stowers, "Paul on the Use and Abuse of Reason," and Bornkamm, "Faith and Reason in Paul," in *Early Christian Experience,* 29-46. "In 1 Cor 1–3 the Apostle speaks about the wisdom of the world and not immediately about reason. . . . The 'wisdom of the world' is a very definite way of thinking, qualified by its content. . . . It is not by chance that the phrases in 1 Cor. 1:18ff. occur in a carefully reasoned relationship" (29-30). "Paul speaks of reason . . . with an elenctic purpose, i.e., to convict the hearer of his guilt before God" (35). "The style of the Pauline sermon is just not that of a revelation-speech but of the diatribe" (36). There is also an appeal to reason in his ethical directives (40-41). Paul values rationality, but knows that it can be misused (41-42, 29-46). Stowers argues with even more force, especially with reference to 1 Corinthians 2.

displays of pomp and applause. To convey Paul's point of emphasis we have, in effect, placed σοφίας in quotation marks. Paul renounces "preaching for effect" in the sense of parading **cleverness** in the eyes of the audience. As the following verses make clear, and as Oke's article confirms, if the audience assents to certain claims for the wrong reason, this may not constitute a lasting work of God's Holy Spirit. The reference to the Holy Spirit contrasts not only with persuasive *linguistic* styles, but more especially with the *self-presentation* and *self-prominence* associated with the "presence" of the sophist (see above, esp. on Winter).

The present participle active καταγγέλλων indeed means **proclaiming** in the full sense of the word. It vindicates the title of Litfin's work as well as his observations on this passage, partly because it is broader than what we think of today as *preaching* (mainly in the context of liturgy or worship by ordained or trained speakers), but mainly because it occurs most characteristically in contexts which carry nuances of solemnity or due weight.[349] In 11:26 those who participate in the Lord's Supper **proclaim** the Lord's death; in Acts 13:5 the word of God is **proclaimed** in the synagogues. In Rom 1:8 Paul tells the church at Rome that their faith is **proclaimed** everywhere, i.e., it is communicated in the public domain as a matter of import. In Acts 26:23 light is proclaimed to the Gentiles.[350] Litfin compares this use of the word with προγράφω, *to show forth, to proclaim,* or *to placard,* which also underlines its place in the *public* domain, so that all may see what is displayed.[351]

S. K. Stowers has argued that Paul is unlikely to have preached "publicly" in the sense of using public buildings or adopting the role of a public orator or street-corner preacher. Since the use of public buildings, or recognition as an orator, presupposes some public status or appropriate social reputation, Stowers concludes that the most probable center of Paul's preaching was that of the household or private home.[352] If this argument can be sustained, it may add force to 2:1, where "self-presentation" and display of the speaker is at issue. For Paul may well be saying that he did not lay claim to the role of public orator. If so, this would then have lowered his status at Corinth. But the proclamation remains "public" in the sense that *it does not communicate esoteric teaching to some inner group of initiates, but an announcement of events and state of affairs to all who would hear.* In this sense the gospel is universal. The central content concerns a declaration of God's deeds in Christ.

We have already touched on the meaning of μυστήριον, *mystery,* in our textual note (above). If the textual alternative μαρτύριον, *witness,* is followed,

---

349. Litfin, *St Paul's Theology of Proclamation* 204-9; cf. 193-203.

350. Cf. BAGD, 409; Grimm-Thayer, 330; MM, 324 (esp. *announcing news*); Lampe, *Patristic Greek Lexicon,* 706 (gospel proclamation and doxology); also Schrage, *Der erste Brief,* 1:227.

351. Litfin, *Proclamation,* 196-97; cf. BAGD, 704.

352. Stanley K. Stowers, "Social Status, Public Speaking and Private Teaching: The Circumstances of Paul's Preaching," *NovT* 26 (1984): 59-82.

whether τοῦ θεοῦ is subjective genitive ("the genitive θεοῦ is that of the author," Godet) or objective genitive (Paul's witness about God and his acts in Christ) may be determined, as Meyer suggests, with reference to our earlier discussion concerning witness of Christ in 1:6.[353] Paul, Godet observes, proclaims "not a system of ideas to be exhibited, but merely a testimony rendered to a fact."[354] Lightfoot also speaks of "plain and simple language as becomes a witness."[355] Unlike Meyer, he distinguishes between an objective genitive in 1:6 (testimony to Christ) and a subjective genitive here (testimony borne by God), not least on the ground that testimony is borne by God to Christ. But in Paul as well as in John the inverse direction of witness is also sometimes implied.

These difficulties are avoided if μυστήριον is taken as original, although Robertson and Plummer and Allo offer a paraphrase which might well be the meaning of either word: either may convey "the message of God's love to mankind declared in the saving work of Christ."[356] Héring considers that if we read **witness** neither the objective genitive is appropriate, since Paul witnesses to Christ and the cross, nor the subjective since if God is the subject it remains unclear to whom the witness is directed.[357] On the other hand, he urges, it is entirely straightforward to speak of Paul's proclaiming the cross as God's mystery, in the sense that it transcends the wisdom of the world but manifests the hidden wisdom of God's eternal purpose.[358] To those whose concerns are merely wrapped up in themselves, the gospel is an enigma.[359]

In secular Greek and in the mystery religions μυστήριον means *a secret, a secret rite, or secret teaching.*[360] But the word is used differently in Paul, most notably when he uses the plural *the mysteries of God* as the content of Christian proclamation in 1 Cor 4:1 (cf. on this Schrage's critique of Fee's argument that this does not bear on 2:1, cited in the Textual Note). In 1 Cor 13:2 the understanding of mysteries is a possibility for believers, but in the NT the term always points to the necessity for divine revelation as a gift, as against human dis-

---

353. F. Godet, *Commentary,* 1:124; Meyer, *First Epistle,* 1:55.

354. Godet, *Commentary,* 1:124.

355. Lightfoot, *Notes,* 170 and 171; cf. Wolff, *Der erste Brief,* 46.

356. Robertson and Plummer, *First Epistle,* 30; Allo, *Première Épitre,* 30.

357. Héring, *First Epistle,* 14. Héring probably overstates the difficulty. As Grosheide observes, "to speak of God is to speak of Christ" (*First Epistle,* 59).

358. Ibid., 15; similarly Lang, *Die Briefe,* 35.

359. Schrage, *Der erste Brief,* 1:226-27.

360. BAGD, 530; cf. MM, 420; Grimm-Thayer, also 420. A vast literature on the mystery religions could be cited. Cf., e.g., R. Bultmann, *Primitive Christianity in the Contemporary Setting* (Eng. trans., London, 1956), 156-61; Günter Wagner, *Pauline Baptism and the Pagan Mysteries* (Eng. Edinburgh: Oliver & Boyd, 1967), 61-267; R. Reitzenstein, *Hellenistic Mystery-Religions: Their Basic Ideas and Significance* (Eng. trans., Pittsburgh: Pickwick, 1978); W. Bousset, *Kyrios Christos* (Eng. trans., Nashville: Abingdon, 1970); the older but in many ways more judicious work of H. A. A. Kennedy, *St Paul and the Mystery Religions* (London: Hodder & Stoughton, 1914); A. J. M. Wedderburn, "The Soteriology of the Mysteries and Pauline Baptismal Theology," *NovT* 29 (1987): 53-72; and F. Cumont, *The Oriental Religions in Roman Paganism* (Eng. trans., Chicago: Open Court, 1911).

covery as a stage of achievement (21 occurrences in Paul); "a mystery too profound for human ingenuity," e.g., Rom 11:25 (partial hardening of Israel, which is both explained yet also lies beyond full explanation); 1 Cor 15:51 (again, partially but not fully explained); Col 2:2 (formerly hidden but now revealed).[361] As Schrage rightly concludes, this theme of revelation in 2:1 matches the verbs of proclamation and announcement and Paul's uses of ἀποκαλύπτεσθαι.[362] "In Jewish apocalyptic literature **mystery** *(raz)* has an eschatological meaning. It designates the salvific events to be revealed in the age to come."[363]

2 We translate **For I did not resolve to know** after careful consideration, since it goes against the tendency of most English versions. The issue is whether the negative οὐ (**not**) is to be construed (i) with εἰδέναι *(not to know),* or (ii) with τι *(to know nothing),* or (iii) as the word order of the Greek seems to us to demand, with ἔκρινα (**I did not resolve**). (i) The AV/KJV *(I determined not to know anything),* NJB *(the only knowledge I would have),* and TEV *(I made up my mind to forget everything)* all implicitly construe οὐ (**not**) with *to know* or *knowledge.* On the other hand, (ii) NRSV *(I decided to know nothing),* NIV *(I resolved to know nothing),* and Barrett *(I would know nothing)* negate τι *(something,* **anything,** translating it as *nothing).* But did Paul steadily resolve to empty his mind (εἰδέναι, perfect infinitive of οἶδα) of everything except the message of the cross? (REB avoids the issue with *I resolve that . . . I would not claim to know anything. . . .*). (iii) Only Collins appears to reflect the third, correct option unambiguously.[364]

As the Greek stands, the act of resolution or of firm, considered decision (BAGD) is qualified by the negative. Paul's firm, considered policy on which he committed himself was only that which concerned **Christ crucified**.[365] Whether or not he spoke of anything else would be incidental; *to proclaim the crucified Christ, and Christ alone, remains his settled policy.* He did not take a vow of excluding everything else, whatever might happen, but he did make a commitment that nothing would compromise the central place of **Christ crucified**. Fee retains Barrrett's syntax, but explains that *nothing* does not mean "nothing" in context.[366] Schrage observes, "Of nothing else does Paul wish to know."[367] P. Lampe is no doubt correct to see this section as part of a rhetorical method of alluding *indirectly* to the self-focused power play of 1:10-12.[368] Paul

---

361. BAGD, 530; cf. MM, 420, and Grimm-Thayer, also 420.

362. Schrage, *Der erste Brief,* 1:227.

363. Collins, *First Cor,* 115.

364. Ibid., 115-18.

365. BAGD, 451-52.

366. Fee, *First Epistle,* 92 (cf. Barrett, *First Epistle,* 63).

367. Schrage, *Der erste Brief,* 1:227.

368. P. Lampe, "Theological Wisdom and the 'Word about the Cross': The Rhetorical Scheme in 1 Cor 1–4," *Int* 44 (1990): 117-31. Conzelmann's allusion to "theological knowledge" (*1 Cor,* 54) appears to miss this point. In support of Lampe, see Bullmore, *Rhetorical Style,* 206-10.

211

resolves to provide a *transparent window onto the cross: not to parade himself.*
Hence *any* "self-preservation" on the part of *any* "leader or name" has no place
in a community founded by and on the gospel.

The background in rhetoric at Corinth therefore overtakes some of the
older comments on the syntax. Lightfoot urges that Paul declares: "I had no intent, no mind to know anything. It does not mean, therefore, 'I steadfastly excluded all other knowledge,' but simply 'I did not trouble myself about the
knowledge of anything else.'"[369] Findlay and Robertson and Plummer make
the same point. They consider the counterargument that often οὐ φημί has the
same sense as φημὶ οὐ. But this is not the case with οὐκ ἔκρινα and ἔκρινα οὐ, or
at very least no evidence exists to imply it.[370] Findlay says tartly, "'I determined not to know' contravenes the order of words."[371] Meyer similarly interprets *I did not resolve* as "did not set it before me as part of my undertaking."[372]
These observations, together with what we now know of the rhetorical background at Corinth, release Paul of any hint of an uncharacteristic or obsessional
anti-intellectualism, or any lack of imagination or *communicative flexibility.*
His settled resolve was that he would do only what served the gospel of Christ
crucified, regardless of people's expectations or seductive shortcuts to success,
most of all the seduction of self-advertisement. Neither then nor now does the
gospel rest on the magnetism of "big personalities."

Many have asked here whether Paul's experience of a less-than-happy result following a more philosophical approach at Athens (Acts 17:22-31) contributed to the boundaries of this resolve. Moffatt points out that in the
Areopagus speech Paul had been leading up to the core of his gospel, namely,
Christ's death and resurrection, when he was interrupted: "There is no hint that
he had felt disillusioned by the Athenian experience."[373] He adds that if a contrast is to be understood, this is not between Paul's past experience and a more
recent policy, but between Paul and certain others who tried to court the approval of their audience. Barrett likewise dismisses this "imaginative picture"
as having "no evidence whatever," while Schrage similarly points to Paul's
practice instantiated in Gal 3:1 of "placarding" Christ crucified.[374]

Several minor details of translation invite brief comment. First, the pronoun τοῦτον, *this person,* is usually rendered "Jesus Christ and *him* crucified."
But the frequent use of this pronoun in Greek is hardly captured by an English
personal pronoun, and a demonstrative pronoun, regularly used in first-century
Greek, would be strained in English. Hence we have repeated the name, which

369. Lightfoot, *Notes,* 171.

370. Robertson and Plummer, *First Epistle,* 30. Even more sharply this is repeated by A. T.
Robertson, *Word Pictures in the NT* (New York: Richard Smith, 1931), 4:82; cf. Findlay, *Expositor's Greek Testament,* 2:775.

371. Findlay, *Expositor's Greek Testament,* 2:775.

372. Meyer, *First Epistle,* 1:55.

373. Moffatt, *First Epistle,* 22.

374. Barrett, *First Epistle,* 63; and Schrage, *Der erste Brief,* 1:229.

conveys Paul's effect: **Jesus Christ, and Christ crucified**. Second, ἐσταυ-ρωμένον is the perfect passive participle of σταυρόω. Clearly we must distinguish between "effects" remaining and "state" continuing. The permanent significance of the past event is in view, and **crucified** is probably the only possible translation. The versions which choose *nailed to the cross* are not wrong, but may draw the mind more closely to the event than to the abiding effects witnessed in tradition. Third, the Greek phrase ἐν ὑμῖν, **among you,** is awkward in English without either an added verb or explanatory clause. The versions which translate *while I was with you,* however, go far beyond the Greek, since Paul's stay of some eighteen months at Corinth must have included teaching and pastoral care as well as evangelism.[375] Fourth, εἰδέναι, **to know,** may seem surprising. We might expect **I did not reach a decision** *to speak* **anything**. But Paul refers to his whole mind-set and stance; hence we translate **decision to know anything to speak among you,** thus attempting to address the third and fourth points together.

3 Fear and trembling has been part of the English language, and translates ἐν φόβῳ καὶ ἐν τρόμῳ adequately, with the intensifier πολλῷ, **much**.[376] Five points call for special comment. (1) Since he makes such play of not seeking the esteem of the audience, we must infer that the root cause of Paul's **much fear and trembling** lay largely in his sense of responsibility before God to fulfill God's call to be an effective messenger of grace perhaps in conjunction with some circumstance which added to his "weakness" about which we can only speculate. (2) On the other hand, the point may also be more general: *Paul disowns the protection of the veneer of rhetorical tricks and routines* which can offer a false self-confidence by turning a solemn proclamation into "going through the motions" of a performance. (3) Yet in the end, **fear and trembling** serves most of all to place an antithetical contrast in view with *the confident self-promotion of the sophist's visit*. Paul is precisely not a visiting orator come to entertain the crowds as an audience-pleasing *performer*.[377]

(4) Albert Schweitzer, followed by Dibelius and Kümmel, speculates about the possible impact of illness on Paul's sense of "weakness."[378] Schweitzer declares, "That he [Paul] suffered from attacks of some kind which were calculated to humiliate him in the eyes of men, we learn from the Epistle to the Galatians."[379] Collins notes: "Paul's self-deprecation is part of his rhetorical ap-

---

375. Further, this would entirely miss Bruce Winter's point about self-promotion *on the arrival* of a sophist orator (see above).

376. Fee correctly applies πολλῷ to both states, not simply to τρόμῳ (*First Epistle,* 93, n. 23).

377. See Winter, *Philo and Paul,* 147-61; Bullmore, *Rhetorical Style,* 212-13 and throughout. The Gk. κἀγώ (καί + ἐγώ), **as for me,** intensifies the contrast with other speakers or other visitors.

378. A. Schweitzer, *Mysticism,* 152-55; and Martin Dibelius and W. G. Kümmel, *Paul* (Eng. trans., London: Longmans, Green & Co., 1953), 42-43.

379. Schweitzer, *Mysticism,* 152.

peal. . . . Nevertheless Paul's description of his weakness may reflect his real situation *as well* . . . (cf. 2 Cor 11:16-29)."[380] (5) L. Hartman has argued that **weakness** is the "anti-rhetor" aspect of Jer 9:22-23 (cf. 1 Cor 1:31).[381] The **weak** glories in the Lord (see below on vv. 4-5).

Schweitzer refers to Gal 4:13-14, where Paul says that he preached the gospel δι' ἀσθένειαν τῆς σαρκός (lit. "weakness" of the flesh, in the sense of "with a physical ailment"). The Galatians "did not despise or spit out, but welcomed me." Schweitzer comments, "It was usual to spit out in the presence of men who had mysterious illnesses in order to protect oneself. . . . The most natural hypothesis is therefore that Paul suffered from some kind of epileptiform attacks," even if this may not have meant that he was "a real epileptic" in the fullest sense.[382] These writers associate with this Paul's language about his σκόλοψ τῇ σαρκί (2 Cor 12:7-10, thorn in the flesh? sharp physical pain?). Schweitzer, Dibelius, and Kümmel further link with this the reference to the Galatians' willingness to offer their eyes to Paul (Gal 4:15, although F. F. Bruce views this as entirely metaphorical), and they explore a possible connection between problems of sight at intervals and acute and chronic migraines.[383]

We cannot be certain, however, that any of this applies to 1 Cor 2:3. Moreover, it would arguably detract from Paul's argument if it did. Paul conveys the *principle* that proclaiming the gospel does not depend on self-confident rhetorical assertion, of the kind which many today mistakenly think of as "speaking with authority." Paul's "authority" lay *not in smooth, competent, impressive, powers of articulation,* but in a faithful and sensitive **proclaiming** rendered operative *not by the applause of the audience, but by the activity of God.* Self-promotion, too, is alien to proclaiming the gospel.

Timothy Savage offers an explanation of **fear and trembling** which would too exclusively and narrowly relate only to the first of our four points above. He writes: "In the Septuagint the term φόβος καὶ τρόμος often depicts one's humble response to the awe-inspiring majesty of God" (e.g., Exod 15:16, LXX; Isa 19:16, LXX).[384] Savage sees this as a more probable background for Paul's comment that he came to Corinth "in profound humility and trepidation" (v. 3). "We can see that Paul is distancing himself from arrogant speech . . ." or

380. Collins, *First Cor,* 116 (my italics).
381. L. Hartman, "Some Remarks on I Cor 2:1-5," *SEÅ* 39 (1974): 109-20.
382. Schweitzer, *Mysticism,* 153.
383. Schweitzer writes, "By the pains which he has to bear Paul comes to be aware that he is a sick man. He explains this as due to an angel of Satan's being permitted to buffet him, in order that he may not be exalted above measure by the privilege of having been rapt into the third heaven (2 Cor 12:6-9). . . . What was the character of his pains and how they were connected with his attacks is not clear. But how greatly Paul must have suffered when he can speak thus of them" (154). The "marks" *(stigmata)* of suffering (στίγματα, Gal 6:17) "mean primarily the brandings by which a slave . . . was made recognizable as his master's property" (143). For a different view of Gal 4:15, cf. F. F. Bruce, *Commentary on Galatians,* NIGTC (Grand Rapids and Exeter: Eerdmans and Paternoster, 1982), 210-11.
384. Timothy B. Savage, *Power through Weakness,* 73.

"the speech of those who are puffed up" (4:19b).[385] While the second set of comments is valid, the first seems in part at variance with what Paul declares elsewhere about deliverance from the πνεῦμα of fear: by his Spirit God has poured out his love: "you have not received the πνεῦμα δουλείας πάλιν εἰς φόβον ἀλλὰ ἐλάβετε πνεῦμα υἱοθεσίας ἐν ᾧ κράζομεν, Αββα ὁ πατήρ" (Rom 8:15; cf. Rom 5:5).

Whether or not he has pressed the "illness" aspect a little further than the evidence, Schweitzer's theological emphasis on "weakness" as sharing with Christ in his humiliation, suffering, and death in order to bring life seems to offer firmer ground.[386] Paul glories in weakness because his work then offers "sure evidence that the power was of God and not of himself."[387] Authentic "apostolicity" entails identification with Christ in his self-giving and a reaching out beyond one's own personal resources (2 Cor 1:9), in a further experience of resurrection power.[388]

The phrase ἐγενόμην πρὸς ὑμᾶς may possibly be construed with **weakness** to mean "I was with (πρός) you in weakness," but more naturally and in view of the context should be construed with πρὸς ὑμας to mean **I came to you in weakness**.[388] **Fear and trembling** may constitute an *escalating experience:* fear betrays itself in a symptom which might seem to inhibit the preaching; in turn this intensifies the fear of falling short for such a heavy responsibility.[390] No doubt, if we draw on the narratives in Acts, the temporary absence of Paul's co-workers Silas and Timothy (Acts 17:15; 18:5) added a psychological dimension of loneliness or isolation which exacerbated Paul's **fear and trembling** (cf. the absence of Titus in 2 Cor 2:13).[391]

4-5 This is a sufficiently well-known crux to invite fuller comments than usual. There are no less than eleven variant readings of v. 4. (1) We may readily dispose of the MSS which insert ἀνθρωπίνης before or after σοφίας, which "are obviously secondary" and have "the appearance of an explanatory gloss inserted by copyists (at different places) in order to identify more exactly the nuance attaching to σοφίας."[392] These variants are found in the corrector of ℵ, A, C, syr^h and cop^bo, as well as later MSS.

(2) A more serious difficulty, however, arises from the difference between the reading πειθοῖς σοφίας λόγοις found in B, D, the first hand of ℵ (although with the misspelling λόγος), and the majority of quotations in Origen, Eusebius, and half in Chrysostom; and the reading πειθοὶς σοφίας found in the very early p^46 (c. AD 200 but

385. Ibid.
386. Schweitzer, *Mysticism,* 101-59.
387. Fee, *First Epistle,* 93.
388. See under "apostle" at 1:1.
389. See Winter, *Philo and Paul,* 147-61.
390. Lightfoot, *Notes,* 172.
391. *Acts of Paul and Thecla,* 3 (c. AD 190-200?) embodies a tradition about Paul's supposedly unattractive appearance, but even if this rested on solid ground it hardly elucidates the points at issue here.
392. Metzger, *Textual Commentary* (2d ed.), 481.

otherwise mainly only in F, G, and 33. Meanwhile a third variant, ἐν πειθοῖ σοφίας λόγου, is found in some of Origen's quotations, while Ambrose presupposes ἐν πειθοῖ ἀνθρωπίνης σοφίας. Of these, the first corresponds to our **enticing** *(persuasive),* **clever words**; the second (NRSV mg.) *persuasiveness of wisdom;* while the third reads the dative singular of the noun *persuasion.* The root problem is that the adjective πειθός, **enticing,** *plausible, persuasive,* is not found in any other Greek text. Hence Weiss, Zuntz, Héring, Fee, and Pogoloff all reject this reading in favor of p[46] mainly on the ground of lexicography, but also because the number of variants which arise signal that the original has been modified.[393] Fee also omits λόγοις under the principle of *difficilior lectio probabilior.*[394] Schrage also has some sympathy with the view that *persuasiveness* of "wisdom" offers a better correspondence with the second half of the verse.[395]

Yet some substantial arguments may be put forward on the other side. Most important, as Conzelmann notes, is that the Greek Fathers do not seem in general to be troubled by the form πειθός, *persuasive,* **enticing.**[396] Second, Heinrici, Lietzmann, and others point out that this form corresponds with expected grammatical conventions for structural transformation of the cognate verb πείθω, *I persuade,* into a related adjective which Barrett thinks Paul may well have coined, or may have been in oral currency.[397] Third, Findlay follows Westcott and Hort in seeing behind πειθός an original πιθός, which stands for πιθανός as an alternative form (although this argument may be double-edged; why did Paul not use πιθανός?).[398] Fourth, the combination of ℵ*, B, D, and 33 is extremely strong as a combined witness from different areas and traditions. Hence, against Weiss, Zuntz, and others cited, but with Edwards, Robertson and Plummer, Findlay, Lietzmann, Grosheide, Barrett, Conzelmann, Wolff, and Metzger, we would give the balance of probability to the UBS 4th ed. text; although, as Metzger explains, it is understandable why this edition reads πειθοί[ς], and gives the reading a "C" ranking to indicate that "the Committee had difficulty in deciding which variant to place in the text."[399] Merklein also considers that either of the two main choices is possible.[400] We have set out the details because this verse is one of several well-known examples of textual difficulty in 1 Corinthians. But the result makes little serious difference for the thrust of the verse.

In accord with subsequent work by Bullmore and Winter, Lim argues in a research article devoted to this verse that Paul's concern here is to distance himself from the kind of rhetoric and orator often expected and appreciated at Corinth.[401]

---

393. Weiss, *Der erste Korintherbrief,* 49; Zuntz, *Text of the Epistles,* 23-25; Héring, *First Epistle,* 15; Fee, *First Epistle,* 88; Pogoloff, *Logos and Sophia,* 137, n. 25.

394. Fee, *First Epistle,* 88.

395. Schrage, *Der erste Brief,* 1:231-32.

396. Conzelmann, *1 Corinthians,* 55 and 55, n. 21.

397. Lietzmann, *An die Korinther,* 11; cf. Edwards, *First Epistle,* 47; Heinrici, *Das erste Sendschreiben,* 103; Barrett, *First Epistle,* 65.

398. Findlay, *Expositor's Greek Testament,* 2:776.

399. Findlay, *Expositor's Greek Testament,* 2:776; also Grosheide, *First Epistle,* 61; Wolff, *Der erste Brief,* 49; Collins, *First Cor,* 119-20, tends to support Zuntz and Fee, adding that the final sigma of πειθοῖς may be due to dittography.

400. Merklein, *Der erste Brief 1–4,* 205.

401. Lim, "'Not in Persuasive Words of Wisdom, but in Demonstration of the Spirit and Power' (1 Cor 2:4)," 137-49.

Paul relies on the power of God to demonstrate, or perhaps to manifest, the Holy Spirit at work in convincing hearts and minds of the truth of ὁ λόγος μου καὶ τὸ κήρυγμά μου, **my speech and my proclamation**. Commentators have expended considerable effort on exploring a possible distinction between ὁ λόγος μου (which Paul uses for *the proclamation of the cross* in 1:17, but also for **clever speech** in 2:1) and τὸ κήρυγμά μου (which he uses for *through the foolishness of what we proclaim,* or *the foolishness of proclamation,* in 1:21). Some (e.g., Aquinas, Grotius, De Lyra, Bengel, and Fascher) propose that λόγος refers to private communication and κήρυγμα to public proclamation.[402] Others (e.g., Lightfoot and Schrage) firmly reject this as without evidence or foundation.[403] Many interpreters distinguish between λόγος as the substance or subject matter (hence Fee translates it as "message") and κήρυγμα as the mode, form, or testimony rendered to the substance.[404] But Conzelmann and others reject any supposed distinction between "form" and "content" or between "private" and "public" discourse, while Bullmore concludes that the form-content contrast has little practical significance and may reflect a hendiadys of terms.[405]

The long-standing contrast between public speaking and private teaching receives a further blow from the research and arguments of Stowers in his study of this subject.[406] He argues that Paul more probably found his opportunities for evangelism in "open" gatherings in private houses than in lecture halls or in official street-corner oratory for which some social or professional status or official patronage would usually (although not invariably) be expected. Schrage convincingly sees λόγος and κήρυγμα as inseparable aspects of a single apostolic activity: "λόγος and κήρυγμα are as little to be distinguished as form and content as they are private and public proclamation. In spite of the double μου, it is an inclusive way of using words for apostolic activity. The intended differentiation has as its goal the contrast with v. 5."[407] Thus speculations by Hodge and by Robertson and Plummer about which is the broader term also add little to the meaning of the text. Others more convincingly see this as "rhetorical duplication" (Conzelmann) and as a single "focus on the proclamatory nature of his mission . . ." (Beaudean).[408] In modern linguistics the importance of "redundancy" is widely accepted in the light of information theory. Any number of

---

402. Bengel, *Gnomon,* 613: λόγος, *sermo, privatus;* κήρυγμα, *praedicatio, publica;* πειθοῖς, *Verbum valde proprium.*

403. Lightfoot, *Notes,* 172; Robertson and Plummer, *First Epistle,* 32; and Schrage, *Der erste Brief,* 1:231.

404. For example, Godet, *First Epistle,* 1:128; Grosheide, *First Epistle,* 61; and Fee, *First Epistle,* 94.

405. Robertson and Plummer, *First Epistle,* 32; Conzelmann, *1 Corinthians,* 54; Schrage, *Der erste Brief,* 1:231; and Bullmore, *St Paul's Theology of Rhetorical Style,* 216; cf. 210-25.

406. Stowers, "Social Status, Public Speaking and Private Teaching," 69; cf. 59-82.

407. Schrage, *Der erste Brief,* 1:231.

408. Conzelmann, *1 Corinthians,* 54; and Beaudean, *Paul's Theology of Preaching,* 116-17. See further Mitchell, "Rhetorical Shorthand," in Jervis and Richardson (eds.), *Gospel in Paul,* 63-88.

good reasons contribute to it: emphasis, clarification, assurance of attention, filling in gaps for rhythmic balance, and so on. We need only think of poetic parallelism in Hebrew or of Cranmer's magnificent liturgy to appreciate the principle.

The explosion of recent work on rhetoric in the Graeco-Roman world and in Paul both sheds light on this verse and also gives it further importance for current debate. In what sense does Paul renounce the use of **enticing words** (AV/KJV) or (if the other reading is followed [see above]) *persuasive wisdom?* Schrage debates whether πειθοῖς (or πειθοῖ) is used positively *(persuasive),* neutrally *(plausible),* or pejoratively (**enticing**).[409] In view of the rarity of πειθοῖς and the textual ambiguity, everything depends on the context, especially if Barrett is right in suggesting that Paul himself coined the term. The mass of literature on rhetoric must be taken into account. The primary emphasis by Pogoloff, Bullmore, and Winter on specifically "Sophistic" applause-generating, consumer-oriented rhetoric must remain a central resource, but other work is also illuminating.[410] We must also arrive at a conclusion in the light of related questions about the precise meaning of the difficult phrase which stands in contrast to it, namely, ἐν ἀποδείξει πνεύματος, translated above as **by transparent proof brought home powerfully by the Holy Spirit** (see below).

We shall now attempt to identify three stable markers to assist our way through a complex debate. Before we examine further details, research on rhetoric in Paul and the ancient world yields two firm markers which guide us toward our exegesis.

(i) First, Witherington, as we have noted, sums up one key point succinctly: "The Corinthians felt that they had the *right to judge Paul* and his message and were evaluating him *by the same criteria by which popular orators and teachers were judged.* Paul disputed this right" (my italics).[411] Timothy Savage takes up the issue of "assertiveness" in the sense of *verbal bullying,* imposing one's force of personality, cajoling, and similar techniques which fea-

409. Schrage, *Der erste Brief,* 1:232.

410. Winter, *Philo and Paul;* Pogoloff, *Logos and Sophia;* Bullmore, *St Paul's Theology of Rhetorical Style;* but cf. also Witherington, *Conflict and Community,* 8-9, 23-24, 39-48; Mitchell, *Paul and the Rhetoric of Reconciliation;* T. Engsberg-Peterson, "The Gospel and Social Practice according to 1 Corinthians," *NTS* 36 (1990): 557-84; P. J. J. Botha, "The Verbal Art of the Pauline Letters: Rhetoric, Performance and Presence," in S. E. Porter and T. H. Olbricht (eds.), *Rhetoric and the NT,* 409-28; Duane F. Watson (ed.), *Persuasive Artistry: Studies in NT Rhetoric in Honour of George A. Kennedy,* JSNTSS 50 (Sheffield: Sheffield Academic Press, 1991); Jeffrey A. Crafton, *The Agency of the Apostle,* JSNTSS 51 (Sheffield: Sheffield Academic Press, 1991); Neil Elliott, *The Rhetoric of Romans,* JSNTSS 45 (Sheffield: Sheffield Academic Press, 1990); Litfin, *Paul's Theology of Proclamation;* Moores, *Wrestling with Rationality in Paul,* rhetoric in the wider Graeco-Roman world; also D. L. Clark, *Rhetoric in the Graeco-Roman World* (New York: Columbia University Press, 1957), esp. 177-261; James L. Kinneavy, *Greek Rhetorical Origins of Christian Faith: An Inquiry* (New York: Oxford University Press, 1987); George A. Kennedy, *Classical Rhetoric and its Christian and Secular Tradition from Ancient to Modern* Times (London: Croom Helm, 1980), 86-132; and Clarke, *Higher Education in the Ancient World.*

411. Witherington, *Conflict and Community,* 47.

ture in the rhetorical handbooks discussed by Clarke (n. 17) and other writers. He declares: "Paul is distancing himself from arrogant speech. . . . The Corinthians *want* assertiveness and demogoguery. . . . He gives them only words of weakness and humility" (my italics).[412] The work of Moxnes and many others on "honor" and "shame" adds further plausibility to these perceptions of the gulf between Paul and some at Corinth.[413]

(ii) Our second fixed marker emerges from the helpful and convincing work of Pogoloff, Bullmore, and Winter. Pogoloff draws firmly on the perceived tradition since the time of Plato and Aristotle between a concern to "use" reason or rhetoric entirely *instrumentally to win an argument* and the more philosophical Platonic-Aristotelian tradition which respected reason as part of a logical *demonstration of truth.* Pogoloff is aware that we cannot commit the anachronism of confusing fifth-century-(BC) Athens with first-century Corinth, but he can readily demonstrate, as writers such as M. L. Clarke conclusively prove, that these distinctions not only survive in the first century but remain greatly influential in Paul's day from Rome to Asia Minor. Everything rests on "Paul's contrast of πειθώ and ἀπόδειξις."[414] In Aristotelian terms, Pogoloff argues, the former depends on "rhetorical methods to sway you to γνῶσις . . . clever arguments based on opinion"; the latter "is grounded on something far more sure . . . the necessary proofs [ἀποδείξεις] of God's spirit and power."[415] Paul wants to let *truth* speak for itself, *not to manipulate rhetoric to sway his audience by appeal to opinions.* Aristotle sets out this contrast in his three books *On Rhetoric* and in the *Topics.*[416] Aristotle agrees with Plato that logical proof should have clear privilege over the dressing up of "opinions" to make them seem convincing.[417]

Pogoloff now combines this contrast with a correlative one which relates to what Bullmore and Winter demonstrate about the self-commendation of the sophist. The schools of rhetorical training were not only highly competitive but also highly conscious of rank and status. *Honor could be gained* by drawing on standard *topoi* and tools of the rhetorical trade to turn *any* argument, *whether true or false,* into a convincing appeal which swayed the audience *to believe it true.* It is precisely here that the tradition of Plato and Aristotle conflicts with that of popular rhetoricians and the second sophists. That is not to include the finest rhetoricians such as Cicero and Quintilian, but it would apply to lesser

---

412. Savage, *Power through Weakness,* 73.

413. Moxnes, "Honor, Shame and the Outside World," *The Social World of Formative Christianity and Judaism,* 207-19; also several specialist works discussed under 1:26-31.

414. Pogoloff, *Logos and Sophia,* 138.

415. Ibid.

416. Aristotle, *Topics,* 1.1 (100a, 18–100b, 23); 1.4 (100b, 11-16); 1.8 (103b, 1-7); 1.11 (104b, 1-3); *Rhetoric,* 1.1-3 (1354a); 1.1.11 (1355a).

417. Kennedy, *Classical Rhetoric and Its Christian and Secular Tradition,* 64; on Aristotle, cf. 60-85; on his *Rhetoric,* 63-82; on his *Topics,* 82-84. Cf. further Clarke, *Higher Education in the Ancient World,* and *Rhetoric at Rome: A Historical Survey* (London: Cohen & West, 1953).

sophistical "schools of rhetoric" in a "university" city such as Athens or Corinth. Pogoloff finds examples of ὑπεροχή (1 Cor 2:1) to mean "rhetorical prestige" which is bound up with social prestige in Diodorus Siculus.[418] He finds in Eunapius a reference to Sosipatra, a woman who "by her surprising wisdom" (ὑπεροχὴν σοφίας) made her own sophist husband Eustathius seem inferior.[419] Even closer to home, Eunapius compares unfavorably the "superabundant eloquence (λόγων ὑπεροχήν)" of a certain Maximus who "scorned all logical proof (ἀποδείξις)" with those who seek truth by demonstrable evidence (ἀποδείξις).[420]

Against this background it seems clear that Paul determines *to let truth speak for itself, confident in the power of the Holy Spirit of God* to bring this truth home to the hearts, minds, and wills of the hearers. *But the price is a renunciation of the status of rhetorician,* for while it is tempting to render ἐν ἀπαδείξει as *exhibiting* or *manifesting* (with Oke) the rhetorical background makes it virtually certain that Paul gives rhetorical or *logical demonstration* or **transparent proof** a distinctive turn by ascribing such **proof** ultimately to the agency of the **Holy Spirit** as effective **power**.[421]

(iii) A third firm marker for interpretation comes not from research on rhetoric, but from the relation between 2:4, 5 and Paul's argument in 1:18-31, especially in *the context of the OT and wisdom traditions in Judaism.* In his relatively brief but fairly recent commentary, Graydon Snyder includes a useful section on this passage under the subheading "the text in its biblical context." He rightly compares and contrasts a different tradition in which "the Lord will defeat all those who wage war against Jerusalem" (Zechariah 14) with that of the suffering servant (Isaiah 53 and Acts 8:26-40) and the way of the cross (Mark 8:31; 1 Cor 1:18-25; 2 Cor 5:21; Gal 3:13; cf. 1 Pet 2:24). Compared with triumphalist militarism and the use of compelling forces, "the wisdom of God, shown on the cross, works in quite another way: power is expressed in weakness."[422] Snyder places this in the context of election and calling: "My father was a wandering Aramaean" (Deut 26:5); God made those who were no people, his people (Exod 19:4-6): "likewise Paul's personal analogy has deep roots in biblical tradition. . . . Moses claimed lack of eloquence (Ex 4:10); Isaiah had unclean lips (Isa 6:5); Jeremiah was too young for public speaking (Jer 1:6). The power of the speaker is a gift of God (Matt 10:19)."[423]

James A. Davis shows that certain sapiential traditions within Judaism come closer to the expectations of Graeco-Roman rhetoric than we might ex-

---

418. Pogoloff, 132; Didorus Siculus, 34/35.5.5.

419. Ibid.

420. Ibid., 133; Eunapius, *Lives of the Sophists,* 466-69 and 475.

421. Cf. Oke, "Paul's Method Not a Demonstration but an Exhibition of the Spirit," 85-86. On the Greek as a technical term in rhetoric, see also Weiss, Robertson, Plummer, and Lim, "'Not in Persuasive Words,'" 137-49, and Merklein, *Der erste Brief 1–4,* 211.

422. Snyder, *First Corinthians,* 32.

423. Ibid.

pect. Paul, he argues, contrasts the two types of authentication: "as Paul makes plain in 1 Cor 2:4 the conclusive and definitive demonstration of inspiration is not found in external manifestations such as eloquence."[424] L. Hartman makes a similar point with reference to Paul's earlier allusion to Jer 9:22-23.[425] Hartman compares Paul's claim to "weakness" with making "the Lord" his sole ground of confidence and boast (1:31).

These three markers together serve to call into question some influential interpretations of these verses. For example, (1) many write here that Paul disowns "philosophy."[426] But Paul probably shares with the Platonic and Aristotelian traditions a *concern for truth* which stands over against the *instrumental* or *manipulative* use of language and opinions which marked sophist or popular rhetoric.[427] In the polarity between philosophy and rhetoric, Paul would almost certainly have shared the philosophers' concern for truth, although not, of course, their worldviews. Especially if ἀποδειξις means **proof** (as it does in the papyri, Josephus, and Philo), it stands in contrast to *persuasion* when evidence is lacking, or when argument lacks integrity and truth.

Further, (2) these factors call into question whether the uses of **Spirit** and *power* allude to external signs and miracles.[428] Origen and Grotius suggest that πνεύματος points to OT oracles and apostolic miracles, but this does not seem to be typical of Origen's interpretation of this passage.[429] Strikingly elsewhere in the same work Origen speaks of apostolic "power" as a style of "life and disposition . . . which struggles even to death for the sake of truth."[430] More generally he says of this verse that "unless power is given to the speaker by God . . . preaching cannot touch the human heart."[431] Chrysostom speaks of signs and miracles here, but at once acknowledges that "the reward of faith is lessened in proportion to the evidence wherewith the miracle is set forth."[432] Lietzmann alludes to "the signs of a true apostle . . . signs and wonders and mighty works (2 Cor 12:12)."[433] But Senft puts for-

424. Davis, *Wisdom and Spirit,* 80; cf. 78-81.

425. L. Hartman, "Some Remarks on 1 Cor 2:1-5," *SEÅ* 39 (1974): 109-20. Cf. further H. K. Nielsen, "Paulus Verwendung des Begriffes *Dunamis.* Eine Replik zur Kreuzestheologie," in S. Pedersen (ed.), *Die Paulinische Literatur und Theologie* (Arhus: Forlaget Aros, 1980), 137-58.

426. Cf. Héring, *First Epistle,* 14.

427. See esp. Clarke, *Higher Education in the Ancient World.*

428. BAGD, 89; cf. *Letter of Aristeas* 102; Josephus, *Antiquities* 17.99; Philo, *De Vita Mosis* 1.95; *Papyrus Oxyrhynchus* 2:257:19 (c. AD 94-95); and further MM, 60-61.

429. Origen, *Against Celsus,* 1:5. This view appears to be favored by Christian F. Kling, *First Epistle of Paul to the Corinthians* (German 1861; English 1868; rpt. Grand Rapids: Zondervan, 1960), 52; and Meyer, *First Corinthians,* 1:58.

430. Origen, *Against Celsus,* 1:63.

431. Ibid., 6:2; cf. *De Principiis,* 4:1:7.

432. Chrysostom, *1 Cor. Hom.,* 6:5.

433. Lietzmann, *An die Korinther,* 11. Among modern writers Lietzmann is anticipated by Beet (1883), and Edwards traces this interpretation in both more sceptical traditions (Lessing) and in those who stress the place of tongues and prophecy (Stillingfleet). Fee views this interpretation as possible but not probable (*First Epistle,* 95).

ward the compelling point that if these two contexts are confused it produces a logical contradiction with the force of Paul's argument in 2:3-5.[434] Conzelmann notes, "Miracles . . . do not prove the truth of the word of the cross, but . . . are subject to the criterion of the cross."[435]

Are the genitives πνεύματος καὶ δυνάμεως objective (Allo, Bachmann) or subjective (Conzelmann, Fee) or both (as Barrett urges)? If the genitive is subjective, "the Divine spirit . . . reveals the truth."[436] If it is objective, the preaching "manifests 'the power of the spirit.' "[437] But Barrett's interpretation coheres well with Paul's wider theology of the Holy Spirit. The Holy Spirit witnesses to his own presence and activity precisely by witnessing to Christ, to the effectiveness of the gospel, and to other effects which are themselves the work of the trinitarian God.[438] Some of the sharp criticisms made against the objective genitive (i.e., Paul's gospel exhibits, or gives proof of, the Spirit) would be valid only if it were not also the work of the Holy Spirit in Paul's preaching that activates and actualizes this witness, exhibition, or demonstration. Collins comments, "The Spirit is the powerful rhetor; Paul is but the spokesperson. . . . **Spirit and Power** . . . is a classic Pauline hendiadys. . . . The epexegetical **and power** identifies the **Spirit** as the powerful **Spirit** of God."[439]

Nevertheless, "hendiadys" does only partial justice to the force of the syntax. The full force is better conveyed by **brought home powerfully by the Spirit**. Considerable debate has taken place about whether πνεύματος καὶ δυνάμεως constitutes a hendiadys for *powerful Spirit*. Edwards, among others, opposes this interpretation; Fee, with a minor qualification, favors it.[440] *Power* is regularly associated with God's *effective action* and *reality* in contrast to mere "words." Paul speaks of the *effectiveness* of the Spirit's witness to his own *effective* work. Moreover, as becomes clear from 2:16–3:4, **Spirit**, in turn, is defined christologically: he points beyond himself to God's work in Christ, even if the presence of the self-effacing Spirit thereby *becomes transparent* as a by-product of the Spirit's work. Only with these qualifications may we render πνεύματος καὶ δυνάμεως as *powerful Spirit*. But this use of "powerful" is so far from the mind-set of today's world that such a phrase could not be used as a

434. Senft, *La première Épitre,* 46.

435. Conzelmann, *1 Corinthians,* 55. Weiss anticipates this view also.

436. Godet, *First Epistle,* 1:129; cf. Fee, *First Epistle,* 95; Senft, *Première Épitre,* 46-47; Bruce, *1 and 2 Corinthians,* 37; and Conzelmann, *1 Cor,* 55.

437. Allo, *Première Épitre,* 24.

438. Barrett, *First Epistle,* 65; cf. Merklein, *Der erste Brief 1–4,* 212. This emphasis is reflected also in Moltmann, *The Spirit of Life* (Minneapolis: Fortress Press, 1992), 1-14, 35-36, 47-51, and 301-6.

439. Collins, *First Corinthians,* 120. Nevertheless we should not lose sight of another aspect. Alluding to the self-effacing aspect of the Spirit, Oke speaks of God's revelation "by shadow and footfall rather than by indubitable presence. An obtrusive God . . . would not be Godlike" ("Paul's Method Not a Demonstration," 86).

440. Edwards, *First Epistle,* 48 (firm rejection of hendiadys); Fee, *First Epistle,* 95: "probably very close to a hendiadys . . . 'the Spirit, that is, Power.' "

translation without almost certain risk of misunderstanding. Hence we propose the translation above.

The language and meaning of v. 5 run on without the need for extended comment. The word πίστις, **faith**, emerges as in other Pauline passages as a response to the proclamation of the gospel which is itself a gift of God. It is no precarious human construct, produced only by the sway exerted by clever rhetoric or manipulative presentations of belief systems. It does not exist (ᾖ, subjunctive of εἰμι) by virtue of all that Paul has placed within the category of "human wisdom" (ἐν σοφίᾳ ἀνθρώπων) and judged deficient under the critique of the cross. This, by contrast, operates ἐν δυνάμει θεοῦ, i.e., by the effective and creative agency [power] of God.

It would be a mistake to define πίστις, **faith**, apart from a given context in which this term functions. Elsewhere I have described it as "a polymorphous concept" (like σάρξ, *flesh,* and ἀλήθεια, *truth*) since any attempt at an abstract definition encounters contexts which will not match some *single* meaning or "essence" of the term.[441] Bultmann, for example, reads *into* πίστις his own Kantian and kerygmatic emphasis on will: "Paul understands faith primarily as obedience . . . the act of faith as an act of obedience."[442] He can readily cite Rom 1:5 and Rom 16:19, but hardly the present passage. Nor does faith in this specific phrase stand first and foremost in opposition to "works" as Weiss and Jeremias define it, *except* insofar as the *whole context* of act of God versus human wisdom which runs through 1:18 to 2:5 constitutes what Ljungmann would call a *presupposition* for its more specific uses.[443] Similarly the meaning of faith as, in effect, "Christianity" may fit Gal 1:23, but hardly this verse.[444] "The nature of faith is given in the object to which faith is directed."[445]

Here, therefore, it means a mind-set which includes both an intellectual conviction of truth (a response to ἀπόδειξις) and a stance of heart and will which exhibits trust in God's salvific act in Christ as the basis of life (as against σοφία ἀνθρώπως). Godet comments, "To be solid, it must be a work of God"; while Deluz also expresses the negative side: "A faith based on human arguments would be built on sand."[446] This does not mean that argument or persuasion can play no role; it means that something more is involved that speaks to the heart as well as to the mind and creates a new reality (δύναμις θεοῦ) for the believer (cf. 1:18).

---

441. Thiselton, *The Two Horizons,* 407-9; cf. 409-15.

442. Bultmann, *Theology of the NT,* 1:314.

443. H. Ljungman, *Pistis: A Study of Its Presuppositions and Its Meaning in Pauline Use* (Lund: Gleerup, 1964), 37-79.

444. Weiss, *Earliest Christianity,* 2:508; J. Jeremias, *Central Message of the NT* (Eng. trans., London: SCM, 1965), 55 and 68; Ljungman, *Pistis.*

445. Bornkamm, *Paul,* 141.

446. Godet, *First Epistle,* 1:130; and Deluz, *Companion,* 22.

C. A REDEFINITION OF "WISDOM," "MATURITY," AND "SPIRITUALITY" IN THE LIGHT OF GOD, CHRIST, AND THE HOLY SPIRIT (2:6–3:4)

1. The Need for "Wisdom," Duly Redefined (2:6-16)

(6) Yet we do communicate a wisdom among the mature, but it is a wisdom which is not of this present world order, nor of the rulers of this world order who are doomed to come to nothing. (7) Well, we speak God's wisdom in discourse too profound for merely human discovery, a wisdom that was hidden, which God marked out beforehand, before the ages, for our glory. (8) None of the rulers of this present world order had come to know this. For if they had known it, they would not have crucified the Lord of glory. (9) However, as it is written, what eye did not see, and ear did not hear, and what no human heart conceived, how very much God prepared for those who love him!

(10) God revealed these things through the Spirit to us! For the Spirit searches out everything, even the depths of God's own self. (11) For who among human beings knows what pertains to the person in view except that person's innermost self? Even so, no one knows what pertains to God except the Spirit of God. (12) Now, as for us, it is not the spirit of the world that we received, but the Spirit who issues from God, in order that we may know the things that were freely given to us by God. (13) These things, further, we communicate not in speech taught out of mere human cleverness, but in language which the Spirit teaches, interpreting things of the Spirit to people of the Spirit.

(14) The person who lives on an entirely human level does not receive the things of the Spirit of God, for they are folly to them, and they cannot come to know them because they are discerned spiritually. (15, 16) "Now the spiritual person sifts out everything, but the person concerned is put on trial by no one." For "Who has come to know the mind of the Lord, that he should instruct him?" But as for us, we have Christ's mind!

Many writers have agreed that the terminology and stance of this section differs so consistently from Paul's more usual vocabulary and concerns as to cast doubts on its integrity with the rest of this epistle (see the Introduction, 36-41, on the unity and integrity of the epistle). But Paul takes up the major catchwords which had become embedded in the life of the church at Corinth, and his most urgent task at this point is neither to reject their validity nor to bypass what was important for his readers, but to reclaim the terms for the gospel by redefining them in the light of the nature of God and of the gospel.

In particular the use of σοφία, *wisdom,* at Corinth had misdirected attention to issues of status and human achievement rather than to wisdom as a sheer gift of God given in and through Christ. Paul has attacked their false "wisdom" in 1:17–2:5, but now he wishes to make it clear that a true wisdom remains both part of his own teaching to Christian believers and an essential mark of a mature Christian community. The initial phrase Σοφίαν δὲ λαλοῦμεν (2:6) is contrastive: **yet we do** [indeed] **communicate a wisdom . . . but it is a wisdom which is not of this present world order.** . . . Paul expounds the theme of σοφία, **wisdom**, mainly in vv. 6-9.

It is probable (although it cannot be proven without any doubt) that τέλειος, **mature** or **spiritually adult,** had also acquired currency at Corinth to support the power bids of a self-styled elite who, perhaps on the grounds of education, social status, or the manifestation of more spectacular spiritual gifts, claimed the rank of inner-circle leaders who possessed this "wisdom" by which they directed others. Just as Paul turned upside down the pretentiousness of claims to "wisdom" based on "cleverness" or status, so he redefined *spiritual maturity and adulthood in terms of Christlikeness.* Whether τέλειος was borrowed by some Corinthian Christians from its use as "initiates into the inner circle" in some of the mystery religions remains a highly technical question which we shall address below. Paul makes it clear, however, that Christian maturity does not entail some "two-stage" view of the Christian life, but the flowering of those qualities which characterize the God who reveals himself in the humiliation of the cross and the love of Christ for others. This aspect receives further elaboration in 3:1-4. "Childish" faith remains self-absorbed and self-centered (cf. 13:1-3, 11, 12). Paul expounds "wisdom" ἐν τοῖς τελείοις, **among the mature** (esp. vv. 14-16).

In much of this section, it is difficult to be certain when Paul is citing slogans about "being spiritual" (πνευματικός) as many Corinthians used the term, and when he is moving toward a redefinition of "spiritual" to mean *reflecting the work of the Holy Spirit of God.* The phrase τὸ πνεῦμα ἐκ τοῦ θεοῦ, **the Spirit who comes forth from God** (2:12), is of the utmost importance. As against immanental notions of "spirituality" as qualities of human religiosity generated by attention to the inner human spirit, true "spirituality" is a creation by the agency of God's *transcendent Holy Spirit who is Other and comes from* (ἐκ) *God alone.* This spirit is "received" (ἐλάβομεν, 2:12), not immanent in the world (πνεῦμα τοῦ κόσμου, v. 12). Paul speaks at times of the "Holy" Spirit as the Spirit who is *Other,* or as "the *Beyond who is within.*" Communicating (λαλοῦμεν) the things of **the Spirit** becomes a special task mainly in vv. 10-13.

When we place together the last paragraph on πνεῦμα and "spirituality" with the previous paragraph about τέλειος, it is scarcely surprising that many interpreters have seen in these verses the influence of the Graeco-Roman or Graeco-Oriental mystery religions. The immediately parallel terms include to the mature (ἐν τοῖς τελείοις, in the mystery religions, to those who are initiates 2:6); in a mystery (ἐν μυστηρίῳ, 2:7); and the difference between ψυχικὸς ἄνθρωπος (2:14) and ὁ πνευματικός (2:15). However, the rest of the epistle draws in parts on a similarly common vocabulary: wisdom, σοφία, in 1:17–2:7; knowledge (γνῶσις) in 8:1 and 13:8; and revealing (ἀπεκάλυψεν, 2:10). Even if no problem is raised by issues of dating, however, these have become general terms used within a variety of religious outlooks.[1]

Once again the comments which Samuel Laeuchli applies to the language of gnosticism also apply here: "There is a tension between the meaning [of the vocabulary] in its original frame and the new frame into which it is inserted."[2] Laeuchli argues that in the case of, e.g., *gnōsis, neos, plērōma, mystērion,* and *sophia* it is not "the terminology" or "the concept" in isolation which conveys the meaning but "the relation in which it stands to other concepts" and how these "chameleon-like terms" are actually used.[3] Even in gnosticism, e.g., *mystērion* is used in more than one way, although all of these uses lose "the christological and theological context" which gives the term a different force in Paul and in the NT.[4] Our exegesis of 2:6-16 will give substance to these claims.

a. Exposition of the True Wisdom (2:6-9)

Bibliography on Issues Relating to *Teleios*, Wisdom, and the Terminology of the Mystery Religions

Aune, D., "Religions, Greco-Roman," in *DPL,* 786-96.

Baird, W., "Among the Mature: The Idea of Wisdom in 1 Cor 2:6," *Int* 13 (1959): 425-32.

Berger, K., "Zur Diskussion über die Herkunft von 1 Kor ii 9," *NTS* 24 (1978): 270-83.

Bockmuehl, M. N. A., *Revelation and Mystery in Ancient Judaism and Pauline Christianity,* WUNT 2:36 (Tübingen: Mohr, 1990).

Burkert, W., *Ancient Mystery Cults* (Cambridge, Mass.: Harvard University Press, 1987).

Cumont, F., *The Mysteries of Mithra* (New York: Dover, 1956).

Davis, James A., *Wisdom and Spirit* (Lanham, Md.: University Press of America, 1984), 83-130.

Delling, G., "τέλιος," *TDNT,* 7:49-87.

Dunn, J. D. G., *The Theology of Paul the Apostle* (Edinburgh: T. & T. Clark, 1998), 266-72.

Du Plessis, P. J., *Teleios: The Idea of Perfection in the NT* (Kampen: Kok, 1959).

Ellis, E. E., *Prophecy and Hermeneutic* (Grand Rapids: Eerdmans, 1978), 23-44 and 213-20.

Frid, B., "The Enigmatic ἀλλά in 1 Cor 2:9," *NTS* 31 (1985): 603-11.

Funk, R. W., "Word and Word in 1 Cor 2:6-16," in *Language, Hermeneutic and Word of God* (New York: Harper & Row, 1966), 275-303.

Hamerton-Kelly, R. G., *Pre-existence, Wisdom and the Son of Man: A Study of the Idea*

---

1. See Pearson, *The Pneumatikos-Psychikos Terminology in 1 Cor,* 27-43.

2. Laeuchli, *The Language of Faith: An Introduction to the Semantic Dilemma of the Early Church,* 19.

3. Ibid., 16; cf. 15-93.

4. Ibid., 50 (*mystērion,* 49-51).

of Pre-Existence in the NT, SNTSMS 21 (Cambridge: Cambridge University Press, 1973).

Hegermann, H., "σοφία," *EDNT,* 3:258-62.

Kennedy, H. A. A., *St Paul and the Mystery Religions* (London: Hodder & Stoughton, 1914).

Laeuchli, S., *The Language of Faith: An Introduction to the Semantic Dilemma of the Early Church* (London: Epworth, 1965), 15-93.

Lieberschütz, J. H. W., *Continuity and Change in Roman Religion* (Oxford: Clarendon, 1979).

Machen, J. Gresham, *The Origin of Paul's Religion* (New York: Macmillan, 1928), 265-77.

MacMullen, R., *Paganism in the Roman Empire* (New Haven: Yale University Press, 1981).

Nock, A. D., *Conversion: The Old and the New in Religion from Alexander the Great to Augustine of Hippo* (London: Oxford University Press, 1933).

Painter, J., "Paul and the πνευματικοί at Corinth," in M. D. Hooker and S. G. Wilson (eds.), *Paul and Paulinism: In Honour of C. K. Barrett* (London: SPCK, 1982), 237-50.

Pearson, B. A., *The Pneumatikos-Psychikos Terminology in 1 Cor,* SBLDS 12 (Missoula: Scholars Press, 1973) 27-43.

Reitzenstein, R., *Hellenistic Mystery Religions: Their Basic Ideas and Significance* (Eng. trans., Pittsburgh: Pickwick, 1978).

Reiling, J., "Wisdom and Spirit: An Exegesis of 1 Cor 2:6-16," in T. Baarda et al. (eds.), *Text and Testimony: Essays in NT and Apocryphal Literature in Honour of A. F. J. Klijn* (Kampen, 1988), 200-211.

Schnackenburg, "Christian Adulthood according to the Apostle Paul," *CBQ* 25 (1963): 254-70.

Scroggs, R., "σοφὸς καὶ πνευματικός," *NTS* 14 (1967-68): 33-55.

Sterling, G. E., "'Wisdom among the Perfect': Creation Tradition in Alexandrian Judaism and Corinthian Christianity," *NovT* 37 (1995): 355-84.

Stuhlmacher, P., "Zur hermeneutischen Bedeutung von 1 Kor 2:6-16," *TBei* 18 (1987): 133-58.

Theissen, G., *Psychological Aspects of Pauline Theology* (Eng. trans., Edinburgh: T. & T. Clark, 1987), 368-74.

Wagner, G., *Pauline Baptism and the Pagan Mysteries* (Eng. trans., Edinburgh: Oliver & Boyd, 1967).

Wedderburn, A. J. M., *Baptism and Resurrection in Pauline Theology against Its Graeco-Roman Background,* WUNT 1:44 (Tübingen: Mohr, 1987).

———, "The Soteriology of the Mysteries and Pauline Baptismal Theology," *NovT* 29 (1987): 53-72.

Wilckens, U., "σοφία," *TDNT,* 7:465-528.

Wilckens, U., *Weisheit und Torheit* (Tübingen: Mohr, 1959), 52-95.

Winter, M., *Pneumatiker und Psychiker in Korinth. Zum religionsgeschichtlichen Hintergrund von 1 Kor. 2:6–3:4,* Marburger theologische Studien 12 (Marburg: Elwert, 1975).

Zaidman, L. B., and P. S. Pantel, *Religion in the Ancient Greek City* (Cambridge: Cambridge University Press, 1992).

Bibliography on "the Rulers of This World Order"

Arnold, C. F., *Powers of Darkness: Principalities and Powers in Paul's Letters* (Downers Grove: InterVarsity Press, 1992).

Caird, George B., *Principalities and Power* (Oxford: Clarendon Press, 1956).

Carr, A. Wesley, *Angels and Principalities: The Background, Meaning and Development of the Pauline Phrase "hai archai kai hai exousiai,"* SNTSMS 42 (Cambridge, Cambridge University Press, 1981).

————, "The Rulers of This Age — 1 Cor. ii:6-8," *NTS* 23 (1976): 20-35.

Cullmann, Oscar, *Christ and Time* (Eng. trans., London: SCM, 1951), 191-201.

Dibelius, Martin, *Die Geistwelt im Glauben des Paulus* (Göttingen: Vandenhoeck & Ruprecht, 1909).

Elliott, Neil, *Liberating Paul: The Justice of God and the Politics of the Apostle* (Maryknoll, N.Y.: Orbis, 1994), 114-24, "Paul and 'the Power.' "

Feuillet, A., "Les 'Chefs de ce siècle' et la sagesse divine d'après 1 Cor 2:6-8," in *Studiorum Paulinorum Congressus Internationalis Catholicus 1961* (Rome: Pontifical Biblical Institute, 1963), 383-93.

Hanson, A. T., "The Conquest of the Powers," in *Studies in Paul's Technique and Theology* (London: SPCK, 1974), 1-12.

Kovacs, Judith, "The Archons, the Spirit, and the Death of Christ: Do We Really Need the Hypothesis of Gnostic Opponents to Explain 1 Cor. 2:2-16?" in Joel Marcus and Marion L. Soards (eds.), *Apocalyptic in the NT: Essays in Honor of J. Louis Martyn,* JSNTSS 24 (Sheffield: JSOT Press, 1989), 217-36.

MacGregor, G. H. C., "Principalities and Power: "The Cosmic Background of St Paul's Thought," *NTS* 1 (1954): 17-28.

Miller, G., "Ἀρχόντων τοῦ αἰῶνος — A New Look at 1 Cor. 2:6-8," *JBL* 91 (1972): 522-28.

Morrison, Clinton D., *The Powers That Be* (London: SCM, 1960).

Newman, C. C., *Paul's Glory Christology: Tradition and Rhetoric,* NovTSup 69 (Leiden: Brill, 1992).

Niebuhr, Reinhold, *Moral Man and Immoral Society* (London: SCM, 1963 [1932]).

Schniewind, J., "Die Archontes dieses Äons, 1 Kor 2:6-8," in E. Kähler (ed.), *Nachgelassene Reden und Aufsätze* (Berlin: Töpelmann, 1952).

Scroggs, Robin, "Paul: Σοφός and πνευματικός," *NTS* 14 (1967-68): 33-55.

Theissen, Gerd, *Psychological Aspects of Pauline Theology* (Eng. trans., Edinburgh: T. & T. Clark, 1987), 374-78 (cf. 368-74).

Whiteley, D. E. H., *The Theology of St Paul* (Oxford: Blackwell, 2d ed. 1974), 23-31, 283-86.

Wilckens, Ulrich, *Weisheit und Torheit* (Tübingen: Mohr, 1959), 52-96.

————, "Zu 1 Kor. 2:1-16," in C. Andersen and G. Klein (eds.), *Theologia Crucis — Signum Crucis: Festschrift für Erich Dinkler* (Tübingen: Mohr, 1979), 501-37.

Wink, Walter, *Engaging the Powers: Discernment and Resistance in a World of Domination* (Minneapolis: Fortress, 1992).

————, *Naming the Powers: The Language of Power in the NT* (Philadelphia: Fortress, 1984).

————, *Unmasking the Powers: The Invisible Forces That Determine Human Existence* (Philadelphia: Fortress, 1986).

Bibliography on "Lord of Glory" and the Jewish Background of 2:6-9

Bockmuehl, M. N. A., *Revelation and Mystery in Ancient Judaism and Pauline Christianity,* WUNT 2:36 (Tübingen: Mohr, 1990).

Newman, Carey C., *Paul's Glory-Christology: Tradition and Rhetoric,* NovTSup 69 (Leiden: Brill, 1992), 17-24, 157-64, and 235-40.

O'Neill, J. C., *Who Did Jesus Think He Was?* BibIntMon 11 (Leiden: Brill, 1995), esp. 42-114.

Stauffer, E., *NT Theology* (Eng. trans., London: SCM, 1955), 120-33.

Stuhlmacher, P., "The Hermeneutical Significance of 1 Cor. 2:6-16," in G. F. Hawthorne and O. Betz (eds.), *Tradition and Interpretation in the NT: Essays in Honor of E. Earle Ellis* (Tübingen: Mohr and Grand Rapids: Eerdmans, 1987), 328-47.

Bibliography on the Possible Citation in 2:9

Berger, K., "Zur Diskussion über die Herkunft von 1 Kor 2:9," *NTS* 24 (1978): 270-83.

Hofius, Otfried, "Das Zitat I Kor 2:9 und das koptische Testament des Jakob," *ZNW* 66 (1975): 140-42.

Nordheim, Eckard von, "Das Zitat des Paulus in 1 Kor. 2:9 und seine Beziehung zum koptischen Testament Jakobs," *ZNW* 65 (1974): 112-20.

Philonenko, M., "Quod oculus non vidit, I Cor. 2:9," *TZ* 15 (1959): 51-52.

Ponsot, H., "D'Isaie 64:3 à 1 Cor. 2:9," *RB* 90 (1983): 239-42.

Prigent, P., "Ce que l'oeil n'a pas vu," *TZ* 14 (1958): 416-29.

Sparks, H. F. D., "1 Kor. 2:9: A Quotation from the Coptic Testament of Jacob?" *ZNW* 67 (1976): 269-76.

Stanley, C. D., *Paul and the Language of Scripture,* SNTSMS 74 (Cambridge: Cambridge University Press, 1992), 188-89.

6 Paul changes the first person singular which has characterized his personal proclamation of the gospel from 1:18 through to 2:5 to the first person plural σοφίαν δὲ λαλοῦμεν ἐν τοῖς τελείοις. Λαλοῦμεν is repeated in vv. 7 and 13. Over against the singular pronoun κἀγώ . . . κἀγώ . . . (2:1, 3), Paul now uses the plural pronouns ἡμῖν ἀπεκάλυψεν ὁ θεός (2:10); ἡμεῖς δέ . . . ἡμῖν (2:12); ἡμεῖς . . . ἔχομεν (2:16). Widmann argues that this change suggests a later interpolation into Paul's text, although this is not his only argument to this effect.[5] Schrage and Collins, however, insist that the plural denotes "a common activity within the community. What the community speaks is the leitmotif of the pericope."[6] "Without doubt ἡμῶν in v. 7b and *we* in v. 12 signify *all* Christians" (Schrage's italics).[7] "The use of the first person plural throughout this section suggests that the *locus operandi* of the Spirit is the fellowship of the Christian community."[8] Widman's argument in favor of a post-Pauline interpolation becomes unnecessary and untenable.[9]

---

5. M. Widmann, "1 Kor 2:6-16: Ein Einspruch gegen Paulus," *ZNW* 70 (1979): 44-53. He thinks that the context contradicts much of 1:18–2:5 and 3:1–4:21.

6. Collins, *First Cor,* 122.

7. Schrage, *Der erste Brief,* 1:248.

8. Orr and Walther, *1 Corinthians,* 166.

9. See Murphy-O'Connor, *Paul: A Critical Life,* 283, and "Interpolations in 1 Cor," *CBQ* 48 (1986): 81-94.

Paul and his fellow believers do indeed, however (contrastive δέ), communicate (λαλοῦμεν, *speak*, in various ways) **a wisdom** (anarthrous form, as against τὴν σοφίαν). In the tradition of Proverbs this denotes *habits of judgment applicable to life*. It concerns *the formation of a Christian mind, which issues in a right action*. In certain contemporary writers, notably in Hans-Georg Gadamer and in Alasdair MacIntyre a parallel occurs with Paul's "two wisdoms" in an opposing contrast between τέχνη *(technē)* used as *instrumental* reason, or a means of gaining achievement in technology, sciences, or techniques (e.g., of persuasion), and φρόνησις *(phronēsis, insight)* to denote ways of thinking and judging with wise insight that brings habits of wisdom to bear on action and human life.[10] Paul associates the use of the term at Corinth with what amounts to a *self-centered, at times childish,* attempt to manipulate things to one's own advantage. True wisdom from God, however, is sought by those who are sufficiently **adult** (τέλειος) *to exercise it responsibly for the good of all*.

Even so, "there is a different shade of meaning in the word σοφία (and σοφός) every time it occurs."[11] In the seventeen uses of **wisdom** in 1 Corinthians Paul used the same word (σοφία) to designate both senses of the term. The reason is twofold. First and foremost, without any doubt, it had become a theological catchphrase at Corinth. We have noted already that seventeen of the nineteen uses of the word in the undisputed Pauline writings occur in this letter (sixteen in 1 Corinthians 1–3).[12] Paul wishes to redefine and thus to rescue an important term. Wisdom (σοφία) must never be equated with information (often γνῶσις, 8:1). Second, σοφία most frequently translates the Hebrew חכמה *(chokmah, **wisdom**)* in the LXX of Proverbs and other Wisdom literature. By contrast, φρόνησις, *insight, frame of mind, understanding, way of judging,* never occurs in this substantival form in the undisputed Pauline epistle, and only once in the wider Pauline corpus (Eph 1:8).[13] Yet the cognate form φρήν *(understanding)* and the cognate verb φρονέω *(to have a certain way of thinking)* occur in Paul in this epistle to signal a contrast, as in this verse, between *childish* (παιδία, νήπιος) and *adult* (τέλειοι) ways of thinking: ἐφρόνουν ὡς νήπιος, *I used to think like a child* (1 Cor 13:11), and μὴ παιδία γίνεσθε ταῖς φρεσίν, ἀλλὰ τῇ κακίᾳ νηπιάζετε, ταῖς δὲ φρεσὶν τέλειοι γίνεσθε. *do not be childish in your ways of thinking, but be adult in your understanding* (14:20)

10. For the lexicography of the NT period, cf. BAGD, 814 and 866; Grimm-Thayer, 581-82; U. Wilckens, "σοφία," *TDNT*, 7:465-528; and for earlier Greek usage, LSJ. On Gadamer, see, e.g., *Truth and Method* (Eng. trans., New York: Crossroad, 2d ed. 1989), pt. 1; on MacIntyre, e.g., *After Virtue: A Study in Moral Theory* (London: Duckworth, 2d ed. 1985), 204-43 and 264-78.

11. Barrett, *Essays on Paul*, 7.

12. 1 Cor 1:17, 19, 20, 21, 22, 24, 30; 2:1, 4, 5, 6, 7, 13; 3:19; and 12:8. Elsewhere once only in Romans (Rom 11:33, perhaps a pre-Pauline hymn) and in 2 Cor 1:12; absent from Galatians, Philippians, and Philemon. It reappears in Col 1:9, 28; 2:3, 23; 3:16; 4:5, and three times in Ephesians. See Barrett, *Essays on Paul*, 6; and MM, 898-99. The adjectival form σοφός, *wise*, also occurs ten times in 1 Corinthians 1–3.

13. In the rest of the NT the Greek word occurs only in Luke 1:17.

This contrast at the level of σοφία, **wisdom**, explains that ἐν τοῖς τελείοις, **among the mature**, retains the double sense common to Paul and to many at Corinth and at bottom means *spiritual adults*. Although in some contexts (cf. Rom 12:2; 1 Cor 13:10) the meaning *perfect* may fit the sense of the word, to translate it as *perfect* in this verse (AV/KJV) is not appropriate. The semantic opposition derives its force from that between babies and adults. We were tempted to translate **spiritual adults** since this would take account of the definite article τοῖς to specify a category within the church at Corinth and would match the same semantic contrast as that which reappears at 1 Cor 3:1, ὡς νηπίοις, in specific contrast to ὡς πνευματικοῖς. The same contrast between feeding a *baby*, νήπιος, with milk, and adults (τελείων) with solid food, occurs in Heb 5:13-14 and τέλειος often means *adult* in first-century Greek writers including Philo and Josephus.[14] Héring comments, "They are not Christians who have arrived at perfection, for that cannot be reached before the obtaining of 'glory.' But they are Christians who are spiritually adult, as is shown by . . . 3:1."[15]

This stands a long way from Irenaeus's interpretation of οἱ τέλειοι as those who manifest such gifts of the Spirit as "speaking in [foreign] tongues."[16] The most frequent translation of ἐν τοῖς τελείοις in English VSS is **among the mature** (NRSV, NIV, Moffatt); *spiritually mature* (TEV); or those who have *reached maturity* (NJB). Those who are *ready* to receive σοφία are those who have attained the spiritually adult perception that wisdom is *not* a "human device and artifice"; it is "dangerous when preachers think they can use it as a substitute for Christ crucified."[17] Spiritual adulthood entails perceiving that wisdom comes from God as a gift in Christ (1:30) which enables the self to *live responsibly and wisely for others* and for the good of the whole community. This brings *adult responsibilities*.

Barrett explains Paul's reference to **the rulers** of the present world order as exercising a σοφία which is a "self-regarding, self-preserving σοφία."[18] But this kind of "wisdom" will prove to be illusory and false, and indeed will not benefit them, for with this set of values they **are doomed to come to nothing**, τῶν καταργουμένων (already discussed in 1:28). The present tense underlines that they are in the process of being reduced to nothing; this process remains continuous as an unstoppable process, i.e., they are **doomed to come to noth-**

---

14. For example, Josephus, *Antiquities* 19.362.

15. Héring. *First Epistle,* 16.

16. Irenaeus, *Against Heresies,* 5:6:1. But we should remember that Irenaeus is concerned to define the word in terms of the fullness of the Holy Spirit as witness to Christ, as against gnostic interpretations of τέλειος as relating to "the Plērōma" (*Against Heresies,* 1:8:4), or the various interpretations which equate "maturity" with following "Valentinus . . . Marcion . . . Cerinthus . . . Basilides . . . or any other opponent who could speak nothing relating to salvation" (*Against Heresies,* 3:2:1).

17. Barrett, *Essays on Paul,* 8.

18. Ibid., 10.

ing, or **doomed to pass away**. We have already discussed how to translate τοῦ αἰῶνος τούτου, **of this present world order**, in 1:20 (see above). In theory either *age* or *aeon* strictly reflects the Greek more specifically, but is open to misunderstanding among modern readers who may be unfamiliar with Jewish apocalyptic and the eschatology which Paul draws from it. Hence **world order** is the nearest modern equivalent for this structural term, while **present world order** adds the apocalyptic or eschatological nuance of a contrast with an *aeon* or *order* yet to come, both alongside it in the present and fully to replace it in God's due time.

PAUL'S USE OF THE TERM τέλειος

The term τέλειος, **mature**, has already received some discussion, but raises one technical point. Did the use of the term at Corinth derive any currency from its use in the Graeco-oriental and Graeco-Roman mystery religions? Whatever conclusion we reach, the pronouncement of Gresham Machen remains valid. He comments: "If it should appear that Paul uses a vocabulary derived from the mysteries, the fact would not necessarily be of any significance whatever in determining the origin of his religion."[19] Indeed, Robert Funk argues that if the Corinthians used the term *mature* or *initiate* in the sense of one initiated into the elite inner circle of one privy to highest mysteries, "Paul has simply *turned their language, and thus their expectations, inside out* in the interests of bringing them face to face *with the work of the cross* (my italics)."[20]

Paul excludes any notion that to be a τέλειος (a mature Christian in the church, or an initiate into an inner circle in the mystery religions) constitutes a source of status as a "first-class" believer in contrast to "second-class" believers. Although at the final day of judgment he wants believers to be presented "complete" or "perfect" in Christ (Col 1:28), there remains an *aim* or *goal* to which even Paul himself has not yet attained (Phil 3:12-14; cf. 1 Cor 13:10).[21] Thus Conzelman distorts the argument when he speaks too readily of "a higher class of believer."[22] But Conzelman believes that, in addition to borrowing hellenistic language from outside the OT and Christian tradition, Paul uses gnostic modes of thought here. Similarly, Lietzmann insists that Paul reserves "true wisdom" for "perfected pneumatics," although he concedes that Paul may use this formula with more than a hint of irony.[23] H. Hegermann moves onto

---

19. Machen, *The Origin of Paul's Religion,* 272; cf. 255-75. Detailed discussions occur in a vast literature (cited elsewhere); cf., e.g., Wagner, *Pauline Baptism and the Pagan Mysteries;* and Wedderburn, *Baptism and Resurrection in Pauline Theology against Its Graeco-Roman Background.* The classic but now dated study is Reitzenstein, *Hellenistic Mystery-Religions: Their Basic Ideas and Significance.*

20. Funk, *Language, Hermeneutics and Word of God,* 300, n. 107. I have put forward similar arguments in "The Meaning of σάρξ in 1 Cor. 5:5: A Fresh Approach in the Light of Logical and Semantic Factors," *SJT* 26 (1973): 204-28, and in "Realized Eschatology at Corinth," *NTS* 24 (1978): 510 26.

21. Du Plessis, *ΤΕΛΕΙΟΣ: The Idea of Perfection in the NT,* 198-99; cf. 175-99.

22. Conzelmann, *I Corinthians,* 60.

23. Lietzmann, *An die Korinther,* 11-12.

more secure ground when he observes: "Paul gives an example of the self-adulation of the Corinthian pneumatics and of this 'wisdom for the mature' (2:6). τέλειος here is a concept from the mysteries that has already become a shared image or metaphor, though it is not yet thought of in Gnostic terms. A pronounced claim of religious power has been made in the name of the power of pneuma. . . . Paul's theology of the cross changes this entirely. Whoever does not perceive God in the word of the cross is spiritually empty and ψυχικός" (i.e., unspiritual).[24]

Orr and Walther convincingly argue that if 2:6-16 were to refer to some "higher" wisdom than 1:18–2:5, this would imply a "wisdom deeper than that of the Christ crucified. [Hence] No . . . new wisdom is offered here."[25] Senft sharpens the point further. The term οἱ τέλειοι *("les parfaits")* comes from the mystery religions and denotes "those who have been fully instructed in secret doctrines and have passed through the rite of initiation, *the initiates.* By analogy the term ought to apply in Paul to the baptized; but this is evidently not the case here. . . . Does Paul make a distinction between two classes of Christians, simple believers who remain at an elementary level . . . and spiritual people . . . of higher status? . . . In reality Paul says something else. . . . The *psychikoí* ["unspiritual," v. 14] are not simple believers who remain content with basics."[26] On the contrary, they are those who do not allow themselves to come under "the word of the cross . . . the Spirit of God," and Paul makes this point by using language about "deeper" knowledge "without risk of compromising the truth of the gospel."[27]

The three most decisive points have already been noted in our introduction to 2:6-16 and our exegesis so far. (1) The sheer occurrence of certain terminology (e.g., τέλειος, σοφία, μυστήριον, πνευματικός, γνῶσις) has little significance apart from its *use* within a given frame and in relation to other terms or concepts (see above on Laeuchli).[28] (2) Schrage, Collins, and others have urged that the language of 2:6-16 reflects "that of all Christians," "a common activity within the community," "the fellowship of the Christian community."[29] (3) Virtually all of the "sensitive" terms were, by around the date of this epistle, part of a common religious vocabulary in the Graeco-Roman world, even if they came to possess an especially privileged currency at Corinth.[30] None of these three points can support an "elitist" or mystery-religion use of these terms as such.

THE MEANING OF "THE RULERS OF THIS WORLD ORDER"

Conzelmann and Carr argue that the above phrase imposes an exclusive choice: we must choose between a "heavenly or demonic powers" interpretation and the "earthly

---

24. H. Hegermann, "σοφία," *EDNT,* 3:260; cf. 258-61.

25. Orr and Walther, *1 Cor,* 163.

26. Senft, *La première Épitre,* 49.

27. *Ibid.* So also Schrage, *Der erste Brief,* 1:249-50.

28. Laeuchli, *The Language of Faith,* 15-93, includes γνῶσις (43-49, including 1 Cor 2:6-9); μυστήριον (49-51), αἰών (59-67), and the loss of Pauline realism (67-93).

29. Schrage, *Der erste Brief,* 1:248; Collins, *First Cor,* 122; Orr and Walther, *1 Cor,* 166.

30. Cf. Pearson, *Pneumatikos-Psychikos,* 27-43; Burkert, *Ancient Mystery Cults,* 1987, and Wedderburn, *Baptism and Resurrection.*

rulers" view.[31] But Cullmann and Caird insist that a combination of both views is more than possible, largely on the basis of traditions in Judaism concerning "angels" as custodians of the nations.[32] We shall advocate a fourth view, namely, that corporate structures entail more than the sum of their parts, but that these "spiritual powers" are not necessarily external to the sociopolitical structures as Cullmann and Caird imply. Since each tradition of exegesis has some roots in ancient thought and also receives strong support among modern writers up to the very present, each deserves serious discussion. We shall consider the four interpretations under separate headings.

(1) **Rulers** (ἄρχοντες) *as demonic powers.* Modern writers claim a substantial patristic tradition for this interpretation, but many of the passages which are confidently cited turn out to be ambiguous or of indecisive significance as possible allusions which remain uncertain. W. L. Knox cites the very early evidence of Ignatius (c. AD 108, but on examination his reference to Christ's being "hidden from the ruler of this world" (ἔλαθεν τοῦ ἄρχοντα τοῦ αἰῶνος τούτου) is an allusion to the virgin birth and death of Jesus our Lord, in which ἄρχοντα is the accusative singular (not plural) and the textual allusion uncertain and unspecific.[33] Ignatius does regularly refer to ὁ ἄρχων τοῦ αἰῶνος τούτου, *the ruler of this world order* in a supernatural sense, but the singular form does not explicitly refer to 1 Cor 2:6, 8 in his various epistles.[34]

Apart from Tertullian's allusion to Marcion, the first unambiguous interpretation of 1 Cor 2:6 as referring "not to human but to invisible power" comes in the Fragments of Origen's *Commentary on 1 Corinthians:* οὐκ ἐστὶν ἀνθρώπων . . . ἀλλὰ δυνάμεων ἀοράτων τῶν καταργουμένων.[35] More general references then occur in Origen's work elsewhere. In his comments on Matthew Origen alluded to Satan's seduction of Judas, which leads to a reflection on how the wisdom of this present world order was of such a nature as to allow the rulers of this world likewise to be seduced into crucifying Jesus.[36] In *De Principiis* Origen contrasts "a wisdom of this world, and a wisdom of the princes of this world, and another wisdom of God."[37] False knowledge is "stirred up by the opposing powers . . . introduced into human minds, and humans led astray, while they imagine that they themselves have discovered 'wisdom.'"[38] "Opposing powers ensnare and injure humans to deceive them. . . . Certain spiritual powers have been assigned the rule over certain nations, who are termed for that reason 'rulers of this world' . . . spiritual powers which bring almost certain effects. . . ."[39]

31. Conzelmann, *1 Corinthians,* 6.1; Carr, "The Rulers of This Age — 1 Cor. ii:6-8," 20-35, and *Angels and Principalities: The Background, Meaning and Development of the Pauline Phrase "hai archai kai hai exousiai."*

32. Cullmann, *Christ and Time,* 191-201; and Caird, *Principalities and Powers: A Study in Pauline Theology.* Cf. further MacGregor, "Principalities and Powers: The Cosmic Background of St Paul's Thought," 17-28.

33. Ignatius, *To the Ephesians,* 19:1; cf. W. L. Knox, *St Paul and the Church of the Gentiles* (Cambridge: Cambridge University Press, 1939), 220 and 220-26.

34. Ignatius, *To the Romans,* 7:1; *To the Magnesians,* 1:3; *To the Ephesians,* 17:1, 19; *To the Philadelphians,* 6.

35. Origen, *Fragments on Comm. 1 Cor,* sect. ix, lines 14-15 (Greek text *JTS* 9 [1908]: 239).

36. Origen, *Commentary on Matthew,* bk. 13, sect. 8.

37. Origen, *De Principiis,* 3:3:1.

38. *De Principiis,* 3:3:2.

39. *De Principiis,* 3:3:3.

On the whole, however, the patristic tradition does not favour this (see under 2). Marcion holds this interpretation, but Tertullian attacks it. The interpretation which views **the rulers of this world order** as demonic forces has become prominent, if not dominant, in modern writers on the basis of two approaches which need not be mutually exclusive. One stresses the influence on Paul of the apocalyptic tradition that the present world order is too severely flawed to be reformed, but necessitates, rather, new creation. This state of fallenness and bondage is confirmed by the plight of the present aeon as characterized by the influence of demonic forces.[40] The other approach stresses the cosmic character of fallenness and redemption found in early trends toward gnosticism.[41] In the history of modern interpretation advocates of this view of 1 Cor 2:6 include Dibelius (1909), Weiss (1910), Lietzmann (1933), Delling (1933), Moffatt (1938), Knox (1939), Héring (1948), Craig (1953), Bultmann (1952), Wendland (1956), Wilckens (1959), Barrett (1968), Conzelmann (1969), Senft (1979), Merk (1980), and Schrage (1991).[42] Many cite what Moffatt calls "strange ideas" in such passages as Col 2:14-15 and Phil 2:9-10 — cf. Rom 8:38.

The strength of this view does not lie in the speculations of Weiss, Lietzmann, and Schmithals about possible gnostic influences. The connection between Jewish apocalyptic and Paul's language about spiritual powers elsewhere in his epistles offers the strongest evidence for this view. Schoeps observes concerning Paul's use of the Jewish eschatology of "two aeons": "Through Christ's death on the cross the world . . . begins to pass away. The old aeon is still in force, but it is already crumbling (1 Cor. 2:6)."[43] A. Schweitzer captures the flavor of this apocalyptic dimension: Jesus Christ gave himself "to pluck us forth from this present evil world" (Gal 1:4), for "Demons and angels exercise power in it."[44] The "strong man" must be bound before

40. This has some influence on the recent exegesis of Schrage and of Collins (see below). Cf. E. Käsemann, "On the Subject of Primitive Christian Apocalyptics," trans. from *ZTK* 59 (1962): 257-84, in *NT Questions of Today* (Eng. trans., London: SCM, 1967), 108-37; J. C. Beker, *Paul's Apocalyptic Gospel* (Philadelphia: Fortress, 1982), 29-54, and *Paul the Apostle* (Edinburgh: T. & T. Clark, 1980), 135-81; A. Schweitzer, *The Mysticism of Paul the Apostle* (Eng. trans., London: Black, 1931), 52-100; H. J. Schoeps, *Paul* (Eng. trans., London: Lutterworth, 1961), 43-47 and 88-110; and J. Marcus and M. L. Soards (eds.), *Apocalyptic and the NT* (Sheffield: JSOT Press, 1989). Cf. further D. S. Russell, *The Method and Message of Jewish Apocalyptic* (London: SCM, 1964).

41. We have already cited literature in connection with γνῶσις, e.g., Dupont, *Gnosis;* Schmithals, *Gnosticism in Corinth;* Horsley, "Gnosis in Corinth: 1 Cor. 8:1-6," 32-51; Rudolph, *Gnosis;* and especially R. McL Wilson, "Gnosis at Corinth," in M. D. Hooker and S. G. Wilson (eds.), *Paul and Paulinism,* 102-14. See further F. O. Francis, "Humility and Angelic Worship in Col. 2:18," in F. O. Francis and W. A. Meeks (eds.), *Conflict at Colossae* (Missoula: Scholars Press, 2d ed., 1975), 163-95; Kovacs, "The Archons, the Spirit and the Death of Christ: Do We Need the Hypothesis of Gnostic Opponents to Explain 1 Cor. 2:6-16?" in Marcus and Soards (eds.), *Apocalyptic and the NT,* 217-36; and E. M. Yamauchi, *Pre-Christian Gnosticism* (Grand Rapids: Baker, rev. ed. 1983).

42. For example, Dibelius, *Die Geistwelt im Glauben des Paulus;* Lietzmann, *An die Korinther,* 11-12; Weiss, *Der erste Korintherbrief,* 53-57; Moffatt, *First Epistle,* 29-30; C. T. Craig, "ἄρχων," *IB,* 10:37-38; Wendland, *Die Briefe,* 27-28; Barrett, *First Epistle,* 70; Bultmann *Theology of the NT,* 1:174-75; Schrage, *Der erste Brief,* 250; Wilckens, *Weisheit und Torheit,* 52-96; Merk, "ἄρχων," *EDNT,* 1:167-68; Collins, *First Cor,* 129. Many compare also Rom 8:38, Phil 2:9-10, and Col 2:14-15.

43. Schoeps, *Paul,* 102.

44. Schweitzer, *Mysticism of Paul,* 55; cf. 52.

Christ can despoil him of his goods by rescuing his people from his sway (Matt 12:22-29).[45] "The destruction of the dominion of the Angels will be completed by the Return of Jesus."[46]

Thus the paean of praise at the conclusion of Romans 8 includes thanksgiving for rescue from the controlling domain of every force which is not of God: οὔτε ἄγγελοι οὔτε ἀρχαί (neither angels nor "powers"), οὔτε ὕψωμα οὔτε βάθος (neither height nor depth, interpreted by Whiteley as astrological forces at given astronomical points), can interrupt the believer's salvation by God's love (Rom 8:38-39).[47] Similarly, Paul speaks of "the god of this world" (ὁ θεὸς τοῦ αἰῶνος τούτου) using the apocalyptic term **this present world order,** or aeon, in 2 Cor 4:4. Here R. P. Martin comments on that verse: "The god of this αἰών, 'age', is Satan . . . the Jewish doctrine of two ages is important for the apostle, so Satan controls this age under God's decree."[48]

(2) **Rulers** (ἄρχοντες) *as earthly political rulers.* The above view has been vigorously attacked by A. Wesley Carr, among others, both in his monograph and in his extensive article on this verse.[49] He regards it as of the utmost importance that most frequently references to any supernatural dimension use the singular ὁ ἄρχων (e.g., John 12:31) not the plural ἄρχοντες. Moreover, ἄρχοντες, **rulers** (in the plural), occurs often in the NT of human political rulers, especially in relation to the crucifixion (e.g., Luke 23:14, 35; 24:20; Acts 3:17; 4:8, 25; 13:27). Thus "the plural carries no demonic sense *per se.*"[50] Even to the Corinthians, Carr urges, "the word ἄρχοντες would have conveyed . . . no immediate demonic sense, *unless we first assume* that the Corinthian Christians were under some gnostic influence in which the word had become a technical term" (my italics).[51] But 1 Cor 2:6-8 is not concerned with "gnosis." Although he does not fully address the issue of apocalyptic themes in Paul, Carr argues that this motif plays no more part in our passage than *gnosis.*

The last point is perhaps the weakest in Carr's argument. Nevertheless, the majority of the Church Fathers and very many modern writers interpret the phrase ἄρχοντες τοῦ αἰῶνος τούτου to mean *political* **rulers** who shape **the present world order.** Tertullian explicitly rejects Marcion's interpretation. He writes: "But he [Paul] did not speak of 'spiritual' rulers; he meant secular ones. . . ."[52] The volumes of *Biblia Patristica* cite some eighty-three references to 1 Cor 2:6 in the writings of Origen. I have checked the majority of them, and only a small minority explicitly appeal to the notion of supernatural demonic rulers, although it does occur explicitly in his commentary on 1 Cor 2:6, and most commentators describe this as "Origen's view."[53]

45. Ibid., 56.
46. Ibid., 65.
47. Whiteley, *The Theology of St Paul,* 24 and 23-31; cf. 283-86; cf. further Lietzmann, *An die Römer* (Tübingen: Mohr, 1938), 88; cf. Plutarch, *Septem Sapientum Convivium* 3.149a; Diogenes Laertius, 8.28 and 6.102. For talk of stars as "deities" see further Plato, *Timaeus* 40a, c-d and 41a; cf. also Arnold, *Power of Darkness: Principalities and Powers in Paul's Letters.*
48. R. P. Martin, *2 Corinthians,* WBC 40 (Waco: Word, 1986), 78-79, and *Reconciliation: A Study of Paul's Theology* (London: Marshall, Morgan, and Scott, 1981), 51-54.
49. Carr, "The Rulers of This Age — 1 Cor ii:6-8," 20-35.
50. Ibid., 23.
51. Ibid.
52. Tertullian, *Against Marcion,* 5:6.
53. *Biblia Patristica,* 3:385; as against his *Commentary,* sect. ix, lines 14-15, and other sources in Origen cited above.

Chrysostom rejects this "supernatural" interpretation. He declares "By 'the rulers of the world', here, he [Paul] means not certain demons, as some suspect, but those in authority, those in power . . . philosophers, rhetoricians . . . leaders of the people," and Calvin shares this view.[54]

Among modern writers of this century those who associate our phrase in this verse with Pilate, Herod, Rome, or other earthly authorities find support in special studies by J. Schniewind and G. Miller as well as Carr.[55] In broad terms the following refer the phrase to political rulers or to humans who hold powers: Heinrici (1880), Findlay (1900), Robertson and Plummer (1911), Parry (1916), Bachmann (1936), Grosheide (1954), Morris (1958), Munck (1959), Feuillet (1963), Thrall (1965), Bruce (1971), Miller (1972), Davis (1984), Fee (1987), Strobel (1989), Kistemaker (1993,) Lang (1994), Witherington (1995), Wolf (1996), Hays (1997), and Horsley (1998) adopt this view.[56] Davis and Fee follow Carr and Miller in stressing (i) lexicography; (ii) the decisive difference between singular and plural uses of ἄρχων, and (iii) the relation to 1:18-25. Fee concludes, "There is no evidence of any kind, either in Jewish or Christian writings until the second century, that the term was used of demons."[57]

(3) **Rulers** *as angelic custodians of nations? Both supernatural and political.* Oscar Cullmann writes, "Paul manifestly means *both* the invisible 'princes of this world' . . . and their actual human instruments, Herod and Pilate" (his italics).[58] Invisible powers *"stand behind what occurs in the world"* (his italics).[59] Martin Dibelius, he asserts, first demonstrated the widespread belief in Judaism "that there is a particular angel for each people."[60] He cites Daniel, Winston Enoch, and the Talmud for this belief in Judaism. In Paul Cullmann cites both the cosmic scope of Christ's Lordship in Phil 2:10, and the ἐξουσίαι, *authorities,* which sustain the state in Rom 13:1. Redemption in Christ embraces cosmic "subjection of the angelic powers."[61] Cullmann finds confirmation of this in 1 Cor 2:6-8. George Caird develops Cullmann's argument further in his *Principalities and Powers* (1956). Various figures in the OT, often mentioned as "sons of God," appear as supernatural agents of God (Gen 6:3; Deut 32:8 [LXX, Heb. "sons of Israel"]; and Job 1).[62] Notably Deut 4:19 speaks of heavenly bodies to whom God "has allotted

---

54. Chrysostom, *Hom. 1 Cor.,* 7:1; Calvin, *First Epistle,* 53.

55. Schniewind, "Die Archontes dieses Äons. 1 Kor. 2:6-8," in *Nachgelassene Reden und Aufsätze,* 104-9; and Miller, "Ἀρχόντων τοῦ αἰῶνος τούτου — A New Look at 1 Cor. 2:6-8," 522-28.

56. For example, Findlay, *Expositor's Greek Testament,* 2:778; Robertson and Plummer, *First Epistle,* 36-37; Grosheide, *Commentary,* 63 ("not . . . magistrates only, since Paul has in mind all those who set the pattern of this world"); Thrall, *1 Corinthians,* 25; A. Feuillet, "Les 'Chefs de ce siècle' et la sagesse divine d'après 1 Cor. 2:6-8," in *Studiorum Paulinorum Congressus Internationalis Catholicus 1961,* 1:383-93; and *Le Christ, Sagesse de Dieu* (Paris: Gabalda, 1968), 37-57; Bruce, *1 Corinthians,* 38; Davis, *Wisdom and Spirit,* 87-92 (largely following Carr), cf. 85-131 on 2:6-16; Fee, *First Epistle,* 104; Kistemaker, *1 Corinthians,* 80; Witherington, *Conflict and Community,* 127; Lang, *Die Briefe,* 42-43; Strobel, *Der erste Brief,* 65-66; Wolff, *Der erste Brief,* 53; Hays, *1 Cor,* 43; Horsley, *1 Cor,* 58.

57. Fee, *First Epistle,* 104, n. 24; cf. Davis, *Wisdom and Spirit,* 90-91.

58. Cullmann, *Christ and Time,* 191.

59. Ibid., 192.

60. Ibid.

61. Ibid., 193.

62. Caird, *Principalities and Powers,* 1-11.

all the peoples," while Daniel 10 is said to allude to a (heavenly) prince (Heb. שׂר, sar; ἄρχων) who has guardianship over Persia (Dan 10:13) and Greece (Dan 10:20). For Caird, followed by Whiteley, Ecclus 17:17 assumes special importance: "He appointed a ruler over every nation, but Israel is the Lord's own portion."[63] According to this view, Paul stands in, or at least draws on, this tradition in Judaism. Christian believers, as God's own people, enjoy the direct protection and care of God. But other super-earthly forces "stand behind" the authorities, leaders, structures, and identity of unbelieving "nations."

We have noted, however, that for Carr, Miller, Davis, and Fee, among a host of others, this view rests on the use of the singular ἄρχων rather than the plural in Septuagintal Judaism, while in terms of lexicography the evidence remains slim. Hatch-Redpath list over thirty-three Hebrew words which ἄρχων translates, and only in the passage cited does שׂר (sar) represent a supernatural ruler. Other writers, including M. Pesce, E. Peterson, J. Munck, and T. Ballarini, agree with Carr that this interpretation aggravates the continuity of argument with 1:18-31, unless we follow W. O. Walker and others in regarding 2:6-16 as a non-Pauline interpolation.[64]

(4) **Rulers of this world order** *as sociopolitical powers in a structural collectivity that transcends given human individuals* (possibly with a hint of demonic overtones). Of the three interpretations considered above, the second has most to commend it, but the resonances of the third cannot simply be swept aside as irrelevant. Paul stands closer to Jewish apocalyptic than to Western individualism from Descartes to the late twentieth century. Humankind is more than a collection of individual entities or agents, but a corporeity within which evil and evil forces become endemic and structural. Moreover, Jesus Christ, for Paul, was not crucified simply by Pilate or Herod or individual leaders, but as a cosmic event on which God addressed *all* forces of evil from which liberation could subsequently come (Rom 8:38-39). We do not have to postulate an explicit reference to "astrological forces" in 8:39 to take the point that forces more than merely the power of individuals are at issue.

Even if Paul's language *denotes* human leaders, *connotations* remain of a structural power either by cumulative inbuilt fallenness or by association with still stronger cosmic forces. This comes close to Theissen's approach, and Reinhold Niebuhr demonstrates that corporate evil takes a qualitative leap beyond the sum of all individual acts of evil.[65]

Can support for this interpretation be found among Pauline specialists? In addition to Theissen's work and that of Kovacs, two writers contribute very important work. First, Walter Wink's three works offer an incisive account of biblical material, including Paul.[66] Wink comments, "Both the argument that the *archontes* in 1 Cor 2:6-8 are human and the argument that they are divine are plausible. . . . Both views are cor-

---

63. Caird, *Principalities and Powers,* and Whiteley, *The Theology of St Paul,* 21.

64. A summary of M. Pesce's *Paolo e gli archonti a Corinto* (1977) is offered by T. Ballarini in *Laurentianum* 21 (1980): 251-72, with observations on 1 Cor 2:6, 8; cf. W. O. Walker, "1 Cor. 2:6-16: A Non-Pauline Interpolation?" *JSNT* 47 (1992): 75-94.

65. Theissen, *Psychological Aspects of Pauline Theology,* 374-78; cf. Niebuhr, *Moral Man and Immoral Society.* The issues could clearly be taken further with reference, e.g., to Rom 1:18-32.

66. Wink, *Naming the Powers: The Language of Power in the New Testament,* esp. 40-45; *Engaging the Powers: Discernment and Resistance in a World of Domination,* and *Unmasking the Powers: The Invisible Forces That Determine Human Existence.*

rect."[67] Second, Neil Elliott's book *Liberating Paul* offers a very constructive discussion of "Paul and 'the Powers'."[68] Wink and Elliott agree with Beker on the significance of the apocalyptic and cosmic background, and that the field of cosmic powers opposed to God "operates as an interrelated whole. . . . No power can be viewed in isolation from the others."[69] Contrary perhaps to a possible emphasis in Colossians, in 1 Corinthians the powers as yet remain unconquered (1 Cor 15:24) although they have begun to crumble and are doomed (2:6). Elliott writes, "there is no good reason to marginalize the clearly apocalyptic viewpoint of 1 Corinthians 2 and 15 within Paul's thinking."[70] The work of J. Kovacs, "Archons, the Spirit and the Death of Christ," underlines the theme of "God's battle with cosmic forces of evil" for 1 Corinthians as a whole.[71] Ortkemper refuses the either/or of Conzelmann and Carr: "Paul formulates a double meaning: while the political powers bring Jesus to death, they show themselves as tools of demonic powers that resist God."[72]

Wink declares especially with reference to Col 1:16, "These powers are both heavenly and earthly, divine and human, spiritual and political, invisible and structural . . . (they) possess an outer, physical, manifestation and an inner . . . corporate culture or collective personality."[73] Elliott views Wink's grammar of power as "compelling," but places stronger emphasis on the continuing battle which 1 Corinthians, with its protest again an illusory, overrealized eschatology, stresses. Elliott rightly relates structural evil to political regimes of violence and to the forces which inspire them and escalate their obsession with self-survival by violent power and oppression. He discusses concretely Ferdinand Marcos and Benigno Aquino in the Philippines, the assassination of Archbishop Oscar Romero in El Salvador, and Jean-Bertrand Aristide in Haiti as "the powers," not merely individuals, associated with "oppression, distress, persecution, starvation, destitution, peril, sword" (Rom 8:35-39).[74] "The Spirit draws Christians into the trauma of a cosmic childbirth. . . . Paul interprets Jesus' death as *the beginning of God's final 'war of liberation' against all the Powers that hold creation in thrall* through the instruments of earthly oppression" (Elliott's italics).[75] Without commenting on the specific examples chosen by Wink and Elliott, the principle which they formulate seems to offer a valid hermeneutic based on careful exegetical argument. Structural and corporate evil is addressed by the cross.

THE INTEGRITY OF THE TEXT OF 2:6-16

Widmann and Walker argue that such are the linguistic and terminological peculiarities of this section (vv. 6-16) that we must seriously consider the case for the view that

67. Wink, *Naming the Powers*, 44.
68. Elliott, *Liberating Paul: The Justice of God and the Politics of the Apostle*, 114-24.
69. Beker, *Paul the Apostle*, 189-90.
70. Elliott, *Liberating Paul*, 115.
71. Kovacs, "The Archons, the Spirit, and the Death of Christ: Do We Really Need the Hypothesis of Gnostic Opponents to Explain 1 Cor. 2:6-16?" in Marcus and Soards (eds.), *Apocalyptic in the NT: Essays in Honour of J. Louis Martyn*, esp. 224-25.
72. Ortkemper, *1 Korintherbrief*, 36.
73. Wink, *Engaging the Powers*, 3.
74. Elliott, *Liberating Paul*, 118-21.
75. Ibid., 123.

Paul did not write it.[76] *Prima facie* these verses might well be an immediate response from those whom Paul attacks in 1:1–2:5. The response then begins, "But *we do* speak a wisdom. . . ." This is not, they reply, destructive, but truly "spiritual." For many years Weiss and others have viewed aspects of 2:15-16, as coming from the lips of the addressees.[77] There are strong counterarguments from Murphy-O'Connor, Mitchell, and others.[78] But if Widmann and Walker are right, more is at issue than Paul's redefinition of "wisdom" in the light of the cross and of Christology. This issue needs to be kept in mind as we proceed with the exegesis of 2:7-16. At all events Paul gives the argument a decisive christological turn in 3:1-4. We remain convinced, in practice, that 2:6-16 are Paul's own words, but that he traces, indeed anticipates, the style of argument which the Corinthian elitists would use, consciously taking up their catchwords to place them in a christological context. The definitive study of how quasi-gnostic terms, or more strictly terms *shared* by Christians and gnostics, convey a different semantic content depending on their context and frame of reference is probably still the excellent but unduly neglected study by Samuel Laeuchli.[79]

It may well be the case that Paul's opponents readily cited "wisdom" traditions from the LXX to support their views, esp. Isaiah 40, 52, and 64. However, it seems difficult to follow Earle Ellis in regarding 2:6-16 as having "the literary form of a midrash or exposition of scripture probably . . . created within a (Pauline) group of pneumatics prior to its use in 1 Cor. 2."[80] Ellis's citing of "the spirit of the world" and "the Spirit who is from God" is entirely double-edged, since the latter offers a correction of the former in line with Pauline thought.[81] On this issue and on the use of the first person plural, see further above.

7 It is difficult to know whether to gloss ἐν μυστηρίῳ, *in a mystery,* as **in discourse too profound for merely human discovery**. The NIV, REB, and NRSV avoid the word "mystery," understanding the term as intensifying **hidden** (ἀποκεκρυμμένην). Hence NRSV translates, *we speak God's wisdom, secret and hidden, which God decreed. . . .* NJB changes JB's *we teach in our mysteries* to *It is of the mysterious wisdom of God that we talk,* while REB translates: *I speak God's hidden wisdom, his secret purpose.*

If Paul is using the word in the sense which matches his theology in the four major epistles and in Colossians, as Bockmuehl argues in his recent monograph on the subject, the emphasis falls on *revealed* mysteries as against human discovery.[82] The problem for modern readers is that *mystery* tends to convey

76. M. Widmann, "1 Kor. 2:6-16: Ein Einspruch gegen Paulus," 44-53; W. O. Walker, "1 Cor. 2:6-16: A Non-Pauline Interpolation?" *JSNT* 47 (1992), 75-94.

77. Weiss, *Earliest Christianity,* 2:511-13: *Der erste Korintherbrief,* 64-70.

78. J. Murphy-O'Connor, "Interpolations in 1 Corinthians," *CBQ* 48 (1986): 81-94.

79. Laeuchli, *The Language of Faith: An Introduction to the Semantic Dilemma of the Early Church.*

80. Ellis, *Prophecy and Hermeneutic,* 25-26.

81. Ibid., 26, n. 17.

82. Bockmuehl, *Revelation and Mystery in Ancient Judaism and Pauline Christianity.* Bockmuehl traces the development of the term in apocalyptic, Qumran, the wisdom literature, Philo, Josephus, and Paul, finding in 1 Corinthians an emphasis on "revealed mysteries," in which his Christology redefines the Jewish usage.

what is impenetrable not because it necessitates revelation but because it can never in principle become coherent or intelligible. The notion of divine "secrets" seems to verge on trivial anthropomorphism, as if God "keeps back" truth, rather than emphasizing that fallen human capacities cannot penetrate God's truth without the event of the cross and the work of the Holy Spirit. Outside its technical use in the mystery religions μυστήριον is that which is *too profound for human ingenuity*.[83] It surrounds such issues as God's "hardening" of Israel (Rom 11:25), the resurrection power of the Holy Spirit to transform whole persons at the parousia (1 Cor 15:51), and indeed God's self-disclosure and identity in Christ (Col 2:2). (See further, above, on 2:1, and below on 4:1, 3; 13:2; 14:2; and 15:51.)

NRSV and NIV construe ἐν μυστηρίῳ, *in a mystery*, with ἀποκεκρυμ-μένην, *hidden (secret and hidden)*, following the syntax assumed by Fee, Schrage, and several others.[84] Some (Meyer, Edwards) construe the phrase with λαλοῦμεν, "we speak as a mystery. . . ."[85] There is little difference, however, in the communicative effect. "The use of 'mystery' also points out that Christ, our wisdom, surpasses our human understanding (cf. 15:15; Eph. 5:32).[86] Schrage reiterates, "God's wisdom . . . is nothing other than the crucified Christ."[87] It is unattainable by "unassisted human reason."[88]

We cannot dismiss the possibility, however, that vv. 7 and 8 (together with two or three later verses in this chapter) could represent arguments of some at Corinth which Paul cites in order to respond to them. In the writings of Tacitus, the Christian worship gatherings were indeed associated with "secret rites" known only to initiates, as in the mystery religions. The arguments of Weiss, Schmithals, Ellis, and others about "pneumatics" could perhaps apply to this verse. This is why, whereas Barrett translates the Greek adversative ἀλλά, *but*, as *"No, we speak . . . ,"* and Collins renders it *"Rather we speak . . . ,"* a strong adversative, we have left the link open-ended by rendering as equivalent the English **"Well, we speak. . . ."**[89] For *well* can be used either to introduce self-justifying argument, or, equally, a merely loose connection embodying a minor pause.

If μυστήριον is used in the sense of initiated elite in a mystery religion or a radically "enthusiast-charismatic" community, the word would signify a knowledge shared exclusively by "insiders," as against that which is human by revelation. The former meaning leads to the technical sense of "secret rites and ceremonies" in the mystery religions, and could carry this currency here

83. BAGD, 530-31.
84. Conzelmann, *1 Corinthians*, 62; Robertson and Plummer, *First Epistle*, 37; Fee, *First Epistle*, 105; Schrage, *Der erste Brief*, I, 250; also Aquinas, Grotius, and Lightfoot.
85. Meyer, *First Epistle*, 1:62-63; also Erasmus and de Wette.
86. Grosheide, *First Epistle*, 64.
87. Schrage, *Der erste Brief*, 1:250.
88. Findlay, *Expositor's Greek Testament*, 2:778.
89. Collins, *First Cor*, 129; Barrett, *First Epistle*, 70.

only if it is a direct quotation from elitist arguments at Corinth, i.e., "when *our* group meets, we speak. . . ." But the issue can only remain speculative, and the triple emphasis falls, at least for Paul, on revelation, on truths beyond intellectual discovery alone, and on Christ as God's wisdom marked out from before all ages.

The verb προώρισεν (προοριπίζω) derives from the word group that pre-dates the Eng. *horizon,* i.e., to determine a boundary from beforehand. In clas-sical Greek it is used of reaching decisions before the event (Demosthenes, 31:4). In Rom 8:30 it became familiar as "predestined" (NRSV) or "foreor-dained" (REB). As in Rom 8:30, the purpose of the verb in which προώρισεν occurs is to emphasize that "God does not leave his purpose to chance. . . . Paul looks at the whole process from the perspective of its successful outcome."[90] In 1 Cor 2:7 the NRSV translates *decreed;* NJB, *predestined;* NIV, *destined be-fore . . . ;* and REB, *a purpose framed from the very beginning.* Moulton-Milligan list no use of the word in the papyri, although ὁρίζω without the com-pound preposition can mean to fix the boundaries (e.g., of land), as well as *to appoint* or *to decree* (cf. Luke 22:22, *London Papyri* 1168:13, AD 18); ὁρισμός means boundary in *BGU* 2:599:2. On the ground that the compound form inten-sifies deciding beforehand, Fee translates to *predestine,* and renders πρὸ τῶν αἰώνων (before the ages) as *before time began.*[91]

Modern readers, however, are inevitably shaped by two thousand years of philosophical tradition, in which "predestination before time began" imposes a supposed fixity on the mode by which the goal is reached, and this may unwit-tingly imply a philosophical agenda which Paul does not address here. *In the context of apocalyptic thought* (rightly emphasized by Wolff, Strobel, and oth-ers), the presence of which is indicated by such terms as *hidden, before the ages,* and *revealed mystery,* decision to *mark out* what belongs to God and his purposes generally takes the form of *sealing* or *naming, which guarantees the security of those who are marked as the Lord's own.*[92] Hence in combination with the intensified compound form of ὁρίζω (with προ-), *to mark out* or *to de-fine boundaries,* the best translation may well be, **God marked out before-hand. . . .** This entails the nuance of predestination, but without the additional resonances which it acquired in philosophical traditions.

This meaning coheres with the profoundly moving phrase εἰς δόξαν ἡμῶν, **for our glory,** construing εἰς with the accusative in the sense of *with a view to.* As Moltmann, Jüngel, and Brümmer well argue, if the love of God is such that he treats the well-being of his people as his own, there can be no com-petition *within the love of God* between what works toward *God's own* **glory**

90. Dunn, *Romans,* 1:485.

91. Fee, *First Epistle,* 105. Cf. Collins, *First Cor,* 121, 123, *God pre-ordained before the ages.*

92. For example, on sealing (σφραγίζω) cf. Rev 7:3, 4, 5, 8; 20:3; 2 Cor 1:22; Eph 4:30; and on name (ὄνομα) Rev 3:12; 14:1; 22:4 (cf. 1 Cor 1:13). Cf. Wolff, *Der erste Brief,* 55 on Bar 14:9; *1 Enoch* 37:2, 3; and 1QS 4:18. Also Strobel, *Der erste Brief,* 66.

and his desire and indeed decree for his people to share that **glory**.[93] It is conceivable, as we have argued, that this could represent Paul's quotation of Corinthian claims to the legitimacy of a triumphalism of **glory**. If so, Paul anticipates Luther's later contrast in this verse between a *theologia crucis* and a false *theologia gloriae*.[94] This corresponds, moreover, precisely with Paul's description of the destiny of Christ's people in 1 Cor 15:40-56. At the resurrection Christians assume a mode of existence characterized by the Holy Spirit by bearing the image of Christ, and by δόξα, *glory* (15:40-41, and esp. 43: ἐγείρεται ἐν δόξῃ, *raised in glory;* cf. Phil. 3:21).

To appreciate the full force of the word δόξα, **glory**, it is necessary to look at the Hebrew which is presupposed and translated as δόξα in the LXX. A classic piece of research on the semantics of Heb. כבוד *(kabod)* and Gk. δόξα *(doxa)* has been provided by Carey C. Newman.[95] He reminds us that the כבד word group occurs about 400 times in the Hebrew Bible. Within this group several distinct theological themes and lexical domains interact, e.g., that of God's presence, to which Newman and Clements have given special attention, and "theophany" and *shekinah* interact with those characteristics which reveal the "weight," majesty, or impressiveness of God's acts and the radiancy of divine glory as light.[96] Indeed, many lexicographical studies of כבוד *(kabod)* begin with the notion of *weight,* or *weightiness,* from which *honour, splendor,* and *reputation* are derived.[97] The Hebrew semantic field may include the more "neutral" aspects of weightiness, but also more "positive" nuances of blessing, bounty, praise, salvation, beauty, wealth or well-being, multiplication, heaven, and the presence of God.[98]

In his section on Pauline lexicographical resources, Newman draws from BAGD and other sources the four major meanings of (i) brightness, radiance, splendor; (ii) magnificence, which might catch the eye (or perhaps the breath); (iii) fame, renown, honor; and (iv) sometimes an "office."[99] Of these, the first appears to constitute the most frequent use. But Newman also shows that a fuller and more sophisticated list of variations occurs in Paul. In conjunction with εἰς with δόξα in the (articular) accusative, and θεός, "praise" becomes focal: εἰς τὴν δόξαν θεοῦ. When θεός is the subject, however, and εἰς is followed by the accusative of δόξα in conjunction with a verb which governs the phrase or the clause, unexpectedly Newman translates the

93. Vincent Brümmer, *The Model of Love: A Study in Philosophical Theology* (Cambridge: Cambridge University Press, 1993), 127-245, esp. 239-40.

94. Luther, *The Heidelberg Disputation,* esp. sects. xx-xxviii (*WA,* 1:361-65); also *Early Theological Works,* 290-95.

95. Newman, *Paul's Glory-Christology: Tradition and Rhetoric,* esp. "Some Semantic Observations on Glory in the Hebrew Bible," 17-24; "Some Semantic Observations on Glory in Paul," 157-64, and "1 Cor. 2:8," 235-40.

96. Ibid., 17-75; cf. R. E. Clements, *God and Temple* (Philadelphia: Fortress, 1965).

97. BDBG, 456-59; L. Köhler and W. Baumgartner, *HALAT,* 2:434-35.

98. See Newman, *Paul's Glory-Christology,* 19, for a useful semantic summary.

99. Ibid., 157. cf. BAGD, 203-5.

only two examples, one of which is προώρισεν ὁ θεὸς . . . εἰς δόξαν ἡμῶν in 2:7 as "for his benefit."[100]

Nevertheless most commentators read the syntax and lexicographical field of 2:7 quite differently. In Conzelmann's judgment it means "with a view to our glory" in the sense of describing "our new being as supernatural."[101] This, he adds, "marks the horizon of the saving knowledge that is proclaimed by those in the know." Fee comments that here "God 'destined' his people for glory (not shame)," while Barrett argues that "God's wisdom leads to *our glory* in so far as it makes us obedient" (his italics).[102] Grosheide writes: "The glory of believers is an essential part of God's decree."[103] Wendland and Schrage stress the eschatological character of δόξαν ἡμῶν (**our glory**) here: Schrage compares it with πρὸ τῶν αἰώνων (**before the ages**) as the *Urzeit-Endzeit* pattern of soteriology, i.e., the final end-time goal at last corresponds to the original point of departure or "primal time" of apocalyptic, while Dahl speaks here of a "revelation schema."[104] Here he also reinforces our observations about the translation of προορίζειν, which carries no allusion to some moment in time, nor necessarily to timeless decrees, but to the priority of God's will and purpose which he accomplishes at the end-goal.

Thus principal commentators of recent years, including Barrett, Conzelmann, Fee, Schrage, Collins, and Merklein, all line up against Newman's colorless rendering, removed from ἡμῶν, **our**, "for his benefit."[105] Bengel and Meyer rightly stress that "the δόξα of believers" (Meyer) is indeed *part of* "the glory of the Lord," but this is to return to our earlier point.[106] Robertson and Plummer see believers as enjoying the foretaste of this glory as the firstfruits of the Spirit (ἀρραβών, 2 Cor. 1:22, first down payment of more to come), "but the eschatological sense is primary."[107]

How, then, do the semantic fields which Newman explored more widely and more convincingly apply here? That which renders *God* "weighty," "impressive," "of high reputation," or "of splendour" is not simply his holy majesty (which is not Paul's focus here) but his free, sovereign, choice (προώρισεν, **he marked out beforehand**) to give himself in mercy and love in the **revealed mystery** of the cross of the Christ. But this "being for others" (Bonhoeffer,

100. Ibid., 159-60 (including 160, n. 14 and n. 15).

101. Conzelmann, *1 Corinthians*, 62.

102. Fee, *First Epistle*, 10; Barrett, *First Epistle*, 71.

103. Grosheide, *First Epistle*, 64.

104. Schrage, *Der erste Brief*, 1:251-52. Cf. N. A. Dahl, "Formgeschichtliche Beobachtungen zur Christusverkündigung in Gemeindepredigt," in W. Eltester (ed.), *Neutestamentliche Studien für R. Bultmann*, 3-9. Paul alludes to "hiddenness" in relation to God's eschatological initiative of grace, not because he draws on a particular formula; cf. Merklein, *Der erste Brief 1–4*, 228-29.

105. For example, Merklein, *Der erste Brief 1–4*, 228-29; Schrage, *Der erste Brief*, 1:251-52. Wolff, *Der erste Brief*, 55, seems to hint at both views; but Grosheide, Wendland, Lietzmann, and Robertson and Plummer support Fee and Schrage.

106. Meyer, *First Epistle*, 1:63.

107. Robertson and Plummer, *First Epistle*, 38.

Jüngel) results in believers sharing in the having-died-with and being-raised-with Christ, as sharing in the radiancy of his self-giving. Thus *benefit* blandly reduces the profound force of Paul's vision, while Conzelmann's *new being as supernatural* equally misses the main target. God shows forth his radiant splendor chiefly in the cross, where for the present it remains largely but not entirely hidden, for the salvation of believers constitutes the preliminary and far from perfect showing forth of this glory in which they share insofar as they share the character of Christ. In 15:44-57 Paul will show how this resurrection to glory into full characterization by the image (φορέσομεν τὴν εἰκόνα) of Christ (15:49), fully shaped by the Holy Spirit (σῶμα . . . πνευματικόν, 15:44), is the demise of this same μυστήριον (15:51 and 2:6).

8 On the phrase **the rulers of this present world order** (τῶν ἀρχόντων τοῦ αἰῶνος τούτου), see under 2:6. A further comment from Wink's *Naming the Powers,* however, in conjunction with Schniewind's work on this passage, develops the relation between the first half and the second half of this verse, i.e., between "the powers" and "the Cross."[108] Wink helpfully allocates the semantic contrast between "we" structures and "they" structures in two columns as follows:

WE		THEY
Our glorification (2:7)	vs.	Rulers of this age (2:6, 8)
Those who love him (2:9)	vs.	Those who crucified the lord of glory (2:8)
The Spirit of God (2:12)	vs.	The spirit of the world (2:12)
The spiritual person (2:15)	vs.	The unspiritual person (2:14)

The "they" group, Schniewind and Wink urge, include "the expert (σοφός, γραμματεύς), influential (δυνατοί), and those of high family status (εὐγενεῖς) in 1:26 (cf. 1:20), whom God will bring to nothing (καταργήσῃ, 1:28), just as all **the rulers of this present world order** are in process of being reduced to nothing (τῶν καταργουμένων, 2:6). In accordance with our argument for a fourth view of **rulers** in 2:6, Wink adds: "The case that the *archons* of 1 Cor. 2:6-8 are human is very persuasive, but . . . Herod, Pilate and the Jewish authorities cannot possibly be made to bear the weight of the phrase 'rulers of this aeon.' . . . Every *archon* involved in Jesus' death is intended."[109] Morrison likewise sees a multilayered meaning here.[110]

This interpretation not only rightly underlines the cosmic conflict between "the spirit of the world" (2:12) and the proclamation of the cross (1:18–2:5), but also places "wisdom" and "the powers" in a context of salvation through Christ which addresses one major argument for viewing 2:1-16 as ei-

---

108. Wink, *Naming the Powers,* 41 (cf. 40-45); and Schniewind, "Die Archontes," in *Nachgelassene Reden,* 104-9.

109. Wink, *Naming the Powers,* 42 and 44.

110. Morrison, *The Powers That Be,* 23-24.

ther non-Pauline or as a later insertion. Paul uses "alien" conceptual fields only in order to bring them new definition in the light of the cross.

All the same, if **the rulers of this present world order** reflect both a human and also a more-than-individual-persons dimension, in what sense does Paul assert their ignorance of the nature of God's revealed mystery with reference to the crucifixion? Jewish and Christian apocalyptic suggests one ready answer. *1 Enoch* 16:1-3 speaks of "destroying" spirits and of "watchers" (cf. Heb. עִיר, *'ir,* with Gk. ἄγγελος, e.g., in Gen 6:1-4; Dan 4:17, 20) to whom it is explicitly said: "All the mysteries have not yet been revealed to you."[111] This theme also finds affinities with *Ascension of Isaiah* 11:24: "How did our Lord descend in our midst, and we perceived not his glory?" (cf. *Jubilees* 1:25; *Asc. Isa.* 8:7; 10:8-12; *Assumption of Moses* 1:12-13).[112] *1 Enoch,* moreover, uses the phrase **the Lord of glory** (ὁ κύριος τῆς δόξης, *1 Enoch* 22:14; 25:3, 7; 27:3, 4; cf. 66:2).

Does this help us to understand Paul? Recently J. C. O'Neill (1995) has daringly argued that pre-Christian Jewish traditions, especially in apocalyptic, reflect "trinitarian formulas."[113] In the *Ascension of Isaiah* all "powers" outside or below "the sixth heaven," i.e., those especially close to God, remain ignorant of the "names" of "the Father, the Beloved Christ, and the Holy Spirit" (*Asc. Isa.* 8:18). In *1 Enoch,* only those spirits whose eyes have been opened can acknowledge "the Chosen One . . . the Son of Man" who receives the Spirit to equip him for his work (*1 Enoch* 62:1-2, 5).[114] Clearly pre-Pauline material in the basic, authentic chapters of *1 Enoch* do speak of fallen angels in allusion to Gen 6:1-8 as a source of evil. There is even a suggestion that these fallen angels instruct people of influence in arts and crafts (*1 Enoch* 10:8). But the "Messianic" passages come in the more problematic *Similitudes of Enoch,* where the dating becomes uncertain. Moreover, in spite of the scope of O'Neill's allusion to multiple traditions, it remains difficult to be certain that the more striking passages have not been corrupted by post-Pauline Christian redaction.[115] Three points, however, remain clear.

111. Cf. Barrett, *First Epistle,* 72.

112. Schrage, *Der erste Brief,* 1:253; cf. Collins, *First Cor,* 131; Lang, *Die Brief,* 43-44; Merklein, *Der erste Brief 1–4,* 230-31.

113. J. C. O'Neill, *Who Did Jesus Think He Was?* BibIntMon 11 (Leiden: Brill, 1995), 42-114 and throughout (quoted phrase, 99).

114. Ibid., 99.

115. This is a standard problem in interpreting the Jewish pseudepigrapha, especially apocalyptic literature. The basic document (earlier chapters) of *1 Enoch* is pre-Pauline, and establishes the theme of revealed mysteries (cf. Enoch as translated to heaven on the basis of Gen 5:24), the role of angels or "watchers" (Gen 6:1-3), and the term "Lord of glory" (*1 Enoch* 22:14; 25:3, 7; 27:3, 4). The "powers" are doomed, but the righteous are saved (*1 Enoch* 10:17). *Jubilees* is also clearly pre-Pauline, and gives an important place to *aeons* (each age or *aeon* is concluded by a year of Jubilee); but the emphasis lies more on the law than on the cosmic concerns of Paul. The messianic references in the *Similitudes of Enoch,* together with a theology of revelation and the Spirit, may be closely relevant, as O'Neill suggests, but we cannot rely on a lack of editing for those passages which are near to Christian motifs. see further Bockmuehl, *Revelation and Mystery.*

(i) As Newman convincingly argues, the title τὸν κύριον τῆς δόξης (**the Lord of glory**), "which occurs nowhere else in the NT," does not depend on "Hellenistic religious speculation" but "should be read against the horizon of early Jewish apocalypses."[116] It forms part of the "throne vision" in such literature, and ἐν μυστηρίῳ (*in* or *by* **revealed mystery**) signals the visionary disclosure of the splendor of God, or in Paul, of God-in-Christ. This is confirmed by Paul's use of the verb ἀπεκάλυψεν, **revealed** (2:10), with διὰ τοῦ πνεύματος, **through the Spirit**. O'Neill rightly notes resonances with hiddenness and unveiling in passages of this kind.[117]

(ii) Newman follows Schniewind and Wink in asserting that Paul sets in contrast "two convictional paradigms — a wisdom of God . . . and a wisdom preferred by ἀρχόντων τοῦ αἰῶνος τούτου (2:6). In their own self-reliant claims to knowledge, gifts, and the Spirit, the Corinthians have been tricked into following *a false wisdom which actually still participates in a "this world" structure* [which] . . . *spells peril* . . ." (my italics).[118] By contrast, God's own wisdom reveals the crucified Christ as **Lord of glory**, i.e., exposes the "poverty" of the structures of **the present world order** as against the glorious radiancy (**glory**) of that which gives "weight" to Christ as the One who gives himself in pure love for others. (On **glory**, see the discussion of the term in v. 6, which supports this exegesis of v. 8.) Peter Stuhlmacher likewise sets out 1 Cor 2:6-16 as a single, coherent argument of this nature.[119]

(iii) "The very ones who were trying to do away with Jesus by crucifying him were in fact carrying out God's prior will."[120] What appeared to wreck God's purpose turns out, through its ignorance of higher purposes, to fulfill them. This blindness, which led to "the powers" being used for saving purposes against their intention, extended to all the corporate structures which stood behind the regimes which led to the crucifixion of Christ as the **Lord of glory**.

One or two points of grammar and syntax remain to be considered. First, **Lord of glory** belongs to a broader contrast in Paul in which **glory** relates to the cross (Gal 6:14). The phrase does not mean "the Lord who dispenses glory" (objective genitive, Augustine, *On the Trinity,* 1:12:24), nor is it a semiticism for "glorious Lord" (adjectival genitive). It means *"the Lord to whom glory belongs"* (genitive of quality), now defined in terms of the wonder of his self-giving in the cross.[121] The worlds divide on the question "self-glory or God's glory," but Jesus reveals God's glory as the glory of the self-giving of the cross

---

116. Newman, *Paul's Glory-Christology,* 236 and 237; see 235-40.

117. O'Neill, *Who Did Jesus Think He Was?* 42-54, 94-101.

118. Newman, *Paul's Glory-Christology,* 239; cf. 236-37 (and on Wink and Schniewind, see above).

119. P. Stuhlmacher, "The Hermeneutical Significance of 1 Cor. 2:6-16," in G. F. Hawthorne and O. Betz (eds.). *Tradition and Interpretation in the NT: Essays in Honour of E. Earle Ellis* (Tübingen: Mohr and Grand Rapids: Eerdmans, 1987), 328-47.

120. Fee, *First Epistle,* 106.

121. Edwards, *First Epistle,* 54.

"in a world intoxicated with its own [glory])."[122] The cross is a triumph which manifests Jesus as **Lord of glory**, for through the cross he absorbed and draws out the sting of death and of the powers (1 Cor. 15:55). The Son is glorified, Stauffer urges, "on Good Friday itself."[123]

Second, the form ἔγνωκεν (v. 8a) (perfect active of γινώσκω), refers to a hypothetical state of knowledge which would have been based on some prior disclosure. The second use of the same verb occurs in the aorist active indicative as the protasis of a conditional sentence: ἔγνωσαν: **if they had known**, i.e., if there had occurred such an event of disclosure (which in the event did not occur), they would not have crucified. . . . If they had had access to God's wisdom which decreed the effects of the cross, or indeed could have known that the cross formed a central place in God's wise purposes, they would not have lent their aid unwittingly to furthering these purposes. *There can scarcely be a clearer statement in Scripture that the cross was no unfortunate historical accident; a mere act of bravery* or political martyrdom *later* turned to good account.

9 The last relative pronoun (accusative before ἡτοίμασεν) is ὅσα in A, B, and a few other MSS, but ἅ in p[46], ℵ, C, D, F, G. On the complex syntax see below.

On the syntax of the Greek of this verse Conzelmann declares, "All attempts to rescue the construction of the sentence are to no purpose."[124] He equally despairs of any way of identifying the quotation. Virtually a special study is devoted to the syntax in Bo Frid's article "The Enigmatic ΑΛΛΑ in 1 Cor. 2:9."[125] Frid calls attention to the three recognized difficulties which have bequeathed to exegetes a variety of possible reconstructions.

(i) The verse lacks a main verb, unless the second use of ἅ (v. 9b) is regarded as representing ὅσα, and ὅσα is interpreted as a pronoun of measure or of degree, as in our translation **how very much**. In this case **God prepared** becomes the main verb. But probably most writers view ἅ in v. 9b as a relative pronoun, meaning *what* **God prepared**.

(ii) Further, the first use of the neuter plural relative pronoun ἅ in v. 9a (translated **what**) performs a double function: it serves as neuter plural *accusative* in relation to the verbs οὐκ εἶδεν, **did not see**, and οὐκ ἤκουσεν, **did not hear**; on the other hand, it appears to function as a neuter plural *nominative* in relation to οὐκ ἀνέβη, *what did not enter the human heart* (translated, for reasons which we shall explain, as **what no human heart conceived**).

(iii) Problems remain regarding the function of the introductory word ἀλλά, normally *but,* translated above as **However**. Frid calls it "enigmatic" because once its contrastive force has been granted, exegetes differ in locating the semantic or rhetorical opposition. Frid argues that this presents such an obsta-

122. Stauffer, *NT Theology,* 121 and 122; cf. 120-33.
123. Ibid., 130.
124. Conzelmann, *1 Corinthians,* 64.
125. Frid, "The Enigmatic ἀλλά in 1 Cor. 2:9," 603-11.

cle as to render the shape of the grammar "almost hopeless" for most commentators. Heinrici perceived the contrast as lying with ἣν οὐδεὶς . . . ἔγνωκεν, *which no one . . . had come to know;* Weiss relates the contrast back to v. 6, mainly between two wisdoms; Allo, probably more convincingly, refers it to λαλοῦμεν, **we speak**.[126] Thus λαλοῦμεν comes to function as the main verb: *We speak . . . what God prepared. . . .*

Frid suggests that the grammar becomes simple and straightforward as soon as we recognize that Paul uses indirect communication through "an elliptical mode of expression."[127] The fundamental contrast expressed by ἀλλά, *but* or **however**, lies between the ignorance of the "powers" and the knowledge that "we know": the missing main verb to be supplied is [ταῦτα] ἐγνώκαμεν, *we have come to know these things.* "Paul in his liveliness leaves this aside and leaps to the statement in v. 10a, connected by γάρ, which gives the reason why it is possible actually to have knowledge of a divine and hidden wisdom."[128]

This interpretation remains perfectly possible and is our second preference if our suggestion fails. But the ambiguity of the two uses of the relative pronouns ἅ, **what** (v. 9a) and probably **how very much** (v. 9b), can be explained. The first use may derive part of its force from the Semitic idiom which lies behind the third phrase. Thus ἅ, **what** (things) functions as an accusative in **what eye did not see** and in **what ear did not hear**, but also as subject or nominative.[129] But the phrase ἐπὶ καρδίαν ἀνθρώπου οὐκ ἀνέβη (lit. *did not go up onto the human heart*) reflects the oral idiom of the Hebrew עלה על לב (*'alah 'al lebh*) to go up onto the heart, i.e. *to enter human thought,* or *to arise on a human agenda.* Although technically Paul uses a Greek surface structure in which the pronoun ἅ, **what**, is forced into the nominative, the deep structure of logic reflects an idiom in which the word takes the place of an implied accusative: **what no human heart conceived**, because a merely *human* agenda gave no place to it. In Hebrew *heart* (לב, *lebh*) includes both "mind" and will to decide, as well as the depths which embody preconscious (or secret) attitudes. Hence we retain **heart** as broader than the English *mind.*

The remaining use of ἅ, strictly *what,* in v. 9b, may well, as many older commentators believe, reflect ὅσα, the neuter plural of ὅσος, which might also be the original reading since it is found in B as well as A. But although ὅσος may mean *how great* or *how far,* BAGD list many instances of its meaning *how much, as much,* or as an indicator of degree (although admittedly usually with τοσοῦτο).[130] Moulton-Milligan cite more fluid uses in the papyri shortly after

---

126. Heinrici, *Das erste Sendschreiben,* 95-100; Weiss, *Der erste Korintherbrief,* 57-58; Allo, *Première Épitre,* 43-44.

127. Frid, "The Enigmatic ἀλλά," 606.

128. Ibid., 607-8.

129. Merklein, *Der erste Brief 1–4,* 232-33, but earlier also in Lightfoot, *Notes,* 176; BDF, sect. 4 (subheading 2 and n. 4), and further in E. Norden, *Die antike Kunstprosa,* 2 Nachtr. 3. They compare the phrase "the thought came to him."

130. BAGD, 586, categorize the word (1) "of space and time"; (2) of quantity and number;

Paul: in papyri shortly after the end of the first century, ὅσα may virtually mean *all*.[131] *Either* (i) we must settle for ὅσα (whether or not represented by ἅ) used as minor ellipses (without, e.g., τοσοῦτο) to function as an exclamation (**how much**) or to mean something like *so much; or* (ii) we must follow Frid's suggestion of supplying *we know; or* (iii) with Conzelmann we must admit defeat and assume that Paul's language drifts into a broken construction. For English to make sense, we probably need **how very much** followed by an exclamation mark.

The form τοῖς ἀγαπῶσιν, is the dative of advantage. Anders Nygren notes how seldom in Paul God becomes the object of ἀγάπη, *love*.[132] It may well be no accident that the only two or three counterexamples (Rom. 8:28; 1 Cor. 2:9; and 8:3) take the verbal, dynamic form as "in progress," in parallel to Paul's more positive use of the verb γινώσκειν, *to know* (God), as against the negative connotations of γνῶσις, to have acquired *knowledge* (of God) as a state which can be "objectified" or "used."[133] The reason for Paul's "direction of flow," Nygren perceptively comments, is that God's own love remains spontaneous, unmotivated by anything outside himself, creative, elective and free, whereas on the contrary human love of God is motivated by the experience of God's love. Hence it has limitations which Paul escapes by usually speaking of trust or faith when this is "toward God."[134]

The difficult problem of identifying Paul's quotation (if this is even possible) remains. Clement of Rome (AD 96) implies that Paul cites the LXX of Isa 64:4 (LXX 64:3). *1 Clement* 34:8 repeats almost exactly Paul's words from Ὀφθαλμὸς οὐκ εἶδεν *(eye did not see)* to ὅσα *(sic)* ἡτοίμασεν *(how much he prepared),* adding κύριος and replacing τοῖς ἀγαπῶσιν αὐτόν with τοῖς ὑπομένουσιν αὐτόν, *what the Lord prepared for those who wait for him.* Lightfoot compares this with a further minor variant in Polycarp, and proposes that an original lay "somewhere between the present LXX rendering in Isaiah and the quotation of St. Paul, though nearer to the latter."[135] The LXX runs ἀπὸ τοῦ αἰῶνος οὐκ ἠκούσαμεν οὐδὲ οἱ ὀφθαλμοὶ ἡμῶν εἶδον θεὸν πλὴν σοῦ καὶ τὰ ἔργα σοῦ. . . . "From eternity *we* did not hear and *our* eyes did not see *God* . . ." as against the Hebrew "*they* have not heard . . . eye has not seen a god." The He-

---

(3) of measure and degree, with καθ' ὅσον πλείονα (Ignatius, *To the Ephesians,* 6:1; cf. Heb 3:3 with κατὰ τοσοῦτο, but without τοσοῦτο in Polybius, 4.42.5, "to the degree that . . .").

131. MM, 461. It certainly covers an *exclamatory* sentence, e.g., "How much trouble I had!" (*Tebtunis Papyrus* 2:378:22, ὅσον κάματον ἤνεγκα: "From this *it is an easy transition to practically the meaning "all,"* as in *Oxyrhynchus Papyrus* 6:898:13 *(ad 123)"* (my italics).

132. A. Nygren, *Agape and Eros* (Eng. trans., London: SPCK, in one volume 1953), 124; cf. 123-33.

133. Ibid., 124, n. 1, and 133-45.

134. Ibid., 125-26; cf. 67-70 and 75-81. This is a *theological* comment on a given *context, not* a defense of some simplistic comments on the Greek word, which have received legitimate criticism. See also J. Moffatt, *Love in the NT* (New York: R. R. Smith, 1930), 154-58; and C. Spicq, under 1 Corinthians 13, below.

135. Lightfoot, *Notes,* 177.

brew idiom of עלה על לב ('alah 'al lebh, lit. "go up onto the heart") occurs in the Greek not here but in Isa. 65:17: οὐκ ἀναβήσεται αὐτῶν ἐπὶ τὴν καρδίαν . . . , but the tense in this second passage is future, not aorist, and it includes αὐτῶν, their. Hence the widespread suggestion that Paul combines Isa 64:4 and 65:17, although possible, seems too imprecise for certainty, even if Paul does combine various quotations in a catena or free collection elsewhere (e.g., in Rom 3:10-18).

Origen believed that Paul's quotation comes from the *Apocalypse of Elijah,* according to his *Commentary on Matthew* (on 5:29). His *Fragments* on 1 Corinthians contain no suggestion about the quotation, and the only reference to the quotation in other works is his use of Paul's words to indicate the glory of the resurrection mode of existence, without reference to any other source.[136] Origen excludes a source within the traditional Hebrew canon ("only in the apocryphon of Elijah"). Clearly the quotation becomes widespread in Christian literature. Jerome, e.g., quotes it several times.[137] It appears in *Ascension of Isaiah* 8:11, a Jewish writing of the first and/or second centuries, but from 3:13 to the end of ch. 11 Christian editing and insertions make the origin of any material in ch. 8 uncertain.

Various speculative suggestions have been made by modern writers. E. von Nordheim proposed a citation from the *Testament of Jacob,* but H. F. D. Sparks and O. Hofius offer several counterarguments, with Sparks concluding that Isa 64:4 offers a more probable alternative.[138] Klaus Berger considers a range of apocalyptic sources, concluding that their field of thought coheres with the notion of God's "preparing" a destiny and "revealing" what is "secret."[139] M. Stone and J. Strugnell argue for an allusion to the *Apocalypse of Elijah.*[140] But only two less speculative possibilities remain. Either Paul begins **It is written** with a phrase or two from Isa 64:4 and 65:17 in mind and then departs from his text, or he offers only allusive resonances which we cannot identify. This would not exclude Kistemaker's proposal to include an allusion to Jer 3:16 with Isa 65:17 and 64:3 (LXX), or Lightfoot's proposals about a variant text in Isa 64:4.[141] Stanley states that the various "solutions" are well documented but all too precarious to meet with widespread approval. To determine the actual text from which Paul quotes "would be presumptuous."[142]

---

136. Origen, *De Principiis,* 3:6:4.

137. Jerome, *Letters,* 3:1 (to Rufinus); 22:4 (to Eustochium); and "Epistola ad Corinthios prima," in Migne, *PL,* 29:785 (including his allusion to the *Ascension of Isaiah*).

138. Von Nordheim, "Das Zitat des Paulus in Kor. 2:9 und seine Beziehung zum koptischen Testament Jakobs," 112-20; criticized by Sparks, "1 Kor. 2:9: A Quotation from the Coptic Testament of Jacob?" 269-76; and Hofius, "Das Zitat 1 Kor 2:9 und das koptische Testament des Jakob," 140-42.

139. Berger, "Zur Diskussion über die Herkunft von 1 Kor. 2:9," 270-83, esp. 278-79.

140. M. Stone and J. Strugnell, *The Books of Elijah,* SBLTT 18 (Missoula: Scholars Press, 1979).

141. Kistemaker, *1 Corinthians,* 85.

142. Stanley, *Paul and the Language of Scripture,* 189.

Probably we have "a pastiche of biblical allusions," including Isa 64:3, which underscore "the radical divide between what humans can know *kata anthrōpon* and the divine mystery known only to God and to those to whom God chooses to reveal it."[143] "The quotation is widespread and occurs in divergent types of material."[144]

b. The Work of the Holy Spirit as Revealer: But of What? (2:10-16)

The following two verses (vv. 10-11) are the most plausible to ascribe to a rejoinder from those elements at Corinthians who appealed to a special wisdom for the inner circle of "spiritual people," if any of the verses are to be understood in this way, together with vv. 13, 15, and perhaps also v. 14. We cannot be certain whether or not Paul is directly quoting their own theological defense, before giving the argument a decisive term with his own decisive reinterpretation of their language in 2:12, 2:16, and 3:1-3.

If the words are Paul's own, however, he stands as close as he can to the terminology of the group at Corinth whom he here addresses, but shows through his utterances in vv. 12, 16 and 3:1-3 that these terms depend for their currency and validity on (i) a thorough appreciation of the nature of God as Other who is not to be transposed into an instrument for self-esteem and self-affirmation (v. 12a); on (ii) an appreciation of God's revelation of himself as sheer gift (v. 12b); or (iii) the christological criterion and definition of "spirituality" or Spirit — revelation (v. 16); and on the redefining of "maturity" (οἱ τέλειοι) in terms of ethical and christological criteria concerning what is "infantile" (ὡς νηπίοις) and what is Christlike (3:1-3). If we grant that these verses decisively identify *Paul's corrective redefinition of "spirituality"* at Corinth, it ceases to remain critical whether vv. 10, 11, 13, 14, and 15 reflect quotations from Corinthian theology, or Paul's bending over backward to endorse as much as he can within the redefining frame of vv. 12, 16 and 3:1-3. B. A. Pearson sums it up: "Paul is accommodating himself to the opponents' terminology, but is radically re-interpreting it."[145]

Bibliography on 2:10-16

Bruner, F. D., *A Theology of the Holy Spirit* (Grand Rapids: Eerdmans, 1970), 267-71.
Bultmann, R., *Theology of the NT* (Eng. trans., London: SCM, 1952), 1:153-64, 190-226, and 330-40.
Davis, J. A., *Wisdom and Spirit* (Lanham, Md.: University Press of America, 1984), 97-131.
Dunn, J. D. G., *Jesus and the Spirit* (London: SCM, 1975), 287-97.

143. Collins, *First Cor,* 132.
144. Pearson, *Pneumatikos-Psychikos,* 34; cf. Schrage, *Der erste Brief,* 1:255-56.
145. Pearson, *The Pneumatikos-Psychikos,* 40.

————, "Spirit, Spiritual," *NIDNTT*, 3:700-707 (cf. 693-700).

————, *The Theology of Paul the Apostle* (Edinburgh: T. & T. Clark, 1998), 413-41.

Ellis, E. E., "Christ and Spirit in 1 Corinthians," in Barnabas Lindars and S. S. Smalley (eds.), *Christ and Spirit in the NT: Studies in Honour of Charles F. D. Moule* (Cambridge: Cambridge University Press, 1973), 269-77; rpt. in Ellis, *Prophecy and Hermeneutic* (Grand Rapids: Eerdmans, 1978), 63-71.

————, *Prophecy and Hermeneutic* (cited above), 23-44, 213-20 (also 63-71 above).

Fichtner, J., "Seele oder Leben in der Bibel," *TZ* 17 (1961): 305-18.

Gaffin, R. B., Jr., "Some Epistemological Reflections on 1 Cor 2:6-16," *WTJ* 57 (1995): 103-24.

Gärtner, B., "The Philosophical Principle 'Like by Like' in Paul and John," *NTS* 14 (1968): 209-31.

Hamilton, N. Q., *The Holy Spirit and Eschatology in St. Paul,* SJT Occasional Papers (Edinburgh: Oliver & Boyd, 1957).

Haykin, M. A. G., "'A Sense of Awe in the Presence of the Ineffable': 1 Cor. 2:11-12 in the Pneumatomachian Controversy of the Fourth Century," *SJT* 41 (1988): 341-57.

————, *The Spirit of God:. The Exegesis of 1 and 2 Corinthians in the Pneumato-machian Controversy of the Fourth Century,* VCSup 27 (Leiden: Brill, 1994), esp. 78-83.

————, "'The Spirit of God': The Exegesis of 1 Cor. 2:10-12 by Origen and Athanasius," *SJT* 36 (1982): 513-28.

Hermann, I., *Kyrios und Pneuma* (Munich: Kösel, 1961).

Hill, David, *Greek Words and Hebrew Meanings,* SNTSMS 5 (Cambridge: Cambridge University Press, 1967), 282-84 (on 1 Corinthians 2); cf. 265-85 (on the Spirit in Paul).

Horsley, R. A., "Pneumatikos vs. Psychikos: Distinctions of Spiritual Status among the Corinthians," *HTR* 69 (1976): 269-88.

————, "Wisdom of Words and Words of Wisdom in Corinth," *CBQ* 39 (1977): 224-39.

Hoyle, R. B., *The Holy Spirit in St. Paul* (London: Hodder & Stoughton, 1927).

Jewett, Robert, *Paul's Anthropological Terms* (Leiden: Brill, 1971), 167-97 and 391-401.

Lampe, G. W. H., "The Holy Spirit and the Person of Christ," in S. W. Sykes and J. P. Clayton (eds.), *Christ, Faith and History* (Cambridge: Cambridge University Press, 1972), 111-30.

Lampe, P., "Theological Wisdom and the 'Word about the Cross': The Rhetorical Scheme in 1 Cor. 1–4," *Int* 44 (1990): 117-31.

Lin, Hong-Hsin, *Die Person des Heiligen Geistes als Thema der Pneumatologie in der reformierten Theologie* (Frankfurt: Land, 1998), 234-45.

Martin, Dale B., *The Corinthian Body* (New Haven: Yale University Press, 1995), 61-65 and 96-102.

Meyer, P., "The Holy Spirit in the Pauline Letters: A Contextual Explanation," *Int* 33 (1979): 3-18.

Moltmann, J., *The Spirit of Life* (Eng. trans., London: SCM, 1992), 31-37, 142-47, 217-29, 270-89.

North, J. L., "'Human Speech' in Paul and the Paulines," *NovT* 37 (1995): 50-67.

Painter, J., "Paul and the πνευματικοί at Corinth," in M. D. Hooker and S. G. Wilson (eds.), *Paul and Paulinism: Essays in Honour of C. K. Barrett* (London: SPCK, 1982), 237-50.

Pearson, Birger A., *The Pneumatikos-Psychikos Terminology in 1 Corinthians: A Study in the Theology of the Corinthian Opponents of Paul and Its Relation to Gnosticism,* SBLDS 12 (Missoula: Scholars Press, 1973).

Reiling, J. "Wisdom and the Spirit: An Exegesis of 1 Cor 2:6-16," in T. Baarda et al. (eds.), *Text and Testimony: Essays in Honour of A. F. J. Klijn* (Kampen: Kok, 1988), 200-211.

Robinson, H. Wheeler, *The Christian Experience of the Holy Spirit* (London: Nisbet. 1928), 62-80 and 223-45.

Schweizer, E., "πνεῦμα," *TDNT,* 6:332-455 (on Paul, 415-37, and on 1 Cor. 2:6-16, 425-27).

———, "Zur Trichotomie von 1 Thess. 5:23 und der Unterscheidung des πνευματικόν vom ψυχικόν in 1 Kor. 2:14; 15:44; Jak. 3:15; Jud. 19," *TZ* 9 (1953): 76-77.

Scott, E. F., *The Spirit in the NT* (London: Hodder & Stoughton, 1923), 165-86.

Scroggs, R., "Paul, Σοφός and Πνευματικός," *NTS* 14 (1967): 33-55.

Stacey, W. D., *The Pauline View of Man* (London: Macmillan, 1956), 121-80 and 211-14.

Stalder, K., *Das Werk des Geistes in der Heiligung bei Paulus* (Zurich: Evangelischer Verlag Zurich, 1962).

Swete, H. B., *The Holy Spirit in the Ancient Church* (London: Macmillan, 1912), 233-39, 244-47, and 266-70.

———, *The Holy Spirit in the NT* (London: Macmillan [1909], 1921), 176-83 and 284-91.

Stuhlmacher, Peter, "The Hermeneutical Significance of 1 Cor. 2:6-16," in G. F. Hawthorne and O. Betz (eds.), *Tradition and Interpretation in the NT: Essays in Honor of E. Earle Ellis* (Tübingen: Mohr and Grand Rapids: Eerdmans, 1987), 328-47.

Theissen, Gerd, *Psychological Aspects of Pauline Theology* (Eng. trans., Edinburgh: T. & T. Clark, 1987), 343-93.

Toussaint, S. D., "The Spiritual Man," *BSac* 125 (168): 139-46.

Whiteley, D. E. H., *The Theology of St. Paul* (Oxford: Blackwell, 1974), 31-44 and 124-28.

Willis, Wendell L., "The 'Mind of Christ' in 1 Cor. 2:16," *Bib* 70 (1989): 110-22.

Winter, M., *Pneumatiker und Psychiker in Korinth. Zum religionsgeschichtlichen Hintergrund von 1 Kor. 2:6–3:4,* Marburger theologische Studien 12 (Marburg: Elwert, 1975).

10 (1) The UBS *Greek New Testament* (4th ed.) reads δέ in v. 10 in spite of the fact that the early 𝔓46 and B, as well as Clement, read γάρ. Metzger argues that γάρ appears to represent a supposed "improvement" in Paul's flow of argument introduced by early copyists, and Zuntz also prefers δέ.[146] The editors of the 4th ed. describe their reading as "almost certain" (i.e., B.). In the 3d ed., however, the editors both had evaluated the reading as B, "some degree of doubt," and classified the reading as old "C," i.e., "a considerable degree of doubt," since δέ is supported by ℵ, A, and C against 𝔓46 and B. Although in the end little of substance may turn on this difference, the variation may also indicate an original possibility of a Corinthian quotation which Paul anticipates, i.e.,

146. Metzger, *Textual Commentary* (2d ed. 1994), 481; and Zuntz, *Text,* 205.

"But God has provided a revelation for us through the Spirit. For the Spirit searches all things, even 'the deep things' of God." On the other hand, γάρ makes the language clearly Paul's own (unless v. 9 is also part of a longer quotation).[147] The safest course for the translator is to follow the NRSV in offering no English equivalent, as against (i) *but* (NIV, AV/KJV, Luther) or (ii) *for* (NEB) or *and* (REB). NJB, *to us, though,* is a good second choice. (2) The variant readings which include αὐτοῦ, *his,* after πνεύματος, *Spirit,* cause less difficulty. The UBS 4th ed. is right to omit αὐτοῦ from the text, since it does not appear in 𝔓46, ℵ (first hand), A, B, C, and a probable reading of 33. In a later corrector of ℵ, the Old Latin and most miniscules, the addition of αὐτοῦ was clarification. Had the word *his* been original, it is difficult to understand both its lack of early support and why it should have been omitted.

If v. 10 embodies Paul's own thought, ἡμῖν, **to us,** refers back to **those who love him** in v. 9 and not to some inner esoteric circle of a privileged category within the church.[148] If the verse reflects thought at Corinth, the ἡμῖν (**to us**) comes first in word order as an emphatic claim: "But it is *to us* that God has revealed . . . the deepest secrets. . . ." If Paul speaks for himself, or if he puts his own construction on a favorite Corinthian theme, the pronoun remains emphatic, but is so because of awe and wonder at God's free choice to bestow such favor. Hence we have tried to capture a degree of emphasis by postponing the pronoun to the end of the clause: **God has revealed these things through his Spirit to us!**

Paul has already referred to **the Spirit** (πνεῦμα) in 2:4 in conjunction with *power* (ἐν ἀποδείξει πνεύματος καὶ δυνάμεως). The word now dominates the thought of our passage (vv. 10, 11, 12, 13, 14), introducing πνευματικός, the adjective *appertaining to the Spirit,* usually ambiguously translated *spiritual* in vv. 13 and 15, with the adverbial form πνευματικῶς *(in a way that relates to the Spirit,* or *spiritually)* additionally in v. 14. As a noun or adjective it occurs in every verse up to the christological definition or qualification of πνεῦμα in v. 16. It is crucial to distinguish between πνεῦμα (**Spirit** or *spirit*) as a Pauline reference to the Holy Spirit or to the Spirit of God from Paul's references to the human spirit or to Stoic or gnostic uses of *spirit* and *spiritual.*[149] This is the point of Paul's emphasis on the divine transcendence of the Spirit in v. 12 as τὸ πνεῦμα τὸ ἐκ τοῦ θεοῦ, **the Spirit from God,** as against "spiritual capacities" in human beings.[150] This becomes critical in 1 Corinthians 15, where *spiritual*

147. See discussion by Frid, "The Enigmatic ἀλλά in 1 Cor 2:9," 603-11 (discussed above under v. 9), of which this subsequent decision forms part.

148. Schrage, *Der erste Brief,* 256.

149. Hoyle, *The Holy Spirit in St. Paul,* 182; cf. Stacey, *The Pauline View of Man,* 128-29; J. D. G. Dunn, *Baptism in the Holy Spirit* (1970), 103; Swete, *The Holy Spirit in the NT,* 169-223; Robinson, *The Christian Experience of the Holy Spirit,* 1-21, 223-45; E. Schweizer, "πνεῦμα," *TDNT,* 6:415-37 (also translated as *Spirit of God,* 54-87); and many other comparable works.

150. Variations in Paul's own uses and exegetical difficulties abound. Does τῷ πνεύματι ζέοντες (Rom 12:11) mean "fervent in spirit" (AV/KJV) or "be aglow with the spirit?" (RSV, NEB), as is far more likely. Another problematic set of passages concerns the so-called psychological uses of πνεῦμα in, e.g., "spirit of bondage" (Rom 8:13), although "Spirit of holiness" (Rom 1:4) and "Spirit of adoption" (Rom 8:15) probably refer to the Holy Spirit. Sometimes Paul uses "be with

body means the *total mode of existence governed by the Spirit* (15:44, σῶμα πνευματικόν).

"Verses 10-16 . . . make up his [Paul's] first sustained reflection on the Spirit," especially as the source of revelation.[151] This section sets a framework for later material on the Holy Spirit in 1 Corinthians 12–14 as well as in the resurrection chapter (15:42-57; cf. 15:12-28, 38-41). In all these passages the work of the Spirit remains inseparable from the work of God as revealed in Christ. By contrast, a wedge was driven by some at Corinth between "spirituality" and Christ crucified. Bultmann convincingly concludes that when he uses πνεῦμα in its most characteristic Pauline sense, Paul always means "divine power that stands in contrast to all that is human," not "spirit" (Germ. *Geist*) in the sense of the inner self of Platonic dualism.[152] Likewise for Schweizer, to be "spiritual" is to appropriate God's saving work through Christ by God's Spirit.[153]

The possibility of an unfortunate ambiguity goes back to Heb. רוח *(ruach)*, which πνεῦμα translates in the LXX. Since *ruach* can mean *breath,* the word has often been understood *immanentally,* as within human persons. But the meaning of *ruach* as *wind* stresses the *transcendent,* powerful element which operates *upon* human persons and which they cannot control or even clearly predict, as Jesus emphasizes to Nicodemus in the wordplay of John 3:8: τὸ πνεῦμα blows where it wills . . . so is everyone who has been born ἐκ τοῦ πνεύματος. Of its OT context Snaith comments that through God's Spirit people can "do those things which of themselves and in their own strength they are incapable of doing."[154] When the Spirit of God gives Israel "rest" in Isa 63:14, this means that his strong warrior-Spirit keeps their cattle secure from marauding bands.

The parallel thought occurs here. Human persons cannot search out the hidden things of God unaided, through their own limited resources of wisdom, knowledge, or stance. The verb ἀπεκάλυψεν is the aorist, not the perfect, of ἀποκαλύπτω, *I reveal, I disclose, I uncover,* and alludes to God's act of removing any barrier which keeps the content of his predetermined purpose secret (v. 9). The associated activity ascribed to God's Spirit by means of the verb ἐραυνάω (third present indicative ἐραυνᾷ, the Alexandrian spelling of the classical ἐρευνάω, ἐρευνᾷ) does not mean searching to discover here, but the activity of exploring God's purposes thoroughly in order to reveal them.[155] Hence Barrett's translation **searches out** is better here than *searches* (NRSV, NIV). The NJB and REB *explores* is equally acceptable.

---

your spirit" to mean no more than "be with you" (Phil 4:23; Philem 25). Weiss rightly sees 1 Cor 2:12 as representing a deliberate distancing by Paul of his own use of πνεῦμα from that of the stoics.

151. Collins, *First Cor,* 132; similarly, Wolff, *Der erste Brief,* 58-59.

152. Bultmann, *Theology of the NT,* 1:153.

153. Schweizer, "πνεῦμα," *TDNT,* 6:436 37 (also *Spirit of God,* 87).

154. N. Snaith, V. Taylor, et al., *The Doctrine of the Holy Spirit* (London: Epworth, 1937), 11. Cf. also C. H. Powell, *Biblical Concept of Power,* 26.

155. See Schrage, *Der erste Brief,* 1:257-58.

The term τὰ βάθη has also invited various translations. The traditional rendering *the deep things* (retained by NIV) depends on taking the neuter plural overliterally. Most English VSS render the word **the depths** (NRSV, NJB, REB, TEV). However, TEV continues further by adding to the genitive τοῦ θεοῦ, **depths of God's purposes**; and REV and NEB, **depths of God's own** *nature;* while NJB, NRSV, and NIV reflect the Greek structure and vocabulary with *of God.* The translation **depths** *of God* cannot be wrong, but v. 11 suggests an analogy that turns on knowledge *of the self.* The REB probably therefore construes Paul's sense as v. 11 explicates it, but the phrase *God's own nature* may suggest metaphysical attributes more akin to Western tradition than to Paul. Perhaps the most neutral and open way of capturing the point is to translate **the depths of God's own self**. God's amazing graciousness is but his very selfhood become exposed to human view **to those who love him** (v. 9) **through his Spirit** (διά + genitive). Nothing lies beyond or beneath God's own selfhood: "**The depths of God** is a comprehensive concept for the ungroundedness *(Unergründliche)* of God," i.e., God is "grounded in" nothing beyond his own selfhood.[156] Today we might speak of the Spirit's revealing *God's inmost heart,* which gives precisely the christological focus toward which Paul is working in 2:16.

11 A superficial reading out of context would suggest that Paul adopts two uncharacteristic standpoints: (i) that he accepts a dualist-Platonic view of human nature as spirit within a human body, or, as Gilbert Ryle dubbed the dualist view, "the ghost in the machine"; and (ii) that he argues on the basis of a natural correspondence between human spirit/human person, and divine Spirit/God, as if **spirit**, πνεῦμα, embodied a natural continuity between the two instantiations of the term.[157] If such a reading were valid, then this would strengthen the argument that the verse represents either a quotation from a piece of Corinthian theology or a post-Pauline editorial interpolation. However, on closer inspection the verse need not, and almost certainly should not, be interpreted in this way.

Admittedly the structure of the Greek word order suggests the translation *For who of human persons* (the fourth word ἀνθρώπων, *of human persons,* must be construed with τίς, *who*) *knows* (strictly a perfect tense meaning *has come to know,* i.e., now *knows*) *the things* (τά, *the affairs*) *of the human being* (genitive singular) *except the spirit of the human person that is within* (τὸ ἐν αὐτῷ, *the within-the-self one*)? But Paul uses spatial language of the human person to indicate *modes or aspects of being.*[158] *The spirit* is *within* not in the sense of loca-

---

156. Wolff, *Der erste Brief,* 58. It is possible that "the depths of Satan" (Rev 2:24) denotes not esoteric satanic knowledge, but a belief in Satan's ontological independence of God, hence a dualist metaphysical system.

157. Gilbert Ryle, *The Concept of Mind* (London: Hutchinson, 1949; Penguin ed. 1963), ch. 1 and throughout.

158. See the detailed discussion of Paul's avoidance of a dualism of inner and outer "parts" of the human person, and the to-and-fro of the history of research into Paul's view of the human

tion, but in the sense of partly hidden stances *of which an outsider or another human person may be unaware unless the person concerned chooses to reveal them by word, gesture, or action.* The point of analogy does *not* turn on human spirit within/divine spirit within, but on the possession of an *exclusive initiative to reveal one's thoughts, counsels, stance, attitudes, intentions,* or whatever else is *"within" in the sense of hidden from the public domain, not* in the sense of *location.*

To insist upon this, as indeed we do, is not to impose modern psychology onto Paul. Indeed, it is the very reverse. It rescues our understanding of Paul from an uncritical embeddedness in a Graeco-Roman tradition which was alien to Paul's OT roots and worldview. As numerous writers over the last fifty years have rightly urged, the largely nineteenth-century idealist view of Lüdemann and others that "human spirit" was a central anthropological category for Paul is simply false.[159] The human spirit is not a "God-related principle of self-consciousness within man which could be directed by the divine spirit to moral activity in opposition to the flesh."[160] Jewett comments: "This conception so dominated exegesis in the latter part of the last century that even scholars who stood in opposition to the liberal theology accepted it. . . . 'Spirit' was not a philosophic category providing continuity between God and man."[161]

In a different tradition from Athanasius to Barth this verse has been understood, rightly, as indicating that, in Barth's words, the issue "God is known through God alone."[162] Athanasius explicitly quotes 1 Cor 2:11-12 and comments, "What kinship could there be, judging by the above [i.e., vv. 11 and 12], between **the Spirit** and the creatures? . . . God is Being (ὤν ἐστιν) and the Spirit is from him (ἐξ οὗ). That which is from God (ἐκ τοῦ θεοῦ) could not be from that which is not (ἐκ τοῦ μὴ ὄντος)."[163] The logic of Paul's thought is that if, by

---

constitution or personhood in Robert Jewett's masterly work *Paul's Anthropological Terms: A Study of Their Use in Conflict Settings,* esp. 167-97 (on πνεῦμα, *spirit*) and 391-401 (on ἔσω/ἔξω ἄνθρωπος, "inner"/"outer man"). See further Bultmann, *Theology of the NT,* 1:153-64, 190-226, and 330-40; Whiteley, *The Theology of St. Paul,* 31-44; cf. 126-28; Robinson, *The Body,* 7-33; and esp. Theissen, *Psychological Aspects,* 356-93.

159. See H. Lüdemann, *Die Anthropologie des Apostels Paulus und ihre Stellung innerhalb seiner Heilslehre* (Kiel: University Press, 1872), 49. With Lüdemann we may also compare the idealist-dualist interpretations of Otto Pfleiderer, *Paulinism* (Germ., 1873; Eng. trans.; 2 vols., London, 1877); Willibald Beyschlag, *NT Theology* (Germ., vol. 2, Halle, 1896; Eng. trans., 2 vols., Edinburgh: T. & T. Clark); and H. J. Holtzmann, *Lehrbuch der Neutestamentlichen Theologie* (Tübingen, n.d.). For an overview cf. Jewett, "History of Research," in *Paul's Anthropological Terms,* and A. Schweitzer, *Paul and His Interpreters* (Eng. trans., London: Black, 1912 and 1956), "From Baur to Holtzmann," 22-99.

160. Jewett, *Paul's Anthropological Terms,* 167.

161. Ibid., 168. See further Schrage, *Der erste Brief,* 2:258-59; Merklein, *Der erste Brief 1–4,* 236-37.

162. Barth, *CD,* 2/1, sect. 27, 179.

163. Athanasius, *Letter to Serapion,* 1:22 (also Migne, *PG,* 26:581). For a recent account of exegetical issues relating to knowledge cf. Gaffin, "Some Epistemological Reflections on 1 Cor 2:6-16," 103-24, esp. 112-13 on vv. 11-14.

analogy, one person cannot know the least accessible aspects of another human being unless that person is willing to place them in the public domain, even so we cannot expect that God's own thought's, God's own purposes, God's own qualities, or God's own self could be open to scrutiny unless his spirit makes them accessible by an act of unveiling them. Athanasius makes this still clearer when he expounds ἐκ τοῦ θεοῦ, **from God**, in v. 12.[164]

Given this theological context, how are we to translate and to understand τὰ τοῦ θεοῦ, variously translated *the things of God* (AV/KJV); *the thoughts of God* (Moffatt, NIV); *the hidden depths of God's purposes* (TEV); *"what is truly God's"* (NRSV); *what God is* (REB); and *the qualities of God* (NJB). We have tried to avoid offering a translation which makes the English more specific and narrow than the Greek, while avoiding rendering the neuter plural of the definite article by the banal *things* or *affairs*. In this context *what pertains to God* points toward the REB or the NJB meaning (which is probable but not explicit) of that which makes God what he is, i.e., his character or Godhood, but also leaving open room for *purposes, thoughts,* and *depths,* none of which can be excluded. The corresponding term of the analogy then becomes **what pertains to the human person in view**, noting that the term is a singular noun made specific by the definite article (in the genitive). In order to convey the positive nuances of πνεῦμα, *spirit,* as that which is *within* carefully defined above, but without the baggage of dualist idealism, we have translated **except that person's innermost self** for εἰ μὴ τὸ πνεῦμα τοῦ ἀνθρώπου τὸ ἐν αὐτῷ (articular genitive singular with explicative adjectival phrase).[165]

The task of translation here takes us beyond linguistics, lexicography, and grammar to judgments of theology, hermeneutics, and rhetorical-historical reconstruction, without which there would *be* no "text" to be discussed "in its own right." We cannot avoid asking: Is this a piece of Corinthian theology, or is it Paul's, or is Paul trying to borrow back their terminology in order to redefine it, as Pearson convincingly argues? Answers to these questions will largely determine translation, in addition to a hermeneutical sensitivity toward diverse understandings of *spirit* in Hebrew-Pauline, Platonic-hellenistic, modern Western, and quasi-postmodern anti-metaphysical traditions.

Yet *provisionally* Paul's language can be expressed relatively simply. All this talk of "wisdom," "secrets," and "being spiritual," he says, amounts to little or nothing — *unless you are open to reappropriate the message of the cross in your innermost being.* Here lies the key to the "secret" of God's being and "wisdom," which can be apprehended *only* as his Holy Spirit shows

---

164. A constructive explanatory exposition of Athanasius's thought on 1 Cor 2:11-12, can be found in Haykin, *The Spirit of God: The Exegesis of 1 and 2 Corinthians in the Pneumato-machian Controversy of the Fourth Century,* VCSup 27 (Leiden: Brill, 1994), 77-83.

165. The complexity of what is at issue in attempting to capture the varied social, communicative, psychological, history-of-religions, and theological dimensions of the language can be judged from Theissen, *Psychological Aspects of Pauline Theology,* 343-93, where some fifty pages concern these issues.

you Christ (2:16–3:3). That gives you the kind of "secret" which makes status-seeking out of place and draws you anew to the cross. Theissen astutely traces the parallel recapitulation of 1:18-25, on the *proclamation of the cross* as a life-changing reality *for all,* and 2:1-16 on the *wisdom of the cross* as a life-changing reality among those who have already perceived its effects but now need "not . . . new contents, but . . . a more profound consciousness *'to' emancipate themselves consciously from the compulsive standards of the world.*"[166] Theissen's *Psychological Aspects* deserves careful study (see below, esp. on chs. 12–14). Meanwhile one of Funk's early essays makes the point well: "Paul is labouring to hear the word [of the cross] anew for himself and for the Corinthians. [Their] *sophia* does not consist . . . of knowledge of the counsels of God. . . . Even the cross can become σοφία if it is divorced from its ground. . . . [Paul seeks] to establish a 'world' in which the Crucified reigns as Lord."[167] The theological presupposition, which Merklein emphasizes more than Funk, however, is the discontinuity between humankind and the transcendence of God which necessitates the active help of the Holy Spirit (cf. Rom 8:16)."[168]

12   The Stoic concept of πνεῦμα as a pervasive, animating, quasi-agent, quasi-substance which permeated everything had become widespread among thinking people of Paul's world. Hoyle suggests the modern analogy of the penetrating capacity of X rays. In this sense, it was a short step to conceive of "God" as a kind of animating world-soul or immanental **spirit of the world**.[169] This belief lay behind Stoic comparisons between πνεῦμα, *spirit,* and fire as that which could pass into whatever it willed and assimilated other entities into itself. We should note, however, that the point of the analogy for Stoic thought has become the very opposite of that which the same analogy suggests in the OT and in the Epistle to the Hebrews. Here the notion of God as "a consuming fire" indicates God's transcendence, otherness, and holiness, in contradistinction from "the world" (Heb 12:29, cf. Exod 3:2; 19:18; Isa 66:15; Jer 5:14; Ezek 1:4, 27; Mal 3:2; Heb 12:18; Rev 1:14; 2:18).

Against this background Weiss adds a second basic point. He declares: "This is the essential difference between the Stoa and Paul. The former thinks of an innate and inborn divine nature; the latter, of a divine, supernatural equipment given. . . . He who processes the Spirit of God can really and truly know God. . . ."[170] Weiss compares Paul's thought in 1 Cor 2:12-16 with that of Epictetus: "Our souls are joined together with God as parts and fragments of him."[171] Paul's near contemporary Seneca writes, "Reason is nothing else than

166. Ibid., 385.

167. Funk, "Word and Word in 1 Cor 2:6-16," in *Language, Hermeneutic and Word of God,* 276, 280 and 284.

168. Merklein, *Der erste Brief 1–4,* 237.

169. Hoyle, *The Holy Spirit in St Paul,* 219.

170. Weiss, *Earliest Christianity,* 2.512.

171. Epictetus, *Discourse* 1.14.6.

a part of the divine spirit sunk in a human body."[172] Marcus Aurelius declares, "The soul is a part, an outflow, a fragment, of God."[173] This mode of thought gained more than a foothold in speculative Jewish thought of Paul's day. Thus Philo speaks of the human soul as "a divine breath that migrated hither from that blissful and happy existence . . . the part that is invisible."[174]

To speak of the influence of Stoic terms and ideas in the popular mind does not imply the mistake of imagining that most Greeks were "philosophers."[175] Further, the early Stoicism of Zeno and Cleanthes must be distinguished from the Middle Stoic thought of the first century BC (which influenced, e.g., Cicero) and the Roman Stoicism of which the very three writers from whom we have just quoted, namely, Epictetus (c. AD 55-135), Seneca (c. AD 1-65), and Marcus Aurelius (121-80) constitute major representations.[176] In all strands the world is conceived of as an organic whole, animated by a rational force called πνεῦμα or *spiritus*. A thing's qualities are constituted by its πνεῦμα, which appears in plants under the mode of nature (φύσις), in animals under the mode of life (ψυχή), and in human persons directly as spirit (πνεῦμα). Thus at death, Epictetus observes, a person passes back "into what is friendly and akin" (εἰς τὰ φίλα καὶ συγγενῆ), whatever is of fire into fire, whatever is of earth into earth, whatever is of spirit into spirit" (ὅσον πνευματίου εἰς πνευμάτιον) (Epictetus, *Dissertations* 3.13.15). Weiss calls attention to this background.[177]

Paul's use of the phrase τὸ πνεῦμα τὸ ἐκ τοῦ θεοῦ, **the Spirit who issues from God** thus stands in semantic opposition or contrast to **the spirit of the world** and conveys more than a simple genitive without ἐκ (from, out of). H. B. Swete compares the parallel notion of the Spirit's "going forth from" (ἐκπορεύεται ἐκ) God in John 15:26-27.[178] John uses παρά as well as ἐκ, as in *from the Father* (παρὰ τοῦ πατρός, 16:27; also of Christ, John 1:14; 6:46; 7:29; 17:8). Swete glosses 1 Cor 2:12 as "issuing forth from God" (cf. Lightfoot's *cometh from;* more dynamic than Collins, *that is from*), and our translation takes up his phrase.[179] This contrast between what is drawn from the world and what has come forth as a freely given gift from God is intensified by the emphatic place of ἡμεῖς as first in the word order of the verse; hence we have translated it **as for us.** . . . We have then preserved the syntagmatic sequence of οὐ τὸ πνεῦμα (**not the spirit**) and the aorist form of λαμβάνω (ἐλάβομεν, second aorist, **we received**) by translating in a contrastive mode, **it is not the spirit of**

172. Seneca, *Letters* 62.12; cf. further 41.2; 31.11.

173. Marcus Aurelius, 5.27.

174. Philo, *Opificio Mundi* 135; cf. 69.

175. J. B. Skemp, *The Greeks and the Gospel* (London: Carey Kingsgate, 1964), 1-10, 45-68, and 95-100.

176. In addition to the references above, cf. Cicero, *De Divinatione* 1.30:64.

177. Weiss, *Der erste Korintherbrief,* 62-70, and *Earliest Christianity,* 2:511-13.

178. Swete, *The Holy Spirit in the NT,* 155; cf. 178-79, 265, and 284-85.

179. Swete, *Holy Spirit,* 285, cf. 178; Lightfoot, *Notes,* 180; Collins, *First Cor,* 121-34; against AV/KJV, "of God."

the world that we received, but the spirit who issues from God.[180] Especially in view of Conzelmann's claim that Paul risks moving from a more historical gospel perspective to the more "timeless" categories of proto-gnostic
thought, it is best to retain the dynamic-action aspect of aorists where possible,
as against the more stative nuances of a perfect. The aorist recalls the moment
when they heard the gospel by faith on the basis of God.[181]

We may now consider Theissen's more speculative but nevertheless constructive exposition of the contrast between **the spirit of the world** and the
Holy **Spirit** whom **God** gives from beyond as Other. He convincingly perceives
a parallel between **the rulers of this present world order** (2:6) and **the spirit
of the world** (2:12). Both stand in contrast to the tradition of **the wisdom of
God** as that which escapes the powerful, the influential, and the experts of the
world order who shape the world to be what it is: "wisdom is withdrawn from
the 'wise and understanding' (Matt. 11:25), from the 'educated, powerful and
well-born' (1 Cor. 1:26). . . . It is scarcely a coincidence that wisdom and
antiwisdom are confronted . . . in the Epistle of James. The community . . . behind James also counts itself among the poor (James 2:5-7); in 3:15-17 it also
opposes . . . 'wisdom which is earthly, unspiritual, devilish . . . where jealousy
and selfish ambition exist . . . disorder. . . . But the wisdom from above is first
pure, then peaceable, gentle, open to reason. . . .'"[182]

The divine Spirit comes from "beyond" to impart a disclosure of God's
own "wisdom." But here Theissen advances a convincing observation about the
relation between 2:12-14 and modern learning theory. The church at Corinth
has already drawn its new life from the proclamation of the cross (1:18–2:5).
But now all this has to be more deeply appropriated (2:6–3:23). Both sections
trace the themes of divine wisdom as "unrecognizable" (1:18-21 and 2:6-8) and
"foolish" (1:22-25 and 2:9-16) when placed within the wrong frame of reference (Jews and Gentiles, 1:22-25; the "unspiritual"; 2:9-16). Both advance to
consider the social dimensions of the context of learning (1:26-30, the modest
social status of the church: 3:1-4, the immaturity of the church). Hence, just as
an appropriation of the message of the cross meant a reorientation of outlook,
so a deeper, reflective, embracing of the lifestyle which the cross brings entails
steady disengagement from the values and traditions imposed by **the rulers of
this present world order** and by **the spirit of the world**. Just as Theissen
rightly rejected the alternative "historical *or* demonic" with reference to **the
rulers** or **archons**, so the reorientation to be open to **the Spirit who issues
from God** and to disengage from **the spirit of the world** involves a *relearning
process of structural and sociocosmic dimensions* which, in turn, invites a
learning environment **among the mature**.[183] Too many commentators reduce

---

180. Schrage emphasizes this aspect of *receiving* as a *gift* (*Der erste Brief*, 1:259-60).
181. Orr and Walther, *1 Corinthians*, 158.
182. Theissen, *Psychological Aspects of Pauline Theology*, 360 and 361.
183. Ibid., 378; cf. 379-86.

the substantive content of **spirit of the world** to a merely negative term of contrast to Spirit of God.[184]

This "wisdom" of 2:6-16, however, is *not* a matter of "new contents" (as *against* a *gnostic* rereading 1:18-25 against 2:6-16), but a deeper grasp of realities which "emancipate [them] . . . from the compulsive standards of this world."[185] Theissen concludes: "In speaking of 'this world', Paul presupposes the existence of a new world. Prior to all 'worlds', God had a plan that leads beyond 'this world'. This plan was realized in Christ. But since Christ did not fit into this world — he was rejected by it — he can be ordered into a meaningful context only as the beginning of a new world."[186] A contradiction appears which demands reorientation in the power of the Holy Spirit of God. "It then appears as no meaningless contradiction but rather opens a more comprehensive horizon of meaning."[187] This happy phrase "a more comprehensive horizon" sheds further light on the meaning content of τέλειος, **mature. Maturity** entails integration of character and a long-term stance toward responsibility and hope.

This coheres wonderfully with the concluding clause of the verse. The revelation by the Spirit unveils **the things that were freely given to us by God**. The neuter plural aorist passive participle of the deponent form χαρίζομαι (as BAGD observe, here in the genuinely passive sense, as in Phil 1:29 and Acts 3:14), *I freely give*, or *I bestow as an undeserved favor*, occurs with the neuter plural definite article to signify what God has chosen to give by grace (χάρις) alone (cf. 1:7 above).[188] Thus it is to enter the "new world" (see on Funk above and on 2:6-9), which is neither of human creation nor governed by "powers" or "rulers" hostile or indifferent to God. Its generous largeness and transformative power are defined by the cross of Christ. This "new world" which God has freely bestowed is not merely an object of speculation or a human projection. **The Spirit who issues from God** was also "given" (the correlate of ἐλάβομεν, **we received**) for the purpose (purposive ἵνα, **in order that**) of our **knowing** it (εἰδῶμεν, subjunctive mood of εἰδέναι, from the perfect stem οἶδα, used with present meaning).

Fee is probably right to call this "the central issue in the whole paragraph" and on this basis to render the connecting link with the previous verse (δέ, *and* or *but*) as a "resumptive" link, which is best translated by the logical

184. For example, Grosheide, *First Epistle,* 70. Barrett holds a middle position. He comments, "Paul does not explain what he means by the spirit of the world. . . . The Qumran parallels are of limited importance, but it is evident that Paul did believe in a spiritual force opposed to God, and connected it with this world (2 Cor. 4:4) . . . hardly . . . distinguished from the wisdom of this age (v. 6) . . . a man-centred planning" (*First Epistle,* 75). Meyer calls this spirit "the spirit proceeding forth from the devil" (*First Epistle,* 1:69).

185. Theissen, *Psychological Aspects,* 385.

186. Ibid., 388.

187. Ibid.

188. BAGD, 876-79, where the connection with χάρισμα, *a free gift,* or more technically in ecclesial contexts, *a free gift for a specific task.* But this latter connection is less certain than that of χάρις, *grace* or *free gift.*

connective **Now**.[189] Héring describes this theme, with its central statements in vv. 12-16, as "the great charter for Christian theologians."[190] This verse alone will hardly support a fully articulate doctrine of "the procession of the Holy Spirit." However, Edwards argues that "though ἐκ does not here express the truth of the Spirit's procession (as Theod. explains) yet it implies it."[191] (On the use of this passage by Origen, Athanasius, and Basil, see the section "Posthistory, Influence, and Reception of 2:10-16.")

13   The dative plural *adjective* πνευματικοῖς, which can strictly be rendered either as a masculine plural, **to people of the Spirit**, or as a neuter plural *(with things of the Spirit)* is read as an *adverb* (πνευματικῶς, *spiritually*) by the important uncial B and by 33. But it is generally agreed that this is likely to reflect an assimilation to the adverbial form in v. 14; the overwhelming MS support favors the UBS 4th ed. reading.

A number of lexicographical and grammatical issues have made this a standard passage for comment. In short, (a) συγκρίνοντες (nominative masculine plural present participle active of συγκρίνω) can have at least three possible different meanings on the basis of lexicography: (i) **interpreting** (above, with NRSV, REB, Moffatt, Luther, NIV mg.); or *explaining* (TEV); or (ii) *comparing* (AV/ KJV); or (iii) *bringing together* either in the sense of *matching* or *fitting* (NJB) spiritual things or language to spiritual people, or in the sense of *expressing* (NIV) or *teaching* (JB) them.[192] On top of this, (b) the dative plural adjective πνευματικοῖς can in terms of grammar alone be either (i) *masculine, to spiritual people,* or (as we have translated it in view of the context of argument) **to people of the Spirit;** or (ii) *neuter, with* (or *to* or *by*) *spiritual things,* which may invite a further range of meanings, e.g., *spiritual subject matter, spiritual language,* or *spiritual truths.* (c) Given that the accusative neuter plural adjective πνευματικά may already mean either **spiritual things** in a general, unspecified sense (as virtually all translations render it) or something more specific (spiritual truths, spiritual revelations, spiritual mysteries . . .), the final *combination* of *possible* renderings of so many variables remains very wide. Schrage warns his readers that the interpretation "is certainly of the greatest difficulty" and yields at least four distinct possibilities.[193]

Robertson and Plummer (in some measure anticipating Schrage) succinctly sum up what they see as the main candidates, as follows.[194]

189. Fee, *First Epistle,* 112 and 112, n. 61.

190. Héring, *First Epistle,* 19.

191. Edwards, *First Epistle,* 60.

192. BAGD, 774-75; MM, 610; LSJ, 1450. The classical connotation stresses *combining* into a compound; the hellenistic and NT era contains the whole range; the papyri tend toward the meaning *compare*. Lightfoot favors *combining,* but then takes the net force to mean "applying spiritual methods to *explain* spiritual truths" (*Notes,* 180, my italics).

193. Schrage, *Der erste Brief,* 1:261.

194. Robertson and Plummer. *First Epistle,* 47. See also Merklein, *Der erste Brief 1-4,* 240; and Collins, *First Cor,* 135.

(i) *If we take πνευματικοῖς as neuter,* we may render:
   a. Combining spiritual things (words) with spiritual things (subject matter)
   b. Interpreting (explaining) spiritual things by spiritual things, meaning:
      (1) interpreting OT types by NT themes
      (2) interpreting spiritual truths by spiritual language
      (3) interpreting spiritual truths by spiritual faculties
(ii) *If we take πνευματικοῖς as masculine* we may render:
   a. Suiting (matching, fitting) spiritual matters to spiritual hearers
   b. Interpreting spiritual truths to spiritual hearers

The range of possible meanings, then, according to Robertson and Plummer, amounts to not less than six on the basis of lexicography and grammar. Everything, then, depends on judgments about the contextual flow of the argument, the situation at Corinth which shapes how Paul would consider his language to be perceived and received, and not least on Paul's own theology of revelation and communication and of the Holy Spirit. Collins, for example, follows (i) (b) and (ii) (b): *interpreting* what God has revealed "for the benefit of *spiritual persons.*"[195]

First and foremost, in the previous verse Paul has underlined the transcendence and otherness of God's Spirit as **issuing from God** (τὸ πνεῦμα τὸ ἐκ τοῦ θεοῦ). We believe that this is a decisive indication that Paul wishes the adjectival form πνευματικός to be understood as meaning **of the Spirit** (of God), and not as the more bland *spiritual,* which allows for the very misunderstandings which Paul wishes to exclude. (This applies later to πνευματικόν σῶμα as *the resurrection mode of existence characterized by the Spirit* in 15:44, as well as to *free gifts of the Holy Spirit* in 12:1–14:40.)

The initial καί after ἅ has the consecutive sense of carrying *further* the logic of v. 12 from "knowledge *(connaissance)* of God's work as a gift of the Spirit" (Senft) to the character of its "announcement" as equally a "Spiritual," not a merely human, matter.[196] Hence we have followed Barrett in translating καί here as **further**. Clearly λαλοῦμεν takes up 2:6, and since Paul turns to issues of a *mode* of discourse as well as its *content* we have taken up his redundant indicator (in the technical sense of *useful* "redundancy" in linguistics), namely, λαλοῦμεν . . . ἐν διδακτοῖς . . . λόγοις by rendering *we speak* or **we communicate . . . in speech taught**. . . . This now permits us to retain Paul's use of *the genitive of origin* for ἀνθρωπίνης σοφίας: **not in speech taught out of mere human cleverness**. It is not *from* (out of) human cleverness (our earlier rendering of σοφία), but *derives from* the Holy Spirit of God.

Although σοφία does indeed point back to the instrumental and illusory "wisdom" discussed in 1:18-31 and 2:1-5, it goes well beyond the text to follow

195. Collins, *First Corinthians,* 135.
196. Senft, *La Première Épitre,* 53; cf. Conzelmann, *1 Corinthians,* 67 and 67, n. 109.

NJB's *human philosophy.* As we argued earlier, Paul's concern for *truth* stood closer to the best traditions of "philosophy" as against his more immediate target of the stances promoted by popular schools of *rhetoric.*[197]

Héring includes an unusually lengthy discussion of the syntax of διδακτοῖς . . . λόγοις . . . which concludes by offering support for the rendering *learned discourse,* with the particular meaning of "learned discourses in philosophy."[198] He translates "amongst people instructed in human philosophy" as a counterpart to "among the mature." But two rejoinders are invited. First, research into rhetorical schools in first-century cities such as Corinth reveals that "learned discourses" occur as models in schools of *rhetoric* with more regularity and more explicit evidence (e.g., cf. Quintilian and Cicero) than in schools of philosophy (see the extensive discussion above). Second, Héring is almost alone in making such heavy weather of an unusual but by no means difficult construction. Héring has to follow Blass in deleting λογοῖς and treats διδακτοῖς as a masculine noun. Lightfoot discusses "the genitive with verbal adjectives of passive force."[199] In the end, Héring's reconstruction makes little difference for exegesis, and should not unduly detain us. Edwards observes, "σοφίας [**cleverness**] and πνεύμαψος [**of the Spirit**] are genitives, as Erasmus saw, not after λόγοις but after διδακτοῖς as in Jn. 6:45."[200]

In the light of the above, the majority rendering of συγκρίνοντες as *explaining* or *interpreting* (with Collins, Fee, Merklein, and others) seems naturally to unfold Paul's argument.[201] The entailments of the divine wisdom of the cross are ever-more-deeply appropriated by Christian openness to the work of the Holy Spirit. Since **interpretating** may entail opening the understanding through *life experience* (Schleiermacher, Dilthey, Ricoeur) and *stance* (Wolterstorff) as well as simply intellectual *explanation* (TEV), **interpret** is preferable to *explain.* At the same time we need not exclude the possibility that Paul consciously utilizes the wordplay of semantic duality with *matching* and *fitting.* For the flow of argument from 2:6 to 3:4 also includes the notion of *readiness* to understand what the Spirit reveals. Paul not only *interprets* whatever the Holy Spirit of God has revealed to those in whose lives **the Spirit** is co-working in applying the revelation; Paul *also matches* "what they are ready to take," or "words which they can hear without misconstrual" to their state of readiness (cf. Calvin, *aptantes, aptare, to adjust or to adapt).*[202] Every pastor knows the crucial importance of *pastoral timing* (not only *what* to say but also *when* to say

197. Pogoloff, *Logos and Sophia,* 99-172, 197-214, and elsewhere.

198. Héring, *First Epistle,* 20.

199. Lightfoot, *Notes,* 180.

200. Edwards, *1 Corinthians,* 61. He adds that διδακτός is especially apt to take the genitive (cf. Sophocles, *Electra* 344). Moreover, other words which govern the genitive have the same construction (2 Pet 2:14; Matt 25:34), sect. 8.

201. Fee, *First Epistle,* 115; Collins, *First Cor,* 135; Merklein, *Der erste Brief 1-4,* 241; Barrett, *First Epistle,* 75-76; also Bengel, *Gnomon,* 615, *interpretantes.*

202. Calvin, *First Epistle,* 60.

it) and matching a mode of discourse to the situation (not just *what* to say, but also *how* to say it).

14   The difficulty of translating ψυχικός into English is notorious. Some older modern commentators take up the adjectival sense of "animal" person from the vulgate *animalis homo* (cf. Lat. *anima, that which breathes,* or *animus, rational soul*), which Collins and NJB take up by translating *the natural person.*[203] Similarly, John Locke (1707) speaks here of "the animal powers, i.e., faculties of the soul unassisted by the spirit or revelation. . . . The things of revelation are discovered or discerned only by the help of revelation."[204] The distinction between ψυχικός and πνευματικός does not necessarily involve, or indeed relate to, any supposed "trichotomous" view of human persons as composed of "body, soul, and spirit" (σῶμα, ψυχή, πνεῦμα), whether or not on the basis of some alleged exegesis of 1 Thess 5:23 "ψυχικός is used of a man whose motives do not rise above the level of merely human needs and aspirations."[205] The noun ψυχή stands for the principle of *life* in the sense of any human existence animated by the power of life which sustains it.

On the other hand, the history of religions and the special background of Gen 2:7 (LXX ὁ θεός . . . ἐνεφύσησεν . . . καὶ ἐγένετο ὁ ἄνθρωπος εἰς ψυχὴν ζῶσαν, God . . . breathed . . . and the human became a living being) add possible complexities. The Hebrew supports what we have said: ויהי האדם לנפש חיה, *wayehi ha'adam lenephesh hayyah,* i.e., ψυχὴν ζῶσαν represents *living (hayyah) being (nephesh).* In Hebrew נפש (*nephesh*) certainly need not mean *soul.* Indeed, in five instances the word means *dead body* (Lev 19:28, 21:1; 22:4; Num 5:2; 6:11). As BDBG confirm, it also means, according to its context, *life, living being, desire, self, soul,* or *person.* The Hebrew overlaps with the Lat. *anima* as *that which breathes* or *the inner being of the self.*[206] BDBG renders the Hebrew in Gen 2:7 as *a living being,* "elsewhere used always of animals, Gen 1:20, 24, 30; 9:12, 15, 16 . . . Ez. 47:9" and further references.[207] Not surprisingly, in the NT the rendering of ψυχή as *life* rather than *soul* (AV/KJV) generated some controversy in such a passage as "what does it profit if a man gain the whole world and lose his own soul? . . . What shall a man give in exchange for his soul?" (Mark 8:36, 37, AV/KJV; par. Matt 16:26).

In 1 Cor 2:13, therefore, the term ψυχικός stands in contrast to that which is animated and motivated by God's Spirit, rather than the contrast with χοϊκός, *material* or *of the dust of the earth* (cf. 15:46-49).[208] Hence in place of NJB *natural,* many versions translate the Greek *unspiritual* (NRSV, REB). One problem with this translation, however, is that the term becomes negative rather than

---

203. Robertson and Plummer, *First Epistle,* 48-49; Collins, *First Cor,* 135.

204. John Locke, *A Paraphrase and Notes on the Epistles of St Paul* (1707; ed. Wainwright, 1987), 1:424.

205. Robertson and Plummer, *First Epistle,* 49.

206. BDBG, 659-61.

207. Ibid., 659, heading 2.

208. Schweizer, "ψυχή," *TDNT,* 9:604-67 (with Dihle, Lohse, Tröger, et al.).

conveying the more value-neutral nuances of *ordinary person* or **person who lives on an entirely human level** (cf. *the man without the Spirit*, NIV); *whoever does not have the Spirit* (TEV). Yet the translation *ordinary* risks quasi-gnostic categorizations into "fleshly material," "psychical soul," and "spiritual elite." The problem is complicated further since, as Pearson stresses, "Paul is accommodating himself to his opponents' terminology, but is radically reinterpreting it."[209]

Irenaeus explicitly tells us that the Valentinians misinterpret Pauline passages, "dressing them up anew" for their own purposes, of which one prime example is to support the gnostic doctrine of "three kinds of persons . . . the material . . . the "psychical" (ψυχικός) . . . of intermediate class . . . and the spiritual (πνευματικός) . . . who belonged to the spiritual class."[210] To press this point, Irenaeus declares, they appeal to such passages as 1 Cor 15:48 (ὁ χοϊκός, man of earth [Adam]; οἱ χοϊκοί ["material" class of humans]; ὁ ἐπουράνιος, heavenly [Redeemer] . . . οἱ ἐπουράνιοι, those of heaven); 1 Cor 2:14-15 (ψυχικὸς ἄνθρωπος, "psychical" person, and ὁ πνευματικός, "spiritual" person).

To move to second-century Valentinianism, however, is to move too far beyond the date at which Paul writes. In Paul's day a process was probably in motion which would end as developed gnosticism, and traces of this trend can be found in embryonic form in the theology of some at Corinth. The exegesis of Gen 2:7 which we find in Philo and Josephus signals a trichotomous understanding of *body, soul* (ψυχή), and spirit (πνεῦμα), which also finds its way into Justin.[211] It is because of these non-Pauline understandings of *spiritual* and *spirituality* that we consistently translate πνευματικός as **of the Spirit, pertaining to the Spirit**, or **characterized by the Spirit**, understanding πνεῦμα as **Spirit of God** or **Spirit who issues from God**, *not* that part of the human person which is "spiritual" or religious."

Pearson believes that the wording of the contrast in v. 13 belongs to Paul's opponents, even if Paul carefully qualifies it and redefines its currency.[212] He sees affinities with the wisdom theology at Corinth and Philo's notion that the πνεῦμα, *spirit*, or νοῦς, *mind*, can become a receptacle for a "fragment" (ἀπόσπασμα) of the deity (Philo, *Quod Deterius Potiori Insidiari Soleat* 90). On the basis of Gen 2:7, God has "breathed" (ἐνεφύσησεν) "the spirit" (τὸ πνεῦμα), which is "received" by "the mind" (ὁ νοῦς), to result in a "union"

---

209. Pearson, *Pneumatikos-Psychikos*, 40. Hays also points our that NRSV's *Those who are unspiritual do not receive the gifts of the Spirit* "runs the risk of suggesting that Paul is talking about 'spiritual gifts' of the sort that he will discuss in chapters 12–14" (*First Cor*, 46).

210. Irenaeus, *Against Heresies*, 1:8:1 (on distorting and "dressing up" passages), and 8:3 (on the three "classes" cited from 1 Cor 15:48 in relation to 1 Cor 2:14-15).

211. Justin, *Dialogues*, 5 and 6:2; Josephus, *Antiquities* 1.34; Philo, *Legum Allegoriae* 1.76; 3.161; *Opificio Mundi* 135; *De Specialibus Legibus* 4.123; and *De Plantatione* 18. A further resonance occurs in Wis 2:2-3 (cf. Wis 15:11). See further Pearson, *Pneumatikos-Psychikos*, 7-12, 18-21, and 37-40.

212. Pearson, *Pneumatikos-Psychikos*, 38.

(ἔνωσις) of the three: divine breath or spirit, human spirit, and human mind. By contrast, Philo argues, the *anima* or ψυχή "could not have thought of God"; only πνεῦμα, *spirit,* and νοῦς, *mind.*[213] Thus, on such a basis it is the human capacity of spirituality (πνευματικός) which makes it possible "to know" (γινώσκειν) God.

Every one of these key terms (πνευματικός, ψυχικός, νοῦς γινώσκειν) recurs in 2:14-16, but with a different meaning from that outlined above. Pearson comments: "These texts [from Philo, Justin, and others] illuminate for us the background of 1 Cor 2:13b-14. . . . The opponents of Paul in Corinth were teaching that they had the potentiality of becoming πνευματικοί within themselves by virtue of the πνευματικός nature given them by God, and that by a cultivation of Wisdom they could rise above the earthly and 'psychic' level of existence and anticipate heavenly glory."[214] Those who had already attained this they viewed as the τέλειοι (*the mature,* the perfect) as against the "babes." R. A. Horsley confirms the point that while certain hellenistic-Jewish texts do not draw a dualism of *spirit* and *soul* from Gen 2:7, they nevertheless sometimes lead to notions of different levels of "spiritual status" focused on Wisdom.[215] Samuel Laeuchli makes this point more broadly and most incisively. In terms of "isolated" concepts, words, and phrases, he argues, Paul and later gnostics use the same vocabulary, which is largely "biblical." But between Paul's "frame" and "the new frame into which it [the language] is inserted," a tension arises: "phrases stand in another light."[216] Laeuchli adds, "The *language* contained in this passage is no different from certain gnostic usages . . . 'a secret and hidden wisdom which God decreed before the ages' . . . 'We have received the Spirit . . .'; but "as a chain, a total expression" Paul's Christocentric language makes a different point (my italics).[217] We have already noted Neil Richardson's forceful case about the centrality of God and Christ in Paul's language. He notes "not only the frequency of the word θεός in 1 Cor 1:18–3:23, but also its often emphatic character."[218]

The arguments in favor of our understanding of ψυχικός as **the person who lives on an entirely human level** are conclusive, and difficult, if not impossible, to translate into any single word. A. Sand points out that such an interpretation does not differ substantially from its meaning in 1 Cor 15:44 and 45 as an "earthly-worldly" body or "the earthly person of the dust," since "in 1 Cor 2:14, too, the ψυχικὸς ἄνθρωπος is the '[merely] earthly-worldly person' who does not understand what can only be understood through the power of the gift of the Spirit."[219] This remains true whether or not gnostic texts "represent the

213. Philo, *Leg. All.* 1.36; cf. Pearson, *Pneumatikos-Psychikos,* 39.

214. Pearson, ibid.

215. Horsley "Pneumatikos vs. Psychikos: Distinctions of Spiritual Status among the Corinthians," 169-88.

216. Laeuchli, *The Language of Faith,* 16 and 19.

217. Ibid., 47; cf. Richardson, *Paul's Language about God.*

218. Richardson, *Paul's Language about God,* 116; cf. 66-73, 95-124, 271-75, and 308-19.

219. A. Sand, "ψυχή, ψυχικός," *EDNT,* 3:503; cf. 500-503.

direct linguistic and conceptual background of the Pauline antithesis."[220]
M. Winter calls into question any gnostic influence on Paul's theology, but, like
Pearson, considers that the thought world of which gnosticism forms (or will
form) a part provides the necessary terminological background for interpreting
1 Cor 2:6–13:4.[221] Finally, in this connection, Stoic terminology and vocabulary, as we have seen, also contributes to the same issue in 2:14-15. J. N.
Sevenster observes in his *Paul and Seneca* that on *pneuma*- and *psychē*-related
terms "they use similar words [with] entirely different meanings."[222]

The perception of the things of God's Spirit as **folly** (μωρία) recapitulates
the parallel theme in 1:23, where the context of **the things of the Spirit**, namely **a
crucified Christ** (1:23) is an **affront** (σκάνδαλον) to Jews and **folly** (μωρίαν) to
Gentiles.[223] This provides the reason why (cf. γάρ, **for** . . .) **the person who lives
on an entirely human level** rejects them. At this stage of the argument Paul says
that such a person **does not receive**, i.e., rejects, **the things of the Spirit**, not at
this point that such a one *cannot* receive them.[224] They are rejected because
within the prior horizons of these preexisting interests and concerns the message
of the cross and the things of the Spirit find no desired relevance or credibility;
they are **folly** unless or until the Spirit moves or expounds those horizons.

This now precisely defines the sense in which a person in this condition
cannot come to know them (οὐ δύναται γνῶναι). First, γνῶναι (second aorist
infinitive active) is used as an ingressive aorist to mean *to get to know, to acquire a knowledge of.* . . . Second, as the above discussion indicates, this **cannot**
is what philosophers term a "logical" rather than an "empirical" **cannot**. The
question *Can you lift it?* refers to a physical, causal, or empirical *can.* But "*can*
God make a stone so big that he cannot lift it?" or "*Can* a triangle have four
sides?" are examples of a *logical "can."*[225] The **cannot** arises from the mutu-

220. Winter, *Pneumatiker und Psychiker in Korinth,* 205-6.

221. Ibid., 231-32 and throughout. Wilckens argues that ψυχικός is used here rather than
"fleshly" because of the use of the term at Corinth (*Weisheit und Torheit,* 89-91).

222. J. N. Sevenster, *Paul and Seneca,* NovTSup 4 (Leiden: Brill, 1961), 78; cf. 26-83. Cf.
further Seneca, *Letters* 120.14; 106.4; although in *Letters* 50.6 he writes, "Quid enim est aliud animus quam quodam modo se habens spiritus?"

223. Theissen, *Psychological Aspects,* 355.

224. Wolff, *Der erste Brief,* 61, and Robertson and Plummer, *First Epistle,* 4, carefully preserve the **does not** of v. 14a as against **cannot** of v. 14b; cf. Erasmus, "He does not accept . . . ,"
with de Wette, Meyer (*First Epistle* 1:75), and others. **Cannot** in v. 14b corresponds with μωρία in
1:18, 21, 23 (Wolff, *Der erste Brief,* 61).

225. The difference between logical "can/cannot" and causal-empirical "can/cannot" is well
brought out in a classic passage on L. Wittgenstein, *Philosophical Investigations* (Oxford: Blackwell, 2d ed. Germ. and Eng. 1967), sect. 497, in relation to sects. 150, 183, and 194. Of more immediate relevance to biblical specialists is my discussion in *The Two Horizons: NT Hermeneutics and
Philosophical Description* (Grand Rapids: Eerdmans, Exeter and Carlisle: Paternoster, 1980, rpt.
1993), 393-98, on, e.g., "how *could* God judge the world?" (Rom 3:6); "Who *can* resist his will?"
(Rom 9:19); "those in the flesh (ἐν σαρκί) *cannot* (οὐ δύνανται) please God" (Rom 8:7, 8); and "no
one *can* call Jesus Lord (δύναται εἰπεῖν κύριος) except by the Holy Spirit" (1 Cor 12:3). (Also Korean trans., Seoul: Chongshin, 1990, 600-610.)

ally incompatible horizons which cannot be engaged interactively by *effort* (causal, empirical *can*), but only by a *change in one of the terms of the equation* (logical *can*). In order to make this very point Paul concludes the verse with a statement which is already *analytic* of the previous sentences: **because they are discerned spiritually**, i.e., discernment of this meaning and sense (that they are not **folly**) entails the work of the Holy Spirit. (On ἀνακρίνω as **discern** see on v. 15.)

We first translated πνευματικῶς as *in a manner determined by the Spirit* in order to maintain the Pauline sense of the adverb **spiritually**. However, since our translation of the adjectival form πνευματικός makes this point more than once, such a translation would have been pedantic and clumsy, as well as missing the wordplay with notions of "spirituality" at Corinth. The distinction of meaning remains all the same, and is as relevant today as it was for ancient Corinth.

15-16 The 4th ed. UBS *Greek New Testament* places τά in square brackets before τάντα to indicate the degree of textual difficulty. The definite article *the* (τά) is supported by the early 𝔓46, together with A, C, and the first hand of D, but it remains absent from ℵ and B (an important combination), the second copyist of D, and many other MSS. A possible complication arises from the insertion (or retention?) of μέν in B and in later copyists of ℵ and D, as well as in 33. But, as Metzger observes, the μέν is almost certainly an addition by "pedantic copyists" who thought that it should serve as a correlate to δέ.[226] The problem of the definite article cannot be ignored because of the early witness of 𝔓46, but its insertion can be explained as an early gloss to ensure that πάντα, **everything**, *all things,* was duly read as a neuter plural, not as a masculine accusative singular which shares the same grammatical form.

We have regularly considered whether any or all of the verses in 2:6-16 could represent either interpolations or quotations by Paul of theological catchphrases used at Corinth. The Greek text, of course, carried no equivalent to quotation marks, and even the much later convention of beginning a quotation with a capital letter is meaningless in early uncial MSS. Quotations most certainly occur elsewhere in this epistle (at the very least, Πάντα μοι ἔξεστιν, " 'All things are lawful' — Yes, but not all things are helpful!" (6:12, repeated in 10:23); πάντες γνῶσιν ἔχομεν, " 'All possess knowledge' — We know that: knowledge inflates you; but love builds" (8:1). I argue that quotations also occur at 7:1 ("it is well for a man not to touch a woman"); 8:4 ("An idol has no real existence"); and probably several others which we discuss (e.g., 6:13; 8:6; 8:8; 11:2). Murphy-O'Connor provides a useful discussion of issues of interpolations, while J. C. Hurd in particular offers a very detailed and in many respects convincing account of this issue of questions, including a chart of the conclusions of twenty-four earlier scholars on eight possible quotations (e.g., twenty-two, plus Hurd, affirm 6:12; every single writer affirms

226. Metzger, *Textual Commentary* (2d ed.), 482.

8:1; twenty affirm 8:4; but only ten affirm 7:1).[227] He omits any consideration of 1 Cor 2:6-16 here, perhaps because, with the notable exception of 6:12, all the quotations may come from the *letter* which Paul received from Corinth, and 6:12 simply anticipates 10:23, which is also part of the letter as Hurd reconstructs it.[228] Hurd's discussion of criteria to distinguish oral information from Corinth from their queries by letter is largely convincing in general terms and invites respect.[229]

We have provisionally treated 2:15 as a quotation, as the quotation marks in our translation indicate, although this by no means implies that Paul necessarily dissents from it, provided that it is contextualized within his wider theology of the Holy Spirit and the Christian life. Witherington's apt comments, together with those of Pogoloff, about rhetoric and "judging" must be seen as part of the background.[230] As "spiritual people," many at Corinth saw themselves as "judging everything" but as "being judged by no one." Johannes Weiss comments, "The 'spiritual' man knows and judges not only the being of God, but everything else, for the Spirit penetrates everything, even the deep things of God (1 Cor 2:15, 10). These are the confessions of a spiritual ('pneumatic') mystic: his feeling of exaltation, his sense of superiority and unassailability are especially asserted in the statement (2:15), 'but he himself is judged by no man.'"[231] While in one sense Paul does not entirely deny this, Weiss urges, Paul's placing whatever privileges the "spiritual person" has under the controlling rubric of *gift* of *grace* (*charisma;* cf. "the *gift* of prophecy and know all mysteries and all knowledge," 13:2) changes the entire perspective of the utterance and modifies its content. Moreover, in v. 16 Paul will give it a decisive christological critique.[232] Schrage compares the assertion of "special gnosis" with Paul's rejoinder in 1 Thess 5:21, "Testing everything."[233] How could Paul imply here that no "testing" of "spiritual" utterance is possible?

The posthistory of the text brings out the enormity of its claims if it is abstracted from the Pauline context. Luther had to cope with appeals about the immunity of "the spiritual" from normal canons of judgment and good sense no less than Paul did. On the other hand, ecclesial regimes have equally appealed to this passage to legitimate their power. As Robertson and Plummer note, it can be a recipe for "either anarchy or tyranny," although Paul's redefinition of terms and contextualization of it allows for neither.[234]

---

227. Hurd, *The Origin of 1 Corinthians,* 68; cf. 61-94. Cf. J. Murphy-O'Connor, "Interpolations in 1 Cor," *CBQ* 48 (1986): 81-94.

228. Hurd, *Origin,* 114-212.

229. A summary is offered in Hurd, *Origin,* 82.

230. Witherington, *Conflict and Community,* 47; and Pogoloff, *Logos and Sophia,* 173-96, 273-75.

231. Weiss, *Earliest Christianity,* 2:513. Cf. Weiss, *Der erste Korintherbrief,* 66-67; on "the pseudo-pneumatic discourse" cf. 12:10, διάκρισις πνευμάτων.

232. Weiss, *Earliest Christianity,* 2:508-13.

233. Schrage, *Der erste Brief,* 1:265.

234. Robertson and Plummer, *First Epistle,* 50.

It is time to explore the meaning of ἀνακρίνω, which we translate as **discern** in v. 14, Weiss translates as *judge* in this verse. NRSV renders the active (v. 15a) as **discern** and the passive (v. 15b) as *are themselves subject to scrutiny;* AV/KJV and Collins translate *judges* and *judged;* the NIV (and approximately REB) *makes judgments* and *subject to any man's judgment;* NJB has *assess* and *be assessed.* In lexicographical terms the range of ἀνακρίνειν is wide. It may mean *to question* (Epictetus, *Dissertations* 1.1.20), *to examine* (as in *examine the scriptures,* Acts 17:11); *to scrutinize* or *to judge, to assess,* **to put on trial** (1 Cor 4:3-4; cf. 9:3; 1 Cor 9:3): *to conduct an examination* (Acts 12:19); BAGD also includes *to discuss* here, against Lightfoot.[235] Collins reminds us that the wordplay of "rhetorical assonance" colors Paul's usage: these may be playful rhetorical nuances of *judging.*[236]

Nevertheless *judge,* **discern,** *assess,* and **put on trial** are different from **sift**. Lightfoot holds that *judge* would invite the simple form κρίνω while *discern* reflects διακρίνω, not ἀνακρίνω. If we translate *judge,* we almost certainly place the slogan on the lips of a "pneumatic." It is possible to leave the attribution more open if we translate to *fathom,* **sift out.** Hence we use **sifts out everything** for the active in v. 15a. Conversely, the passive in v. 15b has the sense of being *scrutinized, fathomed, sifted, assessed,* Findlay proposed *put on trial.*[237] Since this nuance is picked up by the same verb in 4:3-4 and there is also a background of competitive claims of wisdom or cleverness in rhetoric, *put on trial* may be a genuine possibility with a hint of irony. **Put on trial** seems appropriate for the passive, in spite of its losing its symmetry with the first half of the verse.[238] αὐτὸς δέ also is difficult to render in the English: **the person concerned** avoids any gender-specific *translation and preserves the emphatic* singular.

While Paul is correcting pretensions to invulnerability and lack of criticism by certain "spiritual persons," *there remains an important positive sense in which Paul endorses the maxim, while at the same time he qualifies it.* Kistemaker writes: "What a delight for a spiritual person to go directly to God himself, the source of all wisdom (James 1:5)."[239] Interpreting "discernment" here (as Kaiser does) to include "scripture," he continues: "For the believer, the Scriptures are a light on his path and a lamp before his feet (Ps 119:105). He knows that in God's light he sees light (Ps 26:9). . . . He is able to distinguish truth from error . . . and authenticity from pretence."[240] Kistemaker rightly re-

235. BAGD, 56; cf. MM, 35 and Lightfoot, *Notes* 182, where he insists that only κρίνειν means *to judge,* while διακρίνειν means *to discern.*

236. Collins, *First Cor,* 137; also BDF, sect. 488.1.

237. Findlay, *Expositor's Greek Testament,* 2:784.

238. Collins's point about rhetorical assonance cuts both ways. We cannot be certain of the "best" translation.

239. Kistemaker, *1 Corinthians,* 92-93.

240. A special argument for a relevance here to biblical material is put foward by Walter C. Kaiser, "A Neglected Text in Bibliology Discussions: 1 Cor 2:6-16," *WTJ* 43 (1981): 301-19.

fers, however, to the context of the community (see on Schrage et al. under v. 6), for Paul stresses this throughout the epistle, especially in 12:1–14:49. He concludes, "This does not mean that the spiritual man is an expert in every area of life. Rather, with respect to the community in which God has placed him, he is able to appraise all things spiritually."[241] Insofar as the first person plural represents the whole community, Paul can stand behind these words; insofar as they represent an elitist group of "spiritual people" or prophets, Paul disowns what cannot be tested (see notes 7 and 16).

The phrase αὐτὸς δέ ὑπὸ οὐδενὸς ἀνακρίνεται would thus be understood differently by Paul than by some at Corinth. In the view of some at Corinth, it would signify a certain *immunity* or *invulnerability* from correction and critique. For Paul, however, it signifies at the very least that there are depths and dimensions to life in the Spirit which **the person who lives on an entirely human level** (v. 14) simply cannot *fathom*. Aspects of Christian existence remain an enigma, unless others share the same insight of the Spirit of God. Hence they can hardly possess all the material and understanding necessary to have completed an adequate **trial** of what makes the Christian what he or she is. Conceivably Paul's thought even hints at what he will later say in Rom 8:33: τίς ἐγκαλέσει κατὰ ἐκλεκτῶν θεοῦ; Who will bring any charge against God's elect?

Since the quotation in v. 16 is based broadly on Isa 40:13, its use can also be attributed equally to the Corinthian "spiritual persons" and to Paul himself. This is confirmed by Fee's helpful comment concerning its "double intent."[242] The impossibility of **coming to know the mind of the Lord** (again, as in v. 14, *ingressive* aorist of γινώσκω) applies to the ψυχικοί, i.e., those who **live on an entirely human level** (v. 14).[243] This would be firmly enunciated by the church at Corinth, and would not be disputed by Paul, except perhaps with respect at times to the mood with which it was uttered. But the apostle may well be adding a further dimension of his own. In Fee's words, "Who among his detractors, now enamoured with human wisdom and passing judgment on Paul, is so capable of knowing the mind of the Lord that he/she can bypass the very wisdom of God itself as it is revealed in the cross?"[244]

The grammar and syntax of the relative pronoun ὅς requires comment: the relative *who* both picks up the LXX and functions in effect as a consecutive to express result, or more accurately "contemplated result."[245] Hence: **that he**

Héring also implies that the role of the OT quotations significantly differentiates Paul from gnostic uses of the argument (*First Epistle*, 21).

241. Kistemaker, *1 Corinthians*, 93. We recall Schrage's comment on 2:6 that the plural **we** refers to "**all** Christians" (*Der erste Brief,* 1:248); Collins on "a common activity within the community" (*First Cor,* 122); and Orr and Walther on the locus of the Spirit's activity as "the fellowship of the Christian community" (*1 Cor,* 166).

242. Fee, *First Epistle*, 119.

243. On the ingressive or inceptive aorist cf. MHT, 1:109 and Moule, *Idiom Book*, sect. 4.

244. Fee, *First Epistle*, 119.

245. Findlay, *Expositor's Greek Testament*, 2:785; also Barrett, *First Epistle*, 78.

should instruct him? translates the clause. The LXX of Isa 40:13 reads τίς ἔγνω νοῦν κυρίου; καὶ τίς αὐτοῦ σύμβουλος ἐγένετο, ὃς συμβιβᾶ αὐτόν; the quotation thus begins exactly as Paul quotes it (with his addition of **for**), but the middle clause is omitted, since "Who has become his adviser?" (σύμβουλος) is less pointed than the dynamic barb "Who **should instruct him?** The LXX verb can carry the sense of **instruct,** *teach,* or *advise* someone. The LXX regularly uses anarthrous forms (νοῦν κυρίου) where non-Semitic Greek would expect the definite article, and the form represents the classical ἐμβιβάζειν.[246] Isa 40:13 (last clause) is also quoted in Rom 11:34.

The key assertion now comes in v. 16c, with "the Christological application" of the citation.[247] The change from **of the Lord** (κυρίου) to **of Christ** (Χριστοῦ) is, as Schrage indicates, of pivotal importance.[248] Schrage reminds us that up to this point all of the major references to **Christ** have been to **a Christ crucified** (1:17, 23-24, 30; 2:2; cf. 15:3). The Spirit who teaches what it is to know the mind of Christ is no naturalistic "spirit of the world," nor an instrumental "power" to provide some supposed spiritual elite with status, but the Spirit who anointed Christ to die for others on the cross.[249] Throughout this epistle, and not least here, in 12:1–14:49, and in 15:1-11, 44-58, the work of the Spirit is defined in terms of christological criteria.

This becomes still more evident when we recall that the word **mind** (νοῦς) constitutes "not an instrument of thought" but "a mode of thought" or "mind-set" *(Denkweise* or *Gesinnung;* not *Organ des Denkens).*[250] Similarly, νοῦς denotes "a constellation of thoughts and beliefs which provides the criteria for judgments and actions."[251] Jewett speaks of "character or disposition."[252] The view of Reitzenstein that it relates in Paul to mental capacities which offer affinities with the divine spirit has long been discredited. As Allo tartly states, Paul is not a pantheist.[253] In 1 Cor 14:14 νοῦς "is expressly opposed to πνεῦμα."[254] In 2:16, Allo adds, it is because Christ lives in those who have received the Spirit that their stance and outlook can be that of Christ, and in this sense they are "spiritual."[255]

The Hebrew represented by the LXX in any case has רוּחַ *(ruach)* of God, and Paul uses πνεῦμα θεοῦ, *Spirit of God,* and πνεῦμα Χριστοῦ, *Spirit of Christ,* in ways that are at times virtually interchangeable. Rom 8:9 offers one example: "God's Spirit dwells in you, and anyone who does not possess the Spirit of

---

246. BDF, 135, sect. 259 (3).
247. Schrage, *Der erste Brief,* 1:267.
248. Ibid.
249. Ibid., 267-68.
250. Weiss, *Der erste Korintherbrief,* 68.
251. Jewett, *Paul's Anthropological Terms,* 361, with reference to A. Schlatter, *Die Theologie des Judentums . . .* (1932), 27.
252. Jewett, *Paul's Anthropological Terms,* 362.
253. Allo, *Première Épitre,* 105.
254. Ibid.
255. Ibid., 50.

Christ does not belong to Christ." Hanson argues that Paul is aware of this background in 1 Cor 2:16.[256] Thus, when he prays that Christians may reflect "the mind of Christ," Paul cites the self-humiliation of Christ in the existence of a "slave" and the cross (Phil 2:5). "The change of expression from 'Lord' in 16a to 'Christ' in 16b binds the true divine wisdom to the crucified Christ, and thereby excludes the gnostic gospel of a transcendent wisdom."[257] Paul will expound practical entailments of this in 3:1-4.

THE POSTHISTORY, INFLUENCE, AND RECEPTION OF 2:6-16

Introduction

This is one of the key passages for an effective and detailed *Wirkungsgeschichte,* or history of effects, of a Pauline text in this epistle. (1) In the second and third centuries the major exegetical comments of Irenaeus, Clement, and Tertullian engage with gnostic themes and claims. But Tertullian introduces a much larger multiform agenda which includes the OT, christological criteria of "spirituality," the nature of the Spirit, and later his own shift to Montanism. (2) The fourth and fifth centuries witness exegetical work for a theology of the Holy Spirit. Notably Origen, Athanasius, and especially Basil engage with these issues, as well as refining criteria of "spirituality." The medieval period raises issues of ontology through Anselm, while the Reformers extend the agenda onto epistemology and other issues. Finally, the modern period raises issues of relationality within the Godhead, all of which find an exegetical groundwork in 1 Cor 2:10-16. The value of this study is such that it justifies greater detail than elsewhere in this commentary.

Irenaeus alludes to the teaching of the Valentinian gnostics on "three types of people": the material, the *animalis homo* or ψυχικός, and the spiritual or πνευματικός, and their appeal to "the *animalis homo* does not receive the things of the Spirit" (1 Cor 2:14) and "the spiritual person judges all things" (2:15). Irenaeus cites around sixteen passages to which the Valentinians appeal, of which 1 Cor 2:14-15 constitutes the most plausible. Hence Irenaeus cites our passage as one among nearly a score to instantiate how they "abuse the scriptures by endeavouring to support their own system out of them."[258] Their conceptual frame remains so alien to Pauline thought that the coincidence of parallel terminology remains part of what Irenaeus calls their "self-deception."[259] Elsewhere Irenaeus himself takes up the Pauline argument about the incapacity of the *animalis homo* for the things of the Spirit of God in a way which matches Paul's thread of thought in 2:9–3:4. The evidence, he argues, of whether people "receive the divine Spirit" or live as ψυχικοί appears in their practical lifestyle: "Why do you call me Lord, Lord, and do not the things which I say?"[260] He perceives the christological criterion of claims about the Spirit as it applies to stances in life.

---

256. A. T. Hanson, *Studies in Paul's Technique and Theology* (London: SPCK, 1974), 197.
257. Jewett, *Paul's Anthropological Terms,* 377; cf. 358-67 and 375-84.
258. Irenaeus, *Against Heresies,* 1:9:1; cf. 8:3-5.
259. Ibid.
260. Irenaeus, *Against Heresies,* 5:8:4.

Clement of Alexandria distinguishes between a Christian and a worldly philosophy on the basis of the contrast between divine wisdom which comes from God's Spirit, and human wisdom which reflects nothing more than purely human origins, goals, and values. Hence, when Paul says, "The spiritual person sifts out everything, but the person is put on trial by no one" (1 Cor 2:15), this entails the protection of the Christian against the seductions of Epicurean philosophy, "which deifies pleasure."[261] Stoic philosophy reflects only "human traditions" and credits a spiritual God with "pervading lowliest matter."[262] In keeping with Clement's own quasi-gnostic leanings, he stresses that God's "mysteries" are revealed only to the appropriate circle. Revealed truth appears "ludicrous to the masses" since "the ψυχικός person does not receive the things of the Spirit" (2:14).[263]

The theme of divine wisdom, however, permits Clement, he thinks, to find a divine if "slender spark, capable of being fanned into flame, a trace of wisdom and an impulse from God" in true philosophy which avoids mere human sophistry. He appeals to 1 Cor 2:13 for the view that the Spirit can bestow wisdom of this kind.[264] Here we have moved *into a different world from the emphasis of Irenaeus on public lifestyle and Christology.* Indeed, Clement interprets the complex and difficult phrase πνευματικοῖς πνευματικὰ συγκρίνοντες as comparing spiritual things with spiritual *in the sense of using "the method of concealment."*[265] But this does not cohere with the exegesis above. He relates this, instead, to Plato's maxim that the impure should not touch the pure; allegorical interpretation and the perception of revelation as "mysteries" discourage the open declaration in the public domain which is advocated by Irenaeus. The difference between their respective exegeses of 2:10-16 reflects Clement's closer sympathy with "gnostic" themes.

Tertullian relates wisdom in this chapter not to philosophy or to the rational but to *the OT background* in Proverbs, once again true to our expectations. This offers him a path to approach Paul's passage *as doxology.* Wisdom in Proverbs delights in God and in the acts of creating in which Wisdom shares. Such praise can be shared only in knowing "the mind of the Lord. For 'who knows the things of God . . . but the Spirit who is in him?'" (1 Cor 2:11).[266] Tertullian does not, however, equate Wisdom with the Spirit of God, for "the very wisdom of God is declared to be born and created. . . . We should not suppose that there be any being other than God who is unbegotten and uncreated."[267] Still more significantly, like Irenaeus, *Tertullian takes up Paul's christological context which governs revelation by the Spirit.* In the Valentinian system, he says, "the Aeon" longs to know the Father, but "only the Son knows the Father." For the Son came not to do his own will, but the Father's, and this he knew intimately: "for who has come to know the things which are in God, except the Spirit who is in him?" (1 Cor 2:11).[268] Tertullian is rejecting a modalist theology of God as Father, Son, and Spirit, but also defending a trinitarian understanding of God against subor-

261. Clement, *Stromata*, 1:11.
262. Ibid.
263. *Stromata*, 1:12.
264. *Stromata*, 1:17.
265. *Stromata*, 5:4.
266. Tertullian, *Against Hermogenes*, 18.
267. Ibid.
268. Tertullian, *Against Praxeas*, 8.

dinationism. *Hence the relation between God and the Spirit in 1 Cor 2:10-16 as intimate yet distinct becomes important for Christian doctrine,* especially in conjunction with Paul's christological frame in 1:18–3:4.

If Tertullian became a Montanist c. AD 206, about nine years after coming to faith, we should expect to find Montanist resonances in his exegesis of passages about the Spirit in *Against Marcion,* of which bk. 1 probably appeared one year later in 207. Now the allusion to the ψυχικός or "human" person of 1 Cor 2:14 becomes the person who believes that the period of "ecstatic raptures and revelations" ended with the close of the apostolic age. "For when a person is rapt in the Spirit . . . or when God speaks through him, he loses his sensation . . . a point about which there is a question between us and the ψυχικός person."[269] However, in Book I Tertullian continues to retain his earlier Pauline themes of continuity with the OT, revelation, and Christology. Most constructively of all, no one can say that God's nature should be this rather than that, for "no one knows what is in God except the Spirit of God" (1 Cor 2:11).[270]

The Later Patristic Period:
The Nature of the Holy Spirit and of Being "Spiritual"

Origen (c. 185–254) stresses the heart of the Pauline theme in the Fragments of his Commentary.[271] The "matching," "comparing," or "interpreting" of spiritual things with or to spiritual people (πνευματικοῖς πνευματικὰ συγκρίνοντες, 1 Cor 2:13) involves Spirit and Word, or "the mind [stance] of scripture" (ὁ νοῦς τῆς γραφῆς) . . . "taught by the Spirit (διδακτὸς πνεύματος)."[272] The reason why the ψυχικός person does not receive the things of the Spirit (1 Cor 2:14) is that "unless the Spirit opens the words of the prophets the things which are [otherwise] locked up (τὰ κεκλεισμένα) cannot be opened (οὐ δύναται ἀνοιχθῆναι).[273]

Origen also, like Paul, perceives the gift character of "sifting out everything" (1 Cor 2:15) and its relation to a lifestyle "according to the Spirit (τὸ χάρισμα τοῦ θεοῦ, κατὰ πνεῦμα) which issues in "the fruit of the Spirit" (καρπὸς τοῦ πνεύματος) as love, joy, peace, patience, kindness, goodness, faith, gentleness, self-discipline: ὅπου ταῦτα, ἐκεῖ τὸ πνεῦμα, ἐκεῖνος πνευματικός: *where these are, there is the Spirit; that person is a 'spiritual' person.*"[274] Where gifts remain still to come, "that person is not yet (οὔπω) a 'spiritual' person."[275]

In *De Principiis* the same christological and ethical criterion is applied to language about the Spirit in this passage: "We have the mind of Christ that we might know the things freely given to us by him, which we communicate in words . . . which the Spirit teaches (1 Cor 2:12, 13, 16). It is within this frame that Origen speaks, as is so widely known, of "an inner, namely a divine sense revealed by grace alone" in the

269. Tertullian, *Against Marcion,* 4:22.

270. *Against Marcion,* 1:2.

271. Origen, *Fragments of Commentary on 1 Cor,* in *JTS* 9 (1908): 240, sect. 11 (46), lines 10-15.

272. Ibid., lines 21-22.

273. Ibid., lines 25-26; cf. 29-30.

274. Origen, *Fragments, JTS* 9:241, sect. 1, lines 48-50.

275. Ibid., 50-51.

words of Scripture as found, e.g., in the prophets.[276] Origen therefore links the capacity of Scripture to reveal and to speak with the revelatory work of the Spirit which enables the reading community to perceive what the Spirit discloses within it. He uses the simile of constantly trying to plumb the depths with a small receptacle: the Spirit "pours" what he reveals into "those who are capable of understanding the divine wisdom."[277] In *Against Celsus* Origen finds himself on more speculative ground about the nature of πνεῦμα.[278] Yet his added insistence that here we may speak of the incarnation of God is bound up with an implicitly trinitarian discussion of πνεῦμα, πνευματικός, and πνευματικῶς, and the need for understanding through the Spirit.[279] Thus Origen offers an exegetical comment on 1 Cor 2:10-16 in several contexts: the revelation of truth by the Spirit; the christological or cruciform criterion of what is to be a person of the Spirit; the interpretation and operation of Scripture; and Christology with hints of a trinitarian frame. In his fundamental perception of the passage he remains close to Paul, but he extends the history of its effects to several specific situations which he faces.

Athanasius (c. 296–373). 1 Cor 2:10-16 held a place of the utmost importance. If in his earlier work he had been especially concerned with the humanity and true deity of Jesus Christ, Athanasius became increasingly concerned to demonstrate the deity of the Holy Spirit. Hence in his Epistle to Serapion he sets out the doctrine of the divinity of the Holy Spirit, making much of Paul's assertions that the Spirit of God is not the spirit of the world, but is τὸ πνεῦμα τὸ ἐκ τοῦ θεοῦ, *the Spirit who issues from God* (1 Cor 2:12).[280] "What kinship could there be," Athanasius asks, "between the Spirit and his creatures," when Paul says, "no one knows the thoughts of God except the Spirit of God" (2:11)?[281] He undertakes a detailed consideration of ἐκ τοῦ θεοῦ (2:12) as signifying deity, in contrast to that which *issues from nothing* (ἐκ τοῦ μὴ ὄντος) as indicating what is creaturely. But as Haykin correctly comments, his interpretation of ἐκ, *from*, is *not* a statement about *origin* (for we cannot speak of the "origin" of the Holy Spirit) but about the Spirit's status as ὁ ὤν, *Being*, just as God is Being, in contrast to non-being, i.e., the contingency of the finite creature which may contingently be-or-not-be as against the *aseity* of God *as God* (from Lat. *a se*, of [or from] himself).[282]

Later in the same Epistle Athanasius applies the same phrase in Paul (1 Cor 2:12b) to the parallel between the deity of Christ and the deity of the Spirit: "The Holy Spirit is, and is said to be, from God (so said the Apostle). . . . Of necessity the Spirit is not a creature"; but Christ, too, is "not of that which non-being (ἐξ οὐκ ὄντων οὐκ ἐστίν) but from God."[283] This, again, refers not to their origin but to their divine nature. Athanasius sees the phrase "searches the depths of God" (2:10) as confirming all this even more clearly.[284]

276. Origen, *De Principiis*, 4:1:10.

277. Ibid. (Latin text). The Greek text speaks of "countless profound ideas" the comprehension of which cannot merely be "rapid," and the key to which does not lie "with the lawyers."

278. Origen, *Against Celsus*, 6:71.

279. *Against Celsus*, 6:71-75.

280. Athanasius, *Letter to Serapion*, 1:22 (Migne, *PG*, 26:581).

281. Ibid.

282. Haykin, *The Spirit of God: The Exegesis of 1 and 2 Corinthians in the Pneumatomachian Controversy of the Fourth Century*, 79; and Athanasius, *Letter to Serapion*, 1:22.

283. Athanasius, *Letter to Serapion*, 3:2; cf. 2:2-3.

284. Ibid., 3:2.

Indeed, on 2:11 Athanasius goes decidedly further than Paul. Here the Spirit's knowledge of God is thought to imply the unchangeable nature of the Spirit in contrast to the parallel "spirit of man."[285] But while Paul and Athanasius both emphasize the *transcendence* of God and God's Spirit here, as "the Beyond who is within," the concept of *unchangeableness* is an implicate of Athanasius's own system of Being, but is not part of Paul's argument in 2:11-12.[286] The question which Athanasius raises for us is whether Paul's language in 1 Cor 2:10-15, on which he draws heavily, contains *ontological* entailments or operates only to describe *functions*. Athanasius argues that the whole passage within its christological frame points not only to the deity of the Spirit (which seems a genuine entailment of Paul's language), but also to his oneness in being with the Father and the Son.[287] Might this go further than Paul, as Gregg and Groh argue, or does Paul's language at least point in this direction?[288] Father, Son, and Spirit are both one in being and yet distinct, and for Athanasius 1 Cor 2:10-12, 14, and 15 play a major role in reaching this conclusion.

Basil of Caesarea (c. 330-79) also finds in 1 Cor 2:11 the most significant declaration within the NT of the unity of the Spirit with the Father, and less directly with the Father and the Son. He first draws heavily on the Pauline passage in *Against Eunomius,* 1-3 (written c. 363-65), and then in his treatise *On the Holy Spirit* (AD 374). In *Eunomius* 1-3 he draws from 2:10-15 the principle that the Being and nature of God the Father is unknowable to all but the Son and the Spirit; otherwise "God is beyond all understanding and human understanding.... 'No one knows the Father except the Son' [Matt 11:27].... 'The Spirit searches out everything, even the depths of God's own self.... No one knows what pertains to God except the Spirit who is from God' [1 Cor 2:10-11]."[289]

Like Athanasius, Basil interprets 1 Cor 2:10-16 as demonstrating the deity of the Holy Spirit. The Spirit shares the activities of the Father and the Son, including the sharing of knowledge: the Spirit knows the Father and reveals the mind of Christ: "the Spirit shares the ineffable thoughts of God."[290] The analogy of the human spirit (1 Cor 2:11) demonstrates that God remains inscrutable to all creatures, but not to the Son and the Spirit who share deity. As against this, Eunomius had asserted that the Spirit was a creature, neither uncreated nor begotten. But on the law of 1 Cor 2:11 Basil asserts that the Spirit not only shares the nature of God but is even "within God" (parallel to τὸ ἐν αὐτῷ in 2:11a, of the human πνεῦμα).

References to 1 Cor 2:10-12 remain no less pivotal in Basil's treatise *On the Holy Spirit.* The Spirit is no mere "instrument" or "servant," for the "servant does not know what his master does" (John 15:15), whereas the Spirit *intimately knows* God (1 Cor 2:11).[291] Paul's words in 2:11 constitute "the greatest proof of the co-joining of the Spirit with the Father and the Son."[292] The sequence of Paul's argument from 2:9 on-

285. Ibid., 1:26.

286. Haykin (*The Spirit*, 82) cites Athanasius, *Letter to the African Bishops,* 7, and other references, where Athanasius also appeals to Jas 1:17.

287. The cluster of arguments in Athanasius *Letter to Serapion,* 1:20-26 and 3:1-2 need to be taken together to gain their full force.

288. R. G. Gregg and D. E. Groh, *Early Arianism* (London: SCM, 1981), 8-9, 63, 68, 100-107.

289. Basil, *Against Eunomius,* 1:13-14.

290. Ibid., 3:4.

291. Basil, *On the Holy Spirit,* 19:50 (last line).

292. Ibid., 16:40.

ward, and its implications for 1 Cor 12:8, has already been traced.[293] Moreover, *in keeping with Paul, Basil retains an explicitly christological focus in his references to the Spirit:* truly "to know the things of God" (1 Cor 2:12) amounts to understanding that God has graciously given freely all things through his Son (Rom 8:32).[294] Basil pays due attention to the Pauline context. He recognizes that the emphasis on revelation by the Spirit in 2:10 entails an appreciation of the limits and fallibility of human wisdom.[295] Basil stresses that revelation through the Spirit "cannot be divorced from the work of the Father and the Son."[296] Hence *reflection on 1 Cor 2:10-16* now gives birth *to a pastoral approach to trinitarian theology.* Pastoral and theological problems arise *either* if the Spirit is viewed merely as an *"instrument"* to "serve" believers as bringer of blessings; *or* if gifts of the Spirit are *abstracted from their trinitarian context. This seems to be a legitimate explication of the effective history of the text, which remains entirely true to 1 Cor 2:10-16 and to Paul's wider theology.* The influence of Athanasius's exegesis on Basil's agenda reveals a further fundamental aspect of *Wirkungsgeschichte* and its importance for exegesis and hermeneutics.

Chrysostom (347-407) retains the christological focus of language about the Spirit's revelation in 2:10-16. The true wisdom of God enters by his Spirit into the human heart which it works "within," whereas the false wisdom of the world remains external and "makes the cross of no effect."[297] This "wisdom of the Spirit" makes intelligible and credible such otherwise foolish things as the resurrection or the virgin birth of Christ, the child-bearing of Sarah, and creation *ex nihilo* because "spiritual things" must be compared or matched with spiritual (2:13). Again, this is "lest the cross should be emptied of its power."[298] The ψυχικός who does not receive the things of the Spirit (2:14) is like someone who may have good eyes but tries to see in the dark: to such a one only the Spirit of God can bring light. Hence fumbling confusion reigns, and the soul (ψυχή) is even unaware that it is not self-sufficient.[299] It finds itself deceived. With a possible allusion to the Johannine Paraclete, Chrysostom observes in 2:15 that to sift or to discern (ἀνακρίνειν) is necessary to expose (ἐλέγχειν): in this sense things lie open to view for the person of the Spirit.[300] Here to have the mind of Christ is part of what it is for the cross to work its power.[301]

Augustine (354-430) appeals to verses within our passage in at least three contexts. (a) In *City of God* he makes two major points. He recognizes the complexity of the word πνεῦμα and the need for linguistic reflection on 1 Cor 2:11.[302] Further, his comments instantiate our translation of ψυχικός in 2:11-16 as **the person who lives on an entirely human level.** He expounds these six verses in such a way as to underline this point, concluding, with Paul, that the test or sign of being "of the Spirit" is

293. Ibid., 5:10.
294. Ibid., 24:57.
295. Basil, *Homilies*, 20:3.
296. Haykin, *The Spirit of God*, 142.
297. Chrysostom, *Hom. 1 Cor.*, 7:6.
298. Chrysostom, *Hom. 1 Cor.*, 7:8.
299. *Hom.*, 7:9.
300. *Hom.*, 7:11.
301. *Hom.*, 7:12. Sections 14-19 then move away into less disciplined and less exegetical homiletical reflections of a fairly rambling nature, before exegetical discipline resumes at 3:1, with *Hom.* 8.
302. Augustine, *City of God*, 13:24.

negatively the absence of "envy and strife" (3:3) and positively reflecting "the mind of Christ" (2:16).[303] (b) Augustine's psychology of human nature and sin directs his attention to Paul's assertion that only the human spirit within a person, i.e., the *inner self*, fully understands them. Hence he warns his readers against superficial self-assessments and self-deception. There is need for a deeper "searching" of the heart within. Augustine appeals for all this to 1 Cor 2:11a.[304] (c) Under the pressure of the Donatist controversy, Augustine appeals to the axiom that only the spiritual person knows the things of the Spirit (1 Cor 2:14). Since people of the Spirit "sift out all things" (2:15), estrangement from the church invites estrangement from the sphere of the Spirit.[305] The church almost defines the sphere of the Spirit.[306] But this takes us from Paul's theme under pressure of controversy and needs to be reexamined when Augustine considers 1 Corinthians 12, 13, and 14.

The Medieval Period

Anselm (c. 1033-1109) perceives 1 Cor 2:10, 14, and 15 as shedding light on the status of his theology (including his formulation of the ontological argument concerning God) as testimony to the divine wisdom, revealed by the Spirit. "The *animalis homo* does not perceive the things of God (2:14).[307] To be "spiritual" entails not only obedience, but also being nourished by meditation on the Scriptures. Thus, with 2:10-16, he emphasizes the limitations and potentially destructive effects of purely human cleverness, the need for revelation by the Spirit of God, and the criterion of what it is to be "spiritual" as an appropriate stance of discipleship in life.

Thomas Aquinas (c. 1225-74) assigns to 1 Cor 2:12-15 several roles, but we select two as the most significant. (a) Of all his uses of these verses, the most fundamental comes where Thomas discusses the very nature of theology, and it remains of the utmost relevance to current questions about the nature of the knowledge Thomas discusses whether theology is "wisdom" *(utrum haec doctrina sit sapientia)*.[308] In a decisively qualified sense, theology is wisdom only as something above "human wisdom" *(sapientias humanas):* it is directly "from God" *(de Deo),* not derivative from other human sciences or skills. We now reach the heart of the matter. "Having a formed judgment characterizes the wise person *(quod cum judicium ad sapientem pertineat).*[309] But there are two kinds of wisdom (cf. 1 Cor 1:18–3:4). One is a matter primarily of "cognition" *(per modum cognitionis);* the other, "which is classed among the gifts of the Holy Spirit, "takes effect" *when a person who possesses the habit of a virtue rightly commits himself to what should be done in accordance with it* because he is already in sympathy with it *(sicut quit habet habitum virtutis recte judicat de his quae sunt secundum virtutem agenda*

---

303. *City of God,* 14:4.

304. Augustine, *City of God,* 1:26. Cf. further *Letters,* 130:3 (7).

305. Augustine, *On Baptism, Against the Donatists,* 3:18 (23) (c. AD 400).

306. *On Baptism,* 1:15 (23).

307. Anselm, *Letter to Pope Urban II on the Incarnation of the Word,* in E. R. Fairweather (ed.), *A Scholastic Miscellany: Anselm to Ockham,* LCC 10 (London: SCM, 1956), 97.

308. Thomas Aquinas, *Summa Theologiae* (London: Eyre & Spottiswoode, Lat. and Eng., 60 vols.; Blackfriars ed., 1963-), 1:21-25: 1a, Q. 1, art. 6.

309. *Summa,* 1a, Q. 1, art. 6; vol. 1:22 (Lat.), 23 (Eng.).

inquantum ad illa inclinatur). This way, Aquinas concludes, *corresponds with Paul's words that "the spiritual man judges all things (modus judicandi . . . pertinet ad sapientiam quae ponitur donum Spiritus Sancti; secundum illiud 1 Cor, Spiritualis homo judicat omnia)"* (1 Cor 2:15).[310] This precisely applies 1 Corinthians 2 to current debates about the difference between Enlightenment reason (τέχνη) and a more Gadamerian or neo-Aristotelian way of conserving of ethics on theology as *habitus* (Farley), φρόνησις (MacIntyre) "practical reason," "stance" (Wolterstorff), or judgment-based action-in-life.[311] By applying 1 Cor 2:10-16 to a largely Aristotelian agenda about the nature of virtue and of knowledge, and the contrast between wisdom and instrumental sciences, Aquinas has offered a "Reception" of the text which addresses issues of the cultural crises of today. (b) A second theme in the *Summa* which draws on 1 Cor 2:12 anticipates Calvin's point from our passage about Christian *assurance.* In v. 12, Aquinas comments, the Spirit reveals "the things freely given to us."[312] Hence "a person who has received grace through the Holy Spirit therefore knows that grace is given to him."[313]

The Reformation Period

Luther (1483-1546) offers a developing case study on his own. (a) In his earliest works (1517-19) Luther appeals to 1 Cor 2:10, 11, 16 in the context of the problem of knowledge. He writes: "It is not sufficient to know God . . . as philosophers write of his nature. . . . This is a natural knowledge of the senses, harmful to those who do not understand it. . . . No one understands his commands rightly unless he first be illuminated from above. . . . 'Who has known the mind of the Lord . . . ? (1 Cor 2:16). . . . 'The things of God no one knows, only the Spirit of God, but God has revealed them to us by his Spirit' (1 Cor 2:11, 10)."[314] As a pastoral theme this leads to a deeper understanding of divine vocation. The gift of the Spirit comes "to magnify our vision . . . and understand the gifts bestowed on us by God, as St Paul says in 1 Cor 2:12 . . . such gifts are more splendid than heaven and earth."[315] (b) In the period following 1521, Luther's ideas spread so rapidly that Carlstadt, Müntzer, and others were found carrying them to extremes. The "fanatics," as Luther termed them, inspired radicalism in politics, theology, and liturgy. By 1522 the excesses of the "enthusiasts" had much in common with "the people of the Spirit" at Corinth. It is no accident, then, that in 1525, in the course of his

---

310. *Summa*, 22-24 (Lat.); 23-25 (Eng.).

311. Edward Farley, "Theology and Practice outside the Clerical Paradigm," in Don S. Browning (ed.), *Practical Theology* (San Francisco: Harper & Row, 1983), 23 and 30 (on *habitus*); cf. 21-41; Alasdair MacIntyre, *After Virtue: A Study in Moral Theology* (London: Duckworth, 2d ed. 1985), 62-78 ("the failure of the Enlightenment project") and 204-25 (on virtue and tradition); cf. 146-276; and *Three Rival Versions of Moral Enquiry* (London: Duckworth, 1990), esp. 127-48 (on "Aquinas and the Rationality of Tradition"); and N. Wolterstorff, *Divine Discourse* (Cambridge: Cambridge University Press, 1995) 31-36, 52-57, 240-60, and elsewhere.

312. Aquinas, *Summa Theologiae* (vol. 30, 12ae), Q. 112, art. 5, sect. 4.

313. Ibid.

314. Luther, *The Epistle to the Hebrews* (1517) on Heb 6:13, in *Works*, 29 (American ed., Concordia: St. Louis, 1974), and in Luther, *Early Theological Works*, LCC 16 (ed. J. Atkinson; London: SCM, 1962), 126.

315. Luther, *Commentary on 1 Corinthians 15*, in *Works*, 28 (St Louis: Concordia, 1973), 137-38; and *WA*, 36:587.

debate with Erasmus *On the Bondage of the Will,* Luther is fairly dismissive of claims about "the spiritual person judges all things, but is judged by no one" (1 Cor 2:15). This "internal clarity" is given by the Spirit to all Christians, but must be checked against "external" criteria relating "to the public ministry of the Word and to the outward office. . . . All spirits are to be tested in the presence of the Church at the bar of Scripture. . . . The Holy Scriptures are a spiritual light brighter than the sun itself, especially in things that are necessary to salvation."[316] Luther's contrast between a *theologia crucis* and a *theologia gloriae* resonates both with his own attack on the "fanatics" and their claims about the Spirit and with Paul's formulation of a theology of the cross against what Horsley calls "the language of exalted religious status and spiritual perfection" found among some at Corinth.[317]

Calvin (1509-64) begins his exposition of 2:10-16 with a doxological perspective reminiscent of Tertullian's comments. God's revelation by the Spirit in the face of human blindness, he observes, points to God's goodness, while the sentence "the Spirit searches out all things" (1 Cor 2:10) is added "for the encouragement of believers" that they may rest their faith securely in that revelation which the Spirit gives them.[318] However, Calvin's major emphasis falls on the confidence of Christians in the revelatory work of the Holy Spirit, given as a gift of God's goodness and grace. Thus the contrast with "the spirit of the world" (2:12) eliminates the notion that Christians are always in a state of confusion or perplexity. The pastoral issue for Calvin, therefore, is that the guarantee of revelation and the gift of knowing God's ways in Christ protect the believer against "doubt if we are in a state of grace."[319] Faith, therefore, need not be "agitated and hesitant." Although this may not be the central theme of these verses, the emphasis is true to Paul's phrase "that we may know what things have been given to us by God" (1 Cor 2:12b). We noted above that Calvin also draws from 2:13 a confirmation of his principle of accommodation: God "adapts *(aptare)* spiritual things to spiritual, when he accommodates the words to the reality."[320] Plain speech may thus become a vehicle for the Spirit. Likewise we share with Calvin our principle in translation and exegesis that normally "the spiritual refers to the man whose mind is directed by . . . the Spirit," while the ψυχικός is one whose *anima* is "bound up with nature," i.e., motivated by things *on an entirely human level.*[321] Characteristically Calvin interprets the corollary of the need for the Spirit's light to be that otherwise the human predicament is marred by "blindness" and "darkness." Conversely, 2:15, he urges, implies that no human argument can shake the assurance of faith of the believer by assessing his/her status in the eyes of God. In this context Calvin links 2:16 with the theme of ministry which arises from 3:4 to 4:21. Taught by the Spirit, "faithful ministers . . . might speak fearlessly as it were from the mouth of the Lord."[322]

316. Luther, *The Bondage of the Will, WA,* 652-53; also Eng. trans., *Luther and Erasmus,* LCC 17 (ed. E. G. Rupp; London: SCM, 1969), 159.

317. Horsley, "Spiritual Elitism at Corinth," *NovT* 20 (1978): 203-31, esp. 203-5. See further Thiselton, "Luther and Barth on 1 Corinthians 15," in W. P. Stephens (ed.), *The Bible, the Reformation and the Church: Essays in Honour of James Atkinson,* JSNTSS (Sheffield: Sheffield Academic Press, 1995), 258-307.

318. Calvin, *First Epistle,* 57-58.

319. Ibid., 59.

320. Ibid., 60.

321. Ibid., 61.

322. Ibid., 64.

The Enlightenment and Modern Periods

John Locke (1632-1704) interprets "taught by the Spirit" (2:13) as "the words of reve-lation in the Sacred Scripture."[323] He also understood "matching" or "comparing" spir-itual things with spiritual as meaning comparing one part of Scripture with another (v. 13b). This coheres with his own wider program of arguing for a rational, scholarly, commonsense approach to exegesis, as against special pleading of various kinds. On 2:14 Locke concedes that a faith based on biblical revelation cannot be adequately put on trial by "natural faculties" alone.[324] The ψυχικός or *animalis homo* is "the man that supposes such a natural sufficiency in the humane soul in order to its own per-fection and happinesse . . . that there was noe necessity either of divine revelation . . . or of divine grace"[325]

Karl Barth (1886-1968) The theme "No one knows what pertains to God ex-cept the Spirit of God" (2:11) points in the direction of Barth's maxim: "God is known through God alone."[326] Two themes in this passage are fundamental for Barth's theol-ogy: "the knowability" of the word of God, and the lostness of the image of God in hu-man persons which is restored in Christ.[327] This possibility rests solely on grace, "not, then, as a natural capacity in man." Only God's gracious act can give knowledge of "the deep things of God (1 Cor 2:10)."[328] Following Luther, Barth also takes up this passage in connection with vocation: "According to 1 Cor 2:13, 14, vocation as a pneu-matic reality can be known only by men who are themselves pneumatic."[329]

The revelation of the Spirit in 2:10-16 is also implicit in **Jüngel** (b. 1934). Jüngel perceives divine self-disclosure as *address*. Only when human persons become "ad-dressable" does God assume *"conceivability"* . . . as "a God who *speaks out of himself*" (my italics).[330] Moltmann (b. 1928) speaks of the need to retain some sense of "discontinuity between God's Spirit and the spirit of human beings," but without forcing a dichotomy between "God's self-revelation" and "experience." God's revelation is a "making-itself-experienceable through others . . . in the relationship to that Other."[331] Since almost ev-erything about the Spirit in Moltmann's work concerns relationality, 1 Cor 2:6-16 leads to 12:1–14:40, as it does in Paul. "The Spirit allows himself to be known as presence and counterpart"; but even in the case of the Spirit's own personhood "his subjectivity is constituted by his intersubjectivity."[332] 1 Cor 2:10-15 reflects this theme.

Summary

The continuities, discontinuities, developments, and reappropriations of 1 Cor 2:10-16 make this a model paradigm of the value of a *Wirkungsgeschichte* of a Pauline text. A

---

323. John Locke, *A Paraphrase and Notes of the Epistles of St Paul* (ed. A. W. Wainwright; Oxford: Clarendon Press, 1987 [1707]), 1:424.

324. Ibid.

325. Ibid.; cf. 425.

326. Barth, *CD*, 2/1, sect. 27.179.

327. *CD*, 1/1, sect. 4.241.

328. Ibid.

329. *CD*, 4/3/2, sect. 71.502.

330. Jüngel, *God as the Mystery of the World*, 152-53, 155, 158; cf. 152-69.

331. Moltmann, *The Spirit of Life*, 5-6.

332. Ibid., 287 and 289; cf. 268-309.

flood of light is shed in both directions — back onto the text and forward into the world.

c. The Inapplicability of the Term "Spiritual" in the Face of Infantile Status-Seeking (3:1-4)

(1) For my part, my Christian friends, I could not address you as people of the Spirit, but as people moved by entirely human drives, as people who in Christian terms are infantile. (2) I gave you milk to drink, not solid food; for you could not take it. Indeed, even now you still cannot manage it. (3) You are still unspiritual. For where jealousy and strife prevail among you, are you not centered on yourselves and behaving like any merely human person? (4) When someone declares, "I, for one, am one of Paul's people," and another asserts, "I, for my part, am for Apollos," are you not all too human?

The passage from 2:6–2:16 has expounded the visionary consequences of the new worlds which the Holy Spirit can open and reveal to believing Christians. The wonder of what the Spirit can display passes all human experiences of sight and sound, and all human imagining (2:9). The truly "spiritual" person does indeed enjoy intimacy with God, and through knowing what gifts God has bestowed (2:12c) experiences assurance of salvation. In one sense, which is, however, carefully qualified, Paul endorses the Corinthian catchphrase that people of the Spirit sift out everything, while no one else puts spiritual persons on trial or sifts them out (2:15)! However, for Paul the test of whether people are truly "of the Spirit" is whether the Spirit has formed within them the mind-set of Christ (2:16).

However, claims to be Christ-like cannot be sustained among those whose desire for status and self-esteem leads them to rivalries. Where envy and strife are in evidence, Paul is reluctant to use the word "spiritual." He does not deny that committed Christians may behave in infantile ways. The church is a school for sinners, not a museum for saints. But the actual situation at Corinth makes triumphalist claims about being "people of the Spirit" look out of place and rather foolish, at least until they have more deeply appropriated the stance and lifestyle that is the way of Christ and the cross. However, the passage does look forward in confident hope. The addressees are simply **not yet** (οὔπω, 3:2) ready for Paul to address them as "spiritual" people in the full sense of the term. They will grow.

Bibliography on 3:1-4

Bultmann, R., *Theology of the NT* (Eng. trans., London: SCM, 1952), 1:223 and 239-46.
Byrne, B., "Ministry and Maturity in 1 Cor. 3," *AusBR* 35 (1987): 83-87.
Davies, W. D., *Paul and Rabbinic Judaism* (London: SPCK, 2d ed. 1955), 19-35.

Francis, James, "As Babes in Christ — Some Proposals regarding 1 Cor. 3:1-3," *JSNT* 7 (1980): 41-60.

Gaventa, B. R., "Our Mother St Paul: Toward the Recovery of a Neglected Theme," *PSB* 17 (1996): 29-44.

Gerleman, G., *Der Heidenapostel. Ketzerische Erwägungen zur Predigt des Paulus zugleich ein Streifzug in der griechischen Mythologie* (Stockholm: Almqvist & Wiksell, 1989).

Grundmann, W., "Die νήπιοι in der urchristlichen Paränese," *NTS* 5 (1958-59): 188-205.

Holloway, J. O., περιπατέω *as a Thematic Marker for Pauline Ethics* (San Francisco: Mellen, 1992).

Hooker, Morna, "Hard Sayings: 1 Cor. 3:2," *Theology* 69 (1966): 19-22.

Mitchell, M. M., *Paul and the Rhetoric of Reconciliation* (Tübingen: Mohr and Louisville: John Knox, 1992), 68-98.

Maly, Karl, *Mündige Gemeinde. Untersuchungen zur pastoralen Führung des Apostels Paulus im 1 Korintherbrief,* SBM 2 (Stuttgart: Katholisches Bibelwerk, 1967), 49-61.

Plank, Karl A., *Paul and the Irony of Affliction* (Atlanta: Scholars Press, 1987), 25-31.

Rhyne, Thomas, "1 Cor 3:1-9," *Int* 44 (1990): 174-79.

Schnackenburg, R., "Christian Adulthood according to Paul," *CBQ* 25 (1963): 354-70.

Thompson, J. W., "Paideia" and "A Theory of Education," in *Beginnings of Christian Philosophy: The Epistle to the Hebrews* (Washington, D.C.: Catholic Biblical Association of America, 1982), 18-27, 35-40.

Thüsing, W., "'Milch' und 'feste Speise' (1 Kor 3:1f und Hebr 5:11–6:3," *TTZ* 76 (1967): 233-46, 261-80.

Weiss, J., *Earliest Christianity* (New York: Harper, 1937), 2:468-69.

Welborn, L. L., "On the Discord at Corinth: 1 Cor 1–4 and Ancient Politics," *JBL* 106 (1987): 83-113.

Wilckens, Ulrich, *Weisheit und Torheit* (Tübingen: Mohr, 1959), 89-96.

Yarbrough, O. L., "Parents and Children in the Letters of Paul," in L. M. White and O. L. Yarbrough (eds.), *The Social World of the First Christians: Essays in Honor of W. A. Meeks* (Minneapolis: Fortress, 1995), 126-41.

1 Κἀγώ may be translated **For my part** for two reasons. First, some indicator of a return to the singular (καὶ ἐγω) is needed to remind the reader that after the use of the first plural ἡμεῖς, *we,* or λαλοῦμεν, *we speak* (2:6), from 2:6 to 2:16, Paul returns to the personal "I" of 1:1–2:5, especially instantiated in Paul's reference to his personal circumstances in 2:1-5. Second, ἐγώ, **I**, is an indicator of emphasis, for the inflection of the verb alone can identify the subject as first person singular. We might have expected a contrastive **but** (REB) in place of καί, although Findlay suggests that the καί *(and)* points back to 2:14, "A person who lives on an entirely human level does not receive the Spirit."[333] On the difficulty of translating ἀδελφοί with accuracy in today's culture, see on 1 Cor 1:10. This family word also occurs when Paul fears that he needs to offer a rebuke, but wishes to indicate affection and solidarity with the addressees at the same time.

333. Findlay, *Expositor's Greek Testament,* 2:785.

287

On the translation and meaning of πνευματικοῖς (πνευματικός as *spiritual* and/or as **person of the Spirit**), see above on 2:10. Paul makes it clear elsewhere that all Christians receive the Holy Spirit (e.g., 1 Cor 12:3 and Rom 8:9b are decisive); but he cannot *address* them in ways which they might expect on the basis of *their claims to be "spiritual people"* when they have so much still to learn.

The adjectival form σάρκινος, which we have rendered **people moved by entirely human drives** would mean, solely on the basis of a referential theory of meaning, people composed of flesh (σάρξ) or perhaps *people who belong to the realm of the flesh,* as BAGD suggest.[334] Older lexicographers suggest that whereas σαρκικός (3:3) emphasizes a *disposition* of σάρξ (flesh), σάρκινος denotes a *constitution* or *nature* of σάρξ, perceiving the -ικός ending to relate to κατὰ σάρκα εἶναι, *to live according to the flesh,* whereas the -ίνος ending reflects ἐν σαρκὶ εἶναι, *to live an ordinary, earthly life in this world.*[335] Although among more recent commentators Fee retains this contrast, the distinction remains one of morphology rather than semantics.[336] For if Conzelmann and most others are right in explaining σάρκινος in v. 1 as people who behave "as 'natural' men, as ἄνθρωποι, 'humans'," does Paul not explain σαρκικός in v. 3 as "behaving like ordinary human people" (κατὰ ἄνθρωπον περιπατεῖτε)?[337]

Yet the two adjectival forms which derive from σάρξ may carry a nuance different from ψυχικός, derived from ψυχή, in 2:14. In most contexts ψυχικός stands in contrast to persons characterized by the agency of the Holy Spirit, whereas σάρξ and σαρκικός tend to carry a *further overtone of human self-sufficiency* in many (although not in all) contexts. The full theological sense of σάρξ as "human self-sufficiency" or the self in pursuit of its own ends (as Bultmann and J. A. T. Robinson express it) emerges in Rom 8:7: τὸ φρόνημα τῆς σαρκὸς ἔχθρα εἰς θεόν, the mind-set of the "flesh" is hostile to God.[338] In its fullest theological sense, Bultmann comments, "living out of the 'flesh' is the self-reliant attitude of the man who puts his trust in his own strength and in that which is controllable by him." It is "trust in one's self as being able to procure life by the use of the earthly and through one's own strength . . . (Rom. 8:7)."[339]

At the same time the nuances of σάρξ range from "mere man, . . . man in his weakness and mortality" through persons "as part of the whole worldorder" to "human self-sufficiency."[340] In the context of 1 Cor 2:6–3:3, a translation and meaning need to be proposed for σάρκινος which recognizes this extensive

334. BAGD, 743.

335. Lightfoot, *Notes,* 185; Findlay, *Expositor's Greek Testament,* 2:785; Robertson and Plummer, *First Epistle,* 52; Godet, *First Epistle,* 1:166; Weiss, *Der erste Korintherbrief,* 71-72; Edwards, *First Epistle,* 70-71.

336. Fee, *First Epistle,* 121, n. 1.

337. Conzelmann, *1 Corinthians,* 71.

338. Bultmann, *Theology of the NT,* 1:239-46; Robinson, *The Body,* 17-26.

339. Bultmann, *Theology,* 240 and 239.

340. Robinson, *The Body,* 19, 21, and 25.

range of semantic variables and also the move from ψυχικός as a less positive and less colorful contrast to πνεῦμα in 2:14. Hence, as against **on an entirely human level** for ψυχικός (2:14) we propose **people moved by entirely human drives**. *Flesh, fleshly,* cannot avoid nuances of sensuality in the late twentieth century, which is not Paul's point. But may an objection not be made that our translation is anachronistic, owing more to Freud than to Paul? We may reply that σάρξ can denote human persons in respect of their drive toward self-esteem, preservation, or "success," in a sense akin to the rabbinic יצר *(yetser) inclination* or *drive*. On one side, the rabbis urged, human nature was driven by *the-impulse-to*-evil, היצר הרע *(ha-yetser ha-ra).*[341] But this drive or impulse may be complemented by היצר הטוב *(ha-yetser ha-tobh), the-impulse-to-good*. Without these drives, as Rabbi Samuel ben Nathan is said to have observed, "no one would build a house, nor beget children, nor engage in trade."[342] Hence σάρκινος means **moved by entirely human drives**, while σαρκικός means *moved by self-interest.*[343]

Paul appears to use νηπίοις, *young children, babes, infants,* or here metaphorically **those who are infantile**, in semantic contrast to τέλειος, **mature**, *grown up, adult* (2:6). Paul does not doubt that the addressees have received the Spirit because without the Spirit they could not be ἐν Χριστῷ, whether this is understood to mean *in union with Christ,* or **in Christian terms**.[344] But does Paul have in mind the image of children who need to grow, or that of infantile adults who need to adjust their attitude?

(i) The vast majority of commentators perceive the issue as a call to maturity and to *progress*. Moffatt comments that all "had the Spirit, but converts might at first be so uninformed and immature that the Spirit did not yet control

341. Cf. Heb. Sir 15:14; Sir 21:11; 17:5-6; *Genesis Rabbah* 9:7; *Testament of Asher* 1:4-9; *Testament of Judah* 11:1; Further, G. Theissen, *Psychological Aspects of Pauline Theology* (though-out).

342. *Gen. Rab.* 9:7; cf. Moore, *Judaism,* 1:480-91; H. Wheeler Robinson, *The Christian Doctrine of Man,* 22; Williams, *The Ideas of the Fall and Original Sin,* 60-69; Strack-Billerbeck, 3:94-95 and 329-31 and 4:466-67; and esp. W. D. Davies, *Paul and Rabbinic Judaism* (London: SPCK, 2d ed. 1955), 19-35.

343. See Theissen, *Psychological Aspects,* 66-74, 96-114, and 345-52. In later Jewish tradition after Paul, the Mishnah associates the two "impulses" with two "hearts" (Heb. לב, *lebh*) in the sense rightly associated by Bultmann with "the hidden things" which nowadays we call the unconscious or subconscious (Mishnah, *Berakoth* 9:5); cf. Bultmann, *Theology,* 1:223, "it need not penetrate into the field of consciousness at all, but may designate the hidden tendency of the self." See further R. H. Charles (ed.), *The Apocrypha and Pseudepigrapha* (Oxford: Clarendon Press, 1913), 2:343, on *Testament of Asher* 1:4-9 and wider allusions to the *yêtser*.

344. Often Paul uses ἐν Χριστῷ in the full theological sense of *being-in-Christ*. But as J. Weiss has conclusively shown, he uses the phrase in at least five distinct ways, of which the above is only one category (Weiss, *Earliest Christianity,* 2:468-69, esp. n. 22. To translate *in Christ* runs the further risk of seeming to suggest that a Christ-centered faith can yield to a more "advanced" Spirit-centered faith, which is closer to the view of some at Corinth than to Paul, who would utterly reject it. J. Francis suggests, *"from a Christian point of view,"* which approximates Weiss and our **in Christian terms**.

their personalities fully." He then points out that the metaphor of "babes" who need to grow was entirely familiar in the ancient world as an image for development from Pythagoras onward.[345] Collins discusses the widespread use of this imagery with reference to Paul's "maternal image [of] pastoral care . . . of those he has evangelized."[346] Paul's use of analogy and metaphor is well underlined by Gale, and this imagery is widespread in Paul's era.[347]

(ii) Weiss points out that in our passage the main semantic contrast is not between νήπιοι (infants) and τέλειοι (mature adults), but between νήπιοι (in the sense of people who are infantile) and πνευματικοί (people under the control of the Spirit).[348] James Francis develops this contrast in a detailed argument.[349] He states, "We shall argue that Paul is rebuking his readers not because they are babes still, and had not progressed further, but because they were in fact being childish, a condition contrary to being spiritual."[350] Francis sees 1 Cor 13:11 as likewise portraying the huge contrast between the "this-worldly" and the world to come. In 1 Cor 14:20 Paul says that if his addressees insist on being "childish," at least let this be in matters of evil. Like Deluz, Francis diagnoses the problem as relating back to 2:1-5 and the Corinthians' perception of his so-called "milk-and-water" speech in contrast to a "meaty" rhetoric which dazzled his hearers with its wit and wisdom. But it was not *possible* (logical possibility) for Paul to be perceived otherwise, given their infantile obsession with point-scoring rhetoric as against Paul's exclusive focus on proclaiming a crucified Christ. Thus 3:1-3 provides a transitional link between the previous discussion and the following material on ministry. Francis concludes, "Paul at 1:17 and 2:4 seems to be countering a charge that he was a poor orator. . . . We may therefore take 3:1 with 2:1ff as part of his defence."[351]

---

345. Moffatt, *First Epistle,* 36.

346. Collins, *First Cor,* 141, cf. 143; B. R. Gaventa, "Our Mother St Paul: Toward the Recovery of a Neglected Theme," *PSB* 17 (1996): 29-44; and Wolff, *Der erste Brief,* 64.

347. H. M. Gale, *The Use of Analogy in the Letters of Paul* (Philadelphia: Westminster, 1964). Cf. Eph 4:13-14; Heb 5:11-14; and 1 Pet 2:2; also Plato in the "preparatory" *propaideia* (Plato, *Republic* 7.531D, 534D, and 536E, and *Theaetetus* 145); Seneca on the liberal arts as "preparatory teaching" for virtue (Seneca, *Letters* 88.20); Philo on OT characters as "not yet perfect" (*De Specialibus Legibus* 3.244; *De Sacrificiis Abelis et Caini* 7) and on teaching as leading to maturity (*De Fuga et Inventione* 172; *De Mutatione Nominum* 270). The image of mild and solid food occurs in Philo, *Quod Omnis Probus Liber Sit* 160; *De Congressu Quarendae* 15-19; and *De Agricultura* 2 and 9. The imagery occurs in Epictetus, *Dissertations* 2.16.39; 3.24.9; cf. 3.19.6; and *Enchiridion* 51:1, in the light of D. S. Sharp, *Epictetus and the NT* (London: Kelly, 1914), 59-60; and A. Bonhoeffer, *Epiktetus und das NT* (Giessen: Töpelmann, 1911), 62. See also W. Grundmann, "Die νήπιοι in der urchristlichen Paränese," *NTS* 5 (1958-59): 188-205.

348. Weiss, *Der erste Korintherbrief,* 71-74. The exegesis on 71 is supported by a close comparison with other ancient sources on 73-74.

349. J. Francis, "As Babes in Christ — Some Proposals regarding 1 Cor. 3:1-3," *JSNT* 7 (1980): 41-60.

350. Ibid., 43.

351. Ibid., 53 Long before the explosion of research on "rhetoric" G. Deluz also perceived the problem here as one of a perception of Paul as "not eloquent and lacking a commanding pres-

If this argument fits Paul's thought, as we believe that it does, the practical point for readers today is not so much a call to maturity (although this may well be an implicate of these verses), but a warning that *the self-centered competitive naïveté which characterizes young children* who have not yet learned to respect the interests of the Other will lead to *misjudgments about* the *quality and required methods of Christian proclamation and teaching.* A "childish" mind-set may, e.g., place undue value upon the style of a chat-show host, or alternatively the pseudo-learning of a long display of rhetorical theatricals, *above gospel content.* To be spiritually minded is to bring different criteria to the role and style of preachers and teachers.

2 ἔτι, **still**, is omitted by p[45]; B; as Metzger observes, this is doubtless due to an Alexandrian desire to smooth the style, since οὐδέ, **not even**, with the shift from the aorist to the present tense (δύνασθε) makes ἔτι strictly redundant. However, redundancy in everyday speech often adds force, even if at the cost of stylistic elegance, and it is almost certainly Pauline and is included in our translation. D and F also insert καί, *and,* before **not solid food** (so AV/KJV), but early and virtually unanimous MS support for the omission confirms that this is a later addition. (On the grammatical status of καί, cf. BDF, sect. 460 [1].)

The simile of childhood diet for the novice, the immature, or the infantile was widespread (see n. 347 above). The aorist of ποτίζω, *I give* [someone something] *to drink,* and of δύναμαι, *I can,* point back to Paul's earliest arrival and proclamation (as in 2:1-5) and the early period. But time brought no change of stance, and ἀλλά, normally *but,* carries here its effect as an intensifier, which is best translated as **indeed**.[352] Strictly, since ποτίζω refers only to drink, not to food and drink, the use of a single verb to govern two objects when it suits only one constitutes an example of zeugma.[353] As a sense construction it raises no problem, and we often use it today. The sense-construction also necessitates the supply of verbs after ἐδύνασθε and δύνασθε, at least for smooth translation, and we have supplied **take it** and **manage it** as implicit but not explicit in the Greek.

Morna Hooker's article on this verse achieves double importance in view of the reappraisal of v. 1 which J. Francis offers (see above). She urges, convincingly, that the contrast is "not between two quite different diets" in the sense of elementary and advanced Christian doctrine (as in Heb. 5:11-14) but between "the true food of the Gospel . . . (whether milk or meat) and the synthetic substitutes which the Corinthians have preferred."[354] Similarly, against

---

ence. They looked on him as a third-rate philosopher and found his teaching over-simple . . . who fancied themselves as intellectuals . . ." (*Companion to 1 Corinthians,* 33).

352. Barrett, *First Epistle,* 81. Cf. Merklein, *Der erste Brief 1–4,* 251; Collins, *First Cor,* 144.

353. Cf. BDF, sect. 479 (1).

354. M. Hooker, "Hard Sayings: 1 Cor. 3:2," *Theology* 69 (1966): 21; cf. 19-22. This finds a parallel in Wolff, *Der erste Brief,* 64, and is followed by Merklein, *Der erste Brief 1–4,* 249-50.

the stream of most commentaries Fee declares, "The Corinthians do not need a change in diet but a change in perspective."[355] If Paul meant that **even now you still cannot manage** something more complex than **the milk** of proclamation, it is difficult to see what he expects them to make of his rigorous arguments about ethical conduct, marriage and celibacy, the nature of freedom in relation to food offered to idols, the eucharist, spiritual gifts or persons in a corporate setting, and the resurrection. G. Gerleman's speculative arguments to the effect that Paul has two different types of teaching, one of which explores the world of Greek mythology, cannot be substantiated.[356] Paul responds to their accusations that *at the level of rhetoric* his discourse is mere milk-and-water with the reply that *in terms of realities of the Spirit* they need to be *nourished and nurtured,* be it with milk or with something more. The need for *nurture* addresses their self-confident stance that accepting someone else's *ministry,* like it or not, was somehow questionable.[357] It seemed to compromise their status as "spiritual people" who were "free" and "already nourished and reigning" with "knowledge" of their own (2:15; 6:12a; 4:8; 8:1: "all [of us] have knowledge, γνῶσις"). Hence they "cheat themselves" (μηδεὶς ἑαυτὸν ἐξαπατάτω, 3:18) out of the range of ministerial resources which God has given for their nurture.

3 UBS⁴ grades the inclusion of ἔρις, **strife** (v. 3), without the addition of καὶ διχοστασίαι, *and dissensions,* as "almost certain" (B). The longer reading has some weighty support, especially 𝔓⁴⁶, D, G, 33, and Marcion. But 𝔓¹¹(?), ℵ, A, B, C, Clement, and Origen have the shorter reading. The question has to be taken seriously because the early 𝔓⁴⁶ is Alexandrian (as is the important cursive, 33) and D, F, and G are significant Western witnesses. On the other hand, the impressive combination of a damaged 𝔓¹¹ (probable reading), ℵ, A, B, and C with the early Alexandrian Fathers also carries much weight. The general consensus is that the longer reading is almost certainly a Western gloss which draws in the additional word from the parallel in Gal. 5:20. This explanation for the addition is more convincing than any proposal to try to explain the omission.

We have translated the same Greek word, σαρκικοί, differently on each occasion it is used in this verse: first, as **unspiritual**, and then as **centered on yourselves**. It is of pivotal importance to grasp the nuances which distinguish this word in its present context from ψυχικός in 2:14 (translated there as **the person who lives on an entirely human level**) and from σάρκινος in 3:1 (translated there as **moved by entirely human drives**, drawing on the background of καρδία and לב [lebh], *heart,* and יצר [yetser], *impulse, drive*). The three terms ψυχικός (2:14), σάρκινος (3:1), and σαρκικός (3:3) all draw their semantic nuances from their mutual interaction with one another within a single semantic field in which the term of major contrast to all three is πνευματικός, *spiritual* or *pertaining to the Spirit.*

---

355. Fee, *First Epistle,* 125.
356. Gerleman, *Der Heidenapostel: Ketzerische Erwägungen zur Predigt des Paulus.*
357. Byrne, "Ministry and Maturity in 1 Cor. 3," 83-87.

Of the three terms which jointly stand in contrast to πνεῦμα *(Spirit),* (i) ψυχικός (Vulg. *animalis homo,* 2:14) is virtually *neutral.* It means *unspiritual* (NRSV, REB) in the neutral sense of **an entirely human** (unrenewed) nature, without further subtext (cf. AV/KJV, *natural*). (ii) σάρκινος means *unspiritual* in a *descriptive* sense: in 3:1 such a person shows no sign of the presence and power of the Spirit of God, but appears to be motivated **by human, natural drives** alone (cf. REB, *on the natural plane;* NJB, *people living by their natural inclination*), (iii) σαρκικός in 3:3 means **unspiritual** (first translation) in an *evaluative* sense, which carries with it *theological appraisal:* such a person in this context is **unspiritual** in every sense conveyed by σάρξ *(flesh).* In the light of comments from Bultmann and from J. A. T. Robinson we saw (above, v. 1) that this included *human self-sufficiency, life in pursuit of its own ends,* or *being* **centered on the self** (second translation).

To be sure, σάρξ often occurs in other contexts to denote humankind in its weakness and creatureliness. Much depends on the context. Here the explicit meaning is parallel to Paul's evaluation of *the works of the flesh* (τὰ ἔργα τῆς σαρκός) in Gal 5:18, which include the very disposition and behavior mentioned here: **strife** (ἔρις,) **jealousy** (ζῆλος), and the divisiveness denoted in the longer textual reading here and in Gal 5:20 by διχοστασίαι, *dissensions.* Galatians offers a striking and important key for our understanding of σάρξ and σαρκικός. For how can *obsessional zeal for the law* and *self-indulgent license* which disdains the law *both* be "fleshly" attitudes? Jewett writes: "The key to the 'flesh' concept is . . . that it lures him [the human person] to substitute his own good for God's. . . . The Jew sought to gain life through the law. . . . The flesh represents to the libertinist objects of desire which man is to satisfy (Gal 5:16). These objects lure man on. They seem to offer man exactly what the law and circumcision offered — life."[358] This semantic analysis and hermeneutic holds the key for those passages which concern "the Revolt of the σάρξ against the πνεῦμα . . . the independent action of the σάρξ. . . ."[359]

If we place together the acute observations of Bultmann, Robinson, and Jewett, this coheres entirely with Paul's thought in 3:3 that what is at issue is the anomaly of Christians who are nominally or in principle focused on Christ but *in practice and in stance still focused on the interests of the self.* This provides the root explanation for the anomaly of **jealousy** (the desire that the self may have the status, possessions, esteem, or honor supposedly accorded to others) and **strife** (the expression of this desire in active strategies to gain advantage for the self or for the peer group of the self). Both terms are concerned with advancing the claims and interests of the self. (See above on 1:11.)[360]

---

358. Barrett, *First Epistle,* 81.

359. Cf. BDF, sect. 479 (1).

360. Further to the comments on ἔρις offered under 1:11, we may recall Margaret M. Mitchell's incisive analysis of the political significance of this vocabulary. She points out that *quarrels* is far too weak a translation. It denotes political or domestic discord, and Ἔρις is personified as the Greek goddess of discord. It refers "to political **strife** and its causes" (Mitchell, *Paul and the Rheto-*

The notion of *anomaly* appears in Paul's shocked and indignant οὐχὶ . . . κατὰ ἄνθρωπον περιπατεῖτε: **are you not . . . behaving like any merely human person?** Christians who have been reoriented and transformed on the basis of the cross (1:18-25; 2:1-5) are not **like any merely human person** if they are living out the entailments of the cross and the gift of the Holy Spirit. Paul's prepositional phrase κατὰ ἄνθρωπον (κατά with accusative normally means *according to*) stands in contrast to the κατὰ πνεῦμα *(according to the Spirit)* which ought to have characterized their lives. The first draft of our proposed translation read *like people motivated by purely human concerns.* This better expresses the sense, but moves perhaps too far from the Greek vocabulary of the text. The verb περιπατέω, *I walk,* regularly denotes *behavior* in Paul, since the normal word in the Hebrew Bible for *behaving* is *walking.* (Heb. הלכה, *Halakah,* i.e., a body, a material relating to conduct, may be distinguished from *Haggadah* as narrative material.) Paul regularly speaks of how a Christian believer should *walk* in this sense (Rom 13:13; 2 Cor 10:2; Phil 3:17; 1 Thess 4:12; cf. Eph 5:15, walk ἀκριβῶς). J. O. Holloway argues in a full-length study that Paul uses περιπατέω, *walk,* for what he regards as fundamental themes in ethical exhortation. He includes 1 Cor 3:3 among twenty Pauline examples.[361]

To be sure, in many instances an incongruous gap appears between what God has made the Christian's status as a new creation in Christ and the Christian's lifestyle, which may lag behind it. For, as Whiteley points out, Christians are "subject to two sets of 'forces' . . . just as a man who has come out of the cold into a warm room is subject both to the cold which has numbed his hands and to the heat which is thawing them out."[362] The forces of the heat are now decisive, for the room remains his sphere of influence, just as believers are decisively "in" the Spirit and "in" Christ. But incongruous pockets of cold still make themselves felt. However, in the case of many at Corinth, the anomalous aspect assumed undue proportions. Deluz comments, "They were carried away with childish enthusiasm, they set themselves up as enlightened men, they were greedy for ecstatic experiences. Paul show[s] how infantile [νηπίοις] these things are."[363]

4 Paul recapitulates his argument to conclude this section before moving on to consider the true role that God has assigned to Apollos and to himself. The introductory γάρ, *for,* once again links the logical chain of explanatory reasoning, but in English the repetition of *for* on each occasion would make the style seem stilted. Two sets of contrastive indicators, the particles μέν and δέ, and the pronouns τις, **someone,** and ἕτερος, someone else, **another,** invite some recognition in English. Hence, we translate Ἐγὼ μέν and ἕτερος δέ, Ἐγώ . . . as

---

ric of Reconciliation, 81). In conjunction with ζῆλος, she adds, it amounts to "subscribing to earthly and secular values of political glory and strength" (82). This re-inforces our account of σαρκικός as a **self-centered** stance.

361. Holloway, *περιπατέω as a Thematic Marker for Pauline Ethics.*
362. Whiteley, *The Theology of St Paul,* 126-27.
363. Deluz, *Companion to 1 Corinthians,* 35.

"**I for one . . .**" and "**I for my part. . . .**" On the translation of the genitives as **one of Paul's people** and **for Apollos**, see on 1:12, where we have explained the issues in considerable detail especially in relation to the work of Welborn and Mitchell.[364] The use of ὅταν, **when**, with the present subjunctive mood λέγῃ denotes not lack of fact, but what Findlay calls "recurring contingency" amounting to *whenever one says.*[365]

It seems impossible here to improve on the force of the REB: **are you not all too human?** The NIV's *are you not mere men?* and the NRSV's *are you not merely human?* seem anticlimactic when the careful use of the contrastive particles μέν and δέ in addition to γάρ add an escalating dimension which cannot easily be conveyed unless we adopt the intensifying translation of the REB. Paul wishes to underline the utter incongruity to which we alluded at the end of our comment on the previous verse. Christ and the Spirit have become decisive determinants for their lives, and yet they continue as if they had no horizon beyond the merely human. The anomaly is huge, and the addressees must now be disabused of some of the fallacious presuppositions about "Paul," "Apollos," and supposed routes to esteem and prestige on which their incongruous stance rests.

D. THE APPLICATION OF THESE ISSUES TO THE CHURCH MINISTERS, AND MINISTRY (3:5–4:21)

1. Three Explanatory Images: God's Field, God's Building, and God's Holy Shrine (3:5-17)

(5) What then is Apollos? What, now, is Paul? Servants through whom you came to faith, even as the Lord assigned the role to each. (6, 7) I planted, Apollos watered, but God went on giving the increase. So then neither the one who plants nor the one who waters is anything, but God who went on giving the increase. (8, 9) Now the one who does the planting and the one who waters are one in the work, and each will receive their reward in accordance with their own labor. For we are fellow laborers who belong to God, and you are the field which belongs to God. (9c, 10) You are also a building of God's. According to the gracious privilege which God gave to me, as a skilled master-builder I laid a foundation, and someone else is building on it. But let each person take care how they continue the building. (11) For no one can lay down any other foundation than that which has already been laid down, namely Jesus Christ. (12, 13) Now if anyone builds upon the foundation with gold, silver, and costly stones, or with wood, hay, and straw, the work of each

364. See above in detail for a range of literature, including Welborn, "Discord in Corinth," in *Politics and Rhetoric,* 1-42; and Mitchell, *Paul and the Rhetoric of Reconciliation,* esp. 68-98.

365. Findlay, *Expositor's Greek Testament,* 2:787.

will become apparent, for the Day shall reveal it, because it is disclosed by fire; the fire will test what kind of work each has done. (14, 15) If anyone's work which that person built abides, he/she will receive a reward; if anyone's work is burnt up, that person will suffer loss, but such persons themselves will be saved, but as if through fire. (16) Do you not know that you are the temple of God, and that the Spirit of God dwells in you? (17) If anyone destroys God's temple, God will destroy that person. For God's temple is holy, and that temple are you!

The argument flows on from what has been established in 1:18–3:4. In his detailed study of 3:5–4:5 David W. Kuck is right to express doubts about the various theories which treat the passage as an amalgam of shorter, diverse sections, whether or not Paul is supposed to have pressed various homily sources into the service of his argument.[1] The background contrast between "two wisdoms" and the foundational theology of the cross and the Holy Spirit provide two evaluative frames of reference within which assessments of ministers, the ministry, and ministerial activity appear in very different lights. Dale Martin speaks of a "status-reversal strategy." "By the standards of normal society (those of 'this world') (1:20; 2:6; 3:18, 19) [t]he Apostles are only servants (3:5) and farm laborers (3:6-8). . . . The apostles are last, in the position of criminals . . . hungry, thirsty, naked . . . society's 'scum' (4:9-12). But immediately after this graphic portrait . . . Paul uses high-status language . . . he is a father and they are children (4:14). . . ."[2]

Although he presents his arguments in a multilayered way which invites different assessments of the ministry from different viewpoints, Paul does not leave his arguments open in the sense that readers or addressees determine the meaning of ministry.[3] As John Moores comments in his recent and novel approach to Paul's semantic strategy, the "wisdom/folly alternation of 1 Cor. 1–2" shows that "where the audience is not right for the sign . . . semiosis will misfire." But "reader-response" is turned on its head. It is not that the message or identity of the text depends on the readers, but that the identity of the readers is unmasked in their response to a stable text.[4] Paul's message is simply expressed in Rupert Davies' nonspecialist study. Chapters 3 and 4, he states simply, "save us from too high a doctrine of the Ministry — from supposing that the Minister

---

1. Kuck, *Judgement and Community Conflict,* 152-53. He compares the respective claims of Conzelmann, Wendland, Senft, Ellis, Wuellner, and Branick regarding the unity of 1:18–4:5. Mitchell's *Paul and the Rhetoric of Reconciliation* (98-111 and throughout) points in the same direction as Kuck. (Both writers appear to offer independent arguments to the same end at the same time of writing.)

2. Martin, *The Corinthian Body,* 102-3.

3. See further P. Stuhlmacher, "The Hermeneutical Significance of 1 Cor. 2:6-16," in G. F. Hawthorne (ed.), *Tradition and Interpretation in the NT: Essays in Honor of E. Earle Ellis* (Grand Rapids: Eerdmans, 1987), 328-47.

4. John D. Moores, *Wrestling with Rationality in Paul* (Cambridge: Cambridge University Press, 1995), 133-34.

is the person who makes the Church. . . . They save us also from too low a doctrine of the Ministry. Ministers are not just full-time servants of the Church. . . . Ministers are God's agents."[5]

Recent literature on social status and rhetoric elaborates this and raises the stakes. People do not gain status by a close association with some specific minister, apostle, or mode of ministry. On the other side, only worldly status-seeking under the guise of a higher "spirituality" regards Christians as so self-sufficient as not to need the particular gifts assigned by God to those called to minister to them. The central focus remains that of God-in-Christ as source of life and source of growth. A subsidiary emphasis is placed on ministry as a necessary role within the process, like the work of those who plant seeds or tend plants. Meanwhile the evaluative frame of the cross, the Spirit, and the new wisdom receives sharper focus by a reiteration and expansion of the eschatological tone introduced in 1:8-9. The authenticity of all claims and counter-claims will become apparent at the last day. Then it will become apparent on one side whether people can fully mature without ministry in a spirit of independence, and on the other side whether a minister's claim that his/her work is valid and necessary is proved to be bogus or justified.

Paul introduces the general principle that governs the argument in 3:5: ὡς ὁ κύριος ἔδωκεν . . . **as the Lord assigned to each**. He then illustrates and applies the principle in terms of three analogies, the first two of which are metaphors: the image of the field and the fellow laborers (3:6-9a, b); that of building and testing the builders' work (3:9c-15); and that of the people of God as the corporate shrine of the Holy Spirit (3:16-17).

Bibliography on 3:5-17

Barnett, J. M., *The Diaconate* (New York: Seabury, 1981), 13-42.

Branick, V. P., "Sources and Redaction Analysis of 1 Cor. 1–3," *JBL* 101 (1982): 251-69.

Byrne, B., "Ministry and Maturity in 1 Cor 3," *AusBR* 35 (1987): 83-87.

Carson, D. A., *The Cross and Christian Ministry: An Exposition of Passages from 1 Corinthians* (Grand Rapids: Baker and Leicester: Inter-Varsity Press, 1993), 67-90.

Chevallier, M. A., "La constriction de la communauté sur le fondement du Christ (1 Cor. 3:5-17)," in L. de Lorenzi (ed.), *Freedom and Love* (Rome: Pontifical Biblical Institute, 1981), 109-29.

Clarke, Andrew D., *Secular and Christian Leadership in Corinth: A Socio-Historical and Exegetical Study of 1 Cor. 1–6,* AGJU 18 (Leiden: Brill, 1993), esp. 118-22.

Collins, J. N., *Diakonia* (Oxford and New York: Oxford University Press, 1990), esp. 227-44, 338-39.

Cox, L. G., "The 'Straw' in the Believer — 1 Cor. 3:12," *Wesleyan Theological Journal* 12 (1977): 34-38.

Davies, R. E., *Studies in 1 Corinthians* (London: Epworth Press, 1962), 41-48.

Derrett, J. D., "Paul as Master Builder," *EvQ* 69 (1997): 129-37.

---

5. Davies, *Studies in 1 Corinthians,* 42; cf. 41-48.

Didier, G., *Désinteressement du Chétien: la rétribution dans la morale de S. Paul* (Paris: Aubier, 1955).

Dittberner, A., "Who Is Apollos and Who Is Paul? — 1 Cor. 3:5," *BibTod* 71 (1974): 1,549-52.

Donfried, K. P., "Justification and Last Judgement in Paul," *Int* 30 (1976): 140-52.

Draper, J. A., "The Tip of an Ice-Berg: The Temple of the Holy Spirit," *South African Journal of Theology* 59 (1987): 57-65.

Evans, Craig A., "How Are the Apostles Judged? A Note on 1 Cor. 3:10-15," *JETS* 27 (1984): 149-50.

Filson, F. V., *St Paul's Conception of Recompense* (Leipzig: Hinrichs, 1931).

Fishburne, C. W., "1 Cor. 3:10-15 and the Testament of Abraham," *NTS* 17 (1969-70): 109-15.

Ford, J. M., "You are God's 'Sukkah' (1 Cor. 3:10-17)," *NTS* 21 (1974): 139-42.

Fridrichsen, A., "Themelios, 1 Kor. 3:11," *TZ* 2 (1946): 316.

Fung, R. Y. K., "The Nature of the Ministry according to Paul," *EvQ* 54 (1982): 129-46.

Furnish, Victor, "Fellow Workers in God's Service," *JBL* 80 (1961): 364-70.

Gale, Herbert M., *The Use of Analogy in the Letters of Paul* (Philadelphia: Westminster, 1964), 79-94.

Gnilka, J., *Ist 1 Kor 3:10-15 ein Schriftzeugnis für das Fegfeuer?* (Düsseldorf: Triltsch, 1955).

Hanson, A. T., *The Pioneer Ministry* (London: SCM, 1961), 57-64.

Harrington, D. J., "Paul and Collaborative Ministry" *New Theology Review* 3 (1990): 62-71.

Hollander, H. W., "Revelation by Fire: 1 Cor. 3:13," *BT* 44 (1993): 242-44.

———, "The Testing by Fire of the Builders' Works: 1 Cor. 3:10-15," *NTS* 40 (1994): 89-104.

Käsemann, E., "Sentences of Holy Law in the NT," in *NT Questions of Today* (London: SCM, 1969), 66-81.

Kitzberger, Ingrid, *Bau der Gemeinde. Das paulinische Wortfeld οἰκοδομή/(επ)οικοδομεῖν,* FB 53 (Würzberg: Echter, 1986), esp. 64-72.

Kuck, David W., *Judgement and Community Conflict: Paul's Use of Apocalyptic Judgement Language in 1 Cor. 3:5–4:5,* NovTSup 66 (Leiden: Brill, 1992), 150-239.

———, "Paul and Pastoral Ambition: A Reflection on 1 Cor. 3–4," *Currents in Missionary Theology* 19 (1992): 174-183.

Lanci, J. R., *A New Temple for Corinth: Rhetorical and Archaeological Approaches to Pauline Imagery* (New York and Bern: Lang, 1997).

Maly, K., *Mündige Gemeinde* (Stuttgart: Katholisches Bibelwerk, 1967), 61-72.

Martin, Dale B., *The Corinthian Body* (New Haven: Yale University Press, 1995), 102-3.

McKelvey, R. J., *The New Temple: The Church in the NT* (Oxford: Oxford University Press, 1969), 98-102.

Michel, O., "οἰκοδομέω," *TDNT,* 5:140-59.

Mitchell, M. M., *Paul and the Rhetoric of Reconciliation* (Tübingen. Mohr, 1992), 98-111.

Peterson, E., "Ἔργον in der Bedeutung 'Bau' bei Paulus," *Bib* 22 (1941): 439-41.

Pfammatter, J., *Die Kirche als Bau. Eine exegetisch-theologische Studie zur Ekklesiologie der Paulusbriefe,* AnGr 110 (Rome: Pontifical Biblical Institute, 1960).

Proctor, J., "Fire in God's House: Influence of Malachi 3 in the NT," *JETS* 36 (1993): 9-14.

Rhyne, T., "1 Cor. 3:1-9)," *Int* 44 (1990): 174-79.

Riesenfeld, H., "The Ministry in the NT," in A. Fridrichsen (ed.), *The Root of the Vine: Essays in Biblical Theology* (London: Dacre/Black, 1953), 96-127 (esp. 116-27).

Roetzel, C. J., *Judgment in the Community* (Leiden: Brill, 1972).

Shanor, J., "Paul as Master Builder: Construction Terms in 1 Cor," *NTS* 34 (1988): 461-71.

Townsend, J. T., "1 Cor. 3:15 and the School of Shammai," *HTR* 61 (1968): 500-504.

Travis, S. H., *Christ and the Judgement of God* (London: Marshall Pickering, 1986), 113-17.

Vielhauer, P., *Oikodomē, Aufsätze zum NT,* Bd. II, *TBü* 65 (Munich: Kaiser, 1979), 1-168, esp. 74-82.

Watson, N. M., "Justified by Faith; Judged by Works — An Antinomy?" *JTS* 29 (1983): 209-21.

Xavier, A., "Ministerial Images in 1 Cor. 3:5–4:1," *Indian Theological Studies* 24 (1987), 29-40.

5 (1) Some early MSS (p46, C, D, F, G) read the masc. pronoun τίς, *who,* in place of the neuter τί, **what**. Since the masculine would normally be expected in relation to personal names, this represents a later accommodation to more regular usage. Similarly, for predictable reasons some later MSS place the question about Paul before the question about Apollos. But ℵ, A, B, C, D1, 33 et al. read the UBS4 text.

The double-sided point of v. 5 emerges in the dialectic between the neuter singular pronoun **what** and the verbal phrase ὡς ὁ κύριος ἔδωκεν, **as the Lord assigned**. In Dale Martin's socio-anthropological vocabulary, the neuter **what** signifies the low-status vocabulary of things, tools, or instruments, the status of which is entirely to serve the interests of the user.[6] However, the allusion to **the Lord** introduces a high-status aspect, because Apollos and Paul are not merely optional extras for the church's convenience, but those whom God-in-Christ has called to a necessary task or role.

The τί form regularly introduces questions of definition in Socratic dialogues: *What is . . . ?* usually leads into a deeper exploration of what lies hitherto unnoticed behind some overglib prior use of the word or term.[7] Hence it points back to the ζῆλος καὶ ἔρις, **jealousy and strife**, of 3:3 (and 1:10-12) arising from political sloganizing about being **for Apollos** or whatever (3:4). Hence, along the lines of a Socratic dialogue, Paul asks: Now what does all this Apollos-language and Paul-language amount to? What *is* Apollos or Paul? What is their role?

Paul's own answer reveals that what these ministers or **servants** (διάκονοι, cognate with διακονέω, *I serve*) amount to largely depends on the frame of reference within which they are viewed. Paul makes this point in more detail in a string of so-called paradoxes in 2 Cor 6:8-10: "in honour and

---

6. Martin, *The Corinthian Body,* 102. On the servant image see also J. Roloff, *Apostolat-Verkündigung-Kirche* (Gütersloh: Mohn, 1965), 121; and Merklein, *Der erste Brief 1–4,* 259.

7. Merklein, *Der erste Brief 1–4,* 259; and Robertson and Plummer, *First Epistle,* 56.

dishonour" (διὰ δόξης καὶ ἀτιμίας [v. 8], the same contrast as in 1 Cor. 15:43a) . . . in ill-repute and good repute . . . as imposters and yet true (ὡς πλάνοι καὶ ἀληθεῖς) . . . dying and, look, we live . . . poor, yet making many rich . . ." (v. 10).[8] But this dialectic is more than that of the contrast between a this-worldly and other-worldly horizon. The same duality of viewpoint attaches to the identity, or perceived identity, of Christ, from whom the ministry of Paul and Apollos is derived. Christ is only "a descendant of David" (ἐκ σπέρματος Δανίδ) "on a merely human level" (κατὰ σάρκα), but marked (defined?) as Son of God with power within the horizon of the Spirit (κατὰ πνεῦμα, Rom 1:3, 4).[9]

Even though they were **servants**, however, the Corinthian congregation had experienced the role of Apollos and Paul in their being a means through which they **came to faith**. This translation preserves the force of ἐπιστεύσατε as second plural first aorist active indicative of πιστεύω, *I believe, I trust,* as the inception of the event: Schrage rightly calls this an ingressive aorist, indicating the event of coming-to-faith, *"das zum-Glauben-Kommen."*[10] The genitive pronoun with διά (δι' ὧν, **through whom**) indicates the *means* or *channel* of belief, not its source. In this sense ministers *serve God's* good purposes. The evidence for the use of the word to mean *deacon* within the NT is open to question, and at best ambiguous.[11] As Hanson reminds us, in these chapters Paul uses the image of a *servant* (διάκονος); an *attendant,* or someone who renders *manual or other service* (ὑπηρέτης, 1 Cor 4:1); and a household manager or *steward* (οἰκονόμος, 1 Cor. 4:2), to describe the roles of Apollos and himself.[12] On the other hand, John N. Collins develops both NT research and earlier work on the diaconate by Karl Rahner and James Barnett to demonstrate that "serving" in NT ecclesiology does not simply mean "assisting" in some subordinate role but is an integral aspect of *mission.* διάκονοι are not merely agents, but *responsible agents on behalf of others* in whom *the mission of the whole church may find a focus.*[13]

The key factor for Paul remains that of how **the Lord** (ὁ κύριος, equally meaning *also the employer, the boss,* probably as a deliberate semantic play in relation to servant) **assigned** in his sovereign choice. Schrage, following Robertson and Plummer, explicates Paul's condensed Greek as representing

8. Cf. V. P. Furnish, *II Corinthians,* AB (New York: Doubleday, 1984), 346-47.

9. See D. G. Dunn, *Romans 1–8,* WBC 38 (Dallas: Word, 1988), 12-15.

10. Schrage, *Der erste Brief,* 291; cf. 1 Cor 15:2, 11.

11. The ecclesiological meaning is rejected by Lightfoot ("mere servants, not leaders at all"), *Notes,* 187; cf. his dissertation in his *Commentary on Philippians* (London: Macmillan, 1879), 181-269, esp. 190-91.

12. Hanson, *The Pioneer Ministry,* 67.

13. Collins, *Diakonia,* esp. 227-44 and throughout. He argues that Acts 6:1-6 does not refer simply to serving *tables* (social welfare), but serving *persons* by bringing them the gospel. Stephen is at once portrayed as preaching. When *serving* gives rise to an office of *deacon,* this represents a delegated authority for preaching (or prophecy) and *mission.* Barnett and especially Collins have given a new turn to debates on these issues. Cf. Barnett, *The Diaconate,* 13-42.

ἕκαστος ὡς ὁ κύριος ἔδωκεν αὐτῷ. They note that Paul uses ἕκαστος, **each**, no less than five times in 3:5-13.[14] However, whereas Robertson and Plummer stress that "God deals separately with each individual soul," Hanson (followed closely by Schrage, Harrington, and Furnish) resists the tendency of nine-teenth- and earlier twentieth-century commentators "to represent Paul as very much of an individualist; we are shown [i.e., by older commentators] a picture of a man who founded churches by himself, directed and disciplined by him-self, and expected obedience to himself as an individual. . . . But nowhere does he specifically exclude his fellow-workers . . . and in several places he explic-itly includes them, e.g., 1 Cor 3:5; 4:1; 4:9; 2 Cor 1:19."[15] We have already ob-served how important Paul's emphasis on "co-workers" is deemed to be by Holmberg and many others.[16] Paul therefore uses **each** (ἕκαστος) not to argue for an individualistic concept of ministry, but in fact the reverse. Apollos and Paul each perform assigned roles within a corporate ministry.

A. D. Clarke rightly declares that here "the particular rôle, rather than the person, is emphasized."[17] This is part of the broader contrast between secular and Christian leadership styles in Paul's day. Thus Clarke adds: "The task-orientated perception of leadership is clearly to be contrasted with the way in which the Corinthians had been viewing their leadership figures. The discus-sion in both 1 Cor. 1:10-17 and 3:1-4 shows how the Corinthians were focusing their attention on the personalities of the apostles, and taking pride in them as men. Paul, rather, concentrates on the particular task each leader is accomplish-ing."[18] The issue concerns "their role" and "function as servants" (v. 5), each with "different gifts *(Gaben)* and tasks *(Aufgaben)*."[19] These depend on God's free gift of grace *(Gnadengabe)*.[20]

a. The Image of the Field and the Fellow Laborer (3:6-9b)

6-7 The thrust of vv. 6-7 is clear. Chrysostom paraphrases: "I first cast the word into the ground. . . . Apollos added his own part. But *the whole* was of God" (my italics).[21] Similarly, Erasmus comments that what counts is some-

14. Schrage, *Der erste Brief,* 1:291; and Robertson and Plummer, *First Epistle,* 57.

15. Ibid.; and Hanson, *Pioneer Ministry,* 67-68; cf. Harrington, "Paul and Collaborative Ministry," *New Theology Review* 3 (1990): 62-71; Schrage, *Der erste Brief,* 1:290, *"religiösen Individualismus."* See further Furnish, "Fellow Workers in God's Service," 364-70 (discussed fur-ther under 3:9). See above and on ch. 16 for further literature on co-workers and collaborative min-istry.

16. Holmberg, *Paul and Power,* 58-71 and throughout.

17. A. D. Clarke, *Secular and Christian Leadership in Corinth: A Socio-Historical and Exegetical Study of I Corinthians 1–6* (Leiden: Brill, 1993), 119.

18. Ibid.

19. Schrage, *Der erste Brief,* 1:288.

20. Ibid., 1:291.

21. Chrysostom, *Hom. 1 Cor.,* 8:5.

thing to be bestowed by God, not by us *("id Deo tribuendum est, non nobis")*.[22] Whether a minister is **anything** or *something* (τι) depends on whether they play the subsidiary role assigned by God as agents to facilitate God's work, not their own projects. The image of the people of God as a field draws on a well-known tradition concerning Israel, perhaps deriving initially from Israel as God's vineyard (Isa 5:7; Ezek 36:9). Wolff offers extended examples of OT and Jewish pictures of the people of God as "planted by God."[23] It coheres with the concept of God as Creator and Giver of life. Within this primary framework, ministers, like agricultural laborers, perform tasks which remain *conditions for* growth (not *sources of* growth). Thereby both their "low-status" aspect and "high-status" aspect receive simultaneous justification.

The aorist ἐφύτευσα refers to the event of Paul's arrival in Corinth as the initiator of evangelism in that city. The image of watering likewise finds expression through the aorist of ποτίζω, which alludes to the event of Apollos's arrival to continue a work already begun. Once the main point has been made, the metaphor cannot be pressed to imply that Paul did not follow up his evangelism (indeed, he remained in Corinth as pastor and evangelist for some eighteen months). Equally, it does not imply that Apollos never evangelized, especially since 3:5 explicitly states that people **came to faith** through both of their ministries. As always, the nature of ministry turns as much on *timing* as on other aspects of the task. Apollos took up the torch to ensure that the plants received continuing nourishment from God's creative work and word.

The shift from the passing events denoted by the two aorists **I planted, Apollos watered**, to the continuous *imperfect tense* of ηὔξανεν, **God went on giving the increase**, is important.[24] *Ministers come and go, but God's own work continues.* This applies equally both historically at the macrolevel (church, Fathers, Reformers, rationalists, Puritans, charismatics, and others, all come and go as ministers, but God continues to give life and growth); and locally at the microlevel (pastor succeeds pastor, but God continues his work in his own people; cf. the possessive genitive in **church of God** in 1:2). In Attic Greek αὐξάνω is transitive, but it becomes intransitive in many instances in hellenistic Greek. Since the object of the verb here is implicit (the church) but not explicit, **giving the increase** solves the problem of grammar.

The following verse (3:7) recapitulates and reiterates the point. Strictly in the context of the situation at Corinth it provides a crushing rejoinder to those

---

22. *Desiderii Erasmi Opera Omnia,* 7: *Paraphrases in N. Testamentum* (Petri Vander, 1706, rpt. [facsimile ed.] [London: Gregg Press, 1962]), 867, col. 1.

23. Wolff, *Der erste Brief,* 67 adds Exodus 15; 17; Num 24:5-6; Isa 5:1-7; 60:1-3, 21; Jer 2:21; Amos 9:15; *Psalms of Solomon* 14:3-5; H. Riesenfeld, *The Gospel Tradition: Essays* (Eng. trans., Philadelphia: Fortress, 1970), 187-204, on parabolic language in the Pauline epistles, esp. 197-99, traces further roots, and Gale, *Paul's Use of Analogy* (cited above), emphasizes the role of analogy and imagery in Paul.

24. Conzelmann, *1 Corinthians,* 74 and 74, n. 47; cf. Lightfoot, *Notes,* 188; Merklein, *Der erste Brief 1-4,* 260-61.

who sought reflected honor and status by means of association with some esteemed public leader, after the style of patronage and "friendship" in secular
world of Paul's day. "Paul has deliberately inverted the Graeco-Roman scale of
values: those who are being looked up to as patron figures, he is describing
rather as διάκονοι (1 Cor. 3:5)."[25] The emphasis on God and "low-status" language used here of the ministers of God finds forceful expression in Godet's
rhetorical question: "What harvest would have sprung up from the labour of the
two workers without the life which God alone could give?"[26] What does a routine of ministry amount to unless it also constitutes a channel for the creative
work of God?

Bengel presses the contrast with a merely mechanical model of ministry.
Without God's gift of organic "increase," the seed or grain would be "from the
first moment of sowing like a pebble"; i.e., *inanimate: sine hoc incremento
granum a primo sationis momento esset instar lapilli: ex incremento, protinus
tides germinat* (faith springs up).[27]

8-9b   Whereas the Corinthian addressees place each minister in a different category and stand back to evaluate them, Paul places all those who share
authentic ministry as God's channels in **one** *category* (vv. 8-9b): they are **one**
(ἕν); even if the Corinthians are to be distinguished as the **field** (γεώργιον) from
the **fellow laborers** (συνεργοί). Exegetes and translators show some disagreement, however, about whether **one** (ἕν, neuter form of εἷς, μία, ἕν, adjectival singular numeral, **one** [person] . . . **one** [thing]) signifies here one in status (*equal,*
RSV; *there is no difference between . . . ,* TEV) or one in task and goal (*have a
common purpose,* NRSV; *work as a team,* REB; *are working for the same end,*
Basic English). The AV/KJV and RV simply reproduce the Greek, *are one,*
while the NJB has a useful double play in rendering *It is all one who does the
planting and who does the watering.* This flows beautifully, has great force, and
much to commend it since the Greek leaves open whether purpose or status is
in view, and probably embraces both.[28] But NJB unwittingly dissolves the earlier force of v. 5b, **as the Lord assigned to each.** It is *not* "all one" who does
what; each is to do what task **the Lord has assigned** to him or her, and perhaps
also the use of ἴδιον, **one's own** in the last phrase of our present verse. Hence
our translation (above) leaves the Greek open (as NJB does) but without obscuring v. 5 by translating **one in the work.**

Paul has already urged that planting and watering serve the single goal of

25. Clarke, *Secular and Christian Leadership,* 119-20; cf. 31-36 and our comments above
on 1:10-12 with reference to Clarke, Chow, P. Mitchell, and others.

26. Godet, *First Letter,* 1:175.

27. Bengel, *Gnomon,* 616.

28. The semantic scope of *one* (ἕν) is wide in terms of lexicography. BAGD list numerous
instances of *one* in contrast to a plurality; *one* in contrast to disparate, separate parts; *one* in the
sense of "one and the same" (*token* sameness); and *one* in type, character, class, or quality (*type*
sameness); BAGD, 230-32. Robertson and Plummer rightly use the phrase "in one category" here
(*First Epistle,* 58).

facilitating the process of growth which God alone can provide, and now draws out the logical entailment that if both tasks are necessary for the same end, this excludes any notion of rivalry, competition, or ranking. The emphasis lies on "co-operation, solidarity and unity."[29] As Paul will state in greater detail in chs. 12–14, there can be no competition between gifts and tasks that genuinely build the community in different ways, as long as they truly serve this goal and not self-interest or self-fulfillment. A desire for self-fulfillment and recognition is far from a call by God to perform a task for others.

The concept of **reward** (*one's* **own reward**, τὸν ἴδιον μισθόν, v. 8b) has caused much perplexity and discussion. The word μισθός usually means *wages, pay, salary, goods-for-services* in the normal commercial sense. "Paul's present point is not immediately obvious. Probably it emphasizes again [that]. . . . They labor under another who also determines their pay."[30]

(i) If, as we shall argue, **fellow workers who belong to God** (θεοῦ γὰρ ἐσμεν συνεργοί, v. 9a) is understood as we have translated it, interpreting θεοῦ, *of God,* as a possessive genitive, the image of *pay* or **reward** serves primarily to intensify the point that Paul and Apollos are responsible *to God,* their employer, for judgments about their success or failure, not the community. In this sense the μισθός becomes an indication of *worth.* Stipends accorded by the church do not indicate this worth, against the assumptions of a consumer-driven world. *God* knows what they are worth in the work of the kingdom, and the matter must be left in God's hand for God's final verdict. But more must be implied. As Schrage observes, μισθός, *pay,* is repeated in 3:14.

(ii) Images of **reward** and even punishment probably *also* reflect what linguistic philosophers usually call *an internal grammar,* i.e., the effects are built into the work internally as part of what it amounts to. The ineffective, shallow, prayerless minister, e.g., may perhaps never see the "reward" of men and women coming to faith and growing to maturity, however hard his or her labor, and however long his or her hours. On the other hand, an authentic ministry may bring "rewards" of which only God and the minister know. We may doubt, however, whether this exhausts the whole meaning either, even if it is part of it. For in the parallel image of testing the work of ministers as builders (3:9c-15), the final outcome remains hidden until the day of judgment declares it (3:13).

(iii) The concept of μισθός is closely bound up with that of an employer's assessment of the value of the work. The most appropriate explanation is to be found in 3:13-14, and more especially in 4:3-5. There Paul insists that assessments of one's own work are pointless and misleading before all the data are open to view and God has pronounced his definitive verdict at the last day. The **reward** for those who will then have been raised into a mode of existence characterized by the Christ-like transformation brought about fully by the Holy Spirit (1 Cor 15:44-49) will be to discover that work done in one's life has re-

29. Schrage, *Der erste Brief,* 1:292.
30. Fee, *First Epistle,* 133.

mained a condition of some established effect in the new world order of "what abides" as the fruit of the Spirit or as the work of God's kingdom (1 Cor 13:8-13). This will be κατὰ τὸν ἴδιον κόπον, **in accordance with their own labor**, i.e., bear some relation to its nature, authenticity, motivation, and quality.

(iv) This interpretation would have profound consequences for a Christian understanding of selfhood, and in fact these are confirmed in the full-length study devoted entirely to judgment, community-conflict, and apocalyptic-judgment language in 1 Cor. 3:5–4:5 by David W. Kuck. He writes: "κόπος is a favourite word of Paul to describe the effort and hardship which the Christian mission necessitates. . . . Here in v. 8 Paul would seem to be speaking about the individual effort of each servant . . . for 1 Cor. 3:8 it is the individual distinctiveness of Paul and Apollos which is undiscovered by the reference to their eschatological reward."[31] Continuity of a stable self depends on a dialectic between the self and the Other within a sustained temporal narrative of memory, accountability, and hope.[32]

Kuck also alludes to other instances of **reward** as an eschatological phenomenon in the NT, e.g., Matt 5:12 (par. Luke 6:23); 6:1; 10:41-42; Mark 9:41; Luke 6:35; Rev. 11:18; 22:12; cf. *Didache* 4:7; 5:2; *1 Clement* 34:3.[33] Faithful servanthood, he observes, is bound up with accountability and especially with promise. "Rewards" may differ, "although wherein the difference might lie is never made explicit."[34] Probably the dimension of "internal grammar" (see ii above) enters the picture: for example, an amateur musician who has slaved over a piece of music may subsequently derive "more" from hearing the same music played by a top-rank professional than a child invited to the same performance. Whether or not this sheds light on the issue, Paul speaks of gaining a crown (στέφανος, 1 Cor 9:25) or a prize or award (βραβεῖον, 9:24; cf. Phil 3:14).[35]

The remaining issue to be determined is whether **fellow laborers** (συνεργοί, v. 4a) means *fellow workers with God* or, as most English VSS render it, *God's servants working together* (NRSV); *fellow workers for God* (RSV); or *fellow workers in God's service* (REB); cf. *we share in God's work*

31. Kuck, *Judgement and Community Conflict,* 166-67 and 168.

32. Paul Ricoeur, *Time and Narrative* (Eng. trans., 3 vols., Chicago: University of Chicago Press, 1984-88), which begins by drawing on Augustine's notion of time and Aristotle's concept of plot, and more esp. *Oneself as Another* (Eng. trans., Chicago: University of Chicago Press, 1992).

33. Kuck, "Paul and Pastoral Ambition: A Reflection on 1 Cor 3–4," in *Currents in the Theology of Missions* 19 (1992): 174-83. This aspect is also important for F. V. Filson, *St. Paul's Conception of Recompense* (Leipzig: Hinrichs, 1931).

34. Kuck, *Judgement,* 168. Kuck retains a judicious discipline in neither allowing dogmatic questions about justification by grace to influence his exegesis, nor forgetting that Paul held together the two themes. Here his critique of Roetzel's *Judgement in the Community* is especially useful, since Roetzel takes inadequate account of the latter point. Cf. Kuck, *Judgement,* 5-7 and 168-86.

35. Cf. BAGD, 146; Philo, *De Praemiis et Poenis,* 6; *Sibylline Oracles* 2:149; *1 Clement* 5:5.

(NJB). The NIV leaves the issue open with *we are God's fellow workers*. The first interpretation, *fellow workers with God* (implying the point that Paul, Apollos, and God work for the same purpose) is urged by Weiss, partly on analogy with 2 Cor 6:1, partly on the ground of its being "the more simple and natural translation."[36] On the other side, Collins and many others construe the genitive θεοῦ, *of God,* differently. Less hesitantly than Fee and Kistemaker but with them and especially with Furnish and Wolff and Collins, we interpret this as a possessive genitive.[37] Apollos and Paul are **fellow laborers who belong to God** since he has assigned them tasks; his is the work; to him (not to the applause of the addressees) they owe this primary accountability; he will pay their "wages"; for his sake they work on his field as those who toil in hard labor. Furnish argues emphatically that the shared task is "the service of God," while "he who plants is nothing and he who waters is nothing. . . . Paul is concerned about defining the relationship of the apostles *to one another*" (my italics).[38] The verse "introduces a contrast between Paul and Apollos on the one hand and the Corinthians on the other."[39]

Paul concludes this subsection on the image of the field and the fellow laborers by applying the image of **field which belongs to God** (θεοῦ γεώργιον v. 9b). The genitive is also likely to be a genitive of possession (cf. 1:2), which our translation indicates.[40] Whether it is a question about the ministry or an issue about the church, both belong to God, since he has made them what they are: he assigned ministerial tasks, and he gave germination and growth to the seeds. Some interpret γεώργιον as *vineyard* rather than **field**.[41] The OT background draws heavily on analogies between Israel and the vine or vineyard, but as a Jew writing for a Graeco-Roman readership Philo uses γεώργιον to mean field or cultivated land in general, which may or may not include "vineyard" as a subcategory of cultivated ground as the case may be.[42] Thus no genuine conflict of interpretation is involved if we adopt the broader term. The imagery carries with it the

36. Robertson and Plummer, *First Epistle,* 58; cf. Edwards, *First Epistle,* 75 (because they work with God they are one); Weiss, *Der erste Korintherbrief,* 77-78; H.-D. Wendland, *Die Briefe,* 33; Lietzmann, *An die Korinther,* "die mit Gott arbeiten," 15.

37. Wolff, *Der erste Brief,* 68: "As fellow-workers they are participants in God's work of salvation"; more strongly Findlay, *Expositor's Greek Testament,* 2:789: "The συν of συνεργοί [and] the context forbid our referring it to the dependent genitive . . . as though Paul meant fellow-workers *with* God." Cf. Moffatt, *First Epistle,* 39; Héring, *First Epistle,* 23 (their jont responsibility before God); Fee, *First Epistle,* 133-34, rightly comparing the possessive **God's field**; Kistemaker, *First Epistle,* 107; Barrett, *First Epistle,* 86; Collins, *First Cor,* 146: "The results of the work belong to God." (On Furnish, see next note.)

38. Furnish, "Fellow Workers in God's Service," 368 and 369; cf. 364-70.

39. Collins, *First Cor,* 146.

40. Cf. Schrage, *Der erste Brief,* 1:294.

41. Riesenfeld, *The Gospel Tradition,* 197-99; cf. Ezek 17:7; Matt 15:13.

42. For example, Philo, *De Plantatione* 2. Further, the verb γεωργέω means generally to cultivate, while the noun γεωργός means either a farm laborer, a tenant farmer (Mark 12:1-2), a farmer, or a vinedresser (John 15:1), depending on context. Wolff, *Der erste Brief,* 68-69, emphasizes this background.

themes of (i) belonging to God; (ii) inviting growth and fruitfulness; (iii) needing the nurture and care of those who have been assigned to this task by the owner. The metaphor excludes self-sufficiency, mechanistic routinization, and stasis.

b. The Image of the Building and the Testing of the Builders' Work (3:9c-15)

9c-10 J. R. Lanci has recently devoted a monograph to the image of the community as a temple in this epistle. While this applies more closely to 3:16-17, Lanci follows M. M. Mitchell in perceiving the "building" of the Christian community as central and fundamental for Paul's theological and pastoral concern in this epistle.[43] The very image of a **building** (οἰκοδομή), applied to the church, excludes individualism; it is not a single object but a corporate structure, a community.[44] Further, the switch of imagery adds the new dimension that before a building can be erected, a foundation must be laid.[45] Paul brings this point out in his introduction to the new subsection in the present verse (v. 10), and applies this aspect christologically in v. 11. Like the image of the field or vineyard, the description of the community of believers as a building also has a background in Judaism (within which J. M. Ford argues for a special background relating to the Feast of Tabernacles).[46] **Building** in the verbal form denoting the process of "building up" remains familiar within the OT: God appoints Jeremiah (whose call may be compared with Paul's) "to destroy and to overthrow, to build and to plant" (Jer 1:10; cf. 12:16). Paul takes up the verbal, dynamic aspect in the context of love (ἀγάπη) as against knowledge (γνῶσις), but it is not the primary point here, except that Paul and Apollos are now perceived as co-workers in the building enterprise.

V. 10 is part of a chiasmus which finds completion in v. 11: (A) Paul laid the foundation (v. 10a); (B) someone else is building on it (v. 10b); (B) let that person take care how the process goes (v. 10c): (A) the foundation is Christ (v. 11a).[47] Theme (A) relates to the foundation; theme (B) concerns the quality and authenticity of the process of building.

---

43. Lanci, *A New Temple for Corinth: Rhetorical and Archaeological Approaches to Pauline Imagery;* and Mitchell, *Rhetoric of Reconciliation.* Both urge that the motif of "building up" for the common good is central to Paul's rhetoric and argument.

44. Schrage, *Der erste Brief,* 1:295; Conzelmann, *1 Corinthians,* 75.

45. Leo G. Cox, "The 'Straw' in the Believer — 1 Cor 3:12," *Wesleyan Theological Journal* 12 (1977): 34; cf. 34-38.

46. Cf. 1QS 8:5-10 and CD 3:19, among the texts of Qumran. See further Riesenfeld, "Parabolic Language in the Pauline Epistles," in *The Gospel Tradition* (Philadelphia: Fortress, 1970), 199. Ford, in "You Are God's 'Sukkah' (1 Cor. 3:10-17)," *NTS* 21 (1974-75): 139-42, argues that the *sukkah* framework of the constructions made at the Feast of Tabernacles accounts more readily for Paul's allusions to "hay" and "straw" than other analogies. But this hypothesis is neither demonstrable nor necessary and brings its own difficulties (see below).

47. Fee, *First Epistle,* 137.

The detailed imagery of the building invites two complementary comments. On one side J. Shanor (1988) examines the "construction terms," particularly in the light of an inscription dated fourth century BC from Arcadian Tegea, arguing that its details offer "tangible assistance in the interpretation" of 3:9b-17.[48] The inscription takes the form of a legal trade agreement about the contracted *"job"* (ἔργοι) and the nature of the *work* (ἔργον), with clauses anticipating possible *damage* or *hindrances* (ἐφθορκώς) or people *doing damage* (φθήρων) who therefore invite *penalties, losses,* or *fines* (ζαμίαι, ζαμιόντω) to make up necessary work (ἔργα). Allowing for the dating and locality of the earlier Greek dialect, these must remind us of Paul's language about the *job* and the *work* (ἔργον, 3:14, 15); *penalties* and *loss* (ζημιωθήσεται, v. 15); and *damage* (φθείρει, v. 17).[49] From the other side, however, Herbert M. Gale warns us that this is a broad image or analogy, not a point-by-point allegory.[50] Thus building quality does not normally turn on whether materials are combustible, and penalties within contracts do not generally relate to the effects of fire. But the two approaches are not mutually exclusive. Shanor's inscription sheds light on various aspects of the analogy; Gale simply warns us, as Travis confirms, that details should not be pressed uniformly or in isolation from the main points.[51]

Shanor's study sheds light, first, on the term σοφὸς ἀρχιτέκτων, **skilled master-builder**. Contracts were made with individual workers, but because of his professional **skill** one person usually assumed a particular coordinating role, maintaining an overview of the work, but not as paymaster. Even in the case of large buildings, Shanor argues, the number of participants in the actual building process who were contracted was small. Hence the image of a small team coordinated by the ἀρχιτέκτων whose skill was recognized by the others rings true to the application of the analogy to ministry at Corinth. We have already discussed the importance of "co-workers" for Paul (above, 1:1, and on Holmberg, Clarke, and others). In lexicographical terms, ἀρχιτέκτων brings together τέκτων, a worker in wood or stone, i.e., *carpenter* or *mason,* with ἀρχι-, *chief,* or *leader,* here perhaps as first among equals, more probably leading in experience and skill rather than in managerial status.

Most VSS translate Κατὰ τὴν χάριν τοῦ, θεοῦ τὴν δοθεῖσάν μοι as *according to the grace of God given to me* (NRSV), although the RSV translates χάριν as *commission*. This reflects the Greek structure: κατά with the accusative means *according to;* χάρις regularly means *grace;* while δοθεῖσαν functions as an adjectival aorist passive participle. While this is correct, the passive voice is often used by biblical writers of actions of divine agency, and the English active provides a stronger force more succinctly in the receptor language. *Commission*

48. Shanor, "Paul as Master Builder: Construction Terms in First Corinthians," 461; cf. 461-71.

49. Ibid., 462.

50. Gale, *The Use of Analogy in the Letters of Paul,* 79-90, esp. 85-86.

51. Cf. Travis, *Christ and the Judgement of God,* 113-16.

and *grace* both convey valid nuances. Paul combines the thought of God's un-deserved sovereign generosity (grace) with the notion of honoring a master-builder with a privileged commission to undertake a special task. Hence we combine NRSV's *grace* with REB's translation *God gave me the privilege . . . ,* to render: **According to the gracious privilege which God gave to me.** . . . *Foundational work* is *apostolic work* in Paul and in other parts of the NT, espe-cially in Luke–Acts (see on 1:1 and 9:1-3).

The verb ἔθηκα, **I laid,** may be in the aorist since Lightfoot suggests that the perfect tense (read by a few MSS, including D and $\aleph^3$) might hint at arro-gance, stressing the effects of *I have laid* rather than factual event, **I laid.** The form θεμέλιον is technically an adjective implicitly understanding λίθον, *foun-dation stone.* But it comes to mean simply **foundation.** Fridrichsen thinks that the foundation includes the foundation walls.[52] This foundational work of Paul is explicated in 1 Cor 2:2, where the content of foundational proclamation is the apostolic message of *a Christ crucified,* without the addition of various human opinions and evaluations.[53] Its christological and Christocentric character is what makes it the solid foundation without which the building would not stand, and certainly would not stand as *that* building.

The identity and evaluation of ἄλλος δὲ ἐποικοδομεῖ, **and someone else is building on it** (οἰκοδομέω, *I build,* with ἐπί, **on** or *upon*), remain open-ended and neutral.[54] **Someone else** does not exclude Apollos because the person con-cerned is indeed building on the foundation which Paul laid. A serious oppo-nent might be the kind of leader who arrives at a church to dig up all the foun-dation work already carried out, in the belief that it all has to begin again. On the other hand, no minister, including Apollos and Paul himself, remains ex-empt from the apostolic charge: **let each person take care how they continue the building.** βλεπέτω, third singular present imperative, *I see,* or (mentally) *I direct attention to,* is best translated, **I take care** (as, e.g., in the use of the sec-ond plural imperative βλέπετε in Mark 13:33; cf. Col 2:5). The Greek repeats the same verb ἐποικοδομεῖ, which we have translated **continue the building**

---

52. Fridrichsen, "Neutestamentliche Wortforschung: Themelios, 1 Kor 3:11," 316-17.

53. Barrett, *First Epistle,* 87.

54. A considerable amount of further discussion concerns the question of whether Apollos is the referent of **someone else**, or alternatively whether this excludes Apollos. Allo thinks that Paul is reluctantly reconciled to "others" (plural) continuing the work, but with a de-gree of concern (*Première Épitre,* 58); Grosheide and Senft also point to the "impersonal . . . vagueness" of the reference, which "is not to be taken as a sort of reproach. On the contrary a foundation only makes sense if someone else built on it, and that is what Paul hoped would hap-pen" (Grosheide, *First Epistle,* 84). Fee insists, "He does not now intend Apollos or Peter" (*First Epistle,* 138). Fee offers as a reason that Apollos and Paul share a common cause, and that Paul would hardly include Apollos in his warning; but Grosheide, as well as I, suggests that Apollos cannot be excluded, even if he is not the primary or sole referent. Lightfoot's point remains valid: "The reference is not solely to Apollos" (*Notes,* 189). "Paul is exhorting the workers to individ-ual responsibility" (Collins, *First Cor,* 156). Wolff urges, "Paul does not intend any specific per-son by ἄλλος" (*Der erste Brief,* 71).

solely for reasons of English style. The theme of *taking care* is now expounded as the central motif of vv. 11-17 within a Christocentric and eschatological frame.

11 The parallel with the analogy of the field and the fellow laborers becomes clear. Just as the essential thing for the harvest or crop was **God who gives the increase**, so here the one essential thing about the building is that it depends on **Jesus Christ** as the **foundation** of its existence, coherence, and identity. All the same, just as the work of planting and watering were necessary, if subsidiary, conditions for the growth of the field, so the choice of appropriate materials also contributes, even if less fundamentally, to the building. The all-important factor is God-in-Christ, as life-giver and foundation; but planting and watering, and the use of appropriate materials (v. 12), play a necessary part in each case for the completion of the work.

θεῖναι, second aorist infinitive active, denotes the single *act* of **laying down a foundation**, τὸν κείμενον (accusative masculine singular perfect participle middle with passive sense) derives from a different stem κεῖμαι, to denote **that which has already been laid down**. The perfect carries its most distinctive nuance, calling attention to permanent effects of a past act. The gender may be masculine because the foundation is Christ, but more probably because technically θεμέλιον, **foundation**, achieved currency as an adjectival form in conjunction with λίθος, *stone*, i.e., *foundation stone*.[55] The concept of Christ as foundation lies behind the resurrection chapter (1 Cor 15:1-11, including its pre-Pauline tradition, 15:3-8). It gives added force to the interpretation of Matt 16:18 concerning "the rock on which I will build my church" as referring primarily to the christological content of Peter's confession as the foundation stone (rock) of the church.

Any **other** foundation would not merely make the building precarious; it would cease to exist *as that building*. We give παρά with the accusative case its comparative sense **than**, but especially with the genitive or dative the fundamental sense of the preposition is *alongside*.[56] Paul may have meant that no foundation laid "alongside Christ" counts for anything. But in the light of the accusative case he probably uses δύναται in its logical sense (on logical *can* versus causal *can*, see above) to mean: no other foundation is logically possible except Christ himself if the building is truly to be the church of God. Conzelmann's notion that this verse is "paradoxical" in relation to other parts of Paul's theology is as surprising as Fee's contention that it is "an intrusion into the analogy."[57] We explained how it underlined the parallel with the field image in our initial comments on this verse, and Schrage explains the allusion

---

55. A. T. Robertson (*Epistles,* 4:96) suggests that it is the reference to Christ that invites the masculine form, but Findlay cites examples of the masculine in 2 Tim 2:19; Heb 11:10; Rev 21:14, 19, although often neuter in LXX and in Acts 16:26 (*Expositor's Greek Testament,* 2:790-91). ἄλλον (also masculine) confirms the gender.

56. BAGD, 609-11, esp. 3:3, 611, col. 1; and Fee, *First Epistle,* 139, n. 24.

57. Conzelmann, *1 Corinthians,* 75; Fee, *First Epistle,* 139.

back to 1:18-25.[58] Moreover, Gale's distinction between analogy here and allegory elsewhere must be kept in mind.[59] Fee is right to stress, however, that for Paul *Christ himself* is the foundation here, not a particular set of doctrinal formulations *about* Christ. "No other foundation can be laid because the one foundation has ultimately been laid by God (v. 11)."[60]

12-13 (1) Some MSS insert *this* (τοῦτον) after **foundation** in v. 12a, to read **If anyone builds upon** *this* **foundation**. . . . But θεμέλιον is read without the demonstrative pronoun by 𝔭46, the first hand of ℵ*, A, B, C, and various VSS. τοῦτον is a natural clarification, the addition of which can readily be explained, whereas its omission would be difficult to account for. (2) In v. 13 the pronoun αὐτό is placed in square brackets, since its status is difficult to determine. Whether it is included makes no difference to the meaning. Its inclusion is supported by A, B, C, and 33, but it is absent from ℵ, D, a probable reconstructed 𝔭46, the Harclean Syriac, the Vulgate, and the Coptic VSS. On balance it should probably be omitted.

If Paul is partly anticipating his next image (3:16-17) of the community as God's temple, Karl Maly, David Kuck, and others may be right to detect here an allusion to Solomon's building of the temple with "gold for the things of gold, silver for the things of silver, bronze for the things of bronze . . . wood for the things of wood, besides great quantities of onyx . . . all sorts of precious stones and marble in abundance" (1 Chron 29:2; cf. Exod 25:3-7; 31:4, 5; 1 Chron 22:14-16).[61] In this case we can translate λίθους τιμίους with its most usual meaning, *precious stones*. But the addition of **hay** and **straw** (cf. the use of thatch for roofing) makes it far more likely that Paul is using what F. Lang calls a non-specific analogy, in which only *two* categories of materials are envisaged: non-combustible materials which will stand the test of a fire (**gold, silver, costly stones**) and combustible elements (**wood, hay, straw**) which form part of the imagery.[62] In this case λίθους τιμίους should be translated **costly stones** (as above), i.e., of high quality, of which *marble* constitutes the prime example. The overwhelming majority of commentators rightly perceive a qualitative difference between only two types of material, as against six. Even though Paul lists the most costly material (**gold**) first, and proceeds down a list to the cheapest (**straw**), the eschatological "fire" reduces the materials to those which abide

---

58. Schrage, *Der erste Brief,* 1:298. See also Collins, *First Corinthians,* and Strobel, *Der erste Brief* (n. 6).

59. Gale, *Use of Analogy,* 85-86.

60. Collins, *First Cor,* 149; similarly Strobel, *Der erste Brief,* 81, with reference to the OT background (e.g., Ps 118:22-23).

61. Maly, *Mündige Gemeinde,* 68; Kuck, *Judgement,* 177; discussed also by Wolff, *Der erste Brief,* 72-73.

62. To be sure, **hay** and **straw** appear in rabbinic writings and elsewhere to denote especially worthless items, but the role played by fire in the imagery shows that durability is the issue here. As Conzelmann argues, Paul is not categorizing the wider range of materials which play a part in the buildings and temples of apocalyptic speculation or typology (Conzelmann, *1 Corinthians,* 76).

and those which fail to last.[63] The translation **builds . . . with gold** . . . reflects the lexicographical point that χρυσίον, technically a diminutive form, denotes *gold* as metal **with** which objects of gold (χρυσός) are made.[64]

It is hardly convincing to argue, with Kuck, that Paul "seems to mix together two sorts of criteria — intrinsic value and durability in the face of fire."[65] Rather, as Lang insists, Paul expresses his concern as missionary-pastor that all ministerial or church work should be founded on the reality of a Christ crucified and should endure. The "testing by fire" connected with the last judgment simply underlines the subsidiary but important point which Paul elaborates in 4:4 and 5, that such is the opaqueness and duplicity of the human heart that even the builders of authentic work will not know definitively "how they build" until God's own definitive verdict declares this and it becomes publicly visible at the last judgment.[66] Still more to the point, one cannot judge the quality of the work of another builder: others are "either doing that which will last or that which will perish," and only time and the day of judgment will determine this.[67] It is telling that even work which someone genuinely **builds upon the foundation** may still turn out to be of no permanent value. Cox surmises that elements of self-interest or building for applause or self-gain can turn even the Christian's building "upon Christ" into **hay** or **straw**.[68] Such building would not be *Christ-like*.

The two distinct phrases φανερὸν γενήσεται and ἡ γὰρ ἡμέρα δηλώσει make complementary points. The first phrase asserts that only time will tell, and that indeed time will inescapably tell, the nature of the work. The verb γενήσεται is the future of γίνομαι: the nature of the work **will become apparent**, even if the present is marked by ambiguities and hiddenness. But the adjective φανερός, cognate with the active verb φαίνω, *shine, shed light upon,* and the deponent φαίνομαι, *I appear, become visible,* **become apparent**, occurs in eschatological contexts (1 Cor 13:13; 2 Cor 5:10; cf. the verb in 1 Cor 4:5) as well as here and there of present disclosures (1 Cor 11:19; 14:25). Paul gives this point unrestrained emphasis by placing together here the periphrastic form φανερὸν γενήσεται with δηλώσει, ἀποκαλύπτεται, and δοκιμάσει ([the fire] **will test** . . .). The present tense draws attention to the principle as an axiom, the future verbs allude to future events (**shall reveal . . . will test**).[69]

Together these terms carry the sonority and weight of what in English we might think of as an apocalyptic epiphany: a universal disclosure in which all hitherto protective veils of ambiguity and hoping-for-the-best (or, equally, fear-

63. Lang, *Die Briefe,* 53.

64. As noted by Robertson and Plummer, *First Epistle,* 62. The same distinction applies to ἀργύριον, *silver as a metal,* and ἄργυρος, *silver.*

65. Kuck, *Judgement,* 177.

66. Lang, *Die Briefe,* 53.

67. Cox, "The 'Straw' in the Believer — 1 Cor 3:12," 35; cf. 34-38.

68. Ibid., 37.

69. Meyer, *First Epistle,* 1:96.

ing-for-the-worst) are removed in a definitive, cosmic act in the public domain. Chrysostom anticipates Lightfoot's comment that fire purifies the better material more brightly, but consumes the base.[70] Conzelmann rightly interprets ἐν πυρί in its instrumental sense as **with fire** (against Edwards and Meyer).[71] After its destruction by the Romans in 146 BC, the city lay partly or largely in ruins until its refounding as a Roman colony by Julius Caesar in 44 BC, and only then did it begin to regain its eminence. When Corinth rose from its ruins, the observer might well have seen some hovel patched up with clay and stubble or thatch alongside the marble wall. To what extent remnants of the earlier incongruities survived to Paul's day we cannot be certain. But it is more than possible that traces of this kind of anomaly could be found in certain parts of the city. The dread of fire sweeping through a dry Mediterranean city with its mixed building materials would have resonated more deeply with the addressees than with most modern Western readers, for whom fire zones are more easily controlled and contained, and where buildings are all too uniform. Clearly the stage is set for a consideration of the devastating effects of the Day of Judgment. Paul uses ἡμέρα, **the day**, by itself to refer to final judgment in Rom 13:12 and 1 Thess 5:4, as *the day when God judges* in Rom 2:16.[72] Most often he uses the phrase *the day of the Lord* (1 Cor 1:8; 5:5; 2 Cor 1:14; Phil 1:6, 10; 2:16; 1 Thess 5:2; 2 Thess 2:2), while parallel passages speak of the Lord's coming (1 Cor 4:5; cf. 1 Thess 2:19; 3:13). The phrase ἐκείνη ἡ ἡμέρα, *that day*, occurs in 2 Thess 1:10, and frequently in the Gospels.[73] The phrase **the day** without further qualification demonstrates its familiarity in Pauline preaching and teaching.

It is to some degree surprising that many writers through the centuries up to the present speak as if judgment in terms of rewards and penalties were a quite separate matter from judgment as testing. The two are inseparable. For *prior to the last judgment all human evaluations remain corrigible; they depended on unknown factors about additional information, human motivations, and long-term effects. But God pronounces a definitive verdict at the last judgment which cannot be revised, for all factors have been taken into account in a total context.* Thus the verb δοκιμάζω (τὸ πῦρ [αὐτὸ] δοκιμάσει), **the fire will test** (it) should not be thought of on the analogy of a test set by a headmaster or high school principal, but as that which *discloses definitive approval (or otherwise)* in the sense of a disclosure of all the factors which contribute to God's definitive verdict. This may, indeed will, include whether the person concerned shares the rightwised (justified) status of those who are in Christ; but it will also disclose the extent to which their work has produced some lasting effect in God's sight. For if justification by grace means the dissolution of all that is self-

70. Lightfoot, *Notes,* 192; Chrysostom, *1 Cor. Hom.,* 9:5.
71. Conzelmann, *1 Corinthians,* 76. Meyer (*First Epistle,* 1:95) and Edwards (*First Epistle,* 80) refer the subject not to the work but to the Day, to mean *encompassed with fire.*
72. Kuck, *Judgement,* 179.
73. Matt 7:22; 24:36; 26:29; Mark 13:32; 14:25; Luke 10:12; 17:31; 21:34.

centered, sinful, and unworthy, such things by definition will not "survive." On the other hand, what was offered in the strength of the Holy Spirit and in the name of Christ will have effects that eternally abide within the very existence and praise of the redeemed community and the life of God at the last day. This is precisely Paul's point when he writes that the Day will disclose **what kind of work** (τὸ ἔργον ὁποῖον) each has done. This sets the stage for our understanding, further, of vv. 14 and 15.

14-15 The two outcomes of the two *kinds* of (ὁποῖον, v. 13) work consist on one side in (a) permanency (μενεῖ), i.e., remaining unharmed and undamaged as the work survives even the Day of Judgment, and on the other side (b) being thoroughly consumed (κατά intensive with the late hellenistic form of the future passive indicative, i.e., normally in earlier Greek κατακαυθήσεται). Where English uses *up* to express the intensive, **is burnt up**, Greek achieves the same end with *down*, i.e., *is burned down*. The protasis of each conditional occurs in the indicative since it is determined, not indefinite, and English tends to render this by a present tense in place of the Greek future (as NRSV, REB, NJB). W. J. Conybeare well translates *stands unharmed . . . is burned down. . . .* The phrase ὃ ἐποικοδομήσησεν (first aorist indicative active) retains the reference to building a superstructure on the foundation.[74]

The parallels **will receive a reward** (v. 14 where λήμψεται is the future indicative of λαμβάνω) and **will suffer loss** (v. 15, ζημιωθήσεται), should be referred back to the inscription language of the building contract identified and discussed by J. Shanor (see above on 3:10).[75] There if necessary work (ἔργον) was delayed or inadequate, penalty clauses allowed for fines or loss of payment (ζαμίαι, ζαμιότω, allowing for an earlier and different regional dialect form in fourth-century-BC Arcadian Tegae). ζημιόω does not normally mean *to punish,* but *to deprive someone of something.* Only if this imagery is interpreted as point-for-point allegory to be decoded rather than as a broad image to make a forceful point can theoretical issues concerning possible "penalty" be transposed into some kind of postmortem doctrine.[76] (See also above on μισθός in 3:8 and on δοκιμάσει in 3:13.)

The pronoun αὐτός remains emphatic (*He himself,* but we have used the unsatisfactory plural **they themselves** in the face of difficulty posed by gender-neuter translation). For Paul even Christian service seriously flawed by self-interest cannot imperil the Christian believer's salvation. But in the nature of the case flawed work cannot survive the divine verdict at the last day, and fails to find a lasting place among those qualities of love and service which the Spirit has inspired and for which God's servants have been faithful channels and co-

74. Hays, *First Cor,* 54, expounds the anomaly of trying to build on "a new wing," which would necessitate adding to the foundation what would be "founded on wisdom."

75. Cf. Shanor, "Paul as Master Builder," 461-71. The passive form carries a future middle meaning here.

76. See J. Gnilka, *1 Kor. 3:10-15 ein Schriftzeugnis für das Fegfeuer?* (Düsseldorf: Triltsch, 1955).

agents.[77] It is unlikely, although possible, that ὡς διὰ πυρός means simply *like someone who comes through the fire intact.* It is far more likely that the phrase had become a metaphor like "brand plucked from the burning" (Amos 4:11), comparable to "saved by the skin of one's teeth."[78] One of the standard detailed commentaries on Amos interprets 4:11 as "being rescued at the last moment. The expression was a proverbial one" (cf. Zech 3:2).[79] J. Weiss points also to a range of Greek literature (e.g., Euripides) and Latin texts (e.g., Livy) for similar proverbial parallels.[80]

As Fee concludes, this is "not . . . a soteriological statement. . . . He is warning his Corinthian friends. . . . Salvation after all is by grace, not by one's own works. But . . . he expects his warnings to be taken seriously. . . ."[81] Witherington explicitly observes, "This cannot be a reference to purgatory since Paul is referring to what happens on the judgment day . . . after the return of Christ. . . . He is not referring to what happens to a person after death and before the final judgment. . . . 'As through fire' is a metaphor for escaping . . . by the skin of one's teeth."[82]

c. The Temple and the Indwelling Spirit of God (3:16-17)

In this epistle and in Pauline theology as a whole issues about the ministry are inextricably woven with questions about the nature of the church. The ministry exists for the proclamation of the gospel in word and life, and for the benefit and building up of the church. The church can devalue the role of ministry, but, even worse, ministry carried out for reasons of self-esteem, status-seeking, or self-interest can damage the church. This leads Paul to explore the third piece of imagery on which he draws in this chapter.

16 This verse brings us to the heart of Lanci's argument, noted above, concerning the centrality of "building up" and the metaphor of the people of God as God's temple at Corinth.[83] Two Greek words call for special notice. First, while ἱερόν denotes the holy area of the temple as a whole, ναός denotes the temple building itself. Hence it carries forward the previous image, but in a specific way which narrows its focus to the issue of holiness and to God's sanctifying indwelling. There is some justification for those translations which try

---

77. See Schrage, *Der erste Brief,* 1:303-4, where grace and responsibility are emphasized.

78. Fee, *First Epistle,* 144; and Witherington, *Conflict and Community,* 134.

79. R. S. Cripps, *A Critical and Exegetical Commentary on the Book of Amos* (London: SPCK, 1929), 175. Schrage, *Der erste Brief,* 1:303-4, also calls attention to the OT background.

80. Weiss, *Der erste Korintherbrief,* 83, n. 1: Euripedes, *Andromache* 487: διὰ γάρ πυρός ἦλθ') and *Electra* 1182; Livy, 20:35; cf. also Jude 23, ἐκ πυρὸς ἁρπάζοντες, *snatching them from the fire.*

81. Fee, *First Epistle,* 144.

82. Witherington, *Conflict and Community,* 134.

83. Lanci, *A New Temple for Corinth,* cited above (see under 3:9c, 10).

to capture the contrast with ἱερόν by rendering the word here as *shrine* (W. J. Conybeare) or *sanctuary* (Centenary Translation by H. B. Montgomery); but most VSS simply translate **temple** (NRSV, REB, NJB, AV/KJV). We were tempted by *temple sanctuary,* since the consecration of the temple is the central issue, but this would overtranslate the Greek.[84]

Second, the final phrase ἐν ὑμῖν, **in you,** is *plural,* as the Greek makes clear. Here Paul is not saying that each individual Christian is a temple within which God's Spirit dwells, but rather that the Spirit of God dwells in the Christian community *corporately as a community.* However, where Paul speaks of the ethics of individual conduct in 6:12-20, in spite of the use of the plural, there it is entirely legitimate to interpret 6:19 to mean that the Spirit of God dwells in each believer **also** *as an individual:* τὸ σῶμα ὑμῶν ναὸς τοῦ ἐν ὑμῖν ἁγίου πνεύματός ἐστιν, *your body* (singular) *is a temple of the Holy Spirit who is within you* (plural, this second time). Whatever we conclude about 6:19, however, 3:16 refers to a corporate indwelling of the Spirit of God.

The opening phrase οὐκ οἴδατε ὅτι, **Do you not know that . . . ?** occurs some ten times in this epistle. It indicates both Paul's intensity of feeling (surely you know *this!*) and his belief that the principle at issue is axiomatic for the Christian and should not have escaped attention as a cardinal element in the community's thinking.[85] J. C. Hurd sets forth the ten examples as symptomatic of Paul's sometimes even "jarring and aggressive" response to the oral report of failures and scandals at Corinth, in contrast to his more carefully balanced response to their own written questions in which he meticulously sets forth the pros and cons.[86] It was certainly axiomatic in pagan religions of Paul's day that temples reflected the nature and name of their god or goddess (e.g., the temple [here ἱερόν] of Artemis, Acts 19:24). Moreover, the notion that the God of Israel dwells among his people rather than "in temples made with hands" was also axiomatic in hellenistic diaspora Judaism and in the Christian communities whose roots had been in diaspora Judaism (Acts 7:48, Stephen's speech, and 17:24). In Jewish and Christian apocalyptic the sacredness of the temple as radiating God's presence and glory is no less axiomatic (Rev 7:15; 11:19; 14:17; 21:10; cf. 21:22). Thus Paul speaks of the temple "of the living God" (2 Cor 6:16). Its sanctity can be violated by association with idols (2 Thess 2:4; 2 Cor 6:16).

Lionel Thornton draws out the ethical and liturgical implications of this passage in relation to Paul's theology of holiness. He writes: "The Corinthians are God's sanctuary, in which the Holy Spirit dwells. Yet they are threatening this sanctuary with destruction [v. 17] by their sinful divisions. . . . Their vainglory, jealousy and partisanship . . . is treachery to the common life. But worse still, *it is a form of sacrilege*" (my italics).[87] It is sacrilege because in sinning

---

84. O. Michel, "ναός," *TDNT,* 4:880-90; and H. B. Swete, *The Holy Spirit in the NT,* 180-81.

85. See also 5:6; 6:2, 3, 9, 15, 16, 19; and 9:13, 24.

86. Hurd, *The Origin of 1 Corinthians,* 85-87; cf. 75-94.

87. L. S. Thornton, *The Common Life in the Body of Christ* (London: Dacre Press, 3d ed., 1950), 14.

against "consecrated persons" who are corporately God's temple, it defiles the joint sharing in the Spirit who consecrates the temple (κοινωνία). By sinning against the consecrated corporeity, some are sinning against God and committing sacrilege against the Spirit.[88] On the phrase **the Spirit of God** and its theology, see above on 2:10-16, in full detail. Most non-Christian religious worshipers in Paul's day would expect to find an image of the deity in their temple. Hence it is axiomatic that the presence of God through his Holy Spirit consecrates his own temple "not made with human hands."[89] God's presence *constitutes* the temple status of his people, and without it they are no temple, just as in Rom 8:9, 11 the Spirit's indwelling constitutes the identity of the people of God-in-Christ.[90]

17 The Greek employs a play on words with the two uses of *damage, defile,* **destroy** (φθείρω), although it should be noted that the first occurs in the present indicative active, while the second is a contracted future form (φθειρεῖ). It is often observed that a symmetrical wordplay of this form constitutes a supposed expression of *lex talionis.*[91] Indeed, E. Käsemann selects 1 Cor 3:17 as his first example of "sentences of holy law." He comments, "The same verb describes in the chiasmus of the protasis and apodosis both human guilt and divine judgment in order to characterize by this method both the precise correspondence of the two in content and this indissoluble and harsh logical connection. It is evident that the *jus talionis* is being promulgated here: the destruction of the destroyer."[92] Käsemann compares the structure of Gen 9:6, "Whoever sheds the blood of men, by man shall his blood be shed," with a further parallel form of Aeschylus.[93] 1 Cor 14:38 reflects a similar structure: εἰ δέ τις ἀγνοεῖ, ἀγνοεῖται.[94] Also under this heading Käsemann examines 1 Cor 16:22 and 1 Cor 5:3-5, and, admitting a more remote comparison in other examples, 2 Cor 9:6; Rom 2:12; and 1 Cor 14:13, 28, 30, 35 and 37.

Käsemann's argument that these are embedded in a *Sitz im Leben* of prophetic utterance has received incisive criticism.[95] Klaus Berger and David Hill have revealed weaknesses in this aspect of Käsemann's argument.[96] Hill persuasively concludes that this aspect is "at best . . . only a hypothesis . . . which

---

88. Ibid., 13-23; on other parts of the NT cf. 221-52.

89. On this basis some (e.g., J. Moltmann) argue that images are prohibited in the OT not only because God is Other and transcendent, but also because God created *humankind to be his image.*

90. Maly, *Mündige Gemeinde,* 70.

91. Lightfoot speaks of the offender's being "requited in kind" (*Notes,* 194).

92. Käsemann, "Sentences of Holy Law in the NT," in *NT Questions of Today,* 67; cf. 66-81 (German, "Sätze Heiligen Rechtes im NT," *NTS* 1 [1954-55]: 248-60).

93. Aeschylus, *Choephori* 312-13.

94. Käsemann, *NT Questions,* 68-69.

95. Käsemann, *NT Questions,* 76-81, on 1 Cor 3:17, Mark 8:38, and form-critical issues.

96. K. Berger, "Zu den sogenannten Sätzen heiligen Rechts," *NTS* 16 (1969-70): 10-40, and in "Die sogenannten 'Sätze heiligen Rechts' im NT," *TZ* 28 (1972): 305-30; and David Hill, *NT Prophecy* (London: Marshall, Morgan & Scott, 1979), 171-74.

has been elevated to the level of an assumed fact by reason of its frequent reiteration."[97] At the same time a different aspect of Käsemann's argument remains useful. 1 Cor 3:17, he says, is not quite "a threat." "In it a process of being judged is already under way." It "anticipates the verdict of the ultimate Judge."[98] But this is not because Paul's prophetic status achieves this. It is because the destruction of the destroyer is tied to the destroyer's act *by internal logical grammar.* So to damage the church that the work of the Spirit becomes impeded is *thereby* to cut oneself off from the Spirit as one's own source of life. Thus Käsemann's instinct that a quasi-legal formula lies in the background has some validity, but not in the sense which he supposes. As J. L. Austin declared, the cue words *hereby* or *thereby* often indicate quasi-institutional *speech-acts,* in the utterance of which something occurs.[99] Paul warns the addressees that seriously to undo the work of authentic building *thereby* brings destruction upon the person in question, and *thereby also* invites the corroborative verdict of the judgment of God. That person's plight is dreadful indeed.[100]

2. The Limitations of Merely Human Assessments of Ministry and of Manipulative Attitudes (3:18–4:5)

(18) Let no one be self-deceived. If any among you thinks that he or she is wise in terms of this world order, let that person become a fool in order to become wise. (19, 20) For the wisdom of this world is folly beside God. For it is written, "He catches the clever in their craftiness." And again, "The Lord knows that the reasonings of the clever are futile." (21) So then, let no one glory in human persons. (22, 23) For all things are yours: whether Paul or Apollos or Cephas, or the world or life or death, or things present or things to come; all are yours, and you are Christ's, and Christ is God's.

(1, 2) Let a person count us as servants of Christ and estate managers of the mysteries of God. As for the rest, here it is required among estate managers that a person be found trustworthy. (3) It counts for very little with me, however, that I should be judged by you or by any human court of judgment; indeed, I do not even judge myself. (4) I do not have anything on my conscience, but I am not thereby pronounced in the right. The One who judges me is the Lord. (5) So do not pronounce judgments on anything before the proper time, until the Lord comes, who will shed light upon the hidden things of darkness and will disclose the hidden motivations of our lives. Then will recognition come for each from God.

97. Hill, *NT Prophecy,* 174.
98. Käsemann, *NT Questions,* 68.
99. J. L. Austin, *How to Do Things with Words* (Oxford: Clarendon Press, 1962), 6-16. For a more up-to-date account of speech-acts see the Introduction, and N. Wolterstorff, *Divine Discourse* (Cambridge: Cambridge University Press, 1995), 75-94 and throughout.
100. On the judgment aspect see further Merklein, *Der erste Brief 1–4,* 274-77.

Collins observes that 3:18-23 serves as a kind of *inclusio* to give preliminary closure to the argument of 1:10–3:23, alluding to Paul and Apollos, wisdom and folly, this age, and boasting.[101]

The new subsection begins with a reference to self-deception: Μηδεὶς ἑαυτὸν ἐξαπατάτω **let no one deceive** or *cheat himself/herself.* Self-deception about the status of the self as already **mature** or fully **spiritual** may lead to further deception about a lack of need for ministry. Hence it is possible to cheat oneself out of the full range of ministerial resources and support which God has provided. Carson's subheading makes the point accurately: "Factionalists Ignore the Wealth of the Heritage We as Christians Properly Enjoy."[102] "The world tries to impress with its rhetoric and sophistication. . . . The apostles of Jesus Christ prize truth above style and quietly refuse to endorse any form that may prove . . . diversionary . . . [from] gospel truth." Bultmann and especially Theissen have also demonstrated the role that self-deception plays in Paul's theology, long before the era of Freud.[103]

If supposed wisdom leads to people within the church losing out on resources which God has granted, then such wisdom does indeed become unmasked as utmost folly. This is part of the "reversals" of judgment created by the cross. On a merely human level ministers may appear less impressive than rhetoricians, like mere manual **laborers**, but in God's eyes they are channels for the household management of the needs of his community: stewards or **estate managers** of the mysteries of God (4:1). These "two viewpoints" are bound up not with a Platonic dualism between a view "from below" and a vision "from above," but with a temporal contrast between those who have passed through the cross and resurrection and live in anticipation of the verdict of last day, and those who still belong to the old, earlier world order. Hence Paul will introduce the dimensions of Christology and eschatology to ground the practical point in theology.

Bibliography on 3:18–4:5

Barth, K., *The Resurrection of the Dead* (Eng. trans., London: Hodder, 1993), 16-21.

Bassler, J., "1 Cor. 4:1-5," *Int* 44 (1990): 179-83.

Bultmann, R., "καυχάομαι," *TDNT,* 3:645-54.

Bultmann, R., *Theology of the NT* (London: SCM, 1952), 1:242 and 330-33.

Carson, D. A., *The Cross and the Christian Ministry* (Grand Rapids: Baker and Leicester: Inter-Varsity Press, 1993), 84-103.

Clarke, A. D., *Secular and Christian Leadership in Corinth* (Leiden: Brill, 1993), 124-26.

Combes, I. A. H., *The Metaphor of Slavery in the Writings of the Early Church,* JSNTSS 156 (Sheffield: Sheffield Academic Press, 1998), 77-93.

---

101. Collins, *First Cor,* 162-63.

102. Carson, *The Cross and the Christian Ministry,* 84; cf. 84-89.

103. Theissen, *Psychological Aspects of Pauline Theology,* esp. 59-66 (on this passage) but also 57-114 and throughout.

Coune, M., "L'apôtre sera jugé. I Co. 4:1-5," *ASeign* 39 (1972): 10-17.

Eckstein, H.-G., *Der Begriff Syneidesis bei Paulus,* WUNT 2:10 (Tübingen: Mohr, 1983).

Fiore, B., "'Covert Allusion' in 1 Cor 1–4," *CBQ* 47 (1985): 85-102.

Hoffmann, P., "Er ist unsere Freiheit. Aspekte einer konkreten Christologie," *BK* 42 (1987): 109-15.

Kuck, D. W., *Judgement and Community Conflict* (Leiden: Brill, 1993): 188-210.

Léon-Dufour, X., "Jugement de l'homme et jugement de Dieu. 1 Cor. 4:1-5 dans le quadre de 3:18–4:5," in L. de Lorenzi (ed.), *Paolo a uno chiesa divisa (1 Cor. 1–4),* BibEcum 5 (Rome: Benedictina, 1980), 137-53.

Maly, K., *Mündige Gemeinde* (Stuttgart: Katholisches Bibelwerk), 72-79.

Martin, D., *Slavery as Salvation* (New Haven: Yale University Press, 1990), 15-22 and 122-24.

Mitchell, M. M., *Paul and the Rhetoric of Reconciliation* (Tübingen: Mohr, 1992), 91-99.

Pack, F., "Boasting in the Lord," *ResQ* 19 (1976): 65-71.

Pierce, C. A., *Conscience in the NT* (London: SCM, 1955), 60-110.

Pogoloff, S. M., *Logos and Sophia* (Atlanta: Scholars Press, 1992), 214-17.

Ramsaran, R. A., *Liberating Words: Paul's Use of Rhetorical Maxims in 1 Cor 1–10* (Valley Forge, Pa.: Trinity Press International, 1996).

Reumann, J., "'Servants of God' — Pre-Christian Religious Application of οἰκονόμος in Greek," *JBL* 77 (1958): 339-49.

Reumann, J., "οἰκονομία Terms in Paul in Comparison with Lucan *Heilsgeschichte*," *NTS* 13 (1966-67): 147-67.

Richardson, N., *Paul's Language about God,* JSNTSS 99 (Sheffield Academic Press, 1994), 110-16.

Robinson, W. E., "The Church in the World: 'Steward of the Mysteries of God' (1 Cor. 4:1)," *Int* 19 (1966): 412-17.

Roetzel, C. J., *Judgment in the Community: A Study in the Relation between Eschatology and Ecclesiology in Paul* (Leiden: Brill, 1972), 38-41, 68-105.

Schaller, B., "Zum Textcharakter der Hiobzitate in paulinischen Schriftum," *ZNW* 71 (1980): 21-26.

Sevenster, J. N., *Paul and Seneca,* NovTSup 4 (Leiden: Brill, 1961), 109-22.

Stanley, C. D., *Paul and the Language of Scripture: Citation Technique in the Pauline Epistle and Contemporary Literature,* SNTSMS 74 (Cambridge: Cambridge University Press, 1995), 189-95.

Stendahl, K., *Paul among Jews and Gentiles* (Philadelphia: Fortress, 1976, and London: SCM, 1977), esp. 23-40 and 78-96.

Theissen, G., *Psychological Aspects of Pauline Theology* (Eng. trans., Edinburgh: T. & T. Clark, 1987), 59-66.

———, *The Social Setting of Pauline Christianity* (Philadelphia: Fortress, 1982), 75-83.

Weiss, J., *Earliest Christianity* (2 vols., New York: Harper, 1959 [1937]), 2:458-63.

Wire, A. C., *The Corinthian Women Prophets* (Minneapolis: Fortress, 1990), 37-38, 41-43.

Witherington, B., *Conflict and Community in Corinth* (Grand Rapids: Eerdmans and Carlisle: Paternoster, 1995), 135-40.

Wolterstorff, N., *Divine Discourse* (Cambridge: Cambridge University Press, 1995), 76-89.

Zmijewski, J., "καυχάομαι," *EDNT,* 2:276-79.

18 The two third person imperatives give particular punch to the structure, but cause difficulties in English translation if gender-neutral language is required. ἐξαπατάτω is third singular present imperative, with intensive ἐκ to form the compound, while γενέσθω is probably ingressive aorist, stressing the commencement of the act. Gender-neutral English favors the plural: *let them not deceive themselves;* but many VSS reflect the view that we might as well transpose it into a second person imperative: *do not deceive yourselves* (NRSV, NIV, Collins). NJB rightly perceives that Paul presents *self-deception* as a key *concept;* hence *there is no room for self-delusion.*[104] We have tried to combine the third singular imperative gender-neutral pronouns, and the conceptual point identified by NJB with **Let no one be self-deceived**.

Self-deception constitutes the reason why a person who **thinks** (the meaning of δοκέω here), as against *seems* (KJV/AV) **that he or she is wise** (i.e., "wise" as **this world order** counts wisdom, σοφός ... ἐν τῷ αἰῶνι τούτῳ) has to **become a fool in order to become** [truly] **wise**. The second use γίνομαι (second aorist subjunctive γένηται) expresses the purpose clause **in order to become wise**.

At its minimum Paul expresses the well-known maxim of Socrates that recognition of one's own ignorance is the starting point for the acquisition of knowledge or wisdom.[105] Paul endorses this maxim, and asserts no less, even if he asserts also more. Allo and Witherington convincingly refer the principle of "reversal" back to the cross in 1:18-25, which "turns things upside down."[106] Others refer the application of the principle back to 3:16-17, stating that "the danger of sacrilege and of its heavy penalty (vv. 16, 17) is not so remote as some . . . may think."[107] But a long tradition which includes Origen, Cyprian, Chrysostom, Luther, and most modern commentators refers the application forward to the attitude of the church toward ministry.

Some contend that the main burden of warning falls on aspiring teachers. But the context of 3:21b, 22a and 4:3-5, combined with the stress on "order" in 3:23, points to the folly of those who "cheat themselves" out of the ministerial resources which God provides for their assistance and growth (cf. 3:5-7). Either those who were "foolish" wished to dispense with all ministerial agency (cf. those "of Christ" in 1:12) or more probably they used their selected favorites to confirm what they already believed and wished to believe, refusing to be chal-

---

104. This theme is rightly identified, e.g., by Strobel, *Der erste Brief,* 84-85; Collins, *First Cor,* 164-65; also by such earlier writers as Meyer, *First Epistle,* 1:102; Godet, *First Epistle,* 1:195. Merklein, *Der erste Brief 1–4,* 281, connects this self-deception with a self-styled leader whose words or deeds have destructive effects on the "temple" of God's people (v. 17).

105. As Lang, *Die Briefe,* 57, among others, duly notes. Héring argues further that μωρός had a more negative sense of "unsophisticated" in Cynic and Stoic circles, which Paul required Christians to accept in terms of that "world order" (*First Epistle,* 25).

106. Allo, *Première Épitre,* 64; Harrisville, *1 Corinthians,* 63; Schrage, *Der erste Brief,* 1:311; Witherington, *Conflict and Community,* 135 (quoted above).

107. Meyer, *First Epistle,* 1:102; Robertson and Plummer, *First Epistle,* 69.

lenged by the corporate ministry which God had assigned (cf. those of "Peter," or of "Apollos," 1:12). Ministry now becomes an instrument of mere self-affirmation, and the challenge of the cross and the fullness of the Spirit may become distorted or fragmented.

Chrysostom rightly brings out the christological and soteriological dimensions of evaluations of ministry here: the rejection of the standards and criteria of the world is part of what it is "to become, as it were dead to the world; and this deadness harms not at all, but rather profits, being made a cause of life . . . as the cross, though counted ignominious, became the author of innumerable blessings."[108]

19-20   The opening phrase takes up the theme of 1:18, just as the quotation effectively recapitulates 1:19, thereby confirming the close relation of thought with a theology of the cross (cf. above, on 3:18). The preposition παρά with the dative has its distinctive, innate force of **beside**.[109] The NRSV *with* undertranslates, although the NIV *in God's sight,* while possible, loses the vivid force of a quasi-spatial metaphor which turns on being alongside.

Paul draws his OT quotation from Job 5:13, which appears to be the only use of Job within the NT. Paul substitutes ὁ δρασσόμενος for the LXX ὁ καταλαμβάνων, and more notably uses ἐν τῇ πανουργίᾳ, **in their craftiness**, in place of ἐν τῇ φρονήσει, *in their understanding.* The Greek πανουργία derives from the notion of being ready to turn one's hand to anything or everything (παν-), but regularly denotes the negative quality of *cunning, knavery,* or **craftiness**. Hence, although the LXX translates Heb. עָרְמָה (*'armah*) by φρόνησις, Paul's πανουργία seems to be a closer equivalent to the Hebrew. Similarly, δράσσομαι, *to grasp,* **catch**, *lay hold of,* translates קָמַץ (*qamats,* or elsewhere also נָשַׁק (*nashaq*), *to enclose with the hand, to grasp.*[110] While καταλαμβάνω incorporates the κατα-intensive compound and can mean *seize, appropriate, take by surprise,* δράσσομαι with πανουργία more closely, perhaps, reflects the picture in Job as God **catches** *hold of* those who maneuver to and fro in their attempts to counsel leaders. Berndt Schaller argues that Paul's text has close affinities with the Massoretic Text as a probable revision of the LXX text.[111]

C. D. Stanley, however, remains unconvinced by this specific textual theory. He does not agree that πανουργία is a better translation; rather, he argues that while αὐτῶν, **their [craftiness]**, "clearly reflects the wording of the Massoretic Hebrew . . . the presence of the plural article before σοφούς actually moves 1 Cor. 3:19 farther away from the text."[112] He believes that both translations of δράσσομαι and φρονήσει are "beyond question" in their suitability for

108. Chrysostom, *1 Cor. Hom.,* 10:2.
109. BAGD, 610, 2:1 and 2.
110. BDBG, 888.
111. B. Schaller, "Zum Textcharacter der Hiobzitate im paulinischen Schriftum," *ZNW* 71 (1980): 21-26.
112. C. D. Stanley, *Paul and the Language of Scripture,* SNTSMS 74 (Cambridge: Cambridge University Press, 1992), 190.

עֲרְמָה *('armah)*. Stanley concludes that both the LXX and 1 Cor 3:19b "might represent wholly independent translations of the Hebrew text of Job."[113] D.-A. Koch nevertheless adopts Schaller's view.[114]

The quotation from Job is coupled with another from the OT introduced, as is regularly the case, with καὶ πάλιν, **and again**. As Fee helpfully observes, these two verses make the converse point to 1:18-25: there Paul says that what God does in wisdom seems foolish to the world; here he declares that what the world thinks is wise God sees as futile folly.[115] Paul now, therefore, turns to Ps 94:11 (LXX, 93:11). Here, however, he follows the LXX wording, except that he repeats τῶν σοφῶν, **of the clever,** in place of the LXX τῶν ἀνθρώπων, *of human beings*. As Lightfoot urges, **reasonings** both accurately translates διαλογισμούς and properly reflects the thrust of the OT quotation. Psalm 94 stresses that in spite of manipulative and corrupt leadership by those in authority (Ps 94:5-7, 16), the "schemes" of these human persons fail because their best "thinkers" are fallible (Ps 94:11).[116] Since advisers are clearly in view here, Paul's use of τῶν σοφῶν simply explicates their deliberative and advisory role as against τῶν ἀνθρώπων, which stresses their mere humanness. Paul *explicates* an aspect of the meaning; he cannot be said to have *changed* it.

The use of the OT in Paul constitutes a distinct subject in its own right which cannot be explored in detail here. Major discussions have been provided by the six scholars listed below.[117] Numerous further studies can be consulted.[118] The present passage, however, provides special interest through its juxtaposition of two categories of quotation. 1 Cor 3:19 is one of a small group of half a dozen quotations which imply Paul's familiarity with, and use of, the Hebrew text. 1 Cor 3:20 follows the LXX, as Paul does in around sixty instances, using the text which is familiar to his readers and congregations, as Christians outside Israel or Judea. Of about a hundred citations or allusions, (i) some forty follow the LXX where the LXX also matches the Hebrew

113. Ibid., 191.

114. D.-A. Koch, *Die Schrift als Zeuge des Evangeliums* (Tübingen: Mohr, 1986), 71-72.

115. Fee, *First Epistle,* 152.

116. J. W. Rogerson and J. W. McKay, *Psalms 51–100* (Cambridge: Cambridge University Press, 1977), 213-15. Stanley argues that the replacement by σοφῶν can point in more than one direction (*Paul and the Language of Scripture,* 194-95).

117. O. Michel, *Paulus und seine Bibel* (Gütersloh: Bertelsmann, 1929); E. E. Ellis, *Paul's Use of the OT* (Edinburgh: Oliver & Boyd, 1957: rpt. Grand Rapids: Baker, 1981); L. Goppelt, *Typos* (Eng. trans., Grand Rapids: Eerdmans, 1981), 127-52; Koch, *Die Schrift als Zeuge des Evangeliums;* R. B. Hays, *Echoes of Scripture in the Letters of Paul* (New Haven: Yale University Press, 1989); and Stanley, *Paul and the Language of Scripture* (cited above).

118. Cf. J. W. Aageson, *Written Also for Our Sake: Paul and the Art of Biblical Interpretation* (Louisville: Westminster/Knox, 1993); A. T. Hanson, *Studies in Paul's Technique and Theology* (Grand Rapids: Eerdmans and London: SPCK, 1974); R. N. Longenecker, *Biblical Exegesis in the Apostolic Period* (Grand Rapids: Eerdmans, 1975); and D. Moody Smith, "The Pauline Literature," in D. A. Carson and H. G. M. Williamson (eds.), *It is Written: Scripture Citing Scripture: Essays in Honour of Barnabas Lindars* (Cambridge: Cambridge University Press, 1988), 265-91; B. S. Rosner, *Paul, Scripture and Ethics* (cited below).

Massoretic Text; (ii) six are closer to the Hebrew; (iii) seventeen follow the LXX where there is some divergence from the Hebrew text; and (iv) two dozen or so invite more speculative explanations as "free" quotations which are not easy to identify with any single passage closely in either the LXX or the Massoretic Text. Less than a third, therefore, appear to possess the degree of "free" quotation which is often assumed to characterize Paul. Moreover, whether Paul quotes precisely from the LXX or Hebrew, or whether he uses allusive resonances, depends largely on the specific purpose for which he cites the OT material.

One further point may be added. The presence of some nine quotations in Corinthians from categories (i), (ii), and (iii), together with a further six in (iv), i.e., fifteen total, suggests that the theory that Paul appeals to scripture only as an *ad hominem* argument in the quasi-Jewish contexts of Romans and Galatians is difficult to sustain. Indeed, Brian Rosner has recently demonstrated the key role of the OT for Paul's ethics in this epistle.[119]

21 The particle ὥστε introduces a distinctive construction when it is used in its fully consecutive sense, *so that.* Here, however, it serves only as an inferential particle-conjunction, *so,* or **so then**.[120] The negative **let no one glory in human persons** reflects and repeats 1:29: ὅπως μὴ καυχήσηται πᾶσα σάρξ ἐνώπιον τοῦ θεοῦ. which has its positive corollary in 1:31, Ὁ καυχώμενος ἐν κυρίῳ καυχάσθω, **Let the one who glories, glory in the Lord**. This not only recapitulates 1:18-31 from the converse side, but it also directly addresses the "party slogans" or "leader slogans" of 1:10-12.[121] It also partly corroborates the rhetorical function of these verses suggested by Collins (noted in our introduction to these verses).

This passage is fundamental to Karl Barth's early understanding of this epistle and of the resurrection chapter. He writes: "The main defect of Corinthian conditions . . . Paul sees to consist in the boldness, assurance and enthusiasm with which they believe not in God but in their own belief in God and in particular leaders and heroes. . . . They confuse belief with specific human experiences. . . . Against this, the clarion call of Paul rings out: 'Let no man glory in men' (3:21), or expressed in positive form, 'He that glorieth, let him glory in the Lord' (1:31) . . . 'Every man shall have praise of God' (4:5). This 'of God' is clearly the secret nerve of this whole (and perhaps not only this) section."[122]

Barth's perspective on this passage is wholly right. It also partly explains, as Calvin observes, why Paul leaves the resurrection chapter to the end, to clinch the argument about the centrality of God and God-in-Christ.[123] This further helps us to notice otherwise underestimated affinities with major themes in

---

119. B. S. Rosner, *Paul, Scripture and Ethics: A Study of 1 Cor. 5–7* (Leiden: Brill, 1994).

120. A. T. Robertson, *Grammar,* 999, counts 30 such uses in the NT, of which eleven introduce an imperative, as here.

121. Fee, *First Epistle,* 153; Collins, *First Cor,* 162-63; Schrage, *Der erste Brief,* 1:314-15.

122. Barth, *The Resurrection of the Dead,* 17 and 18.

123. Calvin, *First Epistle,* 14 and 312.

Romans.[124] Furthermore, as Karl Plank points out, the allusion to **glorying** also points forward to 4:8-13, where many Corinthians seem to "live it up in glory," i.e., self-glory, while the apostles recognize their status as gladiators in the ring, who strive to exhibit the glory of God for others.[125] Similarly, J. T. Fitzgerald sees Paul and Apollos in 3:5–4:5 as "counterexamples" to the Corinthian tendency to exult in self-ascribed wisdom and glory.[126]

In secular Greek traditions καυχάομαι could be used in a negative sense in the context of warning against self-glory, bragging or illusory boasting (Pindar, c. 490 BC, 9.58, *loud-mouthed;* cf. Aristotle, *Politics* 5.10-16; Herodotus, 7.39; cf. Plautus on self-praise, 2.539ff.) but Homeric heroes may from time to time **glory** in their weapons or in their battle skills in the more positive sense of *taking pride* in them.[127] Paul says that if Christians are *to take pride* in anything, in the sense of **glorying** in it, this is not to be in any feature of the *church or its leaders,* but in God as revealed in Christ, and *in God alone.*[128] Paul's most personal, self-involving declaration rings out in Gal 6:14: ἐμοὶ δὲ μὴ γένοιτο καυχᾶσθαι εἰ μὴ ἐν τῷ σταυρῷ τοῦ κυρίου ἡμῶν Ἰησοῦ Χριστοῦ, *Perish the thought that I should glory in anything but the cross of our Lord Jesus Christ.*

22-23 The list which follows **For all are yours** (v. 22) looks back, as Lang observes, to exclusivist slogans of 1:10-12 which are now purged of their exclusivism and political overtones.[129] We may note the closeness of wording to 1:12, with the intensifying use of the predicate genitive in the sense of "they belong to you." Findlay wonders whether this, too, might be a Corinthian slogan: *this leader belongs to us.*[130] If this is so, we have yet another example of Pauline redefinition, or of what Umberto Eco and John Moores would call *the switching of a semiotic "code"* in order to generate a different meaning by the same signs, i.e., by the same vocabulary and phrases.[131] **Let no one glory in**

---

124. Thiselton, "Luther and Barth on 1 Cor. 15," in W. P. Stephens (ed.), *The Bible, The Reformation and the Church: Essays in Honour of James Atkinson,* 258-89. (See further the note below on καυχάομαι and φυσιόω in Paul.)

125. K. A. Plank, *Paul and the Irony of Affliction* (Atlanta: Scholars Press, 1987), 27-28.

126. J. T. Fitzgerald, *Cracks in an Earthen Vessel* (Atlanta: Scholars Press, 1988), 120 and 120, n. 13.

127. Bultmann, "καυχάομαι," *TDNT,* 3:645-46; cf. 645-54; LSJ, 790; and J. Zmijewski, "καυχάομαι," *EDNT,* 2:276-79.

128. Some fifty-three of sixty uses of the word in the NT occur in Paul. Paul boasts because of the hope God gives (Rom 5:2), boasts in God (Rom 2:17; 5:11), boasts in the Lord (1 Cor 1:31; 2 Cor 10:17), and boasts in Christ (Phil 3:3). On the other side, to boast in the self is the essence of what Paul calls "the mind of the flesh" (σάρξ), and is hostile to God since it transfers the glory due to him to the self and to humankind. Where σάρξ becomes prominent in Romans, φυσίομαι, *to be puffed up, inflated with self-importance,* becomes more central in our epistle (1 Cor 8:1).

129. Lang, *Die Briefe,* 58.

130. Findlay, *Expositor's Greek Testament,* 2:795.

131. Moores, *Wrestling with Rationality in Paul,* 6-10, 25-28, and 132-38; Umberto Eco, *Semiotics and the Philosophy of Language* (London: Macmillan, 1988), and *The Role of the Reader* (Bloomington: Indiana University Press, 1979). In semiotic theory the *code* is distinguished from

human persons effectively withdraws the meaning currency from *this leader is ours*. The words "belong to you" can have *meaning currency and truth if, and only if, three provisos or qualifications are made:*

(i) that the *true ministerial role of the leaders in God's sight* is fully acknowledged, as against this-worldly evaluations of their roles (3:5-20; cf. 1:18-31);

(ii) that each minister is perceived *as part of a comprehensive range of gifts and resources,* all lavished upon them as a corporeity or plurality to be used without picking and choosing the gifts (πάντα, εἴτε . . . εἴτε . . . , **all, whether** . . . 3:22);

(iii) that the chain of gifts which begins with human agents ascends in due course through aspects of grace and providence (κόσμος . . . ζωή . . . **the world** . . . **life** . . .) to embrace an *order in which Christ is Lord* and in which *even Christ has an ordered role* in relation to God within God's economy of action and order. *Theological order* replaces political egalitarianism. (We discuss the claims of A. C. Wire about "hierarchy" at a later point.)

These three constituent elements of Paul's thought *shape the semiotic code* which generates the meaning of catchphrases upon which the Corinthians have seized on the basis of their own sociopolitical code. **All are yours** thus has currency, *provided that it is redefined.* Robertson and Plummer see significance in the ascending sequence of the list. They comment: "His aim is not merely to proclaim how wide their heritage is. . . . They want to make him [or some other leader] a chieftain. . . . The church is not the property of Apostles. Apostles are ministers of the Church."[132] Further, the items on the list are not "ends in themselves" but all jointly serve the Lordship of Christ (v. 23a).

Just as an exclusive obsession with any single minister can cheat the Christian believer out of his or her heritage and freedom, so the next five items make a parallel point. People can allow the world, life, death, the present, or the future to serve as what Fee imaginatively calls "tyrannies of existence."[133] In Rom 8:38 Paul includes precisely four of these: death (θάνατος), life (ζωή), things present (ἐνεστῶτα), or things to come (μέλλοντα) (but substituting there

the *message.* All texts presuppose a code usually dependent on recognized conventions. (i) A map, (ii) medical prescription, or (iii) a sheet of music conveys its "message" through (i) signs about trees, roads, bridges (etc.); (ii) instructions about quantity, timing, compound (traditionally in Latin); and (iii) crochets or semi-quavers placed on a stave with a clef, key signature, and indication of time. These three matrices are *codes* for each type of message. When apocalyptic literature is treated as a time chart, a modern Western objectivist *code* is substituted for that of apocalyptic. On *code* see A. C. Thiselton, *New Horizons in Hermeneutics* (London: Harper Collins; Carlisle: Paternoster; and Grand Rapids: Zondervan, 1992), 80-84; and on Eco, *Semiotics,* 524-29.

132. Robertson and Plummer, *First Epistle,* 72.

133. Fee, *First Epistle,* 154.

ἀρχαί, powers, for κόσμος, the world, and adding δυνάμεις, forces or powers of various kind, together with height (ὕψωμα) and depth (βάθος), as potential tyrannies capable hypothetically of becoming negative forces which can separate the believer from God's love if or when they come to divert attention from God to themselves. Whiteley subscribes to the view that height and depth signify paths of planets which betoken bondage to belief in astrological forces. In 1 Cor 3:22 Paul likewise sees these as unable to defeat the Christian, since once the believer perceives all them, including those who minister in the church, as gifts from God to assist and to enrich them, they constitute positive forces for good which the Christian can "own" as God's gifts, given the three provisos set out above.

The theology here is profound. The Christian shares in the Lordship of Christ whereby creation and the church are restored into cooperative agencies for the well-being of humankind and for the glory of God-in-Christ, set within the providential dimension of the new order in Christ. As Karl Maly writes, here are Paul's concluding remarks about the problem of preachers and preaching at Corinth, concerning which he wants no mistake to be made: "all belong to the Corinthians since they no longer are their own but as his members belong to Christ (cf. Gal. 2:20; Rom. 14:8)."[134] Maly refers to Bultmann's major point that in "belonging to the Lord" (Rom. 14:8) lies the true freedom of the Christian, since Christ has taken over the responsibility for, and care of, the believer: "He lets this care go, yielding himself entirely to the grace of God. . . . The mightiest expression of freedom is 1 Cor. 3:21-23: 'For all things are yours. . . .'"[135]

Bultmann at once adds, "But the concluding clauses are 'and you are Christ's, and Christ is God's,'" pointing out that this coheres with and anticipates Paul's words "You do not belong to yourselves" in 1 Cor. 6:19.[136] In one sense a slave is not free; but in another sense the slave who has been granted privileges can enjoy all the resources of his master's property and all the protection of his master's care. Weiss points here to a fundamental difference between Hebrew and Greek traditions. In Semitic thought to be a servant, messenger, or courtier of a great personage is to be honored; and to carry with one the support and resources of the master. In Greek traditions the free, autonomous individual has status; servanthood and dependency seem ignoble.[137] To be sure, this distinction has become blurred with the intermixture of Roman, Greek and Oriental cultures in the first century, but there remains some truth in Weiss's comment that "what appears in the Greek as ignoble or servile appears in the Semitic as a proud title."[138] "To belong to Christ," he asserts, noting 1 Cor 7:23,

134. Maly, *Mündige Gemeinde,* 77.

135. Bultmann, *Theology,* 1:331. See Hoffmann, "Er ist unsere Freiheit. Aspekte einer konkreten Christologie," 109-15: Jesus is the concrete paradigm of God's freedom-giving action, and Jesus is Lord over the powers.

136. Bultmann, *Theology,* 1:331.

137. Weiss, *Earliest Christianity,* 2:459, n. 9 and 458-59.

138. Ibid., 2:460.

is to be "lord of all," set free to serve others as "a joyful, thankful act. . . . The believer can now rely upon him in every situation."[139]

Dale Martin's approach to this issue draws widely on social theory and social history. Slavery was not always something to be despised; indeed, it could provide a vehicle for "upward social mobility." The status of the master could have positive consequences for the slave. Thus "slavery to Christ" could offer symbolic status to a convert or bestow a level of derived status and authority upon a Christian leader.[140] Household slaves could include "manager slaves." More recently I. A. H. Combes has called into question some of Martin's claims about *perceptions* of slavery.[141] Hence while Martin's work contributes to our understanding it is not perhaps the last word on the subject. Indeed, the residual contrast between the Greek and Hebrew traditions finds expression in the linguistic phenomenon to which Fee, Kuck, and many others allude, namely, that for the first-century Stoic "all things are yours" means something quite different, namely, the free self-sufficiency (αὐτάρκης) of the individual who needs nothing which is beyond his existing resources.[142] J. B. Lightfoot, followed by J. N. Sevenster in his full-length study *Paul and Seneca,* makes similar points, noting that Paul's language about "learning to be content" and being "able to do all things" (Phil 4:11, 18) has an entirely different basis from Seneca's parallel language. The former is on the basis of "incorporation" into "him who strengthens me"; the latter depends on "self-isolation."[143]

The final phrases of 3:23, therefore, remain critical. Kuck observes, "The fact that they all together belong to Christ keeps their Christian liberty from pulling them apart in all sorts of individual directions through judging and boasting. . . . The factional strife in Corinth has been central at least in part by the desire of people to be judged as wise in the eyes of the culture, and to judge others in the church by that same worldly standard. . . . One theme stands out clearly: God as judge."[144]

This theme moves the addressees from **you are Christ's** to **and Christ is God's**. This relation between Christ and God remains a serious theological theme in 1 Corinthians, for the notion that "God is head of Christ" appears in some related form since it occurs not only here but also in 11:3 and 15:28 (see below), with some further resonance in 1:30. James Moffatt propounded the theory that on that basis those Graeco-Roman cults for whom Zeus was a shadowy figure but their cult-lord a more favorite figure, the Corinthian fellowship "gathered round their own favourite . . . divine figure . . . a form of Christ-mysticism which loos-

---

139. Ibid., 2:460 and 461.

140. Martin, *Slavery as Salvation,* 50-85, 145-49, and throughout.

141. Combes, *The Metaphor of Slavery in the Writings of the Early Church,* 79-81.

142. Fee, *First Epistle,* 154; Kuck, *Judgement,* 190-91. Cf. Seneca, *De Beneficiis* 7.1: "We say that all things belong to him, *Omnia illius esse dicimus*"; cf. 7.2.5; 3.2; 4.1.

143. Sevenster, *Paul and Seneca,* 114, 119, 120; cf. 109-22 and further J. B. Lightfoot, *Philippians,* 305.

144. Kuck, *Judgement,* 196.

ened the nexus between God and Christ, till God became less relevant . . . than Jesus the Lord for worship and action."[145] Neil Richardson, however, relates this more especially to the specific failure in all probability of the so-called Christ-party (see above on 1:12).[146] We have noted Richardson's analysis of the "clusters" of emphasis on **God** (θεός) especially at 1:26-28; 2:1, 5, 11, 12, 14; 3:6, 7, 9, 23. He urges on 3:23 (as with 11:3 and 15:28), "Thus θεός has a critical function, and Paul offers a thoroughly theocentric understanding of both the gospel and the Christian life."[147] Richardson more generally concludes, "Paul's language about God and about Christ are thoroughly interdependent, but that interdependence is not reciprocal."[148] At all events the affirmation of ontological "order" in a passage about eschatology (see under 15:28) makes this principle one of more than ecclesiology or a temporary "order" addressing human fallenness.[149]

Does not this lack of reciprocity constitute a reminder to the addressees that even when Christ is one with God, this does not dissolve all differentiation, distinction, or structure as if the gospel dissolves all "order" in an egalitarian assertion of the "rights" of individuals? (See further on 11:2-16.) *As the Lord assigned to each* characterizes ministerial vocation not least because the principle marks the ministry of Christ from which all ministry is derived. Hence there is a finality about the last word of the chapter, θεοῦ, **of God**. This is what holds together freedom, unity, and differentiated purpose. Even Christ does not choose exemption from the principle that God assigns to each his or her calling, even if at the same time this is the Christ-like God who gives "all things" to his people.

Whether or not we adopt this view, it seems likely that a further reason for Paul's asserting the ultimacy of God lay in his opponents' overreadiness to regard Christ as "one manifestation of eternal Wisdom which is the divine . . . in the universe."[150] Just as in 2:10-16 Paul maintained the transcendence of God against claims to be "of the Spirit," so in 3:18-23 he maintains this transcendence in the face of possible claims about "wisdom" as a more immanental figure. More speculative issues, however, are better considered in relation to the posthistory of the text, which we shall consider selectively and briefly after 4:5. Meanwhile, the ending **of God** underlines the ultimacy of the divine verdict for all and on all, while **Paul, Apollos, Cephas, death, the world** . . . remain agents or instruments for the fulfillment of the purposes of God, of which Christians are sharers and inheritors with **Christ**.

---

145. Moffatt, *First Epistle,* 250-51.

146. Richardson, *Paul's Language about God,* 114-15.

147. Ibid., 116.

148. Ibid., 311. We discuss Wire's claims esp. in relation to 12-14 and under 15:28.

149. Fee explicitly rejects "ontological" in favor of "functional." Wolff follows the views of Fee and Barrett, taking a middle view that the differentiation relates primarily to salvation history (*Der erste Brief,* 78). But the *principle* of "ordered distinction" is fundamental to the nature of God, whose work at creation consisted in structuring chaos through "difference."

150. R. G. Hamerton-Kelly, *Pre-existence, Wisdom and the Son of Man,* SNTSMS 21 (Cambridge: Cambridge University Press, 1973), 123, cf. 120-30; and Wire, *Corinthian Women Prophets,* 37-38, 41-43.

THE POSTHISTORY, RECEPTION, AND INFLUENCE
OF CHAPTER 3, ESPECIALLY 3:5-17

The Earlier Patristic Writers: Ministry and Faithfulness and the Spirit

Irenaeus takes up Paul's allusion to the temple of the Holy Spirit (3:16), stressing the holiness of God's temple and defining the term *spiritual,* following Paul, as the quality of sharing in the Holy Spirit.[151] **Clement of Alexandria** accepts that Christian identity entails building on the foundation of Jesus Christ (3:11), but applies "someone else who builds upon it" to a "gnostic superstructure on the foundation of faith in Christ Jesus."[152] Against the grain of Paul's argument here, Clement adds that the true Christian gnostic, however, will construct a superstructure of advanced teaching which has the quality of "gold, silver, precious stones," whereas "'the stubble and wood and the hay' are the additions of heresies."[153] **Tertullian** finds in the "foundation-stone" image a vindication against Marcion of the use of the OT, namely, Isa 28:16, "Behold, I lay in Sion for a foundation a precious stone and honourable, and he who rests thereon shall not be confounded." Moreover, it is the Creator (Marcion's rival demiurge) who evaluates whether the work of the superstructure is "either sound or worthless doctrine."[154] He stresses the doctrine of accountability to the Judge of all at the last day (3:13) which is part of a distinctively Christian belief in life after death.[155]

Origen's main hermeneutical goal concerns *apostolicity and orders of ministry.* Ministers must be fruitful (3:6-8).[156] Paul the apostle alone is truly the ἀρχιτέκτων who proclaimed the gospel of Christ. Moreover, *the concept of a threefold order of ministry now begins to emerge.* For Paul explains (ὁποῖον τὸν ἐπίσκοπον εἶναι πρεσβυτέρους τε καὶ διακόνους), giving due warning about care how one builds.[157] The fact that no one can lay any foundation which is other than Christ now points to the uniqueness of the apostolic ministry: τοῦτον τὸν θεμέλιον ἐν μὲν τῇ Ἰουδαίᾳ οἱ ἀπόστολοι ἔθηκαν, ἐν δὲ τοῖς ἔθνεσιν ὁ ἀπόστολος τῶν ἐθνῶν. To build wood, hay or straw results from overthrowing the truth (ἐσφάλησαν τῆς ἀληθείας). Origen recognizes that to be the temple of the Holy Spirit (3:16, 17) is *to share in the glory (δόξα) of God.* Indeed, the purpose of our being his temple is *"to glorify his name."*[158]

Cyprian *reverses the thrust of Paul's language* about the temple of the Holy Spirit to argue that even a baptized Christian may lose the Spirit's consecration: "him will God destroy. . . . If you forsake him, he will forsake you."[159] Cyprian is only too conscious of those who have fallen away under the Decian persecution (249-51). However, **Basil** draws on 1 Cor 3:16 to pursue his central theme of the deity of the Holy Spirit. The Spirit is the distinctive agent of sanctification; hence only

---

151. Irenaeus, *Against Heresies,* 5:6:1, 2.
152. Clement, *Stromata,* 5:4.
153. Ibid. Cf. 7:13.
154. Tertullian, *Against Marcion,* 5:6.
155. Tertullian, *On the Resurrection,* 3.
156. Origen, *Frag. 1 Cor.* (ed. C. Jenkins; *JTS* 9 [1908]: 243), sect. xiv.
157. Ibid., sect. xi (*JTS* 9 [1908]: 244).
158. Ibid., sect. xvi (*JTS* 9 [1908]: 246, my italics).
159. Cyprian, *Treatises,* 3: *Testimony,* 27.

through the Holy Spirit can God's full salvation be accomplished. Christian believers must not offer "the quarters of a slave" to the God of splendor who deigns to dwell among us. The Spirit is Lord.[160]

The Later Fathers: Origins of Speculation on the "Fire" of Purgatory

Ambrose follows Paul's thought closely (except perhaps on 3:15). He equates "planting" with the proclamation of the gospel, but he adds that to forgive sins and to give the Spirit come from God alone *(peccata autem dimittere, et Spiritum dare, Dei solus)*.[161] God gives the increase; in this respect the human agents are nothing *(nihil)*. The gospel of Christ requires building materials that must match *(congruant fundamento)*.[162] The wood, hay, and straw include *mala . . . et adultera doctrina*.[163] Nevertheless, he is ambivalent about the role of the fire (3:15). A salvation that is *quasi per ignem,* Ambrose comments, is *non sine poena* (not without *payment, penalty, or means of satisfaction*) . . . *ut per ignam purgatus fiat salvus*.[164] While a doctrine of purgatory has not become explicit in Ambrose, this direction has now been taken for future writers. **Chrysostom** avoids the problem: "'the work is destroyed', is the 'builder' to be saved? . . . The discourse is about actions."[165] A man who wears golden armor would pass through a river of fire all the brighter, whereas shoddy materials simply "burn up and become ashes."[166]

The issue of "purgatory" is often associated with **Augustine** on this passage. Eschatology and hope occupy a key place in his thought. Pelagius and the Donatists, both of whom he attacked, "anachronistically demanded a pure church, without spot or wrinkle. . . . What Pelagius failed to allow for, so Augustine wrote, was 'the interim, the interval between the remission of sins . . . and the permanently established sinless state in that kingdom which is to come.'" . . .[167]

Augustine writes that every Christian will build along with the gold, silver, and costly stone "wood, hay, and stubble" (1 Cor 3:13), which, as "attachment to worldly things however lawful these may be in themselves," become lost.[168] But the Christian knows that "the foundation is Christ" (1 Cor 3:11) and that since Christ is all, "he himself will be saved" (3:15), but "the fire which tests" is "the fire of adversity," "a furnace of affliction."[169] The whole of Augustine's *Enchiridion* 68 constitutes an exposition of 1 Cor 3:11-15. But "the furnace of affliction" is not simply "purgatory." *Either* the absence

---

160. Basil, *On the Holy Spirit,* 21, cf. Haykin, *The Spirit of God,* 119-20 and 221-22.

161. Ambrose, *Opera Omnia: In Epistolam b. Pauli ad Cor. Primam,* ed. J.-P. Migne, *PL,* 17:2:2 (Paris: Garnier, 1879), 209.

162. Ibid., 210.

163. Ibid., 211.

164. Ibid.

165. Chrysostom, *1 Cor. Hom.,* 9:4.

166. Ibid., 9:5 and 6.

167. R. A. Markus, "Comment: Augustine's Pauline Legacies," in William S. Babcock (ed.), *Paul and the Legacies of Paul* (Dallas: Southern Methodist University Press, 1990), 222; cf. 221-25, and B. Studer, "Augustine and the Pauline Theme of Hope," 201-20. See also Augustine, *De Gestis Pelagii,* 12:28ff.: *Anti-Pelagian Treatises* (ed. W. Bright; Oxford: Clarendon Press, 1880), 171.

168. Augustine, *Enchiridion,* 68 (throughout).

169. Ibid. Also sects. 5 and 6.

of solid work proves that self-interest so ruled someone's life that they did not build upon Christ at all, *or* some hint of solidity characterizes that life, but much is burned up in the affliction of becoming detached from earthly desires. Tribulation consti- tutes a prime example of being saved "through fire," i.e., *the pain of discovering where solid realities lie.* Those whose work is gold "'receive a reward' — i.e., he shall reap the fruit of his care. 'But if any man's work shall be burned, he shall suffer loss' — for what he loved he shall not retain: 'but he himself shall be saved' — for no tribulation shall have moved him from that stable foundation."[170] Problems arise, however, when Au- gustine *allows himself to speculate* about "the interval of time between the death of this body and that last day of judgment which shall follow the resurrection." Here he does envisage the possibility that to be saved "through fire" may be something close to a doctrine of purgatory, considering a kind of "worldliness that is venial," which may then be consumed in flames. Of such a fire of tribulation "here or hereafter," he comments (perhaps as if with reluctance?), "this I do not contradict, because possibly it is true."[171] Thus he formulates the *possibility* of a doctrine of purgatory on the basis of 1 Cor 3:11-15. The doctrine seems to have become established with Gregory.[172]

Cyril of Alexandria offers a fine example of a pastoral exposition of the church and ministry in 3:5-17. The planting (3:5-8) is a matter of bringing people to faith, but the pastoral task of *nourishing* the church (τρέφουσα) so that it bears fruit (καρποφόρος) remains essential.[173] Growth comes through the Spirit (διὰ πνεύματος). The possessive genitives "God's field; God's building" (3:9) reflect the purchase of the people of God through the precious blood of Christ (ἐξηγόρασεν τῷ τιμίῳ αὐτοῦ αἵματι).[174] As master-builder Paul is first or chief (πρῶτος) beside many other teachers. **Theodoret** comments that as we build we are often ignorant of the secret things of the heart until the coming of the Lord (Greek VS: τὴν ἐπιφανείας τοῦ Σωτῆτος ἡμέραν, Latin VS: *in die adventus Domini*).[175]

The Medieval Period

Ivo of Chartres (d. 1115) achieved special importance for his interpretation of canon law and church discipline. He argues that "the principal intention of all ecclesiastical discipline is this: either to destroy every construction which erects itself against the knowledge of Christ or to construct God's building which stands firm" (1 Cor 3:9-

170. Augustine, *City of God,* 21:26; cf. also 21:1, 2.

171. Ibid. (Schaff's edition, 2:475, col. 1; the discussion begins on 473, col. 2).

172. Some ambiguity also appears in *City of God,* 21:13, which appears both to affirm the doctrine and to express reservations about it, but the passing allusion to prayer for the dead in 21:24 is more telling in favor of Augustine's own belief in purgatory. Pope Gregory officially taught it, ar- guing that the primary pain of purgatory is the deprivation of the vision of God. The Eastern Church prays for the dead, but is less specific about their state than Gregory, Bede, and Thomas Aquinas. The Reformers rejected the doctrine as both unsupported by exegesis and contrary to salvation by grace apart from works. (See Barth's succinct comment.)

173. Philippus E. Pusey (ed.), *Cyrilli Alexandrini, Fragmenta Varia* 3 (Brussels: Culture et Civilisation, 1965), *In Epistolam 1 ad Corinthios,* 258.

174. Ibid., 259.

175. Theodoret, *Opera Omnia: Interpretatio primae epistolae ad Corinthios,* in J.-P. Migne, *PG,* 82 (Tomus Tertius) (1864), 249 and 252 (Greek) and 250-51 (Latin).

11).[176] The materials of the building must reflect truth of faith and morals. **Bernard of Clairvaux** (d. 1153) uses 1 Cor 3:9 to underline the union of divine and human agency, interpreting "God's fellow workers" as "co-operators with the Holy Spirit."[177] But, as we have noted, this departs from the most convincing exegesis of this verse. **Thomas Aquinas** (d. 1274) draws on Paul's image of the skilled (σοφός) master-builder (3:10) as he asks what sacred doctrine might be. He answers that it is the wisdom *(sapientia)* of all wisdoms. Paul applies the term wise *(sapiens)* master-builder to the one who needs to plan the whole structure, as against the artisans who cut the stones and mix the mortar, *sacra doctrina maxime dicitur sapientia.*[178]

The Reformation Era: Ministry and Authenticity

Erasmus offers a sound historical exegesis of 3:5-11: God is our source of life. But as soon as he reaches Paul's allusion to wood, hay, and straw or stubble (3:12), Erasmus at once calls into question phenomena of his times: the gold, silver, and costly stones all redound to *the glory of Christ;* but human persons add questionable man-made regulations, cold ceremonies, superstitions in place of godliness *("addit constitutianculas, de cultu . . . de frigidis ceremoniis . . . degenerent in superstitiosos pro piis . . .").*[179]

Erasmus characteristically calls for purity and innocence *(innocentia),* as against the contagion of selfish power seeking and striving, in those who are the temple of the Holy Spirit.[180] **Luther** takes issue with Erasmus's appeal to 3:7 in his evaluation of the ministry.[181] Paul elsewhere gives the ministry "high praise." Here, "as regards the giving of the growth, the planter and waterer are nothing, but as regards planting and watering they are not nothing, seeing that the supreme work of the Spirit in the church of God is to teach and to exhort. That is what Paul means."[182] Indeed, Paul's analogy fits precisely what Luther wishes to say about freedom, bondage, and grace. "Luther admits, of course, that man has a sort of freedom in respect of what he calls 'things beneath him.'" But humankind is not free "in relation to 'things above him', as Luther calls them, which pertain to eternal salvation or perdition."[183] Thus Paul and Apollos function as active agents in the processes of planting and watering; but in the process of the church's salvation they are mere instruments called by God's grace, and no contradiction exists between the all-sufficiency of God's grace and the subsidiary but necessary roles assigned to Paul and Apollos.[184] "In Christ God has furnished

---

176. Ivo of Chartres, *Decretum (Prologue)* (Eng. trans. in E. R. Fairweather [ed.], *A Scholastic Miscellany,* LCC 10 [London: SCM, 1956], 239; cf. 238-42).

177. Bernard, *Treatise on Grace and Free Choice,* 13:45.

178. Thomas Aquinas, *Summa Theologiae,* 1, Q. 1, art. 6 (Blackfriars ed., 1:20 and 22 (Latin), 21 and 23 (English). On the temple, see Q. 109, art. 9, sect. 3.

179. Desiderii Erasmi, *Omnia Opera: Paraphrasis in Epistulam Pauli ad 1 Cor,* 868.

180. Ibid. and *Enchiridion,* 18th Rule.

181. Cf. Erasmus, *On the Freedom of the Will,* pt. 3, sect. 1; in Gordon E. Rupp and Philip S. Watson (eds.), *Luther and Erasmus: Free Will and Salvation,* LCC 17 (London: SCM, 1969), 78.

182. Luther, *On the Bondage of the Will* (Rupp and Watson [eds.], *Luther and Erasmus*), 286; also *WA,* 18:750-51, and *On the Bondage of the Will,* ed. J. I. Packer and O. R. Johnston (London: Clarke, 1957), 264.

183. Philip S. Watson, "The Lutheran Riposte," in *Luther and Erasmus,* 17-18.

184. Luther, *On the Bondage of the Will* (Rupp and Watson [eds.]), 288; *WA,* 18:753.

us with a foundation on which to stand, but there are various ways in which supposed 'building' comes to nothing and is bogus, like straw, whether these are of sophists 'obsessed with their own speculations' or 'the Enthusiasts' who substitute inner experiences, supposedly of the Spirit, for scripture."[185]

In Luther's mature thought no Pauline text can be used to support any notion of purgatory: "Indulgences, purgatory . . . and similar abominations come tumbling down."[186] Purgatory belongs to "human traditions" and to "the papal kingdom," not to Christ and to Paul.[187] Otherwise justification by grace through faith alone becomes void. However, in his *earliest* thought he had considered 2 Macc 12:43ff. more positively in this connection, and retained a sympathy with Augustine's exegesis of 1 Cor 3:15.[188]

Calvin insists on both the high office of ministers who plant and water (3:5) alongside their lowly status as agents in their own right. Indeed, by "boasting in" given leaders, the Corinthians "deprive them of their true greatness."[189] On one side, "the attentiveness of the farmer is not ineffective"; on the other side, growth is "a miracle of divine grace" (3:6).[190] Thus ministry is described "in two ways" in 3:7-8. On one side, ministers are "ordained by the Lord"; on the other side, "he sometimes thinks of the minister as a servant . . . as an instrument."[191] Their distinctive responsibilities to God exclude their becoming "intoxicated by the glory of the world."[192] To build solidly and lastingly on this foundation (3:11) requires *faithfulness* and the recognition of *Christ's sufficiency*.[193] The materials that survive (3:12) are "in keeping with Christ," whereas the wood, hay, and stubble are "fabricated in men's minds."[194] The disclosure of God's verdict at the day (3:13) stands in contrast with "the favour of men . . . the applause of the world."[195] All human inventions will vanish in the fire.

Calvin addresses the issue of purgatory in two ways. Exegetically, Paul is speaking of *ministers* and *the ministry;* so how can this be generalized into a doctrine of purgatory? Calvin also considers the history of the interpretation of 3:12-15.[196] Most of the Fathers, he urges, offer no such understanding of "the fire" as purgatory. Even the practice of remembering the dead in prayer, Calvin concludes, remained for the Fathers an expression of care and remembrance: "assuredly they made no such assertion about purgatory or implied that they did not hold it to be uncertain."[197]

---

185. Luther, *Table Talk* (Autumn 1532), in *Letters of Spiritual Counsel,* LCC (Eng. trans., London: SCM, 1955), 122; and Luther, *Lectures on 1 Timothy,* in *Luther's Works,* 28 (American ed., St. Louis: Concordia, 1973), 223-24 (on 1 Tim 1:4-5; *WA,* 26:9).

186. Luther, *Lectures on Galatians 1535,* in *Luther's Works,* 25 (American ed., St. Louis: Concordia, 1963), 221; on Gal 3:5 (*WA,* 40:353; also Clarke ed. of 1575 ed., 218).

187. Luther, *Lectures on Galatians 1535,* in *Luther's Works,* 26:135; *WA,* 40:237 (on Gal 2:16).

188. Luther, "Letter to Jerome Weller July 1530," "Letter to V. Hausmann, une 1532," and many examples in *Letters of Spiritual Counsel,* 84-87, 120-21; cf. 82-138.

189. Calvin, *First Epistle,* 68; cf. also 70: ". . . in two ways: ordained by the Lord."

190. Ibid., 69.

191. Ibid., 70.

192. Ibid., 71.

193. Calvin, *First Epistle,* 73-74; *Institutes,* 3:18:1; *First Epistle,* 75.

194. Ibid., 75.

195. Ibid., 76.

196. Calvin, *Institutes,* 3:5:9, 10 (Beveridge ed., 1957, 1:579-82).

197. *Institutes,* 3:5:10 (Beveridge ed., 1:582).

The Enlightenment and Modern Period

Locke reflects the best of English commonsense reasonableness as an exegetical tool. In what sense does the person who builds wood, hay, or straw on the foundation of Christ "suffer loss" (3:15) even if such a person is saved? Locke remarks: "You lose your time and trouble."[198] The Day of 3:12-13 is the last judgement, which may reveal the illusory nature of the superstructure, as not corresponding to true, authentic doctrine.[199] Locke avoids speculations. **Bengel** (d. 1752) retains an eye to pastoral encouragement. The responsibility of ministerial builders is daunting (3:10b), but "even a little grain of gold is permanent" *(mica auri, durum est)*.[200] It is worth including a brief note concerning 3:21 in the writings of **Kierkegaard** (d. 1855). "All are yours" (1 Cor 3:21b) presupposes a context of love, as something that "belongs" but not in any grasping, absolute sense as "mine," as if "my God" or "my loved one" had the same grammar as "my shoes."[201] We noted Shanor's reference to the building inscription from Arcadian Tegea in which the "master-builder" (ἀρχιτέκτων) coordinates work globally and strategically.[202] Karl Barth expounds 1 Cor 3:11 in terms of the need for "integration, or fitting together, of different elements. Thus everything is to be judged by the standard whether it serves this integration."[203] Believers will come in due time to see their lifework "in the eyes of God."[204] Nevertheless, "If our whole work perish" we rejoice to be saved at the last "not because of, but in spite of, the work in which we took such pride."[205]

1-2 In v. 2 ζητεῖται, **it is required**, is a sound reading, including B and all the Fathers. However, 𝔭[46], ℵ, D, and C read the imperative ζητεῖτε, *seek,* which Héring favors.[206] The aural effect would not differ greatly, and most see no reason to doubt ζητεῖται.

Paul again speaks of ministers or of apostles as they are to be truly perceived in the light of God's dealings with the world. The first word which describes this function or office is ὑπηρέτης, which in the first century covers a variety of activities of *service.* In second-century papyri the word may often mean *assistant,* and in the hellenistic Greek of Paul's day it can vary from a *menial household servant* to a *junior officer* who assists his superior. This background lends support to REB, *subordinates.*[207] In classical Greek the word could mean *under-rower* in appropriate contexts, but although Corinth was a seaport the addressees would probably not be expected to think primarily of this meaning. In view

198. John Locke, *A Paraphrase and Notes* (Oxford: Clarendon Press, 1987), 1:427.

199. Ibid., 426.

200. Bengel, *Gnomon,* 617.

201. S. Kierkegaard, *Works of Love* (Eng. trans., New York: Harper & Row, 1962), 250; Further, ibid., 104; and *Christian Discourses* (Eng. trans., Princeton: Princeton University Press, 1971), 137-38.

202. Shanor, "Paul as Master Builder," 465.

203. Barth, *CD,* 4/2 (sect. 67), 1:637.

204. *CD,* 4/3 (sect. 73), 1:928.

205. Barth, *Resurrection of the Dead,* 19.

206. Héring, *First Epistle,* 27.

207. Collins, *First Cor,* 167, translates *assistants* (also 172).

of its range of applications, **servants** remains the nearest equivalent because of its broad semantic scope (as NRSV, NIV, NASB, NJB).[208]

The second main term, οἰκονόμους, is almost universally translated *stewards* (NRSV, REB, AV/KJV, NJB). But NIV recognizes that today *steward* is too often associated with waiters on board ships, and translates *those entrusted with (secret things)*. The nearest equivalent today is *household manager, housekeeper,* or most broadly, especially in contemporary papyri, **estate manager.**[209] This office normally included *responsibility for overseeing* a household budget, purchasing, accounts, resource allocation, collection of debts, and general running of the establishment, *but only as instructed* within guidelines agreed by the employer or the head of the house.[210] Theissen also lists evidence for the further use of the term especially in connection with Erastus as οἰκομόμος τῆς πόλεως *(city treasurer, city administrator,* Rom 16:23), in which he concludes that "the meaning of the word οἰκονόμος varies according to time and place," but as city office "refers to a high position . . . not simply treasurer."[211] It remains an open question whether the οἰκονόμος at Corinth might have been "a person of elevated social status."[212]

On this basis there is justification for Goodspeed's translation *managers,* and in association with πιστός for Charles Williams's rendering *trustees.* In such a position the essential requirement was that the οἰκονόμος remains *faithful* (AV/KJV, NIV, for πιστός) *to the wishes and instructions* of the owner of the estate or employer, and **trustworthy** (NRSV, NJB, TCNT, Williams) *in the administration of resources* which belonged to the employer. The word πιστός includes these double nuances of *faithful* and **trustworthy.** If English possessed a single word which covered both, this would improve on either alone. Like a dispensing chemist who makes up a medical prescription prescribed by a doctor, the requirement is to do the job *as instructed,* and not to try to make self-devised "improvements" of one's own. On μυστηρίων θεοῦ, mysteries of God, see above on 2:7.[213] Collins suggests that *prudence* is also required.[214]

---

208. BAGD, 842-43.

209. MM, 442-43; BAGD, 560 and 559.

210. Examples of performing the acts of οἰκονομέω, *managing,* include arranging transport for barley and wheat *(PS* 1 6:584:17; *BGU* 4:1209:19 [23 BC]); collecting debts or making arrangements relating to debts *(Oxyrhynchus Papyri* 9:1203:27, late first century AD; οἰκονόμος or manager of property *(P. Oxy.* 5:929:25 [2d cent. AD]; possibly in Rom 16:23, *Treasurer,* and in Gal 4:2 *one who has responsibility for a minor.*

211. On the οἰκονόμος as holding a position of trust, see Reumann, "'Servants of God' — Pre-Christian Religious Application of οἰκονόμος in Greek," 339-49, and "οἰκονομία Terms in Paul in Comparison with Lucan *Heilsgeschichte,"* 147-67; and W. E. Robinson, "The Church in the World: 'Steward of the Mysteries of God' (1 Cor 4:1)," 412-17; Martin, "Managerial Slaves," in *Slavery as Salvation,* 15-22.

212. Theissen, *Social Setting,* 79; cf. 75-83. See further Combes, *The Metaphor of Slavery,* 77-93, and the discussion of διακονέω above with reference to the research of Barnett and Collins on the diaconate.

213. Aquinas applies the word to the sacraments at this point.

214. Collins, *First Cor,* 172.

In v. 1 Paul uses λογίζομαι, *I reckon,* **I count as. Counting as** has now come to assume a significant status in speech-act theory and in the philosophy of language. This preempts the regular ctriticism that if such phrases as *reckon as righteous* or **count as** *accepted* are applied to justification by grace through faith, this constitutes some kind of legal fiction (see separate note on "Justification by Grace" under 6:11, below). Among philosophers of language J. L. Austin and John Searle show how such "speech-acts" as *reckoning,* **counting as,** *finding guilty,* or *"I pronounce you man and wife"* move beyond the normal boundaries of assertion (i.e., language which performs an act of asserting) to language which Austin usually terms *verdictive* (acts of giving verdicts) and Searle calls *declarative* (acts of *declaring x as y*).[215] Nicholas Wolterstorff sees the logic of such "performative" acts in language as fundamental to most human discourse, but especially to religious language. Thus it is central to communication to **count** a flashing light in the right of a car *as* the driver's warning that he or she will turn right.[216] It is no more a "fiction" to speak of a divine verdict as *conveying* an act of liberation *in* the saying of the declaration. In 4:1-2, such a *declarative* **counting as** signifies an assigned status and role within an institutional context. Thus *I diagnose* serves as a performative speech-act *in the institutional context* of medicine; *I find you guilty,* in the institutional context of the lawcourt; *I pronounce you man and wife,* in the institutional context of marriage; you are **counted as servants . . . and estate managers,** in the institutional context of apostolic ministry. Wolterstorff calls this "ascribing a standing" of a given kind.[217] The nouns which follow occur in the accusative because they are in apposition to ἡμᾶς, **us,** as objects of **count as** or *reckon.* Wolff argues that the reintroduction of the plural in this section (cf. 3:22) explicitly takes up the allusion to Paul, Apollos, and Peter as examples.[218]

In v. 2 ὧδε means **here,** in the logical sense of *on this matter* rather than in the local sense (with Alford) of *here on earth.* The accusative singular adjectival form λοιπόν is used adverbially as an accusative of reference, or accusative of respect. Since English has no adverb *restly,* **for the rest** conveys this grammatical function, i.e., *with reference to what is left.* The passive form of ζητέω, *I seek,* could be translated *it is sought,* but in this context **it is required**. Finally, the outcome of whether the **estate manager** has indeed been proven **trustworthy** is expressed by εὑρεθῇ (the subjunctive because it follows ἵνα, even although here it is not used in its full purposive sense). Ministers need to ask the question whether they will **found** *honest, faithful, reliable,* or **trustworthy**.

215. J. L. Austin, *How to Do Things with Words* (Oxford: Clarendon, 1962), 4-24, 76-93, 99-119, and esp. 152-63: *Reckon, rank, value,* and *interpret as* are "verdictives" (152); J. R. Searle, *Expression and Meaning: Studies in the Theory of Speech Acts* (Cambridge: Cambridge University Press, 1979), 24-27; cf. 1-129, where Searle prefers "declaratives."

216. Nicholas Wolterstorff, *Divine Discourse* (Cambridge: Cambridge University Press, 1995), esp. 76-91.

217. Ibid., 83-84.

218. Wolff, *Der erste Brief,* 79.

Paul is about to disclaim the capacity to know fully the secrets even of his own heart. *He simply leaves with God in trust how **trustworthy** his work will be **found** to have been in the judgment of God.*

3 This is one of the memorably liberating statements of Paul. δέ is contrastive. Paul has acknowledged the need for **estate managers** to be accountable and responsible. He adds: it is not to you, **however,** that I have to give account. D. W. Kuck's heading for 4:1-5, "The Futility of Premature Human Judgments," correctly complements, but also stands in contrast to Francis and Sampley's heading "It Is the Lord Who Judges."[219] The personal pronoun ἐμοί is a dative of personal interest and corresponds comfortably with Eng. **with me,** in the sense of *as I look at my own case.* The superlative form ἐλάχιστόν is used in its elative (as against comparative) sense to mean *very,* **very little** (as NIV) or *very small* (NRSV, AV/KJV). The translation **it counts for very little** signals the verdictive flavor of the speech-act of pronouncing an evaluation, and is rendered in some way by most versions, e.g., *it is of no importance to me* (NJB), or *to me it matters not at all* (REB). The verb ἀνακριθῶ (aorist passive subjunctive) following ἵνα is readily conveyed as an indefinite or hypothetical act by Eng. **that I should be judged,** i.e., *that I should be placed under judgment **by you.*** Wolff compares Paul's contrast between divine and human evaluations in 2 Cor 1:12 and Rom 9:1.[220]

Two explanations can be found among lexicographers and commentators for interpreting ἀνθρωπίνης ἡμέρας to mean **human court of judgment.** First, the human ἡμέρα stands in contrast to **the day** [of the Lord] in 3:13, i.e., it is to God's day of judgment, not to any human day of judgment, that we look for a valid assessment of our work.[221] Second, in Hebrew and in other languages including very occasionally Greek, a close link exists between *day* and *judgment* or **court** (Heb םוי, *yom*). Possibly the contrast between the hiddenness of night and disclosure in the day played a part, but more probably the notion of a special day set aside for reckoning led to the close relation between **the day** and **the day of reckoning,** with the added urgency of *today.*[222] Whatever the historical route, the semantic meaning is clear and agreed, and need not be ascribed (with Jerome) to Paul's provincial dialect. The normally adversative ἀλλά means *on the contrary* only in the sense of stating the other side of the same coin, and functions as a confirmation: **indeed.** The present indicative ἀνακρίνω could in theory be descriptive, i.e., *I do not undertake judgments on myself,* but more probably serves as an illocutionary speech-act, *I do not pronounce judgment on myself.* Our translation **I do not even judge myself** reflects the openness of the Greek.

This last phrase (v. 3b) has assumed particular importance for Krister

219. Kuck, *Judgement,* 196; Francis and Sampley, *Pauline Parallels,* 116 (sect. 83).
220. Wolff, *Der erste Brief,* 81.
221. Robertson and Plummer, *First Epistle,* 76; LSJ, 648, ii, III.
222. BDBG, 398-401, where an extensive list of nuances is distinguished. Cf. further Germ. *Reichstag.*

Stendahl's interpretation of Paul, which also paved the way for E. P. Sanders's hermeneutic. Stendahl argued that "the Pauline awareness of sin has been interpreted in the light of Luther's struggle with his conscience."[223] But it is "exactly at that point" that a drastic difference emerges between Luther and Paul. Paul, Stendahl argues, was aware of the problem of sin and guilt as an objective state of affairs, but not primarily as the subjective problem of "a troubled conscience." Indeed, he declares that he was "blameless as to righteousness — of the law, that is" (Phil 3:6). "Paul was equipped with what in our eyes must be called a rather 'robust' conscience."[224] He is concerned with the objective status of being declared in a right relation with God, not with the problem of "forgiveness," about which he speaks seldom. As a Pharisee he perceives himself to have been obedient (Gal 1:13; Phil 3:6), and as a Christian to have received grace which was "not in vain" (1 Cor 15:10).[225] Strikingly, Stendahl asserts, Paul declares "I have nothing on my conscience" (1 Cor 4:4).[226] But Western tradition turns Paul into an introspective, guilt-ridden, individual-centered, experience-centered man, misinterpreting the "I" of Rom 7:13-23 as an individual ego in conflict with itself rather than as representative of an objective human condition in relation to divine law and divine grace.[227] The upshot is that whereas Paul stressed justification, the Western tradition stresses forgiveness; where Paul stressed call, this tradition stresses conversion; where Paul ascribed a role to weakness, this historical legacy is obsessed with sin.[228]

The value of Stendahl's approach is both to correct an imbalance and to disengage an obsession with "experience," "relevance," "failure," or even "success" from Paul in exchange for Paul's emphasis on objective acts of God which bring objective consequences for humankind as a social whole. Whether Stendahl can be defended in his further critique of the Lutheran interpretation of "boasting" becomes more problematic, for he concedes that Paul boasts in his "weakness" as against the triumphalism and self-sufficiency of his opponents.[229] His work, however, serves to demonstrate the pivotal importance of 4:3b and 4:4 for Paul's theology. He leaves his successes and failures with God. What has been done is done, and God alone knows and can disclose the worth of it. It must simply be left with God while the servant of God goes on to the next task, at the same moment "judging nothing before the time" (4:5) and "knowing that your labor is not in vain (κενός, *empty, null*) in the Lord" (15:58).

223. K. Stendahl, "The Apostle Paul and the Introspective Conscience of the West" (1961 and 1963); rpt. in *Paul among Jews and Gentiles* (London: SCM, 1977 and Philadelphia: Fortress, 1976), 78-96. Cf. E. P. Sanders, *Paul and Palestinian Judaism* (London: SCM, 1977), 434-47.
224. Ibid., 80-81.
225. Ibid., 89.
226. Ibid., 90-91.
227. Ibid., 86, 92-95; cf. 3-7, 23-40.
228. Ibid., 20-43, 81-82, 86-87.
229. Ibid., 40 and 88.

4 The traditional translation of the first part is *I know nothing against myself* (RV) or *I am not aware of anything against myself* (NRSV). The compound verb σύνοιδα means *to share knowledge with,* and with ἐμαυτῷ, the reflexive pronoun *myself,* denotes *self-awareness.* However, οἶδα is technically the perfect form derived from the stem εἰδ- (subjunctive εἰδῶ, infinitive εἰδέναι), and the noun συνείδησις means *consciousness* (Josephus, *Antiquities* 16.212; Philo, *Quod Deterius Potiori Insidiari Soleat* 146) but most often, arguably in the NT, **conscience.**[230] Hence REB renders, **I have** *nothing* **on my conscience**; NIV, **my conscience** *is clear;* and NJB, **my conscience** *does not reproach me.* The main point is that human judgment remains fallible and inadequate whether it be positive or negative, or whether it be Paul's or another human agent's.[231]

Our understanding of the noun συνείδησις (cognate with the verb σύνοιδα), however, has undergone extensive scrutiny and revision in the 1980s and especially 1990s following the work of Eckstein, Horsley, Gardner, and Gooch. These writers argue forcefully that the noun should be translated not *conscience* but *self-awareness,* at least in 8:7-13.[232]

Although we discuss the term **conscience** in Paul more fully in connection with 8:7, 10, 12, the specific use of **conscience** here coheres well with C. A. Pierce's analysis of conscience as "the painful reaction of man's nature, as morally responsible, against infringements of its created limits."[233] Pierce rightly argues that the sense of remorse or pain consequent on infringing the standards set internally by the conscience can never in Pauline thought be absolute, for *a person's conscience derives its criteria and standards from the character and moral mind-set of the moral agent.* Hence it is like the pointer on a dial which registers *wrong* or *clear depending on how the mechanism has been set.*[234] Thus a person's conscience may be oversensitive and overreact, or undersensitive and underreact. Thus Paul can place no trust in the relativity of human conscience *as over against the absolute verdict of God,* although conscience has value as a *relative* indicator of self-approval or self-disapproval. To be sure, Thrall, Eckstein, Gooch, and others have proposed modifications to Pierce's approach, but these specific points cohere with Paul's emphasis here.[235] Thrall is more concerned with the notion of a "good" conscience in,

---

230. BAGD, 786-87.

231. Schrage, *Der erste Brief,* 1:322.

232. See, e.g., Eckstein, *Der Begriff Syneidesis bei Paulus;* P. W. Gooch, "'Conscience' in 1 Cor 8 and 10," *NTS* 33 (1987): 244-54; and P. D. Gardner, *The Gifts of God* (Lanham, Md.: University Press of America, 1994), 42-54. We have adopted that translation in ch. 8, but it seems difficult to avoid the further sense of **conscience** in 4:4. Rather than anticipate later discussion, see special note on "Conscience or Self-Awareness?" under 8:7, below.

233. Pierce, *Conscience in the NT,* 108; cf. 60-110 and throughout.

234. Ibid., 109; endorsed by Whiteley, *Theology,* 210.

235. In addition to n. 3, see M. Thrall, "The Pauline Use of συνείδησις," *NTS* 14 (1967-68): 118-25; Jewett, *Paul's Anthropological Terms,* 402-46; H. Chadwick, in *RAC* (ed. T. Klauser), 10:1,025-1,107; G. Lüdemann, "συνείδησις," *EDNT,* 3:301-3; and C. Maurer, "συνείδησις," *TDNT,* 7:898-919.

e.g., 2 Cor 1:12, whereas 1 Cor 4:4 turns on "freedom from remorse," as well as objective "blame."[236] The experience of the lack of a bad conscience depends on the prior scale of values out of which a conscience (rightly or wrongly) operates.

The most creative research relevant to this passage comes from Theissen. "Paul contrasts two illegitimate tribunals of judgment with the sole legitimate one. . . . The eschatological judge will bring to light not only hidden deeds (as in 2 Cor 5:10) but also the hidden intentions of the heart (τῶν καρδίων) — precisely what, in view of the preceding claim of innocence, *must have been unconscious*" (my italics).[237] Paul, Theissen urges, allows "for unconscious intentions that could stand in tension with his consciousness. But he is convinced that these unconscious intentions *can no longer existentially endanger him in the judgment* [my italics]. He is 'reconciled' with the unconscious which is unknown to him."[238] *Hence Paul trustfully leaves everything in the hands of God who alone has competency to judge in an absolute, irrevocable sense.*[239] *Neither other people's verdicts nor one's own self-awareness can penetrate unconscious motives and stance: everything, these included, are left with God.*

Paul does not therefore advocate a thick-skinned indifference to public opinion; his point is a different one, namely, its fallibility, relativity, and limits which make it an unreliable guide on which to depend. Everything must be left with God in the last analysis, and one should not give privilege to one's own introspective assessments.

The perfect tense of δεδικαίωμαι, **pronounced in the right**, is used. It intimates "that the case is still pending."[240] The permanence of any verdict prior to the day of God's judgment (expressed by the perfect) is negated. In the light of eschatology we may wonder whether the debate about whether δικαιόω refers here to justification by grace through faith (Melanchthon) or more broadly to a verdict of approval of workmanship or ministry (Chrysostom, Theodoret, Calvin) has genuine relevance here. Only God's verdict remains final and definitive, whether it refers to the justifying of a salvation with God or to the assessment of someone's work as of abiding value and effect. Justification by grace constitutes no less the bringing forward of the eschatological in advance to the present through trustful appropriation than the assurance and trust with which Paul suspends judgments about his ministerial effectiveness, placing both, and indeed everything, simply into the hands of God.[241] The believer, as

---

236. Whiteley, *Theology,* 210-12; and more especially Merklein, *Der erste Brief 1–4,* 294-96; Eckstein, *Begriff Syneidesis,* 212-13; and Theissen (cited below).

237. Theissen, *Psychological Aspects,* 61; cf. 59-66.

238. Ibid., 63.

239. Ibid., 65-66. Cf. Roetzel, *Judgement in the Community: A Study in the Relation between Eschatology and Ecclesiology in Paul,* 68-105, and on ἡμέρα, 38-41.

240. Edwards, *First Epistle,* 99.

241. Collins, however, argues that "declare righteous" has "another connotation" in Romans and Galatians (*First Cor,* 173). This drives an unnecessary wedge between what for Paul is a seam-

341

Moltmann expresses it, avoids both the despair of assuming failure in advance of the Day and the presumption of assuming total success in advance of eschatological judgment.[242]

5 The use of ὥστε, **so**, functions exactly as it does in 3:21 (see above). Clearly κρίνετε is present imperative (not indicative here), and functions as an illocutionary speech-act: **do not pronounce judgments,** *do not make (premature) judgments,* i.e., avoid *definitive* verdicts. It does not demand the suspension of all judgment in the sense of using *discernment* or *discrimination* provided that its fallible and provisional nature before the last judgement is fully recognized.

Oscar Cullmann has made much of καιρός, **the proper time**, as against χρόνος, *duration of time.*[243] While he has been criticized for reading too much into distinctions of lexicography, nevertheless it remains true that in *many* cases (*not,* as his critics urge, in *all* cases) καιρός denotes both a specific time rather than time as duration, and in particular a *favorable* time, the *right* time, **the proper time.** Cullmann writes: "*Kairos* in secular usage is the moment in time which is especially favourable for an undertaking."[244] In history these *favorable moments* constitute times when God's purposes become ripe for action (1 Thess 5:1, 2).[245] Before the Last Supper Jesus tells his disciples, "My *kairos* is near" (Matt 26:18).[246] In the Epistle to the Hebrews the special moment of favorable opportunity is σήμερον, *today* (Heb 3:7; 13:15), just as in Ps 95:7 the church recalls, "*Today* if you will hear his voice, do not harden your hearts."[247] In 1 Cor 4:5 Paul stresses that **the proper time,** *the appropriate moment,* for reaching definitive judgments has not yet arrived, but lies in the future.[248] A straight imperatival injunction is necessary: **do not pronounce judgments on anything** (τι) **before the proper time.** The theme is not peculiar to Paul but reflects "Judge not that you be not judged" (Matt 7:1), where the analogy of the plank and the splinter (7:4) makes it clear that the fallibility, relativity, and limitation of all human judgment, as well as self-interest, vitiates premature verdicts.

The next clause, as it happens, recalls a different aspect of Cullmann's work on a different theme. The key point is "It is **the Lord** who judges." Thus some see a part parallel here with Rom 2:16, "God judges human secrets"; Rom 14:13, "let us no more pass judgment on one another"; and Col 2:16-19, "let no one pass judgment . . . belongs to Christ . . . is from God."[249] In this connection

less whole based upon sheer grace and an eschatology of definitive verdict or last judgment. Merklein notes the interactions within the semantic field (*Der erste Brief 1–4,* 288-89 and 297-98).

242. Moltmann, *Theology of Hope,* 23.

243. O. Cullmann, *Christ and Time* (Eng. trans., London: SCM, 2d ed. 1951), 37-50, esp. 37-43.

244. Ibid., 39.

245. Ibid., 40.

246. Ibid., 41.

247. Ibid., 44.

248. Moltmann's work confirms this approach, if not its lexicographical aspects; cf. *Theology of Hope,* 102-20.

249. Francis and Sampley, *Pauline Parallels,* 116-17.

God-in-Christ alone is the *rightful* judge; and Cullmann argues that in contrast to the word δεσπότης (which conveys overtones of arbitrariness), κύριος denotes one who is **the** *rightful* **Lord**.[250] Again, Cullmann has been criticized with some justice for overpressing a connotation of the word which is often but not always implied; but here it becomes relevant. Since he is Lord, the conditions which need to operate for a verdictive speech-act of definitive declaration fully apply: Christ, or God-in-Christ, alone is the rightful judge, because he alone knows all and pronounces his verdict in the light of his rightful status and universal purposes. This is enacted when **the Lord comes**, i.e., when the entire context of all human action has become complete and definitive in a completed history.

ἕως, **until**, with the aorist subjunctive (here of ἔρχομαι) occurs regularly, either with or without the indefinite particle ἄν, i.e., *whenever this may be.* Werner Kramer has discussed Paul's linking of the term **Lord** with his *coming* at the parousia (2 Cor 1:14; 1 Thess 2:19; 3:13; 4:15; 5:2, 23; cf. 1 Cor 1:7-8; 4:5; 5:5).[251] The two themes, he argues, are closely related, as the Aramaic formula *Marana tha* (1 Cor 16:22) witnesses in the context not primarily of confession but of *acclamation.*[252] Christians *acclaim* Christ as the one with whom they leave all evaluation and verdicts as well as their care, welfare, status, and salvation.

At the day of judgment **the Lord will shed light upon** (future indicative of φωτίζω) **the hidden things** (τὰ κρυπτά) hitherto concealed and protected from scrutiny by **the darkness**. The verb φωτίζω properly means *to shed light upon, not* to illumine *from within.* This accords fully with its use in John 1:9, where the point is not that the Logos or Christ *provides* light, but *casts* light *upon* all things, exposing them to a light of judgment which divides and demands response. Even Jesus in the Fourth Gospel refrains from pronouncing a final verdict (8:15b, *I judge no one*), until the End. The causative -ιζω verb φωτίζω is coupled with a second causative -όω verb φανερόω, in the future, **will disclose**, i.e., make plain, make transparent.

What will become crystal clear at the parousia is τὰς βουλάς, *the wishes, the counsels,* or **the motivations**, in Paul's terminology, *of hearts.* Paul uses τῶν καρδιῶν to signify **the hidden** motives, desires, and interests which may even deceive the self, and of which the self is certainly not fully aware.[253] In the biblical writings, however, *heart* includes not only these hidden depths, but mind, emotion, attitude, stance, and wishes that become will and action.[254] Hence we must translate **the hidden motivations of our lives** to include every

250. O. Cullmann, *Christology of the NT* (Eng. trans., London: SCM, 2d ed. 1963), 196-99 and 207-28; cf. 195-237. See further (esp. on 1 Cor 8:6) J. D. G. Dunn, *Christology in the Making* (London: SCM, 1980), 179-83.

251. Kramer, *Christ, Lord and Son of God* (Eng. trans., London: SCM, 1966), 173-76.

252. Ibid., 99-107 (see further under 16:22 below).

253. Theissen, *Psychological Aspects,* 59-66.

254. BAGD, 281, sect. 1.

aspect of human agency, and not only its feeling, theoretical thought, or capacity for decision and action. Each and all of these are involved.

Most versions translate ἔπαινος as *praise* (AV/KJV, NIV) or *commendation* (NRSV, REB, NJB). But since Paul hardly seems to presuppose that **each** will receive positive *praise* or *commendation* (he does not know the outcome, as he states, let alone for every single person) some versions solve the problem by adding a gloss, e.g., *appropriate commendation* (NJB). However, although *praise* or *approval* is indeed the most frequent meaning of this word, BAGD constructively list **recognition** as part of its semantic range.[255] This matches such passages as *1 Clement* 30:6 (ὁ ἔπαινος ἡμῶν ἔστω ἐν θεῷ), allowing for a positive meaning of the **recognition** of achievement, worth, or salvation, but not excluding the possible recognition of other traits.

Allo concludes that if Paul himself held reserve about his work "in spite of his untroubled conscience, his apostolic illumination, and heavenly revelations, how much more should the Corinthians . . . abstain from making precipitous and imprudent judgements on a matter which certainly went beyond their superficial spirits as 'little infants [or infantile people] in Christ' (3:1-4)?"[256]

3. The Cross as Critique of Triumphalism and of Premature Eschatological Glorying (4:6-21)

(6) I have allusively applied all this to myself and to Apollos on your account, dear members of our Christian family, that you may learn through our case what "Not beyond what is written" consists in, so that one of you be not inflated on behalf of one against another. (7) For who sees anything different in you? What do you have that you did not receive? If, however, you received it, why do you boast as if you did not receive it? (8) Already you have become glutted! Already you have been "made rich"! Without us you came to "reign as kings"! If only you did "reign as kings," so that we, too, could reign as kings with you! (9) For it seems to me that God has put us apostles on display as the grand finale, as those doomed to die, because we have been made a spectacle in the eyes of the world, of angels, and of humankind. (10) We are fools on Christ's account, but you are wise in your Christian existence; we are weak, while you are strong. You are honored, we are disgraced. (11) Up to this very hour we go hungry and thirsty and poorly clothed; we are roughly treated and have no fixed abode. (12, 13) We toil until we are weary, laboring with our own hands. When we are abused, we reply with good words; when we are persecuted, we put up with it; when we are slandered, we appeal to them directly. Up to this very moment we have become, as it were, the world's scum, the scrapings from everyone's shoes.

255. BAGD, 281.
256. Allo, *Première Épitre*, 70.

(14) I do not write all this to bring you into shame, but as a warning to my dearly loved children. (15, 16) For you might have thousands of people in Christ to correct you, but you can hardly have more than one father. For in Christ Jesus it was I who became your father through proclaiming the gospel. I ask you, then, take your cue from me. (17) It is for this reason that I send to you Timothy, who is my very dear child and trustworthy in the Lord: he will bring to your mind the patterns of life which I live in Christ Jesus, even as I teach them everywhere in every Christian congregation.

(18, 19) As though I were not coming to you, however, some have begun to be inflated with arrogance. But I shall come to you soon, if the Lord wills, and I shall discover not the talk of these inflated people, but what they can do. (20) For the kingdom of God is not a matter of talk but of solid efficacy. (21) What do you prefer? Am I to come to you with a stick in my hand or with love and a gentle spirit?

Among the vast quantity of modern literature on 1:1–4:21 special studies also relate in abundance to this passage or to specific verses within it. K. A. Plank (1987), e.g., examines Paul's self-description of his catalogue of afflictions in 4:9-13, arguing that he offers a rhetorical *poiesis* of fundamental irony.[257] M. S. Ferrari also traces an extensive history of research on "catalogues of sufferings" in Pauline and other writings which relates to 4:10-13.[258] J. T. Fitzgerald sees Paul's "list of hardships" as a mark of the authentic sage.[259] However, K. T. Kleinknecht regards 4:8-13 as the climax or "high point" of 1:1–4:21 in that it provides the final step in a cross-centered critique of "boasting in human persons" (1:29-31; 3:18-20; 4:6-7).[260] Kleinknecht convincingly traces how this lay behind the σχίσματα (1:10), ἔριδες (1:11), and ζῆλος (3:3) which gave the community its infantile and un-Christlike qualities, and promoted a triumphalist, overrealized eschatology *which also stood in fundamental conflict with the critique of the cross.* Rather than construing "gifts" as self-affirming vehicles for status-seeking, if only they had fully grasped the necessity *to build* (3:5-17) *toward* the eschatological goal rather than assuming that "spiritual people" had already reached it, the Corinthians would have perceived that "gifts" were to be humbly and gratefully received *for the good of all.*

On this basis the continuity of 4:8-13 is clearly seen not only with the rest of 1:1–4:21, but no less (as against those who see it as a self-contained treatise) with 8:1–11:1 and with 12:1–14:40, as well as underlining why 15:1-58 consti-

257. Plank, *Paul and the Irony of Affliction,* esp. 33-70.

258. Ferrari, *Die Sprache des Leids in den paulinischen Peristasenkatalogen.* With 1 Corinthians 4 he takes up 2 Cor 4:8-9; 6:4-5, 8-10; 11:23-29; 12:10; Rom 8:35; and Phil 4:12. He includes Schrage, Hodgson, and many others (see bibliography).

259. Fitzgerald, *Cracks in an Earthen Vessel: An Examination of Catalogues of Hardships in the Corinthian Correspondence,* esp. 117-48, on 4:8-13, but also throughout for the wider background in the Graeco-Roman world.

260. Kleinknecht, *Der leidende Gerechtfertigte,* 208-304.

tutes the crown of the whole epistle. It also corroborates the point which Schrage makes in his special study of this issue, that the "afflictions" of 4:8-13 relate equally to two key foci of the epistle, namely, on one side to the cross, and on the other side more broadly to the background of apocalyptic and eschatology.[261]

Finally, one or two specific verses have invited a deluge of discussion and research. Of these the most notorious occurs in 4:6, first with the meaning of μετεσχημάτισα, usually translated *I have applied* [all this to myself and to Apollos], and most especially τὸ μὴ ὑπὲρ ἃ γέγραπται, most frequently rendered **not beyond what is written**.[262] To these problems we now turn.

Bibliography on 4:6-21

Bailey, K. E., "The Structure of 1 Cor and Paul's Theological Method with Special Reference to 4:17," *NovT* 25 (1983): 37-58.

Betz, H. D., *Der Apostel Paulus und die sokratische Tradition,* BHT 45 (Tübingen: Mohr, 1972).

————, *Nachfolge und Nachahmung Jesu Christi im NT,* BHT 37 (Tübingen: Mohr, 1967), 153-59.

de Boer, P., *Imitation of Paul: An Exegetical Study* (Kampen: Kok, 1962).

Castelli, E. A., *Imitating Paul: A Discussion of Power* (Louisville: Westminster/Knox, 1991), 97-115.

Clarke, A. D., *Secular and Christian Leadership at Corinth: A Socio-Historical and Exegetical Study of 1 Cor 1–6* (Leiden: Brill, 1993), 122-27.

Colson, F. N., "Μετεσχημάτισα in 1 Cor 4:6," *JTS* 17 (1916): 380-83.

Ebner, M., *Leidenslisten und Apostelbrief,* FB 66 (Würzburg: Echter, 1991).

Ferrari, M. Schiefer, *Die Sprache des Leids in den paulinischen Peristasenkatalogen* (Stuttgart: Katholisches Bibelwerk, 1991).

Fiore, B., "'Covert Allusion' in 1 Cor 1–4," *CBQ* 47 (1985): 85-102.

————, *The Function of Personal Example in the Socratic and Pastoral Epistles,* AnBib 105 (Rome: Pontifical Biblical Institute, 1986).

Fitzgerald, J. T., *Cracks in an Earthen Vessel: An Examination of Catalogues of Hardships in the Corinthian Correspondence,* SBLDS 99 (Atlanta: Scholars Press, 1988), esp. 117-48.

Funk, R. W., "The Apostolic *Parousia:* Form and Significance," in W. R. Farmer, C. F. D. Moule, and R. R. Niebuhr (eds.), *Christian History and Interpretation: Studies Presented to John Knox* (Cambridge: Cambridge University Press, 1967), 249-68; also rpt. in R. W. Funk, *Parables and Presence* (Philadelphia: Fortress, 1982), 81-102.

261. Schrage, "Leid, Kreuz und Eschaton. Die Peristasenkataloge als Merkmale paulinischer theologia crucis und Eschatologie," *EvT* 34 (1974): 141-75. Schrage's work clearly influences Kleinknecht's approach. Both reflect a theological depth not always present in those studies of the phenomena which focus too narrowly on "rhetorical" aspects. See further Thiselton, "Realized Eschatology at Corinth," 510-26.

262. See bibliography for articles by M. D. Hooker, A. Legault, J. M. Ross, D. R. Hall, and others.

Hafemann, S. J., *Suffering and the Spirit: An Exegetical Study of II Cor 2:14–3:3* (Tübingen, Mohr, 1986), 58-64.

Hall, D. R., "A Disguise for the Wise: μετασχηματισμός in 1 Cor 4:6," *NTS* 40 (1994): 143-49.

Hanges, J. C., "1 Cor 4:6 and the Possibility of Written Bylaws in the Corinthian Church," *JBL* 117 (1998): 275-98.

Hanson, A. T., "1 Cor 4:13b and Lam 3:45," *ExpTim* 93 (1982): 214-15.

———, "Reconciliation by Atonement: 1 Cor 4:10-13," in *The Paradox of the Cross in the Thought of St Paul,* JSNTSS 17 (Sheffield: JSOT Press, 1987), 25-37.

Hock, R. F., *The Social Context of Paul's Ministry: Tentmaking and Apostleship* (Philadelphia: Fortress, 1980).

Hodgson, R., "Paul the Apostle and First Century Tribulation Lists," *ZNW* 74 (1983): 59-80.

Hooker, M. D., "'Beyond the Things Which Are Written': An Examination of 1 Cor 4:6," *NTS* 10 (1963-64): 127-32.

Horrell, D. G., *The Social Ethos of the Corinthian Correspondence* (Edinburgh: T. & T. Clark, 1996), 200-204.

Kleinknecht, K. T., *Der leidende Gerechtfertigte: Die alttestamentlich-jüdische Tradition vom 'leidenden Gerechten' und ihre Rezeption bei Paulus,* WUNT 2:13 (Tübingen: Mohr, 1984), 208-304.

Lassen, E. M., "The Use of the Father Image in Imperial Propaganda and 1 Cor 4:14-21," *TynBul* 42 (1991): 127-36.

Legault, A., "'Beyond the Things That Are Written' (1 Cor 4:6)," *NTS* 18 (1971-72): 227-31.

Malan, F. S., "Rhetorical Analysis of 1 Cor 4," *Theologia Viatorum* 20 (1993): 100-114.

Michaelis, W., "μιμέομαι," *TDNT,* 4:659-74.

Mitchell, M. M., *Paul and the Rhetoric of Reconciliation* (Louisville: Westminster and Knox, 1992), 93-99.

Pfitzner, V. C., *Paul and the Agon Motif,* NovTSup 16 (Leiden: Brill, 1967), 62-64, 93-97, and 102.

Plank, Karl A., *Paul and the Irony of Affliction* (Atlanta: Scholars Press, 1987), esp. 33-70, but throughout.

Pogoloff, S. M., *Logos and Sophia: The Rhetorical Situation of 1 Cor,* SBLDS 134 (Atlanta: Scholars Press, 1992), 197-223.

Powell, C. H., *The Biblical Concept of Power* (London: Epworth, 1963), 117-29, 134-42.

Ross, J. M., "Not Above What is Written: A Note on 1 Cor 4:6," *ExpTim* 82 (1971): 215-17.

Saillard, M., "C'est moi qui par l'Evangile vous ai enfantés dans le Christ Jésus (1 Cor 4:15)," *RSR* 56 (1968): 5-41.

Sanders, B., "Imitating Paul: 1 Cor 4:16," *HTR* 74 (1981): 353-63.

Schrage, W., *Die konkreten Einzelgebote in der paulinischen Paränese* (Gütersloh: Mohr, 1961).

———, "Leid, Kreuz und Eschaton. Die Peristasenkataloge als Merkmale paulinischer theologia crucis und Eschatologie," *EvT* 34 (1974): 141-75.

Spencer, W. D., "The Power in Paul's Teaching (1 Cor 4:9-20)," *JETS* 32 (1989): 51-61.

Stanley, D. M., "Become Imitators of Me," *Bib* 40 (1959): 859-79.

Strugnell, J., "A Plea for Conjectural Emendation in the NT, with a Coda on 1 Cor 4:6," *CBQ* 36 (1974): 543-58.

Thiselton, A. C., *Interpreting God and the Postmodern Self: On Meaning, Manipulation and Promise* (Grand Rapids: Eerdmans and Edinburgh: T. & T. Clark, 1995), 3-45 and 121-64.

————, "Realized Eschatology at Corinth," *NTS* 24 (1978): 510-26.

Vos, J. S., "Der *metaschematismos* in 1 Kor 4:6" *ZNW* 86 (1995): 154-72.

Wagner, J. R., "'Not Beyond the Things Which Are Written': A Call to Boast Only in the Lord," *NTS* 44 (1998): 279-87.

Welborn, L. L., "A Conciliatory Principle in 1 Cor 4:6," *NovT* 29 (1987): 320-46 (rev. version in Welborn, *Politics and Rhetoric in the Corinthian Epistles* (Macon, Ga.: Mercer University Press, 1997), 43-76.

Witherington, B., III, *Conflict and Community at Corinth* (Grand Rapids: Eerdmans and Carlisle: Paternoster, 1995), 137-50.

Young, N. H., "Paidagogos: The Social Setting of a Pauline Metaphor," *NovT* 29 (1987): 150-76.

6 The speculative theory that the notorious difficulties of this verse are due to a series of scribal misunderstandings and "corrections" is discussed fully below. There is no textual evidence for this theory. The only attested differences in reading are minimal: (1) D, F, G replace ἅ (neuter plural relative pronoun) by ὅ (singular) before γέγραπται, but p[46], ℵ, A, B, C, 33 etc. read the text repeated in UBS[4]. (2) Some later "correctors" (ℵ[2], D[2]) and later MSS, including the Textus Receptus, insert φρονεῖν, which finds its way into AV/KJV against firm attestation to the contrary.

Once again ἀδελφοί, here translated **dear members of our Christian family,** signals the transition to a new section of the argument. On the difficulty of translating the Greek, see on 1:10 (and the repetition of the difficulty in 1:11, 26; 2:1; 3:1; 10:1; 12:1; 14:6; 15:1). No single solution can be found, hence variations may ease the problem.

Of far greater difficulty and controversy is the meaning and translation of μετεσχημάτισα εἰς, **I have allusively applied [all this] to** (hapax in 1 Corinthians, used only by Paul). Virtually all the English VSS translate this as, *I have applied [all this] to* (NRSV, NIV, REB, NJB). Collins and NJB have changed JB's *I have taken Apollos and myself as an example;* and REB changed NEB *Into this general picture, my friends, I have brought Apollos and myself.*[263] **All this** (ταῦτα, neuter plural, *these things,* NIV) covers all that Paul has hitherto said about their ministerial roles and labors, together with the images of 3:5-17, although Wolff and Vos argue that the pronoun refers only to 3:5–4:5.[264] Four broad approaches to the meaning of μετεσχημάτισα may be distinguished and evaluated, as follows.

---

263. Collins, *First Cor,* 179 endorses BAGD, 513, "1 Cor 4:6 is more or less unique."

264. J. S. Vos, "Der μετασχηματισμός in 1 Kor 4:6," 154-72. Also Wolff, *Der erste Brief,* 84.

a. A Device to Maintain the Anonymity of Accused Parties: "Disguised Form" or "Covert Allusion"

Chrysostom put forward an argument which does full justice to the precise meaning of μετεσχηματίζω as it occurs elsewhere in the NT and in other Greek literature. He writes that so harsh were Paul's criticisms of those specific unnamed leaders at Corinth who, in effect, did not reflect Christ and the cross in their stance that Paul "refrained from drawing up the curtain, and went on arguing as if he were himself the person to whom they were addressed."[265] He thus retains the sense of σχῆμα as *outward form* (τὸ σχῆμα τοῦ κόσμου τούτου, 1 Cor 7:31; σχήματι εὑρεθεὶς ὡς ἄνθωπος, Phil 2:8) with the μετά compound and causative -ίζω signifying an act of *change*. Characteristically, e.g., Paul speaks of Satan as *disguising himself* or *masquerading* (μετασχηματίζεται) as an angel of light (2 Cor 11:14) or of God's transforming the believer's *mode of being* but *not his/her identity* (μετασχηματίσει τὸ σῶμα, Phil 3:21; cf. 2 Cor 11:13, 15). On this basis Chrysostom argues that Paul means to say that he has applied all these images and argument to Apollos and to himself *in a disguised form,* but their underlying reality concerns those anonymous teachers at Corinth who are inflated with self-importance and may even verge on the brink of doing destructive things to God's temple (3:16-17).

In more recent times it was argued that the word signified "a rhetorical artifice by which, either from fear or respect . . . the speaker veiled the allusion to individuals under an allegory or a feigned name."[266] Quintilian uses the phrase *solum schema* to designate this indirect, covert allusiveness.[267] "Covert allusion," Lightfoot declares, "had almost monopolized the meaning of *schema* in Quintilian's day: cf. Martial, iii: 68:7: *"schemate nec dubio sed aperte nominat illam."*[268] Recent advocates for this view include Collins, Fiore, and Winter.[269]

b. The Application of Metaphors and Images: Figurative Application

Many scholars see no evidence that Paul alludes to Apollos and to his own case *in place of* others fictively, or as a subtext rather than *as one example alongside others who are not explicitly mentioned.*[270] They hold that the application of the met-

---

265. Chrysostom, *1 Cor. Hom.,* 12:1 (*PG,* 61:97).

266. Lightfoot, *Notes,* 199; and fully discussed by Schrage, *Der erste Brief,* 1:334, esp. n. 103.

267. Quintilian, 9.2.65 (cited by Schrage and Lightfoot).

268. Lightfoot, *Notes,* 199; cf. also Suetonius, *Domitian* 10 for the use of *figura* in this way. Broadly also Hays, *First Cor,* 68.

269. Collins, *First Cor,* 176; B. Fiore, "'Covert Allusion' in 1 Cor 1–4," 85-102; and B. W. Winter, *Seek the Welfare of the City,* 117, and *Philo and Paul among the Sophists,* 196-201.

270. Barrett, *First Epistle,* 106. Hays, *First Corinthians,* 68, seems to combine the first and second views.

aphors and imagery is sufficient to account for the σχῆμα-aspect of the word: it need not imply disguise, only that figurative application of examples are involved. Barrett translates, *I have for your sake made these things seem to apply to Apollos and myself.*[271] Conzelmann also collects evidence that the verb may denote nothing more than using a figure of speech, and even favors Lietzmann's contention that it sometimes means simply to use an unusual form of presentation.[272] He endorses Morna Hooker's view that Paul refers to his transposing or applying the metaphors of 3:5-17.[273] Fee sees "little sense" in Chrysostom's appeal to a strategy of fiction: Paul "has gone from metaphor to metaphor."[274]

c. Further Allusive References: "Reading between the Lines"

All the same, the last word has not yet been said. Schrage believes that Paul invites his readers "to read between the lines."[275] Indeed, the most forceful argument comes from David R. Hall. He believes that "Paul is referring to a transformation in his argument from statements about something or someone else into statements about himself and Apollos."[276] The strength of Hall's argument is partly lexicographical; partly, that such allusions as that of damaging God's temple hardly apply to Paul or Apollos, if these are part of ταῦτα, *these things* or **all this**, as most believe.[277] Does Paul really wish to include Apollos within the warning "let each take care how he builds" (3:10)? On the other hand, those who reject the hypothesis of fictional application point out that Chrysostom has already moved beyond the evidence in proposing that the names of Paul, Apollos, and Peter are fictional devices in 1:10-12, and that Paul's use of metaphor might adequately reflect the use of the verb.

d. "Instantiation" and Further Evaluations of Possibilities

Commentators and special studies remain divided. On one side, Benjamin Fiore argues that the "figurative" nature of the application fully explains the unusual use of μετεσχημάτισα, and Héring finds the "covert allusion" approach "unacceptable."[278] H.-J. Klauck interprets the word to mean exemplification or

271. Barrett, *First Epistle,* 106.
272. Conzelmann, *1 Corinthians,* 85-86.
273. Hooker, "'Beyond the Things Which Are Written': An Examination of 1 Cor 4:6," 127-32.
274. Fee, *First Epistle,* 166-67.
275. Schrage, *Der erste Brief,* 1:334; also Heinrici, *Das erste Sendschreiben,* 147.
276. Hall, "A Disguise for the Wise: μετασχηματισμός in 1 Cor 4:6," 144; cf. 143-49.
277. Hall cites among lexicographical witnesses Philo, *De Aeternitate Mundi* 79; Plutarch, *Moralia* 680A; and Josephus, *Antiquities* 7.257, as well as NT material.
278. Fiore, "'Covert Allusion' in 1 Cor 1-4," 85-102; and Héring, *First Epistle,* 28.

instantiation *(exemplifiziert),* broadly following Lietzmann.[279] Allo rejects the whole notion of *une fiction diplomatique,* while Colson contends that the combination of tact and imagery allows for the use of the verb without any fictional or "covert" allusion.[280] Numerous commentators from Calvin to Lang follow this approach.[281] On the other side, Chrysostom reflects a strong patristic tradition and has modern advocates.[282]

e. Conclusions Reflected in Our Translation

Hence we translate, **I have allusively applied all this to myself and to Apollos** to convey precisely the balance between probability and openness latent in the Greek. Clearly the examples are *allusive* to those whom Paul does not mention by name; but it goes beyond the evidence to claim that Paul and Apollos themselves are necessarily only *ciphers of rhetorical fiction* whom Paul himself exempts from his own warnings. Indeed, his reference to his own self-knowledge or conscience (4:4) suggests the opposite. Mere *example* undertranslates; *covert* rhetoric overtranslates; **allusive application** identifies the issue.

On your account translates δι' ὑμᾶς, since the preposition with the accusative means *on account of* meaning, "for your better instruction." This probably stands in contrast to "for Apollos and me to take to heart."[283] The phrase ἵνα ἐν ἡμῖν μάθητε, **that you may learn through our case**, is a final (purposive) clause (second aorist subjunctive after Ἵνα). This suggests an instrumental function for ἐν, i.e., *by us, by our example,* or more idiomatically (in English) and pointing more inclusively of all aspects of the apostolic life, **through our case**.

The next clause provides one of the most technically interesting and notorious examples for textual and exegetical discussion. Collins heads it "An Enigmatic Saying" and confesses that it is difficult to understand, while Schrage

279. Klauck, *1 Korintherbrief* (3d ed. 1992), 37; Lietzmann, *An die Korinther,* 19.

280. Allo, *Première Épitre,* 71-72; also Colson, "Μετεσχημάτισα in 1 Cor 4:6," 380-83.

281. Calvin, *First Epistle,* 90; Hodge, *First Epistle,* 70; Barrett, *First Epistle,* 106; Moffatt, *First Epistle,* 46-47; Harrisville, *1 Corinthians,* 70-71; Bruce, *1 and 2 Corinthians,* 48; Hooker, Conzelmann, and Fee, *loc. cit.;* Lang, *Die Brief,* 62-63.

282. Ambrose, *Opera Omnia: In Ep. b. Pauli ad Cor. Primum,* 124D (Migne, *PL,* 17:2:ii, 214-15): *Contentus est tacere: tacito autem nomine si quis audiens . . . dissimulat;* also Theodoret, *Opera Omnia: Interpr. Ep. 1 ad Cor.,* 187B-C (Greek) and 185D and 188A (Latin) is less explicit (Migne *PG,* 82:255 [Latin] and 256 [Greek]). Hall cites only 233, which alludes to the so-called "parties" at 1:12, where Theodoret follows Chrysostom's interpretation of this verse (i.e., 1:12); Photius of Constantinople, in Karl Staab (ed.), *Pauluskommentare aus der Griechischen Kirche* (Münster: Aschendorff, 1933), 545; Erasmus, *Opera Omnia: in Ep. Pauli 1 ad Cor.,* 870 *(fictis nominibus proponere, ut lecta in commune . . . tacitus . . .).* In the modern period Meyer, *First Epistle,* 1:116-17; Edwards, *First Epistle,* 101; Lightfoot, *Notes,* 199 (where the term "covert allusion" is coined); Godet, *First Epistle,* 1:215-16; Robertson and Plummer, *First Epistle,* 81.

283. Findlay, *Expositor's Greek Testament,* 2:799.

also views it as "one of the most difficult places of the whole epistle."[284] In general seven possible interpretations of the phrase invite consideration:

   (i) that the reference to **what is written** rests on a misunderstood scribal gloss (Baljon, Legault, Héring);
  (ii) that **what is written** refers to the OT in general, i.e., the principle of *sola scriptura* (Bengel, Schlatter, Leitzman, Bruce, Barrett);
 (iii) that the phrase means **what is written** in this epistle (Calvin [this or iv]; Cranmer)
  (iv) that it refers to what Paul has quoted as scripture already in the epistle (Hooker, Fee, Kleinknecht, Wolff, Lang);
   (v) that it alludes to **what is written** in church regulations or earlier letters (Parry) or explicit public "church regulations" or "bylaws" (Hanges)
  (vi) that it refers to (ii) or (v) as a familiar or accepted maxim (Godet, Moffatt, Bruce, in the sense of ii; Ross and Welborn in the sense of v)
 (vii) that part of the "childishness" of the addressees is like that of children unable to read letters properly (Ebner).

   (i) The hypothesis of a scribal gloss may have been formulated first by J. M. S. Baljon in 1884 (although F. F. Bruce ascribes it to F. A. Bornemann earlier) and is most strongly advocated by Héring as "the only explanation at all satisfactory."[285] Following Baljon he proposes that the original text simply read: *so that you may learn from our example not to be puffed up . . . one against the other,* i.e., ἵνα ἐν ἡμῖν μάθητε ἵνα μὴ εἷς ὑπὲρ τοῦ ἑνὸς φυσιοῦσθε (omitting *not beyond what is written*). But an early copyist accidentally omitted the μή (**not**) before the word εἷς. To remedy the problem he sandwiched the μή above the α of ἵνα. The *next* copyist, however, was overconscientious. Recognizing the problems of possible misreadings of abbreviated, crowded, or unclear manuscripts, he scrupulously left a marginal note (gloss) for subsequent copyists to explain the state of the text as he received it. In the margin he noted "The μή has been written above the alpha," i.e., τὸ μὴ ὑπὲρ α γέγραπται.
   One problem (if such a thing ever occurred) is that margins could be used for two purposes: *either* for some scribal comment (we noted that *their Lord and ours* at the end of 1:2 was ascribed by a few to the addition of an indignant but pious scribe!); *or,* if there was space, for the insertion of a word or phrase that a copyist had accidentally omitted. Hence a *third* copyist interpreted the gloss not as a comment, but as an accidental omission to be reinserted. The phrase then precisely occurs in our text (while we note that breathings and accents appeared later than the earliest Uncial texts): τὸ ὑπὲρ ἃ γέγραπται. The single reason, therefore, why this is regarded as "the only explanation at all sat-

284. Collins, *First Cor,* 177; Schrage, *Der erste Brief,* 1:334.
   285. Héring, *First Epistle,* 28; Collins, *First Cor,* 180; and Fee, *First Epistle,* 167-68, n. 14, refer it to J. Baljon of Utrecht in his doctoral dissertation of 1884. Cf. Bruce, *1 and 2 Cor,* 48.

isfactory" is that it seems difficult otherwise to account for the unexpected insertion of the definite article τò before μὴ (*the* before **not**). But other more convincing explanations are offered (below).

Legault argues for a *modified version* of this scribal theory in a special study: the phrase owes its origin to the shifting of the μή by one copyist. The addition to the τó, his main argument is that "without these perplexing words the sentence is very clear."[286] Almost simultaneously in a parallel study J. M. Ross urged that the hypothesis lacked any scrap of evidence and was too complicated to be remotely credible. Even those MSS which habitually choose shorter readings where possible include the phrase **not beyond (or above) what is written**. Indeed, Ross (with Barrett, Bruce, Fee, and others) advocates what is the obvious explanation for the unexpected inclusion of the definite article τó, *namely, that it introduces a familiar saying or a quotation.*[287] He concludes that in his view the saying is sufficiently indefinite to permit some such meaning as "that you may learn to 'keep within the rules.'" We cannot simply sweep aside the hypothesis, since many still seek to defend it.[288] Nevertheless it is exceedingly improbable and has little to commend it over other explanations.[289]

(ii) Schrage and many others interpret '**Not beyond what is written**' *to the OT in general* as the scripture of the church.[290] Bengel explicitly comments, i.e., "*in the whole of scripture,* from which some quotations, 3:19, 20, have just been made. . . . We are not allowed to depart from this rule, 2 Cor 10:13 . . . the general principle . . . by which the Lord will judge all persons" (*in tota Scriptura . . . qua Dominus quemvis judicabit*).[291] However, variants of this approach may be found. J. MacRory understands this to refer to the OT, but also more specifically to scriptural teaching on humility.[292] Godet refers it to scripture, but in combination with approach (vi), namely, that Paul cites a familiar principle, probably derived from rabbinic axioms, i.e., the axiom, "*not above scripture.*"[293] Blomberg believes that it may well allude to a general need "to remain within biblical standards."[294] Many of the Church Fathers, with a less developmental view of Paul, Jesus, and "scripture," perceived this as an allu-

---

286. Legault, "'Beyond the Things Which Are Written,'" 230; cf. 227-31. Legault traces the view first to A. S. Peake among English writers.

287. Ross, "Not Above What Is Written: A Note on 1 Cor 4:6," *ExpTim* 82 (1971): 215-17.

288. See further J. Murphy O'Connor, "Interpolations in 1 Cor" (although his theory inclines to interpolation), *CBQ* 48 (1986): 81-94, esp. 84-85; J. Strugnell, "A Plea for Conjectural Emendation in the NT, with a Coda on 1 Cor 4:6," 543-58, esp. 555-58; W. F. Howard, "1 Cor 4:6 (Exegesis or Emendation?)," *ExpTim* 33 (1922): 479-80; cf. also D. R. MacDonald, "A Conjectural Emendation of 1 Cor 15:31-32, or the Case of the Misplaced Lion Fight," *HTR* 93 (1980): 261.

289. Weiss, *Der erste Korintherbrief,* 102-4.

290. Major advocates include Hays, *First Cor,* 69; Barrett, *First Epistle,* 106-7; Schrage, *Der erste Brief,* 1:334-35; and Bruce, *1 and 2 Cor,* 48, "Keep to the Book."

291. Bengel, *Gnomon,* 619.

292. MacRory, *First Epistle,* 53.

293. Godet, *First Epistle,* 1:217.

294. Blomberg, *1 Cor,* 89. However, he concedes that there are various possibilities.

sion to words of Jesus. Chrysostom and Theodoret refer it to **what is written** in Matt 7:3, "Why do you look at the splinter in your brother's eye [Paul's?] but fail to see the plank in your own eye?" and compare "Whoever humbles himself will be exalted . . .," while Theodoret even adds 1 Cor 7:24.[295] Meyer speaks of: "the rule written in the OT" with special allusion to its teaching on humility: "the rule" takes account of the definite article τό adequately.[296] Bruce's "Keep to the Book" would substantiate the "axiom" aspect also.[297]

(iii) It remains a logical option that **what is written** may refer back to what *Paul has already written about not glorying in human status* or in human leaders. Connected with this, however, is the Western (Latin) reading of D, which witnesses to ὃ γέγραπται (the singular for **what**) as against the widespread witness (**א**, B, A, C, etc.) to ἃ (plural). Cranmer took this to mean "beyond that whyche is above wrytten."[298] The plural would just as easily support the interpretation (a neuter subject governs the singular verb in both instances), and Calvin considers this to be one of two possible interpretations, the second being what Paul himself has not only written but specifically quoted in this epistle from scripture.[299] Criteria for a decision are not clear. Indeed, Conzelmann simply gives up trying to make sense of the phrase.[300] But so regularly does γέγραπται, **it is written**, refer to scripture that options (ii), (iv), and (vi) (when vi includes a scriptural maxim) are almost certainly right.

(iv) Several (e.g., Hooker, Wolff, Fee, and Lang) return to Calvin's second option, namely, *what Paul has already quoted from scripture*.[301] The strength of this view is that it carries the force of (ii), including the usual use of γέγραπται, **it is written**, but appeals pointedly to what Paul has already identified as addressing the situation of what the readers need to **learn**, in the quotations used in 1:29, 31 (not to glory in human leaders or status, but in the Lord), and to evaluate things by God's "wisdom," not by human cleverness (1:19; 3:19-20). All this fits admirably with the rest of the verse and its context. We have merely to integrate it with (vi),[302] which Wolff achieves by citing the above verses and proposing that Paul cites an "anti-enthusiast motto."

(v) The definite article may simply introduce a *well-known saying or maxim*. Welborn devotes over 30 pages to this verse and suggests that it offers "a conciliatory principle" by appeal "in the character of a maxim."[303] St John

---

295. Chrysostom, *1 Cor. Hom.*, 12:2; and Theodoret, *Opera Omnia*, 188D (Migne, *PG*, 82:256).

296. Meyer, *First Epistle*, 1:118.

297. Bruce, *1 and 2 Corinthians*, 48.

298. Cited in Godet, *First Epistle*, 1:215-16.

299. Calvin, *First Epistle*, 90.

300. Conzelmann, *1 Corinthians*, 86: "The phrase . . . is unintelligible."

301. Lang, *Die Briefe*, 63; Hooker, "'Beyond the Things Which Are Written,'" 127-32; Fee, *First Epistle*, 167-68; Kleinknecht, *Der Leidende Gerechtfertigte*, 224; and Wolff, *Der erste Brief*, 85.

302. Wolff, *Der erste Brief*, 85.

303. Welborn, *Politics and Rhetoric in the Corinthian Letters*, 74; cf. 43-75.

Parry proposes that it refers to some well-known terms of reference for ministry or leadership within the church, and Ross believes that it alludes to some such maxim as "keep the rules" or "play the game."[304] Hanges claims that there are resemblances to Greek *leges sacrae* in cults, to which a parallel would be a church document which laid out guidelines and axioms for church members.[305] But all the arguments above suggest that Bruce's "Keep to the Book" has all the advantages and none of the problems of this suggestion.

(vi) It is perfectly possible, and indeed broadly convincing, to combine the thrust of (iv) *(what Paul has quoted from scripture)*, with the two broader principles of (ii), i.e., the regular *appeal to the OT* as Christian scripture, and (v), that this has assumed the *status of a maxim,* or what Bruce calls "not, probably, a current proverb, but a saying well known in the Corinthian church, where some were disposed to go beyond the gospel of Christ crucified and risen, which they had received 'in accordance with the scriptures' (15:3, 4)."[306] Morna Hooker makes precisely this point. *Some at Corinth tried to supplement a theology of the cross with a second-stage "Wisdom"-based spirituality.*[307] This harmonizes perfectly with the need to **learn . . . that one of you be not inflated on behalf of one against another**. "Adding to" the cross has this effect. The work of Christ is complete.

(vii) Ebner makes the novel suggestion that **what is written** may allude to *letters,* which a child cannot trace properly, to reinforce Paul's earlier attack on the childish condition of some addressees.[308] However such a hypothesis remains entirely speculative and fails to carry the weight of the three which we favor. In the clause **so that one of you be not inflated on behalf of one against another**, the verb translated **inflated** (often *puffed up,* φυσιοῦσθε) is used only by Paul in the NT, and with the exception of one occurrence in Colossians it is peculiar to this epistle (1 Cor 4:6, 18, 19; 5:2; 8:1; 13:4; cf. Col 2:18). In 8:1 it is γνῶσις which *puffs up* (as against love which builds up); in 13:4 love is *not puffed up;* in 5:2 the addressees are **inflated** with arrogant complacency. In terms of word history the older form φυσάω has a cognate affinity with the noun meaning *a pair of bellows.* This becomes a colorful and vivid metaphor for becoming blown up with self-importance, like the frog in Aesop's Fables. Paul warns the addressees that if they seek to go **beyond what is written**, the misguided attempt to "add to" the gospel of the cross by self-styled wisdom, rhetorical status-seeking, or self-styled "spirituality," the result will be an inflation of mere wind that will lead to taking sides, self-affirmation, and putting one group or its leaders against another.

304. Parry, *Commentary on 1 Corinthians* (Cambridge: Cambridge University Press, 1926); and Ross, *Not Above What Is Written,* 217.

305. Hanges, "1 Cor 4:6 and the Possibility of Written Bylaws in the Corinthian Church," 275-98.

306. Bruce, *1 and 2 Cor,* 48-49.

307. Hooker, "'Beyond the Things Which are Written,'" 127-32; cf. also Kleinknecht, *Der leidende Gerechtfertigte,* 224 and 233-34.

308. M. Ebner, *Leidenslisten und Apostelbrief,* 33-36.

Contrary to Conzelmann's comment that this passage is largely unintelligible, what emerges is the force and relevance of the verse both for Corinth and for today's church. Paul uses (1) *scripture,* especially those passages which address the situation; (2) *tradition,* in the form of accepted "sayings" or maxims, and (3) *reason,* which demonstrates the respective entailments of human wisdom, infantile spirituality, and a trustful faith grounded in the cross; all to address the Corinthian situation. Most of all, he urges *the sufficiency of the gospel of the cross interpreted within the framework of biblical tradition,* as against the misguided and indeed damaging effects of trying to *add* "wisdom" aspects or notions of being "people of the Spirit" without the cross. Christianity without the cross, as Bonhoeffer urges, becomes "cheap grace . . . forgiveness without repentance, baptism without church discipline, and the Christian live[s] like the rest of the world."[309]

7 Since διακρίνω means *to sift out,* or *to separate between,* in strictly linguistic terms the verb in v. 7 may mean either **who** *separates* **you** *from anyone else* or **who** *separates one from another* among **you**? Most English VSS follow some such translation as **For who sees anything different in you?** (NRSV), but NRSV includes the conceivable alternative, *Who makes you different from one another?* as a marginal note. The discussion goes back to the early church and the Reformation era. Ambrose rejects here degrees of difference of status achieved by "adding" particular eloquence or doctrine.[310] No one has anything "that can mark him out as superior to others."[311] "These excellent qualities belong not to you but to God."[312] To the question, *who differentiates you?* Origen, Theodoret, and Grotius envisage the answer, *God.* Paul exposes the inconsistency of "boasting" while accepting a gift.[313] The logical grammar of *grace* is: εἰ δὲ χάριτι, οὐκέτι ἐξ ἔργων, ἐπεὶ ἡ χάρις οὐκέτι γίνεται χάρις (Rom 11:6).[314]

Indeed, the aorist ἔλαβες, **you received,** underlines the event-character of grace as an act of giving-and-receiving which occurred when the addressees became Christians. The sequence εἰ δὲ καί is awkward. Many interpret it to mean *even if,* in the sense of *even if you now possess it.* But λαμβάνω especially in the aorist stresses the receiving, not the possessing. Hence it may be right to interpret the meaning as, *Why, even although you received it, do you still boast?*[315] However, Paul's argument moves too quickly for us to make too much of such a small detail of syntax. The older form καυχᾶσαι, **you boast,** is the uncontracted form. On **boasting** or glorying, see above on 1:29, 31 and 3:21.

---

309. D. Bonhoeffer, *The Cost of Discipleship* (Eng. trans., London: SCM, 1959), 35 and 36.

310. Ambrose, *Op. Omn.: In ep. ad 1 Cor.,* 124D (Migne, *PL,* 17:2.ii, 215).

311. Calvin, *First Epistle,* 91.

312. Chrysostom, *1 Cor. Hom.,* 12:3.

313. Theodoret, *Op. Omn.: Int. prim. ep. ad 1 Cor.,* 188D (Migne, *PG,* 82:256 [Greek], 255 [Latin]).

314. Discussed in Thiselton, *The Two Horizons,* 389; cf. 386-92.

315. Edwards, *First Epistle,* 105.

The negative μή with the aorist participle λαβών and ὡς, **as if you did not receive it**, rounds off the question with a devastating exposure of living out a false assumption. The triumphalist self-important Christian lives ὡς μή . . . **as if** something were the case when it is **not** so. From the viewpoint of the Giver, a parent who gives a gift to a child hopes that the gift will bring joy, but not a reason to gloat over brothers or sisters, or to draw comparisons. The combination of φυσιοῦσθαι and καυχᾶσθαι is devastating. Augustine cites these words on numerous occasions, most characteristically in his attack on Pelagius's view of grace: *Quid enim habebat quod non acceperat.*[316]

8 That Paul uses irony is proved by the juxtaposition of **you came "to reign as kings"** with **if only you did "reign as kings."** It is impossible fully to appreciate the force of this verse without grasping two factors about the Pauline churches: the problem of "overrealized" eschatology; and the effects of perceived conversion experiences within many Graeco-Roman and especially Graeco-Oriental cults. Grant describes how eschatology had become distorted and mistimed (4:4, 5). They changed "the Christian eschatological message . . . believing that eschatology had been 'realized'. The kingdom had already arrived."[317] Together with this, Nock observes that among hellenistic-oriental cults notions of conversion in the first century could be extravagant: a convert could be overwhelmed by a new sense of power, liberation, and status: "Many of the converts, convinced that they were on a new plane of life, felt that they could do anything: they were kings (1 Cor 4:8), they were in the Spirit, they were . . . emancipated. . . . They were altogether superior to the unchanged men around them."[318]

In yet another context, **to be rich** and **to reign** represent catchwords of the Stoics. As Moffatt acutely observes: "Paul . . . pours out his soul. . . . The nearest approach to this caustic description of religious self-satisfaction lies in the prophet John's word to the Christian church at Laodicea (Rev 3:17): "you declare, 'I am rich, I am well off, I lack nothing.' . . . 'Rich' and 'reigning' were catchwords of the Stoics ever since Diogenes, whose tomb was shown at Corinth, had taught a Stoic to maintain, 'I alone am rich, I alone reign as king' in the world."[319] Further, Moffatt points out, in relation to the Greek βασιλένω, **I reign**, at Roman Corinth the Latin *basilicas* could mean *a person of importance.* Finally, the nurture of hope in apocalyptic was to come at last to inherit the kingdom. The supreme irony lies in Paul's expostulation: "So it has all come about already . . . and **without us**," i.e., either *without our cooperation* or *ahead of us,* poor apostles![320]

---

316. Augustine, *De Natura et Gratia,* 24:27 (Latin ed. of W. Bright, 1880, 76); cf. *Letters,* 140:7, 21, 26; 186:4, 10; *On the Spirit and Letter,* 15:9; 50:29; 54:31; 57:33; 60:34.

317. R. M. Grant, *An Historical Introduction to the NT* (London: Collins, 1963), 204.

318. A. D. Nock, *St Paul* (London and New York: Harper, 1938), 174. Cf. also Nock, *Conversion: The Old and the New in Religion from Alexander the Great to Augustine of Hippo* (Oxford: Oxford University Press, 1933 and 1961), 99-121.

319. Moffatt, *First Epistle,* 49; also Collins, *First Cor,* 183 and 186-88.

320. Ibid.

357

The Greek verbs give force to this picture. κεκορεσμένοι ἐστέ is the periphrastic use of the participial form with εἰμί, *to be,* specifically here the perfect participle passive nominative masculine plural of κορέννυμι, normally meaning *satiated, fed-to-the-full,* **glutted,** applying to the "bloated" self-important "people of the Spirit" the farmyard metaphor of overfed animals. Philo and Josephus similarly use it figuratively.[321] Horace satirizes claims to be *dives, liber, honoratus . . .* rex *. . .* regum.[322] Epictetus perceives the Cynic philosopher "as sharing in the kingly rule of Zeus" (ὡς μετέχων τῆς ἀρχῆς τοῦ Διός).[323] All this stands in sharp opposition to 1 Cor 15:25, where "Christ must reign until (δεῖ γὰρ αὐτὸν βασιλεύειν ἄχρι) he lays all his enemies under his feet."

In an earlier study I recognized the implausibility of the hypothesis of Grant and Hurd that most people at Corinth "misunderstood" Paul's eschatology after eighteen months of his ministry with them, although we should not underestimate the growth or addition of new believers after Paul's departure.[324] However, ἤδη, **already,** is a clear signal of an overrealized eschatology, especially in conjunction with χωρὶς ἡμῶν, **without us.**[325] Schrage takes up two closely related themes: the role of the resurrection chapter and a one-sided theology of the Holy Spirit at Corinth. Hence he speaks of the premature triumphalism of the addressees as "the illusion of the enthusiasts," using Luther's term *(die illusion von Schwämern)* for those whose emphasis on the Spirit overlooked the realities of continuing sin and struggle, and the need for discipline and order.[326] By contrast, Paul acknowledges that they had "not yet reached the victory" (Phil 3:12) and that he was still "not as I should be" (Phil 3:13 in Taylor, *Living Letters*).[327]

To sum up: "The Corinthians are behaving as if the age to come were already consummated, as if the saints had already taken over the kingdom (Dan 7:18); for them there is no 'not yet' to qualify the 'already' of realized eschatology."[328] Because of this, Wendland and Wolff add that they transpose the gospel into a mixture of wisdom-gnosis and Spirit-centered enthusiasm *(Gnosis und Enthusiasmus).*[329]

Some earlier commentators even detect this trend in the Greek syntax. The perfect tense of κεκορεσμένοι changes to the aorist in ἐπλουτήσατε and ἐβασιλεύσατε. As our translation **came to reign** indicates, these are ingressive aorists, but Lightfoot adds that "the aorists, used instead of per-

---

321. Josephus, *Wars* 4.3 (4); Philo, *De Sobrietate* 57; BAGD, 444.

322. Horace, *Satires* 1.3.132-33; *Epodes* 1.1.106-7.

323. Epictetus, *Dissertations* 3.22.95.

324. Thiselton, "Realized Eschatology at Corinth," 510-26.

325. Schrage, *Der erste Brief,* 1:338; cf. 339-40.

326. Schrage, *Der erste Brief,* 1:338, n. 137; Thiselton, "Realized Eschatology at Corinth," 523-25.

327. Schrage, *Der erste Brief,* Conzelmann, *1 Corinthians,* 87.

328. Barrett, *First Epistle,* 109.

329. Wendland, *Die Briefe an die Korinther,* 40; Wolff, *Der erste Brief,* 86.

fects, imply indecent haste," while Robertson and Plummer observe, "They have got a private millennium of their own."[330] The irony and pathos emerge poignantly, however, in ὄφελόν γε ἐβασιλεύσατε, where ὄφελον expresses *an unfulfilled wish.* Although ὄφελον is grammatically either the second aorist of the verb ὀφείλω, *I owe, I ought,* without the augment, or (as BAGD virtually alone argue against Robertson and others) a participial form of ὀφείλω.[331] But it became equivalent to an exclamatory particle (usually followed by an aorist) long before Paul. Hence we translate **if only you did**. . . . The compound συμ, **reign with,** coupled with χωρὶς ἡμῶν, **without us,** sharpens and heightens the pathos of the illusion.

Few interpreters capture this ironic contrast more vividly than Deluz: "These Corinthians are lucky. *Already* they enjoy favours that the apostles dare only hope for. They no longer 'hunger and thirst after righteousness'; they are *filled;* in the theory of the Spirit, they have eaten to satiety. . . . In short, the Messianic kingdom seems to have come to Corinth and these people have been given their thrones, while the apostles dance attendance and are placed with the servants."[332] This metaphor is exchanged for that of the gladiatorial ring in v. 9. Further light will be shed on this verse when we compare research of (e.g., Kleinknecht, Fitzgerald, Plank, and Ferrari) on the "catalogue of afflictions" which follow. (See the extended note after 4:13 on "Paul's Catalogue of Afflictions").

9 Paul introduces the metaphor of a great pageant, in which criminals, prisoners, or professional gladiators process to the gladiatorial ring, with the apostles bringing up the rear as those who must fight to the death. δοκῶ, *I think, I am of the opinion,* carries its frequent sense here of **it seems to me** when the speaker wishes to express what an appearance may seem to suggest as against some deeper, underlying reality or truth. The main verb of the sentence is ἀπέδειξεν (aorist of ἀποδείκνυμι, **to put on display**). It is used in the context of displaying theatrical entertainments or gladiatorial shows (cf. 1 Cor 15:32). The cry of the Roman artisans, unemployed, or slaves for "bread and games" runs parallel to the obsession with violence and "thrills" for many popular audiences today, also living out emotions through the sufferings, victories, and brutalities of others.

The Corinthians have a grandstand view of the gladiators from their tiered seats as spectators. But Paul and other authentic apostles are put into the ring as **the spectacle** (θέατρον). Moreover, with a conscious allusion to the premature eschatology of v. 8, Paul explains that the apostles come behind the Co-

330. Lightfoot, *Notes;* Robertson and Plummer, *First Epistle,* 84.
331. BAGD, 599, argue for the participle against almost all other writers. Cf. BDF, sect. 359; and Wolff, *Der erste Brief,* 87: "an unfulfilled wish."
332. Deluz, *Companion to 1 Cor,* 46-47. Wolff speaks (with Wendland) in particular of the combination of exultation in "Wisdom" and in "numerous charismata, above all, ecstatic gifts of the Spirit" (*Der erste Brief,* 86). Blomberg speaks of "rich and regal . . . you have all you want" (*1 Cor,* 90).

rinthians (τοὺς ἀποστόλους ἐσχάτους); indeed, they bring up the rear as **the grand finale** of the gladiatorial show: as the drama intensifies, finally the doomed criminals appear who must fight to the death, **doomed to die** (ἐπιθανατίους) because they cannot win every combat, and their bloodied bodies will weaken until humiliation and death overtake them. The word ἐπιθανατίους occurs only here in the NT, but it appears in the LXX for those thrown to the lions (Bel and the Dragon 31).[333] Schrage relates the "death" here to sharing with Christ as the crucified one, and the public **spectacle** as underlining its cosmic significances before the world and angels (see the extended note after v. 13). The datives of interest, τῷ κόσμῳ καὶ ἀγγέλοις καὶ ἀνθρώποις, may be expressed in English as **in the eyes the world, of angels, and of humanity**.

Paul perceives his apostolic labors as a cosmic spectacle, which, if they are evaluated by Corinthian criteria, **seem** to be **a spectacle** of struggle, failure, and disgrace. The apostles "seem to be of no more importance than the gladiators who shed their blood in the arena to provide an amusing public spectacle . . . surely the Corinthians should be ashamed to lounge in the best seats and just applaud or even boo!"[334]

In research on "catalogues of afflictions" or "*peristalsis* catalogues" in Greek and in Pauline thought, Karl Plank argues that Paul may well consciously overstate the case in 4:8-9 and in 4:10-13 to invite a reappraisal through irony of a lack of realism in Corinthian thought.[335] The seminal source of doubt: "isn't Paul going over the top here?" may well constitute a considered rhetorical tool for inviting the Corinthians on their own active initiative to query: "Have we gone over the top in some of our thinking and lifestyle?" (see Note below at 4:13). John Fitzgerald makes much of the use of "catalogues of hardship" in Greek literature to shed light on 4:7-13 as "the most debated and least appreciated" example in 1 and 2 Corinthians.[336] He discusses the history of research on these "catalogues of affliction," which is expanded in still greater detail in M. Schiefer Ferrari's detailed study of some five hundred pages.[337] Other earlier studies, however, also relate such "catalogues" of suffering to the fate of the righteous in relation to eschatological judgement in Judaism and to justification by grace, the cross, and eschatology in Paul. Kleinknecht and Schrage provide important examples.[338] (See the note below.)

10-11 On the various important nuances of μωρός, *fool,* and μωροί,

333. Cited among others by Wolff, *Der erste Brief,* 87.

334. Deluz, *Companion to 1 Corinthians,* 47.

335. Plank, *Paul and the Irony of Affliction,* 48-52; cf. 33-70 (on 4:9-13), 11-32 (on Corinth), and 71-94 (on rhetoric and wider issues).

336. Fitzgerald, *Cracks in an Earthen Vessel: An Examination of Catalogues of Hardship,* 129; cf. esp. 117-48 (on this passage and Corinth) and 7-116 (on the history of research and *parastaseis* in Greek literature).

337. Ferrari, *Die Sprache des Leids in den paulinischen Peristasenkatalogen,* where he takes up 2 Cor 4:8-9; 6:4-10; 11:23-29; and 12:10, together with Rom 8:35 and Phil 4:12, alongside 1 Cor 4:10-13.

338. See bibliography on 4:6-21 and notes below for full details.

fools, see above on 1:25 (μωρὸν τοῦ θεοῦ), 1:27 (τὰ μωρὰ τοῦ κόσμου), and 3:18 (μωρὸς γενέσθω). The context in those three passages is fundamental for the meaning of **fools** here. 1:25 and 27 relate to God's choice of the supposedly weak and foolish (from a human point of view) which constitutes the heart of the criterion of the cross. In 3:18 Paul may be referring to the Socratic notion that the sage is well aware of the need to perceive his or her own ignorance, and this would fit Fitzgerald's notion of Paul using his own example and that of Apollos as counterexamples of the humility which befits the true sage in the best Greek traditions.[339] But, as we have argued, it is more likely that Paul more deeply grounds 3:18 in a theology of the cross. Hence, as Schrage and Kleinknecht urge, **fools** here belongs to the "negative" axis of a theology of the cross, which leads to transformation and to future eschatological reversals.[340] The force of the preposition διά with the accusative, *on account of,* translated above **on Christ's account** further confirms the links with Christology and the cross in 1:25-27 and 3:18.

Verse 10 embodies three antitheses in the sharpest possible form. Merklein and Plank rightly see these as reversals relating to 1:26-28.[341] Others refer these respectively to "teaching" (**fools** vs. **wise**); "demeanour" (**weak** vs. **strong**); and "worldly position" (**honoured** vs. **disgraced**), and add that the last clause is inverted from **we . . . you** to **you . . . we** so that the content of ἄτιμοι, *without honour* or **disgraced,** can be unpacked in v. 11.[342] But while the second comment is helpful, the first runs counter to a prevailing proposal today that all may be terms of social status or general prestige. (See the Note below.)

The verb γυμνιτεύομεν does not occur elsewhere in the NT or LXX, but, from a background meaning in hellenistic literature of *lightly armed,* comes to mean *poorly* clothed (e.g., Dio Chrysostom, 75 [25].3). The adjective γυμνός, which describes the anonymous young man (sometimes identified as Mark) in Mark 14:52 could mean naked but more probably means without a respectable outer garment. At all events, a respectable or respected person would not normally wish to appear in public γυμνός, exposed to view and to ridicule (Rev 3:17; 16:15; *Testament of Joseph* 8:3, ἔφυγον γυμνός).[343] In Plato the word can refer to a bare soul (Cratylus 20.403A, while its meaning in 2 Cor 5:3 is fiercely debated. Paul states here that their clothing is inadequate, either functionally, in respectability or status, or perhaps both. Collins alludes to the "tattered and threadbare clothing . . . [of] the 'have nots' at Corinth."[344]

---

339. Fitzgerald, *Cracks in an Earthen Vessel,* 3-5 and ch. 2, including esp. the role of the Stoic, the Cynic, and Seneca as a virtual contemporary with Paul, 112-16; cf. further 132-48.

340. Schrage, "Leid, Kreuz and Eschaton. Die Peristasenkataloge als Merkmale paulinischer theologia crucis und Eschatologie," *EvT* 34 (1974): 141-75; cf. Kleinknecht, *Der leidende Gerechtfertigte,* 208-304.

341. Merklein, *Die erste Brief 1–4,* 313-14; Plank, *Paul,* 47.

342. Robertson and Plummer, *First Epistle,* 86.

343. Cf. BAGD, 167-68.

344. Collins, *First Cor,* 190.

The verb κολαφίζω has four possible meanings here.[345] (i) The word often means *to strike with the fist, to punch,* or *to beat.* It may refer to being beaten up, mob violence, or malice, or being *beaten* as a formal punishment (cf. Mark 14:65).[346] (ii) Paul also uses the word metaphorically of the "messenger of Satan" in 2 Cor 12:7, and we noted (on 2:1-5) that in the view of Schweitzer and others Paul may perhaps have suffered from a version of epilepsy, for which this word can be used. Anyone who has suffered violent illness will appreciate how κολαφίζω can apply only too well to such a situation. It could in principle, therefore, include specific bouts of severe ill health (surely for some at Corinth a sign of not being fully "spiritual"!). Today we might speak of being *knocked out* by a period of ill health. (iii) The word clearly means also **we are roughly treated**. It refers to the kind of rough treatment which is symptomatic of the lack of respect (ἄτιμοι, **in disgrace**, v. 10) which Paul is expounding concretely in this verse. Hence, while it may well include (i) and (ii), our translation reflects (iii) as best matching this particular context. Paul's adding **up to this very hour** could support any of these meanings. On one side, he alludes to a specific event at Ephesus in 15:32; on the other hand, the words appear to signify a state which remains continuous and unabated. (iv) Above all, being **roughly treated** should *not be restricted to* specific events of violence, although these are certainly *included.* Victor Pfitzner and R. F. Hock stress the role of *hard manual labor* and *a low social status* determined by toiling as a leather worker or tentmaker in a small, hot workshop "bent over a workbench like a slave and . . . working side by side with slaves . . . thereby being perceived by others and by himself as slavish and humiliated; of suffering the artisan's lack of status and so being reviled and abused."[347]

Ten verbs and four participles trace the catalogue from v. 11 to v. 13. ἀστατοῦμεν, **we have no fixed abode**, not only recalls that Jesus had nowhere "to lay his head" (Matt 8:20; Luke 9:58) but again carries a social implication not entirely unlike that of the nuance of "of no fixed abode" on the witness stand or in the accused dock in English law: respectable citizens usually have residences, telephones, licenses, and insurance numbers. The verb does not occur elsewhere in the NT or LXX but the alpha privative with the Greek stem yields a transparent semantic content. On **weak** (ἀσθενεῖς, v. 10) see above on 1:25 and 1:27, where it relates closely to the cross as criterion and critique; but also below on 8:7, 9, 10; 9:22; 11:30; and 12:22, where it may mean the vulnerable, the oversensitive, people of a specific social status, or a combination of these (but see also the Note below). Merklein and Kleinknecht retain an empha-

345. Cf. BAGD, 441.

346. Collins, *First Cor,* 183, and Merklein, *Der erste Brief 1–4,* 314-15, allude to Paul's physical beating in 2 Cor 12:7 (cf. also Acts 16:21-23; 2 Cor 11:25; 1 Thess 2:2). Fee discusses the range of "deprivations" as a whole (*First Epistle,* 177-79).

347. Hock, *The Social Context of Paul's Ministry,* 67. See further Pfitzner, *Paul and the Agon Motif,* 92-94; and Witherington, *Conflict and Community,* 19-28.

sis on the connection between all this and identification with Christ and the cross.[348]

12-13 The verb κοπιῶμεν signifies *hard toil* to the point of *weariness* or near exhaustion. Hence NRSV renders, *we grow weary from the work of our own hands,* whereas RSV simply translates, *we labour, working with our own hands,* and NIV, *we work hard with our own hands.* Our translation requires both **toil** or *hard work* (κοπιῶμεν, contrasted verb) and **labor** (ἐπγάζομαι, *work,* but explicitly *manual* labour here), with the added dimension of reaching *weariness;* hence **we toil until we are weary, laboring with our own hands.** The lexicography is confirmed by Hock's research on the social, economic, and physical conditions of Paul's trade. Hock concludes that what made Paul seem **weak** (4:10) at Corinth "is identified in the following peristasis-catalog, which contains an explicit reference to his working at a trade (v. 12)."[349] He perceives hunger, thirst, and nakedness as "work-related experiences." "Paul would have been a weak figure without power, prestige, and privilege."[350] Workshops, such as that in which Paul would have plied his trade, "were often noisy, dirty and dangerous. . . . The life of the artisan was in no way easy. . . . His work amounted to 'exhausting toil' (1 Thes. 2:9; 1 Cor. 4:12)."[351] This is why, Hock proposes, the Corinthians were so upset that Paul did not wish them to provide financial support as his patrons, thereby bestowing upon him a superior social status as a professional rhetorician.[352]

The dative χερσίν, **with our hands** (v. 12), is instrumental, and calls attention to the status of manual labor, which was in general despised in Greek culture by those who secured an income in other ways. εὐλογοῦμεν (v. 12b) is almost universally translated *we bless* (NRSV, REB, NIV, AV/KJV) or *answer with a blessing* (NJB). If Plank's claims are valid that Paul heightens the irony by consciously sharing in exaggeration (see the extended note at v. 13), *we bless* may be right. But if Paul's language is descriptive, did he reply piously, or pray for his abusers silently? The regular usage of εὐλογέω outside explicitly religious contexts seems more likely, i.e., **we reply with good words.** This would match the context, and it does justice to the lexical and semantic evidence. **Putting up with** or *enduring* (ἀνεχόμεθα) persecution may nowadays suggest *harassment.* But we have retained **when we are persecuted** since for Paul it probably included more than harassment. Paul follows Jesus' principle of non-retaliation, which, yet once again, was regarded as **weak** or unmanly in the Roman and Graeco-Roman world of Paul's day.

---

348. Merklein, *Der erste Brief 1-4,* 316; Kleinknecht, *Gerechtfertigte,* 231-33.

349. Hock, *Social Context,* 60.

350. Ibid.

351. Ibid., 34-35; cf. 29-39.

352. Ibid., 50-62. The full force of this point is brought home in conjunction with work by others on patronage and reciprocal expectations in "friendship"; cf. Chow, *Patronage and Power* (passim), and Marshall, *Enmity in Corinth.* Nevertheless, the theological dimension urged by Kleinknecht and Schrage must also be kept in view.

Fee observes that while the catalogue up to v. 12a reflects the standard features of deprivation and serves as a series of antitheses to "filled, rich and reigning" (v. 8), "the three antitheses of vv. 12b-13a go beyond the mere cataloguing of hardships to express his response to ill treatment."[353] In the face of **slander** (δυσφημούμενοι, *ill-used,* ill-spoken of, not elsewhere in NT but in 1 Macc 7:41, here as a passive participle) Paul **appeals directly** to the culprits. The Gk. παρακαλοῦμεν (present indicative of contracted verb παρακαλέω) is usually translated into English as one of the following: *we entreat* (AV/KJV); *we speak kindly* (NRSV, NIV; Schrage; or *courteously,* NJB); *try to be conciliatory* (REB; cf. *try to conciliate,* Williams). But παρακαλέω, together with its substantial cognate παράκλητος (*paraclete;* cf. John 14:16, 26; 15:26; 16:7), embraces an exceptionally wide range of semantic nuances. Fundamentally it never quite loses its "transparent" meaning as παρα-καλέω, *I call alongside,* whether to call to one's side by *inviting,* by *calling them to one's side to help,* by *calling them to one's side to listen* (i.e., appeal), by *calling them to one's side for friendship or comfort;* or *calling them to one's side as a prosecuting or defending witness.*[354] Hence in the face of those who **slander** him or *speak ill of him behind his back,* Paul *appeals* to them, but probably face to face, i.e., clarifies misunderstanding with moral courage and *sensitive listening.* Hence we translate, **we appeal to them directly.** Again, taking the trouble to placate someone might well be construed as another sign of being **weak.** It would be quicker to cast aspersions on their character.

The words translated **the world's scum** (περικαθάρματα τοῦ κόσμου) and **everyone's scrapings** (πάντων περίψημα) mean precisely this. Without its compound κάθαρμα means *sweepings* which are swept up from the floor, i.e., the *unwanted dirt.* But with the addition of the compound περικάθαρμα means what is removed as a result of scouring *round* a utensil. Hence the filthy residue is **the scum** which clings to surfaces unwanted. Epictetus refers to *the offscourings of humanity* in this way (*Dissertations* 3.22.78). But although the word does not appear elsewhere in the NT, in the LXX the technical meaning of *scapegoat* emerges in Prov 21:18. Although Lietzmann, BAGD, and Barrett favor *scapegoats* in this passage, Conzelmann and Fee, among others, more convincingly argue for *offscourings, refuse,* or **scum.**[355] Hanson sees in these "very remarkable" words "a strong overtone of expiation."[356] But *scapegoats* or *sacrificed victims* in Greek literature were often regarded as "worthless," and the term remains one of deep insult, whether or not its secondary nuance sur-

---

353. Fee, *First Epistle,* 179.

354. BAGD, 617 and 618; Robertson and Plummer, *First Epistle,* 87-88; Merklein, *Der erste Brief 1–4,* 316-17.

355. BAGD, 647; Barrett, *First Epistle,* 112; Lietzmann, *An die Korinther,* 21; as against Robertson and Plummer, *First Epistle,* 88; Conzelmann, *1 Corinthians,* 90, n. 49; Fee, *First Epistle,* 180.

356. Hanson, *The Paradox of the Cross,* 32; cf. 32-37; Wolff, *Der erste Brief,* 90: "sin offering."

vives.[357] περικαθάρματα are what has to be scrubbed off, περίψημα derives from ψάω, *to wipe, rub,* or *scrape, that which has been scraped off,* i.e., everyone's scrapings. Paul is searching for the lowest, strongest, most earthy language he can find. In an ancient city the most filthy scrapings would be encountered not in the home but in the street, probably **the scrapings from everyone's shoes**. Luther translates *Kehricht, trash,* and Schrage proposes *Drecke, dirt, mud, excrement.*[358]

PAUL'S "CATALOGUE OF AFFLICTIONS" AND ITS RHETORIC (4:8-13)

A series of questions have been posed especially by Schrage (1974), Hodgson (1983), Kleinknecht (1984), Plank (1987), Fitzgerald (1988), and Ferrari (1991) in their research on "Catalogues of Affliction" in 4:8-13. (See details in bibliography.) While Schrage and Kleinknecht are successful in linking the issue with the suffering of the righteous in apocalyptic Judaism as a background to Paul, Fitzgerald offers abundant examples of such catalogues in Greek literature in connection with the endurance of the sage, and the sage's indifference (especially in Stoic-Cynic traditions) to worldly contingencies. As Betz notes (see below), the term *"peristasis* catalogues" derives from the Greek word for *circumstances,* often those which are unpredictable or *harsh.* The dual background is acknowledged by Hodgson, who finds sources in Stoic philosophy, Jewish apocalyptic, the hellenistic Jewish writings of Josephus, and even pharisaic-rabbinic material in the Mishnah, with further hints in early gnostic writings. This vast area of research is surveyed in detail by Ferrari.

(i) Fitzgerald convincingly demonstrates how frequently Paul speaks of afflictions: he "dies daily" (1 Cor 15:30-31), experiences *"a sentence of death"* (2 Cor 1:8-10), recites a catalogue of such circumstances as shipwrecks, muggings, and legal penalties (2 Cor 11:23-28) and sees himself as scum in the eyes of the world and society (1 Cor 4:9-13). This evidence is cited in the other main studies also. But Fitzgerald takes up the challenge of H. D. Betz that the *literary* form and function of these peristasis catalogues require more serious investigation.[359] He sums up his purpose as "an attempt to use Hellenistic material to address *literary* rather than historical or history-of-religion issues."[360] He then argues that Paul draws on *sophos-* imagery. In the history of research Heinrici began a decisive move in his exploration of Epictetus, and others explored the work of hellenistic writers on *peristasis* as "adverse, unfavourable, circumstance."[361] Here from Epictetus (e.g., *Dissertations* 1.24.1) to Chrysostom and John of Damascus, *hardships* included a range of events from shipwrecks to poverty.

In hellenistic philosophy the Cynic's catalogue of hardships and nonpossessions performed "a vital function": the Cynic's reaction to them proves that the life of

---

357. Schrage, *Der erste Brief,* 1:350; Barrett reserves *scum* for this second word, since he has used *scapegoats* for the first (*First Epistle,* 112).

358. Schrage, *Der erste Brief,* 1:350.

359. Betz, *Der Apostel Paulus und die sokratische Tradition,* 98.

360. Fitzgerald, *Cracks in an Earthen Vessel,* 3.

361. Ibid., 37.

the sage does not depend on material prosperity.[362] Hence, in contrast to "boasting" in his philosophical writing, Epictetus writes: "bring on hardships, bring on imprisonment, bring on disrepute, bring on condemnation. This is the proper exhibition . . ." (*Diss.* 2.1.35). As a Stoic thinker contemporary with Paul, Seneca writes of the tortures, burnings, and deaths under Gaius, and of his willingness to die for loyalty (Seneca, *Quaestiones Naturales* 4A, Preface to 14-17; cf. *Letters* 9.8.10; 85.29).[363] Here "self-praise" for "achievements" is regarded as *offensive;* but "self-praise" for endurance amidst bad fortune is *encouraged.*

Fitzgerald sees the catalogues in 1 Cor 4:9-13 as arising from Paul *"admonitions"* in 4:6 and 4:14 as a father responding to "arrogance" on the part of his children.[364] They imagine themselves "wise" (3:18; 4:10), but even in the eyes of the educated Cynic-Stoic rhetorician and philosopher there is an impropriety about claims to wisdom which are associated with comfort, complacency, or lack of proven endurance amidst trials. Hence Paul's list of trials support a claim to "wisdom" more impressively than the claims made at Corinth even on the basis of their own hellenistic traditions.[365] Hence Paul borrows the rhetoric of the hellenistic sage to make the point. **Working with their own hands** (4:11-12) on this basis becomes a "hardship" in the face of which Paul shows his qualities as a *wise* person. By contrast, the Corinthians claim the Stoic quality of **reigning** (4:8) and regard the apostles as **weak** and as **fools** (4:10) and as not sharing in the **reigning-as-kings**, when there is nothing about their lifestyle to substantiate such claims, but rather the reverse, even by Stoic-Cynic standards.[366] The wise man is the "suffering sage."[367] "Power" manifests itself in adversity.[368] In Fitzgerald's view Paul's entire rhetoric in 4:8-13 reflects "the traditions about the sage."[369]

(ii) Karl Plank sheds a different light on this passage. Where Fitzgerald speaks of *admonition,* Plank speaks of *accusation,* although equally here in relation to 2 Corinthians 10–13, as well as 1 Corinthians 1–4. The language of 1 Cor 4:4 relates to judgment and to acquittal.[370] Paul concedes certain forms of **weakness** on his own part (2:1-5) coupled with humiliation and affliction (4:9-13), and it is the charge of "weakness" to which Paul wishes to reply.[371] For Paul, however, power (δύναμις) suggests not authoritarian self-assertion but "the *efficacy* of a word, its capacity to have consequence for those who speak and hear it, and may also point to its divine *backing*" (both Plank's italics).[372] Hence it is the proclamation of *the cross* that reveals *power,* whether or not the mode of communication appears to some as *weak.* The word was not "empty." Here *calling* occupies an important place in determining the power character of the speech.[373] The definitions of Paul and the Corinthians concerning

362. Ibid., 112.
363. Further examples occur in Fitzgerald, *Cracks in an Earthen Vessel,* 113-14.
364. Ibid., 117-18; cf. 204.
365. Ibid., 120-36.
366. Ibid., 135-48.
367. Ibid., 203.
368. Ibid., 205.
369. Ibid., 207.
370. Plank, *Paul and the Irony of Affliction,* 13.
371. Ibid., 14-17.
372. Ibid., 18.
373. Ibid., 25.

"power" and "weakness" differ because of what Bartchy and Plank call "different ways of apprehending reality."[374] We endorsed this approach and developed it further in our commentary on 1:18–2:5 above, as well as on 3:18–4:5.

In 4:8-13, Plank argues, "living it up in glory" is no sign of "power"; for it is "before the time" (4:5). Hence Paul embarks on a "rhetoric of irony" in these verses. The situation is one of *paradox;* but a paradox which reflects those of 1:18-25 and 2:1-5. This paves the way for irony which rests also on an "unexpected co-existence, to the point of identity, of certain contrasts."[375] Irony states *both* what it *appears* to be *and* what it is *not*. Hence it *destabilizes* assumptions about reality. With Kierkegaard, we must distinguish irony from dissemblance. Irony, as Kierkegaard insisted, aims to unmask the real or genuine; dissimulation covers the genuine with a veneer of illusion. In this light Plank sets in contrasts the *unreality* of the Corinthian claims to be **wise**, to **reign as kings**, to have **become rich** (v. 8), and to regard Paul as **disgraced** or at least as **weak** (v. 10). Paul has already shown in 1:26-31 that there were "not many wise" . . . (1:26) but that God chose "the nothings" (1:28) and **the weak** (1:27) to make them "something" (1:27-28). Paul therefore employs both dissimulative irony to unmask pretense and paradoxical irony to restore contact with reality in 4:8-13.[376] Can the addressees really be wealthy monarchs, while the apostles are "scum" living under a death writ?

Here Plank begins to draw constructively on Wolfgang Iser's reader-response theory. The readers have to resolve the tension for themselves, and this very act deconstructs their prior attitudes and projects more appropriate "worlds" of values. Paul adds to the effect by heightening each side of the tensions with "corroborative texts" (1:4-9, they have been enriched; 2:1-4, Paul was "weak"; and 3:21-22 "all are yours") and "conflicting texts" (1:26, "not many influential, of good status"; and 2:4-7, "we do communicate a wisdom among the mature").[377] In Iser's terminology "the conflicting texts create a 'blank' — a break in connections . . . that the readers must fill in their reading."[378] Unlike Fitzgerald, however, Plank rightly relates this to the theological paradox of the cross (1:18-25), namely, that power (δύναμις) emerges from a crucified Christ (1:24) who remains to many a σκάνδαλον, or *disruption,* and μωρίαν, **folly** (1:23).[379]

(iii) This last point brings us precisely to the constructive work of Schrage and Kleinknecht. Kleinknecht interprets the sufferings of the righteous as connected with the inauguration of the kingdom of God in Jewish apocalyptic discourse. Paul develops this in terms of identification with the afflictions of Jesus as the righteous one who is crucified. Christ's rejection as one "dishonored" or "disgraced" by the shame of the cross colors Paul's language in 4:8-13.[380] Schrage similarly perceives this as an issue of identification and fellowship with the crucified Christ. He compares Paul's language in Gal 6:17 about "bearing the marks *(stigmata)* of the crucified One in his own body" (cf. 2 Cor 4:10, also).[381] Like Schweitzer, Schrage links it

---

374. Ibid., 27.
375. Ibid., 40 (with reference to W. Lynch).
376. Ibid., 48-52.
377. Ibid., 48.
378. Ibid., 52.
379. Ibid., 57.
380. Kleinknecht, *Der leidende Gerechtfertigte,* 221-41.
381. Schrage, "Leid, Kreuz und Eschaton. Die Peristasenkataloge als Merkmale paulinischer theologia crucis und Eschatologie," 141-75.

with the afflictions of the righteous in apocalyptic (*2 Enoch* 66:6; *Jubilees* 23:13; 1QH 9; cf. Rom 8:36).

Schrage does not reject the possible relevance of Stoic imagery, which may serve as a theme or *topos* common with his readers and their hellenistic, Roman, and Jewish backgrounds. Nevertheless, "the theme is the reflection of the cross, not heroic autonomy."[382] Here lies the basis of the juxtaposition of δύναμις and ζωή as the manifestation of Christ's resurrection with the present condition of sharing in the cosmic tribulation which finds its focus in the work of Christ. This cosmic dimension explains the phrase "a spectacle to the world and to angels" as well as humankind (4:9).[383] A further support for the approach of Schrage and Kleinknecht comes from Scott J. Hafemann, who perceives 4:10-13 as closely cohering with 2 Cor 1:9 and 2 Cor 2:14-3:3 as a focus of "dying with Christ." He rightly sees 1 Cor 1:10-4:21 as "the *locus classicus* of the Pauline theology of the cross" as "a theological criterion."[384] He agrees with Kleinknecht that in this respect 4:8-13 is the "high point" of the epistle.[385]

We find the arguments of Schrage wholly convincing, and view the work of Plank, Kleinknecht, and Ferrari as useful supplements. Within this theological frame, and only within it, Fitzgerald's work adds a further explanatory dimension concerning the special force of his rhetoric for those at Corinth who prized their Graeco-Roman cultural tradition. However, the foundation of the cross remains the key here, and on this basis, and only on this basis, Plank's explanation of irony in Kierkegaard and the role of the reader in Iser shed further valuable light in Paul's strategy of argumentation. At the center of the stage, however, remains what Schrage alludes to in the sense of Luther's *Heidelberg Disputation,* namely, the contrast between a Corinthian *theologia gloriae,* centered on experiences, beliefs, and the church, and Paul's *theologia crucis,* centered on the cross and on Christ.

14 The square brackets of the UBS 4th ed. in νουθετῶ[ν] (v. 4) indicate a difficult balance of MS readings between νουθετῶ (𝔭46, B, D, F, G, and Vulgate) and νουθετῶν (probable reconstruction of 𝔭11, ℵ, C, 33). The participle *warning,* νουθετῶν, is more probable, since the ν may well have become omitted or obscured (especially if a MS suffered wear or damage). Perhaps the only strong argument for the reverse conclusion is the maxim that the more difficult reading may be the more probable one. But this does not always apply. Hence the text uses brackets. The issue is not one of substance.

I recall translating 4:8-14 in my undergraduate student days, and thinking that if vv. 8-13 did not *shame* the readers, what could? But Paul means, as Plank insists, that his irony is to achieve *realism, not low self-esteem.* Hence, as Plank notes, texts of corroboration and texts of conflict *together* express the "now" and "not yet" of eschatological fulfillment, together with a parallel dialectic between the principle of the cross as a critique and the resurrection as a promise.

382. Schrage, *Der erste Brief,* 1:342.
383. Ibid.
384. Hafemann, *Suffering and the Spirit: An Exegetical Study of II Cor. 2:14–3:3 within the Corinthian Correspondence,* 58.
385. Ibid., 60.

Thus Paul characteristically performs *illocutionary* speech-acts of **warning** (νουθετῶν; cf. 1 Thess 5:12, 14; Rom 15:14; Col 1:28–3:16) in contrast to *perlocutionary* speech-acts of **bringing shame to** his addressees. He does not intend *causally* to demolish their self-respect by mere epideictic rhetoric alone, but to convey acts of warning on the basis of a personal and institutional relationship to the believers as their spiritual father and apostle.

Since he genuinely loves them (ἀγαπητά, *beloved,* or in more suitable current English idiom, **dearly loved**), Paul wants their well-being, not to crush them with self-recrimination or **shame** (ἐντρέπων). This issue is all the more sensitive and intelligible when we recall that the Corinthians lived "within an honor-shame cultural orientation, where public recognition was important"; many were "status-hungry people."[386] "The Corinthians were competing for status."[387] Paul does not wish simply to remove all status, but to redefine what counts as status in terms of glorying in the cross, glorying in the Lord, and perceiving "slavery as salvation," i.e., the honor of being accounted worthy to suffer hardships in the service of their Lord.[388] This "redefinition" is described by John Moores as a readjustment of the presuppositions of the *enthymemes* (implicit, open-ended, incomplete premises) of Paul's arguments or a switch of the *"code"* which generates new meaning through the same words.[389] *The argument up to 4:13 has given them all the material they need to reappraise in what true "wisdom" and true "status" consists.*

The phrase ὡς τέκνα μου, **as my children,** used to read at face value in commentaries up to around 1990. Parental love sometimes entails the unpleasant task of correction for the good of the child, but this is a sign not of indifference but of concern, care, and responsible love. Strangers and even grandparents can afford to be more relaxed about "training"; but parents have to suffer the recriminatory outbursts which sometimes accompany the imposition of discipline, which they enjoy no more than the child. Indulgent parents show a less responsible, less long-term love than those who are consistent in correction and affirming support. However, in recent years Paul has been accused of using the parent-child imagery for manipulative purposes, for self-interest, or at very least in a "paternalist" way. E. A. Castelli explores some of these issues, and they will be better considered in relation to vv. 15-16 (see below).

15-16   The Greek syntax and vocabulary is entirely clear on its own terms, but invites some restructuring if the force and content is to be retained idiomatically in English today. The protasis is introduced by ἐάν, followed by the present subjunctive to signify an indefinite or unfulfilled hypothesis, *for if you may perhaps have . . . ,* which expects a future verb in the apodosis which Paul never states. Most English VSS therefore supply a second *have* in the

---

386. Witherington, *Conflict and Community,* 8 and 24; cf. Pogoloff, *Logos and Sophia,* 196-236, and other literature cited on the honor-shame theme.

387. Pogoloff, *Logos and Sophia,* 203.

388. Martin, *Slavery as Salvation,* 122-23; cf. 50-68.

389. Moores, *Wrestling with Rationality in Paul,* 21-32.

apodosis, and use some device to indicate that the hypothesis is unfulfilled. NIV and NRSV render, *For though you might have ten thousand guardians in Christ, you do not have many fathers,* and NJB also uses *though* and *might* as against the Greek *if.* But once we change the conditional structure *(if)* into a concessive *(though),* it seems preferable to convey the unfulfilled hypothesis as two contrasting statements: **You might have . . . thousands . . . , but . . .** μυρίους strictly means *ten thousand,* but is regularly used for the highest imaginable number, and is equivalent to **thousands of** (in this context) or *millions of,* e.g., in apocalyptic or cosmic contexts. (Ten thousand times ten thousand [Rev 9:16] is a primitive logarithmic "to the power of . . . ," to indicate enormous numbers; just as to forgive "seven times seven" also means "on and on.") In the ancient Graeco-Roman world παιδαγωγός had a definite social meaning and function. This person was usually a *slave* or *paid attendant* who accompanied *the child* (τέκνον, v. 14) for the purpose of protection, guidance, and general supervision of behavior, e.g., to or from school, or on occasions when a parent was absent. The main function was as *guardian,* teacher, and corrector, but the motivation of the παιδαγωγός would be either one of paid duty or one of obedience to the instructions of the slave's master, not love for the child. English does not have a noun for *corrector,* and *supervisor* conveys a different idea. Various VSS choose *tutors* (REB), guardians (NRSV/RSV), *instructors* (AV/KJV), or *slaves to look after you* (NJB), to which BAGD add *attendants* and *custodians.* But in this context the metaphor is already halfway toward being applied by Paul; hence we propose **thousands of people in Christ to correct you,** i.e., they may all *correct* you, but if we do it, it is entirely out of parental love. In intertextual terms, within the canon this resonates with the contrast in the Fourth Gospel between "the good shepherd" who lays down his life for the sheep and the "hired help" who has a different stake in the matter (John 10:11-14).

Three phrases have already been discussed at length. On ἐν Χριστῷ see on 1:30. Its semantic range varies (cf., e.g., 1 Cor 1:2, 4, 30; 3:1; 4:10). The first occurrence in 4:15 probably means *with reference to your life as Christians,* or perhaps *thousands of Christian people;* but the second occurrence in v. 15 probably has the deeper theological meaning of *in union with Christ.* However, since this depends on an exegetical judgment, our translation preserves the open-endedness of the Greek, i.e., **in Christ.** The meaning of παρακαλῶ is of critical importance, and we provided a detailed full-length discussion of the issues above (see note on 1:10). The noun εὐαγγελίον (see on 1:17) needs to be rendered in a verbal mode (**through proclaiming the gospel**) because in this context the reference to Paul's agency as one who brought life to the addressees means *through the gospel-as-proclaimed,* i.e., in the event of Paul's preaching and speaking.

A further lexical comment concerns μιμηταί, often translated *imitators* (NRSV, ASV, Louw and Nida), or *followers* (AV/KJV). REB translates *to follow my example;* NIV, *to imitate;* NJB, *to take me as your pattern.* But while the noun μιμητής and the verb μιμέομαι can indeed mean *imitator* or *to imitate*, these forms also convey a broader, less mechanical meaning, in the sense of *emulate, follow,* or *use as a model.* Moreover, Michaelis (partly supported by W. de Boer and B. Fiore) argues that in contexts such as these in related literature an added dimension of *oversight* is implicit in this use of the noun or verb.[390] Paul's thrust is in part *by your conduct prove your parentage.*[391] If we combine these two insights with other lexical research, the translation which comes perhaps nearest to conveying the nuance of the Greek-in-context is **take your cue from me**. In the light of Kleinknecht and Plank's remarks on 4:8-13, Paul's concern is that the Corinthians' lifestyle should reflect the having-died-with-Christ experience which is demonstrated in the lifestyle of authentic apostles. It is not simply "do as I say," but "do as I do"; but this does not entail wooden "imitation" in every detail of life, as the rest of the epistle shows. On the question of food offered to idols, e.g., there is scope for variation.

MIMESIS AND ALLEGED PATERNAL AUTHORITARIANISM (4:15-16)

We encounter a serious problem about "paternalism" and authoritarianism in 4:16, according to Elizabeth A. Castelli, in her study *Imitating Paul*. We must read this verse, she urges, "in cultural context, that is, in relationship to the nature of the paternal role in Graeco-Roman society — which is a role of possessing total authority over children."[392] Castelli puts forward four main concerns or arguments, among others:

(i) The paternal metaphor becomes especially authoritarian and "political" when it is used in conjunction with a call to *mimesis.* "In relation to mimetic language [it] evokes authority."[393]

(ii) Further, the fact that there is little specificity about the content of the *mimesis* signals not, as de Boer claims, Paul's gentleness, but rather the reverse: it is concerned with imposing a uniform social structure upon a diversified, pluralist community.[394]

(iii) Paul uses a rhetorical strategy which has the effect (whether or not this was the overt intention) of manipulation. For simultaneously Paul claims privilege as the only "father"; while also claiming to step back from personal claims to do all in the name of Christ. Castelli notes in particular 1:17, "Christ did not send me to baptize but to proclaim the gospel . . . lest the cross should be emptied of its power," and describes the simultaneous assertion of authority and self-effacement as "a clever rhetorical strategy."[395]

---

390. Michaelis, "μιμέομαι," *TDNT,* 4:668-69; cf. 659-74. Further, BAGD, 521-22; Willis de Boer, *Imitation of Paul: An Exegetical Study* (Kampen: Kok, 1962); Fiore, *The Function of Personal Example in the Socratic and Pastoral Epistles;* and Castelli, *Imitating Paul: A Discussion of Power,* 97-111; cf. 139 and 142.

391. Cf. Robertson and Plummer, *First Epistle,* 90.

392. Castelli, *Imitating Paul,* 101.

393. Ibid., 111; also 99, 101, 107-10.

394. Ibid., 109-10.

395. Ibid., 99.

(iv) In relation to twentieth-century thought this resonates with Michel Foucault's analysis of what masquerade as claims to truth but serve in reality as bids for power. These are all the more subtle when they appear to relate to benign institutional "order."[396] Foucault speaks of the power of the smiling face in the white coat especially in prisons and in hospitals. Might not Paul's appeal to institutional well-being as "order," including the hierarchy of the family headed by the father, perform the same function? Castelli concedes that Paul may or may not himself be fully aware of this strategy, but concludes that his rhetoric of mimesis has this effect.[397]

I have addressed such problems elsewhere, including a discussion of Foucault.[398] We cannot doubt that Paul has a more positive attitude toward "order" and institutional cohesion than the more freelance, egalitarian "freedoms" demanded at Corinth. He does indeed want "to hold together" a corporate Christian identity founded on the death and resurrection of Christ, which applies Christ and the cross as a *criterion and critique* of freelance claims to be "spiritual persons," or "people of the Spirit."[399] But he seeks neither uniformity, nor self-interest, nor any desire to exercise authority apart from the wider network of apostles and co-workers who not only hold together individual Christians within one local community, but also a range of local communities as the one people of God in Christ.

The problem has an entirely contemporary ring in the twentieth century. Is the local church a loose federation of self-styled "spiritual people," or does it derive its identity from a common reality identified by the cross as criterion? Is the wider church no more than a loose federation of *independent* congregations, or does some larger corporate identity permit an appeal to an adherence to traditions "everywhere in every church" (4:17), or observed "in all the churches" (ἐν ταῖς ἐκκλησίαις πάσαις, 7:17, and similar wording in 14:33). As we shall note in connection with the next verse, Paul lays the foundation for a shared corporate identity which later became known in dogmatic or systematic theology as the four "marks" of the church: as universal (i.e., catholic), apostolic, holy, and one.

This "oneness," however, is not *sameness*. Castelli argues, "By promoting the value of sameness, he [Paul] is also shaping relations of power."[400] In 12:15 Paul declares, concerning his image of the church as Christ's body, "The foot does not say to the hand, 'Because I am not a hand, I do not belong to the body' — that would not make it any less a part of the body" (cf. 12:14-25). Paul promotes a diversity of "gifts, ministries, works . . . infinitely various," as against a "single-cell organism . . . the lowest form of life."[401] He certainly does not endorse the claims of any so-called "Paul group" (1:10-12) and is entirely nondefensive and positive about encouraging an imminent visit from Apollos (see 16:12 and exegesis of this verse).

Castelli overlooks the heart of the issue identified by Senft and by Schrage as a

---

396. Ibid., 35-58.

397. Ibid., 116-17; cf. 30-33, 57-58, and 89-136.

398. Thiselton, *Interpreting God and the Postmodern Self: On Meaning, Manipulation and Promise* (Edinburgh: T. & T. Clark and Grand Rapids: Eerdmans, 1995), 3-45 and 121-64.

399. On ἔξεστιν and ἐξουσία as a claim to "autonomy" or "rights to act as I will," see on 6:12 and 10:23, including Wire's *defense* of this slogan *against* Paul in *The Corinthian Women Prophets* under 6:12, below).

400. Castelli, *Imitating Paul*, 97, 111, and 119.

401. Deluz, *Companion to 1 Cor*, 172.

manner of life which "accords with the crucified Christ."[402] We shall consider this further in connection with the next verse, where we also note W. D. Spencer's convincing argument that Paul's "catalogue of afflictions" (4:9-13), cruciform lifestyle (4:14-17), and costly discipleship (4:18-21) are all of one piece (see under v. 17).[403] Further, Castelli's argument about the indeterminate content of *mimesis* overlooks the research article of Boykin Sanders, which she mentions but does not appear adequately to address, in which he argues that its content derives from all that Paul has said about his role as *servant,* and as *estate manager* who cannot act on his own behalf.[404] If Foucault replies that even "service" can play on manipulative obligation, this simply excludes altruism of any kind and underlines a theology of fallenness.

Paul places his own ministry under the critique and judgment of the cross, no less than that of other ministers and the "groups" and the congregation. Far from defending a "Pauline" group, he calls attention away from *all* leaders and groups with "let no one boast of human beings" (3:21).[405] In short, Castelli's arguments neither engage fully with the detailed exegetical evidence of 1:10–4:21, nor with philosophical and theological questions about manipulation, power, and truth of the kind which emerge in philosophical critiques of Foucault.[406] *Power,* we see repeatedly in these verses, has to do with the *effectiveness* of the gospel in life, not, within the world of the cross, with rhetorical manipulation. Paul's choice of low social status as an artisan turns *power* on its head. Jesus so clearly renounced "glory" that Castelli's view of power would constitute a self-contradictory understanding of *the gospel of Christ crucified.* Both biblical and sociological traditions permit distinctions between *power over* (the possibility of domination) and *power for* (the possibility of resource and transformation).[407]

17 (1) p[46], ℵ, C, syr, and 33 read Χριστῷ ᾿Ιησοῦ, **Christ Jesus,** while A, B, and sah read Χριστῷ, **Christ,** alone. The Western D, G, follow a secondary variant κυρίῳ ᾿Ιησοῦ, which is clearly a scribal corruption, influenced by the previous κυρίῳ. Zuntz, Conzelmann, Barrett, and Schrage, probably rightly, read Χριστῷ ᾿Ιησοῦ, while Allo, Metzger, and Fee see an equal case for the shorter Χριστῷ alone.[408] Often the shorter reading is preferable, but the MS evidence favors including ᾿Ιησοῦ. (2) Some Alexandrian readings, p[11], the first hand of ℵ and 33, include αὐτό after τοῦτο to read **for this** *very* **reason,** but there are inadequate textual or stylistic grounds for its support.

402. Senft, *Première Épitre,* 70; Schrage, *Der erste Brief,* 1:358.

403. W. D. Spencer, "The Power in Paul's Teaching (1 Cor 4:9-20)," 51-61.

404. B. Sanders, "Imitating Paul: 1 Cor 4:16," 354; cf. 353-63.

405. Ibid., 356; Sanders rightly associates this with the catalogue in 4:9-13, including "working with our own hands," 362-63.

406. See J. Baudrillard, *Forget Foucault* (New York: Columbia University Press, 1987); and Thiselton, *Interpreting God and the Postmodern Self,* 12-16, 21, 105-7, 125-34, and 140-47, where the role of the cross as critique is also explored (22-25, 89, 100, and 142-49). On the exegetical aspects see also Clarke, *Secular and Christian Leadership at Corinth,* 122-27. See further C. F. Hinze, *Comprehending Power in Christian Social Ethics,* AARAS 93 (Atlanta: Scholars Press, 1995), esp. 108-45 (Foucault and Arendt).

407. See esp. Hinze, *Comprehending Power* (above), and the Johannine tradition.

408. Allo, *Première Épitre,* 78; Fee, *First Epistle,* 183, n. 6; Zuntz, *Text,* 181; Conzelmann, *1 Corinthians,* 92; Metzger, *Textual Commentary* (2d ed.), 484.

For this reason (διά, *on account of,* with accusative) explains the grounds on which he has sent Timothy to Corinth. These grounds are not that Paul is their father (as Chrysostom and Theophylact interpret the phrase), but that he wants the flesh-and-blood presence of Timothy to instantiate in their presence the flesh-and-blood living out of the gospel of the cross which equally **will bring to your mind** Paul's own **patterns of life**. Almost every word in the first half of the verse sheds light on the rest. As **my very dear child, Timothy** both instantiates the discipleship of someone whom Paul's ministry has brought to faith (in this sense he is μου τέκνον ἀγαπητόν, **my very dear child**) but will also prove himself *faithful* or **trustworthy** as a living exemplification of the gospel lifestyle. Hence it is not simply, or perhaps even primarily, the **he will bring to your mind** (ἀναμνήσει) by intellectual teaching, but by his own very stance and conduct. Arguably this accords with the understanding of ἀναμιμνήσκω as being something more than merely subjective, mental recollection: **to bring to mind** has a more objective nuance. The word ἀνάμνησις is discussed in 11:24 (see below on these complex issues of semantics and theology, as well as the Hebrew background).

The phrase translated **the patterns of life which I live in Christ Jesus** cannot be conveyed by rendering τὰς ὁδούς μου τὰς ἐν Χριστῷ ['Ιησοῦ] simply as *my ways in Christ Jesus*. Many point to the use of the noun ὁδοί to denote an equivalent to the rabbinic *halakhah, walking*. These writers rightly insist that their word conveys a dimension of *moral standards* which the Greek alone, without its Hebrew-Christian biblical background, would fail to convey. A whole corpus of literature makes this point.[409] Thus W. D. Spencer rightly links the contrast between talking and living which follows (4:19) with this present appeal in vv. 15-17 with a lifestyle or **pattern of life** which reflects the reality of the sufferings of the cross and of all that is seen **in Christ Jesus**. Paul remonstrates with those who merely "talk" rather than live out the gospel **pattern of life in Christ Jesus**. The "catalogue of sufferings" (4:9-13), the *mimesis* of Paul's **pattern of life** (vv. 15-17), and the realities of costly discipleship (vv. 18-21) are all of a piece.[410]

The aorist ἔπεμψα, **I sent**, has invited discussion about whether (i) this represents an *epistolary aorist,* i.e., *I am sending* **Timothy** (NRSV mg., NIV) as bearer of this letter (e.g., Conzelmann on the basis of 16:10); or whether (ii) it implies that he had already sent him to Corinth before the letter was written or completed; or whether (iii) Paul has required Timothy to include Corinth among a list of visits for which he had already departed from Ephesus (trans. as

---

409. Schrage, *Die konkreten Einzelgebote in der paulinischen Paränese,* esp. 32-33; Sanders, "Imitating Paul: 1 Cor 4:16," 353-63; Betz, *Nachfolge und Nachahmung Jesu Christi im NT,* 153-59; Spencer, "The Power in Paul's Teaching (1 Cor 4:9-20)," 51-61; Stanley, "Become Imitators of Me," 859-77; and many other sources, including Willis de Boer and Ben Fiore (cited above). On further literature cf. Schrage, *Der erste Brief,* 1:359, n. 280.

410. Spencer, "The Power in Paul's Teaching." See further Schrage, *Der erste Brief,* 1:357-61.

aorist in NRSV, NJB, REB).[411] Barrett regards the epistolary aorist as the least likely since Paul does allude to Timothy at the beginning of the epistle.[412] Moreover, a further difficulty is raised by 16:10: *if* (ἐάν) *Timothy comes* (ἔλθῃ, aorist subjunctive), *see that . . .* , which appears to suggest doubt about whether he will arrive. Either this gives some ground for partition theories of a composite letter, or, more probably, Barrett is right to favor the possibility that Paul has sent Timothy to several destinations, with the hope, but not the certainty, that these will allow time for him to include Corinth.[413] The one remaining possibility is to interpret ἔπεμψα here to mean *I have sent word to Timothy* (who may already be on a different mission in Macedonia). This seems a less probable meaning. These issues are discussed more fully under 16:10, where we also stress Paul's regular pattern of collaborative ministry with a network of co-workers, as well as further discussion of **Timothy**.[414]

According to Funk, Paul used "a consistent pattern" for preparing his communities for his apostolic presence, for which letters and emissaries were merely stopgap substitutes. "In ascending order of significance" Paul speaks of (i) his writing; (ii) his sending of an emissary to represent him; and (iii) his own arrival, coming, or presence *(parousia)* "as the primary medium by which he makes his apostolic authority effective."[415] When he speaks of his emissary Paul uses precisely the formula which occurs in 1 Cor 4:7: (a) for this reason ἔπεμψα ὑμῖν Τιμόθεον *(introductory clause);* (b) my dearly loved child, trustworthy . . . *(credentials clause);* (c) to bring to your mind the pattern of life which I live . . . *(purpose clause).*[416] The very same structure, Funk observes, occurs in 1 Thess 2:2-3 and in Phil 2:25-30, and a modified parallel in 2 Cor 9:3-5 (which omits clause b) and 2 Cor 8:18-23 (which omits clause c, but emphasizes b). Larger contexts concerning the apostolic *parousia* yield parallel features in Rom 1:8-13; 15:14-33; Philem 21-22; 1 Cor 4:14-21; 16:1-11; 2 Cor 8:16-23; 9:1-5; 12:14–13:13; 1 Thess 2:17–3:13; and Phil 2:25-30.[417]

καθὼς πανταχοῦ ἐν πάσῃ ἐκκλησίᾳ, **even as everywhere in every congregation** is not simply an authoritarian bid for regimentation (as Castelli argues), but an assurance that Paul will not require more from Corinth than that which identifies any or every community as *Christian.*[418] All, however, are *ap-*

411. Conzelmann, *1 Corinthians,* 92, n. 19.
412. Barrett, *First Epistle,* 116.
413. Barrett, *First Epistle,* 116 and 390. See also Collins, *First Cor,* 596; Fee, *First Epistle,* 821; Murphy-O'Connor, *Paul,* 292-93, esp. on 16:10.
414. Cf. E. E. Ellis, "Coworkers," *DPL,* 183-89; W. H. Ollrog, *Paulus und seine Mitarbeiter* (Neukirchen: Neukirchener, 1979); D. J. Harrington, "Paul and Collaborative Ministry," *New Theology Review* 3 (1990): 62-71; F. F. Bruce, *The Pauline Circle* (Exeter: Paternoster, 1985).
415. Funk, "The Apostolic *Parousia:* Form and Significance," in W. R. Farmer, C. F. D. Moule, and R. Niebuhr (eds.), *Christian History and Interpretation,* 258; cf. 248-68, esp. 251-53.
416. Ibid., 255.
417. Ibid., 253-54, where Funk proposes thirteen parallel structures.
418. Robertson and Plummer, *First Epistle,* 91.

ostolic, catholic, holy, and *one* in coherent corporate identity. As Calvin comments, the issue is one of *consistency*.[419] This is not to be confused with Castelli's "sameness," although she rightly perceives this as entailing "order."

18-19 As though (ὡς, *as*) introduces a negated (μή), unfulfilled genitive absolute, in which the subject is expressed in the genitive (μου) in apposition to the genitive singular masculine present participle of ἔρχομαι, **as though I were not coming to you**. The aorist passive of φυσιόω, *I puff up, I blow up* with *wind* or *air*, **I inflate**, serves as an ingressive aorist. If the meaning is that on hearing that Timothy, rather than Paul, is likely to visit to Corinth (v. 17), their self-importance and arrogance at once receives a boost, the best translation is **some have begun to be inflated**. If the reference is more generally to the arrogant stance of those who have puffed themselves up with self-importance, a better translation would be, *some have come to be inflated.* Since *being blown up with air* was a more familiar metaphor for arrogant self-importance in the first century than today, a translation probably needs to make explicit what was without question implicit in the well-known metaphor, i.e., **inflated with arrogance** or **inflated** *with self-importance.*

A rude shock now confronts any who were congratulating themselves that they would not need to meet Paul face to face.[420] In fact Paul **will come** *speedily* or **soon** (ταχέως). We have argued on each occasion hitherto in this epistle when Paul uses δύναμις, *power,* that when applied to God, to Christ, or to the gospel the word carries the meaning of valid effects (1:18, of God; 1:24, of Christ; 2:4, of the gospel; 2:5, of God) although the single use of the adjective δυνατοί in 1:26 means having *social effects,* or *influence,* i.e., *influential.* While other meanings do occur later in the epistle, whenever the contrast is with "mere speech" the emphasis lies on *effectiveness in life* as against mere rhetoric, and when the semantic opposition is that of *wind, air, gas bags,* or being **inflated** with these, δύναμις represents *solidarity* or *substance.* In the Hebrew Bible הֶבֶל *(hebel)* means *vapor, breath, vanity, empty air,* or *that which lacks substance.* It applies to wealth gained by deceit rather than solid work (Prov 13:11; 21:6); to idols (Jer 10:15); or to the self-defeating existence of an empty life (Eccl 1:22; 12:8).[421] The term closely resembles the dismissive Yorkshire idiom "they're now't but wind," i.e., *without substance, mere takers who do nothing.* Paul's semantic contrast is similar. When he comes to Corinth, he **will discover** (γνώσομαι, future indicative of γινώσκω) whether those concerned are mere windbags who merely **talk** (τὸν λόγον) or whether these are

419. Calvin, *First Epistle,* 100.

420. It would go beyond the evidence of 16:10 to suggest that Timothy is "timid." The issue turns on the preference of some for a visit *from Apollos* (see 16:12) who refuses to come. See C. R. Hutson, "Was Timothy Timid?" *BR* 42 (1997): 58-73, discussed under 16:10-12.

421. This approach is substantiated, e.g., in Spencer, "The Power in Paul's Teaching," 51-61, where he rightly argues that Paul's "power" lies in his life of suffering and costly witness which reflects the character of Christ and of the cross in life and action, and with effect (see above on 4:16-17). Cf. Barth, *The Resurrection of the Dead,* 18 and 17-29.

solid effects that indicate **what they can do** (τὴν δύναμιν).⁴²² The point is not simply that of illusory size but also lack of solidity, as at 8:1 (love *builds up;* γνῶσις *puffs up*). When Paul arrives, some may find that their public esteem corresponds with that of burst balloons.

20 The translation of ἐν δυνάμει, almost universally rendered into English as *in, on,* or *of power* (NRSV, NIV, REB, NJB, AV/KJV), remains of critical importance. As it stands, the word may convey *power* in the sense ascribed to Paul by Castelli (see above), and postmodern thought readily perceives claims to truth in religion as bids for power. But here Schrage declares, *power* is neither manipulative nor (*pace* Chrysostom) miraculous, but derives its meaning from its contrast with λόγος, **talk.** Its central point is therefore *the ability to carry a deed through effectively (Durchschlagskraft),* or in other words an issue of **efficacy** *(efficacia).*⁴²³ Since the sentence contains no verb (Greek often understands ἐστιν), interpretative judgments are offered by the main translations, e.g., *depends on* (NRSV) or **is a matter of** (NIV and above).

The phrase **the kingdom of God** occurs relatively seldom in the Pauline corpus (1 Cor 4:20; 6:9, 10; 15:24, 50; cf. Rom 14:17; Gal 5:21; Col 1:13; 4:11; Eph 5:5, 2 Thess 1:5; 2 Tim 4:18). Most uses are eschatological (e.g., 1 Cor 6:9-10; 15:50), but Fee points out that the casual use of the term implies that it functioned as part of Paul's thinking.⁴²⁴ As is widely appreciated today (in contrast to late nineteenth-century works) **kingdom** refers in the Gospels to the active, dynamic *reigning* of God as sovereign, even if this reign is in part veiled until its consummation at the *parousia* and last judgment. It is tempting to translate βασιλεία as *reign,* but since the phrase is more characteristic of Jesus than of Paul, it may be best to leave its allusive resonance untouched for the modern reader. Chilton has shown on the basis of research into Targumic studies that *God's power* is at issue in Jesus' use of the term, and this may explain why Paul selects this phrase here.⁴²⁵ When he reaches Corinth, he wants to discover not whether this or that rhetoric prevails, but *what manifests the reality of God-in-Christ and his sovereign deeds.* This is precisely what Karl Barth identifies as the theme of 1:1–4:21. Everything rests on "the understanding or the failure to understand the three words, ἀπὸ τοῦ θεοῦ (from God). Unless everything deceives, that is the trend of Paul's utterance (1 Cor i–iv)."⁴²⁶

21 The verb of the main sentence, ἔλθω, functions as a *deliberative* sub-

422. BDBG, 210-11. The phrase **what they can do** corresponds to the REB.
423. Schrage, *Der erste Brief,* 1:362-63. Chrysostom, *1 Cor. Hom.,* 14:2, contrasts "the pomp of words" with "signs" which manifest "the power of the Spirit." But Schrage rejects this meaning, alluding, among other contextual factors, to the mode in which the Spirit becomes manifest in 2:4; cf. Edwards, *First Epistle,* 118. C. H. Powell speaks of "soteriological power" as the key to Pauline passages such as this, where the cross never stands far away (*The Biblical Concept of Power,* 117-29).
424. Fee, *First Epistle,* 192.
425. B. D. Chilton, *God in Strength: Jesus' Announcement of the Kingdom* (Sheffield: JSOT Press, 1987).
426. Barth, *The Resurrection of the Dead,* 29; the "three words" are from 4:5.

junctive, to be translated, **Am I to come?** (as NRSV, REB, NJB) rather than, *Shall I come?* (AV/KJV, NIV). (The simple future could have been used.) θέλετε may be rendered **prefer** (rather than wish) when two options are introduced by a deliberative subjunctive indicating reflection on a ranking of desires. ῥάβδος, *a staff, rod,* or **stick**, is not the *whip* of the hellenistic schoolmaster (NIV) but the "rod of correction" of OT and LXX traditions. Although normally ἐν with the dative would be likely to be instrumental, here it may well take up the Hebrew idiom which uses the prefix ‎ב‎ (*bᵉ*) *to describe the manner of Paul's coming, reflected in the translation with a* **stick** *or rod* **in my hand** (REB, NJB, and above).[427] Although πνεῦμα does not characteristically occur in Paul to denote a stance or frame of mind, such a use is not exceptional. In Gal 6:1 Paul uses the same phrase in a similar context of correction and restoration: καταρτίζετε τὸν τοιοῦτον ἐν πνεύματι πραΰτητος, *restore* or *heal such a person in a spirit of meekness,* i.e., *with a gentle spirit.*[428]

The allusion to **love,** ἀγάπη, does not entail an exclusive association with gentleness; sometimes correction springs equally from love: "The question is whether love is to be expressed in gentleness or in violence, and this will depend not on Paul's mood, but on the Corinthian response to his admonition (v. 14)."[429] Eva M. Lassen sheds further light on the role of this verse in the context of the father image in imperial Rome and its culture at Corinth. As a Roman colony, she argues, Corinth was less dominated by Greek democratic policies than many assume.[430] The figures of the emperor and of the father of the family were expected to admonish the communities for which they were responsible, but also to seek their welfare. The Corinthians would well understand the question: In which of these two ways am I to come as father?[431] Paul is eager to say that *he* does not *wish* for any confrontation, but if some persist in ignoring the entire argument of 1:10–4:21, they will have made a choice which will leave Paul with no choice.

A *warning* (an *illocutionary* speech-act) is not necessarily a *threat* (a *perlocution*). *Internal processes at Corinth* will determine whether or not his imminent visit will be from the start a happy one for all parties. The matter is in hands other than his, but he cannot let things drift; for that would be to shirk his assigned responsibilities for the welfare of the whole community. Paul is not one of those pastors who relish confrontation; quite the reverse is the case. Nevertheless, he will not allow moral cowardice to relieve him from

427. MacRory, *Epistles of St Paul to the Corinthians,* 60, as against Allo, *Première Épitre,* 80, who follows Robertson and Plummer, *First Epistle,* 92. On the other hand, Allo, and Robertson and Plummer, concede that LXX (e.g., 1 Sam 17:43) may use ἐν as a preposition of "accompaniment" in the phrase ἐν ῥάβδῳ, rather than as a preposition of instrument.

428. Weiss, *Der erste Korintherbrief,* 123.

429. Barrett, *First Epistle,* 119.

430. Lassen, "The Use of the Father Image in Imperial Propaganda and 1 Cor 4:14-21," 127-36.

431. Ibid., 134-36.

taking matters firmly in hand, if such has to be done. As a sensitive pastor, he is reluctant to bring matters to a head, but resolved to do so if there proves to be no other way forward. His appeal to the criterion of the cross is not part of a clever power strategy on his own behalf, but underlines his concern for the welfare of the entire community, and for the effective living out of the gospel principle at Corinth.

III. Moral Issues Which Demand a Clear-Cut Verdict (5:1–6:20)

Although we enter a new major section of this epistle, a link readily emerges with 1:10–4:21 because "the man who committed the act of πορνεία in ch. 5 has contributed to community divisiveness (5:2, 6)."[1] The issue of his expulsion might serve to restore unity, although it also raises questions about community boundaries. However surprising it may seem in our more cerebral age, Paul appears more ready to tolerate "a mixed church" which includes those who have doctrinal problems about the resurrection (15:33-35 is addressed to people within the congregation) than to allow persistent immorality of a notorious kind to compromise the corporate identity of the community (5:5, 7, 13).[2] Further, just as Mitchell identifies a continuing thread from 1 Corinthians 1–4 in terms of the welfare of the community and its unity, so Fee, followed by South, regards 5:1-13 and 6:1-20 as test cases for Paul's authority as it has been implicitly entailed in the allusions to apostleship, fatherhood, planting, coordinating building, and providing a model of cruciform gospel proclamation.[3] In an earlier study I argued for a third link, namely, between the "boasting" which was associated with "freedom from the law" and the realized eschatology of 4:5 and 8:13.[4] From a compositional point of view, various continuities of theme and argument emerge.

On the other hand, this chapter begins a second main block (or a third, if we count 1:1-9 as a block of material) or topic. Chapters 5 and 6 expound what for Paul constitute clear-cut moral and ethical issues. In this respect this main block stands in contrast to the material in 7:1–11:1, which no less concerns matters of ethics, but in the latter case "grey areas" where much depends on situations and circumstances. If 7:1–11:1 legitimate some form of "situation ethics," 5:1–6:20 demonstrate that certain moral principles stand above and beyond situational variables. Depending on the ethical content of the moral issue, therefore, Paul expounds *both* an absolutist ethic *and* a situational ethic. On the first he is unwilling to negotiate; on the second, negotiation, dialogue, and "what if . . . ?" remain all-important. and Paul combines a situational ethic with

---

1. Mitchell, *Rhetoric of Reconciliation,* 112.
2. Witherington, *Conflict and Community,* 151-61.
3. Fee, *First Epistle,* 194-96; and South, *Disciplinary Practices in Pauline Texts,* 25-26.
4. Thiselton, "The Meaning of Σάρξ in 1 Cor. 5:5: A Fresh Approach," 204-28.

pastoral judgment and sensitivity to variations between different cases and case studies.

A. A CASE FOR MORAL DISCIPLINE (5:1-13)

The details of the sexual relationship which Paul regards as not merely immoral but particularly outrageous are considered in the exegesis below. Recent writers have treated the issue in a number of different ways, but interest has shifted from a multiplicity of research articles about excommunication and "the destruction of the σάρξ" (5:5) to reasons for the complacency, smugness, or *arrogance* (πεφυσιωμένοι ἐστε, 5:2) of the community (cf. also καύχημα, *boasting, glorying,* 5:6). Paul condemns this, hardly less than the immorality itself. Hypotheses abound. Dale Martin relates the matter to "invasive" notions of the impurity of the body corporate, with reference to theories of medicine and disease in the ancient world (see bibliography and below). John K. Chow and Andrew Clarke argue that the issue turns on the community's sense of obligations to a wealthy patron whom they felt that they should not antagonize, and whose immoral relationship may perhaps have diverted wealth from the wider family of his parents to himself, of which members of the church may have become indirect beneficiaries thereby. Witherington perceives the issues as turning on a dialectic of Spirit and order, in which the purity of the group must be maintained within relative limits, where the man in question had gone "beyond all bounds." There is force in all of these proposals, including my earlier argument that a sense of "freedom from the law" played a part, if not the whole part. The issue of community boundaries and of the dialectic between a "mixed" church and church discipline as a condition for the corporate identity of the church as Christ's body remains as relevant today as ever it was, as can also be perceived in the history of interpretation. How do they retain a corporate identity as God's holy temple (3:16) and Christ's body (12:27) without manifesting an exclusiveness not characteristic of Christ's own identity?

Bibliography on 5:1-13

Bammel, E., "Rechtsfindung in Korinth," *ETL* 83 (1997): 107-13.

Cambier, J., "La Chair et l'Esprit en 1 Cor. 5:5," *NTS* 15 (1968-69): 221-32.

Campbell, B., "Flesh and Spirit in 1 Cor. 5:5: An Exercise in Rhetorical Criticism of the NT," *JETS* 36 (1993): 331-42.

Chow, J. K., *Patronage and Power: A Study of Social Networks in Corinth,* JSNTSS 75 (Sheffield: Sheffield Academic Press, 1992): 130-41.

Clarke, A. D., *Secular and Christian Leadership at Corinth* (Leiden: Brill, 1993), 73-88.

Cole, G. A., "1 Cor. 5:4 'With My Spirit,'" *ExpTim* 98 (1987): 205.

Collins, A. Y., "The Function of 'Excommunication' in Paul," *HTR* 73 (1980): 251-63.

Déaut, R. le, "Paques et vie nouvelle (1 Cor. 5)," *Assemblées du Seigneur* 22 (1972): 34-44.

COMMENTARY ON 5:1-13

————, "The Paschal Mystery and Morality," *Doctrine and Life* 18 (1968): 262-69.

Derrett, J. D. M., "'Handing Over to Satan': An Explanation of 1 Cor. 5:1-7," in *Revue Internationale des Droits de l'Antiquité* 26 (1979): 11-30.

Fascher, E., "Zu Tertullians Auslegung von 1 Kor. 5:1-5 (*de pudicitia* c. 13-16)," *TLZ* 99 (1974): 9-12.

Forkman, G., *The Limits of the Religious Community* (Lund: Gleerup, 1972), 139-51.

Fowl, S. E., "Making Stealing Possible," in *Engaging Scripture* (Oxford: Blackwell, 1998).

Funk, R. W., "The Apostolic Presence," in *Parables and Presence* (Philadelphia: Fortress: 1982), 81-102; also rpt. from W. R. Farmer, C. F. D. Moule, and R. R. Niebuhr *Christian History* (see above).

Giblin, C. H., *In Hope of God's Glory* (Leiden: Brill, 1970), 136-88.

Goulder, M. D., "Libertines? (1 Cor 5–6)," *NovT* 41 (1999): 334-48.

Gundry-Volf, J. M., *Paul and Perseverance,* WUNT 2:37 (Tübingen: Mohr, 1990), 113-20.

Harris, G., "The Beginnings of Church Discipline: 1 Cor. 5," *NTS* 37 (1991): 1-21.

Harrisville, R. A., "The Concept of Newness in the NT," *JBL* 74 (1955): 69-79.

————, *The Concept of Newness in the NT* (Minneapolis: Augsburg, 1960), 1-70 and 109-114.

Hays, R. B., "Eschatology and Ethics in 1 Cor," *Ex Auditu* 10 (1994): 31-43.

Hill, D., *Greek Words and Hebrew Meanings* (Cambridge: Cambridge University Press, 1967), 265-85.

Horbury, W., "Extirpation and Excommunication," *VT* 35 (1985): 13-38.

Howard, J. K., 'Christ Our Passover': A Study of the Passover-Exodus Theme in 1 Corinthians," *EvQ* 41 (1969): 97-108.

Joy, N. G., "Is the Body Really to be Destroyed? (1 Cor. 5:5)," *BT* 39 (1988): 429-36.

Käsemann, E., "Sentences of Holy Law in the NT," in *NT Questions of Today* (Eng. trans., London: SCM and Philadelphia: Fortress, 1969), 66-81.

Kempthorne, R., "Incest and the Body of Christ," *NTS* 14 (1968): 568-74.

Lampe, G. W. H., "Church Discipline and the Interpretation of the Epistles to the Corinthians," in W. R. Farmer, C. F. D. Moule, and R. R. Niebuhr (eds.), *Christian History and Interpretation: Studies Presented to John Knox* (Cambridge: Cambridge University Press, 1967), 337-62.

MacArthur, J. D., "'Spirit' in the Pauline Usage: 1 Cor. 5:5," in E. A. Livingstone (ed.), *Studia Biblica* 3, JSNTSS 3 (Sheffield: Academic Press, 1978), 249-56.

Malina, B., "Does Porneia Mean Fornication?" *NovT* 14 (1972): 10-17.

Martin, D. B., *The Corinthian Body* (New Haven: Yale University Press, 1995), 153-74.

Menoud, P. H., "L'Écharde et l'Ange satanique," in *Studia Paulina: In Honorem J. de Zwaan* (Haarlem: Bohn, 1953), 163-71.

Minear, P., "Christ and the Congregation: 1 Cor. 5–6," *RevExp* 80 (1983): 341-50.

Mitchell, M. M., *Paul and the Rhetoric of Reconciliation* (Louisville: Westminster and Knox, 1992), 112-16.

Mitton, C. L., "New Wine in Old Wine Skins: iv, Leaven," *ExpTim* 84 (1973): 339-43.

Moore, W. D., "The Origin of 'Porneia' Reflected in 1 Cor. 5–6 and Its Implications to an Understanding of the Fundamental Orientation of the Corinthian Church" (Waco: Baylor Univ. Ph.D. diss., 1978).

Murphy-O'Connor, J., "1 Cor. 5:3-5," *RB* 84 (1977): 239-45.

383

Pfitzner, V. C., "Purified Community–Purified Sinner: Expulsion from the Community according to Matt. 18:15-18 and 1 Cor. 5:1-5," *AusBR* 30 (1982): 34-55.

Roetzel, C. J., *Judgement in the Community: A Study in the Relationship between Eschatology and Ecclesiology in Paul* (Leiden: Brill, 1972), 115-25.

Rosner, B. S., "Οὐχί μᾶλλον ἐπενθήσατε: Corporate Responsibility in 1 Cor. 5," *NTS* 38 (1992): 470-73.

———, *Paul, Scripture and Ethics: A Study of 1 Cor. 5–7* (Leiden: Brill, 1994), 61-93.

———, "Temple and Holiness in 1 Cor. 5," *TynBul* 42 (1991): 137-45.

Sand, A., *Der Begriff 'Fleisch' in den paulinischen Hauptbriefen* (Regensburg: Pustet, 1967), esp. 143-45.

Schrage, W., *Ethik des NT* (Göttingen: Vandenhoeck & Ruprecht, 2d ed. 1989), 170-75.

South, J. T., "A Critique of the 'Curse/Death' Interpretation of 1 Cor. 5:1-8," *NTS* 39 (1993): 539-61.

———, *Disciplinary Practices in Pauline Texts* (Lewiston, N.Y.: Mellen Biblical Press, 1992), 1-88, 181-98.

Thiselton, A. C., "The Meaning of Σάρξ in 1 Cor. 5:5: A Fresh Approach in the Light of Logical and Semantic Factors," *SJT* 26 (1973): 204-28.

———, "Truth, ἀλήθεια," *NIDNTT*, 3 (Grand Rapids: Zondervan, 1978), 874-902.

Thornton, T. C. G., "Satan — God's Agent for Punishing," *ExpTim* 83 (1972): 151-52.

Travis, S. H., *Christ and the Judgement of God* (London: Marshall Pickering, 1986), 79-81.

Vander Broek, L., "Discipline and Community: Another Look at 1 Cor. 5," *RefRev* 48 (1994): 5-13.

Wenthe, D. O., "An Exegetical Study of 1 Cor. 5:7b," *The Spring Fielder* 38 (1974): 134-40.

Yarbrough, O. L., *Not Like the Gentiles: Marriage Rules in the Letters of Paul* (Atlanta: Scholars Press, 1985).

Zaas, P., "Catalogues and Context: 1 Cor. 5 and 6," *NTS* 34 (1988): 622-29.

1. The Problem of the Incestuous Relationship (5:1-8)

(1) It is actually reported that there is an illicit sexual relationship among you: immorality of a kind which is not tolerated even among the Gentiles. Someone is having relations with his stepmother. (2) And you remain complacent! Ought you not rather to have entered into a state of mourning, that the man who has committed this practice be removed from your community?

(3) And for my part, as physically absent, but nevertheless present in the Spirit, I have already pronounced judgment on the man who has perpetrated this act under such circumstances, as effectively present. (4, 5) When you are assembled together in the name of our Lord Jesus, with my spiritual presence, and with the effective power of our Lord Jesus, we are to consign this man, such as he is, to Satan with a view to the destruction of the fleshly, in order that the spirit may be saved at the day of the Lord.

(6) Your self-satisfaction is ill placed. Do you not know that a little leaven leavens all of the dough? (7, 8) Clean out the old leaven, so that you

384

may be a newly begun batch of dough, even as you are indeed without old leaven. For our Passover lamb, Christ, has been sacrificed. So let us celebrate the Passover festival not with old leaven, not with leaven that ferments wickedness and evil, but with the unleavened bread which is purity and truth.

1 𝔭⁴⁶, ℵ*, A, B, C, D, F, G, 33, Vulg, et al. includes no verb with ἔθνεσιν. There is little support for the secondary ὀνομάζεται (𝔭⁶⁸, ℵ², Syriac), which finds its way into the AV/KJV (see below). The addition is easy to explain.

In earlier Greek Ὅλως usually meant *wholly* or *altogether* (reflected in KJV/AV *commonly*), but in the papyri and later literature it also means *really* or **actually** (here and in most English VSS). The passive ἀκούεται signals the continuation of the oral report brought by Chloe's people (1:11, ἐδηλώθη), and underlines that the Corinthians did not even inquire about this problem.[5] The concern shifts from περὶ ὑμῶν, *about you* (1:10) to ἐν ὑμῖν, **among you.**

Paul uses the word πορνεία, *sexual immorality,* or **an illicit sexual relationship,** six times, of which five occur in 1 Corinthians 5–7. NRSV, REB, NIV, and NJB all render the term *sexual immorality* (AV/KJV, RV, *fornication*), because the term is a generic one which includes various subcategories such as μοιχεία, *adultery.* The word covers "every kind of unlawful sexual intercourse."[6] The incestuous relationship is therefore specified as an especially outrageous sub-category of πορνεία, which is of such a kind (τοιαύτη) that **not even** (οὐδέ) **among the Gentiles** can the offense against law and society be **tolerated.** Among the best MSS no verb appears in the Greek sentence (see Textual Note), and we have supplied **tolerated.** South convincingly points out that the verb to be supplied can hardly be *found* (NRSV) or *occurred* (NIV), let alone *named* (AV/KJV) (see Note above), since cases *are* addressed and condemned, but they were not **tolerated** (REB and above) in Roman society or in Roman law.[7] Indeed, numerous commentators from Lietzmann and Héring to Fee and Collins, as well as writers of specialist monographs, including South and Clarke, cite the *Institutes* of the Roman jurist Gaius (c. AD 161) on these cases. He declares, "It is illegal to marry a father's or mother's sister; neither can I marry her who has been *quondam (formerly? at one time? ever?)* my mother-in-law or stepmother."[8] In the first century BC Cicero expresses extreme disgust when "mother-in-law marries son-in-law. . . . Oh, to think of the woman's sin, unbelievable, unheard of. . . . To think that she did not quail!"[9] (We note the resonance with **should you not have**

5. South, *Disciplinary Practices,* 25.
6. BAGD, 693; similarly Grimm-Thayer, 531-32.
7. South, *Disciplinary Practices,* 29.
8. Gaius, *Institutes,* 1: 63; Eng. ed., J. Muirhead, *The Institutes of Gaius and Rules of Ulpian* (Edinburgh: T. & T. Clark, 1880) 24-25; cf. Collins, *First Cor,* 206, 209-10.
9. Cicero, *Pro Cluentio* 5.27; rpt. *Speeches,* Loeb Library (Lat. and Eng., Cambridge, Mass.: Harvard University Press, 1927), 237.

grieved? 5:2.) Even the virtually unshockable Catullus expresses utter abhorrence at such a sexual relationship.[10]

If the Roman world found such a union repulsive, the biblical-Jewish tradition decisively legislates against such a possibility. Again, modern writers unanimously cite such passages as Lev 18:18; 20:11; Deut 23:1; 27:20.[11] In Deut 27:20 it stands under the twelve "curses," and in Lev 18:8, 29, it invites the death penalty. The Mishnah (*Sanhedrin* 7:4) rules death by stoning: "These are they that are to be stoned: he that has connexion with his mother, *his father's wife,* his daughter-in-law, a male, or a beast. . . ."[12] Such judicial language, coupled with the "curse" speech-acts of Deuteronomy 27, provides one (not necessarily the only) important and intelligible background to Paul's judicial and exercitive language in 5:3-5.

The present tense of the infinitive ἔχειν, **is having**, denotes a continuous relationship, as against a single act which would probably invite the aorist.[13] We shall consider the view of Chow and Clarke that this may have taken the form of a married union which involved property rights otherwise held by the family. We cannot be certain about the situation of the father. Lietzmann speaks of "a wild marriage with the escaped or divorced wife of the still-living father."[14] Weiss envisages a relationship consequent upon the father's death or his divorcing the woman.[15] Chrysostom argues that the use of the phrase γυναῖκα τοῦ πατρός, *father's wife,* in place of μητρυία, *stepmother,* is to explicate the gravity of the act.[16] Many modern writers follow this view, and many write as if Godet had first proposed this suggestion rather than drew it from Chrysostom. It is perhaps more likely, however, that Paul uses the longer phrase to reproduce the Deuteronomic or Levitical texts. Conzelmann and E. Schüssler Fiorenza suggest that because of the sanctions of Roman law, co-habitation is more likely than formal marriage, but Chow and Clarke maintain their view about patronage and property against this view.[17] We may conclude that marriage is probable but not certain.[18]

Chow's reminder that in a situation where marriage may take place in

10. Catullus, *The Poems of Gaius Valerius Catullus* 74 and 88-90, Loeb Library (Lat. and Eng., Cambridge, Mass.: Harvard University Press, 1913), 163-65.

11. For example, Wolff, *Der erste Brief,* 100.

12. Translation by H. Danby, *The Mishnah* (Oxford: Clarendon Press, 1933, my italics). See further Wolff, *Der erste Brief,* 100-101.

13. Chow, *Patronage and Power,* 132, argues that whatever form the relationship took "it would be safe to assume it was a long-term one"; cf. 130-41.

14. Lietzmann, *An die Korinther,* 23. Lietzmann also cites Lev 18:7; 20:11; Gaius, *Institutes* 1.63; a, d; Mishnah *Sanhedrin* 7:4.

15. Weiss, *Der erste Korintherbrief,* 125. On ἔχειν Weiss also compares Matt 14:4; 22:28; John 4:18; and 1 Cor 7:2, 29.

16. Chrysostom, *1 Cor. Hom.,* 15:2.

17. Conzelmann, *1 Corinthians,* 96; E. S. Fiorenza, "1 Corinthians," in *Harper's Bible Commentary* (New York: Harper, 1988), 1,174.

18. With Barrett, *First Epistle,* 122.

early years the woman may well have remained attractive and relatively young in the eyes of her husband's son, points to a moral and pastoral purpose in the Levitical "prohibited kinship and affinity relations."[19] Whatever theories spring from anthropological research about tribal kinship systems, Paul endorses a biblical provision which has the effect of protecting marriage and the nuclear family within the larger framework of an extended family. Daily sharing of the same home by a daughter-in-law and a father, a mother and a son-in-law, and so forth, could well lead to attractions toward the supposed charms of an older or younger member of the other sex which could strain existing marriage loyalties unless this direction of thought or desire were so decisively "off-limits" as effectively to remain inconceivable as a possibility even to be imagined by any party. Hence there emerges a further strand to the issue which is relevant equally to Corinth and for today: *in certain cases law ministers to trust and to freedom;* it does not oppose freedom.

Thus the traditional arguments about the relevance of "all things are lawful" (6:12) to the complacency of the community in condoning the act of incest should not be dismissed. This is not a competing hypothesis to Dale Martin's theories about purity or to Chow and Clarke on patronage. Their work adds a constructive dimension to our understanding of the issues, but it does remain more speculative than the issue of order and law as expressed in 6:12 in the text itself. Whatever the sociological origins of Leviticus 18, the Church of England still retains a largely Levitical "Table of Kindred and Affinity" in its Book of Common Prayer (1662), drawn from the list of prohibited relationships (1563) compiled from Calvin's understanding of Leviticus 18. For *pastoral* reasons the Church of England retains the list in modified form as Canon B31 of its fourth (1986) edition of *The Canons.*[20]

2 πράξας is found in ℵ, A, C, 33, and a reconstructed 𝔭[11]. But 𝔭[46], B, D, F, G, and most minuscules read ποιήσας. Metzger explains that the UBS 4th ed. prefers πράξας because the phrase ποιεῖν ἔργον is such a standard one that scribes would be more likely to reproduce it than to change ποιήσας into a secondary πράξας. But the issue is finely balanced and of little material substance.

We translate **remain complacent** to convey the continuous effects denoted by the perfect tense of the passive participle πεφυσιωμένοι. But much hinges on how we interpret this word. On the Greek word and its metaphorical use, see above on 4:6, and 4:18, 19, where we noted that six of its seven occurrences in the NT appear in 1 Corinthians, and its meaning *puffed up, inflated,* i.e., with *pride, self-importance, arrogance, complacency,* or *self-congratulation.* It is possible that this first clause should also take the form of a question: *And can you really show complacency?*[21] The ὑμεῖς, **you,** is emphatic, no doubt looking

19. Chow, *Patronage and Power,* 134.
20. *The Canons of the Church of England* (London: Church House, 1986), 41.
21. Edwards, *First Epistle,* 123.

back to 4:6, 18, 19 and to the earlier passages about *boasting,* with the sense of *not again!*

The whole community, Paul declares through a rhetorical question, should be *grieving* (πενθέω is used intransitively of *being sad, grieving,* or **mourning**, but also transitively with an object to mean *to mourn over*).[22] The first aorist indicative ἐπενθήσατε is likely to carry the nuance of a past act (ingressive) of **entering into a state of mourning**, because although *to grieve* at first sight seems more appropriate as expressing psychological sorrow, a **formal state of mourning** would stamp the life and worship of the church objectively and publicly in a way which would thereby make it intolerable for the offender to remain, and would then in all probability have made his own choice to leave (or to change his lifestyle).[23] He would know that he blighted the church's life (see n. 23). Hence Paul follows the main verb with a final or purposive clause *in order that he might* **be removed**: ἵνα ἀρθῇ, third singular aorist subjunctive passive of αἴρω, *I lift up, I remove.* Pfitzner (followed by South and Rosner) links this ἵνα clause directly with the **state of mourning**: this signals not merely grief at the sin, he argues, but **mourning** for the loss of an unrepentant sinner (if he fails to change) from the community.[24] The intensive compound ἐξαρεῖτε τὸν πονηρόν, **drive out** . . ., in v. 13 is even stronger, perhaps because in the first instance the community's stance *implicitly* leaves him in the cold so that he departs, whereas the more formal act *explicitly* enacts a formal pronouncement as a speech-act of verdict and directive.

A. D. Clarke categorizes three distinct explanations among modern writers concerning the **complacency** or *boasting.* (i) The controlling background may be found in the slogan of 6:12, πάντα μοι ἔξεστιν. As I argued in 1973, following A. D. Nock, part of the problem was that the feeling that "they were on a new plane of life, [and] felt that they could do anything," therefore the flagrant disregard of "law" could be perceived as demonstrating the superiority of their status as "those who reign as kings" and are above struggle.[25] Clarke rightly ar-

---

22. BAGD, 642; cf. Grimm-Thayer, 500, *mourn* in 1 Cor 5:2.

23. Lightfoot translates, "ye ought rather to have put on mourning," i.e., "an outward exhibition of humiliation and grief." The powerful OT tradition of not merely *feeling* regret but *performing a public act* of sorrow, remorse, and repentance found expression in Hebrew life in *clothing oneself with sackcloth* (Heb. אבל, *'abel), to mourn,* frequently with שׂק (saq), sackcloth (LXX σάκκος), e.g., 2 Sam 3:31 and Jer 49:3; cf. further Gen 37:34; 1 Kings 20:31-32; 21:27; 1 Chron 21:16; Esth 4:1-4; Ps 30:11; 69:11; Isa 37:1-2; 50:3; Jer 4:8; Lam 2:10; Ezek 7:18; Dan 9:3. Also Matt 11:21 par. Luke 10:13, Greek loanword σάκκος. Coarse, rough cloth which expresses mourning, sometimes with "ashes," is equally expressive of public penitence i.e. *an act* of penitence. Héring likewise stresses the importance of this background of "the efficacy of mourning and fasting" (*First Epistle,* 35).

24. Pfitzner, "Purified Community," 34-55; South, *Disciplinary Practices,* 32-33; and Rosner, "Οὐχὶ μᾶλλον ἐπενθήσατε· Corporate Responsibility in 1 Cor. 5," 470-73.

25. Thiselton, "The Meaning of Σαρξ in 1 Cor. 5:5," 211; cf. 204-28; and A. D. Nock, *St Paul* (London: Thornton Butterworth, 1938), 174, and *Conversion* (Oxford: Oxford University Press, 1938), 118-21 and throughout.

gues that this is unlikely to constitute the entire explanation, but, together with O. L. Yarbrough, he is too hasty in dismissing its force as a strong contributing factor.[26] Origen closely links the double accusation of pride and the church's tolerance, and a long tradition of such a view is evidenced by the fact that Matthew Poole (1685) cites such a view, even if he rejects it.[27] F. F. Bruce explains why Paul is no less concerned about the arrogance than about the moral sin in these terms: "a significant body of opinion in Corinth (cf. 6:12ff.) thought that this was rather a fine assertion of Christian liberty, of emancipation from Jewish Law and Gentile convention alike."[28] Barrett retains an open mind about this possibility.[29] Craig Blomberg achieves a judicious balance: "They were actually smug over their newfound 'enlightened' tolerance as Christians (v. 2)."[30]

(ii) A second view, which goes back to the patristic commentators, perceives the "boasting" as arising from their accepting the instruction of the man in question, who evidently taught in the church. Chrysostom, Theodoret, Theophylact, and Grotius propose such a possibility.[31] They glory not in his lapse, but in his supposed eloquence or "wisdom." Such a view may seem more plausible if we also follow Meyer (and more recently D. Daube) in speculating that the man "put forward in his own defence . . . the Rabbinical axiom that becoming a proselyte, as a new birth, did away with the restrictions of forbidden degrees (Maimonides, *Jebhamoth,* F.982)."[32] Daube ascribes the complacency or, in his view, elation, to the gaining of a new convert from a Jewish background rather than to a symptom of antinomianism.[33] The hypothesis might perhaps better serve to support the approach of Chrysostom and Theodoret as an impressive piece of "wisdom," but in the end Clarke is surely right to argue that we should expect Paul to address the issue more explicitly (e.g., what is at issue in new creation) if this hypothesis had validity.[34]

(iii) Probably the majority of modern writers interpret the complacency as being *despite* the offender's illicit relationship. Allo, Weiss, and others interpret Paul to mean: even this gross sin does not disturb your complacent, inflated

26. Clarke, *Secular and Christian Leadership,* 74 including n. 6; Yarbrough, *Not like the Gentiles: Marriage Rules in the Letters of Paul* (Atlanta: Scholars Press, 1985), 96-97.

27. Origen, *On 1 Corinthians* (*Fragments,* ed. C. Jenkins, *JTS* 9 [1908]: 363), *Frag.* 23 (on 4:21–5:2); Matthew Poole, *Commentary,* 3:552.

28. Bruce, *1 and 2 Corinthians,* 54.

29. Barrett, *First Epistle,* 122.

30. Blomberg, *1 Corinthians,* 104-5. Collins, *First Cor,* 210, suggests that the plural **you** may include especially their leaders.

31. Chrysostom, *1 Cor. Hom.,* 15:2, "'Puffed up' not with the sin . . . but with the teaching heard from that person"; Theodoret, *Interpretatio ep. ad Cor.,* 191D, Gk. πεπαιδευμένον διδάσκακον ἔχοντες: Lat., 192A, *qui doctorem eruditum habereat.*

32. Meyer, *First Epistle,* 1:140; cf. D. Daube, "Pauline Contributions to a Pluralistic Culture: Re-creation and Beyond," in D. G. Miller and D. K. Hadidian (eds.), *Jesus and Man's Hope* (Pittsburgh: Pickwick Press, 1971), 223-27.

33. Daube, "Pauline Contributions to a Pluralistic Culture" (n. 32 above).

34. Clarke, *Secular and Christian Leadership,* 75.

triumphalism as you live in "the celestial heights."[35] Clarke and Conzelmann stress that this is simply part of the general attitude within the church.[36] Others speak of "their morbid self-importance."[37]

On two issues, however, virtually all modern writers agree. First, Paul attacks two distinct problems: (a) the immoral act of the individual person; and (b) the corporate sin of the community in condoning, accepting, and tolerating the situation, with no overt sign even of concern.[38] Second, unless we accept G. Sellin's problematic argument of a partition on composition between 4:21 and 5:1 (indeed, he isolates 5:1-8 from chs. 1–4 and from 5:9-13, conceding only that it is linked with 6:1-11, 9:26–10:22, and 11:2-34 as the *Vorbrief*), most writers see Paul's concern here for the purity of the community as reflecting his language about the holiness of the church as God's temple, sanctified by the Holy Spirit (3:16-17).[39] Brian Rosner defends this important point, arguing further that the "destruction" of the σάρξ in 5:5 corresponds conversely with the warning about attempts to "destroy" the holy temple (3:17).[40] Campbell and Rosner (in a second article) go further. The issue is one of *corporate responsibility:* what the individual member does is not merely an individual matter.[41] The issue is the responsibility of the whole community.[42]

3 The personal pronoun ἐγώ denotes an emphatic expression of Paul's attitude in contrast to the ὑμεῖς (v. 2) of those who refuse to mourn. Hence Allo and Fee propose **I for my part**, or *quant à moi*.[43] Both note that μέν is not followed by δέ here, because the contrast is with v. 2. The contrastive present participles ἀπών, *being* **absent**, and παρών, *being* **present**, are qualified by two datives which are either modal (in effect adverbial) or locative, i.e., τῷ σώματι, *in body*, i.e., **physically**, and τῷ πνεύματι, the meaning of which remains open to debate. From the nineteenth century to the late 1950s the virtually unanimous interpretation is *in spirit*, i.e., in a *non-bodily* sense, because the semantic contrast between σῶμα and πνεῦμα was assumed to reflect the classical Western

---

35. Godet, *First Epistle,* 1:242; cf. Weiss, *Der erste Korintherbrief,* 133; Allo, *Première Épitre,* 116; Lenski, *1 Corinthians,* 206; Robertson and Plummer, *First Epistle,* 97.

36. Clarke, *Leadership,* 77; Conzelmann, *1 Corinthians,* 96-97; cf. Klauck, *1 Korintherbrief,* 42; and Lang, *Die Briefe an die Korinther,* 70-71.

37. Robertson and Plummer, *First Epistle,* 97.

38. The argument of L. Vander Broek, "Discipline and Community: Another Look at 1 Cor. 5," *RefRev* 48 (1994): 5-13. The argument is valid but hardly distinctive. Most writers make a similar point.

39. Robertson G. Sellin, "1 Kor. 5–6 und der 'Vorbrief' nach Korinth," *NTS* 37 (1991): 535-58.

40. Rosner, "Temple and Holiness in 1 Cor. 5," 137-45.

41. B. Campbell, "Flesh and Spirit in 1 Cor 5:5," 331.42; and esp. Rosner, "Οὐχὶ μᾶλλον ἐπενθήσατε: Corporate Responsibility in 1 Cor. 5," 470-73.

42. South, "A Critique of the 'Curse/Death' Interpretation of 1 Cor. 5:1-8," 539-61; and *Disciplinary Practices,* 33-71.

43. Fee, *First Epistle,* 203.

mind-body dualism of Plato and Descartes. Many others cite Col. 2:5 as a parallel, and instances of such a contrast in Paul cannot be denied.[44]

How secure is this assumption? It is hardly convincing to follow G. Karlsson in regarding the contrast as mere literary convention, even if we can readily imagine (also today) instances of letter writing when we wish to say "I am with you in spirit," i.e., my thoughts and concerns are with you. H.-J. Klauck believes that "we encounter a special letter-formula" which exposes the misguided nature of many other discussions.[45] But more of substance is at stake in Paul's words, and his table of "presence" is not on the same level as that of secular Greek epistolography.[46] South recalls G. P. Wiles's comment: "This striking threefold emphasis on his presence must mean more than a conventional epistolary formula. . . . Rather, his spirit is mediated to them σὺν τῇ δυνάμει τοῦ κυρίου ἡμῶν Ἰησοῦ."[47]

Fee and South point in the right direction by taking seriously the possibility that Paul does not express a mind-body contrast as such, but uses τῷ πνεύματι to refer primarily to the Holy Spirit, even if there is a secondary allusion to πνεῦμα as the human self in its capacity to be open to the Spirit. It is in the power of the Holy Spirit that Paul is present, as one who integrally forms part of the one holy temple at Corinth which is threatened with defilement and destruction (cf. Rosner, above) but is sanctified by the common bond of the Spirit, who indwells the corporate body. South alludes to my earlier study on 5:5 and declares: "Thiselton has demonstrated convincingly that whenever the two terms [there σάρξ and πνεῦμα] stand in contrast to one another, the meaning is seldom (if ever) that of body/spirit."[48] Ambrosiaster adopted this interpretation, and Fee strengthens this case by tracing backward and forward allusions to πνεῦμα as the Spirit of God in corporate contexts, and contexts of bonding, in this epistle.[49] Others are attracted to this view, provided that we do not exclude a double allusion to human spirit or modes of the self as well as to the Spirit of God as the ground for the possibility of Paul's effective presence.[50] This is supported by the anthropological use of πνεῦμα in 5:5.

Otherwise commentators tend either to hedge their bets with a phrase such as "Paul promises that he will be spiritually present" (Héring) or to follow the more traditional dualist interpretation. Allo, e.g., writes that πνεῦμα and σῶμα stand in opposition, in which "in spirit" means "a presence of thought and

44. Schrage, *Der erste Brief,* 1:373, as a point to be conceded, not as a characteristic use.
45. Klauck, *1 Korintherbrief,* 42; cf. G. Karlsson, "Formelhaftes in Paulusbriefen?" *Eranos* 54 (1956): 138-41; and Conzelmann, *1 Corinthians,* 97.
46. Funk, "The Apostolic Presence: Paul," in *Parables and Presence,* 81-102; and South, *Disciplinary Practices,* 33-34.
47. G. P. Wiles, *Paul's Intercessory Prayers* (Cambridge: Cambridge University Press, 1974), 145. South, "A Critique of the 'Curse/Death' Interpretation of 1 Cor. 5:1-8," 552; cf. 539-61.
48. South, "A Critique of the 'Curse/Death' Interpretation of 1 Cor. 5:1-8," 552; cf. 539-61.
49. Fee, *First Epistle,* 203-13; esp. 204-5.
50. Schrage, *Der erste Brief,* 1:373.

intention, nothing more."[51] He recognizes in his extended appendix "the diverse meanings of πνεῦμα."[52]

The perfect indicative active κέκρικα **I pronounce judgement,** implies that Paul has already (ἤδη) reached a settled public verdict, as part of the community, upon **the man** (τόν with the participle) **who has perpetrated such an act.** The participle of κατεργάζομαι, *I work out, I work through,* with the intensive κατ' may be rendered portentously as **perpetrated,** especially in conjunction with Paul's indignant use of the adverb οὕτως, *in this way,* or *thus,* or **under such circumstances**: "The word aggravates the charge."[53] There are important differences of translation in rendering ὡς παρών. Fee, South, and Schrage are right to insist (against almost all English VSS and against most commentaries) that Paul does *not* say *as if* or *as though* I were present, but *being present, as one who is present* (Fee), or **nevertheless present.**[54] This underlines the *logical* tension with ἀπών. Several grammarians have described the participle as concessive, but, as Schrage insists, vv. 4 and 5 demonstrate that Paul does *not* regard his "presence" as merely "fictive" (against NRSV, *as if present;* NIV, *just as if I were present;* AV/KJV, RV, *as though I were present*). It is a mistake to regard the realm of eschatology, the Spirit, and divine verdict as the realm of "as if," and the historical, empirical realm as "reality." I have argued elsewhere that both dimensions are *reality* perceived as part of different frames of reference. For the Christian, it is not the realm of the earthly and contingent that is more "real" if forced (wrongly) into an either-or.[55]

4-5 p[46], B, D, G, and some Syriac MSS include ἡμῶν, **our** (but ℵ and A omit it), while p[46], copyists of D, G, 33, and Vulgate also add Χριστοῦ, *Christ,* but it is omitted by ℵ, A, B, the original of D*, and Vulgate. The argument that copyists are likely to pile up solemn epithets because of the heavy, formal sonority of the whole passage might be thought to cut both ways, in that Paul might well have included them; but on this basis it is difficult to account for their omissions, except on grounds of what might later be perceived as redundancy. On balance the MS evidence favors ἡμῶν, although it is not certain; while Χριστοῦ has too much against it and can hardly be original. Metzger regards the witness of B and D together as tipping the scales for the UBS 4th edition.[56] Further, in v. 5, ℵ adds Ἰησοῦ to **day of the Lord,** while D adds Ἰησοῦ Χριστοῦ. But the shorter reading of B, **day of the Lord,** has the most to commend it, for it is easier to envisage copyists picking up the additions from the previous lines than to explain B's omission unless it is authentic. Again, little of substance is at issue in exegesis.

---

51. Allo, *Première Épitre,* 120.

52. Ibid., 91-101.

53. Lightfoot, *Notes,* 204.

54. Fee, *First Epistle,* 204, n. 39; South, *Disciplinary Practices,* 34; Schrage, *Der erste Brief,* 1:373.

55. A. C. Thiselton, "On the Logical Grammar of Justification in Paul," in *SE* 7 (Berlin: Berlin Academy, 1982), 491-95; and *The Two Horizons* (Grand Rapids: Eerdmans, 1980), 415-27.

56. Metzger, *Textual Commentary* (2d ed. 1994), 485.

Verses 4 and 5 contain a number of well-known problems, which commentators and other modern writers address at length.

(i) The first major question concerns the connection of the phrase ἐν τῷ ὀνόματι τοῦ κυρίου [ἡμῶν] Ἰησοῦ, **in the name of our Lord Jesus**. Origen, Chrysostom, and other Fathers discussed whether the phrase qualified the genitive absolute συναχθέντων ὑμῶν, **when you are assembled together** (genitive), belongs with κέκρικα (v. 3), whether it belongs to the whole series of clauses, or whether it relates more specifically to παραδοῦναι (aorist infinitive), *I hand over*, **I consign**. In the modern period the construction is regularly debated. Allo provides a detailed table listing five options; while Conzelmann includes a series of six possibilities.[57] These include:

(a) Interpreting ἐν τῷ ὀνόματι τοῦ κυρίου, . . . **in the name of [our] Lord**, with the genitive absolute, to mean **when you are assembled together in the name of our Lord Jesus**. Since the time of Origen, followed by Chrysostom, Theodoret, and Theophylact, Matt 18:20 has been cited for evidence of the early tradition that συνηγμένοι εἰς τὸ ὄνομα constitutes a paradigmatic definition of *meeting as a Christian congregation.*[58]

(b) Many interpret **in the name** with *assembling* (as above) and then construe **with the [effective] power of our Lord Jesus** with the act of **consigning the man to Satan** (where παραδοῦναι, infinitive of παραδίδωμι, forms a continuation of the sentence begun in v. 3). Heinrici and Lietzmann argue for this view on grounds of the word order of the Greek, following Chrysostom, Beza, Olshausen, and Ewald.[59]

(c) More convincingly on grounds of context, H. A. W. Meyer sets out a list of four options and exegesis. B. Rosner follows Theodoret, Erasmus, Calvin, Weiss, and others in rendering *gathered together in the name and power of the Lord* (Rosner), i.e., construing **in the name of [our] Lord** with both συναχθέντων and σὺν τῇ δυνάμει.[60] However, for Calvin and others the *corporate* nature of the act of discipline is crucial, and is underlined by this interpretation.

(d) Ambrosiaster and Mosheim seek to go further, by construing (c) above with *the act of* **consigning** (παραδοῦναι), to mean *to consign the man in the name of our Lord and by the power of our Lord. . . .*[61]

(e) Once we enlarge the scope of the model in adverbial clauses as interactive, however, we may as well follow Luther, Estius, and Bengel in interpreting **in the name of our Lord** as qualifying the entire remainder of the two

---

57. Allo, *Première Épitre,* 121-24; Conzelmann, *1 Corinthians,* 97.

58. Chrysostom, *1 Cor. Hom.,* 15:3; Theodoret, *Interp. ep. 1 ad Cor.,* 191B (Gk.), 192B (Lat.); Migne, *PG,* 82:261 and 262.

59. Heinrici, *Das erste Sendschreiben,* 162, esp. nn. 2, 3; Lietzmann, *An die Korinther,* 23.

60. Rosner, *Paul, Scripture and Ethics,* 84; Theodoret, *Interp. ep. 1 ad Cor.,* 191B (Gk.), 192 (Lat.); Calvin, *First Epistle,* 107-8; Weiss, *Der erste Korintherbrief,* 127-33; and Erasmus, *In ep. Pauli ad Cor. 1,* 874.

61. Ambrosiaster, *Commentary,* in CSEL, 81:54.

clauses.[62] Allo argues carefully for this view, and concludes that while ἐν τῷ ὀνόματι τοῦ κυρίου . . . comes first to make a solemn emphasis, and indeed governs the main verb, nevertheless σὺν τῇ δυνάμει τοῦ κυρίου "supplies a co-efficient that is essential to the competency of the tribunal."[63] This has considerable force, not least because it coheres well with the expected logic of a speech-act which is both verdictive (κέκρικα) and exercitive (e.g., the verdict "guilty" [verdictive] is followed by the judge's sentence [exercitive])[64] The **effective power of the Lord** (cf. δύναμις as putting into effect with substance) is *not* the *power* of bare causality, but the *institutional authority* in which the power **of the Lord Jesus** provides "backing" or *legitimation* to the verdict and execution of the act.

(f) Finally, a minority, construe **in the name** with κέκρικα, and separate the second clause in which σὺν τῇ δυνάμει governs **when you are assembled**. This has less support than (c) and (e), which are the two most convincing candidates.

Such is the length of this single convoluted sentence in vv. 3-5 that it is difficult to argue for one view over another.[65] With this caveat, however, we conclude that (e) has most to commend it on the grounds of its status as a speech-act, while (c) also remains convincing as seriously possible, and none (except perhaps [f]) can be excluded with certainty. In both cases, the model function of **assembled together** qualifying the whole makes the speech-act not simply an individual act of Paul, but a corporate act of the whole community, explicitly including Paul as its apostolic focus of unity and "order."[66]

(ii) Just as the translation *with the power* strictly reflects the Greek but could lead to misunderstanding which invites our translating **with the effective power** to preserve the theological nuance in this epistle, so καὶ τοῦ ἐμοῦ πνεύματος strictly means *and my spirit,* but we have tried to anticipate the mistake of reading this through the un-Pauline lenses of Western dualism by translating **with my spiritual presence**. This coheres both with the meaning of v. 3 (see above) and with the fact that Paul's use of πνεῦμα more usually refers ei-

---

62. Yet against Calvin, Bengel affirms that the judicial act was the prerogative of Paul, not of the Corinthians (cf. 2 Cor 13:10): on v. 5: *"id apostoli erat, non Corinthiorum."* On v. 4: *"Paulus de se loquens, Spiritum adhibet; de Christo, potentiam, conf.* 2 Cor. 13:3; Matt. 28:20; 18:20" (*Gnomon,* 622).

63. In much more detail Robertson and Plummer, *First Epistle,* 98-99; and esp. Allo, *Première Épitre,* in a long discussion, 121-24.

64. Collins, *First Cor,* 207, *render judgment,* usefully conveys the speech-act performative dimension.

65. Blomberg, *1 Corinthians,* 105.

66. Calvin emphasizes this strongly. He declares, "It is quite out of keeping with the institution of Christ and the apostles, with the order of the church, and in fact with fairness itself, that there should be put in the hands of one man the right to excommunicate, on his own authority, any person he wants. . . . There is nothing in greater opposition to the discipline of the Christ *(Christi disciplinae)* than tyranny; and the door is wide open to it if all the power is surrendered to one man" (*First Epistle,* 107).

ther to the Holy Spirit or to a mode of human selfhood that is open to the Spirit or is viewed in terms of its capacity to transcend the merely human and earthly. (See above on v. 3 and also on 2:4, 10-14; 3:16; and 4:21; cf. further 2:15 and 3:11 on the adjective.)

(iii) The most controversial clauses are παραδοῦναι τὸν τοιοῦτον τῷ Σατανᾷ εἰς ὄλεθρον τῆς σαρκός, ἵνα τὸ πνεῦμα σωθῇ ἐν τῇ ἡμέρᾳ τοῦ κυρίου, translated above as **we are to consign** (the aorist active infinitive has to be rendered as a finite verb unless the sentence is continued from v. 3, and **we** is clearly the subject of the **assembly** in which Paul is **spiritually present**), **this man such as he is** (τὸν τοιοῦτον) **to Satan with a view to** (εἰς with accusative) **the destruction of the fleshly** . . . (ὄλεθρον τῆς σαρκός . . .), **in order that spiritually he may be saved** (ἵνα followed by the first of σῴζω) **at the day of the Lord**.

(a) Before we pre-judge the meaning of σάρξ, **flesh**, in this verse, we note J. T. South's conclusion that "Paul's intention hinges upon the interpretation of παραδοῦναι τῳ σατανᾷ, a phrase that has led exegetes in many directions."[67] The verb means *to deliver (someone) into custody* (e.g., Matt 10:19), and in connection with Judas Iscariot either *to betray* or *to hand over* (Matt 26:15, 25). In 1 Tim 1:20 the writer speaks of *handing over* or **consigning** Hymenaeus and Alexander to Satan. The noun ὄλεθρον denotes *ruination* or **destruction**. Hence most writers and interpreters understand σάρξ as *the physical body* or *the earthly life,* and assume that **to consign a man such as he is to Satan** means quite simply to pronounce a sentence of *death.* But this leaves a number of difficulties. The most serious one is that Paul explicitly expresses a salvific intention. In South's view, "This can be nothing other than eschatological salvation."[68] Does this suggest, then, that if the man fails to renounce his sin in the face of the impending sentence of death, Paul envisages some kind of postmortal change of stance? Nowhere else in Paul is such a concept hinted at. Or does τὸ πνεῦμα refer only to the corporate salvation of the community, rather than the man? Further, is this a kind of "curse" sentence, as envisaged in Acts 5:5, 10 in the case of Ananias and Sapphira? South rightly exposes the problematic character of such a notion.[69]

(b) There are several explanations of ὄλεθρον τῆς σαρκός. Käsemann believes that this "obviously entails the death of the guilty," and Schneider and Craig also adopt this view.[70] But A. Sand rightly endorses Bultmann's view that σάρξ can mean the whole self as perceived in terms of a specific aspect.[71] Hence its "destruction" can refer to the destruction of the particular aspects or qualities which the term denotes. I spent twenty pages defending this view in

67. South, *Disciplinary Practices,* 35.
68. Ibid., 36.
69. South, "A Critique of the 'Curse/Death' Interpretation of 1 Cor. 5:1-8," 539-61.
70. Käsemann, *NT Questions of Today,* 71; Schneider, "σάρξ," *TDNT,* 5:169; Craig, "First Epistle," in *IB,* 10:62.
71. Sand, *Der Begriff 'Fleisch' in den paulinischen Hauptbriefen,* 143-45.

my article of 1973.[72] Origen anticipates the translation which we offer above: he comments on Paul's phrase, τοῦτ' ἔστι τὸ φρόνημα τῆς σαρκός, i.e., the destruction of the *mind* or *stance* of the flesh.[73] I concluded in 1973 that "the punishment of the offender *may or may not* have included physical suffering in its outworking," but that what is to be destroyed is the "self-glorying or self-satisfaction" of the offender and perhaps also of the community.[74] Both the salvation of the man and the salvation of the community entail orientations or stances which are "the very opposite of self-glorifying or self-satisfaction."[75]

Much of my argument depended on the use of what linguistic philosophers and linguisticians often call *persuasive definition*. This depends on a process of switching between descriptive and evaluative definitions of terms from within different frames of reference. For example, *murder* may denote the same act as *killing* or *withdrawing life,* but in contexts of debates about abortion and euthanasia the evaluative dimensions are often treated as if they *denoted* actions *descriptively* rather than *embodying an evaluation also.* Here the terms *sarx, flesh,* and *pneuma, spirit,* become open to *persuasive* and *evaluative* definitions which may differ between the Corinthians' and Paul's frames of reference respectively.[76] Very recently John Moores has expressed these semantic principles in terms of Umberto Eco's semantic theory of *code switching* and applied it constructively to his modes of argument mainly in Romans but also with allusion to 1 Corinthians.[77]

What is to be destroyed is arguably not primarily the physical body of the offender (although this may or may not be secondarily entailed) but the "fleshly" *stance of self-sufficiency* of which Paul accuses *primarily the community* but surely *also the man.* To my more linguistic and semantic arguments, Chow, South, and others have recently *added the social argument about patronage and perhaps also property.*[78] Perhaps the community's "pride" was nourished by the patronage of one of distinguished status (the offender) whose wealth may even have been enhanced by the illicit marriage. If **consigning to Satan** means excluding him from the community, this spells the end of self-congratulation about their association with such a distinguished patron; while for the offender himself sudden removal from a platform of adulation to total isolation from the community would have a sobering if not devastating effect.

72. Thiselton, "The Meaning of Σάρξ in 1 Cor. 5:5. A Fresh Approach in the Light of Logical and Semantic Factors," 204-28.

73. Origen, *1 Cor. Fragments,* 24:93:12-13 (ed. Jenkins, *JTS* 9 [1908]: 364).

74. Thiselton, "The Meaning of Σάρξ," 225 and 226.

75. Ibid., 226.

76. Ibid., 207-15.

77. J. Moores, *Wrestling with Rationality in Paul,* SNTSMS 82 (Cambridge: Cambridge University Press, 1995), 5-32 and 132-60.

78. Chow, *Patronage and Power,* 130-41, esp. 139-40. Chow observes that Moffatt plausibly viewed the offender as probably "too important or wealthy" for the church to accuse or to identify as a problem (Moffatt, *First Epistle,* 53). Chow believes that "the case of immorality basically concerns a man with material possessions" (139).

(c) This readily explains how παραδοῦναι . . . τῷ Σατανᾷ can have *the purpose* (ἵνα with the subjunctive) *of salvation* (ἵνα τὸ πνεῦμα σωθῇ ἐν τῇ ἡμέρᾳ τοῦ κυρίου). Before reading the arguments of Rosner, Campbell, and especially South, I had long believed that while the text did not necessarily envisage the offender's death (as they, too, argue) the purpose of salvation concerned primarily the man. But these writers have convinced me that the salvific purposes embrace both the community and the man.[79] I concede that this makes the translation of τὸ πνεῦμα difficult. I remain unconvinced by MacArthur's attempt to interpret πνεῦμα as the man's self as he faces the last judgment.[80] After some deliberation I have left the word as it stands: **in order that the spirit may be saved** leaves open, as the Greek does, whether Paul means the *stance of the man, the man under the mode of* his openness to God, the *stance of the church, the animating principle of the church* (which would not be characteristic of Paul, but no writer need always use terms "characteristically"), or simply *that mode of being of the community and the man which is purged of its fleshly, self-sufficient complacency.* Cambier sees πνεῦμα as characterizing "the whole person" here.[81] Only the exegetical context can determine the semantic boundaries and reference of πνεῦμα here.

South provides an admirable and convincing critique of the "curse/death" interpretation of **consigning to Satan for the destruction of the fleshly**. Conzelmann declares that this "can hardly mean anything else but death."[82] C. T. Craig perceives this as the "only" possible meaning.[83] E. von Dobschutz describes this as "a penal miracle."[84] Derrett argues that **consignment to Satan** means handing the man over to the civil authorities for execution.[85] Forkman resists the view that death is at issue, but still interprets the judgment against the background of "curse."[86] Nevertheless, as I argued earlier, South insists that this consigning to Satan means "putting him outside the sphere of God's protection within the church, and leaving him exposed to the satanic forces of evil in hope that the experience would cause him to repent and return to the fellowship of the church. The 'flesh' to be destroyed is thus not his physical body. . . ."[87] The REB translation *the destruction of his body* is unfortunate, and here it is the NIV which comes to the rescue with *that the sinful nature may be*

---

79. Thiselton, "The Meaning of Σάρξ in 1 Cor. 5:5," 204-28; cf. Rosner, "Οὐχὶ μᾶλλον ἐπενθήσατε: Corporate Responsibility in 1 Cor. 5," 470-73; Campbell, "Flesh and Spirit in 1 Cor. 5:5," 331-42; and esp. South, *Disciplinary Practices,* 38-71 and "A Critique of the 'Curse/Death' Interpretation on 1 Cor 5:1-8," 539-61.

80. J. D. MacArthur, "'Spirit' in Pauline Usage: 1 Cor. 5:5," 249-56, esp. 253.

81. Cambier, "La Chair et l'Esprit en 1 Cor. 5:5," 221, 223-24, and 228.

82. Conzelmann, *1 Cor,* 97.

83. Craig, "First Epistle," in *IB,* 10:62.

84. E. von Dobschutz, *Christian Life in the Primitive Church* (New York: Putnam and London: Williams & Norgate, 1904), 46.

85. Derrett, "Handing Over to Satan," 11-30.

86. Forkman, *The Limits of the Religious Community,* 144.

87. South, *Disciplinary Practices,* 43; cf. 44-71.

destroyed (adding n. "Or, *that his body*"). JB attempts a compromise with *his sensual body.*

Tertullian draws a contrast between the fate of the "inflated" and that of the incestuous offender. "The 'inflated' is rebuked; but the 'incestuous' is condemned."[88] In Tertullian's view the power of the Lord, the "angel" of the church, and the "spirit" of Paul together pronounce an effective sentence of condemnation on the man. In the following section this leads into a discussion of the impossibility of absolution after baptism. Hence, historically, this tradition of *death* has its origins in a context which belongs to a prior agenda.

(d) The agency of Satan admittedly is associated with illness and death in various strands of Judaism, traces of which remain in the NT (Job 2:5, 6; *Jubilees* 11:11, 12; 48:2, 3, 49; *Testament of Benjamin* 3:3; 1QS 4:14; CD 2:6; 4:13; cf. sources cited in Strack-Billerbeck, 1:144-49 and 4:501-35; in the NT, Luke 13:11, 16; 2 Cor 12:7). But this is by no means an essential feature of this agency, nor perhaps a systematic or a central one. Paul refers relatively seldom to the agency of Satan (Rom 16:20; 1 Cor 5:5; 7:5; 2 Cor 2:11; 11:14; 12:7; 1 Thess 2:18; 2 Thess 2:9; cf. 1 Tim 1:20; 5:15, i.e., approximately eight times in Paul, roughly eight in the Gospels [only one in John], and eight in Revelation). Some references in Paul have more to do with deception, or with accusation, or the crushing of pride, than with notions of "curse" or "death." None of the Greek "magical" curse formulae cited by Deissmann, Collins, and Conzelmann relate to "handing over to Satan," while Rosner's work on the OT background confirms the notion of exposure to *punishment* rather than to *death.*[89] T. C. G. Thornton goes further. Not only does the outcome fail to entail death, but in 1 Cor 5:5, he argues, as in 1 Tim 1:20 and 2 Cor 12:7, Satan is perceived "not . . . as God's enemy, but rather as God's agent."[90] The OT and Judaism, he contends, offer no systematic or unified role for satanic agency, and we should therefore be reluctant to assume some prior meaning other than that which the context of a verse in Paul demands.

(e) In another study (1974) I argued in detail that extreme caution should be used when considering what specialist writers have claimed about "curse" and its supposedly causal effects in the biblical writings.[91] The older views of such writers as L. Dürr and O. Grether, who interpret biblical blessings and curses as *kraftgeladen,* and even Gerhard von Rad's perception of them as "an objective reality endowed with mysterious power," rest on a failure to understand the conditions which are necessary for the performance or nonperformance of illocutionary speech-acts.[92] The reason why Isaac cannot revoke his blessing, and why it is

---

88. Tertullian, *On Modesty,* 14; cf. also 13 and 15; and Fascher, "Zu Tertullians Auslegung von 1 Kor. 5:1-5," 9-12.

89. South, *Disciplinary Practices,* 44-46; Rosner, *Paul, Scripture and Ethics,* 84-85.

90. Thornton, "Satan — God's Agent for Punishing," 151-52.

91. Thiselton, "The Supposed Power of Words in the Biblical Writings," *JTS* 25 (1974): 283-99.

92. G. von Rad, *OT Theology* (Edinburgh: Oliver & Boyd, 1965), 2:85; cf. L. Dürr, *Die Wertung des göttlichen Wortes im A. T. und im antiken Orient* (Leipzig, 1938), 52, 61, and 71.

believed that neither blessing nor curse can be called back in the story of Balak and Balaam (Num 22:6) has nothing whatever to do with the theory that such words in Hebrew are "like a missile with a time-fuse," or "like a long-forgotten mine in the sea."[93] The notion of *causal* force, as instantiated in primitive word magic, has no place here. Quite apart from the fact that blessings and cursings invoke God as agent, not the speaker, these utterances are illocutionary speech-acts which presuppose *institutional* states of affairs. There is no more in the OT or in Paul a *recognized procedure* for "unblessing" or "uncursing" than there is today for "unbaptizing" (as against unmarrying by divorce or unordaining by withdrawing a license and "unfrocking" the ordained person).[94] It is clear that Käsemann's inclusion of this verse in his examples of "sentences of Holy Law in the New Testament" fails to offer a sufficiently sophisticated account of speech-act theory to be valid. His linguistic distinctions do not utilize the refinements pioneered by Austin, Searle, Recanati, and others. The one point of value in this work is his linking of Paul's language with *verdictives*.[95]

(f) Once we abandon the unhelpful imagery of "missiles with a time-fuse," however, notions that Paul and the congregation have **consigned** the man to a process which *causally* leads on to death have no necessary connection with a proper understanding of the judicial verdictive and directive illocutions which expel him from the congregation. Since Paul explicitly states that the whole purpose is ἵνα τὸ πνεῦμα σωθῇ, unless we restrict this *saving act* to the congregation's purification without reference to the offender at all (which the syntax hardly suggests), no grounds remain for assuming that Paul does not still hope that the offender will abandon his illicit relationship and return to the congregation. Indeed, as South rightly points out, the "messenger of Satan" who acts upon Paul in 2 Cor 12:7-10 causes not his death, but through subduing any sense of self-elation "teaches him lessons of patience and dependence on God."[96] This accords with J. Gundry-Volf's convincing argument that Paul's hope is for the man's change of heart and for his future salvation, rather than for his death.[97] This rightly goes further than Goulder's view that "what is expected is that he will fall ill . . . or conceivably actually die; but the kindly pastor knows that this will be for his eternal good."[98] What Paul hopes will be destroyed is his attitude of self-congratulation, which deprivation from the respect

93. W. Eichrodt, *Theology of the OT* (London: SCM, 1967), 2:69.

94. Thiselton, "Supposed Power," esp. 292-96; cf. H. C. Brichto, *The Problem of Curse in the Hebrew Bible,* SBLMS 13 (Philadelphia: Fortress, 1963), and other literature cited in Thiselton, "Supposed Power," 294, n. 3.

95. Käsemann, "Sentences of Holy Law in the NT," in *NT Questions of Today,* 70-73; cf. 66-81. Käsemann includes from our epistle 1 Cor 3:17 (66-68); 14:38 (68-69); 16:22 (69-70); and 5:3-5 (70-73), with 14:13, 28, 30, 35, 37 as "decretal jussive" rather than strictly "sentences of holy law" (74-75). As we have noted, his speculations about pre Pauline origins (76-80) have been well criticized by my former Sheffield colleague David Hill and others.

96. South, *Disciplinary Practices,* 47.

97. J. Gundry-Volf, *Paul and Perseverance,* WUNT 2:37 (Tübingen: Mohr, 1990), 113-20.

98. M. D. Goulder, "Libertines? (1 Cor 5–6)," *NovT* 41 (1999): 341; cf. 334-48.

and support of the church is likely to bring about. This accords with the double use of σάρξ in Galatians, as Jewett points out, by legalists and libertines alike.[99] Presumably that aspect of σάρξ which includes an illicit sexual stance will also be included in this process of *destruction*. In order to foreclose as little semantic flexibility as possible, we have translated the *destruction of the fleshly*. This leaves room, for example, for Dale Martin's interpretation of the offender as one "whose presence threatens to pollute the entire body."[100]

6 D*, Marcion, the Latin of Irenaeus and Tertullian read δολοῖ in place of ζυμοῖ, **leavens**. But this Western reading arises through the Latin and is not authentic.

To translate οὐ καλόν as *not good* (NIV, AV/KJV) or *not a good thing* (NRSV) understates Paul's words and invites a sense of anticlimax or banality. Paul wishes to express deep shock.[101] The REB's *ill becomes you* rightly takes up the meaning of καλός as *seemly* or *appropriate* (as well as its basic meaning, *good* or *well*), but NJB's *is ill-founded* grasps and conveys Paul's point still more precisely. We try to combine the best of NJB and REB by translating **is ill-placed**. On the cognate verb καυχάομαι, of which καύχημα, *boasting*, **self-satisfaction**, *self-congratulation, glorying, complacency* is the related noun, see above on 1:29, 31; 3:21; and 4:7. In 15:31 Paul also uses καύχησις, and repeats κάυχημα in 9:15 and 16. Paul's one ground of "boasting," we noted, is the cross of Christ (cf. Gal 6:4).

The phrase **do you not know that** occurs ten times in 1 Corinthians and only once elsewhere in Paul's established letters (1 Cor 3:16; 5:6; 6:2, 3, 9, 15, 17; 9:13, 24; and Rom 6:16). Hurd, once again, points out that these carry the notion of exposing what the addressees might be expected to **know** if indeed their claim "all have γνῶσις" (8:1) were actually true![102] They generally allude either to axioms or to maxims, but also to theological principles or to knowledge of the world. Harrisville sums up the use neatly as to "signal a contradiction between what is and what ought to be, between what Corinth knows and does."[103] Here the phrase introduces what is probably a maxim or proverb (although there is little evidence for this) or at least a standard metaphor. Paul similarly quotes it in Gal 5:9. Appeal to the penetrating and influential effects of **leaven** had probably become a standard metaphor (whether in terms of its negative effects, Mark 8:15, par. Matt 16:5; Luke 12:1: "beware of the leaven of the Pharisees," or for a more positive evaluation in Matt 13:33, the kingdom of

99. Jewett, *Paul's Anthropological Terms*, 95-115.
100. Dale B. Martin sees the man as "an invading agent of Satan" who puts the purity of the corporate body of the community at risk. Martin alludes to the dual medical background of one tradition which perceives disease as due to an imbalance within a systemic organism and another which attributes disease to an invasion of some alien influence which must be expelled if the body is to regain its proper health. 1 Cor 5:3-5 falls under the second category (Martin, *The Corinthian Body*, 168 and 139-74).
101. Hurd, *The Origin of 1 Corinthians*, 77.
102. Ibid., 85.
103. Harrisville, *1 Corinthians*, 84.

heaven is like leaven hidden in a batch of dough," as is evident from its other NT parallels).

C. L. Mitton offers a substantial comment in his article on this verse and the meaning of ζύμη, **leaven**. BAGD, Louw-Nida, NIV, and NJB (against most other VSS) treat **leaven** and *yeast* as virtually synonymous, although Grimm-Thayer retains only **leaven** as its meaning.[104] Mitton anticipates part of his 1973 article in an earlier comment on Mark 8:15, "'Leaven' is not quite the same as yeast. In ancient times, instead of yeast, a piece of dough was held over from one week's baking to the next. By then it was fermenting, and so could cause fermentation in the new lot of dough, causing it to rise in the heat. This was a useful practice, but not hygienic, since dirt and disease could be passed on from week to week."[105] In the light of this, once a year the Jews would break the chain and begin all over again with fresh, unleavened dough. Hence the influence of a small amount of material carried over from the past was eradicated, and a new beginning took place. (ζύμη, a relatively late word, derives from the older verb ζέω, *I boil*. In v. 6 the verb ζυμόω appears in the contracted third singular present indicative form ζυμοῖ.)

In his later article Mitton states the principle less tentatively. He sheds light on misguided debates about whether the influence of leaven can be construed as "infection" (it *may* carry infection in certain cases), although we should not "read back" the modern medical sciences of microbiology and immunology. Mitton rightly argues that failure to *distinguish* between yeast and leaven may well generate "confusion."[106] Sometimes **leaven** is used as a symbol of dynamic vitality and as a source of unstoppable effects disproportionate to its size (e.g., Matt 13:33); sometimes it signifies the consequences of these qualities when it has become tainted. Paul sees the *disastrous consequences of letting the church become distorted and misshaped by a tainting element which permeates the whole, and calls for a reshaping based solely on the "new," unleavened bread of the Passover, namely, the body of Christ which absorbed sin and perished* on the cross, to be *raised as a new bodily reality* the likeness of which *gave identity and shape to the church.* Hence, Mitton concludes, any "infected" piece no longer has any influence on the new batch, and through death and resurrection with Christ "the new quality of life awakened in the heart of the new believer" prevails.[107]

Fee and Schrage follow the line of approach opened by Mitton's work.[108] Schrage retains *Sauerteig* (leaven) and avoids *Hefe* (yeast), as Lang and Klauck also do.[109] The Greek ὅλον τὸ φύραμα, *the whole mixed lump,* has been trans-

104. BAGD, 340; Louw-Nida, 2:113; Grimm-Thayer, 273.

105. C. L. Mitton, *The Gospel according to St. Mark* (London: Epworth, 1957), 61.

106. Mitton, "New Wine in Old Wineskins: iv, Leaven," *ExpTim* 84 (1973): 339-43.

107. Ibid., 340 and 342-43.

108. Fee, *First Epistle,* 216, esp. n. 6; J. K. Howard, "'Christ our Passover': A Study of the Passover-Exodus Theme in 1 Cor.," 97-108; and Schrage, *Der erste Brief,* 1:379-85.

109. Schrage, *Der erste Brief,* 1:379-85; cf. Lang, *Die Briefe,* 73-4; and Klauck, *1 Korintherbrief,* 43.

lated **all of the dough**: φύραμα is mixed with water and kneaded. It is more important to note the emphatic position of μικρά, **little**. Paul calls attention to the unstoppable, spreading, disastrous influence on the nature and identity of the whole community which is out of all proportion to what those who were **self-satisfied** evidently imagined could spring from a "little" case of one immoral relationship, even if one of an utterly outrageous nature.

G. Harris has explored several sociological models which shed further light on Paul's concern.[110] He looks initially at the well-known and often over-played work of P. Berger and T. Luckmann on "the social construction of reality." We do not have to endorse their theory of constructivism to agree that any community of values has a systemic aspect which needs to be maintained by some principle of internal "order" or "discipline" if its boundaries are not to disintegrate.[111] More interesting is Harris's use of H. Himmelweit's model of "reaction to deviance."[112] Without doubt Paul regards *both* the incestuous relationship *and* the church's attitude toward it as instantiations of deviance from Christian corporate identity. Equally, however, Harris proposes that the new community had distanced itself from the moral traditions of society and the legal traditions of Judaism as acceptable norms for those "freed from the law." Hence Paul reinforces the "catalogue of vices" in 5:9-11 which is fundamental for Judaism. If deviance remains unchecked, like the influence of **leaven** Himmelweit lists the social consequences as: (a) loss of group cohesion; (b) loss of a membership structure; (c) reduced ability to sustain identity against threats from the wider society outside the community; and (d) further consequences for group norms and tacks. "The more cohesive the group . . . the stronger will be the demand for conforming behaviour and the greater the rejection of deviant members." Similarly, in periods in which "outside threat" is stronger, cohesion and lack of deviance become more urgent.

Harris also draws on K. Burridge's social theory of norms. The openness of the relationship of incest to public view implied that the congregation, unlike Paul, did not view this conduct as infringing a norm of group acceptability or of corporate identity.[113] Harris comments again, "Paul's ambivalent stance towards the Mosaic Law may have contributed to the congregation's attitude."[114] Paul's complex attitude emerges from 1 Corinthians 9, where he speaks of "not being under the law" (9:20), yet also appeals to the principle of Deuteronomic law (9:8-9). Räisänen observes, "1 Cor. 5–6 and 2 Cor. 12:10, 11 are serious indicators of what could happen in a congregation which, by and large, lacked the

110. Harris, "The Beginnings of Church Discipline: 1 Cor. 5," 1-21.

111. Ibid., 1-2; cf. 18-20.

112. Ibid., 3-9; cf. H. Himmelweit, "Deviant Behavior," in *A Dictionary of the Social Sciences,* ed. J. Gould and W. L. Kolh (New York: Free Press, 1964), 196-97.

113. K. Burridge, *New Heaven, New Earth* (Oxford: Blackwell, 1969); and Collins, "The Function of 'Excommunication' in Paul," 253; cf. 251-63.

114. Harris, "The Beginnings of Church Discipline," 11.

moral basis provided by Judaism."[115] Social research traces the sociological pathway by which a "new" community or sect first throws off the rules or norms of the old, initially attempting to sustain its identity "without rules"; then enters a phase of rigid rule formulation to preserve its potentially dissipating structure and identity; and finally achieves a new stability.[116] In 1 Corinthians 5, Harris suggests, we see the Corinthian church remaining at the first "no rules" stage; while Paul finds himself pressed into reacting more closely to the second stage for reasons of necessity at that point in the community's development. However, as chs. 8–10 show, Paul also looks ahead to a more open-textured notion of corporate structure and identity, although certain boundary markers remain. The second phase is necessary because "the case of incest openly contradicted Paul's previous instructions. . . . Paul feared contamination of the whole community."[117] (See also in 5:9-11.)

7-8 These two verses are full of fundamental theology, which provides the basis for ecclesiology and ethics. Some modern writers seem to imply that social concerns and rhetoric provide Paul's first concern, rather than understanding 1 Corinthians 1–2, on the cross, and 15, on the resurrection, as the basis for questions of ecclesiology and ethics. Both approaches are essential, but "social history" should not lead to an unintended marginalization of Paul's central theological concerns.

(i) First and foremost, the ethical becomes operative (**clean out**) *because the theological indicative is true* (**as you are** . . .). Paul uses the imperative **clean out the old leaven** on the ground that **you are indeed without old leaven** (καθώς ἐστε ἄζυμοι). "The imperative . . . not only does not contradict the indicative . . . but results from it. . . . The indicative is the foundation of the imperative."[118] This is no mere adjustment "of doing with knowing," or of "praxis to theory" but "the beating heart of his (Paul's) 'imperative' is promise, good news, because his 'speech' and his 'message' effect what they say . . . calling into existence the things that are nothing. . . ."[119] "Purity" is not simply a matter of social identity and boundaries, but of reflecting a *theological* identity as the temple of the Holy Spirit. (See above on ch. 3.)

(ii) More sharply, the ethical reflects what the Christian community and the Christian believer *will become.* Cullmann and Schrage assert this of Paul with particular force. "Upon the basis of the Holy Spirit . . . man is that which he will become only in the future. . . . The Holy Spirit is nothing else than the anticipation of the end in the present."[120] "Of particular importance is the fact

115. H. Räisänen, *Paul and the Law* (Philadelphia: Fortress, 1983), 117, esp. n. 112.

116. Burridge, "New Heaven, New Earth."

117. Harris, "The Beginnings of Church Discipline," 19.

118. Bultmann, *Theology of the NT,* 1:332 and 333; cf. A. Nygren, *Agape and Eros,* 146-59; Schrage, *Der erste Brief,* 1:379-85; Collins, *First Cor,* 208-9; Lang, *Die Briefe,* 73.

119. Harrisville, *1 Corinthians,* 85.

120. Cullmann, *Christ and Time,* 72 and 75-76; cf. Schrage, *Ethik des NT* (Göttingen: Vandenhoeck & Ruprecht, 2d ed. 1989), 170-75; and *Der erste Brief,* 1:380-82.

that there is also to be found an eschatological interpretation of the unleavened bread, side by side with the historical interpretation and that which relates it to the present. . . . 1 Cor. 5:7b-8 . . . is probably based upon an early Christian passover *haggadah*."[121] The Passover lamb, Jeremias continues, together with the bitter herbs and unleavened bread, signifies that "to be a Christian means to live in the passover, in the deliverance from the bondage of sin."[122]

(iii) The possibility of "ethics" in this specific context depends on the reality of the new life, which in turn is founded on Christ as "the passover lamb . . . the symbol of the Messiah who was sacrificed as the unblemished lamb. The leaven which is removed from all of the houses during the night of Nisan 13/14 is the symbol of the evil and wickedness which characterize the old world. The unleavened bread is interpreted eschatologically . . . as the purity and truth which characterize the new world (1 Cor. 5:8), and as new dough they symbolize the redeemed community (1 Cor. 5:7a)."[123]

(iv) R. A. Harrisville provides an incisive study of the words for **new** (νέος and καινός) in these verses and more broadly in Paul. **New** incorporates the four "elements of contrast, continuity, dynamic and finality."[124] Paul establishes (a) a *contrast* between the **old** (here, τὴν παλαιὰν ζύμην) and the **new** (νέον φύραμα). Christ brings in the new *aeon,* to which believers and the believing community must (imperative) and do in principle (indicative) correspond.[125] However, (b) the new is not unrelated to the old, or it would not be *that* which is made new: the crucified Christ is raised; the person in bondage becomes a new creation (2 Cor. 5:17). (c) A *dynamic* is at work which "crowds out" the old: *"The new asserts itself over against the old, and actually crowds it out of existence.* It is also revealed in the power of the new to perpetuate itself . . . *the power of renewal, in contrast to the old which has the tendency to remain as it is"* (my italics).[126] Hence in this passage the dynamic ἐκκαθάρατε, *thoroughly* **clean out**, plays its part. (d) Finally, the **new** has the eschatological quality of God's untarnished new creation. If any semantic distinction exists between νέος and καινός, this may perhaps be discerned in the notion of God's final, new restored creation as unsullied, pure, and untainted (καινός, generally).[127] If this is true of the church, then even now the Corinthians must **clean out** what holds it back from its promised future.

These four theological foundation principles (i-iv above) find expression

121. J. Jeremias, *The Eucharistic Words of Jesus,* 59.

122. Ibid., 60.

123. Ibid.

124. Harrisville, "The Concept of Newness in the NT," 79; cf. 69-79.

125. Ibid., 73.

126. Ibid., 75-76.

127. Ibid., 71 and 76; cf. Wolff, *Der erste Brief,* 86-87, and the use of καινός in 2 Cor 5:17; Gal 6:15; and ἀνακαινός in 2 Cor 4:16, as against νέος in 1 Cor 5:7 and Col 3:10. The *new* cloth (καινός) in Mark 2:21, par. Luke 5:36, is *unused;* in the Apocalypse of John καινός refers to the *new name* (Rev 3:12), *the new song* (Rev 5:9; 14:3); and a *new heaven and earth* (Rev 21:1) and "all things" (21:5).

in Paul's combination of the metaphor of **leaven**, begun in v. 6, with the expanded imagery of the Passover lamb and the actions of the Passover celebration as initiated in the prescriptions of Exod 12:18-20 and 13:7 and transmitted with modifications in Jewish traditions.[128] In Jewish traditions, partly through an interpretative reading of Zeph 1:12, the purging of the house of all leaven was understood as a symbol of moral purification, with candles to look into corners.[129] By analogy, the church is to **clean out** what defiles its identity and purity. Especially in view of the first person plural in v. 8, Chrysostom and many others interpret the **old leaven** as applying more broadly than to the offender alone, although certainly including the offender.[130] The imperative ἐκκαθάρατε is the first aorist active imperative of ἐκκαθαίρω, in which the compound ἐκ signifies both motion and intensity, and the effective aorist signifies the summons to perform a specific act. It is not too much to perceive in the Greek compound and syntax an implicit urgency about effectively completing this action with thoroughness, especially in its ritualistic context.

Especially in view of the important observations of C. L. Mitton (see above on v. 6) the emphasis lies on *making a fresh start,* which entails a break with a past stance. Harrisville's work on *newness* (see again on v. 6) gives further point to this aspect. **Unleavened** translates -ζυμοι with the α-privative. We should resist imposing a late nineteenth-century neo-Kantian idealism onto this verse, as in the comment that "Paul habitually idealizes . . . exemplifying Kant's maxim that you should treat a man as you would wish him to be."[131] This misses the eschatological, christological, and soteriological basis of the indicative.

Several major English versions translate τὸ πάσχα ἡμῶν as **our passover lamb**, or *our paschal lamb* (NRSV, REB, NIV); as against *our passover* (AV/KJV, NJB). Unless we restructure the sentence, ἐτύθη entails *paschal lamb* or **Passover lamb** as the object of sacrifice, as D. O. Wenthe argues.[132] Just as the Passover festival embraces a series of aspects and events, so the whole work of Christ, including his death and resurrection, includes many aspects. But *the death of Christ* corresponds to the sacrifice of the Passover lamb. Here, for Paul, the old is abolished and the blood of the Passover lamb ratifies the promises of redemption *from* bondage (where "Egypt" symbolizes the bondage of human existence without Christ) *to* a new purity and freedom *by* a costly act. This is not to read *into* Paul any "theory of the atonement," for the transparently clear reference here to *sacrifice* (θύω) is complemented by the language of *re-*

128. On the exegesis of Exod 12:18-20 and 13:7 contextualized in the OT. Judaism, the NT, the patristic period, and historical theology, cf. B. S. Childs, *Exodus: A Commentary* (London: SCM, 1874 and 1977), 178-214, esp. 198-210.

129. Cf. Meyer, *First Epistle,* 1:148-51.

130. Chrysostom, *1 Cor. Hom.,* 15:5.

131. Robertson and Plummer, *First Epistle,* 102, and more adequately Strobel, *Der erste Brief,* 101.

132. Wenthe, "An Exegetical Study of 1 Cor. 5:7b," 134-40. Also Strobel, *Der erste Brief,* 101-2.

demption (ἀγοράζω) in 6:20, and *covenant promise, identification,* and the shedding of *Christ's blood* in 11:25-26. The blood of the Passover lamb, splashed upon the lintel of the door of the redeemed household, *marks the identity* of those who are about to enter a new freedom from bondage to a new purity of service as God's own holy people. This epistle has a very strong doctrine of the work of Christ which is often underplayed by interpreters. Conzelmann's attempt to reduce the force of the imagery on the grounds that it is applied *corporately* seems to betray a prior stance of Western individualism which shapes his expectations.[133] It should not be forgotten that 1:17–2:5 presents a theology of the cross as Paul's major theme.

The converse and complementary theme which parallels the destruction of sin, failure, and decay in Christ's sacrificial death (v. 7) emerges as the celebration of the new life enacted in and through Christ's being raised to new life. Hence the first plural present active subjunctive ἑορτάζωμεν means **let us celebrate the festival**; or if the specific ἑορτή in question is, as here, that of the Passover, **let us celebrate the Passover festival**. "The Community is encouraged to get on with the celebration" when the old has been purged.[134] On its own ἑορτή means simply *a feast,* and in the papyri often means *a joyous festival.* In the NT it is sometimes specified as ἑορτὴ τοῦ πάσχα (Luke 2:41; John 13:1, *the festival of the Passover*) or ἡ ἑορτὴ τῶν ἀζύμων (Luke 22:1, *the festival of unleavened bread*). The continuous present tense offers grounds for Godet's comment that "Our passover feast is not for a week, but for a lifetime."[135] This reflects Chrysostom's observation: "It is a festival, then, the whole time in which we live . . . the whole of time is a festival to Christians, because of the excellency of the good things which have been given. . . . The Son of God . . . freed you from death and called you to a kingdom."[136] Chrysostom compares this with the parables of banquets and celebratory feasts (e.g., Matt 22:1), and some of the Fathers and several modern writers endorse and expound this theme.[137]

In a celebration of the new, therefore (see especially Harrisville's comments above), what **ferments wickedness and evil** has no place. Our word **ferments** simply explicates the objective genitive κακίας, since **leaven** *of wickedness* means **leaven** that *generates, transmits,* or **ferments** it. The image of a *spreading* evil is clear enough. Although several writers distinguish between κακία as **wickedness** in the sense of *malice* (AV/KJV) and πονηρία as the **evil** which results from this stance or disposition, the two terms are used as synonyms on occasion, and any difference of this kind is vague and certainly not uniform. The genitive plural ἀζύμοις may suggest **unleavened** *loaves* (plural); the Greek has no word for *bread* here, but this is understood. It is more difficult

---

133. Conzelmann, *1 Cor,* 99.
134. Collins, *First Cor,* 215; similarly Lang, *Die Briefe,* 74, Strobel, *Der erste Brief,* 101-2.
135. Godet, *First Epistle,* 1:266.
136. Chrysostom, *1 Cor. Hom.,* 15:6.
137. Schrage, *Der erste Brief,* 1:384; Theophylact, 625; Strobel, *Der erste Brief,* 101-2.

to assess the force of ἐν with the datives ζύμῃ παλαιᾷ and ζύμῃ κακίας. If the syntax reflects the metaphorical act, the translation should be **not with the old leaven**. If Paul is already applying the metaphor, ἐν might be understood to mean *not under the influence of the old leaven,* understanding it in a modal sense more broadly rather than more narrowly of the action itself. But the application comes in the explicating clause: **not with the leaven that ferments wickedness and evil**.

The word εἰλικρινείας is rare. εἰλικρινεία occurs in 2 Cor 2:17 to denote **purity** or *transparency* of motive on Paul's part. It also occurs in Wis 7:25, but otherwise only in pre-Socratic texts and the papyri. Its word history is debated, but it seems plausible to consider the notion of judging (κρίνω) in the light of the sun (ἥλιος, allegedly with a variant form εἵλιος), i.e., to see its *transparent* character. But **purity** seems to fit the context best both here and in 2 Cor. 2:17. *Sincerity* (NRSV, REB, NIV, NJB) is basically sound. But the semantic contrast here is between **purity** and what *defiles* the body: *limpid purity,* or *transparency.*[138]

This coheres well with the meaning of ἀλήθεία, **truth**, here. Paul follows Wis 13 and 14 in contrasting **truth** with the self-deception and illusion entailed in both idol worship and moral decline (Rom 1:25). In this theological and moral context Paul speaks in Romans of "suppressing the truth" (Rom 1:18) and of exchanging the truth of God for the falsehoods of mere human opinion (Rom 1:25). Although it is incorrect, as J. Barr has stressed, to argue that truth *means faithfulness* or *stability* simply on the grounds that the Hebrew אמת *('emeth)* can do duty for both Greek words, nevertheless in this context **truth** bears some relationship to remaining *faithful* or *true* to one's individual and corporate identity as Christian people. Hence, as I have argued in considerable detail elsewhere (1978), Paul uses **truth** not only in contrast to falsehood, illusion, and deception but also "in the sense of an honesty or integrity in which word and deed correspond. . . . Hence he exclaims, 'We have renounced disgraceful, underhanded ways; we refuse to practise cunning . . . but by open statement of the truth we commend ourselves . . .' (2 Cor. 4:2)."[139] Here **truth** relates to being true to the Christian's *identity* as sharing in the afflictions of Christ and a *Christian lifestyle*. Hence, here, **purity and truth** means the living out of a Christian life in actions which reflect the identity and reality of the new creation, as against that which is tainted by the self-interest and moral degeneracy, which must be **cleaned out**.

Whether Paul's use of the first plural for **let us celebrate the Passover festival** implies that Paul was writing this epistle from Ephesus at the time of the Passover remains a debated question. Many allude to 16:8, "I will stay in Ephesus until Pentecost," in conjunction with 4:19, "I will come to you soon" (see on 16:8). Carrington in fact regards this epistle as "a Paschal letter, a fact

138. Strobel, *Der erste Brief,* 102; BAGD, 222, *purity of motive.*
139. Thiselton, "Truth, ἀλήθεία," 886 and 874-902.

which is made particularly clear in its use of Exodus-Numbers [10:1-10] or more likely a 'midrash' upon it."[140] Hurd judiciously comments that "the theme of 1 Cor. 5:6-8 may well have been suggested to Paul by the season," and the hypothesis of his writing at the Passover season is adopted by Allo and Klauck among others.[141]

2. Further Reflection on the Holiness of the Congregation and Allusion to the Previous Letter (5:9-13)

(9, 10) I wrote to you in my letter not to mix indiscriminately with immoral people. In no way did this refer to people in secular society who are immoral or grasping or who practice extortion or idolatry, since you would then be obliged to withdraw from the world. (11) As matters stand, however, I am writing to you not to mix indiscriminately with someone who accepts the name of Christian and remains immoral or grasping in their stance or is involved in idolatry, or is characterized as a person of verbal abuse, or a drunkard, or someone who gains by extortionate dealing. With such a person you should not even share your table. (12, 13) For what business of mine is it to formulate verdicts about outsiders? Is it not those inside to whom your verdicts apply? Those outside have God as their judge. "Banish the evil man."

Two kinds of explanations link vv. 9-13 with vv. 1-8. First, Paul writes to explain further the reason for his uncompromising tone in 5:1-8, and to point out that his readers had already received prior warning about the entailment of holiness and purity for those who wished to be part of the Christian congregation. Second, more especially, Rosner has traced the importance of the Deuteronomic background in 5:1-8, and demonstrates how the three themes of covenant identity, corporate responsibility, and holiness characterize both material in Deuteronomy which Paul has in mind (especially Deut 23:1-9) and the recontextualization of this material in terms of community identity in Ezra 9:1, 2 (cf. Neh 13:1-3, 23-27) and in 1 Cor 5:9-13.[142]

9-10 Several of the Church Fathers (followed by Erasmus) interpret ἔγραψα in v. 9 as an epistolary aorist denoting the present act of writing (as in Gal 6:11; Philem 19, 21; and Col 4:8).[143] But this is excluded by ἐν τῇ ἐπιστολῇ,

---

140. P. Carrington, *The Primitive Christian Calendar* (Cambridge: Cambridge University Press, 1952), 42.

141. Hurd, *The Origin of 1 Corinthians,* 139; cf. Meyer, *First Epistle,* 1:152; Allo, *Première Épitre,* 125-27; and Klauck, *1 Korintherbrief,* 43. (Hurd includes a critique of Carrington's view.) Caution is shown by G. Lüdemann, *Paul, Apostle to the Gentiles: Studies in Chronology* (Eng. trans., London: SCM, 1984), 89-90.

142. Rosner, *Paul, Scripture and Ethics,* 61-93.

143. Theodoret, *Interpretatio prim. ep. ad Cor.,* 194 (Migne, *PG,* 82:263 [Lat.], 264 [Gk.]); Chrysostom, *1 Cor. Hom.,* 16:1; Erasmus, *Periphr. in Ep. Pauli ad Cor. 1,* 874.

in my [the] **letter.**[144] The view that this verse makes it certain that Paul wrote "a previous letter" goes back to the early Latin commentator Ambrosiaster, and is endorsed by Calvin, Beza, Estius, Grotius, Bengel, and virtually all modern commentators.[145] Hurd reconstructs the series of events which relate to the previous letter, but many remain justifiably guarded about the notion that the Corinthians could "misunderstand" Paul as seriously as Hurd's later reconstruction supposes.[146] On the other hand, some may maliciously have applied a *reductio ad absurdum* of which Paul now shows himself fully aware.[147]

Paul's choice of the word συναναμιγνύσθαι (the double compound verb συναναμιγνῦμι), translated above with μή, as **not to mix indiscriminately with**, provides lexicographers with much room for debate. It is a late word, occurring only here, in v. 11, and in 2 Thess 3:14 within the NT, and otherwise rarely except in the papyri. In classical Greek few instances of the active voice mean *to mix up together,* while the rare passives mean *to associate with* (Plutarch, *Philopoemen* 21).[148] In their lexicography of the papyri, Moulton-Milligan understand *associate with* as the metaphorical translation of the meaning *mix up together* in 1 Cor 5:9, 11 and 2 Thess 3:14, but suggest a meaning more akin to *inclusion* in the isolated example of *Oxyrhynchus Papyri* 4:718:16 (c. AD 190.[149] Collins endorses *associate with.*[150]

Most English VSS choose *not to associate with* (NRSV, NIV) or *have nothing to do with* (REB, NJB), leaving aside *have no company with* (AV/KJV). But these lose the wry double compound: μίγνυμι + ἀνα + συν- retains its structure in English, *mixed up with,* where the middle denotes not simply personal interest but subjectivity of situation, i.e., **to mix indiscriminately with**. This fits the context better than either *have nothing to do with* (are they to cut them dead in the street?) or *not to associate with* (should they check what meetings or functions they attend?). Schrage applies common sense to the everyday situation, e.g., of slaves.[151] Paul calls for *discrimination* about boundary markers, corporate identity, and the recognition of the Christian community as a corporate witness to overt beliefs, values, and lifestyles. *The addressees are to use their sense about how this works out* so that no one is confused and so that a man such as the immoral offender is well aware of where he stands in relation to the community. On the translation of πόρνοις as **immoral people** and the meaning of πορνεία, see above on 5:1.

The syntax of v. 10 permits two possible interpretations of the relation

144. Schrage, *Der erste Brief,* 1:388; Conzelmann, *1 Corinthians,* 99; Hurd, *Origin,* 50-53.
145. Calvin, *First Epistle,* 111: "The letter to which he refers does not exist today"; cf. Bengel, *Gnomon,* 623: *ante hanc scripta;* Meyer, *First Epistle,* 1:152-54.
146. Cf. Hurd, *Origin,* 50-53.
147. Schrage, *Der erste Brief,* 1:388-89.
148. LSJ, 1,474.
149. MM, 602.
150. Collins, *First Cor,* 216 and 217.
151. Schrage, *Der erste Brief,* 1:389.

between οὐ, *not,* and πάντως, *wholly, entirely, altogether.* The REB interprets the negative as qualifying the adverb, so that Paul is *not* referring to *people in general . . .* but *to Christians. . . .*[152] However, the NRSV and NIV interpret the negative as negating the whole concept expressed in the clause: *not at all meaning. . . .* By inserting an additional *of course* the REB, however, succeeds in hedging its bets. In view of the complacency of those who appealed to γνῶσις (8:1), however, along the problem of spiritual elitism and the query about ascetic practices in 7:1-16, it is likely that, even if both are plausible, Paul wishes to emphasize the impossibility of a Christlike community forming a ghetto.[153] Hence we translate: **in no way did this refer to people in secular society who are immoral** . . . rendering τοῦ κόσμου τούτου *(of this world)* as **in secular society.** The allusion to **this** world implicitly points to a contrast between those whose lives are governed by the here-and-now within the corporate structures of the world and those whose citizenship is "in heaven" (Phil 3:20).

Four terms denoting immoral or illicit conduct occur in v. 10, and six, of which only two terms are new, are repeated in v. 11. "Lists" or "catalogues" of vices are common in ancient literature, including Rom 1:29-31 (twenty-one "vices" from rumormongers and braggarts to God-haters and murderers); Wis 14:25-26 (which Romans 1 reflects probably deliberately to reproduce synagogue homily material to serve Paul's arguments); twelve "vices" in *1 Clement* 35:5; and even longer lists in Philo and in other writings. A number of full-length studies of "catalogues of virtues and vices" have been influential.[154]

Conzelmann insists that these "catalogues" have no model in the OT, and that where they occur in Judaism "Greek influence is at hand." The lists derive in origin, he argues, from Stoic catalogues or tables of the cardinal virtues and vices (as A. Vögtle proposed in 1936) and further back to Plato's work on virtues.[155] While the occurrence of this material in Greek and hellenistic writers is clearly in evidence, the inferences often drawn from the data are a different matter. Conzelmann represents a typical view when he claims that the lists owe more to standard catchphrases than to actual conditions, e.g., at Corinth, which invite attention to specific details. (But see on 6:9-10.) Meanwhile, while it is true that Paul uses "lists" in Rom 1:29-31, Gal 5:19-21, and perhaps in 1 Cor 6:9-10 and 2 Cor 12:20-21, especially in the Corinthians letters we must recall (with Rosner) that Paul draws upon a moral tradition from the OT and Judaism especially from Deuteronomy. Further, Harris's application of this material to

152. Fee, *First Epistle,* 223: ". . . more likely that in a qualified way he did not 'in general' intend what they have taken it to mean." Cf. Parry, *First Epistle,* 92, "not meaning absolutely."

153. The point is underlined by Conzelmann, *1 Cor.,* 100.

154. See S. Wibbing, *Die Tugend- und Lasterkataloge in NT und ihre Traditionsgeschichte,* BZNW 25 (Berlin: Töpelmann, 1959); and E. Kamlah, *Die Form der katalogischen Paränese im NT* (Tübingen: Mohr, 1964); cf. Conzelmann, *1 Cor.,* 100-101, "Excursus."

155. A. Vögtle, *Die Tugend- und Lasterkataloge im NT* (Münster: Aschendorff, 1936), esp. 58-73; cf. Dio Chrysostom, *Orations* 45 (62):2, 6; 56 (73):1; Cicero, *Tusculanae Disputationes* 4.3.5; 4.6.11–14.33; Epictetus, *Dissertations* 2.16.11, and Conzelmann, *1 Cor,* 100-101.

community identity calls in question Conzelmann's bland assumption that the choice of "vices" in 5:10-11 fails to reflect the actual state of affairs at Corinth.[156] In fact, in v. 10 we find a so-called "catalogue" of only four, with only two further additions in v. 11!

Some individual terms invite lexical and contextual examination. (1) We translated the dative plural πόρνοις as **people who are immoral**. Paul ascribes this to the Corinthians situation (5:1), but it also reflects the OT Decalogue (cf. Exod 20:13; Deut 5:17, although LXX μοιεύσεις, *adultery,* is a special subcategory of πορνεία). (2) πλεονέκταις, in the terminology of semantic theory, is a "transparent" compound joining πλέον (cf. πολύς, πλείων), *more,* with ἔχω, *I have,* i.e., *covetous, avaricious,* **grasping** people who always *want more than they have.* To be sure, πλεονεξία occurs in Greek "lists of vices."[157] But this also corresponds precisely with the social analysis of Corinthian society offered by Pogoloff, Witherington, and others, that many at Corinth were obsessed with the *ambition to achieve,* i.e., *to gain more* social status, power, or wealth.[158] This quality is endemic in the Corinthian self-made persons and *nouveau riche* culture, and Paul sees its relegation as a boundary marker for Christian corporate identity. It also reflects the tenth commandment of the Decalogue, "You shall not covet . . ." (Exod 20:17, although LXX uses ἐπιθυμήσεις, as also in Deut. 5:2). (3) ἅρπαξ usually means *swindler,* i.e., one who *robs by cheating* as against the λῃστής, who *robs by violence.* Much more common is the verb ἁρπάζω, *to snatch something and carry it off as one's own.* Perhaps, therefore, our tentative proposal to translate **people who practice extortion** (which approximates REB, *extortioners*) most adequately combines the two nuances of using deceptive methods to snatch something away from someone to make it one's own.[159] We use *extortionate* of those who exploit people who need a commodity or a service *in such a way as to gain speedy and disproportionate wealth at the expense of others.* This, once again, may reflect the entrepreneurial culture at Corinth, whereby to "get rich quick" and to knock others off the ladder was the name of the game. Hence, once again, Paul wishes to distance the Christian community from cultural assumptions that such practices are acceptable. *This difference of stance* constitutes one of many *boundary markers for Christian identity.* Without such explanation, the crude NRSV *robbers* plays into the hands of the type of argument used by Conzelmann and gives an air of unreality to the historical situation, replacing it with a literary convention. By contrast **extortion** instantiates precisely the kind of "stealing" which genuinely

---

156. Harris, "The Beginnings of Church Discipline: 1 Cor. 5," 1-21; cf. Rosner, *Paul, Scripture and Ethics: A Study of 1 Cor 5–7,* esp. 61-93.

157. BAGD, 667; cf. Dio Chrysostom, *Orations* 67 (17):6, 7 as μέγιστον κακόν; Philo, *De Specialibus Legibus* 1.173; Diodorus Siculus, 13.30.4; *1 Clement* 35:12 (a list of twelve "vices," with some others in the rest of the chapter). Cf. Grimm-Thayer, 516.

158. Witherington, *Conflict and Community,* e.g., 24, "status-hungry people"; cf. 22-29 and throughout; and Pogoloff, *Logos and Sophia,* 129-72.

159. Cf. BAGD, 109.

tempted earlier Christians in business or property, who could manipulate rents or charges as a misuse of power without appearing flagrantly to rob in the criminal sense of the term.[160] (4) **people who practice idolatry** (εἰδωλολάτραις) constitutes, Edwards claims, the earliest occurrence of this word.[161] The whole discussion from 8:1 to 11:1 reflects the genuine temptation for Christians living among the Gentiles, to blur boundary markers in such a way as to compromise "the table of the Lord" and that of idols (10:16-23). Hence, 8:1-7 and 10:16-23, as well as other material in these chapters, demonstrate that, against Conzelmann and others, this fourth "vice" reflects the specific situation at Corinth, even if it applies only to some within the church.

We may now return to the arguments of Harris and Rosner.[162] Harris convincingly explains why the "old rules" would too readily be discarded by many at Corinth who sought a new corporate identity. It is difficult to exaggerate the fluidity of the situation at Corinth if the moral tradition of Judaism were either discarded or of little influence.[163] Hence Paul has to reinforce the community boundary markers and moral traditions *before* new "freedoms" can play their proper role. The maxim in 6:12, with Paul's caveat, places the issue in focus.

Rosner also demonstrates the relevance of the Deuteronomic traditions, the Decalogue, and the holiness of the community in 3:16-17 for Paul's thought here. Behind the expulsion of the offender, Rosner argues, lie the prohibitions of Deut 27:20 and 23:1, with the added force of Deut 5:13, 22:22; 23:2-9, and the tradition embodied in Mishnah *Sanhedrin* 7:4, *Jubilees* 33:10-13, Tosefta *Sanhedrin* 10:1, and CD 5.[164] Moreover, what most scholars call "the vice catalogue" is better interpreted in terms of the Deuteronomic covenant identity and convenient obligations. Rosner points out that Paul's terms appear in Deut 22:21 (LXX ἐκπορνεύω, "equivalent to Paul's πόρνος"); 17:3, 7 (LXX εἰδωλολάτρης); and 24:27 (LXX ἅπαξ). The two additional terms introduced in 5:11 occur in Deut 21:20-21 and 19:18-19. Only πλεονέκτης is absent, which Rosner and Leon Morris see as included with ἅρπαξιν and is merely explicating it.[165] Rosner traces equally to the OT background the motifs of corporate responsibility and holiness, as we have already noted.

On top of all this, recently Peter S. Zaas clinches the whole argument. He argues: "The vice catalogues of 1 Cor. 5:10, 11 and 6:9-10 are closely related to the epistolary situation of this part of the letter."[166] There is no evidence for the view that Paul merely repeats traditional material. This issue is of special importance for the ethics of 6:9-10 (see below, further).

---

160. See the excellent chapter, "Making Stealing Possible," in Fowl, *Engaging Scripture: A Model for Theological Interpretation*.

161. Edwards, *First Epistle*, 132.

162. Harris, "Church Discipline," 1-21; Rosner, *Paul, Scripture, and Ethics*, 61-93.

163. We noted above arguments from A. D. Nock, H. Räisänen, and G. Harris to this effect.

164. Rosner, *Paul, Scripture and Ethics*, 82-83.

165. Ibid., 69; Morris, *First Epistle*, 88.

166. P. S. Zaas, "Catalogues and Context: 1 Cor. 5 and 6:2," 623-24, 622-29.

After listing four qualities which characterize those with whom the addressees are **not to mix indiscriminately**, Paul reinforces the absurdity of any notion that he could be understood to include people of their kind *outside the Christian congregation*.[167] Hence he adds as the last clause of the verse: **since you would then** (ἄρα as *then*, of logical consequence, i.e., *in that case*) **be obliged** (ὠφείλετε, imperfect indicative) **to withdraw from the world**. In theory we might have expected some such linguistic indicator as ἄν to signal the indefinite character of the unfulfilled conditional, but in practice the present construction often occurs with verbs of obligation.

11 In v. 10 the syntatical connection between ἔγραψα, *I wrote*, and ἐν τῇ ἐπιστολῇ, *in my letter*, excluded the possibility of interpreting ἔγραψα as an epistolary aorist there. Here, by contrast, νῦν, *now* (i.e., **as matters stand**), has the opposite effect: it suggests that the aorist ἔγραψα is to be understood in this verse in an epistolary sense to mean **Now, however, I am writing**. Commentators and English translations reflect a divided judgment on this. REB and NJB render *I meant,* interpreting the aorist as a past tense (with Conzelmann and Wolff), but the NRSV and NIV (with Collins and Fee) translate more plausibly, **now I am writing**, or *what I now write*.[168] Allo convincingly observes, "What Paul wished to say in his first letter, he now explicates, since he has seen that he needs to do so."[169]

Many of the remaining words of the verse repeat a vocabulary already employed in vv. 9 and 10 and hence require no further comment. On **not to mix indiscriminately** see on v. 9. The verbal adjective ὀνομαζόμενος is passive (Bengel: passive used in a middle sense) but conveys in this context not only *being* named as a brother (ἀδελφός), but the *person's passing himself off as Christian,* i.e., **who accepts the name of Christian**.[170] English VSS convey this nuance in different ways, e.g., *bears the name of brother* (NRSV), *anyone who calls himself a brother* (NIV), *any so-called Christian* (REB), or *anyone going by the name of brother* (NJB).[171] On **immoral, grasping extortion and idolatry**, see the detailed comments on v. 10. We rejected the argument that these are determined only by a standard "catalogue" form without reference to the specific situation at Corinth. On the other hand, these "vices" are indeed listed as *characteristics,* or *continuous practices,* as against lapses from which an offender subsequently turns away. Hence the English translation above draws attention to this aspect by rendering **remains immoral or grasping in their stance**, and in the light of 8:1-7 and 10:16-23 (in the larger context of 8:1–11:1) we translate **involved in idolatry**, for in these verses the issue turns on what counts as "involvement." We explained above (v. 10) how **extortionate**

167. Schrage, *Der erste Brief,* 1:389-90.
168. Conzelmann, *1 Corinthians,* 102, n. 81; Wolff, *Der erste Brief,* 109, against Barrett, *First Epistle,* 131; Fee, *First Epistle,* 230, n. 4; Collins, *First Cor,* 216 and 220-21.
169. Allo, *Première Épitre,* 129.
170. Bengel, *Gnomon,* 623.
171. Similarly Weiss, *Der erst Korintherbrief,* 140.

dealings could feature in an achievement culture. Being an "extortioner" does not refer to being part of a professional occupation; Paul means someone who kicks others down the ladder in order to advance upward at any price.

To the four characteristics of v. 10 Paul now adds λοίδορος ἢ μέθυσος. (5) Paul has already employed λοιδορούμενοι in 4:12 (see above), where we argued that Paul's response of εὐλογοῦμεν did *not* mean that he "blessed" slanderers, but that he met **verbal abuse** with words that were good, courteous, positive, and constructive. Here he refers to people who cannot open their mouths without putting others down in a way *which causes hurt* and implies a *scornful, superior attitude* on the part of the speaker. This can become a habitual style of communication which betrays self-importance and insensitivity, and escalates pain into grievance and a legitimate desire to withdraw from verbal communication on the part of the person to whom **the abuse** is directed. Hence, as Margaret Mitchell argues, while any political or social body contains a "mix" (μίγνυσθαι), "Paul must define the proper boundaries of the new 'mix,' as he does in 5:1-13."[172] Some cannot be included without disrupting the identity and daily cohesion of the congregation.

(6) λοίδορος and μέθυσος, **drunkard**, occur in Deut 19:19 and 20:20-21, where they characterize people who excluded themselves from the covenant community as the holy people of God.[173] Both on theological grounds of the corporate identity of the community and on pastoral grounds of what might cause the community to disintegrate, Paul draws a boundary which defines these qualities as belonging to "outsiders," not to Christians, at least as habitual characterizations of their conduct. **Drunkenness** not only repels others from the company of the **drunkard**; in turn it may lead to **verbal** and even to physical **abuse**. It excludes the possibility of respect and concern for the welfare of others while it holds sway. But ἀγάπη, *respect, regard, love,* for others is a hallmark of Christian identity. What is said about **drunkenness** in the literature of first-century Judaism places more emphasis on the unacceptable behavior to which it gives rise than to the consumption of alcohol in itself.[174]

Paul does not enjoin total abstinence from wine in a "wine culture," but calls for the same attitude of discipline and regard for others as he does in the areas of wealth, sex, and other aspects of social life. It would be anachronistic to expect that first-century culture would have identified the specific medical problem of the alcoholic in today's terms. Hence this additional feature must be taken into account when reflecting on the issues which are implied for today. The debate about the "strong" and the "weak" in the context of idols and meat eating might have more to say in this specific issue, where individual case studies play a part (see 10:23-33). In the ancient world sharing food and drink was of the utmost importance for social bonding. Hence the general principle would

172. Mitchell, *Paul and the Rhetoric of Reconciliation,* 115-16.
173. Rosner, *Paul, Scripture and Ethics,* 82-83.
174. Fee, *First Epistle,* 225-26.

be to fit in with the conventions of the group, but subject to (i) individual situations and circumstances, which include, e.g., issues of personal example, influence on others, or other matters of "exception" (10:23-33); and (ii) that kind of "social drinking" which leads to lack of sobriety, self-control, concern for others and to excess (Rom 13:13). The slogans "taste not, touch not" (Col 2:21) are likely to spring from conservative Judaizing, anti-Gentile tendencies within the NT church. Paul wants Christians to be credible to outsiders as human persons, but in the light of individual situations urges elsewhere, "Allow no one to take you to task over what you eat or drink," i.e., one way or the other (Col 2:16, REB).

The social bonding associated with eating and drinking together helps us to understand μηδὲ συνεσθίειν, *not even to eat with them,* i.e., **you should not even share your table (with such a person).** Although there is a well-known debate about whether Paul refers here to eating together at the Lord's Table or to eating together in houses in everyday social relationships, the use of μηδέ, **not even,** would *not make sense* if Paul were understood to say: they do not belong to the congregation, **not even** to the fellowship of the Lord's Supper. The logical step proceeds in the wrong direction, i.e., would be understandable only if it were to mean exclusions from the Lord's Supper and **not even** more "open" occasions. However, **not even** can be understood in a more constructive, generous sense. If **not even** inviting **such a person** (τῷ τοιούτῳ) home for the social bonding of the family table expressed *the negative limits,* there could be no question of never speaking to such people in the street, or of excluding the *normal courtesies due to acquaintances, but not to friends, associates, or close colleagues.* Paul's μηδέ seems to exclude withdrawal from the normal courtesies of life, but does indeed specify *association, support,* and *compromise of community-identity.*

12-13 (i) p[46], Coptic Bohairic, and the Syriac Peshitta VSS transpose the second clause (v. 12b) from a rhetorical question expecting an affirmative reply, οὐχὶ τοὺς ἔσω ὑμεῖς κρίνετε, into an imperative, omitting οὐχί: you [must take responsibility for being] judge. . . . (ii) Conversely, the Coptic Sahidic VS construed οὐχί with the previous clause to read ἔξω κρίνειν καὶ ἔσω οὐχί, i.e., what business is it of mine to formulate verdicts about outsiders and not those inside? The overwhelming majority of textual witnesses, however, read the text of UBS[4], which is secure. (iii) In the first clause of v. 13, whether a *perispomenon* accent should be placed over the ending of κρινεῖ remains uncertain, since the earliest MSS did not carry accents. The accent interprets κρινεῖ as the contracted future indicative of κρίνω, *God will judge,* whereas κρίνει denotes the present (uncontracted) tense, *God judges.* We can avoid a decision by rendering **have God as their judge,** which may include both present state and future action.[175]

175. Metzger concedes that the balance of probability is fine, but in view of the eschatological flavor of this epistle "the majority of the Committee" (i.e., clearly not all!) considered the future "more appropriate in the context" (*Textual Commentary* [2d ed.], 486). Schrage balances the future judgment of 4:5 (cf. Rom 2:5, 16) against the present situation of community-insiders and the situation of others (*Der erste Brief,* 1:394).

The Greek idiom τί γάρ μοι corresponds with the Latin idiom of the Vulgate, *quid enim mihi,* and Beza's *quid mea interest?* It reminds us of the well-known rhetorical question of Jesus to Mary at Cana, τί ἐμοὶ καὶ σοί, γύναι; (John 2:4). Findlay proposed the excellent idiomatic translation, **For what business of mine is it. . . ?** This is incorporated as it stands into the REB and NIV (also above). NJB, *it is no concern of mine,* is less happy than JB, *it is not my business,* because although μοι is technically a dative of interest *(it is not for me)* it more naturally concerns a *formal role* or *sphere of interest* here than any notion of psychological or spiritual indifference. The central issue is the capacity of Paul in conjunction with the corporate community (5:2-5) to legislate community rules and to execute them with legitimate authority *within* the Christian congregation. Calvin asserts, "In this context Paul is speaking about the special jurisdiction of the Church. . . . This punishment is part of the discipline which is confined to the Church, and does not embrace those outside."[176]

Although κρίνω in general means *I judge,* according to its context it may refer to **formulating verdicts,** *reaching verdicts,* or *enacting verdicts.* Nowadays the raw translation *what have I to do with judging those outside?* (NRSV) reads superficially more like a disclaimer about moralistic judgmentalism, which is not Paul's point at all. He is expressing a profound principle about church polity: the church as a whole has a responsibility to formulate its own house rules for the preservation of its unity, holiness, catholicity, and apostolicity as expressing a distinctively *Christian* (or *Christ*-like) corporate identity which retains cohesion for its witness, nurture, and mission to the world. Bammel's notion of an autonomous community in 1 Corinthians 5 hardly seems to reflect Paul's ecclesiology.[177]

Vv. 12 and 13 constitute complementary aspects of a single theme. The

---

176. Calvin, First Epistle, 115.

177. E. Bammel, "Rechtsfindung in Korinth," 107-13 (although Bammel gives weight to a "change" toward 2 Cor 12:21–13:10). Rosner includes a note on the relation between this passage and Matt 18:13-20 (which in turn reflects Lev 19:17 and Deut 19:15-19). In Matthew, as here, one main concern is for *the restitution of the sinner.* But *in each case the whole church is also involved,* and in each case the sinner's stance rather than a single act is in view (*Paul, Scripture and Ethics,* 89-90). Godet also writes of "the profound analogy which prevails between this chapter and the disciplinary direction given to the Apostles by our Lord" (Matt 18:15-20; in more recent Matthean scholarship writers compare later questions about excommunication from the synagogue). Comparing Matt 5:22, 18:15-20; 2 Thess 3:6, 14, 15 and Rev 2:19-22, we find that common to all are (i) admonition; (ii) an eventual public declaration or verdictive speech-act. See South, *Disciplinary Practices in Pauline Texts,* 23-88 (on 1 Cor 5:1-5), 89-110 (on 2 Cor 2:5-11), 111-38 (on Galatians), 139-58 (on Rom 16:17 and Phil 3:2), and 159-80 (on 2 Thessalonians, Ephesians, and the Pastorals). South concludes: "The exercise of discipline was ultimately for the gain of both the offender and the community" (186). Fee urges that "Paul is not a separtist . . . ," and rightly laments the tendency of churches today to fall into either of the two extremes of diffused loss of identity or tight authoritarian sectarianism (*First Epistle,* 227-28). A. C. Wire interprets the Pauline texts in a way which ascribes to Paul an authoritarianism which is at odds with the Pauline emphasis on holding together structure and freedom (*The Corinthian Women Prophets,* 1990, esp. 26-30 and 76-79; for a contrary perspective see F. F. Bruce, *Paul, Apostle of the Free Spirit* (Exeter: Paternoster, and Grand Rapids: Eerdmans, 1977).

disclaimer about **outsiders** makes sense only as a way of underlining the importance of responsible household rules for **those inside**. Once this has been established, Paul adds that if people wonder about **those outside**, **outsiders** do not escape responsibility for their lifestyles; they **have God as their judge**, but it is not for the church to try to impose its corporate house rules upon them. This does not imply that the church should keep silent about what God has ordained for the welfare of humanity. But it places its imposition of "rules of conduct" for the internal affairs of the church and the external affairs of the world on a different footing. Against the laissez-faire, consumerist culture of today, Paul asserts that to become part of the Christian community is explicitly to place oneself under the discipline of a Christian lifestyle.

The last clause begins with the aorist imperative ἐξάρατε although some MSS read the future indicative active ἐξαρεῖτε, understood as a command, on the basis of the LXX of Deut 17:7, which Paul proceeds to quote: *expel* (imperative) **the evil man**, ἐξ ὑμῶν αὐτῶν, or (LXX), *you shall expel* (future indicative) **the evil man**. . . . The double use of ἐκ (ἐξ) intensifies the injunction, hence REB, *root out the wrong-doer from your community,* as against NIV's *expel,* NRSV's *drive out,* and NJB's **banish**. All of these VSS can be justified, but the double use of ἐκ or ἐξ requires a strong word such as **banish**. Paul has argued that **evil** somehow emanates from a penetrating and spreading source, like *leaven.* In the light of Chow's work on patronage and social networks in Corinth the situation is not difficult to envisage.[178]

The final appeal to Deut 17:7 (LXX) corroborates Rosner's detailed work on the Deuteronomic background to this chapter.[179] C. D. Stanley follows E. Earle Ellis and others in giving little attention to this citation, on the ground that although his quotation is "virtually word-perfect," Paul does not explicitly use any of the standard formulae for identifying it as such for his readers, who therefore may not perceive it in this way.[180] But Hays interprets this lack of a signal for quotation more positively. For Paul "there always has been and will be only one Israel. Into that one Israel Gentile Christians such as the Corinthians have now been absorbed. For that reason Paul can deploy the words of Deut 17:7 (LXX) as a direct word of exhortation to the Corinthians to guard the purity of their community. . . . No introductory formula intrudes between Moses and the Corinthians, no conjunction weakens the command to a simile. Paul could have written, 'Just as Moses commanded Israel to drive out the evil person, so you. . . .' But . . . the scriptural command is treated as a self-evidently valid word addressed immediately to these Gentiles . . . [a] daring hermeneutical posture: they are to stand with Israel and join in the covenant

---

178. Chow, *Patronage and Power,* esp. 123-27 and 130-41.

179. In addition to his main argument on this passage (*Paul, Scripture and Ethics,* 61-93), Rosner evaluates the claims of those who underplay the relevance of the Old Testament, including the use of Deut 17:7 in 5:13, e.g., the claims of E. Ellis, R. Longenecker, H. Ulonska, and P. Zaas that it may be merely an allusion or a parallel (61-64).

180. Stanley, *Paul and the Language of Scripture,* 33-36.

confession. . . . Only for readers who stand within this covenant community does the immediacy of Paul's appeal to Deut 17:7 make sense."[181]

The OT background brings particular coherence and force to 5:1-13. As with the expulsion of Achan, of "infamous" sins it is said, "such a thing is not done in Israel" (Gen 34:7; Deut 22:21; Judg 20:6, 10; 2 Sam 13:12; Jer 29:23). The principle expressed in Deut 17:7 reappears in Deut 13:5; 19:19; and 22:22, 24 (E. Earle Ellis thinks that 1 Cor 5:13 alludes to Deut 22:24). Furthermore, whether the accusation and expulsion are valid or otherwise in a specific case, exclusion, Wolff comments, leaves the person who is expelled *lonely* (יחד, *yachid*), to endure "the misery of segregation and isolation, which imply wretchedness and affliction."[182] This (as I argued earlier and South more recently) is what Paul hopes will lead to the turning and salvation of the offender, and still more urgently to setting things right for the corporate identity and holiness of the congregation, as the people of the new covenant.

B. A SECOND EXAMPLE OF ETHICAL FAILURE LINKED WITH SOCIAL STATUS AND DIVISION (6:1-20)

1. Legal Action by the Socially Influential as an Abuse of Power (6:1-11)

(1) If one of you has a case against another, dare that one seek judgment at a court where there is questionable justice, rather than arbitration before God's people? (2) Or do you not know that "the saints will judge the world"? Well, if it is among you that the world is judged, are you unfit to hold a tribunal for small claims? (3) Do you not know that we shall judge angels; need I add, then, matters of everyday life? (4) If, rather, you hold tribunals concerning matters of everyday life, do you set upon judgment seats those who are viewed in the church as people of no esteem? (5) It is to make you feel ashamed that I say this to you. Has it come to this, that there is found not a single one among you who is sufficiently "a wise person" to be competent to arbitrate between two fellow believers? (6) But must a Christian go to law with a fellow believer, and this before unbelievers! (7) In fact, already it is a total moral defeat for you that you have cases for judgment with one another. Why do you not rather let yourselves be deprived of your rights? Why do you not rather let yourselves be defrauded? (8) But you, as it is, deprive people of justice, and you defraud, and fellow Christians at that.

(9, 10) Or do you not know that people who practice evil cannot inherit God's kingdom? Stop being misled: neither those who practice immoral sexual relations, nor those who pursue practices bound up with idolatry, nor

---

181. Hays, *Echoes of Scripture in the Letters of Paul,* 96-97.
182. H. W. Wolff, *Anthropology of the OT* (London: SCM, 1974), 217; cf. 216-19.

people who practice adultery, nor perverts [or those involved in pederastic practices], nor men who practice sexual relations with men, nor those who practice thievery, nor those who always grasp for more, nor drunkards, nor those who practice verbal abuse, nor people who exploit others in their own interests shall inherit the kingdom. (11) And this some of you used to be. But you were washed clean, you were set apart as holy, you were put right in your standing in the name of the Lord Jesus Christ and by the Spirit of our God.

Three issues, among others, achieve prominence in this passage. First, does the theme of "church order" as identified by G. Harris's article "The Beginnings of Church Discipline: 1 Cor 5," undergo further development in this chapter? Paul states that what in English law today are called "small claims," if they arise between fellow Christians at Corinth, should invite some kind of arbitration procedure within the church itself, not on the part of "outsiders." Thereby both internal issues of institutional order and external questions about community boundaries continue a theme begun in 5:1-13.

Second, the local situation at Corinth was without doubt a major factor in this Pauline reading. For whereas the criminal courts of the Roman government to some reasonable extent could be respected as sources of relative justice (cf. Rom 13:1-7), the local civil magistrate's courts allowed too much room for patronage and vested interest in the stance of local judges or the appointment of juries to reflect anything like even a near degree of integrity in comparison with major criminal courts. The wealthy, "influential," and "clever" could manipulate social networks outside the church to their advantage and thereby, in effect, take advantage of the poor or "weak" within the congregation.

Third, the community identity of the church could be put at risk either by practicing manipulative strategies in full view of Gentile patrons or clever legal advocates, whom wealthy Christians might hire, and the Gentile world be exposed to the sight of believers obsessed with acquisition of property or of their "rights," as against the sacrificial service of others which truly identifies what it is to be "of Christ" and to share in Christ's cross. Hence the specific moral failures of 6:9-11 continue the theme of sacrificing the credibility and meaning of Christian identity for the sake of personal gratification.

The second point invites more detailed reference to some recent literature. A. C. Mitchell laments the dearth of attention to social factors in studies of the passage until recently.[1] The history of exegesis, as traced by Lukas Vischer up to 1955, in large measure confirms his point.[2] Mitchell argues that "higher status people were taking lower status people to court, where the latter were at a disadvantage."[3] Thereby a concern for the unity of the congregation was sacri-

---

1. Mitchell, "Rich and Poor in the Courts of Corinth: Litigiousness and Status in 1 Cor 6:1-11," 562-86.
2. Cf. L. Vischer, *Die Auslegungsgeschichte von 1 Kor 6:1-11*.
3. Mitchell, "Rich and Poor in the Courts of Corinth," 562-63.

ficed to the use of social networks of power and patronage outside the congregation. To succeed at law a person usually needed the right contacts and direct or indirect influence.

Certainly Mitchell is not the only writer to emphasize this important aspect as one of the indispensable keys to unlocking the meaning of the passage and its significance for today. Chow predictably insists, "We must not conclude that the significance of the legal case has been exhausted by investigations into the theological background," citing work by Käsemann, Horsley, Schmithals, Talbert, and some of my own earlier work.[4] A year before the appearance of Mitchell's article, Chow uses almost the same words as Mitchell: "Since inequality was built into the legal system and improper influence could also be exercised . . . it is less likely that the court would be used by the weak and powerless. . . . The litigants, as Paul seems to imply (1 Cor 6:5), and as Talbert and Theissen have suggested, were among the wise and the strong in the church."[5] We readily arrive at issues of *Patronage and Power* and *Social Networks in Corinth* (Chow's title and subtitle). As Chow and Mitchell concede, as long ago as in his essay "Social Stratification in the Corinthian Community" (Germ. 1974; Eng. 1982) Theissen had observed that "litigation would hardly be undertaken by those who have no property. Further . . . numbers of the upper classes generally have greater confidence in receiving justice from a court . . . especially since they can pay for good attorneys."[6] Both writers also allude to preparatory work by Wayne Meeks.

Further, in an illuminating study of this chapter Bruce W. Winter applies a wealth of material about the operation of the courts of Roman magistrates to the situation at Corinth.[7] His major concern is to explain the apparent discrepancy between Paul's positive attitude toward Roman structures of law in Rom 13:1-7 and the extreme reservations which he clearly holds about resorting to the local courts at Corinth in 1 Cor 6:1-8. He agrees that only the socially advantaged would normally initiate litigation, but also shows that the status of the accused cannot be shown decisively to differ from that of the plaintiff. The argument that only one side appealed to patronage or to social networks is less secure than the established fact that panels of jurists were readily influenced to act in the interests of one of the two parties. Around AD 100 Dio Chrysostom speaks of "innumerable lawyers perverting justice"; and in the early period of the Empire "minor civil actions were left in the control of local courts and could be tried by judges or juries."[8] Winter concludes that for Paul there is a fundamental difference between appealing to the morally questionable judges

4. Chow, *Patronage and Power,* 124; cf. 123.

5. Ibid., 129.

6. Theissen, *Social Setting of Pauline Christianity,* 97.

7. Winter, "Civil Litigation in Secular Corinth and the Church: The Forensic Background to 1 Cor 6:1-8," 559-72.

8. Ibid., 564 and 561; Dio Chrysostom, *Orations* 37.16-17. Winter refers to various sources, including J. A. Crook, *Law and Life in Rome* (London: Thames & Hudson, 1967), 79.

and jurists of the local Corinthian courts which tried minor cases of litigation and the valid right of the Roman government to administer criminal law as reflected in Rom 13:1-7.[9]

If Winter's diagnosis of the problem reflects a difference of emphasis from that of Chow and Mitchell, in what lies Paul's sense of outrage in 6:1-8? With Margaret M. Mitchell, Winter perceives the initiation of litigation in secular courts as aligning divisions or splits within the church with cliques or rival networks of influence outside the church and thereby doing double damage: (i) promoting and inflaming division within the church; and (ii) involving the unbridled rhetoric of those outside the church to exacerbate division within and thereby simultaneously disrupting the unity and cohesion of the church and compromising its boundaries of corporate Christian identity.

This provides a more credible link with the flow of thought in 5:1-13 than to argue that the case brought to court involved the illicit relationship of 5:1-5. Moreover, whether we adopt A. C. Mitchell's detailed approach or the details of Bruce Winter's argument, a ready explanation for the link between 6:1-8 and 6:9-11 now emerges. For the issue which now emerges resolves into a general principle: are the "insiders" within the congregation to draw not only their assumptions about "wisdom" and "rhetoric" (1:10–4:21) but also their standards of self-gratification, morality, and manipulation from the secular culture of "outsiders" at Corinth? How distinctive (not how ghetto-like) is the community to be which is founded not on human wisdom or "religion" but on the centrality of Christ and the cross, within the framework of the interpretative and moral tradition of the scriptures? The case study of initiating litigation brings this universal issue to a sharp local focus. Moreover, as Conzelmann observes, in conjunction with 5:1-5, 13 we see the beginnings of an internal jurisdiction within the church, which brings us back to the first main point of this introduction.

Bibliography on 6:1-11

Bailey, K. E., "Paul's Theological Foundation for Human Sexuality: 1 Cor 6:9-20 in the Light of Rhetorical Criticism," *Near East School of Theology Theological Review* 3 (1980): 27-41.

Barton, S. C., "Homosexuality and the Church of England: Perspectives from the Social Sciences," *Theol* 92 (1989): 175-81.

Bernard, J. H., "The Connexion between the Fifth and Sixth Chapters of 1 Cor," *ExpTim* 7 (1907): 433-43.

Boswell, J., *Christianity, Social Tolerance and Homosexuality* (Chicago: University of Chicago Press, 1980).

Burkill, T. A., "Two into One: The Notion of Carnal Union in Mk 10:8, 1 Kor 6:10, Eph 5:31," *ZNW* 62 (1971): 112-20.

Chow, J. K., *Patronage and Power. A Study of Social Networks in Corinth,* JSNTSS 75 (Sheffield: Sheffield Academic Press, 1992), 123-41.

Clarke, A. D., *Secular and Christian Leadership at Corinth* (Leiden: Brill, 1993), 59-72.

9. Winter, "Civil Litigation in Secular Corinth and the Church," esp. 563-64 and 571-72.

Countryman, L. W., *Dirt, Greed and Sex: Sexual Ethics in the NT and Their Implication for Today* (Philadelphia: Fortress, 1988).

Deleur, M., "Les Tribunaux de l'Eglise de Corinthe et les Tribunaux de Qumran," in *Studiorum Paulinorum Congressus Internationalis Catholicus 1961* (Rome: Pontifical Biblical Institute, 1963), 2:535-48.

Derrett, J. D. M., "Judgement and 1 Cor 6," *NTS* 37 (1991): 22-36.

Devor, R. C., "Homosexuality and St Paul," *PastPsy* 23 (1972): 50-58.

Dinkler, E., "Zum Problem der Ethik bei Paulus: Rechtsnahme und Rechtsverzicht (1 Kor 6:1-11)," *ZTK* 49 (1952): 167-200.

Donfried, K. P., "Justification and Last Judgment in Paul," *ZNW* 67 (1976).

Easton, B. S., "NT Ethical Lists," *JBL* 51 (1932): 1-12.

Fuller, R. H., "First Cor 6:1-11: An Exegetical Paper," *Ex Auditu* 2 (1986): 96-104.

Furnish, V. P., *The Moral Teaching of Paul's Selected Issues* (Nashville: Abingdon, 1979), 52-83.

Halter, H., *Taufe und Ethos: Paulinische Kriterien für das Proprium christlicher Moral* (Freiburg: Herder, 1977).

Hays, R. B., "Eschatology and Ethics in 1 Corinthians," *Ex Auditu* 10 (1994): 31-43.

————, "Relations Natural and Unnatural: A Response to John Boswell's Exegesis of Rom 1," *JRE* 14 (1986): 184-215.

Hurd, J. C., *The Origin of 1 Corinthians* (London: SPCK, 1965), 83-89.

Kamlah, R., *Die Form der katalogischen Paränese im NT*, WUNT 7 (Tübingen: Mohr, 1964), esp. 11-14 and 27-31.

Kinman, B. R., "'Appoint the Despised or Judges?' (1 Cor 6:4)," *TynBul* 48 (1997): 345-54.

Lee, G. M., "1 Cor 6:5," *ExpTim* 79 (1968): 310.

Malick, D. E., "The Condemnation of Homosexuality in 1 Cor 6:9," *BSac* 150 (1993): 479-92.

Merk, O., *Handeln aus Glauben. Die Motivierungen der paulinischen Ethik* (Marburg: Elwert, 1968), 91-96.

Mitchell, A. C., "Rich and Poor in the Courts of Corinth: Litigiousness and Status in 1 Cor 6:1-11," *NTS* 39 (1993): 562-86.

Mitchell, M. M., *Paul and the Rhetoric of Reconciliation* (Louisville: Knox and Tübingen: Mohr, 1992), 116-18.

Oropeza, B. J., "Situational Immorality — Paul's 'Vice Lists' at Corinth," *ExpTim* 110 (1998): 9-10.

Osten-Sacken, P. von der, "Paulinisches Evangelium und Homosexualität," *Berlin theologische Zeitschrift* 3 (1986): 28-49.

Petersen, W. L., "Can ἀρσενοκοῖται Be Translated by 'Homosexuals'? (1 Cor 6:9, 1 Tim 1:10," *VC* 40 (1986): 187-91.

Richardson, P., "Judgment in Sexual Matters in 1 Cor 6:1-11," *Nov T* 25 (1983): 37-58.

Rosner, B. S., "Moses Appointing Judges: An Antecedent to 1 Cor 1–6?" *ZNW* 82 (1990): 275-78.

————, "The Origin and Meaning of 1 Cor 6:9-11 on Context," *BZ* 40 (1996): 250-53.

Scroggs, R., *The NT and Homosexuality* (Philadelphia: Fortress, 1983).

Schnackenburg, R., *Baptism in the Thought of St Paul* (Oxford: Blackwell, 1964), esp. 105-12.

Schrage, W., *Die konkreten Einzelgebote in der paulinischen Paränese* (Gütersloh: Mohn, 1961), 147-49 and 262-67.

Siker, J. S. (ed.), *Homosexuality in the Church: Both Sides of the Debate* (Louisville: Westminster-Knox, 1994), esp. Hays (3-17) and Furnish (18-37).

Stegemann, W., "Paul and the Sexual Mentality of His World," *BTB* 23 (1993): 161-66.

Stein, A., "Wo trugen die Korinthischen Christen ihre Rechtshändel aus?" *ZNW* 59 (1968): 86-90.

Strecker, G., "Homosexualität in biblischer Sicht," *KD* 28 (1982): 127-41.

Taylor, R. D., "Towards a Biblical Theology of Litigation: A Law Professor Looks at 1 Cor 6:1-11," *Ex Auditu* 2 (1986): 105-15.

Thiselton, A. C., "Can Hermeneutics Ease the Deadlock: Some Biblical Exegeses and Hermeneutical Models," in T. Bradshaw (ed.), *The Way Forward? Christian Voices on Homosexuality and the Church* (London: Hodder & Stoughton, 1997), 145-96.

Ukleja, P. M., "Homosexuality in the NT," *BSac* 140 (1983): 350-58.

Vasey, M., *Strangers and Friends: A New Exploration of Homosexuality and the Bible* (London: Hodder & Stoughton, 1995), 134-36.

Vischer, L., *Die Auslegungsgeschichte von 1 Kor 6:1-11. Rechtsverzicht und Schlichtung* (Tübingen: Mohr, 1955).

Vögtle, A., *Die Tugend- und Lasterkataloge im NT* (Münster: Aschendorff, 1936).

Wengst, R., "Paulus und die Homosexualität," *ZEE* 31 (1987): 72-80.

Wibbing, S., *Die Tugend- und Lasterkataloge im NT und ihre Traditionsgeschichte*, BZNW 25 (Berlin: Töpelmann, 1959).

Winter, B. W., "Civil Litigation in Secular Corinth and the Church: The Forensic Background to 1 Cor 6:1-8," *NTS* 37 (1991): 559-72; also rpt. in B. W. Winter, *Seek the Welfare of the City* (Carlisle: Paternoster and Grand Rapids: Eerdmans, 1994), 105-21.

Wire, A. C., *The Corinthian Women Prophets* (Minneapolis: Fortress, 1990), 72-79.

Wolff, C., "Exkurs: Zur paulinischen Bewertung der Homosexualitat," in *Der erste Brief des Paulus an die Korinther* (Leipzig: Evangelische Verlagsanstalt, 1996), 119-20.

Wright, D. F., "Early Christian Attitudes to Homosexuality," *Studia Patristica* 18 (1989): 329-34.

———, "Homosexuality: The Relevance of the Bible," *EvQ* 61 (1989): 291-300.

———, "Homosexuals or Prostitutes? The Meaning of ἀρσενοκοῖται (1 Cor 6:9; 1 Tim 1:10)," *VC* 38 (1984): 125-53.

———, "Translating Ἀρσενοκοῖται: 1 Cor 6:9; 1 Tim 1:10," *VC* 41 (1987): 396-98.

Zaas, P., "Was Homosexuality Condoned in the Corinthian Church?" *SBL Seminar Papers,* 1/2 (1979).

Ziesler, J. A., *The Meaning of Righteousness in Paul,* JSNTMS (Cambridge: Cambridge University Press, 1972), 155-63.

1   The very first word, τολμᾷ, identifies another anomaly which causes Paul to experience a further sense of outrage and disappointment, introduced here by means of a rhetorical question. The question carries the force of an exclamatory expression of censure: *How dare you!* We were tempted to follow the REB's excellent, forceful rendering *Does he have the face to . . . ?* But normally τολμάω is used in the positive sense of *courageous, daring,* and *Does he have the face to . . . ?* misses the nuance of ironic, dry humor which may also give a more interpersonal, less confrontational note to the admittedly emphatic rebuke. Misplaced boldness becomes sheer *cheek.* Collins, *have the affrontery,* is excellent.[10]

The phrase πρᾶγμα ἔχων construes the participle of ἔχω with πρᾶγμα, *a matter.* But in a legal context the phrase regularly means **to have a case** against (πρὸς τὸν ἕτερον) another.[11] **Another** (or *the other*) is used elsewhere of seeking the welfare of *the other* (10:24, τοῦ ἑτέρου; cf. 14:17, ὁ ἕτερος οὐκ οἰκοδομεῖται). Bonhoeffer's theology and Ricoeur's philosophy of "the other," or "for others," find a basis in Pauline texts here. Christian identity is bound up with attitudes toward *the other.* The middle or passive infinitive κρίνεσθαι is regularly used in forensic contexts of *going to law,* i.e., **to seek judgment at a court**.

It is notoriously difficult to translate ἐπὶ τῶν ἀδίκων since any translation presupposes an exegesis of the verse. (i) NRSV, *unrighteous,* and AV/KJV, *unjust,* follow the lexicographical meaning of the word in its most usual contexts; (ii) a conscious contextual interpretation leads to REB and to translate *before a pagan court,* or *pagan lawcourts;* (iii) NIV's *ungodly,* NJB's *sinners,* and Moffatt's *sinful pagan court* attempt to achieve the best of both worlds, by preserving both the moral content of ἀδίκων and the semantic contrast between *heathen* (TCNT) and Christian arbitration. REB can readily be defended since δίκαιος could mean *faithful Israelite* in Jewish traditions.[12] Nevertheless, as Moores observes more widely of many Pauline texts, the text contains an unexpressed premise with which the first readers would either already be familiar or alternatively reflect to explicate the unexpressed point.[13] The research on Roman provincial lawcourts to which we referred in the introduction to 6:1-11 (especially with reference to Winter [1991], Chow [1992], and A. C. Mitchell [1993]) is well supported by the work of historians of Roman law.[14] It is safe to conclude that the use of *Roman provincial courts* for *minor* cases and the near certainty of a result of **questionable justice** are virtually *synonymous*. Hence our translation above remains as close as possible to the Greek while conveying the sense of ἐπὶ τῶν ἀδίκων as it would be understood by the first addressees, in

10. Collins, *First Cor,* 224, 227.
11. Wolff, *Der erste Brief,* 114, and Conzelmann, *1 Cor,* 103, n. 1, underline this point; cf. *Oxyrhynchus Papyri* 743:19 and examples in MM.
12. Lightfoot, *Notes,* 211.
13. Moores, *Wrestling with Rationality in Paul,* 5-37.
14. For example, P. Garnsey, "The Civil Suit," in *Social Status and Legal Privilege in the Roman Empire* (Oxford: Clarendon Press, 1970); J. M. Kelly, *Roman Litigation* (Oxford: Clarendon Press, 1966); W. Kunkel, *An Introduction to Roman Legal and Constitutional History* (Oxford: Clarendon Press, 2d ed. 1973); A. H. M. Jones, *The Criminal Courts of the Roman Republic and Principate* (Oxford: Blackwell, 1972); Crook, *Law and Life in Rome;* and K. H. Ziegler, *Das private Schiedsgericht im antiken römischen Recht* (Munich: Beck, 1971). Winter and Mitchell cite firsthand documents and nonliterary sources, e.g., Mitchell, "Rich and Poor," 567-68, n. 20, which includes first-century inscriptions on private arbitration and the Tablets of Herculaneum for the years 1946-55 in *La Parola del Passato* 1 (1946): 373-79 to 10 (1955): 448-77.

an English form intelligible to modern readers. ἄδικος, when referring to persons, means *one who does contrary to what is right.*[15] But the immediate qualification οὐχὶ ἐπὶ τῶν ἁγίων shows that the contrast between *local Roman civil courts* and some means of retaining arbitration in Christian hands remains central to the issue Paul raises.

On the translation and meaning of τῶν ἁγίων, see above on 1:2. In the present context REB's **God's people** conveys the meaning while retaining the nuance of *holy* as *belonging to God.* It is surprising that NRSV and NIV think that *saints* does not convey different nuances today, in contrast to NJB's *God's holy people,* which is no less accurate. We have supplied the word **arbitration**, which is not in the Greek, simply to explicate the meaning which the words already imply. The preposition ἐπί with the genitive otherwise becomes difficult to render, since its meaning *in the presence of* may become formalized as **before** if some such event as a *tribunal* (vv. 2, 4-7) is in view. One further advantage is gained by translating τῶν ἁγίων as **God's people**. On the basis of Exod 21:1, the rabbis argued that it was unlawful for Jews to bring their civil cases before Gentile courts. By the period of Paul, the Romans had granted to Jews a measure of freedom to legislate for their own internal legal affairs.[16] Schrage compares the texts of Qumran (e.g., 1QS 5:1-4, 13-18; 9:7; and 1QSa 1:13-14) while Rosner emphasizes the relevance of Deut 1:12-18.[17]

2 On **do you not know?** (v. 2) see above on 3:16 (cf. also 5:6). It is more than likely that the saying "**the saints will judge the world**" represented a self-congratulatory catchphrase along with language about *being filled to satisfaction, being enriched,* and *reigning as kings* (4:8), especially in the light of the wording of its traditions cited below (Matt 19:28; Rev 20:4).[18] Paul could not have cited this at 4:8 since the issue there was the claim to have anticipated all such glories *in advance,* whereas the theme of the eschatological judgment of the world could not have been brought forward without its losing its meaning. We cannot be sure that this was a catchphrase; but it may at minimum have been "a reminiscence of Wis 3:7, 8," or more probably, as Strobel, Fee, and others suggest, a well-known axiom derived from Dan 7:22 (LXX: "judgment was given to the saints of the Most High").[19]

In Jewish apocalyptic and in the writings of Qumran the theme features regularly, e.g., "God will judge all the nations by the hand of his elect" (1Qp-

---

15. BAGD, 18.

16. Fee, *First Epistle,* 231 n. 11; cf. E. Schürer, *The History of the Jewish People,* ed. G. Vermes et al. (Edinburgh: T & T Clark, rev. ed. 1979), 208-9.

17. Schrage, *Der erste Brief,* 1:408; and Rosner, "Moses Appointing Judges: An Antecedent to 1 Cor 6:1-6?" 275-78.

18. Schrage, *Der erste Brief,* 2:409, where the notion of "reigning" as "spiritual people" may encourage some version of this theme.

19. Weiss, *Der erste Korintherbrief,* 146-47; Strobel, *Der erste Brief,* 107-8; C. H. Dodd, *According to the Scriptures* (London: Nisbet, 1952), 68; Fee, *First Epistle,* 233. The citation from Wis 3:7-8 reads, "They shall judge nations and rule over peoples." On the possible use of Wisdom by Paul, see E. Earle Ellis, *Paul's Use of the OT,* 77-80.

Hab 5:4). It also features in Christian apocalyptic: "to him who is victorious, to him who perseveres . . . I will give authority over (ἐξουσίαν ἐπί) the nations" (Rev 2:26); "Then I saw thrones (θρόνους) and upon them sat those to whom judgment was committed (κρίμα ἐδόθη αὐτοῖς) . . . those who had not worshipped the beast. . . . They reigned (ἐβασίλευσαν) with Christ" (Rev 20:4).[20] The startling saying of Matt 19:28 appears in the Synoptic tradition: "When the Son of Man is seated on his throne in heavenly splendor, you my followers will have thrones of your own, where you will sit as judges (καθήσεσθε . . . κρίνοντες) of the twelve tribes of Israel."[21] This is not peculiar to Matthean eschatology or to his attitude for or against Judaism. Luke offers a parallel: "you shall eat and drink at my table in my kingdom and sit on thrones as judges (καθήσεσθε . . . κρίνοντες) of the twelve tribes of Israel" (Luke 22:30).

It is surprising that modern commentators in general (as against patristic writers) seem to assume that the meaning here is self-evident. In what sense will **the saints judge the world**? If we interpret the principle at its face value, Paul's logic is forceful: "if you think that you will be called to judge the *great issues of the world,* why do you act as if to imply that Christians are not qualified to adjudicate matters of *very little* (ἐλαχίστων), importance?" But in what sense does Paul envisage Christians as "sitting as judges" over the world? Three possibilities may be considered.

(i) Chrysostom, far from alone among the Fathers, insists that "they will *not* indeed judge," in the sense of demanding account. This is the prerogative of God-in-Christ alone. However, just as the experience of the Queen of Sheba "condemned" the unbelief of the generation of hearers who rejected Jesus (Matt 12:42), the possibility of faith and obedience among Christians "will accuse them." Ambrosiaster, Theodoret, Theophylus, Photius, and Erasmus all adopt Chrysostom's view.[22]

(ii) Yet within patristic thought a theological clue is offered concerning what Paul may have in mind. For while the Fathers in general retreat from ascribing a role in the judgment to all Christians, some, e.g., Eusebius, perceive the martyrs as those identified with Christ's afflictions and death, as thereby "These divine martyrs are seated with Christ . . . sharers in his kingdom [reign], partakers of his judgment and judges with him" (μέτοχοι τῆς κρίσεως αὐτοῦ καὶ συνδικάζοντες αὐτῷ).[23] But in Paul's view all Christians (not only martyrs) share in Christ's death and resurrection (Rom 6:3-11). Arguably, then, if one of

20. The link with thrones reminds us of the complex of themes in 4:8; cf. also Collins, *First Cor,* 231, on this apocalyptic context.

21. Chrysostom, *1 Cor. Hom.,* 16:5.

22. Theodoret, *Opera Omnia: Int. ep. 1 ad Cor.,* 194C (Migne, *PG,* 82:263 [Lat.], 264 [Gk.]); Photius (c. AD 858) in Karl Staab (ed.), *Pauluskommentare aus der griechischen Kirche* (Munster: Aschendorff, 1933), 555; (Fragment on 1 Cor 6:1-9). Erasmus, *Periphrasis in Ep. Pauli ad Cor. 1,* 874F-875A: *vos enim estis lux mundae, quae coarguet impiorum errores. Hoc quo pacto fiat, si in vobis ipsius sint tenebrae?.*

23. Eusebius, *Church History,* 6:42:5.

the three great end events, namely, the resurrection, has a corporate dimension in which all are raised because they are *raised-with-Christ* (and "bear the image of the man of heaven," 1 Cor 15:49), so similarly the Christian corporeity cannot but be likewise in the event of judgment, in the sense of its *being-in-Christ* as *Christ* takes his throne and *pronounces judgment.* Chrysostom's concern might perhaps be expressed more accurately by asserting that no Christian will "judge" the world *as an independent individual,* but as one of the corporeity who bears Christ's image and *shares Christ's destiny and likeness* as raised-with-him. All judgment would in this sense remain *Christ's* since those in Christ would reflect only the character of Christ.

(iii) It is possible to imagine that even if Paul himself held either the first view or more probably the second, some of the Corinthians might still hold a more naive, individualist, self-congratulatory view of their role at the last judgment. If so, Paul's argument would retain its full force logically if served as a strictly *ad hominem* argument, with the sense: you think that you are worthy (ἄξιοι) to judge the Roman Gentiles on the last day, do you? So why are you not competent or worthy (ἀνάξιοι) to arbitrate concerning some **very little**, everyday matter? (Erasmus uses the phrase *de rebus frivolis* in contrast to the notion that *tanta res vobis committitur, ut per vos totius mundi, hoc est, omnium impiorum vita damnetur. . . .*)[24] In opposition to any triumphalist view of the church's "judging" the world, Tertullian explains in his *Apology* that the church "shares a common discipline and a common hope," in which the only "wrestling" that relates to the world is a wrestling in prayer for the world's welfare.[25]

Several Greek words require comment, especially κριτηρίων. The UBS *Greek New Testament,* 4th ed.. places the perispomenon (circumflex) accent over κρινοῦσιν to signify the contracted future indicative of κρίνω. Since the earliest MSS lacked accents this is a conjecture, but a justified one; otherwise the verb could be only a "timeless" present: **the saints** *judge* **the world** as a principle revealed in scripture. (See above on 5:13.) The word ἀνάξιοι occurs only here in the NT, but its meaning, **unfit,** seems clear. By contrast the meaning (or more strictly the application or reference) of κριτηρίων (genitive plural of the neuter noun κριτήριον) invites debate. In the singular the usual meaning is *lawcourt* or **tribunal** (from the classical period, e.g., Plato, *Laws* 6.767B, through the first-century hellenistic writers (e.g., Philo, *De Virtutibus* 66) to examples in the papyri (e.g., *BGU* 1054:1). BAGD note that 1 Cor 6:2 may not cohere readily with this usual meaning, but interpret κριτηρίων ἐλαχίστων as *the most insignificant courts* in the sense of "those that have jurisdiction over the petty details of everyday life."[26] They perceive βιωτικὰ κριτήρια in 6:4 as confirming this meaning, i.e., in v. 4, *courts for the matters of everyday life.* Additionally κριτήριον may denote *legal action* or *a lawcourt.*

24. Erasmus, *Church History,* 875A.
25. Tertullian, *Apology,* 39.
26. BAGD, 453.

What kind of *lawcourt* might κριτηρίων denote? The ending -τήριον is generally regarded as indicating a place where judgment is rendered. (i) Chrysostom, Theophylact, and many earlier writers interpret the word as referring to *Roman civil courts which adjudicate minor cases,* rather like the *small-claims courts* introduced over the last few years in English law. Chrysostom comments, "How absurd for one at variance with his friend to take his enemy as a reconciler between them!"[27] But this requires the removal of the question mark and a rather strained use of ἀνάξιοι, i.e., *you are unworthy of civil courts* is not *civil courts are unworthy of you.* (ii) On the other hand, κριτηρίων could refer to *small-claims courts* if the point at issue is the use of *Gentile advocates* in contrast to defending one's own case. This would cohere with C. K. Barrett's rendering: *Are you unworthy to sit in the lowest courts?*[28] Grosheide translates: *courts which have to treat the smaller matters.*[29] With this gloss, a version of Chrysostom's interpretation might have some possibility. (iii) Others interpret κριτρίων ἐκαχίστων as *trivial cases* (Bruce), *petty lawsuits* (Conzelmann), or *minor cases* (Collins).[30] Derrett and several lexicographers insist that the ending form -τήριον clearly denotes *place* of judgment, unless the context positively demands otherwise.[31] (iv) Although (iii) can be supported on the basis of metonymy, the translation **tribunal**, favored by many including Allo and Derrett, appears to do justice to every aspect of the issue.[32] The Corinthian Christians, Paul urges, should **hold a tribunal for small claims** themselves.

This fourth view coheres most closely with Rosner's article on the background of Deut 1:9-17 and Exod 18:13-26.[33] In Deuteronomy Moses expresses concern about the burdens of administration and is instructed to choose out "wise and reputable" persons, and judges are charged: "Give the members of your community a fair hearing, and judge rightly between one person and another, whether citizen or resident alien. You must not be partial in judging." Exod 18:13-26 expounds the same theme. Moses cannot do everything himself; he is to appoint people with integrity "as judges for the people" (18:22). Even if Moses retains "important cases," they are to decide "minor cases" (LXX τὰ δὲ βραχέα τῶν κριμάτων κρινοῦσιν αὐτοί). The LXX κριτήριον translates Heb. דין *(din),* e.g., Dan 7:10, 26 (but in 1 Kings 7:7 it translates *m-sh-p-t*).[34] Rosner

27. Chrysostom, *1 Cor. Hom.,* 16:4.

28. Barrett, *First Epistle,* 136.

29. Grosheide, *First Epistle,* 134, n. 3.

30. Bruce, *1 and 2 Corinthians,* 60; Conzelmann, *1 Cor,* 105 (including n. 20); Collins, *First Cor,* 231-32. Kistemaker also has *lawsuits* (*1 Corinthians,* 181); Fee believes that there is "sufficient evidence" for this translation (*First Epistle,* 234). (Also de Wette and Ewald.)

31. Derrett, "Judgment in 1 Cor 6," 27, n. 11; cf. 22-36. (Also Findlay, and Robertson and Plummer).

32. Meyer, *First Epistle,* 1:166; Robertson and Plummer, *First Epistle,* 112; Allo, *La Première Épitre,* 133 (with reference to the papyri); Findlay, *Expositor's Greek Testament,* 2:814; Lightfoot, *Notes,* 211; and Derrett, "Judgment in 1 Cor 6," 27, n. 11.

33. Rosner, "Moses Appointing Judges. An Antecedent to 1 Cor 6:1-6?" 275-78.

34. Hatch-Redpath (1977 ed.), 2:791.

concludes that a parallel exists between the OT situation and that of Corinth, of which Paul would no doubt be aware. There is a need for internal **tribunals** or *means of arbitration* which not only ensure honest, impartial justice on the part of morally committed persons (i.e., committed to the standards of God's covenant laws), but also to avoid what R. H. Fuller terms "washing their dirty linen in public" rather than settling the issue quietly among God's own people.[35]

Rosner's approach coheres well with two successive articles in *New Testament Studies* (same number) by G. Harris on "The Beginnings of Church Discipline: 1 Cor 5" and by J. D. M. Derrett on "Judgment in 1 Cor 6."[36] Derrett argues that ἐπί with the genitive provides evidence that "some groups held corporate jurisdiction, the contrast being between genuine church members ('saints') and others. . . . Paul makes two complaints: disputes were brought before incompetent (improper) persons; and litigation existed where it should not."[37] Both Harris and Derrett (like Rosner) look to the OT and Jewish background to shed light on this passage. Derrett, however, appeals with great effect to the traditions behind Matt 18:15-17 and Luke 12:13-21. In the case of Matt 18:15-17 we find "a gradation of mediation, conciliation, and expulsion in the case of failure of the previous expedients."[38] In Luke 12:13-21 two brothers are in dispute about an inheritance case. Evidently the weaker claimed the solution of partition, while the stronger resisted this on grounds of reduction of productivity and his own perceived rights. Jesus does not enter into the details of litigation, but "calls their attention to the sin of avarice."[39] Paul follows Jesus in urging a "brother" to make "peace with one's adversary (however wrongheaded)."[40] It would be better "to be wronged" (1 Cor 6:7) than to force the issue.

The **tribunal**, then, may consist not of a series of legal pronouncements by fellow Christians, but of a gathering of appropriate people within the church to attempt mediation, based on a renunciation of avarice and even, if necessary, of "rights" (as Paul does in 9:3-12, "we have not claimed this 'right,'" v. 12). It would be wholly inappropriate, however, for any who have the dispositions characterized in 6:9-11 to count as "insiders" for the purpose of mediating between the parties. Any person deemed grasping or self-indulgent, if they are to remain part of the community at all (which may be in question), certainly cannot belong to the panel of "insiders" who hold the **tribunal**. If the group in 6:9-11 persist in their stance, they, too, may perhaps come under the ultimate sanction of Matt 18:15-17 and 1 Cor 5:1-5, 13. But the plea against avarice (Luke 12:13-21) through an inquiry which places matters on the table with

35. Fuller, "First Corinthians 6:1-11," *Ex Auditu* 2 (1986): 99; cf. 96-104.
36. G. Harris, "Beginnings of Church Discipline: 1 Cor 5," *NTS* 37 (1991): 1-21; Derrett, "Judgment in 1 Cor 6," 22-36.
37. Derrett, "Judgment," 27.
38. Ibid., 25.
39. Ibid., 26.
40. Ibid., 32.

a view to mediation and a willingness not to overpress one's "rights" comes first.[41]

This is reflected in *The Apostolic Constitutions* (attributed to Julian after c. AD 381: "It is good for a Christian to have no dispute with anyone; but if . . . a dispute arises . . . although thereby he be obliged to lose somewhat, let it not come before a heathen court . . . as though we had 'not one wise to judge between his brothers'" (2:45). The elative sense of the superlative form ἐλαχίστων, *very small,* reminds us that these are usually **small claims**, not matters of criminal importance.

3 Although the UBS *Greek New Testament,* 4th ed., has a question mark at the end of this sentence without further comment, the 3d ed. notes helpfully that the *Textus Receptus,* Westcott-Hort, and Nestlé (1898) placed a first question mark after **angels**. This permits the smoother NEB translation: *Are you not aware that we are to judge angels? How much more, then, mere matters of business.* The REB, however, changes the NEB: *Are you not aware that we are to judge angels, not to mention day-to-day affairs?* The force of μήτιγε is to join a question expecting an emphatic negative answer (μήτι) with the particle γε, *at any rate,* or equivalent to some idiom in English which gives sharper point to the rhetorical question. Conzelmann renders, *to say nothing of . . .;* we propose: **need I add, then . . . ?**[42] On **do you not know**, see above on 3:16 (cf. also 5:6; 6:2). The question is repeated in 6:9, 15, 16 and 19. Thus six of Paul's ten uses of the phrases occur in this chapter, or seven if you count 5:1–6:20 as a single unit. (Hurd, we noted, identifies all the occurrences as part of Paul's response to the oral report, and believes that they strike "a jarring note" in Paul's remonstration.)[43]

As Lukas Vischer observes, this argument is an example of the inclusion of the lesser within the greater, which finds a place in the logic of both Aristotle and the rabbis.[44] The "lesser" is expressed as βιωτικά. In the business and official correspondence of the papyri this term regularly means *business matters,* i.e., what enables one *to make a living* (hence NEB, *matters of business*). But outside this narrower context, the neuter plural adjective means *what relates to* βίος, i.e., *earthly life,* or *matters of daily life.* Hence NIV and NJB translate matters or things of this life and NRSV *ordinary matters.* Our **everyday life** combines nuances of *daily life* with the *ordinary.* It is far more difficult to suggest what might be entailed in the phrase **we shall judge angels**.

(i) In Derrett's view this is simply part of the stage scenery of "the myth of the Last Judgment" in which "angels, too will be judged, **the angels** *of nations,* not merely wicked angels."[45] It would fit nicely with Paul's argument about pagan magistrate's courts if he suggests that the **angels** who watch over

41. Ibid., 33-36.
42. Conzelmann, *1 Cor,* 105.
43. Hurd, *Origin of 1 Corinthians,* 85-87; cf. 75-94.
44. Vischer, *Die Auslegungsgeschichte von 1 Kor 6:1-11,* 10.
45. Derrett, "Judgment in 1 Cor 6," 28 (my italics).

the corporate structures of Gentile nations will stand at the last under the judgment of Christians at Corinth. But in spite of the powerful advocacy of this view of **angels** and nations by G. B. Caird and others, when we examined τῶν ἀρχόντων τοῦ αἰῶνος τούτου in 2:8, we saw the complexity of the issues and the difficulties of this view (see above on 2:8).

(ii) Most patristic, medieval, and Reformation commentators and many or most modern writers interpret the reference to **angels** *of wickedness,* or *demons.* Chrysostom adopts this view (after rejecting a curious tradition that the word refers to priests, perhaps on the basis of the "angels" of the seven churches in Rev 2:1–3:22). Chrysostom appeals for clarification to Matt 25:41, "the fire prepared for the devil and his angels"; and 2 Cor 11:15, "disguised as an angel of light." Most pointedly for us today, he identifies them as beings "in contradistinction to what relates to this life."[46] Beings of another nonhuman order exist but do not depend on human βιωτικά. Theophylact and Aquinas, broadly adopt this view, while Bengel simply defines them as *eos qui non sunt sancti.*[47] Erasmus comments on the arrogance of assuming that only humankind comprise the created order, and observes of believers, *vestra pietas illorum impietatem.*[48] Theodoret writes: "'Ἀγγέλους δὲ λέγει τοὺς δαίμονας. *Angelos autem dieit daemonas.'*[49] Calvin applies the sentence to "apostate angels."[50] Conzelmann similarly speaks of "fallen angels" here.[51]

(iii) H. A. W. Meyer argues for a reference to "good" angels. Angels must render account of their service, he argues, in Heb 1:14.[52] But most writers see this allusion as part of "the apocalyptic theme of the judgment of fallen angels (2 Pet 2:4; Jude 6; possibly *1 Enoch* 10:11-14; 67-68.[53] The word "includes bad as well as good."[54]

(iv) We must return to the considerations set out under view (ii) on the previous verse, on **will judge the world**. Godet reminds us that in the climax to this epistle Paul declares that Christ will finally destroy πᾶσαν ἀρχὴν καὶ πᾶσαν ἐξουσίαν (15:24). Christ alone will be sovereign and will yield his kingship to God (v. 24a), and arguably (see above on v. 2) the corporeity of believers characterized by being-in-Christ in this derivative sense share in Christ's acts and declarative speech-acts. That the setting-to-rights of all things includes the nonhuman creation as well as the world is, as Erasmus comments, a less presumptuous assumption than to assume the opposite.

4 Both the word order and the use of the normally contrastive μέν with-

46. Chrysostom, *1 Cor. Hom,,* 16:5.
47. Bengel, *Gnomon,* 625; in addition, Beza, Weiss, and Lietzmann, *An die Korinther,* 25.
48. Erasmus, *Op. Omn.: Ep. Pauli ad Cor.,* 875B.
49. Theodoret, *Interp. Ep. 1 ad Cor.,* 195A (Migne, *PG,* 82:265A, 266A).
50. Calvin, *First Epistle,* 119.
51. Conzelmann, *1 Cor,* 105, n. 22. He cites Jude 6, 2 Pet 2:4, and *1 Enoch* 91:15.
52. Meyer, *First Epistle,* 1:166-67.
53. Collins, *First Cor,* 232, Grotius and de Wette reflect this theme.
54. Barrett, *First Epistle,* 136.

out a contrary δέ make the phrase tribunals concerning **matters of everyday life** very emphatic, especially directly following βιωτικά as the last word of v. 3, which lifted the mind to cosmic dimensions concerning **angels**! The protasis of the conditional is introduced by ἐάν with the present subjunctive of ἔχω. The punctuation at the end of the verse together with the reference of ἐξουθενημένους gives rise to a well-known crux of interpretation.

(i) *Interrogative Interpretation* (NRSV, REB, NJV, NASB, Barrett, Collins)

We have followed the Greek text of the UBS 4th ed., which reads the sentence as a question. In this case, καθίζετε is second plural *present indicative* active of καθίζω, *I cause to sit down, I seat*, **I set**, and the reference of ἐξουθενημένους (for the grammar and meaning of this word see in 1:28) must be to *Gentile* juries or to *Gentile* magistrates who have *no esteem within the community* (ἐν τῇ ἐκκλησίᾳ) *because they are not Christian believers.*

(ii) *Imperatival Interpretation* (NIV, AV/KJV)

Since punctuation marks were added to the text in later years, it is arguable that this sentence should be construed not as a question, but on the basis of parsing καθίζετε as second plural *present imperative* active of καθίζω. In this case, the whole meaning shifts. If this is an imperative, Paul does *not* enjoin his address-ees to set pagan judges over them; but ἐξουθενημένους must now mean, *set those Christians least esteemed among you* as your tribunal. In a recent study B. Kinman argues forcefully for this interpretation, reviewing Paul's rhetorical strategy and presenting a cumulative case.[55] In this case *least esteemed* or *"nothings"* (see on 1:28) can be explained in either of two ways: (a) Paul may be saying drily that even the least able believer is a safer guide than partial Gentiles who are influenced by social pressures; or (b) he may mean that the hyper-"spiritual" can remain at their tongues and worship, while the down-to-earth, ordinary, commonsense members of the congregation may have better usefulness for practical administrative tasks or plain reasoning with the two parties.

(iii) *Indicative Exclamatory Interpretation* (Moffatt, NJB)

In the case of *least esteemed in the church* it would also be possible to construe the sentence as neither a *question* nor a *command,* but as (iii) as an ironic *state-ment* or an *exclamation* (see on Moffatt below). Much depends on whether ἐξουθενημένους can reasonably be understood to apply to people within the congregation, especially since Paul has questioned the standing of the Gentile

---

55. Kinman, "'Appoint the Despised as Judges!' (1 Cor 6:4)," 345-54.

local civil courts and "reversed" the meaning *of no account,* spoken of believers, in 1:28-31.[56] F. F. Bruce considers the issue too finely balanced to invite a conclusion.[57]

Each tradition of interpretation has impressive support. (a) The imperative, with a reference to Christians who are "least esteemed," is adopted by Chrysostom, Theodoret, Augustine, and many modern writers (e.g., Bachmann, Allo, Clarke).[58] (b) Some refer ἐξουθενημένους to pagan juries or magistrates but interpret the sentence as an ironic exclamatory statement: "when you have mundane issues to settle, you refer them to the judgment of men who from this point of view of the church are of no account!"[59] (c) The interrogative indicative (which is very similar in meaning to (b)) is supported by Valla, Luther, Tischendorf, and more recently Fee, Wolff, and Lang.[60] Kinman puts forward five arguments for the imperative: (1) argument from word order (against Fee); (2) counterarguments about the rhetorical flow; (3) issues about the legal background: how can the church "appoint judges"? (4) The characterization of "Gentiles" in terms of this verse (e.g., "despised"); (5) the hypothetical indefinite syntax.[61] Long ago Lightfoot had argued that τοὺς ἐξουθενημένους is "a strong phrase to apply to the heathen."[62] But in favor of the interrogative indicative (i) Fee's points about word order are not decisively answered: the imperative would not be delayed to the end, especially if it is understood as irony;[63] (ii) it is also difficult to apply ἐξουθενημένους to Christians, although this may be an ironic parody of the language of the elitist spiritual enthusiast within the church;[64] (iii) the context about the last judgment may provide the context for applying the "outsider" term to Gentiles.[65] On balance, the interpretation implied by the UBS 4th ed. Greek text (i.e., as a question) may well be correct, but we cannot exclude the alternative with certainty. Although the force of the syntax may well be *interrogative,* the noun may still apply to those *(outside)* whom *the church does not regard as esteemed.*[66]

56. Schrage, *Der erste Brief,* 1:412.

57. Bruce *1 and 2 Cor,* 60.

58. Chrysostom, *1 Cor. Hom.,* 16:6; Theodoret, *Interp. Ep. 1 ad Cor.,* 195A (Migne, *PG,* 82:265-66); Calvin, *First Epistle,* 120; Bengel, *Gnomon,* 625; Edwards, *First Epistle,* 139-40; Lightfoot, *Notes,* 211; MacRory, *Epistles,* 73-74; Goudge, *First Epistle,* 44; Allo, *La Prèmiere Épitre,* 134-35; Kistemaker, *1 Cor,* 181-82; Clarke, *Secular Leadership,* 71; also Derrett, "Judgment," 29.

59. Moffatt, *First Epistle,* 63 and 65; Héring, *First Epistle,* 40; Weiss, *Der erste Korintherbrief,* 148-49.

60. Lietzmann, *An die Korinther,* 26 ("die Heiden"); Orr and Walther, *1 Cor,* 194; Barrett, *First Epistle,* 137; Lang, *Die Briefe,* 77-78; Fee, *First Epistle,* 236; Strobel, *Der erste Brief,* 108; Wolff, *Der erste Brief,* 115; Collins, *First Cor,* 232.

61. Kinman, "'Appoint the Despised as Judges!'" esp. 348-54.

62. Lightfoot, *Notes,* 211.

63. Fee, *First Epistle,* 235.

64. Wolff, *Der erste Brief,* 116.

65. Collins, *First Cor,* 229.

66. This does not fully address Kinman's third point, which is probably his strongest.

5 With the negative οὐκ ἐντρέπων in 4:14 we may note a contrast in the noun form ἐντροπή (v. 5) as a positive objective. Both cognate forms derive historically from the notion of *turning inward* (cf. *entropy* of thermal energy in physics, by later analogy), and with the dative ὑμῖν ἐντροπή convey a middle-voice or reflexive nuance of the objective of making the addressees **feel ashamed** (cf. NJB, *to make you ashamed of yourselves*). Our translation places the word order in the same sequence as the Greek to reflect the emphasis of the syntax. In 4:14 Paul does not interpret the premature triumphalism of the readers as grounds for destroying their self-respect by shame. But here the situation is so blatantly at odds with Christian identity that Paul is quite willing to demolish the self-esteem of the socially influential if it will help them to see the enormity of the attitudes and actions which betray their Christian profession as people of Christ and people of the cross. The *shame* derives from (i) ranking a grasping attitude above the welfare of the church; (ii) resorting to a potentially corrupt use of patronage to serve the interests of the self at the expense of justice or good; and (iii) thereby deepening damaging splits within the community. To these (iv) J. H. Bernard proposes that the legal dispute concerned the sexual issue of 5:1-13, while P. Richardson associates it with the sexual conduct relating to 6:12-19.[67] Chow believes that the general attitudes toward sexual freedom and manipulative patronage have close resonances.[68]

The translation **has it come to this, that there is found** . . . is drawn directly from J. B. Lightfoot's interpretation (followed by that of Senft) of οὕτως as a modal and adverbial demonstrative indicative of the degree of degeneration in the situation and of ἔνι, which represents an intensifying shortened form in place of ἔνεστι, it exists, or it is found to exist.[69] If Chow and many recent writers are correct in identifying those who initiate legal proceedings with high-status, well-connected people, Paul's logic is irrefutable. If there are those in the church who think highly of themselves, how is it that their "wisdom" to arbitrate between fellow Christians remains inferior to that of Gentiles who do not have gifts of "wisdom," "the Spirit," "revelation," or "knowledge" and who "reign as kings"? On the other hand, if being initiated as "persons of the Spirit" makes them superior to the Gentile world around them (4:8-11), might not the very lowliest low-status Christians be better equipped "to sit as judges" than high-status pagans? The addressees really cannot have it both ways!

Immense irony attaches to the future indicative δυνήσεται, *will be* **competent** in the light of κατὰ σάρκα οὐ πολλοὶ δυνατοί (1:26), δύναμις (1:18, 24; 2:4, 5; 4:19, 20) and δύναμαι (2:14; 3:2) compounded with the aorist infinitive διακρῖναι (cf. 4:7; 11:29, 31, 14:29) and διακρίσεις πνευμάτων (12:10). *Could* they "discern" or *could they not* "discern"?[70] The idiom ἀνὰ μέσον makes it

---

67. Bernard, "The Connexion between the Fifth and Sixth Chapters of 1 Cor," 433-43; Richardson, "Judgment in Sexual Matters in 1 Cor 6:1-11," 37-58.

68. Chow, *Patronage and Power,* 129-33.

69. Lightfoot, *Notes* 212; Robertson, *Epistles,* 4:118; and Senft, *La Première Épitre,* 78.

70. See the discussion above by S. Pogoloff, J. Davis, and others on "Wisdom."

clear that what is at issue is a capacity **to arbitrate** within the church between conflicting claims.

A profound link between Christian theology and the sociology of institutional communities emerges here, as Bonhoeffer perceived throughout his *Sanctorum Communio*.[71] The give-and-take of subjecting self-interest and personal desire to a consensus among capable people of integrity (far from necessarily the whole community) is part and parcel of respecting the corporate self-discipline and discernment of the Other-than-self, or other than a closely like-minded group. As Senft observes, here one experiences one of the greatest differences between the stance of the world and the stance expected of Christians.[72] Here the Greek word for *brother* bears its customary sense in this epistle of those who share the family likeness of **fellow believers**.

6 The UBS 4th ed., like the 3d ed., punctuates the sentence (with Conzelmann) as an interrogative (also with NRSV, NJB, and Barrett, continuing the question begun in v. 5; and with AV/KJV, REB, and Collins as a separate interrogative sentence). But Moffatt and NIV punctuate the sentence as a declarative exclamation. Findlay asserts: "This is an *answer* (his italics) to the question of ver 5, not a continuation of it."[73] The Greek gives no assistance on this issue. Against most translations and many modern commentaries, however, Findlay's comment seems to carry considerable weight. Further, the exclamation sharpens the contrastive force of ἀλλά. Edwards notes: "The contrast is threefold: instead of displaying the moderation of wisdom, you wrangle brother against brother; instead of accepting arbitration, you go to law; instead of referring matters to brethren for decision, you bring complaints against brethren before heathen tribunals."[74] Although κρίνεται is present indicative middle of κρίνω, REB rightly uses a *logical* **must**.

The neuter singular accusative demonstrative pronoun τοῦτο, **this**, is an accusative of general reference which marks the climactic, crowning affront of going to law before unbelievers. Often the plural τοῦτα performs this role.[75] The bad becomes worse, and the worse becomes the worst possible scenario by placing the greed and its accompanying manipulative strategies in the public domain for all the pagan world to behold. Christian failures diminish the credibility of the gospel as it is; but to advertise the failures is utter folly and disaster. Paul might have something to say about the manipulative use of media and the published word by Christians who want to score fellow believers, even at the price of heightening the profile of their lack of respect for the other in the eyes of the world. Once again, the gender-neutral translation *brother* causes insoluble problems, but here the term clearly stands in semantic opposition to **unbe-**

71. D. Bonhoeffer, *Sanctorum Communio: A Dogmatic Inquiry into the Sociology of the Church* (Eng. trans., London: SCM, 1963).

72. Senft, *La Première Épitre,* 78.

73. Findlay, *Expositor's Greek Testament,* 2:816 (as against Conzelmann, *1 Cor,* 105).

74. Edwards, *First Epistle,* 140-41.

75. BDF, 151, sect. 290, entry (5).

lievers.[76] Witherington rightly sees this climactic stage as turning on a "bad witness to the world."[77]

7 The use of ἤδη, **already**, as Conzelmann declares, "shows that a Christian court of arbitration is only a concession."[78] This entirely accords with the stance expressed in Matt 18:15-17. The ideal is ὕπαγε ἔλεγξον αὐτὸν μεταξὺ σοῦ καὶ αὐτοῦ μόνου (Matt 18:15). Only if this private face-to-face remonstration fails may the person who feels a sense of grievance seek a further step which entails ἕνα ἢ δύο (18:16); and only as a last resort is the wider group in the church (τῇ ἐκκλησίᾳ, Matt 18:17) involved. To move beyond the first stage of person-to-person dialogue is already ἥττημα, a **moral failure**.

In biblical Greek ἥττημα occurs only here and in Rom 11:12 (also Isa 31:8, LXX, as a cognate of ἥττων, *less;* but the term also has a classical background in which it means *defeat* in semantic contrast with *victory*. The combined nuances of *being less, falling short,* or *failing* with *defeat* invite the rendering **moral failure**, as Héring asserts and as Barrett implies but does not fully state.[79] The use of ὅλως, which could mean either *actually* or *entirely* (in the sense of *on all sides,* or *without qualification*), in 5:1 provides a part parallel, but here *wholly, entirely,* or *completely* may be restructured from an adverbial form to an adjectival English translation to denote **a total moral failure**. We follow Barrett in rendering μὲν οὖν **in fact** (as also NRSV; cf. REB, *indeed*).[80] Although κρίματα usually means *judgments,* interpreters agree that here the word denotes *lawsuits* or **cases for judgment**.

The second part of the verse comes to the heart of the matter. The later discussion of "rights" which features in 8:1–11:1 and reaches a peak in 9:19-23 places into the sharpest focus the priority of letting go what is theoretically a right but which may bring potentially destructive effects (see below, especially on 8:1-13 and 9:19-23). The desire for self-preservation which *lacks the courage to make oneself vulnerable in a first stage of interpersonal, face-to-face* pleading with understanding escalates into a confrontational, self-centered *defense* (a military image) of one's *rights*. But Paul is as hesitant about pressing the absoluteness of personal δίκη (in which an internal grammar of *penalty* and *justice* forces the other to make sacrifices) as he is about the absoluteness of γνῶσις, *knowledge,* which can *inflate* rather than *build* (8:1-2). Hence he turns the issue upside down, just as justice, penalty, and "rights" of the self are turned upside down in the theology of the *cross* (1:18-31) and in the mind of *Christ* (2:16–3:4).

---

76. Hence **fellow believer** (new translation) as against *sibling* (Collins) or *brother(s)* (Barrett).

77. Witherington, *Conflict and Community,* 164.

78. Conzelmann, *1 Cor,* 105.

79. Héring, *First Epistle,* 41; Barrett, *First Epistle,* 138; cf. Findlay, *Expositor's Greek Testament,* 2:816.

80. The particles μέν and οὖν are both included by p[11] (apparent reading), A, B, C, and most MSS, although the early p[46] and the original hands of ℵ and D omit οὖν, as signified by the UBS 4th ed. square brackets.

Paul adds the alpha-privative to the "rights" word: ἀδικέω signifies *being in the wrong.* But is the verb to be understood as a *passive* ἀδικεῖσθε *(you are deprived of your rights, you are injured)* or as a causative-reflexive or "permissive" use of the *middle voice:* **let yourselves be deprived of your rights** (even if this explicitly entails *suffering wrong*)? We suggest that the middle voice precisely matches and reflects Paul's theology of sacrificing one's "rights" in 8:1–11:1, especially 8:1-13 and 9:19-23. This use of the middle is repeated in the next verb.[81]

Indeed, the general principle which has been expressed receives further expression here in **Why do you not rather let yourselves be defrauded?** Like ἀδικεῖσθε, the middle voice of ἀποσερεῖσθε is also a "permissive" middle (here of ἀποστερέω, *to steal, to rob, to deprive,* **to defraud.** In the next verse the direction of this verb will be inverted as an active voice to mean **you defraud** (6:8).

Is Paul's expectation fair or reasonable? It is no more "fair" and "reasonable" than the divine grace which has eclipsed justice in Christ's giving up of his person and his "rights" on the cross, indicating in turn God's surrender of his "right" to pronounce a negative verdict on humankind without transcending justice in costly, generous mercy.

Senft includes a special note here on "Equity" *(Droit),* or "Justice" and Nonresistance.[82] He broadens the principle expressed above with reference to the Sermon on the Mount (esp. Matt 5:38-42). He argues that Paul's appeal to "wisdom" in this section, whether or not it includes ironic overtones, calls for the Christian perception and insight that the foundation of life is itself grounded on something higher and deeper than "law," "justice" and "rights." To renounce a right "ought to be itself a moral act," but it transcends even this *as a free act which bears the image of the grace of God.*[83] *Grace goes the second mile.*[84]

8 The combination of the adversative ἀλλά and the emphatic ὑμεῖς conveys the thought, *"you, Christians though you are. . . ."* Since this would strictly over-translate the Greek, we signal the syntax by **But you, as it is, . . .** On ἀδικέω see above, which conveys a double nuance of *you injure* and *you deprive others of rights,* since it represents an inverted logical, grammatical, and lexical symmetry with the previous verse. But *to deprive of rights* begins to move too far from translation to interpretation, whereas **deprive people of justice** not only reflects faithfully the alpha privative with the -δίκη word group, but also coheres precisely with the claims of Chow and many others about the *eclipse of justice by social networking* and manipulative uses of patronage

81. BDF, 166, sect. 317, includes the middle voice use of "to let oneself be . . ." as a subcategory of causative in reflexive mode. (Robertson and Plummer insist that the verb is "middle, not passive," *First Epistle,* 116.) On the lexicography of the word, cf. BAGD, 17; MM, 10.

82. Senft, *La Première Épitre,* 79-80.

83. Ibid., 79.

84. Calvin, *First Epistle,* 121-23, gives more attention to the delegated authority of magistrates here than to the principle of grace.

which local magistrates' courts (not major criminal courts) regularly invited (see under 6:1-4). If play is made of social influence and/or patronage, the net effect of taking a case to a Gentile court might well be to **defraud** a fellow Christian, especially if the case is brought by the wealthy or socially "strong."[85]

We have also noted above that to sin against fellow Christians is to commit sacrilege against God's holy temple, since God's people constitute the temple of the Holy Spirit. The demonstrative τοῦτο performs a parallel function to that of the same pronoun in v. 6. Since the accusative ἀδελφούς is the direct object of the verbs **deprive of justice** and **defraud**, the easiest way of conveying the syntactic function of τοῦτο is to follow the NRSV, *and believers* **at that**. The phrase "is accordingly not a limitation, but a concretization."[86]

9-10 On **do you not know that** (v. 9), see on 3:16 (also 5:6; cf. 6:2, 3 and Hurd's comments on the ten uses of this phrase in this epistle).[87] REB's *surely you know that* and NJB's *do you not realise that* convey the nuance well, but the force of the more traditional translation has become familiar as an indicator of Paul's deep concern. "These verses are characterized by the direct rhetorical appeal (Paul's use of the second person plural) and their eschatological perspective."[88] Since the attempt to bypass justice by social networks of influence probably lies behind 6:1-8, there are good grounds for translating ἄδικοι as *unjust* (Collins). But most translations reflect a concern not to narrow or to overspecify the semantic range as an introduction to the broad contrast which Paul is about to make. Hence most translate as *wrongdoers* (NRSV, REB), *wicked* (NIV, Moffatt), or *unrighteous* (AV/KJV). NJB, however, plausibly seeks a stronger term for the contrast with v. 11 and renders the adjective with the definite article **people who** *do* **evil**, which we modify, in accordance with Paul's emphasis here on habit or disposition as **people who practice evil**.

The actions of vv. 9 and 10, associated also with the use of μή with the present imperative πλανᾶσθε, urge puting an end to what Paul may perceive as a disturbing "parade" of inappropriate conduct before his eyes, while these verses set in contrast an active lifestyle which contradicts claims to Christian identity (1 John is a paradigm, as Neufeld demonstrates) with stances that characterize the Christlike qualities of the new creation (v. 11).[89]

---

85. **Defrauding** may appear to be a "respectable" version of downright stealing (e.g., in business, commerce, or social relations). See above under **extortionate dealings**; and S. E. Fowl, "Making Stealing Possible," in *Engaging Scripture,* esp. 164-71.

86. Conzelmann, *1 Cor,* 106, n. 29.

87. Hurd, *Origin of 1 Corinthians,* 85-86.

88. Collins, *First Cor,* 229.

89. D. Neufeld, *Reconceiving Texts as Speech-Acts: An Analysis of 1 John,* BibInt 7 (Leiden: Brill, 1994), throughout. Our reference to a disturbing "parade" tentatively takes account of Stanley E. Porter's argument that the present may relate to the aspect of actions as it is viewed *(Aktionsart)* than to a more objective distinction between the continuous and punctiliar. However, we are not as convinced as Porter appears to be about these so often *alternative* accounts of the verbal forms (i.e., aspect versus tense). See S. E. Porter, *Verbal Aspect in the Greek of the NT with Reference to Tense and Mood,* Studies in Biblical Greek 1 (New York: Lang, 1989, esp. ch. 2;

Inherit God's kingdom (θεοῦ βασιλείαν in v. 9) or shall (not) inherit the kingdom of God (βασιλείαν θεοῦ, v. 10) anticipates the theme expressed most explicitly in 15:50.[90] "Flesh and blood cannot inherit the kingdom of God" (15:50) because only transformed humanity can be described as coming fully under God's rule.[91] There is therefore an aspect of "internal grammar" to Paul's pronouncement. *He is not describing the qualifications required for an entrance examination; he is comparing habituated actions, which by definition can find no place in God's reign for the welfare of all, with those qualities in accordance with which Christian believers need to be transformed if they belong authentically to God's new creation in Christ.* Everything which persistently opposes what it is to be Christlike *must undergo change if those who practice such things wish to call themselves Christians and to look forward to resurrection with Christ.* We have therefore translated the first occurrence of the future indicative of κληρονομέω with the negative οὐ as **cannot inherit**, in the *logical* sense of *cannot* (*not* its *causal* sense). No difference in time reference is implied, for as J. D. Hester argues, the word **inheritance** carries with it entailments of continuity and discontinuity which relate the future to the present, and the present to the future.[92] For **people who do evil** to **inherit** God's Lordship is self-contradiction. Hence it entails a tacit invitation *to change. In principle* the old practices lie behind them, belonging to their past. They must (logical *must*) remove these anomalies to prove the authenticity of their calling as *holy people* who *belong to God* (1:2-3).

While the principle expressed in these verses is clear, however, the details are notoriously complex. (i) We noted in 5:9-11 that more needed to be said about "catalogues of vices" in Paul. Are these merely generalized stereotypical material drawn from Stoic traditions of ethics, or do the specified habits relate to specific situations? (ii) Is the general background for interpretation that of the Platonic-Stoic virtues and vices, or is it drawn from hellenistic Judaism, or from the OT and the Decalogue? (iii) How are the individual actions identified to be translated? Here the most notorious and intensive debate concerns whether οὔτε μαλακοὶ οὔτε ἀρσενοηοῖται refers to homosexual relations in general, or more narrowly to male prostitution, sacred male prostitution, pederastic practices, or concepts of maleness and effeminacy in the Greek or Jewish world

---

S.E. Porter and D. A. Carson, *Biblical Greek Language and Linguistics: Open Questions in Current Research,* JSNTSS 80 (Sheffield: Sheffield Academic Press, 1993), esp. 26-45; and B. M. Fanning, *Verbal Aspect in the NT,* Oxford Theological Monograph (Oxford: Clarendon, 1990). For a brief introductory overview cf. S. E. Porter, "Keeping Up with Recent Studies, 17: Greek Language and Linguistics," *ExpTim* 103 (1992): 202-8.

90. Schrage, *Der erste Brief,* 1:426, nn. 151 and 429.

91. J. Jeremias, "Flesh and Blood Cannot Inherit the Kingdom of God" (1 Cor XV:50)," *NTS* 2 (1955): 151-59.

92. J. D. Hester, *Paul's Concept of Inheritance,* SJT Occasional Paper 14 (Edinburgh: Oliver & Boyd, 1968). This useful, succinct study of the term and its semantic field adopts a similar approach to the relation between the present and the future as O. Cullmann's *Christ and Time* and Cullmann's other works on salvation history.

of the day. (iv) Finally, how do Paul's terms relate to more modern understandings of these issues? Is there any risk of historical anachronism in our interpretations? Clearly all this invites, indeed necessitates, an extended note.

VICE LISTS, CATECHESIS, AND THE HOMOSEXUALITY DEBATE (6:9-10)

The Status of So-Called Catalogues of Vices in Paul

On 5:9-11 we noted that such catalogues do occur in Paul: twenty-one specific moral failures are listed in Rom 1:29-31, where the background clearly reflects material often used in the homilies of hellenistic Jewish synagogues as a means of exhorting a difference of status and lifestyle between Jews of the diaspora and pagan society around them. Thus Wis 14:22-26 perceives moral failure to spring from idolatry and proceeds to enumerate some twenty-seven related dispositions or practices. Paul's notion is drawn from Wisdom or Wisdom-type material that ignorance of God turns moral values upside down so that "evils are called peace" (Wis 14:22), and these consequences damage the status of marriage (Wis 14:24) and lead to "adultery . . . murder, theft, fraud, corruption, treachery, riot, perjury . . ." (14:24-25). They bring γάμων ἀταξία, μοιχεία καὶ ἀσέλγεια, for "The worship of idols (εἰδώλων θρησκεία) is the beginning (or origin, ἀρχή) of every evil (κακοῦ) and its cause (αἰτία)" (14:26-27, LXX). Thereby the double sin of reducing God to idols and falling victim to unrestrained evil are closely related both causally and logically (14:30-31).

The link consists in making "God" and other persons manipulable tools to serve self-interest. "Anything goes" because the idols are nameless constructs (Wis 14:27) and moral constraints are thrown up in a process of escalating self-gratification. The major significance of Paul's use of these lists is to take up this tradition of logic, which, in turn, distances these pursuits from the very different styles of life which identify God's people as his holy people committed in covenant to trust and obedience, not simply to please themselves and to create God and life in their own independent image.

In the history of NT research, however, the direction of thought has often taken a very different turn. J. Weiss noted the presence of these catalogues in 1910, and in 1932 B. S. Easton argued that the "catalogues" were primarily derived from the Stoics and their lists of virtues.[93] In 1936 A Vögtle traveled further along the same road, interpreting the lists in terms of a successive expansion of Plato's cardinal virtues (and their opposites) first by the Stoics and then especially by those strands in hellenistic Judaism which utilized Stoic thought.[94] Vögtle's *positive* arguments are valid; examples can be found in Plato's discussion of virtues, in the Stoics, and most especially in hellenistic Judaism. However, he underestimated the role played by OT texts, which we shall subsequently discuss.

---

93. Weiss, *Der erste Korintherbrief,* 140-45 and 152-56, for terminological parallels (e.g., Philo, *Sibylline Oracles,* Plutarch). Weiss studies ethical content in his *Earliest Christianity,* 2:546-94. Cf. Easton, "NT Ethical Lists," 1-12.

94. Vögtle, *Die Tugend- und Lasterkataloge im NT.*

Vögtle's work (1936) on "catalogues" was followed by that of Wibbing (1959), Kamlah (1964), and others, although Wibbing stresses a *Jewish* background and Kamlah a *catechetical* one.[95] But why should these studies be of immediate concern for the exegesis of 1 Cor 6:9-10? The answer is readily explained. On the basis of form-critical work which ascribed a *Sitz im Leben* out of which the catalogue forms arose to Greek, hellenistic, or Graeco-Roman contexts, or to a hellenistic-Jewish tradition which drew decisively from such contexts, Lietzmann, Conzelmann, and Scroggs, among others, put forward the view that the specific moral failures listed in 6:9-10 (and 5:9-11) are *not of individual contextual significance in this epistle,* but should be re-garded as a *generalized form reflecting stereotypical ethical material drawn from Stoic, Cynic, or satirical sources with Graeco-Roman traditions.* Thus Conzelmann urges, "It is drawing on set tradition. The terms of expression . . . are not specifically Pauline."[96] He cannot accept the fact that the individual dispositions or actions are significant indi-vidually, and rejects the view that in 6:9-10 we have "to do with a realistic description of conditions at Corinth."[97] Scroggs utilizes the hypothesis of a Roman setting to ar-gue that the vocabulary traditionally understood to refer to homosexual relations de-notes only *pederasty.*[98] Similarly, Boswell distinguishes homosexual acts, which Paul does not call "morally reprehensible," from *male prostitution.*[99] (See the discussion below.)

We therefore need to review critically the genuine implications of a form-critical approach to the ethical catalogues for an exegesis of our passage. Vögtle ar-gued that the ethical catalogues in Stoic philosophical tradition derive from earlier discussions of the virtues in Plato and in Aristotle. From the different conceptual starting points of Plato on theory of virtue and Aristotle on wisdom and the ethical mean, both merge with a Stoic emphasis on lack of excess and lack of physical self-indulgence. Plato's theory of universal Forms or Ideas offered a framework for his ex-position of *the cardinal virtues* as an aspect of "the soul's" spurning physical passions and appetites of the body. Other virtues emerged as subcategorizations of the four cardinal virtues. Aristotle rejected a point of departure in universal Ideas or Forms, but shared the view that to pursue an ethic of *well-being* (εὐδαιμονία) in the setting of the city-state demanded an avoidance of excess, as articulated in his ethics of the mean. The Middle Platonism of the first century cohered with Stoic traditions from Cleanthes to Epictetus in seeing ethical virtue largely in terms of "living harmoniously with the natural order" (τῇ φύσει ὁμολογουμένως ζῆν, or in Cicero, *cum natura convenienter vivere*).[100] Vögtle readily finds evidence of an ethic which has points of affinity with Philo, Wisdom, and Paul in this respect, in Seneca (c. 4 BC–AD 65), Musonius Rufus (c. AD 30–c. 100), and Epictetus (c. AD 50–c. AD 130), and distinguishes

95. Wibbing, *Die Tugend- und Lasterkataloge im NT;* and Kamlah, *Die Form der katalo-gischen Paränese im NT.*

96. Conzelmann, *1 Cor,* 106; cf. "Catalogues of Virtues and Vices," ibid., 100-102.

97. Ibid., 101.

98. Scroggs, *The NT and Homosexuality,* 85-97; cf. 29-65 and 105-22.

99. Boswell, *Christianity, Social Tolerance and Homosexuality,* 111-14.

100. Aristotle, *Nicomachean Ethics* 1.8.4; 7.13.2; Plato, *Republic* 354A, 444D, 580C, 588C, and *Protagoras* 315C; Cleanthes, *Stoicorum veterum fragmenta* (ed. J. von Arnim), 3.16, 17; Epictetus, *Dissertations* 3.1.24-35 (on the "natural" characteristics respectively of men and women); 3.9.16, 17 (χρείαν αὐτῶν [possessions] οὐκ ἔχω . . . τοῦ κατὰ φύσιν ἔχειν τὴν διάνοιαν, τοῦ μὴ ταράττεσθαι).

between the occurrence of ethical catalogues in later Stoic philosophy, Graeco-Roman satire, and hellenistic Jewish sources.[101]

Yet when all has been said about resemblances, it is arguable, at the very least, that we remain at the level of vocabulary, style and *form,* not how the ethical virtues and vices are integrated with a particular system of thought. Four serious criticisms invite assessment.

(a) C. H. Dodd argued convincingly in his *Gospel and Law* (1951) that *the basis of Paul's ethics is to be* "sharply distinguished from that of contemporary Greek moralists, who from the time of Aristotle have set out to provide a self-contained and self-justifying system of ethics."[102] For while he conceded that a considerable overlap of specific content exists, in Paul and the NT, he also insisted that ethics flows from a response to the gospel which forms part of the identity of Christian believers (including their inheritance of the OT).[103] Evidence of similar patterns of style and parenetic catalogues within the NT (1 Thess 4:1-9; 5:14-18, with 1 Pet 1:13-22; 2:11; Heb 13:1-3) owe more to a common *catechetical Sitz im Leben* than to the hellenistic settings proposed by Vögtle, as the detailed work of P. Carrington and E. G. Selwyn suggests.[104]

This precisely fits the *Sitz im Leben* of 1 Cor 6:9-11 (and 5:9-11), which Paul introduces by **do you not know that. . . ?** It also coheres with Moule's stress on *motivation* as the key to the ethical significance of such material and "obligation."[105] Dodd lists six distinctive themes in such Pauline settings: (1) sitting loose to earthly possessions in the light of eschatology (not in Stoic self-sufficiency; cf. 1 Cor 7:29-34; Rom 13:11, 12); (2) the newness of the new life (1 Cor 5:7; 2 Cor 5:17), often in the context of baptism (or conversion-initiation, see 1 Cor 6:11); (3) corporate solidarity, or "belonging" to one another as a new corporate identity (1 Cor 12:12-27; cf. 1 Cor 6:1-8); (4) the imitation of Christ, or transformation into Christ's image (1 Cor 11:1; 2 Cor 8:9; Phil 2:5-11); (5) the motivation of ἀγάπη instantiated concretely (1 Cor 8:1-3; 13:1-13; Rom 13:8-10); and (6) tacit or explicit allusions or appeals to the words of Jesus (Rom 12:16; 13:7; 1 Cor 7:1-7; 8-11, 12-16; 9:14).[106] *If the background is catechetical, this transforms the significance of such a "list" into guidelines explicit for teaching on the nature of the Christian life.*

---

101. Late, i.e., first-century BC-AD Stoic sources include Musonius, *Fragmenta,* 16; *Cicero, Tusculanae Disputationes* 4.11-27; Epictetus, *Diss.* 3.20.5, 6 (see also above note); cf. further Diogenes Laertius, 7.87, 92-93, 110-12; while satirical authors include Lucian and Horace, *Epodes* 1.1.33-40. On the other hand, some "lists" or "catalogues" are almost too short to merit the name, e.g., the four virtues in Epictetus, *Diss.* 3.20.5, 6, ἐτηρήσεν τὸν φιλόπατριν, τὸν μεγαλόφρονα, τὸν πιστόν, τὸν γενναῖον. See further Vögtle, *Die Tugend- und Lasterkataloge,* 79-88 and elsewhere.

102. C. H. Dodd, *Gospel and Law* (Cambridge: Cambridge University Press, 1951), 10.

103. Ibid., 10-17.

104. Ibid., 18-21; P. Carrington, *The Primitive Christian Catechism* (Cambridge: Cambridge University Press, 1940); and E. G. Selwyn *The First Epistle of St Peter* (London: Macmillan, 2d ed. 1947), 365-466. Both reflect the work of A. Seeberg, *Der Katechismus der Urchristenheit* (Leipzig: Bohme, 1903).

105. C. F. D. Moule, "Obligation in the Ethic of Paul," in W. R. Farmer, C. F. D. Moule, and R. R. Niebuhr (eds.), *Christian History and Interpretation: Studies Presented to John Knox* (Cambridge: Cambridge University Press, 1967), 389-406, esp. 393.

106. Dodd, *Gospel and Law,* 25-31, 31-32, 32-38, 39-42, 42-45, 46-50. On this last point see also D. L. Dungan, *The Sayings of Jesus in the Churches of Paul* (Oxford: Blackwell, 1971), esp. 3-27, 83-101, 146-50.

(b) J. N. Sevenster reveals that countless times "Paul and Seneca . . . use similar words in entirely different meanings."[107] Paul's concern is precisely *not* harmony with the universe, but harmony with the likeness of God in Christ (1 Cor 2:13-16).[108] Seneca repeatedly discusses *virtus;* Paul alludes only once to ἀρετή (Phil 4:8 [apart from the Pastorals]).[109] "Virtue is essentially an anthropocentric notion."[110] Typical is Seneca's praise of bravery *(fortitudo),* whereas ἀνδρεία "does not occur in Paul or in the whole of the NT."[111] In their use of ethical imagery they remain apart.[112] Even *wisdom* has different meanings in each of the two writers: for Seneca, the wise man remains "inwardly inviolable"; "the wise man reigns over the whole world" (cf. 1 Cor 4:8); Paul's concept of wisdom derives from God's ways in Christ (1 Cor 1:24; 1:30; Col 2:3), which are received as a gift rather than achieved as a goal.[113]

(c) This brings us neatly to the contribution with which S. Wibbing seeks to update and to supplement the work of Vögtle. Wibbing, partly followed more recently by O. L. Yarbrough, notes the presence of ethical catalogues *in* Judaism approximately contemporary with Paul and the NT.[114] Admittedly Wibbing is reluctant to view this Jewish material as derived from the OT rather than from Graeco-Roman sources on one side and the settings of its own apocalyptic traditions on the other. However, Wibbing's work provides an advance on the claims of Vögtle, partly in identifying the importance of such sources as *1 Enoch, Jubilees,* and the *Testaments of the Twelve Patriarchs,* but more especially (following his teacher K. G. Kuhn) of the texts of Qumran. Wibbing concedes that the *moral* dualism of Qumran reflects the original "two ways" of obedience and disobedience of Deut 27:15-26 and 30:15ff. Although he rightly calls attention to *1 Enoch* 10:20; 91:6-7; *Jubilees* 7:20-21; 23:14; and *Testament of Moses* 7, his greatest advance is to relate these forms to *"the two ways"* of 1QS 4:9-11.[115] This very point paves the way for a more positive consideration of the relevance of Deuteronomy and the OT for the ethical "catalogue."

(d) E. Kamlah sought to develop the approaches of Vögtle and Wibbing and on this basis cited a similar array of data.[116] But like Dodd, Carrington, and Selwyn, he explored *Christian catechesis* as a major *Sitz im Leben* for the forms. The major weakness of his work upon terminology remains his preoccupation with surface vocabulary and style. He operates almost entirely at the level of *forms*. Without adequate attention to Paul's theological foundation and issues of ethical motivation for a specific lifestyle in concrete situations (in marked contrast to Schrage) Kamlah's work remains

---

107. J. N. Sevenster, *Paul and Seneca,* NovTSup 4 (Leiden: Brill, 1961), 78.

108. Ibid., 52.

109. Ibid., 154.

110. Ibid., 156.

111. Ibid., 158; cf. Seneca, *Epistulae* 37.1, 2; 67.6; 113.27, 28.

112. Sevenster, *Paul and Seneca,* 161-64; cf. Seneca, *Ep.* 82.5; 107.9; 120.12; *De Vita Beata* 15.5.

113. Sevenster, *Paul and Seneca,* 164, 165, 166. Cf. Seneca, *De Vita Beata* 3.3; *Ep.* 94.68; 89.4; 20.5; *De Beneficiis* 7.3.2 (on "reigning").

114. Wibbing, *Die Tugend- und Lasterkataloge im NT und ihre Traditionsgeschichte,* esp. 14-76; cf. O. L. Yarbrough, *Not Like the Gentiles: Marriage Rules in the Letters of Paul,* SBLDS 80 (Atlanta: Scholars Press, 1985), 8-26.

115. Wibbing, *Die Tugend- und Lasterkataloge,* 43-76.

116. Kamlah, *Die Form der katalogischen Paränese im NT,* e.g., 39-53, 104-15, and 171-75, reflects Wibbing, *Die Tugend- und Lasterkataloge,* 27-33, 43-76, and elsewhere.

incomplete.[117] All the same, his work adds to the need for caution in accepting the sweeping claims of Lietzmann, Conzelmann, and Scroggs about the Graeco-Roman setting of stereotypical material for our exegesis of 1 Cor 6:9-10 and similar passages in Paul.

(e) Some interim inferences may be drawn before we move to the next main issue. All the while that Graeco-Roman (as against OT, Jewish, and Christian) frames for "ethical catalogues" are given central prominence, it may simply be assumed that the "lists" reflect little more than culture-relative conventions of the day. Thus it has recently been claimed that Paul merely shares "the Mediterranean consensus" of his day.[118]

Further, when *terminological and formal* parallels are cited without reference to a distinctive theological and conceptual frame which determines their meaning currency, it is all too easy to misread such parallels. In a comparable "catalogue" in Rom 1:26-29, e.g., Paul speaks of same-sex relations as παρὰ φύσιν, *against nature*. But *nature* (φύσις) has no precise equivalent in Hebrew, and at first sight cannot reflect any OT background.[119] It is usually related to the kind of argument put forward by Epictetus that for a man to play the role of a woman, or to wish to act as a woman, is for him to complain against his *nature* (ἐγκαλέσαι σου τῇ φύσει, *Dissertations* 3.1.30). To confuse the life roles (from dress to sex) of male and female is not only to fail to live "in harmony with nature" (φύσει ὁμολουμένως) *(Diss.* 3.1.25); it is to make oneself "weird" or "a prodigy" (ὢ δεινοῦ θεάματος, 3.29). It is then a very short step to argue that modern understandings of what is "natural" for given persons have so radically changed in the light of psychology as to render the whole approach simplistic and absolute and to sweep aside issues of social conditioning, let alone social construction. But is Paul using φύσις (when he does) as Epictetus and the Stoics use it, and does a Stoic world-view or Stoic psychology play any part at all in such passages as 1 Cor 6:9-10?

The Relevance of the OT and Theology Thereby Entailed

(a) Rosner explores the "two ways" motif in Deuteronomy 27 and Deuteronomy 30.[120] This constitutes a convincing background to Wibbing's appeal to the two ways of 1QS 4:9-11, equally instantiated in the claims of Kamlah, Carrington, and Dodd concerning catechesis. Rosner argues in detail for "the Jewish mediation of Scripture to Paul's ethics."[121] Following K. Berger and F. Dexinger, he believes that the influence of the Decalogue (Exod 20:1-17; Deut 5:6-21) "would be difficult to overstate," especially in conjunction with Deut 27:15-26 and Ezekiel 18 and 22.[122]

---

117. Contrast Schrage, *Die Konkreten Einzelbote in der paulinischen Paränese.*

118. Stegemann, "Paul and the Sexual Mentality of His World," 161-66.

119. J. D. G. Dunn stresses that "φύσις, nature, is not a Hebrew concept; the term only comes into the LXX in the later works which originated in Greek (Wisd Sol 3 and 4 Macc). . . . The concept is primarily Greek and typically Stoic" (*Romans 1–8*, WBC [Dallas: Word Books, 1988], 64).

120. Rosner, *Paul, Scripture and Ethics,* 53-55; cf. 46-47, 51-53, and 164-66.

121. Ibid., 55.

122. Ibid., 210.

(b) To turn to details, how do we assess Conzelmann's claim here that the phraseology of 1 Cor 6:9-11 is un-Pauline, as betrayed by the term **the kingdom of God**? J. A. Kirk convincingly explains Paul's use of a phrase which normally he rarely uses in the light of the contextual significance, what the unrighteous **cannot inherit** and the righteous **shall inherit**.[123] **The kingdom of God** is both present and future. But we observed from Hester's work that *the concept of inheritance* carries with it dimensions of continuity and discontinuity in relation to present reality and future promise. This coheres with our comments that exclusion **from the kingdom** is largely a *self-imposed* entailment (a relation of *internal* logical grammar) of dispositions and acts which persistently contradict Christian identity as persons in whom God's reign becomes instantiated. If, however, this is the case, we have entered the semantic domain of OT time, history, and promise, which has little or nothing to do with the "timeless" virtues of the Platonic, Aristotelian, and Stoic traditions. If we press the "un-Pauline" character of the phrase, the OT as primitive pre-Pauline Christian aspects invite emphasis still more strongly. Kirk's linking of **kingdom** with **inherit** in 1 Cor 6:9 and Gal 5:21 (cf. Eph 5:5) is confirmed by Paul's double emphasis in the present (1 Thess 2:12; 2 Thess 1:5; Col 1:13) and the eschatological future (1 Cor 15:24, 50; cf. 2 Tim 4:1).

(c) Whatever may be claimed about the origins of the use of φύσις in Rom 1:26-27 and in 1 Cor 6:9-10, every term finds its place in the LXX translation of Hebrew texts, especially in the context of Levitical and Deuteronomic legislation. Scroggs points out that the four terms listed in 5:10 are expanded into six in 5:11 by the addition of **people who practice verbal abuse** and **drunkards**. In 6:9-10 a further four terms are added (μοιχοί, μαλακοί, ἀρσενοκοῖται, and κλέπται) to complete a "catalogue" of ten.[124] We have discussed the meanings of the earlier six terms above (see on 5:10-11), but here we may note that all have OT backgrounds.

Hatch-Redpath list around fifty uses of πορνεία (of which forty-six come from the LXX of the Hebrew text), three uses of πορνεῖον, nineteen uses of πορνεύειν, and forty-two uses of πόρνη. The three (only) occurrences of πόρνος all come from Wis 23:16, 17, 18, but πορνικός occurs in Prov 7:10 and Ezek 16:24. πορνεύειν generally translates זנה (zanah), as πορνικός does (also זונה [zonah] in Prov 7:10). But πορνεύων also translates קדשׁ (qadesh).[125] Rosner discusses the distinction between the "secular" prostitute (zonah) and the cult prostitute (qadesh) in the OT, noting that the first is condemned in the context of personal moral failure, and the second of disloyalty to God, but that both contradict the call to holy faithfulness on the part of the people of God.[126] Both aspects, he argues, may lie behind 1 Corinthians 6, esp. 6:12-20, and the principle emerges in Deut 22:21 as well.[127]

While the noun πλεονέκτης occurs only once in the Greek Bible (Wis 14:9), the verb πλεονεκτεῖν occurs three times (including Exod 22:27), and πλεονεξία eight times.[128] But Rosner relates the act to the attitude reflected in selling a fellow Israelite for personal gain (Deut 24:7), which fits the context of 1 Cor 6:1-8.[129] He assigns the

---

123. J. A. Kirk, "En torno al concepto del reino en Pablo," *RevistB* 41 (1979): 97-108.

124. Scroggs, *The NT and Homosexuality*, 103.

125. Hatch-Redpath, 2:1194-95.

126. Rosner, *Paul, Scripture and Ethics*, 126-28.

127. Ibid., 93.

128. Hatch-Redpath, 2:1142.

129. Rosner, *Paul, Scripture and Ethics*, 126-28.

background of ἅρπαξ to the same passage in Deuteronomy. The πλεον- stem with ἔχω (as we noted on 5:10-11) denotes always wanting *to have more, an addiction to multiplying possessions by whatever means.* The Greek translates Heb. בצע (*batsa'*, verb, or *betsa'*, noun). ἅρπαξ and ἁρπάζειν translate Hebrew texts in the LXX some forty times, usually Heb. מרף (*mâraph*), in addition to ἁρπαγή (five times in Hebrew, nine times in the LXX only) and ἅρπαγμα (seventeen times). It conveys the nuance of *grasping* or *snatching from another.*[130]

It is scarcely necessary to explicate the OT backgrounds of εἰδωλολάτρης, λοίδορος, and μέθυσος, for which Rosner points us especially to Deut 13:5 (and 17:7); 19:19; and 21:21, respectively. We wait till the next subheading to supply the translation and OT background of the controversial terms distinctive to 6:9-10. In the light of a detailed full-length study of this subject Rosner concludes: "The evidence we have rehearsed supports the conclusion that the Scriptures were an indispensable and formative source for 1 Cor 6:1-11.... Paul ... showed himself to have *Scriptural structures of thought,* such as the notion that *identity must inform behaviour*" (my italics).[131]

If the above discussion were merely to rest on vocabulary alone, we should be guilty of the same semantic and hermeneutical superficiality as those who conclude that the Graeco-Roman background is decisive on the basis of terminological parallels in Epictetus, Musonius, and Seneca among the philosophers and Horace and Lucian among the satirists. But what Rom 1:26-31, 1 Cor 6:9-11, Wis 13:1-19, and Wis 14:22-31 have in common with Deuteronomy 27–30, Hosea, and many parts of the OT is the axiom that idolatry corrupts holy identity, which in turn leads to moral collapse.[132] Once humans have reconstructed God in accordance with its religious and power preferences, as Feuerbach and Nietzsche knew full well, they are free to reconstruct ethics and conduct in accordance with their moral and social preferences. Romans, Corinthians, Wisdom, Proverbs, Hosea, and Deuteronomy all share this single frame of reference, which gives the "catalogues" a currency quite different from Stoic distaste for excess, or Platonic devaluation of the senses, or satirical portraits of the grammar of self-destruction or hypocrisy. Fitzmyer comments in his incisive discussion of the principle in Rom 1:18-32: "Pagan idolatry has become the 'big lie.' ... The condition of pagan humanity results from the moral degradation to which their idolatry has brought them: to the craving ... for moral impurity ... sexual excess (1:24, 26a) and homosexual activity (1:26b-27)."[133]

Admittedly some interpreters remain unconvinced and interpret even the frame very differently. Furnish sees the Pauline approach as colored more decisively by first-century Graeco-Roman society, assumptions about "nature," notions of "activity" and "passivity" in the sexual act, and primitive superstitions about the effects of same-sex relations as leading to sterility.[134] These constitute for him a more decisive frame of interpretation. But Paul's very point in 1 Cor 5:1-13 and in 6:1-20 is that Christian corpo-

---

130. Hatch-Redpath, 1:159-60.

131. Rosner, *Paul, Scripture and Ethics,* 121. Rosner extends this to marriage in ch. 7; cf. 147-76.

132. J. A. Fitzmyer gives a judicious commentary on this in *Romans,* AB (New York: Doubleday, 1993), 270-77 (on Rom 1:18-32).

133. Ibid., 271.

134. V. P. Furnish, "The Bible and Homosexuality: Reading the Texts in Context," in Siker (ed.), *Homosexuality in the Church: Both Sides of the Debate,* 26-28; cf. 18-35.

rate identity *has a distinctive foundation and a distinctive lifestyle* as against Graeco-Roman social, political, and religious traditions. If, as we have argued above, the distinctive *catechetical* frame plays some part in conjunction with OT themes about "a holy people," we may endorse E. Earle Ellis's conclusion regarding "traditions in 1 Corinthians": that these "NT catalogues are closer to one another than to similar lists in Jewish or even more distant Greek philosophical texts.... The NT writers have ... an agreed understanding about moral imperatives for believers...."[135] *The catechetical setting of 6:9-11 makes this an even more important and foundational passage than Romans 1, which contains its own problems, for an evaluation of the ethical contrasts entailed.*

The Translation of Controversial Terms and Their Specific Contextual Relation to Corinth

P. Zaas explicitly attacks the assumption of Scroggs that "any relation between an individual item in a list and the situation addressed was thus, more often than not, nonexistent. Furthermore, the items might well be partially, at least, memorized from a traditional stock of evils."[136] Just as we pointed out (above) that each term came from Hebrew texts, so Zaas argues that each item relates to specific issues at Corinth. In 5:1 Paul describes the issue as πορνεία, **an illicit sexual relationship**; in 5:9 he speaks of πόρνοι, and he uses πόρνος in 5:11.[137] The disposition that reaches expression in action is *desire for what is not one's due*, and it finds expression *no less* in the manipulative ploy of *grasping at* property through *exploiting* social networks by initiating litigation in a local magistrate's court for small claims (see above, with reference to Chow and Winter, on courts and patronage). Paul constantly feels the need to remind the Corinthians that they have not yet arrived (4:8-13); they have yet to **inherit the kingdom** (6:9). Rather that seeing the *extended* list as primary (with Scroggs), Zaas perceives Paul as *beginning with the list of four, then extending it to six*, and finally in 6:9-11 showing the *extended consequences* which pave the way for his insistence that surrendering to bodily liaison with a prostitute is to tear apart the new identity of being-in-Christ which God has created (6:13, 15-18).

The basis for these specific, individual issues is not Stoic or Jewish ethics, but Christian identity as temples of the Holy Spirit (6:19) redeemed at cost to belong to Christ as his (6:20). "You are not your own" (6:19b) is as far from Stoic autonomy as can be imagined. It is not necessary to follow P. Richardson here in identifying the content of the proposed lawsuit as the sexual relationship itself, although Richardson, like Zaas, sees the "list" as containing components which relate closely to the situation.[138]

Two studies convincingly confirm Zaas's claims about the *contextual* basis of the so-called list in the Corinthian situation. First, B. J. Oropeza (1998) urges that Paul "writes these lists to identify what he perceives as disruptive influences in the ... community.... The vices in the Corinthian letters are mostly situational."[139] Paul claims

---

135. E. E. Ellis, "Traditions in 1 Corinthians," *NTS* 32 (1986): 483; cf. 481-502.

136. Scroggs, *The NT and Homosexuality,* 102, Zaas, "Catalogues and Context: 1 Cor 5 and 6," 624; cf. 622-29.

137. Ibid., 625, 626.

138. Richardson, "Judgment in Sexual Matters in 1 Cor 6:1-11," 37-58.

139. Oropeza, "Situational Immorality: Paul's 'Vice Lists' at Corinth," 9; cf. 9-10.

"that *some* in the Corinthian church were also practising these vices . . . (1 Cor 3:3; 4:6, 18-19 . . . 5:1-5; 6:12ff. . . . 11:16-34)."[140] These include sins of self-centered desire, sexual abuses, issues about idols, damaging the weak, and drunkenness at the Lord's Supper. The chapter on love exposes jealousy and verbal abuse (13:4-5; cf. 6:7). This becomes "most cogent in 1 Cor 10:5-10 where he warns against committing idolatry, fornication, tempting Christ and grumbling . . . eating and drinking (10:20, 21)."[141] Both Corinth and the OT allusions behind 1 Corinthians 10 relate to contentions about leadership and desire for power. Citing the work of M. Mitchell and Rosner, Oropeza insists, "The Corinthians were committing most of the vices in these lists . . . and have inherited the same scriptures as their Israelite predecessors."[142]

Second, this theme is expounded in a masterly way by Kenneth Bailey, to whose study we shall refer in more detail again. He points out that of the ten "vices" listed in 6:9-10, five allude to sexual issues, which directly relate to 5:1-13 and 6:12-20; while a further five relate to issues of greed and grasping, eating and being drunk, which are taken up explicitly in 11:17-34.[143] In Bailey's incisive study the specific significance of Paul's "list" for issues at Corinth becomes undeniable.

The four terms which Paul adds as distinctive to 1 Cor 6:9-10 as against the other six include two that go back to the Decalogue and two that are virtually new as Greek words in the NT. Prohibitions against *stealing* and *committing adultery* occur in the Decalogue: οὐ μοιχεύσεις (Exod 20:13; Deut 5:18, LXX) and οὐ κλέψεις (Exod 20:14; Deut 5:19 LXX; MT 5:17). But the remaining two words are controversial. μαλακός outside sexual contexts means *soft*, as in *a soft tongue* (γλῶσσα δὲ μαλακὴ συντρίβει ὀστᾶ, Prov 25:15 LXX); or *soft clothing* (Matt 11:8). In hellenistic literature of the Roman period it may mean *effeminate* when applied to men (Dio Chrysostom, 49 [66]; Diogenes Laertius, 7: 173, and papyri).[144] In 1 Cor 6:9 its syntagmatic relation with ἀρσενοκοῖται influences its semantic range. But this verse may well be the earliest occurrence of ἀρσενοκοῖτης as a compound adjectival form, and thus it has no lexicographical prehistory. Nevertheless, as we shall note, writers are virtually agreed that its component aspects signify *sleeping with*, or *having sexual relations with* (κοῖτης) *males* (ἄρσην, male [noun], ἀρσενικός, male [adjective], usually in a sexual context).[145]

Both terms have received intense lexicographical scrutiny. Scroggs allows that while μαλακός may mean *unmanly* in general terms, more characteristically it is used of "the youth who consciously imitated feminine styles and ways."[146] This all too readily slips into "passive homosexual activity" whether for pleasure or for pay.[147] From the classical period to Philo extreme distaste is expressed in Greek and hellenis-

140. Ibid.

141. Ibid., 9-10.

142. Ibid., 10.

143. Bailey, "Paul's Theological Foundation for Human Sexuality: 1 Cor 6:12-20 in the Light of Rhetorical Criticism," 27-41.

144. BAGD, 488; Scroggs, *The New Testament and Homosexuality,* 62-65 and 105-7; Louw-Nida, 2:156, 1:79-100, and 88-281; Fee, *First Epistle,* 243, n. 22. BAGD, Scroggs, and Fee allude to the *Hibeh Papyri,* no. 54, reproduced in reduced photographic facsimile by A. Deissmann, *Light from the Ancient East* (London: Hodder & Stoughton, 1927), 164.

145. BAGD, 109-10; LSJ, 223-24; see further discussion and sources below; also Hatch-Redpath, 160-61.

146. Scroggs, *The New Testament and Homosexuality.* 106.

147. Ibid.

tic literature for the effeminate male who uses cosmetics and the coiffuring of the hair, for which Philo sometimes uses the term ἀνδρόγυνος, *male-female* (e.g., *De Specialibus Legibus* 3.37). These issues lie behind the astonishing array of English translations in our versions.[148]

In general there is broad (but not unanimous) agreement that μαλακοί in 1 Cor 6:9-10 denotes "the passive . . . partner . . . in male homosexual relations" (Barrett), but whereas Scroggs argues that it refers to the *call boy* who prostitutes his services to an older male, usually for pay, many others tend to regard the evidence for restricting the term to contexts of *pederasty* linked with *male prostitution* as at best indecisive and at worst unconvincing.[149] Scroggs depends for his view on the background of pederastic practices in Graeco-Roman society (whether voluntary, or for payment) and the impact of this culture for the pejorative reactions in hellenistic Judaism (especially Philo).[150] Dale Martin's close study of the role of the body in first-century Graeco-Roman and Pauline thought provides a new twist to the notion of a lifestyle which does not properly express one's own gender in a way suitable, respectively, for females and for males: "every human body, male or female, occupies some position on the spectrum male-female."[151]

We remain on speculative ground *until we consider the two terms in relation to each other.* Here the debate tends mainly to turn on whether the joint use of the two terms signifies *male prostitution* (Boswell; cf. Scroggs), or homosexual relations between the more "passive" and more "active" partner, *without specific reference* to pederasty (Scroggs) or to prostitution (Boswell).[152] Some such translation as **nor perverts** *nor ho-*

---

148. For example, *male sodomites* (NRSV); *male prostitutes, homosexual offenders* (NIV); *catamites, sodomites* (JB, Moffatt, Barrett); *sexual perverts* (REB); μαλακοί as *effeminate* (AV/ KJV, RV); *pederasts* (Scroggs); *Knabenschänder* (Luther).

149. Barrett, *First Corinthians,* 140. Cf. Scroggs, *The New Testament and Homosexuality,* 106. Cf. 29-65, 85-122. Witherington allows for both arguments: "the two terms refer respectively, then, to the leading and following partners in a homosexual pederastic tryst" (*Conflict and Community,* 166). For support for, or agreement with, Barrett's interpretation see the references below to K. Bailey, R. B. Hays, D. F. Wright, P. Zaas, and others. V. P. Furnish argues, "Exactly how Paul is using the two terms remains in dispute. . . . Is he thinking of all kinds of homosexual relationships, or only of pederasty? Or only of male prostitution? For this reason, and also because one is dealing only with a list, *1 Cor 6:9 can be of little help in ascertaining Paul's attitude toward homosexual practice*" (my italics) ("Homosexual Practices in Biblical Perspective," in J. J. Carey [ed.], *The Sexuality Debate in North American Churches 1988-95,* Symposium 36 [Lewiston and Lampeter: Mellen, 1995], 267; cf. 253-86).

150. Scroggs, *The NT and Homosexuality,* 29-65 and 85-122. Cf. Philo, *De Specialibus Legibus* 3.36-37, and the discussion under (i) above.

151. Martin, *The Corinthian Body,* 33; cf. 29-34. "The male-female continuum was always hierarchical. . . . Aristotelian theory held women to be incomplete males" (32). But while Martin's perception of *body* for Paul and for Corinth is constructive, we hesitate to assume to identify Pauline psychology with that of the Greek world. For a contrary analysis see Bailey, "Paul's Theological Foundation for Human Sexuality: 1 Cor 6:9-20 in the Light of Rhetorical Criticism," 27-41; and D. S. Bailey, *Homosexuality and the Western Christian Tradition* (New York and London: Longmans, 1955), and *The Man-Woman Relation in Christian Thought* (New York and London: Longmans, 1959).

152. Boswell, *Christianity, Social Tolerance and Homosexuality,* esp. 107 and 341-44. The meaning "homosexual" is also rejected by Petersen, "Can ἀρσενοκοῖται Be Translated by 'Homosexuals'? (1 Cor 6:9; 1 Tim 1:10)," 187-91, on grounds of language and historical anachronism.

mosexuals (Collins) or perhaps *catamites and sodomites* (Barrett) is broadly supported by the first fourteen writers listed in the note.[153] On one point each side in the debate tends to "talk past" the other. At opposite ends of the spectrum, so to speak, R. Scroggs and D. F. Wright both agree that ἀρσενοκοῖται means the lying-in-bed (-κοῖται) of males (ἀρσεν-), i.e., "one who lies with a male," as this occurs in Lev 18:22 (and Lev 20:13).[154] Scroggs concedes that "the Hebrew is translated faithfully" but also floats the possibility that the plural form is not gender-specific in terms of grammar alone, and hence *may* refer to women prostitutes who have relations with males; but he does not seriously press the point other than to insist on an element of ambiguity.[155] He concedes: "parts of the Greek compound appear in the Septuagint versions of the laws in Leviticus," and in rabbinic legal discussions "lying with a male" *(mishkav zakur)* is "the term most often used to describe male homosexuality."[156]

The issue does not turn in fact on whether a link can be traced between Lev 18:22 (and 20:13) and 1 Cor 6:9-10, but on *whether Paul sees the OT origins entirely through the lenses of hellenistic Jewish recontextualizations in terms of Graeco-Roman society, or whether he interprets the OT as Christian scripture offering direct paradigms for the habituated lifestyle and ethics of God's holy people as a corporate identity.* In terms of the vocabulary of our own day, does Paul use the OT critically in the sense of his being aware of different traditions of interpretation and vocabulary currencies? If so, this would lend support to J. B. de Young's argument that Lev 20:13 and 1 Cor 6:9 include more than one form of male sexual relation with male, and D. F. Wright's case (especially against Boswell) that the language of Lev 18:22, 20:13, and 1 Cor 6:9, each of which he understands as *sleeping with men,* witnesses to the seriousness with which Paul views the OT as Christian scripture. Similarly, even if (which we doubt) the LXX gives a "spin" to the Hebrew in ways proposed by Scroggs and by Boswell, we

---

153. Wright, "Homosexuals or Prostitutes? The Meaning of ἀρσενοκοῖται (1 Cor 6:9; 1 Tim 1:10)," 125-53; J. B. de Young, "The Source and NT Meaning of ἀρσενοκοῖται with Implications for Christian Ethics and Ministry," *Master's Seminary Journal* 3 (1992): 191-215; Malick, "The Condemnation of Homosexuality in 1 Cor 6:9," 479-92; Zaas, "Catalogues and Context: 1 Cor 5 and 6," 622-29; and Zaas, "Was Homosexuality Condoned in the Corinthian Church?" in P. Achtemeier (ed.), *SBL Seminar Papers 1979* (Missoula: Scholars Press, 1979), 2:205-12; R. B. Hays, "The Bible and Homosexuality," in J. S. Siker (ed.), *Homosexuality,* 3-17, 6-7; cf. more broadly Hays, "Relations Natural and Unnatural: A Response to John Boswell's Exegesis of Rom 1," *JRE* 4 (1986): 184-215; Bruce, *1 and 2 Cor,* 61; Senft, *La Prèmiere Épitre,* 80; Moffatt, *First Epistle,* 66; Kistemaker, *1 Cor,* 188; Fitzmyer, *Romans,* 287-88 (on 1 Cor 6:9). Bailey, "Paul's Theological Foundation," 27-41; Barrett, *First Epistle,* 140; Collins, *First Cor,* 236; Wolff, *Der erste Brief,* 119. Schrage softens this view a little by arguing that while both male prostitution and pederasty are probably the major targets of Paul's emphasis, it goes beyond the evidence explicitly to restrict the semantic range of the two terms to these two types of relations between males: it is "not only male prostitution," and Luther's translation *Knabenschänder* is probably too narrow (*Der erste Brief,* 1:431-32). Schrage considers the Graeco-Roman traditions and Philo, but like Hays, Rosner, Zaas, and others perceives the OT texts as most decisive for Paul. In the light of the arguments put forward by these writers, it goes too far to say with Michael Vasey that "there is no real evidence" for the interpretation considered here, Vasey, *Strangers and Friends: A New Exploration of Homosexuality and the Bible,* 135.

154. Scroggs, *The New Testament and Homosexuality,* 85-88 and 106-8; and Wright, "Homosexuals or Prostitutes?" 125-53.

155. Scroggs, *The New Testament and Homosexuality,* 107, n. 10.

156. Ibid., 107-8.

cannot assume that Paul recontextualizes the OT traditions in the way followed by Philo and strands of literature in hellenistic Judaism. Paul does not surrender an emphasis on the holiness and corporate identity of the covenant people of God in favor of Stoic views of "nature" as a basis for ethics. As Fitzmyer comments on Rom 1:18-32, even if Stoic or hellenistic-Jewish notions "color" Paul's notions of "nature," Paul uses the concept in a different way as "the order intended by the Creator, the order that is manifest in God's creation" in this context (even if the meaning in 1 Corinthians 11 comes nearer to notions of "convention").[157]

Kenneth Bailey also seeks to shed light on the issues by a careful structural analysis of 6:9-20 concerning the wider theological basis of sexuality in Paul's thought. He argues that 6:9-20 constitutes a carefully constructed literary whole of five stanzas in which (a) the five sexual failures listed relate especially to ch. 5 and 6:12-20, while (b) the remaining five relate to issues of eating and drinking (cf. 11:17-34, "Some are hungry, some yet drunk").[158] Neither the "sexual" sins nor the "greed, grasping" sins have prior condemnation over the other: both concern *the body*. Nevertheless, each subcategory within each of the two groups remains significant. Hence, Bailey argues, among the sexual failures **being associated with idolatry** opens the door theologically, socially, and ethically to laissez-faire unfaithfulness in principle. Of the remaining four dispositions which are expressed in acts, two are heterosexual and two are homosexual. In the heterosexual context **adultery** concerns married people; while **illicit relationships** may apply to single people. In the homosexual context, one applies to the more "active" or "lead" role, the other to the converse.[159]

We cannot be certain that Bailey's arguments hold, but they are impressive and carry much weight. In our view Zaas and Bailey offer more substance than the attempts of Scroggs and Furnish to place so much weight on assimilations of Graeco-Roman contexts of thought. On the other side, however, overattention to lexicographical, contextual, and historical detail should not blind us to Vasey's reminder that in the society of imperial Rome Jews and Christians saw a "form of homosexuality [which] was strongly associated with idolatry, slavery and social dominance. It was often the assertion of the strong over the bodies of the weak."[160] This no doubt colored Paul's perception, and coheres with certain attitudes related to wealth, status, manipulation, and power at Corinth.

Some Brief Starting Points toward a Hermeneutic

(a) Within the catalogue of ten dispositions which achieve unchecked habituated action in the public domain, only two concern same-sex relations, and these receive no greater emphasis than the other eight. Of the ten, half concern attitudes of grasping for more, an addiction to gain possessions or power at the expense of others. It may well be that this common thread runs through all of the "vices," and any persistent activity cited here should be regarded on an equal footing when issues of church membership, ordination, or related questions are discussed. Constraints are laid upon het-

---

157. Fitzmyer, *Romans*, 286-87.
158. Bailey, "Paul's Theological Foundation," 27 and 29.
159. Ibid., 29.
160. Vasey, *Strangers and Friends*, 132.

erosexual desire, and upon desire for ever increasing power and possessions, as much as upon same-sex relations.

(b) The claims often made that "the issue of 'homosexuality'-psychosexual orientation — simply was not a biblical issue" are confused.[161] Paul addresses every form of "desire," whether heterosexual or materialistic, and distinguishes between passionate longing and action (cf. 7:9). It is true that "homosexual orientation" does not feature as a phenomenon for explicit comment, but to dismiss the parallel, e.g., between heterosexual desire and an illicit habituated heterosexual relationship is itself to isolate same-sex relations from other ethical issues in a way which such writers as Furnish, Scroggs, Boswell, and Nelson rightly deplore. Many also argue that abusive pederasty was the standard form in which Paul encountered male intimacy. But Wolff shows that this is far from the case. Paul witnessed around him *both* abusive relationships of power or money *and* examples of "genuine love" between males. We must not misunderstand Paul's "worldly" knowledge.[162]

(c) On the basis of the distance between the first and twentieth centuries, many ask: "Is the situation addressed by the biblical writer genuinely comparable to our own?"[163] The more closely writers examine Graeco-Roman society and the pluralism of its ethical traditions, the more the Corinthian situation appears to resonate with our own. Some writers believe that Paul simply took over conventions from hellenistic Judaism, while others see him as returning to the OT as a source of a distinctive ethic for a distinctive people. A more substantial problem arises from whether undue attention to the Levitical and Deuteronomic codes would signify a "Judaizing" obsession with law as against gospel. It is a valid observation that Lev 18:22; 19:19, 27, 28; 20:13; and 21:5 include prohibitions against cross-breeding animals, sowing two kinds of seed in a field, and wearing garments made of two different materials, which virtually everyone does today. But some of these passages relate to issues beneath the surface. The prohibitions about reshaping beards and hair (Lev 19:26-28), e.g., probably relate to practices designed to avoid recognition by evil spirits who supposedly hover around a dead body and operate only in the context of such beliefs. Whether principles of differentiation between gender-roles belong merely to ancient worldviews or form part of God's design for his holy covenant people must be judged in the light of patient exegesis and theological reflection. (See on 11:2-16.) What is clear from the connection between 1 Cor 6:9 and Rom 1:26-29 and their OT backgrounds is Paul's endorsement of the view that idolatry, i.e., placing human autonomy to construct one's values above covenant commitments to God, leads to a collapse of moral values in a kind of domino effect. As writers as different from each other in stance as Kenneth Bailey and Dale Martin agree, 1 Corinthians strongly affirms that *the body* and its practices occupies a place of paramount importance for those who are united with Christ.[164]

---

161. J. B. Nelson, "Sources for Body Theology," in Siker (ed.), *Homosexuality*, 80.

162. Strobel, *Der erste Brief,* 109, tends to underplay Paul's level of awareness, whereas Wolff carefully shows that Paul's situation in cosmopolitan pluralist cultures made him aware of what are not simply "modern" shades of distinction ("Exkurs: Zur paulinischen Bewertung der Homosexualität," *Der erste Brief,* 119-20). He cites, e.g., Plutarch, *Moralia* 751A (as a near contemporary of Paul).

163. Nelson, "Sources for Body Theology," 78.

164. Bailey, "Paul's Theological Foundation," 31-40; and Martin, *The Corinthian Body,* esp. 163-228.

(d) Elsewhere I have argued that a hermeneutic of "interest," a hermeneutic of suspicion, and a hermeneutic of "surplus of meaning" play a part for all parties in the debate.[165]

11 Three variants relate to Ἰησοῦ Χριστοῦ. (i) The shortest reading (often the most probable) is Ἰησοῦ alone (A, later hand of D, 88, Harclean Syriac lectionaries). The longest is ἡμῶν Ἰησοῦ Χριστοῦ (B, apparent reading of C, 33, Latin of Origen, Athanasius). The UBS 4th ed. reads Ἰησοῦ Χριστοῦ (apparent p[11], ℵ, first hand of D, majority in Irenaeus and in Tertullian and Cyprian) but concedes "C," i.e., "difficulty in describing." The weight of support is on this as the safest assessment, although Bruce Metzger is personally attracted to the shortest reading.[166]

The most important point about the initial sentence in v. 11 is the continuous imperfect indicative of the form ἦτε. The NRSV, NJB, **this** *is what* **you used to be**, is exactly right, as against REB, AV/KJV, *such were some of you* (NJB changes JB's *were*). While *were* is not strictly incorrect, Paul's reference to *continuous habituation* is implicit in the imperfect (see above on vv. 9-10). The *neuter* plural demonstrative pronoun ταῦτα emphasizes Paul's sense of shock and undermines the unnecessary discussion about lists of qualities versus lists of actions. The English **this** *is the kind of thing that you were* brings together the notion of a state of being with the performance of actions which instantiated it. Paul's τινες avoids stereotyping, e.g., devout Jews or morally upright Gentiles who were among those who came to faith in Christ.

Although NRSV and NIV translate the aorist indicative middle ἀπελού-σασθε as *you were washed,* NJB has reason to translate **you were washed clean**. The primary reason comes from the force of the compound preposition ἀπο-, intensifying λούω to mean *wash away.* The use of the aorist middle may also project the nuance *you had your sins washed away for you.* Although in strictly grammatical terms the verb may be used as a "direct" middle, *you washed yourselves,* the middle voice is far more likely to function as a middle of personal interest, as indicated above.[167] The aorist focuses the *event* of coming to faith. Traditionally these have been called "baptismal" aorists, especially since the notion of *having one's sins washed away* fits a baptismal context in conjunction with the (probably) punctiliar aorist of event. But Dunn rightly insists that we should interpret "baptismal" in the broadest terms as the way of describing the spiritual event of which baptism constitutes the sign, whether or not it coincides chronologically. On 6:11 he declares: "But in fact Paul is not talking about baptism at all; he speaks rather of the great spiritual transformation of conversion. . . ."[168] Dunn's

---

165. Thiselton, "Can Hermeneutics Ease the Deadlock?" in T. Bradshaw (ed.), *The Way Forward?* (London: Hodder & Stoughton, 1997), 145-96, esp. 149-61.

166. Metzger, *Textual Commentary,* (2d ed.), 486.

167. Schrage, *Der erste Brief,* 1:433.

168. J. D. G. Dunn, *Baptism in the Holy Spirit: A Re-examination of the NT Teaching on the Gift of the Spirit in Relation to Pentecostalism Today,* SBT 2 (London: SCM, 1970), 121; cf. 120-23 on this passage, and 116-31 on this epistle.

broader thesis is that "baptism is only one element in the total complex event of becoming a Christian," and that it is therefore misleading to speak too readily of "baptismal contexts." Sometimes Paul speaks of baptism without alluding to the Holy Spirit or to faith (Rom 6:4); sometimes he alludes to faith without mention of the Spirit or of baptism (1 Cor 15:1-2); at other times he speaks of the Holy Spirit without alluding to either faith or baptism (2 Cor 1:21-22). Hence, Dunn concludes, it is better to speak of "conversion-initiation" contexts.[169] Dunn has effectively put an end to an uncritical tradition of interpretation instanced, e.g., in H. L. Goudge's commentary: *"But ye were washed,* i.e., in baptism."[170]

Allusions to a baptismal context, however, if interpreted within the constraints properly imposed by Dunn, nevertheless safeguard a different and complementary point. This **washing clean** is not just the *forgiveness* for which the believer asks day-by-day renewal. It is *a wiping clean of the slate once-for-all* which is associated (as here) with justification by grace which is independent of renewed pardon. Paul does not use the word ἄφεσις, *pardon, forgiveness* but refers to a once-for-all event which corresponds to the once-for-all sufficiency of Christ's deed of salvation. The Church of England's Easter Anthem in the Book of Common Prayer links the feast of the New Passover (1 Cor 5:7) with the unrepeatable nature of Christ's death and resurrection: "he died to sin once" (ἐφάπαξ, Rom 6:10).[171] The "newness" of the Easter anthem conveys the Pauline theme: you have left behind what you used to be once-for-all: celebrate the resurrection existence. This is Paul's point here.

Yet, when all has been said, has the past lost all of its influence and reality? Paul now uses ἡγιάσθητε and ἐδικαιώθητε to signify the once-for-all events when in Christ the readers **were set apart as holy** and **put right in your standing**. In spite of the force of the -άζω and -όω endings, the translations *made holy* and *made righteous* would be misleading since Paul does not deny the continuing datum of sin, moral failure, and remnants of old habits and attitudes among Christian believers (e.g., ἔτι γὰρ σαρκικοί ἐστε. ὅπου γὰρ ἐν ὑμῖν ζῆλος καὶ ἔρις, 3:3). Again, Whiteley's analogy is clearly to the point. Two "sets of forces" still operate, "just as a man who has come out of the cold into a warm room is subject both to the cold which has numbed his hands and to the heat which is thawing them out."[172] But the new forces, like the heat in the analogy, are decisive and *will* crowd out and disperse the old *inevitably.* Moreover, as Whiteley observes on this verse, the believer becomes *united with Christ as one body* in these "baptismal" (Dunn, "conversion-initiation") events. Although Good Friday and Easter Day "were in no sense *repeated* when a man was baptized . . . in his Baptism they were *reflected . . .*" (Whiteley's italics).[173] The

169. Ibid., 104.
170. Goudge, *First Epistle,* 45; cf. Dunn, *Baptism in the Holy Spirit,* 104. Schrage is willing to allude to baptism if the term is understood in an "effective" sense here (*Der erste Brief,* 433).
171. Schrage, *Der erste Brief,* 1:433-34.
172. Whiteley, *The Theology of St. Paul,* 126-27.
173. Ibid., 168-69.

source of being **set apart as holy** and **put right in your standing** is sharing Christ's identity (ἐν τῷ ὀνόματι τοῦ κυρίου Ἰησοῦ) and being "glued" (κολλώμενος, 6:17) to the Lord as one (ἕν, v. 17). Incorporation in *one body* and *one Spirit* (6:17-19) is **by the Spirit of our God** (6:11), interpreting ἐν as a preposition of instrument or agency here.

On ἁγιάζω and ἡγιασμένοις, see the detailed discussion on 1:2 (above). We took up δικαιόω in 4:4. But here it has its full theological sense of *justification by grace through faith.* The Greek word does not occur again in this epistle; hence many have argued that this theme emerges seriously only in the polemical context of Galatians and its further outworking in Romans, where Paul addresses "Judaizing" tendencies. We have noted, however, that in 1:30 Christ was described as ἡμῖν ἀπὸ θεοῦ δικαιοσύνη τε καὶ ἁγιασμός, and I have argued in detail elsewhere that the "gift" character of resurrection, together with its basis in union with Christ as the single, raised, transformed corporeity, performs in our epistle the role ascribed to justification by grace in Romans and Galatians.[174]

The aorist passive ἐδικαιώθητε without doubt has its full meaning of justification by grace: *you were put in a right relation with God,* **you were put right in your standing**. Far from appealing to supposedly narrow imagery of forensic acquittal or of so-called legal fiction, at Corinth the theology combines both the gift character of Corinthian concerns about *status* and *self-worth* (they are *accepted* and given a status of privilege bestowed by grace) and the dual frame of reference which Paul earlier applied to ministry as both high-status (necessary to God's purposes of growth) and low-status (servants, 3:5-6: τί οὖν ἐστιν Ἀπολλῶς; τί δέ ἐστιν Παῦλος; διάκονοι . . . ὁ θεὸς ηὔξανεν·). In close parallel, the Corinthians are indeed *"semper iustus, semper peccator."*[175] Can such an approach be sustained from these limited passages?

JUSTIFICATION BY GRACE IN 6:11 AND IN THE EPISTLE

As the LXX translation of the Heb. צדק (*tsadaq,* verb; *tsaddiq,* noun), in spite of the -όω ending in Greek δικαιόω most frequently means *to account righteous,* not *to make righteous.*[176] It is not a descriptive locution, *but an illocutionary speech-act of declaration and verdict,* operating with the widespread logic in religious language of *pro-*

---

174. A. C. Thiselton, "Luther and Barth on 1 Cor. 15: Six Theses for Theology in Relation to Recent Interpretation," in W. P. Stephens (ed.), *The Bible, the Reformation and the Church* (1995), 258-89.

175. On Luther's language in relation to Paul's, cf. P. Stuhlmacher, *Gerechtigkeit Gottes bei Paulus* (Göttingen: Vandenhoeck & Ruprecht, 1965), 19-23.

176. See Stuhlmacher, ibid.; and J. A. Ziesler, *The Meaning of Righteousness in Paul,* SNTSMS 20 (Cambridge: Cambridge University Press, 1972), 147-63; cf. 18 45. At minimum if צדק *(ts-d-q)* always meant *to make righteous,* such a passage as "For I will not account the wicked righteous" (Exod 23:7) would be impossible; to *make* them righteous would be positive; to *count* them righteous, a perversion of justice in this context; cf. similarly Prov 17:15. See further J. D. G. Dunn, "Justification by Faith," in *The Theology of Paul* (Edinburgh: T. & T. Clark, 1998), 334-89.

nouncing, deeming, seeing as, authorizing, declaring, evaluating. Recently Seifrid has underlined the centrality of the theme in Paul, and Winninge has compared the dynamics of *"status"* and *"transfer"* in Paul with reference to settings in apocalyptic, especially in the *Psalms of Solomon.*[177] Pauline scholarship was shunted onto the wrong track by underplaying the frame offered by apocalyptic or eschatology, and by assuming a disjunction between (a) everyday discourse and (b) legal discourse peculiar to courts of justice. Building on constructive philosophies of language, we can avoid certain blind alleys.

Developing the theories of speech-acts found in Austin, Searle, and an increasing flood of writers, Wolterstorff argues that *every* linguistic or visual sign (or almost every sign) rests on *counting as* and *judgment* for its effect.[178] If a person extends his or her arm out of a car window and moves that hand in a particular way, I have to judge whether this *counts as* a signal to overtake, or a warning not to overtake.[179] In games, what *counts as* a move is presupposed, unless problematic instances invite a *judgment* from an umpire, referee, or linesman. Every sign operates *as* a sign only *within a system* which generates its operational currency. Wolterstorff calls this *count generation.* Winning or losing is not doing what fits some abstract, general concept of winning, but doing what *counts as* winning in a given system. In one setting a boy may speak and act like any other child; but in a specific context the same boy may speak and act as *crown prince.*[180] To suggest that for Prince William to have the status of a "merely ordinary young person" at Eton College, but to have the status of Prince in a state service in Westminster Abbey is not to operate "a legal fiction." This *counting as* would reflect the realities of British life.[181] *All the time we use the language of count generation, and very frequently people are accorded different standings in different contexts.*[182]

This is not to suggest that Wolterstorff provides a comprehensive theory of *counting as;* his is one of many such approaches to these issues, and distinctions can be made between "stronger" and "weaker" examples.[183] I argued this principle earlier with reference to the double context of history and eschatology, sin and justification, and D. D. Evans's notion of *onlooks* in his philosophy of language. To *look on* x as y is not "fiction" but life.[184] Hence when Weiss observes that δικαιόω declares "not . . .

---

177. M. A. Seifrid, *Justification by Faith: The Origin and Development of a Central Pauline Term,* NovTSup 68 (Leiden: Brill, 1992); and M. Winninge, *Sinners and the Righteous,* ConBNT (Stockholm: Almqvist & Wiksell, 1995).

178. N. Wolterstorff, *Divine Discourse* (Cambridge: Cambridge University Press, 1995), 75-94.

179. Ibid., 78-79; cf. 88-91.

180. Ibid., 83-85.

181. Ibid., 83, 85, 90-91.

182. Ibid., 92-94.

183. See S. L. Tsohatzidis (ed.), *Foundations of Speech-Act Theory* (London: Routledge, 1994); D. Vanderveken, *Principles of Language Use I: Meaning and Speech Acts* (Cambridge, Cambridge University Press, 1990); J. R. Searle, *The Construction of Social Reality* (London: Allen Lane, 1995); R. Lundin, A. C. Thiselton, and C. Walhout, *The Promise of Hermeneutics* (Grand Rapids: Eerdmans and Carlisle: Paternoster, 1999), esp. 144-82, 200-209, and 223-40. The contrast between "strong" and "weak" forms first appears in G. J. Warnock, "Some Types of Performative Utterance," in I. Berlin (ed.), *Essays on J. L. Austin* (Oxford: Clarendon, 1973).

184. Thiselton, *The Two Horizons,* 415-22; cf. D. D. Evans, *The Logic of Self-Involvement* (London: SCM, 1963).

what a man is in himself, but it states that he is considered, in the eyes of God, right with God," this is valid except for the need to modify the imprecise words "in himself" and "states."[185] The word *declares* (versus *states*) not the standing which he receives *causally* from his own acts *in history,* but the standing which he *receives eschatologically* at the *last judgment,* as the verdict "everything put right" is *anticipated in the hiddenness of the present by faith on the basis of the gift from God and union with Christ.*[186]

On this basis Käsemann argues (against Stendahl) that if this theme is properly interpreted, there is nothing more Christ-centered and God-centered (not individual centered), for it precisely shifts the believer's ground of confidence and trust from himself or herself to Christ alone.[187] The well-known distinction drawn by Ziesler between the *declarative* force of the verb δικαιόω and the more "ethical" nuance of the noun δικαιοσύνη has partial validity not because Paul is inconsistent, but because it is the verb which performs the illocutionary act of count generation.[188]

To transpose the universe of discourse from "legal status" to speech-act, however, now reveals the claim to drive a wedge between 1 Corinthians and Romans-Galatians as misguided. Count generation does not depend on a polemical context about the law, nor on *ad hominem* appeals to the OT.[189] It exposes *the gift character of God's acts,* who bestows **being right in your standing** as an act of grace in advance of the final day of judgment. What clinches the fundamental part played by this theme in 1 Corinthians is both the theology of *Christ as the believer's righteousness* (and wisdom and status of holiness, 1:30) and more especially the gift of transformed life to the dead who cannot contribute either life or transformation, for they are dead. Resurrection, unlike "immortality," is not an innate capacity of the self, but that which "God gives" (ὁ δὲ θεὸς δίδωσιν αὐτῷ σῶμα καθὼς ἠθέλησεν, 15:38).[190]

In the context of union with Christ the passive voice "Christ was raised" (ἐγήγερται, 15:4, 14) constitutes an essential part of the logic of divine gift which embraces resurrection and justification equally, as by grace alone, without human contribution. In 6:11 the theme of newness of life is thus expressed in the three aorists: ἀπελούσασθε . . . ἡγιάσθητε . . . ἐδικαιώθητε ἐν τῷ ὀνόματι τοῦ κυρίου Ἰησοῦ Χριστοῦ. This applies with particular poignancy to the addressees at Corinth. As we have noted, many were obsessed with problems arising from the thirst for *status, acceptance, and self-esteem.* Paul declares: You are accepted! You belong! You have privileged status! But all this comes from God as his free, sovereign, gift. He tells them (to

185. Weiss, *Earliest Christianity,* 2:499.

186. Ibid., 419-21; cf. Bultmann, *Theology of the NT,* 1:276; C. K. Barrett, *Romans* (London: Black, 2d ed. 1962), 75; Stuhlmacher, *Gerechtigkeit Gottes bei Paulus,* 112-60. Cf. Weiss, *Earliest Christianity,* 2:502, "an occurrence which will take place only on the day of divine judgement" (Rom 2:12-13; Gal 5:5); A. Richardson, *An Introduction to the Theology of the NT* (London: SCM, 1958), 341-44; A. Schweitzer, *The Mysticism of Paul the Apostle,* 205.

187. E. Käsemann, "Justification and Salvation-History," in *Perspectives on Paul* (Eng. trans., London: SCM, 1971), 60-78; cf. also " 'The Righteousness of God' in Paul," *NT Questions of Today* (Eng. trans., London: SCM, 1969), 168-82.

188. J. Ziesler, *The Meaning of Righteousness in Paul,* SNTSMS 20 (Cambridge: Cambridge University Press, 1972), 47-103 and 128.

189. Cf. Schweitzer, *Mysticism,* 220.

190. We return to this theme in 1 Corinthians 15, where we also reconsider my earlier "Luther and Barth on 1 Cor 15," 258-89.

borrow Tillich's phrase) *to accept that they are accepted* as the antidote to the status hunger which drives them to compete, as long as they keep in mind the basis and ground of their acceptance. Justification by grace through faith fits the Corinthian situation no less readily than that of the readers of Galatians and Romans. It speaks equally to their cultural situation, where obsession with achievement and status and, no less, anxiety over low self-esteem compound the ills of society: "but by the grace of God I am what I am" (15:10).

2. Union with Christ and the Theology of the Body (6:12-20)

(12) "Liberty to do all things"; but not everything is helpful. "Liberty to do anything"; but I will not let anything take liberties with me. (13, 14) "Food for the stomach, and the stomach for food; and God will do away with the one and the other." But the body is not for immortality; on the contrary, it is for the Lord, and the Lord for the body. God raised the Lord, and he will raise us up through his power. (15) Do you not know that your bodies are Christ's limbs and organs? Shall I, then, take away Christ's limbs and organs and make them the limbs and organs of a prostitute? Perish the very thought! (16, 17) Do you not know that a person who is united in intimacy with a prostitute is one body with her? For as it is said, "The two shall become one flesh." But the person who is intimately united with the Lord is one Spirit. (18) Keep away from sexual immorality. Every other sin which a person may commit is done outside the body. But the person who sins sexually sins against his or her own body. (19) Or do you not know that your body is a temple of the Holy Spirit who indwells you, whom you received from God, and that you do not belong to yourselves? (20) For you were bought with a price. Show forth God's glory, then, in how you live your bodily life.

This section demonstrates, once again, the inseparability of Christian identity and Christian lifestyle, or of theology and ethics. This third example of illicit conduct turns, like the other two, on the importance of the body and bodily actions, and its relation of union with Christ. Although Fee comments that "how this section relates to what immediately precedes is not at all certain," the connection is clarified when we recall that in 6:9-10 the sin of idolatry, i.e., a context in which exclusive faithfulness to Christ's Lordship becomes compromised, relates to two kinds of moral failures: those categorized as relating to the body in terms of seeking self-gratification, what is off-limits sexually; and those categorized as relating to the body in terms of seeking self-gratification, what is off-limits in terms of justice and property rights. If the subject of litigation also relates to sexual matters, as Bernard and Richardson argue, the theme is even more closely integrated, but we cannot rely on their arguments.

The body of the Christian believer is "for the Lord," not "for" self-gratification (6:13). Paul rejects the quasi-gnostic dualistic notion that "spiritual" issues are "above" matters relating to the body. Quite the reverse is the case. Far from Pauline Christianity being what Nietzsche and the later Heidegger called "Platonism for the people," early Christian theology perceives the body as the temple sanctified by the Holy Spirit (6:19), united-as-one-entity with Christ (μέλη Χριστοῦ, 6:15), and a mode of being through which and in which the Christian self brings glory to God (6:20). Hence Paul dissociates himself from three Corinthian slogans: (1) it is false that whether "everything is permitted" determines criteria of sexual constraints or sexual freedoms; (2) it is false that every sin is ἐκτὸς τοῦ σώμωτος (6:18), and false most of all in respect to sexual relations with a prostitute; (3) it is false that neither the stomach (ἡ κοιλία) and eating nor the body (τὸ σῶμα, 6:13, 14) and sex or greed have significance for future destiny, which in turn gives meaning to the present. A particularly subtle exposition of, and modification to, this argument has been offered by M. D. Goulder. Goulder argues that those whom Paul addresses are not "libertines" but (as we suggest) "spiritual" people who extend freedom about food offered to idols (cf. 6:12; 10:23; 8:1–11:1) to wider issues about "the body." This need not denote actual prostitution but does entail extramarital sexual unions (see further below). As those who belong to Christ by redemptive purchase (6:20), Christians are to live out their bodily existence in union with Christ, indwelt by the Spirit, to the glory of God (6:15-20). A hint of a trinitarian pattern emerges here.

Bibliography on 6:12-20

Bailey, K. E., "Paul's Theological Foundation for Human Sexuality: 1 Cor 6:9-20 in the Light of Rhetorical Criticism," *Near East School of Theology Theological Review* 3 (1980): 27-41.

Batey, R., "The μία σάρξ Union of Christ and the Church," *NTS* 13 (1966-67): 270-81.

Baumert, N., *Frau und Mann bei Paulus. Überwindung eines Missverständnisses* (Würzburg: Echter, 1992).

Best, E., *One Body in Christ* (London: SPCK 1955).

Burkhill, T. A., "Two into One: The Notion of Carnal Union in Mk 10:8, 1 Cor 6:16, Eph 5:31," *ZNW* 62 (1971): 115-20.

Byrne, B., "Eschatologies of Resurrection and Destruction: The Ethical Significance of Paul's Dispute with the Corinthians," *Downside Review* 104 (1986): 288-96.

———, "Sinning against One's Own Body: Paul's Understanding of the Sexual Relationship in 1 Cor. 6:18," *CBQ* 45 (1983): 608-16.

Claudel, G., "1 Kor 6:12–7:40 neu gelesen," *TT* 294 (1985): 20-36.

Combes, I. A. H., *The Metaphor of Slavery in the Writings of the Early Church,* JSNTSS 156 (Sheffield: Sheffield Academic Press, 1998), 77-94.

Dahl, M. E., *The Resurrection of the Body,* SBT 36 (London: SCM, 1962), 59-126.

Dawes, G. W., *The Body in Question: Metaphor and Meaning in the Interpretation of Ephesians 5:21-33* (Leiden: Brill, 1998), 1-80.

Derrett, J. D. M., "Right and Wrong Sticking (1 Cor 6:18)," *EstBib* 55 (1997): 89-106.

Dodd, B. J., "Paul's Paradigmatic 'I' and 1 Cor 6:12," *JSNT* 59 (1995): 39-58.

Fisk, B. N., "πορνεύειν as Body Violation: The Unique Nature of Sexual Sin in 1 Cor 6:18," *NTS* 42 (1996): 540-58.

Fuchs, E., "Die Herrschaft Christi. Zur Auslegung von 1 Kor 6:12-20," in *NT und christliche Existenz. Festschrift für Herbert Braun* (1973), 183-93.

Goulder, M. D., "Libertines? (1 Cor 5–6)," *NovT* 41 (1991): 334-48.

Gundry, R. H., *Soma in Biblical Theology with Emphasis on Pauline Anthropology,* SNTSMS 29 (Cambridge: Cambridge University Press, 1976), 51-80.

Käsemann, E., *Leib und Leib Christi: Eine Untersuchung zur paulinischen Begrifflichkeit* (Tübingen: Mohr, 1933).

Käsemann, E., *NT Questions of Today* (Eng. trans., London: SCM, 1969), 124-37.

Kempthorne, R., "Incest and the Body of Christ: A Study of 1 Cor. 6:12-20," *NTS* 14 (1968): 568-74.

Kirchhoff, R., *Die Sünde gegen den eigenen Leib. Studien zu πόρνη und πορνεία in 1 Kor. 6:12-20,* SUNT 18 (Göttingen: Vandenhoeck & Ruprecht, 1994).

Martin, D. B., *The Corinthian Body* (New Haven: Yale University Press, 1995), esp. 174-78.

————, *Slavery as Salvation* (New Haven: Yale University Press, 1990).

Maurer, C., "Ehe und Unzucht nach 1 Kor 6:12–7:7," *Wort und Dienst* 6 (1959): 159-69.

Miguez, M., "Christ's 'Members' and Sex (1 Cor. 6:12-20)," *Thomist* 39 (1975): 24-48.

Miller, J. I., "A Fresh Look at 1 Cor. 6:16f," *NTS* 27 (1980): 125-27.

Murphy-O'Connor, J., "Corinthian Slogans in 1 Cor. 6:12-20," *CBQ* 40 (1978): 391-96.

Neyrey, J. H., "Body Language in 1 Cor.: The Use of Anthropological Models. . . ," *Semeia* 35 (1986): 129-70.

Omanson, R., "Acknowledging Paul's Quotation," *BibTod* 43 (1992): 201-13.

Porter, S. E., "How Should κολλώμενος in 1 Cor. 6:16-17 Be Translated?" *ETL* 67 (1991): 105-6.

Radcliffe, T., " 'Glorify God in Your Bodies': 1 Cor. 6:12-20 as a Sexual Ethic," *New Blackfriars* 67 (1986): 306-14.

Robinson, J. A. T., *The Body: A Study in Pauline Theology,* SBT 5 (London: SCM, 1957), 7-33, 55-83.

Rosner, B. S., "A Possible Quotation of Test. Reuben 5:5 in 1 Cor. 6:18a," *JTS* 43 (1992): 123-27.

————, "Temple Prostitution in 1 Cor 6:12-20," *NovT* 40 (1998): 336-51.

Sampley, J. P., *"And the Two Shall Become One Flesh": A Study of Traditions in Eph. 5:21-33,* SNTSMS 16 (Cambridge: Cambridge University Press, 1971), 77-85.

Schnelle, U., "1 Kor 6:14 — Ein nachpaulinische Glosse," *NovT* 25 (1983): 217-19.

Shedd, R. P., *Man in Community* (London: Epworth Press, 1958), 157-81.

Stegemann, W., "Paul and the Sexual Mentality of His World," *BTB* 23 (1993): 161-66.

Thornton, L. S., *The Common Life in the Body of Christ* (London: Dacre Press, 3d ed. 1950), 14-21 and 221-87.

Winter, B. W., "Gluttony and Immorality at Elitist Banquets: The Background to 1 Cor 6:12-20," *Jian Dao* [Hong Kong] 7 (1997): 77-90.

12 There can be no question that the initial clause of v. 12 represents a quotation used as a maxim by some or by many at Corinth, in spite of a recent argument to the contrary by B. J. Dodd.[191] The overwhelming majority of modern

191. B. J. Dodd, "Paul's Paradigmatic 'I' and 1 Cor 6:12," 39-58, argues that this is part of Paul's own rhetorical *inclusio* (with 10:23) to urge a balance between freedom and responsibility.

scholars adopt this view, and tables of such writers are readily at hand.[192] Schrage calls it a "Corinthian maxim"; and Collins, "probably a slogan bandied about among some of the Christians in Corinth and used . . . to justify an indiscriminate exercise of their rights (ἐξουσία).[193] The third singular present indicative ἔξεστι (from a theoretical form ἔξειμι, which is not used) will provide a wordplay on ἐξουσία, *a right*.[194] The traditional translation *all things are lawful* (AV/KJV, NRSV) does not mean *all things are sanctioned* by the law, but denotes that which the law *no longer prohibits*, i.e., it is part of the Corinthian theology that Christian believers have been granted **liberty** *from* the law. Hence in lexicographical terms *everything is permissible* (NIV, NJB) is correct. But REB recognizes that impersonal verbs with the dative in Greek and in Latin are often more idiomatically translated by restructuring the dative into a nominative in English: *I am free to do anything*. In many cultural situations, slogans often appeal to *freedom* or **liberty** for their emotive power.

In the Greek there is clearly a conscious wordplay on the two forms derived from ἐκ + εἰμι. ἔξεστι (indicative) relates to ἐξουσία (participle) and hence to the first singular future passive indicative ἐξουσιασθήσομαι, from ἐξουσιάζω.[195] The noun ἐξουσία often *authority*, but means no less *the right to act* because the agent possesses ἐξουσία in the sense of *freedom of choice*. In the active voice ἐξουσιάζω means *to control someone else's rights, power, or freedom of choice*. Hence the passive voice (as used here) can mean *I will not be mastered by* (NIV), or *dominated by* (NRSV, NJB). The REB more clearly brings out the play on words with *I will not let anything make free with me*. But *make free with* perhaps does not frequently occur in the precise sense *to control*. On the other hand, our proposal **"Liberty to do anything" — but I will not let anything take liberties with me** seems to capture all the appropriate nuances, combining Corinthian triumphalism and sloganizing with Paul's related theology of redefined freedom. It is a well-known paradox that if *everyone* claims unqualified autonomy, *no one* can be free, for everyone is threatened by the freedoms of the other.

Paul therefore proposes a change of starting point. He transposes debates about "liberty" and "what is permissible" into the different key of "what is

192. J. C. Hurd lists tewnty-four writers up to his own work of 1965, of whom all but two agree that 6:12 is a quotation from Corinth, as he himself does, bringing the total to twenty-three writers [twenty-seven with the four more recent ones listed below] (*Origin of 1 Corinthians,* 68). Advocates include Allo, Wendland, Lietzmann, Robertson and Plummer, Weiss, Moffatt, Héring, and Jeremias. (The two who either dissent or remain silent are Heinrici [1880] and D. Smith.) More recently Fee calls it "almost certainly a quotation" (*First Epistle,* 251); Senft views it as a slogan used to justify self-indulgent sexual conduct and translates the Greek as *tout m'est permis* (*La première Épitre,* 82); Barrett speaks of "general agreement" that the words are a quotation, to which he subscribes (*First Epistle,* 144). See also Murphy-O'Connor, "Corinthian Slogans in 1 Cor 6:12-20," 391-96.

193. Schrage, *Der erste Brief,* 2:17; Collins, *First Cor,* 243.
194. As in Wolff, *Der erste Brief,* 125; and Schrage, *Der erste Brief,* 16.
195. BAGD, 279; also Schrage, *Der erste Brief,* 2:16.

helpful."[196] The clause οὐ πάντα συμφέρει negates the universality of πάντα: **not everything is helpful**. The verb carries the nuance of bearing (φέρω) together (συν-) for good as a benefit. The issue for Paul is *what helps* and *what hinders* in constituting credible corporate Christian identity as a community in corporate solidarity with Christ. Both a theology of identity and an ethic of social or interpersonal relations are aspects of the unity (Mitchell) at issue.[197] If *freedom* or **liberty** is absolutized without qualification it brings bondage, or at least threatening constraints, to the competing freedoms of others. But *part of the grammar of union with Christ is to share Christ's concern for the well-being of the other, and to let go of his or her own freedoms in order to liberate the other.* The "mind of Christ" (2:16) has to be relearned and rediscovered at Corinth, not least as a basis for ethics and lifestyle.

13-14 As numerous modern writers agree, including Collins and Murphy-O'Connor, Paul now quotes another Corinthian slogan.[198] The purpose of the slogan was to articulate a sense of distance between deeds done in the physical body, especially matters relating to food, sex, or property, and the supposedly "spiritual" level of life, which some would like to think operates on a "higher" plane which can be isolated from the "lower." This supposed dualism of "levels" is foreign to Pauline thought, but commonplace in those circles influenced by a popular form of quasi-Platonic thought. This becomes even more marked if proto-gnostic influences were also at work. The second slogan, therefore, in effect gives further support to the slogan of the previous verse. To be "above" earthly matters coheres with the claim to be "above" the law as spiritual persons.

If this is a quotation, however, at what point does the quotation end? Surprisingly the NRSV, NIV, and a number of translations place the quotation marks at the end of "**food for the stomach, and the stomach for food**." But even given the interpretation of κοιλία as *the digestive system,* this bare quotation on its own seems banal, unless "**and God will do away with one and the other**" is explicitly linked to mean: "all this is transitory and without permanent significance for people of the Spirit such as us." In 1978 I wrote: "We may question whether two of the main English versions, the RSV and the NEB, are correct in closing the quotation marks where they do. . . . More probably the whole on v. 13a constitutes an eschatologically orientated slogan current at Corinth, and Paul only begins his rejoinder with the words, 'The body (τὸ

---

196. See Radcliffe, "'Glorify God in Your Bodies': 1 Cor. 6:12-20 as a Sexual Ethic," 306-14.

197. M. M. Mitchell, *Paul and the Rhetoric of Reconciliation,* 25-39, appeals to Paul's use of a deliberative rhetoric of "advantage" in relation to church unity. This aspect is included, but here Paul also moves beyond this.

198. Murphy-O'Connor, "Corinthian Slogans in 1 Cor. 6:12-20," 391-96. Hurd cites by page fifteen scholars who agree that this is a quotation (up to 1965), and more recently Barrett, *First Epistle,* 146-47; Conzelmann, *1 Cor,* 110; Schrage, *Der erste Brief,* 2:20 (following Weiss, Robertson and Plummer, Morris, Allo, and others); and Collins, *First Cor,* 244-45, concur.

σῶμα) is not meant for immorality', 13b."[199] I then discussed the part parallel of the Christian tradition which finds expression in Mark 7:14-19, and asked what the truncated version of the slogan could amount to on its own. I described as "uninformative" the redundantly repeated tautology. The very same year J. Murphy-O'Connor put forward still stronger arguments to the same effect, and recently Collins has included v. 13a within the Corinthian quotation.[200] The general point may be: "libertines had . . . used the fact that food did not raise a moral issue to support their contention that sexual conduct also had no moral significance. Paul grants that both food and the stomach belong to the transient physical sphere. . . . But . . . the body [σῶμα] is not something transient, but will be raised from the dead."[201]

The Corinthian libertines were not necessarily what Craig calls "gnostic libertines," except insofar as their theology reflects the same kind of dualism as later gnostic systems. The particular uses of κοιλία in first-century Greek literature helps us to understand their three-stage logic: (1) κοιλία often means *the digestive system* rather than a location within the body, i.e., to say *"food is for digestion"* means that it soon passes through and is disposed of; (2) in this respect it stands as a kind of metonym for all things physical and transient; (3) hence, supposedly, on this line of reasoning, God is concerned only with those aspects of selfhood which will survive disintegration at death, i.e., what pertains to the spirit or to the Spirit.[202] Paul interposes a fundamental qualification, however, which interrupts the logic. The σῶμα is not to be equated with the κοιλία, but *somatic* life is absorbed and transformed in the resurrection of the σῶμα in such a way that continuity as well as change characterizes the relation between the present σῶμα, i.e., present life *in its totality,* and the resurrection σῶμα, i.e., the transformation of the *whole* human self as part of the raised corporeity in Christ.[203]

The logic which Paul uses here will be expounded in detail in 1 Cor 15:12-58, where continuity of identity and transformation of mode of being constitute two principles of the resurrection of the σῶμα (see below, on 15:12-58). Hence the body is οὐ τῇ πορνείᾳ (on this word, see above on 5:1 and 6:9-10, n.), but **for the Lord**.[204] Paul's theology of the resurrection of the σῶμα also unfolds in three stages of logical steps: (1) **God raised the Lord** (ἤγειρεν, third singular first aorist indicative active of ἐγείρω). Christ is always the *object* of

199. Thiselton, "Realized Eschatology at Corinth," *NTS* 24 (1978): 517.

200. Murphy-O'Connor, "Corinthian Slogans," 391-96; Collins, *First Cor,* 239.

201. Craig, "1 Cor," in *IB*, 10:73-74.

202. BAGD, 437; cf. MM, 349, although the papyri increasingly use κοιλία as a metonym for greed (e.g., lovers of the κοιλία). The awkward ταυτὴν καὶ ταῦτα reflects the singular of κοιλία and the plural of βρώματα, hence **one and the other** for *this* and *these*.

203. We reserve a full discussion of σῶμα for comments on 15:38-44, and more briefly and in part 6:20. We note, however, M. E. Dahl's comment, "St. Paul's conception of 'body' would transcend and *include* the modern conception. This kind of identity I have called *somatic identity"* (*The Resurrection of the Body;* SBT 36 [London: SCM, 1962], 94).

204. On πορνεία, see on 5:1, above.

God's act of raising, not its subject (cf. the passive in 1 Cor. 15:14, 20 of Christ, and the active in 15:38 of God);[205] (2) Christian believers belong to the *single* ("one") Christ-corporeity as his *"members"* (τὰ μέλη τοῦ Χριστοῦ, 6:15; and ὁ κολλώμενος τῷ κυρίῳ ἕν πνεῦμά ἐστιν, 6:17). (3) **God will raise** (ἐξεγερεῖ, future, 6:14) **us** (ἡμᾶς) as the single in-Christ corporeity, for whom "bodily" existence matters.

Paul will argue in the next few verses that being-in-Christ entails a bonding and binding (κολλάω) which is threatened with a wrenching apart if the body (τὸ σῶμα) is "bonded" with that which contradicts the Christ bonding, or pulls in a different direction. Käsemann offers an important comment on this issue of public "world." He declares, "For Paul it is all important that the Christian life is not limited to interior piety and cultic acts. One of the most remarkable, and at the same time least known sentences of the Apostle runs (1 Cor. 6:13): 'The body belongs to the Lord, and the Lord to the body.' . . . Paul does not mean, as Bultmann would have us believe, man's relation to himself, but that piece of the world which we ourselves are and for which we bear responsibility because it was the earliest gift of our Creator to us. . . . It signifies man in his worldliness [worldhood conveys the idea less ambiguously] and therefore in his ability to communicate [i.e., in his relationality]."[206] Käsemann concludes: "In the bodily obedience of the Christian . . . the lordship of Christ finds visible expression, and only when this visible expression takes personal shape in us does the whole thing become credible as Gospel message."[207]

U. Schnelle argues that v. 14 constitutes a post-Pauline gloss on the grounds that it stands in tension with 15:51-52: πάντες δὲ ἀλλαγησόμεθα. Raised believers will be ἄφθαρτοι.[208] But this is to misread the careful dialectic between continuity and change which runs throughout 15:1-58. To be sure, Paul's resurrection σῶμα is a transformed σῶμα; but it remains the *same self* which *also* retains "somatic continuity," as Dahl well argues. In Käsemann's language, *the network of relationships and public world in relation to which the self is this self and not another* remains of permanent significance as "input" to the transformed mode of existence. We shall return to this in ch. 15. B. Byrne, contrary to Schnelle, constructively argues that Paul's eschatology counters the dualism of those at Corinth who devalue the body by demonstrating how resur-

205. This point is made, rightly, by Schrage, *Der erste Brief,* 2:16 and 24-25, and especially by Dahl, *Resurrection of the Body,* 98-99, where he provides a table of uses with the verb ἐγείρω: in the transitive uses, God is subject of the verb in Paul some fifteen times, of which eleven have Christ as the object (Rom 4:24; 8:11 [twice]; 10:9; 1 Cor 6:14; 15:15 [twice]; Gal 1:1; Col 2:12; 1 Thess 1:10); and the remainder have believers as the object (2 Cor 4:14; 1 Cor 6:14; 2 Cor 1:9; 4:14). There are also approximately fourteen intransitive uses. Transitive uses in which Christ is subject appear in the NT only in John 2:19 (with ἐγείρω) and John 6:39-40 (with ἀνίστημι). The active use in the Fourth Gospel by Jesus constitutes a special case in a different context.

206. E. Käsemann, *NT Questions of Today* (Eng. trans., London: SCM, 1969), 135; cf. 124-37.

207. Ibid., 135.

208. Schnelle, "1 Kor. 6:14 — Eine nachpaulinische Glosse," 217-19.

rection destiny is precisely what gives meaning, responsibility, and significance to bodily existence in the present.[209] Dale Martin's sociocritical emphasis on the importance of σῶμα in Paul as an issue of "health" or "purity," and Derrett's distinctive arguments about "sticking" (κολλάω) remain important, but the frame identified by Käsemann and Byrne remains even more decisive for this point.[210]

15 This is the sixth occurrence of οἴδατε ὅτι in this epistle (see above on 3:16; cf. also 5:6; 6:2, 3, 9). Robinson and Thornton make a major issue of the trite banality to which the word **members** has sunk in the metaphorical image of a **body** of persons in modern thought, in contrast to Paul's meaning in this verse and in related passages in 1 Corinthians.[211] Robinson asserts, "The language of 'membership' of a body corporate has become so trite that the idea that the individual can be a 'member' has ceased to be offensive."[212] We do not have to subscribe to Robinson's theories about the identity of Christ's risen body with the community of the church to accept his valid starting point, "The subject has been both complicated and illuminated by J. A. T. Robinson."[213] The only way to recover Paul's meaning is to search for a translation of the neuter plural μέλη, which Paul uses no fewer than three times in this single verse for emphasis, which has not become a "trite" dead metaphor in English. The nearest single words are **limbs**, *parts, members.*[214] But **limbs** are only one category of bodily *members.* No better alternative can be found in English than to use together the two words selected by REB: **limbs and organs.** For the double context of public action in the world and sexual intimacy belongs integrally to Paul's logic.

Kempthorne and Schrage make the further point that to translate ἄρας as *shall I take* misses its force here as meaning **shall I take away** . . . ?[215] Like Lat. *rapio* it means *to snatch and carry off.* Hence, we noted, Bailey spoke of a "wrenching" when one body became "one" with two independent, incompatible, alien entities. In grammatical terms, ποιήσω may be either future indicative or first aorist active deliberative subjunctive. The latter would be translated *am I to take away . . . ?* which might lend weight to the rhetorical question. But so strong is Paul's language that *deliberation,* even if purely rhetorical, seems out of place. The straightforward **shall I take away. . . ?** invites the immediate emphatic optative wish μὴ γένοιτο, *may it not happen* (optative of γίνομαι); the id-

209. B. Byrne, "Eschatologies of Resurrection and Destruction: The Ethical Significance of Paul's Dispute with the Corinthians," *Downside Review* 104 (1986): 288-98.

210. Cf. D. Martin, *The Corinthian Body,* esp. 168-79; Derrett, "Right and Wrong Sticking (1 Cor 6:18)," 89-106.

211. J. A. T. Robinson, *The Body,* 51-55; Thornton, *The Common Life in the Body of Christ,* 253-57.

212. Robinson, *The Body,* 51.

213. Whiteley, *The Theology of St Paul,* 192; cf. 190-99.

214. BAGD, 501-2.

215. Kempthorne, "Incest and the Body of Christ," 568-74; Schrage, *Der erste Brief,* 2:26, n. 320. Also, earlier, Edwards, *First Epistle,* 148.

iom is hugely emphatic: **perish the very thought**! Other idioms are equally possible: *Unthinkable!;* NIV, *Never!* (The AV/KJV translation *God forbid!* comes from an age before secularization when to invoke God offers the strongest form of a negative wish.)[216]

While it is reading far too much into Paul to construe a theology in such terms as "Christ has no hands but our hands . . . ," Paul does indeed see the public, embodied life of Christ's people as the instantiation of the gospel which points to, and thereby identifies, Christ for the world. In the early years of this century and in the last century with the rise of Tractarianism it became fashionable to speak of the church as an extension of the incarnation. This ascribed too high a status to the visible church and its institutional officers, inviting the notion that to become part of the church is *ipso facto* to belong to Christ. Nevertheless, Protestant scruples about the misuse of the phrase should not blind us to the very specific sense in which the **bodies** of Christians are **limbs and organs** that are quite literally "for" Christ. The Christian cannot claim the privilege of being *redeemed* or **purchased** (6:20) as one who *belongs* to Christ and simultaneously **take away** (back) the **limbs and organs** which have been grafted onto Christ for un-Christlike purposes that wrench them apart again. Robinson perceives the origins of Paul's thinking in Christ's identification with his persecuted people in the words "Why do you persecute *me?*" (Acts 26:14-15; cf. 9:4-5; 22:7-8).[217] Even more powerful, however, is Dale Martin's argument that Paul consciously reverses the hierarchy of values ascribed to "soul" and "body" in the context of religion and the spiritual life.[218]

16-17 A seventh occurrence of **do you not know that . . . ?** in this epistle (v. 16) underlines the strength of Paul's response (see on 3:16). Some discussion has taken place about the appropriate translation of κολλώμενος, the present participle middle of κολλάω, *to join, to bond, to glue, to bind indissolubly,* for which we propose **the person who is united in intimacy**. In classical literature and in papyri outside the NT it frequently means *to glue, to cement, together by a method of bonding.* Thus Liddell-Scott-Jones and Moulton-Milligan offer a different impression of semantic range and examples from that of Bauer-Arndt-Gingrich-Danker.[219] Typically Pindar, Plato, and early papyri

216. A. J. Malherbe, "Μὴ γένοιτο in the Diatribe and Paul," *HTR* 73 (1980): 231-40, alludes to the use of the phrase in Epictetus to set aside a false objection to an argument, like the sweep of a hand.

217. Robinson, *The Body,* 58.

218. The importance of the "ordinary" aspects of bodily behavior, including eating, drinking, enjoying what is at one's disposal, sexual relations, and day-to-day living for "spiritual" life in Paul's view is well argued by Martin, *The Corinthian Body,* 176; cf. 174-79 and throughout.

219. LSJ, 825, cites Plato, *Timaeus* 75D and 82D, on cement or glue; Pindar, *Nemean Odes* 7.115, on inlaid gold; Aeschylus, *Agamemnon* 1566, on binding indissolubly (esp. in middle). MM cite uses in the papyri of "sticking on" the handle of a cup (352-53; they date this BC 279; cf. also *Oxyrhynchus Papyri* 12:1449:15, 20, 23, AD 213-17). Such contexts do not occur in the NT (BAGD, 441), but provide excellent insight into the force of the extended or metaphorical use. This point is well made, e.g., by Edwards, *First Epistle,* 148.

use it of joining or welding metals, or gluing a handle to pottery when it has come apart. In Christian literature the word is used of sexual intimacy (Matt 19:5); love between human persons and God (*1 Clement* 49:5); the union of body and spirit or Spirit (*2 Clement* 14:5); and of hiring oneself out to someone (Luke 15:15). On the basis of the use of κολλάω without the prefix προσ-, J. I. Miller argues that κολλᾶσθαι means *adherence,* and partly on the basis of Luke 15:15 S. E. Porter argues that in this passage it means "the one who sells himself into bondage (i.e., obligates himself)."[220] The word, he argues, reflects the metaphorical currency of economic subordination, which is applied to two mutually exclusive sets of "obligations": the illicit relationship and Christ. But three considerations count against this more specialized meaning: (i) in the LXX κολλάω translates chiefly דבק *(dabaq),* which with the dative (as in Matt 19:5) normally denotes sexual union and intimacy as such; (ii) the context is about to focus on the εἰς σάρκα μίαν of Gen 2:24 (LXX) as its controlling paradigm; and (iii) the arguments of K. Bailey, R. H. Gundry, and J. P. Sampley on "one flesh" offer a more straightforward explanation which is adequate (below).[221] Further, (iv) Derrett's allusion to the Hebrew background זנות *(zenuth), idolatry, unfaithfulness* (overlaps with πορνεία), with its play on זנה *(zanah), to commit adultery,* and זונה *(zonah), harlot,* provides a relevant theological background to "sticking" to God. To whom will the believer "stick"?[222]

The impersonal verbal form φησίν usually denotes oral speech rather than written texts but clearly refers to the quotation of Gen 2:24. Although Ellis's claim that Paul implies "God says" cannot be demonstrated, it remains true that in the LXX φημί chiefly translates נאם *(na'am),* which in its substantival form is regularly used in *oracle of Yahweh,* or *thus says the Lord.*[223] In any case, Stanley's recent research confirms that "The quotation in 1 Cor 6:16 follows the unanimous wording of the LXX tradition of Gen 2:24."[224] However, the Hebrew MT does not include **the two** behind οἱ δύο, even if the words are found in the Samaritan Pentateuch and the Targum of Jonathan. The LXX's **two** does occur in the numerous quotations in Philo and in Mark 10:8, Matt 19:5, and Eph 5:31. Further, following the Hebrew idiom behind the Greek, we translate ἔσονται with most English VSS as **shall become one flesh**, representing והיו לבשר אחד *(wehayu lebasar 'echad),* where the Greek preposition εἰς represents the Heb ל *(le)* to qualify the verb's relation to the noun.

---

220. Miller, "A Fresh Look at 1 Cor 6:16f," 125-27 (appealing to C. F. D. Moule); and Porter, "How Should κολλώμενος in 1 Cor 6:16-17 Be Translated?" 105-6. Numerous scholars address the omission of προσ- as a prefix to κολλᾶσθαι as "not a problem" (e.g., Sampley, *"And the Two Shall Become One Flesh,"* 78, n. 2.

221. Sampley, *"And the Two Shall Become One Flesh,"* 77-85; Gundry, *Sōma in Biblical Theology,* 59-69; Bailey, "Paul's Foundation for Human Sexuality," 27-41.

222. Derrett, "Right and Wrong Sticking (1 Cor 6:18)," 89-106.

223. Ellis, *Paul's Use of the OT,* 23; questioned by Fee, *First Epistle,* 259, n. 47; cf. BDF, sect. 30:4 on the impersonal use of the Greek verb.

224. C. D. Stanley, *Paul and the Language of Scripture,* 195.

Gundry argues that the adversative ὁ δέ, which begins v. 17, contrasts "the physical side of *sōma*" highlighted by **flesh** (σάρξ; בָּשָׂר, *basar*) with Paul's use of πνεῦμα to denote the relationship of intimate union between the believer and Christ: "*Sarka* highlights the physical side, not of *sōma,* but of *man.*"[225] Two points within Gundry's argument, however, must be distinguished. On one side he rightly argues that Paul does not appeal to a superiority of the *pneuma* over the *sōma.* This accords with Dale Martin's powerful argument that Paul "rejects a hierarchical notion of the body . . . as if the body and food are lower on a hierarchical scale of meaningfulness than the human mind or will. . . . Instead of placing the human will or soul on one side, and food and the body on the other, he opposes *porneia* as representative of the estranged cosmos, and God, Jesus Christ, and believers as fully embodied beings. The prostitute (*pornē,* vv. 15-16), therefore, is not a person in her own right, but a representative of the cosmos that is estranged and opposed to God and Christ."[226] This deserves careful consideration, but it entails a different view of *sōma* from Gundry's second, distinct argument, namely, that the *physicality* of *sōma* is more central to Paul's use of the term than his use of σῶμα to mean *the total self.* The question which Käsemann answers more convincingly than Gundry is whether σῶμα stresses the totality of the self in the public domain as "that piece of the world which the person is," or whether Paul retains some aspect of the Greek dualism of soul-body in the sense of nonphysical versus physical.[227]

The force of μέλη, **limbs and organs** (v. 15; see above), seems to endorse Dale Martin's point: "The man who has sex with a prostitute is, in Paul's construction, Christ's 'member' entering the body of the prostitute."[228] Martin allows for the close parallel in first-century thought between σῶμα as the regulated system which constitutes the individual self and the regulated system which constitutes a social organism. In each case identity (and purity) is stabilized by maintaining identity boundaries. The identity crisis which the immoral relationship brings about concerns both the individual identity boundaries of the offender and the corporate identity boundaries of what it is to belong to the people of Christ in union with Christ.[229] This background is explored in particular by J. H. Neyrey, drawing on the work of Mary Douglas, among others.[230] But Martin differs from Neyrey in the rigor of his exegesis and his refusal to

225. Gundry, *Sōma in Biblical Theology,* 68.
226. Martin, *The Corinthian Body,* 176.
227. On Käsemann, see above on the previous verse.
228. Martin, *The Corinthian Body,* 176.
229. The social anthropology of Mary Douglas and others lies behind Martin's work. We need not subscribe to such theories in detail nor impose upon Paul a conscious drawing upon this conceptuality in order to appreciate its place in the scaffolding of ancient thought both in the biblical and Greek worlds. On this point cf. J. D. G. Dunn, *1 Corinthians* (Sheffield: Sheffield Academic Press, 1995), 65-67.
230. J. H. Neyrey, "Perceiving the Human Body: Body Language in 1 Cor," in his *Paul in Other Words: A Cultural Reading of his Letters* (Louisville: Westminster, 1990), 102-46.

draw on generalizations about purity systems. Martin sees the indifference to **the body** in these verses as a characteristic of "the strong" which Paul attacks.[231]

Nevertheless, Paul gives a distinctively theological redefinition (or "code switching") to πνεῦμα. It is doubtful whether Martin can sustain the view that here "The man's body and Christ's body share the same pneuma" in the sense of "the pneumatic life-force of the larger body."[232] Paul is not comfortable with using πνεῦμα in this way, other than in unimportant contexts. Fee is on more secure ground when he writes: "Paul is probably referring to the work of the Spirit, whereby through the 'one Spirit' the believer's 'spirit' has been joined indissolubly with Christ. . . . The way to express that union is in terms of the Spirit."[233] After all, in v. 14 Paul has just appealed to the principle of the act of resurrection, the agent of which is regularly the Holy Spirit in Paul (Rom 8:11; 1 Cor 15:44); he has spoken of the corporeity of believers as the Spirit's temple (3:17) and will explicitly designate τὸ σῶμα ὑμῶν as ναὸς τοῦ ἐν ὑμῖν ἁγίου πνεύματος in v. 19. In simple terms, "In Paul's own thought, the twin thoughts add up to this: the whole man, body and spirit, belongs to the Lord. Therefore illicit union with a harlot, although it is 'merely' physical, as the Corinthians [or "the strong" at Corinth] would say, effects a oneness of physical relationship which contradicts the Lord's claim over the body. . . ."[234]

In spite of the familiar phrase εἰς σάρκα μίαν from Gen 2:24 (LXX), Paul chooses to use the words ἓν σῶμα in v. 16. Quite clearly this paves the way for his statement in 1 Corinthians 12 that just as one Spirit (τὸ δὲ αὐτὸ πνεῦμα in 12:4 is clearly the Holy Spirit) yields a rich diversity of freely given "gifts," so the one body (τὸ σῶμα ἕν, 12:12) has many limbs and organs (μέλη πολλά, 12:12). These are in Christ (12:12). The model of unity-in-difference or differentiation within unity is expounded in detail with reference to different "workings," "ways of serving," and "free gifts" of the trinitarian God (12:4-12), but no less does it embrace the imagery of sexual union in marriage drawn from Gen 2:24. As J. P. Sampley shows, whatever evaluations are offered about the authorship of the classic "one flesh" passage in Eph 5:21-33, Paul not only uses this imagery in 1 Cor 6:12-20, but also tells the Corinthians that some response of "jealousy" is in order at their stance and conduct since "I betrothed you to Christ to present you as a pure bride to her one husband" (2 Cor 11:2-3). This lack of "devotion" to Christ (2 Cor 11:3) contradicts this "marriage pledge" or "betrothal" (ἁρμόζομαι, 11:2, only here in the NT, meaning *to fit together, to join, to give in marriage*).[235]

It is well known that Ephesians expounds a corporate theology of the

231. Martin, *The Corinthian Body*, 176-89; cf. also 277, n. 2.

232. Ibid., 176.

233. Fee, *First Epistle*, 260.

234. Gundry, *Sōma in Biblical Theology*, 69 (Gundry's next [unquoted] sentence may become more problematic).

235. Sampley, *"And the Two Shall Become One Flesh,"* 81-82; cf. 77-85 and 34-66.

church, and some of the arguments against a Pauline authorship depend on a supposed shift of emphasis from Christology to structural ecclesiology. But whatever our conclusions about authorship, the ready shift between the individual and corporate, all against the background of mutual loyalty to a joint or a common solidarity as "one," lends further weight to some of the arguments of Dale Martin, but on theological as well as sociohistorical grounds. The recent work of Dawes takes these issues with a careful account of the dynamics of metaphor and imagery in language about "one body" and "one flesh."[236] We shall return to Paul's understanding of sexuality (as well as the possible background in Hosea) in our comments on the next verse.[237] Even earlier than 1 Corinthians is Paul's insistence that all baptized, committed Christians are "one person in Christ Jesus" (Gal 3:28). Hays rightly argues that *the community is the primary addressee of God's imperatives* (his italics). . . . The primary sphere of moral concern is . . . the corporate obedience of the church."[238]

18 The present imperative φεύγετε is best expressed in translation as **keep away from** (NJB). However, Rosner alerts us to the resonances of "flee" in a possible allusion to the narrative of Joseph's flight from Potiphar's wife (Genesis 39) in Jewish tradition.[239]

Many versions insert **other** into the Greek text (REB, NIV, NJB), although it is not strictly explicit, for the sake of clarification. But it remains an interpretative gloss. This verse in notoriously difficult, except perhaps with reference to its most immediate rhetorical context. Is not such a sin as drunkenness and drug addiction a **sin against his or her own body**, let alone suicide? Does not this support the view of Nietzsche and many others that Christianity is responsible for a negative evaluation of sex, placing it below social oppression or personal greed

236. Dawes, *The Body in Question: Metaphor and Meaning in the Interpretation of Eph 5:21-33,* esp. 150-67 and 168-77.

237. Cf. Burkill, "Two into One: The Notion of Carnal Union in Mark 10:8; 1 Cor 6:16; Eph 5:31," 115-20, which relates the issue to "one God" but also argues some questionable conclusions: notably, Bailey, "Paul's Theological Foundation for Human Sexuality: 1 Cor 6:9-20," 27-41; and G. Klein, "Hos 3:1-3 — Background to 1 Cor 6:19b-20?" *Criswell Theological Review* 3 (1989): 373-75 (on Hosea's marriage as a paradigm of prophecy and covenant).

238. Hay, "Ecclesiology and Ethics in 1 Cor," *Ex Auditu* 10 (1994): 33; cf. 31-43. Other important works which rightly place ethical obligation in the context of the Christian community as "one" body include D. J. Deidun, *New Covenant Morality in Paul,* AnBib 89 (Rome: Pontifical Biblical Institute, 1981); and J. P. Sampley, *Walking between the Times: Paul's Moral Reasoning* (Minneapolis: Fortress, 1991). See further E. Best, *One Body in Christ* (London: SPCK, 1955); J. D. G. Dunn, "'The Body of Christ' in Paul," in M. J. Wilkins and T. Paige (eds.), *Worship, Theology and Ministry in the Early Church,* JSNTS 87 (Sheffield: Sheffield Academic Press, 1992), 146-62; A. Perriman, "'His Body, Which Is the Church . . .': Coming to Terms with Metaphor," *EvQ* 62 (1990): 123-42; and A. J. M. Wedderburn, "The Body of Christ and Related Concepts in 1 Cor," *SJT* 24 (1971): 74-96.

239. Rosner, "A Possible Quotation of Test. Reuben 5:5 in 1 Cor. 6:18a," 123-27. Some ancient writers made much of *fleeing* here. Chrysostom observes, "He does not say 'abstain from fornication', but 'Flee', that is, with all zeal to seek deliverance . . ." (*1 Cor. Hom.,* 18:2). Conzelmann views *shun* as typical of parenesis (*1 Cor,* 112).

for wealth or for power? Some patristic comments do imply such a view.[240] Chrysostom observes: "It was not possible to mention anything worse than fornication," and appeals to the "uncleanness" of the relationship to explain Paul's language.[241] But a rhetorical analysis suggests a different explanation.

Kenneth Bailey proposes a chiasmic structure for the block of material from 6:13 to 20. The first theme corresponds with the last: "the body is for the Lord," or "glorify God in your body" (vv. 13c-14 and 20). The second stage "members of Christ" is first expressed as being μέλη Χριστοῦ and then reflected in the penultimate verse ναὸς τοῦ ἐν ὑμῖν ἁγίου πνευματός (vv. 15 and 19). This leaves the concentrated theological ethics of the central block (vv. 16-18), which is governed by what precedes and follows it.[242] A person can be κολλώμενος τῇ πόρνῃ (and therefore ἓν σῶμα with her v. 16) or can be κολλώμενος τῷ κυρίῳ (and therefore ἓν πνεῦμα with him, v. 17), yielding the corollary that in the former instance a person violates or tears apart ἴδιον σῶμα in two senses. This occurs first because the union of the whole self (*pace* Gundry, but with Käsemann and others) with the Lord is in jeopardy; second, because the application of ἴδιον now becomes problematic. Does he *belong* to himself, another, or the Lord? Bailey's establishing of vv. 16-18 as a centerpiece distinct from vv. 12-15 and 19-20 is pressed further by Bruce Fisk.[243] However, Fisk first raises (with Bailey, see below) the issue of whether v. 18a is another quotation from Corinth.

(1) Those who ascribe v. 18a to Paul himself often cite Paul's dependence on OT sources. Thus Conzelmann holds that he is unduly influenced by an overconcern about prostitution in Proverbs (e.g., 6:25-33). Whereas a thief only "forfeits his goods," a sexual offender "destroys himself" (Prov 6:32). On this basis Paul remains responsible for the kind of comment which we noted in Chrysostom, for this is (in Conzelmann's view) "formulated *ad hoc* . . . plainly taking his cue from a Jewish saying which describes fornication as the direst of sins."[244]

(2) By contrast, many argue that "**every sin . . . is done outside the body**" is a Corinthian slogan which Paul is quoting. Morris and J. Murphy-O'Connor are sympathetic to this, while a recent firm advocate is Roger Omanson.[245] Among such advocates, interpretations of the role of the slogan at Corinth vary. Moule and Thrall perceive those at Corinth as insisting that the

240. F. Nietzsche, *The Antichrist,* e.g., sect. 56 (conveniently with *Twilight of the Idols* [London: Penguin 1968], 175-76).

241. Chrysostom, loc. cit.

242. Bailey, "Paul's Theological Foundation for Human Sexuality," 32-36.

243. Fisk, "πορνεύειν as Body Violation: The Unique Nature of Sexual Sin in 1 Cor 6:18," 540-58.

244. Conzelmann, *1 Cor,* 112; Collins, *First Cor,* 249, has a more positive view of Paul's use of the OT here.

245. Omanson, "Acknowledging Paul's Quotations," 201-13. Cf. also C. F. D. Moule, *Idiom Book of NT Greek* (2d ed.), 196-97; W. J. Conybeare and J. S. Howson, *Life and Epistles of St Paul,* 392, n. 5; Morris, *First Epistle,* 103; Murphy-O'Connor, "Corinthian Slogans in 1 Cor 6:12-20," *CBQ* 40 (1978): 391-96.

offender's personality is not affected.[246] Murphy-O'Connor and Omanson view them as arguing that **the body** is morally irrelevant; sin occurs on a different "level" (see above).[247] Kempthorne understands the Corinthians to say that the church is not affected.[248]

(3) Another group of writers argue that while v. 18 comes from Paul himself, the distinction between sexual sin and other sins lies in comparative generalization, perhaps in terms of its permanent effects, rather than a very sharp absolute of a difference in kind.[249]

(4) Finally, the largest group of writers do see a qualitative difference in Paul's thinking, either in terms of (a) the destructiveness of its effects; or (b) in terms of its intrinsic sinfulness; or (c) its damaging effects specifically upon the self.

A wide range of writers develop versions of this fourth approach, but notably Bruce, Fisk, and Kenneth Bailey (see further below). Meyer, e.g., proposed that whereas drunkenness, greed, and even suicide use means external to the body for the purpose of self-gratification or desire, only sexual acts are entirely and exclusively initiated by, and carried out by means of, the body.[250] Dale Martin revives a variant of this which combines well with Bailey's view (see below).[251] Yet the shadings and hypotheses of interpretation of this verse are almost limitless. Some "acknowledge their inability to find a meaning for the contrast," and even Schrage is cautious about overpreserving this verse in such a way as to single out sexual sin above other sinful actions.[252] Senft rejects the tradition that the contrast here is only one of degree but compares four other views.[253] Allo also notes a wide range.[254]

Fisk carefully compares all the main interpretations of this verse. He shows that τὸ ἴδιον σῶμα means *the man's own body* and (with Bailey) constitutes a centerpiece in relation to vv. 15 and 19-20. In summary, Sir 19:2b provides a close similarity with 6:16a, which introduces the theme of "a sin against oneself."[255] He concludes, "Paul grounds his prohibition of sexual immorality in three distinct but closely related arguments (vv. 15, 16-18, 19-20) relating respectively to Christ-violation, body-violation and Spirit-violation."[256] In com-

---

246. Moule, *Idiom Book,* 196-97; Thrall, *1 and 2 Cor,* 49.

247. Murphy-O'Connor, "Corinthian Slogans," 391-96; Omanson, "Acknowledging Paul's Quotations," 201-13.

248. Kempthorne, "Incest and the Body of Christ," 568-74.

249. Theodore in K. Staab (ed.), *Pauluskommentare aus der griechischen Kirche,* 181; Calvin, *First Epistle,* 181-82; Barrett, *First Epistle,* 150.

250. Meyer, *First Epistle,* 1:185; See also Wolff, *Der erste Brief,* 129-30.

251. Martin, *The Corinthian Body,* 176-78.

252. Godet, *First Epistle,* 1:311, cites Rückert and de Wette; cf. Schrage, *Der erste Brief,* 2:32-33.

253. Senft, *La première Épitre,* 84-85.

254. Allo, *Première Épitre,* 148.

255. Fisk, "Sexual Sin in 1 Cor 6:18," 554-56.

256. Ibid., 557.

mon with the wisdom background of the OT and Judaism Paul "declares sexual sin to be profoundly (and even uniquely) self-destructive."[257] This approach receives support, in effect, from Derrett's ingenious discussion of the Hebrew background concerning זנות *(zenuth)* and זונה *(zonah)* helpfully combines the issue of "sticking" with that of pollution.[258] Kenneth Bailey sees the major force of the verse to be that *since the Christian is now part of Christ,* the practice at issue in these verses is "the tearing of it [the body] away from the body of Christ in both individual and corporate terms."[259] Martin goes further. The Greek phrase εἰς τὸ ἴδιον σῶμα carries the combined force of **against** one's own body and *into* (εἰς with the accusative) one's body: "*Porneia* quintessentially represents the invasion of the body. . . . Christ is [thereby] sexually penetrating the evil cosmos," since the man's **limbs and organs are Christ's** (v. 15) and the wrenching from the **one body** of Christ wrenches the one **body** away from Christ into the domain that is not-Christ.[260] This becomes doubly poignant with the double ambiguity of εἰς (**against** or *into?*) and ἴδιον (**his own** or *Christ's own?* Can it be both, if **you are not your own** [6:20]?). Martin concludes that Paul reverses the supposed hierarchy of bodily and "spiritual" modalities attributed to persons in the psychology of much Graeco-Roman thought, as if "higher things" (as against food, drink, and sex) related more closely to "spirituality." It is precisely in how a person *reveals themselves as what they are in the bodily and everyday life* that what it means to be "in Christ" emerges.

One further approach to this difficult verse (and verses) needs to be considered. We alluded in our introduction to 6:12-20 to Goulder's novel and subtle arguments about this passage.[261] With Goulder we agree that Paul cites catchphrases used by his opponents, which he then caps, and that those whom Paul addresses include those who think of themselves as "spiritual" in the sense of being "of the Spirit."[262] He is also correct to distance Roman Corinth from the extravagant portraits of the Greek city of Aphrodite "as a sink of sexual vice" almost beyond comparison. Since the context of 6:12-20 is less specific and less explicit than those of 5:1-8, or 6:1-8, Goulder proposes that the appeal to "freedom" (or "rights") in 6:12 applies to a broad range of issues, including food offered to idols (cf. 10:33 and 8:1–11:1), and that the kind of sexual union envisaged in 6:12-20 is not that of sexual promiscuity with prostitutes but some such extramarital relationship as that with a concubine or a mistress, which might be supposed not to cause scandal or to merit such rebuke as occurs in 5:1-5 and 6:1-11. Goulder argues, however, that in Paul's view of Gen 2:24 "the sexual sinner unites himself for eternity in one

257. Ibid. Thus Fisk groups himself with those who see a "qualitative difference" here (because of intrinsic difference, Grosheide, Gundry; a destructive effect, Fee, Käsemann).

258. Derrett, "Right and Wrong Sticking," 89-106.

259. Bailey, "Paul's Theological Foundation for Human Sexuality," 37.

260. Martin, *The Corinthian Body,* 178.

261. M. D. Goulder, "Libertines? (1 Cor 5–6)," *NovT* 41 (1999): 334-48.

262. Ibid., 341-45.

flesh with the whore."[263] Gen 2:24 refers "to marital union, but Paul takes [it] to cover all sexual union."[264] Although the most distinctive details of Goulder's thesis remain difficult to substantiate, light is shed on several problems, not least on Paul's singling out the sphere of bodily union as unique.

Hence, far from *devaluing* sex, *the very opposite comes about.* In this area Paul was far ahead of first-century cultural assumptions in perceiving the sexual act as one of intimacy and *self-commitment which involved the whole person;* not the mere manipulation of some "peripheral" function of the body.[265] Broadly like Käsemann with his emphasis on "public world," B. Byrne concludes that σῶμα denotes **the body** under the aspect of "personal communication."[266] Byrne's work supports Bailey's conclusion that in the context equally of union with Christ and of physical union the issue becomes one of fully "giving" oneself to the one to whom one belongs. In the context of marriage Paul can perceive this intimacy of self-giving as making "holy" (7:14) or as "in the Lord" (7:39). This achieves an even clearer profile if Klein is right to perceive a possible background to 6:18-20 in the covenantal relationship which is presupposed in Hos 3:1-3.[267]

19 A and 33 read the plural σώματα in place of the singular σῶμα. But this is an understandable secondary gloss. The singular with the genitive plural ὑμῶν may seem awkward (Kempthorne), while classical Greek sources offer evidence of the distributive use of the singular where a plural meaning might be suggested.[268] The variant is responsible for the Vulgate's *membra vestra.* Our translation follows the punctuation of the UBS 4th ed. But NRSV, REB, NIV, and NJB place a full stop (period) after **belong to yourselves**, and a question mark after **received from God**.

Verse 19 contains the eighth occurrence of the ten **do you not know**? rhetorical devices in this epistle (see above on 3:16; cf. 5:6; 6:2, 3, 9, 15, 16). See also above on 3:16 for the meaning of ναὸς τοῦ ἁγίου πνεύματος. The corporate aspect of the community as the Spirit's temple in 3:16 receives a more individual application here, which arises in the context of the personal lifestyle at issue in this chapter.[269] The universal presence of images of the deities in Graeco-Roman temples would have made the principle more vivid to first-century read-

263. Ibid., 347.

264. Ibid., 346.

265. D. S. Bailey, *The Man-Woman Relation in Christian Thought* (London: Longmans, 1959), 9-10.

266. Byrne, "Sinning against One's Own Body: Paul's Understanding of the Sexual Relationships in 1 Cor. 6:18," 608-16.

267. Klein, "Hos. 3:1-3 — Background to 1 Cor. 6:19b-20?" 373-75.

268. Cf. Kempthorne, "Incest and the Body of Christ: A Study of 1 Cor. 6:12-20," 572-73 (cf. 568-74); Edwards, *First Epistle,* 150, for an allusion to the syntax in Plato; Schrage, *Der erste Brief,* 2.33, n. 360.

269. "What was said in 3:16 of the community . . . is here transferred to the individual" (Conzelmann, *1 Cor,* 112). Alluding to Cerfaux, Conzelmann asserts that the emphasis in 3:16 is "primary as compared with 6:19" (ibid., n. 37).

ers. The image of the god or goddess usually dominated the temple either by size or by number (or both), and Paul declares that the very person of the Holy Spirit of God, by parity of reasoning, stands to the totality of the bodily, everyday life of the believer (σῶμα) in the same relation of influence and molding of identity as the images of deities in pagan temples. Moreover, as we noted above, if believers are consecrated by the Holy Spirit, to sin either against a fellow Christian (6:1-8) or against one's body (6:9-19, esp. 18) is sacrilege and desecration.[270] Finally, there is a conscious tension between εἰς τὸ ἴδιον σῶμα (v. 18) and οὐκ ἐστὲ ἑαυτῶν (v. 19).

The phrase οὖ ἔχετε ἀπὸ θεοῦ emphasizes both the transcendent source of the Holy Spirit who is Other and holy (see above on τὸ πνεῦμα τὸ ἐκ τοῦ θεοῦ, 2:12), and the gracious bestowal of the Holy Spirit as God's free gift of love. Grace and judgment are held together: to desecrate the body is to violate God's gift and to invite an unfavorable and awesome verdict on the part of God himself. H. B. Swete writes on v. 19: "The general lesson is clear: You are God's consecrated shrine, through the Spirit's indwelling, and you are therefore relatively holy; beware lest your relation to the Holy Spirit be your ruin. . . . The body has been sanctified; let it fulfil its proper end, that of bringing glory to God whose temple it is."[271]

20 (1) Some later uncials (C[3], D[2], and some Syriac VSS) add καὶ ἐν τῷ πνεύματι ὑμῶν ἅτινά ἐστι τοῦ φεοῦ to v. 20, which accounts for the AV/KJV *and in your spirit, which are God's,* after *your body.* But this reflects a later ascetic and dualistic attempt to compensate for a loss of understanding of Paul's use of σῶμα to denote *the whole person.* The shorter text (𝔭[46], ℵ, A, B, C, D, Coptic, Irenaeus, et al.) is authentic. (2) The particle δή functions to give intensity to the imperative, translated above as **then**. In transmission and interaction between Greek and Latin versions, it appears that the meaning was linked with ἄραγε (also **then** in the logical sense), which was misread at an early stage as ἄρατε (easily enough in uncials, where T could become Γ). When translated into Latin, this was rendered as *Glorificate et* **portate** *Deum in corpore vestro,* which appears in Tertullian's quotation of Marcion's citation of the verse, in Cyprian, and in Ambrosiaster.[272]

The concept of purchasing a slave from another owner flows logically from **you do not belong to yourselves** as substantiating the ground for the principle. Hence γάρ introduces the explanation for the previous sentence (or previous rhetorical question). The imagery of the purchased slave underpins the point that Christian believers *belong to a new master, or owner,* to whom they must give account for everything. That the main emphasis falls on this point is cor-

---

270. See Thornton, *The Common Life in the Body of Christ,* 14-20 and 136-37. "Treachery to the common life . . . is a form of sacrilege. The holy shrine of God's own Spirit is invaded by a spirit of profanity. . . . The body of the Christian is a shrine of the Holy Spirit. Its misuse therefore would be a form of sacrilege" (ibid., 14 and 15).
271. H. B. Swete, *The Holy Spirit in the NT* (London: Macmillan, 1909 and 1921), 181.
272. Metzger, *Textual Commentary* (2d ed.), 487.

rect, as Conzelmann claims; but his reluctance to infer more from the imagery is misplaced, especially in view of the intensive and detailed work of Dale Martin (1990) and more recently also of Combes (1998).[273]

Deissmann was among the first to show how the metaphor of slavery had become so overlaid with theological and dogmatic nuances as to result in "the total effacement of its ancient significance"; it is "only vaguely understood among us."[274] He attempted to shed light on the ancient practice of slavery and manumission by examining up to a thousand inscriptions at Delphi and elsewhere.[275] At Delphi numerous inscriptions invoked Apollo as party to the transaction, often following such a formula as "Apollo bought a slave named X from Y at **a price** of Z" (e.g., τιμᾶς ἀργυρίου μνᾶν τριῶν) with a witnessed receipt (e.g., τιμὰν ἀπέχει).[276] At first sight Deissmann's pattern appears to offer an important clue to the understanding of 1 Cor. 1:20. He cites, e.g., "sale and purchase" of slaves to Athene at Physcus, to Asclepius at Amphissa, and to Adrastia at Cos.[277] The payment of a **price** (τιμή; genitive of price τιμῆς, older regional dialect τιμᾶς) *to* a god or goddess buys freedom (ἐπ' ἐλευθερίαι in Delphic inscriptions) for the slave. But while Deissmann's work does indeed shed light on the connection between slavery and purchase price, specialists on this subject have increasingly dissented from Deissmann's view that it places 1 Cor 6:20 and related verses in 1 Corinthians 7 in the context of manumission for *freedom*.

Important studies by S. Scott Bartchy and especially by Dale B. Martin, as well as a very large quantity of related research literature, shed a different light on this passage. First, the transaction which involved **a price** here enacts not freedom but *a change of ownership*. Martin declares, "Most scholars have agreed that Deissmann's explanation of **buy** (ἀγοράζειν) to mean redemption *from* slavery by way of sacral manumission must be rejected. *Priasthai,* not *agorazein,* is the word most commonly used in those contracts [as Deissmann's own examples show]. *Agorazein* refers . . . to the ordinary sale of a slave by one owner to another owner. . . . When Christ buys a person, the salvific element of the metaphor is . . . to a higher level of slavery (as the slave of Christ)."[278] This point remains open to misunderstanding, however, until we have established a second point.

---

273. Conzelmann states that "the metaphor is not developed" (*1 Cor,* 113). But this is because "it is obvious from the way Paul suddenly injects the image into his discourse, without introduction or explanation, that his readers must already have been familiar with this kind of language to portray one's becoming a Christian" (Martin, *Slavery as Salvation,* 63). Conzelmann's appeal to Deissmann is dated and flawed, and limits his appreciation of the importance of the image for soteriology. Martin's title is well chosen. See also Combes, *The Metaphor of Slavery in the Writings of the Early Church,* 77-94. Also Bartchy, cited below, n. 275.

274. Deissmann, *Light from the Ancient East,* 319.

275. Ibid., 321.

276. Ibid., 323.

277. Ibid., 322-32.

278. Martin, *Slavery as Salvation,* 63; cf. also xvi-xvii. Wolff, *Der erste Brief,* 131-32, also succinctly notes the shift of emphasis to ownership.

A second fundamental principle now emerges from research on slavery among many writers. Bartchy argues that Deissmann's work on inscriptions concerning sacral manumission tell us nothing at all about Paul's theology of *redemption,* including 1 Cor 6:20 and 7:22-23, for which we should rather turn to the Hebrew and Jewish traditions of what it is to be "slaves of Yahweh."[279] The reason for this (our second principle) is that the relative status of free person, freed person, and slave depended less on these categories in themselves "than the question of *whose* slave or freedman he was or had been . . ." (Ste Croix's italics).[280] Dale Martin argues the same point in detail. The status of a slave, he argues, was exceedingly complex, depending partly on the role of the slave within a given household (in which his or her role could vary from laborer or menial domestic to estate manager, even owning slaves of his own), and still more decisively on the character, status, and influence of the one to whom one belonged as slave.[281] He stresses the significance of the choice of slaves to state this status in inscriptions as "slave of X." He comments: "Slaves and freed persons may have willingly given up this status in order to emphasize their connection with someone higher up in the patronage structure of society."[282] Similarly M. Flory believes that the slave's status was placed in an epitaph "for its prestige value."[283]

It is in this light that we should read *slaves of the Lord* (1 Cor 7:22) and **bought with a price** (6:20; cf. "slaves of God," 1 Pet. 2:16). The genitive of price, τιμῆς, may well be translated *bought for a price* (Moffatt, Martin), or *bought at a price* (REB, NIV, NJB), as well as **with a price** (NRSV, AV/KJV).[284] Cost in some form remains implicit in the use of **price**, although the imagery does not require that speculations are encouraged about *to* whom a price might be paid. The imagery stresses primarily the new ownership, and secondly a costly act on the part of the new owner which makes the believer legitimately and contractually the one to whom the believer now *belongs.* Collins points out that price is important, since this *finalizes* the transaction in the world of Paul's day.[285] On one side, the slave (i.e., the Christian believer) no longer *belongs* either to himself/herself or to powers into whose bondage he/she may have entered. The believer *belongs* to One to whom it is an honor to belong, and who, like the "good" first-century slave owner, accepts responsibility for clothing, housing, feeding, and generally caring for the slave who is the

279. S. S. Bartchy, *Μᾶλλον χρῆσαι: First-Century Slavery and the Interpretation of 1 Cor. 7:21,* SBLDS 11 (Missoula: Scholars Press, 1973, rpt. 1985), 121-25.

280. G. E. M. de Ste Croix, *The Class Struggle in the Ancient Greek World from the Archaic Age to the Arab Conquests* (Ithaca: Cornell University Press, 1981), 175.

281. Martin, *Slavery as Salvation,* 1-49.

282. Ibid., 47-48.

283. M. Flory, "Family in *Familia:* Kinship and Community in Slavery," *AJAH* 3 (1978): 80; cf. 78-95.

284. Martin, *Slavery as Salvation,* 63.

285. Collins, *First Cor,* 249.

master's concern. For a slave to have someone else to take responsibility for these things is a freedom. On the other side, the owner who has bought the slave with a price expects, and has a right (cf. 6:12) to expect, allegiance, faithfulness, loyalty, obedience, and, on the basis of character and provision hitherto, also wholehearted trust.

Hence Weiss observes that what it means to invoke Christ as Lord, what "the Kyrios-faith" amounts to, "in a practical . . . sense will best be made clear through the correlative concept of 'servant' or 'slave' of Christ (Rom. 1:1; 1 Cor. 7:22-23; Gal. 1:10; Phil. 1:1; Col. 4:12)."[286] Ahead of his times, Weiss urges caution about over-stating a Greek love of autonomous freedom as over against an Oriental and Hebrew acceptance of a servile relationship of honor if this is to a great "lord": "Paul had his moments when Greek and Oriental feelings met and mingled."[287] To be engaged in "the Lord's service," he notes, is an honorable status among the hellenistic Christian congregations.[288] Bartchy and Martin endorse this point. An understanding of 1 Cor 7:22-23, Martin insists, "depends on the status-improvement meaning of slavery to Christ . . . depicted as upward mobility within slavery."[289] Those Greek writers who considered the philosophical implications of slave status insisted that "belonging" could leave room for "inner" freedom. Sophocles, Bion, Seneca, Horace, Epictetus, and especially Philo all stress this.[290] Thus on 7:22-23 Martin concludes, "The slave, according to Paul, should not be concerned about his or her current state of slavery. In reality he or she is not the slave of just anyone, but the freedperson of Christ."[291]

We should not allow the wealth of research on first-century slavery to obscure its function as a metaphor within a theology of redemption inherited from the OT. Schrage draws attention to the Hebrew terms פדה (padah) and גאל (ga'al) behind ἀγοράζειν.[292] Redemption is from a state of jeopardy by a costly act to a new state. This should qualify issues about whether a slave was mere property, not a personal agent with the "rights" of a person. A slave "was a thing (res). Owners had the right to bind, torture or kill their slaves."[293] Thus Rabbi Hillel warned that, even within Judaism, to own too many female slaves was to multiply temptations to exploit their bodies, since their bodies were not their own. Paul rejects the notion that a slave has the "right" to do anything (πάντα μοι ἔξεστιν, 6:12). A slave must be useful (συμφέρει, 6:12; Philemon

286. Weiss, Earliest Christianity, 2:458.
287. Ibid., 460.
288. Ibid., 459, n. 9.
289. Martin, Slavery as Salvation, 63.
290. T. Wiedemann, Greek and Roman Slavery (London and Canberra: Groom Helm, 1981), 224-43, contains extracts from Dio Chrysostom, 15; Horace, Satirae 2.7.75-94; Seneca, De Tranquillitate 10.3; Epistulae 47; Beneficiis 3.17.
291. Martin, Slavery as Salvation, 64.
292. Schrage, Der erste Brief, 2:35-36.
293. Ibid., xiii. See further Wiedemann, Greek and Roman Slavery, 167-88, for primary sources.

11). But on the other side, as well as protecting and guarding his own "property," a caring lord would treat his slave as a fully trusted personal agent in appropriate circumstances. Indeed, where he or she found the right potential master, many voluntarily sold themselves into his service for greater security, freedom, and status than as poor, deprived, or oppressed free persons.[294] As Combes reminds, we are dealing with the language (again) of *metaphor*, indeed with "the complex use" of this metaphor in the ancient world and in Paul.[295] Hence it is a valuable resource, but its counterparts in social life should be pressed in every detail.

MAJOR THEMES FROM THE POSTHISTORY, INFLUENCE, AND RECEPTION OF CHAPTERS 5 AND 6

Some of these verses have proved seminal for certain major theological debates within which different parties have appealed to them. We simply note these trends selectively by themes, rather than offering a longer "history" of reception. (1) Paul's language about the body has been utilized in some circles to encourage ascetic practices, but more often to refute negative attitudes toward the body. Tertullian explicitly draws on 6:19 to attack Platonic dualism, while Augustine readily draws on them in his polemic against Manicheanism. (2) Of particular sensitivity down the centuries has been the debate about exclusivity in a "pure" church, or the location of "boundaries" in a mixed church. In the era of the Donatists, Augustine addressed this issue, using these verses; Luther, Calvin, and Bullinger stand in contrast in the sixteenth and seventeenth centuries to Dietrich Philips as one of the first major "Mennonite" figures who insist on a greater withdrawal of a "pure" church from the world. (Many on both sides draw on, e.g., 5:5, 9-11; 6:9-11.) (3) Passages about sin and immorality, especially the image of the leaven (5:6-7), provide material for Augustine, Luther, and others to underline spreading consequences which can bring human persons and institutions into bondage and decay. Nevertheless, 6:12-15 gives grounds for encouragement to self-control. (4) "Christ our Passover" (5:7-8) occurs in multiform interpretive agendas, in issues about the use of the OT (Tertullian), and whether eucharistic language applies closely here (Aquinas) or in a representation or analogical mode (Zwingli).

The Body

Tertullian writes: "In Platonic language indeed the body is a prison, but in the apostle's it is 'the temple of God' because it is in Christ" (1 Cor 6:19; cf. 3:16).[296] Chrysostom is at pains to establish that 6:12-13 attacks not the body, but failure by the mind to exercise restraint: "'I do not blame the body' he [Paul] says but the excessive lack of constraint in the part of the mind." Therefore he declares, "Now the body is . . . for the Lord', for it was not formed for sexual immorality . . . nor to be greedy, but to follow

---

294. The subject is discussed further in relation to 7:21-24.
295. Combes, *The Metaphor of Slavery*, 11-48; cf. also 49-84, 162-72.
296. Tertullian, *Treatise on the Soul* 54:5.

Christ as Head, that the Lord be set over the body."[297] Cyprian calls attention to Paul's positive view of the body in 6:20: "Let us glorify God and bear him in a pure and spotless body with more perfect observance . . . the abode where he dwells."[298] Origen underlines the sanctity of the body on the basis of 6:13: μὴ νομίσῃς ὅτι τὸ σῶμα γέγονε δεὰ συνουσιασμόν . . . ἵνα ναὸς ᾖ τῷ κυρίῳ, i.e., it is a temple for the Lord, not degraded by habituated associations with earthly things.[299] With these comments we may contrast the second-century gnostic "exegesis" of 5:3-5 that since Paul is "spiritual" (πνευματικός) he is present in spirit but not in body: "he lives apart from the body and its concerns."[300] Similarly, for the "spiritual" Paul declares that "all things are authorized" (6:12); indeed, they have authority to rule (6:2-3), and can "regard bodily things with indifference." Sexual union (6:13-15, 17-21) is an allegory for a "spiritual" relationship.[301] In his writings against the Manichaeans, Augustine repeats almost the exact wording of Tertullian: "You blaspheme the temple of God, calling it not only the workmanship of satan [the gnostic demiurge] but the prison-house of God [Platonism, Neo-Platonism]. The apostle, on the other hand, says . . . 'Do you not know that your bodies are the temple of the Holy Spirit who dwells in you?'" (6:19; cf. 3:17).[302] In the last section of his anti-Manichean *Morals of the Church*, Augustine quotes the whole of 6:12-20 and 7:1-7 to substantiate the wholesomeness of God's gifts of everyday life, including marriage.[303]

"Pure" Church or Mixed Church

A strong patristic tradition takes up the plural focus of Paul's rebuke in 5:2-4. Those who "support" the incestuous offender, Ambrosiaster declares, "are not innocent either."[304] Chrysostom urges that Paul leaves to the church no other possible course of action but instant expulsion.[305] Otherwise, like leaven, toleration will spread destructive effects: "those who corrupt households (οἱ οἰκοφθόροι)," Ignatius asserts, "will not inherit the kingdom of God" (5:6, 7; 6:9).[306] Yet Augustine belongs to the mainstream of patristic writers who also believe in the realities of a "mixed" church, within reasonable limits. He addresses the rigorist exclusivism of the Donatists largely by showing that their patron figure, Cyprian, held a realist view. Augustine cites 6:9-10 to show his agreement with Paul on the reality of divine judgment; "but let us not flatter the Catholic Christian, merely because he is a Catholic Christian, to promise him impunity," i.e., there is still sin with the church, and unavoidably so.[307] In spite of Paul's warning in 5:11, "Cyprian used to admit to fellowship with the altar of God colleagues who were

297. Chrysostom, *1 Cor. Hom.*, 17:1.

298. Cyprian, *The Dress of Virgins*, 2.

299. Origen, *Fragment on 1 Cor 6:13;* in Jenkins (ed.), *JTS* 9:370.

300. Cf. *Excerpta ex Theodoto*, 67:1, cited by Pagels, *The Gnostic Paul*, 65.

301. Cited in Irenaeus, *Against Heresies*, 1:21:5; 22:3, 24:4-5; 25:4-5; also *Excerpta ex Theodoto* 52:1-2; Pagels, *The Gnostic Paul*, 65-68.

302. Augustine, *Reply to Faustus the Manichaean*, 20:15.

303. Augustine, *On the Morals of the Church*, 35:78.

304. Ambrosiaster, *Commentary*, cited from CSEL 81:52.

305. Chrysostom, *1 Cor. Hom.*, 15:3.

306. Ignatius, *To the Ephesians*, 16:1.

307. Augustine, *On Baptism, Against the Donatists*, 4:19:27 (c. AD 400).

usurers, and treacherous, and fraudulent, and robbers.... In what manner this may be defended has been sufficently set forth."[308] Citing 6:10, Augustine concedes that many in the Church fall short, but Cyprian endured them with compassion, and likewise Paul "with the same love . . . endured those who were ill-disposed and envious towards him.... Wheat and tares within the Church...."[309] Once we exclude people, where will it end?[310]

The Reformation and Post-Reformation eras provide a still clearer parallel. Dietrich Philips (c. 1560) appeals to 5:13 to support his rigorist view that "if offending members are not cut off, the whole body must perish. If . . . transgressors are not excluded, the whole congregation must be defiled (1 Cor 5:13, 1 Thess 5:14)."[311] The editor C. H. Williams describes Philips as "occupying a place in Mennonitism comparable to that of Melanchthon . . . within Lutheranism."[312] Such a use of 1 Cor 5:13, however, takes us far from Heinrich Bullinger's *Of the Holy Catholic Church* of some ten years earlier. Quoting 1 Cor 5:11, he admits the need for church discipline.[313] Nevertheless, "the holy men do indeed offend or fall, but they do not forsake Christ utterly.... St Peter denies the Lord.... We may gather round the general and orthodox opinion that all who are said to be the Church . . . are not straightway the Church."[314] For "the kingdom of heaven is like a net which draws all manner of things . . . good and bad." John Calvin offers a judicious balance not only in his Commentary on this epistle but in his discussion of the issue with reference to these chapters in the *Institutes*.[315] Even if Matthew 13 urges tolerance, 1 Cor 5:11-12 sets limits: "pastors are not always vigilant" (5:2-4). Nevertheless, "even the good are sometimes affected by this inconsiderate zeal for righteousness," which may even arise from "excessive moroseness . . . a false idea of sanctity, than genuine sanctity itself."[316]

Nature and Effects of Sin

The image of the leaven (5:6) and very forceful warnings (5:1, 5, 9-11; 6:9, 10, 15-18) provide an armory for writers who perceive sin as a power which can bring humankind into bondage. Origen underlines the different degrees of evil which 5:1 implies.[317] Ambrosiaster perceives leaven as representing what corrupts the whole person.[318] Luther brackets 1 Corinthians 5 (esp. 5:6) with Rom 6:6; 7:13; 8:2, urging that sin "is always covetous" (i.e., springs from wrongly directly desire) and constitutes a

308. Ibid., 7:45:89 (translation in NPNF, 4:510).

309. Ibid., 4:11.

310. Augustine, *Letters of Petilian the Donatist*, 2:10:24: What kind of people remain?

311. Dietrich Philips, *The Church of God, 2: Seven Ordinances of the True Church* from *Enchiridion*, rpt. in C. H. Williams (ed.), *Spiritual and Anabaptist Writers*, LCC 25 (London: SCM, 1957), 254.

312. Philips, in Williams (ed.), *Spiritual and Anabaptist Writers*, 226.

313. H. Bullinger, *Of the Holy Catholic Church* (c. 1549-51), in G. W. Bromiley (ed.), *Zwingli and Bullinger*, LCC 24 (London: SCM, 1953), 297.

314. Ibid.

315. The issue is set out in Calvin, *Institutes*, 4:1:7-22.

316. *Inst.*, 4:1:16 (Beveridge ed., London: James Clarke, 1957, 2:294).

317. Origen, *Fragments*, in Jenkins (ed.), *JTS* 9:263.

318. Ambrosiaster, *Commentary on 5:6*, in CSEL, 81:56-57.

"power" or a "tinder" which can spark things off. It cannot be dealt with "like shaving the hair where it will only grow again," but by "the gift of God . . . killing the root" (cf. 5:7-8; 6:19-20).[319] 6:3 also provides room for cosmic forces of evil among those many earlier commentators who regard *the angels* as fallen angels of wickedness. Among the Fathers, Chrysostom, Theophylact, and Theodoret adopt this view; in the medieval period, Aquinas; and in the Reformation era, Erasmus, Calvin, Beza, and subsequently Bengel.[320]

Christ Our Passover (5:7)

Several different interpretative agendas emerge. Tertullian is eager to stress continuity with OT. Not only the Passover but the role of the law (Leviticus 18; cf. 6:9-11) and language about the Day of the Lord all (against Marcion) affirm this continuity in 5–6.[321] Clement of Alexandria stresses the newness of life expressed through the Passover imagery.[322] Thomas Aquinas cites 5:7 and observes: "The paschal lamb prefigured this sacrament *(praefigurabat hoc sacramentum)* under three aspects. . . . It was eaten with unleavened bread . . . by the whole congregation . . . it was through the blood of the paschal lamb that the children of Israel were preserved from the destroying angel. . . . For this reason the paschal life is regarded as the outstanding type or figure of this sacrament *(ponitur figura sacramenti praecipua agnus paschalis)*.[323] Zwingli addresses the same verse (5:7) with the comment that "the Paschal Lamb" represents indeed "the Lord's Passover," but the Lord's Supper no more "is" the Paschal Lamb than later celebrations of the Passover Festival are more than a "figure" of the first passing over. He argues that 5:7 underpins his understanding of 1 Corinthians 11 and Matthew 26, and that the logic is not that of identity but "figurative or metaphorical."[324] An agenda about the eucharist has now arisen which was hardly within Paul's horizon in the writing of ch. 5.

Many other issues might have been addressed, given further space.[325]

319. Luther, *Answer to Latomus, WA,* 8:109-10; J. Atkinson (ed.), *Luther: Early Theological Works,* LCC 16 (London: SCM, 1962), 353.

320. For example, Chrysostom, *1 Cor. Hom.,* 16:5; Theodoret, *Opera Omnia: Interp. ep. 1 ad Cor.,* 195A (Migne, *PG,* 82:265A, 266A); Erasmus, *Periphrasis in Ep. Pauli, ad Cor. 1,* 875B; Calvin, *First Epistle,* 119; Bengel, *Gnomon,* 625.

321. Tertullian, *Against Marcion,* 5:7.

322. Clement, *Stromata,* 3:40:5.

323. Aquinas, *Summa Theologiae,* 3a, Q. 73, art. 6 (reply) in Blackfriars ed. (London: Eyre & Spottiswood), vol. 58: *Eucharistic Presence,* 23

324. Zwingli, *On the Lord's Supper,* in Bromiley (ed.), *Zwingli and Bullinger,* 226-27.

325. The entries in *Biblia Patristica* (6 vols.) are extensive. See further L. Vischer, *Die Auslegungsgeschichte von 1 Kor 6:1-11,* and relevant entries in Lampe, *A Patristic Greek Lexicon.*

IV. Response to Inquiries about Marriage and Related Issues and about Associations with Idols (7:1–11:1)

The tone of 7:1–11:1 differs strikingly from that of 5:1–6:20. The ethical anomalies of the previous two chapters are clear-cut, and all the more serious because the Corinthian community showed no evidence of even wishing to invite Paul's verdict on them. Paul's tone in these previous chapters betrays a sense of keen disappointment and outrage. Hence Paul constantly repeats, "Do you not know. . . ?" "The treatment is direct and one-sided; all is black and white. He condemns the past behaviour of the Corinthians. . . . In general he . . . speaks for himself. He does not discuss or seek to persuade."[1] This is not at all the flavour of 7:1–11:1.

The response which Paul makes to inquiries from Corinth concern grey areas which invite extreme pastoral sensitivity towards specific variable factors and situations. The "previous letter" (5:9, ἔγραψα ὑμῖν ἐν τῇ ἐπιστολῇ . . .) and the Corinthians' written letter to Paul (7:1, περὶ δὲ ὧν ἐγράψατε . . .) are no mere hypotheses of biblical scholarship, but find direct witness in the text of this epistle. Margaret Mitchell is right to express doubt about whether from here on "the structure of 1 Corinthians simply mirrors that of the Corinthians' letter to Paul," and whether περὶ δέ implies περὶ δὲ ὧν ἐγράψατε on each occasion of its use (7:1, 25; 8:1; 12:1; 16:1, 12).[2] She argues that with the single proviso that the topic in question is readily known to both author and readers, the formula is simply "a topic marker" to introduce a new subject. Nevertheless there can be little doubt that 7:1–11:1 as a unit constitutes a reply to the Corinthians' letter. For detailed arguments we refer readers to our Introduction, 32-39, and to Hurd's arguments and general criteria.[3]

The key point in this major block is Paul's pastoral sensitivity to grey areas of difficulty. In particular Clarence E. Glad has recently argued convincingly for Paul's recognition of the need for adaptability in the varied pastoral

1. Hurd, *Origin of 1 Corinthians*, 82; cf. 75-94.
2. M. M. Mitchell, *Paul and the Rhetoric of Reconciliation*, 190-191, and more especially her article "Concerning περὶ δέ in 1 Corinthians," 229-56.
3. Hurd, *Origin of 1 Corinthians*, esp. 61-71.

circumstances which may influence ethical decisions. Paul does not, e.g., merely stereotype "the strong" and "the weak"; Glad sees these terms as denoting varied temperaments and dispositions among all groups of persons, whose spirituality and lifestyle must not merely be imposed by the expectations of others in some uniform way.[4] He is willing to be "all things to all people. . . ," including "the weak" (9:22). This aspect of Paul the pastor differs greatly from portraits of Paul in popular thought.

A. DOMESTIC ISSUES: MARRIAGE, STATUS, CELIBACY, AND WIDOWS (7:1-40)

Bibliography on Marriage, Celibacy, and Widows (7:1-16, 25-40)

Achelis, H., *Virgines Subintroductae. Ein Beitrag zum VII Kapitel des 1 Kor* (Leipzig: Hinrichs, 1902).

Allmen, J. von, *Pauline Teaching on Marriage* (London: Faith Press, 1963).

Balch, D. L., "Backgrounds of 1 Cor. 7: Sayings of the Lord in Q: Moses as an Ascetic θεῖος ἀνήρ in II Cor. iii," *NTS* 18 (1971-72): 351-64.

———, "1 Cor. 7:32-35 and Stoic Debates about Marriage, Anxiety and Distraction," *JBL* 102 (1983): 429-39.

———, "Household Codes," in D. E. Aune (ed.), *Greco-Roman Literature and the NT: Selected Forms and Genres,* SBL Sources 21 (Atlanta: Scholars Press, 1988), 25-50.

———, *Let Wives Be Submissive: The Domestic Code in 1 Peter,* SBLMS 26 (Chico: Scholars Press, 1981).

Baltensweiler, H., *Die Ehe im NT* (Zurich and Stuttgart: Zwingli, 1967).

Barré, M. L., "To Marry or to Burn: *pyrousthai* in 1 Cor. 7:9," *CBQ* 36 (1974): 193-202.

Baumert, N., *Ehelosigkeit und Ehe im Herrn: Eine Neuinterpretation von 1 Kor 7,* FB 47 (Würzburg: Echter, 1984).

Best, E., "1 Cor. 7:14 and Children in the Church," *IBS* 12 (1990): 158-66.

Blue, B. B., "The House Church at Corinth and the Lord's Supper: Famine, Food Supply and the Present Distress," *Criswell Theological Review* 5 (1991): 221-39.

Brown, C., "Separate: Divorce, Separation and Remarriage," in C. Brown (ed.), *NIDNTT,* 3 (Grand Rapids: Zondervan, 1978), 535-43.

Brown, Peter, *The Body and Society: Men, Women and Sexual Renunciation in Early Christianity* (New York: Columbia University Press, 1988).

Bruns, B., "'Die Frau hat über ihren Leib nicht die Verflügungsgewalt, sondern der Mann . . .'. Zur Herkunft und Bedeutung der Formulierung in 1 Kor 7:4," *MTZ* 33 (1982): 177-94.

Byrne, B., *Paul and the Christian Woman* (Collegeville, Minn.: Liturgical Press, 1989).

Cartlidge, D. R., "1 Cor. 7 as a Foundation for a Christian Sex Ethic," *JR* 55 (1975): 220-34.

Cha, J.-S., "The Ascetic Virgins in 1 Cor 7:25-38," *Asia Journal of Theology* 12 (1998): 89-117.

---

4. Clarence E. Glad, *Paul and Philodemus: Adaptability in Epicurean and Early Christian Psychagogy,* NovTSup 81 (Leiden: Brill, 1995).

Collins, R. F., *Divorce in the NT* (Collegeville: Liturgical Press, 1992).

———, "The Unity of Paul's Paraenesis in 1 Thess 4:3-8 and 1 Cor 7:1-7," *NTS* 29 (1983): 420-29.

Countryman, L. W., *Dirt, Greed and Sex: Sexual Ethics in the NT and Their Implications for Today* (Philadelphia: Fortress, 1988).

Deidun, "Beyond Dualisms: Paul on Sex, *Sarx* and *Soma*," *Way* 28 (1988): 195-205.

Delling, G., *Paulus' Stellung zu Frau und Ehe,* BWANT 4/5 (Stuttgart: Kolhammer, 1931).

Deming, W., *Paul on Marriage and Celibacy: The Hellenistic Background of 1 Cor 7,* SNTSMS 83 (Cambridge: Cambridge University Press, 1995).

Derrett, J. D. M., "The Disposal of Virgins," *Man* 9 (1974): 23-30.

Dungan, D. L., *The Sayings of Jesus in the Churches of Paul* (Oxford: Blackwell, 1971), 83-99.

Elliott, J. K., "Paul's Teaching on Marriage in 1 Cor: Some Problems Considered," *NTS* 19 (1972-73): 219-25.

Fee, G. D., "1 Cor. 7:1 in the NIV," *JETS* 23 (1980): 307-14.

Ford, J. M., "St. Paul the Philogamist (1 Cor vii in Early Patristic Exegesis)," *NTS* 11 (1964-65): 326-48.

Garland, D. E., "The Christian's Posture Toward Marriage and Celibacy: 1 Cor. 7," *RevExp* 80 (1983): 351-62.

Genton, P., "I Cor 7:25-40. Notes exégetiques," *ETR* 67 (1992): 249-53.

Greeven, H., "Ehe nach dem NT," *NTS* 15 (1968-69): 365-88.

Gundry-Volf, J. M., "Celebrate Pneumatics and Social Power: On the Motivations for Sexual Asceticism in Corinth," *USQR* 48 (1994): 105-26.

Heth, W. A., "The Changing Basis for Permitting Remarriage after Divorce for Adultery: The Influence of R. H. Charles," *TrinJ* 11 (1990): 143-59.

———, "The Meaning of Divorce in Matt 19:3-9," *Churchman* 98 (1984): 136-52.

———, and G. J. Wenham, *Jesus and Divorce: The Problem with the Evangelical Consensus* (London: Hodder & Stoughton, 1984; and Nashville: Nelson, 1985).

Hierzenberger, G., *Weltbewertung bei Paulus nach 1 Kor 7:29-31. Eine exegetisch-kerygmatische Studie* (Düsseldorf: Patmos, 1967).

Horsley, R. A., "Spiritual Marriage with Sophia," *VC* 33 (1979): 30-54.

Kelly, K. T., "Divorce and Remarriage," in B. Hoose (ed.), *Christian Ethics* (London: Cassell, 1998), 248-65.

———, *Divorce and Second Marriage: Facing the Challenge* (Kansas City: Sheed & Ward, 2d ed. 1996).

Kubo, S., "1 Cor vii:16: Optimistic or Pessimistic?" *NTS* 24 (1978): 539-44.

Kugelmann, R., "1 Cor. 7:36-38," *CBQ* 10 (1948): 63-71.

Laney, J. C., "Paul and the Permanence of Marriage in 1 Cor. 7," *JETS* 25 (1982): 283-94.

Legrand, L., *The Biblical Doctrine of Virginity* (London: Chapman, 1963).

Léon-DuFour, X., "Du bon usage de ce Monde: 1 Cor. 7:29-31," *ASeign* 34 (1973): 26-31.

MacDonald, M. Y., "Early Christian Women Married to Unbelievers," *SR* 19 (1990): 221-34.

MacDonald, M. Y., "Women Holy in Body and Spirit in the Social Setting of 1 Cor 7," *NTS* 36 (1990): 161-81.

Marrow, S. B., "Marriage and Divorce in the NT," *ATR* 70 (1988): 3-15.

485

Meeks, W. A., *The Moral World of the First Christian* (Philadelphia: Westminster, 1986).

Merklein, H., "'Es ist gut für den Menschen eine Frau nicht anzufassen'. Paulus und Sexualität nach 1 Kor 7," in *Studien zu Jesus und Paulus,* WUNT 43 (Tübingen: Mohr, 1987), 385-408; also in G. Dautzenberg (ed.), *Die Frau im Urchristentum* (Freiburg: Herder, 1983).

Mitchell, M. M., "Concerning περὶ δέ in 1 Cor," *NovT* 31 (1989): 229-56.

Moiser, J., "A Re-Assessment of Paul's View of Marriage with Reference to 1 Cor 7," *JSNT* 18 (1983): 103-22.

Murphy-O'Connor, J., "The Divorced Woman in 1 Cor. 7:10-11," *JBL* 100 (1981): 601-6.

Niederwimmer, K., "Zur Analyse der asketischen Motivation in 1 Kor 7," *TLZ* 99 (1974): 241-48.

Osiek, C., "First Cor 7 and Family Questions," *BibTod* 35 (1997): 275-79.

Oster, R. E., "Use, Misuse and Neglect of Archeological Evidence in Some Modern Works on 1 Cor (1 Cor. 7:1-5; 8:10; 11:2-16; 12:14-26)," *ZNW* 83 (1992): 52-73.

Pagels, E. H., "Paul and Women: A Response to Recent Discussion," *JAAR* 42 (1974): 538-49.

Peterman, G. W., "Marriage and Sexual Fidelity in the Papyri, Plutarch, and Paul," *TynBul* 50 (1999): 163-72.

Phipps, W. E., "Is Paul's Attitude toward Sexual Relations Contained in 1 Cor. 7:1?" *NTS* 28 (1982): 125-31.

Pomeroy, S. B., *Goddesses, Whores, Wives and Slaves: Women in Classical Antiquity* (New York: Schocken, 1975).

Richardson, P., "'I Say, Not the Lord': Personal Opinion, Apostolic Authority and the Development of Early Christian Halakah," *TynBul* 31 (1980): 65-86.

Rousselle, A., "Body Politics in Ancient Rome," in P. S. Pantel (ed.), *A History of Women in the West* (Cambridge, Mass.: Harvard, 1992), 296-336.

Ruether, R. R., "Is Celibacy Eschatological?: The Suppression of Christian Radicalism," in *Liberation Theology: Human Hope* . . . (New York: Paulist Press, 1972), 51-64.

Schrage, W., *The Ethics of the NT* (Eng. trans., Edinburgh: T. & T. Clark and Augsburg: Fortress, 1988), 91-98.

———, "Zur Frontstellung der paulinischen Ehebewertung in 1 Kor 7:1-7," *ZNW* 67 (1976): 214-34.

———, "Die Stellung zur Welt bei Paulus, Epiktet und in der Apokalyptik: Ein Beitrag zu 1 Kor 7:29-31," *ZTK* 61 (1964): 125-54.

Scroggs, R., "Paul and the Eschatological Woman," *JAAR* 40 (1972): 283-303.

Tuckett, C. M., "1 Cor and Q," *JBL* 102 (1983): 607-19.

Ward, R. B., "Musonius and Paul on Marriage," *NTS* 36 (1990): 281-89.

Weder, H., "Perspective der Frauen?" *EvT* 43 (1983): 175-78.

Willi, H.-U., "Das Privilegium Paulinum (1 Kor 7:15, 16) — Pauli eigene Lebenserinnerung?" *BZ* 22 (1978): 100-108.

Wimbush, V. L., "The Ascetic Impulse in Ancient Christianity," *TTday* 50 (1993): 417-28.

———, *Paul, the Worldly Ascetic: Response to the World and Self-Understanding according to 1 Cor. 7* (Macon, Ga.: Mercer, 1987).

Winter, B. W., "1 Cor 7:6-7: A Caveat and a Framework for 'the Sayings' in 7:8-24," *TynBul* 48 (1997): 57-65.

———, "Secular and Christian Responses to Corinthian Famines," *TynBul* 40 (1989): 86-106.

Witherington, B., *Conflict and Community in Corinth* (Grand Rapids: Eerdmans, 1995), 170-85.

———, *Women in the Earliest Churches,* SNTSMS 59 (Cambridge: Cambridge University Press, 1988 and 1991), 24-42.

Wolbert, W., *Ethische Argumentation und Paränese in 1 Kor 7* (Düsseldorf: Patmos, 1981).

Working Party Document, *Marriage in Church after Divorce: A Discussion Document Commissioned by the House of Bishops of the Church of England* (London: Church House Publishing, 2000).

Yarbrough, O. L., *Not like the Gentiles: Marriage Rules in the Letters of Paul,* SBLDS 80 (Atlanta: Scholars Press, 1985).

Zimmerman, M. and R., "Zitation, Kontradiktion oder Applikation? Die Jesuslogien in 1 Kor 7:10-11 und 9:14," *ZNW* 87 (1996): 83-100.

Modern literature on these verses is vast in range and quantity. A helpful recent survey up to 1995 has been provided by Will Deming, who is critical of virtually the entire body of literature and offers a brief comment on the main types of approach.[5] We may briefly introduce Deming's approach and then select two or three other approaches by way of example.

(a) *Deming* (1995) relates Paul's arguments closely to those of the Stoics, noting that in the history of thought before modern scholarship only Clement of Alexandria and Hugo Grotius had explored this relationship.[6] The background for Deming lies in "the Stoic-Cynic marriage debate," in which the axiom which the whole debate presupposed was "a basic datum of free Greek society: marriage involved a man in weighty responsibilities."[7] The responsibilities of a father, a householder, and a citizen ensured and required that the married man became active in the social, political, and economic life of his town. Within this frame, the Stoic tradition viewed marriage positively as contributing to the welfare and especially to the stability of society; the Cynic tradition conceded the principle, "but in contrast to the traditionalism of the Stoics, the Cynics denied the importance of the Greek city-states, promoting instead a radical cosmopolitanism. They held that the social structures of marriage, household, and city-state had their origin in mere human convention, not divine purpose, and in their place demanded individualism. . . ."[8]

Within this frame of thought it emerges that what may appear to be an ambivalent attitude on Paul's part, or at least one which qualifies a cautiously positive attitude with "ifs" and "buts," can be found among hellenistic and Roman writers who address this Stoic-Cynic debate. Thus Epictetus, virtually Paul's contemporary, advocates marriage for the ordinary person as "beneficial" in general terms, but for the Cynic devoted to philosophical reflection

5. Deming, *Paul on Marriage and Celibacy: The Hellenistic Background of 1 Corinthians 7,* 5-49.

6. Ibid., 6.

7. Ibid., 52.

8. Ibid., 60.

Deming observes that "he essentially flips everything on its head. What is true for the common men is wrong for the Cynic . . . the Cynic can marry *only* under 'special circumstances'" (Epictetus, *Dissertations* 3.22.76).[9] Even the notion that the person who marries "does well" but the person who foregoes marriage "will do better" (in relation to the situation of 7:36-40) finds a parallel in Epictetus, *Diss.* 4.1.147, where Epictetus concedes that to marry from love is "good" but may distract from "the better."[10]

(b) *G. Delling* (1931). Deming's approach provides a constructive alternative to the influential study by Gerhard Delling to the effect that Paul's own stance on marriage and celibacy is so confused and inconsistent as to give the Corinthians good reasons for their advocacy of celibacy and accompanying perplexities about its application and relative scope.[11] Delling attributes to Paul a negative attitude towards sexuality which, as Deidun and others urge, imposes onto Paul a dualism of "spirit and flesh" which Paul does not hold.[12]

(c) *Vincent L. Wimbush* (1987) allows for Stoic influence on Paul's discussion, and draws a contrast between an ascetic withdrawal from the world among some at Corinth and Paul's simultaneous insistence that while "the things of the Lord" are to be given priority, this does not entail a fully ascetic lifestyle or ethic.[13] Indeed, Wimbush's title *Paul: The Worldly Ascetic* sums up a "middle-of-the-road" stance in which Paul guides the community "in the direction of accepting the world as the *sphere* of the Christian," while also adopting a new self-understanding and lifestyle ὡς μή the world which did not threaten to impose its values and structures on the church.[14] Wimbush argues elsewhere (1993) that this ὡς μή (7:29-31, repeated no less than five times), together with μὴ ἅπτεσθαι (7:1), gave rise to a countercultural, or at least culture-critical, stance within the patristic church.[15] Such an assessment of Paul would be strongly at variance with Deming's conclusion that Paul's discussion and reasoning took place *within* hellenistic-Roman cultural traditions. He urges: "Fully within the parameters of these discussions Paul assesses the value of marriage and celibacy with regard to prevailing circumstances. For him it is not a matter of choosing a lower or higher standard of morality, but of . . . expediency. With the church fathers the focus has shifted

9. Ibid., 85. Epictetus refers to a "special case" which arose out of passionate love: περιστασίν μοι λέγεις ἐξ ἔρωτος γενομένην. He contrasts "ordinary marriages" and "special circumstances": ἡμεῖς δὲ περὶ τῶν κοινῶν γάμων καὶ ἀπεριστάτων ζητοῦμεν. Normally "we do not find that marriage under present circumstances is of first importance for the Cynic" (*Dissertations* 3.22.76). Elsewhere Epictetus states that an unmarried person for most people would undermine the responsibilities of civic life (3.7.19, 26).

10. Deming, *Paul on Marriage and Celibacy,* 210.

11. Delling, *Paulus' Stellung zu Frau und Ehe,* BWANT 4/5 (Stuttgart: Kolhammer, 1931).

12. Ibid., 65; cf. Deidun, "Beyond Dualisms: Paul on Sex, *Sarx* and *Sōma,*" 195-205.

13. Wimbush, *Paul the Worldly Ascetic: Response to the World and Self-Understanding according to 1 Cor 7.*

14. Ibid., 90.

15. Wimbush, "The Ascetic Impulse in Ancient Christianity," 417-28.

to a dualistic understanding of the world . . . demanding a choice between sexuality and spirituality."[16]

(d) *O. Larry Yarbrough* (1985) also takes account of Paul's relation to Stoic tradition and to sociological factors, even if Deming distances himself from certain elements in his work.[17] But he is prepared to place much more emphasis than Deming on the Intertestamental writings and Rabbinic Judaism.[18] Yarbrough dissents from those who interpret 1 Corinthians 7 as an *ad hoc* reaction to the situation at Corinth, and only as that. He discusses Paul's call to holiness of life in 1 Thess 4:2-8 as a formulation for principles later expounded in 1 Corinthians 7: "For this is the will of God, even your sanctification; that you abstain from unchastity, and that each of you know how to take a wife for himself in holiness and honor . . . not like the Gentiles who do not know God" (1 Thess 4:3-5).[19] The Thessalonians passage explains how the new converts are to reorient their lifestyle in Gentile surroundings.[20] The Corinthians' own ascetic slogan in 1 Cor 7:1a initiates an expansion and pastoral application of this holiness theme, which Francis and Sampley also note as "a Pauline parallel."[21] Here, however, Yarbrough anticipates Margaret Mitchell in understanding Paul as perceiving the potential *divisiveness* of a two-tier morality, in which the spiritually "elite" claim a "higher" lifestyle.[22] At precisely this point he also anticipates Deming's point about Stoic views of marriage as an institution which promotes unity and stability for the community.[23] Thus, in M. M. Mitchell's words, the chapter may concern "other issues which are dividing the Corinthian church."[24]

(e) *Antoinette C. Wire* (1990) independently reaches Mitchell's conclusion that for Paul marriage is connected with his appeal for unity, but places this within the entirely different frame of a feminist reading of the status of women prophets at Corinth. Women prophets, she argues, had discovered a new status and indeed claimed "authority to do all things" (πάντα μοι ἔξεστιν, 6:12).[25] The Corinthian women prophets brought to the church a rich diversity of gifts which Paul (who had sacrificed high pharisaic status in exchange for a "low" apostolic one) saw as disruptive of stability, unity, and order. In this chapter "Paul seems to be making the home into a buffer zone for the people's energy. . . . Paul's advocacy of marriage to prevent immorality only makes sense if many have chosen to live without marriage. Women, as the more socially re-

16. Deming, *Paul on Marriage and Celibacy,* 224.

17. Yarbrough, *Not like the Gentiles: Marriage Rules in the Letters of Paul.*

18. Ibid., 8-17 on, e.g., Tob 4:12; *Jubilees* 22:16-20; *Testament of Levi* 9:9, 10; and 17-28 on rabbinic and diaspora traditions against a Gentile background.

19. Ibid., 65-76.

20. Ibid., 76-87.

21. Ibid., 93-96, 117-22. Cf. Francis and Sampley, *Pauline Parallels,* sect. 93 (128-29).

22. Ibid., 96-117.

23. Ibid., 107-10; cf. 32-62.

24. Mitchell, *Paul and the Rhetoric of Reconciliation,* 121.

25. A. C. Wire, *The Corinthian Women Prophets* (Minneapolis: Fortress, 1990), 14.

stricted sex, would have particular advantage in taking on the less sex-specific roles within a community."[26] Thus in the material on the Lord's Supper Paul relocates the meal aspect in the home (11:22), partly to sideline the women back into food preparation. On their side, however, the Corinthian women prophets perceive celibacy whether within marriage or in a single state to constitute a liberation from domination and an expression of their new right (ἐξουσία) to freedom. Wire argues that Paul's need to address a multiplicity of categories (married women, widows, women of marriageable age who did not wish to marry, and women who were separated from their husbands, or contemplating separation) suggests a specific "movement of considerable proportions."[27] Paul's rhetoric, she concludes, appears on the surface to advocate "mutuality" but in practice constrains the freedom of the women prophets.

(f) *Ben Witherington* (1988 and 1995). Witherington's work deserves special consideration for at least two reasons. First, whereas Deming and others have looked primarily to conceptual discussions of marriage in the Graeco-Roman world of philosophy and religion, Witherington has paid special attention to sociohistorical factors in the Roman world. Second, he has provided two complementary studies which relate to this chapter. In *Women in the Earliest Churches* (1988) Witherington discusses 1 Corinthians 7 in the context of wider issues about the role of women in Paul, other NT writings, and the subapostolic period up to the rise of Montanism, while in his *Conflict and Community in Corinth* (1995) he restricts his attention to social and rhetorical factors which influence the exegesis of this epistle.

Witherington agrees with Wire about the radical systemic and structural disadvantages for women in the Roman world, but firmly dissents from her in seeing Paul's language about mutuality in 1 Corinthians not as a rhetorical ploy but to "give women more security in marriage, and to give them freedom to abstain from marriage. . . . It is not necessary to envision a radical group of Corinthian women at odds with Paul's teaching on sexual matters. . . . Most women surely would have welcomed Paul's attempt to reform the patriarchal approach to marriage and singleness."[28] Witherington also takes full account of the role of marriage in Roman society and in Roman Corinth. Tacitus underlines the importance of "arranged marriages" as an aid to social advancement (Tacitus, *Agricola* 6.1). The division between public and "private" spheres was clear-cut, as much of Wire's argument seems to imply. Paul's concept of marriage as providing mutual support and mutual belonging is a far cry from the usual Roman view. Indeed, Paul could hardly stand further away from some *status quo,* traditionalist image against the historical data of Roman society.

Paul's emphasis on equality is genuine. Witherington endorses Bartchy's

---

26. Ibid., 16-17; cf. 80-97.

27. Ibid., 81. On 11:22, cf. 17 On Paul's rhetoric cf. 81-97. For an approach which shares certain themes but with differences cf. Gundry-Volf, "Celibate Pneumatics and Social Power. On the Motivations for Sexual Asceticism in Corinth," 105-26.

28. Witherington, *Conflict and Community,* 177; cf. 170-81.

view that the section on slavery and on circumcision in 7:17-24 is best explained not as an appeal to the *status quo* theory, but because he develops from Gal 3:28 the principle that male-female, slave-free, Jew-Gentile relations undergo a parallel change in understanding the new creation within its frame of eschatology.[29]

(g) *Brian Rosner* (1994). Like Deming, Rosner pays considerable attention to circumstantial issues of expedience, but holds that Paul owes more to OT traditions than to the Stoic-Cynic debate. Two key factors are "contentment in one's life situation" and a positive view of the body: "hatred for the body" would have "denied the goodness of creation."[30] The basic affirmation of intimacy in marriage is qualified only by particular situations or reasons of expediency.

(h) *W. Schrage* (1976, 1982, and 1995), *C. Brown* (1978), *B. Winter* (1989, 1994), and *B. B. Blue* (1991) on *Circumstantial Factors.* Schrage rightly insists that Paul's view of marriage in 1 Corinthians 7 must be seen not as a systematic exposition of his theology of marriage or of singleness, but as what emerges in confrontation with specific and contingent issues in Corinth.[31] Not only is it a mistake to regard 1 Corinthians 7 as Paul's "complete teaching concerning marriage"; we must also recognize that 7:1 constitutes a quotation from Corinth, that "in v. 2 Paul states his own opinion, which opposes this option of sexual abstinence," and especially that most of Paul's commentators mistake the force of his positive view when they caricature his view of marriage as "a necessary evil," a concession to pacify "un-Christian longings," a mere "safety-valve" . . . . "a middle way" between *enkratia* and fornication."[32] In the 1995 volume of his four-volume commentary Schrage reemphasizes that 7:2 is "the central viewpoint" from which the meaning of the issues raised is to be determined.[33] Whatever is meant by διὰ τὴν ἐνεστῶσαν ἀνάγκην in 7:26, Schrage insists that καλόν, *good* (v. 26), applies *both* to his commendation of marriage in 7:2-7 *and* to commendation of celibacy for those who receive the κλῆσις, *calling,* or χάρισμα, special *gift* for a task, in this latter case the celibate life.[34]

Colin Brown equally emphasizes the specificity of the questions and situations which Paul addresses in 1 Corinthians 7.[35] He agrees with other writers that "in principle Paul regards the marriage bond as lifelong (1 Cor 7:10-11, 39; cf. Rom 7:1-3. . . . It is grounded in the creation ordinance of Gen 2:24" (cf. Eph. 5:31).[36] But in 1 Cor 7:1-24 Paul addresses such specific questions as ob-

29. Witherington, *Women in the Earliest Churches,* 26-27.
30. Rosner, *Paul, Scripture and Ethics,* 147 and 153; cf. 147-76.
31. Schrage, "Zur Frontstellung der paulinischen Ehewertung in 1 Kor 7:1-7," 214-34.
32. Further, Schrage, *The Ethics of the NT,* 226; cf. Schrage, *Der erste Brief,* 2:50-74, 154-60, and, more broadly, 50-211.
33. Schrage, *Der erste Brief,* 2:83.
34. Ibid., 156-57.
35. C. Brown, "Separate: Divorce, Separation and Re-marriage," in Brown (ed.), *NIDNTT,* 3:535-43; cf. also H. Reisser and W. Günther, "Marriage," *NIDNTT,* 2:579-84.
36. Ibid., 535.

ligations within marriage and the continuation of mixed marriages. In the latter case separation may be a possible course, but only if maintaining the marriage proves to be a coercive imposition. Brown links ch. 7 closely with serious sexual deviations relating to "the body" in chs. 5 and 6 and urges that "Paul sees the normal married life as the divine provision for man's natural needs."[37] Alternatives relate to special circumstances and gifts. Since a flagrant breach of the covenant bond by adultery would have ended in death in the OT but in excommunication in the church (cf. Lev 20:10-12; Deut 22:22; 1 Cor 5:5, 9-11), and since death terminates the mariage bond (Rom 7:2, 3), Brown argues that on such a basis it is consistent to understand 7:27-28 as encouraging freedom to remarry.[38] "For those who find their marriages broken beyond repair . . . remarriage is not a sin" (1 Cor 7:27-28).[39] "If we have not the gift of celibacy, the unmarried state can be more a hindrance than a help" (vv. 2ff., 5, 9, 36ff."[40] (See the extended note on "Divorce and Remarriage" after 7:16.)

Whether περὶ δὲ τῶν παρθένων (7:25) is understood in its more usual sense of *those who have not as yet married* or in the less usual but still possible sense of *those who at present are unmarried* (whether or not they were previously married), the circumstantial role of 7:26-28 must be taken into account. While ἀνάγκη (v. 26) may mean *pressure, distress* (Collins) or even *dislocation* (Winter), the term may carry eschatological or historical connotations, or perhaps both.[41] Bruce Winter builds up a careful case for the view that it denotes the distress and "dislocation" associated with famines in Greece during the reign of Claudius, one of which can be dated around AD 51.[42] Tacitus alludes to AD 51 as an "ominous year."[43] Without question, food shortages had very considerable effects on city populations, and the only serious objection to Winter's argument may arise from whether the commercial prosperity of Corinth made it immune to such hardship. However, two counterreplies can be offered. First, its very prosperity would have encouraged inflated prices for grain which the poor could not manage; second, J. J. Meggitt's work on the marginal subsistence level of many urban poor reinforces the reality of the plight of the poor at such times.[44] Even granted that the civic authorities would appoint a *curator annonae* or curator of grain to oversee supplies and to arrange subsidies, while wealthy households could afford to buy grain, "non-slave laborers and artisans" would suffer badly in

---

37. Ibid., 536.

38. Ibid., 537.

39. Ibid.

40. Ibid.

41. Collins, *First Corinthians,* 293, rightly observes: "'Distress' *(anagke)* is not necessarily a term with eschatological connotations" (see exegesis below).

42. Winter, "Secular and Christian Responses to Corinthian Famines"; reaffirmed in Winter, *Seek the Welfare of the City,* 53-57; see further 145-64 on "calling."

43. Tacitus, *Annals* 12.43.

44. See the Introduction, 23-29, and the exegesis of 1:26 on the arguments of J. J. Meggitt, *Paul, Poverty and Survival* (Edinburgh: T. & T. Clark, 1998).

such times of "present dislocation."[45] This becomes all the more significant in the light of Cynic-Stoic discussions of marriage by, e.g., Hierocles, Musonius, and Epictetus. Musonius concedes that in spite of the advantages of marriage, its added responsibilities increase "self-imposed poverty."[46] B. B. Blue further underlines (although mainly also in relation to 11:17-34) the probability of allusion to famine in AD 51 when Tiberius Claudius Dinippus was *curator annonae*.[47]

In spite of Blomberg's comment that "it is hard to determine how significant some lingering effects of earlier famines were," a connection between a possible eschatological dimension and historical-contingent events which underline the fragility and vulnerability of the present world order cannot be excluded.[48] (See the note on "Eschatological Imminence" in 7:29-31 below.) Meggitt's claims about the margins of survival for nonslave artisans, together with Deming's arguments about the added weight of married responsibilities (see under [a] above), underline the cumulative effect of specific circumstances relevant to the issues in the middle period of the first century. Epictetus comments on the numerous burdens of obligations which accompany marriage in this context: obligations (Gk. δεῖ) to render services to a father-in-law, to other in-laws and relatives of the wife (συγγενέσι), and to the wife herself, and duties to nurse and to provide for the whole family.[49] Circumstantial issues do indeed enter into Paul's advocacy of that style of life to which a given person has been called.

Summarizing Note: An Overview of the Chapter, Especially Distinctive Concerns about Marriage and Inferences from the Patristic Posthistory of Chapter 7 for Celibacy

1. Marriage. It would be a mistake to regard the whole of ch. 7 as addressing the issues of marriage. 7:10-11, e.g., discusses separation initiated by one married partner; 7:12-16 addresses the issue of Christians married to unbelieving spouses; and 7:39-40 affirms the freedom of the widowed to remarry. Two aspects of marriage are considered under 7:1-7 and 7:8-9: intimacy and mutuality within marriage, and circumstances relating to a decision to marry. In spite of the positive contribution of Balch, Wimbush, Yarbrough, and Deming on overlappings between Paul's approach and Stoic-Cynic debates on the advantages and disadvantages of the married state, one key factor is omitted which

---

45. Winter, *Seek the Welfare,* 55 and 57.

46. Musonius, *Is Marriage a Handicap?* 90:1–92:6. See also O. L. Yarbrough, *Not like the Gentiles: Marriage Rules in the Letters of Paul.* 38-46

47. Blue, "The House Church at Corinth and the Lord's Supper: Famine, Food Supply and the Present Distress," 221-39.

48. Blomberg, *1 Cor,* 151, n. 1.

49. Epictetus, *Dissertations,* 3.22.70-71.

R. B. Ward rightly identifies as distinctive to Paul.[50] Musonius the Stoic argued that sexual or erotic desire (ἀφροδίσια) could be justified within marriage only "for the purpose of begetting children. . . . [It] is unlawful when it is mere pleasure-seeking (ἡδονή) even within marriage."[51]

Without doubt the allusion to abstinence from physical intimacy (the context implies that the reference is to that within marriage) comes not from Paul but from Corinth (7:1). It is part of the topic indicator of explicit response to the letter from Corinth. The suggestion that it represents a quotation from a Corinthian viewpoint is no mere construct of modern critical theories. In the third century Origen argued that the slogan reflected confusion or discord (ἀκαταστασία) in the Corinthian church initiated by those who argued that ascetic abstinence was "a good thing" (καλόν).[52] Origen provides a convincing scenario of the Corinthian ascetic (probably "spiritual") spokesperson: "You are not abusing her, you say, but claiming that you can be chaste and live more purely. But look how your poor wife is being destroyed as a result, because she is unable to endure your 'purity.' You should sleep with your wife, not for your sake but for hers."[53] Paul is concerned that any abstinence should be a mutual decision and only for a short time (7:5).[54]

Ware points out that this attitude toward intimacy as an expression of *needed love* is distinctive to Paul over against most writing of the time (i.e., on marriage) in the Roman world. Ovid the Latin poet believed that "there could be no erotic pleasure *(amor)* between husband and wife because it was a relationship of duty."[55] By contrast, Ward asserts, Paul does not even mention procreation as the dutiful purpose of married love, and far from criticizing erotic desire within marriage urges that it takes its rightful place. As Colin Brown argues (see above), the positive bodily union in this context complements what Paul has said about its necessary absence in nonmarital contexts in 6:12-20, and this emphasis is confirmed indirectly by Goulder.[56] Ward makes a startling assertion on the basis of 7:1-9: "Paul, in effect, redefined marriage as a context for the mutual satisfying of erotic desires" in contrast to traditional ideas that "the purpose of marriage was the procreation of legitimate heirs who would inherit and continue the name, property and sacred rites of the family."[57]

Striking as Ward's comments are, we must not neglect Schrage's circumstantial warning that "we must first avoid the misconception that 1 Corinthians

---

50. Ward, "Musonius and Paul on Marriage," 281-89.

51. Musonius, *Is Marriage a Handicap?* 85:5-6.

52. Origen, *1 Cor, Fragment* 33, in *JTS* 9 (1908): 500-501.

53. Ibid., 501.

54. Cf. Yarbrough, *Not like the Gentiles,* 97.

55. Ward, "Musonius and Paul on Marriage," 285; Ovid, *Ars Amatoriae* 2.585-86; cf. 2.685.

56. M. D. Goulder, "Libertines? (1 Cor 5–6)," *NovT* 41 (1999): 334-48; Brown, *NIDNTT,* 3:535-36.

57. Ward, "Musonius and Paul on Marriage," 286-87.

7 provides something like a complete Pauline teaching concerning marriage."[58] The circumstantial aspects of 1 Corinthians 7 cut both ways on some major questions. Nevertheless, Ward's observations place in their proper context what might otherwise appear to be a grudgingly concessionary tone about "desire" and "self-control" in vv. 2a, 6, 7a, and esp. 9. Indeed, in a second study Schrage urges that τοῦτο δὲ λέγω κατὰ συγγνώμην (*I say this by way of concession,* v. 6) refers not to marrying but only to a temporary agreed abstinence.[59]

Murphy-O'Connor is not quite as positive on this point as Ward and Schrage, but complements their work in one respect. He perceives that in asceticism "there was an element of idealism that struck a chord in Paul. He himself lived a life of sexual asceticism (vv. 7-8), and believed that someone like him [i.e., who had this *charisma,* 7:7] could . . . live a more ordered (v. 35), less anxious (v. 32), less troubled (v. 28) and happier life (v. 40)."[60] However, Murphy-O'Connor continues, Paul "did not fall into the trap of imagining that what was best for him was best for everyone else."[61] We cannot always easily transfer a theoretical ideal "into a concrete situation"; Paul's aim is to inject "a note of realism [into] . . . an exaggerated idealism. Paul simply asks them to look at reality."[62]

Provided that we do not lose the positive evaluations of the sexual and physical underlined by Schrage and by Ward, Murphy-O'Connor offers an equally valid line of approach. In other parts of this epistle Paul will say more about complementarity, mutuality, and reciprocity (see below, e.g., on 11:7-12). Paul's advice to those who have been widowed (7:8-9, 39-40) falls broadly into the patterns of issues set out above. We should recall that in the ancient world disease, lack of hygiene, poverty, and violence often led to a short average life expectancy, even if exceptions occurred. An inscription "In praise of Turia" probably alludes to life span as well as to frequent, often multiple, divorce: "Marriages as long as ours are rare, marriages that are ended by death and not broken by divorce."[63]

2. *Inferences from Patristic Posthistory of Chapter 7 for "Celibacy."* There is general agreement that in 1 Corinthians 5–7 Paul envisages *either* physical union within marriage *or* celibacy. However, the complementary question to that raised about marriage is whether Paul, with some in Corinth, views celibacy as a "higher" calling, or simply that to which some are called, while others are called to marriage. C. H. Giblin places the issue firmly within the

---

58. Schrage, *Ethics of the NT,* 226.

59. Schrage, "Zur Frontstellung der paulinischen Ehebewertung in 1 Kor 7:2-7"; cf. *Der erste Brief,* 2:67-72.

60. J. Murphy-O'Connor, *1 Cor,* 59.

61. Ibid.

62. Ibid., 60. Derrett, "The Disposal of Virgins," 23-30, anticipates this argument with reference to 7:29-30 and 36-38. Fathers should not impose upon their daughters the supposedly "higher" celibacy advocated by some at Corinth.

63. Inscription *Laudatio Turiae* 1:27, cited by Yarbrough, *Not like the Gentiles,* 63.

framework of Paul's insistence that all Christians are one, and every charisma is equally necessary for the church (12:12-31): "Paul implies no 'second rate' Christianity in the area of marriage," but there also exist "a variety of charismatic functions," of which celibacy may constitute one.[64] He concludes that "Paul's counsels on virginity are basically encouragement to participate in his own prophetic and apostolic outlook . . . rather than a concern for the world."[65]

The second sentence, however, goes beyond the first, and is more open to question than the more perceptive first sentence. By contrast, Josephine Massingberd Ford has argued that in 1 Corinthians 7 Paul was not discussing virginity or celibacy but second marriages.[66] The aim of her second article, on the patristic exegesis of 1 Corinthians 7, is to show that in 1 Corinthians 7 and in the earliest churches "consecrated virginity was not a customary way of life."[67] She demonstrates without difficulty that this chapter was not understood to promote this lifestyle in earliest patristic exegesis, and that it began to function as an appeal for, and defense of, this only when at a later period the celibate life became an official vocation. The turning point comes with Cyprian's *De Habitu Virginum* in the mid-third century, together with Pseudo-Cyprian's *De Bono Pudicitiae* and *De Singularitate Clericorum*. By the fourth century Athanasius has five treatises on virginity, and Ambrose has seven.

Clement of Alexandria's very explicit treatise on continence attacks gnostic disparagements of marriage, but his opponents do not appeal to 1 Cor 7:25, 36-38 in support of this view. They use Matt 19:12; 22:30; Rom 6:14; and 1 Cor 7:5, 39-40. On the other hand, Clement appeals to 1 Cor 7:2, 5, and 27 in defense of marriage.[68] It is Clement's recognition of the seeming inconsistency of *let them get married* in v. 36, and *gives in marriage* in v. 38, that appears to J. M. Ford to confirm her suggestion about Levirate marriage in which "a man both gives and receives the same woman in marriage."[69] We have already discussed Origen's reconstruction of the main issue in 1 Corinthians 7 in our Note above. As Ford observes, Origen underlines Paul's concern "to stress equality and justice in the marriage bond."[70] She adds: Origen appears to think that the concession [7:6] refers to second marriages . . . not to first marriage."[71] ἄγαμος, she argues, means *widower*, not *celibate person*, in Paul, and in Origen it may denote *continence* rather than *virginity*.

64. Giblin, "1 Cor 7: A Negative Theology of Marriage and Celibacy?" *BT* 41 (1969): 2,853; cf. 2,839-55.

65. Ibid., 2,855. See further Wolbert, *Ethische Argumentation und Paränese in 1 Kor 7*, 72-134 and 192-202.

66. J. M. Ford, "Levirate Marriage in St Paul," *NTS* 10 (1964): 361-65; and "St. Paul the Philogamist (1 Cor vii in Early Patristic Exegesis)," 326-48.

67. Ford, "St. Paul the Philogamist," 326.

68. Clement, *Stromata*, 3:6; cf. also 3.12.

69. Ford, "St. Paul the Philogamist," 328; "Levirate Marriage in Paul," 364.

70. Origen, *1 Cor, Fragment* 33, in *JTS* 9 (1908): 501; Ford, "St. Paul the Philogamist," 329.

71. Ibid., 330; cf. also H. Crouzel, *Virginité et marriage selon Origèn* (Paris: Desclée de Brouwer, 1962), 80.

An idiosyncratic change of climate emerges with Tertullian, concerning whom J. M. Ford emphasizes the influence of Montanism during the period when he wrote *Ad Uxorem* and *De Monogamia*.[72] Tertullian accepts the creation order of marriage as "one flesh" (Gen 2:21-22).[73] However, in his use of 1 Corinthians 7 Tertullian argues that Paul advises against the remarriage of those who have been widowed, even if it is not forbidden (with the proviso that this is marriage to a fellow Christian).[74] Yet Tertullian also seems to imply that remarriage is forbidden, and Ford concludes that "no decisive conclusion about Tertullian's exegesis of 1 Cor vii" is possible, except that it is "profoundly different from either Clement's or Origen's."[75] A still more decisive move is found in Methodius, who perhaps for the first time understands the commendation of abstinence in 7:1 as Paul's own words, even if he then qualifies them because of human weakness.[76] Methodius argues from 1 Corinthians 7 that Paul enjoins celibacy, with marriage only for those who find it a necessity. Finally, Ambrose "regarded 1 Cor vii as his 'proof text' " on the subject of virginity.[77] Apart from the idiosyncrasies of Tertullian, Ford concludes, the earlier patristic witnesses (Clement and Origen) understand 1 Corinthians 7 to reflect an entirely positive view of marriage. Only with Methodius and Ambrose at the close of the third century and the fourth century does the notion of looking to 1 Corinthians 7 for support for "celibacy" or "virginity" as a "higher" calling emerge.

1. Marriage and Marital Intimacy (7:1-7)

(1) Now for the matters about which you wrote: "It is a good thing for a man not to have physical intimacy with a woman." (2) On the contrary, on account of cases of irregular physical intimacy, let each man hold to his own wife, and let each woman hold to her own husband. (3, 4) Let the husband give to his wife what is due to her, and similarly the wife what is due to her husband. The wife does not have exclusive rights over her own body but the husband: similarly also the husband does not have exclusive rights over his own body but the wife. (5) Stop depriving each other of what is due in marriage, except perhaps by mutual agreement for a specific span of time, that you may find unhurried time for prayer, and then come back together again. The goal would be nullified if Satan went on putting you through trials beyond your self-control. (6) I say this by way of concession, not as a command. (7) To be sure, I should like everybody to be as I myself am too. But each per-

---

72. Dated by Ford about AD 200-206 and AD 217 respectively.
73. Tertullian, *Ad Uxorem,* 1:2.
74. Ibid., 2.2-5.
75. Ford, "St. Paul the Philogamist," 342.
76. Methodius, *Conviviales* [*Symposium*], 3:11-12 (Methodius of Olympus, c. 260-311).
77. Ford, "St. Paul the Philogamist," 344; cf. Ambrose, *De Virginibus,* 1:5:23; 1:6:24; *De Institutione Virginitate* 1:2; *Exhortatio Virginitatibus* 7:46 (Ambrose of Milan, c. 339-97).

son has his or her own gift freely bestowed from God: one person, this kind; another, that kind.

1 We have already considered the relation between the formula περὶ δέ and the Corinthians' letter, with reference to the views of Hurd, Mitchell, and others.[78] The traditional translation *Now concerning* . . . (NRSV, AV/KJV) accurately translates περί with the genitive. But, as Allo observes, the formula signals a new topic for discussion. Hence the translation **Now for** . . . (REB, NIV, NJB) more forcefully conveys the dynamic equivalence which these latter English versions seek, and in this context is to be preferred.

Whether the clause καλὸν ἀνθρώπῳ γυναικὸς μὴ ἅπτεσθαι constitutes a Pauline statement which he will modify, a question form, or a quotation from Corinth is a notorious crux. An increasing consensus inclines towards this last view, and the arguments for it carry convincing weight. Writers who view it as a quotation from Corinth include Schrage, Collins, and Lang ("ein Schlagwort der Korinthischen Schwärmer").[79] Several specialist monographs also regard 7:1 as a quotation from Corinth.[80] This explanation of 7:1b goes back to Origen, who ascribes to a group at Corinth the stance, Ἐγὼ δύναμαι ἐγκατεύεσθαι καὶ ζῆν καθαρώτερον . . . τοιοῦτον τι γέγονεν ἐν κορίνθῳ . . . ἔγραψαν οὖν περὶ τούτου ἐπιστολὴν οἱ ἐν κορίνθῳ τῷ ἀποστόλῳ . . . (*Fragment* 33 [121]:8-14).[81]

The arguments are compelling. (a) A first strong argument in favor of this view, which has been advocated by Schrage and Martin (among others), derives from the structural similarity with the undoubted quotations in 8:1, almost certainly 8:8, and probably also 8:5-6. The twenty-five scholars cited by Hurd for a variety of views are unanimous in ascribing 8:1 to the Corinthians themselves.[82] (b) Second, this view is further supported by additional arguments in articles by Schrage, Merklein, and Phipps.[83] Phipps forcefully argues that the

---

78. See general introduction to 7:1–11:1; Mitchell, "Concerning περὶ δέ in 1 Cor," 229-56; *Paul and the Rhetoric of 1 Corinthians,* 190-91; Hurd, *Origin of 1 Corinthians,* 61-71; Allo, *Première Épitre,* 153: δέ marque ici le passage à un nouveau sujet."

79. Lang, *Die Briefe,* 89; Schrage, *Der erste Brief,* 2:59; Collins, *First Cor,* 252 and 258; Fee, *First Epistle,* 272-77, esp. 276 (cf. Fee, "1 Cor. 7:1 in the NIV," 307-14); cf. also Kistemaker, *1 Cor,* 109; Barrett, *First Epistle,* 154-55; Hurd, *Origin of 1 Corinthians,* 120-23, 163; Moffatt, *First Epistle,* 75; Bruce, *1 and 2 Cor,* 66; Goudge, *First Epistle,* 53; Parry, *First Epistle,* 70; and J. Jeremias, "Die Briefzitate in 1 Kor 8:1-13," a section of his "Zur Gedankenführung in den paulinischen Briefen," in J. N. Sevenster and W. C. van Unnik (eds.), *Studia Paulina in Honorem Johannis de Zwaan* (Haarlem: Bohn, 1953), 151-53.

80. Wire, *Corinthian Women Prophets,* 87; Martin, *The Corinthian Body,* 205; Deming, *Paul on Marriage,* 110-14 and 122; Rosner, *Paul, Scripture and Ethics,* 151; and Yarbrough, *Not like the Gentiles,* 93-96.

81. Text in Jenkins (ed.), "Origen on 1 Cor," *JTS* 9 (1908): 500.

82. Hurd, *Origin of 1 Corinthians,* 68. Collins recently strengthened the argument: the issue was probably "in the air" (*First Cor,* 252-53).

83. Schrage, "Zur Frontstellung der paulinischen Ehebewertung in 1 Kor 7:1-7," 214-34; W. E. Phipps, "Is Paul's Attitude towards Sexual Relations Contained in 1 Cor. 7:1?" 125-31;

slogan can neither be Paul's, nor even a Corinthian slogan with which Paul agrees; but only a slogan from Corinth with which he will express serious disagreement and which he will accept only with very important modifications and qualifications for given situations. (c) Among other arguments, whereas Yarbrough, Kistemaker, and Rosner stress Paul's continuity in this chapter with the OT, as it stands 7:1b would contradict what Paul would regard as a divine ordinance: "It is *not* good for the man to be alone" (Gen 2:18).[84] (d) It is no accident that in the major epistles Paul associates physical union within marriage with σῶμα rather than with σάρξ, to ensure that no hint of any dualism between "the spiritual" and the physical occurs. Paul's language moves "beyond dualisms."[85] (e) This view is no novel insight of modern scholars, but goes back as early as Origen. (f) Finally, Hurd traces a convincing analogy of *content* as well as style in the quotations of 8:1, 6. In each case those at Corinth "had chosen the superior . . . and more dangerous course of action. . . . The Corinthians' attitudes towards idol meat and marital intercourse are entirely consistent."[86]

Against this impressive array of arguments, we can find only one of modest weight, one which is relatively speculative, and one which merely modifies the force of 7:1b to attempt to interpret it as compatible with Paul's outlook.

(a) Conzelmann argues that the use of καλόν with the dative at 7:1, 7:8, and 7:26 establishes this as "Pauline style."[87] But the phrase is too short and too readily taken up from widespread discussions in the Graeco-Roman world to be considered a specific or exclusive indicator of Paul's style. Deming carefully cuts the ground from under this argument, and examples in non-Pauline literature can be cited.

(b) Mitchell's argument that Paul uses it as a rhetorical strategy of appearing to begin "on their side" does admittedly cohere with Paul's practice of using his readers' terminology, only to redefine it or to "switch codes." But the stance changes too abruptly to perceive this as a subtle strategy at this point. She is obliged to describe his rhetoric in this case as "an oscillating argument," which in spite of Blomberg's "Yes, but . . ." argument, which Paul uses elsewhere, places her approach too near to Delling's in contrast to Deming's to sustain conviction.[88]

(c) Most writers who reject the view that 7:1b is a quotation follow Calvin in defining or expounding καλόν in such a way that it virtually dies the death of a thousand qualifications as a serious statement of moral stance. Calvin believed that Paul "teaches first that it would be 'good' if every man kept away from a woman, provided that he has the power to do so. In the second place he modifies

Merklein, "'Es ist gut für den Menschen eine Frau nicht anzufassen': Paulus und die Sexualität nach 1 Kor 7," in Dautzenberg (ed.), *Die Frau im Urchristentum*, 230-31.

84. Kistemaker, *1 Cor*, 209.
85. Deldun, "Beyond Dualisms: Paul on Sex, Sarx and *Sōma*," 195-205.
86. Hurd, *Origin of 1 Corinthians*, 165 and 164.
87. Conzelmann, *1 Cor*, 115, n. 10.
88. Deming, *Paul on Marriage*, 111-13.

this. . . ."[89] But how does this meet the problem that at best makes either (i) marriage or (ii) intimacy within marriage a kind of "second-best," which is at odds with Gen 2:18, which implies "not good"? To be sure, Calvin hastily distances himself from Jerome, who was "swept off his feet by excessive zeal" and defines "good" wholly in pragmatic terms relating to "annoyances and responsibilities."[90] Calvin acknowledges that in Gen 2:18 it is "good" for a man to have the "help" of a companion, but in these more evil days it has become "good but only to a degree." In other words, faced with an insoluble problem, Calvin ends up with a contrast not between "good" and "disadvantageous," but between "good" and "good only to a degree." But in 7:1-7 it appears that *marriage* or *intimacy, not* celibacy, is what is "good, only to a degree."[91]

The spread of English versions offers an interesting commentary by way of summary. NRSV rightly uses quotation marks where RSV previously had none; REB uses quotation marks where NEB had none, although it added a marginal alternative with quotation marks; NJB follows JB in identifying a quotation, but one which Paul endorses: *Yes, it is a good thing for a man. . . .* The AV/KJV has no quotation marks. Surprisingly the NIV also lacks quotation marks, and Fee addresses this.[92]

In the middle voice ἅπτεσθαι with the genitive means *to touch* or *to take hold of,* but it occurs widely in Greek literature as a euphemism for *to have sexual intercourse with,* or **to have physical intimacy with** (here followed by γυναικός).[93] In order to leave open the vexed question of whether the point at issue concerns the beginnings of such a relationship, i.e., marriage (Grosheide), or a relationship of physical intimacy within an existing marriage (Hurd), or any intimacy without specification, we translate γυναικός as **with a woman** (with REB, NRSV, NJB, and most English VSS), but in theory the Greek could mean *with his wife.* On the focus on the conduct of **a man** (ἀνθρώπῳ in contrast here to γυναικός, although often meaning *a person*) Conzelmann suggests that the lack of gender symmetry arises from how the question was formulated at Corinth.[94] Wolff suggests that ἄνθρωπος is used in place of ἀνήρ to include the unmarried as well as the married.[95] Chrysostom concludes that although marriage may be "safe and helpful to your own weakness," in principle "the superior course" is "not to have any connection whatever with a woman."[96]

89. Mitchell, *Paul and the Rhetoric of Reconciliation,* 235-36; cf. 122-23; and Blomberg, *1 Cor,* 133.

90. Calvin, *First Epistle,* 134.

91. Ibid., 136; cf. 134-35.

92. Fee, "1 Cor. 7:1 in the NIV," 272-77.

93. For example, Plato, *Leges* 8.840A; Plutarch (c. AD 50-120), *Anthony* 1.17.13; *Alexander* 21.9; Josephus (c. AD 37-97), *Antiquities* 1.163; cf. R. Grob, *NIDNTT,* 3:859-61; BAGD, 102-3. Grosheide refers the term to marriage, as a figurative use of the term; but Hurd argues against this (in addition to supplying lexicographical evidence).

94. Conzelmann, *1 Cor,* 115, n. 10.

95. Wolff, *Der erste Brief,* 134.

96. Chrysostom, *1 Cor. Hom.,* 19:1.

Although Parry and Héring argue that καλόν means only *pragmatically salutary,* Meyer anticipates much subsequent research in discerning a widespread formula for "a moral axiom, a statement of what is *ethically* salutary" (his italics), although he rejects Jerome's use of the verse to defend "celibacy in general."[97] Allo and Lietzmann interpret it as *a higher good,* in contrast to the view of Jerome and Tertullian that it is an *absolute good.*[98]

2   If, as we have argued, v. 1b is best understood as a quotation from Corinth with which Paul does not wholly agree, the adversative particle δέ needs to be rendered with due force, such as **On the contrary**. We should next note that τὰς πορνείας is an articular accusative noun *in the plural.* Hence it need not be taken to suggest (as the traditional AV/KJV translation *to avoid fornication* may seem to imply) that the main reason for marriage, or for intimacy within marriage, is to provide an alternative to indiscriminate sexual relations, but that **cases** (plural) *of fornication* (Barrett) at Corinth give special point to Paul's injunction here.[99] Indeed, the definite article τάς, while technically it may qualify any abstract noun, here seems likely to imply a specific allusion to **the cases of irregular physical intimacy** which he has identified in 5:1-5, 6:12-20, and possibly indirectly in 6:9-10. REB captures the issue by translating, *Rather, in the face of so much immorality . . .* (although this overtranslates).

Against this background Paul advocates "a full conjugal life" (Rosner) against the background of Gen 2:18 and the Decalogue.[100] Deming rightly declares, "The Judaeo-Christian component of his argument appears most prominently in verse 2."[101] The use of the wide-ranging verb ἔχω (present imperative ἐχέτω) receives its particular nuance from its close syntagmatic proximity with τὴν ἑαυτοῦ γυναῖκα and τὸν ἴδιον ἄνδρα. In the active voice the verb may mean **hold** or *keep* as well as *have,* whether in the sense of *having* a possession, *holding* a weapon, or *keeping* something safely (e.g., Luke 19:20). The force of *keeping* probably does not refer *only to retaining* a prior marriage status, since

97. Meyer, *First Epistle,* 1:193. Jerome asserts: *Si bonum est mulierem non tangere, malum ergo est tangere, Adversus Jovinianum,* 1:4).

98. Allo, *Première Épitre,* 153-54; as against Jerome, *Adv. Jovin.* 1:4, 7, and Tertullian, *On Monogamy,* 3: "'Good', he [Paul] says. . . . For nothing is contrary to good except evil." In *On Monogamy,* 9 Tertullian stresses the concessive status of marriage "by way of allowance" for those who were anxious about whether they could enjoy their married state without guilt.

99. Barrett, *First Epistle.* 155. Edwards, *First Epistle,* 157 similarly takes the plural to refer to "the prevalence of fornication in Corinth," which is part of Paul's "reason" here. But a critical literature has emerged on πορνεία in this kind of context; cf. B. Malina, "Does *Porneia* Mean Fornication?" *NovT* 14 (1972): 10-17; the reply by J. Jensen, "Does *Porneia* Mean Fornication? A Critique of Bruce Malina," *NovT* 20 (1978): 161-84; and Fee, *First Epistle,* 277-78; including nn. 44-47. Malina argues that πορνεία includes a variety of "irregular" or "illicit" acts prohibited by the Torah, including prebetrothed or premarital intercourse; Jensen argues that it means fornication, including sexual abuse; Fee argues that the word points to actual occurrences at Corinth.

100. Rosner, *Paul, Scripture and Ethics,* 149-61; Yarbrough, *Not like the Gentiles,* 3-28; cf. 65-96.

101. Deming, *Paul on Marriage,* 116.

in this case we might have expected κατέχειν.[102] The key to its special nuance lies in the usual force of the middle voice, which has to do with "inner belonging and close association" (BAGD).[103] In this verse this sense is achieved by twice repeating a reflexive pronoun of personal interest: ἑαυτοῦ, **his own**, and τὸν ἴδιον, **her own**. The net effect is a double imperative, **let him hold to his own wife, let her hold to her own husband**, as against the **cases of irregular physical intimacy**. Here πορνείας has more to do with semantic and moral *contrast* than with issues of *causation* in relation to the holiness of the Christian community.

This approach and explanation would receive added confirmation if behind Paul's language there lies the perplexing phenomenon of so-called "spiritual relationships" with virgins vowed to chastity who in the subapostolic and patristic era appear to have cohabited with Christian men on occasion and may conceivably be the subject of 7:36-38 (if certain interpretations of those verses are accepted). In the *Shepherd of Hermas,* while the Shepherd rests in the midst of his visions, Hermas is invited to spend the night "alone with the virgins. . . . 'You will sleep with us,' they said, 'as a brother, and not as a husband' (ὡς ἀδελφός, καὶ οὐχ ὡς ἀνήρ). . . . She [their leader] kissed me. . . . I slept beside the tower. . . . And I without ceasing prayed with them . . . and remained until the next day . . ." (*Similitude* 9:10:6–11:8 dated c. AD 160). H. Achelis has appealed to this kind of example to suggest the notion of "spiritual" quasi-marriages at Corinth.[104] Parallels of some kind appear in Tertullian, Cyprian, and Eusebius.[105] But whether the idiosyncratic Hermas and scattered references of an occasional nature can be read into 1 Corinthians 7 is unclear and doubtful.

On the other hand, the evidence of these writings may indeed suggest *a*

---

102. Edwards, *First Epistle,* 157.

103. BAGD, 331-34, for a multiplicity of context-governed uses, esp. III (334).

104. Achelis, *Virgines Subintroductae: Ein Beitrag zum VII Kapitel des 1 Korintherbriefs,* and Deming's critique in *Paul on Marriage,* 40-47.

105. Tertullian, *On Monogamy,* 16, "What if he pleads the loneliness of his home? [i.e., on the death of his wife]. . . . He has a widow at hand . . . even a plurality it is permitted to have" [but not to raise children]; *Exhortation to Chastity,* 12: " 'In my widowed state a partner in domestic activities is necessary'. Then take some spiritual wife . . . from among the widows, one fair in faith . . . sealed with age. . . . Shall the servant of God yearn after heirs, who has disinherited himself from the world?" (c. AD 200-225); Cyprian, *Epistle,* 61:2, "To Pomponius concerning Virgins": "We should not allow virgins to dwell with men, I do not say to sleep together, but to live together. . . . No one who is near to danger is long safe. . . . They may be separated while they can still be separated in innocence." In other words, Achelis perceives here a situation which presupposes "spiritual" cohabitation but which Cyprian calls into question (c. AD 240-250); Achelis, *Virgines Subintroductae,* 7-9; and Eusebius, *Ecclesiastical History,* 7:30:12: "And there are women, the *'subintroductae'* (συνείσακτοι) [came to mean children born out of wedlock], as the people of Antioch call them, who belong to him [Paul of Samosata] and to the presbyters and deacons who are with him." The Latin and Greek terms may mean those who keep house for celibate priests, but later θυγατέρες συνείσακτοι became a term for children born out of wedlock in a church-related context (cf. LSJ and commentaries on Eusebius).

lack of realism about "spiritual" relationships which may well add a further circumstantial explanatory strand to Paul's διὰ δὲ τὰς πορνείας. In this case *the issue is not two-level morality but pastoral realism,* and has nothing to do with any dualist view of the body or devaluation of marriage as "for the weak." Some see later isolated references to "spiritual" co-habiting as a sign of perennial unrealism among self-styled "people of the Spirit," Balch's suggestion about the practice of celibacy out of a desire to receive divine revelations or visions. If these have a measure of plausibility, weight is added when Blomberg observes, "With prostitutes and mistresses abundantly available (recall 6:12-20) Corinthian men unable to have sex with their wives would often look elsewhere."[106] Peterman has reinforced from the papyri and from Plutarch the double standards of a degree of extramarital relationships in the case of men in the Roman world, in contrast to married women.[107] Paul's moral and pastoral principle remains *either* (a) *monogamy* (with a full relationship for most of the time; cf. v. 5); *or* (b) celibacy; but *not* (c) *irregular* physical relationships.[108] Paul's injunctions to be content with one's situation are not his central point, but offer an antidote to a *Corinthian* desire to change everything with their new-found status.[109]

3-4 The accusative ὀφειλήν, *obligation, duty,* **what is** *one's* **due** (figuratively from *debt*), is without doubt the valid reading (supported by ${\wp}^{11}$, apparent ${\wp}^{46}$, ℵ, A, B, C, D, F, 33, Coptic, Tertullian, Clement, Origen, Cyprian. A later reading found in K, L, many minuscules, and Syriac VSS changes the Greek to due kindness (ὀφειλομένην εὔνοιαν), thereby "spiritualizing" the verse in precisely the way Paul rejects. This gloss may be a misguided attempt at good taste; but it is more likely to reflect a thoroughly un-Pauline attitude to the body and to sex.

On the distinctive emphasis and pattern of Paul's positive attitude toward intimate affection within marriage against a contrasting background in Roman and Corinthian thought, see "Summarizing Note" toward the end of the introduction to ch. 7. Wolff emphasizes Paul's concern for "partnership" in marriage at every level: *"Frau-Mann; Mann-Frau, wird die Totalität partnerschaftlicher ehelicher Gemeinschaft unterstrichen."*[110] If Wire carries credibility in her hypothesis about woman prophets with reference to these verses, part of the mutual expectations **due** in marriage is the sharing of a home, rather than two independent lifestyles in which marriage obligations of mutual support and

---

106. Blomberg, *1 Cor,* 133; cf. Balch, "Backgrounds of 1 Cor vii," 351-64, where he appeals to Philo's *Life of Moses* 2.66-70 for the notion.

107. Peterman, "Marriage and Sexual Fidelity in the Papyri, Plutarch and Paul," 163-72, e.g., *BGU* 1052 (13 BC); Plutarch, *Moralia* 139C, 140B and D.

108. The contrasting situation of polygamy is referred to by Justin, *Dialogue with Trypho,* 134: ". . . for each man to have four or five wives. . . ."

109. Wimbush, *Paul the Worldly Ascetic,* 21.

110. Wolff, *Der erste Brief,* 135. Also Collins, *First Cor,* 255: ". . . focuses on mutuality and on physical communion."

companionship as well as intimacy have been sidelined in the interest of the "rights" (ἔξεστιν, 6:12) of the individual.[111] Wire even considers the possibility that in the Apocalypse of John "Jezebel" the prophetess is described as immoral because "this charge of immorality may be a reference to leaving a marriage or to drawing other women away from sexual relations."[112] The present imperative ἀποδιδότω continues the imperatival structure of v. 2, corroborating that these are jussives, not merely permissive third singular imperatives. The present may imply that the ascetics were not in the majority at Corinth: the believers are to continue the established practice (rather than to return to it, as aorist would imply). On the other hand, the present may simply denote a habitual practice.

Most writers and commentators have drawn attention to ὁμοίως as a signal of Paul's concern for mutuality, reciprocity, or equality in the marriage relationship, not least in this sphere. But Wire views this as deceptive rhetoric: "some people are being manoeuvred back into sexual relations within their marriages."[113] Because Paul does not ask the strong to help the weak but uses a rhetoric of equality, he disguises the gross inequality in his treatment of the woman who has chosen abstinence and the man who lacks "authority over his own desire" (7:37). Paul, she argues, places the avoidance of male immorality above female rights to freedom. Wire's argument depends on three factors, among others. (a) The first is the historical hypothesis that "woman prophets" stand behind almost every issue and every passage in this epistle. (b) The second is the view that new creation in Christ abrogates the creation ordinances of the OT (which Rosner, Yarbrough, and others identify behind much of Paul's theology in 1 Corinthians 5–7). Wire makes much of Paul's personal surrender of "high" pharisaic status (law) for "low" apostolic status (gospel), as against the woman prophets' discovery of a new "high" status (new creation). (c) The wealth of material on social status at Corinth even since the publication of Wire's book may perhaps call into question such a straightforward contrast between "high" and "low" status amidst the ambiguities, crisscrossings, and mobile value systems in Corinthian society. Witherington, e.g., speaks of "status inconsistency."[114]

The translation of v. 4 is difficult. ἐξουσιάζω means *to have a right or a power over something or someone*. ὁ ἐξουσιάζων means *the person in authority* (Eccl 10:4-5; Luke 22:25).[115] But we have already demonstrated that in 6:12 Paul uses a deliberate wordplay between the Corinthian slogan πάντα μοι ἔξεστιν and his reply, οὐκ ἐγὼ ἐξουσιασθήσομαι ὑπό τινος. To make this point we translated *"Liberty to do anything" — but I will not let anything take liberties with me.* The second clause, which embodies the future passive of ἐξουσιάζω, was variously

111. Wire, *Corinthian Women Prophets*, 82-90.
112. Ibid., 83.
113. Ibid., 84; cf. also 90.
114. Witherington, *Conflict and Community*, 23.
115. Cf. BAGD, 279; and Schrage, *Der erste Brief*, 2:65, n. 81.

translated in English VSS as *dominated by* (NRSV, NJB), *let anything make free with* (REB), or *mastered by* (NIV), while ἔξεστι, *are lawful* (NRSV), *permissible* (NJB), becomes an issue of *having rights* in Wire. In 7:4, therefore, NRSV translates *the wife does not have authority over her body, but the husband does; likewise the husband does not have authority over his own body but the wife does.* The REB comes nearer to our proposal with *the wife cannot claim her body as her own; it is her husband's. Equally, the husband . . . ,* and still nearer the NIV, *The wife's body does not belong to her alone, but also to her husband. In the same way. . . .* The major issue, therefore, is whether we are justified in including NIV's *alone* and *also,* which corresponds with our **exclusive**. The traditional interpretation that "each is the other's possession" (Edwards) is important in that the traditional concept in the ancient world that a father *gives* his daughter to the bridegroom as *his* is now qualified by *the reciprocity of mutual giving of the self:* the self (σῶμα), i.e., everything is *given to the other* in marriage. The husband cannot abuse the wife, for his body is no longer his own to use as he wills without her consent; the wife cannot opt out of intimacy permanently, for her body, *similarly,* is not (**exclusively**?) hers.

Bengel calls attention to the "paradox" of calling something "one's own" (ἑαυτοῦ . . . ἴδιον) if one cannot do what one likes with it.[116] Either one must appeal to the logical grammar of a reciprocal gift (above), or it is just possible that the Greek syntax may be construed in a way not hitherto suggested (to my knowledge). Short statements in Greek often imply ἐστι or ἐστιν to mean *there is,* with a complement in the nominative, but in predicative clauses ἐστι is also from time to time omitted (cf. *est* in Latin). Might it just be possible that Paul is declaring: **the wife does not have exclusive rights over her own body, but there is the husband** (also to consider); **similarly, the husband does not have exclusive rights over his body, but there is the wife** (to consider)?

Whichever of these two interpretations is followed, both cohere with Conzelmann's summary statement: "The equality results from the limitation of freedom which is given with the presence of the partner."[117] The notion of "rights" (ἔξεστι) seems foreign to Paul, for whom everything depends on undeserved grace which relativizes "rights," unless (a) "rights" are limited and qualified for the good of all; and/or (b) "rights" belong to the sphere of institutions or laws, in the sense in which Luther distinguished a need for a realm of law outside the reign of grace. This issue, however, should not distract us from the central thesis of this verse. Héring calls v. 4 "the heart of this short pericope . . . bearing upon the ultimate nature of Christian marriage."[118] B. Bruns has devoted a research article entirely to this verse, which contains an ingenious sug-

---

116. Bengel, *Gnomon,* 628: "Hoc cum" potestam non habet elegans facit paradoxon. Jus utrinque est aequale." Collins uses the phrase "physical autonomy" (*First Cor,* 255), which is not without certain difficulties. Does Paul ever promote "autonomy"? His appeal to "equality" and "mutuality" (255-56) is happier.

117. Conzelmann, *1 Cor,* 117; cf. Schrage, *Der erste Brief,* 2:63-66.

118. Héring, *First Epistle,* 50.

gestion. "Gnostic" types of religious people, he proposes, may well have used the notion that ἡ γυνὴ τοῦ ἰδίου σώματος οὐκ ἐξουσιάζει on the ground that physical life is indifferent, unimportant, or "subjugated" by the spiritually redeemed who live on a higher plane. But by adding the words ἀλλὰ ὁ ἀνήρ and ἀλλὰ ἡ γυνή Paul literally brings them down to earth about the value, importance, and obligations of bodily life.[119] Paul thus expounds his Christian theology of the body, according to which σῶμα includes both physical and transphysical existence. In Christian marriage, husband and wife "belong" to each other. But since, as Schrage also argues, this "belonging" is grounded in ἀγάπη, which entails respect for the other, even placing the other first, far from being incompatible with union with Christ, it instantiates the priority of concern for the other which finds paradigmatic expression in Christ's love for his body, the church, for whose good he gave himself up to death on the cross.[120] The precedence of the other over the self links 1:18-31 with 7:1-40. This is a helpful insight, but as Deming insists, it must also be qualified by the emphasis on *mutuality* in the surrounding verses. It does not deprive the self of its active agency, as in the case of **mutual agreement**.[121]

5   Three variants invite notice. (1) To the dative τῇ προσευχῇ ℵ², K, L, 88, some later Syriac readings, and Chrysostom add τῇ νηστείᾳ, *fasting*. The parallel is understandable but entirely secondary. The evidence for **prayer** alone is overwhelming (apparent 𝔭¹¹, 𝔭⁴⁶, ℵ*, A, B, C, D, Ignatius, and Origen among others. (2) Some later readings substitute the more explicit and appropriate συνέρχησθε for the bland ἦτε. The very fact that this "improves" the text suggests its secondary nature, but once again support for ἦτε is early and strong (ℵ, A, B, C, D, F, 33, 88). (3) The important hesitance of the construction εἰ μήτι ἄν is compromised by the omission of ἄν in 𝔭⁴⁶ and B. No allusion to this question seems to occur either in UBS⁴ or in Metzger's *Textual Commentary* (2d ed.) although Westcott-Hort place ἄν in brackets. Even more surprisingly, this (presumably) pro-ascetic omission appears to lie behind an absence of hesitancy in the NIV and REB, which adds to Fee's criticisms of NIV renderings of verses in this chapter.[122] NRSV's *except* **perhaps by** is preferable to NIV, NJB, *except by,* or REB, *except when.* ℵ, C, D, E, and most early MSS include ἄν, and it seems more likely to have been omitted by patristic copyists than inserted by them, given attitudes found in post-Pauline traditions on this subject.

The verb ἀποστερέω, *to rob, to defraud, to deprive,* denotes illegal theft and is used in Mark 10:19 in *do not steal,* and in 1 Cor 6:7 in the passive voice for *being defrauded.*[123] In a marital context it logically matches τὴν ὀφειλὴν

---

119. B. Bruns, "Die Frau hat über ihren Leib nicht die Verflügungsgewalt, sondern der Mann . . .'. Zur Herkunft und Bedeutung der Formulierung in 1 Kor 7:4," 177-94.

120. *Ibid.;* cf. Schrage, *Der erste Brief,* 64, where he compares the "debt" of love in Rom 13:8 and 15:1, 27 with ὀφειλή (note in this light the ἀπο- compound in ἀποδιδότω, v. 3).

121. Deming, *Paul on Marriage,* 121.

122. Fee, *First Epistle,* 281, n. 64; also Schrage, *Der erste Brief,* 2:67.

123. BAGD, 99.

ἀποδιδότω (v. 3) and the theme of "belonging" to each other (v. 4). However, BAGD propose to soften the stridency of the term in this delicate context by translating *do not deprive each other of marital rights,* since *rights* or **dues** with **deprive** conveys the force of taking what is not one's own to take with suitable sensitivity to the subject.[124] **Marital dues** brings out what is implicit but not explicit in the Greek. Although the context makes it clear that physical intimacy is the primary issue, mutual support and companionship cannot be excluded.[125] We may envisage either Wire's "women prophets" or male evangelists placing "God's call" above support for their spouse in various ways, and thereby making either spouse isolated and vulnerable to frustration which could result in problems, except "in special circumstances." Several writers (in spite of more recent work on aspect but still in harmony with the context) understand the negated μή with the present (as against the aorist) imperative μὴ ἀποστερεῖτε to have the customary force of this tense in a prohibition, i.e., **Stop depriving each other.**[126] A significant number at Corinth were already claiming that spiritual priorities took precedence over physical intimacy, whether or not we accept Wire's particular version of this hypothesis as that of the status, freedom, and "rights" of Corinthian women prophets.[127]

The concession for "special circumstances" is expressed hesitantly as εἰ μήτι ἄν.[128] Although ἐκ συμφώνου occurs only here in the NT, the papyri use the phrase to denote **mutual agreement,** as against unilateral decision.[129] Cullmann's broad contrast between χρόνος as time under the aspect of duration and καιρός as **a specific span of time** which may constitute a favorable moment for a particular undertaking has been subject to criticism when it is over-pressed, but here it entirely illustrates the force of the word.[130] The preposition πρός expresses the notion of its being *with a view to* a short time.

Paul introduces the notion of **goal** through his use of the purposive ἵνα. The fact that Fee feels the need to explain the structure of the verse by setting

124. Ibid.

125. Cf. Wolff, *Der erste Brief,* 135; and Collins, *First Cor,* 255.

126. Robertson and Plummer, *First Epistle,* 134: "cease to defraud"; and Fee, *First Epistle,* 281. Fee contends that otherwise Paul would have used a different word. In spite of the force of many (but not all) claims in S. E. Porter, *Verbal Aspect in the Greek of the NT with Reference to Tense and Mood,* and B. M. Fanning, *Verbal Aspect in the NT* (both cited above), here the context seems to suggest that the negation applies to a process already begun, even if we acknowledge the place of "viewpoint."

127. On Wire, see above; and *Corinthian Women Prophets,* 82-90.

128. See above under Textual Notes (3), and BDF, *Greek Grammar,* 191, sect. 376. The particle makes the clause indefinite, "except perhaps in case you may . . ." (Edwards, *First Epistle,* 159).

129. So argue Senft, *La Première Épitre,* 89; Schrage, *Der erste Brief,* 2:67-68; and many others. Cf. Lang's use of Germ. *Einverständnis* (*Die Briefe,* 90).

130. With Cullmann, *Christ and Time* (Eng. trans., London: SCM, 1955), 38-50; cf. BAGD, 394-95. The criticisms concern attempts to read "a theology of time" into the lexicography, rather than the suggestive lexicography itself, which does witness to the idea of "a favorable moment," "the right time." See further Schrage, *Der erste Brief,* 2:68.

forth a series of subordinate clauses, each of which depends on another, suggests that a working translation in modern English necessitates a change of structure in the Receptor language. Rather than pile up successive ἵνα clauses, *in order that you may find leisure to pray and be together again in order that Satan might not tempt you* with a further *because* (διά) clause, we have expressed the first immediate goal (first ἵνα) by **that you may find unhurried time** (second plural inceptive *aorist* subjunctive σχολάσητε) **for prayer**, and ended the first sentence. The second ἵνα is signified by restructuring it as a noun, **the goal**; and the convoluted logic of the μή in the second ἵνα clause is rendered by **The goal would be nullified if Satan. . . .** This provides a signal that the element of **goal** or *purpose* (ἵνα) is cumulative: **then come back together again** (strictly in the best MSS [see textual notes] *that you may be* [ἦτε, second plural subjunctive] *to the same place* [ἐπί with the accusative, τὸ αὐτό, i.e., resume full cohabitation with intimacy]) is included in the first immediate goal of the couple. Their purpose (goal) is *both* to devote time to prayer *and* to return to intimacy. The secondary goal is a negative one which entails a further condition: *in order that* (ἵνα) *Satan might not keep tempting you* (μὴ πειράζῃ ὑμᾶς, third singular *present subjunctive* active) *on account of your lack of self-control* (διὰ τὴν ἀκρασίαν ὑμῶν). We convey the *aorist* of the first subjunctive after the first ἵνα by **that you may find unhurried time**, and the *present* of the second negated subjunctive after the second ἵνα by **The goal would be nullified if Satan went on putting you through trials. . . .** For in addition to the inclusion of the proper effects within each goal, the interpretation must understand inclusive and exclusive negations in their appropriate sense.

We have still to examine the lexical scope of σχολάσητε and πειράζῃ as well as the force of διὰ τὴν ἀκρασίαν ὑμῶν. The general meaning of σχολάζω apart from specific contexts is straightforward. It means *to have time* or *to have leisure;* with the dative it means *to have time for someone or something*. In contrast to businesspeople, craftsmen, and slaves with designated tasks, a scholar had time for his or her studies. It may also mean *to have time to devote oneself to* a specific task.[131] The noun σχολή could mean either *leisure* or *a place where one had time to meet with teachers*, i.e., *a school* (Plutarch, *Moralia* 42A, 519F, 605A; Epictetus, *Dissertations* 1.29.34; Josephus, *Against Apion* 1.53; all Paul's era).[132] But does it mean in this verse *that you may have leisure* **for prayer** (NJB, *make yourselves free for prayer*) or *that you may devote yourselves to* **prayer** (NIV)? Deming observes that Paul uses σχολάζω only here, whereas it is a common term in Stoic-Cynic debate about marriage.[133] Although it ultimately concerns *devotion to* the study of philosophy, in the marriage debate the Cynic philosophers are concerned that marriage *crowds out* the priority status of philosophy. Given that the Stoic-Cynic context entails marital

131. For the range of meanings, cf. BAGD, 797-98; and MM, 619-20.
132. BAGD, 797-98.
133. Deming, *Paul on Marriage*, 112-13.

responsibilities, Deming interprets 7:5 as denoting "mutual consent in order 'to have leisure' for prayer."[134] But we may doubt whether Paul refers solely to *chronological duration.* The use of time is coupled with centers of attention, or what nowadays some call "quality time." Paul perhaps says that if one has excluded certain things both from one's timetable and from one's mind (for a season) one **may find unhurried time** (aorist subjunctive σχολάσητε) in the sense of quality and duration **for prayer.** This would place the issue on an entirely different footing from David Balch's appeal to Philo's *Life of Moses* for the view that ascetic abstinence promotes the capacity for revelations and visions.[135] A better parallel is the notion of abstinence for prayer "at the proper time" (καιρός) in *Testament of Naphtali* 2:9-10. Many writers draw attention to the importance of this parallel.[136]

Superficially ἵνα μὴ πειράζῃ ὑμᾶς ὁ Σατανᾶς διὰ τὴν ἀκρασίαν ὑμῶν looks as if Paul may perceive the goal as that of avoiding temptation on account of your lack of self-control, i.e., you must avoid being tempted because you will not hold out. But this is probably not Paul's main point. As we have argued, it is important to discern Paul's grading and framing of instrumental and final goals, and to disentangle logically, inclusive, and exclusive negations. πειράζω means *to try,* in the sense of *to make trial of, to put to the test,* although in appropriate contexts it may also mean *to tempt.*[137] Two interpretations are possible. Probably Satan is cast into the role of a hostile agent (as in Jewish and early Christian apocalyptic) who causes distress in an objective sense (including accusation) rather than primarily provoking experiences of inner tension.[138] Alternatively, Theissen believes that Paul has in mind "sexual fantasies."[139] At all events, if the καιρός in which the couple cease intimacy is too prolonged, Satan will cash in on it to transform a time of prayer into one of negative trials or harmful fantasy. When voluntary consent begins to degenerate into frustration and the boundaries of self-control begin to collapse into ἀκρασία, the whole experience becomes counterproductive: **the goal would be nullified if Satan went on putting you through trials beyond your self-control.** Paul speaks

134. Ibid., 112.

135. Balch, "Backgrounds of 1 Cor. viii," 354-64; we alluded above to his citation of, e.g., Philo, *De Vita Mosis* 2.66-70. Balch also makes use of the concept of the θεῖος ἀνήρ (358-61), which has often been regarded as problematic in relation to aspects of the NT. Cf. the brief critique in Deming, op. cit., 11-12.

136. The parallels with *Testament of Naphtali* 2:9, 10; 8:1; 8:7-10, esp. 8:8 are striking, and are discussed by Deming, *Paul on Marriage,* 124-26; Lang, *Die Brief,* 90; Collins, *First Cor,* 257; Wolff, *Der erste Brief,* 136-37; Schrage, *Der erste Brief,* 2:68, n. 99.

137. BAGD, 640-41.

138. Cf. Thiselton, "The Meaning of σάρξ in 1 Cor. 5:5," *SJT* 26 (1973): 204-28, esp. 218-21; T. Ling, *The Significance of Satan* (London: SPCK, 1961), 81-92; R. Yates, "The Powers of Evil in the NT," *EvQ* 52 (1980). 97-111. J. A. Fitzmyer describes Satan in the Pauline writings as "the Personification of all evil, disorder, dissension and scandal in the community" in contrast to "the God of Peace" (*Romans;* New York: Doubleday, 1993, 746).

139. Theissen, *Psychological Aspects,* 172.

here more as a pastor and counselor than as a Christian moralist, which precisely introduces his comment to this effect in v. 6.

6 This verse may appear to be too short and innocent to require more than the briefest of comments. But considerable energy has been exhausted on debating the scope of the application of τοῦτο in the first part of the verse, τοῦτο δὲ λέγω κατὰ συγγνώμην. NRSV, REB, NIV, and NJB render συγγνώμην **concession**, and we cannot improve on this. The etymological history of the word illustrates the image of knowing (γνώμη) *with* (συν- or συγ-), i.e., by *mutual consent*. This actually looks back, we shall argue, to the **mutual agreement** in v. 5b. But five views of τοῦτο have been advocated: (i) that it refers to the whole of vv. 2-5; (ii) that it alludes to v. 2; (iii) that it concerns the intimacy of v. 5a or the whole of v. 5; (iv) that it directly applies to the clause of hesitancy which ends v. 5, from εἰ μήτι ἄν only; and (v) that τοῦτο points forward to what follows. Winter advocates this fifth view forcefully.

(i) That τοῦτο refers to the whole of vv. 2-5 is advocated by early writers (e.g., Chrysostom, Peter Lombard, Thomas Aquinas), older modern commentators (Heinrici, Robertson and Plummer), and more recent scholars (e.g., Allo, Merklein, Senft).[140] The sole strong argument appears to be the concessive mood of the passage (although this may be questioned), and Allo and Conzelmann freely admit that in this case "the imperatives must not be pressed," a view which finds expression in such an influential work as Thielicke's *Ethics.*[141] All jussive imperatives become permissive imperatives. This would include not only whether to marry (Grosheide), but intimacy within marriage.

(ii) The proposal that τοῦτο applies to v. 2 would make sense, since it would cohere with Paul's view that marriage is a respected divine ordinance, but not necessarily for everyone. Certainly it is to be preferred over (i), since "vv. 2-4 contain precepts actually obligatory"; or at least it would seem so.[142] Hence Grosheide and others adopt (ii), and Barrett lists it as his second choice in ranking order.[143] It is understandable that Grosheide adopts (ii), since he is among the small minority who consider that the main issue is marriage versus celibacy as against either physical intimacy within marriage or sexual relations in any context (i.e., as the question formulated at Corinth). But the sheer distance between τοῦτο and v. 2 makes the suggestion improbable.[144] Whether Tertullian and Jerome apply the "concession" to marriage or to the clause in

140. For example, Robertson and Plummer, *First Epistle,* 135; Morris, *First Epistle,* 107; Allo, *La Première Épitre,* 159 (in detail); Conzelmann, *1 Cor,* 118; Merklein, "'Es ist gut für den Menschen,'" in Dautzenburg, *Die Frau,* 233-34; Senft, *Première Épitre,* 90; cf. Lightfoot, *Notes,* 223; Heinrici, *Das erste Sendschreiben,* 216. (See also Bengel, Estius, Rücket, Godet, Lietzmann.)

141. Conzelmann, *1 Cor,* 118; cf. Allo, *Première Épitre,* 159, and significantly in H. Thielicke, *Theological Ethics,* 3 (Grand Rapids: Eerdmans, 1964), 3:122-24.

142. Meyer, *First Epistle,* 1:197; Weiss, *Der erste Kor,* 175.

143. For example, Hodge, *First Epistle,* 110-11; Findlay, *Expositor's Greek Testament,* 2:824; Grosheide, *First Epistle,* 158; Barrett, *First Epistle,* 157; also Beza, Grotius, de Wette.

144. Fee, *First Epistle,* 283; Witherington, *Women in the Earliest Church,* 29.

v. 5b is ambiguous, for their main concern is to stress that no physical intimacy is positively commended (see under iv).[145]

(iii) The suggestion that Paul's explicit concession concerns the whole of v. 5, including both the physical intimacy and the mutual agreement to abstain from it on specific occasions, is defended by Barrett, following Meyer.[146] But it seems difficult to reconcile the notion that Paul is merely "advising" in v. 5a, when he has described abstinence on a permanent basis as "defrauding" or **depriving** one's spouse of what is theirs.

(iv) Witherington, Wolff, Schrage, and many others refer the **concession** to the clause at the end of v. 5 only: the couple may abstain from intimacy for a specific time if both of them find this helpful, but this is purely their own decision, and Paul lays down no rule or **command** about this matter.[147] This interpretation is entirely convincing (*pace* Winter) and leaves no apparent linguistic or exegetical difficulty. This explanation also coheres with Paul's affirmation of a full marriage relationship, against the Roman background in which marriages were often mere instruments of convenience, and could be annulled simply with the words *tuas res tihi habeto* ("take your things and go").[148] Against such a background, Weiss sees apostolic injunctions, which Witherington convincingly perceives as about mutuality and reciprocal dues. In *this* context, the concession applies only to the special circumstances of v. 5b.

(v) Can we interpret τοῦτο as pointing to what follows? As Fee insists, its linguistic and exegetical difficulties make this a hypothesis of last resort.[149] On the other hand, Orr and Walther defend this possibility. At the same time Bruce Winter argues a special linguistic case for the prospective function of τοῦτο when it is the object of *saying*. Contrary to most writers he urges that its position shows a forward reference, and that 7:7b offers the framework for Paul's wider discussion. It is difficult to set aside, however, the weight of exegetical and syntactical arguments, which favor the allusion to v. 5b.[150]

---

145. On the general importance of the contrast between **command** and **concession** throughout 7:1-40 for Tertullian, see Tertullian, *To His Wife* (c. 207), 2:1; further, "Paul *permits* marrying but *prefers* abstinence," 1:3. Jerome certainly does not wish to isolate 7:5b as the key "concession" in contrast to 7:1-5 (or 1-40). He finds his way around the problem by asserting that Paul commands prayer at all times (1 Thess 5:17); but "if we are always to pray we must never yield to the claims of wedlock, for as often as I render my due to my wife I cannot pray . . ." (Jerome, *Letters,* 48:15). In *Letters,* 48:16, Jerome explicitly refers Paul's word "concession . . . not command" to entering marriage: "do we still hesitate to speak of marriage as a thing permitted instead of a thing enjoined?"

146. Meyer, *First Epistle,* 1:197; Barrett, *First Epistle,* 157.

147. See Fee, *First Epistle,* 281; Kistemaker, *1 Cor,* 214; Weiss, *Der erste Korintherbrief,* 175; Schrage, *Der erste Brief,* 2:71-72, including nn. 112-15; Witherington, *Women in the Earliest Churches,* 29; Hays, *First Cor,* 117; Wolff, *Der erste Brief,* 137; Yarbrough, *Not like the Gentiles,* 98-100.

148. Witherington, *Conflict and Community,* 171.

149. Fee, *First Epistle,* 283.

150. Orr and Walther, *1 Cor,* 207; Winter, "1 Cor 7:6-7: A Caveat and a Framework for 'the Sayings in 7:8-24," 57-65.

It may be worth adding, in the light of accusations about Paul's supposed obsession with "sameness" and "order" (Wire, Castelli), that ἐπιταγή is merely a general word for **command**.[151] Even if τάξις and τάγμα might suggest "bringing into line," ἐπιταγή has as its cognate ταγή, *decree*, and τάσσω, *appoint*, rather than τάγμα. Further, the negative οὐ κατ' ἐπιταγήν *disengages* Paul from "sameness" as a command, and even his preferences (θέλω, v. 7) depend on χάρισμα. (On the view that Paul in no way gives a merely grudging concession about erotic love and its physical expression within marriage, see the "Extended Note" offering an overview of Paul's distinctive attitude toward the end of the introduction to ch. 7.)

7 𝔭46, ℵ*, D, A, C, F, Coptic Bohairic, certain eds. of the Vulgate, Origen, Tertullian, and Ambrose read δέ, whereas B, ℵ2 and D2, Syriac VSS, and Coptic Sahidic read γάρ. Clearly δέ has earlier and stronger support, and γάρ may perhaps have arisen from a mistaken assumption that v. 7 explicated the τοῦτο of v. 6 (see above). Virtually all writers favor δέ.

Again, on circumstantial issues and on issues of call and gift, see our introduction to this chapter (above). It has been suggested that those at Corinth who argued for abstaining from all physical intimacy had probably cited Paul's own example.[152] If so, the particle δέ would carry the force of **To be sure . . . ,** followed by θέλω in the sense of **I should like** (as REB, NJB) although *I wish* (NRSV, NIV) cannot be ruled out as doing violence to the Greek. Deming's "as I myself also am" (**as I myself am too**) rightly construes the καί with ἐμαυτόν, as against Orr and Walther's "to be even as," which construes καί with ὡς.[153]

Speculation about whether Paul was widowed has continued over the centuries. The usual view takes the form of a syllogism. (a) *Major premise:* from what we know of Paul's pharisaic background, it would be the norm for a leader in pharisaic or rabbinic circles to be married. Various strands of evidence and argument have been put forward. (b) *Minor premise:* but the implication of this verse that Paul is celibate is confirmed by **unmarried as I am** (v. 8) and may find a resonance in vv. 32-34 and 40. (c) *Conclusion:* it would cohere with both premises if (1) Paul had been married but was now a widower.[154] Alternatively (2) Paul or his wife may have parted at his conversion, although his emphasis on "mutual dues" (vv. 2-4) suggests that unless he took a course of action which he later viewed with regret, Paul himself would not have thought it

---

151. Wire, *Corinthian Women Prophets;* E. A. Castelli, *Imitating Paul: A Discourse of Power* (Louisville: Knox-Westminster, 1991), 119.

152. For example, Hurd, *Origin of 1 Corinthians,* 167.

153. Deming, *Paul on Marriage,* 126; Orr and Walther, *1 Cor,* 207. Also Edwards, *First Epistle,* 162, who concludes that *also* is the best construction.

154. Collins, *First Cor,* 260, endorses this, especially the major premise. Cf. J. Jeremias, "War Paulus Witwer?" *ZNW* 28 (1929): 321-23. E. Arens, "Was St. Paul Married?" *BibTod* 66 (1973): 1188-91, e.g., explores the lack of unanimity among the early Fathers, but concludes on the basis of obligations recognized by law-keeping Jews and by the later comments in 1 Cor 7:7-8 and 9:5 that in all probability Paul had been married, but was living a celibate life by the time of 1 Corinthians 7–9.

right to leave a wife to whom he owed responsibilities and support.[155] Deming argues that "the contrast Paul draws in 7:7 is not one between incontinent married Christians, one one side, and continent unmarried Christians on the other, but between those married Christians who are able to forgo sexual relations and those who are not. This is clearly his concern in 7:4-6, at least."[156] But Paul cannot be implying that he himself remains celibate within marriage, for in v. 8 he seems to classify himself as among the ἀγάμοις καὶ ταῖς χήραις.

If his comment sheds little light on Paul's own situation, Deming's observation remains useful as an explanatory comment on ἕκαστος ἴδιον ἔχει χάρισμα ἐκ θεοῦ. On χάρισμα, see above on 1:7 and also below on 12:4 (the word also occurs in 12:9, 28, 30, 31). Rom 1:11 shares some parallel with 1 Cor 1:7; and Rom 12:6 with 1 Cor 12:4, 9, 28-31. All of these references contain the notion of a **gift freely bestowed** to some extent; but this emphasis becomes absolutely central in some occurrences (Rom 6:23, τὸ δὲ χάρισμα τοῦ θεοῦ ζωὴ αἰώνιος), whereas it is merely a part of what the word denotes in others. The notion of a **gift freely bestowed from God** (ἐκ θεοῦ, i.e., of transcendent origin, not a mere "innate human capacity") clearly relates to a specific purpose or task in 1 Cor 12:4, 9, 28-31 and in Rom 12:6; but this aspect is also present here in 7:7. In modern post-Freudian terms we might say that Paul's χάρισμα lay in his capacity to sublimate his sexual drives (rather than in one direction merely repressing them, or in the other direction gratifying them) with the result that his creative energy is poured forth into the work of the gospel at every level of consciousness to great effect, and with no desire for something further (Phil 4:11).

The fact that Paul recognizes differing gifts ὁ μὲν οὕτως, ὁ δέ οὕτως prohibits our referring χάρισμα exclusively to the gift of chastity, unless we try to interpret οὕτως to mean *to this degree* rather than its more customary sense of *in this manner* or *of* **this kind** (adverbial form of οὗτος, *this-ly*, i.e., *thus*). Even granted the theological interest of the Reformers, and in spite of Niederwimmer's argument to the contrary, it is exegetically reasonable for Luther to comment on this verse: "Marriage is just as much a gift of God, St. Paul says here, as chastity is."[157] Yet the parallel is not celibacy versus marriage, but the gift of a positive attitude which makes the most of the freedoms of celibacy without frustration, and the positive attitude which caringly provides the responsibilities, intimacies, love, and "dues" of marriage while equally living out

155. G. Bouwman, "Paulus en het celibaat," *Bijdragen* 37 (1976): 379-90, attempts a speculative argument that Paul was divorced, and questions Jeremias's view that Paul was a widower. Bouwman's case rests basically on the hypothetical reference to expenses for a wife in 1 Cor 9:5-6, which he thinks may have rested on an earlier report of Paul's needs. But the argument against Jeremias is hardly decisive, and Arens, Bouwman, and Jeremias agree that in all probability Paul was married in earlier times.

156. Deming, *Paul on Marriage,* 128.

157. Luther, *Works,* vol. 28 (American ed., St. Louis: Concordia, 1973), 16 (*WA,* 12:104). K. Niederwimmer, *Askese und Mysterium: Über Ehe* (Göttingen: Vandenhoeck & Ruprecht, 1975), 6, argues that "*Marriage for Paul is no grace,* rather, a sign for lack of grace . . . the lack of ἐγκάτεια." But this is to misread 7:1-7.

the gospel. Either state offers rewards or frustrations, depending on varied attitudes, varied situations, and varied gifts. Hence Paul will shortly move on to consider divine vocation, on which these factors depend.

Paul has not left behind the original Corinthian question about physical aspects of human sexuality. He has now contextualized his varied series of replies. The place of physical intimacy depends on the varied situations of marriage, separation, and singleness and widowhood; and even within marriage there may be variables as long as decisions are mutual and reciprocal.[158] Each lifestyle is "good" in the right context and with the right attitude. However, Paul does not hide his own entirely personal preferences based on his own χάρισμα. Not only is he content with celibacy; for him it is preferable: so much so that he **would like everyone** (πάντας ἀνθρώπους) to share his own personal attitude. Deming perceives this expression of preference as "diplomatic" support for, and self-identification with, those who raised the issue at Corinth "enabling Paul to identify with the Corinthians and advise them. A similar manner of persuasion may be found elsewhere in Paul, namely in 1 Cor. 14. . . . Paul expresses both his empathy and his reservations by stating in 14:5, 'I want you all to speak in tongues — but *rather* that you may prophesy' (θέλω δὲ πάντας . . . μᾶλλον δέ . . .), and in 14:18-19, 'I thank God that I speak in tongues more that you all, *but* . . .'" (Deming's italics).[159]

Deming adds that it is scarcely a co-incidence that in 7:7 and in 14:18-19 χαρίσματα are at issue. Certainly we must point out that the occurrence of χάρισμα in 7:7 as a gift which enables one to make the best of celibacy is hardly "spontaneous," rather than a settled attitude which becomes strengthened by a habituated stance. Finally, we should remind ourselves that θέλω is personal, not moral. Whiteley offers an excellent analogy. We are accustomed, he observes, to pray for good ministerial candidates. We may well "say 'It is a good thing for a young man [woman] to offer himself [or herself] as a candidate for the sacred ministry' without for one moment suggesting that there is anything 'wrong' . . . about being a lay [person]."[160] Those of us who value our ordination may add "I wish they were as I am"; but everything would still depend on the varied circumstances of *gift* and *call*.

2. Marriage for the Unmarried? (7:8-9)

(8) To those who are not married and to widows I say that it is a good thing for them if they remain unmarried, as I am. (9) But if they do not have power over their passions, let them get married; for it is better to marry than for their passions to burn.

158. Cf. C. Osiek, "First Cor 7 and Family Questions," 275-79.
159. Deming, *Paul on Marriage,* 128.
160. D. E. H. Whiteley, *The Theology of St. Paul,* 215.

514

8 Since unmarried women constitute a particular category for advice in v. 25, some have suggested that the masculine plural dative τοῖς ἀγάμοις means *unmarried men*, rather than **those who are not married** of both sexes, and that this is complemented by the feminine category ταῖς χήραις. But it is more likely that *either* (a) the masculine is gender-inclusive here, and that Paul states a generalizing principle which is subject to qualifications and to case situations to which he will return, *or* (b) that the term denotes *widowers*, in spite of the claim that the term is "not to be rendered 'widowers' as though corresponding to ταῖς χήραις."[161] Deming applies the verse to "those who have been previously married and are now single."[162] Both he and Schrage cite the use of ἄγαμος for someone formerly married but now separated in 7:11 (less clearly, also 7:34). Fee concedes: "What Paul intended is not clear. . . . One cannot be sure either to whom this is addressed or what is the exact nature of the exception in v. 9."[163] In the end, however, Fee favors the view advocated by Deming, Collins, and Schrage on the ground that Greek seldom used the rare word for *widower,* and that throughout the chapter Paul discusses gender situations "in mutuality" some dozen times: "on balance, 'widower' seems to be the best understanding of the word here."[164] Probably the balance of writers, however, adopt the other view.[165]

On grounds of lexicography alone we might accept the majority view against Schrage and Deming. But none of these "majority" writers appears to mention the strongest reason why the minority view deserves respect. An important volume, *A History of Women in the West* (1992), includes a very useful essay, "Body Politics in Ancient Rome," by Aline Rousselle.[166] Citing numerous ancient sources, she argues that in higher (and probably other) ranks in Roman society *"a widow was expected to remarry within a year"* (my italics), "a divorcee within six months."[167] Pressures on both men and women to remarry

---

161. Lightfoot, *Notes,* 224.

162. Deming, *Paul on Marriage,* 130; cf. Schrage, *Der erste Brief,* 2:93-94.

163. Fee, *First Epistle,* 287.

164. Ibid., 228; also Orr and Walther, *1 Cor,* 210, and in most detail and with most force by Schrage, *Der erste Brief,* 2:94, including n. 240, where he also cites Fascher, *Der erste Brief,* 183, and Bouwman, "Paulus in het celibaat," 379-90.

165. For example, Barrett, *First Epistle,* 160; Héring, *First Epistle,* 51; Witherington, *Women in the Earliest Churches,* 30; Allo, *Première Épitre,* 162; Robertson and Plummer, *First Epistle,* 138; Weiss, *Der erste Korintherbrief,* 177; Bruce, *1 and 2 Cor,* 68; Meyer, *First Epistle,* 1:199; Kistemaker, *1 Cor,* 217; Lang, *Die Briefe,* 91; and Senft, *La Première Épitre,* 91. Luther felt the difficulty of a decision, mainly because he believed that Paul was a widower and here alluded to his personal state. Luther's earlier editions of his German translation translated *den widwehern und witwynnen* (1522). But by 1530 he had changed this to *den ledigen und witwin;* and in 1546 to *den Ledigen und Widwen.* This did not alter Luther's view that with regard to Paul himself "It is likely that he had been a husband."

166. Aline Rousselle, "Body Politics in Ancient Rome," in Pauline S. Pantel (ed.), *A History of Women in the West,* vol. 1: *From Ancient Goddess to Christian Saints* (Cambridge, Mass.: Harvard University Press, 1992), 296-336.

167. Ibid., 316.

were imposed by four considerations: issues about acquiring property; the pro-creation of not less than three children; the use of marriage (or remarriage) to enhance status; and the low life-expectancy of women ("twenty to thirty years"), especially connected with instances of death in childbirth.[168] These factors mean that the issue of "whether to marry" or "whether to have physical intimacy" was a much larger and more widespread issue for widowers and wid-ows than we can easily comprehend today if we merely project our modern sit-uation back into the Graeco-Roman world.[169] Further, the attitude toward re-marriage and children changed during the early years of the Empire under Augustus and Tiberius, when concern was expressed about a decline in birth-rate of the higher ranks of Roman society. At Corinth it may have been bound up with social as well as ascetic factors to determine what policy the church might or might not adopt.

Even so, to say that this constitutes a *large* category of **those who are not married** is not to say that it represents an **exclusive** category. Hence we agree with Kistemaker: "the unmarried are a class of people that includes widowers and both men and women who are single, separated, or di-vorced."[170] Witherington may then be right to read ἀγάμοις as the general term, and καί as meaning *especially*.[171] The very young age of marriage (of-ten twelve for girls) might add force to the pastoral axiom that to stay as one is (at least for the present) is **a good thing**. But we must recall Whiteley's analogy about a call to the ordained ministry (see above). To be ordained is **a good thing**; without prejudice to any evaluation of the Christian status of laypeople. *It is not a comparative evaluation in terms of any negative entail-ment for others.* On ὡς κἀγώ, see the discussion about Paul's possible status as widower, above.[172]

9   Traditional translations of this verse have given rise to a phrase which K. C. Russell uses as a title for a short research article on it: "That Embar-rassing Verse in First Corinthians."[173] The two difficulties which contribute to embarrassment are (i) the translation of οὐκ ἐγκρατεύονται as *if they cannot control themselves* (NIV), or *if they cannot exercise self-control* (RSV, NJB) and (ii) the translation of πυροῦσθαι as *to be aflame with passion* (NRSV); *burn with passion* (NIV); or *burn* (AV/KJV). In popular thought these suggest that Paul ranks marriage as little more than a remedy for a strong sex drive which cannot be controlled. A crude transplant into the world of our own day might

---

168. Ibid., 319; cf. 308-24.

169. Hays, *First Cor,* 111-19, succinctly summarizes some of the differences between an-cient and modern assumptions.

170. Kistemaker, *1 Cor,* 217.

171. Witherington, *Women in the Earliest Churches,* 30; also P. Bachmann, *Der erste Brief.*

172. Further, J. Jeremias, "Die missionarische Aufgabe in der Mischehe (1 Kor 7:16)," in *Abba* (Göttingen: Vandenhoeck & Ruprecht, 1966), 292-98.

173. K. C. Russell, "That Embarrassing Verse in First Corinthians," *BibTod* 18 (1980): 338-41.

perceive it as a recipe for a two-tier system in which *those who cannot control themselves* forestall a series of extramarital affairs by remarriage, while a stalwart band of disciplined believers doggedly pursues celibacy.

Clearly the context excludes any meaning even remotely of this kind. The major problem concerns the meaning of ἐγκρατεύονται, but we should note that the most radical attempts to rescue the verse offer alternative interpretations of πυροῦσθαι. M. L. Barré offers a careful lexicographical study of πυρόω in the LXX, the Qumran writings, and the NT.[174] Barré concludes that in addition to its literal or referential designative of *to burn* (active), *to be on fire* (middle), the verb also has four figurative uses: *tried-and-true, purified, burn in penal fire,* and *be aflame with passion.* Paul, Barré argues, saw physical intimacy outside marriage not as a mere hypothesis but as an occurrence at Corinth (1 Cor. 5:1-5; 6:12-20). Hence he interprets Paul as saying that in such a situation it is better to marry than to burn in the fires of judgment. This is to transpose the verse into a different key from that in which marriage is a *remedium concupiscentiae.*

K. C. Russell presses the same conclusion about the meaning of πυροῦσθαι. This time, however, the emphasis falls on rhetorical strategy rather than lexicography alone. Russell reconstructs the situation in which a group at Corinth exert pressure for celibacy in all circumstances. Paul forces them to consider the realistic implications of this for the probability of irregular relationships and concludes with a shock tactic as a punch line: *it is better to marry than to burn in hell!*[175]

These explanations have not found general favour. Blomberg describes NIV's *burn with passion* as "probably correct (cf. Paul's burning with indignation in 2 Cor. 11:9)." Then he adds: "But it could just possibly mean 'burn in hell' and be parallel to 1 Cor. 6:9-10."[176] Both interpretations could appeal to Jewish traditions. *Burning in judgment,* Fee notes, resonates with 1 Cor 3:15 and perhaps *m. Aboth* 1:5; but *burning with passion* runs parallel to 2 Cor. 11:29 and also Sir. 23:17 (LXX). To be consumed with passion "seems more likely" here.[177] Barrett and Conzelmann write before the appearance of the two articles and do not consider the possibility. Orr and Walther reject Barré as "not convincing."[178] Lang and Schrage consider a possible link with 3:13, but only to reject the notion.[179] Perhaps only G. F. Snyder fully and firmly endorses *than to burn in the endtime.*[180]

---

174. Barré, "To Marry or to Burn: πυροῦσθαι in 1 Cor 7:9," 193-202.

175. Russell, "That Embarrassing Verse," 338-41.

176. Blomberg, *1 Cor,* 134.

177. Fee, *First Epistle,* 289, including nn. 9-14.

178. Orr and Walther, *1 Cor,* 210.

179. Schrage, *Der erste Brief,* 2:96-97; Kistemaker, *1 Cor,* 218; Lang, *Die Briefe,* 91. Cf. also Lang, "πύρ," *TDNT,* 6:948-50.

180. Snyder, *First Corinthians,* 97. The possibility is not considered by Klauck, Senft, Laurin, Harrisville, or Collins.

In fact, πυροῦσθαι as the fires of penalty was considered by Tertullian (c. AD 208). It harmonizes better with Paul's thought, Tertullian believes, "to take forethought for the fires of penalty."[181] But Tertullian holds the very view that is described as "embarrassing." He believes that marriage obstructs prayer and the study of Scripture, and dissipates energies in the responsibilities of a home and children. The ideal is the companionship (or useful help) of "an aged pious widow" who will not rouse any passion to forsake celibacy.[182] The interpretation of Barré and Russell leaves the difficulty as before, unless it is treated as mere rhetorical shock tactic.

We may move forward more constructively in two ways. First, in our introduction to this chapter we noted the positive views of R. B. Ward, Colin Brown, and others (in effect following Origen) about sexual intimacy in marriage as God-given (see details above). Second, it is helpful to explore the meaning of ἐγκρατεύονται. Although very frequently, and especially in Gal 5:23, ἐγκάτεια means self-control, as many writers observe the verb in this verse is a straightforward present indicative and hardly justifies *if they cannot control themselves* (NIV) or *cannot exercise self-control* (NJB).[183] ἐγκράτεια has a long history in Greek, hellenistic, and Roman philosophy from Plato to the first-century Cynic and Stoic traditions. It appears to have been introduced by Socrates (Xenophon, *Memorabilia* 1.5.4), and Plato uses it to mean *judicious moderation* in contrast to over-indulgence or unrestrained self-gratification in matters of food or sex (*Republic* 3.390).[184] But to negate the verb ἐγκρατεύονται *does not imply that self-control has collapsed.* It denotes *the absence of the power to rank one's feelings in relation to strict goal,* for which Paul transparently uses the image of ἐγκράτεια in 1 Cor 9:25. Pfitzner discusses its significance at length. It "provides an illustration of the Apostle's principal [sic]: everything for the sake of the Gospel — including the right use of his liberty in the renunciation of his rights."[185]

In 7:9 Paul envisages a couple for whom mutual love has become so powerful a force that it distracts them from "everything for the sake of the gospel" when they are dominated by unfulfilled longing. Deming astutely points to a parallel in Epictetus where the norm for the Cynic philosopher of "everything for the sake of philosophy" simply cannot work in the case of a particular individual because "out of passionate love" (ἐξ ἔρωτος) he is distracted whether he marries or not; indeed, he will have to adopt the former course if any philosophy is to be done.[186] The traditional notion of persons who *cannot control*

181. Tertullian, *On Modesty,* 16. He returns to 1 Cor 7:9 repeatedly.

182. Tertullian, *On Chastity,* 12; cf. *On Monogamy,* 16; *On Modesty,* 1.

183. On Gal 5:23, see F. F. Bruce, *Commentary on Galatians,* NIGTC (Grand Rapids: Eerdmans and Carlisle: Paternoster, 1982), 255.

184. BAGD, 216; LSJ; MM, 180; and various sources.

185. V. C. Pfitzner, *Paul and the Agon Motif: Traditional Athletic Imagery in the Pauline Literature,* NovTSup 16 (Leiden: Brill, 1967), 87-88; cf. 82-98.

186. Epictetus, *Dissertations* 3.22.76 (also cited above); Deming, *Paul on Marriage,* 131.

themselves (NIV) conveys the wrong idea. We suggest **if they do not have power over their passions**, i.e., to devote themselves to more fundamental priorities. **Power** also resonates with the word history of κρατέω, *to take into custody, to take hold of and grasp,* with ἐν, of the person's inner attitude or mindset. κράτος simply means *power.* κρεῖττον has now become self-explanatory: it invites the act of **getting married** denoted by the third plural aorist imperative γαμησάτωσαν (an ingressive or incipient aorist).

3. A Case for Separation? Its Consequences (7:10-11)

(10, 11) To those who are married I give this charge, which is not mine but the Lord's: a wife should not separate from her husband (but if a separation occurs, she is to remain unmarried or else be reconciled to her husband); and a husband is not to divorce his wife.

10-11   In place of the majority reading χωρισθῆναι (aorist passive infinitive) A, D, F, and G read χωρίζεσθαι (present infinitive). Some argue that the aorist is "more usual after verbs of commanding," whereas Fee speaks of "the more difficult aorist passive" read by p[11] (apparent), ℵ, B, and C.[187] To compound the issue, p[46] reads χωρίζεσθε (present imperative), which transposes the charge from indirect speech to direct speech. Either the aorist intelligibly calls attention to *initiating* a separation or the present understandably stresses *the state of being separated.* Since the aorist passive probably carries a middle-voice sense here, we cannot employ the well-known *difficilior lectio probabilior* dictum. The present imperative would require a different translation, into direct speech, but this is the less probable reading.

The two verses must be taken together, or we lose the mutuality of Paul's categories **a wife . . . a husband.** . . . Further, unless the middle clause is placed as a parenthesis (either by means of dashes, as in UBS 4th ed. Greek text, parentheses, as above), the sense becomes confusing and even risks misleading the reader. D. L. Dungan describes 1 Cor 7:10 and 9:14 as the two examples of undoubted bedrock where Paul quotes the words of Jesus, but adds that at first sight he seems to quote Jesus only to contradict him: "Paul — in the midst of quoting a command of the Lord — applies it in such a way as flatly to contradict it! The Lord's command is: no divorce. But Paul's ruling is: let the woman divorce and remain single. . . . Something is taking place beneath the surface of the text."[188] When he reaches our two verses Dungan interprets them as above: "Between the two clauses . . . there is a parenthesis."[189]

The addressees in this section are clearly identified by the use of the dative plural perfect active participle γεγαμηκόσιν, **to those who are married.**

---

187. Fee, *First Epistle,* 290, n. 1.
188. Dungan, *The Sayings of Jesus in the Churches of Paul,* 82.
189. Ibid., 89.

The perfect denotes the married state consequent on the act of marrying. Further, after the clear-cut moral issues of chs. 5 and 6, this is one of the few instances in 7:1–11:1 of παραγγέλλω in the sense of *order, command,* or **give a charge**.[190] This is because it is **a charge which is not mine but the Lord's** (οὐκ ἐγὼ ἀλλὰ ὁ κύριος). The use of κύριος in contexts of obedience and worship has been noted and discussed, and Collins refers this "charge" to the risen Lord rather than to a saying of Jesus.[191]

The content of **the charge** or *command* from the Lord is that (accusative and infinitive of indirect speech) γυναῖκα ἀπὸ ἀνδρὸς μὴ χωρισθῆναι . . . καὶ ἄνδρα γυναῖκα μὴ ἀφιέναι. If the aorist passive infinitive of χωρίζω carries the force of a middle voice of personal involvement or reflexive action, the meaning is **should not separate from**. . . .[192] In most contexts χωρίζω means *to separate,* while ἀφίημι, to send away, comes to mean *to divorce* in a legal context (as in Herodotus, 5.39; present active infinitive ἀφιέναι).[193] But the difference may partly be explained in terms of the respective gender of each agent: **a husband is not to divorce his wife**. Schrage concludes that between the two terms "there is scarcely a differentiation," as if the first meant "bare separation," while the latter entails a formal judicial divorce.[194] For the very use of the phrase "you are to leave" constituted in Roman law all that was necessary for a husband to divorce his wife. Wire makes the same point, although Witherington argues that ἀφιέναι means *to divorce,* while χωρίζω means *to put asunder.*[195]

To what extent Paul has in mind the words of Jesus in much of his ethical advice as a church teacher remains an issue of controversy. Dungan cites the opposing views of Davies and of Bultmann.[196] Davies believes that "it was the words of Jesus himself that formed Paul's primary source in his work as ethical *didaskalos.*"[197] In addition to the two "pillar" verses, 1 Cor 7:10 and 9:14, he cites 11:23ff.; 14:37; and 1 Thess 4:15-16, among other examples. Other writers strongly affirm the importance of the words of Jesus for

---

190. The word *charge* is used by Héring and Barrett, as against *ruling* (NJB, REB) or *command* (NRSV, NIV, NAB). Most interpreters agree that no substantial difference is entailed, but J. A. Fischer insists that here the Greek falls "somewhere between gnomic exhortation and administrative decision" ("1 Cor 7:8-24 — Marriage and Divorce," *BR* 23 [1978]: 26; cf. 26-36).

191. Collins, *First Cor* 264-65. On the other hand, Collins recognizes the strong attestation to the "saying" of Jesus. See W. W. Kramer, *Christ, Lord and Son of God* (London: SCM, 1966), 65-83, 169-73; Cullmann, *Christology of the NT* (London: SCM, 2d ed. 1963), 207-32. See above on 1:2-10; 1:31; 2:8; and the comments of J. D. G. Dunn and N. Richardson, including Dunn, *The Theology of Paul* (Grand Rapids: Eerdmans, 1999), 245-52.

192. Conzelmann rightly discusses the middle force (*1 Cor,* 119, n. 5; cf. Fee, *First Epistle,* 290; Schrage, *Der erste Brief,* 2:98-100).

193. BAGD, 125-26.

194. Schrage, *Der erste Brief,* 2:99. See above.

195. Witherington, *Women in the Earliest Churches,* 31-32; as against Wire, *Women Prophets,* 84.

196. Dungan, *Sayings of Jesus,* xvii.

197. Davies, *Paul and Rabbinic Judaism,* 138-39.

Paul.[198] Allison and others also trace Paul's use of certain blocks of the Synoptic tradition.[199]

Many writers urge that the saying of Jesus to which Paul refers finds expression in Mark 10:11-12: Ὃς ἂν ἀπολύσῃ τὴν γυναῖκα αὐτοῦ καὶ γαμήσῃ ἄλλην μοιχᾶται ἐπ᾽ αὐτήν. This links the principle with the Decalogue, but concerns remarriage rather than separation or divorce. If this is Paul's major concern here, then Mark 10:11-12 may be the operative saying, but in this case the "parenthesis" ἐὰν δὲ καὶ χωρισθῇ μενέτω ἄγαμος, ἢ τῷ ἀνδρὶ καταλλαγήτω. Many interpreters believe that much of ch. 7 (all of it in Ford's view) concerns remarriage. But the same word as that which Paul uses here also occurs in Mark 10:9: ὃ οὖν ὁ θεὸς συνέζευξεν ἄνθρωπος μὴ χωριζέτω. If this is the primary saying to which he alludes, Paul is declaring that "alienation" between a Christian husband and a Christian wife, or even the desire of the one to leave the other (the converse of καταλλάσσω), should not of itself lead to permanent separation, let alone to remarriage.

PRELIMINARY NOTE ON DIVORCE IN RELATION TO 7:10-11
(But See Also Second Extended Note on
Divorce and Remarriage — after 7:16)

A complex historical and sociological background lies behind these two verses. Hurd relates the marital tension back to the question about intimacy in 7:1, and suggests that the spiritually "enthusiast" or "ascetic" partner wishes to dissolve the marriage in order to be rid of any requirement for intimacy. He quotes Cadbury's phrase about the excesses of "overconversion" from the world. Wire was not at all the first to argue that Christian women perceived their conversion as a route to "rights to be free."[200] Although he addresses both men and women here, Paul dwells on a woman's possible desire to separate, for "Christianity had powerfully stirred the feminine mind at Corinth."[201] Moffatt speaks of "the feminist party in the local church," which "had evidently claimed freedom to desert or to divorce a husband.... Some wives, of an ultra-spiritual temper may have gone ... further...."[202] Less convincingly perhaps, Murphy-O'Connor considers the scenario to be the specific case of an ascetic husband who had divorced his wife, on the ground that she wanted a normal marriage.[203]

---

198. F. F. Bruce, "Paul and the Historical Jesus," *BJRL* 56 (1974): 317-35; D. Wenham, "Paul's Use of the Jesus Tradition: Three Samples," in D. Wenham (ed.), *The Jesus Tradition outside the Gospels,* Gospel Perspectives 5 (Sheffield: JSOT Press, 1985), 7-37.

199. D. C. Allison, "The Pauline Epistles and the Synoptic Gospels: The Pattern of the Parallels," *NTS* 28 (1982): 1-32. In addition to 1 Corinthians Allison cites Romans 12–14, 1 Thessalonians 4–5, and Colossians 3–4 as instances which reflect sources behind Mark 6:6b-13; 9:33-50; and Luke 6:27-38. Cf. also P. Richardson and P. Gooch in D. Wenham (ed.), *The Jesus Tradition outside the Gospels,* 38ff.

200. Wire, *The Corinthian Women Prophets,* 82-97.

201. Findlay, *Expositor's Greek Testament,* 2:825.

202. Moffatt, *First Epistle,* 78.

203. Murphy-O'Connor, "The Divorced Woman in 1 Cor 7:10-11," 601-6.

More fundamental than these speculations, however, is the contrast between the seriousness of marriage for Jesus and for Paul, and the ease with which divorce and remarriage could occur in the Roman world. Admittedly, exceptions can readily be found in the Roman world, but these tend to be exceptions that prove the rule. Thus Seneca speaks tenderly of his wife Paulina of long years and describes unchastity as "the greatest evil of our time."[204] But the absence of this vice in his wife makes her almost unique, and is regarded as old-fashioned by her contemporaries.[205] Few women seem "to blush at divorce," and many "reckon their years not by the number of consuls but by the number of their husbands. They leave home in order to marry, and marry in order to divorce."[206] Similarly, Paul's other near-contemporary Stoic thinker Musonius Rufus praises a wife's stable marriage.[207] Nevertheless, we see from Tacitus that divorce in the Julio-Claudian period and the time of Nero was widespread and readily enacted for a wide range of reasons including social aspiration and personal taste.[208] Witherington and Cantarella remind us, again, that the performative utterance *tuas res tibi habeto* amounted to a legally recognized act of divorce.[209] (See fuller "Extended Note" with further details after 7:16, below.)

The situation in first-century Judaism seems to have been more one-sided, although whether women could initiate divorce is argued positively by B. J. Brooten against strong evidence to the contrary from H. Weder and E. Schweizer.[210] J. Moiser and H. J. Boecker cite evidence that a wife was not permitted to separate unilaterally in Jewish law.[211] The Mishnah (although of later date) states: "The man that divorces is not like the woman that is divorced; for a woman is put away with her consent or without it, but a husband can put away his wife only with his own consent" (*m. Yebamoth* 14:1; cf. *Yeb.* 2:6, 10). The Mishnah tractate *Gittin* legislates on the subject in detail. A man may, e.g., "put away his wife because she was barren . . ." (*m. Git.* 4:8); "If the report goes forth . . . that she is divorced, she is deemed to be divorced provided there is not cause enough to gainsay it" (*Git.* 9:9); "The School of Shammai say: A man may not put away his wife unless he has found unchastity in her. . . . The School of Hillel say: He may divorce her even if she has spoiled a dish for him. . ." (*Git.* 9:10).[212]

It is time to sum up where a consensus lies and where dissent still reigns.

204. Seneca, *Helvia* 16.3; cf. *Ira* 3.36.3 (on his wife's long care and familiarity with his habits); *Epistles* 104:1, 2, 5 (on his gratitude for her concern for his welfare over the years).

205. Seneca, *Helvia* 16.3; 19.2.

206. Seneca, *De Beneficiis* 3.16.2; cf. *Constitutiones* 14.1.

207. Musonius, *Fragment,* 14.94.2-19; cf. 14.92.17; 94.32-33.

208. For example, Tacitus, *Agricola* 6.1.

209. Witherington, *Conflict and Community,* 171; E. Cantarella, *Pandora's Daughters* (Baltimore: Johns Hopkins University Press, 1987), 136-37. See also G. W. Peterman, "Marriage and Sexual Fidelity in the Papyri, Plutarch and Paul," *TynBul* 50 (1999): 163-72.

210. H. Weder, "Perspective der Frauen?" *EvT* 43 (1983): 175-78; B. J. Brooten, "Zur Debutte über das Schneidungs recht der jüdischen Frau," *EvT* 43 (1983): 466-78.

211. Moiser, "A Re-Assessment of Paul's View of Marriage with Reference to 1 Cor 7," 109; cf. 103-22; and H. J. Boecker, *Law and the Administration of Justice in the OT and Ancient Near East* (Eng. trans., London: SPCK, 1980), 110-11.

212. Oster points out, however, that archaeological and historical evidence cannot determine with certainty "the extent and nature of the Jewish presence in Julio-Claudian Corinth" ("Use, Misuse and Neglect of Archaeological Evidence in Some Modern Works on 1 Cor (1 Cor 7:1-5; 8:10; 11:2-16; 12:14-26)," 57; cf. 52-73.

(i) First, in Jewish, Greek, and Roman law a husband could divorce his wife for a variety of reasons, and in Greek and Roman law divorce could be initiated freely from either side.[213] A. Rousselle points out how relatively seldom the same couple would enjoy a mutually lifelong relationship, not least because child-bearing was initially frequent (married at around twelve in Roman society, later in Greek culture; and Corinth, as we have noted, aspired to the former), with one in five pregnancies fatal, and family planning and abortion dangerous.[214] Life expectancy for women in the Roman Empire was on average between twenty and thirty years.[215] *It is little wonder, then, that the notion of a partner for life seemed almost an innovative concept. "To remain as your are" is no conservative "status quo" ethic, but a radical and high evaluation of Christian marriage.*

(ii) Virtually all modern writers regard vv. 10-11 as concerning marriage between Christians. Paul turns to the subject of mixed marriages later. However, Conzelmann's view that ἐάν with the aorist subjunctive χωρισθῇ means "if she has separated herself" (i.e., already) has been widely challenged.[216] Dungan supports Conzelmann, but B. A. Pearson argues in detail that this Greek construction cannot refer to a *past* act.[217]

(iii) Whether the initiative to separate was taken by one specific man (Murphy-O'Connor) or by a group of women (Findlay, Moffatt, Hurd, Wire) cannot be determined with certainty, but the probability is the latter. Schrage makes a forceful case for a combination of asceticism and "eschatological perfectionism" at Corinth.[218] The fact, however, that Paul speaks of either remaining unmarried or **being reconciled** may suggest incompatibility of temperament or mean-mindedness (μικροψυχίας, Chrysostom) could have played as great a part as theological emphasis.[219] But equally it may have been differences of conviction that bred alienation. καταλλαγήτω is the second aorist imperative of καταλλάσσω, which concerns bringing about a change into another (ἄλλος) relationship of reconciliation, harmony, and mutual acceptance in place of tension or alienation. The relationship is restored. The word is used theologically in 2 Cor 5:18-21.[220] Even here, however, the situation is uncertain. Dungan believes that "what the woman wanted was precisely what Paul denied to her — *another marriage . . . a divorce to marry someone else*" (his italics).[221]

(iv) The saying of Jesus may be reflected equally either in Mark 10:11-12 or Mark 10:9. But Dungan, followed by Pearson, argues for the priority of the tradition behind the Matthean exception (Matt 19:9; cf. 5:32), and indeed Omanson considers

---

213. On the "double standard" evidenced from Plutarch and the papyri, however, see Petersen (above). Conzelmann cites a number of further sources (*1 Cor,* 120-21, nn. 19-22).

214. Rouselle, "Body Politics in Ancient Rome," in Pantel, *A History of Women in the West,* 302-10.

215. Ibid., 318.

216. Conzelmann, *1 Cor,* 120.

217. B. A. Pearson, "Jesus' Teachings as Regulations in the Early Church," *Int* 26 (1972): 348-51.

218. Schrage, "Zur Frontstellung der paulinischen Ehebewertung in 1 Kor 7:1-7," 214-34, and *Der erste Brief,* 2:53-103.

219. Chrysostom, *1 Cor. Hom.,* 19:4.

220. Cf. *Papyrus Oxyrhynchus* 104:27 (1st cent. of persons); 2 Cor 5:18 of God (BAGD, 414).

221. Dungan, *Sayings of Jesus,* 92.

the appeal to the saying in effect "an afterthought."[222] Again, opinions are divided. F. W. Beare finds "no parallel" between Mark 10:11-12 and 1 Cor 7:10-11 on the ground that the former concerns divorce and the latter rejects remarriage, while others (e.g., Moffatt) appeal to the tradition behind Mark 10:11-12 for Paul's words.[223] Some interpretations, therefore, soften a *prima facie* "passing *on*" (Robertson and Plummer) of a *command* from the sayings of Jesus into an allusion to the sayings of Jesus as a starting point for a *pastoral concession.* Molldrem argues that Paul is *not* concerned to give a "ruling" but to offer pastoral advice for the benefit of both partners in complex situations, while Spieth believes that Paul's pastoral stance here positively encourages a wife to separate if the marriage has deteriorated into one of abuse.[224] Such interpretations appear difficult to sustain in the light of παραγγέλλω, but on the other side two factors invite respect for, if not agreement with, this shift of emphasis. First, the Corinthian questions and situations are complex, and, unlike 5:1–6:20, 7:1–11:1, looks flexibly at "grey areas" of pastoral concern. Second, marriages were arranged, not usually initiated, by both partners, and such factors as social or material advantage placed higher than modern Western notions of "compatibility," let alone romantic love (in most cases).

(v) Three factors deserve note. It might be possible to argue that once the distinctiveness of the Christian view of marriage as indissoluble has been firmly established in principle against the backgrounds of Roman, Greek, and Jewish assumptions, individual exceptions might be envisaged. But this remains to be discussed more fully in our second "Extended Note of Divorce and Remarriage" (below, 7:16). A careful study of "special circumstances," and Paul's respect for them, remains relevant.[225] (b) Wimbush rightly points out that the notion of **remaining** (μενέτω) in a particular situation *in no way* supports a *traditional status quo ethic: it swam against the stream of Graeco-Roman readiness to change everything to suit personal desire,* and "was designed to *relativize* the importance of all worldly conditions and relationships."[226] *Whereas "pneumatic Christian existence" (cf. 7:1a) saw everything in black-and-white, Paul avoids any sweeping cultural or countercultural attitude which does other than place "the things of the Lord" first in a complex variety of real situations.*[227] Indeed, **remaining** is part of the "not yet" which conflicts with what Schrage calls the "eschatological perfectionism" found in Corinth.[228] (c) Finally, D. R. Cartlidge observes that "1 Cor 7 does not deal with sex alone. . . . In 7:17-20 Paul works with the problem of Jews or Greeks; in 7:21-24, the subject is freemen and slaves. . . . The most famous locus of these 'pairs' is Gal 3:28."[229] Hence

222. R. L. Omanson, "Some Comments about Style and Meaning: 1 Cor 9:15 and 7:10," *BT* 34 (1983): 135-39; Dungan, *Sayings of Jesus,* 107-31, 132-35.

223. F. W. Beare, *The Earliest Records of Jesus* (Nashville: Abingdon, 1962), 192.

224. M. J. Molldrem, "A Hermeneutic of Pastoral Care and the Law," *Int* 45 (1991): 43-54; S. I. Spieth, "Divorce: Under No Circumstances?" *Ashland Theological Journal* 24 (1992): 73-79.

225. Moiser's argument, "In short, Paul offers remarriage to innocent Christians abandoned by their partners," applies to vv. 12-16 ("Paul's View of Marriage with Reference to 1 Cor 7," 109; cf. 103-22).

226. Wimbush, *Paul, the Worldly Ascetic,* 16.

227. Ibid., 17.

228. Schrage, "Zur Frontstellung," 214-34. This convincing account of "not yet" appears in Cartlidge, "1 Cor 7 as a Foundation for a Christian Sex Ethic," 225.

229. Cartlidge, "1 Cor 7 as a Foundation for a Christian Sex Ethic," 221; cf. 220-34.

Witherington is right to place emphasis here on *mutuality* (*pace* Wire) as a Pauline principle.[230] (See further, however, on 7:15 and "Note" following v. 16, and the exegetical debate about the so-called Pauline privilege.)

4. Christians Already Married to Unbelievers (7:12-16)

(12, 13) But to the rest I say (not a saying of the Lord): if any Christian brother has a wife who is an unbeliever and she consents to continue to live with him, he is not to divorce her. And if any woman has a husband who is an unbeliever, and he consents to go on living with her, she is not to divorce her husband. (14) For the husband who is not a believer is made holy through his [Christian] wife, and the wife who is not a believer is made holy through her Christian husband. Otherwise, it follows, your children would not be cleansed; but now in fact they are holy. (15) If, on the other hand, the unbelieving partner takes the step of separation, let the separation take place. The Christian husband or the Christian wife does not remain in slavery in such circumstances. No, God has called you to live in peace. (16) For how far do you know, you who are the wife, whether you will bring your husband to salvation? Or how can you know, you who are the husband, whether you will save your wife?

12-13 The phrase ἐγὼ οὐχ ὁ κύριος is open to misunderstanding if the immediate context of v. 10 is forgotten. The whole of the previous statement about married Christian couples received added point from Paul's citing a tradition concerning **a saying of the Lord** in the context of the previous issue, but on the question of what should be the attitude of a person when one of a married couple comes to faith and the other does not was not a situation addressed in the teachings of Jesus. So Paul now disengages the present pastoral issue from traditions about sayings of Jesus. Paul regularly speaks of Jesus, even the earthly Jesus, as *Christ* (2 Cor 5:16) or by means of his favorite and most characteristic title **Lord**; hence there is no need to speculate here about revelations or otherwise from the risen Lord. **Sayings** of Jesus are the issue.

The traditional translations, e.g., *I say — I and not the Lord* (NRSV), *I say . . . not the Lord* (NIV), *I say this as my own word, not as the Lord's* (REB), give priority to reproducing the structure of the Greek syntax and grammar ἐγὼ οὐχ ὁ κύριος at the expense of inviting logical ambiguity. Tertullian felt compelled to

---

230. Witherington, *Conflict and Community*, 175-77; *Women in the Earliest Churches*, 26-30, 73-75; Witherington judiciously rejects both authoritarian and egalitarian interpretations of Paul, or, rather, asserts that Paul holds a dialectic between the two: "at the same time egalitarian and, in a limited sense, patriarchal" (73). Freedom does not mean lack of responsibility, but Paul certainly liberates women from their more "instrumental" roles in Graeco-Roman society of the day, placing decisions and responsibilities in their hands, but within a framework of Christian ethics, mutual responsibilities, and service to God within certain structures.

enter into a defense of the status of what was not **of the Lord** by relating the words to fulfilling that to which God called his people (v. 16) and Paul's possession of the Spirit (v. 40).[231] But such a debate and its place in the history of interpretation is irrelevant if the logic of Paul's point is protected and clarified by explicitly translating (**not a saying of the Lord**). The misplaced discussion tends unwittingly to treat οὐχ ὁ κύριος as an instance of what logicians call *contrary negation,* or *contrariety,* as if *Paul* and **the Lord** were alternate sources of authority or of disclosure. However, the logic of negation allows for (i) *alternation;* or (ii) *otherness* (as here). First-century Stoics were well aware of the logical difference between *external* negation (exclusivity) and *internal* negation (differentiation from a *component within* the proposition; i.e., only part of the proposition, or only an aspect of a word, is negated).[232] The latter applies *contextually,* as is the case here. Our proposed translation, **to the rest I say (not a saying of the Lord)**, assumes that logical accuracy as determined by the context takes priority over the general grammatical and syntactical structure. All that it presupposes *outside* the context is that, again, ὁ κύριος here (and in v. 10) refers to traditions concerning Jesus of Nazareth's ethical teaching, not to the raised Lord as a source of prophetic utterance. Only a small minority of commentators understand v. 10 in this way, mainly following Bultmann's scepticism about the date and the status of traditions which claim to go back to historical Jesus, on matters of teaching.

τοῖς δὲ λοιποῖς almost certainly means **to the rest** *of those who are married,* i.e., those whose marriages were to those who had not yet come to faith (in contrast to Christian couples, vv. 10-11).[233] If, however, vv. 2-11 are treated in totality as *command* in contrast to *advice,* it is just arguable that τοῖς δὲ λοιποῖς means *to the remaining categories* (who may also have raised questions) *not yet addressed.* This section would represent the fourth "question" identified by Hurd. Hurd suggests that (i) the married asked about physical intimacy; (ii) the unmarried asked about celibacy; (iii) Christian couples asked about separation; and (iv) those married to unbelievers asked for pastoral advice on how to handle their situation.[234] He argues that the further περὶ δέ in 7:25 leads on to a distinct further topic.[235] The Corinthians' statements "show no uncertainty, but are definite and even aggressive."[236]

---

231. Tertullian raised this issue in c. AD 204. What is "permitted" and what is "commanded" in 1 Cor 7 (*Exhortations to Chastity,* 3). Even if Paul admits to no "precept of the Lord," the advice or instruction is from God, for it promotes that to which "God calls" (7:15) and Paul has the Spirit (7:40; Tertullian, *Chastity,* 4). Chrysostom recognizes that sayings of Jesus are involved (e.g., Matt 5:32; 19:9), but agrees that Paul's situation at Corinth is different. Paul's ruling is more than human opinion, however, for it reflects God's creation ordinances (Chrysostom, *On Virgins,* 12).

232. Cf. W. E. Johnson, *Logic* (Cambridge: Cambridge University Press, 1921), pt. 1, chs. 5 and 14.

233. Conzelmann (*1 Cor,* 121) and Fee (*First Epistle,* 298) rightly argue for this (following Robertson and Plummer, *First Epistle,* 141).

234. Hurd, *Origin of 1 Corinthians,* 157-69.

235. Ibid., 169.

236. Ibid., 168.

After the problems which beset the respective identifications of the audience and subject matter in the previous three sections, it is a relief to find virtual unanimity about these issues in this passage. The Christian partner is to remain with his or her spouse, subject to their agreement. We have set forth vv. 12 and 13 together to emphasize, once again, the evenhanded mutuality of Paul's exhortation, which stands in contrast to what we might have expected from a first-century writer, but which coheres with Gal 3:28. συνευδοκεῖ means *seems good* (εὐδοκέω) *together* (σου-), denoting *mutual* **consent**, as also above (v. 5, ἐκ συμφώνου). **Divorce** in both verses (NRSV, REB, NIV, NJB, Collins) is better than *leave* (JB, v. 13) since ἀφιέτω is the third singular present imperative active of ἀφίημι, in other contexts *to send away;* in marital context, **to divorce**, and the same imperative active form is repeated in each verse. *Leave* might be justified only from usage in later papyri, and if the wife had no power to divorce, which was not the case in Roman or Greek society. Whatever the more ambiguous situation in Judaism, we have noted R. E. Oster's comment that to assume a significant Jewish population in Corinth goes beyond the evidence. **A wife who is an unbeliever** properly translates γυναῖκα . . . ἄπιστον, since the masculine ending is regularly used of adjectives with the alpha privative, and the Greek means either *unfaithful* or (here) **unbeliever**, according to its context.

Justin illustrates forcefully the relevance of this issue to church life one hundred years later. His *Second Apology,* addressed to the Roman Senate, tells of the conversion to Christian faith of a woman in whose marriage both had hitherto been "loose," "unbridled," or "promiscuous" (ἀκολασταίνοντι, from ἀκολασταίνω). On becoming a Christian she changed her lifestyle and spoke to her husband of Christ's teachings. They became alienated in due course (cf. καταλλάσσω, 7:11), but in spite of her deep desire to leave him, her friends advised her to stay to try to win her husband. Her husband so declined in unnatural vice, however, that in the end she gave him a writ of divorce. Upon this, her husband reported her to the authorities for her Christian faith. This set in motion a chain of events in which the new Emperor, Marcus Aurelius, became involved (Justin, *Apology,* 2:2; c. AD 161-62).

14 (a) For symmetry, ἐν τῇ γυναικί would expect not ἐν τῷ ἀδελφῷ but ἐν τῷ ἀνδρί. Hence it is not surprising that ℵ², D², and some Syriac readings make this expected change. But ἀδελφῷ is the original reading, and is well supported by p⁴⁶, ℵ*, A, B, C, D*, 33 et al. (b) The Western D, F, and G and the Vulgate add the gloss τῇ πιστῇ to γυναικί for the same kind of reason. It explicates the meaning, but was absent from most early MSS.

Among the English translations REB and Barrett render *through his Christian wife,* as the gloss in D, F, and G seems to require. This is Paul's meaning, since it mirrors τῷ ἀδελφῷ, *her Christian husband.* The dividing line between translation and interpretation is fine and never clear-cut, but since the best Greek MSS have only τῇ γυναικί we have resorted (probably for the only time), to inserting **Christian** in square brackets to signify a combination of absence and implicit presence.

The precise meaning of ἡγίασται constitutes a notorious crux of interpretation: **is made holy** follows the NRSV and Collins, in comparison with *has been sanctified* (NIV, Barrett), *is sanctified* (NJB, AV/KJV) *is consecrated* (Moffatt; Phillips adds "in a sense"); *belongs to God* (REB); and rather desperately *is made one with the saints* (JB), *has become associated with Christ's people* (TCNT).[237] NIV and Barrett's *has been sanctified* endeavors to do justice to the perfect passive indicative form ἡγίασται, but arguably **is made holy** or **is sanctified** incorporate already the notions of some past event on the basis of which the emphasis now falls on the present resultant state. The advantage of **is made holy** is that it leaves open certain options of understanding which *has been . . .* would exclude, especially the dynamic presence of the Christian spouse as a continuing influence. On ἁγιάζω and ἅγιοι see above on the phrases ἡγιασμένοις ἐν Χριστῷ 'Ιησοῦ and κλητοῖς ἁγίοις in 1:2, where we considered the background of the Hebrew קדשׁ *(q-d-sh)*.

The key controlling principle lies in the recognition of the nature of the anxiety which Paul seeks to allay. The believer asks Paul with genuine concern: if I have left behind the old life and become a new creation in Christ, does not my relation with my unbelieving, unrepentant spouse and my entire home atmosphere threaten to pollute and to corrode my purity as one who belongs to Christ? Paul has argued readily enough that relations with a pagan prostitute tear apart the limbs of Christ (6:12-20). How can someone who has been purchased by Christ to belong to him (6:20), who is the Spirit's holy shrine (6:19), also "belong" to a spouse who does not "belong" to Christ?

The REB translation *the husband now belongs to God* admirably answers this anxiety, and in this particular respect is well chosen. But in what sense, if this says everything that Paul intends, are we to understand ἐν τῇ γυναικί . . . ἐν τῷ ἀδελφῷ?

(i) The simplest, but not in the end valid, explanation is to refer to interpretations from A. Schweitzer to J. A. T. Robinson about the *"physical"* or *"quasi-physical"* nature of union with Christ, almost like a contagion. Schweitzer urges that being-in-Christ is "a relation of corporeal union. . . . Paul assumes a similar projection of the being-in-Christ, thought of as quasi-physical, into the natural corporeal union of one human being with another when he asserts that the unbelieving husband is sanctified in the "believing wife."[238] To support his view Schweitzer cites the physical use of κολλᾶσθαι, *to cleave,* in 1 Cor 6:16-17 (cf. Gen 2:24) and the enigmatic "baptism for the dead (15:29) which he attempts confidently to explain on the same principle as that found in 7:14.[239] Further, this "physical" aspect explains, for Schweitzer, why

---

237. Barrett, *First Epistle,* 159 and 164; Collins, *First Cor,* 262 and 271.
238. Schweitzer, *Mysticism of Paul the Apostle,* 285.
239. Ibid., 127, 128, and 280-86.

those who do not maintain union with Christ through the eucharist fall ill and die (1 Cor 10:1-13; 11:29-32).[240] Robinson virtually repeats Schweitzer's arguments a quarter of a century later. "A similar quasi-physical understanding of sacramental relationships within the Body underlies the practice of vicarious baptism for the dead (1 Cor 15:29) . . . the directives he [Paul] issues in 1 Cor 7:12-14 . . . rest on the same basic presupposition. . . ."[241] He observes, "It is almost impossible to exaggerate the materialism and crudity of Paul's doctrine of the Church as literally now the resurrection *body* of Christ" (Robinson's italics).[242]

However, we endorse Whiteley's *critique* of Robinson's views.[243] Even Conzelmann, after acknowledging that "it looks as if holiness is crassly regarded as a thing; it is transferable, without faith. . . . There can in fact be no denying the massively thinglike character of the idea," nevertheless concludes: "the explanations that have so far been suggested are almost without exception unsatisfactory."[244] Along the kind of lines identified by James Barr as "illegitimate totality transfer" Whiteley shows that (a) the body of Christ in his earthly life, (b) his resurrection body, (c) the church, and (d) body in eucharistic contexts maintain semantic boundaries which may at times become blurred but never entirely merge.[245]

(ii) It is quite astonishing that all this talk about "quasi-physical" conceptual schemes directs attention away from the central theme of *relationality*. F. F. Bruce and C. K. Barrett do not warm to any overready identification between belonging to Christ and belonging to a visible church, and Bruce describes this verse as an "extension of the OT principle of holiness by association."[246] To the question "Is not the believing pattern defiled by such close association with an unbeliever?" the reply is, "No, contrariwise, the unbeliever is to this degree (not necessarily in the sense of 1:2; 6:11) in a state of sanctification . . . through association with the believer."[247] Collins observes that the non-Christian husband "participates in God's covenanted people (see 1:2) through her."[248]

(iii) Yet not all has yet been said. In a neglected book, O. R. Jones, an accomplished philosopher of language, produced a significant semantic and conceptual analysis of holiness in biblical material.[249] He demonstrates that the *holy* in the biblical writings *is not a static quality*. Indeed, contrary to Conzelmann, it is not conceptually "thinglike." It is not like a color word or a

240. Ibid., 282-83; cf. 258-60.
241. Robinson, *The Body*, 54.
242. Ibid., 51.
243. Whiteley, *The Theology of St Paul*, 192-98.
244. Conzelmann, *1 Cor*, 121-22.
245. Whiteley, *The Theology of St Paul*, 197; cf. J. Barr, *The Semantics of Biblical Language* (Oxford: Oxford University Press, 1961), 218 and 233; see further, 107-60.
246. Bruce, *1 and 2 Cor*, 69; cf. Barrett, *First Epistle*, 165.
247. Bruce, loc. cit.
248. Collins, *First Cor*, 271.
249. O. R. Jones, *The Concept of Holiness* (London: Allen & Unwin, 1961).

color, but operates with a *dynamic* logic that entails *dispositional responses of "fearfulness," "wholeness," and "separatedness."* In successive chapters Jones explores conceptually what it was for the biblical writers to experience *fear* of the holy, the power of holiness, and to respond to the holy as a manifestation of numinous *separation.* Kuyper and Murphy-O'Connor develop this point in exegetical terms.[250] Kuyper traces the **holy** through Levitical and other cultic texts which use the term to denote, "being set apart for God's service." In 1 Cor 7:14, however, he argues, "the condition or state of holiness is not a static condition, but rather it embraces dynamic possibilities."[251] Murphy-O'Connor goes much further. He rejects Allo's notion that **holy** is used in a merely legal or ritualistic sense, just as he rejects Kümmel's theory that in 7:14 the meaning is unique to this verse alone.[252] He argues for the "ethical dimension of 'holiness' here," partly in terms of contextual factors about "to care for the things of the Lord" and "to please the Lord. . . . For God has called us . . . to holiness."[253] The **holy** is "essentially a dynamic concept . . . the fruit of love in action."[254] What determines that a **husband** *or* **wife who is not a believer is made holy** is "the *willingness of the unbeliever to continue the relationship" which "has had a decisive influence on his or her behavior"* (my italics).[255] The lifestyle of the Christian partner cannot but affect the ethos and to some extent the values and lifestyle of the home, whether this be the husband or the wife. The spouse's example, witness, prayer, and living out of the gospel make the spouse (and the children) *in this sense* **holy**.

If we pursue the line of approach suggested by Jones and Murphy-O'Connor, the equally notorious problem about **your children . . . are holy** has already been solved. If the spouse falls under the influence of the Christian partner's faith, lifestyle, prayer, and living out of the gospel, how much more shall not the children? This *a fortiori* logic is well expressed by ἐπεὶ ἄρα, *since it would then follow* (Robertson and Plummer); "this argumentative ἐπεὶ, '*since otherwise*' (Lightfoot), is strengthened by a logical and perhaps also temporal νῦν δὲ ἅγια, '*but, as it is, they are holy.*'"[256] The aspects of dynamic action and "separateness" in ἅγια mean that even if only one parent is Christian the children will be marked by an element of shaping and "difference" from a wholly pagan environment.

250. L. J. Kuyper, "Exegetical Study on 1 Cor 7:14," *RefRev* 31 (1977): 62-64; J. Murphy-O'Connor, "Works without Faith in 1 Cor VII:14," *RB* 84 (1977): 349-69.
251. Kuyper, "1 Cor 7:14," 63. Cf. also Best, "1 Cor. 7:14 and the Children in the Church," 158-66.
252. Murphy-O'Connor, "Works without Faith," 350-51; cf. Allo, *Première Épitre,* 166; and Kümmel, "Anhang," in Lietzmann, *An die Korinther,* 176-77.
253. Murphy-O'Connor, "Works without Faith," 353.
254. Ibid., 355.
255. Ibid., 358. For a still broader understanding see Deming, *Paul on Marriage,* 134 (linked with "usefulness").
256. Lightfoot, *Notes,* 226; Robertson and Plummer, *First Epistle,* 142.

NOTE ON THE POSTHISTORY AND RECEPTION OF 7:14

The history of interpretation has thrown up some idiosyncratic explanations of **holy**. Of the examples listed below, some tend to reflect too closely the agenda of their own concerns. The last two bring us closer to Paul.

1. *Irenaeus.* Irenaeus compares the dynamic of 7:14 with that of God's command to the prophet Hosea to marry a prostitute (Hos 1:2-3).[257] The context of argument is that God may be known in many ways, not simply through the predictable and ecclesially reputable. Rahab, e.g., received and protected the Israelite spies, with the result that her house was protected as if she were one of God's own people: "Rahab the prostitute was preserved . . . through faith of the scarlet sign."[258] Significantly in the case of Hosea, his son's initial name, "Not-a-People," was reversed: "They shall be called the children of the living God" (Hos 1:6-9; cf. Rom 9:25-26). This principle, Irenaeus observes, explains the dynamic of 1 Cor 7:14: "For this reason Paul declares that 'the unbelieving wife is made holy by the believing husband,'" and on this basis the significance of the children finds a parallel between the promises of God in Hosea and in 1 Cor 7:14. The further parallel of the grafting of the wild olive into the true, cultivated olive (Rom 11:17-19) similarly expounds the parallel of "if the loaf is holy, so is the whole batch; if the root is holy, so are the branches" (Rom 11:16). Irenaeus notes that Paul's treatise on the mystery and generosity of God's unstoppable electing grace focuses on the derivative holiness of Gentiles from Israel's elected, privileged status as the people of God. Similarly, the "union" with the holy makes an inclusive extension of the holy. Irenaeus thereby treats 1 Cor 7:14 in the context of (i) the OT (Abraham, Moses, Rahab, Hosea, the call of "a people who are not"); (ii) the electing, generous grace of God; (iii) cross references with Paul's thought in Romans 9–11; and (iv) the efficacy of "union" instantiated most fundamentally in union with Christ.[259]

2. *Clement of Alexandria.* Clement advocates and encourages marriage and permits second marriage.[260] In this context he compares Paul's citation of Christ's ordinance concerning marriage with his modifying clause, adding further, "Now are they holy" (1 Cor 7:14).[261] Clement points out that holiness may spread either through the agency of a Christian husband or through that of a Christian wife, since the two are "one flesh."[262] However, reference to the children seems to remain implicit rather than explicit. Clement leaves it to the reader to understand a solidarity of holiness through the union, proximity, and intimacy implicit in the relationships, in which the emphasis falls upon the positive and potentially salvific effects of marriage.

3. *Tertullian* devotes a full chapter to 7:12-14, where his main burden is that v. 14 gives no license for Christians to marry unbelievers.[263] If a Christian is *already*

---

257. Irenaeus, *Against Heresies*, 4:20:11.

258. Ibid.

259. Ibid.

260. Clement, *Stromata*, 3:2 (on 1 Cor 7:9), 3:6 (on 7:14 and Matt 19:3; Mark 10:2), and 3:18 (on 7:10-14).

261. Ibid., 3:18, where Clement summarizes Paul from 6:13 to 7:14.

262. Ibid., 3:6.

263. Tertullian, *To His Wife*, 2:2. He strongly compares "in the Lord" in 7:39, understood as "to a Christian" (ibid.). See esp. 2:2:9.

531

married to an unbeliever, the situation is different. Here the encouragement is offered that the unbeliever cannot diminish the sanctity of the spouse or of their children, positively through association or solidarity and "through the *discipline of the institution" (ex institutionis disciplina) of Christian upbringing and education*.[264] Baptism and eschatological destiny play a role: the children are on their way to a holiness to which God has called them. "They are in some sense destined for holiness and salvation."[265] This gives no encouragement, Tertullian insists, *to initiate* a mixed marriage. "The grace of God sanctifies what it *finds* [i.e., already]."[266] Otherwise it remains "impure" and is "not able to be sanctified."[267] Tertullian makes similar points in passing in his firm rejections of second marriages.[268]

4. *Origen.* Surprisingly, Origen seems to miss the very point underlined by his Alexandrian predecessor, Clement, that God's grace of sanctification operates in both directions, from husband to wife and from wife to husband (see above). Origen compares the union of a mixed marriage to the mixing of wine with water: one sanctifies or gives flavor, while the other corrupts or dilutes.[269] This appears to run contrary to what Paul is saying, but he is staying with Paul's point that no Christian should *initiate* marriage with an unbeliever (cf. Tertullian on 7:39).[270] This is not strictly an exegesis of 7:14.

5. *Later Fathers* (except Theodoret, see below). With the exception of Augustine and Chrysostom, in many cases this period offers less exegetical or pastoral insight than earlier or later works. *Jerome* simply repeats and quotes the "weaker" strand in Tertullian (*On Monogamy,* 11:8 and *To His Wife,* 2:2) that children of believers are, "as it were, candidates for the faith."[271] This may allude to Tertullian's constructive emphasis on Christian education, but misses the Pauline context of mixed marriages, which Tertullian addressed. *Severian of Gabala* (c. 400) has a fragment on 1 Cor 7:14 which Staab has preserved. He writes, "When the children are clean and holy, uncorrupted by unbelief, the faith of the parent has won."[272] At the turn of the third and fourth centuries, *holy* seems to have been understood of children primarily in a proleptic or anticipatory sense in this verse. *Chrysostom* explains "holy" in 7:14 in two ways. Primarily it serves in a pragmatic way "to deliver the woman from fear as completely as possible."[273] The proof is that her child is "not unclean." Second, the effect of bodily union has already been stated in 6:15-17.[274] *Augustine* refers to 7:14 in a number of treatises. In *On the Good of Marriage* he refers back to Paul's teaching on the body as the temple of the Holy Spirit (1 Cor 6:19). He infers: "Therefore the bodies of the married are also holy. . . . Even an unbelieving partner does not stand in the way of this sanctity"; the sanctity of the one "profits" the other.[275] Elsewhere Augustine seems to

264. Tertullian, *Treatise on the Soul,* 39:4.
265. Ibid.
266. Tertullian, *To His Wife,* 2:2:9.
267. Ibid.
268. Tertullian, *On Meaning,* 2:8.
269. Origen, *1 Cor, Frag.* 33, in *JTS* 9 (1908): 505.
270. Ibid.
271. Jerome, *Letters,* 85:5.
272. Staab, *Pauluskommentare aus der griechischen Kirche* (already cited), 250.
273. Chrysostom, *1 Cor. Hom.,* 19:4.
274. Ibid.
275. Augustine, *On the Good of Marriage,* 13 (quoting 1 Cor 7:14).

suggest that Paul refers to actual events of families coming to faith, led by one parent.[276]

6. *Cajetan* (d. 1534) and *Melanchthon* (d. 1560) press ἅγια into meaning *legitimate* in the eyes of state law *(de sanctitate civili)*. Several medieval commentators (e.g., Walafrid Strabo, c. AD 808-849 explore this notion on the assumption that if the Christian spouse separates, this will probably result in their children having adulterous parental figures in a new marriage *(adulteri estis, et filii vestri spurii . . . nunc, sancti quia de licitis conjugis nati).*[277]

7. *Bullinger* (1566) and *Matthew Poole* (1685) understand **holy** in 7:14 as *sanctitas federalis*, i.e., *status within the covenant* (not unlike Collins, above), but part of the agenda here is that children within the covenant have the right to the covenant sign, namely, baptism.[278]

8. *Beza* holds the minority view that **holy**, of the children, denotes or presupposes *regeneration* on the basis of election: (4) Bengel combines the earlier interpretation *legitimate* with a "somewhat closer" relation to the church: *non sint spurii . . . sit legitima, non adulterina . . . sed propinquirem aliquam cum ecclesia.*[279]

9. *Theodoret* (c. 458) interprets **holy** in relation to the unbelieving wife in terms of *hope* of salvation, and for the children what seems to be a promised *futurity:* the wife ἔχει σωτηρίας ἐλπίδα (Latin text, *habet spem salutis);* children suggest the notion of σπέρμα . . . τῆς σωτηρίας *(semen illius erit salutis particeps).*[280] However, Theodoret also considers this ὑπερβολικώτερον *(haec autem cum hyperbole)* in order to be persuasive about staying together and maintaining the family.[281] **Holy** is almost used emotively to mean "there is nothing to worry about." Luther grounds this theologically under the rubric "to the pure all things are pure." The faith of the believing partner, Luther urges, can promote a positive stance toward all things, even to adult children who do not share the faith.[282]

10. *Calvin.* Commonsense exegesis comes from Calvin: "The godliness of the one does more to 'sanctify' the marriage than the ungodliness of the other to make it unclean. Accordingly a believer can live with an unbeliever ['not in the contracting of marriages but in maintaining those already entered into'] with a clear conscience."[283] But for Calvin the question about the children invites more speculative considerations about covenant, for which he refers his readers to Rom 11:16.

---

276. Augustine, *Our Lord's Sermon on the Mount,* 1:16:45; "I suppose it had already occurred that some wives were embracing faith by means of their believing husbands, and husbands by means of their believing wives. . . . Now the children were Christians . . . at the instance of one of the parents." This would never have occurred, he adds in relation to 7:14 and its context, if the believer had initiated a separation on coming to faith. Cf. also 1:22:73 and *On the Morals of the Catholic Church,* 35:79.

277. Walafrid Strabo, *Glossa Ordinaria: Epist. 1 ad Cor.,* in *Opera Omnia:* Migne, *Saeculum IX,* Tom. II (1879), 530.

278. Matthew Poole, *Commentary,* 3:560: "not inwardly renewed . . . but in the sense that all the Jewish nation are called a holy people. . . . Counted in covenant with him and have a right to baptism."

279. Bengel, *Gnomon,* 629.

280. Theodoret, *Interp. ep. 1 ad Cor.,* in Migne, *PG,* 82:277 (Gk.), 278 (Lat.), 205B.

281. Ibid.

282. Luther, *Works,* 28:34-35 (*WA,* 12:121); similarly, to some extent, Schrage, *Der erste Brief,* 2:108-9.

283. Calvin, *First Epistle,* 148.

15 𝔭⁴⁶, B, D, א², E, F, G, Ψ, 33, Peshitta, Coptic, Sahidic, and Vulgate read ἡμᾶς in place of ὑμᾶς, which is ranked as "B" by the UBS⁴ text, following א*, A, C, and Coptic and Bohairic. It is surprising that Metzger considers support for ἡμᾶς only "slightly stronger."²⁸⁴ On evidence alone we might prefer **has called us**.²⁸⁵ But Metzger rightly makes the point that scribes often tended to broaden the reference of general aphorisms to include readers, and ὑμᾶς fits Paul's context of argument exactly.

The present indicative middle form χωρίζεται probably has the force of *separates himself/herself*, signifying that the subject of the verb takes the initiative in the act of separation. Hence we translate **takes the step of separation**, since everything depends on making this transparently clear. The argumentative ἐπεὶ ἄρα . . . νῦν δέ of the previous verse is followed by yet another contrastive δέ, and since, again, the contrast of a new situation is fundamental to the sense, we translate εἰ δὲ ὁ ἄπιστος as **If, on the other hand, the unbelieving partner. . . .** Since Paul has addressed husband and wife in mutuality and reciprocity throughout from 7:2, all of the major English translations rightly regard the masculine as gender-inclusive, meaning *unbelieving partner* (NRSV, REB) or *unbeliever* (NIV, NJB). The third singular present imperative middle χωριζέσθω invites a little more than the bare verb *to separate* in English: **let the separation take place**. The present contains an overtone of continuance.

The most crucial words for exegesis and interpretation are οὐ δεδού-λωται, the (perfect passive of δουλόω, *to enslave*). The syntactical meaning is clear: **the Christian husband or wife does not remain in slavery**, *does not remain under bondage* in the present as a result of a past action. But does the referential denotation mean: *not . . . in slavery to remain with the former spouse,* or *not in bondage to the marriage tie which would prevent freedom to remarry? The latter way of understanding Paul has come to be known as* "the Pauline privilege."

(1) Fee argues forcefully against this latter "Pauline privilege" interpretation.²⁸⁶ He argues (i) that since the general thrust of the chapter is against remarriage, it would be strange if Paul sought to make room for it in what was virtually a throwaway line; (ii) the use of δουλόω, *to enslave,* is not a usual way of describing marriage, even in Paul; (iii) in 7:39 it appears that only death can break the marriage bond; (iv) remarriage is disallowed in v. 11, which has parallels; and (v) the general argument in ch. 7 is to remain as one is without actively seeking a change in status. Witherington expresses this view cautiously: "It is doubtful that there is a 'Pauline privilege.'"²⁸⁷

(2) Conzelmann takes the opposite view: "The Christian is not subjected to any constraint. . . . He can marry again."²⁸⁸ Héring is no less emphatic on the side

---

284. Metzger, *Textual Commentary* (2d ed. 1994), 489.
285. Héring, *First Epistle,* 53. But against Nestlé.
286. Fee, *First Epistle,* 303.
287. Witherington, *Women in the Earliest Churches,* 32. But his discussion is very brief.
288. Conzelmann, *1 Cor,* 123.

of the "privilege": "If the pagan leaves the Christian partner the marriage is regarded as having been nullified, and the Christian can marry again . . . with a
member of the Christian Church (ἐν κυρίῳ, 7:39)."[289] Héring might have supported his own view with reference to his particular understanding of **in peace**, ἐν
εἰρήνῃ. He sees the Greek as equivalent here to the Hebrew שָׁלוֹם *(shalom)*. This
means not merely absence of strife with a former spouse, but "complete peace,
outward and inward" (Héring's italics), which might be thought to underline
Conzelmann's theme of freedom in this passage.[290] R. H. Stein also interprets
Paul as anticipating Matthew (5:32; 19:9) in softening the apparent absoluteness
of the tradition of Jesus' words in Mark 10:11.[291] Byron sees a clue to the "Pauline privilege" in Paul's distancing this section from sayings of Jesus by "I say,
not the Lord."[292] Luther also regards the Christian partner as free to remarry.[293]

(3) Other literature, however, reveals greater complexities in the debate.
H.-U. Willi discusses the Jewish background to 7:15 and claims that it reflects
Paul's personal experience of married life before and after his conversion. Willi
combs through a mass of Jewish and rabbinic material and dismisses the hypothesis.[294] Deming pays more substantial attention, however, to the background of εἰρήνη and δουλόω in the Cynic-Stoic literature on marriage and celibacy. If Paul is utilizing Stoic-Cynic terminology (as Deming maintains), it
would be odd to say that a person **does not remain in slavery** (οὐ δεδούλωται)
if Paul envisaged such a person remarrying.[295] Philo, e.g., reports Essene philosophers as stating that a person who marries becomes "a slave (δοῦλος) in
place of a freeperson."[296] Musonius speaks of a married woman who wishes to
study philosophy as already in a slave's role (δουλικά).[297] Stobaeus quotes from
Euripides that children and a wife place a man under "great tyranny."[298] The
language about *reigning as kings* which we find in 1 Cor 4:8, Deming urges,
stands in semantic contrast to all this imagery about *slavery* in Musonius,
Epictetus, and Diogenes Laertius, and reflects common currency in the coinage
of Roman Corinth. Power (ἐξουσία, ἔξεστι, 6:12) is the opposite to being under
someone else's power (ἐξουσιάζομαι) and acting as a slave (δουλεύειν). In the
light of extensive examples, one after another, we must concede that it would be
unwise to follow a number of commentators in assuming that δεδούλωται in
7:15 means bound rather than *under bondage* or *in slavery*.

289. Héring, *First Epistle*, 53.
290. Ibid.
291. R. H. Stein, "Is It Lawful for a Man to Divorce His Wife?" *JETS* 22 (1979): 115-21.
292. B. Byron, "General Theology of Marriage in the NT and 1 Cor 7:15," *ACR* 49 (1972):
1-10.
293. Luther, *Works*, 28, 36-38; *WA*, 12:123-25.
294. H.-U. Willi, "Das Privilegium Paulinum (1 Kor 7:15-16) — Pauli eigene Lebenserinnerung?" *BZ* 22 (1978): 100-108.
295. Deming, *Paul on Marriage*, 131-73.
296. Ibid., 150; Philo, *Hypothetica* 11.3.17.
297. Musonius, *Fragment*, 3:42:8.
298. Stobaeus, 4.494.4, from *Oedipus;* cf. Deming, *Paul on Marriage*, 152.

(4) Yet Deming's arguments cannot be accepted uncritically. For Dale Martin has shown with no less force that in 7:22-23 the central theme is "the status-improvement meaning of slavery to Christ . . . as upward mobility."[299] The two certain effects of Deming's work are (i) to undermine the understanding of οὐ δεδούλωται as *not bound,* on the basis of which Luther and others argued for the possibility of remarriage; but also (ii) to undermine Fee's second argument that *slavery* could hardly be used of marriage. Deming has shown how frequently it was so used, and Martin's research may give this a more positive twist in Paul than Deming finds in Stoic-Cynic sources. Luther's comments (followed more recently by Wimbush) also undermine Fee's fifth point: "remaining" is not a status quo conservatism but demonstrates what Luther calls the capacity to be "free in essence" whatever the "orders or estates" in which Christians may find themselves.[300] Deming also finds this "inner" freedom in Stoic-Cynic discourse.[301]

(5) Ultimately there are arguments on both sides of the question whether v. 15 grants "the Pauline privilege" of the possibility of remarriage in the specific case of prior abandonment by a partner who remained an unbeliever, and to whom the Christian was *already* married at his or her own conversion. Fee's strongest argument against it is an interpretative judgment that the principle expressed in 7:39 (marriage can be dissolved only by death) controls all the cases in the chapter without exception. But does this exclude the "Matthean" exception of a partner's adultery? Most would allow Matthew's exception, and we should need to assert that Paul was unaware of this tradition. On the other side, however, in 7:7 Paul seems to envisage that only those who receive the same χάρισμα as he has are called to the celibate life, but that if a different χάρισμα is given marriage is likely to be the norm. F. F. Bruce concedes that Paul may not explicitly address the issue head-on, but concludes that by inference he defines abandonment in these circumstances as "a state of what amounted to widowhood." He adds: "Presumably remarriage would not be completely excluded for the believer."[302]

This brings us back to Fee's first argument, namely, that the general thrust of the chapter is against remarriage. This is largely true, but not exhaustively so. We might well add that it is interwoven with a second theme, which may be summed up under the rubric "It all depends. . . ." This is perhaps why Paul is quite happy to leave loose ends. As Giblin argues with respect to this chapter, and as Clarence Glad argues of 7:1–11:1 and other parts of this epistle, Paul deals with the good, the possible, the just, the feasible, the constructive, the useful, and the right "and their contraries" in ways which "take se-

---

299. Martin, *Slavery or Salvation,* 63.

300. Luther, *Works,* 28, 39; *WA,* 12:126.

301. Deming, *Paul on Marriage,* 60-73, 86, 131-72. Deming also considers the relevance of 2 Cor 6:14–7:1 (136-40) and of Ben Sira 9:14-16 (140-42 and 148). He diagnoses the main sources for a *Corinthian* view as (i) Stoic thought, (ii) wisdom traditions, and (iii) apocalyptic.

302. Bruce, *1 and 2 Cor,* 70.

riously the contingencies of the addressees' life . . . in an epistolary context which combines dissuasion and persuasion with praise and blame, [and] under-scores . . . Paul's concern with adaptation. . . . The word ἕκαστος draws attention to individual differences."[303] This does not mean that Paul's ethics are always situational ethics. There is nothing "adaptable" about right and wrong in chs. 5 and 6; but in 7:1–11:1 we see Paul the pastor setting forth a dialectic between principles and circumstances.

We should read neither too much nor too little from ἐν εἰρήνῃ, **in peace.** The phrase may denote the result of the separation, or alternatively the hope of a relationship of harmony (see on v. 16). Although Héring is right to allude to the Hebrew background of שָׁלוֹם *(shalom),* it would also be a mistake to read every nuance of the Hebrew word into Paul's contextually conditional use of the Greek here. Probably ἐν with the dative denotes *the sphere of* **peace** in which life is lived (although some argue that with MS abbreviations at the earliest stage we cannot absolutely rule out the possibility that Paul may have dictated εἰς with the accusative). At all events, most agree that the word denotes more than either mere absence of strife between partners or a subjective feeling of inner tranquility. The word describes an objective condition of harmony or reconciliation. Paul greeted the readers with a prayer for **peace** (1:3). God has called the Christian with continuing effect (κέκληκεν, perfect indicative active of καλέω) to a life in which **peace** holds sway (cf. Phil 4:7, peace as guardian).[304]

16   The use of τί expresses not the manner of obtaining knowledge (i.e., not *how do you know . . . ?*) but its *extent* (**how far do you know?**). Once the force of this idiom has been established, its parallel in v. 16b can be rendered more freely as **can you know. . . ?**, but it is the same Greek construction. Yet RSV, NAB, and NIV persist in translating *how do you know?* (RV, *how knowest thou?* AV/KJV, *what knowest thou whether . . . ?*) as against NJB's *how can you tell?* or NRSV's *for all you know.*

These unsatisfactory translations (except NRSV) impose a well-known exegetical dilemma delightfully summed up in Sakae Kubo's title "1 Cor VII:16: Optimistic or Pessimistic?"[305] For the RSV translates, *Wife, how do you know whether you will save your husband? Husband, how do you know whether you will save your wife?* which seems to suggest that it adds encouragement to the separation envisaged in the previous verse with the thought: "It

303. Glad, *Paul and Philodemus: Adaptability in Epicurean and Early Christian Psychagogy,* 246. Cf. also Charles H. Giblin, "1 Cor 7 — A Negative Theology of Marriage and Celibacy?" *BT* 41 (1969): 239-55. Giblin argues that Paul tries to avoid "abstract principles" in the face of the complexities of human life, but seeks to apply the gospel pastorally in such a way that it can be lived out. Glad attempts to extend the principle of "flexibility" to 5:1–11:1, but we remain unconvinced about 5:1–6:20.

304. With Phil 4:7, cf. further Rom 14:19; 1 Thess 5:13; 2 Cor 13:11; and V. Hasler, "εἰρήνη," *EDNT,* 1:396-97.

305. S. Kubo, "1 Cor VII:16: Optimistic or Pessimistic?" 539-44.

is no use hanging on in the hope of converting him/her, because how do you know that this will happen?" The NIV follows the RSV fairly closely, with the same "pessimistic" nuance. On the other side, NAB, JB, TEV, and most explicitly REB are "optimistic." NAB renders the question: *Wife, how do you know that you will not save your husband . . . ?* while REB imposes a clear decision onto the text: *But remember, a wife may save her husband. . . .*

Tertullian, Augustine, Theodoret, Photius, and Theophylact held this "optimistic" view.[306] But from the time of Nicholas of Lyra (c. 1270-1340) a wide range of commentators, with certain exceptions, have held the "pessimistic" view.[307] If the optimistic view is adopted, the connective γάρ surely implies that **God has called you to live in peace** (v. 15c) must refer to a restored relationship with the yet-to-be-converted spouse, which entails knock-on difficulties identified above. The most influential force for reinstating the "optimistic" view, as Kubo points out, is Jeremias's essay on the missionary task in the mixed marriage in which in addition to considering various grammatical factors Jeremias urges that the optimistic interpretation corresponds with Paul's own missionary attitude.[308] Among earlier modern commentators a number defend the optimistic view.[309]

Edwards examines the reason for Nicholas of Lyra's dissatisfaction with the optimistic view.[310] The γάρ most naturally links our verse with Paul's immediately preceding assurance "don't have a bad conscience about the partner's deciding to separate." If the appeal to **can you know** means, *But remember: a wife may save her husband . . .* (REB), v. 15 must now become parenthetical to link v. 16 back to vv. 12-14, and furthermore γάρ, **for**, must be changed into *but* unless v. 15 is placed explicitly in brackets. Nicholas of Lyra does not explicate this in detail (he was a good biblical scholar, with a close knowledge of the history of interpretation and of Hebrew, but apparently not Greek); but he argues that after two reasons for a good conscience in v. 15, v. 16 adds a third reason: "your hope to convert him/her at great personal cost remains hypothetical." The

306. Tertullian, *To His Wife,* 2:2; Augustine, *On Adulterous Marriages,* 1:13; Theodoret, *Interp. ep. 1 ad Cor., Opera Omnia* 206D, in Migne, *PG,* 82:277-78 (ἐλπίσι πόνον, Lat. *bona inquit spe proposita laborem suscipe*); Photius (c. 810-95), in K. Staab (ed.), *Pauluskommentare aus der grieschischen Kirche,* 558; Chrysostom is ambiguous: Jeremias selects from his *Catechumens,* but in *1 Cor. Hom.,* 19:4 he writes, "He [Paul] leaves the matter in suspense."

307. Cf. Kubo, "1 Cor VII:16," 539; Stanley, *Epistles,* 112. The version of Thomas Aquinas on 1 Corinthians associated with his lectures as *Postilla* from Niccolai de Gorram leaves the issue open: *primo spem alienae conversionis; secundo permanentiam in statu propriae vocationis* (in Thomas, *super ep. S. Pauli,* 350).

308. J. Jeremias, "Die missionarische Aufgabe in der Mischehe (1 Kor 7:16)," *Abba, loc. cit.;* cf. also C. Burchard, "Εἰ nach einem Ausdruck des Wissens oder Nichtwissens . . .," *ZNW* 52 (1961): 73-82.

309. Calvin, *First Epistle,* 150, "a word of encouragement"; Hodge, *1 Cor,* 120; Findlay, *Expositor's Greek Testament,* 2:827-28; Lightfoot, *Notes,* 227; Moffatt, *First Epistle,* believes that both "make good sense" but the optimistic version "suits the paragraph better" (84).

310. Cf. Edwards's summary, *First Epistle,* 176-77.

privilege of spiritual peace and single-minded, un-anxious devotion must not be lost simply for a hypothetical hope.

Lyra's view was adopted by Weiss, Robertson and Plummer, Allo, and Héring.[311] But these were writing prior to the essay of Jeremias, which changed the paradigm a second time, as Kubo points out. After Jeremias, scholars of stature can be found on both sides. F. F. Bruce cites the work of Jeremias and calls the optimistic view "indeed preferable"; Schrage echoes Calvin's words that the keynote is "encouragement," not "resignation."[312] Barrett also repeats Jeremias's main arguments, including (i) the translation of εἰ as equivalent to εἰ μή, i.e., *perhaps you will . . . ;* (ii) the patristic tradition; (iii) missionary concern; and (iv) backgrounds of 2 Sam 12:22 (LXX) and Epictetus, *Dissertations* 2.20.28-31; 25.2, for the meaning *how do you know that you will not . . . ?* (as NAB).[313] On the other side, Conzelmann remains unconvinced by Jeremias's linguistic arguments, while Fee points out that Jeremias establishes the *possibility* of the optimistic interpretation, but *not its necessity.*[314] Similarly, Senft addresses the detailed issues and concludes that the "optimistic" view leaves more difficulties than the "pessimistic" one.[315] Senft stresses (i) that in v. 12 Paul envisages two distinct possibilities of life, which depend on "mutual consent" (εἴ τις . . . εἰ δέ . . . cf. v. 15); (ii) if v. 15 becomes a parenthesis, which the Jeremias view demands, the imperative of v. 15a hardly takes its proper place as a serious piece of counsel alongside vv. 12 and 13; (iii) it seems unnatural and indeed uncharitable to try to hold someone to the home who wants to separate when the object is gospel witness, and the chances of winning over to faith a partner who remains in the home grudgingly (or who has been tracked down, to return), almost under duress, seem remote in the extreme![316]

We cannot exclude the "optimistic" interpretation. Fee rightly observes that it would be a pity if the concern expressed here for evangelism within the home were lost from view, since Paul does raise, or respond to, this issue. But when Kubo's critique of Jeremias (and of similar arguments by Burchard) are placed alongside the commonsense observations of Senft, we cannot regard Jeremias as convincing. We have every reason, therefore, to translate the Greek with an eye both to accuracy and to the genuine openness of syntax.

We conclude that (i) Paul's *"open"* point concerns *the limits of human knowledge,* which finds precise expression in the Greek construction τί γὰρ

---

311. For example, Meyer, *First Epistle,* 1:209; Alford, *Greek Testament,* 2:525-26, comments, "Lyra seems first to have proposed the true rendering which was afterwards adopted . . . by Estius . . . Meyer . . . de Wette." The alternative makes v. 15 "parenthetical," which evidently it is not, and forces εἰ to carry the meaning of εἰ μή (against Burchard, above). Cf. further Robertson and Plummer, *First Epistle,* 144; Allo, *Première Épitre,* 169; Héring, *First Epistle,* 53.

312. Bruce, *1 and 2 Cor,* 70; Schrage, *Der erste Brief,* 2:112.

313. Barrett, *First Epistle,* 166-67.

314. Conzelmann, *1 Cor,* 124, including nn. 47 and 48; Fee, *First Epistle,* 305-6.

315. Senft, *Première Épitre,* 95; Orr and Walther, *1 Cor,* 212 and 214.

316. Senft, *Premiére Épitre,* 95.

οἶδας, γύναι, εἰ. . . .[317] (ii) Even closer to Paul's heart than "missionary concern" is *everything is in the hands of God.* With *God* even a seeming negative can still be redeemed: the partner may change his or her mind, or the Christian's words and lifestyle hitherto may yet take effect. But by the same token, the believing partner should not live with anxieties and scruples, which can be handed over *to God.* (iii) Only an *open* construction can make this point; otherwise, to quote Moltmann, "pessimism" presumes un-Christian despair, and "optimism," un-Christian presumption. The right attitude, Paul urges, whatever occurs, is to *leave it with God* **in peace**.[318]

CONTROVERSY ABOUT DIVORCE AND REMARRIAGE FOR CHRISTIANS

We have already provided a "Preliminary Note on Divorce in Relation to 7:10-11" (see the end of the exegesis of vv. 10-11). However, broader questions have been raised by vv. 12-16 (esp. v. 15) and other parts of this chapter. We now attempt to address these broader questions with a particular emphasis on controversy about remarriage for Christians after the collapse of a first marriage.

In the Roman world of the first century divorce was undertaken both frequently and often for selfish, trivial reasons. (See the introduction to ch. 7 above and the earlier "Note.") Thus Seneca scornfully parodies women "who mark the years not by changing Censors but by the acquisition of a new husband."[319] The Stoic ideal expressed by Musonius is that nature has implanted a desire for union between male and female "to devise a way of life in common," in which marriage and the household is like a boundary wall or defense wall around a city.[320] Nevertheless, in practice, as Yarbrough observes, "Divorce . . . was exceedingly frequent."[321] Expectations were often beyond reality and led to frustration. Thus Callicratidas advises men to choose a younger wife who "can be easily moulded and . . . docile," while Plutarch replies to the man who has a preference for homosexual love, complaining that a wealthy woman is determined "to command and to dominate him," that even "a decent woman can be disagreeable and a poor woman can subject a man to her."[322] The idealized portrayals of a wife whose qualities included "loyalty, obedience, affability, reasonableness, industry in working wool, religion without superstition, sobriety of attire, modesty of appearance" must have raised expectations which could only be a source of mutual strain.[323] In funeral inscriptions the phrase "she never caused anyone grief" became so conventional that *"sine ulla querella"* could be understood simply by abbreviation as *"s. u. q."*

Failure to give and to receive such theoretical ideals might therefore be construed as implying a "failed" or "abnormal" marriage, which could supposedly invite

317. In practice this is Chrysostom's view in *1 Cor. Hom.,* 19:4 (see above).
318. Cf. J. Moltmann, *Theology of Hope* (London: SCM, 1967), 23.
319. Seneca, *De Beneficiis* 3.16.2; cf. Juvenal, Satire 6.224-30.
320. Musonius, *Fragments,* 14 (Eng. trans. C. E. Lutz, *Musonius Rufus* [New Haven: Yale University Press, 1947], 93).
321. Yarbrough, *Not like the Gentiles,* 63.
322. Callicratidas, *On Happiness* 10.8-11; Plutarch, *Moralia* 753C.
323. Cited from *Laudatio Turiae* by Yarbrough, *Not like the Gentiles,* 51.

divorce. It is against such a background that we must understand Paul's deeper understanding of marriage as a bond which is not to be dissolved at will. Thus a believer who is already married to an unbelieving spouse does not have grounds thereby to seek or to initiate separation or divorce (1 Cor 7:10-14). Nevertheless, if the unbelieving spouse perceives this as grounds for divorce, it is no use denying this (7:15), although this remains a last resort (7:16). Realism accepts what cannot be changed without damage (cf. vv. 17-24, on which see exegesis below).

Although Paul regards the marriage bond as in principle lifelong (7:10-11, 39; cf. Rom 7:1-3), in the OT provision was made for a husband to initiate divorce (Deut 24:1-4) "if he finds something indecent" in his wife (Heb. עָרְוַת דָּבָר *'erwat dabar*), which destroys his finding "favor" (חֵן, *chen*) in her (v. 1). Heb. עֶרְוָה *('erwah)* often means shameful exposure or nakedness, but in this context "the precise meaning is not clear" and may denote "a physical deficiency such as the inability to bear children."[324] The emphasis of Deut 24:1-4, however, lies not on what grounds for divorce are acceptable, but that, given the tradition of its occurrence, a legal document of divorce is to be formally provided, almost certainly to provide the divorced wife with protection and a formal status under the law, and equally certainly, it would appear, to give her freedom to remarry without the charge of adultery. The specific illegality of remarriage "to the former husband" (v. 4) presupposes the legality of a different remarriage.

Mark 10:2-12 presupposes that the issue of remarriage after divorce remained a live question among the Jewish Pharisees or rabbis. Since the School of Hillel permitted divorce on trivial grounds while the School of Shammai recognized only adultery as due cause, the way in which the Pharisees are said to frame the question in Matt 19:3 (cf. Matt 19:3-12 par.) is more likely to reflect a query about this contention concerning the *grounds* for divorce, although the Markan account presupposes a question which Jesus actually addresses. In summary, Jesus distinguishes between God's will for human persons (i.e., that marriage is indissoluble) and what the law allows "because of the hardness of your hearts" (i.e., in the light of human fallenness, failure, and consequent closing up of the self and the heart).[325]

Paul describes his injunction to those already married in 7:10-11 as **not mine but the Lord's**. We discuss the relation of this appeal to the Synoptic tradition in our exegesis of these verses and a brief note attached thereto (see below). Here we restrict our attention to the debate about the possibility of remarriage where vv. 8-9, 12, and 15 assume distinctive importance. Although R. H. Charles argued on exegetical grounds for the legitimacy of remarriage after divorce for the "innocent" partner in cases of adultery, W. A. Heth has argued against this view.[326] His more recent argument (1990) against what he perceives to be an "evangelical consensus" based on a

324. P. C. Craigie, *The Book of Deuteronomy* (Grand Rapids: Eerdmans, 1976); cf. BDBG, 788-89.

325. Cf M. D. Hooker, *The Gospel according to St. Mark,* Black's series (Peabody, Mass.: Hendrickson, 1991), 234-37; L. W. Hurtado, *Mark,* NIBC (Peabody: Hendrickson, 1989), 159-61 and 166-68; C. E. B. Cranfield, T*he Gospel according to St. Mark* (Cambridge: Cambridge University Press, 1959), 319; D. A. Hagner, *Matthew 14–28* (Dallas: Word, 1995), 545-51. Arguments for the originality of Mark 10 or Matthew 19 over against each other have been put forward on both sides and are discussed below under 7:10-11.

326. Heth, "The Changing Basis for Permitting Remarriage after Divorce for Adultery: The Influence of R. H. Charles," 143-59.

mistaken exegesis of "the Matthean exception" reflects his earlier work (1984) in collaboration with Gordon Wenham.[327] They argue that a Reformation exegesis which
follows Erasmus distorts the absoluteness which Jesus ascribes to the marriage bond.
A "middle" position is adopted by S. B. Marrow, who argues that Jesus in Mark and
Matthew and Paul in 1 Cor 7:10-11 formulate an absolutist view, but then adapt or
modify it in relation to the needs of the audience (Mark 10:12; Matt 5:32; 19:9; 1 Cor
7:12-16).[328] A more positive understanding of the possibility of remarriage is defended by Colin Brown.[329] Brown points out that Gk. τοῖς ἀγάμοις (7:8) and ἄγαμος (vv.
11 and 32) do not exclude those who have previously been married but are now
alone through separation, just as ταῖς χήραις (v. 8) denotes those who were married
but are now separated by death.

Indeed, Brown sees further parallels in view of the penalty for an adulterous
partner being excommunicated from the church (5:1-5) as against the penalty of
death in Levitical legislation (Lev 20:10-12; cf. Deut 22:22). In each case the penalty
functions in parallel to release the "innocent" partner: **The Christian husband or the
Christian wife does not remain in slavery** (οὐ δεδούλωται) in **such circumstances**
(7:15), i.e., tied and trapped there, for marriage ceases at death (7:39). This is closely
connected in Brown's judgment with the entirely positive view offered by Paul of
physical union within marriage as a good gift for human existence, other than for
those called to the celibate life as their χάρισμα (7:7). Thus while he acknowledges
that "marriage is intended by God to be lifelong," four elements suggest "a frank recognition of human needs" on the part of those deserted (geographically or adulter-
ously): (1) the meaning of **unmarried** in vv. 8, 11, and 32; (2) parallels between death
and excommunication (7:39 and 7:2, 3); (3) the allusion to being no longer "bound"
(7:15); and (4) the needs of human nature in relation to God's gifts (7:3-7).[330]

John R. Donahue urges strongly the contextual issues that shape the formulations of Jesus and of Paul. They do not make "the legal form of a declarative pronouncement" an absolutist rule, but "a prophetic defence of marriage in the face of
easy divorce laws. . . . Paul . . . defends marriage against those who would force celibacy or separation upon would-be Christians. . . ."[331] In the history of the interpretation of 1 Corinthians 7, it is not merely the tradition of Erasmus and the Reformation
which Heth has to consider. While Roman Catholic tradition has been "absolutist" (except for the exegetical and pastoral unease of a number of contemporary Roman
Catholic biblical scholars), "the Eastern tradition and Orthodox Churches today believe that a marriage can 'die.' Such a death is seen as tragic, but those who are left
alone as a result of it can still trust in the loving care of God . . . and may still find
salvific life in the loving union of a second marriage."[332] The Anglican–Roman Catho-

---

327. Heth and Wenham, *Jesus and Divorce: The Problem with the Evangelical Consensus;*
cf. also Heth, "The Meaning of Divorce in Matt 19:3-9," 36-52.

328. Marrow, "Marriage and Divorce in the NT," 3-15.

329. Brown, "Separate: Divorce, Separation and Remarriage," in Brown (ed.), *NIDNTT,*
3:535-43.

330. Ibid., 536 and 537.

331. J. R. Donahue, "Divorce: NT Perspectives," *The Month* (1981): 113-20; also rpt. in
Kelly, *Divorce and Second Marriage: Facing the Challenge,* 212-28.

332. Kelly, "Divorce and Remarriage," in Hoose (ed.), *Christian Ethics,* 255; cf. 248-65;
also on the Orthodox tradition B. Häring, *No Way Out? Pastoral Care for the Divorced and Re-
married* (Slough: St. Paul, 1989).

lic International Commission's agreed statement of 1994 (ARCIC II) affirms a common view of the lifelong nature of marriage but notes that, in the view of some Anglicans, where a marriage "dies," the marriage bond has also "died."[333]

Nevertheless, the Church of England House of Bishops Report of 1991 warns that even if marriages fall short, "the sentimental dream of an idyllic, romantic union in which failings, sins, and incompatibilities that mark us all are magically done away" must not be allowed to determine what counts as the norm or life of a marriage.[334] This relates closely to our comments above about the Roman world and its overly ready expectation of *sine ulla querella*. In their 1999 Report the English Anglican Bishops hold together "that marriage is an unconditional commitment for life" and that "a further marriage after a divorce is an exceptional act" to be considered only "with great honesty and circumspection."[335] A fuller document from a Working Party of the Church of England House of Bishops has just appeared, which accepts the view of the 1980 General Synod that "there are circumstances in which a divorced person may be married by the church during the lifetime of a former partner."[336] Nevertheless, this possibility must rest upon certain nationally agreed criteria with the advice of their bishops.[337] It is not a *carte blanche* for separation and remarriage of every kind. This at least attempts to recognize the ethical and pastoral dialectic which a careful exegesis of 1 Corinthians 7 may seem to suggest.

In 1946 the Methodist Conference in Britain accepted the possibility of remarriage in church for the "innocent party" of a divorce. Dissenting ministers, however, were permitted not to officiate on grounds of conscience. Initially this was designed for rare cases, but it is stated that by 1996 62 percent of all marriages in Methodist churches involved at least one divorced person (partly, perhaps, because of requests from those unable to be married in Anglican churches).[338] In 1998 ministers were also relieved of the task of identifying an "innocent party" or the causes of breakdown. Hence the spectrum of ethical and pastoral practice from Roman Catholic through Anglican to Eastern Orthodox and Methodist witnesses to the lack of a clear consensus about the application of NT material, although the dialectic expounded above probably represents the view of a fair range, if not the majority, of Pauline exegetes and NT specialists.

---

333. ARCIC II, *Life in Christ: Morals, Communion and the Church* (London: Church House Publishing and Catholic Truth Society, 1994), 75.

334. *Issues in Human Sexuality: A Statement by the House of Bishops* (London: Church House Publishing, 1991), 28 (sect. 3.23).

335. *Marriage: A Teaching Document from the House of Bishops of the Church of England* (London: Church House Publishing, 1999), 18.

336. *Marriage in Church after Divorce: A Discussion Document from a Working Party Commissioned by the House of Bishops of the Church of England* (London: Church House Publishing and Archbishops' Council, 2000), 50.

337. Ibid., 50-51 and 30-49. Cf. also Church of England General Synod Marriage Commission, *Marriage and the Church's Task* (London: Church Information Office, 1978), of which an extract appears in *Marriage in Church*, 65-86 (Appendix 3).

338. *Marriage in Church*, 30-31.

5. Divine Calling or Improved Status? (7:17-24)

(17) At all events, let each person conduct his or her life as the Lord has apportioned it and as God has called each. So, too, do I lay down this charge in all the churches. (18) If anyone was circumcised already when he was called to faith, let him not cover over his circumcision. If anyone was uncircumcised at the time of his call, he should not be circumcised. (19) Circumcision is nothing and uncircumcision is nothing; what matters is keeping God's commandments. (20) Each person should remain in the situation in which he or she was when God called them. (21) If, when God called you, you were a slave, do not let it worry you. Even if there is a possibility that you might come to be free, rather, start to make positive use of the present. (22, 23, 24) For the slave who was called in the Lord is a freedperson to the Lord; likewise the free person who was called is a slave of Christ. You were purchased with a price. Do not become slaves to human persons. Dear Christian brothers and sisters, let each person remain in whatever his or her situation was when they were called, with God at their side.

This section is usually given some such title as "The Guiding Principle — Stay as One Was When Called."[339] But we noted Cartlidge's comment that in 1 Corinthians 7 Paul works not only with the issues of gender, sex, marriage, and celibacy but also with the parallel "pairs" of Jew and Gentile, slave and free, as he does in the three categories of Gal 3:28. Paul does not want the addressees who may have a lack of realism and unhelpful priorities in the first area to fail to notice how the same stance would impinge on the other two related categories. In this sense F. F. Bruce's provision of a generic title captures Paul's concern well: "Calling and Status."[340]

Dale Martin's novel insights in his *Slavery as Salvation* give pause for thought before we speak too readily of the "remaining in the *status quo*" principle as a key to the issues under discussion. Martin sees slavery in these verses as related to "upward mobility" in a complex dialectic between state and status. He writes: "Paul does not here destroy the divisions between persons of different statuses. He first redefines the arena for status by taking it out of normal discourse and placing it within the symbolic world of the household of Christ. Then he reverses the status within the household, giving higher status within the household to those who held lower status outside the household."[341] If Martin's view carries any weight, the title proposed by Conzelmann, "Eschatological Freedom" is one-sided in one direction, just as "Remain as You Were" would be one-sided in the other direction.[342] Paul calls on the three categories

339. Fee, *First Epistle,* 306.
340. Bruce, *1 and 2 Cor,* 71.
341. Martin, *Slavery as Salvation,* 66.
342. Conzelmann, *1 Cor,* 125.

of sex, race, and class because it is easy to be simplistic if arguments are applied to only one group of these issues. When we consider all three, crosscurrents and complexities prohibit overeasy or overhasty "solutions" to a pastoral and a moral theology that applies the gospel and liberation to a series of differing and changing contexts in the real world.

One practical upshot of Paul's reply to Corinth is to establish the principle that *neither freedom in the new creation nor obedient response to divine call can be compromised by the constraints of a person's circumstantial situation or status in everyday life.* A Christian does not have to seek "the right situation" in order to enjoy Christian freedom or to serve God's call effectively.

Supplementary Bibliography on 7:17-24

The main bibliography on 7:1-16, 25-40 is listed above. These remain important sources for vv. 17-24 (see above). Additionally on vv. 17-24:

Barclay, J. M. G., "Paul, Philemon and the Dilemma of Christian Slave-Ownership," *NTS* 37 (1991): 161-86.

Bartschy, S. S., *Μᾶλλον χρῆσαι: First Century Slavery and the Interpretation of 1 Cor. 7:21,* SBLDS 11 (Missoula: Scholars Press, 1973).

Bieder, W., *Die Berufung im NT* (Zürich: Zwingli 1961).

Bradley, K. R., *Slaves and Masters in the Roman Empire* (New York: Oxford University Press, 1987).

Brockmeyer, N., *Antike Sklaverei* (Darmstadt: Wissenschaftliche Buchgesellschaft, 1979).

Bultmann, R., *Theology of the NT* (Eng. trans., London, SCM, 1952): 1:331-33, 343-44.

Caird, G. B., *The Language and Imagery of the Bible* (London: Duckworth, 1980), 243-71.

Cambier, J., "Paul and Tradition," *Concilium* 10.2 (1966): 53-60.

Combes, I. A. H., *The Metaphor of Slavery in the Writings of the Early Church,* JSNTSS 156 (Sheffield: Sheffield Academic Press, 1998), 49-67 and 77-94.

Dawes, G. W., "But If You Can Gain Your Freedom (1 Cor. 7:17-24)," *CBQ* 52 (1990): 681-91.

Deissmann, A., *Light from the Ancient East* (Eng. trans., London: Hodder & Stoughton, 1927), 319-32.

Deming, W., *Paul on Marriage and Celibacy: The Hellenistic Background of 1 Cor. 7* (Cambridge: Cambridge University Press, 1995), 157-73.

Fischer, J. A., "1 Cor. 7:8-24: Marriage and Divorce," *BR* 23 (1978): 26-36.

Finley, M. I., *Ancient Slavery and Modern Ideology* (London: Chatto & Windus, 1980), 11-66.

Glasswell, M. E., "New Wine in Old Wine-Skins, VIII: Circumcision," *ExpTim* 85 (1974): 328-32.

Gülzow, H., *Christentum und Sklaverei in den ersten drei Jahrhunderten* (Bonn: Hobelt, 1969), 9-56.

Harrill, J. Λ., *The Manumission of Slaves in Early Christianity,* HUT 32 (Tübingen: Mohr, 1995).

————, "Paul and Slavery: The Problem of 1 Cor 7:21," *BR* 39 (1994): 5-28.

————, "Slavery and Society at Corinth," *BibTod* 35 (1997): 287-93.

Hopkins K., *Conquerors and Slaves: Sociological Studies in Roman History* (Cambridge: Cambridge University Press, 1978), ch. 1.

Jones, F. S., *"Freiheit" in den Briefen des Apostels Paulus* (Gottingen: Vandenhoeck & Ruprecht, 1987).

Lyall, L., "Roman Law in the Writings of Paul — The Slave and the Freedman," *NTS* 17 (1970): 73-79.

Martin, D. B., *Slavery as Salvation* (New Haven and London: Yale University Press, 1990), 63-68 and throughout.

Meeks, W. A., "The Circle of Reference in Pauline Morality," in D. L. Balch, E. Ferguson, and W. A. Meeks (eds.), *Greeks, Romans and Christians: Essays in Honor of A. J. Malherbe* (Minneapolis: Fortress, 1991), 305-17.

————, *The First Urban Christians: The Social World of the Apostle Paul* (New Haven: Yale University Press, 1983), esp. 21-25.

Neuhaüser, E., "Ruf Gottes und Stand der Christen. Bemerkungen zu 1 Kor. 7," *BZ* 3 (1959): 43-51.

Roland, G., *Die Stellung des Sklaven in den paulinischen Gemeiden und bei Paulus* (Bern: Lang, 1976).

Rollins, W. G., "Greco-Roman Slave Terminology and Pauline Metaphors for Salvation," in K. H. Richards (ed.), *SBL Seminar Papers 1987* (Atlanta: Scholars Press, 1987), 100-110.

Schweitzer, A., *The Mysticism of Paul the Apostle* (Eng. trans., London: Black, 1931), 187-96.

Schweizer, E., "Zum Slavenproblem im NT," *EvT* 32 (1972): 502-6.

Trummer, P., "Die Chance der Freiheit. Zur Interpretation des μᾶλλον χρῆσαι in 1 Kor. 7:21," *Bib* 56 (1975): 344-68.

Watson, A., *Roman Slave Law* (Baltimore: Johns Hopkins University Press, 1987).

Wiedemann, T. E. J., *Greek and Roman Slavery* (London: Groom Helm, 1981).

————, *Slavery,* Greece and Rome: New Surveys 19 (Oxford: Oxford University Press and the Classical Association, 1997), esp. 1-46.

Wiederkehr, D., *Die Theologie der Berufung in den Paulusbriefen* (Fribourg: Universïtätsverlag, 1963), 148-87 and 112-25.

Winter, B. W., "Secular and Christian Responses to Corinthian Famines," *TynBul* 20 (1989): 86-106.

————, "Social Mobility: 1 Cor 7:17-24," in Winter's *Seek the Welfare of the City* (Grand Rapids: Eerdmans and Carlisle: Paternoster, 1994), 145-63.

————, "St Paul Is a Critic of Roman Slavery in 1 Cor 7:21-23," *Berea* (1997): 337-55.

Wolbert, W., *Ethische Argumentation und Paränese in 1 Kor. 7* (Düsseldorf: Patmos, 1981), 72-170, esp. 107-18.

17 It is scarcely the case that "Paul digresses."[343] Bartchy, Deming, and Cartlidge are right to urge that the three "pairs" of Gal 3:28 (male, female; slave, free; Greek, Jew) have interactive significance which prohibits an unduly simplistic understanding of the implications of the gospel for any category alone.[344] Whereas in Gal 3:28 Paul's primary sphere of discourse is Jew-

---

343. Kistemaker, *1 Cor,* 229.

344. Bartchy, *Μᾶλλον χρῆσαι: First Century Slavery and the Interpretation of 1 Cor. 7:21*

Gentile relations, which he compares with the other two categories, in 1 Corinthians 7 the issues have been those of sex and gender (the former on physical intimacy and celibacy; the latter on mutuality and reciprocity), these issues are protected from a simplistic "everything has changed" or "nothing has changed" by comparisons with slave-free and Jew-Gentile issues. In one sense, the new eschatological reality of the gospel abolishes "human" categorization; but in a deeper and more realistic sense it relativizes and redefines them. The logic of "eschatological perfectionism" (to use Schrage's term) would abolish physical intimacy and prior mutual obligations concerning race, status, and gender. *Paul's difficult pastoral task is to show in what sense this is true and in what sense it is false.*

Deming makes an apt comment: "First . . . no Christian can be enslaved by the circumstances of his or her life, by virtue of God's 'call' to become a Christian. . . . Second, undue concern for changing the circumstances of one's life disregards the efficiency of God's call, and thereby represents a form of slavery in itself. In this way, the pair circumcised-uncircumcised (7:18-19) functions here to illustrate the general principle that outward circumstances are of no consequence to the Christian, and therefore a Christian should not seek to make a change in one way or the other."[345] But the remaining pair, slave-free, goes further by implying that the new creation *reverses* the old situation at a fundamental level.[346] Yet even Deming's approach remains insufficiently subtle to do full justice to Paul's complex thought. For Deming is too eager to ascribe to Paul a notion of "inner" freedom which can be found in Stoic attitudes. Stoic self-sufficiency made a person "free" of outward circumstances, but for Paul life in the body remains the domain in which the gospel is lived out and exhibits its reality. Hence there is a subtle dialectic between the sense in which outward circumstances matter and the sense in which they do not. Thus Deming's parallels from Seneca, Plutarch, and Epictetus shed light on part of the issue, but not on all of it.[347] His strong and important point is that vv. 17-24 cut across Corinthian notions about "bettering oneself" by seeking "better" situations and "better" status. The gospel has already done that.[348] Our "Summarizing Note: An Overview of the Chapter" toward the end of our introduction to ch. 7, however, firmly stresses the importance and *positive significance of varied circumstantial factors for Paul's view of marriage and celibacy which might otherwise appear to be ambivalent or even self-contradictory.*

It is generally agreed that vv. 17 and 24 constitute a parallel beginning

---

(Missoula: Scholars Press, 1973), 140; Cartlidge, "1 Cor. 7 as a Foundation . . .," *JR* 55 (1975): 221-22; cf. 220-34; Deming, *Paul on Marriage,* 157-59.

345. Deming, *Paul on Marriage,* 158.

346. Ibid.

347. Ibid., 161-73; cf. Seneca, *De Tranquillitate Animi* 4.3-4; Plutarch, *Moralia* 829F; 1103D; Epictetus, *Enchiridion* 11 and 15; *Dissertationes* 3.24.98-99; 4.1; (cf. also *Diss.* 1.19.9; 3.22.38-44 and Philo, *Legum Allegoriae* 1.93-95).

348. Deming, *Paul on Marriage,* 159.

and ending of a quasi-chiasmic structure, in which v. 24 returns to the theme of v. 17 by its repetition of καλέω (κέκληκεν ὁ θεός, perfect active indicative with **God** as subject in an emphatic position; ἐκλήθη, aorist passive in v. 24) together with the emphatic conclusion μενέτω παρὰ θεῷ (v. 24). That v. 17 states a principle is well introduced by εἰ μή, which we translate **At all events**. This use of εἰ μή as an elliptical condition occurs, e.g., in 7:5, Gal. 1:7, 9, and Rom. 14:14. Such translations as **At all events**, *only* (RSV, RV, Barrett), *however that may be* (NRSV, REB), or the more colloquial *Anyway* (NJB) serve adequately to reflect a contrastive note of "whatever has gone before, this is the principle. . . ." But NIV's *nevertheless* and AV/KJV's *but* appear to offer an abrupt, even harsh, contrast with the previous sentence, which is not the purpose of the idiom here. It is nearer to πλήν than to ἀλλά.[349]

The key principle ἑκάστῳ ὡς ἐμέρισεν ὁ κύριος finds expression elsewhere in Paul. Negatively, Paul exclaimed in 1:13 has Christ been **apportioned out**? (μεμέρισται). Positively Paul writes in Romans, ἑκάστῳ ὡς ὁ θεὸς ἐμέρισεν μέτρον πίστεως (Rom 12:3; cf. 2 Cor 10:13, similarly). But in the context of ministries, spiritual gifts, and the resurrection mode of existence Paul more often uses δίδωμι, *to give*, than μερίζω, *to assign*, **to apportion out**. With parallel effect ἑκάστῳ ὡς ὁ κύριος ἔδωκεν is used of ministry in 1 Cor 3:5; ἑκάστῳ δὲ δίδοται, of spiritual gifts in 12:7; ὁ δὲ θεὸς δίδωσιν . . . καθὼς ἠθέλησεν, of the resurrection mode of existence in 15:38. The circumstances of daily life are no less a matter what the Lord in his purposes, not ours, assigns to each. This Pauline concept of call and service varies greatly from that of secular modernity, which gives a privileged place to "autonomy," and from that of secular postmodernity, which gives privilege to self-fulfillment and to power interests. These stand nearer to Corinth than to Paul, and give this section fresh relevance to the present.

We have already commented on the words καλέω (here the perfect indicative active κέκληκεν; see on 1:9 and cf. 1:1-2 [κλητός]) and 1:24, 26 [κλῆσις] and περιπατέω (see on 3:3, where the background of the Hebrew הלך [*halak*]), suggests the translation **conduct his or her life**). The syntax of ὡς κέκληκεν ὁ θεός, however, is not easy, as even Barrett concedes.[350] Clearly, as we have already noted above, Paul's most characteristic uses of καλέω and κλητός refer to God's act of having **called** to Christian salvation, which in Paul's case (and not only his) coincided with his call to a task of service. His autobiographical reflection in Gal 1:15 with its connection between καλέσας and ἀφορίσας ἐκ κοιλίας μητρός μου resonates with the call of prophets (especially Jeremiah, Judg 16:17; Jer 1:4, 5) and Israel and the servant (Isa 49:1-2; cf. Ps 21:10-11).[351] Isaiah's use of קרא (*qara*) prepares the way for the notion of the people of God as the **called** in Rom 8:30 and 1QM

349. BDF, 376.
350. Barrett, *First Epistle,* 168.
351. Cf. Munck, *Paul and the Salvation of Mankind,* 11-35.

3:2; 4:10-11.[352] But is there also a secondary sense in which "present circumstances" constitute that to which **God has called** the Christian?

The use of **called** in v. 15b may support either response, but **called** in vv. 18 (a and b), 20b, and 22 is sensitive to the controlling meaning of *when you became a Christian.* To attempt to make the primary meaning coincide with a mere notion of "vocation" to a particular kind of work would risk clouding Paul's meaning, as Barrett urges. Yet in v. 20a τῇ κλήσει comes very close to the notion of a *calling* to a specific state or role. The very use of the phrase ἐμέρισεν ὁ κύριος in v. 17a should make us wary of claiming that Paul did *not* regard some prior role in society as a matter of divine vocation. The Pauline logic seems to be that the **call** of the gospel (in the primary sense) can subsume within it a transposition and sublation of earthly circumstances which make a situation capable of becoming one in which *the call to service* can become (or remain) operative. With this careful distinction in mind, we should not too readily dismiss a dialectic which allows some scope for the interpretative comments of Luther and of Barth on this passage, which perceive divine vocation "in and throughout all orders and estates."[353] Barth's judicious observation that theologically "there can be no question of complete discontinuity or incomparability between the old and the new" matches Wayne Meeks's comment that sociologically "outsiders are often a negative reference group, yet the Pauline stance is not simply countercultural."[354] Meeks adds, "However dualistically Paul can sometimes portray 'this world,' it remains the creation of God that 'groans in travail' for its liberation . . . in which the apostle's efforts and the inner life of the Christian groups are implicated."[355]

Barth's comment that "a man does not live to work; he works to live" forms part of his definition of vocation as "the whole of the particularity, limitation and restriction in which every man meets the divine call and command."[356] God's addressing this person in this way and that person in another is part of "differentiation and specification . . . as God intends."[357] Barth acknowledges that Luther's translation of 7:20 as *Beruf,* vocation, formed part of his polemic against the notion that only monks, nuns, and priests were **called**; but he warns us not to react so strongly against this hermeneutic that we lose the wider point of Paul and of Luther that God calls in *concreto:* "κλῆσις is the call of God . . . the sum of those points at which the divine calling encounters each of us as this ἕκαστος."[358] Paul's thought cannot be far removed from Christology here. The

---

352. The corporate aspect is stressed by W. Bieder, *Die Berufung im NT* (Zürich: Zwingli, 1961).

353. Luther, *Works,* 28, 39 (*WA,* 12:126); Barth similarly discusses "Vocation" as that "with which the commanding God calls each man to the freedom of obedience" (*CD,* 3/4, sect. 56, 595).

354. Barth, *CD,* 3/4 sect. 56, 596; Wayne Meeks, "The Circle of Reference in Pauline Morality," 317.

355. Meeks, "The Circle of Reference," 317.

356. Barth, *CD,* 3/4, sect. 56, 599.

357. Ibid., 600.

358. Ibid., 601, 603, 605.

vocation of the Servant is to serve *through* situations of constraint, in God's freedom, not *in spite of* constraint in bondage to a grudging spirit. Hence Deming's earlier point remains valid: freedom is not dependent on trying to "better" oneself, but to make the best of what and where one is, subject to the remainder of Paul's arguments in vv. 17-24.[359]

Paul's final phrase οὕτως ἐν ταῖς ἐκκλησίαις πάσαις διατάσσομαι reflects the initial concern of 1:2b, σὺν πᾶσιν τοῖς ἐπικαλουμένοις τὸ ὄνομα τοῦ κυρίου . . . ἐν παντὶ τόπῳ, αὐτῶν καὶ ἡμῶν, and the concern expressed later in 11:34. It may be taken as an encouragement: I am not simply saying this to you at Corinth; I say it widely wherever I preach and teach.[360] Or it may (more probably) be understood as a reminder that this (possible) lack of realism or "eschatological perfectionism" is peculiar to this idiosyncratic interpretation of the gospel. Or (*pace* Wire and Castelli) to mean that Paul is not being personally authoritarian, but reflecting the "ordered" realism (τάσσω) of the wider church and its varied congregations. The middle voice is similar to the active, translated above as **I lay down this charge** (since *give* might imply initiating it).

18 Against the early and strong support for the perfect passive κέκληται, a few MSS woodenly repeat the first ἐκλήθη (aorist passive) a second time in v. 18. But the paucity of support and reason for the variant leaves κέκληται without serious challenge.

The UBS 4th ed. *Greek New Testament* punctuates the verse as two hypothetical sentences or clauses (with Tyndale and NJB). But most English VSS follow the AV/KJV in punctuating it as two questions (with NRSV, REB, NIV) which seems more probable: *was anyone circumcised when . . . , let him not. . . .* The difference is merely stylistic and cannot be decisively resolved.

Schweitzer sees this as an absolute affirmation of the *status quo* principle: "This theory of the status quo is again a necessary inference for the doctrine of the mystical being-in-Christ. From the moment that a man is in Christ, his whole being is conditioned by that fact. His natural existence and all the circumstances connected with it have become of no importance. He is like a house sold for breaking up, all repairs to which become irrational."[361] To become "Jewish" or to suppress one's Jewish identity would be like tinkering with repairs.

Yet while Schweitzer's principle about eschatological new creation and the irrelevance of "repairs" remains true to Paul, Paul's dialectic is more complex. To *remain* Jewish or non-Jewish does not spring from general indifference, but from its *salvific* irrelevance. As in the case of gender, such distinc-

---

359. Fee convincingly criticizes Bartchy's interpretation of the perfect tense as "live according to the fact that God has called you" (Bartchy, Μᾶλλον χρῆσαι, 151-55; Fee, *First Epistle,* 310, n. 21).

360. Edwards, *First Epistle,* 179. Cf. the middle in 11:34 and Acts 24:23, with the active in 9:14.

361. Schweitzer, *Mysticism of Paul the Apostle,* 194.

tions are not abrogated wholesale: whether for friendship or for the witness of the gospel there need to be Christian Jews, Christian gentiles, Christian singles, and Christian married (1 Cor 9:17-23). The new creation *transforms* and *relativizes* such distinctions, but they have a place. Certainly the Christian is not to seek change merely to gratify ambition or to be a "better" Christian.

The present middle imperative ἐπισπάσθω comes from the rare ὠπισπάομαι, used in a medical sense only here in the NT.[362] Surgery which might **cover over circumcision** (verb, *to draw over,* Heb. מֹשֵׁךְ, *moshek*) was used by those Jews who wished to hide their Jewish identity in the Greek gymnasium (1 Macc 1:15; Josephus, *Antiquities* 12.5.1). Philo states that in his day (later first century AD) circumcision was "ridiculed by many."[363] Thus this is the first of three examples (the others occur in vv. 21-23a and 23b) where Christians seek social "upward mobility," greater influence, or higher status in the eyes of the world by a change of their social intention.[364]

19 οὐδέν ἐστιν is used succinctly, but the REB's idiom *is neither here nor there* conveys Paul's meaning well, subject to our comments on v. 18. The simple adversative ἀλλά before τήρησις again reflects succinctness of style, but English versions widely reflect the need for a stronger word than *but* (above) in modern English: **what matters is** follows Barrett's suggestion; NRSV has *obeying the commandments of God is everything;* Collins simply retains *but.*

Paul's evaluation of the sign of covenantal Jewishness reflects his axiom in Gal 5:6: ἐν γὰρ Χριστῷ Ἰησοῦ οὔτε περιτομή τι ἰσχύει (has any force, is operative) οὔτε ἀκροβυστία ἀλλὰ πίστις. But here Paul sharpens what becomes a paradox. For if circumcision was *commanded* (Gen 17:10-14, 23-27; cf. Exod 4:24-26), is it not a contradiction to say that circumcision does not matter, but **keeping God's commandments**? In Gal 6:15 Paul repeats οὔτε γὰρ περιτομή τί ἐστιν οὔτε ἀκροβυστία but adds: ἀλλὰ καινὴ κτίσις. The *new creation* occurs not only in Paul but in pre-Pauline material in *Jubilees* 4:26.[365] Here it describes a new cosmic act of God, a new cosmic relationship with God.[366] In the terminology of Pauline studies it affirms an eschatological status on the basis of which issues of circumcision and "Jewishness" have become obsolete.

In this sense Paul's paradox offers both an explicit affirmation of the salvific aspect of eschatological belief at Corinth: yes, the Corinthian believers are part of God's new creation in which former distinctions are placed within a new frame and relativized. But no, this does not mean an eschatological perfectionism in which commands and constraints no longer apply, for the church is

362. The operation is described in the medical handbook by Aulus Cornelius Celsus, *De Medicina* 7:25 (early first century AD).

363. Philo, *De Specialibus Legibus* 1.2; further, Josephus, *Against Apion* 2.13.137.

364. On this issue see esp. Winter, *Seek the Welfare of the City,* 152-54. This places a different emphasis from the link provided by "bondage" emphasized by Combes, *The Metaphor of Slavery,* 82-83. Combes fails to refer to Winter.

365. B. D. Chilton, "Gal. 6:15: A Call to Freedom before God," *ExpTim* 89 (1978): 311-13.

366. G. L. Davenport, *The Eschatology of the Book of Jubilees* (Leiden: Brill, 1971), 75.

still en route to becoming what God has made it to be as the new creation. Hence Schweitzer's axiom about the incompatibility of law and eschatology applies to the salvific role of law, but not to law or "order" as an expression of God's will in the intermediate period when the new has come, but the old is still in process of passing away, as Christians live in the real world of constraint and fallibility.[367] Although we cannot know what proportion of the Corinthian church was Jewish, the Jewish reaction of *difficulty* in accepting that Jewish circumcision did not matter would have stood in sharp contrast to the supposed *ease* which some claimed that marriage or intimacy did not matter.[368] Paul's judiciousness in placing these three "pairs" together as part parallels must have indicated itself in discussions at Corinth. Glasswell observes that the distinction on which 7:19 hinges would be "meaningless for the Jew for whom circumcision was the gateway to keeping the law and a necessary mark of it."[369] If Wire is even partly right about Corinthian women, their surprise would be the converse: do we not belong to the new creation in which old relations, distinctions, and obligations have been abrogated?[370]

20 This verse constitutes the pivotal center of the roughly chiasmic structure which begins and ends with remaining in the situation in which one was **called** to faith (vv. 17 and 24). The first half (vv. 18-19) concerned circumcision; the second (vv. 21-23) slave status. The verse sums up issues already discussed in detail. (See above on vv. 17, 18, and 19.) We have frequently rendered the third singular imperative by its structural equivalent in English, i.e., μενέτω as *let him/her remain.* But a succession of such Greek idioms becomes stilted in English, as well as being mired in the problems of gender-inclusive pronouns. Hence we have varied the restructured **should remain** (REB) with the more traditional *let each of you remain* (NRSV), and also returned to the important individual diversity of ἕκαστος, **each**, as against the generic *everyone* (NJB).

It is strongly tempting to translate ἐν τῇ κλήσει ᾗ ἐκλήθη as *in the calling in which he/she was called* (AV/KJV, RV, Conzelmann, Barrett, Collins), but few modern English versions risk the ambiguity of the post-Luther sense of *calling* as *occupational* calling, even though we have defended this secondary implication of Paul's thought in the light of his use of such words as μερίζω with ὁ κύριος as the subject (v. 17). The meaning of κλῆσις in 1:26 (like κλητοῖς

367. Schweitzer, *Mysticism of Paul,* 52-100 and 177-204, esp. 187-96. It is because he shares Schweitzer's one-sidedness that J. Weiss tends to see the *status quo* principle as absolute in 7:7-24 (*Der erste Korintherbrief,* 185-92; cf. his *Earliest Christianity,* 2:411-16, 433-35, 515-25, 543-45, 549-54).

368. See further Rom 2:25-29.

369. Glasswell, "New Wine in Old Wineskins, 8: Circumcision," *ExpTim* 85 (1974): 329; cf. 328-32. Glasswell seems to conclude that **called** of 7:17-24 refers to *election* of the new covenant people, which constitutes a new beginning.

370. Wire, *The Corinthian Women Prophets,* esp. 82-97: "Apparently God does not call the women of Corinth to remain as they were when called but transforms their social lives through new sexual choices. . . . *This is the God of disruption, not the God of peace and order*" (97, my italics).

in 1:24) is decisive. There Paul clearly means *consider the circumstances that you were in when you came to faith* (see above on 1:26), not *consider what lowly occupations you held.* It is to clarify this point that we have interpreted the aorist passive ἐκλήθη as a so-called divine passive, i.e., **when God called them**. For this reason we follow the modern VSS in avoiding calling for κλῆσει (cf. RSV, NJB, *state;* NRSV, REB, *condition;* Moffatt, *condition of life;* NIV, *place;* Fee, **situation**).

Clearly in this context Paul refers to the respective **situations** of being married, being celibate, being a widow or widower, being separated, being a Jew or a Gentile, and being a slave, freedperson, or freeborn. Hence *place* is narrow if it means location, and it reflects a Bradleyan philosophy of politics if it means "knowing one's place." On the other hand, *state* too broadly includes attitudes, which are emphatically not to remain as they are. **Situations** may remain unchanged if, and only if, attitudes toward those situations undergo change and maturity.

21 Like v. 18 in the converse aspect of the chiasmic structure, this verse may be read as opening with a hypothetical statement (as UBS 4th ed. Greek and hence our translation, with NJB), or alternatively (perhaps better) as a question, *Were you a slave when called? Do not be concerned about it* (NRSV; similarly NIV, AV/KJV). The first half of the verse has straightforward syntax, apart from its punctuation. ἐκλήθης (aorist passive) may again be interpreted as a passive with an implicit reference to **God** as subject: **when God called you**. δοῦλος stands in apposition to the implied personal pronoun **you**, the subject of the passive. μελέτω, the third singular present imperative of the impersonal verb μέλει, usually occurs with a dative (here, σοι) sometimes followed by ὅτι, and means *to be of care or concern to* someone. With the negative μή the imperative here carries the force of *let it not worry you,* or **do not let it worry you**. It releases the addressees from undue care, concern, or anxiety. In modern colloquial parlance, it might almost be rendered *forget it.* The phrase regularly occurs in Stoic writers.

The second half of this verse, however, constitutes yet another notorious crux of interpretation. The phrase μᾶλλον χρῆσαι has actually been adopted as a title by S. Scott Bartchy, which turns largely (but not exclusively) on the meaning of these two words. χράομαι (χρῆσαι, aorist middle imperative) means *to make use of, to employ* (usually with the dative). But Paul leaves the verb hanging *without making explicit what it is* that is *to be made use of.* Further, does μᾶλλον have any special force here, and what significance, if any, is to be attached to the aorist of the imperative? Virtually every commentator since Chrysostom recognizes that this has become a notorious crux, and discusses it. We have therefore summarized the two main views, with two further variants, before comparing the English VSS and in this important case listing the main advocates of each view. For each tradition is supported by weighty writers. Those who supply τῇ ἐλευθερίᾳ (view i below) include patristic and Reformation writers and numerous modern writers from Origen and Jerome to Fee and Wolff. Those who supply τῇ δουλείᾳ (view ii) include patristic, medieval, and post-Reformation writers and numerous modern scholars, from Chrysostom and Peter Lombard to Senft and Collins. Even this, however, does not exhaust the possibilities. The following *four possibilities* emerge: (i) εἰ καὶ δύνασαι ἐλεύθερος γενέσθαι is understood to mean, *if you can gain free status,* and μᾶλλον χρῆσαι as *use the opportunity [for freedom] instead;* (ii) εἰ καὶ δύνασαι is taken to mean, *even if a chance of freedom arises,* and μᾶλλον χρῆσαι to mean *rather, use your position as a slave* i.e., for faithful Christian living;[371] (iii) Bartchy attempts a "middle" view but nearer to (i): *If indeed you become manumitted, by all means live according to God's calling* (i.e., as a freedperson); i.e., the verb (in an unusual sense) is applied to *calling;*[372] (iv) our translation suggests a "middle" view, but inclining a little more to (ii), i.e., **even if some possibility exists** (εἰ καὶ δύνασαι) **of becoming free** (ἐλεύθερος γενέσθαι, second aorist infinitive of γίνομαι), **make positive use** (aorist imperative middle), **rather, of your situation**. The verb is applied to *present situations* (*deliberately unspecified,* as against future hopes).

We shall reserve relevant details about slave status and manumission for a note at the end of this section. Meanwhile, which of these four makes best linguistic and contextual sense? There are distinct parallels with the "optimistic" and "pessimistic" interpretations of 7:16, where one solution appears to cut the ground from under the main thrust of the verses, while the other supposedly coheres more closely with general missionary stance, and where each entails some linguistic difficulties.

(i) *Applying χρῆσαι to freedom.* The AV/KJV and RV imply the first interpretation: *if thou canst become free, use it rather* (RV). The RSV (but *not* the NRSV), TEV, and NIV follow this more explicitly: *if you can gain your freedom, avail yourself of the opportunity* (NIV, *do so*). The REB basically follows this, but more carefully and subtly. It recognizes *(rightly)* that the addressee *must not take the initiative for change* (see note below). But it regards χρῆσαι as applying to the freed status: *if a chance of freedom should come* [correct!], *by all means take it* [more questionable].

In general patristic exegesis rejects this view, certainly in the form found in RSV, NIV, RV. The two apparent exceptions are Origen and Jerome. Jerome relates v. 21 back to marriage with the interpretation, "If you can be free, use it."[373] Origen's *Fragment* likewise relates the verse so closely to the marriage issue that its compressed argument is not altogether clear because he uses *slavery* in a metaphorical sense. But in direction he anticipates Jerome.[374] Erasmus more explicitly understands Paul to mean: *si detur occasio, libertatem arripiat,*

---

371. BAGD, 884; on the wider background of how *slavery* can or could be *used,* see Martin, *Slavery as Salvation,* 63-65 (and throughout).

372. Bartchy, Μᾶλλον χρῆσαι, 155-59; cf. 137-54.

373. Jerome, *Against Jovinianus,* 1:11; cf. also *Letter,* 48:6.

374. Origen, *1 Cor. Frag.,* 38:5-21 (in Jenkins, ed., *JTS* 9 [1908]: 508).

ac mutet servitutem.[375] Luther, Calvin, and Beza expand this view. Of course, Luther asserts, "Being a serf does not hinder him."[376] This includes "all paid servants, maids, . . . workmen, domestics."[377] As an ardent opponent of the Peasants' Revolt and especially its encouragement by the "radical" or "hyper-spiritual" Reformers, Luther could not countenance, nor find in Paul, any notion that the slave initiated freedom without his or her master's consent. All the same, "If you can gain your freedom, avail yourself of the opportunity . . . with the knowledge and consent of your master."[378] Calvin likewise observes: "If, instead of being a slave, you could become even free, it would be more suitable for you. . . . I do not debar you from enjoying your liberty."[379]

Among modern commentators and special studies, two dozen could readily be named, including especially Trummer, Fee, Hays, Rosner, and Wolff, who take this view.[380] Wolff (1) appeals to the ingressive aorist (with Schrage and Fee) to mean *begin to use the new status;* (2) argues that this coheres with the general context of freedom in ch. 7; (3) urges that if even a married person suffers "distractions" from serving the Lord, how much would not a slave![381] To these points (4) Robertson and Plummer add that the καί affects δύνασαι, not εἰ, i.e., not **even if** but *if you can also.* . . . On this basis they dismiss the other interpretation (i.e., ii) as "remarkable."[382] (But we offer a different explanation for the ingressive or inceptive aorist, under iic and iv, below.)

(ii) *Applying χρῆσαι to slavery:* NRSV, *Even if you can gain your freedom make use of your present condition* (cf. NJB, *even if you have the chance of freedom you should prefer to make use of your condition as a slave*). Chrysostom explicitly states: "'if you can become free, use it rather': that is, rather continue as a slave. . . . Slavery is no harm but an advantage."[383] He acknowledges that there is already a tradition of the main alternative interpretation, "But the expression would be very contrary to Paul's manner if he intended this. For . . . some might say, 'What, then, if I am not able . . . ?' . . . A man gets nothing by being freed."[384] With Ambrosiaster, Chrysostom is fol-

375. Erasmus, *Omn. Op.: Periph. in Ep. Pauli ad Cor.,* 881F.

376. Luther, *Works,* 28:42; *WA,* 12:129.

377. Ibid.; cf. *Early Theological Works* (ed. J. Atkinson; LCC), 262-63.

378. *Works,* 28:43 (*WA,* 12:129-30).

379. Calvin, *First Epistle,* 154.

380. P. Trummer attempts a linguistic defense in "Die Chance der Freiheit. Zur Interpretation des μᾶλλον χρῆσαι in 1 Kor 7:21," 344-68. Wolff, *Der erste Brief,* 149-50; Rosner, *Paul, Scripture and Ethics,* 174. See Findlay, *Expositor's Greek Testament,* 2:880; Godet, *First Epistle,* 1:357-61; Lightfoot, *Notes,* 229-30; Craig, "1 Cor," *IB,* 10:83; Moffatt, *First Epistle,* 87; Deluz, *Companion to 1 Corinthians,* 92; Bruce, *1 and 2 Cor,* 72; Fee, *First Epistle,* 315-18; Talbert, *Reading Corinthians,* 42; Blomberg, *1 Cor,* 146; Kistemaker, *1 Cor,* 232-33; Rengstorf, "δοῦλος," *TDNT,* 2:272; Wire, *Women Prophets,* 86 and 86, n. 10; Hays, *First Cor,* 125-26.

381. Wolff, *Der erste Brief,* 149-50; Schrage, *Der erste Brief,* 2:139, Bruce, *1 and 2 Cor,* 72; Fee, *First Epistle,* 317.

382. Robertson and Plummer, *First Epistle,* 147-48.

383. Chrysostom, *1 Cor. Hom.,* 19:5.

384. Ibid.

lowed by Theodoret, Pelagius, and Theophylact and in the medieval period by Photius, Peter Lombard, and probably also Thomas Aquinas (Peter Lombard writes *magis utere servitute*).[385] In the post-Reformation period Estius and Bengel apply the verb to *slavery*, and a flood of modern writers advocate this view, including especially Allo, Barrett, Conzelmann, Senft, Lang, Deming, and Collins.[386]

(a) The arguments for this view have been substantially strengthened by Martin's research in *Slavery as Salvation*, although he tends to endorse Bartchy's view of this particular verse (view iii, below).[387] If Martin is correct in relating the circumstances of slavery to "upward mobility" and to a huge variation in status between a mere piece of property and a highly esteemed manager or administrator who shared in part in the esteemed status of an important master, then we must rethink Lightfoot's assumption that every slave was "fettered at every turn" and Blomberg's comment that Paul could never have countenanced "a form of oppression that displeases God," even temporarily.[388] Almost every recent writer on Roman slavery is at pains both to stress its *variable* condition *and to distance it from resonances with nineteenth-century American slavery.*

(b) The argument that the constraints of slavery leave no room to be free for the Lord backfires. It undermines Paul's reassurance in v. 21a (**do not let it worry you**). Edwards anticipates Deming's citations of Stoic parallels when he observes, "The Apostle's words imply that the Christian slave is more likely than the free man to realize vividly his freedom in the Lord."[389] In any case, freedpersons were by no means "free" from obligations to their former masters.

(c) The strongest argument of view (i) is the use of the aorist imperative rather than present. It signifies "making use of a definite opportunity."[390] But while this *may* account for the aorist, our view (iv) has in common with view (i) the notion that χρῆσαι entails attitude of mind *as well as* behavior. A grudging attitude which resented the constraint invites *not* the injunction *go on using*

385. Ambrosiaster, *Commentary,* in CSEL, 81:79; Theodoret, *Op. Omnia: Int. Ep. 1 ad Cor.,* 207D-208, in Migne, *PG,* 82:279 (Gk.), 280 (Lat.). In the medieval period Photius (c. 810-95), Greek text in K. Staab (ed.), *Pauluskommentare,* 539 (lines 12-20); Thomas Aquinas, *Epistolas s. Pauli,* 1:304 (but *Postilla* glossed by Niccolai de Gorram); Peter Lombard, in Migne, *PL,* 162:1595B.

386. Bengel, *Gnomon,* 630; Meyer, *First Epistle,* 1:214-16; Heinrici, *Das erste Sendschreiben,* 201; Weiss, *Der erste Korintherbrief,* 187-88; MacRory, *Epistles,* 100-101; Bachmann, *Der erste Brief,* 278; Lietzmann, *An die Korinther,* 32-33; Allo, *Première Épitre,* 173-74; Héring, *First Epistle,* 55-56; Wendland, *Die Briefe,* 59-60; Barrett, *First Epistle,* 170-71; Conzelmann, *1 Cor,* 127; Senft, *La Première Épitre,* 97-98; Lang, *Die Briefe,* 96-97; Deming, *Paul on Marriage,* 158-59; Collins, *First Cor,* 285-86; cf. Mitchell, *Rhetoric of Reconciliation,* 124, n. 357, with more caution, as also Orr and Walther, *1 Cor,* 215.

387. Martin, *Slavery,* 198, n. 16, and 60-65 and throughout.

388. Lightfoot, *Notes,* 229-30; Blomberg, *1 Cor,* 146.

389. Edwards, *First Epistle,* 183-84.

390. Bruce, *1 and 2 Cor,* 72.

(present imperative) but *start to use* (aorist), or **start to make positive use** of the present situation, without pre-judging whether or not freedom may eventually come. Strobel understands Paul to say, "Do not be weighed down by care ('Sorge dich nicht!'). . . . Civil freedom or lack of civil freedom are without relevance for the person whose life is from Christ . . . a free person in Christ."[391]

(d) While advocates of view (i) interpret εἰ καί to mean *if you actually have . . .* , in conjunction with the elative use of μᾶλλον as *by all means* (take the opportunity), Barrett and others do not consider that this naturally fits the context.[392] Edwards cites, by contrast, the use of εἰ δὲ ὁ Σατανᾶς, if Satan even, in Luke 11:18, and εἰ καὶ σπένδομαι, if I am offered even, in Phil 2:17, concluding that if he had envisaged applying χρῆσαι to *freedom,* Paul would have omitted καί, as in vv. 9 and 15. In any case, Collins argues that if the grammar seems to point in the other direction, Paul's brachylogy technically leaves the issue open, while the content concerning contentment in any situation is more decisive.[393]

(e) This interpretation coheres best with the words that follow: ὁ γὰρ ἐν κυρίῳ κληθεὶς δοῦλος ἀπελεύθερος. . . .[394] The two categories of the slave as the Lord's freedperson and the free as the Lord's slave occur in v. 22, which expresses consolation and encouragement to those who in outward circumstances remain slaves.

(iii) *Applying χρῆσαι to Christian κλῆσις.* S. S. Bartchy translates: *If indeed you become manumitted, by all means live according to God's calling [as a freedperson].*[395] Grosheide virtually anticipates Bartchy's view precisely twenty years earlier. He writes: "Not slavery but vocation is the main thing. A slave may be a very good Christian. Just so he is called! . . . The first thing is to be a Christian, and that in all possible circumstances."[396] Grosheide rejects the view that χρῆσαι applies to liberty; but neither, he argues, does it properly mean *use your slavery:* "Neither of the opinions is correct."[397] It is neither of these circumstantial conditions that is to be *used:* "This prompts us to supply the words 'your vocation' after *use.*"[398]

Fee argues with Bartchy's rejection of *make use of your slavery* on the ground that a slave had no choice in the matter. But this is entirely to misconstrue Paul's differentiation between *stance toward* one's Christian status and *stance toward* one's circumstantial status. As Klauck, Fascher, and others insist, it is a matter of *attitude.* In this respect an accidental overlap with Stoic

---

391. Strobel, *Der erste Brief,* 124.
392. Barrett, *First Epistle,* 170; Edwards, *First Epistle,* 183.
393. Collins, *First Cor,* 285-86. See also on the linguistic issue Conzelmann, *1 Cor,* 127 and 127, n. 22.
394. Héring, *First Epistle,* 56.
395. Bartchy, *Μαλλον χρῆσαι,* 155-59.
396. Grosheide, *First Epistle,* 170.
397. Ibid.
398. Ibid.

philosophy does occur.[399] Bondage of circumstances need not constrain a person into a grudging, resentful stance, but *the very circumstantial constraint can be used as an opportunity for pleasing the Lord as the slave's real master.* This frame of reference is different from Stoicism, but in differentiating between circumstances and attitude toward them, the language of Teles, Seneca, and of Philo comes to that of Paul.[400] Bartchy can make a tolerable, although verging on marginal, case for understanding χρῆσαι to mean *live according to,* since BAGD cite, e.g., Josephus, *Against Apion* 2.125, for this meaning (with τοῖς νόμοις), as well as a few earlier sources.[401] But Fee and Corcoran convincingly challenge his interpretation of the syntax to mean live according to the fact that God has called you.[402]

(iv) If we draw in all of the positive observations made under (ii) and (iii), including the positive aspects of Bartchy's work (but not his syntax), the first half of the verse **do not let it worry you** is now amplified in v. 21b: **even if** *you can become . . .* is *not* to be understood to mean *even if you can save up and do in all in your power to gain freedom;* for this undermines the principle that it sufficiently *matters* to engage all one's thoughts, energies, and anxieties. Nevertheless, if the *empirical can* is excluded, δύνασαι must have a function, which is that of a *logical can.* **Even if there is a possibility** (δύνασαι) **that you might** (one day) **come to be free** (aorist infinitive γενέσθαι) faithfully reflects the protasis of the conditional. What is the apodosis? It is that which remains the ongoing theme and subtext of the whole of ch. 7, namely, **the present** *circumstances.* Paul has moved from varied circumstance to varied circumstance in ch. 7. *This is why the noun may be left implicit* after χρῆσαι. *Each both matters and does not matter.* These do *not promote or impede spiritual status.* But the gospel is lived out *through* earthly institutions and constraints, *not in spite of* them.

Here we must keep in view the purpose of the so-called digression. Do any of these things "matter"? Paul replies, in effect: consider the apparently varied values placed on physical intimacy, marriage, celibacy, remarriage, circumcision, menial slavery, managerial slavery to an important person, being a freedperson of a patron, and so on. All these things can have some *use* within the context of living out the gospel in the everyday.[403] Neither eschatological perfectionism, which would sweep them all aside, nor ascetic religion, which would value some over others, reflects Paul's gospel of a freedom-realism dialectic. Klauck and Harrisville make this point well.[404] Hope for freedom must

---

399. Klauck, *1 Korintherbrief,* 54; Lang, *Die Briefe,* 96-97; Deming, *Paul on Marriage,* 158-70; Harrisville, *1 Cor,* 115-16; Fischer, "1 Cor. 7:8-24," *BR* 32; cf. 26-36.

400. Teles, *Fragment,* 2.10.65-80; Philo, *De Iosepho* 143-44; Seneca, *De Tranquilitate* 4.3, 4. (For further examples cf. Deming, *Paul on Marriage,* 158-70.)

401. BAGD, 884; Bartchy, *Μᾶλλον χρῆσαι,* 155-59.

402. Fee, *First Epistle,* 310, n. 21; cf. G. Corcoran, "Slavery in the NT, 2," *Milltown Studies* 6 (1980): 69-72.

403. Cf. Wolff, *Der erste Brief,* 149-50.

404. Klauck, *1 Korintherbrief,* 54; cf. Harrisville, *1 Cor,* 115-16.

not be a distraction; one can **use positively** one's present situation. But if, after putting it in perspective and "waiting," freedom comes, then that now becomes the situation to **use**. Paul does not bind his readers to remain in slavery; but neither does he want them unsettled by fantasizing about discipleship as a freedperson. Every **present** circumstance brings its own special privileges and drawbacks as a public sphere for living out the gospel in one's stance toward God, toward others, and toward life. This interpretation will become still more convincing in the light of the note on slavery. The importance of the social background for exegesis cannot easily be exaggerated. (See the Note below.)

22-23a   The most illuminating interpretation of v. 22 comes from Dale Martin.[405] We broadly adopt Martin's translation, since it serves to underline the Pauline emphases which Martin identifies, as against the views of Conzelmann and others. He develops the dialectic which we have sought to preserve throughout 7:19-24, namely that in one sense the distinctions male-female, Jew-Gentile, slave-free have been abrogated, while in another sense they have not. Thus, Martin writes: "Paul is not simply mitigating the pain of slavery by claiming that in Christ all people are in basically the same situation, as if, because all are slave and yet all are free, the external, worldly status of each individual is unimportant."[406] According to such an interpretation, "the differences of status between Christians are annulled in the eschatological levelling of everyone to paradoxical freedom within slavery to Christ."[407]

Much depends here on our understanding of ἀπελεύθερος κυρίου. Conzelmann insists that the translation *the Lord's freedman* "does not really fit. . . . The meaning is rather that if he is in the Lord, if he belongs to him, then he is free in the eschatological sense, free from sin."[408] But does not the lexicographical evidence demonstrate that ἀπελεύθερος means primarily **freedperson** or *freeman?* Yes, Conzelmann concedes, but here this must mean not *freedman in relation to the Lord,* but *freedman in relation to his former slave status to his earthly master.* In Christian terms, Conzelmann follows Lietzmann in emphasizing freedom in the Lord, as against Kümmel's emphasis on service to the Lord.[409] For Conzelmann the decisive Pauline parallels occur in Rom 6:18; 8:2; and Gal 5:1.

Fee follows Conzelmann fairly closely. This verse "gives the theological reason for v. 21 as why the Christian slave should not let his/her social situation be the occasion for distress. . . . Neither slavery nor freedom counts for everything to the one who is called [into] . . . 'freedom' from the bondage of one's former sins."[410] Schrage explicitly endorses the sentence from Conzelmann about ἀπελεύθερος κυρίου which falls under Martin's criticism, while Senft fol-

---

405. Martin, *Slavery as Salvation,* 63-68.
406. Ibid., 64.
407. Ibid.
408. Conzelmann, *1 Cor,* 128.
409. Ibid., 128, n. 29; cf. Lietzmann, *An die Korinther,* 33; Kümmel, "Anhang," 177-78.
410. Fee, *First Epistle,* 318 and 319.

lows the drift of Conzelmann and Fee by calling v. 21 "a sort of commentary on Gal. 3:28."[411] Barrett is among the minority who reflect greater concern about preserving the subtle dialectic identified in 7:17-24 here (above) and instantiated in Martin's incisive analysis.[412]

Martin asserts: "Conzelmann's interpretation, however, does not adequately recognize the complexity of Greco-Roman slavery and the social meanings of Paul's terms. Had Paul wished to emphasize the eschatological freedom of the person in Christ, he would have used the word ἐλεύθερος, not ἀπελεύθερος. The second had definite social significance in that it stressed the relation of the freedperson with the patron."[413] The evidence of tombstones abounds with the use of the status-carrying designation ἀπελεύθερος (followed by name of patron in the genitive) in apposition to the name of the person whom the tombstone commemorates. Sometimes, as Martin observes, the upward-mobility–status theme led to a linked chain of status claims, e.g., "slave of Julia the freedperson of Gaius." Martin decisively states: "By calling the slave 'a freedman of Christ' rather than 'a free man *in* Christ' Paul stresses precisely what Conzelmann denies: that the status of the person is the issue, not eschatological freedom . . . the benefits of clientage to Christ over clientage to a human patron."[414]

To be **a freedperson of the Lord** is a "status improvement" not only in terms of a transition from *slave to freedperson,* but in terms of being **a freedperson to the Lord**, *rather than to another.* Hence we follow Martin in rendering κυρίου **to the Lord**, in English, whether partly as a genitive of *possession (belongs to the Lord)* or in the form of an objective genitive (μαρτύριον Χριστοῦ, 1:6, probably *testimony to Christ*), which BDF link closely with the genitive of *origin.*[415] The English preposition simply arrests attention without violating the genitive meaning. The social background has now paved the way for the *theological* point which Fee and Schrage make: "The slave's real status is not defined by current legal status, but neither is it defined as simply an improved individual condition: freedom. *The slave's real status is determined by his or her placement in a different household entirely: the household of Christ.* The slave is a freedperson of the Lord and *shares in the benefit, status, and obligations* that relationship brings" (my italics).[416] All of this instantiates Martin's fundamental thesis, which he applies to 6:20 and 9:16-18, that Paul uses slave imagery not simply (or even primarily) as a sign of servile, lowly status, but as "a positive metaphor for Christian salvation by upward mobility."[417]

Martin wishes to go one step further. Whereas a re-definition of δουλεία is achieved by what Moores, following Eco, calls "code switching" (see above,

411. Senft, *Première Épitre,* 98-99; Schrage, *Der erste Brief,* 2:142.
412. Barrett, *First Epistle,* 171.
413. Martin, *Slavery as Salvation,* 64.
414. Ibid.
415. BDF, sects. 162 and 163 (89-90).
416. Martin, *Slavery as Salvation,* 65; cf. Schrage, *Der erste Brief,* 2:140-43.
417. Ibid.; cf. 117-35, on 1 Corinthians 9.

325, 369), so what it is to be a **free person** also undergoes a semantic shift and re-contextualization. For the **free person** becomes a slave of Christ (ἐλεύθερος κληθεὶς δοῦλός ἐστιν Χριστοῦ), whereas the slave becomes the Lord's **freedperson** (κληθεὶς δοῦλος ἀπελεύθερος κυρίου ἐστίν). This is precisely *not* an eschatological "leveling," Martin claims, but more akin to a *reversal* of status. It is not a definition of *individual* status as such, but corresponds to Paul's theology of relationships within the body of Christ. We may readily compare the status attitude of those who say "I have no need of you" (12:21) with Paul's rejoinder that in the body "those parts which we think are less honorable we treat with special honor" (12:23, here NIV). Nevertheless to be a **slave of Christ** (rather than of another) outranks any other status in any other "household." This is so fundamentally the case that internal differentiations within Christ's household are as radically relativized as distinctions outside it. Yet in no household are all distinctions of function and care *abolished:* the relativization is part of a sensitive pastoral and theological *dialectic.*

All of this prepares for the understanding of v. 23a, which we have already expounded in our comments on 6:20 (see above). The two words of v. 23a are identical to those of 6:20a (although in reverse order): τιμῆς ἠγοράσθητε. We noted above (see on 6:20) Martin's rejection of Deissmann's elaborate appeals to inscriptions to explain the notion of Christ's purchase of believers *out of* slavery. Rather, **the price** brings the believer into Christ's own possession as his or her Lord, who then takes over the responsibility and care of the purchased one. The Christian *belongs to Christ,* not to himself or to herself. This is status and honor, for the slave represents his or her Lord; and it is freedom, for the believer is placed thereby in the hands of the Lord *for his care, his decisions, his directions, his responsibility.*[418]

23b-24 Verse 23b follows from 23a: if Christ has purchased Christians as his own possession at the price of the event of the cross, believers are not free to sell themselves into bondage under human persons, agencies, or institutions. The clearest comment, however, comes from Winter: v. 23a concerns "Christian slaves who aspired to freedom" (with vv. 21-22); v. 23b concerns "Christian free men willing to sell themselves into slavery for social and financial benefit."[419] Robertson and Plummer anticipate this in some measure.[420] The context suggests that Paul's concern remains that of warning the addressees against obsessive preoccupations about "status-betterment," whether by association with important names (1:10-12?), or with patronage and possessions (1:26–2:5; 5:1-5; 6:1-8; 9:15-18). This coheres with the achievement-oriented and competitive background of Corinth. On the other hand, Scott Bartchy is surely right to suggest that "there are good reasons for finding physical and

---

418. Cf. Weiss, *Earliest Christianity,* 2:458-60; Bultmann, *Theology of the NT,* 1:331-32, 343-44.

419. Winter, "Social Mobility: 1 Cor 7:17-24," in *Seek the Welfare of the City: Christians as Benefactors and Citizens,* 146; cf. 145-77.

420. Robertson and Plummer, *First Epistle,* 149.

spiritual slavery in 7:23."[421] Paul is concerned with *both situations and* attitude; the public world *and* personal stance. Believers are not *to return to the bondage of an honor-shame culture where everything revolves round what status is achieved in human eyes.* But with chs. 1–4, this is the "wisdom" only of the world which is folly with God.

The long-standing problem of a gender-inclusive translation of ἀδελφοί appears yet again in v. 24. Since the context has to do with both the Christian household, mutuality, and a common standing in Christ, Paul probably intends the four aspects of Christian, familial, mutual, and affectionate to be understood; **dear Christian brothers and sisters** seems most appropriate contextually here. The problem of gender-inclusive language also leads some English VSS to substitute *every* or *all* for **each**. But **each** constitutes a recurring emphasis on the diversity of case studies in this chapter. It is essential to flag ἕκαστος in the conclusion to this section. Paul repeats the earlier theme (see above), but adds παρὰ θεῷ. This may mean *in the presence of God* (REB, NJB) or *with God* (AV/KJV, NRSV), but requires a strong rendering which includes the nuance of παρά as *alongside.* Some consider *on God's side* a firm possibility.[422] Hence we render **with God at their side**, to fit the context and to reflect the emphasis of the Greek word order.

SLAVERY IN THE GRAECO-ROMAN WORLD OF THE FIRST CENTURY[423]

This is not the place for a general study. However, the exegesis of 7:21-23 invites corroboration and clarification of selected issues concerning slavery as an institution in the Roman world of Paul's day.

Becoming a Slave

(a) Those who were born as children of a woman in slavery constituted up to around a third of the slave population in major urban centers.[424] (b) A second major source came

---

421. Bartchy, *Μᾶλλον χρῆσαι,* 182 (against cf. Fee, *First Epistle,* 320, n. 58).

422. Robertson and Plummer, *First Epistle,* 150; cf. BAGD, 609-11, esp. sect. 2.

423. Documentation is included for all the relevant claims made in the commentary, but the material below is gathered from the variety of sources cited in the bibliography. Among the main sources consulted are, esp., S. S. Bartchy, K. R. Bradley, Dale B. Martin, H. Gülzow, and T. Wiedemann. In addition to these standard sources, G. Theissen (e.g., *Social Setting*) and Wayne Meeks (e.g., *The First Urban Christian*) draw attention to the decisive importance of such factors as differences between the city and the country, the crisscrossing boundaries, levels of social status, and differences from situation to situation. T. Wiedemann lists primary texts for "sources of slaves" in *Greek and Roman Slavery,* 106-21. These include, e.g., Pliny the Elder, *Natural History* 35, 58; Suetonius, *Augustus* 32; Polybius, 10.17.6-15; Strabo, 14.5.2.

424. O. Patterson, *Slavery and Social Death: A Comparative Study* (Cambridge, Mass.: Harvard University Press, 1982), 105-31, suggests that over 85 percent of the population of Rome were either slaves or of slave origin, with a smaller but not radically smaller ratio in many of the

from those who sold themselves into slavery, often to pay off a debt, but with funds remaining which could form the nucleus for savings or "earnings" through which the person concerned might hope to redeem his or her freedom. Some choice might be exercised within this category of self-sale concerning the identity of the master. In certain circumstances to sell oneself to a prestigious and successful master whose fairness one trusted could even be perceived as an investment for future prosperity and present protection, always, however, with risk.[425] Clement (c. AD 96) actually speaks of Christians who have sold themselves into slavery (παρέδωκεν εἰς δουλείαν) to pay for food for others (*1 Clement* 55:2). (c) The sale and theft of children without protection and kidnapping of adults (cf. kidnapper, RSV; slave-trader, NIV, in 1 Tim 1:10) was an illegal source, but one in practice, and some sold babies who had been left to die of exposure.[426] (d) The capture of prisoners of war and enemy populations occurred from time to time. Philo speaks of Jewish slaves who had been brought as captive slaves to Rome in 62 BC by Pompey, but such wars effectively ceased at the beginning of the Imperial period apart from such sporadic events as the Jewish revolt of AD 66-70, when Vespasian took 6,000 Jews for use as forced labor.[427]

Huge Variations in Role and Status

In strictly legal terms the slave was not a fully personal agent with personal rights but *"a thing" (res)*, i.e., the master's *property*.[428] This view could give rise to the utmost abuse and imposed, oppressive misery in the case of slave-owners without scruple who indulged their every whim and sense of power. Torture and corporal punishment occurred. Slaves, especially women slaves, could be used as mere objects of sexual gratification, and often it was expected that female slaves would be available to sons of the owner. At the other end of the spectrum, many slave owners believed that it was a matter of honor and ethics to treat slaves well who gave good service, and indeed that it was advantageous to all to nurture trust and hopes of manumission for loyal service. A "managerial" slave of a respected owner could enjoy a measure of the respect accorded to the owner outside the household. It has been observed that *to*

---

provinces. If up to a third became slaves through slave birth, this would still account for approximately one in four of the population. The children of slaves became the property of their owners.

425. The price of a young adult male slave without special skills was placed at various levels in the first century, but one marker was the cost of four tons of wheat. This indicates the possible magnitude of a sum. But the risk lay in complete loss of control of one's situation and of all rights as a human agent (see ii). On "responsible" masters cf. Seneca, *Dialogi* 5; *De Ira* 3.29 (and sources in Wiedemann, *Greek and Roman Slavery,* 110-16).

426. Wiedemann, *Greek and Roman Slavery,* 118-21, e.g., *Code of Theodosius* 5.10.1 and 3.3.1; and on Kidnap, cf. Pausanias 5.21.10. See further T. E. J. Wiedemann, *Slavery* (Oxford: Oxford University Press and Classical Association, 1997), 1-46.

427. This reached its height in the late Republic. In Paul's day many would be children of freedpersons (cf. "synagogue of the freedman"). Finley discusses the institutional structure of slave labor (*Ancient Slavery and Modern Ideology* [London: Chatto & Windus, 1980], 67).

428. Even a slave's marriage was not *matrimonium* but *contubernium*. On examples of cruelty, see Wiedemann, *Greek and Roman Slavery,* 167-87, esp. *Code of Theodosius,* 9:12:1; and on the complexities of the varied situations, see Martin, *Slavery as Salvation,* and Wiedemann, *Greek and Roman Slavery,* 2-11.

whom a person was slave was second only to *whether* one was a slave. The status and possible potential for "upward mobility" of a slave would depend on two factors: (a) their role within the household, which might vary from that of menial domestic or agricultural laborer to that of financial manager, general administrator, or secretary, depending on ability and opportunity; (b) movement from one household to another of higher status.[429] Some households were small and relatively modest. The Roman poet and satirist Horace owned three domestic slaves at Rome, and eight laborers on his farm. Some wealthy households had up to several hundred slaves.

Slave Families, Property, and Funereal Inscriptions

It is false to assume that the ancient world knew of nothing in any way comparable with a nuclear family. Evidence of inscriptions on tombstones bear witness to the special status of the relationships between, e.g., husband and wife, or husband, wife, and children. Extended family structures of "households" could still leave room for more intimate family structures within the extended grouping. Although at one level the slave was merely the master's "property" *(res),* in practice slaves usually received very modest wages and were permitted to save, to make purchases, to enter into contracts, and to run property.

Manumission of Slaves

The very large numbers and influence of freedpersons would be proof alone that most or very many slaves hoped to gain their freedom in due course. Relatively few spent their entire lives as slaves for two very different reasons. On one side, many owners felt it a matter of public honor to be known to treat their slaves fairly, and either to reward loyal service with manumission, or to permit the slaves to redeem themselves from the proceeds of savings or commercial sidelines.[430] On the other side, many owners found the provision of shelter, clothes, and food relatively expensive when a slave had aged past his or her prime. Manumissions then became a matter of self-interest for the owner, and in some cases as a freedperson the former slave's standard of living could actually deteriorate.[431] "The reasons were not primarily humanitarian but arose out of self-interest."[432] Manumission had reached a level in the first quarter of the first century AD that led Augustus to impose legislation restricting

---

429. This is argued in detail by Bartchy and especially by Martin. Martin includes a huge list of "slave jobs," from barbers, mirror makers, and goldsmiths to architects, business managers, bureaucrats, and archivists, and the professional roles of "managerial slaves" who could run country estates on behalf of their owners in Rome (*Slavery as Salvation,* 11-22).

430. For example, Suetonius, *Claudius* 25. On the complexity of these issues, see Wiedemann, *Slavery,* and the final section of this note.

431. For example, Dio Cassius 60.29.

432. Winter, "Social Mobility: 1 Cor 7:17-24" (sect. on "Manumission of Slaves"), in *Seek the Welfare of the City* (Grand Rapids: Eerdmans and Carlisle: Paternoster, 1994), 153. Winter cites further evidence from K. Hopkins, *Conquerors and Slaves: Sociological Studies in Roman History,* 1 (Cambridge: Cambridge University Press, 1978); and A. Watson, *Roman Slave Law* (Baltimore: Johns Hopkins University Press, 1987).

the number and ages of those freed.[433] It is widely held on the basis of evidence from inscriptions that most domestic slaves could hope for manumissions by their early 30s. Cicero observed that many could expect freedom in seven years. The freed-person received the status of a free personal agent, with the responsibilities as well as freedoms entailed, but the freedperson might well also retain a relation of client to the patronage of the former owner. Indeed, Winter is not alone in pointing out that continuing obligations of freedpersons to their former master should not be under-estimated in determining the problematic exegesis of 7:21.[434] In an extensive study Harrill concludes that neither 1 Cor 7:21 nor Ignatius, *Letter to Polycarp*, 4:3 can sup-port any suggestion that Christians opposed the liberation of baptized slaves.[435]

Historiography and Hermeneutics

We have space to draw attention to only one major issue. Thomas Wiedemann notes the traditional awareness that slavery reflects "an unequal relationship [which] de-nies the slave any existence as a person independent from that which his master chooses to grant him."[436] This, however, renders it "an ideal subject to which to apply the Structuralist concept of 'marginality'. . . . Things that are marginal are ambivalent, pointing in two directions. This makes the onlooker uncertain into which conceptual category to place them . . . and what practical action to take."[437] For what slaves "are" depends on what lies at the center of social life. In a society the citizen is at the center; the slave represents the opposite pole of minimum participation in humanity. Never-theless, other cultural systems have different "centers." New historical research has made it clear that in a number of situations (e.g., constructions of public buildings), "free and slave craftsmen worked side-by-side, and were paid a wage of money . . . they might not be living in the [master's] *oikos* at all."[438] New historical evaluations (e.g., of their role in leather-working, baking, pottery, wood-working) are still in prog-ress. Slaves shared work as nurses, childminders, barbers, teachers, physicians (i.e., overlapping with today's "professions"), and many aspects and issues yield complexi-ties which are still far from clear. "What has not emerged is a clear picture of the cir-cumstances under which slaves served their masters."[439]

6. Issues for Those Not Yet Married, Especially Unmarried Women (7:25-38)

(25) Concerning those who have not yet married, I have no charge from the Lord. But I give my opinion as someone whom the Lord's bestowal of mercy

---

433. *Lex Aelia Sentia* (AD 4) sets a minimum age of thirty. See further Bartchy, "Slavery," *ISBE*, 4:543-46.

434. Winter, "Social Mobility," in *Seek the Welfare of the City*, 153.

435. Harrill, *The Manumission of Slaves in Early Christianity*.

436. Wiedemann, *Slavery*, 3.

437. Ibid.

438. Ibid., 33.

439. Ibid.

has made worthy of trust. (26) Accordingly I think that it is well on account of the impending severe pressures for a person to remain as he or she is, as a good course. (27) If you have become bound to a woman, do not seek to loose the tie; if the tie has been dissolved, stop seeking to marry. (28) But if you do get married, you have done no sin. If, too, a woman who has not yet married becomes married, she has done no sin. But such married couples will have pressures in everyday life, and I would spare you that.

(29, 30) I affirm this point, dear brothers and sisters: limits have been placed on the critical time. For what remains of this time those who are married should be as though they had no married ties, and those who weep as if they were not weeping, while those who rejoice as if they were not rejoicing; and those who have transacted commerce as though they did not hold possessions. (31) And those who deal with the world must not be as though they were engrossed in it. For the external structures of this world are slipping away. (32, 33) Now I want you to be free from anxieties. The unmarried man devotes his concern to the things of the Lord, how he is to please the Lord. But the man who has married has anxieties about the affairs of the world, how he is to please his wife. (34) And he is pulled in two directions. Both the woman who is currently free of wedlock and the woman who has never married devote their concern to the things of the Lord, in order to be holy both publicly and in the Spirit. But the woman who has become married is anxious about the affairs of the world, how she is to please her husband. (35) I am saying this entirely for your own help, not to throw a tight rein over you; but with a view to what is proper and well suited to undistracted devotion to the Lord.

(36) If anyone thinks that he is not behaving in a proper way toward his betrothed, if it is a matter of undue strain and it seems the right thing, he should do what he wishes. There is no sin: let them get married. (37) Nevertheless a person who stands firm, steadfast in his conviction and not because persons or situations are forcing him, has a full right to make his own decision, and has reached the decision by independent personal conviction to respect her virginity, he will do well. (38) So, then, he who marries his betrothed does well, and he who does not marry will do better.

Supplementary Bibliography on 7:25-40

Allmen, J. J. von, *Pauline Teaching on Marriage* (London: Faith Press, 1963), 11-22.

Balch, D. L., "1 Cor 7:32-35 and Stoic Debates about Marriages, Anxiety and Distraction," *JBL* 102 (1983): 429-39.

Cambier, J.-M., "Doctrine paulinienne du mariage chrétien," *EeT* 10 (1979): 13-59.

Coppens, J., "L'Appel Paulinien à la Virginité," *ETL* 50 (1974): 272-78.

Deming, W., *Paul on Marriage and Celibacy: The Hellenistic Background of 1 Cor 7*, SNTSMS 83 (Cambridge: Cambridge University Press, 1995), esp. 173-210.

Derrett, J. D. M., "The Disposal of Virgins," *Man* 9 (1974): 23-30.

Doulfe, K. G. E., "1 Cor 7:25 Reconsidered (Paul a Supposed Adviser)," *ZNW* 83 (1992): 115-18.

Doughty, D. J., "The Presence and Future of Salvation in Corinth" (on 7:29-31), *ZNW* 66 (1975): 66-74.

Fischer, J. A., "Paul on Virginity," *BibTod* 72 (1974): 1633-38.

Ford, J. M., "Levirate Marriage in St Paul (1 Cor vii)," *NTS* 10 (1963-64): 361-65.

―――, "The Meaning of 'Virgin,'" *NTS* 12 (1966): 293-99.

Gager, J. G., "Functional Diversity in Paul's Use of End-Time Language," *JBL* 89 (1970): 323-37.

Genton, P., "1 Cor 7:25-40: Notes exégétiques," *ETR* 67 (1992): 249-53.

Giblin, C. H., "1 Cor 7 — A Negative Theology of Marriage and Celibacy?" *BT* 41 (1969): 239-55.

Hierzenberger, G., *Weltbewertung bei Paulus nach 1 Kor 7:29-31* (Düsseldorf: Patmos, 1967).

Hurd, J. C., *The Origin of 1 Corinthians* (London: SPCK, 1965), 169-82.

Kümmel, W. G., "Verlobung und Heirat bei Paulus (1 Kor 7:36-38)," in W. Eltester (ed.), *Neutestamentliche Studien für Rudolf Bultmann,* BZNW 21 (Berlin: Töpelmann, 1954), 275-95.

Lake, K., *The Earlier Epistles of St Paul* (London: Rivingtons, 2d ed. 1914), 184-91.

MacDonald, M. Y., "Women Holy in Body and Spirit: The Social Setting of 1 Cor 7," *NTS* 36 (1990): 161-81.

Meeks, W. A., *The First Urban Christians: The Social World of the Apostle Paul* (New Haven: Yale University Press, 1983), 84-107.

Müller, U., *Prophetie und Predigt im NT* (Gütersloh: Gütersloher Verlagshaus Mohn, 1975), 142-62.

Niederwimmer, K., *Askese und Mysterium. Über Ehe, Ehescheidung und Eheverzicht* (Göttingen: Vandenhoeck & Ruprecht, 1975), 13-41.

O'Rourke, J. J., "Hypotheses regarding 1 Cor 7:36-38," *CBQ* 20 (1958): 492-98.

Ramsarin, R. A., "More than an Opinion: Paul's Rhetorical Maxim on First Cor 7:25-26," *CBQ* 57 (1995): 531-41.

Schlier, H., "Über das Hauptanliegen des 1 Korintherbriefes," *EvT* 8 (1948-49).

Schrage, W., "Die Stellung zur Welt bei Paulus, Epiktet, und in der Apokalyptik. Ein Beitrag zur 1 Kor 7:29-31," *ZTK* 61 (1964): 125-54.

Scroggs, R., "Paul and the Eschatological Woman," *JAAR* 41 (1972): 532-37.

Sickenberger, J., "Syneisaktentum im ersten Korintherbriefe?" *BZ* 3 (1905): 44-69.

Williams, T., "The Forgotten Alternative in First Cor 7," *CT* 17 (1973): 6-8.

Wimbush, V. L., *Paul, the Worldly Ascetic* (Macon, Ga.: Mercer, 1987), 1-93.

Winter, B. W., "Secular and Christian Responses to Corinthian Famines," *TynBul* 40 (1989): 106.

Witherington, B., *Women in the Earliest Churches,* SNTSMS 58 (Cambridge: Cambridge University Press, 1988), 26-42.

Wolbert, W., *Ethische Argumentation und Paränese in 1 Kor 7* (Düsseldorf: Patmos, 1981), 72-134.

25   On the issue of "celibacy" in relation to the whole chapter, see our "Note on Celibacy in the Patristic Posthistory of the Text" toward the end of the introduction to ch 7. On περὶ δέ in v. 25 see above on 7:1, and especially the comments of M. M. Mitchell. The formula occurs six times in this epistle (7:1, 25; 8:1; 12:1; 16:1, 12) and usually signals the beginning of a new topic. Mitchell's article, however, becomes more relevant to this reference than to 7:1, since part of her thesis is that "περὶ δέ is not restricted to the answering of epistolary questions," whereas, as she concedes, in 7:1 it does explicitly signal a response to a Corinthian letter.[440] She concludes that most modern scholars have read too much into the phrase: negatively it in no way suggests any partition theory which undermines the unity of 1 Corinthians; but positively it is "our most important clue to understand how Paul, on his own terms, chose to respond to the multifaceted situation at Corinth.[441] Hurd's arguments may carry more force than Mitchell judges. Whether the addressees or Paul first brought up the topic περὶ τῶν παρθένων cannot be answered with certainty. The view that it had been raised at Corinth seems highly likely, and Conzelmann believes that this was "obviously" the case.[442]

A new category is now to be placed alongside married couples (7:2-7), those separated or widowed (7:8-9), people contemplating separation (7:10-11), people married already to those who have not come to faith (7:12-16), those seeking "improvement" in situation or status (7:17-24), and now περὶ τῶν παρθένων. But who are these? At least four possibilities must be explored, and Fee concludes that no major proposal is without difficulty.[443] Initially (1), are the *unmarried women of marriageable* age (in vv. 36-38, those already betrothed but under pressure not to take the step of marriage) *in the same category* as those in v. 24 (hence Moffatt, *unmarried women*)? Or are the women of vv. 36-38 *a subcategory* of the group addressed here (as seems more likely)? In lexicographical terms παρθένος includes "men who have had no intercourse with women" (BAGD). This invites a masculine noun, but the genitive plural form with the definite article τῶν παρθένων offers no indication of gender.[444] It may be second declension feminine or a masculine form used gender-inclusively. Although many allow the meaning of the word in vv. 36-38 to override the lexicography, this simply prejudges the conclusion. Fitzmyer, e.g., asserts: "A distinction must be made between the use of παρθένος in vv. 25-34 and the use of it in vv. 36-38. Vv. 25, 28 and 34 speak generally of παρθένοι."[445] Our own view that vv. 36-38 represent a specific subcategory within the broader group of vv. 25-34 gives us hesitation about assuming that Paul's addressees are exclusively women (cf. his ἀνθρώπῳ, not a marked gender term in v. 26), and to indicate category and subcategory we entitled this section "Issues for Those Not Yet Married, Especially Unmarried Women, 7:25-38."[446]

440. M. M. Mitchell, "Concerning περὶ δέ in 1 Cor," *NovT* 31 (1989): 247; cf. 229-56; see further her *Paul and the Rhetoric of Reconciliation,* 190-91; Hurd, *Origin of 1 Corinthians,* 61-71; Allo, *Première Épitre,* 153 and 196; Wimbush, *Paul, the Worldly Ascetic,* 11-13; and G. Sellin, "Hauptprobleme des Ersten Korintherbriefes," *ANRW* 2:25:4, 2,941-42 (cf. 2,940-3,044).

441. Mitchell, "Concerning περὶ δέ in 1 Cor," 256.

442. Conzelmann, *1 Cor,* 131.

443. Fee, *First Epistle,* 326.

444. BAGD, 627; as also in Rev 14:4.

445. J. A. Fitzmyer, "παρθένος," *EDNT,* 3:40.

446. See above, p. 565.

(i) J. K. Elliott proposes that the whole of 7:25-38 concerns *engaged couples,* but that the term παρθένος means *betrothed women* in this context.[447] In v. 27 Paul advises the man, "Are you engaged to a woman? Do not seek release, i.e., from the engagement. Are you single? Do not seek to marry." But the complexities of the case studies can hardly be simplified, as Elliott in effect proposes, to divorce (vv. 1-24), engagement (vv. 25-38), and remarriage (vv. 39-40).

(ii) J. F. Bound offers a similar exegesis of vv. 26-29, but, following Matthew Black, holds that παρθένος in vv. 25-28 means *virgin man* or *single, celibate male.*[448] This leaves the problem of the feminine ἡ παρθένος in v. 28. Bound resorts to the expedient of proposing that the feminine definite article ἡ is a corrupt MS reading for ὁ. But it would be perfectly arguable that up to v. 28a παρθένος is male, but Paul then follows his established practice of mutuality of address by speaking next to the unmarried celibate woman. A number of writers from Weiss to Schrage reject the feminine meaning.[449]

(iii) Hurd is among those who advocate the relevance of "spiritual marriages" already discussed above (on 7:2). He considers the "engaged couples" hypothesis too complex, as involving the three steps of (a) becoming engaged; (b) becoming converted to an ascetic viewpoint; and (c), instead of dissolving the relationship, establishing it in an ascetic nonintimate basis.[450] But anyone who has close familiarity with pastoral situations in church life will find this less complex than the vicissitudes of younger men and women in relatively small communities, especially where "elders" may also exercise pressures. Nevertheless, Hurd considers the "spiritual marriages" reconstruction plausible. A couple, on this hypothesis, intended to lead an ascetic lifestyle from the first.[451] This remains equally plausible in circles of so-called "eschatological perfectionism" or "enthusiasm," in which realism sometimes becomes a casualty.

In our comments on 7:2 we cited examples of such notions from The Shepherd of Hermas (*Similitudes,* 9:10:6–11:8, c. AD 160), from Tertullian (*Chastity,* 12), Cyprian (*Epistles,* 61:2), and Eusebius (*Ecclesiastical History,* 7:30:12). As Fee observes, there is a lack of hard evidence that these notions can be read back onto first-century Corinth, but the examples suggest that the notion cannot be excluded.[452] On the other hand, the formalized relationships discussed by H. Achelis seem to belong to a later era. At a less institutional

447. J. K. Elliott, "Paul's Teaching on Marriage in 1 Cor: Some Problems Considered," *NTS* 19 (1973): 219-25.

448. J. F. Bound, "Who Are the 'Virgins' Discussed in 1 Cor 7:25-38?" *Evangelical Journal* 2 (1984): 3-15; cf. M. Black, *The Scrolls and Christian Origins* (London: SCM, 1961), 85.

449. Bengel, *Gnomon,* 630: *utriusque sexus;* Weiss, *Der erste Korintherbrief,* 194; Schrage, *Der erste Brief,* 2:156 and 156, n. 592.

450. Hurd, *Origin of 1 Corinthians,* 177.

451. Ibid., 176-80. Achelis, *Virgines Subintroductae. Ein Beitrag zum VII Kapitel der 1 Kor,* remains a detailed extended study, even though it has been seriously overtaken by more recent research.

452. Fee, *First Epistle,* 327.

level than that discussed by Eusebius concerning Paul of Samosata, M. E. Thrall sees in vv. 36-38 "the situation . . . of a man and a woman who have decided to live with each other without marrying and having sexual intercourse."[453] However, to assume that this situation accounts for the whole of vv. 25-38 is to make yet another unproven assumption. Indeed, even Fee tends to lump together the "spiritual marriages" view with the distinct conclusion that παρθένος includes both celibate man and celibate women.[454] But it does not necessarily follow that the men and women who are παρθένοι already live together in vv. 25-35.

(iv) Lightfoot succinctly states a view which comes from a well-established tradition of interpretation. He first argues that the application of παρθένος to celibate men is largely post-Pauline in currency, and that such a use in Rev 14:4 is atypical and needs to be explained there (against Allo but defended by Kümmel). He then argues, by contrast, that Paul addresses the case of celibate men in vv. 26-33. But all this arises, he proposes, because "the Corinthians consulted him about the special case of giving virgin daughters in marriage."[455] This led Paul to offer some generalizations about παρθένοι, but the introduction (v. 25) and main conclusion (vv. 36-38) concern the *unmarried daughters* of the group who raised the query. However, this depends on an exegesis of v. 36 in terms of fathers and daughters which is problematic and no longer widely accepted. For such a convoluted theory, firmer evidence would be needed, in spite of its long and respected tradition.

(v) Many major writers understand the Greek to refer to *unmarried men and women* who may well have become *engaged*. Schrage and Wimbush are advocates of this view applying παρθένοι to *engaged parties*.[456] Collins shares this view, regarding vv. 25 and 35 as forming a rhetorical *inclusio*.[457] The application to male and female distinguishes this view from Elliott's. Wimbush and Deming both interpret Paul as following a Stoic pattern of argument about present circumstances (see below). Wimbush insists that Paul again emphasizes "the relative unimportance of the celibate life as far as status with God is concerned: one who has been single but desires to marry does not sin (v. 28)."[458] Deming cites H. Chadwick's view that "Paul's demand for continence as set within the eschatological framework of Christian thought, fused with Stoic-Cynic ideas about the soul's detachment and ἀταραξία."[459]

453. Thrall, *1 and 2 Cor,* 59.

454. Fee, *First Epistle,* 326-27.

455. Lightfoot, *Notes,* 231.

456. Wimbush, *Paul, the Worldly Ascetic,* 14, 20, and 23-24; Schrage, *Der erste Brief,* 2:155-56; also Fee, *First Epistle,* 326-27; Deming, *Paul on Marriage,* 173-77; Senft, *La Première Épitre,* 98-99; Wolff, *Der erste Brief,* 155.

457. Collins, *First Cor,* 288 and 293.

458. Wimbush, *Paul, the Worldly Ascetic,* 20.

459. Deming, *Paul on Marriage,* 190; H. Chadwick, "'All Things to All Men' (1 Cor ix:22)," *NTS* 1 (1954-55): 268; cf. 261-75.

Fee places more emphasis on the betrothed woman's situation, but equally on the betrothed man as the main addressee. These women, along with their fiancés, "were being pressured by the pneumatics, and were now themselves wondering whether to go through with the marriage."[460] It is entirely convincing to follow Schrage in insisting that παρθένος applies to the celibate of either or both sexes from verse to verse. The situation reconstructed by Fee and Wimbush is plausible as the general background, but flexibility should be retained to allow room (against Fee) for the possibility that this group may well have included a second subcategory of those whose so-called "spiritual marriages" (in whatever form) were beginning to take on an unpredicted attraction. If Fee's allusion to pressure from "pneumatics" is plausible (which it is), this scenario would scarcely be less probable.

(vi) J. M. Ford attempts to argue that παρθένοι refers to young widows and widowers who have been married not more than once.[461] But neither issues about Levirate marriage in OT traditions nor the adjective παρθενική of young Roman women who may have been married can make this proposal convincing. It must be rejected, together with any attempt to restrict παρθένος in these verses to either sex alone, as well as with the older "virgin-daughter" interpretation. In general terms, (v) is correct, with the priviso that variations of individual cases within each category would come within Paul's pastoral concern. He avoids stereotyped "answers" in 7:1–11:1, which fail to address special circumstances.

We turn to the translation. NJB's *people remaining virgin* (JB's *remaining celibate*) accurately renders παρθένων. But while *virgins* may not jar in 1611 or 1881 (AV/KJV and RV) the word today belongs usually to medical discourse or to sexual discourse with prior value-judgments. Yet REB's *the unmarried* does not (as it needs to do) exclude widowed and separated partners, whom Paul addresses elsewhere in this chapter. We dissent from Moffatt's overnarrow *unmarried women*. Either *those who have not married* or **those who have not yet married** seems best for modern English and public reading. The former matches the Greek more closely, but the latter reflects the Greek-in-context more clearly. The English then readily runs parallel to the other categories listed: married couples (7:2-7), the widowed or separated (7:8-9); those contemplating separation (7:10, 11); and so on.

On ἐπιταγὴν κυρίου οὐκ ἔχω, see above on 7:10 (where οὐκ ἀλλὰ ὁ κύριος almost certainly alludes to traditions of a saying of Jesus) and similarly on 7:12 (λέγω ἐγὼ οὐχ ὁ κύριος). Since Paul cites "present circumstances" or some impending event as that which tips the scales if all other things are equal, clearly nothing in the teaching of Jesus corresponds to the contingent event to which, Paul, in a personal and pastoral capacity, gives considerable weight.[462] When

---

460. Fee, *First Epistle,* 327.
461. J. M. Ford, "Levirate Marriage in St Paul (1 Cor vii)," 362; cf. 361-65.
462. Deming and Wimbush both stress the importance of contingent circumstances.

his teaching derives from his own thinking, as against what was becoming an apostolic rule of faith, Paul does not hesitate to say so. Perhaps, as Allo suggests, his plea that he can be trusted is linked to his keen awareness that in earlier times he was unconvinced by the gospel and persecuted the church.[463] However, Ramsaran may well be correct to argue that it is more than "advice," but a rhetorical expression of a maxim (γνώμη). It redefines the Corinthian maxim of 7:1.[464] Characteristically in Paul πιστός means *trustworthy*.[465] To call oneself a person **worthy of trust** seems like self-promotion (which Paul has criticized in 1:26–2:5 and 3:5–4:13). Hence he couples πιστός with a cause outside himself: **as someone whom the Lord's bestowal of mercy has made worthy of trust**.

Virtually all commentators and specialist writers translate γνώμην as **opinion** (NRSV, REB, NJB; cf. NIV, *judgment*). K. G. E. Doulfe attempts to argue on the basis of earlier Greek that γνώμη means *decision*.[466] Paul is not, he argues, an "advisor." The Greek idiom means *I take upon myself to,* with the performative or illocutionary force of a commitment or declaration. But in the view of Deming and Wimbush it precisely fits an appeal to the effects of a "present situation" and an opinion about what would be "fitting" in the light of it. This *is* a matter of opinion. Here Paul genuinely weighs up advantages and disadvantages, as if he were writing in the Stoic-Cynic tradition. We need not accept Deming's arguments wholesale to appreciate that at this point his analysis is valid and illuminating.[467] At the same time Collins underlines the rhetorical weight of γνώμη as meaning more than "personal opinion": Paul is expressing a "principle or rule of conduct."[468] Hence if Dolfe is strong, Deming is probably too weak. There is to be responsible reflection in the light of Paul's guideline or "maxim."

26 The verb νομίζω is neither hesitant nor uncertain but explicates (hence οὖν, **accordingly**, *therefore*) the content of γνώμην in v. 25. The remaining syntax and semantics of the verse, however, are complicated and invite some detailed explanation. διὰ τὴν ἐνεστῶσαν ἀνάγκην means **on account of** (διά + accusative) the ἀνάγκην *(necessity? external circumstances? constraint?)*, which is at once qualified by the adjectival perfect active participle of ἐνίστημι (feminine accusative singular). The verb ἐνίστημι (intransitive meaning, in terms of analytical components *to stand in*) may mean either *present* or **impending**. It therefore matches the notion of *present circumstances* in Stoic-Cynic discourse, to which Deming and Wimbush regularly refer, but, as H.

463. Allo, *Première Épitre,* 177.

464. Ramsarin, "More than an Opinion: Paul's Rhetorical Maxim in First Cor 7:25-26," *CBQ* 57 (1995): 531-41.

465. Barrett, *First Epistle,* 174. The translation *faithful* would not fit the context.

466. Doulfe, "1 Cor 7:25 Reconsidered (Paul a Supposed Advisor)," 115-18. The proposal is suggestive and deserves respect, but raises contextual difficulties.

467. Deming, *Paul on Marriage,* 175-77.

468. Collins, *First Cor,* 289.

Chadwick observes (see above, on v. 25), signifies something of greater urgency or intensity, perhaps within an eschatological frame.

The noun ἀνάγκη carries overtones of *that which pinches,* and Bruce Winter's argument that it refers to famine, or, with ἐνεστῶσαν, fear of impending famine.[469] We have already discussed the claims of Winter's argument (supported also by Bradley Blue) that resonances and effects from the famine of AD 51 might well constitute part of that to which Paul refers. Indeed, in relation to vv. 29-30, famine could well provide *a concrete instantiation of the eschatological question mark which stands over against the supposed stability, security, or permanence of lifestyles available in mid-first-century Roman society.* The suggestions of Winter and of Blue are by no means an alternative to an eschatological dimension, even if they resort to a firm view of eschatological *imminence* an unnecessary hypothesis (see Note on vv. 29-30, below). Moreover, they add a necessary circumstantial aspect to Paul's advice. (See introduction to ch. 7, above.) The word conveys the notion of *necessity, hardship,* or especially of *external circumstances which bring severe constraints* or **severe pressures**. Josephus uses the word for necessity or compulsion (Josephus, *Antiquities* 16.290), and Paul uses it to indicate the God-given *compulsion* or *constraint* which drives him to proclaim the gospel (9:16, below). Yet ἀνάγκη also means *calamity* or *distress,* and is comparable in this respect to θλίψις. Clement speaks of the need for rescue from *calamities* (*1 Clement* 56:8). These two aspects come together in the notion of *the means of compulsion,* i.e., *that which brings about* **the severe pressure**, *distress* or *necessity.*[470] In 2 Cor 12:10 Paul lists his "weaknesses" and says he is "content with weaknesses (ἀσθενείαις), insults (ὕβρεσιν), and things that bring hardship and constraining pressures (ἀνάγκαις)." This would admirably fit the social conditions and dislocations of situations of actual or impending famine, as Winter argues with reference to detailed historical evidence. Winter links this verse with issues about grain supply, and the appointment of Tiberius Claudius Dinippus as curator of supplies at Corinth, as well as with attitudes toward the poor, the dispossessed, and the hungry within the church (11:21, 34). **Pressures** could readily include the phenomenon of famine. This would constitute a model example of Deming's case list of the kind of factors which would constitute "disadvantageous or restricting circumstances" in regular Stoic-Cynic debates about marriage. This *line of reasoning* (γνώμη, νομίζω) would be familiar both to Paul and to Corinth.

Before we return once more to **the impending severe pressures**, the re-

---

469. B. Winter, "Secular and Christian Responses to Corinthian Famines," *TynBul* 40 (1989): 86-106; cf. also B. B. Blue, "The House Church at Corinth and the Lord's Supper: Famine, Food Supply, and the Present Distress," *Crisswell Theological Review* (1991): 221-39. Collins, *First Cor,* 293 sees no difficulty in applying the Greek phrase "to indicate a variety of stressful situations."

470. BAGD, 52, has three distinct headings: (i) *necessity, compulsion;* (ii) *distress, calamity;* (iii) *the means of compulsion* (e.g., use of torture).

maining syntax of the verse also invites comment. ὑπάρχειν is the infinitive of indirect speech which follows νομίζω, with the accusative τοῦτο serving as the subject for which καλόν becomes the predicate: *I think that this is good.* The use of ὅτι then becomes that of ὅτι recitative, which introduces a second καλόν clause. Many render the second καλόν as *best,* but Paul moves from what is thought to be *good* (it is **well**) to the implicit or projected direct-speech content: this is a **good course** *of action.* The practical, circumstantial mood identified by Wimbush and Deming must be maintained in the translation as far as is possible. The convoluted sentence ends with the articular infinitive with οὕτως: τὸ οὕτως εἶναι, *that the being so is good for a person* (τῷ ἀνθρώπῳ). Several translations too readily smooth out Paul's syntax when his aim is to demonstrate practical reasoning in action, and each clause performs its own function. Robertson and Plummer call the syntax "intelligible" but not regular.[471] This receives further support if we follow Jeremias, Barrett, and Hurd in identifying the ὅτι recitative as reflecting a slogan at Corinth which matches the structure of "it is good . . ." in 7:1.[472]

In the light of all these linguistic, stylistic and contextual factors, we can no longer simply assume that "ἀνάγκη, 'distress', is an apocalyptic term."[473] Schweitzer speaks of Paul's "direct allusion to the coming trials of the Times of the End (1 Cor vii:26) and the destruction of the world (1 Cor vii:29, 31)."[474] For this eschatological reason, Schweitzer maintains, Paul "holds up celibacy as the ideal (1 Cor vii:1, 7, 26, 38)."[475] This "renunciation" has nothing to do with empirical practicalities; it is part of "the comradeship of the Elect with the Messiah in His struggle against the evil powers."[476] It derives from sharing in the messianic sufferings that bring in the kingdom of God in which the "pre-Messianic tribulations" which found expression in the cross of Jesus spill over into the living out of union with Christ in the "tribulation" which also affects Christ's people.[477] To bear in one's body the marks (στίγματα) of "having-died-with-Christ" (Gal 6:17; cf. 1 Cor 15:31; Rom 6:4; 2 Cor 4:10, 11) is to experience the overflow of the messianic tribulation which links the cross with the cosmic event of eschatological distress (ἀνάγκη).[478]

Two difficulties, among others, beset Schweitzer's hypothesis. First, while his attention to eschatology performed an indispensable service at the time, and while the link between "following Jesus" in the Synoptic Gospels and sharing in

471. Robertson and Plummer, *First Epistle,* 152, and in more detail A. T. Robertson, *Word Pictures,* 4:131-32.

472. Hurd, *Origin of 1 Corinthians,* 178-79; Barrett, *First Epistle,* 174; J. Jeremias, "Zur Gedankenführung in den Paulinischen Briefen," in *Studia Paulina in Honorem J. de Zwaan* (ed. J. N. Sevenster and W. C. van Unnik), 151; cf. 146-54.

473. Conzelmann, *1 Cor,* 132.

474. Schweitzer, *Mysticism of Paul,* 311.

475. Ibid.

476. Ibid., 312 and 313.

477. Ibid., 57-74, 101-13, 118-40.

478. Further, ibid., 142-45.

the fellowship of his sufferings in Paul remains fundamental, eschatology does not dominate all early Christian thought to the degree claimed by Schweitzer.[479] Whiteley follows Lowe, e.g., in criticizing any overneat scheme about "eschatological imminence" and "development" in Paul.[480] Second, as George Caird has argued with force, eschatological imagery is capable of multiple applications which are often employed in the NT with the logic of metaphor.[481] Therefore Lightfoot's identification of ἀνάγκην with *persecution* and Winter's allusions to *famine* may well represent *concrete instantiations of* the eschatological principle identified by Schweitzer, namely that believers do not march directly from their "natural" condition to resurrection without in some sense *also* sharing in the afflictions, constraints, and difficulties which in a secondary, reflected way are signs that their sharing in Christ's resurrection is inseparable from their sharing, in some sense, in the cross. *Both* a principle of substitution *and* a principle of identification and participation apply to this sharing in Christ's afflictions and his acceptance of **constraints** as part of the ways of God.

In some measure this coheres with F. F. Bruce's comment that a time of increasing tribulation heralds the end of the age "of which signs had already manifested themselves."[482] Thus, arguably the fall of Jerusalem in AD 70 might be a concrete symptom or sign of the eschatological ἀνάγκη. The use of ἐνεστῶσαν (see above for comment on this word) to include the nuance of *both present* (*"present,"* not "imminent," Lightfoot) *and imminent* ("imminent" distress, Conzelman) matches the eschatological tension of eschatology in the Synoptic Gospels. But Bruce's comment is too readily capable of being understood in the sense of an eschatological timetable without the broader theological explanation of our paragraph above. As Deming and Wimbush urge, Paul's pragmatic pastoral criteria do not suggest a theology of eschatological imminence which depends on the conviction that the Pauline communities are the last generation.

The most problematic question is how to retain a dimension of eschatology while making room for such concrete instantiations as persecution, famine, or some unnamed source of distress. Luther argues, e.g., that Christians at all times labor under the possibility of persecution, danger of losing one's possessions, friends, or home, or the general costliness of faithfulness to the gospel. Paul's main ground for advice not to marry, Luther insists, is the involvement of one's family in all this (although later he further concedes the point about divided interests).[483] In v. 29 Luther translates the eschatology of the shortened

479. A. C. Thiselton, "Schweitzer's Interpretation of Paul," *ExpTim* 90 (1979): 132-37; and J. Kreitzer, *Jesus and God in Paul's Eschatology,* JSNTSS 19 (Sheffield: JSOT Press, 1987), 97-99 and 135-39.

480. Whiteley, *Theology of St Paul,* 244-48.

481. G. B. Caird, *The Language and Imagery of the Bible* (London: Duckworth and Philadelphia: Westminster, 1980), 201-71.

482. Bruce, *1 and 2 Cor,* 74.

483. Luther, *Works,* 28:49; cf. *WA,* 12:134-35.

time into existential address to "all Christians," who are "like guests on the earth."[484] We return to this issue when we reach v. 29.

27 The vocabulary, grammar, and syntax are almost deceptively simple, but v. 27a can be interpreted and translated in either of two quite different ways. Like vv. 18 and 21, with which the construction and meaning yield parallels, the Greek in the first half of the verse may also be construed as the protasis of a hypothetical statement (with the Greek of UBS 4th ed. and NJB) or as a question (with NRSV, REB, NIV). The key issue depends on how we understand γυναικί, and especially λύσιν. Most translations follow the majority tradition of referring it to *marriage* and *the dissolution of marriage* (REB; approximately NJB); being *bound to a wife* and not seeking *to be free* (NRSV); or *being married* and *not seeking divorce* (NIV). However, if, as the views of most modern commentators and specialists cited above seem to imply, 7:25-38 primarily concerns παρθένοι *who are betrothed, i.e., in a committed relationship,* might not δέδεσαι γυναικί mean **bound** (i.e., tied or betrothed) **to a woman** (i.e., fiancée)? The case for **woman** meets difficulties, however, since γυνή is the standard word for *married woman,* although not invariably so. In either case, however, might not λύσιν mean *the dissolution of the obligation* or **to loose the tie** rather than *divorce* (NIV) or the *dissolution* of the marriage bond (REB)? To maintain an overview and sense of perspective or balanced wholeness on Paul's advice, see Notes toward the end of our introduction to ch. 7, and additionally "Controversy about Divorce and Remarriage for Christians" (above, end of 7:16).

The lexicography of δέδεσαι (perfect passive of δέω) is not decisive. It is used of the bond between husband and wife in Rom 7:2, but in the papyri it is used of legal obligations. Clement uses it of the *moral commitments of church law* (*1 Clement* 40:5). The physical act of binding is metaphorically extended in various ways.[485] However, while, as a noun, it is relatively rare, λύσις is more significant. It occurs only here in the NT, although the NT contains many references to divorce for which other terms are used.[486] The phrase λύσις τῶν κακῶν means the removal or *resolution of difficulties,* while in Wis 8:8 the noun occurs in the plural to mean *solutions* or *resolutions of riddles* (λύσεις αἰνιγμάτων).[487] More especially Moulton-Milligan list a number of examples from contemporary papyri in which λύσις means *discharge of bonds,* or *discharge of debts* (esp. *BGU* 4:1149; 22 [BC 13] and *Papyrus Oxyrhynchus* 3:510:17 [AD 101]).[488]

How are we to balance the force of λύσις as more likely to mean *dissolving the obligation* (betrothal) against the force of γυνή as more likely to mean *wife* than *women* (marriage)? Numerous uses of γυνή occur without any specific reference to married status (in the NT, e.g., Matt 9:20, 22; 15:22, 28; Mark

---

484. *Works,* 28:52; *WA,* 12:138.
485. BAGD, 127-28.
486. Moulton and Geden, *Concordance to the Greek Testament,* 607; BAGD, 482; Grimm-Thayer, 384, "loosing any bond."
487. Hatch-Redpath, *Concordance to the Septuagint,* 890.
488. MM, 382.

14:3; ἡ γυνὴ ἡ ἄγαμος [probably widow], 1 Cor 7:34); outside the NT BAGD distinguish (i) "any adult female (virgins are included . . .)"; (ii) "wife"; (iii) "bride"; and (iv) "the woman in heaven."[489] Moreover, the single man may be betrothed to a young widow. So this is not a wholly decisive factor. The usual application of λύσις is sufficiently strong to persuade Weiss that it meant liberation from an obligation, and Fee that this account of λύσις fits "on balance."[490] Some held that the word applied to the obligations of betrothal, but others rejected this primarily on the ground that γυνή meant *wife*.[491] Does λέλυσαι in **if the tie has been dissolved** (or in second person, *if you have been released*) refer to the discharge of obligation to the betrothed or to the spouse. But if it is *to the spouse,* then *either* (i) λύω refers to the death of the partner, or (ii) it presupposes a positive interpretation of "the Pauline privilege" (see above on 7:15), *or* (iii) v. 28a cannot follow as an alternative course of action.[492] *Betrothal* would avoid these problems and maintain continuity of topic and argument.

The relation between this verse and vv. 25-26 and v. 28 underlines Paul's desire for a *practical reflection on concrete circumstances.* Paul never devalues rationality and wise reflection, nor are they restricted to "principles of theology" in abstraction from life. Paul the pastor thinks aloud, and expects his communities to do the same. They do not need some "charge from the Lord" when they are free to make responsible decisions about advantages and disadvantages for the kingdom of God, for others, and for themselves.

28 The feminine definite article which identifies ἡ παρθένος as a woman who has not yet married is found in p[15], p[46], ℵ, A, D, K, and most minuscules, but is omitted by B, F, and G. Since the article clearly indicates the sense, it is idle to speculate, but UBS 4th ed. rightly retains it.

Yet again (v. 28) Paul emphasizes the difference between what is required of the Christian and areas of freedom where Christians must take responsibility for their own decisions after weighing carefully the factors which others (including Christian teachers or pastors) have brought to their attention in a nondirective manner. It is no less important to note this aspect of Paul's understanding of his own role as pastor and of the adult responsibilities of Christian people to work things out for themselves, than to allude to the rules and traditions which allow no negotiation.

The protasis ἐὰν δὲ καὶ γαμήσῃς represents the ingressive use of the aorist subjunctive: **But if you get married**. The apodosis οὐχ ἥμαρτες is translated as a gnomic ("timeless") aorist by NRSV, *you do not sin,* and most explicitly gnomic in REB, *you are not doing anything wrong* (cf. NJB, *this is not a sin*). But it

489. BAGD, 168.
490. Fee, *First Epistle,* 352; Weiss, *Der erste Korintherbrief,* 194-96.
491. Meyer, *First Epistle,* 1:221, rejects the proposal of Ewald and Hoffmann.
492. Cf. Edwards, *First Epistle,* 191; and Tertullian, *To His Wife,* 1:7.

is common, as A. T. Robertson notes, to mix the time standpoints of a proleptic apodosis with an ingressive aorist protasis, so that the aorist indicative ἥμαρτες then means that (looking back from the projected "world") **you have done no sin** (NIV, *you have not sinned;* Robertson and Plummer, *There was no sin in that*).[493] The same construction is repeated for ἡ παρθένος. Here, however, γήμῃ is an older classical form of the later Koine aorist subjunctive γαμήσῃ. Predictably some later MSS harmonize the two different forms of the aorist (K and L and in Chrysostom).

There are two ways of understanding θλίψιν. If Paul has in mind τὴν ἐνεστῶσαν ἀνάγκην of v. 26, this may be a specific reference to the *distress* (NRSV), *worldly trouble(s)* (NIV; cf. Moffatt), or *hardships* (REB; cf. NJB) which are caused by such an event as, e.g., persecution (Luther), famine (Winter), or some particular crisis. On the other hand θλῖψις frequently over a long period means **pressure**, in accordance with the cognate verb θλίβω, *to press upon, to squeeze, to restrict,* of which *to oppress* forms only one subcategory. Certainly it does often mean *affliction* or *distress.* If it is specific to v. 26, this may apply here; otherwise **pressures** anticipates very appropriately what Paul will say about an undue spread of interests and energies in vv. 32-35. τοιοῦτοι, *people of such kind,* i.e., **such married couples, will have pressures** τῇ σαρκί, **in everyday life**. Many translations understand τῇ σαρκί to qualify θλῖψιν, hence RSV, *worldly troubles.* But the future verb ἕξουσιν is also adjacent to τῇ σαρκί, and either **everyday life** must qualify both (as NRSV) or the experience itself (as above). One factor which Paul places before the couple is the advantage (cf. Deming's arguments) of being **spared** these **pressures**, or, still worse, possible *distress.*

29-30 (1) The Western D, E, F, and G insert ὅτι after ἀδελφοί, which could be ὅτι recitative, or carry the force of *that* or even *because.* But the reading is insufficiently supported to be even possible. (2) A second issue concerns the punctuation before and after τὸ λοιπόν. We have followed the UBS 4th ed., which accords more closely with Paul's usual use of the term and makes better sense here than construing it with what precedes it. But commentators are divided.

It is fundamental that Paul is not now advocating a moral asceticism of a kind which he has questioned rather than promoted from 7:2 to 7:28. Furthermore, although he undoubtedly appeals to a *theology* of eschatological imminence, this in no way presupposes a *chronology* of eschatological imminence. This distinction between *theological stance* and *chronological estimate* is well underlined by Wimbush and Caird. See below.[494]

The initial phrase τοῦτο δέ φημι, ἀδελφοί, requires translation in a way

493. A. T. Robertson, *Grammar,* 1,020 and 1,023; cf. BDF, sect. 372; Robertson and Plummer, *First Epistle,* 153.

494. Wimbush, *Paul, the Worldly Ascetic,* esp. 23-48; Caird, *The Language and Imagery of the Bible,* 243-71, esp. 269-71; cf. 131-43, 183-97, and 219-42.

which accords (i) due weight to φημι as against, e.g., λέγω; (ii) recognizes that the combination of φημι and ἀδελφοί signals a new turn in the argument which Paul regards as important; and (iii) renders τοῦτο in such a way that it clearly points forward to a principle, maxim, or point that is about to be made. NIV's *What I mean, brother, is . . .* would be reasonably satisfactory, and φημι may carry the force of *I mean.*[495] The word may also introduce a quotation perhaps reflecting a maxim or catchphrase already in currency.[496] But this cannot be certain, and there are insufficient grounds for assuming it.[497] Moreover, we might more naturally expect the more frequently used impersonal third singular φησίν for a quotation, or even the third person plural φασίν (cf. Rom 3:8; 2 Cor 10:10). Unless we accept the translation *I mean* (NRSV, NIV, REB, NJB), which is clearly acceptable (as against *I say,* AV/KJV, RV), *I declare* or **I affirm** gives due weight to above factors, strengthening the role of τοῦτο here by rendering **I affirm this point**.[498] On the repeated problem of translating ἀδελφοί, and its role in this epistle, see above on 1:10, 11, 26; 2:1. It occurs some nineteen times in this epistle, which is more than in any other.

The phrase ὁ καιρὸς συνεσταλμένος ἐστίν has been much debated. Doubtless some will suggest that we have overtranslated the sentence. But Cullmann has argued that (i) καιρός refers to a *specific quality of a particular period of time* as against χρόνος, which has the force of *time as chronological duration,* and, further, (ii) that καιρός often constitutes a **critical** moment in which *much is at stake.* This is often but not always a time of *opportunity* which will not last indefinitely. Cullmann's work is currently unfashionable, since he is associated with the more holistic and uncritical claims of the "biblical theology" movement at its height. But Cullmann's claims about καιρός are wrong only if they are read into every use of the word in the NT. In 7:29 the term carries precisely the sense which Cullmann claimed for it.[499] It is *limited;* it is a **critical time**. We have yet to consider whether this means only **a critical time** of distress (e.g., famine; cf. B. Winter), which may pass; or whether it may include this but also constitute *a time of opportunity.* In the first case, the restrictions (if these are what they are) are temporary and specific to a given situation; in the second case the eschatological context of vv. 29-31 is taken more seriously, and we encounter a permanent *theological* principle of the *relativizing* of all civic, family, and commercial commitments on the basis of eschatological realities. "The Co-

495. BAGD, 856; cf. Schrage, *Der erste Brief,* 2:169-70.
496. Wimbush, *Paul, the Worldly Ascetic,* 35-47.
497. The issues raised by Wimbush are addressed below in the light of Caird.
498. *This I do declare* is the preference of Robertson and Plummer, *First Epistle,* 154.
499. Cullmann, *Christ and Time,* 39-45, 79, 121. Cf. BAGD, 394-95, where a welcome time or favorable moment especially finds a place in 2 Cor 6:2, and difficult times in 2 Tim 3:1. See further 2 Cor 7:8; Gal 2:5; 6:10; Heb 11:15. In LXX, *festal seasons* is used in Exod 23:14, 17; Lev 23:4; Philo, *De Specialibus Legibus* 1.191; cf. "a time to be healed," *2 Clement* 9:7, and the right time, 1 Tim 2:6; *1 Clement* 20:4. The eschatological context appears in Mark 13:33; 1 Thess 5:1; 1 Pet 1:5. Cf. further Plutarch, *Moralia* 549F. Elsewhere cf. Fee, *First Epistle,* 338, n. 12; Parry, *First Epistle,* 120; Schrage, *Der erste Brief,* 2:170-71 and 170, n. 676.

rinthians are to live their everyday lives in security and tranquility, all the while realizing that the aspects of their lives to which the verbs point are but penultimate reality: παράγει γὰρ τὸ σχῆμα τοῦ κόσμου τούτου in v. 31.[500] Special attention needs to be given to the language of so-called eschatological imminence. (We return to v. 30 toward the end of the following Note).

THE LANGUAGE OF "ESCHATOLOGICAL IMMINENCE" (7:29-30)

Our first task is to explore the distinctive work of Caird on the language of eschatology. Caird compares the respective merits of two distinct ways of reading these verses: "Does Paul mean that world history is about to come to an end, or simply that, in a period when the old regime is cracking up, Christians must expect to live under harsh social pressure?"[501] Like Wimbush at a later time of writing, Caird observes, "how half-hearted is Paul's so-called asceticism. . . . The one governing principle is: 'I want you to be free from anxiety' (7:32). It is not just that marriage is a distraction from full-time service. Paul wants to spare his friends the sort of distress which married people are liable to experience in times of emergency (7:28). The one argument he conspicuously fails to use is that they should be ready for the coming of the Lord . . .' I am thinking simply of your own good . . .' (7:35)."[502]

Does this mean that Caird fails to take the eschatological dimension seriously, or that he fails to find it in these verses? Neither is the case. Caird's masterly volume grew out of earlier lectures initially delivered at Oxford in 1968-69, in consultation with his colleague in semantic theory, S. Ullmann. In the first third of his work Caird addresses issues of language and meaning; in the middle third, the role of metaphor; and in the final third, history, myth, and eschatology. In his section on meaning Caird refuses to cash out the language of eschatology either in chronological or in reductive terms. It is not a contradiction to say, "Watch, for it [The End] may happen at any moment," and to say to the same church, "Do not get excited, because it cannot happen yet" (1 Thess 5:1-3; 2 Thess 2:1-8).[503] On metaphor, he observes that some of his hearers at Thessalonica and at Corinth "took literally" what Paul had said about eschatology.[504] In his chapter on eschatology Caird attacks as naive the equation of Paul's use of imminent eschatological imagery with the explicit belief that the *eschaton* would come soon.[505] Caird rejects equally Schweitzer's view that Paul believed in the imminence of the parousia in the near future and Bultmann's view that this language is merely a device to promote a sense of existential urgency, also transposing cosmic into individualist language.

I have explained elsewhere why neither of these views can be accepted, independently of Caird's observations.[506] The amount of weight placed on "we who are

500. Collins, *First Cor,* 291.
501. Caird, *Language and Imagery,* 270.
502. Ibid., 270-71.
503. Ibid., 121.
504. Ibid., 184.
505. Ibid., 250.
506. Thiselton, "The Parousia in Modern Theology: Some Questions and Comments," *TynBul* 27 (1976): 27-54.

alive and remain until the Lord comes" (1 Thess 4:15) verges on the absurd. Any logical analysis will distinguish between "participation" logic and "descriptive" logic, as I have also argued elsewhere.[507] Caird's contribution is to explain in linguistic terms how early Christian writers, including Paul, *regularly used end-of-the-world language meta-phorically to refer to that which they well knew was not the end of the world*" (my italics).[508] This is not because the world will continue as it is indefinitely. Quite the reverse: events such as the fall of Jerusalem, violent attacks on the church by evil forces, and the relativizing question marks which hang over a world order which has no future all constitute partial "end-of-the-world" experiences which come about because the present world order does indeed stand under judgment and does indeed face a cosmic End.[509]

This admirably paves the way for appreciating the force of Wimbush's arguments about the relativizing in vv. 29-35 of (a) the world and its present world order; (b) ascetic practices as well as practices of everyday life; and even (c) language about imminent expectation.[510] Wimbush rightly argues that συνεσταλμένος, the perfect passive participle of συστέλλω (which occurs elsewhere in the NT only in Acts 5:6, of wrapping a corpse in a shroud), means *shortened:* "either God's shortening of the time of distress before the end for the sake of the elect, or, more likely, the traditional expectation of a short period of time before the Parousia."[511] He adds that τὸ λοιπόν usually *begins* sentences in Paul, so here refers to the *remaining time* of the καιρός. In the context of the subjunctive ὦσιν, with Moule and with Salom, Wimbush rightly notes: "ἵνα has an imperatival force."[512] But is this to be understood as a temporal belief (Schweitzer), or as a linguistic-existential device only to induce urgency (Bultmann)?

Wimbush, in the spirit of Caird, argues that "the eschatological affirmation is not developed" and that the emphasis falls on "the relativizing of worldly things, which comes to expression in the ὡς μή exhortations."[513] "Marrying, weeping, rejoicing, doing business, are all typical human worldly activities or responses to stimuli in the world."[514] Most important of all, if we look ahead to v. 31b, through the present tense of the verb παράγει, "the imminence of the End is no longer in focus: the concern seems to be to describe the *perennial* state of affairs in the present order."[515] A question mark is placed over the "everyday" activities of life as "ends" in themselves; but as against Schweitzer's view Paul does not say that they are hardly worth doing, only that they

507. The difference of logical frame is explored in A. C. Thiselton, "The Logical Role of the Liar Paradox in Titus 1:12, 13: A Dissent from the Commentaries," *BibInt* 2 (1994): 207-23. In 1 Thess 4:15 Paul could hardly have said "those of you who are alive" without making a contrary presupposition. While descriptive "spectator" logic would offer an assertion, "participant" logic must choose a standpoint in solidarity with the readers which invites them to take the possibility at issue seriously.

508. Caird, *Language and Imagery,* 256.

509. Ibid., 258-69.

510. Wimbush, *Paul, the Worldly Ascetic,* 50.

511. Ibid., 26.

512. Ibid., 27; also Moule, *Idiom Book,* 145; A. P. Salom, "The Imperatival use of ἵνα in the NT," *AusBR* 6 (1958), 135; cf. BDF, 387; and Fee, *First Epistle,* 338, n. 10.

513. Wimbush, *Paul, the Worldly Ascetic,* 33.

514. Ibid., 30.

515. Ibid., 34 (his italics).

take second place, or a relativized place, to what relates to the cosmic End of God's purposes for the world and for his people. The passive form of συνεσταλμένος, Wimbush
speculates, signals "the theocentric perspective of apocalyptic."[516]

A difference of emphasis between Wimbush and Caird emerges in the importance which Wimbush attaches to identifying vv. 29-31a as a piece of pre-Pauline material influenced by apocalyptic, as against the Pauline "corrective" in v. 31b, and indeed in vv. 31b-35: "Paul himself de-eschatologizes: in 31b he emphasizes instead of
the imminence of the End, the transience of the things of the world."[517] But Caird
would see the inner linguistic dynamic of the tension between the eschatology of vv.
29-31a and the transience-perspective of vv. 31b-35 as *both equally necessary* for
what Paul wishes to say, as appears in similar internal tensions within the Synoptic
Gospel, e.g., Mark 13 and Matt 24. Wimbush and Caird both wish to take seriously the
juxtaposition of the stereoscopic perspective, but where Wimbush sees v. 31b as a
Pauline *correction* or at least *qualification,* Caird would see it as a Pauline *clarification*
or *explanation,* which does not detract from the force of the earlier verses. Wimbush
comes close to Caird in his discussions of the exegesis of Schrage and of Doughty.[518]
He concludes: "The exhortations encourage limited engagement in the world. . . . Ethical posture . . . is not the *primary* consideration."[519]

Witherington's work on eschatology also sheds light on these verses.[520] As we
have already argued, he underlines the point that συνεσταλμένος means shortened,
not short. This adds a dimension of indefiniteness, as well as divine action.[521] In v. 31
"Paul is not speaking of some future apocalyptic event, but of an eschatological process already begun."[522] Although these verses imply an ethic "affected" by the "possible shortness of the time left," the redemptive events which took place in the death
and resurrection of Christ remain "decisive": these have "shortened the time," leaving
believers ignorant of how long they have before the parousia will finally cut short all
activity in this world.[523] Hence "Paul is not advocating withdrawal from, or renunciation of, the world. Rather, the world is the sphere where the believer is called to obey
God's will. The 'as if' here (reflects) . . . a dialectical relationship between a human being and his world."[524]

This comes close to amplifying the points of Caird and Wimbush, except that
Caird might have hesitated to endorse Witherington's view that this dialectic "does
not reflect a tension between present and future."[525]

In Caird's view, this is the ontological ground on which Paul's theology and ethics of urgency are based, even if it does not entail "end-of-the-world" descriptive language concerning any necessarily imminent future. Although Caird wrote in 1980,

516. Ibid., 40.
517. Ibid., 47.
518. Schrage, "Die Stellung zur Welt bei Paulus, Epiktet und in der Apokalyptik," 137; cf.
125-54; and Doughty, "The Present and Future of Salvation in Corinth," 69; cf. 66-74.
519. Wimbush, *Paul, the Worldly Ascetic*, 43 (his italics).
520. B. Witherington, *Jesus, Paul, and the End of the World* (Carlisle: Paternoster, 1992),
27-30.
521. Ibid., 27.
522. Ibid., 28.
523. Ibid., 29.
524. Ibid.
525. Ibid.

few seem to have fully integrated his linguistic insights into eschatology into their interpretation of this passage. On one side, Paul never intended his eschatological language to be understood as a kind of time map bearing the caption "You are Standing Here"; on the other side, it does not reduce present and future to mere instrumental devices to strike a particular posture of ethical urgency. The practical stance of vv. 29-31 arises from the partial mode in relation to which fuller "end-of-the-world" language genuinely alludes to the end of the world. It applies to a situation in which the same language alludes only partially, analogically, or proleptically to the end of the world. A person's "world" comes into question because it is part of the world order which is to pass away in due course. The difference between "participant logic" and "observer logic" (see above), which is fundamental for understanding language about time and the End, also relates to two respective realities of "worldhood." Israel's "world" (arguably) collapsed with the fall of Jerusalem (cf. Mark 13), but the "observer" world is the universal, intersubjective *cosmos*. "My" world collapses at death; "the" world, at the End.

While we may not rule out the possibility that συνεσταλμένος ἐστίν means that the time of tribulation associated with eschatology has been compressed or shortened, καιρός so frequently means *favorable moment of opportunity* that the following interpretation may be suggested. Christians may still with good conscience enter **marriage**, remain in their married state with all that this implies (7:2-7); they may perform the normal conventions of **weeping**, e.g., either in a situation of personal bereavement or of sharing in the mourning customs of others or, as Schrage prefers, participating in the low points and high points of life.[526] Thus they may **rejoice** either in a general sense, or by acts of celebration, or in celebrations arranged by others; and they may **undertake commercial transactions** which involve the transfer of property or **possessions**. But this last example provides a helpful clue to the practical meaning of ὡς μή. Robertson and Plummer note the intensive compound form κατέχω: "ὡς μὴ κατέχοντες 'as not entering upon full ownership' or 'keeping fast hold upon' (xi 2; xv 2; 2 Cor vi:10). . . . Earthly goods are a trust, not a possession."[527] It would be a mistake, however, to ignore the possibility (even probability) that certain specific circumstances instantiated the eschatological question mark over supposed present securities and stability. In our introduction to this chapter and on vv. 26-27 we noted the careful arguments of B. W. Winter and B. B. Blue about the role of famine for those who experienced poverty and the fragility of everyday life. In such circumstances such **pressures**, *constraints,* or *distress* could be intensified by the commitments of marriage (again, see further under the introduction to ch. 7). This could have a negative effect upon a *calling,* whether this alludes more *broadly* to work to which a person is *called* or more *specifically* to a *calling* to the work of the gospel. Such concrete circumstances bring home the crumbling insecurity of a world order which stands under the apocalyptic judgment of the cross.[528]

31 Much of the comment required for this verse has already been made above on vv. 29-30. As Wimbush notes, this completes the five instances of ὡς μή

---

526. Schrage, *Der erste Brief,* 2:174.
527. Robertson and Plummer, *First Epistle,* 156.
528. Cf. A. R. Brown, *The Cross and Human Transformation: Paul's Apocalyptic Word in 1 Cor,* 1-25, 34, and esp. 168-69.

which provides a focus for Paul's thought.[529] The play on the Greek οἱ χρώμενοι and ὡς μὴ καταχρώμενοι seems impossible to reproduce in English without doing violence to Paul's meaning. Any underlying notion of *using* **the world** without *using it up* undoubtedly conveys the contrast between the simple verb and the intensive compound, especially on the basis of an analogy with ἐσθίω and κατεσθίω *(eat it, but don't eat it all up)*. The wordplay reproduced in the AV/KJV, *use . . . abuse* cannot be justified from the Greek. Its origins lie in the Latin translation *non abutentes* or *abuti* in Tertullian, Theodoret, Theophylact, Luther, and Beza, although the Vulgate, Calvin, and Grotius read *using as though not using,* treating the compound (more convincingly) as a stylistic variant which adds a nuance of personal interest.[530]

Luther, however, retains the eschatological flavor of the phrase in a way which ultimately serves the points made by Caird and Wimbush, and noted above. Christians, Luther asserts, should use what is available but "not sink too deeply into it either with love and desire or suffering and boredom, but should rather behave like guests on earth, using everything for a short time because of need. . . ."[531] Calvin preserves the wordplay in the best way available by contrasting χρώμενοι as *using,* with καταχρώμενοι as *making full use of, using to the full.* The thrust now becomes that of "a moderate and disciplined way," which at first seems to lose its eschatological nuance (cf. Luther's "like guests") except that Calvin immediately continues, "such as will not hinder or delay us on our journey."[532] In the sense of stressing the need to sit light to earthly things. Luther and Calvin preserve part of Paul's eschatology. But something of its corporate dimension drops from view, until Calvin expounds σχῆμα (v. 31b) as a facade which as it shifts leaves nothing of its own which is stable or solid.

A lexicographical analysis of χράομαι, however, reveals that it constitutes what philosophers of language term "a polymorphous concept." In many contexts it means *to use;* but in some contexts, the context itself defines the content of what it is to use something. Thus χράομαι τοῖς νόμοις would mean in English *to live according to the laws,* not *to use the laws* (Josephus, *Antiquities* 16.27). χράομαι πολλῇ παρρησίᾳ (2 Cor 3:12) means *to act with much boldness.* χράομαι φίλοις καλῶς means *to treat one's friends well* (Xenophon, *Memorabilia* 1.2.48).[533] Hence RSV translates v. 29 **those who deal with the world**.

A more difficult semantic question concerns the scope and force of the compound καταχράομαι. If it does not mean *use,* can it mean *use to the full* (with Calvin), or does it merely repeat the simple verb as a variant, as RSV's **those who deal with the world** *as though they had no dealings with it?* BAGD

529. Wimbush, *Paul, the Worldly Ascetic,* 29.
530. Theodoret, *Op. Omn. Int. 1 ad Cor.,* 209D (Migne, *PG,* 82, col. 282 [Lat.], *utuutur hoc mundo, tanquam non abutentes;* cf. Luther, *Works,* 28:52 (WA, 12:138).
531. Luther, *Works,* 28:52.
532. Calvin, *First Epistle,* 160.
533. Cf. BAGD, 884.

hedge their bets by asserting that "as a rule the prep gives the simple verb a special colouring *('make full use of,' 'misuse,' 'use up')*," but hastily add that in the NT and early Christian literature "this verb differs little, if at all, from the simple verb *use*." In *Oxyrhynchus Papyri* 494:20 it may mean *to use for one's own needs* (cf. also Josephus, *Antiquities* 3.303; Philo, *De Opificio Mundi* 171).[534] However, in 1 Cor 9:18 Paul clearly employs it to mean *to make full use of my right or authority*. If he had wished to give the compound verb the same force as the simple verb, Paul could simply have written χρώμενοι ὡς μὴ χρώμενοι with no more stylistic inelegance or repetition than κλαίοντες ὡς μὴ κλαίοντες in the previous verse.[535] On the basis of the presence of lexicographical evidence for *to use to the full* we translate **as though they were engrossed in it**, i.e., it had come to occupy their entire attention.[536]

The crumbling of the present world order is indicated by παράγει γὰρ τὸ σχῆμα τοῦ κόσμου τούτου. Most commentators interpret παράγει as signifying the *transience* of the present world order, and point to affinities with the Stoic philosophy of detachment from what is contingent and passing. But Paul's eschatological frame indicates a dynamic cosmic process. Hence we translate, **For the external structures of this world are slipping away**.

The conjunction of παράγει and τὸ σχῆμα τοῦ κόσμου τούτου is highly significant. παράγω means *to pass along,* "like a moving panorama."[537] Hence Héring observes that it picks up allusions to an actor passing across the stage, to disappear into the wings or behind the curtains, having finished his or her part. Thus the outward form (τὸ σχῆμα) of **this world** (i.e., of the present world order and its **external structures**) "passes like an actor leaving the stage."[538] Barrett goes still further. The word σχῆμα, he suggests, means here *outward show* which *is passing away:* "Paul's point is not the transiency of creation as such [note the τούτου in addition to τὸ σχῆμα], but the fact that its outward pattern, in social and mercantile institutions, for example, has no permanence."[539] To combine Barrett's emphasis on social, political, and commercial institutions with the notion of outward appearance with Héring's "disappearing across the stage" we translate the sentence as **For the external structures of this world are slipping away**.

"Paul's words have a Stoic sound, but the context of thought is quite different." Paul is not contradicting his injunction in Rom 12:15 to rejoice with those who rejoice and to weep with those who weep. This is "not . . . Stoic apathy" in vv. 29-31.[540] Schrage and Deming show that Stoic and apocalyptic linguistic parallels can be identified, e.g., in similar language about "buying" or

534. Ibid., 420.
535. Héring, *First Epistle*, 59.
536. Cf. Lightfoot, *Notes*, 233.
537. Robertson, *Epistles*, 4:134.
538. Héring, *First Epistle*, 60.
539. Barrett, *First Epistle*, 178.
540. Ibid., 178.

"not buying" and "rejoicing" or "not rejoicing" in such passages as Ezek 7:12 (LXX); *Apocalypse of Elijah* 2:31; *Sibylline Oracles* 2:327-29; and especially 4 Ezra (2 Esdras) 16:40-44 (cf. chs. 15–16).[541] But Schrage insists rightly that the *motivation* and implied *stance* differ in each case. Deming attempts to combine the elements by interpreting apocalyptic events as circumstances of which the Stoic will take account, and therefore will, equally, sit light to the structures and possessions of the world. But in spite of his mistaken emphasis on temporal imminence, Schweitzer rightly perceives the apocalyptic frame to be different: "In the Stoic view the world is thought of as static and unaltering. The world is Nature. . . . Paul lives in the conceptions of the dramatic world-view characteristic of late Jewish eschatology."[542] παράγει γὰρ τὸ σχῆμα. . . .

32-33 Now signals the shift of emphasis which Wimbush identifies, noting the slightly adversative and transitional force of δέ after θέλω and the second person plural ὑμᾶς, which is absent in effect from vv. 29-31a.[543] The keyword is ἀμερίμνους, **free from anxieties**. The alpha-privative negates the adjectival form of the noun μέριμνα, *anxiety, care,* the cognate verb of which is μεριμνάω, used in the dual sense of (i) **being anxious**, *being unduly concerned,* and (ii) *being properly concerned for,* **devoting concern to**. Thus the third singular present indicative active of the contracted verb μεριμνᾷ probably plays on the double nuance of **devoting his concern** (v. 32) and *worrying about,* or **having anxieties about** (v. 33).[544] The alpha-privative adjective ἀμέριμνος is rare in the NT, but occurs in Seneca as an attribute of celibacy which offers care-free concentration in contemplative philosophy. Collins alludes to parallels in Cynic philosophy.[545] Thus the use of the word group functions against two distinct backgrounds of discourse. It is prevalent in Stoicism as a quality which results from indifference to contingent events; it occurs in the teaching of Jesus as a manifestation of the single-mindedness which trust in God brings about (Matt 6:25, 28; par. Luke 12:22, 26; Matt 10:19). Paul uses the word elsewhere both in the sense of a prohibition against *anxiety* in the light of the peace of God (Phil 4:6) and in the sense of encouraging *concern* for other people (Phil 2:20). Jesus also refers to the *worry* or *worries of the present world-order* (τοῦ αἰῶνος, Matt 13:22; Mark 4:19).[546]

A further tradition emerges from the LXX, where the theme of *anxiety*

---

541. Deming, *Paul on Marriage,* 177-97, contains numerous citations of such sources for "apocalyptic 'circumstances'" (177); cf. Schrage, "Die Stellung zur Welt," esp. 125-30 and 136-39.

542. Schweitzer, *Mysticism of Paul,* 11.

543. Wimbush, *Paul, the Worldly Ascetic,* 49, notes these aspects of syntax as "the sign of a shift . . . in emphasis . . . a significant turn. . . ."

544. Cf. the entries in BAGD, 504-5, and Moulton-Geden. Deming also perceives wordplay (*Paul on Marriage,* 203).

545. Seneca speaks of a mind "beyond reach of fear" (*De Vita Beata* 4.3; cf. 4.2). Cf. Collins, *First Cor,* 291. However, the basis, ground, and motivation for Christian believers remains distinctive (see below).

546. In Mark 4:19 the parable of the sower includes the picture of how the cares or anxieties of the everyday life of this world's commercial and civic structures "choke" the word of God.

seems to include the added component of *striving* for that which may lie beyond one's grasp; cf. Ps 54:22; Prov 27:12; Sir 30:24; 38:29; Wis 12:22;
2 Macc 6:10. Deming also claims that the motif of freedom from distraction
specifically for a unified concern owes even more to Cynic discourse than to
Stoicism. The main Cynic term ἀπερισπάστως, *without distraction,* appears in
v. 35. But he concedes that this adverbial form is rare at this date, and that it occurs in Epictetus and Marcus Aurelius among the Stoics.[547] But as we noted in
the context of v. 31, we need to guard against overhasty inferences from terminological parallels. *Trust in God relativizes* all other concerns; it does not "de-
tach" the Christian believer from them. The universe of discourse is different,
and we should avoid what Moores, following Eco, calls the "code switching"
which would generate confused or even fused meaning.[548]

We cannot translate ὁ ἄγαμος μεριμνᾷ τὰ τοῦ κυρίου as *the unmarried
man is anxious about the things of the Lord,* since Paul wants all of his readers
(θέλω δὲ ὑμᾶς) to be anxiety-free. Barrett constructively points out that since
Paul elsewhere assures the churches that God loves them whatever occurs
(Rom 5:1; 8:38-39) the word could mean *anxious* only if it is a consciously allusive polemic against "anxiety to win God's favor by pleasing him."[549] Perhaps those who advocated ascetic practices at Corinth had become obsessive
about the supposed need to win God's favor by going beyond ordinary requirements. In the end Barrett concludes that Paul advocates the kind of "good anxiety" which casts out "bad anxiety." But in this case, with Deming we should
plausibly interpret Paul as drawing on an established double meaning of
μεριμνάω; here, **the unmarried man devotes his concern to the things of the
Lord**; in v. 33 μεριμνάω denotes **being anxious**.

The common thread which unites the two aspects becomes apparent in
the deliberative subjunctive πῶς ἀρέσῃ τῷ κυρίῳ, best marked by translating
how he is to please the Lord. A to-and-fro deliberation is implied, but a trustful, not anxious deliberation, which is part of Christian maturity. NRSV and
RSV simply translate *how to please . . .,* but several VSS rephrase the clause,
e.g., *his aim is to please the Lord* (REB); cf. *how he can please the Lord* (NJB).
The construction functions, in effect, as an indirect question.[550]

The articular aorist participle ὁ δὲ γαμήσας draws attention to entering
into the change of situation. Robertson and Plummer suggest: *once a man is
married.*[551] **The man who has married** (as against *married man,* REB, NRSV,
NIV; or *is married,* NJB) seems a less distracting compromise. Here Fee under-

547. Epictetus *Dissertations* 1.29.58-59; Marcus Aurelius, 3.6. Cf. Polybius, 2.20.10, and
Deming, *Paul on Marriage,* 199-200.

548. Cf. Moores, *Wrestling with Rationality in Paul,* 5-33, 132-60.

549. Barrett, *First Epistle,* 179.

550. Fee picks up the construction well: "a deliberative subjunctive. . . . It would say, 'How
might I please the Lord?'" (*First Epistle,* 343, n. 32); although "how am I to please the Lord?" might
be even better.

551. Robertson and Plummer, *First Epistle,* 157; cf. Wolff, *Der erste Brief,* 159.

stands μεριμνᾷ in a positive sense: *he cares for the things of the world, how to please his wife.*[552] He "cares for" *both* the Lord *and* his wife. But the very objection which Fee makes to the interpretation of a double meaning (cf. above) for μεριμάω as making the word "mean two different things" applies equally here, except that the difference of meaning has now shifted from the contrast between v. 32b and v. 33 to a parallel contrast between v. 32a and v. 33. In any case, as we shall see (below on v. 34), μεμέρισται means not simply *divided* but **pulled in two directions** (REB).[553]

In his detailed study *Paul and Seneca* J. N. Sevenster repeatedly warns readers "not . . . to be misled by superficial verbal parallels."[554] Whereas Jesus and Paul advocate freedom from anxiety and preoccupation with the self by placing everything in God's hands, in trust, Seneca argues that it is folly to look to God for "what you can acquire from yourself."[555] Lack of anxiety for Seneca becomes a matter of accepting fate: "in noble virtue the willing soul Fate leads; but the unwilling fate drags along."[556] Paul invites, rather, responsible deliberation in trust: how is one to please the Lord? Marriage may be a factor in the situation, but, as 7:28 confirms ("if you do marry, you are not doing anything wrong," REB), marriage is no decisive obstacle to "pleasing the Lord" and is certainly not merely accepted with Stoic resignation or as a Cynic accommodation to special circumstances which take priority over such "distraction."[557] Throughout this section, in spite of Fee's reservations about interpreting μεριμνάω in a double sense (as both positive *concern* and negative *worry*) Moffatt convincingly comments, "Paul plays on the double sense of *anxious* . . . right concern."[558] This point is developed in the next verse.

34 This verse yields one of the most widely known textual problems in the Pauline epistles. Orr and Walther observe that nine variant readings can be traced.[559] The UBS 4th ed. *Greek New Testament* follows the reading which we have translated (in common with the Nestlé text) but ranks it in the "D" category, which the Committee tries to avoid, namely, where they had "great difficulty in arriving at a decision." The UBS 3rd ed. had also ranked it "D," in this case to signify "a very high degree of doubt." The main issue of substance is whether the verb μεμέρισται, translated as the first sentence above, should be construed (as here) as referring to the subject of the previous verse, or whether it points forward to what follows, to yield some such meaning as *There is a difference*

---

552. Fee, *First Epistle*, 344.

553. Cf. Schrage, *Der erste Brief*, 2:178-80.

554. Sevenster, *Paul and Seneca*, 82.

555. Seneca, *Epistles* 41.1; cf. 95.50; and Sevenster, *Paul and Seneca*, 46.

556. Seneca, *Epistles* 107.10-12.

557. Epictetus, *Diss.* 3.22.69; cf. D. S. Sharp, *Epictetus and the NT* (London: Kelly, 1914), 49-50; A. Bonhöffer, *Epiktet und das NT* (Giessen: Töpelmann, 1911), 35-38, 108, 330, and 382-90.

558. Moffatt, *First Epistle*, 94; cf. Fee, *First Epistle*, 343-45, and Schrage, *Der erste Brief*, 2:178-80.

559. Orr and Walther, *1 Cor*, 219.

between the married woman and the unmarried. Many of the nine variants are slips or rationalizations which may be resolved into a smaller number of major variants.[560]

(1) Thus the very early p[46] (c. AD 200) attaches ἡ ἄγαμος to ἡ παρθένος, in a situation which Metzger regards as one of typical scribal conflation. But he accepts that the UBS 4th ed. reading has the support of p[46] (c. 200), p[15] (third century), and B (fourth century) with some minuscules, Vulgate *(et divisus est),* Coptic VSS (from third century), and Eusebius, i.e., both early Alexandrian and Western support. On the basis of external evidence, this reading has much to commend it. (2) The second καί is omitted by D*, and ἡ ἄγαμος is transposed from ἡ γυνή to ἡ παρθένος. Thus the Western tradition D, E, F, G, K, L, some Old Latin MSS, Tertullian, and certain Vulgate MSS read, *There is a difference between the married woman and the woman who has not married.* (3) A third group does not transpose ἡ ἄγαμος, leaving it to qualify ἡ γυνή, while at the time omitting the first καί. It thus connects μεμέρισται with what follows, and yields some such meaning as *The woman is also divided. However.* . . . This reading is supported by ℵ, A, and 33.

Summary: Most translations and writers accept (1). Thus the (1) (UBS 4th ed.) reading is adopted by NRSV, REB, ASV, NIV, NJB, Barrett, Moffatt, Collins, and Luther. (2) The AV/KJV and RV, together with J. B. Phillips, follow the reading of D, E, F, and G: *There is a difference also between a* (AV)/*the* (RV)/*wife and a/the virgin.* (3) The third possibility does not seem to find favor among major translations.

The main objections to construing μεμέρισται with what follows arise from the singular of the verb, and the contention that the passive of μερίζω would not mean "there is a difference."[561] Meyer argues that "μερίζεσθαι is used . . . to denote division into different tendencies, views, party-positions . . ."; and "is in the *singular* because it stands at the head of the sentence."[562] Lietzmann urges that it was the very perception of a lack of parallelism which led to the alteration from the authentic reading in B to the secondary gloss in D and Latin traditions.[563] This, in turn, led to various forms of mixed text in ℵ, A, and other MSS. Godet, Meyer, Lightfoot, and Robertson and Plummer follow not only Tertullian and Ambrose but also Chrysostom, Theodoret, and Luther. But today the majority follow the first view.[564] The older writers did not have access to p[46], and other details are discussed further by Schrage (loc. cit.).

The one remaining problem is easily clarified. Whichever of the two main readings we adopt, the earliest MSS appear to include an unnecessary second ἄγαμος. While the reading is possible, the word may in the first instance have been omitted by a scribe who then placed the omission either in the margin or crammed it above the line. Subsequent scribes then inserted the word at different places.[565] Metzger attributes the problem to the difficulty of distinguishing the various categories within the verse.[566]

560. Metzger, *Textual Commentary* (2d ed. 1994), 490; on the 3d UBS ed. cf. his 1st ed., 555-56.

561. Héring, *First Epistle,* 61.

562. Meyer, *First Epistle,* 1:225-26; cf. Godet, *First Epistle,* 1:382-83.

563. Lietzmann, *An die Korinther,* 34-35, where Tertullian and Ambrose are compared with Clement and Origen.

564. Weiss, *Der erste Korintherbrief,* 202-3; Bachmann, *Der erste Brief,* 280-84; Hering, *First Epistle,* 61; Conzelmann, *1 Cor,* 134, n. 1; Barrett, *First Epistle,* 180; Fee, *First Epistle,* 335, nn. 3 and 5; Collins, *First Cor,* 296; Schrage, *Der erste Brief,* 2:178-79, n. 721.

565. Lightfoot, *Notes,* 233.

566. Metzger, *A Textual Commentary* (2d ed.), 490.

The REB translation is adopted here: **And he is pulled in two directions** (cf. Collins and Moffatt, *he is torn*). In 1:13 Paul used μεμέρισται ὁ Χριστός; to mean not simply, *is Christ divided?* but, *has Christ been apportioned out?* μερίζω is both *to divide into component parts* and *to distribute, deal out, apportion, assign.*[567] The married man finds himself *apportioned* to both his wife and to the Lord; and it is this *parceling out* of time, attention, energies, and tasks that means he is **pulled in two directions**. This solves the problem which Fee tries to resolve by unnecessarily complex arguments about the positive and negative force of μεριμνάω.[568] It is simply a lexicographical fact that the word is used in both senses, and **to be pulled in two directions** is so different from *being anxious* that the meaning of μεμέρισται should not govern our interpretation of μεριμνάω.

The distinction between ἡ γυνὴ ἤγαμος and ἡ παρθένος has been much discussed. But the difference seems to be fairly clear. The former term denotes (usually) a woman who has been married but is now either widowed, divorced, or in a state of permanent separation. Since the latter subcategory is included, we need not be surprised that Paul does not choose to use χῆρα, even if *widows* represent the majority of those included under the broader term. Moreover, in the case of slaves (who would certainly be among members of the church), the wider term would include women who were neither formally married nor virgins (see above on slaves and slavery).[569] We have thus translated the first term **the woman who is currently free of wedlock**. By contrast, ἡ παρθένος raises little difficulty. Strictly the word with the feminine definite article means *women who are virgins,* but generally means *young woman* in this category (i.e., usually between twelve and sixteen). But again the term need not always be limited to the younger age group. Hence we signal the contrast in modern English by (a) **the woman who is currently free of wedlock** and (b) **the woman who has never married**. See "Controversy about Divorce and Remarriage for Christians" (after 7:16), where C. Brown and others address this question in an urgent context for today.

The one complication is the singular verb (unless we add a second complication interpreting παρθένος as *virgin daughters* in v. 38). REB, NIV, and Knox neatly solve the problem by substituting *or* for *and* as the translation of καί, which allows both for a singular and for the possibility that the second term is merely explanatory in relation to the first.[570] But NRSV, ASV, and NJB retain **and**. The singular is readily explained, however, as a *sense construction for the single collective category,* whether or not it technically constitutes a minor grammatical slip.

567. BAGD, 504.
568. Fee, *First Epistle,* 343-45.
569. Barrett, *First Epistle,* 180; and esp. Wire, *Corinthian Women Prophets,* 91; cf. 90-93.
570. Ronald Knox translates **a woman who is free of wedlock**, *or a virgin . . . ,* and we have used his phrase in preference to *a woman who is not currently married.* We cannot translate *the woman who is no longer married* because this would exclude the last subcategory, who would without question exist in a slave culture.

An additional phrase is now added which was not applied to the single or widowed man: ἵνα ᾖ ἁγία καὶ τῷ σώματι καὶ τῷ πνεύματι. Clearly a lesser involvement with "the things of the world" is correlative with being **holy** both in the OT sense of belonging exclusively to God (e.g., קָדוֹשׁ, *qadosh, separate*) and in the sense of devoted attention and service to the Lord. At least two reasons have been suggested for the asymmetrical addition. Moffatt perceives Paul as "vindicating an unmarried Christian woman's position as honourable . . . freeing her from the stigma which was generally attached to spinsters in ancient society."[571] Barrett holds that the association between **being holy** and bodily celibacy is so uncharacteristic of Paul and in conflict with what he has said about the holiness of the family in 7:14 that the phrase must be understood as embodying a direct quotation from Corinth: "We must conclude, therefore, that in *that she may be holy both in body and in spirit* we have words quoted from the Corinthian ascetical party. Paul approves the sentiment, though he would not himself confine it to the unmarried."[572] Wire's study lends support to this view.[573]

The contrast in this clause between τῷ σώματι and τῷ πνεύματι may well add weight to Barrett's suggestion. In spite of Gundry's claims about Paul's use of σῶμα, the term on its own can denote human life in its completeness.[574] As Käsemann urges, for Paul σῶμα *denotes the human person as part of the* **public** *world*.[575] Probably a midway view is the right one, as advocated by Ruef. It was doubtless some of the Corinthians themselves, he argues, who drew a sharp line between *the affairs of the world* and *the affairs of the Lord,* "the kind of distinction which the Corinthians made to their own confusion."[576] Ruef alludes to 6:12-13. Hence we must *either* (a) follow Barrett and use quotation marks with a conventional translation, *in order to be "holy both in body and in spirit." But the woman . . . , or* (b) translate the terms in a way which brings together the public world of the whole person as σῶμα with the transcendent realm of the whole person's intimacy with God as πνεῦμα, or Holy Spirit: **in order to be holy both publicly and in the Spirit**. This parallels the point made earlier about time for prayer in 7:5, and accords with Paul's most usual and characteristic use of πνεῦμα.

The second half of the antithesis (v. 34c) follows the vocabulary and syntax of v. 33, except for the change from τῇ γυναικί (v. 33) to τῷ ἀνδρί (v. 34c), and therefore requires no further comment.

35 For your own help translates the neuter singular adjective σύμφορον with the definite article, which bears the meaning *profitable, advan-*

---

571. Moffatt, *First Epistle,* 95.
572. Barrett, *First Epistle,* 181.
573. Wire, *Corinthian Women Prophets,* 90-97
574. Gundry, *Sōma in Biblical Theology,* 80.
575. E. Käsemann, *NT Questions of Today* (Eng. trans., London: SCM, 1969), 135; cf. also his *Leib und Leib Christi* (Tübingen: Mohr, 1933).
576. Ruef, *First Letter,* 66.

tageous, helpful, in conjunction with the reflexive plural ὑμῶν αὐτῶν.[577] The effect of the reflexive construction is to focus attention on the fact that the help or benefit is **entirely** their **own**; hence the translation makes this explicit. The phrase βρόχον ὑμῖν ἐπιβαλω (second aorist subjunctive) utilizes the image of *throwing a lasso over* the heads of animals, which can then be drawn by a slip-knot into **a tight rein.** Although the papyri contain examples of its being used both for the hangman's noose and for the slipknot of a snare or trap, the phrase occurs within the NT only here, where clearly the established image of the lasso and tight rein is more appropriate to Paul's contextual concern than AV/KJV, *cast a snare upon you.* The literal use of the phrase occurs from Homer through the LXX period to *Oxyrhynchus Papyri* 51:16 for war or for hunting animals, and serves here as a metaphor of firm restraint. Paul's motivation and concern are neither purely authoritarian nor largely ascetic, but to maximize the freedom and lack of anxiety experienced by the addressees in the Lord's work.

The negation of the **tight rein** is amplified by the positive, complementary observation that *on the contrary* (ἀλλά, **but**) it was **with a view to** (πρός with articular accusative) **what is proper.** This last phrase translates εὔσχημον, which means *proper* or *presentable* in 12:24, of parts of the body, and in its cognate adverbial form εὐσχημόνως refers to doing everything **properly,** *decently, appropriately,* or *in good order* (14:40). The word is used in this sense in contemporary Cynic and Stoic writers (Epictetus, *Dissertations* 2.5.23; cf. Josephus, *Antiquities* 15.102; Rom 13:13). It further draws its semantic currency from its contrast with the negative verbal form ἀσχημονεῖν in the next verse (v. 36), *to behave without propriety.*

The very rare adjective εὐπάρεδρος receives only three lines in BAGD, who cite only two references: here within the NT and otherwise only in Hesychius who wrote in the fifth century AD. Nevertheless, in semantic terms the word is "transparent" (in contrast to "opaque"), i.e., it is made up of εὐ, *well, in a good manner,* with πάρεδρος, *sitting beside* (cf. *kath-edral,* [bishop's] *seat*). The concept of *taking a good position beside the Lord* remains (together with τὸ εὔσχημον) governed by πρός, **with a view to,** and NRSV, RSV, NIV follow BAGD in translating it as **devotion to the Lord** (cf. NJB, *attention to the Lord*).[578]

The adverb ἀπερισπάστως receives much attention from Deming, Wimbush, and Yarbrough on account of its role in discussions of marriage and "worldly" affairs in Stoic-Cynic discourse. The emphasis on **undistracted devotion to** the study of philosophy is central in much Cynic discourse, where reservations about marriage have *nothing to do with asceticism* but *everything to do with being without distraction* (ἀπερισπάστως). Yarbrough writes, "As we have seen, Epictetus did not claim that marriage in itself was wrong. Indeed he

---

577. Cf. M. M. Mitchell, *Paul and the Rhetoric of Reconciliation,* esp. 25-39 on τὸ συμφέρον as "advantage" in Paul's use of deliberative rhetoric in 1 Corinthians.

578. BAGD, 324; and Bachmann, *Der erste Brief,* 287.

argued that it was a civic duty which most men were obliged to perform. . . . It was only for the Cynic who had taken up a divine mission that it was inappropriate, since he must devote himself . . . to the performance of that mission (Epictetus, *Dissertations* 3.22.69).[579] Yarbrough, Wimbush, and Deming all perceive a close affinity between Cynic concerns and those of Paul at this point.[580] This is probably the closest point of affinity in this chapter, with the fundamental difference that (i) Paul speaks of **devotion to the Lord**; and (ii) Christian husband and Christian wife can also encourage and enhance each other's **devotion to the Lord**, even though a balance sheet emerges of "distractions" generated by family responsibilities.

36   D, G, and L read the singular γαμείτω in place of the plural γαμειτῶσαν. We discuss this below, since it is bound up with issues of exegesis.

Hurd describes v. 36 as "one of the most difficult and controversial in the NT."[581] Again an unusual lexicographical problem is tied up with exegetical and contextual judgments. On the translation for ὑπέρακμος in this verse (a) Grimm-Thayer offers a clear analysis: ὑπέρ *(beyond)* the ἀκμή *(prime of life, bloom of life, ripe time)* leads to at least two possible types of meaning (cf. Vulgate, *superadultus*).[582] They argue for *overripe,* which when applied to a person's age means *"past the flower of her age,* 1 Cor vii 36," or *past one's prime.* Other lexicographers propose *pertaining to being of an age beyond the prime of life* (in 1 Cor 7:36, *". . . beyond normal marriageable age"*),[583] *past the bloom of youth* as the primary meaning.[584] BAGD allude to being past the ἀκμή, "the highest point . . . of a person's development" (cf. ἀκμή in Plato, *Republic* 5.460E; Philo, *Legum Allegoriae* 1.10) and interpret this verse in this way.[585] If the younger but more mature woman has reached this point, perhaps, after all, she should not delay indefinitely. (b) On the other hand, it is possible to apply ὑπέρ, *beyond,* to *intensity* of life feeling, *passion,* or *vigor.*[586] Although virtually all the major lexicographers argue for temporal span or age, the English translations are divided. Several follow *if his passions are strong* (NRSV, REB, Moffatt), *strong passions* (NJB and Collins), or *oversexed* (Barrett) over against *past the flower of her age* (AV/KJV); *if she is getting on in years* (NIV).

579. Yarbrough, *Not like the Gentiles,* 105. The issue is μή ποτ' ἀπερίσπαστον εἶναι δεῖ τὸν κυνικόν, ὅλον πρὸς τῇ διακονίᾳ τοῦ θεοῦ, "whether the Cynic should be *free from distraction,* wholly for the service of the Lord."

580. Ibid., 101-10; Wimbush, *Paul, the Worldly Ascetic,* 49-71; Deming, *Paul on Marriage,* 199-203: "The logic of 7:32-35 runs parallel to the 'Cynic' position" (199).

581. Hurd, *Origin of 1 Corinthians,* 171.

582. Grimm-Thayer, 640.

583. Louw-Nida, 1:650 (entry 67.158).

584. LSJ, 1,609.

585. BAGD, 839; cf. MM, 652, "of full age"; *Rylands Papyri* 2:105:11 (AD 136); and "ὑπέρακμος," *EDNT,* 3:398.

586. Héring, *First Epistle,* 63.

"PARTHENOS" AND "HYPERAKMOS"

The issue cannot be decided until we have also explored the exegetical issues surrounding the meaning of τὴν παρθένον αὐτοῦ . . . ἐὰν ἦ. . . . The older, traditional interpretation assumed that αὐτοῦ referred to a *father* (not to a fiancé or to a "spiritual" partner) and παρθένον referred to his *virgin daughter*. In this case the subject of the subjunctive verb is the daughter, and the condition for recommending permission for marriage will be one of *age*. But most recent commentators understand τὴν παρθένον to refer to a betrothed woman, and ὑπέρακμος to refer to the man's sense of the pull of passion beyond reasonable limits. It may indeed refer to a mutual sense of a pull which is so strong as to have become counterproductive for **undistracted devotion to the Lord** (v. 35). Héring and Conzelmann apply this to the category of "spiritual" marriages, where proximity has led to strong attraction, and it is better for the couple to marry as husband and wife than to try to sustain the pretense of undistracted detachment.[587] (See above on 7:2 and 7:25.)[588] Since the feminine and masculine forms of ὑπέρακμος remain the same, this matter cannot be decided on purely linguistic grounds, just as the subject of the subjunctive verb also remains ambiguous in the Greek. Apart from making the interpretative judgment that the evidence for viewing αὐτοῦ as a *father* and παρθένον (here) as *virgin daughter* is too weak to carry conviction, we have translated **if it is a matter of undue strain** to yield a meaning which most naturally refers to *the pull of passion or attraction beyond reasonable limits,* without excluding the possibility that **the strain** might have included *sheer length of time* either additionally or instead.

Since Paul is positively encouraging a sense of freedom, Barrett's proposed translation *oversexed* hardly accords with Paul's desire not to offer a negative value judgment on those who wish to marry.[589] Moreover, there is no lexicographical evidence that ἀκμή means anything more than *point, culminating point,* or even (LSJ) *"most fitting time"* (e.g., Sophocles, *Oedipus Tyrannus* 1492; Sophocles, *Philoctetes* 12).[590] Any degree of attraction that passes the line of what fittingly allows **undistracted devotion to the Lord** without marriage undercuts Corinthian ascetic advice not to marry, for such advice (not now as *ascetic* advice, but *circumstantial* advice) at this point defeats its own purpose.[591]

THE MEANING OF ὑπέρακμος

A number of writers include a special appendix in their commentaries on these terms. Allo, e.g., includes a detailed discussion of the views of Achelis, Lietzmann, and others.

587. Ibid., 62-63 and Conzelmann, *1 Cor,* 134-36.

588. Under 7:2 we noted the views of Achelis, *Virgines Subintroductae,* together with allusions in Tertullian, *On Monogramy,* 16 and *Exhortation to Chastity,* 12; Eusebius, *Ecclesiastical History,* 7:30:12, and arguments in Balch and Wimbush.

589. Barrett, *First Epistle,* 173 and 182.

590. LSJ, 48.

591. The concerns of Deming, Wimbush, and Yarbrough to explore Cynic-Stoic affinities, whatever reservations may be entertained over certain aspects of their work all share the merit of rightly pushing Paul's alleged asceticism to the margins as far less central than, e.g., circumstantial factors and issues of "advantage" for different persons in different situations. Barrett's translation is uncharacteristically injudicious.

In summary, three main views, with a fourth scarcely supported option, and a fifth worthy of thought may be considered. By subdividing the fifth, Schrage arrives at six options.[592]

(i) The view that the man and woman in this passage refer to father and daughter is widely said to constitute the normal interpretation among the Fathers. On closer inspection of the actual sources, however, the interpretation is less "universal" than is often claimed. Chrysostom's *Homilies on 1 Corinthians* are not conclusive, but his reference in his *De Virginitate* does adopt the father-daughter view.[593] Ambrose interprets ὑπέρακμος as *si sit ultra pubertatem,* and the comments which he makes on *quod faciat, non peccat, si nubat* . . . seem hardly to restrict the application explicitly to fathers and daughters.[594] On the other hand, Theodore of Mopsuestia does explicitly write εἰ τις εὐθράσει τῇ τῆς θυγατρὸς προαιρέσει, φοβεῖται δὲ μὴ ὑπέρακμος γενομένη . . . , which is said to be the usual patristic view.[595] Augustine also follows this view, and Theodoret's Latin version is equally explicit in its use of *filiam,* just as his Greek version uses τὴν θυγατέρα.[596] Luther also attempts to explain how, if fathers are the subject of inquiry, behaving "in ways not proper" could be at stake. He replies: "if it is the custom in your city . . . that one is ashamed to have his daughters become old maids, one should do as he wishes. . . ."[597] Calvin declares, "Paul now turns to address the parents who had children under their control."[598] In the face of all the talk at Corinth about celibacy, Paul wants the parents to act in the interests of the daughter "when a father has weighed up his daughter's temperament."[599] Chrysostom, Theodore, Augustine, Theodoret, Luther, and Calvin are followed by the writers listed below.[600] Allo places most of the weight on the force of ὑπέρακμος and the transitive use of γαμίζω.[601]

(ii) We have already discussed the hypothesis advocated by Achelis (probably following E. Grafe) about "spiritual" marriages, i.e., couples living together who practiced, and had probably vowed, celibacy. Achelis refers to "pseudo-marriages" (Pseudo-Ehe) of the third and fourth centuries mostly on the part of clergy and finds

---

592. Allo, *Première Épitre,* 191-94; cf. Lietzmann, *An die Korinther,* 35-37; Schrage, *Der erste Brief,* 2:197-99.

593. Chrysostom, *On Virginity,* 73 (Migne, *PG,* 48:586-88), which appears to have been omitted from the library of NPNF in English translation. Chrysostom, *1 Cor. Hom.,* 19:7, is more ambiguous, and indeed a possibly implied allusion to second marriages might be thought to suggest the opposite view.

594. Ambrose, *Opera Omnia: In Epist. 1 ad Cor.,* 138A (Migne, *PL,* 17.2.2, 237).

595. Theodore of Mopsuestia, *1 Kor,* 5 Frag. 271, in K. Staab (ed.), *Pauluskommentare,*183.

596. Theodoret, *Opera Omnia: Interpr. Ep. 1 ad Cor,* 211C (Migne, *PG,* 82:283-84).

597. Luther, *Works,* 28:54 (*WA,* 12:140).

598. Calvin, *First Epistle,* 164.

599. Ibid., 165.

600. Bengel, *Gnomon,* 633: *aliquis, parens;* Bachmann, *Der erste Brief,* 280; Lightfoot, *Notes,* 234; Parry, *1 Cor,* 78; Grosheide, *First Epistle,* 182-84; Edwards, *First Epistle,* 200-201; Allo, *Première Épitre,* 177, 184, and 191-94; Morris, *First Epistle,* 120: "The *man* is a general term for the parent or guardian of a girl . . ."; Robertson and Plummer, *First Epistle,* 158: "The Corinthians had asked him about the duty of a father with a daughter of age to marry"; Snyder, *First Cor,* 115; Goudge, *First Epistle,* 62, alludes to Ecclus 42:9, 10. It was a disgrace for a virgin never to have "a marriage song" (Ps 78:63); Heinrici, *Das erste Sendschreiben,* 211-13.

601. Allo, *Première Épitre,* 191-94.

an allusion in the Synod of Nicea of AD 325.[602] We concluded that we could neither establish nor exclude this possibility (see above on 7:2, 25). To the present verse Weiss, Héring, Conzelmann, and other writers listed below apply this view.[603] Héring produces many arguments against the first view. But a direct, firsthand examination of the ancient primary sources indicates that certain difficulties have been anticipated. Thus Luther explores why it might not be "proper" for a father to withhold consent to marriage by his daughter: as against Héring's doubt about such a reason Luther discusses the social status of the unmarried daughter.[604] Nevertheless, most of Héring's arguments stand, and are strengthened by Hurd's careful list of eight relevant factors (see below). The closest English translation which explicitly supports this view is probably Moffatt's *spiritual bride*.

(iii) A clear majority of twentieth-century scholars interpret v. 36 as referring to *engaged couples*. As against RV, ASV, and TCNT (the AV/KJV probably also, but it has some ambiguity) virtually every modern English translation reflects this view: NRSV, REB, NIV, NJB, Goodspeed, Collins, and Barrett. Among specialist writers, Lietzmann, Kümmel, Wolbert, Senft, Fee, Hurd, Lang, and Schrage argue for the view, while it is also supported or adopted by Bruce, Barrett, Harrisville, Talbert, and Witherington.[605] Fee, Senft, and Schrage argue that the third plural imperative γαμείτωσαν is difficult for the father-daughter view, since now not only an unidentified τις has entered the text, but some third party implicit in the verb.[606] Only by reading the selective D, G, L MS family (not well supported), i.e., the singular γαμείτω, *let her marry* (with NASB) could this be overcome. But the change in MSS is easy to explain as secondary. The indefinite pronoun would hardly refer to a new unidentified subject, and most of the impressive array of thirteen scholars cited above contend that the contextual theme of *engaged couples* in the larger section must be assumed unless there is evidence to the contrary.[607] As Hurd, Lietzmann, and Schrage concede, the only argument which

602. See above on 7:2 and in further detail on 7:25. Achelis, *Virgines Subintroductae. Ein Beitrag zu 1 Kor VII*, 4 and 5 cites the work of E. Grafe (1899) and compares 1 Cor 7:36-38 (6, n. 1). But apart from the reference to Hermas (discussed above) Achelis depends mainly on such later sources as Cyprian and the Acts of Carthage (AD 256) (7-15) and Montanist practices (18-20). His discussion of 1 Cor 7:36-38 (20-33) has been overtaken by more recent research. Some of his sources for the early church remain obscure (41-59), and his arguments speculative (60-75).

603. Weiss, *Der erste Korintherbrief*, 206-9 who refers to E. Grafe's research prior to Achelis, and to the subsequent research of J. Sickenberger in *BZ* 3 (1905): 44-69; Lake, *Earlier Epistles*, 190 (cf. 184-91); Schlier, "Über das Hauptanliegen des 1 Korintherbriefes," *EvT* 8 (1948-49): 469; Thrall, *1 and 2 Cor*, 59; Héring, *First Epistle*, 63; Hurd, *Origin of 1 Corinthians*, 171-80; Conzelmann, *1 Cor*, 134-36. See further G. Delling, *Paulus' Stellung zu Frau und Ehe* (Stuttgart: Kohlhammer, 1931), 86ff.

604. Luther, *Works*, 28:54 (*WA*, 12:140).

605. An early detailed discussion in favor of this view is W. G. Kümmel, "Verlobung und Heirat bei Paulus (1 Kor 7:36-38)," in *Neutestamentliche Studien für Rudolf Bultmann*, 275-95. Kümmel suggests that this view was first proposed by W. C. van Manen in 1874 (*Neutestamentliche Studien*, 277); also Lietzmann, *An die Korinther*, 35-37 (with Kümmel's additional comment, 178-79); Senft, *La Première Épitre*, 105-6, esp. n. 11; Schrage, *Der erste Brief*, 2:197-200; Wolbert, *Ethische Argumentation und Paränese in 1 Kor 7*, 131-32; Lang, *Die Briefe*, 102-3. Support can be found in Bruce, *1 and 2 Cor*, 76; Harrisville, *1 Cor*, 127-29; Barrett, *First Epistle*, 184; Talbert, *Reading Corinthians;* Witherington, *Women in the Earliest Churches*, 41.

606. For example, Fee, *First Epistle*, 352.

607. For example, Senft, *La Première Épitre*, 106, n. 11; Schrage, *Der erste Brief*, 2:197-99.

remains strong in favor of the father-daughter view is the use of the normally transitive verb γαμίζω in v. 38. But Lietzmann appeals to Debrunner and other grammarians for intransitive instances of the verb, and Schrage finds intransitive uses in the LXX.[608] Further, -ιζω endings are not always transitive: ἐλπίζω, *I hope,* represents one example.

(iv) We have already considered the proposal of J. M. Ford that παρθένος refers to the custom in Judaism of Levirite marriage, which can apply, according to the Mishnah, "only when the girl has reached the age of puberty" (Ford's interpretation of ὑπέρακμος).[609] But as we noted in 7:25, (a) lexicographers hesitate to accept that παρθένος could include *a widow;* (b) this meaning of ὑπέρακμος is improbable and in any case speculative; and (c) the influence of customs in Judaism in the church remains problematic. Few specialists, if any, regard this view as possible.[610]

(v) A fifth suggestion offers a variant, but a more convincing variant, of (i). The proposal may be subdivided, as J. O'Rourke, H. J. Klauck, and W. Schrage have outlined, as (v)(a) a reference to *guardians* or *persons unspecified* who are caring for the welfare of an otherwise unprotected virgin; and (v)(b), *the owner of a virgin who is his female slave.*[611] The former subcategory coheres with the interpretation of Peter Lombard and Thomas Aquinas, who speak, without narrower specification, of *"eustodes virginum,"* and of Estius, who alludes only to *"custos."*[612] The latter subcategory is explored by Klauck and Schrage as a historical possibility which would explain the issue about **proper** behavior or conduct toward the girl, and may in principle (depending on linguistic factors) include the notion of the owner's giving permission for her to marry, or just conceivably to let her marry him. But largely because of the syntax as well as the speculative explanation for Paul's otherwise unexplained τις, Schrage firmly chooses the third option above, namely, that the man and woman are already an engaged couple.[613]

Some writers (e.g., Orr and Walther) hold that the issues are too finely balanced and complex to permit any exegetical decision.[614] But Hurd lists eight significant factors which influence the exegesis, of which only one, namely, the use of the normally transitive γαμίζω, counts in favor of (i).[615] But Schrage and Lietzmann have adequately disposed of this problem: it can be used intransitively. Since (iv) is highly improbable and (v) possible but speculative, we are left with (ii) and (iii). Deming's sustained attack on "spiritual marriages" deserves respect, which causes us to favor (iii), but we cannot exclude (ii) and should not forget (v).[616] However, Paul's advice re-

608. Lietzmann, *An die Korinther,* 35-36; Schrage, *Der erste Brief,* 2:198 cites Deut 25:3; Ezek 16:7.

609. Ford, "Levirate Marriage in St Paul (1 Cor vii)," 361-65.

610. Ford alludes to *m. Niddah* 5:6, 7; but see above on 7:25 and the decisive criticisms in Barrett's comment on v. 36.

611. Klauck, *1 Korintherbrief,* 57-58; Schrage, *Der erste Brief,* 2:197-98. Cf. also J. J. O'Rourke, "Hypotheses regarding 1 Cor 7:36-38," 492-98 on master–female slave, adopted ward, guardian. He argues for master-slave.

612. Peter Lombard, *Collectanea,* in Migne, *PL,* 192; Thomas Aquinas, *Super Epist. S. Pauli: ad 1 Cor,* 309, sect. 400 (cf. Nicholas, *Postilla,* ibid.); also Estius (William van Est, c. 1614).

613. Schrage, *Der erste Brief,* 2:197-99.

614. Orr and Walther, *1 Cor,* 224.

615. Hurd, *Origin of 1 Corinthians,* 172-75.

616. Deming, *Paul on Marriage,* 40-47; cf. 206-9.

mains in practice the same, whether (ii) or (iii) is accepted. He offers (1) a positive evaluation of celibacy, but for practical and pastoral, not ascetic reasons; and recognizes (2) that since people and circumstances vary, in certain cases where abstinence would cause **strain beyond reasonable limit** marriage could yield **undistracted devotion to the Lord** more readily than celibacy.

The argument that *special circumstances* may include *a high intensity of love or passion* and could thereby exempt someone from expectations of celibacy for the purpose *solely* of *lack of distraction* finds a precise parallel in Epictetus.[617] Both Paul and Epictetus advocate **what helps** in such "special circumstances," the former in terms of what yields least distraction from **devotion to the Lord**; the latter, in terms of what yields least distraction from *philosophical study* (Epictetus, *Dissertations* 3.22.76; cf. 2.5.23; 4.1.147). Hence Deming renders ὑπέρακμος as *over the limit,* which would be a satisfactory translation if it did not require some contextual explanation.[618] Blomberg is no more ready to offer a judgment than Orr and Walther, but concludes that on any interpretation the message of "Yes, but . . ." characterizes Paul's advice, which again coheres with Deming, Yarbrough, and Wimbush on Paul's rejection of unqualified asceticism in favour of practical considerations.[619]

In the second half of the verse the interpretation of καὶ οὕτως ὀφείλει γίνεσθαι ὃ θέλει ποιείτω depends partly on our view of the options set forth above. On the basis of the second or third view (spiritual marriages or engaged couples), our translation conveys the moral evaluation implicit in ὀφείλει by **and it seems the right thing**, and ποιείτω as the concessive imperative by **he should do what he wishes**. On the other hand, if the father-daughter view is adopted, ὀφείλει becomes more mandatory: it becomes a matter of *obligation* (ὀφείλω, *I owe, I ought*) to permit his daughter to marry if either (a) she is captive to mutual love or passion with a potential husband, or (b) she has reached an age at which an unmarried status begins to raise eyebrows. The plural imperative at the end of the verse, γαμείτωσαν (see above), causes difficulties for this view. But if the subject includes both the παρθένος and (by implication) the betrothed this would be grammatically admissible."

The key phrase, however, is clear in meaning: οὐχ ἁμαρτάνει. Paul not only adopts an *anti-ascetic* stance towards the Corinthian ascetics (or at very least one which Wimbush calls "worldly" asceticism), but is also concerned pastorally *to release those who wish to marry from any sense of sin, failure, or second-class status.*[620] He refuses to allow the voluntary ascetics to regard themselves as a spiritual elite: God's demands remain diverse for different people in different situations.

37 Now that he has established the genuine freedom of the couple to marry or not to marry, Paul does not wish to press the case for marriage too far. The key issue, he argues, is whether marriage or celibacy is chosen as a result of pressure from other people who try to impose celibacy as a higher kind of spirituality, or whether the person in question is inclined in this direction entirely on grounds of personal conviction, with complete freedom from pressure from

617. Ibid., 209.
618. Ibid., 206.
619. Blomberg, *1 Cor,* 155.
620. Again, the "anti-ascetic" stance is urged by Schrage, Deming, and Yarbrough.

outside. Again, however, we cannot yet escape the problem of how we interpret v. 36. For if the father-daughter view is adopted (see above), the conditions for decision which Paul sets out apply to a father or guardian (or perhaps slave owner?) rather than to the man who is trying to decide whether he should marry the potential partner to whom he is betrothed (or, as some argue, whether his "spiritual" partner should formally become his wife). Paul lays down four conditions for complete freedom of decision.

(i) A person must **stand firm, steadfast in his conviction**. ἕστηκεν (perfect active of ἵστημι) has its usual *intransitive* and *stative* meaning: he is in *an established condition of standing*. The Greek καρδία includes both intellectual belief and stance or attitude of will that reaches through the hidden depths beneath the surface of the mind.[621] Many linguistic philosophers would perceive the addition of καρδία, in its full Pauline sense (which reflects the Hebrew לֵב *(lebh)*, as an equivalent to the "dispositional" (as opposed to "mental state") view of belief.[622] It is best translated **in his conviction**, for καρδία in such a context as this carries the four aspects of *intellectual* belief, *emotional* depth, *volitional* commitment, and *total* stance. It might have been translated *through and through* in an adverbial sense. The adjective ἑδραῖος, **steadfast**, further enhances the force. The whole phrase invites comparison with Paul's later use of the same idea in Rom 14:5: ἕκαστος ἐν τῷ ἰδίῳ νοΐ πληροφορείσθω, where the context also concerns the danger of falling prey to the pressure of other people's judgments and pressures.

(ii) The second condition is negative: **not because persons or situations are forcing him**. The Greek is less explicit and more succinct: μὴ ἔχων ἀνάγκην. But to translate simply *not having necessity* would be insufficiently clear. At the very least we need to make clear that Paul means *not under external necessity,* since ἀνάγκη draws its semantic force as the kind of necessity which stands in contrast to inward conviction. The use of παρθένος precludes any notion that the "necessity" has anything to do with a pregnancy. The context indicates that it concerns *the constraints imposed* by other people's beliefs, expectations, and pressures. But *other people* would narrow the reference more explicitly than the Greek. Hence, in spite of its length, the proposed translation reflects what Paul says in this context. Bruce interprets it as *external pressure.*[623]

(iii) Third, the man must have **a full right to make his own decision**: ἐξουσίαν δὲ ἔχει περὶ τοῦ ἰδίου θελήματος. We noted that in 6:12 ἔξεστι had to do with a supposed **right** *to do anything,* in contrast to Paul's desire not to come under the *power of anything* (ἐξουσιασθήσομαι). The noun form first appears here to mean *authority, power,* or **right**, but it occurs again in 8:9; 9:4, 5, 6, 12, 18; 11:10; and 15:24 (nine times in all in 1 Corinthians). The whole phrase, however, can be understood in an entirely different way if ἐξουσία is interpreted simply as *power*

---

621. On καρδία see above on 2:9 and 4:5, where we discuss in particular the research of R. Bultmann, G. Theissen, and R. Jewett, among others (see esp. Jewett, *Paul's Anthropological Terms,* 23-40, 305-33, and 447-48; and Theissen, *Psychological Aspects,* 59-80).

622. The classic study is H. H. Price, *Belief* (London: Allen & Unwin, 1969).

623. Bruce, *1 and 2 Cor,* 76.

in the sense of *control*. Traditionally the exegesis has been *either* (a) the issue of *the right to determine the decision* in the context of the *father-daughter* relationship (*patria potestas* in Lightfoot and others), *or* (b) the issue of *self-control* over one's desires or passions in the context of the *betrothed couple* relationship.[624] Thus Barrett offers "the picture . . . of a young man who is able to master his natural desire to marry his fiancée."[625] But in what sense does Paul use ἐξουσία?[626] It is difficult to see how Paul can expect a man to predict his future degree of "control over his own will." Indeed, this would have been the very mistake that led to hasty vows of celibacy in so-called "spiritual marriages," if such existed in Paul's day. Both in terms of lexicographical evidence for ἐξουσία (see note) and the need to interpret ἀνάγκη in vv. 26 and 37 differently, it is far more likely that a group at Corinth was ready to challenge institutions in the old civic order urging unilateral decisions which might pre-empt the authority, e.g., of secular slave owners, patrons, fathers, or other secular agencies who might hold the issue in their hands.[627] Paul therefore lays down a third condition that the persons addressed are the ones who have the right to formalize the decision.

This may also serve to explain why Paul's usual mutuality of address to male and female appears to be compromised by his addressing only the male fiancé. Even in the context of the father-daughter interpretation, a father who was himself a slave would not have such **a right**.[628] The issue of Roman citizenship may also have been a factor in determining who had **a right** to permit what. Yet after all has been said, Paul may not have restricted **rights** here to civic and legal conditions (see note on ἐξουσία in this verse). The *moral authority* of the person in question may well have included, e.g., the wishes of the partner. Paul insists above on **mutual consent** (7:5, ἐκ συμφώνου; cf. 7:27, 28, and 32-35). It is likely, therefore, that *taking into account the wishes of the prospective partner as well as his social, legal, and civic position* contributed to this third condition of having **a full right to make his own decision**. This need not exclude factors relating to his own self-control and temperament, while τοῦ ἰδίου θελήματος stands in contrast not to the wishes of a potential spouse, but to

624. Lightfoot, *Notes* 234; cf. Findlay, *Expositor's Greek Testament,* 2:837.

625. Barrett, *First Epistle,* 185.

626. On ἐξουσία, see above on ἔξεστι in 6:12, and below on 9:4-6 and 11:10 (with relevant literature, e.g., G. Dautzenberg, *Urchristliche Prophetie* [Stuttgart: Kohlhammer, 1975], 265-69); P. Amiet, "Exousia im NT," *IKZ* 61 (1971): 233-42; W. Foerster, *TDNT,* 2:560-75; I. Broer, *EDNT,* 2:9-12; BAGD, 277-78. Examples are plentiful. They include (a) *right to act,* e.g., *Oxyrhynchus Papyri* 272-73; *BGU* 183:25; 2 Thess 3:9; 1 Cor 9:4-6, 12, 18; (b) *capability, ability, power,* e.g., 2 Macc 7:16; Acts 8:19; John 1:12; Epictetus, *Dissertations* 4.12.8; Josephus, *Antiquities* 5.109; *The Shepherd* (Hermas), 4:1:11; (c) *authority, warrant, commission,* e.g., Acts 26:12; Josephus, *Ant.* 2.90; 20.193; 2 Cor 10:8; Matt 28:18; Wis 10:14; Sir 17:2; (d) *power exercised by virtue of office,* e.g., Josephus, *Wars* 2.140; John 19:10-11; Luke 4:6; 12:11; Wis 6:3; (e) the controversial and problematic meaning in 1 Cor 11:10 (see below).

627. Conceded by Yarbrough, *Not like the Gentiles,* 103; in v. 37 "inability to control one's sexual desires"; in v. 26 "distress," i.e., *external* constraints.

628. See the note on slave, slavery, which follows 7:24.

the pressures imposed by others, presumably the "elitist" ascetic group of "spirituals" in the church.[629]

(iv) The fourth condition is that the man **has reached his decision independently by personal conviction**. The perfect indicative active κέκρικεν indicates a settled judgment which has continuing effects. The two English adjectives **independent** and **personal** have no one-to-one corresponding equivalent in terms of Greek words, but represent the combination of a repeated use of τῇ ἰδίᾳ (cf. τοῦ ἰδίου above) and the highly personal dispositional term καρδία (on καρδία see above) as well as the further addition toward the end of the verse of ἑαυτοῦ to qualify τὴν παρθένον. This string of self-reflexive pronouns with a twice repeated καρδία amounts to what in modern English we would call an **independent personal conviction**.

The use of the Greek verb τηρεῖν, which normally means *to keep* and has τὴν παρθένον as its direct object, cannot be intelligibly translated as *to keep his own virgin* without distorting Paul's meaning. The noun refers to *the-woman-as-virgin* for which in English we should speak of **the woman's virginity**. τηρέω covers a wide semantic area, including not only keep or hold, but also to watch over, guard, preserve, keep unharmed, protect, and pay attention to. In the context of attributes and customs it means, e.g., respecting laws (Josephus, *Against Apion* 273; *Antiquities* 8.395; 9.222; cf. also Sir 29:1; John 9:16 [respecting, keeping, the sabbath]; Mark 7:9 [fasting]; John 14:24 [the words of the prophets]; Philo, *Legum Allegoriae* 3.184).[630] In the light of lexicographical evidence and contextual indicators, it is difficult to improve on REB's **to respect her virginity**.

Just as the thrust of the previous verse was οὐχ ἁμαρτάνει, even so the climax of this verse is καλῶς ποιήσει. Over against Niederwimmer's undue emphasis on ascetic themes, others rightly keep in view the spirit of this verse by stressing Paul's constant concern to be pastorally positive and constructive, while also emphasizing the importance of determining what is helpful in specific cases and circumstances.[631] Paul counsels not withdrawal from the world but "relativizing" it.[632]

---

629. See on 4:8 and 12:1-3, including, e.g., J. Painter, "Paul and the πνευματικοί at Corinth," in M. D. Hooker and S. G. Wilson (eds.), *Paul and Paulinism: Essays in Honour of C. K. Barrett* (London: SPCK, 1982), 237-50; R. Scroggs, "The Exaltation of the Spirit by Some Early Christians," *JBL* 84 (1965): 359-73.

630. Cf. BAGD, 815; and Schrage, *Der erste Brief,* 2:203.

631. K. Niederwimmer, "Zur Analyse der asketischen Motivation in 1 Kor 7," *TLZ* 99 (1974): 241-48. Although he recognizes that Paul limits his asceticism and rejects a two-level morality, Niederwimmer interprets 7:1 as Paul's own maxim, and alongside christological and echatological themes perceives Paul as rather grudgingly permitting "concessions" for marriage for those whose earthly passions are too strong to allow for the ideal of celibacy. The stance of Deming, Wimbush, and Yarbrough is different. Wimbush's notion of Paul as a "worldly" ascetic leaves room to combine a positive view of marriage and interaction with society with the need for single-minded devotion. Cf. Deming, *Paul on Marriage,* 205-20; Wimbush, *Paul, the Worldly Ascetic,* 1-22 and 49ff.; Yarbrough, *Not like the Gentiles,* 31-63 and 93-104.

632. Wimbush, *Paul, the Worldly Ascetic,* 16 and throughout. On the problem of defining "ascetic" see ibid., 1-10, and Witherington, *Conflict and Community,* 174-81.

38 Once again the interpretation which adopts the fathers-daughters view (or master–female slave, or guardian-ward) may translate ὁ γαμίζων in its most usual or more expected sense to mean *he who gives her in marriage* (AV/ KJV, ASV). But virtually all of the major modern VSS understand ὁ γαμίζων in the sense of **he who marries** (NRSV, REB, NIV, NJB). We have already noted the linguistic precedents for this meaning cited by Lietzmann, Schrage, and others (see above). The use of ὥστε to introduce a concluding inference within a logical argument in the sense of *so, then,* occurs also at 3:21 (see above; cf. also 10:12; 11:27, 33; 14:22, 39; 15:58). This chapter provides an excellent example of John D. Moores's account of rationality in Paul, whereby he pursues a chain of inferences, but in such a way that the semiotic code which generates the chain of argument transcends abstract induction or deduction. The switching of codes (here from ascetic elitism to practical freedom from distraction to be devoted to the Lord) "corresponds to that which in the rhetoric of antiquity was the enthymeme . . . the superimposition of one code upon another which is a pervasive feature of sign-production."[633]

This principle entirely governs how we should understand the comparison between καλῶς ποιεῖ, **he does well**, and κρεῖσσον ποιήσει, **he will do better**. To decontextualize these terms from the semiotic code which has been carefully established throughout the previous thirty-seven verses is to risk completely distorting Paul's conclusion by generating his conclusion out of a mis-matched presuppositional code. Only in the light of all that has gone before can we assess the respective currencies of καλῶς the adverb, and κρεῖσσον the comparative adverb. Since he has already explained how much depends on circumstances and personal convictions, he is not damning καλῶς with faint praise. The use of καλῶς must also confirm that 7:1 is a quotation (καλόν . . . μή . . .). Paul's polemic against asceticism is clear. Nevertheless, his personal inclination is still to encourage those who are content to remain celibate, if this is out of conviction about how they may best serve the Lord, and not because of a Corinthian pressure group. Hence both the married and the celibate are to be encouraged positively; but some extra practical support is given to the celibate.[634]

7. Widows and Remarriage (7:39-40)

(39) A wife is bound in marriage for as long as her husband lives. But if her husband dies she is free to get married to whom she wishes — only in the Lord. (40) But in my opinion she is happier if she stays as she is, and I, for one, also think that I have the Spirit of God.

633. Moores, *Wrestling with Rationality in Paul,* 26; cf. 1-32 and 132-60.
634. In addition to works already cited, see also von Allmen, *Pauline Teaching on Marriage,* 11-22, on this chapter.

7:1-24 and 39-40 respond to several distinct questions about marriage, and 7:25-38 addresses questions about the unmarried or celibate.[635] "This passage concerns widows. In the foreground stands the principle (formulated in Jewish terms) which agrees with v. 10," i.e., μὴ χωρισθῆναι, for which appeal to the words of Jesus has been made.[636] But after "death us do part" these two verses "expressly permit remarriage."[637] The very fact, however, that Tertullian devotes space and energy to debating these two verses and the remarriage of widows serves as an indicator that the issue in all probability became a live question at Corinth. Tertullian perceives that on one side to remarry on the death of a spouse is "to throw away an opportunity" for the devotedness of the celibate life; yet it seems as if the bereaved may remarry "in the Lord." However, Tertullian reflects, if the Holy Spirit "prefers that widows and unmarried should preserve their integrity," how genuine is this option?[638] He concludes that in principle a man should have only one wife in his lifetime. However, it is essential to see these verses against a broad background. See the introduction to the chapter, including Notes on marriage and on celibacy, and "Controversy about Divorce and Remarriage for Christians" (at 7:16).

39 The perfect tense of δέω indicates the continuing effects of the past act of marital commitment. As occurs in several cases, Paul will repeat the theme from a slightly different construction in Romans: τῷ ζῶντρι ἀνδρί (Rom 7:2), although there he uses the present construction of commitments to the law: ὁ νόμος κυριεύει . . . ἐφ' ὅσον χρόνον ζῇ (Rom 7:1). Lightfoot describes this as the origin of a metaphor which Paul will work out in a few months' time in Rom 7:1-3.[639]

In early Christian vocabulary *sleep* (κοιμηθῇ) is often used as euphemism for death (as in 11:30; 15:6, 18, 20, 51; cf. 1 Thess 4:13-15). The expression is more than stylistic. Pannenberg and Cullmann, among others, have explored the profound significance of this image of *sleep* for *death* in Paul's writings. Cullmann compares the "wrongness" of death in pre-Christian biblical tradition with the deceptive optimism concerning death as "release" from the body in such Greek thinkers as Socrates. Only after the horror of Christ's death can death "lose its sting." Hence while "with sublime calm Socrates drinks the hemlock. . . . Jesus . . . cries, 'My God, my God, why hast Thou forsaken me?' (Mark 15:37). . . . This is not 'death as a friend'. This is death in all its frightful horror . . . *'the last enemy'* of God" (Cullmann's italics).[640] Because it is God's enemy it separates us from God."[641] But once a person has grasped "the horror

---

635. Hurd, *Origin of 1 Corinthians,* 154-69 (marriage), 169-82 (virgins).

636. Conzelmann, *1 Cor,* 136.

637. Héring, *First Epistle,* 64.

638. Tertullian, *To His Wife,* 2:1 and 2.

639. Lightfoot, *Notes,* 234.

640. O. Cullmann, *Immortality of the Soul or Resurrection of the Dead? The Witness of the NT* (London: Epworth Press, 1958), 24.

641. Ibid.

of death" it becomes possible "to join Paul in the hymn of victory: 'Death is swallowed up — in victory'. O death, where is thy victory? O death, where is thy sting?" (See below in 1 Cor 15:54-55.)"[642] Hence, if a Christian encounters death as an experience which has lost its sting, "the most usual image for Paul is: 'they are asleep'. . . . Death has lost its horror."[643] Pannenberg points out that the logic of "waking" is entailed in the notion of sleep: it promises resurrection: "The familiar experience of being awakened and rising from sleep serves as a parable for the completely unknown destiny expected for the dead."[644]

The principle that if a spouse has died the remaining partner is free to re-marry is qualified by the phrase μόνον ἐν κυρίῳ. Against our inclination we have left the translation as open-ended as the Greek, in order not to pre-judge an interpretation, as far as possible. Most English translations retain **only in the Lord**, although NIV explicates *he must belong to the Lord,* and REB, *within the Lord's fellowship.* For the meaning is disputed. J.-J. von Allmen thinks it means, "without her [the widow who remarries] being excluded from the body of Christ."[645] Most interpreters, however, but not all, see this as a proviso ad-dressed to the widow specifying that the remarriage is legitimate only if it is to a Christian believer. This is the view of many.[646] A small minority insist that "the expression cannot be so pressed. . . . She must remember that she is a member of Christ's body and not forget her Christian duties."[647] But after all that Paul has said about *lack of distraction* such a meaning would be banal, and would contradict any notion that freedom to be devoted to the Lord as a single, celibate person could be balanced against the opportunity to serve the Lord with the mutual support of a Christian spouse. This view is well supported (Senft, Héring, Fee, et al.).[648] The only mixed marriages which Paul counte-nances are *existing* ones; to marry an unbeliever would indeed be to invite a pull in two directions and a lack of unified vision. Bruce believes that marriage to a fellow-Christian is "probably implied."[649] But the principle of "marriage" with a Christian (Senft) or "a Christian marriage" (Héring) is demanded not so much by the syntax of this verse as by the perspective of the whole chapter. The alter-native is "unthinkable" (Fee).[650]

---

642. Ibid., 27.

643. Ibid., 51.

644. W. Pannenberg, *Jesus — God and Man* (Eng. trans., Philadelphia: Westminster Press and London: SCM, 1968), 74.

645. von Allmen, *Pauline Teaching on Marriage,* 24.

646. Tertullian, *Against Marcion,* 5:7; Cyprian, *Testimony,* 3:62; Jerome, *Epistles,* 123:5; Bengel, *Gnomon,* 633; Calvin, *First Epistle,* 168.

647. Lightfoot, *Notes,* 225.

648. Harrisville, *1 Cor,* 129; Senft, *La Première Épitre,* 106; Héring, *First Epistle,* 65; Fee, *First Epistle,* 356. Meyer, *First Epistle,* 1:231; Robertson and Plummer, *First Epistle* 161; Wolbert, *Ethische Argumentation . . . in Kor 7,* 132-34; and Kistemaker, *1 Cor,* 255.

649. Bruce, *1 and 2 Cor,* 77; cf. Barrett, *First Epistle,* 186.

650. Harrisville, Senft, and Héring *First Epistle* (above). Fee (*First Epistle,* 356) rightly asks how Paul could simultaneously stress the nature of marriage as "one body" and contemplate a

40 𝔓¹⁵ and 33 read πνεῦμα, but **Spirit of God** is supported by overwhelming evidence, including 𝔭⁴⁶, **ℵ**, A, B, D, F, G et al. and is authentic.

On τὴν ἐμὴν γνώμην see above on 7:25. We concluded that the translation **opinion** (but in the sense of maxim, not personal opinion only) was correct (in v. 25 with NRSV, REB, NJB; in this verse REB retains **opinion**, as against NRSV and NIV's *judgment,* and NJB's *way of thinking*). The comparative reflects the καλῶς . . . κρεῖσσον of v. 38, on which see above.

One issue, however, takes us beyond previous comment, especially the sentence δοκῶ δὲ κἀγὼ πνεῦμα θεοῦ ἔχειν. A. C. Wire considers this "modest" language about "his own best judgment in God's Spirit (7:6, 12, 25, 40)" where "stress is put on balance" to be a rhetorical strategy or "device."[651] Paul hopes to maintain "a judicious air" to convince "confident people whose position [he] wants to modify."[652] He projects "the rhetoric of equality four times in four sentences."[653] But this is a ploy; he really intends to draw the Corinthian groups into agreeing to stay as they were when they became Christians. It is a "thin cover" for the great difference between "a free Jewish single male — and that of the slave Gentile married woman."[654] The latter may remain repressed by Paul's rhetorical strategy, which concludes by appealing to the possession of the Holy Spirit.

Wire's theory, however, overshoots its goal. For Paul makes it clear that people really are free to reach decisions of conviction, and these must involve mutual consent, and his sticking points mainly address the pressures exercised by a group at Corinth against individuals who may not wish to yield to such pressure. In the language of today's ideologies, we may say that Paul wants justice and mutual respect, but not "affirmative action" or "positive discrimination" on the part of some strident Corinthian group which wants to turn the tables by a conscious role reversal of pre-conversion structures. As Robertson and Plummer observe, δοκῶ δὲ κἀγώ means *not,* "I think that *I also* . . . ," but "*I also think.* . . ."[655] The emphatic ἐγώ after καί uses the kind of language noted in

---

marriage between two people with different value systems, lifestyles, and priorities, which would not nullify the points made in this chapter. Schrage's emphasis on the widow's Christian lifestyle (*Der erste Brief,* 2:205-6) simply makes this point more urgent: how could marriage to an unbeliever allow an undistracted pursuit of such a lifestyle without divided loyalties and division of mind? Calvin similarly holds that **only in the Lord** applies in the first instance to marrying only a Christian believer, but that it also includes more: "that they should enter on this second marriage reverently and in the fear of the Lord" (*First Epistle,* 168).

651. Wire, *Corinthian Women Prophets,* 79.

652. Ibid., 80.

653. Ibid., 85.

654. Ibid., 86.

655. Robertson and Plummer, *First Epistle,* 161. Edwards notes that there is nothing contradictory about working out opinions by rational reflection and perceiving the guidance of the Spirit of God at work in various aspects of life, including such critical reflection (*First Epistle,* 205). The allusion to an ascetic group need not support Augustine's proposal that Paul's "I also think that I have the Spirit" is an ironic allusion to the other "parties" at Corinth (*Gospel of John,* 38). Cf. de

1:12: **I, for one, also think that**. . . . The clear implication is that those who strongly urged ascetic views at Corinth did so in the name of the Spirit. Here Wire may well be right in perceiving them as "Corinthian prophets," although whether they were "Corinthian women prophets" depends on whether the details of Wire's reconstruction are more than conjectural. Paul is not, therefore, claiming a monopoly of the Holy Spirit in order to validate his **opinion**. He is simply saying that if others appeal to the Spirit's action in their lives as a proof of their "wisdom," he, **for one** (i.e., not claiming a monopoly), has hardly received any less a share of the Spirit in whose light he offers his. Oddly, in the face of Wire's arguments, it is precisely in the context of arguing for (i) celibacy, and (ii) individual happiness or well-being, that he makes this appeal. To use **opinion** in vv. 39-40 as part of an elaborate rhetorical strategy when in principle he approves whichever course the couple mutually desire is to use a sledgehammer to drive in a drawing pin. With Robertson and Plummer's linguistic proviso, these particular two verses hardly invite Wire's hermeneutic of suspicion.[656]

To attempt to offer a summary of our comments, or even of the chapter, would lead to replication and to oversimplification. Paul addresses a variety of situations, and circumstantial factors sometimes color his language. The broad issues have been discussed in their most general terms in our introduction to this chapter and in our subsequent Notes. Paul's series of directions and advice respond to a *Corinthian* tendency to undervalue marriage or physical intimacy within it (7:1). Trying to please strong personalities at Corinth by ignoring the natural, God-given desires of love is to find oneself torn apart (cf. 7:34). Most significantly of all, we saw in our introduction that, in contrast to much of the Roman world, Paul viewed *affection and erotic love within marriage* as a *gift* of God, just as he regarded *celibacy* as a *gift*. As in chs. 12–14, Paul stresses that *different people receive different gifts,* and these are to operate, with due regard to practical circumstances, for the good of all, not for the interests of some pressure group. Two earlier comments deserve repetition. In our introduction to this chapter we noted Schrage's comment that Paul views both marriage and celibacy as "good" (καλόν), and that marriage is more than a mere safety valve to pacify supposedly un-Christian longings (cf. also R. B. Ward, above). Second, we noted Murphy-O'Connor's point. Paul believed that for those who were given the charisma that he had received (7:7) "someone like him could . . . live a more ordered (v. 35), less anxious (v. 32), less troubled (v. 28) and happier life (v. 40)" (*1 Corinthians,* 59). However, different Christians receive different charismata and find themselves in different situations.

Wette and Meyer, who speaks of "a touch of irony" (*First Epistle,* 1:232). See further Schrage, *Der erste Brief,* 2:206-7.

656. No less important are the arguments of Deming, Wimbush, Yarbrough, and Wolbert. Deming postdates Wire, and neither Wimbush nor Yarbrough nor Wolbert finds a place in her index of names, nor, it appears, in her arguments in her ch. 4 on 1 Corinthians 5–7 (nor its 23 footnotes, 276-77).

B. QUESTIONS ABOUT MEAT ASSOCIATED WITH IDOLS AND THE PRIORITY OF LOVE OVER "RIGHTS" (8:1–11:1)

We offer a relatively distinctive argument about the unity of Paul's themes from 8:1 through to 14:40. Not only, we argue, does 8:1–11:1 form a coherent unity rather than composite letters offering more "liberal" (ch. 8) or more "conservative" (10:1-22) responses to questions from Corinth; we urge that 11:2-16, 17-34 and chs. 12–14 share with chs. 8–10 an exposition of the themes of love and respect for "the other" in the light of biblical and shared theological traditions. Thus a theological dialectic of oneness and ordered differentiation is found most clearly in (1) Paul's theology of the unity and differentiation of the body, applied to the church (12:12-31a); but no less in (2) issues about the apportionment of gifts of the Holy Spirit (12:1–14:40); (3) love for "the other" as the path to genuine maturity and eschatological destiny (ch. 13); (4) the principle of "building up" the other and discerning differences (ch. 14); and (5) the everyday practical problems of social and religious life at Corinth in relation to pagan cultural or cultic backgrounds (chs. 8–10).

The last category also entailed a number of different themes which achieve coherence in Paul's response. Some case studies relate to (i) whether socially privileged believers (probably "the strong") can continue with good conscience, or with full awareness of what they are doing, to accept social invitations to occasions and events held by their non-Christian colleagues and friends, or as civic occasions, in the precincts of pagan temples (probably 8:4-13). (ii) Other examples concern eating meat purchased through the city markets but in all probability originating from temple outlets to the butchers' shops (10:25-29). (iii) A special case is raised when "strong" and "weak" (less privileged, or oversensitive?) believers find themselves invited to the same pagan household for a meal (10:27-33). (iv) The most extreme difficulty concerns the incompatibility between commitment to Christ pledged in the Lord's Supper and possible participation in more explicitly cultic sacrificial meals or ceremonies in pagan temples (10:1-10, 14-22), especially if put under pressure by colleagues, patrons, or civic duties (10:11-13). (v) In any and every one of these cases Paul rejects the maxim about "knowing my rights" in favor of following his personal example of "foregoing my rights" (ch. 9 and 11:1). Paul's personal example of voluntarily foregoing the acceptance of financial support derives special force from his need to avoid pastoral restriction or favoritism on the basis of expected reciprocal obligations or supposed patron-client relationships.

The central principles so far outlined, i.e., at the heart of 8:1–11:1 (as well as more broadly also 11:2–14:40), serve to explain the coherence of Paul's argument and logic in the face of a differing range of circumstances and case issues. Margaret Mitchell has gone a considerable way in explaining how these issues cohere in terms of "unity" and "building up the whole" (see below), but wider and deeper issues of theology are also involved, including argument on the basis of a shared common tradition (see on Anders Eriksson, below, as well as Schrage's analyses of the issues).[1]

Thus Paul first addresses the second of the issues about which the letter from Corinth raised inquiries by reciting shared material from a common tradition which finds creedal expression in 8:6: **"There is one God, the Father, from whom all things take their origin, and the goal of our existence, and one Lord Jesus Christ, through whom all things come and the means of our existence.** Whatever his reservations about the parade of γνῶσις at Corinth, as if mere theoretical knowledge or theology alone were everything, Paul cannot deny, and does not wish to deny, the common basis of their shared monotheistic creed (see on 8:1-6, below). The next section (8:7-13) begins, however, with a strongly contrastive ἀλλ᾽ οὐκ ἐν πᾶσιν ἡ γνῶσις (v. 7). The tradition is valid, but its *application* has to be qualified and modified in the light of habituated sensitivities on the part of those who are perceived (by "the strong"?) as "the weak" (or, in this case, *the vulnerable* as well as the less influential or socially and intellectually significant). The key is that their standing and need deserve respect and regard, and nothing must be allowed to let them **find destruction** (v. 11) or receive **damaging blows** (v. 12) which **trip them up** and **cause their downfall** (v. 13), as a **brother or sister for whom Christ died** (v. 11).

The "freedom" to which more liberal Corinthians appeal remains parallel with Paul's "freedom" to receive financial support: **Am I not free?** (9:1). However, Paul offers an example of preferring to make himself **a slave for all** (9:19) if thereby the gospel is not hindered but promoted in word and life (9:19-23). Self-discipline has a necessary place in many areas of life, and self-indulgence achieves nothing (9:24-27).

In cases where more extreme "spiritual liberalism" becomes an arrogant belief that believers have **the right to do anything** (10:23, esp. 23b), Paul takes a more severe tone. Any notion of taking part in pagan cultic rites on the ground that "we know" that in reality an **idol is "nothing"** rests upon a half-truth (10:19-20), and such cases come more readily under the heading of participation in **demonic forces** (10:20) and in **idolatry**, which Scripture denounces (10:7, 14). What masquerades as a truth claim about "freedom" really rests on a **craving** concerning which the OT provides **formative models** of danger and ruin (10:6). Even more, those who share **the cup** and **the bread** of the Lord's Supper thereby commit a breach of covenant which is a betrayal and sacrilege (10:14-22). At the same time, issues about eating meat, from whatever source, in the household of a friend or colleague remain matters of an entirely different order (10:25-33). Here it becomes a matter of **taking account of all the interests of everyone, not seeking any advantage of my own** (10:33).

The coherence of these chapters and of Paul's argument may seem vul-

---

1. Eriksson, *Traditions as Rhetorical Proof: Paul's Argumentation in 1 Cor,* 97-99, 106-10, 120-27, and esp. 135-73; cf. Mitchell, *Paul and the Rhetoric of Reconciliation,* 126-49 and 237-58; and Schrage, *Der erste Brief,* 2:211-486, esp. 212-15, 221-26, 253-54, 278-86, 381-87, and 430-35.

nerable *only if passages are removed from their context, or if the varied circumstantial differences between specific cases under review are neglected.* We do not deny difficulties about many details, including the almost untranslatable meaning of συνείδησις (e.g., conscience or self-awareness? 8:10). The lexicographical and contextual meaning of εἰδωλόθυτος or τὸ εἰδωλόθυτον (8:1), traditionally translated as *meat offered to an idol,* offers an example. The meaning may be influenced in part by whether the meaning of ὁ ἀσθενῶν (8:11; cf. τοῖς ἀσθενέσιν, 8:9), *the weak* (cf. (1:25, 27; 4:10; 8:7; 9:22; 11:30; 12:22) has socioeconomic reference (those with low socioeconomic status) or ethnoreligious allusions (the overscrupulous believers, who may include Jewish members).[2]

If (as Theissen urges) *the weak* refers to the socioeconomic poor who seldom have the chance to eat meat except in the context of an invitation to a party which may perhaps be held within the precincts of a pagan temple (or purchased by a host from a temple outlet), the translation *meat associated with idols* is more likely than the more general *idol foods,* which Horsley advocates.[3] On the other hand, Büchsel, Barrett, and Sawyer stress the Jewish context of the word, suggesting that a tacit allusion to a more cautious, overscrupulous "Peter group" may perhaps be at issue.[4] But in a monograph wholly devoted to this subject W. L. Willis argues in detail that "the focus is on the social relationship among the worshipers," while Fee insists that the argument addresses the situation of Gentile, not Jewish, converts to Christian faith and lifestyle, and Witherington restricts the context to cultic meals in the presence of the idol.[5]

At once we can see how the broad and fundamental issue of whether Paul takes sides with "the weak" or "the strong," or remains neutral, engages intimately with such particular details. If the "Peter group" theory had any force, we might expect that Paul is fully endorsing the argument of "the strong" to the effect that "We know that an idol has no real existence" (8:4). However, if "the strong" were the socially privileged who were among the few who could afford meat, and if (as seems conclusive from primary sources) "in Greece the great mass of the people were nourished by food made from flour, such as porridge made of barley flour . . . or bread baked from wheat flour," it may be understandable that two different habituated lifestyles, one of which might be evaluated differently by the other, could give rise to tensions within the community.[6] It would be easy for the privileged to regard misgivings on the part of the poor

2. BAGD, 221 (cf. 4 Macc 5:2; Acts 15:29; 1 Cor 8:1, 4, 7, 10; 10:19; Rev 2:14, 20), and Moulton-Geden, *Concordance to the Greek Testament,* 115-16.

3. Horsley, *New Documents,* 1:36-37; Theissen, *Social Setting,* 125-29.

4. F. Büchsel, "εἴδωλον," *TDNT,* 2:378; C. K. Barrett, *Essays on Paul,* 54; and W. T. Sawyer, "The Problem of Meat Sacrificed to Idols in the Corinthian Church" (Th.D. diss., Southern Baptist Seminary, Louisville, Ky., 1968).

5. Willis, *Idol Meat in Corinth: The Pauline Argument in 1 Cor 8 and 10,* 20; G. Fee, "II Cor vi:14–vii:1 and Food Offered to Idols," *NTS* 23 (1977): 140-61; "Εἰδωλόθυτα Once Again: An Interpretation of 1 Cor 8–10," 172-97; and *First Epistle,* 358-67; Witherington, "Not So Idle Thoughts about *Eidolothuton,*" 237-54.

6. Theissen, *Social Setting,* 126-27.

as due to cultural inadequacy rather than religious sensitivity, and Paul, while affirming the liberty of the wealthy in appropriate circumstances, insists that they limit this freedom when given situations arise.

This bears closely on issues about the integrity of 8:1–11:1 and its coherence as a rhetorical or thematic unity. Such unity or integrity has recently been challenged in detail by Khiok-Khing Yeo.[7] I have discussed in brief the partition theories of various writers elsewhere.[8] Weiss and Schmithals separate 10:1-22 ("Letter A") from the rest of 8:1–11:1 ("Letter B").[9] Héring assigns 8:1-13 and 10:23–11:1 to "Letter A," and 9:1–10:22 to his "Letter B."[10] Sellin separates 9:24–10:22 from 7:1–9:23 and 10:23–11:1.[11] Jewett and Schmithals offer still more complicated arrangements.[12] Kkiok-Khing Yeo interprets 9:24–10:22 along with 6:12-20 and 15:1-15 as "a letter of advice on paganism and resurrection" (Letter B); 8:1-13, 9:19-23, and 10:23–11:1 belong with 1:1–6:11 and 7:1–end of 12–14 to the "mainframe letter" concerning "more targeted issues" (Letter C); while 9:1-18 belongs to a fifth "Letter E," which concerns the nonacceptance of financial gifts.[13] He postulates six letter frames in all.

All this complex theorizing, however, founders on three undoubted facts and two further arguments. (1) First, as I argued in my earlier study, in common with Fee, almost all of the complex partition theories conflict with one another in the specific frames which they supposedly identify.[14] This conspicuous failure to produce a consensus seriously undermines the credibility of these hypotheses.[15] (2) Second, as Schrage and others argue, 9:1-23 offers a personal example (as 11:1 suggests that we should expect) of a person's being theoretically "free" to take advantage of a situation, but choosing to surrender such freedom in the interests of others.[16] Although some brush aside this argument, often on the ground that Paul's appeal to apostolic authority is more central, nu-

7. Yeo, *Rhetorical Interaction in 1 Corinthians 8 and 10: A Formal Analysis with Preliminary Suggestions for a Chinese Cross-Cultural Hermeneutic*, esp. 76-83 and 120-211, summed up on 81-82.

8. A. C. Thiselton, "Luther and Barth on 1 Cor 15," in W. P. Stephens (ed.), *The Bible, The Reformation and the Church*, JSNTSS 105 (Sheffield: Sheffield Academic Press, 1995), 258-89, esp. 275-78.

9. Weiss, *Der erste Korintherbrief*, xi-xliii.

10. Héring, *First Epistle*, xii-xiv.

11. G. Sellin, "Hauptprobleme des ersten Korintherbriefes," *ANRW*, 2:25:4 (1987), 2,964-86.

12. R. Jewett, "The Redaction of 1 Cor and the Trajectory of the Pauline School," *JAAR*Sup 46 (1978): 398-444; W. Schmithals, "Die Korintherbriefe als Briefsammlung," *ZNW* 64 (1973): 263-88, and *Gnosticism in Corinth*, 87-113.

13. Yeo, *Rhetorical Interaction in 1 Cor 8 and 10*, esp. 78-83, but also as cited above.

14. Thiselton, "Luther and Barth on 1 Cor 15," 277.

15. Fee observes, "The very fact that there is so little agreement in these theories suggests that the various reconstructions are not as viable as their proponents would lead us to believe" (*First Epistle*, 15).

16. Schrage, *Der erste Brief*, 2:211-15, 216-35, and 277-350; also Robertson and Plummer, *First Epistle*, xxvi and 174-77.

merous commentators agree with or anticipate Schrage. Our third point (below) makes this decisive. Thus Wolff is entirely correct to entitle 8:1-6 "Knowledge and Love"; 8:1-13, "Knowledge and the Power or Right *(Vollmacht)* to Eat Meat Offered to Idols"; and 9:1-27, "A Personal Example *(Beispiel)* of the Use of Freedom."[17]

(3) Our third appeal is still more decisive. The work of Chow and Clarke on patronage, and that of R. F. Hock and Peter Marshall on reciprocal "favors," friendship, and manual labor, remains fundamental for understanding the special role of ch. 9 in reinforcing Paul's way of addressing the issue of the "rights" of *the strong* to eat meat offered to nonexistent deities which nevertheless should be qualified and tightly restrained in given situations in the interests of *the weak*.[18] Throughout 8:1–11:1 commentators find "contradictions" which lead them to partition different letters or different revisions of Pauline letters. But in ch. 9 Paul explains *that there is a "contradiction" in the entailments of freedom and of love respectively.* He does indeed have the right to receive payment for his apostolic labors. But since the danger of becoming obligated to patrons would cause special difficulties, *he chooses to reject that to which he is entitled.* This is precisely the issue of ch. 8 and ch. 10, which he concludes with the injunction to follow his example (μιμηταί μου γίνεσθε καθὼς κἀγὼ Χριστοῦ, 11:1). We argue under 8:7 that in any case to view "the strong" as those who are *"secure"* both in socioeconomic and in "religious" terms as against "the weak" who are socially, economically, and in terms of religious or moral consciousness *"insecure"* brings together a coherent understanding of the two terms in 8:1–11:1. Hence, further, far from this being an issue of power play, as Castelli seems to suggest, Paul appeals to his own example in the context of the further example of Christ as "for others," and the entire argument serves to defend *the weak* of chs. 8–10 from the social and theological assertiveness of the *strong*.[19] *Freedom* is radically qualified by *love; love*, not for the self, but for *the other*. Hence Paul adds καθὼς κἀγὼ Χριστοῦ (11:1).

Two further points can be added to these three arguments.

(4) The first of these arises from Margaret Mitchell's defense of the integrity of the whole epistle largely on grounds of rhetorical as well as compositional analysis. The divisive potential of "knowledge" (γνῶσις, 8:1-2, 7, 10, 11) stands in contrast to the unifying potential of "love" (ἀγάπη, 8:1; cf. 12-13), and this coheres well with Mitchell's thesis that the whole epistle functions as a "rhetoric of reconciliation." She sees γνῶσις as "contributing to community division."[20] Moreover, she argues that πρόσκομμα (*pitfall, offense,*

17. Wolff, *Der erste Brief,* 168 and 184; cf. 165-208.

18. See Marshall, *Enmity in Corinth,* esp. 173-258; R. F. Hock, *The Social Contexts of Paul's Ministry: Tentmaking and Apostleship* (Philadelphia: Fortress, 1990), throughout; Chow, *Patronage and Power,* 141-57 (on chs. 8 and 10) and 172-75 on Paul's defense in 9:1-23; cf. Clarke, *Secular and Christian Leadership,* 124-26 and 133.

19. Castelli, *Imitating Paul: A Discourse of Power,* 89-118.

20. Mitchell, *Paul and the Rhetoric of Reconciliation,* 126; see 126-49.

cause of stumbling, 8:9; 10:32) is "also at home in factional disputes in antiquity."[21] With regard to 9:1-23 she looks beyond the short-term conflict identified by Peter Marshall to the long-term aim of "non-divisive, conciliatory behavior."[22] Paul does not make use of his "right" (ἐξουσία, 9:12, 18, 23). Willingness to forego "rights" in ch. 9 is precisely what most of 8:1–11:11 is all about: "Political realism dictates that everyone cannot have their way in everything."[23] "Paul has been true to the counsel he offers."[24]

(5) The second additional point is perhaps more hypothetical. Is there a better explanation for "a double tone" in these chapters than partition? Several writers argue that Paul, in effect, supports "the strong" *provided that the context of meat eating remains that of the home,* even if the meat was purchased from a temple-related outlet. However, he attacks the strong and sides with the weak, so the argument runs, *when the context becomes that of eating within the precincts of a pagan temple.* Witherington insists that "the more one knows about the archaeology of Roman Corinth and the religious practices of the Greco-Roman world (the clearer it becomes that) εἰδωλόθυτον was a polemical Jewish-Christian term . . . to warn against the danger of participating in feasts in pagan temple dining rooms. . . ."[25] The factors which we have identified provide cogent evidence for the unity of rhetoric and theme in 8:1–11:1. We might go further. Paul's personal example of "rights" and self-discipline (9:1-23) is then instantiated further with reference to the hellenistic culture of the Isthmian games (9:24-27); and finally with reference to the church's scripture in the events of Israelite history (10:1-13) and to the discipline of contemporary hellenistic Judaism (10:18-22). Paul concludes with an application to various case studies (10:25-29) which reflect the principles established in 10:14-17; 10:23, 24; and 10:29–11:1. The relations between knowledge and love, and between "rights" and self-discipline for the sake of a greater good give coherence to the whole of 8:1–11:1. Many of these arguments are woven together in a forceful presentation of the unity of 8:1–11:1 by John Brunt.[26]

1. Knowledge, Love, and Freedom: Meat Associated with Idols (8:1-13)

(1) Now on the subject of meat associated with offerings to pagan deities: we are fully aware that "All of us possess 'knowledge.'" This "knowledge" in-

21. Ibid., 128.
22. Ibid., 130.
23. Ibid., 131.
24. Ibid., 133; cf. 133-49.
25. Witherington, "Not So Idle Thoughts about *Eidolothuton*," 254; cf. 237-54.
26. J. C. Brunt, "Love, Freedom and Moral Responsibility: The Contribution of 1 Cor 8–10 to an Understanding of Paul's Ethical Thinking," in *SBL 1991 Seminar Papers* (ed. K. H. Richards; Chico: Scholars Press, 1981), 19-33.

flates; love, on the other hand, builds. (2) If anyone thinks that he or she has achieved [some piece of] this "knowledge," they have not yet come to know as they ought to know. (3) But if anyone loves [God], he or she has experienced true "knowing" [is known by him].

(4) To return to the topic of eating meat associated with idols, then, we share your knowledge that "An idol has no real existence," and that "There is no God but One." (5, 6) For even if there really exists, for the sake of argument, so-called gods, whether in heaven of on earth, as indeed there are many "gods" and many "lords," yet for us there is one God, the Father, from whom all things take their origin and the goal of our existence, and one Lord Jesus Christ, through whom all things come and the means of our existence.

(7) But it is not everyone who possesses this "knowledge." Some are still gripped by the idol by force of habit even now, and they eat meat as an actual idol sacrifice. Hence their self-awareness [or conscience], being insecure, is tainted. (8) "Food will not bring us to God's judgment"; neither if we abstain from food do we lose any advantage, nor if we eat do we gain any advantage. (9) Only see that this "right to choose" of yours does not become a cause of stumbling to the less secure. (10) Suppose someone sees you seated at table in the actual place of an idol, you who "possess knowledge": will the insecure person's self-awareness not be "built" into eating meat sacrificed to the actual idol? (11) Then, to be sure, the insecure person finds destruction by being drawn into your "knowledge" — the brother or sister for whom Christ died. (12) But in such a way as this, in sinning against your brothers and sisters by inflicting damaging blows on their self-awareness while it is still insecure, you are sinning against Christ. (13) Therefore, if food so affronts my brother or sister as to trip them up, I will certainly never in any event eat meat in any form lest I cause my brother's or sister's downfall.

Bibliography on 8:1-13

Barrett, C. K., "Things Sacrificed to Idols," in *Essays on Paul* (London: SPCK, 1982), 40-59; rpt. from *NTS* 11 (1965): 138-53.

Borgen, P., "'Yes', 'No', 'How Far?' The Participation of Jews and Christians in Pagan Cults," in T. Engberg-Pedersen (ed.), *Paul in His Hellenistic Context* (Minneapolis: Fortress, 1995), 30-59.

Brunt, J. C., "Rejected, Ignored, or Misunderstood? The Fate of Paul's Approach to the Problem of Food Offered to Idols in Early Christianity," *NTS* 31 (1985): 113-24.

Büchsel, F., "εἴδωλον," *TDNT,* 2:375-80.

Bultmann, R., "γνῶσις," *TDNT,* 1:689-719.

Cohon, S., "The Unity of God: A Study in Hellenistic and Rabbinic Theology," *HUCA* 26 (1955): 425-79.

Cole, S. G., *Theoi Megaloi: The Cult of the Great Gods of Samothrace* (Leiden: Brill, 1984).

Combs, W. W., "Nag Hammadi, Gnosticism and New Testament Interpretation," *GTJ* 8 (1987).

Cooper, E. J., "Man's Basic Freedom and Freedom of Conscience in the Bible: Reflections on 1 Corinthians 8–10," *ITQ* 42 (1975): 272-83.

Cope, L., "First Corinthians 8–10: Continuity or Contradiction?" *ATRSup* 11 (1990): 114-123.

Cullmann, O., *The Earliest Christian Confessions* (Eng. trans., London: Lutterworth, 1949).

———, *Early Christian Worship* (Eng. trans., London: SCM, 1953).

Davis, C. J., *The Name and Way of the Lord: OT Themes, NT Christology,* JSNTSS 129 (Sheffield: Sheffield Academic Press, 1996).

Davis, J. A., "The Interaction between Individual Ethical Conscience and Community Ethical Consciousness in 1 Corinthians," *HBT* 10 (1988): 1-18.

Dawes, G. W., "The Danger of Idolatry: First Cor 8:7-13," *CBQ* 58 (1996): 82-98.

DeLacey, D. R., "'One Lord' in Pauline Christology," in H. H. Rowdon (ed.), *Christ the Lord: Studies in Christology Presented to D. Guthrie* (Leicester: Inter-Varsity Press, 1982), 191-203.

De Lorenzi, L., *Freedom and Love: The Guide for Christian Life* (1 Cor 8–10; Rm 14–15) (Rome: St. Paul's Abbey, 1981).

Dunn, J. D. G., *The Theology of Paul the Apostle* (Edinburgh: T. & T. Clark, 1998), 27-50, 701-6.

———, "Was Christianity a Monotheistic Faith from the Beginning?" *SJT* 35 (1982): 303-35.

Eckstein, H.-J., *Der Begriff Syneidēsis bei Paulus* (Tübingen: Mohr, 1983).

Eriksson, A., *Traditions as Rhetorical Proof: Pauline Argumentation in 1 Corinthians,* ConBNT (Stockholm: Almqvist & Wiksell, 1998), 97-99, 135-73, and 120-27.

Fee, G. D., "Εἰδωλόθυτα Once Again: An Interpretation of 1 Corinthians 8–10," *Bib* 61 (1980): 172-97.

Filorama, G., *A History of Gnosticism* (Eng. trans., Oxford: Blackwell, 1990).

Fisk, B. N., "Eating Meat Offered to Idols: Corinthian Behavior and Pauline Response in 1 Corinthians 8–10 (A Response to Gordon Fee)," *TrinJ* 10 (1989): 49-70.

Gardner, P. D., *The Gifts of God and the Authentication of a Christian: An Exegetical Study of 1 Corinthians 8–11* (Lanham, Md.: University Press of America, 1994).

Giblin, C. H., "Three Monotheistic Texts in Paul," *CBQ* 37 (1975): 527-47.

Gooch, Peter D., *Dangerous Food: 1 Corinthians 8–10 in Its Context* (Waterloo, Ont: Wilfrid Laurier University Press, 1993).

———, "'Conscience' in 1 Corinthians 8 and 10," *NTS* 33 (1987): 244-54.

———, *Partial Knowledge: Philosophical Studies in Paul* (Notre Dame: University of Notre Dame, 1987), 102-23.

Grant, R. M., "Early Christians and Gnostics in Greco-Roman Society," in *The New Testament and Gnosis: Essays in Honour of Robert McL Wilson* (ed. A. H. B. Logan and A. J. M. Wedderburn; Edinburgh: T. & T. Clark, 1983), 176-86.

———, "Gnostic Spirituality," in B. McGinn and J. Meyendorff (eds.), *Christian Spirituality: Origins to the Twelfth Century* (New York: Crossroad, 1985), 44-60.

———, *Gods and the One God* (Philadelphia: Westminster Press, 1986).

Green, H., "Gnosis and Gnosticism: A Study in Methodology," *Numen* 24 (1977): 95-134.

Harris, B. F., "συνείδησις (Conscience) in the Pauline Writings," *WTJ* 24 (1962): 173-86.

Horrell, D. G., *The Social Ethos of the Corinthian Correspondence* (Edinburgh: T. & T. Clark, 1996), 105-9, 145-50.

Horsley, R. A., "The Background of the Confessional Formula in 1 Kor 8:6," *ZNW* 69 (1978): 130-35.

———, "Consciousness and Freedom among the Corinthians: 1 Corinthians 8–10," *CBQ* 40 (1978): 574-89.

———, "Gnosis in Corinth: 1 Corinthians 8:1-6," *NTS* 27 (1980): 32-51.

———, "Pneumatikos vs Psychikos: Distinction of Spiritual Status among the Corinthians," *HTR* 69 (1976): 269-88.

Hurtado, L. W., *One God, One Lord: Early Christian Devotion and Ancient Jewish Monotheism* (Philadelphia: Fortress, 1988).

Jewett, R., *Paul's Anthropological Terms: A Study of Their Use in Conflict Settings* (Leiden: Brill, 1971), 402-46 and 458-60.

———, "The Redaction of 1 Cor and the Trajectory of the Pauline School," *JAAR* Sup 46 (1978): 398-44.

Kern, W., "Mein Glaube — Und die Anderen Biblische Überlegungen mit dem Apostel Paulus," *Geistleib* 52 (1979): 454-63.

Kerst, R., "1 Kor 8.6 — Ein vorpaulinisches Taufbekenntnis?" *ZNW* 66 (1975):130-39.

Kitzberger, I., *Bau der Gemeinde: Das paulinische Wortfeld oikodomē* (Würzburg: Echter Verlag, 1986), 64-117 and 224-70.

Lorenzi, L. de, *Freedom and Love: The Guide for Christian Life (1 Cor 8–10, Rom 14–15)* (Rome: St Paul's Abbey, 1981).

Maurer, C., "συνείδησις," *TDNT,* 7:898-919.

Meeks, W. A., "The Polyphonic Ethics of the Apostle Paul," *Annual of the Society of Christian Ethics* (1988): 17-29.

Meggitt, J. J., "Meat Consumption and Social Conflict in Corinth," *JTS* 45 (1994): 137-41.

Mitchell, M. M., "Concerning περὶ δέ in 1 Corinthians," *NovT* 31 (1989): 229-56.

———, *Paul and the Rhetoric of Reconciliation* (Tübingen, Mohr and Louisville: Westminster/Knox, 1992).

Murphy-O'Connor, J., "Food and Spiritual Gifts in 1 Cor 8:8," *CBQ* 41 (1979): 292-98.

———, "1 Cor viii,6 — Cosmology or Soteriology?" *RB* 85 (1978): 253-67.

———, "Freedom or the Ghetto (1 Cor VIII:1-13, X:23–XI:1)," *RB* 85 (1978): 541-74.

———, *St. Paul's Corinth Texts and Archaeology* (Wilmington: Glazier, 1983), esp. 161-67.

Neufeld, V. H., *Earliest Christian Confessions* (Leiden: Brill, 1963).

Outka, G., "On Harming Others," *Int* 34 (1980): 381-93.

Perkins, P., "Gnostic Christologies and the New Testament," *CBQ* 43 (1981): 590-606.

Pierce, C. A., *Conscience in the New Testament* (London: SCM, 1955).

Probst, H., *Paulus und der Brief. Die Rhetorik des antiken Briefes als Form der paulinischen Korintherkorrespondenz (1 Kor 8–10),* WUNT 2:45 (Tübingen: Mohr, 1991).

Richardson, N., *Paul's Language about God* (cited above), 296-304.

Rudolph, K., "'Gnosis' and 'Gnosticism' — The Problems of Their Definition and Their Relation to the Writings of the New Testament," in A. H. B. Logan and A. J. M. Wedderburn (eds.), *The New Testament and Gnosis: Essays in Honour of Robert McL. Wilson* (Edinburgh: T. & T. Clark, 1983), 21-37.

———, *Gnosis: The Nature and History of Gnosticism* (Eng. trans., San Francisco: Harper & Row, 1983).

Schmithals, W., "The Corpus Paulinum and Gnosis," in *The New Testament and Gnosis: Essays in Honour of Robert McL. Wilson* (cited above), 107-24.

615

———, *Gnosticism in Corinth: An Investigation of the Letters to the Corinthians* (Nashville: Abingdon Press, 1971).

Schnackenburg, R., "Early Gnosticism," in *Jesus in His Time* (Eng. trans., London: SPCK, 1971), 132-41.

Schweizer, E., "Paul's Christology and Gnosticism," in M. D. Hooker and S. Wilson (eds.), *Paul and Paulinism: Essays in Honour of C. K. Barrett* (London: SPCK, 1982), 115-23.

Smit, J. F. M., "1 Cor 8:1-6: A Rhetorical Partitio. A Contribution to the Coherence of 1 Cor 8:1–11:1," in R. Bieringer (ed.), *The Corinthian Correspondence* (Leuven: Leuven University Press, 1996), 577-91.

———, "The Rhetorical Disposition of First Cor 8:7–9:27," *CBQ* 59 (1997): 476-91.

Söding, T., "Starke und Schwache der Götzenopferstreit in 1 Kor 8–10 als Paradigma paulinischer Ethik," *ZNW* 85 (1994): 69-142.

Songer, H. S., "Problems Arising from the Worship of Idols: 1 Corinthians 8:1–11:1," *RevExp* 80 (1983): 363-75.

Spicq, C., *Agape in the NT* (Eng. trans., 3 vols., St. Louis and London: Herder, 1965), vol. 2.

———, "La Conscience dans le Nouveau Testament," *RB* 47 (1938): 50-80.

Theissen, G., *The Social Setting of Pauline Christianity: Essays on Corinth* (Eng. trans., Philadelphia: Fortress Press, 1982), 121-44.

Thrall, M. E., "The Meaning of οἰκοδομέω in Relation to the Concept of συνείδησις (1 Cor 8:10)," in *SE* 4 (Berlin: Berlin Academy, 1969), 468-72.

———, "The Pauline Use of συνείδησις," *NTS* 14 (1967): 118-25.

Thüsing, W., *Per Christum in Deum: Studien zum Verhältnis von Christozentrik und Theozentrik in den paulinischen Hauptbriefen* (Münster: Aschendorff, 1965).

Willis, W. L., *Idol Meat in Corinth: The Pauline Argument in 1 Corinthians 8 and 10*, SBLDS 68 (Chico, Calif.: Scholars Press, 1985).

Winter, B. W., "The Achaean Federal Imperial Cult II: The Corinthian Church," *TynBul* 46 (1995): 169-78.

———, "Theological and Ethical Responses to Religious Pluralism — 1 Corinthians 8–10," *TynBul* 41 (1990): 209-26.

Witherington, B., "Not So idle Thoughts about Eidolothuton," *TynBul* 44 (1993): 237-54.

———, "Why Not Idol Meat? Is It What You Eat or Where You Eat It?" *BibRev* 10 (1994): 38-43 and 54-55.

Yeo, Khiok-khing, *Rhetorical Interaction in 1 Cor 8 and 10: A Formal Analysis with Preliminary Suggestions for a Chinese Cross-Cultural Hermeneutic*, BibInt 9 (Leiden: Brill, 1995), esp. 5-14, 76-211.

a. Free to Indulge "Rights" on the Basis of Knowledge? (8:1-6)

1 The Greek introduces a new topic with the customary περὶ δέ, *now about* (REB, NIV, NJB) or *now concerning* (NRSV, AV/KJV). This reproduces the Greek preposition faithfully, but may fail to convey to English-speaking readers its conventional use as an indicator of a new topic. We accept Mitchell's argument that the preposition need not *invariably* signal a response to the Corinthians' letter to Paul, but it is virtually certain that in most cases, as here, it does serve as such a signal.[27]

εἰδωλόθυτα AND THE SCOPE OF THE CORINTHIAN CATCHPHRASES

(i) τὰ εἰδωλόθυτα

The best translation and broader significance of τῶν εἰδωλοθύτων remain controversial and difficult. (1) The traditional translations differ between *food offered to idols* (RSV) and food *sacrificed to idols* (NRSV, NIV). An explicit allusion to *sacrifice* reflects the Greek θύω in εἰδωλόθυτα, and fits Fee's view that the term "does not refer primarily to marketplace food, but to the eating of sacrificial food at cultic meals in the pagan temples."[28] Fee's view coheres with Paul's "stricter" admonitions against idolatry in 10:14-22, and presumably the term does not then apply to "anything sold in the marketplace" in 10:25. But the research on socioreligious life at Corinth discussed by the five specialist studies listed below seems to suggest a wider reference than Fee suggests.[29] Indeed, the REB translation *meat consecrated to heathen deities* and the NJB's *food which has been dedicated to false gods* come closer, in our view, to Paul's meaning than either of the more traditional translations (cf. AV/KJV, *things offered unto idols* versus RV, *things sacrificed to idols*).

(2) The difference between the REB and NJB translations draws attention to a further, related issue. Does the term allude to *meat consecrated* . . . (REB) or to *food* . . . *dedicated* . . . (NJB)? R. A. Horsley argues that offerings to the gods need not be restricted to *meat* or to animal sacrifices, but could include grain, cereal, or other gift offerings.[30] But if Theissen and the majority of specialist writers are correct in their sociological analysis of the identities of "the strong" and "the weak," the issue of eating *meat*, together with its scarcity for the poor and the variety of social occasions for the rich, has a decisive bearing on Paul's discussion.[31]

(3) The commercial, social, and religious factors were closely intertwined. B. B. Blue asserts simultaneously that "early Christian leaders . . . forbade eating meat sacrificed to idols (Acts 15:20, 29; 21:25; Rev 2:20; Did 6:3)" and that "the idol temple seems to have served both as a butcher shop and as a place for sharing a cultic meal."[32] Büchsel and Conzelmann argue that τὰ εἰδωλόθυτα was a Jewish term, alluding to *idols* in contrast to the Gentile religious term ἱερόθυτον, *meat sacrificed for sacred use*, found once in Paul in 10:28.[33] But the only possible pre-Christian use, depending on

27. Mitchell, "Concerning περὶ δέ in 1 Corinthians," 229-56. See further under 7:1; 7:25; 12:1; and 16:1, 12.

28. Fee, *First Epistle*, 359, and "Εἰδωλόθυτα 'Once Again,'" 172-97.

29. Willis, *Idol Meat in Corinth*, esp. 37-45; Murphy-O'Connor, *St. Paul's Corinth*, 161-67; Horsley, "Consciousness and Freedom among the Corinthians: 1 Cor 8–10," 574-89, and *New Documents*, 1:6; Gardner, *The Gifts of God and the Authentication of a Christian: An Exegetical Study of 1 Cor 8–11:1* (Lanham and New York: University Press of America, 1994), 15-23; and Yeo, *Rhetorical Interaction*, esp. 94-119.

30. Horsley, *New Documents*, 1:36-37.

31. Theissen, *Social Setting*, 121-43.

32. B. B. Blue, "Food Offered to Idols and Jewish Food Laws" in *DPL*, 309; cf. 306-10.

33. Büchsel, "εἴδωλον," *TDNT*, 2:378; Conzelmann, *1 Cor*, 139 and 139, n. 6.

issues of dating, occurs in 4 Macc 5:2 (cf. *Sibylline Oracles* 2:95), which probably post dates Paul.[34] Paul Gardner, supported also by a discussion from Witherington, therefore suggests "that the word was actually coined around the time of the Jerusalem Council and was of *Christian* origin. . . . The word in 8:1 is extremely early and typically expresses Christian abhorrence of pagan sacrifices within the context of the early church debate about the nature of the liberties Christians were allowed."[35]

(4) Even so, the nuances and locations of these "sacrifices" were varied and complex. Willis distinguishes forcefully between (a) a *fully sacramental use, occasion, and understanding of* τὰ εἰδωλόθυτα (which Paul attacks in 10:14-22); (b) a *"communal" understanding* which still retains difficult nuances for all Christians; and (c) a more clearly *"social" aspect in which the emphasis falls not at all upon "conscious worship"* but on "the social relationship among the worshippers."[36] These distinctions help to explain what may otherwise appear to be inconsistencies in Paul's stance more convincingly than hypotheses about multiple letters and partition theories (see the introduction to 8:1–11:1, above). Willis argues for the most part that 1 Corinthians 8–10 presupposes and addresses the "social interpretation" of εἰδωλόθυτα. Willis may well be right to claim that *some* contexts in 1 Corinthians 8–10 may suggest this, but it hardly applies to *all*. Conversely, I find a mirror-image with Witherington's recent article. His insistence that εἰδωλόθυτον *totally excludes* Willis's interpretation but is always "eating in the presence of an idol" again reflects *specific cases* in 1 Corinthians 8–10 (esp. 10:7, 20-21, as Witherington claims), but hardly every passage.[37] We cannot fully rely on the complex historical reconstruction of a relation to Acts 15 which he suggests.

(5) The wealth of archaeological and social data which Theissen, Murphy-O'Connor, and many others have collected supports this broad approach. Murphy-O'Connor observes, "About the only time that meat came on the market was after pagan festivals, and it had been part of the victims sacrificed to the gods."[38] This meat could be purchased for use in private homes, where "the strong" in socioeconomic status could afford it and "the strong" in "knowledge" about the nonexistence of pagan deities could enjoy it without scruple. But this was not the only possible location for a festive meal involving the serving of meat. Murphy-O'Connor provides a sketch of the temple of Asclepius located just inside the north wall of ancient Corinth, to which Pausanias (c. AD 170) alludes explicitly (Pausanias, 4:5). Originally built in the fourth century BC and then damaged in 146 BC, the temple was newly restored in 44 BC by Roman colonists, and at an indeterminate period (probably but not definitely the first century) three dining rooms were built on the east side of the temple courtyard. On the analogy of the adjacent church hall built next to many English parish churches, these could be used for either religious or social events. Just as the vicar or minister of the church might open the event but have minimal connection with it, so

---

34. 4 Maccabees probably belongs to a date between AD 19 and AD 54.

35. Gardner, *The Gifts of God,* 15 and 16 (his italics); Witherington, "Not So Idle Thoughts about *Eidolothuton,*" 237-54.

36. Willis, *Idol Meat,* 10-21, esp. 18-21. In the "sacramental view" the worshipper "appropriated . . . peculiar traits and powers" in union with a pagan deity (18); the "communal" presupposes "the presence and participation of the god" (20); while "the social" emphasizes social friendship, even if with the deity as "more an observer than a participant" (20).

37. Witherington, "Not So Idle Thoughts about *Eidolothuton,*" 245 and 247; cf. 237-54.

38. Murphy-O'Connor, *St Paul's Corinth,* 161.

people could hold birthday celebrations, festive meals to celebrate a family event, or other social occasions under the auspices or patronage of the temple dining facilities.

Archaeological evidence corroborates this. Willis collects numerous examples. Many cite *Papyrus Oxyrhynchus* 1484: "Apollonius requests you to dine at the table of the Lord Serapis on the occasion of the coming of age of his brothers in the temple of Thoeris." Another example comes from *P. Oxy.* 1755: "Apion invites you to dine in the house of Serapis at the table of the Lord Serapis on the 13th at 9 o'clock."[39] Willis sets out the evidence of archaeological remains and inscriptions, and no fewer than five "invitations" to "the table of the Lord Serapis" in the *Oxyrhynchus Papyri* alone (*P. Oxy.* 110, 523, 1484, 1755, 2791), together with *Papyrus Osloensis* 157, *Papyrus Yale* 85, *Papyrus Fouad* 76, and *Papyrus Colon* 2555. He concludes that "the locations vary" and "similarly varied are the occasions stated for meals."[40] Further, the first point, he infers, "suggests a very loose connection, if at all, with the cult's liturgy. . . . The temple might have operated an adjunct restaurant. . . ."[41]

(6) Just as Willis convincingly corrects an overnarrow understanding of τὰ εἰδωλόθυτα, so Gardner warns us that Willis himself tends only to emphasize the "broader" aspect. Gardner insists that we cannot be certain that the "invitation" examples are precisely what occurred in Paul's Corinth, and adds, "Even if they were, they are open to different interpretations."[42] Would a convert *from* the Church of England still want to celebrate family occasions in the local parish church hall? Such a person would have, to apply the analogy to Corinth, a "right" (ἐξουσία) to arrange such events, but would it be appropriate, especially for guests whose conversion might have been costly or traumatic? For one of "the strong," for whom everything had been easy, to impose a social obligation to take part in an event onto a "weaker," more fragile, or more economically dependent church member might be to commit an insensitive and destructive act.

(7) As Theissen and Yeo observe, this would be all the more difficult and seductive for the socioeconomic "weak" or poor, who could not otherwise afford the luxury of eating meat, but were consigned to an endless diet of wheat bread or barley-based cereals.[43] Moreover, the very exceptional character of eating meat would more readily recall the cultic occasion of its slaughter. It is easy, Theissen argues, to understand "the reasons for the opposing attitudes of the weak and the strong. . . . Wealthy people could eat meat more often than others."[44] From 8:7 we can infer that "the weak" did eat meat, but "with a bad conscience."[45] 8:10-13 suggests that "in a cultic setting" this becomes "a genuine temptation" to which they should not be exposed.[46] Although Willis argues that in the "social" context the pagan deity was a mere observer, not a participant, Horsley insists that the general perception is that of eating "in the presence of" the deity, and Gardner endorses this aspect of the situation.[47]

---

39. Willis, *Idol Meat,* 41, where the Greek text is also cited.
40. Ibid., 42.
41. Ibid., 43.
42. Gardner, *The Gifts of God,* 18.
43. Theissen, *Social Setting,* 126-27; Yeo, *Rhetorical Interaction,* 97-98.
44. Theissen, *Social Setting,* 122 and 125.
45. Ibid., 127.
46. Ibid.
47. Gardner, *The Gifts of God,* 19.

(8) This complex situation explains, and paves the way for, the argument in the next few verses about whether an idol "really exists." Because of his conviction that these so-called gods are illusory, Paul draws on the early Christian (or perhaps Jewish) term *idol* in *idol-meat*. But because new converts have genuinely been held under their spell as dominating forces, he also contests the view that their "nonexistence" is all that need be said or thought about them. There is some merit in Yeo's view that "as an apocalyptic thinker" Paul knows that God alone reigns supreme and will triumph over every opposing force, but that while the world is held in bondage to forces beyond its own control "only an apocalyptic thinker like Paul can hold both the power and the vanity of idols in tension."[48]

Since the social, socioeconomic, cultic, and religious dimensions of τὰ εἰδωλόθυτα are so multidimensional and complex, we propose the translation **meat associated with offerings to pagan deities**. This allows for the breadth of locations and settings discussed by Willis, while retaining the importance of **meat** shared by Theissen, Yeo, and Gardner, but also coupling broader **association** with the more sensitive issue of cultic **offering** as "the weak" would all too readily perceive it, and as Paul perceives it as being in the context of 10:14-22. The translation is cumbersome, but it hardly overtranslates a Greek term which is almost impossible to translate into English otherwise without further explanation.

(ii) The Scope of the Corinthian Catchphrase:
(οἴδαμεν) ὅτι πάντες γνῶσιν ἔχομεν

Few doubt that Paul is quoting a Corinthian slogan or maxim. Hurd lists twenty-four commentators (and even then only up to 1965) who unanimously hold this view, although Hurd himself argues that the phrase characterizes Paul's own preaching when he first arrived in Corinth.[49] Subsequent to Hurd's volume, we should add the further ten major writers listed below.[50] A related problem arises from trying to identify whether the Corinthian quotation begins with πάντες or with οἴδαμεν. Willis urges that **we are fully aware that** . . . also belongs to the Corinthian catchphrase.[51] He admits that normally ὅτι functions as ὅτι recitative (i.e., before πάντες), as the equivalent of quotation marks (which do not exist in hellenistic Greek). But he claims that uniquely in this epistle οἴδαμεν ὅτι . . . reflects a non-Pauline or Corinthian style, since Paul normally inserts δέ or γάρ before the ὅτι. He argues that a tension or contradiction between 8:1 and 8:7 (not everyone has this "knowledge") is removed by this reconstruction. This follows a century-old suggestion of W. Lock.[52] But Fee and Gardner

---

48. Yeo, *Rhetorical Interaction,* 101.

49. Hurd, *The Origin of 1 Cor,* 68 and 279: e.g., Heinrici, Weiss, Lietzmann, Allo, and Héring.

50. Barrett, *First Epistle,* "appears to quote . . ." (189); Conzelmann, *1 Cor,* "the quoted slogan" (140); Fee, *First Epistle,* "the opening words of their argument" (363); Senft, *La Première Épitre,* "une phrase de la lettre qu'il a reçue" (109); Schrage, *Der erste Brief,* 2:229; and Wolff, *Der erste Brief,* "des korinthischen Satzes . . ." (169); Gardner, *The Gifts of God,* 22; Collins, *First Cor,* 313-14, 318-19; Lang, *Die Briefe,* 108, "ein Schlagwort der Korinthischen Pneumatiker (cf. 6:12; 7:1; 10:23)"; Hays, *First Cor,* 136.

51. Willis, *Idol Meat,* 67-70.

52. W. Lock, "1 Cor viii:1-9. A Suggestion," *Exp.,* 5th ser., 6 (1897): 65-74.

show that the argument is precarious and narrowly based, and that other explanations can be offered concerning the relation between 8:1 and 8:7.[53] Willis's view neglects the occurrence of οἴδαμεν ὅτι as an established formula. The relation to 8:7 may in any case be softened by transposing οἴδαμεν, *we know,* into Paul's acknowledgment of his awareness of its currency: **we are fully aware that** (as you say) "**All of us possess 'knowledge.'**" This then becomes stance-neutral in relation to "but it is not the case that everyone does possess this 'knowledge'" (8:7). Paul adopts a common starting point, as he so often does. He stands within the projected "world" of the addressees, as I have argued elsewhere, in order to subvert it more convincingly and without unnecessary confrontation.[54] This is a fundamental rhetorical strategy, akin to that of "projected worlds" in the parables of Jesus.

The translation of ἔχομεν as *we have* (REB, NJB, AV/KJV) seems too insipid to reflect the Corinthians' stance. NRSV's "**all of us possess knowledge**" is appropriately stronger as a "claim," perhaps connected with "spiritual gifts" (cf. 12–14). γνῶσις occurs nine or ten times in 1 Corinthians and six times in 2 Corinthians (15 times in the Corinthian correspondence) but only five times in the other generally accepted Pauline epistles (see above). Only eight other occurrences can be found in the whole NT (see 1 Cor 1:5; and cf. 8:7, 10, 11; 12:8; 13:2, 8; and 14:6). Barrett argues, against Schmithals, that Paul usually uses γνῶσις "in a plain, non-technical sense . . . [as] a good thing, but it is inferior to love, and may lead to an exaggerated individualism which loses concern for the neighbour."[55] But if, as is virtually certain from the syntax, context of argument, and rhetorical strategy, the term γνῶσις is borrowed here from the use made of it by the Corinthians themselves, then Schmithals may be correct in detecting un-Pauline nuances in the word in this verse, whether or not "gnostic" turns out to be the most appropriate way to describe these.[56] At all events, the term here needs to be placed within inner quotation marks to denote its specific reference and force at Corinth. This is substantiated by 8:2: "Anyone who claims 'to know' . . . does not yet have knowledge."

It is a mistake simply to draw a contrast between γνῶσις as theoretical and σοφία as more practical, or to suggest that the self-styled theologians at Corinth sought γνῶσις as mere theory. It had very practical effects in providing not only an illusory self-confidence but also more especially division and potential damage. Margaret Mitchell sees it as "contributing to community division" here, particularly "in the justification it provides for certain contro-

53. Fee, *First Epistle,* 365, n. 31; and Gardner, *The Gifts of God,* 22-23.

54. A. C. Thiselton, "The Meaning of σάρξ in 1 Cor 5:5: A Fresh Approach in the Light of Logical and Semantic Factors," *SJT* 26 (1973): 215-18; cf. 204-28.

55. Barrett, *Essays on Paul,* 7; cf. *First Epistle,* 37 and 189.

56. Schmithals, *Gnosticism in Corinth,* 229. Schmithals amplifies his view with reference to his partition theory. In 10:14-22 ("letter Λ"), Paul had attacked worship of idols. But afterward the intellectual gnostics at Corinth worked out a different theological stance in relation to *meat associated with offerings to pagan deities* outside the cultic context. Hence 8:1-13 forms part of a subsequent response ("Letter B").

versial actions."[57] It cannot therefore be exactly equivalent to the γνῶσις for which Paul gives thanks in 1:5. It may well be that the Corinthian "knowledge" had a gnostic, antirealist tinge in perhaps suggesting that to participate in eating **meat associated with offerings to pagan deities** would demonstrate their indifference to, and indeed victory over, demonic forces: "the demons have indeed been conquered. This needs to be demonstrated. The Gnostic is ἰσχυρός [strong]. . . . Highly instructive is the comment of Irenaeus about the Valentinians (1:6:3): 'They eat heathen sacrifices without hesitation and do not believe that they are defiled by it. . . .'"[58] Seen from such a distorted, antirealist standpoint, it becomes a relatively short step to assume that *in the eyes of the Corinthians* (but not in the eyes of Paul) *this* kind of "knowledge" constituted a special charismatic "spiritual gift" as described in 1:5; 12:4, 28-31; and 14:1. Gardner argues for such a view, expressing understandable surprise that the link with these verses "is rarely developed."[59]

Käsemann warns his readers against confusing life in the Holy Spirit with lack of earthly realism.[60] Gardner, however, substantiates his argument by comparing the contrast between "**knowledge**" and **love** in this verse with the parallel contrast between 13:1-13 and the two chapters on "spiritual gifts" which provide its frame.[61] He insists that γνῶσις is *practical;* but its nature and its relation to love can profoundly determine what kind of practical effects it sets in motion.[62]

Gardner's argument reaches its peak with the suggestion, admittedly speculative, that the self-styled "spiritual people" at Corinth aimed "**to build**" people in the church by revelatory "knowledge," he suggests, as "a deliberate policy."[63] This would enhance Paul's response with the utmost irony and wordplay: it is **love** that "**builds**"; "**knowledge**" merely **inflates**! If Gardner is right, this would also explain why the Greek word φυσιόω occurs six times in this epistle (1 Cor 4:6, 18, 19; 5:2; 8:1; 13:4) but only once in the rest of the whole NT (Col 2:18). φυσιόω suggests the self-importance of the frog in Aesop's *Fables,* or something pretentiously enlarged by virtue of being pumped full of air or wind. **Love**, by contrast, builds solidly, and does not pretend to be what it is not. If it gives stature to a person or to a community, that enlargement remains solid and genuine.[64]

Rather than seeking to demonstrate some individualist assertion of free-

---

57. Mitchell, *Paul and Rhetoric,* 126.

58. Schmithals, *Gnosticism in Corinth,* 226.

59. Gardner, *The Gifts of God,* 25, esp. n. 63.

60. E. Käsemann, e.g., "Primitive Christian Apocalyptic," in his *NT Questions of Today* (Eng. trans., London: SCM, 1969), esp. 131-37. See further A. C. Thiselton, "Realized Eschatology at Corinth," *NTS* 24 (1978): 510-26.

61. Gardner, *The Gifts of God,* 25-26.

62. Gardner's discussion is excellent; ibid., 23-27.

63. Ibid., 24.

64. See the introduction to, and exegesis of, 13:1-13.

dom or even victory, **love** seeks the welfare of the other. Hence if "the strong" express **love**, they will show active concern that "the weak" are not precipitated into situations of bad conscience, remorse, unease, or stumbling (see πρόσ-κομμα in 13:7,9). Rather, the one who *loves* the other will consider the effect of his or her own attitudes and actions upon "weaker" brothers and sisters. This is precisely the theology of the church as Christ's "body" which Paul will ex-pound in 12:21-24: "God composed the body, giving to that which feels inferior greater honor" (12:24). The "strong" hands and feet are to protect "unpresent-able" parts of the body (12:23), since the "unpresentable" parts are utterly es-sential to the welfare of the body, even if the supposedly "impressive" parts place themselves on display and imagine that other parts are "dishonourable." Every part of ch. 12 bears on 8:1-13, just as numerous resonances ring out from ch. 13, e.g., love does not brag (13:4); "if I have all 'knowledge' . . . — but after all, may lack love, I am nothing" (13:2). (See below on these passages, includ-ing the discussion of love in Paul by Spicq and Nygren.)

Karl Maly relates 8:1 not only to chs. 12–14 but to the fundamental theme of the whole epistle. Anticipating Margaret Mitchell, he contrasts the individu-alistic concerns about the mode of being ascribed to idols (8:4) to the role of **love** in **building** *up* the community as a whole. Throughout, the Corinthians are fixated with "individual edification" *(Erbauung)* as against "corporate" ("con-struction" *(Aufbau)* of the whole church together.[65] The semantic force of οἰκοδομεῖ, **builds**, in the setting of the church as a community is traced by I. Kitzberger, who discusses the semantic contrast with φυσιόω in these verses, and the correlative opposition between **love** and "**knowledge**."[66] Kitzberger traces the broader uses of (ἐπ)οικοδομέω in Paul (e.g., Rom 14:19; 15:2, 20; 1 Cor 3:5-17; 10:23–11:1; and 14:1-9, 26a, 37-40) and traces its development into the word field of Ephesians.[67] The contrastive semantic terms also include σκάνδαλον, as against ἀγάπη and εἰρήνη.[68]

2   The UBS 4th ed. includes τι after ἐγνωκέναι, together with the translated equivalent in NRSV, NIV, NJB and in more subtle ways by Moffatt, REB and Barrett, whose trans-lation **some piece of** we have accepted but placed in square brackets as uncertain. Conzelmann finds the shorter text attractive but uncertain, while Fee and Zuntz (against Metzger) think that the shorter text is probable. Fee comments: "This . . . reading [with-out τι] fits the context so perfectly that it is either the Pauline original or else the work of an editorial genius."[69] The very early witness of 𝔭46 (about AD 200), coupled with Tertullian and Origen, offers strong evidence for the shorter reading. But this leaves un-answered the awkward question of why ℵ, B, D and other MSS should have included τι.

65. Maly, *Mündige Gemeinde,* 101; cf. 100-104.

66. Kitzberger, *Bau der Gemeinde. Das Paulinische Wortfeld oikodomē/(ep)oikodomein,* 73-78.

67. Kitzberger, *Bau der Gemeinde,* 64-72, 79-117 (on passages in 1 Corinthians).

68. Ibid., 165-206 and 266-70; cf. 224-54 and 304-5.

69. Fee, *First Epistle,* 367; cf. Zuntz, *Text,* 31-32; Conzelmann, *1 Cor,* 139; Metzger sees no need to comment on the UBS 4th ed. text *(Textual Commentary,* 490).

To follow 𝔭⁴⁶ goes against the popular canon *difficilior lectio probabilior*, but it also co-heres with the (here conflicting) canon concerning *brevior lectio* (although recently this has suffered criticism). Nevertheless, an early scribe might believe that τι was needed to qualify a claim to *unlimited* knowledge, and therefore (in the scribe's view) had been ac-cidentally omitted, and should be restored. Thereby an early tradition might have come to include τι. On balance we incline toward the early witness of 𝔭⁴⁶, even if the question cannot be settled. The translations by Moffatt, REB, and Barrett manage to achieve the best of both worlds: *If anyone fancies that he has some kind of knowledge* (REB); or **If anyone thinks he has achieved some piece of knowledge** (Barrett). Since τι does not strictly refer to a qualitative "kind," Barrett's proposal seems to be the more accurate of these two.[70]

We have argued above that the γνῶσις claimed by some or by many at Corinth was a different kind of "knowledge" from that which Paul understands by the same word. Hence in vv. 1 and 2 we have used the phrase **this knowledge**. It is also important to distinguish between the noun γνῶσις, preferred by the Corin-thians as a completed or at least defined "gift," and the verbal form preferred by Paul as denoting *a process of coming to know*.[71] Hence, although different tenses of the verb occur in this verse, we translate the Corinthian version by a noun, **knowledge**, and Paul's concept by verbal forms. It appears that only the REB and NJB reproduce this difference of form, while NRSV even attribute the noun *(the necessary knowledge)* to Paul's *verbal* formulation in v. 2b.

The difference of tense in the Greek is fundamental.[72] The use of the *per-fect* infinitive (ἐγνωκέναι) signifies that the Corinthians, or some of them, per-ceive themselves to have achieved a present state of "having come to know," i.e., having **achieved knowledge**. By contrast *the ingressive use of the aorist* (ἔγνω) represents Paul's correction: *he or she* **has not yet come to know**. The aorist infinitive γνῶναι, which follows καθὼς δεῖ (*as it is necessary*, or **as they ought**), expands the contrast: *just as it is necessary to come to know the differ-ence* between the Christian process of **coming to know** and quasi-gnostic, triumphalist claims **to possess** (v. 1), *the completed process of having come to know*, i.e., **knowledge**, probably as a "spiritual gift" of revelation which is de-finitive. If τι belongs genuinely to the text (which may be doubted; see Textual Note), it cannot logically qualify the verb in the sense of degree *(any knowl-edge)*; but means **has achieved some piece of knowledge**, or **has achieved** *this* **knowledge**.[73]

It is more than likely that Paul's allusions elsewhere to the need to test claims to possess prophetic revelation exemplify the same principle. If all

---

70. Barrett, *First Epistle*, 190.

71. Héring, *First Epistle*, 67-68 makes this point well: "Commentators have not sufficiently attended to the deliberate opposition between the perfect . . . and the aorist (ἔγνω). This aorist is in-ceptive (or ingressive): 'You who claim to be in possession of complete *gnosis* . . . you are not even at the beginning . . .'" (67).

72. Most commentators stress this point, e.g., Schrage, *Der erste Brief,* 2:232-33.

73. Conzelmann attributes the meaning "something worthwhile" to τι (*1 Cor,* 141, n. 16).

Christians are in process of **coming to know** in a dynamic rather than a static sense, claims to **knowledge** remain open to discussion and to possible correction in the light of Scripture, tradition, and the corporate experience of "all the churches." Hence Paul links this principle with "If anyone thinks that he or she is a prophet or a 'person of the Spirit,' let them acknowledge that what I am writing to you is the Lord's command" (14:37). Similarly, Paul has already declared: "If any among you thinks that he or she is wise in terms of this world order, let that person become a fool in order to become wise" (3:18). In 3:18 self-deception and the fallibility of the human heart are not phenomena from which Christians are exempt, and the principle of the cross as "criterion" and "reversal" (Schrage et al.) has to be applied. Similarly, it is implicit for all claims to "knowledge" (8:1-13) or to be "gifted people of the Spirit" (12:1–14:40). So important is this principle in Käsemann's understanding of Paul that he includes 1 Cor 14:37-38 among his so-called Sentences of Holy Law, i.e., within a process of "internal" judgment which amounts to a "decretal jussive."[74] False "knowledge" is "not *acknowledged by* God; that is, he is rejected."[75] This leads on to 8:3.

3 p[46] and Clement of Alexandria omit τὸν θεόν, as well as ὑπ' αὐτοῦ. This makes excellent sense in this context. The verb ἔγνωσται may be construed either as middle (expressing personal interest or the involvement of the subject of the verb in a reflexive sense) or as a passive (known). To retain the ambiguity, we may translate the shorter text: **But if anyone loves, he or she has experienced true "knowing."** Thus ℵ* and 33 also omit ὑπ' αὐτοῦ. Conzelmann describes this shorter reading as "a very pregnant text"; Fee observes that "this shorter text brings Paul's point home so powerfully that it is most likely what he originally wrote"; and Spicq considers it "very probably authentic."[76]

Against p[46] and Clement, p[15], ℵ[2], A, B, D, F, the Latin and Syriac VSS, and Chrysostom, Theodoret, and Augustine include τὸν θεόν and also (except for ℵ* and 33) ὑπ' αὐτοῦ. The UBS 4th ed. accepts the longer reading with an "A" grading. Metzger defends this on the grounds that "the absence of τὸν θεόν . . . was regarded by the Committee to be the result of formal assimilation to ver 2."[77] The omission of ὑπ' αὐτοῦ from ℵ* and 33 is said to be "accidental."[78] Metzger's discussion certainly establishes (with Schrage and Fee) that there can be no certainty about the shorter text. But Zuntz and especially Maly argue more forcefully and convincingly for the shorter text. Maly insists that Zuntz's arguments carry weight, and that all three "longer" readings in 8:2-3 are secondary. The issue here is "not love *toward God,* but love *toward another*" (Maly's italics).[79] The ὑπ' αὐτοῦ is merely added on the basis of analogy with the addition of

---

74. Käsemann, "Sentences of Holy Law in the NT," in *NT Questions of Today,* 74; cf. 66-81. These include 1 Cor 3:17 (66-68); 1 Cor 14:38 (68-69); 1 Cor 16:22 (69-70); 1 Cor 5:3-5 (70-74); and 14:37 (74-75).

75. Ibid., 69 (my italics).

76. Conzelmann, *1 Cor,* 139, n. 3; Fee, *First Epistle,* 368; and C. Spicq, *Agapē in the NT* (Eng. trans., 3 vols., St Louis and London: Herder, 1965), 2:27.

77. Metzger, *Textual Commentary* (2d ed.), 490.

78. Ibid., 491.

79. Maly, *Mündige Gemeinde,* 102-3; cf. Zuntz, *Text,* 32.

God. This meaning, however, would already be implicit if we construe the passive of γινώσκω, as 13:12 demonstrates, and this adds to Maly's suspicion about its originality. Schrage is impressed with Maly's arguments, while Wolff sums up Paul's meaning broadly in terms of our "shorter" translation: "But if anyone loves, that person has true, i.e., genuine (in Paul's sense) knowledge *(wahre Erkenntnis).*[80] Although Senft argues that the reference to God maintains the typically Pauline emphasis on the priority of divine grace, Maly and Héring insist that "true knowledge," especially if the verb is understood as a passive, *presupposes divine election and initiative.* Similarly, Schrage detects Heb. ידע *(yada')* behind ἔγνωσται as an OT allusion to divine election.[81] Although this cannot be decisive, the cumulative arguments for the shorter text remain impressive and deserve respect.

The general meaning and force is clear even if textual uncertainties leave room for doubt in fine-tuning. The kind of "knowledge" which "the strong" use manipulatively to assert their "rights" (cf. ἐξουσία, 8:9; 9:4; and ἔξεστιν, 6:12; 10:23) about meat associated with idols differs from an authentic Christian process of **knowing** which is inextricably bound up with **loving**. While Gardner is right to insist that the contrast involves more than the difference between theory and practice, each kind of "knowledge" has contrasting sets of practical consequences. The triumphalist, manipulative, quasi-gnostic, individualist knowledge can be divisive and even destructive (8:9 and 8:11, "destroyed"); the process of genuinely coming to know and being known entails a stance of active loving and building others by "internal" logical grammar. In other words, it is part of the concept of authentic Christian knowing and being known that love constitutes a dimension of this process. In Schlatter's words, it is "the *kind* of knowledge" which "gives the right direction."[82]

The longer reading, whether it is Pauline or secondary, explicates the foundation of this process in the elective love of God. Senft, Schrage, Maly, and Strobel all perceive this aspect of election either by understanding ἔγνωσται as passive, especially with ὑπ' αὐτοῦ, or alternatively by virtue of what Maly calls "this interdependence of *gnōsis* and *agapē.*"[83] Whichever reading is adopted, however, Fee comments (especially with reference to the shorter text): "True *gnōsis* consists not in the accumulation of so much data, nor even in the correctness of one's theology, but in the fact that one has learned to live in love toward all."[84] He allows for the verb ἔγνωσται to be middle or passive (against, e.g.,

80. Wolff, *Der erste Brief,* 170; cf. Schrage, *Der erste Brief,* 2:232-34, esp. n. 131.
81. Schrage, *Der erste Brief,* 2:234-35; cf. Héring, *First Epistle,* 68; and Senft, *La Première Épitre* 109. This also coheres with Anders Nygren's insistence that although in particular contexts in Paul "God" is the object or recipient of human love, this is uncharacteristic of Paul and occurs only where Paul has specified that God's creative love set the process in motion (see references to Nygren throughout 13:1-13).
82. Schlatter, *Die Korintherbriefe,* 98.
83. Maly, *Mündige Gemeinde,* 103; cf. Schrage, *Der erste Brief,* 2:233-35; Senft, *La Première Épitre,* 109-10; and Strobel, *Der erste Brief,* 135.
84. Fee, *First Epistle,* 368.

Kistemaker's insistence that it is passive).[85] The middle, we have argued, suggests the nuance of active personal stance or involvement; the passive would call attention to "recognition" or election by God. In abstraction from loving concern for others, claims by intellectuals to "more informed" knowledge or claims by pietists to "deep" private or sectarian revelations can do actual damage, especially to "the weak" or vulnerable who may have neither the socioeconomic status nor the confidence to reach an independent view (1 Cor 8:9, 11).[86]

Our proposed translation, **he or she has experienced true knowing**, not only allows for the ambiguity of whether the Greek verb ἔγνωσται is middle or passive (since it can accurately translate either), but also gives point to what Héring calls Paul's "twist" to the Corinthian formula. In 13:12, as in Gal 4:9, Héring notes, "it is explained that no one can know God unless he is already known by God. In our verse there is therefore a kind of ellipsis . . . almost synonymous with 'to have been chosen by him.' . . . Love . . . is therefore the true sign of election."[87] This therefore brings us back to Paul's argument in 4:5. As against claims to be "gifted" by "knowledge" (as Gardner perceives the issue), Paul asks: "What do you have that you have not received? But if you received it [as a gift], why boast as if it were not something received [but achieved]?" (4:7). Thomas Aquinas draws this point from Gal 4:9, "you have known God, or rather are known by God. . . ." Aquinas comments: "He reminds them of the gift received. . . . You were brought to a knowledge of God. . . ."[88] The ellipsis is well summed up by Spicq: "The only perfect knowledge, both loving and practical, is given by God. . . . To be known by God means to belong to him . . . chosen by God. . . . Could there have been a more sure way of showing that this love is really possible than by showing that God himself truly communicated it?"[89]

Once again, then, we find a further example of what I had earlier called (1973) Pauline "redefinition," but which Umberto Eco and John Moores more technically call "code switching."[90] The Corinthian claim to "knowledge," especially knowledge that there is one God (8:4-6) is accepted but "recoded" by means of a "twist" (Héring) which leads the argument now in a new and different direction. Thus J. C. Brunt notes, "Paul treats the question by changing the focus to the issue of Christian love rather than simply giving 'the answer' to the question."[91]

85. Kistemaker, *1 Cor,* 265.

86. See again Gardner's excellent treatment of claims to *gnōsis* here as claims to apply "a spiritual gift" to justify the conduct of "the strong" (*The Gifts of God,* 25-26).

87. Héring, *First Epistle,* 68.

88. Thomas Aquinas, *Commentary on St, Paul's Epistle to the Galatians* (Eng. trans., Albany, N.Y.: Magi Books, 1966), 122.

89. Spicq, *Agapē in the NT,* 27, 28, and 29.

90. Thiselton, "The Meaning of σάρξ," 204-28; Moores, *Wrestling with Rationality in Paul,* 1 28 and 132-60; and U. Eco, *A Theory of Semiotics* (Bloomington: Indiana University Press, 1976).

91. Brunt, "Rejected, Ignored or Misunderstood? The Fate of Paul's Approach to the Problem of Food Offered to Idols in Early Christianity," 115; cf. 113-24.

4 The Syriac addition of ἕτερος to mean "no other God" is a secondary gloss (perhaps reflecting Exod 20:3) which need not detain us.

Margaret Mitchell's claims about περὶ δέ appear to be substantiated by its occurrence in v. 4. She writes, "The formula περὶ δέ, as found in a great variety of ancient Greek texts . . . is simply a topic marker, a shorthand way of introducing the next subject. . . ."[92] Even though the formula often signals a response to a topic raised by the addressees, this need not be so, and no partition theory can be based on this assumption. Clearly the formula marks here a *return to the topic* raised at Corinth after a broader observation about **knowing** and **loving**, and hence the appropriate functional equivalent in idiomatic English would not be another *concerning . . . ,* but **to return to the topic of. . . .**

The Greek word βρῶσις simply means **eating**. Although BAGD translate the whole genitival phrase in this verse *eating of meat sacrificed to idols,* we have argued above (under v. 1) that the term cannot be restricted (as St. John Parry and Lietzmann attempt to narrow it) to participation in cultic meals at which sacrifices necessarily took place.[93] A whole variety of situations may be implied by the phrase, ranging from meat purchased at a butcher's shop which originated from a temple as wholesale supplier to attendance at festivals where meat was available to the poorer classes, probably after a pagan "blessing" or "dedication," or eating in a dining room attached to the temple (cf. J. Murphy-O'Connor), to eating on formal civic occasions "presided over" by one or more pagan deities. Our translation, **associated with idols**, not only allows for this broad variety of situations, but takes up J. C. Brunt's argument that we do not possess conclusive evidence that the term means "food offered to idols" throughout 8:1–11:1, but we do have firm evidence that, as far as "the weak" were concerned, "this *association* of idol-meat with idolatry made them vulnerable" (my italics).[94] A. J. Blasi observes: "Specifically meat was given away to the poor by the well-to-do on religious holidays in honor of one false god or another."[95]

Most writers acknowledge that vv. 4-6 contain quotations either from Corinth or from pre-Pauline catechesis. Wuellner, Kennedy, Mitchell, Fiorenza, and Yeo interpret ch. 8 as largely deliberative rhetoric.[96] Thus Mitchell points

92. Mitchell, "Concerning περὶ δέ in 1 Corinthians," 233-34; cf. 229-56.

93. BAGD, 148; St. John Parry, *First Epistle,* 125-55; Lietzmann, *An die Korinther,* 37-52. Fee ascribes this narrower situation to 8:10 and 10:1-22 but concedes that 8:1-13 may involve broader dimensions, "Εἰδωλόθυτα 'Once Again,'" 172; cf. 172-97 and *First Epistle,* 359-63.

94. Brunt, "Love, Freedom and Moral Responsibility: The Contribution of 1 Cor 8–10 to an Understanding of Paul's Ethical Thinking," in *SBL 1991 Seminar Papers,* 20; cf. 19-33. See also Brunt, "Rejected, Ignored or Misunderstood?" 113-24 (cited above).

95. A. J. Blasi, *Early Christianity as a Social Movement,* 61.

96. W. Wuellner, "Where is Rhetorical Criticism Taking Us?" *CBQ* 49 (1987): 448-63; G. Kennedy, *NT Interpretation through Rhetorical Criticism* (Chapel Hill: University of North Carolina Press, 1984), 87; E. Schüssler Fiorenza, "Rhetorical Situation and Historical Reconstruction in 1 Cor," *NTS* 33 (1987): 399; cf. 386-403; Mitchell, *Paul and the Rhetoric,* 36-37 and 126-30; Yeo, *Rhetorical Interaction,* 182-83.

out that in 10:23–11:1 "Paul overtly and consciously redefines what is τὸ συμφέρον for the Corinthian community."[97] Horsley, Kramer, Murphy-O'Connor and too many authors to cite agree that 8:6 is a confessional formula which "became an important basis for the development of the Christian creed."[98] But what are the limits of the quoted material in 8:4? Does the repeated ὅτι, as some maintain, represent a double occurrence of ὅτι recitative, to signal that "An idol has no real existence" and "There is no God but One" both represent quotations, or does "we know that" also constitute a Corinthian quotation which declares the entailments of their gift of "knowledge"? Most interpreters agree that Paul shares with his readers the confessions of monotheistic belief that 8:4 and 8:6 express, even if there is more to be said. Hence, since we cannot be certain whether οἴδαμεν presupposes Paul or the Corinthians as its grammatical subject, the best way of conveying the meaning and the ambiguity is to translate **we share your knowledge that**. . . . This captures the force of Paul's rhetorical strategy and truth claim. Yeo writes, "By partially quoting the Corinthians' slogan in the first five verses Paul has gained a strong foothold for his persuasion. . . . But Paul does not just quote, he also clarifies."[99]

Are the two quotations about nonexistent idols and about the one God drawn from Corinth? Giblin argues that 8:4b and 4c are both "probably quoting the Corinthians," especially since the ὅτι is repeated and v. 4 is parallel with v. 1.[100] But he also acknowledges that the confession of monotheism embodies biblical roots from the Decalogue and especially Deut 6:4; 32:39; Isa 44:6 and other passages from the OT which reflect "the unique transcendence of the one God."[101] Strobel sees the Decalogue as the background, and Weiss, Schrage, and Wolff allude to the background of the Shema (Deut 6:4).[102] If οὐδὲν εἴδωλον ἐν κόσμῳ is understood to mean "An idol is a nonentity (meaningless thing) in the world," Giblin thinks it likely that this phrase comes especially from the "knowledgeable" at Corinth.[103] But if the point is simply to draw a contrast between false gods and the uniqueness of the one God, this reflects common hellenistic-Jewish and Jewish-Christian tradition which may have wider currency as a formulation than simply at Corinth.[104] Yeo considers discussions about the sources and scope of the various quotations identified by Weiss, Hurd, Willis, and Omanson, but "prefer[s] to describe Paul's use of quotations as the use of many voices in the congregation as dialogical arrange-

97. Mitchell, *Paul and the Rhetoric of Reconciliation,* 36.

98. Horsley, "The Background of the Confessional Formula in 1 Kor 8:6," 130; cf. 130-35. (On other writers, see below on 8:6.)

99. Yeo, *Rhetorical Interaction,* 185; cf. 186-91.

100. Giblin, "Three Monotheistic Texts in Paul," 530; cf. 527-47.

101. Ibid., 328.

102. Weiss, *Der erste Korintherbrief,* 219 (cf. 219-27); Wolff, *Der erste Brief,* 171; Schrage, *Der erste Brief,* II, 237; and Strobel, *Der erste Brief,* 135.

103. Giblin, "Three Monotheistic Texts," 531.

104. Schrage, *Der erste Brief,* 2:237-38.

ment."[105] Those who identify a part or parts of 8:4 as one, two, or three quotations include, e.g., Schrage, Maly, Senft, Strobel, Collins, and Wolff.[106]

Exegetes and grammarians are divided over whether οὐδὲν εἴδωλον should be construed as attributive ("no idol [exists]") or as predicative ("an idol is a nothing . . ."). Murphy-O'Connor, Schrage, and Yeo insist that it is the latter (with Tertullian, Chrysostom, Theodoret, and Calvin).[107] Yeo argues that an attributive construction would stand in contradiction to v. 10. But if the slogan or creed is a *Corinthian* formulation which Paul generally but not precisely endorses, this argument cannot be decisive. Héring (with Meyer and de Wette) favors the attributive understanding because of the parallelism between οὐδὲν εἴδωλον ("no idol exists . . .") and οὐδεὶς θεός ("no God exists except One").[108] But Schrage rejects the adequacy of this argument. The phrase ἐν κόσμῳ may well be equivalent to **real** in **has no real existence** in contrast to that which belongs only to the sphere of concepts, ideas, or imagination. Even if the idol is regarded in educated pagan circles (and certainly in Stoic-Cynic philosophy) as symbolically pointing to a "beyond" which it signifies, Paul insists with the OT and Judaism that it points to nothing that is **real** apart from human concepts or fantasies themselves. This coheres with the history of traditions in the Hebrew OT, in the LXX, and in hellenistic Judaism about idolatry, as Schrage shows in detail (Exod 20:4; Num 33:52; Deut 5:8; 2 Chron 14:5; Jer 9:14; Hos 8:4; cf. 1 John 5:21).[109]

We miss Paul's point, however, if the claim to truth expressed in the Jewish-Christian confession of monotheism is divorced from its existential or self-involving dimension. As Vernon Neufeld and others have conclusively shown, early Christian confessions embodied *both* a *cognitive truth-claiming content* ("*that there is* no God but One") *and* a *self-involving personal stake and personal signature* in my "*world*" (no other lord holds sway over me or over the forces that control that "world": my loyalty and trust are undivided).[110] This will serve to explain how it is that at this existential or self-involving level Paul is concerned in 10:14-22 that a Christian believer can relapse into so redefining

105. Yeo, *Rhetorical Interaction*, 182-83. Cf. Weiss, *Der erste Korintherbrief*, 219-25; Hurd, *Origin of 1 Corinthians*, 68, 120, 129-30, 145, and, in general on 8:1–11:1, 114-49; R. L. Omanson, "Acknowledging Paul's Quotations," *BT* 43 (1992): 201-13. Omanson lists 8:1a-4b, 8a, 9, 10, as well as 10:23 and 10:29b-30. (He also cites 2:15-16a; 4:6; 6:12, 13a, 18; 7:1b, 26b and 34.)

106. For example, Collins, *First Cor,* 313-14 and 318-19; Senft, *La Première Épitre,* 110, "terms of the letter which they had written to him"; Maly, *Mündige Gemeinde,* 105, "the common faith of every member of the community . . . the confession of monotheism . . ."; and Richardson, *Paul's Language about God,* 114-15; Schrage, *Der erste Brief,* 2:236; Strobel, *Der erste Brief,* 135-36; Wolff, *Der erste Brief,* 171-77. Also Weiss, Parry, Allo, Lietzmann, Grosheide, Wendland, and Willis.

107. Yeo, *Rhetorical Interaction,* 188; Schrage, *Der erste Brief,* 2:236. Cf. Tertullian, *Against Marcion,* 5:7; Chrysostom, *1 Cor. Hom.,* 20:4.

108. Héring, *First Epistle,* 68.

109. Schrage, *Der erste Brief,* 2:236-37.

110. Neufeld, *Earliest Christian Confessions.*

his or her "world" that forces beyond his or her control come to usurp the place otherwise uniquely given to God as the One Lord. Neufeld speaks of "the life situation" of these confessions.[111] As Kelly observes in his work on early creeds, from the first, belief, tradition, and truth claim were bound up with preaching, catechesis, stance, and way of life.[112] Cullmann's work on the practical settings-in-life of early Christian confessions and creeds (e.g., situations of faithfulness under persecution; worship; practical witness) confirms the importance of both aspects.[113] Further literature and issues are discussed under "Jesus is Lord" in 12:3.[114]

5-6   (1) Since the introductory καὶ γὰρ εἴπερ at the beginning of v. 5 gives to v. 5 the status of a protasis of a conditional, or perhaps the condition for a concessive, the first word in v. 6, ἀλλ' strictly interrupts the syntax as if v. 5 had already functioned as a main clause. The awkwardness is avoided in 𝔭46, B, 33, and Irenaeus by omitting the ἀλλ'. However, most writers consider this an early "tidying" of what is strictly an anacolouthon. The sense remains clear enough, even if the syntax is not smooth.

(2) It is perhaps not surprising that to a confessional formula acclaiming God the Father and Jesus Christ as Lord, some later MSS should develop this into a Trinitarian creed by adding "and one Holy Spirit, in whom are all things, and we in him." But this is no earlier than the fourth century. Metzger detects the use of the longer form in Gregory Nazianzus.[115]

Much depends on how many parts of these two verses are regarded as quotations, and how much represents Paul's careful qualifications to what he quotes. Willis argues that "Omitting the qualification of v. 5b, the Corinthians' defense is cogently set forth in 8:4-6."[116] "Agreeing with Lock, it seems best to take v. 5 as also a quotation from the Corinthians. In this approach, καὶ γὰρ εἴπερ introduces a qualified assent by the Corinthians to the many gods. They term these gods of their pagan friends λεγόμενοι. Paul's own qualification is the phrase ὥσπερ εἰσὶν θεοὶ πολλοὶ καὶ κύριοι."[117] Willis's view may seem to be supported by our translation of καὶ γὰρ εἴπερ εἰσὶν λεγόμενοι θεοί as **For even if there really exist, for the sake of argument, so-called gods**. In practice, we do not regard Willis's view as firmly established, but propose this translation on the basis of what the Greek seems to demand. Collins alludes to a contrast "on two levels" to capture the mood of hypothetical argument which the vocabulary and

111. Ibid., 60-67.
112. J. N. D. Kelly, *Early Christian Creeds* (London: Chapman, 3d ed. 1972), 6-21, esp. 7 and 16-19.
113. Cullmann, *The Earliest Christian Confessions*.
114. For example, T. Holtz, "Das Kennzeichen des Geistes (1 Kor 12:1-3)," *NTS* 18 (1972): 365-76; W. Kramer, *Christ, Lord and Son of God*, 66-67; W. Bousset, *Kyrios Christos* (Eng. trans., Nashville: Abingdon, 1970), esp. 147; F. W. Danker, *Creeds in the Bible* (St. Louis: Concordia, 1966), 41-46.
115. Metzger, *Textual Commentary* (2d ed.), 491.
116. Willis, *Idol Meat*, 86.
117. Ibid.

syntax signals: "For even granted that there are so-called gods . . . ," and Schrage confirms this hypothetical force.[118] It is possible to understand εἴπερ, with Barrett and BDF, as expressing a concessive relating to a contingent possibility ("though there are . . ."), but as A. T. Robertson argues, the construction "Even if indeed they are" is "assumed . . . for argument's sake."[119]

If this translation is accepted, Willis can argue with some force that it is Paul himself who intervenes between the Corinthian viewpoint and the common Christian creed, **"as indeed there are many 'gods' and many 'lords.'"** The "weak" at Corinth still perceive these as real powers, or at least as genuine sources of corruption, pollution, or compromise, and Paul insists that "the strong" take account of this. Indeed, in 10:14-22 he seems to endorse the view of the weak that sharing in a cultic meal devoted to an idol is tantamount to a return to idolatry involving "sacrifice to demonic powers" and "co-partnership with demonic forces" (10:20). Thus Barrett, Fee, NIV, and JB place **"gods"** and **"lords"** in quotation marks within the clause. Paul states that certainly existentially, but probably also in terms of actual ontological structural forces of evil, there are genuine powers that still shape certain people's lives, although they are certainly not "gods" (for there is no God but one), and no "lords" in any rightful sense.[120]

Although Willis's view finds parallels in some earlier modern commentaries (Parry and Grosheide), most writers (e.g., Fee, Schrage, and Gardner) insist that v. 5 is Paul's formulation, not a quotation from Corinth.[121] Yeo and Wolff interpret it as Paul's broad endorsement of the Corinthian view, which includes, however, a firm qualification in v. 5b that the false "gods" still exercise power, at the very least in an existential or subjective sense, over those who formerly worshiped them.[122] Fee and Yeo pay particular attention to the bipartite structure of the formula in vv. 5 and 6, concerning which Fee comments that, first, the explanatory γάρ "is a strictly Pauline feature," and further that the terms "god" and "lord" in v. 6 "are dependent on the Pauline interruption with its 'gods many' and 'lords many.'"[123] In view of the probability of the use of pre-Pauline material, however, Yeo states the matter more clearly: "The literary form of v. 6 and the anacolouthon of vv. 5-6 suggest that v. 6 is a cited tradition which enhances Paul's argument. Its bipartite form suggests that it is perhaps a pre-Pauline creedal formula from Hellenistic Judaism."[124]

118. Robertson and Plummer, *First Epistle,* 167; Collins, *First Cor,* 315; Schrage, *Der erste Brief,* 2:239.

119. Barrett, *First Epistle,* 191; BDF, sect. 454; Robertson, *Epistles,* 4:138.

120. Fee, *First Epistle,* 369; Barrett, *First Epistle,* 192; as against, e.g., Conzelmann, REB, NRSV, and NJB. See further Murphy-O'Connor, "1 Cor 8:6: Cosmology or Soteriology?" 253-67.

121. Conzelmann, *1 Cor,* 142-43; Fee, *First Epistle,* 371, n. 10 and 371-72; Gardner, *The Gifts of God,* 33-36; Schrage, *Der erste Brief,* 2:221, n. 44 and 239-40.

122. Yeo, *Rhetorical Interaction,* 189-90; and Wolff, *Der erste Brief,* 171-72.

123. Fee, *First Epistle,* n. 10.

124. Yeo, *Rhetorical Interaction,* 190.

The use made by W. Bousset of the phrase θεοὶ πολλοὶ καὶ κύριοι πολλοί is too well known to need rehearsal in detail. It formed part of his now largely abandoned argument that Christians called Christ "Lord" first in the hellenistic communities.[125] We note criticisms of this view in our comments under 12:3, especially his undue separation between "Palestinian" and "hellenistic" Judaism, which Hengel and others have shown to be grossly exaggerated.[126] Bousset's notion of syncretistic development no longer commends general assent. However, the one part of Bousset's research which remains valuable is his discussion of the multiplicity of "*kyrios*-cults" which characterized the Graeco-Roman world of the first century. The emphasis in these cults fell on practical devotion and worship, and in this respect the practical or existential dimension of the confessions and contrasts of vv. 5 and 6 comes forcefully to gain attention for understanding their meaning in this context.

The "strong" at Corinth asserted an ontological and existential monotheism in which the **so-called** (λεγόμενοι) **gods** were nonexistent nothings. Paul endorses their ontological monotheism. Even if these "**so-called gods**" have power over people's lives, they are not **gods** or **God**. Only **God** is *God.* Nevertheless, the fact that *kyrios*-cults **do really exist** means that *habituated patterns of loyalty and devotion* long practiced by new converts before their conversion *cannot simply be brushed aside as no longer affecting their lives and attitudes in the present.* At an existential and psychological level they still leave their mark (cf. Collins's "two-level" contrast, above). Indeed, this may mean even more. Not only do they return a subjective influence; they may also constitute *objective forces of evil which bring destruction, disintegration, and pain.* Unless we adopt a partition theory between 8:1-13 and 10:14-22, Paul appears to associate them with demonic forces.

The texts leaves open some more distinctively modern questions that we may wish to ask. Are these supernatural demonic agencies in the sense of satanic powers? Or are they "demonic" in Paul Tillich's sense of the term, i.e., that whatever fragments life and loyalty into a multiplicity of conflicting directions rather than a single ultimate concern focused on God has destructive force? Murphy-O'Connor, Wolff, and Fee agued that Paul "does not intend that the 'gods' exist objectively . . . they 'exist' subjectively in the sense that they are believed in."[127] Conzelmann expresses the undoubted ambiguity in sensitive and more precise terms. Paul differs from the Corinthian "gnostics" (or "triumphalists," or "strong"), he explains, in holding to a more "existential character of knowledge. . . . The formal knowledge of the fact that there is *one* God is not yet insight

125. Bousset, *Kyrios Christos,* esp. 8-9 and 147.

126. For example, M. Hengel, *Judaism and Hellenism: Studies in Their Encounter in Palestine during the Early Hellenistic Period* (Eng. trans., London: SCM, 1974). See further under 12:3.

127. Fee, *First Epistle,* 373; cf. Wolff, *Der erste Brief,* 172; Murphy-O'Connor, "Freedom or the Ghetto (1 Cor 8:1-13; 10:23–11:1)," in L. De Lorenzi (ed.), *Freedom and Love: The Guide for Christian Life (1 Corinthians 8–10; Romans 14–15)* (Rome: St. Paul's Abbey, 1981), 25; cf. 7-38.

into the truth about the powers of the world. . . . The gods . . . 'so-called' . . . may well be existent in the sense of being 'there' in the world and having a certain power. . . . But they are not gods."[128] Conzelmann alludes to Gal 4:8: "Then, not knowing God, you served those who by nature are not gods." Side by side with this, however, should also be placed 1 Cor 12:2, with its allusion to "dumb" idols to which existentially the converts had once been seduced.

Wendland, Horsley, and Yeo have attempted to express or to explain this ambiguity or tension in other complementary ways. Hurd argues that Paul "believed in the real existence of a variety of spiritual powers, some of them good but most of them evil," and therefore limited the application of an "absolute" monotheism by "the strong" in such a way as to neglect this.[129] Wendland speaks explicitly of an existential "being-there" of "many gods and lords" *(das Dasein* [Heidegger's word] *vieler Götter under Herren)* in conjunction with their being also "cosmic realities" *("aber sie sind 'kosmische' Realitäten").*[130] Gardner points out the Greek verb εἰσίν (**there are**) "is placed forward in both vv. 5a and 5b, which suggests emphasis on the word. . . . Paul's main qualification of what 'the strong' were claiming was that it was only partly true. . . . Paul conceded the real existence of gods but claimed that in the *Christian* context only the one God was recognized."[131]

Horsley paves the way for Yeo's conclusion by arguing that the OT and Judaism embodied two traditions side by side. (a) "In Deutero-Isaiah . . . heathen gods [are] nothings," and *this tradition becomes dominant in the wisdom literature and in hellenistic Judaism.*[132] Examples of this first, more dominant tradition occur in Wisdom 13–15 and in Philo. (b) *On the other hand, apocalyptic writings built upon such OT allusions as Deut 4:19; 29:25; Jer 16:19, and Mal 1:11 to develop the notion that whereas God has chosen Israel as his own people,* "He had subjected the other peoples to the subordinate cosmic powers."[133] The notion that idolatry serves demons or demonic powers emerges, e.g., in *Jubilees* 11:4-6; 22:16-22; *1 Enoch* 19; 99:6-10; *Testament of Naphtali* 3:3-4. Horsley shows how well this second tradition coheres with the emphasis on divine judgment found in 1 Cor 10:1-13 and 10:20-22.[134] K.-K. Yeo holds these two traditions together most illuminatingly with particular emphasis on the second when he concludes: "*Paul* believes in *both the vanity and the power* of the idol because of the apocalyptic tension and ambiguity in his thought. But the 'strong' and the 'weak' hold merely to *the vanity* **or** *the power* of the idol respectively" (my italics).[135] This is the most illuminating comment

128. Conzelmann, *1 Cor,* 143 (his italics).
129. Hurd, *Origin of 1 Corinthians,* 121; cf. 120-23; also Gardner, *Gifts of God,* 35.
130. Wendland, *Die Briefe,* 68.
131. Gardner, *The Gifts of God,* 35.
132. Horsley, "Gnosis in Corinth: 1 Cor 8:1-6," 37-39; cf. 32-51.
133. Ibid., 38.
134. Ibid., 39.
135. Yeo, *Rhetorical Interaction,* 189.

that can readily be made on the meaning of v. 5b in relation to the whole chapter and the wider material.

We may now concentrate entirely on v. 6. Conzelmann claims that "the formula makes use of a Hellenistic type of religious language which has been developed in Stoic pantheism."[136] R. Kerst argues that the confession "is a characteristic document of syncretism: the τὰ πάντα formula is familiar from the Stoa; the εἷς θεός formula is a propaganda-form from Judaism; the κύριος invocation comes from Christianity."[137] The evidence of parallels with Stoicism was collected mainly by E. Norden.[138] Norden cites especially, e.g., Marcus Aurelius, *Meditationes* 4.23, "if you are all things, in you are all things, to you are all things" (ἐκσοῦ πάντα ἐν σοὶ πάντα, εἰς σὲ πάντα), but also Seneca, *Epistula* 65:8, *id ex quo, id a quo, id in quo, id propter quod . . . ;* and Pseudo-Aristotle, *De Mundo* 6, ἐκ θεοῦ πάντα καὶ διὰ θεοῦ συνέστηκε ("from God are all things, and through God they hold together"). Willis, Kerst, Horsley, Dunn, and others cite these and similar sources.[139] However, Kerst acknowledges that these phrases perform a different function in the probable context of a Christian baptismal liturgy. Indeed, Albert Schweitzer insists that the "God-mysticism" of the Areopagus speech, "In him we live and move and exist" (Acts 17:28), is closer to the Stoics than to the authentic or customary Paul, since "in the Stoic view the world is thought of as static and unaltering. The world is Nature. . . . For Paul . . . a . . . process which has for its stages the forthgoing of the world from God, its alienation from him, and its return to him. . . . St Paul lives in the conceptions of the dramatic world-view characteristic of late Jewish eschatology. . . . 'For *from* Him and *through* Him and *unto* Him are all things' (Rom 11:36); but he cannot take a step further and add that all things are *in* God."[140]

This entirely shifts the frame of reference. Indeed, Murphy-O'Connor goes so far as to interpret τὰ πάντα as denoting primarily the new creation in Christ over which "the powers" hold no sway. This confession, he concludes, has more to do with soteriology than with mere cosmological belief; indeed, it has "an exclusively soteriological meaning."[141] Few follow Murphy-O'Connor fully, but it is widely acknowledged that τὰ πάντα alludes either to the origin and purpose of the world or the universe in Genesis 1 and elsewhere in Jewish tradition as this closely coheres with "God's plan of salvation" expounded in 1 Cor 1:18–2:16 (Dunn), or more particularly with the

136. Conzelmann, *1 Cor,* 144.

137. R. Kerst, "1 Kor 8:6 — Ein vorpaulinisches Taufbekenntnis?" *ZNW* 66 (1975): 130; cf. 130-39.

138. E. Norden, *Agnostos Theos* (Leipzig: Teubner, 1913).

139. Cited not only by Norden but by Conzelmann (Aurelius), by Kerst ("1 Kor 8:6," 131, n. 19), by Dunn, *Christology in the Making,* 329, n 64, and by R. A. Horsley, "The Background of the Confessional Formula in 1 Kor 8:6," 130; cf. 130-35.

140. A. Schweitzer, *The Mysticism of Paul the Apostle* (Eng. trans., London: Black, 1931), 6 and 11.

141. Murphy-O'Connor, "1 Cor 8:6: Cosmology or Soteriology?" 253-67.

context in this chapter of the goodness of creation, including what is eaten and enjoyed (Ellis).[142]

Dunn points out that Paul begins with the basic starting point of the Shema (Deut 6:4), but then splits this initial reference between God the Father and Christ the Lord "in a way that has no earlier parallel."[143] His further argument that the second "split" reassigns respective functions to God the Father and to Christ the Lord along the lines of a development from Stoic terminology through Jewish wisdom literature into a "wisdom Christology" is less easy to establish, although Horsley also supports this "wisdom" aspect as essential to the background.[144] But the issues to which Schweitzer and others draw attention remain central and set the stage for our understanding of the fundamental difference between ἐξ οὗ τὰ πάντα, **from whom all things take their origin**, or *derive* or *originate* (i.e., from **one God the Father**), and δι᾽ οὗ τὰ πάντα, **through whom all things come** (i.e., through **one Lord Jesus Christ** as mediate Creator, not originator). As Dunn observes, the third clause refers to Paul, his readers, and the Christian community. Thus in my translation **we** (ἡμεῖς, explicit) (no verb) εἰς αὐτόν, i.e., stand in relation to **God the Father** as **the goal of our existence**; while ἡμεῖς δι᾽ αὐτοῦ sets forth **the Lord Jesus Christ** as **the means** (mediate creator and also redeemer) **of our existence**.

L. Hurtado likewise sees here a Christian utilization of Jewish monotheistic traditions and the Shema (v. 6a), in which Jesus is associated exclusively with the one God of the OT and Jewish tradition, as God's unique agent.[145] This early credal formulation stresses not only monotheism but also (as Dunn expresses it) "the unity of creation and salvation, to prevent a split in the Corinthians' thinking between their experience of spiritual power and their attitude to the material world.... The Lord though whom salvation comes is the Lord through whom all things come.... Salvation for us means that we live *for* the one God from whom are all things and *through* the one Lord ..." (Dunn's italics).[146]

O. Cullmann and N. Richardson note the importance of the different prepositions.[147] They examine the different force of ἐξ αὐτοῦ and δι᾽ αὐτοῦ, and Richardson also examines εἰς with the accusative.[148] With W. Thüsing, he compares the nuances of Rom 11:36 and 1 Cor 8:6.[149] But against Dunn and Hors-

---

142. Dunn, *Christology in the Making,* 182 (cf. 179-83); and E. Earle Ellis, "Traditions in 1 Corinthians," *NTS* 32 (1986): 494 (cf. 481-502); See further Dunn, *The Theology of Paul,* 28-50.

143. Dunn, *Christology,* 180; also *The Theology of Paul,* 28-50.

144. Horsley, "Background of the Confessional Formula" (cited above), 130-35.

145. Hurtado, *One God, One Lord: Early Christian Devotion and Ancient Jewish Monotheism,* 97-99.

146. Dunn, *Christology,* 180.

147. Richardson, *Paul's Language about God* (Sheffield: Sheffield Academic Press, 1994), 296-304; Vincent Taylor, *The Person of Christ in NT Teaching,* 51; O. Cullmann, *Christology of the NT,* 197 and 247.

148. W. Thüsing, *Per Christum in Deum. Studien zum Verhältnis von Christozentrik und Theozentrik in den paulinischen Hauptbriefen* (Münster: Aschendorff, 1965).

149. Richardson, *Paul's Language about God,*.

ley Richardson concludes that "there is very little trace of 'Wisdom Christology' in the undisputed Pauline writings." Indeed, much of Horsley's argument presupposes that 8:6 owes more to Philo, to hellenistic Judaism, and to Corinth than to Paul. This coheres with Willis's view that the whole of the credal formulation in 8:4-6 represents a Corinthian form of words.[150] Nevertheless, these discussions call attention to the placing together of God and Christ, of creation and redemption, in a way which is both Pauline and yet draws upon pre-Pauline credal traditions. Gardner writes, "Possibly it draws on earlier forms of a creed, but it seems to be put together by Paul for this situation."[151] Dunn observes, "The formulation in 1 Cor 8:6 is directed wholly to the situation of the Corinthians," even if the result of vv. 5-6 is both "fascinating and at times puzzling."[152]

It is significant that this view comes to light mainly in specialist studies of the relation between Paul's language about God and his language about Christ, more notably by W. Thüsing and by N. Richardson. As long ago as 1926 E. Peterson proposed that Paul used a monotheistic "acclamation formula" in the tradition of the Shema and the Decalogue.[153] In 1965 Wilhelm Thüsing compared Paul's expressions, acclamations, and confessions of theocentric belief and issues about the centrality of Christ in his theology.[154] Although he confined his attention to Romans, in 1970 Leon Morris argued that the central theme of Romans is "the God theme": Rom 11:33-36 is a "doxology" and declarative "rhapsody" on "the wonder and excellence of God."[155] In 1994 Neil Richardson takes up the theme. He accepts "the Jewish background of the phrase εἷς θεός (8:6a)," but rightly concludes: "His [Paul's] thinking begins and ends with God. Yet between the 'movement' from God and back to God there is Christ. Thus Paul's language about God has been opened up, amplified, explicated, justified, by language about Christ."[156] P. H. Langkammer also concludes, "Paul is the first to outline a sketch of a formal link between Protology [cosmology] and soteriology" which proclaims before the community "God the Father, the originating Ground of all and the end-goal," alongside "the one Lord, the Mediator of the first creation and the Mediator of the reality of salvation."[157] The dynamic sense of movement "from . . . through . . . to" is so perva-

150. Willis, *Idol Meat,* 85-87.

151. Gardner, *The Gifts of God,* 38.

152. Dunn, *Christology,* 181, and *The Theology of Paul,* 36.

153. E. Peterson, Εἷς θεός, FRLANT 23 (Göttingen: Vandenhoeck & Ruprecht, 1926), esp. 219-40 and 253-36.

154. W. Thüsing, *Per Christum in Deum. Studien zum Verhältnis von Christozentrik und Theozentrik in den paulinischen Hauptbriefen.*

155. L. Morris, "The Theme of Romans," in W. Ward Gasque and R. P. Martin (eds.), *Apostolic History and the Gospel: Essays Presented to F. F. Bruce* (Exeter: Paternoster, 1970), 251, 252, 260 (cf. 249-63).

156. Richardson, *Paul's Language about God,* 304.

157. P. H. Langkammer, "Literarische und theologische Einzelstücke in 1 Kor VIII:6," *NTS* 17 (1970-71): 197; cf. 193-97.

sive that Sagnard observes that to try to insert the verb "to be" petrifies Paul's thought in such a way as to distort it.[158] Rom 11:36 underlines this.

Yet complementary observations also need to be made. Collins observes that "Paul's *understanding* of God was affected by his understanding of Christ" (my italics); "Verse 6 is the only passage in the extant letters in which Paul attributes a mediating function in creation to Christ."[159] All of this shows that a static metaphysical monotheism disengaged from discipleship is not enough. Hence the argument of "the strong" that since idols are nothings and one God alone has being is accepted; but it is not accepted as an argument for lovelessly ignoring the anxieties of "the weak." For all things, including Christian existence, **take their origin from God** as a gift, and since **the one God** is **the goal of our existence**, the means by which this comes about is that it is **one Lord Jesus Christ through whom all things come**, and he is **the means of our existence**. Christ-likeness and the shape of the cross mark all that Christian believers are and do. Nevertheless, the argument of "the weak" that forces of evil still hold sway is equally qualified by the reminder that in common Christian confession **all things**, even all food, **take their origin from God** and that we cannot drive a wedge between creation and redemption so as to live in a ghetto, for it is **through one Lord Jesus Christ** that **all things** (the world of creation and the blessings of salvation) *come*.

Horsley succinctly suggests: "8:6 is explainable as Paul's attempt to replace *Sophia,* the source of the Corinthians' *gnosis,* with Christ. . . . Paul borrows one of the particular forms of their Enlightenment theology. . . . Leaving intact their affirmation of God as the source and final cause of all things, he replaces *Sophia* with Christ, applying to him the predicates of the instrument of creation ('through whom are all things') and the instrument of salvation ('through him we'). . . . In three successive steps Paul thus challenges [their] gnosis (vv. 1b-3), contradicts their radical monotheistic principle (vv. 4-5) and finally attempts to replace *Sophia* . . . with Christ (v. 6)."[160] After these three steps Paul can turn to the content of their "liberty" to eat food associated with idols. This in no way undermines Eriksson's belief that 8:6 also constitutes "a tradition Paul had already transmitted to the Christians in Corinth."[161] If he is applying a tradition which he endorses, the compressed logic is readily understandable. A tradition of teaching is presupposed, and Paul argues on this ground with explication related to the situation.

---

158. F. M. M. Sagnard, "A propos de 1 Cor VIII.5," *ETL* 26 (1950): 54-58.
159. Collins, *First Cor,* 315 and 320 (although cf. Col 1:16).
160. Horsley, *1 Cor,* 120.
161. Eriksson, *Traditions as Rhetorical Proof,* 121; cf. 120-27.

b. Freedom, "Rights," Self-Awareness (Conscience), and Love (8:7-13)

7 The UBS 4th ed. grades the reading συνηθείᾳ, *by habituation,* or in our translation **by force of habit**, as "A" since it is strongly supported by p⁴⁶, ℵ*, B, 33, and the Coptic and some Syriac VSS. Several Western texts (D, G, Vulgate, ℵ², and some Latin Fathers) read συνείδησει *(conscious* or *with conscience).* But as Metzger, Schrage, and most others argue, the latter reading is easily explained by assimilation to the subsequent use of the word *conscience* in the last clause of the verse.[162] The exceptions include Maly and Coune.[163]

The word order ἀλλ' οὐκ ἐν πᾶσιν at the beginning of the verse invites emphasis, especially with the strong adversative. It is best translated as: **But it is not everyone who . . .** (as Barrett, Collins, and NRSV; but not REB, NIV, and NJB). On **possesses this "knowledge"** (ἐν πᾶσιν ἡ γνῶσις), see above under 8:1 and 8:1-3. Exegesis turns in large measure on (1) knowledge and habituation, (2) taint or pollution, (3) the meaning of συνείδησις; and (4) the identity of "the weak" and "the strong."

(i) "Knowledge" and Habituation

Habituated attitudes, stances, and patterns of behavior (τῇ συνηθείᾳ [cf. συν + ἦθος]) or **force of habit** still persist in conditioning the outlooks and feelings of **some** (τινές) **even now** (ἕως ἄρτι, *right up to the present*). Hence they eat **as an actual** εἰδωλόθυτον, i.e., *as if it had been sacrificed to an idol as an actual reality,* even if their head, but not their heart, tells them differently. Gardner criticizes Fee's view that the difference here turns simply on the difference between theory and practice: "Theory and experience were not divided in this way. Further, the text does not *say* what Fee suggests. . . . Paul did not suggest that those "weak" people should become more knowledgeable. He said that they did not have *this* knowledge, and so should be treated appropriately. . . . Wrong knowledge involved wrong actions."[164] As we noted in our introduction to this section, Paul may very well side with "the strong" in appropriate, limited situations. But in some contexts "the weak" wanted "to be *seen* to be like the strong, even to the point where they were led into real idolatry."[165] If the context of the **eating** happens to be an actual cultic meal to which a wealthy Christian patron has invited his poorer "client," then "the strong" may cause actual damage

---

162. Schrage, *Der erste Brief,* 2:255, n. 258; Fee, *First Epistle,* 376, n. 1; Metzger, *Textual Commentary* (2d ed.), 491; Weiss, *Der erste Korintherbrief,* 228; Conzelman, *1 Cor,* 146, n. 2; Barrett, *First Epistle,* 194; also Bengel, Westcott-Hort, Godet, and Héring.

163. Cf. M. Coune, "Le problème des Idolothytès et l'education de la Syneidésis," *RSR* 51 (1963): 515-17; and Maly, *Mündige Gemeinde,* 110-11.

164. Gardner, *The Gifts of God,* 40; cf. Fee, *First Epistle,* 379.

165. Gardner, *The Gifts of God,* 45 (his italics). The point is explained further below.

which genuinely **taints,** *pollutes, stains, soils,* or *defiles* (μολύνω) the "weaker" brother or sister in Christ.

(ii) Tainting, Smearing, and Polluting

Moulton-Milligan illustrate the metaphorical force of μολύνω from the papyri (e.g., *Oxyrhynchus Papyrus* 5:840:16, where a *polluted* person walks within a pure sacred area). They compare *pollution* in Rev 3:4 and 14:4 with 1 Cor 8:7.[166] BAGD set forth the semantic field of *stain, make impure, soil, defile, smear, render unclean.*[167] The ritual and ethical nuances of the ancient world may suggest that today *to sling mud at* or *to smear excrement over* conveys the force more incisively. The power of this imagery as symbol which resonates with the effects of evil is well captured and conveyed by Paul Ricoeur's analysis in his volume *The Symbolism of Evil.*[168] In Ricoeur's view these are powerful "double meaning expressions" which open levels of meaning which lie deeply within preconscious processes. But Theissen convincingly equates these preconscious drives in subconscious yearnings with Pauline language about *the heart* (see on 4:1-5; 12:10; 14:20-25).[169] Hence, as we have argued above, the difference between a stance towards idols *in the heart* and knowledge about them in the head entails a far more significant contrast than one between practice and theory. The effect of being projected by "the strong" into a situation which made "the weak" react with alarm, disgust, or guilt, actually **polluted** them and destroyed their innocence. It forced them to connive in a situation of evil.

(3) συνείδησις: CONSCIENCE OR SELF-AWARENESS?

Paul sides neither entirely with "the weak" nor entirely with "the strong" in all respects and in relation to every context or occasion. For the **self-awareness** or **conscience** of *specific persons* (συνείδησις αὐτῶν) does not constitute an infallible guide to moral conduct in Paul's view. If 8:1–11:1 is regarded as a unity (see the introduction to 8:1–11:1, together with Schrage, Wolff, and Brunt), someone's **self-awareness** or **conscience** may be insufficiently sensitive to register negative judgment or appropriate *discomfort* in some contexts (10:6-22), and oversensitive to the point of causing *mistaken* judgment or *unnecessary* discomfort in others (10:23-27). Whiteley may perhaps overstate the point, but he is broadly correct when he observes that συνείδησις (*conscience,* he translates it) often means no more than "remorse" and "tells us how man reacts to his own sin, not how man is constituted."[170]

The word συνείδησις has been the subject of a long history of research in Pau-

---

166. MM, 416.
167. BAGD, 526-27.
168. P. Ricoeur, *The Symbolism of Evil* (Eng. trans., Boston: Beacon Press, 1967).
169. Theissen, *Psychological Aspects of Pauline Theology,* 59-80, 96-114, and 267-341.
170. Whiteley, *The Theology of St. Paul,* 44.

line studies.[171] At the beginning of the twentieth century H. J. Holtzmann argued that Paul borrowed the term from hellenism, where its use was broader than that of *conscience* in medieval and modern moral discourse. A number of lexicographers and commentators separated the preposition from the compound verb to support the argument that the word meant a *knowing* (-εἴδησις) *with* (or together, συν-), as reflected in the Latin *con-scientia, consciousness, knowledge,* or *joint witness* (as in Cicero, Livy, and Tacitus). However, Cicero and Seneca also speak of *conscientia bona, conscientia recta,* and *conscientia mala.* Hence some such notion as *moral consciousness* emerges within the broader area of knowledge. C. Spicq observed that the verbal form may have a relatively broad meaning in 1 Cor 4:4 (as we noted on σύνοιδα).[172] There Paul explicitly states that such "knowledge," "witness," or self-awareness is corrigible, fallible, and provisional on confirmation or disconfirmation at the last judgment (4:1-5).

Research into Pauline uses of συνείδησις passed through several phases.

From Holtzmann (1911) through Spicq (1938) to Bultmann (1948) and Dupont (1948), similarities with the broader uses of the term in Graeco-Roman and Stoic literature tended to be emphasized. It was noted that the term had no precise equivalent in the Hebrew OT and had little or no role in Judaism, except for Jewish writers who were heavily influenced by Greek thought. Bultmann takes up συνείδησις within his section on νοῦς, *mind,* and writes, "συνείδησις ('conscience') is a man's knowledge ('consciousness') of his conduct as his own."[173] However, it does not include intent, but as a second-order process "scrutinizes precisely this intent of one's own mind. Conscience judges, i.e., it is a knowledge about one's own conduct in respect to a requirement."[174] Bultmann finds this exemplified in 1 Cor 8:7-12; 10:25-30.

A second stage of modern research can be traced broadly through the 1950s and 1960s. Two decisive works came from C. A. Pierce (1955) and from J. N. Sevenster (1961), and these are taken up by Whiteley (1964, 2d ed. 1974). Pierce understandably reacted against the notion that if συνείδησις is regarded first and foremost as a source of *knowledge,* as in Seneca and the Stoics, it slid too easily into the notion of knowledge of the moral law as understood in much Christian tradition and in modern ethical theory, which clearly falsifies the emphasis and scope of the term in Paul.[175] Pierce in fact urges that "the assumption . . . of a Stoic origin for the Pauline συνείδησις rests on quite insufficient evidence, and is inherently improbable."[176] It is a "fallacy."[177] Certainly it has nothing to do with an immanent "divine voice" which rests on a non-Pauline, Stoic worldview and pantheism.

Pierce believed that in the Pauline writings the function of συνείδησις was primarily negative. "Conscience" gives rise to "the pain consequent upon the inception of an act believed to be wrong."[178] Thus on 1 Cor 8:7, 10, 12 he comments that Paul at-

171. Jewett, *Paul's Anthropological Terms,* 402-46, provides an excellent discussion.
172. Spicq, "La Conscience dans le Nouveau Testament," 50-80. He emphasizes the common notion of "witness" or "knowledge with," shared by Paul and many Greek writers.
173. R. Bultmann, *Theology of the NT* 1 (German 1948; Eng. 1952), 216-17.
174. Ibid., 217.
175. Pierce, *Conscience in the NT,* esp. 13-20 and 111-30.
176. Ibid., 15.
177. Ibid., 13-20.
178. Pierce, *Conscience in the NT,* 82.

tacks not the oversensitive conscience, but the undersensitive conscience of "the strong" who allow "the weak," who are "the little ones" of Matt 18:3-4, to be hurt and damaged. "The *little ones* ["the weak"] should be protected by the body of which he is a member from the pain called *conscience*.... To offend against love is to sin against Christ himself" (8:12, Pierce's italics).[179] "The words for *defile* and *wound* are not so very different from each other....*Defilement* is painful."[180] Whiteley endorses Pierce's view without reserve, sharing his conclusion that to view "conscience" as anything more than a measure of how "we know that we have already done wrong" springs from Christian tradition after the third century.[181]

More recent writers tend to regard Pierce as having combined insights with overstatement. Sevenster's careful comparison between Paul and Seneca on συνείδησις helps us here.[182] Sevenster has little difficulty in finding a vast range of references to *conscientia* to denote "man's knowledge of his own actions."[183] But conscience can be "our guardian" for Seneca, because "God ... is with you, is within you."[184] Sevenster points out that while both Paul and Seneca call "conscience" knowledge and a witness (2 Cor 1:2; Rom 9:1, 2, 15; cf. Seneca, *Epistula* 43.5; *De Beneficiis* 2.10.2), for Seneca conscience is a *final* judgment, while for Paul it remains *fallible, provisional, subject to correction,* and *relative to a person's prior moral stance* (e.g., 1 Cor 4:1-5).[185] Rom 2:14-15, he urges, does not presuppose "natural revelation." "The promptings of conscience do not possess unconditional validity."[186] Hence in 1 Cor 8:7 Paul does *not* urge "the strong" to obey the promptings of *their* "knowledge" or "conscience"; this is to be determined by the well-being of the "weaker" brother.[187]

The third phase of research begins perhaps transitionally with Margaret Thrall's modifications to Pierce's interpretation (1967-68), and pays increasing attention to the variety of meanings of συνείδησις found in different contexts in Paul.[188] But although she successfully points to counterexamples neglected by Pierce, she reacts too strongly in relocating the term in hellenistic contexts, as Jewett (1971) suggests.[189] Jewett himself not only fully recognizes the differing nuances of συνείδησις in different Pauline letters and passages, but makes full use of his elaborate partition theory of 1 Corinthians to trace a diversity of meanings within our epistle (cf. 8:7, 10, 12; 10:25, 27, 28, 29).[190] This now paves the way for the third main phase: Horsley's interpretation of συνείδησις as "consciousness" or **self-awareness** in 1 Corinthians 8–10 (1978), and for the work of H.-J. Eckstein (1983), Willis (1985), P. W. Gooch (1987), and

179. Ibid., 81.

180. Ibid.

181. Whiteley, *The Theology of St. Paul,* 210; cf. 44.

182. J. N. Sevenster, *Paul and Seneca,* NovTSup 4 (Leiden: Brill, 1961), 84-102.

183. Ibid., 85; cf. 84-92; e.g., Seneca, *Epistula* 59.16; 81.21; 87.23; 97.12-15; 105.7; *De Clementia* 1.1.2, 3; 2.1.3; *De Beneficiis* 3.13.1; 5.17.2.

184. Seneca, *Ep.* 41.1, 2; cf. Sevenster, *Paul and Seneca,* 89.

185. Sevenster, *Paul and Seneca,* 101.

186. Ibid., 100 and 99.

187. Ibid., 99.

188. Thrall, "The Pauline Use of συνείδησις," 118-25.

189. Jewett, *Paul's Anthropological Terms,* 419.

190. Ibid., 421-39. Of twenty uses of συνείδησις in the NT, nearly half occur in 1 Corinthians.

Gardner (1994), among others, who take full account of previous work and Paul's contexts of thought.[191]

Eckstein traces the continuity between Paul's use of συνείδησις and the semantic scope of לב (lebh), heart, in the OT.[192] In the OT heart includes intellectual "knowing" but also transcends the merely cognitive. It denotes the seat of states of feeling (esp. pain, anxiety, fear, trembling, or joy and exultation) but also a stance of will associated with resoluteness, decision, or assessments leading to decision. Thus Eckstein argues that in 1 Corinthians and in Romans, Gk. συνείδησις includes awareness of, reflection on, and evaluation concerning, thought, will, decision, and resultant action.[193] A "**weak**" conscience is one that has become incapable (or never was capable) of fulfilling these tasks. This would cohere with a "**weak**" conscience being associated with lack of knowledge or with merely routinized, unthinking, habituated action. If this is correct, to **wound** the συνείδησις of a fellow Christian by insensitively questioning his or her frame of reference for assessment would amount to reducing its effectiveness by **damaging** it (see exegesis below).[194] Eckstein understands this action of inflicting damaging blows upon it (8:12, see exegesis) as in effect an objective assault upon the whole person: an assault upon more than a subjective aspect or "part."[195] Hence the results of this destructive action are also objective: the weak experience **a cause of stumbling** (8:9), destruction (8:11), and **downfall** (8:13).

Eckstein provides excellent insight into the plight of "the weak." However, Horsley, Gooch, and Gardner develop the scope of the term in such a way as also to explain the situation of "the strong" more clearly as an antithetical term in this context.[196] They argue for the meaning self-awareness (Gooch, Gardner) or perhaps consciousness (Horsley).[197] "The strong" wanted to continue their lifestyle of meeting at festivals and parties where meat was served, and their robust, confident **self-awareness** of their "knowledge" about the nonexistence of idols supported this confidence. "The weak," Gardner continues, "desired to be seen to be like the 'strong', even to the point where they were led into real idolatry (vv. 7b and 10 c); it is quite likely that a 'weak conscience' simply means a 'lack of knowledge of oneself in relation to others.'... Being 'weak' in this sort of self-perception would provide ample motivation to do something known to be wrong. Much-deserved group recognition could easily lead to doing many unwise things" (Gardner's italics).[198] The "weak" were insecure in reflecting on their own actions, and were too easily carried along by the overconfidence of the "strong." Hence they lost their integrity and became **tainted** or stained in their **self-awareness**. Twenty years after his seminal study of 1978 Horsley repeats in 1998

191. Horsley, "Consciousness and Freedom among the Corinthians: 1 Cor 8–10," 574-89; Eckstein, Der Begriff Syneidêsis bei Paulus; Willis, Idol Meat, 89-96; Gooch, "'Conscience' in 1 Cor 8 and 10," 244-54; and Gardner, The Gifts of God, 42-54.

192. Eckstein, Der Begriff Syneidēsis bei Paulus, 35-135.

193. Ibid., 311-14.

194. Cf. J. M. Gundry-Volf, "Conscience," in DPL (1993), 153-56, esp. 154-55.

195. Eckstein, Der Begriff Syneidēsis, 241.

196. Gardner, The Gifts of God, 44-46; Gooch, "'Conscience' in 1 Cor 8 and 10," 244-54; Horsley, "Consciousness and Freedom," esp. 582 and 586: "The 'consciousness' of the Corinthians seems to work in a way contrary to how we conceive of 'conscience' working" (596).

197. Gardner, Gifts, 40-64; Gooch, "'Conscience,'" 244-54; Horsley, "Consciousness," 582. Gooch emphasizes here a "sense of Christian identity" (250).

198. Gardner, Gifts, 45.

commentary, "*Consciousness* would far better render the Greek term *syneidesis* (NRSV *conscience*) both here and elsewhere in Paul's letters."[199] Collins (1999) simply translates the Greek in 8:7 *consciousness*.[200]

The practical lessons here are profound. Paul is *not* advocating the kind of "autonomy" mistakenly regarded widely today as "liberty of conscience." Rather, he is arguing for the reverse. Freedom and "rights" (see on ἐξουσία, below) must be restrained by self-discipline *for the sake of love for the insecure or the vulnerable,* for whom "my freedom" might be "their ruin." This "freedom" may become "sin against Christ" (8:12). Finally, Paul uses here the strategy of redefinition or "code switching" to which we have referred repeatedly. Horsley observes: "Paul . . . is coaxing the enlightened Corinthians along by using their own language, only to give it a very different twist or application."[201]

(4) The Identity of "the Weak" and "the Strong"

On Paul's use of the terms ἀσθενής, **weak** (see above under 1 Cor 1:25, 27; also 4:10; 8:7, 9, 10; 9:22; 11:30; 12:22 [also the verb, 1 Cor 8:11, 12]) and ἰσχυρός, **strong** (see above under 1 Cor 1:25, 27; also 4:10; 10:22, as well as 8:1). Paul uses the terms in 2 Cor 10:10; 11:21, 29. *The particular approach explored by Horsley and Gardner illuminates what seems otherwise to be a puzzling disjunction between two separate meanings of* **the strong** *and the* **weak**. If Theissen is correct to attribute a socioeconomic meaning to these terms, how can they also appear to denote respectively an undersensitive and oversensitive conscience?[202] On the basis of the above exegesis *the two terms denote respectively* **the secure** *(both in socioeconomic status and in "knowledge") and* **the insecure** (again *both in social and economic and patronage terms*), and in a *more confused* **self-awareness** which makes them *vulnerable* to be led along by the pretensions and *superior* social status of "**the strong**." A coherent explanation of these terms has emerged, which corroborates the exegesis.

Yeo's observations about "the strong" as those with "social power, influence, political status and wealth" but also including "a traditional Roman value . . . of ability or competence in a variety of areas" seems to clinch the argument.[203] "The weak," conversely, are not only "of low social standing" but as part of a nondescript "mass of undifferentiated citizens" crave for identity and for recognition and acceptance by "the strong."[204] If "the strong" set an agenda,

199. Horsley, *1 Cor,* 121.
200. Collins, *First Cor,* 321; defended, 324-25.
201. Horsley, "Consciousness and Freedom," 587.
202. Cf. Theissen, *Social Setting,* 121-44. Willis, *Idol Meat,* 92-96, is right to warn us against assimilating references to "the weak" and "the strong" in 1 Corinthians 8–10 with, e.g., the debate in Rom 14:1-2. Willis prefers to relate the term to Paul's "impassioned defense of the weak" in 2 Cor 11:29 (95).
203. Yeo, *Rhetorical Interaction,* 90.
204. Ibid., where Yeo finds further support from an unpublished thesis by Mark Reasoner, "The 'Strong' and the 'Weak' in Rome and in Paul's Theology" (Ph.D. diss., University of Chicago, 1990), esp. 123-27.

"the weak" may be seduced into doing almost anything to gain what they seek, while compounding their own confusions and inner tensions by feeling the "wrongness" of it all at the same time. Their integrity has been compromised, polluted, or **tainted**. In ch. 10 Paul will speak of their being "wounded by blows" (τύπτω).

8 (1) παραστήσει, the *future* tense, **will present**, is read by **א**, A, B, and all the major MSS except for **א**², the Western D, E, and Western Fathers Tertullian and Cyprian. These read the *present* παρίστησι. The latter reformulates a declaration as a maxim. Some argue for the present on the ground that a maxim is being quoted, and therefore "is the most natural sense." Weiss translates *"bringt uns nicht vor Gottes Gericht."*²⁰⁵ Copyists probably changed the future to the present for this reason.²⁰⁶ Most writers accept the future.

(2) **א**, 33, and a few other MSS replace ἡμᾶς, **us**, by ὑμᾶς, **you**. This has too little support to deserve consideration, and since the verse is almost certainly a quotation from Corinth, ὑμᾶς is even less likely.

(3) There is some textual confusion about the sequence of the two halves of the quotation "**if we abstain . . . if we eat.**" Further, the single witness A³ matches this quotation more closely to the first half of the verse to read "We are not better off if we abstain, and no worse off if we eat." This is accepted by Murphy-O'Connor because it precisely captures the theology of "the strong" as Paul quotes it. But Fee and others argue against Murphy-O'Connor's view on the ground that it neglects the weight of textual evidence.²⁰⁷ The translation proposed above follows the sequence of the text adopted by UBS 4th ed. since we regard it as reasonably supported by p⁴⁶, B, and A*, (33*), Vulgate, Coptic VSS; although **א**, D, F, and G reverse the order (with Tertullian, Cyprian, Augustine and Pelagius, Origen, Basil and Chrysostom). Zuntz argues for this latter, D reading, but this reading probably arose to match v. 8a more closely.²⁰⁸

J. Murphy-O'Connor's article on this verse deserves the most careful consideration, while P. D. Gardner's development of, and modification to, his approach offers a novel approach which also carries much weight.²⁰⁹ Our understanding of this pivotal verse depends on a variety of factors, not least on (i) the meaning of οὐ παραστήσει τῷ θεῷ (translated above as **will not bring us to God's judgment**); (ii) whether the whole or part of v. 8 represents a Corinthian quotation or Paul's declaration of a principle; and (iii) whether the addressees are primarily "the strong," "the weak," or the mixed community, and whether the quotation (if quotation is involved) reflects a maxim of "the strong" or of others.

(i) παρίστημι may convey various meanings, depending on its context and use.

(a) The AV/KJV, RV, and RSV, followed by Barrett, translate: *Food will*

205. Weiss, *Der erste Korintherbrief,* 229 and 229, n. 1; also Godet, *First Epistle,* 1:423.
206. Murphy-O'Connor, "Food and Spiritual Gifts in 1 Cor 8:8," 296; cf. 292-98.
207. Fee, *First Epistle,* 377, n. 6.
208. Conzelmann, *1 Cor,* 146, n. 3; against Zuntz, *Text,* 161-62.
209. Murphy-O'Connor, "Food and Spiritual Gifts in 1 Cor 8:8," 296; and Gardner, *Gifts of God,* 48-54.

not commend us to God.[210] This is too restrictively positive for the verb; Senft, Maly, and Schrage note that had the word meant *commend* we should expect συνίστημι rather than παρίστημι, for these two verbs are not usually synonymous.[211] Murphy-O'Connor states that while the RSV "appears limpidly clear . . . in fact it [this clause] abounds in problems."[212]

(b) Most writers draw attention to the lexicographical formation of the compound verb as denoting *to place* (ἵστημι) *beside* (παρά). The most transparent rendering of this sense appears in JB: *Food cannot bring us in touch with God,* or more loosely in NRSV: *Food will not bring us close to God.* However, Schrage, Wolff, and others insist that the verb primarily concerns *social or legal status* in this kind of context, rather than a metaphor of spatial proximity or relationship.[213] Murphy-O'Connor shows that *to bring close to God* originates with a dubious argument from R. Reitzenstein which lacks adequate evidence.

(c) The verb regularly conveys the notion of *introducing* someone, which is well reflected in REB's translation *Food will not bring us into God's presence.* Conzelmann, Senft, and Collins defend this meaning in this verse, and it coheres with other Pauline and NT uses (e.g., to present as a holy bride, 2 Cor 11:2; to present himself alive, Acts 9:14; to present Jesus in the temple, Luke 2:22).[214] But although this may include the nuance of status, this translation loses the primary emphasis. BAGD note that many contexts having to do with *to bring before* are legal, e.g., *to bring before a judge.*[215] Collins translates: *But food will not put us in the presence of God,* after considering the various textual readings and Murphy-O'Connor's arguments *(loc. cit.).*

(d) The most sophisticated studies recognize that the verb probably alludes to *status before God,* although opinion is divided about whether in this verse the meaning is a positive one drawn from "strong" but negated by Paul, i.e., *"Food will not affect our standing before God,"* proposed by P. D. Gardner, or a negative, pejorative sense used as a quotation from "the strong": *"Food will not bring us before (the judgment seat of) God,"* proposed by Murphy-O'Connor.[216] Most

210. Barrett, *First Epistle,* 195.

211. Robertson and Plummer, *First Epistle,* 170; Findlay, *Expositor's Greek Testament,* 2:843; Heinrici, *Das erste Sendschreiben,* 232, n. 3; Edwards, *First Epistle,* 222; Senft, *Première Épitre,* 113, n. 6; Maly, *Mündige Gemeinde,* 115-17; J. Jeremias, "Zur Gedankenführung in den paulinischen Briefen," in J. N. Sevenster and W. C. van Unnik (eds.), *Studia Paulina in Honorem J. de Zwaan* (Haarlem: Bohn, 1953), 151-52; Schrage, *Der erste Brief,* 2:259-60; Weiss, *Der erste Korintherbrief,* 229, esp. n. 1.

212. Murphy-O'Connor, "Food and Spiritual Gifts in 1 Cor. 8:8," 292.

213. Ibid., 297 and 292-98; Gardner, *Gifts,* 48 and 48-54; Schrage, *Der erste Brief,* 2:259-60; Fee, *First Epistle,* 382-83, esp. n. 34; and Wolff, *Der erste Brief,* 179-80, who concedes the variability of the semantic range.

214. Conzelmann, *1 Cor,* 146-48; Senft, *Première Épitre,* 113; cf. BAGD, 627 (category 1b); Collins, *First Cor,* 321 and 325.

215. BAGD, 628 (category 1e), together with Robertson and Plummer *First Epistle;* Murphy-O'Connor, "Food and Spiritual Gifts," 292; Weiss, *Der erste Korintherbrief,* 229.

216. Murphy-O'Connor, "Food," 297; Gardner, *Gifts,* 48.

writers endorse H. A. W. Meyer's view that the issue turns on the religious neutrality of food. Meyer paraphrases: *Food is not the determining element in the Christian's relation to God*' (his italics).[217] Gardner argues a very strong case for the view that "the strong" viewed the spiritual gift of "knowledge," which enabled them to eat meat associated with idols, as a positively authenticating mark of their giftedness and standing before God. It is this, he argues, that Paul denies (see further under ii).[218]

(e) Murphy-O'Connor and Jeremias take up the emphasis reflected in our proposed translation "**Food will not bring us to God's judgment**," viewed as both a negative or pejorative allusion to *being judged* and as a slogan or catchphrase of "the strong."[219] This allusion to judgment already finds expression in Weiss, Robertson and Plummer, and BAGD.[220] In 2 Cor 4:14 the verb presupposes an allusion to God's judgment, and some stress the eschatological reference which is implied in v. 8a. Similarly, Heinrici has little doubt that the issue concerns divine judgement.[221] The difference between (d) and (e) turns on two subtle points: whether v. 8 quotes a catchphrase or is Paul's correction alone; and whether "the strong" claimed that their "boldness" failed to risk God's wrath (Murphy-O'Connor) or, still further, that it constituted an authentic mark of possessing a gifted status as a proven believer (Gardner). We are strongly tempted in Gardner's direction, but Murphy-O'Connor's competing explanation seems to be right.

(ii) Our own translation places quotation marks around v. 8a, which corresponds with the NRSV and with Barrett, but with few other VSS. Our translation of the verb also differs from that of the NRSV. Calvin understands 8a as reflecting a Corinthian view, but not in the sense urged by either Gardner or Murphy-O'Connor.[222] Among modern commentators, this verse is regarded as partly or wholly a quotation of a catchphrase by the eight writers listed below (from Heinrici to Yeo).[223] Yeo suggests that the verse embodies axioms of "the strong" into which Paul inserts οὔτε *(it is not the case that)* in v. 8b to their "gnostic" campaign motto ἐὰν μὴ φάγωμεν ὑστερούμεθα, ἐὰν φάγωμεν περισσεύομεν: *their* principle was "if we do not eat, we fall prey to a lack; if we do eat, we abound." Bruce thinks that v. 8a *"may* be a quotation" (my italics).[224] At the very least, many regard v. 8a and perhaps v. 8b as a paraphrase or echo of

217. Meyer, *Epistles to the Corinthians,* 1:245.

218. Gardner, *Gifts,* 48-54.

219. Murphy-O'Connor, "Food," 297; Jeremias, "Zur Gedakenführung in den paulinischen Briefen," 151-52.

220. Weiss, *Der erste Korintherbrief,* 229; Robertson and Plummer, *First Epistle,* 170; and BAGD, 628.

221. Heinrici, *Das erste Sendschreiben,* 233, n. 3.

222. Calvin, *First Epistle,* 177.

223. Heinrici, *Das erste Sendschreiben,* 229; Weiss, *Der erste Korintherbrief,* 229; Parry, *First Epistle,* 90; Morris, *First Epistle,* 128; Jeremias, "Zur Gedankenführung," 151-52; Grosheide, *First Epistle,* 194; Barrett, *First Epistle,* 195; and Yeo, *Rhetorical Interaction,* 192-93.

224. Bruce, *1 and 2 Cor,* 81.

Corinthian theology on the part of "the strong." Indeed, Gardner's view is not far from Wendland's when the latter asserts: "The Corinthian 'free' and 'strong' openly parade their 'eating' as signs *(als Zeichen)* [Gardner, "authentications"] of their quite special spiritual knowledge. . . ."[225] For Gardner "the gifts" are proofs or evidences of authentic Christian status as gifted Christians. Fee reflects a number of commentators when he observes, "Both sentences reflect what the Corinthians were arguing in their letter, whether they are direct quotations or not."[226]

However, if the Greek of v. 8a is construed as above, v. 8b does not merely repeat the same thought. In our view (following Jeremias and Murphy-O'Connor) the thrust of v. 8a picks up the note of pressure exerted by "the strong" upon "the weak," either in a neutral sense ("enjoy your freedom: eat meat") or in the Wendland-Gardner sense ("show that you too have this gift of knowledge . . ."). Paul then offers a comment, using the deliberative rhetoric which M. M. Mitchell identifies as entailing an appeal to "advantage."[227] The sequence of the bipartite clause reflected in the UBS obviates an expectation of δέ or ἀλλά: **Neither** [is it the case that] **if we abstain from food do we lose any advantage** (ὑστερούμεθα, middle voice as in 1:7) **nor** [is it the case that] **if we eat do we gain any advantage** (περισσεύομεν).[228] If, however, v. 8b means no more than that "eating" is a matter of *indifference* rather than *a cancelling off of advantages,* then it becomes quite possible that the whole of v. 8 constitutes a Corinthian maxim parallel to indifference about the use of the body (τὸ σῶμα) in 6:12-13. The issue may seem finely balanced; but if v. 8b is accorded its proper weight, the arguments of Murphy-O'Connor, Gardner, Mitchell, and Yeo that in v. 8b Paul's position is "clearly stated" carry the day.[229] Yet the thought does remain parallel in some respects with 6:12-13 as the return to the theme of ἐξουσία (appeal to **rights** or just possibly *authority*) in the next verse clearly proves.

(iii) It has already become apparent that whether Paul primarily addresses "the strong," "the weak," or the mixed community depends partly on how we punctuate the verse, i.e., on what parts, if any, of v. 8 reflect views held at Corinth but not by Paul, what are held by Paul but not at Corinth, and what constitutes common ground. In our proposed translation, Paul explicitly responds in v. 8b to the propagandist view of "the strong" in v. 8a, but does so out of pastoral concern for both "the strong" and more especially "the weak" within the community. Although v. 8b offers *a response to "the strong,"* it is also an *address to the whole community.*[230] The one remaining serious query here is

225. Wendland, *Die Briefe,* 70.

226. Fee, *First Epistle,* 383.

227. Mitchell, *Paul and the Rhetoric of Reconciliation,* 25-38; cf. 241-42.

228. The textual reading which includes γάρ cannot be sustained, especially in view of its omission by ℵ, A, B, et al. It is purely Western and Syrian.

229. Mitchell, *Rhetoric,* 242; cf. Yeo, *Rhetorical Interaction,* 193; and Murphy-O'Connor, "Food," 297.

230. Yeo and Gardner point out that the immediately following allusion to ἐξουσία confirms

whether "the men of knowledge [simply] deny that they are in any danger of in-curring the wrath of God" (Murphy-O'Connor) or whether they go one step fur-ther and feel "the need to be *seen* to be God's people [and] . . . were *deliberately* eating this food" to exhibit an authenticating "gift of knowledge" (Gardner; his italics).[231] We cannot exclude either possibility. Murphy-O'Connor seems to be on firmer ground; but Gardner's view coheres well with our picture of the Co-rinthian "strings" theologies.

9 After Murphy-O'Connor's comment that v. 8 "abounds in problems," it is a relief to note Héring's conclusion that "8:9-13 presents no particular diffi-culties."[232] Much of the exegetical discussion and translation concerns the allu-sive character of Greek terms, which allow for more than one meaning. Thus Gardner discusses the force of ἐξουσία and πρόσκομμα over some nine or ten pages.[233]

The translation of ἐξουσία, rendered above as "**the right to choose**" and placed within quotation marks, must be rendered in such a way as to cohere with translations proposed for ἔξεστιν in 6:12 a, b, and 10:23 a, b, and with ἐξουσία in 9:4, 5, 6, 12, 18. Most English VSS render the word *liberty* (AV/ KJV, REB, NRSV) or *freedom* (NIV, NJB). But these versions then usually translate the word in 9:4, 5, 12, 18 as *rights* (REB) or *right* (NRSV, NIV, NJB), which *misses the deliberate resonance* and application of the point made here. If on top of this 6:12 and 10:23 are also translated *free to* (REB), or, worse still, *are lawful* (AV/KJV, NRSV), *the fundamental continuity of the argument and the role of ἐξουσία in the theology of "the strong" falls from view.* The central argument of vv. 9-13 is well summed up by Gardner: "For Paul, the so-called ἐξουσία of the Corinthians is a πρόσκομμα."[234] In turn, πρόσκομμα, translated here as **a cause of stumbling**, looks back to σκάνδαλον in the proclamation of the cross in 1:23; looks ahead to the obstacles in the race which may trip up runners (9:24-27; cf. 10:12); and presupposes the OT background concerning "the stone of stumbling" (Isa 8:14, LXX, λίθος προσκόμματος, Heb. אֶבֶן נֶגֶף, *eben neneph;* also Exod 34:12, מוֹקֵשׁ, *moqesh;* cf. also Rom 9:22, 23; 14:13, 20). The verbal form προσκόπτω regularly means *to stumble* or *to stumble at* in its intransitive use or *to strike against* in its transitive use.

There can be no doubt that in ch. 9 Paul takes up the issue of a **right**, in-deed of a **right to choose**, but that this emphasis falls on the *relativity* and *re-nunciation* of such a right. *If this passage says anything at all to the ethical de-bates of today's world, it addresses not the overworn issue of "conscience" (see above) but the impropriety of giving absolute status to "***the right to choose***," whatever the cost for others.*

that Paul is concerned about assertive and triumphalist claims imposed on "the weak" by "the strong."

231. Gardner, *Gifts,* 54.
232. Héring, *First Epistle,* 73.
233. Gardner, *Gifts,* 54-63.
234. Ibid., 54.

BAGD and most lexicographers confirm this nuance of ἐξουσία in appropriate contexts. BAGD's category 1 offers as an equivalent *freedom of choice* and **right** *to act.*[235] In legal contexts in the papyri, e.g., legal ownership bestows **the right** to dispose of one's property *as one chooses* (*BGU*, 4:1158:13 [9 BC]; *Papyrus Oxyrhynchus* 2:272:13). With the references in 8:9 and 9:4-6, 12, 18, we may compare Heb 13:10, Rev 13:5, and Epictetus, *Diss.* 3.24.70. BAGD distinguish this first category from a second denoting *power* or *capability,* and a third denoting *authority* or *warrant,* which is essentially a derived right bestowed by another.[236]

Against this lexicographical background, which precisely accords with the specific context of 1 Corinthians 8–10, it merely distracts us to explore theories of an explicitly gnostic background (Lietzmann, Reitzenstein), the use of the word in Stoic traditions (Dupont), or even the background in Philo and hellenistic Judaism (Horsley).[237] More is to be gained by noting that Paul describes the ἐξουσία in question as **this "right to choose" of yours** (ἡ ἐξουσία ὑμῶν αὕτη). Nothing could signal more clearly that Paul addresses *the specific use, understanding, and manipulation of a* **right** which characterized *a certain stance at Corinth.* Gardner notes that "the use of ὑμῶν suggests that Paul is not aligning himself with this 'right.' αὕτη emphasizes the particular ἐξουσία being addressed, indicating that Paul was referring back to the Corinthian display of knowledge (8:7)."[238] *This now becomes a warning which addresses an especially sinister aspect of life within certain churches today.* Some manipulate their supposed "gifts" (whether intellectual, structural, or "spiritual") to assume that they have the **right** *to engage in aggressive conduct which may well cause* **the less secure** (in terms of social class, learning, or supposed inferiority in "spiritual gifts") *to face an unnecessary* **cause of stumbling**.

Here, however, as Bultmann urges, **the cause of stumbling** provided by self-centered or assertive conduct on the part of certain Christians must not be confused with the quite different **cause of stumbling** provided by the cross (1:23; cf. 1:18-25).[239] For in the first case, "the weak" or **less secure** are tripped up and damaged *by the self-assertive behavior* of the overconfident; while in the second place it is *putting the other before the self,* manifest in the transformative effect of the cross, which causes the self-sufficient to turn away.

235. BAGD, 277-79; cf. Abbott-Smith, *Manual,* 161-62; MM, 225, *power of choice, liberty of action,* in which similar papyrological sources are cited. For a **right** conveyed by law cf. *Oxyrhynchus Papyrus* 2:237:6:17 and 259:18 [AD 23]. *BGU,* 4:1200:12 [2 BC] corresponds with **right** or *power* of *rule* in Rev 14:18.

236. BAGD, 278, cite Acts 26:12 in the sense of a **right** or *authority* given on the basis of a *commission;* cf Matt 21:27; Mark 11:28, 29; Rev 12:10.

237. R. Reitzenstein, *The Hellenistic Mystery Religions,* 461-62; J. Dupont, *Gnosis,* 301-8; Horsley, "Consciousness and Freedom," 574-89.

238. Gardner, *Gifts,* 55.

239. R. Bultmann, *Jesus Christ and Mythology* (Eng. trans., London: SCM, 1960), 35-36. This does not imply that Bultmann's own method of exposing the "true" stumbling block is entirely correct; cf. Thiselton, *The Two Horizons,* 205-92.

Once again, Gardner is right to press the Christocentric theme of 1:18-31 as the decisive background to issues of "knowledge" and "wisdom," and the "weak" and the "strong," in 8:9-13. True "wisdom" is seen in Christ's concern for the "weak" and **the less secure**, to the point of renouncing his own **rights**, even to the death of the cross. Paul's own lesser example will appear in ch. 9. 8:11-13 confirms this.

10 UBS 4th ed. follows the inclusion of σέ (**see you**) rather than simply *see one who possesses knowledge*), with ℵ, A, D, and the majority of MSS. But p⁴⁶, B, F, G and Old Latin omit it. Metzger defends the UBS reading on the ground that later copyists would be more likely to omit σέ in order to generalize the verse than vice versa.²⁴⁰ Zuntz favors the omission, Yeo more convincingly perceives the singular pronoun as reflecting Paul's rhetorical strategy in addressing an imaginary interlocutor.²⁴¹ This change from plural to singular instantiates rhetorical apostrophe.

Our translation depends on earlier conclusions in this commentary about συνείδησις and ἀσθενής, here translated respectively as **self-awareness** and **insecure person** (see above, under 8:7, with particular reference to Horsley, Gooch, and Gardner). Further, contextual considerations suggest that the entire verse carries allusive intertextual resonances both to earlier axioms, "*we all possess knowledge*" (8:1); to "**knowledge**" (γνῶσις) as "inflating" (φυσιοῖ, 8:1); to a disagreement between Paul and "the strong" about whether "**edifying**" (οἰκοδομέω, 8:1) is achieved by "**knowledge**" or by love for the other; and to the difference between **meat associated with idols** indirectly in nonsacral contexts (e.g., homes or shops) and directly when it is explicitly **meat sacrificed to idols** within the very presence of what **the insecure** still find themselves habituated to perceive as **the actual idol**.

As a rule, we have tried to avoid translations which exclusively reflect "dynamic" or "functional equivalence" without raising additional questions about extralinguistic reference to their historical setting, and similarly to avoid translations which presuppose a decision about a very specific exegesis. However, in this particular verse hard choices are imposed upon us. We have already accepted the arguments of Horsley, Gooch, and Gardner about the problems of translating συνείδησις in this chapter as *conscience*. Furthermore, our exegesis has led to the inescapable conclusion that some of the triumphalist, overconfident "strong" sought to encourage **the less secure** to act on their spiritual gift of **knowledge** as a way of "**building**" an emancipated, informed faith that paraded its **self-awareness** of the **nothingness** of **idols** and the neutrality of the **meat** associated with idol worship. The triumphalists wish **to edify the insecure** into enjoying what was **a right** (ἐξουσία); Paul drily observes that this approach "edifies" them into a return to an improper participation in *cultic* aspects of **eating meat sacrificed to idols**, if the context is that of heathen temples. He will

240. Metzger, *Textual Commentary* (2d ed.), 491.
241. Zuntz, *Text*, 92; Yeo, *Rhetorical Interaction*, 194.

return to this latter distinction in 10:1-22, but "for the first and only time in his letter Paul mentions a temple of an idol in v. 10."[242] Collins adds a comment about the archaeological evidence for remains, e.g., of the sanctuaries of Demeter and Kore on the road to Acrocorinth; the temple of Asklepios; and other sites (see Introduction, 7-8).[243]

Although Paul constantly alludes to the vivid picture of **building** in this epistle (3:9; 8:1, 10; 10:23; 14:3, 4, 5, 12, 17, 26, as both verb and noun), most English VSS lose the wordplay here to translate the passive voice of οἰκοδομέω as *emboldened* (AV/KJV, RV, NIV, REB), or *encouraged* (NRSV, NJB, Collins).[244] Yet a number of commentators have drawn attention to what is missed in the usual translations. "The irony is lost if we render it 'emboldened.'" "He enlightens . . . him to his loss. Fine edification!" Fee speaks of "the ironic use of the verb 'build up,'" and finds "no known parallel" for the translation "emboldened."[245] Strobel insists that we must retain the explicit allusion to "building up" *(erbauen)*, which takes up 8:1.[246]

Yeo clinches this argument. He writes, "The gnostics' [his term] *edification campaign for the 'weak'* is probably a strategy to ask the 'weak' to eat idol food so that the 'weak' might overcome their weak conscience [or insecure self-awareness]" (my italics).[247] Yeo convincingly traces the escalating rhetorical strategy which underlies this chapter until "the question in verses 10-11 evokes irony and leads the audience to accept the rhetor's persuasion."[248] Paul now exclaims, after going along with all the supposedly shared assumptions: So is *this* what the process of *building* and **edifying the insecure** finally achieves? Does it not make their **insecurity** *worse* and their **self-awareness** more confused? Does it not in practice **destroy** (v. 11) the brother or sister, the fellow family member, for whose benefit Christ yielded his life and to whom these people therefore belong?

The translation and meaning of the protasis of the conditional remain less controversial. The hypothesis ἐὰν γὰρ τις ἴδῃ σέ introduces what Schrage calls "the case as one which is possible, but not purely as a hypothetical construction."[249] That is to say, the aorist subjunctive ἴδῃ with ἐάν introduces an indefinite possibility, but the existence of **the insecure** as a group or type at Corinth is itself actual rather than merely rhetorically hypothetical.[250] Hence we follow the NJB in indicating the aorist subjunctive by translating **Suppose someone**

242. Collins, *First Cor,* 322.

243. Ibid. Cf. J. Wiseman, "Corinth and Rome, 1: 228 BC–AD 267," *ANRW,* 2:7:1 (1979), 487-89 (cf. 435-548).

244. Cf. the importance attached to this theme by Mitchell, *Rhetoric of Reconciliation;* Edwards, *First Epistle,* 223; Godet, *First Epistle,* 1:426.

245. Fee, *First Epistle,* 386 and 386, n. 57; Héring, *First Epistle,* 73.

246. Strobel, *Der erste Brief,* 138.

247. Yeo, *Rhetorical Interaction,* 192.

248. Ibid., 194.

249. Schrage, *Der erste Brief,* 2:262.

250. Fee, *First Epistle,* 385; as against Hurd, *Origin of 1 Corinthians,* 125.

sees you. . . . The perfect participle κατακείμενον denotes "reclining at table," but in a changed cultural situation of dining arrangements the translation can only be **seated at table**. The Greek ἐν εἰδωλείῳ regularly means **in the place of an idol**. We have inverted the sequence of this clause with **seated at table** to convey the emphasis which Paul clearly intends, namely, that supposed "**knowledge**" about the alleged neutrality of physical things in more "harmless" contexts (e.g., in shops or in the home) leads on this aggressive program of the overconfident to what amounts to a return to idolatrous practices: **in the [actual] place of an idol . . . sacrificed to the [actual] idol**.[251]

11   The UBS 4th ed. γάρ is attested by ℘⁴⁶, ℵ, B, 33 et al., but A reads οὖ and some MSS read καί in place of it. However, if we accept Conzelmann's explanatory comment on the force of γάρ, the possible difference in force from οὖν is relatively small in effect.

We have followed Conzelmann in translating γάρ, *for,* as **then, to be sure**, as denoting a logical consequence, which should not be mistaken for causal explanation or explication alone. The English *for* combines both functions, but we have made the logical force explicit. Edwards makes the point clearly. This verse is not part of v. 10, "but the answer to it: 'Builded up, did I say? Nay, he is perishing!' "[252]

The translation **finds destruction** is borrowed from Robertson and Plummer for two reasons.[253] First, it requires emphasis as the exact opposite of **building** in the previous verse. Hence *perish* (which would change the imagery) is inadequate. Second, most VSS understand ἀπόλλυται as passive in sense (*is destroyed*, NIV, NRSV, Collins). But if the force of the middle voice is to be preserved, the best translation would be *finds ruin* or **finds destruction**. Although the active (*destroys the weak*, REB) or *passive* (*is destroyed*, NIV; *are destroyed*, NRSV) maintains a forceful dynamism, the middle conveys a nuance of participating self-involvement (**finds destruction**; *is lost*, NJB) which finds expression in the specific choice of the preposition ἐν in the following phrase ἐν τῇ σῇ γνώσει. J. M. Gundry-Volf urges that the verb does not imply eschatological destruction but "existential destruction with both subjective and objective dimensions."[254] This coheres with the proposal that ἐν here denotes "not 'by reason of thy knowledge' but 'by attempting to share in thy knowledge' without making it really his own."[255] To be sure, ἐν with the dative may

---

251. We have already discussed τὰ εἰδωλόθυτα at length (see the Note under 8:1), and cannot share the view that throughout the whole of chs. 8–10 Paul always and only refers to meat sacrificed to idols in a cultic setting. Willis may go too far in the opposite direction, but his arguments cannot be swept aside in all cases. *Here,* however, Paul *does* anticipate the "idolatry" theme in 10:1-22.

252. Edwards, *First Epistle,* 223-24.

253. Robertson and Plummer, *First Epistle,* 172.

254. J. M. Gundry-Volf, *Paul and Perseverance,* WUNT 2:37 (Tübingen: Mohr, 1990), 1:96; cf. 85-97.

255. Edwards, *First Epistle,* 224.

be instrumental; but the context suggests that the **insecure person** finds himself or herself "surrounded by" a frame of "knowledge" to which he or she does not fully subscribe. By *projecting* the "weak" into this "medium" of γνῶσις, the "strong" bring such a person face-to-face with utter **destruction**.[256] What a way to "build" them! This is where all this propaganda about "**the right to choose leads.**"

By contrast, **Christ died** not as an act of self-assertion or claiming **rights**, but as an act of self-giving love for the sake of the other, not least for (διά + accusative) "the weak." Moreover, the appeal to the status of a fellow believer as ὁ ἀδελφός, **brother and sister**, stands in contrast, as Schrage notes, to **you** and **yours** (τῇ σῇ γνώσει), just as love does to **knowledge**. Paul takes up the thought of ch. 3: the "strong" bring face-to-face with **destruction** those who are not "their" group or congregation but those who are *Christ's* by virtue of his redemptive and saving death. Further, to sin against one of Christ's own is *to sin against Christ*. This is precisely the point which Paul next addresses.

12 p46 and Clement omit ἀσθενοῦσαν (the feminine singular accusative present participle active of ἀσθενέω), *being weak,* translated above as **while it is still insecure** (to call attention to the use of the present). But the UBS 4th ed. includes the word as an "A" graded reading, and it is defended by Metzger and most writers.[257] It may have been inserted to explicate the scope of the condemnation, or simply by accident.

The use of οὕτως is emphatic here, and refers back to what Paul has just said.[258] The emphasis invites the translation **in such a way as this**. The participle τύπτοντες also invites careful translation. Most of the VSS translate *wounding* (RV, REB) or wound (NRSV, NIV, AV/KJV, NJB). But nowadays people speak of being *wounded* in a psychological sense, which may be relatively trivialized into *feeling hurt* (at the subjective level) rather than suffering *damage* (in an objective sense). The lexicons and word studies unanimously understand τύπτω to mean **to inflict blows** or *to strike a blow against* someone or something: to hit, to strike, to beat.[259] People can be *struck on* the mouth (Acts 23:2, 3), the head (Mark 15:9), and the cheek (Luke 6:29). Käsemann points out that in 8:9-13 both the *striking* or *wounding* and the stance of *love* are *objective and carry objective effects*.[260] Stählin similarly asserts that "it is actual damage" that is in view.[261] In such a context it is not unreasonable to perceive resonances surviv-

---

256. The emphatic and objective force of the verb is discussed by Schrage, *Der erste Brief,* 2:265-66, who cites the parallel use in 1:18 (also 265, n. 313).

257. Metzger, *Textual Commentary* (2d ed.), 491.

258. The point is well made by Robertson and Plummer, *First Epistle,* 172; Fee, *First Epistle,* 388, n. 63; and many other writers. Cf. BAGD, 597-98.

259. BAGD, 830; MM, 646; Grimm-Thayer, 632; *LSJ,* 1,589-90; G. Stählin, "τύπτω," *TDNT,* 8:260-69; *EDNT,* 3:376. Cf. *London Papyrus* 44;22; *Rylands Papyrus* 2:77;39, et al.

260. E. Käsemann, "Ministry and Community in the NT," in his *Essays on NT Themes* (Eng. trans., London: SCM, 1964), 77 (cf. 63-94).

261. Stählin, *TDNT,* 8:268.

ing from the earlier history of the word as meaning *to stamp or mark,* i.e., *to hit* or *to press* with the result that an *imprint* or *impression* (τύπτος) is left, especially since in *koinē* Greek this meaning of the noun τύπτος remained in currency.[262] Hence we translate **inflicting damaging blows on their self-awareness**.

On συνείδησις, see above, under 8:7: If the translation *conscience* is still preferred, Paul speaks here of its being *damaged*. We translate the accusative adjectival participle ἀσθενοῦσαν as **while it is still insecure** in order to bring to notice the force of the *continuous present process,* which may develop in due course into a clearer or more confident **self-awareness**. (On this understanding of "weak," see above esp. under 8:7.)

Paul reaches the climax of his argument in the declarative pronouncement that *to* **sin against** *Christian* **brothers and sisters** (εἰς τοὺς ἀδελφούς) is *to* **sin against Christ** (εἰς Χριστὸν ἁμαρτάνετε). J. A. T. Robinson is undoubtedly right to see the seeds of Paul's doctrine of the true people of God, the body of Christ (12:12-30), as looking back to the experience on the road to Damascus, "Why do you persecute *me? . . .* I am *Jesus whom you are persecuting*" (Acts 26:14-15; cf. 9:4-5; 22:7-8; Robinson's use of italics).[263] Robinson quotes E. Mersch's comment: Paul "can no longer look into the eyes of a Christian without meeting there the gaze of Christ," and compares 1 Cor 8:12 and Gal 4:14 in this context.[264] It is a pity that Robinson's insight is often lost from view because it forms part of a more problematic claim about the resurrection of Christ "not as an individual but as the Christian community."[265] Whiteley notes that this "has been both complicated and illuminated by J. A. T. Robinson, and seeks to extract the insights from a more problematic theology of the risen body of Christ.[266]

L. S. Thornton also demonstrates the relation between this theme and the corporate solidarity of believers, to use Paul's language more especially in other epistles, "in Christ." Thornton writes, "If Christ identifies himself with each of his disciples, then there must be a sense in which each represents Christ to the others. This may be understood in two ways: (1) He who ministers to a weaker member is ministering to Christ himself [as in this verse]. But (2) he is also ministering on behalf of Christ . . . to one of his brethren."[267] Hence it is all the more a terrible affront and betrayal for a ministry which in principle should reflect the *loving self-giving of* **"rights"** *for the benefit of the other* to degenerate into the very opposite: *an aggressive bruising which bruises* **Christ**. This theme looks back to 3:16-17, where to damage a fellow Christian is to commit

262. Ibid., 260; and L. Goppelt, "τύπος," *TDNT,* 8:246-59.
263. J. A. T. Robinson, *The Body: A Study in Pauline Theology* (London: SCM, 1952), 58.
264. Ibid., from Mersch, *The Whole Christ,* 104 (no date or publisher cited).
265. Ibid.
266. Whiteley, *The Theology of St. Paul,* 192; cf. 192-97.
267. L. S. Thornton, *The Common Life in the Body of Christ* (London: Dacre Press, 3d ed. 1950), 40.

the sacrilege of profaning God's temple sanctified by his Spirit (cf. 6:19) and forward to 12:12–13:13, where love is the animating principle of mutual support within "the body" in which the "strong" protect the less secure, but the "weak" perform utterly vital functions within the body.

It is a mistake to imagine that Romans and Galatians have much more to say about "being-in-Christ" than 1 Corinthians. Union with Christ is "an objective state in the case of every Christian. . . . The Christian is in a new world and is a new creature . . . [even if] the new world has not yet come to pass fully but exists in embryo."[268] Wikenhauser's description of union with Christ in Paul finds all its practical outworkings and its theological basis as a transforming gift throughout this epistle, where it concerns stance and lifestyle and not only a system of belief. Since through participation in the death of Christ crucified the believer becomes *identified with Christ,* **Christ** *identifies himself* with those whom he has consecrated (1:2), enriched (1:5), and purchased as his own (6:20), who are shrines of the Spirit (6:19). The previous verse (8:11) has shown that what is at stake is the self-assertive stance of "the strong" bringing "the weak" for whom Christ died face-to-face with *destruction.* The solemnity and dire seriousness of this emerges in Paul's ringing declaration that οὕτως, **in such a way as this**, they actually **sin against Christ**, who identifies *himself* with "the weak."

13 Several Western MSS omit the second μου, **my**, but apart from the strong textual support for μου the possessive pronoun is implicit in the construction.

διόπερ, **Therefore**, is an emphatic logical connective: *"for this very reason,* i.e., to avoid sinning against Christ."[269] But the next word εἰ, **if** . . ., reminds us that for all the emphatic nature of both the connective and the content of the apodosis (**I will certainly never in any event** . . .) the declaration remains conditional on a given situation, i.e., one in which the protasis (**so affronts my brother or sister as to trip them up**) actually applies. The declaration about *eating* **food** remains null unless the condition holds good. Hence the declaration and principle remain context-specific.

The translation of σκανδαλίζει, **so affronts . . . as to trip up . . .** is difficult to render in a single equivalent English word since the Greek verb carries a double meaning which brings out both aspects here. In 1:23, which describes different evaluations and effects of the proclamation of the cross, we translated σκάνδαλον as **an affront**, since there it meant more than *what* **trips** *someone* **up**. But here the verb deliberately explicates πρόσκομμα, **cause of stumbling** (where it stands in contrast to ἐξουσία; a **right to choose**), and by implication

---

268. A. Wikenhauser, *Pauline Mysticism: Christ in the Mystical Teaching of St Paul* (Freiburg: Herder, 1960), 94. Wikenhauser uses "mysticism" in "an eschatological sense" (95), standing nearer to A. Schweitzer than to the more "psychological" account of A. Deissmann, *Paul* (Eng. trans., New York: Harper, 1957 [2d ed. 1927]), 135-57.

269. Robertson and Plummer, *First Epistle,* 173.

looks forward beyond the coming debate about ἐξουσία in 9:4-6, 12, 18 to the contrast between **obstacles** (for the OT background of *stone of stumbling,* see under 8:9) and the unfettered runner in the Isthmian games (9:24-27). Hence, cumbersome as it may be, our translation seeks to convey both themes as a faithful reflection of the force of the Greek verb in this context.[270] Once we have established the twofold force of the verb, however, we may follow the REB in translating the second occurrence of the verb (in the future tense) as **will not cause** [their] **downfall. Downfall** is suitably stronger than *to stumble.*

The relationship of **brother or sister** (ἀδελφός) receives emphasis no less than four times in vv. 11-13. It reflects both the priority of **love** over "**knowledge**" and over "rights" and the oneness of believers "in Christ" (see under v. 12). On this basis, including especially *Christ's own identification of himself with* these **brothers** and **sisters,** Paul chooses to use an exceptionally emphatic mode of negation, οὐ μὴ φάγω . . . εἰς τὸν αἰῶνα, **I will certainly never in any event.** . . . Fee renders the dimension of duration (εἰς τὸν αἰῶνα) *I will never . . . again as long as I live.*[271] We convey the intensity and qualitative dimension by **certainly never . . . in any event.** The double negative (οὐ μή) with the second aorist subjunctive (φάγω, from ἐσθίω), or sometimes a future indicative, is "the most definite form of negation regarding the future."[272] The phrase εἰς τὸν αἰῶνα, *to eternity,* may be taken (with Fee) in a temporal sense, *while the world lasts,* but may serve as an adverbial clause further to enhance the intensity or quality of the negation. We may compare the strictly ungrammatical but widespread English idiom "Don't ever ever do that 'again,'" for "Never, never do that again!."

Many commentators make much of the shift from βρῶμα, **food,** to κρέα, **meat in any form.** But the point is not (as many mistakenly argue) a shift from **food** in general to **meat** in particular, but the use of the *plural* form κρέα (singular κρέας).[273] When a collective noun (e.g., *cheese, fruit, meat*) is used in the plural *(cheeses, fruits, meats),* this regularly denotes *kinds of* cheese, fruit, or meat. With the negative, therefore, this excludes *different kinds,* i.e., **meat in any form.** That it is to say, although eating **meat** sacrificed to idols *in the actual cultus* is clearly out of bounds, **if** the act **so affronts my brother or sister as to trip them up,** even meat sold in the butcher's shop (which was a temple outlet) eaten at home is also something **certainly never in any event** to be done, i.e., *conditional* on this being in circumstances which damage a fellow Christian.

Chrysostom comments, "It is foolish in the extreme that we should esteem

---

270. Fee rightly insists that the verb reflects the theme of "being destroyed" in 8:9-12 *(First Epistle,* 389, n. 69).

271. Fee, *First Epistle,* 389. Collins renders it, *"until the age (to come)"* (*1 Cor,* 321, 327).

272. BDF, sect. 365 (p. 184). It occurs in the sayings of Jesus, e.g., Matt 26:35 (aorist subjunctive); Matt 16:22 (future indicative); cf. Rev 2:11.

273. Few seem to note this nuance. See, however, Findlay, *Expositor's Greek Testament,* 2:844; although cf. also Schrage, *Der erste Brief,* 2:268.

as so entirely beneath our notice those that Christ so greatly cared for that he should have even chosen to die for them, as not even to abstain from meat on their account."[274] This comment captures very well the key contrast throughout this chapter between asserting one's own "**right to choose**" and reflecting with the motivation of **love** *for the other* what consequences might be entailed for fellow Christians if self-centered "autonomy" rules patterns of Christian attitudes and conduct. It has little or nothing to do with whether actions "offend" other Christians in the modern sense of causing psychological irritation, annoyance, or displeasure at a purely subjective level. It has everything to do with whether such attitudes and actions cause *damage,* or whether they genuinely *build* not just "knowledge" but Christian character and Christian community. The references to **sinning against Christ** and to those **for whom Christ died** appeal to the paradigmatic nature of belonging to the **Christ** who renounced his "**right** *to life*" for the sake of others. Indeed, Allo takes up Chrysostom's point that here to assert one's rights becomes an act of "cruelty."[275] In Chrysostom's words, "'What do I care if a person stumbles?' savors of cruelty and inhumanity."[276]

TWO THEMES IN THE POSTHISTORY AND RECEPTION OF CHAPTER 8

(a) On Creation and the One God (8:4-6)

(1) Patristic Thought

Irenaeus relates confession of **one God** to the first commandment of the Decalogue, and then explains the **so-called gods whether in heaven or on earth** in terms of the prohibition of the second commandment against "graven images" or "idols" on earth, and worship of the sun, moon, or stars in heaven (Deut 5:8; cf. Deut 4:19).[277] *Tertullian* takes up the thought which we have just expressed in connection with Paul's admonition or encouragement to "the weak." He stresses both the *nonexistence of idols or false gods* and (against Marcion) the *unity of creation and redemption* as flowing from the **one God** who is "Creator of **all things**," including the realm of redemption and the **one Lord Jesus Christ**. Indeed, Christ, Tertullian argues, co-works with **God the Father** during the OT period, and creation and salvation flow from **the one** source and **the one** mediator. Since all of God's creation is good and comes from him through Christ, *the prohibition of meat and drink cannot be sustained.*[278]

Origen, like Tertullian, considers 8:5 and 6 phrase by phrase. The **so-called gods** represent *"thrones . . . dominions . . . powers . . . principalities."* But God destines for believers direct access to the **one God**; hence **for us** there is **one God the Father. . . .** "When he shall appear, we shall be like him" (1 John 3:2).[279] **Chrysostom**, by contrast,

---

274. Chrysostom, *1 Cor. Hom.,* 20:11.
275. Allo, *Première Épitre,* 206.
276. Chrysostom, *1 Cor. Hom.,* 20:11.
277. Irenaeus, *Against Heresies,* 3:6:5.
278. Tertullian, *Against Marcion,* 5:7.
279. Origen, *Against Celsus,* 4:29.

denies the reality of the **so-called gods**, except insofar as (like Irenaeus) he understands **so-called gods on earth** to be idols who are actually worshiped, and **so-called gods in heaven** such as the sun, moon, or stars, which are also made objects of worship. Further, like Tertullian *he co-joins the orders of creation and redemption,* alluding to 1 Cor 1:30, "it is from him (ἐξ αὐτοῦ) that you are in Christ Jesus."[280] Chrysostom then enters the third area of the relation between God the Father and Christ the Lord. *Neither term excludes predication to the other agent:* God is also **Lord**; **Christ** is also **God**; hence Paul speaks of **one God**.[281] Chrysostom concludes by noting that the context does not require a reference to the Holy Spirit, but that Paul brings **God the Father** and **Christ the Lord** together with the Holy Spirit in 12:4 and in 2 Cor 13:14.[282] *Basil* also explains that the absence of an allusion to the one Spirit alongside **God the Father** and **Christ the Lord** in 8:6 constituted a proof-text for those who wanted to deny the deity of the Holy Spirit.[283]

(2) The Modern Period

Karl Barth speaks of **God the Father** as originating cause of all existence who "holds us from the abyss of non-Being."[284] Also because he is origin and source, God's *fatherhood* is that from which all notions or experiences of fatherhood are derivative and secondary. **God** is **the** Father. In accord with our exegesis above, *J. Moltmann* is concerned to maintain a careful distinction between "philosophical monotheism" and *soteriological formulations of monotheism.* He is suspicious of the "wisdom" traditions in Philo and hellenistic Judaism: "strict monotheism obliges us *to think of God without Christ, and consequently of Christ without God.*"[285] But this falsifies Paul and the gospel. By contrast *"Christian panentheism"* (Moltmann's italics) sees creation as a "first of God's longing for 'his Other' and for that Other's free response to the divine love."[286] God cannot be conceived of, therefore, other than as creative, and as co-creator with Christ. Even the term **the Father** expresses salvific love: "he is only 'our Father' for his Son's sake."[287] *E. Jüngel* captures the *dynamic* force of 8:5-6 (see exegesis above): "God . . . *goes out of himself,* and only for that reason there is a *difference* between Being and nothingness" (his italics).[288] But this dynamic "going out" (cf. 1 Cor 2:12-15; 8:5-6) goes out creatively and lovingly *"into nothingness"* (Jüngel's italics). Hence a christological dimension and agency comes into play. Jüngel, Moltmann, and Barth, then, in spite of other differences of emphasis, follow Paul in placing **God the Father**

280. Chrysostom, *1 Cor. Hom.,* 20:5.

281. Ibid., 20:6.

282. Ibid., 20:7.

283. Basil, *On the Holy Spirit,* 2:4 and 5:7.

284. K. Barth, *Church Dogmatics,* 1/1, 384-88 and esp. 441-42; cf. 2/1, 454.

285. J. Moltmann, *The Trinity and the Kingdom of God* (Eng. trans., London: SCM, 1981), 131.

286. Ibid., 106.

287. Ibid., 163.

288. E. Jüngel, *God as the Mystery of the World* (Eng. trans., Grand Rapids: Eerdmans and Edinburgh: T. & T. Clark, 1983), 224. Cf. also W. Pannenberg, *Systematic Theology,* 1:308-10. Pannenberg also begins with differences between God and Christ, and moves to a confession of **the One**.

and the **Lord Jesus Christ** side by side as a context which is both ontological and soteriological: "**for us**" there is "**one God . . . one Lord . . .**" God is "the One who he is," but apart from his address as "addressable being" in and through Christ, God is not "conceivable." Hence bare *gnosis* alone cannot find "God" even "thinkable" apart from Christology, salvation, and address.[289]

(b) On Food Offered to Idols in Patristic Thought

A history also emerges concerning the role of εἰδωλόθυτον, **meat associated with offerings to pagan deities**. J. Brunt argues that a "stricter" interpretation and ethic appears in post-Pauline and patristic sources than that of Paul himself.[290]

(1) Brunt reminds us that Revelation 1–3 (esp. 2:12-17 [Pergamum] and 2:18-29 [Thyatira]) not only excludes φαγεῖν εἰδωλόθυτα, but associates it with immorality (πορνεῦσαι). The figures of Balaam and Jezebel emerge as part of the polemic.

(2) The period after the NT maintains the "stricter" line. Justin attacks the compromising stance of Solomon toward idolatry, although this invites Trypho's reply that "Many of those who confess Jesus . . . eat food sacrificed to [associated with] idols, and declare that they are not damaged in self-awareness [or conscience]."[291] This suggests that the debate behind 1 Cor 8:7-13 still continues. Justin offers the counterreply that such Christians "are not teaching Christ's doctrines but those of spirits of error."[292] But it is not entirely clear that Brunt is correct in regarding this as a "stricter" view than Paul's. For Justin shares Paul's concern that in the situation of the Christian church such a practice "causes splits." In this respect, Justin may be seeking to convey the teaching of 8:7-13 within its contextual frame reflected in 1 Corinthians. Indeed, he moves on to designate as the "heretics" (i.e., those who cause the splits) those who style themselves Christians but in practice follow Valentinian, Marcionite, or Basilidian patterns, i.e., have some kinship to certain features shared with "the strong" at Corinth. Justin's final appeal to Christ's blameless suffering resonates with Paul's appeal to those for whom Christ died.

(3) Irenaeus takes up the reference to the Valentinians and to Basilides. The Valentinians "make no scruple about eating food sacrificed to idols, imagining that they thereby contract no defilement."[293] Similarly, Basilides considers eating such food "of no consequence."[294] The important contextual point here, however, is not whether Irenaeus is "stricter" than Paul, but that the ground on which Valentinus and Basilides act is a belief that *the body and the physical* is of no consequence for the gnostic or redeemed, which echoes the view which Paul attacks in 1 Cor 6:12-20. This in turn relates to the centrality of the cross (1 Cor 1:18–2:3. "Jesus [they say] received the form of Simon [of Cyrene] while he stood by and laughed at them."[295]

---

289. Jüngel, *God as the Mystery*, 1522-63.
290. Brunt, "Rejected, Ignored, or Misunderstood? The Fate of Paul's Approach to the Problem of Food Offered to Idols in Early Christianity," 113-24.
291. Justin, *Dialogue*, 35 (cf. 34).
292. Ibid.
293. Irenaeus, *Against Heresies*, 1:6:3.
294. Ibid., 1:24:5.
295. Ibid., 1:24:4.

(4) *Origen* may, in one sense, seem "stricter" than Paul in 8:7-13, but he is strongly influenced by Paul's dire warnings about eating in an explicitly cultic context in 10:18-22: "That which is offered to idols is sacrificed to demons . . . do not share in the table of demons."[296]

(5) *The Valentinian gnostics* utilized the passages which modern research ascribes to the Corinthians rather than to Paul, e.g., 8:8, interpreted from a "gnostic" angle.[297] The *Gospel of Truth* expounds Paul's contrast between "the strong" and "the weak" as one between "the spiritual" or "pneumatic" and "the psychical" ones.[298]

(6) *Novatian* offers a broader discussion.[299]

(7) By the later patristic period. Theodore (d. 428) and Theodoret (d. 466) observe (in harmony with Paul) that whether "damage" occurs depends *contextually* on whether the person concerned has scruples: *what counts is the attitude or mind-set, not eating (φαγόντες) as such,* whatever the origin of the food.[300] Now that the situation is less divisive, a more faithful exegesis of Paul prevails. Later, however, Christian freedom from the law becomes the issue in Reformation theology. Christian believers were free unless issues concerning the gospel were at stake.[301]

2. Second Part of Paul's Response: A Personal Example of Subordinating "Rights" for the Good of the Whole (9:1-27)

The vehement emphasis on apostleship, the apparent introduction of the new subject of "rights" to ministerial financial support, and the series of very forceful rhetorical questions (four in 9:1, followed by twelve more as the chapter proceeds) lead many (e.g., Weiss and Schmithals) to argue that Paul moves to an entirely new topic, or even that 9:1-27 constitutes part of a separate letter from 8:1-13.[1]

Nevertheless, a variety of factors combine to suggest that such an interpretation entirely misses the point. The forceful, almost indignant rhetoric urging "the rights" of apostles to financial support from the church or churches which they serve reaches an anticlimax, if it is read at face value, in Paul's conclusion that he does not, in fact, want to exercise the very "right" which he has been striving to establish. The argument about "rights" and "apostleship" simply runs parallel to Corinthian arguments about *their* "right to choose" (cf.

---

296. Origen, *Against Celsus,* 8:30; cf. 8:28-30; and Clement, *Stromata,* 4:16.

297. Irenaeus, *Against Heresies,* 1:6:3; cf. E. H. Pagels, *The Gnostic Paul: Gnostic Exegesis of the Pauline Letters* (Philadelphia: Fortress, 1975), 70-71.

298. *Gospel of Truth,* 33:22.

299. Novatian, *On Jewish Meats,* 1-7.

300. Theodore, Greek text fragment in K. Staab (ed.), *Pauluskommentare aus der griechischen Kirche,* 184.

301. Cf. Calvin, *Institutes,* 3:19:11.

1. On the integrity of the epistle see Introduction (above, 36-41) and in less detail under 1:1 on letter forms and on Sosthenes as possible amanuensis or even reader. Cf. J. Weiss, *Der erste Korintherbrief,* xxxix-xliii, 211-13; Schmithals, "Die Korintherbriefe as Briefsammlung," *ZNW* 64 (1973): 263-88, and *Gnosticism,* 87-113.

6:12; 8:1-13; 10-23) in order *first to establish the validity of the "right"* so that Paul, in turn, *may choose to relinquish it where it threatens to harm the welfare of others,* or of the church as a whole.

In rhetorical and sociological terms this reading may readily be corroborated. Margaret Mitchell underlines the part played in deliberative rhetoric by *"proof from example."*[2] "Twice in the letter Paul explicitly tells the Corinthians to imitate him" (μιμηταί μου γίνεσθε, 4:16; 11:1).[3] Not only Paul himself, but the soldier, planter, and shepherd take their place as part of a rhetoric which draws on arguments from examples in this chapter (9:7). In Paul's own case, however, this is more than a mere rhetoric of persuasion. It is founded deeply in two theological axioms: first, Paul draws his own lifestyle from that of Christ (μιμηταί μου γίνεσθε καθὼς κἀγὼ Χριστοῦ, 11:1). Christ constitutes the supreme paradigm of one who did not cling to his "rights" but subordinated them freely to the welfare of others (cf. Phil 2:5-11). Second, for Paul as an apostle (as well as for every believer) belief and lifestyle must be intimately interwoven. Hence Paul lives out not only what he preaches in general terms, but also the specific theology of "the right to choose" versus the benefit or harm to others which may be entailed in claiming or renouncing these rights (cf. 8:7-13). Thus "Paul presents himself as the perfect paradigm of the proper use of Christian freedom — which freely surrenders its right to have its own way for the sake of the entire church community and the gospel."[4]

Sociological studies of Paul and Corinth fully explain why, while it could be in everyone's interest for Paul to accept financial support from Philippi or other external sources, it would seriously compromise his obligations to support "the weak" and the equal needs of the whole community at Corinth if he had mortgaged his primary obligations to the "friends" or "patrons" from whom he derived special support. Once again, Peter Marshall's specialist study *Enmity in Corinth* assists our understanding of the extent of the social obligations to which Paul would be understood to have committed himself if he had made use of his "rights" in the Corinthian situation.[5] While Graeco-Roman writers most certainly perceived friendship as a "bond," Seneca is not alone in talking of an explicit return or benefits which even friendship entails.[6] Friendship brings "advantage" *(utilitas),* in Cicero's view.[7] "To regain the advantage, the recipient is obliged not merely to reciprocate but to outdo his benefactor in generosity."[8] If Paul could not provide this in monetary terms, no doubt the rich

2. M. M. Mitchell, *Paul and the Rhetoric of Reconciliation,* 47-50 and 130-38.

3. Ibid., 49-50.

4. Mitchell, *Rhetoric of Reconciliation,* 130.

5. Marshall, *Enmity in Corinth: Social Conventions in Paul's Relation with the Corinthians,* WUNT 2:23 (Tübingen: Mohr, 1987).

6. Ibid., 1-34; cf. Seneca, *De Beneficiis* 1.4.2.

7. Cicero, *De Amicitia* 14.51; cf. Marshall, *Enmity,* 6-9; Cicero, *Ad Familiares* 2.6.1; and A. W. H. Adkins, "'Friendship' and 'Self-Sufficiency' in Homer and Aristotle," *ClQ* 13 (1963): 30-45.

8. Marshall, *Enmity,* 11.

"patron" would expect some *quid pro quo* in terms of status, influence, or leadership role within the church.

What Marshall demonstrates in the case of friendship and its transactional expectations, Chow develops further explicitly in terms of *patronage*. The significance of Chow's work has been discussed above in the context of splits (1:10-12), issues about incest (5:1-5), and especially litigation (6:1-11). Chow gives careful consideration to "Paul and Financial Support" and to "the Rich Patron."[9] He agrees with Robertson and Plummer, W. Willis, and C. H. Talbert (anticipating also Mitchell, Schrage, and our own view) that 1 Corinthians 9 "could serve a paradigmatic purpose" in relation to the request in ch. 8 for the readers "to forego their right to eat meat for the good of others."[10] Since, however, for a missionary worker or teacher to accept "financial support from the rich and powerful might even have been the norm accepted by the Corinthians," the paradigmatic function does not exclude an apologetic motif.[11] Paul has also to defend not *his apostleship as such,* but whether his reluctance to take advantage of an apostle's "right" implied that the "right" itself was in question, i.e., either Paul was not a true "apostle," or he had somehow compromised the leadership role which invited such entitlement.

This explains with complete adequacy why the chapter appears on a superficial reading to constitute a defense of Paul's apostleship but in practice operates at a more fundamental level to support the logic of chs. 8–10. Finally, Paul's appeal to follow his example is fully explained by the above considerations, without resort to the hypotheses about power play explored in outline by E. Castelli.[12]

a. A Personal Example: Paul's Apostleship (9:1-3)

(1) Am I not "free"? Am I not an apostle? Have I not seen Jesus our Lord? Is it not you who are my work in the Lord? (2) If to others I am no apostle, at any rate I am to you. For you yourselves constitute my certificate of apostleship in the Lord.

(3) This is my statement of defence to those who investigate me.

Bibliography on 9:1-3, especially on Apostleship (on 9:4-23, 24-27, see below)

Agnew, E. F., "On the Origin of the Term *Apostolos,*" *CBQ* 38 (1976): 49-53.
——, "The Origin of the NT Apostle-Concept," *JBL* 105 (1986): 75-96.

---

9. Chow, *Patronage and Power,* 107-12 and 130-41.
10. Ibid., 107-8 Cf. Schrage, *Der erste Brief,* 2:280-81.
11. Chow, *Patronage and Power,* 109; cf. 108.
12. Castelli, *Imitating Paul: A Discussion of Power,* 89-118. Cf. Wire, *The Corinthian Women Prophets,* 98-115, and on the nonmanipulatory stance of Paul, Thiselton, *Interpreting God and the Postmodern Self,* 19-32 and 145-63.

Barrett, C. K., "Paul and the 'Pillar' Apostles," in J. N. Sevenster (ed.), *Studia Paulina in Honorem J. de Zwaan* (Haarlem: Bohn, 1953): 1-19.

―――, *The Signs of an Apostle* (London: Epworth Press, 1970), 11-84.

Beardslee, W. A., *Human Achievement and Divine Vocation in the Message of Paul* (London: SCM, 1961), 79-94.

Best, E., "Paul's Apostolic Authority," *JSNT* 27 (1986): 3-25.

Brockhaus, R., *Charisma und Amt die paulinische Charismenlehre auf dem Hintergrund der frühchristlichen Gemeindefunktionen* (Wuppertal: Brockhaus, 1972), 112-23.

Campenhausen, Hans von, *Ecclesiastical Authority and Spiritual Power in the Church of the First Three Centuries* (Eng. trans., London: Black, 1969), 30-54.

―――, "Der urchristliche Apostelbegriff," *ST* 1 (1948): 96-130.

Cerfaux, L., *The Church in the Theology of St. Paul* (Eng. trans., New York: Herder, 1959), 248-61.

Crafton, J. A., *The Agency of the Apostle*, JSNTSS 51 (Sheffield: Sheffield Academic Press, 1991), 53-103.

Ehrhardt, A., *The Apostolic Ministry*, SJT Occasional Papers 7 (Edinburgh: Oliver & Boyd, 1958).

Farrer, A. M., "Ministry in the NT" (esp. "III, Apostles and Elders"), in K. E. Kirk (ed.), *The Apostolic Ministry* (London: Hodder & Stoughton, 1946), 113-82, esp. 133-42.

Frazer, J. W., *Jesus and Paul* (Appleford: Mancham Manor Press, 1974), 63-72.

Fridrichsen, A., "The Apostle and His Message," *Uppsala Universitets Årsskrift* 3 (1947): 3-23.

Furnish, V. P., "On Putting Paul in His Place," *JBL* 113 (1994): 3-17.

Georgi, D., *The Opponents of Paul in Second Corinthians* (Eng. trans., Philadelphia: Fortress Press, 1986).

Hahn, F., "Der Apostolat im Urchristentum," *KD* 20 (1974): 54-77.

Herron, R. W., "The Origins of the NT Apostolate," *WTJ* 45 (1983): 101-31.

Hock, R. F., *The Social Context of Paul's Ministry: Testimony and Apostleship* (Philadelphia: Fortress Press, 1980), 50-68.

Horrell, D. G., *The Social Ethos of the Corinthian Correspondence* (Edinburgh T. & T. Clark, 1996), 204-17.

Holmberg, B., *Paul and Power: The Structure of Authority in the Primitive Church as Reflected in the Pauline Epistles* (Lund: Gleerup, 1978).

Jones, P. R., "1 Corinthians 15:8: Paul the Last Apostle," *TynBul* 36 (1985): 3-34.

Käsemann, E., "Die Legitimität des Apostels," *ZNW* 41 (1942): 33-71; rpt. in K. L. Rengstorf (ed.), *Das Paulusbild in der neueren deutschen Forschung* (Darmstadt: Wissenschaftliche Buchgesellschaft, 1969).

―――, "Ministry and Community in the NT," in *Essays on NT Themes* (Eng. trans., London: SCM, 1964) 63-94.

―――, "A Pauline Version of the 'Amor Fati,'" in *NT Questions Today* (London: SCM, 1969), 217-35.

Kertelge, K., "Das Apostelamt des Paulus, sein Ursprung und seine Bedeutung," *BZ* 14 (1970): 161-81.

―――, *Gemeinde und Amt in NT* (Münich: Kösel, 1972).

Kim, S., *The Origin of Paul's Gospel* (Grand Rapids: Eerdmans, 1981), 56-66.

Kirk, J. A., "Apostleship since Rengstorf: Towards a Synthesis," *NTS* 21 (1974-75): 249-64.

Klein, G., *Die zwölf Apostel: Ursprung und Gehalt einer Idee,* FRLANT 77 (Göttingen: Vandenhoeck & Ruprecht, 1961).

Kredel, E. M., "Der Apostelbegrift in neueren Exegese," *ZKT* 78 (1956): 16-93 and 257-305.

MacDonald, M. Y., *The Pauline Churches: A Socio-historical Study of Institutionalization in the Pauline and Deutero-Pauline Writings,* JSNTSS 60 (Cambridge: Cambridge University Press, 1988), 46-60.

Manson, T. W., "The Apostolate," in *The Church's Ministry* (London: Hodder & Stoughton, 1948), 31-52.

Moltmann, J., *The Church in the Power of the Spirit* (Eng. trans., London: SCM, 1975).

Mosbech, H., "*Apostolos* in the New Testament," *ST* 2 (1949-50): 166-200.

Munck, J., "Paul and the Apostles and the Twelve," *ST* 3 (1950-51): 96-110 (also in the next item).

————, *Paul and the Salvation of Mankind* (Eng. trans., London: SCM, 1959), 11-68 and 168-95.

Nasuti, H. P., The Woes of the Prophets and the Rights of the Apostle: The Internal Dynamics of 1 Cor 9," *CBQ* 50 (1988): 246-64.

Peterson, N., *Rediscovering Paul: Philemon and the Sociology of Paul's Narrative World* (Philadelphia: Fortress Press, 1985), 122-51, 163-70.

Rengstorf, K. L., "ἀπόστολος," *TDNT,* 1:407-47.

Rigaux, B., *The Letters of St Paul: Modern Studies* (Eng. trans., Chicago: Franciscan Herald Press, 1968), 55-67.

Roloff, J., *Apostolat–Verkündigung–Kirche* (Gütersloh: Gutersloher Verlagshaus Gerd Mohn, 1965), 9-137.

Satake, A., "Apostolat und Gnade bei Paulus," *NTS* 15 (1968-69): 96-107.

Schmithals, W., *The Office of Apostle in the Early Church* (Eng. trans., Nashville: Abingdon, 1969).

Schnackenburg, R., "Apostles before and during Paul's Time," in W. W. Gasque and R. P. Martin (eds.), *Apostolic History and the Gospel: Essays Presented to F. F. Bruce* (Exeter: Paternoster, 1970), 287-303.

Schütz, J. H., *Paul and the Anatomy of Apostolic Authority,* SNTSMS 26 (Cambridge: Cambridge University Press, 1975).

Schweizer, E., *Church Order in the New Testament* (Eng. trans., London: SCM, 1961), 97-100.

Stewart-Sykes, A., "Ancient Editors and Copyists and Modern Partition Theories: The Case of the Corinthian Correspondence," *JSNT* 61 (1996): 53-54.

Stuhlmacher, P., "Evangelium–Apostolat–Gemeinde," *KD* 17 (1971): 28-45.

Theissen, G., *The Social Setting of Pauline Christianity* (Eng. trans. Philadelphia: Fortress, 1982), 40-54.

Weiss, J., *Earliest Christianity* (Eng. trans., New York: Harper, 1959), 2:673-87.

Wilckens, U., "Der Ursprung der Überlieferung der Erscheinungen des Auferstandenen: Zur traditionsgeschichtlichen Analyse von 1 Kor 15:1-11," in W. Joest and W. Pannenberg (eds.), *Dogma und Denkstrukturen* (Göttingen: Vandenhoeck & Ruprecht, 1963), 56-95.

Willis, W., "An Apostolic Apologia? The Form and Function of 1 Cor 9," *JSNT* 24 (1985): 33-48.

Young, F., and D. F. Ford, "The Authority of Paul," in *Meaning and Truth in 2 Corinthians* (London: SPCK, 1987), 207-34.

1 (i) The form of the Greek translated **have I not seen** appears in an older form, ἑόρακα in p⁴⁶, A, and B³, but in the more usual form ἑώρακα in ℵ and B*. There is no difference in meaning: ἑόρακα is found in the oldest LXX papyri, but the difference in oral dictation or oral reading would have been small.[13]

(ii) The first two questions are reversed in sequence in D, F, and G, presumably to place what they thought was the theme first. But the UBS 4th ed. text is well attested, e.g., p⁴⁶, ℵ, B, 33, et al.

For the role of this verse in Paul's general argument, see the introduction to 9:1–27. We strenuously urge that to construe this chapter as a "defense of Paul's apostleship" as if this were the central issue in its own right is to miss the point of Paul's theology, ethics, and rhetoric in these verses. Scholars have been seduced along this path partly because of blind alleys in the history of research on **apostle** in a variety of different contexts and partly because the implausibility of the many competing partition hypotheses have only relatively recently been fully grasped. We have argued above that partition theories concerning this epistle founder for three reasons, among others: (a) the complete failure to agree on where supposed units begin and end; (b) the recent argument of A. Stewart-Sykes about the sheer physical constraints on the task of scribes to "cut and paste" papyrus rolls for reductional purposes; and (c) the more convincing compositional analysis offered by such writers as M. M. Mitchell, and the more convincing exegesis to which it gives rise.[14]

Paul is keen to establish the credentials of true apostleship not because they were held in doubt as such, but because his freely chosen decision to renounce "rights" which "the strong" undoubtedly regarded as part of the status and signs of apostleship (forceful, stylish rhetoric and its related "professional status," 2:1–5, and financial support from a patron or patrons, 9:1-27) was perceived to imply thereby something deficient about his status in relation to such "rights." He defends his apostleship only (a) in order to establish the "right" which he chooses to renounce, and (b) because the argument which he is about to offer may otherwise cast doubt on the initial premise which is otherwise accepted. Barrett sums up the point: "'If this man were a true apostle . . . he would not allow himself to be restricted in this way'. . . ."[15] Yet even Barrett, followed by Fee, appears to imply that his apostleship was also questioned in a more general way: "Paul would hardly have spent so long on the question of apostolic rights if his own apostolic status had not been questioned in Corinth," in contrast to Schrage's placing the weight on the role of *example* for the force of 8:1–11:1.[16] Collins calls these

13. Cf. BDF, sect. 68, who drew especially on the work of P. Katz on Septuagintal texts.
14. Stewart-Sykes, "Ancient Editors and Copyists and Modern Partition Theories: The Case of the Corinthian Correspondence," 53-54; as against not only Weiss and Schmithals but also the recent popular study by H. Frör, *You Wretched Corinthians!* (Eng. trans., London: SCM, 1995), 140-43 and throughout.
15. Barrett, *First Epistle,* 200.
16. Ibid.; cf. Schrage, *Der erste Brief,* 2:280-81. Fee even more explicitly states, "A crisis of authority lies behind much of this letter (cf. 4:1-5; 5-6; 14:36-37)" (*First Epistle,* 393; cf. 395). But

verses "his *apologia pro vita sua*."[17] Even if v. 3 seems to imply this, the major thrust of the argument of ch. 9 seems to lie more closely with the principle of 8:1–11:1 which Paul's own life and work instantiates.

The sustained argument is not to establish "authority" as part of a theological ecclesiology, but to offer a serious parallel to the Corinthians' reasoning about the "**right**" to eat **meat associated with idols** in 8:1-13, running parallel with what may have been a lengthy argument from "the strong" about their possession of the gift of **knowledge** (8:1) and the theological and experimental basis for their "rights." Paul stands alongside their rhetoric with his own to establish the comparability of the major premises from which they and Paul infer contradictory conclusions. For the minor premise makes the difference: in the case of "the strong" it explicates entailments of "the right to choose"; in Paul's view it appeals to Christ's dying for all believers, including "the weak" who must not be damaged.

Paul therefore establishes first that he is no less **free**, ἐλεύθερος, than "the strong" or other believers. He includes this rhetorical question among a strikingly forceful series construed with the negatives οὐκ . . . οὐκ . . . οὐχί . . . to invite an emphatically affirmative set of answers: **Am I not free?** *(Of course I am!)* **Am I not an apostle?** *(It could be otherwise!)* But just as **we all have knowledge** (8:1) is affirmed only to be subsequently qualified, so this **freedom** is taken up in 9:19 with the comment: **although I am from all** [people or restrictions?] **I made myself a slave for all** (πᾶσιν ἐμαυτὸν ἐδούλωσα). Many of the older commentators seize on **free** as indicating a Pauline theology of freedom from the Jewish law. But Conzelmann urges, "He does not speak about the freedom of Christians in general, but about his own particular freedom . . . his own particular apostleship."[18] Bengel anticipates this comment: **Liber sum**: *deinde aetiologiam,* **Apostolus sum** . . . *id in substantivo est* ἐξουσία, v. 4."[19] The correlation with ἐξουσία (v. 4), is exactly right.[20] Among older modern commentators, Heinrici also perceives the narrower point.[21]

The initial "qualifications" or initial criteria to be an **apostle** are well expressed in terms of this verse as follows: "The two essential constituents of apostleship were, first, that the Apostle should bear witness to the world of the central fact of Christianity, the resurrection of Jesus Christ; and second, that he should preach the risen Saviour 'in the demonstration of Spirit and of power'" (interpreting the latter phrase in the sense discussed under 2:4).[22] In this context

---

divergences from Paul's instructions or view need not imply doubt about his status as **apostle**, given that the Corinthians sought to play off one leader against another (cf. 1:10-12).

17. Collins, *First Cor,* 328.
18. Conzelmann, *1 Cor,* 152.
19. Bengel, *Gnomon,* 635.
20. Schrage, *Der erste Brief,* 2:287; and Senft, *Première Épitre,* 117.
21. Heinrici, *Das erste Sendschreiben,* 238.
22. Edwards, *First Epistle,* 226. So also Strobel, *Der erste Brief,* 143 (cf. Gal 1:11-15; 1 Cor 15:8-9); Senft, *Première Épitre,* 117; Lang, *Die Briefe,* 114; and Dunn, *Romans,* 1:9.

the perfect indicative ἑόρακα (ἑώρακα) expresses the present effect of Paul's earlier experience of encounter with the raised Christ at the moment of his missionary and apostolic commission on the way to Damascus. The fact that Paul uses Ἰησοῦν rather than Χριστόν, and yet also combines the "earthly" name with τὸν κύριον ἡμῶν, places it beyond doubt that while the reference is to the raised Christ, the identity of Jesus of Nazareth and the raised heavenly Lord are one in Paul's faith and thought.[23] In our discussion under 1:1, however, we argued that a third element was also entailed. Apostles were not merely witnesses in terms of truth claims about status of affairs, and not only preachers who proclaimed a gospel content centered on Christ, but also above all *performed self-involving acts of witness which were transparent in their cruciform and Christocentric lifestyle.*

"Apostolic witness" concerns life as well as word. Hence Paul is not simply appealing to "example" in the rhetorical sense identified by Mitchell, as an instantiation to illustrate or to support an argument. The instantiation of the cruciform, Christlike stance toward others in practical lifestyle constitutes both part of what it is to be an **apostle** *and an instantiation of the Christ-centered principle urged in 8:1-13.*

This reflects the priority of Christology over ecclesiology in Paul. In 1:18-25 we argued that Schrage's theme of "the cross as criterion" was paramount.[24] In modern theology none more strongly than J. Moltmann argues that the very identity of church and apostleship depends on this: "Christian identity" is found "in an act of identification with the crucified Christ."[25] The struggle for "maintenance" and "relevance" is at odds with identification with Jesus as "the One for others" (to borrow Bonhoeffer's phrase).[26] "To build a defensive wall around their own little group" is neither Christian identity nor church identity nor apostolic identity.[27] In this context "a rhetoric of advantage" (as in Mitchell) invites Moltmann's criticism, "we have surrounded the scandal of the cross [1 Cor 1:18-25] with roses."[28] Moltmann develops this as a doctrine of the church and apostleship in *The Church in the Power of the Spirit.* The Spirit leads the church neither into triumphalism nor into exclusivism. It identifies itself with the acts of God in Christ in which "God allows himself to be crucified" even in "love of the enemy" or love of the outsider.[29] Against "the strong" and with Paul, Moltmann insists that apostolic and ecclesial identity does not exist in and for itself. It will be ap-

23. J. D. G. Dunn identifies this identity and continuity as one of the threads which perform a unifying role within the NT, as against many features of diversity in his *Unity and Diversity in the NT* (Philadelphia: Westminster and London: SCM, 1977), underlined in *Theology of Paul,* 183-266.

24. See under 1:18-25; and Schrage, *Der erste Brief,* 1:65-90, *Kreuz als Grund und Kriterium von Gemeinde und Apostel* (165).

25. J. Moltmann, *The Crucified God* (Eng. trans., London: SCM, 1974), 19.

26. Ibid.

27. Ibid., 20.

28. Ibid., 36.

29. Quotation from ibid., 249; cf. *The Church in the Power of the Spirit,* throughout.

parent that this perspective challenges the popular use of the term *apostolic* to mean "in accordance with the church's historical roots" usually as a comment on doctrine in the narrower sense rather than in the proper wider sense of doctrine as that which embraces *ethics and lifestyle.*

This helps us to return to the four meanings of **apostle** which we distinguished under interpretations of 1:1 (see above): (i) **apostle** as "affirmation of authority" (Calvin, Allo, Wire); (ii) **apostle** as pointing *away* from the self to God-in-Christ and to others (Chrysostom, Schrage, Wolff, Crafton); (iii) **apostle** as a *"sign" of living out* the dying-and-being-raised of Christ with him (Barrett, Merklein, Schütz); and (iv) **apostle** as *also* a public, visible *witness* to the truth claims which are lived out in accordance with (ii) and (iii) (V. Neufeld and our own view).[30] Once this transparency of match between truth and life is achieved in an integrated witness, the sense implied in (i) which relates to "authority" emerges as a *derivative* quality of *"foundational"* witness. **Have I not seen Jesus our Lord?** (9:1) instantiates the aspect of being a *unique foundational witness to a truth claim about* **Christ** *and his resurrection.* **Is it not you who are my work in the Lord?** instantiates the lifestyle of witnesses whose words and deeds brought forth fruit under the influence of the Spirit of Christ, which thereby entailed a derivative consequence of occupying a position of apostolic authority in relation to the converts.

However, as we argued in some detail in our introduction to 9:1-27, the Corinthians expected that a "true" **apostle** would manifest the very trappings of status and power which Moltmann perceives as a betrayal of apostolic identity (see above). Hence Paul is drawn, against his will, into not only establishing his apostolic "rights" in parallel with arguments about "knowledge" and "rights" in 8:1-13, but also to reassert the genuineness of his vocation. Part of his argument is existential or experimental. As Strobel indicates, both ὑμεῖς and ἐν κυρίῳ receive some emphasis in the Greek word order.[31] The **you** implies that the Corinthians, least of all, have reason to question what is self-evident, while **in the Lord** counterbalances any suggestion that Paul regards this work (τὸ ἔργον μου) as his own personal "achievement" apart from God's grace in Christ. Hence we translate, **Is it not you who are my work in the Lord?** REB personalizes ἔργον by translating it *my own handiwork.*

SOME MISLEADING FACTORS IN THE HISTORY OF INTERPRETATION OF "APOSTLE"

We have argued above (under 1:1 and 9:1) that the relation between **apostle** and (i) pointing away from the self to God, (ii) offering a sign of what it is to live out the

---

30. V. H. Neufeld does not apply this specifically to apostleship, but his double understanding of *witness* as both *truth*-claiming and a *self-involving life stance* is indispensable for our view of *apostleship.*

31. Strobel, *Der erste Brief,* 143; and Robertson and Plummer, *First Epistle,* 178 (on v. 2).

gospel in a cruciform lifestyle; and (iii) a foundational witness to truth claims and personal stake became unnecessarily subordinated to polemical issues about self-assertive power and ecclesial authority not least because of trajectories in the history of research on the term and the theme. Nevertheless, following Käsemann a turn began to point in a more constructive direction.

(i) In effect the beginnings of modern controversy about Paul's apostleship began with F. C. Baur (1792-1860), whose paper on "the Christ party" (1831) drove a wedge between "Pauline" Christianity and a supposedly "Petrine" or conservative Jewish tradition.[32] In his *Paulus* (1845) he expounded the theory that Paul's claim to "apostleship" served as a necessary criterion for the genuinely Pauline epistles and constituted a polemic to gain equality of power with the narrower Jewish "legalist" traditions of the Jerusalem community. In spite of its patent flaws, Baur's work influenced the kind of approach to the Lord's Supper which we find in H. Lietzmann, where everything hinges on a disjunction between "Pauline" and "Jerusalem" traditions. Yet from around the year of Baur's death, Albrecht Ritschl, who earlier belonged to his circle, began to expose the simplistic and sweeping assumptions which Baur's hypothesis presupposed.

(ii) In 1933 K. L. Rengstorf produced his influential article on apostleship in *TDNT*, 1.[33] He argued that the background in Greek lexicography (ἀποστέλλειν), **to send away, to send out** (i.e., as representative or delegate) was too broad to assist NT interpretation. He turned instead to the *first-century rabbinic background as supposedly reflected in the later Mishnah*. Here reference is made to the local institution of an official representative of שליח (*shaliach*).[34] Rengstorf acknowledges, however, that this does not apply fully to Paul, for whom the prophetic model of the call of Jeremiah offers a better parallel: "Jeremiah was Paul's great predecessor."[35] But the Mishnah does speak of a *shaliach* or agent for a congregation, and states, "A man's *shaliach* is like himself" (*Berakoth* 5:5), i.e., a plenipotentiary representative. Historically this provided material for Dom Gregory Dix (1946), A. G. Hebert (1946, 1963), and others to try to defend a dogmatic doctrine of "apostolic succession" in an institutional sense, which they applied to episcopal succession.[36] Nowadays few defend this quasi-mechanical transmissive theory, but the ecclesiological and doctrinal emphasis had become widely established. T. W. Manson argues for the relevance of the *shaliach* approach, but declares: "the *shaliach* has a definite commission . . . his authority does not extend . . . it lapses when the commission has been executed."[37] The post-Rengstorf attack on the relevance of the *shaliach* has been traced by J. A. Kirk.[38]

---

32. F. C. Baur, "Die Christuspartei in der korinthischen Gemeinde, der Gegensatz des petrinischen und paulinischen Christentums in der ältesten Kirche, der Apostel Petrus in Rom," *Tübinger Zeitschrift für Theologie* 4 (1831): 61-206.

33. Rengstorf, "ἀπόστολος," *TDNT,* 1:407-47; cf. 398-406, 413-20.

34. *TDNT,* 1:400-403, 413-20, 425-30, and 441-42.

35. Ibid., 439.

36. Dom Gregory Dix, "Ministry in the Early Church," in Kenneth E. Kirk (ed.), *The Apostolic Ministry: Essays on the History and Doctrine of Episcopacy* (London: Hodder & Stoughton, 1946), 183-303; and A. G. Hebert, "Ministerial Episcopacy," ibid., 493-533, and 1963, 53; cf. A. M. Farrer's more cautious allusions in "The Ministry in the NT," ibid., 113-81.

37. Manson, *The Church's Ministry,* 37; cf. 31-52.

38. Kirk, "Apostleship since Rengstorf," 249-64.

Writers who reject the relevance of this approach include Mosbeck, Klein, Rigaux, and Hans von Campenhausen.[39]

(iii) To some extent the beginnings of a turning point emerged with E. Käsemann's long essay on apostleship of 1942. He argued that issues about "legiti-mation" and "legitimacy" were raised not, as Baur had implied, by Paul, but by Paul's opponents in 2 Corinthians 10–13. Following Reitzenstein and influencing Schütz, Käsemann identifies Paul's main "opponents" in 1 Corinthians as "pneumatic" enthusi-asts, but sees his adversaries in 2 Corinthians as those who to some extent remain "pneumatics" but also promote a Jewish form of Christianity allegedly under the name of the earliest "primitive" apostles.[40] They accuse Paul of lacking "the signs" of an apostle (2 Cor 12:12). Käsemann believes that they evolve an *ecclesial doctrine of tradition* as the criterion for "legitimation."[41] By contrast, Käsemann interprets Paul's own notion of apostleship as *christological, not ecclesiological:* apostleship is grounded in "the mind of Christ" (1 Cor 2:16), whose sufferings entail "weakness," and the term is correlated with "gospel."

The strength of Käsemann's work lies in his association of the signs of apostle-ship with Christology and the gospel (as we have argued above), rather than with ecclesial or manipulative power. Nevertheless, the weakness of Käsemann's study lies in its retention of an ecclesial (or antiecclesial) dogmatic agenda, which is almost as transparent as that of Dix and Hebert, but with the very opposite goal, namely of at-tacking an institutional or more "catholic" view of apostolicity. Käsemann seeks to perceive Paul as standing midway between institutional legitimation and pneumatic power, taking up the cross against both. Hence in his later essay on ministry in the NT he sees the institutionalization of gifts of grace in the later writings as replacing a the-ology of the cross by what Luther termed a *theologia gloriae,* or a triumphalist, manip-ulative distortion of the *theologia crucis.*[42] "As God's power is . . . the basis of the resur-rection, so weakness is the groundroot of the cross."[43] "The true sign of apostleship is not mighty works, nor ecstatic experiences, but . . . service which lives out the cross."[44]

(iv) Käsemann's former pupil J. H. Schütz begins by reviewing Käsemann's per-spective in the light of Max Weber's contrast between charismatic, routinized, and in-stitutional authority. More recently Margaret Y. MacDonald has approached these is-sues with similar tools.[45] But while on one side Schütz perceives a degree of circularity of Paul's critique of the pneumatics, Schütz also offers the potential for a solution when he takes up Käsemann's theme of the cross.[46] This coheres with our emphasis, shared with Schrage and Moltmann, on the cross as "ground and criterion" (see above, and under 1:18-31; cf. 2:1–4:21).

---

39. Mosbech, "*Apostolos* in the NT," *ST* 2 (1949-50): 166-200; Klein, *Die zwölf Apostel,* 26-30 and 202-10; Rigaux, *The Letters of St. Paul,* 55-67; and Von Campenhausen, *Ecclesiastical Authority and Spiritual Power,* 12-29.

40. Käsemann, "Die Legitimität des Apostels," 33-71; rpt. in K. Rengstorf (ed.), *Das Paulusbild in der neueren deutschen Forschung* (Darmstadt: Wissenschaftliche Buchgesellschaft, 1969), 492.

41. Ibid., 496.

42. Käsemann, "Ministry and Community," in *Essays on NT Themes,* 92.

43. Käsemann, "Legitimät," in *Paulusbild,* 501.

44. Ibid., 520 and 499.

45. MacDonald, *Pauline Churches,* 10-29, 46-60, and 123-58.

46. Schütz, *Anatomy of Apostolic Authority,* 249-86.

(v) A further stage of debate unfolds with Rudolf Schnackenburg's essay of 1970. Among many useful points, two stand out: first "Paul did not know of a uniform concept of apostleship which had clear-cut criteria."[47] Second, "It makes no sense to play the 'charismatic' and 'institutional' concepts of an apostle against one another.... The concept . . . was not carefully defined."[48] Schnackenburg concedes that among the Jerusalem community and perhaps more widely up to Paul's letters, **apostles** were those who had witnessed the resurrection of Christ. But very soon, while it related to "a cohesive group," the term began to develop more broadly. 1 Cor 9:1 and 15:7 do not provide conclusive proof that apostleship in every area at that time depended on being a witness to the resurrection. The group may have become wide enough to include, e.g., Andronicus and Junias, but they may well be described only as "well known among the group of apostles" (Rom 16:7; depending on how we translate ἐπίσημοι ἐν τοῖς ἀποστόλοις.[49] The interrelation of title and function or lifestyle may not have been distinctive of Paul, who asks whether it is lived out. The claim to "credentials" in 2 Corinthians may refer not to letters of authorization, but to letters which witness to apostolic behavior, except that Paul regards these as part of the "deceit" of his opponents and the deviousness of their manipulative methods (2 Cor 3:1-3; 6; 12:11).[50] In the end, everything turns on what is conveyed by their preaching and their life.

(vi) B. Holmberg's study *Paul and Power* (1978) offers a distinctive contribution to the debate. His key point concerns the organic and diffused nature of authority structures or influences in the Pauline churches "where the different constituents are bound to one another in mutual, but not symmetric dependence."[51] Because apostleship is translocal, and for other reasons also, Paul's standing with one community may strengthen or weaken his influence on another. But writers, he claims (whether they utilize Käsemann, Weber, Rengstorf, or Schütz), for the most part fail to note "the complexity of authority in the primitive church — a charismatic form of authority that is continuously being institutionalized and re-institutionalized through the dialectical interaction of persons, institutions and social forces at various levels with the structure of the church."[52]

This gives a quite different meaning from that of more political or "democratic" notions of "shared leadership" in the late twentieth century. These often invite either an inclusive democracy where votes carry the day, or a more exclusive corporate "eldership" in which a sharply defined "inner circle" hardens into a new authoritarian structure, all the worse for being only locally accountable through purely internal criteria. In Holmberg's understanding of Paul there remains room for genuine *leadership,* but *cross-currents of consent and accountability shift in various ways* as a whole host of contextual, theological, and social factors serve to interact and to provide a counterbalance. Hence Paul resists any simplistic, overneat understanding of "leader" or *apos-*

---

47. Schnackenburg, "Apostles before and during Paul's Time," in Gasque and Martin (eds.), *Apostolic History and the Gospel: Essays Presented to F. F. Bruce,* 301; cf. 287-303.

48. Ibid., 302.

49. Ibid., 293-94.

50. Ibid., 297. Schnackenburg agrees, however, that the image "the Twelve" soon began to dominate notions of **apostle** (302).

51. Holmberg, *Paul and Power,* 207.

52. Ibid., 204-5.

tle. He finds a place both for leadership and for mutuality. G. Theissen (1982) and others take some of these issues further in particular directions, but Theissen tends to polarize once again the charismatic and institutional, probably giving too much weight to Weber (as against Schnackenburg).[53] Holmberg probably offers more help.

(vii) More recent approaches may be considered together for convenience. E. Best (1986) presents an important case for disentangling **apostle** from issues of *authority*.[54] Anticipating A. C. Wire, he argues that Paul's leadership role as one in authority derives more directly from his status and role as "founder" and "father" of the Pauline congregations (1 Cor 4:14-21).[55] Hence Paul asks: **"Is it not you who are my work in the Lord?"** This has affinities with Beardslee and Dunn.[56] P. R. Jones brings together foundational, missionary, translocal, and eschatological aspects.[57] Finally, D. Litfin and N. Richardson take this further. Litfin removes the term *apostle* from the agenda of concerns about power in the new rhetoric. He reminds us of the attention which C. K. Barrett gives to Paul's concept of "placarding" Christ. The verb "expresses this non-rhetorical emphasis. . . . Paul's mission was to placard Christ crucified."[58] Neil Richardson concludes, "the σλάνδαλον was re-enacted in the person of the apostle."[59]

(viii) *Conclusions*. Apostleship fundamentally points away from the self (from a self-conscious preoccupation with the status of the apostolic agent) to Christ as crucified and raised. The "grammar" of apostleship rests upon the effectiveness and transparency of this witness to that for the sake of which apostles were commissioned. There is no reason to restrict this witness to apostolic words alone; Paul also appeals to a lifestyle which conforms to the pattern of the cruciform and living Christ. However, the very fact that Paul may also speak of the foundational role of apostolic witness (see on Jones above, under vii) anchors this witness in the earliest kerygma and traditions, especially those concerning the cross and the resurrection. There may be some force in Käsemann's suggestion that an apostolic normativity began to stand in contrast to claims about "spirituality" which were not wholly anchored in Christology. Here the "institutional" commission of apostles by Jesus Christ provides some parallel with the institution of baptism and the Lord's Supper as "anchoring" the gospel in the cross and resurrection (cf. Rom 6:3-11 and 1 Cor 11:23-26). In neither case, however, are the agents or the sacraments self-contained "transmitters" of grace in any reified sense, but agencies or channels through which that which is actualized conforms with the central events of the gospel. Thus Barrett's observation about "placarding" Christ, and Richardson's comment about reenacting the σκάνδαλον of the gospel remain central to the idea. However, (iii) through to (vii) all contribute elements to our understanding of this term.

2   On this occasion we have reproduced G. G. Findlay's translation of the first Greek sentence, for it captures the precise force with grammatical accuracy. It

53. Theissen, *Social Setting*, 40-54, and elsewhere in his writings.
54. Best, "Paul's Apostolic Authority?" 3-25.
55. Cf. Wire, *Women Prophets*, 45-47.
56. Beardslee, *Human Achievement and Divine Vocation in the Message of Paul*, 82, 90, 91; cf. 79-94; and Dunn, *Romans*, 1:9.
57. Jones, "1 Cor 15:8," *TynBul* 36 (1985): 21 and 28-34.
58. Litfin, *St Paul's Theology of Proclamation*, 196.
59. Richardson, *Paul's Language*, 135; cf. 95-138.

is possible to render ἀλλά γε ὑμῖν as *for you at least.*[60] But equally in classical and Koine Greek ἀλλά regularly means **at any rate,** especially in the apodosis of a conditional sentence. REB's *If others do not accept me as an apostle, you at least are bound to do so* captures the force, but it requires such radical restructuring as almost to introduce paraphrase. However, **if** (REB, NRSV, NJB, AV/KJV) is preferable to *even though [I may not]* (NIV) as a translation of εἰ ... οὐκ εἰμί.[61] Findlay's **I am no apostle** conveys the force of the hypothetical thought more strikingly than the more labored *if I am not an apostle* (NRSV). The dative may be a dative of interest (*in the eyes of,* as Héring argues) or a dative of advantage, *for you* (which Héring also includes additionally). With Héring, it should probably be construed as **to you** in the sense of *in your eyes.* Paul often subtly takes account of *perceptions* (as a good pastor) *as well as* objective *realities,* although Schrage places the emphasis entirely on the latter.[62]

Robertson and Plummer observe, "The Corinthians are the very last people who could reasonably question his claim to be an apostle. . . . 'For **my certificate of apostleship**' (ἡ γὰρ σφραγὶς μου τῆς ἀποστολῆς) **are you yourselves** (ὑμεῖς ἐστε) **in the Lord**. Although σφραγίς regularly means *seal,* it also frequently means the *mark* or *stamp,* e.g., of a signet ring in wax which then may carry the force of **certificate** (BAGD) or *attestation of genuineness* or of *confirmation* (Schrage).[63] In Rev 7:3 the elect are "stamped" (σφραγίζω) with God's seal as belonging to him, so that they do not become "lost" within the changes, chances, and ambiguities of the world, but reach their eschatological goal as his own *authentic* people, **certified** *as his* by their *stamp, seal,* or *mark of ownership.* Similarly, when there is apparent ambivalence about status claims and the "signs of apostleship," Paul perceives the genuineness of his mission and pastoral nurture of the addressees as a **certificate** which witnesses to the genuineness of his **apostleship**.[64] Edwards insists that **in the Lord** is construed with **you** rather than with **apostleship**, and also points out that σφραγίς, **certificate** or *attestation,* denotes more than simply σημεῖον, *sign.*[65] As Wolff observes, Paul drily implies that **if** he is **no apostle**, *they deny their own existence* **in the Lord**.[66] Gardner concludes that the word is not only a *seal,* but "a seal indicating a 'legally valid attestation.'"[67]

3   Commentators, lexicographers, and grammarians are divided over

---

60. Conzelmann appeals to BDF, sects. 439 (2), 448 (5), "classical" (*1 Cor,* 151, n. 2).

61. Fee points out that the NIV translation presupposes external challenges from outside the community (cf. 2 Corinthians 10–12) but "nowhere else does 1 Corinthians suggest that the trouble is due to outside agitation" (*First Epistle,* 396).

62. Schrage, *Der erste Brief,* 2:290; Héring, *First Epistle,* 76.

63. BAGD, 796-97, either literally [under 1(d)] **certificate**, *stamp of approval* or [under 2(a)] *that which attests* or *confirms,* as Schrage, *Der erste Brief,* also interprets it.

64. REB translates, *you are the very seal;* NRSV, NIV, NJB, Barrett, RV, and AV/KJV, *the seal.* But **certificate** is corroborated both by lexicography and by exegesis.

65. Edwards, *First Epistle,* 227.

66. Wolff, *Der erste Brief,* 189.

67. Gardner, *The Gifts of God,* 71.

whether αὕτη, **this**, refers back to Paul's statements in vv. 1 and 2, or forward to vv. 4-27. Chrysostom and Ambrose construe the pronoun as referring to what follows, which also gives rise to the paragraph division adopted by the UBS 4th ed. Greek text, the REB, NRSV, and NIV, and to the punctuation (colon) in the AV/KJV. But Robertson and Plummer argue that "it is more probable that it refers to what precedes, 'That I have seen the Risen Lord, and that you are such a Church as you are — there you have my defence when people ask me for evidence of my Apostleship.'"[68] Edwards is still more emphatic: "The word must, therefore, refer to what precedes."[69] Weiss, Allo, Fee, and Collins construe αὕτη as pointing to what follows, although Conzelmann and Barrett concede that either construction is possible, and Wolff argues that this view is rather more probable.[70] But if the Greek construction permits either view, much turns on the many issues about the purpose of ch. 9 and the concepts of apostle which we have discussed in very fine detail above (including the introduction to 9:1-27). However, Schrage shows that the issue is less of an exclusive alternative than we might imagine. For while he concedes that 9:1-2 concerns **apostleship** and v. 4 onward concern **rights** (ἐξουσία), Paul speaks not of **rights** in general (such as human **rights**) but only of those which are specifically bound up with his **apostleship**.[71] Hence, however we construe the Greek, our conclusions about the role of the chapter remain uncompromised.

Both ἡ ἐμὴ ἀπολογία, **my statement of defence**, and the dative participle τοῖς ἐμὲ ἀνακρίνουσιν, **to those who investigate me**, are legal metaphors. The noun ἀπολογία is technically *a speech of defense* (as in Acts 22:1; cf. 1 Pet 3:15, *ready to make a defense to anyone*), but in the context of a semijudicial **investigation** of someone under scrutiny is best translated **statement of defense**.[72] The verb ἀνακρίνω is more difficult, as we noted (2:14, 15 and 4:3, 4; and again under 10:25, 27 and 14:24). Since the word occurs once in the Gospels (Luke 23:14), five times in Acts (4:9; 12:19; 17:11; 24:8; 28:18) and then nine times in 1 Corinthians with no further uses in the NT, clearly, as Gardner urges, it is a "Corinthian" word.[73] Many Corinthians liked to *scrutinize, examine, judge,* or **investigate** other people, but also ascribed a measure of "discernment" to themselves.[74] Gardner observes, "We may deduce that the Corinthians were prematurely adjudging others. . . . Paul was indeed 'in the dark,'" but he chose to put himself there to establish the ground for his subsequent discussion

---

68. Robertson and Plummer, *First Epistle,* 179.

69. Edwards, *First Epistle,* 227.

70. For example, Fee, *First Epistle,* 397; Conzelmann, *1 Cor,* 152, n. 13 and 153; Barrett, *First Epistle,* 202; Wolff, *Der erste Brief,* 189. Cf. Allo, *Première Épitre,* 211; Collins, *First Cor,* 335.

71. Schrage, *Der erste Brief,* 2:290-91.

72. See BAGD, 96, for these meanings.

73. Gardner, *The Gifts of God,* 73-77.

74. See above, esp. in 2:14, 15; and esp. S. Pogoloff, *Logos and Sophia,* on competitive evaluations of "performers" in rhetoric and the status duly earned or ascribed thereby.

of the difference between his view and theirs about "entitlements."[75] We should not allow anything to obscure the force of this chapter for current debates today about "autonomy" and "the **right** to choose."

b. On Rights and Freedoms: Everything for Christ and the Gospel, or "Standing on My Rights"? (9:4-18)

(4) Surely it cannot be that we have no "right" to eat or to drink? (5) Can it be that we have no "right" to take about with us a Christian who is our wife, as the rest of the apostles also have, as well as the brothers of the Lord and Peter? (6) Or do Barnabas and I alone have no right to stop working for our living. (7) Who has ever been known to serve in the army bringing all his own provisions? Who plants a vineyard and eats none of its fruit? Or who tends a flock without using the product of its milk?

(8) You cannot think (can you?) that I am urging this on the level of purely human example. Or does not the law also say this? (9, 10) For in the Law of Moses it is written, "You shall not muzzle an ox while it is treading out the grain." Is it perhaps about oxen that God is concerned? Or is he not certainly speaking in our interest? It was indeed on our account that it was written: "it should be in hope that the one who ploughs does the ploughing; and in hope of a share of the crop that the thresher does the threshing." (11, 12a) If we ourselves have sown the things of the Spirit for you, is it a big issue if we reap material benefits from you? If other people share what you grant them as a right, do not we deserve our due all the more?

(12b) By contrast we did not make use of this right, but put up with everything, in order not to make any cut across a path for the gospel of Christ. (13) Do you not know that those who are employed in sacred duties gain their subsistence from the temple offerings, and those who officiate at the altar have a share of what is sacrificed on the altar? (14) In the same way the Lord commanded that those who proclaim the gospel should derive their living from the gospel.

(15) For my part, I have never availed myself of any of these rights. Nor am I writing all this in order that they may be thus applied in my case. I would rather die than — well, no one shall invalidate my ground for glorying! (16) For simply to proclaim the gospel does not constitute my ground for boasting. For compulsion presses upon me; it is agony for me if I do not proclaim the gospel. (17) If I do this entirely by personal choice, I am in the realm of reward. But if it does not arise from my own initiative, I accept it as one entrusted with a task. (18) What counts, then, as my "reward"? That when I proclaim the gospel I make the good news free of charge, with a view to gratuitously foregoing my right in the gospel.

75. Gardner, *The Gifts of God*, 75 and 76; cf. 67-91.

Bibliography on 9:4-18. See also further list at 9:19 on vv. 19-23, where partial overlap is unavoidable.

Bauckham, R. J., "The Brothers and Sisters of Jesus: An Epiphanian Response to John P. Meier," *CBQ* 56 (1994): 686-700.

Bauer, J. B., "Uxores circumducere (1 Kor 9:5)," *BZ* 3 (1959): 94-102.

Black, D. A., "A Note on 'The Weak' in 1 Cor 9:22," *Bib* 64 (1983): 315-24.

Blinzler, J., *Die Brüder und Schwestern Jesu* (Stuttgart: Katholisches Bibelwerk, 2d ed. 1967).

Bornkamm, G., "The Missionary Stance of Paul in 1 Cor 9 and Acts," in L. Keck and J. Martyn (eds.), *Studies in Luke-Acts: Essays in Honor of Paul Schubert* (London: SCM, 1966), 194-207.

Bosch, J. S., *"Gloriarse" Según San Pablo. Sentido y teleogia de* καυχάομαι, AnBib 40 (Rome: Pontifical Biblical Institute, 1970).

Bowers, P., "Church and Mission in Paul," *JSNT* 44 (1991): 89-111.

Brewer, D. I., "1 Cor 9:9-11: A Literal Interpretation of 'Do Not Muzzle the Ox,'" *NTS* 38 (1992): 554-65.

Brunt, J. C., "Love, Freedom and Moral Responsibility: The Contribution of 1 Cor 8–10 to an Understanding of Paul's Ethical Thinking," in *SBL 1981 Seminar Papers* (Chico: Scholars Press, 1981), 19-33.

Bultmann, R., "καυχάομαι," *TDNT*, 3:645-53.

Caird, G. B., "Everything to Everyone," *Int* 13 (1959): 387-99.

Caragounis, C. G., "*Opsōnion:* A Reconsideration of Its Meaning," *NovT* 16 (1974): 35-57.

Carson, D., "Pauline Inconsistency: Reflections on 1 Cor 9:19-23," *Churchman* 100 (1986): 6-45.

Chadwick, H., "All Things to All Men," *NTS* 1 (1954): 261-75.

Chow, J. K., *Patronage and Power,* JSNTSS 75 (Sheffield: Sheffield Academic Press, 1992), 107-12 and 130-41.

Dautzenberg, G., "Der Verzicht auf des apostolische Unterhaltsrecht. Eine exegetische Untersuchung zu 1 Kor 9," *Bib* 50 (1969): 212-32.

Didier, G., "Le Salaire du Désinteressement (1 Cor ix:14-27)," *RSR* 43 (1955): 228-51.

Dodd, C. H., "Ἔννομος Χριστοῦ," in J. N. Sevenster (ed.), *Studia Paulina in Honorem J. de Zwaan* (Haarlem: Bohn, 1953), 96-110.

Foerster, W., "ἐξουσία," *TDNT*, 2:562-75.

Gale, H. M., *The Use of Analogy in the Letters of Paul* (Philadelphia: Westminster, 1964), 101-8.

Gardner, P. D., *The Gifts of God and the Authentication of a Christian* (Lanham, Md. and London: University Press of America, 1994), 77-96.

Glad, C. E., *Paul and Philodemus: Adaptability in Epicurean and Early Christian Psychagogy,* NovTSup 81 (Leiden: Brill, 1995).

Gooch, P. W., *Partial Knowledge: Philosophical Studies in Paul* (Notre Dame: University of Notre Dame Press, 1987), 102-23.

Gordon, J. D., *Sister or Wife? 1 Cor 7 and Cultural Anthropology,* JSNTSS 149 (Sheffield: Sheffield Academic Press, 1997).

Harvey, A. E., "The Workman Is Worthy of His Hire: Fortunes of a Proverb in the Early Church," *NovT* 24 (1982): 209-21.

Hock, R. F., *The Social Context of Paul's Ministry: Tentmaking and Apostleship* (Philadelphia: Fortress, 1980).

———, "The Workshop as a Social Setting for Paul's Missionary Preaching," *CBQ* 41 (1979): 438-50.

Hofius, O., "Paulus — Missionar und Theologe," in J. Adna, S. J. Hafemann, and O. Hofius (eds.), *Evangelium, Schriftauslegung, Kirche. Festschrift für P. Stuhlmacher* (Göttingen: Vandenhoeck & Ruprecht, 1997), 224-37.

Horrell, D. G., "'The Lord Commanded . . . But I Have Not Used . . .': Exegetical and Hermeneutical Reflections on 1 Cor 9:14, 15," *NTS* 43 (1997): 587-603.

Kaiser, W. C., "The Current Crisis in Exegesis on the Apostolic Use of Deut 25:4 in 1 Cor 9:8-10" *JETS* 21 (1978): 3-18.

Käsemann, E., "A Pauline Version of the 'Amor Fati,'" in his *NT Questions of Today* (London: SCM, 1969), 217-35.

Lee, G. M., "1 Cor 9:9" *Theol* 71 (1968): 122-23.

Marshall, P., *Enmity in Corinth*, WUNT 2:23 (Tübingen: Mohr, 1987).

Murphy-O'Connor, J., "Co-Authorship in the Corinthian Correspondence," *RB* 100 (1993): 562-79.

Nasuti, H. P., "The Woes of the Prophets and the Rights of the Apostle: The Internal Dynamics of 1 Cor 9," *CBQ* 50 (1988): 246-64.

Nickle, K., "A Parenthetical Apologia: 1 Cor 9:1-3," *CurThM* 1 (1974): 68-70.

Richardson, P., "Pauline Inconsistency: 1 Cor 9:19-23 and Gal 2:11-14," *NTS* 26 (1980): 347-62.

Richardson, P., and P. W. Gooch, "Accommodation Ethics," in *TynBul* 29 (1975): 89-142.

Schütz, J. H., *Paul and the Anatomy of Apostolic Authority*, SNTSMS 26 (Cambridge: Cambridge University Press, 1975).

Tassin, C., "Finances et mission selon Saint Paul," *Spiritus* 33 (1992): 452-67.

Theissen, G., "Legitimation and Subsistence . . .," in *The Social Setting of Pauline Christianity* (Philadelphia: Fortress, 1982), 27-54.

Tuckett, C., "Paul and the Synoptic Mission Discourse?" *ETL* 60 (1984): 376-81.

Wilckens, U., "Zur Entwicklung des paulinischen Gesetzverständnis," *NTS* 28 (1982): 154-90.

Willis, W. L., "An Apostolic Apologia? The Form and Function of 1 Cor 9," *JSNT* 24 (1985): 33-48.

4 The rhetorical questions continue to turn on the issue of "having rights" (ἔχομεν ἐξουσίαν) or "entitlements."[76] The use of the double negative μὴ οὐκ ἔχομεν intensifies the rhetorical force of the question by substituting a query about the proposition *p* "we have the right"/"do we not have the right?" for the *negation* of the *negative* proposition *not-p*: **Surely it cannot be** the case **that** (regular use of μή as a question expecting the answer "no" [cf. Lat. *num*]) **we** do *not* **have** *the* **right** (οὐκ ἔχομεν, i.e., **we have no right**). The Vulgate therefore reads *numquid non habemus potestatem*. But NJB, *have we not every right;* REB, *have I no right?;* and NRSV, *Do we not have the right?* (as NIV, AV/ KJV), translate the syntax as if the initial μή were absent, as in v. 1. Collins

76. Gardner, *The Gifts of God*, 77-78; Fee, *First Epistle*, 402.

translates, *Don't we have the right to eat and drink?* which amalgamates two of the negatives.[77]

The aorist infinitives φαγεῖν καὶ πεῖν are understood by most commentators to mean the right to have meals "at the expense of the Church."[78] Barrett, however, concedes that there is "much weight" in the view that "the right to eat" carries the further reference to food which might have come from a cultic setting or initially from a pagan temple through the meat market, thereby taking up 8:7-13 directly.[79] Yet Barrett concedes that the main thrust of 9:4-27 is that of renouncing "rights" in more general terms, and the allusion to food sacrificed to idols remains indirect. Otherwise the force of the argument loses momentum as it moves on to a series of broader examples. Most commentators exclude the narrower allusion.[80] The subsequent appeal to the missionary maxim of Luke 10:7-8 (cf. Matt 10:10) confirms this, as Wolff insists.

The remaining question concerns the shift from the singular in vv. 1-3 to the plural, **we have** (ἔχομεν), here. Wolff asserts that it is the "we" of Pauline apostleship, but Lang and most other writers explain it as anticipating the reference to Paul and Barnabas, which follows in v. 6.[81] In support of Wolff, the plural verb of v. 5 takes the singular *wife* (not *wives*). The allusion to Barnabas in v. 6, however, is not arbitrary. Barnabas disposed of his own source of business income to support the church (Acts 4:36-37), and his introduction of Paul to the missionary staff of the churches (Acts 11:22-26) may have implied that they shared the policy of trying to "pay their way" as part of their joint missionary strategy, whether or not other co-workers did the same. Murphy-O'Connor speculates whether the use of the plural in some part of this epistle may conceivably allude to Sosthenes as co-author, but the context seems to favor the traditional explanation here.[82]

5 Some Western MSS, e.g., F, G, Tertullian, read γυναῖκας, *wives,* as plural in place of the singular γυναῖκα, **wife**, on the assumption that the plural implicit in ἔχομεν is more than formal or literary, and omit ἀδελφήν. Virtually alone, Zuntz supports the omission of ἀδελφήν in spite of good MS evidence.[83] On the significance of ἀδελφή, see the exegesis below.

77. Collins, *First Cor,* 327 and 335. The force of the double negative is well conveyed by Meyer, *First Epistle,* 1:254: "we surely are not destitute of the right to . . . ," and by Robertson and Plummer, *First Epistle,* 179: "Do you mean to say that we have no right?"

78. Héring, *First Epistle,* 76; Schrage, *Der erste Brief,* 2:291 et al.

79. Barrett, *First Epistle,* 202.

80. In addition to Héring and Schrage, see also, e.g., Lang, *Die Briefe,* 115; Wolff, *Der erste Brief,* 190; Senft, *Première Épitre,* 118.

81. Wolff, *Der erste Brief,* 190; Lang, *Die Briefe,* 115.

82. Murphy-O'Connor, "Co-authorship in the Corinthian Correspondence," *RB* 100 (1993): 562-79.

83. Zuntz, *Text,* 138.

The word translated as **Christian** is the noun ἀδελφήν, as it occurs in apposition with γυναῖκα, **wife**. Although the AV/KJV, *to lead about a sister a wife (or as wife)* strictly follows the Greek vocabulary as if each term were context-free, even the 1881 RV renders the Greek to lead about a wife that is a believer (placing "Greek, *sister*" in the margin), all of the major modern translations rightly interpret ἀδελφήν to mean **Christian** (REB, NJB, Collins) or *believing* (NRSV, NIV). For ἀδελφή occurs in the sense of **Christian** *(sister)* in 7:15 and in, e.g., Rom 16:1 and Philem 1. Schrage endorses this as "without doubt," and virtually all major commentators take this view.[84] All except a few also understand γυναῖκα here to mean **wife**. The communities expect to support the married couple, on the assumption that the **wife** shares her husband's Christian concerns and will support him in turn in these concerns. The point is one of substance, since otherwise the inclusion of ἀδελφήν is redundant.

Two variations of meaning are proposed by two or three individual scholars. J. B. Bauer virtually alone argues that περιάγειν, translated above as **to take about** (as BAGD, REB, and Barrett; cf. NIV, Collins, *take along;* NRSV, NJB, *be accompanied by*), refers to the general married relationship in the sense of *go through life with*.[85] But Bauer has to follow the later Western reading (F, G, Tertullian), which includes the plural γυναῖκας and omits ἀδελφ[ας], and BAGD and other sources confirm that the Greek verb regularly means *to take someone about or along with oneself,* i.e., *take about* in 9:5.[86] The second minority variation is that of Allo, who attempts to argue for the view of Tertullian, Clement of Alexandria, and Jerome, that Paul means **taking about with us a Christian** *as a female assistant*.[87] Allo agrees that "it is certain that in our epistle γυνή generally denotes 'wife' (e.g., 7:34) and that ἀδελφή has the general sense of *'sister in the faith,' Christian*" (7:15). Allo disarmingly concedes that his exegesis is bound up with traditions about whether Paul or other apostles were married as viewed through the lenses of the Western Fathers and certain modern Catholic exegesis. He even allows that on these questions "we still hesitate a little to decide on a view."[88] However, in view of evidence about "deaconesses" he thinks it "preferable" to reconstruct 9:6 in this way, even if he concedes that on purely linguistic grounds this meaning is unlikely.[89] Tertullian in practice holds more than one, while Clement of Alexandria believed that an apostle could be accompanied by his wife, but would treat her "as a sister" in the sense of not living

---

84. Schrage, *Der erste Brief,* 2:292; cf. Conzelmann, *1 Cor,* 153, n. 19; Wolff, *Der erste Brief,* 190; Barrett, *First Epistle,* 202-3; Fee, *First Epistle,* 403; Collins, *First Cor,* 336.

85. Bauer, "Uxores circumducere (1 Kor 9:5)," *BZ* 3 (1959): 94-102.

86. BAGD, 645 (as above); Grimm-Thayer, 502, usually with reference to *place*.

87. Tertullian, *On Monogamy,* 8; Clement, *Stromata,* 4:3; Jerome, *Adversus Jovinianum,* 1:26; and Allo, *Première Épitre,* 212-14. Cf. further Augustine, *On the Work of Monks,* 4:5 and Theodoret, in 9:5.

88. Allo, *Première Épitre,* 213.

89. Ibid., 214.

maritally with her (against 7:1-7).[90] Moreover, Héring argues that "if *adelphē* meant here any Christian woman, travelling as a spiritual assistant, the substantive *gunē* would be quite superfluous."[91] The apostles, he concludes, had the right "not only to be married and to be accompanied by their wives on their journeys *(peri-agein)* but also to have them supported by the Church."[92] Few if any among recent exegetes appear to accept Allo's view.

Mark 6:3 (par. Matt 13:56) refers to **the brothers** of Jesus as James, Joses (Joseph), Judas, and Simon; Mark 3:32 (par. Matt 12:46; Luke 8:19-20) speaks in general terms of "your **brothers**"; while Paul alludes to James as τὸν ἀδελφὸν τοῦ κυρίου in Gal 1:19. John 2:12 speaks of the **brother** of Jesus as accompanying him to the wedding at Capernaum, and in John 7:3-10 his brothers urge that he display his miracles at the Feast of Tabernacles. A reference to James also appears in Acts 1:14. Eusebius associates the relatives of Jesus with leadership in the Jerusalem church and mentions James in this context.[93] By the middle or late second century, however, the notion of Mary's perpetual virginity emerged in the pseudopigraphical *Protevangelium of James.* For the first time **the brothers of the Lord** were perceived as half-brothers from a previous marriage of Joseph.[94] Later tradition ascribes to Tertullian the view that they were full brothers, and to Origen and Eusebius the view that they were half-brothers. Thomas Aquinas gives extensive consideration to the phrase *the Lord's brother* in Gal 1:19. He examines several theories and concludes (9:5) with Jerome that **brother** means only *kinsman.* Apart from appeals to uses as *Christian brother,* however, this depends largely on postcanonical traditions which are linked with a doctrine of Mary's perpetual virginity.[95] By contrast, on exegetical grounds alone many (with the notable exception of Richard Bauckham) suggest that the word means simply **brothers** in the usual sense, although many Catholic and some Protestant commentators content themselves with the observation that the "half-brother" hypothesis cannot be excluded with absolute certainty.[96] Other Protestant scholars insist in robust terms that "there

---

90. Clement, *Stromata,* 6:3; Tertullian, *Exhortation to Chastity,* 8, differs from the other source cited above.

91. Héring, *First Epistle,* 77.

92. Ibid.

93. Eusebius, *Ecclesiastical History,* 2:1:10-17; 3:11.

94. *Protevangelium of James* 9:2; 19:1–20:3.

95. Thomas Aquinas, *Commentary on Galatians* (Albany, N.Y.: Magi Books, 1966), 28-30. On literature in Catholic and other thought, see J. Blinzler, *Die Brüder und Schwestern Jesu,* SBS 21 (Stuttgart: Katholisches Bibelwerk, 2d ed. 1967), and useful bibliographical data in H. D. Betz, *Galatians* (Philadelphia: Fortress, 1979), 79. Cf. also J. B. Lightfoot ad loc.

96. Cf. Barrett, *First Epistle,* 203. Jerome insisted that the word could mean no more than "close relatives," probably "cousins." R. J. Bauckham argues that we should take more seriously the Epiphanian view that the "brothers and sisters" of Jesus were the children of Joseph by a previous marriage. He considers second-century evidence which might support this, and emphasizes the significance of the unexpected phrase "son of Mary" of Jesus in Mark 6:3. Bauckham's argument cannot be dismissed. See Bauckham, "The Brothers and Sisters of Jesus: An Epiphanian Response to John P. Meier," 686-700.

are no reasons for arguing, with Catholic thinkers, that James, Joses, Simon and Jude were not true sons of Joseph and Mary. And a similar remark could, of course, be made about their sisters."[97] Since this is the only reference in the NT to the right of **the brothers of the Lord** to receive support from the churches, we know nothing more about the reasons or the role which they may have performed in this context.[98]

As Conzelmann observes, we may understand οἱ λοιποὶ ἀπόστολοι . . . καὶ κηφᾶς in more than one possible way. If we draw our model of apostleship partly from 15:7, the group or category appears to constitute "an essentially closed circle."[99] If, however, the principle at issue, namely, financial support for "workers" in mission (vv. 6-11), controls the meaning of **apostle** as those commissioned for such work and faithful to it in word and lifestyle, then it is conceivable that the contextual meaning in this verse is more "open." If the scope is not certain in this particular verse, however, this should not detract from the uniqueness of apostolic witness as foundational for the church in contexts where it carries its full technical force. This point does not depend on either an acceptance or a rejection of a hypothesis about apostleship in Luke-Acts.

Verse 5 does *not* assert that *all* apostles were necessarily married, but simply that they had the *"right"* to be married; and if they were, to receive additional financial support. It is possible that **Peter** receives explicit mention at the end because it was widely known that he was married (Matt 8:14) or in the light of 1:12 (see above). However, the tradition that *all* of the apostles were married may owe its origin to a later interpolation in the Epistles of Ignatius, and in any case full account needs to be taken of 7:8 and our discussion of 7:8 (above).[100] However, Paul's appeal to an established entitlement would not carry much weight if there were hardly any examples of utilization. Whatever conclusions are urged about the scope of οἱ λοιποὶ ἀπόστολοι here (and in whatever category we place **the brothers of the Lord**), here is a very early Christian witness to the theme of Christian married couples traveling together for mutual companionship and vision in missionary or pastoral work, unless a specific decision is made to the contrary, or other circumstances prevail.

6 On the reference to Barnabas in Acts 4:36-7 and 11:22-26, see above under v. 4 (where Paul introduces the plural). If Acts 13 and 14 provide earlier historical material known among the Pauline communities, the early "missionary journey" of Paul and Barnabas may have offered a well-known model of missionary-pastors who paid their own way rather than drawing financial support from

97. Héring, *First Epistle*, 77, n. 9; similarly, Fee, *First Epistle*, 403: "This refers to Mary's children."

98. How they might relate, if at all, to Theissen's "itinerant charismatic missionaries" remains problematic. If support was as widespread as Theissen claims, especially with its social background, the picture becomes more complex. Cf. Theissen, *Social Setting*, 27-59.

99. Conzelmann, *1 Cor*, 153.

100. See Robertson and Plummer, *First Epistle*, 181.

Antioch or from those to whom they ministered.[101] The present infinitive ἐργάζεσθαι is the usual word for manual labor, and R. F. Hock has expounded in accurate and imaginative detail the discomfort and menial status involved in setting up a booth as a leather worker or tentmaker in a commercial *agora*.[102] With NIV we translate ἐργάζεσθαι as **work for a living** (which is what it means here), and with NJB we translate the negative μή with the continuous present infinitive as **no right to stop working**. . . . NRSV brings out the negated present by *refrain from working,* but REB and other VSS tend to miss the force of the theme of Paul's semiironic allusion to **the right** *to choose* (cf. 8:9-13).

7   The UBS 4th ed. reads τὸν καρπόν, **its fruit**, following א*, A, B, C*, D*, F, G, and 33. Although the early p⁴⁶ reads ἐκ τοῦ καρποῦ, this is generally regarded as an assimilation to ἐκ τοῦ γάλακτος in the next line, and the correctors of א, C, and D have changed it back into what A, B, F, and G read as the original.

As Herbert Gale argues, it is a mistake to assume that whereas the teaching of Jesus contains a multiplicity of images, pictures, analogies, and parables, Paul always remains in the realm of abstract discourse. Gale traces some thirty-three blocks of passages which embody models and concrete pictorial analysis in the four major epistles alone, together with others from 1 Thessalonians. Moreover, he urges, in 9:7 the three analogues of the soldier, the planter of a vineyard, and the shepherd "are not merely illustrative. They are obviously intended to constitute an argument: what is true in these areas of activity ought also to be true for Paul (and Barnabas)."[103]

The verb στρατεύεται regularly means **to serve in the army,** *to serve as a soldier* (cf. 2 Cor 10:3, 4, *to engage in warfare*). The controversial Greek word is ὀψωνίοις, usually translated in English VSS as *expense* or *expenses* (REB, NRSV, NIV, NJB) or *charges* (AV/KJV, RV). But in the papyri and inscriptions it very frequently occurs with the meaning *rations* or *food,* although also to denote a workman's *pay*.[104] Moulton-Milligan argue that here in 9:7 it means *ration money* or *allowance,* but allow that it often means *rations* or **provisions** in Koine Greek.[105] Although Caragounis has argued for the meaning *expense* or *expenses,*

---

101. See J. Jervell, "The Problems of Traditions in Acts," in his *Luke and the People of God* (Eng. trans., Minneapolis: Fortress, 1972), 19-39, argues that the succinct allusive assumption of common knowledge about "the apostles" argues for a widespread familiarity with early traditions; similarly, Fee, *First Epistle,* 404.

102. Hock, *The Social Context of Paul's Ministry: Tentmaking and Apostleship,* and "The Workshop as a Social Setting for Paul's Missionary Preaching," *CBQ* 41 (1979): 438-50.

103. Gale, *The Use of Analogy in the Letters of Paul,* 101.

104. MM, 471-72, trace "this interesting word" first in Menander, then freely in Polybius (e.g., 6.39.12), although banned as unduly colloquial by classical Attic linguists. It means **provisions** in the second-century *Oxyrhynchus Papyrus* 3:531: "pay for the provisions yourself until I send you some money."

105. Ibid. Grimm-Thayer, 471, stress the "corn, meat, fruits, salt," which were "often given to soldiers instead of pay."

his argument concedes that this is not in the sense of monetary pay as such, but in the wider sense of **provisions**.[106] We should have proposed *rations* as best fitting the context of the argument (how could anyone expect a soldier to bring his own *rations?!*), but since a monetary component is probably implied in the word, **all his own provisions** covers both *expenses* and *rations* for the forceful ἰδίοις ὀψωνίοις. (NRSV's *expenses* sounds more like what a salaried executive deducts from tax.) Furthermore, as Grimm-Thayer and Schrage urge, often corn, meat, fruits, nuts, and salt were given to soldiers on active service in place of pay, and on this basis they apply this meaning to this verse.[107] The indefinite ποτέ widens the negation and occurs regularly in indefinite counterfactual hypotheses with the nuance conveyed by REB's *Did you ever hear of a man serving . . . ?* Hence we translate, **Who has ever been known to serve . . . ?** The *application* of the maxim is counterfactual and indefinite, as REB and our translation indicate.

REB continues the indefinite counterfactual indicator to govern the other two examples: *Or planting a vineyard. . . .* This is imaginative and justifiable, but strictly goes beyond the given Greek syntax. In the second example we can either translate *does not eat the grapes* (translating τὸν καρπόν contextually with **vineyard**), or **eats none of its fruit**. For the planter of the vineyard does not necessarily consume *all* of the produce. The image is used in Deut 20:6.[108] In the third analogy, we might have expected *drinks* **the milk**, whereas the Greek has ἐσθίει, *eats*. This is because **milk** for a shepherd would include the combined **product** of the **milk** which today we call *dairy* **produce** (e.g., including cheeses). The Gk. ἐκ with the genitive conveys precisely the double point: partitive (sharing) *and* genitive of origin.

8 Some English idiom has to be found to convey the rhetorical force of μή, i.e., a question which is formulated with the sole purpose of eliciting a participatory "No!" Barrett translates, *you don't suppose, do you. . . ?* Collins has, *I do not say this on human authority, do I?* More difficult is the precise force of κατὰ ἄνθρωπον. This expression occurs in this epistle at 3:3 (you are **behaving like any merely human person**; see above) and 15:32, where it is variously rendered in English VSS (NEB, *as the saying is;* REB, *no more than human hopes;* KJV/AV, *after the manner of men*), as well as in Rom 3:5; Gal 1:11; 3:15. Schrage agrees with the view also adopted by REB that here the phrase "does not have negative connotations" but refers to analogies or examples drawn from human occupations and related methods of argumentation.[109] Thus

---

106. C. C. Caragounis, "ὀψώνιον: A Reconsideration of Its Meaning," *NovT* 16 (1974).

107. See note above; as enforced by Schrage, *Der erste Brief,* 2:296-97; also Caesar, *Bellum Gallicum* 1.23.1; Polybius, 1.66-68; 3.13.8. See further Deissmann, *Light from the Ancient East,* 168; and Findlay, *Expositor's Greek Testament,* 2:847 (even if these predate Caragounis, Schrage does not).

108. The LXX terminology and vocabulary are reproduced exactly by Paul in this verse. Prov 27:18 applies the principle to planting figs. See Gale, *Analogy,* 104-5.

109. Schrage, *Der erste Brief,* 2:297. If Schrage is right, NJB's *that this is merely worldly wisdom* is unnecessarily strong in its negative force here.

while NRSV and Barrett (Collins similarly) translate *with no more than* **human** *authority,* and NIV *from a* **human** *point of view* (neither of which is wrong), it is most probable that Paul used the standard phrase to refer more specifically to (REB) *these* **human** *analogies.* **On the level of purely human example** is intended to express both the mode and method of argument (with Schrage). The Greek plural ταῦτα, *these things,* is very frequently equivalent to **this** in idiomatic English. If the second ταῦτα is accented ταῦτά, it means *the same thing(s).*

The law, ὁ νόμος, refers to the Pentateuch here, as often elsewhere in Paul, and he is about to cite Deut 25:4. The fact that Deuteronomy 25 concerns another analogy, namely, the feeding of oxen, confirms that in v. 8a Paul declares that the argument from analogy drawn from **human** life as such can be supported further by parallel analogies or **examples** from scripture. Only older commentators stress the difference between λαλῶ and λέγει as a more formal utterance, since the distinction belongs more properly to the earlier classical period (see under 14:34). We may note that Paul's method of argument constructively draws upon (i) common experience or rational practice and (ii) scriptural support or coherence with scriptural traditions.

9-10   The UBS 4th ed. κημώσεις follows B*, D*, F, and G. The early 𝔓46, A, B3 and C, K and most minuscules follow the LXX translation of the Hebrew of Deut 25:4 by using the more literary word for muzzle, φιμώσεις. However, Metzger observes that copyists would be more likely to alter the less literary word to the more polished one (which also has familiarity from the LXX) than the other way round.[110] It is likely that Paul uses the more populist term, but C. D. Stanley insists that this argument "has its problems" and cannot be certain. κημώσεις might possibly have arisen as an early gloss to explain the literary word for a less literate readership.

Apart from the change of verb noted above, the quotation follows the negative future indicative form used for prohibitions with βοῦν ἀλοῶντα, which corresponds with the LXX of Deut 25:4. Our translation corresponds with NRSV and REB (against NIV, *do not muzzle*). All three rightly reflect the present participle active as continuous action: **while it is treading out** (against AV/KJV, *that treadeth out*).

PAUL'S USE OF THE OLD TESTAMENT IN 9:8-9

Conzelmann insists that since the function of Deut 25:4 is to serve as "essentially a rule for the protection of animals" this meaning remains "contrary to Paul's exegesis . . . God's concern is with higher things."[111] Conzelmann correctly cites evidence for such a view of the nonhuman creation in Philo and in hellenistic Judaism. Philo as-

110. Metzger, *Textual Commentary* (2d ed.), 492; also Senft, *Première Épitre,* 119; Schrage, *Der erste Brief,* 2:298, n. 119; against Stanley, *Paul and the Language of Scripture,* 195-96, esp. n. 2, with reference to Emil Kautzsch, *De Veteris Testamenti.*

111. Conzelmann, *1 Cor,* 154-55.

serts, "The law does not concern the benefit of creatures without reason (οὐ ὑπὲρ τῶν ἀλλόγων) but the benefit of those who have mind and reason (νοῦν καὶ λόγον)" (De Specialibus Legibus 1.260). Senft follows Conzelmann's view, citing the same passage from Philo.[112]

Schrage offers a detailed account of Paul's use of OT scripture in which he recognizes that Paul very rarely resorts to allegorical interpretation (probably, he argues, only here, in 10:4, and in Gal 4:21ff.).[113] The problem here is that the term "allegorical" can be understood in a variety of ways, and Schrage's discussion is less satisfactory than that of the two excellent discussions by Fee and most especially Richard Hays. The starting point rightly identified by Hays is to look anew at the context of Deut 25:4. Hays notes that many describe Paul's exegesis as "an example of arbitrary prooftexting on Paul's part, but closer observation demonstrates a more complex hermeneutical strategy.... A careful look at the context of Deut 25:4 lends some credence to Paul's claim.... The surrounding laws in Deut 24 and 25 (esp. Deut 24:6-7, 10-22; 25:1-3) almost all serve to promote dignity and justice for *human beings*" (my italics).[114] This comment is simply true to the text: Deut 24:1-4 concerns the implementation of divorce; 24:5-9 concerns exemption from military service on compassionate grounds, the limits of pledges of debt, treating persons as objects of commerce, and protection from disease; vv. 10-22 extend issues about pledges and debt, a minimum wage, and care of the family, resident aliens, orphans, and widows; 25:1-3 regulates legal disputes and restricts punishment to avoid "humiliation"; 25:5-10 concerns Levirate marriage.[115] The unexpected insertion of one verse about threshing coheres most closely with the encouragement of *human sensitivity* and *humane compassion* toward the suffering or defenseless (e.g., the immediately preceding context concerns the plight of widows, orphans, and victims of punishment).

Paul's question, then, **Is it perhaps about oxen that God is concerned?** (i.e., oxen *as such*) genuinely conveys the thrust of the context that constrains the force and direction of 25:4, although in this case it is more likely that μὴ ... θεῷ is the μή used to express a *hesitant* question (**is it perhaps ...?**) rather than the question which invites an emphatically negative answer: *Surely God is not concerned for oxen, is he? Of course not!* The meaning also partly hinges on our understanding of πάντως. NRSV (with NJB) translates this as *entirely: Or does he [God] not speak entirely for our sake?* (v. 10a). NIV, *surely he says this for us, doesn't he?* and REB, *must not the saying refer to us?* avoid the exclusivity which *entirely* in NRSV and NJB implies. BAGD concede that in an explicitly negative sentence πάντως usually means *not at all.* However, there is no negative in the Greek. Hence they categorize for πάντως a first range of meanings as **certainly**, *doubtless, by all means,* and propose **Or is he (not) certainly speaking in our interest?** for 1 Cor 9:10.[116] This second category includes *altogether,* but it also includes *of course* or *above all,* or just possibly even *perhaps.* BAGD provide a number of relevant parallels for **certainly** or *surely.* Findlay shows how this meaning evolves: "The augmentative πάντως (cf.

112. Senft, *Première Épitre,* 119, n. 17.

113. Schrage, *Der erste Brief,* 299-301.

114. Hays, *First Cor,* 151; see also Hays, *Echoes of Scripture in the Letters of Paul,* 165-66.

115. Cf., e.g., P. C. Craigie, *The Book of Deuteronomy* (Grand Rapids: Eerdmans, 1976), 304-15.

116. BAGD, 609. The "not" in brackets conveys not a Greek but an English idiom at this point, which requires insertion if we are to begin with the Greek **Or.**

Rom 3:9) *on every ground . . .* not that 'God is concerned *wholly (exclusively)* for us . . . but *on every account* a provision made for the beasts . . . must hold good, *a fortiori,* for God's proper servants; cf. Matt vi 26ff.; also x 31."[117]

We may return to the excellent analysis by Hays, which receives some support from Straub, Fee, and others. Deut 25:4 "functions as an elegant metaphor for just the point that Paul wants to make: the ox being driven around and around on the thresh-ing floor should not be cruelly restrained from eating the food that his own labor is making available . . . so, too, with apostles."[118] In both of his books which handle this subject, Hays specifies this further by arguing that δι' ἡμᾶς is not simply "synonymous with a more neutral δι' ἄνθρωπους. . . . We should probably understand him to be claiming that the words of the law . . . find their time and primary referent in the finan-cial arrangements pertaining to his own ministry."[119] *"For our sake,* that is [it was writ-ten], for the sake of the church in Paul's own time. The first person plural pronoun of v. 10 has the same implied antecedent as the first person plural pronoun of v. 11: Paul and his associates in ministry: 'If *we* have sown spiritual things . . .' (v. 11)."[120]

To suggest that this is the "true and primary referent" of Deut 25:4 may perhaps overpress a point which is otherwise helpful. No doubt Paul sees Deuteronomy 25 as being written *more* for humankind than for animals (but not exclusively so), just as he perceives the OT scriptures as *more* for the people of the new age of fulfillment than for Israel or for humankind in general (but clearly not exclusively so). Hence the appli-cation to the people of the gospel has a pointed reference to the apostles whose lives and ministry are paradigmatic for the community insofar as they witness to the death and resurrection of Christ (cf. 9:1; 15:3-9). However, to speak of this as "the true" refer-ent hints at an exclusiveness which Hays otherwise succeeds generally in avoiding. If it is taken at face value, we are forced to return to Schrage's claim about allegorizing, if not to Conzelmann's claim about a "contrary" Pauline exegesis. In the sense in which eschatology exhibits a goal and purpose which moves beyond the merely provi-sional, "Paul reflects the same eschatological view of the OT expressed in 10:11, that Scripture *ultimately* exists for those upon whom the end of the ages has come."[121] Nevertheless, as Moltmann and Pannenberg urged, this would by no means imply that *provisional* or *penultimate* events or understandings are invalid, irrelevant, or worthless.[122] Thus Paul can accord value to the OT in its proper context, while seek-ing that which transcends the immediate context. This further or "fallen" dimension often embodies a christological content or an eschatological promise.

---

117. Findlay, *Expositor's Greek Testament,* 2, "1 Cor," 848. On the other hand, Schrage re-jects the "how much more" mode of argument on Paul's part (*Der erste Brief,* 2:299). However, Findlay's understanding of πάντως remains unassailed.

118. Hays, *First Cor,* 151; cf. W. Straub, *Der Bildersprache des Apostels Paulus* (Tübingen: Mohr, 1937), 81-82; Fee, *First Epistle,* 408.

119. Hays, *Echoes of Scripture,* 165-66; cf. *First Cor,* 151.

120. Hays, *First Cor,* 151.

121. Fee, *First Epistle,* 408. Fee's approach is more helpful than Kaiser's attempt to relate the destination to Hirsch's contrast between "meaning" and "significance"; Kaiser, "The Current Crises in Exegesis and the Apostolic Use of Deut 25:4 in 1 Cor 9:8-10," 3-18: "He (Paul) has ex-pertly taken from its temporary wrapping a permanent principle" (15).

122. J. Moltmann, e.g., *The Coming of God* (Eng. trans., London: SCM, 1996), 279-95; and W. Pannenberg, e.g., *Systematic Theology,* 3 (Eng. trans., Edinburgh: T. & T. Clark and Grand Rapids: Eerdmans, 1998), 465-98, 527-54, 580-607.

J. W. Aageson's study *Written Also for Our Sake* coheres with this approach. He associates 1 Cor 9:9-10 with a similar double or extended context in Rom 4:23-24, although he also includes Gal 4:21-31, which may perhaps extend the second context further than in the other two instances. Aageson sees "the force of the scriptural passage" (i.e., Deut 25:4 in 1 Cor 9:9-10) as an aid "in the process of visualizing and defining the nature of the problem that confronts Paul, as well as . . . communicating this vision to his audience."[123] While at one level Paul sees Deut 25:4 as serving "his own purposes," in principle this serves as an *aid* in understanding the situation and God's will for the new community, rather than as legislation exclusively aimed at the church in such a way as to override its first immediate context. Against any anticipation of the second-century heresy of Marcion, Paul affirms the unity of God's concern for the world and for this people in both Testaments. Aageson's use of *Also* in his title legitimately identifies Paul's "merging" of contexts, in his concern "for the common life and unity of a church composed of both Jews and Gentiles."[124] Anticipating Calvin, Paul uses scripture as a *lens through which* to understand the present, *as well as* a light shed upon the past. Other biblical passages corroborate God's concern for the whole of his creation, as Augustine and Barth observe.[125]

Our translation **it should be in hope that** is designed to reflect the emphasis carried by ἐπ' ἐλπίδι (repeated twice) in the text. No labor should be mere drudgery without any "recognition" or incentive, whether this be financial or in kind. Neither human persons nor even animals are to be reduced to mere mechanical instruments serving only the welfare of others without thought for the welfare or encouragement of those who toil and need something more in life than the sheer toil alone. If Paul chooses as a voluntary act to regard his labor of love as itself the "something more," this remains his personal choice. However, **the law**, which here denotes not only the Pentateuch but also God's will for his world, demands something more in normal circumstances, and Deuteronomy stands as a model of humanitarian concern for the daily life of God's created, covenant order.[126] **Hope** invites a forward expectation above and beyond the toils and trials of the present. It brings a perspective and a horizon which can transform the constraints of a present situation.[127] The tradition that "the labourer deserves his wages" (Luke 10:7) is repeated in 1 Tim 5:18, after a repeated citation of Deut 25:4. The genitive articular infinitive τοῦ μετέχειν indicates a **share** in kind of the produce. (Paul will take this up as a "share" in "rights" in v. 12.)

11-12a   The logical emphasis in v. 11 falls upon μέγα. At the time of writing the precise equivalent in current idiomatic English would be: **is it** *any Big Deal* **if we reap** . . . ? In more formal terms μέγα denotes here **a big issue** (NJB, *is it too much to ask that;* NRSV, *is it too much if;* REB, *is it too much to expect . . .*).

123. J. W. Aageson, *Written Also for Our Sake: Paul and the Art of Biblical Interpretation* (Louisville: Westminster/Knox, 1993), 49; cf. 49-53.

124. Ibid., 129 and 130.

125. Augustine and Barth cite such passages as Ps 147:9 (feeding the ravens), Matt 10:29 (the fall of a sparrow), and Matt 6:30 (the grass of the field); cf. Augustine, *Commentary on Matthew,* ad loc.; Barth, *CD,* 3/3, 174.

126. "It is not surprising that Paul would have read this verse [25:4] also as suggesting something about justice in human economic affairs" (Hays, *1 Cor,* 151).

127. BAGD, 252-53; Moltmann, *Theology of Hope.*

Paul applies the cause-effect principle of **sowing** and **reaping**, first, to take up the **we/us** from vv. 9-10, as Hays, following others, argues.[128] Yet, second, it also compares the hugely different scale of **sowing** and **reaping** merely earthly or **material** things (τὰ σαρκικά) with **sowing** and **reaping the things of the** Holy **Spirit** (τὰ πνευματικά), providing "a sudden . . . almost humorous descent . . . to practical common sense. The irony of the transition is slightly marked by the antithetical balance of the two clauses and the use of μέγα."[129] The Gk. τὰ σαρκικά is in this case synecdoche for the **practical** things of life, for which τὰ βιωτικά is used in 6:3. τὰ πνευματικά normally denotes **the things of the [Holy] Spirit** in Paul (cf. 12:1; 15:44). **Material benefits** (as NRSV) simply places the noun in the beneficial context of the effects of **sowing** and **reaping**. Although ministers may be portrayed in terms which correspond precisely with his analysis elsewhere in his letters (serving as a soldier, 2 Cor 10:3-4: planting or sowing the seed of the gospel message, 1 Cor 3:6-8), the use of sowing and reaping may have been suggested to Paul by the imagery of Deut 20:6, together with other OT resonances (e.g., Prov 27:18, 26, 27). In all of these passages "the idea of receiving a return from the work corresponds closely to the Pauline emphasis."[130]

Chow suggests that the allusion to **others** in v. 12 recalls Paul's earlier comment that each receives a μισθός appropriate to the agent in question (3:13-15) and that it is God alone who determines the nature of this "reward" or "recognition" (4:1-5).[131] "While the μισθός which the rival apostles receive . . . appears to be . . . financial aid (1 Cor 9:6, 12a), the μισθός which Paul receives . . . may be that he preaches it free of charge (1 Cor 9:17-18)."[132] To make his point about voluntary relinquishment of a right, however, Paul has to show that like **others** he *could* have availed himself of the ἐξουσία which **others share**. Hock and Chow accurately show that this voluntary constraint on his freedom is bound up with a potentially vulnerable indebtedness to patrons, which could compromise his position as an impartial apostle (cf. 1:12, 13, 14, "Was it in Paul's name that you were baptized . . . ?").[133] Peter Marshall observes: "Whether the leaders of one of the factions [i.e., not all] made the offer to Paul is not indicated. That similar offers were made to others (1 Cor 9:11-12a) who accepted is known; that these recipients were made figureheads of the factions and the means of comparison and opposition to Paul is probable."[134] The difference between *acceptance* and the *authority* or **right** (ἐξουσία) to accept is crucial to

128. Hays, *1 Cor,* 151; *Echoes,* 165-68; cf. Edwards, *First Epistle,* 230-31; also Schrage, *Der erste Brief,* 2:301-2.

129. Edwards, *First Epistle,* 231.

130. Gale, *The Use of Analogy in the Letters of Paul,* 105; cf. 101-8.

131. Chow, *Patronage and Power,* 106-7.

132. Ibid., 107; cf. Hock, *Social Context,* 61-62.

133. However, Chow appears to miss the implication that Paul's "boast" in giving free services becomes humorous or ironic; Chow, *Patronage,* 173-75; cf. Hock, *Social Context,* 61-62.

134. Marshall, *Enmity in Corinth,* 232.

Paul's argument. The *offer* of support on the part of some leading people of influence "was more likely . . . an attempt to get Paul over to their side and thus obligated to them."[135] Thus, if Marshall's analysis of the reciprocal obligations of "friendship" in the Graeco-Roman world is correct, Paul, unlike **others**, refuses a "friendship" or patronage which is offered by *selected people of influence,* rather than as at Philippi the church as a whole. Hence these verses offer a double lesson for today's church: (i) its pastors and leaders deserve material support; (ii) there is no place for that special "friendship" which predisposes pastors or leaders to favor the wishes or inclinations of some against those of others.

The Greek permits more than one possible construction: τῆς ὑμῶν ἐξουσίας μετέχουσιν may allow us to understand the genitive ὑμῶν as a subjective genitive, i.e., **what you grant them as a right**, or as an objective genitive, i.e., *share in rights over you,* which Fee regards as "more likely."[136] Schrage accepts that it may well be a subjective genitive, but on balance believes that since Paul wishes to claim a "right" *over* the Corinthians, it is more probably objective.[137] However, it is doubtful whether this captures Paul's main concern. This chapter is not concerned with "authority" but with *renouncing* "rights." Indeed, if, as Schrage, Weiss and Lietzmann argue, **others** probably includes the so-called apostles or pseudo-apostles of 2 Corinthians, "rights *over* them" characterizes Paul's opponents rather than Paul himself.[138] Héring strongly rejects the interpretation of an objective genitive on grounds of word order as well as meaning.[139]

12b The aorist ἐχρησάμεθα, **we did not make use of**, alludes to Paul's conduct during his eighteen months or so at Corinth, although in v. 15 he uses the perfect to denote a continuing stance derived from this past decision. The verb is used in 7:21, where we discussed the respective arguments about **making use of** (i) freedom; (ii) slavery; (iii) God's calling; and (iv) the opportunities of the situation (see above). In 7:31 Paul introduces a wordplay between χρώμενοι and κατὰ χρώμενοι in which the notion of **making use of** something only if or when this is appropriate and always with self-discipline and restraint coheres well with our present verse (see under 7:31). Since ἐξουσία (cf. also ἔξεστιν in 6:12 and 10:23) is a term especially prominent in Corinthian theology, it would be arguable that we should place **this "right"** in quotation marks. Paul's argument seriously qualifies an ethics of "rights," although he allows it a partial and relative validity within an appropriate value system (most frequently love, but also grace and judgment) which relativizes "rights."

On στέγομεν, translated here **we put up with** (with NJB, REB, NIV; cf.

---

135. Ibid.
136. Fee, *First Epistle,* 410.
137. Schrage, *Der erste Brief,* 2:304, n. 157.
138. Ibid., 304; Weiss, *Der erste Korintherbrief,* 238.
139. Héring, *First Epistle,* 78-79. He also thinks that ἐξουσία functions here as a synonym for οὐσία, *substance* (rejected by Schrage).

NRSV, *endure*), see under 13:7. Dale Martin observes that this **putting up with** to avoid "hindrance" is precisely what the socially "strong" were not prepared to do. "We must recognize that . . . 9:12 is parallel to 8:8-9."[140] The usual translation *obstacle* for τινα ἐγκοπήν (NRSV) is acceptable, as is *any hindrance* (REB). This is the only occurrence of this Greek word within the NT (although the cognate verb, *to hinder,* occurs, e.g., in Gal 5:7 and 1 Thess 2:18). However, whether the metaphor is still live or merely a dead metaphor in Paul's day, the force of the noun derives from *making a cut into* something. The metaphor is drawn from a military context of blocking enemy advance. Yet for Paul there may be a resonance with disrupting the level pathway for the messengers of good news in Isa 40:3-4 ("prepare the way of the Lord . . . make uneven ground level"), which suggests avoiding **any** (τινα) **cut** *(cutting into* or *cutting up)* which roughens the path for **the gospel of Christ**.[141] Paul will take up this theme again in v. 23. Rudolf Bultmann retains at the heart of his work, whatever its unfortunate effects in other directions, a concern that while the cross itself cannot be other than a *skandalon* or *offense,* all possible efforts should be made to "eliminate [every] false stumbling-block" which hinders vision of "the real stumbling-block, the message of the cross."[142] This is the heart of Paul's and Luther's concern about pastoral office.

13 UBS 4th ed. [τὰ] ἐκ τοῦ ἱεροῦ uses brackets for the neuter plural definite article in v. 13. Its inclusion is attested by ℵ and B and the Western D*, F, G, and Coptic, but p46, A, C, and D3 omit the article. Conzelmann, Fee, and Schrage argue for its retention, although some perceive the addition of the article as a very early scribal correction.[143] The article gives the sense **the things of the temple**.

Either Paul was so eager to make the point about voluntary restraint that v. 12b interrupts the argument, or more probably he suddenly remembers a still more compelling argument which does not depend on analogy but on established precedent familiar to the readers, whether drawn from OT or Jewish or Graeco-Roman religious practice.[144] As in other occurrences of **Do you not know . . . ?** the presupposed knowledge is clear or self-evident (cf. 3:16). The OT background can be found, e.g., in Lev 6:9-11, where "cereal offerings donated by lay people could be eaten by the priests" in contrast to offerings made by the priest himself.[145] The practice would have evidential paral-

140. Martin, *Slavery as Salvation,* 120; cf. 117-49.
141. Chrysostom uses ἀναβολή, a mound thrown up to block the road (*1 Cor. Hom.,* 21:7, 8).
142. R. Bultmann, *Jesus Christ and Mythology* (Eng. trans., London: SCM, 1960), 35-36.
143. Conzelmann, *1 Cor,* 156, n. 2; Fee, *First Epistle,* 398, n. 8; Schrage, *Der erste Brief,* 2:307, n. 175.
144. Fee, *First Epistle,* 411.
145. G. J. Wenham, *Leviticus* (Grand Rapids: Eerdmans, 1979), 121; cf. J. Milgrom, "Two Kinds of Hatta'th," *VT* 26 (1976): 333-37; Lev 6:26-28; 7:6, 8-10; 28-36; and further J. Milgrom, *Leviticus 1–16,* AB (New York: Doubleday, 1991).

lels in first-century Temple Judaism and in Graeco-Roman religions. Meyer and Schlatter emphasize the OT background as an argument from Scripture, while several patristic and medieval commentators stress the familiarity of the practice in Graeco-Roman cults.[146] Most commentators (e.g., Barrett) give weight to all three contexts.[147] Although the verb in other contexts frequently means *to labor, to toil,* here οἱ τὰ ἱερὰ ἐργαζόμενοι has the meaning **those who are employed in** *sacred things,* i.e., in **sacred duties,** or *that which pertains to the cultus.*[148]

If we follow those MSS which include the definite article τά before ἐκ τοῦ ἱεροῦ (see above) the next clause refers to *eating the things of* **the temple,** i.e., **gain their subsistence from the temple offerings. Subsistence** is used in many modern contexts (e.g., subsistence farming) to denote precisely living on the basis of benefits in kind, which replicates Paul's imagery. Οἱ τῷ θυσιαστηρίῳ draws on the word history of *sitting down alongside the altar* with the force of "be jealously engaged in" (Conzelmann) and thus **those who officiate at the altar.**[149] They devote their services to it. Hence they **have a share** of (συμμερίζονται) **what is sacrificed on the altar** (if we understand the second use of θυσιαστηρίῳ as a metonym for **what is sacrificed** at the altar of burnt offerings as the LXX uses the term).

Most modern commentators regard the two clauses as broadly parallel in meaning. There is no evidence for the exegesis of Chrysostom and Theophylact which assigns the reference in the first clause to Levites and the second clause to priests.[150] Weiss and Schrage compare the Hebraic *parallelismus membrorum.*[151] Héring argues for the view of Chrysostom and Theophylact, but acknowledges "a close parallelism between the two phrases."[152] Meyer decisively shows the inapplicability of the first clause to Levites.[153]

14 Patristic sources identify this directive of **the Lord** as "the laborer (ὁ ἐργάτης) deserves his food" (ἄξιος . . . τῆς τροφῆς αὐτοῦ, Matt 10:10), or "the laborer deserves his pay" (ἄξιος ὁ ἐργάτης τοῦ μισθοῦ αὐτοῦ, Luke 10:7). Chrysostom identifies the passage without further comment, but Theodore of Mopsuestia calls attention to the Gospels' corollary that only thus can the Twelve in Matthew or the Seventy in Luke "take no bag nor money" but place

---

146. Meyer, *First Epistle,* 1:263, citing Lucian, *Asin* 5; Demosthenes, 1300.6; Ambrosiaster, 101, and Peter Lombard, 1610, anticipates Fee, *First Epistle,* 412, n. 83.

147. Barrett, *First Epistle,* 207. See further H. P. Nasuti, "The Woes of the Prophets and the Rights of the Apostles: The Internal Dynamics of 1 Cor 9," 251-54.

148. This does not exclude the nuance of *laboring at,* but the primary reference concerns a context or mode of employment in parallel occurrences. **Sacred duties** occurs in this sense in 3 Macc 3:21.

149. Cf. Conzelmann, *1 Cor,* 157.

150. Chrysostom, *1 Cor. Hom.,* 22:1; Theophylact, *Epist. Prim. ad Cor.,* in Migne, *PG,* 124:669.

151. Schrage, *Der erste Brief,* 2:306; see further 307, n. 171, for a detailed discussion.

152. Against Héring, *First Epistle,* 79-80.

153. Meyer, *First Epistle,* 1:253.

their trust in God and stay at the first house where they are welcomed without picking and choosing.[154] Luke's context (9:58; 10:3-9) associates this ministerial direction with "the Son of Man has nowhere to lay his head," which is also combined with the motif of urgency for the path of the good news in Matt 8:18-22; 9:37-38; 10:5-14.

That Paul should invoke this passage gives pause about too ready an acceptance of Theissen's overdrawn contrast between the itinerant "wanderers" of Jesus and the "community organizers" of Paul.[155] Horrell notes, "The problem cannot be solved by suggesting, as Theissen does, that Paul rejected financial support only when engaged in his initial evangelism, for he insists that he will *never* burden the Corinthians in such a way (2 Cor 11:9-12; 12:14)" (his italics).[156] As Conzelmann observes, Paul's double argument finds a double counterpart in the gospel tradition. Luke 10:7 underlines "the preacher's right to remuneration," while Matt 10:8-10 develops the theme of giving freely because one has freely received, and freedom from care and false securities.[157] Don Carson applies this principle to the whole notion of support for the ministry in broad terms: "The church does not pay its ministers; rather it provides them with resources so that they are able to serve freely."[158]

15 The reading οὐδεὶς κενώσει, **no one shall invalidate** or *make empty . . .*, is classified as "B" by the UBS 4th ed., but has the support of 𝔭46, ℵ*, B, D*, 33, itd, syr4, Tertullian, and Gregory of Nyssa. The variant readings virtually all provide ways round the occurrence of aposiopesis, i.e., Paul's beginning **I would rather die than** and then breaking off the construction in mid-flow to replace it by another.[159] Of these the alternative in ℵ2, C, and D2 is ἵνα τις κενώσῃ, while A reads οὐθεὶς μὴ κενώσει. Other variants also occur. We have only to recall that Paul is no doubt dictating orally to understand how readily he speaks with such passion that he pauses to resume with a more succinct summary. Thus the UBS reading is likely to be correct. Senft and Robertson (among many) offer reasons for the disrupted syntax (see below), but too many English VSS (apart from NJB) seek to smooth it out.

The use of the emphatic personal pronoun ἐγώ and the resumption of the first singular (cf. first plural in vv. 4-12) require a signal of individuality and emphasis.[160] Hence we translate, **For my part I have never**. . . . Further, the perfect denotes the continuing stance in contrast to the past decision indicated by the

---

154. Chrysostom, *1 Cor. Hom.*, 22:1; Theodore, "1 Kor," in K. Staab (ed.), *Paulus-kommentare*, 184.

155. With G. Theissen, *The First Followers of Jesus* (Eng. trans., London: SCM, 1978), and Theissen, *Social Setting*, 27-67, cf. esp. Horrell, *The Social Ethos of the Corinthian Correspondence*, 126-217.

156. Horrell, *Social Ethos*, 212.

157. Conzelmann, *1 Cor*, 157.

158. D. A. Carson, *When Jesus Confronts the World* (Grand Rapids: Baker, 1987), 125 (cited by Blomberg, *1 Cor*, 176).

159. Cf. Metzger, *Textual Commentary* (2d ed.), 492.

160. As Meyer, *First Epistle*, 1:264, observes.

aorist in 9:12.[161] The plural ταῦτα, *these things,* is usually represented more idiomatically by **this** in English, but "*Nor did I write* **all this**" reflects "all the
pleas which he has been urging (vv. 4-14)."[162] Since ἔγραψα is an epistolary
aorist, the verb has the force of **I am writing** rather than *I wrote.* οὐδενὶ τούτων,
however, is open to more than one understanding and includes "a multitude of
things."[163] Most commentators and VSS interpret the phrase to mean **never ...
any of these rights**, i.e., *none of these prerogatives,* not, as Heinrici proposes,
none of these arguments.[164] The phrase ἐν ἐμοί often means **in my case**.[165]

The occurrence of aposiopesis (see above under the textual note) causes
no surprise. "The apostle passes to a more profound motivation . . . the construction of the phrase is broken asunder *(est rompue)* signifying the apostle's
emotion . . . concerning the subject of *glory* [which] does not contradict the theology of grace."[166] "The tangled syntax . . . reflects the intensity of Paul's feeling in the subject . . . [producing] a violent anacoluthon. Instead of another infinitive (κενῶσαι) after ἤ *(than)* he changes to the future indicative without ὅτι
or ἵνα, 'No one shall make my glorying void.'"[167] We have used **Well,** to mark
the pause as the immensity of the subject overwhelms Paul, followed by his reformulation of a new syntactical beginning. Among the modern English VSS
only NJB has correctly reproduced the aposiopesis and anacoluthon without
smoothing it out into a blander, more "correct" syntax. NJB translates: **I would
rather die than** *that. . . .* **No one shall** *take from me* **my ground** *of boasting.*

It may be easy to misunderstand Paul's use of τὸ καύχημά μου if we forget that Paul's theme is his *glory in the cross* (1:18-31). His thought revolves
around a core contrast between *human boasting* and *glorying in the Lord* (1:30-
31). His rejection of dependency on patronage at Corinth reflects, in accordance with Matt 10:5-14 and the part parallel Luke 10:3-9, the apostolic living
out of trustful dependence on God's grace alone, in which he is able *freely to
give* precisely as his response to his having *freely received.* It does violence to
the NT when the theme of justification by grace is perceived to emerge only in
the polemical contexts of Galatians and Romans, when 1 Corinthians and the
message of Jesus no less clearly declare this central nerve of the gospel. In the
light of this history of misperception it is preferable to translate τὸ καύχημά μου
as **my ground for glorying** rather than *my ground for boasting* (NRSV) or
boast (REB, NIV). **Glorying** calls to mind Paul's theme in 1:31: **let the one
who glories glory in the Lord**. On καυχάομαι, see above under 1:29, 31. Paul
also uses καυχάομαι and καύχημα with negative, pejorative force in 3:21 (let no
one boast in human persons); 4:7 (why do you boast as if you did not receive it

---

161. See above on Horrell's critique of Theissen here (under v. 14 and its n. 2).
162. Robertson and Plummer, *First Epistle,* 188.
163. Meyer, *First Epistle,* 1:264.
164. Heinrici, *Das erste Sendschreiben,* 246-47.
165. Cf. Matt 17:12; Edwards, *First Epistle,* 233.
166. Senft, *La Première Épitre,* 121.
167. Robertson, *Word Pictures, IV: Epistles,* 146.

as a gift?); 5:6 (your boasting is not appropriate).[168] Fee offers an aphoristic summary of Paul's central point: "In offering the 'free' gospel 'free of charge' his own ministry becomes a living paradigm of the gospel itself."[169] Hayes rightly endorses this comment, and Käsemann's fine essay "A Pauline Version of 'Amor Fati' makes the same point in various ways.[170] Käsemann speaks of the "interweaving" of Paul's life and thought in his apostolic witness to the gospel, which does give boundaries to freedom.

The subapostolic *1 Clement* (c. 96 AD) takes up this theme of **glorying** in the Lord: "Let our glorying (τὸ καύχημα ἡμῶν) and bold confidence (ἡ παρρησία) be in him [the Lord]" (*1 Clement* 34:5). Chrysostom affirms that Paul's **ground for glorying** (τὸ καύχημα) is the cross of Christ (*Hom. in Matt.*, 26:39 [3:19B]). Ignatius faces martyrdom, as he seeks to die *not in boastful self-confidence* (μὲν ἐν καυχήσει ἀπόγωμαι) but in looking away glory from self (Ignatius, *To the Trallians,* 4:1). Origen quotes from Paul's refrain of **glorying** (ἡ καύχησις) in the context of human weakness, suffering or death (Rom 5:3-5; 1 Cor 15:32; 2 Cor 1:5; *On Martyrdom,* 41 [Migne, *PG,* 11:617A]).[171] Such texts contribute to what comes to represent a posthistory of the Pauline texts. This reaches a new peak in Luther and in the Reformers' interpretations of Paul.[172] The "Exegetical and Hermeneutical Reflections" on 9:14-15 offered by David G. Horrell confirms the kerygmatic and Christocentric focus shared by the exegesis of Käsemann, Fee, and Hays and the hermeneutical reflections of Origen and Luther. Horrell writes, "For Paul, the self-giving of Christ, his self-emptying and self-sacrifice, is a fundamental ethical resource, a paradigm. . . . In Paul's view, obedient Christian discipleship."[173]

16 The protasis of the conditional clause ἐὰν γὰρ εὐαγγελίζωμαι has the force of **simply to proclaim**. . . . Paul has explained that he can glory or boast only where the principle of "freely you received, freely give" operates, and when a renunciation of "rights" is *entirely voluntary*. This cannot apply in his particular case to the act of preaching alone or to proclamation itself, for, like Jeremiah, in every account of his call Paul insists that *God's* **compulsion presses upon** *him.* This accords precisely with the accounts of Munck and Sandnes (noted elsewhere) of Paul's being "overpowered" (κατελήμφθην, Phil 3:12) and "under compulsion" (ἀνάγκη, 1 Cor 9:16):; "from now on you will have no discharge from . . . service (Acts 26:14, on the basis of the Aramaic be-

---

168. See BAGD, 425-26.

169. Fee, *First Epistle,* 421. Cf. also ibid., 417-20.

170. Hays, *First Cor,* 153; Käsemann, *NT Questions of Today,* 217-35.

171. Cf. further *Apostolic Constitutions,* 3:13:1; Lampe, *Patristic Greek Lexicon,* 739.

172. For example, Luther, *Heidelberg Disputation* (1518), 20 (where Luther cites 1 Cor 1:21), 25 (cites 1 Cor 1:30), et al.

173. Horrell, "'The Lord Commanded . . . But I Have Not Used . . .': Exegetical and Hermeneutical Reflections on 1 Cor 9:14, 15," 600-601; cf. 587-603. However, Horrell's main argument, that Paul can follow Christ only by "setting aside a . . . word of Jesus" (601), becomes more problematic, since the distinction between mandatory and permissive injunctions may imply a different logic from that for which Horrell seems to argue.

hind σκληρόν σοι πρὸς κέντρα λακτίζειν).[174] Paul, like Jeremiah, was set apart for this task from before his birth (Gal 1:15; cf. Jer 1:4-10; 20:7).[175] This exegesis is well elucidated by Wolff as entirely compatible with a theology of grace and lexicographical surveys of ἀνάγκη as "necessity, compulsion of any kind," but here by the will and agency of God.[176] ἐπίκειται is better understood to mean *lies* or *presses upon* than *is laid* (AV/KJV).[177]

The traditional *woe is unto me if I preach not the gospel* (AV/KJV; cf. NRSV) represents the Greek οὐαὶ γάρ μοί ἐάν. . . . However οὐαί denotes pain or displeasure either as an exclamatory *alas!* or with ἐστιν (as here), *misfortune, trouble* (NJB) or **agony for me** (with REB).[178] It is **agony** if Paul tries to escape from the constraints and commission which the love and grace of "the hound of heaven" **presses upon** him. With this further logical step *glorying* (καύχημα) begins to slip back subtly into **boasting**.

17 This verse generates sensitive problems of translation. Although strictly ἑκών means *willingly* or *gladly,* the word stands in semantic opposition to that which is by *force* or *compulsion* and hence denotes *of one's own free will* (as NJB) or **entirely by personal choice**.[179] To translate μισθὸν ἔχω requires no less sensitive care. Paul is expounding not so much an issue of *physical or empirical* cause and effect (for which *I have . . .* would be appropriate) as the *logical grammar* of a contrast between two conceptual fields. Thus lexicons (including BAGD) distinguish between "physical" uses of ἔχω to mean *I have, I possess, I hold in my hands, I own as a possession* and extended, sometimes conceptual uses to mean *I have at hand, I experience, I consider, I view, I have the possibility of, I am situated in relation to. . . .*[180] The flexibility and range of ἔχω in the papyri is striking.[181] Louw and Nida distinguish a semantic domain in which ἔχω relates to content from another in which the verb relates to experiencing "a state or condition."[182] Hence Paul makes a *logical* point that only acts carried out from self-motivation or self-initiative belong to the logical order of "reward"; and thereby his own irresistible commission excludes such logic. One network is **in the realm of reward**; the other is that of **one entrusted with a task** (οἰκονομίαν πεπίστευμαι). It is almost, as it were, like being within a given management chain (οἰκονομία), to which Paul also alludes in 4:1.[183] "The

174. Munck, *Paul and the Salvation of Mankind,* 20-23; cf. K. O. Sandnes, *Paul — One of the Prophets? A Contribution to the Apostle's Self-Understanding,* WUNT 2:43 (Tübingen: Mohr, 1991), 125-29.

175. Munck, *Paul and Salvation,* 24-30; Sandnes, *Paul — One of the Prophets?* 123-24.

176. Wolff, *Der erste Brief,* 200; BAGD, 52. Cf. also Senft, *La Première Épitre.*

177. As Robertson and Plummer, *First Epistle,* 189, observe.

178. Cf. BAGD, 591.

179. Cf. BAGD, 247; Grimm-Thayer, 201; MM, 200.

180. See BAGD, 331-32 (1, entries 1-7; 2, entry 1); and Grimm-Thayer 265-68 (1, a-n, and 2).

181. MM, 270.

182. Louw-Nida, 1:801 (90.27), 807 (90.65); cf. 2:295.

183. See Wolff, *Der erste Brief,* 200-201.

language recalls the appointment of imperial secretaries who as a rule were either slaves or freedmen."[184]

Curiously Héring falls into difficulty by doing precisely what Conzelmann warns exegetes against doing. He sees in this passage the notion of "works of supererogation. . . . What the Apostle does presuppose here . . . is the idea that — salvation apart — Christians will be subject to a kind of grading."[185] Yet, as Conzelmann urges, "it is misguided to remove this rule from the framework of the argument, to regard it on its own . . . thinking in terms of works and deserts."[186] The whole argument hinges on sovereign grace, and that it is in *freely giving* in response to God's free gift that καύχημα, grounds for taking delight in what one gives, becomes possible *only within a framework where pressure and law do not apply:* free gift in response to free gift. It is in *giving* that the believer *receives,* not as some "external" reward, but through the internal grammar of the blessedness of giving which is a stamp of identification with the cross. Hence if Paul cannot "freely" give his apostolic work (since to this he is pressed by God without choice), what is left to give "freely" is his toil and labor as a leather worker and salesman in the commercial agora. This he gives to relieve others of bearing his costs and more especially avoiding the obligations of patronage which might compromise his voice on behalf of less influential groups within the church.[187] In view of the close link with v. 18 and Dale Martin's point about "slavery," freedom, and "the weak," it does not seem that "the argument has gone afield a bit" (Fee), for v. 17 paves the way for v. 18.[188] Collins observes, "'Boasting is a major theme in 1 Cor. . . . The object of Paul's boasting is not the preaching of the gospel. . . . Paul's boast is that he has not made use of the rights to which he is entitled . . . to support himself by the work of his own hands."[189]

18 This verse explicates the point just made above. Only by *gratuitously* proclaiming the gospel *gratis* can Paul go beyond the preaching which God has pressed upon him as an inescapable, not voluntary, task, and thereby go "the second mile." To do this, however, he must forego a right, as he pleads with "the strong" among his readers to do. Dale Martin (against, e.g., G. Bornkamm) insists that Paul does not ask *every* reader to give up a right, but those who have "rights" to give up, i.e., the strong or socially influential: "Paul has been willing to do what the strong have heretofore resisted: he has not made use of his right but has 'endured' everything. . . . Paul calls not the weak but the strong to do this. The term *exousia* refers to a social prerogative and is directly

---

184. Barrett, *First Epistle,* 209.

185. Héring, *First Epistle,* 80 and 81.

186. Conzelmann, *1 Cor,* 158.

187. Cf. our discussions above of Paul's arduous toil with particular reference to Hock, *The Social Context of Paul's Ministry;* and on patronage Chow, *Patronage and Power;* Marshall, *Enmity in Corinth;* and Clarke, *Secular and Christian Leadership in Corinth.*

188. Fee, *First Epistle,* 420 (which predates Martin's comments).

189. Collins, *First Cor,* 346. Collins recognizes that this causes contention.

related to freedom, high status and power. Low-status persons, the weak, by definition have no exousia to surrender. Telling the weak to give up *exousia* is like telling a slave to give up his or her *eleutheria*, 'freedom.'" Paul's pointed surrender of his *eleutheria* and *exousia* (as one of the strong) is therefore . . . directed precisely at those who have these things and resist giving them up, that is, those of higher status."[190] They should relinquish their "right" to eat food sacrificed to idols, or to enjoy privileges which thereby may bring destructive effects upon others just as Paul, as slave of Christ, forgoes some of his own "rights" for the sake of the Christian community *as a whole.*

It would be unwise to base any theology of "rewards" on a use of μισθός which entails a wordplay and reevaluation of that in which μισθός consists. Paul's μισθός comes through his renunciation of μισθός: "reward" or "pay" is "first denied, then asserted . . . he repudiates 'reward' in the mercenary sense, to claim it in the larger, ethical [internal, conceptual] sense."[191]

The future tense θήσω may well carry the sense of *I intend to make the good news . . .* but since this translation would be overspecific we follow the customary *I make the good news. . . .* Similarly, **in the gospel** reflects the Greek construction (with NRSV, AV/KJV), which we reproduce in order to avoid foreclosing either of two more explicit meanings which are both possible: *in preaching it* (NIV) or *which the gospel allows me* (NJB; cf. REB).

c. *"Everything for the Gospel": Paul's Own Strategy and Example in Sharper Focus (9:19-23)*

(19) Free is what I am — no slave to any human person — yet I put myself into slavery to every human person, in order to win all the more of them. (20) To the Jews I made myself as a Jew to win the Jews; to those under the law as one under the law, although I myself am not under the law, in order to win those under the law. (21) To those outside the law, as one outside the law, even though I am not outside God's law but subject to the law of Christ, in order to win those who are outside the law. (22) To the "weak" I made myself weak in order to win the weak. To them all I have become everything in turn so that through every possible means I may bring some to salvation. (23) Now all this I do on account of the nature of the gospel in order that I may have a joint share in it.

These verses form a rhetorical climax to the argument in 9:1-18, and confirm that ch. 9 is no mere digression on the subject of apostleship as such. Whereas

---

190. Martin, *Slavery as Salvation,* 120 and 121.

191. Findlay, *Expositor's Greek Testament,* 2:853. "Thus his 'reward,' as his 'boast,' is to be found in the 'weakness' of working with his own hands so as not to hinder the forward progress of the gospel" (Fee, *First Epistle,* 421). See further Senft, *La Première Épitre,* 122.

vv. 1-18 focus largely on the strategy and personal example of foregoing the "right" to substance, however, these verses show that standing in solidarity with "the other," as against autonomy or self-affirmation, lies at the heart of the gospel. In particular, concern for the diversity of those who are "the weak" constitutes a profound pastoral and missionary strategy which is not built on pragmatic "success" but on the nature of the gospel (v. 23) in which Paul has a part. As Käsemann points out, the whole of this section continues "this interweaving of person and content" which is found especially in vv. 14-18: "Paul is illustrating (over against the enthusiasts) by his personal renunciation the principle that love sets bounds to Christian freedom."[192]

Further research literature sheds considerable light on this section. We refer below once again to Margaret Mitchell's research as well as to Robert Jewett's *Christian Tolerance.* Issues of Paul's consistency are raised by P. Richardson and D. Carson, among others, while these verses reopen the discussion initiated by Theissen about "the weak" as the socially vulnerable who were inhibited by socioeconomic dependency and a sense of insecurity. However, one of the most significant monographs to which we refer in this chapter is Clarence Glad's *Paul and Philodemus.*[193] Glad argues that in 9:19-23 Paul combines two distinct aspects of strategy and stance. First Paul draws on a relatively familiar tradition in the Graeco-Roman world in which educators (or "wise people") recognize the need for flexible and adaptive approaches to others in the light of human diversity; second, he challenges "the strong" at Corinth to act like "the wise" they claim to be, and to allow attentiveness to "the weak" and to others in diverse situations of culture, religion, and status to override their own concerns for self-affirmation and freedom.[194] This reconstruction brings to light a generally insufficiently noticed background and sharpens the issue, but it does not detract from Paul's central mainspring that it is the nature of the gospel which leads to the principles formulated in 9:19-23.

Supplementary Bibliography on 9:19-23
(Additional to Works Cited Above under 9:1-3 and 4-23)

Barton, S. E., "All Things to All People — Paul and the Law in the Light of 1 Cor 9:19-23," in J. D. G. Dunn (ed.), *Paul and the Mosaic Law: The Third Durham-Tübingen Research Symposium,* WUNT 89 (Tübingen: Mohr, 1996).

Black, D. A., "A Note on 'the Weak' in 1 Cor 9:22," *Bib* 64 (1983): 240-42.

Bornkamm, G., "The Missionary Stance of Paul in 1 Cor 9 and in Acts," in L. E. Keck and J. L. Martin (eds.), *Studies in Luke-Acts* (London: SPCK, 1968), 194-207.

Carson, D. A., "Pauline Inconsistency: Reflections on 1 Cor 9:19-23 and Gal 2:11-14," *Churchman* 100 (1986): 6-45.

192. Käsemann, "A Pauline Version of 'Amor Fati,'" in his *NT Questions of Today,* 217 and 218; cf. 217-35.

193. Glad, *Paul and Philodemus: Adaptability in Epicurean and Early Christian Psychagogy.*

194. Ibid., 43-45 and throughout.

Chadwick, H., "All Things to All Men" (1 Cor 9:22)," *NTS* 1 (1955): 261-75.

Daube, D., "κερδαίνω as a Missionary Term," *HTR* 40 (1947): 109-20.

Dodd, C. H., "Ἔννομος Χριστοῦ," in J. Sevenster and W. C. van Unnik (eds.), *Studia Paulina in Honorem Johannis de Zwaan* (Haarlem: Bohn, 1953), 96-110.

Dunn, J. D. G. (ed.), *Paul and the Mosaic Law* (Tübingen: Mohr, 1996).

Glad, C. E., *Paul and Philodemus: Adaptability in Epicurean and Early Christian Psychagogy,* NovTSup 81 (Leiden: Brill, 1995), 43-45, 240-77.

Gooch, P. W., "For and Against Accommodation: 1 Cor 9:19-23," in his *Partial Knowledge* (cited above), 124-41.

Jewett, R., *Christian Tolerance: Paul's Message to the Modern Church* (Philadelphia: Fortress 1982), 33, 49-51.

Käsemann, E., "A Pauline Verson of 'Amor Fati,'" in his *NT Questions of Today* (London: SCM, 1969), 217-35.

Lodge, J. G., "All Things to All: Paul's Pastoral Strategy," *Chicago Studies* 24 (1985): 291-306.

Mitchell, M. M., *Paul and the Rhetoric of Reconciliation* (cited above), 343-49.

Neller, K. V., "1 Cor 9:19-23: A Model for Those Who Seek to Win Souls," *ResQ* 29 (1987): 129-42.

Richardson, P., "Pauline Inconsistency in 1 Cor 9:19-23 and Gal 2:11-14," *NTS* 26 (1980): 347-62.

———, and P. W. Gooch, "Accommodation Ethics," *TynBul* 29 (1978): 89-142.

Roloff, J., *Apostolat–Verkündigung–Kirche,* (cited above), 90-93.

Saillard, M., "Paul, êvangêliste. 1 Cor 9:16-19, 22-23," *ASeign* 36 (1974): 34-37.

Theissen, G., "The Strong and the Weak," in his *Social Setting of Pauline Christianity,* (cited above), 121-43.

Theobald, M., "'Allen bin ich alles geworden . . .' (1 Kor 9:22b). Paulus und das Problem der Inkulturation des Glaubens," *TQ* 176 (1996): 1-6.

Wilckens, U., "Zur Entwicklung des paulinischen Gesetzesverständnis," *NTS* 28 (1982): 154-90.

19 Any translation needs to signal the emphatic place of the first word in the Greek, the adjective ἐλεύθερος, **free**, not least since this is a catchword in sociopolitical and religious aspirations and concerns about status at Corinth. Paul signals the conclusion of vv. 1-18 by placing **free** as the first emphatic word of vv. 19-23. It strikes the keynote for the coda. The present participle ὤν, *being,* is usually translated as a concessive clause (*though I was not a slave,* NJB; *though I am free,* NRSV). We have used the finite verb **I am** with ἐκ πάντων as the parenthetical explication — **no slave to any human person**, followed by a contrastive **yet**. The participle leaves open how we construe best the contrastive force.[195] Since ἐλεύθερος is so strongly emphatic, we may retain the positive term **free** (with almost all VSS) to denote the Corinthian catchword taken up by Paul, but also combine it with NJB's subtle use of the negative *though I was not a slave to any human being, I put myself in slavery to all people,* since this picks up the theme expounded in Martin's *Slavery as Salvation* better than most

195. Cf. REB's *I am free and own no master; but. . . .*

other VSS. Paul very subtly but also emphatically presses in what precise sense Christian believers and Christian leaders are **free** and in what sense voluntary **slavery** performs a wholesome, even essential, saving purpose in Christ-like obedience and love for the other.

I put myself into slavery translates ἐμαυτὸν ἐδούλωσα, followed by the ἵνα of purpose governing κερδήσω. The VSS vary in how they render τοὺς πλείονας: *as many as I could* (NJB); *as many as possible* (REB, NIV); or *more of them* (NRSV). The definite article has the effect of transposing what is strictly the *comparative* form of πολύς, *much* (occasionally, but rarely used in place of the superlative πλεῖστος, *most*), to denote **all the more**.[196] Thus NJB, REB, and NIV are strictly more correct than NRSV, although our translation **all the more** seeks to convey the meaning while retaining the strict form kept by the Greek and the NRSV. Paul explicates his principles of "nothing to hinder the path for the gospel" by using the positive image of doing everything he can, including **putting** himself **into slavery** in a certain sense (i.e., certainly restricting his own options) in order to *gain* or to **win** (κερδαίνω) **all the more** people for the gospel of Christ. The missionary background of *winning* disciples for Jesus Christ occurs in Matt 18:15, although it derives from the commercial background *of gaining an asset* or *making a profit*. Daube shows that it was probably a technical term for "winning a proselyte" in Judaism, reflecting the Hebrew נשכר (*niskar,* the Niphal of *sakar, to hire, to gain*).[197] In the light of the metaphor of building materials and survival (1 Cor 3:12-15), the permanent and eternal effects of this "gain" enhance Paul's notion of what is at issue in voluntary restraint for the greater good. He uses κερδαίνω several times in vv. 20-22.

20 UBS 4th ed. rightly regards μὴ ὢν αὐτὸς ὑπὸ νόμον as authentic, with the support of ℵ, 𝔭[46], A, B, C, D*, F, G, 33, Vulgate, Syriac, Coptic, Chrysostom, Ambrosiaster, and some VSS of Origen MSS. It is omitted by D[2], Byzantine texts, and other VSS of Origen. As Metzger argues, it is easy to see how it "probably fell out by accident in transcription, the eye of the copyist passing from ὑπὸ νόμον to ὑπὸ νόμον."[198]

Although normally we offer a distinctive translation, it seems impossible to improve on NJB here. While ἐγενόμην strictly means *I became* (NRSV, AV/KJV), **I made myself** (NJB, NIV) provides the nuance suggested by the immediate context of argument. On the other hand, *I behaved like* (REB) overtranslates the

196. Findlay, *Expositor's Greek Testament,* 2:853, "'the more' not 'the greater part' (as in 10:5) . . . but 'so much more' than could otherwise be gained (cf. 2 Cor 4:15)." See further BAGD, 689, and Schrage, *Der erste Brief,* 2:339-40, who acknowledges that the precise meaning is not certain here.

197. D. Daube, "κερδαίνω as a Missionary Term," *HTR* 40 (1947): 109-20; BAGD, 429; *EDNT,* 2:283-84; Schrage, *Der erste Brief,* 2:339.

198. Metzger, *Textual Commentary,* 2d ed., 493. *The Textus Receptus* omitted the clause, and, as Héring observes, on both textual and exegetical grounds "it is hard to see how" this could occur (*First Epistle,* 82). Yet Edwards (*First Epistle,* 238) follows Lachmann, Tischendorf, Westcott, and Hort in regarding the clause as an insertion.

verb in too specific a way since, as Mitchell insists, it includes *strategy* as well as behavior.[199] Schrage observes that in v. 20a, Paul specifies and illustrates in parallel propositions the principle πᾶσιν δουλοῦν ἑαυτόν.[200] The substance of Paul's point amounts to what the REB translation suggests, i.e., "in his relation to the Jews, whom he sought to convert, he [Paul] behaved in Jewish fashion observing, e.g., Jewish customs (Acts 16:3; 21:26)."[201] Paul is not alluding to behavior among Jewish Christians, but the Jews whom he is seeking **to win**. The phrase τοῖς ὑπὸ νόμον simply explicates the reference to **the Jews**, although Theodoret interprets it to mean Jewish Christians and Theodore of Mopsuestia understands the phrase to refer to Jewish proselytes.[202] Findlay and Heinrici follow Theodore in regarding the phrase to those under the law as a description which "enlarges the category τοῖς Ἰουδαίοις by including circumcised proselytes."[203] Blomberg includes proselytes and "God fearers."[204] The phrases ὡς Ἰουδαῖος and ὡς ὑπὸ νόμον are especially revealing of Paul's theology of the new creation: "Since Paul was in fact a Jew, this formulation shows how radically he conceives the claim that in Christ he is . . . in a position transcending all cultural allegiances" (cf. Gal 2:15; 3:28; and 1 Cor 12:13).[205]

This passage is widely known as expounding a principle of missionary "accommodation and flexibility" on the part of those who proclaim the message.[206] As we should expect, Robert Jewett and Margaret Mitchell found in these verses a rich source for Paul's concept of "tolerance" (Jewett) and "reconciliation" (Mitchell).[207] Paul's argument about **winning** or "gaining" **all the more** converts coheres precisely with Mitchell's identification of a rhetorical appeal to "advantage": "Paul expounds upon the advantage to be gained from this kind of self-renunciation, and in so doing redefines the μισθός and the κέρδος . . . another . . . proof for the redefinition of τὸ συμφέρον, the advantageous course of action to follow. The common advantage (that of 'the all', 'the many', 9:19, 22) . . . not merely one's own advantage . . . gives the specific application of the exemplary argument to the Corinthian situation."[208] "Paul is not concerned for the Corinthians likewise to work for their living, but rather to be accommodating of one another in all things, but especially in regard to meat-eating practices."[209]

199. M. M. Mitchell, *Paul and the Rhetoric of Reconciliation*, 248, n. 344.

200. Schrage, *Der erste Brief*, 2:340.

201. Meyer, *First Epistle*, 1:271.

202. Theodoret, in Migne, *PG*, 82:297; Theodore in Staab, *Pauluskommentare*, 184.

203. Findlay, *Expositor's Greek Testament*, 2:854, partly by appeal to Gal 5:1-3; Heinrici, *Das erste Sendschreiben*, 250, n. 4.

204. Blomberg, *I Cor*, 184. However, God fearers did not usually embrace all the demands of the law (e.g., circumcision).

205. Hays, *First Cor*, 153. The same point is made in Schrage, *Der erste Brief*, 2:340-41.

206. Schrage, *Der erste Brief*, 2:341.

207. R. Jewett, *Christian Tolerance: Paul's Message to the Modern Church* (Philadelphia: Fortress, 1982), 33, 49-51; M. M. Mitchell, *Paul and the Rhetoric of Reconciliation*, 243-49.

208. Mitchell, *Paul and the Rhetoric of Reconciliation*, 248.

209. Ibid.

Weiss and especially Henry Chadwick relate this missionary strategy to Paul's handling of pastoral situations within the church, where the same need to gain the assent and respect of diverse groups in diverse theological and cultural situations also applies.[210] Both Weiss and Chadwick detect a parallel attempt to stand alongside opposing or diverse groups in Paul's affirmation of both marriage and celibacy in ch. 7. Mitchell, however, considers that this "rhetoric of reconciliation" offers more than "apologetic" (Chadwick) or pastoral strategy (Weiss) but a specific rhetorical strategy based on pastoral and missionary strategy in the course of addressing factionalism. It is more than *behavioral* accommodation.[211]

On the other hand, it is not less than this, as if to imply that these verses applied only to church factions or to large pastoral or missionary strategy. F. F. Bruce observes how closely they also bear on issues of individual Christian conduct. On one side, Paul can accommodate his behaviour to the sensitivities of the Jews (and thereby to issues which face Christians who work and witness among them) by taking part in the discharge of a Nazirite vow in the Temple (Acts 21:23ff.). "If he no longer felt any necessity to comply with Jewish regulations and ceremonies as matters of divine obligation, he did not go to the other extreme and regard these things as forbidden to a Christian. . . ."[212] This Pauline "freedom" lies at the heart of Bruce's expositions of Paul's life and thought.[213] Almost needless to say, Martin Luther repeats Paul's principle in his work *Concerning Christian Liberty:* "a Christian man is the most free lord of all, and subject to none; a Christian man is the most dutiful servant of all, and subject to everyone. . . ."[214]

21 **To those outside the law** translates τοῖς ἀνόμοις, which in other contexts could mean to the *unjust, unrighteous,* or *godless* (cf. Acts 2:23; 3 Macc 6:9; Ezek 18:24 LXX; Luke 22:37) or to the *lawless* or *outlaw* (2 Thess 2:8; νόμος with alpha privative), but clearly in this context denotes Gentiles who are **outside** the revealed **law** of the OT and Judaism (with NRSV, REB, NJB; cf. *to those not having the law,* NIV).[215] The semantic contrast is with **to those under the law** (v. 20). The phrase ἔννομος Χριστοῦ, **subject to the law of Christ**, provides the title for a well-known article on 1 Cor 9:19-22 by C. H.

210. Weiss, *Der erste Korintherbrief,* 242-46; *Earliest Christianity,* 1:329, 2:416-21, esp. 418; H. Chadwick, "All Things to All Men (1 Cor 9:22)," *NTS* 1 (1955): 261-75.

211. Hence Mitchell cannot fully endorse P. Richardson and P. W. Gooch, "Accommodation Ethics," *TynBul* 29 (1978): 89-142.

212. Bruce, *1 and 2 Cor,* 86-87.

213. F. F. Bruce, *Paul: Apostle of the Free Spirit* (Exeter: Paternoster, 1977), 267-73 (on Corinth) and throughout, esp. 458-63, which portray Paul's generosity of spirit and largeness of heart. (This Manchester lecture material is published by Eerdmans under the title *Paul: Apostle of the Heart Set Free.*)

214. Luther, *Concerning Christian Liberty,* in H. Wace and C. A. Buchheim (eds.), *Luther's Primary Works* (London: Murray, 1883), 104; also rpt. in E. G. Rupp and B. Drewery (eds.), *Martin Luther: Documents* (London: Arnold, 1970), 50.

215. Cf. BAGD, 72.

Dodd, and its use by Paul prompts Dodd to reflect further on the relation between ὡς ἄνομος, **as one outside the law**, and ἔννομος.[216] Dodd calls attention to "the special *nuance* of ἄνομος in the mouth of a Jew . . . well illustrated by Acts 2:23. . . ."[217] As he dictates, however, Paul is troubled that to apply ἄνομος to himself "might very well be gravely misunderstood by readers to whom the equivalence of νόμος and Torah was by no means familiar. He must guard his statement carefully against . . . misunderstanding."[218] Hence he states that he is **not outside God's law**. The notion that not to be **under the law** is to be godless or ungovernable presupposes "an unwarranted identity of the Torah as the ultimate law of God. A man may be free from the Torah and yet be loyal to the law of God as it is represented or expressed in the law of Christ."[219] Thus Paul remains **subject to the law of Christ**. Indeed, Dodd points out, 9:14 has already alluded to an "ordinance" of Christ, just as Paul does in 7:10-11.[220] Bruce further relates this to 11:1, where the example of Christ is to be seen as paradigmatic for Christian conduct.[221] On the other hand, as Dodd, Bruce, Heinrici, and Schrage also observe, **the law of Christ** should not be restricted to any specific body of traditional sayings of Jesus. Christians stand under the direction of the gospel as that which witnesses to Christ in a broader and more comprehensive sense (cf. Gal 6:2).

Paul does not understand ὡς ἄνομος to sanction antinomian calls for "autonomy." Nor does it encourage the Marcionite heresy in understanding the OT. Conzelmann corrects what might become an undue overpressing of Dodd's argument when he observes: "His [Paul's] intention is not to suggest that idea of a 'new' law. . . . Cf. the rejection of antinomianism in Rom 7:7ff."[222] The comparison with Romans is also discussed by Barrett, who describes this passage as "one of the most difficult sentences in the epistle, and also one of the most important."[223] Barrett goes so far as to translate ἔννομος as *under legal obligation to Christ*. Paul attacks not the *gift* of the law, which he values as holy and good (Rom 7:12) but its misuse, especially as a means of establishing a false security which distracts people from God's grace in Christ. Whatever the crosscurrents of debate between more traditional supposedly "Lutheran" understandings of Paul on the law and the so-called post-Sanders "new" look, Hays pinpoints the practical issue: "being free from the Law does not mean that Paul runs wild with self-indulgence — a word pointedly spoken to the Corinthians who are

216. C. H. Dodd, "ἔννομος Χριστοῦ," in J. Sevenster and W. C. van Unnik (eds.), *Studia Paulina in Honorem Johannis de Zwaan* (Haarlem: Bohm, 1953), 96-110.
217. Ibid., 997, n. 1.
218. Ibid., 97.
219. Ibid., 99. As Schrage points out, Heinrici virtually anticipates Dodd's argument in 1880: Heinrici, *Das erste Sendschreiben*, 285; Schrage, *Der erste Brief*, 2:345, n. 367.
220. Dodd, "ἔννομος Χριστοῦ," in Sevenster and van Unnik (eds.), *Studia Paulina*, 103-8.
221. Bruce, *1 and 2 Cor*, 88.
222. Conzelmann, *1 Cor*, 161 and 161, n. 26.
223. Barrett, *First Epistle*, 212; cf. 212-15.

proclaiming 'I am free to do anything.' Instead, he lives with a powerful sense of obligation to God, defined now by his relationship to Christ."[224]

This example of strategy is especially for the apostle who consciously regarded his apostolic vocation as having explicit reference "from before my birth . . . to proclaim him [Christ] to the Gentiles (τοῖς ἔθνεσιν, Gal 1:15, 16; also Rom 1:6, "We received grace and apostleship to call people from all the Gentiles). Roloff discusses the notion of a "double" apostleship in which Peter, James, and John are associated with apostleship to the Jews, and Paul and his apostolic co-worker with apostleship to the Gentiles (Gal 2:9; cf. also Acts 18:6).[225] This is all the more remarkable in the light of Paul's strict Jewish pharisaic-rabbinic training (Gal 1:13-15; Phil 3:5-7). The need for restraint, sensitivity, and a measure of accommodation may be demanded by a given calling, sometimes even contrary to a person's own cultural background and traditions. Paul not only lived this out, but also avoided the "inverted" snobbery or "twice-born" reactive arrogance which undervalues the very traditions which that person has been called to relativize.[226]

22 It is tempting to translate τοῖς ἀσθενέσιν as *to the overscrupulous* or *to those who feel insecure* on the basis of the emerging meaning of **the weak** as a technical term in the earlier part of this topic of self-restraint in 8:7, 9, 10. However, to translate it other than in the general sense **weak** risks imposing our exegesis (however accurate) onto the translation and forecloses further possible nuances. NRSV, NIV, REB, and NJB also render **to the weak**. Moreover, if **the weak** in 8:7-10 means *those who feel insecure* (see above on those verses), Paul can hardly be saying that he behaves as if he felt ambivalent about his identity, although on the specific matter of meat eating he may well be warning "the strong" that he is about to side with the overscrupulous (if they cannot overcome their scruples). At the same time we must recall Theissen's point that **the weak** is a designation which derives from how "the strong" *perceive* the social relationship, *in addition to* denoting *an objective social contrast* between the *influential* and the *vulnerable*.[227] In this context **the weak** may mean those whose options for life and conduct were severely restricted because of their dependence on *the wishes of patrons, employers, or slave owners*.

If we consider the strong and the weak who are already Christian believers, many argue that the strong have a firm consciousness of authority and freedom, while the weak have an uneasy conscience, an ambivalent self-identity, or low self-esteem in relation to "high status" Christians. However, Paul is speaking here of **winning** converts (on κερδαίνω, see above under v. 20); he wishes to save some (τινὰς σώσω, i.e., bring some to salvation, with NJB). Hence these

---

224. Hays, *1 Cor,* 154. Cf. E. P. Sanders, *Paul, the Law and the Jewish People* (Philadelphia: Fortress, 1983), and for a recent discussion of approaches and textual material, J. D. G. Dunn, *The Theology of Paul* (Edinburgh: T. & T. Clark, 1998), 128-61.

225. J. Roloff, *Apostolat–Verkündigung–Kirche,* 90-93.

226. Hence the importance of Paul's careful observance of conventions (e.g., in letter forms and rhetoric) alongside his radical, creative call for freedom.

227. Theissen, "The Strong and the Weak at Corinth," in his *Social Setting,* 121-43.

are people who are most probably the vulnerable in sociopolitical terms, forced into dependency on patrons, owners, or employers, which makes decisive initiative or boldness a foreign habit of mind. *Paul behaves, and observes a strategy, which takes account of the inhibited, vulnerable, and dependent. In today's terms, he does not proclaim merely a "success" gospel for extrovert "winners." If these people are too scrupulous in their eagerness "to do the right thing," Paul stands with them.* **The weak** stand in contrast to those with "social power, influence, political status . . . ability or competence in a variety of areas" and by contrast have "low social standing" and crave for identity, recognition, and acceptance.[228] Paul's foregoing of his rights to a "professional" status by functioning as a religious rhetorician for a patron and toiling as an artisan demonstrate his solidarity with **the weak** both as a missionary and pastoral strategist and in Christlike behavior (cf. 11:1). The "Christlikeness" of "weakness" also appears in a different context in 1:25, 27 and 4:10, where it is associated with the cross. Schütz has little difficulty in relating the issue of apostolic "rights" in 9:3-12 and apostolic sensitivity in 9:19-23 to "boasting" in that which is weakness in 2 Corinthians 10–13, esp. 11:10–12:9.[229] "Paul sees his life as making transparent what the gospel tells about, the power and weakness of God acting in those events which constitute the beginning of the new creation . . . through the weakness and power of Christ's death and resurrection."[230]

The interpretation which the AV/KJV and RV phrase "all things to all men" (for τοῖς πᾶσιν γέγονα πάντα) needs to be understood strictly in terms of the exegesis of vv. 19-22a. The change from the aorist to the perfect signifies "the permanent result of his past action."[231] Whether or not this is described as "accommodation" emerges not in questions about terminology but in perceiving the specific content and nuances of these verses as explicated in the exegesis of these pages.[232] The NJB translation, *I accommodated myself to people in all kinds of different situations,* perhaps moves too far from the actual Greek in its valid endeavor to allow the exegetical context to control and qualify the meaning of γέγονα πάντα. However, we have adopted REB's **To them all I have become everything in turn** since this steers a proper middle course between too slavish a replication of the Greek pronouns and the clarification imposed genuinely by the context. The adverbial πάντως may mean here *at least* but more probably carries the meaning **through every possible means** within this context.[233] That there are limits to what we

228. Yeo, *Rhetorical Interaction,* 90; cf. Willis, *Idol Meat,* 92-96; Gardner, *Gifts of God,* 45; Gooch, "'Conscience' in 1 Cor 8 and 10," *NTS* 33 (1987): 244-54; and further literature cited above under 8:7-9.

229. J. H. Schütz, *Paul and the Anatomy of Apostolic Authority,* 232-48.

230. Ibid., 248.

231. Robertson and Plummer, *First Epistle,* 192.

232. Cf. Schrage, *Der erste Brief,* 2:347-48, including nn. 399-405.

233. BAGD, 609, propose either *at least* or *by all means* for 1 Cor 9:22; Schrage, *Der erste Brief,* 348.

should understand by "accommodation" is well argued by D. A. Carson in relation to Gal 2:1-14.[234]

23   Fee rightly comments that "all things for the sake of the gospel" identifies "the singular passion of his [Paul's] life" (διὰ τὸ εὐαγγέλιον, **on account of the gospel**).[235] However, Fee's discussion of whether Paul has as his purpose (ἵνα) to be a fellow participant (συγκοινωνός) in it means "his participation in the *work* of the gospel" (with Schütz) or "his sharing with them in its *benefits*" (Fee's italics) is perhaps less happy.[236] To be sure, NRSV and NIV adopt the latter: *that I may share in its blessings* (also approximately REB), while NJB implies the former in proposing *that I may share its benefits with others*. Fee admits, however, that superficially the purpose of "sharing in its *benefits*" may sound self-serving, and Collins rightly dismisses NRSV and this understanding as "foreign to the ideas that Paul expresses."[237] For once the restraint and literalism of the AV/KJV may serve us better: *that I might be a partaker thereof with you.* In our view (with Collins) the issue is neither that of bringing benefits to others (NJB), nor that of sharing in these benefits as a missionary-pastor (NRSV, NIV, REB, Fee). To stand alongside the Jew, the Gentile, the socially dependent and vulnerable, or to live and act in solidarity with every kind of person in every kind of situation is to have a **share** in **the nature of the gospel**, i.e., *to instantiate what the gospel is and how it operates.* The use of compounds here (συν-) "express[es] various forms of solidarity in Christian existence."[238]

Strangely Fee identified this point with reference to v. 18 but not here: "his own ministry becomes a living paradigm of the gospel itself."[239] Paul, like Jesus, both places himself in solidarity with those **under the law**, but also, like Jesus, experiences "the pattern of Christ's self-sacrificial death on a cross . . . [as] the normative pattern for his own existence," and stands in solidarity with those **outside the law**, in order **to bring them salvation** (vv. 20, 21, 22).[240] Paul's use of the adjective συγκοινωνός with the genitive for that in which he has a share denotes an intimate, organic, reproductive sharing which transcends the original commercial or business setting of being a *shareholder* in a company or a joint venture, i.e., a business partner. In Rom 11:17 the adjective denotes the common share of the rich, life-giving sap which permeates the whole olive tree including its newly grafted branches.[241] There is a parallel here with

234. D. A. Carson, "Pauline Inconsistency: Reflections on 1 Cor 9:19-23 and Gal 2:11-14," *Churchman* 100 (1986): 6-45.

235. Fee, *First Epistle,* 431-32.

236. Ibid., 432; cf. Schütz, *Paul and the Anatomy of Apostolic Authority,* 51-52.

237. Collins, *First Cor,* 356.

238. Ibid.

239. Fee, *First Epistle,* 421.

240. Hays, *First Cor,* 154. An illuminatory understanding of sharing *in solidarity with* Christ can be found in L. S. Thornton, *The Common Life in the Body of Christ* (London: Dacre Press, 1944), 34-187.

241. Unfortunately BAGD speak of *sharing the benefits* rather than *sharing the life* here; 774.

the organic life of the vine imagery in John 15:1-5, and also, as Schweitzer argues, with sharing solidarity with the Son of Man in the Synoptic Gospels (Mark 8:35, 38).[242] Schweitzer cites passage after passage which witnesses to this theme in Paul: the κοινωνία of Christ's sufferings which Paul shares (Phil 3:10-11); "putting on Christ" (Gal 3:27); "carrying about the having-died of Jesus that the life of Jesus may be also transparent in our bodies" (i.e., in our everyday life in the public domain).[243] Believers are "members of Christ" (1 Cor 6:13-19). The στίγματα (Gal 6:17) are like the brands by which Christ's "slaves" are recognizable as his.[244]

Paul does **all** that he does to make transparent by his everyday life in the public domain the character of **the gospel** which he proclaims as the **proclamation of the cross** (1:18-25), which derives its character, and not simply its "benefits," from Christ himself. This is a fitting concluding summary for an argument which begins by alluding to his authentic **apostleship** and develops the theme that a voluntary renunciation of "rights" is part of the conceptual and practical grammar of what it is to live out an apostolic witness to Christ, whether in day-to-day lifestyle as an artisan or in pastoral and missionary strategy by standing alongside those whom he seeks to **win**. Paul's ultimate purpose is to be part of all that; **to have a joint share in it**.[245]

d. A Corroborative Example from Graeco-Roman Competitive Pursuits: The Need for Self-Control (9:24-27)

(24) Are you not aware that while all of the runners in a stadium take part in the race, it is only one of them who receives the prize? Run with this approach, to make the prize yours. (25) Everyone who enters as a combatant exercises self-control in everything: athletes, however, do it in order to win a crown that fades and disintegrates; but we, in our case, to win that which will never fade away. (26) I, for my part, therefore, am so running, as one not distracted from keeping an eye clearly on the goal. I am not like one who shadowboxes into empty air. (27) My day-to-day life as a whole I treat roughly, and make it strictly serve my purposes, lest, after preaching to others, I find myself not proven to stand the test.

Paul's appeal to the principle of forbearance, or to voluntary renunciation of rights or entitlements, receives explication through three categories of examples. In 9:1-23 Paul appeals to his own personal example (cf. 11:1), although

---

242. A. Schweitzer, *The Mysticism of Paul the Apostle* (Eng. trans., London: Black, 1931), 106, 107.

243. Ibid., 121, 122, 126.

244. Ibid., 143; cf. 141-76.

245. Schrage, *Der erste Brief*, 2:348-50, also emphasizes that the "power" of the gospel operates in this way. Without the theme of 1:18-25 there is no ἐξουσία to discuss.

this appeal also embodies analogies and appeals to scripture and to the sayings of Jesus about ministerial maintenance. In 9:24-27 Paul appeals to an example drawn from Graeco-Roman competitive pursuits, namely, the Isthmian games. Straub, Pfitzner, and others agree that the central issue here is the need for ἐγκράτεια, **self-control**, or in some contexts *abstinence* (see below).

After establishing the recognizable need for ἐγκράτεια from GraecoRoman culture and recreation, Paul will turn in 10:1-13 to a third category of example, namely, scriptural warnings which arise from Israel's biblical history. The climactic statement that only one receives the prize has nothing to do with any theology of exclusivism or elitism, but serves as part of the analogical picture which provides the setting for the notion of the urgency and strength of motivation which leads the athlete to surrender lesser goods in order to attain the higher goal. Paul has just defined this highest goal as the gospel and all that the gospel embodies, represents, and brings about. To hinder this by selfindulgence or by standing on one's rights is to be like an athlete who allows distractions to undermine the whole purpose of entering for the race. Theories about the origin and background of Paul's imagery and its relation to Graeco-Roman religion and literature (e.g., by Broneer and Funke) are described below. What is clear is that the prestige and commercial benefit of the Isthmian games to which the analogies doubtless allude would be very familiar to the readers at Corinth.

Bibliography on 9:24-27

Bauernfeind, O., "τρέχω δρόμος," *TDNT*, 8:226-35.

Bowers, P., "Church and Mission in Paul," *JSNT* 44 (1991): 89-111.

Broneer, O., "The Apostle Paul and the Isthmian Games," *BA* 25 (1962): 2-31.

———, "The Isthmian Victory Crown," *AJA* 66 (1962): 259-63.

———, "Paul and the Pagan Cults at Isthmia," *HTR* 64 (1971): 169-87.

———, *Isthmia II: Topography and Architecture* (Princeton: American School of Classical Studies at Athens, 1973).

Dautzenberg, G., "ἀγών," *EDNT*, 1:25-27.

Ehrhardt, A., "An Unknown Orphic Writing in the Demosthenes Scholia and St Paul," *ZNW* 56 (1957): 101-10.

Funke, H., "Antisthenes bei Paulus," *Hermes* 98 (1970): 459-71.

Gale, H. M., *The Use of Analogy in the Letters of Paul* (Philadelphia: Westminster, 1964), 108-16.

Garrison, "Paul's Use of the Athlete Metaphor in 1 Cor 9," *SR* 22 (1993): 209-17.

Glad, C. G., *Paul and Philodemus: Adaptability in Epicurean and Early Christian Psychagogy*, NovTSup 16 (Leiden: Brill, 1995), 247-49 and 281-85.

Grundmann, W., "στέφανος," *TDNT*, 7:615-36.

Merk, O., *Handeln aus Glauben*, 127-29.

Murphy-O'Connor, J., *St Paul's Corinth*, 14-17, 99, and 116-19.

Papathomas, A., "Das agonistische Motif 1 Kor 9:24ff. im Spiegel zeitgenössischer dokumentarischer Quellen," *NTS* 43 (1997): 223-41.

Pfitzner, V. C., *Paul and the Agon Motif*, NovTSup 16 (Leiden: Brill, 1967), 23-35 and esp. 76-109.

Straub, W., *Die Bildersprache des Apostels Paulus* (Tübingen: Mohr, 1937), 89-91.

24 Once again Paul uses οὐκ οἴδατε, *do you not know, are you not aware,* as a rhetorical question which provokes the addressees to notice afresh what they know perfectly well if they take note or reflect. Although ἐν σταδίῳ may be translated **in a stadium** (more regularly) or *in a race,* it alludes to the **stadium** in which the pan-hellenic Isthmian games were held. The **stadium** would include not only foot races (οἱ ἐν σταδίῳ τρέχοντες . . . τρέχουσιν) but also athletic contests of other kinds (e.g., boxing). Murphy-O'Connor discusses the Isthmian games in detail, concluding: "Paul could not have been unaware of the Isthmian games, and was probably in Corinth when they took place; they were celebrated in the spring of AD 49 and 51. Athletic metaphors were a commonplace in the popular philosophy of the period . . . but it can hardly be coincidence that Paul's first sustained development of this theme occurs in a letter to the Corinthians (1 Cor 9:24-27)."[246]

The Isthmian Games were one of the four great pan-hellenic festivals, ranking second only to the Olympic Games and above those of Delphi and Nemea.[247] The prestige of the Games was enhanced by a tradition which went back to the sixth century BC, and they took place every two years, up to 146 BC at Corinth (when the Romans laid Corinth waste). Although for more than a century the Games were held at Sicyon, some six miles to the northwest, after the resettlement of 44 BC the influence of Corinth upon the Games steadily increased until it recovered their administration during the first decade of the first century. The inscriptions made available under the editorship of J. H. Kent provide evidence of financial sponsorship of the Games, including the renovation of buildings and the provision of banquets "for all the inhabitants of the colony" by a Corinthian patron.[248] Both Murphy-O'Connor and Broneer call attention, in the other direction, to the substantial revenue that accrued to the Corinthian tradespeople and entrepreneurs from the huge crowds who stayed in the city and area for the duration of the games every alternate spring. Broneer discusses the archaeological remains of the site at Isthmia, which still offer fascinating details for the modern writer (e.g., the special system of starting the race (the device called *balbides*), the patronage in honor of Poseidon, and implications for a large commercial income for Corinthian businessmen.[249]

The fame of the Isthmian Games is well attested in Greek literature and philosophy. Plutarch discusses the plant material used for the crown or garland

246. Murphy-O'Connor, *St. Paul's Corinth,* 16-17.
247. Ibid., 14; cf. also the various research contributions of Oscar Broneer cited in the bibliography above.
248. J. H. Kent, *Corinth,* VIII/3: *The Inscriptions, 1926-50* (Princeton: American School of Classical Studies at Athens, 1966), 70.
249. Broneer, "The Apostle Paul and the Isthmian Games," *BA* 25 (1962): 2-31. The opportunity to view this site is not to be missed. Cf. also Murphy-O'Connor, *St. Paul's Corinth,* 16-17.

at the games.[250] An account of this biennial celebration and orations is found in Aelius Aristides, *Ovations* 46.20-31, in the third quarter of the second century AD.[251] H. Funke cites the Cynic diatribe traditionally ascribed to Dio of Prusa but in Funke's view to be attributed to Antisthenes as shedding light on Paul's use of the imagery drawn from the Games.[252] The number and types of contest were increased in the era of Tiberius (AD 14-37), and this makes problematic Conzelmann's claim that the reference here to only **one** runner gaining a prize is both moralistic and "out of place."[253] Only a misunderstanding of the function of analogy, or a confusion between analogy and allegory, could suggest that the notion of **one . . . prize** is problematic in terms of *theology*. Papathomas cites a wealth of material from papyri and inscriptions concerning the contemporary background of Paul's metaphor of the athletic contest, the winning of the crown (στέφανος) or prize (τὸ βραβεῖον), and related data and themes.[254]

Pfitzner and Gale discuss more carefully in what specific respect the analogy reflected by οὕτως τρέχετε . . . applies directly. Pfitzner rightly insists that most of the details of the image of v. 24 are to "*set the stage for the theme of* ἐγκράτεια, which follows. All the endeavors of the athlete are in vain if he has not trained his body and abstained from all that may in any way harm his physical condition" (his italics).[255] Gale similarly insists: "It is clearly apparent that Paul does not intend the picture to be applied in all respects. Even the fact that is explicitly mentioned, that 'only one receives the prize,' can have no relevance here, for the reward or prize . . . is not thought by him [Paul] to be given only to 'one.'"[256] Even the intensity of effort demanded of the athlete to **make the prize yours** (ἵνα καταλάβητε) belongs to the stage setting of the picture: an athlete goes through anything, both effort and abstinence, to win, because he or she has an eye on the ultimate goal.[257]

Can the Corinthians, then, not exercise due ἐγκράτεια, **self-control** or *abstinence,* when what is at stake is not a garland made from vegetation, or even the acclaim of the crowd, but "the brother or sister for whom Christ died" (8:11)? This verse does not imply a theology of "Christian struggle," other than struggle for self-mastery to forego indulgence of "rights." We must not confuse the content *(Sachhälfte)* with the imagery *(Bildhälfte).*[258] Hence, although οὕτως strictly means only *thus, so,* or *in this way* (adverbial form of οὗτος), we have translated it **with this approach** to avoid an understanding of οὕτως

---

250. Plutarch, *Quaestiones Conviviales,* 5.3.1-3 (675D-677B).

251. Cited in Murphy-O'Connor, *St. Paul's Corinth,* 115-19.

252. Funke, "Antisthenes bei Paulus," *Hermes* 98 (1970): 459-71.

253. Conzelmann, *1 Cor,* 162.

254. Papathomas, "Das agonistische Motiv 1 Kor 9:24ff im Spiegel zeitgenössischer dokumentarischer Quellen," *NTS* 43 (1997): 223-41, esp. 225-40.

255. Pfitzner, *Paul and the Agon Motif,* 87.

256. Gale, *The Use of Analogy in the Letters of Paul,* 109.

257. For the precise nuance of καταλαμβάνω as *win* or (better here) **make one's own**, see BAGD, 412-13.

258. Straub, *Die Bildersprache des apostels Paulus,* 90.

which Paul does not wish to convey.[259] Even Origen was so troubled about the possible theological force of the pictorial imagery that he resorted to explaining **it is only one . . . who receives the prize** on the ground that **one** denotes the single entity of the church as a corporate whole. However, the posthistory of the text moves beyond Paul's horizon as the patristic era develops, for from the second to the fourth centuries the "athletic contest" or "struggle" comes to be perceived increasingly as "the holy athletes" who "stood alone and naked" as martyrs for the faith.[260] This is not what Paul has in view in 9:24-27. As Eusebius witnesses, the particular resonance here is striving for the "crown" of martyrdom.[261] However, Basil the Great uses the "crown" imagery (v. 25) to return to the Pauline point about *renunciation, self-discipline,* and *self-control.*[262]

25 Many English VSS translate ὁ ἀγωνιζόμενος as *athlete* (NRSV, NJB) as against AV/KJV, *man that striveth for the mastery.* The meaning of the deponent verb ἀγωνίζομαι, however, stands somewhere between these two nuances. As BAGD assert, it denotes (i) literally or figuratively *engaging in a contest,* or (ii), in the context of weaponry, wrestling or boxing, *fighting* or *struggling,* as well as (iii) a more general notion of *exerting oneself.*[263] The major specialist study on the term by Pfitzner, which has not yet been surpassed in judicious research into the background and exegesis, traces the background of the word in competitive contexts of rivalry and sports as a metaphor in moral philosophy in Plato, Aristotle, the Stoics, Cynic philosophy, the mystery religions, Philo, Josephus, and the Pseudepigrapha.[264] Pfitzner rejects the earlier research which seeks to argue for Paul's use of ἀγών and ἀγωνίζομαι as denoting "the Christian's moral task."[265] Such a view rests on ignoring the eschatological and soteriological framework within which Paul uses the term.[266] E. Stauffer, e.g., pays too much attention to the patristic posthistory of the text, which relates the issue more often to martyrdom.[267] A. Ehrhardt also appeals to a second-century Orphic writing for a sense which is foreign to Paul.[268] Paul's meaning is more closely anticipated in Aristotle's moral philosophy. Aristotle uses the *analogy*

---

259. On the other hand we have not reduced the pictorial face in the translation of the image, e.g., the contrastive μέν . . . δέ . . . with εἷς leads us to propose, **it is only one of them who receives the prize**.

260. Eusebius, *Ecclesiastical History,* 8:7:2; cf. 2:3; 5:1:5, 6; Origen, *Exhortation to Martyrdom,* 1:5.

261. Eusebius, 5:1:36: "their martyrdoms . . . plaiting a crown . . . noble athletes having endured a manifold strife and conquered, should receive the crown. . . ."

262. Basil, *Ad Adulescentes,* 6 (Migne, *PG,* 31:580B; as emphasized by Schrage, *Der erste Brief,* 2:366-67.

263. BAGD, 15; cf. *2 Clement* 7:1; Polybius, 1.45.9; 2 Macc 8:16; Col 1:29.

264. Pfitzner, *Paul and the Agon Motif,* 1-75. Pfitzner also reviews the history of earlier research.

265. Ibid., 7.

266. Ibid., 10-11.

267. Stauffer, "ἀγών," *TDNT,* 1:134-41.

268. Ehrhardt, *ZNW* 56 (1957): 101-10 (cited in full above).

of the trained runner or wrestler who avoids immoderate excess; this serves to establish Aristotle's well-known moral philosophy of "the mean" (τὸ μέσον).[269] Moderation, not struggle, is the "point" of the allusion: ὑπερβολή (excess) is to be avoided.[270]

The popularity of the athletic metaphor as a tool in moral discourse flourishes in Epictetus, Seneca, Plutarch, and Marcus Aurelius. Epictetus, a near contemporary of Paul, offers a close parallel to Paul's contrast between the relative futility of athletic success by comparison with moral character.[271] In Seneca (also contemporary to Paul) the form in which the "struggle" is perceived is that of restraint from indulgence and becoming victim to one's passions (i.e., attaining ἀταραξία).[272] Seneca compares the self-discipline of the present with the "greater good" of the final goal *(summum bonum)*.[273] Seneca's emphasis in his use of athletic imagery remains always on the "greater good," not upon competition or competitive struggle. Moreover, this is precisely the emphasis found in Paul's third near-contemporary, Philo. As Pfitzner observes, it "becomes part of Philo's stock vocabulary in picturing the *self-control and renunciation,* practice, toil . . . in the Agon for virtue" (my italics).[274] Allusions in Philo are too numerous to mention.[275]

All of this contributes to the main point that **everyone who enters as a combatant exercises self-control** (ἐγρατεύεται) **in everything** (πάντα, accusative of respect).[276] As Pfitzner notes, "πάντα ἐγκρατεύεται in v. 25 directly takes up the catchword sounded in vv. 12b, 19 and 22b-23 and provides an illustration of the Apostle's principal [sic]: *everything* for the sake of the Gospel — including the right use of his liberty in the renunciation of his rights" (his italics and spelling).[277]

The stage has been well and truly set for the subsidiary point, which is more than part of the image or *Bildhälfte,* namely, that the athlete gives up **everything to win a crown** (στέφανον) **that fades** (φθαρτόν). There is strong evidence that at the Isthmian Games the **crown** or *garland* given to the winner was made first from plastered pine leaves, although perhaps later from "celery."[278] Paul uses the cognate noun ἐν φθορᾷ in 1 Cor 15:42 (cf. also 15:53) to describe

269. Aristotle, *Nichomachean Ethics,* 2.2 (1104A); cf. 5 (1106B).

270. Ibid., 6.1 (1138B); 3.12 (1119B).

271. Epictetus, *Dissertations* 4.4.11-13.

272. Seneca, *De Otio* 6.2; 94.45; cf. M. Aurelius, 3.3.

273. Seneca, *De Vita Beata* 9.3; cf. *Epistulae* 17.1.

274. Pfitzner, *Paul and the Agon Motif,* 40.

275. For example, Philo, *De Specialibus Legibus* 4.99 (ἐγκράτεια) 101; *De Congressu Quaerendae Eruditionis Gratia* 108; *De Migratione Abrahami* 200; *De Vita Mosis* 1.48; et al.

276. On ἐγκρατεύομαι and ἐγκράτεια, see BAGD, 216, and the numerous references in Philo and others cited and discussed by Pfitzner, *Paul and the Agon Motif,* and Schrage, *Der erste Brief,* 2·364-68.

277. Pfitzner, *Paul and the Agon Motif,* 87-88.

278. Plutarch, *Quaestiones Conviviales* 5.3.1 (675 D). See further W. Grundmann, *TDNT,* 7: 615-36; Murphy-O'Connor, *St. Paul's Corinth,* 95 and 99.

the mode of being or σῶμα which decays, in contrast to resurrection ἐν ἀφθαρσίᾳ. The terms φθορά and φθαρτός are themselves cognates of the verb φθείρω, *to destroy, to corrupt* (in the LXX used to translate Heb. הבל *(ch-b-l)*, *emptiness, nothing,* and thus φθαρτός vividly denotes **that which fades and disintegrates**, describing how pine leaves suffer decay and destruction. The alpha privative describes the crown **which will never fade away**. As we noted above, Basil picks up this contrast to make Paul's point in later patristic thought (see under v. 24). The ἡμεῖς δέ occupies an emphatic position of contrast with ἐκεῖνοι μέν, and hence we translate **athletes, however . . . ; but we in our case**. Paul stresses the qualitative differences between the two situations in which people are called to stake **everything**, and invites his readers to draw their own inferences from the comparison.

The tradition of a **crown** of victory stemming from the Greek city-states should be distinguished from a **crown** of royalty in the tradition of monarchies and the kingship of Israel and the kingdom of God or Christ. The widespread NT use of the **crown** for believers (e.g., 1 Pet 5:4; Jas 1:12; 2 Tim 4:8; Rev 2:10) is more likely to signify the **crown** of victory than of that of royalty, although sometimes sharing in the reign of Christ is in view. The four allusions just cited are to *a crown of righteousness,* a *crown of glory* or a *crown of life,* which reflect the contrast in 1 Cor 9:25 between a fading and an enduring crown of victory. The notion of *casting crowns before God* (Rev 4:10) occurs in Eusebius's description of the victory of the martyr who (as in Revelation) wins victory by preferring to die than to renounce the Lord (cited above). The contrast between the transitory crown of the athlete and the lasting crown of mature selfhood is paralleled not only in 1 Pet 5:4, but, as we have noted, in Seneca and Epictetus.[279]

26 ἐγὼ τοίνυν οὕτως τρέχω moves from principle or third-person example to Paul himself, and the Greek construction and use of pronouns and connectives have the force of **I, for my part, therefore, am so running** . . . with an emphatic use of ἐγώ and οὕτως enhanced by τοίνυν, *at any rate, for* **my part**. Weiss argues that to run with (or without) a clear goal (τρέχειν [οὐκ] ἀδήλως) is likely to be already a technical term.[280] The Vulgate *non in incertum* reflects the meaning of ἀδήλως as the adverbial form of the adjective which means *indistinct,* i.e., *uncertainly* in the sense of having *an indistinct* or *unclear* **goal**; not as if to say that a person is unsure what the goal is.[281] Today we might say: I play *with my eye on the ball,* or with *my eye clearly on the target.* If we transpose this imagery from ball games or archery to running, we propose the reading **an eye clearly on the goal**. If this clarity and force of translation is not to be achieved at the price of losing Paul's *double negative* (οὐκ ἀδήλως), we must

279. Cf. Seneca, *Epistulae Morales* 78.16; Epictetus, *Dissertationes* 3:21, and references cited above.

280. Weiss, *Der erste Korintherbrief,* 248, n. 2. He cites Diogenes Laertius, 9:51 and compares Phil 3:14.

281. Pfitzner, *Paul and the Agon Motif,* 90; cf. BAGD, 16.

render **as one not distracted from keeping an eye clearly on the goal**. Collins renders the word *without hesitation,* alluding only to 14:8 for possible support, but Schrage retains the notion of having the *goal* in front of one's eyes.[282]

It is difficult to know whether ἀέρα δέρων means *shadow boxing* or flinging punches in a genuine fight which find no target. Pfitzner and Schmidt find examples of both uses.[283] Although the second meaning underlines the fruitlessness of the exercise, it is more likely that Paul wants to expose "the strong" at Corinth who parade γνῶσις rather than ἀγάπη as all too ready "to go through the motions" of religious profession and routine without real engagement with the daily life-or-death issues arising from love for the other and the need to discipline and to constrain their own indulgences and freedoms. To lay primary stress on the first with a nuance suggesting the second is perhaps best achieved by **one who shadowboxes into empty air**.

27 The overwhelming majority of MSS read ὑπωπιάζω (on the meaning see below). The AV/KJV) *keep under,* rests on the reading ὑποπιάζω adopted only by the later Western F, G, and K, which is clearly a later correction and not to be accepted.

Much discussion surrounds the meaning of ὑπωπιάζω in this context, although its meaning in its "home" contexts is clear. In straightforward physical terms it means *to give a black eye to* someone or, more pedantically, *to strike under the eye.*[284] Many of the older modern commentators therefore perceive this as an extension of the boxing image. Findlay and Robertson and Plummer suggest, *I beat my body black and blue,* and Findlay places vv. 24-27 under the misleading heading "Paul's Asceticism."[285] The lexicons uniformly recognize, however, that this verb is also widely used as a metaphor. BAGD (with Derrett) suggest that the woman driven to desperation in pleading before the "unjust judge" either threatens in the judge's judgment *to fly in his face* or, in a more weakened sense, to *wear him out,* or *annoy him* by pestering (Luke 18:5).[286] In 1 Cor 9:27, however, BAGD favor **treat roughly** or *maltreat.* This allows for Weiss's belief, endorsed by Pfitzner, that in this last verse Paul has abandoned the boxing imagery, and is making a straightforward, nonanalogical comment about his own behavior, stance, and apostolic example. To be sure, Paul accepts the necessity, where it arises, for pain and even death, but this is more, not less, than a boxer's training, and is not to be confused with an "ascetic" lifestyle. He actively enslaves his life to larger apostolic purposes.[287]

282. Collins, *First Cor,* 362; Schrage, *Der erste Brief,* 2:368-69.

283. Pfitzner, *Paul and the Agon Motif;* K. L. Schmidt, "πυγμή," *TDNT,* 6:916-17.

284. BAGD, 648; Grimm-Thayer, 646; et al.

285. Findlay, *Expositor's Greek Testament,* 856 (heading on 855); also Robertson and Plummer, *First Epistle,* 196.

286. J. D. M. Derrett, "Law in the NT: The Parable of the Unjust Judge," *NTS* 18 (1972): 178-91, esp. 189-91; BAGD, 16.

287. Weiss, *Der erste Korintherbrief,* 248-49; Pfitzner, *Paul and the Agon Motif,* 95 (see further below).

This convincing approach leads us to reconsider whether *body* remains the best translation for σῶμα, even if virtually all VSS retain it. NRSV and NJB have, *I punish my body;* REB, *I do not spare my body;* NIV, *I beat my body.* On occasion Paul does indeed use σῶμα to denote the human body (e.g., 1 Cor 5:3; 7:4; 12:16; probably 6:13; and passages especially cited by Gundry).[288] On the other hand, Paul more characteristically uses σῶμα, especially in theological contexts, to denote **day-to-day life as a whole** *in the public domain, the life of the whole person without reduction* (1 Cor 6:19-20; 12:12, 13, 24-27; 15:38-44). We have noted above Käsemann's definition, that for Paul "'Body' . . . mean[s] . . . that piece of the world which we ourselves are and for which we bear responsibility . . . [the sphere of] bodily obedience . . . in the world of everyday [in which] the lordship of Christ finds visible expression . . . and the whole thing become[s] credible as Gospel. . . ."[289] Fee also supports a broader meaning here.[290]

This coheres precisely with the rest of Paul's language in v. 27. The term correlative to *lord* is *slave,* and Paul explicates why he treats his **day-to-day life as a whole roughly** in terms of *rendering it a slave* (δουλαγωγῶ), i.e., to **make it strictly serve my purposes**, *bring it under strict control,* NJB, REB; *enslave it,* NRSV. The whole of life is at issue, including not simply the body's desire to eat meat or to enjoy feasts but wholesale attitudes toward others which determine day-to-day practical stances and conduct which affects others as well as the Christian believer who needs to exercise self-control for their sake. *The whole of everyday life* must be held captive to the purposes of the gospel.

Paul finally notes what an irony it would be if, after all his **preaching to others**, it should turn out to be the case that he himself should find, when all secrets are disclosed at the day of judgment (4:4-5), that he is **not proven to stand the test** (αὐτὸς ἀδόκιμος γένωμαι). Although BAGD and most VSS understand this to mean *unqualified,* as well as *not standing the test,* this ignores the fact that the semantic content of ἀδόκιμος depends on what it is that is tested (δοκιμάζω). Here Paul indicates the test of subordinating **everything** to the gospel.[291] The meaning is confirmed by Grimm-Thayer and by Schrage to mean **not standing the test**, in the sense of that which does not prove itself to be such as it ought *(der die Bewährungsprobe nicht bestanden).*[292] As a meta-

288. R. H. Gundry, *Sōma in Biblical Theology,* SNTSMS 29 (Cambridge: Cambridge University Press, 1976), 34-80, 135-244.

289. Käsemann, in *NT Questions of Today,* 135.

290. Fee, *First Epistle* 439. "His point, after all, is the need for self-restraint, not asceticism (which he thoroughly rejects) or self-flagellation.

291. BAGD, 18, accept that *not standing the test* is a regular meaning elsewhere, but propose *unqualified* for 1 Cor 9:27. This may depend in part, however, on extending the boxing image (with Robertson and Plummer, against Pfitzner and Weiss). Fee accepts *disqualified (First Epistle,* 440), but only as part of the boxing metaphor, in contrast to Pfitzner. Pfitzner insists that Paul's use of δόκιμος and the scope of this passage "speak decidedly against the assumption that the athletic metaphor is here continued" *(Paul and the Agon Motif,* 95).

292. Grimm-Thayer, 12; Schrage, *Der erste Brief,* 2:372. Moulton-Milligan offer no exam-

phor it may be applied to sterile soil (Heb 6:8) or to base or impure metals or coins (Isa 1:22; Prov 25:6). However, Paul does not specify that he would be *not approved* (Grimm-Thayer's second main possibility) as if to imply eschatological rejection or loss of salvation. The notion of *that which does not prove itself to be such as it ought* well captures the notion of purpose in relation to calling and verdict. The **test** reveals failures of an unspecified nature, not utter rejection. *Fail to qualify* (Collins) or *disqualified* (REB, NRSV, NJB) risks such an understanding, although NIV narrows the scope by continuing the metaphor, *disqualified for the prize.*

3. Third Part of Paul's Response to Questions about Meat Associated with Idols (10:1–11:1)

We have already noted that numerous writers argue that parts of 8:1–11:1 constitute separate material from the main body of 1 Corinthians, but that these three chapters themselves lack literary integrity.[1] On the other hand, we endorsed the arguments of Willis, Fee, Schrage, and Mitchell that the three chapters reflected a unified argument. An examination of partition theories over the last thirty years does not suggest complete or even general unanimity about the boundaries of units, as Mitchell points out.[2] However, earlier modern writers do reflect a degree of consensus in designating 1 Corinthians 8 as a "letter A" section; 10:1-22 as a "letter B" section; and 10:23–11:1 as "letter C," following Hans von Soden (although even here there is strong disagreement: Héring, e.g., assigns ch. 8 and 10:23–11:1 to a "letter A," and 9:1–10:22 to a "letter B").[3] Many argue that 8:1-13 and 10:23-33 offer a "weaker," more tolerant response from Paul than the "harsher" approach of 10:1-22.[4]

This would be thoroughly understandable, on the other hand, if these sections address closely related but different issues. If 8:1-13 concerns eating meat

---

ple of the privative form of the adjective and speculate about δοκίμος and δόκιμος (ibid., 167-68). Louw-Nida propose *worthless* for one semantic field but (better for here) also *pertaining to not being in accordance with what is right, appropriate, or fitting* (Louw-Nida, 1:622 [65-73] and 755 [88-111]). The second makes the point which Paul seeks to convey in v. 27.

1. See under 8:1. For example, Weiss, *Der erste Korintherbrief,* xxxix-xliii; W. Schmithals, "Die Korintherbriefe als Briefsammlung," *ZNW* 64 (1973): 263-88, and his *Gnosticism at Corinth,* 87-113; G. Sellin, "Hauptprobleme der ersten Korintherbriefes," *ANRW* 2:24:4 (1987), 2,964-86; also Héring, Walther, and Yeo, loc. cit.

2. M. M. Mitchell, *Paul and the Rhetoric of Reconciliation,* 16-19, 296-304, and throughout.

3. Hans von Soden, "Sakrament und Ethik bei Paulus," in *Marburger Theologische Studien* (Gotha: Klotz, 1931), 1-40, esp. 17-18; Héring, *First Epistle,* xii-xiv; cf. the summary up to around 1965 in J. C. Hurd, *The Origins of 1 Corinthians,* 43-47.

4. For example, Wayne A. Meeks, "'And Rose Up to Play': Midrash and Paraenesis in 1 Cor 10:1-22," *JSNT* 16 (1982): 64; cf. 64-78. Cf. Yeo, *Rhetorical Interaction in 1 Cor 8 and 10,* esp. 1-14 and throughout.

in the precincts of a pagan temple and 10:23–11:1 relates this further to issues arising from this, while 10:1-22 directly addresses "participation" in idolatrous cultic events, then the difference of tone is to be expected. In 10:1-13 "Paul insists that . . . both Israel's flirtation with pagan cults and their punishment for doing so have exemplary importance for the Corinthians, because they also are tempted to such involvement with pagan deities (10:6-13)."[5] 10:14-22 proceeds to demonstrate the mutual exclusivity of "involvements" or "participation" in incompatible commonalities (κοινωνία). Yet, as Willis points out, this alludes directly to arguments of the Corinthian "strong" in 8:4 that "we all 'know' (γνῶσις) that 'an idol is nothing,'" and therefore "participation" in a "nothing" hardly counts as anything. This scenario is immensely strengthened by the forceful arguments of N. Walter concerning the presupposition, which could be carried over from a Gentile background. In a syncretistic, pluralistic religious culture, it might be plausible to imagine that all manifestations of "the sacred" reflected the being of the one God of monotheism. By contrast, Paul insists on the covenantal exclusivism of loyalty to Christ as a definitive revelation of God.[6]

We have consistently argued that 9:1-27 constitutes an integral part of the argument of 8:1–11:1. Paul foregoes his apostolic "rights" for the sake of the gospel and out of loving concern for the whole church, especially "the weak." If there is a "digression," it is 10:1-13, or perhaps 10:1-22, but this remains part of Paul's argument in which he presses a "worst case" scenario, found perhaps in a minority group of extremists among "the strong." In 10:23–11:1 the basic argument is resumed. Here Willis (followed by Mitchell and others) rightly sees close parallels with other Pauline material. In 1 Cor 10:1-12 and Rom 14:10 Paul reminds the addressees of their serious accountability, but "the behavior which Paul positively urges in both Rom 14, 15 and 1 Cor 8–10 is the strengthening of the Christian community, its 'building up' (1 Cor 8:1; 10:23; Rom 14:19; 15:2)."[7] Willis concludes: "In summary the parallel treatment in Romans 14, 15, suggests a unity to Paul's arguments as presented in 1 Cor 8–10."[8]

For today's reader, however, these chapters declare more than the necessity of respect for the "weak," the principle of foregoing "rights" when necessary, and the powerful effects for good or evil of participation in commonalities of cultic or corporate entities: they also serve to underline the continuity of the two Testaments and the importance of scripture for the Christian community. Here one of the classic studies is that presented by L. Goppelt. 10:1-13, Goppelt argues, decisively demonstrates the error of the mistaken assumption that Paul makes a serious appeal to scripture only when he is engaged in polemic in Galatians and Romans. His appeals to scripture "are . . . neither here

5. Willis, *Idol Meat in Corinth*, 271.
6. Walter, "Christusglaube und heidnische Religiosität in paulinischen Gemeinden," 422-42.
7. Willis, *Idol Meat*, 275.
8. Ibid.

nor in other passages simply contextual apologetics, or polemics, or traditional scholarship of the scribes, but a . . . *central means of interpreting the gospel*" (his italics).[9]

a. Warnings and Models from Scripture: "Craving" and Idolatry (10:1-13)

(1, 2) For I do not want you to fail to recognize, my dear fellow Christians, that our spiritual ancestors were all under the cloud and all passed through the sea. All of them had themselves baptized into Moses in the cloud and in the sea. (3, 4) All of them also ate the same spiritual food, and all of them drank the same spiritual drink; for they used to drink from a spiritual rock which went with them: now the Rock was Christ. (5) Nevertheless, on the far greater part of their number God visited his displeasure, for their corpses were strewn over the wilderness.

(6) Now these events occurred as formative models for us, with a view to our not craving for evil things, even as those people craved for them. (7) Do not take part in idol worship like some of them, as it is written, "The people sat down to eat and drink and rose up to virtual orgy. (8) Neither should we indulge in sexual immorality, as some of them did, and in a single day twenty-three thousand fell. (9) Nor should we continue to put Christ to the test, even as some of them tested him and suffered the process of destruction by the snakes. (10) Also stop your querulous moaning just as some of them muttered with complaints, and suffered destruction at the hands of the Destroyer. (11) [All] these things happened in succession to them as formative models of broader patterns. They were written also to serve as warnings for us, upon whom the ends of the ages have come. (12, 13) So, then, whoever thinks that he or she is standing fast, watch out lest you fall. No temptation has fastened upon you except what is part and parcel of being human. Now God is faithful: he will not allow you to be tempted beyond your powers, but he will make an exit path alongside the temptation. His purpose in this is for you to bear up under it.

Goppelt's observation provides an admirable introduction to 10:1-13. At the heart of this section lie issues about the status and interpretation of scripture for the church, where the OT remains definitive for a mixed congregation from a predominantly Gentile background, but where a distinctively Christ-related lens enables scripture to speak and to be heard with a fresh voice. As Goppelt, again, urges, the OT anchors salvation in history (not merely in constructed nontemporal "ideas"), but in such a way that *"the effective (or actual) center of*

---

9. Goppelt, "Paulus und die Heilsgeschichte: Schlussfolgerungen aus Röm iv und 1 Kor x:1-13," 32; cf. 31-42.

719

the Christ-event" (die sachliche Mitte des Christusgeschehens) is retained (Goppelt's italics).[10] Yet other questions crowd in: In what sense, if at all, can Christian church members at Corinth appear to be involved in "idolatry"? How could such "participation" appear to remain an attractive "craving" in temptation?[11] Could there be any truth in the claim that vv. 1-13 constitute a midrash in OT passages which predates this epistle or even Paul?[12]

Bibliography on 10:1-13

Aageson, J. W. *Written Also for Our Sake: Paul and the Art of Biblical Interpretation* (Louisville: Westminster/Knox, 1993), 49-53 and 117-27.

Badke, W. B., "Baptized into Moses — Baptized into Christ . . .," *EvQ* 88 (1988): 23-29.

Baird, W., "1 Cor 10:1-13," *Int* 44 (1990): 286-90.

Bandstra, A., "Interpretation in 1 Cor 10:1-11," *Calvin Theological Journal* 6 (1971): 5-21.

Ciocchi, D. M., "Understanding Our Ability to Endure Temptation: A Theological Watershed," *JETS* 35 (1992): 463-79.

Collier, G. D., " 'That We Might Not Crave Evil': The Structure and Argument of 1 Cor 10:1-13," *JSNT* 55 (1994): 55-75.

Comblin, J., "Le conflit de la liberté et de la charité (1 Cor 10)," *ASeign* 37 (1971): 48-52.

Cullmann, O., *Baptism in the NT* (Eng. trans., London: SCM, 1950), 45-54.

———, "πέτρα," *TDNT,* 6:95-99.

Dabelstein, R., *Die Beurteilung der 'Heiden' bei Paulus,* BBET 14 (Frankfurt am Main: Lang, 1981).

Davidson, R. M., *Typology in Scripture: A Study of the Hermeneutical Typos Structures* (Berrien Springs, Mich.: Andrews University Press, 1981), 191-231, 245-47.

Davies, W. D., *Paul and Rabbinic Judaism* (London: SPCK, 2d ed. 1955), 147-76.

Dunn, J. D. G., *The Theology of the Apostle Paul* (Grand Rapids: Eerdmans and Edinburgh: T. & T. Clark, 1998), 266-93.

Ellis, E. E., "A Note on 1 Cor 10:4," *JBL* 76 (1957): 53-56; rpt. in his *Prophecy and Hermeneutic in Early Christianity* (Grand Rapids: Eerdmans, 1978), 209-12.

———, *Paul's Use of the OT* (Edinburgh: Oliver & Boyd, 1957), 66-70.

Feuillet, A., *Le Christ sagesse de Dieu d'après les épitres Pauliniennes* (Paris: Gabalda, 1966).

Gardner, P. D., *The Gifts of God and the Authentication of a Christian: An Exegetical Study of 1 Cor 8–11:1* (Lanham, Md.: University Press of America, 1994), 111-55.

Goldingay, J., *Models for Interpretation of Scripture* (Grand Rapids: Eerdmans and Carlisle: Paternoster, 1993), 61-66.

Goppelt, L., "Paulus und die Heilsgeschichte: Schlussfolgerungen aus Röm iv und 1 Kor X:1-3," *NTS* 13 (1966): 31-42.

———, "τύπος," *TDNT,* 8:246-60.

10. Ibid., 33.

11. See J. D. Collier, " 'That We Might Not Crave Evil': The Structure and Argument of 1 Cor 10:1-13," 55-75.

12. Meeks, " 'And Rose Up to Play': Midrash and Paraenesis in 1 Cor 10:1-22."

————, *Typos: The Typological Interpretation of OT in the New* (Grand Rapids: Eerdmans, 1982), 127-52 and 209-37.

Hamerton-Kelly, R. G., *Pre-Existence, Wisdom and the Son of Man,* SNTSMS 21 (Cambridge: Cambridge University Press, 1973), 131-44, 192-93.

Hanson, A. T., *The Image of the Invisible God* (London: SCM, 1982).

————, *Jesus Christ in the OT* (London: SPCK, 1965), 11-16.

————, *Studies in Paul's Technique and Theology* (London: SPCK, 1974).

Haykin, A. G., "'In the Cloud and in the Sea': Basil of Caesarea and the Exegesis of 1 Cor 10:2," *VC* 40 (1986): 135-44.

Hays, B., *Echoes of Scripture in the Letters of Paul* (New Haven: Yale University Press, 1989), 91-102.

Hofius, O., "The Lord's Supper and the Lord's Supper Tradition: Reflections on 1 Cor 11:23b-25," in B. F. Meyer (ed.), *One Loaf, One Cup: Ecumenical Studies . . .* (Macon, Ga.: Mercer, 1993), 75-115, esp. 100-102.

Jervis, L. A., "'But I Want You to Know . . .': Paul's Midrashic Intertextual Response to the Corinthian Worshipers (1 Cor 11:2-16)," *JBL* 112 (1993): 231-46.

Koet, B. J., "The OT Background to 1 Cor 10:7-8," in R. Bieringer (ed.), *The Corinthian Correspondence,* BETL 225 (Leuven: Leuven University Press, 1996), 607-15.

Kreitzer, L., "1 Cor 10:4 and Philo's Flinty Rock," *CV* 35 (1993): 109-26.

Lampe, G. W. H., and K. J. Woollcombe, *Essays on Typology* (London: SCM, 1957), 16-69.

Malina, B. J., *The Palestinian Manna Tradition,* AGJU (Leiden: Brill, 1968), 94-99.

Maly, K., *Mündige Gemeinde* (Stuttgart: Katholische Bibelwerk, 1967), 123-27.

Martelet, G., "Sacrements, Figures et exhortation en 1 Cor 10:1-11," *RSR* 44 (1956): 323-39 and 525-59.

McEwen, A., "Paul's Use of the OT in 1 Cor 10:1-4," *VoxRef* 47 (1986): 3-10.

Meeks, Wayne A., "'And Rose Up to Play': Midrash and Paraenesis in 1 Cor 10:1-22," *JSNT* 16 (1982): 64-78.

Osten-Sacken, P. von der, "Die Tora in 1 Kor 10:1-13," in his *Die Heiligkeit der Tora. Studien zum Gesetz bei Paulus* (Munich: Kaiser, 1989), 60-86.

Perrot, C., "Les examples du désert (1 Cor 10:6-11)," *NTS* 29 (1983): 437-52.

Ramsaran, R. A., *Liberating Words: Paul's Use of Rhetorical Maxims in 1 Cor 1–10* (Valley Forge, Pa.: Trinity Press International, 1996), esp. 47-63.

Schnabel, E. J., *Law and Wisdom from Ben Sira to Paul,* WUNT 2:16 (Tübingen: Mohr, 1985).

Schnackenburg, R., *Baptism in the Thought of St Paul* (Eng. trans., Oxford: Blackwell, 1964), 91-95.

Sigal, P., "Another Note to 1 Cor 10:16," *NTS* 29 (1983): 134-39.

Smit, J. F. M., "Do Not Be Idolaters: Paul's Rhetoric in 1 Cor 10:1-22," *NovT* 39 (1997): 40-53.

Walter, N., "Christusglaube und heidnische Religiosität in paulinischen Gemeinden," *NTS* 25 (1979): 422-42.

Willis, W. L., *Idol Meat in Corinth: The Pauline Argument in 1 Cor 8 and 10,* SBLDS 68 (Chico: Scholars Press, 1985), 123-64.

Witherington, B., *Jesus the Sage: The Pilgrimage of Wisdom* (Edinburgh: T. & T. Clark and Minneapolis: Fortress, 1994).

————, "Not So Idle Thoughts about *Eidolothuton*," *TynBul* 44 (1993): 237-54.

Yeo, Khiok-Khing, *Rhetorical Interaction in 1 Cor 8 and 10,* BibInt 9 (Leiden: Brill, 1995), esp. 74-119, 142-79, 212-14.

(1) Warning Models: All Shared; Many Fell (10:1-6)

1-2 Metzger's comment and the "C" grading for the aorist passive ἐβαπτίσθησαν in v. 2 in the UBS 4th ed. may imply that the UBS Committee was divided over whether to accept the aorist passive read by ℵ, A, C, D, G, 33, Basil, and Cyril or the aorist middle ἐβαπτίσαντο, read by p[46c], B, Origen, and Chrysostom. Metzger and Wikgren appear to be the minority on the UBS Committee who would have favored the middle, along with Zuntz.[13] Arguably the UBS 4th ed. favors the passive on the grounds of broader attestation, but the UBS 3d ed., Metzger, and Zuntz judge the transition from an original middle to a later passive to be more probable. Certainly the opposite process would be difficult to explain. In the light of the Jewish practice of baptizing oneself, the OT context, and especially of Conzelmann's comment that although we cannot read too much into the distinction the force of Paul's comment may well be that **all of them had themselves baptized** (middle of self-interest), the middle is more probable and is reflected in our translation.[14] p[46] originally had ἐβαπτίζοντο but corrected it to the aorist middle. As Conzelmann hints, even the passive (if it were accepted) could carry a reflexive meaning as well: they had themselves baptized.[15]

Wayne Meeks argues in detail that the section vv. 1-13 is "a literary unit, very carefully composed prior to its use in its present context. For convenience I shall call it a homily, without wishing to beg the question of its pre-epistolary *Sitz im Leben.*"[16] The argument is not only that it supposedly conflicts in tone and direction with 8:1-13 and 10:23-31 (see the introduction to 10:1-31), but also that it contains a distinctive variety of intertextual resonances with OT passages, themes, and symbols of importance to contemporary Judaism including "the following Rock, the meaning of 'spiritual food' and 'spiritual drink,'" and themes associated with Wisdom, for which the manna and the rock were symbols in Philo.[17] Symbols associated with the Exodus wilderness narratives include **the cloud** (Exod 13:21), **the sea** (Exod 14:21-22), the manna (Exod 16:4, 14-18), the spring (Exod 17:6), and apostasy (Exod 32:6).

In principle it may be entirely reasonable to assume that Paul embodies pre-Pauline or even pre-Christian material in his epistles, for in 1 Cor 11:23b-26 and 15:3b-5 he quotes pre-Pauline Christian tradition; he himself may have composed 13:1-13 while reflecting in Corinth but prior to dictating the letter (see introduction to ch. 13); in Rom 1:18-32 he uses standard or stereotypical

13. Metzger, *Textual Commentary* (2d ed.), 493, esp. the added note; Zuntz, *The Text of the Epistles,* 234. Fee and Schrage favor the middle (*First Epistle,* 441, n. 2; *Der erste Brief,* 2:390, n. 44).

14. Conzelmann, *1 Cor,* 164, n. 1. Even the older modern commentators recognize the probability of the aorist middle: Meyer, *First Epistle,* 1:279.

15. So also Edwards, *First Epistle,* 244.

16. Meeks, "'And Rose Up to Play': Midrash and Paraenesis in 1 Cor 10:1-22," 65.

17. Ibid., 64; cf. 64-78. The following symbols are listed by Conzelmann, *1 Cor,* 165.

sentences or phrases drawn from anti-Gentile synagogue homilies. However, it is no easier to separate the themes of 10:1-13 from the broader thrust of 8:1–11:1 and the epistle as a whole than it is to dislodge the poetic rhythms of 13:1-13 from allusions to the Corinthian situation. Fee rightly observes, "An explanatory 'for' and the vocative brothers [and sisters] indicate that the present argument has close ties with the exhortation and warning that has just preceded. They are to run as those intent on winning; that is, they must exercise self-control in all things. . . . Many commentators either ignore this γάρ . . . or minimize it as a 'loose' connection with what precedes."[18] Schrage also notes the "explanatory function" of γάρ in relation to 9:27 and Paul's concern not to find himself unproven to stand the test (ἀδόκιμος).[19]

At the time the earlier comments of Weiss and others which identified 10:1-5 as "a midrash" underline the character of vv. 1-6 as a unit.[20] Meeks observes that vv. 1-13 are "divided neatly in half by a simple contrast between 'all' of the Israelites, who engaged God's salvation at the Sea of Reeds and his protection in the wilderness. And 'some [most] of them' who rebelled against God and were punished for it. To the five parallel clauses signalled by the repeated πάντες in verses 1-4 correspond five statements about 'some of them' in verses 6-10."[21] The five positive and five negative models are linked with a paraenetic conclusion in vv. 12-13 by means of a rhetorical inclusion in vv. 6 and 11: ταῦτα δὲ τύμοι ἡμῶν . . . (v. 6) and ταῦτα δὲ τυπικῶς . . . (v. 11). Vv. 6-11 will offer a commentary (*midrash*, which resonates with rabbinic traditions about wilderness "tests") on aspects of Num 14:22, 23, 28-30, with further intertextual resonances with, or cross references to, passages in Exodus, Deuteronomy, and Psalms (see below). As Fee observes, resonances with Psalm 78 and Deuteronomy 32 take up the issue of warnings concerning the need for self-control elucidated in 9:1-27.[22]

The phrase οὐ θέλω ὑμᾶς ἀγνοεῖν is a broadly standard formula in first-century Graeco-Roman letters or treatises (cf. Josephus, *Antiquities* 13.354; Epictetus, *Dissertations* 4.8.27; 1 Cor 12:1; 2 Cor 1:8; 1 Thess 4:13; Rom 1:13). However, in many contexts (as here) ἀγνοέω with a second negative οὐ has the force of **fail to recognize** which coheres with the use of ὅτι after the verb in v. 1.[23] Once again, the translation of ἀδελφοί is troublesome both because of the need for a gender-inclusive term which does not obtrude into the text with gender issues (as the cumbersome *brothers and sisters* does) but also because the Greek word includes both blood siblings and intimate colleagues. Hence we vary our translation (see under 1:10) and here propose **my dear fellow Christians**. Al-

---

18. Fee, *First Epistle*, 443 and 443, n. 7. Fee perceives the first failure in Conzelmann and the second in Barrett. His point is fundamental.

19. Schrage, *Der erste Brief*, 2:387 88.

20. Weiss, *Der erste Korintherbrief*, 249-50.

21. Meeks, "'And Rose Up to Play,'" 65.

22. Fee, *First Epistle*, 442.

23. BAGD, 11.

though strictly οἱ πατέρες ἡμῶν means *our fathers,* lexicographical surveys reveal that *forefathers* or **ancestors** is a common usage in biblical Greek, and often denotes **spiritual ancestor** in a sense which denotes not necessarily blood ties but reproduction of character.[24] The key theological point here concerns Paul's use of ἡμῶν, **our,** for Israelites in the Mosaic era as the *fathers* of the Gentile-Christian or mixed Christian community at Graeco-Roman Corinth. Goppelt insists on this point. Whatever the novelties and discontinuities brought about by the new creation in Christ, Israel and the Christian church belong to a single *history* of God's activity and self-disclosure.[25] Irenaeus and other later Church Fathers, especially those who confronted Marcionism, were at pains to cite Paul's insistent theme that the experiences, failures, or lessons drawn from ancient Israel remain "for our instruction."[26] The God of Israel and the God of the Christian church are (against Marcion) "the same God."[27] The definite articles (the cloud) and lack of explanation suggest that OT material is known and used.[28]

Paul now lists the privileges which **all** enjoyed under **Moses**. First, they **all** enjoyed the protection and guidance of **the cloud**, which represented the presence of God to lead them (Exod 13:21; 14:19-20), and **all** experienced the redemptive act of God which brought them *out of* bondage in Egypt *through* the Sea of Reeds *by* God's saving action *to* the new state of existence won for God's covenant people. Because these events constitute a paradigm of redemption (*from* bondage, *by* God's saving act, *to* a new lifestyle and reality, Exod 14:19-22) Paul finds it appropriate to denote this as a **baptismal**-like redemptive experience of grace. The significance of **baptized** in relation to **Moses** is not least to identify the *participating* nature of their status and experience. Baptism signifies *being bound up with* the one in whose name, or in whose sphere of influence, a person is baptized, so that in Paul Christian baptism signifies above all else *identification with Christ,* especially identification with Christ's saving death and resurrection (Rom 6:3-11). This point is made with convincing force by R. Schnackenburg.[29] The coupling of **the cloud and the sea** with

---

24. Cf. Epictetus, *Dissertations* 3.22.82, of Diogenes and the Cynic; Aelius Aristides 47, 425D; but **ancestor** is a common meaning for πατήρ, esp. of Abraham (John 8:39, 53, 56; Acts 7:2; Josephus, *Antiquities* 14.255); of Isaac in Rom 9:10; Jacob in John 4:12; plural οἱ πατέρες as **ancestors** in Josephus, *Ant.* 14.297; Matt 23:30, 32; esp. Heb 1:1, 8, 9, et al. See also BAGD, 635.

25. Goppelt, "Paulus und die Heilsgeschichte," 35-39; cf. 31-42.

26. Irenaeus, *Against Heresies,* 4:27:4.

27. Ibid., 27:1-4.

28. As Conzelmann notes (*1 Cor,* 165).

29. R. Schnackenburg, *Baptism in the Thought of St Paul* (Eng. trans., Oxford: Blackwell, 1964), remains a classic study. Schnackenburg argues that the aspect of "washing" has fairly minimal significance for Paul (ibid., 3-17), but that the two major strands are (i) "assignment to . . . and incorporation in Christ" (1 Cor 1:13; 1 Cor 12:13; Gal 3:27); and (ii) "salvation-event with (σύν) Christ" (Rom 6:1-11), including σύμφυτοι (6:5) and "crucified with" (6:6) (ibid., 30-61). Christ's saving act is the foundation (ibid., 112-21) which I appropriated (121-38) by becoming "included" in the Christ-event of his dying and being raised (154-69, 196-203). The translation points out the convergence of views by a Roman Catholic writer and a Baptist translator and is "sufficiently unusual to call for comment" (G. R. Beasley-Murray, *Baptism in the NT,* ix).

the verb **baptized** underlines the redemptive dimension, just as πάντες underlines participation in, and identification with, those redemptive events.

Those who argue that the Christian sacrament of baptism witnesses to grace rather than to an explicit profession of faith may wish to argue that here **baptized into Moses** means *initiated into* the corporate experiences of the *visible community* of the people of God.[30] Those who hold a "Baptist" view may wish to argue that **baptized** carries here no more than a typological or figurative meaning. Nevertheless, we cannot avoid asking why Paul believed that the term was appropriate in this context, and drawing inferences from our answer. Thus Cullmann comments that 1 Cor 10:1-6 is "a passage which ought to be much more carefully observed in the discussion of child Baptism. It is here quite plain that the act of grace, which is regarded as the type of Baptism, concerns the covenant which God made with the whole people."[31] Schnackenburg believes that "manifestly it [this passage] is an imitation of εἰς Χριστόν (Gal 3:27; Rom 6:3); but confirms that Moses, rather than Christ, is cited as a τύπος. For the Tannaitic midrash *Mekilta* "interprets the dividing of the waters as a kind of archway through water."[32] It would be difficult to translate εἰς τὸν Μωϋσῆν differently from **into Moses** (NRSV, NIV, NJB, although REB, *into the fellowship of Moses,* can also be defended). The phrase may mean **into** his leadership, but if, as is more likely, the meaning is determined by the antitypical εἰς Χριστόν, a number of writers argue (with Schnackenburg) that εἰς represents in effect a shorthand for εἰς τὸ ὄνομα Χριστοῦ signifying not locality, sphere, or movement but *adherence to* the one in whose name the candidate is **baptized**. βαπτίζειν εἰς thus stands in parallel with πιστεύειν εἰς, suggesting "the direction of faith, but it does not express any mystical movement. . . ."[33]

The main point here, however, remains clear. Such is the generosity of God's grace that **all** (πάντες is repeated five times in vv. 1-4) participate in the privileges and blessings of the redeemed covenant people of God, the first two of which are **the** protective **cloud** of God's saving presence and the redemptive crossing of **the Sea** of Reeds (the manna and the spring of water are about to be mentioned). Nevertheless in the face of such divine generosity, less than the **all** will appropriate God's gifts and exercise the self-discipline which will bring them safely through the tests of the wilderness journey.

3-4 p⁴⁶, ℵ*, and A omit the first τὸ αὐτό, **the same**, in v. 3; p⁴⁶ and A also omit the second. If we follow Calvin and Heinrici in understanding the phrase to mean "**the same** as we Christians eat and drink," the omission may be explicable as due to a "high" theology

30. Cf. O. Cullmann, *Baptism in the NT,* 14-15, 23-46, 49-70.

31. Ibid., 45.

32. Schnackenburg, *Baptism,* 92-93.

33. Ibid., 23; cf. 21-29. See also Schrage, *Der erste Brief,* 2:390-91, including nn. 48-51. Calvin underlines this point, noting that εἰς may serve in the place of ἐν with ὄνομα (*First Epistle,* 201).

of the Christian sacraments on the part of an early Christian copyist.[34] Otherwise **the same** is sufficiently well attested (א³, B, C², E, F, G, K, Latin VSS) to be virtually certain and, if it means "**the same** as one another," is already implied by the construction.

The terms τὸ αὐτὸ πνευματικὸν βρῶμα and τὸ αὐτὸ πνευματικὸν . . . πόμα, **the same spiritual food . . . the same spiritual drink**, allude to the manna (Exod 16:4, 14-18) and to the miraculous water which flowed from the rock struck by Moses (Exod 17:6; Num 20:7-13). As we should expect in Paul's use of **spiritual**, the adjective does not mean *immaterial,* but that which is provided by the Spirit of God (cf. 9:11; 12:1; 15:44, 46), with all the 'hallmarks' of what is regarded as a miraculous provision. In spite of numerous claims that **spiritual food and drink** become synonyms for the eucharistic elements in the subapostolic period (e.g., *Didache* 10:3, πνευματικὴν τροφὴν καὶ πότον), such a meaning cannot be read back into Paul. In its OT context "spiritual" food denotes *manna* provided by God as a miracle, while in the NT and especially in Paul πνευματικός denotes that which is of God's Spirit: "gifts of a superterrestrial heavenly origin and nature."[35]

At the same time the immediate referents, *manna* and *water* do not exhaust the fuller references and allusions. It is customary for commentators to interpret a double meaning in which the parallel "visible signs" of the old and new covenants are set alongside each other: *manna* is said to imply (either typologically or in some other way) the **spiritual food** of the Lord's Supper or Eucharist, while the *water* **from** the **rock** is said to signify further the **spiritual drink** of the eucharistic wine of the Lord's Supper. Paul does move explicitly to the Eucharist or Lord's Supper in 10:14-22. However, if he is drawing on traditions in Judaism inherited by the church that God's Wisdom actively conveyed his agency and presence in earlier history, Paul has already identified God's Wisdom with Christ himself (e.g., 1:30). A. T. Hanson declares, "In 1 Cor 10 we have an instance of the real presence of Christ in Israel's history of old."[36] Paul could draw on the rabbinic legend that Moses' rock actually *rolled after, followed,* or *went with* (ἀκολουθούσης πέτρας) if he means to point beyond it to the truth that Christ was their ever new, ever con-

---

34. Calvin, *First Epistle,* 203: "The old sacraments of the law had the same power as ours have today. . . . A sign *(signum)* is indeed a sign and retains its own substance *(substantiam).* . . . The reality of the sacrament was conveyed to the people of old just as much as to us." Calvin attacks "scholastics . . . and men of the Sorbonne" for holding a contrary view. "The difference between us and them [the people of God under Moses] is only one of degree (which) we have more fully *(plenius,* 204)." Also Heinrici, *Das erste Sendschreiben,* 262.

35. Hofius, "The Lord's Supper and the Lord's Supper Tradition," in Meyer (ed.), *One Loaf, One Cup,* 101; cf. 99-103; also cf. Justin, *Apology,* 1:65:5; on *spirit* and **spiritual**, see further esp. R. Bultmann, *Theology of the NT,* vol. 1 (Eng. trans., London: SCM, 1952), 153: "*Pneuma* does not mean 'spirit' in the Greek-Platonic . . . sense, i.e., it does not mean mind in contrast to body . . . *Pneuma* is the miraculous divine power that stands in absolute contrast to all that is human"; also Schrage, *Der erste Brief,* 2:392.

36. Hanson, *Studies in Paul's Technique and Theology,* 100.

stant supply, ever with them.[37] Indeed, Hanson holds that in Paul's understanding **the cloud** alludes to God's presence as it is mediated through the Person of Christ.[38] Christ is "the angel of the Lord" who represents God in the history of Israel in the OT. Christ constitutes "the form in which God was known to Israel of old."[39]

PAUL'S ALLUSION TO THE "ROCK WHICH WENT WITH THEM"

Hanson's comments from three of his books on the use of the OT in the New and its significance for Christology especially in Paul and in Hebrews lead us into a controversial debate. If Hanson is right, Paul's explanatory statement **now the Rock was Christ** serves exactly as an explanatory proposition about *a state of affairs* (for which Findlay well renders ἡ πέτρα δέ as: **Now the Rock . . .**).[40] On the other hand, many writers regard ἦν ὁ Χριστός as a typological comment. In this case, the change from the aorist ἔπιον πόμα (**they drank the same spiritual drink**) to the imperfect ἔπινον (**for they used to drink from a spiritual rock which went with them**) denotes not a constant, renewed nourishment and refreshment from the living source that **was Christ**, but an allusion to "the *following* **rock**" of rabbinic legend which *typologically signifies* Christ. Indeed, Yeo distinguishes in "live scholarly interpretation" (a) the *realistic,* the Rock *is* the preexistent Christ; (b) they are *identical events* (Käsemann, Lietzmann, R. P. C. Hanson); (c) the symbolic: the rock stands for Christ; (d) they are parallel but not the same (Barrett) (e) typological interpretation, i.e., it points to the Christian reality (Wendland). Collins writes that "in Paul's view the rock must have followed the Israelites because Moses was able to strike it more than once."[41] Thus, at the opposite end of a spectrum of views from Hanson, Hayes argues that virtually all the comparisons and parallels are *types* (τυπικῶς, v. 11; τύποι, v. 6) in which **baptized . . . in the cloud and in the sea** becomes "an imaginative construction on the analogy of Christian baptism," and **spiritual food and drink** occurs "prefiguring the Christian Eucharist. . . . The fanciful analogies allow Paul to make the serious point that participation in spectacular spiritual experiences does not relieve the people of God from ethical responsibility. . . . Paul immerses them in startling figurative claims. . . . Paul's metaphors should not be pressed."[42]

---

37. On the semantic scope of ἀκολουθέω as *go along with, accompany,* **go with** (rather than only *follow*), cf. BAGD, 31.

38. Hanson, *Jesus Christ in the OT,* 11-16.

39. Hanson, *The Image of the Invisible God,* 81.

40. Findlay, *Expositor's Greek Testament,* 2:858.

41. Collins, *First Cor,* 369; see also Yeo, *Rhetorical Interaction in 1 Cor 8 and 10,* 167, n. 52. Numerous writers collected material which witnesses to a tradition of rabbinic reflection on Num 21:17 and other verses about the rock which supplied the water and "followed" Israel to give repeated supply (Targum Onkelos [Aramaic translation of] Num 21:17); Midrash Sifre on Num 11:21; *b. Sabbath* 35a, "a moveable well"; *b. Aboth* 5:6; *Midrash Numbers Rabbah* 19:25-26; *t. Sukka* 3:11; cf. Strack-Billerbeck, *Kommentar,* 3:406-7. See further Ellis, *Paul's Use of the OT,* 66-70, esp. 67 and 67, n. 2; Willis, *Idol Meat,* 133-42; and Schnabel, *Law and Wisdom from Ben Sira to Paul.*

42. Hays, *Echoes of Scripture,* 91.

In the use of rabbinic traditions reflected in Targum, Midrash, and most certainly Talmud, issues of dating remain obscure and complex. Ellis reconstructs a coherent rabbinic tradition concerning a movable well, "rock-shaped and resembling a sieve . . . given to the Israelites in the desert . . . one of the ten things created on the evening of the Sixth Day. . . . It rolled along after the wanderers through hills and valleys, and when they camped it settled at the tent of meeting. . . ."[43] Some degree of speculation cannot be avoided about whether Paul uses material even in pretextual form to address Corinth. On the other hand, *the role of the figure of Wisdom in guiding, protecting, and nurturing Israel through the wilderness is very widely attested* in literature in hellenistic Judaism over the century before Paul's writing, in contemporary synagogue homilies, and in Paul's near-contemporary Philo. Both Wisdom 2, the Book of Wisdom, and Philo speak of Wisdom's provision of water to wandering Israel "from a flinty rock ἐδόθη αὐτοῖς ἐκ πέτρος ἀκροτόμου ὕδωρ (Wis 2:4) on which Philo observes: "the flinty rock is the wisdom of God" (Philo, *Legum Allegoriae* 2.86). The point here is that it is clearly and widely recognized that *Paul informs his own Christology by drawing explicitly on traditions of preexistent Wisdom from the OT Wisdom literature* (e.g., Proverbs 8) and hellenistic Judaism of the first century. Certain differences between the rabbinic and Philonic traditions in relation to 1 Cor 10:4 have recently been explored by Kreitzer; his approach underlines the need for caution in drawing too readily or uncritically on widespread assumptions about Paul's sources and his use of them.[44] Paul certainly drew on Wisdom traditions in the LXX; what part is from speculative material in rabbinic traditions or in Philo remains open to serious question.

We cannot readily underplay the role for Paul of **Christ the Wisdom of God** (1:30) when it not only plays a major role in his dialogue with Corinth and "the strong" but also features prominently over the last fifty years of Pauline research from W. D. Davies (1948) to J. D. G. Dunn (1998), including important studies in each decade, e.g., by Feuillet (1966), Hamerton-Kelly (1973), Schnabel (1985), and Witherington (1994).[45] Witherington (with Hays and Fee) is entirely right to insist that complexities of discussion about the precise force of **now the rock was Christ** should not distract us from Paul's main point that "the Israelites had the same sort of benefit as Christians do, even benefits from Christ himself, and even this did not secure them against perishing . . . and losing out. . . ."[46] Nevertheless, Paul could take for granted a back-

---

43. Ellis, *Paul's Use of the OT,* 67; cf. the reference in rabbinic sources cited in the above note.

44. Kreitzer, "1 Cor 10:4 and Philo's Flinty Rock," 109-26. Kreitzer recognizes substantial differences between the role of the rock and the OT passages for Paul and for Philo, not least in terms of "timeless" allegory in Philo and historical typology in Paul. Philo's background alone cannot be used to arrive at the preexistence of Christ, but through Deut 8:5-8 and other passages a covenant motif, Kreitzer argues, emerges.

45. Davies, *Paul and Rabbinic Judaism,* 147-76; and Dunn, *The Theology of the Apostle Paul,* 266-93. See also Dunn, *Christology in the Making* (London: SCM, 2d ed. 1989, and Grand Rapids: Eerdmans, 1996); Feuillet, *Le Christ sagesse de Dieu d'après les épitres Pauliniennes;* Hamerton-Kelly, *Pre-existence, Wisdom and the Son of Man,* 112-54 and 192-96; Schnabel, *Law and Wisdom from Ben Sira to Paul;* B. Witherington, *Jesus the Sage: The Pilgrimage of Wisdom.*

46. Witherington, *Conflict and Community,* 219. Cf. Fee, *First Epistle,* 448: "His interest is not in the water but in its source." "It is doubtful whether he was trying to say something about the sacramental character of the food" (ibid., 447; against Goppelt, *Typos,* 145, and many others, but

ground about the role of divine Wisdom as protector, guide, and nourisher of Israel in the wilderness which could readily be applied to the preexistent Christ, while this background, which was the stock-in-trade of hellenistic Jewish diaspora synagogue sermons, has become unfamiliar now to most modern readers, and hence requires explanation.

In addition to Wis 11:4 numerous allusions to the role of preexistent Wisdom in guiding and sustaining Israel through the wilderness wanderings form a theme which covers several chapters of Wisdom of Solomon. Wisdom "delivered a holy people ... from oppressors ... guided them ... [was] their shelter by day ... their starlight through the night and brought them across **the** Red **Sea**, leading them through immensity of *water*" (Wis 10:15-18). "Overshadowing the camp was **the cloud** (ἡ σκιάζουσα νεφέλη) ... they **all** passed across ... seeing the wondrous miracles (θαυμαστὰ τέρατα; cf. our discussion of πνευματικός, **spiritual**, above; Wis 19:7-8). In other parts of the book, resonances with a Wisdom Christology in 1 Corinthians may perhaps be detected. Wisdom is praised as an active, accessible outflow of God's creative Being," the glory of the Almighty" (Wis 7:25; cf. 7:22–8:1), "permeates all things" (7:24; cf. 1 Cor 2:10-16), and even exercises the gentle and compassionate restraint of forbearance (Wis 11:20–12:18; cf. 1 Cor 8:7–9:27; 10:23–11:1; "... imitators of me," 11:1a; cf. 9:1-23; "... of Christ," 11:1b).

This kind of background may reflect meditation not only on Proverbs 8 but on many other OT passages. On **the rock** Cullmann suggests that some part was played by Deut 8:15; 32:13; Neh 9:15; Isa 48:21; and Pss 78:15-20; 81:16 et al., as well as the Exodus material.[47] Taking all these streams of tradition into account, Dunn observes: "Clearly ... Paul was attributing to *Christ* the role previously attributed to divine Wisdom" (his italics).[48] This is perhaps neither direct identification nor mere "personification." Dunn prefers to use the term "hypostatization," or, better, "the 'metaphor' of Wisdom ... as God's Wisdom" which Paul applies to Christ.[49] He concedes, however, that in 1 Cor 10:4 we may infer that "Paul had in mind a range of reflection which these traditions stimulated in Jewish thought closely contemporary with Paul."[50] How hard the relation or identification between the preexistent Christ and preexistent Wisdom should be pressed remains a matter of debate.[51]

If we take seriously the implications of Paul's Christology (cf. the cosmic "creeded" patterns noted in 1 Cor 8:4-6 and the "trinitarian" pattern of 12:4-6; see loc. cit.), we may fully endorse Witherington's comment on **now the rock was Christ**: "'Was' indicates that the divine Christ was really a part of Israel's history, providing them with life-giving water."[52] A. Bandstra expresses this forcefully: "Christ himself, the pre-existent Christ, was present with the Israelites in their wilderness journey."

---

with Witherington: "He is not arguing that the Red Sea was a sacrament" (*Conflict and Comunity*, 219); cf. Hays, *Echoes of Scripture*.

47. O. Cullmann, "πέτρα," *TDNT*, 6:97.

48. Dunn, *Theology of Paul*, 270.

49. Ibid., 272.

50. Ibid., 279.

51. Ibid., 280. See the degrees of position on a spectrum identified by Willis, *Idol Meat*, 133-42.

52. Witherington, *Conflict and Community*, 218. See further Schrage, *Der erste Brief*, 2:395-96.

Christ was "as much the source of the spiritual food and drink of the Israelites as he is the one present in the Lord's Supper at Corinth."[53]

The long-standing debate about the relation between **the rock** and **Christ** has generated considerable heat, but it is better to allow the exegesis to determine how we understand τύπος than to approach the text with presuppositions about typology. The major difference between *type* and *allegory* is that the former is grounded in *history* and presupposes corresponding *events;* the latter is grounded in a linguistic system of signs or *semiotic codes* and presupposes resonances or parallels between *ideas* or semiotic *meanings.* If we insist on pedantic questions of nomenclature, Paul makes (i) *theological or ontological truth claims* about the agency of the preexistent Christ; (ii) utilizes a *typological context of historical parallels* between *events* in the experience of Israel and *events* in the experience of the church at Corinth; and further *using a suggestive semiotic,* (iii) *may* well be drawing *a cluster of symbolic resonances* as well (if some of the traditions which emerge in Philo and rabbinic sources were widespread as early as Paul's letter).[54] This may suggest, if it is valid, that Paul offers a suggestive "play" which portrays the all-sufficiency of the living Christ who renews his mercies (not merely as a source of a static γνῶσις) as continuous provider, sustainer, and guide (imperfect ἔπινον) for **all** those privileged to participate in these blessings.[55] Schrage is entirely safe to speak of "the analogy" between grace to Israel and the grace of the Lord's supper.[56]

5 The contrast between all ... all ... all (five times in vv. 1-4) and the minority who were left in distinction from τοῖς πλείοσιν αὐτῶν (**the far greater part of their number**) demands an emphatic translation for the Greek contrastive ἀλλ᾽, i.e., **nevertheless** (with NRSV, NIV).[57] REB *yet* underplays the contrast, while NJB, *in spite of this,* while justifiable, goes beyond the Greek. Everything hinges on a sharp, crisply expressed contrast. *To visit displeasure* seems more forceful than a double negative for οὐκ ... εὐδόκησεν ὁ θεός, although we could also perhaps translate, *God's favor did not rest on. . . .* The active effects are implied by Fee's correct observation that NIV's omission of γάρ, **for,** loses the point that the fate of the **corpses strewn over the wilderness** explicates the substance of what οὐκ ... εὐδόκησεν consisted in, as explanation and proof of it.[58] Fee also convincingly defends the translation κατεστρώθησαν as *scattered* or **strewn** since this reflects what the LXX of Num 14:16 (on which the picture

53. Bandstra, "Interpretation in 1 Cor 10:1-11," 14; cf. 5-21. We noted above that this is Calvin's view.

54. This argument is present in Davidson, *Typology in Scripture,* 191-231, 245-47, combining a semiotic approach with an Adventist theological approach.

55. Cf. Aageson, *Written Also for Our Sake,* 123-24; cf. 112-27.

56. Schrage, *Der erste Brief,* 2:393. Schrage also constructively pays attention to the OT background to 10:4 in Num 21:16-18; Exod 17:5-7; and Num 20:11 (in contrast to more speculative "sources") (ibid., 394). He also discusses Ellis's allusions to *pesher* interpretation to explain ἥν (**was Christ**) in Ellis, *Prophecy and Hermeneutic,* 159-61.

57. As Edwards and others point out, οὐκ ἐν τοῖς πλείοσιν has the force of *very few* (*First Epistle,* 247). In Num 14:30 only Joshua and Caleb reach the promised land.

58. Fee, *First Epistle,* 450 and 450, n. 41.

is based) conveys when it uses the same word. **Strewn** with **their corpses** follows REB, against NRSV's *struck down,* although NJB and NIV accept *scattered.*[59] If we were to ignore the LXX nuance of **strewn**, a better alternative might have been to preserve the resonance *suffered catastrophe* (καταστρέφω). Complacency, self-will, and disobedience forfeited the privileges in which **all** had shared.

6   Many interpreters include v. 6 with vv. 7-13, identifying **craving** as the first of *five* specific failures enumerated here.[60] However, in our view **craving** represents the general stance from which the specific *four* failures of vv. 7-13 flow. Again, δέ in this context of introducing a summarizing proposition has the force of the logical **now** in English, with NRSV, NJB, and NIV. Since Paul is considering a correspondence between *events* (as in typology), not merely ideas (as in allegory), and appeals to *history* (as Goppelt insists), ταῦτα is well translated **these events** in REB. In his article on τύπος in *TDNT,* Goppelt urges that although the Greek word means *example* or sometimes *mark* (in the sense of stamp or imprint), or *example as a norm* (Rom 6:17), there also "occurs a new sense peculiar to the NT. In 1 Cor 10:6, Rom 5:14, τύπος is a hermeneutical term for the OT 'type'. A corresponding sense is borne by . . . τυπικῶς in 1 Cor 10:11 and ἀντίτυπος in 1 Pet 3:21."[61] Goppelt also notes the use of the word in the sense of a heavenly "original" in Heb 9:24.

Since the word *type,* however, is largely unfamiliar in these technical senses outside the discourse of students of the Bible, it is tempting to borrow the word *paradigm* or *paradigmatic model* since this is now widespread with almost the precise sense used in 10:6 in philosophy of language and (with T. Kuhn) in the history of science. However, in an illuminating and more recent article on τύπος, G. Schunack suggests that the term **formative model** represents "the exegetically proven use" in such a context as 1 Cor 10:6.[62] This we have adopted. For in Paul's view, corroborated by certain approaches in hermeneutical theory, the function of biblical texts (at the risk of simplistic generalization) is that of spiritual and ethical **formation**, which may also entail *transformation.*[63] As Schunack observes, issues about whether τύπος refers "to the 'real' spiritual meaning of a text or narrated event" misses the main issue: the issues about "typology" have accumulated a non-Pauline agenda in the history of Christian traditions which makes it preferable to avoid translating τύπος

59. BAGD, 419, includes only *to upset, to overturn, to destroy, to ruin.* These are usual but not exhaustive meanings (cf. Matt 21:12, overturned the money changers' tables).

60. For example, Yeo, *Rhetorical Interaction in 1 Cor 8 and 10,* 167-70; and Meeks, "'And Rose Up to Play,'" 69.

61. Goppelt, "τύπος," *TDNT,* 8:248-49; cf. 246-59.

62. G. Schunack, "τύπος," *EDNT,* 3:374; cf. 372-76. Hays argues that the distinctive meaning is *pattern* or *mold* (*1 Cor,* 162).

63. Cf. Thiselton, *New Horizons in Hermeneutics: The Theory and Practice of Transforming Biblical Reading,* esp. 1-35, 272-312, 379-410, 546-620.

as *type.*[64] Hence NRSV, NIV, NJB, AV/KJV, Barrett, and Phillips render the Greek by *examples,* and REB by *warnings* (and surprisingly v. 11 as *symbolic*). *Examples* improves on *types;* however, the word is too weak in the light of such possibilities as *paradigmatic models, paradigms,* or **formative models**. With the realization in the late twentieth century that progress in the physical sciences, human knowledge, and socioethical understanding depends on *models,* or where possible cognitive, imaginative, paradigmatic, or **formative models**, the ground is prepared for a more ready access to understanding Paul's point. On such ground the question "is the τύπος 'real' or merely an example?" loses its point in the context of a more profound grasp of the role of "models" in concept formation and character formation.

This becomes still clearer in the light of some excellent comments from Paul Gardner. He writes: "later revelation from God was not always to be seen as a straightforward *application* of the events to a later generation in some 'spiritual' manner. Rather, God revealed more about how things actually *were.* This new understanding of what happened *then* could now be shown . . . to parallel events of the day in which the reader lived" (his italics).[65]

One further reason why **formative model for us** is an important indicator of Paul's meaning is that whatever the complexities of theories of typology, the value of the notion of typology of which τύπος forms part is that "each biblical story belongs in the setting of the story as a whole, stretching from Beginning to End, with the Christ-event at the centre. . . . The events related in the two Testaments form one story . . . despite Marcion's attempt to understand it [the NT] as a wholly new story."[66] Goldingay sees much of the value of the term "typology" as a "witness to one story," in which there is an "interlinking" of events through their sharing in the common purpose of the God of Israel who is the Father of Jesus Christ. Yet he concedes that the use of typology is fraught with "risk," and that extreme caution must be exercised to avoid self-deception and anachronism.

The purpose clause has the structure of the negative μή with εἰς and the articular infinitive: εἰς τὸ μὴ εἶναι ἡμᾶς, **with a view to our not craving for evil things**. Barrett comments that the use of the noun with εἶναι followed by καθὼς κἀκεῖνοι ἐπεθύμησαν is "harsh" as well as emphatic, and argues (with Hays and others) that it alludes to desire for "the flesh pots of Egypt" in Num 11:4-34.[67] As Findlay observes, "lusting" for the diet of Egypt "hints at the attraction of the Corinthian idol feasts."[68] On the other hand, the specific plural of τύποι should be

64. Schunack, "τύπος," 375. Even Schunack's disagreement with Goppelt about the role of "historical facts . . . persons, deeds, events . . ." becomes problematic, as if Schunack's stress on eschatology were an *alternative* to Goppelt's valid emphasis on history and events.

65. Gardner, *The Gifts of God,* 113; cf. also Lampe and Woollcombe, *Essays on Typology,* 66; and Ellis, *Prophecy and Hermeneutlc,* 166.

66. Goldingay, *Models for Interpretation of Scripture,* 62; see also 61-66.

67. Barrett, *First Epistle,* 224; cf. Hays, *1 Cor,* 162-63.

68. Findlay, *Expositor's Greek Testament,* 2:859.

noted. Blomberg reminds us that the four privileges granted to **all** in vv. 1-5 find parallels in four tests failed by **the far greater part** in vv. 7-10. He specifies these respectively as (1) the privileges of (a) guidance by the cloud; (b) crossing the sea; (c) the provision of manna; and (d) the supernatural water. (2) The disobedient and self-sufficient stance which leads to failure finds expression in (a) idolatry; (b) immorality; (c) putting the Lord to the test; and (d) grumbling or complaint.[69] G. D. Collier argues for the translation **craving** for evil things, urging that the text constitutes a self-contained Midrash on ἐπιθυμία in Numbers 11, which is "opened up" by Exod 32:6 and other OT passages.[70] Paul applies this Midrash to focus the **craving** of the "strong" at Corinth for participation in the cultic feasts and sacral events which constitute idolatrous practices.[71]

(2) Four Specific Formative Models, by Way of Warning, from Scripture (10:7-13)

If Collier is correct about the force and centrality of ἐπιθυμία in this passage, this entirely coheres with Paul's theology of human sin. Pannenberg rightly observes with reference to Paul and historical theology, "The classical significance of Augustine for the Christian doctrine of sin consists in the fact that he viewed and analysed *the Pauline link between sin and desire more deeply* than Christian theology had hitherto managed to do. . . . Many modern treatments have been unsuccessful because they have overhastily dismissed Augustine's teaching" (my italics).[72] It is "absolute self-willing" that alienates human persons from God, not merely a shallow moralism in which sin is equated with acts which fail to correspond with a legal or moral norm.[73] Further, in the Augsburg Confession sin is both lack of a godly fear of God and "lack of trust in him."[74] Augustine uses Lat. *libido* or *cupiditas* for desire or craving as a basic form of sin where Paul uses Gk. ἐπιθυμία.[75] He speaks of the "attractions" which "lead astray" from God, including "to be held in esteem by others . . . gaining power over them . . . feeling things agreeable to the touch . . . fear of losing good things . . . wanting someone's wife or estates . . . defrauding . . . obtaining honour . . . ," indeed, virtually all of the aspects of misdirected human will, craving, and lifestyle which Paul identified in this epistle.[76] All this springs from "an au-

69. Blomberg, *1 Cor,* 191.

70. Collier, "'That We Might Not Crave Evil': The Structure and Argument of 1 Cor 10:1-13," 55-75.

71. On ἐπιθυμία and ἐπιθυμέω, see BAGD, 293, where there are examples of its use to denote "a desire for something forbidden" not only in the NT and LXX but also in Plato and the Stoics.

72. W. Pannenberg, *Systematic Theology,* 2:241 and 242; cf. 238-65.

73. Ibid., 2:261.

74. Schaff, *Creeds,* 3:8; cited by Pannenberg, *Systematic Theology,* 2:241.

75. Augustine, *On Free Will,* 1:3-4; 3:17-19; on perversion of will and desire cf. *On Eighty-Three Varied Questions,* 35:1 (Migne, *PL,* 40:23); *City of God,* 12:8; *Confessions,* 2:5.

76. Augustine, *Confessions,* 2:5, passim.

tonomy of the will that puts the self in the centre and uses everything else as a means to the self as an end."[77]

This is no mere detour into historical theology. It vindicates the fundamental nature of Paul's argument in 10:1-13 for 8:1–11:1 and for the whole of the epistle and of Paul's theology. Moreover, in his nineteenth-century commentary (1885) Edwards goes behind the "four examples" identified by Meeks and others to show that ἐπιθυμία, misdirected *desire*, lies behind all four, while worldly self-indulgence or "sensuality" leads to (i) idolatry and (ii) immorality; and unbelief leads to (iii) doubt which puts God to the test, and (iv) despair, complaint, or "murmuring."[78] The unity of 10:7-13 is no less theological than it is rhetorical or hermeneutical.

7 Meeks embraces within *"rose up to play"* (παίζειν) the list of five failures which he enumerates (see above). However, it arguably prepares for the transition between **taking part in idol worship** and the reference in the next verse to **immorality**. Paul cites as his biblical quotation the episode narrated in Exod 32:6 (cf. 32:1-6) where the story of the worship of the golden calf begins with unrestrained *feasting and* **drinking** which leads, in the absence of Moses, **to virtual orgy**. To translate παίζειν is an almost impossible task. NJB's innocent-sounding *to amuse themselves* probably derives from BAGD's unimaginatively wooden rendering of παίζω as *to play, to amuse oneself*.[79] Strictly this conveys its most frequent meaning, as its cognate relation with παιδία, *childishness*, and παιδίον, παῖς, a *child*, indicates: children *play games*. The word also denotes *dancing*. A wider semantic range, however, is rightly conveyed by Grimm-Thayer and Liddell-Scott-Jones who include *to sport, to jest, to play amorously, to joke, to dance and sing, to play games, to make sport* (cf. Collins, *rose to play*).[80] Bertram explores an even wider range.[81] How, then, can we determine what part of the semantic range is in view?

The answer lies in the force of Exod 32:1-6 (LXX) as Paul would have understood it, and although Paul cites the LXX wording, the LXX παίζειν was presumably chosen as the nearest equivalent to the Hebrew which it translated, namely, צחק (ts-ch-q), here in the form לצחק (l-ts-ch-q). BDB renders the Qal form *to laugh*, but the form used in the context of Exod 32:6 is *to make sport*, allowing for a probably triple meaning: (i) "letting their hair down" in the absence of Moses with nuances of (ii) idolatrous dancing before the golden calf, and (iii) sexual license approaching **orgy** — all in contrast to the theological

---

77. Pannenberg, *Systematic Theology,* 2:243.

78. Edwards, *First Epistle,* 248.

79. BAGD, 604.

80. Grimm-Thayer, 473; LSJ, 1,109, where *to play amorously* is listed under category I, 5. Cf. also Louw-Nida, *Lexicon,* 1:528; cf. Collins, *First Cor,* 363, 370.

81. G. Bertram, "παίζω," *TDNT,* 5:625-30. Since the time of Homer, παίζειν could embody either neutral or erotic overtones, e.g., in the *dancing* of nymphs. Plato uses the term of flippant behavior (*Republic* 10.602b). *Play* may involve regarding persons as *playthings*. The earliest OT allusions concern *dance* and *laughter,* but Wis 15:12 uses the term critically of treating *life* as a *game*.

and ethical restraint and sober *self-control* (cf. 9:24-27) demanded of God's covenant people.[82] This demands a more forceful translation than *to play* (NRSV) and a more sinister nuance than *to revel* (REB). Fee criticizes NIV's *to indulge in pagan revelry* as reading *pagan* into the text, but his criticism overlooks Bertram's exegesis of Exodus 32 in "cultic dancing" or overly harsh in the light of the Hebrew and the context of Exod 32:1-6, where "pagan-*like*" is implicit.[83] The combination "lifting the lid" of control or restraint, fired by **drink**, a party mood, and the absence of the patriarchal figure of Moses led to more than mere *play*. Even though Louw-Nida separate the "semantic domain" of παίζω from that of κῶμος, *drunken orgy* (in Rom 13:13), in 1 Pet 4:3 κῶμος is associated with ἐπιθυμία, and Louw-Nida recognize that a number of scholars understand παίζω in 1 Cor 10:7 "as a euphemism for sex."[84] The two terms overlap. Brevard Childs well captures the mood of Exod 32:1-6. Aaron declares of the human constructs, "These are your gods, O Israel . . . ," and the section concludes with "a burst of frenzied activity. . . . A religious orgy has begun."[85] Only in order to preserve a semantic distinction from κῶμος do we translate **to virtual orgy**, but Paul is obliged to use the LXX word. **Orgy** allows for (i) lack of sober restraint and self-control; (ii) religious or cultic "enthusiasm" which goes beyond reasonable or sober limits; and (iii) probably sexual license. If it were not for the probable cultic dimension, we might try to capture the double meaning in modern English by *got up to have a romp* (cf. *romp in the hay*), or (in quotation marks) *got up to have "fun and games."* Schrage speaks of the "Kultisch-orgiastische Tänze vor dem Goldenen Kalb."[86]

The relevance of Israel's experience to Corinth and the huge force of the sentiment for which *amuse themselves* (NJB) or *play* (NRSV) misses the point can be appreciated only when we fully grasp the intimate connection for the LXX, hellenistic Judaism, and Paul between worshiping religious constructs of human devising and sexual immorality and abandonment of the "censor" to sheer unbridled indulgence. This explains Rom 1:18-31, which reflects Wis 7:25; 11:15; 13:1-19; 14:22-31; 15:18-19 (and in turn Ps 106:20; Isa 44:9-20).[87] In 1 Cor 10:1-13 it is precisely the "turn on" which idolatrous cultic festivals gave to an overrelaxed, psychotic mind-set that leads Paul to tackle the issue so forcefully. Such "participation" could damage and destroy all that the Christian community represented.

For μηδὲ εἰδωλολάτραι γίνεσθε BAGD rightly propose *do not take part in idol worship* both on the ground of the context at Corinth (avoid *participation,*

---

82. BDBG, *Hebrew Aramaic English Lexicon* (1980 ed.), 850.

83. Fee, *First Epistle,* 454, n. 19. See Bertram, "παίζω," 629.

84. Louw-Nida, *Lexicon,* 1:528 (entry 50.8), 773 (entry 88.287).

85. D. S. Childs, *Exodus: A Commentary* (London: SCM, 1974), 566; cf. 564-67. Cf. further Strack-Billerbeck, *Kommentar,* 3:410.

86. Schrage, *Der erste Brief,* 2:398.

87. Cf. Dunn, *Romans 1–8,* 53-76; S. Wibbing, *Die Tugend- und Lasterkataloge im NT und ihr Traditionsgeschichte,* BZNW 25 (Berlin: Töpelmann, 1959); Fitzmyer, *Romans,* 270-90.

taking part in pagan cultic acts) and of language (εἴδωλον + λατρεύω, λατρεία): "What he [Paul] condemns here is the actual participation in idolatrous worship, which he never condones, since he sees it to result in communion with the demons (10:20, 21)."[88] This is a different issue from eating meat which had been supplied by pagan temples for the market (8:1-13; 10:23-33). As Senft states, Paul has in mind "participation at the ceremonies [cultic festivities] at pagan banquets."[89]

Archaeological evidence concerning the Temple of Asclepios (to which Pausanias refers also) provides an excellent example of the difference between attending a meal which might just happen to be located within the precincts of a temple, and accepting an invitation to attend a meal which was devoted to the offering of thanks and praise to Asclepios, the god of healing, for a return of health on the part of the one who arranges the cultic banquet. Vitruvius writes of "the shrines . . . for Asclepios and Salus . . . by whose medical power sick persons are manifestly healed . . . so it will happen that the divinity, from the nature of the site [of the Temple], will gain a greater and higher reputation and authority."[90] It is possible, but not certain, that three dining rooms to the east side of the courtyard of the Temple of Asclepios were in operation in Paul's time. The couches around the walls could accommodate eleven persons, and the blackening of stone suggests that cooking was undertaken there. Murphy-O'Connor makes the fundamental point that "some of the functions would have been *purely social* in character [my italics; cf. 8:1-13; 10:23-33]; but others would have been gestures of gratitude to the god for such happy events as a cure, a birth, a coming of age, or a marriage [cf. 10:1-22]."[91] The wording of an invitation would often indicate whether a religious or cultic dimension was involved. A well-known example is: "Herais asks you to dine in the room of the Serapheion [= Asclepion] at the banquet of the Lord Seraphis tomorrow from the 11th, from the 9th hour."[92]

The excavations of the Asclepion have uncovered terra-cotta representations of heads, hands, feet, legs, eyes, and ears, signifying parts of the body constructed to acknowledge their healing and restoration by the god. Indeed, A. E. Hill has proposed that this contributed to Paul's use of the body imagery, although this view is firmly rejected by Murphy-O'Connor and others.[93] Murphy-O'Connor invites us to imagine the dilemma of "the weak" when the host calls out an invitation to a questionable cultic meal, and the "weak" per-

---

88. Barrett, *First Epistle,* 225; BAGD, 221; similarly, Schrage, *Der erste Brief,* 2:398.

89. Senft, *La Première Épitre,* 130.

90. Vitruvius, *On Architecture,* 1.2.7; conveniently cited in Murphy-O'Connor, *St. Paul's Corinth,* 162.

91. Murphy-O'Connor, *St. Paul's Corinth,* 164 (Murphy-O'Connor provides the above description of the dining rooms, 164).

92. *Papyrus Oxyrhynchus* 110.

93. A. E. Hill, "The Temple of Asclepius: An Alternative Source for Paul's Body Theology?" *JBL* 99 (1980): 437-39.

son sees a "strong" Christian believer already reclining in the dining room. This provides a better framework for understanding the difference between 8:1-13 and 10:23-33 than the very close discussion of the nature of "idol meats" conducted by Fee and others with much speculation and controversy. Friendships and kinship relations could give rise to sensitive difficulties in the area under discussion. As Khiok-khing Yeo observes, "a social obligation such as a marriage, a birth or a graduation party would require friends and relatives to celebrate in the temple, a social club, or a friend's home. Such celebrations often began with a sacrifice and ended with a banquet. . . . The setting of 1 Cor 8 and 10 is explicitly mentioned in 8:10 as the pagan temple, and in 10:23–11:1 as the private home."[94] Willis distinguishes between (i) formal public sacrifice to pagan deities involving cultic meals; (ii) quasi-religious social or political gatherings or state festivals; and (iii) private meals in pagan homes, or in rooms associated with pagan deities.[95] Paul adopts a strict stance toward any setting that may be regarded as **taking part in idol worship**.

N. Walter facilitates our understanding of the position of "the strong."[96] Not only did they wish to avoid appearing "narrow," overscrupulous, and over-sensitive to their families and friends, especially those of influence; they also argued that since "we all know that God is one" (8:3-6) any manifestation of "the sacred" or of "religion" surely reflects the immanent being of the one universal God, who has more than one face. After all, Paul believed that they were not to withdraw from the world.[97] The setting of the private meals causes no problem: the issue concerns εἰδωλόθυτον, but an idol is "nothing." On the other hand, does participation in pagan cultic practices constitute εἰδωλολατρία?[98] For Paul the answer is clear: because he draws on the biblical tradition he believes *both* that idols have no real existence *and* that they represent sinister, demonic powers of evil, not least because gods fashioned by humankind provide religious sanction for all kinds of wishful indulgence.[99] Hence against syncretistic assumptions drawn from the Gentile world, Paul confronts his readers with the scriptural tradition of a covenant loyalty to the God of Israel which is different from Graeco-Roman "religiosity."[100] The Christian sacraments specifically anchor faith to *Christ*.

8 (i) A few minor late variants correct the number to 24,000 to accord with Num 25:9; (ii) D³, K, and L change the first aorist ἔπεσαν to the more usual second aorist ἔπεσον,

---

94. Yeo, *Rhetorical Interaction in 1 Cor 8 and 10,* 95 and 96.

95. Willis, *Idol Meat,* 8-64.

96. Walter, "Christusglaube und heidnische Religiosität in paulinischen Gemeinden," esp. 425-36.

97. Ibid., 422.

98. Ibid., 427.

99. Ibid., 429.

100. Ibid., 430-36; cf. Yeo, *Rhetorical Interaction in 1 Cor 8 and 10,* 100-119.

but the first aorist occurs in the LXX and especially in Alexandrian literature, and there is no reason to doubt its genuineness.

Sexual immorality (v. 8) represents the second of the four failures, or failed tests, which characterized Israel in the OT wilderness traditions. On the precise meaning of πορνεύω, πόρνος, πορνεία, see above under 5:9-11; 6:9 (πόρνος); 6:18 (πορνεύω); 5:1; 6:13, 18; 7:2 (πορνεία); esp. 5:1; 5:9-11; 6:13. In v. 8 these commands apply in general, except that 10:8 is recognized to apply more specifically to temple prostitution.[101] The dual background to this verse must be borne in mind. (i) The first context is the traditions of the OT, hellenistic-Jewish literature (esp. Wisdom of Solomon), and the midrashic traditions which are found in developed form in rabbinic literature and with which Meeks and Collier, among others, associate these verses (see above under 10:6-7). (ii) The second fundamental context is that of the influence of the cults of Aphrodite, Dionysus/Bacchus, Apollo, Isis and Serapis, and Poseidon at Corinth. Archaeological evidence not only establishes, but brings to life, the reality and impact of these cults, many with implications for sexual license for Corinth in its civic, cultural, and everyday life. To be sure, we must note the problem of date. Those who cite the visual impact of the hilltop of Acrocorinth, e.g., long associated with Aphrodite as the protector of the city, often allude to excesses in the earlier pre-Roman period. The earlier Greek period was more responsible than the Roman for the specifically sexual influences of pagan idolatry. Nevertheless, the Roman period is far from innocent of this aspect, and archaeology offers abundant evidence of the influence of Graeco-Roman cults and images at every turn.

Six pagan temples dating from around the first century BC line the west side of the Agora, not far from the series for worship on the northern side, where Paul may have plied his trade as a leather worker during his eighteen months in the city. Whether or not Paul worked there, above the workshops rose the Temple of Apollo, and we have alluded above to evidence concerning the Temple of Asclepios. Yeo (following Williams and Engels) observes that "In Corinth [Aphrodite] was a god of sailors and sacred prostitution and the protectress of the city."[102] Hence business interests and trade were bound up with the welfare of the cult. Yet in OT and Jewish traditions Aphrodite bears direct historical relation to the Assyrian-Babylonian-Persian "Queen of Heaven" denounced in Jer 7:18; 14:18. Coins excavated at Corinth bear the images of Aphrodite and Poseidon more often than those of any other pagan gods.[103] All that

---

101. Wolff, *Der erste Brief,* 219 et al.

102. Yeo, *Rhetorical Interaction,* 109. See further C. K. Williams, "Corinth and the Cult of Aphrodite," in M. A. Del Chiaco (ed.), *Corinthiaca: Studies in Honor of Darell A. Amyne* (Columbia: University of Missouri Press, 1986), 12-24; and D. Engels, *Roman Corinth* (Chicago: University of Chicago Press, 1990), 97-99.

103. Cf. J. K. Kent, *Corinth: The Inscriptions, 1926-1952,* no. 12; Yeo, *Rhetorical Interaction,* 105.

we observed under vv. 6-7 about the relation between idolatry and sexual license receives added point in this context. Moreover, Yeo gives further evidence of the impact of the Bacchic/Dionysiac cult on Corinth, supported by the research of Broneer.[104]

As we have noted, the competitiveness and status-seeking at Corinth suggest parallels with early twentieth-first-century modern/postmodern cultures. Similarly, the cults of Aphrodite, Apollo, and Dionysus invited a "freedom" to dispense with moral restraint and to tolerate everything except any trans-contextual truth claim which might interfere with an individual's "right" to instant self-gratification. All of this resonates with a postmodern ethic which is founded only on "where society is" at the beginning of the twenty-first century.[105] "'And Rose Up to Play'" resonates with treating other human persons as "playthings" in the "play" of cultic and recreational sex (see the Introduction, 11). It is against this background that Paul presses the issue of whether it is the OT as scripture that provides the believers' **formative models** (10:6, 11) or whether they stand instead in solidarity with those of Israel who **fell** and with *degenerate idolatry*.

Paul cites the incident narrated in Num 25:1-9, according to which 24,000 fell (Num 25:9). However, Paul (against LXX, Philo et al.) speaks of **twenty-three thousand**. Commentators have exhausted their ingenuity in trying to explain the numerical "discrepancy." An early tradition found in Grotius suggests that 23,000 fell *in one day,* but 24,000 in all. Calvin speculates: "Moses gives the upper limit, Paul the lower, so there is really no discrepancy."[106] Bengel refines Calvin's proposal, urging that if, e.g., the actual number (we have to assume known to Moses and to Paul) were 23,600, the round number could plausibly be expressed by Paul's retaining the twenty-three (23,000), while Moses rounded it up to the strictly nearest thousand, i.e., 24,000. Bengel disarmingly adds that this avoids "the subtleties of other interpreters"(!)[107] Charles Hodge follows Calvin and Bengel, including a brief defence of biblical "infallibility," in arguing that for people to resort to attacking this doctrine by appealing to a trivial problem which is capable of explanation exposes the weakness of the opposition.[108] Most modern commentators contend that Paul is not troubled to provide an exact memory, and may well have conflated his thought with a further allusion to Num 26:62.[109] Fee concludes that "there is not an entirely satisfactory solution" to "the infamous case of the missing thousand," while Kistemaker reminds us not to draw any in-

---

104. Yeo, *Rhetorical Interaction,* 107 (and 94-119); O. Broneer, "Paul and the Pagan Cults at Isthmia," *HTR* 44 (1971): 182.

105. H. W. House, "Tongues and the Mystery Religions at Corinth," *BSac* 140 (1983): 134-50.

106. Calvin, *First Epistle,* 209.

107. Bengel, *Gnomon,* 639-40.

108. Hodge, *First Epistle,* 178.

109. Conzelmann, *1 Cor,* 168; Wolff, *Der erste Brief,* 219; Schrage, *Der erste Brief,* 2:400; Lang, *Die Brief,* 125.

ference too readily in a case where we cannot be clearly certain what has occurred.[110] It is worth noting that the patristic writers seem to be untroubled by this verse. I can find no discussion of the issue, e.g., in Origen, Chrysostom, or Augustine.[111]

9 (1) Χριστόν is attested by the earliest MS. 𝔭46, together with D, E, F, G, K, and early patristic writers in a variety of local regions: Irenaeus (Lyons); Ephraem (Edessa), Clement (Alexandria), Old Latin, Vulgate, Syriac, Sahidic, and Bohairic. However, ℵ, B, and C have τὸν κύριον, which reflects τὸν θέον (cf. LXX of Num 21:5-6; Deut 6:16, and Ps 77:18 [Ps 78:18]: *They put God to the test in their hearts by demanding food for their own desires*). Before reference could be made to 𝔭46, some older commentators suggested that "we may safely prefer τὸν κύριον."[112] However, more recent writers almost unanimously (but with exceptions) argue for τὸν Χριστόν, including Metzger, Conzelmann, Schrage, Fee, and most decisively Zuntz and the research article by C. D. Osburn.[113] The major arguments in favor of accepting and retaining **Christ** (which UBS 4th ed. ranks as "B," i.e., "almost certain") are (a) that it is easy to understand how an original **Christ** could be changed to *the Lord* because (i) **Christ** presupposes a Christology which identifies the *God* of Israel (or the *angel of the Lord*) with the preexistent Christ;[114] (ii) *Lord* with *put to the test* would be a familiar phrase from the use of Deut 6:16 in the Gospel narratives of the messianic temptations; (iii) *Lord* would be near to LXX Num 21:5-6; Ps 77:18 [78:18]; and (b) that 𝔭46 goes back to around AD 200, and is supported by D and very early second- and third-century patristic witness from locations across the Graeco-Roman world. (2) ἀπώλοντο reflects the better ℵ, A, and B as reading ἀπώλοντο of C, D, and G. Some MSS read ἀπώλλυντο (see below).

The third example or **formative model** (by way of warning) is that of **putting Christ to the test**. A form of μή with the subjunctive is used: μηδὲ ἐκπειράζωμεν. The compound verb with ἐκ occurs in the LXX as well as in relation to Christ in the NT (Matt 4:7; par. Lk 4:12). The present subjunctive may have the force of *let us no longer put,* i.e., **nor should we continue to put Christ to the test**. Although this must not be pressed, the implication is that the addressees were already doing this. While ἐκπειράζω in classical Greek serves as a synonym for πειράζω in Koine Greek, since Paul uses the LXX

110. Fee, *First Epistle,* 456; Kistemaker, *First Epistle,* 330.

111. Chrysostom, *Homilies on 1 Corinthians,* offers no comment; and J. W. Wiles, *A Scripture Index to the Works of St Augustine* (Lanham, Md.: University Press of America, 1993), has no reference, as is the case in D. D. Hannah, *The Text of 1 Corinthians in the Writings of Origen* (Atlanta: Scholars Press, 1997).

112. Robertson and Plummer, *First Epistle,* 205; so also Meyer, *First Epistle,* 1:279.

113. C. D. Osburn, "The Text of 1 Cor 10:9," in E. J. Epp and G. D. Fee (eds.) *NT Textual Criticism: Its Significance for Exegesis: Essays in Honour of B. M. Metzger* (Oxford: Clarendon Press, 1981), 201-12; Metzger, *Textual Commentary,* 2d ed., 494; Zuntz, *Text,* 126-27; Conzelmann, *1 Cor,* 164, n. 2; Fee, *First Epistle,* 450, n. 2 and 457, n. 34; Schrage, *Der erste Brief,* 2:400-401, n. 101. An exception is Senft, *La Première Épitre,* 130.

114. Cf. J. Habermann, *Präexistenzaussagen im NT,* EHS T 23 (Frankfurt am Main, 1990), 219-20; A. T. Hanson, *Jesus Christ in the OT,* 11-16.

term, it is preferable to embody the intensive force of the compound ἐκ in translation, i.e., **put to the test** (with NRSV, REB, NJB) as against *test* (NIV).[115] The LXX sometimes uses ἐκπειράζω (Num 21:4, 5; Ps 77:18) but at other times the simple form πείραζω (Ps 94:9), thereby inviting note when the stronger form occurs.[116]

Our second textual note calls attention to the use of the second aorist middle ἀπώλοντο, which understands **destruction** or *perishing under the aspect of an event.* However, the "vivid" or "graphic" form of the imperfect middle ἀπώλλυντο or the more usual imperfect ἀπώλλοντο (the probable reading) denote **destruction** or *perishing under the aspect of process.* Findlay suggests "lay a-perishing."[117] BAGD propose the bland and insipid *they were killed* for this verse, which NIV and NJB adopt.[118] NRSV and REB have *were destroyed,* which better reflects the powerful verb ἀπόλλυμι (active, *to destroy;* middle, *to perish,* to suffer ruin). The use of ὑπὸ τῶν ὄφεων, **by the snakes,** to express *active agency* with the intransitive middle of the verb has parallels elsewhere and is not irregular. Since Paul uses ἀπόλλυμι with force and significance in this epistle (1:18, τοῖς ἀπολλυμένοις, *to those who are on their way to ruin;* 1:9, ἀπολῶ, *I will destroy the "wisdom" of the wise*), we must retain either *ruin* or **destruction**, but strive to maintain the force of the imperfect as a *process* before the eyes. Hence **suffered the process of destruction by the snakes** (including death throes as the effects become operative).

The theological distinctions between the four examples are profound. We have noted how all flow from ἐπιθυμία (see the introduction to vv. 7-13). (i) and (ii) reflected idolatry and immorality, and vv. 7 and 8 revealed intimate links between these. *The contrast between formative models (iii) and (iv) concerns respectively the sin of presumption and the sin of despair.* By presuming (in Witherington's words) that "they were immune to spiritual danger" and "to spiritual danger at pagan feasts," they put God's love and promise most sorely to the test: Would God not protect them?[119] They *presumed* to force God's hand to preserve them by **putting** his love and salvation **to the** utmost **test**. This entirely reflects the overconfident stance of "the strong," secure, but, as Schrage notes, falsely secure, in their "knowledge" (γνῶσις, 8:1) and abuse of freedom (10:23).[120]

This presumption is incisively and movingly brought out in Jürgen Moltmann's *Theology of Hope.* Drawing on the work of Walther Zimmerli and Gerhard von Rad on divine promise and hope on the OT, Moltmann insists that for Israel in the wilderness, as for the pilgrim church of Christ, the future is promised but not yet. Hence "Presumption is the premature self-willed antici-

115. Cf. BAGD, 243.
116. Schrage, *Der erste Brief,* 2:401.
117. Findlay, *Expositor's Greek Testament,* 2:861.
118. BAGD, 95.
119. Witherington, *Conflict and Community,* 220.
120. Schrage, *Der erste Brief,* 2:401.

pation of what we hope from God; despair is the premature arbitrary anticipation of non-fulfilment."[121] By contrast to each, Christian faith lays hold on divine promise. In this context (1 Corinthians 8–10) it adopts neither the presumptions of "the strong" nor the anxious timidity of "the weak," but moves forward in both wariness and confidence, with self-discipline and trust. Believers, Moltmann asserts (with Paul), live as the "exodus church."[122]

10 The lexicons may well convey the normal semantic range of γογγύζω (v. 10), the onomatopoeic word for *murmuring, grumbling, griping, groaning, whining, whispering, complaining* (especially behind one's hand).[123] However, the OT contexts are decisive in assisting us to grasp what semantic nuances are operative. The bold statement *Don't complain. . . . The angel of death killed them* (W. F. Beck, *The New Testament in the Language of Today*) or even *Neither murmur ye, as some of them murmured and were destroyed of the destroyer* (AV/KJV) implies a questionable theology of God which is out of context. In context the concept is not petty complaints as such, but the constant grudging, carping, **querulous moaning** which transformed the bold, glad self-perception of those whom God had redeemed from Egypt for a new lifestyle into a self-pitying, false perception of themselves as "victims" on whom God had weighed heavy burdens and trials, in contrast to a fantasy life of ideal existence in Egypt or the world.

Whenever Moses called for restraint or discipline, or whenever people within Israel themselves were not involved in leadership or in exalted experiences, the LXX portrays them by the verb γογγύζω, for Heb. לוּן *(lun)*, in Exodus 15–17, esp. 15:24; 16:2, 7, 8, often with עַל *('al)*, for against Moses; in Numbers 14–17, esp. 14:2, 27, 29; 16:11, 41, also with עַל, 14:27, 29, for against God.[124] As Orr and Walther observe, this verse uses γογγύζω as "a summary statement" for the sixteen or so occurrences in the Pentateuch.[125] On the construction ἀπώλοντο ὑπὸ τοῦ ὀλοθρευτοῦ, see above under v. 9. When this is applied to Corinth (as well as to Israel) Grimm-Thayer's comment about fueling *complaining* by covert exchanges in small groups (often against the leadership) becomes highly relevant (see the earlier Note).

Hays, who has carried out special research in this area, concedes that of the four OT examples in 10:7-10, this fourth "is the most difficult to connect to a specific OT text and also the most difficult to relate to any known behavior of the Corinthians. The best guess is that Paul is thinking of Numbers 14, in which the people complain against Moses and Aaron and desire to return to Egypt

121. J. Moltmann, *Theology of Hope* (Eng. trans., London: SCM, 1967), 21.

122. Ibid., 95-154, on promise and hope, covenant, and the Exodus church.

123. BAGD, 164; Grimm-Thayer, 120. The lexicographers agree that the word typically denotes murmuring as a sign of displeasure (e.g., Exod 16:7; Matt 20:11; Num 14:27, to speak complainingly, BAGD). Grimm-Thayer stress the *underground* or secret nature of the complaining often *corporately*.

124. BDBG (1980 ed.), 534.

125. Orr and Walther, *1 Cor*, 246.

(14:2-4).”[126] Since the allusion may be general rather than specific, **the destroyer** (rare word, the destroying one in Exod 12:23 LXX) seems to offer a suitably less specific translation than the angel of death (1 Chron 21:12, 15). Schneider has provided a discussion of this issue.[127] Paul elsewhere refers to OT patterns rather than necessarily to specific verses (cf. 15:4a, b, *according to the scriptures*), which often provide *more* powerful, *not less* powerful, *formative models* than a single passage may do.

11 UBS 4th ed. ranks ταῦτα without πάντα as "B," i.e., "almost certain." This is probably correct. It is possible that Paul wrote **all these things** (with ℵ, D, F, and G, but A, B, and 33 omit **all**, and MSS vary in where they place πάντα.[128] D and G omit τυπικῶς, but (with the possible exception of Zuntz) virtually all regard the inclusion of the word as correct.

Heinrici believes that the meaning of the entire verse remains obscure unless we attend to its major premise, that Christian believers live as those privileged to live *in the last days* (ἐσχάται ἡμέραι, Isa 2:2).[129] However, Weiss (partly followed by Héring) insists on taking seriously the *two* plurals in the phrase τὰ τέλη τῶν αἰώνων, **the ends of the ages**, with NRSV; cf. NJB, *in the last days of the ages* (against REB, *end of the ages*); NIV, *the fulfillment of the ages* (one plural only); AV/KJV, *the ends of the world* (a single but different plural). Weiss envisages *the two ages* of the OT and Jewish thought "touching end to end," i.e., "intersecting," where "the close of the old [age] coincides with the beginning of the new."[130] Anticipating Schweitzer, he alludes to 4 Ezra (2 Esdr) 6:7-10. "All this has been written *'for our sakes'* (Rom 15:4; 1 Cor 10:11 who stand on the borderline of both aeons. In these last times the veil . . . should be lifted . . . (2 Cor 3:14) . . . Christ (2 Cor 1:20) . . . is the real content of the Holy Scriptures (Rom 1:2, 3). . . . Everything in Scripture seems to relate itself to him; all must be related to him. . . . Thus . . . the word 'Lord' appear[s] in a new light."[131]

Héring contends that Weiss pays insufficient attention to the force of the preposition εἰς with the relative pronoun οὕς (**upon whom**) in relation to the meaning of κατήντηκεν, **have come**, which Héring understands in the sense of the middle *they meet one another.* Robertson and Plummer argue that in the NT the Greek καταντάω means *to reach one's destination* but concede that here the meaning is "obscure."[132] Héring interprets Paul to mean: "The

126. Hays, *First Cor,* 165.

127. J. Schneider, "ὀλεθρεύω," *TDNT,* 5:168-70. See further Fee, *First Epistle,* 457-58, who proposes Num 14:1-38 or Num 16:41 (the Korah narrative, where people are destroyed by plague). Heinrici rejects an allusion to Numbers 14 in favor of Numbers 16 *(Das erste Sendschreiben),* 268-69.

128. Metzger, *Commentary,* 2d ed., 494.

129. Heinrici, *Das erste Sendschreiben,* 269.

130. Weiss, *Der erste Korintherbrief,* 254.

131. Weiss, *Earliest Christianity,* 2:436-37.

132. Robertson and Plummer, *First Epistle,* 207.

two ages meet one another at their extremities at the point where we Christians stand. We are at the point of intersection of the two worlds."[133] This does not seem to differ from Weiss as greatly as he appears to claim. However, more important, it fully harmonizes with the "now and not yet" eschatology of Paul and of the NT: "Christians live on the one hand in the last days of the former age, and on the other, in the Kingdom of Christ, which is an anticipation of the future age."[134]

This frame of reference precisely fits the contrast between 10:9 and 10:10 as a Corinthian *theology of presumption or overconfidence* (partly based on overrealized eschatology, partly on the Graeco-Roman attitudes inherited by "the strong") and *a theology of despair or doubt* (reflected perhaps in the insecurities and tendency to self-doubt among some of the "weak").[135] As Moltmann insists (see above), *neither presumption nor despair* can remain compatible with the Exodus pilgrimage of faith on the basis of promise, where the people of God have decisively *crossed the sea* (v. 2) but travel through the wilderness as pilgrims, who still look ahead to the promised land. At one time, especially during the 1950s, it became almost wearisome to read in almost every work on eschatology in Paul and the NT that (in W. Manson's words) it exhibited "an essential bi-polarity. The End has come! The end has not come!"[136] It was almost as if scholars relished a contradiction which flowed from Paul's dependence on "the Hebraic mind" of the "biblical theology movement" or the appropriation of apocalyptic and rabbinic legacies when "Hellenism" was out of fashion. However, Moltmann has demonstrated in modern systematic theology that none of this offers the theoretical stalemate which work from Weiss and Schweitzer to Dodd and Jeremias might seem to imply. Eschatology, especially its dynamic bipolar tension, offers a dimension of theology which has deeply practical implications for all theology and ethics.[137] In Pauline theology practical implications began to emerge in Käsemann's identification of overrealized eschatology and "enthusiasm" with lack of realism about self-discipline and pilgrimage, and with Harrisville's emphasis on "newness" as entailing both continuity and contrast.[138] Increasingly its ethical significance has

133. Héring, *First Epistle,* 89; he also cites Polybius, 4.26.1 for the middle force of the active, when they meet each other (89, n. 23).

134. Héring, *First Epistle,* 89.

135. See above on "the strong" and "the weak"; A. C. Thiselton, "Realized Eschatology at Corinth," *NTS* 24 (1978): 510-26; and E. Käsemann, *NT Questions of Today,* 125-26. On the danger of subsuming Christology under eschatology cf. also A. König, *The Eclipse of Christ in Eschatology* (Grand Rapids: Eerdmans, 1989).

136. W. Manson et al., *Eschatology,* SJT Occasional Papers (Edinburgh: Oliver & Boyd, 1953), 7.

137. Moltmann, *Theology of Hope,* 16 and throughout, and *The Coming of God* (Eng. trans., London: SCM, 1996), esp. 6-46.

138. Käsemann, *NT Questions of Today,* 125-26; R. A. Harrisville, *The Concept of Newness in the NT* (Minneapolis: Augsburg, 1960), 12-29 and throughout; also "The Concept of Newness in the NT," *JBL* 74 (1955): 75-76.

been appreciated, and in 1991 it found expression in J. P. Sampley's *Walking between the Times: Paul's Moral Reasoning.*[139]

We may transpose Sampley's terminology to match the issues which Paul addresses more closely. The "not yet" dimension addresses a *Corinthian theology of presumption,* especially on the part of the "strong"; *freedom* is all; God will not allow us to fall; we belong *wholly* to the age of new creation, no less than our counterparts in Graeco-Roman cults who have been redeemed from the world and elevated to a new plane of existence.[140] People who thought that they "stood" needed to "take heed lest they fell."[141] The "now" dimension addresses *a Corinthian theology of doubt and anxiety,* especially on the part of the "weak," for whom the socioeconomic realities of dependency on the powerful (now often the powerful in the church) seem not to have changed very much. Life goes on. To both Paul explains that they are incorporated within a cosmic story of grace to Israel and to the church in which God decisively redeems his people but also requires that they journey as pilgrims "through" but not "of" the world, with realism about self-discipline and trust in the divine promise.

It is within this eschatological frame that we may ask what sense τὰ τέλη τῶν αἰώνων carries here, and begin to explore (also in the light of our comments on τύποι, v. 6 above) how we should understand the force of ταῦτα δὲ τυπικῶς συνέβαινεν ἐκείνοις. Our discussion of eschatology suggests that to lay all the emphasis (with NIV, REB, and Fee) on the "fulfillment of the ages" (Fee) is inadequate. Paul stresses *not only the contrast* between the age of Israel and the age of the church (i.e., in Christ we perceive the meaning of the OT traditions more clearly) but *also the continuity* with which they lead from one to the other (the church, too, has its "tests" in a pilgrim journey). It is not enough to say "the old is on its way out, the new has begun (2 Cor 5:17)."[142] It is true that for Paul Christians stand in a more direct relation to Christ "toward whom all history has had its goal."[143] However, if Fee is right in also claiming that "although the wording has changed from v. 6, the point is the same in both instances," the relation between **formative models** (τύποι, v. 6) and eschatology is more complex.[144] We respect part of Gardner's excellent comment on τύπος: "Later revelation . . . was not always to be seen as a straightforward *application* of the events to a later generation in some 'spiritual' manner. Rather, God revealed more about how things actually *were.* . . ."[145]

139. P. J. Sampley, *Walking between the Times* (Minneapolis: Fortress, 1991), esp. 7-35, 50-70, 107-19.

140. Cf. A. D. Nock, *St. Paul* (New York and London: Harper, 1938), 174; Nock, *Conversion* (Oxford: Oxford University Press, 1933; rpt. 1961), 1-16, 33-47, 99-137, 193-211; and R. A. Knox, *Enthusiasm* (Oxford: Oxford University Press, 1950), 9-24.

141. Gardner, *Gifts of God,* 149 and 10-12.

142. Fee, *First Epistle,* 459.

143. Ibid.

144. Ibid., 458.

145. Gardner, *Gifts of God,* 113. For the full quotation, see under v. 6.

Paul, however, does *not* say in this verse that the events of the wilderness happened τυπικῶς *to us,* but **these things happened in succession** (continuous imperfect, συνέβαινεν, one by one) **to them** (ἐκείνοις) in the mode (adverb) of their **formative models**. Israel was to shape faith and conduct in the light of *each successive event in a series of patterned occurrences which befell them in their wilderness journey.* The continuous imperfect is significant, for if a single event wiped out all of Israel's people, this would hardly serve as a **formative model for them**. However, Paul hastens to add in the same breath that their narrative functions **also** extend **to serve as warnings for us** (ἐγράφη δὲ νουθεσίαν ἡμῶν). J. W. Aageson's title *Written Also for Our Sake* faithfully reflects Paul's use of δέ. Since he calls attention to the eschatological situation of continuity and contrast between Israel and Christian believers, it is beyond doubt that he wishes this to illuminate in what sense he now uses τυπικῶς. It has become part of its logical grammar *in this context* that it denotes the mode of operation (adverb) of **formative models of broader patterns**, or **formative models** which *also transcend their immediate context.*[146] A translation is needed which recognizes the primary function of *the events* as **formative models** for **them** (Israel), but **also** as no less for **us** (Christians living at the **ends** or meeting point **of the ages**) since they presuppose and instantiate **broader patterns** (see further under v. 6, above). We have retained **the ends** (rather than *meeting point*) for τὰ τέλη since our interpretation should not foreclose the possibility of other nuances of a word that means **ends**.[147]

12-13 With Schrage and Ramsaran we view vv. 12 and 13 as two sides of a whole, under the theme of πειρασμός.[148] Gardner rightly perceives the issue "people who thought they 'stood' needed to take heed lest they fell" as "at the root of the Corinthian problem. Many thought they were 'standing', but were in fact falling."[149] ὥστε with the (third singular) imperative demonstrates the centrality of the directive about to be made, following the formative models and warnings of 10:1-11, and should be translated (with Findlay) **So, then, . . .** (cf. 3:21).[150] Willis notes the regular stylized patterns of imperative and subjunctive (in vv. 7-10 in an A-B-B-A chiastic pattern), which here reaches a climax with the imperative, in which "ὥστε indicates the conclusive character of this sentence."[151]

---

146. Cf. Ramsaran, *Liberating Words:* "happened to them in a patterned fashion" (137, n. 253). It should be noted that τυπικῶς occurs otherwise only in a later papyrus and in ecclesiastical writers. Paul coins the adverb to convey a technical sense here. Cf. BAGD 829; A. T. Robertson, *Epistles,* 4:153-54; MM, 645; Schrage, *Der erste Brief,* 2:403-8.

147. Numerous writers offer an exegesis which leaves a recognized "apocalyptic or eschatological" dimension in virtual isolation from the meaning of τυπικῶς. Even Aageson interprets the latter as "to serve as an example" and the former as "apocalyptic" in the sense of "the end of the age has come." However, this misses the context of presumption and doubt and the dialectic between contrast and continuity which is at issue (cf. Aageson, *Written Also for Our Sake,* 23).

148. Schrage, *Der erste Brief,* 2:409; Ramsaran, *Liberating Words,* 57.

149. Gardner, *Gifts of God,* 149.

150. Findlay, *Expositor's Greek Testament,* 2:862.

151. Willis, *Idol Meat,* 147 and 155; also 155, n. 143.

The perfect infinitive ἑστάναι is also emphatic, signifying *stand firm* or **stand fast**, while ὁ δοκῶν, *the one who* **thinks** (**whoever thinks**) alludes, as Conzelmann notes, to a misplaced *securitas* as "cocksureness."[152] For **to think** that one **stands fast** has overtones of reliance upon God's covenant security. LXX ἵστημι often translates Hebrew עמד (*'āmad*) and כון *(kûn)* in the context of standing firm in the confidence of covenant security (Ps 104:10, LXX).[153] This "presumption" (see above under v. 9) is connected in the case of "the strong" with a "knowledge" (γνῶσις, 8:1) which is deceptive, theoretical, and illusory. In the end they are "gnostic" not in the usual sense advocated by Schmithals and others, but in the sense that their confidence rests in their own theology rather than on a day-by-day reappropriation of divine grace.

Once again Barth's prophetic exegesis is indicated when he speaks of "the boldness, assurance and enthusiasm with which they believe not in God, but in their own belief in God . . . they confuse belief with specific human experiences . . . trends of thought and theories. . . . Against this, the clarion call of Paul rings out: 'let no man glory in man' (iii:21) or . . . 'He that glorieth, let him glory in the Lord' (i:31)."[154] For too long interpreters have looked exclusively to Romans as a vindication of this kind of distinction in Barth when, as a matter of stance, lifestyle, and practice, the "strong" at Corinth are the very paradigm of what Barth calls *homo religiosus.*[155] The second aorist subjunctive πέσῃ with μή expresses negative purpose: **lest you** [strictly *he or she*] **fall**.

Is πειρασμός here to be understood as *trial* (REB, NJB), *testing* (NRSV, Barrett), or **temptation** (NIV, AV/KJV, Phillips)? In terms of lexicography all three translations remain possible in independence of contextual constraints.[156] If we think of the four so-called tests of "standing" which Israel in the wilderness in general failed, especially *putting Christ to the test* (but ἐκπειράζω in v. 9), we may lean toward the meaning *testing* or *trial*. However, Paul is always more concerned with sin as an *attitude, stance, state,* or *orientation of will* than the concrete acts of "falling short" which assume more prominence in the Epistle to the Hebrews. We have already seen that what fuels the *four formative models* which occur as *events* is the attitude of ἐπιθυμία or **craving** (v. 6). Paul here addresses the *craving* in terms of a **temptation** which draws, seduces, beguiles, attracts, and corresponds to the deeper nature of sin which may be found shared by Paul, Augustine, and the recent analysis of historical theology by Pannenberg (see above).

152. Conzelmann, *1 Cor,* 168.
153. See further Gardner, *Gifts of God,* 152.
154. Barth, *The Resurrection of the Dead,* 17.
155. Ibid., 20.
156. BAGD, 640-41; Sir 6:7; 27:5, 7 for *testing;* 1 Pet 1:6; 4:12; Jas 1:2; and Heb 9:7 for *trial;* and Luke 4:13; Jas 1:12; Sir 33:1; 44:20; 1 Macc 2:52; Matt 6:13 (par. Luke 11·4); *Didache* 8·2 for *temptation.* Moulton-Milligan point out that the term is virtually confined to biblical Greek. Liddell-Scott-Jones, 1169, concur. Grimm-Thayer, 498-99, note its use in the LXX to translate מסה *(massah)* — sometimes as the trial of a person's virtue or integrity (1 Pet 4:12); sometimes as temptation or enticement to sin, Luke 4:13; 8:13; 1 Cor 10:13; also as adversity or trouble sent by God to prove one's loyalty.

It is coping with this *craving* (v. 6) which was instantiated in the experience of Israel in the wilderness (vv. 6-11) but is now said to be more extensive, i.e., **part and parcel of being human** (εἰ μὴ ἀνθρώπινος, *falling to the lot of being human*).[157] Hence Paul rebukes the notion that those who are accustomed to *taking part in* cultic meals are victimized. They see themselves as those who (as politicians and Union leaders often claim) "have no choice but to . . . ," i.e., the *craving to be accepted* by the pagan peer-group "strong," and to join the cultic festivals or feasts *seizes* them or **fastens upon** them as special victims (εἴληφεν; perfect tense). BAGD demonstrate that λαμβάνω has an enormous semantic range of meanings, including *chosen from among men* (Heb 5:1), *apprehend, appropriate,* or *make one's own* (Phil 3:12), take up (John 6:21), as well as the more usual *take hold of* or *receive.*[158] If we combine the senses of *seize* and *take hold of* in the context of supposedly being singled out in a special category as a victim, **no temptation has fastened upon you except what is part and parcel of being human** achieves the two points which Paul is making: (i) "the strong" should *not* always try to be the *"special category"* which influenced or educated people often claim for themselves; (ii) God's people are still frail and *all-too-human,* as over against the unrealism of "enthusiasm" and an overrealized eschatology (see under τὰ τέλη τῶν αἰώνων in v. 11). They are still "on the journey" of everyday life, with its vulnerability and need for discipline (cf. 1:7-9; 1:18, etc.).

Against the claim that "the strong" are so seized by pressure that they have no choice, Paul replies that *God always provides his people with a choice:* the situation brings **a temptation**; but **alongside the temptation** God will also provide **an exit path** (ἔκβασις).[159] Although Paul comforts and encourages the addressees by declaring with emphasis **"faithful *is* God"** (emphatic word order: πιστὸς δὲ ὁ θεός), God's very capacity to be trusted, because he is **faithful** demands that (i) the addressees look away from themselves and their seductions to **God**; and (ii) they can be assured that they will be provided with an **exit path**, which will both provide a positive (and better) alternative and take away their alibi. However, as Gardner notes, where the phrase πιστὸς θεός appears in the LXX (surprisingly, it seems, only twice, Deut 7:9 and 34:4) both occurrences arise in the context of *the covenant.*[160] This throws considerable light on whether the covenant is "two-sided."[161] Israel or Christian believers can never

157. Robertson, *Epistles,* 4:154.

158. BAGD, 464-65 (some ten or a dozen subcategories); scarcely less in Grimm-Thayer 370-71, who emphasize the frequency of *lay hold of.*

159. The verb ἐκβαίνω simply means *to go out.* The specific nuance of ἔκβασις as *a successful outcome* (cf. Weiss, *Der erste Korintherbrief,* 255, Conclusion) arises only when it is used with τοῦ βίου (Wis 2:17), *the outcome of one's life.* Otherwise it means *way out,* **exit**, or **exit path** (BAGD, 237-38; Grimm-Thayer, 193). BAGD and Grimm-Thayer cite the meaning **exit** or *way out* in Epictetus. However, Conzelmann, *1 Cor,* 169, associates it with eschatology.

160. Gardner, *Gifts of God,* 154.

161. It is doubtful whether genuine exegesis of this single verse goes as far as D. M. Ciocchi

748

claim that they could not help themselves in the face of pressure to abandon covenant faithfulness, for God will ensure, as part of his own covenant faithfulness, that he will not simply leave them to face impossible odds. His grace provides ever new opportunities for human faithfulness. Yet Paul will not allow this faithfulness to be manipulated by human presumption. The believer must respond not by expecting all **temptation** to be removed, but by taking the **exit path** which God provides, marks, and renders the believer *able* (δύνασθε) to use. For **he will not allow you to be tempted beyond your powers**. If the believer must attend to how it is *removed,* **God** takes care of *what force it can exercise* in relation to the believer's capacities to appropriate divine grace in face of it.[162]

It is wide of the mark, then, when commentators express surprise that Paul offers a crumb of comfort in this verse when 10:1-13a is full of warnings. First, that **temptations** are **part and parcel of being human** is not *in this verse* a comfort, *but a rejection of special pleading by a special group* ("the strong") who perceive *their* **temptations** as exercising *unique force.* Second, God's covenant faithfulness cuts both ways. To the anxious and "weak" it comes as an immense assurance that their insecurity or *self-doubt* will not be fatal. God **will not allow** their own capacities to limit his grace. On the other hand, "the Corinthian gnosis-boasters . . . Paul sternly warns that they should not be so cocky."[163] Gardner sums up the issue well: "Verse 13 is neither simply an 'encouragement' nor a further warning. It serves both ends, but also functions as a reminder of God's covenant faithfulness to his people even when they were being tempted to break that covenant. . . . God's faithfulness helps them '**bear up under**' (ὑποφέρω) the temptation."[164] This reflects the prologue to the letter, where Paul assures his readers that in the interim period of eschatological pilgrimage (ἀπεκδεχομένους τὴν ἀποκάλυψιν τοῦ κυρίου ἡμῶν, 1:7) God will keep them firm . . . unimpeachable at the Day (βεβαιώσει . . . ἕως τέλους ἀνεγκλήτους ἐν τῇ ἡμέρᾳ . . .) because πιστὸς ὁ θεός (1:8, 9a).[165]

claims in addressing conflicts between "Arminian" and "Calvinist" or "compatibilist" arguments about human freedom in response to temptation and grace. On the other hand, our closing comments on this verse (see below) resonate with some of his comments. See Ciocchi, "Understanding Our Ability to Endure Temptation: A Theological Watershed," 463-79 (also below).

162. Allo, *Première Épitre,* 235; Chrysostom, *1 Cor. Hom.,* 24:1 (although Chrysostom speaks of both "patience" and "release").

163. Hays, *First Cor,* 166; cf. Wolff, *Der erste Brief,* 223-24.

164. Gardner, *Gifts of God,* 155. On ὑποφέρω, cf. BAGD, 848. LXX (Mic 7:9; Amos 7:10) conveys this meaning.

165. This reflects the constructive aspect of the research article by Ciocchi, "Understanding Our Ability to Endure Temptation," 463-79. On Luther's, Calvin's, Osiander's, and Spener's comments on this verse see Schrage, *Der erste Brief,* 2:426-29.

4. Exclusive Loyalty to God: Covenantal Allegiance in Sharing in the Lord's Supper (10:14-22)

(14, 15) So then, my very dear friends, flee from idolatry. I appeal to your common sense. Judge for yourselves what I declare. (16) The cup of blessing over which we offer a blessing, is it not a communal participation in the blood of Christ? The bread which we break, is it not a communal participation in the body of Christ? (17) Because there is one bread, many as we are we are one body; for it is the one bread that we all share. (18) Consider Israel of earthly descent: are not those who eat the sacrifices communal participants in the altar of sacrifice? (19, 20) What, then, do I mean to affirm? That the offering of what is sacrificed to idols amounts to anything, or that an idol is anything? Not that! But that when they sacrifice, "they offer sacrifices to demons and not to God." But I do not want you to become communal participants in demonic forces. (21) You cannot drink from the cup of the Lord and the cup of devilish powers; you cannot participate in the table of the Lord and the table of demons. (22) What! Are we in process of arousing the Lord's jealousy? Surely it cannot be that we are "stronger" than he, can it?

The theme of covenant clearly provides the thematic link between 10:1-13 and 10:14-22. This latter passage forms one of two discussions of the Lord's Supper in this epistle (cf. 11:17-34). In the second passage the Lord's Supper constitutes a major topic in its own right; here it remains "an *exemplum* . . . to show the dual aspects of κοινωνία [translated **communal participation** above in 1:9] and μετέχειν [**to share**, or **sharing**, also above in 9:10, 12]: κοινωνία with the body and blood of Christ means *community rather than individual edification,* and κοινωνία and μετέχειν in the body of Christ means the *exclusivity and necessity of being true to God alone*" (my italics).[1] Hence, as Yeo observes, there is a double connection of thought with the rest of 1 Corinthians 8–10. *Community* means concern for "the brother or sister for whom Christ died" (8:11), i.e., who also have a share in his body and blood; *exclusivity* means the pledge of covenant loyalty to the one God, as against the "idols" and other human constructs, which are not to replace God in the Christian's value system or lifestyle and thereby provoke God himself to **jealousy** (10:22; cf. Exod 20:5; Deut 5:9).

The covenant theme which constitutes the major context for the Decalogue (Exod 20:1-17; Deut 5:6-21) receives a distinctively Christocentric or Christomorphic interpretation in 10:14-22 and 11:17-34. The context in Exodus 20, Deuteronomy 5, and 1 Corinthians 10 concerns the incompatibility between what counts as "idolatry" and sharing in God's redemptive acts whereby he makes his people his own (cf. Exod 19:4; Deut 5:1-3; 6:4-15; 1 Cor 10:1-13, 18-22; 11:25, 26). We noted in our discussion of 1:9 that κοινωνία means far more than a Graeco-Roman *societas* of like-minded people. Writers from

1. Yeo, *Rhetorical Interaction in 1 Cor 8 and 10,* 174.

Seesemann and Thornton to Hainz and Smit have insisted that the "vertical" or theological dimension of *sharing in Christ* constitutes the foundation for the derivative "horizontal" or socioecclesial dimension of "fellowship" in a group.[2] Smit notes explicitly that the theological identification with the crucified Christ cannot be reduced to a quasisocial ecclesial dimension, even if the two aspects are certainly not exclusive. However, Paul applies the rhetoric of "disjunctive syllogism" whereby being "sharers" in Christ is clearly exclusive of "sharing" in idolatry: the κοινωνία is primarily "vertical" and then by inference also "horizontal."[3]

We argue that, as in the case of "apostleship," to *participate,* or *to have a share in,* **the body** and **blood of Christ** is neither merely a self-referring allusion to belonging to the church nor an argument which depends on a quasi-physical sacramental theology of the Lord's Supper. Rather, it places at center stage (i) the commonality (with concern for "the other") and (ii) the exclusivity (in the framework of covenant loyalty) of a *cruciform lifestyle* which witnesses to *identification with Christ in the practical stance and lifestyle* of witnessing to the practical entailments of Christ's dying for "others" and being raised by God. Hence Paul sets up a dialectic between sharing in shed **blood** or constituting **one loaf** (10:16, 17) and receiving a **cup** *of thanksgiving* or **a cup for which God be blessed** which together mark the **offering to God** not of the Lord's Supper as such but of the *life and lifestyle* which expresses its Christomorphic, Christocentric orientation in such a way that "you cannot take part in both the Lord's table and the table of demons" (10:21, NIV). William Lane declares that "covenant is the key to Paul's conflict with Corinth."[4]

To compromise covenant loyalty risks the same effect as the warning about divided loyalties with idolatrous practices in the two main accounts of the Decalogue in its covenant setting. It risks or even provokes **the Lord's jealousy** as a betrayal of the covenant bond (10:22; cf. Exod 20:5; Deut 5:9). Gardner sums up the issue well: "A κοινωνία in the blood and body of Christ may mean a sharing in the results of Christ's sacrificial death. . . . What the Corinthians had not realized through arrogance and complacency was the fact that the cup also committed them to covenant judgment when they sinned."[5] 10:14-22 is "not so much . . . about the Eucharist as . . . rhetorical arguments (the argument from *pathos*) from the Corinthians' experience of it."[6] On the other hand, certain inferences can be drawn concerning Paul's understanding of the Lord's Supper (more fully in 11:17-34).

---

2. Thornton, *The Common Life,* esp. 322-55 (but also 34-65, 156-87); Seesemann, *Der Begriff κοινωνία in NT;* Hainz, *Koinonia;* and Smit, "'Do Not Be Idolaters': Paul's Rhetoric in First Corinthians 10:1-22," 40-53.

3. Smit, "'Do Not Be Idolaters,'" 40-53. Cf. also Gardner, *The Gifts of God,* 159-65.

4. Lane, "Covenant: The Key to Paul's Conflict with Corinth," 28; cf. 3-29. On the importance of covenant in this context, see further, below.

5. Gardner, *The Gifts of God,* 162 and 164.

6. Collins, *First Cor,* 375.

Bibliography on 10:14-22

Aalen, S., "Das Abendmahl als Opfermahl in NT," *NovT* 6 (1963): 128-52.

Allo, E.-B., "La synthese du dogme eucharistique chez saint Paul," *RB* 18 (1921): 321-43.

Baumert, N., "Κοινωνία τοῦ αἵματος τοῦ Χριστοῦ (1 Kor 10:14-22)," in R. Bieringer (ed.), *The Corinthian Correspondence* (Leuven: Leuven University Press, 1996), 617-26.

Best, E., *One Body in Christ* (London: SPCK, 1955), 74-114.

Boismard, M. E., "L'eucharistie selon S. Paul," *LV* 31 (1957): 93-106.

Bornkamm, G., "Lord's Supper and Church in Paul," in his *Early Christian Experience* (Eng. trans., London: SCM, 1969), 123-60 (German, *ZTK* 53 [1956]: 312-49).

Campbell, J. Y., "Κοινωνία and Its Cognates in the NT," *JBL* 51 (1932): 352-80.

Casey, P. M., "The Original Aramaic Form of Jesus' Interpretation of the Cup," *JTS* 41 (1990): 1-12.

Cohn-Sherbok, D., "A Jewish Note on τὸ ποτήριον τῆς εὐλογίας," *NTS* 27 (1981): 704-9.

Cope, L., "First Cor 8–10: Continuity or Contradiction?" *ATRSS* 11 (1990): 114-23.

Cullmann, O., *Early Christian Worship,* SBT 10 (Eng. trans., London: SCM, 1953), 26-33.

———, and F. J. Leenhardt, *Essays on the Lord's Supper,* Ecumenical Studies in Worship 1 (Eng. trans., London: Lutterworth, 1958).

Delling G., "Das Abendmahlgeschehen nach Paulus," in *Studien zum NT und zum hellenistischen Judentum. Gesammelte Aufsätze 1950-1968,* ed. F. Hahn et al. (Göttingen, 1970), 318-35.

Dunn, J. D. G., "The Body of Christ in Paul," in M. J. Wilkins and T. Paige (eds.), *Worship, Theology and Ministry in the Early Church,* JSNTSS 87 (Sheffield: JSOT Press, 1992), 146-62.

———, "The Lord's Supper," in his *The Theology of Paul the Apostle* (Edinburgh: T. & T. Clark and Grand Rapids: Eerdmans, 1998), 599-624.

Gardner, P., *The Gifts of God* (Lanham, Md.: University Press of America, 1994), 155-85.

Grayston, K., *Dying We Live* (New York and Oxford: Oxford University Press, 1990), 36-45.

Gressmann, H., "ἡ κοινωνία τῶν δαιμωνίων," *ZNW* 20 (1921): 224-30.

Gundry, R. H., *Sōma in Biblical Theology,* JSNTMS 29 (Cambridge: Cambridge University Press, 1976).

Hainz, J., *Koinōnia: 'Kirche' als Gemeinschaft bei Paulus,* BU 16 (Regensburg: Pustet, 1982).

Higgins, A. J. B., *The Lord's Supper in the NT* (London: SCM, 1952).

Jeremias, J., *The Eucharistic Words of Jesus* (Eng. trans., London: SCM, 3d ed. 1966), esp. 218-62; cf. 41-88.

———, "πασχα," *TDNT,* 5:896-904.

———, "This Is My Body," *ExpTim* 83 (1972): 196-203.

Jourdan, G. V., "*Koinōnia* in 1 Cor 10:16," *JBL* 67 (1948): 111-24.

Käsemann, E., *Essays on NT Themes* (Eng. trans., London: SCM, 1964), 108-35.

———, *Leib und Leib Christi* (Tübingen: Mohr, 1933).

———, "The Theological Problem Presented by the Motif of the Body of Christ," in Käsemann, *Perspectives on Paul* (Eng. trans., London: SCM, 1971), 102-21, esp. 105-14.

Karrer, M., "Der Kelch des neuen Bundes," *BZ* 34 (1990): 198-221.

Kevan, E. F., *The Lord's Supper* (Kovilpatti, South India: SBM, 1960), 21-62.

Kilpatrick, G. D., "Eucharist as Sacrifice and Sacrament in the NT," in J. Gnilka (ed.), *Neues Testament und Kirche* (Freiburg: Herder, 1974).

Klauck, H.-J., "Eucharistie und Kirchengemeinschaft bei Paulus," *Wissenschaft und Weisheit* 49 (1986): 1-14; cf. "Eucharist and Church Community in Paul," *Theology Digest* 35 (1988): 19-24.

————, *Herrenmahl und Hellenistischer Kult* (Münster: Aschendorff, 1982), 258-72.

Lane, W., "Covenant: The Key to Paul's Conflict with Corinth," *TynBul* 33 (1982): 3-30.

Lietzmann, H., *Mass and Lord's Supper: A Study in the History of the Liturgy* (with Introductory Notes by R. D. Richardson; Eng. trans., Leiden: Brill, 1979), 20-29, 177-87, 326-31, 508-9, 596-608, and 685-98.

Maccoby, H., "Paul and the Eucharist," *NTS* 37 (1991): 247-67.

MacGregor, G. H. C., *Eucharistic Origins: A Study of the NT Evidence* (London, 1928).

McDermot, M., "The Biblical Doctrine of *Koinōnia*," *BZ* 19 (1975): 64-77.

Maly, K., *Mündige Gemeinde* (Stuttgart: Katholischer Bibelwerk, 1967), 127-46.

Marion, D., "Communion. L'essence du christianisme," *Esprit et Vie* 102 (1992): 145-50, 157-59.

Marshall, I. H., *Last Supper and Lord's Supper* (Exeter: Paternoster and Grand Rapids: Eerdmans, 1980).

Martin, D. B., *The Corinthian Body* (New Haven: Yale University Press, 1995).

Marxsen, W., *The Lord's Supper as a Christological Problem* (Eng. trans., Philadelphia: Fortress, 1970).

Mazza, E., "L'Eucharistia di 1 Cor 10:16-17 in rapporto a Didache 9–10," *Ephemerides Liturgicae* 100 (1986): 193-223.

Meyer, B. F. (ed.), *One Loaf, One Cup: Eucharistic Studies of 1 Cor 11 and Other Eucharistic Texts,* New Gospel Studies 6 (Macon, Ga.: Mercer University Press, 1993).

Millard, A. R., "Covenant and Communion in First Corinthians," in W. Gasque and R. P. Martin (eds.), *Apostolic History and the Gospel: In Honour of F. F. Bruce* (Exeter: Paternoster, 1970), 242-48.

Moule, C. F. D., "The Judgment Theme in the Sacraments," in W. D. Davies and D. Daube (eds.), *The Background of the NT and Its Eschatology: Studies in Honour of C. H. Dodd* (Cambridge: Cambridge University Press, 1956), 464-81.

Müller, P., *Der Soma-Begriff bei Paulus* (Stuttgart: Brachhaus, 1988).

Murphy-O'Connor, J., "Eucharist and Community in 1 Cor," *Worship* 51 (1977): 56-69.

Neuenzeit, P., *Das Herrenmahl. Studien zur paulinischen Eucharistieauffassung* (Munich: Kösel, 1960).

Neyrey, J. H., "Body Language in 1 Corinthians: The Use of Anthropological Models for Understanding Paul and His Opponents," *Semeia* 35 (Social-Scientific Criticism of the NT and Its Social World): 129-70.

Panikulam, G., *Koinōnia in the NT. A Dynamic Expression of Christian Life,* AnBib 85 (Rome: Pontifical Biblical Institute, 1979), esp. 3-30.

Pesch, R., *Das Abendmahl und Jesu Todesverständnis,* Quaestiones Disputatae 80 (Freiburg: Herder, 1978), esp. 190-93.

Porter, C. L., "An Interpretation of Paul's Lord's Supper Texts: 1 Cor 10:14-22 and 11:17-34," *Encounter* 50 (1989): 29-45.

Prout, E., "One Loaf — One Body," *ResQ* 25 (1982): 78-81.

Robinson, J. A. T., *The Body: A Study in Pauline Theology* (London: SCM, 1952).

Roetzel, C. J., *Judgment in the Community: A Study of the Relationship between Eschatology and Ecclesiology in Paul* (Leiden: Brill, 1972).

Rosner, B. S., "'Stronger Than He?' The Strength of 1 Cor 10:22b," *TynBul* 43 (1992): 171-79.

Schweizer, E., "Die Kirche als Leib Christi in den paulinischen Homologoumena," *TLZ* 86 (1961): 161-74.

———, *The Lord's Supper according to the NT* (Eng. trans., London: SCM, 1967).

———, "σῶμα," *EDNT*, 3:321-25.

———, "σῶμα," *TDNT*, 7:1024-94.

Sebothoma, W. A., "κοινωνία in 1 Cor 10:16," *Neot* 24 (1990): 63-69.

Seesemann, H., *Der Begriff κοινωνία in NT*, BZNW 14 (Giessen: Töpelmann, 1933), esp. 34-56.

Sigal, P., "Another Note to 1 Cor 10:16," *NTS* 29 (1983): 134-39.

Sloyan, G. S., "Primitive and Pauline Concepts of the Eucharist," *CBQ* 23 (1961): 1-13.

Smit, J., "'Do Not Be Idolaters': Paul's Rhetoric in First Corinthians 10:1-22," *NovT* 39 (1997): 40-53.

Soden, Hans von, "Sakrament und Ethik bei Paulus," in his *Urchristentum und Geschichte* (Tübingen: Mohr, 1951), 1:239-75.

Söding, T., "Eucharistie und Mysterien Urchristliche Herrenmahlstheologie und antike Mysterienreligiosität im Spiegel von 1 Kor 10," *BK* 45 (1990): 140-45.

Thornton, L. S., *The Common Life in the Body of Christ* (London: Dacre Press, 3d ed. 1950), 34-65, 156-87, 253-86, and esp. 322-55.

Thurian, M., *The Eucharistic Memorial*, Ecumenical Studies in Worship 8 (Eng. trans., London: Lutterworth, 1961).

Truets, C., "The Eucharist and the Christian Community: Some Pauline and Augustinian Evidence," *LS* 12 (1987): 152-71.

Wedderburn, A. J. M., "The Body of Christ and Related Concepts in 1 Corinthians," *SJT* 24 (1971): 74-96.

Willis, W. L., *Idol Meat in Corinth: The Pauline Argument in 1 Corinthians 8 and 10* (Chico: Scholars Press, 1985), 182-22.

Winter, B. W., "The Lord's Supper at Corinth," *RTR* 37 (1978): 73-82.

Wolff, C., "Exkurs: Das in 1 Kor 10:16 aufgenommene Traditionsstück," in his *Der erste Brief des Paulus an die Korinther* (Leipzig: Evangelische Verlagsanstalt, 1996), 226-29.

Yeo, Khiok-Khing, *Rhetorical Interaction in 1 Corinthians 8 and 10* (Leiden: Brill, 1995), 172-79.

14-15 The UBS 4th ed. begins a fresh paragraph at v. 14. In spite of the fact that many start the section at v. 15, Schrage argues (with the UBS text) that ἀγαπητοί μου, in conjunction with διόπερ, "begins the new section."[7] REB well translates διόπερ as **so then**, since the conjunction is both inferential and argumentative, and constitutes an emphatic connective in an emphatic position.[8]

---

7. Schrage, *Der erste Brief*, 2:435; also Barrett, *First Epistle*, 230; and Conzelmann, *1 Cor*, 170.

8. BAGD, 199; *therefore; for this very reason;* cf. Barrett, *First Epistle*, 230, and Schrage, *Der erste Brief*, 2:435.

However, the usual translation *my dear friends* (REB, NRSV) seems a little distant for the more intimate ἀγαπητοί μου, even if *my beloved one* remains archaic. Hence one compromise is to strengthen the REB-NRSV rendering by translating **my very dear friends**. Chrysostom's reading ἀδελφοί has inadequate textual support.[9] However, Chrysostom's comment that Paul does not say "simply 'depart,' but 'flee' (φεύγετε)" and "to be rid of this sin with all speed" is to the point.[10] He adds that Paul's basis of argument now shifts from that of damaging others to inviting disaster and self-destruction. Nigel Turner argues that the use of the definite article τῆς εἰδωλολατρίας implies "the worship of idols which you know so well."[11] But this strains the construction.[12] More to the point, the preposition ἀπό before the articular phrase conveys a metaphor of location and active flight which picks up the preceding allusion to ἔκβασις in v. 13. The **way out** (v. 13) conjures up the image of an army caught (εἴληφεν) in a defile and urged to flee at all speed through a mountain pass.[13]

Much debate surrounds the force of ὡς φρονίμοις, often translated as *to people of discernment*. Parallels with 3:1 and with 4:10 raise the question of whether Paul uses a degree of irony. But Meyer, Edwards, Conzelmann, and others interpret this as a straightforward **appeal** to the readers to use their natural *intelligence*, and Barrett and Schrage appropriately conclude that Paul appeals to their **common sense**.[14] The full weight of the Greek construction falls on ὑμεῖς, *you yourselves*. Hence we translate κρίνατε ὑμεῖς ὅ φημι, **Judge for yourselves what I declare**. The use of **declare** distinguishes the force of φημι from the less formal, less weighty λέγω, which may include a range of meanings from *I mean* or *I say* to (here) **I appeal**.[15] Paul uses an assertive or declarative speech-act.

16 Some minor Western texts (e.g., F and G) substitute εὐχαριστίας, *thanksgiving,* for εὐλογίας, **blessing**, in v. 16. This probably reflects later liturgical tradition, but may also have been thought to avoid tautology. NIV translates *the cup of thanksgiving for which we give thanks,* but this is no doubt to avoid any misunderstanding of the force of εὐλογίας rather than on the basis of a later textual reading.

Schrage helps to unravel the complexities of this controversial verse by distinguishing between three questions: (a) How are we to understand τὸ ποτήριον τῆς εὐλογίας (usually translated **the cup of blessing**, REB, NRSV, and above, but also as *the blessing cup,* NJB)? (b) What is the force of ὃ εὐλογοῦμεν (usu-

---

9. Chrysostom, *1 Cor. Hom.*, 24:2.
10. Ibid.
11. Moulton-Howard-Turner, *Grammar,* 3:173.
12. As Barrett argues, *First Epistle,* 230.
13. The link is stressed by Schrage, *Der erste Brief,* 2:435 (including nn 310 and 311), and the image is used by Edwards, *First Epistle,* 251-52. So also Robertson and Plummer, *First Epistle,* 211 (although against Weiss).
14. Schrage uses the *English* "common sense" (*Der erste Brief,* 2:433-36).
15. Meyer rightly notes the difference of force (*First Epistle,* 1:294).

ally translated *which we bless,* NJB, or *that we bless,* NRSV; but in NIV as *for which we give thanks,* and above as **over which we offer a blessing**)? (c) How are we to interpret οὐχὶ κοινωνία ἐστὶν τοῦ αἵματος τοῦ Χριστοῦ (variously translated *is it not a means of sharing in the blood of Christ?* REB; *is it not a sharing in . . . ?* NJB, NRSV; **is it not a communal participation in the blood of Christ**? above).[16]

(a) **The cup of blessing** coheres precisely with the context of the Passover meal as the framework for the interpretation of the Lord's Supper, but in other contexts the phrase may also denote **the cup** over which "grace" is said at everyday meals in a Jewish household. The *Mishnah* and other sources provide ample evidence for the practice of using as a grace or thanksgiving at the end of the meal the formula "Blessed be Thou, Lord God, King of the Universe, who created the fruit of the vine" (*Berakoth* 6:1).[17] The *thanksgiving* over **the cup** is Heb. כוס של בוכה (see Extended Note, 758-60, for a fuller discussion). The *Mishnah* also cites variants for thanksgivings for fruit, vegetables, or bread, e.g., "Blessed be Thou, who bringest forth bread from the earth" (*Berakoth* 6:1). In Greek-speaking Judaism, therefore, at grace people did not "bless **the cup**," but blessed *God* (i.e., with thanksgiving) for what God had provided.

Complex questions arise, however, about whether the framework which determines the meaning and force of τὸ ποτήριον τῆς εὐλογίας in this verse is shaped primarily by (i) the background of hellenistic cultic meals; (ii) either everyday meals in a Jewish household or perhaps some supposedly "special" form of Jewish fellowship meals (Lietzmann's notion of the *Haburah,* followed by Dix) or even theories concerning *Kiddush* meals on the sabbath (proposed, e.g., by F. Spitta and P. Batifoll); or should we (iii) (as we ourselves firmly hold) turn to the context of the Passover meal for a decisive understanding of the text. Many writers (e.g., P. Sigal) identify **the cup of blessing** with the third of the four *cups,* although some (e.g., Cohn-Sherbok) argue that it is more likely to denote the fourth cup of the Passover.

THE CUP OF BLESSING (10:16)

(i) This is not the place for a full discussion of claims about the hellenistic origins of Paul's language in this verse. The case has been made out most recently by T. Söding, but at greater length by H.-J. Klauck and earlier by W. Heitmüller.[18] We shall comment

16. Schrage, *Der erste Brief,* 2:436-39.

17. *m. Berakoth* 6:1 (Danby ed., 6); *b. Pesahim* 103a, 106a. See further in Strack-Billerbeck 4:2; 62, 611-39; L. Goppelt, "ποτήριον," *TDNT,* 6:53 (148-60); Jeremias, *The Eucharistic Words of Jesus,* 15-89 and throughout; Marshall, *Last Supper and Lord's Supper,* 19-20; B. Klappert, *NIDNTT,* 2:522.

18. Söding, "Eucharistie und Mysterien. Urchristliche Herrenmahls — theologie und antike Mysterienreligiosität im Spiegel von 1 Kor 10," 140-45; Klauck, *Herrenmahl und hellenistischer Kult,* esp. 258-72; W. Heitmüller, *Taufe und Abendmahl im Urchristentum* (Göttingen: Vandenhoeck & Ruprecht, 1903, 2d ed. 1911); cf. R. Reitzenstein, *Hellenistic Mystery Religions,* 77-78.

further on this in connection with the force of κοινωνία. The major problem which this view encounters is well identified by Käsemann, among others. The formulaic language, which reflects its Jewish or more specifically Jewish-Christian roots, which reflect the Markan and pre-Pauline tradition, together with other factors, means that "the attempt to shed light on Paul's teaching on the Lord's Supper from its links with Hellenistic cult meals has completely broken down."[19] Käsemann does not deny, however, that "analogies" with hellenistic meals allow Paul's argument to assume a certain form "for polemical purposes."[20] G. H. C. MacGregor has addressed the arguments of Heitmüller, and Senft sums up the generally agreed view: "The expression **cup of blessing** is Semitic."[21]

(ii) Although we need to return to the issue in greater detail on 11:20-29, we need to refer briefly to Hans Lietzmann's well-known theory that **the cup of blessing** formed part of a fellowship meal derived from Jewish fellowship groups *(haburoth)* who shared the *Haburah*.[22] Lietzmann's theory does at first sight seem to fit the notion that at Corinth a love feast, or celebratory *Agapē*, remained a reflection of "the breaking of bread" in the earliest churches, where the focus lay on rejoicing in the presence of the risen Christ and on social conviviality, as against Paul's insistence that the Lord's Supper constituted a covenant focus on the Lord's death (11:24-26). Thus Paul rebukes the Corinthians for being so taken up with fellowship and celebration that they ceased to participate in κυριακὸν δεῖπνον rather than *their own* "supper" (11:20). Overtones of solemnity and judgment marked Paul's view of the Lord's Supper (11:27-29).

Nevertheless, as R. D. Richardson acknowledges in his Notes in Lietzmann's large volume, this theory suffers from three major flaws. First, Lietzmann depends largely on Hippolytus for a dubious reconstruction of the middle decades of the first century.[23] Second, "two . . . opposing reconstructions" depend on methods in which "second-century evidence, in all its flux and change, has not been rightly handled."[24] Third, in Marshall's view, shared by many, "there is no evidence whatever that the Jewish haburoth held meals that were in any way different from ordinary Jewish meals."[25] Jeremias makes the same point: "we have an *ad hoc* conjecture for which there is absolutely no evidence."[26]

Jeremias equally firmly excludes speculations about a *Kiddush* meal: "The Kiddush is therefore neither a meal, nor a sacrifice . . . , but it is just a simple blessing."[27] But might the Last Supper have been nothing more than an everyday meal, given special significance by the words of Jesus? Under the section title "The Last Supper —

19. Käsemann, "The Pauline Doctrine of the Lord's Supper," in *Essays on NT Themes,* 108; cf. 108-35.
20. Ibid., 108.
21. Senft, *La Première Épitre,* 133; cf. G. H. C. MacGregor, *Eucharistic Origins: A Survey of the NT Evidence.*
22. H. Lietzmann, *Mass and Lord's Supper: A Study in the History of the Liturgy* (with essays by R. D. Richardson; Eng. trans., Leiden: Brill, 1979), 161-87; cf. 267-68, 623-25, 653. See also Dix, *The Shape of the Liturgy* (1945), 50-70.
23. Lietzmann, *Mass and Lord's Supper,* 160-71.
24. Ibid., 267 (Richardson).
25. Marshall, *Last Supper and Lord's Supper,* 20.
26. Jeremias, *The Eucharistic Words of Jesus,* 30.
27. Ibid., 27.

A Passover Meal!" Jeremias traces fourteen significant points of substance which provide a "convincing argument for the paschal character of the Last Supper. Jesus announces his impending passion at the Last Supper *by speaking words of interpretation over the bread and wine. . . . Interpretation of the special elements of the meal is a fixed part of the passover ritual*" (Jeremias's italics).[28]

(iii) Jeremias argues for *the importance of the Passover context* in more than one study.[29] A number of commentators as well as contributors of specialist studies broadly endorse this view, including I. H. Marshall.[30] The Passover ritual is outlined in *m. Pesahim* 10:1-7. Here a benediction is offered to God over the *first cup;* seasoned food including unleavened bread (cf. 5:7 above) and *haroseth* (paste of nuts and fruit pounded together and mixed with vinegar) is brought before the host; *the second cup* is mixed, and the son asks the father about the meaning of the ritual; "Why is this night different from other nights?" (*Pes.* 10:4). The father begins the recital of God's redemptive acts, including Israel's corporate self-involvement in, and witness to, these events: "A wandering Aramaean was my father . . ." (Deut 26:5ff.; cf. Exod 12:37-39). Bitter herbs are eaten "because the Egyptians embittered the lives of our fathers" (Pes. 10:5). The self-involving character of the narrative becomes explicit in the use of the first person singular in the Mishnah: "It is because of what the Lord did for *me* when *I* came forth out of Egypt" (Pes. 10:5).[31] The *seder* (i.e., set quasi-liturgical order) proceeds with an expected response of praise, using the first part of the *Hallel* (Psalms 113–114 of 113–118), concluded with a blessing, but specifically a blessing (of God) for *redemption* (the גאולה [g'ullah], from גאל [ga'al], to *redeem;* גאולים [g'ulim], *redemption*). Probably the majority of scholars associate **the cup of blessing** in this verse with *the third cup* of the Passover *seder* which now follows. Sharing this cup represents a participation (κοινωνία) in the redemption achieved in this context not by liberation from the oppression of Egypt but the costly purchase of freedom from sin (1 Cor 6:19) won through the "body and blood" of Christ. However, after the third cup, the head of the household or the host leads in further praise by completing the Hallel (Psalms 115–118), usually associated with ὑμνήσαντες of Mark 14:26 (Matt 26:30), and a blessing is finally offered over *a fourth cup.* D. Cohn-Sherbok argues for the view that τὸ ποτήριον τῆς εὐλογίας in this verse denotes this fourth cup, after which there was allowance for further praise.[32]

Before we pursue this subsidiary question, we must put forward an argument which strengthens the allusions to the Passover *seder* by Jeremias, Marshall, Wolff, and others by reemphasizing the key point made in our Introduction to 10:14-22 about

28. Ibid., 55-56; cf. the cumulative argument of 41-62.

29. Jeremias, *Eucharistic Words,* 15-88, and πάσχα, 896-904, esp. 899: ". . . that Jesus clothes his words and gift in the form of an interpretation of bread and wine can hardly be explained except in terms of the Passover ritual."

30. Marshall, *Last Supper and Lord's Supper,* 57-75; and such commentators as Edwards, *First Epistle,* 253; Robertson and Plummer, *First Epistle,* 211; Weiss, *Der erste Korintherbrief,* 256-57; Héring, *First Epistle,* 94; Wolff, *Der erste Brief,* 228-29; Lang, *Die Brief,* 127; Schrage, *Der erste Brief,* 2:436-37; Goppelt, *TDNT,* 6:156; Bornkamm, "Lord's Supper," in his *Early Christian Experience,* 140-43; Collins, *First Cor,* 376 and 379, although Collins adds other resonances.

31. The Mishnah declares, "In every generation each man must so regard himself as if he came forth out of Egypt . . . what the Lord did for *me* . . ." (*Pesahim* 10:5). Cf. Exod 13:8 and H. Danby (ed.), *The Mishnah,* 151, nn. 1-5.

32. D. Cohn-Sherbok, "A Jewish Note on τὸ ποτήριον τῆς εὐλογίας," 704-9.

the covenant context. This section reaches its climactic conclusion with a reference to covenant loyalty, although as a negative counterfactual hypothesis: παραζηλοῦμεν τὸν κύριον; (10:22, *shall we provoke the Lord to jealousy?*).[33] This would be to renege on the covenant pledge of sharing through **communal participation** in the Passover **cup of blessing** of Christ's redemptive **blood**. In addition to the forceful observations of Yeo, Willis and Gardner also argue convincingly for the prominence of the covenantal theme in this context: "κοινωνία [is] a covenant relationship" whereby "the Christian . . . 'receives an interest in the death of Christ.'"[34] W. L. Lane expounds a detailed case for viewing "covenant" as "the key to Paul's conflict with Corinth" with particular reference to 2 Corinthians (especially 2 Cor 3:1–7:1).[35] He compares OT models of covenantal "lawsuit" modes of speech which he perceives Paul as presenting in this epistle, and alludes, e.g., to 3:6, 14; 4:2; 5:18-20; and 6:14–7:1. The parallel between 1 Cor 10:14-22 and 2 Cor 6:14–7:1 is striking, in spite of theories which view the latter as a non-Pauline interpolation. Not surprisingly Francis and Sampley list these as explicit parallels in their *Pauline Parallels*.[36] The **cup of blessing** of covenant participation also finds a parallel with "the metaphor of the betrothal contract" in 2 Cor 11:1-2, both of which combine pledged loyalty with an exclusivist image of judgment.[37] Thus Bornkamm relates 1 Cor 10:16 to "the new covenant," while Käsemann acknowledges the dimension of judgment and speaks of the central importance of διαθήκη.[38]

The combination of all the varied arguments about the Passover setting of the pre-Pauline tradition therefore cohere with Paul's own covenantal emphasis in these verses as underlining the paschal framework which lends decisive meaning to τὸ ποτήριον τῆς λογίας. Even D. Cohn-Sherbok's detailed argument that **the cup of blessing** alludes to the *fourth* cup of the Passover *seder* rather than to the *third* retains the presupposition that it refers directly to the Passover meal. This would even allow for an interpretation of **blessing** which we do not endorse, namely, that, in Cohn-Sherbok's view, "It may well be that Paul was simply specifying the cup that Jesus blessed rather than indicating that a particular blessing was said over it."[39] Calvin among others sees Jesus as the agent of the act of "**blessing the cup**," although Goodspeed goes too far in translating *the consecrated cup*.[40] Morna Hooker also shares the view that if the setting is that of the Passover tradition, **the cup of blessing** is the *fourth* cup.[41]

J. Héring, L. Goppelt, C. Wolff, and P. Sigal, by contrast, associate **the cup of blessing** with *the third cup*, i.e., an expansion of the "grace" (ברכת המזון, *birkat*

33. See the incisive arguments here of Yeo, *Rhetorical Interaction in 1 Cor 8 and 10*, 172-79, e.g., "the Lord's Supper is used as an *exemplum* event in verses 16-21 to show the dual aspects of κοινωνία and μετέχειν" (174).

34. Cf. Willis, *Idol Meat in Corinth*, 205-6 and 208 (the last phrase is a quotation from Barrett, *First Epistle*, 232-33). See further Gardner, *The Gifts of God*, 162-65.

35. Lane, "Covenant: The Key to Paul's Conflict with Corinth," 3-30, esp. 19-20, 23-24.

36. Francis and Sampley, *Pauline Parallels*, 144, sect. 110.

37. Lane, "Covenant," 26.

38. Bornkamm, "The Lord's Supper," in *Early Christian Experience*, 140-43; and Käsemann, "The Pauline Doctrine of the Lord's Supper," in *Essays*, 120 and 130-32.

39. Cohn-Sherbok, "A Jewish Note . . .," 707.

40. Calvin, *First Epistle*, 215.

41. M. D. Hooker, *The Gospel according to St. Mark* (Peabody: Hendrickson and London: Black, 1991), 340-41.

hammazon) rather than the fourth (שׁיר ברכת, *birkat hashir*).[42] Allo, Héring, and Conzelmann explicitly refer to the *third cup* as הברכה כוס (*kus hab'rakah*, **cup of blessing**), which fulfilled the role of blessing God for his good provision at all meals.[43] This is also the most natural implication of Schrage's argument that this giving of praise to God is a synonym for εὐχαρεστεῖν (with Zwingli, Melanchthon, Heinrici, Kistemaker, and NIV, but against Calvin, Meyer, and some others).[44] Robertson and Plummer conclude that we cannot be certain which of the Passover cups is at issue.[45] Whatever the details concerning the third or fourth cup, however, an implicit allusion to the covenantal blood of the Passover provides the most convincing and constructive context within which to understand τὸ ποτήριον τῆς εὐλογίας. This accords entirely with both the present context of loyalty and covenant exclusivity and the explicit language of 11:25 (see below). Gardner concludes: "Given the tendency to link the Exodus, the Red Sea, and the wanderings in Sinai, it should be no surprise that the Passover would recall God's 'covenant' dealings with his people."[46] But Gardner leaves the door open for a wider covenant framework for these verses than that of the Lord's Supper as a Christian Passover meal alone: it is upon covenant rather than upon the Passover meal as such that emphasis derived from the sharing of **the cup of blessing** falls primarily.[47]

(b) The next phrase, ὃ εὐλογοῦμεν, is not "pleonastic" (Lietzmann).[48] (i) Most writers tend to agree with the thought well expressed by Grosheide (with Goppelt): "through the benediction of God, as Christ has prescribed [and is mediated in the pre-Pauline tradition], the cup becomes a special cup," i.e., it is more than a "grace" patterned on Jewish practice or even the Passover *seder* cup in abstraction from the Christocentric focus of the Lord's Supper (cf. 11:23-26).[49] (ii) This phrase also underlines the Godward direction of the blessing. Thus Meyer's translation approximates ours when he proposes: **the cup over which** *the blessing is spoken* (cf. our suggested **over which we offer a blessing**).[50] The context disengages this verse and this passage from traditional discussions about **blessing** as "power-laden" utterances often directed toward persons or even objects.[51] (iii) Schrage and Grosheide also underline the impor-

42. P. Sigal, "Another Note to 1 Cor 10:16," 134-39; cf. also Héring, *First Epistle,* 94; Goppelt, *TDNT,* 6:153-58; Wolff, *Der erste Brief,* 228.

43. Allo, *Première Épitre,* 238; Héring, *First Epistle,* 94; Conzelmann, *1 Cor,* 171, n. 13. Cf. Barrett, *First Epistle,* 231.

44. Schrage, *Der erste Brief,* 2:436; cf. Heinrici, *Das erste Sendschreiben,* 273-75; Calvin, *First Epistle,* 215; Meyer, *First Epistle,* 1:295-96; Kistemaker, *1 Cor,* 341. Cf. also Strack-Billerbeck, 4:72.

45. Robertson and Plummer, *First Epistle,* 211.

46. Gardner, *Gifts of God,* 158.

47. Ibid., 159-72 P. D. Richardson attempts to restrict the Passover aspect to a stage of the common tradition, but his wedge between Paul and the pre-Pauline understanding cannot be convincingly sustained (Lietzmann, *Mass and Lord's Supper,* 327-29).

48. Lietzmann, *An die Korinther,* 48.

49. Grosheide, *First Epistle* 231. Also Goppelt, *TDNT,* 6:153-58.

50. Meyer, *First Epistle,* 1:295.

51. A. C. Thiselton, "The Supposed Power of Words in the Biblical Writings," *JTS* 25

tance of the first person *plural:* to "the fact that the congregation observes the ordinance."[52]

These three points find striking and informative expression in the second-century *Apology* of Justin (AD 110-165). Justin recounts how baptized Christians offer prayers "in common . . . for all . . . in every place" (cf. 1 Cor 1:2-3) and, after a greeting, bring to the president "bread and a cup of wine mixed with water."[53] He takes these, and "gives praise to the Father of the universe through the name of the Son and the Holy Spirit . . . and offers thanks. . . . When he has concluded the prayers and thanksgiving all the people present express their assent by *'Amen,'* which corresponds in the Hebrew to 'so be it' (γένοιτο)."[54] After this, those present *participate communally* in the bread and the wine, and if some are absent it is permitted to carry to them a share. The *Amen* signifies the congregational nature of the act of blessing offered through the lips of "the president"; the *blessing* is addressed to God; the *cup* clearly denotes participation in Christ's redemptive act of giving himself for the blessing of others.[55]

(c) How are we to interpret οὐχὶ κοινωνία ἐστὶν τοῦ αἵματος τοῦ Χριστοῦ, translated above as **is it not a communal participation in the blood of Christ**? The translation **communal participation** for κοινωνία represents no special pleading for this verse. We translated the Greek word in precisely this way in 1:9: ἐκλήθητε εἰς κοινωνίαν τοῦ υἱοῦ αὐτοῦ Ἰησοῦ Χριστοῦ τοῦ κυρίου ἡμῶν. We argued above that *fellowship* fails to convey the "vertical" dimension of Paul's meaning, as if to imply that the emphasis fell on the "horizontal" bonding of a like-minded group in the sense of a Graeco-Roman *societas.*[56] We noted Sampley's view that although the Greek word may bear this more "social" meaning, e.g., in Rom 15:27, in 1:9 (and even more so here in 10:16) it denotes having an active *common share* in the life, death, resurrection, and presence of Jesus **Christ** as the Lord who determines the identity and lifestyle of that in which Christians share. We also alluded in particular to the work of Godet, Thornton, Panikulam, Seesemann, and especially Hainz and Marion.[57] Indeed, Hainz explicitly identifies this participatory and Christomorphic dimension both in 1:9 and in 10:16.

In a recent study Smit specifically compares the two images or metaphors of "horizontal" and "vertical" **participation**. He argues that in this verse the

---

(1974): 283-99; cf. essays in *Semeia* 24 (1982); C. Westermann, *Blessing in the Bible* (Eng. trans., Philadelphia: Fortress, 1978), 113-14.

52. Schrage, *Der erste Brief,* 2:436-37, esp. n. 324; Grosheide, *First Epistle,* 230; Meyer, *First Epistle,* 1:295, n. 1.

53. Justin, *Apology,* 1:65.

54. Ibid.

55. Ibid.

56. Above, under 1:9.

57. Godet, *First Epistle,* 1:60; Sampley, *Pauline Partnership,* 96-97; Thornton, *The Common Life in the Body of Christ,* 71-79, 156-87; Panikulam, *Koinōnia in the NT,* esp. 3-5 and 17-30; Seesemann, *Der Begriff κοινωνία im NT,* esp. 34-56; Hainz, *Koinōnia;* and D. Marion, "Communion. L'essence du christianisme," 145-50 and 157-59.

"vertical" and "theological" have priority of emphasis over the "horizontal" and social.[58] This transposes Lietzmann's agenda into a new key. It is not that Paul recasts the Jerusalem tradition of meals (at which the presence of the raised Christ was celebrated) into a solemn memorial of the cross as a matter of time. It is rather that Paul transposes the reductively *social* dimension at Corinth into a genuine reappropriation of what **communal participation** in the identity and redemptive work of Christ means, as this is focused most sharply and expressively in his suffering for others and redemptive death. Barrett makes this point well. He declares, "*a common* **participation** (both English words are needed to render κοινωνία) **in the blood of Christ**" means "not simply being with him" but receiving "an interest in the death of Christ."[59]

Barrett's insistence that we need two English words to convey the force of the one Greek word κοινωνία in this context is reflected in our translation, which is very close to his. The **communal** aspect cannot be minimized. As Willis notes, κοινωνία has a wide usage which includes "business partnerships, various associations, joint enterprises, social relationships . . . common life."[60] Hence Yeo correctly observes that the flight from idolatry reflects a turning away "from the individual spirituality" of many of the so-called strong at Corinth (Yeo calls them "gnostics") "to the communal solidarity in the body of Christ (ἕν σῶμα)."[61] Weiss, Robertson and Plummer, and Allo emphasize this **communal** aspect.[62] But as Seesemann insists, in addition to the aspects of "community" *(Gemeinschaft)*, "sharing" *(Anteilhaben)* and "communion" *(Mitteilsamkeit)* also denote that in which the participants share.[63] Heinrici makes the point still more strongly. In this verse, he asserts, κοινωνία is *not* "community" *(nicht Gemeinschaft)* nor even "communion" *(auch nicht Mittheilung)* but "**participation** in Christ" *(sondern Theilhaben an Christus)* in which *"his life becomes our life"* (my italics).[64] Similarly, Strobel declares that the construction is *"not* 'fellowship with' *(Gemeinschaft mit)* but 'share in' *(Anteil an)*."[65] Grosheide concludes: "Paul implies that the Christian, because he partakes of the Lord's Supper, is in connection with the death of Christ."[66]

Meyer and Grosheide go to considerable lengths to argue that if the pre-Pauline tradition which Paul endorses (cf. 11:23 and οὐχί . . . ;) goes back to the Upper Room of the Markan tradition, the referential relation between **communal participation** and the **blood of Christ** could not be "physical" in the *his-*

58. Smit, "'Do Not Be Idolaters': Paul's Rhetoric in First Corinthians 10:1-22," 40-53. These terms also appear, however, in Gardner, *Gifts of God,* 161, to make this point.

59. Barrett, *First Epistle,* 230-32.

60. Willis, *Idol Meat,* 168. Cf. his discussion of literature and sources, 168-212.

61. Yeo, *Rhetorical Interaction,* 173.

62. Weiss, *Der erste Korintherbrief,* 258; Robertson and Plummer, *First Epistle,* 212; Allo, *Première Épitre,* 238-39.

63. Seesemann, *Der Begriff κοινωνία in NT,* 24, 99, and 193.

64. Heinrici, *Das erste Sendschreiben,* 274.

65. Strobel, *Der erste Brief,* 158.

66. Grosheide, *First Epistle,* 232.

torical sense "since at the institution of the Supper the body of Christ was not yet slain, and His blood still flowed in his veins."[67] "The shed blood and the broken body of Christ do not exist anymore."[68] But we should not make the opposite mistake. Yeo reminds us that at Corinth Christians were all too ready to assume that "spiritual" salvation had little or nothing to do with the physical realm, tending toward thinking of "the worthlessness of the body."[69] Thus in their view "the right to do what I like" extended from sexual license (6:12-19) to a devaluing of marital intimacy (7:1-7). Certainly, as P. Neuenzeit observes, Paul appeals to a well-known tradition of the Lord's Supper (e.g., οὐχὶ κοινωνία . . . ;).[70] But he does this in order to insist that the Lord's Supper entails not only communal participation in *a covenant pledge of "belonging" and faithfulness* to this bond, but also **communal participation** *in the actual physical lifestyle and stance toward life which* **the blood of Christ** *as the giving of the self to others instantiates and demands.* It signifies *identification with Christ in his death as both the source of redemption and the pattern for life and lifestyle.* This provides the frame of reference which reveals Paul's coherence of thought throughout this chapter, as well as the dual themes of blessing and judgment in 11:23-24.

Once this principle has been recognized and established, the ground of "unity" which the **one loaf** comes to represent can more readily be appreciated. Sharing the mind of Christ, as Traets argues with reference to this verse and to Augustine, becomes the key to the meaning of unity — in the Eucharist.[71] But this should not detract from the centrality of divine grace and of eschatology which makes *corporate solidarity with Christ* the basis of this **communal participation** and unity, even when Christians fail.[72] The use of μετέχειν (10:17) does entail "participation *(Anteilhabe)* in the blood and body of Christ."[73] But, as in 11:29, to have an "interest" in Christ's body and blood is to appropriate for oneself the purpose of Christ's death.[74] D. Marion and J. Hainz therefore appeal to parallels in 1 Cor 1:9, Phil 1:5-6, 2 Corinthians 8–9, but most especially (with Wolff) in Phil 3:10-11, where Paul speaks of sharing in Christ's sufferings and in the glory of the cross and resurrection.[75] Héring even speaks of "a metaphysical union of the believer with Christ," but then misconstrues the allusion to **the blood of Christ** as "regenerating" rather than (more properly) as re-

---

67. Meyer, *First Epistle,* 1:297.
68. Grosheide, *First Epistle,* 231.
69. Yeo, *Rhetorical Interaction,* 173.
70. Neuenzeit, *Herrenmahl,* 59-60.
71. Truets, "The Eucharist and the Christian Community: Some Pauline and Augustinian Evidence," 152-71.
72. Cf. Sebothoma, "κοινωνία in 1 Cor 10:16," 63-69.
73. Schrage, *Der erste Brief,* 2:437.
74. So argues, rightly, Prout, "'One Loaf — One Body,'" 78-81.
75. Hainz, *Koinōnia,* 20-25; esp. Marion, "Communion. L'essence du christianisme en un seul mot," 145-50 and 157-59; similarly, Wolff, *Der erste Brief,* 229. Cf. also Willis, *Idol Meat,* 168.

demptive.[76] The shedding of blood has to do with a costly act of redemption, as Paul implies in 6:20. Once again, this coheres with 11:23-34 (see below). Ortkemper speaks of "solidarity" in suffering.[77] For Gardner it means "a sharing in the results of Christ's sacrificial death."[78] Schrage calls it "a share in the dying of Christ *(Anteil am Sterben der Christus)* and "communal participation with the Crucified One and his death."[79]

There is no need to speculate on hypotheses designed to explain why the allusion to **the cup** and to **the blood** precede, rather than follow, Paul's references to **the bread** and **the body of Christ**: τὸν ἄρτον ὃν κλῶμεν, οὐχὶ κοινωνία τοῦ σώματος τοῦ Χριστοῦ ἐστιν; **The cup** is mentioned before **the bread** in Luke 22:17 and in the *Didache* 9, and is repeated in v. 21. But Paul follows the usual order in 11:23, which expressly quotes the words of institution. Here, as Meyer writes, "Paul names the cup first . . . because he means to speak at more length about the bread."[80] The sequence here simply serves his flow of expression.

Strictly τὸν ἄρτον should appear in the nominative rather than the accusative. Probably it is simply attracted into the accusative by the relative pronoun ὅν, and many argue that the grammatically ambiguous τὸ ποτήριον is also an implied accusative, after the analogy of the second clause, making both examples of *attractio inversa* (where the case of the relative pronoun attracts the noun, rather than vice versa). Although in other respects the substance of the two clauses (i.e., respectively concerning **the cup** and **the bread**), there can be no parallel to ὃν κλῶμεν, **which we break**.[81] However, this need not be interpreted to imply that the phrase **the bread which we break** has no particular significance beyond that of *sharing out* the bread, as the phrase occurred in everyday Jewish household meals (see above). We seldom disagree with the judicious comments of Schrage. But we question whether he is correct in asserting that "the breaking of bread" belongs only to the background of the Jewish meal terminology, applied here to the sharing of the eucharistic elements, and "not as a symbol for interpreting the action through which the body of Jesus came to be broken."[82]

Schrage repeats a widely held view among liturgists, which is also endorsed by Fee. Fee argues that the breaking of the bread "does not mean . . . 'participation in' the 'broken body' of Christ, while Gregory Dix insists that the

76. Héring, *First Epistle*, 94.

77. Ortkemper, *1 Korintherbrief*, 96.

78. Gardner, *Gifts of God*, 162.

79. Schrage, *Der erste Brief*, 2:438 and 439.

80. Meyer, *First Epistle*, 1:295; Robertson and Plummer, *First Epistle*, 213; cf. Conzelmann, *1 Cor*, 171.

81. The point is amplified by Robertson and Plummer, *First Epistle*, 213. *Drinking* is parallel with *eating*, not with *breaking*. Mark 14:24, however, does speak of "my blood of the covenant poured out . . .," although in Luke 22:19-20 "given" and "poured out" are found only in the longer text.

82. Schrage, *Der erste Brief*, 2:439.

bread was "broken simply for distribution and not for symbolic purposes."[83] It is also argued that κλώμενον has poor MS support in 11:24 (א^c, C^3, D^b, syr^p), although it may be implied by the previous ἔκλασεν and the well-attested τὸ ὑπὲρ ὑμῶν (p^{46}, א*, A, B, C*, 33), which can only mean *given* or *broken* **for you**.[84] Orr and Walther construe "the breaking of bread" as a sign that a meal has begun.[85] On the other side, Grosheide writes, "The breaking of the bread is a sign of Christ's suffering on the cross."[86] Vincent Taylor urges that "As the loaf is broken, so his body will be broken in the near future. The words are interpretative and invest the fraction with dramatic significance."[87] Two short articles, one by David Brown and the other by A. R. Winnett, further defend this view.[88] Winnett recognizes that the breaking of bread "was a normal action of the host" at the beginning of every Jewish meal, but this, he argues, does not preclude the view "that Jesus invested the action with a distinctive significance in the special circumstances of the Supper."[89] Even if crucifixion did not literally entail a "breaking of bones" (cf. John 19:36), Jesus (Winnett suggests, following R. Otto) may initially have anticipated death by stoning.[90]

It is not necessary to resort to Otto's speculative hypothesis. Jesus may well have employed this image of "breaking" bread as a creative metaphor which covered more than one meaning. Already in its most prosaic everyday sense "the breaking of bread" operates with more than one meaning: it signals both the beginning of a meal (Orr and Walther) and the communal nature of the meal (Schrage). But the "double meaning" of metaphor (Ricoeur) as well as of κοινωνία (Barrett, Hainz, Smit) carries yet further levels of meaning.[91] Edwards' early comment on κλῶμεν, "The act of breaking the bread . . . represents the sacrificial death of Christ," is corroborated and developed by what is probably the most recent (to date) of the serious, detailed commentaries.[92] Christian Wolff (1996) examines the views of Allo, Hauck, Hahn, Panikulam, Hainz,

---

83. Dix, *The Shape of the Liturgy,* 80; and Fee, *First Epistle,* 469. Fee tends to collapse the imagery into a church-oriented ecclesiology. Hence his commentary is untypically disappointing here.

84. Cf. Metzger, *Textual Commentary* (2d ed.), 496.

85. Orr and Walther, *1 Cor,* 251.

86. Grosheide, *First Epistle,* 232 (fully acknowledged by Schrage, *Der erste Brief,* n. 340.

87. Vincent Taylor, *Jesus and His Sacrifice* (London: Macmillan, 1939), 118.

88. D. Brown, "The Breaking of the Bread," *Theol* 75 (1972); and A. R. Winnett, "The Breaking of Bread: Does it Symbolize the Passover?" *ExpTim* 88 (1977): 181-82.

89. Ibid., 181.

90. Ibid., 181-82.

91. Cf. Paul Ricoeur on "the semantic structure of having a double meaning" in metaphor, "Metaphor and Symbol," in Ricoeur, *Interpretation Theory: Discourse and Surplus of Meaning* (Fort Worth: Texas Christian University Press, 1976), 45-60. Metaphor entails "the productive use of ambiguity," "semantic innovation," and "extension of meaning" (47, 52, 55). Further discussions occur in *The Rule of Metaphor* (Eng. trans., London: Routledge, 1978), and in *Time and Narrative* (3 vols.; Chicago: University of Chicago Press, 1984-88). Cf. also Hainz, *Koinōnia,* esp. 20-25; and Barrett, *First Epistle,* 231-33.

92. Edwards, *First Epistle,* 256.

Klauck, and many others, and reaches the conclusion that the *parallelism of the two clauses* about **the blood of Christ** and **the body of Christ** *reinforces* the christological or Christocentric significance of the language about **the bread**.[93] The *"broken bread"* signifies "the body of Christ as he abandoned it to the cross."[94]

Pressing further all that we have said above about **communal participation** in **the body** and **blood of Christ**, Wolff invites us to compare the force of Rom 7:4, "Likewise, brothers and sisters, you have died . . . through the body of Christ, so that you may belong . . . to him who has been raised from the dead . . ." (cf. also Col 1:22). Whatsoever the details of possible textual variants in 11:24 or the Synoptic tradition, the *"body for you" (Leib für euch)* aspect remains, with sacrificial and soteriological force.[95] This latter point is reflected in some of Morna Hooker's careful comments on Mark 14.[96] We do not have to choose between a quasiphysical "mystical" or unduly sacramentalist interpretation and a reductive "hyper-Protestant" view which refers **body** and **bread** almost wholly to the church.

Meyer, Grosheide, and Conzelmann (with Wolff) try to steer this middle course. Conzelmann's dual claim that "**blood** does not mean blood as a substance" but does refer to "the death of Christ as a saving event" avoids both quasiphysical sacramentalism and a reduction of v. 16 to statements merely about the church.[97] Meyer's language about the physico-historical body of Jesus at the Institution (cited above) does not prevent him from emphasizing the participatory, christological significance of **the** *broken* **bread** in v. 16.[98] If the main feature about **the bread which we break** is that it "picks up the language of the Jewish meal . . . (cf. Acts 2:46; 20:7, 11)" and that what is "unique" is Paul's interpretation of "the bread in terms of the church" (Fee), the contextual logic and theological seriousness of the argument and of the "vertical" dimension of κοινωνία become emasculated.[99] We should not be unduly influenced by the quite different level of meaning at which "the breaking of bread" operates in other contexts. A failure to grasp the issue of polyvalent meaning and to apply Ricoeur's maxim that "the symbols gives rise to thought" doubtless played a part in the steady disappearance of the term *breaking of bread* to denote the Lord's Supper (in spite of the *Didache* and Ignatius) in favor of the term *Eucharist, thanksgiving*.[100]

---

93. Wolff, *Der erste Brief,* 228-30.

94. Ibid., 230.

95. Ibid.

96. Hooker, *The Gospel according to St, Mark,* 338-43, e.g., even the shorter texts stress "the sacrificial interpretation of Jesus' death" (338).

97. Conzelmann, *1 Cor,* 171, n. 14, citing Goppelt, *TDNT,* 6:143, n. 70.

98. Meyer, *First Epistle,* 1:297. See also Kistemaker, *1 Cor,* 341-42, for a broad balance.

99. Fee, *First Epistle,* 468; cf. 469.

100. P. Ricoeur, *Freud and Philosophy* (New Haven: Yale University Press, 1970), 543. See also Thiselton, *New Horizons in Hermeneutics,* 344-78; and Smit, " 'Do Not Be Idolaters,' " 40-53.

Käsemann's work on σῶμα calls attention to what the less adequate approach obscures. In Käsemann's view **body** denotes a person's visible communicative stance *in the public domain:* "that piece of the world which we ourselves are" which manifests our lifestyle.[101] But **communal participation** in the **body** and **blood of Christ** entails manifesting publicly the sacrificial lifestyle of **Christ**, as seen in his **blood** (i.e., his death) and **body** (i.e., self-giving public life). Thus Käsemann affirms that 10:16-17 signifies that this *body* is the *body of Jesus given over to death for us. . . .* The new *diathēkē* is founded on this death."[102] Thus *covenant* takes up the context in which 10:16 occurs. "I" died when **Christ** died (cf. the Passover *seder*): "I cannot share in idolatry." Luther asserts that 10:16 denotes "a share in everything that my body [Christ's body] has and does and suffers . . . by virtue of God's promise."[103]

17 A few later Western texts (D, F, G) add καὶ τοῦ ἑνὸς ποτηρίου. But this doubtless reflects a later liturgical symmetry.

Robertson and Plummer observe that while the sense of this verse is clear, it is difficult to decide on the details of translation.[104] Our translation of the first clause follows Goodspeed's version, which seems to capture the emphasis of the Greek: ὅτι εἷς ἄρτος, ἓν σῶμα οἱ πολλοί ἐσμεν. . . . The word **many** has virtually the force of a subordinate concessive, **many as we are** (cf. REB, *we, though many . . . ,* which seems more clumsy). The more usual *we who are many* (NRSV, NIV) or *being many* (AV/KJV) reduces the clause to mere description, which reduces the force of the point which is being made. **Many** may well also allude to Mark 14:24 in the pre-Pauline tradition.[105] Further, although Robertson and Plummer prefer the AV/KJV *For* rather than **Because** for ὅτι, the Greek word is a strong causal connective. The causal force, however, applies not to the mechanics of bread and eating, but to the principle as an exposition of the previous explanation in v. 16 about the entailments of **communal participation**. The ground of unity is *Christ,* not the oneness of the bread or loaf (ἄρτος) as if to imply that the church would be fragmented if more than one loaf were shared at the one Eucharist.[106] Again Ricoeur's discussion of metaphor, and levels of "double meaning" and "split reference" (see above), needs to be borne in mind.

Similarly, in the second clause the emphasis falls upon the final verb in the Greek: οἱ γὰρ πάντες ἐκ τοῦ ἑνὸς ἄρτου μετέχομεν, **we all share**.[107] Fee

---

101. E. Käsemann, *NT Questions of Today* (Eng. trans., London: SCM, 1969): "in bodily obedience . . . the service of God in the everyday world finds visible expression" (135).

102. Käsemann, "The Pauline Doctrine of the Lord's Supper," in his *Essays on NT Themes,* 130.

103. Luther, *LW,* 36 (American ed., Philadelphia: Fortress, 1959), 283.

104. Robertson and Plummer, *First Epistle,* 214.

105. Schrage, *Der erste Brief,* 2:440, n. 349.

106. In this sense Schrage observes, "the church does not become constituted from the first through the Lord's Supper" (*Der erste Brief,* 2:440).

107. On μετέχω, see BAGD, 514: *share,* **have a share,** *participate* (with genitive), and 9:12.

points out that since the use of ἐκ reflects a semiticism, we should not take undue note of it, and duly observes that the emphasis of v. 17 falls *not* simply on the *unity* of the **one body**, but on "*the solidarity* of the redeemed community as one body in Christ that forbids all such unions."[108]

THE SEMANTICS OF "ONE BREAD . . . ONE BODY" (10:17)

Fee's language about solidarity reflects an earlier emphasis found in J. A. T. Robinson. It is on the basis of the principle of "solidarity," i.e., sharing the privileges, liabilities, commitments, and status of a single corporeity that Robinson declares, "The concept of the body forms the keystone of Paul's theology."[109] He believes that modern language about "membership" in social and legal contexts emasculates our grasp of the fundamental character of "body" language in Paul.[110] However, although this observation is valid and important, and challenges the Western individualism of modernity (postmodernity is more ambivalent), Robinson spoils his work by following A. Schweitzer and L. S. Thornton too readily toward a virtually unqualified or isomorphic identification between the eucharistic community of the fallible church and the body of the raised Christ. We speak of "identification" in the theological and eschatological sense with its ethical entailments found in Rom 7:4 (cf. Wolff, above, under v. 16), but not in terms of a comprehensive correspondence, when the church still sins and Christians still die. Under 12:12 (cf. vv. 12-26) we examine these issues further, noting the meaning of the problems caused by language in Schweitzer, Thornton, and Robinson, and Whiteley's shrewd comment that Robinson's work simultaneously illuminates and overcomplicates Paul's theology.[111]

Thornton's giveaway line that "there is no Christ without the Church" as well as his sacramentalist language about the church as "an extension of the incarnation" invites Ernest Best's rebuke that such language ignores the contexts in this epistle, as well as a sharp attack from Käsemann.[112] Robinson is surely right to detect a determining shaping of Paul's "body" language in his earliest reflection on the words of his conversion and communion: "Saul, why are you persecuting *me?*" (Acts 9:4, 5; 22:7, 8, where "me" also denotes the Christian community).[113] But as Gundry declares, all the evidence confirms that "Paul intended his statement in ch. 10 to be taken as a metaphor."[114]

These considerations, all the same, must not obscure the fundamental point

108. Fee, *First Epistle,* 469.

109. Robinson, *The Body: A Study in Pauline Theology,* 9.

110. Ibid., 51.

111. Schweitzer, *The Mysticism of Paul the Apostle,* 101-40 and 227-92; Thornton, *The Common Life in the Body of Christ,* 310, 315, and 335-37; Robinson, *The Body,* 47-52, 78-79; Whiteley, *The Theology of St Paul,* 192-95.

112. Best, *One Body in Christ,* 96, esp. n. 1. Käsemann does not explicitly address Thornton, but considers the approach of Schweitzer and others in "The Motif of the Body of Christ," in his *Perspectives on Paul,* 102-21, esp. 110-14. (On his *Leib und Leib Christi,* see under 12:12.)

113. Robinson, *The Body,* 58.

114. Cf. Gundry, *Sōma in Biblical Theology,* 238 (cf. 232-44) for some careful and telling arguments.

that **one body** in this verse stands in contrast to the *splits* (1:10-12) which characterized the church at Corinth. The present verse reflects Paul's insistent assertion that Christ cannot be *"apportioned out"* (μεμέρισται ὁ Χριστός; 1:13). Christians at Corinth were baptized in **one** *name* (1:13-17), and the **one** *event* of the cross of Christ constitutes the "foundation and criterion" (Schrage) for the life and lifestyle of *all* (1:18-25). Thus the **one body** (ἓν σῶμα) of this verse looks back *both* to the "political" terminology of splits and unity in 1:10-17 *and* to the christological, soteriological, and covenantal basis of *one, single solidarity* (1:18-25; 10:16).[115] In Margaret Mitchell's view, the use of κοινωνία and ἓν σῶμα "as an argument to advise social unity" complements and entails the corresponding warning of the wider context in 10:14-22 concerning "exclusion of outside cultic associations."[116] Not only Barrett (cited above) but also Kümmel and Marshall perceive the key theme as "that of receiving" an interest in the death of Christ, which, according to Rom 3:25; 5:9, mediates to man the justification and atonement God provides."[117]

The issue of "split-reference" and "double meaning" (Ricoeur) remains fundamental for understanding this "first use of a metaphor which is developed later in ch. 12 when he [Paul] speaks of believers becoming members of one body . . . 'the body of Christ'."[118] Marshall perceives the link between this verse and commitment to corporate responsibility for brothers and sisters "for whom Christ died" (8:11).[119] The importance of "split reference," developed by Ricoeur, seems to be missed by most commentators. In v. 16 the Lord's Supper is a **communal participation in the body of Christ** where **Christ** *becomes implicitly the referent of* **body** (τοῦ σώματος τοῦ Χριστοῦ), while in v. 17 *the church* (**we**) *is beyond doubt the referent of* **body** in ἓν σῶμα οἱ πολλοί ἐσμεν. Paul Ricoeur draws the theory of "split reference" from Roman Jakobson.[120] Applying the principle to metaphor, Ricoeur endorses Max Black's view that it "has the power to bring two separate domains into cognitive and emotional relations by using language directly appropriate for the one as a lens for seeing the other."[121] Here, however, the "lens" redefines the more "obvious" level of reference. If **body** is already an established political term for the unity of a community, as Mitchell argues (cf. Livy, 2.32.12-33; Dionysius of Halicarnassus, *Antiquitates Romanae* 6.85; Plutarch, *Coriolanus* 6.2-6; *Moralia* 426A; Dio Chrysostom, *Orations* 1.32; 3.104-7; 17.19; 50.3; Plato, *Republic* 5.470C, D), it eminently reflects Pauline thought to use **Christ** and his **body** given over on the cross as a "lens" (i.e., "foundation and criterion") to refocus and to enlarge the application of **body** to the church. Conversely, the intimate relationship of **communal participation** in **Christ** by the

---

115. On the "political" nature of "body" terminology cf. M. M. Mitchell, *Paul and the Rhetoric of Reconciliation,* 68-80, 141-42, and 254-56.

116. Ibid., 254.

117. W. G. Kümmel, "Anhang," in Lietzmann, *An der Korinther,* 182; Marshall, *Last Supper and Lord's Supper,* 120 (cf. 118-23); cf. Barrett, *First Epistle,* 232.

118. Marshall, *Last Supper and Lord's Supper,* 121. On Ricoeur on metaphor, see above under v. 16 (n. 91) and also further on v. 17 below.

119. Ibid.

120. Ricoeur, *The Rule of Metaphor* (cited above), 6.

121. Ricoeur, *Interpretation Theory* (cited above), 67; cf. 45, 47, 55, and 60. Ricoeur and Black firmly reject "substitution" and "decorative" theories of metaphor, in favor of an "interactive" account; cf. Max Black, *Models and Metaphors* (Ithaca: Cornell University Press, 1962); and J. Martin Soskice, *Metaphor and Religious Language* (Oxford: Clarendon Press, 1985).

many illuminates levels of meaning generated by the phrase **the body of Christ** depending on whether the context is that of eschatology, status, lifestyle, or the Lord's Supper. We should note that **cup** (v. 16) also has a split reference, as in Mark 10:38, where it refers to Christ's baptism and to the need for disciples to "share" in it.[122] If we are to do full justice to the force of this verse, but with semantic accuracy, both functions of metaphor and contextual variables must be brought into play against the theological and sociopolitical backgrounds of **body** and the exegesis of the previous verse.

While the richness of poetic symbolism must be allowed its force, linguistic and semantic controls must also operate. Thus while *Didache* 10:4-5 generates suggestive beauty ("As this broken bread was scattered upon the mountains, but was brought together and became one [ἐγένετο ἕν], so let Thy church be gathered together . . . but let none eat or drink of your eucharist except those who are baptized"), Meyer insists "the thought of bread having become a unity out of many separate grains of corn is foreign to the connection."[123] Fee notes the chiastic symmetry of the verse: ἄρτος, **bread**, appears in A and A' in the chiasmus A B B' A'.[124] Hence most translations either translate **bread** in both v. 17a and v. 17b (NRSV, AV/KJV) or *loaf* in both parallels (REB, NIV, Barrett). But Meyer's warning that "the unity of the bread [is understood] not numerically . . . but *qualitatively*" (his italics) should make us cautious in assuming that the entire metaphor or symbolism depends on the use of a single *loaf* for distribution at the Lord's Supper.[125] The meaning is more likely to spring from the generic oneness of **bread** as "one kind of thing," unless we understand the force to be "we form a single loaf" (with Senft, as "explicating" v. 16) or alternatively unless the pre-Pauline tradition consciously retained the memory of a direct allusion to the Passover "household."[126] Even if *loaf* carries a more suitable meaning for v. 17b, we have to decide whether it is better to spoil the chiastic symmetry by translating **one bread . . . one** *loaf*, or to use *loaf* twice, which verges on the banal as a christological symbol, and removes the English from a semantic domain into which a variety of symbolic levels and resonances have already been attracted (i.e., **bread**).

As a postscript we may note that Cullmann's link between **the one** and *worship* coheres well with the broader argument about idol worship in 10:14-22 and in 10:1-13. Cullmann urges that it is *"worship . . . that the community assumes in worship the form of the body of the crucified and risen Christ"* (his italics).[127] With the proviso noted above about metaphor, split reference, and multiple meaning, this comment constructively combines *worship* with the emphasis already discussed on *covenant* as the two major thematic links with the context of the chapter. The "vertical" dimension of **communal participation** in the Lord's Supper, underlined by both themes, naturally

---

122. Cf. Gardner, *Gifts of God,* 164; Cullmann, *Early Christian Worship,* 66; J. A. T. Robinson, *Twelve NT Studies* (London: SCM, 1962), 160.

123. *Didache* 10:4-5; Meyer, *First Epistle,* 1:301. Chrysostom, Augustine, and Erasmus, however, assume this connection: "As the bread consisting of many grains is one, so that the grains no longer appear . . . so are we cojoined with one another and with Christ" (Chrysostom, *1 Cor. Hom.,* 24:4).

124. Fee, *First Epistle,* 469.

125. Meyer, *First Epistle,* 1:301, cf. Wolff, *Der erste Brief,* 231.

126. Senft, *La Première Épitre,* 134.

127. Cullmann, *Early Christian Worship,* 74.

spills over into the "horizontal" dimension of lifestyle.[128] As Collins observes, this is the *beginning* of the theme which Paul expounds further in 12:12-26.[129]

18 βλέπετε which means *look at* (Knox translation), regularly means **consider** (NRSV, NIV) in metaphorical contexts. Ἰσραὴλ κατὰ σάρκα means either (i) *physical* Israel, i.e., the historic nation as a physical entity seen in the public domain; or (ii) *outward* Israel, i.e., in the sense in which Paul uses κατὰ σάρκα in 1:26 to denote what people *naturally perceive as* "clever, influential, or well-connected." (Interestingly he uses βλέπετε in connection with κατὰ σάρκα in 1:26 also.) However, as I have argued elsewhere, the range of nuances conveyed by σάρξ is very wide.[130] BAGD include eight main divisions, several of which may be in view here.[131] On the analogy of Rom 4:1 (Ἀβραὰμ τὸν προπάτορα ἡμῶν κατὰ σάρκα), Paul probably means more specifically (iii) **Israel of earthly descent** (placed in this category by BAGD). This use is found in Rom 9:8 (in contrast to *children of promise*); Gal 4:23; and esp. Rom 11:14 (*"my fellow countrymen"*). Conzelmann proposes *earthly Israel* (cf. *the people of Israel,* NIV, NRSV).[132] The main problem with REB's *Consider Jewish practice* is that it presupposes a reference to first-century Judaism, whereas "probably he [Paul] still had in mind the golden calf incident (v. 7)" of the OT.[133] "This verse brings a 'historical' proof (but one extending into Paul's own day). . . . The scriptural foundation is Lev 7:6, 15; Deut 18:1-4."[134]

The historical example can be understood either in a value-neutral sense (with Barrett) or in an entirely negative sense (with Gardner). Barrett cites the privileges and responsibilities (cf. "solidarity" in vv. 16 and 17) of the priests to consume parts of the sacrifices (Lev 10:12-15), and thus become *"partners"* (or **participants**) in what was sacrificed.[135] Gardner argues that Paul takes up his earlier argument from 10:1-13, using κατὰ σάρκα (as he sometimes does of other entities in other contexts) to place "emphasis on the *sin* of Israel" (his italics).[136] Gardner's interpretation offers the advantage that it appears to make better sense of the transition of language and logic to the next verse, namely, a comment on the issues associated with idols (unless one takes the *negative* entailments of v. 19 as the link, i.e., the principle that "idols" belong to a *different category* from OT or Jewish sacrifices).[137]

Gardner's view would cohere with Dale Martin's thesis that 10:14-22

128. Smit, "'Do Not Be Idolaters,'" 53; and Gardner, *Gifts of God,* 165.
129. Collins, *First Cor,* 380.
130. A. C. Thiselton, "The Meaning of σάρξ in 1 Cor 5:5," *SJT* 26 (1973).
131. BAGD, 743-44. Cf. R. Jewett, *Paul's Anthropological Terms,* 49-166.
132. Conzelmann, *1 Cor,* 170; cf. 172.
133. Gardner, *Gifts of God,* 165.
134. Conzelmann, *1 Cor,* 172.
135. Barrett, *First Epistle,* 235.
136. Gardner, *Gifts of God,* 165.
137. A related issue concerns the MS reading τὰ ἔθνη, *the Gentiles* or *the pagans,* in v. 20 (see under v. 20).

turns on the theme of "pollution": "that eating idol-meat meant ingestion of the daimon into the body of the weak Christian," just as "sharing the cup" means "sharing in his blood."[138] But in spite of Martin's careful examination of ancient physiologies of the body, the consistently expounded "physical pollution" aspect seems to move beyond specifically Pauline exegetical evidence in several passages. Gardner's insistence on the constant relevance of the golden calf theme of Deuteronomy 32 in this passage is confirmed by Hays.[139] Yet most commentators follow the view reflected in Barrett. Héring, e.g. (followed by Schrage), argues that κατὰ σάρκα is used here "without any figurative stance."[140] The main difference of emphasis seems to lie in whether the allusion relates to *the people of Israel* in the biblical period (NRSV) or *Jewish practice* (REB) in Paul's time. Senft, Conzelmann, Schrage, and Wendland interpret the reference in terms of Levitical sacrifices (cf. Lev 7:6, 11-15, זבח, *zebach*).[141] On the other hand, Weiss and in part Héring cite the widespread familiarity with theologies of communion sacrifice in hellenistic Judaism (e.g., Philo, *De Specialibus Legibus* 1.131, 229).[142] Nevertheless, the issue cannot be finally decided concerning Gardner's view until we have compared Paul's allusions to Deuteronomy 32 and his language about τραπέζης δαιμονίων in vv. 19-22. Recent arguments by Hays and by Kistemaker lend support to Gardner's view that the allusion to Deuteronomy 32 is better matched by his proposed interpretation of v. 18.[143]

The phrase κοινωνοὶ τοῦ θυσιαστηρίου embodies an objective genitive: **communal participants in the altar of sacrifice** (i.e., not *with* the altar). Since today the word **altar** has been widely used in some circles to denote a Christian Communion Table, the contextual allusion to **an altar of sacrifice** should be retained, especially since the θύω component resonates with the same component in εἰδωλόθυτα, *food sacrificed to idols,* and with τὰς θυσίας, **the sacrifices**. The participant and the participant's group or community appropriate the reality or influence which **the altar of sacrifice** represents and conveys. A broad parallel occurs in Heb 3:14, where disloyalty to the covenant God is excluded by being μέτοχοι of Christ.[144]

19-20 (i) The last clause of v. 19, ἢ ὅτι εἴδωλόν τί ἐστιν, remains, as Schrage concludes, "uncertain." p46, א*, C*, and 33 omit it, and Maly views it as a secondary gloss

---

138. Martin, *The Corinthian Body,* 188; cf. 179-97.

139. R. B. Hays, *Echoes of Scripture in the Letters of Paul* (New Haven: Yale University Press, 1989), 93.

140. Héring, *First Epistle,* 95.

141. Senft, *Première Épitre,* 134; Conzelmann, *1 Cor,* 172; Schrage, *Der erste Brief,* 2:442-43; Wendland, *Die Briefe,* 81.

142. Weiss, *Der erste Korintherbrief,* 260; Héring, *First Epistle,* 96.

143. Cf. Kistemaker, *1 Cor,* 345-50; Hays, *Echoes of Scripture,* 93-94; Gardner, *Gifts of God,* 165-72.

144. Cf. H. W. Attridge, *The Epistle to the Hebrews,* Hermeneia (Philadelphia: Fortress, 1989), 117.

derived from 8:4-6. Metzger and Senft (with Conzelmann leaving it as a question) attribute its inclusion to homoioteleuton, and Schrage believes that Paul's argument runs more smoothly if it is omitted, but K. W. Clark perceives a difference of theological opinion in the different readings.[145] Only because of 8:4-6 can no issue of substance be at stake, since Paul has already addressed the issue in fuller terms in 8:4-6. (But see the discussion of "social constructivism" below.) (ii) In v. 20 τὰ ἔθνη appears after the first θύουσιν, to read *pagans sacrifice* or the *Gentiles sacrifice* (rather than **they sacrifice**) in 𝔭46, ℵ, A, and C. Most recent commentators regard this insertion as a secondary gloss (Schrage, Senft, Gardner, Hays, and, earlier, Bartsch), although some (e.g., Senft) regard the gloss as expressing Paul's meaning, while others (e.g., Gardner, Kistemaker) view it as a mistaken intervention.[146] Only patient exegesis can assist in this decision. However, Gardner points out that the inclusion of τὰ ἔθνη makes the statement effectively a tautology and hardly contributes to the rhetorical force.[147]

On the translation of φημι as **I affirm**, see above. The idiom with τί οὖν is best rendered (with Edwards), **What, then, do I mean to affirm?**[148] (Cf. REB, *What do I imply by this?* But this loses the *declarative* force of φημι as an *act of assertion;* see above under v. 15 on the contrast with λέγω). Robertson and Plummer render: *What, then do I declare?*[149] Paul wishes not only to clarify the scope and entailments of his assertions, but to guard against giving any impression of flatly contradicting what he "declared" in 8:4-6 in credal language.[150] Hence the relation between two sets of *declarative* speech-acts requires further explanation.

In modern conceptual terms Paul means that neither εἰδωλόθυτον nor εἴδωλον possesses *ontological existence* or *metaphysical reality.* In modern and postmodern parlance they constitute *social constructs.* But postmodern literature, whether or not we agree with its worldviews, at the very least exposes that "the social construction of reality," i.e., how groups carve up the world conceptually in terms of categories and typifications (often related to gender, class, and guild) decisively shapes people's lives and what people *count as* "true."[151] Paul expresses this in simple language: ὅτι εἰδωλόθυτόν τί ἐστιν . . . ; NRSV, NIV, and AV/KJV translate simply *is anything;* REB tries to explicate a little by rendering *is anything more than meat.* But it *is* "more than" mere, empirical

145. Schrage, *Der erste Brief,* 2:444, n. 372; Conzelmann, *1 Cor,* 170, n. 4; Senft, *Première Épitre,* 135, n. 13; and K. W. Clark, "Textual Criticism and Doctrine," in J. N. Sevenster (ed.), *Studia Paulina in Honorem J. de Zwaan* (Haarlem: Bohn, 1953), 59-60; cf. 52-65.

146. Schrage, *Der erste Brief,* 445, n. 378; Senft, *Première Épitre,* 135, n. 13; Gardner, *Gifts of God,* 166-67.

147. Gardner, *Gifts of God,:* "No one would even have suggested that *Gentiles* sacrificed to God — self-evidently they did not." *In this context* this assertion seems undeniable.

148. Edwards, *First Epistle,* 258.

149. Robertson and Plummer, *First Epistle,* 215.

150. For the meaning of the phrase see also under 8:4-6, above.

151. On postmodern social construction, cf. A. C. Thiselton, *Interpreting God and the Postmodern Self* (Edinburgh: T. & T. Clark and Grand Rapids: Eerdmans, 1995), 11-19, 33-41, and 121-45, where major bibliographical resources are also cited, 165-72.

meat: it conveys *a "world" of human social constructivism, although not a "world" that is part of God's authentic creation.* Hence we follow NJB's **amounts to anything** as perhaps the best without a more complex gloss. The view that "the εἴδωλον was just so much metal, or word, or stone," presupposed by REB's translation, misses the distinction between nonreality, reality, and social constructivism, i.e., *a contrived quasi-reality for those who share the same sociocultural "world" but not for those outside it.*[152] (The quotation from Robertson and Plummer predates the emergence of modern [or postmodern] sociology of knowledge.) Hence Paul wants to prevent the church from entering the epistemological "world" *within which* (but *only* within which) these things *do* become *real.* Hence perhaps the nearest that Paul can find in premodern vocabulary to express these ideas is his statement in 8:4, οὐδὲν εἴδωλον ἐν κόσμῳ (*is nothing in "the world,"* i.e., in *the created order* as God made it). Jeremias discusses the "contradictions" of 8:1-13 which give rise to assertions followed by ἀλλ' (as here in vv. 19, 20) or invite a dialectic of μέν . . . δέ. . . .[153]

The elliptical transition to ἀλλ' at the beginning of v. 20 causes a headache for translators. Predictably the AV/KJV woodenly clings to the Greek: *What do I say then? that the idol . . . anything? But I say that . . .* Virtually all modern English VSS simply insist on *No* before *but* (NRSV, NIV, REB, Moffatt). NJB and Phillips go still further: *No, not at all!* (NJB), and *Not at all!* (Phillips). But is Paul denying the previous assertion *in every sense?* He still speaks of the *power* or *force* of these "nonrealities" on people's lives, and we have explained that seeming contradiction in terms of the difference between *human social construction* (see above) and *the divinely created order of reality.* Hence it seems more accurate to translate **Not that!** i.e., not the sense that concerns *ontology.* However, the reality of social construction means that idolatry *involves* the **communal participants** (i.e., those who enter the "projected world" at issue) in *actually* becoming κοινωνοὺς τῶν δαιμονίων.

Paul cites the OT traditions of the worship of the Golden Calf as perceived through Deut 32:15-18 (in parallel with his use of the golden calf tradition as interpreted in Ps 106:19-20 in Rom 1:23). Hays offers a superbly constructive comment: "The rhetorical questions and answers in these vv. 18b-20a, with their present tense verbs, not only generalize the application of the figure, but *also project the action of the golden calf worshippers onto the screen of present experience. . . .* The last sentence echoes the Song of Moses in Deut 32:17: 'They sacrificed to demons and not to God; to gods whom they had not known'" (my italics).[154] Paul thus perceives the seductions which face "the strong" at Corinth "in double exposure with Israel's wilderness idolatry. [How-

---

152. Robertson and Plummer, *First Epistle,* 215.

153. Jeremias, "Zur Gedankenführung in den Paulinischen Briefen," in Sevenster (ed.), *Studia Paulina in Honorem Johannis de Zwaan,* esp. 151-52; cf. 146-54.

154. Hays, *Echoes of Scripture in the Letters of Paul,* 93.

ever,] *Paul's intertextual figuration proved opaque to many subsequent Christian readers*" (my italics).[155]

Hays identifies the central issue admirably. Paul *refigures* (to use Ricoeur's phrase as well as that of Hays) the assessment of idol-worship found in Deuteronomy 32 to instantiate what we have called the difference between authentic creation reality and seduction to enter a world of social construction which lays **participants** open to *demons* or to **demonic forces**. The first generation of "subsequent Christian readers" who missed the point were those early Christian scribes who introduced τὰ ἔθνη as the subject of θύουσιν in p[46] (early as it is), ℵ, A, and C (see above under Textual Notes). Against Senft and many others, the emphasis on Deut 32:15-18 urged primarily by Gardner, Hays, and Kistemaker, but also implicitly by Conzelmann and Wolff, gives weight to Gardner's interpretation of Ἰσραὴλ κατὰ σάρκα in v. 17 (see above). Conzelmann is right to place the phrase which Paul draws from Deut 32:17 in quotation marks to signal the quotation, and we have also used quotation marks, "they offer sacrifices to demons and not to God."[156] The LXX reads ἔθυσαν δαιμονίοις καὶ οὐ θεῷ, for which Paul merely changes the tense of θύω to indicate a permanent axiom with a present application. (Even the secondary addition of a second θύουσιν in some MSS suggests an early failure to recognize the quotation.)

Paul's very careful dialectic between the sense in which pagan deities do or do not "exist" should suggest caution in translating τῶν δαιμονίων. That *the* **demonic** is real and powerful Paul never denies. But since he endorses *both* the apocalyptic tradition (reflected in rabbinic Judaism) of **demonic forces** *and* the prophetic tradition reflected in hellenistic Judaism that false gods are "nongods" or "empty" of reality, he is less likely to be thinking of personalized entities than the power of **demonic forces** which reflect powers of evil greater in collective force than human resources.[157] They represent active evil powers which are hostile to God; but they are also "nothings" in themselves. F. F. Bruce comments, "The **demons**, for Paul, were probably not personal beings but impersonal forces which exerted a powerful influence over unregenerate man."[158] Although the word δαίμων occurs regularly in the Synoptic Gospels as personal agencies in the context of exorcisms (e.g., Matt 9:33; Mark 7:26; Luke 11:14; or, in the plural, δαιμόνια, Matt 7:22; 9:34; 10:8; Mark 1:34, 39; 3:15, 22; 6:13; 9:38; Luke 9:49; 11:15, 18, 19), Paul uses the word δαιμόνιον only in 10:20 and 21 (four times in these two verses) in his entire corpus. Collins emphasizes this well: "Only in 1 Cor 10:20-21 does Paul speak about demons. . . . All reality . . . belongs to the one God who has entrusted sovereignty over all things to the one

155. Ibid.
156. Conzelmann, *1 Cor,* 170; and further 173, including n. 34 and n. 35.
157. Cf. W. Foerster, "δαίμων," *TDNT,* 2:1-20; O. Böcher, *Das Neue Testament und die dämonischen Mächte* (Stuttgart: Katholisches Bibelwerk, 1972), which includes a discussion of "victory over demonic powers" and the significance of this theology for today.
158. Bruce, *1 and 2 Cor,* 96.

Lord (8:6; 15:27)."[159] Whereas the Synoptic exorcisms remain signs of the *coming* victory of the death and resurrection of Christ, retrospectively in the light of that victory Paul sees their power as in part real but as *crumbling* (see above on 2:6) and no longer "real" in the sense of retaining an ontological foundation within the new created order.[160] Hence these former agencies have become reduced to *pockets of power* operating where human social "worlds" or value systems still offer them ground and sway. Hence, emphatically, *Christians* must not **participate in** this realm. Bruce adds, "Christ by his victory on the cross has disabled these demonic forces and liberated his people from their influence, but his people might foolishly put themselves in situations where this influence was still potent."[161] (See comments and bibliography under 2:6 and 8:5-6.)

21 The two parallel clauses both signal the parallelism by forming a beginning, a middle term, and the ending with the same Greek words: οὐ δύνασθε . . . κυρίου . . . δαιμονίων (although we have proposed a minor stylistic variation **devilish powers** and **demons** to convey the "double meaning" discussed above).[162] The use of οὐ δύνασθε conveys (i) a *logical* **cannot** (the two possibilities logically exclude each other); (ii) an *empirical* **cannot** (something will be destroyed if you try to do both); and (iii) an *institutional* **cannot** (Christians cannot, and still be *counted as* "Christian").

The parallelism between ποτήριον κυρίου πίνειν and τραπέζης κυρίου μετέχειν is instructive. We noted above the emphasis of Cullmann and Robinson on "sharing Christ's **cup**" (in Mark 10:38, 39) as **communal participation** in the "cup" of *his baptism as Messiah* into suffering, death, and resurrection.[163] It is *impossible* (in all three senses) to participate in Christ, his redemptive act of self-giving in suffering and death, his resurrection mode of existence through the Holy Spirit (15:44; cf. Rom 8:11), and his love for others, and simultaneously to **participate in** the seductive, assertive, manipulative powers of evil which inspire idolatry by substituting themselves in place of God. "With the Christian 'cup' Paul had stressed the covenant identification of those who participated as one body. . . . The contrast Paul built up was not between foods at the respective feasts but between the Lord and demons."[164] κοινωνούς of v. 20 points back to κοινωνοί of v. 18, and both are reflected in μετέχειν in this verse.[165]

In 11:23-31 Paul will relate this more closely to a sharp focus on Christ's

159. Collins, *First Cor,* 380-81.

160. Without an acknowledgment and explanation of the "double meaning" in Paul here and in 8:4-6 writers regard Paul as "curiously inconsistent" (Higgins, *The Lord's Supper in the NT,* 68).

161. Bruce, *1 and 2 Cor,* 96.

162. On the parallelism cf. BDF, 259-60, sect. 490; and Wolff, *Der erste Brief,* 234.

163. Cullmann, *Baptism in the NT,* 23 and elsewhere; J. A. T. Robinson, "The One Baptism" *SJT* 6 (1953): 257-74, rpt. in his *Twelve NT Studies* (London: SCM, 1962), 158-75.

164. Gardner, *The Gifts of God,* 170.

165. Meyer, *First Epistle,* 305.

death, not on the basis of the dubious theories of Lietzmann and Lohmeyer about two types of Lord's Supper, but because, as Thornton urges, all of the Pauline and other NT language about being "partakers of Christ" convey the theme of being *shareholders who have a stake above all in Christ's sufferings:* "Messiahship is rooted in suffering," and Christians "have become partakers in his Messianic status . . ." (cf. Gal 3:26-29 ["put on" like a garment]; Rom 6:2-7 ["baptized . . . into his death"]; 8:33, 34 [". . . as sheep for the slaughter"]; Phil 3:7, 8; Col 1:24; cf. 1 Pet 4:12-14; Heb 11:24-26; 12:22-24; 13:13).[166] "The pattern of the Messianic life is one of suffering and glory."[167] Those who share τραπέζης δαιμονίων manifest the opposite principle: not the giving of the self for the benefit of "the weak" (as is the issue in 8:12, 13) but self-edification, self-fulfillment, or self-enjoyment (cf. Deuteronomy 32) at the expense of others, even if something else is put into the place that belongs to God alone (εἰδωλόν, cf. v. 19).

Tillich designates as "the demonic" anything that fragments the one loyalty and the ultimate concern that belongs to God alone, although he uses the term in a symbolic sense.[168] Christ's death and **the cup of the Lord** constitute a *oneness* of exclusive covenant loyalty to God which is incompatible with the various distractions of idolatrous practices which substitute the many for *the one* which is offered through Christ to God.[169]

By way of postscript two supplementary points emerge. First, Paul's use of argument to press the implications of logical exclusion or self-contradiction should be recalled when people try to underplay Paul's use of rational argumentation. Second the use of **table** here provides scriptural warrant for the term *Communion Table* in the Lord's Supper, although in the context of the OT dispensation τράπεζα can also mean *altar,* as in the background from Malachi which Paul may have in mind (cf. Mal 1:7, 12).[170]

22 The first person plural παραζηλοῦμεν is most naturally understood as a continuous present, although W. F. Howard argues for its status as a deliberative subjunctive: *are we to provoke?* which is tempting to follow but insecure, in spite of REB's and Barrett's advocacy.[171] *Are we provoking?* (NIV) seems to verge on the banal after Paul's relentless argument that such action *is* provocative (as is *do we provoke?* AV/KJV). Moffatt's **What!** *do we intend to rouse the Lord's jealousy?* or NJB's *Do we really want to arouse the Lord's jealousy?* convey the force of the Greek in its context more adequately. In

166. L. S. Thornton, *The Common Life in the Body of Christ,* 34-65 and 69-87.

167. Ibid., 37.

168. Paul Tillich, *Systematic Theology* (3 vols., Chicago: University of Chicago Press and London: Nisbet, 1951, 1957, 1963), 1:14, 15, 17, 42; 2:6-11; 3, pt. iv.

169. A closer Pauline parallel occurs in Rom 1:25, where Paul speaks of worshipping "the creature" (a social construct?) in place of the Creator.

170. Cf. Schrage, *Der erste Brief,* 2:446-47, and Goppelt, "τράπεζα," *TDNT,* 8:148-58.

171. MHT, *Grammar,* 2:196; Barrett, *First Epistle,* 238. REB follows this suggestion. The suggestion appears first to have come from Bultmann (Edwards, *First Epistle,* 262).

Greek rhetoric the opening conjunction ἤ, *or,* must be translated in a way which reflects its rhetorical function in context, for which Moffatt's abrupt exclamatory **What!** well serves the purpose.

παραζηλόω occurs very rarely in Paul (cf. Rom 10:19), and both in Rom 10:19 and in this verse the word clearly alludes to the LXX of Deut 32:21, αὐτοὶ παρεζήλωσάν με ἐπ' οὐ θεῷ. The use of the "jealousy" motif drawn from Deuteronomy 32, esp. 15-21, is discussed definitively by my colleague Richard H. Bell in his volume *Provoked to Jealousy*.[172] Although in Deuteronomy 32 the κύριος is Yahweh, in 1 Cor 10:21-22 κύριος clearly refers to Christ.[173] Bell supports the christological understanding of Deuteronomy 32 found in Paul which A. T. Hanson emphasizes when he calls 10:14-22 "a sort of Midrash on Deut 32:15-31."[174] Deut 32:13-16 speak of Israel's being fed with "oil out of the flinty rock . . . the finest of wheat, and of the blood of the grape you drank wine." Hanson observes: "Here are both bread and wine with a reference to blood, quite enough to point Paul to the Eucharist . . . in 1 Cor 10:14-21."[175] In the very next verse, however (Deut 32:17, cited in 1 Cor 10:20), "they sacrificed to demons who were not gods." Israel's apostasy roused God to jealousy because his covenant people, to whom he had given himself, favored "another people."[176]

Hans von Soden argues that "the strong" reinforced their triumphalist stance of freedom and invulnerability by claiming that *to participate in the Lord's Supper* gave them immunity against any influence from evil powers associated with pagan cults.[177] Hence "the strong," on the basis of combining overrealized eschatology, quasignostic individualism, and an extreme *ex opere operato* sacramentalism, felt that they *could* participate in pagan cultic practices and remain unscathed. This would also cohere with J. H. Neyrey's approach in terms of anthropological models of body language. Against the quasignostic "pneumatics," for Paul "freedom" is not an absolute or overriding value. . . . Paul's regulation of the eating of idol meat and the reasoning which underplay it stand in sharp contrast to the behavior and attitudes of those who would eat in freedom."[178] Paul has argued that this **cannot** be done, and his final argument is that willful disloyalty on the part of *those who have committed themselves to covenant salvation and take part in covenant*

---

172. R. H. Bell, *Provoked to Jealousy: The Origin and Purpose of the Jealousy Motif in Romans 9–11,* WUNT 2:63 (Tübingen: Mohr, 1994), on 1 Corinthians 10, esp. 251-55.

173. Ibid., 254-55.

174. A. T. Hanson, *Studies in Paul's Technique and Theology* (London: SPCK, 1974), 113; cf. 104-25.

175. Ibid., 115.

176. Ibid.; cf. Bell, *Provoked to Jealousy,* 255.

177. Von Soden, "Sakrament und Ethik bei Paulus: Zur Frage der literarischen und theologischen Einheitlichkeit von 1 Kor 8–10," in H. Frick (ed.), *Rudolf Otto Festgruss: Aufsätze eines Kollegenkreises* (Gotha: Klotz, 1931), 1-40 and in his *Urchristentum und Geschichte* (Tübingen: Mohr, 1951), 1:239-75, esp. 261-68.

178. Neyrey, "Body Language in 1 Corinthians," in *Semeia* 35 (1986): 148; cf. 129-64.

ordinances commit a treachery, betrayal, and duplicity that **arouses the Lord's jealousy**.

The last clause is solemn, but it adds a touch of irony if "*the strong* (οἱ ἰσχυρότεροι) so press their self-confidence as to imply that they are **stronger** (ἰσχυρότεροι) **than** God. The ridiculous notion is conveyed by μή as introducing a very hesitant rhetorical question requiring the answer "no": μὴ ἰσχυρότεροι αὐτοῦ (genitive of comparison) ἐσμεν; **surely it cannot be that we are "stronger" than he, can it?**[179] The disloyalty and absurdity of this triumphalist, self-centered theology is exposed.

5. Freedom and Love: Residual Issues and Recapitulation (10:23–11:1)

(23) "Liberty to do all things"; but not everything is helpful. "The right to do anything"; but not everything builds up [the church]. (24) No one should seek his or her own interests but the well-being of the other. (25, 26) Eat whatever is sold in the meat market without asking about it to reach a judgment because of your self-awareness [or just possibly conscience]. For "The earth is the Lord's, and all that is in it." (27) If someone who is an unbeliever invites some of you to a meal and you want to go, make a practice of eating anything that is put before you without asking about it to reach a judgment because of your self-awareness. (28, 29a) If, however, someone should say to you, "This has been offered in sacrifice," make a practice of not eating it, out of regard for the person who informed you and their self-awareness: the self-awareness, I mean, not of one's own, but that of the other person. (29b, 30) For why [you ask] is my freedom being subjected to another person's self-awareness? Well, if I take part in a meal with thanksgiving, why should I suffer defamation of character over that for which I, at least, give thanks. (31, 32) Whether, then, you eat or drink, or whether you do anything different, do it all for the glory of God. Avoid doing damage both to Jews and to Gentiles, as well as to God's Church. (33; 11:1) In just the same way, I on my part strive to take account of all the interests of everyone, not seeking any advantage of my own, but the good of the many, with a view to their salvation. Take me as your pattern, as I take Christ for mine.

Paul has covered most of the ground which he wishes to address in 8:1–11:1. This concluding section addresses issues which arise concerning meat bought from the market, which may well have been resold after earlier use and passage through pagan temples. To what extent, if at all, does what may earlier have been εἰδωλόθυτα acquire a different status for Christian believers when

---

179. "The question is framed so as to demand denial" (Harrisville, *1 Cor,* 172).

it is subsequently sold in the open market perhaps alongside (whether or not indiscriminately; see below, esp. Isenberg) "ordinary" meat on the open market? Should all market meat be abandoned in case its origin is cultic or even unknown? Should attitudes differ depending on whether the context is a believer's own home or whether the believer is a guest in the home of a Gentile friend or colleague? How can the series of principles and case studies examined over virtually three chapters (from 8:1 onward) be summed up and applied to the practical situations of the addressees? Since much of the ground has been covered, little further literature provides resources for this section beyond that cited already, and a number of verses can be clarified by referring back to earlier parallels.

Supplementary Bibliography on 10:23–11:1
(For Most Works, see under 8:1-13 and 10:1-13)

Barrett, C. K., "Things Sacrificed to Idols," *NTS* 11 (1965): 138-53; rpt. in his *Essays on Paul* (London: SPCK, 1982), 40-59.

Betz, H.-D., *Nachfolge und Nachahmung Jesu Christi im Neuen Testament,* BHT 37 (Tübingen: Mohr, 1967).

Cadbury, H. J., "The Macellum of Corinth," *JBL* 53 (1934): 134-41.

Castelli, E. A., *Imitating Paul: A Discourse of Power* (Louisville: Westminster/Knox, 1991), 89-138.

Crafton, J. A., *The Agency of the Apostle,* JSNTSS 51 (Sheffield: Sheffield Academic Press, 1991), 59-102.

de Boer, W. P., *The Imitation of Paul: An Exegetical Study* (Kampen: Kok, 1962), 154-69.

Eckstein, H.-J., *Der Begriff Syneidesis bei Paulus,* WUNT 2:10 (Tübingen: Mohr, 1983), 256-76.

Gardner, P. D., *The Gifts of God and the Authentication of the Christian* (Lanham: University Press of America, 1994), 172-85.

Gill, D. W. J., "In Search of the Social Elite in the Corinthian Church," *TynBul* 44 (1993): 323-37.

————, "The Meat Market at Corinth (1 Cor 10:25)," *TynBul* 43 (1992): 389-93.

Hinz, C., "Bewahrung und Verkehrung der Freiheit in Christo," in K.-W. Tröger (ed.), *Gnosis und NT* (Gütersloh: Mohn, 1973), 405-22.

Horrell, D. G., *The Social Ethos of the Corinthian Correspondence* (Edinburgh: T. & T. Clark, 1996), 145-50.

Isenberg, M., "The Sale of Sacrificial Meat," *Classical Philosophy* 70 (1975): 271-73.

Lohse, E., "Zu 1 Kor 10:26, 31," *ZNW* 47 (1956): 277-80.

Maly, K., *Mündige Gemeinde* (Stuttgart: Katholisches Bibelwerk 1967), 146-56.

MacMullen, R., *Paganism in the Roman Empire* (New Haven: Yale University Press, 1981), 34-42.

Murphy-O'Connor, J., "Freedom or the Ghetto (1 Cor VIII:1-13; X:23-XI)," *RB* 85 (1978): 543-74.

Probst, H., *Paulus und der Brief. Die Rhetorik der antiken Briefes als Form der paulinischen Korintherkorrespondenz (1 Kor 8–10),* WUNT 2:45 (Tübingen: Mohr, 1991), 278-94.

Stanley, D. M., "'Become Imitators of Me': The Pauline Conception of Apostolic Tradition," *Bib* 40 (1959): 859-77.

Watson, D. F., "1 Cor 10:23–11:1 in the Light of Graeco-Roman Rhetoric: The Role of Rhetorical Questions," *JBL* 108 (1989): 301-18.

Webster, J. B., "The Imitation of Christ," *TynBul* 37 (1986): 95-120.

Willis, W. L., *Idol Meat in Corinth* (Chico: Scholars Press, 1985), 229-63.

Yeo, K.-K., *Rhetorical Instruction in 1 Cor 8 and 10* (Leiden: Brill, 1995), 180-211.

23 Some later MSS insert μοι after πάντα in v. 23 to replicate 6:12, but p⁴⁶, ℵ*, A, B, C*, D, F, and G omit it, which is decisive.

For the argument that Paul quotes a slogan current at Corinth and for exegetical comment see under 6:12, where the Greek is virtually identical except for the change from οὐκ ἐγὼ ἐξουσιασθήσομαι ὑπό τινος in 6:12 to οὐ πάντα οἰκοδομεῖ here. There are advantages to translating ἔξεστιν as an issue of **rights** (cognate with ἐξουσία), but the slogan also reflects a concern for **liberty** which no doubt began as an authentic corollary of the gospel degenerated into a manipulative tool for license, self-gratification, and "autonomy." In 6:12 we translate "**Liberty to do all things**" in order to retain Paul's wordplay on ἐξουσιάζω: *but I will not let anything take liberties with me* (6:12b). Here, rather than stress that **liberty** (far from leading to *autonomy*) beguiles a believer into becoming *mastered by the desires which reflect the craving* (ἐπιθυμία of 10:7-13), Paul returns to his earlier theme of **building up** (see above under 3:9; 8:1, 10), which he will develop further in 14:3, 4, 5, 12, 17, 26 (see there the exegetical comments, including allusion to P. Vielhauer's *Oikodomē*).

As we observed under 6:12, οὐ πάντα συμφέρει negates the universality of freedom: **not everything is helpful**. Paul's "appeal to advantage" may well play a part in his epistolary strategy, as Mitchell argues.[1] However, Paul's approach here is negative: unrestrained and undisciplined affirmations of freedom "advantage" no one. This strikes at the roots of a post-Kantian secular ethical liberalism which ranks "autonomy" both as a **right** and as an absolute virtue. To aim at unqualified autonomy may bring about a new bondage and disadvantage the community. As we have noted and will see further (14:3-5, 12-17), **building up** presupposes the logical grammar of **building** *the community;* hence we place [**the church**] in brackets in translation.[2] Paul thinks especially of "the weak," and "to build up . . . usually has a specifically ecclesial reference" (Collins).[3]

24 A later tradition inserts ἕκαστος, *each,* at the end of the sentence (cf. AV/KJV, *every man*); but this has no early MS support and is rightly omitted by UBS 4th ed.

---

1. M. M. Mitchell, *Paul and the Rhetoric of Reconciliation,* 25-39, 256-58: "standard advice to factionalists" (256).

2. Cf. Maly, *Mündige Gemeinde,* 146 also.

3. Collins, *First Cor,* 386.

The diverse situations and case studies examined over the last three chapters now find expression as a "general axiom" or aphorism.[4] Concern for the other remains, in Bonhoeffer's phrase, the Christomorphic pattern of the lifestyle and atoning work of "the Man for Others" (cf. Matt 22:37-40), and Paul will appeal to this in the last verse of this section, 11:1b. It is also, as he states in v. 33 and 11a, a mode of life which he himself seeks to live out, and is a principle of apostolicity (cf. in 1:1; 9:1). The principle also finds expression in 13:5; Rom 14:7; 15:2; Gal 6:2; and Phil 2:1-4, 5-7. Greek often uses the singular **other** when modern English speaks of *others*. However, with the rise of hermeneutical theory in Gadamer, Betti, and Ricoeur, respect for "the otherness of the Other" has entered hermeneutical, philosophical, and ethical vocabulary in precisely this Pauline sense, and hence the singular may be retained as a way of making this specific point.[5] On this basis Barrett rightly questions those who render the other person (τοῦ ἑτέρου) as neighbor because this implies commonality in some degree (e.g., location).[6] Paul's demonstration of how this axiom should operate at Corinth has been set forth in 8:7-13, where concern for the brother or sister for whom Christ died takes priority over one's own concerns for self-affirmation, self-gratification, or self-fulfillment (genuine or imagined). The complementary point about social realities is underlined by Collins: "the Christians at Corinth lived neither in a Christian quarter nor in a ghetto. . . . They had a variety of contacts with those who were not members of the church."[7]

25-26   Paul turns to the subject of what people buy **in the meat market** or butchers' shops. Older modern writers argue that the Greek μάκελλον (only here within the NT) is a late loanword from Lat. *macellum*.[8] In spite of the close relationship of virtual transliteration however, the word can be traced to an inscription of 400 BC at Epidaurus as well as to Ionic Greek, and BAGD insist that it was "not originally a Latin word taken into Greek."[9] Robertson and Moulton-Milligan, among others, however, observe that it also relates to Hebrew, and demonstrate its use in Dio Cassius, Plutarch, the papyri, and inscriptions to mean *market for provisions,* or **the meat market**.[10] Kent shows that of the 104 inscriptions dated prior to the reign of Hadrian, 101 are

---

4. As in Maly, *Mündige Gemeinde,* 147. Conzelmann calls it "a maxim in the style of Wisdom literature" (*1 Cor,* 176).

5. Paul Ricoeur, *Oneself as Another* (Eng. trans., Chicago: University of Chicago, 1992), 4-16 and throughout; Emilio Betti, *Die Hermeneutik als Allgemeine Methodik der Geisteswissenschaften* (Tübingen: Mohr, 2d ed. 1972), 7 and *Allgemeine Auslegungslehre* (Tübingen: Mohr, 1967), 21, 158, 211-13.

6. Barrett, *First Epistle,* 240.

7. Collins, *First Cor,* 383.

8. Findlay, *Expositor's Greek Testament,* 2:867.

9. BAGD, 487.

10. Robertson, *Word Pictures: Epistles,* 4:157; MM, 386, who compare Heb. מכלה (*miklah), enclosure;* cf. Deissmann, *Light from the Ancient East,* 276. In Plautus the Latin has the same meaning.

782

in Latin, and only 3 in Greek.[11] If Latin was used mainly in the early days of Corinth as a Roman colony (from 44 BC onward), in Paul's day Greek would have been the language of trade and commerce, and interaction between the languages was inevitable. The markets, however, may not be identified with the row of shops immediately on the north side of the Agora. They were likely to have been situated between 70 and 100 meters further to the north along the Lechaeum Road.[12] D. W. J. Gill has undertaken recent research on the site of the *macellum* at Corinth, and suggests that Latin inscriptions dating from very shortly before the period of Paul's ministry attest to its presence as a gift from the social elite of the city.[13]

The more important question discussed by Cadbury, Isenberg, and others is whether sacrificial and nonsacrificial meat bought in the *macellum* was readily distinguishable, indiscriminately mixed, or distinguishable only after explicit inquiry.[14] Isenberg argues on the basis of a first-century text, *Vita Aesopi,* that sacrificial and nonsacrificial meats were readily distinguishable, since the sacrificial meat would be valued more highly. He argues that this is also implied by Pliny's *Letter to Trajan* (10.96.10), which seems to stand in tension, he believes, with 1 Cor 10:25. Murphy-O'Connor follows D. E. Smith in concluding that most of the meat which was sold would have originated as sacrificial offerings.[15] However, Paul is not necessarily addressing only those who make the actual purchases rather than also those for whom others may have made the purchases. Conzelmann expresses extreme caution about how applicable to Paul's addressees the evidence which provides apparently large generalizations may be. Arguments of this kind "cannot be maintained in general terms."[16] The work of Gill on food shortages seems to imply that market situations may well have varied from year to year.[17] Nevertheless, Weiss anticipates and Eckstein corroborates the probability underlined by Murphy-O'Connor that "in a city such as Corinth scarcely any other meat would be for sale except for that supplied from the temple."[18]

So much of the above argument has concerned the *qualifications* made about freedom, and the need for restraint, that it may come almost as a surprise to find that Paul's aim here is to release the oversensitive "weak" Christians at Cor-

---

11. Kent, *Corinth, VIII/3: The Inscriptions 1926-1950,* 19.

12. Murphy-O'Connor, *St. Paul's Corinth,* 24-25, 32, 37.

13. Gill, "The Meat Market at Corinth (1 Cor 10:25)," 389-93. He questions the findings of Broneer. See further Gill, "In Search of the Social Elite in the Corinthian Church," 323-37, where he discusses the ownership of flocks and grazing rights.

14. Cadbury, "The Macellum of Corinth," 134-41; and Isenberg, "The Sale of Sacrificial Meat," 271-73.

15. Murphy-O'Connor, *St Paul's Corinth,* 33. He refers to D. E. Smith, "Social Obligation in the Context of Commercial Meals" (Harvard Th.D. diss., 1980), 12.

16. Conzelmann, *1 Cor,* 176.

17. Gill, "In Search of the Social Elite," 323-37.

18. Weiss, *Der erste Korintherbrief,* 263; Eckstein, *Der Begriff Syneidesis,* 257; and with the above caveat, Conzelmann, *1 Cor,* 176.

inth from bondage and inner struggle to a new freedom.[19] As we noted above, this change of mood leads many to formulate partition theories which assign 8:1-13 and 10:23–11:1 to a different letter from that of 10:1-22.[20] However, in the first place this apparent "freedom" remains carefully qualified, even for "the weak" (v. 28 and probably v. 29). In the second place, Eckstein carefully weighs the possibility of two quite different understandings of (1) **eat whatever is sold in the marketplace, without asking about it . . .** (on the translation, see below).[21] (a) One view, advocated by Pierce and followed by Maurer, is that of permissive freedom: *you need not* ask questions, *you are free to eat* **whatever is sold in the meat market**. In Pierce's view Paul seeks to release "the weak" from *unnecessary pain* inflicted on the self by an oversensitive, overscrupulous conscience: hence διὰ τὴν συνείδησιν means literally "*because of conscience* [and the discomfort or pain that it might needlessly inflict] *avoid asking questions* (Pierce's italics).[22] (b) A second, very different line of approach is represented by Jewett. Jewett urges that in this sentence "*He [Paul] places a radical obligation upon 'weak' Christians to overcome their scruples*. . . . In not anxiously examining the origin of the meat they purchase, the 'weak' are to act on the principle that 'the earth is the Lord's and the fullness thereof' " (my italics).[23] "Those with a weak conscience "have no option but to put into practice the gospel freedom of the principle" πάντα μοι ἔξεστιν by not inquiring concerning the origin of what they eat; but the moment they discover it is sacrificial meat [cf. vv. 28-29], they are to desist so as not to contaminate or bruise their conscience."[24]

This difficulty of interpretation is further compounded by two sets of interpretative disagreement. (2) Does διὰ τὴν συνείδησιν refer (a) to the **self-awareness** or *consciousness* (or *conscience?*) of *the person who eats the meat,* or (b) "to the conscience *not of the eater,* or potential eater, but his weak Christian brother" (Barrett, my italics)[25] Pierce, however, believes that what is at issue is the potential pain, damage, or injury done to the conscience of the one who eats.[26] In addition to issue (2), which is already complex, a third disagreement arises. (3) Does συνείδησις mean (a) conscience (Pierce, Sevenster, Thrall) or (b) **self-awareness** (with Gardner, Maurer, Gooch, Horsley); or (c) *consciousness* (Horrell; cf. Eckstein, Willis). An extensive discussion of these views was offered above under 8:7, "Note on Conscience, or Self-

19. Fee, *First Epistle,* 480.

20. See the introduction to 8:1–11:1 above and subsequent comments on this issue, above, on the hypothesis of Schmithals, Jewett, Yeo and others, and the response of Fee, Mitchell, and my own reservations.

21. Eckstein, *Der Begriff Syneidesis,* 257-61.

22. Pierce, *Conscience in the NT,* 75; cf. 60-65 and 75-83; also C. Maurer, *TDNT,* 7:915 (cf. 898-919).

23. Jewett, *Paul's Anthropological Terms,* 428.

24. Ibid.

25. Barrett, "Things Sacrificed to Idols," in his *Essays on Paul,* 46; cf. 40-59 (rpt. from *NTS* 2 [1965]: 138-53).

26. Pierce, *Conscience in the NT,* 75-78, 80-82; cf. Maurer, *TDNT,* 7:915.

Awareness."[27] We concluded our discussion by acknowledging the force of the arguments put forward by Horsley, Gooch, and Gardner.

In the light of 1, 2, and 3 it will become apparent why to translate μηδὲν ἀνακρίνοντες διὰ τὴν συνείδησιν simply as *without raising questions of conscience* (NIV, REB, virtually NRSV); *asking no question for conscience' sake* (AV/KJV), or even *you need not ask questions of conscience first* (NJB) are all to some degree problematic and pre-judge major exegetical and lexicographical issues. In 2:14-15; 4:3-4; 9:3; 14:24 ἀνακρίνω means **to sift evidence, to ask about** (something), or **to reach a judgment** *(not simply to ask about)*. The lexicographical evidence is clear and harmonizes with Fee's comment about Jewish obligations.[28] If Weiss, Conzelmann, and Murphy-O'Connor are right about *most* meat's coming from the temple, this would make it all the more important for Jews and the scrupulous **to ask about** "uncontaminated" supplies **to reach a judgment**. Further, to translate *conscience* transfers the act of *judging* from ἀνακρίνω to συνείδησις, whereas the issue about συνείδησις (see above) is different. It concerns perhaps (a) whether an *oversensitive* **self-awareness** is the root cause (διά) of the problem, i.e., in the sense of troubling too much about "me" rather than "**the Lord**"; or perhaps (b) conversely Paul enjoins "**eat**" because *it has nothing to do with* **your self-awareness**."[29] In practice, (a) and (b) are simply different ways of expressing and explicating διά, and both mean that *too much awareness of self* should not compromise the freedom which comes from letting Christ as **Lord** take responsibility for the self. Too many anxious thoughts about *self* damage Christian *freedom* and threaten a *new bondage to moralism*.[30] The translation **because of your self-awareness** allows for either (a) Gardner's preferred option: "because self-awareness is no longer relevant" or (b), as we propose, "because of too much preoccupation with questions about the self and its scruples."

The quotation from Ps 24:1 performs three functions. (1) It lifts the attention from self and from overscrupulous anxiety to the reminder that the sovereign to whom everything belongs (including the care of the believer) is **the Lord**; (2) It reminds the anxious that even what may or may not have passed through pagan temples still belongs to *the totality of God's creation* over which he (not the so-called gods of 1 Cor 8:1-6) reigns as sovereign.[31] This verse may be compared with Mark 7:19, καθαρίζων πάντα τὰ βρώματα. (3) Most espe-

27. The sources are there documented. However see in particular Horsley, "Consciousness and Freedom . . . 1 Cor 8–10," 574-89; Eckstein, *Der Begriff Syneidēsis,* 257-61; Willis, *Idol Meat,* 89-96; Gooch, " 'Conscience' in 1 Cor 8 and 10," 244-54; Gardner, *Gifts of God,* 42-54 and 174-76; and Horrell, *The Social Ethos of the Corinthian Correspondence,* 105-9 and 146-48.

28. Fee writes, "It was possible in some cases, indeed it was required of the Jews to investigate whether the meat in the *macellum* had been previously sacrificed" *(First Epistle,* 481).

29. Gardner, *Gifts of God,* 175, favors this interpretation of διὰ τὴν συνείδησιν.

30. Whether or not the **self-awareness** relates to *the other* is better left to vv. 28-29, where it becomes explicit. It is unnecessarily complicated to follow Barrett on v. 25: Could the addressees be expected to read the verse in the way which Barrett implies?.

31. Collins, *First Cor,* 387.

cially (with Barrett) it implies that every good gift of God is to be accepted *with gratitude* as **the Lord's** gift. Nothing exists that is not lent or given by **the Lord**. Barrett argues that although there is no evidence that Ps 24:1 was used as a grace in Judaism, nevertheless the implications of the verse were pressed as an argument that grace at meals ought to be said. Τὸ πλήρωμα αὐτῆς, *its fullness* (NRSV) denotes *what it is full of,* i.e., **all that is in it** (with REB). It is sometimes argued that this injunction contradicts the decree of Acts 15. Witherington considers various possible responses, but concludes that in all probability our epistle pre-dates any *public* policy agreement of the kind reflected in Acts.[32] However, he also shows how complex a range of questions is involved, which should invite caution over too hasty a judgment.

27   The second half of the verse replicates the issues discussed under the previous verse in both translation and exegesis (see above). The first half sets the scene for an invitation to a meal, not that of shopping in the market. REB, *if an unbeliever,* or even NIV, *if some unbeliever,* does not entirely convey the possible force of εἴ τις καλεῖ ὑμᾶς τῶν ἀπίστων, since the plural ἀπίστων may serve to remind the addressees that it is not only the status of the host that is a factor, but that the Christian will be entering a pagan household where everything will be prepared and arranged in accordance with the cultural and socioreligious conventions of the day. The meat almost certainly *will* be what had been offered in a temple, especially since the host serves good quality fare. Furthermore, **invites** *you* (NIV, REB, NJB, NRSV) leaves hidden the plural καλεῖ ὑμᾶς, for which Robertson and Plummer suggest "**some of you**," to remind the addressees that Paul has in mind a scenario in which another believer will also probably be present. In this verse the fundamental principle is affirmed of living in gospel *freedom unless either* (i) covenant disloyalty to God *or* (ii) damage to a fellow believer is entailed thereby. **Make a practice of eating** (present imperative) anything that is put before you (πᾶν τὸ παρατιθέμενον ὑμῖν ἐσθίετε) runs parallel with πᾶν τὸ ἐν μακέλλῳ πωλούμενον ἐσθίετε in v. 25, with the replicated addition in each case μηδὲν ἀνακρίνοντες διὰ τὴν συνείδησιν. The exegetical and linguistic issues discussed in v. 25b apply here also, except that the double context of a pagan household and a fellow guest who is a Christian gives rise to the complication which Paul is about to address in the next two or three verses.

28-29a   (1) Later MSS, Chrysostom, and the *Textus Receptus* insert: *for the earth is the Lord's and all that is in it.* Since it is not found in the main early MSS (e.g., ℵ, A, B, C, D, F, G, 33, vg, etc.) it is clearly a gloss derived from v. 26. This also accords with the maxim that the shorter reading is preferred; no good reason for the omission of the quotation has been proposed if it was original.[33] Thus only AV/KJV retain the clause. (2) C,

32. Witherington, "Not So Idle Thoughts about *Eidolothuton*," *TynBul* 44 (1993): 237-54, esp. 252-54. Acts 15 is not the only relevant passage elsewhere in the NT. Cf. Mark 7:19 (cited already above); Acts 10:15, et al.
33. These arguments are put forward in Metzger, *Textual Commentary,* 2d ed., 495; the UBS 4th ed. ranks the shorter reading "A," i.e., it "is certain."

D, E, F, and G read εἰδωλόθυτον for the authentic ἱερόθυτον, but the word which the Gentile host would have used is well attested.

The Greek subjunctive ἐὰν δέ τις . . . εἴπῃ projects a scenario which is only hypothetical or at most perhaps infrequent. Hence we translate, **if, however, someone should say. . . .**[34] The present tense of the negative imperative μὴ ἐσθίετε also deserves note. Since it cannot mean *do not continue to eat,* the Greek present suggests **make a practice of not eating it.**[35]

The main exegetical problem arises from the lack of clarity about the identity of τὸν μηνύσαντα, **the person who informed you.** Many of the patristic writers suggest that this is an unbeliever, some think perhaps the host, largely on the ground that a person of pagan religion would describe as ἱερόθυτον what Jews and Christians call εἰδωλόθυτον, as Origen explicitly observes (comparing his own vocabulary with that of Celsus).[36] Chrysostom, Theophylact, and Erasmus believe that τις here is a pagan Gentile, perhaps acting even with a hostile attempt to embarrass the believer.[37] Weiss insists that "the host it certainly was not, because the τις would not be identified thus," especially not in relation to v. 27.[38] Moreover, he urges, a Christian would understandably use ἱερόθυτον to express a warning in a friendly manner in this context. Heinrici argues for the same conclusion on the ground of the probable meaning of τὴν συνείδησιν, which surely applies to a fellow Christian, and Robertson and Plummer make the same point.[39]

Duane F. Watson sheds further light on this verse by means of a rhetorical approach, in which he shows how closely the logic, structure, and rhetoric tie together the approach of vv. 27-29a with that of v. 25: "the conscience is not concerned" expresses the common thrust.[40] Hence καὶ τὴν συνείδησιν means, as Paul makes clear in v. 29, not that genuine "conscience" on the part of the one to whom Paul addresses his words is involved but only the consciousness (or perhaps conscience) of the person who is concerned about the origin of the meal. The ethical principle involved is therefore not "my conscience" but (as regularly in 8:7-13; 10:23–11:1) *the welfare of the other person.*[41]

---

34. Cf. Meyer, *First Epistle,* 1:309, *If it **should** so happen that **someone**. . . .* Cf. Conzelmann, *1 Cor,* 177.

35. So Robertson and Plummer, *First Epistle,* 222. While more recent writers argue that hellenistic Greek is more fluid, the aorist imperative would otherwise be expected. (The case for a strict parallel with v. 25 would founder on the difference between the indicative [v. 25] and the subjunctive in the protasis.)

36. Origen, *Contra Celsum,* 8:21: Origen would call εἰδωλόθυτα or even δαιμονιόθυτα what Celsus calls ἱερόθυτα, in his ignorance of what is sacred.

37. Chrysostom, *1 Cor. Hom.,* 25:2.

38. Weiss, *Der erste Korintherbrief,* 264-65.

39. Heinrici, *Das erste Sendschreiben,* 287-88; Robertson and Plummer, *First Epistle,* 221.

40. Watson, "1 Cor 10:23–11:1 in the Light of Graeco-Roman Rhetoric: The Role of Rhetorical Questions," 305-6; cf. 301-18.

41. Ibid., 306. Watson is less dismissive of the possibility that this may be a pagan than

This is explicated exactly as we should expect, and thereby confirmed, by Paul's formulation in v. 29a. The concern is *not* with *oneself* (οὐχὶ τὴν ἑαυτοῦ) but with the well-being **of the other person** (ἀλλὰ τὴν τοῦ ἑτέρου). A number of writers regard ἑαυτοῦ as standing for σεαυτοῦ here: *not your own.*[42] However, Barrett plausibly argues **"one's own** . . . the more generalized meaning is better."[43] The translations *the other's conscience* (NRSV) or *not your conscience but his* (REB) take us back to our lengthy debates about whether Pierce, Sevenster, and Jewett or Gooch, Horsley, Eckstein, and Gardner are right about the meaning of συνείδησις. If the latter are correct, Paul is stating that the "weak" fellow Christian could be damaged by a **self-awareness** which suffers conflict, perceives contradiction, or is drawn into an identity crisis. That which his or her consciousness yields about the self must be respected, even if it awaits more confidence through love and instruction. All this remains part of an ethic of *concern for the other, not* the supposed autonomy of "conscience."

29b-30 The problems of vv. 29b-30 have been described by Barrett and Fee as "notoriously difficult" and as "a notorious crux."[44] No fewer than six possible accounts of the verses have been offered by major writers, although in our view the most careful and convincing explanation can be found in an article on the rhetorical function of these questions by Duane F. Watson.[45] Watson examines all the other major proposals, but convincingly concludes that these rhetorical questions serve a multilayered function of recapitulation, argumentation (which focuses the weakness of the position of "the strong"), and a proposal of policy. Once the rhetorical structure and functions have been grasped, and parallels noted, the apparent abruptness of the sudden change from the second person to the first person and supposed ambiguity of the questions cease to remain a problem.[46]

(1) Weiss proposes that these verses are a gloss inserted by a later scribe.[47] This view is widely rejected since it merely ascribed a supposed discontinuity of thought to a different hand. If we could explain the scribe's motivation and purpose, why does it remain more difficult to account for the questions spoken by Paul (unless we assume that they merely represent contradiction of misunderstanding which is a hypothesis of unnecessary last resort)?

(2) A widespread view (Lietzmann, Maly, Merk, Klauck), which is almost convincing, proposes that Paul anticipates an objection on the part of "the

---

Heinrici and Weiss. A pagan might thereby be caused to take the faith less seriously (which comes close to Chrysostom's argument).

42. For example, Edwards, *First Epistle,* 264.

43. Barrett, *First Epistle,* 242.

44. Barrett, *First Epistle,* 242; Fee, *First Epistle,* 486.

45. Watson, "1 Cor 10:23–11:1 in the Light of Greco-Roman Rhetoric: The Role of Rhetorical Questions," 301-18, esp. 308-18.

46. Cf. Fee's comment that of "the variety of solutions" "none is fully satisfactory" (*First Epistle,* 486).

47. Weiss, *Der erste Korintherbrief,* 265-66.

strong" which he expresses in diatribe style.[48] One main difficulty here is that *if* Paul uses the diatribe style, we should normally expect that an "answer" would be provided as the next stage of the rhetoric. However, as Barrett notes, such an answer does not seem to be delivered here.[49] Further, Weiss, Allo, and Schrage find an additional problem in the connective γάρ rather than one of contrast.[50]

(3) A view which is virtually the opposite is carefully argued by Murphy-O'Connor and advocated by Héring, Grosheide, and Richardson, among others. Paul addresses "weak" Christians by way of moderating their scrupulosity: "The conscience of the strong need not feel burdened just because the conscience of the weak is burdened. On the contrary such conscience remains free."[51] In Héring's view "the Apostle seeks to define *limits* for the respect due to the weak" (my italics).[52] Murphy-O'Connor insists that Paul offers warnings equally to "the strong" against their "craving" (esp. 8:7-13; 10:1-22), and to "the weak" whose abstinence gives them a sense of what verges on smug self-righteousness (vv. 29b-30).[53] "The Weak were equally blameworthy insofar as they projected what they felt onto others. 'What good does it do for my freedom to be subjected to the judgment of another's conscience?' (10:29). To assume the worst about others [i.e., "the strong"] is not Christian."[54] Nevertheless, Watson and others find it difficult to reconcile this understanding of the function of these questions with Paul's approval of qualifying freedom in 9:19-23, and more especially his very firm support of "the weak" in 8:11-13 and 10:24.[55]

(4) Paul is explaining that freedom is not lost if a person refrains from eating for the sake of another person's conscience, not because the person concerned has inhibiting scruples. "A free Christian must not allow his own conscience to think that he is doing something evil by the mere fact of eating food. . . . In order not to damage another person's conscience he will refrain from eating; but in his own mind he knows he has a right to eat this food as food. . . ."[56] Meyer and Conzelmann share this approach: "Strictly speaking I can eat anything that I can enjoy with thankfulness. . . . Conscience is under-

48. Lietzmann, *An die Korinther,* 51-52; Wendland, *Die Briefe,* 83-84; Pierce, *Conscience,* 78; Maly, *Mündige Gemeinde,* 152-53; Merk, *Handeln aus Glauben,* 129-30; R. Bultmann, *Der Stil der paulinischen Predigt und die Kynisch-stoische Diatribe,* FRLANT 13 (Göttingen: Vandenhoeck & Ruprecht, 1910), 10-13, 67-68; Klauck, *1 Kor,* 76-77.

49. Barrett, *First Epistle,* 243; Watson, "1 Cor 10:23–11:1," 309; also Willis, *Idol Meat,* 247; and Fee, *First Epistle,* 486, n. 52.

50. Schrage, *Der erste Brief,* 2:471 (Klauck leaves room for Watson's explanation); Allo, *Première Épitre,* 250; Weiss, *Der erste Korintherbrief.*

51. Grosheide, *First Epistle,* 243.

52. Héring, *First Epistle,* 99; so also P. Richardson, *Paul's Ethic of Freedom* (Philadelphia: Westminster, 1979), 129.

53. Murphy-O'Connor, "Freedom or the Ghetto," 543-74, esp. 555-56, 570-71.

54. Murphy-O'Connor, *1 Cor,* 117.

55. Watson, "1 Cor 10:23–11:1," 310.

56. Orr and Walther, *1 Cor,* 256.

stood subjectivistically."[57] This approach has some validity, but also limited validity all the while συνείδησις is understood to mean *conscience* in the Stoic or in the modern sense, and all the while the rhetorical function of the questions is not clarified (see below).

(5) The fifth approach is closely related to this, and depends in part on translating ἱνατί *what good end will be served by . . . ?* or *for what purpose . . . ?* (Findlay), *to what end . . . ?* (Barrett), *for what good will you gain . . . ?* (Godet, Robertson and Plummer), as against *why?* (NRSV, NIV, NJB) or *what . . . ?* (REB). Fee dogmatically asserts, "It does not in fact say, as Findlay translates, 'What good end will be served . . . ?'"; it means, "for what reason?"[58] However, Nigel Turner discusses the huge semantic range of ἵνα from ecbatic and epexegetic to telic, and even C. F. D. Moule's very brief allusion to its meaning *why* concedes that it represents ἵνα τί γένηται, which is the very ground on which Findlay, Robertson and Plummer, and others detect a nuance of "advantage" or "purpose" in the construction here.[59] Further, BDF note that the move to the first person regularly illustrates a universal axiom, which M. M. Mitchell has perceived in this section as a rhetoric of advantage.[60] In our view, *either* **why** (with Collins) *or to what end* provide *equally acceptable translations,* and we choose **why** only to preserve the force of γάρ. Paul's meaning on this basis would be: *what would be the advantage of my exercising my freedom if* I thereby **suffer defamation of character**?[61] *If it genuinely does not matter* whether I eat or not, *why choose the path that raises unnecessary difficulties?* What is the point of "freedom" if I cannot *choose not to cause* problems?

This approach is very well and clearly articulated by Willis, among others.[62] Findlay comments, "Instead of any benefit resulting from the assertion of liberty . . . positive harm ensues."[63] Robertson and Plummer compare Rom 14:16 and 1 Cor 8:8. Fee is correct, however, to note that κρίνεται is an indicative, not a subjunctive. We noted above BAGD's support for translating βλασφημοῦμαι as **suffer defamation of character**. This nuance of the verb is important in the light of the honor-shame categories which were so fundamental in first-century Corinth (see on v. 31, in the context of J. H. Neyrey and others). The **defamation** would arise on the ground that allegedly the Christian is inconsistent in belief and practice.

This fifth approach deserves special respect because of its persistence in

57. Conzelmann, *1 Cor,* 178; cf. Meyer, *First Epistle,* 2:312.

58. Fee, *First Epistle,* 486, n. 52 and 487, n. 55; Findlay, *Expositor's Greek Testament,* 2:869.

59. N. Turner, in MHT, *Grammar,* 3:102-5; Moule, *Idiom Book,* 139; see further Godet, *First Epistle,* 2:98-99; Robertson and Plummer, *First Epistle,* 222-23.

60. BDF, sect. 281.

61. On βλασφημοῦμαι as **to suffer defamation** [**of character**] see BAGD, 142-43.

62. Willis, *Idol Meat,* 249; Hurd, *Origin of 1 Corinthians,* 130-31, speculates that this may allude to Paul's own conduct at Corinth (which would explain the first person in a different way); also Ruef, *First Epistle,* 102-3; Kistemaker, *1 Cor,* 356; Collins, *First Cor,* 388.

63. Findlay, *Expositor's Greek Testament,* 2:869.

the posthistory of the text. Calvin discusses the issues with care, and concludes: "Paul gives serious warning that if we use our freedom just as we like, and thereby cause offence to our neighbours, the result will be . . . that this matchless gift of God will be condemned . . . ruining our freedom by making wrong use of it."[64] As often, but not always, is the case, Calvin follows Chrysostom, and this view can be found in Ambrosiaster, Jerome, Thomas Aquinas, and other writers cited below, including recently also Lang.[65]

(6) D. F. Watson argues convincingly that the dominant genre of 8:10 through to 11:1 is that of deliberative rhetoric, even if judicial and epideictic rhetoric also play a part in ch. 9.[66] 10:1-22 presents a negative warning or *refutatio* of what might have appeared in an illusory way to offer advantage, but the use of rhetorical questions forces the addressees to rethink the issues for themselves. Further rhetorical questions take up and recapitulate what has been said, and also prepare for what follows in 10:31–11:1. As in most deliberative rhetoric (as Mitchell regularly also urges), they introduce reflection which produces a change of policy. In effect, then, Watson's constructive research into the functions of rhetorical questions in Graeco-Roman texts (especially Cicero and Quintilian) and Pauline style (esp. in 1 Corinthians 8–10) provides a new lease on life for the second approach (Lietzmann, Maly, Wendland, and others, i.e., that Paul addresses an objection of "the strong"). It does so in such a way that it can be combined with (5) and thus can account for the connective γάρ (rather than an adversative) and the supposed lack of an "answer" to the diatribe question. With Stowers, he questions how much of Paul's rhetoric is actual *diatribe* in the strict sense. Rather, anticipating M. M. Mitchell, he identifies these rhetorical questions as part of *deliberative rhetoric*, which functions here for the purpose of (i) recapitulation (which can take the form of figures), (ii) argument, (iii) proposal of policy, (iv) interrogation, and sometimes (v) irony.[67] This is why Paul introduces his summary of the main point in 8:7-13; 9; 10:11–11:1 (esp. 10:23–11:1) with γάρ: the questions answer themselves because, as (1) and (5) above indicate, they sum up the thrust of the three chapters, namely, that *while believers are "free,"* concern *for the well-being of the other* has priority over everything else. In particular these verses embody "recapitulation followed by a proposal of policy."[68]

This excludes the need for (1), i.e., the theory of a post-Pauline gloss

64. Calvin, *First Epistle,* 224.

65. Chrysostom, *1 Cor. Hom.,* 25:2; Jerome, *Comm. ad 1 Cor,* in Migne, *PL,* 30:748 C-D: *Hoc est, ad quem profectum ita usor libertate mea, ut me alius reprehendat? . . . Non ideo sub gratia sumus, ut sub libertatis specie occasionem demus infidelibus blasphemandi. . . . Nihil magis agendum est Christiano . . . ;* Thomas Aquinas, *Lect. 1 Cor,* 579-80; Estius, *In omnes D. Pauli epistolas,* 581; Bengel, *Gnomon,* 642 (although his brevity allows equally for [4]); Allo, *Première Épitre,* 250-51; and more loosely Lang, *Die Briefe,* 131-32.

66. Watson, "1 Cor 10:23–11:1," 302-3.

67. Ibid., esp. 311-18.

68. Watson, "1 Cor 10:23–11:1," 318; also Collins, *First Cor,* 388.

(Weiss), and (3), i.e., admonition to "the weak" (Murphy-O'Connor), since this is not the major thrust of the three chapters. In theory (4) might be included, except that, with Gooch, Gardner, Horsley, and others, Watson is rightly reluctant to read into Paul Greek or modern notions of *conscience* when *self-awareness* or *consciousness of self* in a morally neutral sense is more distinctively Pauline and fits the exegesis of these verses very well. It is therefore unnecessary, with Senft, simply to enumerate a variety of views without reaching any conclusion about them, or to share the pessimism of Fee about their difficulty.[69]

Some residual issues, however, still require comment. Chrysostom, Theophylact, Grotius, and many early commentators interpret χάριτι μετέχω to be a reference to receiving divine *grace.* However, the setting in the dining room, together with the earlier quotation *"The earth is the Lord's* and all that is in it" (v. 26; cf. Ps 24:1, which was known, we noted, as one reason why we ought to say grace at meals), make it certain that Paul alludes here *to thanking God for the meal.* In a pagan household, the Christian might not "say grace" aloud, but would eat **with thanksgiving** to God in the heart.[70] The last four words of v. 30, ὑπὲρ οὗ ἐγὼ εὐχαριστῶ repeats the point: if the fellow believer who is overscrupulous cannot give thanks for what is good (or at least morally neutual) because it comes from **the Lord** (not, here, from demons), it is that **for which I, at least** (ἐγώ), **give thanks,** I am free to eat it, because it is part of God's good creation, for which **I, at least,** have blessed God. Paul thereby recapitulates (cf. Watson) all that he has said about "rights" and "freedom" without retracting any of it. All the same, he replies to "the strong," if it is up to you to choose whether to *use* your freedom, you might as well *choose* what does *least harm,* and show *love and respect for the other.* You are *not,* thereby, compromising your freedom by entering into the bondage of the other's scruples. Quite the reverse: you are *using your freedom* to help the other and to serve the gospel. To do otherwise would return you into bondage to your own personal desires and preferences.

This passage has profound implications for the very nature of freedom, debated by Augustine and Pelagius, by Luther and Erasmus, and by people in every generation. Yet by the same token it speaks eloquently to issues as practical as the purchase of large properties, expensive possessions, the use of alcohol in specific situations, and so forth. At one level the Christian is free: it is not other people's judgments, as such, which should determine one's own. On the other hand, always to ask about the impact or effect of these things on the self-awareness (confidence, vulnerability, insecurity, negative

69. Senft, *Première Épitre,* 138; Fee, *First Epistle,* 485-87, esp. n. 52; Schrage, *Der erste Brief,* 2:471-73, comes close to Watson's view but does not appear to make specific reference to the rhetorical issues.

70. The idiom which makes the food the direct object of some such verb as εὐλογέω nevertheless has *God* as the implicit primary accusative: believers *bless God for* his gifts (rather than bless the gifts). The Greek translation of the Hebrew may take a double accusative, in which *God* is sometimes implicit rather than explicit.

reaction) of *the other* must play a part in the believer's decision about how the *freedom* which God has granted is to be *constructively used.* Watson's arguments about rhetoric suggest that Paul does not leave all these thoughts behind when he considers the issues raised in the next chapter. The next four verses explicate all this further.

31-32 D, F, and G place γίνεσθε immediately after ἀπρόσκοποι in v. 31, but it is understandable how this gloss could arise, and the UBS text is authentic.

Collins describes vv. 31-33 as having "the character of a peroration in a deliberative rhetorical appeal."[71] The threefold argument summarizes chs. 8–10. BDF explicitly cite εἴτε τι ποιεῖτε in v. 31 as an example of *ellipsis,* where "the omission of the notion 'other . . .' is specifically Greek . . . (*scil* ἄλλο, 'whatever else') ποιεῖτε.[72] Clearly Paul has just observed that a person who shares *food* or **drink** at table will *bless God* **with thanksgiving** in the heart for these good things. As Augustine insists, God's good creation, on the other hand, is never to become a substitute or counterfeit for which people **crave** (cf. on ἐπιθυμία, above) or *desire* in place of desiring God, or finding in God's gifts a prompting to give God **glory** in, through, and for them. At the same time, Paul has just elaborated a case study where it would be right **to do** *something* **different** which marks a person out from the other. Here, too, he has explained, this should not be done if it is purely determined by the overscrupulosity of "the weak" as a self-contained concern. Only if it is *for the welfare of* **the other,** which constitutes then a proper *use* of gospel freedom (see under v. 30), should **anything different** (in such a case as this) *be done,* i.e., done out of concern to live out the gospel which reaches its clearest focus in Christ's exhibiting the **glory of God** by the fact that God in Christ acts for the good of "the other," "for whom Christ died" (1:30-31; 2:7-8; 8:13).

In this epistle Paul at times uses the word δόξα, **glory,** in its Hebrew sense (LXX translation of כבוד *kabod*) as that which makes something *impressive, weighty,* or *radiant with splendor* (1 Cor 15:40, 41, 43). The semantic range is well set out by C. C. Newman.[73] Yet for Paul, as for John, that which most startlingly displays God's impressive splendor is precisely his self-giving in which the Lord of glory is crucified (2:8).[74] The biblical background is enhanced by the prominence of the categories of honor and shame which characterized Corinthian culture and the Graeco-Roman world.[75] Only by appreciating the extent to which the cross was "shame" (Heb 12:2, αἰσχύνης) for the sake of which

71. Collins, *First Cor,* 384.
72. BDF, 254; sect. 480, example (1).
73. C. Newman, *Paul's Glory Christology: Tradition and Rhetoric,* NovTSup 69 (Leiden: Brill, 1992), esp. 157-63.
74. Cf. E. Stauffer, *NT Theology* (Eng. trans., London: SCM, 1955), 120-22.
75. See V. H. Matthews et al. (eds), "Honor and Shame in the World of the Bible," *Semeia* 68 (1996 [1994]), esp. J. H. Neyrey, "Despising the Shame of the Cross," 113-38.

Christians shared "dishonor" (ἀτιμασθῆναι, Acts 5:41) can Paul's revaluation of what counts as "honor" or **glory** be fully grasped. The Graeco-Roman world were "lovers of honor" (φιλοτιμία); "shame" was associated with loss of face, defeat, and ridicule. Yet for believers, Paul has insisted, "foolishness, weakness and shame in human eyes are wisdom, strength and honor in God's eyes (1 Cor 1:20, 25)."[76] "The life of Jesus is a living doxology. . . . He revealed God's glory in a world intoxicated with its own."[77] As Paul will say in 11:1, to follow this cruciform, Christomorphic pattern is to ascribe **glory** not to the self, but to **God**, in this particular context chiefly by reflecting God's own love which set aside dignity of *one's own* for the benefit of *"the other."* "To bring glory to God was to exalt Christ."[78] In the Fourth Gospel to promote **the glory of God** is seen most clearly of all in the death of Jesus (John 13:31-32; 17:4).[79] Paul's "reversals" in this epistle resonate closely with this doxological theme in John, and help to explain the climax of 8:1–10:33 in 11:1.

The concretization of this general principle is found in the reflection of God's indiscriminate goodness **to both Jews and to Gentiles, as well as to God's Church** (καί . . . καί . . . καί . . . , v. 32), to all of whom the Christian believer must **avoid doing damage** (ἀπρόσκοποι . . . γίνεσθε, *never be a cause of offence,* NJB; *give no offence,* REB), also NRSV; approximately AV/KJV; *do not cause anyone to stumble,* NIV). *Offense* may seem to bring the issue too exclusively into the realm of subjective consciousness of personal reaction (cf. vv. 28-30). NIV's *cause to stumble* is closer to Paul's meaning and picks up 8:13; but he does not use σκανδαλίζω. ἀπρόσκοπος may mean *without offense,* or *causing no offense,* but in more objective terms it denotes (passive) *undamaged* or (active) *causing no damage.*[80] Grimm-Thayer are more explicit and specific than BAGD on the meaning of the word in this verse as *not leading others into sin by one's mode of life.*[81] This is no doubt what Paul wishes the Corinthians to understand, but the word alone is less explicit. Without the alpha privative the noun προσκοπή means *an occasion of stumbling* or *the cause of a fall* (which may also carry resonances of Israel "falling" in the narrative examples, or formative models, of 10:6-13).[82] The word is not identical with πρόσκομμα (8:9), but both words take on similar metaphorical extensions which denote generally destructive qualities, whether it is gospel progress that is damaged or persons themselves. The categorization (with καί) of **Jews, Gentiles,** and the **Church of God,** all alike, looks back to Paul's personal examples in 9:19-23. How any

76. Ibid., 119.

77. Stauffer, *NT Theology,* 120 and 122.

78. Gardner, *Gifts of God,* 180.

79. See further H. Hegemann, "δόξα," *EDNT,* 1:344-48; and H. Schlier, "*Doxa* bei Paulus als Heilsgeschichtlicher Begriff," in *Studiorum Paulinorum Congressus Internationalis Catholicus,* AnBib 17-18 (Rome: Pontifical Biblical Institute, 1963), 1:45-56.

80. BAGD, 102.

81. Grimm-Thayer, 70.

82. Cf. Grimm-Thayer, 546; BAGD, 716.

exegete could seriously propose that 9:1-27 represents "a digression on apostle-ship" is almost beyond comprehension. In 10:1-22 Paul has stressed the conti-nuity of the Church with Israel; the phrase **the Church of God** in this context calls attention at the same time to a discontinuity, as if to imply that "the people of God" are partly redefined, although not in exclusivist terms since their roots and basis of divine promise and covenant remain in continuity with Israel's his-tory. (See Romans 9–11.)

10:23; 11:1   Καθὼς κἀγώ in v. 33 strictly means *even as I . . .* (NIV) or *just as I . . .* (NRSV). However, the length of the Greek sentence with its cumu-lative subordinate clauses has become increasingly foreign and difficult to ab-sorb in modern English. Hence REB begins a new sentence. *For my part. . . .* This takes account of the emphatic ἐγώ. Hence we propose the above to take up the force of both καθώς and the emphatic ἐγώ. The translation of ἀρέσκω is dif-ficult (AV/KJV, *even as I please all men;* NIV and NRSV, *even as I try to please everybody;* as against REB, *I always try to be considerate;* NJB, *just as I try to accommodate everybody).* The lexicographers agree that ἀρέσκω may have the force of either *strive to please, strive to accommodate,* or simply *to please* or *to be pleasing.*[83] Grimm-Thayer are similar to BAGD except that they also specify in more detail *to accommodate oneself to the opinions, desires, interests of oth-ers,* citing 1 Cor 10:33 under this heading.[84] We noted the strengths and weak-nesses of using the term *accommodation* under 9:20-23, where it is both helpful and unhelpful. Instances of word use and contextual factors suggest that Paul most probably means **I on my part strive to take account of all the interests of everyone**. This rendering conveys the notion of his *placing every factor in the equation in relation to the progress of the gospel and the welfare of "the other,"* and translates the *qualitative* or *mortal* πάντα alongside πᾶσιν (dative of advantage) as **all the interests of everyone**. This steers between the flat, bland understatement *try to be considerate* (REB) and the unctuous, self-projecting, overflexible *try to please* (NRSV, NIV). Paul would hardly wish to say the lat-ter, since *try to please* runs flatly against Paul's critique of cheap rhetoric and worldly wisdom which is designed primarily to please the audience, placing *truth* second to *pleasing* people. Witherington, Pogoloff, and others have placed this issue beyond question.[85]

Paul seeks not his **own** personal **advantage** but **the good of the many** (τὸ τῶν πολλῶν). The purpose clause ἵνα σωθῶσιν, *so that they may be saved* (first aorist passive subjunctive), may be given the better broader meaning by render-ing **with a view to their salvation**. This retains a telic force while avoiding a narrower individualistic cause-effect nuance which Paul probably does not in-tend here.

It seems unnecessary, on this occasion, to propose a translation for 11:1

83. E.g., BAGD, 105.
84. Grimm-Thayer, 72.
85. Witherington, *Conflict and Community,* 39-48; Pogoloff, *Logos and Sophia,* 97-172.

which differs from NJB. BAGD suggest *use me as your model* for 4:16 and 11:1, but μιμητής does not necessarily convey the slavish replication which *model* rather than **pattern** might be taken to imply. The **pattern** is that of placing the welfare of *"the other"* before that of oneself, and in this sense Paul himself takes **Christ** as his **pattern** rather than as a *model* of lifestyle in every respect. Willis P. de Boer rightly singles out "humility, self-denial, self-giving, self-sacrifice for the sake of Christ and the salvation of others" as the features of *mimesis* which Paul has in mind.[86] Hans-Dieter Betz notes the relation between mimesis and following a pattern of tradition, but Elizabeth Castelli convincingly questions whether Betz's analysis imposes too uniform an understanding of mimesis in the NT.[87] Castelli's contention that mimesis in 1 Cor 4:16 and 11:1 relates to the kind of "order" which **pattern** would include can be defended, although arguments about "power" may well invite a different interpretation from that which she proposes (see above on 4:16).[88]

Castelli's argument that the parallelism between the Corinthians and Paul corresponds to that between Paul and Christ as both "an act of mediation" and "also a presumptuous move on Paul's part" ignores the frame of reference which dictates the logic which governs this structure.[89] The issue is almost a rerun of the debate about apostleship: does the claim to be called an apostle in 1:1 and 9:1 amount to a power bid, or does it not, rather, constitute a pointing away from self to Christ (with Chrysostom, Calvin, Best, Crafton, and others)? Similarly, if the structure here was embedded within the logic or language game of putting others before the self, even if this was perceived as a disguised power bid, it would disintegrate on sheer self-contradiction. Castelli discusses Foucault here, but this is precisely the kind of logical contradiction (although in Foucault's case it becomes an inverted contradiction) which is pressed by Jean Baudrillard in his critique of Foucault.[90] Indeed, Crafton's study (published in the same year as Castelli's work, 1991), in which he insists that apostolic *agency* points all attention away from . . . self," cuts the ground from under any comparison between Paul and power systems (Crafton's italics).[91] It would make Paul's "transparency" as an apostle who shows forth Christ a radical device of sheer deception, far more sinister than Foucault's "smiling face in a white coat," and to her credit Castelli is reluctant to press such a parallel firmly or radically.

Conzelmann anticipates a similar point to Crafton's. The *contextual* way of understanding **as I take Christ for mine** is not a power claim, but the very

---

86. De Boer, *The Imitation of Paul: An Exegetical Study,* 207; cf. 154-69.

87. Betz, *Nachfolge und Nachahmung Jesu Christi im Neuen Testament,* esp. 3; Castelli, *Imitating Paul: A Discourse of Power,* 28-29.

88. Castelli, *Imitating Paul,* 98 and throughout.

89. Ibid., 113.

90. J. Baudrillard, *Forget Foucault* (New York: Columbia University, 1987).

91. Crafton, *The Agency of the Apostle: A Dramatistic Analysis of Paul's Responses to Conflict in 2 Corinthians,* 62 and 63.

reverse: "His exemplariness consists in the fact that — in himself, objectively, on the basis of his calling — he is nothing. In all the passages on the *imitatio Pauli* the paradox of this exemplariness appears. . . . The imitation of *Christ* takes its bearings . . . in the sense of Phil 2:6-11 — on his saving work."[92] Christ's work, however, brought life to *others* by giving up *himself* to humiliation and to death. This is the **pattern** to which Paul appeals.[93]

92. Conzelmann, *1 Cor,* 179 and 180.

93. It is unnecessary to retrace familiar ground about the use of the term *mimesis* in the context of maintaining traditions inherited from teachers. This is well known, and confirms the inadequacy of *imitate* as a translation.

V. Freedom, Status, Reciprocity, and Respect for the Other in the Ordering of Public Worship and in Attitudes toward "Spiritual Gifts" (11:2–14:40)

It is very surprising how readily virtually all commentators appear to ignore the fundamental continuity between the arguments and themes of 8:1–11:1 and the application of these very same themes to issues concerning public or corporate worship in 11:2–14:40. Just as some view 9:1-27 as a "digression" about apostleship which intrudes into 8:1–11:1, so some view 13:1-13 as an unexpected interruption within 11:2–14:40, when the rhythmic discourse on love sums up the major issue in all parts of 11:2–14:40.

In 11:17-32 "the strong" or wealthy turn the Lord's Supper into a festival meal in the course of which socially deprived or economically dependent late-comers are treated as hangers-on who may have to eat different fare in a different part of the house, thereby undermining the "for others" of the cross itself which the Lord's Supper proclaims (11:26). In 12:1–14:40 the "gifted" seem hardly to care if less "gifted" believers somehow feel estranged or second-class (see below, esp. 12:20-22 and 14:20-22). In 11:2-16 both "rights" to female emancipation and "rights" to male headship receive careful qualification as contributory strands, but by no means the whole picture within a larger, more complex whole, in which respect for "the other" (the other gender and the outside world) remains a fundamental concern. Love modifies "freedom" and "rights" if the good of the whole is thereby better served, and especially if the gospel is more effectively promoted (cf. 9:19-27).

A. MUTUALITY AND RESPECT: MEN AND WOMEN AT WORSHIP IN PUBLIC, AND RICH AND POOR AT THE LORD'S SUPPER (11:2-34)

1. Mutuality and Reciprocity: Self-Respect, Respect for the Other, and Gender Identity in Public Worship (11:2-16)

(2) I give you full credit for keeping me in mind unfailingly, and for continuing to hold fast to the traditions which I, in turn, handed on to you. (3) However, I want you to understand that while Christ is preeminent (or *head? source?*) for man, man is foremost (or *head? source*) in relation to woman, and God is preeminent (or *head? source?*) in relation to Christ. (4) Every man who prays or who utters prophetic speech with his head covered (possibly *with long hair*) shames his head. (5, 6) Every woman who prays or who utters prophetic speech with her head uncovered (less probably, *with long, loose, unbound hair*) shames her head, for it is one and the same thing as a woman whose head had been shaved. For if a woman will not retain her head covering, let her have it cropped close to the head. If, however, to have it cropped close or to have it shaved off brings shame, let her retain her head covering. (7, 8, 9) For a man, for his part, ought not to have his head covered up since man is constituted in the image of God and [manifests] his glory. Woman, on the other hand, is the glory of a man. For it is not the case that man came from woman, but woman was made out of man. For, further, man was not created on woman's account, but woman was created on account of man. (10) Because of this a woman ought to keep control of her head, on account of the angels. (11, 12) Nevertheless, as those in the Lord, although woman is nothing apart from man, man is nothing apart from woman. For just as woman had her origin from man, even so man derives his existence through woman; and the source of everything is God. (13) Come to a decision for yourselves. Is it appropriate for a woman to conduct prayer to God without wearing a hood? (just possibly *with her hair unbound?*) (14, 15) Does not even the very ordering of how things are teach you that if long hair degrades a man, long hair is a woman's glory, because long hair is given as a covering? (16) If anyone is minded to be contentious, we ourselves have no such custom, nor do the churches of God.

Our bibliography for this section alone identifies some eighty publications that invite attention in addition to commentaries and other standard works regularly cited. Yet with a few notable exceptions (see Murphy-O'Connor and others cited below), most writers insist that this passage concerns the clothing (or hairstyle) of *women* rather than (as 11:4 makes clear) of *men and women*. As Roland Barthes among others points out, clothes and hair or beards play a role in a semiotic system which speak volumes about self-perceptions of gender identity, class identity, a sense of occasion, and respect or indifference toward the perception of others. Further, there are multilayered metaphorical and cultural nuances which exclude any understanding of language in these verses in terms of lexicography alone. As Gregory Dawes well argues, it is beside the point to count up how many instances of κεφαλή (11:3-7, 10) mean *head, in the sense of chief;* many denote *source;* and how many denote *head in contrast to body,* if Paul and his readers presuppose metaphorical extension or interactive application of the term.[1]

A further complication arises from the existence of multiple reconstructions of the situation at Corinth. Throughout this commentary we have stressed the importance of looking primarily to Roman cultural and social norms for mid-first-century Corinth, rather than those of Greece which precede 44 BC and steadily return to regain a new peak, after Paul's lifetime, in the age of Hadrian. We refer in the Introduction to the huge preponderance of Latin inscriptions over Greek at Corinth in Paul's day, and even if many flooded into the Roman colony as business people, traders, artisans, or slaves, the main social norms to which Corinthian culture aspired were those of Rome rather than Greece.

Nevertheless, research by classicists demonstrates an unevenness and fluidity in the expectations and status of women in mid-century Roman culture, depending on a variety of factors. Aline Rousselle's essay "Body Politics in Ancient Rome" (1992) assumes great importance for the issue of *head coverings, veils,* or *"hoods"* (cf. κατὰ κεφαλῆς ἔχων, v. 4; ἀκατακαλύπτῳ, v. 5; κατακαλύπτεται, v. 6; cf. Latin [Jerome] by contrast, *nudo capite*).[2] Augustus reformed family law in ways which affected the status of women some three times between 18 BC and AD 9 *(lex Julia de adulteriis; lex Julia de fundo dotali,* et al.). Horace (d. 8 BC) tells us, on one side, that certain *male* attire or hair-styles were deemed effeminate and overtly sexual, while appropriate head coverings for respectable Roman *women* served as a protection of their dignity and status as *women not to be "propositioned."* A. Rousselle and Dale Martin both urge that in the case of respected and respectable women "one sees only the face": "respectable women did nothing to draw attention to themselves. . . . A veil or hood constituted a warning: it signified that the wearer was a respectable woman and that no man dare approach without risking . . . penalties. A woman who went out . . . unveiled forfeited the protection of Roman law against possible attackers who were entitled to plead extenuating circumstances."[3] Rousselle and Martin urge that the point behind Paul's instruction is "to signify that, regardless of their status under other laws, they were untouchable for Christian men."[4]

Public worship was neither the occasion for women to become "objects" of attraction to be "sized up" by men; nor an occasion for women to offer

1. Dawes, *The Body in Question: Metaphor and Meaning in the Interpretation of Ephesians 5:21-33,* esp. 122-49.
2. A. Rousselle, "Body Politics in Ancient Rome," in Duby and Perot (eds.), *A History of Women in the West,* 1: *From Ancient Goddesses to Christian Saints,* 296-337.
3. Ibid., 315; Martin, *The Corinthian Body,* 229-49.
4. Rousselle, "Body Politics," and Martin, *The Corinthian Body,* 229-49.

cryptic "suggestions" to men. As Roland Barthes has convincingly demonstrated, *clothes have usually operated in human cultures as a powerful semiotic system, i.e., they generate ready signs or signals of class, style, modesty, self-promotion, attitude, or whatever.*[5] Similarly, Umberto Eco observes, "*I am speaking through my clothes. If I were wearing a Mao suit, if I were without a tie the ideological connotation of my speech would be changed*" (my italics).[6] Rousselle, still more significantly for our contextual exegesis, concludes that the veil constitutes "also a badge of honour, of sexual reserve, and *hence of mastery of the self*" (my italics).[7] Our point is that this theme of self-discipline which foregoes "rights" dominates 8:1–11:1, including especially 9:23-27, even with additional resonances in ch. 7. We discussed Pfitzner on the *agon* motif above.

How does this relate to language about *head* (κεφαλή)? (i) The laws of Augustus to which we have alluded also modified the system of guardianship *(tutela)* of women inherited from the closing years of the Republic. A guardian could authorize (cf. ἐξουσιάζω) a woman's actions, but after the laws approved under Augustus a woman had the right (ἐξουσία) to take legal action against a guardian whose refusal to give authorization was deemed to be unreasonable. Under Claudius guardianship of freeborn women was abolished, although not for freedwomen.[8] This context raises nuances of meaning about *head* in the sense of *chief,* in relation to mutuality and reciprocity. (ii) Juvenal (c. AD 58-138) shows that by the late first century and early second century women sought quasimale status by going to public baths (Juvenal 6.419-21), by training to fight (1.23), or by hunting (1.247). However, this is the post-Pauline era, and Cantarella notes Juvenal's antifemale bias.[9] On the other hand, there is evidence of earlier debate and practice about gender distinctiveness. In this context Dawes's work on *head* as differentiated from *body* assumes a necessary prominence. (iii) Sarah Pomeroy further shows that women's clothing has an impact on the status of men. She argues that in the early Roman imperial period it was *men,* rather than women, on whom a woman's clothing most reflected. Regulation was required when "men participated in status-seeking by means of the clothing of their women. . . . The usual purpose of honouring women was to exalt the men to whom they were mothers, wives or sisters."[10] In this context language about *glory, source,* and *reciprocity* becomes important.

5. Roland Barthes, *Elements of Semiology* (Eng. trans., London: Cape, 1967), 13-28; cf. *Mythologies* (Eng. trans., London: Cape, 1972).

6. Umberto Eco, "Social Life as a Sign System," in D. Robey (ed.), *Structuralism* (Oxford: Clarendon, 1973), 59; cf. 57-72; and Thiselton, *New Horizons in Hermeneutics,* 80-99.

7. Rousselle, "Body Politics," 315.

8. Cantarella, *Pandora's Daughters: The Role and Status of Women in Greek and Roman Antiquity,* 139; cf. 135-43.

9. Ibid., 141.

10. Pomeroy, *Goddesses, Whores, Wives and Slaves: Women in Classical Antiquity,* 182 and 183.

All these factors and crosscurrents provide a necessary background for an understanding of 1 Cor 11:2-16. The sociocultural factors, however, still represent only part of a wider picture. (iv) If Paul uses *head* (κεφαλή) with more than one nuance, Dawes (1998) is correct in identifying an interactive metaphorical application of the contrast between head and (physical) body as contributing an important focus for *gender differentiation* (whether or not much of Dawes's work concerns the use of the term in Ephesians). (v) Yet perhaps the most seminal study of all is that of Judith Gundry-Volf (1997), who argues that neither merely "egalitarian" nor merely "hierarchical" interpretations do justice to the complexity of the theological issue for Paul.[11] Paul superimposes three "maps" of gender relationships which *together* provide a dialectic between mutuality and "order" or gender differentiation by placing *the whole* within the three "frames" of the order of creation, society and culture, and gospel eschatology. We have yet to take account of a further emphasis identified by J. Murphy-O'Connor (see below under vii).

The most serious mistake of much exegesis has been to interpret each verse or each term atomistically. What *head* means in one specific context is no more than *contributory* to the wholeness of a dialectic of mutuality and order, just as unity and diversity are set in dialectical reciprocity in chs. 12–14 (see below). In the light of research in the 1990s on the dialectical theology, interactive metaphorical force, and dated Roman social background of these verses, we need not entirely share the understandable hesitations expressed by Fee about how to decide between the many variables which face the exegete.[12] A genuine breakthrough is offered (a) by Gundry-Volf's proposal about the need for a wholeness of understanding of Paul's dialectic in the light of three theological superimposed maps; (b) the careful dating of the conventions of what clothing generates signals of respect for Christian women as human persons, not as sexual objects, in public; (c) the interplay between multivalent meanings of κεφαλή and their interactive metaphorical applications; and (d) our own further suggestion that the theme of self-discipline, restraint, and respect for "the other," already prominent in 8:1–11:1, remains central to 11:2–14:40.

(vi) This is confirmed by attention to a sixth contributory factor: Paul's drawing upon the model of the relation between God and Christ (11:3) and his language about *glory*. The relation between God and Christ in this epistle entails both *"order" and differentiation* on one side (cf. 15:28) and *mutuality and reciprocity* on the other. While we cannot read later doctrines of the Trinity onto Paul, it is inadequate to construe this relation as hinging only on "obedience."[13] The one God, the one Lord, and the one Spirit (12:4-6, see below) ex-

11. Gundry-Volf, "Gender and Creation in 1 Cor 11:2-16: A Study in Paul's Theological Method," in Adna et al. (eds.), *Evangelium, Schriftauslegung, Kirche: Festschrift für P. Stuhlmacher* (Göttingen: Vandenhoeck & Ruprecht, 1997), 151-71.

12. Fee, *First Epistle,* 491-98; cf. 502-12, where some of the comments might suggest a different social background.

13. This becomes the focus in M. Thrall, *1 and 2 Cor,* 78-80.

hibit mutuality, oneness, and distinctiveness in a way which is sufficiently close to Paul's dialectic of gender for him to appeal to the nature of God and of Christ in this passage. The simplistic solution of collapsing 11:2-16 into either bare egalitarianism or into an overstated "subordinationism" does justice neither to Paul's view of gender nor to his theology of God and Christ. This is comparable to investing all later trinitarian theology exclusively in "social" or "economic-monarchical" models alone, as if neither needed complementation. On the other side, however, A. C. Wire has argued that subordination is precisely what does characterize Paul's Christology and view of gender in this specific epistle. She appeals to the triple occurrence of "subordination" in 1 Cor 3:21-23, ". . . and Christ is God's"; 11:3; and 15:25-28, "when he hands the kingdom over to God . . . that God may be all in all."[14] Paul presses this Christology into the service of a manipulative argument which begins simply with what linguistic philosophers term "persuasive definition," or in her words "argument from definition" in 11:3, on what counts as the *head*.[15] Wire relates this further to a rhetoric of shame and honor.[16]

Moffatt, however, explains the so-called subordinationism of the God-Christ relationship in this epistle in different terms. He proposes that, surrounded by cozy cult deities of the mystery cults and Graeco-Roman religion, the church at Corinth too readily appropriated a "Lord Jesus" cult mind-set without sufficiently "serious reverence for a supreme deity over the universe," viewing "God" as a shadowing figure in contrast to the passionate, intimate, devotion offered by others to Serapis or Asclepios or by Christians to Jesus as Lord.[17] Moffatt overstates the case, but gives a more convincing explanation for the unusual accumulation of these three references in this epistle. The Greek Fathers' use of the term *perichoresis* well suggests the dialectic of distinctiveness, reciprocity, and oneness which Paul begins to unfold. Phil 2:6-11, as pre-Pauline material which Paul endorses, portrays a voluntary renunciation of "rights" (in this context, genuinely a right). The God-Christ relation has *nothing to do with self-glory* or with affirmation of the self at the expense of the other (cf. the ethical context of Phil 2:6-11; it is *not an involuntary or imposed "subordination," but an example of shared love*). This shared love controls the use of freedom, and thereby each brings "glory" to the other by assuming distinctive roles for a common purpose. This is the context that gives currency to the widespread comment that "the relationship between man and woman is thus in some sense parallelled by that between God and Christ."[18]

14. Wire, *The Corinthian Women Prophets,* 37 and 117; cf. 116-34.

15. Ibid., 23-24; cf. Thiselton, "The Meaning of σάρξ in 1 Cor 5:5 . . .," *SJT* 26 (1973): 204-28, for a more detailed discussion of competing instances of persuasive definition, in this case with reference to the redefinition of "fleshly" and "spiritual" at Corinth.

16. Wire, *The Corinthian Women Prophets,* 19-21, 116-34.

17. Moffatt, *First Epistle,* 250.

18. Hooker, "Authority on Her Head: an Examination of 1 Cor 11:10"; rpt. in her *From Adam to Christ,* 113; cf. 113-20; rpt. from *NTS* 10 (1964): 410-16.

(vii) We have reserved until the end of this introduction a recasting of the force of the passage advocated well by Murphy-O'Connor. Whether or not we endorse his specific argument about κεφαλή as *source,* he convincingly argues that "men figure equally prominently in this section. . . . The problem . . . involved both sexes."[19] Paul's concern is not with subordination but with gender distinction. He expresses no less disquiet (probably indeed more) about men whose style is effeminate with possible hints of a quasihomosexual blurring of male gender than about women who likewise reject the use of signals of respectable and respected gender distinctiveness. We shall return to Murphy-O'Connor's article, which is illuminating and important in its general approach, even if not necessarily in every detail. It supports the genuine mutuality and symmetry of Paul's gender concerns. 11:2-16 is not simply about "the head covering of women," but about *men* and women, freedom and *respect for the otherness of the other in public worship.*

(viii) If in the cultural semiotics of Roland Barthes and Umberto Eco far-reaching significance of clothes as a sign system becomes apparent, we may also need to allude to the social anthropology of C. R. Hallpike and Edmund Leach to inquire about the possible relevance for signals of sex and gender generated by styles of hair. They provide cultural data which associates long hair with undisciplined sexuality, the shaven head with celibacy or "sexlessness," and short hair or covered hair with "restricted sexuality."[20] There are modifications and extensions to an oversimple structural system, but they alert us to wider semiotic issues raised by Paul's allusions to shaving the head and to long hair than is historically-specific to a given period or locality.

Further, a considerable amount of archaeological research on this subject also demands attention. Richard E. Oster's article on the misuse and neglect of archaeological evidence relating to 1 Corinthians (1992) is instructive. Roman customs, as we know, are paramount for understanding the Roman Corinth of Paul's day. Archaeological evidence shows "the widespread use of male liturgical head coverings in the city of Rome, in Italy, and in numerous cities in the Roman East . . . on coins, statues and architectural monuments from around the Mediterranean Basin."[21] "Men covering their heads in the context of prayer and prophecy was a common pattern of Roman piety."[22] Oster finds himself astonished that not only do many writers look far afield to Philo, Tertullian, Gnosticism, and rabbinic sources to try to explain 11:4, but Weiss calls 11:4 "hypothetical," while F. F. Bruce considers the background either "improbable" as an actuality or cited "hypothetically" as

19. Murphy-O'Connor, "Sex and Logic in 1 Cor 11:2-16," *CBQ* 92 (1980): 483; cf. 482-500.

20. Hallpike, "Social Hair," 256-64.

21. R. E. Oster, "Use, Misuse and Neglect of Archaeological Evidence in Some Modern Works on 1 Corinthians (1 Cor 7:1-5; 8:10; 11:2-16; 12:14-26)," *ZNW* 83 (1992): 68; cf. 52-73.

22. Ibid., 69.

"necessary to complete the argument."[23] Even Fee uses the word "speculative" of the implied practice.

(ix) We discussed in the Introduction the issue of the integrity of the epistle. W. O. Walker argues that 11:2-16 is a non-Pauline interpolation, and Trompf sees closer affinities with the material in 1 Tim 2:13-15 than in the earlier authentic Paul.[24] However, Murphy-O'Connor has addressed Walker's arguments convincingly, and they are endorsed by Schrage and the majority of writers.[25] Margaret Mitchell also argues for the integrity of the epistle, and includes a survey of research literature on the authenticity of 11:2-16 as Pauline.[26] Collins also agrees that Murphy-O'Connor and others succeed in demonstrating the "coherent nature of the passage" with "reasonable explanations" of the points made by Walker and Trompf.[27]

Bibliography on 11:2-16

Brown, C., "Head," *NIDNTT,* 2:157-63.

Cantarella, E., *Pandora's Daughters: The Role and Status of Women in Greek and Roman Antiquities* (Baltimore and London: Johns Hopkins University Press, 1987), 90-99 and 135-58.

Carlé, G., *Because of the Angels: Unveiling 1 Cor 11:2-16* (Paraparaumu Beach, New Zealand: Emmaus, 1998).

Cervin, R. S., "Does κεφαλή Mean 'Source' or 'Authority Over' in Greek Literature? A Rebuttal," *TrinJ* 10 (1989): 85-112.

Cleary, F. X., "Women in the NT: St Paul and the Early Pauline Churches," *BTB* 10 (1980): 78-82.

Cope, L., "1 Cor 11:2-16: One Step Farther," *JBL* 97 (1978): 435-36.

Corrington, G. P., "The 'Headless Woman': Paul and the Language of the Body in 1 Cor 11:2-16," *PRS* 18 (1991): 223-31.

Dawes, G. W., *The Body in Question. Metaphor and Meaning in the Interpretation of Eph 5:21-33,* BibInt 30 (Leiden: Brill, 1998), 56-80 and 122-49.

Devor, R. C., "When We're 'Blindsided' by the Gospel," *Encounter* 35 (1974): 368-81.

Dunn, J. D. G., *The Theology of Paul* (Edinburgh: T. & T. Clark, 1998), 588-92.

Edwards, D. R., "Dress and Ornamentation," in *ABD,* 2: 232-38.

Engberg-Pedersen, T., "1 Cor 11:16 and the Character of Pauline Exhortation," *JBL* 110 (1991): 679-89.

Feuillet, A., "La dignité et le rôle de la femme d'après quelques textes pauliniens: comparison avec l'ancient Testament," *NTS* 21 (1973): 157-91.

---

23. Ibid., 68; Weiss, *Der erste Korintherbrief,* 271; Bruce, *1 and 2 Cor,* 104; Fee, *First Epistle,* 506-8.

24. W. O. Walker, "The Non-Pauline Character of 1 Cor 11:2-16," *JBL* 95 (1976): 615-21; cf. Trompf, "On Attitudes toward Women in Paul and Paulinist Literature: 1 Cor 11:3-16 and Its Context," *CBQ* 42 (1980): 196-215.

25. Murphy-O'Connor, "The Non-Pauline Character of 1 Cor 11:2-16?" *JBL* 95 (1976): 615-21; cf. also "1 Cor 11:2-16 Once Again," *CBQ* 50 (1988): 265-74; and Schrage *Der erste Brief,* 2:496-97.

26. M. M. Mitchell, *Paul and the Rhetoric of Reconciliation,* 261-62, esp. n. 417.

27. Collins, *First Cor,* 394.

————, "L'Homme 'gloire de Dieu' et la femme 'gloire de l'homme' (1 Cor XI:7b)," *RB* 81 (1974): 161-82.

————, "Le signe de puissance sur la tête de la femme (1 Cor 11:10)," *NRT* 95 (1973): 945-54.

Fiddes, P. S., "'Woman's Head Is Man': A Doctrinal Reflection upon a Pauline Text," *Baptist Quarterly* 31 (1986): 370-83.

Fiorenza, E. Schüssler, *In Memory of Her: A Feminist Reconstruction of Christian Origin* (London: SCM, 1983), 226-30.

Fitzmyer, J. A., "Another Look at κεφαλή in 1 Cor 11:3," *NTS* 35 (1989): 503-11.

————, "A Feature of Qumran Angelology and the Angels of 1 Cor 11:10," *NTS* 4 (1957-58): 48-58.

————, "*Kephalē* in 1 Cor 11:3," *Int* 47 (1993): 32-59.

Gill, D. W. J., "The Importance of Roman Portraiture for Head Coverings in 1 Cor 11:2-16," *TynBul* 41 (1990): 245-60.

Grudem, W. A., "Does *Kephalē* Mean 'Source' or 'Authority Over' in Greek Literature? A Survey of 2,336 Examples," *TrinJ* 6 (1985): 38-59.

————, "Prophecy — Yes, but Teaching — No: Paul's Consistent Advocacy of Women's Participation without Governing Authority," *JETS* 30 (1987): 11-23.

Gundry-Volf, J. M., "Gender and Creation in 1 Cor 11:2-16: A Study in Paul's Theological Method," in J. Adna, S. J. Hafemann, and O. Hofius (eds.), *Evangelium, Schriftauslegung, Kirche. Festschrift für Peter Stuhlmacher* (Göttingen: Vandenhoeck & Ruprecht, 1997), 151-71.

Hall, D. R., "A Problem of Authority," *ExpTim* 102 (1990): 39-42.

Hallpike, C. R., "Social Hair," *Man* n.s. 4 (1969): 256-64.

Harland, P. J., "Menswear and Womenswear: A Study of Deut 22:5," *ExpTim* 110 (1998): 76; cf. 73-76.

Hasler, V., "Die Gleichstellung der Gattin. Situations-Kritische Reflexionen zu 1 Kor 11:2-16," *TZ* 50 (1994): 189-200.

Holmyard, H. R., "Does I Cor 11:2-6 Refer to Women Praying and Prophesying in Church?" *BSac* 154 (1997): 461-72.

Hooker, M. D., "Authority on Her Head: An Examination of 1 Cor 11:10," *NTS* 10 (1963-64): 410-16; rpt. in her *From Adam to Christ: Essays on Paul* (Cambridge: Cambridge University Press, 1990), 113-20.

Horrell, D. G., *The Social Ethos of the Corinthian Correspondence* (Edinburgh: T. & T. Clark, 1996), 168-76.

Hurley, J. B., "Did Paul Require Veils or the Silence of Women? A Consideration of 1 Cor 11:2-16 and 1 Cor 14:33b-36," *WTJ* 35 (1973): 190-220.

Kroeger, C. C., "The Classical Concept of 'Head' as 'Source,'" in G. Gaebelein Hull (ed.), *Equal to Serve* (London: Scripture Union, 1987) (American title: *Serving Together*).

————, "Head," in *DPL* (1993), 375-77.

Jaubert, A., "Le voile des femmes (1 Cor XI:2-16)," *NTS* 18 (1970-71): 419-30.

Jervis, L. A., "'But I Want You to Know . . .': Paul's Midrashic Intertextual Response to the Corinthian Worshippers (1 Cor 11:2-16)," *JBL* 112 (1993): 231-46.

Keener, C. S., *Paul, Women, Wives* (Peabody, Mass.: Hendrickson, 1992), 19-69.

Kurzinger, J., "Frau und Mann nach 1 Kor 11:11-12," *BZ* 22 (1978): 270-75.

Lefkowitz, M. R., and M. B. Fant, *Women's Life in Greece and Rome: A Source Book in*

Translation (Baltimore: Johns Hopkins University Press and London: Duckworth, 1982), 104-10, 157-71, 181-96, 235-53, 262-79.

Lattke, M., "κεφαλή," *EDNT,* 2:284-86.

Malina, B., *The NT World: Insights from Cultural Anthropology* (Louisville: Westminster/Knox, rev. ed. 1993), 28-62.

Martin, D. B., *The Corinthian Body* (New Haven: Yale University Press, 1995), 229-49.

Martin, W. J., "1 Cor 11:2-16: An Interpretation," in W. Ward Gasque and R. P. Martin (eds.), *Apostolic History and the Gospel: Presented to F. F. Bruce* (Exeter: Paternoster, 1970), 231-41.

Meier, J. P., "On the Veiling of Hermeneutics (1 Cor 11:2-16)," *CBQ* 40 (1978): 212-26.

Meeks, W. A., "The Image of the Androgyne: Some Uses of a Symbol in Earliest Christianity," *History of Religions* 13 (1974): 165-208.

Mercadante, L., "The Male-Female Debate: Can We Read the Bible Objectively?" *Crux* 15 (1979): 20-25.

Merk, O., *Handeln aus Glauben* (Marburg: Elwert, 1968), 131-35.

Mitchell, M. M., *Paul and the Rhetoric of Reconciliation* (Louisville: Westminster/Knox, 1991), 260-63.

Moxnes, H., "Honor, Shame and the Outside World in Paul's Letter to the Romans," in J. Neusner et al. (ed.), *The Social World of Formative Christianity and Judaism* (Philadelphia: Fortress, 1988), 207-18.

Murphy-O'Connor, J., "1 Cor 11:2-16 Once Again," *CBQ* 50 (1988): 265-74.

———, "The Non-Pauline Character of 1 Cor 11:2-16?" *JBL* 95 (1976): 615-21.

———, "Sex and Logic in 1 Cor 11:2-16," *CBQ* 42 (1980): 482-500.

Oster, R. E., "When Men Wore Veils to Worship: The Historical Context of 1 Cor 11:4," *NTS* 34 (1988): 481-505.

Padgett, A., "'Authority over Her Head': Toward a Feminist Reading of St Paul," *Daughters of Sarah* 13 (1986): 5-9.

———, "Paul on Women in the Church: The Contradictions of Coiffure in 1 Cor 11:2-16," *JSNT* 20 (1984): 69-86.

Pagels, E. H., "Paul and Women: A Response to Recent Discussion," *JAAR* 42 (1974): 538-49.

Pella, G., "Voile et soumission? Essai d'interprétation de deux textes pauliniens," *Hokhma* 30 (1985): 3-20.

Perriman, A. C., "The Head of a Woman: The Meaning of κεφαλή in 1 Cor 11:3," *JTS* 45 (1994): 602-22.

Pomeroy, S. B., *Goddesses, Whores, Wives and Slaves: Women in Classical Antiquity* (London: Hale, 1976), 120-89.

Radcliffe, T., "Paul and Sexual Identity: 1 Cor 11:2-16," in J. Martin Soskice (ed.), *After Eve: Women, Theology and the Christian Tradition* (London: Collins/Marshall, 1990), 62-72.

Rousselle, A., "Body Politics in Ancient Rome," in G. Duby and M. Perrot (eds.), *A History of Women in the West,* I: *From Ancient Goddesses to Christian Saints* (Cambridge, Mass.: Harvard, 1992), 296-337.

Schirrmacher, T., *Paulus im kampf gegen den Schleier. Eine alternative Auslegung von 1 Kor 11:2-16,* Biblia et Symbiotica 4 (Bonn: Verlag für Kultur und Wissenschaft, 1993).

Schlier, H., "κεφαλή," *TDNT,* 3:673-82.

Schottroff, L., *Let the Oppressed Go Free: Feminist Perspectives in the NT* (Eng. trans., Louisville: Westminster/Knox, 1993), 109-29.

Schüssler Fiorenza, E., "Women in the Pre-Pauline and Pauline Churches," *USQR* 33 (1978): 153-66.

Stendahl, K., *The Bible and the Role of Women: A Case Study in Hermeneutics* (Philadelphia: Fortress, 1966).

Theissen, G., *The Social Setting of Pauline Christianity* (Eng. trans., Philadelphia: Fortress, 1982), 69-119.

Thompson, C. L., "Hairstyles, Head-Coverings and St Paul: Portraits from Roman Corinth," *BA* 51 (1988): 99-115.

Trompf, G. W., "On Attitudes toward Women in Paul and Paulinist Literature: 1 Cor 11:3-16 and Its Context," *CBQ* 42 (1980): 196-215.

Walker, W. O., "1 Cor 11:2-16 and Paul's Views Regarding Women," *JBL* 94 (1975): 94-110.

————, "The Vocabulary of 1 Cor 11:3-16: Pauline or Non-Pauline?" *JSNT* 35 (1989): 75-88.

Waltke, B. K., "1 Cor 11:2-16: An Interpretation," *BSac* 135 (1978): 46-57.

Weeks, N., "Of Silence and Head Covering," *WTJ* 35 (1972): 21-27.

Wire, A. C., *The Corinthian Women Prophets: A Reconstruction through Paul's Rhetoric* (Minneapolis: Fortress, 1991), 116-34 and 226-28.

Witherington, B., *Conflict and Community in Corinth* (Grand Rapids: Eerdmans and Carlisle: Paternoster, 1995), 231-40.

————, *Women in the Earliest Churches,* SNTSMS 58 (Cambridge: Cambridge University Press, 1988), 78-90.

2 The Western text, D, F, G, K, and 33 insert ἀδελφοί after ὑμᾶς, which finds its way into the AV/KJV. Nevertheless, there is virtually unanimous agreement that the word would be so readily expected at this point that its insertion is readily explained, while its omission from all the main early MSS (e.g., p46, ℵ, A, B, C) would be inexplicable.[28] UBS 4th ed. rightly omits it.

ἐπαινῶ, *I praise,* reflects a change, once again, to the first person. The meaning of the verb remains closer to *praise* (NIV, AV/KJV) than to *commend* (REB, NRSV) or *congratulate* (NJB) since it is a stronger term associated in biblical Greek with *giving praise* to God, or in some contexts with *honoring* a person. In the context of an honor/shame culture some forceful attribution of honor *(praise)* is required, but REB, NJB, and NRSV recognize that to speak of *praising* adults smacks of a patronizing, schoolteacherish paternalism which the Greek would not convey.[29] Since *praise* is status-conferring, we suggest **I give you full credit for**. . . . Similarly, μέμνησθε requires attention to the more forceful, full-blooded, and broader semantic range of μιμνήσκομαι in biblical Greek *(broader than Eng.* **remember***)*; and the nuance of the perfect tense as calling attention to the present state on the basis of past action; **keeping me in mind**

---

28. Zuntz, *Text,* 176; Metzger, *Textual Commentary* (2d ed.), 495; Fee, *First Epistle,* 498, n. 24.

29. BAGD, 281. The word appears only twice in Paul: here and at 11:22.

(with REB) seems to address both factors well.[30] As Schrage and others argue, πάντα is not the object or accusative of the verb, but an adverbial or modal accusative of respect, parallel with ἐν τούτῳ in v. 22.[31] Hence **unfailingly** signals the way of qualifying the process of the perfect of the verb in a general manner.

In patristic and medieval exegesis such lavish *praise* or **credit** *in all things* was understood as ironic by Theodoret, Ambrosiaster, Peter Lombard, and Thomas Aquinas.[32] Allusion is made, by contrast, to 10:32–11:1 and especially 11:22 *(I do not commend you; I do not approve)*. Among modern commentators, Moffatt believes that Paul quotes back the claim of the addressees "with a touch of irony"; Allo is sympathetic with such a view, and Hurd endorses it.[33] Fee and Schrage regard it as a rhetorical *captatio benevolentiae* device to win the readers over.[34] However, Hays offers a more convincing reconstruction. In their letter to Paul the Corinthian Christians express their intention to follow Paul's instructions about the participation of women in the worship, but seek his further advice about an unexpected complication concerning dress (see introduction to 11:2-16).[35] Paul always stands warmly alongside those who admit to perplexity or seek advice. It is when they claim no need of advice, or act unilaterally with complacency rather than consultation, that he becomes sharply polemical.

Barrett helpfully proposes **hold fast to the traditions** and **handed . . . on** for κατέχετε in conjunction with παρέδωκα . . . τὰς παραδόσεις.[36] παράδοσις may mean either *betrayal* (in the active sense of the verb παραδίδωμι) or **tradition** (in the passive sense of the verb), *that which is* **handed on**, including teachings, creeds, narratives, catechesis (cf. 2 Thess 2:15; 3:6, with παραλαμβάνω, also *1 Clement* 7:2; *Diognetus* 11:6). In the same way the verb παραδίδωμι may mean *to hand over* or **to hand on** (cf. 1 Cor 11:23a; 15:3, which are fundamental).[37] In early Christian literature the words soon come to denote an *authoritative tradition of Christian teaching* (Polycarp, *Epistles,* 7:2; Irenaeus, *Against Heresies,* 3:3:4; Clement, *Stromata,* 1:12; Origen, *Contra Celsum,* 4:32).[38] In his study of tradition and tradition terminology Wegenast argues that this epistle provides the first setting within which the notion of a re-

---

30. Cf. BAGD, 522; on the perfect cf. Schrage, *Der erste Brief,* 2:497.

31. Schrage, *Der erste Brief,* 2:499, esp. n. 55; Barrett translates *always,* but comments *"or in all things"* (*First Epistle,* 247).

32. Thomas Aquinas, *Super Ep. S. Pauli,* 344, sect. 584: *in his autem Corinthii deticiebant . . . quasi dicat . . . quasi ad imitandum mea exempla. Non enim possimus illorum exempla imitari, quorum memoriam non habemus.* Cf. Peter Lombard, in Migne, *PL,* 91:1629; Ambrosiaster, CSEL, 81:252.

33. Moffatt, *First Epistle,* 149; Allo, *Première Épitre,* 255; Hurd, *Origin of 1 Corinthians,* 182-83.

34. Fee, *First Epistle,* 500; Schrage, *Der erste Brief,* 2:499.

35. Hays, *1 Cor,* 181-84.

36. Barrett, *First Epistle,* 247.

37. BAGD, 614-15. They give numerous examples of these and other nuances.

38. For further examples cf. Lampe, *Patristic Greek Lexicon,* 1013.

ceived and transmitted doctrine and practice arose (esp. in relation to 11:23 and 15:3-5).[39] This is plausible in the light of the Corinthian tendency to regard their own thought and practice as a unilateral affair (cf. 1:3; 14:36; and elsewhere). Schrage hesitates to regard 11:2-16 as relating to "tradition" in the foundation sense of 11:23 and 15:3-5, since it does not constitute a cross-centered article of faith and life.[40] Nevertheless, the respect or concern for "the other" in 11:2-16 does reflect a cruciform pattern. *Many commentators believe that the tradition for which Paul commends the readers is the eschatological inclusion of men and women as active participants in prayer and prophetic speech, in contrast to the issue of clothing, which Paul believes must still generate signals of gender distinctiveness on the basis of the order of creation, which still holds sway even in the gospel era.*

3 This is only one of three instances, I think, for which we find ourselves compelled to offer an alternative translation or translations in square brackets (cf. 11:4). The translation of this verse has caused more personal agony and difficulty than any other in the epistle, not least because the huge array of research literature and lexicographical data which presses controversially and polemically for diverse translations of κεφαλή, in which each of three main views finds powerful and well-informed advocates. (The decision about *husband* [NRSV] or **man** [REB, NJB, NIV] is of a different order.) NRSV, REB, NJB, NIV, AV/KJV, Moffatt, Barrett, and Collins all translate κεφαλή as *head* (also Jerome, *caput;* Luther, *Haupt;* Luther, Stuttgart 1984 ed., *Haupt*). Out of respect for their strong tradition together with the arguments of Fitzmyer and others we place *head* in square brackets as one clearly possible alternative, but weighty arguments also occur for "source." In the end we are convinced by advocates of a third view, even if barely. The work of Cervin (1989) and more especially Perriman (1994) and Dawes (1998) must be given due weight. Our translation coheres with the recognition by Collins (1999) that Paul deliberately uses a *polymorphous concept,* through a word that has *multiple meanings* (see below).

In whatever way we choose to translate κεφαλή, however, Judith Gundry-Volf formulates the fundamental principle that since Paul is setting up a complex and conscious dialectic between a gender-distinctive creation order and a gospel order of reciprocity and mutuality, neither of these two aspects of the arguments should be selected atomistically and accorded privilege as representing the whole. Paul can appeal "to creation to support instructions which presume a hierarchical relationship of man and woman as well as undergird their new social equality in Christ without denying their difference."[41]

39. K. Wegenast, *Das Verständnis der Tradition bei Paulus und in den Deuteropaulinen,* WMANT 8 (Neukirchen: Neukirchener, 1962), 111.

40. Schrage, *Der erste Brief,* 2:500, n. 61.

41. Gundry-Volf, "Gender and Creation in 1 Cor 11:2-16: A Study in Paul's Theological Method," in Adna et al. (eds.), *Evangelium, Schriftauslegung, Kirche,* 152; cf. 151-71; and the introduction above to 11:2-16.

The history of claims about the meaning of κεφαλή is immense and daunting. It is doubtful whether Fee is entirely correct in suggesting that "all commentaries up to Barrett and Conzelmann" perceive the metaphorical force of κεφαλή as "hierarchical, setting up structures of authority," any more than he can claim so confidently that "nothing in the passage suggests as much [i.e., this view]. . . . Paul's understanding of the metaphor [and] . . . the only one the Corinthians would have grasped is 'head' as 'source', especially 'source of life.'"[42] It does not seem to be the case on careful scrutiny that up until the 1970s the view was virtually always that of "headship," after which virtually all exegetes perceived that κεφαλή really meant *source*. This is open to question because (i) more than one patristic commentator notes the highly open-textured, *multivalent* force of κεφαλή as revolving *metaphorically* around the *physiological head-body contrast;* (ii) the view that κεφαλή means *source* has undergone serious criticism recently. Thus Horrell (1996) observes, "Recent work has cast doubt on the appropriateness of 'source' as a translation of κεφαλή."[43] Even if we hesitate to accept the careful and detailed arguments of Wayne Grudem (1985) and J. Fitzmyer (1989 and 1993) that the word denotes *authoritative headship* (see below), no less important and perhaps still more convincing are the arguments of Richard S. Cervin (1989) and especially A. C. Perriman (1994) that κεφαλή denotes primarily head in contrast to body but more widely (including in 11:3) "that which is most prominent, foremost, uppermost, pre-eminent."[44] The sustained arguments about κεφαλή put forward by Gregory Dawes (1998) confirm these conclusions with sufficient evidence and argument (albeit much relating to Eph 5:21-33) to persuade us to use the three English words **preeminent** (of Christ), **foremost** (of man), and **preeminent** (of God), even if we felt obliged to leave *head* in square brackets as a still arguable translation. Note: A summary and conclusions occur at the end of this discussion for those who wish to bypass the more detailed arguments.

κεφαλή AND ITS MULTIPLE MEANINGS

1. Authority, Supremacy, Leadership

This is the traditional rendering from the medieval period onward. Robertson and Plummer write, "By κεφαλή is meant supremacy. . . . Christ is the head of man; man is the head of woman . . . 3:23; Eph 1:22; 4:15; 5:23. . . . God is supreme. . . . This was a favorite Arian text; it is in harmony with 15:24-28."[45] J. A. Fitzmyer has strongly con-

---

42. Fee, *First Epistle,* 502, 502, n. 41, and 503.

43. Horrell, *Social Ethos,* 171. Against Horrell (1996) Dawes (1998), Perriman (1994), and Hays (1997) defend *source* (earlier Bedale, Barrett, Bruce, and Fee), and this view is still maintained by Schrage (1995), Murphy-O'Connor (1997), and Horsley (1998).

44. Perriman, "The Head of a Woman: The Meaning of κεφαλή in 1 Cor 11:3," 618; cf. 602-22; also Cervin, "Does κεφαλή Mean 'Source' or 'Authority Over' in Greek Literature? A Rebuttal," 85-112.

45. Robertson and Plummer, *First Epistle,* 229.

tended that this view should be reinstated in contrast to the attempts of S. Bedale (1954), Robin Scroggs (1972), and J. Murphy-O'Connor (1980, 1988) to argue for the meaning *source* (see below).[46] Fitzmyer notes that in the LXX κεφαλή translates Heb. רֹאשׁ *(ro'sh) head,* some 281 times, of which the subcategory meaning *leader* occurs in at least 3 places in Exodus and at least 11 times in Judges (e.g., Judg 10:18; 11:8, 9, 11). 2 Sam 22:44 is a key text for this meaning, as Murphy-O'Connor concedes.[47] However, if we understand κεφαλή — רֹאשׁ to include *head* in the sense of English *top,* the numerical ratio is increased.[48] Fitzmyer shows that a wider range of passages than those cited by Murphy-O'Connor bear the meaning *chief, leader, leadership* especially in conjunction with the sense of *preeminent* or *top.* We shall explore these further in the light of the data from Brown-Driver-Briggs (1980 ed.) when we return to our own translation. Fitzmyer concludes: "The upshot . . . is that a Hellenistic Jewish writer such as Paul of Tarsus could well have intended that κεφαλή in 1 Cor 11:3 be understood as 'head' in the sense of authority or supremacy over someone else."[49]

Fitzmyer's work largely vindicates the "traditional" interpretation of Weiss, Robertson and Plummer, Wendland, Allo, Lietzmann and Kümmel, Grosheide, and Héring, whose arguments Murphy-O'Connor and Fee tend to underrate. Héring argues that even in the case of Christ "the term clearly indicates the Son's subordination to the Father."[50] Conzelmann also notes the role of "subordination" but only (rightly) within a broader and more complex frame: "'Head' does not [in the OT] denote the sovereignty of one person over another but over a community. . . . Subordination [in Christology] is also expressed in terms of a totally different complex of ideas."[51] Wolff, however, underlines the Pauline emphasis on the creation "order" as against Corinthian cries for "freedom."[52]

Wayne Grudem provides a survey of 2,336 instances of κεφαλή in the writings of thirty-six Greek authors (based on *Thesaurae Linguae Graecae* from the eighth century BC to the fourth century AD.[53] Of these, over 2,000 denote the "actual physical head of a man or animal," while of the remaining 302 metaphorical uses, 49 apply to a "person of superior authority or rank, or 'ruler', 'ruling part.' No instances were discovered in which κεφαλή had the meaning 'source', 'origin.'"[54] R. S. Cervin offered different conclusions, and hence in 1990 Grudem produced "a Response" to Cervin and to other recent studies which attempt to reinstate "source" or the meaning of "preeminent" or "foremost" without the explicit entailment of "authority over."[55] Here he repeats his conclusions of 1985 and subjects Cervin's methods and conclusions to criticism. Grudem's critique of the proposals about "source" seems convincing, but his

46. Fitzmyer, "Another Look at κεφαλή in 1 Cor 11:3," 503-11.

47. Ibid., 506; Murphy-O'Connor, "Sex and Logic in 1 Cor 11:2-16," 492; cf. 482-500.

48. Fitzmyer, "Another Look at κεφαλή," 506-9.

49. Ibid., 510; cf. BDB (1980 ed.), 910-11. Fitzmyer cites passages from Deuteronomy, 1 Kings, Judges, 2 Samuel, and elsewhere, which BDB also support.

50. Héring, *First Epistle,* 103.

51. Conzelmann, *1 Cor,* 183, n. 21 and n. 26.

52. Wolff, *Der erste Brief,* 248-49.

53. Grudem, "Does κεφαλή ('Head') Mean 'Source' or 'Authority Over' in Greek Literature? A Survey of 2,336 Examples," 38-59.

54. Ibid., 49 and 52.

55. Grudem, "The Meaning of κεφαλή ('Head'): A Response to Recent Studies," *TrinJ* 11 (1990): 3-72.

attempt to insist that the sense of "head" used by Paul necessarily carries with it notions of authority rather than prominence, eminence, representation, or preeminence
is less conclusive, especially when he concedes that some 2,000 of 2,336 occurrences
presuppose the semantic contrast between physical head and physical body.

2. Source, Origin, Temporal Priority

As early as 1954, S. Bedale proposed that κεφαλή could mean *source*.[56] However, he
does not deny, as Murphy-O'Connor was to do, that the Greek word "carries with it the
sense of 'authority'," including its use in 1 Cor 11:3.[57] By contrast, Murphy-O'Connor in
1989 argued that the word "never denotes authority or superiority," while by 1997 he
had softened this to "the instances where 'head' implies superiority are very rare."[58]
F. F. Bruce holds a position between Bedale and Murphy-O'Connor on the same spectrum: "we are probably to understand not . . . 'chief' or 'ruler' but rather 'source' or 'origin' — a sense well attested for Gk. *kephalē*."[59] Bruce bases his argument largely on
the assumption that "source" fits the logic of later verses in this passage, and the role
of Christ as "source" of human existence. Christ "derives his eternal being" from God
(3:23; 8:6).[60] Barrett is perhaps on firmer ground when he argues that since κεφαλή
can denote the part standing for the whole (e.g., head of cattle, see below), this may
extend as a metaphor for the source or origin of the person or object in question.
Barrett then expresses the view which he shares with Bruce, that this sense "is
strongly suggested by verses 8f. Paul does not say that man is the lord (κύριος) of the
woman; he says he is the origin of her being."[61] He argues further, with Bruce, that the
relation between Christ and God "can be understood in a similar way. The Father is
fons divinitatis; the Son is what he is in relation to the Father."[62] R. Scroggs (1972 and
1974) presses the case further. Gal 3:27-28 had already established "the societal-
levelling quality of baptism," and the use of κεφαλή in 1 Cor 11:3 carries no hint of female subordination. Everything hinges on mutual dependence throughout the passage.[63] "In normal Greek κεφαλή does not mean lordship."[64]

John P. Meier also argues that "we have here a later Hellenistic use of *kephalē*
with metaphysical overtones. The idea is 'source' or 'origin,' especially the origin of
something's existence. A chain of sources or emanations is being set up. God is the
source of the Messiah . . . the Son is God's instrument in creation . . . (1 Cor 8:6). Christ is
the source and perhaps also the Platonic archetype of the male. . . . Genesis 2 states
that woman was made from the rib of man. The chain of being, the order of creation,

56. S. Bedale, "The Meaning of κεφαλή in the Pauline Epistles," *JTS* n.s. 5 (1954): 211-15.
57. Ibid., 215.
58. Murphy-O'Connor, *1 Cor,* 121; cf. his comment ad loc. in R. E. Brown, J. A. Fitzmyer,
and R. E. Murphy (eds.), *New Jerome Biblical Commentary* (London: Chapman 1989), sects. 49,
53.
59. Bruce, *1 and 2 Cor,* 103.
60. Ibid.
61. Barrett, *First Epistle,* 248.
62. Ibid., 249.
63. R. Scroggs, "Paul and the Eschatological Woman," *JAAR* 40 (1972): 283-303, and "Paul
and the Eschatological Woman Revisited," *JAAR* 42 (1974): 532-37.
64. Scroggs, "Paul" (1972): 298.

necessarily involves subordination, with set places and roles."[65] Fee also argues for "source," but is closer to Scroggs and Murphy-O'Connor in rejecting the subordinationist aspect. Fee writes: "Paul's understanding of the metaphor, therefore, and almost certainly the only one the Corinthians would have grasped is 'head' as 'source,' especially 'source of life.' This seems corroborated by vv. 8-9."[66] Witherington (1988), Radcliffe (1990), and with more caution Schrage (1995) favor "source."[67] Schrage follows Schlier and Conzelmann in rejecting the notion that κεφαλή can normally denote authority over an individual (although he readily concedes that Heb. שׁאר (ro 'sh) can denote leadership over a group), and rightly insists that the preponderance of uses in this passage denote the physiological *head* in contrast to body (cf. vv. 4a, 5a, 7, 10). He also points out, with J. D. G. Dunn, that since in 11:10 the woman who uses prophetic speech is said to have "authority" (ἐξουσίαν ἔχειν . . .' it is unlikely that the opening propositions serve to establish man's *authority over* woman.[68] Finally, Horsley (1998) advocates *source* on the basis of Philo's use of κεφαλή as progenitor for Abraham (Philo, *De Congressu Quaerendae* 61).[69]

This argument comes up against three problems among others. (a) Is it convincing to ignore the weight of evidence adduced by Fitzmyer about the Hebrew and LXX and by Grudem about uses of κεφαλή in Greek literature? At times the debate degenerates into a confrontation over which meaning is allegedly "rare."[70] Certainly the LXX usage cannot be ignored. Scroggs presents a one-sided and incautious view, while arguably even the ever judicious Murphy-O'Connor may perhaps tend to overstate his case. (b) Granted that (as cannot be denied) the physiological use of κεφαλή hugely preponderates, can a metaphorical extension of the physical head readily mean *source?* We have to envisage a two-stage process in which a direct or level-one metaphor (**preeminence**, *foremost, top*) becomes a second-level metaphor for that preeminence from which other existence flows. However, this does not entail the total eclipse of the **preeminence**, *top-stone* dimension. (c) Much depends on drawing inferences about the christological relation to God in other Pauline passages. Here, although it is true that God is regarded as source (ἐκ τοῦ θεοῦ) in contrast to mediate ground of existence (δι' οὗ τὰ πάντα καὶ ἡμεῖς δι' αὐτοῦ, 8:6), it remains the case for Paul that Christ's work is "for" God as preeminent (3:23; 15:24-28). The *valid* point in all

---

65. Meier, "On the Veiling of Hermeneutics (1 Cor 11:2-16)," 217-18; cf. 212-26.

66. Fee, *First Epistle*, 503. Fee also appeals to P. B. Payne, "Response," in A. Mickelsen (ed.), *Women, Authority and the Bible* (Downers Grove: InterVarsity Press, 1986), 113-32; and Kroeger, "The Classical Concept of 'Head' as 'Source,'" in Gaebelein Hull, *Equal to Serve* (American title *Serving Together* [New York, 1987]).

67. Schrage, *Der erste Brief*, 2:501-4; Witherington, *Women in the Earliest Churches*, 84-85; and Radcliffe, "Paul and Sexual Identity: 1 Cor 11:2-16," in Soskice (ed.), *After Eve*, 66.

68. Schrage, *Der erste Brief*, 2:504; Dunn, *The Theology of Paul*, 589-90; on 11:10 see below; also Gundry-Volf, "Gender and Creation," 159-60.

69. Horsley, *1 Cor*, 153.

70. Puzzlingly, Witherington, e.g., cites H. Schlier, *TDNT*, 3:674-76, to support *source* as "well known in the extrabiblical literature" (*Women in the Earliest Churches*, 84 and 255, n. 37). But when we consult Schlier directly, this is hardly confirmed. Schlier identifies. (1) "first, supreme 'top' or [last in the list and only instantiated two or three times] also 'point', 'point of departure' . . . 'the mouth of a river . . . or also its source'" (Herodotus 4.91), also perhaps in Philo; (2) "'prominent', 'outstanding', 'determinative'"; (3) synecdoche for "the whole man." The Herodotus reference is clear but dates from the fifth century BC; the allusion in Philo is more ambivalent.

of the arguments for "source" is not that κεφαλή *necessarily* means *source* but that (*pace* Grudem) it does *not* seem to denote a relation of *"subordination"* or "authority over."

3. Synecdoche and Preeminence, Foremost, Topmost Serving Interactively as a Metaphor Drawn from the Physiological Head

Whether we scrutinize the use of κεφαλή in Greek literature (including the LXX and Jewish texts) or the Heb רֹאשׁ *(ro'sh),* we find (a) the overwhelming majority of references to physiological head in contrast to body; and (b) a substantial number of occurrences of synecdoche, where *heads* denotes persons or animals (for which the part denotes the whole, as in "head of cattle," or "counting heads"). In theological terms this hints at a representative use: Christ stands for man or humankind in the new order, just as Adam is "head" of the race without the gospel (1 Cor 15:21-24; cf. Rom 5:12-21). This is further corroborated by the language about shame, image, and glory common to 11:4-6 and esp. 11:7 (εἰκὼν καὶ δόξα) and 15:49 (τὴν εἰκόνα τοῦ ἐπουρανίου). This suggests only one nuance of the word, however.

Gregory Dawes devotes eighty pages of his study of this subject to theories of metaphor, including those of M. Beardsley, D. Davidson, Max Black, Janet Martin Soskice, and Paul Ricoeur. He concludes: "If this word is a living metaphor, it can (and should) be translated as 'head.' . . . To *translate* the word as 'source' is to pre-judge an important issue: it is to imply that in this context the word is functioning as a dead metaphor" (his italics).[71] Dawes himself argues that it is a living metaphor that carries neither the sense of "overload" (i.e., the approach under [i] is not fully satisfactory), "nor does it mean 'source' [view (ii)]."[72] He cannot accept Grudem's conclusions on the ground that a word count overlooks the issues concerning metaphorical extension which lie at the heart of Dawes's argument.[73] Rightly, in my view, he asks the question over which I have agonized: in what sense would Paul and his readers use and understand this metaphor which not only elsewhere but specifically in 1 Cor 11:2-16 and in Eph 5:21-33 rests upon the head-body distinction of physiology?

From the side of the hellenistic linguistic background, it is possible to reconstruct a broad medical understanding of κεφαλή in the period from Hippocrates (460-380 BC) to Galen (AD 130-200). Contrary to what is often implied in older modern biblical studies, the ancient world was aware that the brain (ὁ ἐγκέφαλος) constituted a "source." "From the brain and from the brain only arise our pleasures, joys, laughter and jests, as well as our sorrows, pains, griefs . . . ," but the brain also served as a "control": "It makes us mad or delirious, inspires us with dread . . . brings sleeplessness . . . and acts that are contrary to habit. . . . All come from the brain" (ἀπὸ τοῦ ἐγκεφάλου).[74] Dawes cites sources in Pythagorean philosophy which apparently ascribed a "ruling" function to the brain.

Galen opposed the widespread claim that the heart is the source of nervous

71. Dawes, *The Body in Question,* 126.
72. Ibid., 127.
73. Ibid., 128-33.
74. Hippocrates, *De morbo sacro* in *Hippocrates,* LCL (London: Heinemann, 1952), 2:174 and 175.

experience: "the source of all the nerves (τῶν νεύρων) is the brain (ὑπάρχειν τὸν ἐγκέφαλον).[75] Galen perceives that motion and sensation owe their function to the brain: the themes of "source" and of "controlling function" both play a part in medical vocabulary and thought.[76] Within two or three years of the date of our epistle, Seneca writes to Nero that the head is a source of health or well-being: *a capite bona valetudo.*[77] However, Sevenster emphasizes the metaphor of headship and control in these passages, where Dawes focuses more closely on source. As Sevenster notes, the issue in *de clementia* is to plead that as Emperor Nero will, like the head of a body, radiate kindness which will permeate the empire to bring it health, the people will do the same; Dawes cites the parallel in the *Moral Epistles* of Nero as a source of well-being to the "body" of the empire.[78]

From the side of the LXX and Hebrew background, W. J. Martin very well maps a wide semantic field within which *topmost,* synecdoche for *totality,* responsible *eminence,* and *cornerstone* play major roles.[79] Similarly, Dawes concludes that the precise force of the metaphor must be contextually determined: in Eph 5:22-24 it can have no other meaning than "authority over," but this depends on context rather than on lexicography. The problem about translating κεφαλή as *head* in 1 Cor 11:3 remains that, as R. Cervin notes, in English-speaking contexts "the head" almost always implies leadership and authority, as in headmaster, Head of School, Head of Department, head steward.[80] As we noted earlier, Perriman convincingly urges that the equivalent assumption in first-century hellenistic contexts would be to construe the metaphorical force of *head* not as authoritative leader in charge, but as one who is "**prominent, foremost, uppermost, preeminent.**"[81] Senft, Horrell, and in effect Hasler share this view, although Hasler argues that in the context of Paul's deliberative rhetoric a dialectic embraces both the arrangement or "placing" of creation and the new liturgical dignity and equality of the woman who uses prophetic speech within the frame of "glory" received from God.[82] BDB (for Heb.), LSJ (classical Gk.), BAGD, Grimm-Thayer, MM, and Louw-Nida point in this direction (see below).

The multivalency of the term רֹאשׁ *(ro'sh)* for Jewish converts who know the LXX translations should not be forgotten, as Fitzmyer rightly insists (against Scroggs). Of five Hebrew words which κεφαλή translates this is by far the most common.[83] Brown-Driver-Briggs (1980) divide uses into eight categories with subdivisions as follows: (1) *head,* (a) of humans; (b) of animals; (2) *top* (e.g., of rocks, towers, pillars, ladders); (3) *chief,* (a) chief man (see Fitzmyer, above); (b) chief city; (c) chief nation; (d) chief priest; (e) head of family; (4) *front place,* e.g., taken by the leader but *also* used

75. Galen, *On the Doctrines of Hippocrates and Plato,* in *Corpus Medicorum Graecorum* V:4:1, 2 (Berlin: Berlin Academy, 1981), 1.7.55.

76. Galen, *De Usu Partium* 12.4.

77. Seneca, *De Clementia* 2.2.1; cf. *Epistles* 95.52; and *De Ira* 2.31.7.

78. Sevenster, *Paul and Seneca,* 171-72; Dawes, *The Body in Question,* 132-33.

79. Martin, "1 Cor 11:2-16: An Interpretation," in W. W. Gasque and R. P. Martin (eds.), *Apostolic History and the Gospel,* 232-33; cf. 231-41.

80. Cervin, "Does κεφαλή Mean 'Source' or 'Authority Over'?" 87.

81. Perriman, "The Head of a Woman," cf. 602-22.

82. Horrell, *Social Ethos,* 171-72 (cf. 168-76); Senft, *La première Épitre,* 141, "le sommet"; Hasler, "Die Gleichstellung der Gattin. Situationskritische Reflexionen zu 1 Kor 11:2-16," 189-200.

83. Hatch-Redpath, *Concordance to the Septuagint,* 2:760-62.

of priority *in time;* (5) *best;* (6) of an *army* company; (7) *sum* or total; (8) residual nuances.[84] Liddell-Scott-Jones offer a survey of classical Greek uses which is remarkably
similar, beginning with (1) *head* of man or beast; (2) *synecdoche* for the whole person;
(3) *head* of a vegetable; (4) the *capital* or chief place; (5) the *crown* or completion of
something; (6) *chief* (and the idiom κατὰ κεφαλῆς, over the head, e.g., from Homer, *Iliad* 18.24, onward; cf. 11:4).[85]

For the period of NT Greek, BAGD does not differ significantly. The most frequent and prominent, once again, are (1) heads of persons or animals in the physiological sense, e.g., the hairs of the head (Matt 10:30; Luke 7:38; Philo, *De Legatione ad
Gaium* 223); and after this (2) synecdoche (e.g., Rom 12:20, "coals of fire on his head,"
perhaps from a curse formula); (3) head "metaphorically" in contrast to the church as
body (Col 1:18; cf. 2:19); (4) "figuratively" to denote superior rank; (5) also to denote
uppermost part, end, point, keystone (Acts 4:12; 1 Pet 2:7) and either capital or fron-
tier city (Acts 16:12). With Grudem, neither BAGD nor Lattke in *EDNT* nor Grimm-
Thayer appear to propose *source,* even under either "metaphor" (BAGD, 16) or "figurative" use (BAGD's 2a, b).[86] It appears that Louw and Nida also focus on *physiological
head, superior,* or *cornerstone,* but not *source.*[87] Moulton-Milligan stress the occurrence of (1) physiological head; (2) synecdoche, and (3) extremity or topmost in the
papyri, also without apparent mention of *source.*[88] H. Schlier, as we earlier noted,
identifies "first," "prominent," and synecdoche, with only a couple of isolated instances in Herodotus (484-425 BC!). And perhaps in Philo.[89] He does not appear to
propose this meaning for 1 Cor 11:3.

It is significant that in Lampe's *Patristic Greek Lexicon* virtually the only occasion
on which the meaning of κεφαλή is compared with ἀρχή as "equivalent" is with reference to 1 Cor 11:3, on the basis of the application of ἀρχή to God in relation to Christ,
and Christ in relation to the world (but with the important proviso that ἀρχή is also
multivalent as beginning or source, or as first principle, or as ruler, authority).[90] In the
patristic era the emphasis begins to shift from physiological head to the metaphorical use in the ecclesial order as religious superior or bishop (e.g., Athanasius, *Apology*
89), head of the house, or to Christ as head of creation, or as head of the church
(Origen, *John* 1:13). Nevertheless, whether we consult the standard lexicons or the
TLG (with Grudem), this kind of data is insufficiently nuanced contextually to give us a
complete picture.

Here it becomes significant to return to Chrysostom, whom we had in mind
when we initially queried Fee's generalization about eras of study and their related
conclusion. Chrysostom is highly sensitive to the multivalency of κεφαλή in 1 Cor 11:3.
Chrysostom is aware that a parallel between men/women and God/Christ should not
give "the heretics" grounds for a subordinationist Christology. In certain respects

84. BDB (1980 ed.), 910-11.
85. LSJ, 801 (with minor changes to numbering).
86. BAGD, 430. Cf. further Grimm-Thayer, 345. M. Lattke, *EDNT,* 2:284-86, goes further:
he excludes the proposal about *emanation* on the ground of the NT and biblical theme of *creatio ex
nihilo* (285).
87. Louw-Nida, 1:95-96, 739; and 2:141.
88. MM, 342. ἀνεγκέφαλος is used metaphorically to mean "brainless."
89. Schlier, *TDNT,* 3:674; cf. 673-82 (in spite of Witherington's appeal noted above).
90. Lampe, *Patristic Greek Lexicon,* 749; on ἀρχή see BAGD, 111-12.

head denotes a kind of primacy, but both God and Christ on one side and men and women on the other are of the same mode of being. "For had Paul meant to speak of rule and subjection . . . he would not have brought forward the instance of a woman (or wife), but rather of a slave and a master. . . . It is a wife (or woman) as free, as equal in honour; and the Son also, though He did become obedient to the Father, it was as the Son of God; it was as God."[91] While we must avoid reading back patristic doctrines of the Trinity into Pauline texts, Chrysostom (a) reflects Paul's notion that in the context of love between God and Christ, or between man and woman, obedience or response is *chosen, not imposed;* and (b) reflects the endeavor to do justice to *the duality or wholeness* of difference and "order" on one side and reciprocity and mutual dignity and respect on the other.

Chrysostom's one major deviation from Paul's explicit argument in this chapter arises when he distinguishes between woman in creation and woman after the fall. Initially, he comments, woman is "bone of his bone, flesh of his flesh" (Gen 2:23). In creation, he argues, "there is no subjection," but when freedom was misused this status was revised (Gen 3:16). Chrysostom is influenced, it seems, by 2 Tim 2:14 at this point. On the other hand, this observation may be deemed a digression from his main point: "Even to the simple *the difference* is evident" between applications of the word *head* to Christ, to man, and to God (my italics). In the case of the man-woman relationship the physiological head shares "like passions with the body," just as God and Christ share the same nature and being. By contrast the first proportion entails a sharper difference: Christ as *head* of man does share man's order of being.[92] Chrysostom appreciates the sensitivity of the various nuances that may be conveyed.

Tertullian similarly recognizes the interactive force of the metaphor of *head:* "This, to be sure, is an astonishing thing, that the Father can be taken to be the face of the Son (2 Cor 4:6) when he is his head; for 'the head of Christ is God'" (1 Cor 11:3).[93] In effect he anticipates Ian Ramsey's principle that where models conflict or complement each other, unwanted meanings fall away, and the models are thereby qualified.[94] On the other hand, Tertullian goes further. In his specific discussion of the meaning of veils upon the head, he argues that here *head* is used as a synecdoche for the woman herself: "the whole head constitutes the woman."[95] Clearly Augustine is wary of conceiving of *caput* either as head in an authoritarian sense or still more any notion of "source," since he cites 11:3 in his treatise on the Trinity precisely to underline the eternal sonship of Christ and the aseity, equality, and "immortality" of the Trinity: "some things were made by the Father, and some by the Son. . . . The Son is equal with the Father, and the working of the Father and the Son is indivisible. . . . 'Being in the form of God . . .' [Phil 2:6] . . . 'the head of Christ is God' [1 Cor 11:3]."[96]

Fee's general statement may perhaps more readily apply to such patristic writers as Origen and Jerome. Origen is more at ease with a quasi-subordinationist Chris-

---

91. Chrysostom, *1 Cor. Hom.*, 26:2.
92. Ibid., 26:3.
93. Tertullian, *Against Praxeas*, 14.
94. I. Ramsey, *Religious Language* (London: SCM, 1957).
95. Tertullian, *On the Veiling of Women*, 17:2 (on 1 Cor 11:6).
96. Augustine, *On the Trinity*, 1:6:12. Elsewhere Augustine concedes that 11:3 combines the notions of mediator with Christ's being "of the very being of God" (*On the Trinity*, 6:10).

tology, qualifying Col 1:16, 17, with reference to 1 Cor 11:3, "alone having as head God the Father, for it is written 'The head of Christ is God'" (1 Cor 11:3).[97] Jerome comments on 11:3: *"Vir nulli subjectus est nisi Christo, . . . Mulier vero et Christo et viro debet esse subjecta."*[98] However, this misses the subtlety of Tertullian, Chrysostom, Augustine, and several other patristic writers. Patristic writers, as well as modern lexicographical research, encourage the conclusion of Collins: "Paul's rhetorical argument is constructed on the basis of a pun. He plays on the multiple meanings of 'head'."[99]

4. Summary and Conclusions

(a) Head

The value of this translation and interpretation is that it addresses the issues raised by Fitzmyer and the lexicographical survey of *TLG* undertaken by Grudem. If our network of reader expectations in the modern West matched those of first-century Corinth and hellenistic Judaism, this would offer the most open-ended translation to carry the several nuances associated with the metaphorical extension and application of the term, and especially a wordplay with subsequent uses of the physiological *head* seems to be entailed in the following verses. Nevertheless, today's chain of literal and metaphorical associations is so exclusively bound up with institutional authority (witness the use of the term "headship" in late twentieth-century debates) that this translation and interpretation suggest a narrower focus than Paul probably has in mind. It is possible that it is drawn from its use in Corinthian discussion, but we cannot be sufficiently certain to place part of the verse in quotation marks (see below on Schrage's critique of Padgett). If we use the term "head," its multiple meanings from context to context as serving a polymorphous concept must always be kept in view.

(b) Source

This has eminent advocates, including three leading commentators, namely, Barrett, Fee, and Schrage. Yet in spite of claims to the contrary, the paucity of lexicographical evidence remains a major obstacle to this translation. Such contexts of *head of the river* are so *self-evident as a transferred metaphor* that they should be held aside from those contexts where no such clear signal is generated by the immediate context. Arguments from the relation between Christ and God as a parallel "control" in actuality would support all three (or four) translations or interpretations. Oddly, although we ourselves are hesitant to adopt *source*, advocates of this view might have strengthened their case by pointing out more strongly that ἐκ τοῦ ἀνδρός (of source) and διὰ τῆς γυναικός (of "mediate" creation) in 11:12 offers precisely the terminology of 8:6 about God and Christ. This weighs more seriously than broader discussions, and we have to judge whether it is sufficient to make it plausible that Paul *expected* this meaning to be understood by his readers in v. 3, ahead of his argument in v. 12.

97. Origen, *De Principiis*, 2:6:1.
98. Jerome, *Comm. in Ep. 1 ad Cor.*, in Migne, *PL*, 30:749.
99. Collins, *First Cor*, 396; cf. 405-6.

(c) Preeminent, Foremost, and Synecdoche for a Representative Role

This proposal has the merit of *most clearly drawing interactively on the metaphorical conjunction between physiological head* (which is far and away the most frequent, "normal" meaning) and the notion of *prominence,* i.e., the most conspicuous or *topmost* manifestation of that for which the term also functions as *synecdoche for the whole.* The public face is linked with responsibility and representation in the public domain, since *head* is both the part of a person which is most conspicuous and that by which they are most readily distinguished or recognized. These aspects feature more frequently and prominently in first-century Greek texts than either the notions of *ruler* or *source,* although we agree with Fitzmyer and Grudem that a survey of Hatch-Redpath does not corroborate claims that when שׁאר *(ro'sh)* means *rule,* LXX almost always uses a different Greek word.

More striking than links between *source* and the use of Genesis 2 in the immediate context is the total perspective of 1 Cor 8:1–14:40 that Paul corroborates the *theoretical right of the "strong" or "prominent" to exercise their "knowledge" and "freedom,"* but dramatically places *boundaries and qualifications around freedom and knowledge by insisting on the priority of love (as in 13:1-13), most especially love which will respect the self-awareness (conscience??) and self-esteem of the "weak,"* who must not be permitted to stumble. If Paul asserts a theoretical hierarchy, which does indeed correspond with "knowledge" of the creation order, the *foremost* within this order must protect the status and self-respect of "the weak" *for whom they must take responsibility* (synecdoche). The more anyone stresses "prominence," the more that person must ensure that "the other" does *not* experience the self-humiliation expressed in 12:15. "If the *foot* (*sic, πούς*), should say, 'because I am not a hand, I do not belong to the body,' just because of this does it not belong to the body?" Hence women use prophetic speech alongside men. However, at Corinth women as well as men tended to place "knowledge" and "freedom" before love in the Christian sense. Paul does not permit their "freedom" as part of the gospel new creation to destroy their proper self-respect and respect in the eyes of others by taking part in worship dressed like an "available" woman. That is not love, for it brings "shame" on themselves, their menfolk, and on God.

One writer goes a considerable part of the way toward making this point, but exempts gender for the wrong reason. Dale Martin rightly agrees that the appropriate head covering provides a sign of "nonavailability" for respectable women who appear in public, most especially when thoughts are to be focused on God in corporate worship. This "was understood in ancient culture to protect vulnerable women from the penetrating gaze and from dangerous invasion."[100] Throughout this epistle, Martin rightly urges, there is a sense in which Paul "attempts to make the weak strong and the strong weak."[101] Although Martin does not invoke the principle here, this is part of the "reversal" which stems from the role of the cross as "ground and criterion" (Schrage) of Christian life and thought. However, Martin argues that "when it comes to the male-female hierarchy, Paul abruptly renounces any status-questioning stance. . . . This . . . has to do with physiology. The 'stuff' of female nature is differently constituted from that of male nature."[102]

---

100. Martin, *The Corinthian Body,* 242; cf. 233-41.
101. Ibid., 248.
102. Ibid., 248-49.

This is less than convincing, however, in the light of J. Gundry-Volf's more careful arguments about the dialectic between creation, culture, or society and eschatology. *Paul insists on gender distinctiveness.* That goes for the *men* (vv. 4, 7 with Murphy-O'Connor) no less than for the *women* (vv. 5, 6, 7b). However, if love takes priority over freedom, any competitiveness about "authority" becomes obsolete in the new order, even if a reciprocity of relationship allows different inputs to the relation of mutuality; rather, the entailments of protection of, and respect for, "the other" hold greater prominence than issues of "authority" within the wholeness of Paul's dialectic. Here *lexicography, theories of metaphor, exegesis, and the continuity of 8:1–14:14 cohere well together.* Neither "headship," nor "order," nor "equality" alone conveys the complexity and wholeness of Paul's theology. Again, *multiple meaning holds the key.*

Some residual issues in v. 3 deserve brief attention. NRSV translates ὁ ἀνήρ in the middle clause as *husband* (against **man** in REB, NIV, NJB), although it has **man** in the first and third propositions. A few commentators defend *husband,* but the overwhelming majority of writers convincingly argue that the issue concerns gender relations as a whole, not simply those within the more restricted family circle.[103] θέλω δέ should be rendered as an adversative (with NRSV, NJB, REB, Fee, and others; as against NIV, *now . . .*). This also renders still more problematic A. Padgett's argument that the θέλω δὲ ὑμᾶς εἰδέναι wording suggests that Paul is introducing a Corinthian formula in v. 3, a thesis which Fee and Schrage both reject.[104] Perhaps, as Murphy-O'Connor argues, Paul commends the readers for maintaining the tradition that women can be active in prophetic speech, but (δέ) attacks men and women equally for generating signals which blur gender distinctiveness in unacceptable ways by each appearing with inappropriate headgear.[105]

4 The Greek phrase κατὰ κεφαλῆς ἔχων is translated by **with his head covered** in NJB and NIV (also *who keeps* **his head covered**, REB; or *with something on his* **head**, NRSV; but NIV mg. note, or *. . . with long hair . . .*, signals a well-known difficulty). This is all the more important since, as Murphy-O'Connor insists, Paul's first warning against departure from church tradition concerns the clothing or head style of *men,* not women.[106] As we noted at the end of our introduction to 11:2-16, Richard Oster vehemently attacks the suggestions of Weiss, Bruce, and Fee (and Meyer and others could be added) that the notion of men wearing head coverings in the course of preparing or uttering prophetic speech is "hypothetical," together with Fee's conclusion that reconstructions of the situation cannot be more than "speculative."[107] Oster argues

---

103. Orr and Walther, *1 Cor* 259, argue that *husband* is perhaps more likely; cf. also C. S. Keener, *Paul, Women, Wives* (Peabody, Mass.: Hendrickson, 1992), 32-36.

104. Padgett, "Paul on Women in the Church: The Contradictions of Coiffure in 1 Cor 11:2-16," 78-79; (cf. 69-86); criticized by Fee, *First Epistle,* 501, n. 37, and by Schrage, *Der erste Brief,* 2:500, n. 63.

105. Murphy O'Connor, "Sex and Logic," 483.

106. Ibid. (above).

107. Oster, "Use, Misuse and Neglect of Archaeological Evidence in Some Modern Works

that Paul's concern that the church should not retreat into the defensive stance of a sectarian ghetto (cf. 1 Cor 5:10) ensures that the perceptions of society in Roman Corinth mattered to him, and that the church itself would readily have carried with it many cultural norms from Roman society of the first century. Archaeological evidence from coins, statues, and architectural monuments provide an important source for seeking to understand what is at issue here.

THE TRANSLATION OF κατὰ κεφαλῆς ἔχων:
COVERED HEAD OR LONG HAIR? (11:4)

Archaeological evidence from Rome itself to the Roman East is unambiguous, Oster urges, in depicting the "liturgical head covering" of men when they pray or use prophetic speech: "the practice of men covering their heads in the context of prayer and prophecy was a common pattern of Roman piety and widespread during the late Republic and early Empire. Since Corinth was a Roman colony, there should be little doubt that this aspect of Roman religious practice deserves greater attention by commentators than it was received."[108]

Horsley (1998) is one of the most recent writers to argue that Romans and Jews prayed with **heads . . . covered**, in contrast to the Greek practice of praying bareheaded.[109] Yet Oster also insists that it is a third standard "error" to impose "later Jewish practices onto the Corinthian situation."[110] Bruce, Barrett, Kümmel, and Oepke, among others, all appeal to Jewish traditions.[111] We also know from archaeological evidence that there was a Jewish synagogue at Corinth.[112] Nevertheless, Oster argues that neither the OT, nor the LXX, nor Qumran, nor the Gospels, nor Philo, nor Josephus, nor even the *Mishnah* offers any evidence for this. Hypotheses that men wore the traditional Jewish *tallith* or *yarmulke* "distort the historical use of the prayer shawl by Jewish men."[113] The context of wrapping oneself in a cloak "while absolving his vows . . . is not the specific activity that Paul addresses," even if the *Tosefta* mentions such a practice.[114]

---

on 1 Corinthians (1 Cor 7:1-5; 8:10; 11:2-16; 12:14-26)," 68; cf. 52-73, esp. 67-69. Cf. also Weiss, *Der erste Korintherbrief,* 271; Bruce, *1 and 2 Cor,* 104; Fee, *First Epistle,* 506-8; Meier, "On the Veiling of Hermeneutics," 218.

108. Ibid., 69. For evidence cf., e.g., B. S. Ridgway, "Sculpture from Corinth," *Hesperia* 50 (1981): 432-33; and F. P. Johnson, *Corinth,* IX: *Sculpture 1896-1923* (Cambridge Mass.: Harvard University Press, 1931), 70-72; E. Alfoldi-Rosenbaum, *Roman and Early Byzantine Portrait Sculpture in Asia Minor* (London: Oxford University Press, 1966). See further Oster, "When Men Wore Veils to Worship: The Historical Context of 1 Cor 11:4," 481-505, and the statue of Augustus in the Julian Basilica in James Wiseman, *Corinth and Rome* (1979), 1, Plate 8.

109. Horsley, *1 Cor,* 154.

110. Oster, "When Men Wore Veils to Worship," *NTS* 34 (1988): 487.

111. Barrett, *First Epistle,* 249-50; Bruce, *1 and 2 Cor,* 104; A. Oepke, "καλύπτω," *TDNT,* 3:563.

112. For archaeological evidence of the inscription concerning the synagogue, see the reproduction in Wiseman, *Corinth and Rome,* Plate 5, no. 8.

113. Oster, "When Men Wore Veils to Worship," 487.

114. Ibid., 488.

Before we conclude definitively that κατὰ κεφαλῆς ἔχων (down from the head) denotes some form of *material which covers the head,* we must address Murphy-O'Connor's argument that "it would seem more natural to understand the phrase as referring to *long hair*" (my italics).[115] He repeats the point in his short commentary of 1997: "The texts . . . never mention head-gear. The first condemns a man for 'having something hanging from his head' (11:4). The natural interpretation that this means 'long hair' is confirmed by the second reference 'a man who wears his hair long dishonours himself' (11:14)."[116] W. J. Martin, L. B. Hurley, Alan Padgett, and most recently Richard Horsley support this view that *long hair* is the issue.[117] Horsley writes, "'Down the head' in v. 4 is best taken as a reference to *long hair,* which would have been considered disgraceful for a man, particularly when praying or prophesying."[118] Murphy-O'Connor singles out "male homosexuals presiding at liturgy (1 Cor 11:2-11)" as a key element of the report from Chloe's people which "stunned Paul."[119] Nevertheless, Hays (1997) still believes that the issue for men in v. 4 is about "bare heads in worship" even if later in the argument Paul considers the semiotic force of unbound hair which hangs down, whether for men or women.[120] Wolff (1996) also discusses men and "head covering" (*Kopfbedeckung*) with reference to 2 Cor 3:12, 13, although agreeing that there is absence of firm data about Jewish practice for men in Paul's day.[121] Hence we cannot speak of a fresh change in the consensus view.

Murphy-O'Connor argues that κατά with the genitive more naturally denotes *hair which grows "down from" the head* than that which covers it in a more *static* way, i.e., *on the head.* BDF, however, propose equally either "a hanging down from the head" or "on the head," contrasting ἀκατακαλύπτῳ τῇ κεφαλῇ in v. 5, which is no less pertinent (perhaps more so) than Murphy-O'Connor's citing of v. 14 to support his case.[122] We are forced to balance the Roman background forcefully urged by Oster against the ethical-cultural background proposed by Murphy O'Connor in which he perceives resonances of male sexuality or effeminacy, i.e., a homosexual semiotic of the male hair style of long, loose hair, or hair tied into a ponytail. Murphy-O'Connor rightly observes that the Greek phrase does not explicitly mention a *head covering;* but Oster replies that this argument can be applied in the opposite direction: Paul does not explicitly mention *hair style* in v. 4.[123] Murphy-O'Connor can indeed readily cite contemporary sources about men and long hair. Pseudo-Phocylides, a hellenistic Jew who wrote between 30 BC and AD 40, advised parents, "Do not let locks grow on his head. Braid not his crown nor make cross-knots . . . long hair is not fit for men but for voluptuous women . . . *because many rage for intercourse with a man*" (Pseudo-

---

115. Murphy-O'Connor, "The Non-Pauline Character of 1 Cor 11:2-16?" 625.

116. Murphy-O'Connor, *1 Cor,* 122.

117. Horsley, *1 Cor,* 154; cf. J. B. Hurley, *Man and Woman in Biblical Perspective* (Downers Grove: InterVarsity Press, 1981); Martin, "1 Cor 11:2-16," 233; and Padgett, "Paul on Women in the Church," 69-86.

118. Horsley, *1 Cor,* 154.

119. J. Murphy-O'Connor, *Paul: A Critical Life* (Oxford: Oxford University Press, 1997), 279.

120. Hays, *First Cor,* 184.

121. Wolff, *Der erste Brief,* 249-50.

122. BDF, sect. 225, n. on 1 Cor 11:4, col. 2.

123. Murphy-O'Connor, "Sex and Logic," 484.

Phocylides 210-14, my italics).[124] Philo also attacks "the provocative way they [men] curl and dress their hair (τὰς τῆς κεφαλῆς τρίχας ἀναπλεκόμενοι καὶ διακοσμού- μενοι).[125]

From classical to hellenistic times κόμη often denotes *hair* perceived as an or- nament, while θρίξ usually denotes *hair* in a more anatomical sense.[126] But Pseudo- Phocylides uses the former; Philo, the latter. Murphy-O'Connor insists, "Philo's com- ment must mean that homosexuals let their hair grow longer than usual."[127] He sees three parallels in this context between Philo, *De Specialibus Legibus* 7:36-38 and 1 Cor 11:2-16: (i) the blurring of gender identity and distinctiveness, (ii) falsifying the "stamp of *nature*" (Philo; cf. φύσις in 11:14); and (iii) the theme of *shame* or disgrace. Evidence is far wider than Philo and hellenistic Judaism. The Roman satirists Juvenal and Horace also reflect this stance. Juvenal depicts an all-male gathering in which some of the men "filled a golden hair net with prodigious locks *(reticulumque comis auratum ingentibus implet)*."[128] Horace alludes disparagingly to "a well-shaped youth whose long hair is tied in a knot *(longam renodantis comam . . .)*."[129]

We are forced to conclude that although Jerome Murphy-O'Connor's case is strong, we cannot regard it as conclusive, while lexicography and the Roman back- ground cited by Oster, among others, suggests that **with his head covered** remains in the end more probable, but not decisively so. The heat and apparent certainty with which each side seems to press its claims is surprising, and this is one of the only two or three examples in this epistle where we have had to leave an alternative possibility in brackets. Collins cites extensive evidence (e.g., from Musonius, Epictetus, and Strabo) about elaborate and simpler hair styles and the importance attached to them as indicators of status and attitude. He concludes that behind this lies the principle "men should be men and women should be women."[130] Yet he translates "having something on his head" (v. 4) and "her head uncovered" (v. 5) since lack of display is also included under the latter.

The most important point of all, however, can too easily be overlooked. *This re- cent research proves conclusively that 11:4 does not present a merely hypothetical case.* Whether (as is more likely) Paul addressed **every man who prays or utters pro- phetic speech with his head covered** or **every man who prays** . . . *with long hair* (as is also entirely possible), *the first concern of 11:2-16 is about men, not about women.* This section (11:2-16) should not be given the title "The Veiling of Women in Public Worship" (Robertson and Plummer) nor "Die Kopfbedeckung der Frau" (Ortkemper and Wolff), nor "Women in Divine Worship" (Conzelmann), but some such title as "The Subtext behind Issues of Gender Identity and Head Coverings in Public Worship" or

124. Cited in Murphy-O'Connor, "Sex and Logic," 485; and in P. W. van der Horst, *The Sentences of Pseudo-Phocylides* (Leiden: Brill, 1978), 81-83.

125. Philo, *De Specialibus Legibus* 7.36.

126. Cf. Grimm-Thayer, 292 and 354.

127. Murphy-O'Connor, "Sex and Logic," 486.

128. Juvenal, *Satires* 2.96.

129. Horace, *Epistles* 11.28.

130. Collins, *First Cor,* 386-99; Musonius, *Fragments,* 21; Epictetus, *Dissertations* 3.1.14, 24-36, 42-45; Strabo, *Geography* 10.3.8. Witherington, *Conflict and Community,* 232-33, offers important evidence for *head covering* from, e.g., Plutarch, *Regum* 200F; Livy; and the recent work of D. W. J. Gill; but it overstates the issue to dismiss Murphy-O'Connor's arguments as "quite be- side the point" (232).

(as above) "Mutuality and Reciprocity: Self Respect, Respect for the Other, and Gender Identity in Public Worship."[131] Fee also disengages this from an exclusively one-sided gender focus by proposing the title "An Argument from Culture and Shame," although this misses the issues of creation and gospel theology identified alongside culture and shame by J. Gundry-Volf.[132] Barrett rightly heads this section "Men and Women," but most commentators fail to take up this point.[133]

In this verse it is important to note that προφητεύων should not be restricted to the uttering of some supposedly "spontaneous" oracular utterance. In chs. 12–14 we argue (following Hill, Müller, and Gillespie) that it denotes the public proclamation of gospel truth as applied pastorally and contextually to the hearers. This coheres with the contexts in which headgear is discussed in Roman cultural contexts and with issues of representation (see above on κεφαλή, including nuances of synecdoche), but a judgment depends largely on the detailed discussion offered below under προφητεία (see under 12:10; 14:6; 14:22), προφήτης (12:28, 29; 14:29, 32, 37), and προφητεύω (14:1, 3-5, 24, 31, 39). For this reason we avoid the translation *prophesies* (which too often carries modern cultural and ecclesial assumptions) in favor of **utters . . . prophetic speech**. **Prophetic speech** may include *applied theological teaching, encouragement, and exhortation to build the church,* not merely (if at all) *ad hoc* cries of an expressive, diagnostic, or tactical nature, delivered as "spontaneous" mini-messages. The latter debase and trivialize the great tradition of the term in the biblical writings as something altogether more serious, sustained, and reflective (see below on 12:10, 28-29, and on 14:1-5 and 24-39).

The remaining difficulty in this verse concerns the meaning of καταισχύνει τὴν κεφαλὴν αὐτοῦ, translated above as **shames his head**. It has become an axiom of research on this epistle especially in the 1980s and 1990s that the *honor-shame* semiotic contrast permeates the culture of Roman Corinth, much ancient Mediterranean culture, and not least this passage. J. Gundry-Volf observes: "This characterization of the Mediterranean world as a shame/honor society supplies the background for the shame/glory contrast in 1 Cor 11:2-16."[134] Bruce Malina and numerous studies of social or cultural anthropology in relation to the world of Paul underline the point.[135] As Moxnes notes, "Interaction between people was characterized by the com-

---

131. Robertson and Plummer, *First Epistle,* 216; Wolff, *Der erste Brief,* 244; Conzelmann, *1 Cor,* 181; Ortkemper, *1 Korintherbrief,* 102.

132. Fee, *First Epistle,* 498.

133. Barrett, *First Epistle,* 246. The overwhelming majority are one-sided. Even Schrage entitles the section "über die rechte Haartract für Frauen im Gottesdienst" (*Der erste Brief,* 2:487).

134. Gundry-Volf, "Gender and Creation in 1 Cor 11:2-16," 154.

135. Malina, *The NT World: Insights from Cultural Anthropology,* 28-62; Ramsay MacMullen, *Roman Social Relations 50 BC to AD 284* (New Haven: Yale University Press, 1974), 62-109; and H. Moxnes, "Honor, Shame and the Outside World in Paul's Letter to the Romans," in J. Neusner et al. (ed.), *The Social World of Formative Christianity and Judaism,* 207-18.

petition for recognition and the defence of one's own status and honor. To refuse a person's claim for honor was to put the person to shame. . . . Shame and honor . . . represent the value of a person in her or his own eyes but also in the eyes of his or her society."[136]

This background prepares the way for our understanding the double reference of τὴν κεφαλὴν αὐτοῦ here. (i) The Greek refers immediately to the man's physiological **head** both as an anatomical entity and thence as synecdoche for the whole person. In the first place such a man *devalues himself,* i.e., a head covering like that of the Romans before their gods in public devotion (or just possibly a man whose hair style indicated a loose or self-advertising sexuality) *reduced his* **self-respect** (see heading, above) and *shamed his own person.*[137] Since, however, as Moxnes rightly argues, self-respect and personal integrity reflect on other people and especially upon one to whom that person is responsible (employer, patron, slave owner, or God), (ii) this **shames his head** *also* in the sense of appearing thereby to demean *Christ or God as his Lord and Head.*

Barrett argues that **head** refers exclusively in this verse to Christ, who has been described as man's head in the previous verse.[138] However, we have already noted that Barrett approaches this verse almost exclusively within a Jewish or Jewish-Christian context, thereby inviting the criticism of Oster and others on the grounds of their extensive research into archaeological evidence about Roman religion. Allo alludes to a double meaning, noting the discussion of 2 Cor 3:18 where the Christian believer stands in contrast to Moses and his use of a covering.[139] Fee argues that the context of 2 Cor 3:18 is different, and in this he is correct, although his insistence that "there is almost no evidence . . . that men in any of the cultures (Greek, Roman, Jew) covered their heads "runs clearly counter to Oster and the other Roman specialists."[140] In the light of the discussion of honor-shame in cultural anthropology by Moxnes, Malina, and others, we may agree with Allo and with Bruce that in one sense (the more immediate) this is "a denial of man's status" but that no less it also "dishonours Christ."[141] The constant wordplay between physiological and metaphorical uses of head continues in the case of women in vv. 5-16.

This is confirmed by the comments of Murphy-O'Connor and others that (whether we are considering long, unbound hair or inappropriate head covering) what remains common to vv. 4-7 is *that which distracts attention from God or Christ in public worship* by generating a discordant, semiotic clothing code

136. Moxnes, "Honor, Shame and the Outside World," 208.

137. These two meanings of the Greek have been amply demonstrated in the discussion under 11:3 with reference to Dawes and many other writers and textual data.

138. Barrett, *First Epistle,* 250.

139. Allo, *Première Épitre,* 256.

140. Fee, *First Epistle,* 507.

141. Bruce, *1 and 2 Cor,* 104.

or hairstyle code which inevitably draws attention to the self in a way which makes the person's **head** a source of **shame** for his or her own *self-respect, the respect of congregation, and the honor of the Lord who in public worship should be the central focus of thought and attention.* In this *context of worship* Hays's otherwise trivial analogy of attending a formal dinner wearing a baseball cap carries more force than might at first appear: "perceived as rude and irreverent . . . a breach of etiquette . . ." in vv. 4-7 it constitutes attention-seeking behaviour which thereby dishonor God and shames the self.[142]

5-6 A number of the exegetical issues raised by v. 5 have already been addressed above, and the issue of **prophetic speech** is discussed in our extended notes on and exegesis of ch. 14. It is the latter which determines our translation **utters prophetic** speech as less liable to risk ecclesial assumptions drawn from modern church life about "prophesying." Part of the observed *traditions* (παραδόσεις, 11:2) probably included the Christian practice of women leading a congregation in the *Godward* ministry of *prayer,* and leading in *preaching* a pastorally applied message or discourse *from God* (see the Notes on prophetic speech in ch. 14). On the other hand, Anders Eriksson seems to imply that the appeal to traditions looks forward primarily to 11:17-34, as far as Paul is concerned, even if the Corinthians may have appealed to observance of traditions in a more secondary sense.[143] Eriksson reserves *tradition* for "core" theology, although this view might be applied to argue that the role of women in prayer and preaching is by no means contextually conditional but fundamental.

HEAD COVERING (HOODS), GENDER IDENTITY, AND SHAME OR RESPECT (11:5-6)

Head (again, κεφαλή in v. 5) has been discussed exhaustively above. Here its first reference is clearly to the woman's anatomical or physiological head, but (as in v. 4) it is extended in reference to Christ or to God and perhaps arguably (in view of its use as synecdoche) to a guardian, husband, or family *since the cultural issue of the dress code rebounds onto the shame or honour (i.e., respected status) of her family.* The key connection between the need for a *head covering* (Gk. ἀκατακαλύπτῳ, feminine privative adjective **uncovered**) and **shames** (καταισχύνει) finds precise expression in the comments of Aline Rousselle and Dale Martin.[144] The wearing of appropriate head covering (such as a hood) denoted *respect and respectability.* Within the semiotic clothing code of first-century Roman society (see above on Roland Barthes) *"a veil or hood constituted a warning: it signified that the wearer was a respectable woman and that no man dare approach her,"* i.e., as one potentially or actually sexually "available"

---

142. Hays, *First Cor,* 184.

143. A. Eriksson, *Traditions as Rhetorical Proof: Pauline Argumentation in 1 Corinthians,* ConBNT 29 (Stockholm: Almqvist & Wiksell, 1998), 73-134, 174-96, 303-4.

144. See introduction to 11:2-16; Rousselle, "Body Politics in Ancient Rome," 296-337; and Martin, *The Corinthian Body,* 229-49.

(my italics).[145] We postpone for the present whether ἀκατακαλύπτῳ may conceivably denote long hair that is "loosed" down the back, since this would generate the very same signal. If Roland Barthes showed that the semiotics of dress is far from trivial, enormous weight is provided by the context of public worship. We recall again, with Murphy-O'Connor and Richard Oster, that an issue about the semiotic signals generated by *men* at public worship introduces the principle. In vv. 4 (men) and 5 (women) the principle remains the same: self-advertisement, especially if it relates to perceptions of the worship leader as an object of sexual attraction, diverts attention from God who should be the center of undivided attention. *To employ a dress code which hints at sexual availability while leading worship is unthinkable.*

That is not to say, however, that this was the conscious intention of women who attended prophetic speech or prayer at Corinth. It is likely that for them the issue was one of freedom and equality on the basis of the gospel axiom which finds expression in such a passage as Gal 3:28. Sociology of religion confirms that "order" and "tradition" often become overwhelmed where there is a flood of "spiritual" or "charismatic" vitality and dynamism. Hence J. Gundry-Volf may plausibly allude to "the Corinthian pneumatics" praying and prophesying with unfeminine or unmasculine headdress . . . in the worship assembly where outsiders might be present and . . . thus . . . a loss of social acceptability. . . . The pneumatic head-covering practices ignored the social boundaries between male and female and thus brought shame upon themselves and their 'heads.'"[146] In other words, *they confused equality with sameness or lack of gender difference.* Collins writes: "It is probable that the situation was one that resulted from the attitude 'anything goes' (see 6:12; 10:23). . . . [But] because God has created the human genders in different ways a distinction is to be maintained when the community assembles for worship."[147]

This entirely explains why Paul perceives the **shame** of self-advertising dress and sexless, genderless dress (the removal of hair altogether by having **been shaved**) as in effect **one and the same thing**. There are many hypothetical explanations for Paul's reference to having **been shaved**. Depending on context, it may allude to the status of one convicted of prostitution, or sometimes one who has borne the **shame** of being a menial slave, but for the most part the loss of a woman's hair is taken to denote a loss of her *femininity*. By contrast, *covered* hair denotes *self-controlled sexuality.*[148] Precisely the same contrast would be implied by the semantic opposition between long, flowing hair which reaches back over the shoulders and remains unbound as a focus of view and the shaven head. In the context of social anthropology Hallpike correlates the former with "undisciplined sexuality" and the latter with "celibacy" or "sexlessness."[149] Paul states, in effect, that by confusing equality (both male and female may preach and pray in public) with the effective abolition of gender roles and gender identities (as later associated with God's decree for the creation or-

145. Rousselle, "Body Politics in Ancient Rome," 315.

146. Gundry-Volf, "Gender and Creation in 1 Cor 11:2-16," 154.

147. Collins, *First Cor,* 400 and 402. Similarly, Hays, *1 Cor,* 183 writes: "The passage does not require *subordination* of women . . . but a symbolic *distinction* between the sexes" (his italics). Collins discusses *both* head coverings *and* issues of elaborate hair styles on the part of men and women (400-403 and 406-9). Both, he argues, are at issue here.

148. See introduction to 11:2-16, and esp. R. Hallpike, "Social Hair," 256-64.

149. Hallpike, "Social Hair," 256-64.

der) people **bring shame** upon themselves; both shaming an expression of gender identity, shaming the God who decreed it, and perhaps also shaming the person or persons who were perceived as the generally more public associate of the woman (whether husband, guardian, father, or wider family). A. C. Wire may be right: some Corinthian women prophets may have insisted that the private domain of the home restricted their autonomy.[150] That is all very well, Paul replies, but (as in 8:1–11:1) do the consequences for "the other" (husband, father, or other associates) no longer remain your concern? **Shame** is not merely that which attaches to an isolated individual. What kind of preaching or prayer would cohere with bringing shame upon another simply in order to assert one's rights?

The case for interpreting ἀκατακαλύπτῳ (only here and in 11:13 in the NT) to denote *having flowing, loose hair* is not conclusive, although it is possible to envisage, with Hays, a double allusion to loose, flowing hair in conjunction with the lack of a hood or **head covering**. Hays paraphrases the reconstructed report sent to Paul: "some of the women, acting in the freedom and power of the Spirit, have begun to remove their head coverings and loose their hair when they prophesy as a sign of their freedom in Christ."[151] In other words, they want to give socio-symbolic expression to their freedom and equality; Paul insists that a socio-symbolic expression of gender identity cannot be brushed aside in the name of gospel freedom as no longer relevant (cf. Gal 3:28) since (Paul will argue) even the eschatological freedom of the gospel does not revoke expressions of the divine will established in the order of creation, or even sensitivities of perception within a surrounding culture.

Elisabeth Schüssler Fiorenza, however, adopts a radically opposing view. She asserts: "Paul does not argue in 11:2-16 for the 'creational' or 'symbolic' *difference* between women and men despite their equality in Christ, but for the custom of bound-up hair as the symbol of women's prophetic-charismatic power" (her italics).[152] Fiorenza paints a background in which Christian women who spoke as prophets at Corinth perceived "loose and unbound hair [as] a sign of their ecstatic endowment with Spirit-Sophia and a mark of true prophetic behaviour. Paul, on the other hand, is bent on curbing the prophetic frenzy. . . . Women should keep their hair bound up."[153] Such an analysis depends, however, on supposed borrowings by the women of Corinth of notions of prophecy with "dishevelled hair and head thrown back . . . typical for the maenads in the cult of Dionysos . . . Cybele, the Pythia at Delphia . . . in the worship of Isis."[154] In our discussion of prophecy in ch. 14 (see extended notes and exegesis) we shall note the convincing arguments of Christopher Forbes that appeals to such parallels are anachronistic for a first-century Roman colony and largely misplaced.[155]

Forbes carefully examines the classical sources concerning the Pythian priestess, the Delphic oracle, the cults of Dionysus and Cybele, and Virgil's description of the

---

150. Wire, *The Corinthian Women Prophets*, 15-17, 116-34, 220-24.

151. Hays, *1 Cor,* 183.

152. E. Schüssler Fiorenza, *In Memory of Her: A Feminist Theological Reconstruction of Christian Origins* (New York: Crossroad and London: SCM, 1983), 230; cf. 226-30.

153. Ibid., 228.

154. Ibid., 227.

155. See below; and C. Forbes, *Prophecy and Inspired Speech in Early Christianity and Its Hellenistic Environment,* WUNT 2:75 (Tübingen: Mohr, 1995), 103-217.

Sibyl. Euripides (c. 485-407 BC) wrote his powerful work *The Bacchae* in the fifth century BC, in which he did not hesitate to portray the hysteria of this group of almost exclusively female worshippers of Bacchus, in which escape from self-control had nothing to do with "power over the head" but only with sheer abandonment. The ruthless vengeance of Bacchus (Dionysus) upon Pentheus and those who criticized the Bacchae would not only shock a Greek audience but is so utterly removed from the spirit of Christ as to make the suggestion that Christian women perceived such a style as a "model" is frankly incredible, even leaving aside issues of dating and Roman antipathy toward the cult (excluded from Italy in the second century BC). Forbes provides a fuller discussion of the problematic character of such a hypothesis as well as its irrelevance to issues at Corinth.

Equally problematic are the attempts of Fiorenza, Horsley, and others to try to explain the meaning of ἀκατακάλυπτος on the basis of the LXX translation of רוֹשׁ פּוּעַ *(rosh porua')*, the *dishevelled hair* of the leper, in Lev 13:45.[156] In practice Greek and Hebrew lexicographers argue that whether with reference to the Hebrew MT, the LXX, or the NT, רוֹשׁ פּרוּעַ *(rosh porua')* or ἡ κεφαλὴ αὐτοῦ ἀκατακάλυπτος depends on its context for the choice between *to let go* (of hair) or *to uncover* (of head coverings), with a more general leaning toward the latter.[157] The simpler explanations of Aline Rousselle and Dale Martin allude to direct parallels of immediate contemporary practice in Roman society, thereby avoiding speculations about remote Greek or Jewish history. Moreover, the documentation of sources, texts, and inscriptions carefully collected by Mary Lefkowitz and Maureen Fant concerning women in hellenistic and Roman cultures give ample testimony to the relation between appropriate dress, personal achievement, and enjoyment by women of public honor and esteem.[158] The one reservation about Rousselle and Martin is their allusion to "veils," although Rousselle rightly changes this to "a veil or hood."[159] For as Witherington observes, κατὰ κεφαλῆς ἔχων "does not suggest a small or transparent facial veil," while if the allusion were to a heavy veil, it is difficult to imagine that it must be kept in place while the speaker is trying to articulate a public communication: "Paul is interested in a head-covering [i.e., a hood or hooded cloak] not a face covering, hence not a veil *per se*."[160]

Against Fiorenza, but with Gundry-Volf, Murphy-O'Connor, Fiddes, and others, we conclude that Paul insists on gender *difference* without any necessary inference of gender hierarchy. Fiddes sees the parallels with the order which cites God, Christ, man, and woman as primarily one of function and distinctiveness entailing covenant rather than as one of hierarchical status.[161] However, this is not a universal un-

---

156. Horsley, *1 Cor*, 153-54, "loosening a person's head-covering or hair (e.g., in Lev 13:45; Num 5:18; Philo, *Spec. Leg.* 3:60 . . . *unbound hair*," i.e., in 1 Cor 11:5; cf. Schüssler Fiorenza, *In Memory of Her*, 230; Schrage, *Der erste Brief*, 2:507.

157. BDB (1980 ed.), 828-29 on the Hebrew; BAGD, 29, Grimm-Thayer, 21, Louw-Nida, 2:8, on the Greek; with apparently no occurrence in papyri (absent from MM). Cf. further Polybius, 15.27.2.

158. Lefkowitz and Fant, *Women's Life in Greece and Rome*, 104 (sect. 107), 157-60 (sects. 158-69).

159. Rousselle, "Body Politics," 315. H. Frör, *You Wretched Corinthians!* 60, speaks only of "veils."

160. Witherington, *Women in the Earliest Churches*, 83.

161. Fiddes, "'Woman's Head Is Man': A Doctrinal Reflection upon a Pauline Text," 370-83.

derstanding of these verses. Margaret Thrall insists that the issue remains one of "subordination," although here again we need to recall the complexities of the debates about the meaning of **head** (see above).[162] A particular approach is urged by R. T. France: "Injunctions to women to submit to men are not applied to the structures of society (e.g., queens, judges, employers) but to the married relationship."[163] France sees this as conclusive for 1 Cor 14:34-5, 1 Tim 2:11, 12 and Eph 5:23, and *"may"* (his italics) apply here to 11:5-7.[164] France's argument is difficult to support in full detail. At the same time the arguments of Craig S. Keener that a primary (but not exclusive) emphasis falls here upon married women and the effects of their dress style on their husbands deserves serious consideration in the light of the verses which follow.[165] This is a major context, but it does not justify restricting the translation of γυνή to *wife* rather than **woman** (NRSV, NIV, REB, NJB) as if the emphasis were exclusive.

Several explanations have been offered for the last clause of this verse: ἓν γάρ ἐστιν καὶ τὸ αὐτὸ τῇ ἐξυρημένῃ. BDF underline the sense of the woman's being **one and the same as a woman whose head had been shaved**, although Collins stresses the lighter touch of sarcasm here.[166] The two most widespread explanations are: (i) if she really wishes to dissolve the socio-symbolic expression of gender distinctiveness, this is tantamount to adopting the sexless symbolic expression of the shaven head (see above, esp. in Hallpike); (ii) if she is really bent on dressing like a sexually "available" woman, she might as well accept the public humiliation apportioned out to women caught in sexual misdemeanors. No doubt Paul intends this to enact a rhetorical shock: do you really want to **shame** yourself, your family, and your God in such a way? Or alternatively: are you really serious about no longer wanting to be honored as a **woman**, or do you genuinely want to use "gospel freedom" to eradicate *all* that relates to gender distinctiveness? Which of these two interpretations we accept will depend upon our exegesis and understanding of the whole verse and the situation behind it. Fee observes, "The shame seems clearly to be related to her becoming like a man with regard to her hair . . . blurring male/female relationships in general and sexual distinctions in particular."[167] Classical literature contains examples of the blurring of gender complementarity in lesbian relations in the context of "cropped" or "shaved" hair, which coheres with arguments above, including Murphy-O'Connor's allusion to male homosexuality in v. 4.[168]

Verse 6 adds rhetorical force to v. 5 but largely repeats the point, explicating appeal to choice by a deliberative rhetoric concerning future action (for advantage or disadvantage), which nevertheless also embodies an epideictic rhetoric of praise or blame (**shame** or honor) and even a forensic rhetoric of accusation or acceptance (**let her have it cropped close . . . or . . . shaved . . . [or] let her retain her head cover-**

---

162. Thrall, *1 and 2 Cor,* 78-79. See also Ortkemper, *1 Korintherbrief,* 102-3.

163. R. T. France, *Women in the Church's Ministry: A Test-Case for Biblical Hermeneutics* (Carlisle: Paternoster, 1995), 36.

164. Ibid., 47-48.

165. C. S. Keener, *Paul, Women, Wives: Marriage and Women's Ministry in the Letters of Paul* (Peabody, Mass.: Hendrickson, 1992), 32-36.

166. BDF, sect. 194 (1); supported further by Robertson and Plummer, *First Epistle,* 230. Ξυρόω tends to denote **to shave**, whereas κείρω may mean *to cut short.* Cf. Collins, *First Cor,* 409.

167. Fee, *First Epistle,* 511.

168. Fee, *First Epistle,* n. 81, cites Lucian, *Fugitivi* 27 and *Dialogoi Hetairikoi* 5.3.

ing).[169] Paul introduces κείπω as a part synonym for ξυρόω, except that the former denotes the act of **cropping** hair very **close** to the head, whereas the latter denotes **shaving** off all hair.[170] Dio Cassius quotes an aphorism ascribed to Tiberius, "I want my sheep to be sheared (κείρεσθαι), not to be shaved (ἀποξύρεσθαι).[171] Some argue that the former term denotes a "boylike" style, with possible hints of lesbian gender-crossing, while the second denotes the shaven state of one who is either sexless or shamed for uncontrolled behavior. However, the terms sometimes function as virtual synonyms (Acts 18:18, κειράμενος . . . τὴν κεφαλήν, εἶχεν [παῦλος] γὰρ εὐχήν), and allowance must be made for stylistic variation. Robertson and Plummer paraphrase, "If a woman refuses to be veiled, let her be consistently masculine and cut her hair close."[172] The middle voice denotes the agent of action as the woman herself, performing a self-involving or reflexive action. Chrysostom regards this verse as a rhetorical *reductio ad absurdum* which sharpens the point to the axiom "If you cast away the 'covering' appointed by divine law, then cast away the 'covering' appointed by nature. . . . Thereby she falls from her proper honour."[173]

The use of expanded rhetorical repetition here seems to provide a decisive objection to Alan Padgett's view that vv. 4-7 represent a Corinthian statement which Paul rejects.[174] When Paul cites a slogan from Corinth (e.g., 6:12; 8:1[b]; 10:23) he does so succinctly. In any case, Padgett's claims about "coiffure" also remain open to question, for reasons noted above. We should allow the contemporary Roman evidence concerning societal perception (Rousselle, Martin, Lefkowitz, and Flint) to interact with the relevant theological and eschatological dialectic identified above (esp. Gundry-Volf).

7-9   Although normally we have been considering one verse at a time, to guard against an atomistic misunderstanding of each verse we shall examine vv. 7-9 as one theme which draws its force from the role of Gen 1:26-28 and Gen 2:18, 22 in Jewish and Christian traditions, with particular reference to the specific force of εἰκών, **image** (Heb. צֶלֶם, *tselem*) in Gen 1:26-27 (LXX) and the special semantic range of δόξα, **glory** (Heb. usually כָּבוֹד, *kabhodh*) which may also represent ὁμοίωσις, *likeness* (Heb. דְמוּת, *demuth*) in Gen 1:26-27 (LXX). If we give due care to the nuances and force of **image** and **glory** in the biblical writings, esp. Hebrew, it becomes clear that the emphasis falls less on hierarchy as such (although this has a place) than on *relationality*.

169. Cf. M. M. Mitchell, *Paul and the Rhetoric of Reconciliation*, 8-13 and 260-63; also Eriksson, *Traditions as Rhetorical Proof*, 30-63, but with little reference to 11:2-16.
170. BAGD, 427.
171. Dio Cassius, *History of Rome* 15.10.5.
172. Robertson and Plummer, *First Epistle*, 231.
173. Chrysostom, *1 Cor. Hom.*, 26:4.
174. Padgett, "Paul on Women in the Church: The Contradiction of Coiffure of 1 Cor 11:2-16," 69-86.

IMAGE OF GOD, GLORY, AND GENDER DIFFERENTIATION (11:7-9)

Conzelmann rightly includes an extended note on εἰκών as a key to these verses.[175] In classical Greek εἰκών "is an image, work of art, picture . . . also a pattern; also a shadow and a reflected image, an imprinted image."[176] For Plato the cosmos constitutes εἰκὼν τοῦ νοητοῦ θεὸς αἰσθητός (*Timaeus* 92C), i.e., a *visible manifestation* or contingent picture which reflects the otherwise inaccessible but intelligible mind of God. In the LXX there are shifts of meaning, but the notion of *visible model* still remains. In particular the figure of Wisdom manifests, radiates, and mediates the otherwise inaccessible, transcendent reality of God.[177] In the Epistle to the Hebrews Christ is portrayed as "the exact imprint of God's very being," i.e., Christ "makes 'real' the otherwise hidden, mysterious God who is Other and Beyond" on the basis of the author's conflation of the themes of Word, Wisdom, Image, and Glory (cf. John 1:1-3; 1 Cor 8:6; Col 1:16-17; Heb 1:1-3).[178] The OT prohibition of images of God by humankind is fundamental since God's innermost being is not captured by human social construction but through God's self-revelation in word and deed. However, the traditional view that this prohibition serves to prevent humankind from objectifying the living God under static forms (Gerhard von Rad) does not go far enough. J. Moltmann rightly insists that the prohibition is bound up with God's decree that "human persons are to radiate his presence"; humans cannot *construct* images of God, for God purposes that *human lives should manifest the presence and love of God* as actively reflecting and radiating this reality as *themselves* **the image** of God.[179]

In the context of Genesis 1 and 2, therefore, man as male first comes onto the cosmic scene as the **image** which is to manifest God in his life and deeds, since authentic personhood entails living "for" and "in relation to" an Other, not as one centered upon the self. This relationality is then extended in Genesis 2 by the creation of woman **out of** (ἐκ) man, in which man now enjoys a twofold relationality to God and to woman, each as "Other." Woman is both "other" than man-as-male and yet equally reflects or manifests what man is. *For the relationality of human personhood lies neither in absolute difference from, nor in absolute identity with, "the Other."*[180] As Fee argues, a chiasmic structure with v. 10 (or vv. 10-12) underlines the axis of mutuality.[181] Fee lays the groundwork for understanding Paul's use of **glory** in relation to **image** and to the

---

175. Conzelmann, *1 Cor,* 187-88.

176. Ibid., 187.

177. Gerhard von Rad and G. Kittel, "δόξα," in *TDNT,* 2:233-55; also G. Bertram, "ὕπσος," 8:602-14; H. Hegermann, "δόξα," *EDNT,* 1:344-48; F.-W. Eltester, *Eikon im NT,* BZNW 23 (Berlin, 1958).

178. Thiselton, "Epistle to the Hebrews," in J. W. Rogerson and J. D. G. Dunn (eds.), *Commentary 2000* (to be retitled) (Grand Rapids: Eerdmans, forthcoming) on Heb 1:1-3.

179. J. Moltmann, *Man: Christian Anthropology* (Eng. trans., London: SPCK, 1971), 108 and 109.

180. For a modern theological discussion, cf. Thiselton, *Interpreting God and the Postmodern Self* (Grand Rapids: Eerdmans and Edinburgh: T. & T. Clark, 1995), 13, 22-26, 47-58, 73, and 129-30, and esp. P. Ricoeur, *Oneself as Another* (Eng. trans., Chicago: University of Chicago Press, 1992); D. F. Ford, *Self and Salvation* (Cambridge: Cambridge University Press, 1999), esp. 30-72; also, for a distinctive philosophical approach, E. Levinas, *Totality and Infinity: An Essay on Exteriority* (Pittsburgh: Duquesne University Press, 1969).

181. Fee, *First Epistle,* 514.

mutuality of v. 12 when he asserts: "Paul probably means that the existence of the one brings honor and praise to the other. By creating man in his own image God set his own glory in man.... [Yet] man by himself is not complete ... without a companion ... one who is like him but different from him; one who is uniquely his own 'glory.' ...Man ... 'glories' in her.... Paul's point ... is that in the creation narrative this did not happen the other way around. . . ."[182]

This understanding is substantiated and corroborated by the biblical semantic boundaries of δόξα and כבוד (Heb. *kabhodh*). Two definitive discussions by A. Feuillet (1974 and 1975) place the issue in its proper perspective.[183] He rightly rejects the understanding of δόξα as *reflection* in v. 7b (cf. REB, *a woman reflects the glory of man;* and more explicitly NRSV, *woman is the reflection* (or glory) *of man*.[184] Equally, he rejects Moffatt's understanding of δόξα as *supremacy*.[185] **Glory** denotes "a sign of honor."[186] In an objective sense, God's **glory** is "the manifestation of his ... attributes" (although we dissent from Feuillet that this denotes "his power" rather than his mercy, love, or self-giving).[187] In Mal 1:6 Yahweh demands, "if I am your father, where then is my honour [*où donc est my gloire*]." In the creation accounts, however, just as man is to exhibit the attributes of God in his life and role (i.e., give God honor), so the dignity of woman is of such a nature that she complements man with "an incomparably richer reality" which is "irreplaceable" (*une réalité incomparablement plus riche . . . et irremplaçable*).[188] In this sense Paul provides no hint of "inferiority." *Because of women, men is all the more man, just as because of men woman is all the more woman, and as humankind woman and man manifest the divine attributes* (e.g., of power and love but not "stereotypically") *as expressions of God's creative being.* Nevertheless, Feuillet also insists, *there is neither confusion nor precise symmetry,* for "she is different from him," as Paul uses Gen 2:18-25 to emphasize: "that which provides the greatness *(la grandeur)* and dignity of woman is of such a nature as that by which she distinguishes herself from man, that is to say, in her own role which has been specifically assigned by the Creator."[189] Feuillet concludes that this has nothing whatever to do with any supposed "antifeminism" in Paul, for this differentiation is defined in terms of greatness and glory, not inferiority.

Karl Barth returns to this point repeatedly in the four volumes (four "parts") which comprise "Volume 3" of his *Church Dogmatics,* which deal with creation.[190] He writes, "In all that characterizes him as man he will be thrown back upon woman, or as woman upon man. . . . No other distinction between man and man goes so deep as that in which the human male and the human female are so utterly different from

---

182. Ibid., 516 and 517.

183. Feuillet, "L'homme 'gloire de Dieu' et la femme 'gloire de l'homme' (1 Cor XI:7b)," 161-82; and "La dignité et la rôle de la femme d'après quelques textes pauliniens: comparaison avec l'Ancien Testament," 157-91.

184. Feuillet, "La dignité," 159-60.

185. Ibid., 160.

186. Ibid.

187. Ibid., 161.

188. Ibid. and "'L'homme 'gloire de Dieu,'" 161-82.

189. Feuillet, "La dignité," 161; expounded further in "L'homme 'gloire de Dieu' et la femme 'gloire de l'homme,'" 161-82.

190. Barth, *CD,* 3/1, 203-4 (on 1 Cor 11:7), 288-311 (on Gen 2:18-25), 324-29; 3/2, 309-24 (man and woman in Genesis 2); 3/4, 116-240 ("Man and Woman").

each other. . . . Limitation . . . characterizes the encounter between man and woman. . . . Its special glory. . . . Its glory, mystery, significance are disclosed in its limits."[191] Barth is not unaware of the complexities of overlapping masculinity or femininity, yet gender differentiation is part of people acknowledging their sex and not denying it: "he should rejoice in it rather than be a~~~~~~~~~~~~~~"[192] *For the complementarity experienced in encounter with "the other" both on the part of man and on the part of woman arises at the heart of the "glory" manifested in identity, difference, and human creatureliness. This even explains the allusion to Christ and God, who also are more "what they are" in relation to the Other, which in turn becomes more impressively "visible"* (cf. כבוד, Heb. *kabhodh*) *in relation to creaturely humanity.* Full humanness, Barth concludes following Genesis and Paul, is not "male *or* female" but "male *and* female." . . . "They are now a pair. . . . Only in this way is he [man as humankind] genuinely man" (Barth's italics).[193] It is scarcely surprising that, in addition to Genesis, Barth uses 1 Cor 11:2-16 as an exegetical resource. As in 1 Corinthians 15, Barth the theologian explicates a Pauline understanding which partially eludes a number of exegetes, and in this verse coheres with the exegetical arguments of Feuillet as well as with the semantic range and force of δόξα. The heart of the meaning of כבוד–δόξα is that which makes impressive or weighty the person or thing that is glorious. *Hence in John 2 Christ shows his* **glory** *in his disproportionate concern for a humble peasant wedding. Such compassion and implicit humiliation is what for John shows Christ to be Christ in a manifest and visible way.*

In translation, then, it is essential to signal Paul's explicit use of the contrastive μέν and δέ: we render **a man for his part. . . . Woman, on the other hand. . . .** The allusion, which follows, to the sequence of creation moves from Gen 1:26-28 to Gen 2:18-25. We have only to read Philo to observe that in Paul's era this was not necessarily understood as a brute report rather than pointing to socio-symbolic differentiation. Thus Wayne Meeks observes that while ambiguities and loose ends still remain in Paul's account of gender equality and gender difference, for the most part he stresses gender equality in the gospel (cf. Gal 3:28; 1 Cor 7:2-4) but "objects to *symbolic* disregard for sexual differences in the dress of male and female prophets."[194] It would be impossible for a man (or a woman) to glory *in the otherness of the other* if gender differentiation were reduced so that "the other" became "the same"; and it would be impossible for man or woman *to glory* (in the Christian sense) in another human person if they were not accorded dignity and respect as a fellow human being of equal status in the gospel.

With Judith Gundry-Volf (1997) and with P. J. Harland (1998) we conclude that gender differentiation relates to that which God wills, decrees, and expresses in creation or in the creation order. For us a confirmation of this lies in the continuing principle of

191. *CD,* 3/4, 118 and 129.
192. Ibid., 149.
193. *CD,* 3/4, 149 and 150.
194. Meeks, *The First Urban Christians,* 161, and esp. "The Image of the Androgyne: Some Uses of a Symbol in Earliest Christianity," 165-208. In this latter work Meeks argues that in an era when gender differentiation was emphasized (esp. in Roman Imperial times) Paul stresses an equality and mutuality in principle, but insists on the continuing validity of *symbolic expressions* of gender difference. This is clear in 11:2-16 (although Meeks sees 14:33-36 as a non-Pauline rejection of equality and mutuality).

"order" and differentiation expressed in eschatology (see below on 15:24-28). Harland argues this point in relation to the laws of Deut 12:1–26:15 (and not least 22:5): gender differentiation and its expression in the semiotic code of clothes (Deut 22:5) *depends neither on cultus* (cf. A. Phillips on anti-Caananite legislation), nor *issues to do with warfare,* but because of "the order of the world . . . diversity and order . . . characteristic of creation . . . a distinction in the creation of male and female. . . . Man's essence is in two sexes; humanity exists in community . . . centred around the creation of male and female."[195] Judith Gundry-Volf concludes: "Paul's main point is that man and woman are both the *glory of another* and therefore both have an obligation not to cause shame to their 'heads' . . . since they are the glory of *different* persons — man is the glory of God, and woman is the glory of man — they must use different means to avoid shaming their 'heads.' But Paul appeals to creation to show their obligation to bring glory — each to the particular one whose glory they are by creation — which they do through distinctive masculine and feminine hairstyles [or head coverings]" (her italics).[196]

10 A secondary gloss in certain patristic writers and VSS (but not in major uncials) inserts κάλυμμα, *hood, covering,* or *veil,* to explicate the meaning of ἐξουσίαν (e.g., Irenaeus, Tertullian, Jerome, coptic bohairic).[197] However, this is a witness to the early perceptions of the problematic meaning rather than to a genuine textual variant.[198]

Fee regards this as "one of the truly difficult texts in this letter."[199] Nevertheless, although **on account of the angels** has invited speculation since the era of Tertullian (c. AD 200), the problematic status of ἐξουσία arises from generation after generation of interpreters and translators rendering the term *authority.* This lies behind the well-known polarization of opinion between the traditional view that woman's head should *a sign of authority over her* (in which *a sign of* is inserted without any basis in the Greek) and Morna Hooker's now famous "solution" (1964) that *authority on her head* denotes her own active authority to use prophetic utterance as an empowered woman.[200] She writes, "The head-covering . . . also serves as the sign of the ἐξουσία which is given to the woman . . . — authority: in prayer and prophecy. . . ."[201]

195. Harland, "Menswear and Womenswear: A Study of Deut 22:5," 76; cf. 73-76; cf. A. Phillips, *Deuteronomy,* CBC (Cambridge: Cambridge University Press, 1973), 145; C. M. Carmichael, *The Laws of Deuteronomy* (Ithaca: Cornell University Press, 1974), 147-49; C. Houtman, "Another Look at Forbidden Mixtures" *VT* 34 (1984): 226-28; P. D. Miller, *Deuteronomy* (Philadelphia: John Knox, 1990), 161-63; see also Harland, "Menswear and Womenswear," 75, n. 28. Harland applies the principle to the blurring of gender distinctions in homosexuality, and to Houtman's note about "differentiation" in creation between light and dark, water and land.
196. Gundry-Volf, "Gender and Creation in 1 Cor 11:2-16," 157.
197. Irenaeus, in Migne, *PG,* 7:524B; Jerome, in *PL,* 25:439A.
198. Cf. Metzger, *Textual Commentary,* 2d ed., 495; and Héring, *First Epistle,* 107-8.
199. Fee, *First Epistle,* 518.
200. Hooker, "Authority on Her Head: An Examination of 1 Cor 11:10," rpt. in Hooker, *From Adam to Christ: Essays on Paul,* 113-20, from *NTS* 10 (1964): 410-16.
201. Ibid., 119-20.

ἐξουσία: POWER? AUTHORITY? CONTROL? OVER WHAT? (11:10)

It is noteworthy that NJB and NIV have *sign of [the] authority:* NAB has *a sign of submission;* while NRSV has *symbol of authority;* all in contrast to AV/KJV's omission of *sign;* for this cause ought the woman to have power on her head (by 1881 RV inserted a *sign of* in italics).[202] K. N. Taylor's *Living Letters* renders the Greek *a sign that she is under man's authority;* while J. B. Phillips paraphrases, *an outward sign of man's authority.* However, while it retains the intrusive *sign of,* REB clearly follows Hooker by translating, *a woman must have the sign of her [the woman's own] authority on her head,* in contrast to NJB's *a sign of the authority over her;* while NIV remains neutral and can be interpreted either way.

We should note in passing that most patristic commentators saw no problem in understanding ἐξουσία in an active sense as metonymy for *a sign of power over.* Chrysostom observes: "Being covered is a mark of subjection and authority," and Theophylact explicitly understands the metonymic *sign of power.*[203] Irenaeus understands κάλυμμα here.[204] However, Edwards (1885), Ramsay (1907), Robertson and Plummer (1911), and Allo (1956) all anticipate the view for which credit is given to Morna Hooker by comparing "symbol of one's own authority and that of another's" as being linguistically symmetrical and equally possible.[205] Conzelmann follows Kittel and Foerster in seeing an intertextual resonance between the dual meaning of Heb. שַׁלַט *(shalat),* which denotes both *to have power over* and *to conceal,* and Aram. שַׁלְטוֹנְיָה *(shaltonayia)* (sh-l-t-w-nyh) to denote "something like 'headband', 'veil.'"[206] Foerster argues that such a resonance cannot be denied, although he concedes that it remains only conjecture.[207] Kümmel, Barrett, and Schrage, however, offer more penetrating criticisms, including the point that such a resonance would lie entirely beyond the awareness of the Corinthian readers.[208] The fullest discussion of the hypothesis can be found in Allo's extended Note on this difficult verse.[209] Allo traces the complexities of the rabbinic texts but also asks whether Corinthian readers could be expected to appreciate the Semitic background.[210] He concludes that because of the context **on account of the angels** ἐξουσία may signify a woman's *power against* attack by evil angels (along the lines of Tertullian, *Against Marcion,* 5:8) and *On the Veiling of Virgins,* 7); but in the end he follows the argument advocated by Edwards and Ramsay and later developed by Hooker that a veiled or hooded woman has her own power of protection in public because of what she wears.[211]

---

202. However, NRSV points out that *a symbol of* is added, in a footnote.

203. Chrysostom, *1 Cor. Hom.,* 26:5; Theophylact, "Epistulae Primae," in Migne 124:697.

204. Irenaeus, *Against Heresies,* 1:8:2.

205. Edwards, *First Epistle,* 277; W. M. Ramsay, *The Cities of St Paul,* 202-5; Robertson and Plummer, *First Epistle,* 233-34; Allo, *Première Épitre,* 266-67.

206. Conzelmann, *1 Cor,* 189; cf. W. Foerster, "ἐξουσία," *TDNT,* 2:573-74; and G. Kittel, "Die 'Macht' auf dem Haupt (1 Kor 11:10)," in *Rabbinica* (Leipzig, *Arbeiten zur Religionsgeschichte des Urchristentums* 1/3, 1920), 20.

207. Foerster, "ἐξουσία," 574.

208. Barrett, *First Epistle,* 254; Schrage, *Der erste Brief,* 2:513.

209. Allo, *Première Épitre,* 263-68, esp. 164. Allo alludes to the Jerusalem Talmud *Shabbath* 6:8b (on Isa 3:18-21) for the Aramaic and the root שַׁלַט *(shalat).*

210. Ibid., 264.

211. Ibid., 267.

When this view is placed within its proper historical context in Roman society (described above with reference to Dale Martin and Aline Rousselle), this demonstrates how seriously the traditional controversy about "authority" was misconceived and misleading. As A. C. Wire and many others have urged, many women prophets suffered peer-group pressure to throw aside their hoods (or just possibly but less probably the binding of their hair) in the name of gospel freedom and gender equality.[212] Paul insists, however, that they **keep control of** (how people perceive) **their heads**, because the issue here (as throughout 8:1–11:1 or even 8:1–14:40) remains that of assertive autonomy (ἔξεστιν, 6:12, 10:23; cf. ἐξουσία, *I have the right to . . .*) *versus self-control* or an ethic of moderation and restraint (ἐξουσία . . . ἔξεστιν).[213] Although ἔχειν often means *to have,* abundant examples of its use to denote **to keep,** *to hold, to retain,* also occur in the NT.[214] Moreover, ἐπί with the genitive (here ἐπὶ τῆς κεφαλῆς) does not always have the force of power *over;* it often denotes control **of** something as well as (in Hooker's argument) *on* something.[215] If a woman exercises **the control** that exemplifies respectability in Roman society, and retains the semiotic code of gender differentiation in public, "with the veil on her head she can go anywhere in security and profound respect."[216] This extends to the act of using prophetic speech in public worship, but (against M. D. Hooker) is not restricted to being specifically a sign of "authority" to use prophetic speech as such. The *form* of the semiotic code may be culturally variable, but the need to express some kind of semiotic of gender differentiation belongs to the created order. As Gundry-Volf urges, the two principles overlap here.[217]

Much speculation surrounds the interpretation of διὰ τοὺς ἀγγέλους. (1) Ephrem of Syria and Ambrosiaster (followed by Cajetan) interpreted **the angels** respectively as priests *(sacerdotes)* or bishops *(episcopi),* supposedly on the basis of "the angels of the churches" in Rev 2:1, 8, 12, 18; 3:1, 7, 14.[218] (2) Tertullian, as is well known, understands **angels** to refer to angels "fallen from God and heaven on account of their lustful desire for earthly women *(ob concupiscentiam feminarum).*"[219] The *hood* or *veil* protects the women who worship from the gaze of these fallen angels whom Tertullian identifies with the "watchers" of Gen 6:1-2 (i.e., the sons of God who desired the daughters of men). Tertullian ascribes 11:10 to the impropriety of fallen angels in a second passage, this time emphasizing the need for clothing which is not only protective but also modest.[220] (3) Augustine, Peter Lombard, Aquinas, Grotius,

212. Wire, *The Corinthian Women Prophets,* 13-14, 111-13, 131-34, and 181-86.
213. Cf. BAGD, 234-36.
214. BAGD, 331-35; Grimm-Thayer, 265-67.
215. BAGD, 285-89. BDF, sect. 234, seems to privilege "over," but this is circular since it already describes contents of "authority" under (6). Nigel Turner points out that "ἐξουσία ἐπί c gen is exclusively biblical" (*Grammar of NT Greek,* 3:271). See further Grimm-Thayer, 231-36.
216. Robertson and Plummer, *First Epistle,* 232; cf. D. B. Martin and A. Rousselle, above.
217. Gundry-Volf, "Gender and Creation in 1 Cor 11:2-16," 160-71.
218. Ephrem, *Commentarii in ep. d. Pauli* (Venice, 1892), 70; Ambrosiaster in Migne, *PL,* 17.240C, *Angelos episcopos dicit, sicut in Apocalypsi Iohannis.*
219. Tertullian, *On the Veiling of Virgins,* 7.
220. Tertullian, *Against Marcion,* 5:8.

Estius, and others identify **the angels** with *holy angels* who as hosts of heaven participate in the worship of the church. Augustine argues that Paul's allusion to the covering of the head here "is pleasing to the holy angels" on account of the purity and propriety of the heavenly realm.[221] Aquinas cites Augustine's interpretation and records Peter Lombard as following the same view.[222] (4) Theodoret more specifically alludes to the guardian angels, or protecting angels, of Matt 18:10.[223] (5) Another view cites the angels as "covering" themselves in God's presence in Isa 6:2, and proposes that v. 10 means *in imitation of* the angels.

Many modern commentators conflate (3) and (4) either in a general sense of "on display" to "the whole universe" (Fee) or "to glorify God in the company of the heavenly host" (Wire; cf. Schrage).[224] J. Fitzmyer sheds limited light on this verse with reference to the angelology of Qumran.[225] Two passages mention the presence of angels at sacred gatherings: 1QM 7:4-6, in which "holy angels accompany their armies"; and 1QS 2:3-11, in which "holy angels are in their congregation."[226] Because of the presence of the angels, both the volunteer for the holy war in 1QM (the War Scroll), and members of the congregation in 1QS (the Rule of the Congregation or Manual of Discipline) "had to be perfect not only in spirit but also in body."[227] Fitzmyer compares this with Lev 21:17-23, which excludes those with "defects" and suggests a further parallel between "the unveiled head of a woman" and the analogy of "a bodily defect."[228] He concludes, "διὰ τοὺς ἀγγέλους in 1 Cor 11:10 is to be explained in terms of Qumran angelology," not least because this proposed link is not an isolated one between Paul and Qumran.[229]

Although Fitzmyer's approach converges with that of Cadbury and is accepted by Kistemaker, Herbert Braun rejects it by preferring to return to the notion of protection from evil forces, while Héring and Hurd simply regard the proposed parallel as respectively implausible or distant.[230] We have described Fitzmyer's proposal as one of "limited light" because on one side we may doubt the specificity of his suggestion while on the other side we may affirm the more

---

221. Augustine, *On the Trinity,* 12:7:10.

222. Thomas Aquinas, *Super Epistolas s. Pauli Lectura,* sect. 614, cap. 11, lect. 3, 349.

223. Theodoret, in Migne, *PG,* 82:312D-313A.

224. Fee, *First Epistle,* 521; Wire, *Corinthian Women Prophets,* 128; Schrage, *Der erste Brief,* 2:515, n. 167.

225. Fitzmyer, "A Feature of Qumran Angelology and the Angels of 1 Cor 11:10," 48-58 (rpt. in J. Murphy-O'Connor [ed.], *Paul and Qumran* [London: Chapman, 1968], 31-48), rejects this view.

226. Ibid., 41-42.

227. Ibid., 42.

228. Ibid., 43 and 44.

229. Ibid., 44-45.

230. H. J. Cadbury, "A Qumran Parallel to Paul," *HTR* 51 (1958): 1-2; Kistemaker, *1 Cor,* 376-77; H. Braun, "Qumran und das NT," *TRu* 29 (1963): 213-14; Héring, *First Epistle,* 108; Hurd, *Origin of 1 Corinthians,* 184, n. 4.

general point that in NT traditions from Paul to the Revelation of John Christian theology shares the Jewish tradition that Christians worship the transcendent God of heaven in company with the heavenly host.[231] In such a public context of universal cosmic reverence, Paul urges, the axiom "as in heaven, so on earth" should apply to the recognition of respect, reverence, and order which receives symbolic and semiotic expression in the ways indicated. Paul attacks the notion that individual autonomy (questions about "my rights," "my freedom") genuinely remains unqualified in the presence of the otherness of the other (created gender) and the heavenly hosts who perform their due roles and tasks.

One final point may be made. Among the Jewish traditions which find their way into the NT, those in which **angels** are perceived as "guardians of order" as well as "participants in the church's praise to God" provide the best clue to Paul's meaning.[232] Again, this element is noted in the Qumran writings by Fitzmyer, and the role of their "ordering" structures and nations has been emphasized by G. B. Caird among others.[233] In Gal 3:19 Paul observes that the law was put into operation "through angels by a mediator," which coheres with Caird's argument. On the other hand, a recent attempt to argue that in 1 Cor 11:10 Paul alludes to "evil spirit beings" runs against lexicographical evidence for Paul's use of ἄγγελοι, especially with the definite article.[234]

11-12   AV/KJV follows D², K, L, and the Vulgate in transposing the sequence of the clauses in v. 11, but all the early major MSS have the order adopted by UBS 4th ed. and translated here.

No single modern English VS translates the Greek exactly as it stands without addition or modification, if v. 11 is to read as good English. REB eliminates the double negative οὔτε . . . χωρίς (with the genitive) by translating *woman is as essential to man as man to woman.* NRSV and NIV translate, *is not independent of,* but this adds a nuance which goes beyond the adverb χωρίς, which means *separated from,* or *without,* when with a genitive of person. NJB preserves *without,* and with justice renders the οὔτε clause as **is nothing** *without. . . .* We are tempted to follow BAGD's translation, *neither (is) woman (anything) apart from man, nor man from woman.*[235] It seems best to combine BAGD's accurate **apart from** with NJB's idiomatic rendering of the double

231. Cf. Ps 138:1; *Benedicite* (Song of the Three Holy Children), 37; and early Christian liturgies.

232. Hays, *First Cor,* 188.

233. G. B. Caird, *Principalities and Powers,* 17-18.

234. Cf. the rather idiosyncratic and more popular study by Graeme Carlé, *Because of the Angels: Unveiling 1 Cor 11:2-16* (Wellington, N.Z.: Emmaus Road, 1998), 65. Lexicographical evidence is added together from mixed sources. On the other hand, Robertson and Plummer, *First Epistle,* 233, observe that ἄγγελοι "always means good angels" when it is used with the definite article in the NT. Padgett's suggestion about human messengers is also widely rejected.

235. BAGD, 890.

negative, although we then have to add **although** at the price of disturbing the symmetry of οὔτε . . . οὔτε. . . . The emphatic πλήν, **nevertheless**, on the other hand, fully justifies this placing of emphasis by implication.[236]

It is also difficult to translate ἐν κυρίῳ both accurately (as NIV, NRSV, NJB, *in the Lord*) and intelligibly (as REB, *in the Lord's fellowship*). In spite of arguments to the contrary by Barrett and Fee, since he has appealed both to the order of creation and to societal convention, it seems that Paul now uses his third "lens" or "point of reference" as that of eschatology or the order of the gospel.[237] Paul almost certainly means to say that gender differentiation is decreed in creation, expressed in convention, and not abrogated in the order of the gospel, i.e., *in the Lord* in the sense of *among the Lord's people,* or more strictly **as those in the Lord**. On the other hand, Collins understands the phrase to emphasize "similarity" in the Lord, even if "difference" still has a part to play on the basis of creation.[238] Whereas the creation order entails a differentiation that may also embody a hint of priority, at least in terms of the Genesis narrative, Paul adds that in the gospel differentiation is determined more explicitly by a principle of mutuality and reciprocity. *There could be no reciprocity or mutuality unless each was differentiated from the other.* Even so, the very experience of human birth in the natural or created order demonstrates that the principle of mutual interdependence does not originate, Marcion-like, with the new order of the gospel *in the Lord* or **among the Lord's people**. For if the Genesis narratives seem to suggest the priority of man over woman in terms of a primordial decree, at the same time the everyday experience of birth reminds man of his dependence on woman for his very existence in the world.

Fee rightly observes, "With these two sets of sentences, in each of which woman and man are in balanced pairs, Paul qualified the preceding argument."[239] The strong force of πλήν, **nevertheless**, confirms this. Moreover, Fee points out that "a perfect double chiasm" places the two sentences in a close inverted correspondence with the thrust of vv. 8-9; ἀνὴρ ἐκ γυναικὸς ἀλλὰ γυνὴ ἐξ ἀνδρός . . . γυνὴ διὰ τὸν ἄνδρα (vv. 8-9) . . . οὔτε γυνὴ χωρὶς ἀνδρὸς οὔτε ἀνὴρ χωρὶς γυναικός . . . ὁ ἀνὴρ διὰ τῆς γυναικός.[240] Paul's rhetorical artistry is plain to see here. Yet the theology is more vital and breathtaking. In a way that almost anticipates the subtleties of Paul Ricoeur's great work *Oneself as Another* Paul insists that true human relationality entails *otherness* and indeed *respect for the otherness of the other* as a necessary basis for true reciprocity, mutuality,

236. Cf. Gundry-Volf, "Gender and Creation," 163.

237. Ibid., 169. J. Murphy-O'Connor also refers this to the new creation or gospel ("Sex and Logic," 497-98). Barrett, however, understands the phrase in more individualistic terms: *"in the realm of the Christian life; perhaps, in the Lord's intention."* However, he adds rightly that the two themes concern both "the original creation and its restoration" (*First Epistle,* 255); Fee also thinks that Paul still argues "in general terms" (*First Epistle,* 524).

238. Collins, *First Cor,* 403.

239. Fee, *First Epistle,* 522.

240. Ibid., 523.

and relationity that constitutes what it is to be human.[241] Yet he adds that this in turn depends on how these roles are fulfilled in relation to God's will as creator who orders the world (τὰ δὲ πάντα ἐκ τοῦ θεοῦ, **the source of everything is God**) and to God's saving action through Christ as Lord of the church (ἐν κυρίῳ, **among the Lord's people**).

13 The aorist imperative κρίνατε (v. 13) denotes either a punctiliar action which sets a limit to the process of debate, or an ingressive nuance of **coming to a decision**. In either case, κρίνω has the force of *deciding* (NJB) or *making a judgment* (NRSV, NIV, REB) rather than continuing *to consider* the matter, even if lexicography includes either possibility out of a given context.[242] ἐν ὑμῖν αὐτοῖς urges that they take Paul's words to heart and settle the matter among themselves. This seems to confirm our comments above about peer-group pressure on the part of some but not all.

The periphrastic πρέπον ἐστίν may do duty for the more usual πρέπει, but may also call attention more explicitly and deliberately to the issue of what is **appropriate**. The more traditional rendering *seemly* (RV) or *proper* (NIV) is narrower than **appropriate**, and this last translation is to be preferred since, as Schrage urges, Paul is not appealing in this verse to what Godet calls "the instinct of truth which ought to exist in his readers," but to the variety of arguments and principles which apply to this situation.[243] Schrage concedes that Paul appeals to a stance or an orientation of mind, but this is broader than a natural instinct: as in Phil 4:8 Paul appeals to fixing the mind on what is right, true, constructive, praiseworthy, and admirable. Our translation **conduct prayer** for the simple προσεύχεσθαι serves to underline that the context is entirely that of public prayer in the assembled congregation in parallel with using prophetic discourse. "*Proseuchomenos* . . . suggests some sort of verbal activity . . . uttering prayers. . . ."[244]

14-15 א, A, B, 33, 81, Syriac VSS, and most MSS include αὐτῇ after δέδοται in v. 15 (i.e., **given** *to her* . . .). Nevertheless, the early p46 omits it and is followed by the Western tradition D, E, F, and G. While NJB, NIV and NRSV include it (and REB by implication but with careful openness), Zuntz rejects the personal pronoun mainly because its omission makes better sense.[245] The difficulty remains that if Zuntz is correct (as we judge he is) this argument becomes double-edged, for it is also argued that the addition of א, A, and B to explicate the text is more easily explained than its omission. Perhaps for this reason Metzger and UBS 4th ed. find the issue difficult to decide (hence give the pronoun "C" ranking in square brackets).[246] Conzelmann is correct to insist that the read-

---

241. Cf. Ricoeur, *Oneself as Another;* and A. C. Thiselton, "Human Being as Relational in 1 Corinthians, Hebrews, and Western Traditions," in *Ex Auditu* 13 (1997): 76-95.
242. BAGD, 451-52.
243. Godet, *First Epistle,* 2.127; Schrage, *Der erste Brief,* 2:520-21. On the semantic range of πρέπω, cf. BAGD, 699.
244. Collins, *First Cor,* 401.
245. Zuntz, *Text,* 127.
246. Metzger, *Textual Commentary* (2d ed.), 495-96.

ings make little or no difference, but on this occasion our judgment is to follow Zuntz.[247]

No doubt some will attack our translation of οὐδὲ ἡ φύσις αὐτή as **not even the very ordering of how things are** (drawn primarily from Schrage), since in purely lexicographical terms and regularly outside Paul and the NT φύσις simply means *nature*. (We may note the very rare use of οὐδέ in Paul, which strictly carries the force of **not even** in most contexts.) REB translates *nature herself,* similarly *nature itself* in NRSV and NJB. These take account of the emphatic pronoun αὐτή as well as the usual meaning of φύσις. NIV enjoys a rare moment of imaginative vision in avoiding the non-Pauline meaning of the word by translating **the very** *nature* **of things**.

φύσις: NATURE? CUSTOM? ORDERING OF HOW THINGS ARE? (11:14)

One of the most discriminating discussions of ἡ φύσις in this particular verse comes from Schrage. He compares its use here with the occurrences of the term in Rom 1:26; 2:14. To be sure, he observes, unlike the Stoics Paul does not hear "the voice of God from nature" as some competing or alternate source to scripture.[248] In contrast to Cicero, φύσις as "nature" is characterized by "ambivalence and relativity" of a kind unlike the concept among the Stoics.[249] In Paul's sense of the term, "natural" need not refer to a structure inherent in creation but may include "the state of affairs surrounding a convention" or the quality, property, or nature *(Beschaffenheit)* of male or female gender and the order, or arrangement, or system of things as they are *(die Ordnung der Dinge).*[250] Unless we take fully into account "the ambivalence of 'natural,'" we shall find insoluble problems with such historical counterexamples as the custom of Spartan warriors of wearing shoulder-length hair.[251] Paul simply appeals to "how things are" or "how things are ordered" in the period and context for which he is writing. Judiciously Schrage cites Calvin: "Now he means by 'natural' what was accepted by common consent and usage at that time. . . . For long hair was not always regarded as a disgraceful thing in man."[252]

In this history of interpretation four distinct views of ἡ φύσις in this verse may be identified: (1) an intuitive or inborn sense of what is fitting, right, or seemly (Bengel and Meyer); (2) the way humans are created, i.e., their constitution as men and women (de Wette); (3) the physical reality of how the world is ordered (Osiander, Hofius); and (4) the customs of a given society (Chrysostom, Calvin, Grotius, Schrage). Bengel comments on ἡ φύσις, *"natura, ejusque de decoro lumen."*[253] Köster has little difficulty in identifying a multitude of such uses in his extensive lexicographical survey of

---

247. Conzelmann, *1 Cor,* 190, n. 95.
248. Schrage, *Der erste Brief,* 2:521.
249. Ibid.
250. Ibid.
251. Ibid., 522.
252. Calvin, *First Epistle,* 235.
253. Bengel, *Gnomon,* 645. Meyer speaks of "the native, inborn sense and perception of what is seemly" (*First Epistle,* 1:329).

1973.[254] Among the pre-Socratic philosophers, ethics may be defined as each living κατὰ φύσιν (Heraclitus, *Fragments* 1.8, 9). Euripides speaks of the normative character of nature as an expression of the divine.[255] Plato rejects a merely materialist view of nature, but sees ἡ φύσις as the true or essential being of things.[256]

The notion of ἡ φύσις as denoting how things are constituted can be found in Aristotle, i.e., in an ontological sense the essence of something, or how things are.[257] "There is no disorder in it."[258] The Cynic-Stoic philosopher of Paul's era, Epictetus, can appeal to φύσις as *that which rules over all things* and becomes virtually deified.[259] Nevertheless, even in Epictetus ἡ φύσις comes to denote *the order of things* or **the ordering of how things are**. He observes, e.g., that a man who removes hair from his body is complaining against nature that he is a man: "Woman is born smooth and dainty by nature (φύσις); if she is very hairy she is a prodigy (κὰν ἔχῃ τρίχας πολλούς, τέρας ἐστί . . .). But for a man *not* to be hairy . . . if by nature he has no hair (κὰν μὲν φύσει μὴ ἔχῃ) he is a prodigy (τέρας ἐστί). If he removes his hair . . . he is a man who wishes to be a woman. . . . You complain against your nature (σουτῇ φύσις).[260] Among the Roman Stoic philosophical writers this slides into the notion of natural law. Cicero speaks of *lex naturae* or *lex naturalis*.[261] Epictetus also argues that for the more competent or superior to gain advantage over the lower or inferior is simply "a law of nature" (νόμος . . . φυσικός).[262]

Paul would doubtless be aware of these contemporary resonances of the term ἡ φύσις, and the above citations may lend some force to Murphy-O'Connor's claims about long hair and male homosexuality.[263] However, the Hebrew OT does not speak of "nature" in the Stoic sense, but of God's ordering of the world by his command. Hatch-Redpath's *Concordance to the Septuagint* establishes that the LXX uses φύσις only in the books outside the Hebrew canon, e.g., Wis 7:20; 13:1; 19:20; 3 Macc 3:29; 4 Macc I:20; 5:7, 8; 13:27.[264] This point is corroborated and rightly emphasized both by Fitzmyer and by Dunn in their comments in Rom 1:26.[265] Often the word denotes "the order intended by the Creator."[266] Fee, therefore, is entirely right to take up the NIV phrase about the "way things are."[267] *Depending on the context of thought* Paul may use ἡ φύσις sometimes to denote the very "grain" of the created order as a whole, or at other times (as here) to denote "how things are" in more situational or societal terms. With the exception of the first category taken up by Bengel and Meyer, instances of all three remaining

---

254. Helmut Köster, "φύσις," *TDNT,* 9:251-77; cf. also H. Paulsen, *EDNT,* 3:444.

255. Euripides, *Troades* 886; *Bacchae* 896.

256. Plato, *Laws* 10.888E-889C; *Critias* 389B, C; *Phaedrus* 87E, 270C.

257. Aristotle, *Physics* 2.1.

258. Köster, "φύσις," 259; Aristotle, *Physics* 8.1.

259. Epictetus, *Fragments* 469; *Dissertations* 1.146.

260. Epictetus, *Diss.* 3.1.27-30.

261. Cicero, *De Natura Deorum* 1.14.36; *De Officiis* 3.6.27, 30, 31.

262. Epictetus, *Diss.* 3.17.6.

263. Murphy-O'Connor, "Sex and Logic in 1 Cor 11:2-16," 482ff., discussed above.

264. Hatch-Redpath, *Concordance,* 2:1446, col. 3.

265. J. A. Fitzmyer, *Romans,* AB (New York: Doubleday, 1993), 286; and Dunn, *Romans 1-8,* 64.

266. Fitzmyer, *Romans,* 286.

267. Fee, *First Epistle,* 527.

categories can find support in various passages. However, that identified by Calvin and Schrage offers the best understanding of Paul's meaning here.[268]

Bruce succinctly observes: "It is unnecessary to postulate a Stoic source for Paul's present reference to patent physical facts."[269] When we recall that in Rom 11:21 κατὰ φύσιν, according to nature, means "with no human interference" (Fitzmyer), we may see how readily Paul underlines the point that "gender distinction is not something human beings created" (Witherington).[270] This still speaks today when many ascribe gender distinctions largely (although by definition never exhaustively) to social construction.

Commentators seem to have become hopelessly confused by attempting to press the logic in the form of an inverted symmetry between **a covering** (for which Paul now introduces a new Greek term, περιβόλαιον, *covering, wrap, cloak, mantle*) relating to hair and a **covering** in the form of a hood, or the lack of each respectively.[271] Even F. F. Bruce first suggests that Paul is drawing "an analogical inference" from woman's **covering** and man's lack of covering, but then concedes that "readily the opposite conclusion might be drawn from Paul's promise," i.e., that woman then "needs no other head covering."[272] He excludes the latter not on grounds of logic, but because Paul's earlier argument demands this. Such a tortuous problem of logic arises, however, only if we press the argument further than Paul intends. In vv. 14 and 15 his main concern is simply to press the issue of *gender differentiation* and its expression through some semiotic code such as hair or dress. Semiotic code depends on shared conventions, and social norms generally encourage gender differentiation.

Paul has already made out his case in terms of the ordering of creation in accordance with the will of God, and the relation between God's creation decrees and gospel newness. Although, like Conzelmann, he makes too much of "nature," Wolff at least reminds us that Paul is remonstrating with a particular group at Corinth whose "demands" need to be placed in perspective.[273] The force of δέδοται underlines the folly of trying to force people "to go against the grain" of **how things are** and their **very ordering**. (On other phrases and words of vv. 14-15, see above, where they are already discussed.)

16 This constitutes one of the classic examples selected by A. C. Wire of a rhetoric designed, as she expressed it, for the purpose of "dissociating thought from reality," as well as to persuade on the basis of universal church practice.[274] In Wire's view, Paul evokes a strategy "suddenly to deflate" the

268. Conzelmann, *1 Cor,* 190-91 moves too far toward a quasi-Stoic view here.

269. Bruce, *1 and 2 Cor,* 107.

270. Witherington, *Conflict and Community,* 240; Fitzmyer, *Romans,* 286.

271. Cf. BAGD, 646 on the Greek word.

272. Bruce, *1 and 2 Cor,* 108. It is unnecessary to understand ἀντί to mean *instead of* here. The preposition serves the force of **as a covering**, following Basil among the Fathers and most modern commentators. Cf. Edwards, *First Epistle,* 281.

273. Wolff, *Der erste Brief,* 255.

274. Wire, *The Corinthian Women Prophets,* 14-15 and 31-33; cf. further 116-34.

women prophets by suggesting that they base their stance on "mere thought and not reality."[275] As she observes, the interesting Greek word φιλόνεικος derives from the idea of *loving* (φιλο-) victory. Hence she renders it *want to make an issue of this,* although most prefer **contentious**, i.e., striving to contend, or trying to force an argument for the sake of becoming "a winner" rather than primarily to discover truth.[276] The Greek word occurs only here in the NT. Wire argues that having challenged the "right" or "authority" of the women prophets to do as they wish, Paul finds himself in a self-contradictory position by asserting a rival "authority."[277] However, her argument depends on several points of divergence from the exegesis followed above, not least the misleading use of authority in 11:10, a different understanding of the allusion to *glory* (vv. 7, 8), and a particular view of *head* (11:3).

A more promising starting point is to recall our earlier discussion of apostleship in which we argued that authentic apostleship could be perceived in the transparency of witness which focused the pattern of Christ's own self-giving for the benefit of others, or (as here) the corporate building of the community without the hindrance of distraction borne of self-promotion (see above, 1:1; 4:8-13; and esp. 9:1ff.). We noted the work of Roloff, Best, and Crafton in this connection. Where Crafton emphasizes the transparency of apostolic agency, and Best (with Chrysostom and Calvin) its pointing away from self, Roloff emphasizes the link between apostolicity and tradition.[278] The appeal to "all the churches" is bound up with this.[279] Hence δοκεῖ does not have the force of *seems* or even *thinks* here (cf. NJB, NIV, *wants to*), but **is minded to** or *is disposed to* (NRSV), since the word contains a rebuke concerning a disposition or intent in which someone takes pleasure.[280]

It seems self-evident that **the custom** (συνήθειαν) to which Paul alludes concerns gender distinctions in public worship, which, as Murphy-O'Connor urged, are addressed both to men and to women equally. The **custom** is the acceptance of an equality of status in accordance with which woman may lead in public prayer or preaching (see below on *prophecy*) side by side with a recognition that gender differences must not be blurred but appreciated, valued, and expressed in appropriate ways in response to God's unrevoked decree. Chrysostom and Calvin surprisingly argue that the universal church practice to which Paul appeals is a lack of "delight in stirring up quarrels" without "attention to truth."[281] It is because such people are more interested in conflict than truth, Calvin continues, that strictly Paul offers no "answer" to those who bra-

---

275. Ibid., 14.
276. Ibid., 15; cf. A. T. Robertson, *Epistles,* 4:162 similarly, esp. "fond of strife."
277. Ibid., 132-33.
278. J. Roloff, *Apostolat–Verkündigung–Kirche* (Gütersloh: Mohn, 1965), esp. 83-103; cf. 125-37; and J. A. Crafton, *The Agency of the Apostle* (Sheffield: Sheffield Academic Press, 1991).
279. Cf. Merk, *Handeln aus Glauben,* 135.
280. Meyer, *First Epistle,* 1:330-31; Edwards, *First Epistle,* 281; following de Wette.
281. Calvin, *First Epistle,* 255.

zenly stick to their guns, but concludes with an assertion which borders on the dismissive.

All the same, we should not allow the rhetoric of a closing act of pronouncement to obscure the patience and tenacity of Paul's argument. Once again the complexity, subtlety, and care of Paul's argument has been exposed most clearly by Judith Gundry-Volf in her necessarily complex discussion of 11:2-16. She rightly distinguished the three "points of reference," lenses, or "maps" in the light of which Paul conducts the dialogue: the order of creation, custom and propriety, and eschatology or the gospel. Within these three frames Paul uses the contrast between honor and shame, and urges "control over [or of] the head" and a relationship of mutuality, reciprocity, and gender distinctiveness.[282] She opposes "reductionistic explanations of the tension," in the direction of which, we may add, Wire may be in danger of leaning.[283] Only after all this does Paul finally reach a point where, if all else fails, he must resort to a declarative speech-act, or an illocutionary act of apostolic pronouncement, which presupposes the importance of tradition or "catholicity" among Paul's congregations.[284] Yet this does not serve as a substitute for patient argument. Paul *declares* them marginalized only if or because they have chosen to marginalize themselves.

2. Practices concerning "Haves" and "Have Nots" at the Lord's Supper Which Contradict Its Character as a Corporate, Self-Involving Proclamation of the Lord's Death (11:17-34)

(17) Now in giving these directives I cannot continue my commendation because the meetings you hold as a church do more harm than good. (18) First of all, I am given to understand that when you meet together as an assembled church splits occur among you, and to some extent I believe it. (19) For "dissensions are unavoidable," it is claimed among you, in order that those who are tried and true among you may be visibly revealed. (20, 21) Accordingly, when you meet together in the same place, your meeting does not amount to an eating of the Lord's Supper; for at the time of eating each individual devours his or her own meal: one *actually* goes hungry; another is *even* drunk! (22) Surely it cannot be that you have no homes of your own for your eating and drinking, can it? Or do you show contempt for the church which is God's, and put to shame those who have nothing? What am I to say to you? Am I to congratulate you? On this matter I cannot give my approval.

---

282. Gundry-Volf, "Gender and Creation in 1 Cor 11:2-16," 160, 162, and 169.
283. Ibid., 165.
284. Even so, this is a declaration of *internal* logical grammar. If people consistently refuse to listen, they can only end up by placing themselves in the margins.

(23, 24) For, as for me, I received a tradition from the Lord which I have handed on to you, namely, that the Lord Jesus, in the night on which he was handed over, took bread and gave thanks; he broke the loaf and said, "This is my body, which is for you. Do this in remembrance of me." (25) In the same way, with reference to the cup after supper, he said, "This cup is the new covenant in my blood. Whenever you drink it, do this in remembrance of me." (26) For as many times as you eat this bread and drink the cup, it is the death of the Lord that you are proclaiming, until he comes. (27) Consequently, whoever eats the bread or drinks the cup of the Lord in a way that is not fitting will be held accountable for so treating the body and blood of the Lord. (28, 29) On the contrary, a person should examine his or her own genuineness, and only in this way eat from the loaf and drink from the cup. For all who eat and drink eat and drink judgment on themselves if they do not recognize what characterizes the body as different. (30) It is for this reason that many among you are suffering weakness and ill-health, and a good number have died. (31, 32) If, however, we recognize what characterizes us as Christian believers, we should not fall under judgment; but if we are judged by the Lord, we are disciplined by the Lord so that we do not become condemned along with the world. (33, 34) So then, dear fellow Christians, when you gather together for the meal, wait for one another. If any of you is hungry, let that person eat at home, so that when you gather together it will not be to fall under judgment. With regard to the remaining matters, I will set them in order when I come.

The style of this section, together with Paul's redescription of what he understands to be taking place at the Lord's Supper, indicates that he is not responding to a question first raised by the addressees, but initiates the raising of an urgent matter for censure and re-education. This is prompted by oral reports of occurrences and practices at Corinth. Along with 1:10–4:21 and 5:1-13 (cf. also ch. 6), "at 1 Cor 11:18 occurs the third of Paul's explicit references to this oral and unofficial information: '. . . I hear that there are divisions (σχίσματα) among you (11:18). . . . One goes ahead with his own meal, and one is hungry . . .' (11:21)."[1] Whereas he had commended the addressees for observing certain traditions shared by the churches as a whole in v. 2 (ἐπαινῶ ὑμᾶς ὅτι . . . τὰς παραδόσεις κατέχετε, i.e., probably in acknowledging the legitimate role of women under the gospel to lead in public prayer or preaching [see under "prophecy"]), Paul now explicitly retracts such commendation in 11:17: οὐκ ἐπαινῶ ὅτι οὐκ.

Although almost all of 7:1–14:40 (if not also 15:1-58) responds to questions from Corinth, the present topic appropriately comes at this juncture. This

1. Hurd, *Origin of 1 Corinthians,* 78-79; followed by Fee, *First Epistle,* 531, and Hays, *First Cor,* 193. On the other hand, Findlay earlier perceived this as a response to the church's writing "self-complacently" about worship (from 11:2 onward) (*Expositor's Greek Testament,* 2:876).

849

is the case partly because it addresses issues of the assembled congregation at worship (11:2–14:40; cf. also συνέρχεσθαι five times in 11:17, 18, 20, 33, and 34). More especially it is because the theme of *disrupting the community and undermining the nature of the cross by self-affirming insistence on individual or group "freedom," "rights," and "celebration" continues the issue which dominates 8:1–11:1*.[2] In line with the research of Horsley, Gooch, and Gardner on the relation between "self-awareness" (or conscience) and security/insecurity in 8:1–11:1 Bruce Winter urges that those who held "secure" positions at Corinth, whether as host to others in the church or as clients of the patron-host, were too ready to enjoy their group security while leaving those without the protection of a patron to tag along as second-class citizens in the celebrations of the Lord's Supper.[3] Christians who have resources, Winter concludes concerning this passage, should welcome (ἐκδέχεσθε, v. 33) the "have nots" by sharing their food with them at the Lord's Supper.[4] The introduction of the possible role of the host-patron may call into question Fee's contention that the **splits** (σχίσματα, 11:18) of this section are different in kind from the **splits** (same Greek word) in 1:10.[5] Just as in 1:10-12, the groupings caused splits by generating an ethos which came to give the peer group or subgroup more prominence than the "one" Body (cf. 10:16, 17) of the whole church, so the dynamics of the celebrations of the Lord's Supper in house groups in all probability generated the same spirit of focusing on a patron or host to a group rather than exclusively on Christ.

Moreover, by allowing to "the other" only second-class hospitality in the atrium rather than first-class comfort and service in the host's triclinium see below), the proceedings defeated the very proclamation of the Lord, whose death was "for us" and "for the other" as one Body (12:12).[6] It explicitly contradicted and undermined the very purpose of the Lord's Supper (οὐκ εἰς τὸ κρεῖσσον ἀλλὰ εἰς τὸ ἧσσον συνέρχεσθε, v. 17). For the *love for the other, the outsider, and "the weak," which characterized the death of Christ,* was thrust aside.[7] Was their meal still the supper **of the Lord** (v. 20)?

In spite of his tendency to project sometimes speculative imaginative scenarios in his more popular study *You Wretched Corinthians!* Hans Frör well captures the connection between 11:2-16 and 17-34 in the following projected

2. Cf. esp. Hofius, "Herrenmahl und Herrenmahlsparadosis. Erwägungen zu 1 Kor 11:23b-25," 371-408. Hofius argues that lack of hospitality and sharing contradicts the principle of proclaiming the cross of the Christ who died for the sake of others. See also P. Lampe below under n. 7.

3. Winter, "The Lord's Supper at Corinth: An Alternative Reconstruction," 81; cf. 73-82.

4. Ibid., 73-82.

5. Fee, *First Epistle*, 537: "The former divisions were . . . defined as 'quarrels' and 'jealousy' (1:11; 3:4), which are quite missing from this section. . . . In 1:12 Paul mentions at least four names around which the quarrels are taking place. . . ."

6. See Murphy-O'Connor, "House Churches and the Eucharist," 32-38; and *St. Paul's Corinth*, 153-61. Also Pliny, *Letters* 2.6.

7. Lampe, "Das Korinthische Herrenmahl im Schnittpunkt hellenistisch-römischer Mahlpraxis und paulinischer Theologia Crucis (1 Kor 11:17-34)," 183-213.

dialogue initiated by his fictitious barmaid Mara. Mara exclaims: "They're bothering about veils, as though one had only to throw away a bit of material and everyone would be equal at the Lord's table. . . . 'Not slave and free, not poor and rich! That makes me laugh! Clearly the better class gentlemen have been looked after for quite some time in the dining room when our kind comes rushing along. They eat lavishly, drink the finest wines. . . . They mix up the well-laid table of the master of the house with the Lord's table. . . . If we're lucky, all that's left for the shared meal is a bit of bread and a sip of wine. . . . We get the bits."[8]

The focus of **proclaiming the Lord's death**, therefore, serves as a parallel to the central point in 1:18-25: if the cross stands as "the ground and criterion" of what it is to be an apostle and a Christian believer (as Schrage and Moltmann rightly express the point), then the "splits" of chs. 1–4 undermine the heart of the gospel. Similarly, the practices which surround the sharing of the meal which (in Paul's view) points above all to the "for others" of the Lord's death undermine the very heart of why the worshiping community celebrates the Lord's Supper at all. Like apostleship, "remembering" and "showing forth" the Lord's death is a matter of conduct and lifestyle, not simply of words and ecclesial ritual. As in Israel's participation in the Passover, assembled believers are brought "there" to the cross, to allow it once again to reshape their mind-set and their lifestyle.[9]

Two further points should be added by way of introduction to 11:17-34. From the 1920s to the 1960s Hans Lietzmann's work *Mass and Lord's Supper* (first German ed. 1926; successive English eds. from 1953 to 1979) popularized the notion of a contrast between two "primitive types" of Eucharist or Lord's Supper: a so-called "Pauline" type which focused on the death of Christ and finds expression in the Roman liturgy of Hippolytus, and a so-called "Jerusalem" type which reflects a joyous celebration of fellowship meals in communion with the risen Christ as reflected in Acts 2:46 and the early Egyptian liturgy represented in Serapion.[10] Gregory Dix promoted Lietzmann's view in Anglican circles, while A. J. B. Higgins accepted a modified version with the proviso that both "types" go back to earliest times.[11] Even Cullmann regarded Lietzmann's view as unduly neglected, even though he concedes that he was

8. H. Frör, *You Wretched Corinthians!* (Eng. trans., London: SCM, 1995), 59.

9. The intimate connection with the Passover is fundamental and will be explored further below. On the Jewish celebration of Passover, see works cited below, including the Hebrew and English texts of Roth (ed.), *The Haggadah,* esp. 34-48. See esp. Garlatti, "La eucharistia como memoria y proclamación de la muerte del Señor," 321-41; and D. Stanley, "'Do This in Memory of Me' (1 Cor 11:24, 25)," *Studies in Formative Spirituality* 6 (1985): 103-15.

10. Lietzmann, *Mass and Lord's Supper: A Study in the History of the Liturgy,* With Introduction and Further Inquiry by R. D. Richardson, esp. 172 86 on Jesus and the *Haburah* meal; 193-203 in "The Primitive Form of the Lord's Supper," and 203-9 on its development. The early chapters trace details in patristic liturgies.

11. G. Dix, *The Shape of the Liturgy* (London: SCM, 2d ed. 1945 [1943]), 50-70; and A. J. B. Higgins, *The Lord's Supper in the NT* (London: SCM, 1952), 56-73.

"too conscious of the [alleged] gulf separating these two conceptions."[12] At the time Cullmann acknowledges that behind Lietzmann's theory lay the tradition of postresurrection Christophanies which in the radical views of A. Schweitzer, M. Goguel, and A. Loisy assumed the form of "myths of the table-fellowship of the Risen One with His disciples."[13] E. Lohmeyer subsequently argued that a "Galilean" type (which corresponds with Lietzmann's "Jerusalem" type) should be distinguished from a "Jerusalem" type (close to Lietzmann's "Pauline" type).[14]

Lietzmann (followed by Dix) also postulated a parallel between the "Jerusalem" type of the eucharistic tradition and the Haburah meal of "Jewish meals invested with religious solemnity." However, more recent research dismisses such a theory as "an *ad hoc* conjecture for which there is absolutely no evidence."[15] Jeremias's evaluation has been endorsed by I. H. Marshall and others (discussed under exegesis of v. 17). We should not approach vv. 17-34 with any anachronistic preconceptions about "*agapē* (love-feast)" and "Lord's Supper" as reconstructed hypothetically by Lietzmann and his legacy of thought (see below).

The second of the final two points concerns the possibility that the contrast between those who were well provided for and the "have nots" was exacerbated not only by socioeconomic differences of background, birth, patronage, and occupation but also by the specific circumstances of famine (or at least of severe food shortages) around the date of this epistle.[16] B. W. Winter, B. B. Blue, and A. D. Clarke cite the appointment of Tiberius Claudius Dinippus as curator for problems caused by the shortages, although the dating may be a few years later.[17] Donald Engels calculates that even with high yields (e.g., 18 bushels per acre, or 16 hectoliters per hectare) of barley, the 80 square miles (207 square kilometers) of cultivable land which belonged to the agricultural *territorium* of Roman Corinth "would scarcely support 17,600 people" at around 1.2 kilograms (2,600 calories in barley) per day. This figure, even if we include fruit, vegetables, and other crops, represents "absolute maximum."[18] Granted that the city could not be self-supporting, it might well entail relatively small climatic irregularities, especially lack of adequate rain, to cause a degree of scarcity that would raise prices. The effect would be to widen the gap be-

12. Cullmann and Leenhardt, *Essays on the Lord's Supper,* 6. (However, the original German dates from 1936.)

13. Ibid., 9.

14. E. Lohmeyer, "Das Abendmahl in der Urgemeinde," *JBL* 56 (1937): 217-52.

15. Jeremias, *The Eucharistic Words of Jesus,* 30; cf. 29-31.

16. Cf. Winter, "The Lord's Supper at Corinth," 73-82; and "Secular and Christian Responses to Corinthian Famines," 86-106; Blue, "The House Church at Corinth and the Lord's Supper: Famine, Food Supply and the Present Distress," 221-39; and Clarke, *Secular and Christian Leadership in Corinth,* 18-21.

17. Winter, "Secular and Christian Responses," 86-106; and Clarke, *Secular and Christian Leadership in Corinth,* 18 and 140 (Appendix A, no. 38).

18. D. Engels, *Roman Corinth* (Chicago: University of Chicago Press, 1990), 27.

tween the well-to-do who could take price rises in their stride, and those already on the bread line who could not. Suetonius attests several famines or at least shortages during the reign of Claudius (AD 41-54), and Josephus alludes to high prices during this period.[19] Whether or not Blue's reconstruction actually reflects the precise timing of our epistle, the principle of nonagricultural economics and high commercial population at Corinth, as well as a wide range of socioeconomic status, suggests the vulnerability of the poor to shortages. This would make the distinction between first-class and second-class guests at "the Lord's Supper" all the more poignant.

Bibliography on 11:17-34. See also other works listed under 10:14-22.

Aitken, Ellen B., "Τὰ δρώμενα καὶ τὰ λεγόμενα: The Eucharistic Memory of Jesus' Words in First Corinthians," *HTR* 90 (1997): 359-70.

Blue, B. B., "The House Church at Corinth and the Lord's Supper: Famine, Food Supply and the Present Distress," *Criswell Theological Review* 5 (1991): 221-39.

Bornkamm, G., Lord's Supper and Church in Paul," in Bornkamm, *Early Christian Experience* (Eng. trans., London: SCM, 1969), 123-60.

Campbell, R. A., "Does Paul Acquiesce in Divisions at the Lord's Supper?" *NTS* 33 (1991): 61-70.

Casey, P. M., "The Original Aramaic Form of Jesus' Interpretation of the Cup," *JTS* 41 (1990): 1-12.

Chenderlin, F., *"Do This as My Memorial": The Semantic and Conceptual Background and Value of Anamnesis in 1 Cor 11:24-25,* AnBib 99 (Rome: Biblical Pontifical Institute Press, 1982).

Clancy, R. A. D., "The OT Roots of Remembrance in the Lord's Supper," *Concordia Journal* 19 (1993): 35-50.

Coady, C. A. J., *Testimony: A Philosophical Study* (Oxford: Clarendon Press, 1992).

Cullmann, O., *Early Christian Worship* (Eng. trans., London: SCM, 1953), 26-33.

———, *La Tradition. Problème exégétique, historique et théologique,* Cahiers théologiques 33 (Paris: Delachaux & Niestlé, 1953), 29-40.

———, and F. J. Leenhardt, *Essays on the Lord's Supper* (Eng. trans., London: Lutterworth, 1958).

Dunn, J. D. G., "The Lord's Supper," in Dunn, *The Theology of Paul the Apostle* (Edinburgh: T. & T. Clark and Grand Rapids: Eerdmans, 1998), 599-624.

Eriksson, A., *Traditions as Rhetorical Proof: Pauline Argumentation in 1 Corinthians,* ConBNT 29 (Stockholm: Almqvist & Wiksell, 1998), 64-86, 100-106, and 174-96.

Garlatti, G. J., "Las eucharistia como memoria y proclamación de la muerte del Señor," *RevistB* 46 (1984): 321-41.

Gloer, W. H., "Homologies and Hymns in the NT: Form, Content and Criteria for Identification," *Perspectives in Religious Studies* 11 (1984): 115-32.

Gregg, D. W. A., "Hebraic Antecedents to the Eucharistic Anamnesis Formula," *TynBul* 30 (1979): 165-68.

---

19. Suetonius, *Claudius* 18.2; cf. Tacitus, *Annals* 12.43; Dio Cassius, *History* 40.11; Josephus, *Antiquities* 3.320-21. Cf. also Acts 11:29-30.

Gundry-Volf, J., *Paul and Perseverance,* WUNT 2:37 (Tübingen: Mohr, 1990), 99-113.

Higgins, A. J. B., *The Lord's Supper in the NT* (London: SCM, 1952), 13-23 and 64-73, esp. 70-73.

Hofius, O., "Herrenmahl und Herrenmahlsparadosis. Erwägungen zu 1 Kor 11:23b-25," *ZTK* 85 (1988): 371-408; Eng. trans., "The Lord's Supper and the Lord's Supper Tradition: Reflections on 1 Cor 11:23b-25," in B. Meyer (ed.) *One Loaf, One Cup: Ecumenical Studies of 1 Cor 11 and Other Eucharistic Texts* (Macon, Ga.: Mercer University Press, 1993), 75-115.

————, "Tὸ σῶμα τὸ ὑπὲρ ὑμῶν, 1 Kor 11:24," *ZNW* 80 (1989): 80-88.

Horrell, D., "The Lord's Supper at Corinth and in the Church Today," *Theol* 98 (1995): 196-202.

Jeremias, J., *The Eucharistic Words of Jesus* (Eng. trans., London: SCM, 3d ed. 1966).

————, "'This Is My Body,'" *ExpTim* 83 (1972): 196-203.

Karrer, J., "Der kelch des neuen Bundes," *BZ* 34 (1990): 198-221.

Käsemann, E., "The Pauline Doctrine of the Lord's Supper," in Käsemann, *Essays on NT Themes* (Eng. trans., London: SCM, 1964), 108-35.

Klauck, H.-J., "Eucharist and Church Community in Paul," *Theology Digest* 35 (1988): 19-24.

Lampe, P., "The Eucharist: Identifying with Christ on the Cross," *Int* 48 (1994), 36-49.

————, "Das Korinthische Herrenmahl im Schnittpunkt hellenistisch-römischer Mahlpraxis und paulinischer Theologia Crucis (1 Kor 11:17-34)," *ZNW* 82 (1991): 183-213.

Lane, W., "Covenant: The Key to Paul's Conflict with Corinth," *TynBul* 33 (1982): 3-30.

Léon-Dufour, X., "'Prenez': Ceci est mon corps," *NRT* 104 (1982): 223-40.

Lietzmann, H., *Mass and Lord's Supper: A Study in the History of the Liturgy* (Eng. trans., Leiden: Brill, 1979), 20-54, 160-86, 193-208, 596-620.

Maccoby, H., "Paul and the Eucharist," *NTS* 37 (1991): 247-67.

Marshall, I. H., *Last Supper and Lord's Supper* (Grand Rapids: Eerdmans, 1980), 108-23 and throughout.

Martin, R. P., *Worship in the Early Church* (Grand Rapids: Eerdmans, 1974 [1964]).

Mazzo, Enrico, *The Origins of the Eucharistic Prayer* (Collegeville, Minn.: Liturgical Press, 1995), 30-90.

McGowan, A. B., "'Is There a Liturgical Text in This Gospel?' The Institution Narratives and Their Early Interpretative Communities," *JBL* 118 (1999): 73-87.

Merk, O., *Handeln aus Glauben* (Marburg: Elwert, 1968), 135-41.

Meyer, B. F. (ed.), *One Loaf, One Cup: Eucharistic Studies of 1 Cor 11 and Other Eucharistic Texts* (Macon, Ga.: Mercer University Press, 1993).

Moule, C. F. D., "The Judgement Theme in the Sacraments," in W. D. Davies and D. Daube (eds.), *The Background of the NT and Its Eschatology: Studies in Honour of C. H. Dodd* (Cambridge: Cambridge University Press, 1956), 464-81.

Murphy-O'Connor, J., "Eucharist and Community in First Corinthians," *Worship* 51 (1977): 56-69.

————, "House Churches and the Eucharist," *BibTod* 22 (1984): 32-38.

————, *St. Paul's Corinth* (Wilmington: Glazier, 1983).

Neuenzeit, P., *Das Herrenmahl. Studien zur paulinischen Eucharistie-auffassung* (Munich: Kösel, 1960).

Passakos, D. C., "Eucharist in First Cor: A Sociologic Study," *RB* 104 (1997): 192-210.

Paulsen, H., "Schisma und Häresie. Untersuchungen zu 1 Kor 11:18, 19," *ZTK* 79 (1982): 180-211.

Pesce, M., "Mangiare e bere il proprio giudizio. Una concezione culturale commune in 1 Cor e a Sota?" *RevistB* 38 (1990): 495-513.

Pesch, R., *Das Abendmahl und Jesu Todesverständnis* (Freiburg: Herder, 1978).

Pritchard, N. M., "Progression of Faith and Admission to the Communion in the Light of 1 Cor 11 and Other Passages," *SJT* 33 (1980): 55-70.

Popkes, W., *Christus Traditus. Eine Untersuchung zum Begriff der Dahingabe im Neuen Testament* (Zürich: Zwingli Verlag, 1967).

Porter, C. L., "An Interpretation of the Lord's Supper Texts: 1 Cor 10:14-22 and 11:17-34," *Encounter* 50 (1989): 29-45.

Ridderbos, H. N., "The Earliest Confession of the Atonement in Paul," in R. Banks (ed.), *Reconciliation and Hope: NT Essays on Atonement and Eschatology Presented to L. L. Morris* (Exeter: Paternoster, 1974), 76-89.

Roth, Cecil, *The Haggadah: New Edition with Notes* (Heb. and Eng. trans., London: Soncino, 1934).

Schmitz, O., "παραγγέλλω," *TDNT* 5 (1967), 761-65.

Schneider, S., "Glaubensmängel in Korinth. Eine neue Deutung der 'Schwachen, Kranken, Schlafenden' in 1 Kor 11:30," *Filologia Neutestamentaria* 9 (1996): 3-19.

Schrage, W., "Das Verständnis des Todes Jesu Christi im NT," in E. Bizer (ed.), *Das Kreuz Jesu Christi als Grund des Heils* (Gütersloh: Gütersloher, 1969). 49-90.

Schweizer, E., *The Lord's Supper according to the NT* (Eng. trans., London: SCM, 1967).

Theissen, G., "Social Integration and Sacramental Activity: An Analysis of 1 Cor 11:17-34," in *The Social Setting of Pauline Christianity* (Eng. trans., Philadelphia: Fortress, 1982), 145-74.

Thurian, M., *The Eucharistic Memorial* (Eng. trans., London: Lutterworth Press, 1961).

Voegelin, E., "Remembrance of Things Past," in Voegelin, *Anamnesis* (Eng. trans., Notre Dame: University of Notre Dame Press, 1978), 3-13 (on the philosophy and epistemology of *anamnesis*).

von Campenhausen, Hans, "Das Bekenntnis im Urchristentum," *ZNW* 63 (1972): 210-53.

Wainwright, G., *Doxology: The Praise of God in Worship, Doctrine, and Life* (London: Epworth Press, 1980), 182-217.

Wegenast, K., *Das Verständnis der Tradition bei Paulus und in den Deuteropaulinen* (Neukirchen: Neukirchener, 1962).

Wengst, K., "Der Apostel und die Tradition," *ZTK* 69 (1972): 145-62.

Winter, B. W., "The Lord's Supper at Corinth: An Alternative Reconstruction," *RTR* 37 (1978): 73-82.

———, "Secular and Christian Responses to Corinthian Famines," *TynBul* 40 (1989): 86-106.

Witherington, B., *Conflict and Community in Corinth* (Grand Rapids: Eerdmans and Carlisle: Paternoster, 1995), 241-52.

Wolff, C., "Exkurs: Die neutestamentlichen Überlieferungen vom letzten Mahl Jesu," in *Der erste Brief des Paulus an die Korinther* (Leipzig: Evangelische Verlagsanstalt, 1996), 265-73.

17 The MSS reflect some confusion over whether παραγγέλλων and οὐκ ἐπαινῶ should be read respectively as a participle and as an indicative (UBS 4th ed., following א, G, and most MSS), or inverted respectively into an indicative followed by a participle (following A and C*), or even as two participles (following B). Most follow the א and G reading accepted by the UBS 4th ed.

As we noted in our introduction to 11:17-34, Paul's use of οὐκ ἐπαινῶ in this verse signals a deliberate and conscious retraction of his ἐπαινῶ δὲ ὑμᾶς in 11:2.[20] With respect to permitting women to lead in public in prophetic speech or prayer the Corinthian church accorded with the traditions observed among the Pauline churches. However, their mode of sharing, or more strictly of failing genuinely to share, the Lord's Supper transposed it from being *the Lord's* Supper, which proclaimed his giving of himself "for others," into little more than a party meal given for the benefit of some inner group invited by the host of the house (see vv. 20-22). The verb συνέρχεσθε is repeated in vv. 18, 20, 33, and 34, and this specific eucharistic context denotes not simply *assembling together* but **the meeting you hold as a church**. In v. 18 this becomes explicit. It is as one believing community that they meet, not as a group of friends meeting for a private meal. Although they share in solidarity as recipients of divine grace through the cross of Christ (cf. 4:7), the disruptive and divisive nature of their meetings for what amounts to a meal in the house of a wealthy patron **does more harm than good**. This last phrase (REB and NIV) conveys in English idiom the sharpened contrast of Gk. οὐκ εἰς τὸ κρεῖσσον ἀλλὰ εἰς τὸ ἧσσον. We were tempted to follow NRSV's translation of τοῦτο δὲ παραγγέλλων . . . as *Now in the following instructions* (NIV, *the following* **directives**), but for the fact that as eminent an exegete as Barrett insists emphatically that τοῦτο bears its expected meaning as "referring to what precedes."[21] Since examples occur in Greek in which τοῦτο can denote what follows (NRSV, NIV; also by implication NJB), Barrett's view is improbable, but our translation, **these directives**, leaves this issue open (as does REB).

NJB's phrase **the meetings you hold** admirably paves the way for the question: What kind of meetings are these? Are they simply occasions for entertaining those of similar status and background, with hangers on who come because it has the form of a eucharistic memorial by virtue of its framework? Or do these meetings focus on Christ and on a celebration of the New Passover of redemption in which all Christian believers share in solidarity as thankful recipients of God's grace through the work of Christ? As Hays observes, we should be careful to avoid reading back anachronistically the distinction between "the *agapē* (love-feast)" and "the Eucharist" of which Lietzmann made so much.[22] We have already outlined Lietzmann's hypothesis in our introduction to this section, noting its connections with theories of myths of post-

---

20. Also Hays, *First Cor,* 194.
21. Barrett, *First Epistle,* 260.
22. Hays, *First Cor,* 193; Lietzmann, *Mass and Lord's Supper,* 172-86, 193-203, and 203-9.

resurrection Christophanies among such controversial thinkers as Schweitzer, Goguel, and Loisy, its popularization among English-speaking readers by Dix and Higgins, and its subsequent criticism by Jeremias and Marshall, among others.[23] Indeed, the work of Otfried Hofius establishes that the tradition of "remembering" (εἰς τὴν ἐμὴν ἀνάμνησις), especially in the context of Heb. זכר (z-k-r), constitutes a joyful "recalling" or "proclaiming" of God's saving acts (cf. Ps 105:1, 5) which reaches its highest peak in grateful praise and celebration of grace through the cross and identification with Christ ("fellowship," "sharing") as the Crucified and Raised Lord.[24] The two dimensions postulated as "two types" by Lietzmann achieve a historical and theological unity in the more convincing work of Hofius. This does not exclude the various "readings" of the early tradition which express several specific emphases in the liturgies of early centuries.[25]

18 In 1:10-12 we translated σχίσματα as **splits** both to preserve the metaphor of the Greek and to avoid the mistaken notion that the divisions were of a doctrinal nature. REB's *fall into sharply divided groups* may be justified by the exegesis of the whole passage, but goes beyond the Greek of this verse. There is a fundamental difference between 1:10-12 and the point here, however. In 1:10-12 the **splits** seem to reflect tensions between *different ethos of different house groups.* The splits are "external" to given groups, although internal to the whole church of Corinth. Here, however, *the very house meeting itself reflects* **splits** *between the socially advantaged and the socially disadvantaged.* They are "internal" even within a single gathered meeting, i.e., ἐν ἐκκλησίᾳ, when they meet *in one place* **as a church**. However, the Greek phrase should not be interpreted as a locative: it means **as a church**, not *in church* (which would be anachronistic as well as contrary to the normal use of the phrase in this period).[26] If we wish to make the preposition ἐν explicit, we need to follow Robertson and Plummer's *in assembly* as reflecting Heb. קהל *(qahal).*[27] It is possible, but by no means certain, that ἀκούω can be understood as a continuous present, *I continually hear* or *I hear again and again.*[28] However, most English VSS translate either *I hear* (NRSV, NIV, and NJB) or *I am told* (REB). Our translation approximates that of the REB here.

---

23. Jeremias, *Eucharistic Words of Jesus,* 29-31; Marshall, *Last Supper and Lord's Supper,* 20 and 130-33.

24. Hofius, "The Lord's Supper and the Lord's Supper Tradition: Reflections on 1 Cor 11:23b-25," in Meyer (ed.), *One Loaf, One Cup,* 75-115, esp. 103-11; Germ. "Herrenmahl und Herrenmahlsparadosis," 371-408.

25. McGowan, "'Is There a Liturgical Text in This Gospel?' The Institution Narratives and Their Early Interpretative Communities," 73-87.

26. As Héring, *First Epistle,* 112, and Kistemaker, *1 Cor,* 386, argue. The *Didache* (4) also bears this meaning.

27. Robertson and Plummer, *First Epistle,* 239. Unfortunately the AV/KJV follows a MS reading which includes the definite article τῇ.

28. The former is proposed by Robertson and Plummer, *First Epistle,* 239; the latter by Edwards, *First Epistle,* 284.

Commentators make heavy weather of μέρος τι πιστεύω, not least since a variety of understandings are permitted by the Greek. Hays interprets it as an expression of outrage: *I can hardly credit it; I can't believe it.*[29] Robertson and Plummer take the opposite view: Christian hope and charity are always reluctant to believe the worst.[30] Fee argues: "he really does believe it but also acknowledges that his informants are scarcely disinterested observers."[31] Wolff and Kistemaker view this as a case of judicious pastoral "caution": Paul avoids unnecessary confrontation and especially rash, overly hasty speech.[32] This last suggestion is the most reasonable, and is well conveyed by REB, *I believe there is some truth in it.* Our translation, **to some extent I believe it**, assimilates this rendering, together with leaving open what Paul himself probably wishes to leave open, namely that while **splits** on the basis of first-class and second-class guests at dinner clearly occurred, *some* hosts or patrons may have shown more sensitivity than others. The accusation might not have been entirely universal. This strengthens the point noted above about the need for responsible pastoral speech over against rash generalization and the accusation of all and sundry.

19 D*, F, G and Cyprian omit the first ἐν ὑμῖν, and a few MSS omit the second occurrence; but the 4th ed. UBS *Greek New Testament* rightly retains both occurrences.

If our proposed interpretation is accepted, γάρ continues the explanation for the abuses, which are then described further in vv. 20-21. On αἱρέσεις, δόκιμοι, and φανεροί, see BAGD, which accords with our translation.[33] We may begin, however, with Paulsen's argument that Paul is referring here to a saying about the unavoidable process of "dissension" or "division" in the light of an eschatology of judgment.[34] Justin explicitly cites the saying "There shall be splits and dissensions" precisely in such a context of eschatological judgment: "many shall come in My name clothed outwardly in sheep's clothing, but inwardly they are ravening wolves" [Matt 7:15]. . . . "There shall be many false Christs and false apostles . . . [Matt 24:11]."[35] However, while we take up the allusion to a saying probably related to eschatology, we do not accept the view that it is *Paul* who himself appeals to this axiom in this eucharistic context. May it not be that *the educated and sophisticated "strong" at Corinth* had already anticipated and addressed criticism about "divisiveness" by taking up the saying, "Not everyone who claimed to be a believer might be proved to be **tried and true**"; hence all this talk of un-

29. Hays, *First Cor,* 195.
30. Robertson and Plummer, *First Epistle,* 239.
31. Fee, *First Epistle,* 537.
32. Wolff, *Der erste Brief,* 257; Kistemaker, *1 Cor,* 387.
33. BAGD, 23-24, 203, and 852.
34. Paulsen, "Schisma und Häresie. Untersuchungen zu 1 Kor 11:18, 19," 180-211. Many others also argue this point more briefly.
35. Justin, *Dialogue with Trypho,* 34:3. Cf. further *Pseudo-Clementine Homilies,* 16:21:4 and *Didascalia Apostolorum,* 23 (cited by Paulsen and others).

conditional eucharistic "oneness" was debatable. They appealed to the eschatological maxim "**dissensions are unavoidable**."

This meaning of δόκιμος and the eschatological context is supported by
Barrett, Conzelmann, Schrage, and Lang, among others.[36] Kümmel and Conzelmann insist that Paul is neither "ironic" nor merely "resigned." However,
how can Paul otherwise appear to lend support to the very **splits** which he
condemns? Hays sees it as "presumably necessary in the divine plan."[37] Fee,
however, calls this "one of the true puzzles in the letter."[38] He can suggest
only the possibility of "irony," or alternatively an anticipation of Paul's later
allusion to judgment in 11:28-32. This would amount to "resignation in the
face of the inevitable: Paul expected 'divisions' to accompany the End."[39] Yet
Fee is not fully satisfied with his own attempt at an explanation. The suggestion of Weiss and of Robertson and Plummer that **splits** (v. 18) lead to more
serious **dissensions** or *factions* (v. 19) might be plausible for the first half of
the verse, but then the following maxim about **the tried and true** seems to
make a virtue out of a sad necessity. If the second part of the verse indeed
represents Paul's own comments, this sentence remains "one of the true puzzles of the letter" (Fee). However, what Paulsen and many others identify is
likely to have been in circulation among the pre-Pauline churches, and most
probably derives from the sayings of Jesus. Such sayings were cited later to
explain its phenomenon of spurious faith or the danger of Christian presumption, as indeed in the context of Justin's citation.[40] This credibly forms a parenthetical allusion to excuses for a problem of which some at Corinth were
fully aware (cf. comments above on **to some extent I believe it**, v. 18). From
initial remonstration Paul moves to the point that if the dining situation divides participants in the Lord's Supper into a favored triclinium group of
"first class" guests and hangers on in the atrium (see below), this is not **the
Lord's Supper** at all, but a meal in a private house.

If our interpretation is rejected, one possible alternative exists. We may
perhaps follow Horsley in understanding the verse as Pauline irony, although
not in a context of eschatology and judgment. Horsley's own translation makes
clear the possibility of an ironic allusion to the *social categorization* which pre-
vailed: "For of course there must be 'discrimination' among you so that it will
become clear who among you are 'the distinguished ones.'"[41] The reason for

---

36. Schrage, *Der erste Brief,* 3:21-22; Kümmel, "Anhang," in Lietzmann, *An die Korinther,*
185 ("eschatologische Notwendigkeit"; cf. 1 Cor 15:25, 53); Barrett, *First Epistle,* 261-62;
Conzelmann, *1 Cor,* 194 and 194 n. 14; Héring, *First Epistle,* 113: "those who will come through
the test victorious will stand revealed (*dokimoi,* cf. 2 Cor 10:18; 13:7; Rom 14:18)"; Land, *Die
Briefe,* 148 *("notwendigen Prozess . . . das letzte Urteil . . .").*

37. Hays, *First Cor,* 195.

38. Fee, *First Epistle,* 538.

39. Ibid. On vv. 28-32, cf. Gundry-Volf, *Paul and Perseverance,* 99-113.

40. Trypho raises the issue of Christians who eat food offered to idols in the confidence that
nothing destructive can touch them (Justin, *Dialogue,* 34:3).

41. Horsley, *1 Cor,* 159.

ranking this as a second choice is that while it makes good sense and fits the context, it construes Paul's pastoral response as unusually sharp and sarcastic. Admittedly he is sharper and more confrontational when he responds to oral reports than when he replies to the Corinthians' questions.[42] Further, 4:8-13 witnesses to his use of accusatory irony, and the notion that the Lord's Supper is so undermined that it does positive harm and becomes drunken revelry which divides the church into socially accepted and socially second-class is an outrage. Nevertheless, an even better purpose is served if the hypocrisy of self-justification is noted. Either of these two explanations explains what is otherwise regarded as a "puzzle."

20-21 These verses offer a classic and well-known example of how historical and archaeological research can shed a flood of light on the meaning of a biblical text which would not otherwise have been available. Initially with Theissen but then most clearly with Jerome Murphy-O'Connor's application of James Wiseman's archaeological work, a foundation is laid which has transformed exegesis since the early 1980s in such writers as P. Lampe and recent commentators.[43]

Virtually every commentator since the early 1980s rightly alludes to the dining customs and arrangements of the Roman world, which would certainly have a direct bearing on the source of **splits** or **dissensions** when believers met to share a common meal at which the death and risen presence of Christ was celebrated as the New Passover. The two major factors related to issues of space within a large Roman villa and to cultural customs of distinctions between the status of, and respective provision for, guests of the house.

It is possible to visit the site excavated by the American team led in the late 1970s by James Wiseman of the villa dated between AD 50 and 75 at Anaploga.[44] It lies outside the formal boundaries of the site of ancient Corinth beyond the Erastus inscription. In the Museum of Corinth inside the formally contained site of ancient Corinth the impressive mosaic floor of the triclinium (dining room) remains in view and is sufficiently complete to compare its size with the site from which it has been removed. As Murphy-O'Connor observes, the triclinium measures 5.5×7.5 meters, giving a floor area of 41.25 square meters (roughly 24×18 feet). If we allow for the couches on which guests could recline at an appropriate table, it may well be the case that (as Hays sug-

---

42. We noted Hurd's comments on this difference of tone, above.

43. Murphy-O'Connor, *St. Paul's Corinth,* 153-61; also summarized briefly in his *1 Cor,* 128-29. Cf. further his "House Churches and the Eucharist," 32-38. More recent work presupposes, builds on, and develops such work: e.g., Lampe, "Das korinthische Herrenmahl im Schnittpunkt hellenistisch-römischer Mahlpraxis und paulinischer Theologia Crucis (1 Kor 11:12-34)," 183-213; Blue, "The House Church at Corinth and the Lord's Supper: Famine, Food Supply and the Present Distress," 221-39; Hays, *1 Cor,* 195-97; Witherington, *Conflict and Community in Corinth,* 247-52; Schrage, *Der erste Brief,* 3:22-27; and Collins, *First Cor,* 417-19, also allude to H.-J. Klauck's work on comparisons with "fellowship meals" or *symposia* in the Graeco-Roman world.

44. J. Wiseman, "Corinth and Rome I:228 BC-AD 267," in *ANRW,* 528; cf. 438-548; and Murphy-O'Connor, *St. Paul's Corinth,* 155 (and plan of villa on 154).

gests) nine guests may have been a normal maximum for this comfortable dining area.[45]

An entrance vestibule led into a central atrium or courtyard-hallway, which in turn led to four or five other rooms. These included the triclinium (in the Anaploga villa, the first entrance on the right). The atrium measured 5 × 6 meters (approximately 16 × 20 feet). However, the *impluvium* (pool to collect water) stood at its center, thereby diminishing practical floor space. Between twenty and thirty people might be able to squeeze into such a place (up to fifty perhaps in the largest villas excavated, but at a post-Pauline date). If they sat or stood, Hays suggests that between thirty and forty would be possible. It is quite clear that when more than nine or ten people came to dinner, the poorer or less esteemed guests would be accorded space not in the already occupied triclinium but in the scarcely furnished atrium, which functioned in effect as an "overflow" for those who were, in the eyes of the host, lucky to be included at all. The quality of food, drink, service, and comfort would be of a higher order in the triclinium, especially if some in the atrium could arrive only after the best of the meal was over.

A second factor exacerbates such a category distinction. Pliny the Younger describes in detail the categorization of qualities of food and drink as marks of favor to grades of guests: "The best dishes were set in front of himself [the host] and a select few, and cheap scraps of food before the rest of the company. He had even put the wine into very small flasks, divided into three categories . . . one for himself and us, another for his lesser friends (all his friends are graded) and the third for his and our freed persons."[46] The volume of essays *Dining in a Classical Context* takes us still further.[47] According to Booth, only those who assumed the *toga virilis* (i.e., those who were adult males of high status) had authority "to bestow freedom to recline" in a triclinium.[48] Favored boys might sit at the foot of the couch used by a high-status male. The pattern encouraged the notion (even if indirectly by analogy) that to be invited to recline near the host in the triclinium signified a mark of favor from the host which thereby conferred added status upon the recipient of the honor. Seneca readily identifies the connections between luxurious banquets, abuse of pretty *servuli* or "luckless slave boys," and the abuse of power to confer the status of *convivius* on young men.[49] We should not, of course, equate provincial civic life with all that took place in Rome. However, the very use for manipulative purposes of the varying status indicated by food, drink and the possible loca-

---

45. Hays, *1 Cor*, 196. Collins, *First Cor*, 418-19, agrees that the space and arrangement of rooms aggravated the division.

46. Pliny, *Letters* 2.6.

47. W. J. Slater, *Dining in a Classical Context* (Ann Arbor: University of Michigan Press, 1991), esp. A. Booth, "The Age for Reclining and Its Attendant Perils," 105-20.

48. Ibid., 108.

49. Seneca, *Epistles* 95.24; cf. Plutarch, *Quaestiones Romanae* 33; Suetonius, *Augustus* 64.3 and *Claudius* 43; Polybius, 36.25.4.

tions of diners as close friends, second-class friends, hangers on, clients, head persons, youngsters, and servants speaks volumes about the discriminatory conventions presupposed in Graeco-Roman society. This is all part and parcel of the symbolic world of an honor-shame culture.

The foundation for further research on the reliance of such material for our understanding of the present passage emerged largely with Gerd Theissen's essay "Social Integration and Sacramental Activity: An Analysis of 1 Cor 11:17-34," first published in German in 1974.[50] Commenting on vv. 21 and 22, Theissen notes that "have nots" (μὴ ἔχοντες) stand in contrast to those who can have "their own meal, ἴδιον δεῖπνον." This is the primary emphasis of ἕκαστος and τὸ ἴδιον δεῖπνον, although it does not exclude a critique of individualism as well. This issue would assume still sharper proportions if B. B. Blue and B. W. Winter are correct in their assessments of the impact of the famine of AD 51 upon the poor in cities.[51] Followed by Fee, Theissen rightly declares, "ἴδιος and κυριακός refer to questions of ownership": Is it **the Lord's** [own] **supper** which is being held, or *that of the host and his most favored guests?*[52] Who is the focus of attention? For whose benefit is it being held? Indeed, to put it most sharply: *Who, indeed, is "hosting" this meal?*

The Greek vocabulary and syntax entirely invite this understanding of the key issue in vv. 20-22. The genitive absolute with ἐπὶ τὸ αὐτό denotes the act of **meeting together in the same place** as the situational context. The syntactical relationship between οὐκ ἔστιν and the aorist infinitive φαγεῖν expresses a logical definition of what **the act of eating** actually *counts as* in the situation described. Hence we translate οὐκ ἔστιν **does not amount to being** (or, we might suggest, *does not constitute*). From at least the time of Cranmer this has been expressed by many in English as a matter of "logical possibility." Thus Cranmer's Bible has *the Lordes Supper cannot bee eaten,* and Meyer, Edwards, Héring, and Conzelmann (with the RV of 1881) translate, *"It is not possible for you to eat the Lord's Supper."*[53] The difficulty is that *can* or *possible* are also regularly understood not as logical possibility (**it amounts to**; *it constitutes*), but as contingent or empirical capacity. NRSV's *"it is not really to eat the Lord's Supper"* tends to shift the emphasis from logical status to psychological intention.[54] The simpler *It is not the Lord's Supper that you eat* (REB, NIV,

50. G. Theissen, "Soziale Integration . . .," *NovT* 16 (1974): 179-206; English in Theissen, *The Social Setting of Pauline Christianity,* 145-74.

51. See Blue, "The House Church at Corinth and the Lord's Supper: Famine, Food Supply, and the Present Distress," 221-39; and Winter, "Secular and Christian Responses to Corinthian Famine," 86-106; Theissen, *Social Setting,* 148.

52. Theissen, *Social Setting,* 148. Cf. Fee, *First Epistle,* 539 and 539, n. 10: "the Lord's day" (Rev 1:10) has the same force.

53. Meyer, *First Epistle,* 1:335; Edwards, *First Epistle,* 286. Meyer cites the construction of ἔστιν with the infinitive in this sense from classical times (e.g., Thucydides, 8.53; Sophocles, *Philoctetes* 69) to the NT period (e.g., Heb 9:5). Cf. Conzelmann, *1 Cor,* 192, 194; Héring, *First Epistle,* 113.

54. Héring, *First Epistle,* 113 insists that "the idea of purpose . . . is inadmissible."

NJB) at least avoids this possible misunderstanding and adheres closely to the Greek. Conzelmann well comments, "The Corinthians destroy its character by their conduct. It is not the Lord who determines the celebration [i.e., in v. 21] but the individual. Fellowship [joint sharing] is canceled."[55]

The next controversial Greek term is προλαμβάνει (v. 21). Traditionally this has been understood to mean *goes ahead with* (NRSV, NIV, NJB [variant], and Barrett). However, Bruce Winter has argued that here the Greek has the sense of **devours** or *consumes,* and Horsley strongly supports this.[56] The value of this translation is that it places the emphasis on selfish greed rather than on courtesy or manners, and understands the prefix προ- to function as an intensive rather than as a temporal marker. Hays correctly observes that the temporal sense is possible but not demanded.[57] It may refer to the problem of those who are forced to arrive late, but we cannot assume this.[58] Hence, he suggests, *consumes his own supper* offers the best translation, which comes close to REB's *takes his own supper* (against NRSV, NIV, NJB), but rightly conveys the intensive aspect. If the background is that of the further exacerbation of "haves" and "have nots" through food shortage (Winter and others), **devour** or *consume* seems more appropriate to such a context. Fee offers the useful comment that the force of Paul's point (although not a precise translation) may be conveyed by the sense of self-absorption: "each enjoys his 'own supper' instead of the Lord's Supper."[59] Collins translates *takes by preference,* which "may mean starting to eat before others do. . . ." Paul, however, does not stress the temporal aspect of the verb on the only other occasion that he uses it (Gal 6:1).[60]

With regard to one or two remaining Greek phrases, Winter also argues that ἐν τῷ φαγεῖν carries the temporal force of **at the time of eating**.[61] This is convincing and stands in contrast with the less specific anarthrous aorist infinitive in v. 20. The phrase ὃς μὲν πεινᾷ, ὃς δὲ μεθύει seems hardly credible after two thousand years of eucharistic tradition. Actual drunkenness underlines how closely some of the hosts or wealthy adhered to the cultural expectations of private dinner parties among people of high status. The contrastive Gk. μέν . . . δέ . . . always remains difficult to reproduce in English. Paul emphasizes the contrast between the extremes, for which we suggest simply **actually** . . . **even** . . . , since these serve to *intensify* the contrast.

Finally, while we have already noted that κυριακὸν δεῖπνον denotes **Lord's Supper** in the sense of that which *belongs to* the Lord, a further comment may be added. δεῖπνον usually designates the main meal of the day in the Graeco-Roman world. Like the English dinner, it usually denotes an evening

55. Conzelmann, *I Cor,* 194.
56. Winter, "The Lord's Supper at Corinth," 73-82; Horsley, *1 Cor,* 159.
57. Hays, *First Cor,* 197. Thus BAGD, 708, speak of "the temporal sense . . . felt very little."
58. Kistemaker, *1 Cor,* 390; Barrett, *First Epistle,* 262.
59. Fee, *First Epistle,* 540.
60. Collins, *First Cor,* 422.
61. Winter, "The Lord's Supper at Corinth," 73-82.

meal in formal circles, but as in the case of the phrase "Christmas dinner" the emphasis concerns the major event rather than a specific timing. It need not always be an evening meal, although in practice it usually was. It could be translated *meal*. κυριακός denotes whatever *belongs to the Lord,* as in **the Lord's Table** in 10:21 or *the Lord's Day* in Rev 1:10. This is the earliest title for the Eucharist or Holy Communion, and in this context may perhaps equally denote "in honor of the Lord."[62] Since Paul wishes to shift the emphasis from what the community does to the Lord himself, **the Lord's Supper** constitutes a term which denotes the *focus* of thanksgiving, salvation, and sharing. In such a context it may be more appropriate than *Eucharist,* which denotes the community's *activity* of thanksgiving. However, both titles reflect ancient and respected traditions, while *Communion* looks to 1 Corinthians 10.[63]

22 The deliberative subjunctives find expression in most MSS in the two aorists εἴπω and ἐπαινέσω, **what am I to say . . . ? Am I to commend . . . ?** The very early 𝔭[46] and early B read the present indicative ἐπαινῶ in place of ἐπαινέσω (which strictly could be either aorist subjunctive or future indicative). However, this is almost certainly by assimilation to the following ἐπαινῶ, as Fee observes.[64]

The Greek grammar and syntax deserve close attention. The first negative μή introduces a question which anticipates the answer "no," **surely it cannot be . . . can it?** The second negative οὐκ qualifies the statement about having houses. *Could it be (surely not!)* **that you have no homes . . . ?** The use of εἰς with the articular infinitive conveys the sense of *with a view to, for the purpose of. . . .* Hence Paul expostulates that if *what is in view* is a celebratory party or private dinner, they should use *their homes* for such a purpose. Are they really forced by some economic or social factor to hold dual-purpose events in the same house? Hence, **have you no houses for your eating and drinking** takes account of the εἰς τὸ ἐσθίειν construction more explicitly than *do you not have homes to eat and drink in?* (NRSV, REB, NIV; cf., better, *for doing* **your eating and drinking** *in?* (NJB). The genitive τοῦ θεοῦ is doubtless possessive, as it is in 1:2 (see above; cf. also 3:16). The church is more than simply a human society in institution; it belongs to **God.** To show contempt for **the church, which is God's,** is to despise what God has made his own, and on which God has set his love, and therefore given it status and honor in his own eyes.

62. Fee, *First Epistle,* 539-40.

63. δεῖπνον denotes the Eucharist in Chrysostom, *1 Cor. Hom.,* 14:5; *Isa. Hom.,* 6:1; Cyril of Alexandria, *Diverse Homilies,* 10:5; also Dionysius the Areopagite, *De Ecclesias Hierarchiis* 3; 3:1; and Basil, *Regulae Brevius Tractatae,* 310 (with κυριακός) as well as Paul; εὐχαριστία goes back to *Didache* 9:1, Clement of Alexandria, *Stromata,* 4:25, and many other patristic sources; cf. Lampe, *Patristic Greek Lexicon,* 580, κυριακός (see above) of all that pertains to God or more especially to Christ, e.g., *the Lord's house* (Clement, *Stromata,* 3:18), *the Lord's day* as his day of worship (*Didache* 14:1), or *the day of the Lord* as the last day (Origen, *John,* 10:35) cf. Lampe, *Patristic Greek Lexicon,* 786.

64. Fee, *First Epistle,* 535, n. 20.

From the time of Findlay some have translated μὴ ἔχοντας as the **have nots** (taken up, e.g., by B. W. Winter and our heading).[65] Since Paul is concerned about the effect of this selfish, thoughtless, and insensitive conduct upon brothers and sisters in Christ who suffer deprivation in an honor-shame culture, we translate καταισχύνετε as **put to shame** (with NJB; cf. *shame,* REB), although the intensive preposition justifies *humiliate* (NRSV, NIV) as a legitimate alternative. The nuance of the deliberative subjunctives should be preserved: **what I am to say? Am I to congratulate you** (see above on textual note). NJB's **congratulate** adds force to Paul's irony. The second occurrence of ἐπαινῶ, however, signifies the withholding **approval**.

On the contrast between meals in **homes** and **the Lord's Supper** when believers **meet as a church**, see above. It may be the case, as Fee and Horsley argue, that Paul alludes to *having houses* in an explicit reference to *house owners.* Need this mean that, as Fee also urges, we must translate οἰκίας as *houses,* not as *homes* (against NJB, NRSV, NIV, REB, and Hays)?[66] In current English the semantic scope of **home** has expanded to include *home owner,* even though this is technically an abuse of the traditional distinction between *house* and *home.* Here Paul seems to be drawing on a double contrast: (a) if you own a house, you should not assimilate *times when you invite guests to a meal* with your celebrations of **Lord's Supper** when you meet in your house/home with fellow believers *as a church;* (b) the "sacred space" and more especially "sacred time" implicit in the use of a person's home as a gathering for worship should not be confused with domestic utilizations of the same space.[67] As Stephen Barton observes, Paul seeks to reorder "social relations in the church by restricting the intrusion of household-based power."[68] The issue turns at least in part on "where the line is to be drawn between church and household: 1 Cor 14:33b-36 and 1 Cor 11:17-34."[69]

Witherington constructively takes up Barton's point. However, *it is anachronistic and hardly true to Paul to describe Paul's concern for "one body" and "sharing" (κοινωνία) as "more democratic."*[70] A more profoundly theological understanding of Paul's mind is offered by Lionel Thornton.[71] *"Democracy" simply continues the mind-set of modern individualism but within an egalitarian value system.* It does not restore solidarity and care for the other in place of competitive individualism. The Pauline emphasis on "sharing the Lord's death" ex-

65. Findlay, *Expositor's Greek Testament,* 3:879, on the ground that οἱ ἔχοντες often means *persons or property.* Cf. Winter, "The Lord's Supper at Corinth," 73-82.

66. Fee, *First Epistle,* 543; against Hays, *First Cor,* 197; cf. Horsley, *1 Cor,* 157-58.

67. S. C. Barton, "Paul's Sense of Place: An Anthropological Approach to Community Formation in Corinth," *NTS* 32 (1986): 225-46; cf. also Witherington, *Conflict and Community in Corinth,* 242.

68. Barton, "Paul's Sense of Place," 239.

69. Ibid., 225.

70. Witherington, *Conflict and Community,* 242.

71. Thornton, *The Common Life in the Body of Christ,* 5-95, 156-87, 253-87, 322-55, esp. 327-44.

poses the huge hermeneutical gulf that exists between "democracy" and Paul's more radical, transformative, communal, noncompetitive theology of the cross and the one New Creation. Witherington is no less misleading in his comparison with "a Saturnalia," for this again risks imposing alien categories on the nature of the issue at Corinth. Even Barton may go too far in his generally constructive use of sociological models from other cultures and traditions.[72] In contrast to a series of *socially constructed* customs and conventions, Paul as apostle now appeals to the *givenness* of a *specific tradition* **received from the Lord**.

23-24 (1) D replaces the earlier ἀπό before τοῦ κυρίου in v. 23 with παρά. Both mean **from** with the genitive, but D can be explained because Paul usually uses παρά with παραλαμβάνειν, understandably (cf. 1 Thess 2:13; 4:1; Gal 1:12, et al.). It is conceivable that the original difference of preposition calls attention to the reception of a tradition *originally* rather than *"directly"* (in a charismatic sense) **from the Lord**, but this can be suggested not on the basis of any difference between the force of the prepositions, but only in the sense that **received from** occurs here in a slightly different sense from most occurrences of the phrase. The reading ἀπὸ θεοῦ (F and G) is secondary and later. (2) In v. 24 the KJV/AV, the 1662 Book of Common Prayer, and the *Textus Receptus* of the Western tradition presuppose λάβετε φάγετε, *take, eat.* However, this reading is secondary, found in C[3], K, L, P, Old Latin and Vulgate Clementine ed., Syriac witnesses, and many minuscule MSS. Its absence from the early p[46], ℵ, A, B, C*, D, F, G, 33, Coptic, Cyprian, Basil, Chrysostom, et al., together with its occurrence in Matt 26:26 as an obvious source of assimilation, rightly leads Metzger and others to endorse the UBS 4th ed. in categorizing its omission as "A," i.e., "certain."[73] From RV (1881 onward), translators render the clause **which is for you** (RV, REB, NIV, NJB) or *that* **is for you** (NRSV).

(3) Another later variant inserts κλώμενον before ὑπὲρ ὑμῶν, *broken* **for you**, found in ℵ[c], C[3], D[b], G, K, and many Syriac MSS and Byzantine witnesses. Again, however, it is absent from the early p[46], ℵ*, A, B, C*, 33, Origen, Cyprian, et al., and can readily be explained as an explication of ἔκλασεν (v. 24), which is authentic. Hence no issue of meaning other than fuller explication is at issue. Similarly, one other later insertion, διδόμενον, given for you (Vulgate, Coptic), is an assimilation on the basis of Luke 22:19 and is already implicit in Paul's **which is for you**. The concise phrase is characteristic of Paul's style.[74] Among major modern translations, only Moffatt seems to have retained the longer and later *broken for you,* although Marshall holds that the inclusion of Luke's *given (for you)* may reflect the earliest stage of the saying.[75]

Over against the culture-specific issues which undermined the very purpose of sharing in the Lord's Supper at Corinth (v. 17b), Paul appeals to the givenness and universality of a pre-Pauline tradition which originated with **the Lord** himself as a dominical institution and is transmitted as Christian *paradosis* in terms which soon became a formulaic liturgical narrative in the life of the churches. At the time of writing the most recent research of substance and detail on Paul's

72. Barton, "Paul's Sense of Place," 226-28.
73. Metzger, *Textual Commentary* (2d ed.), 496.
74. Ibid.
75. Marshall, *Last Supper and Lord's Supper,* 182.

use of tradition for the purposes of argument comes from Anders Eriksson in a careful and most useful study (although O. Hofius's shorter treatment of the same subject [1993, in oral form 1988] remains also of the utmost importance).[76] The introductory formula ἐγὼ παρέλαβον ὃ καὶ παράδωκα ὑμῖν makes it clear that Paul has delivered this tradition to the Corinthians.[77] The parallelism between the bread-saying and cup-saying and the syntactical role of **the Lord Jesus** (v. 23) render the self-contained "received" character of vv. 23-25 "unproblematic."[78] Jeremias also cites several *"idioms foreign to Paul"* in these verses (his italics), including, e.g., εὐχαριστεῖν used absolutely to designate grace at table, κλᾶν without an object, ἀνάμνησις, and six other examples.[79] Even if the form was not "completely fixed," there can be no doubt whatever that these verses are pre-Pauline and are perhaps "the only place that Paul, *at least in a longer quotation,* betrays his knowledge of the Jesus tradition which later became the synoptic gospels" (italics mine).[80]

The REB (similarly NJB) is entirely justified, therefore, in translating v. 23a as *For the tradition which I handed on to you. . . .* Horsley and Schrage observe, "'Received' and 'handed on' in 11:23 (cf. 15:1-3) were virtually technical terms in Jewish culture for the transmission of important traditions . . . (cf. m. Abot 1:1). Hellenistic philosophies used the same terms in transmitting their standard doctrines. To emphasize the authority of this central . . . tradition Paul identifies it as having come 'from the Lord' . . . focussed on Jesus' death."[81] Moule regards the Greek terms as "naturally apply[ing] to the receiving and transmitting of traditions," while Marshall also sees here "a liturgical formula which he had handed on to the church when it was founded . . . a form of words which was regarded as authoritative in the church generally and was not Paul's own composition. . . . The origin of the Lord's Supper in the explicit command of Jesus as the Lord is thus emphasized."[82] Paul's own willingness to accept and to stand under the authority of this tradition rather than to revise it for his own purposes is underlined by Neuenzeit, and, as McGowan recently argues, this prohibits us from obscuring the reception of this dominical legacy "by the figure of the authoritative apostle."[83] This is not to ignore those scholars who

76. Eriksson, *Traditions as Rhetorical Proof: Pauline Argumentation in 1 Corinthians,* esp. 100-134, on 11:23-25; and Hofius, "The Lord's Supper and the Lord's Supper Tradition: Reflections on 1 Cor 11:23b-25," in Meyer (ed.), *One Loaf, One Cup,* 75-115. See also McGowan, "Is There a Liturgical Text in This Gospel? The Institution Narratives and Their Early Interpretative Communities," 73-87.

77. Eriksson, *Traditions as Rhetorical Proof,* 100.

78. Ibid.

79. Jeremias, *The Eucharistic Words of Jesus,* 104.

80. Eriksson, *Traditions,* 100; cf. Jeremias, *Eucharistic Words,* 103-5.

81. Horsley, *1 Cor,* 160; Schrage, *Der erste Brief,* 29-31.

82. C. F. D. Moule, *Worship in the NT* (London: Lutterworth, 1961), 24 (cf. 18-46); Marshall, *Last Supper and Lord's Supper,* 111 and 112; also Wolff, *Der erste Brief,* 263.

83. Neuenzeit, *Das Herrenmahl: Studien zur paulinischen Eucharistie-auffassung,* esp. 1,033-35; McGowan, "Is There a Liturgical Text in This Gospel?" 78; cf. 73-87. (The question in

claim that the narrative of the institution of the Lord's Supper does not originate from Jesus himself; however, such a view remains in the minority and lacks convincing weight.[84]

We should not assume that the Corinthians ignored this tradition, nor that they doubted its dominical origin. McGowan very constructively links the transmission of traditions with the insights of reader-response theorists (while rightly being aware of their limitations and potential for overstatement). The Corinthian church may well have perceived and interpreted the tradition as an injunction to the performance of thankful celebration of Christ's victory as Lord. "'Do this in memory of me' would seem to lead to 'thanksgiving' (or 'blessing' which was often equivalent) . . . more easily than to recitation of the words 'this is my body which is for you.' . . ."[85] Paul reinterprets the tradition in a way which he perceives to be more faithful to the context in which the words originated. This does not invalidate McGowan's argument that the words of institution did not necessarily constitute words of liturgical *recital* from early times, as may be inferred, he argues, from Justin, Hippolytus, and probably the *Didache*.[86] Marshall, anticipating this more "open" view of the words, states that in the specific quotation of the words of institution Paul gives "a description of what Jesus did at a meal" rather than a legislative account of "what the church ought to do."[87] It is the frame of theology and Paul's allusion to the context of these words that serve to press Paul's point most distinctively.

Eriksson identifies what motivated his constructive 1998 study of Paul's eight uses of common pre-Pauline tradition in 1 Corinthians to promote a distinctive "rhetoric" or mode of argument: "The original impetus of my study was the disturbing fact that the words of institution (1 Cor 11:23-25) and the Gospel summary (15:3-5) seldom in modern commentaries were related to the context in which they are found."[88] Eriksson acknowledges, but expresses dissatisfaction with, the work on relevant Pauline uses of tradition carried out by A. Seeberg (1903), E. Lohmeyer (1927), O. Cullmann (1943 and 1954), Klaus

---

inner quotation marks constitutes an intertextual allusion to Stanley Fish, *Is There a Text in This Class?*).

84. For recent questioning works, see (e.g.) J. Meier, "The Eucharist at the Last Supper: Did It Happen?" *Theology Digest* 42 (1995): 335-51; and J. D. Crossan, *The Historical Jesus: The Life of a Mediterranean Jewish Peasant* (San Francisco: Harper, 1991), 360-67. Against such claims cf. the works cited above by Hofius, Eriksson, and others.

85. McGowan, "'Is There a Liturgical Text in This Gospel?'" 80.

86. Ibid., 75-76, 80-85, citing Justin, *Apology*, 1:66:2, 3, and *Dialogues*, 41:1 and 70:3-4; Hippolytus, *Apostolic Tradition*, 4; cf. M. Metzger, "Nouvelles perspectives pour la prétendue *Tradition Apostolique*," *Ecclesia Orans* 5 (1988): 241-59, and E. Yarnold, "Anaphoras without Institution Narratives?" *Studia Patristica* 30 (1997): 395-410. Cf. the warning of Barrett, *First Epistle,* 264, and Fee's caution, *First Epistle,* 549, n. 22. On the other hand, see Hofius, "The Lord's Supper and the Lord's Supper Tradition: Reflections on 1 Cor 11:23b-25," in Meyer (ed.), *One Loaf, One Cup,* 75-88, for the view that it speedily became fixed in liturgy.

87. Marshall, *Last Supper and Lord's Supper,* 111.

88. Eriksson, *Traditions as Rhetorical Proof,* 4. The other passages are 8:1-6; 10:16; 12:3 (cf. 12:13); 15:3-5; 16:22.

Wegenast (1962), Hans von Campenhausen (1972), K. Wengst (1972), and Hermann von Lips (1991), although rightly he pays tribute to V. H. Neufeld's *The Earliest Christian Confessions* (1963) as among "the most thorough of these studies."[89]

This now throws into relief the importance of Paul's specific allusion to the context of the words of institution as ἐν τῇ νυκτὶ ᾗ παρεδίδετο. The allusion to the meal's being at **night** favors the view that it was a Passover meal (see the Note below). But should the verb (in Koine form) be translated *he was betrayed* (with AV/KJV, 1662 Book of Common Prayer, NRSV, NIV, NJB, Barrett, Conzelmann), or *he was arrested* (REB), or *delivered up* (Rotherham, *The Emphasized NT*), or **he was handed over** (as above with Collins)? BAGD list **hand over**, *deliver*, as their first entry under the active παραδίδωμι, with examples from the Gospels (Matt 25:20, 22), Josephus (*Antiquities* 4.83), and the subapostolic period (*1 Clement* 12:5), as well as from Paul (1 Cor 13:3, "I hand over my body . . ."). However, they also note the use of the verb "especially of the betrayal of Jesus by Judas w. acc and dat Matt 26:15; cf. Mk 14:10; Lk 22:4, 6; Jn 19:11; passive Matt 20:18; Mk 10:33a." They conclude, however, "It is not certain that when Paul uses such terms as 'handing over', 'delivering up', 'arrest' . . . he is thinking of the betrayal of Judas."[90] Moulton-Milligan also suggest **hand over** as "its ordinary meaning," allowing that *deliver up* constitutes an additional area.[91] Within these domains, we may agree, *betrayed* may or may not denote a specific subdomain. Fee observes, "The verb 'betrayed' is just ambiguous enough so that it could mean 'handed over' (as in '. . . over to death')."[92] He concludes that the word "most likely" refers first to the treachery of Judas, but his main reason is simply that an allusion to the betrayal occurs in the Jesus tradition of the announcement of the betrayal at the time of the Last Supper.[93]

Other factors, however, deserve consideration also. First, Hays notes that hardly any commentator or translator takes account of Paul's play on παρέδωκα (**I handed on**, v. 23a) and παρεδίδετο (**was handed over**, v. 23b).[94] Second, the *theological* emphasis of both the *content* and the *context* of the tradition in the Gospels and in Paul (cf. Eriksson's points, above) is that Jesus was "'handed over' *(paredothē)* to death **by God** 'for our trespasses'. . . . God 'gave him up' *(paradōken)* for all of us (Rom 8:32) . . . echoes of the Septuagint's rendering of Isaiah 53:6 ('And the Lord *gave him up* [*paredōken*] for our sins . . .')" (Hays's italics).[95] Hays insists that this theme eclipses the proposed allusion to betrayal by Judas and provides "the background against which 1 Cor 11:23 must be un-

---

89. Ibid., 78. Cf. 77-134 and the bibliography of 11:17-34 for titles of these works.
90. BAGD, 614-15, esp. 614, col. 2. The UBS text rightly reads the Koine form of the verb.
91. Cf. MM, 482-83.
92. Fee, *First Epistle,* 549.
93. Ibid., 549 and 549, n. 26.
94. Hays, *First Cor,* 198.
95. Ibid. Also Schrage, *Der erste Brief,* 3:29-35.

derstood." Third, we recall Eriksson's fundamental argument that Paul uses tradition as a shared presupposition with his readers on the basis of which he may press a specific argument. Here what dominates 11:17-34 is concern for the weak, the other, the despised, as precisely what sharing in Christ's death as the **handing over** of the self to be used for God's loving work of reconciliation and redemption *includes.* Just as the Lord's Supper looks back to the last supper when Jesus was about to be **handed over**, *voluntarily to renounce self-direction and autonomy to place his selfhood and destiny in the hands of God and human persons without any further "say" in what happens,* so, Paul argues, by **proclaiming it** in word, sacrament, attitude, and life.

Eriksson's careful argument is too detailed to reproduce here. However, it coheres precisely with these points. He writes: "What is the behavior prescribed by the words of institution? The answer . . . lies in Paul's use of the tradition in 11:26. . . . Their behavior at the Lord's Supper celebrations is, or at least should be, a proclamation of the Lord's death. For Paul this is a logical consequence of the tradition."[96] This explains precisely why underlying 11:17-34 is a factor which (again) "the majority of interpreters have tended to overlook," namely, "the Corinthians' claim that they deserved praise" (i.e., for *observing* the tradition).[97] "The tradition itself lifts the whole argumentation . . . to a higher plane" which concerns what it is to share in the life and death of "the Lord of the church Himself."[98] The translation of the single word παραδίδετο thus well illustrates the reality of the hermeneutical circle (in its initial sense of the relation between parts and whole in F. Ast and F. Schleiermacher). This detail both influences and reflects our understanding of the whole broader succession of verses.[99]

The participle εὐχαριστήσας may, as Jeremias urges, mean simply, *said grace* (i.e., at table) or **gave thanks.**[100] If, with Fee, we speak of the Jewish practice in which the head of the house would be "giving the traditional blessing over the bread, breaking it, and giving it to those at table," we must avoid any hint that the object of such blessing was the bread, as if to read back an anachronistic parallel with eucharistic "consecration of the elements." The Jewish table grace expressed *blessing God* for God's good gifts. REB's explanatory gloss **gave thanks** *to God* is useful and on this basis perfectly justifiable, although it explicates what is implicit but absent from the text, no doubt because *to God* was quite obviously understood by the readers. If we compare *m. Berakoth* 8:1-5 with *m. Pesahim* 10:2-7, whether the context is grace at meals

---

96. Eriksson, *Traditions,* 186; cf. 179-96.

97. Ibid., 177.

98. Ibid.

99. The detailed discussion of *tradition* above seems to run counter to the view that "the Lord communicated immediately to Paul the truth in question . . . in some . . . visionary way" and to render unnecessary "a possible compromise. . . . Paul received the factual tradition by human means, but received the interpretation of it directly from the Lord" (Barrett, *First Epistle,* 265).

100. Jeremias, *Eucharistic Words,* 104 and 111.

or the blessing of God for the three cups at the Passover meal, "saying the Benediction" uniformly means *blessing God for his gifts, not* "blessing" the gifts.[101] Hence **gave thanks** is an appropriate translation for the verb εὐχαριστεῖν in a Greek-speaking setting, even if Jesus would have *blessed God* as the customary Jewish form of thanksgiving. Such modern versions of "grace" as "bless this food . . ." are not only alien to the meaning conveyed by giving **thanks** to God, whether in the context of Jerusalem, Jesus, or Paul, but also risk imposing at the earliest stage an overly explicit overtone of eucharistic "consecration."

In spite of its later date, the Jewish Passover Haggadah reflects the tradition in question, whether Paul is describing the last supper as an ordinary meal or whether (as the Synoptic Gospels seem to imply, supposedly against the Fourth Gospel) Jesus presided at a Passover meal. The standard form remains, "Blessed art Thou, O Lord, our God, King of the universe, who [e.g.] sustaineth the whole world. . . . He giveth bread to all flesh . . .": **בָּרוּךְ אַתָּה יי אֱלֹהֵינוּ מֶלֶךְ הָעוֹלָם אֲשֶׁר** *(baruk ʾattah y-y ʾeloheynu melek haʿolam ʾasher . . .).*[102] The meaning and translation of εὐχαριστήσας are therefore unaffected by the notorious controversy about whether the last supper constituted for Jesus a Passover meal or simply a fellowship on the eve of the Passover.

On the other hand, the contextual significance of ἄρτον, **bread** (as REB, NIV, AV/KJV, 1662 Book of Common Prayer, or *loaf of bread* (NRSV; *some bread,* NJB), and especially of the key words τοῦτό μού ἐστιν τὸ σῶμα τὸ ὑπὲρ ὑμῶν, does depend to some degree on whether these words were spoken in the context of a Passover meal. Hence a short note must be assigned to this question.

WAS THE LAST SUPPER A PASSOVER MEAL? SIGNIFICANCE FOR EXEGESIS

The question is frequently posed as one of sharp contradiction between the Synoptic Gospels and John. In the three Synoptics to prepare this meal is explicitly described as preparing the Passover meal (Mark 14:12-16; Luke 22:7-13). However, John states that the day of the crucifixion was the day of Preparation of the Passover (John 19:24). The Jewish opponents of Jesus do not enter the Praetorium lest they might be defiled, and so they could eat the Passover (John 18:28). John 13:1 speaks of the supper as "before the Feast of the Passover."[103] Some writers argue that the account of the institution became a self-contained unit so early that we can no longer rely on its setting in either the Synoptics or in John, but such a view has been firmly challenged.[104]

---

101. Cf. Danby, *The Mishnah,* 8-9 and 150-51; Strack-Billerbeck, 4:41-76.

102. Hebrew in Roth (ed.), *The Haggadah: A New Edition* (London: Soncino, 1934 [5694]), 46-67, with notes. These pages are headed "Grace," while 39-43 provide parallel examples for the thanksgivings in the washing, over the bread, the Mazzah, and the bitter herb.

103. Cf. among other sources Marshall, *Last Supper,* 57-75 and his Table 4, 184-85.

104. See n. 84 above on Meir and Crossan, with the replies of Hofius and Eriksson. See also Schweizer, *The Lord's Supper according to the NT,* 29; R. Bultmann, *History of the Synoptic Tradi-*

P. Billerbeck (followed by I. H. Marshall) proposed that two different calendars were in use, each a day out of step with the other, and observed respectively by the Sadducees and the Pharisees.[105] A. Jaubert distinguished between an official lunar calendar observed by the Jerusalem priesthood and presupposed by John, and a calendar (different by one day) used at Qumran and perhaps in Galilee which the Synoptists may have followed.[106] A whole array of further factors have been the subject of hypotheses to explain the apparent durability of the traditions: while "pure" Jews and certainly the Jewish priesthood would have counted the Jewish day as commencing at around 6 p.m. (or related to sunset), the Roman calendar (perhaps followed by Galileans in a more Gentile context, or even, according to H. Hoehner, the Pharisees); others appeal to the fact that δεῖπνον denotes the main meal of the twenty-four-hour period, which may be eaten around noon, in early afternoon, late afternoon, or evening. The timing of the slaughter of the Passover sacrifices also invites consideration.

It would take us beyond our purpose to explore details. In brief, three main hypotheses exist (to which we shall add a fourth). (1) Many accept the Synoptic tradition and view the last supper as a Passover meal, explaining John's framework or comments as underlining his view of Jesus himself as the lamb of the Passover (John 1:29, 36; 19:14). This view is urged by, e.g., G. Dalman, A. J. B. Higgins, F. Leenhardt, and J. Jeremias. See the extended note on "The Cup of Blessing" under 10:16, esp. sect. (iii).[107] (2) Some insist that the Fourth Gospel corresponds more closely with external reasons for dating, and explain the Synoptic tradition as either confused or as referring to a different fellowship meal, perhaps including the *qiddush* prayer said at a festival meal by the head of the household. This view is advocated by J. H. Bernard, G. Ogg, A. Strobel, and R. E. Brown, although Higgins and Kilpatrick urge (against Lietzmann) that Jesus and the Twelve do not form a *chaburah* type religious fellowship. On Lietzmann's view, see the extended note on "The Cup of Blessing" under 10:16, esp. sect. (ii).[108] (3) If more than one calendar system was operative, the traditions need not conflict, and a judgment about the Passover meal must be made on the basis of its content and/or the probable clarity of the Synoptic tradition (P. Billerbeck, J. Klausner, A. Jaubert, I. H. Marshall, D. Chwolson).[109]

---

tion (Eng. trans., Oxford: Blackwell, 1963), 265-67 (with John Meier and J. D. Crossan, cited above), against which see Marshall, *Last Supper,* 35; Dunn, *Theology of Paul the Apostle,* 607-8; Pesch, *Das Abendmahl und Jesu Todesverständnis,* 70-71.

105. Strack-Billerbeck, 2:812-53; cf. Marshall *Last Supper,* 71-72.

106. A. Jaubert, *La date de la Cène. Calendrier biblique et liturgie chrétienne* (Paris: Études biblique, 1957), 105-36. Jaubert's theory is less widely accepted.

107. G. Dalman, *Jesus-Jeschua* (Eng. trans., London: SPCK, 1929); Higgins, *The Lord's Supper in the NT,* 13-23 and 75-78; F. Leenhardt (with O. Cullmann), *Essays on the Lord's Supper* (Eng. trans., London: Lutterworth, 1958), 39-43; Jeremias, *Eucharistic Words,* 15-88; Cf., however, O. Hofius, "The Lord's Supper and the Lord's Supper Tradition," in Meyer (ed.), *One Loaf, One Cup,* 75-88.

108. G. Ogg, "The Chronology of the Last Supper," in SPCK Theological Collections 6, *Historicity and Chronology in the NT* (London: SPCK, 1965), 75-96; A. Strobel, *Ursprung und Geschichte des frühchristlichen Osterkalen-ders* (Berlin: Texte und Untersuchungen 1977); R. B. Brown, *The Gospel according to John* (2 vols.; New York: Doubleday, 1966), 2:556, and more fully in *The Death of the Messiah* (2 vols., London: Chapman, 1994), 2:1356-74.

109. H. W. Hoehner, *Chronological Aspects of the Life of Christ* (Grand Rapids: Zondervan, 1977), 84; Marshall, *Last Supper,* 57-75, 184-85; and Jaubert and others, cited above.

Even if the Johannine chronology were conclusive, however, this would not exclude a fourth explanation, namely, that, as the Synoptists state, Jesus instructed his disciples to prepare *their* Passover meal, thereby integrating the fellowship meal as a redemptive, salvation-participation religious meal bound up with his immediate forthcoming death as the New Passover. In this sense, Leenhardt and Hofius identify a key emphasis. Leenhardt writes, "A few hours before His separation from them, Jesus partook of the traditional Passover meal with His disciples. Why? Shall we say that it is because it happened to be the day, the 14th of Nisan? Perhaps, but this reason is inadequate.... He wanted to introduce into the traditional ritual the most surprising innovation.... He only [?] celebrated the Passover in order to introduce this astonishing change. Jesus uses the tradition as a frame ... the deliverance from Egypt.... According to the Mishnah: 'In every generation a man must so regard himself *as if he came forth himself out of Egypt*' [*m. Pesahim* 10:5, my italics]. Everyone had to participate in the great redemption.... The past reaches and joins the present."[110] The "surprising innovation" which Jesus inserts into this frame is the "totally new element.... Taking the bread, he said: 'This is my body.'"[111]

In spite of his reservations about a clear identification between the last supper and the Passover meal, Hofius also argues that more broadly the words of Jesus, transmitted by Paul, are to be understood as that of "worshipful 'remembering'" of a kind "especially to be met in statements about Passover, which is performed 'in memory of' Israel's redemption from Egyptian slavery."[112] "This is my body" and the word over the cup "both speak of the *expiatory death* of Jesus Christ" (Hofius's italics) and, like the Passover, of covenantal promise.[113] Nevertheless, Hofius adds, such "remembrance" and "participation" is not confined to the Passover alone. On Sabbaths and even in daily prayer "the memory of the foundational saving event ... has its firm place."[114] Hofius explains the importance of this Passover frame for our understanding of several key phrases which follow in 11:24, 25. For example, τὴν ἐμὴν ἀνάμνησιν "can only mean 'in remembrance of' the crucified one, who gave up his body to death for his own and by whose expiatory death (= blood) the economy of eschatological salvation is established.... 'Remembering (z-k-r, Ps 105:5a) is therefore realized in 'proclaiming' (y-d-', v. 1b)."[115] It has nothing to do with "ancient meals in memory of the dead."[116]

Leenhardt rightly insists that only the Passover framework provides the proper contextual guideline (we should wish to say "background" in the technical sense used by John Searle of that which facilitates communicative competency to understand) for the meaning of "This is my body."[117] However, it is E. Ruckstuhl (also with Schrage) who

110. F. J. Leenhardt, "This Is My Body," in O. Cullmann and F. Leenhardt, *Essays on the Lord's Supper* 39-40.

111. Ibid., 40.

112. Hofius, "The Lord's Supper and the Lord's Supper Tradition," in Meyer (ed.), *One Loaf, One Cup,* 104; cf. Exod 12:14; 13:3, 9; Deut 16:3; *Jubilees* 49:7-23; Josephus, *Antiquities* 2:317; *m. Pesahim* 10:37d; 34:17.

113. Ibid., 99.

114. Ibid., 105.

115. Ibid., 103 and 106.

116. Ibid., 104.

117. Leenhardt, "This Is My Body," in O. Cullmann and F. J. Leenhardt, *Essays on the Lord's Supper* 39-40; cf. J. R. Searle, *Intentionality: An Essay in the Philosophy of Mind* (Cam-

most helpfully places "This is my body" explicitly in the context of the Haggadah.[118] In the Haggadah the person who presides explains the various elements, objects, and events which fulfill a redemptive role in the history of God's people, beginning "a wandering Aramean was my father . . ." (Deut 26:5-11; cf. Exod 12:4-39). The *Mishnah* identifies these objects as including a "remembrance" of redemption through Passover, through unleavened bread, and through bitter herbs "as if in every generation he himself came forth from Egypt. . . . He brought us from bondage to freedom (*m. Pesahim* 10:5)." The breaking of the bread is accompanied by the *haroseth* (nuts and fruit pounded together and mixed with vinegar, *m. Pes.* 10:4). In such a context "This is . . ." addresses a horizon of expectation in which the presiding host is about to designate an instrument in the redemptive process. Now, as the "surprise" or "novelty" (Leenhardt) Jesus designates "my body" and "my blood" as the decisive vehicles of redemption.

Hence, the issue of whether or not a Passover frame is presupposed as the framework of interpretation for last supper and the Lord's Supper (and its tradition) has a decisive effect upon the exegesis of vv. 23b-25. In our view, the many factors customarily cited to establish a Passover framework remain utterly convincing.[119] The only serious counter-argument, namely, the witness of the Fourth Gospel, may be explained *either* (1) on the basis of different calendars; *or* (2) on the basis of John's primary concern with the death of Christ (to which the Lord's Supper points and which it proclaims) as the central feature of an integrated Passover theology of redemption; *or* on the basis of the view that Jesus held *his* Passover for the Twelve in advance of the official calendar. The details turn out to be immaterial: Jesus presided at a Passover meal which proclaimed his own broken body and shed blood as the new Passover for Christian believers. "For Paul the Last Supper corresponds to the Passover of Judaism; it is the new Passover . . . εἰς ἀνάμνησιν is the equivalent of *lezeker* (לזכר) . . . of the Haggadah, except that Christ has been substituted for 'the day thou camest forth from Egypt.'"[120] All this coheres with Eriksson's conclusion, "The punch line of Paul's argument is hence the statement: 'Your Lord's Supper celebration is a proclamation of the death of Christ.'"[121] We may now resume our exegesis.

---

bridge: Cambridge University Press, 1983), 19-20, 144-59; also expounded in Thiselton, *New Horizons in Hermeneutics,* 45-46 and 362-63.

118. E. Ruckstuhl, "Zur Chronologie der Leidensgeschichte Jesu," in A. Fuchs (ed.), *Studien zum Neuen Testament und seiner Umwelt* (Linz, 1985), 41-44; cf. 27-61; see also E. Ruckstuhl, *Die Chronologie der letzen Mahles und des Leidens Jesu* (Einsiedeln: Benziger, 1963), and *Jesus im Horizont der Evangelien* (Stuttgart: SBA, 1988), 69-99; also Schrage, *Der erste Brief,* 3:35-45, where *covenant* also receives due emphasis.

119. These include, e.g.: (i) the Last Supper took place in the evening and extended into the night (1 Cor 11:23; cf. Mark 14:17; John 13:30), although apart from the Passover the main meal (δεῖπνον) would more normally be in the afternoon; (ii) at the Passover, people reclined (rather than sat) as a symbol of liberty (cf. John 13:23); (iii) a preliminary dish preceded the breaking of bread (Mark 14:20; Matt 26:23; John 13:26); (iv) at Passover alms were given to the poor (John 13:29); (v) wine was drunk at the Passover; (vi) the Passover and the Last Supper concluded with a hymn (Mark 14:26; Matt 26:30), generally from Psalm 114 or 115–118; and (vii) the words of Jesus entirely cohere with the explanatory narrative of events of the redemptive history of God's people. (See Jeremias; and Hofius, "This Is My Body," 39-40.) Further, in addition to citing "Paschal Features in the Last Supper," Marshall replies to "objections" to this case. Marshall, *Last Supper,* 58-66.

120. W. D. Davies, *Paul and Rabbinic Judaism* (London: SPCK, 2d ed. 1955 [1948]), 252.

121. Eriksson, *Traditions,* 187.

ἔκλασεν (v. 24a) receives particular significance in the light of the words that follow, as the secondary reading κλώμενον [ὑπὲρ ὑμῶν] indicates (see above under Textual Notes, 3). In isolation from the following words of Jesus, however, *breaking bread* has a significance which may vary from social to socioreligious depending on its broader context of discourse. Moule observes: "For the devout Jew there was no meal that was not sacred. Indeed it is an unprofitable question to ask whether 'the breaking' *(Klasis)* means a merely 'secular' act or a ritual 'fraction' of the loaf."[122] In some contexts breaking the bread denotes only "the beginning of the meal."[123] On the other hand, in the context of the last supper and the Lord's Supper all four accounts include the same pair of Greek words ἄρτον . . . ἔκλασεν (Matt 26:26; Mark14:22; Luke 22:19; 1 Cor 11:23b, 24a).

Breaking bread has the communal sense of sharing in solidarity of objective fellowship (κοινωνία, that in which participants or shareholders share, not primarily the subjective feeling associated with this), and this aspect finds expression in 1 Cor 10:16 (τὸν ἄρτον ὃν κλῶμεν; see commentary on 10:16 above) and probably also in Acts 2:42, 46, (although the precise meaning of *breaking bread* in Acts 2 should not be presupposed without careful inquiry).[124] In the *Didache,* however, more clearly the breaking of bread on Sunday is the Eucharist in the full sense of the term: κατὰ κυριακὴν δὲ κυρίου (on the Lord's Day of the Lord, i.e., the double festal and eschatological title) συναχθέντες (cf. 1 Cor 11:17, 18) κλάσετε ἄρτον καὶ εὐχαριστήσατε . . . καθαρὰ ἡ θυσία ὑμῶν ᾖ.[125] Earlier allusions in the *Didache* are even more explicit: giving thanks to God over the cup and "the broken bread" (εὐχαριστοῦμεν σοι, πάτερ ἡμῶν . . . περὶ δὲ τοῦ κλάσματος . . . , *Did.* 9:2, 3). This is followed by the famous prayer, "As this broken bread (τούτο τὸ κλάσμα) was scattered over the mountains but was brought together (συναχθέν, again) and became one (ἐγένετο ἕν), so let your church be gathered together . . . into your kingdom . . ." (9:4). This section concludes by restricting the Eucharist to baptized believers (9:5), and is followed by instruction to conclude the rite with doxology (10:1-6).

He broke the loaf, therefore, constitutes the third component of the shared tradition of a chain of five or six common or replicated elements shared by Matt 26:26-28, Mark 14:22-24, Luke 22:19-20, and (earliest in textual form) 1 Cor 11:23-25. These are: (1) *taking bread,* (2) *giving thanks* to God, (3) *breaking the bread,* (4) saying, *"This is my body,"* (5) [taking] *the cup* (Matt

---

122. Moule, *Worship in the NT,* 19.

123. Conzelmann, *1 Cor,* 197, n. 49; cf. Jer 16:7.

124. See Marshall, *Last Supper,* 126-33. Cf. further literature on 10:16, and Thornton, *The Common Life in the Body of Christ,* 5-95; J. Hainz, *Koinonia* (cited above); and J. Wanke, *Beobachtungen zum Eucharistieverständnis des Lukas auf Grund der lukanischen Mahlberichte* (Leipzig: Erfurter Theologische Schriften, 1973), 19-30, with some justified warnings from Marshall, *Last Supper,* 129-30.

125. *Didache* 14:1; cf. 14:2. The "sacrifice" (i.e., of worship in sharing with Christ) must be "pure"; hence confession of sins precedes the breaking and sharing of the bread.

and Mark "took"; Luke and 1 Corinthians, "likewise"), and (6) depending on whether the longer text of Luke stands (as Jeremias insists it does), reference to *the blood* and to *the covenant*. Already, therefore, the breaking of the bread has come to point from the bread alone to the self-giving of the life of Jesus as a redemptive offering for the restoration of the new community of his Body into one.[126] As Hofius observes, the eucharistic bread has as its significance that of "a share in the σῶμα of Jesus given over to death. . . . The gift of which the word on the bread in 1 Cor 11:24b speaks is a participation in the σῶμα of Jesus. As in Rom 7:4, so here also (and . . . in 11:27 and 29) σῶμα means the body of Jesus Christ given over to death on the cross."[127]

It is essential to understand εἶπεν, τοῦτό μού ἐστιν τὸ σῶμα τὸ ὑπὲρ ὑμῶν within the frame of reference which has been expounded and examined over the pages which follow our translation of this verse. Since intensive controversy over this phrase has divided the church over the centuries, only constraints which genuinely arise from the context can avoid imposing some prior understanding on the basis of special pleading. Once we have grasped the Passover context, it is unnecessary to "defend" any exegesis against permitting a later doctrine of transubstantiation by insisting that, in Fee's words, Paul "means 'this signifies/represents my body.' . . ."[128] It lies beyond both Jesus' intent and the framework within which he and the disciples lived to imagine that some actual change took place, or was intended to take place, in the bread itself." Fee attributes such a view to "Greek modes of thinking."[129] Writers in the Protestant tradition have often appealed to semantics and to logic here. Godet asks, "Does the word *is* denote homogeneity of substance, so that the material of the bread gave place at that moment to that of the body of Jesus. . . ? It is difficult to conceive how the bread could have become the very substance of the hand which offered it. Or might it be His glorified body? But this body was not yet in existence."[130]

Whether or not the outcome of such arguments hit upon truth, the route taken is unnecessary and may sound like special pleading to some ears. In the Passover Haggadah, as we have seen, "In every generation a man must so re-

126. Cf. C. Wolff, *Der erste Brief,* 265-66.

127. Hofius, "The Lord's Supper and the Lord's Supper Tradition," in Meyer (ed.), *One Loaf, One Cup,* 97 and 98.

128. Fee, *First Epistle,* 550. Cf. the longer discussion in Schrage, *Der erste Brief,* 3:35-37.

129. Fee, *First Epistle,* 550.

130. Godet, *First Epistle,* 2:151. Charles Hodge observes, "Probably the history of the world does not furnish a parallel to the controversies occasioned by these simple words." *Is* denotes "the symbol" which we use when we say of a statue that it *"is"* the person "which it represents . . . the sign is the thing of which it is the symbol." Hodge transposes exegesis into comparative doctrine, comparing Rome, Luther, Calvin, and a "Reformed" emphasis on faith (*First Epistle,* 224-26). Even Kistemaker makes what might sound like a pronouncement: "The bread remained bread; it was a symbol that stood for the reality of his body. Much as the dove . . . represents the Holy Spirit . . ." (*1 Cor,* 394). There is a more secure, effective, *historical and exegetical* way to reach a similar conclusion.

gard himself as if he came forth himself out of Egypt. . . . 'What the Lord did for me when I came forth out of Egypt'" (*m. Pesahim* 10:5). "I" was/am "there." The recital of the Jewish Haggadah (Order of the *Seder* Service) begins with doxology: "Blessed art Thou, O Lord, our God, King of the Universe, Creator of the produce of the vine. Blessed art Thou, O Lord, our God, King of the Universe, who has chosen us from all peoples. . . ." Following the benediction, the *karpas* (or hors d'oeuvre characteristic of Passover) is dipped in salt water or in vinegar and distributed, associated with the hyssop dipped in the blood of the first Passover sacrifice, with the words of a further benediction, "Blessed art Thou, O Lord, our God, King of the Universe, Creator of the produce of the earth."[131] The Haggadah then begins: "This is the bread of affliction that our forefathers ate in the land of Egypt." (הא לחמא עניא די-אכלו אבהתנא ברצא דמצרים. *ha' lachma' 'anya' diy-'akalu 'abahtana' be'arats' demitsrayim.*)[132] The "surprise" (to use Leenhardt's imaginative phrase) is that **my body** *now replaces the events or objects of redemption from Egypt made participatory and contemporary.*

It is the event of Calvary, of the atoning death of Jesus as an event within the public domain, that is now appropriated in **This is my body for you. My body for you** (τὸ σῶμα τὸ ὑπὲρ ὑμῶν) precisely resonates with the repeated turn of phrase in the Haggadah: "*We* were Pharaoh's bondmen in Egypt, and the LORD our God brought *us* out therefrom with a mighty hand" (Deut 6:21).[133] "And the LORD heard *our* voice, as it is said, 'And God heard *their* groaning.' . . . And saw *our* afflictions . . . *our* toil. . . ."[134] The Black spiritual "Were you there when they crucified my Lord?" captures the precise resonance of *is* and *remember* (Heb. *z-k-r*). (See further under Note on 10:16.)

The phrase τὸ ὑπὲρ ὑμῶν, *which is* **for you**, characterizes both the early Pauline and the Lukan tradition, and may well reflect the "for you" of Isa 53:12.[135] The work of the Suffering Servant of Isaiah 53 oscillates between *identification* and *substitution,* as does σῶμα here. Hofius, followed by Wolff, cites further OT parallels, especially that of the sin offering in Lev 5:8 (cf. 9:8) and the reversal of the "curses" in Deut 28:23 (cf. 26:11). On this basis Hofius underlines a semitic linguistic background and rejects the theory that τὸ σῶμα τὸ ὑπὲρ ὑμῶν derives entirely from a Greek-speaking background.[136] While he argues that the Pauline text is otherwise closest to that of Mark, G. Bornkamm shares the view of Jeremias that the longer text of the Lukan parallel is early and authentic: "Now, . . . with good reason, most have been convinced . . . that the longer text is the older," which is not necessarily dependent on Paul, but re-

---

131. Roth (ed.), *The Haggadah,* 8 (with note). Cf. further Jeremias, *Eucharistic Words,* 41-62.

132. Roth, *Haggadah,* 9.

133. Ibid., 11.

134. Ibid., 23.

135. Fee, *First Epistle,* 551; and Hays, *First Cor,* 198.

136. Hofius, "Τὸ σῶμα τὸ ὑπὲρ ὑμῶν, 1 Kor 11:24," 80-88; cf. Wolff, *Der erste Brief,* 266.

flects, with Paul, the earliest tradition.[137] Jeremias argues in detail that Luke's shorter text is derived from the longer.[138] Paul regularly uses the preposition ὑπέρ with reference to Christ's death being *for us* or *for our sins* (1 Cor 15:3; Rom 5:6, 8). He does this even where the sacrificial death of Christ is plainly substitutionary (Gal 3:13, γενόμενος ὑπὲρ ἡμῶν κατάρα). Thus, as Hofius observes, while σῶμα, **my body**, initially serves to promote the theme of *sharing, participation, or identification* (cf. "were you *there . . . ?*", discussed above), τὸ ὑπὲρ ὑμῶν, **for you**, speaks of "*the expiatory death* of Jesus Christ" (his italics) enacted to grant "for us" the "forgiveness of sins and communion with God."[139] In the context of the cup Paul will repeat the tradition of the frame of covenantal promise within which this is to be more fully understood.

The theory that **This is my body** may allude either primarily to the church or alternatively equally to the bread and to the people of God, hardly leaves room for the second of these two aspects, in addition to its implausibility, if it genuinely reflects the institution of the last supper.[140] This is not to deny, however, that through the process of identification and participation the broken bread also (secondarily) comes to designate a pledge of eschatological promise that God's fragmented people will finally be gathered as one in the eschatological consummation (cf. *Didache* 9:4; 10:5). However, the Jewish Passover Haggadah, the Synoptic tradition, and the Pauline use of the common tradition all convey a strong eschatological dimension (1 Cor 11:26b; cf. Luke 22:16; Matt 26:29; Mark 14:25).

"IN REMEMBRANCE OF ME"

Only Luke and Paul (on Luke's text see above) include the dominical injunction to repeat the rite (Gk. τοῦτο ποιεῖτε, v. 24b) **do this in remembrance of me** in the context of the bread. Since Paul also includes it in the context of the cup, some have suggested that its absence from Mark and the lack of a second occurrence in Luke cast doubt on its authenticity as part of the common tradition. However, it may well be implicit in Luke's *likewise*.[141] Moreover, Horsley observes, "Mark may have eliminated this command because it did not suit his historical narrative."[142] Discussion of the force of ἀνάμνησις must, once again, be shaped by the horizon of expectation

137. Bornkamm, "Lord's Supper and Church in Paul," in Bornkamm, *Early Christian Experience,* 137; cf. 123-60.

138. Jeremias, *Eucharistic Words,* 138-60; cf. 160-203. Cf. H. Merklein, "Erwägungen zur Überlieferungsgeschichte der neutestamentlichen Abendmahlstraditionen," *BZ* 21 (1977): 88-101 and 235-44; Ruckstuhl, "Zur Chronologie der Leidensgeschichte Jesu," 41-44; and Marshall, *Last Supper,* 46-51.

139. Hofius, "The Lord's Supper and the Lord's Supper Tradition," in Meyer (ed.), *One Loaf, One Cup,* 98 and 99.

140. Dunn's comments on this (*Theology of Paul,* 617) may therefore seem unguarded; but he is also making our next point at the same time in a compressed summary of issues.

141. See Marshall, *Last Supper,* 51-53, and again Jeremias, *Eucharistic Words,* 138-203.

142. Horsley, *1 Cor,* 161.

which the Passover context and OT narrative, prayer, and promise establish. **Remembrance** denotes neither the exclusively subjective mental or psychological process of recollection characteristic of Cartesian or modern thought, nor the often exaggerated, overly objectified claims about "reenactment" associated with the so-called myth-and-ritual school of A. Bentzen, S. H. Hooke, and S. Mowinckel.[143] Bentzen argued in the context of a history-of-religions approach to the OT: "To 'remember' the saving facts of religion means to the ancient world that these facts are tangibly experienced."[144] If this is understood in the sense of "reenactment" of cyclical myth and ritual, this idea should not be imposed onto the biblical tradition with its more complex (in very broad terms, more linear) view of time and history. However, Bentzen's approach retains plausibility because he describes an area which genuinely overlaps with the narrative remembrance of the Passover Haggadah and the Lord's Supper. He rightly declares, "members of the congregation . . . 'become contemporary' with the fundamental act of salvation," although he then appeals to "the Roman Mass and the Lutheran interpretation of the Communion Service" to press his point.[145]

If we press the analogy with the "remembrance" of the Passover in the Haggadah, *making contemporary* is achieved primarily by projecting the reality of the "world" of the Passover and drawing participants of later generations *into* it, then transferring the Passover into the present in a process of reenactment, although these two intersecting "worlds" inevitably both cross boundaries of time. However, the notion in Mowinckel's earlier writings that certain "Coronation Psalms" served in effect to "reenact" God's mythical victory over cosmic forces cannot be applied to the Lord's Supper. Such mistaken "objective" attributions to the "Hebraic mind" as J. Pedersen's notion that to "remember" a name "calls forth the soul it designates" were long since discredited by the work of James Barr and others.[146]

On the other hand, "to remember God's mighty acts" or "to remember the poor" is not simply to call them to mind but to assign to them an active role within one's "world." "To remember" God (cf. Deut 8:18; Judg 8:34; Ps 22:7) is to engage in worship, trust, and obedience, just as "to forget" God is to turn one's back on him. Failure to remember is not absent-mindedness but unfaithfulness to the covenant and disobedience. "Remembering" the gospel tradition (Rom 15:15; 1 Cor 15:3) or "remembering" Christian leaders (Acts 20:31; Heb 13:7) transforms attitude and action. To "remember" the poor is to relieve their needs.

Modern research on the philosophy of "remembering" from Eric Voegelin to Paul Ricoeur reveals how closely the phenomenon is bound up with the establishing and integration of identity.[147] Voegelin urges that *anamnesis* recaptures "living forces in the present constitution of [a person's] consciousness," and in turn offers a renewal

---

143. A. Bentzen, *King and Messiah* (Eng. trans., London, 1955); and S. Mowinckel, *Psalmstudien* (6 vols., Oslo: Kristiania, 1921-24).

144. Bentzen, *King and Messiah*, 12.

145. Ibid., 12 and 80; cf. 72-79.

146. J. Barr, *The Semantics of Biblical Language* (Oxford: Oxford University Press, 1961), 10-20, 25-88.

147. See esp., e.g., E. Voegelin, *Anamnesis* (Eng. trans., Notre Dame and London: University of Notre Dame Press, 1978), esp. 3-35; P. Ricoeur, *Time and Narrative* (3 vols., Eng. trans., Chicago: University of Chicago Press, 1984-88), esp. vol. 1, essays 1 and 2, and vol. 3, 235-40; and *Oneself as Another* (Eng. trans., Chicago: University of Chicago Press, 1992).

of identity within "larger horizons."[148] Consciousness entails attention to the present, but, as Ricoeur insists in detail, this becomes construed in terms of a continuity of personal identity in the linking of past, present, and future in terms of memory and hope, or, in more social, intersubjective terms, in terms of responsibility, promise, accountability, and above all a meaningful "plot" of narrative history. Identity becomes integrative and transformative as "possibility" for change interacts with foundational "givens" as part of a temporal plot which looks back to the past and forward to a new future.[149] A key category for selfhood becomes a temporally conditioned "narrative identity."[150] Appropriate or constructive acts of **remembrance** may recast and reorder the self. None of this deviates from what may be inferred from lexicographical research, still less contradicts it.[151]

When we place *this kind of reflection* alongside the *biblical* traditions concerning **remembrance, do this in remembrance of me** takes on a fuller and more accurate meaning than the inadequate notions that have beset the dated "subjective" versus "objective" debates of the past. **Remembrance** of Christ and of Christ's death (i) retains the biblical aspect of a *self-involving remembering in gratitude, worship, trust, acknowledgment, and obedience* (see biblical examples above). (ii) It also carries with it the experience of *being "there" in identification with the crucified Christ who is also "here" in his raised presence.* However, still further, it embraces (iii) a *self-transforming retrieval of the founding event of the personal identity of the believer (as a believer) and the corporate identity of the church (as the Christian church of God)* as well as (iv) a *looking forward to the new "possibility" for transformed identity opened up by the eschatological consummation* (v. 25). All of this is gathered together in Paul's point that such **remembrance** constitutes a self-involving *proclamation of Christ's death* through a life and a lifestyle which derives from understanding our identity as Christians in terms of sharing the identity of Christ who is **for** the "other."

One further point, at least, demands attention before we leave this verse. Jeremias, as is well known, understands *in remembrance of me* to denote not Christians' or disciples' remembering of Jesus, but "God's remembrance. . . . Something is brought before God . . . *that God may remember*" (his italics).[152] Jeremias's case is based largely on linguistic factors, e.g., that the construction εἰς ἀνάμνησιν is absent as a formula from contexts having to do with memorials for the dead, or commemorative meals.[153] Yet this, Jeremias concedes, relates only to "worldly" memorial feasts, which, as Hofius and Leenhardt argue, are not the point here. Jeremias seeks to find more positive evidence for the use of εἰς ἀνάμνησιν as remembering God or the com-

---

148. Voegelin, *Anamnesis*, 5 and 13.

149. Ricoeur, *Time and Narrative*, 1:522-90, 100-152; 3:60-156, 207-74.

150. Ricoeur, *Oneself as Another*, 17.

151. See ἀναμιμνήσκω, ἀνάμνησις in BAGD, 57-58; e.g., Peter remembered the word (Mark 14:72) in which **remembrance** initiated change of stance, action, and a reshaped identity; similarly, "*remember* the former days . . ." (Heb 10:32) is for identity reshaping, not mere intellectual recall; which is a *reminder of sins* (Heb 10:3) may well denote the *reactivation* of guilt in such a way as to cause a disruption of the new Christian identity. Cf. further Louw-Nida, 1:347-48 (the semantic domain of memory and recall). See also D. Stanley, "Do This in Memory of Me (1 Cor 11:24, 25)," *Studies in Formative Spirituality* 6 (1985): 103-15, on the relevance of imagination and anticipation.

152. Jeremias, *Eucharistic Words*, 248; cf. 237-55.

153. Ibid., 241-42.

mandments of God in the LXX (e.g., Lev 24:7; Ps 69:1, 2; Wis 16:6).[154] He also urges that other NT passages about **remembrance** denote "a memorial before God" (Acts 10:4; probable Mark 14:9).[155]

Jeremias's proposal remains at best controversial. The ensuing debate has been discussed by Reumann.[156] Hays has sympathy with Jeremias but concludes: "However one might speculate about what Jesus himself originally meant, it is clear that Paul thinks of the symbolic action as reminding the *church* of Jesus' death: the proclamation of Jesus' death" (his italics).[157] This would partly address Chenderlin's view that the Godward/humanward direction is ambiguous but not entirely so.[158] Chenderlin believes that only an entirely "open" translation *"as My Memorial"* (without specifying to whom the remembering is directed or who is its primary agent) can do justice to the text. Even Chenderlin's semantic and conceptual explorations, however, which in the main serve negatively to guard against applying "modern" notions to Jesus or Paul, fail to make Jeremias's "Godward" approach convincing.[159] The Pauline passage throughout vv. 23-34 depends on a logic of self-involvement. To "remember" Christ is not only to be "there" at the cross, thankfully to appropriate Christ's death, and to allow this redemptive event to constitute, shape, and transform individual and corporate identity of the persons and community who are his "body" (1 Corinthians 12) with an eschatological goal (see above on these four features); it is also to "remember" in the sense of pleading guilty, and pleading the body and blood of Christ under the weight of judgment and the glory of promise. Only in this derivative sense of "pleading the blood (body) of Christ" is it *also* directed toward God.

As C. F. D. Moule observes in his illuminating but often neglected essay "The Judgment Theme in the Sacraments," "In 1 Cor XI:28-32 δοκιμάζειν, κρίμα, διακρίνειν, κρίνειν and κατακρίνειν are used in quick succession in a very striking way."[160] "Remembering" the Lord's death means "participation in the Lord's Supper [in which] we ought voluntarily to anticipate the Lord's judgment.... If we fail to do so, he will himself judge us, but judge in order to save."[161] "Remembering" is appropriating "this sacramental verdict" in which, through involvement with the atoning death of Christ, believers say "guilty," only to share with Christ God's verdict of "put right"! As Hofius

154. Ibid., 246-47.

155. Ibid., 251.

156. J. Reumann, *The Supper of the Lord: The NT, Ecumenical Dialogues and Faith and Order on Eucharist* (Philadelphia: Fortress, 1985), 27-34.

157. Hays, *First Cor,* 198-99.

158. F. Chenderlin, *"Do This as My Memorial": The Semantic and Conceptual Background and Value of Ἀνάμνησις on 1 Cor 11:24, 25.*

159. As I argued in 1980, a supposed lack of conceptual apparatus in an earlier era should not be regarded as evidence that what today can be expressed more readily cannot be expressed or understood by less direct or purpose-related language in different times or cultures. The relation between biblical and Paul material on the self-deception of the heart and its "secrets" and notions of the unconscious since Freud offers one of many examples. Cf. Thiselton, *The Two Horizons,* 115-42; G. Theissen, *Psychological Aspects of Pauline Theology* (Eng. trans., Edinburgh· T & T. Clark, 1987), 40-114, 271-393, and throughout (and earlier J. Barr, *The Semantics of Biblical Language*).

160. Moule, "The Judgment Theme in the Sacraments," in Davies and Daube (eds.), *The Background of the NT and Its Eschatology: In Honour of C. H. Dodd* (Cambridge: Cambridge University Press, 1956), 470; cf. 464-81.

161. Ibid., 470.

declares, "both [i.e., bread and cup] speak of *the expiatory death* of Jesus Christ" (his italics).[162] Conzelmann painstakingly considers Jeremias's case, including the sources cited from Judaism, and rightly concludes, "This interpretation is in contradiction to the plain wording ... 'in remembrance of me.' ..."[163] This approach, far from offering a theological *alternative* to sociological and archaeological research on the Lord's Supper at Corinth, complements it and makes possible an interactive understanding. P. Lampe's research article, to which we have referred, places the two aspects together admirably. It was precisely because of a self-centered concern for honor, status, or peer group society and because of disregard for "the weak," the despised, or "the other," that the Lord's Supper had come to defeat its very purpose (11:17). For **remembrance** of Christ and of Christ's death "for others" entailed *identification* with the *Christ who denied himself for others* (cf. **for you**).[164] Since this **remembrance** is not mere mental recollection, but a living out of this Christomorphic individual and corporate identity, the collapse of this Christian identity undermines what it is to share in **my body** in such **remembrance**.

25 ὡσαύτως, **in the same way** or *likewise,* explains the succinct, compressed syntax of the rest of v. 25, because **in the same way** urges the parallelism of meaning and action with that associated with the bread. Hence *he took* [the cup] (REB, NIV, NRSV, AV/KJV, Barrett, and Collins) has no precise counterpart in the Greek, although it may be understood.[165] However, NJB preserves the Greek syntax by translating in the same way, *with the cup after supper.* Τὸ ποτήριον may well be accusative as the direct object of an implicit verb *(he took);* but alternatively it may be an *adverbial* accusative or an *accusative of respect* governed by the force of ὡσαύτως.[166] This would explain the point noted by Héring and others about a "lack of exact parallelism" between the two respective actions and utterances over the bread and **the cup**. **In the same way with reference to the cup** would then suggest a more comprehensive parallelism of action than simply *he took*. It leaves room for Héring's argument that this lack of parallelism also "seems to argue for the antiquity of the formula."[167]

The preposition μετά with the aorist active articular infinitive, τὸ δειπνῆσαι, means **after** *taking the main meal* or **after supper.** Pesch and Stuhlmacher regard the phrase as an adjectival or prepositional attributive which

162. Hofius, "The Lord's Supper and the Lord's Supper Tradition," in Meyer (ed.), *One Loaf, One Cup,* 99.

163. Conzelmann, *1 Cor,* 199; cf. 198.

164. Lampe, "Das Korinthische Herrenmahl im Schnittpunkt hellenistisch-römischer Mahlpraxis und paulinischer Theologia Crucis" (1 Kor 11:17-34)," 183-213.

165. Fee, *First Epistle,* 554, states that it is "correctly supplied," following, e.g., Barrett, *First Epistle,* 268; Findlay, *Expositor's Greek Testament,* 2:881.

166. Admittedly the accusative of respect performs a function often performed by the dative in Koine Greek of the first century, but examples in the NT are by no means rare; cf. BDF, 87-88, sect. 160, and N. Turner, *Grammar,* III: *Syntax,* 247. Findlay supplies *he gave, Expositor's Greek Testament,* 2:881.

167. Héring, *First Epistle,* 115.

modifies **the cup** in the sense of *the cup-after-eating*.[168] Hofius agrees that the breaking of bread and thanksgiving occur at the beginning of the meal but disputes the sense in which Pesch and Stuhlmacher understand the syntax. He insists, "'The cup after the meal' in 1 Cor 11:25a is positively excluded," partly on linguistic grounds and partly because Hofius doubts whether **the cup** denotes the third cup of the Passover.[169] In the end, however, he accepts an *"adverbial"* understanding of **after supper . . . the cup**. Hence he challenges not the sequence of events narrated in 11:23-25 as such, but whether this has become *a fixed liturgical ordo which replicates the third cup* of the Passover. As Fee and McGowan observe, even if the narrative of the institution itself recounts a specific sequence, this does not necessarily prescribe a liturgical *ordo* or describe the sequence which actually took place at Corinth.[170]

It is unnecessary to repeat here the detailed discussion about the identity of **the cup** which we pursued in our extended note on "The Cup of Blessing" under 10:16 (see above, esp. sect. iii). We noted that although Lietzmann had attempted to relate the cup of the last supper to the *chaburah* fellowship meal and to establish a polarized distinction between the Jerusalem and Pauline traditions, such arguments are overstated and cannot be sustained. We also concluded that although Cohn-Sherbok identifies **the cup** with the fourth cup of the Passover, there is no reason to doubt that **the cup** in 10:16 and 11:25 denotes *the third cup of the Passover sequence* (with Allo, Barrett, Conzelmann, and Wolff, among many others). As Marshall observes, no sequential significance should be attached to the fact that in 10:16 the cup of blessing occurs in a different order from 11:24-25 since in 1 Cor 10:16 Paul "wanted to make a point about the bread rather than about the cup."[171]

It has often been claimed that the words over **the cup** in Mark (sometimes claimed to be "behind" Paul) cannot go back to Jesus since the Greek form of wording cannot be turned back into Aramaic. A relatively recent article by P. M. Casey shows that, as Marshall also observes, this often amounts to no more than an expression of uncertainty about what the Aramaic might have been, and Casey also shows that Jeremias's reconstruction is wide of the mark, and that J. A. Emerton's "solution" is unsatisfactory.[172] Paul's wording does not replicate the most difficult Greek phrase in Mark from the point of view of Aramaic, i.e., τὸ αἷμά μου τῆς διαθήκης. The use of a suffix in "something like דמי דקימא . . . is not . . . satisfactory Aramaic because a suffix cannot be attached to a noun in the construct state, nor can a noun with a suffix generally

168. Pesch, *Das Abendmahl und Jesu Todesverständnis,* 64; and P. Stuhlmacher, "Das neutestamentliche Zeugnis vom Herrenmahl," *ZTK* 84 (1987): 1-35, esp. 9-10.

169. Hofius, "Lord's Supper and the Lord's Supper Tradition," 82-83; further 80-88.

170. Fee, *First Epistle,* 554; McGowan, "'Is There a Liturgical Text in This Gospel'?" 73-87.

171. Marshall, *Last Supper,* 119.

172. Casey, "The Original Aramaic Form of Jesus' Interpretation of the Cup," 1-12; cf. Marshall, *Last Supper,* 91.

precede ד or די, when this is the standard word for 'of.'"[173] Casey considers Emerton's examples of the possibility of such constructions implausible.

If we allow that the Greek translator *restructured* the receptor language (e.g., by moving ἔστιν from its corresponding equivalent in the host language) an original *Sitz im Leben* of *the third cup of the Passover* becomes perfectly intelligible, over which Jesus "makes the main point, that the wine symbolizes his blood, that is, his forthcoming death. As leader of the Passover group, Jesus had to interpret the main elements of the meal. . . . The giving of this interpretation *after* the wine was drunk will also have helped to make the symbolism dramatic rather than revolting (Mark 14:23-4, altered by Matt 26:26-7 . . .)."[174] Casey concludes, "A natural Aramaic origin of Jesus' word over the cup can be found. . . . Jesus must have said הוא after קימא, [which] puts his interpretation more clearly within the framework of God's covenant with Israel."[175] The Aramaic קים (*qim*) is "the everyday Aramaic equivalent" of Heb. ברית (*berith*), *covenant.*[176]

This brings us to a major second point. In our Extended Note under 10:16 we cited W. L. Lane's important argument that *covenant* constitutes "the key to Paul's conflict with Corinth," although Lane draws most of his exegetical evidence from such passages as 2 Cor 3:1–7:1 and 11:1-2.[177] We also noted that Bornkamm and Käsemann affirmed the centrality of covenantal considerations for 1 Cor 10:16. Schrage underlines its importance here as well.[178] This achieves explicit formulation in the next clause of our verse: τοῦτο τὸ ποτήριον ἡ καινὴ διαθήκη ἐστὶν ἐν τῷ ἐμῷ αἵματι. This reflects the common tradition which Mark 14:24 and Matt 26:28 express as *my blood of the covenant,* and Paul and Luke express as **the new covenant in my blood** (the wording is identical in Luke and Paul except for Luke's omission of ἐστίν).[179] The *new* finds expression in Mark 14:25 (cf. Matt 26:29) in the saying about *"new"* in the eschatological consummation of the kingdom of God. **Covenant** holds together the role of divine promise with that of God's faithfulness to the past and pledge of eschatological newness and well-being. As Luther observed in 10:16, sharing in the body and the blood of Christ entails "sharing in everything that 'my body' has and does and suffers . . . by virtue of God's promise.[180] Yet it is no

173. Casey, "Original Aramaic Form," 1.

174. Ibid., 9-10 (restructuring) and 7-8 (interpretation).

175. Ibid., 10.

176. Ibid., 7; the Aramaic translates the Hebrew in the Targums, and Casey rejects Jeremias's view that it "had not penetrated into everyday speech" (Jeremias, *Eucharistic Words,* 197, n. 3; Casey, "Original Aramaic Form," 6.

177. Lane, "Covenant: The Key to Paul's Conflict with Corinth," 3-30.

178. Cf. Bornkamm, "The Lord's Supper," in *Early Christian Experience,* 140-43; and Käsemann, "The Pauline Doctrine of the Lord's Supper," in *Essays on NT Themes,* 120 and 130-32; Schrage, *Der erste Brief,* 3:37-43.

179. The Synoptic tradition also includes *which is poured out for many,* where Paul's ὡσαύτως may well echo the τὸ ὑπὲρ ὑμῶν of *the body.*

180. Luther, *Luther's Works,* 36 (American ed., Philadelphia: Fortress, 1959), 283.

less true that the death of Christ also constitutes the ratification and validation of God's promise. In Käsemann's words, the theme remains that of "Jesus given over to death for us [and] the new diathēkē is founded on this death."[181]

In the Synoptic Gospels three of the four occurrences of διαθήκη belong to accounts of the *last supper,* and the fourth to God's "remembering" his holy *covenantal promise* (Luke 1:72). In the major Pauline epistles **covenant** refers to the *continuity of God's faithful promises* to Israel (Rom 9:4; 11:27 [from Isa 49:21]), to the *ratification of God's promises* through the free gift of grace made operative in and through Christ (Gal 3:15, 17; 4:24), and to the glory of the **new covenant** (2 Cor 3:6, 14) ratified through *the* **blood** *of Christ* and visibly articulated in the Lord's Supper (1 Cor 11:25). Outside the Pauline corpus, the **new covenant** constitutes "a linchpin" without which the Epistle to the Hebrews would "fall apart."[182] There it denotes the irrevocable nature of the divine promise both in continuity with the OT and in contrast to it as "better" or fully efficacious (Heb 8:7-13; cf. Jer 31:31-34). Given this theological background, it is entirely unnecessary to follow Lietzmann in ascribing the mood of joy and celebration to an emphasis on fellowship and on Christ's risen presence *rather than* his death. It is precisely the death of Christ, **the new covenant in my blood**, which establishes the assurance of redemption, and which permits believers to know where they stand with God, namely, in identification with Christ the vindicated Messiah and exalted Lord on the basis of God's promise duly ratified in the events of Calvary. There is no contrast here between Christ's death and the celebration of his risen identification with the One who gave his **body** and shed his **blood** "for others," i.e., **for you.** Celebration which ignores this identity is hollow and self-contradictory.

Covenant also reflects precisely the major theme which persists from 8:1 to 14:40, namely, that of *constraint,* or the *free choice to forego one's rights.* For *God himself limits his own range of actions by free sovereign choice when he determines to act only in accordance with declared promises of grace.*[183] On such a basis Christian believers may be confident that they are redeemed and accepted. Hence the unwillingness of many of the "strong" at Corinth to permit constraints of their own "rights" for the sake of the weak (cf. 8:7-13; 9:1-12) contradicts not only identification with the Christ who shed his **blood** for others, but also the very principle of divine **covenant** in which the faithful God pledges his faithfulness and thereby also constrains his own "rights" by a voluntary decision of sheer grace.

The repetition of **do this in remembrance of me** in conjunction with ὁσάκις ἐὰν πίνητε underlines the four self-involving aspects which we described in connection with the bread: (1) trust and grateful acknowledgment;

181. Käsemann, "The Pauline Doctrine of the Lord's Supper," 130.
182. S. Lehne, *The New Covenant in Hebrews,* JSNTSS 44 (Sheffield: JSOT, 1990), 11.
183. Cf. E. W. Nicholson, *God and His People: Covenant and Theology in the OT* (Oxford: Clarendon Press, 1986), for the emphasis on divine choice, esp. in Deuteronomy and Hosea, and its relation to divine transcendence.

(2) identification with Christ and his death as those who were "there"; (3) allowing a reshaping of narrative identity in accordance with the founding event which defines the Christian story; and (4) looking ahead to projected eschatological worlds which give meaning to present identity and to present endeavor (see above under v. 24). Whether **whenever you drink it** represents a Pauline redaction "cannot finally be proved."[184]

26 Some MSS understandably add τοῦτον to τὸ ποτήριον, largely to match *this* **cup** with **this bread**, but also perhaps to specify more clearly that **as many times as** applies only to the bread and wine of the Lord's Supper itself (*this* cup). The "improvement" is found as early as in 𝔭46, ℵ2, and D1, but is missing from ℵ*, A, B, C*, D*, F, G, and 33. This omission would be inexplicable, but the early addition is scarcely surprising, especially and perhaps most decisively in view of the attraction of a parallelism in liturgical usage.

The relative adverb ὁσάκις with ἐάν (indefinite) is variously rendered *as often as* (AV/KJV, NRSV, and BAGD), *whenever* (NJB, NIV), or *every time* (REB).[185] Grimm-Thayer attempt to explicate the indefinite force of the adverb with ἐάν by *as often soever as,* which is strictly correct but archaic.[186] *As often as* carries the disadvantage of perhaps seeming to introduce unintended nuances of frequency or regularity, while *every time* seems prosaic and misses the indefinite force of the clause. Findlay's proposal **as many times as** seems to gain the best of all worlds and remains modern as well as accurate. This wording is un-Pauline (and usually late). Yet this alone cannot determine whether it remains part of "the tradition," even if Paul may have taken it up from a pre-Pauline saying which he endorses. Nevertheless, other factors suggest that the isolation of the pre-Pauline tradition in 1 Cor 11:23-25 is unproblematic.[187] We have already noted Eriksson's identification of parallelisms and other features in vv. 23-25 (see above). In accordance with Eriksson's arguments about Paul's use of traditions as a basis for distinctive argument in 1 Corinthians, Paul introduces his application of the common presuppositions by γάρ, which serves as an *explicative* link with the recital of the tradition: **For as many times as**. . . .[188]

The grammar, syntax, and word order place the emphasis on **the death of the Lord** (**it is the death of the Lord that you** . . .), and present καταγγέλλετε clearly as a continous present action: **you are proclaiming**. This not only takes up all that we have said above about the relation between identification with Christ as the One "for others" and a lifestyle that reflects this identification. It goes further. The verb καταγγέλλω regularly means in the NT *to announce or to* **proclaim** *the gospel* (1 Cor 9:14), *to preach the word of God* (Acts 13:5), or *to*

---

184. Fee, *First Epistle,* 556.
185. BAGD, 585.
186. Grimm-Thayer, 456.
187. Eriksson, *Traditions as Rhetorical Proof,* 100.
188. Edwards, *First Epistle,* 295.

preach Christ (Acts 4:2; Phil 1:17, 18).[189] It also carries overtones of *speaking* or *preaching publicly, to publish* or *to promulgate,* or to perform *a declarative speech-act* openly.[190] Hence Paul now further likens what the assembled congregation does in the actions of eating and drinking the bread and wine that makes believers contemporary with the cross *to the recital of the Passover Haggadah* as *gospel proclamation.* However, this is not simply a publishing of the objective event of the cross. It includes this (**the bread is broken** and **the cup . . . in the same way . . .**). Yet like those who recite the Haggadah of the Passover on the understanding that *"in every generation a man must so regard himself as he came forth himself out of Egypt"* (*m. Pesahim* 10:5), it *also* witnesses to *the participant's self-involving appropriation of the cross both for redemption and lifestyle* as those who *share Christ's death* in order to *share Christ's life.*

It is no accident that κατανγέλλετε means **you are proclaiming** or *you are preaching.* By **eating this bread** and **drinking the cup** the whole assembled congregation stands in a witness box and pulpit to proclaim their "part" (cf. κοινωνία in 10:16, objective sharing with a stake; and μετέχειν in 10:17, being an involved participant; see on communal participation under 10:16 and 17, especially under (c), above).[191]

The eschatological dimension, which is firmly part of the common tradition but is expressed in different ways (see above), finds expression here in the phrase ἄχρι οὗ ἔλθῃ. As is now well known, Jeremias attempted to argue that ἄχρι οὗ has a purposive as well as a temporal force, anticipating the *maranatha* tradition articulated in 1 Cor 16:22.[192] However, whether 16:22 represents an Aramaic as an indicative or as an imperative depends on whether we read Μαρὰν ἀθά *(our Lord comes,* or *our Lord has come)* or Μαράνα θά *(our Lord, come)* (see under exegesis of 16:22 more fully, below).[193] Whatever the linguistic force of Jeremias's case (which fails to convince us), the theology of the argument is bound up with his notion that the primary direction of the Lord's Supper is "Godward," i.e., for God to "remember" the plea of Christ's self-offering. This view, however, we also found unconvincing, and the notion that the timing of the parousia is entailed in observances of the Lord's Supper which plead for this consummation finds no echo elsewhere in the NT, whatever other arguments Jeremias may offer. Jeremias falls back on allusions mainly in Jewish prayers to God's "remembering" the Messiah, and thereby of "causes the kingdom to break in by the parousia."[194] The most positive and acceptable

189. BAGD, 409.

190. Grimm-Thayer, 330; cf. Wolff, *Der erste Brief,* 274-75.

191. The discussion above of this aspect (esp. on 10:16-17) under **communal participation** in **the blood of Christ** is extensive, *and necessarily supplements the exegesis of 11:26.* In addition to patristic sources, such modern authors as Thornton, Smit, Strobel, Neuenzeit, Schrage, Hainz, Ortkemper, and Wolff play a decisive part.

192. Jeremias, *Eucharistic Words,* 252-55; cf. Barrett, *First Epistle,* 270-71.

193. See below under 16:22; and Eriksson, *Traditions,* 115.

194. Jeremias, *Eucharistic Words,* 252.

strand in Jeremias's argument is the valid suggestion that embedded in the Lord's Supper is a longing which leads participants to *"pray for its* [the kingdom's] *consummation"* (his italics).[195]

The eschatological tone should not surprise us when in addition to playing a role in the common tradition, eschatology in this epistle serves to remind complacent groups within the congregation at Corinth of their fallibility, vulnerability, and status as pilgrims or travelers still *en route* to their final goal (1 Cor 1:7b-9, 18; 3:13-15, 17, 18; 4:5, 8-13; 6:9-14; 8:1-2, 7-13; 9:24-27; 10:1-5, 12; 11:26; 13:8-13). It would verge on the language of later Christian theology to suggest that the assurance of covenant promise is needed only for the interim period before all fallibility and ignorance is abolished. Yet to await the verdicts of the last day reflects the mind of Paul (4:1-5; 13:8-13). In Calvin's words, "We always stand in need of such an aid as this, as long as we are living in this world."[196]

All the same, Paul means more than this. Just as the full sun outshines any source of illumination otherwise provided in everyday life, so when **he** *(the Lord)* **comes**, this reality will eclipse and outshine the pledges and promises that have hitherto pointed to it. In this sense the fellowship *gathered* around **the table of the Lord** (10:21) provisionally and in partial measure constitutes the pledge and first preliminary imperfect foretaste of the "Supper of the Lamb" of the final consummation to which the Lord's Supper points in promise. Thus, we return to Ricoeur's notion of narrative identity. The founding event of the cross is constitutive for Christian corporate and individual identity. Self-involvement in the story of the cross shapes the story of the self and the Christian church. However, this is not yet the whole of the story. The story does not reach its culmination **until he comes**, and only then will the full meaning of all present moments be disclosed, beyond the need for partial significations.[197]

27 Some later MSS insert τοῦτον to read *this bread,* and a few add *this* to the cup, but p⁴⁶, ℵ, B, C, D, and other earlier texts place UBS 4th ed. beyond question.

ὥστε denotes a logical consequence, i.e., *therefore* (NRSV, NJB), or *it follows that* (REB), or **consequently**, which embraces the full force of result. ὃς ἂν ἐσθίῃ is indefinite *(whoever . . .).* The first major problem concerns the precise meaning of ἀναξίως *(in an unworthy manner,* NRSV, NIV; *unworthily,* REB, NJB, KJV/AV, Barrett). BAGD and Grimm-Thayer propose for this verse *in an unworthy* (or *careless*) *manner.*[198] However, the adjectival form of ἀναξίως in

195. Ibid., 255. Cf. Wolff, *Der erste Brief,* 275-76.
196. Calvin, *First Epistle,* 250.
197. On Ricoeur, see above, pp. 879-80.
198. BAGD, 58; Grimm-Thayer, 40. Fee understandably attacks this translation as "unfortunate," largely on the ground that *unworthy* would more appropriately apply to a person than to *what is being done,* which is Paul's concern. Such a translation has led to a sense of "dire threat" of a moralistic nature especially in pietist circles, and thereby caused "tragedy" (*First Epistle,* 560 and

1 Cor 6:2 conveys the sense of *incompetency,* or *being not good enough* for a task, and this coheres with the adjectival meaning in Epictetus and Philo (although it seems to mean *unworthy* in *1 Clement* 47:6). The adverb clearly stands in semantic opposition to the ἀξίως, ἄξιος, and ἀξιῶ group.[199] Liturgy and song have familiarized Rev 4:11, "*You are worthy,* O Lord . . . to receive glory and honor and power. . . ." However, as BAGD note, in more common parlance the Prodigal Son exclaims, "I am no longer *fit* to be called your son, οὐκέτι εἰμὶ ἄξιος." ἄξιος may be used in a bad sense: *deserving blows* (Luke 12:48), i.e., *fit* to be punished. In the Apocalypse of John, God and Christ are *deserving of* honor; for the adjective most broadly denotes *fitting correspondence* (BAGD) or *appropriate weight* (Grimm-Thayer). Paul's primary point is that attitude and conduct should *fit* the message and solemnity of what is proclaimed. At Corinth these were too often **not fitting**, or, in Meyer's accurate words, "*in a way morally out of keeping with the nature* (10:16) *and design of the ordinance* (11:24-25; his italics).[200] Similarly Wolff, describes this as an "inappropriate" or "unsuitable" attitude *(inunangemessener Haltung).*[201]

The second difficulty arises from how best to translate ἔνοχος ἔσται τοῦ σώματος καὶ τοῦ αἵματος τοῦ κυρίου. Barrett follows the traditional rendering of the AV/KJV and RV, *shall be guilty of* **the body and blood of the Lord**.[202] *Guilty* is also retained for ἔνοχος by REB and NIV, although REB amplifies with *guilty of offending against . . .* (as in Barrett's exegesis); NIV, *quality of sinning against . . . ;* NEB, *quality of desecrating . . . ;* Goodspeed, *quality of profaning. . . .* However, NRSV, NJB, Collins, and Hays translate *will be answerable for . . . ,* which reflects H. B. Montgomery's *must answer for* (Centenary Translation) and Parry's *will have to answer for. . . .*[203] Fee accepts *guilty of* but prefers to emphasize the force of *liable* and rejects NIV's gloss, *guilty of sinning against. . . .*[204] Although we must be extremely cautious about etymology, which usually says more about history than meaning at a later time, Edwards confirms the lexicographical evidence of *liable* with reference to the continuing force of ἐν — ἐχόμενος, *held in,* i.e., *held responsible for.*[205] However, as he also points out, in legal contexts such *liability to* (e.g., the law) usually finds expression with the *dative,* while that which a person is *liable for* (e.g., the crime) is usually expressed by the *genitive* (as here), and then in Koine Greek came to denote the *person against whom the crime is committed.*

560, n. 10). Fee's pastoral concern is shared by Hays, *First Cor,* 200. The Greek is a *hapax legomenon.* Weiss links *unworthiness* with *sacrilege* (*Der erste Korintherbrief,* 290). However, Barrett explains *unworthily* as with "factiousness and greed" (*First Epistle,* 272).

199. BAGD, 78-79; Grimm-Thayer, 52-53.
200. Meyer, *First Epistle,* 1:346.
201. Wolff, *Der erste Brief,* 277; cf. also Klauck, *Herrenmahl,* 324.
202. Barrett, *First Epistle,* 272.
203. Hays, *First Cor,* 200-201; Parry, *First Epistle,* 171.
204. Fee, *First Epistle,* 561-62 and 562, n. 12.
205. Edwards, *First Epistle,* 297-98.

The syntax therefore implies *not a sacrilege against the elements of the Lord's Supper* but answerability or being **held accountable** for the sin against Christ of *claiming identification with him* while using the celebration of the meal *as an occasion for social enjoyment or status enhancement without regard to what sharing in what the Lord's Supper proclaims.*[206] The lexicographical evidence of BAGD, Grimm-Thayer, Louw-Nida, MM, and LSJ confirms these points. BAGD allude to ἐνεχόμενος, *caught in,* where Edwards had spoken of *held in,* but they offer examples of the respective meanings of the adjective to denote *subject to* (with genitive), *answerable* or *guilty* (with dative, but sometimes genitive), in connection with a crime or a punishment or with "the person (or thing) against whom the sin has been committed . . . 1 Cor 11:27. . . ."[207] Grimm-Thayer devote almost a column to the varied uses and contexts, largely in parallel with Edwards, but also describing the word in 11:27 as "guilty of a crime committed against the body and blood of the Lord," which out of context might threaten to undermine Edwards's point.[208] Deissmann claims that the construction in v. 27 represents a Cilician provincialism of Paul, but a range of constructions from legal and political contexts can be found in LSJ and MM.[209] More significant, however, is Collins's observation that vv. 27-32 are "replete with judicial language: 'unworthily . . . answerable . . . scrutinize . . . judgement . . . chastise . . . condemn,' all belong to the semantic domain of the law and the courtroom."[210]

REB, NIV, and NEB, we noted, found it necessary to gloss or to insert a word or phrase for idiomatic English, even though Fee rejected this. If we follow the line of interpretation proposed, we need, similarly, to explicate the Greek by some such insertion as **for so treating**, which the context of discourse clearly implies. Otherwise the original danger identified by Fee and Hays reemerges. Barrett, however, rightly makes a major point here: "That **body** is not to be interpreted here as equivalent to *church* is shown by the addition of **blood**."[211] Exegesis suggests neither, on one side, the notion of sacrilege against the elements themselves, nor, on the other side, mere answerability for social disruption. The focus remains on *Christ, and Christ crucified,* as proclaimed through a self-involving sharing in the bread and wine. If stance and lifestyle make this empty of content and seriousness, participants will be **held accountable for so treating the body and blood of the Lord**.

28-29   The UBS 4th ed. text of v. 29 is rightly ranked as certain ("A"). The earliest witnesses confirm it: 𝔭46, ℵ*, A, B, C*, 33, Coptic (Boh and Sah). However, ℵo, C3, D, G,

---

206. Edwards's patient exposition anticipates remarkably the reconstructions of the situation at Corinth, which sociological and archaeological research from Theissen and Murphy-O'Connor onward has established (*First Epistle,* 298).

207. BAGD, 267-68.

208. Grimm-Thayer, 217.

209. Deissmann, *Light from the Ancient East,* 116; MM, 217.

210. Collins, *First Cor,* 436. He alludes to the literary device of paronomasia here.

211. Barrett, *First Epistle,* 273.

K, most minuscules, and Latin and Syriac VSS insert ἀναξίως from v. 27 after πίνων and add τοῦ κυρίου after σῶμα. The AV/KJV includes both *drinks unworthily* and *not discerning the Lord's body,* with the later Western readings, while oddly the NIV reads *the Lord's* in the second instance. Clearly the longer text explicates and specifies the meaning on the basis of earlier verses, but, as Metzger urges, there would be no reason for the shorter text (with such support) except its authenticity.[212]

The adversative use of δέ introduces the theme of self-examination as a *contrast* (**on the contrary**) to the eating and drinking which is **not fitting** in the previous verse. Paul uses the verb δοκιμάζω to convey more than simple introspective examination alone. The cognate adjective δόκιμοι occurred in 11:19 to mean (in our translation of v. 19 above) **those who are tried and true**, i.e., those who have proved themselves to be *genuine after examination*. This entirely articulates the theme that links the negative of v. 27 with the positive of v. 28: **a person** (ἄνθρωπος) **should examine his or her own genuineness**, i.e., *test* how *genuine* their motives and understanding are.[213]

Only in this way renders the simple οὕτως translated ambiguously as *and so let a man . . .* in AV/KJV, exchanged for the temporal construction *before eating* in REB (also *before we eat* in NIV) and a combination of temporal and perhaps also logical, *and only then eat,* in NJB and NRSV. Clearly the traditional *so* for οὕτως is acknowledged to be ambivalent. οὕτως as the adverbial form which corresponds to οὗτος, *this,* means "thusly" or **in this way** most characteristically with reference to what precedes it, often summarizing the thought just expressed (although it may also refer to what follows). Here Paul clearly means that participants are **only to eat from the loaf** (ἐκ τοῦ ἄρτου) and **drink from the cup** (ἐκ τοῦ ποτηρίου) **in the** way indicated, i.e., by **examining** themselves to confirm that their understanding, attitude, and conduct are **genuine** in sharing (cf. ἐκ) in all that the body and blood of Christ proclaims, both in redemptive and in social terms.

μὴ διακρίνων τὸ σῶμα
AND "EXAMINATION FOR GENUINENESS" (11:29)

This prepares the way for a proper understanding of the much discussed wording κρίμα ἑαυτῷ ἐσθίει καὶ πίνει μὴ διακρίνων τὸ σῶμα in v. 29. We have already noted how readily the theme of eschatology in the sacraments relates to the anticipation of judgment with reference to C. F. D. Moule's classic essay "The Judgement Theme in the Sacraments" (see above under 11:24). Before we take this discussion further, we

---

212. Metzger, *Textual Commentary* (2d ed.), 496.

213. On δοκιμάζω, see BAGD, 202, *to put to the test, examine;* but esp. with reference to the *result* of the examination, e.g., *proving the genuineness of gold by testing;* hence *to accept as proved, to approve.* This is not fully conveyed by *everyone is to examine himself* (NJB) or *examine yourselves* (NRSV), while REB's *everyone must test himself* is also without reference to a positive result.

must note the force that Paul uses in διακρίνω. The verb, according to BAGD, Grimm-Thayer, Lampe, and others, has the force of *to separate, to make a distinction, to differentiate*. Only on the basis of *discrimination* (i.e., *separating x* from *y*) does the word come to mean *to judge* or *judge correctly* (under which BAGD include 1 Cor 11:31) and finally *to recognize* (under which they include our present v. 29).[214] Clearly, therefore, the central motif of *separation* leads to the force of **recognizing . . . what** [is] **different**. However, if we translate simply **to recognize what** is **different** about **the body**, this risks imposing upon Paul a more narrow "sacramentalist" interpretation than the context of thought warrants. As Barrett observes, any thought that the ground of condemnation arises from failure to perceive a difference of substance between the eucharistic elements and ordinary bread "introduces a distinction that does not appear in the context."[215] Expressed differently, Horsley reminds us that the contextual issue remains that of "certain Corinthians' sense of their own importance."[216] This, however, is not merely a "social" matter; as Conzelmann observes in v. 27, it is a matter of *"theologia crucis* as opposed to *theologia gloriae,"* in the sense in which Luther so finely expounds this.[217]

Three broad traditions of interpretation reflect different understandings of the phrase in question: (1) A strong tradition from Justin and Augustine through Thomas Aquinas, Peter Lombard, and even Beza to a number of modern (mainly nineteenth-century) writers, including Heinrici, Weiss, and even (in modified Protestant form) Godet, interpret Paul's words to mean *distinguishing between the sacred eucharistic elements of the Lord's body and ordinary bread from the table.*[218] Godet believes that even Reformed theology can find room for the view that Paul is concerned for proper respect at the Lord's Table, in contrast to merely social gatherings of Christians. Schrage rejects such a view as too narrow, and cites numerous writers in support.[219]

(2) A reaction, represented by such writers as Bornkamm, Käsemann, Kümmel, Schweizer, and earlier Robertson and Plummer, tends, in effect, to understand *discerning the body* as referring primarily *to respect for the congregation of believers as the body of the Lord.*[220] Bornkamm believes that Paul alludes to "'the mystical body of Christ' of the congregation . . . the [united] 'body' of the congregation."[221] Kümmel, in

---

214. BAGD, 185; cf. Grimm-Thayer, 138-39: *to separate . . . discriminate* sometimes with reference to *selection* or to *variation;* also Lampe, *Patristic Greek Lexicon,* 354.

215. Barrett, *First Epistle,* 274. Cf. Robertson and Plummer, *First Epistle,* 252, for a rejection of the "substance" view.

216. Horsley, *1 Cor,* 162.

217. Conzelmann, *1 Cor,* 202. Cf. Luther, *The Heidelberg Disputation,* sects. 20-25 (conveniently in J. Atkinson, *Luther: Early Theological Works,* LCC 16 (London: SCM, 1962), 290-94, e.g., "God is not to be found except in sufferings and the cross . . ." [*WA,* 1:360-64]. "The theologian of glory says bad is good and good is bad. The theologian of the cross calls them by their proper name" (*Heidelberg Disputation,* 21; Atkinson, *Luther,* 291).

218. Justin, *Apology,* 1:66; Augustine, *On John,* sect. 62; and, e.g., Heinrici, *Das erste Sendschreiben,* 338-39; Weiss, *Der erste Kor.,* 291. For a fuller list of sources see also Allo, *Première Épitre,* 283; Maier, Estius, et al.

219. Schrage, *Der erste Brief,* 3:51 and n. 587.

220. Robertson and Plummer, *First Epistle,* 252; Bornkamm, "Lord's Supper and Church in Paul," 148-49; Käsemann, "The Pauline Doctrine of the Lord's Supper," 130-32; and E. Schweizer, "σῶμα," *TDNT,* 7:1,067-69.

221. Bornkamm, "Lord's Supper and Church," 148-49.

the 4th ed. (1949) of *An die Korinther, 1-2,* interestingly dissents from Lietzmann's 3d ed. (1942) in the same series. Lietzmann had spoken of treating the body of Christ as *"profaner Speise."* Kümmel rejects the notion of a contrast between "ordinary food" and the holy elements of the Eucharist; it alludes to "the congregation" of the body of Christ. He approves Moffatt's gloss "without a proper sense of the Body," in the sense that "they forgot what the Body meant as they acted so selfishly towards their humbler fellow-Christians."[222] A flood of modern (often but not always evangelical Protestant) writers follow this approach, often citing (i) a parallel with 10:16-17 and (ii) the use of **the body** here without the addition of *the blood* or *of the Lord.* These arguments are repeated in Witherington, Blomberg, Senft, Horrell, Stanley, and Hays; Collins follows this mainly, but recognizing other nuances.[223] One of the most detailed arguments in support of this comes from Fee, who claims that this verse "makes sense of what is otherwise an unusual short digression in 10:17," where the "one loaf" is identified as the participating solidarity of the community of believers. In v. 29 Paul speaks of this "further sense, the church as that body."[224]

(3) Arguments of this nature (for they are regularly repeated) fail to convince Barrett, Marshall, Hofius, Wolff, Schrage, and the present writer. Barrett argues that the second view "strains the meaning of διακρίνειν" (cf. also Hofius, although this may not be decisive); that it would require τὸ σῶμα to serve with a genitive; and (especially with Marshall) that v. 29 is too far in distance from 10:16-17 for Paul to expect his readers to refer to it as the decisive frame for his meaning.[225] Hofius insists that in this verse "τὸ σῶμα stands *pars pro toto*" for the body and blood.[226] Wolff makes the decisive point. The social is founded on the salvific: the issue is understanding the entailments of "sharing as participants in the death of Jesus 'for you.'"[227] The context of vv. 24 and 27, Wolff rightly urges, is most decisive of all, since it is this that impinges transformatively on believers' attitudes and behavior toward others. Schrage sees v. 31 as an important indicator of the meaning of v. 29. "Right judgment" extends to what it means to be identified with, and involved in, the cross of Christ, in anticipation of judgment.[228] In this sense our verse states that they must **recognize what characterizes the body as different**, i.e., be mindful of the uniqueness of Christ, who is *separated* from others in the sense of giving himself for others in sheer grace. The Lord's Supper, by underlining participation in, and identification with, the cruciform Christ, thereby generates the social transformation, which is Paul's *second* concern. Nevertheless, he never leaves behind *the proclamation of the cross* (1:18-25) as the ground of identity transformation, and it is of the very essence of the Lord's Supper (and of baptism) to keep this anchorage in grace and in the cross in sharp focus.

This becomes corroborated in the remaining allusion to judgment (κρίμα) in

222. Lietzmann-Kümmel, *An die Korinther,* 1/2:59 (Lietzmann) and 186 (Kümmel); cf. Moffatt, *First Epistle,* 171.

223. Witherington, *Conflict and Community,* 252; Blomberg, *1 Cor,* 231; Senft, *La Première Épitre,* 153; Horrell, *Social Ethos,* 153; and "The Lord's Supper at Corinth and in the Church Today," 196-202; Stanley, "'Do This in Memory of Me' . . . ," *Studies in Formative Spirituality* 6 (1985): 103-15; Hays, *First Cor,* 200; and Collins, *First Cor,* 436 and 439.

224. Fee, *First Epistle,* 564.

225. Barrett, *First Epistle,* 275; and Marshall, *Last Supper,* 114.

226. Hofius, "The Lord's Supper and the Lord's Supper Tradition," 114 and 114, n. 224.

227. Wolff, *Der erste Brief,* 279.

228. Schrage, *Der erste Brief,* 3:51-52.

this verse. We need to hold together the observations of Hofius about atonement with those of C. F. D. Moule about judgment and eschatology (above). The cross stands as an anticipation of God's final, definitive judgment which takes the form of a double verdict "guilty" and "justified" (1 Cor 1:30-31). Hence, unless a believer **examines his or her own genuineness** (v. 28) and shares in the Lord's Supper **in this way, what characterizes the body as different** (v. 29) will become lost from view and thereby the very eating and drinking (identification with Christ and sharing in the cross) elicits a verdict of "guilty." In Moule's words, what invites its own judgment is "fundamental blindness."[229] The alternative is to "plead guilty" and thereby pass not only under, but also through, divine judgment.[230] Thus the process of passing through this context of eschatological judgment in advance by "sharing in" the Lord's Supper can be redemptive as well as genuinely threatening to any who become hardened in their self-deception or "fundamental blindness." As Barrett notes, the linguistic and forensic links between κρίμα, διακρίνειν, ἔνοχος, κρίνειν (vv. 31, 32) and κατακρίνειν (v. 32) are easier to see in Greek than to provide in English translation.[231] (On possible pastoral implications for the admission of children to Holy Communion, see also v. 30, and n. 246 under that verse. On the inadequacy of introspective "self-examination" as such, see exegesis of vv. 31-32).

30 Almost alone S. Schneider argues that the three key words ἀσθενεῖς, ἄρρωστοι, and κοιμῶνται are used metaphorically, not physically, to denote *weak in faith, spiritually sick,* and *asleep* or *lethargic,* to convey the cumulative sense of having *a moribund faith.*[232] He cites possible Philonic and patristic parallels. Most commentators, however, perceive a causal connection with v. 29 which reflects, in the phrase used by Allo, a "terrible realism" concerning physical illness and death.[233] Fee believes that Paul draws on a prophetic insight that actual cases of illness, some of them terminal, are linked to attitudes of self-indulgent, manipulatory uses of the Lord's Supper as occasions when they have despised the "have nots."[234] Since he earlier actually mentions *drunkenness* (11:21), it is just conceivable that a serious decline in health could result causally from excess in gluttony and drink which brought its own judgment, especially if a wealthy host saw an opportunity to masquerade sheer excess under the cloak of "doing the Lord's work" by hosting frequent "Suppers of the Lord."

Such lack of *genuineness* (see under v. 28) could well add force to M. Pesce's proposal that this amounts to a breach of covenant or willful sin (cf. Moule's "fundamental blindness") demanding "a sacrifice of reparation" (Num 5:18; cf. 5:11-31), expanded in *m. Sotah* 1:1–4:3 in terms of "the water of bit-

229. Moule, "The Judgment Theme in the Sacraments," in Davies and Daube (eds.), *The Background of the NT and Its Eschatology,* 473.

230. Ibid., 472; cf. 464-81.

231. Barrett, *First Epistle,* 274. See further under M. Pesce in v. 30, below.

232. S. Schneider, "Glaubensmängel in Korinth. Eine neue Deutung der 'Schwachen, Kranken, Schlafenden' in 1 Kor 11:30," *Filologia Neotestamentaria* 9 (1996): 3-19.

233. Allo, *Première Épitre,* 283.

234. Fee, *First Epistle,* 565. Fee is anticipated in Edwards, *First Epistle,* 301.

terness that causes the curse." The breach of covenant is comparable to an adultery in which covenant loyalty is compromised.[235] When she has "finished drinking," "the suspected adulteress" who is being "tested" or "judged" by "drinking the water" either shows immediate signs of serious illness (yellow complexion, bulging eyes, swelling veins) or "if she has any merit this holds her punishment in suspense . . ." (*m. Soṭ.* 3:4). Pesce relates this to the illness and death that befalls the covenant breaker who refuses to be judged by the Lord, or judged by himself, and the one who, in effect, is willing to plead guilty in accordance with vv. 31-32.

This suggestion may shed light on a theological principle, but we cannot be certain that these specific passages were in Paul's mind. It is also worse than speculative to imagine that Paul had not expected deaths to occur before the parousia; this belongs to a discredited view which reads a naïve eschatology of imminence onto Paul on the basis of isolated passages and ignores the point made forcefully by Cullmann and others that, as Paul was fully aware, while Christians are in one (eschatological) sense delivered from sin and death, they still sin and still die.[236] J. Weiss so strongly presses a supernatural "realism" in which he regards the elements of the Eucharist as "solidly sacramental, magical, and miraculous" that he has no problem about their potency for physical damage or benefit.[237] At the same time, he rejects as a later hellenistic development which does not cohere with Paul the Ignatian notion of the Eucharist as "the medicine of immortality" (Ignatius, *Ephesians* 20:2, φάρμακον ἀθανασίας).

Dale Martin combines a social-history approach with theological commentary. On one side he calls attention to the "shocking" nature of the suggestion that "the ingestion of the Eucharist, Christ's body, might under certain circumstances have a toxic effect on the Christian's body. These Corinthians are being poisoned by what should heal them."[238] However, Graeco-Roman medicine and pharmacology reflected a full awareness that φάρμακον, *medical remedy, drug for curing disease* (Philo; Josephus, *Wars* 4.573; *Testament of Joseph* 2:7; Ignatius, *Ephesians*, 20:2 et al.), also denoted *poison* (Josephus, *Antiquities* 16.253; 17.62; *Testament of Joseph* 5:1; LXX; Philo).[239] The verb φαρμακεύω means *to mix a potion, to prepare poison,* or *to practice magic,* while the noun φαρμακεία in LXX and Jewish-Christian literature usually de-

235. M. Pesce, "Mangiare e bere il proprio giudizio. Una concezione culturale commune a 1 Cor e a Sota?" *RevistB* 38 (1990): 495-513. Cf. also Danby (ed.), *Mishnah,* 293-98, with Danby's notes on the text.

236. A. Schweitzer argued that "the case of those who died believing in Jesus was a case not foreseen in the traditional eschatology . . . the first of the problems raised by the delay of the Return of Christ" (*Mysticism of Paul the Apostle,* 92). He accepts, however, that Paul himself was among those who saw the need to come to terms with this "delay."

237. Weiss, *Earliest Christianity,* 2:647; and Weiss, *Der erste Korintherbrief,* 290-91.

238. Weiss, *Earliest Christianity,* 2:648.

239. Martin, *The Corinthian Body,* 191; and BAGD, 854.

notes *sorcery*.[240] The double-sided effect of the same "medicine" resonates with Paul's comment about the apostolic message as a "fragrance" that for some is "a deadly fume" but for others is "a vital fragrance that brings life" (2 Cor 2:14-16).

Many (most?) healing drugs actually operate by injecting "poison" into the system in a mode or degree that proves beneficial. Martin gives a careful account, with documentation, of the assumptions of Graeco-Roman medicine in the ancient world about *the body*.[241] Paul, he argues, "clearly believes that something 'real' happens to the body of the Christian through partaking in the Eucharistic meal."[242] The modern notion of a merely "metaphorical" impact, he argues, is anachronistic. Dale Martin's discussion is suggestive, even if it does not convince us in every detail. The upshot is that it would be entirely intelligible and credible to argue to readers at Corinth that *what could serve as a positive benefit* in a state of "recognizing one's vulnerability to destruction" and "one's contingent status as a member of the larger body of Christ" could also act *as a deadly poison if ingested in the wrong way or in the wrong situation without due understanding, care, attention and caution.*[243]

Several possible explanations for the clear facts (against Schneider) stated in v. 30 are available. There is no need to invoke some theory of magic or a "high" Ignatian sacramentalism. Paul simply states what has occurred. Most commentators understand the effect as "causal" rather than (with Conzelmann) as an act of "punishment."[244] The pastoral concern expressed by Fee, Hays, and others over the harshness of such terms as *unworthily* and *guilty* in v. 27 (while we accept the need for a better translation on *linguistic* grounds) seems to be eclipsed by this more terrifying warning about the consequences of taking part in the Lord's Supper *in a way that it is not fitting.* Héring repeats and endorses Allo's comment that the causal process described in this verse has a "terrible realism."[245] Issues about pastoral and liturgical implications for today are widely debated.[246] C. F. D. Moule places these "judgment" verses in the wider setting

240. BAGD, 854.

241. Martin, *Corinthian Body,* 3-37; 136-62, esp. 146-53; and 191-94.

242. Ibid., 190.

243. Cf. ibid., 194-97. Barrett believes that "those who abused the Lord's table were exposing themselves to the power of demons, who were taken to be the cause of physical disease" (*First Epistle*, 275).

244. Conzelmann, *1 Cor,* 203.

245. Héring, *First Epistle,* 120.

246. The debate is at its most sensitive over the admission to Holy Communion of children from Christian families prior to Confirmation. Some have manipulated the argument in order to detract from the role of Confirmation. However, in relation to these verses, on one side it is suggested that a *fitting way* and a *discerning* or *recognition* of *the body* entails an attitude of open welcome to Christian families who perceive their children as part of *the body* on the basis of baptism and household (v. 33). On the other side, this presupposes an exegesis of *discerning the body* which is not wholly satisfactory (see above), and the risk of inviting children to express their solemn covenant pledge of involvement in all that is proclaimed in the death of Christ may carry potential harm as

of the conviction or judgment (ἔλεγχος) that the work of the Holy Spirit brings as part of the redemptive process, and the contrast between the ἀνάθεμα of judgment on those who do not love Christ and the acknowledgement of Christ as Lord (12:3; 16:22).[247]

31-32 p[46], ℵ, A, B, D, F, G, and 33 have an adversative δέ, which some later texts (ℵº, C, Syriac) change to γάρ.

The translation of διεκρίνομεν must take account of the close proximity of διακρινών only two lines above (v. 29). There we argued that the issue was whether those who take part in the Lord's Supper **recognize what characterizes the body as different**.[248] We need not replicate here the detailed lexicographical and contextual arguments and evidence (see above, under v. 29). This translation, allowing for the replacement of the accusative τὸ σῶμα (v. 29) with the accusative ἑαυτούς, fits the present context exactly. It is not simply a matter of being *critical of ourselves* (NJB) nor even whether *we judged ourselves* (NRSV, NIV, approximately AV/KJV) or *examined ourselves* (REB). Just as v. 29 combines **recognizing** what is the case with *distinguishing* or *identifying* a *separation* or **difference** in *discrimination,* so here Paul speaks not only of *passing a verdict on ourselves* (the verdict may be wrong or inadequate; see 4:1-5, where he rejects this). What is required is **recognizing** *our portion in the cruciform Christ "for us,"* i.e., **recognizing** our status and obligations as **Christian believers**, or, to replicate v. 29, **recognizing what characterizes us as Christian believers**. This is to *discern* our *distinctiveness,* not as individuals, but as *the having-died-and-being-raised-one-body-of-Christ*.

This entirely coheres with Moule's comments about the judgment theme in the sacraments. He concludes, "It depends upon the person's response to that situation whether it proves to be remedial and to be a judgment which will prepare him for salvation at last, or whether it plunges him further into a condition of fatal self-concern."[249] Rightly appropriated divine grace, expressed through "the sacramental verdict," invites and promotes "entry beyond judgment into the life of the age to come."[250]

Our translation misses the reproduction in English of the cognate forms κρίμα, διακρίνειν, κρίνειν, and κατακρίνειν in these verses, which Barrett recog-

---

well as potential good when the circumstances are *fitting*. At the very least these verses should invite pause for very solemn thought. In some circles the admission of "our" children has become something very much like the social status of eating in the triclinium. Pastoral and liturgical practice needs to come to terms with vv. 27-30.

247. Moule, "The Judgment Theme in the Sacraments," in Davies and Daube (eds.), *Background,* 474-75.

248. Barrett regards it as "impossible" to use the same translation (*First Epistle,* 276). But this is because he chooses to use *distinguish* in v. 29 and *examine* in v. 31.

249. Moule, "The Judgment Theme in the Sacraments," in Davies and Daube (eds.), *Background,* 481.

250. Ibid.

nizes cannot be reproduced unless we flatten each into some less nuanced form, probably Eng. *judge*.[251] Fee and Hays note the linguistic advantage of seeking to use related or similar English words which bring into prominence the considerable wordplay on the language of judgment.[252] However, Fee's view that the issue turns on "self-examination" (vv. 28, 31) not only deprives δοκιμάζω and διακρίνω of their proper force as embracing specific effects as well as processes but also substitutes a pietist psychologism for a more robust theological conception of a genuine appropriation of grace anchored in identification with the crucified Christ. Paul's concern anticipates Bonhoeffer's declarations about "cheap grace." Cheap grace is "the preaching of forgiveness without repentance . . . Communion with confession, grace without discipleship . . . Christianity without Christ."[253] By contrast a costly but authentic appropriation of grace entails "taking up the cross . . . sharing Christ's crucifixion . . . the cup of suffering."[254] This is why identification with Christ and the cross in the Lord's Supper is at the same time a dialectical passing through judgment as "guilty" and "accepted" or "rightwised," as 1:18-25, 30-31 paves the way for the Corinthian Christians to perceive.

If "to belong to Jesus Christ means to participate in his giving of himself to God and his kingdom . . . in fellowship with all who are related in this way to the same Lord," then "in right receiving" (11:27) . . . "we judge ourselves *aright*" (my italics) "[and] will not be judged (at the last judgment, v. 31)."[255] For we "pass on ourselves God's verdict."[256] Paul's use of παιδευόμεθα is significant. As in the Epistle to the Hebrews, being **disciplined** (with NRSV, NIV, REB; cf. chastened, AV/KJV; corrected, NJB) performs an educative role (as in Heb 12:7).[257] It should not give rise to doubt of salvation or be endured merely with resignation.[258] It plays a positive role in the process of being conformed to the image of Christ in suffering as well as glory.

33-34 Some later MSS add δέ to the beginning of v. 34 for stylistic reasons, but the UBS 4th ed. reading is certain, supported by 𝔭46, ℵ*, A, B, C, D, F, G, and 33.

On the difficulty of translating ἀδελφοί μου (REB, *my friends;* NRSV, *my brother;* NIV, *my brothers and sisters*), see on 1:10 and other instances. The most problematic Greek word for translation is the key imperative verb ἐκδέχεσθε. In the light of 11:21-22 (which Schrage regards as marking an inclusio with v. 33), lexicography, and the convincing reconstructions by Theissen,

---

251. Barrett, *First Epistle,* 274.
252. Fee, *First Epistle,* 566; Hays, *First Cor,* 201-2.
253. Bonhoeffer, *The Cost of Discipleship,* 38 and 39.
254. Ibid., 71.
255. Pannenberg, *Systematic Theology,* 2:326.
256. Ibid.
257. Cf. Conzelman, *1 Cor,* 203 and 203, n. 117.
258. Rightly, Wolff, *Der erste Brief,* 280.

Murphy-O'Connor, and others, the common translation of the major English VSS, **wait for (one another)** (NRSV, REB, NIV, NJB, Collins with AV/KJV, *tarry*) is entirely correct.[259] However, in Rom 15:7 Paul places similar weight upon a different Greek verb, namely, προσλαμβάνεσθε ἀλλήλους, *welcome one another,* in the context of differences between "the strong" and "the weak," and different cultural or religious observances and ethos within the church. Robert Jewett in a distinctive study regards this as the practical climax of Paul's argument in Romans, and his insistence that both Jews and Gentiles become and remain Christians by sheer grace.[260] Horsley, Hays, and Fee argue that here *welcome, accept,* or *receive* is more than an overtone.[261] On the other hand, the lexicographical evidence is not strong.[262] Edwards points out that the Greek uses this verb for *to receive* only in sense of *receiving from.*[263] The lowly or "despised" are not to be overlooked or made to feel second-class. This is true, but this situation was largely an outcome of the more privileged guests arriving at an earlier time and reclining in the triclinium (see above on 11:21-22). Paul has explained that this violates both the principle of identification with the Christ crucified *"for you"* and participatory sharing in the *one bread* (11:24-25; 10:16-17).[264]

If the well-to-do take their more elaborate meals in their own private houses (ἐν οἴκῳ, at home, as NJB, NRSV), the poor and disadvantaged will not be shamed as they are in the case of current practices.[265] εἰς expresses consequence in the middle of a purpose clause: Ἵνα μὴ εἰς κρίμα συνέρχησθε. "If they satisfy their hunger at home, they can celebrate the Supper together."[266] They can thereby focus their entire attention on the purpose of the Lord's Supper: *to proclaim the Lord's death and their personal and corporate involvement in its salvific and relational consequences as one body, the body of Christ.* The adverbial τὰ δὲ λοιπά, also serving as an accusative of respect, introduces an allusion to other matters which Paul will **set in order** (διατάξομαι) when he visits them.[267]

---

259. Cf. BAGD, 238; Schrage, *Der erste Brief,* 3:56.

260. R. Jewett, *Christian Tolerance: Paul's Message to the Modern Church* (Philadelphia: Westminster, 1982), 23-30, esp. 29.

261. Fee, *First Epistle,* 567-68; Hays, *First Cor,* 202; Horsley, *1 Cor,* 163, seem to rely more on lexicography than on the argument.

262. Meyer traces a tradition of translating the word as *receive* but rightly urges that lexicographical support is inadequate. He lists, e.g., Olhausen, Hofman, Michaelis and Schulz; Meyer, *First Epistle,* 1:351.

263. Edwards, *First Epistle,* 303; Findlay, *Expositor's Greek Testament,* 2:884; Conzelmann, *1 Cor,* 103; Senft, *Première Épitre,* 154.

264. Cf. Wolff, *Der erste Brief,* 280.

265. Theissen, *Social Setting,* 164, argues that Paul permits a "compromise" of retaining "class-specific differences" within the home which he strictly forbids as intolerable in the setting of "gathered," corporate, public worship (συνέρχησθε, v. 34; συνερχόμενοι, v. 33).

266. Conzelmann, *1 Cor,* 203.

267. This is the primary force of the Greek (cf. NJB, *arrange;* REB, *settle*), but it also carries the further force of *give instructions* (NRSV) or *give directions* (NIV). For **set in order,** cf. A. T. Robertson, *Word Pictures in the NT,* 4: *Epistles,* 166.

B. THE GIFTS OF THE SPIRIT FOR SERVICE IN LOVE (12:1–14:40)

Too many writers treat 12:1–14:40 as if it were simply an ad hoc response to questions about spiritual gifts (or spiritual persons) rather than an address to this topic within the broader theological framework of 11:2–14:40 in deliberate continuity with 8:1–11:1, and indeed ultimately with 1:1–4:21. The way in which some ranked their self-perceived "spirituality" or giftedness by the Holy Spirit so as to encourage superior status enhancement which resulted in the attitude "I have no need of you" (12:21-26) provides a close parallel to the status enjoyment of those who enjoyed the more comfortable location and better table fare than the latecomers at the Lord's Supper (11:21-22; see above). We noted this unity of thought and theology in our short introduction to 11:2–14:40 (above). This whole section (11:2–14:40) takes up, in turn, the theme of "respect for the other" which characterizes Paul's demand and plea for "the strong" to put themselves in a position of understanding and respect for "the weak" in 8:1–11:1. Paul himself had offered a model of such concern by foregoing his "right" to financial support from a person or persons to whom he might need to give privileged acknowledgment, in effect, as benefactor(s) or patron(s). The church of God ceases to be the church if it remains no longer characterized by an inclusive mutuality and reciprocity.

The problem of rich and poor, of influential and deprived, however, offers less subtle opportunities for status enhancement and self-deception than issues of "spirituality." Here the temptation to glory in being "one of us" (i.e., those people who are "spiritual") takes a more insidious and ultimately more disastrously damaging form. For it engenders a self-glorying at variance with the reality of divine grace and the transformative proclamation of the cross (1:18–2:5, esp. 1:10, 31). Three-quarters of a century before the work of Dale Martin on glossolalia as a "status indicator," Karl Barth perceived the unity of the whole epistle as turning on the contrast between glorying "in God" and glorying in "their own belief in God and in particular leader and heroes; in the fact that they confuse belief with specific human experiences, convictions. . . . Against this, the clarion call of Paul rings out, 'Let no man glory in man' (3:21), or, expressed in positive form: 'He that glorieth, let him glory in the Lord' (1:31)."[1] Barth acknowledges that chs. 12–14 display an almost dazzling wealth of spiritual and religious life," but observes that "what we are really concerned with is not phenomena in themselves, but with their 'whence?' and 'whether?' To what do they point? To what do they testify?"[2] As soon as their character as *gifts* has been recognized, with all the implications of the logic of that term, the Corinthians in that light only may "covet

---

1. Barth, *The Resurrection of the Dead,* 17; cf. Martin, *The Corinthian Body,* 87-103; and "Tongues of Angels and Other Status Indicators," 547-89.
2. Barth, *Resurrection,* 73 and 80.

the best gifts" (v. 31).[3] The chapter on love, however, underlines that these gifts are given for the mutual building up the whole church inclusively; not for the self, or for the enhancement of any exclusive "spiritual" group within the church. "The criterion by which Paul compares . . . the phenomena. . . . is the idea of mutual and common edification."[4] Yet *edification,* or *building up* in mutuality for the benefit of the whole, also emerges as the theme of chs. 8– 10 and 11, and indeed of the entire epistle, as Margaret Mitchell demonstrates.[5]

Mitchell and Eriksson capture the mood of Paul's starting point in 12:1-3 well. Mitchell writes, "Paul relativizes all claims to greater or less spiritual attainment because of ecstatic gifts by saying that *every Christian is indeed a spiritual person,* because every Christian who makes the common acclamation Κύριος Ἰησοῦς (cf. 8:6) shows that he or she is possessed by the Holy Spirit" (my italics).[6] Eriksson, in accordance with his distinctive method, first identifies premises on the basis of which Paul pursues his argument from the starting point of a shared pre-Pauline tradition (e.g., 12:3, "the kyrios-acclamation 'Lord Jesus'") and provides a wholly convincing account of Paul's rhetorical strategy: "First, Paul treats the finite question of the pneumatics' spiritual status by redefining all baptized Christians as spiritual. Then he continues with the second finite question, the spiritual gifts, by elaborating the charismatic giftedness of all."[7]

These chapters offer a series of specific exegetical and interpretative problems, beginning with the issue of whether Gk. τῶν πνευματικῶν (12:1) should be understood as a masculine genitive plural *(people of the Spirit, spiritual people)* or neuter genitive plural *(spiritual gifts, spiritual matters, spiritual realities, what comes from the Spirit).* Whether the term which Paul himself prefers to use, namely, the gifts that come from the generosity of God's free grace, διαιρέσεις χαρισμάτων (12:4), necessarily entail "spontaneity" rather than simply the diversity of what God chooses to give (see 7:7, ἕκαστος ἴδιον ἔχει χάρισμα ἐκ θεοῦ) remains no less controversial, even if an answer is assumed rather than argued by many. A number of specialist writers on "prophecy" conclude after many pages of discussion that (a) we cannot be entirely certain of its scope; and (b) we have no hermeneutical entitlement simply to read *into* the use of the term in Corinth and by Paul modes of popular understanding of the term today. Moreover, the dialectic of creativity and "order" (κατὰ τάξιν, 14:40) is much more than a mere afterthought placed at the end of the topic. All these issues, however, are more appropriately the subject of detailed exegesis,

3. Ibid., 80-87.
4. Ibid., 94.
5. Mitchell, *Paul and the Rhetoric of Reconciliation,* 241, 248, 256, 258-83.
6. Ibid., 267-68.
7. Eriksson, *Traditions as Rhetorical Proof,* 217. On the identification of pre-Pauline tradition, see 110-14; on the argument of 12:1-11, 217-22; on 12:12-31, 223-31; and on the whole section, 197-231.

not of general introduction. Exegesis will show how closely receiving a gift is bound up with *service* to the other, to all, and to God. Jean-Jacques Suurmond sums up this issue well: "It is not so much a matter of *having* a gift, as of *being* a gift" (his italics).[8]

Hardly any statement about chs. 12 and 14 remains uncontroversial, however, and this understanding of διακονέω has received some modification in a series of publications by J. N. Collins, beginning with his book *Diakonia* (discussed below). The debate is more suitably considered under commentary and exegesis but may be noted in advance.

It is also customary today to offer a comment on the rhetorical structure and strategy of these chapters, even if this often amounts to a more sophisticated version of what more traditional commentators have termed their "argument." Some attempts remain speculative, but in addition to Margaret Mitchell's constructive analysis two accounts deserve particular attention. First, the argument of Eriksson, to which we have already referred, succeeds in relating Paul's strategy, in part at least to his appeal where possible to shared pre-Pauline traditions. His chapter on chs. 12–14 remains constructive and largely convincing.[9] Further, Joop Smit's work on the argument and genre of 12–14 also deserves note.[10] Like Mitchell, he clearly demonstrates the coherence of Paul's argument in chs. 12–14. Although we have emphasized the continuity of thought with 8:1–11:1 and indeed also with 1:10–4:21, Smit points out that γλῶσσα occurs twenty-one times in chs. 12–14, but not elsewhere in the epistle. Similarly, the group προφητεία, προφητεύω, προφήτης occurs twenty times, but otherwise only twice in this epistle (11:4, 5). Smit regards 12:1-3 as an *exordium*, in which he opts for the rhetorical method of *insinuatio* (i.e., the indirect approach in contrast to the overt *principium*).[11] He then expounds two rounds of argumentation: 12:4-30 and 14:1-33a. Within the first, 12:4-6 form a *partitio*, or succinct introduction to promote clarity for the *confirmatio* of vv. 7-30. 14:1-5 provide a *partitio* for the *confirmatio* of 14:6-33a.[12] Smit agrees with Mitchell that the main strategy or genre is that of deliberative rhetoric, an appeal to utility and advantage, especially in 14:1-33a.[13] A detailed analysis is included with which we are in broad agreement, subject to wider reservations about how much is certain and how much can be achieved by such an analysis (expressed above).[14]

---

8. J.-J. Suurmond, "A Fresh Look at Spirit-Baptism and the Charisms," *ExpTim* 109 (1998): 1,105; cf. 103-6.

9. Eriksson, *Traditions as Rhetorical Proof*, 197-231.

10. Schmit, "Argument and Genre of 1 Cor 12–14," in Porter and Olbricht (eds.), *Rhetoric and the NT*, 211-30.

11. Ibid., 212-14.

12. Ibid., 217-21.

13. Ibid., 222-26.

14. Ibid., 227-30.

Main Bibliography on 12:1-11 and 14:1-32
(See Also Bibliographies under 12:1-3; 12:12-31; 13, etc.)

Augustine, *On the Trinity,* 12 (14):22; (15):25; 15 (19):34.

Aune, D. E., *Prophecy in Early Christianity and the Ancient Mediterranean World* (Grand Rapids: Eerdmans, 1983).

Athanasius, *Epistles to Serapion,* 1:30-31 (*PG,* 26 [ed. Migne], 600BC-601A).

Basil, *Against Eunomius,* 3:4 (Migne, *PG,* 29:661B).

―――, *On the Holy Spirit,* 16:30, 38-39.

Best, E., "The Interpretation of Tongues," *SJT* 28 (1975): 45-62.

Betz, O., "Der biblische Hintergrund der paulinischen Gnadengaben," in Betz, *Jesus Herr der Kirche. Aufsätze zur biblischen Theologie,* WUNT 52 (Tübingen: Mohr, 1990), 2:252-74.

―――, and A. C. Thiselton, "Word: λόγος," in C. Brown (ed.), *NIDNTT,* 3:1,078-1,146.

Bittlinger, A., *Gifts and Graces: A Commentary on 1 Cor 12-14* (London: Hodder & Stoughton, 1967).

―――, *Gifts and Ministries* (Grand Rapids: Eerdmans, 1973).

Boring, M. E., *The Continuing Voice of Jesus: Christian Prophecy and the Gospel Tradition* (Louisville: Knox, 1991).

―――, "Prophecy (Early Christian)," in *ABD* 5 (New York: Doubleday, 1992), 495-502.

―――, *Sayings of the Risen Jesus: Christian Prophecy in the Synoptic Tradition,* SNTSMS 46 (Cambridge: Cambridge University Press, 1982).

―――, "What Are We Looking For? Toward a Definition of the Term 'Christian Prophet,'" *SBL Seminar Papers* (Missoula: Society of Biblical Literature, 1973), 142-54.

Brockhaus, U., *Charisma und Amt. Die paulinische Charismenlehre auf dem Hintergrund der frühchristlichen Gemeindefunktionen* (Wuppertal: Brockhaus, 1972).

Bruner, F. D., *A Theology of the Holy Spirit: The Pentecostal Experience and the NT Witness* (Grand Rapids: Eerdmans, 1970), 130-51 and esp. 285-302.

Callan, T., "Prophecy and Ecstasy in Greco-Roman Religion and in 1 Cor," *NovT* 27 (1985): 125-40.

Carson, D., *Showing the Spirit* (Carlisle: Paternoster, 1995 [Grand Rapids: Baker, 1987]).

Collins, J. N., *Diakonia: Reinterpreting the Ancient Sources* (New York and Oxford: Oxford University Press, 1990).

―――, "God's Gifts to Congregations," *Worship* 68 (1994): 242-49.

―――, "Ministry as a Distinct Category among Charismata (1 Cor 12:4-7)," *Neot* 27 (1993): 79-91.

Conzelmann, H., *An Outline of the Theology of the NT* (Eng. trans., London: SCM, 1969), 62-84, 87-89, and 257-65.

Cothenet, E., "Les prophètes chrétiens comme exégètes charismatiques de l'Écriture," in J. Panagopoulos (ed.), *Prophetic Vocation in the NT and Today,* NovTSup 45 (Leiden: Brill, 1977), 77-107.

Crone, T. M., *Early Christian Prophecy: A Study of Its Origin and Function* (Baltimore: St. Mary's University, 1973).

Currie, S. D., "'Speaking in Tongues': Early Evidence Outside the NT," *Int* 19 (1965): 274-94.

Dautzenberg, G., "Glossolalie," in *RAC*, 11 (1981), 221-46.

―――, *Urchristliche Prophetie* (Stuttgart: Kohlhammer, 1975).

―――, "Zum religionsgeschichtlichen Hintergrund der διακρίσεις πνευμάτων (1 Kor 12:10)," *BZ* 15 (1971): 93-104.

Davies, J. G., "Pentecost and Glossolalia," *JTS* 3 (1952): 228-31.

Doohan, H., *Paul's Vision of Church* (Wilmington: Glazier, 1989).

Duquoc, C., and C. Floristan (eds.), *Charisma in the Church* (New York: Seabury, 1978).

Dunn, J. D. G., *Jesus and the Spirit* (London: SCM, 1975), 201-58.

―――, "The Responsible Congregation (1 Cor 14:26-40)," in L. de Lorenzi (ed.), *Charisma und Agape (1 Kor 12-14)* (Rome: Abbey of St Paul, 1983), 201-36.

―――, *The Theology of Paul the Apostle* (Edinburgh: T. & T. Clark, 1998), 418-41 and 533-71.

du Toit, A. B., "Die Charismata," *NGTT* 20 (1979): 189-200.

Ellis, E. E., *Prophecy and Hermeneutic in Early Christianity* (Grand Rapids: Eerdmans, 1978), 23-62 and 129-45.

Eriksson, A., *Traditions as Rhetorical Proof: Pauline Argumentation in 1 Corinthians*, ConBNT 29 (Stockholm: Almqvist & Wiksell, 1998), 110-14 and 199-231.

Farnell, F. D., "The Current Debate about NT Prophecy," *BSac* 149 (1992): 277-303.

Fascher, E., *Prophētēs: Eine sprach- und religionsgeschichtliche Untersuchung* (Geissen: Töpelmann, 1927).

Fee, G., *God's Empowering Presence: The Holy Spirit in the Letters of Paul* (Carlisle: Paternoster and Peabody: Hendrickson, 1994).

Feine, P., "Zungenreden," in Pauly-Wissowa, 21 (1908), 758-59.

Forbes, C., *Prophecy and Inspired Speech in Early Christianity and Its Hellenistic Environment*, WUNT 2:75 (Tübingen: Mohr, 1995).

Friedrich, G., "προφήτης," *TDNT*, 6:781-861.

Fuchs, E., *Christus und der Geist bei Paulus* (Leipzig: Hinrichs, 1932), 36-48.

Fung, R. Y. K., "Ministry, Community and Spiritual Gifts," *EvQ* 56 (1984): 2-20.

Gee, D., *Spiritual Gifts in the Work of the Ministry Today* (Springfield, Mo.: Gospel, 1963).

―――, *Trophimus I Left Sick: Our Problems of Divine Healing* (London: Elim, 1952).

Gillespie, T. W., *The First Theologians: A Study in Early Christian Prophecy* (Grand Rapids: Eerdmans, 1994), esp. 97-164.

Greenspahn, F. E., "Why Prophecy Ceased," *JBL* 108 (1989): 37-49.

Grudem, W. A., *The Gift of Prophecy in 1 Corinthians* (Lanham, Md.: University Press of America, 1982).

―――, "A Response to Gerhard Dautzenberg on 1 Cor 12:10," *BZ* 22 (1978): 253-70; rpt. in *The Gift of Prophecy in 1 Corinthians* (cited above), 263-88.

Grundmann, W., *Der Begriff der Kraft in neutestamentlichen Gedankenwelt*, BWANT 4:8 (Stuttgart, 1932).

Gundry, R. H., "'Ecstatic Utterance' (NEB?)," *JTS* 17 (1966): 299-307.

Guy, II. A., *NT Prophecy: Its Origin and Significance* (London: Epworth Press, 1947).

Hahn, F., "Charisma und Amt," *ZTK* 76 (1979): 4,119-49.

Harrington, D. J., "Charism and Ministry: The Case of the Apostle Paul," *Chicago Studies* 24 (1985): 245-57.

Harris, J. R., "Athena, Sophia and the Logos," *BJRL* 7 (1922): 56-72.

Harrisville, R. A., "Speaking in Tongues: A Lexicographical Study," *CBQ* 38 (1976): 35-48.

Hasenhüttl, G., "Charisma: Ordnungsprinzip der Kirche," in H. Küng and J. Ratzinger (eds.), *Oekumenische Forschungen,* 5 (Freiburg: Herder, 1969).

Haykin, M. A. G., *The Spirit of God: The Exegesis of 1 and 2 Cor in the Pneumatomachian Controversy of the Fourth Century* (Leiden: Brill, 1994).

Heckel, U., "Paulus und die Charismatiker. Zur theologischen Einordnung der Geistesgaben in 1 Kor 12–14" *TBei* 23 (1992): 117-38.

Hill, D., *NT Prophecy* (London: Marshall, 1979).

Hollenweger, W. J., *Conflict in Corinth and Memoirs of an Old Man* (New York: Paulist Press, 1982), 28-31.

———, *The Pentecostals* (Peabody, Mass.: Hendrickson and London: SCM, 1972), 208-13.

Horton, H., *The Gifts of the Spirit* (London: Lamb, 1934; 7th ed. Assemblies of God, 1962).

Hoyle, R. B., *The Holy Spirit in St Paul* (London: Hodder and Stoughton, 1927).

Johnson, L. T., "Norms for True and False Prophecy in First Cor," *ABenR* 22 (1971): 29-45.

———, "Tongues, Gift of," in *ABD,* 6:596-600.

Käsemann, E., "The Cry for Liberty in the Church's Worship," in his *Perspectives on Paul* (Eng. trans., London: SCM, 1971), 122-37.

Käsemann, E., "The Theological Problem Presented by the Motif of the Body of Christ," in Käsemann, *Perspectives on Paul* (Eng. trans., London: SCM, 1971), 102-21.

Kildahl, J. P., *The Psychology of Speaking in Tongues* (New York: Harper & Row, 1972).

Knoch, O., *Der Geist Gottes und der neue Mensch. Der Heilige Geist also Grundkraft und Norm des christlichen Lebens in Kirche und Welt nach dem Zeugnis des Apostels Paulus* (Stuttgart: Katholisches Bibelwerk, 1975).

Kraus, W., *Das Volk gottes: Zur Grundlegung der Ekklesiologie bei Paulus,* WUNT 85 (Tübingen: Mohr, 1996).

Land, S., *Pentecostal Spirituality,* Journal of Pentecostal Theology Supplementary Series 1 (Sheffield: Sheffield Academic Press, 1993).

Lategan, B. C., ". . . Met die oog op wat nuttig is (1 Kor 12:7)," *NGTT* 16 (1975): 314-22.

Macchia, F. D., "Groans Too Deep for Words: Towards a Theology of Tongues as Initial Evidence," *Asian Journal of Pentecostal Studies* 1 (1998): 149-73.

———, "Tongues and Prophecy. A Pentecostal Perspective," *Conc* 3 (1996): 63-69.

———, "Zungenrede und Prophetie. Eine pfingskirchliche Perspektiv," *Conc* 32 (1996): 251-55.

Mack, B. L., *Logos und Sophia. Untersuchungen zur Weisheitstheologie in hellenistischen Jüdentum* (Göttingen: Vandenhoeck & Ruprecht, 1973).

Martin, D. B., *The Corinthian Body* (New Haven and London: Yale University Press, 1995), 87-103.

———, "Tongues of Angels and Other Status Indicators," *JAAR* 59 (1991): 547-89.

———, and P. Mullen (eds.), *Strange Gifts? A Guide to Charismatic Renewal* (Oxford: Blackwell, 1984).

Martin, R. P., *The Spirit and the Congregation: Studies in 1 Corinthians 12–15* (Grand Rapids: Eerdmans, 1984).

McDonnell, K. (ed.), *Presence, Power, Praise: Documents on the Charismatic Renewal*

(3 vols., Collegeville, Minn.: The Liturgical Press, 1980) (documents of major churches and denominational traditions).

Mills, W. E., *A Bibliography of the Nature and Role of the Holy Spirit in Twentieth-Century Writings* (Lewiston and Lampeter: Mellen, 1993).

————, *Charismatic Religion in Modern Research: A Bibliography* (Macon, Ga.: Mercer University Press, 1985).

Mitchell, M. M., *Paul and the Rhetoric of Reconciliation* (Tübingen: Mohr and Louisville: Knox, 1992), 266-83.

Müller, U. B., *Prophetie und Predigt im NT* (Gütersloh: Mohn, 1975).

Nardoni, E., "The Concept of Charism in Paul," *CBQ* 55 (1993): 68-80.

Painter, J., "Paul and the πνευματικοί at Corinth," in M. D. Hooker and J. G. Wilson (eds.), *Paul and Paulinism: Essays in Honour of C. K. Barrett* (London: SPCK, 1982), 237-50.

Panagopoulos, J. (ed.), *Prophetic Vocation in the NT and Today,* NovTSup 45 (Leiden: Brill, 1977).

————, "Die urchristliche Prophetie: Ihr Charakter und ihre Funktion," in *Prophetic Vocation* (cited above), 1-32.

Petts, D., "Healing and Atonement" (University of Nottingham Ph.D. diss., 1993).

Pogoloff, S. M., *Logos and Sophia* (Atlanta: Scholars Press, 1992), 99-172.

Powell, C. H., *The Biblical Concept of Power* (London: Epworth Press, 1963), 101-60 and 180-93.

Prümm, K., *Diakonia Pneumatos* (3 vols., Freiburg: Herder, 1960, 1962, 1966).

Roloff, J., *Die Kirche im NT* (Göttingen: Vandenhoeck & Ruprecht, 1993).

Runia, K., "The 'Gifts of the Spirit,'" *RTR* 29 (1970): 82-94.

Ruthven, J., *On the Cessation of the Charismata: The Protestant Polemic on Post-biblical Miracles,* Journal of Pentecostal Theology Supplementary Series 3 (Sheffield: Sheffield Academic Press, 1993).

Samarin, W. J., *Tongues of Men and Angels: The Religious Language of Pentecostalism* (New York: Macmillan, 1972), 74-128.

Sandnes, K. O., *Paul — One of the Prophets?* WUNT 2:43 (Tübingen: Mohr, 1991).

Schandorff, E. D., *The Doctrine of the Holy Spirit: A Bibliography . . .* (2 vols., Lanham: Scarecrow Press, 1995).

Schatzmann, S., *A Pauline Theology of Charismata* (Peabody, Mass.: Hendrickson, 1987).

Schürmann, H., "Die Geistliche Gnadengaben in den paulinischen Gemeinden," in *Ursprung und Gestalt* (Düsseldorf: Patmos, 1970).

Schweizer, E., *The Holy Spirit* (Philadelphia: Fortress, 1980).

Smit, J., "Argument and Genre of 1 Cor 12–14," in S. E. Porter and T. H. Olbricht (eds.), *Rhetoric and the NT,* JSNTSS 90 (Sheffield: Sheffield Academic Press, 1993), 211-29.

Stendahl, K., "Glossalalia — The NT Evidence," in Stendahl, *Paul among Jews and Gentiles* (London: SCM, 1977), 109-24; also rpt. from M. P. Hamilton (ed.), *The Charismatic Movement* (Grand Rapids: Eerdmans, 1975), 49-60.

Suurmond, J.-J., "A Fresh Look at Spirit-Baptism and the Charisms," *ExpTim* 109 (1998): 103-6.

Talbert, C. H., "Paul's Understanding of the Holy Spirit: The Evidence of 1 Cor 12–14," *Perspectives in Religious Studies* 11 (1984): 95-108.

Tertullian, *Against Marcion,* 5:8.

Theissen, G., *Psychological Aspects of Pauline Theology* (Eng. trans., Edinburgh: T. & T. Clark, 1987), 74-114 and 292-341.

Thiselton, A. C., "The 'Interpretation' of Tongues? A New Suggestion in the Light of Greek Usage in Philo and Josephus," *JTS* 30 (1979): 15-36.

Tugwell, S., *Did You Receive the Spirit?* (London: Darton, Longman & Todd, 1972).

Turner, M., *The Holy Spirit and Spiritual Gifts Then and Now* (Carlisle: Paternoster, 1996), 103-35, 185-302.

Vielhauer, P., *Oikodomē. Das Bild vom Bau in der Christlichen Literatur* (Karlsruhe: Harrassowitz, 1940).

Wedderburn, A. J. M., "The Body of Christ and Related Concepts in 1 Cor," *SJT* 24 (1971): 74-96.

Weinel, H., *Die Wirkungen des Geistes und der Geister im nachapostolischen Zeitalter bis auf Irenaeus* (Freiburg: Mohr, 1899).

Williams, C. G., *Tongues of the Spirit* (Cardiff: University of Wales Press, 1981).

Wire, A. C., *Corinthian Women Prophets* (Philadelphia: Fortress, 1990), 135-58 and 266-28.

Witherington, B., *Conflict and Community in Corinth* (Grand Rapids: Eerdmans, 1995), 253-90.

Wright, G., "Diversity in the Church," *Theological Education* 14 (1983): 64-68.

Zodhiates, S., *1 Cor 12* (2 vols., Chattanooga, Tenn.: AMG Publishers, 1983).

1. All Christians "Spiritual": The Christological Criterion (12:1-3)

(1) Now, about things that "come from the Spirit": my dear Christian family, I do not want you to remain without knowledge. (2) You know that when you were pagans, you used to be carried away to idols that were incapable of speech. (3) Therefore I am imparting to you this "knowledge," that no one who is speaking through the agency of the Spirit of God says, "Jesus is cursed." And no one is able to declare "Jesus is Lord" except through the agency of the Holy Spirit.

Supplementary Bibliography on 12:1-3 against the Background of Chs. 12–14

Albright, W. F., and C. S. Mann, "Two Texts in 1 Cor," *NTS* 16 (1970): 271-76.

Aune, D. E., *The Cultic Setting of Realized Eschatology in Early Christianity,* NovTSup 28 (Leiden: Brill, 1972).

———, *Prophecy in Early Christianity and the Ancient Mediterranean World* (Grand Rapids: Eerdmans, 1983), 195-201, 219-22, 256-58.

Bassler, J. M., "1 Cor. 12:3 — Curse and Confession in Context," *JBL* 101 (1982): 415-21.

Baumert, N., "Zur 'Unterscheidung der Geister,'" *ZTK* 111 (1989): 183-95.

Berggren, E., *The Psychology of Confession* (Leiden: Brill, 1975), 20-35.

Bittlinger, A., *Gifts and Graces: A Commentary on 1 Cor 12–14* (London: Hodder, 1967), 13-22.

907

Bousset, W., *Kyrios Christos* (Eng. trans., Nashville: Abingdon, 1970).

Brox, N., "'Ἀνάθεμα Ἰησοῦς' (1 Cor. 12:3)," *BZ* 12 (1968): 103-11.

Bultmann, R., *Theology of the NT* (Eng. trans., London: SCM, 1952), 1:330-33.

Callan, T., "Prophecy and Ecstasy in Greco-Roman Religion and in 1 Cor," *NovT* 27 (1985): 125-40.

Campenhausen, H. von, "Das Bekenntnis im Urchristentum," *ZNW* 63 (1972): 210-53.

Cerfaux, L., *Christ in the Theology of St. Paul* (Eng. trans., New York: Herder, 1959).

Charles, G. W., "1 Cor. 12:1-13," *Int* 44 (1990): 65-68.

Cullmann, O., *The Christology of the NT* (London: SCM, 2d ed. 1963), 195-237.

—————, *The Earliest Christian Confessions* (London: Lutterworth, 1949).

Dautzenberg, G., *Urchristliche Prophetie* (Stuttgart: Kohlhammer, 1975).

Derrett, J. D. M., "Cursing Jesus (1 Cor. 12:3): The Jews as Religious 'Persecutors,'" *NTS* 21 (1975): 544-54.

Ellis, E. E., "'Spiritual' Gifts in the Pauline Community" and "Christ and Spirit in 1 Corinthians," in Ellis, *Prophecy and Hermeneutic in Early Christianity* (Grand Rapids: Eerdmans, 1978), 25-44 and 63-71.

Eriksson, A., *Traditions as Rhetorical Proof: Pauline Argumentation in 1 Corinthians,* ConBNT 29 (Stockholm: Almqvist & Wiksell, 1998), 110-14 and 217-31.

Fitzmyer, J. A., "The Semitic Background of the NT Kyrios Title," in his *A Wandering Aramaean* (Missoula: Scholars Press, 1979), 115-42.

Foerster, W., and G. Quell, "κύριος," *TDNT,* 3:1,039-98.

Forbes, C., *Prophecy and Inspired Speech in Early Christianity and Its Hellenistic Environment,* WUNT 75 (Tübingen: Mohr, 1995), esp. 20-50.

Führer, W., "'Herr ist Jesus': Die Rezeption der urchristlichen Kyrios-Acclamation durch Paulus Römer 10:9," *KD* 33 (1987): 137-49.

Grudem, W., *The Gift of Prophecy in 1 Corinthians* (Washington, D.C.: University Press of America, 1982).

Gundry, R. H., "'Ecstatic Utterance' (NEB)," *JTS* 17 (1966): 299-307.

Hahn, F., *The Titles of Jesus in Christology* (Eng. trans., London: Lutterworth, 1969).

Holtz, T., "Das Kennzeichen des Geistes (1 Kor 12:1-3)," *NTS* 18 (1971-72): 365-76.

Hurd, J. C., *The Origins of 1 Cor* (London: SPCK, 1965), 186-95.

Kramer, W., *Christ, Lord, Son of God* (Eng. trans., London: SCM, 1966), 65-107, 151-82.

Ladrière, J., "The Performativity of Liturgical Language," *Conc* n.s. 2, no. 9 (1973): 50-62.

Maly, K., "1 Kor 12:1-3. Eine Regel zur Unterscheidung der Geister?" *BZ* 10 (1966): 82-95.

Martin, D. B., *The Corinthian Body* (New Haven: Yale University Press, 1995), 87-103.

—————, "Tongues of Angels and Others Status Indicators," *JAAR* 59 (1991): 347-89.

Martin, R. P., *Worship in the Early Church* (Grand Rapids: Eerdmans, 1974).

Mehat, A. A., "L'enseignement sur 'les choses de l'ésprit' (1 Cor 12:1-3)," *RHPhR* 63 (1983): 395-415.

Neufeld, V. H., *The Earliest Christian Confessions,* NTTS 5 (Leiden: Brill, 1963).

Newman, C. C., *Paul's Glory Christology: Tradition and Rhetoric,* NovTSup 69 (Leiden: Brill, 1992).

Neyrey, J., "Body Language in 1 Cor," *Semeia* 35 (1986): 129-70.

Paige, T., "1 Cor. 12:2: A Pagan *Pompê?*" *JSNT* 44 (1991): 57-65.

Painter, J., "Paul and the πνευματικοί at Corinth," in M. D. Hooker and J. G. Wilson (eds.), *Paul and Paulinism: Essays in Honour of C. K. Barrett* (London: SPCK, 1982).

Patte, D., *Paul's Faith and the Power of the Gospel* (Philadelphia: Fortress, 1983), 306-10.

Pearson, B. A., "Did the Gnostic Curse Jesus?" *JBL* 86 (1967): 301-5.

———, *The Pneumatikos-Psychikos Terminology in 1 Cor* (Missoula: Scholars Press, 1973).

Sanders, J. T., *The NT Christological Hymns,* SNTSMS (Cambridge: Cambridge University Press, 1971), esp. 24-25.

Schmit, J., "Argument and Genre of 1 Cor 12–14," in S. E. Porter and T. H. Olbricht (eds.), *Rhetoric and the NT,* JSNTSS 90 (Sheffield: Sheffield Academic Press, 1993), 21-30.

Scroggs, R., "The Exaltation of the Spirit by Some Early Christians," *JBL* 84 (1965): 359-73.

Searle, J. R., *Speech Acts: An Essay in the Philosophy of Language* (Cambridge: Cambridge University Press, 1970).

Standaert, B., "Analyse rhetorique des chap. 12 à 14 de 1 Cor," in L. de Lorenzi (ed.), *Charisma und Agape* (Rome: Abbey S. Paul, 1983), 23-34.

Sweet, J. P. M., "A Sign for Unbelievers: Paul's Attitude to Glossolalia," *NTS* 13 (1966-67): 240-57.

Van Unnik, W. C., "Jesus: Anathema or Kyrios (1 Cor. 12:3)," in B. Lindars and S. S. Smalley (eds.), *Christ and Spirit in the NT: Studies in Honour of C. F. D. Moule* (Cambridge: Cambridge University Press, 1973), 113-26.

Vawter, B., "The Development of the Expression of Faith in the Worshipping Community," *Conc* n.s. 2, no. 9 (1973): 22-29.

Vos, J. S., "Das Rätsel von 1 Kor 12:1-3," *NovT* 35 (1993): 251-69.

Weiss, J., *Earliest Christianity* (2 vols., Eng. trans., rpt. New York: Harper, 1937), 2:458-63.

Williamson, H., *Jesus Is Lord: A Personal Rediscovery* (Nottingham: Crossway, 1993).

Wolff, C., "Exkurs: Deutungsvorschläge zur Verfluchung Jesu in 1 Kor 12:3," in *Der erste Brief des Paulus an die Kor,* 285-87.

1 On περὶ δέ, see above on 7:1 and 7:25 (this is the fourth occurrence of the phrase, following also 8:1; cf. 16:1, 12). We have endorsed the widespread view that περὶ δέ signals a new topic; we concluded that Hurd's arguments to the effect that it also marked a response to questions from Corinth was probable, although we accepted Mitchell's argument that this cannot be certain in every case.[15]

The translation and meaning of τῶν πνευματικῶν is universally discussed. Since the genitive plural masculine and neuter share the same Greek ending, some understand the Greek to mean *spiritual persons* (modern writers from Heinrici and Weiss to Blomberg and Wire and earlier commentators from Grotius to Locke).[16] Most interpreters, however, believe that the term denotes

15. Hurd, *Origin of 1 Corinthians,* 61-71 and (on 12:1) 186-95; Mitchell, "Concerning περὶ δέ in 1 Cor," *NovT* 31 (1989): 229-56. For the translation **now about**, or *as for,* cf. Moule, *An Idiom Book of New Testament Greek* (2d ed. 1960), 63.

16. Weiss, *Der erste Korintherbrief,* 294; Blomberg, *1 Cor,* 243: "The term probably reflects the prideful way the Corinthian leaders referred to themselves"; Locke, *Paraphrase and*

spiritual gifts (from Tertullian, Novatian, and Cyril of Jerusalem to Conzelmann, Senft, and Lang).[17] This is adopted by AV/KJV, RSV, NRSV, JB, and NIV (cf. NJB, REB, *gifts of the Spirit*). The main argument for the latter view that the Greek "is to be taken in a neuter, not a masculine sense . . . is clear from 14:1 and from the interchange with χαρίσματα."[18] Conzelmann further equates gifts with "ecstatic phenomena," an interpretation which has been questioned by Gundry and recently attacked in detail by Forbes.[19]

A relatively wide range of writers conclude that it is "impossible to find objective ground for a decision between the two possibilities, and little difference in sense is involved — spiritual persons are those who have spiritual gifts."[20] It refers to *either.* But if both the writer and the readers well knew that the Greek ending included *both* genders (i.e., excluded neither), why should the meaning be construed in either-or terms at all? Hence Scrage notes that the masculine may embrace the Corinthians' meaning, while the neuter reflects Paul's preference to substitute χαρίσματα.[21] Meyer rightly cites Chrysostom and Luther as interpreting the Greek to mean *Concerning the forms of action which proceed from the Holy Spirit and make manifest his agency.*[22] The key issue which has been raised (at least the form in which Paul wishes to address it), is this: *What criteria are we to apply for specific people or specific gifts to be considered genuinely "of the Holy Spirit"?* This is what vv. 2 and 3 explicate in terms of a *Christomorphic criterion.*[23] Since it would overtranslate the Greek to render *Concerning what counts as people or as gifts of the Spirit,* we use quotation marks. The church needed clarification about a status-earning buzz slogan: **Now about things that "come from the Spirit,"** i.e., people *say* they do, but

---

Notes, 446: "men assisted and acted by the spirit," in agreement with Grotius against the AV/KJV; Wire, *Corinthian Women Prophets,* 135: "spiritual people" whom Paul "associates with prophets"; Hurd, *Origin of 1 Corinthians,* 194, n. 1; Bruce, *1 and 2 Cor,* 116-17: "more probably 'spiritual persons.'" Cf. also the discussions of Pearson, *Pneumatikos-Psychikos Terminology;* and Gillespie, *The First Theologians,* 97-164.

17. Tertullian, *Against Marcion,* 5:8, "Now concerning spiritual gifts. . . . These were promised by the Creator through Christ . . . the bestowal of a gift . . . from them who made the promise"; Novatian, *On the Trinity,* 29; Cyril of Jerusalem, *Lectures,* 16:1; Robertson and Plummer, *First Epistle,* 259; Héring, *First Epistle,* 122-23; Conzelmann, *1 Cor,* 204; Orr and Walther, *1 Cor,* 278; Lang, *Die Briefe,* 162; Kistemaker, *1 Cor,* 412-13; Grosheide, *First Epistle,* 298; Senft, *La Première Épitre,* 155. Collins, *First Cor,* 446-47, interprets the neuter in a wider sense (see below).

18. Conzelmann, *1 Cor,* 204.

19. Forbes, *Prophecy and Inspired Speech in Early Christianity and Its Hellenistic Environment,* 33-43, 53-57; cf. 124-26, 143-46; see also Gundry, "'Ecstatic Utterance' (NEB)?" 299-307.

20. Barrett, *First Epistle,* 278; Harrisville, *1 Cor,* 205; cf. also Harrisville, "Speaking in Tongues: A Lexicographical Study," 35-48.

21. Schrage, *Der erste Brief,* 3:118-19.

22. Meyer, *First Epistle,* 1:355.

23. Lang, e.g., rightly links v. 1 with the negative criteria of v. 2 and the positive criteria of v. 3; *Die Briefe,* 162. Similarly, Senft reconstructs the question: which of these "spiritual" phenomena have been produced by the Spirit of Christ? (*La Première Épitre,* 155); cf. also Conzelmann, *1 Cor,* 204.

do they? *How are we to know?* Well, Paul replies, **I do not want you to be** *"not knowing"* (ἀγνοεῖν), i.e., **to remain without knowledge**.

The present infinitive is taken by Allo to convey the continuous state: to continue to be ignorant, which also explains, he adds, the γνωρίζω of v. 3.[24] Hence we translate, **I do not want you to remain ignorant**, especially since v. 2 appears to confirm this. There may be truth, however, in Blomberg's perception of a quasi-ironic nuance here: you "spiritual people" surely cannot need to have a state of "ignorance" (ἀ + γνῶσις) remedied.[25]

On the difficulty of translating ἀδελφοί, see above on 1:10, 11, 26 (cf. 2:1; 3:1; 4:6; 7:29; 10:1, where the same accompanying verb ἀγνοεῖν also occurs in the last example). Here we translate **my dear Christian family** especially in the light of the importance of "family" words for the urban Christian communities.[26] Paul is eager to apply the family-likeness which reflects Christ's Lordship over all Christians to the diversity of ways in which this likeness can find creative expression. We cannot always predict how a family likeness will show itself (in the face? in the walk? in the humor?), but members of the same family will exhibit family resemblances or they are not part of *this* family. *Paul begins to set the stage for a dialectic between solidarity and differentiation,* which he is about to introduce in what we must describe as hardly less than trinitarian terms as the foundation of unity-in-diversity, and diversity-in-unity.

2 This verse raises two quite distinct problems. The first arises from its incomplete and ambiguous Greek syntax; the second concerns the nature and degree of significance which is to be attached to the pre-conversion experience of **idols that were incapable of speech** for issues concerning communication in 12:3–14:40.

(i) *Syntax.* If ἤγεσθε is construed as the finite verb within the subordinate ὅτε clause, there is no finite verb for the main clause, in place of which the text has only the participle ἀπαγόμενοι. The simplest way of restoring an intelligible syntax and completing the finite verb is to assume that a final (i.e., second) ἦτε is to be supplied by the readers, thus adding the copula to the participle to transpose it into a periphrastic imperfect passive, **you used to be carried away**.[27] The omission of the copula is a regular example of elliptic construction and is perhaps rendered all the more probable by the fact that ἦτε has already occurred once in the subordinate clause. Alternative hypotheses seem unnecessary. Nevertheless, this has not prevented other, more complex proposals. (a) Westcott-Hort, e.g., conjecture that ποτέ originally stood in place of ὅτε. This would now mean: *at one time you were pagans, carried away . . . however, you were being led.* (b) Weiss attaches the particle

24. Allo, *Première Épitre,* 320.
25. Blomberg, *1 Cor,* 243.
26. Meeks, *First Urban Christians,* 86-88.
27. Robertson and Plummer, *First Epistle,* 259, among others, argue for this. See further Schrage, *Der erste Brief,* 3:120, n. 36, and 122; Weiss, *Der erste Kor,* 294.

ἄν, as a preposition, to ἄγω to form the compound verb ἀνήγεσθε.[28] Further, Héring, in turn, argues that this compound verb can have the technical religious meaning of *snatched away into the invisible world,* i.e., by hostile powers.[29] (c) Terence Paige accounts for the double use of ἀπάγω and (ἀν)άγω in an imaginative suggestion. He rejects the notion that being **carried away** is either mental or metaphorical, or even "spiritual": it refers to the physical act of being caught up and carried along in a festival parade or *pompē*.[30] Collins is sympathetic with this idea, and Paige picks up Wayne Grudem's proposal that travel to idols, not ecstasy, is the point of the reference.[31] The double use of the verb means lead along in the parade and then led up to the silent idol in its temple, where the sacrifice and distributions to participants formed the climax. Hence πρὸς τὰ εἴδωλα means "literally 'to the images.' . . . The *pompē* then symbolizes the ignorance and slavery of the Corinthians' pre-conversion life, in which they simply followed where they were led, like the sacrificial animals in the procession."[32] ἀπαγόμενοι then becomes "a kind of *circumstantial participle* [my italics]: 'whenever you were led [in the procession] you were [really] being carried away captive'. In this way, it is not necessary to read the participle as a pleonastic construction with ἦτε, and the problem of how to relate ἦτε to two predictions . . . disappears."[33]

This novel proposal, following the cue proposed by Grudem, may well shed light on the grammar and meaning; but it cannot readily be proven, in spite of Paige's excellent and full documentation about processions and parades (Paul's Corinth and Paige's Belfast are both thoroughly familiar with processions of one kind and parades of another). Moreover, the iterative use of ἄν with the indicative, which survives from earlier Greek into the NT period (cf. Acts 2:45; 4:35), might be expected more appropriately to qualify *continuously* **being carried away**, rather than *continuously being carried along in the procession* (although *used to be carried along* does make sense).[34] It is a matter of fine judgment whether the distinct easing of the syntax and the plausibility of the reconstruction permit this degree of specificity for purposes of translation. On the principle of Occam's razor, the syntactical difficulties are not insuperable if interpreted along the lines defended by Robertson and Plummer and Schrage, given the frequency of ellipses and periphrastic constructions with participles. Hence we translate: **you used to be carried away to idols that were incapable of speech**, especially since this would not explicitly exclude Paige's explanation as a gloss on what might well lie behind the construction.

(ii) Controversy now falls in the specific sense in which Paul invited re-

28. Weiss, *Der erste Kor,* 294.
29. Héring, *First Epistle,* 123; cf. Luke 4:5; Matt 4:1.
30. Paige, "1 Cor. 12:2: A Pagan *Pompē?*" 8-59; cf. 57-65.
31. Grudem, *The Gift of Prophecy in 1 Corinthians,* 162-64; Collins, *First Cor,* 447.
32. Paige, "1 Cor. 12:2: A Pagan *Pompē?*" 63.
33. Ibid., 64.
34. On the iterative use of ἄν, cf. BDF, 367 and MHT, *Grammar,* 1:167.

flection on, and comparison with, the pre-conversion experience of his address-ees. In very general terms, all interpreters agree that Paul stresses the inade-quacy of any "knowledge" about what constitutes "the spiritual" if it is decisively shaped by expectations and assumptions carried over from pre-conversion days. But can we be more specific?

(a) In a recent study of the rhetoric of 1 Corinthians 12–14, however, Joop Smit seeks to take this further. He argues that these three chapters form a rhe-torical unit introduced by an *exordium* designed to gain a hearing, in which Paul finds himself compelled to use the *indirect approach* known in rhetoric as *insinuatio* (as against the more open and direct *principium*).[35] Smit argues that the real topic at issue is that of tongues and prophecy, since γλῶσσα occurs 21 times in chs. 12–14 and not elsewhere in this epistle, while the προφητεία word group occurs 20 times, and otherwise only at 11:4, 5.[36] Hence, in his use of *insinuatio* Paul cloaks tongues and prophecy under the less sensitive term τῶν πνευματικῶν in v. 1, while Paul's criticism, "for the time being, remains cloaked under an apparently innocent reminder of the past."[37] Verse 3 then in-troduces the centrality of Jesus as Lord.

Smit's line of approach gives a rhetorical stage-setting to what amounts to the standard modern view that Paul's allusion to pre-conversion experience achieves two goals. First, it calls the bluff of any who claim γνῶσις about "what is spiritual" on the basis of some former experience or pre-Christian back-ground. Second, in particular it challenges the widespread assumption in helle-nistic religions that a major criterion of the presence of divine inspiration or di-vine indwelling was the suspension of the rational or the ordinary in ecstatic experiences or ecstatic speech. But this view has been very strongly attacked recently by Christopher Forbes, who believes that it sets us on the wrong track.[38]

(b) The Greek adjective ἄφωνος provides little help that is decisive. In Isa 53:7 (LXX) it translated אלם (*'alam*) for the lamb dumb before its shearers, and it occurs in Wis 4:19, 2 Macc 3:29, and in Josephus, *Antiquities* 6.337. It is used of "dumb animals" (Acts 8:32 reflects Isa 53:7; cf. *1 Clement* 16:7; 2 Pet. 2:16, of the "dumb beast" which spoke in the Balaam story).[39] If we were to follow NJB's *inarticulate*, it would imply perhaps a contrast between an ecstatic state and "putting things into articulate speech," as perhaps implied in 14:13 by ἑρμηνεύειν.[40] But Gundry and Forbes attack such a contrast in these chapters,

---

35. Schmit, "Argument and Genre of 1 Cor 12–14," in Porter-Olbricht, *Rhetoric,* 211-30, esp. 212-14. Schmit compares esp. Cicero, *De Inventione* 1.15.20–15.21.

36. Ibid., 211, n. 1.

37. Ibid., 214.

38. Forbes, *Prophecy and Inspired Speech in Early Christianity,* 20-43, 44-74 on the NT; and 103-81 on evidence in hellenistic sources.

39. Hatch-Redpath and BAGD, 128.

40. Thiselton, "The 'Interpretation' of Tongues? A New Suggestion in the Light of Greek Usage in Philo and Josephus," 15-36.

and it cannot simply be assumed as the background to 12:2.[41] More probably ἄφωνος as applied to the images of pagan deities is an implicit polemic against *self-induced* "spiritual" experiences. **Idols incapable of speech**, by their very silence, provoke their worshipers into uttering "inspired speech" as their mouthpieces. But in addition to the arguments of Gundry and of Forbes, such a suggestion rests on a reconstruction which reads more into the text than the text actually says. It is easy to multiply OT allusions to the contrast between dumb or silent idols and "God who comes and is not silent" (Ps 50:3, with Wolff).[42] Even if we accept the warnings of Gundry and Forbes, Paul's emphasis falls upon *a rejection of all humanly constructed religious "spiritualities"; being "spiritual" depends on the activity of the Holy Spirit,* to which Christomorphic faith, life, and spiritual experience is a *response.* No "construct" can serve as substitute for this, and is counterfeit.

(c) Before we move to the opposite end of the range of possible interpretations to adopt what Fee calls a "minimal" evaluation of Paul's allusion to pre-conversion experience, we should note some possibilities to which Forbes does not appear to allude.[43] Craig does indeed believe that "enthusiastic religious behaviour . . . frenzy" is part of the pre-Christian experience, and this for understandable reasons (see below) Forbes would reject. But Craig rightly notes that this is *not the only* factor which could mislead the Corinthians on the basis of pre-conversion assumptions about "the spiritual." Equally important is the expectation that *certain specific people* within a cult will be regarded as "spiritual" in contrast to others.[44] This relates very closely to the important arguments of Dale Martin, to which we shall refer shortly, about the *status-conferring* significance of the more spectacular spiritual gifts, especially tongues. Many writers contrast a more individualistic emphasis on "being spiritual" both in Judaism (persons equipped by the Spirit of God to perform particular tasks; cf. Judg 3:20; 6:34; 11:29; 14:6; 1 Sam 11:6; 1 Kings 18:12; Ezek 2:2; 3:12; Mic 3:8; *Testaments of the Twelve Patriarchs* Appendix (1), 10:9; *Testament of Benjamin* 8:2) and in hellenistic religions.

(d) Forbes may show more eagerness to suggest a "minimal" evaluation of the pre-Christian allusion behind 12:2 than is strictly necessary for him to establish his arguments against understanding tongues as ecstatic speech or general "inspired utterance." To be sure, Forbes and David Aune are right to argue that there is no hard evidence for interpreting ἀπαγόμενοι as "led away by evil spirits." Aune comments, "Rather, he [Paul] is contrasting the former

---

41. Gundry, " 'Ecstatic Utterances' (NEB)?" 299-307; and Forbes, *Prophecy,* 20-43; 44-74, and 103-81.

42. Wolff, *Der erste Brief,* 283, cites Psalm 50 and numerous other OT sources. But specific citations remain speculative, and we need not depend on issues about hellenistic sources raised by Forbes; cf. the worshipers of the Baalim on Mount Carmel, 1 Kings 18:26-29, esp. against the background of the phrase "dumb idols" in Judaism.

43. Fee, *First Epistle,* 577.

44. Craig, "1 Cor," *IB,* 10:146-47.

enslaved state of the Corinthian Christians in 1 Cor. 12:2 (with no reference to their 'ecstatic' behaviour) with their present state as those who are filled with the Spirit of God."[45] But Forbes seeks to establish more specific points than one which would demand a minimal understanding of the role of pre-Christian experience in v. 2. First, he argues with considerable force and with reference to many sources that common assumptions which link "ecstatic experience" (he rightly has reservations about this term) with, e.g., the Delphic Apollo, the cults of Dionysus and Cybele, and the Magical Papyri all entail problems of dating and precise nature of supposed parallels.[46] Second, he offers more debatable and more specific arguments about the "linguistic" nature of tongues as translatable utterances which, far from detracting from the pre-Christian contrast of 12:2, might, if it could be established, be linked with a defense of authentic as against inauthentic experiences in 12:3–14:40. Part of the issue for Gundry and for Forbes turns on the contrast between the "ecstatic," the rational, and the suprarational or heart-related dimension of the spiritual. On this issue, see our Extended Notes on prophetic speech and on speaking with tongues, below.

(e) The focus of Forbes's attack falls most sharply on the specific interpretation of 12:2 by J. P. M. Sweet and J. Héring, and more broadly that of G. Dautzenberg and B. A. Pearson. Sweet associates the **idols that were incapable of speech** with the "gongs and cymbals" (13:1) of pagan temples, the use of μαίνεσθε in 14:23, and the seductive power (ἀπαγόμενοι) of evil forces or "demons" (10:21), while Schrage discusses the possible role of "demonic 'inspiration.'"[47] Dautzenberg associates πνευματικῶν (12:1) with angelic beings and tongues with angelic speech, which might suggest a contrast in 12:2-3 between good and evil angelic agencies.[48] But as Hill, Forbes, and others argue, such a view brings its own difficulties.[49] Forbes similarly criticizes the selectivity of evidence on which N. I. J. Engelsen depends for a view similar to those advocated by Sweet and by Dautzenberg.[50] Again, Forbes convincingly disposes of narrower, overly specific understandings of 12:1-2, but he does not entirely undermine the broader points made by Earle Ellis and others about the probable connections between 12:1-2 and different understandings of inspired speech and criteria for distinguishing between authentic and evil sources of

45. Aune, *Prophecy in Early Christianity*, 221.

46. Forbes, *Prophecy*, 20-43, 44-74, and 103-81.

47. Sweet, "A Sign for Unbelievers: Paul's Attitude to Glossolalia," 240-57; Schrage, *Der erste Brief*, 3:121. Nevertheless, Schrage recognizes that no specific interpretation can be beyond doubt.

48. Dautzenberg, "Glossolalie," in *RAC*, 11 (1981), 221-46, esp. 227-29; cf. more broadly Dautzenberg, *Urchristliche Prophetie*; cf. Pearson, *Pneumatikos-Psychikos Terminology*, 44-45, and Héring, *First Epistle*, 123.

49. Cf. Hill, *NT Prophecy*, 133-34; and Forbes, *Prophecy*, 19-21, 54-77, and elsewhere.

50. Engelsen's work appears in an unpublished thesis (Yale, 1970) and is discussed by Forbes, *Prophecy*, 19-21, 54-57, etc., who readily shows the selected use of sources in the argument.

"spiritual" (even, for Ellis, angelic) influences.[51] Again, *in our view the pre-Christian and Christian frameworks constitute comparative frames of reference within which respective criteria for what it means to be πνευματικός operate.* Each of these views may offer nuances of the contrast, but Forbes rightly questions whether all of the weight can be placed on the modern consensus view.

(f) In our view, the most important light comes from Dale B. Martin, in conjunction with John Painter's article on the subject. Whether or not "tongues" is the specific focus of 12:3–14:40, there can be little doubt that Martin is convincing *in viewing it as, for many at Corinth, a "high-status indicator."*[52] Whether or not Forbes is right about the need to modify our view of the *content* of the "gifts" of 12:1-2 (see below), the issue remains that in pre-Christian paganism the notion of *status-conferring* "experiences" (like claims to "wisdom") cohered with the cultural, social, rhetorical, and religious climate of Corinth and had found its way into the church. Thus John Painter draws a contrast between the "spirituality" of the πνευματικοί which stressed knowledge, wisdom, and exalted states of consciousness and "the proclamation of the cross as the saving event."[53] While Painter links 12:2 with 1 Cor 1:1–4:21, Martin connects v. 2 with the emphasis on unity-in-diversity in 12:1–14:40.[54] Both point toward the divine act of "status-conferring" in the corporate event of 15:1-58. The contrast with attitudes carried over from paganism thus becomes fundamental and not "minimal."[55]

In summary, v. 2 prepares the way for the christological criterion of "spirituality" which Paul introduces in v. 3 by appealing to the early creed which all believers share as the basis of their new life. With Christ as their Lord, they have no need to construct some "spirituality" as if God were silent. Their varied experiences of the different gifts which God actively apportions out (12:4-11) rest upon his choice and initiative, not upon their own self-generated choices and motivations. Paige's suggestion about the scenario of a parade is attractive but cannot be proven.

3 The transitive verb γνωρίζω means *to make known, to reveal,* **to impart knowledge**, in most contexts (cf. Rom 9:22-23; Luke 2:15; Acts 2:28; 2 Cor 8:1).[56] Occasionally it may be used intransitively, to mean *to know* (Dio Chrysostom 4:33), but not in this verse. Since this is the third consecutive refer-

---

51. E. E. Ellis, "Spiritual Gifts" and "Christ and Spirit in 1 Cor," in *Prophecy and Hermeneutic,* esp. 25 and 70-71; cf. 25-44 and 63-71.

52. Martin, "Tongues of Angels and Other Status Indicators," 547-89, and *The Corinthian Body,* 87-92.

53. Painter, "Paul and the πνευματικοί at Corinth," in Hooker and Wilson (eds.), *Paul and Paulinism,* 245; cf. 237-50.

54. Martin, *The Corinthian Body,* 92-96; cf. 97-103.

55. Hence, Klauck's comment remains very much to the point on v. 2: Paul is concerned with discerning what is "of the Spirit," and thus distinguishes between pre-Christian concerns with exceptional "phenomena" and sees the Spirit in "every genuine manifestation of the Christian life of faith" (*1 Korintherbrief,* 85).

56. Cf. BAGD, 163; Grimm-Thayer, 119.

ence to **knowledge** (ἀγνοεῖν, v. 1; οἴδατε, v. 2), it appears that Paul is taking up the claim of those who style themselves as οἱ πνευματικοί to have γνῶσις (see on 8:1). Hence we place this third reference to **knowledge** in quotation marks.

The preposition with the dative ἐν πνεύματι could denote the sphere of the Spirit of God, understood in effect as a locative, and could be translated *in the Spirit* (NJB) or *under the influence of the Spirit* (REB, JB). But the context and theology of confessional declaration point to the dative of *instrumentality,* or **agency of the Spirit of God**. Schrage and Collins both endorse this, and NRSV, RSV, NIV rightly translate *by the Spirit of God,* which we have simply made more explicit to reflect Paul's double use of the same syntax.[57] We find here a classic model of Wolterstorff's philosophical analysis of human acts of speaking (λαλῶν) which represent speech generated by divine agency (λέγει). Wolterstorff argues that just as the words which a secretary speaks can *count as* words which her employer speaks (if the secretary knows his or her mind and is empowered or authorized to speak on his or her behalf), so human words can in appropriate situations, *count as* "divine discourse." He calls this "double agency discourse."[58] On this basis Paul is asking what content of human speech may be said to *count as* what is spoken *by* the Spirit or **through the agency of the Spirit of God**. Wolterstorff readily shows that, e.g., in the case of ambassadors who speak for a head of state "double-speaking" and "double agency" is entirely intelligible.[59] So Paul asks: Under what conditions does an utterance of a πνευματίκος *count as* an utterance of τὸ ἅγιον πνεῦμα? More broadly, what *experiences and actions, as well as words,* will *count as* manifestations of the Holy Spirit, rather than self-induced experiences, acts, or words, or even those induced by other agencies?

Several points will assist us in understanding the puzzling reference to ἀνάθεμα Ἰησοῦς. First, J. S. Vos offers reasons for regarding 12:1, 2, 3 respectively as *praefatio, narratio,* and *propositio* for the argument and tone of 12:4–14:40.[60] Second, in a careful study to which we shall return T. Holtz shows that in harmony with such confessions as Rom 10:9, Paul brings together word and deed in such a way that the ἀνάθεμα-κύριος contrast is not simply one of mere words but of practical behavioral stance.[61] Holtz also points out that we cannot contemplate a situation in which the bare information "Jesus be cursed" would not be inspired by the Holy Spirit constituted epoch-making or even informative news to the Corinthians, unless something further is at issue beneath the surface. Third, both writers stress convincingly that we cannot find the key to the meaning of ἀνάθεμα Ἰησοῦς without at the same time examining the positive confession **"Jesus is Lord."**

---

57. Schrage, *Der erste Brief,* 3:124-25; Collins, *First Cor,* 448.
58. N. Wolterstorff, *Divine Discourse: Philosophical Reflections on the Claim that God Speaks* (Cambridge: Cambridge University Press, 1995), esp. 1 129. See esp. 38-42 (e.g., secretary analogy), 42-51 ("deputized discourse," e.g., the ambassador and the prophet).
59. Ibid., 45-57 and 75-94 (including "counting as" and "count-generation").
60. Vos, "Das Rätsel von 1 Kor 12:1-3," 251-69.
61. Holtz, "Das Kennzeichen des Geistes (1 Kor xii:1-3)," 365-76.

Astonishing as it may seem, no less than twelve distinct explanations have been offered to try to account for the use of the phrase ἀνάθεμα Ἰησοῦς. Before we briefly list these, it may be helpful provisionally to note the semantic range and lexicographical data which relate to ἀνάθεμα. In classical Greek literature the word regularly means *votive offering* devoted to a deity. In the history of the word the active voice of ἀνατίθημι, *to set up* (i.e., in a temple) or *place upon* (another), takes the middle form ἀνεθέμην, *to lay before*. With the long vowel ἀνάθημα occurs in, e.g., Sophocles, *Antigone* 286; 3 Macc 3:17; Jdt 16:19; *Epistle of Aristeas* 40; Josephus, *Wars* 6.335; *Antiquities* 17.156. The form with the shorter vowel, ἀνάθεμα, assumes: (i) this *votive offering* meaning from its hellenistic background (Plutarch, *Pelopidas* 25.7; Philo, *De Vita Mosis* 1.253); and (ii) the LXX translation for Heb. חרם *(cherem), that which is to be thoroughly destroyed as holy-to-God,* that which is *taboo* and unavailable to human use or contact (Lev 27:28; Josh 6:17; 7:12; Judg 1:17). (iii) In noncultic contexts it then enters ordinary discourse as *cursed* or *cut off,* especially *cut off from God* (Gal 1:8-9; Rom 9:3; 10:1). Schrage and Davis discuss especially (ii) and (iii).[62] The absence of the verb in ἀνάθεμα Ἰησοῦς permits either the imperatival or subjunctive *Jesus be cursed* or the indicative assertion **Jesus is cursed**. We shall argue that the utterance concerning κύριος is a *confession* which combines an assertion about Jesus Christ with self-involvement on the part of the speaker. There need to be compelling reasons for understanding the parallel clause in a different way. This will emerge as we set forth the various possibilities, pausing where more general remarks serve our purpose and evaluation. A final assessment, however, awaits the examination of the κύριος confession.

(i) There is much to be said for Cullmann's view that both utterances serve as *confessions,* characteristically in a *persecution* setting. The curse, Cullmann insists, cannot be related to inarticulate tongues; both utterances are fully "intelligible assertions. . . . The primary theme of the verse is not glossolalia but emperor worship and persecution because of the confession Kyrios Christos." This is probably an allusion, in turn, to the promise of Jesus to give the Spirit in times of persecution, so that **through the agency of the Spirit** those who are "delivered up to councils . . . in synagogues . . . dragged before governors . . ." (Matt 10:17-19) may be able to confess **Jesus is** [my/our/the] **Lord** rather than **Jesus is cursed** or *Caesar is Lord,* "the first proving the working of the Spirit, the second proving the absence of that work."[63] Elsewhere Cullmann shows convincingly that confessions of this nature emerged as primitive credal forms in the settings of *baptism* (Acts 8:37; 1 Pet 3:18-22), *worship* (Phil 2:6-11; 1 Cor 15:3-7), acts of *healing* or (in the subapostolic period) exorcism (Acts 3:13), *persecution settings* (1 Tim 6:12, 13, 16; Rom 10:9; 1 Cor

---

62. Cf. W. H. Davis, "Anathema — Rom. 9:3," *RevExp* 31 (1934): 205-7; Schrage, *Der erste Brief,* 3:123.

63. Cullmann, *The Christology of the NT,* 219; cf. 218-20.

12:3; cf. Matt 10:17-20), and *polemic* against heresy (1 John 4:2; 1 Cor 8:6; 15:3-8).[64] Goudge stresses a persecution setting, Cullmann notes the parallel between ἀνάθεμα Ἰησοῦς and Polycarp's response under persecution that "he had never yet blasphemed Christ (βλασφημῆσαι)," and we may compare Pliny, *Epistles,* 97 in a similar context.[65]

(ii) There is a strong tradition in modern scholarship that both acclamations may pour forth from a state of uncontrolled ecstasy in the context of worship (e.g., Thrall, Schmithals, Weiss, Lietzmann), and Dunn writes, "It is quite likely, though many disagree, that during the Corinthian worship some member(s) of the assembly had cried out under inspiration 'Jesus be cursed!'"[66] Dunn links this with a quasi-gnostic devaluation of the earthly Jesus (see below). Bousset sees the *Kyrios Christos* confession as initially an instance of "brief outcries of prayer, sighs . . . of the overflowing heart which in worship were addressed directly to Jesus. To this category belongs . . . Maranatha. . . . 1 Cor. 12:1-3 presuppose that in the Corinthian community the cry κύριος Ἰησοῦς was a sign and identifying mark of the ecstatic discourses of the prophets in rapture."[67] But is such an interpretation conceivable? Just conceivably "susceptible" charismatic Christians may have picked up the exclamatory shout from Jewish synagogue services either nextdoor or known from pre-conversion experience.[68] These exclamations might well up through the released censor in trancelike experiences. Allo further appeals to the trancelike states of consciousness associated with, e.g., the oracle of the Sibyl.[69] S. Tugwell speaks of the sense of "intoxicating newness and praise" which might produce exalted states of consciousness, which, if authentic prophetic utterance, will accept critical scrutiny (v. 3b).[70] Clearly v. 3a states what for Paul does not stand scrutiny, but it might in principle reflect an expression of the newness of a faith

64. O. Cullmann, *Les Premières Confessions de foi Chrétiennes* (Paris: Presses Universitaires de France, 2d ed. 1948), 13 and in five corresponding sections which trace developments from the NT to the early third century, 14-27. The persecution setting relates ὁμολογέω to μαρτυρέω (19-20), to the parallel with *Kyrios Kaisar* (21-22), and to the assistance of the Holy Spirit as the One who gives speech under persecution (22-24), where ἀνάθεμα Ἰησοῦς is first discussed (23-4) (Eng. trans., *The Earliest Christian Confessions*). Cf. Rev 13:18; Ignatius, *To the Trallians,* 9; Tertullian, *On the Crown,* 11.

65. Polycarp, 9:3; Cullmann, *Premières Confessions,* 22; Goudge, *First Epistle,* 109.

66. Dunn, *Jesus and the Spirit,* 234; also Moffatt, *First Epistle,* 179; Lietzmann, *An die Korinther,* 186-87; Thrall, *1 and 2 Corinthians,* 86; Weiss, *Der erste Korintherbriefe,* 295-97; Scroggs, "The Exaltation of the Spirit by Some Early Christians," 359-73; Simon, *First Epistle,* 123; Evans, *Epistles to the Corinthians,* 129; Morris, *First Epistle,* 168 as "Not beyond the bounds of possibility . . ."; Schmithals, *Gnosticism in Corinth,* 124-32 (discussed below under viii). Cf. further Wilckens, *Weisheit und Torheit,* 121, n. 1.

67. Bousset, *Kyrios Christos: A History of the Belief in Christ from the Beginnings of Christianity to Irenaeus,* 132-33.

68. Findlay, *Expositor's Greek Testament,* 2:886-87. See also Theissen, *Psychological Aspects,* 305-11.

69. Allo, *Première Épitre,* 321-22. See further Wolff, "Exkurs," in *Der erste Brief,* 285-87.

70. S. Tugwell, "The Gift of Tongues in the NT," *ExpTim* 84 (1973): 137-40.

which no longer perceives Jesus of Nazareth as *merely* the historical teacher, rather than the living Christ. Nevertheless, (a) A. Mehat and especially C. Forbes convincingly question the validity of supposed parallels with phenomena like the Sibyl in hellenistic religions (see further, below).[71] (b) T. Holtz, among others, argues that if κύριος Ἰησοῦς represents an intelligible utterance, the same is equally true of ἀνάθεμα Ἰησοῦς: neither yields the inarticulate outpourings of a quasi-trance state, but intelligible declarations.[72]

(iii) Allo and Barrett offer a variant of the above. Allo postulates the situation of believers in the worship assembly who feel an oncoming state of trance or heightened consciousness which they wish to resist, or try to resist. This prompts the ἀνάθεμα utterance.[73] But although he can cite parallels of the desire to resist trance in cultic contexts, the hypothesis must remain sheer conjecture, in spite of the assertion of no less an authority than Barrett that "Allo is probably right."[74] Allo's citation of Cassandra's "cursing" of Apollo and the Sibyl's resisting inspiration in desperate frenzy are hardly close parallels, as Forbes points out in more general terms.

(iv) Numerous writers understand ἀνάθεμα Ἰησοῦς as something like a "cry, so apt to Jewish lips, [which] resounded in the synagogue in response to apostolic preaching."[75] But if Paul is addressing the Christian congregation at Corinth, how would this apply to them? Would it not be self-evident that the polemic against Jesus of Nazareth could not be prompted by Christ's Spirit? This has led to a variety of variants which begin from this starting point.

(v) Bassler argues that Paul may have uttered such a cry in his own rabbinic pre-conversion days: "It is entirely possible that Paul . . . is drawing on his own personal biography to support his argument."[76] Paul had been well aware that the crucified one was "accursed" according to the Torah (Gal 3:13). In fact, Robertson and Plummer anticipated this view in 1911 (2d ed. 1914) when they developed their reconstruction from the point of departure in Judaism, and Witherington considers it possible.[77]

(vi) This means that ἀνάθεμα Ἰησοῦς is a *hypothetical literary device,* i.e., it is used as a hypothetical assertion in contrast to the κύριος Ἰησοῦς confession actually heard in the course of Christian worship. Bassler sees it as in this sense "an ironic understatement" of something that no one ever says who is "spiritual."[78] Thus for Hurd it is "the hypothetical opposite of the cry 'Jesus is

71. Mehat, "L'Enseignement sur 'les choses de l'Esprit' (1 Cor. 12:1-3)," 395-415; C. Forbes, "Early Christian Inspired Speech and Hellenistic Popular Religion," *NovT* 28 (1986): 257-70; and *Prophecy and Inspired Speech in Early Christianity and Its Hellenistic Environment.*

72. Holtz, "Das Kennzeichen des Geistes (1 Kor xii:1-3)," 365-76.

73. Allo, *Première Épitre,* 320-22.

74. Barrett, *First Epistle,* 280.

75. Findlay, *Expositor's Greek Testament,* 2:886; Robertson and Plummer, *First Epistle,* 261.

76. J. M. Bassler, "1 Cor. 12:3 — Curse and Confession in Context," 418; cf. 415-18.

77. Robertson and Plummer, *First Epistle,* 261; cf. Witherington, *Conflict and Community,* 256.

78. Bassler, "1 Cor. 12:3," 418.

Lord.'"[79] Grosheide is regularly cited as supporting (ii), but in fact concludes that Paul uses the formula "without referring to an actual statement" in contrast to the "real confession" of Christ as Lord.[80] Aune, Bruce, and Kistemaker also favor the view that no specific group or occurrence is in view, and Fee views this as one of two possible explanations.[81] But Héring believes, "We feel that the Apostle would not mention this case unless it really had occurred," and Orr and Walther insist that it is "not hypothetical."[82] They cite Acts 26:11, 1 John 4:1-6, and Rev 2:13; 3:8; 12:17; and 17:14 as concrete instances of the text of "an abjuration of Jesus" under Jewish or Gentile persecution. Wendland discusses these issues more broadly.[83]

(vii) A conjectural variant of the Jewish and persecution settings is therefore proposed by J. D. M. Derrett, whose hypotheses are always ingenious.[84] Derrett discusses a proposed OT and Jewish background in Deut 18:17-22, and envisages the situation of a Christian facing imminent expulsion from the Jewish synagogue. The ruler of the synagogue attempts to "tutor" the Christian back by suggesting that to declare ἀνάθεμα ᾽Ιησοῦς would avoid the last step in the process of expulsion. In such a context, Paul asserts, it becomes a decisive test of whether the Spirit is at work. Ingenious as the theory is, however, it rests on no less a degree on conjecture than Allo's proposal about resisting ecstatic consciousness. Yet a broader setting of persecution and the link with Judaism remain plausible components for a reconstruction.

(viii) The hypothesis that the exclamation could occur in an exalted state of consciousness in Christian worship verges on the plausible only in the version advocated by Dunn, namely, that this "spiritual" outlook disparaged the earthly Jesus of history.[85] One specific version of this emphasis is the theory of Schmithals, Wilckens, and Brox about gnostic influence. Schmithals argues that "there were in Corinth people for whom it was not a contradiction to confess the Χριστός and to cry ἀνάθεμα ᾽Ιησοῦς."[86] Such people appear in 1 John 2:22, where they state that ὁ ᾽Ιησοῦς οὐκ ἔστιν ὁ Χριστός. They denied that the Messianic Christ had come "in the flesh" (1 John 4:2). "Thus they were Gnostics who rejected a close connection between the heavenly Pneuma-Christ and the man Jesus."[87] The distinction Χριστὸς κατὰ σάρκα and Χριστὸς κατὰ πνεῦμα is familiar in Paul (Rom 1:3; 9:5), and Paul did not come to belief

79. Hurd, *Origin of 1 Corinthians,* 193.

80. Grosheide, *First Epistle,* 281 (after discussing view ii on 280).

81. Kistemaker, *1 Cor,* 415-16; Bruce, *1 and 2 Cor,* 118; Fee, *First Epistle,* 581; Aune, *Prophecy in Early Christianity,* 221.

82. Héring, *First Epistle,* 125; Orr and Walther, *1 Cor,* 277-78. Also Morris, *First Epistle,* 168.

83. Wendland, *Die Briefe,* 105-7, also alludes to Cullmann's view.

84. Derrett, "Cursing Jesus (1 Cor xii:3): The Jews as Religious Persecutors," 544-54.

85. Dunn, *Jesus and the Spirit,* 234.

86. Schmithals, *Gnosticism in Corinth,* 127; cf. 124-32; U. Wilckens, *Weisheit und Torheit,* 121; Brox, "Ἀνάθεμα ᾽Ιησοῦς (1 Kor 12:3)," *BZ* 12 (1968): 103-11.

87. Ibid.

through Χριστὸς κατὰ σάρκα. Further, Origen tells us that gnostics did not admit persons to their fellowship who "had not first cursed Jesus."[88] Schmithals concludes: "The Christology of the Corinthian 'Christians' which is expressed in the ἀνάθεμα Ἰησοῦς in 1 Cor. 12:3 is the genuinely Gnostic Christology."[89]

The work of Schmithals and Wilckens has been heavily criticized, not least for reading back later gnostic thought into the earlier period of Paul. S. G. Wilson, e.g., concludes after weighing the evidence, "What we have at Corinth, then, is not yet Gnosticism, but a kind of *gnosis*."[90] Nevertheless, Schmithals rightly exposes the link between "spirituality" and Christology here. *We shall indeed argue that Paul consistently sees "Christlikeness" as a criterion for evidence of the action and experience of the Spirit of God, and that the work of the historical Jesus plays a significant part in determining in what this consists.*

(ix) Before we turn to the more christological interpretations of 12:3, we should note two further views. First, some ascribe ἀνάθεμα Ἰησοῦς to undue *openness to evil forces* or to evil spirits when "control" is suspended. This has some importance because *authentic prophecy does* entail "control" and willingness to be examined, scrutinized, and tested.[91] Héring firmly argues that the ἀνάθεμα utterance comes from a charismatic "possessed only by an evil spirit."[92] Ellis takes such a view seriously, Fee finds it "an attractive option," and Witherington considers it possible.[93] But this is an inference which depends more on an interpretative construal than what is explicit in the text. It also assumes the kind of link with an interpretation of v. 2 which Mehat and Forbes heavily criticize.

(x) An allusion to *Gentiles* who attend the Christian worship service is unlikely. For while inquirers or unbelievers may be present (1 Cor 14:23), as Godet observes, how could any reader have been tempted ever to regard this as inspired "by the Spirit"?[94] Paul states the obvious to the point of banality.

(xi) *Christological* explanations have most to be said in their favor, and here W. C. van Unnik proposes an ingenious possibility which deserves consideration and respect. He rejects the explanations of Schmithals and Wilckens about a "gnostic" rejection of the earthly Jesus and in a sense reverses this hypothesis. The speaker who exclaimed ἀνάθεμα Ἰησοῦς endorsed the theology

---

88. Origen, *Against Celsus,* 6:28; cf. Schmithals, *Gnosticism in Corinth,* 128. Less specifically cf. Irenaeus, 1:31:1 and 3:16:1, 8.

89. Schmithals, *Gnosticism in Corinth,* 129.

90. S. G. Wilson, "Gnosis at Corinth," in M. D. Hooker and S. G. Wilson (eds.), *Paul and Paulinism: Essays in Honour of C. K. Barrett,* 112; cf. 102-14. Cf. also Pearson, "Did the Gnostics Curse Jesus?" 301-5.

91. Cf. Tugwell, "The Gift of Tongues in the NT," 137-40; cf. further Grudem, *The Gift of Prophecy in 1 Cor,* 164-73.

92. Héring, *First Epistle,* 125.

93. Ellis, "Christ and Spirit in 1 Cor," in his *Prophecy and Hermeneutic,* 71; cf. 63-71; Witherington, *Conflict,* 256; Fee, *First Epistle,* 579.

94. Godet, *First Epistle,* 2:185.

of expiation or atonement articulated by Paul in Gal 3:13, in conjunction with Deut 21:23 and 27:26: Jesus became *cherem* and κατάρα, accursed under the Law of God "to take away the curse that was on and in the people through the wrath of God, to restore the wholesome situation."[95] Those who confessed ἀνάθεμα Ἰησοῦς confessed a theology of the cross, "but this was not the last word. . . . He not only died, but also was raised from the dead (cf. . . . 1 Cor. 15:3, 4)."[96] However, both ἀνάθεμα and κύριος express not simply what Jesus did; nor do they express an imperatival ἔστω, *let him be.* They demand ἐστίν: **Jesus is cursed . . . Jesus is Lord**.[97] They confess "the status of Jesus," and as such the Spirit witnesses to his status as living, vindicated Lord; Jesus no longer stands in God's curse as a perpetual sacrifice.[98] The confession evoked by the Spirit is a triumphant acclamation of Christ's exaltation over a hostile world. Van Unnik appeals to the context of Rom 10:6-10: his present Lordship brings salvation. The Spirit draws out a "calling upon the Lord" to be saved (Joel 3:5; Acts 2:14-40). The context of this acclamation is Pentecostal: only when eyes are opened by the Holy Spirit can Jesus be seen as a living mediator of salvation.[99] To see him merely as the crucified one from "the earthly side," even in fulfillment of Deut 21:33; 27:26, is not a complete sign of an acclamation prompted by the Holy Spirit, whose work is to glorify Christ.

There is more to be said for this view than many acknowledge, since it is all too plausible that the expression could be one of "religious" praise by persons who had merely worked out an intellectual theology of salvation, without being genuinely open to the fullness of the gospel and the presence of the Spirit. It also rightly perceives Christology as the test of "spirituality," or of what it is to experience **the agency of the Spirit**. But the main problem at Corinth seems to have been triumphalism, which implies that the persons to whom allusion is made were not the main group. However, Paul states in 1 Cor 15:12 that **some** (τινες) deny the resurrection, and this ἀνάθεμα, therefore, may well refer to worship exclamations from such a group. It helps to explain, moreover, why those who deny the resurrection would still belong to a *Christian* congregation, which is otherwise extremely puzzling.[100] A variant of this view is offered by D. Patte, who thinks that the "curse" alludes to a theology of the atonement which overpresses the notion of propitiating an angry God.[101] But there is little in the specific context of Corinthian theology to support this specific understanding of the problem.

95. Van Unnik, "Jesus: Anathema or Kyrios (1 Cor. 12:3)," in B. Lindars and S. S. Smalley (eds.), *Christ and Spirit in the NT: Studies in Honour of C. F. D. Moule,* 120; cf. 113-26.

96. Ibid., 121.

97. Ibid., 115.

98. Ibid., 121.

99. Ibid., 123.

100. Witherington stresses the "some": *Conflict,* 295 and 299.

101. D. Patte, *Paul's Faith and the Power of the Gospel* (Philadelphia: Fortress, 1983), 306-10.

(xii) The *contrast* between the two confessions explicates a *christological criterion* of what it is to experience **the agency of the Spirit**. As Hill observes, it is "a test . . . but it is not a test for true and false prophecy."[102] Indeed, we would go further and, following Godet, Holtz, (in part) Bittlinger, and Deluz, refer it to more than "a test of inspired *speech*" (my italics).[103] Bittlinger argues that *the logic of the passage* presupposes that those addressed "do not regard the expressions 'Jesus be cursed' and 'Christ is Lord' as contradictory," i.e., they separated "the historic Jesus from the pneumatic Christ."[104] But this does not imply that Schmithals on one side and Van Unnik on the other offer more than the right starting point. T. Holtz insists (rightly, with Van Unnik, Wolff, and Schrage) that we must take seriously the confessions of Jesus as *Kyrios* in 12:3c and Rom 10:9. These confessions entail (a) *belief that* Jesus has the status and identity in question, and (b) a *heart orientation of stance and will* which constitutes the *performative, self-involving, and illocutionary nature of a confession from the lips and the heart.*[105]

Confession with words which signal the *stance of the heart* (Rom 10:9) relates, as does the whole of 12:1–14:40, to "the service of God *in life*" (my italics).[106] Rom 10:9 precisely reflects Deut 30:14, where "the word . . . is in your mouth and in your heart *so that you can do it.*" We must interpret the contrastive ἀνάθεμα Ἰησοῦς . . . as the "antithesis . . . in form and content . . . an antithetical picture by analogy," i.e., a turning of one's back upon all that the earthly Jesus represents.

Bittlinger, like others, compares the person who professes "Christ" but denies that Christ "came in the flesh" (1 John 4:2, 3), and rightly adds that such a confession "was more than a formula."[107] But Dietmar Neufeld incisively demolishes the notion of Bultmann and others that this concerns primarily an intellectual belief, namely, doceticism. It is "a self-involving speech-act . . . that the author has committed himself to."[108] The antithesis "depicts two contrasting spheres made up of two types of people who in their confessing, denying, and believing make plain to what sphere they belong."[109] The utterances are "commissive and expressive" of dispositions, stances, and lifestyles.[110]

Our consideration of this range of twelve aspects of understanding v. 3a *brings us to focus more specifically on the confession κύριος Ἰησοῦς.* All that

102. Hill, *NT Prophecy,* 135.

103. Ibid.

104. Bittlinger, *Gifts and Graces: A Commentary on 1 Cor 12–14,* 17.

105. Holtz, "Das Kennzeichen des Geistes (1 Kor xii:1-3)," 365-76, esp. 374; Schrage, *Der erste Brief,* 3:123-24; Wolff, *Der erste Brief,* 286-87.

106. Holtz, "Das Kennzeichen des Geistes," 375.

107. Bittlinger, *Gifts and Graces,* 18; Wolff, *Der erste Brief,* "Exkurs," 286-87, well emphasizes the christological dimension.

108. D. Neufeld, *Reconceiving Texts as Speech-Acts: An Analysis of 1 John,* BibIntMon 7 (Leiden: Brill, 1994), 117 and 131.

109. Ibid., 132.

110. Ibid., 134.

has been said above under (i), (xi), and (xii), among other points, applies especially to the arguments of Cullmann about life settings, Holtz and Neufeld about actions, stances, and lifestyles, and a number of writers about Christology. J. Weiss observes that what it means to confess Jesus as Lord "in a practical sense will best be made clear through the correlative concept of servant or slave of Christ."[111] Kennedy asserts that to call Jesus Lord involves for Paul "surrender, reverence, trust and grateful love."[112] "The *Kyrios* confession can be understood only by the pious simplicity of silent devotion."[113] If the acclamation of Christ as *Kyrios* is a test of the Spirit's agency in the human heart (cf. Rom. 10:9), it must entail more than having "right beliefs," for salvation no more depends on "right thoughts" than "right deeds." C. A. Scott, anticipating Schrage and Eriksson, rightly identifies *"the acknowledgment that 'Jesus is Lord'"* as *"the one audible profession of faith which Paul requires for a would-be Christian, the only and sufficient condition for participating in salvation* (Rom 10:9; cf. 10:8, τὸ ῥῆμα τῆς πίστεως . . . 'the formula which expresses faith' . . . when it is understood as due to the working of the Holy Spirit (1 Cor. xii:3; cf. Matt. xvi:17)" (my italics).[114]

Those arguments which associate the *Kyrios* confession with life and worship rather than with abstract statements, are convincing for further reasons. Kramer calls it "acclaiming his majesty"; an acclamation less part of preaching than "proclaimed with a shout."[115] It is less certain that some of the more specific theories about given aspects of worship, especially eucharistic worship, can be sustained, especially in the form advocated by Lietzmann (discussed above on 11:17-34).[116]

The same kind of difficulty confronts W. Bousset's arguments. According to Bousset's history-of-religions approach, whereas the earliest Jewish-Christian communities had focused largely on Christ as eschatological Son of Man, among the hellenistic communities they carried over and applied to Christ their pre-conversion experience of θεοὶ πολλοὶ καὶ κύριοι πολλοί, to which Paul alludes in 1 Cor 8:5.[117] In his Preface to the fifth edition of Bousset, Bultmann (1964) recognizes that forceful criticisms have been brought against Bousset's argument that Christ was "first characterized and addressed as Lord not in the primitive community but in the Hellenistic community."[118] Nevertheless, he urges "the correctness of Bousset's total view and of his representation of the

111. Weiss, *Earliest Christianity,* 2:458.

112. H. A. A. Kennedy, *The Theology of the Epistles* (London: Duckworth, 1919), 84.

113. Deissmann, *Paul,* 194.

114. C. A. A. Scott, *Christianity according to St. Paul* (Cambridge: Cambridge University Press, 1927), 250 and 250, n. 1; Schrage, *Der erste Brief,* 3:125; Eriksson, *Traditions as Rhetorical Proof,* 110-14.

115. Kramer, *Christ, Lord, Son of God,* 66-67.

116. H. Lietzmann, *Mass and Lord's Supper: A Study in the History of the Liturgy* (Eng. trans., Leiden: Brill, 1979), 205-11.

117. Bousset, *Kyrios Christos,* 147.

118. Ibid., 8.

cultic Kyrios worship in Hellenistic Christianity."[119] On 1 Cor 12:3 Bousset perceives the transposition of "outcries of prayer, sighs of the oppressed and overflowing heart which in worship were addressed to Jesus."[120] To this category belongs Maranatha (1 Cor 16:22). "The eschatological outlook of the primitive community, the yearning for the Lord who is to come, forcibly set precedents in such ecstatic cries."[121]

Bousset thus postulates a quasi-syncretistic process, which Paul modified by insisting on certain christological and ethical constraints. Nevertheless, apart from the general validity of an emphasis on practical worship and devotion, Bousset's theory founders at numerous points, not least on an outdated separation between "Palestinian" and "Hellenistic" compartments of culture, speculations about the nature, scope, and dating of mystery cults, and the issue of theological continuity with the Jerusalem church which appears never to have taken issue with this christological "development."[122] The best that can be drawn from Bousset's work is the proper recognition, shared by form criticism and by speech-act theory, that **Jesus is Lord** is no mere "floating" fragment of descriptive statement or abstract proposition, but is *a spoken act of personal devotion and commitment which is part and parcel of a Christ-centered worship and lifestyle.* Further, Bousset's emphasis in the pre-Pauline community anticipates the valid emphasis of writers from Cullmann to Eriksson that Paul here *bases his argument on the premise of a shared tradition.*[123]

The term also expresses the practical recognition that the speaker *belongs to Christ* as Christ's purchased slave (6:20; 7:23) and that therefore *Christ has the care of the believer.* Paul applies the term κύριος to Jesus Christ some 220 times as "clearly his favorite title for him": "We preach Christ Jesus as Lord" (2 Cor 4:5).[124] On one side, Christ takes responsibility for the believer as his or her *Kyrios;* on the other side, the Lord is the authority to whom the believer is responsible and from whom the believer derives his or her lifestyle and ethics.[125] We have already noted Dale Martin's discussion about whether such "belonging" constitutes "high-status" or "low-status" identity (see on 6:20 and esp. 7:27).[126] Eriksson (as we noted) sees the function of this acclamation in 12:3 as

119. Ibid., 9.

120. Ibid., 133.

121. Ibid.

122. Most notably Martin Hengel, *Judaism and Hellenism: Studies in Their Encounter in Palestine during the Early Hellenistic Period* (Eng. trans., London: SCM, 1974) and, further, Hengel, *The Son of God: The Origins of Christology and the History of Jewish-Hellenistic Religion* (Eng. trans., London: SCM, 1975). Further, I. H. Marshall, *The Origins of NT Christology* (Leicester: Inter-Varsity Press, 1976). J. D. G. Dunn, *Christology in the Making* (London: SCM, 1980): and G. Wagner, *Pauline Baptism and the Pagan Mysteries* (Eng. trans., Edinburgh: Oliver & Boyd, 1967), 268-76 and throughout.

123. Eriksson, *Traditions as Rhetorical Proof,* 111-14 and 217-22.

124. A. M. Hunter, *Paul and His Predecessors* (London: SCM, 2d ed. 1961), 142.

125. Kramer, *Christ, Lord, Son of God,* 181.

126. In addition to Martin's *Slavery as Salvation,* cf. Weiss, *Earliest Christianity,* 2:460.

"fully coherent" with the following argument of 12:4-11, *not least by redefining all baptized Christians as spiritual*" (my italics).[127]

One concluding comment must be added. *Homologia* of the form **Jesus is Lord** occurs in several places in Paul: Rom 10:9; 1 Cor 12:3; Phil 2:11; 1 Cor 8:5-6; Eph 4:5; cf. 1 Tim 2:5. Vernon Neufeld identifies other related confessions in Rom 8:34; 2 Cor 13:4; 1 Thess 4:14; Rom 4:24, 25; 14:9; 1 Cor 15:3-5.[128] Neufeld, however, discusses not only the practical *life setting* of **Jesus is Lord**, but its *belief setting* as contextually linked in regular patterns with Christ's death and resurrection (Rom 14:9), the Lord's coming (1 Thess 4:15), or his humiliation and exaltation (Phil 2:5-11).[129] The *belief that* certain events have occurred and that *certain states of affairs are true* lies behind "the life situation of the *homologia*."[130] The *life-action* of worship does indeed provide the setting for κύριος Ἰησοῦς, but only because the words, deeds, and identity of Christ, and above all their divine indication and corroboration in the resurrection of Christ, *have occurred. Lordship* has its *cash currency* in the church's practical trust and obedience, but it is not *established* by the human existential stance of "building him a throne." That, Paul would say, is God's work; but as an aphoristic motto for a correlative lifestyle the words have understandable if also questionable currency. According to the primitive kerygma, "God made him both Lord and Christ" (Acts 2:34-36).

In his "life settings" section on Paul's use of *homologia* Vernon Neufeld takes up all of Cullmann's categories: baptism, acclamation in worship, oath of loyalty in persecution, controversy, and polemic.[131] But in his conclusion he insists that it equally embodies the cognitive belief that Jesus, the one who lived and died and was crucified, is **Lord** "of the Christian and of the Church by virtue of his resurrection from the dead."[132] The same point is made forcefully in the small book *Creeds in the Bible* by F. W. Danker.[133] What is essential to the confession is (a) the belief; and (b) the acknowledgment in terms of an appropriate lifestyle. In philosophical terms, defining or wearing *one's colors* constitutes a *propositional content;* and *nailing them to the mast* an *illocutionary force, a personal signature.* It is "a personal declaration of faith."[134] Thus Cerfaux insists that Christ's Lordship depends on enthronement *by God,* even if the currency of confession is best perceived by its effects in human life.[135]

---

127. Eriksson, *Traditions as Rhetorical Proof,* 217.

128. Neufeld, *The Earliest Christian Confessions,* 43-49; cf. Schrage, *Der erste Brief,* 3:125; and Eriksson, *Traditions,* 111-14 and 217-22.

129. Neufeld, *Confessions,* 51-60.

130. "Life-situation" is discussed in Neufeld, *Confessions,* 60-67.

131. Ibid., 60-67.

132. Ibid., 67.

133. F. W. Danker, *Creeds in the Bible* (St. Louis: Concordia, 1966), 41-46 (on 1 Cor 12:3 and Phil 2:6-11; cf. Acts 7:59). He speaks of "recognition," and considers Deut 26:5-10; 27:9; Rom 1:3, 4; 1 Cor 15:3-5.

134. Neufeld, "The Function of the *Homologia*," in *Confessions,* 144.

135. Cerfaux, *Christ in the Theology of St. Paul,* 465. On confession see further Von

2. Diversity Grounded in Unity:
Varied Gifts from One Source (12:4-7)

(4, 5) There are different apportionings of gifts, but the same Spirit. There are varieties of ways of serving, but the same Lord. (6) And there are different apportionings of what activates effects, but the same God who brings about everything in everyone. (7) To each is given the public manifestation of the Spirit for common advantage.

Interpreters differ in placing emphasis on unity or on diversity in this chapter. But Dale Martin, Harrington, and Lategan argue convincingly that in these verses, at least, Paul places his emphasis on the unity of source which lies behind a diversity of phenomena. In spite of G. Wright's arguments that Paul here portrays God as a God of diversity, Martin observes, "Thus in 12:4-11 Paul continually stresses unity in diversity in order to overcome divisiveness owing to different valuations being assigned to different gifts, with tongues as the implied higher-status gift."[1] Lategan argues that the body imagery which expresses a careful balance between unity and diversity here undergoes revision and qualification in the light of **the same Spirit . . . the same Lord . . . the same God** (vv. 4-6) in order to stress that the diversity is secondary to the unity.[2] The cohesive bestowal of the gifts ensures their fundamental unity. Thus both contextually and theologically the unity constitutes the major emphasis in vv. 4-11, since "building" provides the cohesive goal and purpose of the gifts, whatever their variety. Harrington stresses unity of source where Lategan stresses unity of goal and Martin underlines the unity of community. The "one

---

Campenhausen, "Das Bekenntnis im Urchristentum," 210-53, where he argues that the earliest confessions originate from Jesus' saying about confessing and denying in Matt 10:32. **Jesus is Lord**, he argues, comes from cultic settings in the hellenistic and Pauline churches, whereas *Jesus is the Christ* has a closer connection with traditions of witnesses. The confessions in 1 John have a third-level function of polemic. But we saw from Dietmar Neufeld that 1 John cannot be isolated and intellectualized in this way. Since Von Campenhausen appreciates the anti-docetic stance of both 1 John and Ignatius (Ignatius, *To the Ephesians,* 7:2; 18:2; *To the Smyrnaeans,* 1, 2), it is a pity that he designates each stage as a "new four" (four stages in all), rather than recognize that all the examples reflect the same combination of belief content and illocutionary, self-involving force. A further *linguistic* contrast may be drawn between "confession" in the sense of declarative witness or creed and "confession" in the sense of confession of sins. As is clearly shown in a standard work on the psychology of religious confession, Berggren, *The Psychology of Confession,* this kind of confession is *expressive* and entreats an authority figure to "hear" it. Berggren cites the example of Pusey's request to Keble to take this part (20-24); cf. 25-35.

1. Martin, *The Corinthian Body,* 87. By contrast, Wright, "Diversity in the Church," 64-68, argues that diversity characterizes the work of God. This point is made in 15:38-41, and perhaps in 12:12-30, but it is not the main point here.

2. Lategan, ". . . Met die oog op wat nuttig is (1 Kor 12:7)," *NGTT* 16 (1975): 314-22. The maxim "for some useful purpose" cited in 12:7 and in the title expresses the cohesive organizing principle that gives unity to the variety of gifts. All serve "to build" in accordance with coherent purpose and pattern.

source" is not only the one Spirit (12:1-3), but God as giver of grace through Christ and the Spirit.[3] Hence the Corinthian elitist talk of πνευματικῶν (12:1) is transposed by Paul into unifying speech about χαρισμάτων (12:4). Collins also argues that "the same Spirit" holds the unit together, and the principle finds a parallel in Rom 12:6-8 and in Paul's own example as one who constantly alludes to grace.[4]

We may also recall that Joop Smit identifies vv. 4-6 as a *partitio,* or succinct introduction of the issue, which paves the way for the *confirmatio* of 12:7-30 (see the introduction to 12:1–14:40 above).

4-5 The word διαιρέσεις occurs only here in the NT and means either *differences, distinctions,* or **apportionings**, *dealings out.* The use of the verbal form διαιροῦν in v. 11, however, alludes to the sovereignty of the Spirit of God in *apportioning out* gifts **to each as the Spirit wills.**[5] Although **different apportionings** may seem stilted or clumsy, *varieties* (NRSV, RSV, REB), *different* (NJB), or *even different kinds* (NIV) does not seem to bring out the idea of *what is allotted* by God. One does not question what is freely given as one's portion.[6]

Surprisingly, while he recognizes BAGD's proposal to translate the word here as *allotments* (also Collins), Barrett's *distributions,* Parry's *variety of gifts assigned,* and even the link with *apportion* in v. 11, Fee simply states without arguments that *difference* or *variety* "is also well established; the context rules in favor of the latter here."[7] But this may appear to carry weight only because, against the views of Dale Martin, M. M. Mitchell, Harrington, Best, Lategan, and Collins, Fee places a heavier emphasis on variety than unity, entitling 12:4-31 as a whole as "The Need for Diversity."[8] Although Wright and Lang follow this approach, Conzelmann and Allo put the other side of the case in more detail.[9] Allo draws a contrast between the *human construct* of differences which become *divisions* (1:10–4:21) and the *divine allocation* of distinctions as *"distributions."*[10] Conzelmann also argues that while the parallel in Rom 12:6 may seem to favor *distinction,* 1 Cor 12:11 decisively points to *assignment,* but grounds this rightly in Paul's theology of grace. Paul's change of the Corinthian term πνευματικά, *spiritual things,* to χαρίσματα, **spiritual gifts,** *"gifts of grace,"* calls attention to God's generous act of *freely* **apportioning** different gifts to different recipients.[11] Once again, grace through the cross governs

---

3. Harrington, "Charism and Ministry: The Case of the Apostle Paul," 245-57.
4. Collins, *First Cor,* 449; Harrington, "Charism and Ministry," 245-57.
5. Cf. the argument to this effect in Robertson and Plummer, *First Epistle,* 262-63.
6. Moreover, the word frequently occurs in the LXX, and it reflects the tradition of "allocating" the share of the Spirit initially given to Moses alone to the seventy elders.
7. Fee, *First Epistle,* 586, n. 13, and 583: "Diversity, not uniformity, is essential. . . ."
8. Ibid., 582.
9. Wright, "Diversity in the Church," 64-68; Lang, *Die Briefe,* 168.
10. Allo, *Première Épitre,* 322.
11. Conzelmann, *1 Cor,* 207.

ecclesiology and ministry. Ideally, as Héring argues, a translation which stresses both aspects is best of all, but the link with apportioned *gift* (χάρις, χάρισμα) remains at the center.[12]

On χάρισμα, see above on 1:7; 7:7. The word occurs most frequently within the NT in Paul, esp. in 1 Cor 12:4, 9, 28, 30, and 31 and Rom 12:6. Ellis rightly insists that χάρισμα is not merely synonymous with πνευματικόν, especially since in Rom 1:11 Paul qualifies χάρισμα by πνευματικόν.[13] However, he is on less certain ground when he seeks to restrict πνευματικόν to "gifts of inspired perception, verbal proclamation and/or its interpretation."[14] Indeed, in my view the situation is virtually the reverse of Ellis's suggestion in terms of semantic range. The Corinthians used πνευματικόν very widely for a range of "religious" feeling-states and observable phenomena. By the application of *persuasive definition* or *code switching* Paul redefines what *counts as spiritual* by talking about what God **freely gives**, on his own initiative, and in his own sovereign choice (12:11) as empowerments (ἐνεργημάτων, v. 6) through the agency of the Holy Spirit for practical service of God and of other persons (διακονιῶν, v. 5).[15] In Rom 11:29 the word denotes the privileges freely given to Israel, where, again, the sovereignty of divine choice and gift for the purpose of service come into view. In Rom 6:23 τὸ χάρισμα τοῦ θεοῦ is eternal life, and in 2 Cor 1:11 it is a gift of rescue from danger. Outside Paul, for whom it is intimately related to χάρις, *grace,* the word occurs rarely; cf. 1 Pet 4:10; *1 Clement* 38:1. In the Pastoral Epistles it is a gift for service visibly identified with a particular office or role by the laying on of hands (1 Tim 4:14; 2 Tim 1:6). The lexicographical convention of distinguishing "general" from "special" gifts already imports distorting pre-judgments into a subtle rhetorical strategy on the part of Paul which is intended to shift the focus from human status claims about πνεῦμα to more humbling realities about God's **different apportionings of gifts** (cf. Collins, *allotments of gifts*).

Zodhiates carefully brings out the link between this aspect and τὸ δὲ αὐτὸ πνεῦμα. He observes: "The most striking element of these statements [i.e., in vv. 4-6] is the one recurring word 'the same.' . . . No one is to say that he has more of the Holy Spirit because he has more gifts. The same Spirit distributes the small or the large gift, not because He favors one Christian less or more than another, but because of His sovereign purposes. . . . The Giver, not the

---

12. Héring, *First Epistle,* 125. The stronger arguments include esp. Robertson and Plummer, *First Epistle,* 262-63.

13. Ellis, "'Spiritual' Gifts in the Pauline Community," in his *Prophecy and Hermeneutic,* 24; cf. 23-44.

14. Ibid.

15. Schrage rightly compares a larger range of instances, including 1 Cor 7:7, *Der erste Brief,* 3:137-41. On persuasive definition see Thiselton, "The Meaning of σάρξ in 1 Cor. 5:5 . . .," *SJT* 26 (1973) 204-28, and on code switching, see above and Moores, *Wrestling with Rationality in Paul,* 5-32. Collins translates simply *gifts* (*First Cor,* 448). Schrage also warns us against anachronistic readings back in terms of Max Weber and his modern sociological theories (*Der erste Brief,* 3:140).

Gift, is what accomplishes anything."[16] Hence v. 6 embodies the phrase "who works everything in everyone." The contrastive δέ marks the difference of emphasis not only between "difference" and unity, but more especially between phenomenon and source. This reflects the point noted above: "What we are concerned with is not the phenomena in themselves, but their whence? and whither? To what do they point?"[17]

We shall reserve our comments about the trinitarian nature of Paul's language in vv. 4-6 to the climax of his argument in v. 6. Whiteley finds here "traces of a Trinitarian ground plan," although Collins expresses caution about this point.[18] Meanwhile, just as διαιρέσεις χαρισμάτων are associated with the agency of the Holy Spirit (v. 4), equally appropriately διαιρέσεις διακονιῶν are associated with **serving . . . the same Lord**. On ὁ αὐτὸς κύριος see above, especially on 12:3. To understand the currency of *lordship,* we argued, we begin by exploring what it is to obey, to trust, and **serve** as a *slave.* Hence Barrett disengages διακονιῶν from "'ministry' in the technical sense; *gifts* are not occasions for boasting but opportunities for service. . . . Christians are his [Christ's] slaves" (his italics).[19] Just as the obedience of the slave demonstrates in the public domain what confessing Christ as Lord amounts to in terms of practical lifestyle, so, Bittlinger observes, *services* in all their apportioned variety (διαιρέσεις διακονιῶν) exhibit "the way in which the gifts become real in practice."[20] It is not a matter of "humiliation," but of "willing action . . . not a matter of waiting until something 'comes over me,'" in Suurmond's memorable phrase (cited in our introduction to this section). "It is not so much a matter of *having* a gift as of *being* a gift" (his italics).[21]

Paul's first definition of specific ministry on the part of Apollos and of himself is that they are *servants:* τί οὖν ἐστιν Ἀπολλῶς; τί δέ ἐστιν Παῦλος; διάκονοι δι᾽ ὧν ἐπιστεύσατε (3:5). Paul even adds the further thought explicated here: καὶ ἑκάστῳ ὡς ὁ κύριος ἔδωκεν. Although all Christians are called to serve, among the **varieties of ways of serving** apostolic and "official" or representative ministry is quite properly called *ministry* or *servanthood.* Thus although here the term covers a broad range, it is possible that the term narrowed later. Yet just as no χάρισμα implies a monopoly of the Spirit, since **the same Spirit** apportions out gifts in variety and degree in accordance with divine purposes, even so no one type of **ways of serving** signifies some special claim to

---

16. Zodhiates, *1 Cor 12,* 1:68-69.
17. Barth, *The Resurrection of the Dead,* 80.
18. Whiteley, *The Theology of St. Paul,* 129; Collins, *First Cor,* 449.
19. Barrett, *First Epistle,* 284.
20. Bittlinger, *Gifts and Graces,* 20.
21. Ibid., 21. Suurmond, "A Fresh Look at Spirit-Baptism and the Charisms," 105. Suurmond's argument about allusions to the atonement fails to convince us since it depends on a closer link between baptism and washing or cleansing than Paul's emphasis seems to allow (see above, esp. on R. Schnackenburg on this subject). However, his argument on "charisms as expressions of love" (ibid., 105-6) is constructive.

extol Christ's Lordship, since **the same Lord** commissions **varieties of ways of serving**. "Gifts, ministries, and works are infinitely various."[22] This practical dimension of practical trust and obedience to the one who nevertheless initiates the call and gift underlines how close Paul's thought remains to the teaching of Jesus about the kingdom, or active reign, of God, which encounters men and women in and through Jesus Christ himself as Lord.

The work of N. J. Collins since 1990 has brought fresh issues into the study of **ways of serving**. In his book *Diakonia* (1990) he argues that "serving" on the part of the Seven in Acts 6:1-7 did not mainly allude to social welfare, to food distribution, or to financial administration, but to furthering the apostolic gospel on behalf of the apostles and the church. It was distinguished from apostolic authority in that it rested upon a derived authority, but like that of apostles it concerned mission rather than only daily practicalities.[23] In his articles of 1992, mainly on 2 Corinthians, Collins perceived the work of Paul as *diakonos* as that of mediating divine revelation, again as a derived but authoritative mediating agency.[24] In 1993, he urged that **service** in 1 Cor 12:4-7 denotes a work commissioned by the Lord and (as in his book *Diakonia*) applied officially to the work of preachers, of apostles, or of apostolic representatives. They thus form a subspecies within a wider genus of spiritual gifts.[25] Like other gifts, they serve the common good. This view has not remained without criticism. Raymond F. Collins, e.g., points out that the construal of the syntax that links vv. 4 and 5 in terms of genus and species "demurs from the *opinio communis*."[26] Most commentators argue that the multiplicity of gifts *all* count as "services." *All* Christians; Schrage insits, exercise διακονία.[27] Thus the two most substantial commentaries of 1999 (Collins and Schrage, vol. 3) dissent from J. N. Collins. Again, to quote Martin, "In 12:4-11 Paul continually stresses unity in diversity in order to overcome divisiveness owing to different valuations being assigned to different gifts."[28] But the issue is also broader than the status-ranking of "spiritual gifts." It also embraces supposed rankings about **ways of serving**. Predictably Margaret Mitchell makes much of this aspect: "12:4-6 reverberates back to 8:6 in its emphasis on Corinthian unity in the same spirit, the same Lord and the same God."[29] The unity reflects a common "belonging to Christ."[30]

6   On the translation of διαιρέσεις (v. 6) as **different apportionings**, see

22. Deluz, *Companion to 1 Corinthians,* 172.

23. J. N. Collins, *Diakonia: Reinterpreting the Ancient Sources.*

24. J. N. Collins, "The Mediatorial Aspect of Paul's Role as *Diakonos*," *AusBR* 40 (1992): 34-44.

25. J. N. Collins, "Ministry as a Distinct Category among Charismata," 79-91.

26. R. F. Collins, *First Cor,* 452.

27. Schrage, *Der erste Brief,* 3:144.

28. Martin, *The Corinthian Body,* 87.

29. Mitchell, *Rhetoric of Reconciliation,* 268; cf. 267-70.

30. E. Best, *One Body in Christ* (London: SPCK, 1955), 96-97.

above on v. 4. We consciously chose the variant translation **varieties** for the same word in v. 5 to call attention to the secondary as well as to the primary force of the term in this context. It is not quite adequate to say, with Fee, that "gifts," "services," and "workings" fully represent the Greek, or that "most likely they are simply three different ways of looking at what in v. 7 Paul calls 'manifestations' of the Spirit."[31] To be sure, Bruce asserts that these are not "distinct categories."[32] They are not different entities; not different experiences. But more than a difference of aspect is entailed, on the part of the subject or the reader's observation. We noted above in what specific sense χάρισμα differs from πνευματικόν (against, e.g., Ellis); and the relation between διαιρέσεις διακονιῶν and the currency of yieldedness to Christ's Lordship in the public domain. Now the stress falls on διαιρέσεις ἐνεργημάτων as **different apportionings of what activates effects**, in the sense of *God's activity* within the community and within the self which *activates gifts* for *service*. Paul completes the argument that *different gifts* imply no ranking of "having the Spirit" in greater or lesser degree, since **the same Spirit** is active in all according to God's own purposes which determine their **apportioning**. Similarly, **different ways of serving**, if they are genuine, all honor **the same Lord**. Finally, *whatever* **activates effects** *"activity"* (the usual meaning of ἐνέργημα, according to BAGD; cf. Collins, *activities*) of a spiritual nature which constitutes a work of **the same God who brings about everything in everyone**. Collins agrees that the point is "the actualization of power."[33] This is valid, but "power" in this kind of Pauline context usually denotes *effectiveness,* as against mere talk.

The verbal participle ἐνεργῶν, from ἐνεργέω, may carry an intransitive meaning of *to be at work* or *to operate,* but also serves as a transitive verb to mean *to produce effects,* **to bring about** *results.* Since here the participle governs the accusative plural τὰ πάντα, the meaning is that **God . . . brings about everything**. The definite article indicates a cosmic sweep of vision. But on this basis, the word ἐνεργημάτων in the first clause implies *activities of God;* hence we must either translate it as *divine activities,* or, applying the logic implicit in the second half of the verse, translate **apportionings of what activates effects**, for this is the kind of "activity" which Paul means. It is *not self-induced activity* but activity *activated* by God. Calvin again refers this back to divine grace: "Men have nothing good or praiseworthy except what comes from God alone."[34] Such a comment is appropriate: divine grace relativizes all claims or anxieties about supposed status differences in experiencing God's power in dif-

31. Fee, *First Epistle,* 587.

32. Bruce, *1 and 2 Cor,* 118 (also noted by Fee, *First Epistle,* n. 18).

33. BAGD, 265. Collins, *First Cor,* 452-53. See also Schrage, *Der erste Brief,* 3:145 (modes of power which spring from the Almighty-ness of God). Wolff, *Der erste Brief,* 289, reflects a similar emphasis. The noun ἐνέργημα occurs only at 12:6 and 12:10 in the NT, but the verb ἐνεργέω appears in Rom 7:5; 1 Cor 12:6, 11; 2 Cor 1:6; 4:12; Gal 2:8; 3:5; 5:6; Phil 2:13; Col 1:29; 1 Thess 2:13; 2 Thess 2:7; four times in Ephesians and in Matt. 14:2; Mark 6:14; and Jas 5:16.

34. Calvin, *First Epistle,* 261.

ferent ways. As Senft observes, the word does not indicate "miraculous" power here; with Schrage, it points to v. 11, where God *activates* believers through his gifts.[35]

The "Trinitarian ground plan" (as Whiteley calls it) constitutes an outstanding feature of 12:4-6. In his recent study devoted to language in Paul about God and Christ, Neil Richardson writes: "In 12:4-6 . . . we encounter the only place in Paul's writings where πνεῦμα, Χριστός, and θεός occur in consecutive and closely parallel statements. . . . Although repeated references to the Spirit now follow . . . the *theo*centric character of the Spirit is understood by the use in v. 11, with the Spirit as subject, of the same verb used in v. 6 with ὁ θεός as subject: πάντα δὲ ταῦτα ἐνεργεῖ τὸ ἓν καὶ τὸ αὐτὸ πνεῦμα. . . ."[36] Richardson argues that whereas in the epistles as a whole the pattern of Paul's language varies, most frequently in 1 Corinthians Paul's arguments either begin or end with an appeal to God. He cites as examples "the weighty theological affirmations" in which 6:14-15 provides an appeal for 6:12-20; 8:6, for 8–10; 11:3, for 11:2-16; and 12:4-6, for 12–14.[37] These provide "a warranting function" for Paul's language. "God is the *alpha* and *omega* of the Christian's existence." While he accepts the monotheistic emphasis upon God as the one Source from whom "all Christians are charismatics," Collins is more doubtful about the extent to which we can perceive trinitarian elements here.[38]

The unity and grace of God as one, who nevertheless dispenses his gifts in variety through Christ as Lord by the Holy Spirit calls attention to God as "author, authorizer, destiny and judge . . . (Rom. 12:1-2; 13:1-4; 1 Thess. 4:3; 1 Cor. 6:13-14; 8:6; 12:4-6). 1 Cor. 7 in particular shows the Pauline tendency 'to trace everything back to God.'"[39] In Barrett's view, "the Trinitarian formula is the more impressive because it seems to be artless and unconscious."[40] While Richardson's work may serve to question whether it is "unconscious," the point remains that it carries no marks of artificial *contrivance*. While the trinitarian stance is implicit in 2 Cor 13:13 and Eph 4:4-6, here we encounter the earliest "clear" trinitarian language.[41]

These verses were of immense importance for Athanasius. He believed that Paul's intimate association of the Spirit with the activity of the Father and the Son "means that there exists an essential unity between the three."[42] On the basis of this passage (12:4-6) Athanasius draws out the profound truth that all persons of the holy Trinity participate in a unified activity which may be

---

35. Senft, *La Première Épitre,* 158; Schrage, *Der erste Brief,* 3:141-42.
36. Richardson, *Paul's Language about God,* 217 and 218.
37. Ibid., 218-19.
38. Ibid., 219; Collins, *First Epistle,* 453.
39. Richardson, *Paul's Language about God,* 237.
40. Barrett, *First Epistle,* 284.
41. Fee, *First Epistle,* 588.
42. Haykin, *The Spirit of God: The Exegesis of 1 and 2 Cor in the Pneumatomachian Controversy of the Fourth Century,* 94.

thought of as the action of the whole Godhead as Trinity. Athanasius comments on 12:4-6, "The gifts which the Spirit divides to each are bestowed from the Father (παρὰ τοῦ πατρός) through the Word (διὰ τοῦ λόγου). For all things that are of the Father are of the Son also; therefore those things which are given from the Son in the Spirit are gifts of the Father. And when the Spirit is in us, the Word also, who gives the Spirit, is in us, and in the Word is the Father."[43] In the exegesis of Athanasius, Paul views the Father as the source of spiritual gifts (*from* God); the Son, Christ, as their mediator (*through* Christ as Lord); to be "activated" by the agency of the Holy Spirit (*by* the Spirit). In the same passage Athanasius compares 2 Cor 13:13 (*Letter to Serapion,* 1:30-31). Only as believers "share" (μετέχοντες) the Spirit can they experience the love of the Father and the grace of the Son. Thus *in the experience of the believer* the persons of the Trinity are inseparable, even if apart from such experience distinctions of personhood can be made.

Even if this goes further than Paul explicates, we cannot deny its implicit coherence with 12:3, where the criterion of claims about the agency of the Holy Spirit is explained in terms of the Spirit's witness to Christ's Lordship, while this depends, in turn, on God's raising him as Lord from the dead (cf. Rom 10:9). In this sense, Athanasius concludes, "The Spirit is not outside the Word. . . . And so the spiritual gifts are given in the Triad . . . the same Spirit and the same Lord and the same God 'who produces all in all' (1 Cor. 12:6)" (Athanasius, *Letter to Serapion,* 3:5).[44] Basil the Great, as we might well predict, makes parallel points about 1 Cor 12:4-6: "It is the same God . . . the distributer . . . the sender . . . the source."[45] The persons of the Trinity, Basil writes, share a common being or unity.[46] By the time of Leo, a greater emphasis had fallen upon assigning distinct roles to specific Persons of the Trinity, even though "the co-operation of the Persons of the Godhead" was also stressed.[47] But Leo went further than Paul in this respect, as if only the Spirit "set people on fire with love."[48] In exegetical terms we are on firmer ground with J. D. G. Dunn's comment that vv. 4-6 speak of "a *power* which is *divine* and which bears *the character of Jesus the Lord*" (his italics).[49] This accords with the criteria of 12:3. Thus Dunn concludes that "the charismatic Spirit" gives "consciousness of grace."[50]

7 In J. Smit's rhetorical analysis (see the introduction to 12:4-11) Paul

43. Athanasius, *Epistles to Serapion,* 1:30; *PG,* 26 (ed. Migne), 600B; cf. *Ep. Serap.* 1:31; *PG,* 26:600C-601A.

44. Athanasius, *Ep. Serap.,* 3:6, moves on to consider 2 Cor 13:13. Cf. Migne, *PG,* 26:633A-B.

45. Basil, *On the Holy Spirit,* 16:37.

46. Basil, *Against Eunomius,* 3:4 (Migne, *PG,* 29:661B; cf. 664A-B).

47. Leo, *Sermons,* 77; cf. 75 and 76.

48. Ibid.

49. Dunn, *Jesus and the Spirit,* 324.

50. The title of Dunn's chapter, mainly on 1 Corinthians 12–14 (ibid., 199-258); cf. 259-300 on "the Body of Christ."

moves here from *exordium* to *confirmatio.* The present passive indicative δίδοται, **is given,** presupposes the agency of God. The noun φανέρωσις is mainly a late word found in the papyri, the NT (2 Cor 4:2 and here), and the Hermetic writings (11:1). In 2 Cor 4:2 it means *open* or *public proclamation,* and the cognate adverbial form φανερῶς means *publicly, openly* (2 Macc 3:28; Mark 1:45) as against ἐν κρυπτῷ or κρυπτῶς. Hence we translate this relatively rare word **public manifestation** rather than simply as *manifestation* (NRSV, NIV, Collins; cf. NJB, *particular manifestation;* REB, *is seen at work*). The genitive πνεύματος may perhaps be subjective (what the Spirit manifests), but it is much more probably objective (the operation which manifests the Spirit in public).[51] Thus the animating power and purpose is *one,* even if phenomena in the public domain take diverse forms. Typically, in accordance with her sustained argument about Paul's use of sociopolitical rhetoric and rhetorical terms, Margaret Mitchell argues for understanding πτὸς τὸ συμφέρον as **for common advantage** rather than less explicitly as *common good* (NRSV, NIV, Collins) or *general good* (NJB; cf. *useful purpose,* REB).[52] This is parallel to 10:33, *do not seek individual advantage,* and to 10:23, where *building up* constitutes the common advantage (cf. also 6:12; 7:35).

To the primary criterion of pointing to the Lordship of Christ or Christlikeness (12:3) as a mark of being authentically activated by the Spirit, Paul now adds a second criterion: the Spirit is at work where **the public manifestation** serves the **common advantage** of others, and not merely self-affirmation, self-fulfillment, or individual status. The Spirit produces visible effects for the profit of all, not for self-glorification. If the latter is prominent, suspicion is invited. δίδοται reflects both a continuous process of giving, and the sovereignty of God in choosing and in freely giving.[53]

3. The Gifts of the Spirit (12:8-11)

(8) To one person, on his or her part, God bestows through the Spirit articulate utterance relating to "wisdom"; to another, inaccordance with the same Spirit, discourse relating to "knowledge." (9) To a different person faith by the same Spirit; to another, gifts for various kinds of healing by the one Spirit. (10) To another, actively effective deeds of power; to another, prophecy; to another, discernment of what is "of the Spirit"; to another, species of tongues; and to another, intelligible articulation of what is spoken in tongues. (11) All these things one and the same Spirit activates, apportioning as he wills to each person individually.

---

51. Robertson and Plummer, *First Epistle,* 264.

52. Mitchell, *Rhetoric of Reconciliation,* 146.

53. As in 1 Cor 15:38, *God gives it a* σῶμα, esp. in the comments of Barth, Kennedy, and Deluz (see below).

Numerous attempts have been made to "classify" the nine instances of gifts which Paul now enumerates. Weiss and Allo are among those who perceive a triad of triads here, while Collins argues for a 2 + 5 + 2 chiasmus.[1] Bengel and Meyer divide the list into three: (a) gifts which relate to "*intellectual* power": λόγος σοφίας, λόγος γνώσεως (v. 8); (b) those which depend on "special *energy* of faith": πίστις, ἰάματα, δυναμεῖς, προφητεία, διακρίσεις πνευμάτων (vv. 9-10a); and (c) "Charismata which have reference to the γλῶσσαι: γένη γλωσσῶν, ἑρμηνεία γλωσσῶν (v. 10b)" (Meyer's italics).[2] Tertullian began similarly by marking off (a) the first two gifts as *sermo intelligentiae et consilii;* but then subdivided (b) πίστις as *spiritus religionis et timoris Dei* from (c) ἰάματα and δυνάμεις as *valentiae spiritus;* and finally (d) προφητεία, διακρίσεις πνευμάτων, γένη γλωσσῶν and ἑρμηνεία γλωσσῶν.[3]

Different "lists" of instantiations of gifts in Paul assume various shapes and sizes. Four lists occur in Rom 12:6-8; 1 Cor 12:8-11; 12:27-28; and Eph 4:11. On this basis Dunn prefers to distinguish thematically between gifts which relate respectively to miracles, revelation, inspired utterance, and service, perceiving all of them to proceed from divine grace.[4] Above all, "*charisma* is always an event, the gracious activity (ἐνέργημα) of God through a man."[5] The word "event," however, may be open to question. Paul's *charisma* of living a celibate life without distraction no doubt entailed a continuous divine sustaining. In his earlier work Dunn's use of "event" slides too readily into assumptions about "spontaneity," but in his volume on Paul's theology (1998) he fully recognizes that these gifts include "more humdrum tasks and organizational roles, as the more eye-catching. . . . The grace was in the giving, we might say, not in the form of the manifestation."[6] He adds: the "event" character should not be "overpressed. . . . 1 Cor 14:26-32 suggests a mixture of *prepared* contribution and some spontaneous utterance" (my italics).[7] Such gifts as *teaching* and *critically evaluating* can hardly be "spontaneous," but are *habits of trained judgment* marked precisely by a *continuity* of the Spirit's *giving as a process over time* (cf. Rom 12:7-8; 1 Cor 12:27; Eph 4:11). "Almsgiving" and "works of mercy" (Rom 12:8) may well seem "more excellent" if the *use* of the gifts is planned, deliberate, and entails a conscious act of will and service rather than a spontaneous welling up of a gesture without reflection. We shall note the importance of Theissen's claims (in effect, against Dunn) that "tongues," e.g., far from being merely spontaneous, may reflect "socially learned behavior."[8]

---

1. Weiss, *Der erste Korintherbrief,* 299, has three talks comparing 12:8-10 with 12:28 and Rom 12:6-8; cf. Allo, *Première Épitre,* 324-25; and Collins, *First Cor,* 451.

2. Meyer, *First Epistle* 1:361; Bengel, *Gnomon,* 651.

3. Tertullian, *Against Marcion,* V:8.

4. Dunn, *Jesus and the Spirit,* 201-58.

5. Ibid., 254. See, however, Dunn's more recent view in *The Theology of Paul* 552-64.

6. Dunn, *The Theology of Paul,* 556.

7. Ibid., 558.

8. Theissen, *Psychological Aspects of Pauline Theology,* 292; cf. 292-341 and 74-114. Both

This issue is discussed further with reference especially to **healing** and to **prophecy**.

a. Articulate Utterances Relating to "Wisdom" or to "Knowledge" (12:8)

8 We insert **on his or her part** to provide a gender-inclusive way of communicating the contrastive particles which qualify the distribution or apportionment of gifts: ᾧ μέν . . . ἄλλῳ δέ. . . . It is quite unsatisfactory to translate λόγος as *word,* even if in Christian circles "a word" has become informal shorthand for a message. λόγος means *word* in certain (mainly linguistic) contexts, but more usually it indicates a rational statement, proposition, or sentence. However, it is not restricted to cognitive propositions. Hence the best translation is **utterance** with a nuance of intelligibility or rationality best conveyed by the compound phrase **articulate utterance**. In John 1:1 the inexpressible, transcendent, holy God becomes enfleshed as God's *articulate utterance* of his being and action in the embodied life and action of Jesus Christ. The fifteen or so sections listed under λόγος in BAGD confirm the frequency of conjunctions between *discourse* and *articulate speech,* with the proviso that λόγος can also mean *question* (Diogenes Laertius, 2.116; Josephus, *Antiquities* 12.99; Matt 21:24), *prayer* (Matt 26:44; Mark 14:39), or story or account (Josephus, *Ant.* 19.132; Mark 1:45; Luke 5:15).[9] In Col 2:23 λόγον ἔχειν σοφίας alludes to *human precepts that have a [mere] appearance of wisdom.* I have discussed the semantic range of λόγος more fully elsewhere.[10]

Our proposed translation **relating to "wisdom"** reflects two points. First, the genitive σοφίας may be either subjective genitive, **articulate utterance** *derived from (God's) wisdom,* or objective genitive, **articulate utterance** *about (God's) wisdom.* Second, σοφία was clearly a catchword or slogan in the Corin-

---

Theissen and Martin, *The Corinthian Body,* 87-103, argue convincingly that status issues which cause divisiveness lie behind the whole discussion of "gifts" and "tongues" in 12:4–14:40. As against W. J. Hollenweger, who associates "tongues" and more "miraculous" gifts with the less literate at Corinth (*Conflict in Corinth;* New York: Paulist Press, 1982, 28-31), Martin identifies them with "the strong," i.e., socially influential with a thirst for esoteric "wisdom" and "knowledge" (cf. 8:1). Cf. also Martin, "Tongues of Angels and Other Status Indicators," 547-89. Also against Dunn and the many who speak of "miraculous" gifts, Martin convincingly warns us that the modern pre-packaged "dichotomies like natural/supernatural, physical/spiritual . . . did not exist in the ancient world **as** *dichotomies*" (my italics; Martin, *The Corinthian Body,* 3). Martin shows how far-reaching for hermeneutics the difference between respective starting points and assumptions in the ancient world and today (e.g., about *body, individual, status,* and so forth) becomes in relation to these and other chapters in 1 Corinthians. We explore these claims elsewhere in this volume, including our comments on 12:8-10 (below).

9. BAGD, 477-79. Cf. H. Ritt, "λόγος," *EDNT,* 2:356-59; Mack, *Logos und Sophia;* Pogoloff, *Logos and Sophia,* 99-172; Harris, "Athena, Sophia and the Logos," 56-72.

10. O. Betz and Thiselton, "Word: λόγος," in C. Brown (ed.), *NIDNTT,* 3:1,078-1,146.

thian community (see above on 1:17, 19, 20, 21, 22, 24, 30; 2:1, 4, 5, 6, 7, 13; 3:19; sixteen times in this epistle, out of only two further uses in the four major epistles, Rom 11:33 and 2 Cor 1:12; six instances in Colossians [1:9, 28; 2:3, 23; 3:16; and 4:5]; and three in Ephesians). Hence we place it in quotation marks. The background which controls the exegesis, therefore, derives from the contrast between the pretentiousness and competitive status-seeking of human wisdom (1:17-22; 2:1-5; 3:19) and the gift of divine wisdom (1:24-31; 2:6-13). Since the emphasis in 12:8 falls entirely on gift, clearly *divine wisdom* as a gift of the Spirit lies in view here. Kistemaker offers an exegesis which coheres with these factors: "The gift is the ability to speak divine wisdom which believers receive through the Holy Spirit (cf. 2:6-7). Divine wisdom is contrasted with human wisdom (1:17, 20, 25)."[11] Similarly, Zodhiates defines this gift as "an intelligent utterance of God's wisdom." Wolff, Collins, and Schrage convincingly insist that any interpretations of this phrase must allude to "Paul's lengthy discussion on word and wisdom (1:18–4:21)" (Collins).[12]

Wisdom, in this context, becomes an evaluation of realities in the light of God's grace and the cross of Christ. It is part of a response to grace.[13] Dunn compares 2 Cor 1:12 in this context: "not by human wisdom but by the grace of God."[14] But it is the **articulate utterance** of this **wisdom**. Hence it relates to "God's plan of salvation" and its articulation or communication. Schatzmann and Schrage confirm this point. First, Paul emphasizes "the actual utterance of wisdom which becomes a shared experience because it results in the upbuilding of the body"; second, "From 1 Cor. 1–3 it is almost certain that Paul identified the wisdom from God with God's saving deed in the crucified Christ, particularly in the proclamation of the saving event."[15] It relates primarily to "the revelation of God in the cross."[16]

Some popular interpretations of this phrase are therefore clearly far more individualistic and pragmatic than the above comments suggest. Kistemaker, Dunn, Schatzmann, and Schrage broadly view the articulation of "wisdom" as the intelligible communication of the purposes of God, as focused in the "reversals" of the cross (1:26-31), for the world and for the *common advantage* of all believers. We can but speculate whether this could include "inspired messages" for specific individuals; certainly there is no firm evidence to warrant such an

11. Kistemaker, *1 Cor,* 421.
12. Zodhiates, *1 Cor 12,* 1:121; Collins, *First Cor,* 453; Wolff, *Der erste Brief,* 290; and Schrage, *Der erste Brief,* 3:148-50.
13. J. A. Davis, *Wisdom and Spirit* (Lanham, Md.: University Press of America, 1984), esp. 71-149, on Paul's distancing from "achievement" in wisdom traditions; and Harrington, "Charism and Ministry: The Case of the Apostle Paul," 245-57. Cf. further Runia, "The 'Gifts of the Spirit,'" 82-94; Zodhiates, *1 Cor 12,* 113-24; Dunn, *Jesus and the Spirit,* 217-21; du Toit, "Die Charismata," 189-200, where du Toit argues that *charismata* belongs to the context of a broad spectrum of God's grace, not a few spectacular gifts.
14. Dunn, *Jesus and the Spirit,* 220.
15. Schatzmann, *A Pauline Theology of Charismata,* 36.
16. Schrage, *Der erste Brief,* 3:149.

understanding. If we interpret the phrase to reflect Paul's other uses of σοφία in this epistle, such an utterance seems more than likely to allude to Christ-centered gospel wisdom. It would not, in other contexts, denote simply some convenient communication without any implicit christological connection. The introductory formulae in 12:1-3 and in 12:4-7 also lead us to expect such a function and content. Wisdom relates to building up the community for the *common advantage of all* through appropriation of the power and lifestyle of Christ. Craig goes so far as to allude to 1 Corinthians 1–4 to urge the conclusion that the first two of the nine "gifts" (and probably several others) refer to "the teaching ministries of the church."[17]

A hint from Chrysostom might seem to imply a different understanding. Chrysostom regards the "spiritual gifts" in general in 12:1-11 as "such as used to occur but now no longer take place."[18] Further, whereas he comments in detail on 12:1-7, he simply repeats the text of vv. 8-10 without comment, as if to imply that we can know nothing about the meaning of these gifts, which, he seems to imply, have ceased.[19] Tertullian, however, returns to christological perspectives. The utterance which relates to wisdom is "the Spirit of wisdom" to which Isaiah alludes: the messianic anointing of Isa 11:1-3 anticipates the christological counterparts in 1 Cor 12:8-11.[20] Wisdom and knowledge, for Tertullian, is gospel wisdom and gospel knowledge.[21] Clement of Alexandria stresses the unity and diversity of the gifts rather than their content, except to comment that they are "apostolic," i.e., reflect the "knowledge, life, preaching, righteousness, purity and prophecy" of the apostles, concerning especially "faith in Christ and the knowledge of the gospel."[22] Origen is quite clear that "in the catalogue of charismata bestowed by God, Paul placed first λόγος σοφίας . . . because he regarded proclamation (λόγος) as higher than miraculous powers."[23]

Among older modern writers Godet and Heinrici echo the same point. Godet stresses an intellectual grasp of gospel principles; Heinrici interprets λόγος σοφίας as knowledge of salvation communicated to others.[24] Allo stresses the compatibility between the agency of the Holy Spirit and intellectual insight, citing the interpretation of this verse by Thomas Aquinas.[25] Allo's understanding borders on permitting a more individualistic view, as entailing knowledge of God's intimate purposes, but the emphasis remains on the intellectual. On the other hand, Héring points out that **wisdom** in the LXX tradition

17. Craig, "1 Cor," *IB,* 10:151.
18. Chrysostom, *1 Cor. Hom.,* 29:1.
19. Ibid., 29:5.
20. Tertullian, *Against Marcion,* 5:8.
21. Tertullian, *Writings against Heretics,* 14.
22. Clement of Alexandria, *Stromata,* 4:21.
23. Origen, *Against Celsus,* 3:46.
24. Godet, *First Epistle,* 1:195.
25. Allo, *Première Épitre,* 325.

includes especially *moral* guidance for life.[26] Yet in the light of James Davis's study of Jewish sapiential traditions, this must not be understood to take us into the domain of "achievement" rather than of divine grace.[27] We have already noted the kerygmatic aspect urged by Wolff, Collins, and Schrage.

There is no consensus whatever about any clear distinction between (1) λόγος σοφίας . . . and (2) λόγος γνώσεως. "**Knowledge**" (γνῶσις) is no less a Corinthian catchphrase than "**wisdom**" (see above on 1:5; 8:1, 7, 10, 11; also on 13:2, 8 and 14:6). Of twenty uses of the noun γνῶσις in Paul (excluding Ephesians and the Pastorals) no less than seventeen occur in 1 and 2 Corinthians, of which nine appear in 1 Corinthians, while only nine or ten further uses occur through Ephesians, the Pastorals, and the rest of the NT (three in 2 Pet. 1:5, 6; 3:18). In his initial thanksgiving (1:4-9) Paul gave thanks that the Corinthians had been made rich ἐν παντὶ λόγῳ καὶ πάσῃ γνώσει, while in 8:1 the fundamental contrast is set up between ἀγάπη as that which builds up and γνῶσις as that inflates. Hence, just as **wisdom** occurs in this epistle both in a pejorative sense of human status seeking and achievement and in a positive sense as the divine wisdom of the cross, so **knowledge** in a "proto-gnostic" or "standing-on-one's-rights" frame means "the static, cognitive epistemology of the gnostics" and in a positive, relational, christological frame "a dynamic affectional relationship from knowledge of God to being known by God" (Yeo).[28] Moreover, "wisdom and knowledge appear together among the basic elements of the spirit of the children of light in 1QS 4:3-4. The Qumran text lists them at the end . . ." (Collins).[29]

Bengel assigns a more theoretical role to **articulate utterance relating to "wisdom"** and a more practical role to **discourse relating to "knowledge"** *(sapientiae . . . cognitionis . . .);* for "knowledge relates to things to be done; wisdom to things eternal; hence wisdom is not said to pass away (13:8) and knowledge occurs more frequently."[30] Paul speaks of these gifts as if they were daily events for the Corinthians *(quae Corinthiis sint quotidianae);* but today we encounter ambiguity about the force of the words and their distinction *(hodie de ipsarum vocum vi et differentia ambigimus).* Meyer, however, takes an opposing, even a reverse view, anticipating Yeo about the *relational* significance of γνῶσις.[31] Augustine observes that for Paul "in Christ Jesus are hidden all the treasurers of wisdom and knowledge" (Col 2:3); hence in 1 Cor 12:8, although wisdom may relate to "divine things" and "knowledge to human things," both aspects concern the believer's relationship to Christ, activated through the Spirit.[32]

---

26. Héring, *First Epistle,* 126.

27. Davis, *Wisdom and Spirit,* 113-37; cf. 16-27.

28. Khiok-khing Yeo, *Rhetorical Interaction in 1 Cor 8 and 10,* BibInt 9 (Leiden: Brill, 1995), 186-87.

29. Collins, *First Cor,* 453.

30. Bengel, *Gnomon,* 651.

31. Meyer, *First Epistle,* 1:363-64.

32. Augustine, *On the Trinity,* 13:(19)24.

Elsewhere Augustine comments that Paul "certainly distinguishes these two things, although he does not there explain the difference, nor in what way one may be distinguished from the other."[33] In yet another reference Augustine relates **wisdom** to the intellectual understanding of *eternal* realities, and **knowledge** to "rational cognizance of *temporal* things," which come as gifts from the Holy Spirit who is beyond the merely earthly.[34] If in *On the Trinity,* 5:4, he stresses the unity and sovereignty of the Spirit, in John 21 Augustine draws attention to the definitive nature of God's apportioning of gifts to one (e.g., λόγος σοφίας) and differently to another (e.g., λόγος γνώσεως) as no more a person's business than Peter's query "Lord, what about this man?" (John 21:21) and Jesus' reply "What is that to you? You go on following me" (21:22).[35]

All this comes close to Dunn's conclusion: "*Gnōsis* and *sophia* . . . present us with special difficulties . . . because in the Corinthian letters in particular they are not Paul's own choice of expression; his use of them has been determined in large measure by the situation which he addresses at Corinth. . . . This is why *gnosis* keeps recurring within the Corinthian letters and only rarely elsewhere."[36] After this introduction, however, Dunn hazards the view that since **knowledge** in 8:1, 4, concerns idols and monotheism, "knowledge here, then, is an insight into the real nature of the cosmos. . . . '**Utterance of knowledge**' may therefore quite properly be understood as a word spoken under inspiration giving an insight into cosmical realities and relationships."[37] On the other hand, Dunn perceives a "broad parallel" between **wisdom** and "revelation and grace," and his later book on Paul's theology constructively relates these two gifts to Rom 12:6-8 in terms of a general gift of speech for "prophecy, teaching, encouraging" in contrast to gifts which relate specifically to action.[38]

While his account of **knowledge** contains elements of conjecture for interpreting 12:8, Dunn makes the valid point that Paul's focus on the **utterance** or **discourse** of **wisdom** and **knowledge** suggests that the gift character of the Spirit's activation includes the moment and mode of their use: "The charisma of God is no possession of man to be used at his will."[39] However, in his earlier work he also argues, "only in the act and moment for uttering it."[40] I firmly agree that since **utterances** are speech-acts in time, the *temporal* dimension is fundamental to the character of the gift as gift. But in this early work Dunn too readily translates this into modern notions of "spontaneity." In my view, these gifts are *not*

---

33. Ibid., 12:(14)22. Similarly, in 5:4 Augustine does not expound the gifts, but stresses only the active and sovereign role of the Spirit.

34. Ibid., 12:(15)25.

35. Augustine, *Harmony of the Gospels,* 4:20.

36. Dunn, *Jesus and the Spirit,* 217; cf. 217-22.

37. Ibid., 218.

38. Ibid., 221; and *The Theology of Paul,* 555.

39. Dunn, *Jesus and the Spirit,* 221.

40. Ibid.

given primarily *in* the moment of their use, but *for* such a moment. Part of the sovereignty of God and of God as Spirit consists in his giving gifts **for the common advantage** of all which find visible expression *at the right moment of pastoral timing.* But this in no way contradicts the notion of a *trained, habituated disposition, shaped and nourished by the Holy Spirit for use at the moment of God's choice.* This is different from popular assumptions about "flashes of insight" into this or that particular situation. While the text does not exclude this, it offers no evidence for it.[41]

Bittlinger tends to overlook the specific issues which concern **wisdom** and **knowledge** in the Corinthian situation. Nevertheless, his link with Jesus' promise of the Spirit to provide intelligible or **articulate utterance** in difficult situations, such as that of persecution, provides a convincing allusion to pre-Pauline traditions of the words of Jesus.[42] Our earlier comments suggest that this would apply especially to the articulation of the gospel. However, Bittlinger's attempts to distinguish this from "the word of knowledge" remain more speculative and less contextually determined.[43] His comments about the situational dimension of utterance serve to underline our observation about God's choice of timing of the use of gifts, which have molded the believer's disposition to respond to situations in appropriate ways. This relates the gift of utterance to holiness and to Christlikeness, as we should expect if they are Spirit-given.

Senft views both as "gifts of theological reflection."[44] This is a helpful counter-balance against ad hoc notions of spontaneous intuition, but it offers only one component within the larger framework explored here. We must not neglect the weight of scholarship, which emphasizes the reflective and dialectic nature of the gift as a habit of mind or a bestowed skill. Thus Banks interprets λόγος γνώσεως as the gift of "understanding the Old Testament, Christian tradition, and the capacity to expound them correctly."[45] But H. Schürmann insists

---

41. Some modern writers tend to cite patristic sources within a framework of supposed "spontaneity" of prophecy which the text does not necessarily imply. One standard example is Justin, *Dialogue,* 39. To be sure, Justin explores with Trypho the prophetic experience of "standing outside or beside oneself" (cf. ec-stasy). But this does not predetermine whether all the gifts of "understanding, counsel, strength, healing, foreknowledge, teaching, and reverence for God" are at issue. Indeed, *teaching* and *reverence* are by definition *habituated* characteristics which entail training. Only a dualistic *Deus ex machina* worldview would suggest that this any *less* reflects *divine agency* than supposedly "spontaneous" manifestations. There is much confusion between *spontaneous* in the sense of *not merely self-induced* and *spontaneous* in the sense of *unprepared* or *ad hoc.* The former applies to the *charismata;* suppositions about the latter are in some cases speculative and in other cases excluded by the nature of the gift (e.g., *teaching, contented celibacy*). The issue about God's purpose as involving *God's timing* is further suggested by Paul's phrase κατὰ τὸ αὐτὸ πνεῦμα, **in accordance with the same Spirit.** Edwards discusses the case for understanding this as either according to the will of the Spirit, or according to the measure of the Spirit, arguing for the probability of the latter (Edwards, *First Epistle,* 315-16).

42. Bittlinger, *Gifts and Graces,* 27-30.

43. Ibid., 30-32.

44. Senft, *La Première Épitre,* 158.

45. Banks, *Paul's Idea of Community,* 96.

that as a "gift of the Spirit" who works in the depths of the human heart the phrase denotes "pneumatic understanding, from the depth of the human spirit, directed more toward the practical."[46] Nevertheless, the rediscovery of a wisdom-related rationality embedded in historical and practical life which has emerged since the 1960s in such writers as H.-G. Gadamer, B. Lonergan, A. MacIntyre, and Paul Ricoeur may help us here.[47] They may save us from allowing our exegesis to be shaped by imposing upon the text an illusory alternative: *either* abstract rationalist reflection based on the model of Enlightenment philosophy *or* an interactive search for creative spontaneity based on the model of pietism and Romanticism. This passage poses no such false alternative. Paul does not seek the wisdom of the Sophists, but neither does he disparage practical reflection and judicious evaluation.[48] Gifts of **articular** communicative **utterance** may draw on **wisdom** and **knowledge** from God especially when this serves both "the common good" of all and the proclamation of the cross. (This is a far cry from some modern notions about coded messages for the welfare of individuals.)

9   The best textual support favors ἑνί, **one**, in the final phrase **by the one Spirit** (A, B, 33, 81, Old Latin, Vulgate, Ambrose, Hilary). Not surprisingly some MSS witness to scribal assimilations to the repeated ἐν τῷ αὐτῷ πνεύματι in the previous clauses (א, C³, Dᵍʳ, F, G, K, some Syric and Sahadic and Bohairic Coptic MSS). Probably simply "through an oversight" p⁴⁶ reads simply ἐν τῷ πνεύματι, *by the Spirit.*[49] But the UBS 4th ed. evaluation of their proposed reading as "A" remains valid, and is accepted and presupposed by NRSV, RSV, REB *(the one Spirit);* NJB *(this one Spirit);* and NIV *(that one Spirit),* and RV *(in the one Spirit),* as against AV/KJV *(by the same Spirit).*

b. Faith as a Special Gift and Gifts
for Various Kinds of Healing (12:9)

ἕτερος means strictly (although certainly not always) *the other of two,* and hence stands in place of the contrastive μέν . . . δέ . . . in v. 8. It can therefore be translated either as *another person* or **a different person**.[50] The latter seems to convey Paul's contrastive concern. It is universally agreed, or virtually so, that in this verse πίστις, **faith,** cannot therefore refer to *saving faith,* or to appropriation of salvation by grace through faith, since Paul explicitly attributes to the

46. Schürmann, "Die Geistliche Gnadengaben in den paulinischen Gemeinden," in *Ursprung und Gestalt,* 256.

47. For example, A. MacIntyre, *After Virtue* (London: Duckworth, 2d ed. 1985); and esp. H.-G. Gadamer, *Truth and Method* (Eng. trans., New York: Crossroad, 2d ed. 1989).

48. Cf. Winter, *Philo and Paul among the Sophists;* and S. K. Stowers, "Paul on the Use and Abuse of Reason," in D. L. Balch et al. (eds.), *Greeks, Romans and Christians: Essays in Honor of A. J. Malherbe* (Minneapolis: Fortress, 1990), 253-86.

49. Metzger, *Textual Commentary* (2d ed.), 497.

50. BAGD, 315.

Spirit the apportioning of this gift ἑτέρῳ, i.e., to someone who is *different* from, or *other* than, certain Christians or even the majority of believers. It is a specific gift reserved *for specific persons.* By definition, therefore, it cannot designate that faith through which all who are believers (cf. Paul's semantic opposite to *believer* as ἄπιστος, 7:13) are indeed "believers" or Christians. Bruce observes: "not the saving faith which is basic to all Christian life, but a special endowment of faith for a special service (cf. 13:2b)," while Collins calls it "something different from the faith that characterizes all believers."[51]

This admirably sums up the point. But some wish to be more specific. Conzelmann thinks that it should be linked to the next two of the nine gifts: "accordingly, not faith, but apparently the ability to perform miracles (13:2) and thus akin to the χαρίσματα ἰαμάτων, "gifts of healing."[52] Fee offers an intermediate proposal: "It probably refers to a supernatural conviction that God will reveal his power or mercy in a special way in a specific instance."[53] Bittlinger acknowledges that this gift is not "saving faith," but then appeals to instances (e.g., Hebrews 11) which are offered as paradigms of faith in general.[54] According to the writer of the Epistle to the Hebrews, all faith entails a willingness to act or to venture in the present on the basis of a reality which has yet to become fully visible when it finally occurs. Thus Luther defines saving faith as "a living, daring confidence in God's grace, so sure and certain that a man would stake his life upon it a thousand times. This confidence in God's grace . . . makes men glad and bold. . . ."[55] But this is no different from the notion of staking one's life on God's promise; whether it be on the model of Abraham in Rom 4:13-25 or of Noah, Abraham, and Moses in Heb 11:6-29. We must resist the temptation to make "saving faith" so passive a gift that anything bold or trustful is associated with this specific gift. A distinction here remains essential.[56] Schatzmann thus speaks of "charismatic faith" (following Hasenhüttl) but adds: "provided it does not imply a relegation of justifying faith to a lesser degree of spirituality."[57] This may perhaps include "a mysterious surge of confidence."[58]

Much exegesis becomes speculative because the verse is read through the lens of modern Western individualism. In a community situation, certain specific persons often come onto the scene as "gifted" with a robust confidence

51. Bruce, *1 and 2 Cor,* 119; Collins, *First Cor,* 454. One rare exception is Gillespie, *The First Theologians: A Study in Early Christian Prophecy,* 113. It is of course true that Paul does not imply "one gift" only for "one believer," but this does not fully address the problem. Cf. Turner, *The Holy Spirit and Spiritual Gifts Then and Now,* 275-77.

52. Conzelmann, *1 Cor,* 209.

53. Fee, *First Epistle,* 593.

54. Bittlinger, *Gifts and Graces,* 32-34.

55. Luther, "Preface to the Epistle to the Romans," *Works,* 35:370.

56. O. Merk, *Handeln aus Glauben* (Marburg: Elwert, 1968), 142.

57. Schatzmann, *A Pauline Theology of Charismata,* 37; and Hasenhüttl, *Charisma. Ordnungsprinzip der Kirche,* in Küng and Ratzinger (eds.), *Oekumenische Forschungen,* 144.

58. Schatzmann, *Charismata,* 37; cf. Dunn, *Jesus and the Spirit,* 211; Barrett, *First Epistle,* 285.

that becomes supportive for the entire community. This may or may not presuppose some specific situation of crisis. The second problematic factor is a dualistic worldview which places each gift either too readily in the *"supernatural" Deus ex machina* category or else views it too naturalistically and reductively as merely an enhanced *natural capacity*. It seems unwise and unnecessary to impose onto Paul dual models of "natural" and "supernatural" which fell into two only after the rise of English Deism and mechanistic worldviews around the end of the seventeenth century and beginning of the eighteenth century. We must at the same time leave the door open to include inexplicable, prodigious acts of faith, such as "faith to move mountains," whatever the metaphorical status of this image (Matt 17:20; 1 Cor 13:2). However, rather than focus on the category of miracle, it is more helpful to consider the conceptual entailments of faith in the God who is Almighty and sovereign in relation to his own world. This links **faith** here with λόγος γνώσεως (v. 8).[59] We shall next consider issues about **healing**, but this will bring us back to further questions about **faith** (see below).

The plural χαρίσματα ἰαμάτων denotes **various kinds of healing**. This use of the plural occurs in English when people speak, e.g., of *fruits* or *cheeses.* Since the singular already denotes more than singularity of instance, the plural becomes a device for carrying the notion of *more than one kind* of what the word in question conveys.[60] Justin, writing in the second century, alludes to the ministry of Christian persons who "perform exorcisms in the name of Jesus Christ . . . who have healed and do heal . . . those who could not be cured . . . by those who use incantations and drugs."[61] This gift of **various kinds of healing** does not appear in the comparable samples of gifts in Rom 12:3-8 and Ephesians 4:11. Indeed, the specific noun ἴαμα, **healing**, occurs in the NT only here and in 12:28, 30, although the cognate verb ἰάομαι occurs nineteen times in the Gospels (including twelve times in Luke), four times in Acts, and once each in Hebrews, James, and 1 Peter. The verb does not occur in Paul. The main alternative word for *to heal,* θεραπεύω, occurs some forty times in the Gospels and Acts, but not in Paul, and elsewhere in the NT only twice (in Rev 13:3, 12). Under the semantic domain of healing, Louw and Nida list only ἰάομαι, to heal, to cause a change from an earlier state, to cure; ἴαμα (only in 1 Cor 12:9, 28, 30); ἴασις (only in Luke 13:32 and Acts 4:22, 30); θεραπεύω (discussed above); and certain special uses of καθαρίζω (e.g., of a leper, Matt 8:2), and ἐγείρω (as a metaphorical extension of *restoration,* e.g., Jas 5:15).[62]

---

59. Among Pannenberg's many writings on this subject cf. *Systematic Theology,* 1 (Eng. trans., Edinburgh: T. & T. Clark, 1991), 63-118 and esp. 327-448; also G. Van der Brink, *Almighty God: A Study in the Doctrine of Divine Omnipotence* (Kampen: Kok-Pharos, 1993). A huge number of commentators use the word "supernatural" here (e.g., Allo and Weiss).

60. Edwards, *First Epistle,* 316, adopts this view; it is also stressed by Zodhiates, *1 Cor 12,* 1:152.

61. Justin, *Apology,* 2:6.

62. Louw and Nida, *Greek-English Lexicon of the NT Based on Semantic Domains* (2 vols.,

With the exception of 1 Cor. 12:9, 28, and 30, Paul appears not to refer to healing at all in his epistles, except implicitly in 2 Cor 12:8, where he writes that three times he prayed that God would remove his *thorn in the flesh* or *sharp physical pain* (σκόλοψ τῇ σαρκί . . . ἵνα με κολαφίζῃ), but rather than a χάρισμα of healing God gave him ἡ χάρις μου as his *sufficiency* (ἀρκεῖ σοι), leaving his *weakness* (ἀσθενεία) without special healing. We discussed above issues about Paul's illness with reference to the hypotheses of Dibelius, Deissmann, and Schweitzer (see above on 2:3, *I came to you in* **weakness** . . .). Collins argues that Paul "does not claim for himself the gift of healing."[63] On the other hand, Turner subsumes "healings" within Paul's claim to preach "with 'signs and wonders' (Rom 15:18, 19; cf. 1 Thess 1:5) . . . 1 Cor 2:2-5."[64] (See further below, toward the end of this section.)

Nevertheless, other parts of the NT associate healing either with God's sovereign choice alone or sometimes with the special kind of faith to which the first part of this verse alludes. Jas 5:15 declares that "the prayer of faith (ἡ εὐχὴ τῆς πίστεως) will save (σώσει) the sick or ill person, and the Lord will restore him to health (ἐγερεῖ αὐτόν). Hence Allo, Senft, Kistemaker, and Lang associate the special **faith** of v. 9a with **kinds of healing** (v. 9b).[65] Bruce, Héring, and Barrett offer virtually no comment on *healings,* presumably believing that everything is self-evident. Schrage refers the use of the plural to traditions of healings performed by Jesus.[66] But if the majority associate *healing* with the **faith** cited in the first part of the verse, and if this **faith** is a sovereign gift given to specific, chosen persons and not to all believers, *Paul may not expect that all believers who need* **various kinds of healing** *will necessarily manifest the gift of* **faith** *with which healing may be associated.* This is given to ἑτέρῳ, **a different person**, or *another.* Fee's comment that the manifestation of the gift is given to the healer, not to the healed, leaves this principle intact.[67] Moreover, if **faith** is said to be a condition for healing, this makes it awkward that the special **faith** is given to ἑτέρῳ, and χαρίσματα ἰαμάτων to ἄλλῳ. It is not necessarily *the healer* who receives the gift of special **faith**.

This underlines the *corporate* rather than individual dimension of these gifts and of Paul's understanding of the apportionment of the Holy Spirit to the church. There is a place for efficacious *corporate faith within the community* which may influence the effectiveness of the entire community. In other words, to cite Moffatt's understanding of the gift of **faith**, "an indomitable assurance that God can overcome any difficulties and meet any emergencies" may be

---

New York: United Bible Societies, 2d ed. 1988), 1:157 (13.66), 269 (23.136-41), and 2:295. The substantial gap left by Louw-Nida is to omit σῴζω from the semantic domain here.

63. Collins, *First Cor,* 454.

64. Turner, *The Holy Spirit and Spiritual Gifts,* 252.

65. Lang, *Die Briefe,* 169; Kistemaker, *1 Cor,* 422; Allo, *Première Épitre,* 325-26; Senft, *La Première Épitre,* 158.

66. Schrage, *Der erste Brief,* 3:151, e.g., Mark 9:23; 10:52. See also ibid., n. 211.

67. Fee, *First Epistle,* 594.

granted to a specific individual in such a way that this radiant confidence in God's grace and sovereignty may pave the way for another to advance processes of healing, and yet another to be restored.[68] Even so, we must not forget that such counter-examples as Paul's "thorn in the flesh" and probable problems with health (1 Cor 2:3-5; 2 Cor 12:8; Gal 4:15) indicate that the final decision lies with God's sovereign choice. Would Paul entirely provide warrant for Max Turner's principle about "expecting" healing as joyful anticipations of "the holistic nature of God's eschatological salvation" in the light of his eschatology in 1 Cor 4:8-13?[69]

The plural, which implies **various kinds of healings**, should also be given its full scope. The **kinds** may appear to include sudden or gradual, physical, psychosomatic, or mental, the use of medication or more "direct" divine agency, and variations which are not to be subsumed in advance under some stereotypical pattern of expectation.[70] From within the Pentecostal tradition even if W. R. Jones perceives these nine gifts of vv. 8-10 to be hallmarks of Pentecostal doctrine, nevertheless Donald Gee declared that **kinds of healings** should "not preclude" what he called "the merciful and manifold work of medical healing."[71] Bengel, too, insists that while these gifts in vv. 9-10 *include* the miraculous, *they do not thereby exclude* "natural remedies" *(per naturalia remedia).*[72] It is indeed doubtful whether Conzelmann's mere allusion to hellenistic parallels of miraculous healings as listed in G. Delling's *Antike Wundertexte* assists us in understanding this verse.[73] Godet, Meyer, Robertson and Plummer, Goudge, Carson, and Schatzmann confirm the point initially drawn from Edwards that the plural denotes **various kinds of healings** enacted in a diversity of ways to address a variety of conditions, and not a uniform stereotypical ministry performed by a permanently endowed "healer."[74]

Healers are given varied gifts at varied times for varied tasks, and we should not impose a post-eighteenth-century dualism of "natural" and "supernatural" upon the ways in which God chooses to use, or not to use, regular physical means.[75] As the Pentecostalist writer Donald Gee points out in relation

---

68. Moffatt, *First Epistle,* 181.

69. Turner, *The Holy Spirit and Spiritual Gifts,* 254-60.

70. This kind of attitude may owe more to supposed parallels in the mystery religions, suggested by Reitzenstein and Weiss.

71. W. R. Jones in P. S. Brewster (ed.), *Pentecostal Doctrine* (Cheltenham: Brewster, 1976), 47-62; and D. Gee, *Spiritual Gifts in the Work of the Ministry Today* (Springfield, Mo.: Gospel, 1963). This reworks and revises D. Gee, *Concerning Spiritual Gifts* (Stockport: Assemblies of God in Great Britain and Ireland, 1928 and 3d ed. 1937).

72. Bengel, *Gnomon,* 652.

73. Conzelmann, *1 Cor,* 209, n. 28; G. Delling, *Antike Wundertexte* (Berlin: de Gruyter, 2d ed. 1960); cf. also A. Oepke, "ἰάομαι," *TDNT,* 3:205-13.

74. Godet, *First Epistle,* 2:197; Meyer, *First Epistle,* 1:364; Robertson and Plummer, *First Epistle,* 266; Goudge, *First Epistle,* 110; Carson, *Showing the Spirit,* 39; Schatzmann, *Charismata,* 37.

75. The most widely known exponent of this kind of warning is Hans Frei, *The Eclipse of*

to the Pastoral Epistles, in 1 Tim 5:23 Paul (or a Pauline writer) enjoins Timothy to gain healing of the stomach by drinking wine rather than the more dubious water supply but in 2 Tim 4:10 he leaves Trophimus sick at Miletus.[76] The illness of Epaphroditus is also mentioned (Phil 2:27).

Parry reminds us that "this is the only passage where S. Paul refers to these 'gifts of healing'."[77] Hence it remains all the more surprising that many writers offer virtually no comment whatever on this phrase. Even Fee, subsequent to a relatively brief comment in his commentary, adds little in his more recent volume of around a thousand pages on the Holy Spirit in Paul's Letters. He writes: "*Gifts of Healings.* What this refers to needs little comment."[78] He then adds that for Jesus, Paul, and the early church, healing of a physical nature was a "regular expectation" largely, or at least "in part," based on "OT promises that in a Messianic age God would 'heal' his people."[79] Although he concedes that "healing" also refers to salvation, Fee places weight on Matthew's use of Isa 53:4 as a "promise for physical healing" in Matt 8:17, supposedly to shed light on the meaning of 1 Cor 12:9. At Corinth, however, the modern visitor has only to witness the astonishing display of body parts recovered from the Temple of Asklepios, the Greek god of healing, to begin to understand the importance of prayers for "supernatural" healing by a god in the daily life of Corinth.[80]

At a minimum, however, the issue is far more complex than Fee and several other writers allow. In a Ph.D. thesis (1993) David Petts allows that for Matthew himself the healing miracles of Jesus are perceived as a fulfillment of Isa 53:4: "he bore our infirmities." But, writing from within a Pentecostal tradition, Petts nevertheless demonstrates that any universal "claim" by believers to be covered by, or to participate in, the atonement of the cross remains of a different order in kind from requests for healing which may (to use Fee's phrase) be "expected," but are certainly not always granted.[81] The very fact that the gifts of the Spirit are apportioned out differently to one and to another, and that

Biblical Narrative (New Haven and London: Yale University Press, 1974). But Frei's view of referential meaning is inadequate, and his notion of fictive meaning requires clarification in the light of N. Wolterstorff, *Divine Discourse* (Cambridge: Cambridge University Press, 1995). Nevertheless, the basic issue about shifts of worldview remains; cf. further H. Thielicke, *The Evangelical Faith* (3 vols., Grand Rapids: Eerdmans, 1974-82), esp. vol. 1.

76. Gee, *Trophimus I Left Sick: Our Problems of Divine Healing.* On Donald Gee's theology, see Hollenweger, *The Pentecostals,* 208-13. Gee adopted a different approach from that of his fellow Pentecostalist, Harold Horton, *The Gifts of the Spirit.* Against Horton, but like most of the Fathers, Gee recognizes the rational teaching content of, e.g., "Word of knowledge" or of "wisdom."

77. Parry, *First Epistle,* 181.

78. Fee, *God's Empowering Presence: The Holy Spirit in the Letters of Paul,* 168.

79. Ibid.; see also n. 320.

80. In addition to works on archaeology (see below on *the body*), see also Collins, *First Cor,* 454-55, on the significance for this verse.

81. Petts, "Healing and Atonement," argues this central thesis with a wealth of exegetical detail.

their bestowal and use is temporally conditioned by God's sovereign choice, precludes any precise parallel from being drawn.

Moreover, no "gift" can be *claimed* unless it is *promised*. Reconciliation with God and justification by grace constitutes a *universal promise* to all who appropriate it through acceptance or "through faith" in the Pauline writings. No such *universal promise* relates to **various kinds of healings**, subject to *fallible human judgments* about the "promises" which may be suggested in religious consciousness or personal experience. That these gifts are sometimes (rightly or wrongly) *perceived as* promises by given communities or individuals need not be denied. But the authentication of such suppositions partly depends on the corporate spread of other gifts in the church, such as *teaching, wisdom,* and *discernment.*[82]

An exegetical scrutiny leaves open the possibility of **gifts of various kinds of healings** in whatever mode, through whatever instrument or human agent, and at whatever time God may choose, as one of many specific **gifts** (χαρίσματα ἰαμάτων). Perhaps it is no accident that χαρίσματα, which is otherwise omitted in connection with the other gifts in this list, appears explicitly here. Tertullian and Cyril of Alexandria make particular play of the connection between these gifts (including healing) and the anointing of Jesus Christ by the Holy Spirit in the Spirit's sevenfold apportionings within the framework of Isa 11:1-3.[83] This serves further to modify any simplistic view of healing. On one side, as Tertullian and Cyril stress, Christ is raised by the Father as Lord and "has dominion." *The fallenness of the fallen world with all of its ills stands under his sovereign victory as crumbling in its power. Yet on the other side, Christ's victory entailed the acceptance of constraints and the limitations of flesh-and-blood vulnerability within the created order. Hence eschatological timing becomes one factor: when is victory complete?* The relationship between participation (sharing Christ's sufferings as a reflection of identification with Christ in his redemptive work) and substitution (Christ wins the victory on behalf of his people) constitutes another factor. Hence Paul stresses the role of the Spirit as a sovereign given, who works unfathomable designs which cannot fully be penetrated until that design is complete at the last day (1 Cor 2:10-16; 4:5).

This christological and eschatological perspective is found in Augustine and in Basil, who relate the Spirit's gifts primarily to the purposes of God in Christ in terms of the process of salvation for the world.[84] The advance of the gospel in the power of the Spirit steadily transposes a variety of evils into goods, and gifts of knowledge, wisdom, healing, and prophetic utterance be-

---

82. See, e.g., Basil, *Letters,* 204:5.

83. Tertullian, *Against Marcion,* 5:8; and Cyril of Alexandria, *Fragmenta: In Ep. 1 ad Cor.,* 288. Cf. Theodoret, *Interp. Ep. 1 ad Cor.* (Migne, *PG,* 82:323-24), 244D.

84. Augustine, *On the Trinity,* 12 (14):22; (15)25; 15(19):34; cf. also *Confessions,* 13:18:23; *Psalms,* 84:11; *Harmony of the Gospels,* 4:10:20; Basil, *On the Holy Spirit,* 16:39; cf. 16:38; the comments of T. F. Torrance, *Divine Meaning: Studies in Patristic Hermeneutics* (Edinburgh: T. & T. Clark, 1995), 384-86; and Basil, *Letters,* 204:5.

long to this holistic, cosmic context of gospel transformation. They are not individualistic universes of self-contained reality.[85] It is difficult to exaggerate how much part of a post-Enlightenment modern world-view some of the popular religious literature is, when dualistic "laws of the supernatural" are spuriously applied as supposed exegesis. As Peter Mullen observes, Francis McNutt's claim that "it is always God's normal will to heal," together with "eleven reasons why God does not always heal," is in a very different world from Paul's.[86] The very notion of God's "normal will" owes more to scientific notions of regularity than to the unfathomable depths of Paul's Ὦ βάθος πλούτου καὶ σοφίας καὶ γνώσεως θεοῦ· ὡς ἀνεξεραύνητα τὰ κρίματα αὐτοῦ καὶ ἀνεξιχνίαστοι αἱ ὁδοὶ αὐτοῦ (Rom 11:33).

The Pauline context of Christology, eschatology, and corporate "building" is well articulated in the Joint Statement "Gospel and Spirit," documented in K. McDonnell (ed.), *Presence, Power, Praise.*[87] On the gift of **healings** the statement declares: "All true wholeness, health, and healing come from God. We do not therefore regard 'divine healing' as being always miraculous. We also look forward to the resurrection, knowing that only then shall we be finally and fully freed from sickness, weakness, pain and mortality [cf. 1 Cor. 15:44 and comment on this view below]. At the same time we welcome the recovery by the Church of a concern for healing . . . but also wish to express caution against giving wrong impressions and causing unnecessary distress through (i) making it appear that it is sinful for a Christian to be ill; (ii) laying too great a stress and responsibility upon the faith of the individual who is seeking healing. . . ."[88] The statement appears to reflect the exegetical arguments presented above.

---

85. Novatian lacks the historical and cosmic vision of continuity found in Augustine and Basil, but nevertheless gives due place to the christological foundation of the Spirit's gifts. Cf. Novatian, *Treatise concerning the Trinity,* 29.

86. P. Mullen in Martin and Mullen (eds.), *Strange Gifts? A Guide to Charismatic Renewal,* 100; cf. 97-106; and F. MacNutt, *Healing* (Notre Dame: Ave Marie and New York: Bantam, 1972), followed by MacNutt, *The Power to Heal* (Notre Dame: Ave Marie, 1977; and New York: Bantam, 1979). Cf. further J. S. McEwen, "The Ministry of Healing," *SJT* 7 (1954): 133-52.

87. "Anglican Church, Great Britain, 1977: *Gospel and Spirit: A Joint Statement,*" in McDonnell (ed.), *Presence, Power, Praise: Documents on the Charismatic Renewal,* 2:291-306.

88. Ibid., 305. On, e.g., Methodism, cf. *Presence, Power, Praise,* 2:22-36, 182-220, and 270-90 (in Australia, Europe, Britain, and the United States respectively); on Pope Paul VI, 3:11-13 and 70-76, and on samples of Roman Catholic traditions in different areas, 2:82-83, 98-113, 358-76, and 490-515; on the Baptist Union of Great Britain and Ireland, 2:379-90; on the Southern Baptists, USA, 2:114-15; on the Dutch Reformed Church, South Africa, 391-428; on the Reformed Church in America, 68-81; and on Lutheran traditions, 2:15-21 and 307-24 (Missouri Synod), 268-69 (Germany), 429-52 (Lutheran Council, USA). All dates in vol. 2 are approximately 1975-79. A mass of bibliographical material largely but not exclusively from the Pentecostal tradition is available in Schandorff, *The Doctrine of the Holy Spirit: A Bibliography,* esp. 2:1,054-55 (on healing); and Mills, *A Bibliography of the Nature and Role of the Holy Spirit in Twentieth-Century Writings,* and *Charismatic Religion in Modern Research: A Bibliography* (Macon, Ga.: Mercer University Press, 1985).

c. Actively Effective Deeds of Power (12:10a)

10a Each phrase has, alas, to be translated into terms which already presuppose a particular interpretation of no less than six terms or phrases, each of which bristles with controversial exegetical possibilities and judgments. Unless we specify a variety of options for the translation above, all that we can do is to set forth the arguments for the various alternatives and explain why we have reached the conclusions implicit in the above translation.

On ἐνεργήματα δυνάμεων Schrage points both forward to 12:28 and backward to the use of the term δύναμις as a word related to salvation elsewhere in the epistle.[89] It is usually translated as *the working of miracles* (NRSV, NJB, AV/KJB, Barrett, in effect Collins) or as *miraculous powers* (REB, NIV, Moffatt). The RV margin recognizes that *miraculous* is not explicit in the Greek, which it renders *workings of powers*. Needless to say (we hope), **deeds of power** (which stresses the plural of δύναμις and the place of this gift among *deeds of action* [**healings**] as against *words of utterance* [**utterance relating to "wisdom," discourse relating to "knowledge"**]) *does not exclude the miraculous, but neither does it narrowly specify it* as the entire content and range of these **deeds of power**. The mere use of the plural alone does not guarantee that the word designates *only* the miraculous. On the other hand, as Barth urges throughout *The Resurrection of the Dead,* in this epistle **power** (whether singular or plural) characteristically designates what is **effective** against any obstacle or constraint because it is validated by God in contrast to human aspirations, which may fail.[90]

We have already discussed the meaning of ἐνεργήματα (see above on v. 6). The link with the genitive δυνάμεων, however, remains disputed. Many assume that it is a *subjective* genitive, *workings of powers,* which, in abstraction from the considerations discussed above on vv. 6-10, would imply that only *workings of miracles* fully avoids tautology. But Calvin among the Reformers, Hodge among post-Reformation writers, and H. Thielicke among modern theologians follow a very widespread patristic tradition of interpretation in regarding δυνάμεων as an *objective* genitive. Calvin doubts whether it means *power to effect miracles:* "I am however inclined to think that it is the power *(virtutem)* which is exercised against demons and also hypocrites."[91] Rightly he views ἐνεργήματα as *effective working* (cf. above) and more speculatively compares Paul's bringing of judicial blindness on Elymas the magician (Acts 13:11) and Peter's juridical speech-act which led to the death of Ananias and Sapphira (Acts 5:1-11). Hodge takes up this theme, and Thielicke similarly understands this gift of the Spirit as "authority over the powers." He recognizes

89. Schrage, *Der erste Brief,* 3:152.
90. Barth, *Resurrection of the Dead,* 18; cf. also 24, 26, 49, 52, 75, 79-82, 115, and 190. But see the subsequent discussion of δυνάμεις.
91. Calvin, *First Epistle,* 262.

that only relatively rarely does δύναμις mean *forces of evil,* but considers that the use of the plural here (which is unusual in the NT) is "used of ungodly forces . . . a power given *over* the powers" (his italics), and compares the reference to "handing over to Satan" in 1 Cor 5:5.[92]

It remains open whether δυνάμεων is intended to be read as an objective or a subjective genitive. Collins rightly makes room for the term *activities* in his translation *the activities of working miracles,* but the text leaves open whether these *powers* or **deeds of power** are *restricted* to the "miraculous" or simply may *include* the miraculous where otherwise they would not be **effective** ones.[93] Our proposed translation, therefore, allows for all these possibilities, except that while in formal grammatical terms **deeds of power** assumes technically a subjective construction of the genitive, in terms of content it allows room for the force of the phrase advocated by Calvin, Thielicke, and many early Fathers. Hence our translation is by no means reductionist or critical of the possibility of what we think of as "miracle," but it avoids pre-judging and narrowing the scope of terms which convey a broader semantic range than is implied by all of the major English versions.

On these matters patristic evidence and arguments deserve serious attention. Chrysostom perceives both overlap and contrast with **healings:** "He who had a gift of healing used only to do cures; but he who possessed ἐνερήματα δυνάμεων used to punish also . . . even as Paul imposed blindness and Peter brought death" (Acts 13:11; 5:1-11).[94] Ambrose (c. AD 397) includes the power to cast out demons, or to perform "signs": *potestatem dari significat in ejiciendis daemoniis, aut signis faciendis.*[95] Similarly, Cyril of Alexandria understands this gift as ἐξουσίαν κατὰ πνευμάτων ἀκαθάρτων ὥστε ἐκβάλλειν αὐτά.[96] But in addition to giving its meaning as "casting out unclean spirits," Cyril quotes the words of the Gospels to extend the list to "healing the sick, raising the dead, cleansing lepers, casting out demons: freely you have received; freely give" (Matt 10:8).[97] Theodoret remarks succinctly that this χάρισμα, for which request is often made, is instantiated "in depriving Elymas of his sight and the death of Ananias and Sapphira."[98] Thomas Aquinas differ-

92. H. Thielicke, *The Evangelical Faith* (3 vols., Grand Rapids: Eerdmans, 1974-82), 3, "Theology of the Spirit," 79; cf. Hodge, *First Epistle,* 247.

93. Collins, *First Cor,* 455. On the use of δύναμις in the plural and its varied meanings, see BAGD, 207-8; MM, 171-72; G. Friedrich, "δύναμις," *EDNT,* 1:355-58; O. Betz, *NIDNTT,* 2:601-6; W. Grundmann, *TDNT,* 2:284-317; and Grundmann, *Der Begriff der Kraft in neutestamentlichen Gedankenwelt;* Karl Prümm, *Diakonia Pneumatos,* 2:2, 243-327; V. K. Robbins, "*Dynameis* and *Sēmeia* in Mark," *BR* 18 (1973): 5-20; Powell, *The Biblical Concept of Power,* esp. "*Dynamis* and Miracle," 107-16, but also 101-60, 180-93.

94. Chrysostom, *1 Cor. Hom.,* 29:5.

95. Ambrose, *Opera: In Ep. 1 ad Cor,* 151D (Migne, *PL,* 17:211, 259).

96. Cyril of Alexandria, *Fragmenta: In Ep. 1 ad Cor,* 288 (1965 Pusey ed.).

97. Ibid.

98. Theodoret, *Opera Omnia: Int. Ep. 1 ad Cor,* 245A (Migne, *PG,* 82:324-25 [Greek text] and 323 and 326 [Latin text]).

entiates **healings** *(possit sanare infirmitatem)* from the broader *operatio virtutum* which ranges from the redemptive act of dividing the sea (Exod 14:21) or even halting the sun (Josh 10:13) to God's working miracles through the Spirit in the church (Gal 3:5).[99] Grotius also speaks here of *potestas puniendi. . . .*[100]

On close inspection of the primary patristic and medieval texts, the reason for an emphasis on *powers over the powers of evil* appears to emerge largely to differentiate a subcategory of gifts of *effective action* from the curative effects of **healings**. They remain linked to the plural δυνάμεις in the broad sense of *mighty works* which also serve as *signs* in the Gospels and in Acts (e.g., Matt 11:21, 23; 13:58; Mark 6:2; Luke 10:13; Acts 8:13). But the Gospels also use the plural δυνάμεις for *the powers of heaven* (Matt 24:29; par. Mark 13:25; Luke 21:26). The singular form usually denotes *the effective power of God* in Paul (Rom 1:4-16; 1 Cor 1:18, 24; 2:4, 5; 4:20; 6:14), but in the Gospels and in Paul the singular may denote *authority* or *force* as well as divine power (Mark 9:1; 12:24; Luke 5:17; 9:1; 1 Cor 15:24; 2 Cor 1:8; 6:3), or even serve as a circumlocution for God himself (Matt 26:64; par. Mark 14:62; Luke 22:69; Acts 1:8; 6:8). *Mighty works* are (i) unusual and visible in their intensity and general unexpectedness; (ii) fully effective in achieving their purpose; and (iii) pointers to or signs of some greater salvific reality. *Miracles,* by contrast, raise issues about worldviews and relations to natural means concerning which δυνάμεις remain more open-ended, presupposing simply the almighty sovereignty of God both *over, in,* and *through* his creation.[101] In what these acts consist in 12:10 corresponds "to the wants of different situations," which may or may not include "judgments on unfaithful Christians or adversaries, such as Ananias or Elymas."[102]

Among specific studies of "power" in the modern period, C. H. Powell writes separate chapters on "Acts of Authority," "*Dynamis* and Miracle," and "Power in Cross and Resurrection," while developing overlapping themes entailed in δυνάμις and δυνάμεις.[103] Prior to the cross, the promises of God appeared to point to "days of God's power" in the sense of portents that would visibly vindicate faith and waiting.[104] But in and through the cross, **power**, and even **deeds of power**, became transposed into that which made actively effective the loving and salvific purposes of the heart of God, as revealed in Christ's

99. Thomas Aquinas, *I ad Corinthos Lectura,* 728 (371-72).

100. Grotius, *Opera Omnia Theologica,* 2:2 ad loc.

101. Kistemaker's surprising comment (*1 Cor,* 423) that "Throughout the Scriptures, miracles are supernatural acts that occur contrary to the laws of nature" not only contradicts the maxim of Augustine and Aquinas that God's unexpected acts still occur *per naturam,* not *contra naturam,* but imposes a historically anachronistic schema onto the text unnecessarily. The key point is the plasticity of the world to God's sovereign will, which began to take on fresh coloring after the era of Isaac Newton.

102. Godet, *First Epistle,* 2:197-98.

103. Powell, *The Biblical Concept of Power,* 101-29.

104. Ibid., 77-100, esp. 92-98.

acceptance of constraints and renunciation of force and spectacle in his messianic temptations. Commenting on the grain of wheat which falls to the earth and dies in order to bring life (John 12:24), Powell declares: "At no point is the difference between the concept of *power* in Old Testament and New so pronounced."[105] We therefore find in 1 Cor 12:10 a dialectic between the power which is effective but cruciform in 1 Corinthians 1–4 and in most of this epistle, and some continuity with visible "signs" to which δυνάμεις often but not always alludes. However, we have noted above (esp. on 1 Cor 1:18–2:5) that authentic "signs" indeed reflect the cross and are derived from a christological foundation.

As an accommodation to tradition and Synoptic usage we translate **actively effective deeds of power** (i.e., *mighty works*); but this may already concede too much to expectations of the spectacular.[106] Dunn recognizes the difficulty of assessing how much weight should be given to the meaning of δυνάμις in the plural in the Synoptic Gospels for an exegesis of Pauline texts, especially 1 Corinthians 12.[107] Anticipating Wolff, he concedes that Paul perhaps thinks here of exorcisms: "yet demon possession as such does not feature prominently in Paul's thought (cf. 1 Cor. 10:20, 21; Eph. 2:2); he thinks rather of spiritual powers in heaven operating through the (personified) power of sin, law and death, and behind the pagan cults and authorities. . . . Liberation from their dominion comes only through the power of the Spirit."[108] But freedom from such

---

105. Ibid., 117.

106. Fee, *God's Empowering Presence,* 169, insists on retaining the dualistic term "kinds of supernatural activities," although he concedes "the word translated 'miracles' is the ordinary one for 'power.'" This places an interpreter in a difficult position if, like the present writer, he does not wish to deny the utter plasticity of the created world to the sovereign will of God, but also wishes to acknowledge the unnecessary problems of a "God of the gaps" theology and to disengage such a modern counter-Enlightenment polemic from Paul, who did not address this specific agenda in these terms. Dunn attempts to adopt a middle ground by making it clear that what for Paul constitutes δυνάμεις is what we should today regard as "*the actual miracle, or miracle-working power operating effectively in a particular instance*" (his italics; *Jesus and the Spirit,* 210). Still more cautious is the documentation of the major traditions collected in McDonnell (ed.), *Presence, Power, Praise* (see notes on previous verse). The document *Gospel and Spirit: A Joint Statement* begins to state that "we all agree that miracles can occur today," but at once concedes the problematic nature of speaking of "miracles" in a linguistic currency that is adequate. It perceives the gift under discussion in 12:10a as "occurrences of an unusual kind which bring awareness of the close presence of God. . . . However, we are never in a position to demand a miracle since we may never dictate to our sovereign Lord how he shall work in answer to our prayers. Our business is to rest upon and claim his promises . . . but to leave the means of the answer to his wisdom" (*Presence, Power, Praise,* 2:304). The Anglican "Joint" Group included "charismatic" and "other" traditions. All concluded: "Our concentration on the miraculous can blind people to the manifold and wonderful everyday working of God in the world. . . . [But] on the precise degree of expectation of miracles which is appropriate today, we are not, however, completely agreed" (ibid., 305). This is entirely understandable, since neither Paul nor other NT writers explicitly address this issue, and no amount of exegetical discussion of our passage would yield a clear answer.

107. Dunn, *Jesus and the Spirit,* 209-10.

108. Wolff, *Der erste Brief,* 291; Dunn, *Jesus and the Spirit,* 210. Dunn appears not to focus

---

dominion is the heritage of all believers; not simply a gift for some. It is therefore essential to regain *the collective and corporate* framework of these gifts
"to some . . . to another." *Specific human agents (not all) may receive a particular gift from the Spirit to advance the gospel against oppressive forces, for the
benefit of all.*

Although he rightly designates such gifts as "visible" in operation or effect, I see no grounds for Dunn's assumption that they are also "a nonrational
power."[109] This would undercut much that has been observed concerning the interpretation of 12:6-10, including the discussions in footnotes. The term *suprarational* might be more acceptable. We must remind ourselves again that for
Augustine and many of the early Fathers such gifts as λόγος σοφίας and λόγος
γνώσεως constituted knowledge of things human and divine, closely connected
with rational reflection on transmitted teaching. Similarly ἐνεργήματα
δυνάμεων concerns **effective deeds** which **actively** operate with **power**,
whether rational or suprarational, whether to overcome spiritual or earthly
forces of opposition, and whether by means of self-sacrifice and the witness of
an outstanding life or by some more spectacular and (in the modern sense) "miraculous" working. The victorious Christ, who was nevertheless crucified and
raised, bestows through the Spirit a gift of victory which may draw its **power**
both from the pattern and reality of the cross (with all its constraints and
"weakness") and from the pattern and reality of the resurrection.

"PROPHECY": A FIRST NOTE IN THE CONTEXT OF CHAPTER 12 (12:10)

The Greek for **to another, prophecy**, is ἄλλῳ προφητεία. What was **prophecy** in the
NT? Bittlinger uses the well-known catchphrase: "Prophecy is not in the first instance
foretelling, but rather forth-telling — light for the present."[110] The address to a present situation retains an expected strand of continuity with *prophet* and **prophecy** in
the OT, and, as Bittlinger adds, in the NT as well as in the OT prophets may often allude
to past and to future events insofar as they shed light on the present or entail promise as a basis for present action or understanding. Rev 1:3 refers to John's apocalyptic
discourse as "this **prophecy**" (cf. also Rev 19:10; 22:10, 19; 1 Tim 1:18; 4:14; 2 Pet 1:19;
1 Cor 13:2). Yet much else which is claimed about NT prophecy remains too often
speculative. Barrett, untypically without offering any evidence for the claim, suggests
that NT prophecy, especially in 1 Cor 12:10, "was uttered in ordinary though probably
excited, perhaps ecstatic, speech."[111] Although he alludes to 1 Cor 14:1-5, his exegesis
of these verses (or on 11:4, 5) adds little or nothing to our understanding of **prophecy**
here.

specific attention on the phrase in his later *The Theology of Paul* except to speak of vv. 9-10 as including "healing and miraculous activities" (556). However, he demystifies the gifts of 12:28 in
terms of "helpful deeds" and "giving guidance" (loc. cit.).

109. Dunn, *Jesus and the Spirit,* 556.
110. Bittlinger, *Gifts and Graces,* 42.
111. Barrett, *First Epistle,* 286.

The verb προφητεύειν, *to prophesy,* occurs some 13 in the Gospels and Acts, but mainly with reference to OT prophecies. In Paul the verb occurs ten times, but *exclusively in this epistle* (11:4, 5; 13:9; 14:1, 3, 4, 5, 24, 31, 35, 39). There are two references in Rev 10:11 and 11:3, and two in 1 Peter and Jude (1 Pet 1:10; Jude 14). The noun προφήτης, *prophet,* is the most common form of the word group in the NT, occurring 144 times. It occurs 37 times in Matthew (reflecting a Matthean interest), six times in Mark, 30 times in combined Luke-Acts, 14 times in John, and, by comparison 14 times in the Pauline corpus (which includes three in Ephesians and one in the Pastorals). Of these, five occur in 1 Corinthians (1 Cor 12:28, 29; 14:29, 32, 37), three in Romans (Rom 1:2; 8:21; 11:3), and the others in 1 Thess 2:15, together with four in Ephesians and Titus (including the "list" in Eph 4:11). The noun προφῆτις occurs twice in the NT; but these two allusions are to Anna (Luke 2:36) and to Jezebel (Rev 2:20), in spite of other implicit allusions to prophecies through women (cf. Acts 2:17; 21:9; and 1 Cor 11:5). The specific term προφητεία, **prophecy,** used in 12:10, occurs five times in 1 Corinthians and seven times in Revelation (1 Cor 12:10; 13:2, 8; 14:6, 22; Rev 1:3; 11:6; 19:10; 22:7, 10, 18, 19); but also in Paul in Rom 12:6 and 1 Thess 5:20 (cf. further 1 Tim 1:18; 4:14). In 2 Pet 1:20 and in Matt 18:14 the term refers to OT prophecy.[112]

With such an apparently wide spread of material, we might suppose that certain stable features would emerge beyond the general comment of Bittlinger concerning the content and nature of NT prophecy. But apart from the fact that many NT references allude to the OT or to distinctive contexts, the mass of modern literature on NT prophecy reveals that the embarrassment of lexicographical riches outside the NT adds to, rather than diminishes, the problems of seeking to discover hard evidence for the meaning. It is essential to compare and to evaluate the work of certain key standard studies. Many, but not all, of the standard studies are cited below.[113]

a. Hellenistic Background?

Fascher and Crone may be viewed as examples of writers who seek to shed light on NT **prophecy** from the standpoint of research into the hellenistic background. Fascher examines a huge variety of uses of προφήτης, προφητεύειν, and προφητεία in secular and religious Greek texts. Here *prophet* is not only "a person who speaks on behalf of a god," an *announcer,* or a *spokesperson,* but also in hellenistic religions an

112. The statistics which can be found in Moulton-Geden, 870-72, are amplified in G. Friedrich, "προφήτης," *TDNT,* 6:781-861.

113. Aune, *Prophecy in Early Christianity and the Ancient Mediterranean World;* Boring, *Sayings of the Risen Jesus: Christian Prophecy in the Synoptic Tradition;* Dautzenberg, *Urchristliche Prophetie;* Fascher, *Prophêtês: Eine sprach- und religionsgeschichtliche Untersuchung;* Hill, *New Testament Prophecy;* Müller, *Prophetie und Predigt im NT;* Forbes, *Prophecy and Inspired Speech in Early Christianity and Its Hellenistic Environment;* Wire, *The Corinthian Women Prophets;* Grudem, *The Gift of Prophecy in 1 Corinthians;* Crone, *Early Christian Prophecy: A Study of Its Origin and Function;* G. Friedrich, *TDNT,* 6:781-861; Gillespie, *The First Theologians: A Study in Early Christian Prophecy,* esp. 97-164; Turner, *The Holy Spirit and Spiritual Gifts,* 185-220; Panagopoulos (ed.), *Prophetic Vocation in the NT and Today,* including Panagopoulos, "Die urchristliche Prophetie," 1-32; Ellis, "Prophecy in the NT Church and Today," in *Prophecy and Hermeneutic in Early Christianity,* 46-57; and Cothenet, "Les prophètes chrétiens comme exégètes charismatiques de l'Écriture," in *Prophetic Vocation in the NT and Today,* 77-107.

official of the cult who functions as *keeper of an oracle*. Although Reitzenstein associates Christian prophets with ecstasy and miracle in the later hellenistic cults of the papyri, Forbes, Boring, and others have little difficulty in showing that Reitzenstein appeals only to highly selective data from a multiplicity of very varied hellenistic phenomena. Forbes incisively attacks widespread assumptions about "ecstatic" consciousness and language on the basis of primary hellenistic texts.[114] Fascher's study uncovers such a wide variety of possibilities that it virtually defeats its purpose, serving in effect to demonstrate the fruitlessness of seeking light on NT **prophecy** from the direction of supposed hellenistic parallels. Crone's attempt to build on Fascher merely lends lexicographical force to this point. As Hill observes, an impression is conveyed that the mere occurrence of the words holds the key to understanding the phenomenon.[115]

b. Apocalyptic Background?

By contrast, Dautzenberg and (with serious modifications and differences) Aune look to the revelation traditions of Jewish apocalyptic discourse for the roots of an understanding of early Christian prophecy. Dautzenberg examines the concept of *mystery* or *riddle* in Jewish apocalyptic (cf. Dan 2:18, 19, 27-30; 4:9, Aram. רז, pl. רזנ *ran, ranin;* LXX, μυστήριον; 1 *Enoch* 9:6, 10:7: 4 Ezra 14:5) and in Philo (*Quaestiones in Genesin* 4:8; *Legum Allegoriae* 3.100), and understands **prophecy** in this context as the explanatory communication of these revealed mysteries to those who are intended to receive them.[116] In this connection Dautzenberg's volume takes up and amplifies his earlier article on διακρίσεις πνευμάτων as connected with prophecy in 1 Cor 12:10 and 14:29. Here he divides the list of nine "gifts" into four groups: (i) λόγος σοφίας and λόγος γνώσεως; (ii) πίστις, χαρίσματα ἰαμάτων, and ἐνεργήματα δυνάμεων; (iii) προφητεία and διακρίσεις πνευμάτων; and (iv) γένη γλωσσῶν and ἑρμηνεία γλωσσῶν. Next, Dautzenberg argues that διακρίνω and διάκρισις mean *interpret, interpretation*. The verb can mean *solving riddles* (e.g., in Josephus *Antiquities* 8.148) and *interpreting dreams* (e.g., Philo, *On Joseph* 90, 104, and 143).[117] He concludes on this basis that it becomes equivalent to Heb.פשר (*pashar,* verb, or *pesher,* noun). Thus, third, the phrase traditionally translated *the discernment of spirits* (NRSV) or *the ability to distinguish true spirits from false* (REB) is perceived by Dautzenberg to mean *the explanatory communication of prophecies,* while **prophecy** means *the revelation of hidden spiritual mysteries now communicated* or explained.

Wayne Grudem, however, has provided a devastating critique of each stage of Dautzenberg's argument.[118] He attacks Dautzenberg's groupings in 12:8-10; exposes

114. Forbes, *Prophecy,* 53-57, 281-88 and throughout. Cf. Reitzenstein, *Hellenistic Mystery Religions,* 297-301.

115. Hill, *NT Prophecy,* 232.

116. Cf. further Dautzenberg, "Zum religionsgeschichtlichen Hintergrund der διακρίσεις πνευμάτων (1 Kor 12:10)," 93-104.

117. Ibid., 99-102.

118. Grudem, "A Response to Gerhard Dautzenberg on 1 Cor 12:1," 253-70; and *The Gift of Prophecy in 1 Corinthians,* in which his *Biblische Zeitschrift* article of 1978 is reprinted as an appendix, 263-88.

the selectivity and paucity of his linguistic evidence especially in Philo and Josephus; concludes that "διάκρισις and διακρίνα are never used in Jewish or Christian literature to refer to the interpretation or possible explanation of prophecies"; and rejects Dautzenberg's dependence on history-of-religions arguments rather than on contextual exegesis of 1 Corinthians 12–14.[119] He concludes, rightly, that Dautzenberg's thesis "lacks historical confirmation."[120]

This does not entail the rejection of research into the background of apocalyptic, however, as one way forward among others. David Aune reminds us that "early Judaism had a variety of different prophetic types: apocalyptic literature (produced by visionaries), eschatological prophecy (. . . by individuals concerned with millennial movements), clerical prophecy (closely associated with the priesthood), and sapiential prophecy (associated with the sage, holy man or true philosopher). Early Christianity began as a sect within Palestinian Judaism, a Judaism which had been penetrated by pagan influences . . . for many centuries."[121] Hence it becomes essential to differentiate between components drawn from an Israelite-Jewish background and those associated with Graeco-Roman paganism. Aune partly anticipates C. Forbes's more detailed critique of H. Bacht's characterization of the Graeco-Roman background as largely self-induced frenzy or quasi-magical spectacle. It is "in many respects . . . a synchronic caricature."[122] However, this forces us back to evaluate what counts as *Christian* **prophecy** virtually in terms of content alone. Each of the phenomenological backgrounds, Aune concludes, betrays deficiencies, and "I have no proposal to suggest in their place. . . . *Christian prophecy produced no distinctive speech forms which would have been readily identifiable as prophetic speech*" (Aune's italics).[123] Aune's study, however, is far from merely negative. It leaves open the possibility that *provided that the content of utterance is appropriate,* the possibility of one or more of the four subcategories in early Judaism identified above could well come under the heading of *Christian* **prophecy**.

c. Scriptural and Apocalyptic Background

Earle Ellis examines Christian **prophecy** in this epistle both contextually and in relation to an apocalyptic background.[124] Like Dautzenberg, he appeals to a background in Daniel (Dan 1:4, 17; 2:21, 22), Qumran (1QpHab 7:4, 5; 1QH 12:11-13; 2:13, 14; 1QS 4:20, 22), and the Revelation of John for the importance of this background. Grudem's critique of Dautzenberg may serve to call in question some of his claims, but his fundamental stance coheres with positive elements in Aune's work and stands up to scrutiny. However, Ellis also emphasizes the role of scriptural exposition and creative application in prophecy. Further, a different kind of bridge between **prophecy** in the Pauline epistles and apocalyptic emerges from the work of Ulrich Müller. Where Ellis addresses the *revelation* of hidden wisdom, Müller takes up the apocalyptic theme of *oracles of judg-*

---

119. The quotation comes from Grudem, *The Gift of Prophecy,* 277.
120. Ibid., 286.
121. Aune, *Prophecy,* 230.
122. Ibid.
123. Ibid., 231.
124. Ellis, *Prophecy and Hermeneutic in Early Christianity,* esp. 57-62; cf. also 23-62 and 129-45.

ment.[125] Such oracles may embody "teaching" as well as announcement or pronouncement on the prophetic preaching of judgment and grace. The major criteria here, however, now concern not the more traditional emphasis on theological content (Aune),
but the *goals of prophetic speech-acts to challenge to repentance and to build up* the community *to salvation.* This "building up" finds a place in the work of Sandnes (see below).
However, it is most notably E. Cothenet who takes up the emphasis on the biblical background but in terms of "charismatic exegesis." Cothenet emphasizes the use of scripture by the Christian prophets, but by "charismatic" he often seems to mean what today
we might call the appeal to a *sensus plenior,* e.g., the identification of the Lord in the OT
with Christ, or placing the OT within a christological frame of reference.[126]

d. Function as "Pastoral Preaching"?

In what respects, however, does this differ from what we more usually think of as
preaching gospel-truth to move present hearers to repentance, change, consolation, or
the full appropriation of salvation? This is precisely how David Hill (together with
J. Héring and T. H. Gillespie) views **prophecy** in Paul: "Necessity is laid upon me. Woe to
me if I do not preach the gospel!" (1 Cor. 9:16) reflects precisely the constraint laid upon
the prophet, almost against the prophet's own choice or will (cf. Isa 49:1-6; Jer 1:4, 5).[127]
In this sense, on the basis of their call, function, and task, "we may have to say that the
apostles are the real successors of these [OT] prophets."[128] On the other hand, *prophets*
becomes a broader term than *apostles.*[129] The utterances of prophets are to be respected, but always tested (1 Thess 5:19-21). That a *prophet* is a person specifically appointed as such must be the case unless the phrase "if anyone *thinks* that he is a
prophet . . ." is to become "meaningless."[130] A *prophet* might prophesy *"on occasion."*
But the apparent assumption at Corinth that this was expected to entail an ecstatic
state of consciousness stands "in tension" with Paul's own view. Hill rejects
Dautzenberg's theory about abnormal states. The issue in 1 Corinthians 12–14 concerns
the relation between *responsible* and *irresponsible* utterances. Hill accepts Friedrich's
carefully argued conclusion that the prophet is a Spirit-endowed person "whose
preaching contains admonition and comfort, the call for repentance and promise" and
who also counsels, as a pastor, and "blames and praises. That, we submit, may be legitimately called a ministry of pastoral teaching and instruction. . . . Christian prophets exercised a teaching ministry in the Church which included pastoral preaching."[131]

Hill is not alone in adopting this approach. Héring observes that since we know
that "the aim of prophecy is to edify, exhort and encourage, it coincides therefore to a
large extent with what we call a sermon today."[132] All the same, it would be a serious

125. Müller, *Prophetie und Predigt im NT,* esp. 47-108.
126. Cothenet, "Les prophètes chrétiens comme exégètes charismatiques de l'Écriture," in
Panagopoulos (ed.), *Prophetic Vocation in the NT and Today,* 77-107.
127. Hill, *NT Prophecy,* 115; cf. 112.
128. Ibid., 116.
129. Ibid., 118.
130. Ibid., 120-21.
131. Ibid., 131; cf. 110-40.
132. Héring, *First Epistle,* 127; similarly, G. Friedrich, *TDNT,* 6:855.

mistake to read back onto Paul modern styles of pastoral preaching. Few churches appear "to test" preaching from the pulpit, and nothing suggests that early Christian prophecy was a sustained, uninterrupted, twenty-minute monologue delivered by a "trained" speaker. Moreover, prophetic preaching differed from *teaching* in that virtually all studies of the subject agree that it addressed issues of the moment, albeit by bringing teaching and gospel truth to bear on the present. Yet Gillespie's joining of (1) the reinterpretation of a *tradition;* (2) continuity with prophetic *declaration and argument in the OT* (especially the proclamation of *judgment and of grace*); (3) its *intelligibility* in contrast to glossolalia; and (4) its function of *edification, exhortation, and encouragement* all corroborate Hill's view that "the proclamation of the prophet is *pastoral preaching.*"[133] The work of K. O. Sandnes, which underlines Paul's prophetic role, and that of P. Vielhauer, which emphasizes the activity of solid "building up" through sober prophetic discourse, further underline the relationship between prophecy and *preaching* found in Hill and Müller.[134] *Prophets preach grace and judgment*, and their work may *win the unbeliever* (14:24) as well as build the church.

Surprisingly, Max Turner dismisses these careful works as "dubious arguments," while on his part he can offer only the evidence that "prophecy in Judaism was stereotypically oracular *speech*" (his italics).[135] First, he gives no account of differences between declarative speech-acts and "oracular" utterance. Second, he uses the term "direct" speech in a value-laden way which fails to take account of earlier discussion of "supernatural" notions and related problems about dualist worldviews (see above under "Healings"). Strobel more realistically speaks of the "struggle" which the OT prophets had to undergo with speech *("Kämpfer des Wortes")* their "critical control"; and lack of sheer subjectivity.[136] The "oracular" model is only *one* model of prophecy, more relevant to earlier prophecy than to, e.g., the reflective wrestlings of Jeremiah. (See further under Second Note at 14:3: "oracular" may refer to speech-acts of declaration, verdict, or direction and need not be "spontaneous").

e. Prophetic Leadership, Freedom, and Women Prophets

We postpone until its more immediate relevance to the issues in ch. 14 a discussion of A. C. Wire's work on women prophets at Corinth.[137] It deserves mention here, however, because in our review of the main approaches to the subject, Wire introduces a necessary dimension in discussing the *leadership role* of prophets. Paul names Christian prophets alongside apostles as sharing such a leadership role. On the other hand, Wire's contentions about women prophets as spokespersons for a *charismatic freedom in opposition to a Pauline emphasis upon "order" and authority* is more debatable.

Wire perceives the call to prophesy as a means by which Christian women at Corinth could achieve an otherwise unattainable freedom and leadership role. They

---

133. Gillespie, *The First Theologians,* 130-50 (Gillespie endorses Hill's conclusion on 141).

134. Sandnes, *Paul — One of the Prophets?;* Vielhauer, *Oikodomē. Das Bild vom Bau in der Christlichen Literatur.*

135. Turner, *The Holy Spirit and Spiritual Gifts,* 207; cf. 206-12.

136. Strobel, *Der erste Brief,* 190.

137. Wire, *The Corinthian Women Prophets,* 135-58 and 226-28.

could speak "divine mysteries in prophecy, prayer, wisdom, knowledge, revelation and tongues" and claim comprehensive "spiritual" status thereby.[138] Wire draws attention to the opportunity which this afforded to escape the more subordinate and domestic roles imposed within the privacy of the home and family (see above on ch. 7). Paul, by contrast, is perceived by Wire as imposing a hierarchical level of a "higher" apostolic authority and a return to "order" which inhibited and compromised this new-found freedom, especially by narrowing the scope of prophecy and giving it privilege over tongues (ch. 14).[139]

No doubt Wire captures the mood of some of the women prophets at Corinth, but her account of Paul's motivations and her transposition of the issue into what amounts to a power struggle is less convincing when we review Paul's theology and Christology as a whole. Further discussion, however, must await a more careful exegesis of ch. 14.

f. Prophetic Consciousness, Fallibility, and Testing

Prophecy, as Dunn asserts, plays its role "in building it [the community] up . . . prophecy is a word of revelation."[140] But on what grounds does Dunn also assert, "It does not denote the delivery of a previously prepared sermon"?[141] Why must "revelation" be instantaneous rather than the result of sustained prayer and sustained prayerful contemplation, meditation, and rational reflection? Prophecy and revelation are indeed closely related in 14:26-32. But Dunn's admission that "prophecy as revelation may of course overlap with prophecy as exhortation and consolation" seriously compromises the notion that the most effective exhortation and comfort occurs as that which is "spontaneous" in the sense of instantaneous. Indeed, in his later work *The Theology of Paul* Dunn recognizes the role of *self-conscious control* (14:32) and *habituated "experience"* of passing on prophetic discourse and of testing.[142] In his book *The Mystery of Preaching* James Black records the tart response of a senior pastor to a younger colleague who preferred "inspiration" to preparation. He is alleged to have responded: "That is not inspiration, but desperation." All that we have said about worldviews and a "God of the gaps" under **healings** in v. 9b applies readily here. That it may *also include* "unprepared" utterance is not to be doubted. The Spirit is promised for occasions of necessity (cf. Mark 13:11, "say whatever is given to you at the time; for it is not you speaking but the Holy Spirit" [NIV]).

Wayne Grudem, like David Hill, traces more fundamental criteria about authority and inspiration for **prophecy** in Paul. He rightly insists that a prophet's subjective evaluation of his or her authority must be distinguished clearly from evaluations reached by the church as a whole, or by others, as against the possibility of self-deception. This issue appears in the OT as well as the NT (cf. 1 Kings 22:1-28). Grudem

---

138. Ibid., 136.
139. Ibid., 137-48.
140. Dunn, *Jesus and the Spirit*, 228; cf. 227-33.
141. Ibid., 228-29.
142. Dunn, *The Theology of Paul*, 580-82; cf. *Jesus and the Spirit*, 229-30. See further our discussion about the different senses of "spontaneous" above, under **healings**, v. 9b, in our introduction.

agrees with Dunn, Hill, Boring, and others that the prophet does not simply speak the prophet's own words, but is "called" or "sent" for the task (Deut 18:18-20; Jer 14:14). On the OT he draws extensively on J. Lindblom's work.[143] Aune and others have shown, however (*pace* Käsemann), that no specific prophetic *form* (such as "I" pronouncements on behalf of God) applies in the case of NT prophecy. Like Hill, Grudem sees NT apostles as the most preeminent example of those who speak with prophetic authority, because they are "messengers of Christ."[144] Paul stands among the prophets in 1 Cor 14:6; the two roles therefore overlap here.

Grudem's most distinctive thesis, apart from his critique of Dautzenberg, is his attempt to distinguish between *levels of prophetic authority*. Thus the women prophets of 11:5 and elitist prophets of 14:37-38 appear to remain subject, at least in Paul's view, to Paul's authority. The prophets at Corinth "were not accorded an absolute divine authority by others. In 14:29 it seems that the prophet's words could be challenged and questioned, and that the prophet could at times be wrong."[145] Yet *to experience self-deception on occasion, or to make a "mistake," does not thereby make the person concerned a "false" prophet.* "Primary" prophetic authority might seem to lie, for Grudem, in such instances as Matt 10:19-20; 1 Cor 14:6; and Rev 1:3, but "secondary" levels in 1 Cor 14:37-38; Acts 2:9; 19:6; 21:4; and 1 Thess 5:19-21.[146]

A more valuable, if less distinctive point, may spring from Grudem's examination of "the psychological state of the prophet."[147] Although his view remains in accord with Dunn's to the effect that the perception of the revealed message *may* be "spontaneous," Grudem is rightly cautious about the use of the category "miraculous" to exclude natural human processes. The Holy Spirit works in various ways, and we must not impose "an extrabiblical concept of 'miracle' . . . on the text."[148] The prophet "did not lose his self-control . . . did not speak things that made no sense to him . . . should not be termed 'ecstatic' . . . [uttering] speech which is made possible by the Spirit without depriving the speaker of his individual volition in deciding what to say."[149] This appears effectively to address Dunn's arguments about "spontaneity," and no less strongly Fee's more explicit version of Dunn's case. Fee claims: "It [**prophecy**] consisted of spontaneous, Spirit-inspired, intelligible messages, orally delivered in the gathered assembly."[150] But even if this occurs, as Fee claims, in 1 Corinthians 14, do *all* manifestations of **prophecy** reflect this pattern?

g. Limits of Certainty and Interim Conclusions Prior to Note at 14:3

Prophecy is for *edification and encouragement and does not necessarily exclude teaching and doctrine* (14:3, 31). It depends on revelation, and is sometimes closely related

---

143. Grudem, *The Gift of Prophecy in 1 Cor* 7; cf. J. Lindblom, *Prophecy in Ancient Israel* (Oxford: Blackwell, 1962).

144. Grudem, *Prophecy*, 43-54.

145. Ibid., 72-73.

146. Ibid., 110-11.

147. Ibid., 115-80.

148. Ibid., 179 and 136-37.

149. Ibid., 180.

150. Fee, *God's Empowering Presence*, 170.

to prayer (11:4-5). The allusion to the cessation of prophecy in 13:10 refers only to the Lord's return.[151] If we were tempted to complain that the definitions of NT prophecy by David Hill, Gillespie, Aune, Müller, or Friedrich were too broad, Grudem concludes with an even broader comment: "Paul defines the function of prophecy very broadly in 1 Cor. 14:3: its functions could include any kind of speech activity which would be helpful to the hearers."[152] "The NT does not lead us to expect to find any distinctive speech forms for prophecy."[153]

The recent study by Christopher Forbes presses home Grudem's claim that prophecy is not necessarily, if at all, ecstatic utterance, and corroborates Aune's critique of overdependence on supposed parallels in hellenistic texts. The merit of Forbes's work is a painstaking examination of the texts at first hand, which demonstrates that the well-known allusions to Bacchic frenzy in Euripides, *Bacchae* 142, 446, 725, 748-68, and 1051-1136, or to the ecstatic state of the oracle of the Sibyl in Virgil, *Aeneid* 6.46-100 are hardly representative of hellenistic understandings of **prophecy**.[154] Indeed, numerous counterexamples are given for every passage cited by Reitzenstein, Leisegang, Conzelmann, Weiss, Bacht, and others who advocate a history-of-religions approach through hellenism.

M. Eugene Boring explores the office of *prophet* on the assumption that explorations of forms and functions of prophetic speech lead only to the vaguest of results. *For the purpose of an exegesis of 1 Cor 12:10, his most important claim is that Paul's own view of the prophet does not correspond with expected notions at Corinth.*[155] Paul owes more to the foundations of Scripture and Jewish tradition than to the floating concepts which probably influenced assumptions at Corinth. Unfortunately, he concludes, Paul's polemic against the danger of eclipsing genuine prophecy with the gift of tongues dominates the epistle too overtly to permit a close understanding of prophecy in this epistle. Nevertheless, **prophecy** remains the only "constant" in the varied instantiations of gifts of the Spirit in 1 Cor 12:8-11, 28-30; 13:1, 2; and Rom 12:6-8.[156]

We should not despair of making some sense of προφητεία in 12:10. We have no reason to doubt the conclusion of Hill, Müller, Gillespie, and Friedrich that **prophecy**, as a gift of the Holy Spirit, combines pastoral insight into the needs of persons, communities, and situations with the ability to address these with a God-given utterance or longer discourse (whether unprompted or prepared with judgment, decision, and rational reflection) leading to challenge or comfort, judgment, or consolation, but ultimately building up the addressees.[157] On the basis of 12:10 (in isolation from

---

151. Grudem, *Prophecy,* 219 (cf. also this emphasis in H. A. Guy, to whom we allude in n. 210.

152. Ibid., 229.

153. Ibid., 230.

154. Forbes, *Prophecy,* 126-43 on the Bacchae, the Sibyl, and the Delphic Oracle; 142-48, on Philo; and 149-81, on popular hellenistic religion and on Corinth.

155. This is an important point in assessing Wire, who may well capture how some of the women prophets at Corinth wished to regard prophecy in contrast to Paul's genuine beliefs about its nature.

156. Boring, *The Continuing Voice of Jesus: Christian Prophecy and the Gospel Tradition;* also "What are We Looking For? Toward a Definition of the Term 'Christian Prophet,'" *SBL Seminar Papers,* 142-54; and "Prophecy (Early Christian)," in *ABD* 5:495-502.

157. Guy, *NT Prophecy: Its Origin and Significance,* is slight in its treatment of the subject, but consistently presses this function of *building up* as the key feature of Christian prophecy.

14:1-25; see under 14:3) more cannot be said with certainty. While the speaker believes that such utterances or discourses come from the Holy Spirit, mistakes can be made, and since believers, including ministers or prophets, remain humanly fallible, claims to **prophecy** must be weighed and tested. It would go beyond the limits of exegesis to assume that the gift of **prophecy** belongs any more *permanently* to some specific individual as an "office" than the gifts of **faith** or **kinds of healings**. The epistle remains silent on this matter. Equally, it offers no evidence that **prophecy** ceases before the return of Christ at the eschaton (see on 13:10). Finally, as J. Panagopoulos insists, prophecy is not to be isolated from tradition, from its OT background, and from the function of announcing and proclaiming the gospel of Jesus Christ.[158] Nothing links it with "trivial" messages to individuals.

d. Discerning What Is of the Spirit (12:10b)

10b Controversial debate concerns the NRSV translation *the* **discernment of** *spirits,* but we have already noted G. Dautzenberg's different account of this gift, together with Grudem's incisive critique of Dautzenberg's proposal. In summary (to recapitulate), Dautzenberg argues (i) that διακρίσεις πνευμάτων is coupled closely with **prophecy**; (ii) that διάκρισις and διακρίνω mean *interpretation* and *to interpret* (on the basis, e.g., of Josephus, *Antiquities* 8.48 and Philo, *On Joseph* 90, 104, and 143); (iii) that this corresponds with the apocalyptic tradition instantiated at Qumran of פשר *(pesher)* interpretation of prophecy; and further (not discussed above) (iv) that *discerning spirits* (or however we translate the Greek) in John 4:1-6, or *testing prophecy and prophets* in 1 Thess 5:19-21 and *Didache* 11:7, reflects a supposedly different situation from that presupposed by 1 Cor 12:10, especially since 12:3 has already provided such a "test."[159] More recently Helmut Merklein has retraced and broadly accepted Dautzenberg's conclusions.[160] Nevertheless, we considered Grudem's critique important and in many respects convincing, even if Conzelmann also appears to suggest an understanding close to Dautzenberg's.[161]

Grudem interprets the plural πνευμάτων as denoting both beneficial and demonic agencies between which **discernment** or distinguishing needs to be

158. Panagopoulos, "Die urchristliche Prophetie. Ihr Charakter und ihre Funktion," in Panagopoulos, *Prophetic Vocation in the NT Today,* 1-32, esp. 17-21. See further Schrage, *Der erste Brief,* 3:155-56.

159. Dautzenberg, "Zum religionsgeschichtlichen Hintergrund der διακρίσεις πνευμάτων (1 Kor 12:10)," 93-104.

160. H. Merklein, "Der Theologe als Prophet. Zur Funktion prophetischen Redens im theologischen Diskurs des Paulus," *NTS* 38 (1992): 402-29. Grudem, *Prophecy,* 263-88, reprinted from *BZ* 22 (1978): 253-70.

161. Cf. Conzelmann, *1 Cor,* 209: the phrase "is explained by 14:24, 25: speaking with tongues (and translating of tongues)."

162. Grudem, *Prophecy,* 58-60.

made.[162] For example, "was an evil spirit causing someone to interpret preaching or teaching or worship services (cf. Acts 16:16-18)?"[163] He is content to understand διακρίσεις πνευμάτων in 12:10 as *distinguishing,* while in 14:29 the word denotes *evaluating* or *judging* prophecies: "Paul uses διακρίνω in several senses. In 11:31 he uses it to mean 'evaluate'; in 11:29, to mean 'distinguish' (or 'evaluate'); in 6:5, to mean 'give a legal judgment'; and in 4:7, to mean 'distinguish'. In Rom. 14:1 he apparently means 'arguments' or 'disputes.'"[164] Hence Grudem contends that in 12:10 *testing* prophets or spirits is inadequate. He is more sympathetic with Robertson and Plummer's "gift of discerning in various cases (hence the plural) whether extraordinary spiritual manifestations were from above or not."[165]

Robertson and Plummer's explanation for the plural of πνευμάτων matches Paul's normal uses of πνεῦμα more readily than the contrast between good and evil spirits assumed by Grudem, or E. Ellis's contrast between angelic and demonic spirits: "Paul . . . associates angelic (and demonic) spirits with prophets and/or 'spiritual' gifts."[166] The fact of the matter is that *the use of πνεῦμα or πνεύματα to denote evil spirits appears either to be absent or to be virtually absent from Paul.*[167] To be sure, in *1 Enoch* 15:4; 15:6-10; and 106:13, 14, 17, πνεύματα can refer to fallen angels, and *evil spirits* occurs in *Jubilees* 10:7-11.[168] More especially *two opposing spirits,* "the spirit of truth" and "the spirit of wickedness," appear in Qumran (1QS 3:18, 19; 4:23-25). A "spirit of light" is opposed by a spirit or angel of darkness (1QM 13:10, 11). *Evil spirits* become a plurality (1QH 3:18; 1QS 3:14). This development continues in the Jewish pseudepigrapha (*Testament of Judah* 20:1; *Testament of Levi* 5:6; *Testament of Dan* 1:6, 7). In the NT, *Mark* uses the explicit phrase πνεῦμα ἀκάφαρτον with the adjective 14 times. Matthew prefers δαιμόνια except for *one use only* of πνεύματα in this sense in Matt 8:16. Paul uses πνεῦμα most characteristically of *the Spirit of God,* although the term also denotes a human stance or direction of influence in his epistles. Schweizer includes no category for *evil spirits* (πνεύματα) in Paul in his extensive and detailed survey.[169] The one possible loophole left by Schweizer is his comment that "the Holy Spirit affects the whole man, and cannot be explained psychologically. This enables Paul to adopt popular ideas quite freely. . . . It can be a parallel for ψυχή (Phil. 1:27)."[170] Yet Schweizer's only reference to 1 Cor 12:10 rightly concerns the

---

163. Ibid., 60.

164. Ibid., 59.

165. Robertson and Plummer, *First Epistle,* 267.

166. Ellis, "Christ and Spirit in 1 Cor," in his *Prophecy and Hermeneutic,* 71; cf. esp. 70 and 63-71.

167. Subject to correction, I have scanned Moulton-Geden, BAGD, and E. Schweizer, "πνεῦμα," *TDNT,* 6:332-435.

168. Cf. *TDNT,* 6:375-76, nn. 214-22.

169. On Paul above, see *TDNT,* 6:415-37.

170. Ibid., 434-35.

transcendent source of the gifts, and gives 12:3, not 12:10, the role of offering "a criterion by which they (the Corinthians) can distinguish the expressions of the Spirit from those of other derivation, namely confession of Jesus as Lord (1 Cor. 12:2, 3)."[171]

Two possible ways forward may be proposed. In his extensive and detailed study of related issues in Paul's vocabulary, Robert Jewett suggests that the notion of a plurality of spirits occurs as Paul's way of insisting on "a critical distinction between the various spirits" among the "Corinthian Gnostics, [who] did not distinguish between various spirits."[172] This does not commit Paul to their view, but means that "this entire construction would have been shaken by Paul's polemic insertion of a distinction between the divine and the human spirits." "Human spirit" becomes distinguished from what marks the divine, transcendent Spirit, as (we urged strongly on 2:11-16) the phrase τὸ πνεῦμα τὸ ἐκ τοῦ θεοῦ (2:12, see above) indicated. Either additionally or alternatively, Jewett also points out that in Paul πνεῦμα "is pictured as opening up the possibility of a particular type of action for the Christian . . . the determination of the believer's existence by God."[173] Ernst Fuchs makes this same point, emphasizing the contrast between the divine Spirit and the human spirit and the varied modes of divine work, while the lexicographical research of R. B. Hoyle confirms it.[174] If we place together these two proposals, the gifts of **discernment** or *discrimination* include (a) a *critical capacity to discern the genuine transcendent activity of the Spirit* from merely human attempts to replicate it; and (b) a *pastoral discernment of the varied ways in which the Spirit of God is working,* in such a way as to distinguish various consequences and patterns. The basic criterion for assessing the difference between the Spirit and forces of evil appears to operate more broadly in the public domain, having to do with whether the phenomena in question promote and witness to the sovereign Lordship of Jesus Christ (v. 3).

Arguments about a "special" gift concerning evil angelic forces retain their own logic. Thus Augustine observes that "it is hard for humans to say what angels can do and not do except by the gift of discernment from God."[175] But does this comment belong to Paul's world and to his concept of πνεῦμα as this occurs in his major or earlier epistles? As Neufeld conclusively shows, criteria about true and false claims in 1 John are to be tested in the public domain

---

171. Ibid., 423. I have also cross-checked variations in the text and indices in Schweizer, *Spirit of God* (London: Black, 1960), which is A. E. Harvey's earlier translation of the article translated by G. W. Bromiley in *TDNT,* VI. The corresponding pages in *Spirit of God* are 84-85, 65, and 65, n. 5 (and 54-87 on Paul).

172. Jewett, *Paul's Anthropological Terms,* 188.

173. Ibid., 170; cf. 167-97.

174. E. Fuchs, *Christus und der Geist bei Paulus,* 36-48, esp. 41 and 46. Cf. also Hoyle, *The Holy Spirit in St Paul.* Hoyle shows detailed differences between Paul and the Greek world of the day.

175. Augustine, *On the Trinity,* 3:9:18.

with reference to a Christlike lifestyle (cf. esp. 1 John 4:1-2).[176] This concern about conduct which "backs" authentic speech in no way detracts from the issue of sober rational reflection in contrast to a human stance uninformed by the mind.[177] As Dunn observes, the gift offers "some kind of control."[178]

Chrysostom defines "discernings of spirits" constructively as a starting point in his comment on this verse: it is "knowing who is spiritual, and who is not: who is a prophet, and who a deceiver, as he [Paul] said to the Thessalonians (1 Thess. 5:20, 21), 'respect prophesyings, but test everything; hold fast to the good!'"[179] Yet to move more explicitly beyond 12:3, our detailed proposals above under (a) and (b) invite fuller consideration. Dunn offers an interpretation which is very close to that of Chrysostom, even though he concedes that "the use of πνεῦμα in plural . . . and the related plurals of 14:12, 32 . . . have caused some perplexity," and that "the precise sense Paul intends by each of the words is not entirely clear."[180] I am strongly inclined toward his hypothesis that Paul may be using πνευμάτων (spirits) "in the sense of πνευματικῶν" (spiritual gifts, or those things which pertain to the Spirit).[181] After all, Dunn observes, Paul can use χάρις and χάρισμα synonymously. But in the end he concludes that the gift concerns "*an evaluation . . . a testing, a weighing of the prophetic utterance* by the rest (of the assembly or of the prophets)" (Dunn's italics).[182] Schatzmann dissents from this as "a narrow conception," since (against Dautzenberg and with Grudem) there is no evidence that this *evaluating* or **discerning** applies only to claims to utter prophecy rather than to all claims to be "of the Spirit" in various gifts, lifestyles, actions, or thoughts.[183] Schatzmann perhaps spoils his case by returning to notions of "a demonic spirit" without linguistic justification in the light of Paul's lexicography, but he rightly alludes to the possibility of a broader application of three criteria which Dunn elsewhere restricts primarily to claims for prophecy: "does it exalt Jesus? (1 Cor. 12:3). . . . Does it manifest love? (1 Cor. 13:4-7). . . . Does it build up? (1 Cor. 14)."[184]

These three criteria are fundamental for Paul's theology of the Holy Spirit and his notions of gospel and community. However, they are reasonably transparent in the public domain. Our proposals above take up these broader

176. D. Neufeld, *Reconceiving Texts as Speech-Acts: An Analysis of 1 John,* BibInt 7 (Leiden: Brill, 1994), 113-35 and throughout.

177. Jewett, *Paul's Anthropological Terms,* 367-73.

178. Dunn, *The Theology of Paul,* 556, n. 134.

179. Chrysostom, *1 Cor. Hom.,* 29:5.

180. Dunn, *Jesus and the Spirit,* 233; cf. 233-36.

181. Ibid., 233.

182. Ibid., 234.

183. Schatzmann, *Theology of Charismata,* 41.

184. Ibid., 42; and Dunn, "Prophetic 'I' Sayings and the Jesus Tradition: The Importance of Testing Prophetic Utterances in Early Christianity," *NTS* 24 (1978): 175-98. D. A. Carson also speaks of "demonic forces" in relation to this verse (*Showing the Spirit,* 40); but cf. the linguistic work of Schweizer, Hoyle, and Jewett discussed above.

principles in relation to a particular gift of critical capacity and pastoral insight which may be mediated to the community through *one* or **another** rather than all. Although the kinds of instantiations of the gift to which exegetical, Pentecostal, and modern charismatic literature often allude (e.g., Peter's perception of the deceit of Ananias and Sapphira, Acts 5:1-11) may be included within gifts of the Spirit as a whole, there is a risk of individualizing and even trivializing *Paul's more corporate and strategic concerns about discerning the ways of the Spirit.* If we wish to consider data in Acts, perhaps the perception of certain difficulties or obstructions as "being prevented *by the Holy Spirit* from preaching in Asia" (Acts 16:6) comes no less under this heading. The gift certainly concerns salvation, the church, and the world rather than relatively trivial individual experiences. Thus Thielicke relates the reception and use of this gift to ensure the cohesion and consistency of the witness of fallible believers to the work of the Holy Spirit as a witnessing community faithful to the gospel.[185] This entirely reflects Paul's concern in these verses for *unity* (not, as Fee argues, *variety*) by **one spirit**.[186] Exegetical and contextual factors assume immense importance in the light of a vast literature on the phrase, only certain items of which pay adequate attention to lexicography, exegesis, and hermeneutics.[187] Thielicke rightly compares the gift of wisdom and right judgment, as instantiated in the messianic Spirit who anointed Jesus Christ prior to his distinctively messianic temptations. *In these evil masqueraded as good: the quotation of Scripture; the urge to bring overwhelming numbers to belief by shortcuts* and spectacles which were contrary to the messianic mission, i.e., "seductive skills with the help of quotations of scripture" *which would distort and imperil the heart of the gospel* and God's strategy for mission.[188]

All this belongs to a different world from popular appeals to use this gift to arbitrate in small-scale controversies between individuals in local communities, or minor variants between traditions of interpretation. Wolff concludes that whether the gift concerns *discerning* and *testing* or (with Dautzenberg and Merklein) *explaining* and *classifying* what is at issue is the *genuine effect of the Holy Spirit,* in continuity with such passages as 2 Thess 2:1-2 (not being unsettled by "some prophecy" that the day of the Lord has already come"); and 1 John 4:1 ("do not believe every spirit, but test the spirits to see whether they

---

185. Thielicke, *The Evangelical Faith,* 3:79.

186. Fee emphasizes "diversity" as the key theme not only in his commentary but again in *God's Empowering Presence,* 159. The different evaluations of unity and diversity respectively have consequences of a sociological and theological nature which find expression throughout Wire, *Corinthian Women Prophets.*

187. Virtually at random, cf., e.g., J. Guillet et al., *Discernment of Spirits* (Eng. trans., Collegeville, Minn.: Liturgical Press, 1970); W. Dantine, *Der Heilige und der unheilige Geist* (Stuttgart: Radius, 1973); M. T. Kelsey, *Discernment: A Study in Ecstasy and Evil* (New York: Paulist Press, 1978); C. Floristan (ed.), *Discernment of the Spirit and the Spirits* (New York: Seabury, 1978); L. Boros, "Discernment of the Spirit," in C. Duquoc and C. Floristan (eds.), *Charisma in the Church* (New York: Seabury, 1978), 78-86.

188. Thielicke, *The Evangelical Faith,* 3:80.

are of God").[189] In other words, is a *"spiritual"* claim one which comes from the *Holy Spirit?*

e. Species of Tongues and Their Intelligible Articulation (12:10c)

10c γένη γλωσσῶν, **species of tongues**, and ἑρμηνεία γλωσσῶν, **intelligible articulation of tongues-speech**. These two gifts of the Spirit must be considered together, since our exegesis and understanding of each relates to our interpretation of the other. Our starting point must be to take γένη, *kinds, sorts,* **species**, with full seriousness. Recent literature on this subject makes this abundantly clear. C. Forbes, e.g., lists a variety of "major views" of what **tongues** is thought to denote, or, rather, is thought to have denoted in the Pauline churches or for Paul.[190] "One major view describes it as a form of inspired prayer and praise to be identified (at least in 1 Cor.) with praying or singing 'in the Spirit' (14:15)."[191] There can be no doubt whatever that whereas prophecy denotes primarily speech-acts *from* God *to the community* or *to individuals* within the assembled church, **tongues** are addressed *from* believers *to* God (14:2: *to* God, *not* to human persons), as against prophecy "to human persons" (14:3). But why does Forbes categorize the role of **tongues** as "a sign" as another or "a second view" of the same phenomenon rather than the manifestation of some different *kind* or **species of tongues**?[192] Too much literature seeks to identify *glossolalia* as "one thing" when Paul specifically takes pains to refer to *different* **species**.

Yet there are "family resemblances" between different **species of tongues** which mark them off from **prophecy** and from other gifts of the Spirit. In the papyri which are nearly contemporary with Paul, γένος regularly means **species**, as in **species** of plants (*BGU* 1119:27 [first century BC], 1120:34, 1122:23; cf. *Papyrus Oxyrhynchus* 8:1134:13; *P. Oxy.* 4:727:20 [AD 154]). The word may also mean *parentage* in the first-century-BC to second-century papyri, e.g., *BGU* 1:140:26; *P. Oxy.* 9:1202:20; or *offspring,* in Acts 17:28.[193] Its semantic field relates more closely to *races, families, relatives, tribes, descendants,* and **species** than to *types, classes,* and *categories,* although it may include the latter. In what lies the difference? For the philosopher Ludwig Wittgenstein the distinction is fundamental. *Classes* are logically inclusive or exclusive, but "a network of similarities overlapping and crisscrossing" in vari-

---

189. Wolff, *Der erste Brief,* 292-93; cf. Schrage, *Der erste Brief,* 3:155-57; Collins, *First Cor,* 455 (except that Collins tends too narrowly to confine the issue to prophecy, without argument); Lang, *Die Briefe,* 169-70 (with a brief comment on Dautzenberg); and Strobel, *Der erste Brief,* 190-91 ("testing").

190. Forbes, *Prophecy and Inspired Speech,* esp. 92-102.

191. Ibid., 92.

192. Ibid., 93.

193. MM, 124; BAGD, 156; Grimm-Thayer, 113-14.

ous ways, not always neatly, has "no better expression to characterize these similarities than 'family resemblances.'"[194] How and why we spot a family resemblance may vary and transcend fixed scientific or logical categories.

We cannot overstate the importance of this fact. *A cluster of generic characteristics* mark off **tongues** from **prophecy**: *in one context,* the contrast between *articulate* speech and *unintelligible* sounds (14:2b, 5, 7-9, 11, 19); *in another context* the contrast between being addressed *to God* and being addressed *to other human persons* (14:2a; 14:15); in *yet another context* the distinction between communicative discourse in the *ordinary public domain* and something so exalted as to be associated with *angelic utterance* (13:1); *in one more context* capable of making some believers feel like exiles or strangers *"not at home"* in the community of believers (14:23a) and repellent to unbelievers (14:23b); in other situations that which *benefits the tongue-speaker* and for which he or she can give thanks (14:4a, 5a, 18). *Any generalizing definition will founder on semantic contrasts which constitute counterexamples.* On the other hand, *one or more* of the above characteristics or family traits give adequate grounds for the use of **tongues**, provided that they are "given" by the Holy Spirit and not self-induced.

This may be one reason why a *phenomenology* of **tongues** is no easier to define than some specified speech-form which defines **prophecy** (see above, esp. on Hill, Aune, Héring, and Boring). Certainly the main thrust of Christopher Forbes's warnings against assuming that **tongues** denotes *ecstatic speech* on the basis of overly selective and unrepresentative examples of "inspired speech" in Graeco-Roman texts should be heeded and accepted. The instances of irrational frenzy described by Euripides concerning the Dionysiac cult in *The Bacchae* and similar phenomena concerning the frenzied antics of the Sibyl in Virgil's *Aeneid,* often familiar from classes in school should not be taken as models for an understanding of 1 Corinthians 12–14 (see above on 1 Cor 12:2).[195] Forbes suspects the approach of history-of-religion writers since Reitzenstein of special pleading, and his wide review of primary sources in Graeco-Roman literature entirely vindicates his scepticism.[196]

In the light of the careful comparisons between the use of the singular γλῶσσα, the plural γλῶσσαι, and the presence or absence of λαλεῖν in the LXX, other Intertestamental literature, Mark, Acts, and Paul in the lexicographical survey undertaken by R. A. Harrisville, Witherington's explanation of "a kind of tongues" as a semilanguage (a kind of language, but not language in the usual sense) is most unlikely to account for γένη.[197] In any case Witherington uses "kind" in the singular, while Paul uses γένη, *kinds* or **species**, in the *plu-*

194. L. Wittgenstein, *Philosophical Investigation* (Eng. and Germ., Oxford: Blackwell, 2d ed. 1967), sects. 66-67.
195. Forbes, *Prophecy,* 126-39; cf. Euripides, *The Bacchae,* 1051-75, 1095-1136; Virgil, *Aeneid* 6.42-155.
196. Forbes, *Prophecy,* 103-62; cf. 279-315.
197. Harrisville, "Speaking in Tongues: A Lexicographical Study," 35-48.

ral.[198] Writers who accept that **species of tongues** may denote more than one of some six "family resemblances" ascribed to **tongues** are on more solid ground than those who invest everything in a single category of description. Even Turner's recognition that **tongues** may have been understood differently by Paul and at Corinth does not appear to be related to Paul's recognition of **species**.[199]

Harrisville shows, moreover, that the lexicographical background in the NT, the LXX, Greek sources, Qumran, and the post-NT period remains at best inconclusive. Although 35 references occur in the NT, 28 of these belong to 1 Corinthians, of which 23 occur in 1 Corinthians 14 and the remainder in 1 Corinthians 12 and 13 (12:10, 31; 13:1; 14:2, 4, 5, 13, 18, 19, 21, 23, 27, 39).[200] The ratio of Paul to Acts and the (spurious) "longer ending" of Mark is four to one.[201] Holtzmann regarded 1 Corinthians 12–14 as the classic source for the terminology; Weiss believed that Paul borrowed it from Corinth; Paul Feine argued that Paul was responsible for the Christian use of the term, allowing for only magical influence from Judaism.[202] Harrisville examines the seven uses of γλῶσσα with λαλεῖν in the LXX and declares: "We cannot conclude without further ado that the Septuagint usage has in any way influenced the NT."[203] In secular Greek we encounter barely a single use of γλῶσσα with λαλεῖν, namely, in *Papyrus Oxyrhynchus* 11:229:199-200, while the plural form in Galen, Pyrrho, and Lucian is shown to be of doubtful relevance by Forbes.[204] The literature in Qumran and the *Testament of Job* is also problematic, although it is taken up by Ellis and by Dautzenberg (see below). Most of the post-NT references occur in commentaries, homilies, or notes on 1 Corinthians 12–14 (e.g., in Origen, Chrysostom, Theodore, Cyril, Theodoret, and Photius). This cannot be accidental. The one writer who suggests "ecstatic" consciousness is Tertullian during his Montanist period.[205] On exegetical and largely contextual grounds the following approaches may be distinguished, and are not mutually exclusive in every case (although they are in some cases).

i. Tongues as Angelic Speech

Ellis and Dautzenberg argue for this view, and Witherington and Barrett express sympathy with it. The main argument in its favor rests on whether Paul

---

198. Witherington, *Conflict and Community*, 258.

199. Turner, *The Holy Spirit*, 227; cf. 221-39.

200. Harrisville. "Speaking in Tongues," 35.

201. Ibid., 36.

202. Feine, "Zungenreden," in Pauly-Wissowa, 21 (1908), 758-59; Weiss, *Der erste Korintherbrief*, 335; Harrisville, "Speaking in Tongues," 36-37.

203. Harrisville, "Speaking in Tongues," 39.

204. Ibid., 39-40; Forbes, *Prophecy*, 108-23, 137-43, 208-17.

205. Cf. Harrisville, "Speaking in Tongues," 47-48, BAGD, 162; MM, 128. In the papyri most references are to eating **tongue** as part of the menu, or less frequently to linguistic dialectics. The **tongue** is the "organ of speech" (BAGD).

(or Corinth) was influenced by the role of angels in apocalyptic or in Qumran, most especially by the *Testament of Job* (first century BC) and by what weight we give to enigmatic references about "rapture" in 2 Cor 12:1-5 (esp. 2 Cor 12:4), to 1 Cor 13:1, and to 1 Cor 14:2, 28.[206] In *Testament of Job* 48:1–50:3 Job's enraptured daughters "no longer mind the things of earth but utter a hymn in the angelic language . . . to God according to the angels' psalmody . . . speaking in the language of the heights. . . . She spoke in the language of the Cherubim . . ."; cf. *Jubilees* 25:14; *Testament of Judah* 25:3; *1 Enoch* 40 and 71:11; and 4 Macc 10:21. Barrett as well as Ellis and Dautzenberg alludes similarly to 1 Cor 13:1, viewing "unintelligible" speech as heavenly.[207] This citation of *Testament of Job* 48:1–50:3 and 1 Cor 13:1 is not new. Heinrich Weinel expounded this theory in 1899 (partly against Reitzenstein here) on the death of their father as one daughter sings to God "in the hymnology of angels"; the second, in the language of the "Archontes"; the third daughter in the speech of the cherubim.[208]

This view is criticized by Allo, who argues that this slides more readily into the traditions of the Montanists than that of Paul and the Fathers.[209] Turner sets out several objections to the "tongues of angels" view, most notably that Paul would not have implied that "they belong only to our pre-resurrection childhood."[210] Grudem points out, also, that *tongues of angels* in 1 Cor 13:1 is at once correlated with *human tongues* in the same phrase. Quite properly, as we have argued already above, Grudem rejects Ellis's understanding of the plural πνεύματα as angelic powers. In 14:32, e.g., he rightly understands the Greek to mean not "spirits of the prophets," but "manifestations of the Holy Spirit at work in prophets."[211] We may also add that the notion of *angels' speech* as being among that which passes away at the parousia (13:8) would be most curious. This is one of the least plausible proposals. Other reasons for the unintelligibility and transcendent, God-directed nature of **tongues** more readily suggest themselves, especially on the analogy of "sighs too deep for words" (Rom 8:26).

ii. Tongues as the Miraculous Power to Speak Other Languages

It is usually claimed that the most widespread pre-modern view held among the Fathers, medieval writers, and Reformers perceives **tongues** as *the miraculous*

---

206. Dautzenberg, "Zum religionsgeschichtlichen Hintergrund," 93-104; and Ellis, "Christ and Spirit in 1 Cor," in *Prophecy and Hermeneutic,* 63-71. Ellis sees prophets as guarded by angelic armies and cites the "spirits" material in Qumran (e.g., 1QS 4:21-22; 1QH 12:11-12; and associates 1 Cor. 13:1 with 11:4, 10).

207. Barrett, *First Epistle,* 286.

208. Weinel, *Die Wirkungen des Geistes und der Geister im nachapostolischen Zeitalter bis auf Irenaeus.*

209. Allo, *Première Épitre,* 377. Cf. 355-56 and Excursus XV, "Glossolalie," 374-84.

210. Turner, *The Holy Spirit,* 228.

211. Grudem, *Gift of Prophecy,* 120-29; quotation from 128. This follows Godet, Ellicott, Barrett, Hodge, Wendland, Goudge, Schlatter, and Chrysostom.

power to speak unlearned foreign languages. Among the Fathers, it is generally claimed that Origen, Chrysostom, Theodore, Cyril, and Theodoret held this view; among medieval writers and Reformers, Thomas Aquinas, Photius, Estius, and Calvin; among modern writers especially J. G. Davies, Robert Gundry, and Christopher Forbes. Jerome's Latin text reads *alii genera linguarum, alii interpretatio sermonum,* but this does not take us very far.[212] When we examine the sources themselves, **tongues**, *as such,* often *lacks* this meaning. Origen's *Fragments on 1 Corinthians* fails to yield any clear comment on **species of tongues**. The allusion in his treatise *Against Celsus,* 7:9, to which Allo and others refer is at best enigmatic. Origen speaks of self-styled, "inspired people" who, as Celsus reports the matter, use first-person utterances, "I am God . . . I am the Spirit"; but he firmly rejects these reports.[213] Chrysostom consciously places more emphasis in his comment on Acts 2 on the content of the "wonderful things" spoken at Pentecost rather than **tongues** in any linguistic sense, and comments on 1 Cor 12:10 or 14:2, 5 virtually ignore the subject.[214] The *Fragments* of Theodore of Mopsuestia on 1 Corinthians in K. Staab's *Pauluskommentare aus der Griechischen Kirche* hardly touch on the issue in 12:10 or on 14:2-36.[215] Cyril of Alexandria addresses his concern to the sign character of **tongues**, and describes **tongues** as utterances which the speaker did not yet understand.[216] Theodoret explains the purpose of **tongues** in 1 Cor 12:10 as ἵνα τὸ κήρυγμα πιστευθῇ, i.e., for the purpose of *evangelical mission.*[217]

How, then, can modern writers speak of *the miraculous power to speak unlearned languages* as the widespread or "main" patristic exegesis? The answer can only depend on their lumping together the comments of the Fathers on ἑρμηνεία γλωσσῶν, **intelligible articulation of what is spoken in tongues**. Thus Theodoret explains that these two gifts serve the *kerygma* or *gospel* together because one person might know only the language of Greece (γλῶσσαν) but after another has spoken in Scythian or the tongue of Thrace could explain the discourse "according to the same spirit everywhere" (πανταχοῦ).[218] *Everywhere* (πανταχοῦ) shows the geographical context of mission. In relation to this ninth gift Cyril of Alexandria now anticipates 14:21: "by foreign languages I shall speak. . . ."[219] Indeed, it is precisely because he elevates the ninth gift as a service gift to support the gospel that in some way Chrysostom ranks apostleship and prophetic proclamation as more primary gifts.[220] Although Peter

212. Jerome., *S. Pauli Ep. 1 ad Cor, Opera Omnia* (Migne, *PL,* 29:794B).
213. Origen, *Against Celsus,* 7:11, "Celsus speaks falsely."
214. Chrysostom, *Acts: Hom.* 4; *1 Cor. Hom.,* 19.
215. Theodore, in Staab (ed.), *Pauluskommentare,* 190 and 192-93.
216. Cyril, *Fragmenta in Ep. 1 ad Cor* (ed. Pusey), 289.
217. Theodoret, *Interp. Ep. 1 ad Cor,* 245A (Migne, *PG,* 82:325 [Greek]; 326 [Latin]), *ut praedicationi fides haberetur.*
218. Ibid.
219. Cyril, *Fragmenta in Ep. 1 ad Cor,* 89.
220. Chrysostom, *1 Cor. Hom.,* 29:5.

Lombard hesitantly alludes to wider phenomena of "inspiration," this becomes the main medieval view.[221] Thus for Thomas Aquinas "the excellence of the gifts corresponds with the order in which they are enumerated," and in Isa 11:2, 3 and in 1 Cor 12:8-10, **wisdom** and **knowledge** because the rational and contemplative are fundamental for knowing God, prior even to action and emotion.[222] Erasmus now speaks of the gift, *dotem, ut idem variis linguis loquatur. . . .*[223] Similarly, Calvin comments (not on **tongues** but on ἑρμηνεία γλωσσῶν), "Interpreters translated the foreign languages into native speech."[224] Those who simply received **species of tongues** "often did not know the language of the people with whom they had to have dealings."[225]

By the time of Hodge, this linguistic capacity has come to be ascribed to **tongues**. Hodge describes this gift as "the ability to speak in languages primarily unknown to the speakers. The nature of this gift is determined by the account given in Acts 2:4-11. . . ."[226] In more recent scholarship advocates for this view include J. G. Davies, S. Tugwell, R. H. Gundry, and Christopher Forbes. Gundry's main concern, like that of Forbes and Turner, is to attack the view that **species of tongues** can embrace "ecstatic utterances" (NEB).[227] However, his "linguistic" view depends largely on understanding ἑρμηνεύω and διερμηνεύω to mean *to translate,* and "the other presupposition underlying Paul's words about the unintelligibility of tongues is that in the ordinary church meeting at Corinth" some would be present who would not know Greek or Latin and would require a translation.[228] As we should expect, Gundry also discusses the significance of "languages" in Acts 2:4-13, together with whether the charge of "drunkenness" serves to indicate symptoms of an ecstatic state.[229]

Forbes covers similar ground, including references to the Cornelius episode in Acts 10:46 and the disciples of the Baptist at Ephesus at Acts 19:6, although in books on the subject these two passages are regarded as notoriously controversial, and relate to new stages of missionary advance in Luke's theological history.[230] Forbes, as we have noted, rejects the application of "ecstasy" as "one of the most misused terms in the vocabulary of NT scholarship." While Turner attacks NT specialists who have not studied the sociology and psychology of ecstasy,[231]

221. Peter Lombard, *Glossa,* in Migne, *PL,* 192:99.

222. Thomas Aquinas, *Summa Theologiae,* Ia and IIae, Q. 68 (Blackfriars ed., vol. 24), art. 7.

223. Erasmus, *Opera Omnia: In Epist. Pauli ad 1 Cor,* 898.

224. Calvin, *First Epistle,* 263.

225. Ibid.

226. Hodge, *First Epistle,* 248.

227. Gundry, "'Ecstatic Utterance' (NEB)?" 299-307; cf. Davies, "Pentecost and Glossolalia," 228-31; Tugwell, *Did You Receive the Spirit?* With Gundry, cf. Turner, *Holy Spirit,* 227-38; Forbes, *Prophecy,* 51-65.

228. Gundry, "'Ecstatic Utterance' (NEB)?" 300 and 303.

229. Ibid., 304.

230. Forbes, *Prophecy,* 51.

231. Ibid., 53; cf. Turner, *Holy Spirit,* 237-38.

Forbes rejects the "angelic speech" view of Ellis and Dautzenberg, together with the notion that **tongues** denotes a poetic medium embodying idiosyncratic or archaic language (see below).[232] He then considers in detail my own earlier arguments that ἑρμηνεία γλωσσῶν and more especially ἵνα διερμηνεύῃ in 14:13 denote *the power to put something into* **articulate speech**, not *to interpret* or *to translate*, in the context of 1 Cor 12:10–14:40.[233] I appealed to uses of the word in Philo and in Josephus to mean the capacity to express in *words* or **articulate speech** wonders which had otherwise left a person speechless, or able to react only emotively with awe or joy. I had observed that "no less than three-quarters of the uses [of διερμηνεύω and διερμήνευσις in Philo] refer to the articulation of thoughts or feelings in intelligible speech."[234] By contrast, the verb means to *translate* only when the context clearly relates to translation.

The only effective rejoinder that Forbes offers is that when ἑρμηνεύω is considered alongside its compound forms the ratio between the two possible meanings shifts.[235] But I am only arguing that the verbs *can* mean *to produce* **articulate speech** in appropriate contexts, and that 1 Corinthians 12–14 provides such a context. His four-page discussion of my exegesis still leaves several questions unanswered, not least the string of difficulties which I did not mention but to which we now turn. Turner also applies such value judgments as "unconvincing" and "misunderstanding" to my argument, but ultimately everything rests upon (a) his insistence that Paul disparages only *uninterpreted* tongues (in fact, it is tongues *in public*); and (b) the hugely different presuppositions which result from (i) failure to work out the implications of a virtually universal understanding of Greek for proclamation; and (ii) appeals to the "normal" use of γλῶσσα to mean *language* (e.g., in Behm) when we are hardly discussing "normal" uses of the term![236]

The most powerful objections to the "linguistic translation" view come from Edwards, H. A. W. Meyer, and L. T. Johnson. Forbes ignores Meyer, refers to Edwards only in another context, and does not discuss Johnson's article of 1992. Turner appears to cite none of these. Moreover, the heart of the problem is implicit in our review of patristic, medieval, and Reformation interpretations. Edwards declares: "*It is evident that the Corinthians did not use their gift of tongues to evangelize the heathen world.* They spoke with tongues in their Church assemblies, and not once does the Apostle urge them to apply the power to the purpose for which it would be so eminently serviceable" (my italics).[237] If there were any hint of this use, Paul *could* not have said "the person who

232. Forbes, *Prophecy,* 57-65.

233. Thiselton, "The 'Interpretation' of Tongues? A New Suggestion in the Light of Greek Usage in Philo and Josephus," 15-36.

234. Ibid., 18; cf. 20; discussed by Forbes, *Prophecy,* 65-72.

235. Forbes, *Prophecy,* 66-68.

236. Turner, *The Holy Spirit,* 227 ("normal" meaning); 229 ("*uninterpreted* tongues" (his italics) and lack of allusion to Greek medium for evangelism.

237. Edwards, *First Epistle,* 319.

speaks in a tongue speaks not to people but to God" (14:2), let alone, "the person who speaks in a tongue builds up only himself/herself (ἑαυτόν, 14:4). But we saw that insofar as Chrysostom, Cyril, Thomas, and most especially Theodoret and Calvin were concerned, the whole point of using *foreign languages* was strictly *to serve the proclamation of the gospel as part of mission to the world.* But if we decontextualize the gift from mission (as Paul clearly does in 1 Corinthians 14), the basis for the gift has disappeared, except for a handful of twentieth-century interpreters. Collins adds that Paul "also compares speaking in tongues with the inarticulate sounds of musical instruments (14:8)."[238] This hardly describes a language system awaiting "translation."

Again, *pace* Forbes, if this is *not* the purpose of the gift, one wonders *what kind of God* gives these gifts. Paul does appeal to Corinthian understandings of *God* for their interpretation of such issues as, e.g., the resurrection (15:34), the role of "wisdom" and rhetoric (1:20, 21, 24-25), the nature of the "spiritual" (2:11), ethics (6:19), and order (11:3). So to ask whether the gift of translation is merely self-edifying (and at the risk of hermeneutical anachronism, apparently not usually given to overseas missionaries or to ordinards learning Greek and Hebrew) seems *prima facie* odd. Edwards in fact holds that **tongues** are no less likely to relate to "tongues of fire" than to "tongues of speech" as the determinative background.[239] Again, Collins urges that "12–14 is different from the disciples' experience at Pentecost (Acts 2:5-13)."[240]

Meyer develops this point.[241] The consequences of this view, he declares, would be: (1) that 14:2 would be false; (2) that we cannot explain why γένη φωνῶν (14:10, 11) is distinguished from γένη γλωσσῶν; (3) the contrast shifts between one language and another rather than between language and some other form of expression which is not intelligible or articulate (cf. 14:15); (4) 14:28 becomes inexplicable since all commonsense persons recognize the everyday phenomenon of translation issues if this is really what is at issue; (5) in 14:18 Paul states that he himself has the gift of **tongues** but chooses not to use it publicly in church. If Gundry is right in claiming that non-Greek-speakers might be present, how or why would Paul not wish to use his gift? (6) Paul would have discussed the use of this gift in quite a different way if it served as Gundry, Turner, and Forbes claim. Meyer adds two further objections, which need not detain us.[242]

L. T. Johnson adds yet further problems, if any further factors were needed to discredit the theory. (1) In Acts 2:4-13, if it is relevant to 1 Cor 12:10–14:40, *the miracle is not that of speaking but of hearing* (2:8). *The "gift" is to hear* in one's own language; not a simultaneous translation process of twelve concurrent utterances. This gift is not given to all the bystanders (2:13).

238. Collins, *First Cor,* 455-56.
239. Ibid., 323; cf. 318-24.
240. Collins, *First Cor,* 456.
241. Meyer, *First Epistle,* 1:366-67.
242. Ibid., 367.

(2) Paul, moreover, "could hardly make clearer his conviction that tongues are an intrinsically noncommunicative form of utterance (1 Cor. 13:1; 14:2, 4, 7-9, 16-17, 23)."[243] (3) The use of ἑρμενεύω and its cognate forms to mean **to bring to articulate expression** or *to put into words* fits the context better and has lexicographical justification. (4) If we may compare modern phenomena without hermeneutical anachronisms, the linguistic research of W. J. Samarin demonstrates that recordings of *modern* glossolalia are "language-like" but *not "linguistic"* in structure.[244] All that Turner seems able to reply to Samarin is that "this verdict perhaps oversimplifies" and offers anecdotal evidence from the late twentieth century which may or may not relate to what Paul discusses with Corinth.[245]

iii. Tongues as Liturgical, Archaic, or Rhythmic Phrases

A third proposal concerns **tongues** as *archaic or novel verbal idioms, usually with music, poetry, and rhythm* (Bleek and Heinrici). This offers a halfway house between "languages" and "inspired utterance" in its approach. Bleek noted that Greek grammarians often used γλῶσσα, **tongue**, to denote *archaic words* or dialects, provincial idioms, or, as in the present context, probably a mixture of ancient, quasi-Semitic *liturgical words or phrases,* perhaps spoken in poetic or exalted rhythms.[246] In spite of the recent work of Forbes, appeal was made to precedents in oracular speech in hellenistic religion. Bleek argues the case in detail and takes up a point of departure already noted by J. G. Herder and J. A. Ernesti.

A detailed advocacy of this view comes from C. F. G. Heinrici.[247] Following Bleek, he appeals to the historical uses of the word in Greek literature and in relation to allusions to ecstatic expressions of joy and praise in Dionysius of Halicarnassus, Sextus Empiricus, and Plutarch.[248] More especially, however, the term is used to denote "unfamiliar" or *out of the ordinary* words and phrases which often (but not necessarily) spring from such contexts, including *poetic* turns of phrase and rhythms.[249] Sometimes provincial dialects or ornamental metaphors might be used here.[250] At the other end of the linguis-

243. Johnson, "Tongues, Gift of," in *ABD,* 6:597; cf. 596-600.

244. Samarin, *Tongues of Men and Angels: The Religious Language of Pentecostalism,* 74-128.

245. Turner, *The Holy Spirit,* 307-10, 312-14. His allusion to Macchia (312, n. 42) is entirely positive and helpful.

246. F. Bleek, "Über die Gabe des γλώσσαις λαλεῖν in der ersten christlichen Kirche," in *Studien und Kritiken* (1829): 3-79.

247. Heinrici, *Der erste Sendschreiben,* 376-94.

248. Ibid., 381.

249. Ibid., 382 and 383.

250. Cf. Dionysius of Halicarnassus, 2:82; Plutarch, *Isis* 375B; and Bleek, "Über die Gabe des γλώσσαις λαλεῖν," 42; Heinrici, *Der erste Sendschreiben,* 382-85. See further Quintilian, *Institutio Oratoria* 1:14.

tic spectrum, these idiosyncratic expressions might come about through coining *new words,* which in turn points to the enigmatic reference in the longer ending of Mark about "speaking with new tongues" (Mark 16:17).[251]

A close association of these idioms not only with poetry and liturgy, but also with music and rhythmic songs of praise belongs, for Heinrici, to the "various kinds of tongues" which differ from straightforward, distinctly articulated, intelligible prose forms of traditional or ordinary language.[252] The connection between rhythmic music and the language of divine worship appears in Greek literature from earliest times.[253] Heinrici then quotes the kind of material in Plato and Virgil alluding to the Sibyl and the Pythis about which Forbes has recently formulated the criticisms noted above.[254] However, he does not depend on a history-of-religions background. On the contrary, his fundamental approach is linguistic, and he is no less concerned to cite Aristotle on language and grammar to support his case.[255] Allo commends Heinrici for avoiding the history-of-religions assumptions found in Reitzenstein and in Weiss.[256]

It is almost universally agreed that reference to modern Pentecostal and charismatic phenomena cannot be used as an exegetical test for proposed interpretations of Paul and Corinth. This would be to presuppose the validity of one specific tradition of interpretation in a circular fashion. However, the modern phenomena do have at least marginal relevance on the *prima facie* plausibility of provisional suggestions. In this context C. G. Williams's discussion of Pentecostalist phenomena is of interest. He quotes H. Horton's description within Pentecostalism of "rising from understood words and rhythms to mystic words and rhythms. . . . It is marrying mystic meanings and mystic cadencies in a glorious rhapsody of adoring worship. . . . Words and music soar infinitely beyond the compass of mere understanding."[257]

On the other side, however, Godet reminds us that many at Corinth were tradespeople, artisans, sailors, or menial slaves. Among such, he observes, "it is impossible to imagine why . . . the most profound emotions of the saved soul should have found expression either in ancient and unusual words, or by means of compositions formed of wholly new terms."[258] He also asks whether this could result if the "understanding" had become secondary. But a reply can be suggested. If Godet's view is placed beside those of Bleek and Heinrici, this lends added force to recent arguments from Dale Martin that the use of species

251. Heinrici, *Der erste Sendschreiben,* 384-86.

252. Ibid., 386-87.

253. Homer, *Iliad* 1.403; 14.291.

254. Plato, *Cratylus* 391D; *Politica* 290E; *Phaedrus* 244A; Plutarch, *Moralia (De Musica)* 1142D, 1144D on music, poetry, and rhythm; Heinrici, *Der erste Sendschreiben,* 388-90 and 388 n. 4.

255. Aristotle, *Poetica* 1457B, 3; *Rhetorica* 1404B, 8.

256. Allo, *Première Épitre,* "Glossolalia," 380.

257. Williams, *Tongues of the Spirit,* 78; he quotes from H. Horton, *What Is the Good of Speaking with Tongues?* (London: Assemblies of God, n.d., rpt. 1960), 21-22. Williams receives perhaps predictable criticism from Turner, *Holy Spirit,* 238, n. 65.

258. Godet, *First Epistle,* 2:202-3.

of tongues could become "status indicator" or a *sign of social elitism.*[259] Only the well-educated could experience wellings up of well-turned poetic phrases and metaphors in exalted or joyous states, and thereby gain admiration and corroborration of their sociospiritual status. Such a possibility would be *divisive,* even if no division had been intended.

Hence, we conclude that while we cannot identify the view of Bleek and Heinrici firmly with **tongues**, it is more than possible that something along these lines featured *among various* **species of tongues** at Corinth, *alongside others.* If comparisons with charismatic phenomena today are hermeneutically permissible, the association of certain states and experiences with rhythmic music, drumbeats, and quasi-dance idioms may offer some parallel, while such cries as "Hallelujah!" might instantiate uses of ancient linguistic (Hebraic!) liturgical formulae! In Heinrici's sense of metaphor and poetic ornamentation, even the chanted choruses, in which the same lines of the simplest content are endlessly repeated and replicated in everincreasing cycles of psychological buildup, may just conceivably offer some broad analogue. This would certainly account for the ambivalence with which Paul seems to affirm the phenomena with one hand and express reserve with the other, as authentic praise which tends, however, too readily to leave the mind on one side, while releasing the deep emotions of gratitude, joy, and celebration (14:2, 5, 14, 15, 20). *But this phenomenon could not account for 14:8-13 and 21-25.* Hence *other* **species of tongues** must have (also) operated at Corinth.

iv. Tongues as "Ecstatic" Speech

We have discussed at length the objections of R. H. Gundry, M. Turner, and C. Forbes to this understanding of **tongues.**[260] However, what Forbes proves conclusively and beyond doubt is not that this approach has no relevance whatever as one **species of tongues** but that (a) if this theory rests on history-of-religions appeals to supposedly parallel phenomena in the Graeco-Roman world, it must fall; (b) that this approach cannot account for *every* type of instantiation of **tongues** in 1 Cor 12:10–14:40; and (c) that the term *ecstasy* is empty and misleading unless or until it is explained in precise terms that can receive exegetical and contextual justification in the NT. We doubt, however, whether either the NEB translation *ecstatic utterances* (replaced by REB's *the gift of tongues of various kinds*) depends *entirely* on (a) above, even if it is a large part of the supposed justification for this understanding of the term. Further, neither Gundry nor Turner seems to have addressed fully the range of courses and details set forth above, as well as the claims of Dale Martin, Anders Eriksson, and others about Paul's rhetorical goals in chs. 12–14.

---

259. Martin, *The Corinthian Body,* 102.
260. Forbes, *Prophecy,* 103-181 and throughout; Gundry, " 'Ecstatic Utterance' (NEB)?"; Turner, *Holy Spirit,* 221-39.

Exponents of this view often begin with Tertullian. In *Against Marcion,* 5, Tertullian takes his reader through 1 Corinthians as a whole, beginning with wisdom and the cross (5:5), moving on through issues of the Spirit and ministerial "building" (5:6), marriage, and idol foods (5:7), to women and prophecy, the Eucharist and spiritual gifts (5:8), prior to considering the resurrection (5:9, 10) and 2 Corinthians (5:11-12). Hence while it is a valid criticism to associate his comment about ecstatic utterance with his Montanist period, on the other hand Tertullian approaches the subject both as a contextual exposition and to demonstrate (against Marcion) the continuity of these themes with their roots in the OT. Thus he sees the root of all the spiritual gifts in the messianic anointing prophesied in Isa 11:1-3 and dispensed by Christ (Eph. 4:8 relates, in his view, closely to 1 Cor 12:4-11). After expounding or enumerating the gifts, Tertullian concludes with a contrast between Marcion and authentic inspiration from the Spirit of God: "Let Marcion produce a psalm, a vision, only let it be by the Spirit in an ecstasy, that is, a rapture, whenever 'interpretation of tongues' has come to him (Lat. *dumtaxat spiritualem, in ecstasi, id est amentia, si qua linguae interpretatio accessit*)."[261]

It is Tertullian, therefore, not simply "the vocabulary of NT scholarship in our era," who introduces the term *in ecstasi* and even the explanatory *id est amentia* in the context of *linguae interpretatio. Amentia* usually means *madness* (in Cicero, Ovid, and others) and can also come to mean *folly* (in Horace) because it also means *"being out of one's mind."*[262] Admittedly most of *Against Marcion* must be dated around AD 207, which marks the point at which Tertullian began to fall under the spell of Montanism. However, he did not formally join a Montanist sect until six years later: Forbes calls this still "his pre-Montanist days."[263] Yet Forbes calls attention not to Tertullian's use of *in ecstasi* or *amentia* but to his witness to the continuing existence of *glossolalia.* He also alludes to Tertullian, *Apology* 18, where the context is "translation" of the LXX.[264] In his Montanist period he wrote a treatise *On Ecstasy,* which has not survived.[265]

Among modern writers, those who take seriously the nature of **tongues** as *ecstatic speech* include especially J. Behm, H. Kleinknecht, S. D. Currie, N. I. J. Engelsen, H. W. House, and in modified form M. E. Boring, L. T. Johnson, as well as a number of other writers. Behm does draw on arguments about common patterns between hellenistic and Christian phenomena. He writes: "Paul is aware of a similarity between Hellenism and Christianity in respect of

261. Tertullian, *Against Marcion,* 5:8 (near concluding lines).
262. W. Smith and J. F. Lockwood, *Latin-English Dictionary* (London: Murray, 3d ed. 1933), 41.
263. Forbes, *Prophecy,* 79.
264. Ibid., 224.
265. On Tertullian's theology of the Spirit, see J. P. Burns and G. M. Fagin, *The Holy Spirit: Message of the Fathers of the Church* (Wilmington: Glazier, 1984), 45-60; H. B. Swete, *The Holy Spirit in the Ancient Church* (London: Macmillan, 1912), 110-15.

these mystical and ecstatic phenomena."[266] But he does not restrict his argument to hellenism. He alludes to "the ecstatic fervor" of Hebrew prophets in 1 Sam 10:5-7; cf. 19:20-22, 1 Kings 18:29, 30; 2 Kings 9:11.[267] On the other hand, he identifies a different tradition in Acts 2:4-13, which he regards as more "linguistic." Behm and Kleinknecht both allude to Plato's notion of "mantic" prophecy in Timaeus 71e-72a, and Kleinknecht also appeals to parallels with oracular speech at Delphi.[268] The latter issue is taken up by Currie, while Engelsen argues that Paul was the first to conceive of a distinction between inspired ecstatic speech and inspired intelligible speech. Forbes has little difficulty in showing that the arguments of all of these writers embody a lack of precision and selectivity in the use of Graeco-Roman sources.[269]

Nevertheless, some writers argue for an "ecstatic" understanding, at least with reference to some **species of tongues**, without resort to Greek parallels. L. T. Johnson notes the presence of *some* "mantic" phenomena in certain hellenistic sources (Plato, *Ion* 534 A-D, *Timaeus* 71E-72B; Plutarch, *De Defectu Oraculorum* 417C; cf. 412A) but places more weight on Paul's word choice in 1 Cor 14:23 (οὐκ ἐροῦσιν ὅτι μαίνεσθε;).[270] Johnson argues that Paul floats the hypothesis that if all speak in **tongues**, an observer would conclude that the congregation was "raving": "In context, this can only mean 'you are prophesying the way all other cults do, in a frenzy.'"[271]

We must reserve more specific comments on 14:23 for our consideration of this verse (see below). This passage has been understood in various ways. It is time to point out that several relatively recent writers, J. D. G. Dunn, Wayne Grudem, C. G. Williams, and by implication G. Theissen, contend that a straight choice between "ecstatic" and "nonecstatic" or "linguistic" does not and cannot do justice to Paul. Grudem points out that a wide variety of quite specific terms are used in the NT for what might be thought less helpfully and less precisely to come under the heading of either ἔκστασις, which can range in meaning from trance (Acts 10:10; 11:5; 22:17) to amazement caused by mighty works (Mark 5:42; 16:8; Luke 5:26; Acts 3:10), or ἀποκάλυψις which he claims is seldom associated with quasi-ecstatic phenomena in the NT as such (although he recognizes 2 Cor 12:1 and Rev 1:1).[272] The verbal form ἐξίστημι usually means *to be amazed* or *to be fearful* in the NT.[273] But even here we should be cautious about differences between *Paul* and *Corinth*. Andrew T. Lincoln provides an important study of 2 Cor 12:1-10 which demonstrates that Paul's

266. J. Behm, "γλῶσσα," *TDNT,* 1:724; cf. 722-24; H. Kleinknecht, "πνεῦμα," *TDNT,* 6:345-48; Currie, "'Speaking in Tongues': Early Evidence outside the NT," *Int* 19 (1965): 274-94.

267. Behm, "γλῶσσα," *TDNT,* 1:724.

268. Kleinknecht, "πνεῦμα," *TDNT,* 6:345-46 and 348.

269. Forbes, *Prophecy,* 17-25 and throughout.

270. Johnson, "Tongues," *ABD,* 6:597-98.

271. Ibid., 598.

272. Grudem, *The Gift of Prophecy,* 132-34.

273. Ibid., 133, n. 30.

allusion to his own "out of body, out of mind" visionary experiences is precisely *not the basis of his apostleship or of his belonging to Christ.*[274] He was granted a glimpse of paradise yet-to-be as a sheer gift. It has nothing to do with what Cyril of Alexandria and Theophylact expected of **tongues**, but which Paul denies to **tongues**. It is a gift for the self, but does not serve the common good or authenticate the gospel.

Cyril Williams, therefore, attempts to hold two aspects together. On one side, "I discover no compelling reasons to abandon the widely held view that the Corinthian phenomenon is unintelligible glossolalia, which in this case was attended by excessive and uncontrolled behavior."[275] This is closely akin to "ecstatic" status. Nevertheless, he rightly adds: "The interpretation of 1 Cor. 14 is not a simple choice of regarding tongues as either ecstatic incoherent utterances or speaking in real languages. Ecstasy is much too vague a term to employ. . . . There are many degrees of it, ranging from mild dissociation to extreme uncontrollable rapture."[276] It is almost inconceivable that *some* **species of tongues** did not fall at *certain* points within the spectrum, but the scope of this spectrum cannot be identified with the scope of **tongues**, without more ado. We must keep sight of the fact that "in many cases the utterances were unintelligible events to those who made them (xiv:11-15)."[277]

Finally, Dunn also affirms the meaning "ecstatic utterance" in his *Jesus and the Spirit,* since it may include "mindless utterance (14:15, 19) . . . confusion and disorder, with a substantial number of the congregation evidently working themselves up into a state of spiritual ecstasy, endeavouring to become vehicles of inspired utterance."[278] Dunn (*pace* Forbes) does allude to the Pythia at Delphi as involving features of which Corinth was "too reminiscent." Yet Dunn qualifies these remarks: "Mindless ecstasy . . . should not characterize Christian worship (12:2); glossolalia is to be strongly discouraged in the assembly (14:5-12, 19). Nevertheless he [Paul] allows glossolalia a role in the assembly (14:27-28, 39)."[279] Paul ranks it as "a gift which appeals to the child more than the man (14:20; cf. 13:11). Nevertheless he does regard it as a charisma . . . and is very willing for the Corinthians to experience this charisma (14:5)."[280] It is "ecstatic only in the technical sense of being automatic speech in which the conscious mind played no part, but not ecstatic in the more common sense of 'produced or accompanied by exalted states of feeling, rapture, frenzy.'"[281]

---

274. A. T. Lincoln, "'Paul the Visionary': The Setting and Significance of the Rapture to Paradise in II Cor xii:1-10," *NTS* 25 (1979): 204-20.

275. Williams, *Tongues of the Spirit,* 30.

276. Ibid. Williams reviews the NT data, 25-45, and then turns to the development of Pentecostal and charismatic phenomena.

277. Goudge, *First Epistle,* 134; cf. his "Note," 134-37.

278. Dunn, *Jesus and the Spirit,* 242. There is relatively little comment in his later *The Theology of Paul* on this issue.

279. Ibid., 243.

280. Ibid.

281. Ibid.; cf. 242-48.

Again, where the boundaries lie between the **species** of Paul's own gift (14:18), a glossolalia which seems controlled (14:28), and that which brings confusion, repugnance, and divisive status division, is hidden within the phrase **species of tongues**, in which one aspect shades off into another in which the positive and negative, grace and sin, may become mixed, like every other phenomenon in the life of the Christian church which still sins but is *in process of* being saved (1:4-9).

v. Proposed Modification from Theissen: Conscious, Unconscious, and a Release (Cf. Rom 8:26)

Gerd Theissen has produced one of the most incisive and innovative treatments of **tongues** available in any language in his major study *Psychological Aspects of Pauline Theology*. He argues that **tongues** are "the language of the unconscious which becomes capable of consciousness through interpretation."[282] In his chapter "Tradition Analysis" relevant to 1 Corinthians 12–14, however, he does defend *certain specific ways* **tongues** relate to ecstatic states. It is extremely disappointing that neither Forbes nor Turner sees fit to address this very important work with seriousness since Theissen also works firsthand not only with Euripides, Virgil, Plato, and Philo but also with apocalyptic and Paul as well as social psychology. Turner has pleaded for such skills.[283] In Euripides, *The Bacchae,* e.g., "unconscious aggressive impulses develop in the ecstatic state and overcome deeply rooted moral inhibitions" which result in the death of Pentheus at the hands of his mother.[284] Theissen discusses the classic work of E. R. Dodds on this subject. Similarly, in Plato, *Phaedrus* 265A, ecstasy entails "divine release from the customary habits," while in *Ion* 533D-535A inspiration entails "being put out of one's senses."[285] To be filled by God *(enthusiasm)* entails relinquishing one's own thoughts to make room for God (Plato, *Ion* 534E). Philo takes up this "ecstatic filling" from Plato. "The light of God shines when human light sets" and thus "divine possession and madness fall upon us" (Philo, *Quis Rerum Divinarum Heres* 263-65).

Although he notes Origen's insistence that this view is not "Christian," Theissen traces themes in 1 Corinthians 12–14 which allow him to see elements of both *angelic tongues (Testament of Job* 48:1-3; 49:2; and 50:2) and *ecstatic utterance* as *aspects* included in *various* **species of tongues**.[286] Nevertheless,

---

282. Theissen, *Psychological Aspects of Pauline Theology,* 79; cf. 59-114, and esp. 276-341.

283. It was precisely Turner's plea that NT scholars should work from these varied backgrounds, including social psychology (*Holy Spirit,* 237-38). Turner cites Theissen only once, and then in a different book on gospel miracles (246). Yet his work appeared twenty years earlier in German and seven years earlier in English

284. Theissen, *Psychological Aspects,* 277-78.

285. Ibid., 282 and 283.

286. Ibid., 276-341.

he agrees with those who regard this as no more than a starting point for further inquiry, *in which radical differences between the three respective stances of Paul, Corinth, and the hellenistic world clearly emerge.*

vi. Tongues as Language of the Unconscious Released in "Sighs Too Deep for Words" (from the Depths of the Heart)

We have already established with detailed argument on 4:3-5 (above) that *the secrets of the heart* (4:5) and *inarticulate groans* associated with longings of *heart* or *our inmost being* (Rom 8:26, Gk. *heart,* and REB, *inmost being*) relate to Bultmann's observation that often Paul uses heart for that which "need not penetrate into the field of consciousness at all, but may designate the hidden tendency of the self."[287] The specific work of the Holy Spirit in actualizing inarticulate yearnings directed toward God from the depths of the heart of the believer in Rom 8:26-27 forms a retrospective summary from Paul's point of view of the phenomenon which occupies many verses in 1 Cor 12:10–14:40 but very few elsewhere in the NT. It is in no way anachronistic to associate Paul's language about *the heart* or what transcends cognitive consciousness *(the mind)* with modern notions of the *preconscious, subconscious,* or *unconscious.* Paul simply used available terminology for *depths of the human self* which may now be described in the more developed language of modern psychology. The conclusions of Bultmann, Jewett, Stendahl, Theissen, and others establish this claim beyond all reasonable doubt. The one proviso is, once again, to heed our own warning that of various **species of tongues**, in principle some manifestations may fall outside this category.

Stendahl also begins his essay on "Glossolalia" in the NT in the same place as that which is emphasized by a more "Pentecostalist" writer, F. D. Macchia. Both focus on a study of "unspeakable groanings" or "Sighs Too Deep for Words" and "he who searches the hearts . . . the Spirit" in Rom 8:26 and 27.[288] The "groaning" is a longing for the eschatological completion of redemption to take place, prompted *by* the Spirit *through* Christ *to* God, like all authentic Christian prayer. This befits the believer's experience of weakness. To be sure, E. Käsemann, whose "antienthusiastic" polemic is well known, discusses Rom 8:26-27 in his essay "The Cry for Liberty in the Worship of the Church," and concludes that for Paul prayer is never "wordless" although it may be "unspeakable." Käsemann writes: "In an unmistakably Pauline paradox the apostle describes as sighs what the church considers and praises as the manifestation of heavenly tongues, and thus compares them with the sighs of the creature and sighing for redemption from bodily temptation *(Anfechtung)*

287. Bultmann, *Theology of the New Testament,* 1:223.
288. Stendahl, "Glossolalia — The NT Evidence," in his *Paul among Jesus and Gentiles,* 111; cf. 109-24; rpt. from Hamilton (ed.), *The Charismatic Movement,* 49-60; see also Macchia, "Groans Too Deep for Words: Towards a Theology of Tongues," 47-73.

which is familiar to every Christian. To break up this paradox is to miss the theme of the text."[289] But Käsemann fully recognizes that both Rom 8:26-27 and 1 Cor 14:21-22 (and 13:1) allude to the promise that in the end time the language and fulfillment of heavenly bliss will be fully revealed, while that time is "not yet" amid the pressures, temptations, and pilgrimage of the present situation. Glimpses of a promised future sustain the church in times of temptation *(Anfechtung),* suffering, longing, and building. As in 1 Cor 1:18–2:5, the *theologia gloriae* of Corinthian enthusiasts is viewed by Paul within the framework of the *theologia crucis.*[290] Käsemann diagnoses the situation as one of contrast between Corinthian "religiosity" and Paul's understanding of Christian doxological worship as "in solidarity with creation."[291]

It is striking to find Stendahl and Käsemann, who differ so radically on some fundamental issues in Paul, agreeing that "the gift of glossolalia is not a sign of spiritual accomplishment" which is "not suited for evangelism or for publicity. It can become divisive. . . ."[292] It may be "wise to let glossolalia gush forth . . . so that those who are not professional in the shaping of words are free to express freely their overwhelmed praise to the Lord."[293] On the other hand, "few human beings can live healthily with high-voltage religious experience over a long period of time."[294] Stendahl attempts not only to show the nature of the contrast between articulate and inarticulate expression, but also to show how this coheres with the theme of the body and limbs in 1 Cor 12:12-31. He writes, "Thus *we* need *them*" [Stendahl means that the literate and articulate need warmly committed charismatic enthusiasts] and *they* need *us* [enthusiasts need the literate and articulate for growth and development; Stendahl's italics]." "The eye cannot say to the hand, 'I have no need of you . . .'" (12:21; cf. 12:29-31). While we cannot be certain that this is the precise application of 12:21, in a broad sense the principle constitutes a coherent whole, in Stendahl's account of the issues.

Without doubt, however, Theissen's treatment is the most detailed, incisive, and innovative, and sheds much light on the issues. He shows beyond doubt that *Paul, glossolaliasts at Corinth, and inspired speech in the external Graeco-Roman world are all to be viewed and understood differently, but with points of overlap.*

(a) Paul and the Corinthians agree that **tongues** have "a personal value for the individual. One who speaks in tongues edifies oneself (1 Cor. 14:4)."[295]

289. Käsemann, "The Cry for Liberty in the Church's Worship," in his *Perspectives on Paul,* 132; cf. 122-37.

290. Ibid., 135-36; cf. also his *Commentary on Romans* (Eng. trans., London: SCM, 1973), 242.

291. For a critical appreciation of Käsemann's view, see D. V. Way, *The Lordship of Christ: Ernst Käsemann's Interpretation of Paul's Theology* (Oxford: Clarendon Press, 1991), 269-76.

292. Stendahl, "Glossolalia," 111 and 113.

293. Ibid., 122.

294. Ibid., 123.

295. Theissen, *Psychological Aspects,* 304.

"Feelings of happiness" or of release, intimacy with God, or other "positive inner consequences are then a motive for repetition of the behavior."[296] But here Paul, unlike many at Corinth, feels unease. For the main need is *the common good,* and **tongues**, at least in public, can become divisive.

(b) **Tongues** can become divisive for at least three reasons. First, they can become specific to a given group within the church (cf. do all **speak in tongues?** 12:30). This can lead to "an emotional bond," and **tongues** can become a badge of membership in a subgroup within the church, with "a tendency to make glossolalia the decisive criterion of belonging to the group."[297] Hence its visibility as a gift which can be misused to this effect accounts for an apparent contradiction between 14:22 and 14:24-25. Second, Theissen links this phenomenon with what J. P. Kildahl identifies as a "dependency syndrome": "I belong to Paul," "I belong to Apollos . . ." (discussed above on 1:12 largely in the sociopolitical terms advanced by Chow, Mitchell, Witherington, and Pogoloff).[298] Hurd suggests that Paul himself may have more of this gift in his earlier ministry than he now wishes he had.[299] While caution should be observed about "reading back" any characteristics identified in modern Pentecostal or charismatic movements onto the Pauline text, E. Best has urged that to ignore possible affinities and aids to understanding would be to deprive the interpreter of a needed tool, provided that judicious care is retained.[300] Third, and most important, W. J. Hollenweger, followed by Theissen and Dale B. Martin, argues for the *social status* significance of **tongues** as a major factor at Corinth.[301] The church, we have noted above, embodied widely differing social stratification. Hollenweger portrays the educated, literate property owner or even slave secretary readily appealing to scripture and to argument, while nonliterate slaves or menial free persons might prefer to invoke the findings of heightened consciousness in **tongues**.

Even if we dismiss rival appeals to Word and Spirit as speculative, there can be little doubt that factors of temperament, gender, and social status played some role in the bonding of subgroups within the church. Theissen writes: "The 'strong' who were free with regard to ancient food taboos . . . who favored openness to the world in eating would probably also feel repelled by an esoteric group language. Conversely, glossolalia could have exerted great attraction for the less educated and 'the weak.'"[302] Theissen also anticipates Wire in arguing that "glossolalia occurred more frequently in women," partly as an inference from 14:33b-36.[303]

---

296. Ibid.
297. Ibid., 294.
298. Ibid., 299; cf. 297-300, and Kildahl, *The Psychology of Speaking in Tongues,* 44-50.
299. Hurd, *Origin of 1 Corinthians,* 243-44, partly on the basis of 2:4 as against 13:11.
300. Best, "The Interpretation of Tongues," 45-62.
301. Hollenweger, *Conflict in Corinth and Memoirs of an Old Man,* 28-31; Martin, *The Corinthian Body,* 87-103.
302. Theissen, *Psychological Aspects,* 301; cf. 300-304.
303. Ibid., 302.

Tongues may then be viewed as "the language of the unconscious" because it is unintelligible (unless it is "interpreted") not only to others but also to the speaker.[304] In 14:11 "foreign language" is unintelligible to the listener but intelligible to the speaker. But this represents "a logical jump." Paul prepares to urge "*the speaker, not the listener*" (my italics) "to pray for the power to interpret," i.e., to articulate what he or she utters, bringing it up from levels of unconscious depths to those of cognitive consciousness.[305] This is precisely the understanding of 14:13 which I proposed in 1979, drawing both on exegesis and on lexicographical explorations of διερμηνεύειν in Philo and in Josephus.[306] Paul does not say that the glossolalist *does* understand his or her utterances, but that he *wishes* that they would, and urges them to pray for this further gift.[307] Usually the gift of **tongues** is given "to one," and **intelligible articulation of tongues-speech** "to another" (12:10). But ideally "one and the same person can possess both gifts," as 14:27-28 probably presupposes, and as I argued in my 1979 article.[308] Theissen convincingly concludes that "glossolalia is language of the unconscious — language capable of consciousness."[309]

Glossolalia, therefore, makes "unconscious depth dimensions of life accessible," which may involve "reassumption of a more primitive level of speaking" to which many at times regress as "a return to egocentric use of language" and is likely to constitute "socially learned behavior."[310] Theissen appeals to 14:4, 20 (cf. 13:11; 14:21). We must postpone further comments until our exegesis of 14:2-38. However, we shall see that it lends further plausibility, over against a publicly reinforced, learned behavior which becomes a socially public habit, to Paul's triple strategy: first, to establish a hierarchy of gifts based on Christomorphic service to others and love for others; second, to "privatize" glossolalia in the home (as both Theissen and Wire stress); and, third, to encourage prayer for the gift of articulating buried longings, yearning, and emotions. Paul does not appear to endorse a view found in some modern churches that public tongues-speech is attractive and melodious; again, assumptions of a one-to-one match between ancient and modern phenomena remain speculative. Meanwhile, Paul see **tongues** as a genuine gift of the Spirit which can help the individual, but subject to the three factors outlined above. Rom 8:26-27 should be kept in mind.

11 Virtually every Greek word and phrase takes up the vocabulary of 12:4-7, to recapitulate the principles articulated in vv. 4-7 and to summarize the

---

304. Ibid., 304; also 79.

305. Ibid., 305.

306. Thiselton, "The 'Interpretation' of Tongues? A New Suggestion in the Light of Greek Usage in Philo and Josephus," 15-36.

307. Theissen, *Psychological Aspects,* 305.

308. Ibid.; and Thiselton, "Interpretation," 33-36. Many VSS intrude a Greek τις into 14:13 which is not in the text.

309. Theissen, *Psychological Aspects,* 306.

310. Ibid., 306, 312, 313, and 292.

trinitarian theology behind 12:4-10. The key phrase καθὼς βούλεται recalls the gift character of the Spirit's endowments, and the divine decision of grace as against human preferences or strivings. "The Spirit chooses what gift shall be given to each Christian, so that none has occasion for boasting, or for a sense of inferiority."[311] The principle anticipates the variety of modes of existence discussed in 15:38 in the context of resurrection: ὁ δὲ θεὸς δίδωσιν αὐτῷ σῶμα καθὼς ἠθέλησεν, καὶ ἑκάστῳ . . . ἴδιον σῶμα. While Fee, Wright, and Maly stress the variety of God's gifts of the Spirit, Lategan, Theissen, and D. B. Martin see a still more important emphasis on the unity.[312] But this dialectic precisely reflects the outworking in the life of Christian believers as part of creation (Käsemann) of the trinitarian pattern πνεῦμα . . . κύριος . . . θεός . . . expounded in vv. 4-6. God is essentially **one**, as an "ordered" being, but manifests himself in acts of the Spirit, acts of the Lord, and acts of God, both jointly and in differentiated ways. Any account of "spiritual gifts" which is merely Spirit-centered rather than Christomorphic (12:3) and trinitarian (12:4-6) is untrue to Paul. Nevertheless, the Spirit has an especially close association with the nine gifts (12:7-10).

Since Paul has already used the vocabulary in vv. 4-6, little more need be added on specific words. πάντα δὲ ταῦτα needs to be translated in a way which recognizes its emphatic position in Paul's word order. On the translation **activates** (as also NRSV), see above on v. 6, where ἐνεργεῖ occurs in a different grammatical form. The neuter singular participle διαιροῦν, **apportioning**, occurs in the form of the plural noun διαιρέσεις in v. 4, where it also means *distributions, allocations,* or **apportionings** (see on v. 4). The phrase τὸ δὲ αὐτὸ πνεῦμα, **the same Spirit**, also occurs in v. 4 (see above, where some MS variants insert ἕν, probably through assimilation with this verse in scribal memories). To each, ἑκάστῳ, also occurred in v. 7 (cf. 15:38). The one fresh word, apart from **as he wills**, is ἴδια, which is used here in its adverbial sense to mean *privately* or **individually**. If no single individual is likely to receive the full range of the gifts of the Spirit, **each** needs others also; hence 12:12-31 expound this principle.

4. The Image of the Body of Christ and Its Dual Rhetorical Function (12:12-30)

(12) For just as the body is one, and has many limbs and organs, and all the limbs and organs of the body, although they are many, constitute a single body, even so this is the case with Christ. (13) For we were all baptized by one Spirit into one body, whether Jews or Gentiles, whether slaves or free people. Of one Spirit were we all given to drink our fill. (14, 15) For the body is not a

---

311. Barrett, *First Epistle*, 286.
312. See on previous verse, and Maly, *Mündige Gemeinde*, 240-41; cf. 240-47.

single entity but many. If the foot should say, "Because I am not a hand, I do not belong to the body," just because of this does it not belong to the body? (16, 17) And if the ear should say, "Because I am not an eye, I do not belong to the body." On that score does it any the less belong to the body? If the whole body were an eye, where would be the hearing? If the whole were an ear, where would the nose be? (18) But as it is, God placed the members, each single one of them, in the body as it seems good to him. (19) But if all were a single organ, in what would the body consist? (20) As it is, on the contrary, many limbs and organs, on one side, constitute a single body. (21) The eye cannot say to the hand, "I do not need you," or, again, the head cannot say to the feet, "I have no need of you." (22) On the contrary, even more to the point, those limbs and organs of the body which seem to be less endowed with power or status than others are essential. (23) And on what we deem to be less honorable parts of the body we invest with greater honor, and our un- presentable private parts have greater adornment to make them presentable. (24) Our presentable parts do not need this. But God composed the body, giv- ing to that which feels inferior greater honor. (25) He purposed that there should be no split within the body, but that its limbs and organs might share the same concern for one another. (26) So if one limb or organ suffers, all the parts of the body suffer with it; or if one limb or organ is praised, all the members of the body share in the congratulations.

(27) Now you yourselves are Christ's body, and each of you, for his or her part, limbs or organs of it. (28) And God has placed in the church, first, some who are apostles; second, prophets; third, teachers; then effective deeds of power, then gifts of healing, various kinds of administrative support, ability to formulate strategies, various kinds of tongues. (29, 30) All are not apostles, are they? Surely all are not prophets? Could all be teachers? Do all perform effective deeds of power? Does everyone have gifts to heal in various ways? Surely all do not speak in tongues, do they? Do all put the deepest se- cret things into articulate speech?

Few terms have undergone so many twists and turns in the history of Pauline scholarship than *body* and *body of Christ*. At first sight the logic of Paul's argu- ment clearly develops the theme of unity-with-diversity (Lategan) or diversity- in-unity (Fee) already established in 12:4-11. The so-called "weak" must not feel that if they happen not to have received certain gifts, they are somehow not a genuine part of the body: "If the foot should say, 'Because I am not a hand, I do not belong to the body,' that would not make it any less part of the body" (12:15). Paul reassures those who are anxious about comparisons with suppos- edly more "gifted" members, and underlines their role, status and welcome. On the other side, he rebukes "the strong" who seem to think that only those of similar social status and similar spiritual gifts are "real" Christians: "The eye cannot say to the hand, 'I have no need of you' . . ." (12:20-21). Deluz observes, "Having spoken to those who have an inferiority complex, Paul now turns to those who are convinced that they know best and want to get everything into their own hands."[1] With Mitchell, this argument concerning mutuality and reciprocity is identified by J. Smit as "the deliberative genre" with its appeal to advantage (cf. 12:7, πρὸς τὸ συμφέρον) for the whole body (see above).[2]

Yet an earlier era of Pauline scholarship from A. Schweitzer to J. A. T. Robinson suggested that Paul uses far more than a metaphor or analogy. For them, μέλη πολλά and ἕν σῶμα *are* ὁ Χριστός (12:12). Schweitzer writes: "In the whole literature of mysticism there is no problem comparable to this of the mystical body of Christ. How could a thinker come to produce this conception of the extension of the body of a personal being?"[3] He adds: "All attempts to distinguish in the relevant passages between the personal (historical) and mystical body of Christ are initially doomed to failure. The obscurity was intended by Paul."[4] On this basis a number of writers, especially in English Anglo-Catholicism from the 1920s to the 1950s, spoke frequently of the church as "the extension of the incarnation" or of "no Christ without the Church . . . his mystical body."[5] J. A. T. Robinson sees the origin of Paul's identifying the Christian community with Christ's raised body in his conversion experience: "Saul, why are you persecuting *me?*" (Acts 9:4-5; 22:7-8). The resurrection body of Christ is revealed *"not as an individual, but as the Christian community"* (Robinson's italics).[6] Certainly, for Robinson, the language of **members** must be disengaged from the modern meaning of *members of a social group.*

Thus the ecclesiological-pastoral emphasis of Deluz and most of the older modern commentators became transposed into a rhetoric which depended not on analogy or metaphor with *body* as such, but specifically with *Christology.* No one must disinherit or tear away limbs of Christ, and no subgroup can claim to be "the whole Christ." But from 1955, with the work of E. Best, followed in 1964 and 1971 by that of D. E. H. Whiteley and others, these approaches of Schweitzer and Robinson were deemed to overpress their approach, and perhaps to fail to attend sufficiently to the context of argument in 1 Corinthians (Best) and "to complicate" at least as much as "illuminate" Paul's arguments (Whiteley).[7] Not least, Robinson appealed too readily to a "Hebraic" cast of mind and paid little attention to any Graeco-Roman background. Käsemann's later work attacks the kind of approach explored by Robinson and Schweitzer, even if his earlier work was marred by overattention to gnosticism.[8] Best allows that Paul offers a christo-

---

1. Deluz, *Companion to 1 Cor,* 180-81.

2. Mitchell, *Paul and the Rhetoric of Reconciliation,* 268-70; Smit, "Argument and Genre of 1 Cor 12–14," in Porter and Olbright (eds.), *Rhetoric and the NT,* 224-25; cf. 211-30.

3. Schweitzer, *Mysticism of Paul the Apostle,* 116; cf. 101-40.

4. Ibid., 118.

5. Thornton, *The Common Life in the Body of Christ,* 310; cf. 315.

6. Robinson, *The Body,* 58; cf. also 78-79.

7. Best, *One Body in Christ,* 96, esp. n. 1; Whiteley, *Theology of St. Paul,* 190-98, esp. 192-95.

8. Käsemann, "The Motif of the Body of Christ," in *Perspectives on Paul,* 102-21, esp. 110-14; cf. his earlier *Leib und Leib Christi,* which relies too heavily on gnostic sources.

logical foundation for his argument, but returns to a dialectic between diversity (gifts in the church) and unity (Christ).[9] Where more recent writers associate *unity* with "rhetoric," however, Best draws on "corporate personality" in the OT. On the other hand, recent writers continue to engage with Robinson's approach alongside that of Käsemann. Schrage, e.g., gives space to their ecclesiology.[10]

We need not trace every twist and turn since Best and Whiteley. A more recent emphasis is represented most constructively and distinctively by M. M. Mitchell and D. B. Martin, who perceive this not simply as a rhetoric of belonging, harmony, and unity-in-diversity, but as a term or turn of phrase *loaded with a political history.*[11] However Paul may have wished to utilize the language for theological purposes, it would be *heard by the addressees* as language traditionally used to argue for *unity on the basis of a hierarchical political structure.* However, earlier commentators had also noted the Graeco-Roman background. Thus Heinrici (1880), e.g., cites "among the parallels" the parable or allegory of Menenius Agrippa's address to the rebel workers in Livy, *Ab Urbe Condita* 2.32; Cicero *De Officiis* 1.35; Marcus Aurelius, 4.40; 7.13; Seneca, *Epistles* 95, among Latin writers alone.[12] Best had examined such sources, together with Käsemann's hypothesis about gnostic influences, but had concluded: "the presence of the metaphor in Greek culture is not the occasion of Paul's description of the Church as 'Body of Christ.'"[13] However, for Mitchell and Martin the history of the term as *sociopolitical rhetoric* is what leads them to a new appraisal of the impact of its background.

Margaret M. Mitchell, with Collins and Wolff, traces back the use of the term *body* as a rhetorical appeal for *harmony and interdependence* in political life from the fifth and fourth centuries BC (including Plato's *Republic*) through to the first and second centuries AD (including Dio Chrysostom's *Orations*).[14] The parallels with detailed parts of the imagery in Paul in the late first-century writers Plutarch and Epictetus are especially noteworthy. Plutarch cites the interdependence and mutual benefit of the *eyes, ears, hands,* and *feet* of the *body* (cf. 1 Cor 12:15, *hands* and *feet;* 12:16-17, *eyes* and *ears*).[15] Epictetus speaks of the mutual *advantage* (τὸ συμφέρον, 1 Cor. 12:7) of the harmonious function of the whole body.[16] Mitchell notes that even in Dionysius of

---

9. Best, *One Body in Christ,* 96-104.

10. Schrage, *Der erste Brief,* 3:210-16, for a detailed discussion (including speculations about an Adam figure).

11. Mitchell, *Paul and the Rhetoric of Reconciliation,* 68-83 and 157-64; Martin, *The Corinthian Body,* 38-68 and 87-103.

12. Heinrici, *Das erste Sendschreiben,* 396-97, esp. n. 1.

13. Best, *One Body,* 85.

14. Cf. Mitchell, *Rhetoric of Reconciliation,* 158-60, esp. nn. 556-76; and, e.g., Dio Chrysostom, *Orations* 1.32; 3.104-7; 17.19; 34.23; 50.3; Plato, *Republic* 5.470C-D and 2.370A-B; cf. 1.352E-54. Similarly, see Collins, *First Cor,* 458-60; Wolff, "Exkurs: Die Gemeinde als 'Leib,'" in *Der erste Brief,* 301-5, esp. 303.

15. Plutarch, *Moralia,* 478D; cf. 812C-E; 819C; and Dio Chrysostom, *Orations* 1.32; 39.5.

16. Epictetus, *Dissertations* 2.10.4–10.5: a citizen is not to treat the matter merely for "pri-

Halicarnassus (c. 30 BC) personifications of the parts of the body occur, as in 1 Cor 12:15-16, "If the foot should say, 'Because I am not the hand, I do not belong to the body.' . . ."[17] She concludes, "Paul's uniformity of use of this metaphor with ancient political writers applies even to the details."[18] In 1 Corinthians, she urges, the image in 1 Corinthians 12 looks back directly to the main proposition or rhetorical thesis of the epistle, namely, what she perceives as a *polemic against factionalism* in 1:10. The theme of σχίσμα (1:10) is explicitly taken up in 12:25 as the climax of the application of the *body* image. This use of body is a common rhetorical *topos, or a set example* for the purpose. The emphasis falls on *unity* (with Martin and Lategan, against Fee).

Dale B. Martin not only endorses Mitchell's arguments, but presses them further. Both the human body and the political body are "a hierarchy, with different members (. . . classes) assigned by Nature to positions in the body and to particular roles."[19] "*Homonoia* speeches always assume that the body is hierarchically constituted and that illness or social disruption occurs when that hierarchy is disrupted."[20] A *locus classicus* is thus the use of the *body topos* by Livy, who places it on the lips of the Senator Menenius to persuade the plebeians, who have gone on strike, to return to work.[21] The active *members* or *limbs* (the workers or plebs) fail to feed the *belly* (*patres* or governing classes). But if the belly dies, the whole body dies. Hence, Martin concludes, the *topos* is a typical "high-status" argument for each to have a proper place within a conservative system. Polybaenus (c. AD 162) likewise uses the *topos* for "ideological" purposes.[22] Martin has not yet stated *his conclusions* about how Paul *applies* this ideological rhetoric. Paul utilizes it, in a sense, to turn it upside down, just as he turns a status system upside down in 1:18–2:5.[23] But this is the appropriate point of departure for an exegesis of our passage.

An archaeological display at the museum of ancient Corinth provides an unforgettable presentation of an extensive collection of terra-cotta models of disjointed, isolated parts of the human body found on the site of the Asklepion. G. G. Garner is among those who have drawn attention to the significance of this collection for our appreciation of Corinthian attention to body parts in this context, although his speculative suggestion that the Temple of Asklepios (Asclepius) might have suggested to Paul the metaphor of "disjointed" parts is unlikely in view of the use of the metaphor widely in an-

---

vate profit," as if he or she were "a detached unit," but to act like the foot or hand . . . with reference to the whole."

17. Dionysius of Halicarnassus, *Roman Antiquities* 6.86.2; cf. Mitchell, *Rhetoric of Reconciliation,* 159.

18. Mitchell, *Rhetoric,* 159.

19. Martin, *The Corinthian Body,* 39.

20. Ibid., 40.

21. Livy, *Ab Urbe Condita* 2.32.7-11; Martin, *The Corinthian Body,* 93.

22. Polybaenus, *Stratagems of War* 3.9.22; Martin, *The Corinthian Body,* 93-94.

23. Martin, *The Corinthian Body,* 94-103; cf. 38-63. Cf. further Wire, *The Corinthian Women Prophets,* 135-49.

cient literature.[24] Collins is on safer ground in calling attention to the collection to underline the self-awareness of "members of the body" at Corinth to which the cult of Asklepios contributed.[25]

Supplementary Bibliography on 12:12-30. (See also above on 12:1–14:40.)

Amiot, F., *The Key Concepts of St Paul* (Eng. trans., Freiburg: Herder, 1962), 204-30.

Archer, K. L., "Pentecostal Hermeneutics: Retrospect and Prospect," *Journal of Pentecostal Theology* 8 (1996): 63-81.

Barth, M., "A Chapter on the Church — The Body of Christ: Interpretation of 1 Corinthians 12," *Int* 24 (1958): 131-56.

Best, E., *One Body in Christ* (London: SPCK, 1955), esp. 74-114 (95-114 explicitly on 1 Cor 12:12-27).

Bonnard, P.-E., "L'Église corps du Christ dans le paulinisme," *RThPh* 8 (1958): 268-82.

Bruner, F. D., *A Theology of the Holy Spirit: The Pentecostal Experience and the NT Witness* (Grand Rapids: Eerdmans, 1970), 56-129, 286-301.

Cerfaux, L., *The Church in the Theology of St. Paul* (Freiburg: Herder, 1959), 262-87.

Dawes, G. W., *The Body in Question: Metaphor and Meaning in the Interpretation of Eph 5:21-33,* BibInt 30 (Leiden: Brill, 1998), 1-78.

Dunn, J. D. G., *Baptism in the Holy Spirit* (London: SCM, 1970), 107-17 and 127-31.

———, "The Body of Christ in Paul," in M. J. Wilkins and T. Paige (eds.), *Worship, Theology and Ministry in the Early Church,* JSNTSS 87 (Sheffield: JSOT Press, 1992), 146-62.

———, *The Theology of Paul the Apostle* (Edinburgh: T. & T. Clark, 1998), 548-52, 582-84.

Eriksson, A., *Traditions as Rhetorical Proof: Pauline Argumentation in 1 Corinthians,* ConBNT 29 (Stockholm: Almqvist & Wiksell, 1998), 127-34 and 223-30.

Fee, G., *Paul, the Spirit, and the People of God* (Peabody, Mass.: Hendrickson, 1996).

Flemington, W. F., *The NT Doctrine of Baptism* (London: SPCK, 1957), 55-59.

Fung, R. Y. K., "Ministry, Community and Spiritual Gifts," *EvQ* 56 (1984): 3-20.

Garner G. G., "The Temple of Asklepius at Corinth and Paul's Teaching," *Buried History* 18 (1982): 52-58.

Gundry, R. H., *Sōma in Biblical Theology,* SNTSMS 29 (Cambridge: Cambridge University Press, 1976).

Hill, A. E., "The Temple of Asklepius: An Alternative Source for Paul's Body Theology," *JBL* 99 (1980): 437-39.

Irvin, D. T., "Drawing All Together in One Bond of Love," *Journal of Pentecostal Theology* 6 (1995): 27-32.

Jewett, R., *Paul: Anthropological Terms* (Leiden: Brill, 1971), 201-304.

Käsemann, E., *Leib und Leib Christi* (Tübingen: Mohr, 1933).

———, "The Theological Problem Presented by the Motif of the Body of Christ," in *Perspectives on Paul* (London: SCM and Philadelphia: Fortress, 1971), 102-21.

Macchia, F. D., "Tongues and Prophecy: A Pentecostal Perspective," *Conc* 3 (1996): 63-69.

24. Garner, "The Temple of Asklepius at Corinth and Paul's Teaching," *Buried History* 18 (1982): 52-58. Cf. also Hill, "The Temple of Asklepius: An Alternative Source for Paul's Body Theology," *JBL* 99 (1980): 437-39.

25. Collins, *First Cor,* 462.

Martin, D. B., *The Corinthian Body* (New Haven and London: Yale University Press, 1995), esp. 3-61 and 94-103.

Merk, O., *Handeln aus Glauben* (Marburg: Elwert, 1968), 141-45.

Mitchell, M. M., *Paul and the Rhetoric of Reconciliation* (Tübingen: Mohr, 1991).

Moltmann, J., "The Knowing of the Other and the Community of the Different," in Moltmann, *God for a Secular Society* (Eng. trans., London: SCM, 1999), 135-52.

Moule, C. F. D., *The Origins of Christology* (Cambridge: Cambridge University Press, 1978), 47-96.

Neyrey, J. H., "Body Language in 1 Cor: The Use of Anthropological Models . . .," *Semeia* 35 (1986): 129-70.

Perlewitz, M. F., "The Unity of the Body of Christ," *BibTod* 18 (1980): 384-92.

Perriman, "His Body, Which Is the Church . . . Coming to Terms with the Metaphor," *EvQ* 62 (1990): 123-42.

Robinson, J. A. T., *The Body: A Study in Pauline Theology* (London: SCM, 1952).

Schnackenburg, R., *Baptism in the Thought of Paul* (Oxford: Blackwell, 1964), 83-91.

Schweitzer, A., *The Mysticism of Paul the Apostle* (London: Black, 1931).

Schweizer, E., "The Church as the Missionary Body of Christ," *NTS* 8 (1961-62): 1-11.

———, "Die Kirche als Leib Christi in den paulinischen Homologoumena," *TLZ* 86 (1961): 161-74.

———, "σῶμα," *TDNT,* 7:1,024-94.

Smit, J. F. M., "Two Puzzles: 1 Cor 12:31 and 13:3: Rhetorical Solution," *NTS* 39 (1993): 246-64.

Wedderburn, A. J. M., "The Body of Christ and Related Concepts in 1 Cor," *SJT* 24 (1971): 74-96.

Wolff, C., "Exkurs: Die Gemeinde als 'Lieb,'" in *Der erste Brief des Paulus und die Korinther,* 301-5.

12   We have already noted the use of **body** (τὸ σῶμα) as a common *topos* in political rhetoric (see above, under introduction to 12:12-30). We noted parallels not only in Plato but also in Livy, Plutarch, Cicero, Dionysius of Halicarnassus, Epictetus, and other writers. It would be beyond doubt that the Corinthian addressees would be familiar with the ideological nuances of the image as one of order and hierarchy, given the understanding of **body** in the era of Paul. The older modern commentators miss the point if or when they interpret Paul's use of σῶμα as due to an inadequate conceptual expression for *person* in the ancient world.[26] The conjunction καθάπερ regularly introduces an analogical comparison, and means *even as* or **just as.**

We might more naturally expect the main clause which applies the analogical comparison to read **this is the case** (Gk. οὕτως, thus, so) *with the body of Christ,* rather than, as Paul states it, **this is the case with Christ** (οὕτως καὶ ὁ Χριστός). This difference lies behind the insistence of Schweitzer and Robinson that we are confronted here with more than an analogy or a metaphor,

---

26. Edwards tends to point the reader in the wrong direction, as against Martin, when he writes, "Thinkers in ancient times had a difficulty to express the notion of personality" (*First Epistle,* 325). This is not the reason for his use of *body.*

namely, an ontological identification between Christ and the church (see above, introduction to this passage). But the argument of 12:12-30 as a whole does not sustain this approach, as Best and Whiteley among others have well shown.[27] Käsemann carefully takes up the point: "Ecclesiological metaphysics are read even into the Pauline statements in a highly dangerous way. . . . To put the matter somewhat too epigrammatically, the apostle is not interested in the church *per se.* . . . He is only interested in it in so far as it is the means whereby Christ reveals himself on earth and becomes incarnate in the world through his Spirit."[28] This emphasis is what accounts for Paul's choice of syntax οὕτως καὶ ὁ Χριστός. While Robinson and Schweitzer overstate a christological metaphysic, it must be conceded that Mitchell and Martin (and most "rhetorical" approaches to these chapters) seriously understate the christological focus. Martin comes near to rescuing Christology, however, by rightly associating rhetorical "status reversals" in 12:12-30 with the argument of 1:18–2:5 (see below), and Schrage (see n. 27) tries to hold together Christology and analogy.

It is partly to emphasize this christological point that, just as we translated μέλη Χριστοῦ as **limbs and organs** *of Christ* in 6:15, so here *members,* as Robinson urges, cannot easily be disengaged from the modern notion of being *members* of a corporate social institution, which is precisely *not* Paul's thought (cf. also REB's *many* **limbs and organs**). On the other hand, REB's **Christ** *is like a single body* . . . seems to pre-judge a particular interpretation of the verse. Although our translation may entail a minor circumlocution for οὕτως καί, **even so this is the case with Christ** seems the best way of conveying Paul's emphasis after the elaboration of the **"for just as . . ."** comparison. It is the use of the *political body–rhetoric* that is the object of comparison; **Christ** remains the main *subject* whom the rhetoric serves, as an analogy which later will be given an unexpected twist by "code switching" what appears to be an unqualified hierarchy. (On code switching, see on Eco and Moores, above.) Christ retains an emphatic position as a nominative at the end of the long sentence; next in emphasis is the *unity* of the **one body** (τὸ σῶμα ἕν ἐστιν); only in third place comes the variety or plurality of the **limbs and organs** or *members* (τὰ μέλη). This is what we should expect regarding the priority of *unity* in the light of the comments of Lategan, Mitchell, and Martin (see above). Probably the participle ὄντα, *being many,* functions as a concessive clause: **although they are many**, though conceivably it functions neutrally or contrastively to mean *while they are many.*

---

27. Cf. Best, *One Body in Christ,* 96-104, and the introduction to 12:12-30. Together with Schweitzer and Robinson, Cerfaux moves too far in this direction (*The Church in the Theology of St. Paul,* 262-87). As Barrett urges, an "identification" would be "unthinkable" for Paul, who has just stressed Christ's Lordship over the church (12:3) and thereby his implicit distinction from it (*First Epistle,* 288). Schrage (*Der erste Brief,* 3:213) concedes that this functions as analogy, but contends that other uses of **body** as the body of Christ in Paul press this further.

28. Käsemann, "The Motif of the Body of Christ," in his *Perspectives on Paul,* 110 and 117; cf. 102-21. Certainly Paul's placing Christ at the center marks off his use of *body* from Stoic appeals to "natural" order alone (Héring, *First Epistle,* 130).

13 A well-known decision which translators and interpreters are required to make is whether to understand ἐν ἑνὶ πνεύματι (v. 13) as *locative* indicating sphere *in the one Spirit* (NRSV, JB, Collins); *in one Spirit* (RV, REB, Barrett); or *in a single Spirit* (NJB); or as *instrumental* indicating agency: **by one Spirit** (AV/KJV, RSV, NASB, NIV, Moffatt [although NIV adds a footnote, *with* or *in*]). All the main modern translations render εἰς ἓν σῶμα as **into one body** (NRSV, REB, NIV, NJB). One of the most careful and meticulous writers on baptism in Paul, however, namely R. Schnackenburg, recognizes that ἐν here might mean either *with,* **by,** *in,* or even *for* (although for himself he chooses an instrumental translation) and that εἰς, while it may be translated **into,** often signifies "direction of faith" rather than "movement."[29] Conzelmann and others seem to think that *in one Spirit* better anticipates the notion that the aorist passive ἐποτίσθημεν in v. 13b means *drenched in, plunged in, saturated, imbued,* or *submerged in,* the Spirit as a kind of baptismal medium.[30] Weiss, Lietzmann, Parry, and Allo favor this interpretation.[31] Yet even if this interpretation is adopted, the probability that ἐν with the dative denotes *agency* carries no less force. Moreover, the meaning of ἐποτίσθημεν brings its own problems with it. In the ancient church Cyril of Alexandria, in the medieval period Thomas Aquinas and Estius, among the Reformers Luther, and in the modern period Cerfaux, Wendland, Heinrici, and Käsemann argue for the view set forth above.[32] Calvin and Conzelmann consider this view possible but not certain.[33] We shall return to this word. Meanwhile, the instrumental force of ἐν, **by one Spirit**, is supported by Oepke, Moffatt, Cullmann, Cerfaux, Flemington, and others.[34]

The fundamental sense of the verse is clear. The previous verse had concluded with ὁ Χριστός as the focus of unity. Paul amplifies this unity by speaking of the common agency and experience of **one Spirit** and **one body** as focused in the very baptism that proclaimed and marked their turning to Christ and their new identity as people of the Spirit. But **all** participated in this, whatever the variety and difference of their pre-Christian status (or "natural" status) as **Jews** or **Gentiles**, or as **slaves** or **freepeople**. *Any theology that might imply that this one*

---

29. Schnackenburg, *Baptism in the Thought of St. Paul,* 22-24 and 83-86.

30. Conzelmann, *1 Cor,* 212, esp. n. 17.

31. Robertson and Plummer, *First Epistle,* 272; Weiss, *Der erste Korintherbrief,* 303-4; Lietzmann, *An die Korinther,* 63; Allo, *Première Épitre,* 329-30, and "Excursus," 91-112; Parry, *First Epistle,* 184; Kling, *First Epistle,* 254.

32. Cf., e.g., Cyril of Alexandria, *Frag. in Ep. 1 ad Cor.* (Lib. 5), 290-91; also Migne (ed.), *PG,* 74:889A-B (although this is partly by assimilating 1 Cor 12:13 with John); Thomas Aquinas, *1 ad Cor. Lect.,* 374, sects. 734-35; Cerfaux, *Church,* 171-72; Heinrici, *Das erste Sendschreiben,* 400-402; Wendland, *Die Briefe,* 111-12.

33. Calvin, *First Epistle,* 265, observes, "It is not certain whether here he is speaking about baptism or the Lord's Supper"; cf. Conzelmann, *1 Cor,* 212, n. 17.

34. Oepke, "βαπτίζειν," *TDNT,* 1:539; Moffatt, *First Epistle,* 186; Cullmann, *Baptism in the NT,* 30; Cerfaux, *The Church in the Theology of St. Paul,* 302; Flemington, *The NT Doctrine of Baptism,* 56-57. (For exponents of the locative view, see above.)

baptism in 13a in which believers were **baptized by** [or *in*] **one Spirit** *might mark off some postconversion experience or status enjoyed only by some Christians attacks and undermines Paul's entire argument and emphasis.* Paul's constant use of ἕν, **one**, and πάντες, **all**, *constitutes a direct onslaught against categorization or elitism within the church.* As Mitchell and Martin (among others) have decisively shown, this argument picks up the categorizations which Paul attacks in 1:10-12. The **all** and the reference to transcending the Jew-Gentile, male-female, slave-free divisions of Paul's day reflect the reference to baptism in Gal. 3:27-28. Dunn demonstrates links between these three major passages.[35]

"SPIRIT-BAPTISM" IN RELATION TO 12:13 IN PENTECOSTAL TRADITIONS

This specific verse has particular importance within Pentecostal thought because it is the only verse in the NT which explicitly uses the phrase **baptized by** (or *in*) [**one**] **Spirit**. Donald Dayton and other historians of the Pentecostal movement identify the "four themes" of (i) salvation; (ii) baptism in the Holy Spirit; (iii) healing; and (iv) looking for the final ("second") coming of Christ as "well-nigh universal within the movement."[36] Especially if Charles Parham is regarded as the founder of Pentecostalism, followed by William Seymour, "the baptism of the Holy Spirit" was already central as a distinctive defining doctrine by 1899.[37] The main biblical material cited by way of comparison, however, is John 20:22 (the Spirit as anointing for apostolic preaching) and Acts 2:4. Speaking in tongues was regarded as, in effect, empirical evidence of baptism in (or of) the Holy Spirit. William Seymour, Parham's student, came to emphasize a glossolalia that was transethnic, transnational, and transeducational.[38] Seymour argued that glossolalia constituted *one* of the signs that verify Spirit-baptism alongside love and the fruit of the Spirit (Gal 5:22-23).[39] Holiness now becomes, in effect, a presupposition or condition for Spirit-baptism. The linchpin now becomes the issue of a replication of the experience on the day of Pentecost in Acts 2:1-2. Thus the Pentecostal writer T. B. Barratt argues: "What distinguishes us . . . (i.e., baptism with the Holy Spirit) is our definite claim to be baptized in the Holy Ghost in the same way as the 120 on the day of Pentecost, a Spirit-baptism accompanied by the speaking in tongues" (cf. Acts 2:1-12; 10:44-48; 11:15-18; 19:1-7).[40]

35. Dunn, *Baptism in the Holy Spirit,* 109-13, 117-20, and 127-31.

36. D. W. Dayton, *Theological Roots of Pentecostalism* (Metuchen, N.J.: Scarecrow Press, 1987), 22. In addition to primary sources listed in Brunner, *A Theology of the Holy Spirit: The Pentecostal Experience and NT Witness,* 346-76, I am also indebted to my doctoral research student, Mrs. Sarah Ahn.

37. Sarah Parham, *The Life of Charles F. Parham* (Joplin, Mo.: Hunter, 1930), 39; J. R. Goff, *Full White unto Harvest: Charles F. Parham and the Missionary Origins of Pentecostalism* (Fayetteville: University of Arkansas, 1988), 51-55.

38. Irvin, "Drawing All Together in One Bond of Love," 27-32; and C. M. Robeck, "William J. Seymour and 'the Biblical Evidence,'" in G. B. McGee (ed.), *Initial Evidence* (Peabody, Mass.: Hendrickson, 1991), 81.

39. Robeck, "William Seymour," 81.

40. N. Bloch-Hoell, *The Pentecostal Movement: Its Origin, Development and Distinctive Character* (Oslo: Universitetsforlaget, 1964), 1-2.

There is a growing recognition among more recent Pentecostal writers that the status of Acts as narrative (in Conzelmann's view, uniquely idealized narrative) and exegetical problems raised by the Pauline writings may call for a sophisticated hermeneutic, designated by Strondstad as a "pragmatic" hermeneutic.[41] While the stage of development at Azusa associated with Seymour coheres very well with the emphasis on unity in 1 Cor 12:12-30 as this has been explicated in terms of the contextual rhetoric surrounding 12:13 among such writers as Mitchell, Dale Martin, and Eriksson, the notion that **we were all baptized by one Spirit into one body** (v. 13) hardly coheres with reaching a prior level of practical holiness, still less with the second or third stage of a "full" gospel appreciated and experienced by some Christian believers but not others. Indeed, it appears to reverse the force and direction of Paul's rhetoric, reinforcing the *differences* claimed by those who called themselves "people of the Spirit" (πνευματικοί) at Corinth. This is not to question the authenticity of experiences which are given such names as "Spirit-baptism" or "speaking in tongues." It is to question whether this tradition can gain any terminological support from the single passage in the NT which employs this term. Meanwhile, the resultant problem of how research into Luke-Acts relates to a different situation addressed by Paul has become a hermeneutical issue which is increasingly recognized and appreciated among informed Pentecostal writers.

Whether Paul could or would have singled out the "four marks" of salvation, Spirit-baptism, healing, and a sense of eschatological imminence becomes dubious on the basis of 1 Corinthians 12–14. That he endorsed the notion of a dynamic experience of the Holy Spirit which transcended boundaries of race, class, culture, and status cannot be doubted.

One of the most constructive Pentecostal theological writers who emphasizes this aspect is F. D. Macchia. Macchia also engages with the exegetical work of James Dunn on Paul, and recognizes the significance of Rom 8:26 for a more ecumenical and psychologically credible understanding of "speaking in tongues."[42] Macchia recognizes the limitations of a disjunction between evidential appeal to Luke-Acts and appeals to "private devotion" in Paul. He concedes that while Paul does not cancel or invalidate Luke-Acts, Pauline exegesis sets limits on how Luke-Acts may be interpreted.[43] However, in relation to the early notion of "four marks," see especially below on the logic of 12:16-18.

Dunn writes, "As the one passage which speaks explicitly of baptism in the Spirit, 1 Cor. 12:13 is crucial for the Pentecostal."[44] He examines the counterarguments in favor of a "special" experience put forward by D. J. du Plessis, W. F. P. Burton,

---

41. R. Strondstad, "Trends in Pentecostal Hermeneutics," *Paraclete* 22 (1988): 1-3; cf. Fee, *Gospel and Spirit* (Peabody, Mass.: Hendrickson, 1991), 85-86; Archer, "Pentecostal Hermeneutics: Retrospect and Prospect," 63-81. On the broader hermeneutical issue a defense of postmodern pluralistic ethical pragmatism is defended by D. Patte, *Ethics of Biblical Interpretation: A Reevaluation* (Louisville: Westminster-Knox, 1995) and attacked by B. J. Malina, "Bible: Witness or Warrant: Reflections on Daniel Patte's *Ethics of Biblical Interpretation*," *BTB* 26 (1996): 82-87. In parallel, H. Räisänen, "Liberating Exegesis," *BJRL* 78 (1996): 193-204 attacks E. Schussler Fiorenza's pragmatic hermeneutic of "usefulness" in her reading of Revelation.

42. F. D. Macchia, "The Tongues of Pentecost: A Pentecostal Perspective on the Promise and Challenge of Catholic Dialogue," *JES* 35 (1998): 1-18, 127; see further reference above, n. 35.

43. Macchia, "Tongues and Prophecy: A Pentecostal Perspective," *Conc* 3 (1996): 63-69.

44. Ibid., 127.

K. Southworth, and M. C. Harper, but concludes: "In short, once the initiatory and incorporative significance of the metaphor is grasped, the Pentecostal arguments fall to the ground."[45] Dunn is well aware that some strands of Pentecostal traditions, especially in neo-Pentecostal or charismatic theologies, have abandoned this view. Further, "on the other side" he resists uncritical assumptions that water-baptism and the dawn of faith as a conversion experience are always temporally synonymous. "βαπτίζειν in itself does not specify *water*-baptism" (Dunn's italics).[46] Dunn has performed an important service in disengaging assumptions in NT scholarship which appear to tie the Spirit *invariably* to water-baptism, and the supposition that water-baptism *invariably* marks the beginning of the Christian life in Pauline thought. Fee also underlines this point in his comments on this verse.[47] Nevertheless, *within its historical context at Corinth* Paul doubtless regards such a link as a *general* norm, which brings together the four elements of his argument in 12:12-13: **Christ, one Spirit, one body**, one single new *status,* in which **all** believers share.

It is inadequate to consider the so-called Pentecostal understandings of 12:13, however, in isolation from other major Pauline epistles. For some appeal to the verb ἐποτίσθημεν in v. 13b to support some "second" decisive experience of the Spirit which may be associated with a so-called baptism of the Holy Spirit. Dunn combs through all the relevant passages and offers an observation on Gal 3:1-5, 14 which invites repetition here. He writes: "These verses are a crushing rejoinder to Pentecostalist ideas about the reception of the Spirit. The reception of the Spirit is the beginning of the Christian life (3:3-5). . . . The gift of the Spirit and justification are two sides of the one coin. . . . The gift of the Spirit is what makes us . . . sons of God. . . ."[48] Similarly, Gal. 3:26-27 concerns "a metaphor drawn from the rite of baptism to describe the entry of the believer into Christian experience."[49] In the context of baptism or of Christian experience (apart, we might suggest, from any specific gift for some specific ministry or task) "there is no talk of a subsequent coming of the Spirit."[50]

Apart from this the aorist passive ἐποτίσθημεν remains that which **all** (πάντες) believers without exception experience. In our view it is clearly epexegetic or explanatory of the preceding aorist passive ἐβαπτίσθημεν. The verb ποτίζω regularly means *to give someone something to drink* (Matt 25:35, 37; Mark 15:36; Rom 12:20) and was used in 1 Cor 3:2 of *giving the Corinthians milk to drink.* But in 1 Cor 3:6-8 its meaning was extended (as it is elsewhere) to *watering* or *irrigating* a field, and in 3:6-8 as a metaphor for nurturing the church in teaching and preaching.[51] In strictly linguistic terms it may therefore here denote either *being* **given the Spirit to drink** or *being*

45. Ibid., 129. On baptism in Paul, see also above on 6:9-11, 14.
46. Ibid.
47. Fee, *First Epistle,* 604-5.
48. Dunn, *Baptism,* 107-8.
49. Ibid., 109.
50. Ibid., 115. While Paul and the NT expound experience of the Holy Spirit primarily in terms of a permanent endowment which unites believers with Christ and guarantees future resurrection as an eschatological firstfruits and pledge, the OT often speaks of temporary endowments by the Spirit for specific tasks in an individual rather than corporate sense. Although in the NT the former aspect dominates, the latter scheme continues alongside union with Christ in terms of special endowments for ministries and tasks. But this is quite different from the classic Pentecostal notion of a "baptism in the Holy Spirit" for a group of Christians subsequent to becoming believers.
51. Cf. BAGD, 695.

watered, saturated, or *drenched in* **the Spirit**. Since Paul's emphasis lies on the *completeness and equality* of the redeemed and sanctified status of **all** who have been grafted into **Christ** (v. 12b) **by one Spirit** (i.e., "you all shared *the same* life-giving divine, saving action), we take up the subsidiary nuance of *drenching* (while avoiding any materialist sacramentalism extraneous to Paul) by translating **Of the Spirit were we all given to drink our fill**. This *excludes* an un-Pauline reading of the verse, and conveys his thought. Divisive antagonisms, Schrage concludes, are not to be brought back into the new world of Christ's body.[52]

Heinrici and Wendland are far from convincing in their attempt to argue that while v. 13a refers to water-baptism, v. 13b denotes the Lord's Supper. ποτίζω supposedly denotes "made to drink" of the cup of the Eucharist or Lord's Supper. Even if the aorist is understood to be gnomic rather than alluding to a single past event, a "timeless" aorist remains ravingly inappropriate for repeating the memorial of the Lord's Supper, which is not "timeless," but reenacts a temporal recital of a temporal event. Chrysostom, Bengel, de Wette, Meyer, and Godet more than counter the vague allusions of Cyril of Alexandria, the inclination but by no means firm conviction of Calvin, and the arguments of Heinrici and Wendland. Heinrici and Wendland tend to assume a theology of the two Dominical sacraments here, but without adequate grounds.[53] Godet, among others, asserts: "the expression to drink the Holy Spirit in the Supper is utterly foreign to the language of Scripture."[54] The connection of the whole verse with the baptismal theology of Gal. 3:27-28 in relation to the one new status of **all** (no subsequent experience necessary) and to the Christocentric and Christomorphic character of **the body** as derived through **Christ by the Spirit**, not by human initiative, is readily confirmed by E. Best and more recently by F. Lang.[55]

14-15 The interrogative form (v. 15) is doubtful. (The issue is discussed in the last paragraph of the exegesis.)

Although some commentators and other writers (Fee and G. Wright) stress the theme of variety throughout most of this chapter, while others stress Paul's focus on unity (Lategan, Mitchell, Martin), yet a third group perceive 12:1-13 as expounding the theme of unity, while 12:14-30 turns to the theme of variety (Conzelmann, Héring).[56] But while the principle that "all organic life manifests

52. Schrage, *Der erste Brief,* 3:217.
53. Heinrici, *Das erste Sendschreiben,* 400-401; Wendland, *Die Brief an die Korinther,* 112; Schrage, surprisingly, is sympathetic with the notion of an allusion either to water-baptism or the Lord's Supper, and finds this question difficult (*Der erste Brief,* 3:216). Collins speaks of a "Spirit-inspired ritual baptism as the act of incorporation into the one body" (*First Cor,* 463). Wolff alludes more generously to the moment of entry into the Christian community (*Der erste Brief,* 298).
54. Godet, *First Epistle,* 2:210.
55. Lang, *Die Briefe,* 171-72; Best, *One Body,* 96-98.
56. Conzelmann, *1 Cor,* 212; Héring, *First Epistle,* 130.

diversity" (Bittlinger) is true and is implicit in v. 14, the rhetorical history of **body** identified by Mitchell and Martin continues to influence the way in which Paul makes his main point in vv. 14-30.[57] We have already noted that in Plutarch's allusions to a **body's** having **hands** and **feet**, and in the personified dialogue between parts of **the body** in Dionysius of Halicarnassus, the context in each case is "a polemic against factionalism" (Mitchell) or an "ideological rhetoric" of "hierarchy" (Martin).[58] It is precisely *not* a late twentieth-century or early twenty-first-century "postmodern" assurance that within certain boundaries everyone "does one's own thing." The respective functions of hands, feet, (v. 15), ears, and eyes (v. 16) *coordinate* the organism as **one**. If each did not play his or her *assigned role,* the **one** body would collapse into a chaotic nonentity. Hence, v. 15 not only reassures those who feel inferior that they do indeed belong to **the body**, but also asserts the *necessity* for the *coherent unity* of the body both of those who feel inferior and to those who devalue others.

The logic of v. 14 can thus be understood in theory in either of two radically different ways. The post-Enlightenment and postmodern reading which seems most "natural" (i.e., expected) is to read the verse as a reassurance that plurality is in order. But the established use of **the body** as a *topos,* or set example, precisely in Paul's own first-century era, suggests that Paul means that unless the **many** perform their assigned functions, however diverse, the **one** body would not exist as **a single entity** but as a chaotic array of conflicting forces, without focus or coherence.

Hence the protasis of the conditional sentence uses an aorist subjunctive to express an unfulfilled hypothesis: ἐὰν εἴπῃ ὁ πούς means **if the foot should say** (as NIV) or *if the foot were to say* (NJB), or (in a different structure) *suppose the foot were to say . . .* (REB). The apodosis οὐκ εἰμὶ ἐκ τοῦ σώματος, *I am not of the body* may be rendered in more idiomatic English, **I do not belong to the body** (as NRSV, REB, NIV, NJB). An important note is struck by Gk. παρὰ τοῦτο. Strictly it carries the sense of *alongside of this* (cf. 4 Macc 10:19); but thereby it occasionally also bears the meaning which it conveys here, namely, **just because of. . . .** C. F. D. Moule suggests *on that score* or *for that reason.*[59] Paul's point is that the merely *subjective feeling* of "I do not belong" has no validity *alongside* the *objective fact*. It is not *in fact* the case that it does not belong **just because** it expresses its own doubts.

The overwhelming majority of VSS and English translations assume that v. 15 is to be punctuated as a statement (NRSV, REB, NIV, NJB, RV, RSV, TEV, Moffatt, Barrett). The 4th ed. UBS *Greek New Testament* and Collins punctuate it as a rhetorical question, returning to AV/KJV and to older many nineteenth-century commentators (e.g., de Wette, Hodge and Alford,

---

57. Bittlinger, *Gifts and Graces,* 58.

58. Mitchell, *Rhetoric of Reconciliation,* 68-83 and 157-64; Martin, *The Corinthian Body,* 38-63 and 94-103. See above, introduction to 12:12-30.

59. Moule, *Idiom Book,* 51; cf. BDF, sect. 236, subsect. 5: "That is no reason why. . . ."

also Estius).[60] Edwards and Findlay observe that we should expect μή, not οὐ, for a question which is either hesitant or anticipates negative exclusion.[61] Since the 3d UBS ed. of the Greek (1975) and the 2d Nestlé ed. (1958) both read vv. 15 and 16 as statements, it is surprising that no comment appears in the 2d ed. (1994) of B. M. Metzger's *Textual Commentary,* to defend the UBS 4th ed. reading. However, the meaning of v. 15 remains virtually the same, and the issue is exegetical rather than one of early MS punctuation.

16-17   Verse 16 requires no further comment since the syntax, exegetical issues, and translation are identical with those discussed under v. 15. This time we have substituted Moule's **on that score** (see above) for stylistic variation. Similarly, for stylistic variation we have borrowed REB's *none* **the less,** which becomes **any the less** if we follow the interrogative punctuation of UBS 4th ed. Greek text, by which, however, we remain unconvinced.

In the semantic sense of meaning, v. 17 is also clear and requires little comment. However, the force for the readers becomes more evident when we note the *application* of the distinction between functions of the body which are wonderful and necessary, and the absurdity of conceiving of the whole body as functioning in that way. It is a deceptively seductive step to move from prizing the sight given by **an eye** (or in the application, preaching, prophecy, wisdom, or tongues) as a most precious and wonderful gift, to the assumption that this is what really makes **the body** the body that it is. Paul primarily addresses those whose gifts have been regarded as "inferior" by others, but his logic equally anticipates his rebuke to the self-sufficient "quasi-gnostics" (who prize "knowledge"), or "spiritual people" (who prize more visible, unusual phenomena of the Spirit), or social patrons (who provide prestige and practical support), who may think (or even implicitly say), "I have no need of you" (v. 21).

Most English translations render ὄσφρησις *sense of smell* (NRSV, NIV), *smell* (REB, JB), or *smelling* (AV/KJV, RV). The word occurs regularly in classical and hellenistic Greek but not elsewhere in the NT. It often means *sense of smell* (Plato, *Phaedo* 3B; Philo), but also simply **nose** (Marcus Aurelius, 10:35; Diogenes Laertius, 6:39).[62] Since ἀκοή also means either *the act of hearing* or *the organ of hearing,* and Paul is distinguishing *organs* of the body, **nose** seems marginally preferable as a translation.

18   The phrase νυνὶ δέ expresses a logical *now, then* in a contrastive mode signaled by δέ. The hypothesis and the analogy is over and done with: now for realities as **God** has arranged them. Hence we translate **But as it is** . . . ὁ θεὸς ἔθετο and καθὼς ἠθέλησεν carry the emphasis of the verse (cf. καθὼς βούλεται, v. 11; and καθὼς ἠθέλησεν, 15:38). H. A. A. Kennedy calls this an

---

60. Collins speaks of "two rhetorical questions" which are parallel, and translates in this way (Collins, *First Cor,* 463).

61. Edwards, *First Epistle,* 327; Findlay, *Expositor's Greek Testament: 1 Cor,* 2:891.

62. BAGD, 587; MM, ad hoc.

aorist of divine sovereignty as reflecting divine decision and decree.[63] ἔθετο is the second aorist middle indicative of τίθημι, which retains its active sense of *put, place, lay, make.*[64] To translate ὁ θεὸς ἔθετο as *God arranged* (NRSV; cf. NIV), *God appointed* (REB), or even *God set* (AV/KJV, RV) weakens the sense in which divine election or the call to Christian existence is inextricably bound up with his purposes for an individual within (ἐν with the dative) the church. The meaning is **God placed the members** (Robertson and Plummer), or *God put all the separate parts* (NJB, JB).[65]

To try to rank some gifts as "more essential" than others, let alone as necessary marks of advanced status to which all should aspire, is to offer a blasphemous challenge to God's freedom to choose whatever is his good will for his people both collectively and individually. The unexpected ἓν ἕκαστον αὐτῶν, which in a different context might seem redundant, here intensifies the emphasis **each single one of them** (thus inviting **single** as a comparably redundant intensifying device in English). How dare anyone either boast or exult in his or her own gifts as if these were a status symbol, or devalue other people's gifts, as if **God** had not chosen them for the other?

Deluz admirably applies a hermeneutic based on good exegesis. He observes: "Christians must give up anxiously comparing themselves with each other. . . . It leads to jealousy [cf. 1:10-12; 3:1-4] and discouragement. . . . They complain that they are not like so-and-so. . . . They develop an inferiority complex and lose all the joy of salvation. The foot grumbles because it walks in the dust and carries the whole weight of the body. . . . Others would like to be the eye which oversees or [especially!] the mouth which speaks. . . . God knows why he has made each one of us as we are; he knows what use each one of us can be."[66]

19-20 As commentators agree, these two verses add no fresh thought to the argument, but bring the logic of 12:12-20 to a summarizing recapitulation. Paul's use of ποῦ to ask rhetorically, *Where is* **the body**? denotes its *logical* inconceivability, if the protasis of the conditional were to be fulfilled. Our translation calls attention to the *logical status* of the question by using the conceptual terminology often rendered by *where* in Greek philosophical discourse by the modern English philosophical equivalent **in what would the body consist?**[67] Again, as in the parallel in v. 18, νυνὶ δέ expresses the logical status of a

63. On Kennedy, see under 15:38; on Barth, see *The Resurrection of the Dead,* for whom this is a major theme throughout the epistle. Barth convincingly makes this case (see below).

64. Cf. BAGD, 815-16; BDF, sect. 316, (i); Robertson, *Grammar,* 804-5.

65. Robertson and Plummer comment, "From the very first it was ordered so, as part of a *plan;* therefore 'placed' rather than 'set'" (*First Epistle,* 274).

66. Deluz, *Companion to 1 Cor,* 179-80. Deluz's comments rightly have in view those who feel "not needed" or "not belonging"; but we have noted that already Paul paves the way for a rebuke to the high status seekers who reject those with "inferior" gifts. Paul will shortly turn the entire logic of status claims upside down.

67. Edwards, *First Epistle,* 327-28: ". . . necessary to the very being of the body." Cf. the use of δεῖ in Aristotle, *Politica* 8.3.6. Collins's notion of a "rare unreal period" *(sic)* distracts from,

given state of affairs in reality, in a contrastive mode; hence: **As it is, on the contrary**. . . .

We have noted Robinson's point that too often μέλη is too readily understood in a modern, social sense, hence, following REB's *many different organs* (rather NRSV, *many members*), we take up REB's earlier rendering **many limbs and organs**, since μέλη is broader than *organs*. Although the translation of μέν and δέ *(on the one hand . . . on the other hand)* is usually found only in the wooden literalism of the school classroom, some way of explicating the contrast is called for, untypically, here. For the principle of v. 20 has the force of a proverb or *axiom:* **Many limbs and organs (on one side); a single body** (on the other). The proverb would be more pithy if the verb **constitute** were omitted (as it is in the Greek). But clarity might suffer unduly if force were the only consideration. Barrett clearly interprets v. 20 as a contingent fact rather than as a logical axiom by translating, *But in fact there are many members and one body.*[68] But it functions as "a concise epigram."[69]

21 Paul now makes utterly explicit what had lain implicitly in his earlier rhetoric. Not only does the rhetoric of the body reassure those with supposedly "inferior" or "dispensable" gifts that they do indeed belong fully to the body as essential limbs and organs, but *this rhetoric now explicitly rebukes those who think that they and their "superior" gifts are self-sufficient for the whole body, or that others are scarcely "authentic" parts of the body, as they themselves are.* It is hardly mere speculation to imagine that those who perceived themselves as possessing the "high-status" gifts of knowledge and wisdom, or of the power to heal or to speak in tongues, could be tempted to think of themselves as *the* inner circle on whom the identity and function of the church really depended. In modern times, the tendency to select either one or more of the "gifts" in 12:8-10, or to interpret the baptism by or in the Spirit in 12:13 as the sign of "advanced" status, comes perilously near to the Corinthian heresy which Paul explicitly attacks.

It is not sufficient to follow many modern commentators in interpreting these verses merely as a legitimation of variety. No doubt the passage carries the corollary that no single type of gift or experience should be used as a measure for other believers. But the political rhetoric traced by Mitchell, Martin, and others (see above) shows that much more is at stake. No subset of gifts or experiences constitutes the *esse* of the church, any more than some selected form of ministerial office represents the *esse* of the church. Both the *esse* and the *bene esse* lie in mutual respect for, and acceptance of, what God has chosen

rather than clarifies, the logical nature of the point (*First Cor,* 464). Hays rightly speaks of "the necessity of diversity" but does not distinguish between *contingent necessity* (vv. 14-17) and *logical necessity* (v. 18) (*First Cor,* 215). Wolff and Schrage simply hurry over these verses, in spite of Wolff's "Excursus."

68. Barrett, *First Epistle,* 290; as also Godet, *First Epistle,* 2:214, "actual fact."
69. Findlay, *Expositor's Greek Testament: 1 Cor,* 2:892; cf. Meyer, *First Epistle,* 1:376; and Roberston and Plummer, *First Epistle,* 274.

(12:11) as that which promotes the Lordship of Christ (12:3) and the building up of the church for the common good (12:7), in an equality of *status* of those who owe their being in Christ to the gracious agency of the Holy Spirit as a gift for **all** (12:13). The sin of "autonomy," *self-sufficiency,* or "the right to do what I like" (6:12) is precisely the "fleshly" attitude within the church (3:1-4), which Paul finds alien to Christlike existence "for others," but reflects much secular culture (whether inside or outside the church) at the beginning of the twenty-first century. Paul defines self-sufficiency here as **having no need** of another or of others.

22 The introductory ἀλλά carries its full adversative force to mean *No,* **on the contrary**. Similarly, πολλῷ μᾶλλον (ignored by a number of English translations) expresses the *a fortiori* argument *by much more,* or (more idiomatically) *it is much more the case that. . . .* But the phrase does **not** apply to *degrees of necessity,* which Paul excludes. Hence we need to translate **even more to the point. . . .**[70] The most crucial word for translation and exegesis is ἀσθενέστερα, the comparative form of the adjective ἀσθενής. We have already discussed the meaning of τὸ ἀσθενὲς τοῦ θεοῦ in 1:25 (see above) and τὰ ἀσθενῆ τοῦ κόσμου in 1:27, where *the weak* were the objects of God's elective salvation (see above). The contrast between ἀσθενεῖς and ἰσχυροί was further discussed under 4:10 in relation to cruciform versus triumphalist ministries, and the relation between "the weak" and "the strong" in 8:7, 9, and 10. There, we noted, Theissen and others view ἀσθενής as a designation of lower social status, while Clarence E. Glad regarded the term as denoting neither people of some specific social or spiritual status nor "theological positions" but as "dispositions of character . . . psychological dispositions or character types revealing different aptitudes . . . and . . . maturity."[71] Glad perceives this meaning especially in 8:1-13 and 10:24–11:1, but also in 9:19-23 and here in 12:22.[72] (On 8:1-13 and 9:19-23, see above.)

In the light of the *social analyses* of ἀσθενής, *weak,* undertaken by Theissen and others, the modification and important revaluations offered by Glad in terms of *disposition of character* and finally the work of Martin in showing special nuances in this verse, we can hardly follow NRSV, NIV, NJB, and JB in translating ἀσθενέστερα as *weaker* or *weakest* without inviting serious misunderstanding of Paul's point.[73] The RV and AV/KJV *more feeble* does

70. Collins applies **all the more** to the end of the clause: *. . . all the more necessary* (*First Cor,* 457, 464).

71. C. E. Glad, *Paul and Philodemus: Adaptability in Epicurean and Early Christian Psychagogy,* NovTSup 81 (Leiden: Brill, 1995), 333.

72. Ibid., 277-97 (on 8:1-13); 43-45 and 240-77 (on 9:19-23); 297-315 (on 1:25-31 and 4:10); and 210-13 (on 12:22).

73. Important points are made very well by Martin, *The Corinthian Body,* 92-96. The classic social analysis by G. Theissen which is the starting point for all subsequent discussion appears as "The Strong and the Weak in Corinth: A Sociological Analysis of a Theological Quarrel," in Theissen, *The Social Setting of Pauline Christianity* (Philadelphia: Fortress, 1982), 121-44, first published in German in *EvT* 35 (1975): 155-72.

not help, and the REB *more frail* goes only part of the way to meet the problem. Our modern idioms and vocabulary-stock force us to express the point by negating the semantic opposite. Paul refers to people in the church whose role, or more probably temperament, or perhaps both, present them as **less endowed with power or status than others**. The "strong" or the "gifted" perceived them as not providing much effective *weight* or *power* in the church's mission, and not much *confidence* borne of *status*. They were insufficiently impressive to count for much, either socially or spiritually, within the church, or in terms of what "contacts" or ability they might show for mission or for speaking with wisdom and knowledge to outsiders. Probably they never did effective mighty works or healing, seldom or never prophesied, and perhaps never spoke in tongues. In v. 23 they are spoken of as *less attractive* and less *"presentable"* (εὐσχημοσύνην).[74]

Martin puts his finger on the issue with remarkable astuteness. Noting that the list of terms in vv. 22-23 looks back to themes in the epistle such as *esteemed* (τὰ δοκοῦντα; cf. 1:26-31; 4:9-13; 6:4-5), *weaker* (ἀσθενέστερα; cf. 1:25-27; 4:10; 8:7-10; 9:19-23), *less honourable* (ἀτιμότερα, v. 23; cf. 4:10; 11:14), and *lacking* (ὑστερουμένῳ, v. 23; cf. 1:7; 8:8), Martin asserts: "The most remarkable thing about Paul's imagery is not his use of status terms . . . but *his claim that the normally conceived body hierarchy is actually only an apparent surface hierarchy*" (my italics).[75] *This accords precisely with Paul's "status reversals" between 1:26-29 and 1:30-31, between 2:1-5 and 2:6-11, and most of all between 1:18-22 and 1:23-25.* Martin does not make as much of these links as he might, for the implicit strategy of Paul is not merely body-rhetoric alone, but *the application of the critique of Christ and the cross to the church.* The "rhetorical" approaches of Mitchell, Witherington, and Martin do not place adequate emphasis on this theology. For this we need to turn to such a volume as Karl Barth's *The Resurrection of the Dead,* or, in more exegetical terms, to Schrage's commentary (to date, only up to 11:16). This is not, however, Barth's imposing dialectical theology onto Paul. The key climax of the "reversals" begins with ὁ δὲ θεὸς δίδωσιν αὐτῷ σῶμα καθὼς ἠθέλησεν (15:38) and finds expression in the resurrection reversals of 15:43-44 (see below).

Meanwhile, before speaking of the *attention and priority* given to "less presentable" parts of the body (v. 23), in this verse Paul first further establishes that **it is much more the case that those . . . less endowed with power or status . . . are essential** (ἀναγκαῖα). Normally we should translate the Greek as *necessary,* since ἀνάγκη usually means *necessity* or *compulsion.* But since the "superior" or "strong" groups see themselves as the *essence* of the church, the wordplays implicit in vv. 22 and 23 may be best served by rendering it **essential**. The Fathers made much of these verses. Chrysostom readily explicates the parallel: "What is meaner than the foot? What is more honorable than the head?

---

74. Martin, *Corinthian Body,* 94-95.
75. Ibid., 94.

For this, the head, more than anything, is the man. Nevertheless . . . it could not do everything on its own. . . . The greater have need of the less. . . . For nothing . . . is dishonorable, seeing it is God's work."[76] In patristic thought the theme recurs that believers *need* those to whom they can show active care, protection, support, and love; otherwise they cannot serve as Christ served "for others." Bonhoeffer brings out this point in his integral connection between Christology, church, and ethics in modern theology.[77] The Reformers, especially Luther and Calvin, further expound the Pauline theme that only through human weakness can the people of God fully "glory" in God alone.[78] Tertullian similarly links Paul's thought here with "I have come to save the lost" (Luke 19:10); "His strength is made perfect in weakness" (2 Cor 12:9); and "those who are whole do not need a physician" (Luke 5:31).[79] J. C. Wand's *bon mot* that the church is a school for sinners, not a museum for saints, underlines that a church made up only of self-styled "gifted" elite would not be the church *of Christ.*

23   Almost every Greek word here permits a play on words which enhances and focuses Paul's compelling rhetoric. We have endeavored to preserve the wordplay where English permits, and in other cases to make explicit the two aspects by two separate but related words. (a) περιτίθεμεν we translate as **invest**, since περιτίθημι means *to place around* in two senses: it regularly means *to bestow* or *to confer* (Prov 12:9, LXX), but also means *to garland* or *to place a piece of clothing or cloth band around* (as in Matt 27:28; Mark 15:17).[80] The English word **invest** admirably conveys (i) *bestowing,* or *investing with,* honor; and (ii) *investing,* in the sense of placing a *vestment* or *cloth* around something. Similarly, (b) the semantic contrast between τὰ ἀσχήμονα (σχῆμα, form, with alpha privative) and εὐσχημοσύνην (σχῆμα, form, with εὖ, *well*) embodies two semantic oppositions (i) between *ugly* and *beautiful* or *adorned;* and (ii) between *private parts* of the body and *publicly "presentable"* limbs and organs. The only way to preserve the wordplay in English seems to be to explicate both double aspects: **our unpresentable private parts have greater adornment to make them presentable**. In v. 22 *necessary part* or **essential** *part* was sometimes used for the private male organ, while Robertson cites the mother's breast and other female organs as among that to which v. 23 alludes.[81] Cultural conditioning leads to a modest hiding of what is most essential for creation and nurture, while we display parts of the body which play a less indispensable function in such terms.

76. Chrysostom, *1 Cor. Hom.,* 31:1, 2.

77. D. Bonhoeffer, *Christology* (Eng. trans., London: SCM, rpt. 1978); cf. also his work *The Communion of Saints: A Dogmatic Inquiry into the Sociology of the Church* (Eng. trans., New York: Harper & Row, 1963), and *Ethics* (New York: Macmillan, 1965).

78. Calvin, *First Epistle,* 268; Luther, *The Heidelberg Disputation* (1518), esp. sects. 20-25 (conveniently Luther, *Early Theological Works,* trans. J. Atkinson [London: SCM, 1962], 290-94).

79. Tertullian, *On the Resurrection,* 9.

80. BAGD, 652; Robertson, *Epistles,* 4:172; and especially Martin, *The Corinthian Body,* 94-95. Cf. further Weiss, *Der erste Korintherbrief,* 305-6. More questionably, Allo speaks of this wordplay as "allegorical" (*Première Épitre,* 330); but cf. Edwards, *First Epistle,* 329.

81. Robertson, *Epistles,* 4:172.

Yet, paradoxically, our very embarrassment over the so-called "less presentable" parts leads to care and attention in how we cover or even adorn them. Moltmann even argues that the disabled constitute a "gift of the Spirit" to the church through their offering of weakness.[82] This seeming paradox admirably illustrates Paul's point about the church as Christ's limbs and members. Those whom the church likes to put on "on display" as our "best" people (whether because of their supposed wisdom and knowledge, or more visible gifts of the Spirit such as tongues or "mighty works") are far from being the essence of the church. There are those who are needy and know of their need (cf. Matt 5:3-10, οἱ πτωχοί, *the poor;* οἱ πενθοῦντες, *those who mourn;* οἱ πραεῖς, *the meek; . . .* οἱ δεδιωγμένοι, *the persecuted . . .*). Paul virtually anticipates Bonhoeffer's point about the Sermon on the Mount. Unlike status seekers "on display" in the church, who have absorbed the competitive spirit of secular Corinth, Jesus, Bonhoeffer observes, calls "blessed" the one who is "refusing to be in tune with the world, or to accommodate oneself to its standards. Such people mourn for the world, for its guilt, its fate and its fortune. While the world keeps holiday . . . , they mourn. . . . The world dreams of power. . . . The meek . . . renounce every right of their own and live for the sake of Jesus Christ. When reproached, they hold their peace. . . . They will not go to law to defend their rights. . . . They are determined to leave their rights to God alone."[83] Every phrase of Bonhoeffer's on Matt 5:3-10 resonates with Paul's language in this epistle: the "reversals" of status in 1:26-29 and 1:30-31; the contrast between the way of the cross and triumphalism in 1:18-25 and 4:7-13; even the issue about lawcourts and "the right to do what I like" in 6:1-8, 12; 11:20-22. Quasi-gnostic triumphalism (8:1-13) reminds us of Bonhoeffer's words about cheap grace: "Cheap grace is the preaching of forgiveness without requiring repentance, baptism without church discipline . . . grace without the cross, grace without Jesus Christ."[84]

All this constitutes a "beauty of holiness" which is Christlike in its self-effacing being "for others." But the status seekers at Corinth within the church perceive such humility as "less presentable" and even an embarrassment, while the gifted ones (socially, spiritually, or in self-confidence of disposition) perceive themselves as the "essential" core of the church. Paul's reaction, **On the contrary** . . ., is expounded by means of an unexpected twist in the standard political rhetoric of the body. Those whom "the strong" wish to hide away as second class perform vital functions which the more confident, well-off, or "spiritual" can never perform. All are needed.

24 ℵ*, A, B, C, and 33 read the middle or passive ὑστερουμένῳ as against 𝔓46, D, F, and G, which read the active form of the participle ὑστεροῦντι. Were it not for the early

---

82. Moltmann, *The Spirit of Life* (section on *charismata*); cf. also Moltmann, "The Knowing of the Other and the Community of the Different," in *God for a Secular Society* (Eng. trans., London: SCM, 1999), 135-52.

83. D. Bonhoeffer, *The Cost of Discipleship* (London: SCM, 6th ed. 1959), 98-99.

84. Ibid., 36.

𝔭⁴⁶, the middle is clearly original, since Paul speaks of those who **feel inferior** or *feel* lacking; not of those of *are* inferior, which would contradict his argument. An early error in 𝔭⁴⁶, however, could simply be reflected in D, F, and G, and against Zuntz we follow Robertson and Plummer, Fee, and the UBS 4th ed. *Greek New Testament* in favoring the middle voice.[85] The only argument for the active reading is that this form sometimes means to be in need rather than to be lacking or to be inferior. But in 1:7 Paul has already said that such a perception would be illusory and subjective. The middle fits the argument; the active does not.

The further reference to **presentable parts** requires no substantial additional comment, in the light of our detailed discussion of v. 23. It simply explicates a further aspect of the point. Those who think themselves already "gifted," "attractive," "essential," or "presentable" are precisely *not* those who should be seeking still further attention and applause. By contrast, **God** (emphatic nominative here) has determined how the church is **composed**. The verb συνεκέρασεν is the first aorist indicative of συγκεράννυμι, which is used of a painter *mixing and blending* colors, of **composing** a harmonious work or substance, or of *compounding the various elements which together* form the human body (Plato, *Timaeus* 35A, Τρίτον ἐξ ἀμφοῖν ἐν μέσῳ ξυνεκεράσατο οὐσίας εἶδος. Cf. also Heb. 4:2 on the hearers' appropriating the word as a constituent element of the *compound* speech-act).[86] The picture is of a craftsman *mixing a compound,* or of a musician **composing** *a harmony,* or of a divine agency creating a body by *combining elements to form a compound.* At all events, it is **God** who decides what or who forms part of a hidden foundation beneath the earth, or an ornamental spire or tower (more showy, but less fundamental) in the case of a building; which parts of a painting shine and which yield dark shadow; or which parts of a body are on display and which parts perform utterly essential functions for the survival of the whole.

No role or way of mixing the compound lies outside the sovereign choice of God. It is only God's **giving** (δούς, aorist participle of δίδωμι) that provides objective grounds for one's place within *the body.*

25 The ἵνα clause with the subjective verb is clearly purposive. Hence it may be rendered as a separate sentence within an overlong flow for modern English by expressing the purpose of *God's composing* in v. 24 as **He purposed that there should be no split**. . . . We fully discussed the meaning of σχίσμα as *rent, tear, dissension,* or **split** under 1:10 (see above). In 1:10 the correlative verb was καταρτίζω, *to mend, repair,* or *knit back together.* Hence we need a word which combines the political rhetoric of *dissensions* with the vivid metaphor of *tearing apart* the body limb from limb. As in 1:10, **split** conveys the

85. Robertson and Plummer, *First Epistle,* 276; and Fee, First *Epistle,* 608, n. 2; as against Zuntz, *The Text of the Epistles,* 128. Collins notes that Paul "has a predilection for compound verbs with *syn* (*First Cor,* 465).

86. BAGD, 773; Edwards, *First Epistle,* 330; and Heinrici, *Das erste Sendschreiben,* 405-6, n. 5, on the verb in Plato and Plutarch. Cf. further Plato, *Timaeus* 69B, 80B; Plutarch, *Numa* 3.

two connotations of politics and pain (cf. also Collins, *bodily rupture*). Once again, we continue to accept Robinson's warning that for modern readers *members* (μέλη) has lost its original force through the modern social meaning of *body*, and continue to use **limbs and organs** as the modern equivalent, especially in relation to σχίσμα. The obsession with groups and with status *tears* and **splits the body** of Christ, **limb** from **limb** and **organ** from **organ**. To have reserved the choice of gifts to God alone without further ado would have prevented the disruption of the purposed unity.

As it is, the *care* or **concern** (μεριμνῶσιν, subjunctive of μεριμνάω) of a given individual or group should have been directed not at their own standing or role, but equally at the standing or role of the whole **body**.[87] In Matt 6:25, 27, 28, and 31 μεριμνάω denotes *anxious care,* while in 1 Cor 7:32, 33, and 34 it denotes **concern** which absorbs the attention (see above on 7:32-34). In modern psychological terms we might say, "Sublimate your preoccupations with your own gifts and status by transferring them equally to all others within the community." Τὸ αὐτό, **the same**, is emphatic. E. Best points out that one *means* whereby **God** *bestows* or **invests honor** to the "**less presentable**" (v. 24) is "through us," i.e., *through* the concern and compassion expressed by the *more confident* (C. E. Glad) toward those who *"feel inferior"* (Robertson and Plummer).[88]

26   From 12:12 to 12:17 it was vital to appreciate the history of rhetoric concerning the politics of the body identified by Mitchell and Martin, and the range of parallels noted earlier by Heinrici, Weiss, and others. But at this stage of the argument it constitutes more of a distraction to note, e.g., Plato's language to the effect that the pain of a finger is the pain felt by the self.[89] To be sure, Plato uses the image to stress the mutuality of the parts or members of the body. But by now, Paul has already given the political-rhetoric *topos* a decisive twist, or *unexpected application, which has effectively turned it upside down* (see above). Now he has prepared the way for a deeper understanding of the mutuality and empathy that marks the common status and common bond of all believers.

The four key verbs are πάσχει and συμπάσχει (v. 26a), and δοξάζεται and συγχαίρει. The first two present no difficultly for translation. Although συμπάσχειν, **to suffer with**, occurs within the NT only here and in Rom 8:17 (where it denotes *suffering with* Christ), the two terms regularly mean **to suffer** in a medical context in Hippocrates and in Galen. The effects of disability on

87. Wolff, *Der erste Brief,* 300-301.

88. Best, *One Body,* 103; cf. Glad, *Paul and Philodemus,* 210-13 and 333; Martin, *The Corinthian Body,* 94-96; Robertson and Plummer, *First Epistle,* 276.

89. Plato, *Republic* 5.462; cf. the Stoic writer Sextus Empiricus, *Adversus Mathematicos* 9.78-79; Josephus, *Wars* 4.406-7. Best, *One Body,* 104, n. 1, also cites Strack-Billerbeck, 3:448-49. Weiss cites numerous sources, including Philo, *De Migratione Abrrahami* 180 (Weiss, *Der erste Korintherbrief,* 307, n. 1). On Mitchell and Martin on the *political rhetoric* of the body, see above, esp. introduction to 12:12-30.

the part of a specific limb or organ (μέλος) on the body as a whole appears widely in ancient writers. Chrysostom, e.g., compares the pain caused to the system merely by a sharp thorn in the foot.

The translation of δοξάζεται and συγχαίρει pose a larger problem. The noun δόξα can mean *splendor* or *glory,* but also *renown, fame,* or *honor.* The verb δοξάζω can mean **to praise**; but if the OT background lends any semantic coloring to the Greek, *to glorify* is *to deem weighty* or *impressive.*[90] NRSV, NIV, NJB, RV, and AV/KJV all follow this last meaning with *is honored;* but REB seeks a closer semantic opposition to *suffer* by rendering the word by the English *flourishes.* But the correlative συγχαίρει, frequently *rejoice with* (as in the parables of the sheep lost and found and the coin lost and found, Luke 15:6, 9) also has an established meaning of **sharing in congratulations**. The REB seems to overstretch the image into an allegory if the separate parts of the body *all rejoice together* (REB) at the health of a particular organ or limb. On the other hand, if the ear and fingers of a musician are **praised**, or if the hands and feet of an athlete are **praised**, a person receives **congratulations** for his or her coordination *as a whole.* The whole person is described as a good musician or as a good athlete, and indeed some intrusive bodily distraction could wreck the performance.

Lionel Thornton does not overstate Paul's argument when he observes: "It follows that in the Body of Christ there are, strictly speaking, no private sufferings. All are shared because there is one life of the whole. Accordingly, wrong done to one member is wrong done to the whole Church, and therefore to Christ himself."[91] Those at Corinth who make others feel inferior merely to enhance their own status thus ultimately demean themselves, and Christ. Or in E. Best's words, "What affects one member affects all. . . . One member of the Church uses his spiritual gift as God intended its use, and the whole Church rejoices, one member misuses his gift and the whole Church sorrows."[92] Ambition, envy, and status-seeking have no place in the commonality of the body and its interdependence.[93] By contrast, a concern for "the suffering and straying members" as a needed part of the whole body finds resonance in Polycarp.[94]

27 D reads ἐκ μέλους in place of ἐκ μέρους, and the Vulgate follows this, to mean *member joined to member.* But against ℵ, A, B, C, this is "obviously a mistake in copying or dictation."[95]

Collins sees vv. 27-31a as a distinct epistolary unit, with vv. 27 and 31a in the second person plural.[96] The syntax of the verse fittingly combines singular and

90. BAGD, 203-4.
91. Thornton, *The Common Life in the Body of Christ,* 36; cf. 34-65, 156-87.
92. Best, *One Body,* 104.
93. Cf. Deluz, *Companion to 1 Cor,* 182, Lang, *Die Briefe,* 173.
94. Polycarp, *Epistle to the Philippians,* 11.
95. Héring, *First Epistle,* 132, n. 20.
96. Collins, *First Cor,* 467.

plural. Our translation adds **yourselves**, which is not strictly in the Greek (although it is emphatic) because it is difficult otherwise to signal in English that ὑμεῖς is *plural.* NJB's *Christ's body is yourselves* reverses the subject and predicate. We follow Luther, Meyer, Weiss, and Conzelmann in understanding ἐκ μέρους to mean *for his own part,* or **for his or her part.**[97] The phrase means *separately,* or *part by part,* and the usual translation *individually* (NRSV; cf. AV/KJV, *in particular;* RV, *severally*) is not wrong. However, the argument has been self-involving: what is my part/their parts in the body? Hence Weiss's *for his own part* conveys a nuance which REB's *each of you* does not quite capture, while NJB goes rather too far beyond the Greek with *Now Christ's body is yourselves, each of you with a part to play in the whole.* In this respect, this verse "ties all the preceding pieces together.[98]

28 This verse is an exegetical and lexicographical minefield. These key questions loom large: (1) do πρῶτον . . . δεύτερον . . . τρίτον . . . ἔπειτα . . . ἔπειτα . . . denote gradations of rank, importance, or indispensability, or simply ways of checking off a long list? (2) While the meaning of ἀποστόλους . . . προφήτας . . . δυνάμεις . . . ἰαμάτων, and γένη γλωσσῶν . . . has been discussed in detail above, we have yet to examine more fully διδάσκαλοι, ἀντιλήμψεις, and κυβερνήσεις. (3) Why does Paul in some cases use abstract nouns denoting the various activities involved, while in other instances he appears to use adjectival titles for persons who perform specific functions or (some argue) offices? (4) Finally, how are we to understand the syntax which relates to οὓς μέν . . . when the contrastive δέ never appears and the construction appears to proceed differently?

(1) *Does the enumeration or sequence imply any kind of "ranking"?* F. F. Bruce argues that enumeration first . . . second . . . third . . . "mark these out as exercising, in Paul's estimation, the three most important ministries. In Eph 4:11 these are also enumerated, together with evangelists, in the order (a) **apostles**, (b) **prophets**, (c) evangelists, (d) pastors and **teachers**, as given by the ascended Lord to equip his people '. . . for building up the body of Christ.'"[99] In the same vein, Grosheide argues that **prophets** are second to apostles because, although both proclaim the gospel, "their office is not . . . as universal as that of the **apostles**" and hence "not as important."[100] Robertson and Plummer perceive **apostles** as "the first order in the Church," since elsewhere in Paul and in Acts it is an essential qualification for the apostolate to have seen the raised Lord (1 Cor. 9:1, 2; 15:7; cf. Acts 1:8, 21-23).[101] Dunn concedes that **apostles**

97. Meyer, *First Epistle,* 1:380; Weiss, *Der erste Korintherbrief,* 307; Luther's Bible, *nach seinem Teil;* Conzelmann, *1 Cor,* 214, n. 39. Chrysostom, Theodoret, Bengel, and Erasmus interpret this as an allusion to the fact that Corinth was itself only a *part* of Christ's body. But as Meyer comments, "this would not fit Paul's" *contextual* concern.

98. Fee, *First Epistle,* 617.
99. Bruce, *1 and 2 Cor,* 122-23.
100. Grosheide, *First Epistle,* 298.
101. Robertson and Plummer, *First Epistle,* 279.

represent in Paul a wider circle than the Twelve, but believes that they still constitute a special group of "founder members" who are personally commissioned on the basis of such passages as Rom 1:5; 11:13; 1 Cor 3:5-10; 9:1, 2; 15:7-11; Gal 1:1 and 1:11, 15-17).[102] The **apostles** are **first** not least in the sense that the church does not "raise up" its apostles, but responds to the apostolic witness. A term like "church founders" might be implied, although Paul asserts categorically that Christ alone is the foundation. Among the most recent commentators, Lang offers a similar evaluation to that of Bruce: "Paul begins with the three most important functions of proclamation: **first** of all, the **apostles**; **second, prophets, third, teachers**."[103]

Other commentators tend to imply a ranking of some kind which is less explicit. Barrett shares with Bruce and Lang the view that "this threefold ministry of the word is, according to Paul, the primary Christian ministry. By it the church is founded and built up. Other activities . . . can occupy only a secondary place. . . . The numerical sequence is pursued no further."[104] Senft, however, is emphatic that the difference between the list in 12:8-10 and the structure of this list "is of extreme importance: it clearly sets out the specifically Pauline conception of the gifts of the Spirit (cf. vv. 4, 5)" as against "the Corinthian definition of 'pneumatic' traits" in 12:8-10.[105] As in Rom 12:6-8, when Paul looks back retrospectively to his Corinthian experience, he places the emphasis on a gradation of "what edifies" the church as a whole, where *service* (as he will explicate in 1 Corinthians 13) becomes the touchstone of importance and ministerial character. Like Conzelmann, Senft urges that "the chief forms of service" are deliberately listed first.[106] Finally, Allo argues that "the adverbs 'firstly', 'secondly', 'thirdly' are to be understood with all the force that they can have: that which is the first. . . ."[107]

To those who know at first hand of the work of "the judicious Richard Hooker" it may come as no surprise to learn that he interprets this verse in terms of a "middle" position. The "Apostles [are] first because unto them was granted the revelation of all truth from Christ immediately."[108] Prophets, he argues, had "some knowledge" of the same kind, and teachers are necessary to build and to instruct. But otherwise "nothing is meant but sundry graces, gifts and abilities which Christ bestowed," and Paul does not have in general view "questions about degrees and offices of ecclesiastical calling."[109]

The single strong argument against an "order" of priority or necessity lies

102. Dunn, *Jesus and the Spirit,* 273-74.

103. Lang, *Die Briefe,* 174.

104. Barrett, *First Epistle,* 295.

105. Senft, *La Première Épitre,* 164.

106. Ibid., 164-65; Conzelmann, *1 Cor,* 215.

107. Allo, *Première Épitre,* 333.

108. Richard Hooker, *Works* (3 vols., ed. J. Keble [7th ed. ed. R. W. Church and F. Paget], Oxford: Clarendon Press, 1878), 5:78:8 (*Of the Laws of Ecclesiastical Polity,* 5 [2:477]).

109. Ibid., 5:78:8 (2:478).

in Martin's incisive argument that Paul has used a rhetoric of political hierarchy only in order to turn it upside down. But this argues for oneness of status and for interdependency of function. Hence the more "egalitarian" interpretations of Godet and of Fee have limited, although perhaps relative, value. Godet asserts: "All have their part to play"; all of the gifts have dignity and value.[110] However, when Fee denies that any of these gifts or roles are "ranked," this is not strictly the case.[111] The comments of Bruce, Dunn, Senft, Hooker, and Schrage remain valid, and interestingly come from Brethren, Methodist, French-language Protestant, Anglican, and German Protestant writers respectively. But perhaps more still should be said. If Martin is correct about his "reversals" (and he surely is), should we not give due weight to Chrysostom's assertion "Because they thought highly of themselves in respect of the tongue, he [Paul] sets it last everywhere. For the terms 'first' and 'secondly' are not used by him at random, but in order by enumeration to point out the more honourable and the inferior."[112]

If this should be thought to reflect only a later patristic reading, we may note that in his discussion of the role of presbyters within the church (c. AD 185) Irenaeus places their ministry among that of the prophets and teachers in Paul's list, observing that "God has placed in the church first apostles, second prophets, third teachers" because an authentic ministry of presbyters must be apostolic, i.e., founded on, and derived from, the apostles.[113] For patristic writers the list is far from random in sequence, whether we consider Origen, Augustine, or others. Indeed, Augustine propounds to Pelagius the ingenious view that no single individual can possess the full range of the gifts of the Spirit (or the body rhetoric would collapse) except apostles, since we can find instances of each gift in Paul's apostolic ministry.[114]

(2) The meaning of the remaining three of the eight gifts of the Spirit not already discussed. (a) On **apostles** see the extended discussion under 1:1. In this context Dunn helpfully notes that Paul alludes to "a limited circle of individuals (though much wider than the 'the twelve')" who are "apostles of Christ rather than delegates of a church . . . commissioned personally by the risen Christ . . . missionaries and church founders. . . . Theirs was a distinctively and decisively eschatological role (Rom. 11:13ff; 15:15-16; 1 Cor. 4:9; 15:8; Eph. 3:5)."[115] "*Eschatological* apostles" (Dunn's italics) had no successors, and Paul uses the term in this sense in 12:28.[116]

110. Godet, *First Epistle,* 2:221.

111. Fee, *First Epistle,* 619; and still more strongly in *God's Empowering Presence,* 190. Collins notes that only here does Paul use *first . . . second . . . third* (*First Cor,* 470), while Schrage contends that the contextual allusion to "greatest gifts" (v. 31a) underlines a dimension of ranking or evaluation and notes the foundational reference of 3:10 (*Der erste Brief,* 3:231-35).

112. Chrysostom, *1 Cor. Hom.,* 32:2.

113. Irenaeus, *Against Heresies,* 4:26:5.

114. Augustine, *On the Proceedings against Pelagius,* 32. Cf. also Origen, *1 Cor. Frag.,* x/viii, in *JTS* 10 (1909): 31-32.

115. Dunn, *Jesus and the Spirit,* 273.

116. Ibid., 273-74.

(b) On **prophets**, see above under 12:10 (προφητεία, προφήτης). There we noted that Paul uses this word only in this epistle (11:4-5; 13:9; 14:1-5, 31, 35, 39). We compared the claims of Aune, Boring, Dautzenberg, Müller, Hill, Grudem, Forbes, and others and concluded that it is difficult to be more specific than Hill and Aune in identifying it as *the proclamation of revealed truth in relation to a pastoral situation.* (See "Prophecy: A First Note" at 12:10 and "Prophecy: A Second Note" at 14:3.) We took issue with Dunn and Grudem about supposed evidence for its "spontaneity," and our further examination of Theissen's careful work on **tongues** as "socially learned behavior" more than confirms these arguments.[117] Their **second** position suggests a possible parallel with presbyterial function. More content, however, can be given to this term in relation to (c) **teachers**.

(c) **Teachers** (ἔθετο ὁ θεός . . . τρίτον διδασκάλους). Again, it is not entirely clear on what basis Dunn draws a firm distinction between "charismatic" and "spontaneous" teachers who taught "*particular* teachings" (Dunn's italics, 1 Cor 14:6, 26; Rom 12:7) and a "noncharismatic sense" of "a body of teaching" (Rom 6:17; 16:17).[118] The verb διδάσκω, **to teach**, occurs only five times in the four major epistles (Rom 2:21; 12:7; 1 Cor 4:17; 11:14; Gal 1:12); the noun διδαχή, **teaching**, only four times (Rom 6:17; 16:17; 1 Cor 14:6, 26, with the related διδασκαλία only in Rom 12:7 and 15:4); and finally διδάσκαλος, **teacher**, in Paul only in Rom 2:20; 1 Cor 12:28-29 (cf. also Eph 4:11; 1 Tim 2:7; 2 Tim 1:11; 4:3).[119] Dunn's contrast becomes difficult to sustain in the narrow range of examples in Romans, 1 Corinthians and Galatians, and even more difficult on the basis of a wider lexicographical survey of hellenistic sources.[120] Barrett observes, "Presumably they [teachers] were mature Christians who instructed others in the meaning and moral implications of the Christian faith (cf. Gal. 6:6); possibly (as some think) they expounded the Christian meaning of the OT."[121] Fee comments that "all attempts to define this ministry from the Pauline perspective are less than convincing since the evidence is so meagre."[122]

117. Cf. Theissen, *Psychological Aspects,* 292-94. Theissen's attention to learning theory alongside psychodynamic expressions of the unconscious or "secrets of the heart" should be examined with care before dismissing them as mere "secular" or "modern" theory. They carry *at least as much weight* as dubious assumptions that the situation in 1 Corinthians 14 presupposes spontaneity. Any tape recording of a "controlled" cognitive conversation reveals how often speakers "interrupt" or speak "at the same time," as any dubbing editor knows.

118. Dunn, *Jesus and the Spirit,* 237; cf. 236-38.

119. διδάσκαλος, **teacher**, also occurs in Acts 13:1, Heb 5:12, Jas 3:1, and some fifty times in the four Gospels; διδακτός, *taught,* occurs in John 6:45 and 1 Cor 2:13; διδάσκω, *teach,* also in Eph 4:21; Col 1:28; 2:7; 3:16; 2 Thess 2:15; 1 Tim 2:12; 4:11; 6:2; 2 Tim 2:2; Tit 1:11.

120. Cf. Josephus, *Antiquities* 13:115; Philo, *Embassy to Gaius* 53; *Didache* 15:1, 2: "Appoint bishops and deacons . . . meek . . . truthful and approved (δεδοκιμασμένους), who also undertake the ministry of prophets and teachers (τὴν λειτουργίαν τῶν προφητῶν καὶ διδασκάλων). The uses of **teacher** as a title of respect in the Gospels also serve to establish the regular meaning of the term in Christian circles.

121. Barrett, *First Epistle,* 295.

122. Fee, *First Epistle,* 621.

Fee rejects Dunn's inclusion of "passing on the tradition" as part of the teaching office.[123] But in this lies the clear and fundamental difference between **prophets** and **teachers**. It is not the case that the first is "spontaneous" as against the second, the result of reflection (still less that the second is also sometimes "spontaneous"). Rather, **prophets** *perform speech-acts of announcement, proclamation, judgment, challenge, comfort, support, or encouragement*, whereas **teachers** *perform speech-acts of transmission, communicative explanation, interpretation of texts, establishment of creeds, exposition of meaning and implication*, and, more *cognitive, less temporally applied communicative acts*. Dunn recently rightly reaffirms his emphasis upon "retaining, passing on and interpreting the congregation's foundation traditions."[124] This helps to explain why Paul uses first . . . second . . . third . . . of these first three gifts, roles, or functions.

The discussion by NT specialists has been vitiated by a failure to appreciate the conceptual difficulties and entailments of the term *revelation* (even though it is true that both **prophets** and **teachers** handle what has been *revealed*), and construe communication largely in terms of conveying information, not of speech-acts. Both points receive detailed attention from Nicholas Wolterstorff. Wolterstorff asserts: "Divine discourse differs from divine revelation. If we assume that illocutionary actions, such as asserting, commanding, promising and asking are a species of revelation, they will elude our grasp. It is true that in promising . . . one reveals various things. . . . But the promising does not itself consist of revealing something. . . ."[125] What speech-act theory from Austin through Searle to Wolterstorff clearly establishes is that effective *acts* of, e.g., *judging, promising, naming, assessing* (the many varied illocutions characteristic of **prophets**) can be operative *only on the basis of certain states of affairs being the case*, as *presuppositions* for the acts to be effective. Hence it is the work of **teachers** *to expound and explain what is the case about God's dealings with the world through Christ by the Spirit*, on the basis of which the *pastoral* and *situational* speech-acts of **prophets** can have their effect.

In several other places I have expounded the principle with reference to transforming speech-acts and Christology.[126] The *liberating* prophetic speech-act "You are hereby forgiven through Christ" depends on the presupposition that Jesus Christ is indeed the one through whose person and work forgiveness

123. Ibid., n. 21. Fee makes the identical set of comments in *God's Empowering Presence*, 192 and 192, n. 407.

124. Dunn, *The Theology of Paul*, 582.

125. Wolterstorff, *Divine Discourse*, 19; cf. 19-36 and 75-129.

126. Thiselton, "Christology in Luke, Speech-Act Theory and the Problem of Dualism in Christology after Kant," in Joel B. Green and Max Turner (eds.), *Jesus of Nazareth, Lord and Christ: Essays on the Historical Jesus and NT Christology in Honor of I. H. Marshall* (Grand Rapids: Eerdmans and Carlisle: Paternoster, 1994), 453-72; also "Authority and Hermeneutics: Some Proposals for a More Creative Agenda," in P. E. Satterthwaite and D. F. Wright (eds.), *A Pathway into Holy Scripture* (Grand Rapids: Eerdmans, 1994), 107-42; and *New Horizons in Hermeneutics*, 283-312; and (with R. Lundin and C. Walhout) *The Promise of Hermeneutics* (Grand Rapids: Eerdmans, 1999), 200-240.

may be mediated to those who believe and appropriate his promises, or that his words stand as God's words. But *whether the state of affairs is that which is presupposed falls within the task of* **teachers** *to establish;* while on the basis of the presupposition the Christian **prophets** may direct *speech-acts of liberation, release, consolation, or exhortation to believe and trust.* This does not impose a modern theory onto Pauline texts. In 1 Cor 14:3, the utterances of **prophets** *operate with effect to build;* and 14:5 repeats this point. In 14:31 the content of a revelation is subdivided into *instruction* and *encouragement.* Paul's language about **prophets'** "inspiration" here need not imply a *Deus ex machina* event, but the *pastoral insight inspired* by instruction set forth by **teachers**. The two experiences of finding an insight *revealed* and being *instructed* in 14:6a are correlated in 14:6b with *prophecy* and *instruction* — we urge *respectively.*

Joseph Fitzmyer brings out these roles well in his comments on Rom 12:6 and 7. The prophet in Rom 12:6 enacts "inspired preaching, as in 1 Cor. 12:10, 28 . . ."; the teacher in Rom 12:7 is "the one who instructs, either in catechesis (1 Cor. 14:19; Gal. 6:6) or in the interpretation of Scripture."[127] As against Fee's scepticism concerning both aspects, Fitzmyer states precisely what Paul means consistently in his allusions to **teachers**. The two primary sources of *teaching* are the OT scriptures and the primitive creeds of the early church. The latter begin, as Cullmann, Hunter, and many others show, as "pre-Pauline formulae" and become developed into full-bodied common *teaching.*[128]

By the time of Irenaeus *teaching* of this kind begins to be recognized as what amounts to the beginnings of a Christian NT canon of scripture. Thus Irenaeus stresses the integral role of *the four canonical Gospels* as a cardinal and authentic source of teaching, while the earliest commentators begin to reiterate their common body of what is to be taught through *creed* and *catechesis.*[129] If teaching can be said to "develop," it is by the threefold process of sifting and reintegrating by **teachers**, fresh pastoral applications by **prophets**, and continuous testing against the fundamental criteria laid down by **apostles**. All that has shifted is a switch from **prophets** to *pastorally gifted preachers* who announce God's dealings with his people and with individuals among them. Along with this, people speak more readily of *testing* prophecy than (as they should) of *testing* preaching.

(d) **Effective deeds of power** and (e) **gifts of healing** have already been discussed in exhaustive detail under 12:10. We are left with the need to comment on (f) **various kinds of administrative support** and (g) **ability to formulate strategies**. We have already examined thoroughly **various kinds of**

127. Fitzmyer, *Romans,* 647 and 648.
128. See Cullmann, *Les premières confessions de foi chrétiennes* (Paris: Universitaires de France, 1948); V. H. Neufeld, *The Earliest Christian Confessions* (Grand Rapids: Eerdmans, 1963); A. M. Hunter, *Paul and His Predecessors* (London: SCM, 2d ed. 1961), 15-78, 108-15, 116-50.
129. Irenaeus, *Against Heresies,* 2:32:1-4 and 3:11:1-9, on the fourfold number of the Gospels, e.g., "it is not possible that the Gospels can be either more or fewer in number than four" (3:11:8; c. AD 185). This "teaching" stands as a safeguard against "pseudo-prophets" (11:9).

tongues, not least with reference to Gundry, Forbes, Dautzenberg, and especially Theissen (see Extended Notes and further in ch. 14).

(f) ἀντιλήμψεις strictly means *helps* (plural), but we argue that the plural denotes **kinds of** *help,* and that in the light of its context and its use in the papyri it probably means **kinds of administrative support**. In biblical Greek the noun often means *help* in the singular (Ps 21:20 [LXX]). In 2 Macc 8:19 the plural ἀντιλήμψεις simply means *acts of help* on a number of occasions when the Jews were at war with Sennacherib, Babylonia, and Macedonia. Dunn therefore understands the Greek to mean *helpful deeds.*[130] The verbal form ἀντιλαμβάνομαι is used in the LXX of divine *help* (Isa 41:9), as it is also in the NT (Luke 1:54). In Rom 8:26 the verb denotes the Holy Spirit's activity of *helping* the believer's prayer. G. Delling insists that in 1 Cor 12:28 ἀντίλημψις "is not to be understood as the assumption of office (as in *Papryus Oxyrhynchus* 900:13), since we have here a list of specific offices; what it means is 'help'"; its differentiation from gifts that precede it lies in "the fact that it does not have a miraculous character, and this leads to those that follow."[131] But Delling ignores the fact that tongues follows κυβερνήσεις, and gives no evidence for sheer statement.

A comparison between the various meanings instantiated in BAGD, Liddell-Scott-Jones, Grimm-Thayer, Moulton-Milligan, and similar sources makes it clear that the term ἀντιλήμψεις (or ἀντιλήψιος) may have various meanings in the plural, most of which are either general or else very context-specific.[132] Thus in *horticultural* contexts it means *taking hold* in the sense of *taking root* (of plants, Theophrastus, *De Clausis Plantarum* 3.6.6; cf. 2.18.2, of a vine); in *medical* contexts it means *offering support* in the sense of *bandages* (Hippocrates, *De Officiis* 743; in the context (especially in the papyri) of *royal petitions, duties,* and *institutions* (mainly in the singular) the word comes to mean *enabling assistance* (*Paris Papyri* 26:40 [BC 163-2]; *Amherst Papyri* 2:35:87 [BC 132]; *BGU* 4:1187:27 [not earlier than the first century BC]; *Fayyum Papyri* 296 [AD 113]). The verbal form ἀντιλαμβάνομαι, which often means *to lay hold of,* comes to mean *to undertake,* especially in commercial business or organizational contexts (e.g., *London Papyri* 301:6-8). In *Papyrus Oxyrhynchus* 9:1196: 12-14 it means *to take up* or *to undertake* an office of responsibility, which in *P. Oxy.* 8:1123:9 (AD 158) means *administering* registered land.

There are three clear choices in the translation and meaning of the word in 12:28. Either it means (i) *helpful deeds* (as in BAGD and Dunn) in the most vague and general sense; or it means (ii) the *help* and *support for those in need* traditionally associated in later church history with the ministry of deacons (as in Grimm-Thayer, Chrysostom, Calvin, Meyer, Heinrici, and Lang) (but

130. Dunn, *The Theology of Paul,* 556.
131. Delling, "ἀντιλαμβάνομαι, ἀντίλημψις," *TDNT,* 1:375; cf. 375-76.
132. Grimm-Thayer, 50; MM, 47 and 48; LSJ, 144; BAGD, 74 and 75. BAGD translate the term as *helpful deeds* in 1 Cor 12:28. The noun occurs in either of the two forms ἀντίληψις or ἀντίλημψις; the latter is the more hellenistic form.

against J. N. Collins); or (iii) its context in the rhetorical function of *body* means support in the sense in which in modern cultures we speak of *support staff,* i.e., in the plural **kinds of administrative support** (as, in effect, Robertson and Plummer). In actual practice this was broadly (*pace* J. N. Collins) *the work of the seven appointed to serve* (διακονεῖν) in Acts 6:2-6. The Twelve express the wish to devote themselves to preaching and to prayer while the church set aside seven with Greek names to support or assist the apostles, partly (with J. N. Collins) for mission, but also (against J. N. Collins) to *administer the funds* set aside for *the support* of Aramaic-speaking and Greek-speaking widows in the earliest organizational development witnessed in Acts (on Collins, see above under 12:5 and 5-11). In our judgment this gift is coupled with κυβερνήσεις exactly because both concern *practical administrative tasks* essential in any concept of *the body* as both a sociopolitical and a theological entity. Margaret Mitchell makes this point forcefully for κυβερνήσεις.

Dunn follows BAGD's meaning *helpful deeds,* but rejects *administration* on the grounds that it presupposes that all too soon the churches had become "administrative structures."[133] But the development of the church in Acts 6:1-6 shows how all too readily an issue about whether funds were *fairly administered* arises from the very first, and the apostles concede that they are too busy with "the real work" to be sidetracked into administration (!). Even if this is treated (with Conzelmann and Haenchen) as a mere later "reading back," anyone familiar with the funding and management of even the smallest, most informal, most "charismatic" group throws up questions about "what was agreed" or how we go about "implementing what was decided." It is unthinkable that Corinth as a church needed no infrastructure within weeks of its coming into being, and that those who are willing and able to organize such matters fairly and efficiently are among the most necessary *kinds of help* which both church and leaders need and which certainly require *special gifts* or χαρίσματα of the Spirit. Thus Robertson and Plummer rightly urge that this gift of "general management" belongs with the next, and Conzelmann renders "administration."[134]

Finally, the second meaning, advocated by Grimm-Thayer, Chrysostom, and Meyer, should certainly be *included within* the third, and Chrysostom provides an unexpected link with recent sociological scholarship. Stating that "to help the weak" is certainly a gift of God, Chrysostom instantiates the *support of a patron* (προστατικόν εἶναι).[135] The nouns προστάτης and προστάτις cover the range of *helper, protector, patron,* and *patroness.* Such a person, Moulton-Milligan show, is often an officeholder in many references among the papyri,

133. Dunn, *Jesus and the Spirit,* 252; cf. *Theology of Paul,* 556; and Fee, *First Epistle,* 621, as also in *God's Empowering Presence,* 193.

134. Robertson and Plummer, *First Epistle,* 280. (Robertson was Bishop of Exeter; and Plummer, Master of University College, Durham.) Similarly, H. Balz and G. Schneider refer to "organizational work in the church" (*EDNT,* 1:110).

135. Chrysostom, *1 Cor. Hom.,* 32:3.

and certainly combines help with *patronage*.[136] Perhaps Paul is here saying not only that good management skills are a gift of the Spirit, but also that those who could support people or work as patrons had a God-given task, as long as (like the other gifts, including **prophets** and **tongues**) the gift was not abused and used for self rather than for others.[137] Heinrici sums up the matter: God's gift provides the wisdom, ability, and power to give the needed assistance.[138] Here any notion that *every charisma* must be "spontaneous" reaches its greatest height of absurdity.

(g) Finally, we translate κυβερνήσεις as the **ability to formulate strategies**. To be sure, κυβερνήσεις in the singular often means *leadership*. Collins understands the term to denote *leaders* with "some kind of directive activity."[139] Hence the plural, *forms of leadership* (NRSV), is broadly acceptable on grounds of Greek lexicography and reflects AV/KJV's and RV's *governments*. But is this translation sufficiently context-specific, given the nuances of the word in various texts? One aspect, namely the one discussed under (f), is expressed by NIV's *administration,* and it is useful, if not entirely adequate, to find this component underlined in the NIV. It is utterly without warrant for Fee to comment that "'administration skills' . . . is probably a far cry from what Paul had in mind."[140] Again, the more a person longs to preach and to teach, the more conscious he or she becomes of the need for others to give structural support (e.g., who will "follow up" what events, and when, and has it been done?) however primitive the structures or small the community.

Fee is entirely correct to point out, however, that the additional nuance of *steersman* or *pilot* is important (cf. Acts 27:11; Rev 18:17), with the emphasis on guidance (Prov 1:5; 11:14; 24:6, LXX).[141] Collins calls it "a nautical metaphor."[142] But Margaret Mitchell calls attention to an aspect of this point which Fee leaves aside. The term, she agrees, "is a common metaphor for rulership in antiquity," but in the context of a rhetoric of concord there comes into prominence "the ship captain and his task to keep a ship afloat" amid rocks and shallows of "factionalism."[143] Here she draws especially on the research of E. Hilgert.[144] Plato appeals to the role of the pilot or helmsman alongside his

---

136. MM, 551; cf. BAGD, 718.

137. Chrysostom's view is supported by Calvin, *First Epistle,* 272; Meyer, *First Epistle,* 1:382; Lang, *Die Briefe,* 174-75; and as probable by Bruce, *1 and 2 Cor,* 123. See also Moltmann's emphasis on charismata and the disabled (above). But, with J. N. Collins, we should not regard this as *excluding* the gift if assisting in preaching and *especially in mission. Mission and outreach* require *planning and execution.*

138. Heinrici, *Das erste Sendschreiben,* 409.

139. Collins, *First Cor,* 469.

140. Fee, *God's Empowering Presence,* 193 (virtually word for word the same as his *First Epistle,* 622, although Mitchell and Martin published their work during the seven-year interval).

141. Ibid. (the same language in both of Fee's books).

142. Collins, *First Cor,* 469.

143. Mitchell, *Paul and the Rhetoric of Reconciliation,* 163.

144. E. Hilgert, *The Ship and Related Symbols in the NT* (Assen: van Gorcum, 1962), esp. 25.

body rhetoric in *The Republic* on the harmony of the city-state.[145] Dio Chrysostom notes that by the latter half of the first century the image of the κυβερνήτης or *steersman* had become a *topos,* or standard example in rhetoric, in appeals for unity and concord.[146] Dio himself uses the analogy of a failed attempt by a leader to bring about sociopolitical harmony with the work of an inept pilot (κεβερνήτης).[147] Mitchell compares application of κυβερνήσεις in 1 Cor 12:28 to directing "the ship of state" in such a way that its "governance structure" keeps it from falling apart or foundering.[148]

This is based on more solid research than the pejorative judgment about "administration" which we have noted above. It has nothing to do with more modern individualist notions of "seeking personal guidance," and it is more specific than "leadership." It refers to **the ability to formulate strategies** which will pilot the ship of the community through the choppy waters of strife and status seeking within, and dangers and potential persecutions without. It is a gift for *strategic statesmanship* to see the larger picture (the pilot's charts) and to use pastoral sensitivity to "steer through" the sins and follies which threaten shipwreck of any church community from time to time. This combines Conzelmann's "administration" with H. W. Beyer's interpretation of the word in this verse as "gifts which qualify a Christian to be a helmsman to his congregation, i.e., a true director of its order and therewith of its life. . . . No society can exist without some order and direction."[149] Weiss also speaks of "order," but the term **strategy** better combines *piloting* and *leadership.*[150] Again, there is no thought of "spontaneous" guidance. As Lang observes, "The quality of a gift of the Spirit depends for Paul not on its coming from some ecstatic form, but on its source from God's Spirit and grace and its function of serving."[151] The Spirit gives "practical insight" especially for "the inner life of the community" (Heinrici).[152]

29-30 It is important to render the rhetorical questions in in English idioms which take full account of the use of μή to express hesitant questions which demand negative answers. The translation *Are all apostles? Are all prophets? Are all teachers? . . .* (NRSV, NIV, AV/KJV, RV) merely renders the

---

145. Plato, *Republic* 6.488A. See further LSJ, 854; MM, 363.

146. Dio Chrysostom, *Orations* 34.16: "Even if this comparison is made repeatedly, still it is your duty not on that account to disregard it" (cited by Mitchell, *Rhetoric of Reconciliation,* n. 596).

147. Dio Chrysostom, *Orations* 48.14.

148. Mitchell, *Rhetoric of Reconciliation,* 164.

149. Conzelmann, *1 Cor,* 215; and H. W. Beyer, "κυβέρνησις," *TDNT,* 3:1,036; cf. 1,035-37.

150. Weiss, *Der erste Korintherbrief,* 308.

151. Lang, *Die Briefe,* 175.

152. Heinrici, *Das erste Sendschreiben,* 409. Although Dunn's allusion to "wise advice to puzzled individuals" may well be included, the context identified by Mitchell and others confirms that the *primary* application is to the corporate life of the local or translocal church (cf. Dunn, *Jesus and the Spirit,* 252). As we noted, H. Balz and G. Schneider refer both (f) and (g) to "organizational work in the Church" (*EDNT,* 1:110).

Greek as if these were open questions; thus it is inadequate. The REB and NJB give a gentle (but perhaps not sufficiently explicit) signal in the omission of the verb after the first question: *Are all apostles? All prophets? All teachers? . . .* Idiomatic English will also avoid stylistic boredom which deprives subsequent phrases of their force by repeating the same structure, even if this is acceptable for Greek where the parallel structure compensates for repetition (as it does not in English). Hence we have (a) produced stylistic variations, (b) used forms which give appropriate weight to μή as a question which predetermines an emphatic negative answer, and (c) translated each phrase and term, e.g., **effective deeds of power** (for δυνάμεις), **put the deepest secret things into articulate speech** (for διερμηνεύουσιν), in ways which accord with our detailed exegetical discussions above.

Yet again Fee's repeated comment that Paul's "concern throughout has been the need for diversity" conflicts with much of our argument and detailed research and exegesis.[153] Paul is not saying, "Look at how varied your gifts are." No, he is asserting, "since none on his or her own receives this extensive range of necessary gifts, *you need others, and others need you.*" All have their place in a single body which shares *the same status in Christ.* However, if any talk goes on about "the most presentable" parts of the body which authenticate its status as "spiritual," this is not **tongues** or **kinds of healing**; rather, it is **first of all** whether it coheres with the proclamation of Christ through **apostles**, next, whether it builds up like the pastoral preaching of *prophets,* and, third, whether it coheres with what **teachers** expound from the OT and from apostolic tradition. But even if **all are not apostles . . . prophets . . . teachers** the other gifts are no less authentic **gifts** from God, which **all** have an honored and respected place within the body of Christ.

Witherington draws on Dale Martin's helpful work to bring the chapter to a forceful conclusion. He writes: "It takes all kinds of parts to make up a body. To think otherwise is to criticize God, because, as v. 18 indicates, it is God who has placed the various members in the body. . . . No particular body member can devalue another or declare it to be of no worth. . . . D. B. Martin rightly concludes that Paul's use of body imagery is at variance with the usual use. . . . Paul uses it to relativize the sense of importance of those of higher status, making them see the importance and necessity of the weaker, lower status Corinthian Christians . . . the 'less presentable' members."[154] But to see the point fully, we must bear in mind that in 4:1-13 it emerges clearly that for the Corinthians "high status" gifts were the triumphalist ones of exultation and visible, demonstrative "success"; the apostles were "dirt," struggling in the arena while the Corinthians sat in seats of honor and watched their bloodied humiliation.[155] Is it

153. Fee, *First Epistle,* 622; repeated in *God's Empowering Presence,* 194.
154. Witherington, *Conflict and Community,* 258-59.
155. This point is transparent in Luther, Calvin, and Barth; cf. Thiselton, "Luther and Barth on 1 Cor 15: Six Theses for Theology in Relation to Recent Interpretation," in W. P. Stephens (ed.),

exultation in the Spirit or humiliation with Christ which identifies Christ's body? Is it self-edification or edification of others? Only when Paul has reflected on the meaning of love for the other (12:31–13:13) and applied it to the assembled church (14:1-40) will he then go on to show the timing and nature of true "spirituality" and of triumphant victory in the Spirit (15:1-58). Even 15:58 returns to ὁ κόπος ὑμῶν, which is οὐ κενὸς ἐν κυρίῳ.

Transitional Verse (12:31)

(31) Continue to be zealously concerned about the "greatest" gifts. Yes, an even greater way still I am going to show you.

We noted above the arguments of Collins for viewing 12:27-31a as a rhetorical unit, with v. 31b beginning the argument of ch. 13. However, the most significant study of this important transitional verse is the 1993 article in *NTS* by J. F. M. Smit.[156] Although commentators traditionally link either the whole of v. 31 or at least v. 31b with ch. 13 rather than with ch. 12, I have become convinced that to do this is to deprive the verse of its integral rhetorical and logical force with the argument which Paul has steadily built up from 12:19-30 and prepared for in 12:12-18. We have seen that there was a *zealous concern,* even a *striving,* for the gifts of the Spirit that were deemed to be **greatest** in the sense of their supposedly constituting a mark of a *high social and/or spiritual status.* Once again Paul uses redefinition or "code switching" (see above on Moores and Eco). Paul rejects their view of "high status" gifts utterly. But, he argues, tongue-in-cheek (Smit, with "sharp irony"), *do not stop being* **zealously concerned about the "greatest" gifts**, provided that you follow me in transposing and subverting your understanding of what counts as **"the greatest."**[157] The **"greatest"** are not those that minister to status or to self, but those which *serve* the good of others and *build* the community. **I now show you** that what is **an even greater way still** is the way of *love.*

As Smit notes, ζηλοῦτε may be technically either indicative or imperative, but in 14:1 and 14:39 it occurs as an imperative among other imperatives and here is "unmistakably imperative."[158] G. Iber and Bittlinger understand it as indicative, but only because they rightly cannot conceive of Paul's urging them *to strive* either for "gifts" (since all depends on God's sovereign choice)

The Bible, The Reformation and the Church: Essays in Honour of James Atkinson, JSNTSS 105 (Sheffield: Sheffield Academic Press, 1995), 258-89; and further, e.g., Luther, *Works,* 28:94-95 and 192 (*WA,* 36:665); Calvin, *First Epistle,* 14 and 312; and Barth, *Resurrection,* vol. 2, and throughout.

156. J. F. M. Smit, "Two Puzzles: 1 Cor 12:31 and 13:3: Rhetorical Solution," *NTS* 39 (1993): 246-64; cf. Collins, *First Cor,* 467-68.

157. Smit, "Two Puzzles," 255.

158. Ibid., 247.

or, worse, the **greatest** gifts.[159] But ζηλόω need not mean *strive,* and Paul redefines **greatest** in a way which pulls the rug from under the feet of the status-
seeking elitists. It is unnecessary, therefore, to assume a more forced indicative,
or that Paul is using a quotation from their own theology. Many commentators
seem to flounder in this discussion: Conzelmann seems ill at ease, and Fee's
statement that "it is not 'love versus gifts'" would never even arise as something to deny on the basis of Smit's reading of this verse.[160] An imperative is
understood by Heinrici, Orr and Walther, Barrett, Conzelmann, Fee, Senft,
Schrage, and Collins.[161] Robertson and Plummer stress the continuous
imperatival present: **continue to be zealously concerned** . . . , which gives
added point to Smit's exegesis.[162]

The meaning of ζηλοῦτε is also disputed. Our various lexicographical
sources list a variety of uses: in a positive sense *to strive, to desire earnestly, to
exert oneself,* or in a negative sense *to envy* or *to covet.*[163] Hence English VSS
employ *strive for* (NRSV), *eagerly desire* (NIV), *desire earnestly* (RV), and
covet (AV/KJV). REB skillfully tries to remove the pejorative sense of envy or
covet by translating *prize,* while NJB translates *set your mind on.* . . . But
BAGD and especially Grimm-Thayer note that *to be deeply concerned about,*
or **zealously concerned about**, can convey the meaning of the Greek usually
when the accusative or object of concern is *personal.* Here the **gifts** of the Holy
Spirit are inseparable from the very presence and personal action of the Spirit
of God. Indeed, Paul urges that the desire for *"spirituality"* is no religious technique but *experience of the Spirit.* Paul thus enjoins them to **continue** their
zealous concern about the "greatest" gifts, provided that they let him redefine what "**greatest**" amounts to in practice. It means here *being busy at what
is of deep concern.*[164]

While strictly μείζονα is the comparative of the adjective μέγας, *great*
(μέγιστος occurs as a superlative in 2 Pet 1:4), this form very frequently represents a superlative, as indeed it does here.[165] Hence it is to be translated **great-**

159. G. Iber, "Zum Verständnis von 1 Cor. 12:31," *ZNW* 54 (1963): 43-53; Bittlinger, *Gifts
and Graces,* 73-75 (following Iber). Bittlinger does concede "a touch of irony" (74).

160. Conzelmann, *1 Cor,* 215-16; Fee, *First Epistle,* 625. Fee's discussion of three possible
interpretations (624-25) lacks his usual clarity and incisiveness.

161. For example, Orr and Walther, *1 Cor,* 288; Barrett, *First Epistle,* 296; Findlay, *Expositor's Greek Testament,* 2:896; Edwards, *First Epistle,* 336; Senft, *Première Épitre,* 165; Heinrici,
Das erste Sendschreiben, 411, n. 3; Collins, *First Cor,* 466 and 471; Schrage, *Der erste Brief,*
3:240.

162. Robertson and Plummer, *First Epistle,* 282.

163. BAGD, 338; Grimm-Thayer, 271.

164. As Grimm-Thayer observe, ζηλόω in the LXX translates קָנָא *(qinne'), to burn with
zeal,* and the metaphor of *burning* or *boiling* denotes *intensity of desire or concern.* In personal concerns, this need not denote *striving,* but rather *being busy about what is of concern* (Grimm-Thayer,
271, entry 2a), or about what is of *deep concern* (BAGD, 338).

165. The point is not generally disputed. Smit is among those who adopt this view ("Two
Puzzles," 247).

est. But we have placed it in quotation marks to make explicit the exegesis convincingly expounded by Smit. The phrase καθ' ὑπερβολήν occurs five times in the NT, exclusively in Paul.[166] Again, it is not a matter of controversy that Paul here uses the phrase to mean *surpassing, excellent.* Although ἔτι could in theory be used in a temporal way to mean *now,* in this context it "may enhance the comparative," and with καί it adds further enhancement, which Smit renders, **yes, even.** . . .[167] However, while Smit prefers, **yes, an even still** *more excellent way,* since the word *excellent* has such a diverse range of quasi-technical meanings in modern English, as well as colloquial ones, it seems best to refer back to the point of the comparison (μείζονα), and to translate **Yes, an even greater way still.** . . . We follow Barrett's rendering of the present tense of δείκνυμι: **I am going on to show you.**[168] Smit clinches his argument with a careful and detailed survey of relevant rhetorical devices, which Paul picks up in 13:3 with καυχήσωμαι, **I may boast.**[169]

5. Love, the Essential and Lasting Criterion (13:1-13)

(1) If I were to speak with human or angelic tongues, but if I had not love, I would have become only a resonating jar or a reverberating cymbal. (2) And if I should have the gift of prophecy, and if I penetrate all the depths too profound for mere human discovery, and have all "knowledge," and if I possess the gifts of every kind of faith sufficient to remove mountains — but, after all, may lack love, I am nothing. (3) Even if I should divide up all my possessions to feed the needy, and if I hand over my body that I may glory, but have not love, it counts for nothing.

(4) Love waits patiently; love shows kindness. Love does not burn with envy; does not brag — is not inflated with its own importance. (5) It does not behave with ill-mannered impropriety; is not preoccupied with the interests of the self; does not become exasperated into pique; does not keep a reckoning up of evil. (6) Love does not take pleasure at wrongdoing, but joyfully celebrates truth. (7) It never tires of support, never loses faith, never exhausts hope, never gives up.

(8) Love never falls apart. Whether it be prophecies, these will be brought to an end; if it be tongues, these will stop; if it be "knowledge," this

---

166. Rom 7:13; 1 Cor 12:31; 2 Cor 1:8; 4:17; Gal 1:13.

167. Smit, "Two Puzzles," 247-48.

168. Barrett, *First Epistle,* 296.

169. Smit, "Two Puzzles," esp. 250-64. Smit recognizes the textual problem of 13:3 (see below). In his view "1 Cor. 12:31–13:13 is a depreciatory speech drafted entirely in accordance with the rhetorical rules of the *genus demonstrativum*" (251). "Irony has its regular place among the rhetorical devices" (e.g., Quintilian, *Institutio Oratoria* 8.6.54-58; 9.2.44-53). . . . "Another signal is contextual contradiction . . ." (251). We fully endorse Smit's view of 12:31, but have strong hesitations about the supposed continuation of irony into ch. 13.

will be rendered obsolete. (9) For we know in fragmentary ways, and we prophesy part by part. (10) But when the completed whole comes, what is piece by piece shall be done away. (11) When I was a child, I used to talk like a child, form opinions like a child, count values like a child; when I reached adulthood, I turned my back on the things of childhood. (12) For we are seeing the present only by means of a mirror indirectly; but then it will be face to face. For the present I come to know part by part; but then I shall come to know just as fully as I have been known. (13) So now, there remain faith, hope, love, these three. But the greatest of these is love.

Spicq observes that this chapter "contains the word *agapē* ten times" and "is undoubtedly the most important in the entire NT concerning charity."[1] Spicq himself entertains no doubt that Paul himself is the author of this chapter, although he acknowledges that many argue to the contrary, partly on the ground that it appears to constitute a literary rather than an epistolary style, and that supposedly it interrupts the flow of chs. 12–14 on gifts within the church. But he rightly urges that it precisely fits its context, and remarks tartly that anyone who has done any preaching will know full well that on occasion a preacher draws on a more lyric expression, perhaps to return later to a more prosaic, conceptual, or cognitive communicative mode.[2] "He [Paul] varies his style constantly . . . doctrinal, catechetical, moral, sapiential, and even juridical. . . . Chapter 13 . . . is a necessary link in the argument putting charisms in their proper place."[3] It also takes its place among the themes which concern worship, from idol foods (chs. 8–10), dress in worship (11:2-16), and the Eucharist (11:17-34) to the use of charisms during worship (12:1–14:40). "The whole presentation begins with a summons to *agapē* (8:1)."[4] We shall argue that this perception is entirely valid.

One of the most sustained attacks on the contextual integrity of the chapter comes from J. Weiss. Weiss argues that the material is a polemic against gnostics and gnosticism, and that it belongs with 8:1-13, not with 12:1–14:40. The statement that love is not "puffed up" (οὐ φυσιοῦται, 13:4) belongs with 8:1, "Knowledge puffs up (ἡ γνῶσις φυσιοῖ), but love builds up (ἡ δὲ ἀγάπη οἰκοδομεῖ)."[5] Weiss further argues that ἀγάπη does not occur in 12:1-30 and 14:1-40, and that this is a further symptom of displacement. Héring, Senft, Schmithals, Titus, and Conzelmann all take up and develop these arguments.[6]

---

1. Spicq, *Agapē in the NT,* 2:139.

2. Ibid., 140-41.

3. Ibid., 140.

4. Ibid.

5. Weiss, *Der erste Korintherbrief,* 309-16; *Earliest Christianity,* 2:569-71; and "Beiträge zur paulinischen Rhetorik," in *Theologische Studien* (Göttingen: Vandenhoeck and Ruprecht, 1897), 196-200; cf. 165-247.

6. Héring, *First Epistle,* 134; Senft, *Première Épitre,* 165-66; Schmithals, *Gnosticism in Corinth,* 90-96, esp. 95-96, n. 23; E. L. Titus, "Did Paul Write 1 Cor 13?" *JBR* 27 (1959): 299-302; and Conzelmann, *1 Cor,* 217.

But among these writers, only Titus appears to exclude Pauline authorship; whereas even Schmithals, who proposes that Paul wrote nine letters to Corinth, (of which thirteen or perhaps even fourteen fragments make up our present 1 Corinthians), opts for the view that a copyist simply made a mistake in inserting omitted material in the wrong place.[7]

Against this Margaret Mitchell argues convincingly that "the objection that 1 Cor. 14 does not fit with chap. 13 because the word ἀγάπη is not used there is easily refuted because in the syllogism of 8:1 Paul had already explicitly equated ἀγάπη with οἰκοδομή, which figures prominently in the argument in chap. 14."[8] Further, alongside his detailed attention to compositional questions, J. C. Hurd asserts that "1 Cor. 13, moreover, manifests the same interest as ch. 14."[9] In practice, ch. 13 takes up the themes of γνῶσις, *knowledge* (13:2, 8, 9; cf. 13:12), γλῶσσαι, *tongues* (13:1, 8), and προφητεῖαι, *prophecies* (13:2, 8, 9), which are central to chs. 12 and 14. This point is firmly made also by Allo, Bruce, Grosheide, Fee, Moffatt, and Hays and conclusively answers the objection of the previous paragraph.[10] Grosheide comments, "Chapter 13 is not to be regarded as interrupting the discourse concerning the charismata. On the contrary, it is a necessary link in the argument which has as its purpose to assign the glossolalia its rightful place."[11] Schrage also sees ch. 13 as a "criterion" (cf. our heading) which explicates 12:31 and indeed 12:1–14:40.[12]

Grosheide's argument is correct, except that Paul's target concerns all kinds of self-centered "spirituality," *including* the public use of glossolalia, *especially as a perceived status indicator.* Just as Spicq's study of *Agapē in the New Testament* constructively informs his exegesis, even so Moffatt's *Love in the New Testament* gives him insight into the role of 1 Corinthians 13, and (in accordance with the hermeneutical circle) vice versa: Moffatt produced both a commentary on 1 Corinthians (1938) and a full-length study of love in the NT (1929). Both are full of good sense. Moffatt urges that even if Paul did not compose "the lyric on love" in the midst of his dictation, nevertheless "This 'Hymn of Love' was written out of a close and trying experience. *If it is a rhapsody, it is the rhapsody of a realist who has come safely through contact with the disenchanting life of the churches* . . . wrung from long intercourse with *ordinary Christians, especially those at Corinth*" (my italics).[13]

Moffatt hits the center of the target here. Indeed, best of all is C. T.

---

7. Schmithals, *Gnosticism,* 95-96, n. 63; cf. his "Die Korintherbriefe als Briefsammlung," *ZNW* 64 (1973): 263-88.

8. Mitchell, *Rhetoric of Reconciliation,* 270.

9. Hurd, *Origin of 1 Cor,* 189.

10. Allo, *Première Épitre,* 340-42; Bruce, *1 and 2 Cor,* 124-26; Grosheide, *First Epistle,* 303; Mitchell, *Rhetoric,* 270-71; Fee, *First Epistle,* 626-28, esp. 626, nn. 5-8; Hays, *First Cor,* 221-22; Collins, *First Cor,* 471, calls it "a digression" but does not question its integrity.

11. Grosheide, *First Epistle,* 303.

12. Schrage, *Der erste Brief,* 3:276-77.

13. Moffatt, *Love in the NT,* 182; cf. also his *First Epistle,* 191.

Craig's comment: "On closer examination it is seen that *almost every word in the chapter has been chosen with this particular situation at Corinth in mind.* . . . The mood is instructive fully as much as lyrical" (my italics).[14] The one hindrance to imagining its being dictated is the polished metrical nature of the phrases, vocabulary, and rhythm, which Hitchcock, among others, sees as the fruit of careful composition.[15] But F. F. Bruce and C. T. Craig paint exactly the right picture. Might not the composition have come to Paul as he churned over in his mind, before writing this part of the letter, the stances at Corinth which "**inflated** the self" (cf. 8:1); which claimed the thrones and **tongues of angels** (4:7-13; 6:3); which prized **knowledge** above concern for the weak (8:1-13; 12:8); which showed **jealousy** over high status (3:1-3; 13:4-7); and which held a *triumphalist overrealized eschatology* without a *theologia crucis* (1:18-25; 4:8-13; 13:8-13)? If Spicq can respond to Weiss about the experience of preaching in various styles, what of the experience of mulling over the next day's sermon during a sleepless night? At all events, if the chapter was composed before the dictation, it must have been composed with the Corinthian situation bubbling in the mind.

The mass of "comparisons" and "parallels" collected by Conzelmann, Sigountos, and others should not distract us from the force of these factors. If this chapter is to be viewed as a rhetorical *encomium* with a patterned rhetorical format or structure, Paul is using it for his own ends as well as for Corinth. It would not distract from the chapter if resonances of rhetorical images and devices from, e.g., popular repetitions of part of Plato's *Symposium* or 1 Esdras 3 informed Paul's conscious or subconscious mind.[16] Carson and Fee are among those who offer warnings about attaching too much importance to parallels of this kind.[17] But the issue, in a sense, is value-neutral. Neither too little nor too much should be inferred from the fact that, as Spicq observes, for Paul to be "inspired" to produce "the musical effect of pleasant-sounding words; the choice of images; the balance and parallelism of its propositions; the use of antithesis, chiasmas, hyperbole, and anaphora; and above all its lyric tone . . . and elevated thought," is it any less "Paul's own" if he draws on imagery and rhetoric from Jewish wisdom literature or from Graeco-Roman philosophers or poets (whether consciously or unconsciously)?[18] "There is no evidence of direct borrowing," however, even if it *might* occur.[19] We need not therefore enter into speculative debates about whether or not this chapter can be called a hymn, or

14. Craig, "1 Cor," *IB,* 10:165.
15. Hitchcock, "St. Paul's Hymn of Love," *Theol* 26 (1933): 65-75; cf. also his "Structure of St. Paul's Hymn of Love," *ExpTim* 34 (1922-23): 488-92.
16. Sigountos, "The Genre of 1 Cor 13," 246-60, argues for close parallels esp. with Plato, *Symposium* 197 C-E, and with 1 Esdr. 3:34-40. This need not imply Paul's *direct* knowledge of the *Symposium,* although we need not exclude the possibility either.
17. Fee, *First Epistle,* 626; Carson, *Showing the Spirit* (Grand Rapids: Baker, 1987), 52.
18. Spicq, *Agapē,* 2:141-42.
19. Ibid., 142.

epideictic rhetoric, or an encomium, or a "word of wisdom."[20] M. M. Mitchell's conclusion that it is "deliberative rhetoric" designed to persuade is sufficiently broad to remain acceptable, but no single language function should obscure its multilayered character.[21] Most writers on the structure perceive a chiasmic form, which clearly divides into three blocks: (a) vv. 1-3, (b) vv. 4-7, and (c) vv. 8-13. Some also argue for a three-fold movement within each of the main parts.[22]

Bibliography on 13:1-13

Barr, J., "Words for Love in Biblical Greek," in N. T. Wright and L. D. Hurst (eds.), *The Glory of Christ in the NT,* Festschrift for G. B. Caird (Oxford: Oxford University Press, 1990), 3-18.

Blair, H. J., "First Corinthians 13 and the Disunity at Corinth," *Theological Education* 14 (1983): 69-77.

Bockmuehl, M., *Revelation and Mystery in Ancient Judaism and Pauline Christianity,* WUNT 2:36 (Tübingen: Mohr, 1990).

Bornkamm, G., "The More Excellent Way (1 Cor. 13)," in his *Early Christian Experience* (Eng. trans., London: SCM, 1969), 180-93 (largely from German of 1933, with revisions on 13:13 rpt. in his *Gesammelte Aufsatze* 1 [1937], 93-112).

Caragounis, C. C., "'To Boast' or 'To Be Burned'? The Crux of 1 Cor 13:3," *SEÅ* 60 (1995): 115-27.

Dautzenberg, G., *Urchristliche Prophetie,* BWANT 104 (Stuttgart: Kohlhammer, 1975), 149-225.

Dunn, J. D. G., *The Theology of Paul the Apostle* (Edinburgh: T. & T. Clark, 1998), 634-42 and 658-61.

Elliott, J. K., "In Favour of καυχήσομαι at 1 Cor. 13:3," *ZNW* 62 (1971): 297-98.

Fishbane, M., "Through the Looking Glass: Reflections on Ezek. 43:3, Num. 12:8 and 1 Cor. 13," *Hebrew Annual Review* 10 (1986): 63-75.

Ford, D. F., "Facing," in *Self and Salvation: Being Transformed* (Cambridge: Cambridge University Press, 1999), 17-29.

Furnish, V. P., *The Love Command in the NT* (London: SCM, 1973), 91-131.

Gerhardsson, B., "1 Kor 13. Om Paulus och hans rabbinska Bakgrund," *SEÅ* 39 (1974): 121-44; also in German in *Donum Gentilicium* (1978): 185-209.

Holladay, C. R., "1 Cor 13: Paul as Apostolic Paradigm," in D. L. Balch, E. Ferguson, and W. A. Meeks (eds.), *Greeks, Romans and Christian — In Honor of A. J. Malherbe* (Minneapolis: Fortress, 1990), 80-98.

Harris, W. V., "'Sounding Brass' and Hellenistic Technology," *BAR* 8 (1982): 38-41.

Hitchcock, F. R. M., "St. Paul's Hymn of Love (1 Cor. xiii)," *Theol* 26 (1933): 65-75.

———, "The Structure of St. Paul's Hymn on Love," *ExpTim* 34 (1922-23): 488-92.

Horsky, R., *Jesus and the Spiral of Violence* (San Francisco: Harper, 1987).

Houghton, M. J., "A Re-examination of 1 Cor 13:8-13," *BSac* 153 (1996): 344-56.

---

20. Astonishingly, such is the fashion of rhetorical theory in NT studies that some spill blood on the carpet to defend or to attack these categories.

21. Mitchell, *Rhetoric of Reconciliation,* 273.

22. Collins, *First Cor,* 472; cf. Mitchell, *Rhetoric of Reconciliation,* 165-67, 274; and Wischmeyer, *Der höchste Weg. Das 13 Kapitel des 1 Kor,* 205-8.

Johansson, N., "1 Cor 13 and 1 Cor 14," *NTS* 10 (1963-64): 383-92.

Joly, R., *Le Vocabulaire chrétien de l'amour, est-il original?* (Brussels: University of Brussels, 1968).

Kieffer, R., *Le primat de l'amour. Commentaire épistémologique de 1 Cor 13,* LD 85 (Paris: Cerf, 1975).

Klein, W. W., "Noisy Gong or Acoustic Vase? A Note on 1 Cor. 13:1," *NTS* 32 (1986): 286-89.

Maly, K., *Mündige Gemeinde* (Stuttgart: Katholisches Bibekwerk, 1967), 193-98.

Martin, R. P., "A Suggested Exegesis of 1 Cor. 13:13," *ExpTim* 82 (1970-71): 119-20, and 351.

Miguens, E., "1 Cor. 13:8-13 Reconsidered," *CBQ* 37 (1975): 76-97.

Mitchell, M. M., *Paul and the Rhetoric of Reconciliation* (Tübingen: Mohr, 1992), 165-71 and 270-79.

Moffatt, J., *Love in the NT* (London, 1929 and New York: Richard Smith, 1930), esp. 168-93.

Mortley, R., "The Mirror and 1 Cor 13:12 in the Epistemology of Clement of Alexandria," *VC* 30 (1976): 109-20.

Nygren, A., *Agapē and Eros* (Eng. trans., London: SPCK, 1957), 61-145, esp. 133-45.

O'Brien, J., "Sophocles' Ode on Man and Paul's Hymn on Love," *Classical Journal* 71 (1975-76): 138-51.

Petzer, J. H., "Contextual Evidence in Favor of καυθήσωμαι in 1 Cor. 13:3," *NTS* 35 (1989): 229-53.

Sanders, J. T., "First Cor 13: Its Interpretation Since the First World War," *Int* 20 (1966): 159-87.

Sanders, T. K., "A New Approach to 1 Cor. 13:1," *NTS* 36 (1990): 614-18.

Schmidt, K. L., "κύμβαλον," *TDNT,* 3:1,037-39.

Schmithals, W., *Gnosticism in Corinth,* 90-96.

———, "Die Korintherbriefe als Briefsammlung," *ZNW* 64 (1973): 263-88.

Schutz, K., "Stückwerk bleibt unser Tun Von der 'Relativität' der Charismen," *Geist und Leben* 45 (1972): 241-45.

Seaford, R., "1 Cor. 13:12," *JTS* 35 (1984): 117-20.

Sigountos, J. G., "The Genre of 1 Cor 13," *NTS* 40 (1994): 246-60.

Smit, J. F. M., "The Genre of 1 Cor 13 in the Light of Classical Rhetoric," *NovT* 33 (1991): 193-216.

———, "Two Puzzles: 1 Cor. 12:31 and 13:3: A Rhetorical Solution," *NTS* 39 (1993): 246-64.

Söding, T., "Das Wortfeld der Liebe im paganen und biblische Griechisch. Philologische Beobachtungen an der Wurzel 'ἀγάπη,'" *ETL* 68 (1992): 284-330.

Spicq, C., *Agapē in the NT* (3 vols., Eng. trans., London and St. Louis: Herder, 1963), 2:139-81.

Standaert, B., "1 Cor 13," in L. de Lorenzi (ed.) *Charisma und Agape (1 Kor 12–14)* (Rome: St Paul's Abbey, 1983), 127-47.

Stauffer, E., "ἀγάπη," *TDNT,* 1:35-55.

Strobel, A., "Exkurs: Der Begriff der Agape im NT," in *Der erste Brief an die Korintherbrief* (Zürich: Theologische Verlag, 1989), 206-8.

Stuart, E., "Love Is . . . Paul," *ExpTim* 102 (1991): 264-66.

Waters, C. J., "'Love Is . . . Paul' — A Response," *ExpTim* 103 (1991): 75.

White, R. F., "Richard Gaffin and Wayne Grudem on 1 Cor. 13:10 . . . ," *JETS* 35 (1992): 173-81.

Wischmeyer, O., *Der höchste Weg. Das 13 Kapitel des 1 Kor* (Gütersloh: Mohn, 1981).

———, "Traditionsgeschichtliche Untersuchung der Paulinischen Aussagen über die Liebe *(Agapē)*," *ZNW* 74 (1983): 222-36.

Yeung M., "A Comparison of Faith in Jesus and Paul" (Unpub. Ph.D. diss., University of Aberdeen, 1999).

We follow the widely accepted division into 13:1-3, vv. 4-7 and vv. 8-13 (or vv. 8-12, with v. 13 as a climax).[23] Our proposed headings approximate those of Bornkamm, which are also broadly followed by Craig.[24] In Barth's words, (a) "love . . . alone decisively determines human life. . . . It is love alone that counts"; (b) "love alone . . . triumphs"; (c) on the basis of "the promise which has eternal content . . . it is . . . love alone that endures."[25]

a. The Fruitlessness of All "Gifts" without Love (13:1-3)

1 Although λαλῶ and ἔχω could be indicative *(if I speak . . . if I do not have),* the use of μή rather than οὐ, coupled with ἐάν rather than εἰ, establishes that Paul uses the subjunctive. The hypothesis is indefinite rather than contingent, and (especially since Dautzenberg and others draw inferences from ἀγγέλων) is perhaps best translated as, **If I were to speak in human or in angelic tongues, but if I had not love, I would have become.** . . . REB achieves the same result by recasting the syntax: *I may speak in tongues . . . but if I have no love . . .* (as against NRSV, RV, and NIV, *if I speak . . . ;* AV/KJV, NJB, *though I . . .*). Conzelmann is correct to observe, "It is . . . a vitally important point that Paul begins with values that are significant in the community at Corinth: speaking with tongues, prophecy, etc."[26] This makes the indefinite syntax all the more important pastorally. It is not an open attack: *if I speak with tongues, but do not have love . . . ,* but *at this point* the more deliberative category of rhetoric advocated by M. M. Mitchell: *suppose that this situation were to arise . . . what would it amount to?* (i.e., you tell me!). In hermeneutical language, it invites reader response.

---

23. O. Wischmeyer, *Der höchste Weg,* 205-8, in fact distinguishes the common form of 13:1-3 and 8-13, in which the worth or *usefulness* of love is praised, with the different formal style of vv. 4-7 as a series of *confessions (Bekenntnisreihe)* of the general ethical character of love. Similarly, Mitchell sees vv. 1-3 and 8-13 as "deliberative rhetoric," and vv. 4-7 as "a very brief encomium on love" with positive and negative epithets *(Rhetoric,* 274; cf. 165-67).

24. Bornkamm suggests, "vanity of all values without love . . . ; the nature and reign of love . . . ; the immortality of love" ("The More Excellent Way," in his *Early Christian Experience,* 180-93). Craig proposes: "the superiority of love . . . the nature of love . . . the permanence of love" ("1 Cor," in *IB,* 10:167, 172, and 185). But an emphasis on the gifts in vv. 1-3, on the dynamic character of the verb in vv. 4-7, and on eschatological permanence in vv. 8-13 is also required.

25. Barth, *Church Dogmatics,* 4/2, sect. 68.825; cf. 727-840.

26. Conzelmann, *1 Cor,* 221.

The dative is a straightforward instrumental use: **to speak with human or angelic tongues**. The distinction between **human** and **angelic** could either (i) reflect a difference of view at Corinth as to whether speaking in or with **tongues** signified inspired human utterances or a "language of heaven"; or (ii) it could refer to human gifts ἐν παντὶ λόγῳ (1:5, *speech*) and also (secondly) to speaking in or with **tongues** (12:10); or (iii) it may refer to **tongues** with an added hyperbole (following Sigountos): *yes, even if these tongues were to be* **angelic** *language itself* (as some seem to think!).[27] On the meaning of **tongues** and *speaking with* **tongues**, see above. Here in our view Paul begins with the notion of **tongues** as that which gives expression to the secret yearnings and praise of the depths of the **human** heart, and escalates to a hypothesis considered at Corinth but not necessarily endorsed by Paul, that **tongues** is the **angelic** language of heaven. See above on 12:10, where these views relate to the work of Theissen and of Dautzenberg. A full discussion of this phenomenon occurs above at 12:10.

Any translation must allow the emphasis to fall upon ἀγάπην (with δέ and μή): **but if I had not love**. In the index to his second volume of *Agapē in the New Testament,* which is almost entirely on the Pauline corpus (with Hebrews and 1 Peter), Spicq lists over a hundred "activities," qualities, or effects of ἀγάπη.[28] The vast majority of writers agree that the noun ἀγάπη, **love**, is relatively rare in Greek literature outside the NT and early Christian writings. But the verb ἀγαπᾶν is more frequent, and indeed very frequent in the LXX. These lexicographical observations may be confirmed not only from linguistic sources (e.g., LSJ, Hatch-Redpath, BAGD) but also from specialist studies from Wischmeyer and Stauffer to Nygren, Moffatt, and Spicq.[29] In particular R. Joly stresses the frequency of the verb ἀγαπᾶν outside the NT.[30] Nygren and Moffatt argue that Paul is concerned to disengage **love** in his own theology from Greek and other pagan ideas of love as primarily emotional, sexual, or ecstatic. They write that "to speak of God's force of love is in itself a credo" (Moffatt), and "Agape comes to us as a quite new creation of Christianity. . . . Without it nothing that is Christian would be Christian" (Nygren).[31] Nevertheless, uses of the *word* must not be confused with Paul's theological emphasis. The worst thing that could happen, Nygren continues, is for Christian uses of ἀγάπη to become confused with non-Christian notions of love through which

---

27. Sigountos, "The Genre of 1 Cor 13," 252; cf. 246-60. See further Senft, *La Première Épitre,* 167.

28. Spicq, *Agapē in the NT,* 2:445-47.

29. Hatch-Redpath, 1:5-7; LSJ, 6; BAGD, 4-6; Wischmeyer, *Der höchste Weg,* 23-26; and her "Vorkommen und Bedeutung von Agapē in der ausserchristlichen Antike," *ZNW* 69 (1978): 212-38; E. Stauffer, "ἀγαπάω," *TDNT,* 1:21-55; A. Nygren, *Agapē and Eros,* 53-67; Moffatt, *Love in the NT,* 4-63; Spicq, *L'agape de 1 Cor XIII, Un example de contribution á la semantique á l'exégèse NT* (Paris: Gabalda, 1955); cf. further W. Harrelson, "The Idea of *Agapē,*" *JR* 31 (1951): 169-82; Louw-Nida, 1:293-96; W. Günther, "Love," *NIDNTT,* 2:542-50.

30. Joly, *Le vocabulaire chrétien de l'amour, est-il original?*

31. Moffatt, *Love in the NT,* 5; Nygren, *Agapē and Eros,* 48.

"the new idea can be drained away from within . . . by the other. . . . Agape entered into a world that had already received the impress of Eros."[32]

One problem with Nygren's identification of ἀγάπη as a distinctive "motif" is the possible confusion between *words* and *concepts*. As Barr reminds us, it is one thing to claim that *conceptual uses of* the word in Paul and the NT are distinctive; it is quite a different matter to suggest that the *word* ἀγάπη itself is distinctive.[33] This has flawed so many parallel claims in "biblical theology" that the temptation is to rebound away from Nygren's important account of Paul's *theological uses* of the word in certain contexts. As a *theological construct based on selected contexts,* his claim remains *profoundly true* that when Paul uses ἀγάπη of God it is "unmotivated"; "indifferent to [prior] value" on the part of the loved one; "creative" of value; and characterized by a fellowship or relationality that reflects God's elective relation with the world, and, we might add, God's trinitarian nature.[34] But to read such qualities back into every occurrence of ἀγάπη, in Paul, would be to commit what Barr terms "illegitimate totality transfer," imposing an accumulation of meanings from various passages onto every specific use of the word.[35]

We have cleared the way, however, to appreciating why Paul wishes to disengage ἀγάπη from the sensual, emotive, erotic, or even ecstatic nuances which the noun ἔρως, *passionate love,* and less often the verb ἀγαπᾶν can convey in secular or non-Christian religious Greek texts. ἀγαπᾶν enters Paul's thinking as the usual LXX translation for Heb. אהב *('aheb), to love,* of which Hatch-Redpath cite around 130 occurrences in the LXX, and the noun ἀγάπη translates אהבה *('ahabah),* **love,** sixteen times in the LXX.[36] In an interesting research article B. Gerhardsson sees ch. 13, especially 13:8-13, as a rhetorical-didactic poem (not a hymn) drawing on wisdom traditions associated with אהב *('aheb)* mediated through rabbinic tradition associated with Hillel.[37] Even more ingeniously, M. Fishbane argues for midrashic wordplays in 13:12 reflecting Ezek 43:3 and Num 12:8, which we shall consider when we comment on that verse.[38] Together with the OT tradition, however M. M. Mitchell argues forcefully that while Paul may distance himself from Gk. ἔρως, one strand in Greek uses of ἀγάπη or ἀγαπᾶν remains closely relevant to 1 Cor 13:1-13. She provides instances where φιλία and other words for love denote the mutual respect or reconciliation which follows the restoration of concord after division and

32. Nygren, *Agapē and Eros,* 53.

33. J. Barr, *The Semantics of Biblical Language* (Oxford: Oxford University Press, 1961), 215-43; cf. 206-14. See more specifically Barr, "Words for Love in Biblical Greek," in Wright and Hurst (eds.), *The Glory of Christ in the NT,* 3-18.

34. Nygren, *Agapē and Eros,* 75-81.

35. Barr, *Semantics,* 218; cf. 70-71 and 216-19.

36. Hatch-Redpath, 1:6-7.

37. Gerhardsson, "1 Kor 13. Om Paulus och hans rabbinska Bakgrund," 121-44 (also in German in *Donum Gentilicium* [1978], 185-209).

38. Fishbane, "Through the Looking Glass: Reflections on Ezek 43:3, Num 12:8, and 1 Cor 13," 63-75.

strife.[39] This may well contribute to Paul's use of the word, in which ch. 13 belongs integrally to 12:1–14:40.

Nevertheless, whereas Nygren's otherwise excellent work risks our reading too much into every use of the word ἀγάπη, in our view Mitchell's correct attempt to contextualize the meaning of **love** in 1 Corinthians 13 risks, equally, narrowing it too specifically. Clearly it is *much deeper and more fundamental in theology* for Paul than any *rhetorical* context about concord might suggest. At least two themes determine a distinctive theological emphasis which the word itself carries in 13:1-13. First, **love** represents "the power of the new age" breaking into the present, "the only vital force which has a future."[40] **Love** is that quality which distinctively stamps the life of heaven, where regard and respect for the other dominates the character of life with God as the communion of saints and heavenly hosts. The theologian may receive his or her redundancy notice; the prophet may have nothing to say which everyone else does not already know; but **love abides** as the character of heavenly, eschatological existence.

Second, as we have noted, **love** (ἀγάπη) denotes above all a *stance* or *attitude* which shows itself *in acts of will* as *regard, respect, and concern for the welfare of the other.* It is therefore profoundly *christological,* for *the cross* is the paradigm case of the act of *will* and *stance* which *places welfare of others above the interests of the self.* Here Moltmann and Jüngel rightly relate this to the *self-giving grace of the cruciform, Christomorphic God.* We cannot read the Johannine "God is love" onto Paul, but in fact it is already there in Paul, and the biblical exegete has no need to compromise the distinctive witness of each biblical source or tradition. It lies at the heart of Paul's theology of grace, and hence *by means of these considerations* Nygren's points carry *indirect* weight for 13:1-13. Nygren's work has particular value for the emphasis of v. 5 (see below).

This is confirmed by the specific and explicit contrasts in 13:1-3. Whereas **tongues** (v. 1) (in certain contexts) minister primarily to the self (14:4, ἑαυτὸν οἰκοδομεῖ), and **knowledge** (γνῶσις) may inflate the self rather than build the other (8:1b), and even good deeds without love can amount to **self-glorification** (13:3), **love does not seek its own personal good** (13:5) but the welfare of *the other.*[41]

Every word of the entire clause which makes up the apodosis of the conditional provides much interest: γέγονα χαλκὸς ἠχῶν ἢ κύμβαλον ἀλαλάζον. The general sense is clear enough: "No matter how exalted my gift of tongues, without love I am nothing more than a resounding gong or a clanging cymbal. This value judgement is meant to be shocking. . . . It is not the gift of tongues

39. Mitchell, *Reconciliation,* 165-71; cf. Aristotle, *Nicomachean Ethics* 8.1.4 (of φιλία); 4 Macc 13:23-26 (φιλανθρωπία); cf. *1 Clement* 49, esp. *1 Clem.* 49:5.

40. E. Stauffer, "ἀγαπᾶν," *TDNT,* 1:51.

41. See Vielhauer, *Oikodomē* (Karlsruhe: Harrassowitz, 1940), esp. 85-88, and his comments on 14:4 (see below).

that is only a resounding gong . . . but I, myself" (Carson).[42] But each word or phrase invites detailed comment.

χαλκὸς ἠχῶν is the subject of a research article by W. Harris under the title "'Sounding Brass' and Hellenistic Technology."[43] Harris discusses the phenomenon of acoustic resonance systems to which Vitruvius alludes in his work *On Architecture* (c. 30 BC). Material of *bronze* (χαλκός) was constructed in such a way as to amplify sound by functioning as an **acoustic resonator** or **resonating acoustic jar**, rather than as some kind of musical instrument or *gong*. Hence ἠχῶν means *sounding* in the sense of *sound producing: not* of *pitching* a sound. This matches uses of ἠχέω to mean *not to pitch* sound, but *to transmit and to resonate sound,* e.g., the roar of the sea or thunder. Paul uses the continuous present participle (Himerius, *Orations* 40; Ps 45:4, LXX; cf. the noun ἠχῶ, *sound,* in Wis 17:18).[44] ἠχῶν therefore does not make ἀλαλάζον redundant, but conveys the notion of *endlessly continuing resonances which have no musical pitch.*

Vitruvius, Harris demonstrates, speaks of **resonating jars** or *bronze vases,* which were placed in niches around the periphery of an auditorium. Such a system seems to have operated at Corinth in the second century BC, although the Roman governor Lucius Mummius later had them removed and sold to raise public funds. Harris concludes that whether or not the Corinthians replaced "the acoustic amplifying system," Paul's readers would know of **resonating** *acoustic bronze* **jars** used to project the voices of actors on stage and music.[45]

William W. Klein supports and develops Harris's view, against virtually all the standard translations and commentaries.[46] **Noisy** *gong* occurs in NRSV, NASB, Goodspeed, and Moffatt, while *gong* is found with a different adjective *(resounding gong)* in NIV, and *(gong booming)* in NJB. Neither *clanging bronze* (Barrett) nor *blaring brass* (Phillips) conveys the primary notion of resonance, although Knox's *echoing bronze* comes near, and AV/KJV's *sounding brass* (followed by Collins) is not a bad translation. Klein notes that Lenski and Grosheide view it as an instrument, and Moffatt's suggestion that it was *a gong* used in pagan temples, especially in the cults of Dionysius and Cybele, has attracted wide support.[47] This last suggestion, however, has been vigorously and strenuously rejected by C. Forbes, partly with reference to Klein's study.[48]

---

42. Carson, *Showing the Spirit,* 59.

43. W. Harris, in *BAR* 8 (1982): 38-41.

44. Cf. BAGD, 349.

45. In addition to *BAR* 8; cf. *Journal of the Acoustical Society of America* 70 (October 1981): 1,184-85.

46. Klein, "Noisy Gong or Acoustic Vase? A Note on 1 Cor. 13:1," 286-89.

47. Moffatt, *First Epistle,* 192. Followed by J. P. M. Sweet, "A Sign for Unbelievers: Paul's Attitude to Glossolalia," *NTS* 13 (1966-67): 240-57.

48. C. Forbes, *Prophecy and Inspired Speech* (Tübingen: Mohr, 1995), 38-39, 135-36; cf. also 20.

Klein infers: (a) that we must relinquish the supposed temple context of pagan religious ecstasy; and (b) that *tongues without love* are still, however, merely "a reverberation, an empty sound coming out of a hollow, lifeless vessel."[49]

Klein agrees with virtually all lexicographers and commentators that κύμβαλον ἀλαλάζον denotes "a musical instrument."[50] I can find no evidence for R. L. Laurin's assertion that it "referred to metal castagnettes" (our modern castanets); K. L. Schmidt includes an article on it in *TDNT* arguing for *cymbal*, but the word occurs only here in 13:1 within the whole of the NT.[51] It derives from κύμβη, a hollow vessel or hollow dish, and denotes a shallow, metallic rounded dish, which is struck against its partner to give out a resounding note. In the LXX it translates Heb. מְצִלְתַּיִם *(metsilttaim)* from the verb צָלַל *(tsalal) to clash, crash, clang,* which verges on the onomatopoeic (mainly 1 and 2 Chronicles, Ezra, Nehemiah, e.g., 1 Chron 13:8). Although the AV/KJV image of a *tinkling cymbal* is the subject of mirth, it is just arguable that in 1 Kings 18:6 the term atypically refers to a three-cornered instrument such as a *triangle,* while Zech 14:20 might denote *bells.*[52] For the bells of a harness might include bosses, and cymbals also could have bosses. Modern musicologists distinguish the *crotal,* which goes back thousands of years and is a thick metal plate, from the modern *orchestral cymbal,* which is of Turkish origin. The *crotal* had "a definite pitch" and could be hit head-on (unlike the modern orchestral cymbal) or struck by a club or hammer.[53] This latter method may account for the singular **a cymbal** here. (If so, *clash,* NJB, is questionable.)

Paul couples with κύμβαλον the adjective ἀλαλάζον. This also is onomatopoeic from the tradition of wailing loudly in lament. Like ἠχῶν it is technically a present participle of continuous action rather than an adjective. The verb ἀλαλάζω means *to wail loudly* in its only other occurrence in the NT (Mark 5:38). A lexicographical search reveals that, according to the occasion (and the agents?), *loud noise* and the action of continuous **reverberating** can be *either majestic and splendiferous* (Ps 145:4, 5, LXX), bringing together τύμπανον, probably *kettle drum,* and κύμβαλον, *crotal* or (broadly) *cymbal,* with ἀλαλαγμοῦ, *sonorous* or *intrusive, invasive and self-important* (BAGD interpret the verbal form τυμπανίζω to mean "to torture with the τύμπανον").[54]

49. Klein, "Noisy Gong or Acoustic Vase?" 288.

50. Ibid., 287.

51. Laurin, *First Cor,* 228; Schmidt, "κύμβαλον," *TDNT,* 3:1,037-39.

52. Schmidt, "κύμβαλον," 3:1,037.

53. S. Kruckenberg, *The Symphony Orchestra and Its Instruments* (New York: Crescent and Gothenberg: AB Nordbook, 1993), 193-95. The modern orchestral cymbal must be struck quasi-horizontally because of the resistance of air pressure, with its larger size (14-22 inches). It would also be anachronistic to assume that even if (wrongly) χαλκός were to be translated *gong,* this was to be equated with the modern orchestral *tam-tam.* This has a diameter of up to five feet (150 centimeters), and even if Hollywood directors project these back into ancient Greece or into ancient Egypt, such overwhelming *fortissimo* seems to have emerged only in the Romantic period of the last 125 years (e.g., with Respighi or Wagner), although it may indeed use bronze.

54. The array of lexicographical entries speak for themselves. Cf. esp. BAGD, 34 and 829.

This issue becomes controversial in a further recent study by T. K. Sanders, which seeks to reevaluate all previous interpretations of this verse, on the basis of the meaning of ἀλαλάζον and the work of Klein. Sanders argues that the Greek participle ἤ, (translated above and elsewhere as **or**) means *rather than*. He proposes the meaning: *I have become* **only a resonating acoustic jar** *rather than a flourish of* **cymbals**.[55] Sanders accepts and defends the empty, noisy, negative character of **mere resonating acoustic jar**. But he rejects the view that ἀλαλάζω refers in most cases to *a loud wailing:* "the interpretation of κύμβαλον ἀλαλάζον as discordant cacophony is inconsistent with the discriminating tastes of antiquity."[56] He therefore turns his attention away from the two pairs of adjectives and nouns to explore ἤ as "a particle denoting comparison," which is "equivalent to the English 'than.' "[57] He concedes that either **or** or *than* is in theory a possible translation, but concludes that since κύμβαλον ἀλαλάζον is more likely to denote "a sound which was pleasant to Paul's readers," *than* is the obvious "solution" to speculations about χαλκός and ἀλαλάζον.[58] The cry ἀλαλαί, he urges, appears in the LXX as one of joy and enthusiasm (e.g., when the walls of Jericho fall, Josh 6:20; when David triumphs, 1 Kings 17:52; cf. Ps 42:2; 65:1; 80:2; 97:4, 6). This accounts for the translation proposed by Collins: *I have become sounding brass rather than a resounding cymbal,* with the latter viewed as a metaphor "for harmonious sound."[59]

The argument of Todd Sanders is innovative and ingenious and deserves respect. He uses Hatch-Redpath, Josephus, other sources, and works on music in the ancient world.[60] But his thesis fails to take adequate account of three factors and a fourth consideration. First, the Graeco-Roman converts who prized "wisdom," "speech," "rhetoric," and social position, even though many spoke with tongues and all were exposed to the OT as the church's scripture, would be unlikely to regard *the crash of cymbals* as the height of their ambition. To be sure, they are triumphalist (4:8), but to build the rhetorical focus of a carefully designed didactic poem on an introductory contrast between **acoustic bronze** and **reverberating cymbals**, even *celebratory, festal,* "good" **cymbals**, hardly accords with the rhetorical and lyric weight of all the other images and contrasts. Second, what is majestic and impressive in one context (especially, as we noted above, the louder cymbals and kettle drums) becomes, as the lexicographers rightly have it, "torture" in another context. When the Queen opens the Church of England General Synod in Westminster Abbey, one's spirit may soar with the decibels of the organ's thunder, while the same level of decibels would

55. Sanders, "A New Approach to 1 Cor. 13:1," 614-18.

56. Ibid., 616.

57. Ibid.

58. Ibid., 617.

59. Collins, *First Cor,* 471 and 475.

60. Cf. his use of I. H. Jones, "Musical Instruments in the Bible, I," *BT* 37 (1986): 108, 109; A. Sendrey, *Music in the Social and Religious Life of Antiquity* (Rutherford-Madison: Fairleigh Dickinson University, 1974); and K. Rengstorf, *Complete Concordance to Josephus.*

for some be sheer torture coming from a local amateur music group. To identify "good" contexts does not mean that noise is always good. Third, to interpose a logical disjunction of a reflective nature in one line of this rhythmic stanza places too much cognitive weight on a supposed pause in the flow.

The alternative proposed by Harris and Klein leaves no difficulty. For the fourth factor is that to which D. A. Carson drew our attention (noted above).[61] Paul is not simply saying that if **love** is absent, *tongues* are hollow and mere noise. He is suggesting that in cases where a tongues speaker might be without love in his or her lifestyle, *the persons themselves* **would have become merely a resonating jar or a reverberating cymbal**.[62] The perfect tense γέγονεν in place of an expected future suggests: "look at what such a person **would have become**." Empty, noisy reverberations go on and on. In Yorkshire idiom in the north of England, they are "now't but wind and rattle."

2 Paul has considered the highest conceivable evaluations of the gift of **tongues** as either the expression of the yearnings of the human heart or part of the praise of heaven, but concluded that even a person so gifted is mere noise without love. Now he turns to communicative and "wisdom" gifts of **prophecy** and **knowledge**, and to the action gift of **faith** of a special kind which produces dramatic effects. We follow the syntactical subdivision of **prophecy, knowledge**, and **faith** proposed by Heinrici and Spicq except that whereas Heinrici links the knowledge of "mysteries" or **the depths too profound for human discovery** with **prophecy**, we argue that this belongs, in terms of Corinthian aspirations, more readily with γνῶσις (**knowledge**).[63] Moreover, "the verb εἰδῶ controls both nouns, 'all mysteries' and 'all knowledge'" (Fee).[64]

Our proposed translation endeavors to bring out the indefinite character of the conditional, the escalating protasis, and the contrastive apodosis which Paul introduces by ἀγάπην δέ . . . to conclude, not *I am no one,* but, with the neuter singular οὐθέν, **I am nothing**. We have tried to convey the anticlimactic fall after the escalating protasis by adding **after all** to the Greek, which is not explicit (but remains implicit) in the text. The subjunctives invite the opening signal **And if I should** . . . , but it would be heavy-handed to labor them further. We use **penetrate** (as NJB) for εἰδῶ, the perfect subjunctive of οἶδα used in a present sense. To translate *if I know* would not only be stylistically repetitive, but it would fail to convey the perfect subjunctive *have come to know* (NRSV, *understand;* NIV, *fathom;* REB, *have knowledge of*).

On the sensitive and major word μυστήριον, translated above as **the depths too profound for mere human discovery**, see above on 2:1 and more especially 2:7 (also used in 4:1; 14:2; 15:51; Rom 11:25; 16:25; 2 Thess 2:7; six times in Ephesians, four times in Colossians, and twice in 1 Timothy). Un-

---

61. Carson, *Showing the Spirit,* 59.

62. In our note on Pentecostal writings on Spirit-Baptism under 12:13, we observed that recent Pentecostal writers have also underlined this point.

63. Heinrici, *Das erste Sendschreiben,* 416-17; Spicq, *Agapē,* 2:144-45.

64. Fee, *First Epistle,* 632, n. 34.

der 2:7 we noted Marcus Bockmuehl's careful argument that at its heart the term denotes a contrast between **mere human discovery** and that which lies beyond unaided human powers and initiatives.[65] Almost any other translation tends to fall either into ambiguity or blandness, when we recall that what constitutes a μυστήριον may well have been at issue between Paul, some at Corinth, and their non-Christian religious environment which may have involved the mystery religions.[66] Our translation at least holds in common Corinthian perceptions and Pauline theology. Logically one use of πάντα relates to the other: Paul escalates the entailments of the gifts *wisdom, revelation,* and **knowledge** to the utmost. **To penetrate** τὰ μυστήρια πάντα (**all the depths**) opens the door to **all "knowledge"** (γνῶσις).

We have placed the term **knowledge** in quotation marks to signal a Corinthian catchword; see above on 1:5 and 8:1 (also used in 8:7, 10, 11; 12:8; 13:8; 14:6). As we noted above, out of about 26 occurrences in the NT, 22 occur in Paul, and of these, 15 occur in 1 and 2 Corinthians, i.e., more than half of the entire collection of uses of γνῶσις in the NT are addressed to Corinth. Furthermore, even at Corinth and in Paul's mind **knowledge** is used in various ways. In one sense πάντες γνῶσιν ἔχομεν (8:1); in another sense, ἀλλ' οὐκ ἐν πᾶσιν ἡ γνῶσις (8:7).[67] It would not be adequate if we failed to place an explicit marker against **knowledge** as a major semantic competitor to love. Nygren observes, "In 1 Cor. xiii there is a definite opposition, a contrast, between two different 'ways,' two different kinds of fellowship with God: on the one side, the Gnostic-mystical 'vision of God' typical of Hellenism; and, on the other, the primitive-Christian and Pauline way of Agape. . . . 'Gnosis puffs up, Agape builds up.'"[68] In what sense is one related to Christ and to the cross, while the other not? Nygren declares: *"Gnosis is egocentric, Agape theocentric"* (his italics).[69]

A pattern now begins to emerge. For Paul's major critique of the *way* in which **tongues** were used as a *public* gift is that **tongues** *build up (only) the self* (14:4); similarly γνῶσις, **knowledge**, unless it is controlled by love, also ministers *to the self* (cf. Nygren's "egocentric"). By contrast, just as Christ lived and died "for others" supremely in the cross, **the way** of the *cross* and **the way** of **love** equally serve *others;* they are *"for others,"* as Paul will unfold in 13:4-7.[70]

---

65. Bockmuehl, *Revelation and Mystery in Ancient Judaism and Pauline Christianity;* also Wolff, *Der erste Brief,* 315. See further Hays, *First Cor,* 224, on Corinth and apocalyptic "mysteries."

66. Cf. the different approaches in, e.g., R. Reitzenstein, *Hellenistic Mystery-Religions* (Eng. trans., Pittsburgh: Pickwick Press, 1978); H. A. A. Kennedy, *St. Paul and the Mystery-Religions* (London and New York: Hodder and Stoughton, 1913); and G. Wagner, *Pauline Baptism and the Pagan Mysteries* (Edinburgh: Oliver & Boyd, 1967).

67. Cf. Glad, *Paul and Philodemus,* 283-85.

68. Nygren, *Agapē and Eros,* 134; cf. 134-45.

69. Ibid., 143.

70. On the contrast, see Vielhauer, *Oikodomē,* on self-edification in "tongues," and Strobel, *Der erste Brief,* 199-200, on love for "the other."

On **faith** (πίστις) see above on 12:9. We noted that there is virtually unanimous agreement among commentators and theologians of every era that this *gift of* **faith** in 12:9 must be distinguished from *saving faith* through which all Christians appropriate the saving work of Christ as "for them" or "for us." We argued that "miraculous faith" betrays not only an overly dualistic worldview which belongs more to Kant and to the Enlightenment than to biblical traditions, but also an overly wooden understanding of **to remove mountains**. *An especially robust, infectious, bold, trustful faith may well be a special gift that performs a special task within a community faced with seemingly insuperable problems.*

To remove mountains is an echo of a tradition that appears in Mark 11:23-24 and Matt 17:20 (cf. Matt. 21:21) as a saying of Jesus.[71] In her commentary on Mark, Morna D. Hooker comments, "Moving a mountain appears to have been a proverbial saying for doing difficult tasks."[72] Similarly, R. T. France describes the Matthew saying as "a proverbial expression for the most improbable occurrence."[73] This is how Paul uses the phrase. Just as **knowledge** transcends **mere human discovery**, so the kind of **faith** which is a gift here transcends mere human capacity and expectation. But there is no need either to defend or to attack worldviews relating to "miracle." The verb μεθιστάνειν means **to remove** an object from one place and to transfer it to another, here used as part of the proverbial imagery. Finally, πᾶσαν τὴν πίστιν is likely to be a generic use of **all: gifts of every kind of faith**. But it may signify either an *ideal* (Godet), i.e., *all possible faith,* or an ultimate, i.e., *absolute faith* (Moffatt, Héring).[74]

The anticlimactic οὐθέν brings the readers back from triumphalist fantasies of glory to the real world. If I can **penetrate all the depths too profound for human discovery . . . have all "knowledge"** . . . and be known by the congregation to have the kind of **faith** that can soar above anything and overcome all difficulties, if I still **lack love**, I myself as a person am simply **nothing**. *To*

71. The Greek vocabulary and syntax of Matt 17:20 and Mark 11:23-24 are different, but the image is the same. On Paul's use of the sayings of Jesus, see esp. F. Neirynck, "Paul and the Sayings of Jesus," in A. Vanhoye (ed.), *Apôtre Paul: Personalité, style et conception du ministère* (Louvain: Leuven University, 1986), 265-321. Neirynck finds only two instances of "an explicit reference to a command of the Lord, in 1 Cor. 7:10-11 and 9:14, but there is no 'quotation'" (320). But Neirynck is prepared to accept that there are a number of "allusions." See further D. Wenham, "Paul's Use of the Jesus Tradition: Three Samples," in D. Wenham (ed.), *Gospel Perspectives, 5: The Jesus Tradition outside the Gospels* (Sheffield: JSOT, 1985), 7-35; and S. Kim, "Jesus, Sayings of," in Hawthorne and Martin (eds.), *DPL,* 474-92. D. L. Dungan appears not to address this verse in his *The Sayings of Jesus in the Churches of Paul* (Oxford: Blackwell, 1971). Barrett, *First Epistle,* 301, doubts whether v. 2 alludes to the Jesus tradition, but clearly the matter cannot be proved. Cf. also Yeung, "A Comparison of Faith in Jesus and Paul."

72. M. D. Hooker, *The Gospel according to St. Mark* (Peabody: Hendrickson and London: Black, 1991), 269.

73. R. T. France, *Matthew* (Grand Rapids: Eerdmans and Leicester: Inter-Varsity Press, 1985), 266.

74. Godet, *First Epistle,* 2:239; Moffatt, *First Epistle,* 192; Héring, *First Epistle,* 135.

all these imagined pretensions: "it falls like a chopper" (Senft).[75] If the charismatic has no charity, he is spiritually zero" (Spicq).[76]

3 This verse constitutes one of the most widely known examples of a crux of textual criticism in the NT. The 4th revised ed. of the UBS *Greek New Testament* (1993) reads ἵνα καυχήσωμαι, **that I may glory**, but classifies it as "C," i.e., "the Committee had difficulty in deciding which variant to place in the text." The UBS 3d ed. (1975) also read καυχήσωμαι and ranked it "C," but the 1975 "C" denoted "a considerable degree of doubt whether the text . . . contains the superior reading" (as against "D," which denoted "a very high degree of doubt" in the 3d ed.).[77] In general, four readings are considered by most critical editions and textual critics: (i) p[46], ℵ, A, B, 6, 048, 33, Sahidic and Bohairic Coptic, Clement, Origen, and Jerome (Latin and Greek) read ἵνα καυχήσωμαι, **that I may glory**; (ii) ἵνα καυθήσομαι, *that I should be burned,* is found in C, D, F, G, L, Clement *Stromata,* 4:8, Basil, Chrysostom, Cyril, and Theodoret; (iii) a closely related grammatical variant of (ii) which carries in effect the same meaning, καυθήσωμαι (late future subjunctive, rare in the first century), is found in K, Ψ, Old Syriac, fourth-century Gothic, fifth-century Armenian VSS, Ethiopic (Praetorius), Tertullian, and Cyprian; (iv) καυθήσεται, the third singular future indicative passive of καίω, *to burn,* which has virtually no support (basically, 1877, fourteenth century, and 2492, thirteenth century) and "nobody seems to take seriously."[78] But while he reads **that I may glory**, of the other three readings Héring asserts that *that it [my body] might be burned* is more likely than (ii) or (iii).[79]

Metzger lists "several very evenly balanced considerations."[80] The external evidence for **that I may glory** is "both early and weighty": (a) p[46] is usually dated c. 200 AD, and its combination with ℵ, A, and B seems exceedingly strong, even if D, F and C diverge. (b) It is also easy to understand how the escalation to martyrdom by fire might be read as the highest possible sacrifice over which even love takes priority. The UBS Committee gave weight to these two arguments together with the fact that (c) ἵνα καυθήσομαι becomes cumbersome, if not clumsy, after παραδῶ τὸ σῶμά μου, which already essentially makes the point. On the other hand, καυθήσομαι, **that I should be burned**, has strong support especially in patristic tradition. "If the motive for giving up life is pride and self-glory," the allusion to love becomes "superfluous."[81]

For these last reasons *to be burned* is favored by Bachmann, Weiss, Lietzmann, Bruce, Barrett, Conzelmann, and Collins and especially in research articles by Caragounis and by Elliott.[82] Elliott and others perceive the minor difference between

75. Senft, *Première Épitre,* 167, where the French *tombe comme un couperet* comes into its own for eloquence!.

76. Spicq, *Agapē,* 2:147.

77. UBS 3d ed., xiii, 4th ed., "Introduction 3*."

78. Petzer, "Contextual Evidence in Favour of καυχήσωμαι in 1 Cor. 13:3," 230; cf. 229-53.

79. Héring, *First Epistle,* 137.

80. Metzger, *Textual Commentary* (2d ed. 1994), 497; cf. 497-98.

81. Ibid., 498.

82. Elliott, "In Favour of καυθήσομαι at 1 Cor. 13:3," *ZNW* 62 (1971): 297-98; Caragounis, "'To Boast' or 'To Be Burned'? The Crux of 1 Cor 13:3," 115-27; also Grosheide, *First Epistle,* 305; Godet, *First Epistle,* 2·241-43; Morris, *First Epistle,* 180-83; Bachmann, *Der erste Brief,* 388-96; Weiss, *Der erste Kor,* 314-15; Robertson and Plummer, *First Epistle,* 290-91; Bruce, *1 and 2 Cor,* 124; Lietzmann, *An die Kor,* 65; Conzelmann, *1 Cor,* 217, n. 1; Barrett, *First Epistle,* 302-3; Collins, *First Cor,* 476. Cf. A. Souter, *Novum Testamentum Graece,* 2d ed. 1956; and also Zuntz, *Text,* 35-37.

καυθήσομαι (first passive indicative) and καυθήσωμαι (passive subjunctive) to be of merely scribal significance and thus to represent a single combined group of witnesses. Collins argues that the sight and sound of the two main readings are so similar that scribal error could readily account for the variant, and the allusions to burning are "explicable" especially in the light of Caragounis's work.[83]

Arguments in favor of καυχήσωμαι, however, are in our view stronger. For one thing, as Héring notes, at this early date reference to martyrdom by fire is "improbable . . . this punishment was unknown in the Graeco-Roman world [at this date]. It would seem rather strange, then, for Paul to select just this one case [i.e., the tradition of Dan 3:28 or 2 Macc 7:37] as his example."[84] The most readily conceivable use of *burn* would be that of selling oneself into slavery to provide funds for the poor, and thus to be branded by a hot-iron. But would Paul use such a specialized example in this genre for this purpose?

A more decisive study, however, comes from J. H. Petzer.[85] After considering the state of the discussion, Petzer bases his arguments on (a) the parallelism and climactic structure in vv. 1-3; and (b) the literary and semiotic phenomenon of defamiliarization. We have already established the issue of parallelism and climax: the familiar part of each protasis focuses on the respective gifts of **tongues** (v. 1), and on **prophecy, knowledge**, and **faith** (v. 2). Now Paul uses the "shock effect" of defamiliarization "to put even more emphasis on ἀγάπη."[86] *Defamiliarization* entails rereading what had appeared *familiar or ordinary* in a context which transposes it into the *no longer familiar* and *no longer ordinary,* to produce *reappraisal by shock.*[87] "Defamiliarization" is regarded as a function of distinctively literary texts which present the otherwise familiar in a new light by breaking "rules" of descriptive presentation. Thus the reader is forced (or seduced) *to rethink* or *to reread* the familiar. Petzer argues that 13:1-3 operates in this way, "in particular by the exaggeration of the issue which is being addressed *ad absurdum.*"[88] Here he suggests that the "absurdity" would be to portray the motivation "that I may glory" as an impure one. Being accorded "glory" is, he argues, an implicitly divine action, whereas giving one's body to be burned remains a purely human action. But such an interpretation of **that I may glory** is unnecessary and misleading. In spite of such weighty support as that of those already cited, we believe that καυχήσωμαι is the more probable reading on both external and internal grounds.[89] Lang shares with Petzer the view that **may glory** is used in

83. Collins, *First Cor,* 476-77.

84. Héring, *First Epistle,* 137. The tradition is discussed by Schrage, *Der erste Brief,* 3:291, including the notion of branding as a slave.

85. Petzer, "Contextual Evidence in Favour of καυχήσωμαι," 229-53.

86. Ibid., 238.

87. Although the concept or device was first explored in Russian formalism, its use in literary theory in the diagnosis of the dynamics of textual forces is now widespread. I have discussed it elsewhere from its origins in V. Shklovsky to its use by J. D. Crossan and others in interpreting the parables of Jesus: Thiselton, *New Horizons in Hermeneutics,* 117-20. When pressed further and coupled with a postmodern stance, it leads to deconstruction (ibid., 120-32).

88. Petzer, "Contextual Evidence," 233; cf. further 237-52, esp. 244-45.

89. Fee, *First Epistle,* 629, n. 18, and 634-35 rightly stresses the excellent quality of the Egyptian tradition; K. W. Clark, "Textual Criticism and Doctrine," in J. N. Sevenster (ed.), *Studia Paulina: In Honorem J. de Zwaan* (Haarlem: Bohn, 1953), 61-62; cf. 52-65; Orr and Walther, *1 Cor,* 291; Lang, *Die Briefe,* 183.

a positive sense (cf. Phil 2:16). Schrage agrees with Wischmeyer that Paul takes up the theme of self-glorying as "nothing" which can profit.[90]

The first word κἄν is *crasis* for καὶ ἐάν, **even if**. This signals the escalating rhetoric to which we have already given attention. The verb ψωμίσω (first aorist subjunctive active of ψωμίζω) functions again as an indefinite protasis, and a lexicographical comment on ψωμίζω is necessary. The noun ψωμίον means *a small piece of bread* or *morsel of food*. If the emphasis of the cognate verb lies on *breaking up* a piece of bread into small morsels, ψωμίζω means to *divide into small pieces* (esp. to give away), or even *to fritter away*. If the emphasis lies on the *bread*, ψωμίζω primarily means *to give someone food, to feed* (as clearly in Rom 12:20). BAGD and M. R. Vincent note the double meaning.[91] We attempt to capture both aspects of what may well be a conscious wordplay by proposing **Even if I should divide up all my possessions to feed the needy**.

παραδῶ (second aorist subjunctive active of παραδίδωμι) means to **hand over**. **Handing over** one's **body** could in theory refer to selling oneself into slavery in order to provide the funds for the needy to which allusion has just been made. But especially in view of 7:17-24, even as a scenario this seems too specific. Paul means putting one's whole being, including the physical body, at the disposal of others. Presumably Paul imagines that this may be done out of a sense of duty rather than out of concern for others' welfare. Lang, Petzer, and Orr and Walther insist that this need not imply selfish motives. Orr and Walther assert, "Paul's ambivalent attitude towards 'boasting' is plain in 9:15-16 . . . cf. II Cor. 11:16-30," while Lang alludes to Phil 2:16.[92] To appreciate fully Paul's logic and meaning, we need to recapitulate in summary the thrust of vv. 1 and 2, especially in the light of Petzer's comments on parallelism, ascending climactic structure, and defamiliarization (see under Textual Comment, above).

It is not necessary to endorse all of Petzer's proposals to accept the link which he maintains between 13:1-3 and allusions to spiritual gifts in chs. 12–14. We have already argued that each parallel in vv. 1 and 2 takes up the "gifts of the Spirit" in sequence: (i) gifts of worship and spiritual exultation, **tongues**; (ii) gifts of speech, wisdom, and communication, **prophecy, knowledge**; (iii) unusual gifts resulting in visible consequences, **faith**. But each pursues a climactic escalation from gifts-as-they-are *to scenarios or imagined projections of the utmost that they could be:* (i) **tongues** are not only (a) expressions of the deepest yearnings and praise which constitute subconscious "secrets of the **human** heart" (Theissen), but also (b) imagined participation in **angelic** worship speech of heaven (Dautzenberg), which Paul takes up from notions discussed at Corinth but does not necessarily agree with or endorse. (ii) **Prophecy** is not

90. Schrage, *Der erste Brief,* 3:290, esp. n. 72; Wischmeyer, *Der höchste Weg,* 84.

91. BAGD, 894; M. R. Vincent, *Word Studies in the NT* (London: Scribner, 1887; and Grand Rapids: Eerdmans, 1946), 3:263; Meyer, *First Epistle,* 1:390-91.

92. Orr and Walther, *1 Cor,* 291-92; Lang, *Die Briefe,* 183; Elliott, "In Favour of καυθήσομαι," 297-98.

only (a) wise, reflective, inspired pastoral preaching which includes announce-ments of judgment and grace, but also (b) leads on to the next gift: (iii) **knowl-edge**, which is not only (a) **knowledge** of God's self-revelation as the one God (8:1-13) and other gospel truth, but also (b), in the view of those who aspired to the greatest heights at Corinth, ability **to penetrate everything too deep for merely human discovery**, thus embracing **all** (conceivable) **knowledge**; (iv) **faith** is not (a) a special, robust, infectious confidence in God which over-comes great difficulties and helps the congregation to do so, but also (b) *achieves the "impossible."*

Now Paul moves to (iv) the relatively familiar (Petzer) phenomenon of (a) **dividing up all my possessions to feed the needy**, which escalates to (b) an imagined scenario of **handing over my body**, perhaps selling myself into slav-ery to gain funds for further provision of funds. If such a person no longer has control of any possessions, or even of his or her own body, is not that (c) real **glory**? It ranks with **angelic tongues, all knowledge**, and **removing** impossible **mountains**. The fourth group, Petzer argues, even begins the sense of shock by proposing a costly action that seems to outrank the individual "gifts" explicated in 12:8-10 and 28. Yet the most comprehensive possession of gifts, even when these are extrapolated into triumphalist fantasy (Petzer uses the term *reductio ad absurdum,* but they are not [yet] "reductions"), ends up (i) as the noise of resonating acoustic jars (v. 1), or (ii) as simply nothing (v. 2), "spiritually zero" (Spicq); and (iii) what counts as nothing (v. 3), if love does not provide the mo-tivation, context, and goal.[93]

The phrase οὐδὲ ὠφελοῦμαι is difficult: the passive of ὀφείλω, *I owe, I ought,* with an accusative. The traditional rendering *it profiteth me nothing* (AV/ KJV, RV) is reflected in the majority of translations (*I gain nothing,* NRSV, REB, NIV; cf. Collins, *it is not to my advantage*). This does tend, however, to presup-pose that the reading *that I may boast* (NRSV) is negative self-glory (REB and NIV presupposed *to be burned,* with NJB). Admittedly the notion of *financial debt* or *moral debt* lies at the heart of uses of ὀφείλω. But this word also has ex-tended uses.[94] There is much to be said in favor of R. Knox's translation *it goes for nothing.* But a hint of the idea of financial or moral debt or evaluation may be conveyed by a compromise proposal, **it counts for nothing**. The first person sub-ject is now merely implicit, but the reference is clear enough from the context. The *logical* (as against *grammatical*) subject is the series of acts which build up from the familiar to a projected climax: *all this* **counts for nothing**. Petzer's anal-ysis of defamiliarization applies. What seemed *ordinary* and obvious now ap-pears in a new, *unfamiliar* light, which produces *shock.*[95] These wondrous gifts and triumphant victories all amount to **nothing**, unless **love** directs them, with its Christlike concern and regard for "the other."

93. Petzer, "In Favour of καυχήσωμαι," 240; cf. esp. 237-45.
94. BAGD, 598-99; cf. Findlay, *Expositor's Greek Testament,* 2:898.
95. Petzer, "In Favour of καυχήσωμαι," 233-34.

b. The Nature and Action of Love (13:4-7)

One important grammatical point affects our understanding of these four verses. Most English translations render the Greek as if it used *adjectives* to describe the *nature* of love "timelessly," e.g., *love is patient; love is kind; love is not envious or boastful or arrogant or rude* (NRSV). But "the nature of love is expressed by Paul in a *series of verbs, the active character of which may not be fully indicated by . . . adjectives . . .*" (Craig) (my italics).[96] Hence we have added the word *Action* to our subheading.

4 The third occurrence of ἀγάπη is ranked "C," and the UBS 4th ed. places it in square brackets as incapable of a clear decision. It is omitted by 𝔭46, B, and 33, but "the majority of the Committee was impressed by the weight of witnesses that include the words" (Metzger).[97]

Our translation strives to preserve the verbal structure of the Greek, as against the adjectival structure of many English versions. The verb μακροθυμέω may mean *to be patient* or *to have patience*. The older English *suffereth long* (AV/KJV, RV) more strictly conveys the compound form made up of μακρός, *long* (in time or in extended space), and θύμος, which may denote either *passionate longing* or *wrath,* resulting in the translation *long-tempered* (curiously absent in English, as opposed to its opposite *short-tempered*); colloquially "with a very long fuse" if θύμος means *wrath;* but **waits patiently** if θύμος means *passionate longing.*[98] In the LXX μακροθυμεῖν may translate האריך אף (*he'erik aph*), *to be slow to anger* (Prov 19:11) but also to take time patiently (Prov 25:15; Eccl 8:12, Heb. ארך (*'arak*).[99] More notably, in Eccl 7:8, *those who are patient in spirit* or in disposition-to-act (LXX, μακρόθυμος . . . πνεύματι, Heb. ארך, *'arek*) are better than the proud in spirit (LXX, ὑψηλόν); hence, *do not be quick to anger* expresses the negative parallel (Eccl 7:9). Similarly, Paul enjoins believers to give their support to "the weak" and to act patiently (μακροθυμεῖν) toward all (1 Thess 5:14). Elsewhere in the NT the word occurs only in Jas 5:7-8 (**wait patiently**, *therefore, brothers and sisters,* ἕως τῆς παρουσίας τοῦ κυρίου); Matt 18:26, 29, **wait patiently** *for me, and I will pay you everything;* Luke 18:7, Heb. 6:15, and 2 Pet. 3:9. In 2 Pet 3:9 the *patience* of the Lord is exhibited in his *waiting for the time appropriate* for the readers themselves, not in mere delay in fulfilling a promise; while similarly in Heb 6:15 the writer commends

---

96. Craig "1 Cor," *IB,* 10:172.

97. Metzger, *Textual Commentary* (2d ed. 1994), 498-99. Metzger may be right. The third ἀγάπη is supported, e.g., by ‭א A, C, D, F, G, Ψ, 048, Origen, and other witnesses. But nothing other than stylistic rhythm is at stake, and no degree of certainty is possible. Cf. Zuntz, *Text,* 68, who argues for "love is patient, love is kind; love does not envy. . . ."

98. BAGD, 488; cf. also 365.

99. Hatch-Redpath, 2:893. Strobel calls attention both to the OT background and to the Christlike nature of this quality in contrast to apocalyptic notions of a warrior Messiah (*Der erste Brief,* 203).

Abraham as a model of one who **waits patiently** for God's *timing,* leaving that to God. Traditions which attempt to stress "eschatological urgency" need to ensure that this quality is not undermined.

Love, Paul urges, **waits patiently** not only because it deals patiently with the loved one but also because it recognizes that *the right timing* plays a huge part in securing the welfare of the other. Love does not blunder in. The Corinthians, by contrast, were all too ready to jump the gun both in their assumptions about Paul and other ministers (1 Cor 4:5) and in anticipating their own triumphs (4:8). George Herbert (1593-1633) captures the notion of love as **waiting patiently** for the understanding of the beloved:

"Love bade me welcome, yet my soul drew back,
   Guilty of dust and sin.
But quick-ey'd Love, observing me grow slack
   From my first entrance in,
Drew nearer to me, sweetly questioning
   If I lack'd any thing.

'A guest,' I answered, 'worthy to be here.'
   Love said, 'You shall be he.'
'I, the unkind, the ungrateful? Ah my dear,
   I cannot look on thee.'
Love took my hand, and smiling did reply,
   'Who made the eyes, but I?'" (Herbert, *Love,* stanzas 1 and 2)

The verb χρηστεύεται, **shows kindness**, occurs only here within the NT, and otherwise only in Christian literature in Clement of Rome (c. 96 AD) and in Eusebius. The use in *1 Clement* 14:3, ὡς χρηστεύεσθε, οὕτως χρηστευθήσεται ὑμῖν, *as you show kindness, so kindness will be shown to you,* underlines the verb as dynamic action, **to show kindness,** as against the more static adjective *is kind.*[100] The adjectival form χρηστός, *kind, kindly, benevolent,* was used widely in the first century (e.g., Philo, *Embassy to Gaius* 67; Josephus, *Antiquities* 6.92; 9.133; cf. *Papyrus Oxyrhynchus* 642; Dio Cassius 66:18), but not the verb. Findlay thinks that Paul may have coined the verb for his purpose.[101]

The cognate noun χρηστότης, *kindness, generosity, uprightness,* however, occurs regularly along with the adjective in hellenistic literature. Hence (a) there is no doubt about the meaning of the verb; and (b) the choice of the dynamic verbal form is deliberate, even if only to play its part in a chain of active temporal processes. Spicq observes that the word "suggests the warm, generous welcome the Christian always gives his brothers . . . does his utmost to be thoughtful, helpful and kind, always in a pleasant way . . . , and confirms the element of magnanimity in *agapē.*"[102] In his commentary on this verse Origen ex-

100. Schrage, *Der erste Brief,* 3:295-96, also stresses the active character of the word.
101. Findlay, *Expositor's Greek Testament,* 2:899; cf. BAGD, 886.
102. Spicq, *Agapē,* 2:151.

pounds the verb as showing "sweetness to all persons" (γλυκὸς πρὸς πάντας τοὺς ἀνθρώπους).[103] Chrysostom perceives **love** here as that which breaks the spiral of passion, anger, and resentment by **showing kindness**: "not only by enduring nobly, but also by soothing and comforting do they cure the sore and heal the wound of passion."[104]

On the meaning ζηλόω, see above on 12:31, where we commented on ζηλοῦτε δὲ τὰ χαρίσματα τὰ μείζονα. There we observed in a footnote that in the LXX ζηλόω translates קַנֵּא (qinnē') and applies the notion of *burning* or *boiling* metaphorically to *burning or boiling emotions, stance, or will* for *earnest striving,* for *passionate zeal,* or for **burning envy.** Whether it is constructive *zeal* or destructive **envy** depends on the context. Again, Paul chooses the verb: **does not burn with envy.** BAGD translate the verb "to be filled with jealousy or envy," but *burning* conveys the intensity more precisely than the hydrodynamic metaphor of *filling.*[105] Only the translation by Charles B. Williams, *Love never boils with jealousy,* seems to retain this nuance explicitly. Clearly the word alludes to 3:3: ὅπου γὰρ ἐν ὑμῖν ζῆλος καὶ ἔρις. . . . The **envy** which is carried over from a status-seeking, non-Christian Corinthian culture into the Christian church is not "of the Holy Spirit" (1 Cor 3:1-3), and is deemed to be incompatible with **love,** which *does not begrudge the status and honor of another, but delights in it for the sake of the other.* How accurately, once again, the "didactic poem" addresses Corinth appears from the socio-rhetorical studies of Corinthian culture by Pogoloff, Witherington, Clarke, and others (see above on passages relating to rhetoric and status).

Most English translations render οὐ περπε ρεύεται as [love is] not *boastful* (NRSV, REB, NJB; cf. AV/KJV, RV, *vaunteth not itself;* NIV, *does not boast;* Collins, *is not conceited*). Moffatt has *makes no parade.* But lexicographical research, together with special attention to first-century literature including Stoic texts, makes it certain that Barrett's translation (also in Spicq) **does not brag** precisely captures the semantic-force primary connotations of the verb.[106] Again, Moffatt, Barrett, and NIV (against Collins) convey the dynamic force of the choice of a verb rather than an adjective. This is the earliest occurrence of the verb περπερεύομαι, but it also occurs in Epictetus, *Dissertations* 2.1.34 and 3.2.14, in Polybius 32.2.5 and 39.1.2, and later in Marcus Antoninus 5.5, clearly to express the verbal action cognate with the form πέρπερος (cf. Lat. *perperus*), *braggart.*[107] An even better translation might be that of Moulton-Milligan and of Robertson and Plummer: [Love] *does not play the braggart.* But this seems too heavy and convoluted for the rhythm and the

103. Origen, *1 Cor. Frag.,* 51:6-7 (text in *JTS* 10 [1909]: 34, ed. Jenkins).

104. Chrysostom, *1 Cor. Hom.,* 33:1.

105. BAGD, 338; further Schrage, *Der erste Brief,* 3:296.

106. Barrett, *First Epistle,* 303; and Spicq, *Agape in the NT,* 2:153.

107. MM, 510 (In addition to the Epictetus sources cited by others, they also cite Basil, *Regulae,* 49:423A; LSJ, 1204; Robertson, *Word Pictures,* 4:178; BAGD, 653; Robertson and Plummer, *First Epistle,* 293.

relatively crisp sequence of verbs. Again the verb underlines the issue of status seeking and triumphalism at Corinth. Even believers seemed to come to act the part of braggarts, which was at odds with cruciform, Christlike **love**.

In the context which has steadily been built up, οὐ φυσιοῦται is best rendered by combining the metaphor **inflating** (cf. AV/KJV, *is not puffed up*) with the implicit emphasis on **its own importance** (cf. Moffatt and Goodspeed, *gives itself no airs;* NRSV, *arrogant;* REB, NJB, *conceited;* Collins, *inflated*). NIV, *proud,* is too wooden and loses the metaphor. For once our proposal comes near to J. B. Phillips's extended paraphrase: *nor does it cherish* **inflated** *ideas of* **its own importance**. For a detailed comment on the verb φυσιόω see above on 4:6, 18, 19; 5:2; and 8:1: "The word φυσιόω is a key term of the letter" (Craig).[108] Of the seven uses of this verb in the entire NT, six occur in these references in the epistles. (The other is Col 2:18.) Paul hammers home the incompatibility of **love** as respect and concern for the welfare of the other and obsessions about the status and attention accorded to the self. How much behavior among believers and even ministers is actually "attention seeking" designed to impress others with one's own supposed importance? Some "spiritual songs" may appear to encourage, rather than discourage, this preoccupation with the self rather than with others and with God. Here is Luther's antithesis between *theologia crucis* and *theologia gloriae,* and in part why Paul leaves ch. 15 to the end. "Ostentation is the chief idea" (i.e., which Paul rejects).[109] Paul sets in contrast with **love** "the thoughtlessness" of "all things are permissible" (Spicq).[110]

5 On οὐκ ἀσχημονεῖ, **it does not behave with ill-mannered impropriety,** see above on 7:36, which is the only other use of the verb in the NT. There we translated the verb as: *if anyone thinks that* **he is not behaving in a proper way** *toward his betrothed.* The adjective ἀσχήμων occurs in the NT only at 12:23, where Paul alludes to **unpresentable** parts of the body, i.e., those which good taste and public respect expect to be clothed. In all three contexts the contrast defines the opposition between on one side *courtesy, good taste, good public* **manners**, and **propriety**, and on the other side thoughtless pursuit of the immediate wishes of the self regardless of the conventions and courtesies of interpersonal life. Thus *"Agapē* is not **ill-mannered"** (Spicq).[111] Love does not act in ways which are "contrary to the requirements of propriety and good order, committed by some ill-mannered members" (Héring).[112]

This paves the way for the contrastive force of εὐσχημόνως, where Paul urges that worship services should be conducted *with "propriety,"* i.e., with order, good taste, courtesy, and lack of an egocentric concern to draw attention to one's own gifts and rhetoric at the expense of the decorum of the

108. Craig, "1 Cor," *IB,* 10:175.
109. Robertson and Plummer, *First Epistle,* 293.
110. Spicq, *Agapē,* 2:153.
111. Ibid., 2:154.
112. Héring, *First Epistle,* 139.

whole.[113] **Love** does not elbow its way into conversations, worship services, or public institutions in a disruptive, discourteous, attention-seeking way. Insofar as courtesy (versus discourtesy) and politeness (versus impoliteness) relate to what is deemed publicly pleasing or displeasing, **love** does not rush in to impose its idiosyncrasies on those for whom bad manners are offensive. 14:40 applies this to *worship,* as well as to life. "Jesus did not make a virtue out of nonconformity. . . ."[114]

The background here may allude to the intrusion of tongues or prophecies at inappropriate moments (cf. ch. 14). But today it may also include any kind of monopolizing of a congregation's time and attention in the service of the self: in the tone, style, and vocabulary adopted in notices or sermons, or, worst of all, the minister as overfamiliar chat-show host or "prophet" of ill-mannered rebuke. Paul asks, *What do respect and* **love** *for the other* actually invite? As Bonhoeffer observed, a theological doctrine of the church and of grace implies its own sociology of the church as a society.

The traditional AV/KJV, [Love] *seeketh not her own,* correctly conveys the structure of the Greek οὐ ζητεῖ τὰ ἑαυτῆς. Yet most modern translations prefer a more explicit reference to **the self**: hence, *is never selfish* (REB, Moffatt); *is never self-seeking* (TCNT); *does not pursue selfish aims* (O. M. Norlie); *is not self-seeking* (NIV); *does not insist on its own way* (NRSV). To seek the affairs of one's own self (reflexive pronoun), however, also conveys the idea of *seeks its own advantage* (NJB). Ever since the rise of the Frankfurt School, Critical Theory, and J. Habermas, the term **interest** says it all within the setting of a postmodern, turn-of-the-century culture today. Hence **is not preoccupied with the interests of the self** conveys to our culture what the Greek conveyed to first-century readers, combining *self-centeredness* with *self-interests* (neuter plural τά). Collins translates *does not seek its own interests,* which captures the main idea.

The lexicography, however, brings us back to the profound point which Nygren and others underline for Paul's *theology.* Love as *Eros* does indeed seek its own satisfaction: *Eros* seeks to "possess" the object of love; in myth, *Eros* is the suitor, ever in need of the gratification of its own desires. By contrast, Nygren writes, *Agape* in Paul stands in *"opposition to all that be called 'self-love'"* (his italics).[115] "It is thus the direct opposite of acquisitive love. . . . '*Agape* seeketh not its own' (1 Cor 13:5), but this is a self-evident consequence of the theocentric nature of his [Paul's] idea of love. Agape spells judgment on the life that centres round the ego and its **interests** [my italics]. . . . For when

---

113. Spicq, *Agapē,* 2:154. Hays, *First Cor,* 226 insists that *rude* (NRSV, NIV) is weak; it is a "stronger term referring to shameful behaviour."

114. Deluz, *Companion to 1 Corinthians,* 190. Deluz uses strong language about Christians who excuse themselves from "rules of propriety and social conventions, the polite behaviour customary in their own world" (loc. cit.). To do this on grounds of "freedom" or "knowledge" is precisely to commit the error of Corinth with which Paul wrestles here.

115. Nygren, *Agapē and Eros,* 130.

God's *Agape* is shed abroad in a man's heart through the Holy Spirit (Rom 5:5) his life thereby gains a new centre. The emphasis is transferred from his own ego to Christ."[116] It is because Eros does "seek its own interest" that Eros-Cupid is depicted in Graeco-Roman myth not only as a suitor, but as one with "cunning, seductive and winning ways. That is why Love is shown as armed with bows and arrows. He is a clever hunter."[117] Even the love of Eros piety, Nygren and Deluz conclude, seeks to grasp the object of its own desire.[118]

Spicq makes the same point in a different way. If love is "disinterested" (i.e., without personal interests for advantage), "there is no greater sign of a pure love than that."[119] He alludes to Matt 5:38-42, where the giving up of "rights" corresponds with Paul's injunctions about "rights" to do anything (1 Cor 6:12). *"Gnosis,"* Spicq observes, also operates on a different level. "Knowledge" and Eros have to do with the *mastery* of an object. "Agapē is not looking for its own advantage, but for the good of others. . . . 'Christ did not please himself' (Rom 15:3). . . . 'No one should look after his own advantage, but after that of his neighbor' (1 Cor 10:24)."[120] Spicq compares "the interests of the other" in Phil 2:4 and 2:21. Existentialist philosophy of the kind expounded by G. Marcel and Martin Buber focuses the ways in which Eros love can transpose a person, a Thou, into an object, an "it" of possession where love becomes possession, domination, and lust. Hence Paul will speak in due course of the personal reciprocity of "knowing and being known."

The coupling of **behaving with ill-mannered impropriety** and **not pre-occupied with the interests of the self** alludes to such conduct at Corinth as (i) insisting on one's way about idol food (10:24, 33); (ii) rushing ahead with the Lord's Supper in a "better" room (the triclinium) while the latecomers are squeezed into the atrium (11:21-22); (iii) interrupting speakers with supposed "instant revelations" during worship, or alternatively carrying on at an inordinate length when someone else has an important contribution to make (14:29-33); and imposing unintelligible tongues into a sequence of worship when the utterance cannot be communicated but remains a purely individual welling up of pre-cognitive expression (14:27-28). Agapē-prompted worship and social relations become contaminated and distorted by Eros piety, in which self-affirmation is disguised as religion. Nietzsche offers an incisive analysis of this attitude, e.g., his aphorism "The 'salvation of the soul' — in plain English [German] 'the world revolves around me.'"[121] As Nygren, Spicq, and others urge, these verses exclude such a notion from Paul.[122]

---

116. Ibid., 130-31.

117. Deluz, *Companion to 1 Corinthians,* 190-91.

118. Nygren, *Agapē,* 30-34, 41-58, 75-81, 115-33; Deluz, *Companion,* 130-32.

119. Spicq, *Agapē,* 2:155.

120. Ibid., 2:155-56.

121. Friedrich Nietzsche, *Collected Works* (18 vols., London: Allen & Unwin, 1909-13), 16, *The Antichrist,* 186, aphorism 43.

122. I have offered a detailed critique of Nietzsche's incisive critique in A. C. Thiselton, *In-*

It is easier to express the force of παροξύνεται through a series of descriptive sentences than to propose a succinct translation. The heart of the word conveys the semantic force of **to exasperate**, *to irritate*, as metaphorical extensions of *to make sharp, to make pointed, to make acid.*[123] Moulton-Milligan cite examples in the papyri for the traditional translation *is not easily provoked* (AV/ KJV). In one example a wife complains that her husband is *being provoked into anger* against her by her sister.[124] Some insist that especially here the issue is that of being provoked into "irritation rather than rage."[125] This distinction depends on context, since lexicography yields both meanings. In the LXX the verb can mean to provoke to anger (Prov 6:3), and in the only other instance of παροξύνομαι to occur in the NT (besides 1 Cor 13:5) Paul is *"provoked to anger* (REB, *outraged*) to see the city so full of idols" (Acts 17:16). However, "the kindred noun παροξυσμός, in Acts xv:39, describes the *irritation* which arose between Paul and Barnabas" (Vincent's italics).[126] Barrett's succinct translation *is not touchy* does indeed convey readiness to overreact on one's own behalf. But it does not adequately portray the process of being on the receiving end (passive voice) of provocative or irritating behavior which, where there is **love that shows patience** (13:4), a person cannot be *goaded into the sharp retort of irritation.*

Virtually every lexicon and primary source indicates the notion of reaching a level of **exasperation**. But how does this express itself? The English **pique** combines the same range of nuances as the Greek: something *between irritation and anger* which takes offense because one's *self-regard has been dented, wounded, or punctured by some sharp point.* **Love**, Paul urges, **does not become exasperated into pique**, partly because **patience** delays *exasperation* and partly because lack of **self-interest** diverts a sense of self-importance away from reacting on the grounds of wounded pride: "it is not embittered by injuries, whether real or supposed."[127]

At Corinth, one group paraded their gifts and status with **ill-mannered impropriety** because they thoughtlessly ignored the well-being and feelings of others; the less gifted or less status-endowed group allowed themselves to become **exasperated into pique** at the aggressive triumphalism and ostentation of the others because they were more wrapped up in their own feelings than in sharing the sense of joy or liberation of others. Many local churches and many

---

terpreting God and the Postmodern Self: On Meaning, Manipulation and Promise (Edinburgh: T. & T. Clark and Grand Rapids: Eerdmans, 1995), 3-45 and 121-64.

123. Rightly, Spicq, *Agapē*, 2:156; cf. BAGD, 629; LSJ, 1158; MM, 496; Edwards, *First Epistle*, 345; Meyer, *First Epistle*, 1:392; Fee, *First Epistle*, 638-39; Bittlinger, *Gifts and Graces*, 86.

124. MM, 496; cf. *BGU* 2:588:7.

125. Craig, "1 Cor," *IB*, 10·178

126. Vincent, *Word Studies in the NT*, 3:265.

127. Robertson and Plummer, *First Epistle*, 294; cf. Schrage, *Der erste Brief*, 3:298-99, where he compares the LXX and Hebrew background further.

theological colleges contain *some who parade their "gifts" while others nurse their "hurts." Does either side, Paul asks, genuinely put the other before the self?*

The verb λογίζομαι means both **to reckon** in a theological sense (Rom 2:26; 3:28; 4:3-11, of justification by grace through faith); to *count as* in an evaluative sense or the "count-generation" (as in Wolterstorff), which ascribes roles, status, or responsibilities (Rom 6:11; 8:36; 1 Cor 4:1; 2 Cor 3:5); and (as here) **to reckon up**, as in the context of accountancy. BAGD interpret the verb in this verse to mean *love does not take evil into account.*[128] They reach this conclusion largely on the ground that in the LXX λογίζομαι can mean *to count something against someone* (e.g., Zech 8:17). On the basis of the LXX, however, Spicq suggests that it might mean *love thinks no evil.* This might mean, in turn, either that love "does not suspect its neighbour of evil or that it does not think about committing evil itself."[129] Spicq further understands Zech 8:17 in the sense of *plotting an evil scheme.* Love, by contrast, remains "innocent of any of the machinations or plots." Although he prefers *love takes no note of injury,* he declares that "once more it is hard to decide exactly what the verb means."[130]

There may be a link, however, between Spicq's interpretation and the notion of **reckoning up**. He observes: "Instead of nursing the memory of an injury . . . charity refuses to notice that anything has happened" (cf. 2 Cor 3:5; Phil 4:8).[131] Conzelmann favors the sense of **reckoning up** by translating *it keeps no score of wrongs* (as also REB; cf. NIV, *keeps no record of wrongs;* NJB, *does not . . . store up grievances*). The NRSV *resentful* presumably seeks to compromise between *thinketh no evil* (AV/KJV) or *taketh no account of evil* (RV) and a gesture toward *keeps no score.* But the NRSV lacks the dynamic pictorial imagery in which every verb depicts an action or stance, usually under the guise of a metaphor or pictorial image. Thus we have encountered, e.g., images of *boiling* or *burning* (ζηλόω), *inflating* or *filling with air* (φυσιόω), behaving in *unpresentable, ill-mannered* ways (ἀσχημονέω), being *probed with a sharp spike* to provoke someone (παροξύνομαι), and now *an accountant* **reckoning up** *accounts* (λογίζομαι). Most English translations, especially NRSV and often NIV, simply abstract the conceptual content of the metaphor from its forceful emotive imagery. F. F. Bruce agrees that **reckoning up** plays a part, but as a matter of "paying the offender back in his own coin."[132] Conzelmann argues for *keeps no score* on the ground that "λογίζεσθαι corresponds to חשׁב *(chashabh),* 'to set to someone's account.'"[133] He is not alone in this view.[134]

128. BAGD, 475-76. Similarly, Collins, *First Cor,* 481, *nor does it calculate evil* (cf. Prov 25:21-22), "makes use of a commercial term sometimes used in political discourse."

129. Spicq, *Agapē,* 2:156.

130. Ibid.

131. Ibid., 157.

132. Bruce, *1 and 2 Cor,* 127.

133. Conzelmann, *1 Cor,* 224; hence Collins's observation (see above).

134. Cf. H. W. Heidland, "λογίζομαι," *TDNT,* 4:284-92; in part Robertson and Plummer,

Love does not have "the habit still widespread even among Christians of keeping a reckoning of the faults of others."[135] Wolff points out that "not keeping a score" which is **reckoned up** coheres well with *counting* attitudes or actions *as* evil, and invites the *double* meaning.[136]

6 We have supplied the English subject **Love,** which serves as the subject of the verb implicitly rather than explicitly in the Greek, simply because modern English style increasingly demands shorter cues. The preposition ἐπί with the dative τῇ ἀδικίᾳ is best translated **at wrongdoing**. Apart from the force of ἐπί, *in wrongdoing* would miss the point and verge on tautology: someone else's **wrongdoing** is at issue. Several writers insist that ἀδικία in Paul has its full theological sense of *unrighteousness* rather than moral *injustice* (cf. Rom 1:32).[137] But along with virtually every other declaration in these verses, Paul probably alludes to a situation of contrast at Corinth. This could either be (i) the sense of inflated self-importance and complacency (πεφυσιωμένοι) with which people at Corinth viewed the **wrongdoing** of the incestuous men in 5:1-5, especially if patronage, property, or social status was involved (see above on 5:1-5); or (ii) the tacit or overt approval of the **injustice** entailed in seeking to use the manipulative machinery of a local Gentile magistrate's court for the acquisition of property rights (see above on 6:1-11); or (iii), more broadly, to the competitive, status-seeking culture at Corinth which would encourage taking **pleasure at** the loss of esteem suffered by another if their complicity or involvement in some **wrongdoing** came to be exposed (see above, Introduction, 12-17, and on 1:12–2:5).

Contextual factors suggest that **wrongdoing** embraces a wider range of possibilities than theological *unrighteousness* or moral *injustice*. Further, these factors suggest that F. F. Bruce's interpretation (with Moffatt) in terms of *Schadenfreude, malicious joy* or *gloating,* i.e., *over people's failures* covers much of the ground but probably not all of it.[138] Barrett believes that, in addition to the issue of "superiority," part of the matter concerns "being censorious."[139] If we genuinely love a person, we should **not take pleasure at** conduct which gives us the opportunity to lecture them or to rebuke them about their **wrongdoing.** Here, again, may be an allusion to overly ready pleasure in *prophetic rebuke* and *pronouncing judgment* on failures within the congregation. Does such a prophet or preacher genuinely **love** those whose welfare he or she claims to cherish if this gives **pleasure**?

First Epistle, stores up no resentment; but esp. Allo, *Première Épitre,* 346, *"elle ne tient compte du mal"* (Loisy).

135. Héring, *First Epistle,* 139.

136. Wolff, *Der erste Brief,* 319-20.

137. Notably, Robertson, *Epistle,* 4:178, for the semantic range of BAGD, 17-18, and Meyer's critique of Chrysostom, Theodoret, and medieval and Reformation commentators (*First Epistle,* 1:392-93).

138. Bruce, *1 and 2 Cor,* 127. Cf. Moffatt, *Love in the NT,* 180-81: "it does not discuss a scandal with gloating."

139. Barrett, *First Epistle,* 304.

Many commentators appear to miss Paul's point about **truth**. Fee contends that the term stands in opposition to evil in the sense of "the gospel and all that is opposed to it . . . behaviour that reflects the gospel."[140] But this use of truth occurs mainly in the later writings of the NT and abruptly introduces a fresh idea without preparation.[141] Moffatt simply equates **truth** with *goodness.*[142] Would the addressees interpret this verse in either of these ways, and would Paul expect them to do so? Wolff alludes to the joining of ἀδικία and ἀλήθεια in 3 Ezra 4:33-39, which may shed some light on the relationship.[143] However, Spicq comes nearer to the heart of the matter when he explores the reason for the compound verb συγχαίρει, translated above as **joyfully celebrates**. With Barrett and Fee, Spicq sees the συν- (συγ-) prefix as primarily intensive: "it shows the intensity and expressiveness of the joy in truth."[144] But rightly he goes beyond Barrett and Fee in understanding the *"with"* aspect of συν- to denote "active participation," with the classical meaning of "congratulate . . . felicitate . . . applaud. . . . Agape's fundamental meaning 'to acclaim' is plain here."[145]

What is it that love **joyfully celebrates** or *acclaims?* At one level Chrysostom convincingly contrasts *the truth* about someone's well-being with reports about their supposed failure. Love "feels pleasure with those who are well spoken of," as against enjoying someone's loss of standing.[146] But probably the disinterested character of ἀγάπη is even more clearly at issue. The proximity between postmodernity after Nietzsche and Derrida and the rhetorical stances applauded at Corinth places us in a better position to appreciate Paul's meaning than commentators from the medieval period to the 1980s. Postmodern philosophers and critical theorists perceive as clearly as Paul did that virtually every action and stance bears some relationship to the power interests of the self, or to one's peer group. Genuine **love**, as I argue as my main thesis in *Interpreting God and the Postmodern Self,* alone *decenters* the power "interests" of the self and of its peer group, and in recentering them in the Other (primarily in God, but also in the other person) disengages from self-interest.[147] Only now can **truth** emerge as disengaged from a power agenda. True disinterested integrity is free to seek **truth**, without anxiety about what it helps or hinders in one's personal agenda. **Love**, Paul says, has discovered *integrity:* As Nygren constantly declares, because it

140. Fee, *First Epistle,* 639.
141. On *truth* in the NT and in modern thought, see A. C. Thiselton, "Truth, ἀλήθεια," in C. Brown (ed.), *NIDNTT,* 3:874-902. See also J. Murphy O'Connor, "Truth: Paul and Qumran," in *Paul and Qumran,* 179-230.
142. Moffatt, *Love in the NT,* 181.
143. Wolff, *Der erste Brief,* 320. Schrage, *Der erste Brief,* 3:300, n. 128, cites many more passages from the LXX and inter-Testamental literature.
144. Spicq, *Agapē,* 2:158.
145. Ibid.
146. Chrysostom, *1 Cor. Hom.,* 32:4.
147. Thiselton, *Interpreting God and the Postmodern Self,* 3-45 and 121-64.

is disinterested and creative of value, it delights in **truth**.[148] The definite article with the abstract noun, τῇ ἀληθείᾳ, does not commit us to the translation *the* **truth**, although admittedly it cannot be excluded. If the article is translated, it probably denotes *the truth* in this or that situation rather than gospel truth *as such*.

The practical thrust of *love* **joyfully celebrates truth**, then, is that love does not use manipulative devices and subtexts to protect itself from **truth** or from *the* **truth**. It is honest and open, not defensive, for it has placed the good of the other above the good of the self. Theology enters the picture in a different way from that envisaged by most commentators. As Karl Rahner observes, the person who has placed everything in the hands of God has no need to fear, or to hide from, the truth. For God already knows it and has accepted the believer as he or she is.[149] The symmetry of v. 6a and v. 6b is now apparent. No taint of evil can enhance or give pleasure to love, where love is genuine. Love takes no pleasure in someone else's failure, and delights in integrity and reality. If the situation is bad, love wants to help; if the situation is good, love wants to celebrate. It wants no hidden interests which disguise truth as something which it is not. Deluz links this verse with the thought of v. 7 that love "does not exaggerate, but it . . . tries to understand . . . bears with it."[150]

7   Our translation restructures the Greek syntax for two reasons, both of which concern the distinction between a logic of inclusion and a logic of exclusion in conveying the force of Paul's fourfold repetition of πάντα, *all things*. First, this fourfold πάντα serves to convey "the absence of all limits" (Héring).[151] It thus *excludes* the *limits* of ἀγάπη rather than defining an *all-inclusive* content. The REB is the only major VS to appreciate that this is best rendered in modern English by negating a series of negations: *There is nothing love cannot face; there is no limit to its faith, its hope, its endurance.* Even Collins produces an all-inclusive translation: *"It bears everything, believes everything, hopes everything, endures everything."*[152]

Second, the traditional translations invite the kind of misunderstandings of Paul and indeed of Christianity which fuel the critiques of Feuerbach, Marx, Nietzsche, and Freud. The well-known AV/KJV and RV rendering *beareth all things, believeth all things, hopeth all things, endureth all things* appears to support Marx's notion of Christianity as the opium of the people, or Nietzsche's concept of Christianity as "servile mediocrity." Paul's notion of the cross and of love, Nietzsche asserts, "has sided with everything weak, low and botched; it has made an ideal out of antagonism towards . . . strong life . . . the will to noth-

148. Nygren, *Agapē and Eros*, 77-78.

149. K. Rahner, "On Truthfulness," in *Theological Investigations*, 7 (Eng. trans., London: Darton, Longman & Todd, 1971), 229-59. Cf. W. Pannenberg, "What Is Truth?" in *Basic Questions in Theology*, 2 (London: SCM, 1971), 1-27.

150. Deluz, *Companion*, 193.

151. Héring, *First Epistle*, 141.

152. Collins, *1 Cor*, 478.

ingness sanctified. . . ."[153] For Nietzsche, Paul was "full of superstition and cunning," for by reinterpreting language about the law he became "the destroyer of the Law" and thereby of criteria other than self-construed outlooks: "Morality itself was blown away, annihilated. . . . 'I am above the Law,' thinks Paul."[154] If Paul enjoins his readers to bear, believe, hope, and endure *everything,* Nietzsche can say that "truth has been turned topsy-turvy . . . transvaluation of all values!" while Michel Foucault can perceive it as the promotion of conformist "docility," Marx as "opium," and Freud as a projection derived from inner conflicts resolved by wishful thinking which "believes all things" in order to "endure all things."[155]

None of this, however, accords with Paul. It is Corinth which coins the slogan "All things are lawful"; "We reign as kings." It is Paul who insists on discrimination and differentiation, especially in prophecy and worship. Moreover, ἀγάπη is precisely *not* "docile" or conformist; it does not seek a quiet life by "servile mediocrity." Nygren's exposition of Paul's theology reveals the reverse: it is creative, innovative, transforming, and indifferent to "returns" in the sense of lacking the very "interests" on which the analyses of Feuerbach, Marx, Nietzsche, and Freud depend. Therefore we must use the semantic strategy of protecting Paul's meaning by using a logic of negation as the least ambiguous way to exclude the partial, as we shall also explore in 15:43 and 44, where similar logical and linguistic problems await us. Paul declares: *Love* **never tires of support, never loses faith, never exhausts hope, never gives up**. The fourfold **never** with four negative actions provides rhetorical force to Paul's fourfold *all things* (πάντα), which clearly invites misunderstanding by readers in a post-Freudian, post-Nietzschean world. The REB offers a good precedent for the basic strategy.

Yet again the precise semantic range of at least one of the verbs remains in question. The meaning of στέγει remains open to debate. Lexicographers and exegetes generally agree that the cognate noun στέγη, *roof* (as in Mark 2:4), offers a starting point. But this may be connected with the verb στέγω in one of several ways. It may mean *to cover,* as a *roof covers* a house. In biblical Greek the verb occurs only (apart from here) in Ecclus 8:17 (LXX), in 1 Cor 9:4, and in 1 Thess 3:1, 5. In Ecclus 8:17 λόγον στέξαι means *to conceal the matter.* This would then accord with the maxim *"Charity shall cover (καλύψει) the multitude of sins"* (1 Pet 4:8, AV/KJV). Conzelmann uses *cover* in his translation and suggests in his exegesis that στέγει means either "(a) 'draw a veil of silence over'; [or] (b) 'bear.'"[156] The latter receives some support from Paul's use of

153. F. Nietzsche, *Works — XVI: The Antichrist,* 130 (aphorisms 5 and 6), 131 (aphorism 7), and 146 (aphorism 18); cf. 142-50 (aphorisms 16-21).

154. Nietzsche, *Works, IX: The Dawn of Day,* 67-70 (aphorism 68; cf. 66-71).

155. Nietzsche, *Works, XVI: The Antichrist,* 138 (aphorism 12) and 231 (aphorism 62); cf. M. Foucault, *Discipline and Punish* (Eng. trans., New York: Pantheon, 1977), e.g., in medicine, religion, or the penal system (190ff.).

156. Conzelmann, *1 Cor,* 224; also 224, n. 64 and 225, n. 65.

the verb in 1 Cor 9:4, where it means *to bear* in the sense of *to put up with*. But it is generally agreed that this is not a frequent meaning of the verb. BAGD conclude that "perhaps" in 13:7 στέγει means "love throws a cloak of silence over what is displeasing in another person" (Harnack).[157] Peter Lombard and many medieval interpreters adopt this meaning in the belief that Paul offers a model of God's love to persons.

Several versions associate στέγει with *roof* in the sense *to protect* rather than *to cover*, i.e., *bearing* in the sense of *carrying* or **supporting** rather than of *to put up with*. NIV renders *always protects;* NRSV plays a lexicographically safe but theologically dangerous game with *bears all things;* NJB expands the "covering" theme with *it is always ready to make allowances,* which embodies a notion of **support**. G. H. Whitaker attempted to preserve the roof imagery by suggesting "Love springs no leak."[158] Godet, following Bengel, urges that *to bear,* in the sense of *to put up with,* is tautologous in relation to ὑπομένει and hence means *to cover* in the sense of *to excuse*.[159] Spicq and more recently Lang have put forward exactly this argument, to conclude that it means *cover*.[160] Our understanding is closest to that of H. A. W. Meyer, Barrett, and Schrage. Citing the Vulgate *suffert,* Meyer proposes a distinction between στέγει and ὑπομένει. The latter sustains its support in *putting up with everything* for a limitless *duration;* the former **supports** a limitless *load:* "holds out under them *(suffert)* without ceasing to love — all burdens, privation, trouble, hardship, toil occasioned by others"; Schrage links *suffert* with *sustinet*.[161] **Support** well conveys this, with a clearer hint at the structure which supports the roof than *bear*. Barrett adds yet further weight to **support** by appealing to the tradition of the Jewish Mishnah stemming from Simeon the Just (third century BC) that *service* is **support** of the world.[162] Kierkegaard's analogy of a mother's love which ceaselessly gives **support** to her child is helpfully noted by Schrage (see below).

Before we complete our interpretation of the remaining verbs, Meyer's exegesis and our proposed translation lend weight to the assumption which lies behind the debate between Elizabeth Stuart and C. J. Walters that here "Love is Paul," i.e., Paul perceives himself as so manifesting his love and concern for Corinth as the Other that this love **never tires of support, never loses faith, never exhausts hope, never gives up**.[163] Neither writer considers this chapter in the detail explored here. Basically Stuart finds a manipulative strategy in

---

157. BAGD, 765-66.

158. Whitaker, "Love Springs No Leak," *Exp.* 21, 8th ser. (1921): 126.

159. Godet, *First Epistle,* 2:247.

160. Lang, *Die Briefe,* 185; and Spicq, *Agapē,* 2:159. Also Senft, *Première Épitre,* 169.

161. Meyer, *First Epistle,* 1:393; Schrage, *Der erste Brief,* 3:341. Schrage also compares the readings of Calvin and Kierkegaard, where the latter compares how a mother *supports* her child in limitless practical ways.

162. Barrett, *First Epistle,* 304; *m., Aboth* 1:2.

163. Stuart, "Love Is . . . Paul," *ExpTim* 102 (1991): 264-66; and Walters, "'Love Is . . . Paul' — A Response," *ExpTim* 103 (1991): 75.

Paul: by defining "love" in terms that relate more closely to his own values than those of the "gifts" at Corinth Paul effectively claims to be *the* paradigm through whom God's love is experienced. Walters attacks and rejects the argument about manipulation, mainly on the ground that Paul associates love with *truth* and disinterested concern *in principle* rather than in personal terms. But neither disputes that Paul himself seeks to live out what he ascribes to **love** in 1 Corinthians 13.

Stuart's approach, it need hardly be said, brings us back to power issues shared by A. C. Wire, E. Castelli, and M. Foucault. Wire asserts, "Paul's sharp contrast of this love to the exercise of all spiritual gifts suggests that the Corinthian prophets' highest value may be seen by reversing these verbs. They no longer suffer but zealously pursue a new life, not orientating themselves kindly on others' needs, but rejoicing in what the spirit has done in them."[164] Thus Wire returns to reading Paul as Feuerbach and Nietzsche do: Paul is the dull proponent of servile mediocrity, while the Corinthian women prophets "dare to exhibit the spirit's creativity."[165] "The women prophets of Corinth [are] on another social trajectory than Paul, and with a different experience of Christ . . . a different social practice and theological integrity."[166] Castelli does not directly address 1 Corinthians 13, but if Wire, Stuart, and others are right (as we agree) in discerning a barely veiled description of Paul's own goals in 13:7, then all of Castelli's observation about the links between Pauline *mimēsis* and Foucault's notions of power and conformity come into play.[167] However, it must be emphasized that the traditional translations of 13:7, especially in AV/KJV, RV, RSV, and NRSV, add fuel to the fire and give more hostages to their arguments than is necessary. At all costs we must hold to the demonstration, primarily in Nygren but also in Spicq, that for ἀγάπη to be manipulatory and concerned for its own interests would be a logical contradiction of huge proportions.

For further considerations about Paul's personal relation to this verse, we refer to the discussions of O. Wischmeyer, H. J. Blair, and others.[168] To translate πάντα πιστεύει as **never loses faith** meets Calvin's point (repeated by Lang): "not that a Christian . . . strips himself of wisdom and discernment . . . not that he has forgotten how to distinguish black from white!"[169] But in the absence of our explicating a logic of negated exclusion rather than universal inclusion even Calvin speaks of being rid of "ill-founded suspicion," and Spicq of "giving a favorable interpretation of everything."[170] Augustine, too, interprets

164. Wire, *Corinthian Women Prophets,* 139.
165. Ibid.
166. Ibid.
167. Castelli, *Imitating Paul,* 97-115 and throughout. She discusses Foucault on 35-58 and 119-24.
168. Wischmeyer, *Der höchste Weg;* and Blair, "First Corinthians 13 and the Disunity at Corinth," 69-77.
169. Calvin, *First Epistle,* 278; cf. Lang, *Die Briefe,* 185.
170. Ibid.; and Spicq, *Agapē,* 2:159.

this as "believing the best" about all people.[171] But Barrett writes: "Not 'always believes the best about people', but 'never loses faith'."[172] Whether we accept Heinrici's interpretation as belief in "the invincible power of good" depends on whether this implies human good (which would be *Eros*) or the transformative power of divine ἀγάπη which does provide grounds for **never loses faith** in Paul's thought.[173] The closely parallel phrase **never exhausts hope** scarcely requires further explanation. **Faith** and **hope** come to be associated with **love** in vv. 8-13 (see below). Finally, ὑπομένει refers to an *endurance* of setbacks and rebuffs which **never gives up** on people, whatever they do. This again bears the stamp of Paul's enduring concern for the people of Corinth. This is ἀγάπη, Deluz observes; "Like Christ on the cross, love endures scorn, failure, ingratitude. . . . At the end shines out the light of Easter. For *love never ends*."[174]

c. The Eschatological Permanence of Love (13:8-13)

The end of v. 7 readily leads into the main thrust of this section. If love *"always perseveres"* or **never gives up** (above; ὑπομένει), what applies at an interpersonal level is now applied at a "deeper" (Carson) level, i.e., at the *cosmic* level of Pauline and Christian eschatology.[175] ἡ ἀγάπη οὐδέποτε πίπτει. The explicit comparison with "spiritual gifts" now also becomes eschatological and temporal.

8 (1) D reads ἐκπίπτει, together with many other Western texts, but the early p[46], together with the overwhelming witness of ℵ*, A, B, C, 048 (fifth century), and 33 read πίπτει **falls**. The latter is the firm reading. (On the difference of nuance, see below.) (2) While other witnesses read γνῶσις for **knowledge**, A reads the plural γνώσεις. This is probably for stylistic symmetry with the plurals **prophecies** and **tongues**, but may reflect a gloss for human *acts* of knowledge.

Since Paul has consciously used images and metaphors of burning or boiling, inflating, bad manners, having a sharp point stuck into one, and reckoning up accounts, it seems a pity to reduce πίπτω, *to fall down, to fall to the ground, to collapse,* **to fall apart**, of its grounding in physical, pictorial imagery by the abstract *fails* (NIV) or *faileth* (AV/KJV, RV) or even *comes to an end* (REB, NJB) or *ends* (NRSV). The Western reading ἐκπίπτει retains the vividness of *falling off,* like a leaf which has decayed and lost its life (cf. Job 13:25, LXX; Jas 1:2; 1 Pet 1:24). The established reading πίπτει means *falls to the ground* in a literal

171. Augustine, *Confessions,* 10:3. However, in *Freedom and Letter* 32 Augustine explains it as belief in the word of God.

172. Barrett, *First Epistle,* 305.

173. Heinrici, *Das erste Sendschreiben,* 421.

174. Deluz, *Companion to 1 Corinthians,* 193.

175. Robertson and Plummer, *First Epistle,* 296; and Carson, *Showing the Spirit,* 66.

and metaphorical sense, often with the added force of *collapsing* or **falling apart**.[176] We regularly use the term **fall apart** of the disintegration and demise of something or someone hitherto apparently robust. The power of Paul's language is best conveyed by this word, which accurately reflects both the cognitive denotation and emotive connotation of the Greek. A strong rendering of the present with **never**, Wolff observes, introduces and enhances Paul's emphasis on love's permanence.[177]

BDF underline the contingent, almost pejorative, force of εἴτε, **whether**, best conveyed in the absence of a verb as "**whether it be**. . . ."[178] Robertson and Plummer declare, "The repeated εἴτε is depreciatory; it suggests indifference to the gifts of which the use was at best temporary: 'But as to prophesyings. . . .'"[179] But too much should not be read into the conditional conjunction; BDFs emphasis on bare contingency makes the point well enough. The gifts are contingent, just as the cosmos is contingent; love participates in eschatological reality in a way which transcends such contingency.

On καταργηθήσεται, **will be brought to an end**, see the discussions of καταργήσῃ in 1:28 (translated there as [God] **brings to nothing**); and of καταργουμένων in 2:6 (where we translate the participle as doomed **to come to nothing**). The intensive compound κατ- with ἀργός, *idle, useless, ineffective*, is very strong, and here the future passive does not suggest simply that **prophecies** melt away of their own accord as they are fulfilled, but that the cosmic, eschatological, public deed of divine judgment **brings them to an end**. How can preachers and prophets have anything to say when the last judgment not only reveals, but evaluates and pronounces judgment upon, everything. The sermons of prophets and the "knowledge" of theologians *are rendered redundant,* while the character and fruit of **love does not fall apart**. To prophesy would be like switching on a torch in the full light of the noonday sun.

The same fate befalls **tongues**. Here, however, we find the future middle παύσονται, *to cease,* **to stop**. *This must surely call into question the notion that* **tongues** *are either,* in Paul's view, *a language of heaven, or a paradigmatic way of expressing exalted intimacy with God.* If this were so, why should they cease at the *eschaton?* Rather, it confirms Theissen's view (see above on 12:10) that **tongues** primarily (although not perhaps exclusively) serve to express inarticulate preconscious longings, yearnings, and wellings up of praise prompted by the activity of the Spirit (Rom 8:26), but as yet "raw" and in need of communicative, intelligible, conscious communication.[180] **Tongues** will evaporate as readily as tears when a resurrection σῶμα allows the believer to come face to face with God without the limitations and hidden conflicts of the mode of this

---

176. BAGD, 659-60.

177. Wolff, *Der erste Brief,* 321-22.

178. BDF, 237, sect. 456, col. 2, entry 3; cf. BAGD, 220, entry 6:13.

179. Robertson and Plummer, *First Epistle,* 296.

180. This is taken up in the long, extended discussion of tongues under 12:10; cf. Theissen, *Psychological Aspects of Pauline Theology,* esp. 292-341.

present life in its earthly σῶμα. There is no need for them to be **brought to an end**; their cause will have disappeared. Interpersonal communication represented by the term *language* (singular) in contrast to either *languages* (plural) or *glossaolalia* is *not* said to cease at the *eschaton*.[181]

Reformation, post-Reformation, and modern theology have tended to obscure the major thrust of Paul's concern by imposing two questions onto Paul's agenda which he did not envisage. Calvin discusses the difficulty caused by some writers in the medieval Western tradition who attempt to appeal to this verse to legitimize the notion that the departed saints pray for the present living.[182] If love is permanent and eschatological, they argue, the concern of those who have died for those who follow them remains active. But huge assumptions about the logic of time and postmortal consciousness prior to the resurrection and last judgment are to be made if this inference is to be drawn, as Calvin implies. In particular I have endeavored elsewhere to develop Gilbert Ryle's distinction between the logic of the participant (first-person logic) and the logic of the observer (third-person logic) in ways which apply to this issue.[183] In first-person terms Paul states elsewhere that to be with Christ is the believer's "next" experience after death (Phil 1:23); but in terms of third-person "observer" logic, i.e., in terms of cosmic, not existential, description, the dead achieve raised awareness when, like a sleeping army, they are awakened by the last trumpet (1 Cor 15:52). The sleeping army is raised to its feet. The permanence of love hardly addresses the issues of prayers by or for the departed.

Similarly, **if it be tongues, these will cease** hardly addresses the debate between Reformed and neo-Pentecostalist writers about "tongues will cease" after the close of the canon or at a given stage of individual or historical maturity. *Here* Paul states that, like prophetic preaching and "knowledge," they will become redundant at the last day. As Carson observes, too much discussion of this issue directs us away from Paul's main point.[184] This issue must be determined on other grounds than exegetical discussions of this verse.

One of the most substantial discussions of this issue in broader terms is Jon Ruthven's book *On the Cessation of the Charismata* (1993).[185] Ruthven

181. Schrage, *Der erste Brief,* 3:343, including n. 420.

182. Calvin, *First Epistle,* 278-79.

183. Gilbert Ryle, *Dilemmas* (Cambridge: Cambridge University Press, 1966 [1954]), 36-53; Thiselton, "The Logical Role of the Liar Paradox in Titus 1:12, 13," *BibInt* 2 (1994): 214-19 (cf. 207-23); and "The Parousia in Modern Theology: Some Questions and Comments," *TynBul* 27 (1976): 27-54. For a broader discussion of "solidarity with the departed" see also J. Moltmann, *The Coming of God* (London: SCM, 1996), 96-128.

184. Carson, *Showing the Spirit,* 66.

185. J. Ruthven, *On the Cessation of the Charismata: The Protestant Polemic on Postbiblical Miracles,* Journal of Pentecostal Theology Supplementary Series (Sheffield: Sheffield Academic Press, 1993); cf. also, e.g., R. L. Thomas, "'Tongues . Will Cease,'" *JETS* 17 (1974): 81-89; S. Schatzmann, *A Pauline Theology of Charismata* (Peabody, Mass.: Hendrickson, 1987), 77-80; W. J. Samarin, "Glossolalia as Regressive Speech," *Language and Speech* 16 (1973): 77-89; G. W. Workman, *Has 'That Which Is Perfect' Come? An Exposition of 1 Cor 13:8-13* (Abilene,

lists about twenty books or articles which support what he terms "the cessationist polemic" against neo-Pentecostalist and related views. This "holds that miracles or 'extraordinary' charismata were terminated at or near the end of the apostolic age."[186] He points out that in historical context "cessationists" are linked historically with the Reformers' suspicions of Roman Catholic claims about miracles in the sixteenth and seventeenth centuries (notably Calvin), and the period of the Hume, Kant, and Enlightenment debate concerning miracles. In the Reformed tradition he cites among recent representatives R. B. Gaffin, N. L. Geisler, J. F. MacArthur, R. L. Thomas and J. F. Walvoord.[187] It more especially reflects an older Calvinist tradition in the systematic theologies of A. A. Hodge, Charles Hodge, and A. H. Strong and in the work of B. B. Warfield.[188] Ruthven concedes that Origen, Chrysostom, and Ambrosiaster reflect "cessationist" views, but attributes the origins of their approach to the excesses of Montanism. Montanism, we admit, damaged the profile of both preaching and concerns about the Spirit among the sober-minded. Augustine, however, moved from a "cessationist" view to a recognition of experiences of miracles (*City of God,* 22:8). But it was Thomas Aquinas, Ruthven concludes, who "ordered the pattern of cessationist tenets which dominated the church until the 20th Century."[189]

The one important point to make here is that few or none of the serious "cessationist" arguments depends on a specific exegesis of 1 Cor 13:8-11. Charles Hodge, e.g., leans toward "cessationist" views in his *Systematic Theology.*[190] But while he expresses some uncertainty about "tongues" in his *Commentary* on 12:10, Hodge makes no play of 13:8-11 in his *Commentary* to support the view of "gifts" or "miracles" which he holds on other grounds.[191] The same holds true for Calvin, who makes no use of 13:8-11 to support his view.[192] Similarly, Thomas Aquinas interprets the cessation of tongues in 13:8 as due both to the dissolution of the physical body *(usum linguae corporeae)* and to the perfection of knowledge at the eschaton, *unde non erit necessarium variis*

Tex.: Quality, 1971); K. Stendahl, "Glossalalia: NT Evidence," in M. P. Hamilton (ed.), *The Charismatic Movement,* 49-60 (rpt. from *Paul among Jews and Gentiles*). This verse offers less potential relevance than perhaps 13:9-11.

186. Ruthven, *On the Cessation of the Charismata,* 15, n. 2.

187. Cf. Thomas, "'Tongues . . . Will Cease,'" 81-89; N. L. Geisler, *Signs and Wonders* (Wheaton: Tyndale Press, 1988); J. F. MacArthur Jr., *Charismatic Chaos* (Grand Rapids: Zondervan, 1992), 106-27, 194-245, 291-96; J. F. Walvoord, *The Holy Spirit* (Grand Rapids: Zondervan, 3d ed. 1977). MacArthur offers a valid, incisive polemic against a distorted "power-success" gospel, whatever his other views.

188. A. A. Hodge, *Outlines of Theology* (New York: Scribner, 1879), 278-79; C. Hodge, *Systematic Theology* (3 vols., New York: Scribner, 1871), 1:635-36; A. H. Strong, *Systematic Theology* (Philadelphia: Judson Press, 1907), 128; but most especially B. B. Warfield, *Counterfeit Miracles* (New York: Scribner, 1918). Ruthven's book is largely an attack on Warfield's arguments.

189. Ruthven, *Cessation,* 13 (v).

190. C. Hodge, *Systematic Theology,* 1:635-36.

191. C. Hodge, *First Epistle,* 271-73; on 12:10, 247-52.

192. Calvin, *First Epistle,* 280-81.

linguis loqui.[193] *These verses should not be used as a polemic for either side in this debate.* All that is clear is that the gifts cease at the eschaton. It may be natural *to assume* that they continue *up to* the eschaton, since "prophecy" and "knowledge" belong together with "tongues." But the assumption does *not* become an *explicit statement* about tongues rather than a *possible allusion* to them.

Karl Barth recaptures Paul's thrust, alluding to Luther's translation *Die Liebe höret nimmer auf.* Love is 'the one form of Christian action which does not require, and is not subject to, transformation or absorption into another, higher, and future form."[194] Everything else is subject to "relativization in the light of its glorious future. . . . But this relativization will not overtake love. . . . Even in the best of cases the same cannot be said of . . . prophecy, tongues and theology in themselves and as such."[195]

9 On Paul's uses of ἐκ μέρους, see above under 12:27. In 12:27 we translated the words *for his or her part* (limbs and organs of Christ's body). The idiom has the force of *piece by piece, bit by bit,* or **part by part** in many contexts, including here. The static adjective *partial* with the static noun *knowledge* (REB), or the static adverbial phrase *in part* (NRSV, NIV, Collins), or even *imperfectly* (NJB) fails to convey the process described here adequately. γινώσκομεν means both **we know** and *we come to know,* and Paul conveys the pictorial image of "building up" knowledge by trying to fit together bits and pieces a part at a time. Luther uses the word *patchwork (das Stückwerk).* Arguably, *part by part* might well invite ἀνὰ μέρος, but a survey of sources suggests that ἐκ μέρους offers a more intensive or emphatic alternative.[196]

We need to recall, in this anti-metaphysical era, that Hegel's notion that only *the whole* is real stems from pre-Socratic debates from Parmenides onward about how *Being* can be grasped without its disintegrating into paradoxes or even apparent contradictions when it is perceived little by little within temporal processes. It is quite astonishing that virtually only with Pannenberg has the importance of "knowledge of the whole" through revelation of the End reentered Christian theology. Paul shares the view explored in the Hegelian tradition that piece-by-piece knowledge may lead to partial and mistaken judgments which set in motion endless processes of correction and recorrection.

In Paul's view any "absolute" of revelation is anchored in the cross and the resurrection within the framework of OT revelation and further disclosures as anticipation of the End when the whole picture becomes unveiled at the last judgment. Only then does "knowledge" become definitive, unrevisable, and no longer corrigible. For stylistic reasons we translate the first ἐκ μέρους as **in**

193. Thomas Aquinas, *Super Epistolas S. Pauli: 1 ad Cor.,* 385, sect. 789.
194. Barth, *CD,* 4/2 (sect. 68), 837.
195. Ibid., 837-38.
196. BAGD, 506, entry c; Grimm-Thayer, 400-401.

fragmentary ways, and the second ἐκ μέρους as **part by part**. Pannenberg faithfully reflects Paul when he urges that we find a dialectic in which, on one side, we "find in the history of Jesus an answer to the question of how 'the whole' of reality and its meaning can be conceived"; but on the other side, also "without compromising the provisionality and historical relativity of all thought . . . on the way and not yet at the goal."[197] But this awaits further clarification in v. 10.

10 The climactic τὸ τέλειον includes the double meaning **the complete** (NRSV) and **wholeness** (REB). Depending on the specific force required by the context the word may also mean *perfection* (NIV, NJB) or *perfect* (AV/KJV, RV). On the lexicography of the word, see above on 2:6, where it clearly carries the different sense of *mature* (usually of persons), as it does in its one remaining use in this epistle, ταῖς δὲ φρεσὶν τέλειοι γίνεσθε (14:20). However, here there is also a further hint of τέλειος as denoting a *goal*. For just as in 2:6 the wisdom for *the mature* is not for those who exhibit childish self-centeredness and immediacy, even so here Paul is about to draw the same contrast with being *infantile* or *childish* or *childlike* in v. 11a and the *goal* of mature adulthood. Hence it combines the two related notions of *fulfillment* or *goal* and the *completed whole*. No English word alone can fully convey the meaning in this context. To translate solely as *the end* (Collins) is barely adequate.[198]

Paul does not wish his readers to be deceived by the apparently immanental process which ἔλθῃ, **comes**, might be thought to imply on its own. Human persons do not simply "progress" to *perfection* or **completion**, as gnostics might propose; for the eschatological act of definitive divine judgment which evaluates everything in the light of the whole **does away with piece-by-piece** knowledge *in a cosmic act of God*. Thus in this context καταργηθήσεται (future passive of the intensive compound καταργέω) has its full force. Moltmann expresses this issue clearly in a way which reflects Paul's eschatology accurately: "What is new announces itself in the judgment of what is old. It does not *emerge* from the old; it makes the old absolute. It is not simply the old in new form. It is also a new creation."[199] Revelation in history and in Christ offers an "anticipatory reaching out to the new future which God has promised to create. . . . The category *novum* dominates the eschatological language of the whole NT." Like the resurrection of Christ and of believers, this new wholeness "does not develop . . . ," even though continuity coexists with contrast.[200]

---

197. W. Pannenberg, *Basic Questions in Theology* (London: SCM, 1969), 1:181. See further Thiselton, "Authority and Hermeneutics," in P. E. Satterthwaite and D. F. Wright (eds.), *A Pathway into the Holy Scripture* (Grand Rapids: Eerdmans, 1994), 117-41; R. Kieffer, *Le primat de l'amour. Commentaire épistémologique de 1 Cor 13,* LD 85, might be expected to address such questions. But help is tangential and verges on the idiosyncratic.

198. Collins, *First Cor,* 483.

199. J. Moltmann, *The Coming of God* (Eng. trans., London: SCM, 1996), 27 (his italics).

200. Ibid., 28.

Harrisville has well expounded this principle, and Paul will do so throughout much of ch. 15 on the resurrection.[201]

11 In 𝔭⁴⁶ the word order is different, placing ὡς νήπιος *before* its verb.

The vocabulary and grammar call for special comment. νήπιος occurred in 3:1 (see above), in contrast to τέλειος, which Paul has just used in v. 10a. But it had a more clearly pejorative meaning in 3:1, where we translated it as *infantile*. Here it serves also in contrast to *maturity,* but in the more value-neutral sense of **child**. The imperfect tenses of, e.g., ἐλαλοῦν signify continuous past processes: **I used to talk like a child**. φρονέω often means *to think,* but it is doubtful whether Paul has in mind the nature of mental processes. The verb also regularly means **to form an opinion** or *to hold* **an opinion**, or alternatively *to set one's mind upon,* which here would denote having childish *interests and concerns*. Since all three meanings are equally possible on the basis of Greek lexicography, we must reach a judgment by considering the context. Since the major contrast turns on **child** versus **adult**, and since λογίζομαι is about to be used for *calculative evaluation,* the most probable candidate seems to be **I used to form opinions like a child**. This would also cohere with the Corinthian concern for rhetoric as shaping **opinion** by persuasion. But, Paul continues, if one *used to reckon, calculate, count as, value,* or **count values** (ἐλογιζόμην, imperfect middle) **like a child**, this dovetails with **talking** and **forming opinions** like a child.[202] NRSV's and REB's *spoke . . . thought . . . reasoned* (similar to NIV) misses the force of the imperfect, and risks losing the contrast between φρονέω and λογίζομαι. The NJB is much better: *I used to talk like a child, see things as a child does, and think like a child.*

The next stretch of grammar and vocabulary is no less important. The perfect active indicatives γέγονα ἀνήρ and κατήργηκα τὰ τοῦ νηπίου stand in contrast with the imperfects of process (i.e., a process of growing). γέγονα means **reached adulthood**, with no going back, and the strong force of καταργέω, *to make ineffective, to render inoperative, to abolish, to wipe out* (κατ- intensive with *idle,* see above), needs to be translated by a strong and forceful English equivalent. AV/KJV's *put away* is too bland; NRSV's *put an end to,* and REB's *I finished with* are improvements in terms of force and color. But the finality of the perfect state and the nuance of *rendering idle* in καταρέω suggest *closing the door upon,* or (following St John Parry) **have done away with** or **turned my back on the things of childhood** to retain the force and completeness of the verb.[203] Moffatt's *I am done with childish ways* and Collins's *I abandoned childish ways* offer good alternatives.

201. Harrisville, *The Concept of Newness in the NT* (Minneapolis: Augsburg, 1960), esp. 1-28, 93-105.

202. Barrett, *First Epistle,* 306: "the thought of calculation, estimation, seems inseparable from it," i.e., from λογίζομαι.

203. Parry, *First Epistle,* 195. See above on 1:28; 2:6; 6:13, and 13:8, 10: Edwards, *First Epistle,* 350, proposes *has brought that period of life to a close.*

Many refer "childhood" to the use of tongues on the basis of 14:20, where this gift is related to a contrast between childish and adult thinking. Moffatt and Barrett consider this a possibility, and Bengel thinks it is the probable meaning.[204] Heinrici and Wolff relate λαλεῖν to tongues, φρονεῖν to prophecy, and λογίζεσθαι to gnosis.[205] Fee rejects interpretations which turn on "growing up" and the use of spiritual gifts since Paul is speaking of the eschatological consummation when these gifts will no longer be needed.[206] But a middle view has much to commend it. As Conzelmann, Lang, and others insist, this metaphor for *maturity* was well known in Paul's world.[207] Further, the use of νήπιος in 3:1 relates precisely to the issue of childishness versus maturity (Allo).[208] Paul is alluding not simply to the *experience* of spiritual gifts, but to how they are *expressed* (λαλεῖν), what **opinions** are held about them (φρονεῖν), and how they are **valued** or *evaluated* (λογίζεσθαι).

A child, as Augustine reflects, inevitably views life with a *self-centered* set of "interests" which steadily develop into *concern for the other;* chaotic drives address, for the child, the gratification of the *immediate present,* whereas the adult *coherently orders strategies* which serve *long-term goals* with *self-discipline.* Bornkamm speaks here of "the child that is moved by dreams and wishes."[209] Although she attacks Paul's emphasis on "order," A. C. Wire has well formulated the issue. From one viewpoint Paul's concern for "order" spoils the liberty and sheer "fun" of the Corinthian [women?] prophets: "not orientating themselves on others' needs, but rejoicing in what the spirit has done in them."[210] From the opposite viewpoint, it is time for a more mature ordering of priorities which places first the welfare of the whole over the "rights" of the individual enthusiast (6:12). Hays observes that "Paul's argument is impeccable within the eschatologically determined symbolic world of the gospel. The Corinthians, however, seem to have lost hold of the future temporal orientation of Paul's preaching. They have moved into a frame of reference that thinks only in spatial categories of 'above' and 'below.'"[211]

12 The major contrast turns on ἄρτι, *just now,* or **for the present**, and τότε, **then** (in the temporal rather than the logical sense). The two terms are repeated, each time with the contrastive δέ, **but**. The introductory γάρ, **for**, signals that Paul uses this imagery to explain what has gone before (in vv. 9-11). Two exegetical decisions have to be made concerning δι' ἐσόπτρου and ἐν αἰνίγματι. (i) Does διά with the genitive mean *through* **a mirror** (as if the image appears to

---

204. Moffatt, *First Epistle,* 200; Barrett, *First Epistle,* 306.
205. Heinrici, *Das erste Sendschreiben,* 423; Wolff, *Der erste Brief,* 323, believes that Heinrici's proposal "exactly" fits the situation.
206. Fee, *First Epistle,* 646. But see Spicq, *Agapē,* 2:161-62.
207. Conzelmann, *1 Cor,* 226; Lang, *Die Briefe,* 187.
208. Allo, *Première Épitre,* 348.
209. Bornkamm, *Early Christian Experience,* 185.
210. Wire, *Corinthian Women Prophets,* 139.
211. Hays, *First Cor,* 229.

be "behind" it); or **by means of a mirror** (as describing medium or means of perception)? (ii) Does ἐν αἰνύγματι allude to *obscurity* or *distortions* or *puzzles* caused by the limitations of **mirrors** in the ancient world (cf. AV/KJV, *darkly*); or to **indirectness** as signifying the difference between secondhand reflections and interpretations, and direct, **face-to-face** vision and complete knowledge?

Corinth was well known for the production of good quality bronze mirrors, by the standards of the day. Although Robertson and Plummer correctly observe that the custom of frequently producing concave or convex mirrors led to "somewhat distorted reflexion," nevertheless to describe the resulting image as *puzzling, obscure,* or *enigmatic* would be to overstate their relative inadequacy by modern standards.[212] Polished bronze can offer quite reasonable images, even if, as the AV/KJV's *darkly* suggests, a deterioration of brightness is entailed. But this does not express Paul's main point, as Héring, Senft and Fee argue.[213] At best it would allow the translation *indistinctly,* which BAGD regard as possible.[214]

Tertullian believes that ἔσοπρον can denote a semitransparent, translucent pane of horn *through* which vague shapes on the other side can be perceived.[215] But ἔσοπρον normally means **mirror** in hellenistic Greek, and its material is polished metal, ideally polished bronze. If these *mirrors* yielded only *puzzling reflections,* it is difficult to understand why there was a lively trade for the purpose of "looking at one's face in a mirror" (Jas 1:23; cf. Josephus, *Antiquities* 12.81; Philo, *De Migratione Abrahami* 98).[216] On the other hand, BAGD's inclusion of *indistinct* means "soft focus." Barrett, Conzelmann, and others, however, retain the notion of *obscure* or *enigmatic* knowledge not on the basis of the properties of Corinthian bronze mirrors, but on that of a probable allusion to Num 12:8 in which God speaks *clearly* to Moses (LXX, ἐν εἴδει) but to others *through riddles,* or *through obscure* or *enigmatic* words (δι' αἰνιγμάτων).[217] Conzelmann, Spicq, and Fishbane go further, detecting a wordplay in the Hebrew behind the Greek where the same form מראה (mar'ah) can be read to mean either *clearly* or **mirror.** Even if this does not provide evidence of a background, Conzelmann concludes, the notion of *obscurity* stands in contrast to face-to-face knowledge.

Michael Fishbane develops these allusions to the Hebrew with reference also to Ezek 43 under the punning title "Through the Looking Glass: Reflections on Ezek 43:3, Num 12:8 and 1 Cor 13:12" (1986).[218] He identifies a triple

---

212. Robertson and Plummer, *First Epistle,* 298.

213. Héring, *First Epistle,* 142; Senft, *Première Épitre,* 171; Fee, *First Epistle,* 647-49.

214. BAGD, 23.

215. Tertullian, *On the Soul,* 53: *velut per corneum specular obsoletior lux* (light illuminates what comes in upon the soul in a confused manner as if through a window of horn); cf. *Against Praxeas,* 14.

216. BAGD, 313.

217. Barrett, *First Epistle,* 307; Conzelmann, *1 Cor,* 226-28.

218. Fishbane, "Through the Looking Glass: Reflections on Ezek 43:3, Num 12:8 and 1 Cor 13:12," 63-75.

wordplay on מראה *(m-r-'h)* where Ezek 43:3 uses *mar'eh* and *mar'ot,* while Numbers 12 involves a pun on *mareh, vision,* and *mar'ah,* **mirror.** 1 Cor 13:12 is then a midrash on Num 12:8. This compounds the problem of whether διά means *through,* **by means of,** or (as in Greek syntax) both! Yet alongside this suggestion other backgrounds have been proposed. Since one usually views only oneself in a mirror, whereas Paul speaks of viewing reality or images of reality, Héring believes that he refers to the "magic" mirrors used by sorcerers for "conjuring up in a mirror persons or scenes distant in space or time."[219] Spicq believes that the connection with *prophecy* and the participation of *children* as a "medium" render this just possible, but such a background seems insufficiently prominent to be introduced or presupposed without further explanation. Far more common in Graeco-Roman first-century thought is the use of **mirror** as a metaphor for **indirect** knowledge.

Although only philosophical thinkers should be called "Platonists" in the strict sense, and although even among philosophers Epicurean and Stoic philosophies were no less widespread than Platonism, Plato's contrast between the **indirect** perception of an *image* and *direct* apprehension of *Ideas* lay behind much Graeco-Roman thought, however tacitly. Plato speaks of "a mirror which receives impressions and provides visible images" (Plato, *Timaeus* 71B; cf. Philo, *De Decalogo* 105). Fee correctly perceives Paul's use of the **mirror** metaphor to indicate **indirect** knowledge.[220] Here the limitations, fallibility, and "interests" of the observation and inference can lead to *mistaken* judgments and opinions. Senft sums up succinctly three conclusive arguments for this view: (i) the metaphor of a **mirror** more often denotes *clarity* than obscurity in ancient literature of the period (e.g., Cicero, *De Finibus* 5.22.61); (ii) mirrors are usually envisaged as instruments of self-knowledge (e.g., Philo, *De Iosepho* 16); and (iii) in the Platonic tradition "the mirror symbolizes indirect vision, which perceives only a reality which is derived, i.e., the image."[221] Thus Philo, in particular, argues that we can compare and evaluate only "representations" concerning which we can make mistakes (Philo, *De Specialibus Legibus* 1.2). Senft concludes: "It is evidently to this tradition that Paul's text refers."[222] However, he adds, Paul is not offering a theory of knowledge as such; Paul simply uses the imagery from this universe of discourse to underline the difference between **present** fallible understanding and future **face-to-face** knowing and being known. The metaphor, like all metaphors, is limited to making a particular point and should not be pressed.

On the translation and meaning of ἐκ μέρους, **part by part,** see above on v. 9. Paul repeats the clause of v. 9a. The quasimechanical attempt to put together *fragments* or **parts** of knowledge derived indirectly from various sources

219. Héring, *First Epistle,* 142.
220. Fee, *First Epistle,* 646.
221. Senft, *Première Épitre,* 171.
222. Ibid.

and experiences stands in utter contrast to the perfection of uninterrupted personal intimacy with God (implied by the passive) which is πρόσωπον πρὸς πρόσωπον, **face to face**, following the continuous βλέπομεν, **we are seeing**. The syntax reflects Heb. פָּנִים אֶל־פָּנִים *(panim 'el-panim),* e.g., Gen 32:31. Both the Greek and especially its Hebrew equivalent mean **face** and/or *presence.* When God's **face** "shines upon" his people, his presence radiates his glory and his saving presence. David Ford provides an illuminating and valuable discussion of the significance of *face* in 2 Corinthians 3 and for theology.[223] "The uniqueness of each face" is part of it all.[224] Here, as elsewhere, the idiom denotes intimacy of relationship and access. πρός in the sense of *facing toward* plays a major part in the grand opening of the Fourth Gospel: ὁ λόγος ἦν πρὸς τὸν θεόν: the Word was (intimate) with God. This intimacy is what holds out as characterizing the eschatological goal for believers. **Then I shall come to know** (ἐπιγνώσομαι, future of ἐπιγινώσκω) **just as fully as I have been known** (καθώς, *even as, exactly as,* indicating quality and measure in this context — **just as fully as** [NJB] with the aorist passive ἐπεγνώσθην). Paul regularly uses what H. A. A. Kennedy calls "an aorist of sovereignty" for divine decision and divine knowledge.[225] This is the measure and nature of the full knowledge.[226] "The consummation consists in the fact that the cleft between knowing and being known by God is abolished" (Bornkamm).[227] Bornkamm adds that this is not the individualistic "union with God" achieved by *gnosis* in quasi-gnostic mystery religions. Indeed, the very fact that "knowing" occurs in a full personal sense only at the eschaton in the context of God's knowing his people excludes the role of *gnosis* found in the earliest gnostic texts.

Barth relates the **indirect** perception **by means of a mirror** as against **coming to know just as fully as I have been known** to a most *profound dialectic concerning knowing God.* On one side, "knowing in part is already knowing." An element of continuity exists between our fragmentary piece-by-piece understanding and the full light of day. In both modes God "presents himself." But, on the other side, the **mirror** constitutes "an element and medium foreign to the object [Object] itself; in the form of human perceptions and concepts; in an earthly history visible in earthly terms . . . even the life of the man Jesus."[228] Nevertheless, "the revelation of God in Jesus Christ will mean that we 'see him as he is' (1 Jn 3:2) directly, unparadoxically and undialectically."[229] Barth, like

---

223. Ford, *Self and Salvation: Being Transformed,* 17-29.

224. Ibid., 20; also "capacities for differentiation, many-levelled communication . . ." (21). See also below on the resurrection mode of existence, 15:44-51.

225. See under 15:38.

226. Robertson and Plummer comment, "It is difficult not to believe that here the compound [i.e., ἐπιγινώσκω] is not meant to indicate more complete knowledge than the simple verb . . . a bold way of expressing the completeness of future illumination" *(First Epistle,* 299).

227. Bornkamm, "The More Excellent Way," in *Early Christian Experience,* 185.

228. Barth, *CD,* 4/2 (sect. 68), 839.

229. Ibid.

many exegetes, believes that behind Paul's language there may well lie the thought of Num 12:8, "With him will I speak mouth to mouth." Is it fanciful to think of the intimacy and self-giving of a kiss at the climax of a dialectic poem on love?

13 This verse presents the notorious difficulty that Paul has spent the entire chapter expounding the eschatological permanence of love alone, only to conclude, apparently, that faith and hope also last forever. It would be easy to justify *the theology* of such a proposition. Just as love will never become obsolete, so where God is the living God his presence continues always to invite trust and confidence, as well as forward-looking hope in the living, ever-ongoing God who does new things, even in the perfection of heaven. But does such a thought, *even if it coheres with Paul's theology (which it does),* also cohere with *the immediate context* (which is doubtful)?

Before we list the standard explanations, we may note what is at issue in the translation. NRSV uncompromisingly translates νυνὶ δὲ μένει πίστις, ἐλπίς, ἀγάπη as *And now* **faith, hope** *and* **love** *abide.* REB is even more explicit: *There are three things that last for ever:* **faith, hope and love.** (AV/KJV and RV are similar to NRSV.) But NJB and NIV allow for a different understanding: *As it is, these* **remain: faith, hope,** *and* **love** (NJB; NIV is virtually the same, beginning *And now . . .*). We also propose (with Collins) **there remain**, since Paul's syntax allows for *two* possible meanings. (i) One meaning is that of an eschatological assertion: these three *abide* or **remain**. (ii) The other is that of a *logical* summary providing the stage setting for v. 13b (as Parry urges): **So now** (logical use) **there remain**, out of all the gifts and experiences compared and considered, **faith, hope and love**. *These are still on the table.* **But the greatest of these** (for reasons which include, among other things, its eschatological permanence) **is love**.[230] For translation, it is essential not to pre-judge by exclusion which of these two meanings Paul wishes to convey. Hence **remain** is preferable to *abide,* since without comment it allows for either or both meanings as the Greek μένει does. The singular of μένει may also suggest the list as a collective agenda.[231]

(i) There appears at first sight to be a strong patristic tradition that all three dispositions or qualities *abide* in eschatological terms, but this impression is deceptive. Irenaeus rightly distinguishes theologically between that which is within human control and that which must be "left in the hands of God." He then concludes that at the end, according to Paul, God will do away with everything except "these three; **faith, hope, love** shall endure."[232] Tertullian appears

---

230. Parry argues strongly for the logical meaning (*First Epistle,* 197).

231. Interestingly, Robertson and Plummer offer a different explanation for the singular (1914) from that which Robertson offers in his own work (1931). Robertson and Plummer argue that the singular "is not a slip in grammar; the three virtues are a triplet" (*First Epistle,* 300). This would support our point, except that they proceed to identify their commonality as consisting in their endurance: "the triplet will survive the second advent." Later, Robertson attributes the singular to its link with πίστις as the singular noun which first governs it (*Word Pictures,* 4, 180).

232. Irenaeus, Against *Heresies,* 2:28:3.

to make this point initially, but his subsequent comments demonstrate that he singles out **love** as that which alone endures after the eschaton. Tertullian quotes 13:13, and then comments: "Rightly [is love the greatest]. For faith departs when we are convinced by vision, by seeing God. And hope vanishes when the things hoped for come about. But love both comes to completion and grows more when the perfect has been given."[233] Chrysostom shares Tertullian's view: "When the good things believed and hoped for have come, faith and hope cease. . . . 'For hope that is seen is not hope' (Rom 8:24). . . . So these cease when those appear, but then love becomes most exalted. . . . '**The greatest of these is love**' (1 Cor 13:13)."[234] Calvin also follows this view: "Faith does not continue after death."[235]

(ii) Meyer correctly argues that Paul cannot be using μένει to mean *remains until the parousia,* as if to distinguish this triad from spiritual gifts that fall away as the church matures, for then he would be omitting prophetic preaching, teaching, and knowledge, which the church needs throughout its history.[236] Spicq's exegesis of *lasts* in the Corinthian situation is not widely supported.[237]

(iii) In what sense, then, would **faith, hope, love,** remain "on the table" in a logical or rhetorical sense? Reitzenstein floated the theory that Paul uses the triad in contrast to a "gnostic" quartet of **faith,** *knowledge,* **love,** and **hope.** He claims: "It was occasioned by the fact that such a four-part formula actually is found in a later pagan author, Porphyry (*ad Marcellam,* 24)."[238] But "later" is the operative word. There is no evidence for a fourfold formula around AD 55. On the other hand, as Weiss and Craig urge, Paul himself has already begun to group **faith, hope,** and **love** in 1 Thess 1:3 and 5:8. "The triad is a favourite one with Paul: it is found in his earliest preserved letter [as cited] and also in one of his latest (Col 1:4, 5)."[239] Wolff insists again that the polemic remains: **faith, hope,** and **love** are in view; *prophecy, speaking in tongues,* and *knowledge* no longer feature in the agenda.[240]

(iv) In practice, in theological terms, as we have noted, the views of Tertullian and Chrysostom have relative but not compelling force. Confident trust in God and appropriation of his grace remains an aspect of **faith** which is to be distinguished both from faith in contrast to sight, and from infectious, ro-

233. Tertullian, *Who is the Rich Man?* 38.

234. Chrysostom, *1 Cor. Hom.,* 34:5.

235. Calvin, *First Epistle,* 283.

236. Meyer, *First Epistle,* 1:398.

237. Spicq, *Agapē,* 2:169-70.

238. Reitzenstein, *Hellenistic Mystery Religions,* 488; cf. 487-89.

239. Craig, "1 Cor," in *IB,* 10:195; cf. Weiss, *Der erste Brief,* 320. Also argued by Conzelmann, *1 Cor,* 229, who has strong reservations about Reitzenstein's theory. Indeed, he notes the emergence of a version of the triad in Judaism before Paul (4 Macc 17:2, 4; πίστις . . . ἐλπίς . . . , but ὑπομονή rather than ἀγάπη). See further Gal 5:6: faith working through love; 5:22, faith and hope; and Eph 1:3-5, 15-18; 1 Tim 6:11; 2 Tim 3:10.

240. Wolff, *Der erste Brief,* 325.

bust faith as a special charismatic gift. Similarly, after the resurrection new hopes concerning fresh creative purposes need not be excluded. As I have strongly argued elsewhere, **faith** and **hope** are "polymorphous concepts": depending on their contextual currency as meaning more than one thing, they both "cease" and "abide."[241] Our question is, rather, Paul's meaning *in this present context.* Barrett assists us here. **Faith** ceases, he argues, if the context is that of what he calls "miracle-working faith" in 13:2. But in the sense used when Paul asserts "whatever is not of faith is sin" (Rom 14:23), "the life of the age to come will rest on faith as completely as does the Christian life now."[242] Similarly, unless we conceive of heaven as a "closed" or static state, the openness of the heavenly life towards the future maintains the relevance of hope. Heinrici similarly holds together the two aspects.[243]

(v) Granted all this, then, does νυνὶ δὲ μένει return to a temporal or eschatological status rather than a logical one? Conzelmann tentatively, Lang with qualifications, and Parry and Strobel with conviction, even with passion, argue for the logical meaning. For Lang, **there remain** in the sense that this triad is constitutive for "being-in-Christ." But **love** still abides when **faith** and **hope** have reached their fullness.[244] Parry first shows why νυνὶ δέ must be logical, not temporal.[245] So far, Parry continues, *the entire chapter has set* **love** *in contrast to all other dispositions and gifts.* There is "something of disappointment and even of bathos in putting as a climax to these contrasts the statement that in this present state faith, hope, love abide."[246] Strobel insists that the **now** of v. 13 is one of "logical conclusion."[247] However, if νυνὶ δὲ μένει means "taking all into account," Paul does not yet quite part with the importance of faith in the God revealed and "hope in the ever-growing revelation." τὰ τρία ταῦτα, **these three** things, "will just hold the mind for a moment," though not *in this context* as "abiding qualities," even if they are "constitutive" ones (Lang).[248] The comparative μείζων, regularly used as a superlative (which is virtually obsolete in later hellenistic Greek), has been defined by all that has gone before.[249] **Love** reflects the concern for others and the Other of which Christ is the paradigm case (cf. 1:18-25), and it will never become obsolete, for it is the very stuff of the heavenly life and the good of heavenly maturity.

Barth concludes his study of these verses by taking up a closely related

241. Thiselton, *The Two Horizons,* 407-12 (on faith), and *Interpreting God and the Postmodern Self,* 145-52 (on hope).

242. Barrett, *First Epistle,* 308-9.

243. Heinrici, *Das erste Sendschreiben,* 425-30.

244. Lang, *Die Briefe,* 188.

245. Parry, *First Epistle,* 196-97; Robertson and Plummer firmly agree with this (*First Epistle,* 300).

246. Parry, *First Epistle,* 196-97.

247. Strobel, *Der erste Brief,* 210.

248. Ibid., 198.

249. Spicq observes, "all commentators agree that 'greater' (μείζων) stands for 'greatest' (μέγιστος)," *Agapē,* 2:170.

theme. Love is "the future eternal light shining in the present. It therefore needs no change of form."[250] In one sense faith and hope abide also, but in forms in which faith becomes assimilated into sight, and hope absorbed into the perfect, even though this is an active perfection. Thus in a subtle sense love alone abides forever in the form in which Christ and the cross has revealed it: "it is that which continues."[251] Thus, if there is any heavenly counterpart to the qualities and dispositions of the earthly life of the church, its worship, its understanding, its faith, and its hope will all undergo modification under new conditions. The teacher, theologian, pastor, and evangelist become redundant in the sense in which their work is currently carried out. But learning to love, to have respect and concern for the Other above the self, is grounded in the nature of God as revealed in Christ, and this will never become redundant, obsolete, or irrelevant. The future thus provides the model for the present in working out priorities at Corinth and in the church at large. *Agapē* is much more than a "moral virtue."[252]

6. Love for the Other and Ordered Differentiation in Evaluating "Prophecy" and "Tongues" (14:1-40)

The key to an accurate understanding of Paul's arguments and declarations in this chapter depends on a full appreciation of two factors initially. (a) vv. 1-25 relate integrally to what Paul has said about *love* in 13:1-13; (b) vv. 26-40 reflect the concerns about *differentiation and ordering* which Paul has expounded in 12:4-31. The first section concerns respect for the needs of *others;* the second half explicates the differentiation and order which characterize the activity of God himself as one God, one Lord, and *one Spirit* (12:4-6).

(a) Each stage of argument in 14:1-25 focuses on the building up of the other. This not only reflects back on 13:1-13 but also on concern for "the brother or sister for whom Christ died" in 8:7-13, as Gardner has rightly stressed. Love of this kind tests what Gardner terms "The Gifts of God and the Authentication of a Christian."[1] Hence the stages of argument turn on: (i) vv. 1-5: the use of "spiritual gifts," or perhaps in a worship context "the gifts of authentic utterance inspired by the Spirit" (τὰ πνευματικά, 14:1) as given for *the service of others,* not for self-affirmation (ἑαυτὸν οἰκοδομεῖ . . . ἐκκλησίαν οἰκοδομεῖ, v. 4a and v. 4b). (ii) vv. 6-12: the profitless nature of *unintelligible noises* as far as a fellow Christian ("the other") is concerned. Far from a coherent building up, a disintegrating barrier which makes one appear as an outsider or foreigner (βάρβαρος, v. 11) is set up, which jars like a discordant note (vv. 7, 8). (iii) vv. 13-19: Intelligible communication remains es-

250. Barth, *CD,* 4/2 (sect. 68), 840.
251. Ibid.
252. Nygren, *Agapē and Eros,* 137.
1. Gardner, *The Gifts of God and the Authentication of a Christian: An Exegetical Study of 1 Cor 8–11:1* (cited above).

sential in the context of the worshiping community, which necessarily entails the use of the mind (τῷ πνεύματι . . . καὶ τῷ νοΐ, v. 15). It is not a sign of love to exclude those who cannot share enough to say "Amen" to the utterance (v. 16), even if Paul himself knows what it is to allow his inner self to well up "in tongues" in private devotions (v. 18).

(iv) A fourth stage of argument, vv. 20-25, is sometimes placed with (b) vv. 25-40 in this chapter, but most interpreters, rightly, understand it as a corroboration and reinforcement of vv. 1-19. Paul takes up the emphasis on using the mind as a sign not only of concern for others in love (with 8:7-13 and 13:1-13), but also of personal maturity. This neatly places some at Corinth in a dilemma. If D. B. Martin is correct in perceiving "tongues" at least in part as a supposed "status indicator" at Corinth, how does this square with their simultaneous insistence that the rhetoric of polished speech (λόγος, or even speech καθ' ὑπεροχὴν λόγου, 2:1) could or should be a sign of mature, sophisticated, "professional" leaders? Paul urges that they replace naïve passivity of the mind (μὴ παιδία γίνεσθε, v. 20a) with energetic thought on behalf of others. To be sure, this is not a use of the mind for competitive "cleverness" or "one upmanship" (τῇ κακίᾳ νηπιάζετε, v. 20b), but for mature adulthood (τέλειοι γίνεσθε, v. 20c) which appreciates how self-indulgent uses of unintelligible noises make even believers (as well as any unbeliever present) feel as if they did not belong, or as if they stood under judgment. For "unintelligible speech" or "strange tongues" in the scriptures represent a sign of judgment upon Israel in exile for their unbelief (vv. 21 [citing Isa 28:11-12, LXX] and 22). Believers will experience a misplaced sense of "being foreign" when they should feel that they belong, while unbelievers will witness what appears to them to be bizarre religious phenomena, not a clear declaration of the gospel (vv. 23-24). They will never become "converted" that way (v. 25)!

(b) Paul summarizes the position about worship by insisting that the congregation cannot simply leave everything to supposed "inspiration" or to "spontaneity" alone. This leads simply to anarchy, whereas it is the nature of God, and of the Spirit of God, to bring "order" or "peace" out of chaos or "disorder" (ἀκαταστασίας, v. 33; κατὰ τάξιν, v. 40; cf. Gen 1:2, 3, 7, 14, 18, 26; see below; and 1 Cor 12:4-6; see above). *If worship is "ordered," this allows for a more caring concern for others, even if, as in 8:7–11:1, self-constraint is the corollary of love for the vulnerable.* Further, if it is claimed that this worship is *"spiritual," i.e., characterized by the presence, agency, and action of the Holy Spirit of God, God himself exercises his governance precisely through rational or coherent processes of timing and differentiation.*

Contrary to widespread popular uses of this chapter to assume an intimate connection between being inspired by the Holy Spirit and "spontaneity," the chapter as a whole places the issue of concern for the other and communicative intelligibility at the center of the discussion, and perceives the Spirit of God as "allocating" both "allotted time" and "differentiation" (terms which are prominent in Karl Barth) as that which reflects God's own mode of self-giving in freedom conditioned by covenantal concern for the other.[2] Thus "order" is not, as most or many modern writers claim, a symptom of authoritarianism (whether or not such sections as vv. 33b-38 are deemed to be non-Pauline interpolations) but arise because, if the Spirit is genuinely inspiring the worship, patterns of worship will be characterized by the nature of God as one gives himself to the other in modes governed by temporal purposiveness, not by anarchy or by activities which minister largely to self-esteem.

This at once coheres with a reasonable (but not yet decisive) consensus reflected by Hill, Müller, Gillespie, and others that, in Hill's words, "The proclamation of the prophet is *pastoral preaching* which, by its very nature, offers guidance and instruction to the community" (his italics).[3] Gillespie traces Paul's explicit argument in this chapter that to prophesy is (i) *to build up* (οἰκοδομέω, 14:4, 5, 17; also cf. 8:1, 10, and 10:23, of love for the other); (ii) *to exhort, plead with, or comfort* (παρακαλέω, 14:31, noun παράκλησις, 14:3; cf. 4:13, 16; 16:12, 15); and (iii) to encourage or to console (παραμυθέομαι, here as a noun παραμυθία, linked with παράκλησις, 14:3; cf. 1 Thess 2:11).[4] Most writers agree that "building up" or "edification" constitutes the key theme, which is also linked with Christian prophecy. Here Vielhauer offers a perceptive and important comment in his special study of this subject. He argues that "building up" has negative and positive implications or nuances for Paul. On one side, it excludes a self-sufficient, indulgent, religious individualism and egoism which can lead to the disintegration of the community; on the other side, it entails helping the other person since thereby the whole community is built up as a cohesive and mutually supportive whole.[5] Hence the verb is closely associated with gospel preaching itself, whether to unbelievers or to believers, placing them under the judgment, grace, promise, and direction of the cross anew.[6]

On this basis the significance of the key contrast between prophecy and tongues in this chapter becomes transparent. Paul does not disparage the *private* use of tongues (14:5a). Indeed, he values such a gift for himself personally (14:18). However, in *public,* especially in corporate worship, five intelligible words carefully thought through to help others are worth more than tongues unlimited (14:19). So strong is Paul's emphasis on the use of mental reflection and control that it is inconceivable (in our view) that most writers are correct to

2. Barth, *CD,* 2/1, sects. 25 and 28-31, esp. 298-99, 450-57, 665-73, where differentiation is a condition of purposive action. Resonances with the theme in Hegel emerge in this volume.

3. Hill, "Christian Prophets as Teachers or Instructors in the Church," in Panagopoulos (ed.), *Prophetic Vocation in the NT and Today,* 111, n. 11; cf. 108-30; Hill, *NT Prophecy,* 131; cf. 110-40 and 193-213; Müller, *Prophetie und Predigt im NT;* and Gillespie, *The First Theologians: A Study in Early Christian Prophecy,* 129-64.

4. Ibid., 142-50. See extended notes at 12:8 and at 14:3 on **prophecy.**

5. Vielhauer, *Oikodomē. Das Bild vom Bau in der christlichen Literatur vom Neuen Testament bis Clemens Alexandrinus,* 91-98.

6. Ibid., 86-87.

assume that prophecy is necessarily or uniformly "spontaneous." True, spontaneous prophecy may occur; but to insist that it is always or necessarily so is to fail to do justice to the text before us. Even Dunn repeats this popular assumption on the basis of 14:30: "It is a spontaneous utterance . . . to be delivered as it is given (14:30)."[7] However, to assume that because this *sometimes* may have occurred it constitutes a *necessary or even usual* characteristic of prophecy is a leap beyond logic and beyond exegesis. We argue this point in greater detail below (as we have already done under 12:8-10).

To define the nature of "tongues" with any degree of certainty is no more straightforward (see the detailed notes above under 12:10, 28, and 30 for full and extended discussion). In an illuminatingly frank and bold comment (since he openly states that he comes from a Pentecostalist tradition) Gordon Fee concedes in a recent work that not only is it unlikely that tongues constitute an earthly language, but more especially that whether today's "charismatic phenomena" replicate what is described in these chapters is also "most probably irrelevant. There is simply no way to know."[8] It is widely agreed, however, that ch. 14 sets prophecy and tongues in contrast throughout "in antithetical parallelism," e.g., "One who speaks in a tongue speaks . . . to God (v. 2); one who prophesies speaks to people (v. 3); one who speaks in a tongue edifies himself, but one who prophesies edifies the church (v. 4). . . ."[9] The overall frame which we introduced at the beginning of our introduction to 14:1-40, however, must not drop from view. Sections (a) and (b) relate respectively to issues about *love for the other* (8:7-13; 13:1-13) and to the way in which the God of love who gives his Holy Spirit acts through *differentiation, temporality, and order* (cf. 12:4-31).

Supplementary Bibliography on 14:1-40. (For the Main Bibliography on 12:1–14:1-32, See Also at 12:1.)

Alison, R. W., "'Let Women Be Silent in the Churches' (1 Cor 14:33b-36): What Did Paul Really Say, and What Did It Mean?" *JSNT* 32 (1988): 27-60.

Arichea, D. C., "The Silence of Women in the Church: Theology and Translation of 1 Cor 14:33b-36," *BT* 46 (1995): 101-12.

Aune, D. E., *Prophecy in Early Christianity and the Ancient Mediterranean World* (Grand Rapids: Eerdmans, 1983), esp. 189-232, 247-346.

Beare, F. W., "Speaking with Tongues," *JBL* 83 (1964): 229-46.

Best, E., "The Interpretation of Tongues," *SJT* 28 (1975): 45-62.

———, "Prophets and Preachers," *SJT* 12 (1959): 129-50.

Bjerkelund, C. J., *Parakalō: Form, Funktion und Sinn der Parakalô-Sätze in den paulinischen Briefen* (Oslo: Universitetsforlaget, 1967).

---

7. Dunn, *Jesus and the Spirit,* 228. We noted under 12:8-9 that this view is softened a little in his more recent *Theology of Paul* (see above).

8. G. Fee, *Paul, the Spirit and the People of God* (Peabody, Mass.: Hendrickson, 1996), 1970; cf. 169.

9. Gillespie, *The First Theologians* 130; cf. 129-32; cf. Maly, *Mündige Gemeinde,* 199-201; more broadly 202-17.

Boring, M. E., *The Continuing Voice of Jesus: Christian Prophecy and the Gospel Tradition* (Louisville: Knox/Westminster, 1991).

Boyer, J. L., "The Office of Prophet in NT Times," *Grace Journal* 1 (1960): 13-20.

Brockhaus, U., *Charisma und Amt* (Wuppertal: Theologischer Verlag Brockhaus, 1972).

Bruner, F. D., *A Theology of the Holy Spirit: The Pentecostal Experience and the NT Witness* (Grand Rapids: Eerdmans, 1970).

Callan, T., "Prophecy and Ecstasy in Greco-Roman Religion and in 1 Corinthians," *NovT* 27 (1985): 125-40.

Carson, D. A., *Showing the Spirit: A Theological Exposition of 1 Cor 12–14* (Grand Rapids: Baker, 1987).

Cothenet, E., "Les prophètes chrétiens comme exégètes charismatiques de L'Écriture," in J. Panagopoulos, *Prophetic Vocation* (cited below), 77-107.

Crone, T. M., *Early Christian Prophecy: A Study of Its Origin and Function* (Baltimore: St. Mary's University, 1973).

Currie, J. D., "'Speaking in Tongues': Early Evidence outside the NT," *Int* 19 (1965): 274-94.

Dautzenberg, G., *Urchristliche Prophetie,* BWANT 104 (Stuttgart: Kohlhammer, 1975). See esp. 226-300.

Davies, J. G., "Pentecost and Glossolalia," *JTS* 3 (1952): 228-31.

Dayton, D. W., *Theological Roots of Pentecostalism* (Grand Rapids: Francis Asbury Press, 1987).

Dunn, J. D. G., *Jesus and the Spirit* (London: SCM, 1975), 205-300.

———, "Prophetic 'I' Sayings and the Jesus Tradition: The Importance of Testing Prophetic Utterances within Early Christianity," *NTS* 24 (1977-78): 175-98.

———, *The Theology of Paul the Apostle* (Edinburgh: T. & T. Clark and Grand Rapids: Eerdmans, 1998), 552-64 and 580-98.

Ellis, E. E., *Prophecy and Hermeneutic in Early Christianity* (Grand Rapids: Eerdmans, 1978), 23-62 and 129-45.

Engelbrecht, E. A., "'To Speak in Tongues': The OT and Early Rabbinic Background of a Pauline Expression," *Concordia Journal* 22 (1996): 295-302.

Eriksson, A., "'Women Tongue Speakers Be Silent': A Reconstruction through Paul's Rhetoric," *BibInt* 6 (1998): 80-104.

Fascher, E., *Prophḗtes. Eine sprach- und religionsgeschichtliche Untersuchung* (Giessen: Töpelmann, 1927).

Fee, G., *God's Empowering Presence: The Holy Spirit in the Letters of Paul* (Peabody, Mass.: Hendrickson, 1994).

———, *Paul, the Spirit and the People of God* (Peabody, Mass.: Hendrickson, 1996).

Flanagan, N. M., and E. H. Snyder, "Did Paul Put Down Women in 1 Cor 14:34-36?" *BTB* 11 (1981): 10-12.

Forbes, C., "Early Christian Inspired Speech and Hellenistic Popular Religion," *NovT* 28 (1986): 257-70.

———, *Prophecy and Inspired Speech in Early Christianity and Its Hellenistic Environment,* WUNT 2:75 (Tübingen: Mohr, 1995).

Friedrich, G., et al., "προφητεύω (κτλ)," *TDNT,* 6:781-861.

Gale, H. M., *The Use of Analogy in the Letters of Paul* (Philadelphia: Westminster, 1964), 129-34.

Gillespie, T. W., *The First Theologians: A Study in Early Christian Prophecy* (Grand Rapids: Eerdmans, 1994).

————, "A Pattern of Prophetic Speech in First Corinthians," *JBL* 97 (1978): 74-95.

Graham, S. R., "'Thus Saith the Lord': Biblical Hermeneutics in the Early Pentecostal Movement," *Ex Auditu* 12 (1996): 121-35.

Greeven, H., "Propheten, Lehrer, Vorsteher bei Paulus," *ZNW* 44 (1852-53): 1-43.

Grudem, W. A., "1 Cor 14:20-25: Prophecy and Tongues as Signs of God's Attitude," *WTJ* 41 (1979): 381-96.

————, *The Gift of Prophecy in 1 Corinthians* (Lanham, Md.: University Press of America, 1982).

————, *The Gift of Prophecy in the NT and Today* (Westminster, Ill.: Crossway, 1988).

Gundry, R. H., "'Ecstatic Utterance' (NEB)?" *JTS* 17 (1966): 299-307.

Gunkel, H., *The Influence of the Holy Spirit* (Eng. trans., Philadelphia: Fortress, 1979).

Guy, H. A., *NT Prophecy: Its Origin and Significance* (London: Epworth, 1947).

Hafemann, Scott J., *Suffering and the Ministry of the Spirit: Paul's Defense of His Ministry in 2 Cor 2:14–3:3* (Grand Rapids: Eerdmans, 1990).

Harrisville, R. A., "Speaking in Tongues: A Lexicographical Study," *CBQ* 38 (1976): 35-48.

Heschel, A. J., *The Prophets* (2 vols., New York: Harper & Row, 1962).

Hill, D., "Christian Prophets as Teachers or Instructors in the Church," in J. Panagopoulos (cited below), 108-30.

————, *NT Prophecy* (London: Marshall, 1979), esp. 110-40 and 193-213.

Jervis, L. A., "1 Cor 14:34-35: A Reconsideration of Paul's Limitation of the Free Speech of Some Corinthian Women," *JSNT* 58 (1995): 51-74.

Johnson, B. C., "Tongues, A Sign for Unbelievers? A Structural and Exegetical Study of 1 Cor XIV:20-25," *NTS* 25 (1979): 180-203.

Johnson, L. T., "Norms for True and False Prophecy in First Corinthians," *ABenR* 22 (1971): 29-45.

————, "Tongues, Gift of," in *ABD,* 6:596-600.

Käsemann, E., "Sentences of Holy Law in the NT," in *NT Questions of Today* (Eng. trans., London: SCM, 1969), 66-81.

Keilbach, W., "Zungenreden," *RGG* (3d ed.), 6, cols. 1940-41.

Kildahl, J. P., *The Psychology of Speaking in Tongues* (New York: Harper & Row, 1972).

Kock, W. J. de, "Empowerment through Engagement — Pentecostal Power for a Pentecostal Task," *Ex Auditu* 12 (1996): 136-46.

Lanier, D. E., "With Stammering Lips and Another Tongue: 1 Cor 14:20-22 and Isa 28:11-12," *Criswell Theological Review* 5 (1991): 259-85.

Macchia, F. D., "Groans Too Deep for Words: Towards a Theology of Tongues as Initial Experience," *Asian Journal of Pentecostal Studies* (1998): 149-73.

————, "Sighs Too Deep for Words: Toward a Theology of Glossolalia," *Journal of Pentecostal Theology* 1 (1992): 47-73.

MacGorman, J. W., "Glossolalic Error and Its Correction: 1 Cor 12–14," *RevExp* 80 (1983): 389-400.

Maier, W. A., "An Exegetical Study of 1 Cor 14:33b-38," *CTQ* 55 (1991): 81-104.

Maly, K., *Mündige Gemeinde* (Stuttgart: Katholisches Bibelwerk, 1967), 198-229.

Martin, D. B., *The Corinthian Body* (New Haven: Yale University Press, 1995), 88-103.

————, "Tongues of Angels and Other Status Indicators," *JAAR* 59 (1991): 547-89.

Martin, R. P., *The Spirit and the Congregation* (Grand Rapids: Eerdmans, 1984).

Merk, O., *Handeln aus Glauben* (Marburg: Elwert, 1968), 145-48.

Merklein, H., "Der Theologe als Prophet: Zur Funktion prophetischen Redens im theologischen Discurs des Paulus," *NTS* 38 (1992): 402-29.

Michel, O., "οἰκοδομή," *TDNT,* 5:119-59.

Mills, Watson E., *A Theological/Exegetical Approach to Glossolalia* (Lanham, Md.: University Press of America, 1985).

Montague, G. T., *The Spirit and His Gifts: The Biblical Background of Spirit-Baptism, Tongue-Speaking and Prophecy* (New York: Paulist Press, 1974).

Müller, U. B., *Prophetie und Predigt im NT* (Gütersloh: Mohn, 1975).

Munro, W., "Women, Text and the Canon: The Strange Case of 1 Cor 14:33-35," *BTB* 18 (1988): 26-31.

Naccum, C., "The Voice of Manuscripts on the Silence of Women: The External Evidence for 1 Cor 14:34-35," *NTS* 43 (1997): 242-55.

Nadeau, D. J., "Le problème des femmes en 1 Cor 14:33b-35," *ÉTR* 69 (1994): 63-65.

Odell-Scott, D. W., "Let the Women Speak in Church: An Egalitarian Interpretation of 1 Cor 14:33b-36," *BTB* 13 (1983): 90-93.

Panagopoulos, J., ἡ ἐκκλησία τῶν προφητῶν (Athens: Historical Publications, 1979).

———— (ed.), *Prophetic Vocation in the NT and Today,* NovTSup 45 (Leiden: Brill, 1977), esp. Panagopoulos, "Die urchristliche Prophetic. Ihr Charakter und ihre Funktion," 1-32.

Percy, M., *Words, Wonders and Power* (London: SPCK, 1976).

Petzer, J. H., "Reconsidering the Silent Women of Corinth — A Note on 1 Cor 14:34-35," *ThEv* 26 (1993): 132-38.

Pinnock, Clark H., *Flame of Love: A Theology of the Holy Spirit* (Downers Grove, Ill.: InterVarsity, 1996).

Poythress, V. S., "The Nature of Corinthian Glossolalia," *WTJ* 40 (1977-78): 130-35.

Rebell, W., "Gemeinde also Missionsfaktor im Urchristem. 1 Kor 14:24f als Schlüsselsituation," *TZ* 44 (1988): 117-34.

Richardson, W., "Liturgical Order and Glossolalia in 1 Cor 14:26c-33a," *NTS* 32 (1986): 144-53.

Robeck, C. M., Jr., "The Gift of Prophesying in Acts and Paul," *Studia Biblica et Theologica* 5 (1975): 15-54.

————, "Prophecy, Prophesying," *DPL* (1993), 755-62.

Roberts, P., "A Sign — Christian or Pagan?" *ExpTim* 90 (1978-79): 199-203.

Robertson, O. P., "Tongues: Sign of Covenantal Curse and Blessing," *WTJ* 38 (1975): 43-53.

Samarin, W. J., *Tongues of Men and Angels: The Religious Language of Pentecostalism* (New York: Macmillan, 1972), 74-128.

Sandnes, K. O., *Paul — One of the Prophets? A Contribution to the Apostle's Self-Understanding,* WUNT 2:43 (Tübingen: Mohr, 1991).

————, "Prophecy — A Sign for Believers (1 Cor 14:20-25)," *Bib* 77 (1996): 1-15.

Schatzmann, S., *A Pauline Theology of Charismata* (Peabody, Mass.: Hendrickson, 1987).

Sigountos, J. G., and M. Shank, "Public Roles for Women in the Pauline Church: A Reappraisal of the Evidence," *JETS* 26 (1983): 283-95.

Smit, J. F. M., "Tongues and Prophecy: Deciphering 1 Cor 14:22," *Bib* 75 (1994): 175-90.

Stendahl, K., "Glossolalia: The NT Evidence," in *Paul among Jews and Gentiles* (London: SCM, 1977), 109-24.

Sweet, J. P. M., "A Sign for Unbelievers: Paul's Attitude to Glossolalia," *NTS* 13 (1967): 240-57.

Theissen, G., *Psychological Aspects of Pauline Theology* (Eng. trans., Edinburgh: T. & T. Clark, 1987), 59-114 and 292-341.

Thiselton, A. C., "The 'Interpretation' of Tongues? A New Suggestion in the Light of Greek Usage in Philo and Josephus," *JTS* 30 (1979): 15-36.

Van Unnik, W. C., "A Formula Describing Prophecy," *NTS* 9 (1962-63): 86-94.

Vielhauer, P., *Oikodomē: Das Bild vom Bau in der christlichen Literatur vom Neuen Testament bis Clemens Alexandrinus* (Karlsruhe: Harrassowitz, 1940).

Williams, C. G., *Tongues of the Spirit* (Cardiff: University of Wales Press, 1981).

Wire, A. C., *The Corinthian Women Prophets* (Minneapolis: Fortress, 1990), 135-58.

a. Intelligible Utterance to Build the Whole Community (14:1-25)

(1) Pursue love, but be eager for gifts of the Spirit [for utterance], most particularly that you may prophesy. (2) For the person who speaks in a tongue does not communicate to human beings but speaks to God. For no one understands anything, but he or she utters mysteries in the Spirit. (3) However, when a person prophesies to other people, the speaker thereby builds them up, encourages them, and brings them comfort. (4) For the person who speaks in a tongue "builds up" himself or herself; whereas the one who prophesies builds up the church community. (5) I take pleasure in all of you speaking in tongues, but I would rather that you prophesy. The person who prophesies is of greater importance than the one who speaks in tongues unless that person articulates the utterance intelligibly for the church community to receive this "building up."

(6) Well now, dear fellow believers, suppose that when I come to you I come speaking in tongues. What shall I profit you unless I speak to you in terms either of a disclosure or of knowledge, or of prophetic speech or of teaching? (7) Similarly, with reference to an inanimate musical instrument: in the case of either a flute or a lyre, unless these yield distinct differences of pitch, how can what is produced by wind or by string be recognized? (8) Further, if the trumpet produces a sound which is ambivalent as a signal, who will prepare for battle? (9) Even so, if you yourselves do not produce through speaking in a tongue a message which is readily intelligible, how shall what is being said be comprehended? For you are speaking into empty air. (10, 11) It may be that there are varieties of languages within the world, and none fails to use sound. Yet it follows that if I do not know the force of the sound, I shall be an alien to the speaker, and the speaker will remain an alien to my eyes. (12) You yourselves are in this situation. Since you have a burning concern about the powers of the Spirit, direct this eagerness toward the building up of the church community, to excel in this.

(13, 14) Hence the person who prays in a tongue should pray that he or she may put what they have uttered into words. For if I pray in a tongue, my innermost spiritual being prays, but my mind produces no fruit from it. (15) So what follows? I will pray with my deepest spiritual being, but I shall also pray with my mind. I will sing praise with the depths of my being, but I will also sing praise with my mind. (16) Otherwise, if you bless God from the depths of your being only [or "in the Spirit"], how can the uninitiated person speak his or her "Amen" to your thanksgiving since he or she does not know what you are saying? (17) For you, on your side, may be giving thanks well enough; but the other, on his or her side, is not being built up. (18, 19) Thank God, I am more gifted in tongues than any of you, but all the same in the assembled congregation I would rather speak five intelligible words to communicate instruction to others than thousands upon thousands in a tongue.

(20) My fellow Christians, do not continue to be like little children born yesterday in how you think. On the contrary, be a child in matters of wickedness, but in matters of the mind be mature adults. (21) In the Law it is written: "By people of a foreign tongue and by alien lips shall I address this people, and not even then will they hear me, says the Lord." (22) So then, tongues serve not as a sign for believers, but as a sign for judgment for unbelievers; while prophetic speech signals not people who do not believe but those who come to faith. (23) If, therefore, the whole church community comes together and everyone is speaking in tongues, and people who are uninitiated or unbelievers enter, will they not say that you are out of your mind? (24, 25) Suppose, by contrast, that everyone is using prophetic speech, and someone who is an unbeliever or an uninitiated person enters and undergoes conviction and judgment by all that is said. The secret depths of their very being become exposed, and thus they fall to their knees in obeisance and worship God, confessing, "God is indeed really among you."

i. Self-Affirmation or Use of Gifts of Utterance for Others? (14:1-5)

1 The verb διώκετε means **pursue** here (NRSV) as in 1 Thess 5:15, as in the case of a hunter chasing after prey. The present tense, Allo argues, "Signifies the continuing of an action already begun."[10] REB, NJB, *make love your aim,* is less forceful and dynamic, while KJV/AV, NIV, *follow* or *follow after,* conveys less urgency. Similarly, ζηλοῦτε denotes cultivating *a stance of eagerness.* **Be eager for** permits a corporate concern for the well-being of *the community,* i.e., that these gifts may operate in the church, which is Paul's horizon of concern. By contrast, NIV's *eagerly desire* suggests a more individualist concern which Paul does not encourage, while NRSV's *strive for* positively conflicts with Paul's insistence that these are "gifts of grace" (as in 12:31, χαρίσματα) which *God chooses to give* or to withhold in his sovereign freedom to "order" the

---

10. Allo, *Première Épitre,* 355; cf. BAGD, 201, on **pursue.**

church as he wills (12:18). To read *strive for* can be pastorally misleading and theologically doubtful. Collins reserves *strive for* for διώκετε in v. 1a, which he views as the last clause of the previous unit (cf. v. 13), and *avidly desire* for ζηλοῦτε.[11] But *striving for love* suggests as oxymoron not entirely consonant with the tone of 13:4-7. Smit's rhetorical analysis retains v. 1a as part of the *argumentio* of ch. 14, of which vv. 1-5 constitute the *partitio:* zeal for love in relation to the gifts.[12]

Competing translations of the particle δέ offer greater difficulty, since *context* has to determine whether it means *and* or **but**. Similarly, τὰ πνευματικά normally means *spiritual gifts* (i.e., gifts from, or characterized by, the Holy Spirit) but in this specific context it may well mean more specifically *spiritual utterances* or **gifts of the Spirit for utterance** within contexts of worship. Thus Gillespie plausibly observes, "The 'greater gifts' are now specified as 'spiritual utterances' *(ta pneumatika),* particularly prophesying."[13] This meaning seems to be required by the context, but the use of brackets may be necessary to indicate that this translation assumes a greater degree of interpretative judgment than the Greek alone in strict terms explicitly bears. However Conzelmann confirms this meaning: "The tenor is now different: no longer a critique of . . . 'spiritual gifts' in general. . . . Now it is only speaking with tongues and prophecy that are discussed as spiritual gifts."[14]

Some commentators regard the force of δέ as resumptive. Hays observes: *and be eager for . . ."* picks up the same verb *(zēloute)* used in 12:31a, now specifying more closely the proper aim of such desire."[15] However, Chrysostom, Theodoret, and Theophylact, followed by modern writers from Heinrici onward, reject the resumptive *and* in favor of the adversative **but**, and are followed by many modern commentators.[16] The interpretation depends on whether we presuppose that both the readers and Paul himself were aware of the potentially competitive and individualistic nature of concerns to display gifts of utterance, especially tongues. If so, Paul is likely to have felt the need to explain: **pursue love, but be eager for gifts of the Spirit for utterance**, because Paul is about to show that these gifts of utterance can *serve others in love,* and *no longer* remain a means of self-affirmation and cause of disruption.

The last clause of v. 1 begins this demonstration or argument. If the readers will pay particular attention (μᾶλλον) to the activity of **prophesying** (in

---

11. Collins, *First Cor,* 488, 491-92.

12. Smit, "Argument and Genre of 1 Cor 12–14," in Porter and Olbricht (eds.), *Rhetoric and the NT,* 229 (211-30).

13. Gillespie, *The First Theologians,* 129-30.

14. Conzelmann, *1 Cor,* 233.

15. Hays, *First Cor,* 235; Fee appears to favor the resumptive (*First Epistle,* 654); also Allo, *Première Épitre,* 355; Kistemaker, *1 Cor,* 476.

16. Chrysostom, *1 Cor. Hom.,* 35:1; Meyer, *Epistle to the Corinthians,* 2:3; Heinrici, *Das erste Sendschreiben,* 430; Edwards, *First Epistle,* 357; Barrett, *First Epistle,* 312.

contrast to speaking with tongues, v. 2), this will serve the good of others, since Paul will show that the aim and effect of authentic prophesying is (i) to build up the whole community (vv. 4, 5, 17; cf. 8:1, 10; 10:23); (ii) to exhort or to comfort (vv. 3 and 31; cf. 4:13, 16; 16:12, 15); and (iii) to console or to encourage (v. 3; cf. 1 Thess 2:11; see introduction to 14:1-40, above). We noted above Vielhauer's contrast between *building up* the community into a cohesive, dynamic whole, and the self-sufficient indulgent religiosity which provides mainly individual satisfaction.[17] In these verses Paul insists that **to prophesy** is to perform intelligible, articulate, communicative acts of speech which have a positive effect on others and, in turn, on the whole community.

We shall argue (with Hill, Müller, and Gillespie, as these verses proceed) that here prophecy amounts to healthy preaching, proclamation, or teaching which is pastorally applied for the appropriation of gospel truth and gospel promise, in their own context of situation, to help others.[18] Indeed, Sandnes argues that Paul understands his own commission to preach the apostolic gospel to the Gentiles in prophetic terms. Gal 1:15-16, e.g., which is widely agreed to reflect Jeremiah's call "from before birth" to prophetic witness (cf. Jer 1:5), stands in continuity with 1 Cor 2:1-16, 2 Cor 4:6, Rom 1:1-5, and Rom 10:14-18 in pointing to the prophetic character of Paul's own apostolic commission to proclaim the gospel of Christ in intelligible communicative action.[19] Sandnes points out that in postcanonical Judaism the term *prophet* denoted a wide range of leadership activities: the famous hymn in honor of leaders which begins "let us now sing the praises of famous men . . ." (Sir 44:1) includes Moses, Nathan, Elijah, Zerubbabel, and others who by their intelligible communicative action lead the people to give praise to God for his saving acts (Sirach 44–50). Paul himself, Sandnes insists, stands in this prophetic tradition. Hence the exhortation μιμηταί μου γίνεσθε looks back to apostolic lifestyle in 4:16, and in 11:1 it provides the transition from concern for the other in the issue of food offered to idols (8:1–11:1) to parallel concern for the welfare of the other in the context of worship (11:1–14:40). Prophets, above all, *build up* the community (8:1, 10; 10:23; 14:4, 17).[20]

2   Although λαλέω and ἀκούω are regularly translated broadly to mean respectively *to speak* and *to hear*, the issue in these verses clearly turns on intelligible communication or effective communicative action between speakers and listeners. Hence NRSV, REB, NIV, NJB, and KJV/AV (in agreement with BAGD)

---

17. Vielhauer, *Oikodomē,* 86-98; see above.

18. The evidence is best reviewed toward the end of the cumulative exegetical examination of Paul's argument. This view coheres with where Paul wishes to place the emphasis, and stands in continuity with prophecy as it is understood in the canonical prophets of the OT, in contrast to theories about prophecy in the Graeco-Roman world or in earlier Israelite religion. However, we include a second special Note at 14:3.

19. Sandnes, *Paul — One of the Prophets? A Contribution to the Apostle's Self-Understanding.*

20. Vielhauer, *Oikodomē,* 86-90; Gillespie, *The First Theologians,* 142-44.

correctly translate οὐδεὶς γὰρ ακούει as **no one understands**. . . .[21] It would even be legitimate to follow BAGD, section 3, and translate *no one learns,* which would be more forceful and appropriate although perhaps overly specific for the Greek.[22] Calvin uses the analogy of preaching to empty air: "He preaches to himself and to the walls."[23] Paul will expound the central theme that the church is built and sustained through the communicative word of the gospel of the cross and resurrection and its many entailments, promises and directives. By contrast, ὁ λαλῶν γλώσσῃ οὐκ ἀνθρώποις λαλεῖ (i.e., to the fragile, vulnerable fellow human beings who need to be built up and encouraged) ἀλλὰ θεῷ. **To speak in a tongue** in this chapter almost always denotes an upwelling of praise or prayer or praising, joyful acclamation **to God** (see above on 12:10 for an extensive discussion; also 14:14-16, 28). We may recall Theissen's comparison with the "Abba" cry of Rom 8:26-27, which "permits the conjecture that unconscious contents break through in ecstasy," even if a measure of "social learning" through environmental factors in a congregation cannot be excluded.[24]

The nature of the unintelligibility and of the related term μυστήρια, here translated **mysteries** (with NRSV, REB, NIV, KJV/AV; cf. NJB, *the meaning is hidden*), remains controversial. Elsewhere Paul often uses this Greek word to denote what was once hidden but has now been disclosed in the era of eschatological fulfillment (cf. 2:1, 7; 4:1; 15:51). However, every writer uses terminology in context-dependent ways that may modify a more usual meaning, and Paul's usual meaning cannot make sense here without undermining his own argument. Dautzenberg needlessly complicates the issue by arguing that since this utterance **to God** is **in the Spirit** the content hardly differs from that of prophecy, except for its status as the eschatological language of angels.[25] However, if prophecy entails building, encouragement, promise, or a declaration of the deeds of God in a pastoral context, it seems inappropriate to think of this as "spoken back to God" in these verses, if at all.[26] It is highly significant that Gordon Fee, who acknowledges a Pentecostalist background of personal spirituality, agrees that the utterance not only "lies outside the understanding" but also constitutes "communing with God" in contrast to the notion "quite common in Pentecostal groups" of referring "to a 'message in tongues' [for which] there seems to be no evidence in Paul."[27] In a more recent work Fee reasserts:

21. As in virtually all major commentators, e.g., Senft, *La première Épitre,* 174; Conzelmann, *1 Cor,* 232-34; Calvin, *First Epistle,* 286.

22. BAGD, 32, cols. 1 and 2, e.g., Matt 14:13, "when Jesus learned about it" [the death of John the Baptist], i.e., *to become informed about.*

23. Calvin, *First Epistle,* 286.

24. Theissen, *Psychological Aspects of Pauline Theology,* 287-88, 293-315. See also F. D. Macchia, "Groans Too Deep for Words: Towards a Theology of Tongues as Initial Evidence," *Asian Journal of Pentecostal Studies* 1 (1998): 149-73, which more or less develops Macchia, "Sighs Too Deep for Words," *Journal of Pentecostal Theology* 1 (1992): 47-73.

25. Dautzenberg, *Urchristliche Prophetie,* 234-37; cf. 226-300.

26. Cf. Fee, *First Epistle,* 656.

27. Ibid.; repeated in Fee, *God's Empowering Presence,* 218.

"At no point in 1 Corinthians 14 does Paul suggest that tongues is speech directed toward people; three times he indicates that it is speech directed toward God (14:2, 14-16, 28)."[28]

In spite of Gundry's arguments about the regular use of γλῶσσα to denote communicative languages which are not necessarily linked with exalted or ecstatic states of consciousness, "It is highly unlikely that tongues signify known languages in these contexts [i.e., 13:1 or 14:2]."[29] Without any contextual indicator, γλῶσσα may denote simply an organ of speech. However, the context of chs. 12–14 provides "antithetical parallelism" between tongues and prophecy in which "the most obvious characteristic of tongues is its unintelligibility," which becomes elaborated in the analogy of reverberating musical instruments as against those with differential pitch, rhythm, and tempo (vv. 7-8).[30] Although Chrysostom interprets **mysteries** more positively, Calvin more convincingly perceives the term to denote that which is "unintelligible, baffling, enigmatic, . . . as if Paul had written, 'Nobody understands a word he says.'"[31] Some modern commentators understand πνεύματι to refer to *the human spirit,* largely on the basis of the occurrence of this meaning in vv. 14 and 32.[32] Many commentators before the 1950s were unduly influenced by a view of human personhood dominated by idealist or Cartesian dualism, and πνεῦμα as human spirit plays a very minor role in Paul. Almost always it denotes the Holy **Spirit**, except in those specific contexts (14:14 and 32) where semantic contrasts clearly indicate otherwise. As in 15:44, to confuse human "spirituality," let alone "immateriality," with that which is characterized by the agency of the Spirit of God is to invite serious misunderstanding of Paul's theology. NRSV, REB, and NJB (against NIV, AV/KJV) rightly translate **the Spirit**.

3 The Greek participle with the definite article ὁ δὲ προφητεύων may be translated *the person who prophesies,* which would preserve the parallel with **the person who speaks in a tongue** (v. 2a). However, Paul is setting in contrast the role of one who speaks in tongues with the effects of prophesying as a dynamic communicative activity, and this invites an emphasis on the *action* in question rather than on the status or role of any specific *person,* in accordance with Paul's concerns and his use of the verb. The use of the definite article with the present participle may convey either habituation (*the person who prophesies;* cf. NRSV, NIV, NJB) or a temporal-conditional contingent clause (*when

28. Fee, *Paul, the Spirit and the People of God,* 148. Similarly, cf. Wolff, *Der erste Brief,* 328-29.

29. Williams, *Tongues of the Spirit,* 26; cf. Gundry, "'Ecstatic Utterance' (NEB)?" 299-307; and BAGD, 162.

30. Gillespie, *The First Theologians,* 130 and 150-51.

31. Calvin, *First Epistle,* 286; cf. Chrysostom, *1 Cor. Hom.,* 35:1, which in part anticipates Dautzenberg's approach.

32. Kistemaker, *1 Cor,* 477; Edwards, *First Epistle,* 357; Meyer, *Cor,* 2:5. However, these writers hastily modify their claim by insisting on the importance of the Spirit's agency at the same time. Robertson and Plummer make no qualification (*First Epistle,* 306). But for **the Spirit** cf. Fee, *First Epistle,* 656-57; and Conzelmann, *1 Cor,* 234.

or *if a person prophesies,* as REB). The latter also paves the way more readily for the proleptic accusatives οἰκοδομήν, παράκλησιν, and παραμυθίαν as reflected in the Vulgate construction *ad aedificationen.*[33] "'What is *in effect*' is the meaning" (Robertson and Plummer's italics).[34] Our use of **thereby** functions to make this point. Other exegetical issues in v. 3 are covered in the following note, especially under b1, 2, and 3. Meanwhile, "the noun οἰκοδομή functions as a *Leitmotif* in what follows and in v. 26."[35]

PROPHECY: A SECOND NOTE IN THE CONTEXT OF CHAPTER 14

In "Prophecy: A First Note" under 12:10 we sketched broad differences of interpretative approaches and took the discussion as far as 12:10 allowed without the benefit of engaging with Paul's major concerns in 14:1-25 (cf. also vv. 29-35). This cleared the ground and illuminated a number of issues. **Prophesying** plays its part, we noted, among the variety of gifts of the Holy Spirit apportioned out by God *for the corporate benefit of the whole community and beyond.* We also distinguished presuppositions or preunderstandings which certain interpreters bring to the text sometimes as firm assumptions, and sometimes as heuristic tools.

(1) Seven Distinctions Which Shape Interpretative Frames of Reference

The seven distinctions made in our first note remain relevant to this second stage of discussion and therefore need to be recapitulated in summary: (i) the use or overuse of supposed parallels from *Hellenistic religions* (Reitzenstein; critically by Fascher and Crone; sharply criticized by Boring and especially Forbes); (ii) appeals to *revelation–heavenly-mystery discourse in Jewish apocalyptic* (Dautzenberg; criticized by Grudem and decisively modified by Ellis and Aune); (iii) links between *apocalyptic discourse and scriptural exposition* (Ellis, Cothenet; partly criticized by Forbes) or between apocalyptic and verdictive *judgment pronouncements* (Müller); (iv) the convincing and close association between **prophesying** *and pastoral preaching* (Hill) or *pastoral and kerygmatic preaching* (Sandnes, Vielhauer, Gillespie); (v) more speculative claims about *freedom and authority* in prophecy (Wire); (vi) the compatibility between levels of inspiration, authority, and necessary *testing for fallibility* (Grudem); and (vii) the limitations of any study which failed to engage seriously with the *goals of prophesying as expressed in 14:1-25.*

(2) Building Up, Encouraging, and Bringing Comfort

(a) Building up (noun, οἰκοδομή, 14:3, 5, 12, 26; cf. 3:9; verb οἰκοδομέω, 14:4, 17; also 8:1; 10:1, 23, ἐποικοδομέω, 3:10, 12, 14). In Paul but outside 1 Corinthians, cf. Rom 14:19;

33. Edwards, *First Epistle,* 358.
34. Robertson and Plummer, *First Epistle,* 306.
35. Schrage, *Der erste Brief,* 3:386.

15:2, 20; 2 Cor 10:8; 12:19; 13:10; Gal 2:18; 1 Thess 5:11 (Eph 4:12, 16, 29). We consistently urge that 8:1-13 and 13:1-13 remain fundamental for understanding 12:1–14:40, and under 8:1 we noted Kitzberger's central semantic contrast between the solidity and ordered permanence of **building up** by ἀγάπη, and the illusory and superficial hollowness of φυσιόω, *to inflate* through γνῶσις without love.[36] The major study of Vielhauer briefly occupied our attention under 14:1, where we noted his convincing contrast between **building up** as a cohesive activity for the benefit of others and a negative sense of affirming mere self-esteem, which we consider further under 14:4.[37] Vielhauer and more recently Sandnes further associate the commission **to build up** with Paul's own personal apostolic commission with which Paul explicitly compares Jeremiah's prophetic call **to build up** (Gal 1:15-16; Jer 1:5, "before birth"; Jer 1:10, "to build and to plant"; cf. 1 Cor 3:6, 10, "I planted. . . . I laid a foundation like a skilled master builder . . .").[38] Citing further arguments to this effect from Schütz, Gillespie concludes: "Essential is the notion that *oikodomē* and the proclamation of the gospel are both *functionally* and *materially* related" (his italics).[39] In 14:26 "**prophesying**, as a cultic event, is subject to this norm."[40]

(b) *Encouraging or exhorting/challenging (παράκλησις).* It is essential to recover the multiform character of παράκλησις if we are to understand the nature of prophecy and prophetic preaching in Pauline theology. It is not the bland communication of information as such, but a varied range of illocutionary speech-acts which plead, exhort, encourage, challenge, brace, console, or provide comfort on the basis of "institutional facts" (in the sense used by philosophers of language), e.g., covenant promises mediated by human agents called and gifted by God for this task through the Holy Spirit. Ulrich Müller rightly understands it as *a correlate of gospel preaching in judgment and grace,* just as Grabner-Haider rightly calls attention to *its active role as exhortation.*[41] On the other hand, those who regard "prophecy" as a rare phenomenon in the churches largely perhaps restricted to the NT era and Pentecostal traditions in the modern era might note that the verb and noun occur some 109 times: "On the basis of statistics alone παρακαλέω/παράκλησις are among the most important terms for speaking and influencing in the NT."[42] Although not every example of *paraklēsis* is **prophesying**, sufficient functional overlap occurs to warrant Fitzmyer's comment that in the gifts listed in Rom 12:6 "the first gift [προφητεία] is inspired Christian preaching, as in 1 Cor 12:10, 28; 13:2; 14:1, 3-6, 24, 39; 1 Tim 4:14. . . . It denotes one who speaks in God's name and probes the secrets of hearts (1 Cor 14:24-25)."[43]

The pastoral dimension is underlined not only by the contextual particularity

36. I. Kitzberger, *Bau der Gemeinde. Das paulinische Wortfeld oikodomē/(ep)oikodomein* (Würzburg: Echter Verlag, 1986), esp. 73-78. See above on 8:1.

37. For references, see above under 14:1.

38. Vielhauer, *Oikodomē,* 77-98; Sandnes, *Paul — One of the Prophets?*

39. Gillespie, *The First Theologians,* 142; cf. Schütz, *Paul and the Anatomy of Apostolic Authority,* 224-25.

40. Gillespie, *The First Theologians,* 144. See also Schrage, *Der erste Brief,* 3:386-89, 396, and 443-48.

41. Müller, *Prophetie und Predigt im NT,* 118-30, 162-233; A. Grabner-Haider, *Paraklese und Eschatologie bei Paulus. Mensch und Welt im Anspruch der Zukunft Gottes,* NTA n.s. 4 (Münster im Westfalen: Aschendorff, 1968), 5 and 116-28.

42. J. Thomas, "παράκλησις," *EDNT,* 3:23; cf. 23-27.

43. J. A. Fitzmyer, *Romans,* AB (New York: Doubleday, 1992), 647.

which distinguishes **prophesying** from *teaching* (which may be more doctrinal or general), but the careful arguments put forward by Bjerkelund that παρακαλέω frequently rests on a *personal relationship* between the speaker and addressees (see under 1:10).[44] The everyday sense of being a "helper" through this activity picks up the overtones of "helping the other" from συμφέρει in 6:12; 10:23 and from concern to sustain the other in 8:7-13. Sometimes, however, it requires honest exposure, challenge, or bracing exhortation "to help" in long-term rather than short-term ways.[45] When the source of address is the Holy Spirit, judgment may become an avenue for the appropriation of grace. Hence the varied nuances of **encouragement** and *exhortation* or *challenge* are not in the least contradictory. The opposite of love is not correction but indifference. "Paul's use of *parakalein* and *oikodomein* in 1 Thess 5:11 suggests that exhortation connotes a sense parallel with gospel proclamation. Evidence of this is provided by 1 Thess 2:2-3, where Paul reminds the community of his initial gospel preaching."[46] Gillespie clearly shows that the term includes gospel preaching, ethical instruction, and applied theology in Paul's letters.[47]

(c) *Bringing comfort* (παραμυθία). The noun in this form occurs only here in the NT (and in variant form in Phil 2:1), but the verbal form appears in 1 Thess 2:11 and 5:14 (also of **comforting** the bereaved sisters of Lazarus in John 11:19, 31). **Comfort** is adopted by NIV and KJV/AV (*consolation*, NRSV); *encourage*, REB; *reassurance*, NJB. The six NT uses of the cognate forms suggest the bracing, strengthening, supportive activity of the older English which reflects the Latin components *com-fort*. Malherbe identifies the term closely with the attitude and activity of *pastoral care*.[48] He addresses in particular 1 Thess 5:14-15 in the light of concern for the weak in the better moral philosophy of the Graeco-Roman world of the day. Seneca, Plutarch, and Philodemus, e.g., caution that while exhortation and persuasion would not be swept aside, sensitivity to the variety of individual personal circumstances for which support is required must be addressed by a close personal understanding of these varied and specific situations.[49] The everyday life of the church at Thessalonica, Malherbe concludes, "required comfort . . . from the earliest days of the church's existence," and the complementary activities of warning and comforting form part of the pastoral process of "nurturing communal relationships."[50] "Paul always παραμυθεῖσθαι or its cognates in conjunction with some form of παράκλησις (5:14; 1 Cor 14:3; Phil 2:1)," and this gives his pastoral preaching and pastoral care a distinctive touch not exhausted by either term alone, although the dual emphasis also occurs in moral philosophy in the Graeco-Roman world.[51]

Such a pastoral concern brings together the OT tradition of prophetic contextual application to particular circumstances and claims by Hill and others that **proph-**

44. C. J. Bjerkelund, *Parakalō. Form, Funktion und Sinn der parakalō-Sätze in den paulinischen Briefen* (Oslo: Universitetsforlaget, 1967), esp. 188-90; cf. 34-58, 109-11.

45. Cf. BAGD, 618, and, by analogy, the Paraclete passages in John.

46. Gillespie, *The First Theologians*, 145.

47. Ibid., 144-48.

48. A. J. Malherbe, "'Pastoral Care' in the Thessalonian Church," *NTS* 36 (1990): 375-91 (main *SNTS* paper, Dublin, 1989).

49. Seneca, *De Ira* 1.6.3; *Epistulae* 64.7-10; 82.23; Plutarch, *Quomodo Adulator* 67B, 73A-C, 74DE; Philodemus, *Peri Parrēsias* 38.

50. Malherbe, "'Pastoral Care,'" 388 and 389.

51. Ibid., 387.

esying has *pastoral preaching* at its center. "Preaching," however, is to be understood not as a flat homily of information or instruction alone, but as a multioperational speech-action of **building up, encouraging** and *challenging,* and **bringing comfort** alongside *exhortation.* Indeed, the opening of what is probably the most outstanding "model" pastoral sermon in the NT (Heb 1:1-4) brings **encouragement** and **comfort** to its addressees by performing multiple acts of acclamation, biblical exposition, promise, doctrinal confession or creedal affirmation, and joyful celebration all through the same multilayered language.[52] As in the Epistle to the Hebrews, "'One who prophesies speaks . . . encouragement to people' (1 Cor 14:3)."[53]

(3) Creative Reinterpretation of Scripture?

Earle Ellis helpfully finds continuities between **prophesying** in the Pauline churches and the OT and Judaism rather than in hellenistic backgrounds. He argues that "the understanding of παράκλησις as the specific ministry of a prophet is supported in the Pauline literature by 1 Cor 14:2, 3," citing Stählin for further support.[54] However, since scripture remains the definitive source of παράκλησις (cf. Rom 15:4-5), Ellis urges that "the interpretation of Scripture, usually in the synagogues, is a key feature of the missions of Paul and Barnabas, Paul and Silas, as well as of Peter and other Christian leaders [i.e., in Acts]."[55] "The interpretation of Scripture as an activity of a prophet was not unknown in the first century since it was explicitly ascribed to Daniel (9:2, 24)."[56] As the argument proceeds, however, Ellis is led toward an increasing overlap with the gift of the ministry of teaching. This invites a speculative, perhaps even misleading, turn. For Ellis finds the most important difference between prophet and teacher in that this can be seen "only by the manner in which it [the teaching] is given or by the recognized status as 'prophet' of the one who is teaching."[57] This may be found, in Ellis's view, largely by appealing to what he seeks to identify as characterizing "pneumatics." This not only invites the danger of circular arguments by "reading in" selective evidence (e.g., in "the Angelic 'Spirits' of the Prophets"), but rests on even more ambivalent assumptions about "mysteries" and creative reinterpretation on analogy with the hermeneutics of Qumran.[58]

Christopher Forbes offers a careful critique of some of these assumptions, alongside that of a related approach adopted by E. Cothenet.[59] Cothenet helpfully associates the role of expounding scripture within the context of the believing commu-

---

52. Cf. A. C. Thiselton, "The Epistle to the Hebrews," in J. D. G. Dunn and J. W. Rogerson (eds.), *Eerdmans Commentary on the Bible* [title to be revised] (Grand Rapids: Eerdmans, forthcoming), ad loc.

53. Gillespie, *The First Theologians,* 149.

54. Ellis, "The Role of the Christian Prophet in Acts," rpt. in his *Prophecy and Hermeneutic in Early Christianity,* 131-32; cf. 129-44; and G. Stählin, *TDNT,* 5:82.

55. Ibid., 132.

56. Ibid., 133.

57. Ibid., 141.

58. Ellis, "'Spiritual' Gifts in the Pauline Community," in *Prophecy and Hermeneutic,* 23-44.

59. E. Cothenet, "Les prophètes chrétiens comme exégètes charismatiques de l'écriture," in Panagopoulos (ed.), *Prophetic Vocation,* 77-107.

nity at worship. However, Forbes convincingly argues that nowhere can it be demonstrated that either didactic of "free" exposition of scripture "was a defining characteristic" of prophesying for Paul.[60] We are on safer ground to remind ourselves, following Aune, that "the early Christian application of the designation prophêtês . . . was originally determined by the prevalent conception of the prophetic role in the OT. In early Judaism the term 'prophet' *(nabi`* or *prophētēs)* was rarely applied to those who were not OT prophets or eschatological prophets."[61] Whether or not we subscribe to the older maxim that the major prophets were reformers, not innovators, their central theme of faithfulness to the covenant God of Israel presupposed a certain continuity of tradition in which the concept of being faithful depended. Hence Gillespie is correct to relate Pauline prophecy to a continuity of gospel promise, and even to a tradition.[62] In this sense the role of scripture and a sense of the coherence of the work of God's Spirit as one who remains faithful to his promise can never be far away. This would have remained part of the bedrock against which claims to prophesy were "tested" (14:29b; cf. 14:36-38; 1 Thess 5:20-21, δοκιμάζετε). Cothenet's chosen title for his essay "charismatic exegesis" (comme exégètes charismatiques de l'écriture") does not entirely do justice to what he proposes.[63] If what is at issue remains the prophetic gift of the Spirit for the interpretation of scripture, this coheres entirely with our own views.

(4) "Spontaneous" or Also Involving Rational Reflection? Pastoral Preaching?

Dunn, Turner, and Forbes remain among the many who claim, or who merely assume, that Pauline prophecy was "spontaneous." Max Turner writes, "For Paul prophecy is the reception and subsequent communication of spontaneous, divinely given *apokalupsis.*"[64] Dunn asserts, "For Paul prophecy is a word of revelation. It does not denote a previously prepared sermon. . . . It is a spontaneous utterance . . . (14:30)."[65] Dunn's main grounds for this are that prophecy cannot be summoned to order, and that in v. 30 the first prophet is to stop if another received "a revelation." Forbes declares that "according to Luke and Paul, Christian prophecy was the reception and immediately public declaration of spontaneous, (usually) verbal, revelation. . . ."[66] It is hereby to be distinguished from preaching, in Forbes's view, for preaching is not *"a charisma,"* whereas in prophecy "revelation is normally spontaneous."[67] These arguments, however, invite serious question, under the following subheadings.

(i) We have already alluded to the problem that it is utterly impossible to regard all "spiritual gifts" *en bloc* as "spontaneous." We argued under 12:8-10 and 28-30 that these could include an ability to lead the church with strategic, statesmanlike vi-

---

60. Forbes, *Prophecy and Inspired Speech,* 235.
61. Aune, *Prophecy in Early Christianity,* 195.
62. Gillespie, *The First Theologians,* 132-36.
63. Cothenet, "Les prophètes chrétiens," 77-107.
64. M. Turner, "Spiritual Gifts Then and Now," *VoxEv* 15 (1985): 10; cf. 7-64.
65. Dunn, *Jesus and the Spirit,* 228, (although see above on his *Theology of Paul).*
66. Forbes, *Prophecy and Inspired Speech,* 229 and 236.
67. Ibid., 229. However, see the discussion on Prophecy and Healings above at 12:8.

sion (κυβερνήσεις; see under 12:28); to provide administrative support skills (ἀντιλήμψεις, v. 28) which entail organization; to exercise a sustained, buoyant, optimistic, pioneering stance of trustful faith (πίστις, under v. 9); to provide a reflective ministry of teaching (διδάσκαλοι, under v. 29, linked closely with prophecy); commission to sustained apostolic witness on the basis of past and present identification with the raised Christ (ἀποστόλους, v. 29; cf. 9:1); to share in healing either by miracle or by medical skills (plural χαρίσματα ἰαμάτων, under 12:9); or to receive a sustained, settled χάρισμα ἐκ θεοῦ to live the celibate life without frustration (7:7). To claim that to be "gifted" to be a *teacher* as a *charisma* cannot involve sustained reflection and preparation is farfetched. Yet this "gift" appears in the same lists and terms as προφῆται. It also goes against the grain of all that Paul says about critical testing to imagine that διακρίσεις πνευμάτων (12:10) is also "spontaneous."

(ii) Too much influence has been exercised by form-critical identifications of "prophecies" within the NT itself. Here, as Müller argues, the influence of Reitzenstein and those who appeal to hellenistic sources has not yet been entirely dissipated.[68] Oracular forms are only one possible form of prophecy, although Aune's major study has the unfortunate effect of identifying numerous fragmentary oracular *forms* as models or paradigm cases of prophetic *functions*. However, the key writer here is David Hill, who almost alone puts the issue into due perspective. He fully accepts that *at Corinth itself* prophesying may have been "only a series of short ejaculatory words of revelation unconnected with one another."[69] *Yet Paul wishes to correct this.* By restricting prophesying to "two or three," he not only urges a coherent ordering which better reflects the nature of God himself as Spirit, but thereby achieves a *"greater coherence of message."*[70] Now, in the light of Paul's reordering of worship, παράκλησις (which **builds up**, **encourages** *or exhorts*, and **brings comfort** (v. 3) "is expressed in sustained utterance," or of what Hill calls pastoral preaching.[71] "Oracular," we noted, should be explicated in terms of a sufficiently sophisticated theory of speech-acts which distinguishes declarative, verdictive, directive, and other forms of illocution which have nothing to do with the presence or absence of prior preparation or reflection. This "oracular" argument rests upon a category mistake.

(iii) The argument based on an appeal to v. 30 rests on the assumption about exalted states of mind which Müller exposes as without secure evidence. The first prophesying must stop if or when a second person receives a "revelation" (ἐὰν δὲ ἄλλῳ ἀποκαλυφθῇ καθημένῳ, v. 30). Yet what is at issue in this "disclosure" other than the *insight* of another, given by God, that the first speaker has begun to indulge in *self-deception, distraction, or sheer error, or a fertile integration* with resources of wisdom or scriptural knowledge which enables the second speaker *to take the theme forward* more imaginatively, accurately, or deeply than the first?

(iv) The assumption that the Spirit himself wearies of the first subject and "falls upon" the second for a fresh vision is more reminiscent of the period *before* the canonical prophets, when the purposive unitary framework within which God could and did still surprise had not yet been fully grasped. Hence "prophecy" in the ninth

---

68. Müller, *Prophetie*, 14. Why, Müller asks, do we merely *assume* that "revelation" implies enhanced, even ecstatic consciousness, rather than an informed mind which lies open to God?

69. Hill, *NT Prophecy*, 123.

70. Ibid.

71. Ibid., 123 and 131.

century BC showed "charismatic" signs absent from Amos, Hosea, or Jeremiah. To restrict "revelation" to a kind of *Deus ex machina* worldview is to impose notions which
owe more to the struggle between theology and secular modernity than they do to
Paul himself. Paul does not specify whether the revelation in v. 30 entails reflective or
critical processes, but his reference to "judging" prophecies suggests that a dimension of critical reflection is highly probable. Nothing remains of the "spontaneity" argument except assumption and conjecture. It is reasonable to infer that both spontaneity and critical reflection may operate at different times in God's providence. A
more sophisticated theory of knowledge might suggest that "insight" given by the
Spirit of God has little to do with issues of temporal duration.

(5) Is Prophesying Limited to Addressing Fellow Believers or May It Also Entail a Wider Audience?

C. M. Robeck insists that prophecy is addressed strictly to the believing community,
and must not be confused with kerygma or gospel preaching.[72] However, this overlooks several points.

(i) Müller perceives the prophetic pronouncements of judgment and grace to
combine the promise of salvation with pastoral exhortation, forming inseparable aspects of a whole.[73] If the church and the world both stand under the judgment of the
cross with the possibility of the grace of transformation, prophetic declaration, prophetic announcement, prophetic verdict, and prophetic exhortation combine to
bring about appropriation, acceptance of judgment, and change in this *Bussrede*.[74]

(ii) Further 14:24-25 explicitly extends to unbelievers the power of the prophetic word to plumb the secrets of the heart, to expose evil or self-centeredness, and
to generate belief through the Spirit's gift. Hill observes, "By including, intentionally,
outsiders and non-believers in this discussion, Paul demonstrates his desire to affirm
the missionary function of the word, even of the inspired prophetic word spoken in
worship. According to 14:24f the effects of prophesying . . . on an unbeliever who happens to visit a service of worship will be to bring about conviction, conversion and acknowledgment of the divine presence in the midst of the assembled congregation. . . . The secrets of his heart are disclosed."[75] (See on 14:24-25.) Since for Paul, no
less than for modern systematic theology, Christ himself is God's prophetic word in a
primary sense (cf. 1:18-25), the church and the world alike can but stand under the
judgment and grace of that word. Believers do not cease to need the gospel word; indeed, this epistle preaches the cross as the criterion for "spirituality" without which a
person is not "of the Spirit."

(iii) Finally, we return to Paul's own prophetic call and consciousness. We have
no need to recapitulate the arguments of Vielhauer and of Sandnes. Paul might
have been surprised and disconcerted to learn that a number of studies identify only
small segments and fragments of his utterances, pronouncements, pleas, arguments,

---

72. C. M. Robeck, "The Gift of Prophecy in Acts and Paul," *Studia Biblica et Theologica* 5
(1975): esp. (2) 39-54; cf. (1) 15-38.

73. Müller, *Prophetie*, 24-26.

74. Ibid.; cf. 12-46.

75. Hill, *NT Prophecy*, 123-24.

and requests as "prophetic." As in 14:3, the prophetic task is **to build**, to **encourage/**
challenge/exhort, and **to bring comfort**. This does *not* logically entail the conclusion
that wherever these three occur, the utterance is prophetic; but it invites caution over
narrowing down the phenomenon to categories which match prior assumptions
about what the modern world, or the Greek world, might expect. It would be like excluding Amos for his supposed "ordinariness," and including only "oracles" in the form
נְאֻם יהוה (Heb. *n'um Yahweh*)

In summary, *prophesying* in Paul's theology and in his argument in this chapter
*is the performing of intelligible, articulate, communicative speech-acts, the operative cur-
rency of which depends on the active agency of the Holy Spirit mediated through human
minds and lives to build up, to encourage, to judge, to exhort, and to comfort others in the
context of interpersonal relations.* Such a definition is not comprehensive. It allows for
short utterances or, in accordance with Paul's own wishes, for longer stretches of
speech to which the nearest modern parallel is probably that of an informed pastoral
sermon which proclaims grace and judgment, or requires change of life, but which
also remains open to question and correction by others. We may note that Zwingli
(1484-1531) and Bullinger (1504-75) used the term "prophesyings" loosely in this way,
although with a greater emphasis on the place of "Bible readings" as generating the
"prophesyings."[76] However, just as many unduly restrict prophecy to the "spontaneous," we should avoid the converse mistake of insisting that prophecy could not in
any circumstance take the more "oracular" form often identified as such today. In the
end our view will be determined by a dialogue between careful exegesis and a theology of the nature of God and of God's ways of action in the world.

4   Since edification or **building up** (οἰκοδομέω) remains a central issue, Paul
applies the term alike to the individualism of the use of tongues and the community effects of prophecy as a fundamental contrast. We have placed the first
use of **builds up** (v. 4) in quotation marks first to indicate that Paul takes it up
as a catchword for the dialogue, and second because whether this first use is
positive (i.e., *edifies* the self) or negative (i.e., ministers to *self-esteem* or *self-
affirmation*) remains acutely controversial. Against a pejorative view Fee insists that "Paul intended no such thing. The edifying is not self-centeredness,
but the personal edifying of the believer that comes through private prayer and
praise."[77] Fee's view is anticipated by Chrysostom, Myer, and others.[78]
Conzelmann and Senft adopt a middle view that, whether or not the individual
is edified, Paul attacks a concern for the individual in contrast to the wider
whole of the church community (ἐκκλησίαν, in the anarthrous form).[79]
P. Vielhauer, however, followed largely by Schrage, makes a strong case for

76. For sources, see below. As an introduction cf. G. W. Bromiley (ed.), *Zwingli and Bullinger: Selected Translations,* LCC (Philadelphia: Westminster and London: SCM, 1963), 27. Hermeneutics in early Pentecostalism took a different turn; cf. S. R. Graham, "'Thus Saith the Lord':
Biblical Hermeneutics in the Early Pentecostal Movement," *Ex Auditu* 12 (1996): 121-35.

77. Fee, *First Epistle,* 657; quoted identically in Fee, *God's Empowering Presence,* 219.

78. Meyer, *Epistles,* 2:6, as against Wetstein's "feels" that he is edified; cf. Chrysostom,
1 Cor. Hom., 35:1.

79. Conzelmann, *1 Cor,* 235; Senft, *La Première Épitre,* 175.

Paul's deliberately using οἰκοδομέω as a double wordplay which may mean *self-sufficiency* or *self-affirmation* in some contexts and genuine **building up** of other people in other contexts. The former use, he argues, is firmly egoist and self-indulgent.[80] Schrage links with this 10:23-24 and Paul's contrast between seeking good for the self and good for "the other," and, in more general terms, the direction of argument is supported by Hill, Cullmann, and Maly.[81] Moreover, if Chrysostom is positive, Theodore of Mopsuestia is distinctly negative in tone.[82]

The strength of Vielhauer's argument lies in his identifying οἰκοδομέω with the apostolic task of building up by proclaiming the cross and resurrection and its practical implications to others. It is not mere "spirituality," but a Christlike, cruciform concern for others which entails costly action. In the picture or model *(das Bild)* of building "we have to think of the love of Christ who must win the real wholeness of the church community."[83] Nevertheless, we cannot wholly dismiss Fee's appeal to the edifying effects of praise and prayer, especially since Paul never denies that **speaking in a tongue** (some late MSS read the plural *tongues* here) comes as a gift from the Holy Spirit, even if some argue that no one can profit from what they cannot understand.[84] The best explanation is that while the positive evaluation adopted by Fee may apply to tongues *specifically used in private,* the *public* use of tongues becomes so bound up with perceived status and self-affirmation that *in public* (but not in private) the negative effects come to outweigh the otherwise positive. However, a firm exegetical judgment remains provisional on how we understand this chapter as a whole, including several difficult verses within it.

Both aspects must be kept in view: **speaking in a tongue** may well reflect an authentic welling up of otherwise inexpressible praise to God (cf. v. 2a); but this activity was probably also construed at Corinth (but not by Paul) as "the ultimate sign of their [the speakers'] spiritual power and maturity," which promoted a negative side-effect for the speakers themselves.[85] "Esoteric speech . . . is usually considered a high status activity *except* in western, rationalist societies where tongue-speaking is taken as evidence of ignorance, lowly origins, and a susceptibility to 'enthusiasm.'"[86] Horrell expresses cautious support for this view.[87] Ronald Knox points out that if Paul does conceive of a hier-

---

80. Vielhauer, *Oidodomē,* 91-98.

81. Schrage, *Der erste Brief,* 3:388 (including nn. 62 and 63; Hill, *NT Prophecy,* 122; Maly, *Mündige Gemeinde,* 199, who also cites Cullmann as well as Vielhauer.

82. Theodore, 2:76r, cited in K. Staab (ed.), *Pauluskommentare aus der griechischen Kirche,* 192. Theodore uses φθέγγεται, he utters loud sounds, also used of speaking "bombastically" (cf. BAGD, 857).

83. Vielhauer, *Oidodomē,* 92.

84. Edwards, *First Epistle,* 358.

85. Hays, *First Cor,* 233; cf. D. B. Martin, "Tongues of Angels and Other Status Indicators," 547-89; and Martin, *The Corinthian Body,* 91-92.

86. Martin, "Tongues of Angels," 556.

87. Horrell, *The Social Ethos of the Corinthian Correspondence,* 177-78; cf. 63-125.

archy of gifts "it is not altogether the hierarchy which the Corinthians would have expected: the apostles come first, then the prophets, then (without any claim to miraculous powers) those engaged in teaching."[88] Healing and tongues are mentioned "in the same breath . . . with works of mercy and church finance" (12:28-30).[89]

Yet the more positive aspect of tongues used in private devotion should not be overlooked. Frank D. Macchia writes from a Pentecostal perspective when he asks: "Could it be that prayer as a rational, articulated response to God does not exhaust the human response . . . ? Poetry, song, dance and silence have always been offered as examples of in-depth responses to God. . . . Glossolalia is certainly one such response to God."[90] However, Macchia recognizes that a christologically oriented experience of "the mystery and freedom of our own beings *coram Deo*" differs in kind from "an empty and self-centered emotional euphoria."[91] If the latter was sought at Corinth, Vielhauer's interpretation is valid. Yet glossolalia, presumably as Paul practiced it in private, "is to be understood Christologically. Hence, the cross becomes the path to glory: glossolalia as groaning for the bound creation becomes the path to glossolalia as praise."[92] We shall argue that it is this experience which genuinely constitutes the *charisma* of tongues; while the further step of articulating the content of such a mysterious experience in communicative speech constitutes a further, distinct gift which may or may not be added to, for use in edifying others in public.

5   The translation of θέλω . . . is notoriously difficult. KJV/AV, *I would that . . . but rather . . .* becomes *I would like . . . but even more* (NRSV); *I would like . . . but I would rather . . .* (NIV); *while I should like . . . I would much rather . . .* (NJB); and perhaps best of these five main examples: *I am happy for . . . but happier still for . . .* (REB). Many commentators regard the θέλω clause as conciliatory or (with NJB) as concessive. Thus Conzelmann comments, "He allows them their speaking in tongues," and in a note compares v. 18 and θέλω in 7:7; while Héring goes further: "'*thelō*' does not express an order, but a concession in the form of a wish unlikely to be fulfilled (cf. 7:7)."[93] Collins translates the verb *I wish,* but takes the point to be that Paul does not "disdain" the gift; while Bruce comments: "He goes as far as he can with those whom he criticizes before interposing a *caveat.*" He then endorses Henry Chadwick's comment "The entire drift of the argument . . . is such as to pour a douche of ice-

88. R. A. Knox, *Enthusiasm* (Oxford: Clarendon Press, 1950), 22.

89. Ibid.

90. F. D. Macchia, "Sighs Too Deep for Words: Toward a Theology of Glossolalia," 47-73. Developed further in his "Groans Too Deep for Words: Towards a Theology of Tongues as Initial Experience," 149-73.

91. Macchia, "Sighs Too Deep for Words," 72.

92. Ibid.

93. Conzelmann, *1 Cor,* 235; cf. Wolff, *Der erste Brief,* 329, "not a pure negative"; and Héring, *First Epistle,* 146.

cold water over the whole practice."[94] Such an interpretation of θέλω . . . μᾶλλον is rejected by Fee, who argues that θέλω means *I wish*, while Kling calls it "a hearty wish and not an unworthy concession."[95]

The use of θέλω to mean simply the permissive *I am willing* does not do justice to the force of the verb, as Schrage confirms. Even in the classical era the verb "implying purpose or design" stands in contrast to the less purposive βούλομαι, although usually in the form ἐθέλω.[96] The force may be softened, however, when, as here, issues of comparative preference shape the semantic domain. Moreover, "the change from infinitive [θέλω δὲ πάντας ὑμᾶς λαλεῖν γλώσσαις] to ἵνα [μᾶλλον δὲ ἵνα προφητεύητε] is perhaps meant to make the wish more intense," and its conjunction with μᾶλλον δέ makes this intensity overwhelming.[97] Thus Kistemaker understands *wish* to govern the whole, but mainly the fulfillment of Num 11:29 when Moses deliberately rejects the individualism and elitism of any exclusive bestowal of the Spirit, expressing the self-effacing wish that "all the LORD's people should be prophets," far from expressing any competitive jealousy that Eldad and Medad were prophesying "in the camp."[98]

Kistemaker has surely identified the source in the OT which lies behind Paul's formulation of his argument and his use of θέλω. *Since he himself uses tongues in private (v. 18, unless this is a quoted slogan), Paul no more wishes to monopolize this gift than he wishes any elitist monopoly of anything at Corinth.* Nevertheless, he clearly states in 12:29-30 that **all** (v. 29, μὴ πάντες ἀπόστολοι; . . . ; v. 30, μὴ πάντες γλώσσαις λαλοῦσιν; cf. 14:5, πάντας ὑμᾶς) will not *be apostles* or **speak in tongues**. The solution to the supposed enigma lies in the observation of BAGD that in first-century *koinē* Greek, among the various constructions which modify the force of θέλω when it occurs with the infinitive, it may denote **I take pleasure in**, as in Mark 12:38, "the scribes **take pleasure in** walking up and down in long robes" (not *wish*).[99] This comes close to REB, *I am happy for . . . ,* which I had proposed in a first draft before consulting REB. However, *to be happy for* seems to retain the permissive force which Fee attacks and which does appear to underplay the verb. Paul does not, I conclude partly on the basis of 12:29-30, *wish* that every member of the church at Corinth may speak with tongues; it is the Holy Spirit alone who wills how his gifts are apportioned,

94. Bruce, *1 and 2 Cor,* 130, citing H. Chadwick, "All Things to All Men," *NTS* 1 (1954-55): 268; Collins, *First Cor,* 493.

95. Fee, *First Epistle,* 658-59; Kling, *First Epistle* (Lange's Commentaries), 10:ii, 284.

96. LSJ, 411 (under ἐθέλω; no entry for θέλω). Schrage, *Der erste Brief,* 3:389, n. 67, distances himself from Weiss and Conzelmann in their more concessive understanding: *"he wishes."*

97. Robertson and Plummer, *First Epistle,* 307.

98. Kistemaker, *1 Cor,* 481.

99. BAGD, 355, sect. 4 under θέλω; cf. par. Luke 20:46. θέλω is the regular *koinē* word from as early as 250 BC, and in the papyri comes to express most often wishes expressed in letter forms, e.g., γινώσκειν σε θέλω. However, often the word is used for θεῶν θελόντων, the gods being willing, and in 1 Cor 15:38, ὡς ὁ θεὸς ἠθέλησεν (cf. *BGU* 1:27:11; 1 Cor 12:28), where the divine sovereign will express "God's sovereign pleasure." For parallels in the papyri cf. MM, 286.

and egalitarianism is as much an undifferentiated dullness as arbitrary hierarchy ministers to authoritarianism and elitism. Paul **takes pleasure in** the sense of intimacy, liberation, and prayerful doxology that those who speak in tongues enjoy. However, their pleasure is very solemnly and seriously constrained by two things: first, that this gift is used only *privately;* second, that proclaiming the gospel of Christ, or **prophesying** for the building up of *others,* holds priority and privilege as an "apostolic" or Christlike, cruciform mode of ministry. Calvin makes this two-sided point. Paul gives "approval to tongues" in principle, but the way in which the gift is used at Corinth makes it "valueless and to some extent harmful"; hence the approval is conditional upon "correcting this fault."[100]

The comparative force of μᾶλλον is crucial for the argument. Paul's pleasure in, and preference for, the use of the gift of **prophesying** (see Note on Prophecy, above) is expressed in this word which denotes both *to a greater degree* (as in Phil 1:12) and also a preferential **rather** (as in 1 Cor 7:21) in the dual sense of *more* and *instead of* (as in Matt 10:6), where the latter is frequently marked by μᾶλλον δέ (as here).[101] This is strengthened by the following description of **the person who prophesies** as **greater** (NRSV, NIV; μείζων), which NJB rightly contextualizes as denoting here not greater in status but, in accordance with the logic of Paul's argument, **of greater importance than the one** (Greek singular) **who speaks in tongues.**

THE "INTERPRETATION" OR "ARTICULATION" OF GLOSSOLALIA?

We have not yet exhausted the issues of controversy in v. 5. Substantial issues hang on how we understand the clause εἰ μὴ διερμηνεύῃ in this context of argument. NRSV's *unless someone interprets* is, in our view, disastrously misleading. *The Greek does not mention any agent other than* **the one who speaks in tongues,** *who remains the subject of the verb. The insertion of someone rests on a particular understanding of* ἑρμηνεία γλωσσῶν (12:10; see above on this verse) and the significance of ἄλλῳ δέ in conjunction with this phrase in 12:10, as if a special agent was "an interpreter" who "interpreted" tongues. However, as I argued in 1979, frequent occurrences of ἑρμηνεύω and διερμηνεύω can be found in which these verbs mean not *to interpret* but **to put into words,** i.e., *to render in articulate intelligible speech,* what is difficult to express.[102] I argued that 14:13 similarly refers to the person who speaks in tongues: "He who speaks in a tongue should pray for the power to produce articular speech."[103]

An illuminating parallel occurs when Josephus is trying to convey to his Roman or Graeco-Roman readers the wonders of Herod's palace. These are "beyond words" (παντὸς λόγου κρείσσων, Josephus, *Jewish Wars* 5.176). The walls, towers, and banquet-

---

100. Calvin, *First Epistle,* 287.

101. BAGD, 489, sects. 1, 2, 3, esp. 3d, col. 2. Cf. Plutarch, *Moralia* 634; Philo, *De Aeternitate Mundi.* 23; Rom 8:34; Gal 4:9. BAGD cite 1 Cor 14:5 under this last category, rightly.

102. Thiselton, "The 'Interpretation' of Tongues? A New Suggestion in the Light of Greek Usage in Philo and Josephus," 15-36.

103. Ibid., 16.

ing hall defy description (ἀδιήγητος, 5.178). When he moves on to the cloisters, gardens, and lavish decorations he exclaims: ἀλλὰ γὰρ οὔθ' ἑρμηνεῦσαι δυνατὸν ἀξίως τὰ βασίλεια (5.182: it is impossible **to put it into words** adequately!). Here *to interpret* or *to translate* simply does not fit.[104] Similarly, when he reflects on Moses' request that Aaron should be his "mouth" (στόμα), Philo observes that what Moses required was someone who could **put into words** of intelligible, articulate communication what Moses felt himself unable to express adequately.[105] Aaron's role is *to produce articulate speech* (ἑρμηνεύω, *Quod Deterius Potiori Insidiari Soleat,* 15), with a view to **putting into words** (πρὸς ἑρμηνείαν, loc. cit. 39) what Moses found overwhelming or difficult. For Aaron to be his "mouth" (στόμα) is also to be his "mouthpiece" (ἑρμηνέα, loc. cit. 39). The evidence for humans' becoming capable of reasoning, Philo urges, can be found in their use of syntax of nouns and verbs **to put things into words** that are intelligible and articulate (ἑρμηνεὺς εἶναι, Philo, *Legum Allegoriae* 1.10). What is at issue is the intelligible expression of ideas (*Leg. Alleg.* 1.74). Philo is all too familiar with "writer's block": thoughts start to flow, but then one cannot get hold of the next idea to put it into words (*De Migratione Abrahami* 21, 35).

Why do we need to appeal to those other and different uses of ἑρμηνεύω and its compound form διερμηνεύω, which denote *translation* or *interpretation* when the meaning identified here utterly coheres with Paul's argument? There is no "interpreter" standing by. Paul declares that **the person who prophesies is of greater importance than the one who speaks in tongues unless** some specific condition is fulfilled: the tongue speaker who is overwhelmed with the presence and love of God to the extent that praise and prayer flow forth in inarticulate sounds uttered by the tongue (γλῶσσα) finds that, after all, he or she can **put into words** the ground of praise, prayer, joy, or longing, and thereby **the church community** as a whole can similarly **receive** (λάβῃ) this public ministry of **building up** (ἵνα ἡ ἐκκλησία οἰκοδομὴν λάβῃ).

This understanding of these verses has recently been attacked by Christopher Forbes.[106] Forbes concedes that the meaning **to put into words** occurs in "a reasonable number of cases," and indeed the 1979 article cites numerous examples where *translate* will not fit, and where *interpret* misses the point. Yet in a way reminiscent of approaches before the 1961 work of James Barr, Forbes appeals to Dunn's view that "to explain," "to translate," or "to interpret" is "the basic meaning of the word."[107] He then argues that even if, as I claim, up to three-quarters of the uses of διερμηνεύω in Philo mean **to put into words**, if we survey uses of ἑρμηνεύω without the διά prefix, the proportion is reversed. However, (i) Paul shows that he is using ἑρμηνεύω with a nuance that is synonymous with διερμηνεύω in these verses (cf. 14:5, 13, 27, 28, διερμηνεύω and διερμηνευτής); and (ii) it is only necessary for our argument to conclude that both English meanings may in principle apply, and that contextual considerations in the light of the Corinthian situation and Paul's argument become decisive for a judgment between them.

104. Ibid., 21.

105. Philo, *Quod Deterius Potiori Insidiari Soleat* 15, 16; cf. Thiselton, "The 'Interpretation' of Tongues," 20-25.

106. Forbes, *Prophecy and Inspired Speech,* "Thiselton's Challenge," 65-72.

107. Ibid., 65; cf. Dunn, *Jesus and the Spirit,* 247; cf. J. Barr, *The Semantics of Biblical Language* (Oxford: Oxford University Press, 1961), 36-39, 133-35, and esp. 163-66 on the fallacy of "basic" or "fundamental" meanings abstracted from specific contexts.

On the exegetical issues Forbes acknowledges that we cannot allow the controversial interpretations of Acts 2 to determine our interpretation of 1 Corinthians 12–14. Quite apart from issues about the perspectives of Luke and Paul, since virtually all the diaspora Jews present in Jerusalem on the day of Pentecost would know Greek renders problematic what kind of "translation" is at issue, and in any case it is presented not as miraculous *speech (the speakers were perceived to be under the influence of alcohol)* but as miraculous *hearing* or *understanding*. However, he fails to address the issue of how speaking in tongues relates to "translation" if it is addressed to God as praise and prayer, and not as a "message" to be decoded and transmitted. He also fails to explain why such a precious gift of "translation" did not play a wider role among those wrestling with missionary proclamation to other cultures, or (if we are permitted to cite claims made in our own era) the gift of tongues (if it *were* to involve "translation") is withheld from seminary students learning Greek. The traditional understanding, represented in extreme form in NRSV's *unless someone interprets,* imposes onto the epistle an ecclesial tradition of assumptions which does not allow Paul to speak for himself. The very insertion of *someone* into the Greek indicates the lengths to which some will go to sustain a specific interpretative tradition.

On *speaking in tongues* as a welling up of pre-conscious yearnings of praise, glory, joy or longing, see Notes in detail above under 12:10, with particular reference to the work of Stendahl and Theissen. This experience of release and liberation is valued by Paul as a gift of the Spirit. However, its association with the transmission of encoded messages is at the very least not demanded by the text. The one point which Forbes makes with validity in this section of an otherwise helpful study is that it is possible to combine the meaning proposed here with the lexicographical sense of *explaining.* For, as long as we note that most typically tongues are addressed to God, the REB rendering *unless indeed he can explain its meaning, and so help to build up the community* retains close affinities with our own proposals. The use of *interprets,* by contrast (NIV, NJB, KJV/AV), generates a signal which has become tied in modern thought to the overly specific exegesis which seduces the NRSV. We may conclude these reflections by noting that recently Gordon Fee, writing from an explicitly Pentecostal perspective, openly and courageously acknowledges that whether "tongues" constitute an actual earthly language "is a moot point, but the overall evidence suggests no," and that whether today's "charismatic phenomena" replicate those of the Pauline churches is also "moot and probably irrelevant. There is simply no way to know."[108] Certainly, he concludes, tongues are directed to God, and Paul holds their private use in high regard.[109] In our earlier Note we allude to some movement of emphasis among certain Pentecostal writers themselves, not least on "Pentecostal hermeneutics."

ii. The Uselessness of Unintelligible Noise: Four Examples (14:6-12)

Paul now introduces a series of examples to substantiate his theme. As we have noted above, Margaret Mitchell notes the regularity with which Paul appeals to "what profits" (cf. 13:3 in this main section) as part of a strategy of deliberative

---

108. Fee, *Paul, the Spirit and the People of God,* 169 and 170.
109. Ibid., 161 and 169.

rhetoric, and this coheres, as she also observes, with the use of examples drawn from personal behavior and from life (cf. 11:1).[110] While attention to rhetoric has become fashionable, relatively few writers have taken up H. M. Gale's neglected work on Paul's use of analogy.[111] Paul uses many more analogies, models, and illustrative or creative pictures than those who portray him as a more abstract thinker recognize. Here he instantiates his argument by a picture of his arrival at Corinth, only to utter inarticulate noises; and a second picture of a melody in which varied pitch becomes confused and hence unrecognized, and a bugle sound where rhythm and/or pitch is so unintelligible as a signal that it cannot promote appropriate action.[112] A fourth example is the experience of language barriers.

6 The translation of νῦν δέ as **Well now** reflects Héring's careful comment that the phrase is neither adversative nor used in a conclusive sense but to mean "'well now', i.e., 'let us look at the facts and take a concrete example.'"[113] Paul's examples are entirely hypothetical scenarios which remain unfulfilled: ἐὰν ἔλθω is an example of the aorist subjunctive used as "third class condition, supposable case."[114] This is well captured by REB's *Suppose, my friends, that when I come to you . . .* , which we have adopted on grounds of grammar, syntax, and meaning. **In terms of** conveys the adverbial mode denoted by ἐν: "The ἐν expresses the form in which the λαλεῖν takes place."[115] **What shall I profit you** (τί ὑμᾶς ὠφελήσω) takes a double accusative, which is by no means rare. ἀποκάλυψις has already been discussed with reference to the **disclosure** or *revealing* of the Lord at the last day (see under 1:7). Although in politics and in the media the term which most closely reflects the Greek, namely unveiling, has once again come into vogue, this use is more usually applied to announcements of governmental, political, or commercial strategy. Conversely, we have avoided *revelation* because it now carries a dead weight of theological and philosophical controversy. **Disclosure** seems to combine the force and relative innocence which the word would carry at Corinth, leaving entirely open whether it also carries some "technical" sense in the context of worship, which remains open to question (see below on 14:26; 14:30). 14:26 is the only other occurrence of the noun in our epistle together with 1:7 and 14:6 (the verb occurs at 2:10, 13 and 14:30).

We have already discussed the force of γνῶσις extensively (see under 1:5; 8:1, 7, 10, 11; 12:8; 13:2, 8). These nine occurrences, together with six in 2 Corinthians (2:14; 4:6; 6:6; 8:7; 10:5; 11:6) compare with only three in Romans, one in Philippians, none in Galatians, and one in Colossians, i.e., this term mat-

---

110. Mitchell, *Paul and the Rhetoric of Reconciliation,* 20-60, esp. 58-59.
111. Gale, *The Use of Analogy in the Letters of Paul.*
112. Ibid., 129-34, esp. 130-31.
113. Héring, *First Epistle,* 147. Meyer's "But so" is hardly idiomatic (*Epistles,* 2:6); cf. Collins, *now, then* (*First Cor,* 494).
114. Robertson, *Epistles,* 4:181.
115. Robertson and Plummer, *First Epistle,* 308.

tered greatly at Corinth. Hence Paul's insistence that inarticulate sounds could not convey γνῶσις would have been especially sharp and poignant to these addressees. In this context the term denotes *cognitive* **knowledge**, so prized in 8:1-11 by "the strong" at Corinth, and REB's looser *enlightenment* conveys the cultural flavor. On **prophetic speech** or *prophecy* see the Extended Note above at 14:3. The inclusion of **teaching** (διδαχή) confirms the point that one spiritual gift cannot be permitted to militate against others which are "for the common good" (12:7-11; see on 28-30, where **teachers** [v. 28] follow *apostles* and *prophets*). Paul's first example (a supposed visit for a purpose) now leads to a second.

7 We follow BAGD, BDF, Jeremias, Héring, and Fee (against Weiss, Edwards, Allo, and several others) in understanding ὅμως (which in non-Pauline texts means *nevertheless* or *all the same*) to represent ὁμῶς, **similarly**.[116] BDF point out that Paul uses this word only twice (here and in Gal 3:15) where οὕτως also follows suggesting "the earlier ὁμῶς 'equally,' and it is therefore to be translated . . . 'likewise.'"[117] As Héring reminds us, accents would occur neither in Pauline texts nor in such early uncials as p[46] and A, and even if ὁμῶς is of an earlier date, the consistency of the two rare uses in Paul suggest that his employment of the adverb remains distinctive, equivalent to ὁμοίως.

The syntax is ambivalent. διδόντα . . . πῶς is usually understood as a nominative active present participle governing not only φωνήν but also leading to the πῶς clause. However, Paul's deliberative style of rhetoric in these verses may permit us to regard it as functioning perhaps as an accusative of reference in apposition to τὰ ἄψυχα, as our translation may suggest. This allows us to understand πῶς as introducing a rhetorical question, which sustains the incisive rhetorical style better than a statement. The privative form ἄψυχα occurs only here in the NT, but regularly means inanimate in old literature and by its negation of ψυχή, life. Although αὐλός strictly denotes flute (as in LXX) and κιθάρα means either lyre or early harp (as in Philo, Josephus, and Rev 5:8; 14:2), the point here is that the principle applies equally in the case of wind instruments and stringed instruments.[118] Collins's elaborate theory that Paul may use *"life-less"* (cf. *inanimate*) to denote synagogue instruments not in current use is too narrow and too speculative, and bypasses the more usual meaning of the word.[119] It serves to offer a contrast with the two examples of interpersonal communication.

---

116. BAGD, 569; BDF, 234, sect. 450 (2), citing also Wilke on *1 Clement;* Héring, *First Epistle,* 147, in some detail; J. Jeremias, "ὅμως, 1 Kor 14:7; Gal 3:15," *ZNW* 52 (1961): 127-28; Fee, *First Epistle,* 663, n. 20. For other views, see Weiss, *Der erste Korintherbrief,* 324, including n. 1; Edwards, *First Epistle,* 360; and Allo, *Première Épitre,* 358, although he concedes the difficulty and his comment is brief; also Meyer, *Epistles,* 2:7-8.

117. BDF, col. 2. Chrysostom understands ὅμως in a concessive sense, "although they are inanimate instruments."

118. BAGD, 121 and 432; see further Wolff, *Der erste Brief,* 330.

119. Collins, *First Cor,* 495-96.

J. D. Moores pays particular attention to these verses (14:7-8) as a classic discussion of "the different ways in which semiosis comes to misfire."[120] He observes, "It is remarkable that Paul thinks of musical sound in connection with meaning at all."[121] In the first parallel (v. 7) semiosis is envisaged in terms of "recognition," but this depends on the principle of "difference" (διαστολή), as Ferdinand de Saussure would enunciate it in his *Course in General Linguistics* first published in 1913: "The semantic scope of γινῶσκω, moreover, allows for a reading that would find him [Paul] envisaging semiosis as recognition."[122] Moores rightly perceives that most English VSS miss the point by translating the Greek simply as *know what is being played* (NRSV, NIV, KJV/AV, Fee; as against **recognized** in NJB and Knox). διαστολή regularly means **difference** or *distinction* in LXX, Philo, and other writers including the papyri, and the nuance of *differential* (which then enters legal and accounting records) permits BAGD to translate "clear distinction" in this verse, and to provide grounds for our intensive **distinct differences**.[123] **Difference** (French *différence*) has become a technical term in semiotics from Saussure to J. Derrida, and makes precisely Paul's point, as Moores notes, "remarkably."

Robertson and Plummer miss and distort Paul's meaning when they attribute "difference" as that of different melodies "to guide people to be joyous, sorrowful, or devout" respectively at festivals, funerals, and worship.[124] Even Fee's comment about failure to produce "a pleasing melody" misses the heart of the issue.[125] The point is not that notes are produced badly or inappropriately, but that untuned strings or overblown wind produces mere noise where there is no "difference" in Saussure's sense of linguistic or semiotic "difference" as the very basis of conveying *anything* articulate or communicable. Prior to Saussure's work, Meyer's commentary perceives this point. Φωνή, he argues, is regularly used of the "voice" of musical instruments (e.g., Sir 1:16; 1 Macc 5:31; Plato, *Timaeus* 47C; *Politica* 3.397A, μουσικὴ φωνή) but an instrumental "voice" without *intervals* (*ex intervallis sonorum,* Cicero, *Tusculanae Disputationes* 1.18.41) is mere *noise* or mere *sound* (unmodulated φωνή, which is not actual "music" at all), and it cannot be "**recognized**."[126] Hence Meyer concludes that "the analogy in v. 7 would be unsuitable, if Paul had been thinking of *foreign languages,* since there would not have lacked the διαστολή of the sounds. . . . It is its *distinctness* [in the sense of Saussure's "difference"] . . . in virtue of which it expresses a melody."[127]

120. J. D. Moores, *Wrestling with Rationality in Paul,* SNTSMS 82 (Cambridge: Cambridge University Press, 1995), 135; cf. 132-38.

121. Ibid., 136.

122. Ibid.; cf. F. de Saussure, *Cours de linguistique générale* (Paris: Payot, 1978); the English translation is acknowledged to have deficiencies; see further Thiselton, *New Horizons in Hermeneutics,* 83-87; and *The Two Horizons,* 115-34.

123. BAGD, 188; cf. MM, 154.

124. Robertson and Plummer, *First Epistle,* 308.

125. Fee, *First Epistle,* 664.

126. Meyer, *Epistles to the Corinthians,* 2:8.

127. Ibid., 9.

Edwards rightly concludes: "διαστολήν . . . used as synonymous with διάστημα, a musical 'interval' . . . the difference in pitch between two sounds."[128]

8 Paul now provides a third example. Again, the issue is not that the **sound** of **the trumpet** (REB, NJB) or the *bugle* (NRSV; σάλπιγξ) is simply unclear (ἄδηλον) in the sense of being faint or below high performance, but that *without differentiations of pitch, rhythm, or length of note* the sound is mere noise rather than a *communicative* **signal to prepare for battle**. Our translation of ἄδηλον . . . φωνήν as **a sound which is ambivalent as a signal** is an accurate translation based on lexicographical research, not a paraphrase or gloss. For Grimm-Thayer's 4th ed.'s rendering of ἄδηλος as *obscure* (also *indistinct*) reflects the alpha-privative of δῆλος, *clear, evident,* which in turn belongs to the cognate verb δηλόω, which means not only *to make manifest,* but also, more frequently, as in 1 Cor 1:11, *"to give one to understand, to indicate, signify"* (cf. Col 1:8; Heb 12:27; 2 Pet 1:14), or *to point to* (1 Pet 1:11), i.e., to *serve as a communicative act* or **signal**.[129]

That the precise force of ἄδηλος depends largely on contextual considerations also is evident from Moulton-Milligan's restriction of the adjectival form to only two occurrences in the papyri, while they cite the positive adjectival form δῆλος as relating primarily, or most often, to clear communication, e.g., of the intention or scope of laws (*Papyrus Oxyrhynchus* 8:1101), although again "the word is by no means common."[130] On the other hand, the verb form δηλόω is indeed common in the papyri, and regularly means *to communicate clearly* or *to convey an intelligible, articulate message* (*P. Oxy.* 2:237:6, AD 186; 10:1293, AD 117-38). The meaning "let me know" (i.e., "send a signal") is "typical of a great many occurrences."[131] Whether in personal, social, institutional (as in 14:8), or legal communications, "it is largely used . . . to denote 'informing.'"[132] Hence BAGD's translation of this verse as *give out an indistinct sound* reflects only part of the semantic range of the word group, although this is followed by most English VSS (NRSV, *distinct;* REB, NIV, *clear*). On the other hand, NJB has utterly rightly and properly *a call which is unrecognizable.*[133] Louw and Nida also consider both meanings of δηλόω and categorize ἄδηλος as either *not evident* or as *unmarked* and *unperceived by any of the senses.* (They compare "unmarked graves," Luke 11:44, as those which convey no **signal** of their existence.)[134]

The apodosis of the conditional clause, expressed as a question, τίς

---

128. Edwards, *First Epistle,* 361.

129. Grimm-Thayer, *Greek-English Lexicon of the NT,* 11 and 131; also Schrage, *Der erste Brief,* 3:393.

130. MM, 9 and 144.

131. Ibid., 144, col. 2.

132. Ibid.

133. BAGD, 16. NJB improves significantly on JB's "no one can be sure which call. . . ."

134. Louw and Nida, *Greek-English Lexicon of the NT,* 1:25 (24-95); cf. also 1:340 (28-42) and 2:57.

παρασκευάσεται εἰς πόλεμον; reinforces the point that intelligible Christian utterance has operative currency which changes attitudes and conduct on the part of others (as well as that of the speaker). Again this highlights the "profitless" nature of tongues *in public* when the concern embraces effects upon *others*. What the trumpeter does when "off-duty" is another matter. Moores relates this to semiotic impacts on "dispositions" to respond.[135]

9 The key word is εὔσημος, **readily intelligible**. Our translation is supported by BAGD, who propose *easily recognizable* or *clear* as the routine meaning but recognize that 14:9 denotes **intelligible** *speech*.[136] The compound adjective εὐ, *well*, **readily**, with σῆμα, *sign*, which belongs to the word group σημαίνω, *to communicate, to signify*, and σημεῖον, *sign, distinguishing mark* (by which something is known), σημειόω, *to mark, to note down*, vividly uses what semanticists call a "transparent" term to indicate the communicative or *semiotic* principle.[137] Communicative acts of speech entail a transactive engagement between speaker, writer or "sender," and addressee, hearer, or "receiver." If the receiver cannot comprehend (γινώσκω) the content of what is being said (τὸ λαλούμενον), communication does not occur. Paul incisively sums up modern communicative and hermeneutical theory in a terse, succinct aphorism, ahead of his time. In such a case, the sender is merely **speaking into empty air** (εἰς ἀέρα). The speech-event is fruitless and pointless, except as self-affirmation or as a benefit to the speaker at the expense of generating negative effects for others (vv. 4a and 11).[138] Fee compares the idiom to "talking to the wind."[139] To be **comprehended** or *recognized* and *understood*, "vocables [must be] ordered, articulate, and conformed to usage. Now this is what the Corinthian Glossolalia was *not*" (Findlay's italics).[140]

10-11 Paul now reaches his fourth example, drawn from the communication barrier which exists where, even when an intelligible language *is* used, if the speaker's and addressee's languages are not known to each other, each will effectively remain **an alien** (βάρβαρος) to the other. A long tradition of modern commentators from Meyer to Conzelmann, Fee, and Wolff suggest that Paul uses γένη φωνῶν rather than γλῶσσα to denote foreign languages, in order to avoid confusion with the "tongues" of glossolalia.[141] This experience of being and feeling **alien** or *foreign* (neither is one understood nor does one understand the language around one) is a common theme in several writers. Heinrici cites Ovid's complaint, *"barbarus hic ergo sum, quia*

---

135. Moores, *Wrestling with Rationality*, 137 and 189, n. 23.
136. BAGD, 326.
137. Ibid., 747-49; also Schrage, *Der erste Brief*, 3:393.
138. Cf. Meyer, *Epistles to the Corinthians*, 2:10, "uselessness."
139. Fee, *First Epistle*, 644, n. 33.
140. Findlay, *Expositor's Greek Testament*, 3:905.
141. Meyer, *Epistles to the Corinthians*, 2:11; Conzelmann, *1 Cor*, 256; Fee, *First Epistle*, 665, n. 36; Wolff, *Der erste Brief*, 331.

non intelligor ulli . . . der Fremdheit und Roheit. . . ."[142] Paul develops this into a major point when he expounds and applies the experience of "not belonging" to which Isa 28:11-12 witnesses as a sign of judgment when he argues in 14:21-22 that this experience should not be illegitimately imposed upon believers who *do* belong and *should feel "at home"* in the worship of the Christian community.

In v. 10 ἄφωνος may mean "without language" (with Conzelmann) in purely lexicographical terms, but this misses the sharp focus of the argument. However, the most probable force in the syntax and grammar is to understand the aorist optative of τυγχάνω in a conditional protasis as **it may be**, carrying the force of rhetorical anticipation of a defense of "foreign" (i.e., unintelligible) speech: *even if it happens that.* Paul further grants that every language uses **sound**, i.e., *makes a noise.* However, *this is no defense of making unintelligible noises in corporate worship.* For the example proves the opposite: when people find themselves amid a babel of unintelligible sound, what strikes them is both their own feeling of **being an alien**, where they do not feel "comfortable" or "at home," and indeed fellow believers seem somehow **alien** to them when in fact they are brothers and sisters in the Lord. A built-in "wrongness" characterizes the whole situation in both subjective terms (perceptions and feelings) and objective reality (artificial barriers have been unwittingly set up). Paul will press the point with biblical warrant in vv. 21-22. There may even be a further nuance of the irritating effect of "foreign" speech in the very word βάρ-βάρ, as in Eng. *"Blah-blah-blah."*[143]

12 The syntax of οὕτως καὶ ὑμεῖς has been construed in more than one way, but most amount to Fee's rendering "So it is with you."[144] Meyer sees the ὑμεῖς as related more closely to the disasters of the previous examples than to the eagerness for spiritual experiences, i.e., you are in this absurd situation, so take fresh stock and reorder your priorities.[145] Most relate it to the following clauses. Hence we adopt a translation which leaves open both possibilities, as well as the emphatic nominative οὕτως, **you yourselves**. Since οὕτως conveys the sense of *thus, so,* usually referring to what precedes (but occasionally to what follows), **in this situation** serves to link "this-ly," "in this manner" most closely with all the examples that precede, but not exclusively so.[146] It provides a further link, even if a weaker one, with what follows.

142. Heinrici, *Das erste Sendschreiben,* 438, n.; cf. Ovid, *Tristia* 5.10. *Barbarus* was used as a pejorative term by the Romans and Greeks of those who were ignorant of Graeco-Roman languages and cultures, but earlier it was the Egyptians who described those who did not speak their language as "barbarous."

143. Conzelmann rightly construes the dative ἐν ἐμοί as meaning "in my eyes," and reminds us that the onomatopoeic or semantically transparent term βάρβαρος (i.e., a speaker whose utterances sound like *bar-bar* [Eng. *blah-blah-blah*]) means "gibberish" (*1 Cor,* 236). On the use of the word see n. 7.

144. Fee, *First Epistle,* 665; *God's Empowering Presence,* 226.

145. Meyer, *Epistles to the Corinthians,* 2:11-12.

146. See BAGD, 597-98, for the emphasis and for examples.

ζηλόω regularly means *to be* **eager** *for* (as in our translation of its second occurrence in this verse), but also to be deeply **concerned about** when the object is personal or has close personal associations.[147] As we noted above, in LXX it translates Heb. קנא *(qinnē'), to burn with zeal, to become heated* (see above on 13:4 and 14:1). Here in the first clause **a burning concern** probably best conveys the force of the Greek. A more serious problem is that whereas it normally governs an accusative, in this verse it is followed by the genitive πνευμάτων, *spirits* (not even πνευματικῶν, *spiritual things*). It is unlikely that even the Corinthians sought inspiration from a plurality of spirits; rather, they sought a plurality of manifestations (as many as possible) from God's Holy Spirit. Conzelmann rightly perceives this as a concern about *phenomena*.[148] We try to convey the mood and content by translating neither *gifts of the Spirit* (REB) nor *spiritual gifts* (NRSV, NIV), since these routine or regular phrases do not signal the strange and unexpected plural of πνεῦμα, but (following NJB's *spiritual powers*), **powers of the Spirit**. It is best to retain **Spirit** wherever possible, since Paul never speaks of "spirituality" in the sense widely used today without implicitly alluding to the Holy Spirit as what makes "spirituality" *spiritual*. It is not a disposition of the human mind or heart, but, as Paul and the Corinthian Christians would agree together, a formation, gift, or phenomenon which reflects the agency, operation, and presence of the Holy Spirit.

Where Paul diverges from the Corinthians is in his insistence that since the Spirit is also the Spirit of Christ, and since Christ gave himself *for others,* any claims about "spirituality" or **powers of the Spirit** become problematic if they have more to do with self-enhancement than with the welfare and benefit of others. Hence all this **burning concern** about **powers of the Spirit** must be redirected into a more Christlike **eagerness** for the **building up** (on οἰκοδομή see above, e.g., 8:1; 14:4) of the **church community** as a corporate whole (cf. the body-of-Christ language in 12:12-30, esp. 12:27).[149] The four examples of 14:6-11 have been sharpened into an incisive and irrefutable application in v. 12.

iii. Communicative Intelligibility and the Use of the Mind in the Context of Public Worship (14:13-19)

13-14 Collins rightly stresses the strong force of διό, *wherefore,* or **hence**, as gathering up the point of the previous examples about intelligible communication.[150] In order to avoid repetition, on διερμηνεύω meaning **to put into words**

---

147. Cf. BAGD, 338; Grimm-Thayer, *Lexicon,* 271.

148. Conzelmann, *1 Cor,* 237: "The application of the examples to the *phenomena* is followed by their application to the Spirit-inspired *church*" (his italics). Cf. Lang, *Die Briefe,* 193: "*die auf sensationelle, ekstatische Geistesäusserungen. . . .*"

149. Strobel, *Der erste Brief,* 217; Wolff, *Der erste Brief,* 331.

150. Collins, *First Cor,* 509.

see above in 14:5. In spite of the insistence of many on trying to force τις, *someone,* into the text at 14:5 (e.g., Héring, against the proper judgment of Heinrici and others that no second party is involved), *all the main English VSS appear to ascribe the act* of **putting into words**, or in most VSS *interpreting* (AV/KJV, NRSV, REB, NJB), *to the one who prays in a tongue.*[151] Here Paul uses the singular γλώσσῃ, but he seems to oscillate between singular and plural without any clear difference of nuance. (We normally reproduce in translation the number used in the Greek.) **Should pray** is the idiomatic way of conveying the force of the Greek third person present imperative προσευχέσθω. This verse reinforces that even when this is (mis)understood as assuming some second act by an "interpreter" of tongues, this is not a "message *to* the congregation" but an act of **praying** to God. The present subjunctive after ἵνα "often serves as a periphrasis for the infinitive" but may perhaps include a hint of a possible potential on the part of the subject or agent of the verb.[152]

"TONGUES" AND COMMUNICATIVE LANGUAGE

Our main treatment of "Species of Tongues and Their Intelligible Articulation" (970-88) offered a discussion under five subheadings in which we considered: (1) tongues as angelic speech; (2) tongues as miraculous power to speak other languages; (3) tongues as liturgical or archaic phrases; (4) tongues as "ecstatic" speech, and (5) tongues as the language of the pre-conscious released in "sighs too deep for words" from the heart. The argument of 14:1-25, however, addresses further considerations which supplement an evaluation of (2) and (5).

Whatever conclusion is proposed about the precise phenomenology of speaking in tongues (and Fee reminds us that this can never be more than speculative, without confirmation or direct evidence), v. 14 appears to endorse the arguments of G. Theissen and K. Stendahl that these utterances well up, in experiences of wonder and praise as the Holy Spirit releases inhibitions and censors, in ways which reflect pre-conscious, pre-cognitive yearnings, sighings, or "building up" which evade cognitive objectification and formulation.[153] This understanding is not incompatible with Käsemann's view that these "ejaculations of prayer are interpreted, at least by the Pauline congregation [i.e., not necessarily by Paul], as speaking with heavenly tongues."[154] All three writers, together with the Pentecostal writer F. D. Macchia, asso-

---

151. Cf. Heinrici, *Das erste Sendschreiben* 433: *"ausgenommen wenn er dolmetscht. . . . Die Dolmetschung erst ermöglicht für die Glossenrede dieselbe Wirkung und giebt ihr denselben Werth, welcher die Prophetie auszeichnet."*

152. BDF, 186, sect. 369; cf. also 187; and N. Turner, *A Grammar of NT Greek,* 3: *Syntax,* 106-8. More especially also Thiselton, "The 'Interpretation' of Tongues? A New Suggestion in the Light of Greek Usage in Philo and Josephus," 15-36; attacked by C. Forbes, *Prophecy and Inspired Speech,* 63-72.

153. Stendahl, "Glossolalia: The NT Evidence," in his *Paul among Jews and Gentiles,* 109-24; Theissen, *Psychological Aspects,* 267-342; cf. Fee, *Paul, the Spirit and the People of God,* 170.

154. Käsemann, "The Cry for Liberty in the Worship of the Church," in his *Perspectives on Paul,* 132; cf. 122-37.

ciate the experience with the intercession prompted by the Holy Spirit "with sighs too deep for words" (στεναγμοὶ ἀλάλητοι) in Rom 8:26-27.[155] Like the acclamatory cry *"Abba,"* this results from a co-witnessing with the Spirit (συμμαρτυρεῖν τῷ πνεύματι, Rom 8:15-16) Käsemann insists that, like the ἄρρητα ῥήματα of 2 Cor 12:4, these are "wordless" not in the sense of "unspoken" but "unspeakable; they are not directly re-producible and shroud mysteries in heavenly language."[156]

The cumulative effect of Paul's four examples of a communicative barrier in vv. 6-11 seem to confirm the implausibility of the notion that speaking in tongues takes the form of a foreign language which an "interpreter of tongues" can translate. The first example (v. 6) not only suggests even a lack of potential communicative content, but also the Greek syntax (see exegesis above) is explicated in terms of the second ex-ample (v. 7) in which musical instruments produce *noise* rather than *notes of a given pitch.* It is not that there is a melody which cannot (yet) be recognized; there is an ab-sence of the very intervals between the pitch of notes (see exegesis above) which *constitutes* them *as "music"* rather than raw sound. Paul anticipates modern language theory that communication presupposes *"difference"* (from Saussure) onward). The third example (v. 8) underlines and develops the point: it is *not* that an unknown sys-tem generates a signal not yet understood, but that nothing counts as a *signal* in prin-ciple. The fourth example (vv. 9-11) comes nearest to suggesting *xenolalia,* but the point of it rests in *inarticulate expression* which does *not* constitute a *communicative act.* Indeed, it has the effect of making Christians within the family feel *alien* within their home, like "outsiders."[157]

Paul neither criticizes nor questions the authenticity of speaking in tongues (especially in the sense of v. 5 above and vv. 18-19). However, he requests *either* of *two* conditions: *either* (a) "private" use (see exegesis of vv. 16-23), i.e., outside the context of public worship; *or* (b) effective prayer that the speaker will be able to express in ar-ticulate communicative speech the wondrous perception of God or the gospel which is otherwise "too deep for words." *No "second" agent* is envisaged; *a second "gift" is in-deed needed,* i.e., the gift of being able *to put it into words.*

The first part of Käsemann's claim seems to cohere with 14:13. However, neither Rom 8:15-16, 26-27 nor 1 Cor 14:5, 13 explicitly describes "a heavenly language"; only that a genuine insight which generates praise exceeds cognitive or conceptual ex-pression. The tongue-speaker may need to step back and reflect, and with the Spirit's grace could benefit the whole community by findings words which, even if they re-main inadequate, at least allow the *corporate* expression of praise which the insight or experience generates, since this fulfills the purpose of a corporate "coming together" for *common* worship (κοινωνία). Käsemann is on stronger ground when he argues that "the context of glossolalic prayer" precisely explains the specific sense in which be-

155. Ibid., 125-31; Macchia, "Sighs Too Deep for Words," 47-73; and "Groans Too Deep for Words," 149-73.

156. Käsemann, "The Cry for Liberty," 130. See further on 12:8-10 above, and, e.g., Schatzmann, *A Pauline Theology of Charismata,* 442-43; Fitzmyer, *Romans,* 518-19 (on 8:26); and Dunn, *Romans 1–8,* 492-93.

157. See J. F. M. Smit, "Tongues and Prophecy: Deciphering 1 Cor 14:22," *Bib* 75 (1994): 175-90; Thiselton, "The 'Interpretation' of Tongues?" 15-36; Macchia, "Sighs Too Deep for Words," 47-73; Aune, *Prophecy,* 19-21; Lang, *Die Briefe,* 204; exegetical literature on 14:1-25 in footnotes, and esp. the discussion of the subject at 12:8.

lievers "do not know" how to pray in Romans 8. The urge, yearning, and direction is there, but as yet it cannot be formulated cognitively. This, we conclude, is why some have the gift of tongues (which liberate and release innermost sighs to God), and others have a *further* gift of enabling which allows them to reflect and to put the content of the experience which had generated the inarticulate sign of the Spirit at work into an articulate communicative signal from which all could benefit. Presumably only those who were not content to use tongues only in private were those whom Paul specifically enjoined to pray for this further gift, or otherwise to remain self-disciplined in public worship. Either course of action would help others, but not the current practice which Paul addresses. Thus the theme of *the regulation of worship* begins to emerge from here on.[158]

The history of Western philosophical and Christian theological tradition makes it misleading to translate τὸ πνεῦμά μου as *my spirit,* although in abstraction from cultural traditions this reflects Paul's choice of expression. As Robert Jewett points out, already in 1 and 2 Thessalonians and in Galatians Paul had opposed νοῦς/νουθετέω terminology, i.e., terms to do *with the use of the mind* in a polemical context where he felt impelled to rectify a lack of common sense brought about by "pneumatic enthusiasts."[159] A lack of cognitive reflection had led to "the enthusiasts' claim that the parousia had already come"; this had shaken them from a right mind (ἀπὸ τοῦ νοός, 2 Thess 2:2).[160] 1 Thess 5:14 is linked with this theme, while excesses of zeal or antinomianism among the Galatians led Paul to address them as ἀνόητοι, *not using their minds* (Gal 3:1).[161] In such contexts τὸ πνεῦμα, *spirit,* does service as standing in semantic opposition to νοῦς, *mind.* Nevertheless, today it is agreed widely, perhaps almost universally, that τὸ πνεῦμα in the major Paul epistles carries a largely negative role of being distinguished from some "other" when it is used as a human capacity. Paul prefers to reserve τὸ πνεῦμα for the Spirit of God, and to use πνευματικός for that which appertains to the Holy Spirit. Even 1 Cor 2:11 serves to distinguish an immanental Stoic view of "spirit" from the transcendent Holy Spirit who proceeds ἐκ τοῦ θεοῦ, *from God.*

As Jewett demonstrates, in its strictly human sense, the history of research into the meaning of the human spirit in Paul has become entangled in philosophical idealism, which has elevated it as a "point of contact" with God's Spirit in un-Pauline ways and with existentialist approaches which have imported an alien individualism into Paul.[162] We need a term which is readily recognized to denote a sphere or mode of human personhood which may be associated with the deepest work and activity of God as Holy Spirit but also stands in contrast to *mind.* In an earlier draft I translated *heart,* but since Paul does use καρδία elsewhere, and not here, this seems overly bold, although it conveys the mood and the issue. All in all, the best compromise may be **my innermost spiritual being.** This risks a misunderstanding in the direction of Plato or of Idealist or Cartesian dualism, but takes up Paul's word and seeks to protect it with appropriately qualifying indicators of Paul's meaning.

---

158. As Fee points out, *God's Empowering Presence,* 228, and *First Epistle,* 669.

159. Jewett, *Paul's Anthropological Terms,* 369; cf. 367-74.

160. Ibid., 368.

161. Ibid., 373-74.

162. Cf. Jewett's wide-ranging discussion in *Paul's Anthropological Terms,* 167-200 and 451-53. Barrett discusses three possible meanings of *my spirit,* but concludes that "Paul's language lacks clarity" because he is compressing several ideas in a short space (*First Epistle* 320).

Paul's use of ἄκαρπος precisely clinches his point. However, many translations spoil it with such renderings as *my mind is barren* (REB), *my mind is unfruitful* (NIV) or *my mind derives no fruit from it* (NJB). As Käsemann insists, Paul's point is *not* that *the tongue-speaker* misses out, but that the *church community* misses out.[163] Of the major translations NRSV's *my mind is unproductive* is best at this point since *produce* can serve others. The same might be said of Collins's translation *useless*. However, it may perhaps still more clearly convey Paul's logic to translate **but my mind produces no fruit from it**, i.e., means by which to benefit others. Käsemann concludes concerning Paul's correction of the individualism that marked assumptions about tongues at Corinth, "It is impossible to demythologize the *theologia gloriae* [of Corinth] into the *theologia viatorum* [of Paul] more thoroughly."[164]

15 Paul argues equally against uncritical "enthusiasm," uncritical "renewal" traditions, or uncritical mysticism on one side and against gnostics, theological theorists, or any who seek to intellectualize Christian faith into a mere belief system on the other. Christians are confronted *not by an either . . . or . . . but by a both . . . and* — **my deepest spiritual being** (τῷ πνεύματι, repeated twice, taking up its further use in v. 14) **but also** (προσεύξομαι δὲ καί . . .) **my mind** (τῷ νοΐ). The connecting phrase τί οὖν ἐστιν; links the logic with the previous verse, almost certainly with the sense of **So what follows?** (Cf. Conzelmann, *What is the conclusion from this?*)[165] Strictly, however, the Greek allows a less specifically consequential force, i.e., *what does this amount to?* REB's and NJB's *What then?* seems too abrupt; while NRSV's and NIV's *What should I do then?* tends to go beyond the Greek in attempting to explicate one aspect of the question.

For the translation of πνεῦμα as **my deepest spiritual being** see on v. 14. We have replaced **innermost** (v. 14) with **deepest** (v. 15a) and **depths** (v. 15b) to try to avoid any hint of Platonic or Cartesian dualisms, while retaining **spiritual** in two of the three instances to retain the resonance with πνεῦμα. However, any translation is likely either to leave the meaning unprotected against the assumptions of Western modernity *(my spirit)* or to reflect interpretative judgments about Paul's precise meaning (e.g., BAGD, *"sing praise in spiritual ecstasy and in full possession of one's mental faculties"*).[166] We might have been content with BAGD, were it not for those research articles which explicitly, and with some force, attack the use of the term *ecstasy* in these contexts, partly on the basis of overly hasty associations with Greek religions.[167] Aune usefully explores in what sense we might speak of "altered states of consciousness" rather

163. Käsemann, "The Cry for Liberty," 132; cf. 122-37.
164. Ibid., 136.
165. Conzelmann, *1 Cor,* 233.
166. BAGD, 891 (under ψάλλω).
167. For example, Gundry, "'Ecstatic Utterance' (NEB)?" 299-307; cf. also Forbes, *Prophecy and Inspired Speech* 53-65, 104-6; Aune, *Prophecy,* 20-21, 230; Dunn, *Jesus and the Spirit,* 242-43; C. G. Williams, "Glossolalia as a Religious Phenomenon: Tongues at Pentecost and Corinth," *Religion* 5 (1975): 21.

than the crude, overly broad, and more questionable *ecstasy,* or the bare alternative *ecstatic versus nonecstatic.*[168] However, he here discusses "ancient prophecy" in relation to "vision trance" or "possession trance" as modes of oracular speech, and leaves us with an open question about whether the terms used in social anthropology can assist us. Certainly there is no evidence whatever, as we have regularly urged, that Paul alludes primarily, if at all, to "oracular" speech, and this would be inapplicable to the present passage, which concerns prayer and praise.[169] Arguments about "ecstasy" and "trance" do not take us forward constructively, but may serve to make a negative point. Thus T. Callan argues that Paul's prophetic speech does not involve trance, whereas tongues do, since 1 Corinthians 14 turns on communicative intelligibility.[170] On the other hand, Engelsen's argument that since prophecy and tongues are both subject to conscious controls "one is not more ecstatic than the other" rests on a circular definition of ecstasy.[171] It is best to follow Lang here, whose reference to "inarticulate sound" (v. 15, *in unartikulierten Laute;* cf. vv. 7 and 8) coheres with our view above.[172]

If we are to venture into modern theories, the well-established phenomenon in psychological observation of the distinction between alpha and beta brain waves seems to apply most clearly, since any *critical reflection* at once raises our consciousness from an alpha state. Anyone who suffers from sleepless nights when "churning" problems and who uses some technique for "relaxation" (i.e., reducing beta waves to alpha waves) will know this from experience. Yet even here this offers no more than a hypothetical scenario for first-century Corinth and Paul. As Forbes observes, in 14:13-15 "the speaker in a tongue is, like the listener, unaware of the sense of his or her own utterance. Equally clearly, in Paul's view such utterance is and ought to be under conscious control."[173]

A disastrous move, however, is to confuse πνεῦμα as a noncognitive or "spiritual" human capacity with *Spirit* as the Holy Spirit of God. There are at least two different reasons. First, Pauline specialists generally agree that Platonic or Idealist notions of the human spirit as a point of "divine contact" are alien to Paul and plainly alien to the explicit thrust of 1 Cor 2:10-12. Second, to read this into 14:15 is to fall into the very trap to which the Corinthians and many today fall prey, namely, of associating the operation of the Holy Spirit

168. Aune, *Prophecy,* 19-21.
169. Cf. further R. Wilson, "Prophecy and Ecstasy: A Re-examination," *JBL* 98 (1979): 321-27; Callan, "Prophecy and Ecstasy in Greco-Roman Religion and in Corinthians," 125-40; Carson, *Showing the Spirit,* 77-79; and Poythress, "The Nature of Corinthian Glossolalia: Possible Options," 130-35.
170. Callan, "Prophecy and Ecstasy," 125-40.
171. N. I. J. Engelsen, "Glossolalia and Other Forms of Inspired Speech" (Yale Ph.D. thesis, 1970, cited by Forbes, *Prophecy and Inspired Speech,* 56).
172. Lang, *Die Briefe,* 204.
173. Forbes, *Prophecy and Inspired Speech,* 55, n. 22.

more closely with noncognitive "spontaneous" phenomena than with a self-critical reflection upon the word of God as that which addresses the understanding and thereby transforms the heart (cf. 14:23-25). Contrary to his usually more judicious assessments Fee repeats this disastrous confusion explicitly in his commentary and in his two more recent volumes: "my S/spirit prays."[174] A third factor is noted by Héring and Barrett. Barrett writes that he might have been sympathetic with this understanding, but for the fact that in v. 14 Paul uses the phrase **my** *spirit,* **my innermost spiritual being** (τὸ πνεῦμά μου, v. 14), thereby disengaging the term from *Spirit of God:* "To describe the Holy Spirit as in any sense *mine* is intolerable, and certainly not Pauline" (his italics): it denotes "part of my psychological make-up."[175] Héring is equally emphatic.[176]

Paul declares that being "spiritual," i.e., of the Holy Spirit, occurs "when the Holy Spirit controls both the spirit and the mind."[177] If only the mind is active, everything remains at a theoretical level; if only the heart is active, the door lies open to self-deception and credulity. If both are open to the Holy Spirit, the result can build up the community and bear the fruit (v. 14a) of love for the other. Is it too speculative to see in ψαλῶ (contracted future of ψάλλω) the combination of words and melody that express respectively the praise of mind and heart as a unity?[178] It is easy to imagine Paul encouraging the church today to combine melody that expresses the praise of the heart with words that genuinely reflect an intelligent expression of gospel truth.[179] Robertson and Plummer observe: "It is possible that the ecstatic utterances [or however we understand the term] sometimes took the form of an inarticulate chant, songs without intelligible words or definite melody."[180] The same A. T. Robertson comments elsewhere, "Solos that people do not understand lose more than half their value in church worship."[181] The concern of the Reformers for public intelligibility in worship reflects Paul's stance, and led to their addressing both traditionalists committed to Latin and enthusiasts committed to individual autonomy of expression.

174. Fee, *1 Cor,* 670; *God's Empowering Presence,* 229-30; cf. *Paul, the Spirit and the People of God,* 148.

175. Barrett, *First Epistle,* 320. Conzelmann also translates *my spirit,* but does not exclude a possible allusion to singing "in the Spirit" (*1 Cor,* 233, 238). This may indeed be the net effect, but it cannot be restricted to the first part of each pair of clauses.

176. Héring, *First Epistle,* 150: "*pneuma* cannot mean here "spirit of God." Many commentators fail fully to address this issue, in this case even Schrage. Schrage (*Der erste Brief,* 3:399-400) and Strobel (*Der erste Brief,* 218) focus mainly on Paul's rejection of an either/or here in favor of both . . . and. . . .

177. Kistemaker, *1 Cor,* 491.

178. BAGD, 891, *to sing praise,* as in the LXX, sometimes *in* or *with your heart.* The earlier classical meaning was only *to play,* but the NT uses follow the LXX, *praise* (Eph 5:19).

179. Cf. Lang, *Die Briefe,* 204.

180. Robertson and Plummer, *First Epistle,* 312.

181. Robertson, *Word Epistles,* 4:183.

16 The aorist subjunctive εὐλογήσῃς is read by 𝔭⁴⁶, F, G, K, and L, with Textus Receptus (cf. KJV/AV, *when thou shalt bless*) as against the widespread reading of the present subjunctive εὐλογῇς. As Fee observes, however, changes to the aorist in such constructions do occur, and the present is virtually certain.[182] The UBS 3rd and 4th ed. *Greek New Testament*s adopt the present without serious question.[183]

The syntax and especially the vocabulary have invited controversy. ἐπεὶ ἐὰν εὐλογῇς, **Otherwise, if you bless God**, is straightforward since ἐπεί takes some such meaning as *in that case* or more explicitly **otherwise** before questions implying a negative (as NJB, NRSV, and Weiss).[184] Similarly, while εὐλογέω is seldom used in a religious sense in secular Greek, in the NT it regularly reflects the LXX usage, which in turn translate Heb. בָּרַךְ *(barak),* **to bless** (in contexts of worship) **God**.[185] Blessing God is virtually synonymous with offering a **thanksgiving** in this context, even if theologically **blessing God** may include both *praise* and **thanksgiving**, which are not identical in other contexts.[186]

Controversy continues to bedevil Paul's use of πνεῦμα when it probably refers to the human capacity or disposition that stands in contrast to cognitive apprehension. On the translation **the depths of our being**, see above (under vv. 14 and 15). Since it stands implicitly in contrast to the mind (explicitly later in the verse), the addition of **only** is required to explicate the force of the term πνεῦμα here. However, it is just possible that Paul is now taking up terminology drawn from Corinth about "uttering blessings in the Spirit." πνεῦμα might therefore denote the Spirit of God if, and only if, Paul draws the term from Corinth, i.e., it is placed in quotation marks. We use square brackets to indicate that this cannot be excluded but is improbable.

The most controversial discussion arises over the meaning of ὁ ἀναπληρῶν τὸν τόπον τοῦ ἰδιώτου, which we have translated in broad and open-ended terms as **the uninitiated person** (with NJB and Héring; cf. NRSV, *anyone in the position of an outsider* [Collins broadly similarly]; REB, *an ordinary person;* KJV/AV, *he that occupieth the room of the unlearned;* J. B. Phillips, *those who are ungifted*). The general thrust of the issue is clear enough: the person who occupies the place or position of an ἰδιώτης is embarrassed and excluded by being unable to join in the corporate response of affirmation, τὸ Ἀμήν, to an acclamation of praise or to a prayer which is unintelligible. It is

---

182. Fee, *First Epistle,* 667, n. 2.

183. Metzger, *Textual Commentary,* does not trouble to comment.

184. Weiss, *Der erste Kor,* 329.

185. Conzelmann, *1 Cor,* 238, n. 58; Weiss, *Der erste Kor,* 329; Kistemaker, *1 Cor,* 493; Meyer, *Epistles to the Corinthians,* 2:15.

186. Most commentators agree that this use of **thanksgiving** and **blessing** cannot be seriously imagined to represent the eucharistic thanksgiving and blessing at the Lord's Supper (see above on 10:16 and 11:24). Cf. Grosheide, *First Epistle,* 326-27; Robertson and Plummer, *First Epistle,* 313: "It is obvious that εὐχαριστία here cannot mean the Eucharist. The minister of that service would not speak in tongues." They add that the "Amen" has no special eucharistic significance here.

1114

also clear that ἴδιος, *one's own,* i.e., that which *belongs to a specific individual* (in contrast to what is common or shared), encourages the inference that in broad lexicographical terms ἰδιώτης denotes *a private person,* perhaps *self-taught,* in contrast to an *expert* who is trained in a common expertise.[187] In this respect it is possible to support *ordinary person* (REB), *unlearned* (KJV/AV), or *outsider* (NRSV). Normally, however, a person who is still *a private individual* in a context such as this carries the meaning of **the uninitiated person** (NJB).[188] The problem is caused by the phrase a *person who held the position of, fills the place of* (ὁ ἀναπληρῶν τὸν τόπον τοῦ ἰδιώτου). This looks like a more technical category. Hence many have suggested that it denotes a *layperson* or *proselyte,* or more plausibly a *catechumen* under instruction before admission to full church membership. This would account for the use of τόπος as suggesting some formal status, and ἀναπληρῶν as denoting a specific group. Moffatt points out that if we translate *outsider,* this is to be understood *not* as an unbeliever, but as an "outsider" *in the view of "the gifted,"* i.e., *an ordinary Christian.*[189]

Robertson and Plummer convincingly argue that especially in the case of early or small house groups "it is unlikely that . . . there was a portion of the room set apart for the ἰδιῶται, or that these were laymen as distinct from officials. . . . Here 'unlearned' or 'inexperienced' may be the meaning; but RV margin is probably right; 'without gifts', i.e., having no gift of tongues. . . . It would therefore be somewhat like ἀμύητος, 'uninitiated.'"[190] Héring therefore regards the ὁ ἀναπληρῶν τὸν τόπον clause as indicating that these "have a definite place in the assembly. . . . They are not pagans present by chance, but sympathizers who are yet unbaptized, or quite simply 'ordinary' Christians who do not possess any gifts of inspiration. The Apostle is afraid that they might be repelled by unintelligible . . . speech."[191] This well sums up the issue, while **uninitiated** avoids any overly technical meaning at the same time as permitting the nuance *ungifted.* Schrage notes that while broadly the Greek word denotes a *nonspecialist* or *layperson,* here it denotes someone who is "not an insider" *(der Nicht-Eingeweihte).*[192] Hence it may suggest a Corinthian term for one whom the "spiritual people" do not regard as "gifted" (like them) with "tongues."

Amen transliterates both Gk. Ἀμήν and Heb. אמן *('amen).* The LXX regularly reflects the transliteration of the Hebrew, e.g., 1 Chron 16:36; Neh 5:13; 8:6; Tob 8:8; 3 Macc 7:13. The use of the liturgical term here to signify en-

187. BAGD, 370; and Grimm-Thayer, 296-97.
188. As in Héring, *First Epistle,* 151.
189. Moffatt, *First Epistle,* 220.
190. Robertson and Plummer, *First Epistle,* 313. They compare Acts 4:13, with the meaning *without special training.* Tyndale and Coverdale use *unlearned* here, but *lay people* in Acts 4:13 in contrast to Jewish scribes or rabbis. In Aramaic הדיוט means *lay* as opposed to *rabbi* (Strack-Billerbeck, *Kommentar zum NT aus Talmud und Midrasch,* 3:463).
191. Héring, *First Epistle,* 151.
192. Schrage, *Der erste Brief,* 3:401.

dorsement or solemn assent to the praise or prayer of another occurs in Num 5:22; Deut 27:15; 1 Chron 16:36; Neh 5:13; 8:6, and our verse reflects the appropriation of this use in the earliest Christian churches. The word is also used more frequently in the NT at the end of the speaker's own ascription of praise or act of prayer (e.g., Rom 1:25; 11:36; 15:33; Gal 1:5; Eph 3:21; Phil 4:20; 2 Tim 4:18; 1 Pet 5:11; Rev 1:6). These liturgical uses are different from the use of the term exclusively in the Gospels to affirm a solemn declaration with the introductory signal *truly* (Matt 5:18; Mark 3:28; or doubly repeated in John 1:51; 3:3; 5:19, et al.). The responsive use in worship as signifying endorsement or solemn assent became prominent in the subapostolic and early patristic periods (e.g., Justin, *Apology,* 1:65-67; Tertullian, *De Spectaculis,* 25), and is also a regular feature of synagogue worship (e.g., 1QS 1:18-20; *m. Berakoth* 8:8). **Amen** concludes doxologies (Rom 11:33-36; Eph 3:20-21) or petitions (Heb 13:21-22).

As we noted above, the nuance conveyed by the Hebrew verb in the niphal, *to be firm,* may be retained by the notion of an endorsement which *not only expresses formal agreement* but also thereby *nails our own colors to the mast.*[193] Jesus, as himself the One who is true, is called **the Amen** in Rev 3:14. Paul uses the term also in the context of his own commitment in action to what he has spoken in words (2 Cor 1:15-22), which in turn reflects God's faithful promise to remain true to what he has spoken (2 Cor 1:18, 20).[194] Worship and prayer, Paul emphasizes, should be *intelligible and corporate,* whether or not any additional issue arises in the context of private devotion. Murphy O'Connor comments on this passage: "The goal of corporate worship is not a personal thrill, but the building up of the Body of Christ . . . leaps of faith . . . had to be consistent with the core of what was already accepted. Such consistency was recognized by the community shouting 'Amen' . . . 'this is true and valid.'"[195]

17 This verse simply explicates and applies the principle established in the previous verses, but it places it in the context of the theme of **building up** which Paul has taken up in 8:1, 10; 10:23; 14:3, 4, 5, and 12, and will repeat in 14:26. The connective γάρ, **for,** confirms the logical link. The occurrence of σὺ μέν . . . with ἀλλ' ὁ ἕτερος (where ἀλλά is even stronger than δέ) signals an emphatic contrast which we have indicated by **you on your side . . . but the other on his or her side**. . . . Paul trenchantly attacks the individualism and egocen-

193. See esp. Neufeld, *The Earliest Christian Confessions,* 51-68 and 140-46; and G. P. Wiles, *Paul's Intercessory Prayers,* SNTSMS 24 (Cambridge: Cambridge University Press, 1974), 68-70.

194. Cf. F. Hahn, "Das Ja des Paulus und das Ja Gottes," in H. D. Betz and L. Schottroff (eds.), *Neues Testament und Christliche Existenz: Festschrift für Herbert Braun* (Tübingen: Mohr, 1973), 229-39; and Wolff, *Der erste Brief,* 333. A vast quantity of literature concentrates upon the use of *Amen* by Jesus (e.g., J. Strugnell, "'Amen, I Say Unto You' in the Sayings of Jesus," *HTR* 67 [1974]: 1977-82; and B. D. Chilton, "'Amen': An Approach through Syriac Gospels," *ZNW* 69 [1978]: 203-11; but this takes us in a different direction from 1 Cor 14:16. The work of J. Jeremias and K. Berger have undergone certain criticism).

195. Murphy-O'Connor, *1 Cor,* 154 and 155.

tric horizons which assume that corporate worship is simply about "God and *me*," rather than "God and *all of us*." On οἰκοδομέω perhaps in a dual sense see above especially 14:4 (with reference to Vielhauer), but even more important, 8:1 uses the verb to introduce the wider issue of Christlike concern for "the other" (ὁ ἕτερος), whether in daily life (8:6-13) or in church worship (14:1-40). We have noted the importance of οἰκοδομέω in Margaret Mitchell's work.

18-19 (1) ὅτι, *that*, is inserted after εὐχαριστῶ τῷ θεῷ in F, G, and many Latin MSS (cf. NRSV, NJB, NIV, *I thank God that . . .* as against REB, **Thank God, I am more gifted**. . . . (2) KJV/AV reads *I thank my God,* but ℘⁴⁶, ℵ, B, and D omit μου, followed by Westcott-Hort (RV) and other VSS. (3) ℵ, A, and D read γλώσσῃ, *in a tongue,* while B, K, and L read γλώσσαις, **tongues**, with the UBS 4th ed. (4) All the main MSS (except A) read λαλῶ, while K and L read λαλῶν (participle); A omits the verb. (5) Most early MSS read τῷ νοΐ, *with my mind* (instrumental); a variant is διὰ τοῦ νοός μου, *through my mind*. None of these affects the substance of vv. 18 and 19, and they reflect stylistic variations which express the same implicit themes or ideas.

Our translation, **Thank God, I am more gifted in tongues than any of you**, replicates the REB. Apart from the omission of ὅτι (see Textual Notes), the REB reflects the point at issue as turning on "giftedness" (in contrast to ἰδιώτης, v. 16), not the sheer frequency of the use of the gift or the duration of the times when the gift is used, i.e., it is a *qualitative* rather than a *quantitative* use of μᾶλλον, **more**.[196] Paul establishes personal credentials before offering a critique of that in which he himself not only shares but is especially gifted.

Virtually all commentators appear to agree that ἐν ἐκκλησίᾳ has the force of **in the assembled congregation**.[197] Hence it is astonishing that the contrast between the respective contexts of public worship and private devotion seem so often to be neglected when it is asked in crude terms whether or not Paul is "in favor of" tongues, or, more surprisingly, that he inconsistently criticizes what he values. It is transparently clear that Paul expresses thanks for a gift given "for private use" (*privat Gebrauch;* cf. v. 28b).[198] In public the use of this gift may do more harm than good, constituting a distracting and intrusive self-advertisement (or group advertisement) into "public worship," i.e., the intelligible communication of doxology, prayer, scripture, probably creed, and proclamation of the word of God.

Confusion has arisen simply from the imposition of a non-Pauline understanding (or at least an understanding for which there is no conclusive evidence) that tongues in public are acceptable if a second gift of "interpretation of

196. So, rightly, Kistemaker, *1 Cor,* 496; cf. Meyer, *Epistles to the Corinthians,* 2:16, "in a higher degree," but against Barrett, *First Epistle,* 321, although Barrett allows for both quantity and quality.

197. Conzelmann, *1 Cor,* 239; K. L. Schmidt, "ἐκκλησία," *TDNT,* 3:506; Barrett, *First Epistle,* 321; Meyer, *Epistles to the Corinthians,* 2:17; Fee, *First Epistle,* 675; Schrage, *Der erste Brief,* 3:403-4.

198. Wolff, *Die Briefe,* 333.

tongues" can be provided as a two-stage operation. But we have shown above that neither the list of gifts in 12:8-10 nor 14:9 nor 14:13 envisages anything more than a tongue-speaker finding the means of building up the community at worship by praying for the gift of sharing that which causes his or her exaltation or exalted awareness by "putting it into intelligible words." Paul does not approve of uttering unintelligible noises in public worship, whether or not someone purports subsequently to "decode" them. Moreover, since the "tongue" would normally be addressed *to God* (14:2, 15, 16), the notion of interpreting glossolalia as a "message" of prophecy addressed *to the congregation* (14:3, "prophesies . . . to other people") owes more to pietist traditions than to exegesis of this epistle. Our arguments are set forth above, and are corroborated by Paul's allusion to Isaiah in vv. 20-25.

The numbers **five** (πέντε) in **five words** (NRSV, NJB) or **five intelligible words** (REB, NIV) and *ten thousand* (μυρίους λόγους ἐν γλῶσσῃ, NRSV, NIV, NJB) are *not* numerical quantifiers (see also above on μᾶλλον as **more gifted**). **Five** is "a round number for 'several'" (Luke 12:6; 14:9).[199] Similarly, μύριοι denotes *ten thousand* as a noun in statistical contexts, but the adjective μυρίους (here in accusative plural form in apposition to λόγους) means *countless, innumerable* (as in 1 Cor 4:15, *1 Clement* 34:6, Philo, *De Legatione ad Gaium* 54), or *myriad*.[200] It is an extravagant term for the highest number conceivable: today, billions to the power of billions; REB, *thousands;* our translation **thousands upon thousands in a tongue**. The Revelation of John uses μυριάς in the plural in μυριάδες μυριάδων (Rev 5:11; 9:16), where any statistical interpretation misses the point and destroys the vision of innumerable millions of redeemed and worshiping people of God.

iv. Maturity as Love for the Other: Gospel and Home for Believers and Outsiders (14:20-25)

This is the fourth section of vv. 1-25, although some prefer to regard it as a first section within vv. 20-40. We argued in the introduction to this chapter that it is best understood as a corroboration and reinforcement of the cumulative argument of vv. 1-19. The use of the mind and communicative intelligibility reflects love for the other (ὁ ἕτερος, v. 17) which takes up the themes of 8:7-13 and 13:1-13. The use of gifts excludes any notion of "cleverness," status, or competitive evaluations of privilege (cf. 2:1-5 with 14:20). "Unintelligible speech" served as a sign of judgment, of not-belonging, in Isa 28:11-12 (LXX), for unbelief. Such speech places both believers and unbelievers in positions which are inappropriate or self-defeating. The believer may feel "alien" even within the

---

199. Conzelmann, *1 Cor,* 240, n. 74; G. Kittel, "Die Füntzahl als geläufige Zahl," in Kittel, *Rabbinica,* 1, 3 (Leipzig: Hinrichs, 1920) 39-47; Strack-Billerbeck, *Kommentar,* 3:461.

200. BAGD, 529 (cf. Rev 5:11; 9:16 for μυριάς, with *Sibylline Oracles* 4:139; Josephus, *Antiquities* 7.318; Dan 7:10).

worshiping community, while it is prophetic proclamation of the gospel, not tongues, that will bring the unbeliever who may be present to Christian faith.

20 Nowhere does Paul state more clearly than in v. 20 that the way in which speaking in tongues is used at Corinth ministers to childish love of display or thoughtless self-centeredness. It is utterly pointless to seek to disengage references to childishness in ch. 13 from issues about tongues when the connection here is transparent and explicit. On the other hand, Paul does not say that speaking in tongues is childish; only that *their public use* and their tendency to minister at Corinth to *self-advertisement at the cost of concern for others* betrays the thoughtless, self-centered horizons of the child who has not yet learned to put himself or herself in the place of others and to seek to see themselves through the eyes of others. Paul uses the noun παιδία, **children** (all major modern VSS), and the negative present imperative μή . . . γίνεσθε suggests **do not continue to be**. . . . A survey of the lexicographical evidence reveals that so often does παιδίον denote very young infants of a few days old or newborn that the English idiom **children born yesterday** serves as a legitimate intensifier.[201] The metaphor of mental childishness also occurs elsewhere.

Paul bids his **fellow Christians** (ἀδελφοί) to retain the innocence of young **children** but to avoid their tendency toward attention seeking and lack of mature thought, especially for others. Although κακία is translated *evil* in NRSV, REB, **wickedness** (NJB) has much stronger lexicographical support.[202] The difference of translation seriously affects the meaning of an important maxim. To be innocent in matters of *evil* may imply remaining aloof from seeking to understand the evil forces which contend against the good. However, to be innocent of **wickedness** entails rejecting knowledge of devious strategies which may promote one's own evil purposes, including here perhaps a hint that even religious contexts can offer subtle temptations to manipulate them on behalf of self-interests in ways which ultimately may come to be *wicked.*[203]

The Corinthian Christians are to bring to bear all the claims to be "wise" and "mature" (Paul takes up their term τέλειοι, **mature adults**, cf. 2:6, as against νηπίοις, *babies,* in 3:1-2) *to build up others,* not to win applause for themselves or to use strategies of self-fulfillment or self-promotion (cf. 14:4). We translate the dative plural ταῖς φρεσίν, **in matters of the mind**, since this is a dative which denotes reference or sphere.[204] The noun φρήν occurs only here in the NT (thus only in the plural), but in Plutarch and in Philo it clearly denotes

---

201. The diminutive παιδίον regularly means *little children, young children,* or *very young babies* (in Gen 17:12 a baby of eight days). *Newborn children* are denoted in Matt 2:8, 9, 11, 13; Luke 1:59, 66; Heb 11:23; cf. Exod 2:2, 3, and the word can be used metaphorically of *infantile minds:* BAGD, 604; Grimm-Thayer, 473.

202. Cf. BAGD, 397.

203. As I have argued in dialogue with Nietzsche, Foucault, and Niebuhr in *Interpreting God and the Postmodern Self,* 3-27 and 127-36.

204. As Edwards, *First Epistle,* 371, argues.

the sphere of *thinking,* or *judgment,* or *understanding.*[205] **Mind** recalls its cognate relation with φρόνησις and φρονέω. Bertram rightly perceives the issue to be one of *taking adult responsibility for others,* as against "childish" self-concern.[206] Deluz relates the outlook of **children** to overvaluing the spectacular: "Children love anything that shines or moves or makes a noise. . . . Many modern Christians have the same mentality. . . . They would rather be made to feel than to think . . . fall too easily under the spell of virtuosi . . . anyone with charm. . . . It shows lack of maturity in the things of the Spirit."[207]

21 With certain modifications to explicate the force, Paul quotes scripture broadly from Isa 28:11-12. **The Law** may be used to denote the whole of Jewish and Christian scripture in the OT, not just the Pentateuch (Rom 3:19; cf. also John 10:34). It remains authoritative for the young church, no less than for Jewish synagogues. The quotation, however, reflects precisely neither the LXX nor the Hebrew. C. D. Stanley observes in his specialist study: "Determining the precise relationship between the wording of 1 Cor 14:21 and the text of the LXX is one of the greatest challenges in the entire corpus of Pauline citations."[208] Whereas some variants in the LXX tradition often account for some changes, Paul's quotation, according to Stanley, cannot be explained so easily. It remains distinct from both the LXX and from the Hebrew MT. However, (i) Origen does claim to have encountered the Pauline wording in Aquila's version (*Philocalia,* 9); (ii) if this remains uncertain, we argue that Paul combines exegesis and application in a way which addresses the differences identified in the next paragraph.

The main differences include (1) Paul's choice of ἐν ἑτερογλώσσοις καὶ ἐν χείλεσιν ἑτέρων for the LXX's διὰ φαυλισμὸν χειλέων διὰ γλώσσης ἑτέρας, (2) a shift to the first person singular λαλήσω, (3) Paul's omission of LXX's λέγοντες . . . σύντριμμα . . . , (4) the shift to the future tense of εἰσακούω, (5) the addition of λέγει κύριος as if it were part of the text, and (6) the substitution of οὐδ' οὕτως for οὐκ. Some tortuous explanations have been offered for such a variety of minor alterations, other than the use of memory or versions no longer extant. Dietrich-Alex Koch's is perhaps the most complex.[209]

The technical issues assume due proportion only in the light of understanding how Paul superimposes the parallel situations of Corinth and Isaiah 28

205. BAGD, 865-66, cite Plutarch, *Moralia* 116a; see further G. Bertram, "φρήν," *TDNT,* 9:220-35.

206. Bertram, "φρονέω," *TDNT,* 9:230.

207. Deluz, *Companion to 1 Cor,* 203.

208. Stanley, *Paul and the Language of Scripture,* 198. Stanley devotes nine pages of his study to this passage: 197-205.

209. D.-A. Koch, *Die Schrift als Zeuge des Evangeliums* (Tübingen: Mohr, 1986) 123; cf. also 64 and 151. Koch argues that one factor which contributes to the absence of a parallel between Corinth and Israel is that Corinth has not shut itself from "hearing" the word, and Paul therefore modifies aspects to address this. However, his arguments become more complex, and Stanley offers a critique which exposes this speculative nature. See further on Maly (below) and Sweet (under v. 22).

onto one another with the effect that the genuine force of OT scripture speaks creatively to a new situation. Ronald Clements explains the situation which Isaiah addressed. "Isaiah found himself in conflict with certain priests and prophets of Jerusalem": their self-indulgence in festivities and drink had confused their speech and their thinking, and led them to mock the serious declarations of Isaiah about divine action.[210] "Isaiah turns back their mockeries on their own head by warning of the way God himself will punish them (v. 11) . . . [with] the coming of the Assyrians."[211] "Whom will he teach knowledge?" (28:9) alludes to Isaiah's wasting his time because the scoffers are too drunk, confused, and self-confident to care. The Hebrew of 28:10 suggests "onomatopoeic . . . representation of the din made by the revellers" who found Isaiah's rebuke "foolish and childish," while in 28:11 "the reference is clearly to the harsh-sounding Assyrian language which . . . 'this people' would soon be hearing. . . . [These foreigners] would soon be teaching them a lesson. . . ."[212] Bruce, Kistemaker, Allo, and Schrage paint a similar background.[213]

The two contexts match well. Those who are "wise" and "gifted" in their own eyes dismiss the plain message as "childish," when in reality it is the supposedly wise who think and act like children. Divine judgment, as so often occurs in life, has a dimension of "internal grammar," i.e., God permits the seeds of its own fall to operate. The disdain of plain speech comes home with a vengeance: if they want something other than intelligible speech, they can have it; however, it will serve as an uncomfortable judgment, for it will place many of God's own people for whom they ought to care in the position of *aliens and outsiders*.[214] As we shall see from our exegesis of v. 22, commentators differ in their judgment of where the emphasis lies. Fee and many others argue that Paul's main concern is the effect of tongues on unbelievers: "in Paul's context this refers to the outsiders of v. 23."[215] This misses the subtlety of Paul's *dual* point: (i) tongue-speaking in public worship is inappropriate in the first place because *it places many of God's own people in the situation of feeling like foreigners in a foreign land and "not at home" in their own home;* (ii) second, tongue-speaking, contrary to some mistaken assumptions about "spirituality"

210. R. E. Clements, *Isaiah 1–39*, NCBC (Grand Rapids: Eerdmans and London: Marshall, 1980), 226.

211. Ibid.

212. Ibid., 228.

213. Bruce, *1 and 2 Cor*, 132; Kistemaker, *1 Cor*, 499; Allo, *Première Épitre*, 365-66. Bruce writes, "They mocked him for using baby-like talk: *sâw lâ-sâw qaw lâ-qâw* (Isa 28:10) . . . imitations of glossolalic utterance . . ."; Schrage, *Der erste Brief*, 3:405-6.

214. "If unintelligible speech was a symbol of the Divine retribution under the shadowy and ceremonial dispensation, much more is it so when we have a fuller revelation of God's truth. . . . Disobedient Israel is, therefore, a type not only of the childish Christian but also of the unbelieving . . ." (Edwards, *First Epistle*, 372).

215. Fee, *First Epistle*, 677 and 680; for a different view of v. 21, cf. Conzelmann, *1 Cor*, 242. A modified version is adopted by Kistemaker, *1 Cor*, 499-500 (see under v. 22 for B. C. Johanson's suggestion that Isa 28:11 was used by speakers in tongues to affirm their value).

in Hellenism, *will not bring the message of the gospel of Christ home to unbelievers.* The cross is more than "religion" or "religious phenomena."

This now accounts for many of the similarities to, and apparent divergences from, the LXX text of Isa 28:11-12, *for Paul is simultaneously quoting and applying the passage.*[216] (1) The repetitive use of ἕτερος as an adjective or as part of a compound faithfully conveys the force of 28:11, but resonates with the wordplay between disdain for "the other" and concern for "the other" (cf. 4:6; 6:1; 14:17, disdain; 10:24, 29, concern).[217] (2) The use of the first person λαλήσω is intensified by perceiving the prophet or apostle in a context of divine agency by the addition of (see [5] above) λέγει κύριος. (3) Some aspects of 28:11 do not directly apply to the situation, and parts of quotations are often omitted. (4) The future tense embraces the consequences which will follow if people persist in their love of the esoteric or unusual at the expense of the welfare of "the other," for whom Christ died (cf. 8:6-13). In sum, such a situation served "to confirm scepticism, instead of arousing an inspiring faith."[218]

22 This is acknowledged to be one of the most difficult verses in our epistle. Chrysostom writes, "The difficulty at this place is great, which seems to arise from what is said."[219] Hays finds "great confusion" since v. 22 "seems to stand in direct contradiction to the explanation that follows in vv. 23-25. . . . Paul's argument here is somewhat garbled."[220] Kistemaker notes that "this text has been problematic for every interpreter," while Ruef and Sweet acknowledge their perplexity.[221] Héring asks why speaking in **tongues** is "a 'sign for unbelievers' and prophecy a 'sign for believers' (to follow the usual translation)? The exact opposite would be expected."[222] Uncharacteristically we receive little help from Conzelmann.[223] As Senft observes, "everything depends on the sense which we attribute to the obscure εἰς σημεῖόν εἶναι . . . **a sign for.**"[224] After considering difficulties and possibilities, however, Senft returns to "the ancient solution of Bengel": "Prophecy makes believers of unbelievers; the speaking tongue leaves the unbeliever to himself" *(quatenus prophetia ex infidelibus credentes facit; lingua loquens infidelum sibi relinquit).* Bengel adds that when tongues are in evidence *infideles . . . infideles manent: sed prophetia ex*

216. See the more subtle discussion in Maly, *Mündige Gemeinde,* 206-11, esp. 208-9 (on the theory of Ellis and Sweet about a tradition of anti-Jewish polemic based on this passage, see under v. 22).

217. Grosheide, *First Epistle,* 330, "The reason for this quotation . . . must be in the twice-repeated *other.* . . . The middle term of the comparison is that in both "other" sounds are uttered. . . . But Israel disregarded this grace of God *(even thus)."* See also Maly, *Mündige Gemeinde,* 206-11. Conzelmann observes, "Unintelligibility is present as a linking motif *(1 Cor,* 242, n. 19).

218. Moffatt, *First Epistle,* 223.

219. Chrysostom, *1 Cor. Hom.,* 36:2.

220. Hays, *First Cor,* 239-40.

221. Kistemaker, *1 Cor,* 500.

222. Héring, *First Epistle,* 152.

223. Conzelmann, *1 Cor,* 242.

224. Senft, *Première Épitre,* 179.

infidelibus fideles facit.[225] It is unusual for Bengel to repeat himself. He recognizes that even this is only a broad match: *sermo Pauli est indefinitus.*

Our translation therefore is designed to indicate that εἰς σημεῖον carries a different force in each of its different contexts. Yet Smit does not press the issue far enough, as his paraphrase suggests. As Barrett and many lexicographical specialists recognize, the prepositional phrase almost certainly means **serves as a sign**, while σημεῖον may denote **a warning sign**, **a sign**, *an outward indicator,* or **signal** for judgment, warning, identification, or benefit.[226] We have to choose between a wooden translation which conveys contradiction, and one which brings out the force of Paul's point. In our survey of views we begin with our own approach. We agree with Sandnes that Paul invites the Corinthians to evaluate the respective *effects* of tongues and prophecy: what signal does each convey?[227] Love for the other will always take account of *perceptions* and *effects* in relation to *others.*

(1) Paul has just stated in v. 21 that the experience of being surrounded by the "tongues" of the Assyrians **served as a sign** (cf. εἰς σημεῖόν εἰσιν, v. 22) (that Israel had been placed under God's **judgment**) for unbelief. Nevertheless, this was an inappropriate situation for the people of God, who had been misled by the "people of influence" who expressed scepticism about Isaiah's message. **Tongues serve as a sign . . . for unbelievers** (τοῖς ἀπίστοις, dative of disadvantage). Hence Christian believers should not have such a "sign" marking their community worship and thereby generating a sense of "wrongness" or "strangeness" more appropriate to what *unbelievers* might be expected to feel. *Believers should feel "at home" in their own corporate worship.* Conversely, where **prophetic speech** operates with effect, this *signals* the presence and action of God in nurturing **people of faith**. *Unbelievers* do not produce **prophetic speech** which communicates gospel truth. Hence on one side **prophetic speech** characterizes the believing *church at worship;* **tongues**, on the other side, constitute *negative* **signs** (at least in public and in their effect) generating barriers and alienation inappropriate for **believers**.

The history of effects *(Wirkungsgeschichte)* of interpretation, however, has set up *horizons of expectation* which presuppose that the series of datives are all *datives of advantage,* signifying *propriety or benefit* rather than external *reference, disadvantage,* or a context of indicative *judgment.* J. B. Phillips thus entirely reverses Paul's point by translating "That means that 'tongues' are a sign of God's power, not for those who are unbelievers but to those who already believe." However, there is no textual MS support for reversing the sequence of the terms.

225. Bengel, *Gnomon,* 659.

226. Barrett, *First Epistle,* 323; BDF, sect. 145; BAGD, 747; Grimm-Thayer, 573-74; MM, 577-78; K. Rengstorf, *TDNT,* 7:200-269, esp. 258-60; O. Betz, *EDNT,* 3:238-41: in 1 Cor 14:22 "*sign* . . . to the extent that they do not recognize it as . . . prompted by God, and reveal . . . their own stubbornness" (240).

227. Sandnes, "Prophecy — A Sign for Believers (1 Cor 14:20-25)," 1-15.

(2) B. C. Johanson treats the first part of the verse as a rhetorical question posed not initially by Paul but initially at Corinth.[228] In effect, v. 21 expresses a view held by some at Corinth, which Paul corrects in vv. 22-23: (a) large numbers of commentators express perplexity about the respective role of *unbelievers* and *believers* in relation to tongues; (b) σημεῖον may be used in either "a positive sense" or "a negative sense"; (c) the quotation from Isa 28:11-12 presents difficulties, although Origen's testimony to an earlier form in Aquila should not be ignored; (d) "unintelligible tongues will be ineffective in causing 'This people to listen to the Lord'"; (e) certain supposed solutions put forward by A. T. Robertson and A. Plummer and by O. P. Robertson contain flaws.[229]

Johanson's next claim is crucial. (f) In the context of the rhetorical structure the role of **as a sign for** should be expressed "in terms of *function*. . . . Function is indicated by εἰς σημεῖον. . . ."[230] At this point, however, Johanson introduces "a new solution," which is problematic, although the thesis that the words already constitute an earlier maxim had been proposed by Sweet.[231] Johanson suggests that we may understand σημεῖον in a positive sense in v. 22a, but that "to do so we would have to attribute the assertions in v. 22 to someone other than Paul." This is partly indicated by ὥστε, **so then**, but within the frame of a rhetorical question: "Are tongues, then, meant as a sign not for believers but for unbelievers. . . ?"[232] The absurdity of what some of the "glossolalists" at Corinth had apparently believed or argued emerges in Paul's comments in vv. 23-25: "Then comes his swift rebuttal in vv. 23-25, showing that for the non-Christian tongues are madness, while it is rather prophecy that convicts the heart."[233] Paul expounds his critique in terms of the "childishness" of the "glossolalist" view which is in question, which in turn alludes back to his critique in 1:10–4:21, especially in relation to τέλειος (2:6) and νήπιος (3:1; cf. also 13:10-11; 14:29). A "sophist-glossolalist" group were probably using **tongues** as a **sign** that "God was among them."[234]

In our view, Paul's appeal to the experience of making those who do not share glossolalia feel "alien" among aliens, like the exiled to whom Isaiah refers, provides sufficient explanation of v. 21 without resort to Johanson's hypothesis. Our explanation coheres with the points made under (3) and (4) below. However, it has the merit of consistency and plausibility. Moreover, if any

228. Johanson, "Tongues, A Sign for Unbelievers? A Structural and Exegetical Study of 1 Cor 14:20-25," 180-203.

229. Ibid., 180-86.

230. Ibid., 190.

231. Sweet, "A Sign for Unbelievers: Paul's Attitude to Glossolalia," 240-47. He argues, following E. E. Ellis, that the theme of Isa 28:11-12 was drawn from an early Christian polemic against the unbelief of Jews, and that this may have entered the Corinthian congregation to defend the status of tongues as a sign. Paul turns this argument on its head. Williams favours Sweet's argument (*Tongues of the Spirit,* 41, n. 23).

232. Johanson, "Tongues, A Sign for Unbelievers?" 193.

233. Ibid., 194.

234. Ibid., 195-201; quotations from 200.

parallels whatever are permitted between Corinth and phenomena today, no doubt glossolalia is indeed promoted in some circles today as a **sign** of God's "power" ministry to reach outsiders as well as authenticate the tongue-speakers.[235] Further, deep in the origins of the Pentecostal movement, and reemphasized today, tongues are seen as "a bond of love" as well as a "fullness of divine power," awakening faith "like a bell."[236] The exegetical and hermeneutical problem is whether this narrative experience has any close relationship with the exegesis of 1 Corinthians 12–14.

(3) C. K. Barrett understands **sign** in the negative sense, namely, as a sign of judgment: "When they are not met with faith (cf. Heb 4:2) tongues *serve* to harden and thus condemn the unbeliever (cf. verses 23f.) [although] they will at least not offend a Christian assembly that understands what is going on" (his italics).[237] The first part of Barrett's claim coheres well with Paul's argument. However, his entire argument elsewhere in this chapter seems to imply that speaking in tongues within the assembled church community has more negative than positive consequences for "the other," whether "the other" is a visiting unbeliever or an "ordinary" or "uninitiated" Christian. Hence only the first part of this suggestion is entirely satisfactory.

(4) A number of research articles, e.g., by Grudem (1979), Lanier (1991), and Smit (1994), as well as work by Rengstorf (1965; Eng. 1971) and Horn (1992), stress the effect of the **sign** as **serving as a sign** of *judgment* upon **those who are unbelievers**: "His [Paul's] point is that speaking in tongues not only does not open up access into the mysteries of God for the ἄπιστος, but actually bars this."[238] Grudem concludes that tongues without interpretation are a sign to unbelievers of God's judgment and displeasure, whereas prophecy ministers to the experience of God's presence and blessing.[239] Lanier similarly argues that Paul follows on logically from the condemnatory force of Isa 28:11-12 to argue for the judgmental significance and hence damning effect of tongues

---

235. Sources relating to Toronto Airport Church and The Association of Vineyard Churches include, e.g., Guy Chevreau, *Catch the Fire: The Toronto Blessing* (London: Marshall Pickering, 1994), esp. 27; Bill Randler, *Weighed and Found Wanting* (Cambridge: St Matthew Publications, 1995), 119; John Wimber, "Association of Vineyard Churches Notice of Withdrawal from the Toronto Airport Vineyard," December 13, 1995; David White, "The Toronto Blessing — Report for Open Distribution" (York: St. Michael le Belfrey Church, 1995); Sue Hope, "The Fruit of Toronto," *Anglicans for Renewal* 70 (1997); W. Boulton, *The Impact of Toronto* (Crowborough: Monarch, 1995); more critically, Martyn Percy, *Words, Wonder and Power* (London: SPCK, 1996); S. E. Porter and P. J. Richter, *The Toronto Blessing — Or Is It?* (London: Darton, Longman & Todd, 1995); D. Martin and P. Mullen (ed.), *Strange Gifts* (Oxford: Blackwell, 1984).

236. D. T. Irvin, "Drawing All Together in One Bond of Love," 40-41; cf. R. Stronstad, "Trends in Pentecostal Hermeneutics"; J. R. Goff, *Fields White unto Harvest: Charles F. Parham and the Missionary Origins of Pentecostalism* (Fayetteville, Ark.: University of Arkansas Press, 1988).

237. Barrett, *First Epistle,* 323.

238. K. Rengstorf, "σημεῖον," *TDNT,* 8:259; cf. 258-60, and for the whole lexicographical survey, 200-269.

239. Grudem, "1 Cor 14:20-25: Prophecy and Tongues as Signs of God's Attitude," 381-96.

upon **those who are unbelievers**.[240] Smit also links the meaning of **sign** directly with the Isaiah quotation. Paul portrays **speaking in tongues** as a **sign** which inexpert **unbelievers** (rightly or wrongly) associate with, and interpret as, pagan μανιά, and thereby are pushed yet further away into judgment. On the other hand, **prophetic speech** brings genuine conviction (ἔλεγχος) of truth, and hence **faith**.[241]

Virtually all of these four views contribute factors which illuminate the text and obviate the despair of some of the commentators with whose observations we began. While Bengel caught the general tone of Paul's concern, we can perhaps be more specific. With (3) and (4) we may agree that in the public worship of the church the transference of experience of being alien prefigured in Isaiah 28 constitutes a **sign of judgment** rather than of grace; it is **prophetic speech** which proclaims grace. With (2), we may concede with Johanson that if all else fails, we must take seriously the possibility of the use of a Corinthian maxim (as in 6:12, 10:23, and elsewhere). However, (1) coheres perhaps most closely with the precise nuance of Paul's argument not only in vv. 20-25, but also earlier in this chapter.

23 The hypothetical clauses which paint an all-too-possible scenario build up to a climax with the keyword μαίνεσθε (v. 23), **you are raving and out of your mind**. We have carefully traced the nuances of μαίνεσθαι through the LXX (e.g., Wis 14:28; 4 Macc 7:5; 8:5; 10:13), the NT (cf. Acts 26:24, 25), the papyri (e.g., *Papyrus Oxyrhynchus* 1:33), Philo and Josephus (e.g., *Wars* 1.352), and in the classical Greek background, notably in Euripides, *Bacchae* 690-711, 748-68, 1095-1136, since, although this stems from the fifth century BC, this last work made a lasting impact on hellenistic understanding of the verb in the context of religion which was emotionally "high" or out of control.[242] Without doubt most references convey the notion of being *mad* (as REB, KJV/AV), *insane,* or **out of your mind** (as NRSV and NIV). However, the verb often applies, as here, to the production of sounds while someone is **out of his mind**; hence NJB translates **that you were all raving** (also proposed, especially by Grimm-Thayer, below). To exclude either of these two nuances is to diminish the force of the verb; hence it hardly overtranslates to use (as is sometimes necessary) two English terms: **raving and out of your mind**. This need not commit us to any specific theory of a conscious equivalence to Bacchic frenzy, as Forbes rightly insists. However, the term carries the double meaning of emotional lack of self-control, expressed as **raving**, and an unattractive, even frightening loss of rational *sanity.*[243]

240. Lanier, "With Stammering Lips and Another Tongue: 1 Cor 14:20-22 and Isa 28:11-12," 259-85.

241. Smit, "Tongues and Prophecy: Deciphering 1 Cor 14:22," 175-90.

242. See further BAGD, 486; Grimm-Thayer, 386; MM, 385; Hatch-Redpath, 2:892; Forbes, *Prophecy and Inspired Speech,* 126-33. The claim of Hays that the word need not be pejorative makes matters worse (see below).

243. Forbes makes useful points about the limited significance of some texts from hellenis-

The buildup of clauses is deliberately impressionistic. In accordance with frequent uses of πάντες, *all*, Paul does not enumerate a statistical totality (explicitly denied in 12:30, μὴ πάντες γλώσσαις λαλοῦσιν; i.e., **all do not speak with tongues, do they?**) but uses the kind of impressionist description that we use when we say, "**everyone** was laughing" or "**everyone** was shouting. . . ." The same point must be made about the phrase ἡ ἐκκλησία ὅλη. Some have used this to infer that the *entire* community could squeeze into a single large house or villa, including sympathetic inquirers or catechumens and unbelievers. Paul is concerned, however, to float a *scenario* which will sum up his argument of 14:1-25.[244] Conzelmann rightly warns us that "even . . . the high tension of spiritual inspiration here cannot be presumed to be normal. We shall have to beware of generalizations."[245]

Hays argues that the use of μαίνεσθε "does not necessarily have the pejorative sense that this translation [*you are out of your mind,* NRSV, NIV] suggests for readers today."[246] However, this makes Paul's painting of a "worst scenario" even more serious: "Outsiders . . . will think that this . . . is simply one more mystery cult that whips its partisans into a frenzy of frothy enthusiasm. . . . It does not mean that the persons in question are crazy."[247] This does indeed run up against the criticisms put forward by Forbes. Yet again, to endorse Conzelmann's warning against generalization, why should we *stereotype* **the uninitiated or unbeliever**? Some (not all) might well dismiss what is going on as yet another "hyped-up" religious cult; others (not all) more probably found a lack of sober proclamation unattractive, unhelpful, and emotionally self-indulgent. In cosmopolitan Corinth, whatever the more specific reason, it contradicted Paul's evangelistic maxim (1 Cor 9:20-23) that he would gladly restrain whatever "rights" or "freedoms" were theoretically his, if thereby he could win for Christ the varieties of "other," be they social elite or socially deprived, or of any specific cultural prejudice.[248] On the meaning of ἰδιῶται, **uninitiated**, see the detailed discussion above under v. 16.

24-25 The use of ἐὰν δέ with the present subjunctive προφητεύσωσιν projects a scenario which the English idiom **suppose, by contrast, that** . . . (used by NJB in v. 23). Again, πάντες, *all people,* is impressionist rather than numerical (see above under v. 23) and therefore should be rendered **everyone**,

---

tic religion. However, it is a *non sequitur* to argue that on this basis the outsider would not perceive the church so described as "raving" (*Prophecy and Inspired Speech,* 174; cf. 124-81). The point is that the *word* frequently combines *insanity* or *mind* with *raving* or *wild* speech (cf. lexicography above). Forbes demolishes a spurious argument which many appeal to for this meaning, but this is *not* the *only* argument for this meaning.

244. Cf. further Maly, *Mündige Gemeinde,* 211-12: Paul uses a *reductio ad absurdum.*

245. Conzelmann, *1 Cor,* 243 and 243, n. 5.

246. Hays, *First Cor,* 238.

247. Ibid.

248. Deluz, *Companion to 1 Cor,* 205: "This speaking in tongues to unbelievers . . . irritates and disturbs and is a sign of unfriendliness . . . gives . . . a feeling of being strangers. . . . They will be shocked, repelled. . . ."

everybody (NIV); as against *all* (NRSV, REB). The indefinite τις ἄπιστος, **someone who is an unbeliever**, maintains the mode and mood of a projected possible scenario. The present passives ἐλέγχεται and ἀνακρίνεται express the heart of this verse: the person in question **undergoes conviction and judgment**. The Greek ἐλέγχω means *to bring to the light, to expose*, especially in classical contexts, but in the NT and often in the papyri it denotes both *conviction of sin* and *conviction of truth*, most especially in the Fourth Gospel, where the agent who brings home this conviction is Jesus Christ or the Spirit-Paraclete (John 8:9, 46; 16:8; cf. Acts 6:10; Philo, *De Specialibus Legibus* 3.54; Jas 2:9; *Papyrus Oxyrhynchus* 1032:30; *BGU* 1138:13). The meaning rendered in our translation coheres with parallel contexts in the NT and in first-century literature.[249] NRSV's *reproved* is too narrow; NIV's *convince* unnecessarily loses some force; while NJB's *put to the test* allows contextual factors too much influence in determining a special use within the lexicographical evidence. As Calvin and Barrett note, the sense is closely parallel to that which John 16:8 ascribes to the work of the Holy Spirit–Paraclete (see below, n. 249).

Undergoes judgment coheres with this reconstruction for ἀνακρίνω, although we concede that in lexicographical terms the verb has two distinguishable meanings: (i) *to question, to examine;* (ii) **to judge**, *to discern, to call to account.*[250] However, even the first meaning generally occurs in settings of accusation or judicial hearings, even if not always so. The outcome in the present context is the same: the words of the prophets bring home the truth of the gospel in such a way that the hearer "stands under" the verdict of the cross (cf. 1:18-25). The reaction portrayed in v. 25 makes it plain that the hearers perceive themselves as falling under judgment, whether for their unbelief or for their conduct, or most probably, in their eyes, for both. The word of God in Paul and in most strata of the NT brings **judgment**, grace, and promise.

It is important for our discussion of **prophetic speech** and *prophecy* (see above at 14:3) to remind ourselves that v. 25 stands in the path of C. M. Roebeck's claim that prophecy is addressed only to the believing community and must not be confused with kerygma or gospel proclamation.[251] On the contrary, this verse corroborates the arguments of Hill, Gillespie, and most especially Müller that prophetic speech enacts judgment and grace, and combines a speech-act of gospel promise with pastoral exhortation.[252] Both the church and the world stand under a prophetic announcement of judgment and

---

249. See BAGD, 249; Godet, *First Epistle,* 2:296; F. Buchsel, "ἐλέγχω," *TDNT,* 2:473-76; F. Porsch, "Pneuma und Wort," *Frankfurter theologische Studien* 16 (1974): 279-89; also in *EDNT,* 1:427-28: "characterizes the convicting and edifying activity of the prophets endowed by the Spirit." Further (with reference to John 16:8) Calvin, *First Epistle,* 298-99; and Barrett, *First Epistle,* 326.

250. BAGD, 56.

251. Robeck, "The Gift of Prophesying in Acts and Paul," 39-54.

252. Müller, *Prophetie und Predigt,* 24-26; Cf. Hill, *NT Prophecy,* 123-24; Gillespie, *The First Theologians,* 134-50.

grace in the mode of warning and promise, as indeed was the case in the OT. Müller uses the term *Bussrede*.[253] The prophetic word, Hill and Müller insist, plumbs the secrets of the inner being of the self to generate both awareness of self-centeredness and belief.[254] (See further the second note on Prophecy, especially section (5), where we also note the significance of the work of Vielhauer, and especially the claims of Sandnes about Paul himself [1093-94].) Since in Paul's theology it is God, especially God the Holy Spirit, who knows the secrets of the heart (cf. Rom 8:27), it is more probable that ὑπὸ πάντων (grammatically either masculine or neuter plural) embraces **all that is said** in the most inclusive sense (both prophets and the prophetic message) rather than exclusively the prophets only, especially since Paul's antecedent is not the noun *prophets* but the verb προφητεύωσιν (indefinite present subjunctive), **everyone is using prophetic speech**.

We translate τὰ κρυπτὰ τῆς καρδίας αὐτοῦ, v. 25 (*the secrets of his heart*, REB, NJB, most VSS) as **the secret depths of their very being** since the use of *heart* to convey all that Heb. לֵב *(lebh)* behind καρδία denotes has steadily become less adequate in our own culture, as *heart* becomes increasingly associated with feeling, romantic attraction, or mere innerness as opposed to the pre-conscious tendencies which drive habituation, volition, acts of judgments, and deep feeling as an integrated totality.[255] This confrontation with the unmasking, exposing power of the divine word and divine Spirit is well described by Theissen: "The step toward uncovering the unconscious is undertaken where the interpersonal limit of understanding becomes an intrapersonal limit, where one stands over against oneself in as strange a manner as to a strange person . . . accepting it as part of oneself."[256] Bultmann reminds us that in Paul καρδία, especially in its deliberative and volitional sense, "need not penetrate into the field of consciousness at all, but may designate the hidden tendency of the self."[257] "*Krupta tes kardias* (secrets of the heart) include unconscious contents. . . . What comes to light is what is hidden in the heart."[258]

Those who **undergo conviction and judgment** (the meaning agreed by Bultmann and Theissen) **fall to their knees in obeisance and worship God**. The Greek πεσὼν ἐπὶ πρόσωπον does indeed mean *to fall down on his face* (NJB, KJV/AV) in first-century language and culture. However, since this is a conscious act of worship (προσκυνήσει . . . ἀπαγγέλλων ὅτι ὄντως . . .), this *falling down* (NIV, REB) must not be confused with neo-Pentecostalist phe-

---

253. Müller, *Prophetie und Predigt,* 12-46.

254. Hill, *NT Prophecy,* 123-24.

255. Cf. Jewett, *Paul's Anthropological Terms,* 305-33, esp. 328; Bultmann, *Theology of the NT,* 1:220-27, esp. 223-24; cf. 1 Cor 4:5; Schrage, *Der erste Brief,* 3:412.

256. Theissen, *Psychological Aspects,* 88; cf. 59-95.

257. Bultmann, *Theology,* 1:223.

258. Theissen, *Psychological Aspects,* 78; we do not, however, follow Theissen in his inferences about the access of the prophets themselves to another person's innermost depths.

nomena often described as being "slain in the Spirit." *To throw oneself to the ground* (in prostration) was used in the OT and in the first century "as a sign of devotion, before high-ranking persons or divine beings especially when one approaches with a petition . . . Matt 2:11; . . . Rev 5:14; 19:4; 22:8 (in all these places closely connected with προσκυνεῖν).[259] NRSV attempts a Western cultural parallel by translating *a person will bow down before God,* which avoids certain pitfalls but loses force. Those who undergo **conviction and judgment** in today's terms **fall to their knees** both "in shame that the hidden sins of their heart should have been brought to light," and in *petitioning* God (see BAGD) for forgiveness and performing an act of worship, i.e., **falling to their knees in obeisance.**[260] Although προσκυνέω takes the accusative in classical Greek and the LXX, in the NT it regularly takes the dative, probably more often but not exclusively. As Chrysostom observes, the aim is "not to astonish . . . bringing a suspicion of madness" but "to draw people from vainglory to . . . wonder and worship."[261]

In this context ἀπαγγέλλω denotes the declarative speech-act of **confession** or worshiping acknowledgment. The convicted persons now understand that what they had hitherto brushed aside as mere "religious phenomena," or "going through the motions" of a religious cult, are **indeed really** the case. The adverb ὄντως, formed from the adjectival participle ὤν, *being,* is generally translated *really* or *certainly,* but in modern English these words have become thinned down by overuse ("I am really pleased to say . . .").[262] Here the portentous nature of this profound revaluation and new grasp of truth invites a more weighty, even sonorous rendering. In this context the words convey some such confession as *in all reality,* or, to maintain **really**, the insertion of **indeed** captures the note of revised conviction. In all **reality** they encounter not simply human religion which constructs or projects a god; they encounter **God**, who draws forth authentic worship as he is authentically active and present among the believers.[263] "God's word effects its entrance . . . and then creates conviction. . . . It bears witness to a profound sense of unworthiness, as well as of the immediate presence of God."[264] Allo suggests that the conviction brought about by prophetic speech stands in contrast to the Corinthian claim that it is speaking in tongues that provides the necessary sign of authenticity.[265]

---

259. BAGD, 659. Cf. also Josephus, *Antiquities* 10.213, after Gen 17:3, 17; Num 14:5; Dan 3:5; Rev 4:10; 5:8.

260. Edwards, *First Epistle,* 377; cf. Conzelmann, *1 Cor,* 243-44, n. 33; Schrage, *Der erste Brief,* 3:413-14.

261. Chrysostom, *1 Cor. Hom.,* 36:2, 3.

262. Hence the adverb often serves to denote a mode or quality which is *genuine* or *authentic;* BAGD, 574.

263. In contrast to the theories of projection formulated by Ludwig Feuerbach and taken up by Don Cupitt, *Taking Leave of God* (New York: Crossroad and London: SCM, 1980).

264. Barrett, *First Epistle,* 326-27. Barrett rightly rejects the notion of a prophet's "miraculous gift of thought reading" (ibid., 326; against Héring, *First Epistle,* 152).

265. Allo, *Première Épitre* 367-68; cf. Schrage, *Der erste Brief,* 3:414.

b. Does the Spirit Create Order or Anarchy?
Controlled Speech and Building Up (14:26-40)

(26) What follows, then, my dear friends? Suppose that when you assemble together each contributes a hymn, an item of teaching, something disclosed, or speaks in a tongue, or puts the tongues language into words, the point remains: "let everything serve the building up of the community." (27) If it is in a tongue that someone speaks, let only two or at the most three speak in turn, and let the one who speaks put it into words. (28) However, if he or she cannot put it into words, let them remain silent in the assembled congregation, and address God privately. (29) In the case of prophets, however, let two or three speak, and let the others sift what is said. (30) If something is disclosed to another person who is sitting down nearby, the first speaker should stop speaking. (31, 32) For you have the power for it to be one by one, every one of you, when you prophesy, in order that all may learn and everyone be encouraged or exhorted. And the spiritual utterances of the prophets are subject to the prophets' control. (33a) For God is a God not of disorder but of peace.

(33b, 34) As in all the churches of God's holy people, when congregations meet in public, the women should allow for silence. For there exists no permission for them to speak [in the way they do (?)]. Let them keep to their ordered place, as the law indicates. (35) If they want to learn anything, let them interrogate their own husbands at home. For a woman to speak thus in public worship brings disgrace. (36) Or was it from you that the word of God went forth? Or are you the only ones to whom it came?

(37, 38) If anyone thinks that he or she is a prophet or a person "of the Spirit," let them recognize that what I write to you is [a command] from the Lord. If anyone does not recognize it, he or she is not [to be?] recognized. (39, 40) So then, my dear friends, continue to be zealously concerned about prophetic speech and do not forbid speaking in tongues. Only, everything should happen fittingly and in an ordered manner.

The term "controlled speech" constitutes a recurrent refrain in William R. Baker's recent volume on personal speech-ethics.[266] Baker discusses the significance of "controlled speech" as an ethical issue in Wisdom literature, the OT, the Apocrypha and Pseudepigrapha, Qumran, rabbinic literature, Graeco-Roman texts, Philo, and parts of the NT, all of which provide a background for the issue in James.[267] The Babylonian Counsels of Wisdom perceive "order" as dependent on such axioms as "let your mouth be controlled and your speech guarded."[268] In OT Wisdom literature "A person of knowledge uses words with

---

266. W. R. Baker, *Personal Speech-Ethics in the Epistle of James,* WUNT 2:68 (Tübingen: Mohr, 1995).

267. Ibid., 23-104; cf. 105-38, 222-42, and 278-90.

268. *Counsels of Wisdom* 26 (cited by Baker, *Personal Speech-Ethics,* 23).

restraint" (Prov 17:27), while unethical, wicked people are characterized by "a loose mouth" (cf. Ps 50:19; 59:7; Prov 25:28). Josephus observes that the Essenes stress the importance of controlled speech for order and mutual respect: "let there be no shouting . . . allow each to speak in turn" (Josephus, *Wars* 2.8.6). Revealed knowledge especially merits control in the Qumran writings; this is to be communicated only "with discretion" (1QS 10:24) and "within a firm boundary" (10:25). Plato compares the ethics of speech with the kind of control that "runs in" (ἀναλαμβάνω) utterances as one would a spirited horse (Plato, *Laws* 701C). Plutarch appeals to the symbolic "fence of teeth in front of the tongue" as a guard for the ethics of speech.[269] Philo sees the control of the tongue as a paradigm case of self-discipline (*De Specialibus Legibus* 2.195). Without this "chaos and confusion enter everything" (Philo, *De Abrahamo* 21.29, cf. *De Vita Mosis* 2.198).

Whereas some perceive Paul as merely imposing an authoritarian hierarchy or a paternalist polemic against the freedom of "enthusiasm," more attention should be paid to the background of an ethic of **controlled speech in traditions of speech-ethics** from the OT to hellenistic Judaism and Philo as a corollary of "order." Together with this, Paul's earlier emphasis expounds an **ordered dialectic between unity and differentiation** as in 12:4-31 (see introduction to 14:1-40, above). As we have noted, the role of **love** (8:7-13; 13:1-13) also plays an important part. Just arguably the dialectic of oneness and differentiation implies a trinitarian perspective in 12:3-6, and at the very least it is grounded in the character and will of God.

i. General Principles and Their Practical Application to Various Cases (14:26-33a)

26   ℵᶜ (i.e., latest corrector), D, F, G, K, L, most minuscules, Vulgate, Syriac Peshitta, and in general Western texts include ὑμῶν after ἕκαστος to make **each** *of you* specific to the addressees. The Alexandrian p⁴⁶, ℵ*, A, B, 33, and Sahidic as well as Coptic Bohairic omit the pronoun. We agree with Metzger, Fee, and Kistemaker that the shorter text is more likely to be the earlier.[270] KJV/AV follows the Western reading.

Virtually all commentators and VSS agree that τί οὖν ἐστιν (v. 26) carries some such sense as "*What does this imply?:* a question inserted in diatribe style to quicken the interest, as in v. 15: anaphora" (cf. NRSV, *What should be done, then, my friends?* REB, *To sum up, my friends;* NJB, *Then what should it be like?*).[271] Once again we vary the rendering of ἀδελφοί in the search for a gen-

---

269. Plutarch, *Moralia* 15.89. Cf. esp. Baker, *Personal Speech-Ethics,* 27-33, 43 6, 49-52, 60-64.

270. Metzger, *Textual Commentary* (2d ed.), 499; Kistemaker, *1 Cor,* 507; Fee, *First Epistle,* 689; as also Conzelmann.

271. Conzelmann, *1 Cor,* 244.

der-inclusive equivalent, which escapes precise translation by any single English word or phrase.

(1) The first main difficulty arises from how to translate and to understand ὅταν with the present subjunctive; this is closely followed by a second major difficulty over the meaning and translation of ἔχει. NJB uses **suppose** for ἐάν with the aorist subjunctive in 14:6 and 23, but arguably the present subjunctive here with ὅταν signifies repetition: *whenever you assemble together.*[272] Dunn believes that this verse provides "the *description* of a *typical gathering for worship*" (my italics).[273] However, while the ἔκαστος ἔχει clauses represent possible scenarios, or, in the language of Heidegger and Ricoeur, projections of "possible worlds," the repetitive reiterative function of ὅταν συνέρχησθε falls not upon the hypothetical scenarios but on the main axiom, that "the overriding aim is to build up the congregation."[274] This purpose of **building up the community** has cumulatively become a refrain or axiom in 14:3, 5, 12, and 26 (where v. 12 not only uses the identical phrase πρὸς τὴν οἰκοδομήν but also adds the implicit τῆς ἐκκλησίας, which 1 Cor 3:9 made explicit by describing the congregation as θεοῦ οἰκοδομή). The use of the verb οἰκοδομέω in 8:1, 10; 10:23; 14:4, 17 confirms this point (see above). Lietzmann is so convinced of the importance of understanding where the relationship between the indefinite hypothesis and the definite principle engages the force of the sentence that in effect he changes the strict syntax of the Greek: ἔκαστος ἔχει signifies a projected thought world serving as "surely an indirect expression of the wish 'so should it be'. Alternatively the sentence is downright clumsy in stylistic formulation and intends to say *(will sagen):* 'Everyone who presents a psalm or a piece of instruction . . . should do it for the purpose of building people up.'"[275] Lietzmann's diagnosis of the problem is right, even if he overpresses it into a change of syntax.[276] "Edification must once more be insisted on as the true aim of them all."[277]

BDF observe that ἄν with the subjunctive of repeated action in the present time stands as near the conjunction or relative as possible.[278] Hence the temporal force of *whenever* governs the **assembling together**, not the ἔκαστος ἔχει clauses, which need to be disengaged from definite description to formulate hypothetical scenarios. **Suppose that when you assemble** seems to offer an acceptable solution without radically recasting the Greek, as Lietzmann does, to achieve this purpose.

(2) The second major problem concerns the meaning and force of

272. As in Robertson, *Word Pictures,* 4:184.

273. Dunn, *The Theology of Paul,* 583.

274. Horrell, *Social Ethos,* 183; cf. Barrett, *First Epistle,* 327.

275. Lietzmann, *An die Korinther,* 73. See also Wolff, *Der erste Brief,* 338-39.

276. As against those who, like Hodge, interpret the actions as an *actual state of affairs* which needs to be *corrected* (Hodge, *First Epistle,* 300-301).

277. Findlay, *Expositor's Greek Testament,* 911-12.

278. BDF, 185, sect. 367.

ἕκαστος. We have already discussed the impressionist (as against numerical) understanding of πάντες λαλῶσιν in v. 23 (see above). As Conzelmann urges, followed by Senft (but against Fee), in the same way ἕκαστος "naturally must not be pressed to the effect that every single individual has one of the gifts mentioned, but means: one has this — another has that."[279] The hypothetical εἴτε γλώσσῃ in the very next verse confirms this. The meaning of ἔχει is difficult to determine. At first glance, *has* seems obvious (NRSV, NIV, KJV/AV, Barrett, Collins, Luther [*hat*]). However, Lietzmann uses *vortragen,* which means either *presents* or *performs,* while NJB renders it *brings;* REB, **contributing** (followed here by Phillips and the NT in Modern English by Montgomery). *Has* reveals how much is pre-judged by Weymouth's explication *there is not one of you who is not ready either with. . . .* Do the worshipers *bring* a pre-chosen, pre-prepared choice of *psalm* or **hymn** (either or both properly translate ψαλμόν), their **item of teaching** (διδαχήν), or something disclosed (ἀποκάλυψιν)?

In our view some of these gifts are by definition *brought* in the sense that **teaching** arises out of processes of reflection over a time span, even if an event may also trigger some more sudden insight. (Against Barrett and especially Fee, Wolff argues that the choices of psalm and teaching are "not spontaneous *(nichts Spontanes)* but an enabling by God's Spirit for reflection of what is handed down *(Überlieferungen).*"[280] The text simply does not specify whether a worshiper *brings* a choice of *psalm* (NJB) or *has* (has composed or is in process of composing) a **hymn** (NIV).[281] We use the broader translation since the latter may include the former, whereas the former *(psalm)* is more specific. On the other hand, it seems odd to try to imagine "bringing" **speaking in tongues**, since this appears to represent an upsurge of deep Godward yearning, longing, or celebrating praise which seizes the worshiper in the context of worship. Hence REB's **contribute** avoids assuming that all the named phenomena are "brought," or that all emerge on the spot as gifts which worshipers "have" during the process of worship.

HERMENEUTICAL METHOD IN THESE VERSES

A general comment on method is invited here. It is difficult to avoid the influence of the so-called hermeneutical circle by virtue of which exegetical decisions tend to be influenced by hypothetical reconstructions of the larger picture, but the larger pic-

279. Conzelmann, *1 Cor,* 244; Senft, *Première Épitre,* 181; against Fee, *First Epistle,* 684 and 690.

280. Wolff, *Der erste Brief,* 339; against Barrett, *First Epistle,* 327; Fee, *First Epistle,* 684 and 690-691. Schrage discusses the issue of spontaneity and preparation at length (*Der erste Brief,* 3:444-45). Clearly preparation is not of the *whole,* but each contribution may be "brought" or, in some cases, *ad hoc.* The phrase used by Collins, *"had something to say,"* rightly leaves this open (*First Cor,* 517).

281. Barrett insists on "hymn" as "a fresh, perhaps spontaneous, composition" (*First Epistle,* 327), but see Wolff and Schrage.

ture rests, in turn, on exegetical decisions. Here the difference of exegetical judgment between Lietzmann, Conzelmann, Wolff, and the present writer on one side, and Fee (with, e.g., Hays) on the other becomes apparent. In his commentary of 1987 and his later work of 1994, supported by his smaller study of 1996, Fee perceives the Pauline communities as "charismatic" and "congregational." Thus he draws from vv. 23 and 26 the following conclusions: (i) "all the believers from all the house churches met together in some way"; (ii) "this worship was 'charismatic' . . . a general participation of all members . . ."; (iii) and "charismatic" also in the emphasis on "the more spontaneous gifts of utterance";[282] (iv) "All" speak in tongues and prophesy, since the apparent negation of this in 12:29-30 was merely "to discourage 'all' from doing so" in actual practice, even if all could if they were permitted."[283] Paul's use of **each** underlines this, even though Lietzmann, Conzelmann, Schrage, and Wolff view this only as a projected scenario, while Hodge regards it as a *de facto* situation which Paul is eager to correct. (v) **Hymn** may include extempore prayer or an "interpretation" of tongues, but Fee rejects the strong possibility that, grounded in biblical tradition, the earliest hymns were probably from the Psalms of the OT. (vi) No leadership is mentioned: "the community appears to be left to itself and to the Holy Spirit."[284] In his study of 1996 Fee sees this verse as among "the most noteworthy available evidence [for] the free, spontaneous nature of worship in Paul's churches . . . with the (potential) participation of everyone (1 Cor 14:26). . . . Spontaneity does not mean lack of order."[285]

The points carefully outlined above, including the contributions of Lietzmann, Conzelmann, and Wolff, are not adequately addressed (although Wolff [German 1996] and Schrage [German 1999] postdate Fee's two books). It is essential to allow for a distinction in translation and meaning between those gifts which can hardly be other than spontaneous (e.g., tongues), those which are likely to require sustained biblical reflection (e.g., **item of teaching**), and those which resist exclusion from either category (**prophetic speech, something disclosed**). Wolff's attention to tradition in Paul is confirmed elsewhere in this epistle.[286] Bengel retains a judicious balance. In addition to recognizing that gifts may be reflective or spontaneous, he also questions the numerical or literal understanding of *all*, but adds, "Then was more fruitful than today when one single person *(unus)* . . . fills up the time with a sermon."[287]

(3) The third main difficulty concerns the meaning and translation of ἀποκάλυψιν and more especially of ἑρμηνείαν. Again, *a revelation* (NRSV, REB, NIV, NJB, KJV/AV) seems to suggest an act of divine disclosure on the spot. The word may indeed include this, but it does not exclude the communication of what came to be revealed by God through some experience or through biblical reflection prior to the act of worship itself. NJB covers this eventuality by *bring . . . a revelation,* but then this excludes the implied

---

282. Fee, *First Epistle,* 683 and 684. Unrevised (1994) in *God's Empowering Presence* 242-43. Cf. also *Paul, the Spirit and the People of God,* 154-62; further Hays, *First Cor,* 241.

283. Fee, *First Epistle,* 684 and 690; *God's Empowering Presence,* 243 and 248.

284. Fee, *First Epistle,* 690-91; *God's Empowering Presence,* 249.

285. Fee, *Paul, the Spirit and the People of God,* 154-55.

286. Bengel observes that the "psalm" may be *"habitu vel actu, vel paulo ante, vel jam modo";* it may or may not be *"a Spiritu cantica extemporalia" (Gnomon,* 660).

287. Ibid., 660.

contemporaneity of NIV's *has . . . a revelation.* In Gal 1:12, 16 Paul uses ἀποκάλυψις of the revelation of God's Son which he had received at his call, albeit with ongoing consequences and entailments. In 1 Cor 1:7 the term denotes the future appearance of Jesus Christ. In 14:6 "ἀποκάλυψις . . . is distinguished from glossolalia and grouped together with 'knowledge or prophecy or teaching'; it is thus . . . something presented in an understandable fashion."[288] Hence **something disclosed** avoids either foreclosing the temporal scope of the term or becoming distracted by modern philosophical and theological controversy about "revelation."[289] The disengagement from later theological traditions runs parallel with the rendering of διδαχή as *a piece of* **teaching** (Barrett), *instruction* (REB, NIV, NJB), or *lesson* (NRSV), in contrast to the older KJV/AV, *a doctrine.*

The most controversial problem arises from the meaning of ἔχει ἑρμηνείαν, translated above as **puts the tongues language into words** but translated elsewhere as *has . . . an interpretation* (REB). Without question what is interpreted or put into words is that which is potentially but not actually articulated in the speaking in tongues, as the use of the precise phrase ἑρμηνεία γλωσσῶν in 12:10 confirms. Barrett translates interpretation, but also affirms "of a communication made in a tongue."[290] Yet we have already questioned in what sense, if any, the preconscious or sublinguistic experience which prompts sounds described technically as **tongues** serves as an actual rather than potential communication. Wittgenstein wrestles continuously with the relation between thought and language, and between experience, stance, and "self-awareness" (cf. συνείδησις in 8:7-13). He observes, "Meaning is as little an experience as intending. But what distinguishes them (sublinguistic "private," dormant, inoperative meanings) from experience? They have no experience-content. For the contents (images for instance) . . . are not the meaning. The intention *with which* one acts does not 'accompany' the action any more than the thought 'accompanies' the speech. . . . 'Talking' (whether out loud or silently) and 'thinking' are not concepts of the same kind."[291] "Talking" becomes communicative only in relation to a given context and semiotic code which presupposes a shared competency between speaker and hearers. Without the latter, "if God had looked into our minds he would not have been able to see there whom we were speaking of."[292] However, a directed longing, a praising stance, an overflowing heart, all these con-

---

288. T. Holtz, *EDNT,* 1:131.

289. Even some conservative writers find negative nuances in the persistent return to this word as a technical theological term; cf. N. Wolterstorff, *Divine Discourse* (Cambridge: Cambridge University Press, 1995), ch. 2, "Speaking Is Not Revealing," 19-36.

290. Barrett, *First Epistle,* 327.

291. L. Wittgenstein, *Philosophical Investigations* (Oxford: Blackwell, 2d ed. Germ. and Eng. 1967), 217, sect. 2.11. On thinking, meaning, understanding, and language cf. sects. 327-49 and throughout.

292. Ibid., 217.

stitute realities which Wittgenstein's hypothetical "God" *could* "see," even if not as "meanings" to be communicated.

It is difficult, unless this analysis is wildly wrong, to understand what is "there" for another human agent, albeit through the Spirit, to interpret as a communicative message. However, it is entirely plausible that, like waking from a scrambled dream, or raising one's threshold of brain waves from the alpha waves of contemplation to the beta waves of meditation, in this very experience meaning emerges as the transnormal experience and attains intelligibility within a context of behavior or events for the speaker, who may then put it into words. Far from causing insurmountable problems, therefore, our understanding of this Greek phrase supports and coheres with our exegesis of 14:2, 4, 6-11, 13 and 18-22 (see above for exegesis of and Notes on these verses, including a response to the counterarguments of Christopher Forbes).

The principles of **the building up of the community** now receives full weight and expression. It is in the first place "a general rule" *(la règle générale)* (cf. v. 12).[293] We have already considered arguments for explicating what is implicit in **building up**, namely, **building up the community**. Barrett confirms these arguments: "The last three words are not in the Greek, but repeatedly (e.g., v. 4) Paul chooses to apply the metaphor of edification to the whole body of Christians rather than to the individual."[294] Our translation of this phrase, therefore, replicates Barrett's.

27 Once again, most VSS and most commentators envisage an agency *additional* to the person or persons who speak(s) in tongues as providing an interpretation of the processes which have overwhelmed the speaker or speakers. However, we have argued consistently that all (or at least virtually all) the relevant passages in 12:1–14:26 which use διερμηνεύω or ἑρμηνεύω (especially 14:6 and 14:13) are more likely to refer to the persons who speak in tongues as themselves articulating what had otherwise been inexpressible in everyday speech. We may recall that Luther and Heinrici hold this view especially of 14:13.[295] The syntax makes this understanding entirely compatible with this verse, even if on its own the Greek could be understood either in the traditional way or in the terms proposed here.

First and foremost, both BDF and BAGD, together with H. D. Betz in *EDNT,* firmly agree that the numeral εἷς (here translated **the one who speaks**) passes regularly "from the force of a numeral (*one* as opposed to several) to that of τις (indefinite article) . . . parallelled in English ["one speaks . . ."], German, and the Romance language [reaching] its climax in modern Greek. The model for the NT was also Hebrew אֶחָד [*'echad*] and Aramaic חַד [*chad*]."[296] The numeral may serve to denote "*someone . . . exactly the same thing as the indef.*

293. Senft, *La Première Épitre,* 181; cf. Horrell, *Social Ethos,* 183.

294. Barrett, *First Epistle,* 327.

295. Heinrici, *Das erste Sendschreiben,* 440, citing and endorsing Luther's translation *wer mit Zungen redet, der bete also dass er es auch auslege.* See 440, n. 3.

296. BDF, 129, sect. 247 (2); cf. BAGD, 231; Betz, *EDNT,* 1:399.

art. . . . someone, . . . Mk 10:17; εἰς ὀνόματι κλεοπᾶς Lk 24:18 . . . perhaps Hebraistic (cf. Num 1:1; 2 Esdr 10:17)."[297] "In koine Greek the use of εἷς is extended so that it increasingly takes the place, e.g., of the indefinite pronoun τις. . . . Also significant is the influence of Semitic usage."[298] It might be thought that its syntagmatic relation to **two or at the most three** would ensure a numerical meaning, and this is what the standard translations assume. However, in a seriatim group εἷς τις ἐξ αὐτῶν (Luke 22:50) can be used to refer back to antecedents (v. 49, οἱ περὶ αὐτόν . . .). Here, therefore, εἷς may refer back in syntax to the τις of the first clause within the verse, varied not only for stylistic reasons but *also to emphasize the preference for a single speaker,* albeit with a concession for **two** or **at the most** (expressing the reluctance of this concession) **three**. It is noteworthy that Fee allows that εἷς here "could refer to one of the . . . tongues speakers.[299]

Second, Conzelmann, Findlay, and NRSV render καὶ ἀνὰ μέρος *"and* **in turn**, [or "by turns] . . . not all confusedly speaking at once," against Edwards' notion that "they speak antiphonally (ἀνὰ μέρος "in turns") until they come to the end of the utterance," passing into antiphonal church music "by an easy and apparently rapid gradation."[300] REB and Barrett's *one at a time* conveys the same idea. Presumably two speakers felt so convinced that they were inspired that they felt "impelled" to speak even if they overrode another. If several are overwhelmed by feelings or experiences that find initial expression in **tongues**, these are to cease to let **one** or **two** (never more than three) make these feelings or experiences communicable so that the community may be edified by joining in with the prayer or praise, aware of its grounds and content. However, these utterances are to remain firmly within "the ethics of controlled speech" (see above, introduction to 14:26-40).[301]

Wolff helpfully compares a parallel "rule" for the avoidance of "confusion" in worship in the Qumran community (1QS 6:8-10).[302] The "rule" at Qumran in the Manual of Discipline ensures that worshipers listen properly to their neighbors before bursting forth into speech. Fee observes that unlike pagan "ecstasy," Christian inspiration of either tongues or prophetic speech "is not 'out of control.' . . . The Spirit does not 'possess' or 'overpower' the speaker."[303] Even so, Paul limits these "interventions" because, as Héring

297. BAGD, 231. See also Schrage, *Der erste Brief,* 3:448.

298. Betz, *EDNT,* 1:399. Against Weiss, Conzelmann also supports this exegesis (*1 Cor,* 245, n. 43).

299. Fee, *First Epistle,* 692, n. 18.

300. Findlay, *Expositor's Greek Testament,* 2:912; cf. Conzelmann, *1 Cor,* 244; against Edwards, *First Epistle,* 379. Findlay tartly observes that exalted or "ecstatic" utterance would be very different from antiphonal chants, even if the syntax favored the idea.

301. **If it is in a tongue that someone** . . . attempts to take account of an emphasis which may perhaps be implied in the Greek word order, where **in a tongue** occurs immediately after **if** or *whether.*

302. Wolff, *Der erste Brief,* 339.

303. Fee, *First Epistle,* 692.

notes, if tongue-speaking in public has to be articulated in plain words, and if on top of this prophetic speech has to be tested, by the time that one adds Bible readings, psalms, prayer, and so forth it might be "necessary to dam these floods of eloquence."[304] On the other hand, we need not suppose that the status of every prophetic declaration was necessarily determined and foreclosed on the spot, as Héring implies. Craig asks (if an "interpreter" is an additional agent), "Can it be that Paul is giving here a permission on the basis of conditions which could not often be met? How could anyone know in advance that another would have the gift. . . ?"[305] For, as Fee concedes, "interpreter of tongues" is not a habituated personal gift comparable with "teacher" or "prophet." Thus, either Paul is very negative, or the verb denotes the tongue-speaker's gift to use intelligible words for the experience.

28 The lack of clear distinction between ἑρμηνευτής and διερμηνευτής is suggested by the minor variants between B, D*, F, and G (the Western texts read the former) and A, E, K, and L, who read the latter while D* and G have the article before the noun. However, Forbes makes this distinction a major one in his critique of my exegesis of 14:13 ("Thiselton's Philological Argument," in his *Prophecy and Inspired Speech*, 65-68).

Schrage discusses the hypothetical nature of the scenario on vv. 28-29, while Heinrici, Weiss, Lietzmann, and Conzelmann helpfully allude here to 14:2 and to those parts of this chapter which draw a firm contrast between encouraging speaking in tongues "at home" and discouraging and restricting the use of tongues "in public."[306] Lietzmann and Edwards understand the subjunctive ᾖ to stand for παρῇ (cf. *sit* for *adsit* in Latin), i.e., *if* **none is** *present who can . . .* or, in their words, *if no interpreter is present.*[307] Weiss, on the other hand, understands ᾖ not as an impersonal *there is,* nor as *he is present,* but as denoting the habituated agency of the subject: *but if he is not an interpreter,* i.e., **if he or she** (the speaker in tongues) **cannot put it into words. . . .**[308] The latter may perhaps cohere more readily with Paul's use of the present imperative σιγάτω, which is best translated **let them** [him or her, singular] **remain silent** (in contrast to *become silent*).

As most of the German commentators recognize, the idiomatic use of ἑαυτῷ, the reflexive pronoun *to* (or *for*) *himself* picks up the resonance of 14:2 (Heinrici, Lang, Wolff) and v. 4 in addition to v. 2 (Weiss, Schrage).[309] With the exception of Strobel, most of these German commentators hold that Paul en-

304. Héring, *First Epistle*, 153.

305. Craig, "1 Cor," *IB*, 10:208.

306. Heinrici, *Das erste Sendschreiben*, 455; Lietzmann, *An die Korinther*, 74; Conzelmann, *1 Cor*, 245; Weiss, *Der erste Korintherbrief*, 339-40; cf. 535-39; Schrage, *Der erste Brief*, 3:447-49.

307. Edwards, *First Epistle*, 379.

308. Weis, *Der erste Korintherbrief*, 339-40.

309. Heinrici, *Das erste Sendschreiben*, 455; Lang, *Die Briefe*, 1,989; Wolff, *Der erste Brief*, 339; Schrage, *Der erste Brief*, 449.

courages the use of tongues only "at home."[310] However, in the light of 14:2, 4, there seems little doubt that Paul uses ἑαυτῷ not in the negative sense of "for self-affirmation" proposed by Vielhauer in the context of 14:2-4, but to mean **privately**. Robertson and Plummer observe "to *himself* . . . that is, in private, not in the congregation. It cannot mean that he is to 'commune with his own heart' in *public* . . ." (their italics).[311] Bruce similarly concludes that Paul's instruction is: "reserve it for private devotion" in such circumstances.[312]

29 Virtually all commentators note Paul's change of tone. There is no reluctance about "at most" three, but a positive and unqualified encouragement to speak. Conzelmann's rendering of the first clause is therefore excellent: **In the case of prophets, however** . . . , which takes up the contrastive use of δέ here.

The most significant Greek word for comment is διακρινέτωσαν, **let them sift.** . . . Although many translate *test* (Barrett), NRSV follows Goodspeed's *weigh,* while KJV/AV and *NT in Basic English* have *judge;* Phillips has *think over;* and REB, *exercise their judgment.* However, as BAGD and other lexicographical studies make clear, the most frequent and most characteristic force of διακρίνω in the active voice is *to differentiate* or to *distinguish between.*[313] The problem is quite simply that it is not idiomatic English to translate the Greek as a hanging intransitive: "let the others *distinguish between.*" However, this is Paul's meaning. **The others** are to **distinguish between** (i) *prophetic speech which is God-given and coheres with the gospel of Christ and the pastoral situation* and (ii) *speech which is merely self-generated rhetoric reflecting the speaker's disguised self-interests, self-deceptions, or errors,* albeit under the guise of supposed "prophecy." We have argued above, following Hill, Müller, Gillespie, and others, that this includes a claim to communicate *gospel preaching pastorally contextualized.* The authentic is to be **sifted** from the inauthentic or spurious, in the light of the OT scriptures, the gospel of Christ, the traditions of all the churches, and critical reflections. Nowhere does Paul hint that preaching or "prophecy" achieves a privileged status which places them above critical reflection in the light of the gospel, the Spirit, and the scriptures. *It is never infallible.*

The others clearly stand in contrast to the two or three who communicate intelligible prophetic speech. In general this task is a corporate one undertaken by the congregation. However, in his discussion of gifts bestowed by the Holy Spirit Paul there specifies that *apostles* and *teachers* have a special role alongside *prophetic speakers,* and that some (ἄλλῳ) are especially equipped by the Spirit for διακρίσεις πνευμάτων (see under 12:10, where this last phrase occurs). In this connection we noted Dautzenberg's distinctive and unusual under-

310. Against Strobel, *Der erste Brief,* 222.
311. Robertson and Plummer, *First Epistle,* 321.
312. Bruce, *1 and 2 Cor,* 134.
313. BAGD, 185. The nuance of *testing* becomes more prominent in the papyri; cf. MM, 150.

standing of this gift of *discernment,* which he viewed against the background of apocalyptic to mean *to interpret.* With respect to 14:29 he therefore explicitly rejects *weigh what is said* (RSV, NRSV), arguing for the meaning "let two or three prophets speak and let the others *interpret.*"[314] However, this is largely because he regards as untenable any notion of "a judicial evaluation of prophets' revelations in the congregational assembly (cf. 1 Cor 14:6, 26, 30)," and because he regards prophetic speech in these passages as that which reveals "mysteries" in the terms of apocalyptic (Dan 9:4; 4 Ezra 12:11-12; 1QpHab 2:8).[315] This speculative explanation is more complex and difficult than the understanding suggested above. Weiss and Friedrich regard οἱ ἄλλοι as referring to **the others** among the *prophets,* but, as we have noted, it would be surprising if *teachers,* let alone *apostles,* were excluded; the term is used in a general way, neither restricted to **prophets** (with Friedrich) nor excluding any particular role on the part of leaders (as Fee implies).[316] Traditions concerning elders, teachers, and a chairperson or president are likely to have been carried over from synagogue tradition, but Paul draws no hard-and-fast line between different categories here.[317] Allo similarly understands **the others** "principally" (but not exclusively) as "the leaders of the congregation *(les chefs de l'assemblée).*"[318]

It is essential to note how rapidly the early church came to hold a different view from that of Paul, at least in some circles. The early subapostolic *Didache* (date uncertain, but perhaps the end of the first century or more probably early second century, perhaps c. AD 117 to c. AD 130) declares, "You shall not test or examine (οὐ πειράσετε οὐδὲ διακρινεῖτε) any prophet who is speaking in the Spirit (ἐν πνεύματι)" since blasphemy against the Spirit "will not be forgiven" (*Didache* 11:7). However, the church soon discovered that it could not simply allow all claims to prophetic speech or prophetic status to go unchallenged. Hence the *Didache* substitutes for Paul's *theological* discrimination a testing that concerns the *lifestyle* of those who claim prophetic inspiration. This writing has to concede, "But not everyone who speaks ἐν πνεύματι [under the guise of speaking 'in the Spirit'?] is a prophet, unless such a one exhibits the life-style (ἐὰν ἔχῃ τοὺς τρόπους) of the Lord" (*Didache* 11:8). I argue elsewhere that concern about lifestyle explains the otherwise self-contradictory utterance on a parallel subject in Titus 1:12-13.[319]

30 Whereas we argued that the earlier allusion to a *disclosure* or *revelation* need not be confined to insight given by God at the very moment of corporate worship, the use of the aorist passive subjunctive ἀποκαλυφθῇ suggests

---

314. Dautzenberg, *Urchristliche Prophetie,* 128-29; and *EDNT,* 1:306.

315. Ibid.

316. Weiss, *Der erste Korintherbrief,* 340; G. Friedrich, "προφήτης," *TDNT,* 6:851; cf. 848-61; Fee, *Paul, the Spirit, and the People of God,* 169-75.

317. Greeven, "Propheten, Lehrer, Vorsteher bei Paulus," 1-43.

318. Allo, *Première Épitre,* 370.

319. A. C. Thiselton, "The Logical Role of the Liar Paradox in Titus 1:12, 13: A Dissent from the Commentaries," *BibInt* 2 (1994): 207-23.

that the light of disclosure dawns with fresh understanding during worship, contemplation, or reflection on the biblical reading or on a previous word of preaching. As Gadamer stresses throughout his work on understanding, frequently a fresh and creative understanding of a "third" context emerges as a to-and-fro of dialogical sharing provides conditions for new insight to "emerge."[320] We should not disengage the workings of God's Holy Spirit from the Spirit's use of human processes such as these which in no way compromise the "gift" or divine origin of the disclosure. As Bengel observes (above under v. 26), a single input of a one-person sermon does not always provide such a "fruitful" or productive stimulus.[321] In relation to the concerns of the *Didache* noted above, Gadamer speaks of a creative understanding which, unlike the more propagandist declarations of one speaker, cannot be "a possession at the disposal of one speaker" for manipulatory purposes, but transforms speaker and hearers alike as the horizons of communal or common understanding are shared together.[322]

The ethics of controlled speech, with which we began our introduction to vv. 25-40 (see above) come to a sharp focus in Paul's insistence that even prophetic monologue must have controlled boundaries. It is quite conceivable that what is **disclosed** or *revealed* to the second speaker is that the first has now unwittingly drifted into self-deceptive, manipulative, mistaken, or merely self-important discourse and has ceased to communicate what God's Spirit has revealed. Whether the disclosure takes this form or the revelation of a quite different insight, Wolff observes that prophetic speech is not exempt from the same constraints of controlled utterance as mark Paul's instructions about speaking in tongues: in both cases the speakers must not give rise to "confusion" or "muddle" *(kein Durcheinander geben).*[323] For this does not witness to the coherent and purposive nature of the sovereign God who *orders* creation and redemption through the purposive agency of his Holy Spirit (see v. 33). In modern theology we might refer here to a trinitarian economy of coherent divine action and relationality.

To another person who is sitting down nearby may seem too specific for the dative present participle ἄλλῳ . . . καθημένῳ. However, NRSV's *sitting nearby* (AV/KJV, NJB, *sitting by*) reflects a subcategory listed in BAGD in association with this verse, where a specific place or location may be envisaged.[324] More to the point, does the verb denote here **sitting down** in semantic

320. H.-G. Gadamer, *Truth and Method* (2d Eng. ed. from 7th Germ ed.; London: Sheed & Ward, 1989), 369-79.

321. Bengel, *Gnomon,* 660.

322. Gadamer, *Truth and Method,* 378-79; cf. also Gadamer, *Dialogue and Dialectic* (New Haven: Yale University Press, 1980); R. R. Sullivan, *Political Hermeneutics: The Early Thinking of Hans-Georg Gadamer* (University Park: Pennsylvania State University Press, 1989), 25-29, 140-81; and Thiselton, *Interpreting God,* 11-27, 67-73.

323. Wolff, *Der erste Brief,* 340.

324. BAGD, 389, entry 1a, second and third categories.

contrast to *standing?* REB avoids implying this contrast by translating *someone else present.* Edwards and Fee suggest that whereas rabbinic teachers and synagogue listeners remain **sitting down** (even for teaching as well as listening) those who read biblical portions, or who pray, or who utter *prophetic speech,* stand up to do so.[325] In this case, the one who is **sitting down nearby** may well have stood to indicate his readiness to communicate what was disclosed to him for the congregation. At that signal the first speaker should **stop speaking** (third person imperative, σιγάτω, *let him be silent*). Nevertheless, while this contrast of posture is probable, as REB indicates, we cannot press this scenario beyond all possible doubt.

31-32 Our translation of v. 31 ensures that the force of δύνασθε γὰρ . . . πάντες is construed in the way that is demanded by the immediate context of argument. The dispute here is not whether all or some may prophesy; it is whether **everyone** who has the gift of using prophetic speech also has the reflective and critical self-awareness and control to begin and especially **to stop** (v. 30) when the circumstances which are going on outside the speaker's immediate prophetic awareness warrant it. Paul insists that there are no exemptions to the rule that prophetic speech, like speaking in tongues, *remains subject to the ethics of controlled speech,* even if this necessitates a critical awareness of what one is doing, and what others are doing, when one's utterance is "inspired" or "given" by God.[326] Perhaps some felt that they were so privileged by their own status as to be *either consciously unwilling or allegedly unable* to stop, on the ground that God had seized and overwhelmed them by his Spirit, and the Spirit must not be hindered. Against this Paul insists that the principles of **one by one** (here the distributive καθ' ἕνα, but also equivalent in effect to ἀνὰ μέρος, **in turn**, of tongues in v. 27) must apply to **everyone**. Hence it is indeed possible to translate *you can all prophesy, one at a time* (NRSV) or *you can all prophesy in turn* (NIV), provided that the *all* and *can* is perceived to apply to the phrase *one at a time,* not (at least here) to the act of prophetic utterance, since it is the former, not the latter, that represents the point of Paul's insistence.

It is virtually impossible to translate the last word of v. 31, παρακαλῶνται, by a single English verb, although NRSV translates **be encouraged** (NJB, *receive encouragement*). However, REB and NIV rightly recognize that παρακαλέω denotes a wide range of meanings, even as prophetic preaching, of which *encouragement* is only one. Hence they render it *instruction and encouragement* (REB) or *instructed and* **encouraged** (NIV). To us, however, *instruction* seems more closely related to teaching (although the broad term **learn**, μανθάνω, occurs in this verse). **Exhorted** or even *warned* seems more charac-

---

325. Edwards, *First Epistle,* 379; Fee, *First Epistle,* 695, n. 35.

326. Fee observes that Paul aims his words particularly "at those who might tend to dominate the meeting, although this is not certain" (*First Epistle,* 695). He rightly adds that the key comment for the meaning of this verse is that "neither the tongues-speaker *nor* the prophet is out of control" (Fee's italics, loc. cit.).

teristic of prophetic speech alongside **encouraged**. See above, "Prophecy: A Second Note" under 14:3, especially (2) (b and c), Building Up, Encouraging and Bringing Comfort, and the literature cited there.[327] This experience of **everyone's learning** and recurring *paraklesis* is expressed in a purpose clause (ἵνα with subjunctive) as the goal which is served by the ethics of controlled speech. This deferring to the other not only replaces irreverent confusion by a respectful order but also allows **everyone** to benefit and none to miss out because of the self-importance or supposed "possession" of a particular speaker.

The concluding clause, v. 32, raises difficulties for translation although the thrust and force are clear. We have already discussed the difficulty of recovering Paul's precise meaning when πνεῦμα is uncharacteristically used of the human spirit, since he uses the term neither after the fashion of hellenistic or Cartesian dualism, nor in the sense of prophetic "inspiration" which in certain Graeco-Roman or oriental religious cults (but not in Paul) are deemed to be independent of reflective consciousness, or the mind. Findlay projects the scenario of an indignant reply from a prophet of Corinth who overdraws the picture: "How can I prophesy *to order?* . . . How restrain the Spirit's course in me?"[328] Paul insists, by way of anticipating this kind of objection, that even **the spiritual utterances of the prophets**, i.e., even what the Spirit of God inspires, remains **subject . . . to control** in the interests of serving the purposes of the Holy Spirit himself, namely, that **everyone** (v. 31) **may learn and be encouraged or exhorted**. Such **control** is no less a part of the Spirit's work than the content of the utterance, but (like the utterance, at least in Paul's view) it also involves the active and responsible agency of the prophet.

The clearest and most transparent word here is ὑποτάσσεται. In the active voice, the verb means *to subordinate,* including subordinating "someone or something to someone."[329] In the passive it means *to be made subject* (cf. Rom 8:20; 1 Cor 15:28). In this verse the present indicative middle has the sense of *to subordinate oneself, to be subjected, to place oneself under* **control**. Hence Paul states that *the ethics of controlled speech* apply to the responsible and critical initiative of the prophetic agent consciously to **control** *where, when, and for how long* to speak, even if the utterance is genuinely **spiritual**, i.e., inspired by the Spirit. For Paul is about to make the point that the Holy Spirit does not undermine his own work by inconsistency and confusion. It cannot be the case that the Spirit purposes to inspire prophets in such a way as to allow some to dominate, while others miss important utterances. Thus the **prophets' control** over their own speech is essential, not least for serving the Spirit's own work

327. Cf. esp. Müller, *Prophetie and Predigt im NT,* 118-30, 162-233; Grabner-Haider, *Paraklese und Eschatologie bei Paulus,* 116-28; and Kitzberger, *Bau der Gemeinde,* 73-78.

328. Findlay, *Expositor's Greek Testament,* 2:913 (his italics).

329. BAGD, 848. It is worth noting the very tempting REB translation, *It is for prophets to control prophetic inspiration.* This excellently conveys the force, but perhaps wanders unnecessarily far from the actual vocabulary and structure of the Greek. However, it is an acceptable rendering of Paul's point.

and for understanding the nature of prophetic "inspiration." Needless to say, any notion of a community "working itself up" by psychological autosuggestion or repetitive devices designed to heighten emotion would be entirely alien to Paul's ethics of controlled speech. "All these directives presume that the gift is in some sense under the speaker's control. One can *choose* whether to speak out in tongues [or in prophetic speech] or to remain [or to become] silent" (Hays's italics).[330] (See above also on Theissen's notion of "learned behavior," especially in the discussion at 12:8).

33a Our translation follows Moffatt and NJB, which is also that of NRSV, REB, and NIV except for the word order of the negative *(God is not a God of disorder . . .)*. We have searched in vain for a stronger, more colorful word than **disorder** for the negated intensive compound word ἀκαταστασία. KJV/AV renders it *confusion,* which is acceptable lexicographically and reflects the Corinthian situation. Similarly, BAGD and other lexicons offer *disturbance, commotion,* and *unruliness* alongside **disorder**, which would cohere with the theme of God's sovereign rule and the semantic contrast with **peace**.[331] However, chs. 12–15 portray the *ordered* nature of God's purposive action in apportioning gifts and in creation and in resurrection, and Paul's larger point is that this **order** in the nature of the God who acts coherently, faithfully, and without self-contradiction should be reflected in the lifestyle and worship of the people of God. Thus a gift given by the Holy Spirit to benefit everyone (vv. 28-32) would be undermined in a self-contradictory and chaotic way if the Spirit himself "fell upon" this or that individual in such a way that responsible processes of ministry were disrupted and confused, and some missed out on part of what the Holy Spirit was communicating through responsible human agents.

This perspective is confirmed with reference to the close affinity of the Greek words in a parallel expression of thought in Jas 3:16-17. The competitive jealousy and strife (ζῆλος καὶ ἔρις) which bedeviled church life at Corinth and rendered it self-centered ("fleshly," σαρκικοί, 3:3; cf. 1:11 [ἔριδες], 12) are paralleled by the jealousy and strife (ζῆλος καὶ ἐριθεία) which bring *unruliness* or **disorder** (ἀκαταστασία) in Jas 3:16. James sets this in contrast to the wisdom which comes from God (ἡ δὲ ἄνωθεν σοφία), which brings **peace** (εἰρηνική, v. 17). In his book on the ethics of controlled speech in James and in the biblical, Jewish, and hellenistic background, W. R. Baker notes how the reciprocity of controlled speech and openness to listen and to learn in meekness and in modesty reflect the wisdom which characterizes the providence of God and God's dealings with the world in divine wisdom: "A mature Christian knows how and when to deliver this powerful word for God's good purposes. . . . James 3:18 bears witness to the integral part that peace and actions which promote it [including silence and refraining from speech] play in James' hopes for

---

330. Hays, *First Cor,* 241-42.
331. BAGD, 30. MM, 17.

the Christian community and even society at large."[332] The source of this "wisdom," however, is God himself: it is "the perfect gift from God (1:17), whose nature such controlled order expresses and reflects."[333]

Yet the aspect of *disturbance* and *commotion* is not lost from view. "The God who gives the inspiration is not on the side of disorder and turbulence, but on that of peace. He cannot be the promoter of tumult, and therefore cannot inspire two people to speak simultaneously to the same audience. Inspiration is no excuse for conflict and confusion, and jealousies and dissensions are not signs of the presence of God (v. 25)."[334] It is far more important to read ch. 14 in the light of the earlier chapters and of chs. 12–13 than to impose upon it a lens forged out of modern controversies surrounding charismatic renewal and theologies of church order as "ecclesiologies." Paul insists on "order" not as self-contained "doctrine of the church," but because the church must reflect the nature of God and respect for "the other."

ii. A Particular Case (14:33b-36)

The translation and exegesis is immensely complex. Contextual factors are vital, including presuppositions about what the addressees were *assumed* to understand by language of which we know only Paul's part of the dialogue. Nevertheless, the main themes of "controlled speech" and "order" (14:24-40) continue. We also note below the problems caused by issues of whether parts of these verses are un-Pauline, either by interpolation of by allusive quotation.

Supplementary Bibliography on 14:33b-36 (but See Also on 14:1-40)

Allison, R. W., "'Let the Women Be Silent in the Churches' (1 Cor 14:33b-36): What Did Paul Really Say, and What Did It Mean?" *JSNT* 32 (1988): 27-60.

Barton, S. C., "Paul's Sense of Place: An Anthropological Approach to Community Formation in Corinth," *NTS* 32 (1986): 225-46.

Ellis, E. E., "The Silenced Wives of Corinth (1 Cor 14:34-35)," in E. J. Epp and G. D. Fee (eds.), *NT Textual Criticism and Its Significance for Exegesis: In Honour of Bruce Metzger* (Oxford: Clarendon, 1981), 213-20.

Fitzer, G., *Das Weib schweige in der Gemeinde,* TEH 10 (Munich: Kaiser, 1963).

Flanagan, N. M., and E. H. Snyder, "Did Paul Put Down Women in 1 Cor 14:34-36?" *BTB* 11 (1981): 10-12.

Harrington, W., "Paul and Women," *Religious Life Review* 25 (1986): 155-63.

Horrell, D. G., *The Social Ethos of the Corinthian Correspondence* (Edinburgh: T. & T. Clark, 1996), 184-95.

Klauck, H.-J., *1 Korintherbrief* (Würzburg: Echter, 1992), "Das Schweigen der Frau," 104-6.

Kroeger, C. and R., "Strange Tongues or Plain Talk?" *Daughters of Sarah* 12 (1986): 10-13.

---

332. Baker, *Personal Speech-Ethics in the Epistle of James,* 103 and 181.
333. Ibid., 11; cf. 102, 175-76, 183.
334. Robertson and Plummer, *First Epistle,* 323-24.

Maier, W. A., "An Exegetical Study of 1 Cor 14:33b-38," *CTQ* 55 (1991): 81-104.

Manus, C. U., "The Subordination of Women . . . 1 Cor 14:33b-36 Reconsidered," *Review of African Theology* 8 (1984): 183-95.

Munro, W., "Women, Text, and the Canon: The Strange Case of 1 Cor 14:33-35," *BTB* 18 (1988): 26-31.

Nadeau, D. J., "La problème des femmes en 1 Cor 14:33b-35," *ETR* 69 (1994): 63-65.

Niccum, C., "The Voice of the Manuscripts on the Silence of Women: The External Evidence for 1 Cor 14:34-35," *NTS* 43 (1997): 242-55.

Odell-Scott, D. W., "In Defence of an Egalitarian Interpretation of 1 Cor 14:34-6 . . . ," *BTB* 17 (1987): 100-103.

———, "Let the Women Speak in Church: An Egalitarian Interpretation of 1 Cor 14:33b-36," *BTB* (1983): 90-93.

Osburn, C. D., "The Interpretation of 1 Cor 14:34-35," in Osburn (ed.), *Essays on Women in Earliest Christianity* (Joplin: College, 1993), 1:219-42.

Payne, P. B., "Fuldensis, Sigla for Variants in Vaticanus, and 1 Cor 14:34-35," *NTS* 41 (1995): 240-62.

Petzer, J. H., "Reconsidering the Silent Women of Corinth . . . 1 Cor 14:34-35," *ThEv* 26 (1993): 132-38.

Ross, J. M., "Floating Words: Their Significance for Textual Criticism," *NTS* 38 (1992): 153-56.

Rowe, A., "Silence and the Christian Women of Corinth . . . 1 Cor 14:33b-36," *CV* 33 (1990): 41-84.

Sigountos, J. G., and M. Shank, "Public Roles for Women in the Pauline Church," *JETS* 26 (1983): 283-95.

Wire, A. C., *The Corinthian Women Prophets* (Minneapolis: Fortress, 1990), 149-58.

Witherington, B., *Conflict and Community in Corinth* (Grand Rapids: Eerdmans, 1995).

———, *Women in the Earliest Churches,* SNTSMS 59 (Cambridge: Cambridge University Press, 1988), 90-104.

Wolff, C., *Der erste Brief des Paulus an die Korinther,* "Exkurs," 341-47.

33b-34 Judgments about translation become immensely difficult because they are inextricably bound up with Paul's assumption that the Corinthian readers would interpret and understand such words as σιγάτωσαν (*let them be silent; let them hold their peace; let them stop speaking; let them not interrupt*) and λαλεῖν (*to speak, to speak in the way just described, to speak in the way they do*) in accordance with *the context of situation* known both to the author and to the addressees. Here an "abstracted" rendering on the basis of word-for-word lexicography alone could actually violate *contextual* understanding. All this is further compounded by the fact that many view these verses (or some verses) as a non-Pauline interpolation by a copyist; others view them as a quotation of a Corinthian view which Paul rejects; yet others perceive them as a pre-Pauline tradition which Paul accepts and adapts. We must first set forth the facts about the textual evidence (or lack of it) for claims that these verses constitute a non-Pauline interpolation. However, most writers who regard these verses as un-Pauline do so only partly on the grounds of textual variants. These various complexities give rise to the research literature cited above, of which the select bibliography represents only a portion of recent studies. Hays regards v. 33b as belonging to the previous unit (vv. 26-33), but Collins and most other writers more convincingly understood it as the introductory principle for vv. 34-36.[335]

(1) The UBS 4th ed. *Greek New Testament* classifies vv. 34-35 as "B," i.e., "the text is almost certain," although the UBS 3d ed. also used "B" but in that earlier edition this classification indicated "some degree of doubt." The basic facts are that the Western, D, E, F, G, the later 88*, and fourth-century Ambrosiaster displace vv. 34-35 to after v. 40. However, the very early $\mathfrak{p}^{46}$ (Chester Beatty, c. AD 200, together with ℵ, B, A, 33, 88 mg, Vulgate, Old Syriac, and most other MSS) read these verses in their normal, accepted place. Many writers (including Weiss, Conzelmann, Klauck, and Senft) use this displacement in the Western text as *part* of an argument for the view that these verses are an interpolation, but we must keep our textual judgments distinct from arguments of other kinds. Surprisingly, Fee is one of those who place most weight on the textual variants, indicating "a very early marginal gloss that was subsequently placed in the text at two different places," and that these verses were "not part of the original."[336] This variant displacement "may not be shunted aside."[337]

While others agree that vv. 34-35 (or vv. 33b-36) are an interpolation, few place the weight that Fee does on a textual variant which Wire, with meticulous scholarship, shows to rest on a single MS tradition (see below). Metzger and Zuntz in fact find it entirely understandable that an early copyist should move vv. 34-35 to the end of the chapter for any of several reasons.[338] Fee's claims about the paucity of evidence for this type of displacement in the NT where the displacement is artificial seems to be answered by the range of evidence put forward by J. M. Ross.[339] A thorough assessment is offered by A. C. Wire. She points out that every "displacement" MS is either a Greek-Latin bilingual or a Latin text, that E is a direct copy of D, and that F and G are so close to each other that it is widely agreed that they copied the same edited text. In practice only D and G remain as two witnesses, which in turn almost certainly come from "a single common archetype."[340] This distinctive Western text gives rise only to the appearance of a variety of Latin text-types, since these depend on the same single tradition. Wire further explains why the anomalous twelfth-century 88* reading is not a survival of earlier pre-Latin texts, but reflects a reactive scribal activity. Finally, in contrast to Fee, and with Metzger, she offers several possible reasons why the D tradition should have displaced the original authentic sequence which occurs in our texts (UBS 3d and 4th eds.). One relates to errors in copying (e.g., haplography) and their correction; a second, to an attempt to "improve" the text; a third, to ideological interests on the part of a corrector: "it is not scientific to exclude *a priori* the possibility of a translator's or scribe's ideological decision to displace or omit a passage silencing

335. Hays, *First Cor,* 244 (also Hays, *Moral Vision of the NT,* 59, n. 82; Collins, *First Cor,* 520. Schrage expresses uncertainty about v. 33b, along with problems about the Pauline authorship of the new unit (*Der erste Brief,* 3:443 and 457).

336. Fee, *First Epistle,* 699.

337. Ibid., 700.

338. Metzger, *Textual Commentary* (2d ed.), 499-500; Zuntz, *The Text of the Epistles,* 17.

339. Ross, "Floating Words . . .," *NTS* 38 (1992): 153-56.

340. Wire, *The Corinthian Women Prophets,* 149; cf. 149-52 (on text) and 152-58.

women."[341] She cites the period of Montanism and Tertullian as a possible background for such changes.

The debate has become intensified by two highly detailed and meticulous studies by Philip Payne (1995) and by Curt Niccum (1997), each of which reaches different and opposing conclusions: Payne argues on the basis of the Vaticanus "bar umlaut and/or umlaut text-critical sigla . . . of the textual variations" that new textual and internal evidence "strengthens an already strong case that 1 Cor 14:34-35 is an interpolation"; Niccum reviews every aspect of the debate (including Wire and Payne), and concludes, "No extant MS offers evidence for an original omission of 1 Cor 14:34-35. . . . No other reading has claim to being 'original' other than that of preserving the traditional sequence of verses."[342] Payne urges that Metzger overlooked the textual evidence of Codex Fuldensis as an important witness to the omission of the verses. Niccum attacks Payne's appeal to "bar umlauts" marks as at best confused and as postdating the fourteenth century. The earliest known witness to a transposition of sequence in the passage is Ambrosiaster (late fourth century). He cites good reasons for a later reapplication of "in all the churches." Niccum's pages are packed with powerful and succinct arguments which prove convincing.

Further arguments concerning the strictly *textual* issue are urged by others mainly in the same direction as Wire (anticipating Niccum) but sometimes with Fee. Horrell defends Fee's position, arguing that Wire has failed to address the issues fully.[343] Earle Ellis argues that vv. 34-35 constitute a *marginal note added by Paul himself* after reading through the draft of 1 Corinthians.[344] Stephen Barton accepts and develops this idea further.[345] On the other side, however, even Conzelmann, who believes that the verses are an interpolation on *internal* grounds (i.e., exegetical and theological, not textual), concedes that the Western readings are themselves "no argument for the assumption of an interpolation."[346] Witherington expresses strong scepticism about the weight of the textual arguments: "Displacement is no argument for interpolation. Probably these verses were displaced by scribes who assumed that they were about household order, not order in worship, scribes working at a time when there were church buildings separate from private homes."[347] (The earliest Western text witness is around AD 375.) Again, many of Fee's points seem to be amply addressed by J. M. Ross, who categorizes different types of displaced or "floating" texts within the NT. He argues that if the verses were an interpolation, this would be "very early, almost before any copies had been made, certainly before the writing of 1 Tim

341. Ibid., 152.

342. Payne, "Fuldensis, Sigla for Variants in Vaticanus, and 1 Cor 14:34-35," 259-60 and 240; cf. 240-62; and Niccum, "The Voice of the Manuscripts on the Silence of Women: The External Evidence for 1 Cor 14:34-35," 254-55; cf. 242-55. Both articles are impressive, but Niccum's seems overwhelmingly convincing.

343. Horrell, *Social Ethos,* 186-89.

344. Ellis, "The Silenced Wives of Corinth," in *NT Textual Criticism* (cited above), 219-20.

345. Barton, "Paul's Sense of Place . . . ," *NTS* 32 (1986): 229-31; cf. 225-46.

346. Conzelmann, *1 Cor,* 246, n. 16. Conzelmann adds, with many others, that the boundaries of what D, E, F, and G displace do not coincide with the scope of what many regard as an interpolation. Craig similarly opts cautiously for an interpolation view, but argues that more depends on internal than on external textual evidence ("1 Cor," *IB,* 10:212-13).

347. Witherington, *Conflict and Community in Corinth,* 288; see also his *Women in the Earliest Churches,* 91-92 (cf. 90-104).

2:11-13. . . . We are bound to accept the unanimous testimony of the manuscripts, however deeply we may regret that Paul expressed this opinion."[348]

(2) A textual note should include mention of a less significant minor variant also. D, F, G, K, and Old Syriac insert ὑμῶν after γυναῖκες. This may have been an attempt to localize the rule and is perhaps not entirely unrelated to the Western tradition discussed under (1). However p[46] (probable reading) and firmly Sinaiticus, A, B, C, 33, Vulgate, and Coptic have the shorter text, which is clearly right.

WHICH WOMEN? WHAT KIND OF SILENCE?
WHAT KIND OF INTERROGATION? (14:33B-35)

(1) A Non-Pauline Interpolation?

It is impossible to explicate the nuances of the words of the text independently of judgments about what verses, if any, constitute non-Pauline interpolations. Those who argue for the view that either vv. 34-35 or vv. 33b-36 represent an interpolation include, e.g., Schmiedel, Weiss, Dautzenberg, Conzelmann, Fitzer, Strobel, Klauck, Fee, Hays, Senft, and Schrage, as well as more cautiously Moffatt and Barrett.[349] Before we consider the various arguments in detail, it may be helpful first to gain an overview. Senft and Schrage provide a helpful outline of five main arguments: (1) The verses allegedly differ from the main theme or themes of 12:1–14:40; (2) they supposedly interrupt the flow of instructions about the prophets, as the Western copyists perceive (and a few MSS place them after 14:40, e.g., D, F, G); (3) the verses contradict 11:5; (4) to appeal to "the law" to endorse or to validate church discipline is "non-Pauline"; (5) "the expression 'the church of the saints' [ταῖς ἐκκλησίαις τῶν ἁγίων, translated above as **the churches of God's holy people**] is foreign to Paul."[350]

Most, if not all, of these arguments (e.g., especially the relation to 11:5) become clarified in the light of patient exegesis. Collins rightly considers this collection of arguments as "not weighty" and traces the themes and vocabulary which precisely reflect Paul's concerns in 14:25-40.[351] Any attempt to assess these arguments, however (especially the relation to 11:5), must also take account of a further complication. Many argue that vv. 34-35 represent a *Corinthian slogan or piece of Corinthian theology which Paul quotes, only to reject it.* Such a view is not farfetched, for Paul appears to do precisely this in 6:12; 7:1; 10:23; and perhaps elsewhere (e.g., in 8:1-6).

348. Ross, "Floating Word . . . ," 155-56.

349. P. W. Schmiedel, *Die Briefe an die Thessalonischer und an die Korinther* (Tübingen: Mohr, 1892), 2:181-82; Weiss, *Der erste Korintherbrief,* xli and 342-43; Dautzenberg, *Urchristliche Prophetie,* 253-300; Conzelmann, *1 Cor,* 246; G. Fitzer, "'Das Weib schweige in der Gemeinde'. Über den unpaulinischen Charakter der mulier-traceat-Verse in 1 Kor 14," *TEH* 110 (Munich: Kaiser, 1963); Strobel, *Der erste Brief,* 222-25; Klauck, *1 Kor,* 104-6; Moffatt, *First Epistle,* 233-34; Barrett, *First Epistle,* 330-33; Fee, *First Epistle,* 700; Senft, *La Première Épitre,* 182-83; Schrage, *Der erste Brief,* 3:481-87; and Hays, *First Cor,* 244.

350. Senft, *Première Épitre,* 182-83; Schrage, *Der erste Brief,* 3:481-87 (placed after 14:40).

351. Collins, *First Cor,* 516; cf. 515-17 and 520-21.

(2) Does Paul Quote a Corinthian View Which He Rejects?

D. W. Odell-Scott is perhaps most widely associated with this view, both in an article of 1983 and a further response to Jerome Murphy-O'Connor in 1987.[352] However, Manus, Flanagan and Snyder, and Allison all offer variants of this view also (see below). Odell-Scott regards the key particle ἤ, **Or**, at the beginning of v. 36, as offering a resounding rhetorical rejoinder to the conservative patriarchal rule expressed by a group at Corinth in the words of vv. 34-35: **Or was it from you that the word of God went out?** (v. 36). According to Odell-Scott, since this can be understood as a strong rebuttal of vv. 34-35, the passage emphatically endorses the authority of women to speak in the public congregation.

This view also finds expression in slightly different terms in C. Ukachukwu Manus. He understands it as Paul's rebuttal of a male sexist group at Corinth who insisted on a strong subordination of women especially here within marriage.[353] This approach, however, develops a view which was formulated more tentatively in 1981 by N. M. Flanagan and E. H. Snyder.[354] More recently in 1988 R. W. Allison provided perhaps the most detailed development of this same approach. He regards vv. 33b-36 as coming from an earlier letter from Paul to Corinth, in which vv. 34-35 represent the hierarchical view of a conservative group at Corinth, v. 33b is an editorial link, and v. 36 introduces Paul's indignant rhetorical questions following the disjunctive particle ἤ.[355] He suggests an original setting in which Paul argued for eschatological freedom. "Paul's rhetorical questions are his sarcastic rebuttal of his opponents' position."[356]

Horrell finds the view of Odell-Smith and Allison "implausible" not least because, as Conzelmann also notes, v. 36, which attacks the self-important claims of some at Corinth to be "different," then leaves v. 33b *either* as part of the Corinthian slogan, which would not cohere with our knowledge of Corinth, *or* as simply hanging without continuation until after an overly long quotation, *or* as belonging to vv. 26-33a, which, apart from Barrett, KJV/AV, RV, Alford, and Phillips, is widely accepted as belonging with vv. 34-37 (as UBS 4th ed., NRSV, REB, NIV, NJB, Conzelmann, and most writers).[357] "The point about the particle . . . makes most sense when v. 36 is linked with v. 33."[358] Witherington offers stronger and more detailed arguments why the hypothesis of Odell-Scott and Flanagan and Snyder are open to doubt. In sum, because of such phrases as **as in all the churches of God's holy people**, and because 6:12; 10:23; 7:1 et al. represent not "rebuttals" but circumstantial qualifications "they raise more questions than they answer."[359] With a deft turn, he adds: "In all probabil-

---

352. Odell-Scott, "Let the Women Speak in Church: An Egalitarian Interpretation of 1 Cor 14:33b-36," 90-93; and "In Defence of an Egalitarian Interpretation," 100-103.

353. C. U. Manus, "The Subordination of Women in the Church: 1 Cor 14:33b-36 Reconsidered," 183-95.

354. Flanagan and Snyder, "Did Paul Put Down Women in 1 Cor 14:34-36?" 10-12.

355. Allison, "Let the Women Be Silent in the Churches (1 Cor 14:33b-36): What Did Paul Really Say and What Did it Mean?" 27-60.

356. Ibid., 47.

357. Horrell, *Social Ethos,* 187-88. Héring, Bruce, Conzelmann, and Witherington all place v. 33b with what follows: cf. Witherington, *Women in the NT,* 91-92 and 258-59, n. 107. Among older modern commentators we may also cite de Wette and Meyer.

358. Horrell, *Social Ethos,* 188.

359. Witherington, *Women in the NT,* 99.

ity Paul is anticipating the response he expected to get (v. 36) when the Corinthians read his argument (vv. 34-35)."[360] The decisive objection, however, arises under the next heading.

(3) Paul's Use of Contextual Terms: "Speaking," "Silence," "Order," and "Churches"

(a) Speaking

We strongly contend, as Earle Ellis and Ben Witherington do, that vv. 34-35 take up "a large amount of significant vocabulary" from the verses which immediately precede them.[361] The four key terms (as Witherington rightly asserts) are λαλέω (repeatedly from 14:14 to 32), σιγάω (14:28, 30, 34), ἐν ἐκκλησίᾳ (14:28, 35; cf. 34); and ὑποτάσσω (14:32, 34). Ellis stresses that the use of σιγάω, *to be silent,* **to stop speaking, to refrain from speaking**, is "the catch-word connection between verses 28, 30, 34," which is overlooked by theories of interpolation.[362] It is this that constrains and shapes our translation, as we indicate in the brief introduction to vv. 33a-36. Against the argument that the use of οὐ γὰρ ἐπιτρέπεται, **there exists no permission**, is not Pauline, several writers refer with approval to S. Aalen's argument that the key word is drawn here by Paul from a rabbinic formula used in the context of biblical texts, especially in the Pentateuch, which express a principle often introduced with ὁ νόμος λέγει, **the law indicates**.[363] BAGD, Moulton-Milligan et al. and Grimm-Thayer provide instances of the verb in the sense of *it is permitted* (sometimes with the perfect stative sense, **there exists permission**) in the papyri, Josephus, and other first-century sources.[364]

(b) Silence

The verb σιγάω, depending on context, means either **to stop speaking** (as in v. 30, also REB), or *to hold one's tongue,* or *hold one's peace,* or **to refrain from** *using a particular kind of speech,* or *speech in a presupposed context.*[365] Hence while KJV/AV translates *keep silence* (v. 34) NEB has *should not address the meeting,* although REB returns to *should keep silent,* even though it translates λαλεῖν as *have no permission to talk.* On the other hand, vv. 29-33 clearly concern **prophetic speech**, and v. 29b especially the **sifting** of **prophetic speech**. We must therefore firmly keep in view that since 11:5 makes it clear that Paul approves of women using **prophetic speech** their *silence* may allude either to **stopping speaking** or more probably to the possibility of sitting in

---

360. Ibid.

361. Ibid., 91.

362. Ellis, "'Spiritual' Gifts in the Pauline Community," in his *Prophecy and Hermeneutic in Early Christianity,* 27, n. 25. See further his "The Silenced Wives of Corinth (1 Cor 14:34-5)," in Epp and Fee (eds.), *NT Textual Criticism,* 213-20.

363. S. Aalen, "A Rabbinic Formula in 1 Cor 14:34," *SE* 2 (Berlin: Berlin Academy, 1964), 513-25.

364. BAGD, 303; MM, 249; Grimm-Thayer, 245.

365. Grimm-Thayer, 574; BAGD, 749; MM, also 574; W. Radl, *EDNT,* 3:242; G. Fitzer, *Das Weib schweige. . . .*

judgment over prophetic speech which may come from their husbands, i.e., **sifting prophetic speech**, or to a constant intervention of **questions** (cf. v. 35) under the guise of **sifting** what has been said. To provide a balance between contextual constraints and unknown factors, we propose a general term in keeping with Paul's own in the previous verses, namely, **should allow for silence**.

(c) Order

The contextual character of ὑποτάσσω is constrained by an explicitly double context. In v. 32 the verb is used in the middle voice to denote *self-control,* or **controlled speech**. Paul may be insisting on a specific extension of this to a group who saw reflective critical control as reimposing an oppressive "order" from which they had been liberated. A. C. Wire, from the standpoint of a feminist critique of Paul's antiegalitarianism, paints a plausible scenario for such a group. In this case Paul has to extend his principle of *"order"* (τάσσω) to those who might genuinely perceive such an imposition as an apostolic power bid to quench the Spirit and to curb legitimate liberty.

A second context of "order," then, is also introduced. This is larger than speech-ethics or ecclesiology. The Pentateuch (ὁ νόμος) declares the *ordered character of creation and human life* and the regulative character (especially Leviticus, Deuteronomy, Numbers) of *boundaries* or *differentiations*. REB well captures this second context by translating ὑποτασσέσθωσαν as they *should keep their place as the law directs* (against NRSV), *should be subordinate,* or, worse, NIV, *must be in submission*. These are quite different in force from the theological context of **keep their ordered place**.

NRSV and NIV presumably rest partly on lexicography and partly on the exegetical tradition which sees **the law** here as referring to Gen 3:16, the "subordination" of Eve. Chrysostom, Bengel, Godet, Grosheide, Robertson and Plummer, and Orr and Walther are among those who support this tradition.[366] F. F. Bruce, however, shows the difficulty of this view and offers a series of constructive comments. He agrees with most commentators that **the law** is likely to refer to the Pentateuch (cf. 9:8), but nevertheless rejects the widespread view that it refers specifically to Gen 3:16. He observes: "This is unlikely, since in MT and LXX Gen 3:16 speaks of a woman's instinctive inclination . . . (Heb. תְּשׁוּקָה [teshuqah]; Gk [LXX] ἀποστροφή) towards her husband, of which he takes advantage so as to dominate her. The reference is more probably to the creation narratives. . . ."[367] We may take this much further. The patterns of **order** demonstrated in divine actions of creation through differentiation and order and in the Levitical and Deuteronomic codes are integral to the Pentateuch. The prior state of "the earth" was "without form and void" (Heb. תֹהוּ וָבֹהוּ, *tohu*

366. Chrysostom, *1 Cor. Hom.,* 37:1; Bengel, *Gnomon,* 661, "*subjici . . . submittant,* Gen 3, 16"; Godet, *First Epistle,* 2:311, "the words, as saith the law, refer to Gen iii.16, 'Thy husband shall rule over thee'"; Grosheide, *First Epistle,* 343; Robertson and Plummer, *First Epistle,* 325, "The reference is to . . . Gen iii.16"; Orr and Walther, *1 Cor,* 312. Augustine curiously explains the command of Jesus to the Samaritan woman to fetch her husband (John 4) as alluding to 1 Cor 14:34 in that Jesus wanted to teach her through her husband (*Treatise on John,* 15:18 on 4).

367. Bruce, *1 and 2 Cor,* 136. We may note a parallel mistake when the promise or expectation of the resurrection of Christ "according to the scriptures" is tied to some specific (problematic) verse rather than to the pattern of divine action witnessed by the OT more broadly in thematic examples of vindication of his obedient servant (see on 15:4).

wabohu, almost onomatopoeic for chaotic abyss, Gen 1:2). God then "divides" or "separates" light from darkness (Gen 1:4) and heaven from earth (1:6-8) to give each "form." This principle of **order** and *differentiation* (Heb. בדל, *badal*, 1:4, 6, 7, 14, 18; LXX διεχώρισεν, vv. 4, 6, 7, διαχωρίζειν, vv. 14, 18, διαχωρίζον, v. 6) occurs in the standard creation parallels in Babylonian and Egyptian texts.[368]

This conviction that God the Holy Spirit creatively transforms chaos into **order** runs throughout the scriptures, and as Stephen Barton reminds us, anthropological and biblical research cohere and converge in exposing the importance of "boundaries" and "markers" for determining what is "out of place" or suitably "in place" in the life of **God's holy people**. Barton himself argues that the specific central issue in 14:33b-36, as it is also in 11:17-34, arises from "conflict . . . between Paul and the Corinthians about *where the line is to be drawn between church and household*" (Barton's italics).[369] However, "the social importance of boundaries," which also relates to issues of "sacredness" and "power," is not confined, in our view, to that between church and household in this passage.[370] Barton cites the standard work of E. Leach, Mary Douglas, Clifford Geertz, and V. W. Turner among others on the anthropological background, and Wayne Meeks, G. Theissen, and E. Schüssler Fiorenza on related issues in the NT.[371] Philo, as Barton notes, relates male-female boundaries to boundaries of place, especially the contrast between public space and the home (Philo, *De Specialibus Legibus* 3.169-71).[372]

What seems surprising is the extent to which writers tend to overspecify the particular aspect of boundaries of "order" which Paul has as his main concern: husbands versus wives; public space versus the home; speech versus silence; controlled speech versus uncontrolled "inspired" or "ecstatic" speech. Although her work defends the emancipated women prophets against an insecure authoritarian Paul, A. C. Wire is surely right to identify the very large issue of *whether "order" still applies to a charismatic gospel community.*[373] *In the eyes of many at Corinth, it did not; in Paul's view, such a claim undermines the very unity of God by making the God of the Spirit of the new age contradict the God who revealed his ordered ways through scripture* (cf. **the law** in a way which would later be called Marcionite or Montanist). Indeed, Wire explicitly argues that Paul's "rhetoric" depends largely on a (male) logic of differentiation: thought versus reality (3:18; 8:2, 3; 10:12; 11:16; 14:37-8); private versus public (7:2, 8-9, 36; 11:5a, 21-22a; *14:18-19a, 28, 34-35;* 16:2); self-benefit versus community benefit

368. *Babylonian Creation Epic: Enuma Elish,* 4:136-38; cf. *ANET* (1950): 3-155; W. G. Lambert, "A New Look at the Babylonian Background of Genesis," *JTS* 16 (1965): 287-300; and A. R. Millard, "A New Babylonian 'Genesis' Story," *TynBul* 18 (1967): 3-18. The Greek word is also familiar (BAGD, 191). On the Hebrew for chaos, cf. BDB, 96 and 1062.

369. Barton, "Paul's Sense of Place: An Anthropological Approach to Community Formation in Corinth," 225; cf. 225-46.

370. Ibid., 226; cf. 227-28.

371. Cf. Meeks, *The First Urban Christians,* 74-163; Theissen, *Social Setting,* 145-74 (cf. also 69-120); Fiorenza, *In Memory of Her,* 86-90, 176-77, and elsewhere. Classic anthropological sources include Mary Douglas, *Purity and Danger* (London: Routledge, 1966), *Natural Symbols* (London: Barrie & Jenkins, 1973), and *Implicit Meanings* (London: Routledge, 1975); and E. Leach, *Social Anthropology* (Glasgow: Fontana, 1982).

372. Barton, "Paul's Sense of Place," 244, n. 32.

373. Wire, *The Corinthian Women Prophets,* throughout (e.g., 13-38, about to be discussed).

(1:10; 3:3; 8:9-11; 9:22; 10:24, 28-29, 32-33; 11:21-22; 12:7, 24b-25; 13:5b; 14:3, 4, 12); shame versus honor (1:26, 27; 4:10, 14; 11:3-7, 13-15, 21-22; 12:23a; *14:34-35;* 15:42, 43a); and human versus divine (2:12-15; 3:1, 3; 6:15-17; 7:32-34; 10:21-22; 11:7, 20-21; 15:50): "Paul's rhetoric in 1 Corinthians again and again stresses . . . dissociation . . . antithesis. . . . [The Corinthians, especially their women prophets,] do not expect the Lord's Spirit to produce resolution . . . an ordered meal in contrast to strife, disorder. . . . Rather, the spirit seems to be known for generating multiple authorities in contrast to a world of stated authority."[374] Paul integrates these differentiations, Wire argues, by appeals to unifying definitions, justice, scripture, argument, God's calling, the Lord's command, structures of reality, and "universal church practice."[375] Wire is not alone in ascribing a special sense of "emancipation" to women's opinion at Corinth, which generated a specific theology of liberation.[376]

All of these points seem to substantiate our understanding and translation of ὑποτασσέσθωσαν as **let them keep to their ordered place**. It is extremely important to distinguish this from *submission* based on Gen 3:16 (see Bruce's comment above), since this then confuses the Christian believer's role within *the created order* with a role still unresolved within *fallen* creation, which then appears to conflict with Gal 3:28. Thus Kistemaker rightly understands the issue as one of "respect" in God's order, in which, Witherington observes, "women are not being commanded to submit to their husbands, but to the principle of order" (although he unduly adds, "in the worship service").[377] The proof of the permanence of the principle of **order** even within an eschatological mode emerges in 1 Cor 15:28. When everything has been properly ordered (ὑποταγῇ . . . τὰ πάντα, Jesus Christ, *the Son, will also resume his ordered place* (ὁ υἱὸς ὑποταγήσεται) in relation to the God who orders all things (τῷ ὑποτάξαντι . . . τὰ πάντα). This exhibits an "ordered" Trinity, not a "subordinationist" Christology.[378]

(d) The Church and Speech

Wire is right about Paul's concern that Corinth does not make unilateral local decisions which are at odds with **all the churches** since these are no less the *one* **holy people of God**. The context makes it quite clear why Paul uses ἁγίων (against those who mistakenly urge that this phrase is "non-Pauline"). In contrast to Babel, the Spirit of God brings God's people together as one holy people. Paul anticipates the later so-called "marks of the church" in classical theology as "one, holy, catholic, and apostolic Church" as many confess Sunday by Sunday in the Nicene Creed. This verse looks back to 1:2, "called as holy (κλητοῖς ἁγίοις) with *all* those who call upon the name of our Lord Jesus Christ in every place — their Lord as well as ours."

It is essential to ask what Paul means by **speaking** *in this context* of church practice. Since Paul expresses no reservation at all about a woman's praying (προσευχομένη) or using prophetic speech (ἢ προφητευουσα) in 11:5, **speaking** cannot

---

374. Ibid., 22; cf. 13-23 for the contrasts.

375. Ibid., 31; the principles emerge in 23-38.

376. Cf., e.g., Maly, *Mündige Gemeinde*, 222-25, although Maly (against Wire) has more sympathy with Paul.

377. Kistemaker, *1 Cor,* 512; and Witherington, *Women in the Earliest Churches,* 102-3.

378. See below on 15:28.

denote speaking *of any kind without qualification*. It is possible that the universal practice was more "strict," and that Paul cites it with broad approval, subject to the qualification enunciated in 11:5 (see below).[379] However, it is likely that the *contextually presupposed* understanding which does not need to be explicated for the addressees is either *a failure to stop speaking* (if Wire's hypothesis about a more "liberated" and "spiritual" women's group is valid, i.e., they would be resistant to the notion of giving priority to an ethic of controlled speech over spiritual inspiration), *or more probably the disruptive **sifting** of prophetic speech (as in v. 29), which might involve (1) repetitive interruption with questioning; and (2) the possibility of wives cross-examining their husbands, especially if, as is developed in the Didache, issues of contextual lifestyle are part of the sifting.* This scenario becomes more plausible when we review the remaining issues.

Fee observes that, apart from those who regard vv. 34-35 as a non-Pauline interpolation, the majority of (especially Protestant) commentators regard it as axiomatic that Paul refers either to some form of *disruptive speech*, or, as a possible alternative, that 14:34-35 is a more formal *church* setting than 11:2-16.[380] The latter is not easy to sustain, since Paul at once goes on to discuss the Lord's Supper in 11:17-33, where the immensely solemn wording about self-examination (11:28) and drinking judgment on oneself (v. 29) precludes the notion that ch. 11 is like being "at home" (ἐν οἴκῳ, v. 34). What emerges, however, is that neither *silence* nor *speech* nor *church* is used in a generalized, context-free way. Thus Bruce interprets the issue as one of "forbidding them to interrupt proceedings. . . ."[381] In what sense they might "interrupt," however, awaits further comment.

(4) Residual Issues: A Pre-Pauline Rule? Relation to 11:5? Jewish and Greek Backgrounds? A Scenario

(a) If we concur with Witherington and others that what is at issue is not "speech" as much as *"abuse of speech,"* a probable scenario begins to emerge.[382] All of Paul's language is context-specific, although he also appeals to the established tradition of the churches in general that respect for order entails silence in the kind of context that is under discussion. Ellis's suggestion, reformulated by Eriksson but which Fee scarcely pauses to consider, that Paul takes up a *pre*-Pauline tradition and adds it in the margin to otherwise wholly context-relative argument, is defended by Barton as cohering with, and supporting, Paul's sense of place, thereby allowing for Paul's endorsement of a wider principle which can be contextually applied and would account for supposedly non-Pauline phrases *without* regarding them as *post*-Pauline.[383] This is a pos-

379. Fee observes that in 11:2-16 "it is assumed without reproof that women pray and prophesy in the assembly, not to mention that such is also assumed in the repeated 'all' of vv. 23-24 and 31" (*First Epistle*, 702).

380. Ibid., 703. Cf. esp. Barrett, *First Epistle*, 331-33; Maly, *Mündige Gemeinde*, 223; Bruce, *1 and 2 Cor*, 135.

381. Bruce, *1 and 2 Cor*, 135.

382. Witherington, *Women in the Earliest Churches*, 104 (my italics).

383. Barton, "Paul's Sense of Place," 229-30: Eriksson, *Traditions as Rhetorical Proof: Pauline Argumentation in 1 Cor*, 214-16 (cf. Fee, *First Epistle*, 699, n. 4).

sibility, but it remains an unnecessary hypothesis in the light of our discussion above on the relation between **the law** and *respect for* **order** which permeates the Pentateuch. There is nothing whatever "un-Pauline" about the allusion to **the law**, once we have grasped the exegetical issues. We shall return to **there exists no permission** shortly.

(b) Most of the hypotheses about "reconciling" 11:5 with 14:33b-36 remain unnecessary. The widespread notion that whereas 11:2-16 speaks of prophetic speech, the use of λαλεῖν refers to *chatter* in these verses ignores first-century lexicographical evidence and the context of discussion in 14:27-40. Deluz writes: "Paul, then, is not forbidding women to undertake 'ministry of the word'; he is forbidding them to indulge in feminine chatter which was becoming a considerable nuisance."[384] Moffatt asserts, "*Keep quiet* means even more than a prohibition of chattering. Worship is not to be turned into discussion groups. ..."[385] This view seems to have gained currency from Heinrici, who, together with Héring, cannot imagine Paul's silencing "inspired" or "liturgical" speech, but can see him as calling to order "ordinary members of the congregation."[386] C. and R. Kroeger argue that Paul forbids either "chatter" or, at the other end of the spectrum, "frenzied shouting."[387] C. K. Barrett, however, soundly dismisses the faulty lexicography to which such interpretations of λαλεῖν often appeal. The meaning *to chatter* does occur in classical Greek of the earlier centuries, "but in the NT and in Paul the verb normally does not have this meaning, and it is used throughout chapter xiv (vv. 2, 3, 4, 5, 6, 9, 11, 13, 18, 19, 21, 23, 27, 28, 29, 39) in the sense of inspired speech."[388] Fiorenza's argument that 11:2-16 refers to women as such, but 14:33b-36 refers only to married women is also possible (especially since γυναῖκες may mean *married women,* or *wives,* as well as *women*) but remains speculative and not perhaps the most obvious explanation if no contradiction between 11:2-16 and 14:33b-36 arises from a contextual exegesis.[389]

(c) A short research article by D. J. Nadeau (1994) reminds us that in this polemical and contextually constrained situation Paul is deeply concerned to avoid any confusion between the emerging Christian churches and marginal Graeco-Roman or oriental cults in which women exercised more prominent roles than in the synagogues which formed the Jewish roots of the churches.[390] Paul expresses his missionary or evangelistic concern in his allusions to what unbelievers will make of tongues (14:23) and his hopes for their conversion under sober prophetic communication (14:24, 25). In 9:19-23 he has stated that he himself is willing to undergo voluntary restraint and control, even of that to which he has a "right," if it enhances his attempts to win others for Christ. Controlled speech reflects the traditions of the Bible, the synagogue, and the early churches. Perhaps this is why he uses the rabbinic formulations concerning whether **permission exists** and what **the law** indicates. Nadeau has well noted one major strand in Paul's concerns, although he has not set forth the whole picture, as Paul's unqualified support for prayer and prophetic speech

---

384. Deluz, *Companion to 1 Cor,* 215.
385. Moffatt, *First Epistle,* 233.
386. Heinrici, *Das erste Sendschreiben,* 456-61; Héring, *First Epistle,* 154.
387. C. and R. Kroeger, "Strange Tongues or Plain Talk?" 10-13.
388. Barrett, *First Epistle,* 332.
389. Schüssler Fiorenza, *In Memory of Her,* 230-31.
390. Nadeau, "Le problème des femmes en 1 Cor 14:33b-35," 63-65.

by women in 11:5 demonstrates. However, if a form of speech or timing of speech other than prayer or proclamation is involved which may generate more hellenistic than Jewish resonances, then Nadeau has taken us forward in some measure.

(d) With Witherington, we believe that the speaking in question denotes the *activity of* **sifting** *or weighing the words of prophets, especially by asking probing questions about the prophet's theology or even the prophet's lifestyle in public.*[391] This would become especially sensitive and problematic *if wives were cross-examining their husbands about the speech and conduct which supported or undermined the authenticity of a claim to utter a prophetic message,* and would readily introduce Paul's allusion to reserving questions of a certain kind for home. The women would in this case (i) be acting as judges over their husbands in public; (ii) risk turning worship into an extended discussion session with perhaps private interests; (iii) militate against the ethics of controlled and restrained speech in the context of which the congregation should be silently listening to God rather than eager to address one another; and (iv) disrupt the sense of respect for the orderliness of God's agency in creation and in the world as against the confusion which preexisted the creative activity of God's Spirit.

The issue of whether "order" merely attaches to worship services and ecclesiology or to larger questions about God, the Spirit of God, and divine governance which is to be reflected in **God's holy people** appears to represent a point of divergence from Witherington's otherwise helpful analysis.[392] Wire's analysis of the situation, whether our own theology lies with the Corinthian women prophets or with Paul, should not too easily be brushed aside. Two different understandings of God and of the divine Spirit are at issue. Even if the broader picture is rejected, however, to understand **speaking** as **sifting prophetic speech** takes thorough account of the earlier context of vv. 32-33, and of that to which these verses lead on in v. 37. Otherwise v. 37, **If anyone thinks that he or she is a prophet under the influence of the Spirit** . . . loses its contextual meaning and leaves a worse case of "Pauline authoritarianism" than vv. 34-35!

(5) What Kind of Interrogation? (14:35)

Most of the fundamental exegetical issues have already been discussed above. In different ways Stephen Barton and Antoinette Wire clarify the importance of boundaries between public and private space in relation to the issues under discussion. In Wire's view Paul wishes to disempower the women by confining their "place" to the home.[393] For Paul, however, the concern is not to disempower women, but (i) to reflect in life and worship the dialectic of creativity and order which reflects God's own nature and his governance of the world; (ii) to keep in view the missionary vision of

---

391. Witherington, *Women in the Earliest Churches,* 102: "Paul would be turning from a more general exhortation to orderly procedure in regard to weighing prophecy (vv. 32-33) to the more specific case of women weighing or questioning prophecy." This would explain v. 37 (whether prophets as in 30-33a, or prophetesses as in 33b-36).

392. In his last paragraph of this section Witherington is so eager to disengage "order" from issues of family life that in effect he restricts it to the church at public worship only (*Women,* 104). Wolff, *Der erste Brief,* 345-46, takes a similar approach.

393. Wire, *Corinthian Women Prophets,* 157-58; cf. also esp. 16-17 and elsewhere.

how any Christian activity, whether corporate or individual, is perceived in the world still to be reached by the gospel (cf. 9:19-23; 14:23-25); and (iii) to avoid a merely localized or brazenly unilateral self-regulation which nurtures the false sense of corporate self-sufficiency of what Calvin calls here "a church . . . turned in on itself, to the neglect of others."[394] This verse thus comes in between the allusions in vv. 33b-34 to **all the churches of God's holy people** (v. 33) and **when congregations meet in public** (v. 34), and in v. 36 to the apostolic origin and shared currency of **the word of God**.

If, as we believe, Witherington is right in asserting that the context of discourse refers most particularly to the **sifting**, *weighing, testing,* or *discerning* of prophetic speech, it has even been the case that "a prophet is not without honour except in his own homeland and in his own home" (ἐν τῇ οἰκίᾳ αὐτοῦ, Matt 13:57); or still further in Mark 6:4, 5: "a prophet is not without honour (ἄτιμος) except in his own homeland and among his relatives (καὶ ἐν τοῖς συγγενεῦσιν αὐτοῦ) and in his home (καὶ ἐν τῇ οἰκίᾳ αὐτοῦ) and he could do no work of power there."[395] The fact that this saying occurs in all four Gospels (cf. Luke 4:24; John 4:44), and that a version of the axiom seems to occur also in the *Gospel of Thomas* 31, suggests that an early authentic saying of Jesus may have become virtually a proverb in the early church as the experience of the fate of Jesus was replicated for early Christian preachers.[396] On Matthew, Hagner comments: "Jesus was widely held to be a prophet (cf. 21:11, 46). The people of his own home town, however, and even his own household or family (cf. Mark 3:21) were outraged and indignant at the pretensions of one who was to them so familiar and hence thought to be ordinary . . . (with wider scope . . . John 1:11)."[397] We have only to recall the debates at Corinth about the status of "people of the Spirit" as against those who were deemed "ordinary" to understand the immense piquancy and sensitivity when a person uttered **prophetic speech**, and as it was **sifted**, or even perhaps to initiate a "sifting," a wife or close relation might interrogate the speaker in public about how the prophets matched their spiritual state or their lifestyle in daily situations as part of the "testing." If even the intimate family of Jesus found his implicit status a *cause of stumbling* and **affront** (σκάνδαλον, Mark 6:3; 1 Cor 1:23), we need not find any difficulty in envisaging the same **affront** caused by the implication that an irritating husband might be regarded as "spiritual" in this context. Does *his* life really suggest that the Holy Spirit of God prompts what he says? This calls for **sifting** indeed!

We therefore suggest that ἐπερωτάτωσαν means something more than *let them ask their (own) husbands* (NRSV, REB, NJB). In Mark 14:60-61 the high priest *cross-examined* or **interrogated** Jesus (ἐπηρώτησεν τὸν Ἰησοῦν) while in v. 61 the same verb moves from judicial investigation to virtual accusation.[398] In hellenistic literature the word may be used of questioning the gods sometimes in the LXX sense of inquiring

394. Calvin, *First Epistle,* 307.

395. The parallel in Luke 4:24 is introduced as solemn words by Jesus with Ἀμὴν, λέγω ὑμῖν ὅτι οὐδεὶς προφήτης δεκτός ἐστιν, "truly I tell you, no prophet is accepted in his own homeland." Mark recounts that while elsewhere people took the ministry of Jesus with seriousness, his hometown, relatives, and immediate family found the prophetic claims of "the carpenter, the son of Mary, the brother of James and Joses . . .," to be a *cause of stumbling* or an **affront** (6:3; 1 Cor 1:23).

396. Morna D. Hooker, *The Gospel according to Mark* (London: Black and Peabody, Mass.: Hendrickson, 1991), 153: "a proverbial saying."

397. Donald A. Hagner, *Matthew* (2 vols., Dallas: Word, 1993), 1:406.

398. BAGD recognize and include this use, 285, category 1b.

into God's will.[399] Even in examples concerning *asking questions* in everyday life. Grimm-Thayer note the mood of **interrogation** which can still apply in their first entry: *to accost one with an enquiry,* to *put a question to . . .* to **interrogate**.[400] They convincingly explain the compound ἐπί as having a *directive* force, which governs an accusative (here in v. 35 τοὺς ἰδίους ἄνδρας). They cite the quasi-legal context of *cross-examination* in Mark 11:29, where Jesus **interrogates** "the chief priests and the scribes" about the basis on which they simultaneously *reject his authority* while purporting to *accept the authority* of John the Baptist. If anywhere the Marcan narrative has to do with **sifting** authoritative speech, it is surely here. Thus the noun ἐπερώτημα oscillates between *inquiry* and *demand,* with overtones of earnest intensity. By contrast, without the directive compound, the *simple* verb ἐπωτάω means more generally *to ask,* in an "open" sense.[401]

In contrast to the *honor* which Jesus associated with the recognition of a prophet (see above), the embarrassing and humiliating cross-examination or **interrogation** of a prophet by a close relative (especially in Jewish or Jewish and Roman cultural context by a wife or close relative who is a **woman**) brings not *honor* but humiliation and **disgrace**. The importance of the honor-shame universe of discourse for first-century Corinth (in contrast to the purity-guilt contrast of the post-Augustan West) stands in the foreground here.[402] J. K. Chance asserts the importance of the honor/shame contrast especially in contexts of *kinship or gender,* both in the biblical writings and in anthropological research.[403] Gender and kinship raise the stakes to "highly emotional" levels, where what is "local" (not merely general) intensifies and personalizes issues.[404] Over the centuries, however, *shame* has become almost merged into *guilt,* in contrast to more public or intersubjective aspects of the *respect, approval, or disapproval of others,* especially in the family, community, or state. The best equivalent in modern English is to *win approval* or **disgrace**. If we restructure the adjective αἰσχρός, *shameful, disgraceful, dishonorable, unbecoming,* the force of Paul's words may be most accurately conveyed by to **speak thus in public worship** (ἐν ἐκκλησίᾳ stands in semantic contrast to ἐν οἴκῳ) **brings disgrace**. Paul emphasizes **disgrace** by placing αἰσχρόν as the first word of v. 35b; English achieves the same effect by placing it last in the sentence.

We may note in passing that whether or not the allusions to **silence** and to **disgrace** in Titus 1:11 consciously look back to our verses, those who are enjoined to be **silent** in Titus 1:11-13 are the broader category of the *leaders* rather than the *women,* even if the issue of disruption and disgrace remains the same. A loud mouth and insistent, polarized argumentation confound the force of the gospel and undermine mutual

---

399. BAGD, category c, Herodotus 1:53; Josephus, *Antiquities* 6.123; cf. Isa 65:1. Of course the word also means simply *to ask a question* (BAGD, 1a), but the nuance depends on the context.

400. Grimm-Thayer, 230. On the context of situation in 1 Cor 14:29-36, see further J. M. Hurley, *Man and Woman in Biblical Perspective* (Leicester: Inter-Varsity, 1981), 185-94.

401. Grimm-Thayer, 252.

402. See esp. *Semeia* 68 (1994): *Honor and Shame in the World of the Bible* (ed. V. H. Matthews et al.); and J. G. Peristiany (ed.), *Honor and Shame: The Values of Mediterranean Society* (Chicago: University of Chicago Press, 1966).

403. J. K. Chance, "The Anthropology of Honor and Shame," *Semeia* 68, 139-51, esp. 143-45.

404. Ibid., 144-45.

respect when what is required is a lifestyle which respects the need for self-control in the ethics of speech. Once again, I have elaborated this point with reference to Titus 1:12 and 13 or elsewhere, since the role of these verses in relation to the argument of the epistle is often misunderstood.[405] Kierkegaard comments on these verses to extol the virtue of silence in just such a broader context: "Silence is just what is needed so that the Word of God may work its work in us. . . . We can only hear the word of God in silence."[406] Witherington also broadens the issue to all people: "The Corinthians should know that the OT speaks about a respectful silence when a word of counsel is spoken (Job 29:21)."[407] However, the context constrains the scope of the meaning and application when the issue is more specifically that of women and silence. An early example of decontextualization in the posthistory of the text can be found in Tertullian. In his work *On Baptism* Tertullian contrasts Paul with the pseudonymous Paul of the apocryphal *Paul and Thecla*. Paul himself, he argues, gives no license for women to teach or to baptize, and cites 1 Cor 14:35 in support of this.[408] We must keep in mind, however, our introduction on "controlled speech" in biblical traditions (see above).

36 Witherington offers two useful observations on v. 36. First, he perceives the point of Paul's rhetorical questions to lie in the scenario that "it appears the Corinthians are trying to make up their own rules, and perhaps thinking their own word is sufficient or authoritative or even *the word of God for themselves* (cf. v. 36)" (my italics).[409] Fee rightly adds, "Has God given them a special word that allows them both to reject Paul's instructions . . . and to be so out of touch with the churches?"[410] Second, a further affinity between v. 33 and v. 36 exists in the contrast between **all** and **only** *you*. Thus Witherington comments, "This summary statement [question] applies to *all*, not just women, for he [Paul] uses the word μόνους instead of μόνας probably to indicate a mixed audience."[411] Robertson and Plummer identify misleading nuances in the AV/KJV: the *from* and *unto* cannot be left as possible alternatives, and *only* must be rendered **only ones** or *only people* (here, as we have noted, inclusive masculine plural), to mean: "Were you the starting point of the Gospel? Or were you its only destination?"[412] This accords, again, precisely with Paul's overture to the whole letter in 1:2: *called . . . with all who call upon the name of our Lord Jesus Christ in every place — their Lord and ours too!* Hence, *has Christ been apportioned out?* (1:13).

405. Again, "The Logical Role of the Liar Paradox in Titus 1:12, 13," *BibInt* 2 (1994): 207-23.
406. Cited by Deluz, *Companion to 1 Cor,* 210: from Kierkegaard, "Touching an Examination of Conscience." Cf. *Either/Or* (Eng. trans., Princeton: Princeton University Press, 2d ed. 1959), 71.
407. Witherington, *Women,* 103.
408. Tertullian, *Treatise on Baptism,* 17:3. As against the apocryphal writing *Paul and Thecla*, "which goes wrongly under Paul's name," Tertullian insists that Paul gives "no license for women's teaching and baptizing . . . let them be silent and at home consult their husbands." Hence, Tertullian observes, people appeal to the spurious example of Thecla.
409. Witherington, *Women in the Earliest Churches,* 98.
410. Fee, *First Epistle,* 710.
411. Witherington, *Women,* 259.
412. Robertson and Plummer, *First Epistle,* 326.

To follow Conzelmann in regarding any "ecumenical" concern as a "bourgeois consolidation of the church" and hence a post-Pauline interpolation (he concedes that no textual reading affects this verse) is to impose a developmental theory upon Paul which does violence to the unity of Paul's thought in this epistle.[413] It is significant that while he rightly sees all of these verses as turning on "what it means to be *pneumatikos*" Fee cites "twofold" rather than "threefold" criteria here. He includes: (1) the variety of the Spirit's gifts; and (2) the criterion of "edification"; but omits (3) the self-coherence and unity of the Spirit's gifts and agency which Christian lifestyle and church order must equally reflect.[414] It is a tragedy of church life that some are so weighed down by history that church activity becomes mere replication and routinization, while others are so concerned with novelty and "relevance" that historical roots do not receive the respect that they deserve as part of a corporate memory and corporate identity.[414] "Some regard must be had to church practice elsewhere (cf. 11:16; 14:33b) including places which were evangelized before Corinth. . . . There may be an implication that, in fulfilment of the prophecy of Isa 2:3/Mic 4:2, it is from Jerusalem (as in Rom 15:19) that the word goes forth."[416] Bruce's comment takes up the OT references also cited by C. H. Kling, who anticipates the point: "Are you the original church, so that your wisdom is to set the standard of propriety . . . at liberty to stand alone?"[417]

iii. A Particular Warning and a General Encouragement (14:37-40)

37-38 (1) Some textual variants assume particular importance, not least because this is one of Käsemann's four most celebrated examples of "sentences of Holy Law in the NT," which favors the reading of the indicative ἀγνοεῖται, **he/she is not recognized (א***, probably A*, D*, G, 33, 1739, it^d, Syriac, Coptic VSS, Vg, Origen's Greek text, and Ambrose), as against the third person imperative ἀγνοείτω, **he/she is to be recognized** or *let him be ignorant* (early p^{46}, B, D^{b,c} [A^2], most later MSS).[418] Many modern VSS and some textual specialists are divided. Thus Metzger, NIV, and NJB favor the passive

---

413. Conzelmann, *1 Cor,* 246. While Fee argues that vv. 34-35 are an interpolation, he criticizes Conzelmann for including v. 36 with 34-35 (*First Epistle,* 710, n. 7).

414. Fee, *First Epistle,* 709. We noted above Fee's one-sided emphasis in ch. 12 where Paul argues on behalf of diversity in one section and on behalf of the unity of the Spirit in another. Paul realized that such unity applies "vertically" to time and history (or idiosyncratic developments of doctrine and ethics would hardly call for responsive action) as well as "horizontally" to geography, as in the case of Corinth.

415. On the tension between history, pragmatism, and Christian truth, see R. Lundin, A. C. Thiselton, and C. Walhout, *The Promise of Hermeneutics* (Grand Rapids: Eerdmans and Carlisle: Paternoster, 1999).

416. Bruce, *1 and 2 Cor,* 136.

417. Kling, *First Epistle,* 6:297. Cf. Chrystostom, *1 Cor. Hom.,* 27:2.

418. See E. Käsemann, "Sentences of Holy Law in the NT" (originally Germ. in *NTS* 1 [1954-55]: 248-60); Eng. in his *New Testament Questions of Today,* 66-81, esp. 68-69.

indicative, Zuntz, NRSV (but not RSV), REB, ASV, and KJV/AV favor the imperative.[419] However, the overwhelming majority of modern commentators support the reading of the indicative (including, e.g., Conzelmann, Barrett, Bruce, Grosheide, Fee, Lang, Klauck, and Hays).[420] Although the imperative has earlier and stronger MS support, exegetical considerations in the light of parallels in Paul suggest an early correction by $\mathfrak{p}^{46}$ of a reading deemed to be "difficult" in the sense of unduly harsh, especially if the passive indicative is taken to mean **not recognized** by God; not known by God.

(2) The word *command* (ἐντολή) in v. 37 is omitted by D*, G, Old Latin, and Origen, and Zuntz considers this to be the original text, i.e., **recognize that what I have written is of the Lord.** Would copyists wish to harden or to soften an original? $\mathfrak{p}^{46}$, B, $\aleph^c$, and 33 read ἐντολή, but some Western traditions read the plural ἐντολαί, *commands.*[421] On this basis Zuntz and Barrett view **command** as a later intruder which generated variants.[422] Most follow $\mathfrak{p}^{46}$, B, and $\aleph^c$ (including UBS 4th ed.) as the better-supported reading, but we cannot be certain which is the original. Either can be defended.

The content of vv. 37-38 serves to add force to the exegesis of vv. 34-36 as continuing the theme of **sifting** or *discriminating* between authentic prophetic speech "given" to a prophetic speaker by the Holy Spirit of God and utterances which had diverged from the Spirit's impetus, or perhaps were simply self-generated by autosuggestion, self-deception, or simply error. In our account (with Witherington) of an **interrogation** of someone who had uttered speech which seemed "prophetic" (at least in the first instance to the speaker, and perhaps was indeed authentic prophecy) the issue of **recognizing** and **being recognized** (or possibly *knowing* and *being known*) is entirely pertinent. Once again, those who are all too ready to regard Paul as authoritarian, and equally those who underestimate the role of *coherence* in **sifting** prophetic speech, tend to pay attention to the wrong thing in these verses. Paul's axiom is entirely logical. God's Spirit does not contradict himself. He does not undermine his own prior disclosures and thereby cause "confusion" or disorder (v. 33a). If a prophet's utterance contradicts *apostolic* utterances (let alone biblical tradition), does not that of itself disenfranchise the currency of the prophetic utterance?

What Käsemann here unnecessarily objectifies as "sentences of holy law" amount to what philosophers of language perceive to be the irresistible logic of "internal grammar." All four of Käsemann's key examples come from this epistle: 1 Cor 3:17; 14:38; 16:22; and 5:3-5.[423] Käsemann writes: "The same verb describes in the chiasmus of the protasis and apodosis both human

419. Metzger, *Textual Commentary* (2d ed.), 500, although with the recognition of some degree of uncertainty; against Zuntz, *Text,* 107-8.

420. For example, Fee, *First Epistle,* 709, n. 4, and 712; Lang, *Die Briefe,* 201; Klauck, *1 Kor,* 107; Bruce, *1 and 2 Cor,* 136-37; Hays, *First Cor,* 244-45; Barrett, *First Epistle,* 314, n. 3; Conzelmann, *1 Cor,* 246; also Orr and Walther, *First Epistle,* 314-15; Kistemaker, *1 Cor,* 518.

421. Cf. Zuntz, *Text,* 139-40.

422. Barrett, *First Epistle* 333-34. Conzelmann places the phrase in brackets (as above; *1 Cor,* 241).

423. Käsemann, "Sentences of Holy Law," 66-72.

guilt and divine judgment in order to characterize by this method both the precise correspondence of the two in content and their *indissoluble and harsh logical connection*" (my italics).[424] It may well be correct that such examples as 1 Cor 5:3-5 do entail a "harsh" judgment, although I have argued elsewhere that judgment in this case is to lead to salvation.[425] In 1 Cor 3:17 and 14:38, however, *internal logic* is entailed: one cannot simultaneously destroy the church, claim to be of the church, and fail to destroy oneself (3:17). One cannot dismiss apostolic disclosure as not of the Spirit of Christ (to whom apostleship by its nature points) and claim simultaneously to be "of the Spirit" (πνευματικός) without exposing self-contradictions before God. Lang prefers to translate ἀγνοεῖται as *is not known* on the basis of the close parallel with 8:1-3: "If a 'pneumatic' does not know — as Paul expresses it in the form of a word-play, then he shows *thereby* that he is not known by God, i.e., that the Spirit of God does not dwell in him" (my italics).[426] Indeed, against the later argument of Wire and others, Chrysostom argues that Paul uses this form precisely to show that *neither compulsion nor high-handed confrontation are in Paul's mind.*[427] *The inauthentic, obstinate "prophet" has exposed his or her own status as "not known," i.e., not recognized by God whose judgment is final.*

Collins makes the point well. "Paul appeals to those who think themselves prophetic types and/or spiritual persons. He confronts them in their self-inflation. . . ."[428] Nevertheless, "internal grammar" should not be seen as a way of disengaging the self-generated effects of self-absorption or sin from divine judgment. Thus Collins continues with reference to Paul's apostolic *ethos.* The well-known argument of Paul, taking up hellenistic Jewish sermon material in Rom 1:18-32, demonstrates that here *personal divine judgment* consists in *"giving up" persons* to suffer *the inbuilt or "internal" consequences* of their obstinate self-absorption. Hence Hays cites parallels from the OT, the Gospels and (like Käsemann) Paul: "Those who are ashamed of me . . . of them shall the Son of Man be ashamed" (Mark 8:38); "You have rejected the word of the LORD, and the LORD has rejected you" (1 Sam 15:26); "If he does not acknowledge this (cf. our translation **recognize**), God does not acknowledge him" (1 Cor 14:38); "if anyone among you thinks himself wise, let him become a fool in order to become wise" (1 Cor 3:38); "if anyone thinks himself to 'know' something, he does not yet 'know' as he ought; if anyone loves God, he is 'known' by him" (1 Cor 8:2, 3).[429] Paul is not saying (as NRSV implies) that *the community* should not recognize the self-confident prophet in 14:38 (NRSV, this is not *to be recognized*).[430]

424. Ibid., 67.
425. See above on 5:3-5 and "The Meaning of σάρξ in 1 Cor 5:5," *SJT* 26 (1973): 204-28.
426. Lang, *Die Briefe,* 201.
427. Chrysostom, *1 Cor. Hom.,* 27:3; cf. Wire, *Corinthian Women Prophets,* esp. 14-15.
428. Collins, *First Cor,* 517.
429. Hays, *First Cor,* 244-45.
430. Ibid., 244. It is surprising that, having apparently grasped the axiomatic character of

A. C. Wire, however, adopts a very different approach to 14:37-38, together with 1 Cor 3:18; 8:2, 3; 11:16, which, like Käsemann, Hays, and others, she associates with our present verses.[431] In her judgment Paul uses a rhetorical device which permits him to associate "reality" with his own apostolic stance and to dismiss that of the Corinthian (women) prophets as mere "thought," pretense, or subjective truth claim. Thus to *think* one is wise (εἴ τις δοκεῖ σοφὸς εἶναι, 3:18a) is set in contrast to *being* or *becoming* wise *in reality* (μωρὸς γενέσθω, ἵνα γένηται σοφός, 3:18b). Similarly, **if anyone thinks that he or she is a prophet** (εἴ τις δοκεῖ προφήτης εἶναι) **or 'of the Spirit'** (14:37a), such a person is **to recognize** the *reality* (ἐπιγινωσκέτω) that **what Paul writes is [a command] from the Lord** (v. 37b). If the prophet (or self-styled prophet) does not *know* or **recognize** this (i.e., if he or she deems Paul's claim to be not reality but merely Pauline opinion), that person's opinion is disengaged from reality: **he or she is** (in actuality) **not recognized** (i.e., as a prophet *by God*). Wire argues that this characterizes Pauline rhetoric in relation to the "spiritual" (largely but not exclusively women) prophets at Corinth: "This provoking of confident boasts, suddenly to deflate them as mere thought and not reality, is found only twice elsewhere in Paul's letters (Gal 6:3; Phil 3:4)."[432] In Wire's view, in the passage about silence, for which this forms the climactic summary, "women prophets, among others, must be intended."[433]

The parallel between a disjunction between thought and reality occurs close by in the disjunction between private and public. Hence, Wire presses further, women's "sphere of power" (if any) is to be relegated to the private sphere of the home (ἐν οἴκῳ, v. 35).[434] She associates 14:35 with "private" tongues (14:18, 19, 28), providing meals "at home" (μὴ γὰρ οἰκίας οὐκ ἔχετε εἰς τὸ ἐσθίειν . . . , 11:22); the private invitation (10:24-33); and Paul's exhortation to maintain a married state rather than to leave home for "single" (prophetic) ministry (7:2, 8-9, 36). The chief threat to "Paul's gospel and leadership," Wire insists, is in the case of Corinth "its prophesying women."[435] "At several points Paul proposes that the Corinthians do at home activities that he considers disrupting or difficult when they gather. . . . He may be trying to send back home a Pandora's box of women's spiritual and physical energy that has given the church the richness and disruptiveness of a home."[436]

We must beware of mixing together (i) a hypothesis about women prophets

---

the principle, Hays should comment, "Paul now seems to be running out of patience." Chrysostom points out that (as we have argued with reference to Titus 1:12, 13, see above) such passages as 1 Cor 11:16; 6:9-11; Gal 5:2 avoid "contention" by explicating an inevitable consequence of the action in view.

431. Wire, *The Corinthian Women Prophets,* esp. 14-15.
432. Ibid., 14.
433. Ibid., 15.
434. Ibid., 16.
435. Ibid., 15.
436. Ibid., 16, 17.

with (ii) sentences of internal grammar which bring together logical contradiction and divine judgment as expressed in and through such contradiction. Wire herself (whether consciously or unwittingly) effectively makes the point by listing as Paul's third "rhetorical device" the disassociation of "self-benefit" from "community benefit."[437] If Paul formulates a criterion of the good of the other (conceded or identified by Wire in 1:10; 3:3; 8:9-11; 9:22; 11:21-22; 12:24-25; 13:5; 14:3-4, 12), it becomes transparent that this is not a mere rhetorical strategy designed in the interests of gender, but constitutes part of Paul's theology of the cross (cf. 1:18-25). If Christ is "for others" (cf. the *pre-Pauline traditions* of τὸ σῶμα τὸ ὑπὲρ ὑμῶν, 11:24; and Χριστὸς ἀπέθανεν ὑπὲρ τῶν ἁμαρτιῶν ἡμῶν, 15:3), then a criterion of authenticity cannot be other than the "community benefit" which encapsulates the love for the other which characterizes the christological basis and character of the agency and gifts of the Holy Spirit.

If the work of the Spirit is to promote the practical Lordship of Christ in every area of life (12:3-6), it becomes transparent that whatever does not cohere with practical witness to the Christlikeness of the God who does not undermine his own work and gifts cannot (logical *cannot*) be **recognized** (v. 38) as authentically "of the Holy Spirit of God" (πνευματικός, v. 37). What has been said above about the convergence between logic and an appeal to divine reality does not require revision in the light of Wire's comments, even if these raise other relevant issues.

39-40 (1) On the MSS which place vv. 34-35 after vv. 39-40, see above under v. 34. (2) 𝔓46, B2, D*, F, G, and many Western MSS omit μου. UBS 4th ed. places the possessive pronoun in brackets. On one side, it is probably more convincing to argue (with Zuntz) that it should be retained, as it is in 11:33. On the other side, it might be argued that a copyist had 11:33 in mind when writing out his verse. This is far from being the only example of an ambivalent reading of μου. **My** probably expresses Pauline affection and concern for the readers.

Yet again ἀδελφοί is almost impossible to translate into modern idiomatic English. As we note above, we vary our translation to indicate this, here **my dear friends**. More controversial is our translation of the present imperative ζηλοῦτε, usually translated as *be eager to* (NRSV, REB, NIV, NJB; cf. KJV/AV, *covet to*). We considered the meaning of this term in 12:31 as ζηλοῦτε δὲ τὰ χαρίσματα τὰ μείζονα. For our detailed arguments that the most accurate rendering in the parallel verse (and hence also here) is **continue to be zealously concerned about**, see under 12:31, and also the supporting research article by Smit.[438] (We also argue

437. Ibid., 17-19. See further Wire's more detailed discussion of ch. 14 to which we have already referred, 138-58.

438. J. F. M. Smit, "Two Puzzles: 1 Cor 12:31 and 13:3: Rhetorical Situation," *NTS* 39 (1993): 246-64. Allo, *Première Épitre,* 374, believes that if the verb is translated *be eager* this makes it "perhaps ironic," since tongue-speaking is merely "tolerated." However, if prophetic speech includes *pastoral preaching* and not merely spontaneous oracular utterance, Paul's encour-

there for the continuous force of the present imperative.) The accusative χαρίσματα in 12:31 is replaced by the accusative articular infinitive τὸ προφητεύειν in v. 39a, which leads, in turn, to a second articular infinitive construction in v. 39b, τὸ λαλεῖν. The emphasis thus falls not on "being a prophet" but on the speech-act of **prophetic speech**. Similarly, the emphasis falls not on "tongues" but on **speaking** in this mode, i.e., their *use*. Paul is summarizing all of the arguments of ch. 14 (or at least 14:26-38). Hence these directions are to be understood and applied with all the constraints and encouragements with which Paul has already qualified them. Thus **continue to be zealously concerned about prophetic speech** almost certainly includes not only the *production* of prophetic speech or discourse but also its **sifting** and its use **in an ordered manner**.

The last verse of the chapter sums up **everything** (πάντα) that pertains to whatever **takes place** (γινέσθω) in public worship on the part of the assembled congregation, whether Paul happens to have mentioned it specifically here or not. The verb used here (γίνομαι) most often has the force of *to come about,* **to happen**, although it may also mean *be created, be made,* less frequently. In spite of the fact that most VSS translate *should be done* (NRSV, REB, NIV), the present force is *let all things be carried on* without a specific reference to agency.[439] The δέ qualifies the specific reference to the encouragement of issues relating to **prophetic speech** and to the permissive status of **speaking in tongues**, and Robertson and Plummer's translation **only** brings out its function more adequately than the more usual *but* (NRSV, NIV).[440]

The punch line of much of the chapter is expressed in the adverb εὐσχημόνως and the adverbial phrase κατὰ τάξιν. The adverb is rendered *decently* or *becomingly* by BAGD, who then propose *properly* for this verse.[441] *Properly* would be excellent if idiomatic English still used *proper* in its more classic sense of *with due decorum*. The cognate noun εὐσχημοσύνη clearly means *propriety, decorum, what is presentable in public,* and we do not doubt that Paul has in mind both *reverence and dignity appropriate to address to and from God,* and a *missionary or evangelistic* rather than strictly aesthetic dimension. The adjective εὐσχήμων means what is **fitting** in 1 Cor 7:25, and what is *publicly presentable* in 1 Cor 12:24.[442] In other contemporary writers the term also means *reputable.*[443] If we take full account of both the lexicographical evidence for Paul's period, Paul's own uses of this and related terms, and contextual factors, **fittingly** perhaps best conveys the Greek.

---

agement is genuine, with the proviso that it refers to concern about all that relates to it, *including its sifting and control.* Collins presses for the traditional notion of "eager pursuit" of prophecy, "not to the neglect of tongues" (*First Cor,* 517).

439. As in Findlay, *Expositor's Greek Testament,* 2:917; Robertson and Plummer, *First Epistle,* 328.

440. Robertson and Plummer, *First Epistle,* 328.

441. BAGD, 327.

442. In addition to BAGD, cf. examples in MM, 266.

443. Cf. Plutarch, *Moralia* 37.7; *Florentine Papyri* 61:61 (AD 85).

The prepositional phrase κατὰ τάξιν is a metaphor drawn from a military universe of discourse. The cognate noun τάγμα means *that which is* **ordered**, especially in literal terms of a body of troops drawn up in **ordered** *ranks*.[444] Notably Clement of Rome, who addresses his letter from Rome to Corinth around AD 95 to correct partisanship and (again) disunity, presses into his service the metaphor or image of fighting God's enemies (cf. Heb 1:13) in God's army "serving our leaders (or generals, ἡγουμένοις) *in a good order* (εὐτάκτως) . . . *being subject to control* (ὑποτεταγμένως). . . . Not all are prefects nor tribunes nor centurions . . . but *each in his own rank* (ἕκαστος ἐν τῷ ἰδίῳ τάγματι . . .)."[445] Paul uses τάγμα of the purposive and **ordered manner** of the resurrection as the action of God and of the Spirit of God (1 Cor 15:23-24). The abstract noun τάξις is then used to denote *fixed succession or order*, while the prepositional phrase κατὰ τάξιν means *in an orderly manner*.[446] *1 Clement* moves on from Clement's argument about military order to follow the themes of 1 Corinthians in terms of mutual help and communal benefit (*1 Clem.* 38:1-4); creative order and wisdom (39:1-9); and corporate worship in which we ought to do *everything* **in an ordered manner** (πάντα τάξει ποιεῖν ὀφείλομεν) . . . at ordered times (κατὰ καιροὺς τεταγμένους, *1 Clem.* 40:1).[447] Clement's next chapter considers diversity, but again, each in his or her own "order" (ἐν τῷ ἰδίῳ τάγματι).[448] **Fittingly and in an ordered manner** well expresses the climax of ch. 14, especially in relation to 12:3-6, 12-18, 28-31; 13:1, 9-10; 14:1-33 (see above).

---

444. BAGD, 802-3; cf. MM, 624.

445. *1 Clement* 37:2, 3.

446. BAGD, 803, col. 2, entry 2; cf. MM, 625, entry 1. Barrett, *First Epistle,* 334, translates, *in an orderly manner.*

447. *1 Clement* 40:1-5.

448. *1 Clement* 41:1. Ch. 42 relates this to trinitarian order (εὐτάκτως, 42:2).

VI. The Resurrection of the Dead (15:1-58)

Seventy-five years of research on 1 Corinthians 15 have provided no convincing reason for disputing the validity of Karl Barth's verdict on this chapter. This fifteenth chapter, he writes, "forms not only the close and crown of the whole epistle, but *also provides the key to its meaning from which light is shed onto the whole,* and it becomes intelligible . . . as a unity" (my italics).[1] This is because it brings to a climax the theme of *grace* as God's sovereign free gift through the cross to which "the dead" contribute no particular "knowledge" or "experience," but do indeed undergo transformation of life and lifestyle through "God, who gives life to the dead" (Rom 4:17) *on the basis of promise.*[2] This is mediated not only through union with Christ but also more specifically through identification with Christ in his death (1 Cor 11:17-34). The cross, to use the phrase applied by Moltmann and by Schrage, remains "the ground and criterion" of Christian existence and Christian identity (1:18-25).[3] This culminates in the future removal of ambivalence and falling short when transformation by the Holy Spirit into that resurrection mode of existence, which is fully characterized by the unhindered operation of the Holy Spirit himself, reaches eschatological fulfilment at the last day.[4]

Luther and Calvin were no less certain that the resurrection chapter addresses issues central to the gospel and to the whole epistle. If a person does not believe in the resurrection, Luther asserts, "he must deny in a lump the Gospel and everything that is proclaimed of Christ and of God. For all of this is linked together like a chain. . . . Whoever denies this article must simultaneously deny far more . . . , in brief, *that God is God*" (my italics).[5] What could be more central to this epistle than that God is *God?* Paul is concerned "about the kind of

---

1. Barth, *The Resurrection of the Dead,* 11.

2. The theme of grace receives attention in Moxnes, *Theology in Conflict,* 231-82, esp. 253-82. He compares Romans 4 with 1 Cor 1:26-31 (277); Rom 4:14-16 with 1 Cor 1:17, 18 (263); and the "reversals" of 1 Cor 1:21-25, 26-31 with 1 Cor 15, esp. 15:14 (260). However, he emphasizes Paul's "reinterpretation" of the theme of "calling into existence the things that are not" by applying this to the *new community of Gentiles;* see on 15:4b.

3. Moltmann, subtitle of *The Crucified God;* Schrage, *Der erste Brief,* 1:165.

4. Expanded in Thiselton, "Luther and Barth on 1 Cor 15: Six Theses for Theology in Relation to Recent Interpretation," in Stephens (ed.), *The Bible, the Reformation and the Church,* 258-89.

5. Luther, *Luther's Works XXVIII: Commentaries on 1 Cor 7 and 15,* 94 and 95.

God God is, but mostly [also] with what God does."[6] Barth speaks of "this 'of God'" (cf. 1 Cor 4:5) as "the secret nerve" of the whole epistle.[7] In an older modern work on Paul's eschatology H. A. A. Kennedy argues that for Paul the only organic link between γυμνὸς κόκκος, *the bare grain* which is nothing in itself, and the σῶμα of glory which is to come is simply and exclusively "the sovereign power of God," who "gives . . . as he wills" (ἠθέλησεν, the aorist expressing God's definitive and sovereign will "determining the constitution of our nature").[8] In contrast to many writers who drive a wedge between 1 Corinthians 15 and 2 Corinthians 5 (ascribing to the latter the quite different notion of "the immortality of the soul"), Kennedy finds the same emphasis on God in 2 Corinthians 5, where "we have a building from God" reflects "sure possession" as a "repetition in another form of . . . 1 Cor 15:38, 'God gives it a body.'"[9]

Calvin, likewise, regards ch. 15 as addressing more than one problem among others, namely, the nature of belief in postmortal existence. It is about God and the nature of the gospel; this is why Paul "refers to the doctrine of the resurrection as the Gospel."[10] This prompts Calvin to address the long-debated question: if the issue is a comprehensive and central one, why does Paul postpone it until almost the end of the epistle? His answer tends toward an over-moralistic and over-ecclesial way of formulating a fundamentally or broadly valid answer. He postpones it, Calvin suggests, "until he had subdued their pride" and fully established his apostolic credentials.[11] J. Moltmann expresses the point less moralistically. The grammar of hope and the logic of resurrection, he shows, arises from looking to God from within "the abyss of nothingness." . . . Resurrection with Christ by the promise of God "annihilates the total *nihil*."[12] The concept loses its current except in dialectical relationship with identification with the crucified One, on the basis of an act of God "*extra se* in the God who creates life and new being out of nothing . . . in the deadliness of death as compared with the promised life . . . not as a mere return to life . . . but as a conquest of the deadliness of death."[13]

Moltmann, like Moxnes, understands this as calling "into being things that are not" in agreement with Rom 4:15, 17.[14] Hence, "unless it apprehends the pain of the negative, Christian hope can never be realistic and liberating."[15]

6. Leon Morris argues with respect to Romans (as well as, by implication, 1 Corinthians) that these epistles even more emphatically concern the nature of God than Christ or Christology ("The Theme of Romans," in W. W. Gasque and R. P. Martin [eds.], *Apostolic History and the Gospel: To F. F. Bruce* [Exeter: Paternoster, 1970], 263; cf. 249-63).

7. Barth, *Resurrection,* 18.

8. Kennedy, *St Paul's Conception of the Last Things,* 243.

9. Ibid., 264 and 265.

10. Calvin, *First Epistle,* 312.

11. Ibid.

12. Moltmann, *Theology of Hope,* 172 and 198.

13. Ibid., 210 and 211.

14. Ibid., 145.

15. J. Moltmann, *The Crucified God* (Eng. trans., London: SCM, 1974), 5. Cf. 46.

This shares common ground with the exegetical work of Moxnes on Romans 4, cited above. Paul could not introduce a theology of the resurrection before the notion of the cross as the "ground and criterion" of Christian identity and life-style had been fully reappropriated. A context of religious triumphalism and complacency leaves no conceptual space for the "transformative reversal" of death and resurrection. Resurrection epitomizes 1:31, "let the person who glories, glory in the Lord." Divine action is directed toward the *dead,* who cannot contribute to their welfare. This underlines both divine sovereignty and divine grace.

Such an approach to, and evaluation of, the resurrection chapter might be predictable, some may argue, on the part of such writers as Luther, Calvin, Barth, and Moltmann. Other modern exegetes, however, do share this perspective and maintain the integrity of the epistle as well, as against Conzelmann's view that "chap. 15 is a self-contained treatise on the resurrection."[16] Harrisville (1987) perceives this chapter as "the heart or hub of the letter from which everything has radiated."[17] It is integrally related to the cross (1:18-25 and throughout) not at all as a "happy ending" but because "the proclamation of the resurrection is at the same time and in the same breath the word of the cross," just as "the word of the cross is at the same time and in the same breath the proclamation of the resurrection. . . . How this can be so, Paul will show in this remarkable chapter."[18] M. C. de Boer (1988) likewise reflects precisely the perspective shared by Barth, Moxnes, and Harrisville when he observes that "Christ's resurrection from the dead signifies that human beings are powerless to effect their own salvation and have no grounds for boasting except in the Lord (1:31). Paul's argument . . . for the resurrection of the dead with his cosmological-apocalyptic understanding of death is thus an extension of his theology of the cross. . . . 'Thanks be *to God* who *gives* us the victory through . . . Christ' (v. 57)" (de Boer's italics).[19]

The problem of partition theories is a familiar one, and is discussed in the Introduction above, 36-41. The supposed shifts in "subject matter, time, and situation" lead not only Conzelmann but also Jewett, Weiss, Schmithals, Héring, Dinkler, Goguel, Walker, and Sellin to doubt its integrity with the rest of the epistle.[20] In our Introduction, however, we set out the convincing counter-

16. Conzelmann, *1 Cor,* 249.

17. Harrisville, *1 Cor,* 247.

18. Ibid., 248.

19. De Boer, *The Defeat of Death: Apocalyptic Eschatology in 1 Cor 15 and Rom 5,* 140; cf. 93-140.

20. The quotation comes from Jewett, *Paul's Anthropological Terms,* 23; see further Jewett, "The Redaction of 1 Cor and the Trajectory of the Pauline School," *JAAR Suppl* 46 (1978): 298-444; Weiss, *Der erste Korintherbrief,* xxxix-xliii and 343-45; W. Schmithals, "Die Korintherbriefe als Briefsammlung," *ZNW* 64 (1973): 263-88; *Gnosticism in Corinth,* 87-113; and other references in the Introduction.

arguments of Mitchell, Fee, Allo, Barrett, and others concerning the coherence of the epistle and the lack of decisive evidence to the contrary.[21]

Before we set forth the rhetorical and logical structure of Paul's argument in this chapter, is there any reasonable consensus about the precise nature of the problem over the resurrection of the dead which Paul addresses? The first eleven verses do not seem to take the form of a "reply" introduced by identifying a topic, although the problem becomes more clearly identified in 15:12 with reference to a group or groups within the church at Corinth (ἐν ὑμῖν τινες, v. 12, not outsiders) who λέγουσιν . . . ὅτι ἀνάστασις νεκρῶν οὐκ ἔστιν. Several theories overlap and crisscross once writers try to be more specific than state that "some" at Corinth denied the reality or possibility of the resurrection of the dead. In broad terms, surveys of the reconstructions follow the same identification of different possibilities in monographs or essays by Wilson (1968). Spörlein (1971), Plank (1981), Sellin (1986), Wedderburn (1987), M. C. de Boer (1988), G. Barth (1992), my own discussion (1995), Joost Holleman (1996), and A. Eriksson (1998, followed in outline by Collins, 1999).[22]

(i) Although we cannot delineate clear boundaries between these rough-and-ready categorizations, some scholars argue that a group at Corinth found themselves *unable to believe in any kind of postmortal existence.* Over the centuries patristic, Reformation, nineteenth-century, and more recent writers have compared the philosophy of the Epicureans in the Graeco-Roman world with the traditions of the Sadducees even within Judaism, and have emphasized that belief in life after death was less widespread in the first century than is often supposed. Appeal has been made to several classical specialists for this view.[23] This view was held by G. Estius (1613), H. Grotius (1645), and subsequently especially by W. M. L. de Wette (1845) and more recently W. Schmithals (Eng. trans. 1970).[24] Calvin and Heinrici are often credited with this view, but Calvin concludes that in the end he is "undecided," and Heinrici also combines more

21. Especially Mitchell, *Paul and the Rhetoric of Reconciliation;* Fee, *First Epistle,* 15-165; Allo, *Première Épitre,* lxxix-lxxxv and 387-88; Barrett, *First Epistle,* 12-17. Cf. further the literature cited in Saw, *Paul's Rhetoric in 1 Cor 15,* 180-83, esp. n. 13; and Thiselton, "Luther and Barth on 1 Cor 15," 275-78.

22. Wilson, "The Corinthians Who Say There Is No Resurrection of the Dead," 90-107; Spörlein, *Die Leugnung der Auferstehung. Eine historisch-kritische Untersung zu 1 Kor 15,* esp. 7-19; Plank, "Resurrection Theology: The Corinthian Controversy Re-examined," 41-54; Sellin, *Der Streit um die Auferstehung der Toten,* 17-37; Wedderburn, *Baptism and Resurrection,* 6-15; de Boer, *The Defeat of Death,* 96-105; G. Barth, "Zur Frage nach der in 1 Kor 15 bekämpten Auferstehungsleugnung," *ZNW* 83 (1992): 187-201; Thiselton, "Luther and Barth on 1 Cor 15," 268-74; J. Holleman, *Resurrection and Parousia: A Traditio-Historical Study of Paul's Eschatology in 1 Cor 15,* 35-48; Eriksson, *Traditions as Rhetorical Proof,* 232-78 (cf. Collins, *First Cor,* 525-28).

23. Especially R. MacMullen, *Paganism in the Roman Empire* (New Haven: Yale University Press, 1981); cf. M. Nilsson, *Geschichte der greichischen Religion* (2 vols., Munich: Beck, 1955 and 1961), 1:220-21.

24. W. M. L. de Wette, *Kurze Erklärung der Briefe and die Korinther* (Leipzig: Weidmannische Buchhandlung, 2d ed. 1845), 7; and Schmithals, *Gnosticism in Corinth,* 156.

than one approach.[25] Such writers regularly appeal to Paul's use of the Epicurean maxim "let us eat and drink, for tomorrow we die" (15:32b) and to the notion that for those who deny the belief in question faith is empty or futile (15:17); if in this life only they have hope, they deserve only pity and are still in their sins (15:17, 19). Spörlein believes that this view of 1 Corinthians 15 typified the period of F. C. Baur, de Wette, and the 1840s, although Schmithals and others have also urged it more recently.[26]

Schmithals emphatically asserts, "Paul is of the opinion that the Corinthians were denying any hope of the hereafter. Such beliefs were not strange to his time."[27] Bultmann agrees that this was Paul's perception, but questions its validity: "Paul, one must admit, misunderstands his opponents in attributing to them the view that with death everything is over (1 Cor 15:19, 32)."[28] Bultmann appeals to such passages as 15:29 to argue that the Corinthian view was different. However, a greater majority of writers argue that 15:29 and other passages which speak of Corinthian action or belief on the basis of some kind of future hope suggest *not* that Paul has misunderstood the situation, but that this first theory overstates and oversimplifies the problem.[29] The "denial" was more specific. Moreover, as Wedderburn urges, even if de Wette's evaluation might apply to one small group, Paul may well allude to a different group in 15:29.[30]

(ii) A second proposed reconstruction goes back to Chrysostom and to Luther: the group "alleged that the resurrection had taken place a long time ago," i.e., that *resurrection has already occurred* (2 Tim 2:18).[31] If Christian believers have already been raised with Christ to a new mode of life, all that happens at death is the dissolution of the physical body, while the already existing "pneumatic" or "spiritual" nature continues its existence without the husk of the body. In various forms this approach is linked with an overrealized eschatology and sometimes with spiritual enthusiasm or alternatively a high sacramentalism by such writers as Heinrici (1880), Hans von Soden (1931), J. Schniewind (1952), and thereafter in chronological sequence Munck, Wilckens, Grant, Käsemann, Shires, Barrett, Wilson, Bruce, Becker, Bünker, and Martin.[32]

25. Calvin, *First Epistle,* 312; Heinrici, *Das erste Sendschreiben,* 463-71.

26. Spörlein, *Die Leugnung,* 7, n. 3.

27. Schmithals, *Gnosticism,* 156.

28. Bultmann, *Theology of the NT,* 1:169.

29. For example, de Boer, *Defeat of Death,* 96-97; Holleman, *Resurrection and Parousia,* 36; Fee, *First Epistle,* 716; Spörlein, *Leugnung,* 9-12; G. Barth, "Zur Frage nach der in 1 Kor 15."

30. Wedderburn, "The Problem of the Denial of the Resurrection in 1 Cor 15," 229; cf. 229-41.

31. *Luther's Works,* vol. 28, 59 (Germ. *WA* 36:482); Chrysostom, *1 Cor. Hom.,* 38:1.

32. Heinrici, *Das erste Sendschreiben,* 463-71; Hans von Soden, "Sakrament und Ethik bei Paulus," in H. Frick (ed.), *Marburger Theologische Studien,* 1 (Gotha: Klotz, 1931), 23; cf. 1-40; J. Schiewind, "Die Leugnung der Auferstehung in Korinth," in *Nachgelassene Reden und Aufsätze* (ed. E. Kähler; Berlin: Töpelmann, 1952), 110-39; Munck, *Paul and the Salvation of Mankind,* 165; Wilckens, *Weisheit und Torheit,* 11; Grant, *Historical Introduction,* 204;

Within these views, however, we must draw some important distinctions or subcategorizations. Schniewind leaned heavily upon a theory of gnostic influence for the view that a fully "spiritual" existence had begun now, in which believers were raised already above the realms of the merely sensuous. Wilckens draws on broadly similar notions, arguing that on this "higher" plane the "gnostic" has left judgment behind. The view that 1 Corinthians reflects a realized eschatology at Corinth should be carefully distinguished from outdated theories about the supposed influence of "gnosticism" as early as around AD 55.[33] Moreover, the argument that an overrealized eschatology serves to link together such apparently diverse themes as undervaluing the cross, misunderstanding the role of ministry and ethics, abusing the Lord's Supper, and regarding "spiritual gifts" as a sign of status need not carry with it such a specific reconstruction of the grounds for denials of the resurrection of the dead.[34] A sober balance is provided by David W. Kuck. He accepts the point behind J. M. Robinson's allusion to a "turgid fanaticism of those who have already risen and are living it up in glory" (cf. 4:8-13) and recognizes the force of Käsemann's arguments about pneumatics or *Schwärmer* "for whom 'the end of history has already arrived . . . everything which apocalyptic still hopes for has already been realized,'" and for whom no "theological relevant future hope" still remains.[35]

Kuck points out, however, that 15:12 "gives neither a reason for their denial nor a clue to whatever belief they did hold about the dead."[36] Popular philosophical beliefs as well as everyday notions about "the soul" are no less likely to cause difficulties which turn on the contrast between the resurrection of the *body* (σῶμα) and the immortality of the soul.

(iii) Numerous writers focus on difficulties about belief in the resurrection *of the body* on the part of some or many at Corinth. Chrysostom, in practice, combines the identification of this difficulty with our second category. More explicitly, J. Weiss (1910), followed in chronological sequence by Lietzmann, Deluz, Hoffmann, Sider, Murphy-O'Connor, Perkins, Sellin,

---

Käsemann, *NT Questions,* 125-26; Shires, *The Eschatology of Paul in the Light of Modern Scholarship,* 53-54; Wilson, "The Corinthians Who Say There Is No Resurrection," 90-107; Barrett, *First Epistle,* 109; Bruce, *1 and 2 Cor,* 49-50; Becker, *Auferstehung der Toten im Urchristentum,* 74-76; Bünker, *Briefformular und rhetorische Disposition in 1 Kor,* 72; and Martin, *The Spirit and the Congregation,* 109-10.

33. Cf. A. C. Thiselton, "Realized Eschatology at Corinth," *NTS* 24 (1977): 510-26.

34. Ibid.; cf. Kuck, *Judgment and Community Conflict,* 24.

35. Kuck, *Judgment,* 23; cf. 23-31; J. M. Robinson, "Kerygma and History in the NT," in J. M. Robinson and H. Koester (eds.), *Trajectories through Early Christianity* (Philadelphia: Fortress, 1971), 33-34; and Käsemann, *NT Questions of Today,* 106 and 131.

36. Kuck, *Judgment,* 27. Stronger attacks in the "realized eschatology" approach come from E. Earle Ellis, "Christ Crucified," in R. Banks, (ed.), *Reconciliation and Hope* (Exeter: Paternoster, 1974), 73-74; Horsley, "Pneumatikos versus Psychikos," 269-88; Wedderburn, "Problem of the Denial," 231-33; Marshall, *Enmity in Corinth,* 206-9; and P. J. Doughty, "The Presence and Future of Salvation in Corinth," *ZNW* 66 (1975): 61-90.

Strobel, and Dale Martin, emphasizes the problematic character of this contrast for the Corinthian group, as well as for theological and philosophical issues today.[37] Contrary to notions of immortality inherent in the soul as that which belongs to Plato's timeless realm of Ideas or Forms, Pheme Perkins declares that even today "Resurrection cannot be made philosophically coherent without distorting some of its fundamental commitments."[38] Belief in the resurrection of the body (σῶμα) belongs to the logical grammar, universe of discourse, or language game in which it is intelligible to rest trust in "God, who gives life to the dead and calls into existence the things that do not exist" (Rom 4:17).[39]

Yet just as the previous theory embodied two different aspects (gnosticism and overrealized eschatology), so this third approach demands differentiation between the issue of (a) belief in the sovereign power of God to create out of nothing (ἐκ τῶν νεκρῶν) and to raise the σῶμα to a transformed (15:42-44) mode of "somatic" existence; and (b) the notion that the *body* (σῶμα) cannot be a vehicle for this transformed mode of existence which enters the kingdom of God (15:50-54).[40] The former aspect lies behind the comment of G. Deluz: "They confused this pagan doctrine of immortality with Christian teaching on the resurrection."[41] The latter aspect lies behind Dale Martin's ingenious and suggestive hypothesis that whereas ordinary, unsophisticated Christians at Corinth ("the weak") might accept a hierarchy of essences which could make broad sense out of Paul's teaching, "the strong" could only view the notion of resurrection ἐκ τῶν νεκρῶν as an unacceptably primitive concept of raising rotting corpses.[42]

The issues here will come to a head in our exegesis of 15:42-44 and 50-54. For we reject not Martin's correlation between cultural groupings and readiness to find certain beliefs harder or easier, but his return to a highly questionable understanding of σῶμα πνευματικόν as *body which participates in the sphere of spirit* rather than as *made of full communicative existence characterized by the Holy Spirit*.[43] However, Martin's is not the only version of this approach, and his inquiry about whether *some* (τινες, 15:22) reflects the outlook of "the strong" deserves exploration. Pearson and Horsley argue that the group

---

37. Weiss, *Der erste Korintherbrief,* 344; Lietzmann, *An die Korinther,* 79; Deluz, *Companion to 1 Cor,* 225; P. Hoffmann, *Die Toten in Christus* (Münster: Aschendorff, 1966), 241-43; Sider, "St. Paul's Understanding of the Nature and Significance of the Resurrection in 1 Cor 15:1-19," 137; Murphy-O'Connor, *1 Cor,* 137; Perkins, *Resurrection: NT Witness and Contemporary Reflection* (London: Chapman, 1984), 221-27 and 431-46; Sellin, *Der Streit um die Auferstehung,* 79-189 and 290; Strobel, *Der erste Brief,* 226-27, 240-43; Martin, *The Corinthian Body,* 104-36.

38. Perkins, *Resurrection,* 438.

39. Cf. Moxnes, *Theology in Conflict,* 231-82: "God Who Gives Life to the Dead," 231-82.

40. Dahl, *The Resurrection of the Body,* insists that we cannot try to translate *sōma* and must use the adjective "somatic."

41. Deluz, *Companion to 1 Cor,* 225.

42. Martin, *The Corinthian Body,* 130, 132, 135-36.

43. Martin, *Corinthian Body,* 132.

at Corinth holds a view similar to that of the immortality of the soul, but use terminology which draws much of its currency from Jewish wisdom traditions, of which Philo is one representative among others. Clearly Paul's reversal of the order of the first and last Adam in 15:45-49 may well reflect a Philonic type of speculation.[44]

Another variant of the view that *the body* proves to be a major cause for doubt at Corinth arises from the work of G. Sellin.[45] Sellin argues that a dualist understanding of being human may have influenced some at Corinth. To be "spiritual" is to experience inspiration of the soul by the spirit. Paul, in Sellin's view, counteracts this view by drawing on an apocalyptic view of resurrection at the end time which entails new creation. Most important of all, the judgment theme in apocalyptic, and its theology of the two ages, ensures an emphasis on discontinuity as well as continuity in God's eschatological act of new creation. This discontinuity, all the same, is experienced in part in identification with Christ in the cross. Thus the resurrection corroborates the need for changes of ethical lifestyle now (v. 58).

(iv) It is difficult to deny that both the second and the third approaches contain important elements which seem convincing, even if not as exclusive or comprehensive accounts of the problem. It may well be the case that Luther anticipated the most plausible argument (found currently in, e.g., Mitchell and Eriksson) when he proposed that *some* (τινες, v. 12) *may allude to more than one group which was beset with more than one problem*).[46] Most writers concede that we have insufficient evidence to specify one solution in such a way as decisively to exclude others.[47] Most commentators believe that few if any denied the resurrection of *Christ;* but some failed to follow through the eschatological and ethical entailments of what it meant to share in Christ's resurrection, not least corporately as his body.

Our final consideration in this introduction to ch. 15 concerns the rhetorical structure and logic of Paul's argument. In very recent years a vast amount of material has been produced on Pauline rhetoric, and not least his rhetoric in 1 Corinthians 15.[48] Saw, Eriksson, and Mitchell all stress the appeal to the com-

---

44. Cf. Philo, *Legum Allegoriae* 1.31 and 2.4 with Gen 1:27; 2:7 and 1 Cor 15:45-53. See B. A. Pearson, *The Pneumatikos-Psychikos Terminology in 1 Corinthians,* SBLDS 12 (Missoula: Scholars Press, 1973), 82; and Horsley, "Pneumatikos versus Psychikos: Distinctions of Spiritual Status among the Corinthians," 269-88.

45. Sellin, *Der Streit um die Auferstehung,* 79-189.

46. *Luther's Works,* 18:59 (Germ. *WA* 36:482); also Mitchell, *Paul and the Rhetoric of Reconciliation,* 177 and 287; Eriksson, *Traditions,* 236-37; and Thiselton, "Luther and Barth on 1 Cor 15," 268-69.

47. Cf. Spörlein, *Die Leugnung,* 9-12; and Wolff, *Der erste Brief,* 349-52.

48. Cf., e.g., Saw, *Paul's Rhetoric in 1 Cor 15: An Analysis Utilizing the Theories of Classical Rhetoric;* Eriksson, *Traditions as Rhetorical Proof,* esp. 232-78; Mitchell, *Paul and the Rhetoric of Reconciliation,* 175-77 and 283-90; Bünker, *Briefformular und rhetorische Disposition im 1 Kor;* Watson, "Paul's Rhetorical Strategy in 1 Cor 15," in Porter and Olbricht (eds.), *Rhetoric and the NT,* 231-49.

monality of tradition, which functions for Saw as "proponent" alongside Paul's general use of deliberative rhetoric.[49]

We are no less concerned with the *logical* structure of Paul's argument, although, insofar as good rhetorical studies include an identification of communicative strategy (a subcategory within hermeneutics), attention to classical and Pauline rhetorical methods and aims assists us in this task (see the Introduction, 41-52). The chapter is so well presented as a powerful discourse which unfolds distinct stages in a progressive argument that it is understandable that Conzelmann (who, as we have noted, doubts its integrity with the rest of the epistle) regards ch. 15 as "a self-contained treatise."[50] Virtually all writers accept the unity of 15:1-58, and its rhetorical coherence is underlined by Mitchell, Eriksson, and Watson among others.[51] Eriksson perceives a use of *inclusio* whereby the theme of *emptiness or futility* marks its beginning in v. 2 (εἰκός) and ending in v. 58 (κενός).[52]

There is also virtually universal agreement about the distinct stages of argument.[53] The section on *the resurrection of Christ* (15:1-11) embodies the common pre-Pauline tradition (probably vv. 3-5) which constitutes "the first part of the *narratio* [i.e., vv. 1-11], provides the statement of the case, and is the common ground between Paul and the Corinthians."[54] This accords, in rhetorical terms, with Cicero's definition of "the statement" as an explanation of facts "as . . . a base and foundation for the establishment of belief."[55] Normally a *narratio* has the qualities of brevity, clarity, and plausibility. What many who offer a rhetorical analysis overlook, however, is that the second part of the *narratio* (vv. 8-11) states the reality of *God's creative, sovereign, undeserved grace* (τῷ ἐκτρώματι . . . v. 8, χάριτι δὲ θεοῦ εἰμι ὅ εἰμι, v. 10) *alongside the reality of Christ's resurrection.* Divine grace and the person and work of Christ provide the foundation for the rest of the chapter.

The first *refutatio* (15:12-19) begins to explain the dire consequences of denying the resurrection: If the resurrection of the dead is in principle impossible, how could Christ have been raised (15:12-14, 16)? Paul then uses deliberative rhetoric to underline the disadvantages or (here) disastrous consequences of such a denial: faith is empty; the apostles are false witnesses; there is no release from sin; dead believers are lost (15:15-19). This is followed by a first *confirmatio* (15:20-34): but in fact Christ was raised as the firstfruits of the resurrection of

49. For example, Saw, *Paul's Rhetoric,* 183-201; cf. Eriksson, *Traditions,* 89-97; Mitchell, *Rhetoric,* 283-88.

50. Conzelmann, *1 Cor,* 249 (discussed above).

51. Mitchell, *Rhetoric of Reconciliation,* 284; Eriksson, *Traditions,* 233; Watson, "Paul's Rhetorical Strategy," 231-49.

52. Eriksson, *Traditions,* 233.

53. Together with studies already cited, e.g., Fee, *First Epistle,* 713-809; Hays, *First Cor,* 252-77; Ortkemper, *1 Kor,* 143-67; Horsley, *1 Cor,* 197-220; Klauck, *1 Kor,* 107-23; Harrisville, *1 Cor,* 247-84; Wolff, *Der erste Brief,* 349-426; Allo, *Première Épitre,* 387-454.

54. Ibid.

55. Cicero, *De Partitione Oratoria* 9.31.

those who share his life and death (vv. 22-23), as God's purposes unfold in an orderly way (vv. 24-38), as Christian action tacitly implies (vv. 29-34).

The third main block within this chapter concerns *the logical possibility or conceivability of the resurrection of the dead* (15:35-58). In rhetorical terms Eriksson designates its two subsections as the *second refutatio* (15:35-49) and the *second confirmatio* (15:50-57), after which a very brief *peroratio* (v. 58) sums up and concludes the argument.[56] Once again, however, just as they often miss the centrality of grace-as-gift in 15:8-11, a number of writers concerned with rhetorical (rather than more strictly logical) analysis too often overlook the fundamental role of the transitional verse (v. 34) identified by Barth, Kennedy, and other more theological writers as the linchpin which provides the logical force: some (τινες) have no knowledge of *God* (ἀγνωσίαν γὰρ θεοῦ τινες ἔχουσιν), which matches γνωρίζω as the first Greek word of the chapter (v. 1). The ground for belief in the *possibility* of resurrection, therefore, becomes not some inherent human capacity, but the infinite resourcefulness and creativity of the sovereign and gracious God to *give* (v. 58) whatever appropriate σῶμα God wills, just as he has already demonstrated in the resourcefulness which gave rise to the infinite varieties and glories of creation (vv. 39-41). This paves the way for a theology of *transformation* (15:42-57).

Transformation, in turn, entails not only the ultimate necessary cause (source) of the sovereign grace of God and the efficient cause of the activity of the Holy Spirit (vv. 44-45), but also the mediate cause and final cause of being transformed into the image of Christ as the last Adam. The earlier allusion to Christ as the first sample sheaf of the harvest, or firstfruits (ἀπαρχή) of man to come (vv. 20, 23), is corroborated and expanded by the Adam typology of vv. 45-49, in which believers *will bear the image of the last Adam* (v. 49). Thus Joost Holleman's analysis of the logic is confirmed: "(a) Jesus has been raised as *the first* of those who have fallen asleep . . . ; (b) Jesus has been raised as *the representative* of those who will be raised" (his italics).[57] Nevertheless, as M. E. Dahl is at pains to emphasize, the active agent of resurrection for Christ and for Christian believers remains the sovereign *God* in his gracious decision to do so.[58]

Main Bibliography on 15:1-58

This main bibliography includes most literature on the whole chapter, but especially on 15:1-11. Supplementary bibliographies are also included at 15:12 on 15:12-34, and at 15:35 on 15:35-58.

Barrett, C. K., "Immortality and Resurrection," in C. Duthie (ed.), *Resurrection and Immortality* (London: Bagster, 1979), 68-88 (rpt. from *London Quarterly Holborn Review* [1965]: 91-102).

56. Eriksson, *Traditions,* 275.
57. Holleman, *Resurrection and Parousia,* 1. Cf. also Pate, *The Glory of Adam and the Afflictions of the Righteous: Pauline Suffering in Context.*
58. Dahl, *The Resurrection of the Body,* 96-100 and throughout.

Barth, G., "Zur Frage nach der in 1 Kor bekämpfen Auferstehungsleugnung," *ZNW* 83 (1992): 187-201.

Barth, K., *The Resurrection of the Dead* (Eng. trans., London: Hodder & Stoughton, 1933).

Bartsch, H.-W., "Inhalt und Funktion des urchristlichen Osterglaubens," *NTS* 26 (1980): 180-96.

Becker, J., *Auferstehung der Toten im Urchristentum* (Stuttgart: Katholisches Bibelwerk, 1976).

Beker, J. C., *Paul the Apostle* (Edinburgh: T. & T. Clark, 1980), 135-81.

———, "Paul the Theologian: Major Motifs in Pauline Theology," *Int* 43 (1981): 352-65.

Benoit, P., and R. Murphy (eds.), "Immortality and Resurrection," *Conc* 60 (1970).

Binder, H., "Zum geschichtlichen Hintergrund von 1 Kor 15:12," *TZ* 46 (1990): 193-201.

Boismard, M.-É., *Our Victory over Death: Resurrection?* (Eng. trans., Collegeville, Minn.: Liturgical Press, 1999).

Boer, M. C. de, *The Defeat of Death: Apocalyptic Eschatology in 1 Cor 15 and Rom 5,* JSNTSS 22 (Sheffield: JSOT Press, 1988).

Bruce, F. F., "Paul on Immortality," *SJT* 24 (1971): 457-75.

Bünker, M., *Briefformular und rhetorische Disposition in 1 Kor* (Göttingen: Vandenhoeck & Ruprecht, 1983).

Bultmann, R., "Karl Barth: The Resurrection of the Dead," in Bultmann, *Faith and Understanding* (Eng. trans., London: SCM, 1969), 1:66-94.

Cambier, J., "Paul and Tradition," *Conc* 10:2 (1966): 53-63.

Carnley, P., *The Structure of Resurrection Belief* (Oxford: Clarendon, 1987).

Cavallin, H. C. C., *Life after Death: Paul's Argument for the Resurrection of the Dead in 1 Cor 15,* ConBNT 7 (Lund: Gleerup, 1974).

Collins, R., "From Good Friday to Easter: A Call for Metanoia," *Emmanuel* 98 (1992): 125-29.

Conzelmann, H., "On the Analysis of the Confessional Formula in 1 Cor 15:3-5," *Int* 20 (1966): 15-25 ("Zur Analyse der Bekenntnisformel 1 Kor 15:3-5," *EvT* 25 [1965]: 1-11).

Cullmann, O., *Immortality of the Soul or Resurrection of the Dead* (Eng. trans., London: Epworth Press, 1958).

———, *Les Premières Confessions de Foi Chrétiennes* (Paris: Universitaires de France, 1948).

———, *La Tradition,* Cahiers Théologiques 33 (Paris: Delachaux & Niestlé, 1953); Eng. trans., "The Tradition," in Cullmann, *The Early Church* (London: SCM, 1956), 59-99.

Daalen, D. H. van, *The Real Resurrection* (London: SCM, 1962).

Dahl, M. E., *The Resurrection of the Body* (London: SCM, 1962).

Davis, S. T., *Risen Indeed: Making Sense of the Resurrection* (London: SPCK, 1993), 1-6, 191-209.

Davis, S., D. Kendall, and G. O'Collins (eds.), *The Resurrection: An Interdisciplinary Symposium* (Oxford: Oxford University Press, 1997).

De Margerie, B., "Le troisième jour selon les Ecritures il est ressuscité. Importance théologique d'une recherche exégétique," *RSR* 60 (1986): 158-88.

Dunn, J. D. G., *The Theology of Paul the Apostle* (Edinburgh: T. & T. Clark, 1998), 163-81, 235-66.

Eriksson, A., *Traditions as Rhetorical Proof: Pauline Argumentation in 1 Cor,* ConBNT 29 (Stockholm: Almqvist & Wiksell, 1998), 86-97 and 232-78.

Fischer, K. M., *Das Ostergeschehen* (Göttingen: Vandenhoeck & Ruprecht, 2d ed. 1980 [1978]).

Fiorenza, E. Schüssler, "Rhetorical Situation and Historical Situation in 1 Cor," *NTS* 33 (1987): 386-403.

Harris, M. J., *Raised Immortal* (London: Marshall, Morgan & Scott, 1983).

Hasler, V., "Credo und Auferstehung in Korinth. Erwägungen zu 1 Kor 15," *TZ* 40 (1984): 130-41.

Hill, D., "On the Third Day," *ExpTim* 78 (1966-67): 266-67.

Hoffmann, P. (ed.), *Zur neutestamentlichen Überlieferung von der Auferstehung Jesu* (Darmstadt: Wissenschaftliche Buchgesellschaft, 1988).

Holleman, J., *Resurrection and Parousia: A Traditio-Historical Study of Paul's Eschatology in 1 Cor 15,* NovTSup 84 (Leiden: Brill, 1996).

Horsley, R. A., "'How Can Some of You Say That There Is No Resurrection of the Dead?': Spiritual Elitism in Corinth," *NovT* 20 (1978): 203-31.

———, "Pneumatikos versus Psychikos: Distinctions of Spiritual Status among the Corinthians," *HTR* 69 (1976): 269-88.

Johnson, A., "Firstfruits and Death's Defeat: Metaphor in Paul's Rhetorical Strategy in 1 Cor 15:20-28," *WW* 16 (1996): 456-64.

Jones, P. R., "1 Cor 15:8: Paul the Last Apostle," *TynBul* 36 (1985): 5-34.

Kearney, P. J., "He Appeared to 500 Brothers (1 Cor 15:6)," *NovT* 22 (1980): 264-84.

Kegel, G., *Auferstehung Jesu–Auferstehung der Toten* (Gütersloh: Mohn, 1970).

Kennedy, H. A. A., *St Paul's Conceptions of the Last Things* (London: Hodder & Stoughton, 1904), 222-341.

Kloppenborg, J., "An Analysis of the Pre-Pauline Formula in 1 Cor 15:3b-5 in Light of Some Recent Literature," *CBQ* 40 (1978): 351-67.

Kreitzer, L., "Adam as Analogy: Help or Hindrance?" *New Blackfriars* 70 (1989): 278-84.

———, "Christ and Second Adam in Paul," *CV* 32 (1989): 55-101.

———, *Jesus and God in Paul's Eschatology,* JSNT 19 (Sheffield: JSOT, 1987).

Kuck, D. W., *Judgment and Community Conflict: Paul's Use of Apocalyptic Judgment Language in 1 Cor 3:5–4:5,* NovTSup 66 (Leiden: Brill, 1992).

Künneth, W., *The Theology of the Resurrection* (Eng. trans., London: SCM, 1965).

Lindars, B., "Jesus Risen: Resurrection but No Empty Tomb," *Theol* 89 (1986): 90-96.

———, "The Sound of the Trumpet: Paul and Eschatology," *BJRL* 67 (1984-85): 766-82.

Lindemann, A., "Paulus und die korinthische Eschatologie. Zur These von einer 'Entwicklung' im paulinischen Denken," *NTS* 37 (1991): 373-99.

Lüdemann, G., *Die Auferstehung Jesu* (Göttingen: Vandenhoeck & Ruprecht, 1994).

Luther, M., *Commentaries on 1 Cor 7 and 15, Luther's Works,* 28 (ed. H. Coswald; St Louis: Concordia, 1973) (Weimar ed., 36:482-696).

Martin, D. B., *The Corinthian Body* (New Haven: Yale University Press, 1995), 104-36.

Marxsen, W., "The Resurrection as a Historical and Theological Problem," in C. F. D. Moule (ed.), *The Significance of the Resurrection for Faith in Jesus Christ* (London: SCM, 1968), 15-50.

———, *The Resurrection of Jesus of Nazareth* (Eng. trans., Philadelphia: Fortress, 1970).

McArthur, H. K., "On the Third Day," *NTS* 18 (1971-72): 81-86.

Moiser, J., "1 Cor 15," *IBS* 14 (1992): 10-30.

Moltmann, J., *The Coming of God: Christian Eschatology* (Eng. trans., London: SCM, 1996), 49-256.

————, *Is There Life after Death?* (Milwaukee: Marquette University Press, 1998).

————, *Theology of Hope* (Eng. trans., London: SCM, 1967).

Moore, A. L., *The Parousia in the NT,* NovTSup 13 (Leiden: Brill, 1996).

Moxnes, H., "God Who Gives Life to the Dead," in *Theology in Conflict: Studies in Paul's Understanding of God in Romans,* NovTSup 53 (Leiden: Brill, 1980), 231-82.

Munck, J., "Paulus tanquam abortivus, 1 Cor 15:8," in A. J. B. Higgins (ed.), *NT Essays: Studies in Memory of T. W. Manson* (Manchester: Manchester University Press, 1959), 180-95.

Murphy-O'Connor, J., "Tradition and Redaction in 1 Cor 15:3-7," *CBQ* 43 (1981): 582-89.

Nickelsburg, G. W. E., "An *ektrōma,* Though Appointed from the Womb: Paul's Apostolic Self-Description in 1 Cor 15 and Gal 1," *HTR* 79 (1986): 198-205.

————, *Resurrection, Immortality and Eternal Life in Intertestamental Judaism* (Cambridge, Mass.: Harvard University Press, 1972).

Oberlinner, L. (ed.), *Auferstehung Jesu — Auferstehung der Christen. Deutungen des Osterglaubens* (Freiburg: Herder, 1986).

Pannenberg, W., *Systematic Theology* (3 vols.; Eng. trans., Edinburgh: T. & T. Clark and Grand Rapids: Eerdmans, 1991, 1994, 1998), 2:343-72, 3:375-80, and 555-646.

Pate, C. M., *The Glory of Adam and the Afflictions of the Righteous: Pauline Suffering in Context* (Lewiston, N.Y.: Mellen, 1993).

Perkins, P., *Resurrection: NT Witnesses and Contemporary Reflection* (London: Chapman, 1984).

Plank, K. A., "Resurrection Theology: The Corinthian Controversy Re-examined," *PRS* 8 (1981): 41-54.

Price, R. M., "Apocryphal Apparitions: 1 Cor 15:3-11 as a Post-Pauline Interpolation," *JHC* 2 (1995): 69-99.

Radi, W., "Der Sinn von γνωρίζω in 1 Kor 15:1," *BZ* 28 (1984): 243-45.

Saw, Insawn, *Paul's Rhetoric in 1 Cor 15: An Analysis Utilizing the Theories of Classical Rhetoric* (Lewiston, N.Y.: Mellen, 1995).

Schenk, W., "Textlinguistische Aspekte der Strukturanalyse, dargestellt am Beispiel von 1 Kor xv.1-11," *NTS* 23 (1977): 469-77.

Schütz, J. H., "Apostolic Authority and the Control of Tradition: 1 Cor 15," *NTS* 15 (1968-69): 439-57.

Schweitzer, A., *The Mysticism of Paul the Apostle* (Eng. trans., London: Black, 1931), 219-26 and 294-97.

Sellin, E., *Der Streit um die Auferstehung der Toten* (Göttingen: Vandenhoeck & Ruprecht, 1986).

Shires, H. M., *The Eschatology of Paul in the Light of Modern Scholarship* (Philadelphia: Westminster, 1966).

Sider, R. J., "St. Paul's Understanding of the Nature and Significance of the Resurrection in 1 Cor 15:1-19," *NovT* 19 (1977).

Spallek, A. J., "The Origin and Meaning of Εὐαγγέλιον in the Pauline Corpus," *CTQ* 57 (1993): 177-90.

Spörlein, B., *Die Leugnung der Auferstehung. Eine historisch-kritische Untersuchung zu 1 Kor 15* (Regensburg: Pustet, 1971).

Stanley, D. M., *Christ's Resurrection in Pauline Soteriology,* AnBib 13 (Rome: Pontifical Biblical Institute, 1961), 108-27.

Thiselton, A. C., "Luther and Barth on 1 Cor 15: Six Theses for Theology in Relation to Recent Interpretation," in W. P. Stephens (ed.), *The Bible, the Reformation and the Church: Essays in Honour of J. Atkinson,* JSNTSS 105 (Sheffield: Sheffield Academic Press, 1995), 258-89.

Verburg, W., *Endzeit und Entschlafene. Syntaktische-sigmatische, semantische und pragmatische Analyse von 1 Kor 15,* FB 78 (Würzburg: Echter, 1996).

Von der Osten-Sacken, P., "Die Apologie des paulinischen Apostolats in 1 Kor 15:1-11," *ZNW* 64 (1973): 245-62.

Vorster, J. N., "Resurrection Faith in 1 Cor 15," *Neot* (1989): 287-307.

Wagner, G., "If Christians Refuse to Act, Then Christ Is Not Risen. Once More, 1 Cor 15," *IBS* 6 (1984): 27-39.

Watson, D. F., "Paul's Rhetorical Strategy in 1 Cor 15," in S. E. Porter and T. H. Olbricht (eds.), *Rhetoric and the NT,* JSNTSS 90 (Sheffield: Sheffield Academic Press, 1993), 231-49.

Webber, R. C., "A Note on 1 Cor 15:3-5," *JETS* 26 (1983): 265-69.

Wedderburn, A. J. M., *Baptism and Resurrection: Studies in Pauline Theology against Its Graeco-Roman Background,* WUNT 44 (Tübingen: Mohr, 1987).

————, "The Problem of the Denial of the Resurrection in 1 Cor 15," *NovT* 23 (1981): 229-41.

Wilckens, U., *Resurrection: Biblical Testimony to the Resurrection: An Historical Examination and Explanation* (Eng. trans., Edinburgh: St Andrew's Press, 1977), 1-26, 112-32.

Wilson, J. H., "The Corinthians Who Say There Is No Resurrection of the Dead," *ZNW* 59 (1968): 90-107.

Zimmer, C., "Das argumentum resurrectionis in 1 Kor 15:12-20," *LB* 65 (1991): 25-36.

A. The Reality of the Resurrection of Christ (15:1-11)

(1) Now I want to restore to your full knowledge, dear brothers and sisters, the gospel that I proclaimed to you; the gospel which in turn you received and on which you have taken your stand. (2) Through this gospel you are in process of being saved if you hold fast to the substance of the gospel that I proclaimed to you — unless you believed without coherent consideration.

(3, 4, 5) For I handed on to you first and foremost what I, in turn, received, namely: "Christ died for our sins according to the scriptures; he was buried; he was raised on the third day according to the scriptures; he appeared to Peter and then to the Twelve."

(6) Then he appeared to more than five hundred of our Christian people on a single occasion, most of whom are still alive, although some have died. (7) Then he appeared to James, then to all the apostles. (8, 9) Last of all, he appeared also to me, as if to an aborted fetus. For I am the very least of the

apostles; I am not competent to be called an apostle because I persecuted the church of God. (10) But by the grace of God I am what I am, and his grace which he extended to me has not proved fruitless. On the contrary, I labored to an even greater degree than all of them, yet not I but God's grace working with me. (11) Whether, anyway, it is they or I, it is this that we proclaim and it is this that you came to believe.

1   The translation of γνωρίζω is more difficult than might appear. In 12:3 Paul uses the verb to mean *I give you to understand*. Most major modern English VSS translate it as *remind* (REB, NRSV, NIV); but NJB has, *I want to make quite clear to you;* RV (1881), *I make known,* and (less plausibly) AV/KJV, *I declare*. The usual meaning in most contexts is *to make known* (or *to know*), and on this basis W. Radi argues that it should retain this force not least because it refers not simply to the already known common tradition of vv. 3-5, but to vv. 1-11 and to **the gospel** in the wider sense of all that has been revealed to Paul.[59] In lexicographical terms γνωρίζω does acquire a derivative force of *remind,* but primarily in the sense identified by Grimm-Thayer: "to recall to one's mind as though what is made known had escaped him, 1 Cor xv.1."[60]

Wolff firmly rejects an equivalence to ἀναμνήσκειν, and endorses the comment of Robertson and Plummer that it is as if "he has to begin again and teach them an elementary fact, which they had already accepted."[61] Indeed, Robertson and Plummer (following de Wette and Meyer) translate simply, *I make known*. With Edwards they ascribe the incorrect *remind* to Theodoret and Chrysostom in origin.[62] However, Collins understands the content of these verses as "something which the community already knows," and similarly Findlay argues that *I give you to know* carries "a touch of blame."[63] What clinches the matter for us is not only a comparison with the meaning of the word in 12:3 (cf. Rom 9:22, 23; 2 Cor 8:1; Phil 1:22; 4:6) but also the part played by the theme of *ignorance* and **knowledge** at certain key points in this chapter (esp. ἀγνωσίαν . . . θεοῦ, v. 34; but also ἄφρων, v. 36; μυστήριον, v. 51; εἰδότες, v. 58), not least if there is any truth in Dale Martin's claim that Paul addresses especially "the strong" who are proud of this **knowledge** in this chapter.[64]

Once again on the troublesome translation of ἀδελφοί, see above under 1:10, 11; 2:1; 3:1; 4:6, et al. In addition to serving as a term of affection and a degree of intimacy as members of the Christian family (although it is not exclusive to Christian relationships in this sense), the term introduces a new topic

---

59. W. Radi, "Der Sinn von γνωρίζω in 1 Kor 15:1," 243-45. He alludes to Gal 1:11 in this connection.

60. Grimm-Thayer, 119, col. 2; cf. BAGD, 163.

61. Wolff, *Der erste Brief,* 354. He also endorses Radi's article.

62. Robertson and Plummer, *First Epistle,* 331; Edwards, *First Epistle,* 389; Meyer, *First Epistle,* 2:39.

63. Findlay, *Expositor's Greek Testament,* 2:918; Collins, *First Cor,* 533.

64. Martin, *The Corinthian Body,* 104-36.

and serves as a topic indicator. We cannot convey all this in English, let alone avoid clumsiness in a gender-inclusive rendering. However, **now** (logical **now**) serves as a topic indicator. We use a variety of possible translations in view of the difficulty which takes account of context. In rhetorical terms Paul is encouraging attention and goodwill.

Fee follows Edwards and Findlay (against Héring) in identifying "an A-B-A-B" structure in vv. 1-2 in which "A" first states and then repeats the past communication of **the gospel** as **proclaimed**, while "B" first expresses the Corinthian response and then serves as a negative counterpoint to indicate the net result.[65] Edwards, however, explains the practical thrust of this fourfold analysis more clearly. In today's terminology we should say that "A" reflects **the gospel** as announcing *states of affairs,* especially *acts of God;* "B" conveys the *self-involving dimension* which the *declarative* or *proclamatory* speech-acts entail: the stability of Christian existence, the experience of salvation, and the implication of coherent appropriation (on εἰκῆ see under v. 2).[66] Both aspects explicate the nature of **the gospel**.

The term **the gospel** (τὸ εὐαγγέλιον), as Dunn argues in a recent extended consideration of the word, is predominantly Pauline (60 out of 76 occurrences in the New Testament).[67] It is a key word in Romans (Rom 1:1, 15; 15:20), and Paul is "not ashamed" of the gospel (Rom 1:16; cf. 1 Cor 1:18-25, where "shame" is set in contrast with effective power to save, in both contexts). It is wretchedness and shame for Paul if he cannot proclaim the gospel (1 Cor 9:16; cf. v. 23). His conversion and call was specifically to preach this gospel among the Gentiles (Gal 1:16). Dunn underlines the absence of the term both from the LXX and (in any Pauline sense, if at all) from Greek texts of the period, although the verb εὐαγγελίζομαι occurs in Isa 40:9; 52:7; 61:1-2, and in an echo of these Isaiah passages in *Psalms of Solomon* 11:1: "It is probable that it was Paul himself who coined the usage as a new technical term for his own proclamation."[68] This does not detract from the continuity with the tradition of Jesus' applying the verbal form to his own preaching in the context of Isa 61:1-2 (Luke 4:16-21; cf. Matt 11:5; Luke 7:22).[69] We must understand **the gospel** in 15:1, therefore, to denote more than the message of the resurrection, but not less. It denotes *the message of salvation;* in vv. 3-4 Paul endorses the shared pre-Pauline tradition which both *proclaims the death and resurrection of Christ*

---

65. Fee, *First Epistle,* 720; broadly also Strobel, *Der erste Brief,* 227.

66. Edwards, *First Epistle,* 390; reformulated in my terminology.

67. Dunn, *"Euangelion,"* in his *The Theology of Paul,* 164-69. See also, e.g., J. A. Fitzmyer, "The Gospel in the Theology of Paul," in *To Advance the Gospel* (New York: Crossword, 1981), 149-61; L. A. Jervis and P. Richardson (eds.), *The Gospel in Paul,* JSNTSS 108 (Sheffield: Sheffield Academic Press, 1994); P. T. O'Brien, *Gospel and Mission in the Writings of Paul* (Carlisle: Paternoster, 1995).

68. Dunn, *Theology of Paul,* 168; also 167.

69. Cf. C. K. Barrett, "I Am Not Ashamed of the Gospel," in *NT Essays* (London: SPCK, 1972), 116-43.

and interprets it in terms of the saving and transforming power of God as this receives explanation and intelligibility within the frame of reference provided by the [Old Testament] *scriptures.*[70]

As Eriksson urges, there is still more to be said. Paul declares the gospel as that which is not only revealed (cf. Galatians 1 and 2) but is also "both transmitted and received" and therefore in principle constitutes "the premises of the audience" which provide the foundation on the basis of which Paul will develop his argument about the resurrection of the dead.[71] The readers have **in turn . . . received** it. This is a happy rendering by the NRSV to indicate transmission of a tradition for which the thrice-repeated καί is scarcely accidental. With Wolff, we understand ἐστήκατε to function as a present perfect (with NRSV, against NJB, *took their stand*).[72] REB's **have taken your stand** indicates *present* stability on the basis of past action as well as present state.

2 In place of the authentic UBS 4th ed. εἰ κατέχετε some Western MSS (D*, F, G) read ὀφείλετε κατέχειν. The change is understandable, so even if Zuntz were correct in arguing that one version of p[46] also has the secondary reading, this would not alter the weight of probability (*Text,* 254-55).

Commentators agree that the continuous present σῴζεσθε is to be explicated: it denotes "what is being done for them for the future."[73] The heaping up of relative pronouns required the repetition of **through this gospel** for the Gk. δι' οὗ. The translation of τίνι λόγῳ is difficult to render idiomatically. With what Greek clause should we construe *in what word(s) I proclaimed the gospel to you* (εὐηγγελισάμην ὑμῖν). Some argue that it still depends on γνωρίζω (Bengel, Edwards, A. T. Robertson). However, the distance from the beginning of v. 1 and the addition of other themes make this unlikely.[74] τίνι λόγῳ is probably instrumental and is used here as if it were a relative, as it occurs frequently in the papyri.[75] Any difficulty dissolves (*pace* Conzelmann, see note) as soon as we recall that λόγος often denotes not simply *word, message,* or *act of speaking* but also the *content* or **substance** *of a declaration, assertion, proposition, or other communicative act.*[76] The verb εὐαγγελίζομαι already means **to proclaim the gospel**; hence Paul refers to **the substance of the gospel that I proclaimed to you**.

---

70. See further under 9:16, 23; and Meyer, *First Epistle,* 2:39.

71. Eriksson, *Traditions,* 241.

72. Wolff, *Der erste Brief,* 354; Strobel, *Der erste Brief* 227.

73. Robertson and Plummer, *First Epistle,* 331; Findlay, *Expositor's Greek Testament,* 2:918; Fee, *First Epistle,* 720, n. 32.

74. Findlay is convincing here (*Expositor's Greek Testament,* 2:919).

75. MHT, 1:93-94.

76. BAGD, 477-78; Grimm-Thayer, 380-82. Conzelmann, *1 Cor,* 248, n. 4, makes very heavy weather out of the numerous possibilities of syntactical construction, listing no fewer than six possible views represented respectively by Kümmel, Weiss, BDF, Lietzmann, Heinrici, and his own, which assumes a dependence on γνωρίζω. Collins understands it to mean *the gospel* here (*1 Cor,* 533).

To translate εἰκῇ as *in vain* (NRSV, REB, NIV, NJB, AV/KJV, Collins) causes needless difficulties and forces Paul into an aggressive irony that undermines his seeking common ground by appealing to the shared tradition, calling the readers ἀδελφοί and establishing the previous points. There is firm lexicographical evidence for the meaning *without due consideration,* or *in a haphazard manner* (e.g., Epictetus, *Dissertations* 1.28.28; 6.7) or *thoughtlessly* or *at random* (*1 Clement* 40:2).[77] Here Paul envisages the possibility of such a superficial or *confused* appropriation of the gospel in which no **coherent** grasp of its logical or practical entailments for eschatology or for practical discipleship had been reached. *Incoherent* belief is different from believing *in vain.*

3-5 Both variants (in vv. 3 and 5) say more about the theology of the witnesses than about the text. (1) Marcion predictably omits ὃ καὶ παρέλαβον to avoid any implication that Paul depends on apostolic tradition rather than direct revelation of his "Pauline" gospel. (2) Certain Western readings, D*, F, G and many Latin VSS seek to heighten *Peter's* status in v. 5 by replacing εἶτα, **then,** with μετὰ ταῦτα, *after this,* probably to imply not only precedence but also that the tradition ends with the appearance to Peter; but 𝔭46, B, D2 reflect the authentic text (as does UBS 4th ed.) even if ℵ, A, and 33 have ἔπειτα (drawn from v. 7). (3) In v. 5, D*, F, G, the Vulgate, and some Syriac and Latin VSS (with Eusebius and Jerome) "introduce the pedantic correction ἕνδεκα," *eleven,* "instead of recognizing that δώδεκα is used here as an official designation" (Metzger, *Textual Commentary,* 2d ed., 500).

REB's **first and foremost** well captures the logical rather than temporal force of ἐν πρώτοις in this context, i.e., *of first importance* (as NRSV, NIV).[78] NJB's *handed on to you in the first place* too readily suggests sequence, but does have the advantage of retaining the double meaning which the word *first* can convey in both Greek and English, depending on its context. REB explicates the relative pronoun ὅ by Eng. *the tradition,* which was indeed implied by the two verbs (see above and on 11:23), but in view of the mistakenly negative overtones generated by the notion of *tradition* by those who have not yet been liberated from the worst aspects of Enlightenment rationalism it may be better not to import the word unnecessarily here. Paul does, however, refer to a continuity of **handing on** and **receiving** which constitutes, in effect, an early *creed which declares the absolute fundamentals of Christian faith and on which Christian identity* (and the experience of salvation) *is built.*

The number of studies on Paul and tradition are too many to list. Among influential works in the earlier part of the second half of the twentieth century, Oscar Cullmann (French 1953, English 1956) states in relation to this verse, "The very essence of tradition is that it forms a chain. . . . It is sometimes Paul,

---

77. BAGD, 221-22; Grimm-Thayer, 174.

78. Fee argues that the preposition with the plural "seems especially to point in this direction" (*First Epistle,* 722, n. 45); cf. Robertson and Plummer, "foremost place" (*First Epistle,* 332); and Wolff, *"wichtigsten Stücke"* (*Der erste Brief,* 355). *In the first instance* (Collins) seems to slip back into a temporal mode (*First Cor,* 534).

sometimes the Church which 'received'. The word καί must be particularly noticed, for it certainly belongs to the formula derived from the *paradosis* terminology . . . in 11:23 and . . . in 15:3, but also in 1 Cor 15:1. . . . 'I received the tradition in the same way as I handed it on to you — by *mediation*'" (Cullmann's italics, last quotation cited from E.-B. Allo).[79] The relation between "fragments of Creeds" in 1 Corinthians 15 and elsewhere in Paul and the steady development of early Christian creeds is traced by Hans von Campenhausen and also by J. N. D. Kelly. Kelly argues that 1 Cor 15:3-6 is "manifestly a summary drawn up for catechetical purposes or for preaching: it gives the gist of the Christian message in a concentrated form."[80] As Kelly observes, we should not assume that 1 Cor 11:23-25 and 15:3-5 provide the only such examples from Paul. From 1 Corinthians, we noted Eriksson's identification of pre-Pauline tradition in 8:6; 8:11b; 10:16; 12:3; 13 (and also 16:22); Kelly also compares Rom 1:3-4; 4:24; 8:34; Gal 1:4; 1 Thess 4:14; 5:9; and from later material 1 Pet 3:18-20 and 1 Tim 2:5-6, 8 and 6:13-14. *The juxtaposition of confession in the saving efficacy of the cross and the divine vindication or glorification of Christ in the resurrection feature in virtually all of these passages as an emergent core pattern of the earliest Christian confessions or creeds within the pages of the New Testament.*

The importance of this parallelism is confirmed by the examples cited by Vernon Neufeld. It is possible, Neufeld argues, that the series of verbs ἀπέθανεν . . . ἐτάφη . . . ἐγήγερται . . . ὤφθη (15:3-5) represent a *paradosis* which runs parallel with a form without the precise descriptive phrases found in, e.g., Rom 4:24, 25; 8:34; 10:9; 14:9 (cf. Rom 1:3, 4; 2 Cor 13:4; Gal 3:20; Eph 4:8-10).[81] In many cases a participial construction or use of relative clauses may introduce credal material, but the salvific context of Christ's death and his resurrection or status as "Lord" (1 Cor 12:3) are no less striking than stylistic features. These are "usually . . . bipartite," often but not always with phrases to indicate that they are not adversative but "complementary."[82] Rom 4:34 is adversative; Rom 4:24-25 has the bipartite components in parallel; 1 Cor 15:3-5 clearly demonstrates its early "primitiveness" but embodies qualifying descriptive phrases which place Christ's death and resurrection within a scriptural, salvific, and self-involving frame of reference.[83]

All of these earliest confessions simultaneously assert truth claims about God's action in and through Christ and speak of "the integral relationship between Jesus Christ and the Christian, both as an individual and as a member of

---

79. Cullmann, *La Tradition,* 16; also Eng. trans., "The Tradition," in Cullmann, *The Early Church,* 63-64; cf. 59-99. See also Cullmann, *Les Premières Confessions de Foi Chrétiennes,* 25-27, 33, 43-44; and Cambier, "Paul and Tradition," *Conc* 10:2, 53-63.

80. J. N. D. Kelly, *Early Christian Creeds* (London: Longmans, Green, 1950), 17; cf. 16-29; and Hans von Campenhausen, "Bekenntnis im Urchristentum," *ZNW* 63 (1972): 210-53.

81. V. H. Neufeld, *The Earliest Christian Confessions* (Leiden: Brill, 1963), 42-51.

82. Ibid., 45.

83. Ibid., 47-48 (and throughout on the duality of truth claims and self-involving stance).

the body of believers."[84] 1 Cor 12:3, 15:58, and 16:22 confirm this dual aspect.[85] There is a very close relationship between the dimension of *proclamation* or *kerygma* which declares a gospel truth claim and the dimension of *confession* or *self-involvement* which declares a personal stake in what is asserted. This is fundamental in view of a disastrous dichotomy between an existential approach which perceives *only* a confession of *personal faith* here and a conservative counterreaction which sometimes perceives *only* a statement of *bare fact* here. Since the death and resurrection of Christ are both states of affairs or events *extra nos* and transforming events which shape faith, both aspects are fundamental for 15:3-5. As J. L. Austin long ago observed, such speech-acts as "I do" in a marriage ceremony or a legal oath "presuppose lots of things"; "For a certain performative utterance to be happy [i.e., valid, operative] certain statements have *to be true*" (his italics).[86] Hence foundational confessions in the pre-Pauline and Pauline churches serve *both* as declarative acts of truth claims in the context of proclamation and teaching *and* as an oath of loyalty in baptism, the Eucharist, or times of persecution.

Seeberg viewed 15:3-5 as an early catechism, and Hans von Campenhausen linked it with baptismal confession, while even Bartsch is prepared to emphasize the proclamatory dimension in the τὸ εὐαγγέλιον ὃ εὐηγγελισάμην of v. 1.[87] He relates the background not only to the LXX but also to Luke 23:34 in connection with the appearance of Christ to Peter. V. Hasler, who interprets the appearance of Christ to the five hundred witnesses (v. 6, see below) as an appeal to a firm corroboration of a truth claim, stresses the kerygmatic aspect with reference to the following argument from v. 12 onward. The self-involving identity and hope of believers as that of which Christ constitutes the firstfruits, would make no sense beyond wishful thinking unless Paul regarded this Christology as a firm truth claim.[88]

Most writers agree that the commonality of the pre-Pauline tradition which Paul cites and endorses does indeed constitute what Eriksson calls a shared presupposition or an agreed basis for further argument. Eriksson speaks of "Traditions as Corinthian Premises."[89] P. von der Osten-Sacken attempts to argue that this serves primarily to introduce a defense of Paul's apostleship, but

84. Ibid., 53.

85. Ibid., 55-57.

86. J. L. Austin, *How to Do Things with Words* (Oxford: Clarendon Press, 1962), 51 and 45 respectively. For a more sophisticated discussion see J. R. Searle, *The Construction of Social Reality* (London: Allen Lane, 1995), 1-112; his *Expression and Meaning: Studies in the Theory of Speech Acts* (Cambridge: Cambridge University Press, 1979); D. Vanderveken, *Meaning and Speech Acts*, I: *Principles of Language Use* (Cambridge: Cambridge University Press, 1990); and S. L. Tsohatzidis (ed.), *Foundations of Speech-Act Theory* (New York: Routledge, 1994).

87. A. Seeberg, *Der Katechismus der Urchristenheit* (Munich: Kaiser, 1966 [1903]), 45-57; Bartsch, "Inhalt und Funktion des urchristlichen Osterglaubens," 180-82; cf. 180-96; von Campenhausen, "Bekenntnis im Urchristentum," 210-53.

88. Hasler, "Credo und Auferstehung in Korinth. Erwägungen zu 1 Kor 15," 12-33.

89. Eriksson, *Traditions*, 73-96 and 300.

he has entirely misconstrued the function and emphasis of 15:8, which calls attention to divine, sovereign grace as the mainspring of the principle of resurrection (see on v. 8, below).[90] This view, together with the claims of Wilckens and Kloppenborg that the vocabulary, fourfold ὅτι, and other factors question the unity of vv. 3-5, are well addressed by Murphy-O'Connor and Mitchell.[91] Murphy-O'Connor rightly appeals to the demonstrable convention of using ὅτι to denote quotation marks, with καί to add emphasis.[92] He convincingly sees vv. 3b-5 as a unit, with v. 6 performing the function of adding corroborative verification in the public domain and providing a Pauline transition to the important v. 8. This performs the kind of function which Mitchell in part subsequently identifies.[93] The composite vocabulary suggests not doubt about its unity, but a commonality of traditions which probably reflects both earliest Aramaic elements and a hellenistic-Jewish-Christian tradition which entirely accords with Luke's attributing to Jesus himself the foundational exposition of the meaning of his death and resurrection **according to the scriptures** (Luke 24:25-27 and 44-46).[94] In Luke Jesus explains **the scriptures** in terms of his own work (v. 45) and his own death and resurrection in terms of **the scriptures** (vv. 26-27), in the context of commissioning the hearers as *witnesses* (v. 48).[95]

The *content* of this early declarative, self-involving, descriptive, and commissive credal confession is now expressed by the four parallel components, each of which is introduced by ὅτι or καὶ ὅτι, which effectively serve as the equivalent of quotation marks. The difficulty of otherwise indicating quotation marks in an uncial text without an appropriate verb to introduce the quotation should be borne in mind, with the discussions of BDF, Nigel Turner, and Murphy-O'Connor.[96]

(1) *The first clause expresses the heart of the gospel,* as Paul confirms by his description of the gospel ὁ λόγος ὁ τοῦ σταυροῦ in 1:18 (cf. διὰ τῆς μωρίας

---

90. Von der Osten-Sacken, "Die Apologie des paulinischen Apostolats in 1 Kor 15:1-11," 345-62.

91. U. Wilckens, "Der Ursprung der Überlieferung der Erscheinungen des Auferstanden . . . 1 Kor 15:1-11," in W. Joest and W. Pannenberg (eds.), *Dogma und Denkstrukturen. Festschrift für E. Schlink* (Göttingen: Vandenhoeck & Ruprecht, 1963), 36-95; cf. Wilckens, *Resurrection*, 6-26; Kloppenborg, "An Analysis of the Pre-Pauline Formula in 1 Cor 15:3b-5 in Light of Some Recent Literature," 351-67. Against these: Murphy-O'Connor, "Tradition and Redaction in 1 Cor 15:3-7," 582-89; and Mitchell, *Rhetoric of Reconciliation,* 285-89, including nn. 557-78.

92. Murphy-O'Connor, "Tradition and Redaction," 582-89.

93. Mitchell, *Rhetoric of Reconciliation,* 285-89.

94. The literature is too vast to cite. Cf. Jeremias, *Eucharistic Words,* 101-3, on possible Aramaic elements; and Conzelmann, "On the Analysis of the Confessional Formula in 1 Cor 15:3-5," 15-25, on Greek elements and the LXX. Eriksson argues for a *Sitz im Leben* in the Jerusalem church (*Traditions*, 90-91).

95. See Wolff, *Der erste Brief,* 361.

96. BDF, sect. 470. See also N. Turner in MHT, 3:325-26, on the development and use of this marker and its relation to Heb. כִּי *(kiy)* and Aramaic דִּי "before direct speech" and often colloquial contents (does Mark reflect oral traditions in this respect?). See also Murphy-O'Connor, cited above.

τοῦ κηρύγματος σῶσαι τοὺς πιστεύοντας, 1:21; ἡμεῖς δὲ κηρύσσομεν Χριστὸν ἐσταυρωμένον, 1:23; Χριστὸν θεοῦ δύναμιν, 1:24). The *Sitz im Leben* of proclamation cannot be doubted; Wengst, Kramer, and Hans von Campenhausen (as we have noted) link this with the baptismal motif of being baptized into (or in or in the direction of) Christ's death (Rom 6:3-11).[97] Seeberg's early proposals about such a clause being learned and transmitted as catechism remain plausible and possible.[98] *All of these modes of currency define the bedrock of earliest Christian life, theology, and worship.*

The phrase ἀπέθανεν ὑπὲρ τῶν ἁμαρτιῶν ἡμῶν may perhaps reflect an allusion to the LXX of Isaiah 53 (perhaps 53:5-6, or vv. 11-12).[99] However, in view of the generality of the principle expressed by the phrase κατὰ τῆς γραφάς it is neither convincing nor necessary to isolate any single specific biblical reference, still less to speculate about an allusion to a Targumic VS of Isa 53:5.[100] Stanley, e.g., makes no reference to this passage in his work *Paul and the Language of Scripture* other than a passing mention in the course of his discussion of Gal 3:13.[101] What is at issue is the affirmation "that this atoning death fulfilled the scriptures" of which one instantiation among others is "the classic passage . . . Isa 53, the great description of the redemptive suffering of the servant of the Lord," although "Psalm 22 . . . has a number of details appropriate to a notable victim of public rejection," while the promise of Deut 18:15, 18 and the sorrow of Lam 1:12, 18 cannot be excluded as irrelevant.[102] The key points in the phrase **according to the scriptures**, as Barrett observes, are (1) the continuity of the cross of Christ with the history of the saving purposes of God as revealed in the Old Testament, which find their climax and fulfillment in the saving work of Christ; and (2) understanding the meaning of the saving role of the death of Christ by means of "interpretation in OT categories — for example, of sacrifice . . . atonement . . . sufferings . . . the good time to come."[103] The work of C. H. Dodd in this area remains of permanent value.[104] Blomberg com-

97. Klaus Wengst, *Christologische Formeln und Lieder der Urchristentums* (Gütersloh: Mohn, 1972), 47; cf. "Der Apostel und die Tradition," *ZTK* 69 (1972): 145-62; W. Kramer, *Christ, Lord, and Son of God* (Eng. trans., London: SCM, 1966), 64; Von Campenhausen, "Bekenntnis," 210-53.

98. Seeberg, *Der Katechismus der Urchristenheit*, 45-57.

99. Fee, *First Epistle*, 724.

100. Wolff warns against such speculation (*Der erste Brief*, 359); cf. Hays, *1 Cor*, 256.

101. Stanley, *Christ's Resurrection in Pauline Soteriology*, 246 (cf. 205-6, where he moves from 1 Cor 14:21 to 15:27).

102. Orr and Walther, *1 Cor*, 320.

103. Barrett, *First Epistle*, 338-39. Cf. the multiplicity of OT allusions to facilitate and to guide understanding of the cross (again, Luke 24:25-27, 44-46), although Acts 8:30 again alludes to Isaiah 53.

104. C. H. Dodd, *According to the Scriptures* (London: Nisbet, 1952). Dodd shows how the early church used OT texts to elucidate the kerygma. This entailed not so much citing isolated "proof-texts" as using extended portions of textual units as wholes, especially from Isaiah, Jeremiah, Psalms, and some of the prophetic books. In a coherent and patterned way, these served to provide "regulative ideas" for the "substructure" of NT theology (e.g., *According to the Scriptures*, 127).

ments that "the first Christian writers saw all of the Scripture pointing to Christ."[105]

This prepares the way for us to take with full seriousness the nuances of the words ὑπὲρ τῶν ἁμαρτίων ἡμῶν, a phrase which Paul uses in identical form in Gal 1:4 in explication of why Christ *gave himself* **for our sins** (τοῦ δόντος ἑαυτὸν ὑπὲρ τῶν ἁμαρτιῶν ἡμῶν) is explained as *rescue out of the present wicked age as our God and Father willed* (Gal 1:4, REB). Paul seldom uses the plural **sins**, which underlines this context of tradition here, as Collins notes, while Wolff and Strobel find a further allusion to Isa 53:4, 5, 12; in view of this scriptural frame of reference, is Edwards (and in part Wolff) justified in observing that while a simple **for** *us* (ὑπὲρ ἡμῶν) could mean simply *for our advantage,* **for our sins** "involves with ὑπέρ *the notion of expiation*" (my italics)?[106] Since περὶ ἁμαρτίας in the LXX may denote a sin offering (Lev 5:11; 7:37), Edwards (following Calvin) sees in this verse "a distinct statement of the doctrine that Christ's death was a propitiatory sacrifice for sin 'as' an essential aspect of the gospel (cf. 1:17; 2:2; Gal 3:1; Rom 4:25). . . . The word ὑπέρ expresses the same notion as τιμῆς [bought with a price] in 6:20. . . . Here, therefore, as in 2 Cor 5:21, ὑπέρ is synonymous with ἀντί" (see above on 6:19, 20).[107] Edwards's introduction of the term "propitiation" would seem to many to go beyond the text. However, given that, in Pannenberg's words, "the traditional formula in Paul (1 Cor 15:3) . . . *undoubtedly* means that *he made expiation for our sins*" (my italics), the two technical terms both qualify and complement each other.[108] *Expiation* denotes a means of dealing with sin, but risks a merely de-personalized mechanical model of the act or process; *propitiation* emphasizes that the act is both from God and to God, but risks distortion when Christ is substituted for God as the ultimate source and initiator of the action. After conceding that it is difficult to decide between atonement offering or expiation *(Sühnopfervorstellung)* and representation or substitution *(Stellvertretungsgedanken),* Wolff concludes that each entails the other.[109] This verse

---

105. Blomberg, *1 Cor,* 301.

106. Edwards, *First Epistle,* 392; Collins, *First Cor,* 534; Strobel, *Der erste Brief,* 229; on Wolff, *Der erste Brief,* 362, n. 32. In his detailed excursus Wolff compares Rom 4:25, Gal 3:13, and a variety of OT backgrounds (*Der erste Brief,* 359-62).

107. Edwards, *First Epistle,* 392-93. Calvin goes further: "**For our sins**. That is to say, He took our curse upon himself . . . a sacrifice for the expiation of our sins . . ." (*First Epistle,* 310).

108. Pannenberg, *Systematic Theology,* 2:418. Pannenberg rightly expounds this theme in close connection with, e.g., Rom 4:25; 8:22; 1 Cor 11:24; Gal 2:20, et al.

109. Wolff, *Der erste Brief,* 362; see *"Exkurs"* on 15:3b-5, 355-64. It is unfortunate that much heat has been generated by failing to realize that each model *qualifies* the other in the sense expounded by Ian T. Ramsey in his numerous works (e.g., in *Religious Language;* London: SCM, 1957). *Propitiation* leads to disastrous distortion only if we fail to emphasize that God himself is the *source* of the action, not that Christ "propitiates" an angry and reluctant God. *Expiation* may be a "safer" term, but invites scepticism about the status of abstract principles of justice, as if God were tied by these, rather than recognizing that any notion of *"must* suffer" rests purely on *divine self-consistency in faithfulness to his decrees and promise,* which God has chosen by his own will.

must be viewed in conjunction with others, especially from pre-Pauline traditions.

Whether ὑπέρ functions with the force of ἀντί rests mainly on *contextual* considerations, since while it *sometimes* serves in this way, it *need not* do so on purely linguistic grounds, as the wide range of examples cited by BAGD show.[110] On the other hand, the Greek grammarian A. T. Robertson argues that while ὑπέρ often means *on behalf of,* it may denote "even *instead of* (Gal 3:13) where used of persons. But here much in the sense of περί (Gal 1:14), as is common in *Koinē.* In 1 Pet 3:18 we have περὶ ἁμαρτιῶν."[111] Finally, under v. 3 we should note the aorist ἀπέθανεν: **Christ died** denotes a single past event (as Paul underlines elsewhere; cf. Rom 6:9, "never to die again").

(2) The second clause of the credal confession καὶ ὅτι ἐτάφη (v. 4a) *underlines not only the reality of Christ's death but also the reality of his resurrection: had he not been* **buried**, *the genuine occurrence of either or both might lie more readily open to question.* Further, Calvin observes: "The reality of death [i.e., death as such] . . . is brought out more vividly by mentioning his burial also."[112] Weiss follows Calvin in regarding death-burial-resurrection as a single all-inclusive concept in this context of thought.[113]

Significantly even by the time of the epistles of Ignatius (around AD 108), Ignatius alludes to those who claim that Christ's sufferings were merely "apparent," "seeming," or "in semblance" (λέγουσιν τὸ δοκεῖν αὐ τὸν πεπονθέναι).[114] This tendency to *docetism* was a threat, then, from virtually the first century, and against it Ignatius declared that Christ suffered "for us" (δι᾽ ἡμᾶς) . . . truly (ἀληθῶς ἔπαθεν) just as he truly (ἀληθῶς) underwent resurrection.[115] In his attack on gnostic dissociation between "Jesus" the man and the exalted heavenly "Christ" Irenaeus quotes the Pauline and pre-Pauline tradition exactly as it stands here, including the claim **he was buried**.[116] Docetic Christology is ascribed to Cerinthus c. AD 120-30. Tertullian gives us several examples of an emphasis on Paul's words **he was buried**, in some contexts to underline the reality of death; in others, to stress the reality of the resurrection.[117] *The Epistle to Rheginus* (or the treatise *De Resurrectione,* from Nag Hammadi) appears to dissociate "the psychic preaching which he shares with the other apostles" from a more "spiritual" Pauline "gnostic" understanding.[118]

110. See BAGD, 838-39, esp. under 1(e) and contexts of *suffering.*

111. Robertson, *Epistles,* 4:186-87; see further Meyer, *First Epistle,* 2:42-43.

112. Calvin, *First Epistle,* 314.

113. Weiss, *Der erste Korintherbrief,* 342-47; Calvin, *First Epistle,* 314.

114. Ignatius, *Letter to the Smyrnaeans,* 2:1.

115. Ibid., except that Ignatius replaces Paul's passive for *truly raised himself.*

116. Irenaeus, *Against Heresies,* 3:18:3.

117. Tertullian, *On the Resurrection of the Flesh,* 48 ("he was buried according to the scriptures") and *Against Marcion,* 5:9. Pagels, *The Gnostic Paul,* 82, cites the merely "psychic" understanding of the resurrection as "a literal past event"; the gnostic "spiritual" meaning is the resurrection *of the church.*

118. *Epistle to Rheginus,* 43:33-44; and Pagels, *Paul,* 80.

The allusion to burial in part also addresses the earliest theory which sought to deny the resurrection on the grounds of the theft of the body (Matt 28:13; Origen, *Against Celsus,* 2:56). This theory was revived by H. M. Reimarus in 1778.[119] H. E. G. Paulus (1828) and D. F. Strauss (1835) revived the later theory of the "non-death" of Jesus. Paulus sought to argue that Jesus experienced no more than a state of near-death perceived as death, although he supposes that the "burial" (a cool cavity within the rock and aromatic spices) revived him. Strauss denied the burial itself, suggesting that the body was put into a receptacle into which bodies of criminals were thrown, with the result that he could reappear later to the disciples.[120] The point at issue is that the role played by **he was buried** in the kerygmatic, confessional, credal tradition is to assert the double reality of the genuine death and authentic resurrection of Jesus Christ. The history of subsequent debate vindicates the importance of this clause. Indeed, R. J. Sider argues that it probably alluded to the reality of the *empty tomb* (see further below).[121]

(3) *The third clause* (v. 4b) *formulates the reality of the event of the resurrection of Jesus Christ by means of the perfect passive verb* ὅτι ἐγήγερται, and places this *within an explanatory frame of reference:* τῇ ἡμέρᾳ τῇ τρίτῃ κατὰ τὰς γραφάς, where **according to the scriptures** serves as a broad context of understanding and promise, just as it did in the first clause (see above). M. E. Dahl is utterly and entirely right to insist that we take the *passive force* of the verb seriously.[122] Dahl notes (also anticipating Barrett and Ortkemper). "*God* is practically always the subject of 'resurrection' verbs in the NT. The only instances of explicit statements that *Christ* (*not* his resurrection) causes our resurrection are John 6:39, 40, 54. These could mean that Christ as the divine Logos is the Cause. . . . The vast majority of texts containing ἐγείρω and ἀνίστημι . . . in a transitive, active sense have God as subject and Christ or man as object (Acts 3:15; 4:10; 5:30; 10:40; 13:30, 37; Rom 4:21; 8:11 [*bis*]; 10:9; 1 Cor 6:14; 15:15 [*bis*]; 2 Cor 4:14a; Gal 1:1; Col 2:12; 1 Thess 1:10. . . . In nearly all other cases the verb is in the passive — or middle —

119. H. M. Reimarus, "On the Intention of Jesus and His Disciples," in C. H. Talbert (ed.), *Reimarus Fragments* (London: SCM and Philadelphia: Fortress, 1971 [1778]), pulls no punches about the alleged duplicity of the disciples.

120. D. F. Strauss, *The Life of Jesus, Critically Examined* (Philadelphia: Fortress, 1972); but Strauss's *Das Leben Jesu* (1835) then passed through several different editions: 1838, 1840, and radically in 1864. Neither theory accounts for how Jesus supposedly lived on in this-worldly conditions of secrecy and isolation. Moreover, Paulus and Strauss approach the theory by virtually opposite assumptions about historical method. Paulus imposes a positivistic-rationalistic worldview onto historical inquiry, while Strauss draws upon G. W. F. Hegel's notion that myth constitutes a loose narrative form of representation *(Vorstellung)* in ancient religion, as against the role of the concept *(Begriff)* which allows for a more critical currency in philosophy.

121. Sider, "St. Paul's Understanding of the Nature and Significance of the Resurrection in 1 Cor 15:1-19," 124-41.

122. Dahl, *The Resurrection of the Body,* esp. 96-100; cf. also Moxnes, *Theology in Conflict,* 231-82; Barrett, *First Epistle,* 341; Ortkemper, *1 Kor,* 145.

voice."[123] The effectively single counterexample has to do with a distinctive issue in Johannine Christology and belongs to a different soteriological logic from Paul's normal formulation. Dahl's linguistic tables confirm the data.[124] Rom 8:11 summarizes the Pauline logic formulated more fully in 1 Corinthians 15: "if the Spirit of *him who raised Jesus from the dead* dwells in you, then *the God who raised Christ Jesus from the dead* will also *give life to your mortal bodies* through his indwelling Spirit" (REB, my italics). God will raise *the in-Christ corporeity who are identified with Christ* in the event in which *God raised Christ*.

This coheres with a strong tradition of understanding union with Christ in Paul as "mysticism" only within a firmly eschatological and corporate context. Weiss, Schweitzer, and in a broader sense Thornton and Wikenhauser all sustain this approach.[125] Thornton writes: "Those 'who belong to the Messiah' (Rom 8:23) will one day share with him that risen state to which he has already attained."[126] "The hope of Israel went down into the grave. . . . When he rose [i.e., was raised] from the tomb . . . the Church rose [i.e., is raised/will be raised] from the dead."[127]

Among recent writers, this is the logic which Joost Holleman rightly presses on the dual ground that "(a) Jesus has been raised as *the first* of those who have fallen asleep . . . (vv. 20, 23); (b) Jesus has been raised as *the representative* of those who will be raised . . . (vv. 21-22) . . . through participation in Jesus' resurrection" (his italics).[128] This applies equally to passing through death with Christ: "One has died for all; therefore all have died" (2 Cor 5:14; cf. 2 Cor 5:20; Rom 5:9-10).[129] This brings out a further link between **he was buried** and the passive force of **he was raised**. As Moxnes explains in detail, the *promise* of God which remains steadfast (Rom 4:16) depends entirely on *God's sovereign will and gift of grace to give life to the dead* (Rom 4:17), who *as the dead* have no power to create or to resume life as *God's chosen community*.

More than new existence, however, is at issue. To be sure, "God *calls into existence* things *which do not exist.*"[130] Philo expounds Gen 17:17 (to which Paul alludes) similarly: "To God all things are possible, even to change old age into youth."[131] The Old Testament tradition which stands behind Romans 4 and 1 Corinthians 15 witnesses to the "God who kills and makes alive" (2 Kings

123. Dahl, *Resurrection,* 96-97; cf. Barrett, *First Epistle,* 341; Ortkemper, *1 Kor,* 145. This theme is expounded in detail in Künneth, *The Theology of the Resurrection,* 111-49.

124. Dahl, *Resurrection,* 98-100.

125. Weiss, *Earliest Christianity,* 2:463-71; Schweitzer, *Mysticism of Paul,* esp. 141-74; Thornton, *Common Life,* 34-65, 127-87, and 253-86; A. Wikenhauser, *Pauline Mysticism* (Eng. trans., Freiburg: Herder, 1960), 17-108.

126. Thornton, *Common Life,* 266.

127. Ibid., 282.

128. Holleman, *Resurrection and Parousia,* 1; cf. 1-4, 49-58, 131-63.

129. Ibid., 181.

130. Moxnes, *Theology in Conflict,* 231-33.

131. Philo, *Quaestiones et Solutiones in Genesin* 3.56.

5:7).[132] Yet, Moxnes argues that Paul reinterprets this motif: the transfer "from death to life" thereby provides *a new identity for a new community:* God can "raise up" children of Abraham from the stones (Matt 3:7-10). Hence Paul uses this figure of the "nothingness" of death to expound the establishing of the divine *promise* of life and identity *to the nothings, to the disinherited, to the Gentiles.*[133] This, in turn, brings us face to face with *the theme of grace.*[134] Moxnes rightly perceives this as a (perhaps the) key link between Romans and 1 Corinthians.

This paves the way for our understanding the particular nuance of the phrase **according to the scriptures** when it is applied as a context for understanding the resurrection of Jesus Christ. (a) First, it does indeed relate this divine act of vindication and sovereign action to *the theme of promise.* Its occurrence rests not only on divine power and divine grace, but also on *divine faithfulness* to vindicate his obedient messianic agent. (b) Second, therefore, it would amount to *unintended reductionism and constraint if we seek to isolate some specific individual text* (e.g., Ps 2:7; 16:9, 10; or Hos 6:2) rather than understanding the resurrection of Christ as the witness to a climactic fulfillment of a cumulative tradition of God's promised eschatological act of sovereignty and vindication in grace. In this respect the phrase operates in precise parallel with its use in relation to Christ's death **for our sins** in v. 3.[135] (c) Third, it bears witness to the *character of God whom* **the scriptures** *portray as a giving and gracious* as well as a sovereign, faithful creator. If creation itself is God's gift, the new creation which begins with Christ's resurrection and promises the resurrection of believers is no less so. That is why it serves to sharpen all that Paul has said about grace (1:4, 26-31; 3:5, 22; 4:7; 6:20; 8:13; 9:13; 10:16; 11:24; 12:4; 15:8-10). 15:8-10 especially will take up this theme.

Some writers, admittedly, try to identify specific Old Testament passages on several possible grounds. (a) Senft notes that Hos 6:2 conveys the promise that "after two days he will revive us; on the third day, he will restore us, that we may live in his presence." With Orr and Walther he sees this allusion as "probable."[136] Kistemaker believes that this allusion functions alongside that of the reference to Jonah's being inside the fish for three days (Jonah 1:17), partly on the basis of the explicit reference to the sign of Jonah in Matt 12:40. As Delling and Wolff show, the role of Hos 6:2 becomes highly complex, since while the LXX uses ἐν τῇ ἡμέρᾳ τῇ τρίτῃ καὶ ἀναστησόμεθα καὶ ζησόμεθα . . . *(on the third day we shall be raised up and we shall live . . .),* the Targum

132. Moxnes, *Theology,* 240.

133. Ibid., 241-53.

134. Ibid., 253-82.

135. Héring works toward this conclusion after a consideration of various specific OT texts (*First Epistle,* 158-60). Bruce believes that a variety of texts may be involved, fewer if **on the third day** is part of the allusion *(1 and 2 Cor,* 139-40).

136. Senft, *Première Épitre,* 188. Cf. the discussion in Wolff, *Der erste Brief,* 365-67; Orr and Walther, *1 Cor,* 321; and Lang, *Die Briefe,* 211.

changes this to *in the day of the resurrection of the dead he will raise us up that we may live.* Yet Delling asks whether this may reflect post-Christian alterations to counter Christian uses of Hos 6:2, and argues for the probability of an allusion to Hos 6:2 in 1 Cor 15:4.[137] (b) Grosheide cuts across these arguments by applying the test of whether a textual candidate serves this role elsewhere in the New Testament. He concludes: "Most probably Paul has in view Jonah 1:17 (= Heb and LXX 2:1). . . . Hos 6:2 cannot be understood of Christ's resurrection."[138] Godet and Allo, however, combine the two references, anticipating Kistemaker.[139] (c) Weiss and others refer to the popular Jewish view that corruption besets the body after three days. On this basis D. Hill supports an allusion to Ps 16:9-11 (LXX), which is cited explicitly in the sermon on the day of Pentecost in Acts 2:27: "Thou wilt not abandon me to Hades, nor let thy Holy One see corruption" (διαφθοράν; cf. also 1 Cor 15:43-44).[140]

In the end, however, much depends on whether we construe **according to the scriptures** specifically as qualifying **on the third day** or more generally as providing a frame for interpretation and understanding in the context of divine grace and promise, for **he was raised.** Barrett, Héring, Hays, and many others argue for the latter, which reflects the parallel with line 1.[141] Héring disparagingly speaks of the flow of ink spilled on speculation about certain passages when (as we noted with C. H. Dodd and Blomberg in connection with the first confessional clause) the tradition appeals to patterns of promise and grace of which this constitutes the climax and which they serve to interpret. Nevertheless, this still leaves the question of the role of the inclusion of **on the third day** in this early creed, confession, catechism, or tradition. Wolff discusses no less than seven theories in his special excursus.[142] The major and probably most widespread view is that after the death of Jesus it was **on the third day** that witnesses *experienced the first appearances* of Christ as raised, *or* it was **on the third day** that the first witnesses *discovered that the tomb was empty.*[143]

Several of the other six theories are taken up with speculation about such passages as Hos 6:2 (see above), and others draw on improbable and irrelevant hypotheses about alleged parallels with the mystery cults (e.g., of Osiris). G. Wagner has exposed the fallacies of such theories.[144] Wolff notes that in the

137. G. Delling, "ἡμέρα," *TDNT,* 2:949; cf. 943-53; discussed also by Wolff, "Exkurs: Die Tagesangaben in den Auferstehungs-zeugnissen," in *Der erste Brief,* 364-68, esp. 366, para. 6.

138. Grosheide, *First Epistle,* 350.

139. With the proviso that the syntax connects **the scriptures** with **the third day** (Godet, *First Epistle,* 2:332; Allo, *Première Épitre,* 391).

140. Hill, "On the Third Day," 266-67.

141. Barrett, *First Epistle,* 340; Hays, *First Cor,* 256; Héring, *First Epistle,* 158-60; cf. B. M. Metzger, "A Suggestion concerning the Meaning of 1 Cor xv:4b," *JTS* 8 (1957): 118-23.

142. Wolff, "Exkurs," in *Der erste Brief,* 364-68.

143. Sider, "The Nature and Significance of the Resurrection," 136-39 (cf. 124-41); Weiss, *Der erste Korintherbriefe,* 349.

144. G. Wagner, *Pauline Baptism and the Pagan Mysteries* (Eng. trans., Edinburgh: Oliver & Boyd, 1967).

background lies the belief that corruption had set in decisively by **the third day**, which complements, rather than contradicts, the explanation of historical memory above. The only other theory which deserves note is K. Lehmann's linkage with Old Testament traditions of divine action *(das Eingreifen Jahwes)* on the third day in such passages as Exod 19:11, 16 (cf. also Gen 22:4; 2 Kings 20:5, 8; Esth 5:1; Hos 6:2), including later midrashic material on such passages.[145] This need not, however, represent some contrived "competing" explanation. It may just as readily denote a consistent pattern of divine action as any artificial attempt to read Old Testament passages into New Testament truth claims. The tradition goes back to earliest days, and is more than a "reading back" on the basis of the Synoptic tradition concerning sayings of Jesus (Mark 9:31).[146]

"HE WAS RAISED . . . HE APPEARED . . .": DAWN OF FAITH OR ALSO AN EVENT IN THE PUBLIC DOMAIN?

Does the conjunction of line 3, **he was buried**, and line 4, **he was raised** . . . , allow for, or even suggest, *a bodily resurrection in which the appearances of Christ are complemented by an entailment of the empty tomb?* A full answer must await discussion of the interpretation of v. 5 pressed by W. Marxsen and others (see below). Meanwhile, we may note that many interpret vv. 3b-5 as, in Paul's view, *presupposing the empty tomb tradition,* even if it does not state it explicitly. A. Oepke writes, "Paul accepts the empty tomb (ἐτάφη, 1 Cor 15:4)" even if later apologetic interests "incline the evangelical and post-canonical tradition in a more material direction."[147] R. J. Sider certainly perceives the formula as implying the empty tomb.[148] W. Pannenberg makes four careful and fundamental points: (1) "The first Christians could not have successfully preached the resurrection of Jesus if his body had been intact in the tomb. . . . We must assume that the tomb was in fact empty."[149] All the same, (2) "Paul's mention of the burial of Jesus in 1 Cor 15:4 tells us nothing regarding his knowledge of the finding of the empty tomb. From the fact that he does not expressly mention the empty tomb, we cannot infer that he did not know about it," i.e., only that it played no decisive theological role in his specific arguments as such. "This is not surprising if for Paul the empty tomb was a self-evident implication of what was said about the resurrection of Jesus."[150] The empty tomb could never in itself constitute a "proof," for it could be explained in a variety of ways. (3) However, the empty tomb tradition does create difficulties for attempting to interpret the appearances as "mere hallucinations."[151]

145. K. Lehmann, *Auferweckt am dritten Tag nach der Schrift,* QD 38 (Freiburg: Herder, 2d ed. 1969), 176-81 and 262-90; also followed by Lang, *Die Briefe,* 211.
146. See Wolff's discussion of his "second" theory *(Der erste Brief,* 365) and his broader comments, 364-68.
147. A. Oepke, "ἐγείρω," *TDNT,* 2:335 (cf. 333-39).
148. Sider, "Resurrection," 136-39.
149. Pannenberg, *Systematic Theology,* 2:358 and 359.
150. Ibid., 359.
151. Ibid.

(4) Above all, the resurrection of Jesus constituted a transformative event, *"yet the event took place in this world, namely in the tomb of Jesus in Jerusalem before the visit of the women. . . .* Any assertion that an event took place in the past implies an historical claim and exposes itself to testing" (my italics).[152] This applies, Pannenberg concludes, to the assertion "**He was raised on the third day**" after his death.

(5) *Our understanding of the fourth line,* "**He appeared to Peter and then to the Twelve**" (v. 5), *cannot be isolated from all of these major considerations set forth already on the basis of vv. 3b and 4.* Nevertheless, a wide range of literature and considerable controversy has been generated in particular by how we are to understand the force of καὶ ὅτι ὤφθη Κηφᾷ. In strictly linguistic terms ὤφθη is the first aorist passive indicative of the defective ὁράω. *I see, I see with the eyes* (cf. 1 Cor 9:1, above). Although the aorist passive indicative often means *was seen,* the passive voice also regularly conveys the force of *he became visible* or **he appeared** (as in REB, NIV, NJB, NRSV, RV, and our translation above; as against AV/KJV, *was seen*). *He appeared* occurs with the dative Κηφᾷ in this reflexive sense, but also occurs regularly in the LXX and other religious texts for "exceptional supernatural apparitions" or theophanies as well as for appearance to the eyes and other senses.[153]

It is here that controversy begins to arise. Grimm-Thayer explicitly place 1 Cor 9:1 (active indicative) under the heading *to see with the eyes,* but also catalogue many New Testament uses under *to see with the mind* (e.g., Rom 15:21, where *they shall see* stands in poetic parallelism with *they shall understand;* Col 2:18, REB, *access to some visionary world*); while yet others are understood to denote "to experience, to come to know by experience" (e.g., with ζωή).[154] On the other hand, they suggest that the passive most frequently denotes *I showed myself, I was seen,* or *I appeared,* especially with the dative of person (Luke 24:34; Acts 9:17; 1 Cor 15:5-8). In the Greek of this period outside the New Testament, the active or passive may be used at one end of the spectrum of events or persons visible to witnesses; at the other end of supernatural manifestations (*Papyrus Oxyrhynchus* 1:3; 120:4; Hermas, *The Shepherd,* 12:2, 4; 4 Macc 4:24; 9:30; Philo, *De Migratione Abrahami* 46). The nonliterary often use the verb for *seeing in dreams* or *seeing God,* as well as *to perceive.*[155] Louw-Nida classify one "semantic domain" as (i) *see* under "sensory events and states" (in which they place 1 Cor 15:6); (ii) a second "semantic domain" under *"experience"* ("figurative" extension of "to see"); (iii) another under *"visit"* (as in "to see a friend," Heb 13:23); and four other subcategories.[156]

Although we need to bear in mind the possible impact of a Semitic influence (see below) a search of LXX uses in Hatch-Redpath confirms the contention of H.-W. Bartsch that here ὤφθη with the dative regularly refers to the **appearance** of God, an angel of God, or God's glory. He notes that such **appearances** may be identified characteristically with three specific periods of salvation history: that of Abraham, Isaac, and Jacob; that of Moses and the wilderness; and that of David and Solomon. In such a context, Collins adds, this language for a transcendent "manifestation of the divine did not imply physical sight"; rather, as Bartsch emphasizes, the Psalms and Prophets look forward to a time of restored saving appearance as the fulfillment of the divine

---

152. Ibid., 360.
153. Findlay, *Expositor's Greek Testament,* 2:920; BAGD, 577-78; Grimm-Thayer, 451-52.
154. Grimm-Thayer, 451-52.
155. MM, 455; cf. BAGD, 577-78.
156. Louw-Nida, 1:277 (sect. 24.1), 808 (sect. 90.79), 453 (sect. 34.50).

promise of eschatological glory.[157] An analysis of 1 Cor 15:5 as witness for primitive Christian faith suggests that in the light of this background **appearing** marks the claim of the end of the time of waiting for eschatological and transcendent glory. Christ's risen presence serves as God's eschatological self-manifestation.

One difficulty which this approach might encounter and which might challenge it is the possibility that the Greek reflects a Semitic idiom. This possibility is discussed below (with reference to Bruce and Jeremias). However, Newman has recently taken up Bartsch's analysis to argue that it "situates the appearance of Jesus to Paul within the narrative sequence of God's visitations of Glory" and confirms that in Jesus Christ "the promises for a revelation of eschatological Glory have been proleptically inaugurated."[158] However, while the continuity with earthly history clearly belongs to Paul's frame of thought in 1 Cor 15:3-5, Newman's description of this appearance as "Paul's private Christophany" undermines the very point cited from Pannenberg to the effect that Paul understands Jesus' appearance **to Peter and to the Twelve** as having its basis in *events in the public domain* (see above).

This sharpens the debate for a comparison between the respective understandings of ὤφθη represented by, e.g., W. Marxsen and W. Pannenberg. Marxsen agrees that there is nothing controversial, within the common Christian tradition, about part of the third line: **Christ has been raised.** However, he argues that the force of ὤφθη remains *highly ambiguous concerning the mode in which* **he appeared.** All that is stated without ambiguity, Marxsen claims, is that "the activity of the same Jesus" goes on.[159] First, Marxsen challenges the traditional understanding that those *to whom* Christ appeared have the status primarily of *witnesses* to an event or state of affairs: "this designation is only correct if [= correct only if] one means by it that they all *proclaim* the resurrection. They did not experience it. Their experience is described as seeing Jesus" (Marxsen's italics).[160] Second, "the appearance to Peter is not *described:* it is simply mentioned" (Marxsen's italics).[161] However, Matthew does not mention the Peter appearance; Mark and John narrate an appearance first to Mary Magdalene (Mark 16:9; John 20:2-18; so that for E. Schüssler Fiorenza she becomes "the *apostola apostolorum*"); while Luke, it is argued, has special reasons for emphasizing the distinctive role of Peter.[162] Nevertheless, Marxsen claims, a multiple tradition that Peter was the first to believe must be distinguished from "the detailed account of *how* he came to do so (John 21). . . . The appearance to the disciples sparked off their commission" (his italics). "There is therefore no reason to doubt that Peter was the first to believe in Jesus after Good Friday," but this "finding faith" is not bound up ex-

157. Bartsch, "Inhalt und Funktion der urchristlichen Osterglaubens," 180-96, esp. 184-85 (Abraham), 185-87 (Moses), 187-88 (the Kings), 189-92 (eschatological glory); Collins, *First Cor,* 535.

158. C. C. Newman, *Paul's Glory Christology: Tradition and Rhetoric,* NovTSup 69 (Leiden: Brill, 1992), 192. See further below under the critique of Marxsen.

159. Marxsen, *The Resurrection of Jesus of Nazareth,* 72.

160. Ibid., 81.

161. Ibid., 82.

162. E. Schüssler Fiorenza, *In Memory of Her: A Feminist Reconstruction of Christian Origins* (New York: Crossroad and London: SCM, 1983), 332. Fiorenza tends to drive a wedge between the "feminist" tradition of John in which Mary Magdalene is the primary apostolic witness, the pre-Pauline tradition adopted by Paul, and Luke (315-34). See further below (commentary on v. 5), where Künneth anticipates an alternative explanation, apparently not considered by Fiorenza.

clusively with "aiming *to report the number* of the appearances" (Marxsen's italics); in the case of Peter "seeing Jesus resulted in mission," and the purpose of the appearances tradition is to focus primarily not on "report" but on the *evoking of faith which led to mission.*[163] Third, in line with an emphasis on divine revelation and a perspective about "not a thing of the past at all, but . . . the present," even Paul's experience on the Damascus road, Marxsen urges, rests not on "the precise nature of his experience" but that *"God* did something to me" (his italics).[164] *Present* function, rather than *past* history, takes center stage (1 Cor 9:1; Gal 1:15-16; Matt 28:16; John 20:19-21).

On the basis of these three broad contentions, Marxsen concludes with a fourth. We must abandon talk about "an objective vision"; or at least accept that the weight is placed on "the subjectivity . . . of my own faith," although certainly with the fundamental proviso that for Paul (or Peter) *"the impulse to faith came from outside himself"* (my italics).[165] The focal point of the resurrection and what is "seen" is that "God endorses Jesus *as the person that he was"* (his italics).[166] However, "we still do not know what the raising of Jesus is. We still do not know how people came to speak of the raising of Jesus at all."[167] "Jesus is Lord" is "realized in concrete terms in my own case."[168]

Out of the flood of literature on this issue we have selected Bartsch and Marxsen as reflecting, respectively, linguistic and existential-theological arguments for the view that καὶ ὅτι ὤφθη Κηφᾷ εἶτα τοῖς δώδεκα is not the language of "report," although it does signal an impluse to faith "from outside oneself" in which *God* discloses the Lordship and continuing presence and activity of Jesus Christ of Nazareth whose work is endorsed and vindicated. Nevertheless, we must ask whether this existential or self-involving interpretation embodies the conceptual rigor which *can do justice to two lines of thought which we have explored above:* (a) *research on the earliest creeds and confessions* and more especially on the *basis for the effective currency of self-involving* or *commissive language* suggests that Marxsen's account of the relation between "commission" and states of affairs, or between present experience and past event, does not hold water. We need only recall a history of research from Cullmann, Hans von Campenhausen, and especially Neufeld in relation to the philosophy of language with reference to speech-acts in Austin, Searle, Vanderveken, and others to perceive the *conceptual looseness* of Marxsen's argument.

(b) Research on the relation between history and faith, preeminently in W. Pannenberg, establishes that the pre-Pauline tradition and its subsequent developments are far from being "private" notions of how I experience the Lordship of Christ "in concrete terms of my own case" (even if this is included). Tradition, as Irenaeus stressed over against, e.g., Clement of Alexandria and the gnostics, above all concerns *events which take place in the public domain.* Hence **he was buried** plays a

---

163. Marxsen, *Resurrection,* 82, 83, 95.
164. Ibid., 77 and 106.
165. Ibid., 116 and 117.
166. Ibid., 125.
167. Ibid.
168. Ibid., 124-25. It might be tempting to try to "explain" Marxsen by citing an analogy with Bultmann's view of the Jesus of history in terms of a bare "that" rather than a descriptive content. However, there is even less "objectivity" in Marxsen's scenario, and such an analogy, even if suggestive, would be misleading.

formative role in the earliest tradition alongside **he was raised on the third day**. Moreover, **according to the scriptures** places the resurrection events not in the "private" domain of how I live out the Lordship of Christ "in my own case," but how a pattern of intelligible divine action and human response over a sustained historical period long enough to make sense of divine faithfulness to promise emerges as the frame of reference for understanding.[169] Criticism of the legacy of Bultmann in tending to substitute existential pre-understanding for a "pre-understanding" shaped by the Old Testament has some relevance here. We return to Pannenberg's four key points, in the course of which he concludes, "The event [of the resurrection] took place in this world, namely in the tomb of Jesus in Jerusalem before the visit of the women" (see above).

This should not be taken to imply that those who follow Marxsen "do not believe in the resurrection." Rather, they argue that the New Testament leaves the *mode* of resurrection so open ended that we should not impose unduly "historical" modes of thought onto the text. However, Marxsen's view does leave out of full account details of exegesis and logic and issues of philosophy of language which permit us to describe this as a view which is less than adequate and indeed reductive in the sense of damaging the logic of Paul's argument as a whole in 15:1-58. Moreover, the "openness" of the meaning of ὤφθη claimed by Marxsen fits only the LXX and Greek lexicographical background described above. Bruce follows Jeremias in detecting reflections of an early Semitic background "in the sense of the Hebrew 'tolerative Niph'al'; he 'let himself be seen'. . . the eyewitness evidence for the resurrection is stressed."[170] The context gives it, therefore, a sharper, more "public" meaning than Marxsen's notion of a mere dawning of individual faith in some private manner, like that of a mental or spiritual perception. In our discussion of 9:1, moreover (see above), we understand **have not I seen Jesus our Lord**? as part of "a *unique foundational witness to a truth claim about Christ*" which is bound up with *apostolicity* (my italics; see on 9:1, above). Marxsen's citing of this verse to sustain his argument has a reverse effect, unless we share his view that only Luke-Acts perceives *apostleship* in this sense. Apostolic witness is (against Marxsen) uniquely different from that of the witnessing church in later generations.[171] This is the very point of Paul's citing the pre-Pauline apostolic tradition which he himself is able to endorse.

By way of concluding this section of our discussion we may compare two earlier writers whose approaches are more radical, on either side, than those of Marxsen or of Pannenberg respectively. R. Bultmann insists that the resurrection of Jesus of Nazareth was not an objectively historical event *(ein historisches Ereignis);* belief in the resurrection is "the same thing as faith in the saving efficacy of the cross."[172] It is not to be established *"als objektives Faktum."*[173] *Can this seriously apply to 1 Corinthians 15? In a striking*

169. See A. C. Thiselton in R. Lundin, Thiselton, and C. Walhout, *The Promise of Hermeneutics* (Grand Rapids: Eerdmans, 1999), 223-39.

170. Bruce, *1 and 2 Cor,* 140; see further Jeremias, *Eucharistic Words,* 101-3 (also cited below).

171. See Wilckens, *Resurrection,* 122.

172. R. Bultmann in H.-W. Bartsch (ed.), *Kerygma and Myth* (2 vols., London: SPCK, 1962-64), 1:38 and 41; Germ. *Kerygma und Mythos* (6 vols., Hamburg: Reich & Heidrich, 1948), 1:47.

173. Ibid. (Germ. 49; Eng. trans. 39).

observation Bultmann is forced to concede: "Paul is betrayed by his apologetic into contradicting himself" (my italics).[174] For in Bultmann's view his appeal to witness in 15:1-19 conflicts with his otherworldly language in 15:20-22 and beyond. For vv. 1-11 do represent "an attempt to make the resurrection of Christ credible as an objective historical fact *(ein objektives historisches Faktum)*" against all his better judgment.[175] Luke-Acts, Bultmann believes, portrays the resurrection as bodily (physical?) reality (*Leiblichkeit,* Luke 24:39-43), but Paul's language is existential or self-involving. However, we have already seen that this polarization does violence to an intelligent philosophy of language which comes to terms with multiple and overlapping language functions in early Christian creeds and confessions. Bultmann's need to resort to the charge of Pauline self-contradiction within the same chapter says it all. The entirely positive point pressed by Bultmann and by Marxsen (with Paul) is well identified by Ulrich Wilckens: "It is the ever-new and ever different form of the *reality* of encounter with Christ. . . . This is an essential motif in the history of modern Protestant piety" (his italics).[176] Nevertheless, Wilckens adds, this is *not* the concern of 1 Cor 15:3-8, which speaks of "unique acts" relating to "legitimation" concerning "the first basic witnesses."[177] Wilckens rightly discusses the issue as one of *foundation:* "It was the appearances . . . which inspired belief . . . and led to the founding of the primitive community."[178]

Among earlier twentieth-century writers, the most forthright is perhaps Walter Künneth (1933, 3d ed. 1991, Eng. trans., 1965). He rejects appeals to "myth" of the kind to be pressed by Bultmann, as well as the kind of "Resurrection myth" cited by E. Lohmeyer in a history-of-religions context.[179] Noting (with Barth) the centrality of the *"of God"* in 1 Corinthians 15, he observes: "Myth is expression of anthropocentric religion"; the human and universal rather than a *particular* act of *God.*[180] Künneth anticipates Paul's logic in vv. 34-42a by comparing Christ's resurrection to "primal miracle, like the creation of the world . . . a new and final creation."[181] There is a "qualitative difference" between such ecstatic experiences as that of 2 Cor 12:2-3, and the appearance of Christ to Paul and the other apostles.[182] That "the account of the empty tomb was definitely included in the apostolic tradition" is "as good as certain."[183] Theology must take this "seriously." Anticipating Dahl, Barrett, and Ortkemper (see above), Künneth stresses "God's action in Christ in the resurrection" (cf. the passive in vv. 3b-5).[184] Like Bultmann and Marxsen, he stresses the *present* experience of Christ's continuing action and Lordship, but insists that it is *God's action in and on the world* in Christ's resurrection that serves "to *ground its salvation*" (my italics).[185] Rather than

174. Ibid., 1:83.

175. Ibid., 83; Germ. 54.

176. Wilckens, *Resurrection,* 122.

177. Ibid.

178. Wilckens, "The Tradition of the Resurrection," in C. F. D. Moule (ed.), *The Significance of the Message of a Resurrection for Faith in Jesus Christ* (London: SCM, 1968), 73 (cf. 53-76).

179. Künneth, *The Theology of the Resurrection,* 40-53.

180. Ibid., 57.

181. Ibid., 75.

182. Ibid., 84.

183. Ibid., 93.

184. Ibid., 117; also 97 and 111-49.

185. Ibid., 153.

being disengaged from history publicly, through crises and promise it provides "the focal point of history and meaning."[186]

Künneth does not write with the conceptual precision of Pannenberg, and his work begins to take us too far from 15:4-5. Nevertheless, he provides a constructive example of a further difference of perspective from Marxsen and Bultmann to provide fuller background against which the claims of Pannenberg and others may be viewed. With respect to v. 5, a purely linguistic account of the Gk. ὤφθη, **he appeared**, even in the light of its Septuagintal background, must be supplemented by such contextual considerations as those set forth above. Otherwise, with Bultmann, we begin to force apart the coherent logic of 15:1-58.

The use of the dative Κηφᾷ, *to Cephas,* after the verb has led some to argue that since *Cephas* represents *Paul's* usual name for **Peter** (see above on 1:12; also 3:22; 9:5; Gal 1:18; 2:9, 11, 14), the common pre-Pauline tradition may have ended either at the close of v. 4 or after **he appeared** (v. 5a).[187] We earlier noted, however, that the majority of writers regard the tradition as at least *including* v. 5, whether or not it continued to v. 7.

Eriksson offers an ingenious compromise on the basis of stylistic, structural, and rhetorical analysis. He postulates three types of material. (i) A specific credal tradition runs from vv. 3b-5a inclusive. However, (ii) vv. 5b, 6b, c, and 7 embody "four traditional christophanies" formulated "with the help of a chiasm" of which the center is (iii) v. 6a, an interpretative comment of Paul's own which he then duly follows with other Pauline comments in vv. 8-11. "This structure, where the first line of the chiasm connects with the last line of the ὅτι clauses, indicates that Paul has arranged and redacted pre-Pauline tradition."[188] Over the first half of the twentieth century, perhaps most writers understood vv. 3b-7 as a fixed tradition.[189] Even in this earlier period, however, there was doubt or dissent, and in the second half of the twentieth century the most widely accepted view has been to regard vv. 3b-5 inclusive as the probable boundary of the earliest confession, even if parts of vv. 6-7 come from pre-Pauline sources or traditions.[190]

Barrett points out that any weight given to the use of the Aramaic form *Cephas* (in contrast to the Gk. **Peter**) is more than outweighed by the otherwise non-Pauline use of the fixed phrase **the Twelve**. Indeed, the traditions about **Peter** (Luke 24:34; cf. Mark 16:7; Matt 16:18; and the early chapters of Acts)

---

186. Ibid., 253.

187. The latter view is represented by, e.g., Bartsch, *Kerygma and Myth;* the latter by Héring, although admittedly as no more than "probable" (*First Epistle,* 158).

188. Eriksson, *Traditions,* 89; cf. 86-97.

189. Weiss, *Der erste Korintherbrief,* 350; Bachman, *Der erste Korintherbrief,* 436; Moffatt, *First Epistle,* 237-38; Meyer, *First Epistle,* 2:44-45.

190. Findlay opts for vv. 3-5 (*Expositor's Greek Testament,* 2:920); Robertson and Plummer are uncertain (*First Epistle,* 335-36); more recently Conzelmann, *1 Cor,* 251, Fee, *First Epistle,* 722-29; Bruce, *1 and 2 Cor,* 140-41; Hays, *1 Cor,* 257; Horsley, *1 Cor,* 198; Barrett, *First Epistle,* 341-42; Lang, *Die Briefe,* 212-13; Strobel, *Der erste Brief,* 233; Wolff, *Der erste Brief,* 355-70.

would hardly have been something to which Paul himself would choose to draw attention in view of issues about a Peter group at Corinth (1:12). Jeremias observes that in place of **the Twelve** Paul prefers to use the expression *the apostles,* and goes so far as to claim that vv. 3b-5 inclusive contain "signs that the core of the kerygma is *a translation of a semitic original*" (his italics).[191] If Jeremias is right (and here we cannot be certain), this readily explains also the retention of *Cephas* rather than the Gk. **Peter.** Both **Peter** and **the Twelve** come to have formalized roles as foundational witnesses in early traditions.

E. Schüssler Fiorenza argues that Mark and John offer an entirely different view from that of prominence to the pre-Pauline tradition. Mark portrays *the women* as the unexpected "first" historical witnesses (Mark 16:9), while John sees Mary Magdalene as *the primary apostolic witness* for the Johannine community.[192] Along with Mary of Nazareth and Martha and Mary of Bethany, Mary Magdalene (as "first" among these women) becomes a "paradigm of apostolic discipleship."[193] This Johannine tradition "challenged the Petrine tradition" whch found expression in the pre-Pauline creed of 1 Cor 15:3-6.[194] Künneth, by contrast, understands the inclusion of **Peter** as "first" in the pre-Pauline common tradition because Peter had publicly *denied Jesus.* The paradigm of resurrection combines witness to Jesus with reversal of the "future" of the cross; with transformation and restoration on the basis of sharing in the death and resurrection of Jesus Christ. *It is the common experience of grace and reversal that gives both Peter and Paul a particular shared role as witnesses of the resurrection.*[195] This experience, Künneth concludes, is integral with *"the founding of the apostolate"* (his italics).[196] Since vv. 8-10 will expound precisely this theme of *grace,* it is not surprising that Paul cites the ready-made Petrine tradition about the appearances in this context.[197] Finally, on the Western reading ἕνδεκα, *eleven, in place of the authentic* δώδεκα, **twelve,** see the Textual Note before the exegesis of v. 3 (above). Since Judas was no longer present, some of the Fathers speculated that **Twelve** must have included Matthias (e.g., Origen, Chrysostom, Eusebius, Theophylact, and Photius; in the post-Reformation period, Bengel).[198] Héring (followed by Metzger) regard this

191. Jeremias, *Eucharistic Words,* 102; cf. 101-3.

192. E. Schüssler Fiorenza argues that Luke seeks to suppress the role of the women as proclaimers of the Easter kerygma by saying that the disciples perceived their words "as an idle tale" (Luke 24:11). In contrast to Luke and the pre-Pauline tradition, Mark and John stress their importance: Mark as witnesses, John by placing Mary Magdalene as *"apostola apostolorum"* (*In Memory of Her,* 315-34).

193. Ibid., 333.

194. Ibid., 332.

195. Künneth, *The Theology of the Resurrection,* 86-91.

196. Ibid., 89.

197. This offers a more convincing explanation of differences in traditions than to turn everything into an issue of gender.

198. Origen, *Against Celsus,* 2:65; Bengel, *Gnomon,* 662, *"Probabile est, Matthiam tum quoque interfuisse."*

as a "pedantic" preoccupation with numbers, rather than recognizing that **the Twelve** became a formal title for the corporate apostolic witness of those who had also followed Jesus during his earthly life, and who therefore underlined the continuity of witness to the One who was both crucified and raised.[199] Paul uses the term **the Twelve** only here, preferring the term *the apostles,* which (as we have noted) confirms the pre-Pauline origin of this tradition.[200] Since Paul regularly cites apostolic traditions (see above, esp. Eriksson), it is quite unconvincing to argue that these verses cannot be Pauline on the ground of his claims about direct revelation in Gal 1:1, 11, and 12. These are not competing truth claims.[201]

6 The inclusion of the phrase ἐξ ὧν οἱ πλείονες μένουσιν ἕως ἄρτι "is clearly calculated to provide further evidential support for the resurrection of Jesus; anyone who is disposed to be sceptical will find a formidable gallery of witnesses wanting to testify that they have seen him alive."[202] Hays adds that this shows that Paul did not think of the resurrection "as some sort of ineffable truth beyond history; rather, it was an event . . . for which historical eyewitness testimony was readily available."[203] In the Epistle to the Hebrews ἐφάπαξ conveys the important theological force that the sacrifice of Christ was *once for all* (Rom 6:10). However, the word also denotes *"all at once"* or **on a single occasion** (NRSV, *at one time;* REB, *at once;* NIV, NJB, *at the same time*).[204] Fee argues that the adverb is not to be taken at face value as a temporal or sequential indicator, but merely "as an attempt to indicate the reality and objectivity of the appearances. . . . Beyond that, in terms of time and place, all is speculative."[205] Meyer, however, points out if this word excludes a possible reference to visionary experiences a temporal force is entailed, i.e., we should find it difficult to conceive of "upwards of 500 visions occurring at the same time and place."[206] What indicates the reaility further is the round number: a few people might base their faith on confused perceptions, but hardly such a large cross-section of believers. Collins points out that ἔπειτα, **then**, "is a Pauline term: ten of its sixteen NT occurrences are in Paul. . . . Rhetorically the series of 'then' clauses assures the readers that nothing has been left out."[207]

Kearney reconstructs this verse as a doxology in part by translating ἐπάνω, *above,* in the sense of **more than** to denote *above* in a spatial sense, *he*

199. Héring, *First Epistle,* 161, and the overwhelming majority of commentators.

200. Cf. Conzelmann, *1 Cor,* 257, n. 78, for further literature; and Wolff, *Der erste Brief,* 368-70, esp. on the biblical material.

201. Against Price, "Apocryphal Apparitions: 1 Cor 15:3-11 as a Post-Pauline Interpolation," 69-99.

202. Hays, *First Cor,* 257; also Fee, *First Epistle,* 729-30.

203. Hays, *First Cor,* 257. Cf. also Horsley, *1 Cor,* 199.

204. Grimm-Thayer, 264; BAGD, 330.

205. Fee, *First Epistle,* 730.

206. Meyer, *First Epistle,* 2:45.

207. Collins, *First Cor,* 535. On the difficulty of such mass self-deception, cf. Allo, *Première Épitre,* 395-97; and Murphy-O'Connor, "Tradition and Redaction in 1 Cor 15:3-7," 586.

appeared above to. . . .[208] This looks back to a tradition to which Chrysostom alludes when he writes: "Some say that *above* (ἐπάνω) is above from heaven."[209] Nevertheless, most writers suggest that if this were what Paul said, the word ἄνωθεν would have been used, although Kearny alludes to a possible semitic background.[210] Neither Kearny's theory nor any supposed identification with the crowds on the day of Pentecost is generally accepted, and most (with Fee) "leave open" what this occasion might be.[211]

Allo provides an extensive discussion in a detailed excursus on the appearances and concludes, "We identify, then, with moral certainty, 1 Cor 15:6 and Matt 28:16-20."[212] He has examined the history of views in the Fathers and up to the first half of the twentieth century. Robertson and Plummer also regard this identification as "probable."[213] Many rule it out, perhaps most emphatically Meyer: "Matt 28:16ff. has nothing to do with our passage . . . [which] applies only to the eleven."[214] However, it is part of Matthew's distinctive ecclesiology that the Great Commission, which belongs to this unit (vv. 16-20), is addressed *to the eleven* as authoritative leaders and teachers. It is beyond question, on the other hand, "that traditional elements underlie at least some of the material," as the parallels with resonances from Luke, John, and the longer ending of Mark clearly exist (cf. Luke 24:38, 47, 49, 52; John 20:21; Mark 16:17).[215] Although it cannot be identified with certainty, this example is sufficiently plausible to allay fears that 15:6 could find no possible place in the traditions which find their way into the gospel narratives.

Conzelmann places a different emphasis on the verse, namely, "on the fact that some have already died."[216] This does indeed anticipate issues raised later in the chapter, but this aspect cannot be more than a secondary, even if also constructive resonance. Conzelmann's view finds favor mainly with those writers who do not accept that Paul has an interest in the corroborative character of these verses. It is not widely accepted. Even so, it is likely that Paul is still drawing on elements of earlier traditions, even if the formal "creed" terminated with v. 5b. The translation of ἀδελφοῖς provides the usual nightmare for modern English. Since Jesus appeared to the women, it is virtually certain that NIV's *brothers and sisters* is correct, but the Greek does not say this, and if it is gender-inclusive, it is also gender-intrusive. We propose, therefore, **our Christian people** (see above on 1:10, et al.). The metaphor of *falling asleep* (ἐκοι-

208. Kearney, "He Appeared to 500 Brothers" (1 Cor 15:6)," 264-84.

209. Chrysostom, *1 Cor. Hom.,* 38:5.

210. Cf. Wolff, *Der erste Brief,* 370, n. 115.

211. Lang, *Die Briefe,* 213; Strobel, *Der erste Brief,* 233; Ortkemper, *1 Kor,* 147; Héring, *First Epistle,* 161; Wolff, *Der erste Brief,* 370-71; Barrett, *First Epistle,* 342.

212. Allo, *Première Épitre,* 396; cf. 394-98.

213. Robertson and Plummer, *First Epistle,* 337.

214. Meyer, *First Epistle,* 2:44-45.

215. D. A. Hagner, *Matthew,* 2: *Matt 14–28* (Dallas: Word, 1995), 881, and 880-89.

216. Conzelmann, *1 Cor,* 258.

μήθησαν) to denote the death of Christian believers carried with it the grammar of being *awakened* at the resurrection (see under 15:51).

7   Although it makes little or no difference to the sense of the second **then**, UBS 4th ed. εἶτα, becomes ἔπειτα in 𝔭⁴⁶, ℵ*, A, F, G, and 33, whereas ℵ², B, and D retain the UBS reading (see under exegesis).

NRSV, NIV, and NJB translate as above; REB has **then** . . . and *afterward.* This may perhaps reflect the reading ἔπειτα (see Textual Note), but since a comparison of examples of the meanings of the two words respectively in BAGD reveals little practical difference, the issue remains theoretical in textual or linguistic terms.[217] (Whether in theological terms a break should be marked between the last witness before Paul and all the apostles is perhaps a different matter.) Most writers consider it virtually certain that the **James** in question is James the brother of Jesus.[218] There is no explicit reference to this *appearance* (ὤφθη, again) in the canonical Gospels, although the group to which Acts 1:6-9 alludes may have included James. Paul speaks of him as "the Lord's brother" (Gal 1:19); as a "pillar" of the Jerusalem church (Gal 2:9); and as a participant in the conference (conferences?) at Jerusalem (Gal 2:1-10; cf. Acts 15:1-20). It is widely agreed that the figure described in Galatians 1 and 2 is the James of Acts 12:17; 15:13; 21:18 (also Mark 6:3; par. Matt 13:55; Jas 1:1).

Two particular comments may be made. First, *there is a parallel with Peter and Paul in terms of divine grace.* Just as Künneth underlined the importance of Peter and Paul as witnesses of the resurrection in the light of *Peter's denial,* turn, and restoration, and *Paul's persecution* of the church and call and commission, so James, too, appears *not to have been a follower of Jesus before the crucifixion.* Bruce, therefore (with Robertson and Plummer), compares the conversion of James to discipleship with that of Paul himself: "That . . . Jesus **'appeared to James'** . . . evidently produced in James a revolutionary effect comparable to that which a similar experience later produced in Paul himself."[219] Second, while James of Jerusalem who was the Lord's brother must (as "James the Less") be distinguished firmly from James the son of Zebedee, one of the Twelve, who was martyred very early (around AD 44), we have independent evidence that *Paul clearly regards James the Lord's brother as an apostle.* Bruce notes: "In saying that he 'saw none of the other apostles except James' [Gal 1:18-21], Paul certainly indicates that he re-

---

217. BAGD, 233 and 284.
218. A helpful discussion of the role of James in relation to this verse and within the early church is F. F. Bruce, "James and the Church of Jerusalem," in Bruce, *Men and Movements in the Primitive Church* (Exeter: Paternoster, 1979), 86-119. Cf. also W. Schmithals, *Paul and James* (Eng. trans., London: SCM, 1965); G. Howard, "Was James an Apostle? A Reflection on a New Proposal for Gal 1:19," *NovT* 19 (1977): 63-64; and R. J. Bauckham, *Jude and the Relatives of Jesus in the Early Church* (Edinburgh: T. & T. Clark, 1990).
219. Bruce, "James," 87. Cf. Robertson and Plummer, *First Epistle,* 338.

garded James as an apostle."[220] This anticipates the point that for Paul the term *apostle* is always wider than *the Twelve*.[221] Indeed, in Gal 2:9 James, Cephas and John are described as the three "pillars" of the Jerusalem church. A tradition from Josephus suggests that James probably died in AD 62.[222] Jerome alludes to an account of the appearance of the postresurrection Jesus Christ to James in the apocryphal *The Gospel according to the Hebrews*.[223]

The word order in τοῖς ἀποστόλοις πᾶσιν suggests that the emphasis falls on **the apostles**, not on **all** (with Turner, Barrett, et al.; curiously against Conzelmann).[224] It denotes "the apostolic body as a whole."

Even if Paul uses **apostles** regularly in a wider sense than *the Twelve*, as foundational witnesses there is also a limit or boundary to those who are designated by this term. (On *apostle*, see above, 1:1, esp. 9:1, together with, e.g., 12:29, "are all apostles?" [also 4:9; 9:5; 12:28].) It is likely that the purpose of the phrase is to pave the way for v. 8: the entire apostolate are bound up together in witnessing to Christ's saving work and resurrection: with his reference to his own calling in v. 8, this will complete the list and establish this common foundational apostolic witness to the reality of the resurrection as one of the cardinal elements of the gospel (15:3).

8-9 The emphasis lies not simply on Paul's place among the witnesses, and it is not primarily, if at all, a defense of his apostleship as such (against P. von Osten-Sacken; with Murphy-O'Connor and Mitchell).[225] The emphasis lies in the *undeserved grace of God* (explicated further on v. 10), who chooses to give life and new creation to those reckoned as dead, or, in Paul's case, both a **miscarried, aborted foetus** whose stance had been *hostile* to Christ and to the new people **of God**.

The well-known exegetical crux of v. 8 turns on our understanding and translation of the phrase ὡσπερεί (NRSV), *as to one untimely born;* REB, *it was like a sudden, abnormal birth;* NIV, *as to one abnormally born;* NJB, *as though I were a child born abnormally;* AV/KJV, *as of one born out of due time;* Barrett, *as to one hurried into the world before his time;* Moffatt, *by this so-called "abortion" of an apostle).* Munck begins his careful and well-argued study of the Greek word in question by observing that "the term ἔκτρωμα in 1 Cor 15:8 is difficult to interpret. This is its sole appearance in the NT, and the

220. Bruce, "James," 89.
221. Ibid., 90.
222. Josephus, *Antiquities* 20.200-201.
223. Jerome, *De Viris Illustribus,* 2.
224. As Robertson and Plummer, *First Epistle,* 338; and Barrett, *First Epistle,* 343, agree. Conzelmann, by contrast, claims: "πᾶσιν, 'all' is emphatic by reason of its position," and cites BDF, sect. 575 (5). However, as N. Turner writes, "If πᾶς is placed after a noun with the art., special stress is laid upon the noun, e.g., 1 Cor 15:7 . . ." (MHT, *Grammar,* 3:200).
225. Von der Osten-Sacken, "Die Apologie des paulinischen Apostolats in 1 Kor 15:1-11," 245-62; against which Murphy-O'Connor, "Tradition and Redaction," 582-89, and Mitchell, *Rhetoric,* 285-89, do better justice to the context of grace. P. R. Jones's otherwise useful article, "1 Cor 15:8: Paul the Last Apostle," veers too closely toward "apostleship" and away from "grace" (3-34).

context gives no clear indication of its significance."²²⁶ Earlier interpretations, Munck points out, stressed "the suddenness and violence of Paul's call," but more recently writers have focused on the Greek word as a term of abuse applied to Paul by his opponents. Munck argues convincingly for a third option, namely, the meaning "a prematurely born dead foetus" which reflects a use found in the LXX to denote dire human wretchedness.²²⁷ Arguably he could and should have gone one step further: *grace gives life to* **the dead**.

Broadly we may distinguish between the following claims: (i) Because Paul's call came out of the blue when he was set against the church, ἔκτρωμα denotes the contrast between this sudden, disruptive, violent experience and the steady nurture of faith accorded to Peter and the Twelve. Hence it denotes *one born abnormally* (NIV, REB, NJB; and in effect NRSV, AV/KJV, and Barrett). Calvin, Grotius, Heinrici, and Schneider understand it as a reference to *sudden birth*.²²⁸ (ii) A. Fridrichsen and G. Björck argue that the Greek word may be used as a term of abuse. Perhaps the early Christian believers called him *a monster* in the days when he persecuted the church. Anticipating v. 9, Paul states that the resurrected Jesus Christ appeared to him who was a monster. Björck notes that in modern Greek the word denotes a *monster* or *freak* and traces back its semantic history.²²⁹ (iii) Weiss and Parry take up the use of the term as one of abuse, but suggest that some at Corinth applied the term to Paul in contrast to, e.g., Peter and Apollos.²³⁰ Weiss, however, retains the more traditional meaning *miscarriage (Fehlgeburt)*, even when it is used as a term of abuse (*Schimpfwort*, almost swear word). Collins follows Weiss with *miscarriage*, after examining its LXX backgrounds.²³¹ (iv) Although it is not his first choice, Munck believes that there could be a play in words between παῦλος, *the small one*, and ἔκτρωμα, *of short stature*. This would then serve as an explication of ἔσχατος (v. 8), **last**, and especially ὁ ἐλάχιστος, **least**, in v. 9. *He is* **last** *and* **least**; *the dwarf*. This has the merit of harmonizing with most patristic exegesis in understanding this as a term of humility.²³² (v) However, many early writers hold that the humility arises from a comparison, i.e., "as unworthy to be called an apostle as an abortion to be considered a fully human person."²³³ (vi) The

226. Munck, "Paulus Tanquam Abortivus," in *NT Essays in Memory of T. W. Manson,* 180 (180-93).

227. Ibid., 183.

228. Calvin, *First Epistle,* 315; Heinrici, *Das erste Sendschreiben,* 480; and J. Schneider, "ἔκτρωμα," *TDNT,* 2:466; cf. 365-67.

229. G. Björck, "Nochmals Paulus abortivus," *ConNT* 3 (1938): 3-8.

230. Weiss, *Der erste Korintherbrief,* 351-52; Parry, *First Epistle,* 218.

231. Collins, *First Cor,* 537-38.

232. Munck, *NT Essays,* 188-90. Augustine, however, seems to be the only major exegete in this period who explicitly suggests *of short stature.*

233. Theodoret, Estius, Bengel, de Wette, Meyer, Alford; e.g., Bengel, *Gnomon,* 662: *Articulus vim habet. Paulus se unum sic appellat . . . ut abortus non est dignus humano nomine . . . ;* Meyer, *First Epistle,* 2:46-47, "*the untimely foetus,* LXX Num 12:12; Job 3:16. . . . Figuratively, *inferior.*"

view advocated here coheres with that of Luther and the Reformers. Luther observes that Paul compared himself with "a dead child . . . decayed fruit . . . until I was reborn by Christ," while Calvin also notes: "This abortive birth makes the grace of God all the more evident in Paul's case than if he had grown up in Christ little by little, step by step."[234] Munck has no difficulty in showing that in the LXX "a man in the depths of misery is compared to a stillborn child" (cf. Num 12:12; Job 3:16; Ps 57 [58]:9; Isa 14:9 [Symmachus]).[235] Munck concedes, however, that he cannot decide between his two most favored interpretations ([iv] and [vi]) because sometimes the Greek appears to denote a child born dead, often before its time, but in other instances it may denote the birth of a deformed child, whether or not this is also an abortion.[236] Given Paul's association of his encounter with the resurrected life as one of new creation (2 Cor 4:6; cf. Gen 1:3-5), it seems most probable that Paul perceives himself as one who was unable to contribute anything to an encounter in which God's sovereign grace was all, even to the extent of giving life to one who was humanly beyond all hope. This precisely reflects the theme of resurrection as God's sovereign gift of life to the dead (not to those who already possess capacities of self-perpetuating survival) throughout this chapter. Finally it coheres well with G. W. E. Nickelsburg's arguments that Isa 49:1 (as well as Jer 1:5) and Gal 1:15 play an important part in this "apostolic self-description." Paul is appointed *before birth* by God's grace.[237]

Although we dissent from those who see 15:8-10 as part of a "defense" of Paul's apostleship, Peter Jones is correct to understand Paul's use of **last of all** (especially in relation to **all the apostles** of v. 7) as indicating not only that Paul implicitly included himself within this apostolate but also that "he is conscious of being called to bring the apostolic gospel to completion. . . . The closure with Paul of the apostolic circle" reflects "a solemn claim concerning his apostolic ministry that is grounded . . . in revelation. . . ."[238] On the other hand, as Mitchell points out, to make Paul's apostleship, let alone a "defense" of it, part of 1 Corinthians 15 overlooks the very point that Paul is making: "Paul is not the subject of 1 Cor 15"; this "subject" is *God;* God's *grace* or *gift* of new creation; and *resurrection.*[239]

Some translations reduce the *theological* force of Paul's self-effacement and his use of the superlative (not elative) ἐλάχιστος, **the very least** (v. 9), by

234. Luther, "1 Cor 15," *Luther's Works,* 28:83 (*WA* 36:509); and Calvin, *First Epistle,* 315.
235. Munck, *NT Essays,* 184.
236. Ibid., 187. On further linguistic data, cf. BAGD, 246.
237. Nickelsburg, "An *ektrōma,* Though Appointed from the Womb: Paul's Apostolic Self-Description in 1 Cor 15 and Gal 1," 198-205.
238. Jones, "Paul the Last Apostle," 28 and 33. Jones notes that such a claim runs counter to certain trends in the claims of some Christian denominations, as well as counter to the trend in NT studies to stress the "charismatic" side of Paul in contrast to the Paul who is concerned with "the deposit" of faith in the Pastorals. He rightly applies a hermeneutic of suspicion to the influence of fashions.
239. Mitchell, *Rhetoric of Reconciliation,* 285.

proposing a moralizing translation of ἱκανός, **I who am not competent to be called an apostle**. ἱκανός denotes (with the negative) *insufficiency of human resources* (another key theme of ch. 15 and resurrection as against "natural" immortality). Hence NIV's *do not even deserve to be called* is misleadingly moralistic, while *I am not fit* (NJB, REB; NRSV, *unfit*) risks possible misunderstanding of Paul's point (cf. AJ/KJV, *am not meet*). Paul genuinely laments that he is **least**, in the light of his privilege at being included within the apostolate. This makes it virtually certain that this is not the context in which a wordplay with ἔκτρωμα as *short of stature* would be appropriate. It would suggest an entirely inappropriate self-parody. ἱκανός suggests Paul's *theological* awareness that *he cannot "reach up to" or "aspire to" his calling; he accepts it as a gift of grace.*[240] As Munck and others have shown, Paul's persecuting the church underlines the sovereign initiative of God's grace as intervening gift and allows no room for so-called psychological explanations concerning supposed subconscious guilt feelings which "contribute to the experience of sovereign call." Paul compares this call to that of Jeremiah "before birth" (cf. Gal 1:13-17 and 1 Cor 9:16-18).[241] The relative pronoun ὅς is not *used* as a relative (AV/KJV, *that am,* i.e., *who am*) but in a causal sense, to represent ἐπεὶ ἐγώ.[242]

10 (1) The Western D*, F, and G substitute πτωχή (Ambrose, *pauper*), *poor,* for κενή, *void, in vain* (v. 10), clearly to avoid the thought that divine grace could ever be conceived of as *fruitless* or *empty* in content or effect. (2) More significantly the UBS 4th ed. reading [ἡ] σὺν ἐμοί is ranked "C" by Metzger and the editors (i.e., "the Committee had difficulty in deciding which variant to place in the text").[243] On the principle that the more probable reading is a more "difficult" one, the occurrence of ἡ εἰς ἐμέ in v. 10b, even in as early a MS as 𝔭46 (also with some Syriac texts and Theodoret), almost certainly reflects an unintentional assimilation to the ἡ εἰς ἐμε which occurs at the end of v. 10a. On the other hand, a second difficulty concerns the omission of ἡ from ℵ*, B, D*, F, G, and the Vulgate. It may have been omitted by accident; but equally 𝔭46 and other witnesses (e.g., ℵ2, A, D1) may have inserted it to match the earlier clause which it parallels. The Committee thus places [ἡ] in square brackets. Our translation presupposes the UBS text.

We come to the heart of Paul's point. Undeserved, unmerited **grace** (χάρις) which springs from the free, sovereign love of God alone and becomes operative in human life not only determines Paul's life and apostolic vocation but also characterizes all Christian existence, not least the promise of resurrection and the reality of the activity of Christ as Lord. "The double εἰμί is firmly assertive — 'I am what I am' is the *favour,* utterly undeserved, that summoned Saul of Tarsus . . . (Gal 1:13ff.)."[244] The gist of Paul's point is twofold: (i) God has

---

240. See Robertson and Plummer, *First Epistle,* 341, on "reaching up to."

241. Munck, *Paul and the Salvation of Mankind,* 11-35; and Seyoon Kim, *The Origin of Paul's Gospel* (Grand Rapids: Eerdmans, 1981), 32-99, esp. 55-61.

242. As, e.g., Edwards, *First Epistle,* 399 argues, and most modern English VSS assume.

243. Metzger, *Textual Commentary* (2d ed.), 501.

244. Findlay, *Expositor's Greek Testament,* 2:921-22.

made him what he is as sheer gift; (ii) in addition to *being operative toward or on* him, this grace has also been *operative through* him in making him an apostolic agent for the benefit of others. The usual meaning of κενός is *without content, without substance,* or *empty.* However, BAGD show (with examples) that it also means *without result, without effect, to no purpose* (as indeed in 15:58).[245] Hence with Robertson and Plummer and with Conzelmann (against Findlay) we translate **fruitless**.[246]

The disjunctive ἀλλά carries the force of **on the contrary**. However, Paul's **laboring** (ἐκοπίασα, *heavy, exhausting toiling*) must not be permitted to shift the emphasis away from **God's grace** (ἡ χάρις αὐτοῦ) **extended to me** (ἡ εἰς ἐμέ; a little more than *given to me,* NJB; and clearly more than merely *to me,* REB, NIV; *toward me,* NRSV, is perhaps the best of these four). The comparative adverb περισσότερον (with genitive of comparison αὐτῶν πάντων) derives from the adjectival form περισσός, which may indeed mean *remarkable, abundant,* but strictly denotes *that which exceeds the usual number.* Hence the comparative adverb *even more,* or (here) **to an even greater degree**.[247] Such **labor** becomes possible only because **grace** has made, and makes, Paul the person he is; *not* because in himself he is "that kind of person anyway." If God called him from *before birth* (Gal 1:15; cf. Jer 1:9), **grace** has shaped his entire life and character as an apostolic agent *through whom* God chooses to reach and to transform others. Luther observes: "It is not within man's doing or ability to be or to make a pastor . . . but a heavenly gift. . . . 'Whatever I am and can do, whatever I have and present, is and shall be nought but the grace of God.'"[248]

The emphasis on **labor** reminds us that difficulty and cost in Christian work, far from suggesting an absence of **God's grace**, presupposes the gift of such grace to prosecute the work through all obstacles (see 2 Cor 11:23-27). The theme of grace in and through "weakness" is one which Paul constantly urges to Corinth.[249] The "absoluteness" of grace (Conzelmann) finds a parallel in 9:16.[250]

11 Paul is not "returning from a digression," since his combined emphasis on resurrection, witness, and grace was all of a piece and he did not digress to "defend" his apostleship (see above).[251] Conzelmann identifies the

---

245. BAGD, 427.

246. Findlay argues it means "not *void of result* (that is, ματαία) but *void of reality*" (*Expositor's Greek Testament,* 2:922); but BAGD's examples show that this cannot be sustained (with Robertson and Plummer, *First Epistle,* 341). Conzelmann, *1 Cor,* 260 stresses "result." Collins has the traditional *in vain* (*First Cor,* 538).

247. A series of examples under the cognate terms offers decisive lexicographical evidence; BAGD, 651.

248. Luther, "1 Cor," *Luther's Works,* 28:89 (*WA* 36:517-18).

249. Cf. T. B. Savage, *Power through Weakness: Paul's Understanding of the Christian Ministry in 2 Cor,* SNTSMS 86 (Cambridge: Cambridge University Press, 1996), 130-90; Clarke, *Secular and Christian Leadership;* and Litfin, *St Paul's Theology of Proclamation,* 147-212.

250. Conzelmann, *1 Cor,* 260.

251. Even Fee speaks of a "short digression" (*First Epistle,* 736).

central connection of thought. In the light of *grace* (vv. 8-10) "Paul relativizes the *human* differences in favor of the essential thing, proclamation and faith" (his italics).[252] In other words, **whether** we are talking about how God's grace became operative through other apostles (e.g., Peter or the Twelve) **or** we are considering Paul as an example of one who received grace and witnessed Christ's appearance, the apostolic *kerygma retains the common basis* to which the *common tradition* (vv. 3b-5; corroborated by vv. 6-7, and further instantiated by vv. 8-10) bears united witness. This clearly looks back to 1:10-12, 18-25, and forward to 15:12-58. There is no **is** in the Greek: the implied verb is one of logic, *not of past description.*[253] NJB's rendering of the connective οὖν as **anyway** admirably picks up the resumptive force of the logical consequence.[254]

The Gk. οὕτως is emphatic, which we try to convey by **it is this that we proclaim**. Although the Greek is strictly adverbial *(thus, in this manner),* NIV, REB, and NJB render it as a demonstrative pronoun: *this is what we all proclaim* (REB); *this is what we preach* (NJB), although NRSV leaves the construction open to an adverbial understanding: *so we proclaim and so you have come to believe.* The context suggests that the *context* of the *kerygma,* not its mode of communication, is what is at issue. **This** is therefore entirely appropriate not least because οὕτως may in any case be used as an adjective.[255] On the other hand, although **this** is more probable for **that you came to believe**, an adverbial *thus, in this way* would be no less possible as a translation (with AV/KJV). The change from the present **we proclaim** to the aorist **you came to believe** need not *of itself* imply "that the Corinthians were beginning to waver somewhat in their belief."[256] It is probably an ingressive aorist which, as Wolff notes, looks back at the end of this unit (vv. 1-11) to vv. 1-2.[257] Paul concludes this first foundational section of the resurrection chapter by asserting, *This is what matters: whether you are proclaiming the gospel or responding to it as a Christian believer.* Margaret Mitchell is right to stress both the unifying dimension of these verses and, no less, that the basis for such common faith remains the gospel of the death and resurrection of Jesus Christ: "Paul emphasizes the importance of the things all Christians share: a common faith in the same received παράδοσις."[258] "Ecumenicity" is not the lowest common denominator in a miscellany of individual experiences. For Paul it is defined by the *common kerygma* of a *shared, transmitted gospel tradition,* anchored in the death and resurrection of Jesus Christ as ἐν πρώτοις (15:3).

252. Conzelmann, *1 Cor,* 260.

253. Against *was* in NRSV, REB, NIV and NJB, Fee is right: a temporal allusion misses the nuance of *logical* indifference; cf. Fee, *First Epistle,* 736.

254. Cf. Meyer, *First Epistle,* 2:49.

255. BDF, sect. 434; BAGD, 598, sect. 5.

256. Edwards, *First Epistle,* 401.

257. Wolff, *Der erste Brief,* 375.

258. Mitchell, *Rhetoric of Reconciliation,* 287.

B. THE DIRE CONSEQUENCES OF
DENYING THE RESURRECTION —
FIRST *REFUTATIO* AND *CONFIRMATIO* (15:12-34)

1. The Unacceptable and Disastrous Consequences of Denying the Currency of the Very Concept of Resurrection — First *Refutatio* (15:12-19)

(12, 13) Now if Christ is proclaimed as raised from the dead, how can some of you claim that there is no resurrection of the dead? But if there is no resurrection of the dead, neither can Christ have been raised. (14, 15) Yet if Christ has not been raised, it follows that our proclamation of the gospel is hollow, and empty, also, is your faith. We, too, shall be exposed as liars in what we witness about God, because we gave testimony against God that he raised Christ when, if, as they say, it were the case that the dead are not raised, he did not raise him after all. (16, 17) For if the dead are not raised, neither can Christ have been raised. But if Christ has not been raised, your faith is without effect, and you are still in your sins. (18) It also follows, then, that those who were laid to sleep in Christ are lost for good. (19) If in this life we have placed hope in Christ with nothing beyond, we are more to be pitied than all human beings.

On the rhetorical form and structure of the argument see the introduction to 15:1-58 (above, before bibliography to ch. 15). Paul has concluded "the statement" of vv. 1-11 *(narratio)* in which a rehearsal of the common tradition concerning the death and resurrection of Jesus Christ provided (a) *a base and foundation;* and (b) *a shared presupposition* to be utilized for further argument.[1] The themes of divine sovereignty and *grace* have also emerged *alongside the exposition of the reality of the resurrection of Christ* (see above).

The first *refutatio* now addresses what in the language of deliberative rhetoric would be called the "disadvantages" (or, for Paul, dire, unacceptable consequences) of any attempt to deny the possibility or applicability of resurrection as a reality or concept in principle. Such a denial would entail the unimaginable claim that Jesus Christ himself had not been raised from the dead. If *the universal principle has no currency,* by deductive logic *a particular instance of it has no currency either.* Any possible sense of confusion for the modern reader arises because *the resurrection of Christ is also regarded* (in vv. 20-34) *as the paradigm case of resurrection in reality.* Hence it may appear that Paul is turning an anticipated argument upside down. In practice, however, *these two approaches* represent *different and complementary arguments: there is no contradiction of logic between vv. 12-19 and 20-34,* providing that we

---

1. Cicero uses such terms as *base* and *foundation,* while Eriksson has convincingly expounded Paul's use of *narratio* and *tradition* as shared premises for further argument (see above).

keep in mind their different methods and aims. The first subsection (vv. 12-14, with v. 16) sets forth a twofold argument: (i) if resurrection in general is impossible, how can it be claimed that Christ was raised? (ii) Conversely, if we do proclaim Christ as raised, how can it make sense to deny "the resurrection of the dead"? Paul begins with the second in v. 12. Fee argues that vv. 12-13 reflect a chiastic structure that may be detected in other forms throughout this section.[2]

Supplementary Bibliography on 15:12-34
(Additional to General Bibliography on 15:1-58 above at 15:1)

Barth, G., "Erwägungen zu 1 Kor 15:20-28," *EvT* 30 (1970): 515-27.

Bauckham, R., *The Fate of the Dead: Studies on the Jewish and Christian Apocalypses,* NovTSup 93 (Leiden: Brill, 1998).

Brandenburger, E., *Adam und Christus* (Neukirchen-Vluyn: Neukirchener, 1962).

DeMaris, R. E., "Corinthian Religion and Baptism for the Dead (1 Cor 15:29): Insights from Archaeology and Anthropology," *JBL* 114 (1995): 661-82.

Ford, J. M., "Rabbinic Humour behind Baptism for the Dead (1 Cor XV:29)," in F. L. Cross (ed.), *SE* (Berlin: Berlin Academy, 1968), 2:400-403.

Forschini, B. M., "'Those Who are Baptized for the Dead': 1 Cor 15:29," *CBQ* 12 (1950): 260-76 and 379-88; also 13 (1951): 46-78, 172-98, and 276-83.

Hamilton, N. Q., *The Holy Spirit and Eschatology in Paul, SJT* Occasional Papers (Edinburgh: Oliver & Boyd, 1957), 19-25 and 31-33.

Heil, Uta, "Theologische Interpretation von 1 Kor 15:23-23," *ZNW* 84 (1993): 27-35.

Hill, C. E., "Paul's Understanding of Christ's Kingdom in 1 Cor 15:20-28," *NovT* 30 (1988): 297-320.

Howard, J. K., "Baptism for the Dead: A Study of 1 Cor 15:29," *EvQ* 37 (1965): 137-41.

Lambrecht, J., "Paul's Christological Use of Scripture in 1 Cor 15:20-28," *NTS* 28 (1982): 502-27.

Lassen, E. M., "The Use of the Father Image in Imperial Propaganda and 1 Cor 4:14-21," *TynBul* 42 (1991): 127-36.

Lindemann, A., "Parusie Christi und Herrschaft Gottes. Exegese von 1 Kor 15:23-28," *Wort und Dienst* 19 (1987): 87-107.

Malherbe, A. J., "The Beasts at Ephesus," *JBL* 87 (1968): 71-80.

Marcus, J., and M. L. Soards (eds.), *Apocalyptic and the NT* (Sheffield: JSOT Press, 1989).

Moltmann, J., *Is There Life after Death?* (Milwaukee: Marquette University Press, 1998), 47-55.

Muller, R. A., "Christ in the Eschaton: Calvin and Moltmann on the Duration of the *Munus Regium,*" *HTR* 74 (1981): 31-59.

Murphy-O'Connor, J., "'Baptised for the Dead' (1 Cor XV:29): A Corinthian Slogan?" *RB* 88 (1981): 532-43.

Pannenberg, W., *Systematic Theology,* 1:308-19 and 259-336.

Raeder, M., "Vikariastaufe in 1 Cor 15:29?" *ZNW* 46 (1955): 258-61.

Reaume, J. D., "Another Look at 1 Cor 15:29, 'Baptized for the Dead,'" *BSac* 152 (1995): 457-75.

---

2. Fee, *First Epistle,* 739.

Rissi, M., *Die Taufe für die Toten,* Abhandlung zur Theologie des A und NT 42 (Zurich: Zwingli Verlag, 1962).

Schnackenburg, R., "Baptism for the Dead," in *Baptism in the Thought of Paul,* 95-103.

Wilcke, H.-A., *Das Problem eines messianischen Zwischenreichs bei Paulus* (Zürich: Zwingli, 1967), 85-92.

White, J. R., "'Baptized on Account of the Dead': The Meaning of 1 Cor 15:29 in its Context," *JBL* 116 (1997): 489-99.

Witherington, B., *Conflict and Community in Corinth,* 295-312.

Wolff, C., "Exkurs: Deutungsvorschläge zu 1 Kor 15:29," in *Der erste Brief der Paulus an die Korinther* (Leipzig: Evangelische Verlag, 1996), 392-96.

12-13 We discussed the precise form which the claim **there is no resurrection of the dead** (v. 12) may have taken at Corinth in some considerable detail in our introduction to 15:1-58. (To avoid undue replication, see above.) We alluded to the useful surveys of possible views in Wilson, Spörlein, Sellin, Wedderburn, de Boer, G. Barth, and Holleman.[3] In summary we distinguished between four broad diagnoses of the problem which **some** *at Corinth* (τινες ἐν ὑμῖν) experienced: (i) a lack of belief in any form of postmortal existence, perhaps similar to certain Epicurean attitudes (W. M. L. de Wette, W. Schmithals, and [on the basis of Paul's misunderstanding their problem] Bultmann); (ii) belief that the resurrection was "inner" or "spiritual" and had already occurred in the case of "spiritual" believers (Heinrici, Schniewind, Wilckens); (iii) specific doubts about the possibility of "bodily" resurrection, whether because of the nature of "body" or because of a confusion with the immortality of a continuing "soul" (Weiss, Sellin, Dale Martin); and (iv) the view that **some** may represent one problem, and **some** another (Mitchell, Saw, Erickson, Luther). The strengths and weaknesses of these theories are discussed above (see the introduction to 15:1-58).

As D. F. Watson observes, at all events "In his refutation Paul momentarily agrees with the proposition and then shows that its natural consequences include conclusions the Corinthians are not willing to grant" (cf. 13-19).[4] The fundamental *kerygma* has as its content **the raised Christ** (the force of the perfect passive ἐγήγερται is that Christ *was raised and continues to live:* present state on the basis of past event). Hence, to deny the possibility of resurrection as such is to knock the bottom out of what constitutes a central article of Christian faith (ἐν πρώτοις, 15:3). It recalls the aphoristic warning made by Wittgenstein about the *logical* trap of cutting the ground from under the scaffolding of our thoughts: "I must now saw off the branch on which am sitting."[5] By way of illustrative analogy (but

3. For example, Wilson, "The Corinthians Who Say There Is No Resurrection of the Dead," 90-107; Spörlein, *Die Leugnung der Auferstehung,* esp. 7-19; Sellin, *Der Streit um die Auferstehung,* 17-37; Barth, "Zur Frage," 187-201; Wedderburn, *Baptism and Resurrection,* 187-201; de Boer, *Defeat of Death,* 96-105; Holleman, *Resurrection and Parousia,* 35-48.

4. Watson, "Paul's Rhetorical Strategy in 1 Cor 15," 239.

5. L. Wittgenstein, *Philosophical Investigations* (Germ. and Eng. trans., Oxford: Blackwell, 2d ed. 1967), sect. 55. See further his observations in *On Certainty.*

not as an identical issue) Robertson and Plummer mention the unthought-through pronouncement of a Christian who has moved in positivist circles pontificating "miracles *don't* happen" as a supposed *a priori,* when it can be nothing of the kind for a theist who believes in divine action in the world.[6] Hence, πῶς, **how**, is "an expression of astonishment: how is it yet possible that. . . ?" (Cf. 14:7, 16; Rom 3:6; 6:2; 8:32; 10:15; Gal 2:14.)[7]

Dale Martin and Wolff pay special attention to the phrase ἐκ νεκρῶν. Martin believes that "the strong" at Corinth, "influenced by popular philosophy to deprecate the body, opposed the idea of a resurrected body. Indeed they heard Paul's language about 'resurrection of the dead' (νεκρός) as referring to the resuscitation of a 'corpse,' the normal meaning of νεκρός, and they found such a view philosophically ridiculous."[8] By contrast, "uneducated people might readily have accepted early Christian preaching about resurrected bodies, even if they did not understand by such language precisely what Paul intended."[9] Martin's view may well identify a social difference at Corinth in relation to eschatological belief, but his lexicographical claim about νεκρός may also be overstated. In the LXX (the Bible of the church at Corinth) the Greek term often means *the dead* without necessarily alluding to a rotting corpse: BAGD and Grimm-Thayer may be more helpful than the classical Greek allusions which he cites almost exclusively from Liddell-Scott-Jones.[10] The standard English VSS also distinguished between **raised from (ἐκ) the dead** (ἐκ νεκρῶν ἐγήγερται) in v. 12a, and the resurrection **of the dead** (ἀνάστασις νεκρῶν, without ἐκ) in v. 12b (NRSV, REB, NIV, NJB, AV/KJV).

The connective δέ (v. 13) carries on the chain of inferences, this time by contrast (**But**). Here οὐδὲ Χριστὸς ἐγήγερται expresses the *logical corollary,* perhaps best indicated by translating **then neither can** (*logical* **can**, *not* **can** of *empirical* possibility) **Christ have been raised**. Meyer identifies an interesting implication for Christology which, however, he fails to press. Older dogmaticians had appealed here to "the higher nature of Christ" (e.g., Rückert), but Meyer points out that if Paul had not viewed Jesus of Nazareth as representatively human, the logic to which he appeals here would have lost some of its force.[11] An *a priori* denial of the possibility of resurrection thereby *logically excludes* the resurrection of Christ. These verses underline *Paul's expectation that believing Christians will respect logical coherence and rational thought.* He does not hesitate to appeal to it.

6. Robertson and Plummer, *First Epistle,* 346.

7. Meyer, *First Epistle,* 2:50.

8. Martin, *The Corinthian Body,* 107-8; Wolff, *Der erste Brief,* 377-78; Epictetus, *Dissertations* 1.5.7; 9.33; Lucian, *Menippus,* 17, 18.

9. Martin, *Corinthian Body,* 108.

10. LSJ should be compared with BAGD, 534-35 and Grimm-Thayer, 423-24. In practice a *metaphorical* or "spiritual" view might be more strongly encouraged by lexicographical frequency alone.

11. Meyer, *First Epistle,* 2:50.

14-15 (1) Most MSS (e.g., ℵ, A, D², F, G, Syriac, Coptic, et al., with UBS 4th ed.) read ἡ πίστις ὑμῶν, **your faith**, at the end of v. 14, but B, D*, and 33 read ἡμῶν, *our faith*. This could easily be an assimilation to the previous ἡμῶν, as Metzger notes, and the UBS editors classify the text presupposed in our translation as "B," i.e., "almost certain." This is confirmed by the undisputed reading of v. 17.[12] (2) καί is placed in square brackets in the UBS 4th ed. (and UBS 1979 and Nestlé) texts between ἄρα and τὸ κήρυγμα. It occurs in ℵ*, A, D, F, G, 33, against p⁴⁶, ℵ², and B. In v. 18 a similar construction denotes an additional factor, but unless the syntax is understood to attempt to convey *both . . . and . . .* (as Godet understands it) its inclusion here is surprising, and may be no more than a scribal anticipation of v. 18.[13] With p⁴⁶, ℵ², B, and Syriac it should probably be omitted.[14] (3) D, Tertullian, and a few other MSS omit εἴπερ ἄρα νεκροὶ οὐκ ἐγείρονται. But doubtless the eye of the scribe slipped to the identical three words at the beginning of v. 16.

The connective δέ continues the unfolding logic with another contrast, which in v. 14 ἄρα performs, of indicating a clear logical consequence: *then, therefore,* or **it follows that**, where the force is strong, as here. Κενόν and κενή, **hollow**, **empty**, *without substance,* or *void* (cf. Wolff's *inthaltslos;* on the word, see above), are found in positions of emphasis, hence with the καί we translate **and empty also is your faith**. τὸ κήρυγμα ἡμῶν in this context (already defined in 15:3b-5) denotes neither simply *our preaching* (NIV), nor **our proclamation** (NRSV) but specifically **our proclamation of the gospel** (cf. REB, **our gospel**): it looks back to the κηρύσσομεν of v. 11 and refers to the content of what is proclaimed (with REB). So central are the truth claim and event of the resurrection of Christ that if the linchpin is removed a multitude of dependent derivatives collapses: (i) the content and currency of the gospel; (ii) the authenticity of Christian faith; (iii) the truthfulness of testimony to the acts of God (v. 15); (iv) liberation from the destructive and damaging power of sin (v. 17); and (v) the irretrievable loss of believers who have died (v. 18). In philosophical terms we may therefore regard the resurrection of Christ as having, in Paul's view, a certain "basicality" which should cause us to hesitate to discard what is known in theories of knowledge as a "soft" or "modest" foundationalism as against either "strong" foundationalism (Descartes) or nonfoundationalism (postmodernity). Paul agrees that many Christian beliefs are *mutually* supportive, but gives a degree of primacy (ἐν πρώτοις . . . παρέλαβον . . . κατὰ τὰς γραφάς, vv. 3-5).[15]

12. Metzger, *Textual Commentary* (2d ed.), 501.

13. Godet, *First Epistle,* 2:345 is puzzling, for he seems to attribute the *insertion* of καί, after ἄρα, to B, rather than its omission.

14. With Robertson and Plummer, *First Epistle,* 348n.

15. The debate about "basicality," "mutuality," and "nonfoundational" beliefs has recently achieved a new prominence in philosophical theology. See, e.g., A. Plantinga and N. Wolterstorff (eds.), *Faith and Rationality: Reason and Belief in God* (Notre Dame: University of Notre Dame Press, 1983); W. Jay Wood, *Epistemology: Becoming Intellectually Virtuous* (Leicester: Apollos, 1998), 77-174; and Thiselton in *The Promise of Hermeneutics,* 209-23.

In accordance with the aim of a rhetorical *refutatio* Paul pushes the opposing axiom to its further disastrous ("disadvantageous" in deliberative rhetoric) consequences: the apostles became **exposed as liars** (the practical force of Gk εὑρισκόμεθα, *we shall be found,* i.e., *discovered* to be, *revealed* to be, ψευδομάρτυρες, *false witnesses,* i.e., **liars in what we witness concerning God**).[16] The objective genitive for τοῦ θεοῦ, **concerning God**, seems to fit the context better than a subjective genitive *(in God's service).*[17] ὅτι has causal or explanatory force: **because we gave testimony against God** (κατὰ τοῦ θεοῦ) **that he raised Christ when if, as they say, it were the case.** . . . Barrett (with Edwards) explains the otherwise difficult syntax: **as they say** represents a classical use of ἄρα (BDF, sect. 454).[18] The preposition κατά with the genitive retains its proper meaning **against** and cannot be reduced to περί, *concerning.*[19] Paul traces a downward spiral of devastating consequences. Those who accept the counterproposition or opposing axiom to that of the *kerygma* find themselves in open opposition to God by denying the veracity of his vindication of Christ and initiation of new creation in Christ's resurrection.

As in 15:9 (ὃς οὐκ εἰμὶ ἱκανός . . .), the relative pronoun in Χριστόν, ὃν οὐκ ἐγήγερται . . . functions as a connective of logical explication preceding εἴπερ, *if so be that* (NJB, **Christ** . . . *whereas, if* . . . ; although NRSV retains the relative pronoun as such: *Christ whom he did not raise if* . . .) Barrett renders it **Christ — *whereas,* if, as they say.** . . . The logic may seem overly complex to express the point: "Either Christ was raised from the dead, or we lied in affirming," but Paul shows that more is at stake than merely false witness as such. A whole theology is at stake. Hence, as Wolff notes, v. 15 takes up v. 12; v. 16 takes up v. 13; v. 17 takes up v. 14; and these form an intensifying chain in which the counterthesis depends on the climactic and emphatic εἴπερ . . . ἄρα, **if** *really* **as they** *indeed* **say.**[20]

16-17 B and D* add ἔστιν after **your faith** in v. 17, but this is already understood.

No further comment is needed on v. 16, for it repeats, in effect, the argument of v. 13 (see above). The repetition serves to intensify the cumulative and increasingly devastating chain of consequences which the counterproposition would entail. Of the two consequences identified in v. 17 the force of ματαία to denote the first, **your faith is without effect**, differs in some degree *from your faith is empty* (κενή) in v. 14b. The former (here) concerns the *fruitlessness* or *pointlessness* (NJB) of Christian faith if there is no resurrection and therefore no res-

16. Fee, *First Epistle,* 742, n. 21, rightly detects the force of *found out* here. Collins, *First Cor,* 544, also draws attention to the classical Greek background of the term *false witness* in Demosthenes and other later hellenistic authors.

17. With most commentators but against Edwards, *First Epistle,* 404.

18. Barrett, *First Epistle,* 348; Edwards, *First Epistle,* 405.

19. Against Robertson and Plummer (*First Epistle,* 348-49).

20. Cf. Wolff, *Der erste Brief,* 378; and Edwards, *First Epistle,* 405.

urrection of Jesus Christ (NRSV, *futile;* REB, *your faith has nothing to it*); the latter (v. 14b) concerns its lack of content (REB, *null;* NJB, *without substance*). The second consequence in v. 17, **you are still in your sins**, confirms that without the resurrection of Christ, Christ's death alone has no atoning, redemptive, or liberating effect in relation to human sin.

This underlines the need for a *substitutionary* model of the atonement always to be complemented by the theme of *identification* with Christ. J. K. S. Reid observes that here there is "a rule of contrariety. . . . Christ wins benefits for us, who himself had no need of them" (forgiveness, justification, reconciliation) and "a rule of correspondence: 'because he lives, we shall live also'" (resurrection to a new mode of existence).[21] Other models (Christ as the last Adam, Christ as despoiler of principalities and powers) would also lose their force if there were no resurrection. On all counts believers at Corinth would still (ἔτι) remain **"in your sins"** (ἐν ταῖς ἁμαρτίαις ὑμῶν). It is unusual for Paul to use **sins** in the plural, since he more regularly views sin as an attitude, stance, or state, in contrast to a mere series of actions. But the preposition ἐν, **in**, underlies this more structural aspect.[22]

18 The use of ἄρα καί (v. 18) underlines Paul's identification of further logical consequences in this *refutatio* of the counter-axiom. The metaphor **sleep** for death on the part of believers who are "in Christ" was important in earliest Christian faith, for the logical "grammar" of **sleep** (κοιμάω) carries with it the expectation of *awaking to a new dawn and a new day,* i.e., the expectation of resurrection and the gift of renewed life and vigor (cf. v. 51).[23] It also anticipates the triumphant hope of the removal of *the sting* (τὸ κέντρον, v. 55) of death when God through Christ has dealt with sin (v. 56).[24] Pannenberg adds: "The familiar experience of being awakened and rising from *sleep* serves as a parable for the completely unknown destiny expected for the dead."[25] The new day brings its surprises as well as its new life.

In 1 Corinthians 15, Cullmann argues, "life" would be negated by "the sting of **sin**" as "the enemy" because the effect of sin is separation from God the Life-giver, unless sin has been covered and destroyed (1 Cor 15:19, 54-57).[26] Moltmann also urges that the metaphor of **sleep** should not be pressed in such a way as to exclude the room for "development to completion" allowed by such Pauline phrases as "Lord of the dead and the living" (Rom 14:9) and "life

21. J. K. S. Reid, *Our Life in Christ* (London: SCM, 1963), 90-91.

22. See Pannenberg, *Systematic Theology,* 2:231-76, for an excellent discussion of "the misery of humanity," esp. "forms of sin," 238-52, for the Pauline and Augustinian recognition of human bondage in contrast to secular (and Corinthian) aspirations toward an illusory "autonomy."

23. Strobel, *Der erste Brief,* 245.

24. Cullmann writes, "Paul's joyous exclamation, 'Death, where is your sting?' (15:55) belongs together with his trustful assurance 'Whether we live or die, we are the Lord's' (Rom 14:8)" (*Immortality of the Soul or Resurrection of the Dead,* 55).

25. Pannenberg, *Jesus — God and Man,* 74.

26. Cullmann, *Immortality of the Soul,* 24.

is hidden with Christ in God" (Col 3:3).[27] However, **sleep** regularly denotes the experience of death for Christians as pregnant with hope and becomes a standard term (John 11:11; Acts 7:60; 13:36; 1 Cor 7:39 [see above]; 11:30; 15:6; 2 Pet 3:4; *1 Clement* 44:2; Hermas, *The Shepherd,* 4:4; Ignatius, *Letter to the Romans,* 4:2, and others).[28] If "development" occurs after the resurrection, both aspects may perhaps be explained together. The articular aorist passive participle οἱ κοιμηθέντες ἐν Χριστῷ has the force of **those who were laid to sleep in Christ** (neither NRSV, *those who have died in Christ,* nor NIV, NJB, AV/KJV, *those also who have fallen asleep in Christ,* nor REB, *those who have died within Christ's fellowship,* seems to convey the Greek as well as Findlay and Robertson and Plummer, whom we follow here).[29] The emphatic ἄρα καί is conveyed by **it also follows then that.** . . .

We discussed the force of the middle of ἀπόλλυμι (in the active voice, *to destroy, to bring ruin*) in its present participial form in 1:18: those who are *on their way to ruin* (see above on 1:18). Here we find the second aorist middle indicative ἀπώλοντο, regularly *they have perished* (as NRSV); but Paul has in mind the emptiness and waste of *irretrievable loss* (cf. κενός, above) as in REB, *utterly* **lost**, or, above, **lost for good**.[30] They will never "awake" from **sleep**.

19 Most VSS (NRSV, REB, NJB, Collins) but *not* Barrett render the Greek with μόνον in a way that permits a simple English translation: *if for this life only* (NIV, *only for this life*). It is possible to construe **only** in this way, but the adverb comes at the very end of the clause after the periphrastic perfect ἠλπικότες ἐσμέν *(we are the having-placed-our-hope ones who still hope).*[31] Since strictly **only** qualifies the whole clause (Barrett, Wolff, Robertson), we should not exclude this aspect by an easy English option.[32] Paul carefully portrays someone **who has placed hope in Christ with nothing beyond**, i.e., *only so*. ἐλεεινότεροι denotes *more pitiable,* **more to be pitied**, followed by the genitive of comparison πάντων ἀνθρώπων, **than all human beings** (not simply πάντων).[33] Fee rightly points out that Paul is saying far more than that Christians are to be pitied if there is no postmortal existence.[34] Since Paul builds up *an intensified cumulative logic* in which he *gathers up the whole refutatio,* what

---

27. Moltmann, *Is There Life after Death?* (Milwaukee: Marquette University Press, 1998), 47-55. Moltmann well expounds Luther on "the sleep of the soul" (47-48), but insists that this is not the whole picture, noting Calvin's hesitations (56).

28. In addition to BAGD, 437-38, cf. Lampe, *Patristic Greek Lexicon,* 759-60.

29. Robertson and Plummer, *First Epistle,* 350; Findlay, *Expositor's Greek Testament,* 2:926. NRSV and REB miss the logic of the metaphor, while NIV, NJB, and AV/KJV fail to indicate that a metaphorical force is being used; none draws out the nuance of the passive voice.

30. Cf. also BAGD, 95.

31. On the intensive force of the periphrastic perfect, Wolff, *Der erste Brief,* 380.

32. See the discussions, esp. in Barrett, *First Epistle,* 349-50, and Wolff, *Der erste Brief,* 380. Barrett translates, *in Christ — that and nothing more — then.* . . .

33. NRSV, NJB, and NIV translate *all people.*

34. Fee, *First Epistle,* 741. Fee rightly urges more than is implied by the allusion to *2 Apocalypse of Baruch* 21:13, which is cited by Collins, *First Cor,* 545.

would make Christians pitiable if there is no resurrection is the whole chain of consequences in vv. 13-18 which follow the counteraxiom of v. 12: (i) the gospel has no substance; (ii) faith is ineffective; (iii) the witnesses are liars; (iv) sin retains its destructive and damaging control; and (v) believers who have died are irretrievably lost. On this cumulative and irreversible disaster, see above on vv. 13-18. Thus Paul concludes his *first refutatio:* the *unacceptable and disastrous consequences of denying the currency of the very concept of resurrection.* As an instance of deliberative rhetoric it is a *tour de force.*[35]

2. The Resurrection of Christ as the Foundation of Present Life and Eschatological Promise for Christian Believers — First *Confirmatio* (15:20-34)

(20) In reality, however, Christ has been raised from the dead, the firstfruits of the harvest of the dead. (21, 22) For since through a human being death came, so also through a human being comes about the resurrection of the dead. For just as all die in Adam, even so all will be brought to life in Christ. (23) But each in the proper arranged order: Christ the first fruits; then afterward, at his coming, those who are Christ's. (24, 25) Then is the End, when he hands over the rule to him who is God and Father when he shall have annihilated every rule and every authority and power. For he must reign until he has put all his enemies under his feet. (26, 27) The last enemy doomed to be brought to nothing is death. For "he has placed all things in subjection under his feet." But when it says "all things are in subjection," it is clear that "all things" excludes the One who has brought all things into submission to him. (28) But when all things have been subjected to him, then will the Son himself also be made subject to the One who placed all things in subjection to him, so that God may be all in all. (29) Otherwise what do those people think they are doing who have themselves baptized for the sake of the dead? If the dead are really not raised, what is the point of being baptized for them?

(30, 31) Why do we, too, let ourselves be put at risk every hour of the day? From day to day I court fatality — oh yes, by all the pride in you that I hold dear in Christ Jesus our Lord, I so affirm! (32) If it was only within human horizons that I have battled with wild, bestial creatures at Ephesus, what profit could there have been for me? If dead people are not raised,

"Let us eat and drink,
For tomorrow we die."

(33, 34) Stop being seduced. "Belonging to bad gangs ruins reputable lifestyles." Come to your senses; wake up and sober up! Leave sin alone.

---

35. See Eriksson, *Traditions,* 244-45; cf. Bünker, *Briefformular und rhetorische Disposition,* 62-63.

"Some people," you see, have an utter lack of **"knowledge"** of God, I tell you this to shame you.

After refuting the counteraxiom of the denial by ruthlessly exposing its unacceptable logical consequences Paul reverses the direction of argument to establish the remarkable consequences for which the axiom of resurrection, and in particular the resurrection of Jesus Christ, stands as the foundation.[36] Again, in terms of deliberative rhetoric, he unfolds a series of "advantages," i.e., fundamentals of Christian life and eschatological promise. After he has addressed the "conceivability" of future resurrection (vv. 35-37), Paul will return to this practical dimension in his conclusion to the whole argument in v. 58.

20 Some Western texts insert ἐγένετο to read *and became* **the firstfruits**. It is absent from 𝔭46, ℵ, B, A, and there is no major textual support for this secondary addition.

BAGD confirm with examples that the adverb νυνί may be used to denote not only a temporal or a logical *now* but also "introducing the real situation after an unreal clause or sentence, *but as a matter of fact*" (Heb 9:26; 1 Cor 5:11; cf. NRSV, *But in fact,* REB, *But the truth is . . .*).[37] The further contrastive δέ calls for a clear marker, e.g., **however**. On **raised from the dead** see above on vv. 4, 12, 14, et al. Paul continues to use the *perfect passive,* as Dahl, Barrett, Ortkemper, de Boer, and others emphasize.[38]

Three writers in particular demonstrate the importance of ἀπαρχή, **the firstfruits of the harvest**, for Pauline thought. Hamilton offers some useful short sections on the Holy Spirit as a gift of whom "more to come" is promised.[39] More relevant to this verse, M. C. de Boer and Joost Holleman regard the word in this verse as pivotal for Paul's Christology and for his argument in this chapter. De Boer argues that the image of **the firstfruits** is "derived from the OT where it denotes the first portion of the crop (or flock) which is offered in Thanksgiving to God. As such, *the term signifies the pledge of the remainder,* and concomitantly, *the assurance of a full harvest . . .* the first instalment and that part which includes, as by synecdoche, the whole" (my italics).[40] Holleman goes further. **Firstfruits** in v. 20, he argues, embodies two ideas: a *temporal* logic and a *representative* logic. As firstfruits Christ is the *"first one"* to have been raised: "the first or best part of belongings or possessions" in lexico-

36. Eriksson, *Traditions,* 261-67; Watson, "Rhetorical Strategy," 240-44; Mitchell, *Rhetoric of Reconciliation,* 288-89. Collins perceives "the familiar chiastic A-B-A′ pattern" in vv. 12-19, 20-28, and 29-34 (*First Cor,* 547).

37. BAGD, 546; Grimm-Thayer, 430-31.

38. The significance of the passive for Paul's logic cannot be overemphasized. See above on 15:4 and introduction to 15:1-58, and Dahl, *Resurrection of the Body,* 96-100; Barrett, *First Epistle,* 341; Ortkemper, *1 Kor,* 145; de Boer, *Defeat of Death,* 105-9; further Moxnes, *Theology in Conflict,* 231-82; and Holleman, *Resurrection and Parousia,* 49-57.

39. Hamilton, *The Holy Spirit and Eschatology in Paul,* 19-25 and 31-33.

40. De Boer, *Defeat of Death,* 109.

graphic usage (vv. 20-23). As such, however, Christ is also "a *representation* of the rest" (my italics).[41] This prepares the way for Paul's theology of Christ as the last Adam (vv. 21-22).

Paul uses ἀπαρχή, other than in the present passages, most significantly in Rom 8:23 and 11:16. In Rom 8:23 Christians receive "the first instalment" of the gift of the Holy Spirit of whom their reception now is a pledge of a greater and fuller eschatological experience of the Spirit. This directly coheres with our exegesis of 1 Cor 15:44 (see below). Rom 11:16 alludes to the ritual of the Feast of Weeks: if **the firstfruits** offered to God are holy loaves of bread, the rest of the whole dough shares in this quality of holiness. Both of these examples share with **firstfruits** in our verse (1) prior *temporality;* (2) *representation* of the same quality or character; and (3) *promise* or *pledge* of *more of the same kind to come.*[42] In these respects there are clear parallels with the force of ἀρραβών, *down payment in guarantee of more to come,* applied to the Holy Spirit in 2 Cor 1:22 and 5:5. The metaphor of **firstfruits** is also used in a weaker and less theological sense of the household of Stephanas as the ἀπαρχή of Achaia (i.e., the first converts of the region holding out the promise [in a looser sense] of others, 1 Cor 16:15); and similarly of Epaenetus as the ἀπαρχή of Asia (Rom 16:5). In other contexts the Greek word may sometimes carry the formal legal meaning of birth certificate, which again relates to genuineness and status.[43]

This ordered sequence of temporality, representation, and promise or pledge of what is to come begins *Paul's demonstration of a divine purposive order.* Most commentators emphasize the *existential assurance* of vv. 20-25: because **Christ was raised**, those in Christ will be raised, since he is the **firstfruit** *of the whole* **harvest** *still to come.* This is valid. However, vv. 20-25 *prepare the way for vv. 26-28, which is about God and God's purposes, as is this whole chapter* (as Barth urges). Edwards therefore rightly perceives the key as *the order of things* in which "there is no τάξις without ὑπόταξις."[44] In other words: God has acted and God will act; *but everything in God's time in God's way: order* (τάξις) entails *submission* (ὑπόταξις) to the sovereign will of our gracious God: *we will be made alive* (v. 22), *but each in his or her own order* (v. 23). The unfolding of the resurrection order depends on divine *sovereignty,* divine *grace,* and divine *promise* (see above, especially introduction to 15:1-58).[45]

21-22 It is essential to hold the double set of parallels together since the two respective referents of ἀνθρώπου in v. 21 are explained at once in v. 22 as (i) **Adam** and (ii) **Christ**. As the double γάρ, **for**, indicates, Holleman's emphasis on *representation* (vv. 21-22) as *complementing temporal priority* and

---

41. Holleman, *Resurrection and Parousia,* 49; cf. 49-50.

42. Cf. Holleman, *Resurrection,* 50; Hamilton, *Holy Spirit,* 20-21.

43. BAGD, 81. The role of *firstborn* (πρωτότοκος, Col 1:18; Rev 1:5) should also be compared.

44. Edwards, *First Epistle,* 409.

45. See also Thiselton, "Luther and Barth on 1 Cor 15," 258-89.

promise in firstfruits (v. 20) finds classic expression here. In Bruce's words, "Paul now draws an analogy between two uniquely representative men: **Adam**, head of the old creation, in whom **all die**, and **Christ**, head of the new creation, 'the first-born from the dead' (Col 1:18; cf. Rev 1:8) in whom **all** are to be *made alive* in resurrection."[46] **Adam** is, for Paul, both an individual and a corporate entity: "he was what his Hebrew name signifies — 'mankind'. The whole of mankind is viewed as originally existing in Adam."[47] These verses may appear more logically problematic in the light of modern Western individualism and supposed autonomy than they are. Today, with globalization and international economics, it should be clearer than ever before that humanity as a whole is "bound up in a bundle of created existence" (Robinson's phrase), i.e., of *structural and corporate sin and fallenness.* (However, see the warning note of Fitzmyer, below).[48] In continuity with the promises of the OT Paul thinks of **Adam** and of **humankind** *both* in structural-corporate *and* individual terms, just as the language concerning the righteous Suffering Servant in Isaiah 40–55 oscillates between depicting the Servant as an individual and as a corporate people.[49] Even so, the argument that humanity is, simply as a brute fact, bound up in the solidarities, vulnerabilities, and consequences of the life and destiny of **Adam** finds its saving parallel in the gospel assurance that the new humanity is bound up in the solidarities, atoning work, and resurrection victory and promise of **Christ** as the "last" (i.e., eschatological) **Adam** (see 15:45). J. A. T. Robinson observes, "Solidarity [jointly sharing liabilities and advantages] is the divinely ordained structure in which personal life is to be lived."[50] Davies further claims that "Paul accepted the traditional Rabbinic doctrine of the unity of mankind in Adam." But Fitzmyer adds a note of warning: none of the rabbinic passages "says a thing about the 'inclusion' of all humanity 'in' the body of Adam in the manner of 1 Cor 15:22."[51]

Although it is generally assumed that Rom 5:12-21 provides Paul's most significant treatment of "in Adam . . . in Christ . . . ," the earlier and no less important expositions of this theme in Paul come in 1 Cor 15:21-22 and 45-59. In Rom 5:12-20 Paul uses the typological parallel to explain that although all humanity is trapped in the corporate and structural consequence of sin, the corpo-

46. Bruce, *1 and 2 Cor,* 145.
47. Ibid., 145-46.
48. Contrast even Luther's emphasis on what seems "so absurd and false to the world" ("1 Cor 7 and 15," 116-17); J. A. T. Robinson, *The Body: A Study in Pauline Theology* (London: SCM, 1952), 21; cf. 8-33 and 58-60.
49. Cf. W. D. Davies, *Paul and Rabbinic Judaism* (London: SPCK, 2d ed. 1955), 36-57; K. Barth, *Christ and Adam* (Edinburgh: Oliver & Boyd, 1956); Morna Hooker, "Adam," in *From Adam to Christ: Essays on Paul* (Cambridge: Cambridge University Press, 1990), 73-101 (mainly on Romans 1 and Phil 2:6-11); Brandenburger, *Adam und Christus,* 15-131; G. Barth, "Erwägungen zu 1 Kor 15:20-28," 515-27; J. Lambrecht, "Paul's Christological Use of Scripture on 1 Cor 15:20-28," 502-27.
50. Robinson, *The Body,* 9.
51. Davies, *Paul,* 57; and Fitzmyer, *Romans,* 412.

rate and structural grace "in Christ" exceed even the former in the radical nature of its consequences. Here Paul shows that corporate and structural dimension of "being human" that characterizes the reign of sin and death all the more guarantees that **all** who are **in Christ** will share in solidarity with him the reality of **the resurrection of the dead**. Gerhard Barth therefore calls these verses (15:20-28, esp. 20-22) "the high point of the whole epistle."[52] Similarly, G. Sellin urges that this passage "deals with the central part of Paul's argumentation."[53] As Wolff notes, it prepares the way for all that follows in 15:24-58.[54] In essence "the unity with Adam leads to death; the unity with Christ leads to resurrection" (Holleman).[55]

Whereas Paul's use of Abraham typology (e.g., Romans 4) underlines the continuity of God's faithful acts, "the Adam typology," Beker observes, "operates not in terms of continuity but in terms of discontinuity. Here the last (eschatological) Adam reverses radically what the first Adam has initiated in world history (Rom 5:12-17; 1 Cor 15:20-22), so that the . . . apocalyptic thrust of the Adam typology underscores the radical newness of God's act in Christ."[56] The background to this typology is therefore the apocalyptic background of the two ages with its "ontological antithesis of death and life."[57] Beker works out the implications of this apocalyptic background convincingly and in detail.[58] Building on the work of P. Vielhauer and Klaus Koch, he shows that for Paul "the final resurrection is total renewal in an apocalyptic sense: 'the new world' . . . so that the resurrection of Christ announces the . . . dawn of the general resurrection to come.[59] In Becker's view it was failure to grasp "the apocalyptic connection" that constituted the heart of the problem at Corinth, and hence "constitutes the basis of Paul's argument (15:20-28)."[60] The resurrection is not less than, but far more than, "the enthronement of Christ as 'Lord.' . . ." Thus Beker concludes, in 1 Cor 15:22 we might "expect 'For as by a man came death, by a man came also *life*,' but instead we read 'by a man has come also *the resurrection of the dead*'" (his italics).[61]

This apocalyptic approach has been developed more recently, but with some distinctive modifications, by M. C. de Boer and by J. Holleman. The former cites J. L. Martyn's comment, with his additional reference to Galatians, that an apocalyptic turning point marks "the death of one world, and the advent of another."[62] In line with Schweitzer, Koch, Käsemann, Brandenburger, and

52. G. Barth, "Erwägungen," 516.
53. Sellin, *Der Streit um die Auferstehung*, 261.
54. Wolff, *Der erste Brief*, 382.
55. Holleman, *Resurrection and Parousia*, 53.
56. Beker, *Paul the Apostle*, 100.
57. Ibid.
58. Ibid., 135-81 and throughout.
59. Ibid., 153.
60. Ibid., 168.
61. Ibid., 168 and 170.
62. De Boer, *Defeat of Death*, 34; cf. 32-35 on Beker.

others, de Boer pays attention to such apocalyptic works as *4 Ezra* and *2 Baruch*. However, he focuses (with Brandenberger) on the phenomenon of death: in *4 Ezra* death is seen as "an all-embracing reality of the present aeon," and even in *2 Baruch* "the world is determined by a sentence of death imposed on Adam."[63] The role of Adam varies in the two writings, however. Each stresses structural and corporate aspects: "O Adam, what have you done? Though it was you who sinned, the fall was not yours alone, but ours too who are your descendants" (*4 Ezra* 7:118); "O Adam, what have you done to those who were born from you . . . (*2 Baruch* 48:42). On the other hand, "Adam is not the cause, except for himself only; each of us is his/her own Adam" (*2 Bar.* 54:19).[64] Moreover, we must heed Fitzmyer's warning about care in dating rabbinic and apocalyptic texts, and note the role of Adam also in hellenistic Jewish texts (e.g., Wis 2:24 and Philo).[65]

Provided that we heed Fitzmyer's warnings, it is unnecessary as well as unconvincing to list hypotheses about the ultimate origins of Paul's Adam-Christ typology. As we shall see in vv. 45-49, Paul's eschatological Adam is *not* the "second" Adam of Philo; he does not allude to a myth of a primal man.[66] The legacy of apocalyptic underlines Paul's belief that the old "order" lies trapped within a destructive spiral of sin, the law, and death (cf. Rom 1:18–5:20) and that only a divine act of *new creation* (not "religion") can provide *a new "order" in which God will be all in or to all*. Thus Holleman observes that "**all** (for Paul) participate in the order of death, as 'represented' **in Adam** (v. 22a); with regard to the participation in Jesus' resurrection (v. 22b) Paul speaks about Christians only, since only Christians may consider themselves as being *represented* by Jesus" (my italics).[67] It is characteristic of the apocalyptic emphasis upon *human bondage and its universality* to stress that "death held sway (or reigned) from Adam . . ." (Rom 5:14) and that *new creation alone, which cannot be achieved but can be received only as a gift from beyond the human realm* (Rom 5:15), can reverse and redeem an otherwise insoluble plight. The parallel between Rom 5:12-16 and 1 Cor 15:21-22 is close, but whereas the *former* stresses the *"how much more" of divine grace* (Rom 5:15), our passage

63. Ibid., 75 and 81; also Brandenburger, *Adam und Christus,* 58.

64. Cf. *2 Baruch* 4:3; 17:2; 18:2; 23:4; 48:62; 54:15, 19; *4 Ezra* 3:30, 21, 22, 26.

65. Fitzmyer, *Romans,* 412, where he clearly shows that Davies is misleading at certain points.

66. Against Conzelmann, *1 Cor,* 268-69. Conzelmann argues that the myth of the "primal man" occurs both in Judaism and beyond Judaism in gnosticism. Yet the telltale phrase is that this occurs "above all" in gnosticism. Cf. F. H. Borsch, *The Son of Man in Myth and History* (London: SCM, 1967); Stanley, *Christ's Resurrection in Pauline Soteriology,* 122-24; and esp. Dunn, *Romans,* 277-79, for an incisive critique of the history-of-religions hypothesis.

67. Holleman, *Resurrection,* 55; see his further comments on 52-54. He offers a similar comment in *First Epistle,* 750; also Luther, "1 Cor," 114; and Ortkemper, *1 Kor,* 154. This is *not* to define who might be included under the term *Christians;* it is, however, to contextualize the sense in which **all** is used in v. 22b, i.e., *not* necessarily here in an absolute, unqualified sense. A universalist exegesis is prepared by Origen, *De Principiis* 1:6.

stresses *the pledge of new creation as the promise of* **the resurrection of the dead** on the basis of being **in Christ**, also, however, by *divine grace.*[68]

The implications for Christology are startling: in accordance with the *passive* voice of **raised** when it is applied to Christ, Paul underlines the common *humanity* which Jesus shares with Adam and with all humankind, except that Christ remains God's *righteous* agent of salvation. In this respect alone Stanley's statement "Christ possessed the same human nature as Adam" invites qualification.[69] On the other hand, it implies a no less startling entailment of the same death. For, as 2 Cor 5:20-21 makes explicit, Christ's becoming *one with human sin* in the sense of identification entailed his death being "not . . . merely physical death," but also a *participation in the emptiness of the "eschatological death" which reigns from Adam onward.*[70] Moltmann wrote in his classic study *Theology of Hope,* "Because God and his promise are life, the real bitterness of death lies not merely in the loss of life, but also in the loss of God, as in god-forsakenness. . . ."[71] The proper context for hope (we might add, in contrast to notions of "spirituality" at Corinth) is the "undisguised harshness [of] the deadlines of death as compared with the promised life, received from the promise of God . . . a wholehearted, unrestricted . . . assent to life . . . the victory of praise and therewith of life over death . . . as a conquest of the deadlines of death."[72] This is "a new totality which annihilates the total *nihil*. The two experiences stand in a radical contradiction to each other . . . death and life, nothing and everything, godlessness and the divinity of God."[73]

Here is the full theological justification for Beker's argument that the Adam-Christ typology in 15:22 is one of *contrast* and *reversal*. Yet it also presupposes that Jesus Christ was willing to place himself under the reign of death, in its fullest and most terrifying sense, that spread throughout humanity from the first turning away from God. Robertson and Plummer comment, "Christ leads the way in resurrection, as Adam did in death."[74] But we must not hurry too quickly over Christ's sharing in the horror of this death in order to lead the way in resurrection. As Cullmann among others reminds us, the death which Jesus faced was not the "stingless" death which he has won for others, but the horrifying "God-forsakenness" of the *nihil* (Moltmann).[75] By the same token, it is irrelevant to allude to the probable existence of "death" in the cosmos in the animal kingdom prior to Adam: Adam brought death-as-related-to-sin, a death

68. On Rom 5:12-16, see Fitzmyer, *Romans,* 411-20; Dunn, *Romans,* 270-80.

69. Stanley, *Christ's Resurrection,* 123.

70. Ibid. See also the powerful expositions of this theme initially in Cullmann, *Immortality,* and then esp. in Moltmann, *The Crucified God: The Way of Jesus Christ,* and in Pannenberg, *Systematic Theology,* 2, esp. 416-37.

71. Moltmann, *Theology of Hope,* 208.

72. Ibid., 210 and 211.

73. Ibid., 198; cf. 139-229; also Moltmann, *The Coming of God.*

74. Robertson and Plummer, *First Epistle,* 352.

75. Cullmann, *Immortality.*

which has been described as "a sacrament of the wrath of God," which Christ underwent to deliver his people from this terrible experience. "The evil which arose through a human author is by divine arrangement removed also through a human author" (ἐστί has to be supplied).[76] In v. 22 ἐν τῷ Χριστῷ is identified as this ground and cause.

That ζῳοποιηθήσονται, **shall be brought to life** (future passive, v. 22b), has an eschatological meaning here is shown by its parallelism with ἀνάστασις νεκρῶν (v. 21b). The late Greek verb ζῳοποιέω may mean simply *to restore to life*, but unlike, e.g., the "raising" of Lazarus in John 11, the resurrection of Jesus was not to restore life in the conditions of continuing earthly existence (and eventual death) but to initiate a transformed mode of existence as the **firstfruits** (v. 20) of the eschatological new creation. This theme is explicated further in vv. 23-26. The introductory ὥσπερ (v. 22a) means **just as** . . . (as in Rom 5:12), which is followed by correlative καὶ οὕτως, **even so**. . . . The stress is not on πάντες but on ἐν τῷ Ἀδάμ and ἐν τῷ Χριστῷ, as that in which the respective experiences and destinies are *grounded*.[77]

23 "In vv. 23-28," Lindemann declares, "Paul employs a little apocalyptic drama to develop his assertion of vv. 21b, 22b."[78] The word τάγμα, *that which has been* **arranged**, thing placed in its **proper order**, hence in a military context a *corps, troop division,* or *rank* of troops, underlines both the purposive activity of God and the apocalyptic context of thought.[79] To avoid the gender-exclusive *each in his own order* (NRSV) for ἕκαστος δέ ἐν τῷ ἰδίῳ τάγματι, NJB renders *all of them in their proper order,* but this *all* seems to presuppose more than two groups (as Weiss, Héring, and some others do; see below, v. 24). REB uses *proper* in *proper order* to represent a gender-neutral ἰδίῳ, *one's own*. Drawing in the specific force of τάγμα, we may intensify the particularity by **in proper arranged order** without overextending ἐν τῷ ἰδίῳ τάγματι. This **proper arranged order** explicates both (a) the logic of **firstfruits** (v. 20) as temporally prior to *the rest of the harvest* and (b) the actual situation that **Christ has been raised** (perfect, 15:4, 12, 14, 16, 17, 20), whereas **those in Christ will be raised** (future, 15:22, 49, 51, 52, 54). ἔπειτα indicates a firmly marked sequence: **then** or **afterward**; but may carry more emphasis: *thereafter,* **then afterward**, since it is often used in deliberate "enumerations . . . of time and order."[80]

Those who are Christ's (οἱ τοῦ Χριστοῦ, NRSV, REB, NIV, *those who belong to him*) confirms the soteriological scope of **all** in v. 22b (with Holleman, Fee, and Ortkemper; see above). The Greek background to ἐν τῇ παρουσίᾳ, **at his**

76. Meyer, *First Epistle,* 2:57.

77. Well emphasized by Findlay, *Expositor's Greek Testament,* 2:926. Collins sees vv. 21 and 22 as standing in "synonymous parallelism" (*First Cor,* 548).

78. Lindemann, "Paulus und die korinthische Eschatologie: Zur These von einer 'Entwicklung' im paulinischen Denken," 383; cf. 373-89.

79. Grimm-Thayer, 613; BAGD, 802-3.

80. Grimm-Thayer, 230.

coming, is almost too well known to bear repetition. Although in lexicographical terms παρουσία often denotes *presence,* even *bodily presence* (2 Cor 10:10; Phil 2:12), in eschatological and theological contexts as well as in everyday contexts (2 Cor 7:6, 7) the word also denotes **coming**. As is well known, it may also be used to denote **the coming** *of a person of high rank,* e.g., the visit of an emperor or governor to a province.[81] Recently, however, Moltmann has argued forcefully that *the* **coming** *of God* reflects more accurately than mere *futurity* or *presence* the dynamic nature of the God who *is,* who *was,* and who *is to come* (ὁ ἐρχόμενος, Rev 1:4).[82] God is "in the move and coming. . . . *Futurum* means what will be; *adventus* means what is coming. . . . *Adventus* [cf. *Zukunft*] is . . . a rendering of the Greek word *parousia.*"[83] "What is new . . . does not *emerge* from the old. . . . It is also a new creation . . . creation out of nothing . . . *creatio nova.* . . . Just as the raised Christ does not develop out of the crucified and dead Christ, the *novum ultimum* . . . [although] it is not without analogy. . . . What is eschatologically new creates its own continuity, since it does not annihilate the old but gathers it up and creates it anew" (his italics).[84] This theological background serves to confirm and to give added point to Holleman's exegetical conclusions that in 1 Cor 15:20-28 and elsewhere in Paul the eschatological resurrection of believers takes place at the *parousia.*[85] With regard to v. 23 Holleman simply asserts that here Paul speaks of "two categories. . . . Jesus forms the first category. . . . He will be followed by the second category, those of Christ, at the end of time . . . 'at (the time of) his coming.' . . ."[86]

24-25 (1) παραδιδῷ (as in UBS 4th ed., v. 24, present active subjunctive) reflects 𝔓⁴⁶, A, D; but ℵ reads παραδῷ (aorist subjunctive), while B and G read παραδιδοῖ (which might be indicative, but BDF regard it as subjunctive).[87] The present active subjunctive is sufficiently indefinite with ὅταν to be entirely appropriate, and there is no reason to doubt the UBS text (especially if B is also subjunctive). (2) In v. 25 A and G insert αὐτοῦ after ἐχθρούς to make the **his** of **his enemies** more explicit, but this does not change the meaning and reflects a later addition.

We noted above A. Lindemann's comment that in vv. 23-28 Paul "employs a little apocalyptic drama" as a development of vv. 21b and 22b. He further argues (rightly and with most commentators) that τὸ τέλος in v. 24a does not denote

---

81. References to appropriate literature under each heading occur in BAGD, 629-30.

82. Moltmann, *The Coming of God,* 23.

83. Ibid., 23 and 25. Cf. also Wolff, *Der erste Brief,* 385-86.

84. Moltmann, *The Coming of God,* 27, 28, 29; cf. 22-29. See R. Bauckham (ed.), *God Will Be All in All: The Eschatology of Jürgen Moltmann,* for a critical dialogue between Moltmann and other contributors.

85. Holleman, *Resurrection and Parousia,* 45-47, 56-65, and throughout.

86. Ibid., 52. See further Lindemann, "Paulus und die korinthische Eschatologie," 383; also Lindemann, "Parusie Christi und Herrschaft Gottes. Zur Exegese von 1 Kor 15:23-28," 87-107; Hill, "Paul's Understanding of Christ's Kingdom in 1 Cor 15:20-28," 297-320.

87. BDF, sect. 95.

"the rest" and "thus cannot signify a resurrection of non-Christian human-kind."[88] Lietzmann and Weiss argue the contrary view on two grounds: (a) that the syntax denotes a succession of three events; (b) that Paul alludes to the general resurrection of all expected at the last day.[89] However, it is generally agreed by way of reply that (a) this view does not reflect the lexicographical scope of τὸ τέλος; (b) the syntax and use of εἶτα is far from decisive; (c) Jewish apocalyptic expectation concerns the final resurrection not of all humans but of all "the righteous." A huge mass of commentators from Chrysostom onward through Bengel to the modern era support the view advocated by Lindemann, of which Conzelmann, Wilcke, and Holleman argue the case decisively.[90]

As we observed under Textual Notes to these verses, ὅταν with the present subjunctive παραδιδῷ (or παραδιδοῖ) (or even the aorist subjunctive παραδῷ) leaves the timing unspecific and open-ended. The messianic intermediate reign lasts until two future conditions are fulfilled: (a) Christ **hands over the rule to God** who is also **the Father**; and (b) **he has annihilated** (καταργήσῃ) **every rule and every authority and power.** On καταργέω see above on 1:28 and 2:6 (cf. also 6:13; 13:8, 10, 11 in an eschatological context). The κατά intensive jointly with the alpha privative gives particular force to the notion of *rendering nonoperative,* i.e., **annihilate.** Strictly the Greek syntax τῷ θεῷ καὶ πατρί does *not* mean *to God the Father* (NRSV, REB, NIV, NJB) unless perhaps we understand *to God, even the Father* (AV/KJV), but either *to his God and Father* or **to him who is God and Father** (Barrett).[91] Robertson and Plummer speak of "a reverent reticence and reserve" about an event which is "beyond our comprehension," but they nevertheless make the key point that "sovereignty has been committed to the Son for a definite purpose."[92] Since Christ **died and has been raised**, it remains part of his entailed exaltation to "see through" the consequences of his saving, atoning, and victorious work for the crumbling away not only of individual sin and guilt, but of the hugely serious structural and corporate evil which holds the alienated world under its sway as a consequence of its turning away from God the source of love, justice, and life in illusory self-sufficiency. It is important, however, to recognize that since God and Christ as Lord are "One," this emphasis is not upon a "discontinuation" of Christ's Lordship as such, but upon its culmination within the terms of its purpose for this world and Christ's kingdom here.

88. Lindemann, "Paulus und die korinthische Eschatologie," 383.
89. Weiss, *Der erste Korintherbrief,* 357-58; Lietzmann, *An die Kor,* 1/2:81.
90. Wilcke, *Das Problem eines messianischen Zwischenreichs bei Paulus,* 85-92; Conzelmann, *1 Cor,* 270-71; also Fee, *First Epistle,* 753-54; Barrett, *First Epistle,* 356-57 (with Allo, Héring, Kümmel, and most others). See Holleman, *Resurrection,* 52-55. A longer list occurs in Sellin, *Streit un die Auferstehung,* 264, n. 12; Cf. Collins, *First Cor,* 548: "The parousia of Christ is the end"; and further 552.
91. See Conzelmann, *1 Cor,* 271, n. 79; Weiss, *Der erste Kor,* 358-59; Robertson, *Epistles,* 2:191; Robertson and Plummer, *First Epistle,* 355; Meyer, *First Epistle,* 2:65.
92. Robertson and Plummer, *First Epistle,* 355.

Paul's use of πᾶσαν ἀρχὴν καὶ πᾶσαν ἐξουσίαν καὶ δύναμιν reflects what originally denotes the superhuman agencies of apocalyptic, including demonic powers, but may in Paul indicate *every structural power* against which the individual *qua individual* is helpless and held in bondage as victim. Paul neither asserts nor denies that "demonic" or "supernatural" power may be included, for he sees all oppressive structures which hinder God's purposes or entrap the human person as instruments which, in effect, represent forces which are hostile to God (see above on 2:6 and 2:8).[93] Corporate and structural sin and evil are "bigger" and more sinister than the sum of individual acts and attitude, since they form an oppressive network and godless ethos which holds individual persons in a grip of bondage and evil influence.

Witherington argues in detail that in 15:24b and 28 the destruction of "**all rule, power, and authority** . . ." is probably "counting imperial eschatology . . . which may explain his stress on the fatherhood of **God**, because in the imperial propaganda the emperor was portrayed as not only divine but also as 'father of the fatherland' *(pater patriae)*."[94] He appeals to the work of E. M. Lassen concerning the strength of this image in Roman propaganda not only in Rome and in Italy, but in Roman colonies of which Corinth was a notable example.[95] "Paul is trying to supplant the imperial eschatology which was clearly extant in Corinth and which looked to the emperor as the father and benefactor . . . with an eschatology that involves Christ and a truly divine Father."[96] Without doubt this approach sheds light on Paul's emphasis here. However, it is neither the entire explanation nor an alternative to a more comprehensive understanding of **every rule and every authority and power**, which embodies *any* kind of structural opposition to God, whether social, political, economic, ethical, spiritual, or even (to use a problematic term) "supernatural," i.e., possible agencies beyond this world, although unspecified as such.[97]

Chrysostom understood such **rule** to be simply "that of devils," citing Eph 6:12.[98] Origen identifies the *rulers* of 1 Cor 2:6 as "spiritual powers," while Cyril of Alexandria identifies *rule* in 15:24 with ἀρχῆς ἀπάσης τῶν ἀκαθάρτων πνευμάτων.[99] On the other hand, Calvin explains these as "the legitimate powers which have been ordained by God," and A. Wesley Carr (as we

---

93. 1 Cor 2:6 uses closely similar vocabulary with a nuance of timing which coheres with 15:24, τῶν ἀρχόντων τοῦ αἰῶνος τούτου τῶν καταργουμένων. See also Rom 8:38; Col 1:16; 2:10-15; and material in Eph 1:21; 3:10; 6:12. Hays, *1 Cor,* 265, describes these as "cosmic spheres or forces arranged in opposition to God."

94. Witherington, *Conflict and Community,* 304-5.

95. Lassen, "The Use of the Father Image in Imperial Propaganda and 1 Cor 4:14-21," 127-36, esp. 133.

96. Witherington, *Conflict and Community,* 305. Cf. 295-312.

97. So Meyer, *First Epistle,* 2:64-66, concludes after an extensive review of the history of exegesis.

98. Chrysostom, *1 Cor. Hom.,* 39:6.

99. Origen, *De Principiis,* 3:3:1-3; Cyril of Alexandria, *Fragmenta in Ep. 1 ad Corinthios,* 3:305; also Origen, *Fragments on 1 Cor,* sect. ix, lines 14-15 (on 2:6).

noted in the context of 2:6) advocates an allusion to earthly rulers only.[100] However, Cullmann, Caird, and many others insist that the two views are not mutually exclusive.[101] Conzelmann accepts that apocalyptic implies *demonic powers,* but insists that Paul has "demythologized" these.[102] At all events, the apocalyptic background remains significant as indicating forces from whose power individual human persons cannot extricate themselves through mere determination of will or ethical reform.[103]

From the Church Fathers to the present, writers have asked in what sense Christ, who already rules as exalted *Lord (he has been raised),* does not yet, it appears, have **every rule** under his full control. Luther argues that during this intermediate period "this is a kingdom of faith in which He rules through the Word, and not in a visible, public manner. It is like beholding the sun through a cloud. One sees the light, but not the sun itself. But after the clouds have passed, both light and sun are viewed simultaneously."[104] When the kingdom is **handed over to the Father**, "he [Paul] means to say that He [Christ] will discontinue faith and the hidden essence and present His own to God the Father . . . openly. . . ."[105] Meanwhile "God has hidden himself in Christ, so that we must now seek . . . God only in Him" until we come at the last to see "Him with the Father in divine majesty."[106] Pannenberg describes the contrast less in terms of hiddenness than in terms of scope: "Although he is already Ruler of the world, only at his coming again will Christ annihilate all that possesses lordship, claims power, and exercises force (1 Cor 15:24)."[107]

As Conzelmann observes, the use of δεῖ, **he must** (v. 25), underlines the apocalyptic context of thought: nothing can hinder God's sovereign purposes, and when and how he chooses to enact them.[108] Two issues of translation arise in this verse. First, most English VSS translate θῇ as *(he) has put* (NRSV, REB, NIV, AV/KJV; cf. NJB, *he has made . . .*). The Greek is indeed the second aorist active subjunctive of the verb, but the function of the aorist here is not to indicate time or tense; it is an effective aorist for climax.[109] ἄχρι οὗ θῇ serves to indicate *indefinite future* time: **until he put**. The second issue of translation concerns the subject of the verb: is this *God* (REB) or *"he"* (alluding to *Christ* as

---

100. Calvin, *First Epistle,* 324; A. Wesley Carr, *Angels and Principalities,* SNTSMS 42 (Cambridge: Cambridge University Press, 1981). Grotius also speaks here of "the empires of the world."

101. Cullmann, *Christ and Time,* 191-201; Caird, *Principalities and Power* (throughout).

102. Conzelmann, *1 Cor,* 271-72: "The nonmythological sense is evident from . . . Rom 8:38."

103. Marcus and Soards (eds.), *Apocalyptic and the NT;* D. S. Russell, *The Method and Message of Jewish Apocalyptic* (London: SCM, 1964); and other works cited under 2:6.

104. Luther "1 Cor 7 and 15," *Luther's Works,* 18:124 (*WA,* 569).

105. Ibid., 125 (*WA,* 571).

106. Ibid., 126 (*WA,* 571).

107. Pannenberg, *Systematic Theology,* 3:605.

108. Conzelmann, *1 Cor,* 272; cf. Fee, *First Epistle,* 755, n. 45.

109. Cf. Robertson, *Epistles,* 2:191.

grammatical antecedent, with NRSV, NIV, NJB, AV/KJV)? Barrett and Wolff argue for the former (with some hesitation); Weiss, Conzelmann, and Fee argue for the latter, with fuller and more detailed arguments.[110]

Although it is logical to place the "ultimate" lordship with *God* (Wolff) and to give due weight to the allusion to Ps 110:1, in which *God* is the subject (Barrett), and *Christ* is the one to whom the enemies are subjected in vv. 27-28 (Weiss); the use of Ps 110:1 is an allusion, not a quotation (Conzelmann); and "we must go with the grammar here and see Christ as the subject" (Fee).[111] Since the OT passage is merely allusive, and not an explicit citation, v. 25 does not feature in C. D. Stanley's study of "the language of scripture" in Paul, but R. B. Hays, *Echoes of Scripture,* comments that in 15:25-27 Paul "alludes to Ps 110:1 and Ps 8:6 as prophecies of Christ's enthronement at the right hand of God and ultimate authority over all creation. Thus Paul offers the earliest documentation of a christological exegesis of these psalms."[112] These came to hold a position of importance and influence in the early church (Acts 2:33-36; Heb 1:13; 2:5-9; Eph 1:20-22; Mark 12:35-37).[113] The next three verses explicate the sense of v. 25 further.

26-27 p[46], B, 33, the Vulgate, and some other Latin MSS omit ὅτι before πάντα in v. 27, but ℵ, A, D, F, G, and the Syriac retain it. The case is difficult but of little significance.

It is difficult to do justice to the present passive καταργεῖται in translation. As it stands, the Greek states, **The last enemy** *is being* **annihilated**, *(namely)* **death** (v. 26). It is arguable that Paul uses the present to denote the *process* of annihilation *already set in motion* by Christ's (past) death and resurrection. Thus the "stingless" death experienced by Christians *already represents a partial annihilation of* **death** in its fullest, most terrifying absolute sense (see above). Yet all the main English VSS translate, **The last enemy** *to be destroyed* (NRSV, NIV); *to be deposed* (REB); *to be done away with* (NJB); *that shall be destroyed* (AV/ KJV). The usual explanation for the present is that it expresses the certainty of what lies ahead. Unless we translate it as a process, some such marker as **doomed to be brought to nothing** must be used to indicate that this is not future but at minimum a futurist or "prophetic" use of the present. If, with Barrett, we speak of *robbing death of its efficacy,* the present emphasis more clearly remains.[114] However, Wolff sees this verse as an attack on the Corinthians' obses-

---

110. Barrett, *First Epistle,* 358; Wolff, *Der erste Brief,* 387-88; Conzelmann, *1 Cor,* 272-73; Fee, *First Epistle,* 755-56; Weiss, *Der erste Kor,* 359.

111. Loc. cit., as above.

112. Hays, *Echoes,* 84; cf. Stanley, *Paul and the Language of Scripture,* 206, n. 85.

113. It is impossible to exaggerate the importance of Psalm 110 for the Epistle to the Hebrews. See my commentary on Hebrews in J. W. Rogerson and J. D. G. Dunn (eds.), *Eerdmans Commentary on the Bible* (to be retitled) (Grand Rapids: Eerdmans, forthcoming).

114. Barrett, *First Epistle,* 358; cf. Edwards, *First Epistle* 417-18, on the present.

sion with "now."[115] Thus ἔσχατος is in an emphatic position: death is both an **enemy** (ἐχθρός) and the **last** sequentially to be fully overcome in every sense for all people. Death "forms an obstacle to the all-mightiness of God . . . the empire of death."[116]

Paul now quotes from Ps 8:6 to explain the dynamics of how ἄνθρωπος (as in v. 22), through whom **death** came, can come to receive "dominion over **all things**."[117] Ps 8:5-8 provides a commentary on the creation of humankind in the image of God as God's vice-regent over the earth (Gen 1:26-30). As in Heb 2:5-8, the glorious destiny of humankind to be "crowned with glory and honor" and to receive "dominion over the works of thy hands" (Ps 8:5, 6a) reaches its climax in "Thou hast put all things under his feet" (Ps 8:6b; Heb 2:6a). Heb 2:6b adds, "God left nothing that is not made subject." The author to the Hebrews explains that whereas humankind *qua humankind* failed to achieve what God purposed, through *Jesus* the original role was reacquired, and the sovereignty described in Psalm 110 (LXX Psalm 109) was restored. Paul conjoins the same two psalms in vv. 24-27 here: "Christ as the last Adam, the 'son of man' . . . retrieved the situation which the first Adam lost."[118] Psalm 8 and Psalm 110 stand together not only in Hebrews but also in Eph 1:20-22.

Stanley notes that Paul converts the second person verb of the LXX (πάντα ὑπέταξας, second person aorist active indicative) to the third person first aorist active πάντα (γὰρ) ὑπέταξεν — **he has placed all things in subjection** — and substitutes ὑπὸ τοὺς πόδας αὐτοῦ, **under his feet**, for LXX ὑποκάτω τῶν ποδῶν, which retains the same meaning. After considering other possible explanations, Stanley concludes that Paul is simply making a small change in wording "to conform to his own linguistic usage."[119] The final phrase of the quotation **under his feet** corresponds exactly with the last words of v. 25b. The verb ὑποτάσσω occurred in 14:32 and 34, and is usually translated **put in subjection** (NRSV, REB) but sometimes *put under* (NIV, NJB).[120] The important point, however, is its connection with τάσσω and τάγμα or τάξις, *that which is ordered,* with ὑπό, i.e., *sub-ordinate.* Collins notes "overtones" of military imagery to underline "order" in vv. 24-28.[121]

It might be supposed that in seeking to identify the subject of ὑποτάσσω we need only replay the arguments of Weiss, Conzelmann, Fee, and Collins

115. Wolff, *Der erste Brief,* 388; cf. 1 Cor 3:21, 22.

116. Héring, *First Epistle,* 168. Cf. Isa 25:8; *4 Ezra* 8:53; Rev 6:8; 20:14.

117. Wolff, *Der erste Brief,* 388-89.

118. Bruce, *1 and 2 Cor,* 147.

119. Stanley, *Paul and the Language of Scripture,* 206-7.

120. BAGD, 847-48; Grimm-Thayer, 645. Cf. Rom 13:5; Eph 1:22; Phil 3:21; Heb 2:5, 8b; 1 Pet 3:22; *1 Clement* 2:1. *Subordinate* and *subordination* would more accurately translate the compound verb ὑπό + τάσσω (τάγμα), but attempts to reproduce this in translation result in clumsy and ambiguous English and would not fit all the NT occurrences. Edwards's maxim "there is no τάξις *(order)* without a ὑπόταξις" remains faithful to Paul's thought (*First Epistle,* 409, on v. 20, cited above).

121. Collins, *First Cor,* 553.

(Christ) against those of Barrett and Wolff *(God)*. But, as Fee perceives, this is more than a replication of v. 25b. The subject of ὅταν is not *Christ* either. This second aorist subjunctive need not be taken to denote more than what "it" (i.e., *scripture* or *the psalm*) **says**, in an indefinite context.[122] However, it is also an advance on the argument, for here *God* is implicit in the argument of v. 28, *as well as* the quotation's looking back in corroboration of v. 26.[123] Paul's main point here is that **the last enemy, death**, cannot remain, for then **all things** would *not* have been **placed in submission under his** (Christ's) **feet**. The emphasis lies in πάντα. However, it remains the case also that "δῆλον ὅτι κτλ is a very important point, no mere parenthetical thought. . . . Paul designates God as the *subjecting subject*" (Meyer's italics).[124] Allo cites with approval Barth's particular perspective in vv. 26-28: "Death is the peak of all that is contrary to God in the world, the last **enemy**. . . . That God is all in all . . . must **become** true. . . . To bring about the 'God who is all in all' *such* is the mission and significance of Christ" (Barth's italics).[125] Thus *God* remains the source and goal; *Christ* remains the means through which the goal which God purposes comes to be brought about. This coheres with the emphasis on *the God and Father* (vv. 24 and 28) which Moffatt diagnoses as especially necessary for Corinth, with their emphasis on more "cosy" cult *kyrioi*.[126] (We shall consider Moffatt's approach further under v. 28.)

28 (1) UBS 4th ed. places καί after τότε (before the Son himself) in square brackets. It is omitted by B, D*, F, G, 33, and the Vulgate, but included by ℵ, A, D², and Tertullian. This is finely balanced, and Westcott-Hort also place καί in brackets. If it is included, it may mean either **then** *even* **the Son himself** or **then . . . the Son himself also** (i.e., along with everything else). (2) Tertullian and Ambrosiaster omit ὁ υἱός and leave αὐτός as the subject of the verb, which is clearly secondary and probably theologically motivated.

The "little apocalyptic drama" of vv. 23-28 now reaches its grand climax as Paul discloses the ultimate purpose of the salvific and eschatological "ordered" process.[127] *Christ the firstfruits of the harvest* (v. 20) receives *unlimited dominion,* thereby fulfilling the destiny promised for humankind in Ps 8:6-7 (cf. also Ps 110:1). Nevertheless, not only does "unlimited" exclude God himself (v. 27b); this verse also forms "the frame" with v. 24 by linking **when he hands over the rule to the One who is God and Father** . . . (v. 24) with **that God may be all in all**.[128] We have earlier discussed the relative emphasis which Paul

---

122. Lietzmann, *An die Kor,* 1/2:81; also Conzelmann, *I Cor,* 274. Meyer also suggests that the indefinite construction may carry the force of "a typical declaration" (*First Epistle,* 2:67).

123. Cf. Fee, *First Epistle,* 758, for a careful argument, broadly in these terms.

124. Meyer, *First Epistle,* 2:68-69.

125. Barth, *Resurrection of the Dead,* 178 and 179; cf. Allo, *Première Épitre,* 409.

126. Moffatt, *First Epistle,* 249-51.

127. Lindemann, "Paulus und die korinthische Eschatologie," 383.

128. Harrisville, *1 Cor,* 268.

places in this epistle on *Christ* and **God** who is *Father* (see above, e.g., on 3:23; 11:3; and 15:24). Hays observes, "It is impossible to avoid the impression that Paul is operating with what would later come to be called a subordinationist christology."[129]

Moffatt, however, contextualizes this Pauline emphasis with reference to Corinth. Paul discourages any "notion of a cult of Jesus the divine Lord as practically *everything to every member* [**all in all**] with some vague mysterious idea of God in the background."[130] He argues that in the surrounding Graeco-Roman culture religions "gathered round their own favourite hero or divine figure, Asclaepius, Serapis, and so forth, to whom they offered passionate adoration and with whom they really felt at home, safe and sheltered in their special rites."[131] By contrast, such devotion "hardly ever included any serious reverence for a supreme, central deity over the universe, like Zeus."[132]

Neil Richardson detects such a tendency not necessarily in the church as a whole at Corinth, but probably in the "Christ group" of 1:12.[133] Hence we noted Richardson's examination of "clusters" of passages which emphasize the sovereignty and role of **God**: e.g., 1:26-28, 30; 2:1, 5, 11, 12, 14; 3:6, 7, 9, 23. "All things come from God, including the salvation of the Corinthians (1:30; 8:6; 11:30). . . . All things are destined for God (8:6; 15:28). Christ himself comes from God (1:30; 11:3) and owes allegiance to God (3:23; 11:3; 15:28). The Spirit is the Spirit of *God* (2:10-14; 3:16; 6:11; 7:40; 12:3).[134] The word θεός occurs not only with great frequency but with "often emphatic character."[135] The theme of **God's** power as *choosing, shaming,* or *bringing to nothing* paves the way for ch. 15 in the context of the power of the cross in 1:21, 27, 28 (καταργήσῃ).[136] Paul's thanksgiving "begins and ends with God."[137] With W. Thüsing, Richardson concludes that 15:24 and 28 "are in line with Paul's theology elsewhere."[138]

While all of this may be affirmed, such comments make sense and fail to mislead *only* when we recall that the purposes of **God** and of *Christ* remain *one,* and that any differentiation occurs within the framework of a source, mediate cause, agency, means, and goal which *do not compete* but belong to what Paul and other NT writers (not least John) express as a shared purpose. Hence we should not understate the extent to which such passages as 1 Cor 12:4-7 (cf. 8:6) genuinely reflect what in Christian tradition we call a "trinitarian" perspec-

---

129. Hays, *1 Cor,* 266.
130. Moffatt, *First Epistle,* 250.
131. Ibid.
132. Ibid.
133. N. Richardson, *Paul's Language about God,* JSNTSS 99 (Sheffield: Sheffield Academic Press, 1994), 114-15.
134. Ibid., 115.
135. Ibid., 116.
136. Ibid., 119.
137. Ibid., 304.
138. Ibid., 303; and W. Thüsing, *Per Christum in Deum,* 244.

tive. In general an overreaction against an earlier naïve dogmatics has made us too timid in what we claim for Paul's respective understandings of Christ, the Holy Spirit, and **God**. Twenty centuries of reflection have hardly made it easier for us today *both* to assert the primacy of **God** as source and goal *and* to maintain the mutuality and reciprocity which characterizes God's own self-differentiation as an aspect of his gracious respect for the otherness of the "other" whom the One loves as the self.[139]

Not surprisingly the exegesis of this verse featured prominently in the controversies of the third, fourth, and fifth centuries. Origen expounds this verse in the context of the temporality of the world, which has God as its Source and End.[140] However, he has also to correct the view of "the heretics" who regard the verse as ascribing a "demeaning" subjection to the Son: the emphasis, Origen replies, is on the triumph of God in which the "subjection" of all things is "extremely rational and logical" if God is God and if all things have been restored to their proper order.[141] Chrysostom spreads his comments on v. 28 over what amounts to the equivalent of nearly a dozen columns.[142] This verse, he insists, cannot contradict Christ's exaltation in Phil 2:9. Paul does not say that Christ will cease to reign, only that his reign will not cease before all things have been set to right: Christ will not be "without power."[143] **That God may be all in all** means that **all things** may be "dependent on him."[144] This change of emphasis reflects a history of debate in which Arians appealed to this verse for a subordinationist Christology. Augustine is still more emphatic. "We should not think that Christ will so give up the kingdom to God, even the Father, that he shall take it away."[145] In 1 Cor 15:24-28 "he must reign" determines the relativity of "until." Thus *when he hands over the rule to God* (v. 24) means "when he shall have brought believers to the contemplation of God," while "subjection" to God (v. 28) means change from "the substance of a creature" (in the incarnation) to "become the substance of God."[146] Augustine's treatise *On the Trinity* ends with the acclamation of "the one God, the Trinity," as He who remains "**all in all**."[147]

It is understandable that the posthistory of these verses especially in the

---

139. See Pannenberg, "The Reciprocal Self-Distinction of Father, Son and Spirit as the Concrete Form of Trinitarian Relations," in *Systematic Theology,* 1:308-19 and 259-336; J. Moltmann, *The Trinity and the Kingdom of God* (Eng. trans., London: SCM, 1981), 61-65 and throughout, and *The Spirit of Life* (Eng. trans., London: SCM, 1992), 58-81 and 289-310; and E. Jüngel, *The Doctrine of the Trinity* (Eng. trans., Edinburgh: Scottish Academic Press, 1976).

140. Origen, *De Principiis,* 3:5:6.

141. Ibid., 3:5:7.

142. Chrysostom, *1 Cor. Hom.,* 39:7-17.

143. Ibid., 39:8 and 9.

144. Ibid., 39:11 (with Theophylact and Photius).

145. Augustine, *On the Trinity,* 1:8:16.

146. Ibid., 1:8:15.

147. Ibid., 15:28:51. Ambrosiaster, Athanasius, and Theodoret argue (cf. 12.12) that Christ identifies himself with his church in such a way as to appropriate the "subjection" of the church.

patristic period should invite extreme caution about the possible imposition of later doctrine onto 15:27-28. However, we should not overreact. It is possible to do full exegetical justice to the Pauline passages in the light of the many factors that historically and theologically shape Paul's thought in this specific context.

The purpose clause ἵνα ᾖ ὁ θεὸς πάντα ἐν πᾶσιν requires further comment. **That God may be all in all** (NRSV, NIV, NJB, AV/KJV, Barrett; cf. *will be all,* REB) is the usual translation, understanding ἐν πᾶσιν as probably neuter plural, not least in the light of the parallel in Rom 11:36.[148] Moffatt and Collins, however, translate **so that God may be** *everything to everyone* (taking ἐν πᾶσιν as masculine to mean "with nothing to impair the communion between the Father and all who belong to Christ his Son."[149] **All,** however, should be interpreted not only in the light of the later parallel in Rom 11:36 (ὅτι ἐξ αὐτοῦ καὶ δι' αὐτοῦ καὶ εἰς αὐτὸν τὰ πάντα) but also the specific content of 15:54b-58: death, sin, the law, and the emptiness of fruitless activity. Hence M. C. de Boer and Wolff regard πᾶσιν is neither exclusively neuter (although **all things** are involved) nor exclusively masculine (although **all** concerns the domain of human as well as cosmic life) but "*the totality* of the world experienced by human beings . . . 'all things' *vis à vis the human world* . . . the universe in which all human beings live (cf. 8:6; Rom 11:36; Col 1:16)" (de Boer's italics).[150]

Although the expression τὰ πάντα was used in Stoic thought to denote the universe and "the All," the dynamic, eschatological movement of Pauline thought precludes any affinity with Stoic pantheism. Far from identifying God with "the All," Paul sees God as the source and goal of a world in need of reconciliation and salvation through (δι' αὐτοῦ, Rom 11:36) God in Christ.[151] Schweitzer comments that whereas "in the Stoic view the world is thought of as static. . . . The world is Nature. . . . Paul lives in the conception of the dramatic world-view characteristic of the late Jewish eschatology. . . . He concludes . . . 'For *from* Him and *through* Him and *unto* Him are all things' (Rom xi:36); but he cannot . . . add that all things are *in* God" (his italics).[152] Into this frame of reference Schweitzer places 1 Cor 15:26-28, with its conscious emphasis on succession and purposive process.[153]

If such dynamism characterizes the living **God,** will his purposive action cease even when he is **all in all**? As de Boer affirms, this **all** relates to "our"

148. With Robertson and Plummer, *First Epistle,* 358: "must be neuter"; Findlay, *Expositor's Greek Testament,* 2:930; Conzelmann, *1 Cor,* 275; Fee, *First Epistle,* 759-60; Strobel, *Der erste Brief,* 253; Senft, *Première Épitre,* 200.

149. Moffatt, *First Epistle,* 249; Collins, *First Cor,* 547 and 555; also Meyer, *First Epistle,* 2:69-70. Collins includes God's "enemies" in the masculine gender, as those reconciled.

150. De Boer, *Defeat of Death,* 125-26; also Wolff, *Der erste Brief,* 390.

151. Cf. Marcus Aurelius, 4.23.2; de Boer, *Defeat of Death,* 224, n. 109; Senft, *Première Épitre,* 200; Héring, *First Epistle,* 168-69.

152. Schweitzer, *Mysticism of Paul,* 11. If this is overpressed, it drives a wedge between the Paul of the major epistles and the Paul of Acts 17; but as a provisional generalization it indicates Paul's characteristic stance.

153. Ibid., 12-13.

universe. Moltmann and Bauckham discuss in what sense succession and temporality (but not "human" time) may continue beyond the End (see on 15:44-45).[154]

29 D² and Peshitta replace the final αὐτῶν with τῶν νεκρῶν, but this is clearly late and secondary.

In vv. 29-34 Paul turns from his majestic contemplation of God's ordered eschatological, sovereign purposes to resume his emphasis on the *consequences of denying the resurrection*. The thought begun in v. 20 confirmed the *cause and ground* for such belief; vv. 29-34 focus on the *consequences* of belief or unbelief in terms of a consistency and ethics of lifestyle: (a) baptism for the sake of (or for) the dead would be senseless if resurrection is denied (v. 29); (b) Paul's own sacrifice of his life would be equally pointless and stupid (vv. 30-32a); (c) why not go the whole way and relapse into a lifestyle concerned only for pleasure in this life (vv. 32b-34)?

Verse 29 is a notoriously difficult crux: the most "hotly disputed" in the epistle (Conzelmann); "it is not clear precisely what this practice was" (Dale Martin); "everything must be understood as tentative" (Fee); a variety of understandings emerge "given the enigmatic nature of the practice" (Collins).[155] By 1887 Godet had counted "about thirty explanations" for **baptized for the dead**," while B. M. Foschini and R. Schnackenburg allude to "more than forty."[156] Wolff's commentary includes seventeen subcategories with seven issue-centered general approaches.[157] A vast literature stretches from the second century to the present day. Mathis Rissi devoted an entire book to this one verse, categorizing a mass of views on the history of interpretation under four main groups, with variations in each group. (a) One category adds σωμάτων to ὑπὲρ τῶν νεκρῶν, and identifies **the dead** with those who are being **baptized**. (b) A second view understands **baptism** as the suffering and death of *martyrdom*. (c) A third interprets **baptism** broadly as *washing* (where the Hebrew but not the Greek may use a common word). (d) The fourth understands this as *vicarious baptism* on behalf of people who are **dead**. Rissi rejects the "sacramentalism" often implied in this.[158]

One problem arises from how we understand Gk. ποιέω in τί ποιήσουσιν,

154. R. Bauckham (ed.), *God Will Be All in All* (Edinburgh: T. & T. Clark, 1999), esp. Bauckham, "Time and Eternity" (155-226), and Moltmann's response (227-32).

155. Conzelmann, *1 Cor,* 275; Martin, *The Corinthian Body,* 107; Fee, *First Epistle,* 767; Collins, *First Cor,* 559.

156. Foschini, "'Those Who Are Baptized for the Dead': 1 Cor 15:29," *CBQ* 12 (1950): 260-76 and 379-88; also 13 (1951): 46-78, 172-98, 276-83; Schnackenburg, "Baptism for the Dead," in Schnackenburg, *Baptism in the Thought of Paul,* 95-103.

157. Wolff, "Exkurs: Deutungsvorschäge zu 1 Kor 15:29," in *Der erste Brief,* 392-96.

158. Rissi, *Die Taufe für die Toten.* The literature beyond 1962 is also vast, and still continues, e.g., White, "'Baptized on Account of the Dead': The Meaning of 1 Cor 15:29 in Its Context," 487-99.

but the key issues depend on the force of ὑπέρ with the articular genitive plural noun τῶν νεκρῶν. Other major issues concern possible connections of thought with what precedes or follows, and speculations about possible punctuation.

The semantic range of ποιέω is vast, as the sheer column-inches in BAGD and Grimm-Thayer bear witness, although proportionally much less space is devoted to the word in Liddell-Scott-Jones or Lampe's *Patristic Greek Lexicon*.[159] The relevant possibilities for exploration in this verse may be summarized as (a) *achieving, bringing about;* (b) intransitive *doing* as an activity; (c) *fashioning,* perhaps in an indulgent, self-generating way; and (d) *doing* with a future to indicate the subjective dimension also implicit in (c), i.e., doing *in terms of what one* **thinks** *one is* **doing**. (i) NJB's *What are people up to who . . . ?* is very tempting and could be right. We included it as our translation in an earlier draft, but it misses the *subjective* dimension which several writers perceive (probably rightly) here. Worse in this respect is (ii), *What do they achieve . . . ?* (cf. Grotius, *"quid efficient?"*). P. Bachmann, A. Schlatter, and Barrett (in part) argue for this view, but Meyer comments that a notion of "achievement" by baptism would be "a thought foreign to the apostle. He wished to point out the subjective absurdity of the procedure."[160] (iii) Weiss understands τί ποιήσουσιν as "indeed of course a mode of logical future," but renders it, "What should they resort to. . . . What will they do in the future?"[161] This accords with Barrett's second point that the future may convey the force of, *What will they do next?* (i.e., when it is discovered that there is no resurrection).[162] Barrett agrees that the net force is subjective or self-involving: "Will not these people look fools when . . . ?" (iv) NRSV, NIV, *what will they do . . . ?* (with Wolff and Collins) is similar, but loses both the logical and subjective force.[163] (v) Curiously REB underlines the subjective aspect, but transfers this to the readers rather than those to whom the text refers: *What do you suppose they are doing?* (vi) Moffatt can find more lexicographical support than we might imagine for *What is the meaning of people getting baptized . . . ?* and is a possible way forward. (vii) All in all, **What do those people think they are doing who . . . ?** does justice to (a) the use of the future as a *logical* present; (b) the *subjective* or self-involving aspect; (c) an open-ended appeal to them to reflect on their *self-consistency* of thought and action; and (d) the *wide semantic range* of the word.

159. BAGD, 680-83; Grimm-Thayer, 524-27; cf. LSJ, 1,234-35; and Lampe, *Patristic Greek Lexicon,* 1,107-8.
160. Schlatter, *Die Korintherbriefe,* 201-22, although he concedes that "there is no certain meaning; Meyer, *First Epistle,* 2:72; Barrett, *First Epistle,* 362.
161. Weiss, *Der erste Kor,* 365.
162. Barrett, *First Epistle,* 362.
163. Wolff, *Der erste Brief,* 396; Collins, *First Cor,* 556.

MULTIPLE INTERPRETATIONS OF "BAPTISM FOR THE DEAD" AND OUR CONCLUSION

We must now enumerate the main interpretations of the notorious phrase ὑπὲρ τῶν νεκρῶν, translated *on behalf of* **the dead** in NRSV, REB, NJB, and Barrett, or **for the dead** (NIV, AV/KJV), or **for the sake of the dead**, our translation, following Findley, Raeder, Howard, Collins, and Schnackenburg.[164] (If **for** is understood in its "final" sense, this is also acceptable.) It would detain us unduly to enumerate the many which scarcely deserve thought, but we shall cite (A) *ten which are on the whole unconvincing,* together with (B) *a further three which are either widespread* (11, 12) or (in the last case) *highly probable* (13).

(A)(1) Theodore Beza (d. 1605), Heinrich Bullinger (d. 1575), and J. Cocceius (d. 1669), followed in modern times by J. M. Ford, understand οἱ βαπτιζόμενοι as *"qui ablutione utuntur,"* i.e., *washing.*[165] Beza forced the Greek syntax to mean who wash their dead [for burial]"; Cocceius, "who wash themselves from ceremonial defilement by touching a dead body." Neither the syntax nor the context nor (here) lexicography can support this.

(A)(2) John Lightfoot (d. 1664) understood τῶν νεκρῶν to refer to the dying martyrs, and interprets *baptism* metaphorically to refer to *the baptism of suffering and martyrdom.* This would fit Paul's point about resurrection and also 15:30, but strains τῶν νεκρῶν unduly. Wolff observes that no such role is ascribed to martyrs at such an early time.[166]

(A)(3) Thomas Aquinas and Nicholas de Lyra (d. 1349) identify ὑπὲρ τῶν νεκρῶν with *mortal sins,* for the sake of which people are baptized, but this is anachronistic and violates exegetical criteria.

(A)(4) Luther, followed in the modern period by H. Ewald and in part by F. Grosheide, understand ὑπέρ in its local sense of *above,* and interpret **the dead** as representing *the tombs* or *the graves of the dead.* Grosheide observes, "**The dead** in our context always represents the group of the dead as a whole, not individual dead persons." He considers it possible, but not certain, that "some at Corinth had themselves baptized above the graves, namely of relatives who had died in Christ."[167] Luther first considers "vicarious" baptism and rejects it. The background is "escorting the dead to their graves with honor" as the joint context with baptism as a sign of the reality of the hope of resurrection.[168] However, this local use of ὑπέρ is less common in Koine than in classical Greek and apparently foreign to the NT, and there is no evidence of any special attention to tombs of Christians in c. AD 54-55.[169]

(A)(5) Bengel, Flacius, and Calvin follow Epiphanius in regarding the context as probably that of *the deathbed.* Bengel comments on the variety of theories, and con-

164. Findlay, *Expositor's Greek Testament,* 2:931; Raeder, "Vikariastaufe in 1 Cor 15:29?" 258-61; Howard, "Baptism for the Dead: A Study of 1 Cor 15:29," 137-41; Schnackenburg, "Baptism for the Dead," 102; Collins, *First Cor,* 556.

165. Ford, "Rabbinic Humour behind Baptism for the Dead (1 Cor XV:29)," in Cross (ed.), *SE,* 400-403; cf. Wolff, *Der erste Brief,* 394, sect. 4.

166. Wolff, *Der erste Brief,* 392, sect. 1 (c).

167. Grosheide, *First Epistle,* 372 and 373.

168. Luther, "1 Cor 15," *Luther's Works,* 28:151-52 (*WA* 36:605).

169. Cf. the criticisms of Meyer, *First Epistle,* 2:74 and 75; Wolff, *Der erste Brief,* 392, sect. 1(b); and in M. Rissi, *Die Taufe.*

cludes: *"Nec martyria, nec baptismi super sepulcris, etc . . . sed eo tempore quum mortem ante oculos positam habent . . . vel decrepitam aetatem . . . vel per martyrium."*[170] Calvin concedes that he changed his mind about the meaning. "I used to think that Paul was pointing out the all-embracing end of baptism here, for the benefit of baptism is not confined to our life here." But closer study, Calvin argues, suggests that Paul has in mind those "who have given up hope of life," perhaps especially catechumens who had fallen ill and were "clearly in imminent danger of death."[171] Calvin's allusion to "the Fathers" who report the infiltration of superstition well fits the allusion to this verse in Epiphanius. Epiphanius explains it as the *clinici,* catechumens on their death-bed.[172] P. Bachmann supports this view, but Meyer insists that this forces the Greek of v. 29.[173]

(A)(6) H. Olshausen (see also in Preisker, below) offers at first sight what hardly seems to be a serious view, but Edwards and others regard it as linguistically and exegetically possible. He interprets the Greek "who are baptized to fill the place of the dead": a definite number (πλήρωμα) need to be baptized.[174] If Edwards is correct about the force of ὑπέρ, the one conceivable merit here is continuity with the eschatological drama of vv. 22-28. Yet this idea seems foreign to Paul, and very few accept it in the end.

(A)(7) John Edwards (1692) interprets this verse as referring to **people who have themselves baptized** as converts because they have witnessed the radiant confidence and courage of the martyrs.[175] Paul witnessed the martyrdom of Stephen in this way. Yet many argue that the force of ὑπέρ becomes strained, and it is not clear why Paul should use οἱ βαπτιζόμενοι rather than οἱ πιστεύοντες.[176]

(A)(8) Chrysostom, Theophylact, Photius, and Erasmus understand τῶν νεκρῶν as an ellipsis reflecting *the baptismal creed* in faith: τοῦ νεκροῦ σώματος ἀνάστασιν πιστεύων, i.e., *believes* and *expects* the resurrection **of the dead**.[177] **The dead** refers to "soon to be" dead bodies. Chrysostom utterly rejects the view of "baptizing *in place of the departed*" as a *Marcionite heresy* fit for "people out of their mind . . . and exceedingly simple."[178] Such would be an easy solution, if it did not import into the Greek an additional phrase which is absent: this seems hardly an "elliptic" use of τῶν νεκρῶν without further explanation. Nevertheless, it carried favor in the patristic era.[179]

(A)(9) W. E. Vine repunctuates the verse to give it a different meaning, following a proposal by Sir Robert Anderson (1905) to read: *Otherwise, what shall they do who are baptized? It is for dead persons if the dead do not rise.*[180] A full stop or period separates ὑπὲρ τῶν νεκρῶν from οἱ βαπτιζόμενοι, and more especially from ποιήσουσιν. This

170. Bengel, *Gnomon,* 667.
171. Calvin, *First Epistle,* 330.
172. Epiphanius, *Against Heresies,* 28:3.
173. Meyer, *First Epistle,* 2:74; Bachmann, *Der erste Brief,* 457.
174. Olshausen, *Biblischer Commentar über sämmtliche Schriften des NT* (1840), ad loc.
175. Edwards, *Enquiry into Four Remarkable Texts* (1692).
176. See Edwards, *First Epistle,* 422-23, for the criticisms.
177. Chrysostom, *1 Cor. Hom.,* 40:2.
178. Ibid., 40:1.
179. See further Fee, *First Epistle,* 766.
180. Howard, "Baptism for the Dead: A Study of 1 Cor 15:29," 138; and Sir Robert Anderson, *The Bible or the Church* (London, 1905), 234.

is suggestive but strains the syntax.[181] As Fee observes, "none [of these] is compelling."[182]

(A)(10) J. Murphy-O'Connor refers to the early tradition of understanding baptism as sharing in Jesus' "cup" of suffering and death (Mark 10:39; cf. Luke 12:50; Rom 6:3). In line with the possible jibe against Paul as a "dead foetus" (or however we translate ἐκτρώματι in 15:8), the "spiritual elite" at Corinth use derogatory slogans about Paul which here he seeks to turn around against them to support his argument about resurrection.[183] **Baptized for the dead** originated as an anti-Pauline slogan concerning Paul's suffering and support for an inferior class of believer who is **dead** to true "wisdom." Ironically Paul asks whether such work would continue if there were no resurrection. The strongest arguments for this are (a) the close link with v. 30; (b) the close connection between baptism and death (cf. Mark 10:39 and the work of Cullmann and others on such passages); and (c) the Corinthian use of slogans, e.g., clearly 6:12; 10:23, and several others); and (d) Paul's delight in turning round the slogans against them. Against Murphy-O'Connor's view is its speculative nature and lack of clear linguistic support. Although recently J. L. White has argued that the phrase may allude to the apostles, Wolff, on the other side, draws attention the the awkward syntax of καὶ ἡμεῖς in v. 30 if Paul is an implicit referent behind the allusion of v. 29.[184] The idea deserves serious thought, but fails to carry conviction. White correctly points out that the immediate context refers to dangers which Paul faces (vv. 30-31), but it is more precarious to suppose that he defines "apostle" as one of "the dead" in the present verse.

(B)(11) A large number of writers insist that v. 29 concerns *vicarious baptism.*[185] *This is the first of the three views (under B) which deserve more prominence* **either** *because, as with (11) and (12), they are widespread and influential,* **or** *because, with (13), they are the most probable and relatively convincing.* Conzelmann declares, "The wording is in favor of the 'normal' exposition in terms of 'vicarious baptism': in Corinth living people have themselves vicariously baptized for dead people." Collins offers a similar view.[186] This shows the "sacramentalism" prevailing in Corinth, and "Paul does not criticize the custom but makes use of it for his argument."[187]

(B)(11)(a) Schmithals is so confident about this view, especially in the light of al-

181. Cf. Bachmann, *Der erste Brief,* 457.

182. Fee, *First Epistle,* 766.

183. Murphy-O'Connor, "'Baptized for the Dead' (1 Cor XV:29): A Corinthian Slogan?" 532-33.

184. Wolff, *Der erste Brief,* 395; cf. White, "'Baptized on Account of the Dead': The Meaning of 1 Cor 15:29 in Its Context," 487-99.

185. This is supported by Conzelmann, Schmithals, Lietzmann, Weiss, Oepke, Wendland, Parry, Hays, Allo, Collins, and many others. But we must distinguish between (i) Schmithals' basis in gnosticism; (ii) Hans von Soden's sacramentalism; (iii) Preisker's nonsacramentalist "Jewish" approach in terms of the blood of the martyrs; and (iv) a careful softening by Hays and restriction by Allo which puts this view just within the bounds of remote possibility.

186. Conzelmann, *1 Cor,* 275; Collins, *First Cor,* 559, proposes "some sort of transferred application of benefits, a vicarious effect (cf. 11:24)." Collins appeals to the arguments of R. E. DeMaris about the part played by death in first-century Corinthian thought, but DeMaris's work may equally argue for (B)(13), which (following Raeder and Howard) is our own view (see under (B)(13) below).

187. Conzelmann, *1 Cor,* 275.

leged gnostic influence and that of the hellenistic mystery religion, that he asserts: "It is absurd to dispute this, as Bachmann and Schlatter, for instance, have attempted to do in a more than dubious fashion."[188] In the light of such an immoderate statement, it is scarcely surprising that Conzelmann describes this verse as "hotly disputed." This "baptism by proxy," Schmithals observes, "was common among Gnostics" (and apparently may occur in some form in Mormon circles on occasion today).[189] Indeed, in Gnosticism, Schmithals claims, baptism for the dead has greater significance than for the living.[190] "The effect of the baptism for the dead was magical in nature," and such gnostic texts as *Pistis Sophia,* Schmithals concludes, offer parallels with 15:29.[191] Weiss, Lietzmann, and Wendland argue for vicarious baptism, citing allusions in Tertullian, Chrysostom, and Epiphanius to the practice among Marcionites and other sects.[192]

(B)(11)(b) Some have attempted to argue for vicarious or "proxy" baptism in a sense which depends less on a history-of-religions context than that urged by Schmithals. Wedderburn sees it as baptism on behalf of unbaptized Christians.[193] However, the *opus operatum* "sacramentalism" postulated by Hans von Soden has lived on until the last few years, when the tide has turned.[194] Horsley retains the view that some "were baptized vicariously on behalf of deceased friends and relatives."[195] However, H. Preisker finds a different apocalyptic background in, e.g., 4 Ezra 4:35; 1 Enoch 47:4; Rev 7:2-4 which leads him to declare, "Vicarious baptism is thus not sacramental, but an eschatological use."[196] Preisker argues that the connection lies with the apocalyptic verses 24-28, and therefore presupposes a background of the resurrection of the righteous. Those standing "near" to them could benefit from their deeds by proxy. This view is rightly criticized by Schnackenburg as "unacceptable."[197] Parry more generally concludes: "The plain and necessary sense of the words implies the existence of a practice of vicarious baptism at Corinth, presumably on behalf of believers who died before they were baptized."[198]

(B)(11)(c) Some softening of what constitutes a version of this view comes from Allo and from Hays in different ways. Allo cites the very case of catechumens who, in their own baptism, wish to be identified with the dead of their family in near or actual Christian faith, i.e., without an "official" baptism but with "a baptism of desire."[199] In this one specific instance, it might be understandable if for pastoral reasons Paul refrains from questioning what has been done. This makes further possible sense if,

188. Schmithals, *Gnosticism in Corinth,* 257; cf. 257-59.

189. Ibid., 258.

190. Ibid.

191. Ibid., 259.

192. Weiss, *Der erste Kor,* 363; Lietzmann, *An die Kor, I/II,* 82; and Wendland, *Die Briefe,* 150.

193. Wedderburn, *Baptism and Resurrection,* 288-89.

194. Hans von Soden, "Sakrament und Ethik," esp. 22-40.

195. Horsley, *1 Cor,* 206-7.

196. H. Preisker, "Die Vakariatstaufe 1 Cor 15:29 — ein eschatologischer — nicht sakramentaler Brauch," *ZNW* 23 (1924): 298-304.

197. Schnackenburg, "Baptism for the Dead," in *Baptism in the Thought of Paul,* 97.

198. Parry, *First Epistle,* 228.

199. Allo, *Première Épître,* 411-14, citing Chrysostom, Tertullian, and Bachmann, as well as wider patristic material.

with Hays, we call to mind the "less individualistic" view of Paul than that of modern Protestant thought: "the community can act meaningfully on behalf of those who are not able to act on their own behalf."[200] This specific principle is *in part* instantiated in Anglican and Protestant traditions which practice infant baptism, and Hays also notes that Paul does not "commend" vicarious baptism: he merely points out that to practise it while doubting the resurrection would be self-contradictory.[201]

Many remain unconvinced by this view, both in the patristic era and in recent years, as well as among the Reformers. Murphy-O'Connor declares: "The difficulty . . . is that Paul's understanding of the way the sacraments work would never have permitted him to condone such superstition in any of his churches. . . . The dead cannot make the act of faith that saves (Rom 10:9)."[202] Further, although many argue that Paul does not necessarily approve of this practice, the transition to v. 30 through καὶ ἡμεῖς seems to suggest a continuity of practice which has Paul's approval, and this is scarcely conceivable, even if we grant that the "special case" proposed by Allo might well merit a pastoral blind eye. *The ferocity with which Tertullian and especially Chrysostom view such a practice and characterize it as bizarre among heretics should not too easily be forgotten or swept aside.*

As Kistemaker observes, if those for whom baptism is received by proxy are *dead Christian believers,* how can this salvation be doubted *if they are indeed believers,* whether or not they have been formally baptized?[203] Paul nowhere stipulates that baptism is a *necessary condition* of salvation; only that it is a *normal and appropriate* visible mark of union with Christ and of sharing in Christ's death and resurrection through grace in the wider experience of conversion-initiation. Perhaps few writings have done more to disengage the actual rite of baptism from *absolute identification with the wider complex of conversion-initiation* than James Dunn's work on baptism and on "baptism in the Holy Spirit." He observes, "It is clear from Rom 6:4 that the rite of baptism *usually played a part* in helping bring about the reality depicted by the metaphor of being baptized. . . . 'Baptized in Spirit' is even more clearly an *initiatory* metaphor . . . baptized in Spirit *into Christ.* . . . Paul's correction of elitist spiritualities in Corinth . . . almost reads like a correction of some of the similar misconceptions in modern Pentecostalism. . . ."[204] Without doubt, 1 Cor 15:29 alludes to the *practice,* not the *metaphor,* of baptism; but the wooden literalism that ascribes to Paul indifference to a practice of proxy baptism as "achieving" something for dead believers (let alone for dead *unbelievers*) sidesteps recent research on Paul's broadly nuanced understanding of baptism (see also on 1:14-17, above, which is relevant here).

Above all, it is those who hold a *high* view of the rite of baptism who find baptism for the dead most difficulty: would not Paul deeply care if this important rite, with all its *self-involving role as an effective sign of grace,* is reduced to a mere *in-*

---

200. Hays, *1 Cor,* 267.

201. Ibid., 267 and 268.

202. J. Murphy-O'Connor, *1 Cor* (Oxford: Albatross, 1997 ed.), 178. It is noteworthy that this outspoken comment comes from a Catholic biblical scholar. Cf. also Murphy-O'Connor, "'Baptized for the Dead' (1 Cor XV:29)," cited above.

203. Kistemaker, *1 Cor,* 559.

204. J. D. G. Dunn, "The Birth of a Metaphor — Baptized in Spirit," *ExpTim* 89 (1978): 175; cf. 134-39 and 173-76; and esp. Dunn, *Baptism in the Holy Spirit* (London: SCM, 1970).

strumental mechanism?[205] This emerges in the detailed study by M. Rissi to which we have referred.[206] If baptism entails a serious appropriation of the grace of identification with Christ in his death and resurrection, how can the context be other than that of believers, or (in a later second-generation context) an initiating plea for grace on the presupposition of nurture within a Christian home and family? The state of the dead hardly seems to allow for a serious understanding of what baptism represents and entails. E. Stauffer's countersuggestion that the rite would represent an "intercessory" baptism for the dead on the analogy of "offering (or atonement) for the dead" by Judas Maccabaeus (2 Macc 12:45; cf. vv. 39-44) is too slender and tenuous to bear the weight of such an extension of the theology of baptism.[207] Downey's counterargument about baptismal protection from "principalities and powers" in the afterlife also goes beyond Paul's own theology of salvation and its sacraments.[208]

(B)(12) A variant of the above (which might have been categorized as [11][d]) is advocated most clearly and sharply by H. Alford (1881), although rather differently expressed by Heinrici and in part by Rissi. Alford declares, *"The only legitimate reference* is to a practice . . . not mentioned here with any approval by the Apostle . . . in use by some of the survivors allowing themselves to be baptized on behalf of (believing?) Friends who had died without baptism. . . . But . . . Paul does *not* mention it without a slur on it" (his italics).[209] Needless to say, Alford refers to references in Tertullian, Chrysostom, and Epiphanius in which the Fathers repudiate the practice as non-Christian or heretical.[210] Since the practice (if it existed) "dwindled away," it may be inferred that this is something "with which he [Paul] could have no real sympathy."[211] This is confirmed by the nuance of τί ποιήσουσιν; (see above): "There is in these words a tacit reprehension of the practice about to be mentioned, which it is hardly possible to miss."[212] Heinrici is far less emphatic than Alford about the nature of Paul's reserve, but it features in his argument.[213] Senft cites this approach as originating with Ambrosiaster.[214] However, once again, Rissi looks at Paul's theology of baptism and the work of Christ as a whole, and like Murphy-O'Connor cannot concede that Paul would be indifferent to some instrumentalist view of its nature in isolation from a

---

205. Is it a coincidence that Murphy-O'Connor and Schnackenburg are among the most emphatic critics of this view while many liberal Protestants from the early or mid-twentieth century readily accept it.

206. Rissi, *Die Taufe für die Toten,* emphasizes the reality of *dying with Christ* in the context of *baptismal confession.*

207. Cf. E. Stauffer, *NT Theology* (Eng. trans., London: SCM, 1955), 202 and 299.

208. J. Downey, "1 Cor 15:29 and the Theology of Baptism," *Euntes Docete* 38 (1985): 23-35.

209. H. Alford, *Greek Testament,* 4 vols. (London: Rivingtons and Cambridge: Deighton, Bell, 1881), 2:612.

210. Tertullian, *On the Resurrection of the Flesh,* 48; *Against Marcion,* 5:10; Chrysostom, *1 Cor. Hom.,* 40; Epiphanius, *Against Heresies,* 6. Chrysostom is more condemnatory than Tertullian, who simply asks whether, given their beliefs at Corinth, there could be any benefit from such a practice.

211. Alford, *Greek Testament,* 2:613.

212. Ibid., 611.

213. Heinrici, *Das erste Sendschreiben,* 513-18.

214. Senft, *Première Épitre,* 202.

more adequate context.[215] The difficulties which beset (B)(11) also apply, even if less forcefully, to this proposal, together with an apparently more abrupt switch to the positive in v. 30.

(B)(13) In 1955 Maria Raeder (following G. G. Findlay) explicated more clearly than before a view which had been hinted at in earlier theories, namely that **baptism for the sake of (ὑπέρ) the dead** *refers to the decision of a person or persons to ask for, and to receive, baptism as a result of the desire to be united with their believing relatives who have died. This presupposes that they would share the radiant confidence that they would meet again in and through Christ at the resurrection of the dead.*[216] As a pupil of J. Jeremias, Maria Raeder was well aware of linguistic issues and argues convincingly that this coheres well with uses of the preposition ὑπέρ, in the "final" sense of *for*, i.e., **for the sake of**. Indeed, it is regularly so used in the context of the work of Christ and the earliest kerygma, and coheres well with Robertson and Plummer's proposed baptized out of consideration for the dead.[217] If we consider such a scenario as that of a godly parent who longs for a son or daughter to come to faith, the nuance of ὑπέρ as *for the sake of* (in pragmatic terms) makes sense.

Our Conclusion

J. K. Howard fully supports and develops this view against those which favor vicarious baptism. He writes that **baptism for (for the sake of) the dead** is "not in order to remedy some deficiency on the part of the dead, but in order to be reunited with them at the resurrection."[218] Schackenburg agrees that "the argument does not step outside the frame of primitive Christian views and above all fits excellently into the resurrection chapter."[219] The linguistic force of ὑπέρ, **for the sake of**, is preserved, together with a convincing nonmetaphorical meaning for both τῶν νεκρῶν (**the *Christian* dead**) and the middle-voice force of οἱ βαπτιζόμενα, **those who have themselves baptized**. We may return to G. G. Findlay's succinct and careful comments. After exposing the fallacy of some competing views, he observes, "Paul is referring rather to a much commoner, indeed a normal experience, that the death of Christians leads to the conversion of survivors, who in the first instance 'for the sake of the dead' (their beloved dead) and in the hope of re-union, turn to Christ — *e.g.*, when a dying mother wins her son by the appeal 'Meet me in heaven!' Such appeals, and their frequent salutary effect, give strong and touching evidence of *faith in the resurrection*" (Findlay's italics).[220]

The supposed objection that such conversion would depend on mixed motives in the first place merely finds replication over the centuries in many pastoral situations, and, second, should not obscure the focus of the confident witness to Christ and to the resurrection which such a plea transparently presupposed. From a dying loved one, this would carry enormous weight. There is no room for pretense or self-

215. Rissi, *Die Taufe*.
216. Raeder, "Vikariastaufe in 1 Kor 15:29?" 258-61.
217. Robertson and Plummer, *First Epistle*, 345 (cf. 359-60).
218. Howard, "Baptism for the Dead: A Study of 1 Cor 15:29," 140-41; cf. 137-41.
219. Schnackenburg, "Baptism for the Dead," 102.
220. Findlay, *Expositor's Greek Testament*, 2:931.

interest on a deathbed: the sincerity and transparency of faith and witness become overwhelming. Of two recent articles, the work of R. E. DeMaris on archaeological evidence concerning the importance of the world of **the dead** in mid-first-century Corinth carries weight, but may in effect count equally in favor of the "vicarious baptism" view or this final argument.[221] For the more significant the fate of the dead, the more important and effective would be the plea of the deathbed Christian, with a view to reunion in the afterlife. On the other hand: most of the arguments against view (11) still apply. J. D. Reaume's recent article, however, confirms the direction of our own arguments.[222] *We see no reason to reject this view* (B)(13) *as the least problematic and most convincing of all.*

30-31 (1) In v. 31 a number of important early MSS include the vocative ἀδελφοί after καύχησιν, i.e., ℵ, A, B, as well as 33, Coptic, and the Vulgate. However, it is omitted by the earlier 𝔭46, together with D, F, G, L, the Syriac, and Ambrosiaster. On the ground that its insertion is so much easier to explain than its omission, and the combination of 𝔭46 and the Western text, most writers regard the 𝔭46 reading as correct. UBS 4th ed. places it in square brackets (as does the 1979 ed. of the Nestle-Aland text). Metzger explains that "the Committee was reluctant to drop it from the text altogether" because of its inclusion in ℵ, A, and B; but ranked it as "C," i.e., difficult to decide upon with certainty.[223] NRSV, NIV, and REB retain it (NRSV, NIV, *brothers and sisters;* REB, *my friends);* but NJB (surely rightly) omits it (as does AV/KJV). Why should this term of affection have been omitted by the varied traditions from which it is absent, unless they reflect the text? (2) The objective use of ὑμέτεραν (pride in which I hold you) was misunderstood by some scribes, and thus A and some miniscules read ἡμέτεραν in its place to reflect the subject or active agent.[224] The UBS 4th ed. is well attested, and it is correct as it stands. (3) D* with Ambrosiaster omits ἡμῶν after τῷ κυρίῳ. In spite of Zuntz's defense of the shorter form, it is universally agreed that the text as it stands, *Christ Jesus our Lord,* is correct.[225]

καὶ ἡμεῖς should be construed together as **we, too** or *we also;* καί does not qualify the sentence as a whole but specifically **we**.[226] **We** may refer primarily to **we** *apostles,* but Paul does not explicitly restrict it to one category of Christian work or witness. κινδεύνω means *to be in danger, to stand in jeopardy,* or (in this context) **to let our lives be put at risk**.[227] πᾶσαν ὥραν emphasizes the un-

---

221. DeMaris, "Corinthian Religion and Baptism for the Dead (1 Cor 15:29): Insights from Archaeology and Anthropology," 661-82. Recent firsthand observation of archaeological data and museums at Corinth and elsewhere in Greece convince us of the general point, but not that it counts against (13) above.

222. Reaume, "Another Look at 1 Cor 15:29, 'Baptized for the Dead,'" *BSac* 152 (1995): 457-75.

223. Metzger, *Textual Commentary* (2d ed.), 501; cf. Zuntz, *Text,* 176-77.

224. Cf. Fee, *First Epistle,* 761, n. 3, for an excellent assessment, with literature.

225. Cf. Zuntz, *Text,* 182, against Fee, *First Epistle,* 761, n. 4, and others.

226. As Barrett, *First Epistle,* 364, insists.

227. Grimm-Thayer, 347; Robertson and Plummer, *First Epistle,* 360-61; and others well underline the passive or middle sense of the active form.

interrupted nature of the experience: **every hour of the day**, *all hours, hour by hour, on an hourly basis.*

In v. 31 καθ' ἡμέραν, *every day, day by day,* **from day to day**, carries the same emphasis. ἀποθνῄσκω is difficult to translate accurately. If this carries forward the theological allusion implicit in baptism, it might mean: *I continue to die, my process of death goes on.* We may compare 2 Cor 4:10, πάντοτε τὴν νέκρωσιν τοῦ Ἰησοῦ ἐν τῷ σώματι περιφέροντες, *always carrying about the dying of Jesus in my body.* On the other hand, in 2 Cor 1:9 *we have the sentence of death in us* seems contextually to allude to the physical, psychological, and spiritual experience of *coming to the end of ourselves,* i.e., *our life and strength are gone, everything depends on God alone who raises us from the dead.* The connection with vv. 30 and 32 suggests that here, too, the **dying** is more than metaphorical in the sense of relating to events in the public domain of the world. We might have translated *every* **day** *we are at death's door.* NRSV, NIV, and Collins keep the options open but remain relatively uninformative by replicating the Greek: *I die every day* (as also REB, *every day I die*), which has the merit of faultless accuracy but without contextual explication. NJB therefore risks *I face death every day,* which is faithful to v. 30 as its parallel clause but seems to carry less force than *I die.* After considerable lexicographical and exegetical research, we propose **From day to day I court fatality**, since this combines (a) *facing death* (v. 30), (b) living out an *identification with the death of Christ* voluntarily assumed, and (c) accepting the *vulnerability and fragility* of life in Christian service in the confident expectation of sharing in Christ's resurrection and *being raised* at the last day.[228]

Paul uses an idiom associated with taking an oath or with "affirming" in a quasi-legal sense. Grimm-Thayer notes concerning νή: "a particle employed in affirmations and oaths (common in Attic) and joined to an acc of the pers (for the most part, a divinity) or of the thing affirmed or sworn by . . . [often best translated as] **by** . . . 1 Cor 15:31 (Gen 42:15, 16)."[229] BAGD's entry is similar: "strong affirmation," with examples from Epictetus and the papyri.[230] The accusative that denotes what Paul **affirms** *or* swears **by** (νή) is τὴν ὑμετέραν καύχησιν, *the [act of] glorying in you* (see Textual Note [2] above). Robertson and Plummer approve of Rutherford's "*I assure you* **by the** [brotherly; see Textual Note (1)] **pride** *in your faith with which I am possessed* **in Christ Jesus our Lord**.

How can this be communicated in modern idiomatic English? The *New Oxford Dictionary of English* (1998) offers examples of current usage which include *I swear* **by all that I hold dear** *that . . . ,* which seems to reflect precisely

---

228. Cf. Hays, *1 Cor,* 268, "Paul has repeatedly put his own life and health at risk in order to proclaim the gospel (see, e.g., 4:11-13; 2 Cor 4:8-12; 6:3-10; 11:23-33). If there is no resurrection, why should he bother?" Wolff also compares "a daily death" in 2 Cor 4:10-11, which is more than physical but not less (*Der erste Brief,* 397-98).

229. Grimm-Thayer, 425.

230. BAGD, 537; Epictetus, *Dissertations* 2.20.29; *Papyrus Oxyrhynchus* 939:20. Cf. BDF, sect. 149.

Paul's parallel idiom.[231] Simultaneously he "**affirms**" (as if by a formal oath) that (a) the **risks** and **fatality** to which he alludes are no mere rhetorical exaggeration, but a reality of life grounded in a reality of theology; and (b) the thing that is most **dear** to him [not in the Greek] is his **pride** in what they are **in Christ Jesus our Lord**, and thus it is **by** them and their status in God's grace and shared Christ-union with Paul that he chooses "to affirm." People *swear* or **affirm** only by divinity of **by** something of *ultimate importance* to them.[232] Here is a succinct pastoral theology of the *risks, fragility,* and *dearest, deepest concerns* of a pastor who is willing to sacrifice all for the gospel in the light of the gathering together of all at the resurrection.[233]

32 κατὰ ἄνθρωπον is placed first for emphasis within the protasis of the conditional. It is more likely that it qualifies ἐθηριομάχησα than the apodosis τί μοι τὸ ὄφελος (the latter in the older 2d ed. of the RSV and REB; the former with NRSV, NIV, NJB, AV/KJV, although REB attempts to let it govern the whole sentence). NRSV renders κατὰ ἄνθρωπον as *with merely* **human** *hopes* (in effect also REB); NIV has **human** *reasons.* NJB is better with **human** *perspectives,* since the Greek simply calls attention *to the limitation of the* **human**, even if *hopes* is implicit in the resurrection context and *reasons* in the subsequent reference to *gain* or **profit**. However, the proper term for denoting the *limitations* of a merely human view is **only with human horizons**, i.e., *with horizons that reach neither beyond the grave nor beyond human capacities to the power of God* (see vv. 34 and 38, which focus *precisely on this latter issue, not* simply the former).[234]

Fighting with wild beasts (θηριομαχέω) occurs in the aorist, normally to depict a past event, but since Paul writes from Ephesus, **I have battled** becomes the normal English equivalent.[235] Some allude to being forced to fight with wild animals as a punishment for an alleged or actual crime (Diodorus Siculus, 3.43.7 [first century BC]; Josephus, *Wars* 7.38; Ignatius, *Letter to the Ephesians,* 1:2; *Letter to the Trallians,* 10). However, Ignatius uses the compound verb both literally (as above) and metaphorically: from Syria to Rome I fight with wild beasts, bound to ten leopards, that is a detachment of soldiers (Ignatius, *Letter to the Romans,* 5:1).[236] Luther and Calvin discuss in detail forms of per-

---

231. *New Oxford Dictionary* (Oxford: Clarendon, 1998) 1873, col. 1, under "swear." Compare Fee's correct comment, "He swears by that which is dearest to him, their own existence in Christ, which also came about by labors that had exposed him to such dangers" (*First Epistle,* 770).

232. The AV/KJV *I protest* makes sense only with the presupposition that Paul vividly imagines that he can actually hear a denial or objection. REB and NJB offer no connective, but NRSV and NIV render, *is as certain* or *just as surely.* We have inverted the negative of the AV/KJV to read **oh yes —** . . . .

233. See Luther, "1 Cor 15," *Luther's Works,* 28:152-54: "I am not doing this for honour. . . ." (cf. 1 Cor 4:9); *WA,* 36:608-9.

234. As Robertson and Plummer comment, "the exact meaning of κατὰ ἄνθρωπον (3:3; 9:8; Rom 3:5; Gal 1:11; 3:15) depends on the context" (*First Epistle,* 361).

235. Edwards, *First Epistle,* 428.

236. Cited by BAGD, 360-61.

secution at Rome which entailed battling with wild beasts, but these historically belong to a later date than around 54-55.[237] Weiss and Héring regard the allusion as literal but also as merely hypothetical, which seems to reduce the force of an argument which rhetorically demands a climax or peak.[238] On the other hand, Héring's argument that as a Roman citizen Paul could not have been submitted to such a punishment equally points in the direction of metaphor. The catalogue of sufferings in 2 Cor 11:23ff. also makes no mention of this experience. Even if Weiss and Héring can overcome the grammatical problem of the indicative, most understand it as metaphor. Fee contends that it "must be" metaphor, while Collins sees a metaphorical allusion to the *agōn* motif as more probable than some hypothetical event.[239] Tertullian regarded it as a metaphorical allusion to the tumult narrated in Acts 19.[240] R. E. Osborne and A. J. Malherbe consider alternatives and conclude that metaphor is clearly used here.[241] Wolff compares the experience of Paul's coming to this end of himself (or "receiving a sentence of death"): "we even despaired of life" (2 Cor 1:8-11).[242] In 1 Cor 16:9 Paul alludes to continuing opposition at Ephesus.

Paul asks what **profit** (τὸ ὄφελος) could be derived *for him* (μοι, **for me** as a dative of advantage) **if dead people are not raised**. This emphatically does *not* mean: "if I will not survive to see the result and gain a reward." Paul's thinking is neither so individualist nor so pragmatic nor so self-centered. The **profit** which he seeks as "the dead foetus" raised to life (15:8) is to have a share in the gathering around the throne of God when the whole reconciled people of God shall enter fully into the purposed eschatological salvation. *Suffering* has its role in this eschatological and corporate context. Otherwise everything becomes empty, fruitless, and profitless, and his tenacity was for nothing. The Greek contains no verb behind our English **could there have been**. A verb has to be supplied, and **could** emphasizes the *logical* force of the *conditional* assertion.

Paul now quotes words of despair about a life with nothing beyond the dissolution of personal existence as the end. Is he quoting from Isa 22:13, or from an Epicurean slogan, or from an anti-Epicurean slogan which offers an ironic overstatement of Epicurean philosophy? C. D. Stanley does not include the quotation in his *Paul and the Language of Scripture.*[243] Although he omits it

237. Luther, "1 Cor 15," *Luther's Works,* 156 (*WA,* 36:612-13); Calvin, *First Epistle,* 332-33.

238. Weiss, *Der erste Kor,* 365-55, with a lengthy discussion of nearly two pages; Héring, *First Epistle,* 171, "A further hypothetical element . . . 'Suppose that I had fought against beasts. . . .' The indicative would be used to express an unfulfilled condition."

239. Fee, *First Epistle,* 770; Collins, *First Cor,* 557.

240. Tertullian, *Resurrection,* 48.

241. R. E. Osborne, "Paul and the Wild Beasts," *JBL* 85 (1966): 225-30; and A. J. Malherbe, "The Beasts at Ephesus," *JBL* 87 (1968). 71-80. Malherbe compares hellenistic material from Cynic ethics. Osborne refers to a Jewish background (1QpHab 11:16–12:5 et al.).

242. Wolff, *Der erste Brief,* 398-99; also Wolff, *Zweiter Kor,* 25.

243. On the other hand, Stanley's criteria are rigid.

from his *Echoes of Scripture in the Letters of Paul,* Hays observes in his commentary that such scepticism as is envisaged would lead the readers to act "like the frenzied inhabitants of Jerusalem who faced siege and annihilation at the hands of the Assyrians (Isa 22:12-14): instead of facing their fate with repentance and weeping, they decided to 'party like [i.e., as if] there were no tomorrow' . . . quoted from Isa 22:13."[244] In practice virtually all major commentators assume or argue that Paul quotes from this passage.[245] The question which arises is simply whether this quotation *also* coincides with a quotation from hellenistic philosophical or ethical controversy. Epicureanism in its sophisticated form is more than crude materialism, but its opponents readily characterized it as such, especially in popular Stoic-Cynic circles. As Fee reminds us, Plutarch speaks of a life of "**eating and drinking**" as a dissolute and empty life, with an anti-Epicurean *Tendenz*.[246]

The two sources together form an admirable, logical, and rhetorical bridge to vv. 33-34, as Eriksson points out. Both Isa 22:13 and "contemporary anti-Epicurean polemic" equally "designate the libertinist life. . . . Paul uses it to point to the utter futility of a life without the motivation given by the resurrection of Christ."[247]

33-34   The UBS 4th ed. text rightly reads ὑμῖν λαλῶ, **I tell you**, at the end of v. 34. A, F, and G contain a scribal change to λέγω on the assumption that the latter would be more appropriate for a solemn utterance. Clearly, however, then, words serve as synonyms in most contexts for Paul.

These two verses, especially v. 34, express the *theological* heart of the chapter and the hinge of the argument. *Knowledge of* **God** (God's resources, God's grace, God's transformative action through Christ) holds the key to understanding what the resurrection is actually about.[248] The interrelationship between this knowledge of **God** and daily **lifestyle** is also fundamental. These verses also provide a magnificent workshop for demonstrating significant nuances of grammar and vocabulary.

The first negative imperative is in the present tense, μὴ πλανᾶσθε, which generally (unless the context suggests otherwise) means *cease to err; no longer be led astray;* or **stop being seduced**. It has the force of "*do not go on* **being seduced**." πλανάω also means more than *going wrong* in this context, as the next quotation indicates.

---

244. Hays, *1 Cor,* 268. *Echoes of Scripture* is not intended to be comprehensive in its work on Paul.

245. For example, Wolff, *Der erste Brief,* 399; Fee, *First Epistle,* 772; Conzelmann, *1 Cor,* 278; Weiss, *Der erste Kor,* 366; Héring, *First Epistle,* 172; Barrett, *First Epistle,* 367.

246. Plutarch, *Moralia* 1098C, 1100D, 1125D, well cited by Fee, *First Epistle,* 770.

247. Eriksson, *Traditions as Rhetorical Proof,* 266.

248. This emphasis dominates Barth, *Resurrection of the Dead,* esp. 17-18, 113, 127, 179, 189-97, and is strongly defended in Thiselton, "Luther and Barth on 1 Cor 15," in Stephens (ed.), *The Bible, the Reformation and the Church,* 258-89.

Jerome seems first to have attributed the quotation to Menander's comedy, but there is clear evidence that it had also become a popular maxim.[249] Paul may well have heard it cited more than once as a maxim, and we may infer neither knowledge nor ignorance of Greek literature on Paul's part from this quotation. ὁμιλίαι deserves a carefully nuanced translation. It does indeed denote *association, intercourse, company,* and then by extension a *speech* or *sermon.*[250] However, it conveys the notion of a *clique,* a *group,* or a *"gang"* who regularly do things together and to which people "belong." Hence we translate **belonging to bad gangs** for ὁμιλίαι κακαί. The usual translation is **bad** *company* (NRSV, REB, NIV, NJB; as against AV/KJV, *evil communications*). But this loses the force of the peer pressure experienced from an "in" group with which a person's life has become closely bound.

The next translation issue concerns the force of ἤθη in the phrase ἤθη χρηστά. Here the English VSS do follow different paths: *good morals* (NRSV, Collins), *good character* (REB, NIV, Moffatt), *good ways* (NJB, Barrett), good manners (AV/KJV), *good habits* (W. F. Beck). The use of ἤθος (singular) or ἤθη (plural) to denote *custom* or *habit* is found from early classical Greek (Herodotus, Hesiod) through the Pauline period (Philo, *De Specialibus Legibus* 2.104) to the subapostolic period (*1 Clement* 21:7) and in the papyri (*Papyrus Oxyrhynchus* 642).[251] However, with χρηστά, *good habits,* or a *habituated good disposition,* is, in Greek and in modern ethics, what we call (and the Greek called) a *good character.* Both *habits* (Beck) and *character* (REB, NIV) can be defended. On this basis the habit of practising the *good* may also be perceived as a matter of *morals* (NRSV). The factor which has been neglected, however, remains that of the *expression* of *character* or *habit* in the public domain, which argues for *good ways* (NJB and Barrett's first preference; his second choice is *character*).[252] Since the date of many of these discussions the term **lifestyles** has emerged in common English usage to denote a combination of virtually all of these aspects, including *morals, character, habits,* and *ways.* It even includes the attitude of respect or disrespect for others (cf. 1 Corinthians 8–10) which AV/KJV conveys in the older sense of *manners.* Hence we propose our translation above.

We cannot know whether Paul has in mind a **bad gang** of complacent and sceptical "strong" within the church (Héring; cf. D. B. Martin) or whether he is concerned about the infiltration of non-Christian values through heightened social intercourse and influence from outside.[253] Either or both of these provide

---

249. Menander, *Thais,* Fragment 218; cf. also Euripides, *Fragments* 1,013; Diodorus Siculus, *History* 16.54.4 (period of Augustus); Philo, *Deterius Potiori Insidiari Soleat* 38.

250. BAGD, 565.

251. See the standard range of lexicons, e.g., BAGD, 344.

252. Barrett, *First Epistle,* 367.

253. Héring sees "no need" to look beyond Christians in negative groups within the church (*First Epistle,* 173), while Martin argues precisely that the resurrection issue "divided the Corinthian church along social status lines. The Strong, influenced by popular philosophy to deprecate the body, opposed the idea of a resurrected body" (*The Corinthian Body,* 107; cf. 104-36).

practical pastoral warnings based on good social psychology for today. The pressures imposed by "in-groups" are very strong, and a climate of so-called postmodernity encourages such groups to assume that no shared arbitration is possible or necessary within some larger frame of rationality or worldview.

ἐκνήψατε δικαίως also allows more than one possible translation (cf. *come to a sober and right mind*, NRSV; *wake up from your stupor as you should*, NJB). The verb ἐκνήφω, of which this is the aorist imperative, occurs only here within the NT. But its regular meaning in Greek occurs in the LXX in the sense of *returning to one's self from drunkenness, becoming sober* (Grimm-Thayer), as in Gen 9:24; Joel 1:5; or to mean *to come to one's sens*es (BAGD) in Plutarch, Demosthenes, and other Greek authors.[254] The coupling of δικαίως with *rousing oneself from drunken stupor* has been understood in two quite distinct ways, in accordance with the fact that the Greek relates *either* (a) to moral or relational *rightness* or (b) to *conformity to an appropriate norm* which need not always be specified. On the basis of the second meaning Barrett rightly observes: "*Wake up properly* (δικαίως, not *righteously;* for this sense see Kümmel). . . ."[255] The metaphor requires an English rendering which somehow combines (a) *waking* to a clear *mind* after drunken stupor; (b) waking up to reality, i.e., *coming to one's senses, in place of a fantasy, escapist world;* (c) regaining a necessary, *proper sobriety.*

The meaning of δικαίως is more likely to be *properly* (Barrett, Collins), *as you ought* (NIV), or *as you should* (NJB), than *rightly,* or *with a righteous resolve* (Robertson and Plummer). In this context *properly* is shown to depend for its substance on proper accordance with *the norms of realism and sobriety,* as against triumphalism, complacency, or fantasy about anticipation in the present of all spiritual power and status. Horsley speculates about the "bad conversations" of *gnosis* and the awakening from dreams about *Sophia.*[256] Lang more convincingly alludes to the fantasies of the *intoxicated "highs"* of those who styled themselves as "people of the Spirit (*das schwämerische Hochgefühl der korinthischen Pneumatiker . . . ;* cf. 4:8)" against which Paul calls for "true eschatological 'realism.' "[257] To be "drunk with the Spirit" may be a critic's perception of an undue elation which devalued sober argument and attention to rational truth claims grounded on common traditions as against "the experiences of our group." If such is the case, δικαίως denotes *with due sobriety* (cf. REB) after a "drunken" away trip. Recognizing the combined force of the aorist imperative and intensive adverb we translate: **Come to your senses; wake and sober up**.

The aorist stands between two negative continuous present imperatives. Each cannot but emphasize the other. Hence the meaning of μὴ ἁμαρτάνετε is

254. BAGD, 243; Grimm-Thayer, 198.
255. Barrett, *First Epistle,* 367.
256. Horsley, *1 Cor,* 208.
257. Lang, *Die Briefe,* 231.

cease to sin, stop doing wrong, or (impossible to improve upon, with NJB) **leave sin alone**. Most English VSS retain Paul's theological word **sin** (rightly) since here an attitude toward **God**, other people, credal issues of faith, and conduct of life are all at issue. Paul regularly regards **sin** less in terms (if at all) of *acts* (plural) of commission or omission than as an *attitude, stance, and state* in which the human will is granted "autonomy" to turn away from God and to seek self-gratification as the chief end of human life.[258]

"**Some people**" simply represents τινες, but picks up the resonance to the Greek ear of the **some** of 15:12 who have, in effect, been the "opponents" for the whole of the treatise from 15:1 up to this point. The first word (before γάρ) in the key clause is ἀγνωσίαν. Whatever our theories about *gnosis,* **knowledge**, in this epistle, it is clearly a favorite word of "the strong" at least. *"We all have gnosis"* (8:1, in our group?) is characteristically followed by *"But it is not the case that everyone* [in the church at Corinth] *has 'knowledge'"* (8:7). Some (τινες) remain more vulnerable (8:8-13). It would be easier to translate simply **some have** utter ignorance of **God**, which would preserve Paul's word ἀ-γνωσίαν and its emphasis. But the alpha privative ἀ γνωσίαν permits the word-play on **knowledge** to be recognized (e.g., in Eng. *unknowledge* or *non-knowledge; ignorance* loses the resonance). To add weight to the solemnity of Paul's ringing indictment we translate γάρ, *for,* after τινες as **you see** (i.e., in a *logical* sense **"some people," you see, have an utter lack of "knowledge" of God**). We need some such word as **utter** (not in the Greek) because ἀγνωσίαν ἔχειν "means more than ἀγνοεῖν" in Paul and in much biblical tradition. It is often synonymous, Edwards notes, with a darkened pre-Christian state (*1 Clement* 59). Since it often characterizes the Gentile mind, the thought seems to be, "Some of you are cherishing that ignorance of God which belongs to the heathen."[259]

Knowledge of God is the linchpin of Paul's whole argument. As we have observed, in Barth's view "This 'of God' [cf. 1 Cor 4:5] is clearly the secret nerve . . ." (cf. 1 Corinthians 1-4 and the whole epistle, not least 1 Corinthians 15).[260] Kennedy notes that the only link between *bare grain* or a "rotting corpse" (15:37) and the whole resurrection σῶμα (15:58) is "the sovereign power of God."[261] *The infinite resourcefulness of God* as already demonstrated in his sovereign power and wisdom as creator is the only answer to the "conceivability" of resurrection "bodies" (15:35-45). A dead person cannot contribute to his or her own *"being brought to life."* Even the resurrection of Jesus of Nazareth was enacted by the sovereign power of God (see above, esp. on

258. Even if Pannenberg, *Systematic Theology,* 2:231-76 (cf. also 218-31), is strictly part of a "systematic theology" of the late twentieth century, few writers have more accurately captured and conveyed Paul's perspective than Pannenberg in these pages. See esp. 232-40 on Paul prior to the constructive examination of Augustine.

259. Edwards, *First Epistle,* 430.

260. Barth, *Resurrection,* 18 (Germ. *Auferstehung,* 4).

261. Kennedy, *St Paul's Conceptions of the Last Things,* 243.

the passive voice of the verb). Everything depends on God, "who gives life to the dead and calls into existence the things that do not exist" (Rom 4:12).[262] I have argued for the centrality of this theme for the logic of ch. 15 elsewhere.[263]

Not surprisingly Paul makes this an issue of what mattered perhaps most of all in a culture oriented to the scale of *honor and shame* (see above on 6:5, *it is to make you ashamed that I say this to you*). We have only to recall the importance of honor and self-praise, instantiated in rhetoric, benefactions, and monuments, to recall how sensitive the readers (esp. "the strong") would be to praise in their honor or to accusations which would bring **shame**. Bruce Winter includes an illuminating set of contrasts placed on the honor-shame scale with reference to 1 Cor 1:26-28: "Status in secular Corinth: σοφοί, δυνατοί, εὐγενεῖς" (versus τὰ μωρά . . . τὰ ἀσθενῆ . . . τὰ ἀγενῆ . . . τὰ ἐξουθενημένα . . . τὰ μὴ ὄντα), side by side with the Sophists' list which begins ἔνδοξοι, πλούσιοι, ἡγεμόνες . . . up to twelve terms.[264] Andrew Clarke similarly, as we have noted above, demonstrates "self-praise" as "a widely accepted practice. . . ."[265] Almost nothing could have brought home to the group or groups in question in ch. 15 the enormity of their attitude on their own ground. This verse thus forms the hinge to vv. 35-58, where Paul argues on the basis of the reality of God's creative and sovereign agency through Christ by the Spirit.

C. HOW CAN "THE RESURRECTION OF THE BODY" BE INTELLIGIBLE AND CONCEIVABLE? — SECOND *REFUTATIO* AND *CONFIRMATIO* (15:35-58)

(35) Nevertheless, someone will voice the objection: How are the dead raised? With what kind of body can they come? (36, 37) You nonsense person! What you sow is not brought to life unless it dies. And as to what you sow: it is not the body which is to come about that you sow but a bare grain, perhaps of wheat, or something else. (38) But God gives to it a "body," just as he purposed, that is, to each of the various kinds of seeds its own perishable body. (39, 40) All flesh is not the same flesh. There is human flesh; a different flesh that pertains to animals, another to birds, and another to fish. There are also super-earthly bodies, and bodies for beings of earth. But what gives to super-earthly bodies their particular splendor is one thing; while that of the bodies of those who live on earth is quite another. (41) The splendor of the sun is one particular thing; the splendor of the moon is another; and the stars

---

262. As in Wendland, *Die Briefe,* 151; Lang, *Die Briefe,* 231.

263. Thiselton, "Luther and Barth on 1 Cor 15," in Stephens (ed.), *The Bible, the Reformation and the Church,* 258-89.

264. B. W. Winter, *Philo and Paul among the Sophists,* SNTSMS 96 (Cambridge: Cambridge University Press, 1997), 192 and 193.

265. Clarke, *Secular and Christian Leadership,* 98.

have yet another splendor of their own. For one star differs from another star in splendor. (42) Thus it shall be with the resurrection of the dead. What is sown in decay is raised in decay's reversal. (43) It is sown in humiliation; it is raised in splendor. It is sown in weakness; it is raised in power. (44) It is sown an ordinary human body; it is raised a body constituted by the Spirit. If there is a body for the human realm, there is also a body for the realm of the Spirit. (45, 46) In this sense it is written, "The first human being," Adam, "became a living human person." The last Adam became a life-giving Spirit. However, it is not the One who is of the Spirit that came first, but the one who was purely human, and after that the One of the Spirit. (47, 48) The first man is "from earth's soil, made from dust"; the second man is from heaven. The one from dust is the model for people of dust; the One from heaven models those who pertain to heaven. (49) Even as we have worn the image of him who was formed from earth's dust, so we shall wear also the image of the heavenly one. (50) This I affirm, my dear friends: flesh and blood cannot inherit the kingdom of God; neither can decay come into possession of that which is free from decay. (51, 52) Look! I am telling you a mystery. Not all of us humans will fall asleep in death, but all of us will undergo transformation: in an instant, in the blinking of an eye, at the sound of the last trumpet. For the trumpet will give its signal, and the dead will be raised without degenerating decay, and we shall be transfigured into another form. (53) For this body which is subject to decay must become clothed in that which cannot wear out, and this mortal body shall put on what is incapable of dying. (54, 55) When this body subject to decay comes to put on that which will not decay, and when this mortal body comes to put on what cannot die, then shall come into force the declaration of scripture: "Death has been swallowed up in victory. Death — where is your victory? Death — where is your sting?" (56) Now the sting of death is sin, and the power of sin comes from the law. (57) But thanks be to God, who gives us the victory through our Lord Jesus Christ. (58) Therefore, my very dear fellow Christians, stand firm, immovable, abounding more and more without measure in the work of the Lord always, knowing that your labor is not fruitless in the work of the Lord.

Eriksson's recent rhetorical analysis coheres well with emphases identified in some older modern works (Weiss, Kennedy, and Robertson and Plummer) and in some more recent works (M. M. Mitchell, D. F. Watson, and Wolff).[1] Eriksson writes: "A new round of argumentation with *refutatio* and *confirmatio* starts in 15:35. . . . The question concerns the nature of the resurrection, the stasis of quality signaled by πῶς. . . . The question is more closely specified as ποίῳ δὲ

---

1. Eriksson, *Traditions as Rhetorical Proof,* 267-75; Weiss, *Der erste Kor,* 367-70; Robertson and Plummer, *First Epistle,* 365-73; Kennedy, *St Paul's Conceptions of the Last Things,* 239-62; Mitchell, *Rhetoric of Reconciliation,* 289-90; Watson, "Paul's Rhetorical Strategy in 1 Cor 15," in Porter and Olbricht (eds.), *Rhetoric and the NT,* 244-49; Wolff, *Der erste Brief,* 401-12.

σώματι ἔρχονται; this puts the emphasis on the definition of the resurrection body."[2]

The second *refutatio* (vv. 35-49) exposes the fallacy of the argument that bodily resurrection is logically unintelligible, and in any case inconceivable, by two refutations:

(1) The *exclamatio* (not merely an emotive outburst, ἄφρων σύ, v. 36a) rejects the false assumption that the transformed resurrection "body" (σῶμα) is the same as the body which is sown in death, any more than a flower or fruit is like its seed (even through its identity remains as *this,* not *that*); and (b) the *exclamatio* picks up the allusion to utter lack of knowledge of God (v. 34b) and refutes the notion that intelligibility or conceivability could have any logical currency *apart from the frame* (cf. the logical *enthymeme* that *God the creator gives it* the appropriate σῶμα determined by *his* purpose, wisdom, and resourceful design, not by the limits of human imagination, v. 38).[3]

These two themes of (a) *differences between "bodies"* and (b) the *infinite resourcefulness of the sovereign God already observable in creation* run throughout vv. 35-49, where the climax of the *refutatio* is found both in the transformative role of the Holy Spirit (v. 44) and the contrast between the first Adam of the old order and the last Adam whose image believers will bear (vv. 45-49). Weiss, Watson, and Wolff also note the important role of πῶς, **how**, in the mouth of the opponent or objector (ἀλλὰ ἐρεῖ τις . . .), while Mitchell, Kennedy and Robertson and Plummer (also with Wolff and Watson) note the key role played in Paul's rhetoric or enthymic logic by ὁ δὲ θεὸς δίδωσιν αὐτῷ σῶμα καθὼς ἠθέλησεν.[4]

(2) The second *confirmatio* is identified by Eriksson with vv. 50-57, although Watson argues that the *confirmatio* begins at 44b. Eriksson contends that v. 49 summarizes vv. 35-48 by applying the Adam-Christ analogy to the question of the resurrection body. This is confirmed, in our view, by its reflecting the climax of the "contrast" argument of the *refutatio*. The second *confirmatio* (vv. 50-57) then expounds the *gospel principle of transformation* in terms of *the future*. Eriksson believes that "the cutting edge of Paul's argument is directed to those who maintain a present resurrection."[5] He also rightly accepts the special importance of Jeremias's article on the *propositio* of v. 50 in which *flesh and blood* (which cannot as they stand inherit the eschatological kingdom of God) await *transformation* from their frail, vulnerable, sinful state marked by decay (ἡ φθορά) and "wake" to a transformed condition of glory in which "we shall all be *changed*" instantaneously, as when a sleeping army is

---

2. Eriksson, *Traditions,* 267.

3. On Paul's use of enthymemes, see Moores, *Wrestling with Rationality in Paul.*

4. Mitchell, *Rhetoric of Reconciliation,* 289; Watson, "Rhetorical Strategy," 245; Kennedy, *Last Things,* 242-47; Wolff, *Der erste Brief,* 402-3; Weiss, *Der erste Kor,* 367. Cf. also Bünker, *Briefformular,* 59-72. Kennedy observes that καθὼς ἠθέλησεν, **as he wills**, is in the *aorist* to denote the final act of God's sovereign will (following Edwards, *First Epistle,* 434) to determine its nature.

5. Eriksson, *Traditions,* 272.

roused by the signal of the trumpet (v. 52). The concluding paean of praise embodies a theology of victory over sin, death, and bondage to the effects of past actions (i.e., the law, vv. 54-56), the ground of which remains God's sovereign grace through Christ (v. 57). The final verse (v. 58) returns to *holding fast* to the gospel translation (15:3-6) in theology and in everyday lifestyle as a consequence (ὥστε) of vv. 3-57.[6] On this basis nothing is "in vain."

Supplementary Bibliography on 15:35-58 (Additional to Bibliographies at 15:1 and 15:12)

Altermath, F., *De corps psychique au corps spirituel. Interprétation de 1 Cor 15:35-49 par des auteurs des quatre premiers siècles,* BGBE 18 (Tübingen: Mohr, 1977).

Bonneau, N., "The Logic of Paul's Argument on the Resurrection Body in 1 Cor 15:35-44a," *ScEs* 45 (1993): 79-92.

Burchard, C., "1 Kor 15:39-41," *ZNW* 74 (1983): 233-52.

Carrez, M., "With What Body Do the Dead Rise Again?" *Conc* 10:6 (1970): 92-102.

Cavalin, H. C. C., *Life after Death: Paul's Argument for the Resurrection of the Dead in 1 Cor 15,* ConB 7 (Lund: Gleerup, 1974).

Clavier, H., "Brèves Remarques sur la Notion de σῶμα πνευματικόν," in W. D. Davies and D. Daube (eds.) *The Background to the NT and Its Eschatology: Studies in Honour of C. F. D. Moule* (Cambridge: Cambridge University Press, 1956), 342-62.

Cullmann, O., *Immortality of the Soul or Resurrection of the Dead?* (London: Epworth, 1958).

Davies, J. G., "Factors Leading to the Emergence of Belief in the Resurrection of the Flesh," *JTS* 23 (1972): 448-55.

Dunn, J. D. G., "1 Cor 15:45 — Last Adam, Life-Giving Spirit," in B. Lindars and S. J. Smalley (eds.) *Christ and Spirit in the NT: In Honour of C. F. D. Moule* (Cambridge: Cambridge University Press, 1973), 127-41.

————, *The Theology of Paul* (Edinburgh: T. & T. Clark, 1998), 199-204, 208-12, 241-65.

Ford, D. F., *Self and Salvation: Being Transformed* (Cambridge: Cambridge University Press, 1999).

Gillmann, J., "A Thematic Comparison: 1 Cor 15:50-57 and 2 Cor 5:1-5," *JBL* 107 (1988): 439-54.

————, "Transformation in 1 Cor 15:50-57 and 2 Cor 5:1-5," *ETL* 58 (1982): 309-33.

Goppelt, L., *Typos* (Eng. trans., Grand Rapids: Eerdmans, 1982), 129-36.

Gundry, R. H., *Sōma in Biblical Theology,* SNTSMS 29 (Cambridge: Cambridge University Press, 1976), 159-83.

Hollander, H. W., and J. Holleman, "The Relationship of Death, Sin and the Law in 1 Cor 15:56," *NovT* (1993): 270-91.

Jeremias, J., "Ἀδάμ," *TDNT,* 1:141-43.

————, "'Flesh and Blood Cannot Inherit the Kingdom of God' (1 Cor 15:50)," *NTS* 2 (1955): 151-59 (also rpt. in Jeremias, *Abba* [Göttingen, 1966], 298-307).

Kreitzer, L. J., "Resurrection," *DPL,* 805-12.

Morisette, R., "La condition de ressucité. 1 Cor 15:35-49," *Bib* 53 (1972): 208-28.

6. Eriksson alludes back to "the Gospel Tradition in the *Peroratio*" of v. 58 (ibid., 275).

Pamment, M., "Raised a Spiritual Body: Bodily Resurrection according to Paul," *New Blackfriars* 66 (1985): 372-88.

Perriman, A. C., "Paul and the Parousia: 1 Cor 15:30-37 and 2 Cor 5:1-5," *NTS* 35 (1989): 512-21.

Rahner, K., "Ideas for a Theology of Death," in *Theological Investigations* (London: DLT and New York: Seabury, 1975), 13:169-86.

————, *On the Theology of Death* (Eng. trans., New York: Herder & Herder, 1961).

————, "The Resurrection of the Body," in *Theological Investigations* (Eng. trans., London: DLT and New York: Seabury, 1963), 2:203-16.

————, "The Scandal of Death" and "He Descended into Hell," in *Theological Investigations* (London: DLT and New York: Seabury, 1971), 7:140-51.

Sand, A., *Der Begriff "Fleisch" in den paulinischen Hauptbriefen,* BU 2 (Regensburg: Pustet, 1967).

————, "σάρξ," *EDNT,* 3:230-33.

Schneider, B., "The Corporate Meaning and Background of 1 Cor 15:45b," *CBQ* 29 (1967): 450-67.

Schweizer, E., "χοϊκός," *TDNT,* 9:472-79.

Sider, R., "The Pauline Conception of the Resurrection Body in 1 Cor 15:35-54," *NTS* 21 (1975): 429-39.

Thiselton, A. C., "Eschatology and the Holy Spirit in Paul with Special Reference to 1 Cor" (Unpublished M.Th. thesis, University of London, 1964), 189-239, 245-48.

Usami, K., "'How Are the Dead Raised? (1 Cor 15:35-38)," *Bib* 57 (1976): 468-93.

35 In spite of Paul's accusation of lack of knowledge of God, which he makes to their shame (v. 34), a counterreply emerges, introduced by the strong contrastive ἀλλά, **nevertheless**, voiced as an objection (Greek simply ἐρεῖ, but elsewhere also used by Paul as expressing a reply, counterreply, or objection) on the part of **someone** (τις; cf. 15:12, 34). As Weiss, Lang, and most others insist (against Collins), the focus and force of the objection falls on πῶς, **how**, more in the sense of *"how is it possible?"* than in the sense of "in what manner?"[7] It is *both logical* (primarily) *and contingent* (secondarily). Although the objection is genuine and not merely a rhetorical device, this use of πῶς "often introduces a rhetorical question that calls an assumption in question or rejects it altogether."[8]

There has been much discussion about whether the two questions are distinct and separate, or whether the second amplifies and explicates the first. Since, as Wolff stresses, vv. 35-41 center on the theme (in practice one of *two* themes; see introduction to 15:35-58 above) of *"bodily-ness" (Leiblichkeit)* mainly on the basis of "**body**" as it is perceived to be in the old (empirical) creation, it is natural to infer that the *conceptual difficulty* expressed by **how** draws

7. Weiss, *Der erste Kor,* 367, and Lang, *Die Briefe,* 232; cf. Wolff *Der erste Brief,* 402 (against Collins, *First Cor,* 563, who draws questions about "clothing" and "travel" from apocalyptic speculations about the body).

8. Watson, "Rhetorical Strategy," in *Rhetoric,* 245, n. 50; also BAGD, 732.

its cutting edge from **with what kind of** (ποίῳ) **body**. . . ?[9] The force of δέ has been claimed as an argument against this view but equally as an argument which substantiates it. Thus Meyer urges: "The δέ places πῶς and ποίῳ δὲ σώματι in such a parallel relation that it does not, indeed, mean *or again* (Hofmann) 'but explicates' the scope of the question 'how. . . .'"[10] "This second question is made in support of the first."[11] Fee and Lang concur.[12]

Robertson and Plummer hit the nail on the head with their paraphrase "Can we *conceive of* such a thing? We cannot be expected to believe what is *impossible and inconceivable*" (my italics).[13] This is all the more sharply focused when they cite evidence from Jewish apocalyptic which presupposes a view that the resurrection **body** is an organism composed of particles reassembled from those of the rotting or rotted corpse: "In what shape will those live who live in Thy day? . . . He answered and said to me. . . . The earth shall then assuredly restore the dead [which it now receives in order to preserve them]. *It shall make no change in their form* but as it has received, so it will restore them" (*2 Baruch* 49:2; 50:1-2 [my italics]).[14]

R. H. Charles observes that whereas some of the Pharisees prior to *2 Baruch* (i.e., *Apocalypse of Baruch,* dated c. AD 75-100) believed in a transformed mode of resurrection existence, *2 Baruch* insists on a crudely materialist view according to which "the earth preserves the body intact, as committed to it."[15] On the other hand, Charles's note should not be taken to imply an even greater crudity than exists. Sometimes "the earth" is replaced by the notion that the earthly forms are preserved unchanged in *Sheol* (*4 Bar.* 21:23; 30:2-5, although *2 Baruch* is probably a composite document). The key points are: (i) The *questions* of *2 Bar.* 49:2 are *closely similar* to those of 1 Cor 15:35; but (ii) the emphasis on *no change* of *2 Bar.* 50:2 is *utterly in contradiction to* Paul's "we shall all *be changed*" (15:51) and "what you saw is *not the body that shall be*" (15:37a).[16]

9. Wolff, *Der erste Brief,* 401-12; Strobel, *Der erste Brief,* 257; Collins, *First Cor,* 565, sees the second question as a new one.

10. Meyer, *First Epistle,* 2:85.

11. Robertson and Plummer, *First Epistle,* 368.

12. The second question is "elaborating" the first (Fee, *First Epistle,* 780); also Lang, *Die Briefe,* 232. The major exception is Jeremias, "'Flesh and Blood Cannot Inherit the Kingdom of God' (1 Cor 15:50)," 151-59, who distinguishes between (i) how the resurrection takes place, and (ii) the nature of its "bodilyness."

13. Robertson and Plummer, *First Epistle,* 368.

14. Translation from R. H. Charles, *Apocrypha and Pseudepigrapha of the OT,* II: *Pseudepigrapha* (2 vols., Oxford: Clarendon Press, 1913), 2:508; (not Robertson and Plummer's). Charles uses square brackets where the text is uncertain (as against the latter).

15. Charles, *Pseudepigrapha,* 508, notes on 50-51 and 50-52. The date of the Syrian translation of the Greek is, of course, a different issue.

16. Jewish thought in the first century AD reflected a variety of conceptions. 4 Macc 7:3; 9:22; 13:17; 14:5-6; 17:12, 18, 19 replaces resurrection with a more hellenistic notion of immortality begun at the moment of death (cf. Wisdom 1–6 also). *Psalms of Solomon* speaks of "rising to eternal life" (3, 13), but without elaboration Josephus distinguishes (a) immortality of the soul

The use of the word **come** (ἔρχονται) may seem unexpected and even puzzling: "Paul is probably thinking of real *coming* — out of graves, with Christ" (Barrett's italics).[17] However, we must not forget that the issue is that of *conceptual and logical possibility* in the mouth of the objector (probably real, possibly rhetorical). Hence it is helpful to use the English *logical "can"*: **With what kind of body can they** [*possibly*] **come**? REB's *in what kind of body* simply refuses to take Paul's use of **come** seriously (cf. *do they come,* NRSV, Collins; *will they come,* NIV; *do they have when they come,* NJB). "The real concern behind their denial . . . was an implicit understanding that they meant the re-animation of dead bodies, the resuscitation of corpses."[18]

36-37   The rare future participle τὸ γενησόμενον is correct; p[46], F, and G appear to read γεννησόμενον.

After long earlier debate about whether σύ belongs with ἄφρων or with ὃ σπείρεις, recent research on rhetoric has firmly established the rhetorical (not simply emotive) force of ἄφρων σύ.[19] The phrase functions as an *exclamatio* to intensify the argument, as Quintilian's work on rhetoric suggests.[20] Several English VSS tone down the force of **you**: REB, *What stupid questions!* NJB and NIV, *How foolish!* (as against Barrett and NRSV, *Fool!;* Moffatt, *Foolish man!* Collins, *You fool!*). Gk. ἄφρων means more strictly *senseless, without sense,* i.e., alpha privative with adjective φρόνιμος. All of these factors together suggest that **You nonsense person!** precisely conveys the force of the *exclamatio* while allowing for an ironic overtone which overcomes the apparent downright rudeness (in English) of *Fool!* as well as the less personal circumlocution *what stupid questions!*[21]

Paul uses the model of **sowing** in the ground to underline the universal connection between being **brought to life** *as the crop or fruit* and *transformation of form* or *different mode of existence in continuity of identity.* The same model is used by Jesus in the Fourth Gospel (John 12:24) to denote the contrast between "letting go of self in death" ("unless a grain of wheat falls into the ground and dies, it remains that and nothing more," REB) and a new, glorified state ("but if it dies, it bears a rich harvest. Whoever loves himself is lost . . . ,"

among Essenes; resurrection of the body among Pharisees; and an unbelief in postmortal existence among the Sadducees (*Jewish Wars* 2.8.11, 14: *Antiquities* 18.1.3-5; cf. Mark 12:18-23). The speculations cited by Collins (*First Cor,* 563) largely refer to later rabbinic literature, e.g., *b. Ketubot* 11a; *b. Sanhedrin* 90b; et al.

17. Barrett, *First Epistle,* 370.

18. Fee, *First Epistle,* 776.

19. Eriksson, *Traditions,* 268.

20. Quintilian, *Institutio Oratoria,* 9:2:26, 27 (Quintilian's dates are c. AD 35-95. He cites, e.g., Cicero, *Pro Murena* 6.14, "What madness is this!" See further J. Martin, *Antike Rhetorik. Technik und Methode* (Munich: Beck, 1974), 282, on *exclamatio.*

21. The Greek is severe, but we may assume that "the objector plumes himself in his acuteness" (Robertson and Plummer, *First Epistle,* 369), as well as the rhetorical convention.

vv. 24, 25a, REB). Here in 15:36, however, Paul is not emphasizing the necessity of death, but "the fact of transformation through death and revivification."[22] The grammatical conditional ἐὰν μὴ ἀποθάνῃ underlines the logical and contingent condition of *discontinuity* in order to allow for a *meaningful and conceivable continuity*. Harrisville has shown how these two principles operate in Paul's concept of *newness,* and *they encapsulate the very heart of the dynamics of the gospel itself.*[23]

Paul uses the relatively rare articular future participle of γίνομαι with σῶμα: **it is not the body which is to come about that you sow. Come about** represents the active and dynamic rather than stative force of γίνομαι. The grammar and syntax do not flow smoothly, partly because, in effect, Paul repeats **what you sow** twice; or, more accurately, the first ὃ σπείρεις can be construed in either of two possible ways. Paul probably dictates: **And what you sow — it is not the body which is to come about that you sow but a bare grain**. He breaks off the construction, and begins again to emphasize **what you sow**, understanding ἐστι to be supplied. However, it is equally possible to construe the relative pronoun as an accusative of respect: **And as to what you sow: it is not the body which is to come about that you sow**. . . . The term **bare grain** (γυμνὸν κόκκον) now carries what Paul Ricoeur calls "the double meaning" and "split reference" of all creative or tensive metaphor. In its application to wheat or to crops, the force of *bare, naked seed* should not be pressed beyond its obvious meaning. However, Paul already has in mind the second application of that which lacks the "clothing" of the raised σῶμα described in 15:43-44. This coheres with the parallel in 2 Cor 5:3 (in spite of unconvincing arguments in some quarters to the contrary). εἰ τύχοι, *if it should chance,* may be rendered **perhaps** (with NRSV, REB, NIV; cf. NJB, *I dare say*), e.g., **of wheat or something else**.

38 In this verse Barth, Kennedy, and others find one of the high points of the whole argument. If, writes Kennedy, we ask what is the link between the **bare grain** of the old creation or old order and the "**body**" (σῶμα) of the new, Paul provides "the only one [answer] we can expect him to give. . . . 'The sovereign power of God.' 'He giveth it a body according as he willed' (ἠθέλησεν); 'the aorist denotes the final [i.e., purposive] act of God's will, determining the constitution of nature', so Edwards *ad loc.* admirably."[24] The present force of δίδωσιν stands in contrast to the aorist of ἠθέλησεν. The aorist in this context denotes "not 'as he wills' (according to his choice or liking) but in accordance with his past decree in creation, by which the propagation of life on earth was determined from the beginning (Gen 1:11, 12; for the verb cf. . . . 12:18)."[25]

22. Barrett, *First Epistle,* 370.

23. R. A. Harrisville, "The Concept of Newness in the NT," *JBL* 74 (1955): 69-79.

24. Kennedy, *St Paul's Conceptions of the Last Things,* 243 (quoted in part already above, on v. 34; also (part) Edwards, *First Epistle,* 434; cf. Barth, *Resurrection,* 18; Wendland, *Die Briefe,* 151; Lang, *Die Briefe,* 231.

25. Findlay, *Expositor's Greek Testament,* 2:934.

Thus REB's *of his choice* is too bland; NIV's *as he has determined* is better, recalling the decrees of creation, but misses the *purposive* aspect, which will be explicated in vv. 39-42. God's decree was made in the light of the purpose or role which he assigned **to each** of his creatures. A broad comparison with examples in BAGD but more especially a comparison with the issue of how God apportions gifts to believers within the body of Christ's church καθὼς ἠθέλησεν (12:18) will corroborate this point (see above on 12:18). Differentiation in accordance with God's sovereign decree in relation to his future purposes remains a fundamental principle of the *"ordering"* (15:24-28; 14:40; 12:4-11), whether of the old creation or the new. The use of καθώς underlines the comparative explication: **just as he purposed**.[26] The position of ὁ δὲ θεός at the beginning of the sentence is properly emphatic: *it is* **God** who **gives** (to) **it a body**. . . .

The καί before ἑκάστῳ also has an explicative force, denoting *namely* or **that is** *(i.e.)*. It is important to note that "the singular [of σπέρμα, seed] is used collectively" of grains or kernels sown; hence when the plural occurs (as here) it often denotes **kinds of seeds**.[27] English offers parallels in such words as *cheese* or *fruit* where novelists will often write of *cheeses* or *fruits* to denote a bountiful provision of *kinds of fruit* and *types of cheese*. The use of ἴδιον σῶμα, **its own particular body** (with REB; cf. *its own body,* NRSV, NIV; but *its own kind of body,* NJB), ranks almost equally in emphasis with **God**. The key phrase remains **God gives to it a body just as he purposed**, but the second principle is that of *contrast, differentiation, and variety* which simultaneously promotes a *continuity of identity*. This is one reason why "order" becomes so important for chs. 12, 14, and 15: genuine *differentiation and variety* reflects the will of God, provided that it does not collapse into sheer confusion and the loss of the very identity which preserves *the otherness of the other as other* and not a mere replication or projection of "the strong" within any group. If, as Cullmann declares, "the Spirit is the anticipation of the End in the present," it is not difficult to see why the parallel between 15:38 and 12:18 is so important.[28]

Conzelmann well expresses Paul's thought in contrast to a hybrid mixture with Cartesian dualism. Paul's thought is not that "a naked soul" needs to be "clothed" with a σῶμα; this idea remains captive to Western dualism. Rather, "The new life is a *new* creation, a gift bestowed 'as God will' (Gen 1:11) . . . regarded in terms of faith's understanding of it as in each several instance *my* life: ἴδιον, own particular" (his italics).[29] Further on "**body**," see below, especially vv. 43-44. As Wolff comments, the "**body**" is a "new whole," and the parallel between the old creation and new creation shapes Paul's focus here.[30] The issue is if *no human mind can predict or conceive the shape or form of the as-yet-*

---

26. BAGD, 391; also on θέλω, 354-55.
27. Grimm-Thayer, 583, where the point is clear.
28. O. Cullmann, *Christ and Time,* 72; cf. Rom 8:23; 2 Cor 1:22; 5:5.
29. Conzelmann, *1 Cor,* 281.
30. Wolff, *Der erste Brief,* 404; cf. Hays, *1 Cor,* 270.

unseen σῶμα of the resurrection, as long as all of this lies in the hands of God the giver who has his own sovereign purposes, the matter is firmly in hand.

39-40 (1) Some later MSS insert σάρξ after ἄλλη μέν both to make **human flesh** more explicit and to match the repetition of **flesh** for **animals** and birds. The addition is unnecessary. (2) D*, F, and G change πτηνῶν to the more customary πετεινῶν, but this is a later "improvement." (3) F, K, and L transpose the sequence of **birds** and **fish** to reflect the sequence of Gen 1:25 (from lower to higher orders). The point is that AV/KJV follows the secondary, later readings.

It is difficult to find a better translation of σάρξ than **flesh** (as in virtually all English VSS), but the semantic range of the Greek is far wider than Eng. **flesh**. In Paul σάρξ does not primarily denote the physical and material *in contrast to* **soul** *or* **spirit**, even though it may be used (as here) to denote *"the material that covers the bones of a human or animal body."*[31] It is not used in a sense compatible with Platonic or Western dualism. Paul's multiform uses of the word substantially overlap with Heb. בָּשָׂר *(basar),* which regularly denotes humanity in its creatureliness and vulnerability. Only rarely (as in this verse) does Paul use σάρξ to denote *flesh-substance common to human persons and to the animal kingdom.* With LXX, he usually prefers to use κρέας for animal meat (Rom 14:21; 1 Cor 8:13). Rather than referring to some "part" of a person, σάρξ denotes "the whole person, considered from the point of view of his external, physical existence. Thus Gal 4:13f ('. . . an infirmity of the flesh . . .') (and) 2 Cor 12:7 ('. . . A thorn in the flesh') . . . refer generally to physical distress."[32]

This emerges not least in Paul's assimilation of the LXX translations of Heb. בָּשָׂר *(basar),* which finds its most characteristic meaning not in terms of a semantic contrast with an "inner" soul but in terms of a contrast with what is strong on the transcendent, e.g., "The Egyptians are only human, not God; and their horses are *basar,* not *ruach*" (Isa 31:3). A. Sand well sums up the matter both in his specialist monograph and in his lexicographical study: "The range of meaning extends from the substance *flesh* (both human and animal), to the human body, to the entire person, and to all humankind" (cf. "**flesh** *and blood*") in 15:50.[33]

At the same time Jewett endorses E. D. Burton's thesis that seven distinct uses of the word **flesh** occur in the major Pauline epistles, and that confusion results when these are not held apart.[34] Bultmann is not imposing a supposedly Lutheran theology upon Pauline texts when he notes that in such passages as Rom 8:7 and 8 a heavily theological and ethical use of **flesh** denotes a human

31. BAGD, 743; also Sand, *Der Begriff "Fleisch,"* 144.
32. Robinson, *The Body,* 17-18 and 19, where he also cites Isa 40:6; Ps 36:4; 78:39; Job 34:15; cf. esp. R. Jewett, *Paul's Anthropological Terms* (Leiden: Brill, 1971), 49-166 and 453-56; BAGD, 743-44; E. Schweizer, "σάρξ," *TDNT,* 7:125-36; cf. 98-151.
33. Sand, *Der Begriff "Fleisch" in den paulinischen Hauptbriefen;* quotation from Sand, "σάρξ," *EDNT,* 3:230; cf. 230-33. Cf. Rom 6:19; 1 Cor 5:5; 7:28; 2 Cor 7:1, 5; Gal 4:13.
34. Jewett, *Paul's Anthroplogical Terms,* 63, alluding to Burton's commentary on Galatians.

mind-set of "trust in oneself as being able to procure life by the use of the earthly and through one's own strength and accomplishment."[35] This use is far more characteristic of Paul, and in Galatians a *"fleshly"* mind-set can denote equally self-indulgent libertinism and making "religion" an end in itself for self-advantage (cf. Gal 3:3; 5:19-26; 6:1-6, 13, 14). In Gal 5:19 and 20 "the works of the **flesh**" include attitudes and actions which are not restricted to the realm of the physical or the sensual. Since, as I have argued elsewhere, flesh in Paul does *not* denote any *"one general thing,"* it serves as "a *polymorphous concept*," i.e., its meaning is always heavily context-dependent and variable.[36] *Hence Paul's exposition of the varied context-dependent meanings even of flesh as substance (both human and animal, v. 39) paves the way admirably for his forceful argument that* **body** (σῶμα) *also depends on contextual and purposive factors for its meaning (v. 40).*

Meanwhile, the first stage of this part of the argument is conclusively to confirm the thrust of v. 37: the **body** that rots in the grave is emphatically *not* the **body** of the future resurrection. Already the created order demonstrates the diversity of **flesh**-*substances* and **bodies** which the infinite resourcefulness of the Creator God has provided. Can it, then, be doubted that the *raised* **body**, *too,* will be different in kind and in nature or "substance" from the **body** that has died, according to its new sphere and purpose? In response to the question **how** (v. 35) Paul insists "that the resurrection of the dead is ontologically possible."[37]

The shift from σάρξ (v. 39) to σῶμα (v. 40) is marked by the introduction of δόξα and the allusion to **bodies** that are super-earthly. Whereas **flesh** had emphasized the diversity of the *"stuff"* of creation, **body** now calls attention to diversities of *form and character.*[38] In Calvin's words, the comparisons of v. 39 serve the same purpose as those of vv. 37-38 but add the implication that "whatever diversity we perceive in any particular kind *(in quoqua specie)* is a sort of foreshadowing of the resurrection. . . ."[39] Chrysostom, Theodoret, Ambrosiaster, and Augustine construe vv. 39 and 40 as already anticipating the distinctions supposedly implied by v. 41b, i.e., differences in "honor" even between individual believers at the resurrection, but this goes beyond the explicit sense of these verses.[40] Tertullian, too, sees Paul's argument here (vv. 39-40) as a decisive logical repudiation of Marcion's wish to substitute a notion of the soul's

---

35. Bultmann, *Theology of the NT,* 1:239; cf. 1 Cor 1:29; Phil 3:3-7; Gal 6:13, 14; and Jewett, *Paul's Anthropological Terms,* 95-103.

36. Thiselton, *The Two Horizons,* 408-11. See also Thiselton, "The Meaning of σάρξ in 1 Cor 5:5 . . .," *SJT* 26 (1973): 204-28.

37. Conzelmann, *1 Cor,* 281.

38. Broadly with Conzelmann, *1 Cor,* 282. Fee's chiasmic analysis of differences of "kind" (vv. 39a and 41b), "differences within genus" (vv. 39b, and 41a), and a general contrast (v. 40a, and 40b) seems overly elaborate (*First Epistle,* 783). Did Paul really pause to work out such a chiasmus?

39. Calvin, *First Epistle,* 336.

40. For example, Chrysostom, *1 Cor. Hom.,* 41:43.

immortality for bodily resurrection: "Does he not guarantee that the resurrection shall be accomplished by that God from whom proceed all the examples," i.e., of diversity within creation and of transformation.[41] Tertullian rightly places the emphasis upon *God and God's's resourcefulness as Creator* as the ground of this faith.

The meaning of σώματα ἐπουράνια (v. 40) has been debated since the patristic era. The Greek simply means *existing in heaven* in contrast to ἐπίγεια, existing on earth (ἐπί + γῆ, ἐπί + οὐρανός). But οὐρανος includes (1) the sky above the earth; (2) the sphere of clouds and stars; (3) the abode or sphere of God and angels; and (4), in conjunction with *earth,* that which denotes the whole universe as a complete entity created by God. BAGD provide instances of authors and texts which demonstrate each.[42] Thus ἐπουράνιος in lexicographical terms includes (1) the dwelling or sphere of God or Christ (esp. 1 Cor 15:48-49; cf. Heb 12:12); and (2) the sphere in which the sun, moon, and stars are located (BAGD cite 15:40 in the light of 15:41); as well as (3), more widely or generally, heavenly things or heaven (2 Cor 12:2; Heb 8:5).[43] In the light of v. 41, it might seem obvious that v. 40 alludes to the sphere of the sun, moon, and stars. However, some interpreters object that Paul would not use σῶμα of an impersonal entity, and that to apply this to astronomical "bodies" either imports a modern meaning of σῶμα or presupposes a view of astral bodies as quasi-personal, as reflected in some non-Christian first-century religions. Meyer and Findlay, among others, argue this forcefully, insisting that Paul alludes to bodies of angels in v. 40, appealing to supposed parallels in Matt 22:10 and Luke 20:36.[44]

Héring ascribes a primitive cosmology to Paul here which enables him to combine the two views: " 'heavenly bodies', i.e., the living bodies of certain angels which appear to us in the form of stars, and are of other matter than earthly bodies."[45] But this overlooks our earlier distinction between **flesh** as denoting different *substances* (v. 39) and **body** as denoting different *natures, characters, or forms* within different *spheres* or in relation to different given purposes or functions. Paul consciously extends the normal meaning of **bodies** because the context makes quite clear how this extended meaning is to be understood. What Paul aims to set before his readers is the *conceivability, on the basis of a theology of God as creator of diverse orders of being, of a "sort of body . . . entirely outside our present experience."*[46] Wolff constructively suggests some such background of thought as Sir 43:1-10: "The pride of the higher realms is the

---

41. Tertullian, *Against Marcion,* 5:10.
42. BAGD, 593-95.
43. BAGD, 305-6.
44. Meyer, *First Epistle,* 2:87. Findlay, *Expositor's Greek Testament,* 2:935, insists that "σῶμα is never used elsewhere in Bib Gk and rarely in cl Gk of inorganic bodies." He notes v. 41, but contends that the former arguments "preponderate."
45. Héring, *First Epistle,* 174.
46. Hays, *1 Cor,* 271.

clear vault of the sky as glorious to behold as the sight of the heavens. The sun . . . proclaims as it rises what a marvellous instrument it is, the work of the Most High . . . a furnace . . . bright rays. . . . Great is the Lord who made it. . . . The moon . . . marks the changing seasons . . . the sign for festal days. . . . The glory of the stars is the beauty of heaven. . . ."[47] Wolff rightly appeals to v. 41 as the context of understanding for v. 40.

In view of the debate, we have translated the controversial Greek term as **super-earthly bodies** to allow for the wide semantic range of the Greek and the natural contextual influence of v. 41 (cf. NRSV, NIV, NJB, REB, *heavenly bodies*). However, if (1) we follow Schweizer in insisting that in 15:38 **body** "comes close to meaning *'form,'*" (2) we accept that Paul replies to his objectors at this point in terms of the currency which they use, and (3) we recognize that **body** is used on occasion of inorganic or impersonal entities in Greek writers of Paul's own day, this leaves no problem in assuming that the primary reference of **super-earthly bodies** is stars and planets, even if Paul does not explicitly exclude possible allusion to angelic beings.[48] We remain unconvinced, however, by Dale Martin's proposal that Paul alludes to heavenly bodies in the sense found in certain traditions of Greek philosophy from the pre-Socratics to Origen, namely, that of immortal souls clothed in a substance of glory akin to that of the sun or the stars.[49] In the *Timaeus* Plato speculates about a rearrangement of the elements of earth, water, air, and fire in such a way that fire now dominates.[50] A first-century inscription does indeed read, "Do not weep for me. . . . For I have become an evening star among the gods."[51] Martin compares this with the "shining" of the righteous in Dan 12:3. Nevertheless, two objections among others are substantial. (1) As we commented in relation to Héring, the issue moves from substance in v. 39 to form in vv. 40-41.[52] (2) In vv. 42-57 it becomes clear that spiritual does not mean "composed of spirit" (in the sense of substance) but transformation in accordance with the moral and theological character of the Holy Spirit within the context of sin, salvation, and the splendor of holiness. Martin's analysis leaves no room for the decisive turn of Paul's argument in v. 44 (see below) and misconstrues the nature of *glory* or splendor for Paul.

The meaning of δόξα (NRSV, AV/KJV, Collins, *glory,* or REB, NIV, NJB, and above, **splendor**) is heavily dependent for Paul and the rest of the NT on the Hebrew behind the LXX occurrences, namely, כבוד *(kabod).*[53] The Hebrew de-

---

47. Wolff, *Der erste Brief,* 405.

48. Schweizer, *TDNT,* 7:1,060; cf. 1,055 and 1,062-64; also Philo, *Opificio Mundi* 36, 49, 102; *Confusione Linguarum* 190; *Quis Rerum Divinarum Heres?* 72.

49. Martin, *The Corinthian Body,* 117-20 and 123-36.

50. Plato, *Timaeus* 31B-C2.

51. Arcesine, *Inscriptiones Graecae* 12:7:123, 5-6; cited by Martin, *Corinthian Body,* 274, n. 56.

52. See further Sellin, *Streit um die Auferstehung,* 220; and Strobel, *Der erste Brief,* 258.

53. BDB, 458-59, list (1) *abundance,* (2) *honor, glory,* **splendor**, e.g., of Joseph in Egypt

rives from a cognate network of terms concerning *weight* or *weightiness* and denotes *what makes something weighty* or *impressive.* When he declares in 1 Cor 3:21, "let no one *glory in human persons*," or in 1 Cor 1:31, "let the person who glories, *glory in the Lord*," Paul urges readers to *find what they deem to be impressive, wonderful, full of* **splendor**, *and a source of elation, in Christ, not in human leaders.*[54] For Paul what makes even *God weighty, impressive,* a transcendent source of *delight and* **splendor**, is *not simply* his sheer majestic *radiance or "luminosity"* but (as he deliberately "turns" the image in 2 Cor 4:6) the *"light"* which is "knowledge of *the glory of God in the face of Jesus Christ*" (REB), i.e., in *his self-giving grace.* David Ford observes that all the abundance, all the "flowing brook of delights . . . their countenance full of radiance . . . a fountain of delight," finds its definitive expression in "a glorious face," the "face of Jesus Christ," which "attracts trust, adoration, love, joy, repentance" as the focus of "such multifaceted abundance" which is the glory of God.[55] In other words, it is not simply the raw power and majesty of God which is his *glory* or **splendor**, but his self-giving in gracious love in and through Christ.

These observations overcome any supposed difficulty about ascribing **splendor** or *glory* to **the bodies of those who live on the earth**, even if δόξα has to be understood and supplied in the last clause of v. 40. Robertson and Plummer provide an excellent comment: "As there are differences on the earth, so also in the sky. There is a wide difference (ἑτέρα) between terrestrial and celestial bodies; and there is a further difference (ἄλλη) between one celestial body and another. The God who made these myriads of differences in one and the same universe can be credited with inexhaustible power . . . he has found a body fit for fish, fowl, cattle and mortal man: why not for . . . [raised] man? Experience teaches that God finds a suitable body for every type of earthly life and every type of heavenly life. Experience cannot teach that there is a type of life for which no suitable body can be found."[56]

41 The background of Sir. 43:1-10 clarifies our understanding of **splendor** further.[57] **The splendor of the sun** (i.e., what makes it impressive; see above on the Hebrew background) may indeed lie in "its burning heat . . . a fur-

(Gen 45:13); *wealth and splendor* (1 Chron 29:12, 28); splendor of a throne (1 Sam 2:8; Isa 22:23); priestly robes (Exod 28:2-40); the temple (Hag 2:13); theophanies (Exod 33:18, 22), e.g., in a thunderstorm (Ps 29:3), in the heavens (Ps 19:2); (3) *dignity of position* (Num 24:11); as not appropriate to fools (Prov 26:1); (4) *honor, reputation* (of character) (2 Chron 26:18; Prov 21:21); and (5) *honor due to God* (Isa 42:8; 43:2).

54. K. Barth, *Church Dogmatics,* 4/1, 514 and 524; and *Resurrection,* 68. Cf. Thiselton, "Luther and Barth on 1 Cor 15," in Stephens (ed.), *The Bible, the Reformation, and the Church,* 265 and 288-89.

55. Ford, *Self and Salvation: Being Transformed,* 24-28 and 171-76. Dale Martin's notion of "luminosity" takes second place.

56. Robertson and Plummer, *First Epistle,* 371. Cf. Senft, *Première Épitre,* 205-6: diversity which expresses different types of beauty in which neither the quality nor the essential nature is the same.

57. As Wolff notes (*Der erste Brief,* 405).

nace . . . searching the mountains. . . . Its bright rays blind the eyes" (Sir 43:3-5). The notion of δόξα as *radiance* may well apply here. But this is so only because this is the purpose for which "the LORD . . . made it" (Sir 43:5). **The splendor of the moon** is of a different order: "It governs the times . . . the sign for festal days. . . . It wanes and renews itself; how marvellous it is *in this change*" (Sir 43:6-8, my italics). *This* glory or **splendor** (i.e., *change*) takes a different form in relation to *the fixed but multiform stations of the stars.* "The glory of the stars is the beauty of heaven, *a glittering array.* . . . On the orders of the Holy One *they stand in their appointed places;* they never relax their watches" (Sir 43:9-10). Each is deemed to be "impressive" in relation to the capacities of its σῶμα or *form* to perform **its own** respective function within God's's "ordering" of creation. This corresponds with *each in its own order* (ἐν τῷ ἰδίῳ τάγματι, v. 23) in response to God's "ordering" or "subjecting" (ὑπέταξεν, v. 27; cf. v. 28) of the hierarchy of all beings.

Even **stars** are not interchangeable: each has **its own** position and brightness or magnitude. Thus **one star differs from another star in splendor**, i.e., in what gives it its particular "weight" or impressive capacity to be what God requires of it. Some patristic writers interpret this allegorically of the different glories of different raised believers. But this is not Paul's point, even if it suggests the broad principle of dynamic diversified life in the resurrection mode of existence (see on v. 44b). The verb διαφέρει underlines the inexhaustible wisdom of God to promote differentiation within his coherent purposes (as in his apportioning of "gifts" in 1 Corinthians 12–14).

42 **Thus** takes up and presupposes the whole context of vv. 37-41 concerning (a) the *discontinuity* between the old body which is "**sown**" (v. 37) and the new body which is **raised** (v. 42); (b) the sovereign power of God to enact far-reaching transformation of his own devising, however unimaginable this may be to human mortals now (v. 38); (c) the *variety* of modes of existence that lie within the sovereign capacity of God to create; and (d) the *continuity of identity* suggested by such terms as *each . . . its own* body (v. 38). All of these aspects are implicit in οὕτως, **thus**, *in this manner, in this way.* Since divine decree is entailed in these four aspects, and since the verb has to be supplied in this verse, we propose supplying **it shall be** (as against *it is,* REB, NJB, NRSV; *it will be,* NIV). If we retain *it is,* the argument for this would be that this represents of *logical* or *conceptual "is,"* i.e., defining the nature and "grammar" of the resurrection mode of existence. The use of ἡ ἀνάστασις may support this, except that nothing can be inferred from Paul's not using ἔγερσις since Paul never uses this abstract noun derived from the verb ἐγείρω.

The first major *contrast* or component of *discontinuity* is marked by ἐν φθορᾷ . . . ἐν ἀφθαρσίᾳ. It is customary for exegetes to understand this simply as a contrast of *duration: perishable . . . imperishable* (NRSV, REB, NIV, NJB); *in corruption . . . in incorruption* (AV/KJV): *in mortality . . . in immortality* (Collins). This entirely reflects the meaning of ἀφθαρσία in lexicography, where most instances denote *incorruptibility, immortality,* e.g., in Philo, Plutarch, Ignatius, and LXX (Wisdom, 4 Maccabees).[58] However, since 1964 I have consistently held that φθορά is the term within the semantic opposition that carries the decisive content, in relation to which the contrast is signaled by the alpha privative. φθορά denotes "decreasing capacities and increasing weaknesses, issuing in exhaustion and stagnation," i.e., in a state of **decay**.[59] In the LXX φθορά regularly translates either of two Hebrew words: שחת *(shachat)* and חבל *(chebel)*. The force of שחת and its cognate forms conveys not only *destruction* or *termination* but also *mutilation*. In the Niph'al it may denote *to be marred, spoiled,* while the Hiph'il form means *to pervert* or *to corrupt* (in a moral sense).[60] The semantic contrast to such **decay** would *not* be *permanence* or *everlasting duration,* but *ethical, aesthetic, and psychosocial flourishing and abundance,* even perhaps *perfection,* and certainly *fullness of life.* The second Hebrew word, חבל, denotes a semantic range beginning with *vapor* or *breath* and extending through to *vanity, emptiness, fruitlessness.* The full force of the word finds expression in Isa 49:4: "I have labored in vain; I have spent my strength for nothing and vanity" (NRSV).[61] The semantic contrast now lies with the *purposive progression of dynamic life-processes,* in which *satisfaction or delight* is based on what is *substantial and solid.*

In the light of these considerations, the life of the new **raised body** is not merely *incorruptible* (AV/KJV, Vulgate, *incorruptio*) or *imperishable* (REB, NRSV, et al.) but **decay's reversal,** i.e., *a solidity of progressive, purposive flourishing in fullness of life.* This is entirely compatible with two theological considerations: (a) First, *bodily* or *somatic* (Dahl) existence is *not a reduction or "thinning down"* of a supposedly bodiless mode of being; this is the "bloodless, juiceless existence" of *Sheol.* **Body** provides the vehicle of *communicative flourishing and identity recognition in the public, intersubjective domain of community.*[62] (b) Second, to be **raised** by and through *God* in the power of *the Holy Spirit* entails a dynamic of being that corresponds with the dynamic of the *living* God who acts purposively in ongoing ways, never "trapped" in a timeless vacuum from which all experience of succession is excluded (see further on v. 44).[63] This is more than *imperishability* (NRSV, REB, NIV, NJB) or *immortality* (Collins).[64]

58. Wis 2:23; 4 Macc 9:22; 17:12; Ignatius, *Letter to the Philadelphians,* 9:2; *To the Magnesians,* 6:2; cf. BAGD, 125.

59. Thiselton, "Eschatology and the Holy Spirit in Paul with Special Reference to 1 Cor" (M.Th. thesis, University of London, 1964), 229; cf. 189-96 and 208-39. Cf. also Rom 8:21.

60. BDB, 1,007-8; cf. Thiselton, "Eschatology," 250.

61. Cf. Isa 30:7 and BDB, 210-11.

62. Cf. E. Käsemann, "Primitive Christian Apocalyptic," in *NT Questions of Today,* 135. Käsemann sees "body" as a "gift" which entails solidarity with others and "ability to communicate." Christ's Lordship finds "visible [i.e., public] expression" and "takes personal shape" in the *sōma (ibid.).*

63. Of a huge literature on God and temporality cf. especially the dialogue between R. Bauckham and J. Moltmann in R. Bauckham (ed.), *God Will Be All in All: The Eschatology of Jürgen Moltmann* (Edinburgh: T. & T. Clark, 1999), 155-231.

64. Collins, *First Cor,* 567.

43   The semantic opposition of the first half of v. 43 does not merely negate and affirm precisely the same quality or disposition, and the contrast between ἀτιμίᾳ and δόξῃ can be misunderstood in more than one way. While the Greek negative noun often means dishonor, disgrace, shame (BAGD) and is usually translated *dishonor* (NRSV, NIV, AV/KJV), many German commentators associate the word more specifically with **humiliation** or *a lowly position* (Lang, *Niedrigkeit*), with misery, pitifulness (Wolff and Lange, *Jämmerlichkeit*), or with troublesomeness, lamentation, and complaint (Wolff, *Kläglichkeit*).[65] However, Fee and REB rightly recognize that **humiliation** includes *either or both* of the two distinct senses that may stand in contrast to *glory* or to **splendor**: (a) that which corresponds to Paul's use of τὸ σῶμα τῆς ταπεινώσεως ἡμῶν, *the body of our* **humiliation**, i.e., *of our lowly state,* in Phil 3:21 (the same context of pre-resurrection and post-resurrection modes of existence); and (b) the *shame-honor* contrast which we might expect in opposition to δόξα, **splendor**.[66] The former understanding includes the sense of mourning, sorrow, frailty, and grief which finds a paradigm in sudden death and bereavement in the midst of life. The latter calls attention to association with sinful desires and habituated actions which were performed in the "old" body, but from which the **raised** body will be entirely free. NJB's *contemptible* too readily permits a dualist devaluation of the body, or else commits us exclusively to (b). However, it is likely that broader nuances are at issue, for which **humiliation** offers the most appropriate understanding, and Liddell-Scott-Jones provide instances of this wider meaning of the Greek outside the New Testament.[67]

On the meaning of **splendor**, see above on 15:40-41 (also on 2:7-8; 10:31; 11:7, 15). If **splendor** denotes that which renders someone or something *weighty* (Heb. כבוד, *kabod*) or *impressive* (Gk. δόξα), in this context the nuance of *radiant light* or *luminosity* misses the mark.[68] *Radiance,* however, does enter the picture, for a *radiant* σῶμα (like a radiant face) is one suffused with joy on such occasions as the meeting of a loved one after a long absence; the child on Christmas morning; the bride or bridegroom at a "happy" wedding; the meeting of lovers; and especially the eschatological, face-to-face union of God-in-Christ and the Spirit-filled believer (see under v. 44). Negatively, this **splendor** demonstrates the absence of the last cloud of sin and guilt (vv. 44, 52, 54-57); positively, it expresses the climax of transformation into full Christlikeness (vv. 49, 57).

The second semantic opposition of this verse (which is the third of the four in vv. 42-44) raises less difficulty. The contrast between ἀσθένεια and

---

65. Lang, *Die Brief,* 234; Wolff, *Der erste Brief,* 407; BAGD, 120.

66. On Phil 3:21, see G. F. Hawthorne, *Philippians* (Dallas: Ward, 1983), 172. See also Fee, *First Epistle,* 785; although he simply writes, ". . . 'dishonour' (better, 'humiliation') with no further discussion, Collins relates the term to human fallenness (*First Cor,* 567).

67. LSJ, 270-71.

68. O. Pfleiderer, *Paulinism* (2 vols., Eng. trans., London: Williams & Norgate, 1877 and 1891), 1:201, regards *glory* here as the radiance displayed by "celestial pneuma-substance." Dale Martin sees links with "astral soul" theories (*The Corinthian Body,* 126).

δύναμις is equivalent to Eng. **weakness-power**. **Weakness** explicates further the theme of **decay** (v. 42) and **humiliation** (v. 43a). Decreasing capacities in psychophysical life begin from the moment brain cells die and habituated conduct blocks capacities to re-create and to move in novel directions. The insight of existentialist philosophers that human persons experience limitations through their own past decisions coheres entirely with Paul's understanding of created personhood. Just as **power** in this epistle repeatedly denotes the capacity to carry through purposes or actions with operative effectiveness, so **weakness** denotes an incapacity to achieve such competency and the spiral of consequent frustration and deenergization through maximal unsuccessful effort and distraction.[69] In Paul's analysis of the human condition in this epistle, aspirations toward self-affirmation become self-defeating unless they stand within the sphere which is transformatively energized by the power of the cross. In the preresurrection mode of existence, however, the new creation always remains tarnished and weakened by imperfections in realizing this goal with finality.

An analogy might serve to underline the impropriety of a fully "realized eschatology" for Paul, while acknowledging the decisive significance of the death and resurrection of Christ once for all in the past and the status of the body of believers as already "a new creation" (2 Cor 3:17). A person who is suffering from the **weakness** of a wasting disease may be *decisively transferred* into medical care and the hospital (these new forces *will* prove *to have been* decisive), but en route to full recovery (cf. the eschaton) the patient remains beset with **weakness** until the process of medication and care is complete. Loss of autonomy and handing over the self to the care of Another is the decisive act of the past; the certainty of complete recovery lies in the future. Meanwhile Paul uses past, present, and future tenses of "salvation," of which he employs the present (for the most part) in 1 Corinthians.[70] To describe the preresurrection *sōma* as **sown in weakness** expresses Paul's realism about the *frailty, fragility, vulnerability, and constraints* of human existence (including that of Christians) without diminishing the power of the cross, which is the presupposition for the triumph of the resurrection mode of existence.

Power explicates further **decay's reversal** (v. 42) and the **splendor** (v. 43a) which characterizes the gifts, activity, and agency of the *Holy* **Spirit** (v. 44). Throughout this epistle the word has been associated with (a) the capacity *to effect or to activate* what the agent in question determines to do; (b) that which has *solidity and purposive* effect as against frustrated endeavors; and

---

69. Cf. 1 Cor 1:18, 24; 2:4, 5; 4:19, 20 ("the kingdom of God is not a matter of talk but of *solid efficacy*"); 5:4; 6:14; 12:10; 14:11; 15:24, 46.

70. The classic exposition of Pauline theology as (1) "Salvation as a Fact of the Past," (2) "Salvation Is a Progressive Experience," and (3) "Salvation: Its Consummation in the Future" occurs in C. A. Anderson Scott, *Christianity according to St Paul* (Cambridge: Cambridge University Press, 1927), 26-97, 134-234, and 236-42 respectively; cf. also Thiselton, "Realized Eschatology at Corinth" in "Eschatology and the Holy Spirit," 250.

(c) a *transformative dimension* which creates new worlds of perception, projection, or reality. We observed these aspects in relation to 1:18, 24 (especially in the light of work by Alexandra Brown and Raymond Pickett); 2:4, 5; especially 4:19, 20; 15:24; and other passages.[71] If **weakness, humiliation**, and **decay** represent the pathos of the dominating *decrescendo* of human mortality, **power** denotes not a static source of competency, but an energizing *crescendo* of equipment and capacities for **splendor** and perhaps unimagined tasks and service yet to come. Such a mode of existence, however, remains *somatic* or *bodily* in the sense described under vv. 42 and 44.

44 The key issue hinges on the respective understandings (and respective translations) of the major contrastive Greek words σῶμα ψυχικόν and σῶμα πνευματικόν. I have no doubt whatever that Paul uses the adjective πνευματικός in its regular Pauline sense to denote *that which pertains to the Holy* **Spirit** *of God.* However, a number of VSS and writers suggest different conclusions. One of several relevant factors concerns the relation between this verse and v. 50. Traditionally it was often assumed that the acknowledgment that *flesh and blood cannot inherit the kingdom of God* (v. 50) presupposed the problem of how "physical" bodies could enter the sphere of heaven. Jeremias convincingly disposed of this mistaken understanding in his well-known study of this verse when he argued that *flesh and blood* here refers not to a corrupted human corpse, but to *human nature as such in its frailty and in its sinfulness.*[72] The Hebrew phrase often refers to human nature in its frailty, whether alive or dead, in rabbinic sources.[73] Neither the living nor the dead can take part in the reign of God *as they are,* i.e., *without salvific transformation.* In this light it can be seen that NRSV's rendering (also REB's, surprisingly) of the semantic contrast as *sown a physical body . . . raised a spiritual body* prejudices and probably distorts our interpretation of *spiritual* (i.e., *spiritual* versus *physical*) as against NIV and NJB's infinitely preferable *natural body . . . spiritual body* (i.e., *spiritual* [beyond nature] versus *natural*).

The contrast between ψυχικός ἄνθρωπος and ὁ δὲ πνευματικός in 2:14 and 15 (and πνεῦμα in 2:10-16) decisively prepares the ground for Paul's use of the two terms in 15:44.[74] In 2:14 we translated ψυχικός ἄνθρωπος as *a person who lives on an entirely human level.* The Vulgate rendering *animalis homo* finds subsequent expression in John Locke's "the animal powers, i.e., faculties

71. Brown, *The Cross and Human Transformation;* Pickett, *The Cross in Corinth;* Savage, *Power through Weakness;* Crafton, *The Agency of the Apostle;* see passages cited above.

72. Jeremias, "Flesh and Blood Cannot Inherit the Kingdom of God," 151-59.

73. Cf. Strack-Billerbeck, 1:730-31; cf. also Gal 1:17.

74. See above on 2:10-16, esp. 2:14, 15, where we entered into conversation with various sources, including, e.g., Hoyle, *The Holy Spirit in St Paul,* esp. 182; Schweizer, *TDNT,* 6:415-37; Swete, *The Holy Spirit in the NT,* 169-223; Bultmann, *Theology of the NT,* 1:153-64, 330-40; Theissen, *Psychological Aspects,* 356-93; Dunn, "Spiritual," *NIDNTT,* 3:700-707; Horsley, "Pneumatikos vs. Psychikos," *HTR* 69 (1976): 269-88; Pearson, *The Pneumatikos-Psychikos Terminology in 1 Corinthians;* and Stalder, *Das Werk des Geistes in der Heiligung bei Paulus.*

of the soul unassisted by the spirit or revelation," and Robertson and Plummer's "animal" person in the sense of not rising "above the level of merely human needs and aspirations."[75] In 2:13 ψυχικός stands in contrast *not* to the human spirit but to that which pertains to *God's Holy* **Spirit**. Hence in that verse NRSV, REB, and NJB rightly translate the Greek as *unspiritual*. Senft discusses the varied uses of the Greek term in an excursus and distinguishes the Pauline uses from those of gnostic texts.[76]

THE NATURE OF THE RESURRECTION "BODY" (15:44)

Three possible views of σῶμα πνευματικόν now emerge, of which the first two do not stand up to close scrutiny.

(a) The late nineteenth-century view of πνεῦμα as "a transcendent physical essence, a supersensuous kind of matter" was promoted in 1877 by Otto Pfleiderer, and developed by Johannes Weiss in terms of a "heavenly light substance."[77] Recently it has found a new advocate in Dale Martin in connection with different worldviews held by the "strong" and the "weak" in Corinth. Philosophers of the time, he argues, would speak of the soul as some kind of "stuff," and astral "bodies" were those in which the element of fire predominated over air, earth, and water.[78] In the four canonical Gospels, Martin continues, the nature of the resurrection body of Jesus Christ was not at all clear, whereas for Paul the resurrection mode of existence is to be identified with "the heavenly bodies" which, in the light of vv. 44-49, recall "popular beliefs about the composition and hierarchy of heavenly bodies."[79] At all events, his adjectives describe "their substance and composition" which prove to be "similar" to notions of the actual soul in popular philosophy. *Pneuma* is an "entity held in common by human beings and the stars . . . a pneumatic body . . . not . . . composed of the heavier matter of the earth . . . the substance of stars."[80]

One major difficulty which besets this view is that, as Jeremias argues concerning v. 50, Paul is not primarily addressing the question of the *composition* of the "**body**." (i) Apart from the broader hermeneutical issue, the parallel three contrasts, especially the negatives **decay** (v. 42), **humiliation**, and **weakness** (v. 43), do not denote "substances" but *modes of existence or of life*. This is confirmed by (ii) the generally accepted *modal* use of ἐν in the sets of contrasts, as well as (iii) the widely accepted (although not decisive) lexicographical distinction between -ινος endings, which often, perhaps regularly, denote *composition,* in distinction from -ικος endings, which regularly denote *modes of being* or *characteristics.* Kennedy, Robertson and Plummer, and more recent writers provide decisive arguments against "compo-

---

75. John Locke, *Paraphrase and Notes,* 1:424; Robertson and Plummer, *First Epistle,* 49.

76. Senft, *Première Épître,* 206-7.

77. Pfleiderer, *Paulinism,* 1:201; and J. Weiss, *Earliest Christianity,* 2:535; also *Der erste Kor,* 371-73, where Weiss accepts the contrast with *natural,* but appeals to the hellenistic background concerning a "heavenly or pneumatic body" (372), with further allusions to Stoic texts (372-73).

78. Martin, *The Corinthian Body,* 115 and 118.

79. Ibid., 124-26.

80. Ibid., 126-27.

sition."[81] (iv) Further, Louw and Nida distinguish no fewer than eleven semantic domains for πνεῦμα (including πνευματικός), of which in Pauline material πνευματικός most frequently and characteristically means "pertaining to being derived from, or being about, the Spirit."[82] Thus πνεῦμα refers to both *spiritual* gifts and gifts *from the Holy Spirit* (12:1; cf. 2:13; Rom 1:11; cf. Eph 1:3; 5:19 — hymns inspired by the Holy Spirit, not produced by celestial or actual wavelengths). On rare (always non-Pauline) occasions in the New Testament, πνεῦμα may denote a ghost or spirit being (almost exclusively Mark 14:26; Luke 24:37; Acts 23:8), but such a use is generally avoided because of its association with evil spirits (Mark 9:25; cf. Mark 1:34, δαίμων).[83] Paul is speaking in v. 44 of a *mode and pattern of intersubjective life directed by the Holy Spirit.*

(b) Even less convincing is the theory that σῶμα πνευματικόν means simply a *nonphysical "body."* This would offer a concession (as would [a]) to hellenistic thought, but misses Paul's point entirely. (i) Again, as Fee observed, "the transformed body is not composed of 'spirit'; it is a *body* adapted to the eschatological existence that is under the ultimate domination of the Spirit."[84] All of the objections to (a) apply here. (ii) Further, as M. E. Dahl consistently argues, "σῶμα ψυχικόν = the totality of man as created and *capable* of eternal life . . . σῶμα πνευματικόν = the totality of man redeemed by the new dispensation of the Spirit and actually *endowed* with eternal life (v. 44)" (his italics) on the grounds of the difficulties of alternative views and the understanding of human persons as *totalities,* shared by the Old Testament and Paul.[85] Neither a purely "nonphysical" nor merely "bodily" (in any quasi-physical sense) explanation offers an adequate account of 15:44. To express it in crude terms, *the totality of the mode of life of the resurrection existence in the Holy Spirit is more than physical but not less,* i.e., the equivalent capacities to aesthetic and empirical satisfaction (including, with Käsemann, communicative recognition and differentiation in an intersubjective, public domain) *cannot be less* than those of earthly physical life if this mode of existence embraces the "more" of the agency of the Holy Spirit and the love of the Creator God. Heaven is not *Sheol,* where earthly existence is perceived to be "thinned down."

Startlingly, since all the exegetical, theological, and lexicographical evidence is against it, Louw and Nida astonish us by placing 15:44 almost alone in a short sub-category under the heading "pertaining to not being physical."[86] Perhaps they are unduly influenced by other foreign-language cultures, for some of which they propose "a body which will not have flesh and bones," since even a "body" under the direction of the Spirit is perceived to be physical unless the nuances of Greek and Paul are explained. Elsewhere, however, they rightly note on the basis of 1 Cor

---

81. See Findlay, *Expositor's Greek Testament*, 937; Robertson and Plummer, *First Epistle*, 372-73 (the adjectives mean *"formed to be the organ of,"* not *"made of"* (372; my italics); Pearson, *Pneumatikos-Psychikos Terminology*, 7-26; Lang, *Die Briefe*, 234-5; Kennedy, *St Paul's Conception of the Last Things*, 253, n. 1; Dahl, *The Resurrection of the Body*, 53-57, 59-73, and esp. 125-26. More broadly, see Clavier, "Breves Remarques sur la Notion de σῶμα πνευματικόν," in Davies and Daube (eds.), *The Background of the NT and Its Eschatology*, 346; cf. 342-62.

82. Louw-Nida, 141-43 (sects. 12-18, 12-21) and 509 (sects. 40.41; cf. 79.86).

83. Ibid., 509 (sects. 40-41).

84. Fee, *First Epistle*, 786.

85. Dahl, *Resurrection*, 126; cf. 20-73 and throughout.

86. Louw-Nida, 1:694, sect. 79-3.

3:1 that πνευματικός denotes "a pattern of life controlled and directed by God's Spirit."[87]

(c) The allusion to 1 Cor 3:1 provides an admirable starting point for confirmation of the third understanding which we have been urging. We translated the contrast between πνευματικός and σάρκινος ... σαρκικός in 3:1, 3 as "people of **the Spirit** ... people moved by entirely human drives ... unspiritual...." Thus Barrett understands v. 44 to refer to "the new body animated by the Spirit of God."[88] Bruce hints at the dimension of Christology and character by alluding here to the life-giving Spirit of v. 45.[89] The natural body deserves its character from the Adam of creation; the body which is raised derives its character from the last Adam, Christ, who is both Lord of the Spirit and himself raised by God through the Spirit (Rom 8:11). Wolff declares, "The spiritual body of the resurrection *(der pneumatische Auferstehungsleib)* is through and through a body under the control of the divine Spirit, according to v. 45 a creation of Christ (cf. also vv. 21-22) who is 'the life-giving Spirit.'"[90]

This provides a constructive connection between the salvific and ethical character of the body directed by the Holy Spirit and the character of Christ's own raised body in later traditions of the canonical Gospels as "more" but not "less" than an earthly physical body. In these resurrection traditions Jesus Christ was not always immediately "recognized" (John 20:14, 15; 21:12; Luke 24:13-20) but his personal identity was recognized in terms of sociophysical gestures and characteristics (Luke 24:31; John 20:16, 20, 27-28; action, voice, hands, side). In the tradition of Luke-Acts Jesus "ascended" above the clouds (Acts 1:9, 10), but in the Johannine tradition Jesus appears to have shared in the meal of fish (John 21:12, 13).[91] Paul's analogies concerning the created order are the corresponding match between bodily form and purposive function (birds, fish, sun, moon, stars), which strongly, indeed surely conclusively, suggests that *what counts as a* **body** *(sōma, form,* in relation to a *public context) depends precisely upon its immediate environment and purpose.* When Jesus Christ appeared within the environment of our world's space-time for the purpose of providing visible and tangible (John 20:27) evidence of his identity to witnesses as Jesus of Nazareth both raised and transformed, this "bodily" mode verged on, but also transcended, the

---

87. Ibid., 1:509, sects. 40-41. A large body of literature confirms that this is the most characteristic use of the term by Paul. J. Weiss observes, Paul "could not imagine a disembodied soul ... a 'naked' existence after death" (*Earliest Christianity,* 2:534). The relation between 15:35-44 and 2 Cor 5 is complex but coherent and consistent. Even if we follow Earle Ellis in understanding *naked* in 2 Cor 5:2 as "naked in guilt and shame," this simply substantiates our reading of 15:43-44 in soteriological rather than cosmological terms (E. E. Ellis, "2 Cor 5:1-10 in Pauline Eschatology," *NTS* 3 [1959-60]: 211-24; rpt. in Ellis, *Paul and His Recent Interpreters,* 35-48).

88. Barrett, *First Epistle,* 372.

89. Bruce, *1 and 2 Cor,* 152.

90. Wolff, *Der erste Brief,* 407.

91. For a summary and brief discussion of issues in the Lukan and Johannine traditions see Perkins, *Resurrection: NT Witness and Contemporary Reflection,* 149-94. "Some think that Luke is already confronted with a naïve docetism that denied the bodily character of the resurrection. Luke's entire account ... presents the resurrection as an event that affects Jesus' body," but this need not be an antidocetic construction; it identifies the risen Christ with the earthly Jesus (164). See further R. J. Dillon, *From Witnesses to Ministers of the Word: The Tradition and Composition in Luke 24* (Rome: Biblical Institute Press, 1978); cf. R. E. Brown, *The Gospel according to John* (Garden City, N.Y.: Doubleday, 1970), 2:995-1,092.

physical. In the event of the ascension (whether we regard this as a genuine event or as an event within a projected narrative world) the "body" would transcend physical limitations. However, we must not become re-seduced into construing Paul's purpose in these verses as describing the *composition* of the *sōma*. The point is, rather, that a resurrection mode of existence characterized by the **reversal of decay, splendor, power**, and being constituted by (the direction, control, and character of) **the** (Holy) **Spirit** would be expected *not to be reduced in potential from the physical capacities which biblical traditions value, but enhanced above and beyond them in ways that both assimilate and transcend them.*

Body, therefore, affirms the biblical tradition of a positive attitude toward physicality as a condition for experiencing life in its fullness, but *also assimilates, subsumes, and transcends the role of the physical in the public domain of earthly life.* Hence it would be appropriate to conceive of the **raised body** as a form or mode of existence of the whole person including every level of intersubjective communicative experience that guarantees both the continuity of personal identity and an enhanced experience of community which facilitates intimate union with God in Christ and with differentiated "others" who also share this union. If the marriage bond, e.g., ceases at death, this is also not because the resurrection **body** offers any "less," but because interpersonal union is assimilated and subsumed into a "more" that absorbs exclusivity but "adds" a hitherto unimagined depth. Such mutuality of union and respect for difference, however, presupposes a *"pattern of existence controlled and directed by the* [Holy] **Spirit**" (BAGD, above), and a *mode* of existence designed by God for the new environment of the eschatological new creation. This may imply philosophical issues about how the **raised** community will freely choose such holiness of disposition, but these would take us too far beyond the text.

On the other hand, the three pairs of contrasts — **decay** and its absence or reversal, **humiliation** and **splendor**, and **an ordinary human body** and a **body constituted by the Spirit** — give solid ground for conceiving of the postresurrection mode of life as a *purposive and dynamic crescendo of life,* since the *living God* who acts purposively decrees this fitting mode, rather than envisaging some static ending in which the **raised body** is forever trapped, as if in the last "frozen" frame of a film or movie. In the biblical writings **the Spirit** is closely associated with ongoing *vitality,* which Paul takes up in v. 45b.

Many begin a new paragraph with v. 44b.[92] However, the second half of v. 44 merely signals the reader, if any doubt should still remain, to reflect back upon *what has been said already* about the created order and the infinite resourcefulness of God as Creator. If God can create **an ordinary human body** (v. 44a) among a myriad of other forms and species, is it not logical to suppose that just as there is **a body for the human realm** (v. 44b, σῶμα ψυχικόν, the same Greek term as v. 44a, even if translated differently into English) **there is also a body for the realm of the Spirit** (ἔστιν καὶ πνευματικόν, same Greek as v. 44a)? The one necessary exegetical caveat is to note that **realm of the Spirit** (i.e., πνευματικόν) does *not* mean *primarily* the nonphysical realm (although it certainly includes this), but what befits the transformation of character or pattern of existence effected by the Holy Spirit. Here the biological analogies of transforming a bare seed or grain into fruit, flower, or harvest may take on an aes-

---

92. For example, REB, NIV, and NJB (against NRSV) and Barrett, Héring, and Collins (against Conzelmann and Fee).

thetic dimension for illustrative purposes to underline (a) contrast; (b) continuity of identity; and (c) full and radical transformation of form and character.

Theissen notes that in contrast to the Corinthian tradition that Paul corrects in vv. 44-45 "the pneumatic is to be understood as goal, not as origin.... The conferral of Pneuma signifies an expansion of consciousness beyond the familiar 'psychic' limits.... Paul presupposes the existence of a new world."[93] The dynamic, ongoing, purposive nature of this "new world" is underlined by Paul's insistence that it is characterized by *love* as the one disposition that survives the eschaton (13:8-13), which he already defined as purposive dynamic habituated action (13:4-7; see above on these verses). The **raised body** provides conditions for the meaningful experience of receiving and giving this creative love. As J. Cambier reminds us, v. 44 sums up the transformation which is introduced in vv. 37-38 — "what you sow is not the body which shall be . . . God gives . . ." — and turns neither on two "compositions" nor on two "states," but on "two tendencies, two forces. . . ."[94] Paul is concerned with how the new, raised "body" is "oriented"; and "the principal enemy" which he targets is the reduced existence of the soul-shade in the "Sheol-Hades" of both Jews and Greeks.[95] Hence he leads on to the triumph of v. 55: "Where, O death, is your victory?"

By way of contrast, gnostic texts read Paul as using *spiritual* here in the hermeneutical sense of a "spiritual" or "allegorical" (i.e., metaphorical) reading of the resurrection of the "**body**."[96] Irenaeus attacks such a view decisively. After quoting 1 Cor 15:36, 41-44, he alludes to the Valentinian view as understanding something different from Paul: Paul does not refer to "immortal spirits" but to those in Christ who, just as Christ was raised bodily, will be made alive in "bodies" different from bodies that decompose.[97] Tertullian distances himself from Marcion's devaluation of the body, and Marcion's related reading of 1 Cor 15:42-44, in the same way.[98] Thomas Aquinas understands the **raised body** to function with a multiplicity of organs or "parts."[99] However, Luther captures Paul's perspective well: "It is really the work of God.... it will not be a body that eats, sleeps, and digests, but ... has life in Him ... lives solely of and by the Spirit."[100] Christ, Luther adds (on vv. 48-49), is our prototype, who devours the poison of the sin that corrupts (vv. 54-55), and **the raised body** therefore will be "endowed with a more beautiful and better form than the present one."[101] "Be content to hear what God will do. Then leave it to Him"; "it will be strong and vigorous, healthy and happy ... more beautiful than the sun and moon.... We shall all have spiritual gifts."[102] This is entirely in conflict with

93. Theissen, *Psychological Aspects,* 365 and 388.

94. Cambier, "Brèves Remarques sur la Notion de σῶμα πνευματικόν," 346 and 347-48.

95. Ibid., 351 and 360-61.

96. Cf. *Treatise on the Resurrection,* 45:20-28 and esp. 45:39–46:2; 47:4-8; and 49:25-28, M. L. Peel (ed.), *Epistle to Rheginos,* 186; E. Pagels, *The Gnostic Paul,* 84-85; and Pagels, "Conflicting Versions of Valentinian Eschatology," *HTR* 67 (1974): 35-44.

97. Irenaeus, *Against Heresies,* 5:7:1, 2.

98. Tertullian, *Against Marcion,* 5:10 (throughout).

99. Aquinas, *Summa Theologica,* pars. 3, Q. 84:1:1; cf. also 83:1.

100. Luther, *Works,* 28:187-92; *WA,* 36:657-65.

101. Ibid., 28:181; cf. 196-213; *WA,* 36:648; cf. 670-96.

102. Ibid., 28:180 and 142; *WA,* 36:647 and 593-94. On Luther's exegesis, see Thiselton, "Luther and Barth on 1 Cor 15," in Stephens (ed.), *The Bible, the Reformation, and the Church,* 258-89.

a countertradition that can be traced back to Justin: "we expect to receive again our own bodies, though they be dead and cast into the earth."[103] In Irenaeus and in Tertullian there is ambivalence in this direction, and it conflicts with Paul's argument explicitly in 15:36-38, 42-44, 50-54.[104]

45-46 B, K, and some minuscules omit ἄνθρωπος since it appears to replicate Ἀδάμ (see below).

The citation is from Gen 2:7: καὶ ἐγένετο ὁ ἄνθρωπος εἰς ψυχὴν ζῶσαν (LXX), but Paul has inserted the word πρῶτος.[105] Some regard the introductory οὕτως as marking an acknowledgment that Paul does not cite the LXX *verbatim*.[106] On the other hand, there is much to be said for REB's *it is **in this sense** that scripture says*. . . . The Septuagintal (and Pauline) use of εἰς in εἰς ψυχὴν ζῶσαν simply reflects the Hebrew use of the equivalent ל *(le)*. The whole of the Hebrew original, however, includes the word **Adam**, which LXX translates ἄνθρωπος: ויהי האדם לנפש חיה *(wayehi ha'adam lᵉnephesh chayyah; and man/Adam became [for] a living nephesh/ψυχή/person)*. C. D. Stanley rightly sees this as fruitful for comparing Paul's usual citations of the LXX with his possible use of the Hebrew: "Nothing in either Greek or Hebrew textual traditions offers any reason to think that Paul might have the word πρῶτος in his *Vorlage* of Gen 2:7."[107] However, the addition formalizes "the fundamental contrast between Adam and Christ as the πρῶτος and ἔσχατος Adam (v. 46b) that forms the backbone of the ensuing argument."[108] The insertion of Ἀδάμ, however, may not be due entirely to the shape of Paul's argument. Theodotion and Symmachus read ὁ Ἀδὰμ ἄνθρωπος in their own LXX texts. As Stanley observes, since Heb. אדם *('Adam)* serves either as a generic term for humankind or as a proper name for a male person, a dual word order in Paul and in Theodotion/Symmachus would be entirely possible and understandable: "Paul may not have added the proper name Ἀδάμ to his text of Gen 2:7."[109] (This also underlines that the correct MS reading in v. 45 is not that followed by B and K; see above under Textual Note).

The Adam-Christ typology has already been introduced in 15:21-22, where it closely anticipates the better-known typology of Rom 5:12-19. Morna Hooker points out that in spite of difficulties of syntax, "the parallels and con-

103. Justin, *Apology,* 1:8; cf. *Dialogue,* 81.
104. The materialist aspect emerges in Tertullian more strongly in his *Resurrection of the Flesh,* e.g., *Resurrection,* 35, where hair and teeth are supposedly restored. Cf. Davies, "Factors Leading to the Emergence of Belief in the Resurrection of the Flesh," 448-55. Davies cites (a) the appearance tradition; (b) millenarianism; (c) antignostic polemic; (d) partial hellenistic dualism.
105. On whether he also inserts *Adam,* see below.
106. For example, Edwards, *First Epistle,* 442.
107. Stanley, *Paul and the Language of Scripture,* 208.
108. Ibid.
109. Ibid., 209.

trasts between Adam and Christ [in Rom 5:12-19] are clear: five times over, first negatively and then positively, everything which happened 'in Adam' is more than counterbalanced by what happens 'in Christ.'"[110]

The contrast plays a fundamental part not only in this chapter (15:20-22, 45-49) but in the whole of Paul's theology. James Dunn discusses several passages where the first and last Adam lie at the heart of Paul's thought and argument, naming especially Rom 5:12-21; 1 Cor 15:20-22, and 15:45: "Paul deliberately sets Jesus alongside Adam. . . . Adam is clearly understood in some sort of representative capacity. Adam is humankind, an individual who embodies or represents a whole race of people . . . so also does Christ. Adam is 'the type of the One to come' (Rom 5:14) . . . the eschatological counterpart of the primeval Adam. . . . Each begins an epoch, and the character of each epoch is established by their action."[111]

Paul uses the shorthand *those in* **Adam** and *those in Christ* to express this nexus of thoughts (15:22; see above). As Holleman notes, the framework of thought is representative, soteriological, and apocalyptic: "Jesus has been raised as *the representative* of those who will be raised" (his italics; see above on 15:20-22), ". . . a 'representative figure' who formed a unity with his people."[112] Holleman compares Adam's role in Rom 5:12-21; 1 Cor 15:21-22, 43-49, with that of Abraham as representative in Gal 3:8-9. The contrast between the effects of Adam's representative failure through self-exaltation and Christ's representative victory through voluntary self-humiliation lies behind Phil 2:6-11. That the "old" creation requires not merely "correction" but a new beginning in new creation lies at the center of apocalyptic understandings of human bondage, fallenness, the limits of the law, and divine agency to intervene decisively for salvation.

The corporate and representative role of Adam, however, is not exclusive to Paul or even apocalyptic, but emerges in hellenistic Wisdom texts and Philo.[113] Nevertheless, "the main difference between Paul and Philo arises in relation to the eschatological role of the firstborn heavenly man which also underlies Paul's phrase ἔσχατος Ἀδάμ (v. 45)."[114] As Goppelt observes, late Judaism had already established "the destructive power of Adam" which provides the apocalyptic and soteriological backcloth for Paul "to demonstrate the sav-

---

110. Hooker, "Interchange and Atonement," in *From Adam to Christ,* 28; cf. 26-41, and 13-101. These seven essays of Parts 1 and 2 include Romans 1 and Phil 2:6-11.

111. Dunn, *The Theology of Paul,* 200; cf. 199-204, 208-12, and 241-42.

112. Holleman, *Resurrection and Parousia,* 1 and 21.

113. Sellin, *Der Streit um die Auferstehung der Toten,* 79-189; Weiss, *Der erste Kor,* 374-76; Wis 2:23; 9:2; 10:1, and allusions to Wisdom 12 and 13 in Hooker, *From Adam to Christ,* 75-78; Sir 17:1; 49:16; and notably *Apocalypse of Moses* 7:2-3; 8:2; 9:2; 10:2; 14:2; 21:1-6; 37:1-6; 39:1-3; 41:3; Philo, *Opificio Mundi* 47.136-41.

114. Jeremias, *TDNT,* 1:143; cf. 141-43. See further E. Brandenburger, *Adam und Christus,* 68-157; J. Muddiman, "'Adam, The Type of the One to Come,'" *Theol* 87 (1984): 101-10; Scroggs, *The Last Adam;* M. Black, "The Pauline Doctrine of the Second Adam," *SJT* 7 (1954): 70-79; Goppelt, *Typos,* 129-36; and Pearson, *Pychikos-Pneumatikos,* 17-23.

ing power of Christ."[115] "Paul rejects the kind of speculation about an *ideal* original man that is found in Philo with a remark that he inserts into . . . his argument (1 Cor 15:46). He accepts the order revealed by scripture and redemptive history. . . . According to Gen 2:7, the *first* man is *from the earth,* whereas the *second* man is *from heaven*" (my italics).[116] Each "imprints his likeness on those under his headship (1 Cor 15:48)."[117]

Although **the first Adam** and **the last Adam** share this representative and character-forming role, in other respects the *contrast* between them cannot be exaggerated. **The first Adam** was merely a **living human being** (Gen 2:7). ψυχή, like Heb. שֶׁפֶנ *(nephesh),* denotes earthly life which can be lost in death; indeed, שֶׁפֶנ *(nephesh,* normally *that which breathes)* is also possessed by the animals (Gen 1:20, 24, 30; 2:10), can be used to denote simply a human being (often equivalent to a personal pronoun, Num 23:10; Judg 16:30), and is even used to refer to a person who has died or to a corpse (Num 6:6).[118] Similarly, ψυχή typically describes "one's earthly life as it publicly observable" and can be readily lost.[119] As we have seen, the adjective ψυχικός frequently has negative nuances in Paul (see on 2:14, above). By emphatic contrast, **the last Adam** is not merely **living** but **life-giving**.

First-century speculative interpretations of **Adam** and Genesis 1 agree with Paul in describing **Adam** as the parent of humankind, as **the first man** (Philo, *De Abrahamo* 56; 1 Cor 15:47). However, Philo is sufficiently influenced by Plato's theory of Forms or Ideas to associate the two creation accounts in Genesis 1 and Genesis 2 with *two* concepts of **Adam**. That which bears the stamp of *God's image* (1:26) is πνεῦμα: *spiritual and heavenly.* The prototype of *Ideal Adam* is οὐράνιος ἄνθρωπος . . . κατ᾽ εἰκόνα θεοῦ γεγονώς. . . . However this *"heavenly man"* who bears "God's image" is different from the Adam who is *"earthly"* (γήϊνος) and was *"made out of bits of matter"* (ἐκ σποράδος ὕλης), which Moses calls *"clay"* or **"soil"** (ἣν χοῦν κέκληκεν) in *Legum Allegoriae* 1:31-32. As in Plato's philosophy, **first** comes the *eternal heavenly Idea* or *Form;* second comes the *empirical, contingent, earthly copy* which seeks to approximate the Form or Pattern from which it was derived. For Philo, *humankind* or *"man"* in Gen 2:7 is an admixture of the *contingent,* an object of *sense* data (αἴσθητος . . . ἐκ σώματος καὶ ψυχῆς συνεστώς), and a reaching up to the *incorporeal* (ἀσώματος) and *incorruptible* (ἄφθαρτος). On this basis, "spirituality" could be perceived as the opposite of how Paul views it. For Paul *new creation* and *transformation came from beyond and were constituted by the agency of the Holy Spirit,* not an immanent human spirit.

115. Goppelt, *Typos,* 129-30.
116. Ibid., 134. Goppelt compares "the Son of Man who assumed our flesh when he came from heaven (cf. Rom 8:3) and he will come again in a transfigured heavenly body (cf. Phil 3:20)" (*Typos,* 129-30).
117. Ibid.
118. BAGD, 659-61.
119. Jewett, *Paul's Anthropological Terms,* 448.

It is important to note that "whether Paul read Philo" has little bearing on the issues. Philo, in spite of all his own idiosyncrasies as no "representative" thinker, nevertheless was in touch with, and often reflects, religious philosophies of the day which, especially in Jewish or Christian circles, become attractive when they appear to combine sophisticated concepts with possible readings of scripture.[120] Recently Elaine Pagels has looked again at "the cluster of logia that interpret Genesis 1" in the *Gospel of Thomas* and the Gospel of John. What is presupposed, she urges, is not some single "gnostic myth" but a "widely known and varied . . . exegesis [which] connects the *eikon* of Gen 1:26-27 with the primordial light . . . to show . . . the way back to . . . primordial creation" (Gen 1:3).[121] Pagels perceives the Fourth Gospel as directing "polemics against a type of Genesis exegesis used by a wide range of readers, both Jewish and Christian," and it is *not* farfetched to detect such a concern in Paul.[122]

It seems probable, then, that Paul's explication of the eschatological "order" (cf. on vv. 23-28 above) and purposive sequence serves a dual purpose. (a) It underlines the need to look ahead: believers will be transformed fully into that mode of existence which characterizes Christ as **Spirit** (i.e., both beyond earthly horizons of imagination and beyond the destructive effects of weakness and sin). (b) It also serves as a probable polemic against any Christology which draws on the Archetypal Man theme (found perhaps among some of the more sophisticated "strong") based on scraps of religious philosophy originating from hellenistic or hellenistic-Jewish "wisdom" traditions or perhaps Philo's world of thought.[123] Adam is no archetypal model who represents Ideal Humanity; he stands for all that is fallen and destructive. This is the very background that makes an understanding of *the proclamation of the cross* (1:18-25) utterly central and the ground of all hope. The cross brings *reversal* (cf. 1:26-31), not simply degrees of "advance." Hence v. 46 underlines the contrast between the two orders of being represented respectively by **the first Adam** and **the last Adam**, but the *resurrection carries with it no "myth of eternal return" but the promise of new creation.* Paul does not devalue the physical, which is God's gift, but the natural is bound up with human sin and bondage, and there is no hope of full salvation without *transformation* by an act of the sovereign God which entails the mediate agency also of Christ and **the Spirit**.

Predictably, Schmithals regards the supposed interruption of v. 46 as fur-

120. Cf. further G. J. Warne, *Hebrew Perspectives on the Human Reason in the Hellenistic Era: Philo and Paul,* Mellen Bible Press 35 (Lewiston: Mellen, 1995).

121. E. H. Pagels, "Exegesis of Genesis 1 in the Gospels of Thomas and John," *JBL* 118 (1999): 488; cf. 477-96.

122. Ibid., 492. Cf. Hays, *1 Cor,* 273; and Brandenburger, *Adam und Christus,* 68-157.

123. Certainly "there is no direct evidence that Paul had read Philo" (Barrett, *First Epistle,* 375). However, there were common stocks of speculative thought of which both writers were probably well aware. Certainly educated readers would be familiar with Plato's philosophy of Forms or Ideas of which everyday contingent objects were shadows or copies. Fee points out that "not/but" suggests an assertion "over against the Corinthians themselves" (*First Epistle,* 791). See further Lang, *Die Briefe,* 236, and more briefly Collins, *First Cor,* 571.

ther evidence of gnostic influence at Corinth.[124] We have already noted the problems which beset this view. Although we concede that it is possible to overstress the problem of "Realized Eschatology at Corinth," nevertheless this verse links gospel-grounded transformation with eschatological horizons grounded in Christ.[125] A surprising number of late-nineteenth-century commentaries allude here to "a law of progress," perhaps reflecting a relatively "new" theological acceptance of evolutionary angles of understanding.[126] However, an eschatology which focuses on *new creation* is precisely *not* based on "a low view of progress." All the same, an allusion to "law" remains acceptable if by this we mean the "order" of the divine purpose which Paul underlines in vv. 23-28: *everything in its proper order.*[127] *Eschatological discontinuity* implies that the Corinthians cannot yet live as if the triumph is complete: **first**, *the natural, everyday order of life with all its constraints and contingencies,* i.e., **the purely human**, *continues;* only **after that** does "Christlikeness," i.e., bearing the imprint of **the last Adam**, become wholly transposed into following Christ in the realm of the **Spirit** without constraint or qualification.

Because this very fine point relates so closely to the Corinthian view of salvation, it is scarcely surprising that the allusion to **Spirit** caused considerable perplexity in patristic exegesis. Ambrosiaster (followed by Grotius, Estius, and Heinrici) sees this as referring to the empowering of Christ at his resurrection by *the* **Spirit**.[128] Theophylact regards this as denoting the messianic anointing by *the* **Spirit**, and the use of τὸ ζωοποιόν may have influenced the formulation of the article on the Holy Spirit as "the Lord, the Giver of Life" in the Niceno-Constantinopolitan Creed. The explanation offered above, however, takes full account of Paul's context of situation and the force of his argument at this specific point. Robertson and Plummer better convey Paul's thought: "There is nothing final in the universe except God."[129]

47-48   Three variants are at issue. (1) Marcion changed **the second man** to *Lord* (κύριος), for reasons of theology. Tertullian explicitly attacks Marcion's changing of the text for his own purposes: "If **the first** was a *man,* can there be a second unless he were a *man* also? Or if **the second** is *'Lord,'* was **the first** also *'Lord'?*"[130] Here is an early witness to textual issues. (2) The AV/KJV phrase *the Lord from heaven* is based on the reading of ℵ[3], A, D[2], K, L, and Syriac VSS. Against this, however, is ranged a decisive plurality of early text-types:

124. Schmithals, *Gnosticism,* 169-70; cf. Jewett, *Anthropological Terms,* 352-56.

125. Thiselton, "Realized Eschatology at Corinth," in "Eschatology," 250.

126. Surprisingly, e.g., Edwards, *First Epistle* (1885), 445; Meyer, *First Epistle* (Germ. 4th ed. 1862, Eng. 1884), 2:95, "the law of development." Similarly, Findlay, *Expositor's Greek Testament,* 2:938: "A development from lower to higher."

127. Kennedy, *St Paul's Conceptions of the Last Things,* rescues the point precisely in this way (255-57).

128. Heinrici, *Das erste Sendschreiben,* 538-39, where he also cites Theophylact.

129. Robertson and Plummer, *First Epistle,* 374. Cf. also Burchard, "1 Kor 15:39-41," 243; also 233-52; and Wolff, *Der erste Brief,* 410.

130. Tertullian, *Against Marcion,* 5:10.

א*, B, C, D, Coptic, Bohairic (Sahidic often follows A and various Latin MSS); all rightly omit κύριος. (3) p⁴⁶ reads ἄνθρωπος πνευματικός, but is virtually unsupported. The common assumption is that an early scribe was influenced by having just copied this phrase in v. 46. The UBS 4th ed. text is therefore not to be doubled.[131]

Several themes are interwoven in these succinct, syntactically abbreviated verses. (1) One major strand, the fundamental one, continues to expound the theme of *somatic* forms: humanity as such finds its model in the **first** *Adam,* who was created **from earth's soil** (Gen 2:7, Hebrew and LXX) and shares the mortality and fragility of what belongs to those whose σῶμα is **made from** that which disintegrates into **dust** in the grave (on the Greek and Hebrew, see below). The *raised Christ,* however, belongs to, indeed provides the model for, a different order of existence. Raised by God through the agency of the Holy Spirit, **the second man** exhibits those qualities that come **from heaven** and shape the character and nature of the form in which those "in" Christ (see above) will be raised. (2) A second, less central strand takes up the background of thought which we discussed under v. 46 about the potential for misunderstanding invited by non-Christian speculation about two Adams of a different kind in the type of thought on which Philo draws (whether Paul knew his writings or not). Above all, *spiritual* levels of existence do *not* mean those which draw their character from the *human spirit within, but from the Spirit of God* who is both within and beyond: *the Beyond who is within.* (3) Although Barrett, among others, warns us not to interpret these verses as a matter of moral likeness to Christ, the pronouns οἷος . . . τοιοῦτοι, twice repeated, are "correlative pronouns of character or quality" which enhance more than mere somatic form.[132] On this basis we use Eng. **model/models** (cf. REB, *is the pattern . . . is the pattern* [v. 48]; NJB, *is the pattern;* NRSV, NIV, Collins, *as . . . so . . .*). The resurrection mode of existence, for Paul, is decisively shaped and directed by the Holy Spirit in accordance with transformation into the image of Christ as well as a new "form" (15:44, 45, 49, 50-57). (4) Paul appeals to the first half of Gen 2:7 (cf. the second half in v. 45).

According to E. Schweizer, Paul coined the term χοϊκός, **made from dust**, since it is "only possible on the basis of the LXX translation of Gen 2:7."[133] This is possible because it is a rare word that appears not to predate the time of Paul. The LXX uses the noun form χοῦς. The LXX of Gen 2:7a reads: ἔπλασεν ὁ θεὸς τὸν ἄνθρωπον χοῦν ἀπὸ τῆς γῆς. Paul alludes to part of this, but by changing the specific verbal forms to ἐκ γῆς χοϊκός.[134] Before we examine the Greek, we need to note what Hebrew terms the LXX translates. The Hebrew begins *God formed,* and continues אֶת־הָאָדָם עָפָר מִן־הָאֲדָמָה *(eth-ha'adam*

---

131. Metzger, *Textual Commentary* (2d ed.), 501-2.

132. Robertson, *Epistles,* 4:197; also Fee, *First Epistle,* 792; "quality," not "origin."

133. E. Schweizer, *TDNT,* 9:472, 472-79.

134. Conzelmann perhaps exaggerates the extent to which Gen 2:7 is "completely reinterpreted" (*1 Cor,* 284). This claim depends in part on our exegesis.

'aphar min-ha'adamah); it thus includes both עָפָר *('aphar), dry earth,* **dust,** *loose earth,* or sometimes *surface of the ground,* and אֲדָמָה *('adamah),* **earth's soil,** either dry *(dust)* or wet *(mud)* or both *(humus).*[135] **Dust** (esp. עָפָר, *'aphar,* but also sometimes חֹמֶר, *chomer)* suggests that which may have perished but for a time artificially maintains its earlier form *only to disintegrate into* **dust** *or powder* if it is touched or exposed to the wind or air. It therefore calls to mind the burial of the grave: "From dust humankind came; to dust it returns" (Gen 3:19). Humankind is also said to be created from *clay* (another nuance of חֹמֶר, *chomer,* Job 33:6). The LXX tends to use the noun χοῦς (not the later adjective χοϊκός, which was probably not yet at hand) to denote *earth's soil, dry earth,* or **dust,** and πηλός to translate חֹמֶר *(chomer).* It also uses the wide-ranging γῆ for **earth, soil,** *land,* or *ground.*[136] Often the latter translates אֶרֶץ *('erets), earth* or *land.* γῆ can be used of *life on* **earth** as the pre-eschatological period of testing and temptation, especially in Luke (Luke 21:23, 25), while in John it is used characteristically to denote an order of being or person who is **from the earth** (John 3:31).[137]

Hence a background is inherited in the first-century world of those familiar with scripture which projects subtle and multivalent nuances on which Paul plays. (a) **Earthly** stands implicitly in contrast to being *of the Holy Spirit* in 15:47. (b) The allusion to the material **dust** describes the σῶμα which is laid in the grave in weakness and sorrow, to disintegrate into bones and *powder.* (c) The whole string of nouns and adjectives with ἐκ + genitive of source or efficient cause provides a contrast in the clearest terms between the characteristics of two modes of existence represented respectively by ὁ χοϊκός and ὁ ἐπουράνιος. The latter can best be translated by **what pertains to heaven.** For heaven is not a locality as such, but the realm characterized by the immediate presence and purity of the living God in and through Christ and the Spirit.[138] Further, *the spiritual Man* or *the heavenly Man* smacks of the dubious "heavenly man" speculation.[139] Even the allusion suggested by Barrett to the Son of Man as a heavenly figure in Dan 7:13 and *1 Enoch* 46:1-3 is so fraught with complexity in contemporary debate as to be at best an uncertain background.[140]

In spite of its speculative character also, parallels with Jewish and Christian exegesis of Genesis 1-2 in the first century are more likely to be behind Paul's choice of wording both here and in vv. 45-46 (see above, especially our

135. BDBG, 9-10 and 779-80. אֲדָמָה *('adamah)* denotes *soil* or *land to be tilled* (Gen 2:5, 9; 3:17, 23; 4:2); sometimes *a piece of ground* (Gen 47:18-20); more often *earth as a substance, soil* as a *wet or dry medium* (2 Sam 17:12; 1 Kings 17:11; 18:1). עָפָר *('aphar)* denotes **dust,** *dry earth, loose earth.*

136. Schweizer, *TDNT,* 9:472; BAGD, 884.

137. Also H. Sasse, *TDNT,* 1:677-81; A. Kretzer, *EDNT,* 1:246-47.

138. Cf. the popular slogan, "It is not that in heaven we find God, but that in God we find heaven"; and BAGD, 305-6, on the adjective.

139. Cf. Conzelmann, "Excursus: Adam and Primal Man," *1 Cor,* 284-87; and Brandenburger, *Adam und Christus,* 68-157.

140. Barrett, *First Epistle,* 375-76.

allusions to discussions by Pagels and Brandenburger, and our citation of Greek and English from some of Philo's texts). We discussed above Philo's contrast between the earthly (γήϊνος) Adam of contingent matter (ὕλη) made from soil or dust (χοῦς) and the Adam who bears the image of God (εἰκών) who is the heavenly man (οὐράνιος ἄνθρωπος).[141] Philo stresses the perfection of the heavenly Adam.[142] Again, even if he is often idiosyncratic and unrepresentative of wider thought, he is not alone in portraying the "beauty" of Adam prior to the fall.[143] This relates to the second theme which we identified in our first paragraph on vv. 47-48. Such a perspective could well encourage some at Corinth to look to the realm of *the human spirit and mind* within (especially among "the strong") rather than beyond the whole self to a transformation of *the whole self in its totality* through the agency of the *Holy Spirit* and the discontinuity or "reversal" of eschatological new creation.[144]

Finally, Paul calls for eschatological realism. Humankind remains *human and fragile* prior to the resurrection of the last day. Already the new order has begun a transformation at the level of Christlikeness or being "from the Holy Spirit" in a limited sense that still leaves fallibility and constraint. Those at Corinth must not think and act as if they were already "there." Above all, however, the model of the raised mode of being of the raised Christ constitutes a form (σῶμα) and total self (σῶμα) **from heaven,** i.e., grounded in the reality of God and the new creation. This renders the resurrection "body" which lies in the future yet more credible and conceivable, and binds together the *somatic* and the process of *growth in holiness* as *inextricably* the mark of a mode of existence *directed by the divine Spirit, anticipated in Christ's raised life, and decreed by God* (cf. 1 Cor 2:11-15; 3:1-3; 15:21-28, 38-44).[145] It is in the future that "Christians are destined to become heavenly in the image of the heavenly Man," i.e., the man **from heaven.**[146]

49 Whether we read the future indicative φορέσομεν, **we shall wear,** or the aorist subjunctive, *let us wear,* reflects a long-standing crux. The subjunctive is supported by a wide range of early texts: p⁴⁶, ℵ, C, D, F, G, Latin VSS, Coptic, Bohairic, Clement, the

---

141. Philo, *Legum Allegoriae* 1.31-32; cf. 3.161 and *Opificio Mundi* 69.
142. Philo, *Opificio Mundi* 47.136-41.
143. Sir 49:16.
144. The theology of the resurrection can never be expounded in abstraction from *the "reversals" of the cross* (cf. 1:18-31). The cross is more than a way of making it possible to enter God's presence by grace, forgiving, or union with Christ. The fundamental principle of *discontinuity* (dying with Christ) is indispensable for the related themes of *continuity of identity* and radical *transformation* (15:36, 37, 50, 52). On the *future* emphasis, see Wolff, *Der erste Brief,* 411.
145. As we noted above, the correlative pronouns οἷος . . . τοιοῦτοι . . . of each of the two "orders" denote quality characterization. Hence we may question Barrett's exclusion of the dimension of being "morally like Christ," even if we agree that this is not the primary point of these verses (Barrett, *First Epistle,* 377). Fee comments constructively on the unavoidable constraints of being human, which are relevant to Corinth (*First Epistle,* 793).
146. Héring, *First Epistle,* 179.

Latin of Irenaeus, Origen, and Gregory of Nyssa. The UBS 4th ed. text has the future indicative, supported only by B and a few minuscules, with the Coptic, Sahidic, Gregory Nazianzus, and a few other minor sources. NRSV, REB, NIV, NJB, RV, AV/KJV, and Barrett all follow the indicative reading, but some VSS (NRSV, NIV, RVmg, and Barrett) with a note recording the variant reading of the subjunctive. It is symptomatic of the intensity of the debate that while Conzelmann observes, "the context demands the indicative," Fee reads the subjunctive, declaring, "The UBS committee abandoned its better text-critical sense," on the ground that if the B reading makes such better sense, it is difficult to see why such a large range of texts, including the Alexandrian, should have changed it.[147] Metzger supports the UBS Committee's categorization of the indicative as "almost certain, 'B,'" on exegetical grounds: the text is *didactic.*[148] The debate began in the early centuries. Tertullian argues against Marcion: "He says, 'let us wear [or bear]' as a precept; not 'we shall wear [or bear] in the sense of promise."[149] Chrysostom, Cyprian, and Basil appear to read the subjunctive.[150] Yet Theodoret decisively and probably Theodore favor the indicative, and Cyril of Alexandria appears to oscillate.[151] Although he follows the Latin subjunctive reading *portemus,* Thomas Aquinas cites Rom 8:29 for the promissory nature of *we shall. . . . Quos praescivit et praedestinavit conformes. Sic ergo debemus conformari,* i.e., *we ought to be because we shall be. . . .*[152] The key point recognized in modern scholarship, however, is identified by Barrett: the "short" *o* of the indicative and the *omega* of the subjunctive varied little, if at all, in Greek *pronunciation* (e.g., in dictation, or in public reading), *hence "only exegesis can determine the original sense and reading"* (my italics).[153] Thus the majority of modern commentators stand with Barrett and Conzelmann.[154] However, the issue cannot be closed when Heinrici, Allo, Sider, Collins, and Wolff stand with Fee.[155] In our view, the indicative has the probability of the textual issue, which is closely parallel to Rom 5:1, *we have peace with God. . . .*

The verb φορέω which Paul uses should not be confused with φέρω. Both of these verbs can mean *to bear* or *to carry.*[156] However, in contrast to φέρω, *bear, carry, put up with, bring, produce, lead,* φορέω has the metaphorical force of Fr. *porter,* **to wear**, and regularly applies to *clothes*. Even *to bear* has a more metaphorical sense, e.g., *to bear a name*. Hence it does better justice to Paul to retain the metaphor: **we shall wear** the image or likeness (like a badge, coat of

147. Conzelmann, *1 Cor,* 280, n. 3; against which, see Fee, *First Epistle,* 787, n. 5.

148. Metzger, *Textual Commentary* (2d ed.), 502.

149. Tertullian, *Against Marcion,* 5:10.

150. Chrysostom, *1 Cor. Hom.,* 42:2; Cyprian, *Against the Jews,* 10.

151. Theodore of Mopsuestia in K. Staab (ed.), *Pauluskommentare aus der Griechischen Kirche,* 195.

152. Thomas Aquinas, *1 ad Cor, Lectio* 7, sect. 998 (424).

153. Barrett, *First Epistle,* 369, n. 2.

154. For example, Meyer, *First Epistle,* 2:98; Héring, *First Epistle,* 175 and 179; Edwards, *First Epistle,* 448; Weiss, *Der erste Kor,* 377; also Bachmann, Loisy, Barth.

155. Allo, *Première Épitre,* 429-30; Heinrici, *Der erste Sendschreiben,* 542-44; Sider, "The Pauline Conception of the Resurrection Body in 1 Cor 15:35-54," 434; cf. 428-39; Wolff, *Der erste Brief,* 405-6, n. 339. Collins appeals to the axiom of *lectio difficilior* (*First Cor,* 572).

156. See BAGD, 855 and 864-65.

arms, or *symbolum*) (with REB, as against *bear* in NRSV, NIV, and NJB). The issue anticipates Rom 8:29, as Thomas Aquinas notes (see above): God decreed that those "in Christ" should "share the likeness of his Son" (συμμόρφους τῆς εἰκόνος τοῦ υἱοῦ αὐτοῦ) with a view to (εἰς τὸ + infinitive) Christ's being the πρωτότοκος of the new family likeness.

Meanwhile, the Corinthians are to remember the two sets of forces which operate. They are still *human;* indeed, they are *vulnerable, fallible, and fragile* as **wearing the image of him who was formed from earth's dust** (on the Greek vocabulary, see above). They are not yet purely "people of the Spirit" but share the constraints and limitations of *being human* (cf. 1 Corinthians 8–10 and 12– 14). Nevertheless, they are *en route* to a mode of existence wholly like that of the raised Christ in glory. Then, as Luther writes, believers "become completely spiritual . . . live[s] solely of and by the Spirit. . . . We shall divest ourselves of that image . . . and receive another's, namely the celestial Christ's. Then we shall have the same form and essence which He now has since His resurrection."[157]

50 (1) The Western D, F, G, and Tertullian substitute γάρ for δέ, which would provide a logical link with v. 49. However, exegesis is likely to confirm the authenticity of δέ as marking a transition to a further distinct thought (see below, on Jeremias). (2) A, C, D, the Syriac witnesses, Vulgate, and Irenaeus read the plural of the verb *to be able* (i.e., δύνανται) in the place of the authentic UBS 4th ed. singular δύναται, which treats **flesh and blood** as synonymous with weak (even fallen?) humanity as a single entity, not as denoting two components of a person. (3) Whereas the correct text, supported by ℵ, B, Clement, and Origen, reads the infinitive κληρονομῆσαι, with the verb δύναται, **can,** *is able,* F and G, together with variants of C, D, Vulgate, and Bohairic, read the future indicative κληρονομεῖ.

It is tempting to follow REB in interpreting τοῦτο δέ φημι as *what I mean,* **dear friends,** *is* **this**. φημί bears the sense of *I mean* (BAGD, sect. 2) arguably in 1 Cor 7:29; 10:19 (also followed by ὅτι).[158] This, however, makes it explanatory or explicatory of the previous verse (cf. the reading γάρ, in place of δέ, discussed above), whereas Weiss, Jeremias, Collins, and others stress the beginning of a new pericope.[159] Jeremias argues that it is likely that vv. 35-49 ask and address the question *how* (πῶς) in relation to the σῶμα as a postresurrection mode of existence, while vv. 50-53 ask and address the question *how* in relation to seeing God and being granted the beatific vision.[160] Weiss makes a similar point about the related but different theme of vv. 50-57, also rejecting the reading γάρ for exegetical as well as textual reasons.[161] Hence we follow BAGD's

157. Luther, *Works,* 28:192 and 196 (*WA,* 36:664 and 670-71).
158. BAGD, 856.
159. Collins, *First Cor,* 573-74, esp. on rhetorical grounds, e.g., the use of chiasm. An exception is Héring, *First Epistle,* 179-80.
160. Jeremias, "'Flesh and Blood Cannot Inherit the Kingdom of God' (1 Cor 15:50)," 151- 59 (also rpt. in his *Abba,* 298-307).
161. Weiss, *Der erste Brief,* 377; also Lang, *Die Briefe,* 238-39; Hays, *1 Cor,* 274.

first category: *say*, **affirm**. However, rather than translating (with NRSV, approximately NJB) *What I am saying, brothers and sisters, is this* (which still maintains the link called into question by Weiss and Jeremias), it coheres better with the flow of argument and with the frequently declarative use of φημί regularly, as if ὅτι were ὅτι recitative in place of quotation marks, to translate **affirm** (cf. NIV, *declare*) and to place a colon after the introductory clause (with Conzelmann): **this I affirm, my dear friends: flesh and blood cannot**. . . .[162] This gives full weight to the solemn theological axiom that Paul formulates as a basic affirmation.[163]

The LXX regularly uses **flesh and blood** to denote humankind in its weakness and vulnerability, and in this sense Paul declares elsewhere that his revelation of gospel truth comes not from "flesh and blood" but from God.[164] However, Jeremias's study sheds light on a critical issue. Although this term frequently calls attention to human weakness, far more is at stake than the view of many older modern commentators that "Man . . . is too weak to wield the sceptre over the vast and mighty forces of the other world."[165] It is not simply that "our present bodies, whether living or dead, are absolutely unfitted for the Kingdom."[166] Collins rightly underlines the apocalyptic framework of thought here, even though he dissents from Jeremias over the nature of the parallelism between the two halves of this present verse.[167] Apocalyptic emphasizes "a radical incompatibility between the present condition of human existence and the resurrected condition. . . . Transformation is necessary."[168] Indeed so, but this entails not only transformation from weakness to power (vv. 43-44) but also new creation in terms of full deliverance from sin to a disposition of holiness. It is an axiom of Jewish-Christian theology that only the pure and holy can rest in the immediate presence of God.

Hence Jeremias is correct to detect a parallelism that is more than merely synonymous between v. 50a and v. 50b. Each part takes up (in inverse order) the two aspects of the change described in vv. 43-44. A σῶμα constituted by the presence and direction of the Holy Spirit entails: (i) holiness in place of sin (v. 50a); and (ii) the reversal of weakness, degeneration, and decay (v. 50b). The verb **to inherit** is often used **of coming into possession of** eschatological existence, with all that this implies. Paul has already designated the end time or the last day as that in which God will be All in all. This synonymous parallelism can be found in apocalyptic, including a beautiful passage in the *Apoca-*

---

162. Cf. Conzelmann, *1 Cor*, 288-89.

163. φημί expresses the notion of "affirming in order to correct a misapprehension" (Edwards, *First Epistle*, 449). Cf. also Lang, *Die Briefe*, 238, and the chiastic structure identified by Collins.

164. Weiss, *Der erste Kor*, 377.

165. Edwards, *First Epistle*, 449.

166. Robertson and Plummer, *First Epistle*, 376.

167. Collins, *First Cor*, 573-74 and 579-80.

168. Ibid., 573-74.

lypse of Baruch: "Everything will pass away that is corruptible. . . . And there will be no remembrance of the present time which is polluted by evils. . . . That time is coming which will remain forever; and there is a new world which does not carry back to corruption thou who enter into its beginning. . . . They will inherit this time . . . the promised time."[169]

Much patristic exegesis is far nearer to Paul's mind here than many late nineteenth-century and earlier twentieth-century commentaries. Novatian insists that Paul is not addressing the nature of the σῶμα here, but "the guilt which was caused by humanity's deliberate and rash rebellion."[170] Chrysostom urges that "the body" does not constitute the major problem as such, but "it is because of our wickedness that we cannot inherit the kingdom of God."[171] Admittedly this was often based on a misinterpretation of **flesh and blood**, as in the case of Jerome's attributing the meaning to "the works of the flesh."[172] Further, in some cases patristic exegesis "spiritualizes" Paul's emphasis on public somatic existence. However, Augustine, among others, recognizes that fully to enter into *the reign of God* there must be a resolution of the inner conflict which arises from self-will: "There will be no further conflict within ourselves . . . just as there will be no more external enemies to bear with."[173]

Once again Paul underlines the necessity for transformation as the prerequisite for **inheriting** God's active reign in the postresurrection realm. Whereas the first half of the parallelism is concerned with the need for new creation, the second explicates this further in terms of the impossibility of **decay** somehow achieving its own reversal (see above on v. 42), or even negation by its own capacities without divine transformation. ἀφθαρσία here may simply denote the *cessation of degeneration* or of **decay**, or if it carries forward the probable semantic overtones of its contrastive function in v. 42, perhaps its *reversal*, since this is implicit in the *splendor* of a mode of existence directed by the living and active Holy Spirit (v. 44).

The passage (esp. vv. 48-54) is strikingly close to Paul's similar declaration in Phil 3:21, where Paul uses μετασχηματίζω for *transformation* or *transfiguration*, with τὸ σῶμα τῆς ταπεινώσεως ἡμῶν (cf. 15:46-48) and σύμμορφον τῷ σώματι τῆς δόξης αὐτοῦ (cf. 15:49), adding that this transfiguration in similarity with, or according to mold of (NJB), his glorious body is "by that power which enables him to make all things subject to himself" (REB; Gk. ὑποτάξαι αὐτῷ τὰ πάντα; cf. 15:23-28, esp. v. 27, πάντα γὰρ ὑπέταξεν . . . ὑποτέτακται . . . τοῦ ὑποτάξαντος . . .). It is as if, after reflecting on the details of 15:23-54, Paul summarizes and reaffirms this theology succinctly in Phil 3:20-21, thereby casting into further doubt, if any existed, supposed changes of outlook between 1 Corinthians 15 and 2 Corinthians 5.

169. *2 Apocalypse of Baruch* 44:8-13 (cited in this context by Collins, *First Cor,* 576).
170. Novatian, *The Trinity,* 10.
171. Chrysostom, *1 Cor. Hom.,* 42:2.
172. Jerome, *Homily* 54, in Psalm 143.
173. Augustine, *Enchiridion,* 23:91.

51-52   The textual variants reflect complex concerns of theology, and Conzelmann and Fee have detailed notes on them.[174] The text followed by the UBS 4th ed. is doubtless correct and evaluated as "certain" ("A").[175] The UBS text follows B, D^c, K, Syriac, and Coptic. The problem faced by scribes was that since Paul and his generation had died, the reading πάντες οὐ κοιμηθησόμεθα *we shall not all sleep* (i.e., in death) seems false as it stands, and therefore to invite suspicion and correction. In fact, Paul almost certainly alludes to humankind inclusive of "we" as believers, and their anxiety was misplaced (see exegesis below). As it was perceived, however, the problem gave rise to a series of corrections, as follows: (1) ℵ, C, and 33 transfer the negative to the following clause, πάντες (μὲν) κοιμηθησόμεθα, οὐ πάντες δὲ ἀλλαγησόμεθα; (2) The early date of the first alteration can be seen, as Metzger observes, from the fact that the early p^46, followed by A^c and Origen, conflates both readings to arrive at: *we shall not all sleep, and we shall not all be changed;* (3) A* follows ℵ, C, and 33 in removing the first negative, but replaces the οὐ with οἱ, to read οἱ πάντες μὲν κοιμηθησόμεθα. Finally (4), the Western D*, Vulgate, and Tertullian and Marcion substitute ἀναστησόμεθα, *we shall all be raised,* for the first clause, and *but we shall not all be changed* for the second.[176] It is generally agreed (Metzger, Conzelmann, et al.) that this is a polemical affirmation of the resurrection of all, in the context of the times. ℵ and C (accepted by Augustine) also reflect the "average view" that all must die, i.e., they actually preclude the possibility that the parousia will arrive during the lifetime of the readers. Paul, in our view, leaves this issue open (see below), but clearly the early copyists understood the verse as implying an eschatology of imminence that needed correction, on the assumption that Paul could not have been wrong. Prior to the UBS 4th ed. and recent commentators, Westcott-Hort, Meyer, and Heinrici accept the correct reading.

The major question raised by πάντες οὐ κοιμηθησόμεθα turns on Paul's view of eschatological imminence: strictly it could mean either (i) *none of us shall sleep,* i.e., the parousia will intervene before any believer dies; or (ii) *not all of us shall* (as some of us shall) *sleep,* i.e., the parousia will come in the lifetime of some of us; or (iii) **Not all of us humans shall sleep**, i.e., the parousia will interrupt human history at some point *sooner or later* (time unspecified). The first is clearly excluded by Paul's comments about some of the Corinthian Christians having died already (especially 15:29; cf. also 11:30, which presumably alludes to premature death from "weakness or sickness"). The second view is usually associated with a theory of radical development in Paul's theology from an imminent eschatology in the earlier letters to a quasi-realized eschatology supposedly from 2 Corinthians onward. The stock-in-trade for this approach is usually the phrase "we who are alive and remain" (1 Thess 4:15), together with a questionable exegesis of 1 Cor 7:29 (see above) and this verse. It is a pity that it is necessary repeatedly to call attention to J. Lowe's decisive demolition of the developmental theory of Paul's eschatology as long ago as 1941.[177] Lowe demonstrates that the

---

174. Conzelmann, *1 Cor,* 288 and 289, n. 1; Fee, *First Epistle,* 796, n. 3.

175. Metzger, *Textual Commentary* (2d ed.), 502.

176. Tertullian, *On the Resurrection of the Flesh,* 42, *resurgemus.*

177. J. Lowe, "An Examination of Attempts to Detect Developments in St Paul's Theology," *JTS* 42 (1941): 129-42.

polarities of "eager expectation" and of an emphasis on eschatological nuances in the present occur in earlier and later epistles without clear distinction. Whiteley and others have endorsed his study.[178] The third view reflects Paul's major concern in vv. 51-52: in Whiteley's words, "It is perfectly clear that here, as in 1 Thess, St Paul ascribes to survivors and deceased the same ultimate fate," i.e., *all humans, whether alive or dead at the last resurrection,* **will undergo transformation.**[179]

Paul does indeed want Christians to "sit light" to the world, as eschatological pilgrims ready for the call home, or for the parousia, at any moment. This remains a theme in the earlier 1 Thess 4:13-18 and the later Phil 3:20-21 equally. Philippi, like Corinth, was a Roman colony on Greek soil; both communities would understand the allusion to a heavenly πολίτευμα ἐν οὐρανοῖς ἐξ οὗ καὶ σωτῆρα ἀπεδεχόμεθα κύριον Ἰησοῦν Χριστόν, ὃς μετασχηματίσει τὸ σῶμα τῆς ταπεινώσεως ἡμῶν. Paul no more asserts that the Thessalonians or the readers of 1 Corinthians are *necessarily* that last generation (although they might be) any more than the Philippians, who also *eagerly wait for the Savior, the Lord Jesus Christ* (see above on 1:4-9). Karl Mannheim's view that the "chiliastic mentality" is "always on tiptoe waiting for the propitious moment" (the *kairos*) is well captured by the understandings of Paul's mind-set by Albert Schweitzer and Martin Werner.[180] It is true that there is a link between κυριακὴ ἡμέρα and ἡμέρα τοῦ κυρίου, that Paul holds a dynamic worldview with his eyes upon the End, and that in general institutional concerns arise only in the service of the gospel.[181] Nevertheless, as Arthur Moore also observes, "On the thesis of Consistent Eschatology [i.e., the view that history contradicted the early kerygma] it remains a problem why the Christian sect did not go the way of other disappointed apocalyptic groups when the chosen Messiah had failed them . . . finally dying out."[182] Paul does see "the whole [waiting] on tiptoe . . ." (Rom 8:19, J. B. Phillips's gloss-translation). But this mind-set rests not upon *a statement about eschatological imminence* but upon *a presupposition concerning its genuine possibility.*

Elsewhere I have argued emphatically that the logical grammar of *eschatological expection* concerns (following Wittgenstein) *a stance and appropriate behavior,* not a set of chronological beliefs.[183] In 1 Thessalonians 4 and in 1 Corinthians 15 the exclusion of *we* or **not all** would simply denote a *lack of seri-*

178. Whiteley, *The Theology of St Paul,* 244-48; cf. 241-58.

179. Ibid., 253.

180. Schweitzer, *The Mysticism of Paul the Apostle,* 36-39 and 90-99 (but Paul is not addressing "the otherwise insoluble problem of the fate of believers who have died," 95; even if it remains the case that "he cannot regard 'the resurrection' of Jesus as an isolated event," 98); M. Werner, *The Formation of Christian Dogma* (Eng. trans., London: Black, 1957), 14-15, 31-37; also cf. K. Mannheim, *Ideology and Utopia* (London: Routledge, 1960), 195.

181. Werner, *Formation of Christian Dogma,* 32.

182. Moore, *The Parousia in the NT,* 47.

183. Thiselton, *The Two Horizons,* 383-85, and in "The Logical Role . . .," *BibInt* 2 (1994): 207-23 (on first-person utterances).

ousness in regarding the issue as genuinely possible as well as open: Paul's major concern is *God's orderly plan for humankind* as a corporeity, and for believers as the corporate body of Christ. *It does not matter, he urges, whether you have died or are still alive at the end time: all of us (equally)* **will undergo transformation.** "There can, to his [Paul's] mind, be no distinction between the two groups."[184] Further, "transformation and resurrection are seen as two parts of the same event."[185] This part of Paul's declaration serves to give assurance equally that those who have died lose nothing that will be experienced by those who will still be alive at the parousia, and conversely assures those who might survive that they, too, like the dead, share in the same experience of resurrection-transformation. In spite of arguments by some to the contrary, Paul offers this double assurance, with the proviso that no one can be exempt from the utterly necessary transformation. Paul uses the future passive indicative of ἀλλάσσω, *to change, to alter,* or in the passive, to *have one's condition or form changed.* M. E. Dahl argues that in some respects this is a weak word for change. This is so, however, because it denotes *change of form* following an earlier incorporation into the new creation.[186] At the same time the context confirms that we should not underrate its force.[187]

There may be two distinct nuances to Paul's use of μυστήριον in v. 51a. It would accord with his use of the term elsewhere to denote what was once hidden but has now been disclosed by divine revelation. On the other hand, many interpreters explain it in a way which is closer to its modern meaning in English. Paul cannot and does not say more about the precise nature of the change. He knows that Christ's own resurrection mode of existence provides the model (cf. also Phil 3:20-21), but much more than this we cannot know. It may be that Paul uses this word consciously to convey both senses of the term. Alternatively the latter nuance may sufficiently account for its use.

The change or transformation will be instantaneous, ἐν ἀτόμῳ (τέμνω, *I cut,* with alpha privative), denoting that which is indivisible, i.e., **in an instant,** *the smallest conceivable moment of time.* ἐν ῥιπῇ ὀφθαλμοῦ indicates very rapid eye movement. Most frequently it denotes a rapid, darting glance out of the corner of one's eye, but since ῥίπτω simply means *to throw,* it may have a wider meaning as well. With different nouns, outside the New Testament it can denote the *rapid wing movement* which causes the *buzz of a gnat* or the *twinkling* (cf. AV/KJV) *of a star.* This is the only occurrence of the word in the New Testament, and although NRSV, NJB, REB, and NIV follow AV/KJV's *twinkling of an eye,* this translation depends on modern recognition of the phrase as itself a

---

184. Kennedy, *St Paul's Conceptions of the Last Things,* 261.
185. Holleman, *Resurrection and Parousia,* 168.
186. Dahl, *The Resurrection of the Body,* 103-5.
187. The important point safeguarded by Dahl is that *change* does not disrupt or destroy *continuity of identity.* Nevertheless, the force of **transformation** or *change* is clearly entailed; cf. BAGD, 39; Grimm-Thayer, *"to cause one thing to cease and another to take its place,"* in 1 Cor 15:51-52, **"to transform"** (28).

metaphor for instantaneousness. Strictly the sparkle or change of light of an eye is a process, and rests on transferring the metaphor of a twinkling star. Collins translates **in the blinking of an eye**, which preserves the creative metaphor but avoids dependence on a tradition of understanding.[188]

The last trumpet intensifies the metaphor of suddenness, adding the dimension of divine decree and ordered signal. In both Testaments (Exod 19:16; Zech 9:14; 1 Thess 4:16) manifestations of God are associated with the sound of **the trumpet**. Additionally, however, **the trumpet** awakens a sleeping army to be urgently roused to activity, including possible battle when *the alert* is sounded. In view of its military background, with which readers would be entirely familiar, *sound* would be universally interpreted less as the sound of a musical note than as a *loud* **signal** for all to hear. The trumpet *announces the moment of change,* in accordance with the *timing of God's* royal decree. The form of the future σαλπίσει is late Greek (σαλπίζεται is not used). In apocalyptic literature **the trumpet** is a standard image for announcing a new beginning decreed by God (cf. Rev 11:15). As Collins (closely with Wolff) writes, "'**Last**' may not suggest so much last in a series (cf. Rev 8:2; 11:15), as the source of the final, eschatological trumpet sound . . . the passing of the present order of reality."[189] Ambrosiaster understands the trumpet sound as a sound of triumph when the battle is over.[190] Bruce cites similarly the "great trumpet" for the return of the exiles in Isa 27:13 (cf. Matt 24:31) and that of the year of Jubilee (Lev 25:9), as well as the apocalyptic trumpet for the Lord's descent from heaven in 1 Thess 4:16-17.[191] Augustine also alludes to 1 Thess 4:16: it denotes "a clear signal" which Paul elsewhere calls "the voice of the archangel and the trumpet of God" (1 Thess 4:16).[192]

Once again we encounter ἄφθαρτοι as characterizing the raised mode of existence. In v. 42 we translated this as **decay's reversal** on the ground that it stood in semantic opposition to φθορά, which in turn translated in the LXX the Hebrew terms for *emptiness, fruitlessness,* and *degeneration* or *corruption.* The negation of this, we argued, is *not simply a static state of incorruption,* but a *dynamic process of ethical, aesthetic, and psychosocial flourishing, purpose, and abundance* (see above on v. 42). Although the semantic opposition is not explicit here, *incorruption* does not adequately convey what the absence of this destructive process entails for a *process* directed by the Spirit. The σῶμα will be

---

188. Collins, *First Cor,* 573. Augustine, however, speaks of "the glance of an eye" which reaches all objects simultaneously (*Letter to Deogratias,* 102).

189. Ibid., 580. Wolff uses virtually the same language: "not the last of a series . . . but an eschatological signal (Joel 2:1; Zeph 1:16; 4 Ezra 6:23), unlike the series of the book of Revelation (*Der erste Brief,* 415). "When the signal is sounded, then follows in the shortest possible time the resurrection of the dead (believers) in their new bodily form (cf. v. 42)" (Wolff, *Der erste Brief,* 415).

190. *Commentary on Paul's Epistles* in CSEL, 81:183.

191. Bruce, *1 and 2 Cor,* 155.

192. Augustine, *Letters,* 34.

raised **without degenerating decay** at the very least; perhaps Paul means also here *the reversal of decay,* i.e., *flourishing.*

53 Ronald Sider is entirely correct to underline the importance of the fourfold use of τοῦτο, **this** (twice in v. 53, twice in v. 54), as indicating *clear continuity of identity* (**this body**) even in the midst of radical transformation.[193] The same identifiable, recognizable, and accountable identity (see above on σῶμα) is transfigured into a *radically different form,* but remains **this** *created being in its wholeness.* δεῖ once again underlines the sheer necessity of change, urged repeatedly but especially in vv. 50-52. **This body which is subject to decay** (τὸ φθαρτὸν τοῦτο) is to put on, like a new set of clothes (ἐνδύσασθαι, ingressive aorist middle infinitive [**become clothed**]), ἀφθαρσία. If we continue Paul's metaphor, this ἀφθαρσία denotes **that** which **cannot wear out**, and it corroborates the aspect of σῶμα as (here) denoting *a form* which is *incapable of degeneration.*

In our own era after the turn of the millennium, when medicine has prolonged life beyond all earlier imagination, it is important not to lose sight of Paul's emphasis on *release from degenerating capacities* which the more philosophical, abstract *incorruption* (AV/KJV), or even the more static, metaphysical *imperishable* (REB, NIV, NJB), or *imperishability* (NRSV), may perhaps convey less forcefully and less explicitly as the semantic opposite of τὸ φθαρτόν. Similarly, *immortality* (REB, NIV, NRSV, NJB, AV/KJV) is correct but misses part of the added force provided by the use of the two terms *liable to death* and **incapable of dying** in deliberate semantic opposition. Of all the Church Fathers, it is Ambrose who best captures and conveys the dynamic and positive content of ἀφθαρσία and ἀθανασία in concrete terms: "The blossom of the resurrection" is these; "What is richer . . . ? Here is the manifold fruit, the harvest, whereby man's nature grows more vigorous and productive after death."[194]

Augustine also captures the logical basis to which Paul's "of God" constantly calls attention: "People are amazed that God, who made all things from nothing, makes a heavenly body from human flesh. . . . Is he who was able to make you when you did not exist not able to make over what you once were?"[195]

54-55 (1) The UBS 4th ed., which is generally more optimistic than the 3d ed., categorizes the longer reading of v. 54 (above) as "almost certain" ("B"). The 3d ed. (1966) had classified this reading less convincingly as having "a considerable degree of doubt" ("C," in 3d ed. terms). A shorter reading begins with the second clause, ὅταν δὲ τὸ θνητόν τοῦτο ἐνδύσηται τὴν ἀθανασίαν, and has the support of the early 𝔓⁴⁶, ℵ*, and probably C*, MSS of Old Latin, Vulgate, Coptic (Sah and Boh), and Latin VSS of

---

193. Sider, "The Pauline Conception of the Resurrection Body in 1 Cor 15:35-54," 437; cf. 428-39.

194. Ambrose, *On His Brother Satyrus,* 2:54.

195. Augustine, *Sermons for the Feast of the Ascension,* 264:6.

Irenaeus, Origen, Ambrosiaster, and Hilary. The longer reading (above and UBS 4th ed.) is supported by B and D, with possible deciphering of an unclear C, in part K, Syriac, and Byzantine readings, and the Greek of Origen, Athanasius, and Chrysostom. Two clear canons of textual criticism conflict: (1) Very often the shorter reading is more probable (since copyists are more likely to add than to subtract): (2) the phenomenon of homoioteleuton readily explains an omission of a clause or a phrase when the eye of the copyist readily moves from one occurrence of a similar word or phrase to another. In this case, the second axiom carries far more weight in this verse in spite of early support for the shorter reading. Conzelmann simply states, "p⁴⁶ . . . is a result of homoioteleuton."[196] As a result of the early divergence of readings, other, later variants also occur, but these need not detain us.[197] (2) p⁴⁶, B, D*, and Tertullian, read νεῖκος, *strife,* in place of νῖκος, **victory**, but this is generally ascribed to aural error in misunderstanding dictation.

The argument now proceeds to the next and final stage. Paul picks up the point already made in v. 53, repeating it as his point of departure for vv. 54b, 55, and then vv. 56-57. Ronald Sider's point that the fourfold occurrence of τοῦτο underlines the continuity of identity that survives the transformation of the mode of being receives further emphasis in v. 54a (see on v. 53, above). On the translation and force of φθαρτόν . . . ἀφθαρσίαν . . . θνητόν . . . ἀθανασίαν, see also under v. 53 above. Our translation does not necessarily replicate our earlier English precisely; it is an axiom of linguistics that contextually synonymous forms initially always find a place in, e.g., English (cf. Cranmer's rendering in the Book of Common Prayer); but they convey the force identified above. The aorist middle ἐνδύσηται with the indefinite ὅταν, **when** *(ever),* leaves open any temporal specification, but it does not leave open the sequence, result, or consequence. The aorist with the indefinite is perhaps best conveyed by **when this body . . . comes to put on** . . . (cf. NRSV, *When this . . . body put on . . .*). *When this . . . body . . . has been clothed* (REB, NIV; cf. NJB, *after this . . . nature has put on*) conflicts with A. T. Robertson's rejection of the *futurum exactum.*[198]

Chrysostom understands γενήσεται ὁ λόγος to mean "the word shall be fulfilled" (cf. γίνεσθαι in the sense of to be fulfilled in Matt 6:10; Mark 11:23). This is probably the only loose citation (if citation rather than paraphrase it is) in which fulfillments of scripture to which Paul alludes have not already taken place in Christ. His point, however, remains true to the christological principle: by virtue of the cross and Christ's resurrection the fulfillment is guaranteed, but a later time. Hence γενήσεται bears some such sense as "shall become operative," or "shall come into force."

Most commentators agree that Paul cites, or alludes to, Isa 25:8, probably

---

196. Conzelmann, *1 Cor,* 289, n. 3; Collins, *First Cor,* 582, accepts this reading as "preferable."

197. For example, G omits the entire double ὅταν clause, while A transposes the sequence of the two clauses.

198. Robertson, *Epistles,* 4:198.

in conjunction with Hos 13:14.[199] C. D. Stanley gives detailed attention to how Paul uses and molds this combined quotation.[200] First, Stanley notes, Paul combines parts of Isa 25:8 and Hos 13:14 in such a way as to give "no indication that vv. 54b-55 might represent anything other than a continuous quotation from a single biblical passage."[201] There is no evidence to suggest that these had been combined prior to Paul's use of them together. Stanley urges that the combined use is the fruit of thought and care, not the by-product of careless citation.[202]

Isa 25:8 takes a different form in both the Hebrew and the LXX from Paul's own wording, however. The Hebrew text reads בלע המות לנצח (billaʿ hammaweth lanetsach), he will **swallow up death** forever. The LXX reads κατέπιεν ὁ θάνατος ἰσχύσας, **death** has drunk up in it strength, but the Greek VSS of Aquila and Theodotion read εἰς νῖκος, **in victory** (although Symmachus reads εἰς τέλος). The LXX thus turns **death** (המות, hammaweth, object in Hebrew) into a nominative (which does not fit the surrounding verses; 25:6a, 8b) and interprets לנצח as if it were nearer to the cognate Aramaic verb to overcome than to the Hebrew idiom forever. This explains why Aquila, Theodotion, and Symmachus all have differing variants: all three revisers were trying to correct a faulty LXX rendering of the Hebrew.[203] Paul's version takes up elements from all three, but especially the text of Theodotion: κατεπόθη, **Death has been swallowed up**; with εἰς νῖκος, **in victory**.[204] As Stanley suggests, doubtless there was a common tradition behind these Greek translations and revisions which Paul knew and used.[205]

Paul's citation of, or allusion to, Hos 13:14 also differs both from the LXX and from the Hebrew. The Hebrew of v. 14 reads אהי דבריך מות אהי קטבך שאול (ʾehiy debareyka meweth ʾeh qattabeka sheʾol) Where, O Death, are your plagues? Where, O Sheʾol, is your destruction? The LXX reads ποῦ ἡ δίκη σου θάνατε; ποῦ τὸ κέντρον σου ᾅδη, **Where, O Death, is** your judgment (or penalty)? **Where, O Hades, is your sting**? Paul's citation, therefore, changes the LXX's judgment or penalty to **victory**; and Hades, to **Death**. There is also a change in word order for rhetorical purposes.

---

199. For example, Edwards, *First Epistle,* 456; Hays, *1 Cor,* 275; Grosheide, *First Epistle,* 393; Lang, *Die Briefe,* 240; Fee, *First Epistle,* 803; Collins, *First Cor,* 577-78; Wolff, *Der erste Brief,* 417; Senft, *Première Épitre,* 213-14; Bruce, *1 and 2 Cor,* 156; Conzelmann, *1 Cor,* 292-93; Héring, *First Epistle,* 181-82; Barrett, *First Epistle,* 382-83; Strobel, *Der erste Brief,* 261; Allo, *Première Épitre,* 434-35.

200. Stanley, *Paul and the Language of Scripture,* 209-15.

201. Ibid., 209.

202. Ibid., 209-10.

203. Stanley's view, among others (ibid., 210 and 210, n. 100).

204. Symmachus also uses the passive form καταποθῆναι, while Aquila also reads εἰς νῖκος, **in victory**. κατεπόθη is the aorist passive of the old Gk. καταπίνω, while νῖκος is a later Greek form (e.g., *Sibylline Oracles* 14:334; Vettius Valens, 358:5, second century) of the more usual νίκη, *victory,* as usually in New Testament (1 John 5:4; Josephus, *Antiquities* 6.145 et al.).

205. Stanley, *The Language of Scripture,* 211.

What is significant is the inappropriateness of the LXX ἡ δίκη, whether *judgment, penalty,* or *lawsuit,* to translate Heb. דֶּבֶר *(deber), plague,* in the first place. Hence, Stanley argues, "the possibility of a non-Masoretic *Vorlage* for the primary LXX reading cannot be ruled out," as well as the possibility "that Paul found τὸ νῖκος [**victory**] already in his Greek *Vorlage.*"[206] **Victory** does indeed offer a close rhetorical link between the two citations.[207] With regard to the substitution of **Death** for *Hades,* the two function as rhetorical synonyms; death without the resurrection of the body is a reductive demotion to the realm of the shades, or *She'ol* presented in its Greek form. At all events, the Pauline personification of Death is drawn from Hos 13:14. Stanley and Collins agree that Paul intends that each Old Testament text sheds light on the understanding of the other.[208]

Important as they are, however, these more technical questions about the Old Testament texts used by Paul should not distract us from engaging with the profound theological content which his citations serve to explicate. Paul projects an eschatological vision of a *stingless death* precisely because *Jesus Christ has himself absorbed the sting* on the basis of how his death and resurrection addresses the problem of human sin and the law (vv. 55-57). Oscar Cullmann has well portrayed the contrast between optimistic views of death exemplified in Socrates and Plato as mere release of "the soul" from the "prisonhouse" of the body, and Hebrew-Christian traditions of death as a tragedy apart from the transformation of death brought about by Christ. Nevertheless, he argues, the agony of Gethsemane as Jesus faces the prospect of death as a cruel God-forsakenness, as a sacrament of the wrath of God, should be kept before our eyes as an reminder of what **death's sting** entails apart from the victory won by Christ.[209]

Gk. κέντρον denotes the **sting** or *bite* of a venomous animal or insect (e.g., bees, scorpions: σκορκίος . . . τὸ κέντρον, **the sting** in the *scorpion's tail,* which is *deadly;* Ctesias, *Indika* 7 [4th cent. BC]; also figuratively, Aesop, *Fables* 276). It also denotes the sharp *iron goad* used not only by cattle drovers but also for punishment or torture.[210] In Rev 9:10 the term applies to *the sting of locusts* or *scorpions.* Death is like a serpent with poison fangs; but the poison can be removed. Then it is harmless. Cullmann argues that, in effect, the illusory optimism of Socrates and many Greeks that death is merely a harmless portal to a higher order of being remains (as Hebrew-Christian thought perceived) baseless; but that with **the victory** of Christ over death and sin, this "harmless" death now becomes a genuine and well-founded reality for Christian believers. Hence Paul states that

---

206. Ibid., 212 and 213. Stanley recognizes the complexity of each hypothesis and explores all serious counterarguments and alternatives (212-14).

207. Ibid., 214.

208. Cf. Collins, *First Cor,* 577-78; Stanley, *The Language of Scripture,* 211.

209. Cullmann, *Immortality of the Soul or Resurrection of the Dead?* (the three respective stances are explored in each of the three chapters).

210. BAGD, 428; Grimm-Thayer, 344; Euripides, *Bacchae* 795; Acts 26:14; The verb κεντρέω means *to pierce, to prick.*

death has been swallowed up not only *forever* (Isa 25:8, Heb.) but also **in victory** (Theodotion, Aquila; LXX *Vorlage?*). To press home the powerlessness of death to damage, to intimidate, or to dismay, Paul uses the vocative of address as a *taunt,* like a taunt to a hostile but disarmed, bound, and powerless attacker: **Death — where is your victory? Death — where is your sting?**[211]

56 Findlay offers the delightfully succinct comment that this verse "throws into an epigram the doctrine of Rom iv–vii and Gal iii respecting the interrelations of Sin, Law and Death."[212] Bengel, as might be expected, is no less succinct: *Si peccatum non esset, mors nil posset . . . sine lege peccatum non sentitur; sub lege, peccatum dominatur* (Rom 6:14).[213] Cullmann, as we noted above, explains the terror of **death** in terms of the loss of good, including the loss of the divine presence in God-forsakenness and even the experience of divine wrath. But it is **sin**, the human turning away from God to become centered upon the self, that has turned **death** into such deadly poison, so that it hurts and kills like a **sting.**

Bultmann argued that any causal connection between sin and death is objectified, premodern *myth,* since death is a biological process of nature. Indeed, he held that Paul "objectifies" the relation between **sin** and **death** in two quite different ways: in one conceptual scheme *(Begrifflichkeit) "death is the punishment for the sin a man has committed;* sinners are 'worthy of death' (Rom 1:32, KJV) . . . sin pays her slave his 'wage' with death (Rom 6:16, 23)" (Bultmann's italics).[214] Yet in other Pauline passages "death grows out of fleshly life like a fruit — organically, as it were . . . (Rom 7:5). Death is the 'end' of the 'fruit' of sinful life (Rom 6:21) . . . 'a sōma of death' (Rom 7:24). . . . Human striving . . . pursues life and yet only garners death . . . (Rom 7:7-25)."[215] Elsewhere I have sought to untangle the repeated "code switching" by which Bultmann uses "myth" now as analogy, now as an obsolete prescientific worldview, now as imagery that generates cognitive or propositional contradiction, now as the objectification of human attitudes or social constructs.[216] The fact of the matter is that each conceptual scheme serves a different and complementary purpose. The "organic" image demonstrates the utterly self-defeating and destructive inevitability of sin in destroying the very "good" which it seeks to grasp solely on its own terms without reference to God. In this sense, **sin** arms the power of death with its poison of self-contradiction; it ends in the dust and

---

211. As Fee observes, the change in word order from Hos 13:14 LXX (in addition to word substitutions) "emphasizes the personification [lit. 'Where your, O death, victory?'], which replaces LXX's 'where the penalty of you, O death?'" (*First Epistle,* 804).

212. Findlay, *Expositor's Greek Testament,* 2:942.

213. Bengel, *Gnomon,* 673: "if there were no sin, there could be no death. . . . Without the law sin is not experienced [as sin]; under the law sin reigns supreme."

214. Bultmann, *Theology of the NT,* 1:246; cf. "NT and Mythology," in H.-W. Bartsch (ed.), *Kerygma and Myth* (various eds., e.g., London: SPCK, 1962-64), 1, esp. 1-15.

215. Ibid., 1:247.

216. For example, Thiselton, *The Two Horizons,* 205-92, esp. 252-92.

ashes of disappointment and nothingness. The self chooses self and ends up with the *nihil* of isolation and hence of death. The "judicial" image anchors this process in the decree of God in validating the very process which is part of the eschatological "ordered-ness" of the sovereign Creator who acts in faithfulness to his own word of warning or promise without self-contradiction.[217] To speak of a divine declarative verdict as an anchor of reality is not mere conceptual "objectification," but a validating truth claim.

Paul can therefore urge Christian believers who have been placed in a right relationship with God through the work of Christ to consider themselves (i.e., to be determined by the eschatological projected world in which they are) "dead to sin" and "alive to God" (Rom 6:11), as those freed from death (6:13). A reversal of the process of "wasting," "degenerating," being "on the way to ruin" (τοῖς ἀπολλυμένοις, 1 Cor 1:18) has been taken in hand with the work of Christ, and reaches its ultimate goal in the final transformation of the resurrection. This addresses Paul's question concerning corporate humanity: "Who shall deliver me from the body of this death?" (Rom 7:24).[218] Beker writes, "Death is the primal power: it is 'the last enemy' (1 Cor 15:26) within the field of interlocking forces. The antithesis between the two ages can be summed up as 'the reign of death' as opposed to the 'reign of life' (Rom 5:17, 21). And death remains in some way the signature of the world, even after its allies — the law, the flesh, and sin — have been defeated in the death and resurrection of Christ."[219] "The alliance of sin and death is intimate indeed."[220]

The law, in spite of its being "holy and good" (Rom 7:12, 13) and designed to bring life, comes to perform the very opposite effect in the context of human fallenness, sin, and bondage. Rom 1:18–2:29 and 5:12-21 underline human culpability, which the law appears to intensify as a kind of slavery (Rom 3:20; 6:20; cf. 7:7). However we interpret Rom 7:7-25, and the still sharper critique of Galatians 3–5, a major part of the work of Christ in establishing the new creation "under grace" is that "Christ redeemed us from the curse of the law, being made a curse for us."[221] Again, however we interpret Rom 10:4, Christ as the "end," "goal," or "termination" of the law "initiates a new eschatological life, where God and humankind meet under new conditions. And yet . . . Christ satisfied the righteous requirement of the law (Rom 8:4) as expressive of his holy will, in order to establish a new relationship to God 'apart from the law' (Rom 3:21)."[222]

---

217. The broader issues alongside careful exegesis of Paul within a valid framework of a recognition of Paul's use of apocalyptic themes are constructively set forth in Beker, *Paul the Apostle,* 182-234.

218. Cf. Kennedy, *St Paul's Conception of the Last Things,* 108-30; cf. also Beker, *Paul the Apostle,* esp. 189-98 and 204-15.

219. Beker, *Paul,* 190.

220. Ibid., 215. See further de Boer, *The Defeat of Death,* 17-18, 167-80, 185-88.

221. On this verse see Beker, *Paul,* 186 and 182-212.

222. Ibid., 186. See further Whiteley, *The Theology of St Paul,* 79-86; and Dunn, *Theology,* 128-61.

In seeking to understand Paul, it is worth bearing in mind the three distinct conceptual grammars of ὁ νόμος determined contextually: (i) **The law** *(Torah)* as "God's supreme self-revelation . . . God's gift" (e.g., Rom 7:12-13); (ii) **the law** as "a moral indicator, making it possible to realize the gravity of sin" (e.g., Rom 3:20, "law brings only the consciousness of sin"); and (iii) **the law** used in the sense of a broader principle or rule of cause and effect, which may apply to all humankind, or even to "the law of the Spirit."[223] The major problem about a judicial or *de facto* "law" of cause and effect is that it *ties* a human being to the effects of his or her *past actions*. Consequences of destruction, self-contradiction, guilt, and ultimately **death** are set in train. Both for this reason and on the ground of the second conceptual grammar of "moral indicator" ἡ δὲ δύναμις τῆς ἁμαρτίας ὁ νόμος in this way arms **death** with its deadly κέντρον. However, once the work of Christ has *liberated* the believer from this causal changing which bound him or her to the fruit of past sin and guilt (Gal 3:13a), that person is free to live *for the future*. Indeed, "redemption" in biblical usages (e.g., at the Exodus) follows precisely this pattern: release *from* plight and bondage; *by* a salvific act; *to* a new future which takes a new form of life. This, indeed, well prepares us for the next verse!

57 Here is a classic illocutionary speech-act (an act performed *in* the saying of an utterance): Paul gives thanks for the gracious gift of victory over death and over death's empowerment by sin and by the law in alliance. It is an *act* of thanksgiving; a verbal equivalent to throwing one's arm around someone in gratitude; or like throwing one's hat in the air *in sheer exultation*. Paul's τῷ δὲ θεῷ χάρις is parallel to his paean of exultant thanksgiving in Rom 7:25, χάρις δὲ τῷ θεῷ. Both passages express thanks **to God through our Lord Jesus Christ** (διά with the genitive; in Rom 7:25, **through** *Jesus Christ our Lord*).[224]

The use of δέ is adversative here: **the sting of death** . . . (v. 56). **But thanks be to God** . . . (v. 57). The parallel in Rom 7:25 may suggest that **through our Lord Jesus Christ** is the adverbial mode of the giving of thanks, although it is no less true that the **giving** of **the victory** is equally **through our Lord Jesus Christ**: "The believer's 'victory' lies in deliverance through Christ's propitiatory death (Rom 3:23-24) . . . from the condemnation of the law, and . . . 'the power of sin' and thereby from the bitterness of death."[225] This "chain" could be broken

223. The first two categories and quotations are from Whiteley, *Theology of St. Paul,* 79-82; the third is a modification of his third category, 82-83. Needless to say, the so-called post-Sanders "new look" on Paul and the law strongly emphasizes the first of the three conceptual categories; cf. E. P. Sanders, *Paul and Palestinian Judaism* (London: SCM, 1977), esp. 84-124 and 442-543; *Paul, the Law and the Jewish People* (Philadelphia: Fortress, 1983); and *Jesus, Paul and Torah: Collected Essays,* JSNTSS 43 (Sheffield: Sheffield Academic Press, 1992); and Dunn, "The Law," in the *Theology of Paul,* 128-61. Dunn, alluding to this verse, concedes that the law was "a calculated risk on God's part. . . . But it hastens the destruction of death" (159).

224. See R. Deichgräber, *Gotteshymnus und Christushymnus in der frühen Christenheit* (Göttingen: Vandenhoeck & Ruprecht, 1967), 43-44.

225. Findlay, *Expositor's Greek Testament,* 2:943.

only by the "effective operative power" of the cross (see above on 1:18-25).[226] Several commentators (e.g., Wolff) call attention to the present participle τῷ διδόντι: even if the last resurrection is still future, the basis of the victory is a present gift, providing grounds for present exultation and thanksgiving.[227] It is not a mere present of future certainty about resurrection; it also expresses the present gift of grace to believers for whom the destructive potential of sin, the law, and death as a terrifying prospect has been broken.[228] The present reality is that the sting of death has been drawn out by Christ's victory. Believers already in some measure share in this victory, even though the final appropriation of all that this entails has yet to be appropriated and experienced fully at the last day.[229] This God-given **victory** comes as a gift of grace: "The unit ends [i.e., before v. 58] on a note of joyous celebration . . . 'gives *us* the victory' contains the message of chapter 15 in a nutshell: When God raised Jesus, the benefit was not for him alone: rather, all of us in . . . the body of Christ share in the victory. . . . We too can expect to be raised from the dead."[230]

58 The *peroratio,* introduced by ὥστε, "therefore," sums up the whole argumentation and applies it directly to the Corinthians in a building metaphor which forms an exhortation to be "steadfast and immovable."[231] As Eriksson also notes, this conclusion picks up the theme of the *exordium* of 15:1-2: it is a matter of their **taking their stand in the gospel** (ἐν ᾧ καὶ ἑστήκατε, v. 1) and of not believing in a *haphazard, confused* way **without coherent consideration** (εἰκῇ, v. 2).[232] In contrast to εἰκῇ in v. 2, however, κενός in this verse may mean either empty, i.e., without content (BAGD, 2a) or fruitless, i.e., without result, to no purpose (BAGD, 2b). The latter accords with Paul's earlier application of the building metaphor to Christian work in 3:9b-16. **Stand firm** (REB, NIV) seems preferable to *keep firm* (NJB), for ἑδραῖοι γίνεσθε (see also under 7:37 for the Greek word) means not "continue to be" but "become, prove yourselves to be" (cf. 10:32; 11:1).[233]

Once again we face the usual problem with a gender-inclusive translation for ἀδελφοί μου, which we have regularly discussed above. Since the Greek is already used as a term of affection for those of kindred interests, or friends, the addition of ἀγαπητοί invites double emphasis on these bonds of affection, as well as a suitably weighty rhetorical marker: hence **my very dear fellow Christians** (which also identifies the capacity in which Paul addresses them here).[234]

---

226. Also Brown, *The Cross and Human Transformation,* 1-64, 149-69, and throughout; less directly Pickett, *The Cross in Corinth.*
227. Wolff, *Der erste Brief,* 419.
228. Edwards, *First Epistle,* 459; rightly against Meyer, *First Epistle,* 2:107.
229. Cf. Barrett's balancing of present and future, *First Epistle,* 384.
230. Hays, *First Cor,* 276.
231. Eriksson, *Traditions as Rhetorical Proof,* 275.
232. BAGD, 427-28.
233. As Robertson and Plummer insist (*First Epistle,* 379); cf. BAGD, 217.
234. On ἀδελφοί in these contexts, see above on 1:10, 11, 26; 2:1; 3:1; 4:6; 12:1 et al.

On one side, the Corinthians must not allow a confused or sceptical attitude toward the resurrection of the body leave them unsettled. They must not oscillate or be tossed about (ἀμετακίνητοι combines the alpha privative with μετά + κινέω, *to shift* or *to remove,* i.e., **immovable**).[235] On the other side, there is nothing static about Christian living and service in **the work of the Lord**. The verb περισσεύω conveys two interrelated nuances. The primary force is that of **abounding**. This accords with a distinctive emphasis in modern Christian theology associated especially with David Ford. Ford calls for the recovery in Christian theology and life of "the notes of *abundance, celebration,* and even *extravagance* and *excess . . .* an overflow. . . ."[236] The new Christian self and the self's relation to God and to others "is all taken up into that dynamic of abundance . . . evoked by the language of wealth, *immeasurability,* fulness, *overflowing,* glory, praise, thanks . . . culminating in the vision of God" (my italics).[237] The secondary nuance, to which Ford's language has already alluded, is that of *excess.* In its intransitive uses, περισσεύω denotes (a) "*be* **more** *than enough*" as well as (b) "*be present in abundance,*" and especially (of persons) (a) *to excel, to progress* **more and more**, as well as (b) *to have an abundance, to be rich.*[238] Grimm-Thayer also stress *to exceed a fixed number or measure, to be over and above a certain . . . measure,* so as to *overflow in abundance.*[239]

It is not a matter of cumulatively adding meanings from different contexts (to commit the error rightly identified by James Barr as "illegitimate totality transfer") to infer that Paul consciously draws on this established range of meanings because in Greek this single verb is capable of conveying these plural nuances the same time.[240] As Ford notes, this "totality" is entirely faithful to Paul's perception of the nature of the new, transformed self on the way to full transformation and the beatific vision of the fullness of God. Because the *gift* of *grace* identified in vv. 54-57 is theirs, believers may spend and be spent without limit in **the work of the Lord**, knowing that this response to overflowing grace produces solid, lasting effects.

Most writers who examine the rhetoric in ch. 15 agree with the verdict on v. 58 expressed by Duane Watson: "This is the *peroratio* or conclusion for all of ch. 15. Like the *peroratio* of an entire work it recapitulates the main points of the argumentation of ch. 15 and arouses emotion. A key topos of the chapter 'vain' (κένος) is repeated. . . . The *peroratio* is a proposal of policy (προαίρεσις) as is common to the *peroratio* of deliberative rhetoric."[241] Curiously, Insawn

235. BAGD, 45.
236. D. F. Ford, *Self and Salvation: Being Transformed,* 44 and 112.
237. Ibid., 117 and 222. Cf. the works of Daniel Hardy for a similar emphasis.
238. BAGD, 650-51.
239. Grimm-Thayer, 505.
240. J. Barr, *The Semantics of Biblical Language* (Oxford: Oxford University Press, 1961), 206-38, esp. 217-19.
241. Watson, "Paul's Rhetorical Strategy in 1 Cor 15," 248.

Saw regards the conclusion of v. 58 as "not a logical one, but an exhortation."[242] However, Mitchell, Eriksson, and others endorse Watson's point. As Mitchell observes (anticipating Eriksson), the Greek translated firm and immovable denotes "attributes of a well-grounded, immovable building, metaphorically a well-established and unchangeable polity which withstands the encroachment of destructive and divisive forces."[243] Understanding of the realities of the resurrection of the body (Christ's as an established basis; that of believers as an assured, grounded promise) facilitates confidence in the worthwhile and responsive character of the work of the Lord, which is not grudgingly measured but given *with abundance* and *more and more* "pressed and shaken down and running over" (Luke 6:38) without stint.

THE POSTHISTORY, IMPACT, AND ACTUALIZATION OF CHAPTER 15

(1) The Second Century

In the second century less attention was given to historical or logical grounds for belief in the resurrection of Jesus Christ (respectively 15:1-11 and 12-19) than to issues regarding (a) the fate and destiny of Christians or of humankind; (b) the role of "the body" in salvation and the nature of "bodily" resurrection; (c) whether resurrection assumes or contradicts the human capacity for immortality (esp. 15:35-49): Was the soul naturally immortal?[244] Clearly the background of Plato's philosophy of the immortal soul and gnostic devaluations of the physical body (even, in effect, domain) forms the major background to second-century exegesis of ch. 15.[245]

(a) **Ignatius of Antioch** (d. AD 107 or 108) faithfully reflects Paul's language about Christ as *the firstfruits of the harvest* (15:2, 23) when he declares that the Father who raised up Christ *will raise up in the same manner* those who believe in him (ἐγείραντος αὐτὸν τοῦ πατρὸς αὐτοῦ κατὰ τὸ ὁμοίωμα ὃς καὶ ἡμᾶς τοὺς πιστεύοντας αὐτῷ οὕτως ἐγερεῖ ὁ πατὴρ αὐτοῦ ἐν Χριστῷ Ἰησοῦ; Ignatius, *Letter to the Trallians*, 9:2). One possible allusion to ch. 15 concerns the eagerness of Ignatius to face martyrdom when he speaks of "struggles with wild beasts": "I am fighting with wild beasts" (Ignatius, *Letter to the Romans*, 5:1, 2; cf. 1 Cor 15:32). This bears implicitly on the subject, for Ignatius bases his confidence in the worthwhile character of such a fate on the certainty of resurrection faith. There is a hint of Paul's thought in 15:51-53, that the "fleshly" cannot put on that which is of the Spirit without transformation, although the phraseology equally reflects 1 Corinthians 2: οἱ σαρκικοὶ τὰ πνευματικὰ

242. Saw, *Paul's Rhetoric in 1 Cor 15*, 238.

243. Mitchell, *Paul and the Rhetoric of Reconciliation*, 109; cf. Eriksson, *Traditions as Rhetorical Proof*, 275.

244. On the second century see esp. François Altermath, *Du corps psychique au corps spirituel. Interprétation de 1 Cor 15:35-49 par les auteurs chrétiens des quatre premiers siècles* (Tübingen: Mohr, 1977), 52-94; and Perkins, *Resurrection: NT Witness and Contemporary Reflection*, 331-90.

245. Cf. J. Dillon, *The Middle Platonists* (London: Duckworth, 1977); E. H. Pagels, *The Gnostic Paul: Gnostic Exegesis of the Pauline Letters* (Philadelphia: Fortress, 1975); and S. Laeuchli, *The Language of Faith* (London: Epworth, 1965).

πράσσειν οὐ δύναται, οὐδὲ οἱ πνευματικοὶ τὰ σαρκικά (Ignatius, *Letter to the Ephesians*, 8:2). It remains important for Ignatius that Jesus Christ "ate and drank as a being of flesh (ὡς σαρκικός) after the resurrection, even if his mode of existence was also "spiritual" (καίπερ πνευματικῶς, *Letter to the Smyrnaeans*, 3:3).

(b) **Polycarp** (d. c. 155) places the resurrection in the context of 1 Cor 15:20-28. As in Ignatius, the resurrection of Christ is the guarantee of the resurrection of believers: ὁ δὲ ἐγείρας αὐτὸν ἐκ νεκρῶν, καὶ ἡμᾶς ἐγειρεῖ (Polycarp, *Letter to the Philippians*, 2:2; cf. also Rom 8:11). Yet this is placed in the setting of God's ordered, sovereign purpose, *according to which God raised Christ from the dead* (as in Paul's use of the active verb ἐγείρω and the accusative τὸν κύριον ἡμῶν Ἰησοῦν Χριστόν [see above on M. E. Dahl]) *and gave him glory, "to whom are subjected all things"* (ᾦ ὑπετάγη τὰ πάντα), as in 1 Cor 15:28 (Polycarp, *Letter to the Philippians*, 2:1). There is also a link with Paul's allusion to having knowledge of God (15:34), for Polycarp bases the assurance of future resurrection on *divine promise:* "He promised us" to raise us from the dead" (*Letter to the Philippians*, 5:2).

(c) The **Didache** (probably early second century, but uncertain) alludes to the future resurrection only in the apocalyptic setting suggested by the imagery of 1 Cor 15:51-52: *The resurrection of the dead* is inaugurated by *the sound of the trumpet* (*Didache* 16:6). This coincides with the final parousia of Christ (16:8).

(d) **1 Clement** (AD 96) may be grouped with other Apostolic Fathers, in spite of his early date. Clement of Rome uses the argument about Christ as *the firstfruits* of the resurrection of believers (*1 Clement* 24:1). More significantly he uses the analogy of the seed to explain resurrection transformation: the seed is "parched and bare" (γυμνά, Paul's word in 1 Cor 15:37); but out of its decay and dissolution "the providence of the master raises them up" (ἀνίστησιν αὐτά) and they *bring forth fruit* (ἐκφέρει καρπόν, *1 Clement* 24:5; cf. 1 Cor 15:34, 36, 37, 38, 42, 43). On the other hand, he also moves speculatively beyond Christian tradition with an appeal to the legend of the Phoenix (*1 Clement* 25:1-5; cf. *2 Enoch* 12:1-3). Yet again the metaphor of waking at dawn from sleep (*1 Clement* 24:3) and of being awakened to enjoy God's presence (*1 Clement* 26:2, 3) replicated imagery found in Paul (1 Cor 15:51; cf. Rom 13:12 of new creation).

(e) **Justin Martyr** (d. c. 165). Justin knew Platonism and Stoicism from the inside before his conversion. His *First Apology* (addressed to Emperor Antoninas Rius, c. 155, and his heir Marcus Aurelius) includes the subject of the resurrection in terms of possible continuities and discontinuities with notions of immortality in pagan philosophers. Earlier he engaged in debate with Trypho the Jew (c. 135) at Ephesus, and in his *Dialogue with Trypho* his short comments on future resurrection more narrowly reflect biblical eschatology. Trypho asks whether the righteous of the Old Testament will share in the future resurrection (*Dialogue*, 45:1, 2). Justin replies that those who live acceptably will be raised from the dead "at the second coming of Christ himself" when some will undergo judgment and condemnation while others are "freed from corruption" when they are raised immortal (45). The *First Apology* is more subtle. Justin rejects the argument that the principle of resurrection is to be denied "because you have never seen a dead man rise again" (*Apology*, 1:19). Strictly in accordance with Paul's logic in 15:35-38 (see exegesis above), Justin asks his readers whether they genuinely claim that "even God himself" can do only what we can conceive of; indeed, "God . . . can do anything we are unable to conceive . . . even what is impossible to our own nature and to humankind. . . . 'What is impossible with men is possible with God'

[Matt 19:26]." Justin therefore follows Paul in ascribing everything to what Barth calls "the secret nerve of the epistle . . . the 'of God'" (*Apology*, 1:19; cf. Barth, *Resurrection*, 18). What God has wrought in nature makes such an argument not unreasonable (cf. 1 Cor 15:36-41). If everything created suffers permanent dissolution, what does this say about God's power?

(f) **Relation to Gnostic Themes.** (i) Two main issues arise. Laeuchli sums up one problem succinctly when he observes that for Paul the goal and climax of future resurrection and the eschaton is the reversal of sin's entry into the world (1 Cor 15:21) and the conquest of sin is death's "sting" (1 Cor 15:56), whereas for most gnostic writers of the second century it is the annihilation of ignorance or error (πλάνη) in the revelation of knowledge (γνῶσις).[246] The transformation on which 1 Corinthians hinges is transformation into the image of Christ in terms of a mode of existence characterized by the direction of the Holy Spirit (see exegesis of vv. 44-50); it does not hinge on a qualitative change in knowledge as γνῶσις. (ii) The problem of the σῶμα, however, remains no less a major one. Pagels observes that while the apostles preach "future, bodily resurrection . . . the gnostic initiate rejects this preaching as crude literalism . . . 'the faith of fools.'"[247] Pneumatic and gnostic Christians understood all this "symbolically: Christ's resurrection signifies the 'resurrection of the ecclesia'": on the "third" day because the "hylic" and "psychic" (ψυχικός) days are over for pneumatic-gnostics.[248]

The Treatise on the Resurrection from the Nag Hammadi Library clearly states: "You already have the resurrection" (49:15, 16). The Master's replies to his pupil Rheginus never doubt that Jesus Christ is the basis for this "resurrection" existence, and in this sense there may seem to be a superficial resonance with 1 Cor 15:12, 13 (cf. *Treatise on the Resurrection*, 43:37; 48:8-10). But this is "the way of immortality" (45:14-39) in which the gnostic is led into the immutable realm of middle Platonism, freed already the corruptible sphere of contingency and change (48:20-27). Hence, as Laeuchli observes, gnostic texts are reluctant to use the central transformative, dynamic, verbal language of Paul: "in Christ shall we all be made alive" (1 Cor 15:22).[249] "Death" means participation in the "psychic" (ψυχικός) mode. Paul's analogy of the seed sown is forced to denote the two categories of psychical and pneumatic seed sown by Sophia, which result in the contrasts of 1 Cor 15:42-44.[250] Hence Paul's language about transformation into a somatic mode of existence under the direction of the Holy Spirit is utterly transposed into an entirely different meaning.[251]

(g) **Irenaeus** (d. c. 200). Since he explicitly attacks gnosticism, the previous section sets forth an agenda which shapes the approach of Irenaeus to 1 Corinthians 15. His exegesis follows the main contours of what (broadly) emerged from our exegesis above. (i) Human beings are a psychosomatic unity (even if he tends to view body and soul as "parts"), and "spiritual" persons are those who accept the direction of Holy Spirit (*Against Heresies*, 5:6:1). "They are spiritual because they share in the Spirit, not because their flesh has been stripped off" (6:1). (ii) The issue of belief in the possibility of resur-

246. Laeuchli, *The Language of Faith*, 45 and 45, n. 43.
247. Pagels, *The Gnostic Paul*, 81.
248. Ibid., 82; cf. Tertullian, *On the Resurrection*, 19.
249. Pagels, *The Gnostic Paul*, 81.
250. Laeuchli, *The Language of Faith*, 216. See further Perkins, *Resurrection*, 357-60.
251. See Perkins's documented dialogue with sources (*Resurrection*, 386-89, nn. 61-81).

rection turns on whether we "consider the power of him [God] who raises it up (the σῶμα) from the dead. For if he does not give life to the mortal . . . He is not a God of power" (*Against Heresies,* 5:3:2). Has he not already created eyes for seeing, ears for hearing, hands for feeling and working? "Numbers would fail to express the multiplicity . . ." (3:2; cf. 1 Cor 15:38-41). (iii) Irenaeus explicitly underlines the transformative dimension of 1 Cor 15:54, "the mortal shall put on the imperishable," but disengages it from gnostic transpositions into language about the Pleroma (*Against Heresies,* 1:10:3). It has nothing to do with "error," lack of knowledge, or aeons. As Pheme Perkins observes, "like the Gnostics Irenaeus will speak of the corruptible being swallowed up, but he will mean something quite different by it (Adv. Haer. 3:19:1)" (where Irenaeus sees union with Christ as the ground of "incorruptibility" through adoption as sons).[252]

The second century has provided a laboratory or workshop in which we have seen, first, particular Pauline themes from ch. 15 taken up for particular purposes; then manipulated to support a non-Pauline framework of ideas; and finally, with Irenaeus, brought into a coherent pattern of exegesis which broadly follows Paul's own logic and argumentation.

(2) The Third Century

(a) **Tertullian** (d. c. 225).[253] Tertullian's two major targets of attack were Marcion and Valentinian gnosticism, although issues relating to "Praxeas" and later to Montanism also arise. Hence we would expect that his writings on the resurrection should emphasize (a) continuity with the God of promise of the Old Testament active in Christ (against Marcion); (b) a concern to give due place to "bodily" resurrection (against Valentinianism); and (c) heightened eschatological expectation and the immediacy of the Holy Spirit in his later period of Montanism. We find at least the first two themes in his treatise *On the Resurrection of the Flesh (De Resurrectio Carnis)* as well as in *Against Marcion,* 5:10. The latter closely follows 1 Cor 15:12-53, tracing Paul's thought with his own distinctive glosses; the former engages with a wider range of biblical writings including John, Romans and 2 Corinthians, although toward the end it addresses more specifically 1 Corinthians 15.[254] Regularly, however, Tertullian argues for the incompleteness of any notion of resurrection that is not of the body.[255]

(i) Tertullian appeals first to the wider context of 1 Corinthians: "Glorify God in your body" (6:20; *On the Resurrection,* 16). The resurrection mode of existence must be capable of feeling "pleasure or pain," which presupposes more than the survival of a mere "soul" (*On the Resurrection,* 17). This coheres with "the destiny of the body of the Lord" (although Tertullian here cites the Gospels rather than 1 Corinthians 15). Against the gnostics he asserts that biblical language about resurrection is not merely figurative or allegorical, but literal (*On the Resurrection,* 20, 21).[256] All of this is

252. Perkins, *Resurrection,* 363.
253. Cf. T. P. O'Malley, *Tertullian and the Bible: Language — Imagery — Exegesis* (Nijmegen: Van de Vegt, 1967); Brian E. Daley, *The Hope of the Early Church: A Handbook of Patristic Eschatology* (Cambridge: Cambridge University Press, 1991), 34-37.
254. Tertullian, *On the Resurrection,* esp. 48-55.
255. *On the Resurrection,* esp. 16-21 and 34-38.
256. The theme reappears in *On the Resurrection,* 24, 26, 27.

more explicit and emphatic in *Against Marcion:* "It is the *body (corpus)* that becomes *dead*. . . . For Marcion it is only the salvation of the soul which he [Paul] promises. . . . 'With what body do they come?' [1 Cor 15:35] . . . *ipso facto* proclaimed in the argument that it was a *body* which would rise again" (*Against Marcion,* 5:10). The *"entire human being"* will be raised (*On the Resurrection,* 34).

(ii) In both texts Tertullian follows Paul in regarding the creative sovereign power of God in Christ as the ground of the future resurrection σῶμα, and he denies that the resurrection is a past "inner" event. He compares 1 Cor 15:51-55 with 2 Thess 2:9-19.[257] Like the dry bones of Ezek 37:1-14, the dead have no natural capacity to be restored to life, but resurrection depends on God (*On the Resurrection,* 29). Once the seed has been cast into the ground and suffers dissolution "to God will belong the work of re-vitalizing the body" (*Against Marcion,* 5:10). "Tertullian's explanation of the possibility of resurrection is based on the now standard appeal to God's power: if God is capable of creating us out of nothing, he is surely able to reassemble us out of a state of material disintegration."[258]

(iii) Tertullian is more ambiguous than Paul about *transformation*. On one side, he appears to argue for the identity of the resurrection body with the present body. He uses 1 Cor 15:53 to argue that *"this* mortal body shall put on incorruptibility" (*On the Resurrection,* 51; cf. 52, 53). This, however, leads him into conflict with 15:37, "What you saw is not the body that shall be." However, on the other side, he concedes that a transformation in terms of a "spiritual" mode of existence as living *through the Holy Spirit* is involved. While this is constructive and faithful to Paul's use of *spiritual* (see above on the exegesis of 15:44), Tertullian restricts the dimension of transformation to the creative work of the Spirit of God acting upon (it seems) the same *"body."* There is a duality of insight and undue narrowness concerning Paul's view of τὸ σῶμα πνευματικόν here.

In summary, *Against Marcion,* 5:9, 10 provides virtually a section-by-section exposition of 1 Corinthians 15 which expresses many, but not all, of Paul's themes, while *On the Resurrection of the Flesh* seeks to relate a doctrine of the future resurrection to wider biblical material. (i) and (ii) are becoming firmly embedded in exegetical tradition, while (iii) remains an issue of contention. The controversy with Marcion and Valentinianism serves to sharpen perceptions of (i) and (ii), but leads to an overreaction on (iii).

(b) **Clement of Alexandria** (d. c. 215). The extreme contrast between Tertullian and Clement of Alexandria, between the anti-gnostic and the quasi-gnostic, instantiates H. R. Jauss's analysis of Reception History (see the Preface, xvii). In contrast to Tertullian, Clement regards with favor the capacity of "the soul" to be free from passions and feeling, and in the context of his passages on martyrdom he sees the dissolution of the body as a blessed release and "liberation for the Lord" of the immortal soul.[259] He cites Plato more frequently than 1 Corinthians 15. Indeed, it is almost only Paul's words about *differing degrees of glory* (1 Cor 15:41) that seem to engage Clement: human beings will receive differing degrees of glory insofar as they have trained themselves for "impassibility . . . gnostic perfection," i.e., fullness of *knowledge*.[260] The argument of 1 Corinthians 15 is effectively set aside in favor of a Chris-

---

257. *On the Resurrection,* 24.
258. Daley, *Hope,* 34.
259. Clement, *Stromata,* 1:27:6; 4:2; 7:3:1; 4; 13:1.
260. *Stromata,* 6:13:1.

tianized Platonism which celebrates the capacities of "the soul." Knowledge can anticipate hope to such an extent that "the future is . . . already present." It would be useless to allude to the body of Jesus Christ, since for Clement it remains ἀπαθής, impossible.

(c) **Origen** (d. 254). If Clement promotes the natural capacities of the soul and a realized eschatology, Brian Daley insists that, even granted the controversial nature of Origen's view of the resurrection, "with only a touch of anachronism one might characterize Origen's eschatological thought as an attempt to de-mythologize the accepted apocalyptic tradition of the Scriptures and popular Christian belief," even if in constructive pastoral contexts.[261] Yet this view is one-sided. In his main exposition of future resurrection and especially of σῶμα πνευματικόν (1 Cor 15:44) in *De Principiis*, 2:10, esp. 1-3, Origen takes Paul's text with full seriousness. Indeed, he uses the very argument of Tertullian that if *a body* died, it is *a body* that is raised.[262] (i) First, Origen argues that the *continuity* of the resurrection body is especially important: believers "will be clothed with no other than our own."[263] (ii) At the same time a σῶμα πνευματικόν is *different from the body which was part of the order of nature:* the σῶμα ψυχικόν is that of the physical or natural order, which was "sown into the earth." Indeed, Origen comes as near as a third-century thinker might in discussing σῶμα as a mode of existence or form under which the self apprehends its environment. Precisely in this sense he urges, "there is human flesh; a different flesh that pertains to animals; another to birds, and another to fish. . . . The splendor of the sun is one particular theory; the splendor of the moon is another. . . . So it shall be with the resurrection of the dead" (1 Cor 15:39-42a).[264] (iii) The dynamic concept which holds (i) and (ii) together is that of *transformation.* The natural body is "to be changed by the grace of the resurrection and to become a spiritual one: 'sown in weakness, raised in power'" (1 Cor 15:43). Indeed, the heart of the matter is stated by Paul in 1 Cor 15:51: we shall all be changed (πάντες δὲ ἀλλαγησόμεθα).[265] (iv) This transformation is determined by divine decree: "God gives it a 'body' just as he purposed" (1 Cor 15:38).[266]

These are precisely the themes which emerged in our exegetical discussion above, formulated by Origen with a greater degree of sophistication than his predecessors. On what basis, then, does Daley claim that Origen "demythologizes" the future resurrection? To be sure, Origen regards much of the apocalyptic imagery which surrounds Paul's modes of expression as figurative. For example, if the raised body cannot decay, he asks, how can it suffer the destructive "fires" of judgment? Thus it is the "fire" of shame and remorse as a person is "pierced by his or her own goads."[267] Moreover, when he addresses not the resurrection in 1 Corinthians 15 but the apocalyptic discourses in Matthew 24, Origen distinguishes between the "literal" material relating to false prophets and to the fall of Jerusalem and cosmic apocalyptic which uses symbols inviting present responsibility.[268] The Antichrist is a symbol for all false

261. Daley, *Hope,* 48.
262. Origen, *De Principiis,* 2:10:1.
263. Ibid.
264. Ibid., 5:10:2. See also ibid., 2:9:3.
265. Ibid., 10:3.
266. Ibid.
267. Ibid., 10:4.
268. Origen, *Commentary on Matthew,* 32-60 (on Matt 24:3-44).

doctrine and lack of virtue. Further, some of Origen's statements about the soul *(anima)* are ambivalent. Yet even here a chapter on the Holy Spirit in *De Principiis* prepares the way for a Pauline, rather than gnostic, contrast between πνευματικός and ψυχικός.[269] Finally, we have already observed some of the perceptive comments implied by the *Fragments* of Origen's *Commentary on 1 Corinthians* edited by C. Jenkins (above).[270] Origen is pastorally and theologically aware of the need for "caution" in such subjects as the last judgment and "eternal fire," especially in terms of failing to appreciate that "Gehenna" belongs to the realm of analogy and imagery.[271]

(3) Trajectories in the Fourth Century

Material on the resurrection now becomes less explicitly an engagement with 1 Corinthians 15 than a selection of doctrinal themes. A detailed study would add little to the purpose of this study of impact and actualization beyond that observed in the second and third centuries. Basil of Caesarea, e.g., tends to follow the complexity of paths laid out by Origen.

(a) **Gregory of Nyssa** (d. 394) expounds the *resurrection of the dead* largely in terms of (i) *restoration (ἀποκατάστασις) of the fallen to their original state:* "Now the resurrection promises us nothing else than the restoration of the fallen to their ancient state . . . bringing back again to Paradise the one who was cast out from it."[272] Such a mode of existence corresponds to that of the angels.[273] The ground of the resurrection hope is the resurrection of Christ; Gregory cites 1 Cor 15:12 explicitly here.[274] This entails a change which leads to a recovery of the divine image. (ii) This last thought prompts a theme in which Gregory hints at the full development of human capacities in the light of the divine act of resurrection. This may well be a theme that has to wait for Moltmann before it is explored in depth.[275] Although Daley points out that Gregory is partly motivated by an anthropology that is not entirely Pauline, *transformation at the sound of the last trumpet* (1 Cor 15:51-52) leads on to a divine enabling of the raised human being to *reach his or her full capacities,* which comes about only when they *fully bear the divine image* (cf. ἡμεῖς φορέσομεν καὶ τὴν εἰκόνα τοῦ ἐπουρανίου, 1 Cor 15:49).[276] Human development of all that is possible can be complete only in the "pristine perfection" of the divine likeness.[277]

(b) **John Chrysostom** (d. 407). We have followed Chrysostom's exegesis throughout our commentary, since we have his continuous *Homilies on 1 Corinthians,* each section of which usually begins with solid exegesis before moving to more

269. *De Principiis,* 2:7:1-4; cf. 8:1-5.

270. C. Jenkins in *JTS* 10 (1909): 29-51 (cf. also *JTS* 8 [1908]: 231-47, 353-72, and 500-514).

271. *Comm. on Matt,* 16. Even his language about universal salvation arises in the context of NT language about "restoration."

272. Gregory, *On the Making of Man,* 17:2.

273. Ibid.

274. Ibid., 25:13.

275. Moltmann, *Is There Life after Death?* 5-20, 51-60; and *The Coming of God,* 96-128.

276. Daley, *The Hope of the Early Church,* 87-89.

277. Gregory, *On the Soul and the Resurrection* (esp. NPNF, ser. 2, 5:461), and *On the Making of Man,* 22:6.

homiletical application to his own times. He carefully follows Paul's logic. This begins when he succinctly expounds the heart of the matter in Paul's brief allusion to future resurrection in 1 Cor 6:14. The power of God raised up Christ, and "through his power," since Christ has been raised, God will raise those who are "members of Christ" (*1 Cor. Hom.*, 17:2). On ch. 15 Chrysostom calls attention to the two principles of continuity of identity and transformation on the basis of divine power (*1 Cor. Hom.*, 41:2:3 [1 Cor 15:36-38]; 41:5 [on 15:43-44]; 62:3, 4 [on 1 Cor 15:51-57]). Further details may be seen under our exegesis of ch. 15 above. In summary, the contours of an exegesis that is broadly the major exegetical tradition of ch. 15 has become stabilized, except for specific insights which will emerge over the centuries.

VII. Further Matters of Concern (16:1-24)

Commentators broadly group the subject matter of ch. 16 into three (sometimes four, or occasionally five) sets of issues. Our title for the chapter approximates that proposed by M. M. Mitchell.[1] These sets of concerns include: (A) The Collection for God's People (16:1-4), which carries far more theological and pastoral importance than is often superficially perceived to be the case; (B) Travel Plans (16:5-12), which include the issue of pastoral sensitivity concerning visits on the part of Timothy and Apollos; and (C) Concluding Exhortations and Greetings — *Peroratio* (16:13-24). Fee devotes a separate section to diplomacy about Apollos (v. 12, included in our section B), while Wolff distinguishes the section of Admonitions (*Ermahnungen,* 16:13-18) from concluding farewells (vv. 19-24).

In comparative terms, this chapter raises far fewer controversial debates than most earlier ones, especially ch. 15, on which the research literature is around forty times that of ch. 16 in terms of sheer numbers of monographs and research articles. Nevertheless, questions about the collection have received specialist attention in several monographs, notably those by K. Nickle (1966), by Dieter Georgi (Germ. 1965; Eng. 1992), and more broadly by H.-D. Betz (1985).[2] Georgi offers an interesting link between ch. 15 and 16:1-4. By emphasizing *bodily* resurrection, he suggests, Paul paves the way for an "area of responsibility." Moreover, the link with the historic witnesses of the resurrection underlines a "historical indebtedness" on the part of later Gentile Christians to the first witnesses and their communities.[3] "Saints" or "God's people" (v. 1) denotes the congregation at Jerusalem. With Nickle and Vassiliades, Betz urges that in accordance with Gal 2:10 the collection constitutes a pledge of solidarity with Jewish believers, although this does not exclude the latter's emphasis upon equality and justice.[4] Paul's concerns for mutuality, reciprocity, and solidarity make this much more than a mere postscript or appendix to this

---

1. Mitchell, *Paul and the Rhetoric of Reconciliation,* 177, proposes "Final Matters of Concern."

2. Nickle, *The Collection;* Georgi, *Remembering the Poor: The History of Paul's Collection for Jerusalem,* esp. 49-79; cf. 93-109 and 122-65; and Betz, *2 Cor 8 and 9.*

3. Georgi, *Remembering the Poor,* 51-52.

4. Cf. Vassiliades, "Equality and Justice in Classical Antiquity and in Paul: The Social Implications of the Pauline Collection," 51-59.

theological and practical epistle. Indeed, 2 Corinthians 8–9 shows how profoundly it is bound up with life under the Lordship of Christ, who, "though he was rich, yet for your sakes he became poor" (2 Cor 8:9). The very use of the word περισσεύω in the last verse of the previous chapter (see under 15:58) underlines the connection between motivations for giving and what David Ford calls "the Economics of Abundance" in his work on 2 Corinthians.[5] This issue was for Paul "a major undertaking" in (at least) the churches of Galatia, Macedonia, and Achaia.[6]

In addition to including an important emphasis on giving and mutuality among Christians who transcend any single ethnic constituency, this chapter also contains an allusion to the early role of Sunday, "the first day of the week," in contrast to (or perhaps alongside) the Sabbath or seventh day (16:2). The chapter also gives examples of judicious pastoral wisdom: official procedures are initiated for the transportation of the collection by independently appointed, trustworthy agents (16:3, 4); issues of timing prove that Paul is no "flying evangelist" who stirs people up and leaves others to pick up the pieces (16:7); personal details provide invaluable data for dating and identifying a time and place of writing (16:8). Respect for co-workers as Christian leaders is enjoined (16:10-11), and Paul's and Apollos's *mutual respect* for each other is underlined by Paul's "strongly encouraging" Apollos to revisit Corinth (in spite of his "fans"), while in turn Apollos has no desire to fuel the fire (16:12). *Pastoral timing* is everything: *when* he visits ("when the time is right," 12b) is no less important than *whether* he visits.

The persons mentioned in 16:13-24 reflect a warm vitality of mutually supportive Christian relationships. These people bring the reality of daily church life at Corinth home to us: believers exchange warm greetings, and Paul pleads for respect for those leaders who, like Stephanas, labor for the common good (16:15-18).[7]

A. THE COLLECTION FOR GOD'S PEOPLE (16:1-4)

(1) Now concerning the collection for God's people, as I directed the churches of Galatia, even so you should do likewise. (2) Every Sunday each of you should put aside at home an accumulation of savings in accordance with how you may fare, so that collections are not left to whatever moment I may come. (3) But whenever I arrive, I will send by means of letters of autho-

5. Young and Ford, *Meaning and Truth in 2 Cor,* 171-85.

6. Hays, *First Cor,* 284.

7. An attempt to bring the persons and community to life in popular imagination is offered by Hans Frör, *You Wretched Corinthians! The Correspondence between the Church in Corinth and Paul* (London: SCM, 1995). Like most "docu-dramas," this often catches the imagination but also interweaves some speculative fiction with solid insights.

rization whatever delegates you approve as tried and true to carry your gift to Jerusalem. (4) If it seems right for me to go as well, they can accompany me.

Bibliography on 16:1-12

Bacchiocchi, S., *From Sabbath to Sunday: A Historical Investigation of the Rise of Sunday Observance in Early Christianity* (Rome: Pontifical Gregorian University Press, 1977).

Banks, R., *Paul's Idea of Community* (rev. ed., Peabody, Mass.: Hendrickson, 1994), 139-69.

Beckwith, R. T., and W. Stott, *This Is the Day* (London: Marshall, 1978).

Betz, H. D., *2 Cor 8 and 9: A Commentary on Two Administrative Letters of the Apostle Paul,* Hermeneia (Philadelphia: Fortress, 1985).

Carson, D. A. (ed.), *From Sabbath to Lord's Day: A Biblical, Historical and Theological Investigation* (Grand Rapids: Zondervan, 1982), esp. 221-98 by R. J. Bauckham.

Dockx, S., "Chronologie paulinienne de l'année de la grande collecte," *RB* 81 (1974): 183-95.

Ford, D. F., "The Economy of God," in F. Young and D. F. Ford, *Meaning and Truth in 2 Corinthians* (London: SPCK, 1987), 166-85.

Funk, R. W., "The Apostolic Presence: Paul," in *Parables and Presence* (Philadelphia: Fortress, 1982), 81-102.

Georgi, D., *Remembering the Poor: The History of Paul's Collection for Jerusalem* (Nashville: Abingdon, 1992).

Holmberg, B., *Paul and Power: The Structure of Power in the Primitive Church,* ConBNT 11 (Lund: Gleerup, 1978), 35-57.

Hutson, C. R., "Was Timothy Timid? On the Rhetoric of Fearlessness (1 Cor 16:10-11) and Cowardice (2 Tim 1:7), *BR* 42 (1997): 58-73.

Laansma, J. C., "Lord's Day," in *Dictionary of the Later NT and Its Developments* (Downers Grove: InterVarsity, 1998), 679-86.

Lüdemann, G., *Opposition to Paul in Jewish Christianity* (Minneapolis: Fortress, 1989).

———, *Paul, Apostle to the Gentiles: Studies in Chronology* (London: SCM, 1984).

Mitchell, M. M., "Concerning περὶ δέ in 1 Cor," *NovT* 31 (1989): 229-56.

Munck, J., *Paul and the Salvation of Mankind* (Eng. trans., London: SCM, 1959): 282-308.

Murphy-O'Connor, J., *Paul: A Critical Life* (Oxford: Oxford University Press, 1997), 164-65, 199, 291-332, and 343-48.

Nickle, K. F., *The Collection: A Study of Paul's Strategy,* SBT 48 (London: SCM, 1966).

Rordorf, W., *Sabbat und Sonntag in der alten Kirche* (Zürich: Theologischer Verlag, 1972).

———, *Sunday: The History of the Day of Rest and Worship in the Earliest Centuries of the Christian Church* (Eng. trans., London: SCM, 1968), 193-96.

Vassiliades, P., "Equality and Justice in Classical Antiquity and in Paul: The Social Implications of the Pauline Collection," *St. Vladimir's Theological Quarterly* 36 (1992): 51-59.

1　On the introductory phrase περὶ δέ, see above on 7:1, 25; 8:1; 12:1. In this chapter Paul uses it here and at 16:12, relating to the Apollos issue. Whether or not it necessarily introduces a new topic, even if it usually does, has been discussed in detail by Margaret Mitchell, together with whether it necessarily sig-nals a "reply" to a query raised by the readers.[8] Here it introduces a new topic and is chosen at this "intersection of rhetorical and epistolary employment."[9]

The genitive which follows περὶ δέ, namely τῆς λογείας, is of particular interest. ἡ λογεία, **the collection** (i.e., of money), is found only in papyri and in-scriptions, and only here in the New Testament. Moulton-Milligan confirm A. Deissmann's research on the use of the word in papyri to denote *financial contributions,* especially "irregular local contributions as opposed to regular taxes" (e.g., *Papyrus Oxyrhynchus* 2:239:8 [AD 66], "I swear that I have levied *no contributions* in the above village"; also *BGU* 2:515:7 [AD 193], a *collection for religious purposes*).[10] A Theban ostracon dated 4 August 63, cited by Deissmann, witnesses to the use of the word for a *religious collection* for the priests of Isis: "I received from you four drachmae, I obol, being **the collection** of Isis for public works" (τὴν λογίαν Ἴσιδος περὶ τῶν δημοσίων).[11] A first-cen-tury inscription on a marble tablet from Smyrna also speaks of a religious pro-cession (πομπὴν τῶν θεῶν) at which a **collection** was taken.[12] Grimm-Thayer's comment that the word is not found outside Jewish or Christian writers (among "profane" authors) requires correction in the light of extensive examples from the papyri, inscriptions, and ostraca, as BAGD recognize.[13] The translation **col-lection** reflects the linguistic connection with the force of λόγος in nonbiblical Greek as "collectedness."[14]

This research is not simply of interest to lexicographers. It suggests that Paul avoids more usual words because he wishes to avoid any implication that it is to be regarded as a kind of "tax," and certainly not as a repeated tax. It is possible that the term was used by the Corinthians themselves; but Paul chooses his words for **the collection** carefully.[15] Sometimes Paul refers to this **collection for God's people** *in Jerusalem* as *a gift of kindness* or *of generosity* (χάρις, v. 3; and 2 Cor 8:7); sometimes as *an act of service* (διακονία, 2 Cor 8:4; 9:1, 12, 13; Rom 15:25, 31); sometimes as an act of *fellowship, partnership, sharing,* or *solidarity* (κοινωνία, Rom 15:26); sometimes as bringing *a blessing* (εὐλογία, 2 Cor 9:5); and yet further as an act of *service to God* (λειτουργία, 2 Cor 9:12).[16]

---

8. Mitchell, "Concerning περὶ δέ in 1 Cor," 229-56.

9. Mitchell, *Rhetoric of Reconciliation,* 204, n. 103. See further Horrell, *Social Ethos,* 90.

10. MM, 377.

11. A. Deissmann, *Light from the Ancient East,* 104-5. λογία is an alternative form of λογεία, entered by MM as "λογ(ε)ία."

12. Smyrna, *Sylloge* 583:26, cited by Deissmann, *Light,* 105, n. 10. Cf. also *London Papyri* 3:7 (146 or 135 BC); *Giessen Papyri* 1:61:7 (AD 119); *BGU* 3:891:12 (AD 144). Cf. MHT, *Grammar,* 2:82.

13. Grimm-Thayer, 379; BAGD, 475.

14. This nuance receives major emphasis in the later works of M. Heidegger.

15. Fee contends that the use of the term was "most likely a reflection of the Corinthian let-ter," on the assumption (since questioned by Mitchell) that περὶ δέ nearly always indicated a reply to a question from the addressees.

16. Many commentaries list the various terms, e.g., Fee, *First Epistle,* 810; Edwards, *First*

A whole theology of giving is implicit both in these terms and in their various contexts. As Collins observes, each of Paul's longer or major epistles makes reference to giving, finance, and collecting contributions (1 Cor 16:1-4; Rom 15:25-28; 2 Corinthians 8–9; Gal 2:10).[17] In Gal 2:10 it expresses tangibly a recognition of mutual care, responsibility, and sharing on the part of different ethnic or economic statuses within the worldwide church (Jew and Gentile). This "sealed" the agreement with James of Jerusalem, Peter, and John about the Gentile mission (Gal 2:1-10).

Nevertheless, much more than this is involved. In 2 Cor 4:5-7 the gospel itself is a "treasure," and the issue of the collection is interwoven inseparably with a basic reformulation of the gospel: "For you know the grace of our Lord Jesus Christ, that for you he became poor, though he was rich, so that you might become rich through his poverty" (2 Cor 8:9). David Ford argues that Paul "plays" with and upon this theme to let "the economy of God" speak to the practical financial dealings of Christians.[18] "Resources, work, production, distribution, value and exchange, together with the processes and relationships that these involve," provide in one direction powerful metaphors for the nature and operation of the gospel, but then in turn come to speak back to the Christian's own attitude toward his or her own resources, work, production, value, exchange, reciprocity, mutuality, giving.[19] At the heart of it all is "the economics of abundance": God in Christ has given everything: "the theme of abundance and overflow runs all through the letter" (i.e., 2 Corinthians).[20]

In this light, it is theologically entirely appropriate to speak of **the collection** not as a mundane chore of "maintaining" the church in any routinized mechanistic sense, but of "maintaining" (in the sense of *nurturing*) others by passing on *freely received grace,* χάρις (see above); by tangibly and publicly expressing mutuality and reciprocity in κοινωνία or *partnership;* and by *serving* (διακονία) others, even as Christ has yielded up his riches *to serve.* All of this brings *blessing* (εὐλογία) alike to the one who gives and to the one who receives, "for it is more blessed (even) to give than to receive." Again, in 1 Cor 16:1-4 περισσεύω, *to abound more and more,* is picked up from 15:58. "All human relations of reciprocity are relativized by the God who 'enables every grace to overflow into you, so that you in every way . . . may overflow into every act of goodness' (2 Cor 9:8). . . . The embodiment of grace is Jesus Christ."[21]

Epistle, 462; cf. Collins, *First Cor,* 585 and 588; and Ford "The Economy of God," in *Meaning and Truth in 2 Cor,* 176-77.

17. Collins, *First Cor,* 585 and 588.

18. Ford, "The Economy of God," 170.

19. Ibid., 171. See further Georgi, *Remembering the Poor,* 82-84.

20. Ford, "The Economy of God," 172.

21. Ibid., 178. Ford's exposition of chs. 8–9 as part of the wider theology of grace in 2 Cor carries more weight contextually than Betz's arguments *(2 Cor 8 and 9)* for the separation of ch. 8 from 2 Corinthians 1–7 and for the separate identity and destination of ch. 9. See further Merk, *Handeln aus Glauben* (Marburg: Elwert, 1968), 148.

Keith Nickle well sums up the theological significance of the collection under three headings: "(1) the realization of Christian charity, (2) the expression of Christian unity; (3) the anticipation of Christian eschatology."[22] Fee and Nickle rightly reject Karl Holl's implication that Paul acts out of a sheer imposed deference to the Jerusalem church, disguised as a plea for generous charity. Modified support for Holl can be found in Bengt Holmberg: "Holl infers that not only 'the saints' (οἱ ἅγιοι) but also 'the poor' (οἱ πτωχοί) was a well-known, self-designation of the Christians in Jerusalem. This 'holiness' and God-pleasing 'poverty' were the foundation of the *legal* claim of these Christians on other churches" (my italics).[23] Holl and Holmberg argue that Jerusalem remains the "centre" or "pillar" of the church, with what Holl (but not Holmberg) calls a "right of taxation," parallel with support for the temple from hellenistic Jews.

This view has little credibility, and no firm evidence (see above on the word for **collection**, which has a different force). Two points, however, remain historically significant. First, *Jews* made charitable provisions and *collections* for *impoverished Jews,* and as a witness to Jews (if for no other reason) it would be unthinkable for Christian believers to do any less for Jews in Jerusalem who were also believing Christians, and therefore no longer able to receive support from fellow Jews. Second, as Weiss observes, the voluntary selling of possessions to which Acts 4:32, 34-36 refers would have entailed the ruin of many small businesses in the Jerusalem area, thereby impoverishing not only the donors but the whole church there of income from its own charitable members.[24] That this "obligated" other churches to help them is true only in the sense that any inequality has to be addressed. As Dieter Georgi argues, here a link with the resurrection chapter emerges in two ways: (a) "bodily" existence entails taking responsibility for the corporeity of believers in the everyday public domain; and (b) a debt to the communities founded by the first witnesses of the resurrection may be implied by the moral debt to their "founding" role.[25]

Paul's allusion to his directions (διέταξα) **to the churches of Galatia** establishes not only the solidarity between those who give and those who receive but also the co-solidarity of the wider community of givers in their common recognition of the need for support for the Jerusalem church. **Galatia** almost certainly means the Roman Province of Galatia, which included the communities founded by Paul in Antioch of Pisidia, Iconium, Lystra, and Derbe during

---

22. Nickle, *The Collection,* 100; Fee, *First Epistle,* 810, n. 3.

23. Holmberg, *Paul and Power,* 36; cf. 35-57. Holl's work was first published in 1921 and then reprinted in Holl, *Gesammelte Aufsätze zur Kirchengeschichte,* 2 (Tübingen: Mohr, 1928), 44-67.

24. Weiss, *History of Primitive Christianity* (Harper ed. *Earliest Christianity*), ad loc. on the early Jerusalem church.

25. Georgi, *Remembering the Poor,* 51-52. Georgi's comments about "reward . . . for . . . cultic practice" are more problematic (53).

his so-called First Missionary Journey (Acts 13-14).[26] διατάσσω entails un-avoidable inferences about apostolic authority (on this use of this verb see above under 7:17; cf. also 9:14 where ὁ κύριος is the subject, and the broader force in 11:34). Although Collins translates τοὺς ἁγίους as *the holy ones,* this loses some intelligibility in modern English for some readers, even if *the saints* (NRSV) may be misleading in seeming to apply for some readers believers who acquire a certain degree of habits of holiness (more seriously than 1:2, where goal may also be implied).[27] **God's people** (above) is adopted by REB and NIV (with **God's** *holy* **people** in NJB, equally acceptable). In view of the Old Testament background those who argue that this term applies in particular to the Jerusalem community of believers may have an arguable case, but Paul seems to use the term more widely to denote Christian believers as such. Only the context can determine the semantic scope here.

2 (1) The UBS 4th ed. σαββάτου is well attested (A, B, C, D, F, G, ℵ[1], 33, Syriac, Sahidic), and it is not surprising that some later MSS (ℵ[2], K, L, M, Syriac, Bohairic) should provide σαββάτων (plural) as a supposed correction. (2) εὐοδῶται is a rare word (in the New Testament only here and in Rom 1:10) and may be either present passive subjunctive or perfect passive indicative (Moulton, Findlay, and Robertson and Plummer propose perfect passive subjunctive [see below]).[28] In view of such uncertainty in the grammatical form, some MSS read εὐοδῶθη, first aoristive pass subjunctive (supported by ℵ[2], A, C, K. However, εὐοδῶται receives solid support, e.g., ℵ*, B, D, F, G, and may be accepted.

Verse 2 provides a very early explicit reference to **every Sunday** as a worship day (strictly, *every first day of the week;* Gk. κατὰ μίαν σαββάτου). In accordance with regular LXX rendering of the Semitic idiom in the Hebrew text, Paul uses the cardinal numeral μίαν in place of the more strictly correct ordinal πρώτην. Similarly, the Synoptic Gospels allude to Mary Magdalene and the other women visiting the tomb of Jesus τῇ μιᾷ τῶν σαββάτων (Mark 16:2; cf. Luke 24:1).[29] κατά occurs in its distributive sense to denote **every** (as in καθ' ἡμέραν elsewhere). σαββάτου more usually occurs in the plural to denote *week* (as in Mark 16:2), but sometimes the singular form is used elsewhere in the New Testament (e.g., Luke 18:12, νηστεύω δὶς τοῦ σαββάτου, *I fast twice a week*).

Sunday not only looks back to the Easter event of the resurrection but

---

26. We need not discuss the respective merits of the well-known debate about a "South Galatian" reconstruction (the Roman Province) and a "North Galatian" hypothesis. The former is more convincing (cf. F. J. Matera, *Galatians,* SacPag 9 [Collegeville: Liturgical Press, 1992], 19-24, and numerous other debates). A very helpful reconstruction appears in Murphy-O'Connor, *Paul: A Critical Life,* 159-66.

27. Collins, *First Cor,* 585.

28. J. H. Moulton, *Grammar,* 1: *Prolegomena,* 54, following Findlay, *Expositor's Greek Testament;* also Robertson and Plummer, *First Epistle,* 385.

29. Cf. Robertson, *Grammar,* 672.

also (as *the Lord's Day,* κυριακὴ ἡμέρα, Rev 1:10) looks forward to *the Day of the Lord* (ἡμέρα τοῦ κυρίου), which Werner regards as its "paraphrase."[30] *The Lord's Day* (Rev 1:10) is more usually described as "the first day of the week" (cf. John 20:1, 19; Acts 20:7; *Didache* 14:1), but the title soon came to denote the day observed in honor of the risen Lord.[31]

How quickly the full principle of Sabbath observance was actually *replaced* by **Sunday** (with all the force of the fourth commandment of the Decalogue) is disputed. R. T. Beckwith and W. Stott argue that this occurred during the apostolic age.[32] On the other hand, S. Bacchiocchi and K. A. Strand understand the few New Testament allusions as merely beginning a longer process which achieved the status of a "replacement" for the seventh-day Sabbath only with the intensification of anti-Jewish polemic in the second century.[33] It must be admitted that κυριακὴ ἡμέρα appears only in Rev 1:10 in the New Testament, although thereafter it is found in the early second century (*Didache* 14:1; Ignatius *Letter to the Magnesians,* 9:1; cf. also *Gospel of Peter* 35:50; Irenaeus, *Fragments,* 7).[34] Rordorf's view that κυριακὴ ἡμέρα (Rev 1:10) grew out of κυριακὴ δεῖπνον, *Lord's Supper* (1 Cor 11:20), remains no more than speculative.[35] J. C. Laansma concludes that although the earliest evidence retains some ambiguity, it is probable that *the first day of the week* very soon became the special day for the celebration of the Lord's Supper or Holy Communion even if this did not become universal in apostolic times (cf. further Acts 20:7). A full-scale "replacement" of the Sabbath by Sunday, he argues, more probably belongs to the period of the second century.[36] By around AD 112 more solid evidence emerges (perhaps in Pliny's correspondence with Trajan *Stato die, Letters,* 10.97) but more explicitly in Justin (*Apology,* 1:65-67). Justin explicitly uses the Roman name *Day of the Sun* (τῇ τοῦ ἡλίου λεγομένη ἡμέρα).[37]

As Laanasma observes, although traditionally 1 Cor 16:2 has been regarded as *presupposing* that **Sunday** was a special day for Christians, one major objection to this view arises from the *private* nature of the *collecting,* especially if παρ' ἑαυτῷ τιθέτω is understood to mean *let him or her* **put aside** *at home.* . . . However, in a sense he also hedges his bets: "This point . . . can be made to prove too much if it is made to suggest that the church did not meet on

30. M. Werner, *The Formation of Christian Dogma* (Eng. trans., London: Black, 1957), 32. "Lord's day" in Rev 1:10 points to "Day of the Lord," as in Joel 2:31 (LXX).

31. J. A. Fitzmyer, "κύριος, κυριακός," *EDNT,* 2:331.

32. Beckwith and Scott, *This Is the Day.*

33. Bacchiocchi, *From Sabbath to Sunday;* K. A. Strand (ed.), *The Sabbath in Scripture and History* (Washington, D.C.: Herald, 1982).

34. See further BAGD, 458; LSJ, 1,013; W. Stott, *NIDNTT,* 3:411-12, and esp. Carson (ed.), *From Sabbath to Lord's Day,* esp. R. J. Bauckham, in *From Sabbath to Lord's Day,* 221-50 and 251-98.

35. Rordorf, *Sabbat und Sonntag in der alten Kirche,* and esp. *Sunday.*

36. Laansma, "Lord's Day," in *Dictionary of the Later NT and Its Developments,* 679-86.

37. Similarly, Tertullian, *Ad Nationes,* 1:13: *Die Solis, Sun-Day.*

that day."[38] As he adds, Paul's use of *the first day of the week* almost as a throw-away line without explanation "takes for granted that the choice . . . would have made sense to the Corinthians (as it had to the churches in Galatia)."[39] In our view this is hardly likely to relate to budgetary principles: payment would seldom be in advance, and in any case the clause ὅ τι ἐὰν εὐοδῶται is retrospective, not prospective. The replacement of the Jewish Sabbath by the Christian *Lord's Day, first day,* or **Sunday**, has, it seems, begun to be *in process* within the New Testament period, although the evidence is not decisive before the second century.

The Greek grammar and syntax of the rest of the verse assists our exegesis. τιθέτω is present imperative, as we should expect, to underline the continuous and regular nature of the process of **putting aside** savings for the needs of fellow Christians in Jerusalem. ὅ τι ἐὰν εὐοδῶται, furthermore, has an indefinite force. The rare verb εὐοδόω (only in Rom 1:10, 3 John 2, and here in the New Testament) derives from journeying on a *good* (εὐ) *way* or *road* (ὁδός); hence in Sophocles, LXX, and the papyri *to be led along a good road, to get along well, to prosper* (Prov 28:13; Josh 1:8; 2 Chron 18:11; *1 Enoch* 104:6).[40] In 3 John 2 the writer prays that "all may go well with you." It is questionable, however, whether *profit* (Barrett) or *gain* (BAGD and Collins) remains appropriate, in contrast to *whatever he can afford* (REB) or *as each can spare* (NJB). Since the early uncials and even other early MSS did not carry Greek accents, it is uncertain whether the form is present passive subjunctive (most likely), just possibly perfect passive indicative, or (with Moulton and Findlay) perfect passive subjunctive (see under Textual Note). The problem about specifying *prospers* or *earns* is that we cannot exclude a negative understanding of the indefinite clause, i.e., in the sense of *unless, perchance, he or she is too hard up.* It seems most faithful to Paul's indefinite force to translate **in accordance with how you may fare.**[41] **Fare** combines the notion of *journey* or *travel* with a broader metaphorical meaning in English, as in the Greek.

Fee suggests that NIV, *in keeping with his income,* is "a bit too modern," but it has the advantage of avoiding the notion of giving only when one is making a *profit* (Barrett, Collins, BAGD), or deciding what a donor can *spare* (NJB) or *afford* (REB).[42] In spirit, the tradition of the widow's mite lies behind Paul's phraseology: "Whoever sows sparingly will also reap sparingly, and whoever sows generously will reap generously. . . . God loves a cheerful giver . . ." (2 Cor 9:6, 7; cf. 2 Cor 8:1–9:15). It is just possible that the Greek verb includes more than financial capacity. For the emphasis on glad response to overflowing divine grace in 2 Corinthians 8–9 may be anticipated in the sense of "in keeping

---

38. Laanasma, "Lord's Day," 680. Laanasma's work is based in part on a doctoral thesis (Ph.D. dissertation, University of Aberdeen, 1995).

39. Ibid.

40. BAGD, 323.

41. Robertson and Plummer, *First Epistle,* stress the "neutral" character of the word.

42. Fee, *First Epistle,* 814.

with how God has blessed you on your journey." Perhaps both aspects are applicable.[43] θησαυρίζων, *storing up,* anticipates our notion of "savings" but may be better conveyed by the compound **accumulation of savings**. It is not entirely clear why this collection should take place **at home** (παρ' ἑαυτῷ, *at his or her own house*). Some suggest it was to avoid the offense of an act of giving or receiving on the Jewish Sabbath, but this is already avoided by specifying **every Sunday**.[44] Perhaps sensitivities about patrons, the wealthy, and relations with other churches suggested a quiet, noncompetitive strategy on pastoral grounds. The last clause clinches the specific purpose of the arrangement. There is to be no last-minute, superficial scraping around for funds as an unplanned off-the-cuff gesture. Still less is it to depend on Paul's own personal plea to "the wealthy" as an emergency. **Each** is to play his or her part *in a planned strategy of regular giving* in weekly response to God's blessing and his financial provision, for the benefit of those who suffer deeper poverty and in mutuality and solidarity with a local church community. Further, "Paul is seeking to avoid the unpleasant necessity of launching a fund drive when he arrives in Corinth. . . . The money is not for *him.*"[45]

3 𝔭[46] reads the straightforward present indicative δοκιμάζετε after οὕς, *those whom you approve.* Other MSS, however, read ἐὰν δοκιμάσητε, the aorist subjunctive, probably reflecting the force of *whatever people you may choose.* The latter is in effect certain.[46] The sense is hardly affected.

Once again Paul's judicious pastoral strategy emerges. If Corinth raises a substantial sum, its transmission to the Jerusalem recipients must be by *those whom the Corinthians themselves fully trust, whose integrity is above suspicion at Corinth.* It is not enough for Paul to trust them. Findlay translates: *those whom you accredit by letter,* and in theory δι' ἐπιστολῶν, **by means of letters [of authorization]**, could refer to δοκιμάσητε, *[delegates]* whom **you approve**.[47] Most writers, however, more convincingly construe the **letters of accreditation** with the main finite verb πέμψω, **I will send,** which regularly occurs in syntagmatic semantic relation with **letters**.

Purists may insist that δοκιμάζω means simply **to approve**, not **to approve as tried and true**. However, we have already discussed lexicographical concerns under 3:13 and 11:28 and under δόκιμος in 11:19. The verb conveys not simply *approval,* but being **tried** and *tested* and found to be **true** or *authentic.* Paul is alluding to the *trusted integrity* of those who can serve on

43. Chrysostom believes that Sunday is appropriate on this ground: it is the day when Christians review God's blessings (*1 Cor. Hom.,* 43:2).

44. Cf. the discussion in Edwards, *First Epistle,* 464. The Synoptic tradition also embodies the words of Jesus about giving in secret.

45. Hays, *First Cor,* 285.

46. Metzger, *Textual Commentary,* does not even trouble to comment here.

47. Findlay, *Expositor's Greek Testament,* 2:946.

behalf of a potentially suspicious congregation in which there are already "splits" and perhaps competing patrons. His directive will work without back-firing only if these representatives who carry delegated responsibility for substantial funds amidst the hazards and perils of a long journey are utterly approved as **tried and true**, i.e., with the application of the full force of the verb as denoting *both process and result.*[48] Murphy-O'Connor argues that the moneys collected would be likely to be reduced to the smallest volume, namely, gold, and that Paul's greatest concern would be that of security.[49] Similarly, the word **letters** often carries with it an implicit functional understanding derived from the context, e.g., **letters** *of commendation,* **letters of authorization** or of *accreditation.* NJB, NIV, and REB have **letters** *of introduction,* which may be equally possible (but see below), while NRSV renders simply **letters**, which cannot be faulted. Barrett translates *authorized by letter,* on the ground that such "commendatory letters were well-known form[s] in antiquity."[50] See also 2 Cor 8:16-24.

Although Paul significantly uses the indefinite construction ὅταν δὲ παραγένωμαι (second aorist middle subjunctive), this provides a second example of his firm intention to revisit Corinth (cf. 4:18-21). Any indefinite aspect concerns not "whether" but "when." Robert Funk makes a careful comparison between 4:14-21 and 16:1-11 with eleven other instances in the Pauline epistles of apostolic "presence" (parousia) or the sending of "an apostolic emissary."[51] Funk compares the "power" of apostolic presence, for which letters of emissaries are only a pastoral substitute, with the "power" of apostolic presence in Acts 5:1-11. His discussion lacks the more subtle sophistication of many more recent studies found in his original 1967 text (see, e.g., Schütz, Crafton, or Savage), but it serves to give added point to the role of the proposed **letters of authorization**. These witness to Paul's own apostolic pledge and participation as well as establishing the credentials of the delegates from Corinth. Thus *letters of introduction* (REB, NJB) may in actuality identify only part of the purpose of these letters. χάρις here may denote simply **gift** (NRSV, REB, NIV, NJB, and above), but may also mean *generosity* (Barrett's translation) or *bounty* (as perhaps in 2 Cor 8:4-9), and might equally be translated as *generous* **gift**. Its use to denote God's *grace* would hardly escape the awareness of the readers.

4 𝔭46, ℵ1, A, B, C, 33, and Latin VSS include the full text. ℵ*, D, F, and G omit ἄξιον ᾖ, reading simply *If I go as well.* Presumably some later scribes thought that **seems right**

48. Robertson also supports this meaning (*Epistles of Paul,* 201, as in Phil 1:10). Hence Collins renders this, *those whom you hold in high regard* (*First Cor,* 585).

49. Murphy-O'Connor, *Paul: A Critical Life,* 345-46.

50. Barrett, *First Epistle,* 387. Findlay, *Expositor's Greek Testament,* 2:946, speaks of *credentials.*

51. Funk, "The Apostolic Presence: Paul," in Funk, *Parables and Presence,* 81-102; rpt. from W. R. Farmer, et al. (eds.), *Christian History and Interpretation* (Cambridge: Cambridge University Press, 1967), 249-680.

somehow compromised Paul's authority or decisiveness. There could be no reason for its mistaken addition.

Meyer, Parry, Robertson and Wolff construe ἄξιον with *the gift,* as if to suggest: *if the result of the collection deserves it* (is *worthy,* is **right**), *I shall go as well.*[52] Most recent writers, however, understand ἄξιον, *fit* or **right**, to apply to "circumstances at Jerusalem."[53] Chrysostom writes as if the size of the gift would decide whether Paul was actually "needed" to assist in its conveyance.[54] Conzelmann translates: "if it should be your mind," i.e., it depends on the Corinthians' decision.[55] Allo rejects this as implausible.[56] Fee concludes that Paul deliberately leaves open what factors may determine his decision.[57] This has much to commend it. ἄξιος conveys *what* **seems right** (REB) or *fit* (less obviously *worth my going,* NJB) in relation to timing situation, other needs, and pastoral strategy. By the time he wrote 2 Cor 1:15-16, Paul had firmly decided to accompany the party, and according to Rom 15:26-27 **the collection** was duly made ready. Given the hazards and dangers of travel in the ancient world, going in reasonable numbers assisted safety, security, and mutual support. J. Murphy-O'Connor observes: "Paul could have decided not to return to Jerusalem. His participation in the delegation was not imperative. . . . His decision to persevere, despite mortal danger . . . underlines how deeply he felt about the relationship between Jewish and Gentile churches."[58]

B. TRAVEL PLANS (16:5-12)

(5, 6) **I shall come to you when I have passed through Macedonia, for I plan to go through Macedonia. It may be that I shall stay with you for a time, or even spend the winter with you, so that you can send me wherever I go next with practical support. (7) For it is not my wish to see you just in passing, for I hope to spend some time with you, if the Lord permits. (8, 9) But I shall remain at Ephesus until Pentecost. For a great and effective door stands open to me, and many opponents stand against me. (10, 11) Whenever Timothy comes, take care that he is free from fear when he is with you. For he continues the Lord's work, just as I do. Let no one belittle him as a nobody. Help him on his way with practical support and in peace, for his return to me. For**

52. Meyer, *First Epistle,* 2:112; Parry, *First Epistle,* 246; Morris, *First Epistle,* 239; Robertson, *Epistles,* 201; and Wolff, *Der erste Brief,* 430.

53. Bruce, *1 and 2 Cor,* 159; cf. Collins, *First Cor,* 589-90; Allo, *Première Épitre,* 457; Barrett, *First Epistle,* 387.

54. Chrysostom, *1 Cor. Hom.,* 43:4-5, "if it be such as to require my presence."

55. Conzelmann, *1 Cor,* 294 and 294, n. 5.

56. Allo, *Première Épitre,* 457.

57. Fee, *First Epistle,* 816.

58. Murphy-O'Connor, *Paul: A Critical Life,* 343.

I am waiting for him, with the brothers and sisters. (12) Now concerning our brother Apollos: I besought him earnestly to travel with the others to be with you, but he was fully determined not to go yet. He will go as soon as the time is right.

The difficulty of reconstructing precisely how many times Paul revisited Corinth is widely recognized. One of the clearest surveys of probabilities is offered by Murphy-O'Connor.[59] 2 Cor 12:14 might be translated, "This is the third time I am making preparations to come to you," or "I am ready to come to you for the third time." 2 Cor 13:1a is also ambivalent, while 2 Cor 13:2 is a complex sentence allowing more than one possible meaning.[60] Murphy-O'Connor believes that initially Paul sent Timothy on his behalf with considerable misgivings and anxiety about how he would be received (1 Cor 4:14-21, esp. 17-18), and hence paves the way for this in 16:10-11. "The agitated affection of Paul for his younger colleague culminated in a verbal threat. . . . Paul's surprise visit to Corinth . . . was motivated by Timothy's report."[61] While he was at Ephesus, however, Paul believed that his converts at Philippi were in danger from "Judaizers?" (cf. Phil 3:2–4:1). Hence he perceived a need to visit Macedonia, i.e., Philippi and Thessalonica (1 Cor 16:3).[62] However, if Corinth itself were to be threatened by the same danger, a visit first to Corinth would be a priority. This concern lies behind the plan reflected in 2 Cor 1:15-16.

On the other hand, if dangers of this kind were not apparent at Corinth, a breathing space might have some merit, and he would then plan to come to Corinth via Macedonia (1 Cor 16:5-6). In any event, Murphy-O'Connor suggests, Paul did visit Corinth first, "because of the unique importance of Corinth in his eyes."[63] In the end, he went from Corinth to Macedonia and thence back to Ephesus (2 Cor 2:12-13).[64] He would have taken not less than around three weeks to travel the overland route of some 363 miles from Corinth to Thessalonica if he managed an average of 20 miles per day. However, in poor physical condition he may have "walked slowly into Thessalonica sometime around mid-July AD 54," after passing through the great plain of Thessaly, "in summer . . . one of the hottest places in Europe."[65] On his arrival in Thessalonica and in Philippi, however, the trouble which he had dreaded had not, he found, materialized. Thus Philippi and Thessalonica (his bases in Mace-

59. Murphy-O'Connor, *Paul*, 291-332 and 341-51.
60. Ibid., 291-92.
61. Ibid., 292 and 293.
62. Ibid., 294.
63. Ibid., 296.
64. On this there is reasonable consensus: ibid., 296; R. P. Martin, *2 Cor* (Waco: Word, 1986), 24; Barrett, *Second Epistle to the Corinthians* (London: Black, 1973), 7; G. Lüdemann, *Paul, Apostle to the Gentiles: Studies in Chronology* (London: SCM, 1984), 94.
65. Murphy-O'Connor, *Paul*, 297; also with dangers in the mountains from bears, wolves, and wild boar (Apuleius, *Metamorphoses* 4.13; 7.22-24).

donia), Ephesus (his base in Asia Minor), and to a large extent Corinth in the end (his base in Achaea) had stood firm. Paul's major concern is the gospel, supported by pastoral concern and activity through apostolic "parousia," or by letter when his presence is impossible.[66] Other hypotheses (e.g., that of J. Weiss) are too complex and receive criticism.[67]

The issue of the visit of Timothy (vv. 10-11) is a highly sensitive one (see below), made all the more so because many at Corinth would have preferred a visit from Apollos. Paul uses pastoral wisdom and tact, probably in addition to the subgenre of a letter of recommendation.[68]

5-6 p[46], א, A, C, D, Latin, and Syriac (Harcl) read παραμενῶ, **I shall stay**. p[34] and B read καταμενῶ, *I shall stay behind*. This is less likely.

At the time of writing Paul still plans to make Corinth his base for departure, probably but not certainly with the delegation to Jerusalem (see on this Murphy-O'Connor's comments and reconstruction in the introduction to 16:5-12 above). The verb προπέμπω (here προπέμψητε), translated **send me . . . with practical support** is often used as a technical term to denote "*help on one's journey* with food, money, by arranging for companions . . . etc."[69] The verb is the same as that used (in another grammatical form) in 2 Cor 1:16 (there, προπεμφθῆναι). This gives further support to Murphy-O'Connor's double claim that since Paul need not have returned to Jerusalem, the intention to do so underlines "how deeply he felt about the relationship between Jewish and Gentile churches," and, furthermore, if he could feel that he was *sent on his way with warm support* from Corinth, this reflects "the unique importance of Corinth in his eyes" (see above).[70]

The present διέρχομαι has the force of "imminent purpose" (Findlay), or "firm intention" (Barrett), i.e., **I plan to go through**.[71] **Macedonia** alludes primarily to Thessalonica and Philippi (see above in the introduction to vv. 5-12), although Wolff includes Beraea. πρὸς ὑμᾶς certainly means coming **to you**, but it may also imply interactive relationship (as in John 1:1).[72] The American phrase *visit with* may offer a better parallel than the English *visit,* or **come to you**. A possible reason for Paul's concern about Macedonia is discussed above (introduction). τυχόν is technically the neuter accusative second aorist participle of τυγχάνω used as an adverb, *perhaps,* or **it may be that** . . . παραχειμάζω (here in the future) is a late verb providing a compound made up of παρά,

66. Cf. Funk, "The Apostolic Presence," 81-102; and Collins, *First Cor,* 590-91.

67. See Conzelmann's critique of Weiss's reconstruction, *1 Cor,* 296-97, esp. n. 25.

68. Cf. Kim, *Form and Structure of the Familiar Greek Letter of Recommendation.*

69. BAGD, 709; Grimm-Thayer, 541, also include *escort.* Also Fee, *First Epistle,* 819.

70. Murphy-O'Connor, *Paul,* 296 and 343, as cited above.

71. Findlay, *Expositor's Greek Testament,* 2:946-47; Barrett, *First Epistle,* 389; also Edwards, *First Epistle,* 466; Robertson, *Epistles of Paul,* 201.

72. As Edwards claims, *First Epistle,* 466.

alongside, and χειμών, **winter**, or stormy winter weather. χειμάζω is *to impede by severe weather.*[73] Paul hopes that he may combine a pastorally productive period with waiting for appropriate weather to travel. "The plan to spend the winter follows from the conditions of travel in those days: the winter is not time for journeys, above all by sea."[74]

As a complement to our earlier argument that not all of the so-called spiritual gifts in 12:1–14:42 are necessarily "spontaneous," but may include organization and planning (e.g., a gift of strategic insight, κυβερνήσεις, 12:28), it is clear that Paul also leaves room for an experience of divine "ordering" of his plans when the time is right. Hence later the Corinthians over-readily criticize his readiness to change his plans as fickleness rather than as spiritual and pastoral sensitivity to changing situations (cf. 2 Cor 1:17). Although he expects to move on to Jerusalem from Corinth, Paul leaves open the indefinite nature of the future by the construction οὗ ἐὰν πορεύομαι, **to wherever I go next**.

7 The UBS 4th ed. *Greek New Testament* rightly reads γάρ for the beginning of the second (explanatory) clause (with 𝔭[46], ℵ, A, B, C, D, F, G, 33, et al.). Some Vulgate MSS and Syriac (Harclean) read δέ, which accounts for *but* in the AV/KJV and is clearly secondary (γάρ is untranslated in the NIV).

The Greek idiom ἄρτι ἐν παρόδῳ precisely anticipates the double sense of Eng. **just in passing**, i.e., it may mean *just in passing* in the sense of *incidentally* (while something more important is in view) or it may also denote *just while we happen to pass each other* (like ships passing in the night, i.e., a *fleeting visit*).[75] It is a mistake to think of Paul as an evangelist only, rather than as a missionary-pastor.[76] The proviso ἐὰν ὁ κύριος ἐπιτρέψῃ reinforces the indefinite οὗ ἐὰν πορεύομαι at the end of the previous verse and would be later misperceived as vacillation or fickleness. Paul both reflects critically and sensitively on the varied factors of the situation *and* leaves the final resolution and outcome in the hands of **the Lord** in trust and obedience.

8-9 Most VSS translate the Greek in accordance with UBS 4th ed. ἐπιμενῶ, future, **I shall remain**, but some MSS read the present ἐπιμένω, *I am remaining*. This does not strictly constitute a "Textual Note," however, since the earliest MSS are without accents. Paul's words confirm that this epistle was written from Ephesus, sometime around the middle of spring. Although Paul uses the term **Pentecost** (only here in Paul) drawn from Jewish calendar of festivals, the significance of the season may lie at least in part in that it is a favor-

---

73. Cf. BAGD, 879.

74. Conzelmann, *1 Cor,* 297; cf. Acts 27:9-12.

75. Cf. Robertson, *Epistles,* 201-2. Strictly it means *in a passageway.* Cf. Collins, *First Cor,* 593.

76. See Munck, *Paul and the Salvation of Mankind,* 66-67; also J. Weiss, *Earliest Christianity,* 2:422-45 and N. Elliott, *Liberating Paul* (Maryknoll, N.Y.: Orbis, 1994), 181-214.

able season for travel, as in vv. 5-7.[77] Since he both (1) enjoys a **great door** *of opportunity* (cf. Eng. *window of opportunity*) which **stands open** (ἀνέῳγεν is second perfect active indicative of ἀνοίγω, used intransitively here: *it stands wide* **open**), and (2) still faces opposition which might threaten the work, Paul sees no need to hasten his departure at the earliest possible moment. **Door** is a metaphor for opportunity also in 2 Cor 2:12 and Col 4:3. There is general agreement that ἐνεργής should be translated **effective** here (NRSV, REB, NJB, Barrett, Collins). The Greek word occurs only here and in Philemon 6 in Paul. However, we have discussed the force of the cognate terms ἐνεργέω and more especially ἐνέργημα above (see under 12:6, 10, 11). Findlay understands μεγάλη to denote the *wide scope* of the **door**, and ἐνεργής to denote the effective *influence* gained by entering it.[78]

The ἀντικείμενοι πολλοί may be related to 15:32 ("fought with wild beasts at Ephesus"), the (later?) riot narrated in Acts 19. As a noun ἀντικείμενοι denotes *those in opposition, adversaries,* **opponents**.[79] But the forces of the components of the compound, clearly transparent to readers, mean *forces of opposition lined up against me.* Bengel observes that as often as there is good, evil arises against it at the same time.[80]

10-11   Some argue that ἐὰν δὲ ἔλθῃ is indefinite and should not simply be translated, *If Timothy comes* (with NRSV, REB, NJB, Collins). However, Conzelmann, Fee, and Collins rightly point out that since Paul explicitly states that he has sent Timothy to Corinth (4:17), the indefinite construction refers to the uncertainty not of the event, but of his time of arrival. With some support from BAGD they propose, **Whenever Timothy comes**, which is surely right.[81]

Paul is deeply concerned about how Timothy will be received at Corinth. Again, Fee identifies a key point: Timothy is to "remind them of Paul's ways" (4:17), and he is portrayed here as **continuing the work** (τὸ ἔργον . . . ἐργάζεται, continuous present) which Paul himself began (ὡς κἀγώ).[82] Hence any hostility toward Paul would be likely to rub off onto Timothy as Paul's "delegate," "representative" or co-worker.[83] They may perhaps have preferred to welcome Apollos rather than Timothy.[84] In Acts 19:22 Paul sends Timothy and Erastus into Macedonia, and Barrett dates the allusion at roughly the same period.[85] Paul's concern is that at Corinth Timothy may be *regarded as of little*

---

77. Collins rightly urges that this need not imply any intention actually to celebrate Pentecost as a festival in Ephesus, just as people today might say "until Christmas" simply as a way of broadly identifying a time of year (*First Cor,* 593). Christians at Ephesus were largely of Gentile origin.

78. Findlay, *Expositor's Greek Testament,* 2:947.

79. BAGD, 74.

80. Bengel, *Gnomon,* 674.

81. Conzelmann, *1 Cor,* 297; Fee, *First Epistle,* 821; Collins, *First Cor,* 596.

82. Fee, *First Epistle,* 821.

83. Cf. Murphy-O'Connor, *Paul,* 292-93; Holmberg, *Paul and Power,* 79-82.

84. Hays, *First Cor,* 286-87.

85. Barrett, *First Epistle,* 392.

or no account (μή τις οὖν αὐτὸν ἐξουθενήσῃ). In 1:28 Paul referred to **the no-bodies** (τοὺς ἐξουθενημένα) or *nothings* (neuter) whom God chose, while in 6:4 **the nobodies** (τοὺς ἐξουθενημένους) in the church might better judge civil cases than civil magistrates who had been linked or influenced by favors from the wealthy. Corinth must not regard Timothy so.[86]

As Hutson has recently argued, there is no evidence in either Paul's epistles or in Acts to suggest that Timothy was in any way timid.[87] According to Acts 16:1-2, Timothy was a native of Lystra, the son of a Jewish mother and Greek father, who was chosen by Paul during his second missionary journey to accompany him, as one *well spoken of* by other Christians (Acts 16:2-3). He became Paul's regular associate or co-worker and trusted emissary. His name stands alongside that of Paul in 1 Thess 1:1, 2 Cor 1:1, Phil 1:1, and Philem 1 (cf. Col 1:1). Phil 2:20-22 witnesses to his special relationship to Paul. On Paul's journeys at times he accompanies Paul together with Silas (Acts 16:6-40; cf. 17:10-14; 1 Thess 2:2). Along with Paul and Silvanus he preached at Corinth (2 Cor 1:19), and 16:10-11 may, Hutson argues, suggest his courage rather than the reverse. Paul's directions to the Corinthian church now are that they should **take care that** (one clear meaning of βλέπετε, i.e., *see to it that . . .*): (a) Timothy is **free from fear**; he has *no need to be apprehensive;* (b) he is not to be *despised* or undervalued but *receives due respect;* and (c) his return journey to Paul at Ephesus is facilitated by the *practical support of necessary provisions and other practical needs.*[88] On the technical force of προπέμπω, see above under v. 6.

All this serves to establish the role of Timothy among Paul's co-workers. Earle Ellis observes: "Co-workers are almost always present with Paul, and they participated in his mission in a variety of ways. . . . Some opened their homes for the services of a local congregation (Rom 16:3-5; 1 Cor 16:19; Phlm 2). . . . Most important were those gifted co-workers who were Paul's associates in preaching and teaching and those who were secretaries, recipients of, and contributors to his letters" (see 1:1, under Sosthenes).[89] **Peace** includes general *well-being.*

This is one of the minority of instances where we have translated τῶν ἀδελφῶν as **the brothers and sisters**. For in this case we simply do not know whether Paul means *friends, fellow Christians,* or some specific *group.* It is also unclear from the syntax whether they are **waiting** along with Paul for Timothy's arrival or whether Paul is waiting for their arrival alongside Timothy's.[90]

---

86. See above on 1:28 and 6:4.

87. Hutson, "Was Timothy Timid? On the Rhetoric of Fearlessness (1 Cor 16:10-11) and Cowardice (2 Tim 1:7)," 58-73.

88. On βλέπω, BAGD, 143, category 4a; so also Collins, *First Cor,* 596, as 10:12.

89. E. E. Ellis, "Coworkers, Paul and His," in *DPL,* 187; cf. 183-89; F. F. Bruce, *The Pauline Circle* (Exeter: Paternoster, 1985); D. J. Harrington, "Paul and Collaborative Ministry," *NTR* 3 (1990): 62-71; W. H. Ollrog, *Paulus und seine Mitarbeiter* (Neukirchen: Neukirchener, 1979); and works cited above, including Holmberg and under 1:1.

90. Collins favors the latter view (*First Cor,* 597), as probably does NRSV; but NJB takes the former view, and REB retains the ambiguity.

12 א*, D*, F, G insert δηλῶ ὑμῖν ὅτι before πολλὰ παρεκάλεσα αὐτόν, but this is clearly secondary.

The issue of Apollos was always a highly sensitive one for Paul in his relations with Corinth. Paul makes it utterly transparent that they see eye to eye in the work of the gospel, and perform complementary not competitive roles (see above under 3:5-9a, esp. v. 8: ὁ φυτεύων (Paul) καὶ ὁ ποτίζων (Apollos) ἕν εἰσιν, i.e., **one** *in the work*. He never rebukes the Apollos group (1:12) for any specific attitude distinctive to them; at least not in connection with Apollos. Yet the fact that an "Apollos group" existed at Corinth (1:10-12) with resultant "splits" (σχίσματα, v. 10), with each group in effect trying to "apportion out" Christ into competing group attitudes on ethos (μεμέρισται ὁ Χριστός; 1:13) demonstrates that the problem of an Apollos following was a very serious one. As we have just observed, Paul's anxieties about Timothy's reception may have owed something to hopes and preferences in some quarters for a visit from Apollos instead.

On the nature and grounds of a so-called "Apollos ethos," see above under 1:12. There is no need to rehearse the details here. Hurd follows Weiss, as we noted under 1:12, in associating this following with a "Wisdom" theology, but a number of alternative hypotheses have been floated. The key point underlined by Barrett and Schrage is that Paul never suggests any difference between Apollos and himself, and Apollos was not responsible for the Corinthians' misperceptions.[91] It may well be the case, as some have suggested, that Apollos's very reluctance to visit Corinth, indeed his being **fully determined not to go yet** (πάντως οὐκ ἦν θέλημα ἵνα νῦν ἔλθῃ), arose from his disgust that some at Corinth had manipulated his name as a slogan to promote the claims of a so-called Apollos group. As Wolff observes, Apollos does not appear explicitly to send his greeting along with Aquila and Prisca (v. 19), although it is likely that Apollos was with Paul at Ephesus betweeen AD 52 and 54.[92] According-ing to Acts 18:27 Apollos had "greatly helped those who through grace had be-lieved," and, as Hurst and others suggest, the group at Corinth lionized Apollos as a focus of personal loyalty. His name occurs at least six times in the main section on splits in the church and the role of ministers (1:1–4:21).[93] Hence it is imperative for Paul to disclaim any hand in Apollos's decision. Indeed, he in-sists that the reverse is the case. Paul *pleaded with* him, *urged* him, or **besought** him (παρεκάλεσα) **earnestly** (πολλά) to go to Corinth, but Apollos had made up his mind not to do so.

The Gk. πολλά might just possibly mean *many times* (Collins, *repeat-edly*), but its use with the aorist and its more probable use as an adverb of mode

91. Schrage, *Der erste Brief,* 1:143-44; Barrett, *First Epistle,* 43.
92. Wolff, *Der erste Brief,* 433-34; on whether Apollos was involved in the writing of He-brews during this period at Ephesus, see the critique of H. Montefiore's hypothesis by L. D. Hurst, "Apollos, Hebrews and Corinth: Bishop Montefiore's Theory Examined," *SJT* 38 (1985): 505-13.
93. Hurd, *Origin of 1 Cor,* 97-99.

or quality more convincingly suggest *strongly* (NRSV, REB, NIV) or (with **be-sought**) **earnestly** (NJB). καί without doubt has an adversative force.[94] We have already discussed the possible force of περὶ δέ (under 7:1, 25; 8:1; 12:1; 16:1). If it denotes a topic raised by the addressees, Robertson and Plummer would be correct to argue that the Corinthians had actually requested a visit from Apollos rather than from Timothy.[95] However, we have noted Margaret Mitchell's persuasive arguments that this need not always be the case.[96] Finally, Ἀπολλῶ τοῦ ἀδελφοῦ probably needs to be translated, if woodenly, as **our brother Apollos** (NRSV, NIV, NJB), because while *our friend* (REB) is perhaps more likely as a true equivalent, **brother** can include not only *friend,* but also *colleague, fellow Christian, co-worker,* or *associate,* and *which* is not specified.

C. CONCLUDING EXHORTATIONS AND GREETINGS — *PERORATIO* (16:13-24)

(13, 14) Keep alert; stand firm in the faith; show mature courage; increase in strength. Let everything you do be done in love. (15, 16) I have another request to ask you, dear Christian brothers and sisters. You know that the Stephanas household was the first of more converts to come in Achaia, and that they assigned themselves to the service of God's people. You yourselves should please be subject to such people as these and to everyone who shares in hard toil in our common work. (17, 18) I am delighted that Stephanas and Fortunatus and Achaicus have arrived because they have made up for my missing you here. They have raised my spirits, just as they do yours. You should show due recognition, then, to people of such a kind. (19) The churches of Asia send greetings to you. Aquila and Prisca send warm greetings to you in the Lord, together with the church that meets in their house. (20) Greetings from all your fellow Christians! Greet one another with a holy kiss. (21) The greeting in my — Paul's — hand. (22-24) If anyone does not love the Lord, let that person be anathema. "Our Lord, come!" The grace of the Lord Jesus be with you. My love be with you all in Christ Jesus.

In 1:1-3 we noted that Paul used the conventional epistolary opening common to letters of the hellenistic and early imperial Roman periods but that he also filled these conventional forms with a distinctive Christian content. The same principle applies to the closure of the letter.[97] Hellenistic writers often closed their letters with some such wish as *be strong* or *may you prosper,* and Paul repeats the general

94. Cf. BAGD, 392, sect. 2g, and 5:2; 2 Cor 6:9.
95. Robertson and Plummer, *First Epistle,* 392.
96. Mitchell, "Concerning περὶ δέ in 1 Cor," 229-56.
97. See Weima, *Neglected Endings — The Significance of the Pauline Letter Closings.* Cf. also Hays, *First Cor,* 288; Fee, *First Epistle,* 825-27; Witherington, *Conflict and Community,* 318-24.

sentiment with the addition of **in the faith** (v. 13). The use of a series of short, terse exhortations at the end of a letter is characteristic of Paul's style (cf. Rom 16:17-19; 2 Cor 13:11; Phil 4:8-9; 1 Thess 5:12-22). Two verses (vv. 13-14) embody five imperatives of their kind. It is peculiar to this epistle and its situation, however, to stress the importance of **love** three times in closing (vv. 14, 22, 24; cf. 1:10 and 13:1-13). Other unusual and distinctive features include the **anathema** of v. 22 (elsewhere only in Gal 1:8-9) and the postscript (v. 24) after the final **grace** (v. 23). "Nowhere else in his correspondence does Paul assure the community of his love in a fashion as solemn as he does in 1 Corinthians."[98]

Throughout the closing form, Mitchell argues, runs the theme of reconciliation: "The unifying force of the plea is made once again with πάντες — my love is with *all of you,* and is grounded in a final appeal to Christ Jesus, the one Lord shared by all" (Mitchell's italics).[99] Thus, in spite of sharing and using various Graeco-Roman letter-writing conventions mainly at the formal level, Paul's distinctive content provides what Weima has called a hermeneutical spotlight that highlights the central concerns of the letter.[100] W. Wuellner therefore perceives Paul as exemplifying the rhetorical axiom of Quintilian that the *peroratio* of a speech ought to take up in very succinct form some of the issues previously stated, coupled with an appeal to the heart (Quintilian, *Institutio Oratoria* 6.1.1). It includes a "recapitulation of the basic thesis *(propositio)*" to which a final appeal is added.[101] The strongest and most sophisticated account of the gathering up of themes from the whole letter as a *peroratio* comes from Eriksson (see esp. on vv. 21-24, below).[102]

Supplementary Bibliography on 16:13-24

Albright, W. F., and C. S. Mann, "Two Texts in 1 Cor," *NTS* 16 (1970): 271-76.

Banks, R., *Paul's Idea of Community* (rev. ed., Peabody, Mass.: Hendrickson, 1994), 139-69.

Bjerkelund, C. J., *Parakalō. Form, Funktion and Sinn* (Oslo: Universitetsvorlaget, 1967), 35-111, 141-48, and 188-90.

Black, M., "The Maranatha Invocation and Jude 14, 15 (1 Enoch 1:9)," in Barnabas Lindars and S. S. Smalley (eds.), *Christ and Spirit in the NT: Studies in Honour of C. F. D. Moule* (Cambridge: Cambridge University Press, 1973), 189-96.

Bornkamm, G., "The Anathema in the Lord's Supper Tradition," in *Early Christian Experience* (Eng. trans., London: SCM, 1969), 169-79.

Bruce, F. F., *Paul: Apostle of the Free Spirit* (Exeter: Paternoster, 1977), 248-63, 298-99, 398-99, and 457-58.

Dunphy, W., "Maranatha: Development in Early Christology," *ITQ* 37 (1970): 294-308.

---

98. Collins, *First Cor,* 601.

99. Mitchell, *Rhetoric of Reconciliation,* 179.

100. Weima, *Neglected Endings.*

101. Wuellner, "Greek Rhetoric and Pauline Argumentation," in Schoedel and Wilken (eds.), *Early Christian Literature and the Classical Intellectual Tradition,* 183; cf. 177-88.

102. Eriksson, *Traditions as Rhetorical Proof,* 279-98, including a superb account of vv. 22-24, often overlooked by commentators in terms of detail.

Emmerton, J. A., "Maranatha and Ephphatha," *JTS* 18 (1967): 427-31.

Eriksson, A., "Maranatha in the Letter's *Peroratio,*" in his *Traditions as Rhetorical Proof: Pauline Argumentation in 1 Corinthians,* ConBNT (Stockholm: Almqvist & Wiksell, 1998), 279-98.

Gielen, M., "Zur Interpretation der paulinischen Formel *'hē kat' oikon ekklēsia,'*" *ZNW* 77 (1986): 109-25.

Käsemann, E., "Sentences of Holy Law in the NT," in *NT Questions of Today* (Eng. trans., London: SCM, 1969), 66-81, esp. 68-70.

Kim, Chan-Hie, *Form and Structure of the Familiar Greek Letter of Recommendation,* SBLDS 4 (Missoula: Scholars Press, 1972).

Klassen, W., "The Sacred Kiss in the NT: An Example of Social Boundary Lines," *NTS* 39 (1993): 122-35.

Luke, K., "Maranatha (1 Cor 16:22)," *Biblebhashyam* 10 (1984): 54-73.

Malherbe, A., *Ancient Epistolary Theorists,* SBL Sources 19 (Atlanta: Scholars Press, 1988).

Meeks, Wayne A., *The First Urban Christians* (New Haven: Yale University Press, 1983), 53-63.

Moule, C. F. D., "A Reconsideration of the Context of Maranatha," *NTS* 6 (1959-60): 307-10.

Murphy-O'Connor, J., *Paul: A Critical Life* (Oxford: Oxford University Press, 1997), 164-65, 291-332, 343-48.

———, *Paul the Letter-Writer: His World, His Options, His Skills* (Collegeville: Liturgical Press [Glazier], 1995).

Richards, E. R., *The Secretary in the Letters of Paul,* WUNT 2:42 (Tübingen: Mohr, 1991).

Robinson, J. A. T., "Traces of a Liturgical Sequence in 1 Cor 16:20-24," *JTS* 4 (1953): 38-41.

Schulz, S., "Maranatha und Kyrios Jesus," *ZNW* 53 (1962): 125-44.

Spicq, C., "Comment Comprendre φιλεῖν dans 1 Cor XVI:22?" *NovT* 1 (1956): 200-204.

Stählin, G., "φιλέω, φίλημα," *TDNT,* 9:113-71, esp. 138-46.

Stirewalt, M. L., *Studies in Ancient Greek Epistolography* (Atlanta: Scholars Press, 1993).

Thraede, K., "Ursprunge und Formen des 'heiligen Kusses' im Frühen Christentum," *Jahrbuch für Antike und Christentum* 11/12 (1967-68): 124-80.

van Unnik, W. C., "*Dominus Vobiscum:* The Background of a Liturgical Formula," in A. J. B. Higgins (ed.), *NT Essays: Studies in Memory of T. W. Manson* (Manchester: Manchester University Press, 1959), 270-305.

Weima, J. A. D., *Neglected Endings: The Significance of the Pauline Letter Closings,* JSNTSS 101 (Sheffield: JSOT Press, 1994).

Wiles, G. P., *Paul's Intercessory Prayers,* SNTSMS 24 (Cambridge: Cambridge University Press, 1974), 114-22 and 150-55.

Witherington, B., *Conflict and Community in Corinth* (Grand Rapids: Eerdmans and Carlisle: Paternoster, 1995), 318-24.

White, J. L., "Ancient Greek Letters," in D. E. Aune (ed.) *Greco-Roman Literature and the NT,* SBL Sources 21 (Atlanta: Scholars Press, 1988).

———, *Light from Ancient Letters* (Philadelphia: Fortress, 1986).

Wuellner, W., "Greek Rhetoric and Pauline Argumentation," in W. R. Schoedel and R. L. Wilken (eds.), *Early Christian Literature and the Classical Intellectual Tradition* (Paris: Beauchesne, 1979), 177-88.

13-14 Findlay comments that the four imperatives of v. 13 are aimed respectively against "heedlessness, fickleness, childishness, and moral enervation."[103] It is important to try to convey Paul's use of four *present* imperatives. He does *not* say *wake up, stand up on your feet,* but *stay watchful,* or **keep alert; stand firm**. The first two verbs are derived from older perfect forms but function as presents: γρηγορεῖτε, στήκετε (from γρηγορέω, not ἐγείρω, and from στήκω, not from ἵστημι (although derived from these cognate forms of which they reflected the perfect in earlier Greek). Some VSS translate ἐν τῇ πίστει, **in** *your* **faith** (NRSV); others render the phrase **in the faith** (REB, NIV, NJB). In favor of the former is that the use of **the faith** to denote *the gospel* tends to be more characteristic of later epistles, especially the Pastorals; but Paul is more likely to be speaking of *the gospel* common to all Christian communities in an objective sense than of a quasi-psychological state of faith among Corinthian believers. Thus Conzelmann, Fee, and Wolff rightly understand the latter: the gospel faith "should remain the foundation of the community."[104] The exhortation to **keep alert** need not be understood as primarily or exclusively referring to eschatological watchfulness (as in 1 Thess 5:6, 10; cf. Mark 14:34-38; Matt 24:42-43; 25:13). Paul diagnoses much of the problem of misperception of the resurrection as caused by an absence of alert, coherent reflection (15:2, 33-34). Once they have given alert attention to such matters, they must **stand firm** or *stand fast* in the gospel.

The translation of ἀνδρίζεσθε has probably become unnecessarily sensitive. In lexicographical terms the meaning clearly turns on "masculine" writers stereotypically associated with ἀνήρ (gen ἀνδρός). BAGD propose *conduct oneself in a manly or courageous way,* especially with κραταιοῦσθαι (as here).[105] Classical translations often render *be a man!* (cf. AV/KJV, *quit you like men,* for this verse). Most modern English VSS translate it *be courageous* (NRSV, NIV; cf. *be brave,* NJB, or, better, *be valiant,* REB). But here the gender issue threatens to obscure the force of *be a man!* ἀνήρ has *two* semantic oppositions, not one: it does not simply pose a contrast with supposedly "feminine" qualities; it also stands in contrast with *childish ways,* as strikingly in 1 Cor 13:11: ἐφρόνουν ὡς νήπιος *(I had a childish mind-set, attitude)* but I set all this aside ὅτε γέγονα ἀνήρ *(when I became a man).* Hence the Greek suggests *both maturity and courage:* **show mature courage**. This reflects, in the closure of the letter, Paul's earlier rebukes that their notions of *"the spiritual"* were *immature and childish* (3:1, ὡς νηπίοις; 13:10, 11; 14:20; regularly in the context of defining "spiritual").

It is no accident that a similar duality of nuance attaches to κραταιοῦσθε,

103. Findlay, *Expositor's Greek Testament,* 2:949.

104. Wolff, *Der erste Brief,* 435; cf. Fee, *First Epistle,* 827 and 827, n. 11. Curiously Fee seems to cite Barrett as favoring *your faith;* but Barrett declares himself neutral (Barrett, *First Epistle,* 393). *Your faith* is defended by Parry, *First Epistle,* 249; and Grosheide, *First Epistle,* 402, renders, "by the power of faith."

105. BAGD, 64; also Grimm-Thayer, 43.

although we must not lose sight of the connection with the previous verb cited by BAGD. κραταιόω in the active means "to strengthen," but in the passive "to become strong" (cf. Philo, *De Agricultura* 160; *Quod Omnis Probus Liber Sit* 27; Ps 30:25; Eph 3:16).[106] In the LXX it may translate Heb. חזק *(chazaq)* or the Greek passive, also אמץ *('emets), to make strong,* **to increase in strength**.[107] In view of the conjunction of four imperatives in the continuous present, this last translation seems most appropriate to Paul's concerns about his readers' stability and maturity.

As Paul has argued earlier, *childishness* often takes the form of self-centered concern and short-term gratification. Hence he pleads that whatever the Corinthian Christians do, the motivation and attitude should be that of **love**, i.e., a concern for the good of "the other" which embodies *respect* and seeks to *build them* up in the long term (cf. 8:7-13; 13:1-13).[108]

15-16 In v. 15 א[2] and D insert *and Fortunatus* after *Stephanas,* while C*, F, G, and some VSS *also* insert *and Achaicus;* but this is a secondary reading in anticipation of v. 17.

παρακαλῶ δὲ ὑμᾶς, ἀδελφοί replicates the *parakalô* formula of 1:10, concerning which we entered into detailed discussion. Although most translators suggest *I urge* (NRSV, REB; NJB; in effect NIV), or *I exhort* (Collins), we argued for **I ask** (1:10) (i.e., making a **request**) on the basis of a full-length monograph on παρακαλῶ by Bjerkelund.[109] In contrast to those who regard it as a term which introduces deliberative rhetoric, Bjerkelund shows that in many examples of contemporary Greek it serves to introduce a request on the basis of a specific personal or institutional relationship between the sender and addressee, sometimes of friendship, sometimes of commerce, often of some official standing (see further above under 1:10).

It remains the case that the *epistolographic forms* of vv. 15-18 closely resemble those found frequently in *letters of recommendation* in the hellenistic letter forms of Paul's day.[110] In the introduction to 1:1-9 we cited over forty research items of modern literature on these letter forms of which those by Kim, White, Stirewalt, and Malherbe repay special attention.[111] Some of the so-called criteria for identification of patterns, it must be conceded, could hardly be other than predictable, e.g., the name of the person commended, a participial clause identifying or describing them, a statement of their relationship to the

---

106. BAGD, 448; Grimm-Thayer, 358-59.

107. Grimm-Thayer's translation of the LXX use, 358-59.

108. On **love** as a distinctive theme of this closing section, see the introduction to 16:13-24 above.

109. Bjerkelund, *Parakalō: Form, Funktion und Sinn,* esp. 35-111, 141-48, and 188-90.

110. See esp. Kim, *Form and Structure of the Familiar Greek Letter of Recommendation.*

111. See above, not least White, *Light from Ancient Letters;* "Ancient Greek Letters," in Aune (ed.), *Greco-Roman Literature and the NT,* and in *Semeia* 22 (1981): 1-14 and 89-106; Stirewalt, *Studies in Ancient Greek Epistolography;* and Malherbe, *Ancient Epistolary Theorists.*

writer, and so on. However, it remains the case that, as in the introduction to the letter (1:1-9), Paul follows normal custom and convention where he can, even if he cannot avoid adding distinctively Christian touches or content.

The first issue of major exegetical contention is the meaning in this context of ἀπαρχὴ τῆς Ἀχαίας generally translated *the* **first** *converts in* **Achaia** (NRSV, REB, NIV; cf. Rom 16:5) or more closely to the Greek lexicography and more strictly *the firstfruits of* **Achaia** (NJB, Barrett). Edwards challenges the customary understanding *the* **first** *converts in the province of Achaia* on the ground that according to Acts 17:34 Dionysius and Damaris had already become Christian converts in Athens, the other leading city of Achaia.[112] It is possible that since Corinth was the capital city of Achaia since AD 27 and Paul's unrivaled major base of operations for the Province, they are regarded as in effect the first converts, especially since Paul explicitly declares in 1:16 that he himself baptized the Stephanas household as part of his (initial?) ministry in Corinth. Later other believers might baptize new converts, including (after the first?) his co-workers.[113] However, even those writers who accept the meaning *first converts* also urge that ἀπαρχή, *firstfruits,* derives its main significance not primarily from being *first* in a sequential sense, but *first* in the sense of constituting a *sample, pledge,* or *promise of* **more to come.**[114]

Since **Stephanas** and his **household have assigned themselves** or *devoted themselves* to **the service of God's people**, it seems likely that Paul perceives them not only as the *first converts* as such but more especially as the *core base of mature, long-standing believers: as those* whose loyal work and witness holds *promise of more believers* **to come,** i.e., *to be added* to the Christian church **in Achaia.** This accords with Paul's use of ἀπαρχή in 15:20, 23. On the other hand, Rom 16:5 does seem to speak of Epaenetus as the *first convert* (ἀπαρχή) in the Province of Asia (NIV). If we combine the two ideas, embodying Paul's special interest in Corinth, **Stephanas** appears as "co-worker . . . in founding a church" (Banks).[115] Hence perhaps the two nuances should be combined: **the first of more converts to come in Achaia.**[116]

The use of τάσσω in εἰς διακονίαν τοῖς ἁγίοις ἔταξαν ἑαυτούς has more to do with *appointing* or **assigning** to a task, office, or position than *have devoted themselves* (NRSV, REB, NIV, NJB) might seem to suggest.[117] τάγμα (15:23),

112. Edwards, *First Epistle,* 471.

113. Barrett concedes that first converts "fits ill with" Acts 17:34, but thinks that Paul may be thinking of Corinth only; cf. Rom 16:5 (*First Epistle,* 393).

114. Fee, *First Epistle,* 829 and 829, n. 18.

115. Banks distinguishes between co-workers who have a part in "founding" a local church and who remain loyal to Paul and "itinerant colleagues," placing Stephanas in the first category (*Paul's Idea of Community* [rev. ed., Peabody, Mass.: Hendrickson, 1994], 164-65).

116. Collins understands Paul to mean "a harbinger of things to come . . . a sign of hope" (*First Cor,* 604).

117. Cf. BAGD, 805-6, e.g., *appoint, determine, assign;* Grimm-Thayer, 615: to *place in a certain order, to assign a place, to appoint on one's own authority* (middle). Collins (*First Cor,* 605) also favors **assigned themselves.**

τάξις (14:40), and ὑποτάσσω (14:32, 34; 15:27, 28; 16:16) play a significant part in this epistle in which "rights" and "freedom" feature in Corinthian thinking. The problem is that *appointed themselves* has the nuance of the very self-centered forwardness that troubles Paul, whereas ἔταξαν ἑαυτούς is clearly commended here. Robertson and Plummer understand "appointed themselves" as "a self-imposed duty."[118] *Devoted themselves* must be understood in the sense of *set themselves aside* for this work. Today we might speak of their loyal *commitment* to this work of service and ministry.

Paul enjoins *a mutuality and reciprocity of respect.* Those who have **assigned** or *committed* their energies and time to serving or ministering deserve the honor due to such devotion. Indeed, the church at Corinth should **be subject** to such leaders or ministers who serve them. **Please** conveys the continuation of the syntax introduced by παρακαλῶ (cf. Bjerkelund's comments), and the use of ἀδελφοί, here certainly **brothers and sisters** (denoting inclusiveness and reciprocal equality) as well as συνεργοῦντι, *co-workers* **sharing** in **common work**, underlines *mutuality and complementarity.* Authentic leadership and service entail **hard toil** (κοπιῶντι), which in turn deserves respect and honor.[119] Wolff rightly links this theme of mutuality, recognition, and respect with the theme of love in ch. 13: "Love does not seek its own interests" (13:5).[120]

17-18 p46, ℵ, A, and K read ὑμῶν in place of τὸ ὑμέτερον in v. 17b (with B, C, D, and other MSS). But there is no effective difference in meaning.

A letter form in the hellenistic world of Paul's day would regularly express personal pleasure or joy at some feature or event which related to the recipients.[121] χαίρω is probably the most frequent Greek word for such an expression of pleasure, and today the equivalent would not be the archaic *I rejoice* (NRSV) but **I am delighted** (NJB); *I am glad* (NIV) is perhaps weaker, and *it is a great pleasure* (REB) lacks the warmth which Paul seeks to express.

Yet again the theme of "the apostolic presence," in which ἡ παρουσία denotes both **arrival** and *presence,* makes itself felt in this context.[122] As is also the case in eschatological contexts, the same Greek word denotes both *presence* and *advent.*[123] We have discussed the probable role of **Stephanas** as a co-worker with Paul in founding, or at least nurturing the beginnings, of the church at Corinth and its outreach, and his dual status as a local leader and a loyal associate or colleague of Paul's. We know nothing about **Fortunatus** and **Achaicus**

118. Robertson and Plummer, *First Epistle,* 392 (anticipated by Tyndale's translation).
119. As against more self-assertive attitudes among some at Corinth, Paul attempts to convey a dialectic of subjection and equality in which "orderedness" is sustained by love, not by compulsion or by manipulation. Christ's relation with God (3:23; 15:24-28) provides a model.
120. Wolff, *Der erste Brief,* 435.
121. There is no need to rehearse the mass of literature already cited above and in the bibliography to this section, including, e.g., Weima, White, and Stirewalt.
122. See Funk, "The Apostolic Presence," in his *Parables and Presence,* 81-102.
123. Cf. J. Moltmann, *The Coming of God* (Eng. trans., London: SCM, 1996), 22-28.

except that since they bear Latin names (cf. **Stephanas** as a Greek name) they may well have been freedmen, or of freedmen's stock from the Roman colonists.[124] The name **Achaicus** might also seem to suggest that he had not always lived in Corinth, since "the Achaian" would make little sense as a name *in Achaia.*[125]

Paul states that **the arrival** of these three from Corinth made up for (ἀνεπλήρωσαν) the ὑστέρημα, *absence, deficiency, lack,* left by the distance between Paul and the Corinthian church itself. In modern English idiom Paul seems to say that they *compensate* for his **missing** his dear Christian brothers and sisters there. The three arrivals help *to fill up* (ἀνα + πληρόω) *the hole* which their absence leaves. This combines *affection* for the Corinthian church with *appreciation* for their three representatives. BAGD seem to imply that it is *Paul's* absence from Corinth **for** *which* **they make up.**[126] Robertson and Plummer argue that "my want of you" and "your want of me" are both possible, and that both make good sense.[127] However, NRSV, NIV, NJB, and Collins all presuppose the exegesis proposed here. Edwards supports this decisively, and even Robertson and Plummer plausibly comment: "They were a little bit of Corinth, and as such a delight to the Apostle."[128] A more difficult issue is whether we should follow Barrett and REB in understanding τὸ ὑμέτερον ὑστέρημα as *they have done what you had no chance to do* (REB [*supplied what you could not do for me* (Barrett)]).[129] This is possible, but seems to go further than the Greek. In the absence of firmer evidence, it is wise to assume that the themes of *presence* and *absence* determine the meaning (as translated above): "An antithesis is intended between παρουσία and ὑστέρημα."[130]

Paul sums up the effect of the **arrival** and *presence* of the three as ἀνέπαυσαν γὰρ τὸ ἐμὸν πνεῦμα. Paul seldom uses πνεῦμα to refer to *spirit* in the more modern psychological sense, although he does so occasionally. Schweizer cites 1 Cor 7:34 *(in body and spirit)* and 2 Cor 7:1 *(flesh and spirit)* as clear examples of such a use.[131] But most recent Pauline specialists agree that this is an entirely uncharacteristic and secondary use. Emphatically Paul "never reckons with the salvation of a mere soul" or with πνεῦμα as the major point of contact for salvation.[132] In 1 Corinthians πνεῦμα is the divine Spirit

---

124. See Meeks, *The First Urban Christians,* 53-63, esp. 56. **Fortunatus** was a common name (almost "Lucky") and is hardly likely to be the person of that name in *1 Clement* 59.

125. Ibid.; also Collins, *First Cor,* 603 (unless perhaps the name was inherited). Héring observes that since slaves were often named after their country of origin, **Achaicus** might have been the slave of **Stephanas** (*First Epistle,* 186).

126. BAGD, 849.

127. Robertson and Plummer, *First Epistle,* 396.

128. Ibid.; Edwards, *First Epistle,* 472.

129. Barrett, *First Epistle,* 395.

130. Edwards, *First Epistle,* 472.

131. E. Schweizer, "πνεῦμα," *TDNT,* 6:435; 434-36 on "human" spirit in Paul; 332-435 for the whole article.

132. Ibid., 435, n. 491.

who communicates revelation (1 Cor 2:6-15) or who characterizes the resurrection mode of existence (15:42-44).[133] Jewett sees parallels between πνεῦμα in 16:18 and "loose parallels in Rabbinic Judaism. But [he adds] Paul's concept of the spirit is not typically Rabbinic.[134] Where Jewett underlines the limitations of Paul's use of "human spirit," Dunn explicates Paul's more central and characteristic understanding of πνεῦμα.[135] One of the most useful comparisons between Paul and uses of πνεῦμα in the hellenistic world of Paul's day remains the unduly neglected study by R. B. Hoyle.[136] The classic use for *human spirit* occurs when Paul wishes to set some form of supracognitive or subcognitive mode of experience in contrast to that of rational reflection (1 Cor 14:14-15; see above). However, this is not in view in 16:18. Hence it causes least misunderstanding to follow REB's **they have raised my spirits** rather than the traditional *refreshed my spirit* (NRSV, NIV). NJB finds an alternative way forward: *They have set my mind at rest,* which is still preferable to NRSV and NIV, depending on the force of the verb.

Hence we come to the verb ἀνέπαυσαν. Without doubt ἀναπαύω often means *to cause to rest, to give rest,* whether in the LXX (1 Chron 22:18; Prov 29:17), hellenistic-Jewish first-century literature (Josephus, *Antiquities* 3.61), or in the New Testament (Matt 11:28) the promise of Jesus *to give rest* to those who are heavy-laden.[137] Thus NJB, *set my mind at rest,* is justifiable. The problem then is how it might apply to καὶ τὸ ὑμῶν in 16:18, unless their carrying communications to Paul had this effect.[138] However, the verb also means to cause to cease from movement of any kind, especially that of labor, or whatever brings exhaustion or weary spirits.[139] Grimm-Thayer emphasize pause *for recovery* and *to collect new strength.* This may apply to the words of Jesus as well as to the present verse. Hence to Paul, wearied and anxious amidst the burdens of ministry and leather working and sales at Ephesus, the arrival of the three **raised his spirits** (REB) and gave him not only *refreshment* but also *new heart.* NJB's proposal, however, cannot be excluded.

On the above issue hangs our understanding of the compressed phrase καὶ τὸ ὑμῶν. In view of the inferential sentence which follows, **just as they do yours** (NJB, **just as they** *did* **yours**; NRSV, *as well as yours;* REB, *and no doubt yours too*) seems the most probable and least forced understanding of the Greek. The Corinthian church **should show due recognition, then**

---

133. Ibid., 426-32; cf. 422-25.

134. Jewett, *Paul's Anthropological Terms,* 185.

135. Ibid., 167-97; Dunn, *The Theology of Paul,* 413-41.

136. R. B. Hoyle, *The Holy Spirit in St Paul* (London: Hodder, 1927) (missing from most of the standard bibliographies and dicussions, but still very useful); cf. T. Paige, "Holy Spirit," in *DPL,* 404-13.

137. This is the main meaning of the active in BAGD, 58-59.

138. Theophylact interprets this to mean, "They refreshed your spirit by refreshing mine." Grotius argues: "by bringing my epistle to you."

139. Grimm-Thayer, 40-41.

(ἐπιγινώσκετε οὖν), in the sense of *appreciation* (NJB), **of people such as these** (τοὺς τοιούτους). Fee rightly comments that NIV's *such men deserve recognition* captures the broad sense but fails to communicate Paul's use of the imperative and inferential conjunction: **You should . . . , then. . . .** (The same criticism applies to REB, which follows NIV.)[140] It is a live issue in the church today to what extent, if at all, Christian congregations wish to "honor" leaders in the Christian sphere.[141] Such *respect* or **recognition** has more to do with *attitude* than financial provision, although sometimes the latter is a symptom of the former. However it is shown, Paul urges its propriety; indeed, he *directs* that it be shown. This may apply at any level of service to the church, where often loyal hard work is simply taken for granted rather than publicly and consciously **recognized**.

19   (1) The authentic Pauline reading **Prisca** occurs in 𝔭⁴⁶ (in the form πρείσκας) and also in ℵ, B, 33, Vulgate, Coptic, et al. (πρίσκα). A, C, D, F, G, and Syriac, however, read the more familiar diminutive form of the name, *Priscilla*. Through D (etc.) and the *Textus Receptus* that is the form found in AV/KJV. It is used in Acts (18:2, 18, 26), but not in Paul, and is doubtless a secondary reflection of the name used in Acts in A, C, D, and F. (2) D, F, G, and Pelagius also add a gloss after the names, παρ᾿ οἷς καὶ ξενίζομαι, *with whom I also am lodging.*

Sending greetings is yet another standard and expected part of hellenistic letter forms in Paul's day (see the substantial literature cited above on letter forms). Moulton-Milligan declare, "The papyri have shown conclusively that this common NT word (ἀσπάζομαι) was the regular *term techn* for conveying the greetings at the end of a letter."[142] Their numerous examples include *BGU* 4:1079:83-4 (from AD 41); *BGU* 2:423:18-20 (2d cent.), and *Papyrus Oxyrhynchus* 7:1067:25. The semantic range may vary from conveying *warm personal greeting* to some such equivalent as *pay one's respects to.*[143] Although he was writing specifically from Ephesus (16:8), Paul used this city (the capital of the Province of **Asia**) as a missionary and pastoral "base" for wider contacts and interaction with **the churches of Asia** throughout the Province (cf. Acts 19:10, 26). The Province of **Asia** is mentioned also in 2 Cor 1:8, Rom 16:5, and 2 Tim 1:15.

Aquila and Prisca, we may infer, are now with Paul in Ephesus, and it is natural for them to send **warm greetings** to Corinth. If we put together the New Testament evidence with the reconstructions offered by Murphy-O'Connor, Banks, Bruce, and others, a coherent picture of this husband-and-wife team

140. Fee, *First Epistle,* 832.
141. The lavish hospitality shown to me recently, e.g., by Christians in Singapore was, in their words, *an expression of "honoring" a visiting leader;* by contrast, what some Western (esp. British) churches perceive as "sacrificial" may be perceived as an absence of due "honor" to Christian leaders by Christians from the Far East who visit British churches.
142. MM, *Vocabulary,* 85.
143. Ibid., 85-86.

emerges. Paul explicitly describes them as his co-workers (Rom 16:3-5). They were probably freedpersons of Jewish origin who left Rome in AD 49 when the Emperor Claudius closed down a Roman synagogue (cf. Acts 18:1-3) because of continuous disturbances centering on the figure of Christ.[144] They may well have been converted in Rome, and then came directly to the Roman colony of Corinth to set up their small shop in which to sell leathercraft among the commercial developments off the Lechaeum road. When Paul arrived in Corinth, Aquila and Prisca were already Christian believers, and Murphy-O'Connor convincingly paints a picture of Aquila and Prisca having their home in the loft of one of the shops around the market square (approximately 13 ft. × 13 ft. × 8 ft. without running water) "while Paul slept below amid the tool-strewn workbenches and the rolls of leather and canvas. The workshop was perfect for initial contacts, particularly with women. While Paul worked on a cloak, or sandal or belt, he had the opportunity for conversation. . . ."[145] 1 Cor 16:19 demonstrates that they had been in Corinth and that they were particularly close to Paul, and on this basis we have no reason to doubt the fuller touches of Acts 18:2-3 which introduce them as Paul's hosts.[146] The Alexandrian text of Acts 18 confirms that they were of the same trade.

When Paul traveled to Ephesus in the summer of AD 52, once again it was Prisca and Aquila (Acts 18:24-28) who were there ahead of him to prepare a welcome.[147] Together with Paul, they look back with warm affection to their time spent at Corinth, especially with those who were now fellow Christians, and **send warm greetings in the Lord** (ἐν κυρίῳ πολλά) to them. NRSV's *greet you warmly* (also NIV) interprets πολλά correctly as an adverb of mode or quality, as against REB's *many greetings* (unless we take the latter to mean that *seriatim* they greet many people whom they know). NJB's more formal *best wishes* hardly envisages the intimate affection felt by Christians who had seen their prayers answered in people for whom they deeply cared coming to faith. σὺν τῇ κατ' οἶκον αὐτῶν ἐκκλησίᾳ cannot mean other than **together with the church [that meets] in their house**. However, Gielen points out that this is not a "house church," as if to suggest that it bore an identity of its own in contrast to the main congregation, but the whole church and its corporate identity, or part of it, which meets in the house.[148] Barrett suggests that their various moves (Rome to Corinth, Corinth to Ephesus, and probably Ephesus back to Rome, when Claudius's edict was relaxed in AD 54) imply "that they were not without money."[149] Travel was either for the wealthy or for those with productive busi-

---

144. Murphy O'Connor, *Paul,* 263; similarly, F. F. Bruce, *Paul, Apostle of the Free Spirit,* 250-51 and 381; cf. Suetonius, *Life of Claudius* 25.4: an expulsion *"impulsore Chresto."*

145. Murphy-O'Connor, *Paul,* 263.

146. Ibid., 261.

147. Ibid., 171-72.

148. Gielen, "Zur Interpretation der paulinschen Formel *'he kat' oikon ekkēsia,'*" 109-25. Cf. Rom 16:5; and J. M. Peterson, "House Churches in Rome," *VC* 23 (1965): 264-72.

149. Barrett, *First Epistle,* 396.

ness prospects. Hence it is by no means surprising that by around late AD 52 or AD 53 they had acquired a house large enough to accommodate meetings for worship.

In **Aquila and Prisca** we see a combination of true Christian devotion and sacrifice, a vision for the spread of the gospel, deep affection for Paul, and affection for communities of Christians in a network of locations that was growing into a worldwide church. F. F. Bruce observes that it was probably during this period of the Ephesian ministry that Prisca and Aquila "risked their necks" for Paul's life (Rom 16:4).[150] Bruce points out that this corrects the picture of an "unlovable" Paul so often promoted in modern secular mythology, as well as the mistaken notion that Christian faith simply serves self-affirmation.[151] Finally, **Prisca** (or in Acts *Priscilla*) sometimes receives mention *before* as well as *alongside* her husband **Aquila**. Most writers infer that she is the more prominent, and Banks suggests that her inherited or social status may have been higher.[152] At all events, for Bruce this is another confirmation that it becomes still more difficult to imagine that **Prisca** would encourage "risking their necks" for someone who was supposedly an awkward misogynist.[153]

20 **All** may perhaps allude to any other Christians who had links with Corinth and who lived in the Province of Asia, or perhaps other Christians in Ephesus or the wider area who did not meet specifically in the house of Aquila and Prisca. Murphy-O'Connor suggests that Prisca and Aquila had explicitly asked Paul to send their warm greetings by name, which then obliges Paul to add **everyone** *sends their greetings,* to avoid any complaint that he has omitted those who would like to be included.[154] If so, the pastoral sensitivities of the church resonate between the first century and today, with the corresponding need for pastoral tact. Fee understands the reference to be to "all the brothers presently with him," although he also concedes that it may simply constitute a redundant repetition of those mentioned in v. 19.[155]

ἀσπάσασθε ἀλλήλους ἐν φιλήματι ἁγίῳ occurs in identical form in Rom 16:16 and with only minor variations in 2 Cor 13:12 and 1 Thess 5:26, as well as in 1 Pet 5:14 (there **with a kiss** *of love,* ἐν φιλήματι ἀγάπης). The **kiss** has been widely described as a sign of respect, affection, or reconciliation not only in Judaism but also more widely in the ancient world (cf. Mark 14:45; Luke 7:45; 15:20; 22:48).[156] We shall shortly *question whether such an assumption squares with the evidence.* Meanwhile in *Christian* circles *to greet with a* **holy**

150. Bruce, *Paul,* 298.
151. Ibid., 457.
152. Banks, *Community,* 154.
153. Bruce, *Paul,* 457.
154. Murphy-O'Connor, *Paul the Letter-Writer,* 105.
155. Fee, *First Epistle,* 835-36.
156. See G. Stählin, "The Kiss in the NT," *TDNT,* 9:138-41 and "The Kiss in the Post-NT Period," *TDNT,* 142-46, under φιλέω, φίλημα, *TDNT,* 113-71.

kiss occurred not only in Paul's own communities of Thessalonica and Corinth, but also in Rome (independently of Paul) and in the congregation to whom 1 Peter was addressed. The qualifying adjective **holy** might indicate either (i) its solemnity, or (ii) its specific use as a sign of affection and respect between fellow Christians, or (iii) a liturgical context.[157] By the time of Justin, it had assumed a formal liturgical status as *"the kiss of peace"* in the Eucharist or the Lord's Supper (Justin, *Apology,* 1:65).[158] However, as Fee and Dunn insist, in the absence of clear evidence that Paul explicitly molds his epistolary ending to form part of a Eucharist, it is too specific, if not anachronistic, to follow NEB and REB in translating **holy kiss** as *kiss of peace.*[159] It remains entirely possible, at the same time, to understand **holy kiss** as a *kiss of peace* in a non-eucharistic (or not specifically eucharistic) sense. Thus Ambrosiaster understands the **holy kiss** as a sign of peace which does away with discord.[160]

The evidence of the Gospels may seem to suggest that **the kiss** usually denoted *regard, respect,* and *honor,* whether or not it also denoted affection. The kiss of Judas (Luke 22:47) accorded with the convention according to which a servant or pupil greeted a master *with honor.*[161] Similarly, a host would kiss an honored guest (Luke 7:45). The parting kiss of the Ephesian elders (Acts 20:37) expresses gratitude and respect for Paul as well as affection. Although a number of writers have linked the present allusion in 16:20 to so-called liturgical formulae in 16:22-23, as van Unnik convincingly urges, phrases such as *Dominus Vobiscum* initially owe more to a dynamic soteriology than to liturgical repetition, even if the latter subsequently provides an entirely appropriate setting.[162] Indeed, considerable caution should be observed in assessing the claims of Robinson and Bornkamm about the "eucharistic" setting of 16:20-24.[163]

Nevertheless, recent research by William Klassen (1993) turns some of these assumptions upside down, although he cites the same New Testament evidence.[164] Drawing partly on the earlier research of Klaus Thraede (1967), Klassen notes that in the Old Testament and in Graeco-Roman society, the role of **the kiss** remains varied and ambivalent.[165] By the first century devout Jews

---

157. Stählin, "The Kiss in the NT," *TDNT,* 9:138-41; and Dunn, *Romans,* 2:898-99. See further Wolff, *Der erste Brief,* 438-39.

158. Thereafter, e.g., also Hippolytus, *Apostolic Tradition,* 4:1; 22:3; Tertullian, *Orations,* 18.

159. Dunn, *Romans,* 2:898-99; Fee, *First Epistle,* 836.

160. Ambrosiaster, *Commentary on Paul's Epistles,* in CSEL, 81:193.

161. Stählin, "The Kiss in the NT," *TDNT,* 9:139.

162. Van Unnik, *"Dominus Vobiscum:* The Background of a Liturgical Formula," in Higgins (ed.), *NT Essays: Studies in Memory of T. W. Manson,* 270-305.

163. Robinson, "Traces of a Liturgical Sequence in 1 Cor 16:20-24," 38-41; Bornkamm, "The Anathema in the Early Christian Lord's Supper Tradition," in *Early Christian Experience,* 169-79.

164. Klassen, "The Sacred Kiss in the NT: An Example of Sacred Boundary Lines," 122-35.

165. K. Thraede, "Ursprunge und Formen des 'heiligen Kusses' im frühen Christentum," in *Jahrbuch für Antike und Christentum* 11/12 (1967-68): 124-80.

did not see the kiss "as a merely formal act."[166] In Graeco-Roman society the role of the kiss varies with geographical location and one's place or level in society: "Graeco-Roman society treated the public kiss . . . with considerable reticence," although in some cases it "serves . . . as confirming reconciliation."[167] It becomes a public sign for a "religious community," Thraede and Klassen insist, *only with the emergence of Christianity*.[168] In all probability "It began as a practice which expressed the closeness of people who were coming from many different social classes and who were transcending gender, religious, national, and ethnic divisions and finding themselves one in Christ."[169]

A **holy** kiss appropriately greets another of the *holy people* of God. To be sure, it is never intended to be erotic, although since everything or anything can be abused, Clement of Alexandria warns Christians against a "shameless" use of the **kiss**, while Athenagoras (c. AD 176) warns against "evil thought" which leads on to a second kiss because it is enjoyable.[170] Nevertheless, Klassen concludes that whether or not some biblical passages seem to confirm the role of the kiss as a sign of respect, however, and reconciliation, the basic function was a celebration of *oneness and solidarity and mutuality in Christ that transcended all boundaries of class, gender, or race.* This readily explains, if it is correct, why the Eucharist or Lord's Supper very quickly became the major setting for the "kiss of peace," as the sharing of "One Bread," but it was not (arguably) the *initial* setting.

Klassen's research carries much weight, but does not necessarily detract from more traditional explanations of the **kiss** in the New Testament. We conclude that it constituted *a physical sign in the public domain* of *respect, affection, and reconciliation* within the Christian community, and that its distinctive use among fellow believers *underlined and nurtured the mutuality, reciprocity, and oneness of status and identity which all Christians share across divisions of race, class, and gender.* It was clearly open to abuse, as patristic sources demonstrate, and a counterpart is needed today that offers an effective sign in the public domain that accords with these aims.

21 We have adopted Barrett's translation.[171] The articular noun ὁ ἀσπασμός (arguably *this greeting,* NRSV, REB, NJB) is followed by τῇ ἐμῇ χειρὶ Παύλου, *with the* **hand** *of me,* **Paul,** i.e., **in my — Paul's — hand.** REB offers a satisfactory alternative: *This greeting is in my own hand — Paul;* but NRSV's *I, Paul, write this greeting with my own hand* changes the structure without obvious improvement. Paul similarly writes ἔγραψα (epistolary aorist) τῇ ἐμῇ χειρί in Gal 6:11. This is clear evidence, if any further evidence were

---

166. Klassen, "The Sacred Kiss in the NT," 125.
167. Ibid., 126 and 127.
168. Ibid., 130.
169. Ibid., 132.
170. Athenagoras, *Supplicatio* 32.
171. Barrett, *First Epistle,* 398; similar to Collins (*First Cor,* 607), *A greeting in my own hand, the hand of Paul;* see also Murphy-O'Connor, *Paul the Letter-Writer,* 104.

needed, that Paul dictates his letters to a scribe or secretary, as was the common practice of letter writers in the Graeco-Roman world of Paul's day. "Most letter writers in antiquity used a professional secretary and the Apostle was no exception. . . . The fact is beyond question."[172] In addition to 16:21 and Gal 6:11 we may compare 2 Thess 3:17; Philem 19 and Col 4:18. Tertius makes his secretarial role known in Romans: "I, Tertius, the writer of this letter, greet you in the Lord" (Rom 16:23).

Nevertheless, while it was common in Paul's day to use a scribe or secretary, the convention of adding a personal signature had not yet gained currency, even often in legal documents. Hence although Paul may have added his signature in part to assure his readers of the authenticity of the letter, more probably the personal handwritten signature or note should be understood as a sign of affection and indication of his desire and longing for personal presence in Corinth (see above on *parousia*). It is generally agreed that 1:1 through to 16:20 would have been penned by Sosthenes, while 16:21-24 would be in the different handwriting (probable "larger letters," Gal 6:11) of Paul. Changes of handwriting at, or following, a personal signature with or without a note as a postscript are attested in papyrus letters.[173] Sometimes a short personal note is added in the margin as an afterthought. Paul Schubert notes the inclusion of a hasty last-minute "softener" by an angry wife who writes (through her secretary) of "her disgust" that her husband has not yet come back home.[174] As Fee observes, the personal epistolary touch makes it less likely than some have assumed that vv. 21-24 belong to an original "liturgical" setting.[175] If we cannot entirely exclude the unlikely possibility that the form of vv. 22-24 reflects Paul's envisaging that his letter be read publicly when the church gathered around the Lord's Table, the "Lord's Supper setting" hypothesis is decisively criticized by Eriksson (see under 22-24).[176]

22-24   (1) In v. 22 (a) μαράνα θά seems to be supported by p[46], א, A, B*, C, and D*, and is probably correct. (b) μαρὰν ἀθά has the support of B[1], D[2], probably D*, while (c) the single-word form μαραναθα occurs in F. While there is a difference in meaning between (a) and (b) in the Aramaic, replicated by the Greek (see below), the spacing of words and letters in crowded early MSS remains problematic. (2) In v. 23 the shorter reading Ἰησοῦ is found in א*, B, 33, Vulgate, and Old Latin; but a longer reading, Ἰησοῦ Χριστοῦ, is adopted by א[2], A, C, D, F, G, and Syriac. In Metzger's view the shorter reading is to be preferred.[177] The presence of the longer reading in other Pauline benedictions, however, is

---

172. Murphy-O'Connor, *Paul the Letter-Writer,* 7; cf. 7-9, 104-6, and 110-13; cf. further Richards, *The Secretary in the Letters of Paul.*

173. Cf. Barrett, *First Epistle,* 398; Murphy-O'Connor, *Letter-Writer,* 36 and 110-13; White, *Light from Ancient Letters,* 159-62.

174. Schubert, *Form and Function of the Pauline Thanksgivings,* 161 (from *London Papyri* 42; 168 BC).

175. Fee, *First Epistle,* 836-37; also underlined by R. Y. K. Fung, "Curse," in *DPL,* 200.

176. Eriksson, "Maranatha in the Letter's *Peroratio*," in his *Traditions as Rhetorical Proof: Pauline Argumentation in 1 Cor,* 279-98.

177. Metzger, *Textual Commentary* (2d ed.), 503-4.

double-edged (cf. Rom 16:24; 2 Cor 13:13; Gal 6:18; Phil 4:23; 1 Thess 5:28). As Metzger argues, it is likely that scribes expanded the shorter reading in accordance with their memory of other epistles. On the other hand, the longer reading is more characteristic of Paul. On balance, nevertheless, the maxim about shorter readings applies: why should *Christ* have been omitted by ℵ* and B unless it was because Paul wrote only **of the Lord Jesus**? (3) In v. 24 a liturgical ἀμήν is added after **in Christ Jesus** at the end of the last line by ℵ, A, C, D, Syriac, and other witnesses. The text is supported in effect only by B, F, 33, and a few VSS and other miniscules. The UBS 4th ed. classifies the UBS text (without *Amen*) as "almost certain" (4th ed. "B"). Again, the addition of *Amen,* even as a scribe's own testimony, is utterly predictable, while its omission would be difficult to explain. It might have been added at a very early stage, reflecting its early public reading.

In a masterly concluding chapter to his very helpful *Traditions as Rhetorical Proof: Pauline Argumentation in 1 Corinthians* Anders Eriksson offers one of the very few convincing exegetical accounts of these final three verses, so crucial that Paul chose to pen them in his own hand as his final note.[178] The verses, as Eriksson shows, must be held together and expounded as a single unit if we are to make sense of the separate parts. It would be a mistake to try to comment on each verse as if it were a separate text in its own right, for each verse draws meaning from its place among the other two. Indeed, Eriksson urges that vv. 22-24 make sense only as part of the *peroratio* of the whole letter. He criticizes many of the standard commentaries for undue haste over 16:13-24, as if the nature of epistolary and rhetorical material were less important than other parts of the letter, and with equal justice laments that many treat vv. 22-24 as *either* to be seen in strictly *epistolary* terms, *or* to be understood mainly in *rhetorical* terms, *or* (worst of all) to be approached in *genetic* terms, when many are distracted by issues of origin into floating hypotheses of eucharistic settings.[179] Against all this, Eriksson insists on a synchronic approach which treats *epistolary and rhetorical aspects together* as a way of understanding Paul's aims and strategy.

Lietzmann (probably following A. Seeberg) and subsequently Robinson, Bornkamm, Käsemann, and many others (see above) developed the hypothesis that the occurrence of ἤτω ἀνάθεμα, Μαράνα θά, and perhaps ἡ χάρις τοῦ κυρίου Ἰησοῦ in this context, together with the *kiss* (v. 20) as "a *kiss of peace,*" signals a eucharistic context; but this is firmly rejected by Moule and Eriksson, and questioned by Fee.[180] The hypothesis gained initial currency not least be-

178. Eriksson, "Maranatha in the Letter's *Peroratio,*" in his *Traditions as Rhetorical Proof: Pauline Argumentation in 1 Cor,* 279-98.

179. Ibid., 279-90. Strobel, *Der erste Brief,* 269-72, e.g., gives three pages out of 272 to 16:13-24; Lang, *Die Briefe,* 248-50, devotes two pages out of 250; Senft, *La Première Épitre,* has three pages (222-25) out of 225 on these twelve verses (vv. 13-24).

180. Moule, "A Reconsideration of the Context of Maranatha." Cf. H. Lietzmann, *Mass and Lord's Supper: A Study in the History of the Liturgy* (Leiden: Brett, 1979), 186. Lietzmann associates this with a "non-Pauline" Eucharist of the Jerusalem tradition (204-15); also O. Cullmann, *Early Christian Worship* (Eng. trans., London: SCM, 1953), 13-14; Robinson and Bornkamm (cited above); and Käsemann, "Sentences of Holy Law in the NT," in *NT Questions of Today,* 66-81, esp. 69-70; also Cullmann, *Christology of the NT,* 210.

cause of the occurrence of μαρὰν ἀθά in the later *Didache* 10:6, alongside εἴ τις ἅγιος ἐστιν, ἐρχέσθω· εἴ τις οὐκ ἔστι μετανοείτω, while 9:1 (περὶ δὲ τῆς εὐχαριστίας) and 10:7 (εὐχαριστεῖν) provide the context for the Lord's Supper and eucharistic prayers. This "reading back" of the eucharistic setting of the *Didache* appeared to be confirmed by a summons to self-examination "as a staple part of the eucharistic liturgy" in which cursing and blessing are actions "beyond private space" and resonate with parallels in 1 Cor 11:27-34 and 14:38.[181]

Moule asks, "How much of this is really cogent?" μαράνα θά occurs only here in the New Testament: "why is there so little trace of this in other NT epistles? Why does . . . maranatha in 1 Cor xvi:22 come at this particular point *before* the grace? . . . Is there sufficient evidence to suggest that it was meant to lead into the eucharist proper? And is there anything obviously eucharistic in the context of Rev xxii?"[182] In fact, he concludes, there is nothing eucharistic about "Come, Lord Jesus" in Rev 22:20.[183] Anticipating one part of Eriksson's argument, Moule argues that the key to the meaning of *Marana tha* lies in its relation to *anathema,* serving in part as its sanction. It reinforces the ban. W. Dunphy's study corroborates such a connection within one stream of patristic interpretation. Amandus, e.g., declares excommunicate any who would tamper with his resting place and adds: *et sit anathema maranatha . . . in adventu Domini nostri.*[184] Even if we grant a "eucharistic context" to the book of Revelation, Dunphy adds, "is this sufficient ground for understanding the cry 'Come, Lord!' as a *call to the Lord to be present among the community which already had reason to believe in that presence,* rather than as a *request for the final coming?*" (my italics).[185]

C. F. D. Moule adds one more piece of evidence to support his claim that μαράνα θά or μαραναθά as the Aramaic formula for **Our Lord, come!** applies to the hope of the future parousia, not to the eucharistic presence. He cites from Moulton and Milligan an inscription from Salamis which links the sanction of an ἀνάθεμα with ἤτω μαρὰν ἀθάν.[186] This sepulchral inscription has more to do with eschatology and final judgment than with the Eucharist. Matthew Black endorses Moule's arguments and takes them further.[187] He cites (it seems for the first time) the quotation of *1 Enoch 1:9* paralleled in Jude 14-15: ἰδοὺ ἦλθεν κύριος ἐν ἁγίαις μυριάσιν αὐτοῦ ποιῆσαι κρίσιν κατὰ πάντων καὶ ἀπολέσει πάντας τοὺς ἀσεβεῖς (*1 Enoch* has ἔρχεται).[188] Black notes that this clear refer-

---

181. Käsemann, "Sentences," 68-70.

182. Moule, "Reconsideration," 307.

183. Ibid., 308.

184. Dunphy, "Maranatha: Development in Early Christology," 294; cf. 294-308.

185. Ibid., 296.

186. MM, ἀνάθεμα, 33; on μαραναθά, MM, 388.

187. Black, "The Maranatha Invocation and Jude 14, 15 (1 Enoch 1:9)," in Lindars and Smalley (eds.), *Christ and Spirit in the NT: Studies in Honour of C. F. D. Moule,* 189-96.

188. Ibid., 194-95.

ence to the final parousia circulated in its form in *1 Enoch* 1:9 in Aramaic, which may be reconstructed as *Maranatha.* "If such a possibility is conceded, then the original setting of the *maranatha* formula . . . not only supports the Parousia reference in the NT but can also account for its use as a reinforcement of the ἀνάθεμα: no formula would lend itself more to the purpose of . . . a ban."[189] Even if we insist on understanding the Aramaic as a perfect, "the reference is to the future expressed by a perfectum futuri, here virtually equivalent to a prophetic perfect."[190] In Black's view (as an acknowledged Aramaic specialist of international standing) the Aramaic formula means *either* (a) "The lord *will* (soon, surely) come," i.e., at the parousia; *or* (b) perhaps as an imperative as in terms of the Greek transliteration: "Lord, come," also referring to the parousia.[191]

Eriksson's method is to discard all "genetic" speculations about original pre-Pauline settings, and he would therefore presumably remain unimpressed by the allusion to *1 Enoch* 9:1. However, on all other points his work takes what Moule and Black claim about the parousia and about the semantic mutuality of **anathema** and *Marana tha* as his major area of agreement and point of departure. Eriksson's own approach, however, combines epistolographic and rhetorical research. First, he shows conclusively how the six themes of 16:13-24 take up in turn the key themes of the whole epistle. In 16:13, e.g., γρηγορεῖτε recapitulates this theme of eschatology: the readers are to be alert for the expectation of the parousia. The second imperative στήκετε ἐν τῇ πίστει reintroduces the stability of building for the welfare of the church and its future. The other imperatives perform similar functions in relation to other major themes.[192] "The last part of the *peroratio* is the *postscriptum* in 16:21-24," which sums up the key covenantal relationship with God in terms of covenant curse and covenant blessing: "Both the concept 'loving the Lord' and the curse belong to covenantal terminology."[193]

This conclusion, however, rests upon an intermediate stage of Eriksson's forceful argument. *Marana tha,* **Our Lord, come!** forms the centerpiece of this *postscriptum,* preceded by the conditional clause, **If anyone does not love the Lord, let that person be anathema**. We discussed above the category of *enthymemes,* which John Moores explores from Aristotle in the light of Umberto Eco to shed light on "rationality" in Paul.[194] *Enthymemes* are incomplete syllogisms; their conclusions rest upon premises which are often embedded in a tradition and usually presupposed rather than declared. Eriksson points

189. Ibid., 195.

190. Ibid., 196.

191. Black acknowledges that this runs counter to Kuhn's exclusion of a future meaning (K. G. Kuhn, "μαραναθά," *TDNT,* 4:466-72). Black's evidence contradicts Kuhn.

192. Eriksson, *Traditions,* 289-90, and above on 16:13.

193. Ibid., 291 and 292; cf. 293.

194. Cf. Aristotle, *Rhetoric* 2.21.2 (1394a); and Moores, *Wrestling with Rationality in Paul,* 1-32 and 132-60.

out that Aristotle suggests our asking the question "Why?" to reconstruct the premise of the enthymeme.[195] If we ask what "can provide a reason for a conditional curse" and how it relates to "a prayer for the Lord's return," the foundational presupposition emerges when we perceive that "both the concept of '**loving the Lord**' and the curse [**anathema**] belong to covenantal terminology and point to covenant as the context for the enthymeme."[196] "The commandment to love God is the focal point in the *Shemaʿ*. . . . The consequence of breaking the covenant is curses, and for keeping the covenant, blessings."[197] **Love** here denotes covenant loyalty. 1 Cor 16:22 provides a parallel not only with Gal 1:8-9, but with "No man can serve two masters."[198]

Eriksson is now in a position to explain the normally non-Pauline phrase φιλεῖ τὸν κύριον of v. 22. This is a *hapax legomenon* within the New Testament, and Paul would normally use ἀγαπάω, if he were to speak of *loving God*. Here Eriksson follows Spicq in regarding εἴ τις οὐ φιλεῖ τὸν κύριον (v. 22a) as denoting "not simply an absence of love; it is a *litotes,* analogous to οὐκ οἶδα ὑμᾶς expressing rejection and reprobation . . . *positive opposition*" (my italics).[199] Thus Paul's handwritten afterword to his beloved Corinthians is the love command in a covenantal setting which gives blessings for those who follow and curses for those who do not. *Paul has repreached the kerygma of the cross and the content of the gospel through the array of pastoral, ethical, and theological issues that bubble away at Corinth: "Come on, he concludes; are you 'in' or 'out'?"*

Finally, Eriksson adds one more piece of confirmation to this understanding of the text. He has considered the *epistolary* issues; those of *rhetoric* confirm this conclusion. "The *peroratio* has two main functions: recapitulation and emotional appeal."[200] The speech (or in this case the letter to read aloud in public) must end on a "high." What more heightened climax can be envisaged than the vision of the return of Christ, when, to cite Spicq's allusion to the gospel tradition, **the Lord** who **comes** will say either "Go from me, you who bear the anathema" (πορεύεσθε ἀπ᾽ ἐμοῦ κατηραμένοι . . .) or "Come to me, you who bear the blessing (δεῦτε οἱ εὐλογημένοι τοῦ πατρός μου), inherit the kingdom that was prepared for you from the foundation of the world" (Matt 24:34 and 41).[201] "The future dimension is especially stressed by Paul in 7:26-31; 11:26; 15:24, 51-57."[202] Eriksson not only concludes that Paul's ending follows rhe-

---

195. Aristotle, *Rhetoric* 2.21.2.
196. Eriksson, *Traditions,* 292.
197. Ibid., 293.
198. Ibid., 294.
199. Spicq, "Comment Comprendre φιλεῖν dans 1 Cor XVI:22?" 200-204. Also Edwards, *First Epistle,* 474, "hates."
200. Eriksson, *Traditions,* 283, also 296-97; cf. Quintilian, *Institutio Oratoria,* 6:1:1; Aristotle, *Rhetoric* 3.19.1-6.
201. The parable of judgment also turns on love for "the other"; cf. 1 Cor 8:7-13.
202. Eriksson, *Traditions,* 287.

torical patterns by inviting fear and pity, love and longing, but also that "the *maranatha* effectively stirs the other deliberative emotion, which is hope. *Maranatha* is a prayer for the Lord's return and as such it stresses the eschatological hope for those who love Christ and have not forsaken the Gospel."[203] "The traditional μαράνα θά plays a key role in the *peroratio* and therefore also in the whole letter."[204] In practical terms it shifts attention from "charismatic giftedness" to "the covenant theme, the christocentric emphasis; the eschatological tension and love."[205]

The unusual form ἤτω need not detain us: it is a late form standing for ἐστω. Further, we should not read too much into how *maranatha* is segmented or spaced. The Aramaic noun (מרן) means **Lord**, and the verb אתא *('atha')* means **to come**. If ה *(tha)* stands on its own, this is probably imperative: **Our Lord, come!** The form אתא *('atha')* would probably be indicative: *comes* or possibly *has come* or *will come*. However, the exegetical issues discussed above are decisive, since issues of word spacing and even of dialect in Aramaic remain uncertain (see Textual Note). The part parallel in Rev 22:20, "Amen. Come, Lord Jesus," seems to confirm the imperative.[206]

The final two verses express Paul's characteristic emphasis on **grace** (χάρις) as an unmerited, freely given gift from **the Lord**, while to this church above all he closes with a final wish concerning **love** (ἀγάπη). μεθ᾽ ὑμῶν (v. 23) and μετὰ πάντων ὑμῶν (v. 24) express more than a simple dative (cf. 1:3). Paul has prayed for the stability of the community, and explained to them that love is not a transient feeling but an enduring attitude (13:4-13). To conclude with a "wish-prayer" for **the grace of the Lord Jesus** to be **with** them reflects Paul's regular practice (2 Cor 13:13; Gal 6:18; Phil 4:23; 1 Thess 5:28; Philem 25; cf. Rom 16:24).[207] However, whereas the opening greetings retain a more uniform pattern, "variations are found in the wording of the final grace-wish ranging from the shortest . . . (1 Cor 16:24) to the long 'trinitarian' form . . . (2 Cor 13:14). But except for this long form the gift which is offered is always . . . one — grace."[208] This form may add further weight to the view that Paul expects his letter to be read aloud to the church assembled, probably for worship. **Grace** marks this epistle from one end (1:1-3) to the other (16:21-24). "God's grace seemingly has encompassed everything — a fitting conclusion to Paul's message."[209]

---

203. Ibid., 297.
204. Ibid., 298.
205. Ibid.
206. As Hays, *First Cor,* 292-93, also argues, but Hays tends to promote a liturgical setting above that of eschatology.
207. See Murphy-O'Connor, *Paul the Letter-Writer,* 99-102. The inclusive term "wish-prayer" is regularly employed by Wiles, *Paul's Intercessory Prayers,* 22-155.
208. Ibid., 114; cf. 114-22; "The basic formula is 'Grace with you'" (Murphy O'Connor, *Paul the Letter-Writer,* 100).
209. Hays, *First Cor,* 293.

Nonetheless, Paul wishes to assure his readers that whatever have been the stresses and strains within a vibrant, articulate, overly self-centered church, he never doubts the work of God's grace within them (cf. 1:4-9), and he holds them in his heart with genuine **love**. It is not mere rhetorical strategy that leads him to end on this final note: the so-called letter form is already complete.[210] Perhaps the only half-hidden subtext emerges from μετὰ πάντων ὑμῶν. He loves **all** of them, not simply "the weak" nor the most gifted, nor "Paul's group" (1:12). It is as he sees them as One Body ἐν Χριστῷ Ἰησοῦ that he sends them his genuine **love** to be **with** them **all**.

---

210. This is not to deny Fee's thought that Paul is concerned "to soften" what at times had been some hard blows (*First Epistle,* 840). Nevertheless, as Wolff asserts, **grace** and **love** are genuinely "foundational" for the community (*Der erste Brief,* 440-41).

Index of Subjects

Abraham typology, 945, 1195

Acclamation, acclamation formula, 78, 343, 637, 901-27, 901-27

Accommodation. *See* Adaptability

Accusative of reference, of respect, 337, 810, 882

Acrocorinth, 2, 20, 652

Achievement, wisdom as, 102-3, 182-83, 187, 189, 205, 260-61, 941. *See also* Wisdom; Rhetoric

Adam, last Adam, 268, 816, 1176-78, 1224-29, 1235, 1259, 1278, 1281, 1283

Adaptability, 383, 536-37, 699-708

Administration, administrative support, 336, 428, 1019-21

Adult, maturity, 230-33, 263, 289, 1066-68, 1118-30. *See also* Child, childishness

Adultery, 451, 467, 895

Advantage, argument from. *See* Rhetoric: deliberative

Aedile, 8-9, 202

Affront, cause of stumbling, 13-16, 20-22, 67, 160, 169-72, 186, 197, 270, 643, 649, 656-57

Ages, two, 147-48, 154-56, 165, 235, 244, 246, 743-49. *See* Apocalyptic

Aktionsart, 438-39n.89

Alien, alienated, 1105-7, 1121-26

Allegory, allegorical interpretation, 124, 311, 686-87, 711, 730, 731

Ambrose, 497

Amen, 761, 1075, 1115-16

Analogy, Paul's use of, 258-59, 290, 308, 310-11, 683, 709-12, 727, 757, 771, 1086

Anamnesis, 374, 857, 871-91. *See also* Remembering, remembrance

Anaploga villa, 7, 860-61

Anarchy, confusion, 1138-46

Anathema, 907-9, 917-25, 1348-52

Angels, 235, 246, 398, 807, 837-41, 966, 1033, 1085; guardians, 839-41; holy, 840-41; of the nations, 430-31, 432; participating in church's worship, 839-41; of wickedness (fallen), 431, 482, 839-40

Antinomianism, 131, 382-84, 389, 458-65. *See also* Freedom

Antithesis, 46-48, 142-50, 153-56, 245, 364, 591, 924, 1155

Anxiety, 533, 556-57, 580, 586

Aorist: aspect (vs. tense), 262, 437-39n.89; "baptismal," 453; effective, 166-67; epistolary, 374-75, 408-9, 413, 1346; event, of, 90, 302, 356, 453; gnomic, 577-78; ingressive, 270, 300, 321, 358, 376, 519, 555, 843

Apocalyptic, apocalypse, 147-53, 159, 165, 189, 211, 232, 235, 239, 242, 244, 246, 305, 311, 367, 425-26, 431, 456, 509, 574, 582, 583-86, 620, 743-49, 775, 956, 958-60, 973, 984, 1171, 1174, 1223-40, 1282, 1295-1301, 1307

Apollo, 6-7, 476, 738-39

Apollos, Apollos group, 31-33, 70-71, 121-25, 140, 155-56, 295, 299-312, 322, 346, 348-52, 1315-16, 1328, 1330, 1332

Apostle, apostleship, 55-56, 64-69, 126-31, 335-44, 359, 371, 375, 610-11, 663-76, 751, 796, 847-48, 867-68,

1356

marks of the, 60-61, 72-80, 322, 376, 401-8, 416, 419, 1008, 1155; ministry of, 109-13, 129-33, 302-5; order, polity, 352, 382-408, 419, 479-81, 995-1024, 1153, 1168; temple of Holy Spirit, 315-17. *See also* "Congregationalist" autonomous communities; Ecclesiology; Excommunication; Gifts of the Spirit; Holy Spirit; Lord's Supper; Ministry; Prophecy, prophet; Unity, building up

Cicero, 219, 261, 266, 385, 565, 641

Circumstantial factors (esp. in marriage) 488, 491-93, 507-12, 537, 543, 553, 557-59, 572-74, 577

Claudius, 17, 30-31, 129, 802, 853, 1343

Cleverness, clever rhetoric, 130-32, 144-46, 162-66, 208-9, 265, 1075. *See also* Preaching, proclamation; Rhetoric, rhetorical strategy; Sophists; Wisdom, wisdom of God

Clothing, clothing code, 800-809, 811, 828

Cloud, 725-29, 733

Code switching, 43, 154, 173-75, 240, 325-26, 369-400, 469, 499-500, 560-61, 587, 602, 627, 644, 930, 996, 1024. *See also* Redefinition

Coins, coinage, 6-11, 738-39, 805, 823

Collection, the, 1315, 1318-26

Communal participation. *See Koinonia*

Communication barrier, 1074-75, 1105

Communicative acts, discourse, 971, 1084-98. *See also* Articulate speech; Speech-acts

Communion, Holy. *See* Lord's Supper

Competitive mind-set. *See* Consumerism; Individualism; Rhetoric, rhetorical strategy; Status, status-conferring, status-seeking

Complacency, 355, 382-84, 387. *See also* Boasting; Self-sufficiency, self-centeredness, self-glorying

Conceivability, 285, 1223; of resurrection, 1261-81

Confession, 629-38, 907-9, 917-27, 1186-97, 1200. *See also* Speech-acts

Confirmatio, 47, 50, 149-50, 902, 929, 936, 1177-78, 1258-59

Confusion, chaos, 1138-46, 1154

"Congregationalist" autonomous communities, 56, 66, 73-75, 134

Conscience, 339, 639-44, 705, 779-81, 787-90. *See also* Self-awareness, self-knowledge; "Strong, the"; Weak, "the weak," weakness

Consciousness, 260, 340-44, 641-44

Constraints, 574-75, 599, 689, 950, 955-56

Consumerism, 11, 13-17, 20-21, 108, 159, 218, 291, 417

Controlled speech, control of the tongue, 922, 968, 1131-68

Convention, conventional formulae, 44, 55, 57-59, 63-64, 81, 84-88, 389, 391, 487, 803

Corinth, 1-29, 72-81, 175-95, 710, 738-39; archaeology, archaeological museum, 6-12, 20-21, 28-30, 618-20, 710-11, 736-38, 782-83, 805-6, 822-24, 827, 860-63; commercial activity and prosperity of, 1-17, 23-29, 863, 782-83; culture of, 4-29, 602, 801-9; geography and history of, 1-6, 6-23; Paul's ministry in, 29-41, 204-24, 358, 1327, 1331; Roman colony, 3-12, 313, 357, 612, 618, 782-83, 801-9, 830, 861, 1339-40; social conditions, 1-17, 23-29, 801-9. *See also* Catchphrases, catchwords at Corinth; Oral reports from Corinth; Self-promotion; Slogans, at Corinth; Status, status-conferring, status-seeking; "Strong," the; Weak, "the weak," weakness

Corporate identitiy, personality, 372, 381, 390, 412, 462, 468, 469, 992, 1282

Counting as, count-generation, 337-38, 456-57, 862, 919, 1053. *See also* Speech-acts

Courtesy, 414-15, 863, 899, 1049-50, 1052

Courts of law, 8-9, 338, 418-38

Covenant, 412, 492, 551, 718, 724-25,

Didache, 764, 766, 770, 868, 875, 878, 965, 1141

Differentiation, 469, 911, 929-36, 1103-4, 1154-55

Difficilior lectio, 72-73, 519, 624

Digressions, alleged, 149, 546, 558, 799. *See also* Integrity of the epistle; Partition theories

Diolkos, 1-2, 20

Dionysus/Bacchus, 738-39, 831, 915, 971, 978, 1002, 1036

Discern, discernment, 271, 273, 434, 958, 965-70, 1140-41

Discerning prophecy. *See* Prophecy, prophet, prophetic speech

Discord. *See* Splits

Dishonor. *See* Honor, honor-shame culture values

Dispositio, 47

Divisions. *See* Splits

Distraction (from worship), 590-98, 604, 827-29

Divorce; divorce and remarriage, 492, 519-25, 527, 534-40, 576-77

"Do you not know that?" 316, 400, 425, 430, 442, 466, 474

Donatism, Donatists, 282, 479

Double meaning, 239, 640

Doxology, 794, 1098

Dress code, 828-37

Drugs, 470, 946, 986

Drunkards, drunkenness, 414-15, 419, 445, 470, 472, 860, 863, 894

Dualism, 180, 257, 391, 462, 464, 488, 499, 1176, 1265. *See also* "*Deus ex machina* worldview"

Eating and drinking judgment, 849-98

Ecclesiology, 33, 300, 382-408, 470, 671, 887-88, 992, 995-1024. *See also* Church

"Ecstatic" experience, speech, 908, 912-13, 972, 1111-12. *See also* Gifts of the Spirit

Edification. *See* Build, building, and building up

Egalitarianism, 108, 329, 372, 1098

Eidolothuta. See Meat associated with idols

Election, divine, 250, 626-27, 1004

Elite, spiritual, 108, 232, 240, 240, 242, 274, 709, 929, 980, 998

Ellipse, 208, 249, 250, 911-12

Emperor worship, imperial cult, 918-21

Empty tomb, 1193, 1197-1203

End, end-time. *See* Eschatology

"End of the World" language, 581-83

Enlightenment rationalism, worldview, 283, 638, 944, 951-55, 1041

Enthusiasm, enthusiasts, 241, 383, 358, 432. *See also Schwärmer,* spritual "enthusiasts"; "Spiritual" person, spirituality, claims to

Enthymeme, 369, 602, 1214-18, 1259, 1350-51. *See also* Reason, rationality; Rhetoric, rhetorical strategy; Tradition, pre-Pauline tradition

Entrepreneurs, 11-12, 20, 411, 710

Ephesus, 1, 28, 31, 121, 374, 1048, 1251-52, 1328, 1331-32, 1342-43

Epictetus, 78, 261, 273, 358, 364-66, 444, 446, 478, 487-88, 493, 508, 535, 539, 547, 587, 598, 723, 825, 845-46, 889, 992

Epicureanism, 277, 1172, 1253

Epistemology, 13-17, 147-48, 156-57, 166, 175, 253, 774

Epistolography, 48-49, 52, 62, 69-72, 113, 391, 1334-35, 1337, 1342, 1346-48, 1350

Equality, 491, 496, 504-5, 829

Erastus, 9, 860, 1330

Eros, 1034, 1050-51

Eschatology, 77, 100-105, 165, 231, 232, 305, 341, 357, 377, 395, 493, 551, 559, 743-49, 763, 778, 803, 842, 878, 948, 959, 1035, 1060, 1065, 1155, 1169, 1320, 1349, 1352; existential vs. ontological conceptual grammar of, 1062; glory, 1198-99; imagery, 565, 580-81; imminence (logical grammar of), 493, 574-83; 580-94, 895, 1293; realism, reality, 341, 547, 579; overrealized eschatology, 90, 95-96, 98-106, 239, 345-48,

Hardships, catalogues of. *See* Catalogues of hardship, affliction

Have-nots, 361-64, 852-55, 862, 894. *See also* Lord's Supper; Poverty, poor

Head: vs. body, physiological, 801, 812, 818, 820-21, 827; as chief, leader, 800-809, 812-14, 819; covering, 801-9, 822-37; as source, origin, 814-16, 819; as synecdoche with physiological background, 800-809, 816-22

Healing, 944-51, 953

Heart, 248, 249, 257, 341, 343, 599-601, 640, 643, 985-87

Hebrew text. *See* Old Testament, use of and quotations from

"Hellenistic" Judaism, 439, 633, 637, 1092

Hellenistic Jewish synagogues, 440-43

Hellenistic parallels (women prophets), 830, 952-58, 964

Hermeneutics, 259, 339, 451-53, 565, 866, 870, 937-38n.8, 988, 1028, 1125, 1134

Hierarchy, 803, 1015

"High status," 419-20, 705, 1005-12, 1023-24

Hippocrates, 816, 1011

History of religions approach, 879, 925-26, 959, 971, 979

Holy: logical grammar of, 529-30; people, 103-5, 260, 315-18, 381-84, 401-9, 447, 528-32, 591, 1320, 1346

Holy Spirit: believers as temple of, 315-18, 449, 656; deity of, 103-4, 279-81, 659, 761; eschatology and, 403-8, 1224, 1265, 1269-81, 1286; "fellowship" of, 103-5; gifts of the Spirit, 900-988, 1075-1131; life-giving, 1278-80, 1283; procession of, 261, 264; as revealer, 204, 217-20, 252-76, 283-85, 605-6, 1141-46, 1166-68; "spirituality" and claims to be "spiritual," 131-33, 225-26, 286-88, 296-97, 333, 358, 606, 931-36; as transcendent, 204-5, 225-26, 256-63, 279-81, 475; wisdom from, 166, 390-92, 434, 605. *See also* Gifts of the Spirit; *Koinonia;* "Spiritual" persons(s), spirituality, claims to; Wisdom, wisdom of God

Home, houses: as against alien, 1118-30; as "private" domain, 830, 864-65, 899; women in the, 490, 528, 830, 962, 1158, 1165. *See also* House, church in

Homosexuality, 419, 439-53, 824-25, 832

Honor, honor-shame culture values, 8-15, 182-92, 219, 243, 303, 361-63, 369, 562, 802-9, 826-27, 835, 865, 1008, 1160, 1342, 1345

Hoods, 801-9, 828-37, 846

Hope, 688, 1071-73, 1170-71

Horace, 446, 478, 801, 825

Hoti recitative, 574, 629

Horizon of expectation, 874, 878

House, church in, 108-9, 857, 1343

Household, 28, 121, 135-36, 140-44, 336, 561, 564, 1338

"How do you know?" (optimistic or pessimistic), 537-40

Human drives, 288-94

Humanness, 747-48, 835-36

Identity: Christian, corporate, 158, 372; continuity of, 1259; new, 447, 463. *See also* Gender, gender differentiation: signals of identity

Idol(s), idolatry, 6-8, 316, 412, 440, 446, 452, 634-36, 719-49, 750-51, 762, 767, 771, 777; idol food, idol meat, food offered to idols, 499, 607-60, 778

"Illegitimate totality transfer," 529, 1305

Illocutions, 43, 50-52, 63-64, 112, 146-47, 338, 342, 369, 378, 398-99, 522, 572, 637, 924-27, 1017, 1088. *See also* Speech-acts

Illness, 398, 894-96, 947-49, 951

Image, 290, 308, 317, 470, 475, 689, 833-37, 912, 1235, 1283

Immature. *See* Adult, maturity; Child, childishness

Inarticulate noises, sounds, 977, 985, 1100-1111

Old Testament, use of and quotations
from, 126, 159-66, 195-96, 229, 232,
248-52, 258, 273-75, 322-24, 352-54,
356, 417-18, 452, 471, 479, 586, 649,
685-88, 785-86, 792-93, 1120-26,
1189, 1235; as Christian scripture,
160, 355-56, 450, 471, 686-88, 718-
49, 943, 959-60, 1189; ethical tradition, source of, 324, 386, 398-400,
417, 440-47, 491, 501, 1132; formative models from, 687-88, 719-49;
frame of reference for gospel, 81-82,
126, 160, 356, 378, 408-10, 429-30,
478-79, 630, 1097, 1189-97, 1234;
Hebrew, text of, 160, 237, 249, 251,
275, 322-24, 816-17, 1068-69, 1286-
87, 1299-1301; Septuagint, 214, 237,
243, 322-24, 428, 517, 539, 586,
730-31, 816-17, 845, 869, 913, 918-
19, 972, 1120-21, 1191, 1196, 1235,
1281, 1286, 1299-1301; typological
interpretation of, 731-49. *See also* Allegory, allegorical interpretation;
Decalogue; Deuteronomic traditions
One body, 768-71, 776, 899
One flesh, 466-71
One God, 629-38
Ontology, 276, 282, 329, 659-60, 730,
774, 776, 845, 996, 1165. *See also*
Postmodernity, postmodernism; Truth
"Oracular" forms, 957-61, 1092, 1112
Oral reading of letters, 44, 46, 62-63,
72
Oral reports from Corinth, 32-41, 120-
23, 272, 316, 385, 430, 849, 860
Order in creation, order as purposive divine decree, 74-75, 321, 326, 382-84,
387, 400-418, 451, 552, 845, 901-36,
961, 989, 1131-68, 1229-30, 1307;
and differentiation, 803, 1074-81,
1131-46; and hierarchy, 995-98,
1001-18, 1022-24; ontological, 329
Origen, 197-98, 201, 234, 236, 251,
278-79, 321, 330, 494, 532, 658, 661,
681, 787, 940
Other, otherness, and respect for, concern for, 120, 159, 244, 252, 260,
262, 291, 305, 426, 435, 494, 505,

526, 611, 659, 668, 699, 782-822,
830, 834, 836, 841, 850-52, 870,
1009, 1035, 1074, 1095, 1111-17,
1122, 1337
Outsiders, 1074, 1127. *See also*
Gentiles
Oxymoron, 172-75

Papyri, 25, 56, 78, 85, 97, 101-2, 114,
242, 249-50, 335-36, 385, 406, 409,
503, 527, 576, 666, 711, 818, 936,
957-58, 970, 1019, 1103, 1318, 1342
Papyri, Oxyrhynchus, 409, 576, 584,
592, 619, 640, 650, 970, 972, 1104
Paradosis, terminology. *See* Tradition,
pre-Pauline tradition
Parakalo-form, 63-64, 110-14, 1029,
1077, 1337; *paraklesis,* 1088-90,
1143-44
Parallel, parallelism, 148-49, 153-60,
175, 730, 766, 776, 780, 796. *See
also* Analogy, Paul's use of; Antithesis; Reversals; Rhetoric, rhetorical
strategy
Parousia, 241, 343, 375, 580, 1230,
1284-96. *See also* Day of the Lord,
Last Day, Judgment; Eschatology
Parthenos. See Betrothed couples; Celibacy; Unmarried people, state; Virgins
Participation, communal participation.
See Koinonia
Particles, Greek (of contrast), 122, 132-
33, 154, 229, 230, 431-32, 501, 534,
596, 891, 931, 1140
Partition theories, 36-41, 239-40, 375,
390, 610-12, 642, 666, 717-18. *See
also* Integrity of the epistle
Passover, Passover meal and Lord's
Supper, 401-8, 482, 752-68, 851,
856, 871-75, 882-87, 866-88;
covenantal, 758-60; lamb, 404, 479,
482; recital, with cups and haggadah,
758-59, 877-80; self-involving projection into event, 758-59. *See also* Covenant
Pastor, pastoral care, 17-25, 28-29, 39,
41-52, 290, 483-84, 1316, 1324,

Servant, service, 300, 335-44, 931-34, 1014. *See also* Estate manager; Slave, slavery

Sexual relations, 381-417, 419, 434, 440-78, 484-514, 594-605, 739; sexual availability, 805, 828, 832; sexual intimacy, 467, 469, 493-94, 500, 503, 505-12. *See also* Gender, gender differentiation; Marriage

Shame, lack of respect for self and others, 8-15, 182-88, 434, 822-44. *See also* Honor, honor-shame culture values

Sibyl, 919-20, 971, 979

Sift, sifting, 273, 1152-53, 1158-61, 1163-66

"Sighs too deep for words," 973, 985-89

Sign(s), signal, 95, 170-72, 221, 953-55, 1104-5

Signature, 927, 1347

Silas, Silvanus, 19, 1331

Silence, 1146-62

Sin, 77, 98-99, 102, 282, 339, 342, 385, 418, 429, 577, 654-55; among Christians, 77, 98-99, 102; against the self, the body, 470-74; as state or attitude, or orientation of will, 747-49; theology, nature, and effects of, 481-82, 733-37, 747-48, 955, 1220-21, 1301-4

Slave, slavery, 186, 188, 194, 327-28, 370, 459-60, 475-79, 508, 544-46, 553-60, 562-65, 1044; becoming a slave, 562, 63; of Christ, 478, 561; condition, the, 534-40; families and property, 564; financial benefit of, 561-63; manumission, 476-79, 564-65; marginality, 565; metaphor of, 476-79; varied status of, 328, 477, 563-65; voluntary, 700-703

Sleep, metaphor of, 603, 1206-7, 1220, 1293-95

Slogans, at Corinth, 120-23, 224, 324, 458, 461, 471, 489, 494, 498-501, 574, 620, 629, 647, 781, 910-11, 938-39. *See also* Catchphrases, catchwords, at Corinth; Quotations

Social anthropology, 123, 805, 826, 829

Social constructionism, 13-17, 402-33, 444

Social networks, 419-20, 437-48, 447

Social status, stratification, 20-30, 127-28, 179-88, 987. *See also* Status, status-conferring, status-seeking

Sociology, social theory, sociological models, 183, 328, 387, 402-3, 489, 802-9, 829, 866; socio-symbolic expressions, 156, 162-63, 198, 544, 832

Socrates, Socratic tradition, 156, 162-63, 198, 299, 321, 346, 518

Sophia, 124, 143-45, 148-50, 160-62, 203-4, 230, 260, 638, 830. *See also* Wisdom, wisdom of God

Sophists, 13-17, 27, 66-67, 144-46, 162-66, 182, 205, 219-20. *See also* Cleverness, clever rhetoric; Folly, fool, foolish; Postmodernity, postmodernism; Wisdom, wisdom of God

Sosthenes, 56, 59, 62-63, 69-72, 1347

Soul, beliefs concerning, 261, 268, 466, 1265, 1306

Sources of Paul's information 32-36

Sovereignty, of God. *See* God: sovereignty of

Sowing, imagery of, 1263-65

Speaking in tongues. *See* Tongues, gift of speaking in

Speech-acts, 41-52, 63-64, 78, 81, 84-88, 102, 108-9, 112, 318, 338, 342; behavitive, 81, 84-88; commissive, 881, 1189; confession, 1130; declarative, 102, 325, 337, 431, 455, 887, 890, 924-27, 961, 1017, 1092, 1189, 1302; directive, 399, 1092; exclamatory, 423, 432-33; exercitive, 394; illocutionary, 43, 50-52, 63-64, 81, 84-88, 108-9, 112, 146-48, 369, 378, 398-99; multiple, 81, 85-86, 394, 455, 1188-89; of acclamation, of ascription 78, 85-86; perlocutionary, 51, 108-9, 146-48, 369; verdictive, 101-2, 337, 338, 392-94, 399, 455, 881, 1017, 1092, 1302. *See also* Counting as, count-generation; Illocutions

Spirit. *See* Holy Spirit

Tongues, gift of speaking in, 957-89,
1062-64, 1094-1130; angelic language, 915, 972-73, 976; archaic language, 978-80; earthly language, 915,
971, 973-78, 1107-11; hermeneutical
distance, 937-38n.8; lexicography,
971-72; and "messages," 1085-86,
1108; tongues, interpretation or articulation of, 1094-1101, 1107-11; as
welling up of preconscious sighs of
praise and longings, 970, 984-89,
1108-9, 1111-26
Topic marker, 483, 494, 498, 568, 616-
17, 628, 909. *See also Peri de*
Tradition, pre-Pauline tradition, 42-46,
50-52, 74-75, 128, 356, 523-24, 608-
17, 628-38, 726, 757, 760, 762, 810-
11, 828-29, 847-48, 866-71, 902,
908, 926, 943, 964-65, 1016-18;
common apostolic, arguments from,
74-75, 608-17, 884-86; and Scripture
as basis of argument, 1188-89;
Transformation, 41-52, 145-47, 154,
175, 294, 373, 439, 463, 464, 650,
688, 731, 880, 1175, 1198, 1259-81,
1284-1301, 1305
Travel plans, 1326-34
Triclinium and *atrium,* 859-62, 899
Trinity, trinitarian perspective, 246, 277-
81, 459, 631, 803, 819
Triumphalism, 325, 339, 344-48, 357-
60, 390, 427-34, 626, 923, 1006,
1038, 1041, 1052, 1171, 1255
Trumpet, last, 1104-5, 1296
Trust, 478, 587-88, 630, 694
Truth, 13-17, 94-95, 266, 273, 407, 630,
795, 1055-57, 1059, 1218
Twelve, the, 1203-8
Two-tier morality, 489, 500, 503, 517
Type, 727, 730, 731-32
Typology, 727, 730, 731-49, 1226-28,
1281-90

Unconscious, 340-44, 984, 985, 988,
1129
Unintelligible speech, 1074-75, 1085-87
Unity, unity with diversity, 111-34, 763,
769, 803, 928-36, 984, 990-1012

Unleavened bread, 401-8
Unmarried people, state, 492, 515-19,
542, 565-602
Upward mobility, 328, 544, 551, 556,
560, 564
Use, make use of, 553-59, 690

Veil. *See* Head: covering; Hoods
Verbal abuse, 363-64, 414, 419, 445
Verbal aspect, 438-39n.89
Verbal bullying, 218-19
Vices, catalogue of. *See* Catalogues of
vices (and virtues)
Victory, of and over death, 99, 198,
248, 358, 776, 1171, 1260, 1300-
1304
Vineyard, analogy of, 306, 684
Virgins, 495-97, 502-3, 590, 593-98
Virtue, 282, 410, 440-43
Vocation, 513-14, 557. *See* Call, calling
Washed, 419, 453-54
"We" sections, 19, 70-72, 229-30, 245,
337
Weak, "the weak," weakness, 28, 65-67,
182-88, 204-5, 213-15, 361-63, 414,
418-28, 420, 451, 484-87, 607-17,
632, 638-45, 654-56, 658, 699-705,
736-37, 783-95, 850-51, 870, 885,
899, 900, 987, 990, 1046, 1175, 1274
Western text, 100-101, 292, 354, 392,
578, 656, 679, 691, 809, 843, 866,
891, 1149, 1211, 1223
Widows, widower, 484-87, 493, 495,
513-15, 577, 590, 602-6
Wife and husband, 494, 500, 519-25,
528-29, 540; of apostle, maintained,
679-83. *See also* Marriage; Mutuality; Separation (from marriage);
Women (at Corinth), women prophets: mutuality and reciprocity with
husbands, with men
Wirkungsgeschichte. See Posthistory of
texts, examples of
Wisdom, wisdom of God, 20-22, 123-
25, 134-95, 143-45, 160-62, 189-93,
224-32, 230, 241, 266, 358, 369, 434,
437, 625, 722, 728, 834, 1332; as
achievement, 13-17, 123-25, 134-95,

Index of Modern Authors

Index of Ancient Sources

1396

4:13	1115n.190	13:5	209, 886	18:17	70, 132,
4:18	115	13:11	952, 953		182n.180
4:22	946	13:27	236	18:18	833, 1342
4:30	946	13:30	1193	18:18-19	28
4:32	1320	13:37	1193	18:19-22	31
4:34-36	1320	15	129	18:23	31
4:35	912	15:1-20	1207	18:24	145, 155
4:36-37	679, 682	15:13	1207	18:24-28	1343
5:1-11	952, 953, 969,	15:20	617	18:26	182n.180, 1342
	1325	15:23	81	18:26-28	123
5:6	581	15:29	609n.2, 617	18:27	31, 1332
5:28	115	15:39	1052	19	31n.160, 1252,
5:30	1193	16:1-3	1331		1330
5:40	115	16:3	702	19:1a	31
5:41	794	16:6	19, 969	19:1-7	998
6:1-6	300n.13	16:6-40	1331	19:6	963, 975
6:1-7	932	16:10	19	19:10	1342
6:2-6	1020	16:12	818	19:22	1330
6:8	954	16:16-18	966	19:24	316
6:10	1128	16:18	115	19:26	1342
7:2	724n.24	16:21	30	19:29	28
7:48	316	16:21-23	362n.346	19:42	1342
7:59	927n.133	16:26	310n.55	20:7	766, 1322
7:60	1221	17	1239n.152	20:11	766
8:13	954	17:5-7	19	20:31	879
8:19	600n.626	17:7	30	20:37	1345
8:26-40	220	17:10-14	1331	21:4	963
8:30	1190n.103	17:11	273, 675	21:9	957
8:32	913	17:15	215	21:18	1207
8:37	918	17:16	1052	21:23ff	703
9:4-5	190, 466, 655,	17:22-31	212	21:25	617
	768, 990	17:24	316	21:26	702
9:14	646	17:28	635, 970	22:1	675
9:17	1198	17:34	1338	22:7-8	466, 655, 768,
10:4	881	18	9		990
10:10	982	18:1-3	1343	22:17	982
10:15	786n.32	18:2	182n.180, 1342	23:2-3	654
10:40	1193	18:3	23	23:8	1277
10:44-48	998	18:5	215	24:8	675
11:5	982	18:6	705	24:23	550n.360
11:15-18	998	18:7	30, 182n.180	26:11	921
11:22-26	679, 682	18:7-8	132	26:12	600n.626,
11:26	71	18:8	27, 141, 181,		650n.236
11:29-30	853n.19		182n.180	26:14	55, 69, 190, 695,
12:17	1207	18:11	23, 28		1300n.210
12:19	273, 675	18:12-17	30	26:14-15	466, 655
13–14	19, 682, 1321	18:15-17	69	26:23	209
13:1	1016n.119			26:24-25	1126

1432